FEDERAL WHITE COLLAR CRIME

CASES AND MATERIALS

Seventh Edition

■ ■ ■

Julie R. O'Sullivan

Professor of Law
Georgetown University Law Center

AMERICAN CASEBOOK SERIES®

WEST ACADEMIC PUBLISHING

American Casebook Series is a trademark registered in the U.S. Patent and Trademark Office.

© West, a Thomson business, 2001, 2003, 2007
© 2009, 2012 Thomson Reuters
© 2016 LEG, Inc. d/b/a West Academic
© 2019 LEG, Inc. d/b/a West Academic
      444 Cedar Street, Suite 700
      St. Paul, MN 55101
      1-877-888-1330

West, West Academic Publishing, and West Academic are trademarks of West Publishing Corporation, used under license.

Printed in the United States of America

ISBN: 978-1-64242-098-2

This book is dedicated to
the memory of my Father, Daniel Edward O'Sullivan,
and my Mother, Rosemary Elizabeth O'Sullivan,
and to the apple of my eye,
Daniel Atticus (Sarastro) O'Sullivan

*

Preface to the Seventh Edition

———

Throughout the book, statistics have been updated (e.g., on sentencing, corporate cases v. PDAs; recoveries in FCA cases, FCPA prosecutions and recoveries, etc.), relevant caselaw added, and current scholarship cited or quoted. With respect to specific changes:

Chapter 2 (*Mens Rea*): I added a note on the rule of lenity.

Chapter 3 (Sentencing): I added something on *Rosales-Mireles v. United States*, 138 S.Ct. 1897 (2018) to a footnote; and added a note on *Nelson v. Colorado*, 137 S.Ct. 1249 (2017).

Chapter 4 (Entity Liability): I inserted a note on the "identification" theory of corporate liability; summarized the Yates Memo rather than including it in its entirety; inserted the updated Principles of Federal Prosecution of Business Organizations, which includes some points from the Yates Memo; included mention of the new policy embodied in U.S.A.M. 1-12.100; inserted notes on Jennifer Arlen & Marcel Kahan, *Corporate Governance Regulation through Nonprosecution*, 84 U. Chi. L. Rev. 323, 326-27 (2017) and Jennifer Arlen, *The Potentially Perverse Effects of Corporate Criminal Liability*, 23 J. Legal Stud. 833, 835-37 (1994); inserted a footnote referencing Veronica Root's work on monitorships; omitted dated statistics on the organizational sentencing guidelines; rearranged the sections so that discussion of internal investigations comes after the sections on sentencing and DPAs; and added a notes on *United States v. HSBC Bank USA, N.A.*, 863 F.3d 125, 129, 137 (2d Cir. 2017), *United States v. Fokker Servs., B.V.*, 818 F.3d 733 (D.C. Cir. 2016), and *Logos v. United States*, -- U.S. --, 138 S.Ct. 1684 (2018).

Chapter 5 (False Statements): I referenced *Universal Health Servs. v. United States ex rel. Escobar*, 136 S.Ct. 1989 (2016) in a footnote and added material to the False Claims/*Qui Tam* discussion, including reference to the leaked DOJ confidential January 10, 2018 memorandum and the 2018 Brand Memo.

Chapter 6 (Obstruction): I added notes related to the obstruction investigation apparently underway by the Special Counsel.

Chapter 7 (Fraud): I added *McDonnell v. United States*, 136 S.Ct. 2355 (2016); took out the section on congressional inaction on conflicts of interest post-*Skilling*; changed the charging policy discussion to take into account A.G. Sessions' Memorandum to Federal Prosecutors from U.S. Attorney General Sessions, Department Charging and Sentencing Policy (May 10, 2017); discussed *United States ex rel. O'Donnell v. Countrywide Home Loans, Inc.*, 33 F.Supp.3d 494 (S.D.N.Y. 2014), *rev'd*, 822 F.3d 650 and *United States v. Weimert*, 819 F.3d 351 (7th Cir. 2016), in notes; and added *Shaw v. United States*, 137 S.Ct. 462 (2016) to the bank fraud discussion.

Chapter 8 (Corruption): I amended the "official acts" discussion to reflect *McDonnell*; added a note on 18 U.S.C. § 201(b)(1)(C); amended the discussion of the "stream of benefits" theory of *quid pro quo* to reflect *McDonnell* and the Menendez prosecution; added notes on *United States v. Ocasio*, 136 S.Ct. 1423 (2016), and *United States v. Taylor*, 136 S.Ct. 2074 (2016) to the Hobbs Act section; included a note on the Second Circuit's decision in *United States v. Hoskins*, 2018 WL 4038192 (2d Cir. 2018), in the FCPA section; and reproduced the DOJ's FCPA Corporate Enforcement Policy (U.S.A.M. 9-47.120).

Chapter 9 (Securities): I replaced *Dirks v. SEC*, 463 U.S. 646, 655, n. 14 (1983) with *Salman v. United States*, 137 S.Ct. 420 (2016) (with brief mention of *United States v. Martoma*, 894 F.3d 64, 68 (2018)) and adjusted the notes accordingly; and created a new section for "tipping" liability in recognition of the apparent fact that the same rules apply to classical and misappropriation cases.

Chapter 10 (Conspiracy): I added discussion of the Special Counsel's indictment of various Russian nationals on a defraud clause theory.

Chapter 11 (RICO): I added a note on extraterritorial application of RICO after *RJR Nabisco v. European Community*, 136 S.Ct. 2090 (2016); and added references to *Honeycutt v. United States*, 137 S.Ct. 1626 (2017) and *Luis v. United States*, 136 S.Ct. 1083 (2016) in the forfeiture section.

Chapter 13 (Grand Jury): I added a brief note on *Carpenter v. United States*, -- U.S. --, 138 S.Ct. 2206 (2018); and reference to the Clarifying Lawful Overseas Use of Data (CLOUD) Act, amending the Stored Communications Act.

Chapter 14 (Discovery): I added a cite to *Turner v. United States*, 137 S.Ct. 1885 (2017) in the *Brady* section.

Chapter 15 (Fifth Amendment, testimony): I added a note on *United States v. Allen*, 864 F.3d 63 (2d Cir. 2017).

Chapter 17: (Privileges): I added reference to the Yates Memo in the discussion of *Upjohn* warnings.

Chapter 18 (Representation): I referenced the Yates Memo's effect on hiring of separate counsel and JDAs; and put in a short discussion of *Turner v. United States*, 885 F.3d 949 (6th Cir. 2018) (*en banc*), *cert. filed*, No. 18-106 (July 24, 2018), on the question of whether suspects have a Sixth Amendment right before charging.

Chapter 19 (Plea Bargaining): I changed the charging policy discussion to take into account of A.G. Sessions' Memorandum to Federal Prosecutors from U.S. Attorney General Sessions, Department Charging and Sentencing Policy (May 10, 2017), added *Class v. United States*, 138 S.Ct. 798 (2018) to a footnote; mentioned *Turner* (above); and replaced the Duncan plea agreement with Lt. General Michael Flynn's Plea Agreement and Statement of Offense.

Chapter 21 (Transnational): With apologies, I completely rewrote the first section of the chapter dealing with the extraterritorial application of federal criminal law because I thought that what appeared in the last edition was unnecessarily long and confusing; excerpted *United States v. Allen*, 864 F.3d 63 (2d Cir. 2017); added short notes on the European Union's General Data Protection Regulation (GDPR), which took effect on May 25, 2018, and differences among countries in privilege rules (discussing *The Director of the Serious Fraud Office v. Eurasian Natural Resources Corp., Ltd.* [2018], EWCA Civ. 2006), corporate criminal liability standards, and ethics rules.

Acknowledgments

I am indebted to many family members, friends, and colleagues for their assistance and encouragement during this project. Special thanks go to generations of research assistants (and most especially Maggie Whitney), without whose dedicated efforts this volume would *never* have reached the publisher. Thanks, too, to my friends and colleagues who practice and teach in this area for their advice, insights, corrections, and the like.

I also appreciate the unflagging help and support of the Georgetown University Law Center library and administrative staff, particularly Faculty Manuscript Editor Anna Selden. This seventh edition was produced in print-ready format, meaning that Betsy Kuhn worked hard getting it just right. As always, many thanks to Michele Roberts and Bob Muse, without whose subtle and nimble minds this work would have been much impoverished.

Finally, I would like to thank the following authors, publishers, and copyright holders for their permission to reproduce excerpts from their works in the many different editions of this casebook, including:

TASK FORCE ON FEDERALIZATION OF CRIMINAL LAW, AMERICAN BAR ASSOCIATION CRIMINAL JUSTICE SECTION, THE FEDERALIZATION OF CRIMINAL LAW (1998), Copyright 1998: American Bar Association, Criminal Justice Section. Reprinted with the permission of the American Bar Association.

ABA Task Force Opposes Requiring Lawyers to Report Suspicious Financial Transactions, 71 CRIM. L. REP. (BNA) 648 (Sept. 11, 2002). Reproduced with permission from the American Bar Association and the Bureau of National Affairs, Inc. (BNA). Reproduced with permission from ABA/BNA's Lawyers' Manual on Professional Conduct, Vol. 18, No. 19, pp. 559-560 (Sept. 11, 2002).

Elkan Abramowitz & Barry Bohrer, *Andersen Jury Instructions: A New Collective Corporate Liability?*, N.Y. L.J. (July 2, 2002). This article is reprinted with the permission from the July 2, 2002 edition of the New York Law Journal. © 2002 NLP IP Company. All rights reserved. Further duplication without permission is prohibited.

Sara Sun Beale, *Comparing the Scope of the Federal Government's Authority to Prosecute Federal Corruption and State and Local Corruption: Some Surprising Conclusions and a Proposal*, 51 HASTINGS L.J. 699 (2000), Copyright © 2000 Hastings College of the Law; Sara Sun Beale. Reprinted from the Hastings Law Journal, Vol. 51, No. 4, pp. 699, by permission of the publisher and the author.

Frank O. Bowman III, *Departing is Such Sweet Sorrow: A Year of Judicial Revolt on Substantial Assistance" Departures Follows a Decade of Prosecutorial Indiscipline*, 29 STETSON L. REV. 7 (1999), Copyright © Frank O. Bowman, III, 1999. All Rights Reserved. Reprinted with the permission of the Stetson Law Review and the author.

Stacy L. Brainin & David B. Reece, *From Thornburgh to McDade-Ex Parte Contacts with Corporate Employees During Government Investigations*, in ABA WHITE COLLAR CRIME 2000, Copyright © 2000 American Bar Association. All Rights Reserved. Reprinted by permission of the American Bar Association and the authors.

H. Lowell Brown, *Vicarious Criminal Liability of Corporations for the Acts of Their Employees and Agents*, 41 LOY. L. REV. 279 (1995), Copyright © 1995 by the Loyola University Loyola Law Review; H. Lowell Brown. Reprinted with the permission of the Loyola Law Review and the author.

Steven D. Clymer, *Unequal Justice: The Federalization of Criminal Law*, 70 S. CAL. L. REV. 643 (1997), Copyright © 1997 University of Southern California; Steven D. Clymer. Reprinted with the permission of the Southern California Law Review and the author.

John Coffee, *"No Soul to Damn: No Body to Kick": An Unscandalized Inquiry Into the Problem of Corporate Punishment*, 79 MICH. L. REV. 386 (1981), Copyright © 1980 John C. Coffee, Jr. Reprinted with the permission of the author.

Lance Cole, *The Fifth Amendment and Compelled Production of Personal Documents After United States v. Hubbell–New Protection for Private Papers?*, 29 AM. J. CRIM. L. 123 (2002)

ETHICAL IMPLICATIONS OF JOINT DEFENSE/COMMON INTEREST AGREEMENTS, COMMITTEE ON PROFESSIONAL RESPONSIBILITY OF THE ASSOCIATION OF THE BAR OF THE CITY OF NEW YORK (1996). Reprinted with the permission of the Association of the Bar of the City of New York.

Sharon L. Davies, *The Jurisprudence of Willfulness: An Evolving Theory of Excusable Ignorance*, 48 DUKE L.J. 341 (1998), Copyright © 1998 Duke Law Journal; Sharon L. Davies. Reprinted with the permission of the Duke Law Journal and the author.

Lucian E. Dervan, *International White Collar Crime and the Globalization of Internal Investigations*, 39 Fordham Urb. L.J. 361 (2011).

Robert Fabrikant & Glenn E. Solomon, *Application of the Federal False Claims Act to Regulatory Compliance Issues in the Health Care Industry*, 51 ALA. L. REV. 105 (1999), Copyright © 1999 University of Alabama; Robert Fabrikant, Glenn E. Solomon. Reprinted with the permission of the Alabama Law Review and the authors.

Stanley Z. Fisher, *In Search of the Virtuous Prosecutor: A Conceptual Framework*, 15 AM. J. CRIM. L. 197 (1988), Copyright © 1988 The University of Texas School of Law. Reprinted with the permission of the American Journal of Criminal Law and the author.

Brent Fisse, *Reconstructing Corporate Criminal Law: Deterrence, Retribution, Fault, and Sanctions*, 56 S. CAL. L. REV. 1141 (1982), Copyright © 1982 by Brent Fisse. Reprinted with the permission of the Southern California Law Review and the author.

Robert J. Giuffra, Jr., *E-Mail: The Prosecutor's New Best Friend*, 10 No. 6 Bus. Crimes Bull. 1 (July 2003) Reproduced with the permission of the publisher. Published by Law Journal Press, a division of ALM. © Copyright ALM Properties, Inc. All rights reserved. Copies of the complete work may be ordered from Law Journal Press, Book Fulfillment Department, 105 Madison Avenue, New York, New York 10016 or at www.lawcatalog.com or by calling 800-537-2128, ext. 9300.

John Stewart Geer, *Representation of Multiple Criminal Defendants: Conflicts of Interests and the Professional Responsibilities of the Defense Attorney*, 62 MINN. L. REV. 119 (1978), Copyright © 1978 by the Minnesota Law Review Foundation. Reprinted with the permission of the University of Minnesota Law School.

Hon. John Gleeson, *Supervising Criminal Investigations: The Proper Scope of the Supervisory Power of Federal Judges*, 5 J.L. & POL'Y 423 (1997), Copyright © 1997 Brooklyn Law School, Brooklyn, New York. Reprinted with the permission of the Journal of Law and Policy and the author.

Jack L. Goldsmith, *The Internet and the Legitimacy of Remote Cross-Border Searches*, 2001 U. CHI. LEGAL F. 103. Reprinted with the permission of the University of Chicago Law School *Legal Forum*.

Howard W. Goldstein, *'Vinyard' Raises Issues Regarding Mail Fraud, Private Employment: Tort or Crime?*, BUSINESS CRIMES BULLETIN 3 (Dec. 2001) Reprinted with the permission of the author. Reproduced with the permission of the publisher. Published by Law Journal Press, a division of ALM. © Copyright ALM Properties, Inc. All rights reserved. Copies of the complete work may be ordered from Law Journal Press, Book Fulfillment Department, 105 Madison Avenue, New York, New York 10016 or at www.lawcatalog.com or by calling 800-537-2128, ext. 9300.

John Hasnas, *Ethics and the Problem of White Collar Crime*, 54 Am. U. L. Rev. 579 (2005), Copyright © 2005 American Univ. Law Review, John Hasnas. Reprinted with permission of the American Univ. Law Review and the author.

Peter Henning, *Defense Discovery in White Collar Criminal Prosecutions*, 15 GA. ST. U. L. REV.

601 (1999), Copyright © 1999 Georgia State University Law Review; Peter J. Henning. Reprinted with the permission of the Georgia State University Law Review and the author.

Graham Hughes, *Agreements for Cooperation in Criminal Cases*, 45 VAND. L. REV. 1, 29-40 (1992), Copyright © 1992 Vanderbilt Law Review, Vanderbilt University School of Law; Graham Hughes. Reprinted with the permission of the Vanderbilt Law Review and the author.

William H. Jeffress, *The New Federal Witness Tampering Statute*, 22 AM. CRIM. L. REV. 1 (1984), Copyright © 1984 by the American Bar Association; William H. Jeffries, Jr. Reprinted with the permission of the American Bar Association and the author.

John Calvin Jeffries, Jr., *Legality, Vagueness, and the Construction of Penal Statutes*, 71 VA. L. REV. 189 (1985), Copyright © 1985 by the Virginia Law Review Association; John Calvin Jeffries, Jr. Reprinted with the permission of the Virginia Law Review Association and the author.

John C. Jeffries, Jr., and Hon. John Gleeson, *The Federalization of Organized Crime: Advantages of Federal Prosecution*, 46 HASTINGS L.J. 1095 (1995), Copyright © 1995 by University of California, Hastings College of the Law; John C. Jeffries, Jr., John Gleeson. Reprinted from Hastings Law Journal Vol. 46, p. 1095, by permission of the publisher and the authors.

Dan M. Kahan, *Ignorance of Law is an Excuse--But Only for the Virtuous*, 96 MICH. L. REV. 127 (1997), Copyright © 1997 Michigan Law Review Association; Dan M. Kahan. Reprinted with the permission of the Michigan Law Review Association and the author.

Dan M. Kahan, *Is* Chevron *Relevant to Federal Criminal Law?*, 110 HARV. L. REV. 469 (1996), Copyright © 1996 Harvard Law Review Association; Dan M. Kahan. Reprinted with the permission of the Harvard Law Review Association and the author.

Neal Kumar Katyal, *Conspiracy Theory*, 112 YALE L.J. 101 (2003). Reprinted by permission of the author and The Yale Journal Company and William S. Hein Company from The Yale Law Journal Vol. 112, pages 101-192.

WAYNE R. LaFAVE, CRIMINAL LAW (West 2000), Copyright © 2000 by West Group. All rights reserved. Reprinted with the permission of the West Group and the author.

DONALD C. LANGEVOORT, INSIDER TRADING: REGULATION, ENFORCEMENT, AND PREVENTION (West Group 1999), Copyright © 1999 by West Group. All Rights Reserved. Reprinted with the permission of the publisher and the author.

Richard J. Lazarus, *Meeting the Demands of Integration in the Evolution of Environmental Law: Reforming Environmental Law*, 83 GEO. L.J. 2407 (1995), Copyright © 1995 by the Georgetown Law Review Association; Richard J. Lazarus. Reprinted with the permission of Georgetown University Law Center and the author.

Laurie L. Levenson, *Good Faith Defenses: Reshaping Strict Liability Crimes*, 78 CORNELL L. REV. 401 (1993), Copyright © 1993 by the Cornell University; Laurie L. Levenson. Reprinted with the permission of the Cornell Law Review and the author.

David Luban, *The Publicity of Law and the Regulatory State*, 10 J. OF POL. PHIL. 296 (2002). Reprinted with the permission of the author and by Blackwell Publishing.

David Luban, The Conscience of a Prosecutor, 46 Val. U. L. Rev. 1 (2010). Reprinted with the permission of the author.

Hon. Gerard E. Lynch, *Our Administrative System of Criminal Justice*, 66 FORDHAM L. REV. 2117 (1998), Copyright © 1998 Fordham Law Review; Gerard E. Lynch. Reprinted with the permission of Fordham Law Review and the author.

Hon. Gerard E. Lynch, *RICO: The Crime of Being Criminal, Parts I & II*, 87 COLUM. L. REV. 661 (1987), Copyright © 1987 by the Directors of The Columbia Law Review Association, Inc.; Gerard E. Lynch. Reprinted with the permission of the Columbia Law Review Association and the author.

Hon. Gerard E. Lynch, *RICO: The Crime of Being Criminal, Parts III & IV*, 87 COLUM. L. REV. 920 (1987), Copyright © 1987 by the Directors of The Columbia Law Review Association, Inc.; Gerard E. Lynch. Reprinted with the permission of the Columbia Law Review Association and the author.

KENNETH MANN, DEFENDING WHITE-COLLAR CRIME: A PORTRAIT OF ATTORNEYS AT WORK (Yale Univ. Press 1985), Copyright © 1985 by Yale University Press. All rights reserved. Reprinted with the permission of the Yale University Press and the author.

Money Laundering: Through the wringer, THE ECONOMIST 64-66 April 14, 2001. © 2001 The Economist Newspaper Ltd. All rights reserved. Reprinted with permission. Further reproduction prohibited. www.economist.com.

Jennifer Moore, *Corporate Culpability Under the Federal Sentencing Guidelines*, 34 ARIZ. L. REV. 743 (1992), Copyright © 1992 by the Arizona Board of Regents; Jennifer Moore. Reprinted with the permission of the author and the Arizona Board of Regents. Reprinted by permission.

Ilene H. Nagel & Winthrop M. Swenson, *The Federal Sentencing Guidelines for Corporations: Their Development, Theoretical Underpinnings, and Some Thoughts About Their Future*, 71 WASH. U. L.Q. 205 (1993), Copyright © 1993 by the Washington University; Ilene H. Nagel and Winthrop M. Swenson. Reprinted with the permission of the Washington University Law Quarterly and the authors.

Julie Rose O'Sullivan, *Extraterritorial Jurisdiction* in 1 Reforming Criminal Justice: Introduction and Criminalization 229 (Erik Luna ed. 2017) by permission of Erik Luna.

Julie Rose O'Sullivan, *Professional Discipline for Law Firms? A Response to Professor Schneyer's Proposal*, 16 GEO. J. LEGAL ETHICS 1 (2002).

Julie R. O'Sullivan, *In Defense of the U.S. Sentencing Guidelines' Modified Real-Offense System*, 91 NW. U. L. REV. 1342 (1997), Copyright © 1997 by Northwestern University, School of Law, Northwestern Law Review. Reprinted with the permission of the Northwestern University School of Law and the author.

Julie R. O'Sullivan, *The Federal Criminal "Code" Is a Disgrace: Obstruction Statutes as Case Study*, 96 J. Crim. L. & Criminology 643 (2006).

Julie R. O'Sullivan, *The Last Straw: DOJ's Privilege Waiver Policy and the Death of Adversarial Justice in Criminal Investigations of Corporations*, 57 DePaul L. Rev. 329 (2008).

Julie R. O'Sullivan, *Does the DOJ's Compelled-Voluntary Privilege Waivers Policy Threaten the Rationales Underlying the Attorney-Client Privilege or the Work Product Doctrine? A Preliminary "No"*, 45 Am. Crim. L. Rev. 1237 (2008).

Ellen S. Podgor, *Criminal Discovery of Jencks Witness Statements: Timing Makes a Difference*, 15 GA. ST. U. L. REV. 651 (1999), Copyright © 1999 Georgia State University Law Review; Ellen S. Podgor. Reprinted with the permission of the Georgia State University Law Review and the author.

Ellen S. Podgor, *International Computer Fraud: A Paradigm for Limiting National Jurisdiction*, 35 U.C. DAVIS L. REV. 267 (2002). This work, copyright 2002 by Ellen S. Podgor, was originally published in 35 U.C. Davis L. Rev. 267 (2002), copyright 2002 by the Regents of the University of California. Reprinted with permission.

Harvey L. Pitt & Karl A. Groskaufmanis, *Minimizing Corporate Civil and Criminal Liability: A Second Look at Corporate Codes of Conduct*, 78 GEO. L.J. 1559 (1990), Copyright © 1990 by the Georgetown Law Journal Association; Harvey L. Pitt and Karl A. Groskaufmanis. Reprinted with the permission of the publisher, Georgetown University and Georgetown Law Journal. © 1990, and the authors.

Hon. Jed Rakoff, *The Federal Mail Fraud Statute (Part I)*, 18 DUQ. L. REV. 771 (1980). Reprinted with the permission of the author.

Daniel C. Richman, *Grand Jury Secrecy: Plugging the Leaks in an Empty Bucket*, 36 AM. CRIM. L. REV. 339 (1999), Copyright © 1999 by the Georgetown University Law Center;

Daniel C. Richman. Reprinted with the permission of the publisher, Georgetown University and American Criminal Law Review © 1999 and the author.

David A. Sklansky, *Starr, Singleton, and the Prosecutor's Role*, 26 FORDHAM URB. L.J. 509 (1999), Copyright © 1999 Fordham University School of Law; David A. Sklansky. Reprinted with the permission of Fordham Law Review and the author.

Hon. Thomas G. Snow, *The Investigation and Prosecution of White Collar Crime: International Challenges and the Legal Tools Available to Address Them*, 11 Wm. & Mary Bill of Rights J. 209 (2002).

William J. Stuntz, *The Uneasy Relationship Between Criminal Procedure and Criminal Justice*, 107 YALE L.J. 1 (1997), Copyright © 1997 Yale Law Journal Company, Inc.; Williams J. Stuntz. Reprinted by permission of The Yale Law Journal Company and Fred B. Rothman & Company from The Yale Law Journal, Vol. 107, pages 1-76, and the author.

Winthrop M. Swenson, *The Organizational Guidelines' "Carrot and Stick" Philosophy, and Their Focus on "Effective" Compliance* 1-3, *reprinted in* U.S. SENTENCING COMMISSION, MATERIALS FOR PROGRAM ON CORPORATE CRIME IN AMERICA: STRENGTHENING THE "GOOD CITIZEN" CORPORATION (Sept. 7, 1995), reprinted with the permission of the U.S. Sentencing Commission and the author.

Hon. Stephen S. Trott, *Words of Warning for Prosecutors Using Criminals as Witnesses*, 47 HASTINGS L.J. 1381 (1996), Copyright © 1996 Hastings College of the Law. Reprinted from 47 Hastings L.J. 1381 (1996), by permission of the publisher and the author.

Richard H. Underwood, *Perjury! The Charges and the Defenses*, 36 DUQ. L. REV. 715 (1998), Copyright © 1998 Duquesne University; Richard H. Underwood. Reprinted with the permission of the Duquesne Law Review and the author.

Ernest L. Ten Eyck & Laureen Ryan, *How Does Financial Statement Fraud Occur? Is Something Rotten in the Accounting Department?*, 1438 PLI/Corp. 9 (July 2004).

James Vorenberg, *Decent Restraints in Prosecutorial Power*, 94 HARV. L. REV. 1521 (1981), Copyright © 1981 by the Harvard Law Review Association; James Vorenberg. Reprinted with the permission of the Harvard Law Review Association and Mrs. Vorenberg.

Gregory J. Wallance, *Can You Represent Both Company & Employees After Receiving Grand Jury Subpoenas?* 6 BUSINESS CRIMES BULLETIN No. 10, at 1 (Nov.1999), Reproduced with the permission of the publisher. Published by Law Journal Press, a division of ALM. © Copyright ALM Properties, Inc. All rights reserved. Copies of the complete work may be ordered from Law Journal Press, Book Fulfillment Department, 105 Madison Avenue, New York, New York 10016 or at www.lawcatalog.com or by calling 800-537-2128, ext. 9300.

Dan K. Webb & Steven F. Molo, *Some Practical Considerations in Developing Effective Compliance Programs: A Framework for Meeting the Requirements of the Sentencing Guidelines*, 71 WASH. U.L. Q. 375 (1993), Copyright © 1993 by the Washington University; Dan K. Webb and Steven F. Molo. Reprinted with the permission of the Washington University Law Quarterly and the authors.

DAN K. WEBB, ROBERT W. TARUN & STEVEN F. MOLO, CORPORATE INTERNAL INVESTIGATIONS (Law Journal Press 2006), Reproduced with the permission of the publisher. Published by Law Journal Press, a division of ALM. © Copyright ALM Properties, Inc. All rights reserved. Copies of the complete work may be ordered from Law Journal Press, Book Fulfillment Department, 105 Madison Avenue, New York, New York 10016 or at www.lawcatalog.com or by at calling 800-537-2128, ext. 9300. Also reprinted with the permission of the authors.

DAVID WEISBURD, STANTON WHEELER, ELIN WARIN & NANCY BODE, CRIMES OF THE MIDDLE CLASSES (Yale Univ. Press 1991), Copyright © 1991 by Yale University

Press. All rights reserved. Reprinted with the permission of the Yale University Press and the authors.

Joe D. Whitley & William H. Jordan, *Computer Crime*, 2 OTTO G. OBERMAIER & ROBERT G. MORVILLO, WHITE COLLAR CRIME: BUSINESS AND REGULATORY OFFENSES (Law Journal Press 2002), Copyright © 1990, 1991, 1992, 1993, 1994, 1995, 1996, 1997, 1998, 1999, 2000 NLP IP Company, Law Journal Press, a division of American Lawyer Media, Inc., New York, New York. Reprinted with the permission of the publisher from Chapter 20, "Computer Crime" by Joe D. Whitley and William H. Jordan as it appears in White Collar Crime: Business and Regulatory Offenses by Otto G. Obermaier and Robert G. Morvillo, published and copyrighted by Law Journal Press. All rights reserved. Future copies of the complete work may be ordered from Law Journal Press, Book Fulfillment, 345 Park Avenue South, New York, New York 10010. Also reprinted with the permission of the authors, Joe D. Whitley and William H. Jordan.

John Shepard Wiley Jr., *Not Guilty by Reason of Blamelessness: Culpability in Federal Criminal Interpretation*, 85 VA. L. REV. 1021 (1999), Copyright © 1999 Virginia Law Review Association; John Shepard Wiley, Jr. Reprinted with the permission of the Virginia Law Review Association and the author.

Dr. Stephan Wilske & Teresa Schiller, Esq., *International Jurisdiction in Cyberspace: Which States May Regulate the Internet?*, 50 FED. COMM. L.J. 117 (1997). Reprinted with the permission of the authors and the original source, the Federal Communications Law Journal. Copyright © 2002 Federal Communications Bar Association.

Jonathan M. Winer, *How to Clean Up Dirty Money*, FINANCIAL TIMES (March 22, 2002). Reprinted with the permission of Jonathan M. Winer, Former U.S. Deputy Assistant Secretary of State for International Law Enforcement, who now practices international regulatory law at Alston & Bird LLP and who can be reached at jwiner@alston.com.

Jonathan M. Winer, *Illicit Finance and Global Conflict*, Programme for International Cooperation and Conflict Resolution Fafo Report 380 (March 2002). Reprinted with the permission of Jonathan M. Winer, Esq., Alston & Bird LLP, jwiner@alston.com. Mr. Winer is a former U.S. Deputy Assistant Secretary of State for International Law Enforcement.

Ellen Yaroshefsky, *Cooperation With Federal Prosecutors: Experiences of Truth Telling and Embellishment*, 68 FORDHAM L. REV. 917 (1999), Copyright © 1999 Fordham Law Review; Ellen Yaroshefsky. Reprinted with the permission of the Fordham Law Review and the author.

Fred C. Zacharias, *Structuring the Ethics of Prosecutorial Trial Practice: Can Prosecutors Do Justice?*, 44 VAND. L. REV. 45 (1991), Copyright © 1991 by the Vanderbilt Law Review, Vanderbilt University School of Law; Fred C. Zacharias. Reprinted with the permission of the Vanderbilt Law Review and the author.

Fred C. Zacharias & Bruce A. Green, *The Uniqueness of Federal Prosecutors*, 88 GEO. L.J. 207 (2000), Copyright © 2000 Georgetown Law Journal Association; Fred C. Zacharias and Bruce A. Green. Reprinted with permission of the authors and the publisher, Georgetown University and Georgetown Law Journal. © 2000.

Bruce Zagaris, *Gatekeepers Initiative Seeking Middle Ground Between Client and Government*, 16 CRIMINAL JUSTICE 26 (Winter 2002). Reprinted with the permission of the author, Bruce Zagaris, a partner at Berliner, Corcoran & Rowe, Washington, D.C.; founder and editor-in-chief of the International Enforcement Law Reporter.

Summary of Contents

PREFACE v

ACKNOWLEDGMENTS vii

Chapter 1. Introduction.. 1
A. Definition: Selecting Statutes for Study in "Substantive" Portion of the Course 3
B. Recurring Themes in Examining "Substantive" Federal Law 6
C. Practice: Selecting "Procedural" Topics Relevant to White-Collar Crime 25
D. Professional Responsibility 37

Chapter 2. Mens Rea... 57
A. The Model Penal Code 58
B. The Public Welfare Doctrine 60
C. Awareness of Legal Requirements 87
D. Other Doctrines and Defenses.. 94

Chapter 3. U.S. Sentencing Guidelines... 107
A. Real- Versus Charge-Offense Sentencing 110
B. Guidelines Structure... 116
C. Constitutional Analysis... 122

Chapter 4. Entity Liability 143
A. Criminalizing Corporate Conduct.. 144
B. Principles of Liability... 155
C. Department of Justice Charging Policies.. 180
D. U.S. Sentencing Guidelines: Organizational Sentencing.................................. 198
E. Deferred Prosecution Agreements.. 211
F. Corporate Internal Investigations... 230
G. Managerial Liability: "Responsible Corporate Officer" Doctrine 240

Chapter 5. Perjury, False Statements, and False Claims 257
A. Perjury.. 257
B. False Statements.. 268
C. False Claims 291
D. Charging Considerations: Double Jeopardy... 311

Chapter 6. Obstruction of Justice **323**
A. The "Omnibus" Clause of 18 U.S.C. § 1503.. 324
B. Obstruction of Proceedings Before Congress and Federal Agencies
    Under 18 U.S.C. § 1505 350
C. Witness Tampering Under 18 U.S.C. § 1512....................................... 352
D. Sarbanes-Oxley Act of 2002 Prohibition of Destruction of Records and Whistleblower
    Provisions: 18 U.S.C. §§ 1519, 1520, 1513, 1514a 366

Chapter 7. Mail and Wire Fraud..**383**
A. The Mailing or Wiring in Furtherance Element.................................. 385
B. Scheme to Defraud Element... 394
C. Permissible Objects of a Scheme to Defraud...................................... 415
D. Mail/Wire Fraud Exercise 462

Chapter 8. Public Corruption...**465**
A. Federal Bribery and Gratuities Under § 201 466
B. Extortion Under Color of Official Right § 1951 (The Hobbs Act)....... 485
C. Federal Program Bribery, Theft, and Fraud Under § 666................... 503
D. The Foreign Corrupt Practices Act... 515

Chapter 9. Securities Fraud..**547**
A. Rationale for Insider Trading Prohibition... 549
B. Traditional Theory... 552
C. Misappropriation Theory.. 558
D. Tipper/Tippee Liability.. 570
E. Securities Fraud Under 18 U.S.C. § 1348 577
F. Accounting Fraud... 578
G. Dodd-Frank Whistleblower Program.. 599

Chapter 10. Conspiracy...**605**
A. Practical Consequences of a Conspiracy Charge................................. 606
B. Elements/Principles of Liability... 610
C. U.S. Sentencing Guidelines: Conspiracy Exercise 638

**Chapter 11. The Racketeer Influences and Corrupt Organizations Act
("RICO")**...**641**
A. Elements/Principles of Liability... 644
B. Prosecutorial Powers and Policies 677
C. U.S. Sentencing Guidelines: RICO Exercise 682

Chapter 12. Money Laundering **683**
A. "Transaction" Offenses Under § 1956(a)(1) and § 1957 686
B. "Transportation" Offenses Under § 1956(a)(2) 699
C. Non-Banking Systems: Challenges for Future?................................... 710
D. Money Laundering: Case Study in Institutional Interaction
    in Sentencing.. 713

Chapter 13. Grand Jury..**717**
A. Grand Jury Function... 718
B. Rules Controlling Grand Jury Operation: Fed. R. Crim. P. 6........... 722
C. Investigative Function.. 729
D. Judicial Policing and Prosecutorial Misconduct 744

Chapter 14. Discovery..**757**
A. "Brady" Material 759
B. Pretrial Discovery: Fed. R. Crim. P. 16...................................... 782
C. Jencks Act or "3500" Material: Witness Statements 788
D. Witness Lists... 790
E. Trial Subpoenas: Fed. R. Crim. P. 17... 791
F. Discovery Hypothetical.. 793

Chapter 15. Fifth Amendment: Testimony and Immunity...............**795**
A. Formal Immunity Pursuant to 18 U.S.C. §§ 6002-05.................... 795
B. Proffers 813
C. Informal Immunity Agreements 823

Chapter 16. Fifth Amendment: Documents and Tangible Objects..............**833**
A. Natural Persons (and Sole Proprietorships) 833
B. What Constitutes "Compulsion".. 835
C. The Continuing Viability of the Collective Entity Doctrine After *Fisher*................. 845
D. What Constitutes a "Testimonial Communication"....................... 849
E. How "Incriminating" Must the Communication Be......................... 854
F. "Act of Production" Immunity: *Fisher* Revisited.......................... 856
G. "Required Records" Exceptions... 864

Chapter 17. The Attorney-Client Privilege and the Work Product Doctrine in a Corporate Setting...........................**871**
A. Qualifying for Protection... 873
B. Losing the Privilege: Waiver 884
C. DOJ's "Compelled-Voluntary" Waiver Policy 905
D. Losing the Privilege: Crime/Fraud Exception 913
E. Privileges of Governmental Actors 920

Chapter 18. Representation Issues..**927**
A. Ethical Rules.. 927
B. "Multiple" or "Joint" Representation.. 930
C. Pre-Indictment Sixth Amendment Protection? *United States v. Stein*.............. 942
D. "Joint Defenses" 956

Chapter 19. Plea Bargaining and Cooperation Agreements...........**975**
A. Plea Bargaining: Constitutional Standards................................. 977
B. Fed. R. Crim. P. 11 and Guidelines Bargaining 998
C. Cooperation Agreements 1010

Chapter 20. Parallel Proceedings..**1035**
A. Constitutionality 1035
B. Fifth Amendment Implications 1040
C. Obtaining a Stay of Civil or Administrative Proceedings.....................1051
D. Obtaining a Protective Order in Civil or Administrative Proceedings....................1052
E. Use of Grand Jury Materials..1058
F. Collateral Estoppel 1061
G. Global Settlements..1063
H. Double Jeopardy and Excessive Fines Provisions 1064

Chapter 21. Extraterritorial Application of Federal Criminal Law...........**1071**
A. Extraterritorial Application of U.S. Criminal Statutes............................1074
B. Transnational Internal Investigations.................................1094
C. Obtaining Evidence Abroad and Extradition.........................1103

INDEX 1133

Table of Contents

PREFACE v

ACKNOWLEDGMENTS.. vii

SUMMARY OF CONTENTS xiii

Chapter 1. Introduction... 1

A. Definition: Selecting Statutes for Study in "Substantive" Portion of the Course 3

B. Recurring Themes in Examining "Substantive" Federal Law 6

    1. Criminalization... 7

        18 U.S.C. § 3553 7

        Richard J. Lazarus, *Meeting the Demands of Integration in the Evolution of Environmental Law: Reforming Environmental Law*, 83 Geo. L.J. 2407, 2441-45 (1995)... 7

    2. Overcriminalization; Federalization; Judicial Role; Prosecutorial Function 9

        Julie R. O'Sullivan, *The Federal Criminal "Code" Is a Disgrace: Obstruction Statutes as Case Study*, 96 J. Crim. L. & Criminology 643 (2006)........................... 9

C. Practice: Selecting "Procedural" Topics Relevant to White-Collar Crime 25

D. Professional Responsibility 37

    1. Prosecutorial Role.. 38

        a. Federal Prosecutors' Duty to "Do Justice"....................................... 39

        b. Applicable Ethical Standards... 42

        c. Case Study.. 43

        David Luban, *The Conscience of a Prosecutor*, 45 Val. U. L. Rev. 1 (2010)............. 43

        Note 55

    2. Defense Challenges 55

        Kenneth Mann, Defending White-Collar Crime: A Portrait of Attorneys at Work 16-17 (Yale Univ. Press 1985)....................... 55

Chapter 2. Mens Rea.. **57**

A. The Model Penal Code.. 58

    Model Penal Code § 2.02. General Requirements of Culpability........................... 58

B. The Public Welfare Doctrine... 60

    United States v. International Minerals & Chemical Corp. 60

    Notes 61

    Staples v. United States 66

    Notes 73

    United States v. Weitzenhoff 79

    Notes 85

C. Awareness of Legal Requirements 87

    Bryan v. United States 87

    Notes 93

D. Other Doctrines and Defenses.. 94

    1. Specific and General Intent.. 94

    2. Good Faith Defense 96

    3. Good Faith Reliance on Counsel Defense... 97

    4. "Willful Blindness," "Conscious Avoidance," or "Ostrich" Instructions 98

Global-Tech Appliances, Inc. v. SEB S.A. 101
Notes 103

Chapter 3. U.S. Sentencing Guidelines **107**
A. Real- versus Charge-Offense Sentencing 110
B. Guidelines Structure 116
C. Constitutional Analysis 122
    United States v. Booker 122
    Notes 133
    Jones v. United States 139
    Notes 140

Chapter 4. Entity Liability **143**
A. Criminalizing Corporate Conduct 144
    Harvey L. Pitt & Karl A. Groskaufmanis, *Minimizing Corporate*
    Civil and Criminal Liability: A Second Look at Corporate Codes of Conduct,
    78 Geo. L.J. 1559, 1562-74 (1990) 144
    Brent Fisse, *Reconstructing Corporate Criminal Law: Deterrence,*
    Retribution, Fault, and Sanctions, 56 S. Cal. L. Rev. 1141, 1145-67 (1982) 146
    Julie Rose O'Sullivan, *Professional Discipline for Law Firms? A Response to*
    Professor Schneyer's Proposal, 16 Geo. J. Legal Ethics 1 (2002) 151
B. Principles of Liability 155
    1. "Within the Scope of Employment" Requirement 155
    New York Central & Hudson River R.R. Co. v. United States 155
    Notes 158
    2. "Intention to Benefit the Corporation" Requirement 161
    United States v. Sun-Diamond Growers of California 162
    Notes 164
    3. Liability Where Criminal Action is Contrary to Corporate
        Policy/Orders 165
    United States v. Hilton Hotels Corp. 165
    Notes 167
    Amicus Brief for the Association of Corporate Counsel, et al. in
    United States v. Ionia Management S.A., 555 F.3d 303 (2d Cir. 2009) 170
    Note 174
    4. Difficulties Where Responsibility Is Defused 174
    United States v. Bank of New England, N.A. 175
    Notes 178
C. Department of Justice Charging Policies 180
    USAM § 9-28.000: Principles of Federal Prosecution
    of Business Organizations 181
    Notes 198
D. U.S. Sentencing Guidelines: Organizational Sentencing 198
    1. Background 198
    2. Key Features 201
        a. Part B—Remedying the Harm From Criminal Conduct—
            Restitution 201
        b. Part C—Fines 201
        c. Part D—Organizational Probation 208
    3. Effective Compliance Program: The *Caremark* Decision 209
E. Deferred Prosecution Agreements 211
    Julie R. O'Sullivan, *How Prosecutors Apply the "Federal Prosecutions of*
    Corporations" Charging Policy in the Era of Deferred Prosecutions, and What

That Means for the Purposes of the Federal Criminal Sanction,
51 Am. Crim. L. Rev. 29 (2014).. 212
Notes... 226
F. Corporate Internal Investigations.. 230
Julie R. O'Sullivan, *The Last Straw: The Department of Justice's Privilege*
Waiver Policy and the Death of Adversarial Justice in Criminal
Investigations of Corporations, 57 DePaul L. Rev. 329 (2008) 230
Julie R. O'Sullivan, *Does DOJ's Privilege Waiver Policy Threaten*
the Rationales Underlying the Attorney-Client Privilege and the
Work Product Doctrine? A Preliminary "No,"
45 Am. Crim. L. Rev. 1237 (2008) 233
Notes... 239
G. Managerial Liability: "Responsible Corporate Officer" Doctrine.............. 240
United States v. Park.. 242
Notes... 248
United States v. Brittain.. 249
United State v. MacDonald & Watson Waste Oil Co. 251
Notes... 254

Chapter 5. Perjury, False Statements, and False Claims........................257
A. Perjury... 257
1. Elements/Principles of Liability.. 258
2. Defenses 259
a. Recantation 259
b. "Literal Truth" and "Ambiguity" 260
Bronston v. United States... 261
Notes... 264
B. False Statements... 268
1. Elements/Principles of Liability.. 269
a. False Statements and Affirmative Concealment of Material Facts.............. 269
b. Materiality.. 271
c. "Jurisdiction" 272
d. The "[E]xecutive, [L]egislative, or [J]udicial [B]ranch" 274
e. *Mens Rea* 279
f. Federalization... 283
United States v. Herring 283
Notes... 285
2. Defenses 286
Brogan v. United States.. 286
Notes... 291
C. False Claims 291
1. Criminal False Claims Cases Under § 287 292
2. Civil False Claims Cases: *Qui Tam* Litigation...................................... 294
a. Practical Issues.. 298
b. Constitutional Questions... 300
Riley v. St. Luke's Episcopal Hospital 301
D. Charging Considerations: Double Jeopardy.. 311
1. Multiple Punishments for the Same Offense 311
United States v. Woodward.. 311
Notes... 313
a. Multiplicity 315
b. Duplicity.. 316
2. Successive Prosecutions for the Same Offense 317
3. Dual Sovereignty 320

Chapter 6. Obstruction of Justice **323**
A. The "Omnibus" Clause of 18 U.S.C. § 1503 324
    United States v. Aguilar 324
    Notes 329
    United States v. Cueto 337
    Notes 344
B. Obstruction of Proceedings Before Congress and Federal Agencies
    Under 18 U.S.C. § 1505 350
C. Witness Tampering Under 18 U.S.C. § 1512 352
    Arthur Andersen LLP v. United States 353
    Notes 358
D. Sarbanes-Oxley Act of 2002 Prohibition of Destruction of Records
    and Whistleblower Provisions: 18 U.S.C. §§ 1519, 1520, 1513, 1514a 366
    Yates v. United States 366
    Notes 374
    Appendix 379

Chapter 7. Mail and Wire Fraud **383**
A. The Mailing or Wiring in Furtherance Element 385
    Schmuck v. United States 385
    Notes 389
B. Scheme to Defraud Element 394
    1. Materiality and Reliance 394
       Neder v. United States 394
       Notes 396
       Bridge v. Phoenix Bond & Indemnity Co. 399
       Notes 402
    2. Intent to Defraud: Intent to Injure? 404
       United States v. Regent Office Supply Co. 404
       Notes 407
    3. Varieties of Fraud 409
       United States v. Siegel 410
       Notes 413
C. Permissible Objects of a Scheme to Defraud 415
    1. Property 416
       McNally v. United States 416
       Notes 422
    2. Intangible Property 425
       Carpenter v. United States 425
       Notes 428
    3. "Honest Services": Section 1346 434
       Julie R. O'Sullivan, *Honest-Services Fraud: A (Vague) Threat to*
       Millions of Blissfully Unaware (and Non-Culpable) American Workers,
       63 Vand. L. Rev. En Banc 23 (2010) 434
       Skilling v. United States 441
       Notes 448
       McDonnell v. United States 453
       Notes 461
D. Mail/Wire Fraud Exercise 462
    United States v. Blackmon 462

Chapter 8. Public Corruption **465**
A. Federal Bribery and Gratuities Under § 201 466

United States v. Sun-Diamond Growers of California 466
Notes 471
United States v. Alfisi 478
Notes 484
B. Extortion Under Color of Official Right § 1951 (The Hobbs Act) 485
Evans v. United States 485
Notes 493
Sekhar v. United States 498
Notes 501
C. Federal Program Bribery, Theft, and Fraud Under § 666 503
Fischer v. United States 504
Notes 509
Sabri v. United States 510
Notes 513
D. The Foreign Corrupt Practices Act 515
United States v. Kay 518
Notes 526
U. S. Attorney's Manual, 9-47.120-FCPA Corporate Enforcement Policy 538
Notes 541

Chapter 9. Securities Fraud **547**
A. Rationale for Insider Trading Prohibition 549
Donald C. Langavoort: Insider Trading: Regulation, Enforcement, and
Prevention § 1:2 to 1:6, at 1-8 to 1-17 (West 2002) 549
B. Traditional Theory 552
Chiarella v. United States 552
Notes 556
C. Misappropriation Theory 558
United States v. O'Hagan 558
Notes 566
D. Tipper/Tippee Liability 570
Salman v. United States 570
Notes 575
E. Securities Fraud Under 18 U.S.C. § 1348 577
F. Accounting Fraud 578
Ernest L. Ten Eyck & Laureen Ryan, How Does Financial Statement
Fraud Occur? Is Something Rotten in the Accounting
Department 1438 PLI/Corp 9 (July 2004) 578
United States v. Ebbers 590
G. Dodd-Frank Whistleblower Program 599
SEC Adopts Rules to Establish Whistleblower Program 601

Chapter 10. Conspiracy **605**
A. Practical Consequences of a Conspiracy Charge 606
1. Fed. R. Evid. 801(d)(2)(E) 606
2. Joinder 607
3. Venue 608
4. Statute of Limitations 609
B. Elements/Principles of Liability 610
1. Defraud and Offense Clauses 610
United States v. Arch Trading Co. 610
Notes 612
2. Agreement 614
a. Plurality 614

United States v. Stevens 614
Notes 616
b. Intent, Impossibility, and Withdrawal 618
United States v. Recio 618
Notes 619
c. Defining the "Essential Nature" of the Agreement 620
United States v. Stavroulakis 620
Notes 623
3. Defining the Scope of the Conspiracy 624
United States v. Gatling 624
Notes 628
4. Overt Acts 630
5. *Pinkerton* Liability 631
Pinkerton v. United States 631
Notes 634
Rosemond v. United States 635
C. U.S. Sentencing Guidelines: Conspiracy Exercise 638

Chapter 11. The Racketeer Influenced and Corrupt Organizations Act ("RICO") **641**
A. Elements/Principles of Liability 644
1. Enterprise 644
United States v. Turkette 644
Notes 647
Cedric Kushner Promotions, Ltd. v. King 649
Notes 652
2. Pattern of Racketeering Activity 656
H.J. Inc. v. Northwestern Bell Tel. Co. 656
Notes 660
3. Conduct of Enterprise's Affairs 662
Reves v. Ernst & Young 662
Notes 664
4. RICO Conspiracy 668
United States v. Elliot 668
Notes 672
Salinas v. United States 675
B. Prosecutorial Powers and Policies 677
1. Charging and Evidentiary Considerations 677
2. Criminal Forfeiture 678
3. DOJ Approval Requirements and Charging Directions 680
C. U.S. Sentencing Guidelines: RICO Exercise 682

Chapter 12. Money Laundering **683**
A. "Transaction" Offenses Under § 1956(a)(1) and § 1957 686
1. "Concealment" Offense Under § 1956(a)(1)(B)(i) 686
United States v. Campbell 686
Notes 690
B. "Transportation" Offenses Under § 1956(a)(2) 699
1. "Promotion" Offense Under § 1956(a)(2)(A) 699
United States v. Piervinanzi 699
Notes 705
C. Non-Banking Systems: Challenges for Future? 710
Hawala and Underground Terrorist Financing Mechanisms,
Prepared Statement of Mr. Patrick Jost, SRA International,

U.S. Senate Committee on Banking, Housing, and Urban Affairs,
Subcommittee on International Trade and Finance (Nov. 14, 2001) 710
Note 713
D. Money Laundering: Case Study in Institutional Interaction
In Sentencing 713

Chapter 13. Grand Jury **717**
A. Grand Jury Function 718
Daniel C. Richman, *Grand Jury Secrecy: Plugging the Leaks in an Empty Bucket*,
36 Am. Crim. L. Rev. 339 (1999) 721
B. Rules Controlling Grand Jury Operation: Fed. R. Crim. P. 6 722
1. "Disclosure" of Grand Jury Materials 723
2. "Matters Occurring Before the Grand Jury" 724
In re Sealed Case No. 99-3091 (Office of Independent Counsel Contempt Proceeding) 724
Notes 727
3. Enforcement of Rule 6(e)(2) Secrecy Rules 728
4. Supplementation of Rule 6(e)(2) Secrecy Rules 729
C. Investigative Function 729
1. Rules Applicable to Witnesses 730
Notes 732
2. Rules Applicable to Documents/Tangible Objects 734
United States v. R. Enterprises, Inc. 734
Notes 737
Robert J. Giuffra, Jr., *E-Mail: The Prosecutor's New Best Friend*, 10 Bus. Crimes
Bull. 1 (July 2003) 737
Notes 739
3. Evidentiary Rules 742
Notes 743
D. Judicial Policing and Prosecutorial Misconduct 744
Bank of Nova Scotia v. United States 744
Notes 748
United States v. Williams 749
Notes 755

Chapter 14. Discovery **757**
A. "Brady" Material 759
Brady v. Maryland 759
United States v. Bagley 759
Notes 767
United States v. Ruiz 778
Notes 781
B. Pretrial Discovery: Fed. R. Crim. P. 16 782
Notes 783
C. Jencks Act or "3500" Material: Witness Statements 788
D. Witness Lists 790
E. Trial Subpoenas: Fed. R. Crim. P. 17 791
F. Discovery Hypothetical 793

Chapter 15. Fifth Amendment: Testimony and Immunity **795**
A. Formal Immunity Pursuant to 18 U.S.C. §§ 6002-05 795
1. Constitutional Standards 795
Kastigar v. United States 795
Notes 801

Hon. Stephen S. Trott, *Words of Warning for Prosecutors Using Criminals as Witnesses*, 47 Hastings L. J. 1381 (1996) 808
    2. Defense Witness Immunity 810
B. Proffers 813
    1. Rationale 813
    2. Fed. R. Crim. P. 11(f) and Fed. R. Evid. 410 816
    3. Sample Proffer Agreement 816
    Notes 817
    United States v. Velez 818
    Notes 822
C. Informal Immunity Agreements 823
    1. DOJ Policy 824
    Notes 828
    2. Sample Agreement 829
    Notes 830

Chapter 16. Fifth Amendment: Documents and Tangible Objects **833**
A. Natural Persons (and Sole Proprietorships) 833
B. What Constitutes "Compulsion" 835
    Fisher v. United States 837
    Notes 842
C. The Continuing Viability of the Collective Entity Doctrine After *Fisher* 845
    Braswell v. United States 845
    Notes 847
D. What Constitutes a "Testimonial Communication" 849
    Doe v. United States 849
    Notes 854
E. How "Incriminating" Must the Communication Be 854
    Hoffman v. United States 854
    Notes 856
F. "Act of Production" Immunity: *Fisher* Revisited 856
    United States v. Hubbell 856
    Notes 861
G. "Required Records" Exception 864
    United States v. Chabot 864
    Note 869

Chapter 17. The Attorney-Client Privilege and the Work Product Doctrine in a Corporate Setting **871**
A. Qualifying for Protection 873
    Upjohn Co. v. United States 873
    Notes 878
B. Losing the Privilege: Waiver 884
    1. Who May Waive? 885
    2. Fed. R. Evid. 502 888
    Notes 890
    3. Inadvertent Waiver 891
    Note 893
    4. Partial Waiver 893
    Note 896
    5. Selective Waiver 897
    6. Court Orders and Confidentiality Agreements 899
    Notes 900
    7. Individuals' Attempts to Claim the Corporate Privilege 902

8. *Upjohn* Warning......903
C. DOJ's "Compelled-Voluntary" Waiver Policy......905
Julie R. O'Sullivan, *The Last Straw: Department of Justice's Privilege Waiver Policy and the Death of Adversarial Justice in Criminal Investigations of Corporations,* 57 DePaul L. Rev. 329 (2008) 909
D. Losing the Privilege: Crime/Fraud Exception 913
In re Sealed Case 913
Notes......916
E. Privileges of Governmental Actors......920
In re Grand Jury Investigation 920
Notes......924

Chapter 18. Representation Issues......**927**
A. Ethical Rules......927
B. "Multiple" or "Joint" Representation......930
1. Constitutional Issue......930
Wheat v. United States 930
Notes......936
2. Multiple Representation Decisions in the Corporate Context......938
Gregory J. Wallance, *Can You Represent Both Company and Employee After Receiving Grand Jury Subpoenas?* 6 Bus. Crimes Bull. 1, 5-6 (Nov. 1999)......939
Note 941
C. Pre-Indictment Sixth Amendment Protection? *United States v. Stein*......942
United States v. Stein......943
Notes......954
D. "Joint Defenses" 956
Ethical Implications of Joint Defense/Common Interest Agreements, Committee on Professional Responsibility of the Association of the Bar of the City of New York (1996) 957
Notes......965
In re Grand Jury Subpoena et al.......967
Note 974

Chapter 19. Plea Bargaining and Cooperation Agreements **975**
A. Plea Bargaining: Constitutional Standards......977
Brady v. United States 977
Notes......979
Bordenkircher v. Hayes......985
Notes......987
Ricketts v. Adamson 990
Notes......992
B. Fed. R. Crim. P. 11 and Guidelines Bargaining 998
1. Fed. R. Crim. P. 11......998
2. Guidelines Bargaining......1001
a. Acceptance of Responsibility 1004
b. Charge Bargaining......1004
c. Guidelines "Fact" or "Factor" Bargaining......1007
d. Sentence Bargaining 1008
e. Enforcement 1009
C. Cooperation Agreements 1010
1. Policy Discussion: *United States v. Singleton*......1010
2. U.S.S.G. 5K1.1 1017
3. Sample Agreement......1022

Notes 1033

Chapter 20. Parallel Proceedings **1035**
A. Constitutionality 1035
    United States v. Mahaffy 1037
B. Fifth Amendment Implications 1040
    1. Waiver 1040
    2. Adverse Inference and Other "Penalties" 1043
    LaSalle Bank Lake View v. Seguban 1044
    Notes 1048
C. Obtaining a Stay of Civil or Administrative Proceedings 1051
D. Obtaining a Protective Order in Civil or Administrative Proceedings 1052
    In re Grand Jury Subpoena Served on Meserve, Mumper & Hughes 1052
    Notes 1056
E. Use of Grand Jury Materials 1058
    Douglas Oil Co. of California v. Petrol Stops Northwest 1059
    Notes 1060
F. Collateral Estoppel 1061
G. Global Settlements 1063
H. Double Jeopardy and Excessive Fines Provisions 1064

Chapter 21. Extraterritorial Application of Federal Criminal Law **1071**
A. Extraterritorial Application of U.S. Criminal Statutes 1074
    1. Recent Supreme Court Extraterritoriality Cases 1074
    2. Extraterritoriality in Criminal Cases 1079
    Julie Rose O'Sullivan, *Extraterritorial Criminal Jurisdiction*, 1 Reforming
    Criminal Justice: Introduction and Criminalization 229
    (Erik Luna ed. 2017) 1079
    Notes 1091
B. Transnational Internal Investigations 1094
    Lucian E. Dervan, *International White Collar Crime and The*
    Globalization of Internal Investigations, 39 Fordham Urb. L.J. 361 (2011) 1094
    Notes 1101
C. Obtaining Evidence Abroad and Extradition 1103
    1. The Prosecution 1103
    Hon. Thomas G. Snow, *The Investigation and Prosecution of White*
    Collar Crime: International Challenges and the Legal Tools Available
    to Address Them, 11 Wm. & Mary Bill of Rights J. 209 (2002) 1103
    United States v. Allen 1116
    Notes 1121
    2. The Defense 1123
        a. Domestic Criminal Process: Fed. R. Crim. P. 17 Subpoena Power 1124
        b. Letters Rogatory 1125
        c. Deposition to Preserve Evidence under Fed. R. Crim. P. 15 1127
        d. Fifth and Sixth Amendment Objections/Arguments? 1128
        e. Extradition 1130

INDEX 1133

FEDERAL WHITE COLLAR CRIME

CASES AND MATERIALS

Seventh Edition

Chapter 1

INTRODUCTION

Why should one study federal white-collar crime? Federal criminal cases, though increasing in volume,[1] represent a small percentage of the total number of criminal actions pursued in the United States, and drug and immigration prosecutions, not white-collar cases, presently dominate the federal docket. Why, then, should students' scarce time be devoted to the study of federal white-collar crime? A number of factors make this subject worthy—practically and pedagogically.

Because of federal criminal law's high "visibility, geographic spread and symbolic value, it can be argued that federal enforcement operations comprise the single most important criminal enforcement system in the country."[2] White-collar criminal enforcement is particularly vital given the national toll such crimes exact. The most obvious harm flowing from white-collar crime is financial: most estimates indicate that the dollar loss attributable to white-collar crime dwarfs the monetary harms caused by all other types of offenses combined.[3] Dollars, however, do not begin to measure the total impact of this type of criminal conduct. Many white-collar offenses, such as environmental crimes, also threaten the physical well-being of individuals and the public generally. Finally, the "financial loss from white collar crime, great as it is, is less important than the danger to social relations. White collar crimes violate trust and therefore create distrust, and this lowers social morale and produces social disorganization on a large scale."[4] In the words of former FBI Director William Webster, "[w]hite-collar crime strikes at the very fiber of our society by undermining trust and confidence in our political, governmental, and financial systems."[5] Recent white-collar

---

[1] *See, e.g.*, Sara Sun Beale, *The Many Faces of Overcriminalization: From Morals and Mattress Tags to Overfederalization*, 54 A.U. L. Rev. 747, 755 (2005) (noting that between 1980 and 2003 "the number of cases and defendants in the federal system had more than doubled, with the number of criminal cases increasing 240% and the number of criminal defendants increasing 230%").

[2] Norman Abrams & Sara Sun Beale, Federal Criminal Law 2 (2d ed. 1993).

[3] "The true extent and expense of white-collar crime are unknown," in part because of data collection and compilation difficulties. Cynthia Barnett, U.S. Dep't of Justice, FBI CJIS Division, *The Measurement of White-Collar Crime Using Uniform Crime Reporting (UCR) Data*, at http://www.fbi.gov/ucr/whitecollarforweb.pdf; *see also* Sally S. Simpson, Making Sense of White-Collar Crime: Theory and Research, 8 Ohio St. L.J. 481 (2011). Many white-collar crimes are also not reported. *See, e.g.*, James William Coleman, The Criminal Elite: Understanding White Collar Crime 9 (5th ed.).

[4] Edwin H. Sutherland, White Collar Crime: The Uncut Version 9 (1983).

[5] William H. Webster, *An Examination of FBI Theory and Methodology Regarding White-Collar Crime Investigation and Prevention*, 17 Am. Crim. L. Rev. 279 (1980).

sentencing practices reflect the seriousness of the harms posed. "Particularly in the last several years, it has become common for a federal district court judge to impose a sentence of imprisonment on a white collar offender that is measured in double-digit years, and not infrequently in decades."[6]

Adopting a unified—in this case, federal—frame of reference facilitates an evaluation of the virtues and vices of a system of criminal justice working as a whole; seeing how the parts interact should provide a better perspective in evaluating those parts singly and together. For example, given that approximately 95% of defendants in federal cases plead guilty, and given the circumstances that enhance prosecutors' power to force a plea, students may conclude that defendants should be given more "process" prior to the plea in order to ensure just results. With that in mind, students may come to question the factors that lend prosecutors such enormous power, the judicial precedents declining to review most prosecutorial charging choices, the paucity of pre-trial discovery made available to defense counsel, and the degree to which the grand jury is capable of fulfilling its historic role as an independent body standing between the defendant and the government.

It should also be remembered that most of the issues raised and examined within are not unique to federal practice (or even to litigation; corporate practitioners would be well advised to internalize many of the lessons contained within). Were one to prosecute or defend state law white-collar cases one would encounter many of the same problems. Thus, even where the rules applicable to state practice differ from those applicable in the federal sphere, much can be learned by exploring the legal and policy implications of those problems. In this sense, despite the fact that this book covers only federal law while general criminal law casebooks might reference the law of various jurisdictions, the books' missions are the same. It also may be that those interested in state white-collar practice, which is extensive, will find that the applicable legal rules are not in fact very different. Federal statutes, practices, and precedents often serve as models for state actors. This trend may continue and perhaps intensify as Congress and prosecutors "federalize" much of traditionally state law practice and as the resources committed to federal law enforcement continue to escalate.[7]

---

[6] Samuel W. Buell, *Is the White Collar Offender Privileged?*, 63 Duke L.J. 823 (2014); *see also* United States v. Okum, 453 Fed. Appx. 364 (4th Cir. 2011) (per curiam) (affirming 100 year sentence for "Ponziesque" scheme resulting in losses exceeding $125 million).

[7] As the ABA reported:

> ... Empirical data verifies a growing federal presence in the criminal justice system. Although part of this growth may be explained by greater societal attention to crime, the increase in federal expenditures is disproportionately greater than comparable increases in state criminal justice costs, indicating that at least some part of federal growth is attributable to an expanding federal role. For example, between 1982 and 1993, overall federal justice system expenditures increased at twice the rate of comparable state and local expenditures, increasing 317% as compared to 163%. The number of federal justice system personnel increased by 96% from 1982 to 1993, while state personnel increased at a significantly lesser rate, 42%. Over a twelve year period, the number of federal prison inmates rose by 177%, as compared to a lower increase in state prison inmates, 134%. Putting aside personnel at the Department of Justice headquarters in Washington, the regional U.S. Attorneys' Offices (which litigate the bulk of federal criminal cases) have grown in just the past 30 years from approximately 3,000 prosecutors to about 8,000.

Task Force on Federalization of Criminal Law, American Bar Association Criminal Justice Section, The Federalization of Criminal Law 13-14 (1998).

Finally, by concentrating on a subset of criminal prosecutions in a particular jurisdiction, students may come away with a better a sense of the type of skills and thinking that make for a successful practitioner—in any area of specialization. The intent underlying the selection of the subjects covered is, in part, to illustrate for students how various policy, practical, and legal considerations interact and build upon one another. For example, as the chapters slip by, students should be able to inventory and perhaps prioritize the myriad considerations that affect prosecutors' charging choices—from evaluations of the defendant's relative dangerousness and culpability, to the elements of substantive crimes, to double jeopardy, joinder, venue, and like rules, to evidentiary imperatives, to instrumental needs, to conclusions regarding jury appeal and sentencing considerations. Similarly, after studying such subjects as privilege and representation issues in the corporate context, parallel proceedings, and the sentencing guidelines, students should be able to appreciate the judgment calls and stakes facing defense counsel in the course of conducting internal corporate investigations.

These materials should bring home to students the fact that "spotting" issues, finding applicable law, and writing intelligibly are necessary but by no means sufficient skills for safeguarding clients' interests. Further, students should come to recognize that there oftentimes are no clearly "right" answers to the thornier problems confronting counsel. Recognizing this, these materials are intended to challenge students to think strategically, to hone their advocacy skills, to internalize ethical standards, and to begin to develop the judgment that is ultimately the hallmark of the excellent lawyer.

This book is divided roughly between materials relevant to the study of statutes under which white-collar defendants may be prosecuted and other issues relevant to "substantive" criminal law (Chapters 2-12) and "procedural" issues of importance in this practice area (Chapters 13-21). In Part A, below, I will attempt to define "white-collar crime" for purposes of explaining my choice of the federal criminal statutes included in this casebook. I then explore, in Part B below, some of the recurring themes that will arise in the study of these substantive provisions. Part C, *infra*, describes white-collar practice, and how its attributes differ from other types of criminal investigations and prosecutions, so that readers may understand why certain "procedural" questions of interest were identified for coverage in this volume. Finally, in Part D, we begin to examine questions of professional responsibility—with respect to both the prosecution and the defense functions—to provide background for later explorations of the ethical issues that arise in white-collar practice.

A. DEFINITION: SELECTING STATUTES FOR STUDY IN "SUBSTANTIVE" PORTION OF THE COURSE

What *is* "white-collar crime"? This casebook is more concerned with educating students regarding the challenges faced in a certain type of criminal practice than with arriving at a rigorous definition of "white-collar crime" suitable for use in criminologists' or empiricists' work. Even with such a forgiving mandate, it is necessary to formulate some rough description of the practice to be examined. In consulting the work of academics and researchers, one learns that:

[a]n examination of the various definitions of "white collar crime" and their actual usage in the literature yields fundamental inconsistencies and incompatibilities. It is unclear whether the term characterizes acts or actors, types of offenses or types of offenders; or whether it refers to the social location of deviant behavior, the social role or social status of the actor, the modus operandi of the behavior, or the social relationship of victim and offender. There are frequent disputes over whether the

phenomenon is necessarily "white collar," and even more serious disagreement over whether the behavior is criminal. In this respect, the label is clearly a misnomer.[8]

There also appears to be no single definition used in the practice community. The greatest consensus seems to relate to the core federal crimes involved in white-collar prosecutions (*e.g.*, false statements, false claims, mail and wire fraud, conspiracy, Racketeer Influenced and Corrupt Organizations Act (RICO) and tax violations, securities fraud, tax and antitrust offenses, many environmental and money laundering offenses, Foreign Corrupt Practices Act violations, perjury, many types of obstruction, bribery and gratuity offenses, and non-forcible extortion) and to certain attributes of the actual practice, described further within.

The imprecision of the term in actual practice may relate to the fact that "white-collar crime" originally was a construct generated by social scientists, not a term created by lawyers to describe a certain category of crime.[9] Noted sociologist Edwin H. Sutherland coined the term "white-collar crime" more than sixty years ago to attack the dominant criminological theories of the day that stressed poverty and social disorganization as the primary roots of crime. His detailed documentation of corporate violations was intended to demonstrate that "healthy upbringings and intact psyches had not served to deter monstrous amounts of lawbreaking by persons in positions of power."[10] Consistent with this purpose, Sutherland defined "white-collar" crime as wrongdoing (whether or not technically a crime) "committed by a person of respectability and high social status in the course of his occupation."[11]

During the early 1970s white-collar crimes became the focus of great public attention, and federal authorities responded in part by devoting increased resources to this area of enforcement. In this period, the U.S. Department of Justice undertook to translate Sutherland's sociological concept into a legal one. Not surprisingly given its mission, the Justice Department did not share Sutherland's willingness to identify types of corporate wrongdoing as crimes even when they were not proscribed by criminal statute. It also rejected Sutherland's emphasis on status, occupation, and organization. The Department chose instead to focus on the nature of the (clearly) criminal activity involved when defining "white-collar crime." As then Deputy Attorney General Benjamin Civiletti explained in testimony before Congress:

> Th[e] traditional academic approach does not accurately reflect the type of offenses and offenders encountered by the criminal justice system. Our experience has demonstrated that white-collar offenses are regularly committed by members of all social classes and are not the exclusive domain of the rich and powerful. ... The traditional approach was further rejected because it implicitly raises the specter of

---

[8]Susan P. Shapiro, U.S. Dep't of Justice, Thinking About White Collar Crime: Matters of Conceptualization and Research 1 (1980). For comprehensive analyses of extant definitions, see Samuel W. Buell, "White Collar Crimes," in The Oxford Handbook of Criminal Law (Markus D. Dubber & Tatjana Hornle eds. 2014); Gerard Cliff & Christian Desilets, *White Collar Crime: What It Is and Where It's Going*, 28 Notre Dame J. L. Ethics & Pub. Pol'y, 481 (2014); Stuart P. Green, *The Concept of White Collar Crime in Law and Legal Theory*, 8 Buff. L. Rev. 1 (2004); J. Kelly Strader, *The Judicial Politics of White Collar* Crime, 50 Hastings L.J. 1199, 1204-11 (1998-99); David T. Johnson & Richard A. Leo, *The Yale White-Collar Crime Project: A Review and Critique*, 17 Law & Soc. Inquiry 63 (1993).

[9] *See, e.g.*, Shapiro, *supra* note 8, at 1; David Weisburd, Stanton Wheeler, Elin Warin & Nancy Bode, Crimes of the Middle Classes 3 (Yale Univ. Press 1991).

[10] Gilbert Geis & Colin Goff, *Introduction* to Edwin H. Sutherland, White Collar Crime: The Uncut Version at ix (1983).

[11] Sutherland, *supra* note 4, at 5.

large enforcement agencies targeting whole segments of society for special enforcement emphasis.[12]

An additional reason for reexamining the Sutherland focus is that "[w]hen Sutherland was writing, white-collar work was uniformly high-status work. Today, because of the explosive growth of low-status clerical and technical jobs in American society, white-collar work is no longer synonymous with high social standing and financial success."[13] Given the evolution of workplace demographics, a focus on social status, class, occupation, or even rank in an organization seems misplaced if one is attempting to describe the white-collar practice that most practitioners would recognize.

Accordingly, I adopt the Justice Department's focus on the type of activity involved and see no harm in employing the fairly amorphous working definition of white-collar crime the Department formulated in 1977: "White-collar offenses shall constitute those classes of non-violent illegal activities which principally involve traditional notions of deceit, deception, concealment, manipulation, breach of trust, subterfuge or illegal circumvention."[14]

Recognizing that this definition does not exactly paint a vivid picture of the types of cases students may expect to see in white-collar practice, perhaps some further explication is appropriate. Most obviously, white-collar crime does not include organized crime or "street crimes" (defined to include drug, immigration, and gun violations, forcible extortion, terrorism, murder, rape, burglary, robbery, and commonplace thefts or penny-ante frauds). As a definitional matter, white-collar crime is non-violent in the sense that physical coercion is not used as a means of committing the crime, but it is important to note that the consequences of white-collar crimes such as environmental and Food, Drug and Cosmetic Act violations may well threaten public health and safety. Although the broadest definitions would include virtually any non-violent crime in which some element of deception is present, it is also worth stressing that the overwhelming majority of white-collar crimes will be motivated, directly or indirectly, by a desire for monetary gain or professional advancement.[15]

Although the lines may blur, for example in cases involving the activities of professional con men, the laundering of drug money, or economic crimes perpetrated by organized crime groups, the bulk of white-collar crime generally can be described as non-violent, largely financial, commercial, or business crime (primarily frauds, swindles,

---

[12] Tony G. Poveda, *White-Collar Crime and the Justice Department: The Institutionalization of a Concept*, 17 Crime L. & Soc. Change 235, 242 (1992) (quoting Hearings on White-Collar Crime Before the Subcomm. on Crime of the House Comm. on the Judiciary, 95th Cong. 65 (1979)); *see also* Weisburd, *et al.*, *supra* note 9, at 53-54.

[13] Weisburd, *et al.*, *supra* note 9, at 53-54 (footnote omitted).

[14] Poveda, *supra* note 12, 241 (quoting U.S. Dep't of Justice, National Priorities for White-Collar Crime 5 (1977)).

[15] In this regard, the definition of white-collar crime offered by Herbert Edelhertz has descriptive resonance: in his view, white-collar crime is "an illegal act or series of illegal acts committed by nonphysical means and by concealment or guile, to obtain money or property, or to obtain business or personal advantage." Herbert Edelhertz, U.S. Dep't of Justice, The Nature, Impact and Prosecution of White-Collar Crime 3 (May 1970) (emphasis omitted); *see also* U.S. Dep't of Justice, Dictionary of Criminal Justice Data Terminology 215 (2d ed. 1981) ("Nonviolent crime for financial gain committed by means of deception by persons whose occupational status is entrepreneurial, professional or semi-professional and utilizing their special occupational skills and opportunities; also, nonviolent crime for financial gain utilizing deception and committed by anyone having special technical and professional knowledge of business and government, irrespective of the person's occupation."). There are, of course, exceptions to this generalization. For example, computer crimes (such as hacking) may be committed to demonstrate a defendant's prowess with a keyboard or to inflict harm on persons with whom the defendant has a grievance.

embezzlements, and paper thefts) that is not perpetrated by professional criminals. Further, though it is not a requisite, many significant white-collar cases contain elements that harken back to Sutherland's focus. Thus, it will often be the case that "white collar violations … involve the use of a violator's position of significant power, influence, or trust in the legitimate … order for the purpose of illegal gain, or to commit an illegal act for personal or organizational gain."[16] Certainly one large segment of the white-collar practice—political corruption cases—falls into this important category.

The Department of Justice's definition's emphasis on deception and concealment is also worth stressing. A great many white-collar cases involve attempts to deceive the government about a range of matters including compliance with regulatory requirements, entitlement to government jobs, privileges, or program benefits, and monies owed to or by the government. Actionable deceit may be addressed to private persons, as well as governmental actors, for example in matters dealing with telemarketing, credit card, computer, real estate, financial, and many other types of fraud.

A final category of cases concern individuals' attempts to evade or obstruct justice through a variety of (for our purposes) non-coercive means, such as lies to investigators, destruction of documents, perjury in official proceedings, and attempts to compromise the evidence in others' possession.

With this general conception in mind, I selected for study in the "substantive law" portion of these materials offenses that clearly fall within the rubric of white-collar practice. The offenses included obviously do not exhaust the possibilities. For a number of reasons I omitted two obvious but fairly specialized white-collar candidates, antitrust and tax offenses. Studying the offenses selected should be helpful in the "real world" because of the frequency of the statutes' use in federal prosecutions. At the same time, the choice of these statutes was intended to allow readers to examine a variety of theoretical and practical issues worthy of consideration. To ensure that students have access to the most current versions of the statutes studied, as well as to ease the burden on their pocketbooks, I will be posting edited versions of relevant code provisions on the website for this text, which can be found at http://www.federalwhitecollarcrime.org. (NB: that is ".org" *not* ".com").

B. RECURRING THEMES IN EXAMINING "SUBSTANTIVE" FEDERAL LAW

Particularly in examining the "substantive" portion of the class materials, readers should be aware of certain recurring themes as to which more background, provided in the following subsections, may be helpful: (1) criminalization (*i.e.*, where should the line be drawn between criminal and tortious (or simply immoral) conduct?); (2) federalization (*i.e.*, if one is satisfied that the conduct at issue should be pursued criminally, what principles should control the allocation of cases between federal and state enforcement authorities?); (3) judicial role (*i.e.*, where the content of the criminal prohibition at issue is uncertain, how should courts respond?); and (4) prosecutorial discretion (*i.e.*, what is the value of prosecutorial discretion and how should it be exercised or, where necessary, constrained?). The following readings are designed to give readers some context regarding the foundations of these "themes."

---

[16] A. Reiss & A. Biderman, U.S. Dep't of Justice, Data Sources on White Collar Law Breaking 4 (1980).

1. CRIMINALIZATION

Throughout the course, the reader should be asking: "Should this be pursued criminally?" For future prosecutors, this question should be arising with some frequency given the breadth of prosecutors' enforcement discretion. In thinking about this issue, consider the following section of the United States Code that sets forth Congress's definition of the purposes of federal criminal punishment and a summary by Professor Richard Lazarus of some of the core distinctions between criminal and civil law.

18 U.S.C. § 3553

The court shall impose a sentence sufficient, but not greater than necessary, to comply with the purposes set forth in paragraph **(2)** of this subsection. The court, in determining the particular sentence to be imposed, shall consider—

...

  (2) the need for the sentence imposed—

    (A) to reflect the seriousness of the offense, to promote respect for the law, and to provide just punishment for the offense;

    (B) to afford adequate deterrence to criminal conduct;

    (C) to protect the public from further crimes of the defendant; and

    (D) to provide the defendant with needed educational or vocational training, medical care, or other correctional treatment in the most effective manner.[17]

* * *

Richard J. Lazarus, *Meeting the Demands of Integration in the Evolution of Environmental Law: Reforming Environmental Law*
83 Geo. L.J. 2407, 2441-45 (1995)

At some level of abstraction there may be "no distinction better known, than the distinction between civil and criminal law," but in practice the precise dividing line between the two has become increasingly blurred. Civil sanctions seem more and more like criminal sanctions in their severity and harshness. Moreover, at the federal level, Congress has virtually criminalized civil law by making criminal sanctions available for violations of otherwise civil federal regulatory programs. An estimated 300,000 federal regulations are now subject to criminal enforcement.

Notwithstanding this modern blurring of civil and criminal law, criminal law retains certain distinguishing core features. The most significant is its sanction, from which most of criminal law's other features flow. Criminal sanctions are no longer unique simply because their purpose is to punish; civil sanctions have long included a punitive dimension (e.g., punitive damages in tort law), which has dramatically increased with the inclusion of civil penalty provisions (e.g., civil fines) in most federal regulatory programs. Criminal law's uniqueness instead derives from its invocation of society's harshest sanctions, including the loss of liberty that results from incarceration, death, and the moral stigma associated with a criminal conviction. The long-term effect of this stigma on an individual can be the most severe. In fact, when applied to corporate entities that

---

[17]*But see* 28 U.S.C. § 994(k) ("The [Sentencing] Commission shall insure that the guidelines reflect the inappropriateness of imposing a sentence to a term of imprisonment for the purpose of rehabilitating the defendant or providing the defendant with needed educational or vocational training, medical care, or other correctional treatment."); 18 U.S.C. §3582(a); Tapia v. United States, 564 U.S. 319 (2011) ("Section 3582(a) precludes sentencing courts from imposing or lengthening a prison term to promote an offender's rehabilitation.").

cannot be incarcerated, stigma can be the only meaningful justification for the choice of criminal prosecution rather than the less socially burdensome option of civil enforcement.

Virtually all of criminal law's distinguishing features derive from the need to identify the circumstances that justify the use of criminal sanctions. Such justification entails both carefully defining the human behavior warranting the sanction, as well as attaching procedural safeguards to the criminal proceeding to ensure a fair and accurate adjudication of culpability. Moreover, because moral stigma is one of a criminal conviction's essential features, such careful definitions and procedural safeguards are critical to the viability of the sanction. For the moral stigma of the criminal sanction will attach in the long term only if the public is persuaded both of the moral culpability of the proscribed conduct and of the reliability of the adjudication of the defendant's guilt. In this respect, the criminal law exhibits unavoidable circularity: criminality turns on morality, yet morality may itself turn on criminality. Hence, one of the features that makes criminal law unique—the moral stigma associated with a criminal conviction—is not self-executing. It can be lost over time by overreaching.

The defendant's "moral culpability" is the feature most frequently invoked to justify the severe sanctions of criminal law. What makes conduct more or less morally culpable turns, in the first instance, on the actor's state of mind. The more culpable the state of mind, the harsher the corresponding punishment ought to be. Culpability in this context turns on the defendant's purpose, the extent of the defendant's knowledge of the circumstances surrounding her conduct, the conduct itself, its results, and the reasons for the defendant's behavior.

Other major factors contributing to moral culpability include the nature of the conduct at stake, as well as the kind and amount of resulting harm (either created or threatened). A morally culpable state of mind alone is generally not considered sufficient to warrant criminal sanction; there must be some action (or inaction) in conjunction with that state of mind. There also usually needs to be some concrete harm with a public dimension that is realized or threatened as a direct result of the action. Criminal misconduct is a crime against society; it is not just a private wrong.

Because of these prerequisites, criminal law is more appropriate for redressing violations of absolute duties, whereas tort law is better suited for redressing violations of relative duties. Ideally, criminal standards should be clear and determinate in defining these duties. Absent clarity, criminal law cannot serve well its deterrent function. Nor does societal retribution in the form of a criminal sanction seem fair when society has not given fair notice of what conduct warrants such an extreme sanction. In addition, clarity indicates that lawmakers have squarely focused on the propriety of invoking society's most severe sanction in particular circumstances. There is an "instinctive distaste against men languishing in prison unless the lawmaker has clearly said they should."

Criminal standards also tend to reflect settled societal norms of conduct, rather than sharply disputed matters. "Moral" culpability justifies criminal sanction, which in turn brings the "moral" stigma associated with that form of societal condemnation. The criminal law, then, seeks principally to reflect morality, including more newly settled norms, not to create it. Thus, even though the concept of morality is necessarily elusive and the precise boundary between moral and immoral conduct inevitably debatable, criminal standards risk losing their legitimate claim to moral force when they seek to promote certain utilitarian preferences rather than to condemn conduct that is not morally debatable.

A final distinguishing feature of criminal law is that it imposes a more exacting burden of proof on the government and otherwise provides the defendant with significant additional procedural guarantees. The government must establish the defendant's guilt beyond a reasonable doubt and not, as in civil enforcement actions, by a mere preponderance of the evidence. Moreover, there are a host of evidentiary and procedural rules applicable only to criminal proceedings that are intended to enhance the reliability of the evidence before the factfinder and to preclude consideration of unduly prejudicial information. ...

2. OVERCRIMINALIZATION; FEDERALIZATION; JUDICIAL ROLE; PROSECUTORIAL FUNCTION

Julie R. O'Sullivan, *The Federal Criminal "Code" Is a Disgrace: Obstruction Statutes as Case Study*
96 J. Crim. L. & Criminology 643 (2006)[18]

Any discussion of federal penal law must begin with an important caveat: There actually *is* no federal criminal "code" worthy of the name. A criminal code is defined as "'a systematic collection, compendium, or revision' of laws."[19] What the federal government has is a haphazard grab-bag of statutes accumulated over 200 years, rather than a comprehensive, thoughtful, and internally consistent system of criminal law. In fact, the federal government has *never* had a true criminal code. The closest Congress has come to enacting a code was its creation of Title 18 of the United States Code in 1948. That "exercise, however, accomplished little more than sweeping a host of internally-disorganized statutes containing fragmentary coverage into a series of chapters laid out in ... alphabetical order."[20] Readers should be cautioned, then, that my use of the term "federal criminal code" within this Article is simply a shorthand for an "incomprehensible,"[21] random and incoherent, "duplicative, ambiguous, incomplete, and organizationally nonsensical" mass of federal legislation that carries criminal penalties.

Once this caveat is understood, I can state my (by now obvious) thesis: The so-called federal penal "code" is a national disgrace. Let us first understand why the public should care. Professor Herbert Wechsler, the prime mover behind the Model Penal Code, articulated the stakes best in a passage worth reprinting in its entirety:

> Whatever view one holds about the penal law, no one will question its importance in society. This is the law on which men place their ultimate reliance for protection against all the deepest injuries that human conduct can inflict on individuals and institutions. By the same token, penal law governs the strongest force that we permit official agencies to bring to bear on individuals. Its promise as an instrument of safety is matched only by its power to destroy. If penal law is weak or ineffective, basic human interests are in jeopardy. If it is harsh or arbitrary in its impact, it works a gross injustice on those caught within its toils. The law that carries such responsibilities should surely be as rational and just as law can be. Nowhere in the entire legal field is more at stake for the community or for the individual.[22]

---

[18] Although this article sets forth the majority view, others have weighed in to the contrary. *See, e.g.,* Susan R. Klein & Ingrid B. Grobey, *Debunking Claims of Overfederalization of Criminal Law*, 62 Emory L.J. 1 (2012); Samuel W. Buell, *The Upside of Overbreadth*, 83 N.Y.U. L. Rev. 1491 (2008). *But see* Julie R. O'Sullivan, *The Federal Criminal "Code": Return of Overfederalization*, 37 Harv. J.L. & Pub. Pol'y 57 (2014).

[19] [Author's footnote 1:] Robert H. Joost, *Federal Criminal Code Reform: Is It Possible?*, 1 Buff. Crim. L. Rev. 195, 210 (1997) (*quoting* Black's Law Dictionary 256 (6th ed. 1990)). *See generally* Douglas Husak, Overcriminalization: The Limits of the Criminal Law (Oxford Univ. Press 2008).

[20] [Author's footnote 3:] Ronald L. Gainer, *Federal Criminal Code Reform: Past and Future*, 2 Buff. Crim. L. Rev. 45, 93 (1998) [hereinafter Gainer, *Federal Criminal Code Reform*].

[21] [Author's footnote 4:] Ronald L. Gainer, *Report to the Attorney General on Federal Criminal Code Reform*, 1 Crim. L.F. 99, 100 (1989) [hereinafter Gainer, *Report to the Attorney General*].

[22] [Author's footnote 7:] Herbert Wechsler, *The Challenge of a Model Penal Code*, 65 Harv. L. Rev.

In such circumstances, our failure to have in place even a modestly coherent code makes a mockery of the United States' much-vaunted commitments to justice, the rule of law, and human rights. And this is not news. Distinguished academics, codifiers, judges, former prosecutors, defense lawyers, politicians (including a number of Presidents and Attorneys General), and others have been expressing outrage over the state of federal criminal law for many decades. ... [O]ur society's apparent disinterest in remedying this universally-acknowledged default, [then,] is doubly disgraceful.

To begin with the optimal, an effective and just system of penal laws should be: drafted by elected representatives to be as clear and explicit as possible so that citizens have fair notice of that which will subject them to criminal sanction; public; accessible; comprehensive; internally consistent; reasonably stable; rationally organized to avoid redundancy and ensure appropriate grading of offense seriousness; prospective only in application; and capable of uniform, nonarbitrary, and nondiscriminatory enforcement. No code drafted by human beings and produced by political institutions can meet all of these criteria. What is shameful about the state of federal penal law, however, is that *none* of these characteristics can be claimed by our "code" *and* our elected officials have made no serious effort to correct that glaring fact for decades. I will attempt to substantiate this proposition generally in Part I ....

Although previous code reform efforts in the 1960's through the 1980's failed, they did yield something that made the deficiencies of the substantive code more tolerable: the U.S. Sentencing Guidelines. [I]n pre-Guidelines practice, judges had vast discretion in sentencing criminal offenders; their choice of sentence was constrained only by the statutory maximum Congress set for the offense of conviction (e.g., 0-10 years). Because prosecutors often could choose among a variety of overlapping charges, many of which carried different statutory maximums, prosecutors' discretionary charging choices greatly affected the defendant's sentencing exposure. So, for example, a prosecutor could choose a five-year count (e.g., obstruction of justice under 18 U.S.C. § 1505) rather than a twenty-year count (e.g., obstruction of justice under 18 U.S.C. § 1512(c)).

In the Sentencing Reform Act of 1984, Congress delegated to the U.S. Sentencing Commission the task of making more uniform, proportional, and rational federal sentencing through promulgation of *mandatory* guidelines that directly constrained the sentencing discretion of judges. The mandatory Sentencing Guidelines provided sentencing formulas to be applied to the facts of offenders' cases and *required* judges to sentence offenders within the narrow sentencing range (e.g., 15-21 months) dictated by those formulas absent extraordinary circumstances. The statutory maximums still operated to cap defendants' sentencing exposure, but in most cases the maximums were sufficiently generous that they did not impose a significant limitation on Guidelines sentencing ranges.

The Sentencing Commission recognized the many deficiencies of the code—including the power that its redundancy and irrational grading gave prosecutors to manipulate sentencing results and thus create sentencing disparities. The Commission attempted to address these concerns and others by adopting a modified "real offense" sentencing system—that is, a system where the sentence an offender received was based on the "real" circumstances of his case, often regardless of what charge(s) the prosecutor chose to pursue. One aspect of this "real" system was the Sentencing Commission's decision to create its own classification system based on the type of harm or threat posed by the offense committed by the defendant, not on the chaotic array of statutes available or irrational statutory maximums set by Congress. For example, the same sentencing calculus would apply to arrive at a given sentencing range for defendants charged with *either* § 1505 or § 1512(c). Prosecutors' ability to choose between overlapping and randomly graded offenses, then, often had no impact on the final sentence the judge was required to impose.

Some have gone so far as to suggest that prosecutors' vast discretion in selecting among elastic and redundant code provisions, combined with the mandatory Sentencing Guidelines, rendered the substantive code largely irrelevant. Certainly the Guidelines shifted the critical focus and energies of commentators and public officials from substantive law to sentencing for decades. In 2005, however, the Supreme Court held the *mandatory* Sentencing Guidelines unconstitutional in *Booker v. United States*.[23] It reasoned that augmentation of a defendant's sentence by *mandatory* judicial determination of the "real" facts of the case at sentencing violated defendants' jury trial rights. The Court ruled, however, that augmentation of sentences based on judicial findings in a *discretionary* system did not offend the Sixth Amendment. Accordingly, the Court decreed that, henceforth, the U.S. Sentencing Guidelines should be considered in formulating criminal sentences but they would be advisory only.

This means that, once again, judges have enormous sentencing power because their discretion, though informed by the Guidelines, is limited only by the applicable statutory maximum(s). Prosecutors, too, will have great power to influence sentencing results through their choice of charge, which sets the statutory maximum(s) and thus the effective sentencing range. More than anything else, however, *Booker* means that statutory maximums will once more be the critical limiting factor in sentencing; the code's redundancies, internal inconsistencies, and irrational grading will once more be highly visible and undoubtedly much criticized. The *Booker* Court, then, could be said to have restored the substantive code—with all its problems—to its former prominence. To the extent that a galvanizing event was necessary to refocus reform efforts, *Booker* was it.

The first step in creating a code reform movement must be to publicize the problem, promoting a "widespread understanding, not merely on the part of academics carping from the sidelines, but also on the part of practicing lawyers, judges and even political figures, that the criminal law" of the United States is in shameful condition. ...

I. INDICTMENT OF THE FEDERAL CRIMINAL "CODE"

A.   The "Code" Is a Chaotic Mass of Laws So Vast and Sprawling that Repeated Efforts to Compile a Complete Listing of Federal Crimes Have Come to Naught

At the most basic level, the above-described attributes of an effective and fair code presuppose that we should be able to *identify* the penal laws of the United States. It is a shocking fact, however, that the federal "code" contains a profusion of laws so complex and sprawling that the laws susceptible to criminal sanction *cannot even be counted*. While a count of 3,000 federal crimes was made in about 1989, an ABA Task Force on the Federalization of Criminal Law chaired by former Attorney General Edwin Meese found this number outmoded by 1998. The Task Force tried to come up with a systematic count and finally was forced to give up the effort, concluding instead that "[s]o large is the present body of federal criminal law that there is no conveniently accessible, complete list of federal crimes." ... This ... *excludes* federal regulations that may be criminally enforced. The ABA Task Force projected that, as of 1998, if regulations were included, the number of criminal offense would top 10,000. Other sources, however, estimated in the mid-1990's that there were *300,000* such regulations on the books.

As may be obvious from the above, the code is disorganized and incoherent. And it is not a compulsion for tidiness that underlies the screaming need for *organization* of federal penal statutes. Rather, as Roscoe Pound said, "a satisfactory *administration* of criminal

---

[23] [Author's footnote 18:] 543 U.S. 220 (2005).

justice must rest ultimately on a satisfactory *criminal law*." Without a *system* of offenses, it is impossible to make a collection of random laws work together to serve the purposes of punishment identified by Congress: just deserts, crime control, and (where incarceration is not an option) rehabilitation. One cannot weed out the archaic sections or winnow the code to that which truly deserves incarceration. Thus, criminal prohibitions on knowing transportation of water hyacinths or use of aircraft to hunt wild burros remain cheek by jowl with federal laws punishing arson and assault. One cannot identify internal inconsistencies, gaps, or redundancies in coverage. ... For present purposes it may be sufficient to note that so chaotic was the code that no one noticed that the assassination of a President was not a federal offense until President Kennedy was killed. Perhaps more shocking, Congress neglected to specify *the purposes of criminal punishment* now reflected in 18 U.S.C. § 3553 until 1984.

Absent effective organization, one also cannot assure that offenses are graded in terms of their relative seriousness, as reflected, among other things, in sentencing consequences. Thus, for example, the statutory maximum [punishment] for fleeing enforcement agents at an INS checkpoint in excess of the speed limit, and possession of a depiction of animal cruelty with the intent to mail that depiction for commercial gain— five years—is the same as the penalty prescribed for female genital mutilation of girls under eighteen. "Discriminations that distinguish minor crime from major criminality, or otherwise have large significance for the offender's treatment and his status in society, reflect a multitude of fine distinctions often turning upon factors that have no discernable relation to the ends the law should serve."[24]

This lack of any *system* to the code's organization is not only rife with the possibility of injustice but is also inarguably ineffective in combating crime. As Ronald Gainer, a veteran of earlier code reform wars, asserts: "the existing morass of statutory provisions and judicial decisions is so complex, and so confusing to law enforcement officers as well as to the public, that it could scarcely have been designed to be less efficient."[25] ... [P]rosecutors and judges have to fight their way through a maze of legislation to identify the applicable code section(s) and the elements of the offense(s), and often get it wrong. That time would be better spent pursuing and adjudicating more cases. For example, Ronald Gainer has estimated that if investigators, prosecutors, defense counsel, and judges could reduce by 10% the amount of time they spend wrestling with, and litigating about, confusions in the federal code, that 10% of added time would mean that roughly 4,000 more offenders could be prosecuted each year. Finally, "[a] more efficient criminal justice system would soon be perceived by the public to be more effective. This would promote a greater degree of deterrence of criminal conduct, which in turn could somewhat lessen the future caseload, and thereby hold promise of still greater efficiency and still more deterrence."[26]

B. The "Federalization" and "Overcriminalization" Phenomena Translate into Federal Overreaching into Areas of Traditional State Competence and the Trivialization of the Criminal Sanction

The unfairness and inefficiency flowing from the code's lack of organization is exacerbated by the overly ambitious scope of federal legislation. First-year law students know that the Constitution contemplates a limited role for federal criminal law, but federal officials appear to have only a limited awareness of this constitutional fact. No doubt the breadth of federal penal law would astound the framers. The "federalization"

---

[24] [Author's footnote 38:] [Herbert Wechsler, *A Thoughtful Code of Substantive Law*, 45 J. Crim. L. Criminology & Police Sci. 524, 526 (1955).]

[25] [Author's footnote 39:] Gainer, *Report to the Attorney General*, *supra* note [21], at 107.

[26] [Author's footnote 41:] [*Id.* at 101.]

of criminal law—that is, Congress' increasing penchant for making federal crimes of offenses that traditionally were matters left to the states—has been well documented and much lamented. The ABA Task Force on Federalization of Criminal Law issued a report in 1998 that focused on, and criticized, Congress' role in "federalizing" crime. It noted that the impetus for the increased federal presence in law enforcement did not appear to be one grounded on considerations of respective federal and state competence:

> New crimes are often enacted in patchwork response to newsworthy events, rather than as part of a cohesive code developed in response to an identifiable federal need. Observers have recognized that a crime being considered for federalization is often "regarded as appropriately federal because it is serious and not because of any structural incapacity to deal with the problem on the part of state and local government." There is widespread recognition that a major reason for the federalization trend—even when federal prosecution of these crimes may not be necessary or effective—is that federal crime legislation is politically popular. ... [27]

The ABA Report focused on persuading Congress to consider more carefully its apparent proclivity to respond to important criminal issues through knee-jerk (or politically expedient) federalization. Many observers believe, however, that this battle has been lost, and that the real war lies elsewhere. Professor John Jeffries and Judge John Gleeson have argued that—like it or not—federalization of the substantive criminal law is "largely an accomplished feat."[28] What this means is that, "[w]ith legislation covering virtually any crime they might plausibly wish to prosecute, federal prosecutors pick their targets and marshal their resources, not in response to the limitations of the substantive law but according to their own priorities and agendas."[29]

Like "federalization," the federal "overcriminalization" phenomenon has also been widely discussed. As Professor Erik Luna has pointed out, this one phenomenon actually comprises a number of problems: "(1) untenable offenses; (2) superfluous statues; (3) doctrines that overextend culpability; (4) crimes without jurisdictional authority; (5) grossly disproportionate punishments; and (6) excessive or pretextual enforcement of petty violations."[30] It is almost too easy to find statutory examples: federal criminal statutes sanction using the insignia of the "Swiss Confederation" as a commercial label; knowingly using the character of "Woodsy Owl" without authorization and for profit; transporting alligator grass across a state line; unauthorized use of the slogan "Give a hoot, don't pollute"; wearing a postal worker's uniform in a theatrical production that tends to discredit the postal service; pretending to be a 4-H club member with intent to defraud; and including a member of the armed forces in a voter preference poll. The same sad political considerations that gave us the federalization fashion are also are responsible for this phenomenon: "[a]s a rule, lawmakers have a strong incentive to add new offenses and enhanced penalties, which offer ready-made publicity stunts, but face no countervailing political pressure to scale back the criminal justice system."[31]

---

[27] [Author's footnote 43:] [Task Force on Federalization of Criminal Law, Criminal Justice Section, Am. Bar Ass'n, The Federalization of Criminal Law 14-15 (1998) [hereinafter ABA Task Force Report].]

[28] [Author's footnote 45] John C. Jeffries, Jr. & Hon. John Gleeson, *The Federalization of Organized Crime: Advantages of Federal Prosecution*, 46 Hastings L.J. 1095, 1125 (1995).

[29] [Author's footnote 46:] *Id.*

[30] [Author's footnote 48:] Erik Luna, *The Overcriminalization Phenomenon*, 54 Am. U. L. Rev. 703, 716 (2005).

[31] [Author's footnote 52:] [*Id.* at 718.]

"Overcriminalization" of "essentially innocuous conduct has contributed materially to the trivialization of the concept of criminality ...—a trivialization that erodes the respect for, and hence the deterrent impact of, the criminal law generally."[32] On a more concrete level, the effect of "overcriminalization" is primarily to empower law enforcement officials: "[T]he more crimes on the books, the more behavior that is restricted (and restricted in more ways), and the more punishment for a particular offense, the more clout police and prosecutors can exercise in the criminal justice system."[33]

The "federalization" and "overcriminalization" trends show no sign of abating. "Whatever the exact number of crimes that comprise today's 'federal criminal law,' it is clear that the amount of individual citizen behavior now potentially subject to federal criminal control has increased in astonishing proportions in the last few decades." The ABA Task Force's research revealed that "[m]ore than 40% of the federal criminal provisions enacted since the Civil War have been enacted since 1970." The Federalist Society, in its Report, noted that this "explosive" growth has "continued unabated"; indeed, it concluded that the number of statutory provisions susceptible to criminal enforcement had increased by one-third since 1980.

C. The "Code" Is Redundantly Repetitive, Thereby Increasing the Power of Prosecutors in Charging, Plea-Bargaining, and Determining the Actual Scope of Federal Criminal Law

One aspect of the "overcriminalization" phenomenon deserves particular emphasis. Congress is able to legislate in such numbers and at such a pace over what would seem to be a limited criminal subject-matter because it repeats itself—and often. As Attorney General Griffin Bell testified in 1977, the federal criminal law "now, in many ways, can be described as a nonsystem or nonset of laws because there is so much overlap." To give this "overlap" meaning, numbers may help. Professor Joost notes that "in the mid-1970s there were approximately 159 sections in the United States Code pertaining to offenses involving false statements to government officials, 134 pertaining to theft and fraud, 89 pertaining to forgery and counterfeiting, and 84 pertaining to arson and property destruction."[34] In sum, the federal "code" had 466 sections to cover these four crime categories. But Congress was not finished: by Ronald Gainer's count in 1998, the "code" had grown to include 642 sections covering these categories: 232 statutes pertaining to theft and fraud, 99 pertaining to forgery and counterfeiting, 215 pertaining to false statements, and 96 pertaining to property destruction.[35] To give a sense of how unnecessary this is, one earlier, doomed effort at code reform consolidated these 642 sections into 19 sections, which amply covered the four crime categories at issue.

The reason for the redundancies again can be traced largely to the political desire to react to a given scandal—for example, the destruction of Enron audit records by persons within Arthur Andersen LLP ("Andersen")—by enacting a "new" section that simply repeats existing prohibitions (*and* by jacking up statutory maximum penalties to underscore congressional resolve). Sometimes Congress creates new offenses that are simply more specialized models of old statutes—for example, by passing specific prohibitions on bank, health care, and securities fraud that augment the existing general prohibitions on fraud. Sometimes Congress adds new prohibitions within existing sections that are not specific to the subject-matter of the scandal but can be claimed to be

---

[32] [Author's footnote 53:] Gainer, *Federal Criminal Code Reform, supra* note [20], at 78.

[33] [Author's footnote 54:] Luna, *supra* note [30], at 722.

[34] [Author's footnote 59:] Joost, *supra* note [19], at 197-98.

[35] [Author's footnote 60:] Gainer, *Federal Criminal Code Reform, supra* note [20], at 62.

responsive to it. … [T]hese random additions can make the rag-tag offenses on the books even more incoherent.

The redundancy of the Code, to the extent it helps anyone, helps prosecutors. They have the ability to pick and choose among a smorgasbord of statutes that might apply to given criminal conduct. Some of the statutes will offer prosecutors important advantages over others—in terms of such matters as venue, proof, evidentiary admissibility, or sentencing impact. Often a prosecutor may choose a general statute over a statute that is more specifically tailored to a particular context—by choosing mail fraud or the general conspiracy statute, for example, rather than another statute that has more complicated proof requirements. The effect of these choices is to give prosecutors substantially greater bargaining power vis-á-vis the defense.

The code's redundancy also empowers prosecutors vis-á-vis Congress. The breadth of the penal laws subject to federal sanction all but ensures that federal enforcement officials, despite substantial increases in funding in the last few decades, will be unable to enforce them all. Prosecutorial choices regarding enforcement priorities will mean that some sections of the code may be significantly underenforced, while a very select few sections receive a great deal of attention. For example, according to the U.S. Sentencing Commission, in fiscal year [2017, 30.8% of federal criminal offenders were convicted of a small selection of drug offenses. Immigration offenses accounted for another 30.5% of offenders, firearms offenses for 12.1%, and fraud for 9%. Thus, these four fairly narrow crime categories accounted for just over 82.5% of all cases pursued. And these four offense categories have constituted the vast majority of federal cases for at least the past decade.] Effectively, then, prosecutors could be said to be creating their own code within a code—emphasizing drug, immigration, and fraud cases—and nullifying congressional penal choices in thousands of other available statutes through non-enforcement. Although such choices arguably undermine the legislative role in crime definition, courts cannot second-guess such choices unless (as is virtually impossible to prove) they arise out of unconstitutional motives.

D. Much of the "Code" Consists of Vague, Overbroad, or Internally Inconsistent Laws

Congress' penchant for speaking only in very broad and vague terms in criminal legislation may raise more far-reaching and profound issues than does its habit—reflected in the federalization and overcriminalization debates—of speaking often, repetitively, and over a wide range of subject-matters. Drafting criminal statutes concededly is difficult because of an inherent tension between, on the one hand, creating statutes sufficiently open-ended to address new ways of committing the offense and prevent defendants from evading liability by relying on technical "loopholes" in very specific prohibitions, and, on the other, making criminal prohibitions sufficiently specific to provide citizens fair notice of that which is outlawed, avoid delegation of law-making power to judges, and constrain the charging discretion of prosecutors. While accommodating this tension can be challenging, it is not a challenge that federal draftsmen even appear to recognize: Federal statutes consistently and seriously err on the side of over-inclusiveness. In addition to being overbroad, many statutes lack definition—that is, they are vague. In recognition of the grievous lack of specificity in many statutes subject to criminal sanction, courts regularly add definitions, or even elements, to existing offenses to "cure" any due process difficulties.

1. Mens Rea

One of the areas in which congressional drafting has been most deficient is in specifying the mental element, or *mens rea*, necessary to support a criminal conviction.[36] Criminal liability is normally founded on the concurrence of two factors, "an evil-meaning mind [and] an evil-doing hand." This is often expressed as a requirement that some degree of *mens rea* (guilty mind) must attend the *actus reus* (guilty act or non-action where there is a duty to act) to warrant the imposition of a criminal stigma. Unfortunately, as Professor George Fletcher observed, "[t]here is no term fraught with greater ambiguity than that venerable Latin phrase that haunts Anglo-American criminal law: *mens rea.*"

Part of the ambiguity is founded upon the fact that a seemingly endless variety of terms have been used to describe the guilty mind necessary to prove federal offenses. Federal statutes, for example, provide for more than 100 types of *mens rea*. Even those terms most frequently used in federal legislation—"knowing" and "willful"—have, according to judges, different meanings in different contexts; judges adjust the definitions according to what they believe is the correct level of *mens rea* given the conduct at issue and are able to do so because of congressional inaction. Another layer of difficulty is attributable to the fact that Congress may impose one *mens rea* requirement upon certain elements of the offense and a different level of *mens rea*, or no *mens rea* at all, with respect to other elements. Often, the law at issue does not specify a *mens rea* requirement or, far too frequently, is ambiguous as to which elements an express intent requirement modifies.

The lack of statutory specificity regarding the applicable level of the *mens rea*, and the definition of any potentially applicable *mens rea*, is most troubling where Congress enacts a statute that prospectively "criminalizes" regulations Congress has asked a federal agency to produce. This appears to be done almost as a matter of course these days. In pondering the significance of this drafting default, recall that no one has yet come up with an accurate count of the number of regulations so "criminalized," but estimates range up to *300,000*. Some of these "regulatory" crimes are properly regarded as *malum in se*—wrong in and of themselves independent of law. More often, however, the subject-matters of these regulations concern conduct designed to achieve a regulatory end and are not something that most of the public would know—by reference to societal moral norms—are criminal. Most of these crimes, then, are more properly characterized as *malum prohibitum*—wrong because prohibited. For example, it unlikely that most people would know that criminal sanctions may attach to such activities as walking a dog in a government building, mixing two kinds of turpentine, or violating an instruction in the twenty-two pages of OHSA regulations pertaining to construction of ladders and scaffolding.

Why is this default troubling? I will once again turn to Professor Wechsler to explain:

> Criminal liability imports a condemnation, the gravest we permit ourselves to make. To condemn when fault is absent is barbaric. It is the badge of tyranny, the plainest illustration of injustice. Correct me if I overstate this but I do not think I do. Indeed, we are reluctant—very properly—to condemn action as criminal merely because the actor should have known of its offensive quality. We seek so far as possible to insist that he really must have known. When he knew and acted nonetheless, we feel real confidence that we have our man.

---

[36] [Ed.: *See also* Brian W. Walsh & Tiffany M. Joslyn, *Without Intent: How Congress Is Eroding the Criminal Intent Requirement in Federal Law* (April 2010), available through the Heritage Foundation or the NACDL.]

Nonetheless, the federal courts regularly permit *felony* criminal convictions, in *malum prohibitum* cases, to rely on a species of strict liability. In these so-called "public welfare" cases, Congress passed statutes that state that a "knowing violation" of the regulations can be criminally prosecuted. The plain language might indicate that the defendant must know that he is violating the regulation at issue. Federal courts, however, have consistently read this language to mean, in cases where "deleterious devices or products or obnoxious waste materials" and thus the "public welfare" are at issue, people dealing in such materials should be on notice that their activity is subject to regulation. Accordingly, courts have often decided that persons are criminally culpable if they knew the nature of the material with which they were dealing, even if they were not aware of the regulations at issue and, if they were aware, did not know they were violating them.

That is, of course, unless the courts decide that this shockingly (in a felony case) low level of *mens rea* would "criminalize a broad range of otherwise innocent conduct," in which case courts pump up the *mens rea* required. The judgment of what constitutes "innocent" behavior is made by judges. So, for example, the Ninth Circuit held in *United States v. Weitzenhoff* that persons working in wastewater treatment plants may be held criminally liable for discharging pollutants in excess of the permitted amount as long as they knew (as they had to, given the nature of the business in which they were engaged) that they were discharging pollutants (even if that activity itself—discharging pollutants—was lawful within permitted amounts).[37] The rationale in such cases is that these individuals know that they are dealing with a substance dangerous to human health and thus are responsible for ensuring that their conduct conforms to legal requirements. The *Weitzenhoff* court held that the defendants *did not* need to be aware that they are discharging in excess of permitted amounts—that is, they need have no knowledge regarding the *actus reus* of the crime and no culpable state of mind with respect to the alleged wrongdoing. This decision essentially made "designated felons" of anyone working in the wastewater industry, leaving it to prosecutorial discretion to decide who in a given plant will go to jail when unintended discharges in excess of permitted amounts occur.

By contrast, the Supreme Court held in *Staples v. United States* that semiautomatic weapons are not sufficiently dangerous to put their owners on notice of the regulated nature of such gun ownership.[38] Thus, the Court said, for purposes of prosecuting someone for unlicensed possession of a fully-automatic weapon, it is not sufficient that the government prove that the defendant knew of the dangerous character of the gun he had; rather, to avoid entrapping "innocent" owners of machineguns, the government had to prove that the defendant knew that his semiautomatic weapon had been converted to fully-automatic firing. As *Staples* may indicate, it is difficult to sort out just what criteria the courts are using (aside from their own personal experience and morality) in determining what they consider "innocent" behavior worthy of an elevated *mens rea*.

Should *courts* be able to subject persons violating *malum prohibitum* provisions to felony criminal sanction with only the most negligible showing of *mens rea* (e.g., they knew that they were dealing with a dangerous or deleterious device)? Professor Green identifies arguments many of us would agree with, when he writes that "applying criminal sanctions to morally neutral conduct is both unjust and counterproductive. It unfairly brands defendants as criminals, weakens the moral authority of the sanction, and ultimately renders the penalty ineffective. It also squanders scarce enforcement resources and invites selective, and potentially discriminatory, prosecution."[39] Whatever one might believe is

---

[37] [Author's footnote 76:] [United States v. Weitzenhoff, 35 F.3d 1275 (9th Cir. 1993) (*en banc*).]

[38] [Author's footnote 77:] [Staples v. United States, 511 U.S. 600, 610 (1994).]

[39] [Author's footnote 79:] Stuart P. Green, *Why It's a Crime To Tear the Tag off a Mattress: Overcriminalization and the Moral Content of Regulatory Offenses*, 46 Emory L.J. 1533, 1536 (1997). Consider, too, the following thought from Henry M. Hart, *The Aims of the Criminal Law*, 23 Law &

the *correct* answer as a matter of criminal law policy, this is a sufficiently troubling basis for liability that courts have no business making it. The failure of the criminal code to be specific and clear about the critical *mens rea* element in these regulatory cases is, in short, simply appalling.

Judges' willingness to tinker with the *mens rea* applicable to criminal offenses in the "public welfare" line of cases is anything but aberrational. Judges often undertake to supply missing *mens rea* elements, fill in gaps, or correct ambiguities through "interpretation" (some would say common lawmaking). Sometimes they get it right, and sometimes ... they most assuredly don't. I do not question their good faith in doing so, but I do question the wisdom of such lawmaking. In any case, even were judges able effectively to patch up specific statutory provisions, they cannot do that which is necessary: create a small number of defined and consistent *mens rea* terms to be used with care throughout the United States Code. ...

E. The Penal Laws of the United States May Be Nominally Public, But They Are Not "Accessible," Do Not Provide "Fair Notice," and Invite Arbitrary or Discriminatory Enforcement

This lack of clarity [in many vaguely-worded, and potentially broadly applicable federal criminal statutes] has a number of consequences. First and most obviously, we have both a "fair notice" and an "accessibility" problem. ... Without reference to the—often conflicting—federal case law and, sometimes, volumes of federal regulations, one cannot know the law.

Problems of practical accessibility are compounded by the sheer bulk of federal criminal statutes and the random way in which they are organized, all of which "make[s] it difficult to ferret out the applicable law even in the age of electronic databases. It is particularly hard to find important offenses because they are often surrounded by trivial ones." Once one (or more likely, several) potentially applicable code sections are identified, it is not infrequently the case that the statutory language is difficult to parse. While many statutes are well-drafted, many others are very "plainly deficient either in their conception or in their amenability to application." Consider, for example, that "[m]any of the sentences in current title 18 run over 200 words," and one statute, 18 U.S.C. § 793, contains a lead sentence that is approximately 700 words long. Further, given that different draftsmen over 200 years were responsible for the present code, it is not surprising that there is a great deal of inconsistency in language and structure among statutes pertaining to the same subject-matter. These overlaps in coverage among different sections, then, mean that the code is not only redundant but also internally inconsistent. In short, these statutes may be "public" in the sense of being available in print or on-line, but the "code" is not by any stretch "accessible" to the average citizen.

A lack of precision in statutory drafting fails due process vagueness standards not only when the statutory provision at issue cannot be said to provide "fair notice." An even more important consideration is whether "the legislature [has] establish[ed] minimal guidelines to govern law enforcement."[40] The test is whether the statute "permit[s] 'a

---

Contemp. Probs. 401, 431 n.70 (1958):

> In relation to offenses of a traditional type, [the Supreme Court seems to say], we must be much slower to dispense with a basis for genuine blameworthiness in criminal intent than in relation to modern regulatory offenses. But it is precisely in the area of traditional crimes that the nature of the act itself commonly gives some warning that there may be a problem about its propriety and so affords, without more, at least some slight basis of condemnation for doing it. ... In the area of regulatory crimes, on the other hand, the moral quality of the act is often neutral; and on occasion, the offense may consist not of any act at all, but simply of an intrinsically innocent omission, so there is no basis for moral condemnation whatever.

[40] [Author's footnote 105:] Kolender v. Lawson, 461 U.S. 352, 358 (1983).

standardless sweep [that] allows policemen, prosecutors, and juries to pursue their personal predilections.'"[41] ... The Supreme Court has cautioned that "[i]t would certainly be dangerous if the legislature could set a net large enough to catch all possible offenders, and leave it to the courts to step inside and say who could be rightfully detained, and who should bet set at large."[42] Yet that is precisely what ... many ... code sections do. ...

F. The Above Characteristics Have Fundamentally Changed the Traditional Understanding of the Appropriate Roles of Judges and Prosecutors

The above discussion has highlighted the fact that Congress' default has empowered judges and prosecutors to an extraordinary degree. By leaving to prosecutors and judges the determination of the contours of these vague and overbroad statutes, Congress has effectively delegated its responsibility to determine the content of substantive federal criminal law. Let us turn, then, to the institutional consequences of this delegation.

1. *Judges*

The Supreme Court has decreed that federal crimes "are solely creatures of statute."[43] Arguably a central myth of federal criminal jurisprudence is that there are no "federal common law crimes."[44] To be sure, in a technical sense, federal judges are not creating a federal common law of crime because they always ultimately found their decisions regarding the content of a criminal rule on a statute or regulation. As Professor Jeffries has noted, "[t]oday, no court would invoke the unadorned rubrics of the common law, and the exigencies of law enforcement do not require resort to such authority. Penal legislation exists in such abundance that wholesale judicial creativity is simply unnecessary."[45] And it is worth recalling that "[e]very code will inevitably contain ambiguous language that will be interpreted by judges. A legislature's obligation is to reserve that delegation of judicial authority to the instances in which it is not reasonably avoided." The fact that federal courts clearly engage in interstitial "lawmaking" in the course of interpreting positive law does not raise serious constitutional concerns. Even those most committed to traditional constitutional separation of powers principles acknowledge that "no statute can be entirely precise, and that some judgments, even some judgments involving policy considerations, must be left to the officers executing the law and to the judges applying it."[46]

However, the line between common lawmaking and statutory interpretation is one of degree. Given the complete lack of definition in some important federal statutes, courts are in fact engaging in lawmaking in determining that such statutes in fact apply to varied fact situations when the statutes themselves do not in any intelligible terms speak to those situations. ... [An] excellent example is the rules that govern organizational criminal liability. *There is no generally applicable statute in the federal criminal code that defines when*

---

[41] [Author's footnote 106:] *Id.*

[42] [Author's footnote 107:] *Id.* at 348 n.7.

[43] [Author's footnote 109:] Liparota v. United States, 471 U.S. 419, 424 (1985).

[44] [Author's footnote 110:] *See* United States v. Hudson & Goodwin, 11 U.S. (7 Cranch) 32, 34 (1812).

[45] [Author's footnote 112:] John Calvin Jeffries Jr., *Legality, Vagueness, and the Construction of Penal Statutes*, 71 Va. L. Rev. 189, 202 (1985 (criticizing rule of strict construction because it does not serve stated goals).

[46] [Ed.: for further discussion of the separation of powers concerns implicated by congressional delegations of lawmaking power, see then-Judge Gorsuch's dissent from denial of rehearing *en banc* in United States v. Nichols, 784 F.3d 666, 667 (10th Cir. 2015).]

corporations can be held liable for crimes. Courts have created the black-letter law of organizational liability: a corporation is liable for the criminal misdeeds of its agents acting within the actual or apparent scope of their employment or authority if the agents intend, at least in part, to benefit the corporation. In 1909, the Supreme Court rejected a due process challenge to application of this *respondeat superior* formula when it was *included in a criminal statute*,[47] but courts since that time have simply assumed that this standard applies regardless of whether the criminal statute involved explicitly provides for such liability. Courts have also embroidered on the basic standard, for example, by rejecting a corporate "due diligence" defense—which would relieve organizations of criminal liability where their agents' actions were contrary to organizational policy or express organizational orders—based on what they infer *would be* congressional intent were Congress to speak. Courts have in fact massaged the corporate liability standard to allow for corporate criminal liability where, under traditional *respondeat superior* liability principles, it would not be appropriate. Indeed, given the way that courts have applied these principles, it is difficult to find a case in which a corporation *cannot* be tagged for the activities of its agents—and all on the say-so of judges, rather than Congress. ...

The bar on judicial law-making in the criminal realm is not a theoretical nicety. It is founded in a number of very basic principles—separation of powers being one. "Enlightenment theoreticians decreed that liberty is most secure when power is fractured and separated."[48] It would be a dangerous concentration of power for life tenured judges to both propound the law and to preside over its interpretation and administration. More fundamentally, "[a]s the branch most directly accountable to the people, only the legislature could validate the surrender of individual freedom necessary to formulation of the social contract."[49]

The bar on judicial crime-creation is also founded on "*the* first principle" of criminal law—the principle of legality—which outlaws the retroactive definition of criminal offenses.

> It is condemned because it is retroactive and also because it is judicial—that is, accomplished by an institution not recognized as politically competent to define crime. Thus, a fuller statement of the legality ideal would be that it stands for the desirability in principle of advance legislative specification of criminal misconduct.[50]

The legality principle has been identified as the most basic of human rights in a myriad of international treaties and declarations.

This requisite is, in part, operationalized in U.S. law in the due process vagueness doctrine, which "requires that a penal statute define the criminal offense with sufficient definiteness that ordinary people can understand what conduct is prohibited and in a manner that does not encourage arbitrary and discriminatory enforcement."[51] "[A] statute which either forbids or requires the doing of an act in terms so vague that men of common intelligence must necessarily guess at its meaning and differ as to its application, violates the first essential of due process of law."[52] The vagueness doctrine's "connection

---

[47] [Author's footnote 116:] N.Y. Central & Hudson River R.R. Co. v. United States, 212 U.S. 481 (1909).

[48] [Author's footnote 122:] Jeffries, *supra* note [45], at 202.

[49] [Author's footnote 123:] [*Id.*]

[50] [Author's footnote 125:] [*Id.* at 190.]

[51] [Author's footnote 128:] [*Kolender*, 461 U.S. at 357.]

[52] [Author's footnote 129:] Connally v. Gen. Constr. Co., 269 U.S. 385, 391 (1926).

to legality is obvious: a law whose meaning can only be guessed at remits the actual task of defining criminal misconduct to retroactive judicial decisionmaking."[53]

As the above discussion demonstrates, however, judges have (in this author's view) all too infrequently attended to the allocation of lawmaking responsibility demanded by our democratic system, by separation of powers, by the principle of legality, and by human rights and due process guarantees. Again, it is important to emphasize that I am not questioning their good faith. Many judges may decide that, to do justice in individual cases, they have no choice but to do *something* to clarify the law at issue, given elected officials' demonstrated unwillingness to attend properly to the dismal state of the federal criminal code generally. My view, however, is that by attempting to carry Congress' water through piecemeal fixes, they have in fact made a morass out of a mess. Moreover, if judges were more consistent in requiring Congress to fix what ails many statutes, perhaps Congress would be more willing to address the morass through comprehensive code reform.

2. *Prosecutors*

The same principles that demand that Congress take the laboring oar in identifying the conduct that will be subject to penal sanction—beforehand and with reasonable specificity and clarity—also, of course, bars prosecutorial law-making. And, as noted above, Congress' penchant for federalization, overcriminalization, and speaking in overbroad and vague terms has had the direct effect of empowering prosecutors with vast discretion. Federal prosecutors exercise a very broad—and for the most part unreviewable—discretion in selecting cases and charges. They can also fundamentally change the content of a vaguely worded criminal statute by pursuing novel theories of prosecution. ... Prosecutors "make law," then, by exercising their discretion to make enforcement decisions that functionally determine the real shape of the federal code and to formulate theories of prosecution that expand the accepted understandings of the reach of certain criminal statutes. In these respects, prosecutors are allied with judges in determining the true content of federal penal laws.

Some prosecutorial discretion is inevitable, and it *can be* a positive. Most codes will provide prosecutors with some flexibility in enforcement; as noted above, statutes that are *too* specific may irrationally foreclose the prosecution of persons who knowingly imposed criminal harm on others. And most common law justice systems include some provision for selectivity in prosecution. Otherwise, the social and economic costs of full enforcement of the code would be oppressive. Finally, as Judge Gerard Lynch put it,

> [s]o long as our criminal codes contain too many prohibitions, the contents of which are left to be defined by their implementation, or which cover conduct that is clearly not intended to be punished in every instance, or which provide for the punishment of those who act without wrongful intent, prosecutors must exercise judgment about which of the many cases that are technically covered by the criminal laws are really worthy of criminal punishment.[54]

Again, I believe that most prosecutors act in the good faith belief that they are "doing justice." And I also believe that they sometimes *do* "do justice" by stretching the code. ...

The problem is that there is *too much* discretion available to prosecutors. Prosecutorial discretion flows from a number of circumstances in addition to those noted above. First and foremost is the fact that the number of crimes worthy of investigation

---

[53] [Author's footnote 130:] Jeffries, *supra* note [45], at 196.

[54] [Author's footnote 132:] [Gerard E. Lynch, *Our Administrative System of Criminal Justice*, 66 Fordham L. Rev. 2117, 2136-37 (1998).]

outstrips the resources available to pursue them. Prosecutors' flexibility in responding to these constraints is augmented by the availability of alternative civil and regulatory sanctions; thus prosecutors can decline a case with some confidence that the misconduct involved will be addressed through alternative civil and regulatory action. Much of what is subject to federal prosecution is also subject to prosecution under state law. Accordingly, prosecutors can use their judgment regarding what does and does not deserve federal criminal action.

I view this as the "natural" discretion imbedded in the job given the overabundance of crime and the availability of alternative remedies. That "natural" discretion, however, is exaggerated in a potentially dangerous way by the state of the code. The "code" allows prosecutors to bring cases that would not be warranted under a clean and rational system, and it permits them choices that simply leverage their bargaining power vis-á-vis the defense but … serve no legitimate penal purpose. I have no problem with plea bargaining—it often serves the interests of the government *and* the defense. If, however, prosecutors are given undue power to pressure defendants into pleading because of code irrationalities, the result may be disparate treatment of similarly situated defendants based on the idiosyncratic choices of prosecutors.

A more fundamental concern is that prosecutors, in plea bargaining, can offer defendants such a stark choice between a lenient plea offer (say a five-year count) and a threat of harsh charges if the plea is rejected (the potential for a twenty-year sentence after trial) that risk-averse but innocent defendants will be coerced into a guilty plea. In some white-collar cases, where the issue is less about what happened or who "did it" (the drug deal, assault, etc.) and more about what the defendant's state of mind was at the time or whether the conduct at issue should be sanctioned under an expansive theory of the law, the issue is more subtle. Where a defendant's culpability—even on the facts—is arguable, prosecutors can avoid the adjudication of novel theories or of difficult questions of intent by pressuring a plea. The cases may not involve a complete "innocent," but they may be ones where formal adjudication would reveal that what the defendant did (or what he thought while doing it) should not be criminally sanctioned or should be sanctioned much less stringently than charged.

In sum, the overbreadth, vagueness, and redundancy of the code give prosecutors power that they are not supposed to have in a decently-functioning system of justice. While it would be impossible—and counterproductive—to attempt to stamp out all prosecutorial discretion, there is clearly a point beyond which the code's empowerment of prosecutors is harmful, whether measured in the language of "efficiency" or of "justice." And the overwhelming majority of those familiar with the federal code—including many former prosecutors like me—believe that we have passed that tipping point by a substantial margin.

The fact that prosecutors have such (in my view, outsized) discretion has in part contributed to a reality of prosecutorial functioning that is fundamentally at odds with the traditional conception of prosecutors as advocates in a system of justice where convictions are obtained through adversarial testing. It is more accurate to characterize prosecutors as "administrators" or "quasi-judicial" actors than as advocates. This re-conceptualization of the prosecutorial role is warranted because of the simple truth that the outcome in most cases is determined not by a court or a jury but by the prosecutor. Prosecutors have broad power to pick and choose among cases and, because of the state of the code, to secure indictments and force dispositions; the fact that somewhere around *95% of all federal criminal cases are resolved by guilty plea* demonstrates that criminal law is increasingly an administrative system in which the prosecutor reigns supreme (with occasional "appeals" to the jury).

The costs of *undue* prosecutorial power are many. I have discussed above the concerns that undue prosecutorial discretion may well result in arbitrary and discriminatory enforcement decisions. In addition, as a matter of separation of powers, prosecutors' broad discretion allows them to usurp Congress's role in determining what should and should not be sanctioned criminally. One may further assert that prosecutors, using their discretion to act as administrative adjudicators in declining some cases and plea bargaining away others, are usurping the role of courts and juries. Some contend that prosecutors are not competent—given their adversarial orientation, selection, and training—to dispense the type of neutral justice contemplated by such a role, and that politics and other improper considerations may well taint their exercises of discretion. Certainly, because prosecutorial discretion is largely exercised outside the public eye, it is difficult to document, let alone to regulate or check. The existence of this broad power also "relieve[s] pressure on the public and the legislature to make important and painful decisions."[55] Instead of requiring that hard policy and political choices regarding the allocation of scarce criminal justice resources be debated openly and made publicly, this discretionary power allows prosecutors to make hidden resource decisions.

Most fundamentally, the quantity of unreviewed or unreviewable discretion vested in federal prosecutors obviously raises fundamental questions regarding fair process and equal treatment. As Professor James Vorenberg argued,

> prosecutors are not held to anything remotely like what due process would require if they were engaged in an acknowledged rather than a hidden system of adjudication. No uniform, pre-announced rules inform the defendant and control the decisionmaker; a single official can invoke society's harshest sanctions on the basis of ad hoc personal judgments. Prosecutors can and do accord different treatment— prison for some and probation or diversion to others—on grounds that are not written down anywhere and may not have been either rational, consistent, or discoverable in advance.[56]

The risk of unequal treatment created by standardless discretion is troubling not only as a threat to due process but in its own right as well. Giving prosecutors the power to invoke or deny punishment at their discretion raises the prospect that society's most fundamental sanctions will be imposed arbitrarily and capriciously and that the least favored members of the community—racial and ethnic minorities, social outcasts, the poor—will be treated most harshly.

In short, although it is probably beneficial and certainly inevitable that federal prosecutors exercise *some* discretion in deciding when and how to bring cases, there are substantial costs to investing prosecutors with *too* much discretion. Among the suggestions made for restraining prosecutorial discretion or making prosecutors more accountable for its exercise are: instituting formal guidelines to control prosecutors' choices; legislative oversight; increased judicial activism in reviewing prosecutorial decisions; increasing the public visibility of prosecutorial choices; making governing ethical standards more stringent and specific; and educating prosecutors on their duties and the ramifications of their choices. All of these suggestions have merit. All except perhaps the last, however, are in my view unlikely to come to fruition. In sources too numerous to recount, commentators have documented the ever-increasing discretion vested in federal prosecutors and almost universally bemoaned this increase in prosecutorial power as a pernicious development—but none of these reforms has been seriously considered. The final suggested "fix" is code reform. Although it may, if properly done, be the most effective in appropriately cabining prosecutorial discretion, it is, in the view of many, also the least likely to happen. ... [M]y view is that the potential for code reform is higher than it has been for decades as a result of the Supreme Court's *Booker* decision.

---

[55] [Author's footnote 137:] James Vorenberg, *Decent Restraints in Prosecutorial Power*, 94 Harv. L. Rev. 1521, 1559 (1981).

[56] [Author's footnote 138:] *Id.* at 1554.

G. The Final Cost of Code Irrationality Is Loss of Public Respect For, and Voluntary Compliance With, Criminal Norms

I have traced in the above discussion some of the costs of code irrationality: inefficiency and ineffectiveness in enforcement of the criminal law, "fair notice" and accessibility issues, the potential for arbitrary and discriminatory enforcement, the undue delegation of law-making authority to judges and prosecutors, and the consequences that delegation has for the code and for the traditional roles of judges and prosecutors in the administration of criminal law. All of these are fairly specific, and even potentially measurable. A perhaps greater but harder to quantify cost is the affect that a chaotic code has on societal confidence in the criminal justice system.

A traditional criminal code has a dual audience. First, it speaks to lawyers, judges, jurors and other participants in the criminal system in defining the rules they must employ to decide whether a defendant should be criminally liable, and for what. As noted above, the inefficiency of the code obviously means that those involved in criminal cases—judges, prosecutors, defense lawyers, defendants, and others—will needlessly expend time and energy to deal with poorly drafted, organized, or conceptualized criminal provisions. But the inefficient and ineffective enforcement of criminal law has reverberations far beyond opportunity costs expressed in terms of resources. A code's second audience is the general public, and its purpose in this regard is to "announce[] the law's commands to those whose conduct it seeks to influence."

Obviously, if the law is in a real sense inaccessible, people cannot make the rational calculation necessary for effective deterrence. A code correctly perceived to be irrational, moreover, will undermine faith in the criminal justice system as a whole, thus encouraging the view that "beating the system" is neither immoral nor antisocial. The most unique feature of the penal law is its ability to impose upon wrongdoers the moral stigma of a criminal conviction. Criminal law is critical in assisting in the "building, shaping, and maintaining of [moral] norms and moral principles." If criminal law

> earns a reputation as a reliable statement of what the community, given sufficient information and time to reflect, perceives as condemnable, people are more likely to defer to its commands as morally authoritative and as appropriate to follow in those borderline cases where the propriety of certain conduct is unsettled or ambiguous in the mind of the actor.[57]

This expressive function is particularly important in a complex, multi-cultural and multi-ethnic society such as ours. Obviously, law's expressive function, and criminal law's moral stigma, are only effective where the public is in fact persuaded of the moral culpability of offenders. "In this respect, the criminal law exhibits unavoidable circularity: criminality turns on morality, yet morality may itself turn on criminality. Hence, one of the features that makes criminal law unique—the moral stigma associated with a criminal conviction—is not self-executing. It can be lost over time with overreaching."[58]

"[T]he main goal of penal reform is to promote respect for the law by making law respectable." Public compliance with the law—whether through fear (deterrence) or example (reinforcement of moral norms)—is critical because resource constraints mean that enforcement efforts cannot alone reduce crime rates. To induce the necessary public voluntary compliance with the law's requirements,

---

[57] [Author's footnote 144:] [Paul H. Robinson, *Reforming the Federal Criminal Code: A Top Ten List*, 1 Buff. Crim. L. Rev. 225, 233 (1997).]

[58] [Author's footnote 145:] [Richard J. Lazarus, *Meeting the Demands of Integration in the Evolution of Environmental Law: Reforming Environmental Criminal Law*, 83 Geo. L.J. 2407, 2441-42 (1995).]

the criminal laws and the criminal process must be, and must be publicly perceived to be, sensible, certain, impartial, and efficient. A nation can achieve neither the reality nor the perception of these qualities if the laws themselves are confusing and complex, if important legal consequences turn on accidents in legislative drafting, and if just disposition of offenders often rests as much on chance as on design.[59]

C. PRACTICE: SELECTING "PROCEDURAL" TOPICS RELEVANT TO WHITE-COLLAR CRIME

We turn now to an introduction to the "procedural" issues covered in this volume, which necessitates first some description of white-collar practice. White-collar criminal enforcement is not a new phenomenon; such cases have long been brought and defended in federal courts. It is generally thought, however, that white-collar practice came into being as a discrete calling in the early 1970s.[60] At that time, "[t]he disclosures of corruption at the highest levels of government, evidenced in the Watergate scandals, investigations of American corporations for bribery of foreign officials, and prosecutions of major American manufacturers for the production of unsafe products for consumers shocked the American public. Concern for white-collar crime exploded, enough so that it could fairly be labeled a social movement."[61] "As federal agencies and federal prosecutor offices increased their investigations into white-collar crime, more persons found themselves in need of legal counsel to help them. Particularly because government investigators focused on corporations, officers in corporations, and major political figures, a larger and more influential pool of clients was created."[62] Thus, as of the 1980s, the newly minted field of white-collar criminal defense was said to be "the fastest growing legal specialty in the United States."[63] Many of those joining this growing cadre were former federal prosecutors who increasingly identified themselves as white-collar defense specialists.[64] A recent history of the development of this practice area confirms that today virtually all of the 200 U.S. law firms with the highest grossing revenues boast a white-collar practice.[65] Federal white-collar practice can be "enormously lucrative," in part because this area "is not susceptible to the same type of cost controls that in-house counsel typically seek to implement in other litigation."[66] The majority of lawyers concentrated in this specialty in large firms are former prosecutors. They are also "overwhelmingly" male.[67] The reasons for this distressing disparity are not entirely clear, but it is evident that one cause is hiring disparities within DOJ. Firms tend to recruit white-collar partners from the

---

[59] [Author's footnote 147:] Gainer, *Federal Criminal Code Reform, supra* note [20], at 55-56.

[60] *See* Kenneth Mann, Defending White Collar Crime: A Portrait of Attorneys at Work 19-26 (Yale Univ. Press 1985).

[61] Weisburd, *et al., supra* note 9, at 6-7 (footnote omitted).

[62] Mann, *supra* note 60, at 21.

[63] Paul R. Conolly, Chairman of the Section on Litigation of the ABA (1977), *quoted in,* Malcolm Feeley, The Process is the Punishment (1979).

[64] *See* Mann, *supra* note 60, at 21-26.

[65] Charles D. Weisselberg & Su Li, *Big Law's Sixth Amendment: The Rise of Corporate White-Collar Practices in Large U.S. Law Firms,* 53 Ariz. L. Rev. 1221 (2011).

[66] *Id.* at 1249.

[67] *Id.*

government and markedly fewer women than men serve in the Criminal Division of U.S. Attorneys Offices in the top-five legal markets.[68]

Although the degree of priority accorded to this crime classification by various Administrations has waxed and waned to some degree, the field itself is now well-established. There is tremendous political pressure on the Department of Justice to concentrate its power on violent and drug crime cases. Immigration matters consume a large portion of the DOJ's docket. In the aftermath of the September 11 attack, greater emphasis was placed on terrorism investigations, incidentally including white-collar offenses—such as money laundering—that may support terrorist networks. That said, each few years seems to bring a new species of white-collar disaster: from the Savings and Loan fiasco to the accounting shenanigans of the Enron era to the most recent financial fraud crisis involving mortgage financing. These raise the visibility of white-collar crime and, with it, public and congressional pressure to turn DOJ resources to these matters. Whether white-collar crime will compete successfully with terrorism, violent, immigration, and drug crimes in any particular year for scarce investigative and prosecutorial resources is difficult to forecast. Current levels of white-collar prosecutions (as of mid 2018) are the lowest in 20 years. "Overall, the data show that prosecutions are down 31.3 percent from … 2008 and down 40.8 percent from … [those] reported in 1998."[69] But at the very least, one can assert with some certainty that white-collar crime itself will be growth industry, even if white-collar criminal enforcement is not a consistent priority.

To understand why the incidence of white-collar crime is likely to increase over the years, it is helpful to refer to a 1991 empirical study conducted under the auspices of the Yale White-Collar Crime Project, which attempted to shed some light on the characteristics of white-collar crimes and criminals. It defined its study sample by reference to eight criminal violations that seemed to be clearly "white-collar" in nature, and contrasted those cases with a sampling of federal "common crime" cases, defined as simple non-violent financially-oriented crimes.[70] The Yale Project concluded that such notorious "securities mega-crimes as those charged against Ivan Boesky and Michael Milken … may be symbolically important for what they convey about the nation's business and financial leadership, and they are surely the stuff of which novels and popular movies are made. But, as important as these cases are individually, and as influential as they may be within the business and financial community, they comprise only a tiny portion of the white-collar cases processed in the federal court system."[71]

---

[68] *See id.* at 1289.

[69] Trac Reports, White Collar Prosecutions Fall to Lowest in 20 Years, *available at* http://trac.syr.edu/tracreports/bulletins/white_collar_crime/monthlymay15/fil/ (last visited July 8, 2018).

[70] Weisburd, *et al.*, *supra* note 9, *passim.* The study was published by David Weisburd, Stanton Wheeler, Elin Waring, and Nancy Bode in *Crimes of the Middle Class.* Generally consistent with the Department of Justice's approach, the researchers selected for study not types of offenders but rather types of offenses, focusing on eight specific statutory violations included in most conceptions of white-collar crime—securities fraud, antitrust violations, bribery, bank embezzlement, postal and wire fraud, false claims and statements, credit- and lending-institution fraud, and tax fraud. The authors studied the pre-sentence investigation reports for a sample of offenders convicted of one of these eight crimes in seven federal districts over a two-year period. In comparing this sample with a comparison group of nonviolent, financially-oriented "common criminals"—specifically those prosecuted federally for postal theft and postal forgery—the study revealed important differences between "white-collar" offenses and common financial crime, some of which are discussed within.

[71] *Id.* at 45.

The Yale study reveals that, in sharp contrast to common criminals, the overwhelming majority of white-collar offenders it examined were employed and held jobs in "white-collar" positions (i.e., technical, clerical, or managerial occupations) that carried higher prestige than those held by the general population.[72] The white-collar offenders studied were also better educated and better off financially than common-crime defendants and the general public, although many offenders "have the material goods associated with successful people but may barely be holding their financial selves together" because of the extent of their liabilities.[73] While the general run of white-collar offenders are more privileged in material and other respects than the common criminal and certainly (one would assume) than the general run of drug and violent crime offenders, the Yale researchers stressed that white-collar practice overwhelming involves pursuing "the very broad middle of the society, much above the poverty line but for the most part far from elite social status. Like the offenses they commit, the offenders are mostly commonplace, not unlike the average American in most respects, though perhaps more often with personal lives that are in some state of disarray. The single quality that most distinguishes them from other Americans is that they have been convicted of a federal crime."[74]

Why does this discussion of the nature of white-collar crime indicate that it is likely to be a growth industry? As is indicated in the description of the typical white-collar offense, these are not crimes that one need be wealthy, socially well-placed, particularly skilled or even highly educated to perpetrate. "[F]raud and deceit and dishonesty, and the crimes based on them, [are] … the kinds of offenses that *every person* may commit. They do not take the physical skills and dexterity of many forms of street crime, or even the consummate skills of con artists. … Many of the crimes require not much more than the ability to read, write, and fill out forms, along with some minimum level of presentation of a respectable self."[75] Further, as the Yale Study concluded:

> We believe that ordinary people are committing white-collar crime in increasing numbers. One reason is that ordinary people now have greater access to the white-collar world of paper fraud. For example, more and more men and women work with computers, a technology that barely existed forty years ago, but one that now has a permanent place in national and international life. More and more white-collar computer employees find their jobs attached to some form of banking or company finance, and the potential to cheat is great. Since the nation's financial community and its stock markets are linked by computers, there is little doubt that fraud is a major concern, but one financial leaders dislike discussing publicly.
>
> … [T]he people we studied are the core American criminals, whose ranks will grow as the society becomes ever more middle class, as credit cards and credentialing grow, as television continues to hammer home the message of consumption. … Some members of this broad-based group have access to organizational resources required to commit the most substantial crimes, whereas others do not. Whether or not such resources are used, the skills required for most of these crimes are minimal, and

---

[72] *Id.* at 63-64.

[73] *Id.* at 65.

[74] *Id.* at 73; *see also* Pamela Bucy, *et al.*, *Why Do They Do It?: The Motives, Mores, and Character of White Collar Criminals*, 82 St. John's L. Rev. 401 (2008); Kathleen Daly, *Gender and Varieties of White-Collar Crime*, 27 Criminology 769 (1989).

[75] Weisburd, *et al.*, *supra* note 9, at 182.

many of the crimes seem mundane. Yet this is also why we believe that these are in many ways the prototypical American forms of crime.[76]

Many members of the public seem to labor under the misapprehension—formed no doubt by the media—that white-collar practice consists of a stream of high-profile cases. To some extent this misapprehension rests on a failure to recognize that the caseloads of many practitioners—including most prosecutors, public defenders, and appointed defense counsel—are dominated by the "commonplace" crimes and criminals described above. The rarified practice of privately-retained, specialized criminal counsel most closely resembles the glamorous practice of public impression. Yet the work of these lawyers is defined not by how "sexy" the case is or by the importance or status of the client, but rather by the client's ability to pay—individually or through corporate funding—for what is often an exceedingly time-intensive and thus expensive defense effort.[77] It may not be surprising that in the Yale study the majority of white-collar offenders retained their own counsel (in contrast to 16 percent of the common criminals sampled), but what is surprising is that approximately 40 percent of white-collar criminals relied on public defenders or court-appointed counsel.[78] This private practice, then, while challenging, prestigious, lucrative, and extremely interesting, is more limited than many suppose.

In the (for lack of a better term) "procedural" portion of the casebook, I attempt to focus on subjects that are of particular importance in white-collar practice. I have tried to concentrate on areas pertinent to prosecutors and to defense counsel, to those who deal with the more "mundane" types of cases as well as to those whose practices are followed by the popular press. The following contrast between federal white-collar practice and other types of criminal practice may provide the reader with some sense of why these subjects were selected as well as some insight into the general nature of the practice. (These generalizations regarding the differences between the practice of law in the white-collar crime area and the defense or prosecution of street crimes are, being generalizations, only true more often than not):

1. *Complexity, Scope, and Magnitude:* The Yale researchers concluded that, in the cases they studied, federal white-collar crimes were much more likely than cases involving federal common crime to spread across county, state, and national boundaries, to involve large dollar losses, to target multiple victims, to involve five or more coconspirators, to demonstrate a pattern of offending, and to extend over a substantial period of time.[79] As a consequence, the practical challenges facing white-collar prosecutors and defense counsel in investigating and marshaling the facts may be considerable. Such investigations, if done properly, will consume much more time, money, and attention than most street crime cases.

The subject-matter of these wide-ranging investigations also often demand more business acumen than the typical street crime. For example, rather than mastering the mechanics or techniques of drug dealing, the prosecutor may be called upon to figure out the intricacies of the commodities markets in order to determine how a

---

[76] *Id.* at 183-85; *see also* Stephen Labaton, *Downturn and Shift in Population Feed Boom in White-Collar Crime*, N.Y. Times, June 1, 2002, A1 (noting that white-collar cases were increasing *during* as well as after the economic boom cycle for a number of reasons including the facts that technological advances substantially contributed to the rate of financial crimes, the aging of the boomer generation meant that they are more likely to use a computer than a gun in robbing a bank, the increased education level of society made possible more sophisticated crimes, and executive compensation schemes tied to stock performance created unfortunate incentives).

[77] *See* Mann, *supra* note 60, *passim*, for an excellent and thorough study of this practice.

[78] *See* Weisburd, *et al.*, *supra* note 9, at 100.

[79] *See id.* at 43-45.

fraud was accomplished or concealed. "Follow the money" is the exhortation one often hears in white-collar investigations. But following the money may be quite difficult given the financial sophistication of some white-collar offenders. Certainly, bank embezzlement by a teller or simple non-reporting of income in a tax case may not require a great deal of factual analysis or mastery of accounting principles. But in many cases the methods of operation of white-collar criminals may be difficult to distinguish from normal commercial behavior; it is only through extensive familiarity with the business context that a crime may be detected and proved. Thus, for example in many antitrust, securities, tax, and fraud cases, counsel will need to submerge themselves in the business at issue in order effectively to make a convincing case or to formulate a defense theory.

2. *Investigation*: There are major differences in the ways in which white-collar and street crimes are investigated. Prosecutors increasingly are using investigative methods formerly reserved for street crime in white-collar cases. Thus, for example, the use of search warrants and wiretaps, once unheard of in business crime investigations, is now not infrequent. That said, the grand jury is still the primary investigative force in white-collar cases. The use of formal or informal immunity grants to secure testimony from individuals who assert their Fifth Amendment right are also primarily employed in the white-collar area. By their nature, grand jury investigations necessitate that prosecutors work closely with investigating agents in exploring the facts and developing a case because it is the prosecutor (generally speaking) who actually generates the grand jury subpoenas and certainly it is the prosecutor who runs the show in the grand jury itself. Use of the grand jury, immunity grants, and other traditionally white-collar investigative techniques may be increasing in street crime cases and many such cases may require that agents consult with attorneys, for example to obtain search warrants or wire tap approval. However, it remains true that in street and common crime cases the bulk of the investigative work is done by agents and takes place outside the grand jury.

White-collar cases generally will involve extensive pre-indictment use of grand jury subpoenas for the production of banking, credit, telephone, and travel records, computer-maintained information, business, tax, securities, and accounting documentation, and a variety of other materials. The grand jury investigation may stretch on for quite some time as the subpoenaed materials are produced and analyzed, often prompting yet more subpoenas. Prosecutors and investigating agents reviewing the subpoenaed records may be required to seek expert assistance or to develop accounting, financial, or other industry-specific expertise. Federal agents, and in some jurisdictions and cases, prosecutors, will likely interview a wide spectrum of individuals, from witnesses to (counsel permitting) targets of the inquiry. The grand jury's work may also require that numerous civilian witnesses be called to testify, in contrast to many street crime cases where the grand jury is often asked to indict based upon the testimony of a single law enforcement witness.

3. *Defense Counsel Role*: The critical stage of defense activity in most street crime cases is post-charge but pre-trial, when counsel's challenge is generally (given plea rates) to negotiate a disposition of a case that has already commenced against his client or to get ready for trial. By contrast, the critical stages of a white-collar case from the defense perspective are often the pre-charge and, if the case goes forward, the sentencing phases.

The most obvious difference between white-collar and other criminal practices is the important role that defense counsel will play during the course of the investigation. In street crime cases, counsel generally is not retained or consulted until the defendant is arrested. By contrast, given the overt nature of white-collar investigations and the resources available to many white-collar targets, defense counsel often will be hired when the first subpoenas fly or when an agent appears asking for a few words with a witness. *It cannot be overemphasized that the battle in many white-collar cases is perceived to be lost or won at the indictment stage.* As a consequence, defense counsel's initial focus is on gathering information regarding the subject-matter and likely direction of the investigation—from counsel's client, the prosecutor, other subjects or targets of the investigation, witnesses, hostile sources, and public records. "But above all, and this is the central theme of the white-collar crime defense function, the defense attorney works to keep potential evidence out of government reach by controlling access to information."[80] As one practitioner explained, "[m]y own belief is that the more information you control as [a] defense lawyer, the more effective you are, meaning that the only weapon you have as a defense lawyer in my view is control of information."[81]

In the pre-charge stage, then, the challenges facing defense counsel are (1) divining, without the benefit of formal discovery or other means of compelling the production of most types of information, what the government is investigating; (2) tracing or, with luck, keeping a step ahead of the government in learning the facts; (3) limiting, consistent with ethical and legal constraints, government access to incriminating evidence; and (4) using the facts, law, and equitable arguments to persuade the government to decline prosecution.

Defense counsel's role in the pre-charge period is presumptively (although perhaps not overtly) combative. His strategy of information control is essentially one of non-cooperation with the government even though that may not be the way counsel would explain it to the prosecutor. Throughout this period, however, counsel must be considering whether it is in his client's interest to abandon this approach and to commence negotiating a plea, cooperation, or immunity deal with the government. The earlier a deal is struck, the more advantageous it is likely to be from the defense's perspective. Yet "[a]n attorney who starts negotiations is communicating to the government that the client he represents is guilty of something and that the attorney thinks that the government will be able to prove it."[82] Obviously, this communication is likely to severely prejudice any hopes the defense has of persuading the government that a declination is the only just result. Counsel therefore must constantly evaluate the information he gathers about the evidence the government does and does not have to decide whether the point has come to work with the government rather than against it. Excellent judgment in this respect, as well as finely-honed negotiation skills, are critical to successful white-collar practice.

Because the length or type of criminal sentence is often a cardinal factor in the bargaining process, both sides must know how to use (and some say abuse) the federal sentencing guidelines. Although, after *Booker*, the guidelines are advisory, the federal courts continue to follow their direction most of the time. Post-*Booker*, it appears that, for the most part, judges are following the "advisory" guidelines range—or are deviating from it at the request of the government—in about 76-80% of cases, which is about 10-14% lower than the conformance rate prior to *Booker*. It should be noted that the conformance rate dropped each year after the *Booker* decision but appears to have stabilized at about 76%.[83] (Because there is a great variation around the country

---

[80] Mann, *supra* note 60, at 5; *see also id.* at 8 ("What is distinctive in white-collar cases is the centrality of information control strategies to defense work: they are fundamental modus operandi constituting a basic defense plan, rather than merely tactics in a broader strategy.").

[81] *Id.* at 171.

[82] *Id.* at 14.

[83] *See* "Conformance" is measured by adding the percentage of within-range sentences to the percentage of sentences that were below the range due to government-sponsored downward departures. In the pre-*Booker* period, from about October 2002 through mid-2004, the average nationwide "conformance" rate was a little over 90%. *See* U.S. Sentencing Comm'n, Final Report on the Impact of *United States v. Booker* on Federal Sentencing at vi-vii & n.9 (March 2006). The following summarizes how these percentages have changed over time, as derived from Sentencing Commission Reports and Sourcebooks: 2008, in-guidelines range (59.4%) plus government-sponsored downward departures (25.6%)=conformance rate

in the extent to which judges are following the guidelines, however, this average conformance figure is somewhat misleading.) While familiarity with the guidelines is important in any federal criminal practice, white-collar cases raise different, and probably more extensive, federal sentencing guidelines issues than do street crime cases.

The pre-indictment focus of the practice puts a premium on experience and specialization. Because legal and factual issues are often negotiated and resolved without resort to formal adjudication, much of the "precedent" upon which practitioners rely is unpublished. Effective counsel rely upon their familiarity with dispositions they, or others whom they know, have negotiated in like cases and their knowledge of informal local prosecution policies and practices to ensure that they make the best case possible on behalf of their clients. Some would argue that this focus also means that counsel's reputation and relationship with the prosecutor's office matters more in the white-collar area. The perceived experience, credibility, and integrity of counsel will make a difference when that counsel represents that all the relevant documents, facts, or witnesses have been made available—something that is not generally an issue where, as in street crime cases, the evidence is secured not by subpoena but by seizures or other means. These attributes of counsel may also make a decisive difference when that counsel argues that, given the facts, law, equities, and government policies and dispositions in like cases, no charges should be levied.

If, despite counsel's pre-charge efforts, the government determines to go forward to indictment, defense counsel is very likely to negotiate some sort of disposition. Such dispositions may involve a negotiated plea or some sort of cooperation or immunity deal. Around 97% percent of all federal criminal cases (and over 90% of cases involving organizational defendants) are resolved by guilty pleas. Although empirical evidence on this score is scarce, the common wisdom is that white-collar cases are less likely to go to trial than are drug prosecutions, which dominate the federal criminal caseload.

When these cases do go to trial, the trials are likely to be lengthy relative at least to trials of most street crimes. Given the resources available to many white-collar defendants, such trials are often hard and well fought. The trials will be notably paper-intensive in two respects. First, the evidence likely to be introduced will usually include volumes of paper. Second, where money permits, defense counsel will often make all manner of motions designed to secure any number of important objectives, for example: dismissal of the case; suppression of evidence; exclusion of witnesses; preservation of an issue for any possible appeal; discovering the government's evidence and legal theory; educating the judge on the defense's theory and the problems with the government's case; and (some would say) distracting and burdening the Assistant U.S. Attorney while she prepares for trial. Trial skills are certainly necessary, again for any number of reasons, including: (obviously) to litigate those cases that do go to trial; to maintain the credibility of defense threats to take a case to trial; and to provide some basis for making critical judgments in separating those winnable cases that should go to trial from those less promising cases that

---

of 85.0%; 2009: in-guidelines range (56.8%) plus government-sponsored downward departures (25.3%)=conformance rate of 82.1%; 2010: in-guidelines range (55%) plus government-sponsored downward departures (25.4%)=conformance rate of 80.4%; 2011: in-guidelines range (54.5%) plus government-sponsored downward departures (26.3%)=conformance rate of 80.8%; 2012: in-guidelines range (52.4%) plus government-sponsored downward departures (27.8%)=conformance rate of 80.2%; 2013: in-guidelines range (51.2%) plus government-sponsored downward departures (27.9%)=conformance rate of 79.1%; 2014: in-guidelines range (46%) plus government-sponsored downward departures (30.4%)=conformance rate of 76.4%; 2015: in-guidelines range (47.3%) plus government-sponsored downward departures (29.3%)=conformance rate of 76.6%; 2016: in-guidelines range (48.6%) plus government-sponsored downward departures (28.2%)=conformance rate of 76.8%.

clients would be well advised to plead out early. That said, because of the importance of pre-indictment advocacy skills and motion practice, a white-collar lawyer's writing skills are as important as his trial technique.

4. *Organizational Presence*: In most street crime cases, one commonly will deal exclusively with individuals or with organizations organized for criminal or corrupt purposes. In white-collar cases, by contrast, counsel will often have to deal with issues relating to the presence of a legitimate business or governmental entity in the case—either as a victim, an innocent instrumentality of wrongdoing, or a potential defendant. The Yale study discovered that, of the cases it examined, "[n]early all of our white-collar crimes involve some form of organizational victimization,"[84] in contrast to common crimes in which organizational victims were rare. Further, white-collar crimes were disproportionately "more likely than common crimes to use an organization in their commission."[85] Finally, the researchers concluded that:

> The most consequential white-collar crimes—in terms of their scope, impact, and cost in dollars—appear to require for their commission that their perpetrators operate in an environment that provides access to both money and the organizations through which money moves. The status or prestige of the organization, or of the individual who inhabits it, is only an incidental feature, for the key factor is location in the organization where money is to be found.[86]

This organizational presence introduces a number of interesting legal and business considerations into white-collar practice. For defense counsel, the involvement of an organization, usually a corporation, in the mix will mean that representation issues are a virtual certainty. One or more lawyers or law firms will represent the corporation. Although it is more efficient and may be in the corporation's best interests for counsel to represent both the corporation and all of its present or former officers, directors, employees, or agents with any involvement in the matter, fundamental and immediate issues of conflict of interests may preclude such blanket representation. If separate counsel is engaged for the individuals, a critical question arises whether the corporate and individual clients should enter into a joint defense agreement. Joint defenses, which are viewed by some prosecutors as nothing more than organized obstruction of justice, are often critical to successful white-collar defense practice for three principal reasons.

First, as noted, the focus of much of white-collar defense advocacy is in the pre-indictment period. Second, during that period, subjects and targets of the investigation have no formal discovery rights. Thus, to perform their information gathering and control function effectively, defense counsel must often depend upon others potentially within the investigatory scope to assist them in determining the government's focus and the evidence it has (and has not) uncovered. Finally, such sharing obviously would be dangerous if it could be discovered by the grand jury. Normally, work product protections and the attorney-client privilege are waived when covered materials are disclosed to third parties. Courts have, however, extended work product and attorney-client protections to certain materials shared pursuant to a joint defense agreement. Such agreements may in many cases be the principal vehicle counsel have for obtaining and controlling information, but they do not come without potential problems, ranging from participants' unauthorized use of shared materials to the perception that might be created in some prosecutors' minds

---

[84] Weisburd, *et al.*, *supra* note 9, at 43.

[85] *Id.* at 44.

[86] *Id.* at 60.

that the parties to the agreement are culpable or are even conspiring to obstruct the investigation.

Defense counsel will also be required to look beyond strictly legal concerns and focus on business considerations when advising their clients. The mere fact that a company is subject to a criminal investigation may negatively impact the company in a variety of ways. "In the days after the *New York Times* first reported that Wal-Mart faced charges for FCPA violations in Mexico, for example, its stock value initially declined 4.7 percent, knocking $18 billion off of its market capitalization."[87] Counsel and their clients must also be mindful of regulatory disclosure obligations regarding the status of the investigation, the serious collateral consequences that may flow from certain criminal dispositions (*i.e.*, debarment from government contracting), and the economically onerous restitution, fine, and organizational probation provisions of the federal organizational sentencing guidelines. Finally, defense counsel may be required to consider public relations concerns. Although defense against criminal prosecution or regulatory action should be counsel's cardinal consideration, the client may demand that those goals be met to the extent possible in ways that do not damage the organization's image.

The law permits corporations to be held liable for the misconduct of their agents acting within the scope of their employment and at least in part for the benefit of the corporation, even if the agents are acting contrary to express corporate policy. As stated and as applied, this standard opens the door wide for the imposition of the criminal stigma on corporations and other legal entities. Prosecutors, then, must consider when it is not just possible but also appropriate to charge a corporation for the acts of its employees and whether a plea by the corporation can or should mean that individuals need not be further investigated or prosecuted (and vice versa).

The case involving the indictment of Arthur Andersen LLP for obstruction—and the role that indictment had in the demise of the partnership and the accompanying loss of employment for approximately tens of thousands of workers—generated a great deal of controversy over that exercise of prosecutorial discretion. This controversy resulted in a new approach in organizational crime cases: the federal government's consistent practice of disposing of big-business cases by using so-called "Deferred Prosecution Agreements" (DPAs) or "Non-Prosecution Agreements" (NPAs).[88] These agreements generally provide that, in return for fulsome corporate cooperation in the investigation and prosecution of the individual wrongdoers within an organization (and other consideration), the government will, after a probationary period, dismiss or forego criminal charges against the organization. Deferred prosecution agreements were the norm for many years after the Andersen debacle, but the pendulum may be swinging back. Thus, in 2014 through 2017 the Justice Department forced a number of big banks (Credit Suisse, Citicorp, JP Morgan Chase, Barclays, The Royal Bank of Scotland, and UBS AG) to plead guilty to felony charges, and pay billions in criminal fines, for a variety of offenses including rigging interest rates and manipulating the market for U.S. dollars. In 2018 non-financial firms Volkswagen AG and Tyson Poultry, Inc. also pleaded guilty to federal crimes. Throughout that period, however, most Foreign Corrupt Practices Act cases continued to be settled through DPAs and NPAs.[89]

---

[87] Thomas J. Bussen, *Midnight in the Garden of* Ne Bis In Idem: *The New Urgency for an International Enforcement Mechanism*, 23 Cardozo J. Int'l & Comp. L. 485, 505 (2015).

[88] *See* Julie R. O'Sullivan, *How Prosecutors Apply the "Federal Prosecutions of Corporations" Charging Policy in the Era of Deferred Prosecutions, and What That Means for the Purposes of the Federal Criminal Sanction*, 51 Am. Crim. L. Rev. 29 (2014); Brandon L. Garrett, *Structural Reform Prosecution*, 93 Va. L. Rev. 853 (2007); Leonard Orland, *The Transformation of Corporate Criminal Law*, 1 Brook. J. Corporate Financial & Comm'l L. 45 (2006).

[89] For a comprehensive accounting of corporate dispositions, check the Corporate Prosecution

As we shall see, the government's organizational charging policy demands that, to secure a deferred prosecution agreement, organizations cooperate fully with government investigators, remedy any damage caused by the wrongdoing, and act aggressively to prevent recurrence of the objectionable behaviors. In many cases, the price of cooperation credit may be a waiver of the protections of the attorney client privilege or the work product doctrine—either explicitly or through the operation of privilege rules relating to the consequences of disclosing protected material to adversaries.

5. *Parallel Proceedings*: In many white-collar cases there may be a variety of governmental and private actors seeking to hold the subject of an ongoing criminal investigation accountable. A number of proceedings—brought by state, local, or federal regulatory agencies, shareholders, *qui tam* "relators," or alleged victims—may therefore proceed at the same time as the federal criminal case, or before or after it. "Government and private civil sanctions for the matter under criminal investigation … constitute a major threat to certain clients. They occupy the defense attorney's … attention more than any other collateral concern of the client's. Protection against civil suit is a vital client interest that the attorney must attend to even if he does not or will not represent the client in parallel civil proceedings."[90]

The possibility of parallel proceedings creates enormous challenges for the criminal lawyer. Obviously, such proceedings may consume valuable time and constitute a serious distraction for the client and for counsel. More important, they create difficult strategic issues, particularly where the imperatives of an effective criminal defense conflict with what may be the best strategy in the collateral cases. For example, generally speaking, very damning adverse inferences may be drawn in non-criminal cases from a party's assertion of the Fifth Amendment privilege against self-incrimination. Absent such an assertion, however, admissions may be made and information provided that can be used to great advantage against the party in the ongoing criminal case. At the very least, choices in one arena, such as a decision to disclose a piece of exculpatory evidence at the risk of a privilege waiver, may have disadvantageous consequences or foreclose certain options in another proceeding. The existence of parallel civil proceedings may well complicate efforts to settle the criminal action—especially where the defendant is less concerned about jail time than the monetary consequences of the litigation. For example, a corporation may conclude that the economic fallout of pleading guilty is simply too great to countenance when it considers that its admission of guilt may have collateral estoppel effect in subsequent civil suits. In short, the possibility of parallel proceedings in white-collar defense work means that counsel must constantly be alert to the effects that a decision in one proceeding may have on the interests of the client in a number of other areas.

6. *Multiple Actors*: In some cases—particularly where the criminal conduct at issue concerns the failure of an entity to meet its regulatory responsibilities—assigning criminal responsibility to a single actor or even a discrete group of actors may be difficult. For example, it may be hard in some cases to identify a single corporate agent who should go to jail where the corporation has shipped misbranded drugs or a bank has neglected to make currency transaction reports on covered transactions. In white-collar cases in particular, then, practitioners must wrestle with issues of causation, vicarious liability, and the applicability of traditional requirements of criminal *mens rea* (an evil mind or criminal intent) and *actus reus* (a culpable act).

7. *Centrality of Mens Rea*: Many white-collar cases come down to one question: whether the defendant possessed the requisite evil intent (*i.e.*, *mens rea*). For example, *mens rea* questions may predominate where an individual has filed a tax return

---

Registry,   available   at   http://lib.law.virginia.edu/Garrett/corporate-prosecution-registry/browse/browse.html.
[90] Mann, *supra* note 60, at 44.

misstating his income, a corporation has filed a claim for payment by the government to which it is not entitled, a public official has filed a required ethics disclosure document that excludes material information, or a witness misstates the facts under oath at a trial or a congressional hearing. In all these cases liability may well turn on whether the defendant *knew* that the tax return, claim, document, or testimony was false or whether the defendant *intended* to deceive or defraud or obstruct justice. Intent can be proved directly—for example, by a co-conspirator's testimony that the defendant told the witness that he was attempting to evade his tax obligations. More often, however, it is proved inferentially, by asking the jury to conclude from the facts shown that the defendant must have acted knowingly or with wrongful intent. Careful development of the facts, and skillful arguments regarding the likely inferences that should be drawn from them, are essential in such cases.

8. *Number and Vagueness of Statutory Standards*: As discussed above, the federal white-collar code is sprawling, and its provisions are often redundant and vague. At the very least, this indeterminacy in many of the most frequently-invoked white-collar statutory provisions means that this practice presents challenging legal and policy issues that may not be present in street crime cases. For example, it is generally clear that an assault is an assault, and a drug deal is a drug deal; the question in such cases will most often be not whether the act is criminal but whether the defendant committed it. In a white-collar investigation, however, defense counsel is more often able to argue that the uncontested facts do not and should not constitute a crime. This is a fairly common objection, and, perhaps surprisingly, may sometimes be successful—both in dissuading prosecutors from indicting and in persuading courts to overturn a conviction.

Additionally, white-collar offenses tend to be more "morally ambiguous" than street or other crimes. As Professor Stuart P. Green, has explained:

> …[I]n a surprisingly large number of cases there is a genuine doubt as to whether what the defendant did was in fact morally wrong. In such cases, the issue is not, as it is with necessity, whether the defendant was confronted with some extraordinary choice between obeying the law, and allowing significant harm to occur, or violating the law, and preventing such harm. Rather, the question is whether the conduct engaged in was more or less acceptable behavior that should not have been subject to criminal sanctions in the first place.[91]

It is not infrequently difficult to "differentiate, for example, between criminal fraud and 'sharp dealing,' insider trading and 'savvy investing,' bribery and 'horse trading,' tax evasion and 'tax avoidance,' extortion and 'hard bargaining,' witness tampering and 'witness preparation,' and perjury and 'wiliness on the witness stand.'"[92]

What makes arguments to white-collar prosecutors perhaps unique in criminal practice is their substance. One may actually be able to use to practical effect all the theory and policy one absorbed in law school to argue that a statute should not be extended to cover a defendant's conduct. One can make the case that that which the defendant did was not morally wrong, let alone illegal. In the judicial arena, courts predictably are reluctant to overturn convictions based on arguments that what is clearly "bad" conduct is not proscribed by statute. In white-collar cases more than any other criminal area, however, courts do on occasion accept defense counsel's invitation, particularly where prosecutors are perceived to have stretched the law to invade state prerogatives, where the conduct at issue could conceivably be characterized as aggressive but not necessarily immoral business behavior, or

---

[91] Stuart P. Green, *What is Wrong with Tax Evasion?*, 9 Hous. Bus. & Tax L.J. 221, 223 (2009).

[92] Stuart P. Green & Matthew B. Kugler, *Public Perceptions of White Collar Crime Culpability: Bribery, Perjury, and Fraud*, 75 Law & Contemp. Probs. 33, 33 (2012).

where the government's theory is sufficiently expansive that it may be used in future cases to sanction protected (*e.g.*, political) activity.

9. *Alternative Avenues for Redress*: Much of what is subject to federal white-collar prosecution is also subject to prosecution under state law. Rather than "piling on" and having more than one jurisdiction address the criminal conduct at issue, generally some allocation of responsibility will be made between federal and state actors. Similarly, in many cases, white-collar crimes can be redressed by civil as well as criminal remedies. Thus, it is not always necessary for a criminal case to be made for alleged misconduct to be officially addressed.

10. *Breadth of Prosecutorial Discretion*: Again, as discussed at length above, prosecutors in white-collar cases exercise a very broad—and for the most part unreviewable—discretion in selecting cases and charges. Attorney General, Nuremberg prosecutor, and Supreme Court Justice Robert H. Jackson famously asserted that "[t]he prosecutor has more control over life, liberty, and reputation than any other person in America."[93] "Because the prosecutor has 'responsibility for deciding whether to bring charges and, if so, what charges to bring against the accused, as well as deciding whether to prosecute or dismiss charges or to take other appropriate actions in the interest of justice ... the character, quality, and efficiency of the whole system is shaped in great measure by the manner in which the prosecutor exercises his or her broad discretionary powers.'"[94] As Professor Pamela Bucy, a former federal prosecutor, has explained:

> [As a new AUSA without law enforcement experience,] I learned much. ... Of everything, ... the most startling revelation was the amount of power I and every prosecutor had. There were plenty of experienced prosecutors and agents to guide, advise, and help, and they did, but bottom-line, the decisions—good and bad—were mine: who, when, how to investigate; who to indict, when, and for what charges; what plea offer to extend; and how to conduct my trials, which witnesses to call, and how to present the evidence. The hundreds of decisions I and other AUSAs made every day changed the lives of others forever. When I began at the Department of Justice ... I was eager and aggressive. When I left seven years later, I was humbled by the power of the Office.[95]

The extent of their powers necessitate that all federal prosecutors have a firm handle on, *inter alia*, their unique professional responsibilities and the ethical rules that bind them (considered below).

---

[93] Attorney General Robert H. Jackson, *The Federal Prosecutor*, 24 Judicature 18, 18 (1940).

[94] H.R. Rep. No. 101-986, at 3 (1990) (quoting prepared statement of William W. Taylor III, on behalf of the Am. Bar Ass'n before the Subcomm. on Gov't Information, Justice, and Agriculture, Comm. on Gov't Operations, U.S. House of Representatives, concerning prosecutorial authority (May 10, 1990)); *see also* David Alan Sklansky, *The Nature and Function of Prosecutorial Power*, 106 J. Crim. L. & Criminology 473 (2016); U.S. Dep't of Justice, United States Attorneys Manual § 9-27.001 (Office of Law Enforcement-U.S. Attorneys Manual Project ed., 1997) [hereinafter USAM] ("The manner in which Federal prosecutors exercise their decision-making authority has far-reaching implications, both in terms of justice and effectiveness in law enforcement and in terms of the consequences for individual citizens. A determination to prosecute represents a policy judgment that the fundamental interests of society require the application of the criminal laws to a particular set of circumstances ..."); U.S. Comptroller General, Report to Congress: U.S. Attorneys Do Not Prosecute Many Suspected Violators of Federal Laws (Feb. 27, 1978).

[95] Pamela H. Bucy, *Moral Messengers: Delegating Prosecutorial Power*, 59 S.M.U. L. Rev. 321, 321-22 (2006).

D. PROFESSIONAL RESPONSIBILITY

The U.S. Attorney General heads the U.S. Department of Justice in Washington D.C. (sometimes referred to as "Main Justice"), which is responsible for criminal litigation on behalf of the United States. Within the Department, supervision of criminal enforcement resides primarily in the Criminal Division, although some responsibility for criminal prosecutions rests in other divisions such as the Antitrust Division, the Environmental and Natural Resources Division, the Civil Division, and the Tax Division. The Criminal Division directly undertakes the investigation and prosecution of select cases but the bulk of actual criminal litigation is performed by the U.S. Attorneys Offices (which are actually not within the DOJ's Criminal Division).

There are 94 U.S. Attorneys Offices (USAOs), one of which is located within each of the federal judicial districts. A U.S. Attorney heads each office. The U.S. Attorneys are appointed for four-year terms by the President and confirmed by the Senate. Within each district, the U.S. Attorney is the chief federal law enforcement officer and also handles civil litigation in which the United States has an interest. The U.S. Attorney generally controls the hiring, training, and direct supervision of the Assistant U.S. Attorneys (AUSAs) who actually conduct the day-to-day litigation for each office (although the AUSAs are actually appointed by the Attorney General and are subject to discipline through the Department). Offices of U.S. Attorneys range in size from those with a few assistants to offices of more than 200 AUSAs.

Although the Attorney General and DOJ are part of the executive branch, they are supposed to be above partisan politics.[96] Thus, it is against the law and long-standing DOJ practice to consider political affiliation when hiring career prosecutors to fill positions not classified as "political appointments."[97] Obviously, prosecutorial decisions regarding the persons and crimes to be targeted for investigation and prosecution should never be influenced by political affiliation.[98]

Two of the major federal investigative agencies, the Federal Bureau of Investigation (FBI) and the Drug Enforcement Administration (DEA), are within the Department of Justice. The Attorney General is also responsible for supervising the Bureau of Prisons and the U.S. Marshal's Service. Other federal investigative agencies, such as the U.S. Postal Inspection Service, the Internal Revenue Service, and the U.S. Secret Service are not directly accountable to the Justice Department but work with department attorneys and AUSAs to investigate and prosecute criminal cases.

---

[96] For exploration of the relationship between DOJ and the USAOs, as well as the relationship between the DOJ generally and Congress and the President, see Daniel Richman, *Political Control of Federal Prosecutions: Looking Back and Looking Forward*, 58 Duke L.J. 2087 (2009). For an analysis of the dynamics of the interactions between federal prosecutors and enforcement agents, see Daniel Richman, *Prosecutors and Their Agents, Agents and Their Prosecutors*, 103 Colum. L. Rev. 749 (2003).

[97] That is not to say that this law and policy are never violated; the DOJ career hiring decisions were politicized under Attorney General Alberto Gonzalez. But the resulting furor may prove that this was the exception, not the rule. *See* Office of the Inspector Gen. & Office of Prof'l Responsibility, U.S. Dep't of Justice, An Investigation of Allegations of Politicized Hiring by Monica Goodling and Other Staff in the Office of the Attorney General (2008).

[98] Again, there have been instances in which the DOJ has improperly used partisan political criteria in making prosecutorial decisions. Some allege that this, too, occurred in President George W. Bush's Justice Department. *See* Office of the Inspector Gen. & Office of Prof'l Responsibility, U.S. Dep't of Justice, An Investigation Into the Removal of Nine U.S. Attorneys in 2006 (2008).

1. PROSECUTORIAL ROLE

The materials in this casebook focus to a large degree on the functioning of prosecutors, in part because prosecutors act in a capacity that is unique in the legal system and is rarely explored in depth in other courses. Rule 3.8, the ABA Model Rule of Professional Conduct provision addressed to the "Special Responsibilities of a Prosecutor," provides as follows:

The prosecutor in a criminal case shall:

(a) refrain from prosecuting a charge that the prosecutor knows is not supported by probable cause;

(b) make reasonable efforts to assure that the accused has been advised of the right to, and the procedure for obtaining, counsel and has been given reasonable opportunity to obtain counsel;

(c) not seek to obtain from an unrepresented accused a waiver of important pretrial rights, such as the right to a preliminary hearing;

(d) make timely disclosure to the defense of all evidence or information known to the prosecutor that tends to negate the guilt of the accused or mitigates the offense, and, in connection with sentencing, disclose to the defense and to the tribunal all unprivileged mitigating information known to the prosecutor, except when the prosecutor is relieved of this responsibility by a protective order of the tribunal;

(e) not subpoena a lawyer in a grand jury or other criminal proceeding to present evidence about a past or present client unless the prosecutor reasonably believes:

> (1) the information sought is not protected from disclosure by any applicable privilege;
>
> (2) the evidence sought is essential to the successful completion of an ongoing investigation or prosecution; and
>
> (3) there is no other feasible alternative to obtain the information;

(f) except for statements that are necessary to inform the public of the nature and extent of the prosecutor's action and that serve a legitimate law enforcement purpose, refrain from making extrajudicial comments that have a substantial likelihood of heightening public condemnation of the accused and exercise reasonable care to prevent investigators, law enforcement personnel, employees or other persons assisting or associated with the prosecutor in a criminal case from making an extrajudicial statement that the prosecutor would be prohibited from making under Rule 3.6 or this Rule.

(g) When a prosecutor knows of new, credible and material evidence creating a reasonable likelihood that a convicted defendant did not commit an offense of which the defendant was convicted, the prosecutor shall:

> (1) promptly disclose that evidence to an appropriate court or authority, and
>
> (2) if the conviction was obtained in the prosecutor's jurisdiction,
>
>> (i) promptly disclose that evidence to the defendant unless a court authorizes delay, and
>>
>> (ii) undertake further investigation, or make reasonable efforts to cause an investigation, to determine whether the defendant was convicted of an offense that the defendant did not commit.

(h) When a prosecutor knows of clear and convincing evidence establishing that a defendant in the prosecutor's jurisdiction was convicted of an offense that the defendant did not commit, the prosecutor shall seek to remedy the conviction.

Readers should also reference the American Bar Association's Criminal Justice Standards for the Prosecution and Defense Functions, which were revised in 2015.

To set the stage for further discussion of the prosecutorial role, readers should be aware of two issues that may color much of that functioning: prosecutors' unique obligation to "do justice," and the myriad ethical standards—federal and state—that now apply to federal prosecutors.

a. Federal Prosecutors' Duty to "Do Justice"

The United States Attorney is the representative not of an ordinary party to a controversy, but of a sovereignty whose obligation to govern impartially is as compelling as its obligation to govern at all; and whose interest, therefore, in a criminal prosecution is not that it shall win a case, but that justice shall be done. As such, he is in a peculiar and very definite sense the servant of the law, the twofold aim of which is that guilt shall not escape or innocence suffer. He may prosecute with earnestness and vigor—indeed, he should do so. But, while he may strike hard blows, he is not at liberty to strike foul ones. It is as much his duty to refrain from improper methods calculated to produce a wrongful conviction as it is to use every legitimate means to bring about a just one.[99]

This widely-quoted passage reflects the prevailing view that federal prosecutors have a special role in the adversary process.[100] Although this obligation to "do justice" is not stated in the text of Rule 3.8, the commentary to that ethical standard states that "[a] prosecutor has the responsibility of a minister of justice and not simply that of an advocate. This responsibility carries with it specific obligations to see that the defendant is accorded procedural justice and that guilt is decided upon the basis of sufficient evidence. Precisely how far the prosecutor is required to go in this direction is a matter of debate and varies in different jurisdictions."

The ABA Standards for Criminal Justice, which, although not legally binding, are often relied upon in discussing the duties of criminal counsel, provide the following standard for the function of the prosecutor:

The prosecutor is an administrator of justice, a zealous advocate, and an officer of the court. The prosecutor's office should exercise sound discretion and independent judgment in the performance of the prosecution function. ... The primary duty of the prosecutor is to seek justice within the bounds of the law, not merely to convict.[101]

By contrast, the Standards describe the function of defense counsel as follows:

The primary duties that defense counsel owe to their clients, to the administration of justice, and as officers of the court, are to serve as their clients' counselor and advocate with courage and devotion; to ensure that constitutional and other legal rights of their clients are protected; and to render effective, high-quality legal representation with integrity.[102]

---

[99] Berger v. United States, 295 U.S. 78, 88, (1935).

[100] *See generally* Bruce A. Green, *Why Should Prosecutors "Seek Justice"?*, 26 Fordham Urb. L.J. 607 (1999). B*ut see* Kevin C. McMunigal, *Are Prosecutorial Ethics Standards Different?*, 68 Fordham L. Rev. 1453 (2000) (arguing that overemphasis on uniqueness of prosecutorial ethics standards is "misleading because it fails to convey that in many, perhaps most, instances the standard of conduct for the prosecutor is identical to the standard for the criminal defense lawyer and the civil advocate").

[101] ABA Standards for Criminal Justice: The Prosecution Function Standard 3-1.2(b), (c) (2015).

[102] ABA Standards for Criminal Justice: The Defense Function Standard 4-1.2(b) (2015). This is not to say that defense counsel may not at times face difficult conflicts in the course of his

What is striking about the above description of the ethical prosecutor's role, especially in contrast to the description of defense counsel's role?

The adversarial structure of the American justice system makes the lawyer's zealous advocacy on behalf of the client the linchpin of the process. Yet, the ethical rules that govern the legal profession single out prosecutors as the only participants who must adhere to a special duty beyond that of representing zealously their "client." This higher duty has been variously phrased to require the prosecutor "to seek justice, not merely to convict," and "to serve as a minister of justice and not simply [as] an advocate." The recurrent theme is justice, although the codes do not furnish any guidance about what that means or even whose perspective determines whether a particular result is just.[103]

The "do justice" requirement is an integral part of the self-definition of most federal prosecutors.[104] But what does it mean to "seek justice"? Consider the following discussion by Professor Stanley Z. Fisher:

…The duty to "seek justice" might be construed in a positivist sense, as merely enjoining prosecutors from violating independently articulated restrictions (whether substantive or procedural) on prosecutorial power. The message would be that while performing as an advocate, one should not violate specific ethical prohibitions, court rules, statutes, or the defendant's constitutional rights. In this view, the ethical command has no independent content. …

…But the duty to "seek justice" implies a normative conception of the prosecutor's duty according to which "justice" has some independent meaning. Even if this duty is not enforceable as such, it need not be entirely meaningless. Its very prominence in the professional rhetoric suggests that it says something meaningful to prosecutors, at least about how to apply other, more specific norms. But what is that "something"?[105]

Does that "something" mean that prosecutors must do what they subjectively believe is right or moral in a given situation or a particular case? So read, this obligation would seem to create a great risk of unequal treatment and divergent results depending upon the training, perspective, and judgment of individual prosecutors. Does the fact that the

---

representation, for example where the defendant asks him to do something that runs counter to law or counsel's ethical obligations. In such situations, the Standards provide that "[d]efense counsel has no duty to execute any directive of the accused which does not comport with law or … standards [of professional conduct.] Defense counsel is the professional representative of the accused, not the accused's alter ego." *Id.* at 4-1.2(e).

[103] Peter J. Henning, *Prosecutorial Misconduct and Constitutional Remedies*, 77 Wash. U. L.Q. 713, 727 (1999).

[104] *See, e.g.,* Green, *supra* note 100, at 607; Gerard E. Lynch, *Our Administrative System of Criminal Justice*, 66 Ford. L. Rev. 2117, 2150-51 (1998); Kenneth J. Melilli, *Prosecutorial Discretion in an Adversary System*, 1992 B.Y.U. L. Rev. 669, 669-70; David A. Sklansky, *Starr, Singleton, & the Prosecutor's Role*, 26 Fordham Urb. L.J. 509 (1999).

[105] Stanley Z. Fisher, *In Search of the Virtuous Prosecutor: A Conceptual Framework*, 15 Am. J. Crim. L. 197, 218-19 (1988); *see also* Laurie L. Levenson, *Working Outside the Rules: The Undefined Responsibilities of Federal Prosecutors*, 26 Fordham Urb. L.J. 553, 553 (1999) ("Prosecutors seeking justice often must go beyond the boundaries of the law in an effort to create informal procedures for justice that will apply where the law is silent."); Casey P. McFaden, Note, *Prosecutorial Misconduct*, 14 Geo. J. Legal Ethics 1211 (2001) (identifying and outlining caselaw surrounding Rule 3.8).

obligation to "do justice" appears to be distinct from prosecutors' obligation of zealous advocacy imply an obligation at times to temper the zeal of their advocacy so as to achieve a more "just" result? This reading would seem, on occasion, to present the prosecutors with a sizeable conflict in the exercise of their basic role.[106] It may also present a sizable conflict as a matter of human psychology; some suggest that it is exceedingly difficult, as a practical matter, for prosecutors effectively to operate simultaneously as dispassionate administrators of justice and as zealous advocates.[107]

Perhaps this "justice" obligation simply means, as the commentary to the Model Rules suggests, that prosecutors must not commence a case unless they have a good faith belief that they have the evidence to prove a defendant guilty and that prosecutors must ensure that the adversarial system works as it should—that is, they must work toward "procedural justice."[108] The quantum of personal assurance prosecutors must have before bringing a criminal case is subject to some dispute in the literature,[109] although all agree that the minimum standard is probable cause. This does not seem a particularly controversial aspect of the do-justice obligation, but it also only addresses one decision of the many that face prosecutors daily. The question of how prosecutors must ensure that the justice system's procedures work as they should seems both more difficult and more important from a practical point of view, applying as it does to prosecutors' investigative, charging, trial, plea bargaining, and sentencing responsibilities. This definition of the prosecutor's obligation seems again to raise the question how prosecutors can "correct" systemic defaults, such as bad defense lawyering, without tempering their zeal. Does the resolution of this question depend upon the justifications provided for the duty—whether it is founded upon the gross imbalance of power between prosecutors and defendants or instead on the prosecutor's professional role as a representative of a sovereign?[110] If the latter, how does one define the interests of the sovereign "client" one is required to zealously further?[111] What is the consequence if those interests conflict in a given case?

---

[106] Note that this potential conflict may have important consequences for the prosecutor. Depending upon the definition of the do-justice requirement, she may well feel that she is between a rock (fulfilling the basic role definition under discussion) and a hard place (Justice Department disapproval for failure to exercise sufficient zeal). For example, in 1997, the Justice Department concluded that a Department attorney in three cases had, among other things, "failed to zealously represent the United States by unjustifiably (and without authorization) reducing felony charges to misdemeanors." U.S. Department of Justice, Office of Professional Responsibility, Fiscal Year 1997 Annual Report 6.

[107] *See, e.g.*, H. Richard Uviller, The *Neutral Prosecutor: The Obligation of Dispassion in a Passionate Pursuit*, 68 Fordham L. Rev. 1695 (2000).

[108] *See* Fred C. Zacharias, *Structuring the Ethics of Prosecutorial Trial Practice: Can Prosecutors Do Justice?*, 44 Vand. L. Rev. 45 (1991) (proposing that prosecutors' obligation to "do justice" has two fairly limited prongs, (1) prosecutors should not prosecute unless they have a good faith belief that the defendant is guilty; and, (2) prosecutors must ensure that the basic elements of the adversary system exist at trial and discussing the meaning of these prongs in the context of prosecutorial trial practice).

[109] *Compare, e.g.*, H. Richard Uviller, *The Virtuous Prosecutor in Quest of an Ethical Standard: Guidance from the ABA*, 71 Mich. L. Rev. 1145 (1973) (arguing against requiring a heightened standard of personal prosecutorial certainty with respect to guilt prior to charging), *with* Melilli, *supra* note 104, at 669.

[110] *Compare* Zacharias, *supra* note 108, at 45 (superior power rationale), *with* Green, *supra* note 97, at 607 (representative of sovereign rationale).

[111] *See* Green, *supra* note 100, at 634 (interests of sovereign include "enforcing the criminal law by convicting and punishing some (but not all) of those who commit crimes; avoiding punishment of those who are innocent of criminal wrongdoing...; ... affording the accused, and others, a lawful, fair process"; "treat[ing] individuals with proportionality"; "treat[ing] lawbreakers with rough equality").

b. Applicable Ethical Standards

The Citizens Protection Act (CPA) provides:

§ 530B. Ethical Standards for Attorneys for the Government
(a) An attorney for the Government shall be subject to State laws and rules, and local Federal court rules, governing attorneys in each State where such attorney engages in that attorney's duties, to the same extent as other attorneys in that State.
(b) The Attorney General shall make and amend rules of the Department of Justice to assure compliance with this section.[112]

This statute is sometimes referred to as the "McDade Amendment"—a reference to its chief sponsor, Congressman Joseph McDade, who was acquitted of federal criminal charges after trial and who complained throughout his case about the excesses of federal prosecutors. The Amendment was proposed at a time when the Department of Justice was battling with state bar organizations (and others) about federal prosecutors' obligations to comply with state and federal court ethical rules. The specific ethics rules involved in the debate were the long-standing bar on lawyers contacting represented parties (the "no-contact" rule)[113] and a rule limiting prosecutors' ability to subpoena lawyers.[114] The first Bush Administration by internal memorandum (the "Thornburgh Memo")[115] and the Clinton Administration through regulation (the "Reno Rule"),[116] took the position that federal prosecutors were exempt from state ethics rules and local federal court rules that adopted them. While Attorney General Reno stated that the Justice Department would generally voluntarily adhere to state standards of conduct,[117] the Justice Department's stand was not well received by state officials and the defense community. The Department's position also generated litigation attacking its claims that the Supremacy Clause authorized the preemption of state ethics rules and that separation of powers concerns barred federal courts from applying state rules to federal prosecutors. Who *should* be entrusted with formulating and enforcing the ethical rules that bind federal prosecutors?[118]

---

[112] 28 U.S.C.A. § 530B(a)-(b).

[113] *See* Model Rules of Professional Conduct Rule 4.2 (1983) [hereinafter Model Rules]; Model Code of Professional Responsibility DR 7-102 (1969) [hereinafter Model Code].

[114] *See* Model Rules Rule 3.8(f).

[115] S*ee* Richard L. Thornburgh, Memorandum from Attorney General to all Justice Department Litigators 1 (June 8, 1989) (Thornburgh Memorandum), *reprinted in In re* Doe, 801 F.Supp. 478, 489 (D.N.M.1992); *see also* Richard L. Thornburgh, *Ethics and the Attorney General*, 74 Judicature 290 (1991) (justifying Thornburgh Memorandum).

[116] 28 C.F.R. § 77 (1994), *explained in* Communications With Represented Persons, 59 Fed. Reg. 39,910 (1994) (Reno Rule).

[117] *Id.*

[118] *See, e.g.*, Bruce A. Green & Fred C. Zacharias, *Regulating Federal Prosecutors' Ethics*, 55 Vand. L. Rev. 381 (2002); Jennifer Blair, *The Regulation of Federal Prosecutorial Misconduct by State Bar Associations: 28 U.S.C. § 530B and the Reality of Inaction*, 49 U.C.L.A. L. Rev. 625 (2001). There is an excellent and growing literature concerning the optimal source, form, and content of ethical regulations for prosecutors. In addition to the sources cited throughout, see, e.g., Frank O. Bowman, III, *A Bludgeon by Any Other Name: The Misuse of "Ethical Rules" against Prosecutors to Control the Law of the State*, 9 Geo. J. Legal Ethics 665 (1996); Bruce A. Green, *Whose Rules of Professional Conduct Should Govern Lawyers in Federal Courts and How Should the Rules Be Created?*, 65 Geo. Wash. L. Rev. 460 (1996); Rory K. Little, *Proportionality As an Ethical Precept for Prosecutors in Their Investigative Role*, 68 Fordham L. Rev. 723 (1999); Rory K. Little, *Who Should Regulate the Ethics of Federal Prosecutors?*, 65 Fordham L. Rev. 355 (1996); Fred C. Zacharias, *Who Can Best Regulate the Ethics of Federal Prosecutors, or, Who Should Regulate*

The McDade Amendment's application to violations of the "no-contact" rule is clear,[119] but its potential effects are not confined to that context. As Professors Fred C. Zacharias and Bruce A. Green have noted, a number of other state ethics rules might affect federal prosecutorial practices: (1) a number of states have adopted ethics rules that limit prosecutorial authority to subpoena lawyers to give unprivileged information; (2) "some state ethics rules expand prosecutors' obligation to disclose evidence to the defense, require prosecutors to expose exculpatory evidence to grand juries, require prosecutors to discourage public statements by law enforcement personnel, and limit the prosecutor's (but not the defense's) ability to discourage witnesses from cooperating with their adversaries"; (3) "several states have adopted ethics rules that forbid lawyers to compensate fact witnesses for their testimony... [and] a reasonable argument can be made that plea bargaining inducements do constitute 'compensation' under the state ethics rules"; and (4) "state bar organizations have recently begun to consider whether general prohibitions against 'misrepresentations' by attorneys should be applied to prosecutors," which would affect undercover investigations conducted under a prosecutor's supervision, as well as prosecutorial efforts to induce confessions or cooperation by defendants by making threats that they do not intend to carry out as well as misrepresentations about the facts.[120] The McDade Amendment has drawn a deal of negative commentary[121] and the DOJ has repeatedly sought its repeal—thus far without success.

c. Case Study

David Luban, *The Conscience of a Prosecutor*
45 Val. U. L. Rev. 1 (2010)

...

Two years ago, a startling story appeared in the New York Times: a veteran prosecutor in New York City's District Attorney's ("D.A.'s") office, Daniel Bibb, was assigned to reexamine two men's murder convictions because of new evidence.[122] The men had been in prison for more than a decade, and the new evidence showed that they might be victims of a horrible case of mistaken identity, as defense lawyers and a tenacious police detective had maintained for years. After an exhaustive twenty-one-month investigation, Bibb became convinced they were not guilty. But he could not persuade his superiors to drop the cases, so he went in to the hearing and, in his words, he threw the case. "I did the best I could," Bibb said, "To lose." ...

---

the Regulators?: Response to Little, 65 Fordham L. Rev. 429 (1996).

[119] See, e.g., United States v. Koerber, 966 F.Supp.2d 1207 (D. Utah 2013) (granting motion to suppress upon a finding that prosecutors and investigators violated Utah's no-contact rule and thus the Citizens Protection Act).

[120] Fred C. Zacharias & Bruce A. Green, *The Uniqueness of Federal Prosecutors*, 88 Geo. L. J. 207, 215-23 (2000); *see also* Paula J. Casey, *Regulating Federal Prosecutors: Why McDade Should Be Repealed*, 19 Ga. St. U. L. Rev. 395 (2002) (discussing controversial Oregon Supreme Court decision holding that rule barring misrepresentations applied to federal prosecutors, thus ending their participation in undercover investigations).

[121] See, e.g., Gregory B. LeDonne, Note, *Revisiting the McDade Amendment: Finding the Appropriate Solution for the Federal Government Lawyer*, 44 Harv. J. on Legis. 231 (2007). *But see* Larry D. Thompson, *McDade Law Is Good for the Profession*, Champion, Apr. 2001.

[122] Benjamin Weiser, *Doubting Case, a Prosecutor Helped the Defense*, N.Y. Times, June 23, 2008, http://www.nytimes.com/2008/06/23/nyregion/23da.html?r=1&pagewanted=al [hereinafter Weiser, Doubting Case].

Before turning to issues of ethics and theory, it will be useful to understand the facts of the case. It began in 1990 at an East Village nightclub called the Palladium on Thanksgiving night. A bouncer punched a man in the face and expelled him from the club. The man decided to take revenge and returned with friends and guns. In the wee hours of the morning, two of the gunmen opened fire on bouncers standing outside the club, killing 23-year-old Mark Petersen and wounding a second bouncer.

How did police come to arrest [the two men later exonerated] David Lemus and Olmedo Hidalgo for the Palladium murder? The two men claimed they did not even know each other; Hidalgo said he had never been to the Palladium, and Lemus said he had been there only once in his life, a year before the shooting. But both had prior arrests that got their photos into police files and led to eyewitnesses picking them out of photo arrays that detectives showed them. At trial, multiple eyewitnesses were able to identify Lemus and Hidalgo.

There was one other damning piece of evidence against Lemus: he bragged to a woman named Delores Spencer that he had committed the Palladium killing. She told a friend who told the police. Police had Spencer tape subsequent phone calls with Lemus. This is what the jury at the 1992 trial heard on the tape:

> David Lemus: "If you're scared, just say you're scared."
> Delores Spencer: "Why should I be scared of you?"
> Lemus: "Because you know that I know that you know." [3 short puffs]

Lemus and Hidalgo's attorney did not put on any witnesses, and after a day's deliberation, the jury convicted the men of second-degree murder. They each drew sentences of 25 years to life.

That might have been the end of the story except for a series of coincidences. Around the time the jury convicted Lemus and Hidalgo, New York City detective Robert Addolorato was investigating a Bronx drug and extortion gang called C&C. One of his informants told him that two C&C members named Joey Pillot and Thomas "Spanky" Morales—not Lemus or Hidalgo—were the real Palladium shooters.

Addolorato reported what he heard to the Manhattan D.A.'s office but was told that it did not match the known facts. Understanding quite well that snitches sometimes lie, Detective Addolorato let it drop until 1996, four years later. By that time he was working with federal prosecutors in the C&C investigation, and they arrested none other than Joey Pillot and Spanky Morales. Pillot agreed to cooperate, and his lawyer worked out what prosecutors call a "queen for a day" agreement: Pillot would sing, and none of what he said could be used to prosecute him.

Pillot told the investigators that he and Morales were indeed the real Palladium shooters. Furthermore, he provided details that matched the facts: he remembered that his own gun had jammed and that he ejected a cartridge—and police in fact found an ejected cartridge on the scene. Additionally, Morales drove a blue Oldsmobile, with a license number containing an 8 and a 1. Eyewitnesses had told police that the shooters escaped in a blue car whose license number included an 8 and a 1.

Addolorato went back to the D.A.'s office, and, after some initial resistance, the D.A. agreed to a new hearing on the Palladium shooting: a so-called "440 hearing," referring to section 440.10(g) of the New York Code, which provides for motions to vacate a judgment when new evidence is discovered. But the D.A. argued that the new information, which might well incriminate Spanky Morales, did not show that Lemus or Hidalgo were innocent—and the judge agreed. Even back at the original trial, prosecutors had raised the possibility of a third perpetrator. Justice Gold found Pillot's claim that he and Morales were the sole perpetrators "entirely unworthy of belief."

Then, in 2000, an inmate named Richie Feliciano read a news story about the Palladium case. In early 2001, he told federal prosecutors that he had been at the Palladium that night, just a few feet away when Spanky Morales shot the bouncers.

Feliciano had been the "mediator" attempting to defuse the conflict between Morales and the bouncers—or perhaps the decoy distracting the bouncers. In fact, Feliciano said he was the one who drove Morales's car away from the scene. It seemed increasingly likely that the case against Hidalgo and Lemus was a gigantic miscarriage of justice.

The two convicted men were represented pro bono by a lawyer named Steve Cohen. Cohen is a former federal prosecutor, and back in 1996 he was present during Joey Pillot's queen-for-a-day revelation that he and Spanky Morales had committed the Palladium murder. As Cohen explains it, his initial interest as a prosecutor

> was not that two innocent men were in jail, but that we wanted to use Joey as a witness in the C&C prosecution. I was concerned that we would need a state plea agreement as well as a federal agreement, because we couldn't fold the Palladium murder into a RICO charge.

But the Manhattan D.A.'s office rebuffed Cohen when he and Addolorato alerted them about Pillot's confession. When Cohen went into private practice as a litigator at the New York law firm Kronish Lieb Weiner & Hellman (now Cooley Godward Kronish), the case continued to weigh on his mind. "This is the only case I left behind that keeps me up at night, that plays on my conscience," Cohen told a reporter in 2000. After Lemus's mother began calling him, Cohen agreed to represent Lemus and Hidalgo pro bono. Addolorato, the police detective who first heard Joey Pillot's information, also stuck with the case for sixteen years, and he was in the courtroom when Lemus was ultimately acquitted. In Cohen's view, Addolorato was the true hero in the Palladium case.

Word of Feliciano's admission soon got to Cohen and to Lemus's trial lawyer, Eric Sears; as Cohen observes, the New York City criminal bar is a small world. In 2003, they went back to the Manhattan D.A.'s office and spoke with ADA Stephen Saracco, the head of the Cold Case Unit who had argued the state's side at the 440 hearing. Cohen urged Saracco that it was time for a new trial. Saracco asked, "Are you saying that these guys are actually innocent, or that they have a right to a new trial?" Cohen replied that they were actually innocent. Saracco agreed to open a new investigation, which he thought would take six weeks and lead to a new 440 hearing. But Saracco retired, and the D.A.'s office assigned the investigation to Daniel Bibb. …

Bibb's investigation took … years. Bibb describes the investigation as follows: "Two detectives from the Manhattan South Homicide Squad and I ultimately interviewed over 60 people in connection with the investigation. Interviews were conducted in at least fifteen states, three New York State prisons, eight federal prisons and one county jail, all of which were spread across the country." By the end of the investigation, Bibb was convinced that Lemus and Hidalgo had nothing to do with the Palladium shooting.

Then why had Lemus told Delores Spencer that he was involved? According to Lemus, it was simply a pathetic story of talking big to impress a woman. He was twenty-two years old at the time, and Spencer was thirty—a married mother of three children who, in Lemus's words, "liked the gangster type and thugs." Lemus wanted to show Spencer that he was a tough guy and a player, not just a "knucklehead with a bus pass." He had seen the news about the Palladium shooting on television, and it was the first thing that came to his mind. …

Meanwhile, we can only guess what conversations were going on between Bibb and his superiors in the Manhattan D.A.'s office, but they must have been tense and difficult. Bibb, quite properly, will not talk about confidential office conversations.

The D.A.'s office did not dispute that Morales was the shooter. Rather, along the lines of the third-perpetrator theory, they told Bibb to defend the convictions and argue that all the men were in cahoots. Bibb, on the other hand, was convinced that Lemus and Hidalgo had nothing to do with Morales and Pillot.

Why not prosecute Spanky Morales? This was a question the judge asked Bibb, and his answers hint at some of the disagreements that must have been going on in the D.A.'s office:

> Judge Roger Hayes: "It is something that is puzzling to the court."
> Bibb: "It is the subject of continuing discussion within my office."
> Judge Hayes: "In other words, if your theory is correct, why is that person unprosecuted?"
> Bibb: "That also has been the subject of continuing discussions in my office."

Bibb explains that cases in which prosecutors delay indictment are extremely vulnerable to speedy trial and due process motions, and by this time the D.A.'s office had collected significant evidence against Morales in the Palladium case for many years.

Bibb says that he personally had no problem charging Morales, and in fact he was pushing for the indictment. As he puts it: "I always thought that in a homicide it's better to prosecute and lose on a motion than not to prosecute at all. No dead body should go unpunished." Presumably others in the office disagreed because they concluded that the indictment would be dismissed.

Finally—a few weeks before the new 440 hearing—police arrested Morales for his role in the Palladium homicide, and Bibb drew the assignment to prosecute him. As the D.A.'s office foresaw, when Spanky Morales was finally indicted the judge dismissed the case on a … speedy trial motion. Because of double jeopardy, Morales was safe and could testify in David Lemus's retrial. Defense attorney Cohen believes that the reason the office finally indicted Morales is obvious: his apparent guilt was going to come out in a matter of months at Lemus's and Hidalgo's 440 hearing, and it would look awful if prosecutors had allowed Morales to go unindicted.

The Palladium case was already an embarrassment to the D.A.'s office as news stories over the years, including Dan Slepian's NBC Dateline special, had painted the convictions as a spectacular miscarriage of justice. It was embarrassing enough to become an issue in the re-election campaign of District Attorney Robert Morgenthau. Palladium was an embarrassment as well because of items that turned up in the case file. First, as mentioned earlier, back in 1990 an anonymous tipster phoned a hotline to say that Spanky Morales was the shooter. No one ever pursued that lead, but the note was in the file. Second, soon after the shooting, Morales's sister-in-law told police that Spanky was involved. Third, three of the state's own eyewitnesses had identified Morales from a photo array. However, Police Detective Victoria Garcia explained that she did not write a report about the photo array or a wanted card for Morales because it would weaken the state's case against Lemus and Hidalgo. It seemed that the police had bungled the investigation and then ignored evidence in its own files.

All this led Lemus's and Hidalgo's attorneys to argue that the state had committed *Brady* violations by not revealing the evidence showing that Morales was the guilty man. Here, however, Bibb was not inclined to play along with the defense. In his own words, he "fought the *Brady* allegations tooth and nail," cross-examining Lemus's attorney, Eric Sears, for two full days. Bibb argued that prosecutors told the defense lawyers about Morales in a timely fashion, and the defense withdrew that portion of their *Brady* claim. Thus, whatever ways Bibb "threw the case," admitting police misconduct was not one of them.

Bibb was clearly less comfortable advancing the state's theory that Morales, Lemus, and Hidalgo were all involved. That is not surprising because, as we now know, Bibb was convinced that they were not. "I came to believe that Hidalgo wasn't there. And if he wasn't there, he certainly couldn't have done it." At one point, the judge asked Bibb, "Is there any information in your possession that ties the defendant with each other or the C and C gang[?]" and Bibb responded "Only in the most tenuous way." The men had all grown up in the same neighborhood and hung out at the same bars, but there was no evidence that Lemus and Hidalgo had anything to do with the gang. "Absent that," Bibb stated, "I've been able to find no other connections." Bibb elaborates:

> Many of the witnesses that Lemus and Hidalgo called at the hearing were cooperating with me in the prosecution of Morales. They included at least a half dozen witnesses who Morales admitted his participation to. As I explained when we spoke, the admissions Morales made to these witnesses ... placed him in the role that Lemus was identified by the eyewitnesses as playing, that of the person hit by the bouncer and thrown out of the club. You definitely cannot have two people playing the exact same role in a crime. This is one of the reasons I was and remain convinced that Lemus was misidentified and Morales actually played that role.
>
> For the sake of completeness, I am convinced that the four people involved in the crime were Thomas Morales aka Spanky (hit by [the] bouncer and thrown out of the club, gunman and active shooter), Joseph Pillot aka Joey (gunman whose gun misfired), Ramon Callejas aka Peachy (third gunman who did not fire his weapon and who looks a lot like Morales) and Richard Feliciano aka Richie (employed as a distraction so Spanky could try to get back into the club to kill the bouncer who actually hit him and threw him out of the club). Lemus may very well have been there but, if he was, he was not involved. Hidalgo was not there and was most likely having Thanksgiving dinner with a friend and his friend's wife.

These are the tangled events that led Bibb to throw the case. Contrary to news reports, he never "coached" or "strategized" with defense attorneys—by this time, Lemus and Hidalgo were represented not only by Steve Cohen's firm Cooley Godward Kronish but also by pro bono attorneys from Dickstein Shapiro—but he did speak with them about "the evidence I had uncovered and my view as to what the evidence meant ... On a number of occasions, when they did not understand the import of a particular piece of evidence, I explained it to them." Gordon Mehler, one of Lemus's lawyers, confirmed Bibb's account when he told a reporter that "If I make a mistake in my interpretation of what he said, he'll correct me ... If there's a piece of evidence that [bore] on another piece of evidence I'm talking about, he'll remind me of it. That's not something that a prosecutor typically does." Bibb also made sure that "reluctant witnesses (and some were very reluctant) appeared and all the witnesses Lemus and Hidalgo called to testify on the newly discovered evidence issue were prepared and testified truthfully." Bibb not only prepped the defense witnesses, he told them what he was going to ask them in his cross-examination. Bibb comments:

> Did that feel weird? Sure it did—but not that weird, because I've prepared witnesses to testify a thousand times. I always tell witnesses what questions to expect from the other side. This time, I told them what questions to expect from the defense on direct, then I said "Here are the questions you're going to get on cross." A couple of the witnesses figured out what was going on. They asked who was going to be crossing them, and I told them that I was.

Bibb did not try to undermine the eyewitnesses in his cross-examination. Both he and Cohen point out that he had a pragmatic reason for preserving their credibility; namely, that they would also be witnesses in his pending prosecution of Spanky Morales. But according to Bibb, his basic motive was that he wanted to lose.

Cohen disputed that Bibb "shot over the heads of the enemy":

> [T]he notion that the ADA "threw the case" is not accurate and belied by [Bibb's] conduct at the hearing and the positions he took before the judge. Frankly, there was no[t] a prosecutor in the DA's Office who could have preserved those

convictions. To suggest otherwise does a disservice to the men and woman, esp[ecially] Detective Addolorato, who worked so hard to see justice done.

Cohen nevertheless agrees that Bibb went through a genuine crisis of conscience, and adds: "I did come to like and respect Dan Bibb. He was an honorable person caught in a terrible situation." ...

Why did Bibb handle the case the way he did? Here is his own explanation, in a letter to bar disciplinary authorities:

> I felt that I had a number of choices. The first was to resign. While I am sure it would have garnered a lot of press coverage, it would not have moved the matter along to a just conclusion. In fact, it most likely would have substantially delayed the matter, resulting in the continued incarceration of two innocent men. The next was insubordination, refusing to do the hearing and risk being fired. Practically speaking, neither of these was an option because I have a wife, three children, and a mortgage and college tuition to pay and could not afford to be out of work. The last was to do exactly what I did.

He adds: "In this matter I did what every prosecutor should do, worked to ensure a just result consistent with my conscience, ethical principles and the evidence." Bibb recalls the events leading to his decision:

> Up until the day I was ordered to do the hearing I was confident that I would prevail in my efforts and that there would never be a hearing. I truly believed that common sense would prevail. ... The day I was ordered to do the hearing was the worst day of what was then a 22 year career as a prosecutor. After I left work that day I called a friend who is a civil engineer (and knows about the criminal justice system only what he sees on TV) and got together for a 'few' drinks with him. ... I mulled over and discussed with my pal resigning in protest, refusing to walk into the courtroom and letting them fire me or throwing the hearing. ... I decided then that's what I would do. That was in the first week of April 2005, a few weeks before the hearing began.

II. Ethics and Prosecutors

There is no doubt that what Dan Bibb did was unusual. And there is no doubt that he violated the usual role expectations of the adversary system, where lawyers never try to help the other side make their case even when they think the other side is right. But did Bibb do anything wrong?

Stephen Gillers, a nationally-renowned legal ethics expert, thought he did and predicted that Bibb might face professional discipline. "He's entitled to his conscience," Gillers wrote, "but his conscience does not entitle him to subvert his client's case ... It entitles him to withdraw from the case, or quit if he can't." Bibb, on the other hand, said that he didn't withdraw because "he worried that if he did not take the case, another prosecutor would—and possibly win."

Now I have great admiration for Stephen Gillers (with whom I have co-authored), but in this case I think he was wrong. Daniel Bibb deserves a medal, not a reprimand.

Before I explain why, let's see what the ethics case against Bibb might look like. Imagine that a private lawyer representing a private client does the same thing. She locates truthful but adverse witnesses and persuades them to testify. As a matter of fact, she reveals her cross-examination to them. Not only that, she goes beyond minimally complying with her opponents' discovery requests—the civil counterpart to minimally fulfilling a prosecutor's *Brady* obligations. She points out connections between pieces of evidence to the opposing lawyers. The lawyer does it because she thinks the other side was right, and her client loses.

There is no question that the lawyer could and would be sued for malpractice. As for ethics violations, the lawyer could be charged with several: violating the requirement of competency; the requirement that the client, not the lawyer, sets the goals of the representation; the requirement of diligence (also known as "zeal," although the Model Rules do not use that word in their text); and the conflict of interest provision forbidding lawyers from taking cases where the lawyer's representation of the client will be "materially limited" by "a personal interest of the lawyer." Conceivably she could also be charged with using client confidences against the client's interests, if any of her conduct was based on confidential information from the client. And, if the lawyer kept her strategy secret from her law firm—which expected her to zealously represent the client's position—she was engaging in deceit, which the ethics rules prohibit.

In short, the lawyer in private practice would face a mountain of ethics charges.

All the same prohibitions apply to a prosecutor, but there is one crucial difference: prosecutors are not supposed to win at all costs. In a time-honored formula, their job is to seek justice, not victory. This is a mantra that appears in all the crucial ethics documents. It appears in a comment to the current ABA Model Rules of Professional Conduct: "A prosecutor has the responsibility of a minister of justice and not simply that of an advocate." It appears in the Model Rules' predecessor, the ABA Code of Professional Responsibility: "The responsibility of a public prosecutor differs from that of the usual advocate; his duty is to seek justice, not merely to convict." The same language appears in the ABA's Standards for the Prosecution Function. [Ed.: The author's quotation of the *Berger v. United States* dictum omitted.] ...

This is a very different way to think about a lawyer's role in the adversary system than we are used to in other contexts. It is especially different from the criminal defense attorney's role, which most lawyers and scholars agree requires maximum zeal on the client's behalf. Now in one way, this stark difference between the prosecutor's mission and the mission assigned to other advocates in the adversary system is obvious: the criminal justice system would be a travesty if a prosecutor, holding years of someone's life in her hands, cared about nothing but notching another victory.

But I do want to point out that the *Berger* dictum, with its "seek justice not victory" formula, runs entirely against the grain of popular anti-crime sentiment as well as the way people commonly think about the adversary system. In popular sentiment, criminals are by definition bad guys, prosecutors who lock them up are, for that reason, good guys, and defense lawyers live under a perpetual cloud of suspicion, reflected in endless griping about clever lawyers who get crooks off on technicalities. Criminal defenders constantly face the question "[h]ow can you represent people like that?"—or the more sophisticated law student's version, "I understand why the system needs defense lawyers, but personally I could never do that kind of work." As for our conventional understanding of the adversary system, it envisions complete symmetry of obligation between the two sides: they are both supposed to fight as hard as they can to win.

The "seek justice not victory" formula, coupled with the view that criminal defense requires the maximum level of zealous advocacy, presents an entirely upside down model. Now, we have asymmetrical obligations: the defender is supposed to seek victory, not justice, while the prosecutor is constrained to seek justice, not victory. Prosecutors, it seems, are simply not supposed to fight to win the way defenders are.

Admittedly, there is a delphic quality to the "seek justice not victory" formula. Justice is a grandiose and vague word. Oliver Wendell Holmes famously said "I hate justice, which means that I know if a man begins to talk about that, for one reason or another he is shirking thinking in legal terms." The formal ethics rules—as opposed to aspirational standards like the ABA's Standards for the Prosecution Function—take a pretty minimalist view of the prosecutor's obligations. Prosecutors should not proceed without probable cause, they should make a reasonable effort to ensure that the accused has been informed of his rights, they should not try to get an unrepresented person to waive rights, and they should do timely *Brady* disclosures. They should not subpoena defense lawyers unless they have to. And they should refrain from inflammatory public comments about their cases—a rule all too often honored in the breach. In most jurisdictions, that is the extent of their ethical obligations. These rules leave loads of leeway for prosecutors to seek victory regardless of justice, without facing even a whiff of professional discipline. As Bibb notes, "I could have done a lot of things both inside and outside the courtroom that would have been perfectly legal and ethical to frustrate their [the defense lawyers'] efforts. The fact is that I didn't do them ..."

Fred Zacharias, in a leading scholarly article on the "seek justice not victory" formula, thinks that the justice prosecutors seek "has two fairly limited prongs: (1) prosecutors should not prosecute unless they have a good faith belief that the defendant is guilty; and, (2) prosecutors must ensure that the basic elements of the adversary system exist at trial." The formal ethics rules do not go even that far.

And yet I have spoken with a lot of prosecutors who take "seek justice not victory" seriously, even if they are not 100% confident they know exactly what it requires. At the very least, as Zacharias's first point indicates, they know you should not try to keep people behind bars if you think they didn't do it.

In 2008, the ABA House of Delegates agreed. The ABA added two Model Rules to deal with prosecutors' obligations when new evidence suggests that they obtained wrongful convictions. One requires a prosecutor who learns of "new, credible and material evidence creating a reasonable likelihood that a convicted defendant did not commit an offense of which the defendant was convicted," to disclose the evidence to the proper authorities as well as the defendant and to initiate an investigation. If the evidence is clear and convincing, the prosecutor must "seek to remedy the conviction." Two prominent scholars have argued that these rules do not go far enough because evidence that a convicted person is probably innocent should impel a conscientious prosecutor to try to remedy the injustice, even if the evidence is not clear and convincing.

These rules are rather new, and to date only three states have adopted them. Furthermore, it seems perfectly clear that the ABA was not thinking of Bibb's unorthodox tactics as the way a lawyer should "seek to remedy the conviction." But what, after all, did Bibb do wrong? He persuaded reluctant witnesses to show up in court and testify against the state. Think for a moment about the alternative. Bibb was assigned to investigate the Palladium case, and he went on an odyssey to track down the witnesses: sixty interviews, fifteen states, eleven prisons, one county jail. Once he had the evidence, he was under an obligation to turn it over to the defense if it was exculpatory—which he did.

The alternatives: don't investigate the case very well for fear you will find out that the men doing 25-years-to-life are innocent; or, having investigated it, don't turn over the exculpatory evidence to the defense, violating your constitutional and ethical obligations; or, having turned it over, put the defense to the difficulty of locating the witnesses and getting them to court—so, if the defenders do not succeed, the truth stays buried. That is the ethical obligation of a public prosecutor?

I hope your answer to my rhetorical question is no, but it may not be. A great many lawyers think that putting the other side to the effort and expense of getting witnesses to court is exactly what the adversary system contemplates. Sometimes, people quote a line from the Supreme Court's decision in *Hickman v. Taylor*, that "a learned profession" is not supposed "to perform its functions ... on wits borrowed from the adversary."

I think the Palladium case is a good illustration of how absurd this dictum is. Bibb persuaded reluctant witnesses—not all of whom were solid citizens—to testify truthfully. Would not doing so have impeded the search for truth? ... Steve Cohen believes that the favorable result in the 440 hearing was "pre-ordained," but Bibb responds, "I am sure you know that nothing is pre-ordained in the criminal justice system." It really doesn't matter who is right. Bibb feared a grotesque injustice—otherwise he had no motive to hold his fire any way—and for a lawyer facing such a situation, thinking the result is pre-ordained is a luxury you cannot afford, whether or not it is true. Getting key witnesses onto the stand is exactly what was required to seek justice not victory in this case.

One hundred and eighty years ago, John Stuart Mill criticized jurists who looked at the adversary system through "fox-hunting eyes," as if it were nothing more than "a sort of game, partly of chance, partly of skill." That fox hunter's outlook seems to be the Supreme Court's in *Hickman v. Taylor*, and it is also the outlook of anyone who thinks the prosecutor's job is to stand pat and let the defense get the witnesses to testify—if they can. Years ago, when I first began studying the adversary system, I thought that if this is what lawyering in an adversary system means, it is a large strike against the adversary system. I still think so. But even if you are a bigger fan than I am of the adversary system, you should agree that standing pat in this case would have violated the prosecutor's special responsibility to seek justice not victory.

Admittedly, it is odd to have the prosecutor discuss with the defense how the evidence fits together, and odder still to tell witnesses what he plans to ask them on cross-examination. Notice something important, though: in this case, Bibb's tactics advanced the search for truth and the protection of rights. These are precisely the two values that defenders of the adversary system argue it is there to promote.

In truth, Bibb's conduct may not be so extraordinary. A former federal prosecutor tells me that it is not unusual for prosecutors to throw cases at the grand jury stage because they think the case stinks, but they are under pressure to take it to the grand jury. That is less conspicuous than Bibb throwing the case at a public hearing, but morally it is hard to see the difference.

An important point is lurking in the background here. One reason some lawyers feel uncomfortable with the adage "seek justice not victory" is that there is no consensus about what justice is, and we have every reason to doubt there ever will be. Philosophers who spend their lives thinking about the theory of justice don't agree about whose theory is right. But you do not need a philosophical theory of justice to recognize gross injustice when you see it. Our sense of injustice is more basic, less controversial, and less dependent on philosophical arguments than propositions about justice. "Avoid injustice" might be a more useful imperative than "seek justice," even if it is less catchy and less inspirational. It is probably what prosecutors actually do when they take "seek justice not victory" seriously.

III. Why Should Prosecutors Seek Justice, Not Victory?

Scholars have advanced two theories for why the prosecutor's job is to seek justice not victory. One points to the power differential between the state and the accused individual. The state has tremendous resources: police to investigate cases, crime labs to examine evidence, and-of course-the charging power to flip witnesses and induce plea bargains. The accused typically has an overworked defender with little or no capacity to investigate; in many cases, the accused is in jail. Even the names attached to criminal cases show the power imbalance: *State v. Defendant, People v. Defendant, United States v. Defendant*. Because of the power imbalance, it is essential that prosecutors not take victory as their sole goal. Call this the power theory.

The other theory focuses not on the power imbalance between the government and the accused, but on the special duty of the executive to govern justly and impartially. That is the theory in the *Berger* case, which I quoted earlier: the prosecutor "is the representative not of an ordinary party to a controversy, but of a sovereignty whose obligation to govern impartially is as compelling as its obligation to govern at all." Call this the sovereignty theory.

In my view, neither theory tells the whole story. The sovereignty theory does not explain why prosecutors, seeking victory in an adversary contest where the defense is doing the same, are not governing impartially. Why isn't procedural justice within in the adversary system all the justice prosecutors need to seek? Surely part of the explanation is the power imbalance: giving the state most of the cards in a purely competitive contest, where the only goal is victory, means that it will win even when the defense would prevail in a more even context. So the sovereignty theory needs the power theory to back it up—otherwise, it does not adequately explain why prosecutors should seek justice not victory.

Conversely, the power theory does not explain what is wrong with a pro-government power imbalance, which, after all, many people think is the best way to fight crime. The answer must be that we want more from government than fighting crime: we want government to bend over backwards to achieve fairness and avoid collateral damage to the innocent in the war against crime. In other words, the power theory needs the sovereignty theory to back it up.

In short, each theory needs the other. But even combining them leaves out something essential: the stakes are so much higher in criminal law than anywhere else. We have one of the world's harshest criminal justice systems, with lengthy sentences, draconian conditions of confinement, little if any interest in rehabilitation, loss of rights to convicted felons even after they serve their time, and stigma that follows convicts forever, blighting their chances to make a fresh start. As everyone knows or should know, the United States currently has more people locked up than any nation in history, both per capita and in absolute numbers.

But the United States also has a constitution built on principles of limited government and individual rights. It is an interesting puzzle how the same country that traditionally fears government abuse and rallies around the libertarian slogan "don't tread on me!" can at the same time be so addicted to harsh punishment—but this is not the occasion to address the puzzle.

Instead, I want to emphasize that the protection of individual rights from government abuse is a key part of our political tradition, and the harshness of our punishments makes the protection of rights in the criminal process a matter of life and death. That is why the power imbalance in the criminal justice system and the government's commitment to impartiality are so important. "Seek justice not victory" weaves together all three concerns. Prosecutors should not exploit the power imbalance, and they should care immensely about the rights of the accused, including the substantive right to stay out of jail when you are innocent, because of the enormously high stakes in these cases. Every good prosecutor understands that she holds years of a person's life in her hands.

Obviously, prosecutors are not responsible for mass incarceration—they deal with criminal cases retail, not wholesale, and legislatures' addiction to ratcheting up punishments is not the prosecutor's fault. But the prosecutor is the gatekeeper of the system, the one who decides which cases go from the paddy wagon to the courtroom. The prosecutor's conscience is the invisible guardian of our rights, just as the defense lawyer is the visible guardian. What made Bibb's conduct in the Palladium case so remarkable is that here, the invisible guardian became visible.

IV. Is Hierarchy Process?—or, Who Decides What Justice Is?

I hope I have adequately explained why prosecutors must seek justice, not merely victory. But to this point, I have left out one crucial piece of the story: Bibb was working in a law office, and his superiors in the chain of command disagreed with him. Granted that prosecutors must seek justice, who decides what justice is? Isn't that a decision for the boss rather than an Assistant D.A.?

When I blogged about Bibb and the Palladium case in 2008, several ethics experts objected that I was wrong to ignore the hierarchy of the D.A.'s office. John Steele, a founder of the blog Legal Ethics Forum, put it this way:

Suppose . . . a subordinate lawyer thinks that the evidence doesn't meet the high threshold a prosecutor should have before trying a defendant—but the supervisory lawyer disagrees. . . .

Should the subordinate lawyer accede to the supervisor's orders and try the case, ask to be moved to another case, resign from the organization, or secretly subvert the supervisor's orders while pretending to follow them?

The only answer I can't support is the last one. It's deceit on the supervisor, deceit on the organization, and deceit on the court.

Law professor Marty Lederman, a former Deputy Assistant Attorney General in the Department of Justice's Office of Legal Counsel, agrees:

The prosecutor here was the elected Manhattan D.A., who chose to go ahead with the prosecution. . . .

. . . [L]et's assume, as we must here, that the D.A. was not persuaded by Bibb, and concluded that the defendant was guilty beyond a reasonable doubt.

At that point, Bibb is acting as an agent of the D.A. If he firmly believes his supervisor was wrong, Steele is correct that he can—perhaps should—ask to be removed from the case, or resign. If he thinks the D.A. is willfully acting unlawfully, perhaps he should even make a stink about [it] to the relevant authorities or in public.

But act as an unfaithful agent? . . .

This may not be an ethics violation—but it's a violation of one's contract with the principal, a violation of agency principles, and, as you concede, a fraud on the D.A.

And Stephen Gillers wrote this:

Morgenthau speaks for the client, the People. He was elected not Bibb. It is analogous to a CEO or Board speaking for the company. ...

... Would David support a Bibb-like act in the next case if another assistant threw the case honestly convinced that it is what justice required, ignoring contrary instruction, and it turned out that the freed person really was factually guilty? We law professors have the luxury of living in a more or less hierarchy-free world, but in the 'real life' of big law offices, including government ones, hierarchy is process.

It would take another lecture as long as this one to fully respond to these comments, but my basic answer is very simple. I agree that if you work in an organization—at any rate a decent organization—you should generally respect the chain of command. And if your supervisors reach a different conclusion than you about the same evidence, you should earnestly consider whether their judgment might be better or more objective than yours.

But sometimes it may happen that your certainty remains unshakeable, even when you have tried as hard as you can to see it their way. And sometimes the magnitude of the injustice is intolerable. Lastly, once in a great while, nobody can stop the injustice but you. At that point, the demands of conscience, and indeed of human decency, prevail over the office hierarchy. ...

The basic problem with viewing hierarchy as process is that organizations, including good organizations, can malfunction badly. The record of the Palladium case ... shows astonishing resistance to the truth in the police and the D.A.'s office stretching over many years. Detective Garcia had information that Morales and Pillot were the shooters virtually from the beginning of the investigation but did not properly memorialize it. The D.A.'s office repeatedly rebuffed Detective Addolorato and, later, Cohen. At the first 440 hearing, the office pressed the third-shooter theory, despite the lack of evidence of any connection between Lemus, Hidalgo, and Morales. ...

What explains the evident dysfunction in a generally impressive office? Cohen provides background about why the D.A.'s office was originally resistant to his information about Joey Pillot's confession: there was a long-standing rivalry between the D.A.'s office and the Eastern and Southern Districts' U.S. Attorney's offices (and, he adds, the FBI). "The complexity was that we [the U.S. Attorney's office] were bringing gang cases [when Cohen was involved in the federal investigation of C&C]. Manhattan thought we were treading on their turf; they had the expertise—and in part they were right about that. We had resolved this friction in the Bronx, but not in Manhattan." Then, over the years, as the injustice to Lemus and Hidalgo became greater, it became harder rather than easier for the office to admit error or incompetence—a familiar psychological dynamic in which people become invested in their own earlier decisions.

Cohen writes, "During my years dealing with the Palladium case, I was continually reminded of the work of Stanley Milgram and Philip Zimbardo, the social scientists who conducted obedience experiments. Unfortunately, (I fear) what might be learned from this tragedy is missed time and again." The experiments he refers to are classics of social psychology, studying the dynamics by which structures of authority and role undermine moral judgment. In Milgram's obedience experiments, subjects ordered to administer escalating, possibly lethal electrical shocks to other subjects (who were actually confederates of the experimenter—and the shocks were fake) found it very hard to break off. Indeed, two-thirds of them went all the way to the highest voltage. Milgram's explanation was that "if he breaks off, he must say to himself: 'Everything I have done to this point is bad, and I now acknowledge it by breaking off.' But if he goes on, he is reassured about his past performance." This may well have been the psychology in the D.A.'s office. Even if hierarchy is process, it can be a terribly flawed process: good when it works, but incapable of self-correction when it does not.

V. The Socratic Ideal

I now turn to my final question, perhaps the hardest question in legal ethics. What role does conscience play in lawyer's ethics, when conscience presses one way but the professional rules press the other? ...

The basic principle of Socratic ethics is that it is worse to do wrong than to suffer wrong. In the Apology, Socrates reminds his jurors of two episodes that nearly cost him his life. Once, when he held a public office, the Athenians wanted to put some generals on trial illegally, and Socrates was the only one to oppose them. "I thought I must run the risk to the end with law and justice on my side, rather than join with you when your wishes were unjust ..." On another occasion, the dictators of Athens ordered Socrates and some others to arrest a man named Leon and bring him to be illegally executed. As Socrates reminds the jury, "when we came out of the rotunda, the other four went to Salamis and arrested Leon, but I simply went home .... "

Both times, Socrates defied public authority to avoid participating in wrongful criminal punishments. The examples no doubt infuriated his jurors, because of course Socrates was arguing that his own conviction would be unjust, and the examples were an ironic rebuke to those who were about to convict him. Ironic or not, the examples show us something crucial: the paradigm case of conscience lies in refusing to acquiesce in the wrongful conviction of the innocent.

Of course I am not comparing Dan Bibb to Socrates. Bibb is an unpretentious, plainspoken lawyer, and he would undoubtedly find the comparison embarrassing and absurd. Hopefully any of us would. My point is the striking fact that when Socrates illustrates his conscience at work, he picks examples where public authorities wanted him to participate in wrongful convictions. You might say that these are the original conscience cases. ...

At one point, Bibb remarked to me, "I've become a case. It's the worst thing in the world—being known for just one thing. Forget all the good I did, all the prosecutions over the years, all the bad guys I put behind bars." I did not quite know what to say, because of course the Palladium case was the reason I was talking with him. But I got his point, and it is an important one. Conscience is not the special property of moralists and saints. It is not the property of humanitarians with refined sensibilities—prosecuting felonies is not the career choice of delicate people. If you are lucky, you may never encounter a conscience case, although I suspect that prosecutors encounter them more often than they recognize. The test of character is whether, when you do, you can be stubborn enough and creative enough to rise to the occasion.

Note

1. David Luban reports that New York disciplinary authorities filed a complaint against Bibb based on the above-described events but he was cleared of disciplinary charges and is currently in private practice. Olmedo Hidalgo was deported to the Dominican Republic. David Lemus was acquitted by a jury and released after spending fourteen years in prison. Subsequently, he sued New York City for wrongful imprisonment, and the city settled for $1.2 million. Hidalgo also sued, and reportedly settled for more than twice that amount.

2. DEFENSE CHALLENGES

The ethical obligations of defense counsel in white-collar cases are the same as they are in all other criminal cases. As discussed above, however, the practice does have its unique aspects, and thus may present novel ethical problems. At the least, certain ethical issues will occur more often and perhaps in a more aggravated fashion. Some of these recurring issues will be covered in ensuing chapters; for example, representation issues will receive close attention. The following raises one set of issues that pervades the practice:

Kenneth Mann, Defending White-Collar Crime: A Portrait of Attorneys at Work
(Yale Univ. Press 1985), at pp. 16-17

When an attorney decides that his main defense strategy will be to keep information out of the forum of legal argument, a fundamental ethical question emerges: "How far," he must ask himself, "can I go in my effort to keep facts from being revealed to my opponent?" This problem is a common one for attorneys who handle cases early in an investigation and are presented with opportunities to influence clients, witnesses, and the disposition of documents. The attorney must determine the proper standard of conduct when faced with two goals that may conflict with each other, one compelling him to create maximum control over information, the other to avoid committing an offense himself while attempting to help his client.

The attorney is mandated by the principles of the adversary system to be zealous in pursuing the interest of his client and to resolve doubt in his client's favor. A critical question then is how close to the margin of legitimate action he can go before violating ethical proscriptions. He must decide, for instance, how much he can help clients to understand which documents not to turn over to the government, when the relevant ethical rules state that an attorney shall not "conceal or knowingly fail to disclose that which he is required by law to reveal," or "knowingly make a false statement of law or fact," or "counsel or assist his client in conduct that [he] knows to be illegal or fraudulent"; and he must decide how far to go in secreting information he receives about a client's ongoing crimes or new crimes committed to cover up past crimes, when the relevant ethical rules state that the attorney shall "not knowingly reveal a confidence or secret of his client," but that he *"may* reveal the intention of his client to commit a crime and the information necessary to prevent the crime" (emphasis added). He must decide whether he can influence a client to persuade his employees, associates, or other persons to keep silent, when the relevant ethical rule states that an attorney "shall not give advice to a person who is not represented by a lawyer other than the advice to secure counsel, if the interests of such persons are or have a reasonable possibility of being in conflict with the interest of his client." ...

Chapter 2

MENS REA

Criminal liability is normally founded on the concurrence of two factors, "an evil-meaning mind [and] an evil-doing hand."[1] This is often expressed as a requirement that some degree of *mens rea* (guilty mind) must attend the *actus reus* (guilty act or non-action where there is a duty to act) to warrant the imposition of a criminal stigma. Unfortunately, as Professor George Fletcher observed, "there is no term fraught with greater ambiguity than that venerable Latin phrase that haunts the Anglo-American criminal law: *mens rea*."[2]

Part of the ambiguity is founded upon the fact that a seemingly endless variety of terms have been used to describe the guilty mind necessary to prove an offense. Federal statutes, for example, provide for more than 100 types of *mens rea*.[3] Even those terms most frequently used in federal legislation—"knowing" and "willful"—do not have one invariable meaning. Particularly with respect to judicial interpretation of the term "willful," the precise requirements of these terms depend to some extent on the statutory context in which they are employed.[4] Another layer of difficulty is attributable to the fact that Congress may impose one *mens rea* requirement upon certain elements of the offense and a different level of *mens rea*, or no *mens rea* at all, with respect to other elements.

Finally, the law at issue may not specify a *mens rea* requirement or, more commonly, is ambiguous as to which elements an express intent requirement modifies. In the materials that follow, the courts focus on the appropriate construction of a number of different statutes. By necessity, the analysis is specific to the statutory language at issue and, in some instances, the level of *mens rea* identified by Congress (*e.g.*, "willful" or "knowing"). Leaving to one side their specific context, however, the cases should shed light on the basic interpretative approaches used by federal courts in wrestling with the question of what level of *mens rea* is appropriately applied in cases where the statute is silent or ambiguous.

In many white-collar cases, questions of intent predominate. The presumptions, canons of statutory construction, and doctrines that emerge from these precedents should be of assistance when answering the central question in these cases—whether the defense can successfully assert that the requisite *mens rea* is missing. The terms in which this defense is couched vary. Sometimes it is stated simply that the government does not have proof of the requisite intent—for example, that the proof does not demonstrate that the defendant made a false statement on a tax return "knowing" that the statement was false. In other instances, it is asserted that the prosecution should fail because of a defendant's ignorance or mistake of fact

---

[1] Morissette v. United States, 342 U.S. 246, 251 (1952).

[2] George P. Fletcher, Rethinking Criminal Law 398 (1978).

[3] William S. Laufer, *Culpability and Sentencing of Corporations*, 71 Neb. L. Rev. 1049, 1064-65 (1994).

[4] *See, e.g.*, Ratzlaf v. United States, 510 U.S. 135, 141 (1994) ("'Willful,' this Court has recognized, is a 'word of many meanings,' and 'its construction [is] often ... influenced by its context.'") (*quoting* Spies v. United States, 317 U.S. 492, 497 (1943)).

or law. Thus, a defendant accused of possessing an unregistered fully automatic firearm may contend that he did not know that the weapon he possessed was capable of fully automatic firing (*i.e.*, may, as in *Staples v. United States, infra*, rely upon an asserted ignorance or mistake of fact). A defendant accused of disposing of pollutants in excess of permitted amounts may claim that he did not know that the conceded discharges of pollutants did in fact exceed legal limits (*i.e.*, may, as in *United States v. Weitzenhoff, infra*, rely upon ignorance or mistake of "legal fact"). A defendant accused of consciously avoiding certain regulatory reporting or registration requirements may argue that he did not know that avoidance of such requirements was proscribed by law (*i.e.*, may, as in *Bryant v. United States, infra*, rely upon a mistake of law). Generally, the terms in which the defense is expressed should not change the analysis. As Professor LaFave has explained:

> No area of the substantive criminal law has traditionally been surrounded by more confusion than that of ignorance or mistake of fact or law. [But i]n actuality, the basic rule is extremely simple: ignorance or mistake of law is a defense when it negatives the existence of a mental state essential to the crime charged. ... Instead of speaking of ignorance or mistake of fact or law as a defense, it would be just as easy to note simply that the defendant cannot be convicted when it is shown that he does not have the mental state required by law for commission of that particular offense.[5]

The following materials focus on two lines of cases that have particular relevance in the white-collar area: (A) cases involving assertions that the offense at issue is a "public welfare" violation to which a very low level of *mens rea* should be applied (such that liability is founded on a species of strict liability and honest and reasonable mistakes as to the underlying facts or law may not prevent liability); and (B) cases involving assertions that a very high level of *mens rea* should be applied (such that ignorance that the conduct at issue was proscribed by law *is* a defense to prosecution).

A. THE MODEL PENAL CODE

The federal code does *not* use the Model Penal Code's definitions of the four levels of culpable *mens rea*. Indeed, the federal code contains no generally applicable definitional section for culpable mental states of the sort reproduced below. Nor does the federal code incorporate the Model Penal Code's default rules on construing statutes (for example, the presumption that the legislature intends that a stated *mens rea* apply to all material elements of an offense). Nonetheless, Model Penal Code § 2.02's General Requirements of Culpability are reproduced below because they provide us at the very least a starting vocabulary for such terms as "recklessness" and "negligence." Also, the Supreme Court sometimes references the Model Penal Code, for example in defining "willful blindness." Finally, students should consider whether the Model Penal Code's default rules on construction ought to be used by federal courts in construing the culpability requirements in ambiguous statutes.

MODEL PENAL CODE § 2.02. GENERAL REQUIREMENTS OF CULPABILITY

(1) *Minimum Requirements of Culpability*. [Except with respect to offenses defined by statutes other than the Code, insofar as a legislative purpose to impose absolute liability for such offenses or with respect to any material element thereof plainly appears,] a person is not guilty of an offense unless he acted purposely, knowingly, recklessly or negligently, as the law may require, with respect to each material element of the offense.

---

[5] Wayne R. LaFave, Criminal Law § 5.1(a), at 432-33 (West 3d ed. 2000).

(2) *Kinds of Culpability Defined*

(a) *Purposely.* A person acts purposely with respect to a material element of an offense when:

(i) if the element involves the nature of his conduct or a result thereof, it is his conscious object to engage in conduct of that nature or to cause such a result; and
(ii) if the element involves the attendant circumstances, he is aware of the existence of such circumstances or he believes or hopes that they exist.

(b) *Knowingly.* A person acts knowingly with respect to a material element of an offense when:

(i) if the element involves the nature of his conduct or the attendant circumstances, he is aware that his conduct is of that nature or that such circumstances exist; and
(ii) if the element involves a result of his conduct, he is aware that it is practically certain that his conduct will cause such a result.

(c) *Recklessly.* A person acts recklessly with respect to a material element of an offense when he consciously disregards a substantial and unjustifiable risk that the material element exists or will result from his conduct. The risk must be of such a nature and degree that, considering the nature and purpose of the actor's conduct and the circumstances known to him, its disregard involves a gross deviation from the standard of conduct that a law-abiding person would observe in the actor's situation.

(d) *Negligently.* A person acts negligently with respect to a material element of an offense when he should be aware of a substantial and unjustifiable risk that the material element exists or will result from his conduct. The risk must be of such a nature and degree that the actor's failure to perceive it, considering the nature and purpose of his conduct and the circumstances known to him, involves a gross deviation from the standard of care that a reasonable person would observe in the actor's situation.

(3) *Culpability Required Unless Otherwise Provided.* When the culpability sufficient to establish a material element of an offense is not prescribed by law, such element is established if a person acts purposely, knowingly or recklessly with respect thereto. (No negiegence)

(4) *Prescribed Culpability Requirement Applies to All Material Elements.* When the law defining an offense prescribes the kind of culpability that is sufficient for the commission of an offense, without distinguishing among the material elements thereof, such provision shall apply to all the material elements of the offense, unless a contrary purpose plainly appears. ...

(7) *Requirement of Knowledge Satisfied by Knowledge of High Probability.* When knowledge of the existence of a particular fact is an element of an offense, such knowledge is established if a person is aware of a high probability of its existence, unless he actually believes that it does not exist.

(8) *Requirement of Wilfulness Satisfied by Acting Knowingly.* A requirement that an offense be committed wilfully is satisfied if a person acts knowingly with respect to the material elements of the offense, unless a purpose to impose further requirements appears.

(9) *Culpability as to Illegality of Conduct.* Neither knowledge nor recklessness or negligence as to whether conduct constitutes an offense or as to the existence, meaning or application of the law determining the elements of an offense is an element of such offense, unless the definition of the offense or the Code so provides. ...

B. THE PUBLIC WELFARE DOCTRINE

UNITED STATES v. INTERNATIONAL MINERALS & CHEMICAL CORP.
402 U.S. 558 (1971)

Mr. Justice Douglas delivered the opinion of the Court.

The information charged that appellee shipped sulfuric acid and hydrofluosilicic acid in interstate commerce and "did knowingly fail to show on the shipping papers the required classification of said property, to wit, Corrosive Liquid, in violation of 49 C.F.R. 173.427."

Title 18 U.S.C. § 834(a) gives the Interstate Commerce Commission power to "formulate regulations for the safe transportation" of "corrosive liquids" and 18 U.S.C. § 834(f) states that whoever "knowingly violates any such regulation" shall be fined or imprisoned.

Pursuant to the power granted by § 834(a) the regulatory agency promulgated the regulation already cited which reads in part:

> "Each shipper offering for transportation any hazardous material subject to the regulations in this chapter, shall describe that article on the shipping paper by the shipping name prescribed in § 172.5 of this chapter and by the classification prescribed in § 172.4 of this chapter, and may add a further description not inconsistent therewith. Abbreviations must not be used."

49 CFR § 173.427.

The District Court ... ruled that the information did not charge a "knowing violation" of the regulation and accordingly dismissed the information. ...

Here as in *United States v. Freed*, 401 U.S. 601 (1971), which dealt with the possession of hand grenades, strict or absolute liability is not imposed; knowledge of the shipment of the dangerous materials is required. The sole and narrow question is whether "knowledge" of the regulation is also required. It is in that narrow zone that the issue of "*mens rea*" is raised; and appellee bears down hard on the provision in 18 U.S.C. § 834(f) that whoever "knowingly violates any such regulation" shall be fined, etc. ...

There is no issue in the present case of the propriety of the delegation of the power to establish regulations and of the validity of the regulation at issue. We therefore see no reason why the word "regulations" should not be construed as a shorthand designation for specific acts or omissions which violate the Act. The Act, so viewed, does not signal an exception to the rule that ignorance of the law is no excuse ....

The principle that ignorance of the law is no defense applies whether the law be a statute or a duly promulgated and published regulation. ... [W]e decline to attribute to Congress the inaccurate view that that Act requires proof of knowledge of the law, as well as the facts, and that it intended to endorse that interpretation by retaining the word "knowingly." We conclude that the meager legislative history ... makes unwarranted the conclusion that Congress abandoned the general rule and required knowledge of both the facts and the pertinent law before a criminal conviction could be sustained under this Act.

So far as possession, say, of sulfuric acid is concerned the requirement of "*mens rea*" has been made a requirement of the Act as evidenced by the use of the word "knowingly." A person thinking in good faith that he was shipping distilled water when in fact he was shipping some dangerous acid would not be covered. ...

There is leeway for the exercise of congressional discretion in applying the reach of "*mens rea*." *United States v. Murdock*, 290 U.S. 389 (1933), closely confined the word "willfully" in the income tax law to include a purpose to bring about the forbidden result:

> "He whose conduct is defined as criminal is one who *willfully* fails to pay the tax, to make a return, to keep the required records, or to supply the needed information.

Congress did not intend that a person, by reason of a bona fide misunderstanding as to his liability for the tax, as to his duty to make a return, or as to the adequacy of the records he maintained, should become a criminal by his mere failure to measure up to the prescribed standard of conduct. And the requirement that the omission in these instances must be willful, to be criminal, is persuasive that the same element is essential to the offense of failing to supply information."

In *United States v. Balint*, 258 U.S. 250 (1922), the Court was dealing with drugs, in *United States v. Freed*, 401 U.S. 601 (1971), with hand grenades, in this case with sulfuric and other dangerous acids. Pencils, dental floss, paper clips may also be regulated. But they may be the type of products which might raise substantial due process questions if Congress did not require, as in *Murdock*, "*mens rea*" as to each ingredient of the offense. But where, as here and as in *Balint* and *Freed*, dangerous or deleterious devices or products or obnoxious waste materials are involved, the probability of regulation is so great that anyone who is aware that he is in possession of them or dealing with them must be presumed to be aware of the regulation. ...

Notes

1. In the authorizing statute, the defined *mens rea* requirement, "knowingly," is an adverb that modifies the verb "violate." Does the Court adopt the most natural reading of this language?

As was discussed in Chapter 1, the bar on judicial crime-creation is in part founded on the first principle of criminal law—the principle of legality—which outlaws the retroactive definition of criminal offenses. "It is condemned because it is retroactive and also because it is judicial—that is, accomplished by an institution not recognized as politically competent to define crime. Thus, a fuller statement of the legality ideal would be that it stands for the desirability in principle of advance legislative specification of criminal misconduct." John Calvin Jeffries Jr., *Legality, Vagueness, and the Construction of Penal Statutes*, 71 Va. L. Rev. 189, 190 (1985). One of the ways the legality principle is operationalized is through the rule of strict construction, often referred to as the rule of lenity. The rule of lenity requires that "when choice has to be made between two readings of what conduct Congress has made a crime, it is appropriate, before [the Court chooses] the harsher alternative, to require that Congress should have spoken in language that is clear and definite." United States v. Universal C.I.T. Credit Corp., 344 U.S. 218, 221-22 (1952). The rule is founded first on notice concerns: "a fair warning should be given to the world in language that the common world will understand, of what the law intends to do if a certain line is passed. To make the warning fair, so far as possible the line should be clear." McBoyle v. United States, 283 U.S. 25, 27 (1931). Second, legitimacy concerns reflected in separation of powers principles justify lenity. "[B]ecause of the seriousness of criminal penalties, and because criminal punishment usually represents the moral condemnation of the community, legislatures and not courts should define criminal activity." United States v. Bass, 404 U.S. 336, 348 (1971). "Lenity promotes th[e] conception of legislative supremacy not just by preventing courts from covertly undermining legislative decisions, but also by forcing Congress to shoulder the entire burden of criminal lawmaking even when it prefers to cede some part of that task to courts." Dan M. Kahan, *Lenity and Federal Common Law Crimes*, 1994 Sup. Ct. Rev. 345, 350 (1994). Lenity requires that if two readings of an ambiguous statute are equally plausible, courts should endorse the construction that is most defense-favorable. If "knowingly violate" was in any way ambiguous, why did the Court not apply the rule of lenity?

The rule of lenity applies only in criminal cases. Are there other differences in the canons of construction applicable in civil versus criminal cases? *See, e.g.*, Whitman v. United States, -- U.S. --, 135 S.Ct. 352 (2014) (Scalia, J., respecting the denial of certiorari) (arguing against applying *Chevron* deference to an agency's interpretation of a law that contemplates both civil and criminal enforcement.)

2. Is the Court's reading of the statutory language influenced by context—that is, by the difficulties of proof a contrary reading may create for effective enforcement of the regulations?

Should the fairness of this resolution to the individual defendant affect the Court's disposition? In this regard, it may be worth noting that the regulations at issue required shippers like the International Minerals defendant to provide both the cargo's name as required by one regulation and the cargo's classification in accordance with another. "[T]he defendant apparently had written the correct name of 'sulfuric acid' on the form, for the government charged the defendant only with failing also to give the approved classification: 'Corrosive Liquid.' A good faith and reasonable error could account for this lapse, yet be irrelevant to a criminal charge" under the Court's reading of the statute. John Shepard Wiley Jr., *Not Guilty by Reason of Blamelessness: Culpability in Federal Criminal Interpretation*, 85 Va. L. Rev. 1021, 1054 (1999).

3. The Court's statutory analysis is largely confined to its assertion that it will not assume that Congress would intentionally abandon the basic principal that "ignorance of the law is no excuse." What is the rationale for this principal? Consider the following discussion by Professor Dan Kahan:

> The conventional understanding of the mistake of law doctrine rests on two premises. ... The first is *liberal positivism*. As a descriptive claim, liberal positivism holds that the content of the law can be identified without reference to morality: one needn't be a good man to perceive what's lawful, Holmes tells us; one need only understand the consequences in store if one should choose to act badly. The normative side of liberal positivism urges us to see the independence of law from morality as a good thing. In a pluralistic society, the law should aspire to be comprehensible to persons of diverse moral views. What's more, it should avoid embodying within itself a standard of culpability or blame that depends on an individual's acceptance of any such view as orthodox; in a liberal society, even the bad man can be a good citizen so long as he lives up to society's rules.
>
> Liberal positivism supports denying a mistake of law defense when combined with a second premise: the *utility of legal knowledge*. Under the liberal positivist view, the law disclaims any reliance on the moral knowledge of citizens, as well as any ambition to make them value morality for its own sake. Accordingly, to promote good (that is, law-abiding) conduct, it becomes imperative that citizens be made aware of the content of the law and the consequences of breaking it. Hence, the law shows no mercy for those who claim to be ignorant of what the criminal law proscribes, a position that maximizes citizens' incentive to learn the rules that "the law-maker has determined to make men know and obey."
>
> I want to challenge the accuracy of this account of why ignorance of law does not excuse. In its place, I'll suggest an alternative understanding, which rests on premises diametrically opposed to the Holmesian aphorisms that undergird the classic account.
>
> The first premise of this anti-Holmesian conception is *legal moralism*. This principle asserts that law is suffused with morality and, as a result, can't ultimately be identified or applied without the making of moral judgments. It asserts, too, that individuals are appropriately judged by the law not only for the law-abiding quality of their actions but also for the moral quality of their values, motivations, and emotions—in a word, for the quality of their *characters*.
>
> The second premise of the anti-Holmesian view can be called the *prudence of obfuscation*. Moral judgments are too rich and particular to be subdued by any set of abstract rules; as a result, law will always embody morality only imperfectly. That means that from the standpoint of legal moralism, private knowledge of the law *isn't* unambiguously good. The more readily individuals can discover the law's content, the more readily they'll be able to discern, and exploit, the gaps between what's immoral and what's illegal. The law must therefore employ strategies to discourage citizens from gaining knowledge for this purpose. One is to deny an excuse for ignorance of law. Punishing those who mistakenly believe their conduct to be legal promotes good (that is, moral) behavior less through encouraging citizens to learn the law—an objective that could in fact be more completely realized by excusing at least some mistakes—than by

creating hazards for those who choose to rely on what *they think* they know about the law. By denying a mistake of law defense, the law is saying, contra Holmes, that if a citizen suspects the law fails to prohibit some species of immoral conduct, the only certain way to avoid criminal punishment is to be a good person rather than a bad one.

This anti-Holmesian account, I'll argue, not only offers a superior explanation of why ignorance of the law is *not* ordinarily regarded as an excuse; it also does a better job in explaining why it sometimes *is*. Sometimes it's a crime to engage in an act—for example, omitting to file a tax return or failing to report certain financial transactions—that wouldn't be viewed as immoral were it not for the existence of a legal duty. Crimes of this sort are often referred to as *malum prohibitum*—wrong because prohibited—and are distinguished from crimes that are *malum in se*—wrong in themselves independent of law. *Malum prohibitum* crimes are the ones most likely to be interpreted as permitting mistake of law defenses. This aspect of the doctrine defies both premises of the classic position: to distinguish *malum prohibitum* crimes from *malum in se* ones, courts must employ moral judgments of the sort that liberal positivism forbids; and by allowing a mistake of law defense for *malum prohibitum* crimes, courts relax citizens' incentives to learn the law. Excusing someone for ignorance of a *malum prohibitum* crime makes perfect sense, however, under the anti-Holmesian view: since morality abstracted from law has nothing to say about the underlying conduct, a person can't be expected to rely on her perception of morality rather than her understanding of what such laws prohibit; because even a good person could make that kind of mistake in such circumstances, the defendant is excused.

A final advantage associated with the anti-Holmesian understanding of mistake of law is that it more completely defends the doctrine from the standard criticism made of it. Denying a mistake of law defense, it is said, sanctions punishment of the morally blameless. The classic conception demurs: "[J]ustice to the individual is rightly outweighed by the larger interests on the other side of the scales." But the anti-Holmesian conception goes further, showing that the standard criticism rests on a truncated understanding of when punishment is just: a person is rightly condemned as a criminal wrongdoer not only for knowingly choosing to violate the law, but also for exhibiting the kind of character failing associated with insufficient commitment to the moral norms embodied in the community's criminal law.

Dan M. Kahan, *Ignorance of Law is an Excuse—But Only for the Virtuous*, 96 Mich. L. Rev. 127, 127-30 (1997) (footnotes omitted); *see also* John Shepard Wiley Jr., *Not Guilty by Reason of Blamelessness: Culpability in Federal Criminal Interpretation*, 85 Va. L. Rev. 1021 (1999); Sharon L. Davies, *The Jurisprudence of Willfulness: An Evolving Theory of Excusable Ignorance*, 48 Duke L.J. 341, 353-56 (1998).

4. Given the competing rationales for the principle that "ignorance of the law is no excuse," when, if ever, should exceptions to that rule be recognized? What circumstances would Justice Holmes or Professor Kahan isolate as relevant? Should application of the doctrine depend on how reasonable the presumption is that everyone does or could know the law? For example, should the applicability of this principal depend to some extent on who makes the law and how available and clearly defined it is? Should it depend to some extent on the types of entities or individuals to whom the regulations are addressed?

Obviously, the "anti-Holmesian" view believes that the moral content of the law or regulation at issue will be important in determining whether ignorance of the law should be excused. Many commentators who argue that criminal sanctions are improperly used for regulatory offenses involving morally neutral conduct contend that

applying criminal sanctions to morally neutral conduct is both unjust and counterproductive. It unfairly brands defendants as criminals, weakens the moral authority of the sanction, and ultimately renders the penalty ineffective. It also squanders scarce enforcement resources and invites selective, and potentially discriminatory, prosecution.

Stuart P. Green, *Why It's A Crime to Tear the Tag Off a Mattress: Overcriminalization and the Moral Content of Regulatory Offenses*, 46 Emory L.J. 1533, 1536 (1997). If the perceived "moral" content of a given regulation is relevant, how should that moral evaluation be done—by reference to the defendant's malicious intent, or the social or moral harmfulness of the action proscribed, or some other criteria? Does the societal consensus, to the degree one exists, matter? *See id.* (evaluating these questions and others). Who should be performing this evaluation?

5. The *International Minerals* Court does not read the "knowing" requirement out of the statute entirely; it determines only that the government is not required to prove that the defendant knew that the way in which he shipped the hazardous materials contravened regulatory requirements. The Court's discussion indicates that it *would* recognize a defense in the case of a defendant's mistake of fact—that he thought he was shipping water and not a dangerous substance.

6. According to the Court, precisely what fact(s) must the government prove that the defendant "knew"? Stated another way, ignorance of what fact(s) would permit the defendant to escape liability? Must he know simply that he is dealing with dangerous substances? Or must he know that he is shipping in this case materials of the precise character that subject him to regulation—the corrosive liquids of sulphuric acid and hydrofluosilicic acid? This is an important distinction in practice as well as in theory, particularly in the area of environmental enforcement. As Professor Richard Lazarus explains:

> In the environmental law context, requiring knowledge of the facts that make the defendant's conduct unlawful could be a very exacting standard, given that the factual predicates for liability are often highly complex, technical, and indeterminate. The facts that determine lawfulness involve fine distinctions of degree, not kind.
>
> For instance, the factual inquiry under the Clean Water Act would not simply be whether the person knew that she was emitting pollutants into water. Instead, the issues would be whether the defendant knew precisely how much was being emitted, where and when it was being emitted, how discernible and discrete the manner of emission was, and in a wetlands case, what kinds of vegetation predominated in the area at certain times of the year. ...
>
> There is textual statutory support for the proposition that such factual knowledge is required for criminal culpability. Virtually all of the environmental criminal penalty provisions require in some fashion that the defendant "knowingly" commit a violation: in each of these provisions, "knowingly" modifies either "violates" or "in violation of," or refers to the particular conduct in which the defendant was engaging (e.g., "knowingly treats, stores, or disposes of any hazardous waste identified or listed under this subchapter without a permit"). The question the courts have faced, in light of this statutory language, is what *facts* a defendant must know about her conduct to be convicted of a "knowing" violation. Does criminal culpability turn on the defendant's awareness of facts with the level of precision actually determinative of the lawfulness of the defendant's activity?
>
> Courts have addressed this issue in a variety of environmental law contexts. Their virtually uniform answer is that no such rigorous proof of the defendant's knowledge of relevant facts is required. Some factual knowledge is necessary—liability is not entirely strict. Yet, given the breadth and depth of relevant facts of which the government need not prove knowledge, liability for knowing violations could be fairly dubbed mostly strict (if such a characterization is not an oxymoron).
>
> In most contexts, the courts essentially require knowledge of enough facts to alert the defendant to the *possibility* of environmental regulation. Once that standard is met, the defendant, in effect, acts at her own peril. For example, she need not know all of the facts relevant to determining precisely how much waste is being discharged at a particular time; ... to identifying "wetlands" under the Clean Water Act; to distinguishing between "point" and "nonpoint" sources under the Clean Water Act. ... The court, of course, has to determine whether, as a matter of law, the *actual* facts satisfy those legal standards. But the

defendant need not know those facts, even though they determine the lawfulness of her conduct.

Richard J. Lazarus, *Meeting the Demands of Integration in the Evolution of Environmental Law: Reforming Environmental Criminal Law*, 83 Geo. L.J. 2407, 2471-73 (1995) (footnotes omitted). Is this *mens rea* sufficient in a criminal case? *See* Brian W. Walsh & Tiffany M. Joslyn, Without Intent: How Congress is Eroding the Criminal Intent Requirement in Federal Law (Heritage Found. & NACDL April 2010).

7. Although it was not the first case of its type, *International Minerals* is often cited as the foundation of the so-called "public welfare" line of cases. In particular, as we shall see, subsequent cases often employ language taken from the last sentence of the opinion reproduced above as a test of legislative intent: when reading a statute that does not explicitly provide a *mens rea* or where the *mens rea* requirement is ambiguous, courts will impute to Congress the intent to impose a lower *mens rea* requirement (or strict liability) where "dangerous or deleterious devices or products or obnoxious waste materials are involved." Is this a principled use of the Court's language? In this passage, was the Court stating a rule of legislative interpretation intended to separate "public welfare" offenses (where a lesser *mens rea* requirement is appropriate) from other cases in which a presumption of *mens rea* is normally applied? For a critique of courts' misuse of *International Minerals,* particularly in the environmental enforcement realm, see Lazarus, 83 Geo. L.J. at 2474-84.

8. What is the rationale for the "public welfare" doctrine, which courts use to justify reading statutes to impose strict criminal liability or criminal liability based on a very low level of *mens rea*? Consider the following explanation from Professor Laurie Levenson:

There are several reasons the strict liability doctrine is used to redress invasions of the public welfare. First, the doctrine is employed for these offenses because it shifts the risks of dangerous activity to those best able to prevent a mishap. For example, a pharmaceutical manufacturer is in a unique position to know and control product quality. Strict liability holds the manufacturer liable if that product becomes contaminated for any reason. The risk of mishap is shifted to the manufacturer who can be assured of avoiding liability only by not engaging in the particular high risk activity.

Yet, this reason alone cannot justify the doctrine. The strict liability doctrine is not the only possible method for shifting risk onto the manufacturer. A criminal negligence standard also shifts the risk to the party engaging in the activity and punishes those who act carelessly. ...

... While both negligence and strict liability shift the burden of risk avoidance to the defendant, only under strict liability are individuals imprisoned even if they take all possible precautions to act reasonably. The sole question for the trier of fact is whether the defendant committed the proscribed act. The jury may not decide whether the defendant could have done anything else to prevent the unlawful act.

Thus, there must be additional reasons for selecting the strict liability doctrine over the negligence standard. Among these reasons is the need by the legislature to assure that juries will treat like cases alike when judging conduct involving public welfare. Juries may be ill-suited to decide what is reasonable in complex high-risk activities. ... Moreover, jurors may be swayed by sympathies or prejudices of a particular case. By dictating what is *per se* unreasonable, an individual jury cannot reassess the standard of reasonableness. Accordingly, a second reason for using the strict liability doctrine is that it assures uniform treatment of particular, high risk conduct.

A third justification often offered for the strict liability doctrine is that it eases the burden on the prosecution to prove intent in difficult cases. Strict liability is based largely on the assumption that an accident occurs because the defendant did not take care to prevent it. No showing of intent or negligence is required, because the fact that a prohibited act occurred demonstrates the defendant's negligence. As with most irrebuttable presumptions, the legislature believes individual inquiries are unnecessary because the overwhelming majority of cases will show that the defendant acted at least negligently. Seen in this light, strict liability is a procedural shortcut to punish those who would be culpable under traditional theories of criminal law.

Fourth, even if the presumption is incorrect in a particular case, legislatures determine that this risk is outweighed by the need for additional protection of society and expeditious prosecution of certain cases. For example, driving in excess of a posted speed limit is typically a strict liability crime. With nearly 398,000 annual traffic cases in one state alone, processing these cases as quickly as possible is important. The most efficient way to process such cases is to presume defendants drive carelessly when exceeding speed limits. The presumption is generally accurate and, even when it is not, the need for public safety and the relatively minor punishment minimizes any concern about injustice.

Finally, the strict liability doctrine is attractive as a powerful public statement of legislative intolerance for certain behavior. By labeling an offense as strict liability, the legislature can claim to provide the utmost protection from certain public harms. By affording no leniency for defendants causing harm, the legislature affirms society's interest in being protected from certain conduct. In this sense, strict liability expresses emphatically that such conduct will not be tolerated regardless of the actor's intent.

Laurie L. Levenson, *Good Faith Defenses: Reshaping Strict Liability Crimes*, 78 Cornell L. Rev. 401, 419-22 (1993) (footnotes omitted) (arguing that strict liability, as presently employed, does not further the purposes of criminal punishment, particularly where defendants are convicted despite honest and reasonable mistakes of fact and proposing "a good faith defense to strict liability crimes"); *see also* John Shepard Wiley Jr., *Not Guilty by Reason of Blamelessness: Culpability in Federal Criminal Interpretation*, 85 Va. L. Rev. 1021, 1078-1101 (1999).

STAPLES v. UNITED STATES
511 U.S. 600 (1994)

JUSTICE THOMAS delivered the opinion of the Court.

The National Firearms Act makes it unlawful for any person to possess a machinegun that is not properly registered with the Federal Government. Petitioner contends that to convict him under the Act, the Government should have been required to prove beyond a reasonable doubt that he knew the weapon he possessed had the characteristics that brought it within the statutory definition of a machinegun. We agree and accordingly reverse the judgment of the Court of Appeals.

The National Firearms Act (Act), 26 U.S.C. §§ 5801-5872, imposes strict registration requirements on statutorily defined "firearms." ... [A]ny fully automatic weapon is a "firearm" within the meaning of the Act.[6] Under the Act, all firearms must be registered in the National Firearms Registration and Transfer Record maintained by the Secretary of the Treasury. Section 5861(d) makes it a crime, punishable by up to 10 years in prison for any person to possess a firearm that is not properly registered.

Upon executing a search warrant at petitioner's home, local police and agents of the Bureau of Alcohol, Tobacco and Firearms (BATF) recovered, among other things, an AR-15 [assault] rifle. [The AR-15 is, unless modified, a semiautomatic weapon. Petitioner's AR-15 had been converted in such a way as to be capable of fully automatic firing.] ... BATF agents seized the weapon. Petitioner subsequently was indicted for unlawful possession of an unregistered machinegun in violation of § 5861(d).

At trial, BATF agents testified that when the AR-15 was tested, it fired more than one shot with a single pull of the trigger. It was undisputed that the weapon was not registered as

---

[6] [Court's footnote 1:] As used here, the terms "automatic" and "fully automatic" refer to a weapon that fires repeatedly with a single pull of the trigger. ... Such weapons are "machineguns" within the meaning of the Act. We use the term "semiautomatic" to designate a weapon that fires only one shot with each pull of the trigger, and which requires no manual manipulation by the operator to place another round in the chamber after each round is fired.

required by § 5861(d). Petitioner testified that the rifle had never fired automatically when it was in his possession. He insisted that the AR-15 had operated only semiautomatically, and even then imperfectly, often requiring manual ejection of the spent casing and chambering of the next round. According to petitioner, his alleged ignorance of any automatic firing capability should have shielded him from criminal liability for his failure to register the weapon. He requested the District Court to instruct the jury that, to establish a violation of § 5861(d), the Government must prove beyond a reasonable doubt that the defendant "knew that the gun would fire fully automatically."

The District Court rejected petitioner's proposed instruction and instead charged the jury as follows:

> "The Government need not prove the defendant knows he's dealing with a weapon possessing every last characteristic [which subjects it] to the regulation. It would be enough to prove he knows that he is dealing with a dangerous device of a type as would alert one to the likelihood of regulation."

Petitioner was convicted and sentenced to five years' probation and a $5,000 fine. ...

Whether or not § 5861(d) requires proof that a defendant knew of the characteristics of his weapon that made it a "firearm" under the Act is a question of statutory construction. As we observed in *Liparota v. United States*, 471 U.S. 419 [(1985)], "[t]he definition of the elements of a criminal offense is entrusted to the legislature, particularly in the case of federal crimes, which are solely creatures of statute." Thus, we have long recognized that determining the mental state required for commission of a federal crime requires "construction of the statute and ... inference of the intent of Congress."

The language of the statute, the starting place in our inquiry, provides little explicit guidance in this case. Section 5861(d) is silent concerning the *mens rea* required for a violation. It states simply that "[i]t shall be unlawful for any person ... to receive or possess a firearm which is not registered to him in the National Firearms Registration and Transfer Record." Nevertheless, silence on this point by itself does not necessarily suggest that Congress intended to dispense with a conventional *mens rea* element, which would require that the defendant know the facts that make his conduct illegal. On the contrary, we must construe the statute in light of the background rules of the common law in which the requirement of some *mens rea* for a crime is firmly embedded. As we have observed, "[t]he existence of a *mens rea* is the rule of, rather than the exception to, the principles of Anglo-American criminal jurisprudence." ...

There can be no doubt that this established concept has influenced our interpretation of criminal statutes. Indeed, we have noted that the common-law rule requiring *mens rea* has been "followed in regard to statutory crimes even where the statutory definition did not in terms include it." Relying on the strength of the traditional rule, we have stated that offenses that require no *mens rea* generally are disfavored, and have suggested that some indication of congressional intent, express or implied, is required to dispense with *mens rea* as an element of a crime. *[presumption against no mens rea]*

According to the Government, however, the nature and purpose of the [National Firearms] Act suggest that the presumption favoring *mens rea* does not apply to this case. The Government argues that Congress intended the Act to regulate and restrict the circulation of dangerous weapons. Consequently, in the Government's view, this case fits in a line of precedent concerning what we have termed "public welfare" or "regulatory" offenses, in which we have understood Congress to impose a form of strict criminal liability through statutes that do not require the defendant to know the facts that make his conduct illegal. In construing such statutes, we have inferred from silence that Congress did not intend to require proof of *mens rea* to establish an offense. *[Argue falls under 1st cat.]*

For example, in *United States v. Balint*, 258 U.S. 250, 254 (1922), we concluded that the Narcotic Act of 1914, which was intended in part to minimize the spread of addictive drugs by criminalizing undocumented sales of certain narcotics, required proof only that the defendant knew that he was selling drugs, not that he knew the specific items he had sold were "narcotics" within the ambit of the statute. Cf. *United States v. Dotterweich*, 320 U.S. 277, 281

(1943) (stating in dicta that a statute criminalizing the shipment of adulterated or misbranded drugs did not require knowledge that the items were misbranded or adulterated). As we explained in *Dotterweich, Balint* dealt with "a now familiar type of legislation whereby penalties serve as effective means of regulation. Such legislation dispenses with the conventional requirement for criminal conduct—awareness of some wrongdoing."

Such public welfare offenses have been created by Congress, and recognized by this Court, in "limited circumstances." Typically, our cases recognizing such offenses involve statutes that regulate potentially harmful or injurious items. Cf. *United States v. International Minerals & Chemical Corp.*, 402 U.S. 558, 564-565 (1971) (characterizing *Balint* and similar cases as involving statutes regulating "dangerous or deleterious devices or products or obnoxious waste materials"). In such situations, we have reasoned that as long as a defendant knows that he is dealing with a dangerous device of a character that places him "in responsible relation to a public danger," he should be alerted to the probability of strict regulation, and we have assumed that in such cases Congress intended to place the burden on the defendant to "ascertain at his peril whether [his conduct] comes within the inhibition of the statute." Thus, we essentially have relied on the nature of the statute and the particular character of the items regulated to determine whether congressional silence concerning the mental element of the offense should be interpreted as dispensing with conventional *mens rea* requirements.[7]

The Government argues that § 5861(d) defines precisely the sort of regulatory offense described in *Balint*. In this view, all guns, whether or not they are statutory "firearms," are dangerous devices that put gun owners on notice that they must determine at their hazard whether their weapons come within the scope of the Act. On this understanding, the District Court's instruction in this case was correct, because a conviction can rest simply on proof that a defendant knew he possessed a "firearm" in the ordinary sense of the term.

The Government seeks support for its position from our decision in *United States v. Freed*, 401 U.S. 601 (1971), which involved a prosecution for possession of unregistered grenades under § 5861(d). The defendant knew that the items in his possession were grenades, and we concluded that § 5861(d) did not require the Government to prove the defendant also knew that the grenades were unregistered. To be sure, in deciding that *mens rea* was not required with respect to that element of the offense, we suggested that the Act "is a regulatory measure in the interest of the public safety, which may well be premised on the theory that one would hardly be surprised to learn that possession of hand grenades is not an innocent act." Grenades, we explained, "are highly dangerous offensive weapons, no less dangerous than the narcotics involved in *United States v. Balint*." But that reasoning provides little support for dispensing with *mens rea* in this case.

As the Government concedes, *Freed* did not address the issue presented here. In *Freed*, we decided only that § 5861(d) does not require proof of knowledge that a firearm is *unregistered*. The question presented by a defendant who possesses a weapon that is a "firearm" for purposes of the Act, but who knows only that he has a "firearm" in the general sense of the term, was not raised or considered. And our determination that a defendant need not know

---

[7] [Court's footnote 3:] By interpreting such public welfare offenses to require at least that the defendant know that he is dealing with some dangerous or deleterious substance, we have avoided construing criminal statutes to impose a rigorous form of strict liability. See, e.g., *United States v. International Minerals & Chemical Corp.*, 402 U.S. 558, 563-564 (1971) (suggesting that if a person shipping acid mistakenly thought that he was shipping distilled water, he would not violate a statute criminalizing undocumented shipping of acids). True strict liability might suggest that the defendant need not know even that he was dealing with a dangerous item. Nevertheless, we have referred to public welfare offenses as "dispensing with" or "eliminating" a *mens rea* requirement or "mental element," see, e.g., *Morissette v. United States*, 342 U.S. 246, 250, 263 (1952); *United States v. Dotterweich*, 320 U.S. 277, 281 (1943), and have described them as strict liability crimes. While use of the term "strict liability" is really a misnomer, we have interpreted statutes defining public welfare offenses to eliminate the requirement of *mens rea*; that is, the requirement of a "guilty mind" with respect to an element of a crime. Under such statutes we have not required that the defendant know the facts that make his conduct fit the definition of the offense. Generally speaking, such knowledge is necessary to establish *mens rea*, as is reflected in the maxim *ignorantia facti excusat*.

that his weapon is unregistered suggests no conclusion concerning whether § 5861(d) requires the defendant to know of the features that make his weapon a statutory "firearm"; different elements of the same offense can require different mental states. Moreover, our analysis in *Freed* likening the Act to the public welfare statute in *Balint* rested entirely on the assumption that the defendant *knew* that he was dealing with hand grenades—that is, that he knew he possessed a particularly dangerous type of weapon (one within the statutory definition of a "firearm"), possession of which was not entirely "innocent" in and of itself. The predicate for that analysis is eliminated when, as in this case, the very question to be decided is *whether* the defendant must know of the particular characteristics that make his weapon a statutory firearm.

Notwithstanding these distinctions, the Government urges that *Freed*'s logic applies because guns, no less than grenades, are highly dangerous devices that should alert their owners to the probability of regulation. But the gap between *Freed* and this case is too wide to bridge. In glossing over the distinction between grenades and guns, the Government ignores the particular care we have taken to avoid construing a statute to dispense with *mens rea* where doing so would "criminalize a broad range of apparently innocent conduct." *Liparota*, 471 U.S., at 426. In *Liparota*, we considered a statute that made unlawful the unauthorized acquisition or possession of food stamps. We determined that the statute required proof that the defendant knew his possession of food stamps was unauthorized, largely because dispensing with such a *mens rea* requirement would have resulted in reading the statute to outlaw a number of apparently innocent acts. Our conclusion that the statute should not be treated as defining a public welfare offense rested on the commonsense distinction that a "food stamp can hardly be compared to a hand grenade."

Neither, in our view, can all guns be compared to hand grenades. Although the contrast is certainly not as stark as that presented in *Liparota*, the fact remains that there is a long tradition of widespread lawful gun ownership by private individuals in this country. Such a tradition did not apply to the possession of hand grenades in *Freed* or to the selling of dangerous drugs that we considered in *Balint*. In fact, in *Freed* we construed ... § 5861(d) under the assumption that "one would hardly be surprised to learn that possession of hand grenades is not an innocent act." Here, the Government essentially suggests that we should interpret the section under the altogether different assumption that "one would hardly be surprised to learn that owning a gun is not an innocent act." That proposition is simply not supported by common experience. Guns in general are not "deleterious devices or products or obnoxious waste materials" that put their owners on notice that they stand "in responsible relation to a public danger."

The Government protests that guns, unlike food stamps, but like grenades and narcotics, are potentially harmful devices. Under this view, it seems that *Liparota*'s concern for criminalizing ostensibly innocuous conduct is inapplicable whenever an item is sufficiently dangerous—that is, dangerousness alone should alert an individual to probable regulation and justify treating a statute that regulates the dangerous device as dispensing with *mens rea*. But that an item is "dangerous," in some general sense, does not necessarily suggest, as the Government seems to assume, that it is not also entirely innocent. Even dangerous items can, in some cases, be so commonplace and generally available that we would not consider them to alert individuals to the likelihood of strict regulation. As suggested above, despite their potential for harm, guns generally can be owned in perfect innocence. Of course, we might surely classify certain categories of guns—no doubt including the machineguns, sawed-off shotguns, and artillery pieces that Congress has subjected to regulation—as items the ownership of which would have the same quasi-suspect character we attributed to owning hand grenades in *Freed*. But precisely because guns falling outside those categories traditionally have been widely accepted as lawful possessions, their destructive potential, while perhaps even greater than that of some items we would classify along with narcotics and hand grenades, cannot be said to put gun owners sufficiently on notice of the likelihood of regulation to justify interpreting § 5861(d) as not requiring proof of knowledge of a weapon's characteristics.

On a slightly different tack, the Government suggests that guns are subject to an array of regulations at the federal, state, and local levels that put gun owners on notice that they must determine the characteristics of their weapons and comply with all legal requirements. But regulation in itself is not sufficient to place gun ownership in the category of the sale of narcotics in *Balint*. The food stamps at issue in *Liparota* were subject to comprehensive regulations, yet we did not understand the statute there to dispense with a *mens rea* requirement. Moreover, despite the overlay of legal restrictions on gun ownership, we question whether regulations on guns are sufficiently intrusive that they impinge upon the common experience that owning a gun is usually licit and blameless conduct. Roughly 50 percent of American homes contain at least one firearm of some sort, and in the vast majority of States, buying a shotgun or rifle is a simple transaction that would not alert a person to regulation any more than would buying a car.

If we were to accept as a general rule the Government's suggestion that dangerous and regulated items place their owners under an obligation to inquire at their peril into compliance with regulations, we would undoubtedly reach some untoward results. Automobiles, for example, might also be termed "dangerous" devices and are highly regulated at both the state and federal levels. Congress might see fit to criminalize the violation of certain regulations concerning automobiles, and thus might make it a crime to operate a vehicle without a properly functioning emission control system. But we probably would hesitate to conclude on the basis of silence that Congress intended a prison term to apply to a car owner whose vehicle's emissions levels, wholly unbeknownst to him, began to exceed legal limits between regular inspection dates.

Here, there can be little doubt that, as in *Liparota*, the Government's construction of the statute potentially would impose criminal sanctions on a class of persons whose mental state—ignorance of the characteristics of weapons in their possession—makes their actions entirely innocent. The Government does not dispute the contention that virtually any semiautomatic weapon may be converted, either by internal modification or, in some cases, simply by wear and tear, into a machinegun within the meaning of the Act. Such a gun may give no externally visible indication that it is fully automatic. But in the Government's view, any person who has purchased what he believes to be a semiautomatic rifle or handgun, or who simply has inherited a gun from a relative and left it untouched in an attic or basement, can be subject to imprisonment, despite absolute ignorance of the gun's firing capabilities, if the gun turns out to be an automatic.

We concur in the Fifth Circuit's conclusion on this point: "It is unthinkable to us that Congress intended to subject such law-abiding, well-intentioned citizens to a possible ten-year term of imprisonment if ... what they genuinely and reasonably believed was a conventional semiautomatic [weapon] turns out to have worn down into or been secretly modified to be a fully automatic weapon." As we noted in *Morissette*, the "purpose and obvious effect of doing away with the requirement of a guilty intent is to ease the prosecution's path to conviction."[8] We are reluctant to impute that purpose to Congress where, as here, it would mean easing the path to convicting persons whose conduct would not even alert them to the probability of strict regulation in the form of a statute such as § 5861(d).

The potentially harsh penalty attached to violation of § 5861(d)—up to 10 years' imprisonment—confirms our reading of the Act. Historically, the penalty imposed under a statute has been a significant consideration in determining whether the statute should be construed as dispensing with *mens rea*. Certainly, the cases that first defined the concept of the

---

[8] [Court's footnote 11:] The Government contends that Congress intended precisely such an aid to obtaining convictions, because requiring proof of knowledge would place too heavy a burden on the Government and obstruct the proper functioning of § 5861(d). Cf. *United States v. Balint*, 258 U.S. 250, 254 (1922) (difficulty of proving knowledge suggests Congress did not intend to require *mens rea*). But knowledge can be inferred from circumstantial evidence, including any external indications signaling the nature of the weapon. And firing a fully automatic weapon would make the regulated characteristics of the weapon immediately apparent to its owner. In short, we are confident that when the defendant knows of the characteristics of his weapon that bring it within the scope of the Act, the Government will not face great difficulty in proving that knowledge. Of course, if Congress thinks it necessary to reduce the Government's burden at trial to ensure proper enforcement of the Act, it remains free to amend § 5861(d) by explicitly eliminating a *mens rea* requirement.

public welfare offense almost uniformly involved statutes that provided for only light penalties such as fines or short jail sentences, not imprisonment in the state penitentiary. ...

... "[F]elony" is, as we noted in distinguishing certain common-law crimes from public welfare offenses, "'as bad a word as you can give to man or thing.'" Close adherence to the early cases ... might suggest that punishing a violation as a felony is simply incompatible with the theory of the public welfare offense. In this view, absent a clear statement from Congress that *mens rea* is not required, we should not apply the public welfare offense rationale to interpret any statute defining a felony offense as dispensing with *mens rea*.

We need not adopt such a definitive rule of construction to decide this case, however. Instead, we note only that where, as here, dispensing with *mens rea* would require the defendant to have knowledge only of traditionally lawful conduct, a severe penalty is a further factor tending to suggest that Congress did not intend to eliminate a *mens rea* requirement. In such a case, the usual presumption that a defendant must know the facts that make his conduct illegal should apply.

In short, we conclude that the background rule of the common law favoring *mens rea* should govern interpretation of § 5861(d) in this case. Silence does not suggest that Congress dispensed with *mens rea* for the element of § 5861(d) at issue here. Thus, to obtain a conviction, the Government should have been required to prove that petitioner knew of the features of his AR-15 that brought it within the scope of the Act.

We emphasize that our holding is a narrow one. As in our prior cases, our reasoning depends upon a common-sense evaluation of the nature of the particular device or substance Congress has subjected to regulation and the expectations that individuals may legitimately have in dealing with the regulated items. In addition, we think that the penalty attached to § 5861(d) suggests that Congress did not intend to eliminate a *mens rea* requirement for violation of the section. ... "Neither this Court nor, so far as we are aware, any other has undertaken to delineate a precise line or set forth comprehensive criteria for distinguishing between crimes that require a mental element and crimes that do not." We attempt no definition here, either. We note only that our holding depends critically on our view that if Congress had intended to make outlaws of gun owners who were wholly ignorant of the offending characteristics of their weapons, and to subject them to lengthy prison terms, it would have spoken more clearly to that effect. ...

JUSTICE STEVENS, with whom JUSTICE BLACKMUN joins, dissenting.

To avoid a slight possibility of injustice to unsophisticated owners of machineguns and sawed-off shotguns, the Court has substituted its views of sound policy for the judgment Congress made when it enacted the National Firearms Act (or Act). Because the Court's addition to the text of 26 U.S.C. § 5861(d) is foreclosed by both the statute and our precedent, I respectfully dissent.

The Court is preoccupied with guns that "generally can be owned in perfect innocence." This case, however, involves a semiautomatic weapon that was readily convertible into a machinegun—a weapon that the jury found to be "'a dangerous device of a type as would alert one to the likelihood of regulation.'" These are not guns "of some sort" that can be found in almost "50 percent of American homes." They are particularly dangerous—indeed, a substantial percentage of the unregistered machineguns now in circulation are converted semiautomatic weapons. ...

"Public welfare" offenses share certain characteristics: (1) they regulate "dangerous or deleterious devices or products or obnoxious waste materials," see *United States v. International Minerals & Chemical Corp.*, 402 U.S. 558, 565 (1971); (2) they "heighten the duties of those in control of particular industries, trades, properties or activities that affect public health, safety or welfare," *Morissette*, 342 U.S., at 254; and (3) they "depend on no mental element but consist only of forbidden acts or omissions." Examples of such offenses include Congress' exertion of its power to keep dangerous narcotics, hazardous substances, and impure and adulterated foods and drugs out of the channels of commerce.

Public welfare statutes render criminal "a type of conduct that a reasonable person should know is subject to stringent public regulation and may seriously threaten the community's health or safety." *Liparota v. United States*, 471 U.S. 419, 433 (1985). Thus, under such statutes, "a defendant can be convicted even though he was unaware of the circumstances of his conduct that made it illegal." Referring to the strict criminal sanctions for unintended violations of the food and drug laws, Justice Frankfurter wrote:

"The purposes of this legislation thus touch phases of the lives and health of people which, in the circumstances of modern industrialism, are largely beyond self-protection. Regard for these purposes should infuse construction of the legislation if it is to be treated as a working instrument of government and not merely as a collection of English words. The prosecution ... is based on a now familiar type of legislation whereby penalties serve as effective means of regulation. Such legislation dispenses with the conventional requirement for criminal conduct—awareness of some wrongdoing. In the interest of the larger good it puts the burden of acting at hazard upon a person otherwise innocent but standing in responsible relation to a public danger." *United States v. Dotterweich*, 320 U.S. 277, 280-281 (1943).

The National Firearms Act unquestionably is a public welfare statute. *United States v. Freed*, 401 U.S. 601, 609 (1971) (holding that this statute "is a regulatory measure in the interest of the public safety"). Congress fashioned a legislative scheme to regulate the commerce and possession of certain types of dangerous devices, including specific kinds of weapons, to protect the health and welfare of the citizenry. To enforce this scheme, Congress created criminal penalties for certain acts and omissions. The text of some of these offenses—including the one at issue here—contains no knowledge requirement.

The Court recognizes:

"[W]e have reasoned that as long as a defendant knows that he is dealing with a dangerous device of a character that places him 'in responsible relation to a public danger,' he should be alerted to the probability of strict regulation, and we have assumed that in such cases Congress intended to place the burden on the defendant to 'ascertain at his peril whether [his conduct] comes within the inhibition of the statute.'"

We thus have read a knowledge requirement into public welfare crimes, but not a requirement that the defendant know all the facts that make his conduct illegal. Although the Court acknowledges this standard, it nevertheless concludes that a gun is not the type of dangerous device that would alert one to the possibility of regulation.

[The Court erroneously relies] upon the "tradition[al]" innocence of gun ownership to find that Congress must have intended the Government to prove knowledge of all the characteristics that make a weapon a statutory "firear[m]." We held in *Freed*, however, that a § 5861(d) offense may be committed by one with no awareness of either wrongdoing or of all the facts that constitute the offense. Nevertheless, the Court, asserting that the Government "gloss[es] over the distinction between grenades and guns," determines that "the gap between *Freed* and this case is too wide to bridge." As such, the Court instead reaches the rather surprising conclusion that guns are more analogous to food stamps than to hand grenades. Even if one accepts that dubious proposition, the Court founds it upon a faulty premise: its mischaracterization of the Government's submission as one contending that "*all guns* ... are dangerous devices that put gun owners on notice ..." Accurately identified, the Government's position presents the question whether guns such as the one possessed by petitioner "are highly dangerous offensive weapons, no less dangerous than the narcotics" in *Balint* or the hand grenades in *Freed*.

Thus, even assuming that the Court is correct that the mere possession of an ordinary rifle or pistol does not entail sufficient danger to alert one to the possibility of regulation, that conclusion does not resolve this case. Petitioner knowingly possessed a semiautomatic weapon that was readily convertible into a machinegun. The "character and nature" of such a weapon is sufficiently hazardous to place the possessor on notice of the possibility of regulation. No significant difference exists between imposing upon the possessor a duty to determine whether such a weapon is registered, and imposing a duty to determine whether that weapon has been converted into a machinegun. ...

Notes

1. What are the positions of the parties regarding the appropriate *mens rea* applicable to the statute? Even if one adopted the government's position, or the instruction of the district court, would this be a strict liability offense? Note that in this case the Court found insufficient the general level of factual knowledge that Professor Lazarus states has uniformly been found sufficient to support criminal liability in environmental cases (where the statutes at issue contain an express "knowing" *mens rea*)—that is, knowledge of the generally hazardous and regulated nature of the substance at issue. Why should this be enough to support criminal liability in the environmental area but not in the gun regulation area?

2. The defendant in *Staples* contended that he was mistaken as to the nature of the gun he concededly possessed—that is, he argued that he was ignorant of the qualities that would have subjected the gun to the registration requirements of the statute. Should the fact that he is arguing that his was a mistake of fact, not a mistake of law, make a difference in assessing what level of *mens rea* should be accorded? Does the Court distinguish in its discussion of the applicability of the "public welfare" precedents between mistakes of law and fact?

3. Could one argue that there may be due process limits to use of strict liability where the question is whether the defendant knew the *facts* that could subject him or her to criminal liability? For a discussion of possible due process limitations on the use of strict liability in criminal cases, see Richard Singer & Douglas Husak, *Of Innocence and Innocents: The Supreme Court and Mens Rea Since Herbert Packer*, 2 Buffalo Crim. L. Rev. 859, 943 (1999) (surveying cases and concluding, like Packer, that *mens rea* "is not constitutionally mandated, except sometimes"). If there is no such due process limitation, and defendants may in some cases be subjected to criminal liability even though they were entirely mistaken or ignorant of the facts that subject them to regulatory requirements, in what cases should such strict liability be imposed? *See* United States v. DeCoster, 828 F.3d 626 (8th Cir. 2016) (rejecting due process challenge to strict liability crime).

4. Despite the complete absence of an express *mens rea* requirement in the statutory language, the Court reads into the statute a "knowing" requirement, relying on the presumption of *mens rea* embedded in Anglo-American jurisprudence. Can you justify the Court's use of different statutory interpretation aids and assumptions regarding congressional intent in this case than it did in *International Minerals*? The Court states that at least with regard to crimes having their origin in the common law, it applies an interpretive presumption that *mens rea* is required. Is this presumption appropriately applied in this case? Common law crimes are normally ones that fall in the *malum in se* category, such as theft, fraud, and the like. Does gun regulation fall into this category? Could you make an argument that this presumption is backwards if applied to *malum in se* cases but not cases where the offense is simply *malum prohibitum*? Consider the following thought from Henry M. Hart, *The Aims of the Criminal Law*, 23 Law. & Contemp. Prob. 401, 431 n.70 (1958):

> In relation to offenses of a traditional type, [the Supreme Court seems to say], we must be much slower to dispense with a basis for genuine blameworthiness in criminal intent than in relation to modern regulatory offenses. But it is precisely in the area of traditional crimes that the nature of the act itself commonly gives some warning that there may be a problem about its propriety and so affords, without more, at least some slight basis for condemnation for doing it. ... In the area of regulatory crimes, on the other hand, the moral quality of the act is often neutral; and on occasion, the offense may consist not of any act at all, but simply of an intrinsically innocent omission, so there is no basis for moral condemnation whatever.

5. Why did the Court choose a "knowing" standard? In *Elonis v. United States*, -- U.S. --, 135 S.Ct. 2001, 2010 (2015), the Supreme Court instructed that "[w]hen interpreting federal criminal statutes that are silent on the required mental state, we read into the statute 'only that *mens rea* which is necessary to separate wrongful conduct from 'otherwise innocent conduct.'" Should the *Staples* Court instead have chosen a negligence or recklessness standard?

In *Elonis*, the defendant was convicted of transmitting in interstate commerce "any communication containing any threat … to injure the person of another," 18 U.S.C. § 875(c), by posting some very violent threats against his ex-wife and others on his Facebook page. *See, e.g.*, 135 S.Ct. at 2016 ("There's one way to love you but a thousand ways to kill you. I'm not going to rest until your body is a mess, soaked with blood and dying from all the little cuts"). The district court instructed the jury that "[a] statement is a true threat when a defendant intentionally makes a statement in a context or under such circumstances wherein a reasonable person would foresee that the statement would be interpreted by those to whom the maker communicates the statement as a serious expression of an intention to inflict bodily injury or take the life of an individual." *Id.* at 2007. The Supreme Court reversed the conviction, finding this instruction to be incorrect.

Noting first that the statute does not specify a mental state, the *Elonis* Court cited the general presumption in criminal law that "wrongdoing must be conscious to be criminal." *Id.* at 2009. The defendant does not have to know his conduct is illegal, but he generally must know the facts that make his conduct a crime. The Court then reasoned:

> Section 875, as noted, requires proof that a communication was transmitted and that it contained a threat. The "presumption in favor of a scienter requirement should apply to *each* of the statutory elements that criminalize otherwise innocent conduct." The parties agree that a defendant under Section 875(c) must know that he is transmitting a communication. But communicating *something* is not what makes the conduct "wrongful." Here "the crucial element separating legal innocence from wrongful conduct" is the threatening nature of the communication. The mental state requirement must therefore apply to the fact that the communication contains a threat.
>
> Elonis's conviction, however, was premised solely on how his posts would be understood by a reasonable person. Such a "reasonable person" standard is a familiar feature of civil liability in tort law, but is inconsistent with "the conventional requirement for criminal conduct—*awareness* of some wrongdoing." Having liability turn on whether a "reasonable person" regards the communication as a threat—regardless of what the defendant thinks—"reduces culpability on the all-important element of the crime to negligence," and we have long been reluctant to infer that a negligence standard was intended in criminal statutes. Under these principles, "what [Elonis] thinks" does matter.

Id. at 2011. Justice Alito, concurring in part and dissenting in part, argued for a recklessness standard. The majority, stating that the question whether recklessness suffices for liability under § 875 had not been briefed, declined to address the issue, instead remanding it for further consideration below.

In his separate opinion, Justice Alito noted his agreement with the Court that under the traditional background rules of criminal law, the majority correctly applied a presumption of *mens rea* and ruled out a negligence standard. He then contended:

> Once we have passed negligence, however, no further presumptions are defensible. In the hierarchy of mental states that may be required as a condition for criminal liability, the *mens rea* just above negligence is recklessness. Negligence requires only that the defendant "should [have] be[en] aware of a substantial and unjustifiable risk," ALI, Model Penal Code § 2.02(2)(d), while recklessness exists "when a person disregards a risk of harm of which he is aware," Model Penal Code § 2.02(2)(c). And when Congress does not specify a *mens rea* in a criminal statute, we have no justification for inferring that anything more than recklessness is needed. It is quite unusual for us to interpret a statute to contain a requirement that is nowhere set out in the text. Once we have reached

recklessness, we have gone as far as we can without stepping over the line that separates interpretation from amendment.

There can be no real dispute that recklessness regarding a risk of serious harm is wrongful conduct. In a wide variety of contexts, we have described reckless conduct as morally culpable. Indeed, this Court has held that "reckless disregard for human life" may justify the death penalty. Someone who acts recklessly with respect to conveying a threat necessarily grasps that he is not engaged in innocent conduct. He is not merely careless. He is aware that others could regard his statements as a threat, but he delivers them anyway.

Accordingly, I would hold that a defendant may be convicted under § 875(c) if he or she consciously disregards the risk that the communication transmitted will be interpreted as a true threat. Nothing in the Court's non-committal opinion prevents lower courts from adopting that standard.

Id. at 2015-16 (Alito, J., concurring in part and dissenting in part).

Note that the Supreme Court, despite the language in *Staples*, *Elonis*, and other cases seemingly requiring some level of *mens rea*—and some consciousness of wrongdoing—for criminal convictions, has on occasion been satisfied with a far lower standard. Thus, for example, in *Dean v. United States*, 556 U.S. 568 (2009), the Court accepted an interpretation of a statute whereby even negligence was not required for a criminal conviction. The *Dean* case involved 18 U.S.C. § 924(c)(1)(A)(iii), which imposes a mandatory minimum sentence of 10 years for "discharg[ing]" a firearm during and in relation to any violent or drug trafficking crime. The defendant contended that the discharge of a firearm he had used while committing a robbery was accidental and that this sentence was only warranted when the defendant intends to discharge the firearm. The Supreme Court rejected his argument, reasoning that the language and structure of the statute evidenced that Congress had not required proof of intent. The Court then responded to the defendant's reliance on the presumption of *mens rea* applied in cases like *Staples* as follows:

It is unusual to impose criminal punishment for the consequences of purely accidental conduct. But it is not unusual to punish individuals for the unintended consequences of their *unlawful* acts. The felony-murder rule is a familiar example: If a defendant commits an unintended homicide while committing another felony, the defendant can be convicted of murder. …

Blackstone expressed the idea in the following terms:

"[I]f any accidental mischief happens to follow from the performance of a *lawful* act, the party stands excused from all guilt: but if a man be doing any thing *unlawful,* and a consequence ensues which he did not foresee or intend, as the death of a man or the like, his want of foresight shall be no excuse; for, being guilty of one offence, in doing antecedently what is in itself unlawful, he is criminally guilty of whatever consequence may follow the first misbehaviour." 4 W. Blackstone, Commentaries on the Laws of England 26–27 (1769).

Here the defendant is already guilty of unlawful conduct twice over: a violent or drug trafficking offense and the use, carrying, or possession of a firearm in the course of that offense. That unlawful conduct was not an accident. The fact that the actual discharge of a gun … may be accidental does not mean that the defendant is blameless. The sentencing enhancement in subsection (iii) accounts for the risk of harm resulting from the manner in which the crime is carried out, for which the defendant is responsible. An individual who brings a loaded weapon to commit a crime runs the risk that the gun will discharge accidentally. A gunshot in such circumstances—whether accidental or intended—increases the risk that others will be injured, that people will panic, or that violence (with its own danger to those nearby) will be used in response. Those criminals wishing to avoid the penalty for an inadvertent discharge can lock or unload the firearm, handle it with care during the underlying violent or drug trafficking crime, leave the gun at home, or—best yet—avoid committing the felony in the first place.

Id. at 575-76.

6. According to the *Staples* Court, what are the factors or distinguishing features that justify treating a law as a "public welfare" enactment that presumptively contains a lesser *mens rea* requirement? The *Staples* Court, as it has in prior cases, emphasizes the "innocence" of the individuals subject to regulation. Isn't this circular reasoning? After all, isn't the question that the Court is charged with answering just what is necessary to prove potential defendants guilty?

The *Staples* Court cites a case called *Liparota v. United States*, 471 U.S. 419 (1985), when discussing "the particular care we have taken to avoid construing a statute to dispense with *mens rea* where doing so would 'criminalize a broad range of apparently innocent conduct.'" *Staples*, 511 U.S. at 610. In *Liparota*, the Court rejected application of the "public welfare" doctrine. At issue was a federal statute governing food stamp fraud which provided that:

> Whoever knowingly uses, transfers, acquires, alters, or possesses coupons or authorization cards in any manner not authorized by the statute or the regulations is subject to fine and imprisonment.

The question at issue was "how far down the sentence" the "knowingly" requirement went—that is, whether the defendant had to know only that he was using, transferring, acquiring or possessing food stamps *or* whether he *also* had to know that he was doing so in a manner not authorized by the statute or the regulations.

The *Liparota* Court rejected the government's argument that a defendant is guilty if he knew that he acquired or possessed food stamps and if in fact that acquisition or possession was in a manner not authorized by statute. Instead, the Court held that an individual only violates the statute if he knows that he has acquired or possessed food stamps *and* if he also knows that he has done so in an unauthorized manner. One could argue that the *Liparota* Court rejected the most natural reading of the plain language of the statute (that "knowingly" modifies the verbs that immediately follow (possess or acquire)). Did the Court also disregard the hallowed principle that "ignorance of the law is no defense"?

The *Liparota* Court invoked, in resolving the case, the rule of lenity and the background presumption of our criminal law requiring *mens rea*. As the *Staples* Court indicates, the major force motivating this result (and thus these interpretive aids) was the *Liparota* Court's fear that to construe the statute otherwise would "criminalize a broad range of apparently innocent conduct." Does the Court's use of interpretative aids, such as the presumption of *mens rea*, the rule of lenity, and the like, seem principled? Or are the canons relied upon simply a means to the end of justifying the result reached by reference to the Justices' view of who is a *moral* "innocent"? If the perceived *moral* "innocence" of the activity is the key to resolving these *mens rea* issues, why doesn't the Court simply use that "test," without trotting out other interpretive rules?

Professor David Luban has argued that Liporata was hardly a "moral" innocent:

> Liporata's "innocent" activity consisted of buying food stamps from poor people for less than face value and then reselling or redeeming them at full price. Plainly, this amounts to stealing from the government: the government gives a poor person $200 worth of coupons to purchase food; Liparota buys them for $150 and redeems them for face value, and in this way he diverts $50 of government money to his own pocket.

David Luban, *The Publicity of Law and the Regulatory State*, 10 J. Pol. Phil. 296, 310 (2002). In *International Minerals*, the defendant's activity was *not* morally culpable, yet the Court refused to recognize an exception to this same rule in that case. Can we reconcile these results?

7. In *Flores-Figueroa v. United States*, 556 U.S. 646 (2009), the Supreme Court was asked to interpret the federal statute that outlaws aggravated identity theft, 18 U.S.C. § 1028(a)(1). The

defendant, a native of Mexico, came to the United States and, to secure employment, provided his employer with counterfeit Social Security and alien registration cards; these cards bore the defendant's name but the numbers on both cards were in fact numbers assigned to other people. He was prosecuted under § 1028(a)(1), which makes it a crime to "knowingly ... possess[], or use[], without lawful authority, a means of identification of another person." The issue in the case was, again, how far down the sentence the "knowing" requirement ran—that is, whether the defendant had to know that the numbers on the cards were assigned to other people as opposed to simply made-up. The Supreme Court held, relying on "ordinary English grammar" and *Liparota v. United States*, that the government indeed had to prove knowledge that the identification in fact belonged to another person. *Id.* at 657. In so doing, the majority noted that "courts ordinarily read a phrase in a criminal statute that introduces the elements of a crime with the word 'knowingly' as applying that word to each element." *Id.* at 652. This provoked Justice Scalia, joined by Justice Thomas, to file a concurrence noting their disagreement with this statement, to the extent it was normative as opposed to descriptive. Justice Alito also filed a concurrence, noting that "[i]n interpreting a criminal statute such as the one before us, I think it is fair to begin with a general presumption that the specified *mens rea* applies to all elements of an offense, but it must be recognized that there are instances in which context may well rebut that presumption." *Id.* at 660 (ALITO, J., concurring in part and concurring in the judgment). Would the public welfare offenses fall within Justice Alito's exception? One exception is applied where the element at issue does not go to culpability but rather provides only the statutory "hook" for federal jurisdiction. *See, e.g.*, United States v. Prince, 647 F.3d 1257, 1267 (10th Cir. 2011); *see generally* Leonid Traps, Note, *"Knowingly" Ignorant: Mens Rea Distribution in Federal Criminal Law After* Flores-Figueroa, 112 Colum. L. Rev. 628 (2012).

8. Professor Luban classifies *International Minerals* and *Liporata* as examples of the Court's "signaling theory," in which the Court uses the word "innocent" as "a term of art to denote conduct that, roughly speaking, raises no eyebrows." *Id.* at 302. He explains:

> Used in this way, the word carries no moral connotations. There is nothing immoral about a chemical manufacturer shipping sulfuric acid—doing so is morally innocent behavior—but sulfuric acid is dangerous stuff, and so shipping it is the sort of thing one should expect will be regulated. ... Here, "innocent" is the antonym of "regulable," not of "guilty." ...
>
> In effect, the line of cases including *Balint, Freed, International Minerals & Chemical*, and *Liporata* ... instructs us to range conduct on a continuum from the innocent to the non-innocent and draw a line on the continuum. Conduct is innocent in this sense when it is neither immoral (malum in se) nor regulable-in-se. Everything on the non-innocent side of the line will be presumed to send a signal telling us that we should check the regulations before acting; everything on the innocent side of the line will be presumed to send no such signal, so that before we can be convicted of violating regulations through innocent conduct the government will be compelled to prove that we knew we were breaking the law and thus acted with specific intent to break the law.

Luban, *supra*, at 302-03. If this is correct, why does *Staples* come out the way it does? Owning a gun may not be *malum in se*, but given the current debates raging about gun regulation and control, can anyone truly argue that this activity does not send a signal that it is or may well be "regulable-in-se"? What does the *Staples* Court look to in deciding that certain activity is neither immoral nor "regulable-in-se"? Does the fact that the item is inherently dangerous appear to be determinative? Is the pervasiveness of the regulation of a given item sufficient to place that item in the "public welfare" category? If it is not sufficient to show that an item is both dangerous and highly regulated to fit that item in the "public welfare" category, what actually suffices? What is the defining inquiry?

9. In declining to apply the public welfare doctrine and instead imposing a "knowledge" standard, the *Staples* Court seemed to believe that, in addition to the "usually licit and blameless" nature of gun ownership, the *commonplace, widespread* character of the activity at

issue—broadly described as (any) gun ownership—somehow puts this conduct in the category of "innocent" conduct. Is the Court assuming that the fact that certain conduct is "widespread" or "commonplace" means that it also sends no signals? Does "ordinary" mean "unregulated"?

Consider the Court's car example. It stated that "[i]f we were to accept as a general rule the Government's suggestion that dangerous and regulated items place their owners under an obligation to inquire at their peril into compliance with regulations, we would undoubtedly reach some untoward results. Automobiles, for example, might also be termed 'dangerous' devices and are highly regulated at both the state and federal levels. Congress might see fit to criminalize the violation of certain regulations concerning automobiles, and thus might make it a crime to operate a vehicle without a properly functioning emission control system. But we probably would hesitate to conclude on the basis of silence that Congress intended a prison term to apply to a car owner whose vehicle's emission levels, wholly unbeknownst to him, began to exceed legal limits between regular inspection dates."

Is this argument persuasive? *Would* people be surprised to learn that there might be criminal penalties for auto-emissions violations *because of the commonplace nature of car ownership*? Or, as Professor Luban argues, would they be surprised because they know that cars are heavily regulated and therefore acquaint themselves with applicable regulations; in other words, motorists are not surprised that there is no such rule because "it is common knowledge among motorists that an emissions-violation is *not* a criminal offense, any more than illegal parking is a criminal offense"? *Id.* at 304.

10. Professor Luban posits that *Staples* is better explained as a case in which the court employs a "*social cognition* conception of innocence." *Id.* at 305. He argues:

> Our perceptions of risk depend crucially on framing; "dangerous" means "abnormally dangerous" compared with some cognitive baseline—and cognitive baselines are set by the people around us. The commonplaces of our culture (like automobile ownership and, in much of America, gun ownership) are, by definition, not abnormally dangerous, because everyone does them. Thus, they send no signals. ...
>
> [W]hen society is divided over an issue, the social cognition argument is never just an empirical, social-psychological claim that culture shapes our perception of innocence by setting baselines. It is also a political claim about whose culture *should* set the baselines. It is a normative, not merely a descriptive, argument.
>
> ... Implicit in the social cognition argument is the thought that if an activity is "licit and blameless conduct," then the law has no business regulating it. That is, our intuitions about which activities are regulable-in-se, socially reinforced by the similar intuitions of our neighbors and peers, will inevitably be colored by our theory of what the government may *rightly* regulate.

Id. at 305, 307. Do you agree that this "culture-war" view best explains Justice Thomas's analysis, and the tone of his opinion? *See id.* at 307.

11. The *Staples* Court finally seems to find very important, if not determinative, the punishment available for violations of the statute. Why should the potential sentence matter in such cases?

12. According to Justice Stevens' dissent, when is the "public welfare" doctrine applicable? Would Justice Stevens' approach mean that a potentially vast range of regulation could be read to carry only minimal *mens rea* requirements?

13. In other cases in which the Court has examined the appropriate degree of *mens rea* to be accorded a statutory scheme, rather than dwelling on whether the activity at issue is "commonplace," the Court has emphasized the nature of the regulation at issue. It has on this basis refused to hold individuals strictly liable under regulatory regimes in which the line between acceptable conduct and criminally or civilly sanctionable conduct are not clearly drawn or intuitively obvious. For example, in *United States v. United States Gypsum Co.*, 438 U.S. 422, 440-42 (1978), in which the Court imposed an intent requirement in prosecutions for

price-fixing offenses under the Sherman Act, 15 U.S.C. § 1, the Court explained the necessity of a *mens rea* requirement as follows:

> ... With certain exceptions for conduct regarded as *per se* illegal because of its unquestionably anticompetitive effects, the behavior proscribed by the [Sherman] Act is often difficult to distinguish from the gray zone of socially acceptable and economically justifiable business conduct. Indeed, the type of conduct charged in the indictment in this case—the exchange of price information among competitors—is illustrative in this regard. The imposition of criminal liability on a corporate official, or for that matter on a corporation directly, for engaging in such conduct which only after the fact is determined to violate the statute because of anticompetitive effects, without inquiring into the intent with which it was undertaken, holds out the distinct possibility of overdeterrence; salutary and procompetitive conduct lying close to the borderline of impermissible conduct might be shunned by businessmen who chose to be excessively cautious in the face of uncertainty regarding possible exposure to criminal punishment for even a good-faith error of judgment. Further, the use of criminal sanctions in such circumstances would be difficult to square with the generally accepted functions of the criminal law. The criminal sanctions would be used, not to punish conscious and calculated wrongdoing at odds with statutory proscriptions, but instead simply to *regulate* business practices regardless of the intent with which they were undertaken. While in certain cases we have imputed a regulatory purpose to Congress in choosing to employ criminal sanctions, the availability of a range of nonpenal alternatives to the criminal sanctions of the Sherman Act negates the imputation of any such purpose to Congress in the instant context.

See also Screws v. United States, 325 U.S. 91, 101-02 (1945) (plurality opinion) (holding that conviction under 18 U.S.C. § 20, which made it a misdemeanor to "under color of any law, statute, ordinance, regulation, or custom, willfully [to] subject[] ... any inhabitant of any State ... to the deprivation of any rights, privileges, or immunities secured or protected by the Constitution and laws of the United States," required proof of a specific intent to deprive the victim of a right which had been made specific by the express terms of the Constitution or laws of the United States or decisions interpreting them).

14. At the extremes, where the requirements of the law governing the defendant's actions are very unclear, the defense may have a due process objection to the prosecution on vagueness grounds. *See, e.g.*, United States v. Mallas, 762 F.2d 361 (4th Cir.1985); United States v. Dahlstrom, 713 F.2d 1423 (9th Cir.1983). Often courts will find, however, that the *mens rea* element of a statutory scheme saves it from attack on vagueness grounds and may in fact use the possible vagueness of the statute in absence of a high level of *mens rea* to justify reading such a heightened *mens rea* into the statutory scheme. *See, e.g.*, McFadden v. United States, -- U.S. --, 135 S.Ct. 2298, 2307 (2015) ("Under our precedents, a scienter requirement in a statute 'alleviate[s] vagueness concerns'"); Posters 'N' Things, Ltd. v. United States, 511 U.S. 513, 526 539 (1994) ("'[T]he Court has recognized that a scienter requirement may mitigate a law's vagueness, especially with respect to the adequacy of notice ... that [the] conduct is proscribed.'") (citation omitted); Boyce Motor Lines, Inc. v. United States, 342 U.S. 337, 342 (1952); Screws v. United States, 325 U.S. 91 (1945).

UNITED STATES v. WEITZENHOFF
35 F.3d 1275 (9th Cir.1993) *(en banc)*

FLETCHER, CIRCUIT JUDGE:

Michael H. Weitzenhoff and Thomas W. Mariani, who managed the East Honolulu Community Services Sewage Treatment Plant, appeal their convictions for violations of the Clean Water Act ("CWA"), 33 U.S.C. §§ 1251 *et seq.*, contending that ... the district court misconstrued the word "knowingly" under section 1319(c)(2) of the CWA ....

In 1988 and 1989 Weitzenhoff was the manager and Mariani the assistant manager of the East Honolulu Community Services Sewage Treatment Plant ("the plant"), located not far from Sandy Beach, a popular swimming and surfing beach on Oahu. The plant is designed to treat some 4 million gallons of residential wastewater each day by removing the solids and other harmful pollutants from the sewage so that the resulting effluent can be safely discharged into the ocean. The plant operates under a permit issued pursuant to the National Pollution Discharge Elimination System ("NPDES"), which established the limits on the Total Suspended Solids ("TSS") and Biochemical Oxygen Demand ("BOD")—indicators of the solid and organic matter, respectively, in the effluent discharged at Sandy Beach. During the period in question, the permit limited the discharge of both the TSS and BOD to an average of 976 pounds per day over a 30-day period. It also imposed monitoring and sampling requirements on the plant's management. …

The evidence produced by the government at trial showed that [waste activated sludge ("WAS")] was discharged directly into the ocean from the plant on about 40 separate occasions from April 1988 to June 1989, resulting in some 436,000 pounds of pollutant solids being discharged into the ocean, and that the discharges violated the plant's 30-day average effluent limit under the permit for most of the months during which they occurred. Most of the WAS discharges occurred during the night, and none was reported to the [Hawaii Department of Health ("DOH")] or the [Environmental Protection Agency ("EPA")]. DOH inspectors contacted the plant on several occasions in 1988 in response to complaints by lifeguards at Sandy Beach that sewage was being emitted from the outfall, but Weitzenhoff and Mariani repeatedly denied that there was any problem at the plant. In one letter responding to a DOH inquiry in October 1988, Mariani stated that "the debris that was reported could not have been from the East Honolulu Wastewater Treatment facility, as our records of effluent quality up to this time will substantiate." One of the plant employees who participated in the dumping operation testified that Weitzenhoff instructed him not to say anything about the discharges, because if they all stuck together and did not reveal anything, "they [couldn't] do anything to us."

Following an FBI investigation, Weitzenhoff and Mariani were charged in a thirty-one-count indictment with conspiracy and substantive violations of the Clean Water Act ("CWA"), 33 U.S.C. §§ 1251 *et seq*. At trial, Weitzenhoff and Mariani admitted having authorized the discharges, but claimed that their actions were justified under their interpretation of the NPDES permit. The jury found them guilty of six of the thirty-one counts.

Weitzenhoff was sentenced to twenty-one months and Mariani thirty-three months imprisonment. …

Section 1311(a) of the CWA prohibits the discharge of pollutants into navigable waters without an NPDES permit. 33 U.S.C. § 1311(a). Section 1319(c)(2) makes it a felony offense to "knowingly violate[ ] section 1311, 1312, 1316, 1317, 1318, 1321(b)(3), 1328, or 1345 …, or any permit condition or limitation implementing any of such sections in a permit issued under section 1342."

Prior to trial, the district court construed "knowingly" in section 1319(c)(2) as requiring only that Weitzenhoff and Mariani were aware that they were discharging the pollutants in question, not that they knew they were violating the terms of the statute or permit. According to appellants, the district court erred in its interpretation of the CWA and in instructing the jury that "the government is not required to prove that the defendant knew that his act or omissions were unlawful," as well as in rejecting their proposed instruction based on the defense that they mistakenly believed their conduct was authorized by the permit. Apparently, no court of appeals has confronted the issue raised by appellants.

… "In construing statutes in a case of first impression, we first look to the language of the controlling statutes, and second to legislative history." … If the district court was correct in its interpretation of the statute, then it did not err in giving the instruction it did or refusing to submit appellants' mistake of law defense to the jury.

As with certain other criminal statutes that employ the term "knowingly," it is not apparent from the face of the statute whether "knowingly" means a knowing violation of the law or simply knowing conduct that is violative of the law. We turn, then, to the legislative history of the provision at issue to ascertain what Congress intended.

In 1987, Congress substantially amended the CWA, elevating the penalties for violations of the Act. Increased penalties were considered necessary to deter would-be polluters. With the 1987 amendments, Congress substituted "knowingly" for the earlier intent requirement of "willfully" that appeared in the predecessor to section 1319(c)(2). The Senate report accompanying the legislation explains that the changes in the penalty provisions were to ensure that "[c]riminal liability shall ... attach to any person who is not in compliance with all applicable Federal, State and local requirements and permits *and causes* a POTW [publicly owned treatment works] to violate any effluent limitation or condition in any permit issued to the treatment works." Similarly, the report accompanying the House version of the bill, which contained parallel provisions for enhancement of penalties, states that the proposed amendments were to "provide penalties for dischargers or individuals who knowingly or negligently violate *or cause the violation of* certain of the Act's requirements." Because they speak in terms of "causing" a violation, the congressional explanations of the new penalty provisions strongly suggest that criminal sanctions are to be imposed on an individual who knowingly engages in conduct that results in a permit violation, regardless of whether the polluter is cognizant of the requirements or even the existence of the permit.

Our conclusion that "knowingly" does not refer to the legal violation is fortified by decisions interpreting analogous public welfare statutes. The leading case in this area is *United States v. International Minerals & Chem. Corp.*, 402 U.S. 558 (1971). In *International Minerals*, the Supreme Court construed a statute which made it a crime to "knowingly violate[] any ... regulation."... The Court held that the term "knowingly" referred to the acts made criminal rather than a violation of the regulation, and that "regulation" was a shorthand designation for the specific acts or omissions contemplated by the act. ...

[We do not agree with Weitzenhoff that *Staples v. United States*, 511 U.S. 600 (1994) calls into question our analysis.] The specific holding in *Staples* was that the government is required to prove that a defendant charged with possession of a machine gun knew that the weapon he possessed had the characteristics that brought it within the statutory definition of a machinegun. But the Court took pains to contrast the gun laws to other regulatory regimes, specifically those regulations that govern the handling of "obnoxious waste materials." It noted that the mere innocent ownership of guns is not a public welfare offense. The Court focussed [*sic*] on the long tradition of widespread gun ownership in this country and, recognizing that approximately 50% of American homes contain a firearm, acknowledged that mere ownership of a gun is not sufficient to place people on notice that the act of owning an unregistered firearm is not innocent under the law.

Staples thus explicitly contrasted the mere possession of guns to public welfare offenses, which include statutes that regulate "'dangerous or deleterious devices or products or obnoxious waste materials,'" and confirmed the continued vitality of statutes covering public welfare offenses, which "regulate potentially harmful or injurious items" and place a defendant on notice that he is dealing with a device or a substance "that places him in 'responsible relation to a public danger.'" "[I]n such cases Congress intended to place the burden on the defendant to ascertain at his peril whether [his conduct] comes within the inhibition of the statute."

Unlike "[g]uns [which] in general are not 'deleterious devices or products or obnoxious waste materials,' that put their owners on notice that they stand 'in responsible relation to a public danger[,]' *Dotterweich*, 320 U.S. at 281," the dumping of sewage and other pollutants into our nation's waters is precisely the type of activity that puts the discharger on notice that his acts may pose a public danger. Like other public welfare offenses that regulate the discharge of pollutants into the air, the disposal of hazardous wastes, the undocumented shipping of acids, and the use of pesticides on our food, the improper and excessive discharge of sewage causes cholera, hepatitis, and other serious illnesses, and can have serious repercussions for public health and welfare.[9]

---

[9] [Court's footnote 7:] In *Staples*, the Court also noted that the penalty attached to a violation of a

The criminal provisions of the CWA are clearly designed to protect the public at large from the potentially dire consequences of water pollution, and as such fall within the category of public welfare legislation. *International Minerals* ... controls the case at hand. The government did not need to prove that Weitzenhoff and Mariani knew that their acts violated the permit or the CWA. ...

KLEINFELD, CIRCUIT JUDGE, with whom CIRCUIT JUDGES REINHARDT, KOZINSKI, TROTT, and T.G. NELSON join, dissenting from the order rejecting the suggestion for rehearing en banc.

... The statute at issue makes it a felony, subject to three years of imprisonment, to "knowingly violate[] ... any permit condition or limitation." 33 U.S.C. § 1319(c)(2)(A). Here is the statutory scheme, with the portion applied in *Weitzenhoff* in boldface:

> "Any person who ...
>   "negligently violates [various sections of the Clean Water Act] ... or any permit condition or limitation ... [commits a misdemeanor]. 33 U.S.C. § 1319(c)(1)(A);
>   "negligently introduces into a sewer system or a publicly owned treatment works any pollutant or hazardous substance which such person knew or reasonably should have known could cause personal injury or property damage or ... which causes such treatment works to violate any effluent limitation or condition in any permit ... [commits a misdemeanor]. 33 U.S.C. § 1319(c)(1)(B);
>   **"knowingly violates [various sections of the Clean Water Act] ... or any permit condition or limitation...[commits a felony]. 33 U.S.C. § 1319(c)(2)(A);**
>   "knowingly introduces into a sewer system or into a publicly owned treatment works any pollutant or hazardous substance which such person knew or reasonably should have known could cause personal injury or property damage or ... which causes such treatment works to violate any effluent limitation or condition in a permit ... [commits a felony]. 33 U.S.C. § 1319(c)(2)(B);
>   "knowingly violates [various sections of the Clean Water Act] ... or any permit condition or limitation ... and who knows at that time that he thereby places another person in imminent danger of death or serious bodily injury ... [commits a felony punishable by up to 15 years imprisonment]. 33 U.S.C. § 1319(c)(3)(A).

In this case, the defendants, sewage plant operators, had a permit to discharge sewage into the ocean, but exceeded the permit limitations. The legal issue for the panel was what knowledge would turn innocently or negligently violating a permit into "knowingly" violating a permit. Were the plant operators felons if they knew they were discharging sewage, but did not know that they were violating their permit? Or did they also have to know they were violating their permit? Ordinary English grammar, common sense, and precedent, all compel the latter construction.

As the panel opinion states the facts, these two defendants were literally "midnight dumpers." They managed a sewer plant and told their employees to dump 436,000 pounds of sewage into the ocean, mostly at night, fouling a nearby beach. Their conduct, as set out in the panel opinion, suggests that they must have known they were violating their National Pollution

---

criminal statute in the past has been a relevant factor in determining whether the statute defines a public welfare offense. The Court recognized that public welfare offenses originally involved statutes that provided only light penalties such as fines or short jail sentences, but that modern statutes now punish public welfare offenses with much more significant terms of imprisonment. *E.g.*, *International Minerals*, 402 U.S. 558 (1971) (ten years imprisonment if death or bodily injury results from violation); *United States v. Freed*, 401 U.S. 601, 609-10, (five years imprisonment for possession of unregistered grenade). While the *Staples* opinion expresses concern with this evolution of enhanced punishments for public welfare offenses, it refrains from holding that public welfare offenses may not be punished as felonies.

Discharge Elimination System (NPDES) permit. But we cannot decide the case on that basis, because the jury did not. The court instructed the jury that the government did not have to prove the defendants knew their conduct was unlawful, and refused to instruct the jury that a mistaken belief that the discharge was authorized by the permit would be a defense. Because of the way the jury was instructed, its verdict is consistent with the proposition that the defendants honestly and reasonably believed that their NPDES permit authorized the discharges.

This proposition could be true. NPDES permits are often difficult to understand and obey. The EPA had licensed the defendants' plant to discharge 976 pounds of waste per day, or about 409,920 pounds over the fourteen months covered by the indictment, into the ocean. The wrongful conduct was not discharging waste into the ocean. That was socially desirable conduct by which the defendants protected the people of their city from sewage-borne disease and earned their pay. The wrongful conduct was violating the NPDES permit by discharging 26,000 more pounds of waste than the permit authorized during the fourteen months. Whether these defendants were innocent or not, in the sense of knowing that they were exceeding their permit limitation, the panel's holding will make innocence irrelevant in other permit violation cases where the defendants had no idea that they were exceeding permit limits. The only thing they have to know to be guilty is that they were dumping sewage into the ocean, yet that was a lawful activity expressly authorized by their federal permit.

The statute says "knowingly violate[s] ... any permit condition or limitation." "Knowingly" is an adverb. It modifies the verb "violates." The object of the verb is "any permit condition or limitation." The word "knowingly" is placed before "violates" to "explain its meaning in the case at hand more clearly." Congress has distinguished those who knowingly violate permit conditions, and are thereby felons, from those who unknowingly violate permit conditions, so are not. The panel reads the statute as though it says "knowingly discharges pollutants." It does not. If we read the statute on the assumption that Congress used the English language in an ordinary way, the state of mind required is knowledge that one is violating a permit condition.

This approach has the virtue of attributing common sense and a rational purpose to Congress. It is one thing to defy a permit limitation, but quite another to violate it without realizing that one is violating it. Congress promulgated a parallel statute making it a misdemeanor "negligently" to violate a permit condition or limitation. 33 U.S.C. § 1319(c)(1)(A). If negligent violation is a misdemeanor, why would Congress want to make it a felony to violate the permit without negligence and without even knowing that the discharge exceeded the permit limit? That does not make any sense. It would deter people from working in sewer plants, instead of deterring people from violating permits. All dischargers acting lawfully pursuant to a permit know that they are discharging pollutants. The presence or absence of that knowledge, which is the only mental element determining guilt under the panel's decision, has no bearing on any conduct Congress could have meant to turn into a felony. The only knowledge which could have mattered to Congress, the only knowledge which distinguishes good conduct from bad, is knowledge that the discharge violates the permit. That is what the statute says, "knowingly violates," not "knowingly discharges." There is no sensible reason to doubt that Congress meant what it said and said what it meant.

The panel reaches its surprising result in surprising ways. First, it says that the statute is ambiguous. ... As explained above, a grammatical and sensible reading of the statute leaves no room for ambiguity. But for the sake of discussion, suppose that the statute is ambiguous, as the panel says. Then the rule of lenity requires that the construction allowing the defendant more liberty rather than less be applied by the courts. "[L]enity principles 'demand resolution of ambiguities in criminal statutes in favor of the defendant.'" The reason is the need for "fair warning."

Instead of applying the rule of lenity, as it was required to do, the panel, after identifying the ambiguity, said "[w]e turn, then, to the legislative history of the provision at issue to ascertain what Congress intended." That is not an appropriate way to resolve an ambiguity in a criminal law. "Because construction of a criminal statute must be guided by the need for fair warning, it is rare that legislative history or statutory policies will support a construction of a statute broader than that clearly warranted by the text." We cannot fairly put sewer plant workers in peril of prison if they do not read House and Senate committee reports. ...

The panel then tries to bolster its construction by categorizing the offense as a "public welfare offense," as though that justified more aggressive criminalization without a plain statutory command. This category is a modernized version of "*malum prohibitum.*" Traditionally the criminal law distinguishes between *malum in se*, conduct wrong upon principles of natural moral law, and *malum prohibitum*, conduct not inherently immoral but wrong because prohibited by law. To put this in plain, modern terms, any normal person knows murder, rape and robbery are wrong, and they would be wrong even in a place with no sovereign and no law. Discharging 6% more pollutants than one's permit allows is wrong only because the law says so. Substitution of the modern term "public welfare offense" for the traditional one, *malum prohibitum*, allows for confusion by rhetorical suggestion. The new term suggests that other offenses might merely be private in their impact, and therefore less serious. The older set of terms made it clear that murder was more vile than violating a federal regulation. The category of *malum prohibitum*, or public welfare offenses, makes the rule of lenity especially important, most particularly for felonies, because persons of good conscience may not recognize the wrongfulness of the conduct when they engage in it.

Staples v. United States, 511 U.S. 600 (1994), reminds us that "offenses that require no *mens rea* generally are disfavored." *Mens rea* may be dispensed with in public welfare offenses, but the penalty is a "significant consideration in determining whether the statute should be construed as dispensing with *mens rea.*" ... If Congress makes a crime a felony, the felony categorization alone is a "factor tending to suggest that Congress did not intend to eliminate a *mens rea* requirement. In such a case, the usual presumption that a defendant must know the facts that make his conduct illegal should apply." In the case at bar, "the facts that make his conduct illegal" are the permit violations, not the discharges of pollutants. Discharge of pollutants was licensed by the federal government in the NPDES permit. Under *Staples*, it would be presumed, even if the law did not plainly say so, that the defendant would have to know that he was violating the permit in order to be guilty of the felony. ...

The panel cites *United States v. International Minerals & Chem. Corp.*, 402 U.S. 558 (1971) ... in support of its reading. ... Because of the syntactically similar statute at issue in that case, it is the strongest authority for the panel's decision and raises the most serious question for my own analysis. ... *International Minerals* expressly limits its holding to "dangerous or deleterious devices or products or obnoxious waste materials." The Court distinguished materials not obviously subject to regulation:

> Pencils, dental floss, paper clips may also be regulated. But they may be the type of products which might raise substantial due process questions if Congress did not require ... "*mens rea*" as to each ingredient of the offense. But where, as here..., dangerous or deleterious devices or products or obnoxious waste materials are involved, the probability of regulation is so great that anyone who is aware that he is in possession of them or dealing with them must be presumed to be aware of the regulation.

International Minerals would have much persuasive force for *Weitzenhoff*, because of the grammatical similarity of the statute, if (1) the Clean Water Act limited pollutants to "dangerous or deleterious devices or products or obnoxious waste materials;" (2) the crime was only a misdemeanor; and (3) *Staples* had not come down this term. But all three of these conditions are contrary to fact. The pollutants to which the Clean Water Act felony statute applies include many in the "pencils, dental floss, paper clips" category. Hot water, rock, and sand are classified as "pollutants" by the Clean Water Act. Discharging silt from a stream back into the same stream may amount to discharge of a pollutant. For that matter, so may skipping a stone into a lake. So may a cafeteria worker's pouring hot, stale coffee down the drain. Making these acts a misdemeanor is one thing, but a felony is quite another, as *Staples* teaches.
...

The panel, finally, asserts that as a matter of policy, the Clean Water Act crimes "are clearly designed to protect the public at large from the dire consequences of water pollution."

That is true, but the panel does not explain how the public is to be protected by making felons of sewer workers who unknowingly violate their plants' permits. Provision for sanitary sewage disposal is among the most ancient laws of civilization. Deuteronomy 23:12-13. Sewage workers perform essential work of great social value. Probably nothing has prevented more infant mortality, or freed more people from cholera, hepatitis, typhoid fever, and other disease, than the development in the last two centuries of municipal sewer systems. Sewage utility workers perform their difficult work in malodorous and dangerous environments. We have now imposed on these vitally important public servants a massive legal risk, unjustified by law or precedent, if they unknowingly violate their permit conditions.

Nor is the risk of prison limited to sewage plant workers. It applies to anyone who discharges pollutants pursuant to a permit, and unknowingly violates the permit. The panel suggests that criminalizing this innocent conduct will protect the public from water pollution. It is at least as likely that the increased criminal risk will raise the cost and reduce the availability of such lawful and essential public services as sewage disposal. We should not deprive individuals of justice, whether the judicial action would serve some desirable policy or not. It is by no means certain that the panel's construction will advance the underlying policy it attributes to Congress. We should apply the words Congress and the President promulgated as law, leaving the difficult policy choices to them.

We undermine the foundation of criminal law when we so vitiate the requirement of a criminal state of knowledge and intention as to make felons of the morally innocent. ...

Notes

1. Where on the spectrum from fact to law does the issue in this case fall? What are the parties' positions regarding the *mens rea* that must be shown to sustain a conviction? Even if one were to accept the government's position, would this be a strict liability offense?

2. The court relies on the "public welfare" doctrine to justify its result. What test does the majority employ in order to justify that classification? The *Weitzenhoff* majority's best argument stems from the *International Minerals* Court's reading of identical statutory language not to require knowledge of the applicable regulations. As defense counsel, how would you attack the prosecution's reliance upon *International Minerals* in this case?

3. As in *International Minerals*, and unlike *Staples*, the element as to which the court is determining *mens rea* is a "legal fact"—that is, it is a fact as to which the knowledge of law is relevant. Why is the doctrine that "ignorance of the law is no excuse" not invoked here? Does the court assume that such a discussion is unnecessary because *International Minerals* was based on that doctrine? The "ignorance of the law is no excuse" rule would seem to be the ultimate foundation for this decision. One could potentially argue, however, that an exception to this doctrine recognized in the Model Penal Code may be applicable in this and other regulatory contexts.

The Model Penal Code provides that ignorance or mistake as to a matter of law is a defense if it negatives the *mens rea* applicable to a given material element of the offense but only if the law as to which the defendant is ignorant or mistaken is not the law defining the offense but rather pertains to some "other" legal rule. *See, e.g.*, ALI, Model Penal Code § 2.04(1)(a), 2.02(9) & Comment to § 2.02. For example, if a defendant is prosecuted for malicious destruction of property that he honestly but mistakenly believed belonged to him, he may have a defense premised upon his mistake of law. In such circumstances, his mistake concerns not the criminal law under which he is being prosecuted (*i.e.*, is destruction of property a crime) but rather the property law that is made an attendant circumstance by the criminal prohibition (*i.e.*, is this property his or does it actually belong to another). Could one defend *Weitzenhoff* by arguing that the terms of the permit were in fact "other law" as to which an honest mistake should constitute a defense?

4. The Ninth Circuit's treatment of this issue is consistent with federal courts' general treatment of such issues in the environmental area. As Professor Richard Lazarus notes:

Knowledge of the law denotes two different kinds of knowledge. It may mean that the defendant must know both that the criminal prohibition exists and that she is violating it. Or, it may mean only that when, as often occurs, a criminal provision incorporates by reference a standard of conduct from another source of law (either a different statutory provision or implementing regulations), the defendant must know that there is a standard of conduct and that she is violating it. Under this second, broader meaning, the defendant need not know that such a violation is subject to criminal sanction.

In environmental criminal law, the issue of the defendant's knowledge of the law is confined to the second meaning. None of the criminal penalty provisions requires the government to prove the defendant's knowledge of the criminal status of her conduct. There is, however, textual support for the view that the defendant must possess some knowledge of the environmental standards external to the criminal penalty provision that serve as the basis for prosecution. Because many of the provisions impose criminal penalties on any person who "knowingly violates" a statutory or regulatory requirement, the juxtaposition of "knowingly" and "violates" presents a facially strong argument that Congress has made knowledge of the violation an element of the offense.

Many federal courts have addressed the question whether the government must prove the defendant's knowledge of the environmental standard, the violation of which served as the underlying basis for the criminal prosecution. Without exception, the courts agree that the criminal penalty provisions in the Clean Air Act, Clean Water Act, Federal Insecticide, Fungicide, Rodenticide Act, and Toxic Substances Control Act that require that a person "knowingly violates" do *not* require the government to prove that the defendant was actually aware of the applicable environmental standard.

Richard J. Lazarus, *Meeting the Demands of Integration in the Evolution of Environmental Law: Reforming Environmental Criminal Law*, 83 Geo. L.J. 2407, 2468-69 (1995) (footnotes omitted). Some have argued that because the only distinction between unlawful conduct and conduct that may be attacked civilly is the requirement of a "knowing" violation, the dilution of the "knowing" standard in environmental law means that "the criminal and civil regulatory structures essentially collapse into each other, and almost every environmental violator may be criminally prosecuted." David A. Barker, Note, *Environmental Crimes, Prosecutorial Discretion, and the Civil/Criminal Line*, 88 U. Va. L. Rev. 1387, 1390 (2002). The blurring of the civil/criminal line in turn gives prosecutors a great deal of discretion in determining what cases to pursue criminally, and gives enforcement officials similarly broad discretion to pursue either criminal or civil penalties. *See id.* at 1391.

5. Do the asserted justifications for the public welfare doctrine justify this result? Do we need to use the criminal sanction to create appropriate regulatory incentives or disincentives in this and other environmental cases? Who should be making this judgment, and on the basis of what record? Who is making this judgment, and on the basis of what record?

6. As noted in the dissenting opinion, the Clean Water Act also makes certain violations a federal misdemeanor if committed negligently. "The potential reach of these criminal negligence provisions is extremely broad. For example, any violation of a national pollutant discharge elimination system (NPDES) permit, or spill of a pollutant into waters of the United States attributable to negligent operations, training, or supervision, may theoretically meet the elements of the crime." Steven P. Solow & Ronald A. Sarachan, *Criminal Negligence Prosecutions Under the Federal Clean Water Act: A Statistical Analysis and an Evaluation of the Impact of* Hanousek *and* Hong, 32 E.L.R. 11153 (Oct.2002) (footnote omitted). In *United States v. Hanousek*, 176 F.3d 1116 (9th Cir.1999), the Ninth Circuit broadened even further the potential reach of the negligence provisions. The *Hanousek* court held that the appropriate standard of liability in a misdemeanor Clean Water Act prosecution was *simple* negligence, meaning that the defendant may be convicted upon proof that he failed to use reasonable care. *Id.* at 1120; *see also* United States v. Ortiz, 427 F.3d 1278 (10th Cir. 2005). A recent empirical analysis demonstrated that the government has "brought negligence-based CWA prosecutions only in rare and clearly defined circumstances." Solow & Sarachan, *supra.* It is unclear whether *Hanousek*, and a case in which negligence liability was upheld under a "responsible corporate officer" theory (*United*

States v. Hong, 242 F.3d 528 (4th Cir.2001), discussed *infra* Chapter 4 (Entity Liability; Managerial Liability), will prompt a change in the government's charging policies.

7. Assume you represent a major trade association of waste disposal companies. Would you support these defendants' efforts to have the Supreme Court grant certiorari in this case? What strategic considerations might inform the government's decision whether to oppose any review by the Supreme Court?

C. AWARENESS OF LEGAL REQUIREMENTS

As the above materials indicate, "[t]he general rule that ignorance of the law or a mistake of law is no defense to criminal prosecution is deeply rooted in the American legal system."[10] Sharon Davies explains, however, that courts,

> "have also deviated from the maxim, just as their forebears had done, when evidence of bona fide ignorance or mistake has made criminal conviction (to them) unfathomable, or the law itself has required forgiveness of an accused's legal error. Thus, the courts have sometimes (though not uniformly) held that an accused's ignorance of or mistake about a law is excusable if she fairly relied on some erroneous advice from an official responsible for interpreting or enforcing that law.[11] Ignorance or mistakes of law might also be forgiven if it is determined that the accused reasonably relied on a statute or judicial precedent later repealed or overturned, or if the legislature failed to make the law adequately known or knowable.
>
> An additional important subset of cases deviating from the maxim ... consists of decisions in which courts countenance ignorance or mistake of law claims because the claims disprove an element of the offense the prosecution is obligated to establish. These cases make clear that ignorance of the law will excuse if the law itself permits it to do so. Put another way, the law itself may impose upon a prosecutor the obligation to prove an accused's knowledge of the law as a specific element of a particular offense before a conviction may stand for its violation. For this reason, the statement "ignorance of the law does not excuse" is decidedly deceptive. A more precise statement of the maxim would be: "ignorance of the law is no defense *unless the law under which an accused is prosecuted makes knowledge of the law an element of the offense*."
>
> Determining when the law does this can be a formidable task. ...[12]

BRYAN v. UNITED STATES
524 U.S. 184 (1998)

JUSTICE STEVENS delivered the opinion of the Court.

Petitioner was convicted of "willfully" dealing in firearms without a federal license. The question presented is whether the term "willfully" in 18 U.S.C. § 924(a)(1)(D) requires proof that the defendant knew that his conduct was unlawful, or whether it also requires proof that he knew of the federal licensing requirement.

---

[10] Cheek v. United States, 498 U.S. 192, 199 (1991).

[11] [Ed.:] *See, e.g.*, United States v. Pennsylvania Industrial Chem. Corp., 411 U.S. 655 (1973) (holding that party should have been permitted to put on defense that it had been affirmatively misled into believing that its conduct was not criminal by long-standing, official agency interpretation of regulatory requirement); John T. Parry, *Culpability, Mistake, and Official Interpretations of Law*, 25 Am. J. Crim. L. 1 (1997); *see also* John Sifton, *United States Military and Central Intelligence Agency Personnel Abroad: Plugging the Prosecutorial Gaps*, 43 Harv. J. Legis. 487 (2006).

[12] Sharon L. Davies, *The Jurisprudence of Willfulness: An Evolving Theory of Excusable Ignorance*, 48 Duke L.J. 341, 357-59 (1998) (footnotes omitted).

In 1968 Congress enacted the Omnibus Crime Control and Safe Streets Act. 82 Stat. 197-239. In Title IV of that Act Congress made findings concerning the impact of the traffic in firearms on the prevalence of lawlessness and violent crime in the United States and amended the Criminal Code to include detailed provisions regulating the use and sale of firearms. As amended, 18 U.S.C. § 922 defined a number of "unlawful acts;" subsection (a)(1) made it unlawful for any person except a licensed dealer to engage in the business of dealing in firearms.[13] Section 923 established the federal licensing program and repeated the prohibition against dealing in firearms without a license, and § 924 specified the penalties for violating "any provision of this chapter." Read literally, § 924 authorized the imposition of a fine of up to $5,000 or a prison sentence of not more than five years, "or both," on any person who dealt in firearms without a license even if that person believed that he or she was acting lawfully.[14] As enacted in 1968, § 922(a)(1) and § 924 omitted an express scienter requirement and therefore arguably imposed strict criminal liability on every unlicensed dealer in firearms. The 1968 Act also omitted any definition of the term "engaged in the business" even though that conduct was an element of the unlawful act prohibited by § 922(a)(1).

In 1986 Congress enacted the Firearms Owners' Protection Act (FOPA), in part, to cure these omissions. The findings in that statute explained that additional legislation was necessary to protect law-abiding citizens with respect to the acquisition, possession, or use of firearms for lawful purposes. FOPA therefore amended § 921 to include a definition of the term "engaged in the business,"[15] and amended § 924 to add a scienter requirement as a condition to the imposition of penalties for most of the unlawful acts defined in § 922. For three categories of offenses the intent required is that the defendant acted "knowingly;" for the fourth category, which includes "any other provision of this chapter," the required intent is that the defendant acted "willfully."[16] The § 922(a)(1)(A) offense at issue in this case is an "other provision" in the "willfully" category.

The jury having found petitioner guilty, we accept the Government's version of the evidence. That evidence proved that petitioner did not have a federal license to deal in firearms; that he used so-called "straw purchasers" in Ohio to acquire pistols that he could not have purchased himself; that the straw purchasers made false statements when purchasing the guns; that petitioner assured the straw purchasers that he would file the serial numbers off the guns; and that he resold the guns on Brooklyn street corners known for drug dealing. The evidence was unquestionably adequate to prove that petitioner was dealing in firearms, and

---

[13] [Court's footnote 2:] The current version of this provision, which is substantially the same as the 1968 version, is codified at 18 U.S.C. § 922(a)(1)(A). It states: "(a) It shall be unlawful ... (1) for any person...(A) except a licensed importer, licensed manufacturer, or licensed dealer, to engage in the business of importing, manufacturing, or dealing in firearms, or in the course of such business to ship, transport, or receive any firearm in interstate or foreign commerce."

[14] [Court's footnote 3:] § 924. Penalties: "(a) Whoever violates any provision of this chapter...shall be fined not more than $5,000 or imprisoned not more than five years, or both."

[15] [Court's footnote 5:] "Section 921 of title 18, United States Code, is amended... (21) The term 'engaged in the business' means... (C) as applied to a dealer in firearms, as defined in section 921(a)(11)(A), a person who devotes time, attention, and labor to dealing in firearms as a regular course of trade or business with the principal objective of livelihood and profit through the repetitive purchase and resale of firearms, but such term shall not include a person who makes occasional sales, exchanges, or purchases of firearms for the enhancement of a personal collection or for a hobby, or who sells all or part of his personal collection of firearms ...."

[16] [Court's footnote 6:] Title 18 U.S.C. § 924(a)(1) currently provides: "Except as otherwise provided in this subsection, subsection (b), (c), or (f) of this section, or in section 929, whoever (A) knowingly makes any false statement or representation with respect to the information required by this chapter to be kept in the records of a person licensed under this chapter or in applying for any license or exemption or relief from disability under the provisions of this chapter; (B) knowingly violates subsection (a)(4), (f), (k), (r), (v), or (w) of section 922; (C) knowingly imports or brings into the United States or any possession thereof any firearm or ammunition in violation of section 922(l); or (D) willfully violates any other provision of this chapter, shall be fined under this title, imprisoned not more than five years, or both."

that he knew that his conduct was unlawful. There was, however, no evidence that he was aware of the federal law that prohibits dealing in firearms without a federal license.

Petitioner was charged with a conspiracy to violate 18 U.S.C. § 922(a)(1)(A), by willfully engaging in the business of dealing in firearms, and with a substantive violation of that provision. After the close of evidence, petitioner requested that the trial judge instruct the jury that petitioner could be convicted only if he knew of the federal licensing requirement, but the judge rejected this request. Instead, the trial judge gave this explanation of the term "willfully":

> "A person acts willfully if he acts intentionally and purposely and with the intent to do something the law forbids, that is, with the bad purpose to disobey or to disregard the law. Now, the person need not be aware of the specific law or rule that his conduct may be violating. But he must act with the intent to do something that the law forbids."

Petitioner was found guilty on both counts. On appeal he argued that the evidence was insufficient because there was no proof that he had knowledge of the federal licensing requirement, and that the trial judge had erred by failing to instruct the jury that such knowledge was an essential element of the offense. The Court of Appeals affirmed. It concluded that the instructions were proper and that the Government had elicited "ample proof" that petitioner had acted willfully. ... *[handwritten:] Procedural History*

The word "willfully" is sometimes said to be "a word of many meanings" whose construction is often dependent on the context in which it appears. See, *e.g., Spies v. United States*, 317 U.S. 492, 497 (1943). Most obviously it differentiates between deliberate and unwitting conduct, but in the criminal law it also typically refers to a culpable state of mind. As we explained in *United States v. Murdock*, 290 U.S. 389 (1933), a variety of phrases have been used to describe that concept.[17] As a general matter, when used in the criminal context, a "willful" act is one undertaken with a "bad purpose."[18] In other words, in order to establish a "willful" violation of a statute, "the Government must prove that the defendant acted with knowledge that his conduct was unlawful." *Ratzlaf v. United States*, 510 U.S. 135, 137 (1994).[19]

Petitioner argues that a more particularized showing is required in this case for two principal reasons. First, he argues that the fact that Congress used the adverb "knowingly" to authorize punishment of three categories of acts made unlawful by § 922 and the word "willfully" when it referred to unlicensed dealing in firearms demonstrates that the Government must shoulder a special burden in cases like this. This argument is not persuasive because the term "knowingly" does not necessarily have any reference to a culpable state of mind or to knowledge of the law. As Justice Jackson correctly observed, "the knowledge

---

[17] [Court's footnote 12:] "The word often denotes an act which is intentional, or knowing, or voluntary, as distinguished from accidental. But when used in a criminal statute it generally means an act done with a bad purpose; without justifiable excuse; stubbornly, obstinately, perversely. The word is also employed to characterize a thing done without ground for believing it is lawful, or conduct marked by careless disregard whether or not one has the right so to act." 290 U.S. at 394-95.

[18] Court's footnote 13:] *See, e.g.,* ... 1 L. Sand, J. Siffert, W. Loughlin, & S. Reiss, Modern Federal Jury Instructions 3A.01, p. 3A-18 (1997) ("'Willfully' means to act with knowledge that one's conduct is unlawful and with the intent to do something the law forbids, that is to say with the bad purpose to disobey or to disregard the law").

[19] [Ed.:] In *Ratzlaf v. United States*, 510 U.S. 135 (1994), decided the same Term as *Staples*, the Court held that to commit the crime of "willfully violating" the law against structuring cash transactions to evade currency reporting requirements, the defendant has to know that his conduct was unlawful. The Court reasoned that there might be entirely innocent reasons why an individual might structure his or her cash transactions to evade the reporting requirements. Thus, absent this heightened intent requirement, the statute would criminalize apparently innocent behavior committed without criminal motive. Congress subsequently acted to remove the requirement, imposed in *Ratzlaf*, that the prosecution prove that the defendant know that his structuring to evade reporting requirements is unlawful. *See* Money Laundering Suppression Act of 1994, Pub. L. No. 103-325, Section 411, 108 Stat. 2150, 2253 (1994); H.R. Conf. Rep. No. 103-652 (1994); *see also* United States v. Beidler, 110 F.3d 1064, 1066 n. 1 (4th Cir.1997).

requisite to knowing violation of a statute is factual knowledge as distinguished from knowledge of the law." Thus, in *United States v. Bailey*, 444 U.S. 394 (1980), we held that the prosecution fulfills its burden of proving a knowing violation of the escape statute "if it demonstrates that an escapee knew his actions would result in his leaving physical confinement without permission." And in *Staples v. United States*, 511 U.S. 600 (1994), we held that a charge that the defendant's possession of an unregistered machine gun was unlawful required proof "that he knew the weapon he possessed had the characteristics that brought it within the statutory definition of a machine gun." It was not, however, necessary to prove that the defendant knew that his possession was unlawful. See *Rogers v. United States*, 522 U.S. 252, 254-55 (1998). Thus, unless the text of the statute dictates a different result,[20] the term "knowingly" merely requires proof of knowledge of the facts that constitute the offense.

With respect to the three categories of conduct that are made punishable by § 924 if performed "knowingly," the background presumption that every citizen knows the law makes it unnecessary to adduce specific evidence to prove that "an evil-meaning mind" directed the "evil-doing hand." More is required, however, with respect to the conduct in the fourth category that is only criminal when done "willfully." The jury must find that the defendant acted with an evil-meaning mind, that is to say, that he acted with knowledge that his conduct was unlawful.

Petitioner next argues that we must read § 924(a)(1)(D) to require knowledge of the law because of our interpretation of "willfully" in two other contexts. In certain cases involving willful violations of the tax laws, we have concluded that the jury must find that the defendant was aware of the specific provision of the tax code that he was charged with violating. See, *e.g.*, *Cheek v. United States*, 498 U.S. 192, 201 (1991).[21] Similarly, in order to satisfy a willful violation in *Ratzlaf*, we concluded that the jury had to find that the defendant knew that his structuring of cash transactions to avoid a reporting requirement was unlawful. Those cases, however, are readily distinguishable. Both the tax cases[22] and *Ratzlaf*[23] involved highly technical statutes that presented the danger of ensnaring individuals engaged in apparently innocent conduct.[24] As a

---

[20] [Court's footnote 15:] *Liparota v. United States*, 471 U.S. 419 (1985), was such a case. We there concluded that both the term "knowing" in [7 U.S.C.] § 2024(c) and the term "knowingly" in § 2024(b)(1) ... literally referred to knowledge of the law as well as knowledge of the relevant facts.

[21] [Court's footnote 17:] Even in tax cases, we have not always required this heightened *mens rea*. In *United States v. Pomponio*, 429 U.S. 10 (1976) (*per curiam*), for example, the jury was instructed that a willful act is one done "with [the] bad purpose either to disobey or to disregard the law." We approved of this instruction, concluding that "[t]he trial judge ... adequately instructed the jury on willfulness."

[22] [Court's footnote 18:] As we stated in *Cheek v. United States*, 498 U.S. 192, 199-200 (1991)

> The proliferation of statutes and regulations has sometimes made it difficult for the average citizen to know and comprehend the extent of the duties and obligations imposed by the tax laws. Congress has accordingly softened the impact of the common-law presumption by making specific intent to violate the law an element of certain federal criminal tax offenses. Thus, the Court almost 60 years ago interpreted the statutory term 'willfully' as used in the federal criminal tax statutes as carving out an exception to the traditional rule [that every person is presumed to know the law]. This special treatment of criminal tax offenses is largely due to the complexity of the tax laws.

[23] [Court's footnote 19:] See *Bates v. United States*, 522 U.S. 23, 31, n. 6 (1997) (noting that *Ratzlaf*'s holding was based on the "particular statutory context of currency structuring"); *Ratzlaf*, 510 U.S., at 149 (Court's holding based on "particular contex[t]" of currency structuring statute).

[24] [Court's footnote 20:] *Id.*, at 144-145 ("[C]urrency structuring is not inevitably nefarious ... Nor is a person who structures a currency transaction invariably motivated by a desire to keep the Government in the dark"; Government's construction of the statute would criminalize apparently innocent activity); *Cheek*, 498 U.S., at 205 ("[I]n 'our complex tax system, uncertainty often arises even among taxpayers who earnestly wish to follow the law,' and '[i]t is not the purpose of the law to penalize frank difference of opinion or innocent errors made despite the exercise of reasonable care.'" *United States v. Bishop*, 412 U.S. 346, 360-361 (1973) (*quoting Spies v. United States*, 317 U.S. 492, 496 (1943)); *Murdock*, 290 U.S., at 396 ("Congress did not intend that a person, by reason of a bona fide misunderstanding as to his liability for the tax, as to his duty to make a return, or as to the adequacy of the records he maintained, should

result, we held that these statutes "carv[e] out an exception to the traditional rule" that ignorance of the law is no excuse and require that the defendant have knowledge of the law. The danger of convicting individuals engaged in apparently innocent activity that motivated our decisions in the tax cases and *Ratzlaf* is not present here because the jury found that this petitioner knew that his conduct was unlawful.

Thus, the willfulness requirement of § 924(a)(1)(D) does not carve out an exception to the traditional rule that ignorance of the law is no excuse; knowledge that the conduct is unlawful is all that is required. ...

JUSTICE SCALIA, with whom THE CHIEF JUSTICE and JUSTICE GINSBURG join, dissenting.

Petitioner Sillasse Bryan was convicted of "willfully" violating the federal licensing requirement for firearms dealers. The jury apparently found, and the evidence clearly shows, that Bryan was aware in a general way that some aspect of his conduct was unlawful. The issue is whether that general knowledge of illegality is enough to sustain the conviction, or whether a "willful" violation of the licensing provision requires proof that the defendant knew that his conduct was unlawful specifically because he lacked the necessary license. On that point the statute is, in my view, genuinely ambiguous. Most of the Court's opinion is devoted to confirming half of that ambiguity by refuting Bryan's various arguments that the statute clearly requires specific knowledge of the licensing requirement. The Court offers no real justification for its implicit conclusion that either (1) the statute unambiguously requires only general knowledge of illegality, or (2) ambiguously requiring only general knowledge is enough. Instead, the Court curiously falls back on "the traditional rule that ignorance of the law is no excuse" to conclude that "knowledge that the conduct is unlawful is all that is required." In my view, this case calls for the application of a different canon—"the familiar rule that, 'where there is ambiguity in a criminal statute, doubts are resolved in favor of the defendant.'"

Title 18 U.S.C. § 922(a)(1)(A) makes it unlawful for any person to engage in the business of dealing in firearms without a federal license. That provision is enforced criminally through § 924(a)(1)(D), which imposes criminal penalties on whoever "willfully violates any other provision of this chapter." The word "willfully" has a wide range of meanings, and "'its construction [is] often ... influenced by its context.'" In some contexts it connotes nothing more than "an act which is intentional, or knowing, or voluntary, as distinguished from accidental." In the present context, however, inasmuch as the preceding three subparagraphs of § 924 specify a *mens rea* of "knowingly" for *other* firearms offenses, see §§ 924(a)(1)(A)-(C), a "willful" violation under § 924(a)(1)(D) must require some mental state more culpable than mere intent to perform the forbidden act. The United States concedes (and the Court apparently agrees) that the violation is not "willful" unless the defendant knows in a general way that his conduct is unlawful.

That concession takes this case beyond any useful application of the maxim that ignorance of the law is no excuse. Everyone agrees that § 924(a)(1)(D) requires some knowledge of the law; the only real question is *which* law? The Court's answer is that knowledge of *any* law is enough—or, put another way, that the defendant must be ignorant of *every* law violated by his course of conduct to be innocent of willfully violating the licensing requirement. The Court points to no textual basis for that conclusion other than the notoriously malleable word "willfully" itself. Instead, it seems to fall back on a presumption (apparently derived from the rule that ignorance of the law is no excuse) that even where ignorance of the law *is* an excuse, that excuse should be construed as narrowly as the statutory language permits.

I do not believe that the Court's approach makes sense of the statute that Congress enacted. I have no quarrel with the Court's assertion that "willfully" in § 924(a)(1)(D) requires only "general" knowledge of illegality—in the sense that the defendant need not be able to

---

become a criminal by his mere failure to measure up to the prescribed standard of conduct").

recite chapter and verse from Title 18 of the United States Code. It is enough, in my view, if the defendant is generally aware that the *actus reus* punished by the statute—dealing in firearms without a license—is illegal. But the Court is willing to accept a *mens rea* so "general" that it is entirely divorced from the *actus reus* this statute was enacted to punish. That approach turns § 924(a)(1)(D) into a strange and unlikely creature. Bryan would be guilty of "willfully" dealing in firearms without a federal license even if, for example, he had never heard of the licensing requirement but was aware that he had violated the law by using straw purchasers or filing the serial numbers off the pistols. The Court does not even limit (for there is no rational basis to limit) the universe of relevant laws to federal *firearms* statutes. Bryan would also be "act[ing] with an evil-meaning mind," and hence presumably be guilty of "willfully" dealing in firearms without a license, if he knew that his street-corner transactions violated New York City's business licensing or sales tax ordinances. (For that matter, it ought to suffice if Bryan knew that the car out of which he sold the guns was illegally double-parked, or if, in order to meet the appointed time for the sale, he intentionally violated Pennsylvania's speed limit on the drive back from the gun purchase in Ohio.) Once we stop focusing on the conduct the defendant is actually charged with (*i.e.*, selling guns without a license), I see no principled way to determine *what* law the defendant must be conscious of violating.

Congress is free, of course, to make criminal liability under one statute turn on knowledge of another, to use its firearms dealer statutes to encourage compliance with New York City's tax collection efforts, and to put judges and juries through the kind of mental gymnastics described above. But these are strange results, and I would not lightly assume that Congress intended to make liability under a federal criminal statute depend so heavily upon the vagaries of local law—particularly local law dealing with completely unrelated subjects. If we must have a presumption in cases like this one, I think it would be more reasonable to presume that, when Congress makes ignorance of the law a defense to a criminal prohibition, it ordinarily means ignorance of the unlawfulness of the specific conduct punished *by that criminal prohibition*.

That is the meaning we have given the word "willfully" in other contexts where we have concluded it requires knowledge of the law. See, *e.g.*, [*Ratzlaf v. United States*, 510 U.S. 135, 149 (1994)] ("To convict Ratzlaf of the crime with which he was charged, ... the jury had to find he knew the structuring in which he engaged was unlawful"); *Cheek v. United States*, 498 U.S. 192, 201 (1991) ("[T]he standard for the statutory willfullness requirement is the 'voluntary, intentional violation of a known legal duty.' ... [T]he issue is whether the defendant knew of the duty purportedly imposed by the provision of the statute or regulation he is accused of violating"). The Court explains these cases on the ground that they involved "highly technical statutes that presented the danger of ensnaring individuals engaged in apparently innocent conduct." That is no explanation at all. The complexity of the tax and currency laws may explain why the Court interpreted "willful" to require some awareness of illegality, as opposed to merely "an act which is intentional, or knowing, or voluntary, as distinguished from accidental." But it *in no way* justifies the distinction the Court seeks to draw today between knowledge of the law the defendant is actually charged with violating and knowledge of *any* law the defendant could conceivably be charged with violating. To protect the pure of heart, it is not necessary to forgive someone whose surreptitious laundering of drug money violates, unbeknownst to him, a technical currency statute. There, as here, regardless of how "complex" the violated statute may be, the defendant would have acted "with an evil-meaning mind."

It seems to me likely that Congress had a presumption of offense-specific knowledge of illegality in mind when it enacted the provision here at issue. ...

If one had to choose, therefore, I think a presumption of statutory intent that is the opposite of the one the Court applies would be more reasonable. I would not, however, decide this case on the basis of any presumption at all. It is common ground that the statutory context here requires some awareness of the law for a § 924(a)(1)(D) conviction, but the statute is simply ambiguous, or silent, as to the precise contours of that *mens rea* requirement. In the face of that ambiguity, I would invoke the rule that "'ambiguity concerning the ambit of criminal statutes should be resolved in favor of lenity,'"

"The rule that penal laws are to be construed strictly, is, perhaps, not much less old than construction itself. It is founded on the tenderness of the law for the rights of individuals; and on the plain principle that the power of punishment is vested in the legislative, not in the judicial department." *United States v. Wiltberger*, 5 Wheat. 76, 95 (1820).

In our era of multiplying new federal crimes, there is more reason than ever to give this ancient canon of construction consistent application: by fostering uniformity in the interpretation of criminal statutes, it will reduce the occasions on which this Court will have to produce judicial havoc by resolving in defendants' favor a Circuit conflict regarding the substantive elements of a federal crime. ...

Notes

1. As Judge Learned Hand noted with respect to the difficulties presented by the liberal use of the "willful" *mens rea* in federal criminal law: "[Willfully is] a very dreadful word... It's an awful word! It is one of the most troublesome words in a statute that I know. If I were to have the index purged, 'wilful' would lead all the rest in spite of its being at the end of the alphabet." United States v. Starnes, 583F.3d 196, 210 n.7 (3d Cir. 2008) (quoting ALI proceedings). That said, the following may provide students with a general sense of the three levels of intent that, in different contexts, mean "willful":

> "Willfully" ... is a "notoriously slippery term," a "chameleon word" that "takes color from the text in which it appears." The cases delineate at least three levels of interpretation of the term. In some contexts, "willfully" may denote "'an act which is intentional, or knowing, or voluntary, as distinguished from accidental.'" [*Bryan v. United States*, 524 U.S. 184, 191 n.12 (1998)]. But when "willfully" is used in a criminal statute, and particularly where the term is used in conjunction with "knowingly," ... it usually requires the government to prove that the defendant acted "not merely 'voluntarily,' but with a 'bad purpose,'" that is, with knowledge that his conduct was, in some general sense, "unlawful." *Id.* at 193-93; *see also* Third Circuit Model Crim. Jury Instructions § 5.05 (providing that "willfully" requires the government to prove beyond a reasonable doubt that a defendant "knew that [his or her] conduct was unlawful and intended to do something that the law forbids"). And in some rare instances involving highly technical statutes that present the danger of ensnaring individuals engaged in apparently innocent conduct, such as the federal criminal tax and antistructuring provisions, "willfully" has been read to require proof that the defendant actually knew of the specific law prohibiting the conduct. *See Bryan*, 524 U.S. at 194-95, discussing, among other cases, [*Ratzlaf v. United States*, 510 U.S. 135, 138 (1994)] (antistructuring statutes) and *Cheek v. United States*, 498 U.S. 192 (1991) (criminal tax statutes)).

Id. at 210-11. The federal courts, in construing statutes, generally employ the second formulation of the meaning of "willful"—the one the Court adopted in *Bryan*. *See, e.g.*, United States v. Bishop, 740 F.3d 927 (4th Cir. 2014) (Arms Export Control Act). *But see* United States v. Blankenship, 846 F.3d 663, 671-74 (4th Cir. 2017) ("reckless disregard" can satisfy statutory "willfulness" element).

2. What does the government have to prove to secure a conviction under the statute at issue in *Bryan*? Is the Court correct that this result is consistent with the rule that ignorance of the law is no excuse—*is* knowledge of the law irrelevant?

3. How does the Court distinguish the two lines of cases—the tax cases and the *Ratzlaf* decision—where it imposed an even higher degree of *mens rea*? Does the Court's concern about conviction of the "innocent" ring any bells? Consider the following thesis propounded by Professor John Shepard Wiley Jr., which is founded upon analysis of, among other cases, *Staples* and *Ratzlaf*:

The best explanation for the Court's [recent statutory interpretation results] ... is that the Court now routinely assumes that Congress believes that criminal liability should follow moral culpability: When reading statutes, the Justices today suppose that Congress does not want blameless people to be convicted of serious federal crimes. This interpretive method makes moral culpability mandatory for criminal conviction in federal court—even though courts have yet to say so in so few words.

The Court's new rule of mandatory culpability appears to have three basic steps. First, use conventional interpretive material—statutory text and context, legislative history, statutory comparisons and analogies, and so forth—to list the crime's candidate elements. Second, analyze as a hypothetical matter whether morally blameless people could violate these candidate elements. If they could not, these elements satisfy the rule: The interpretation is final, and the court should reject efforts to add superfluous elements. If a morally blameless person could violate these candidate elements, however, a third step is necessary: formulate an additional and minimally sufficient element about mental state to shield blameless conduct from criminal condemnation. This approach to interpretation operates to ensure that only the culpable can be criminals. This notion is old-fashioned, low-tech, and vastly important.

John Shepard Wiley Jr., *Not Guilty by Reason of Blamelessness: Culpability in Federal Criminal Interpretation*, 85 Va. L. Rev. 1021, 1023 (1999). Is this what the Court is doing in such cases as *Staples*, *Ratzlaf*, and *Bryan*? Does this reflect a signal shift in the Court's view of the appropriate role of prosecutors, the courts, and Congress in the elucidation of criminal standards?

With respect to the role of prosecutors, could one argue that the Court's recent decisions evidence a reevaluation of the value of prosecutorial discretion in avoiding sending the blameless to prison? As Professor Wiley notes, "[e]arlier in this century ... the Justices embraced a strict criminal liability on an implicit faith that prosecutorial discretion was to be the bulwark of justice. ... Today, not a single Justice can be found even to *voice* that extreme argument—even in badly divided opinions with lengthy and strenuous dissents." *Id.* at 1024.

With respect to courts, one could argue that this theory contemplates a fundamental adjustment of judges' roles. "The culpability rule raises two concerns about the judicial role: whether the rule requires 'judicial legislation,' and whether judges are competent to render moral judgments the rule requires." *Id.* at 1068. With respect to the former, the argument is that "reading culpability elements into a statute may 'rewrite the statute' in an improper way." *Id.* With respect to the latter, Professor Wiley notes:

> By assuming that Congress does not want to criminalize "apparently innocent" behavior, the Court has required federal judges to decide what is innocent and what is not according to moral standards that come from neither statutes nor the Constitution. Can unelected judges validly ascertain and apply an unwritten moral code? Or should the problem of moral subjectivity deter courts from making the effort?

Id. at 1071. He concludes that "the culpability rule does not require improper judicial legislation, and that judges indeed are competent to render the necessary moral analysis, so long as they remain aware of the perils of the process and tailor their analysis accordingly." *Id.* at 1068. Do you agree?

D. OTHER DOCTRINES AND DEFENSES

1. SPECIFIC AND GENERAL INTENT

As noted at the inception of the chapter, a variety of terms have been used to express the level of intention that the government must prove to secure a conviction under the federal criminal code. Two *mens rea* terms—"specific" and "general" intent—do not appear in the code, are outdated and confusing, have been rejected by the Supreme Court,[25] and yet appear with sufficient frequency in federal judicial opinions that they must be addressed.

The term *"mens rea"* has two general uses. First, *mens rea* is used to describe a general wicked state of mind or intention, suggesting that the defendant committed a particular action with a morally blameworthy state of mind. This has been described as the "culpability" meaning of *mens rea*.[26] Second, *mens rea* means the particular mental state required to be proved by the statutory offense. This has been labeled the "elemental" meaning of *mens rea*[27] and is the use of the term that has been explored in these materials.

[margin note: Two uses of "Mens Rea"]

Today's statutes generally include some type of express *mens rea* element, but this is a modern development. The historical meaning of "specific" versus "general" intent reflects the fact that statutes formerly did not specify the mental state necessary to be proved. Thus, "general intent" meant that the crime required a *mens rea* in the culpability sense of a blameworthy state of mind. "Specific intent" was a designation reserved for those offenses that required proof of a particular, additional state of mind.

Because modern statutes, and courts interpreting them, at least attempt to specify a particular level of "elemental" *mens rea*, the continuing meaning of the distinction between "general" and "specific" intent is questionable; indeed, there appears to be no commonly accepted definition of these terms. "Generally speaking, however, a 'specific intent' offense is one in which the definition of the crime: (1) includes an intent to do some future act, or achieve some further consequence (*i.e.*, a special motive for the conduct), *beyond the conduct or result that constitutes the actus reus of the offense*; or (2) provides that the actor must be aware of a statutory attendant circumstance. An offense that does not contain either of these features is termed 'general intent.'"[28]

[margin note: Specific intent]

An example of a crime described in (1), above, would be a false statements prosecution under 18 U.S.C. § 1001. Under § 1001, in addition to the "knowing" *mens rea* that attends the *actus reus* (the defendant had to make a statement knowing it to be false), some courts require that the defendant harbor the further, "specific" intent to deceive the recipient of the statement. An example of a crime described in (2), above, would be a money laundering prosecution under 18 U.S.C. § 1956(a)(1). Under that statute, a person is guilty of money laundering if (in short) he conducts a financial transaction with the proceeds of unlawful activity with the intention to hide the nature, source, or ownership of those proceeds or to promote the carrying on of unlawful activity. Conducting the financial transaction is the *actus reus* of the offense; however, to be found guilty, the statute requires that defendants have knowledge of the *attendant circumstance* that the property involved in a financial transaction represents the proceeds of some form of unlawful activity.

If one is attempting to place the terms "specific" and "general" intent in the landscape of the Model Penal Code, probably the closest analogues are "purposely" and "knowingly." A person who causes a particular result is said to act "purposely" if "he consciously desires that result, whatever the likelihood of that result happening from his conduct,"[29] while he is said to

---

[25]*See* Liparota v. United States, 471 U.S. 419, 433 n.16 (1985) (stating that jury instructions concerning specific intent have "been criticized as too general and potentially misleading" and courts should "eschew use of difficult legal terms like 'specific intent'"); United States v. Bailey, 444 U.S. 394, 403-06 (1980) (distinguishing between specific and general intent "has been the source of a good deal of confusion"). "Each of the jury instruction committees of the circuit courts of appeals have followed suit and discouraged the use of jury instructions on specific intent." Kevin F. O'Malley *et al.*, Federal Jury Practice and Instructions § 17.03 (5th ed.2000).

[26] Joshua Dressler, Understanding Criminal Law 102 (Matthew Bender & Co.1995).

[27] *Id.* at 103.

[28] *Id.* at 119.

[29] United States v. Bailey, 444 U.S. 394, 404 (1980); *see also* ALI, Model Penal Code § 2.02(2)(a) ("[i]f the element involves the nature of his conduct or a result thereof, it is his conscious object to engage in conduct of that nature or to cause such a result").

act "knowingly" if he is aware "that the result is practically certain to follow from his conduct whatever his desire may be as to that result."[30] As the Supreme Court has said, "[i]n a general sense, 'purpose' corresponds loosely with the common-law concept of specific intent, while 'knowledge' corresponds loosely with the concept of general intent."[31]

Even if these terms are difficult and outdated, the distinction between specific and general intent is not without ongoing importance. For example, the rules on when mistakes of fact or law will constitute a defense traditionally were said to differ with the type of intent involved. Thus, if the crime is a general intent crime, only reasonable mistakes of fact or law will create an effective defense; by contrast, even unreasonable mistakes of fact or law may be sufficient to defeat a prosecution for a specific intent crime.[32] Federal courts also often indicate that two important defenses—the good faith defense and the reliance on counsel defense discussed below—are available only to defeat charges of specific intent crimes.

2. GOOD FAITH DEFENSE

Where the government bears the burden of proving a specific intent—to defraud, for example—defendants will often defend by asserting that their actions or statements were made in good faith. "A good faith defense is the affirmative converse of the government's burden of proving ... intent to commit a crime. Acquittal ... is mandatory because a finding of good faith precludes a finding of fraudulent intent."[33] As the Ninth Circuit explained:

> One who expresses an opinion honestly held by her or belief honestly entertained by her is not chargeable with fraudulent intent even though her opinion is erroneous or her belief is mistaken. And similarly, evidence which establishes only that a person made a mistake in judgment or an error in management or was careless does not establish fraudulent intent. While the term "good faith" has no precise definition, it means among other things a belief or opinion honestly held with an absence of malice or ill will and intention of taking unfair advantage of another.[34]

A defendant will not necessarily succeed in securing a separate "good faith defense" jury instruction because some courts conclude that an instruction on the requisite *mens rea* necessarily encompasses the good faith defense.[35]

It is worth reiterating that the good faith belief that may defeat a prosecution for a specific intent crime need not be objectively reasonable, at least in certain categories of cases (*e.g.*, tax). For example, in *Cheek v. United States*,[36] the defendant was charged with failing to file a tax return and tax evasion. The Supreme Court noted that these tax offenses "are specific intent

---

[30] *Bailey*, 444 U.S. at 404; *see also* ALI, Model Penal Code § 2.02(2)(b) ("[i]f the element involves the nature of his conduct or the attendant circumstances, he is aware that his conduct is of that nature or that such circumstances exist; and ... if the element involves a result of his conduct, he is aware that it is practically certain that his conduct will cause such a result").

[31] *Bailey*, 444 U.S. at 405.

[32] Wayne R. LaFave, Criminal Law § 5.1 (West 2000); *see also* Cheek v. United States, 498 U.S. 192 (1991).

[33] United States v. Cavin, 39 F.3d 1299, 1310 (5th Cir. 1994).

[34] *See, e.g.,* United States v. Sayakhom, 186 F.3d 928, 940 (9th Cir. 1999); *see also* United States v. Migliaccio, 34 F.3d 1517 (10th Cir. 1994).

[35] *See, e.g.,* United States v. Koster, 163 F.3d 1008, 1011 (7th Cir. 1998); *see also* United States v. Pomponio, 429 U.S. 10, 13 (1976) (*per curiam*) (after instructing the jury on willfulness, "[a]n additional instruction on good faith was unnecessary").

[36] 498 U.S. 192 (1991).

crimes that require the defendant to have acted willfully."[37] It explained that "[w]illfulness, as construed in our prior decisions in criminal tax cases, requires the Government to prove that the law imposed a duty on the defendant, that the defendant knew of this duty, and that he voluntarily and intentionally violated that duty."[38] The government bears the burden of proving that the defendant knew of his duty, and that burden may (where a defendant raises the claim) require "negating a defendant's claim of ignorance of the law or a claim that because of a misunderstanding of the law, he had a good-faith belief that he was not violating any of the provisions of the tax laws."[39]

The *Cheek* Court held that the defendant's claimed good-faith belief need not be objectively reasonable to be considered by the jury as negating the government's evidence purporting to show the defendant's awareness of the legal duty at issue.[40] The Court's holding, however, was limited to situations in which the defendant claims a lack of knowledge regarding the specified legal duty. It ruled that where a defendant is aware of that duty but believes that it is unconstitutional, the defendant is not entitled to have a jury consider his views about the validity of the tax. In such circumstances, it concluded, a defendant "is in no position to claim that his good-faith belief about the validity of the Internal Revenue Code negates willfulness or provides a defense to criminal prosecution" under the failure to file or evasion statutes.[41]

3. GOOD FAITH RELIANCE ON COUNSEL DEFENSE

Federal courts often take the position that the reliance on counsel (and other experts) defense applies to "specific intent" crimes.[42] This reliance defense is often discussed as a simple variant of the good faith defense in that if the requisites of the "good faith reliance on counsel" defense are satisfied, no finding of the requisite *mens rea* is possible.[43] For example, in *United States v. Eisenstein*,[44] the defendant was prosecuted for willful violation of the currency reporting requirements. The court affirmed the existence of a good faith reliance upon counsel defense to negate the requisite intent:

> A defendant charged with violating the reporting statute can attempt to negate proof of specific intent by establishing the defense of good faith reliance on advice of counsel. In order to take advantage of this defense, the defendant must show that he relied in good faith after first making a full disclosure of all facts that are relevant to the advice for which he consulted the attorney. When the defendant presents evidence that he disclosed all relevant facts to his attorney and relied on the attorney's advice based on the disclosure, the trial court must instruct the jury on the defense of good faith reliance on counsel.[45]

Choosing to employ a reliance on counsel defense to a specific intent charge is not without risk; it can often result in a waiver of attorney client privilege. In *United States v.*

---

[37] *Id.* at 195.

[38] *Id.* at 201.

[39] *Id.*

[40] *Id.* at 203; *see also* United States v. Montgomery, 747 F.3d 303 (5th Cir. 2014).

[41] 498 U.S. at 206.

[42] *See, e.g.*, United States v. Condon, 132 F.3d 653 (11th Cir. 1998); United States v. DeFries, 129 F.3d 1293 (D.C. Cir. 1997); United States v. Walters, 913 F.2d 388 (7th Cir. 1990).

[43] *See, e.g.*, United States v. Joshua, 648 F.3d 547, 554-55 (7th Cir. 2011).

[44] 731 F.2d 1540 (11th Cir. 1984) (cited with approval in *Ratzlaf v. United States*, 510 U.S. 135, 141 (1994)).

[45] *Id.* at 1543-44; *see also* Williamson v. United States, 207 U.S. 425, 453 (1908).

Bilzerian,[46] involving a prosecution for securities fraud, the defendant sought to introduce evidence regarding his allegedly good faith efforts to comply with the securities law in order to negate the element of intent. The court held that

> the attorney-client privilege cannot at once be used as a shield and a sword. A defendant may not use the privilege to prejudice his opponent's case or to disclose some selected communications for self-serving purposes. Thus, the privilege may implicitly be waived when defendant asserts a claim that in fairness requires examination of protected communications. This waiver principle is applicable here for Bilzerian's testimony that he thought his actions were legal would have put his knowledge of the law and the basis for his understanding of what the law required in issue. His conversations with counsel regarding the legality of his schemes would have been directly relevant in determining the extent of his knowledge and, as a result, his intent. [47]

4. "WILLFUL BLINDNESS," "CONSCIOUS AVOIDANCE," OR "OSTRICH" INSTRUCTIONS

1. *The Instruction.* A typical jury instruction on what "knowingly" means states:

> When the word "knowingly" or the phrase "the defendant knew" is used in these instructions, it means that the defendant realized what she was doing and was aware of the nature of her conduct and did not act through ignorance, mistake or accident.[48]

To ease their burden to show that the defendant actually, subjectively "knew," federal prosecutors often seek to satisfy a statutory requirement of "knowledge" by using an alternative theory, variously called a "willful blindness," "conscious avoidance," or "ostrich" theory. "All of the … circuits with criminal jurisdiction have approved such [jury] instructions for a wide range of criminal offenses, although the courts' rationales vary, as do the wording of the instructions and the limits on the doctrine's proper use."[49] The following language has frequently been employed (in different combinations), although these instructions should be redrafted in light of the Supreme Court's decision in *Global-Tech Appliances, Inc. v. SEB, S.A.*, excerpted *infra*:[50]

> A. "The element of knowledge may be satisfied by inferences drawn from proof that a defendant deliberately closed his eyes to what would otherwise have been obvious to him. A finding beyond a reasonable doubt of a conscious purpose to avoid enlightenment would permit an inference of knowledge. Stated another way, a defendant's knowledge of a fact may be inferred from willful blindness to the existence of the fact." [51]
> B. "Willful blindness may constitute knowledge of a fact only if you should find that the individual to whom knowledge is sought to be attributed was aware of a high probability that that fact existed."[52]

---

[46] 926 F.2d 1285 (2d Cir.1991).

[47] *Id.* at 1292; *see also In re* County of Erie, 546 F.3d 222, 229 (2d Cir. 2008) (holding that to imply a waiver based on a reliance on counsel defense, there must be a showing that the party relied on privileged advice from his counsel to make his defense); *cf.* United States v. White, 887 F.2d 267 (D.C. Cir. 1989).

[48] United States v. Alston-Graves, 435 F.3d 331, 336 (D.C. Cir. 2006).

[49] *See, e.g., id.* at 338 (footnotes omitted).

[50] 563 U.S. 754 (2011). *See* Dane C. Ball, *Improving 'Willful Blindness' Jury Instructions in Criminal Cases After High Court's Decision in* Global-Tech, 89 Crim. L. Rep. 426 (June 15, 2011).

[51] 1 Devitt & Blackmar, Federal Jury Practice and Instructions § 17.09 (4th ed. 1992).

[52] United States v. St. Michael's Credit Union, 880 F.2d 579, 585 n.1 (1st Cir. 1989); *see also* United States v. Heredia, 483 F.3d 913 (9th Cir. 2007) (*en banc*); United States v. Freeman, 434 F.3d 369, 378

C. "It is entirely up to you as to whether you find any deliberate closing of the eyes, and the inference to be drawn from any such evidence."[53]

D. "A showing of negligence or mistake is not sufficient to support a finding of willfulness or knowledge."[54]

E. Knowledge is not established by proof of a defendant's awareness of a high probability of the existence of the fact in question if the defendant "actually believes it does not exist."[55]

Courts often *say*, at least, that they are "wary of giving a willful blindness instruction, because of the danger they perceive in it allowing the jury to convict based on an *ex post facto* 'he should have been more careful' theory or to convict on mere negligence ('the defendant should have known his conduct was illegal')."[56] Unless carefully restricted, the instruction also carries the danger "of shifting the burden to the defendant to prove his or her innocence."[57] Many courts therefore state that willful blindness instructions are appropriately given only in "rare circumstances"[40] (although it should be noted that the instruction is in fact widely used and its invocation is in the overwhelming majority of cases approved by the courts of appeals).[58] It is often stated that a willful blindness instruction is warranted only if the defendant claims lack of knowledge and the government has introduced affirmative evidence to support an inference that the defendant consciously engaged in a course of deliberate ignorance.[59]

In contesting the provision of any willful blindness charge, defense counsel will often contend that there are insufficient "red flags" in evidence to warrant such a jury instruction.[60] If the court determines to give a willful blindness charge, defense counsel will ask the court to underscore that the test is a subjective one—requiring at least a finding that the defendant deliberately took affirmative steps to avoid knowledge—and not an objective one—perhaps leading to convictions for negligence. How the defense fared in these requests depended upon the circuit.[61]

(5th Cir. 2005).

[53] Devitt & Blackmar, *supra* note 51, at § 14.09.

[54] *Id.*; *see also Heredia*, 483 F.3d 913; United States v. Carrillo, 435 F.3d 767, 779-80 (7th Cir. 2006).

[55] United States v. Jewell, 532 F.2d 697, 704 n.21 (9th Cir. 1976).

[56] *See* United States v. Demmitt, 706 F.3d 665, 675 (5th Cir. 2013); United States v. Mancuso, 42 F.3d 836 (4th Cir. 1994); *see also* United States v. Sanchez-Robles, 927 F.2d 1070 (9th Cir. 1991).

[57] United States v. de Francisco-Lopez, 939 F.2d 1405, 1411 (10th Cir. 1991).

[58] *See Alston-Graves*, 435 F.3d at 337-38.

[59] *See* United States v. Nektalov, 461 F.3d 309, 314 (2d Cir. 2006); United States v. Gabriele, 63 F.3d 61, 66 (1st Cir. 1995); *Mancuso*, 42 F.3d 836; *de Francisco-Lopez*, 939 F.2d at 1411; *Lara-Velasquez*, 919 F.2d at 951; United States v. Hiland, 909 F.2d 1114, 1130 (8th Cir. 1990).

[60] *See, e.g.,* United States v. Ferguson, 653 F.3d 61, 78-79 (2d Cir. 2011); United States v. Ciesiolka, 614 F.3d 347, 353 (7th Cir. 2010); *Gabriele*, 63 F.3d at 66; *St. Michael's Credit Union*, 880 F.2d at 585; *see also* Stanley S. Arkin & Howard J. Kaplan, *How Many 'Red Flags' are Sufficient, if Ever, to Establish Mens Rea?*, Bus. Crimes Bull. (Oct. 2011).

[61] *Compare* United States v. Feroz, 848 F.2d 359, 360 (2d Cir. 1988) (requiring "high probability" and "actual belief" language in instructions), *with* United States v. Prince, 214 F.3d 740, 760 (6th Cir. 2000) (upholding jury charge that did not contain the "high probability" language and that failed to instruct that "carelessness or negligence or foolishness" is insufficient); United States v. Stewart, 185 F.3d 112, 126 (3d Cir. 1999) (holding that specific language that a defendant must have a "subjective awareness of a high probability that something is amiss" is not required as long as charge is sufficient to guard against conviction based on an objective standard of willful blindness); *Hiland*, 909 F.2d at 1130 (rejecting contention that jury instruction must specifically state that a defendant has knowledge of a certain fact only if he is aware of a high probability of its existence).

Why has this theory "spawned a great deal of commentary and a somewhat perplexing body of caselaw"?[62] All the circuit courts appeared to endorse the "[t]he substantive justification for the rule," which is that "deliberate ignorance and positive knowledge are equally culpable."[63] And certainly one way of conceptualizing it is as authorizing circumstantial inferences from the facts proven; as one court explained, the instruction's purpose is "to inform the jury that it may consider evidence of the defendant's *charade* of ignorance as circumstantial proof of guilty knowledge. '[T]he instruction is nothing more than a refined circumstantial evidence instruction properly tailored to the facts of a case.'"[64] But, when attempting to reconcile this instruction with the textual requirement of "knowledge," the circuits demonstrated considerable confusion regarding extent *mens rea* concepts:

a. Recklessness: Some courts, especially in the Seventh Circuit, seemed to argue that it is in essence the defendant's failure, in the face of evidence of wrongdoing, to investigate sufficiently that is the basic problem with the "ostrich" defendant.[65] This approach sounded in recklessness—the defendant is culpable for his conscious failure to satisfy his duty to learn the facts and thus avoid criminality.[66] Other circuits rejected any attempt to found willful blindness culpability on a recklessness theory[67]—and in doing so were clearly correct because, after all, this is a theory that is addressed to crimes requiring at least "knowledge."

b. Model Penal Code's "Knowing": "The trend in favor of allowing a willful blindness instruction may have been accelerated by ... the Model Penal Code, which ... defines knowledge of a fact to include a situation in which 'a person is aware of a high probability of [the fact's] existence, unless he actually believes that it does not exist.'"[68] This conceptualization is "susceptible of several well-founded attacks,"[69] for example that

---

[62] *Heredia*, 483 F.3d at 915.

[63] *Jewell*, 532 F. 2d at 700; *see also Alston-Graves*, 435 F. 3d at 338 n.3.

[64] *Lara-Velasquez*, 919 F.2d at 951 (emphasis added).

[65] *Hiland*, 909 F.2d at 1130 ("'The purpose of a willful blindness theory is to impose criminal liability on people who, recognizing the likelihood of wrongdoing, nonetheless consciously refuse to take basic investigatory steps.'") (quoting United States v. Rothrock, 806 F.2d 318, 322 (1st Cir. 1986)). *But see* United States v. L.E. Myers Co., 562 F.3d 845 (7th Cir. 2009).

[66] *See Prince*, 214 F.3d 740 (noting that the court has upheld a jury instruction that stated that the element of knowledge may be inferred from evidence that the defendants acted with a "reckless disregard for the truth or with a conscious purpose to avoid learning the truth about the unlawful transaction"); United States v. Ramsey, 785 F.2d 184, 189 (7th Cir. 1986) ("If a person with a lurking suspicion goes on as before and avoids further knowledge, this may support an inference that he has deduced the truth and is simply trying to avoid the appearance (and incurring the consequences) of knowledge. Alternatively the evidence would support an inference of criminal recklessness, which is the legal equivalent of knowledge.").

[67] *de Francisco-Lopez*, 939 F.2d at 1411 ("the form and content of the jury instruction may not suggest to the jury that the defendant's conduct is based on negligence or recklessness"); United States v. Kelm, 827 F.2d 1319, 1324 (9th Cir. 1987) (stating that to obtain conscious avoidance instruction, "[t]here must be evidence that the defendant purposely avoided learning all the facts in order to have a defense in the event of being arrested and charged. It is not enough that defendant was mistaken, recklessly disregarded the truth, or negligently failed to inquire."); United States v. Hanlon, 548 F.2d 1096, 1101-02 (2d Cir. 1977) (condemning use of the word "reckless" in a deliberate ignorance jury instruction).

[68] *Id.* at 339 (quoting § 2.02(7) of the Model Penal Code); *see also Jewell*, 532 F.2d at 700 (stating that "the textual justification [for the ostrich instruction] is that in common understanding one 'knows' facts of which he is less than absolutely certain. To act 'knowingly,' therefore, is not necessarily to act only with positive knowledge, but also to act with an awareness of the high probability of the existence of the fact in question. When such awareness is present, 'positive' knowledge is not required"); Ira P. Robbins, *The Ostrich Instruction: Deliberate Ignorance as a Criminal Mens Rea*, 81 J. Crim. L. & Criminology 191 (1990).

[69] *Nektalov*, 461 F.3d at 311.

"it is hard to see how ignorance, from whatever cause, can be knowledge. A particular explanation of why a defendant remains ignorant might justify treating him as though he had knowledge, but it cannot, through some mysterious alchemy, convert ignorance into knowledge."[70]

Despite these critiques, this explanation at least found a principled basis in the Model Penal Code's *mens rea* typography and it is the explanation that "received at least nodding approval by the Supreme Court in *Leary v. United States*."[71] As we shall see, the Supreme Court has recently endorsed this standard in *Global-Tech*, although it added an additional element to it.

c. <u>Purposely or Willfully</u>; Language in some cases, particularly in the Ninth Circuit, would lead one to believe that the willfully blind defendant must be less "ostrich" than "fox."[72] Under this conception, the defendant chooses to remain ignorant of facts "so he can plead lack of positive knowledge in the event he should be caught."[73] "The grand-scheming Fox, who aims to do wrong and structures his own ignorance merely to prepare a defense, has the same level of culpability as any other willful wrongdoer—the highest level, in the Model Penal Code schema."[74] This conceptualization took a body blow in 2007 when the en banc Ninth Circuit, in *United States v. Heredia*, rejected the argument that an ostrich jury instruction must provide that the "defendant's motive in deliberately failing to learn the truth was to give himself a defense in case he should be charged with a crime."[75]

d. *Global-Tech*: MPC's "High Probability" and "Deliberate Actions": The Supreme Court recently set forth its understanding of the requisites of a "willful blindness" charge, adopting the Model Penal Code's standard—with one additional element. Although it did so in the context of determining the *mens rea* applicable in a civil copyright inducement case, the Supreme Court relied on what it understood to be the content of the standard in criminal cases. Thus, in *Global-Tech Appliances, Inc. v. SEB S.A.*,[76] the Court held that a civil plaintiff, SEB, S.A., suing another company, Pentalpha Enterprises, Ltd., for induced infringement of a patent under 35 U.S.C. § 271(b) must show that the defendant knew that the induced acts constituted patent infringement. In the *Global-Tech* case, the dispute came down to whether Pentalpha had known of SEB's patent. The Court evaluated in what circumstances such knowledge could be demonstrated through willful blindness, eventually finding that although the court below had applied the incorrect standard, the evidence was sufficient to find that Pentalpha willfully blinded itself to the infringing nature of sales it encouraged.

GLOBAL-TECH APPLIANCES, INC. v. SEB S.A.
563 U.S. 754 (2011)

[Ed.: The Federal Circuit below had held that § 271(b) requires a "plaintiff [to] show that the alleged infringer knew or should have known that his actions would induce actual infringements" and that this showing includes proof that the alleged infringer knew of the patent. SEB, S.A. v. Montgomery Ward & Co., 594 F.3d 1360, 1376 (Fed. Cir. 2010).

---

[70] *Id.* at 311 n.1 (*quoting* Douglas N. Husak & Craig A. Callender, *Wilful Ignorance, Knowledge, and the "Equal Culpability" Thesis: A Study of the Deeper Significance of the Principle of Legality*, 1994 Wis. L. Rev. 29, 52); *see also Alston-Graves*, 435 F.3d at 337 n.1.

[71] United States v. Jacobs, 475 F.2d 270, 287 (2d Cir. 1973) (Friendly, J.) (referring to Leary v. United States, 395 U.S. 6, 46 n.93 (1969)).

[72] *See* David Luban, *Contrived Ignorance*, 87 Geo. L.J. 957, 968-69 (1999).

[73] United States v. Restrepo-Granda, 575 F.2d 524, 528 (5th Cir. 1978); *see also de Francisco-Lopez*, 939 F.2d at 1409.

[74] Luban, *supra* note 72, at 969.

[75] *Herodia*, 483 F.3d 913.

[76] 563 U.S. 754 (2011).

Although the record contained no direct evidence that Pentalpha knew of SEB's patent, the Federal Circuit found adequate evidence to support a finding that "Pentalpha deliberately disregarded a known risk that SEB had a protective patent." *Id.* at 1377. Such disregard, the court said, "is not different from actual knowledge, but is a form of actual knowledge." *Id.* The Supreme Court held that the Federal Circuit applied an incorrect standard for willful blindness, explaining as follows.]

The doctrine of willful blindness is well established in criminal law. Many criminal statutes require proof that a defendant acted knowingly or willfully, and courts applying the doctrine of willful blindness hold that defendants cannot escape the reach of these statutes by deliberately shielding themselves from clear evidence of critical facts that are strongly suggested by the circumstances. The traditional rationale for this doctrine is that defendants who behave in this manner are just as culpable as those who have actual knowledge. It is also said that persons who know enough to blind themselves to direct proof of critical facts in effect have actual knowledge of those facts. See *United States v. Jewell*, 532 F.2d 697, 700 (C.A. 9 1976) (en banc).

This Court's opinion more than a century ago in *Spurr v. United States,* 174 U.S. 728,[77] while not using the term "willful blindness," endorsed a similar concept. The case involved a criminal statute that prohibited a bank officer from "willfully" certifying a check drawn against insufficient funds. We said that a willful violation would occur "if the [bank] officer purposely keeps himself in ignorance of whether the drawer has money in the bank." Following our decision in *Spurr,* several federal prosecutions in the first half of the 20th century invoked the doctrine of willful blindness. Later, a 1962 proposed draft of the Model Penal Code, which has since become official, attempted to incorporate the doctrine by defining "knowledge of the existence of a particular fact" to include a situation in which "a person is aware of a high probability of [the fact's] existence, unless he actually believes that it does not exist." ALI, Model Penal Code § 2.02(7) (Proposed Official Draft 1962). Our Court has used the Code's definition as a guide in analyzing whether certain statutory presumptions of knowledge comported with due process. And every Court of Appeals—with the possible exception of the District of Columbia Circuit—has fully embraced willful blindness, applying the doctrine to a wide range of criminal statutes.

Given the long history of willful blindness and its wide acceptance in the Federal Judiciary, we can see no reason why the doctrine should not apply in civil lawsuits for induced patent infringement under 35 U.S.C. § 271(b). …

While the Courts of Appeals articulate the doctrine of willful blindness in slightly different ways, all appear to agree on two basic requirements: (1) the defendant must subjectively believe that there is a high probability that a fact exists and (2) the defendant must take deliberate actions to avoid learning of that fact. We think these requirements give willful blindness an appropriately limited scope that surpasses recklessness and negligence. Under this formulation, a willfully blind defendant is one who takes deliberate actions to avoid confirming a high probability of wrongdoing and who can almost be said to have actually known the critical facts. See G. Williams, Criminal Law § 57, p. 159 (2d ed. 1961) ("A court can properly find wilful blindness only where it can almost be said that the defendant actually knew"). By contrast, a reckless defendant is one who merely knows of a substantial and unjustified risk of such wrongdoing, see ALI, Model Penal Code § 2.02(2)(c) (1985), and a negligent defendant is one who should have known of a similar risk but, in fact, did not, see § 2.02(2)(d).

The test applied by the Federal Circuit in this case departs from the proper willful blindness standard in two important respects. First, it permits a finding of knowledge when there is merely a "known risk" that the induced acts are infringing. Second, in demanding only "deliberate indifference" to that risk, the Federal Circuit's test does not require active efforts by an inducer to avoid knowing about the infringing nature of the activities. …

---

[77] [Court's footnote 6:] The doctrine emerged in English law almost four decades earlier and became firmly established by the end of the 19th century. In American law, one of the earliest references to the doctrine appears in an 1882 jury charge in a federal prosecution. In the charge, the trial judge rejected the "great misapprehension" that a person may "close his eyes, when he pleases, upon all sources of information, and then excuse his ignorance by saying that he does not see anything."

Notes

1. *Global-Tech* was initially perceived as a victory for criminal defendants. First, the Court expressly required a state of mind higher than recklessness for a finding of willful blindness. Prior to *Global-Tech*, some circuits had, as noted above, equated willful blindness with recklessness. And very few had, in their pattern jury instructions, excluded recklessness. The instructions expressly instructed juries that a conviction could not be based on mere "negligence" or "mistake" but did not mention recklessness.

Second, the opinion requires that the government prove that the defendant took "deliberate *actions*" to avoid positive knowledge. (Emphasis added.) Prior to *Global-Tech*, circuit courts regularly upheld jury instructions that did not require positive "actions," but rather asked only that, conscious of a substantial probability that a culpable fact existed, the defendant deliberately "closed his/her eyes," First Circuit Pattern Crim. Jury Instr. 1st Cir. 2.14, "deliberately avoided learning about [it]," Mod. Crim. Jury Instr. 3d Cir. 5.06, "deliberately ignor[ed] the obvious," Pattern Crim. Jury Instr. 6th Cir. 2.09, "deliberately avoided learning the truth," Model Crim. Jury Instr. 9th Cir. 5.7, or "deliberately blinded himself to the existence of the fact," Pattern Crim. Jury Instr. 5th Cir. 1.37A, Pattern Crim. Jury Instr. 10th Cir. 1.37; *see also* Fed. Crim. Jury Instr. 7th Cir. 4.10. These formulations imply that if the defendant, while aware of a high probability of a fact, failed to take affirmative steps to investigate the recognized risk, he is culpability willfully blind. Not taking any action— and in particular a failure to investigate—was culpable before *Global-Tech*, but now cannot be reconciled with the plain language of that opinion.

Perhaps it is not surprising that the lower federal courts have largely ignored *Global-Tech* given that the Supreme Court said in that case that it was simply restating the doctrine articulated by the federal circuit courts. *See, e.g.*, Barry Gross & Stephen G. Stroup, *Has the Legal Threshold for "Willful Blindness" Really Changed Since* Global-Tech?, 96 Crim. L. Rptr. (BNA) 533 (Feb. 18, 2015). Many courts rely on existing circuit law affirming the traditional formulation without reference to *Global-Tech*. *See, e.g.*, United States v. Hansen, 791 F.3d 863, 870 (8th Cir. 2015) ("'Ignorance is deliberate if the defendant was presented with facts that put her on notice that criminal activity was particularly likely and yet she intentionally failed to investigate those facts'") (citation omitted); United States v. Mathauda, 740 F.3d 565, 568-69 (11th Cir. 2014); United States v. Demmitt, 706 F.3d 665, 675-76 (5th Cir. 2013) (failure to investigate suspicions constitutes conscious avoidance). A number of circuits to address the case take the position that *Global-Tech* did not in fact change anything. *See, e.g.*, United States v. Goffer, 721 F.3d 113, 128 (2d Cir. 2013). In particular, these circuits note that their instructions' requirement that the defendant "deliberately ignored" or "deliberately closed his eyes" to what was obvious is the same as the Supreme Court's requirement that the defendant must take "deliberate actions" to avoid learning the facts. *See, e.g.*, United States v. Brooks, 681 F.3d 678, 703 (5th Cir. 2012); Pattern Crim. Jury Instr. 6th Cir. 2.09 (2013). And the Eleventh Circuit has even questioned whether *Global Tech* applies outside of the civil patent-infringement context in which it was decided. *See* United States v. Clay, 832 F.3d 1259, 1313-14 & n.28 (11th Cir. 2016).

But *Global-Tech did* change the law (whether the Supreme Court meant to or not) in one important respect: absent a statutory duty to investigate, a defendant's failure to investigate in the face of substantial suspicions does not, alone, constitute willful blindness. *See* United States v. Macias, 786 F.3d 1060 (7th Cir. 2015). And this is obviously correct—and indeed should have been the law all along.

First, the Supreme Court explicitly required deliberate "actions," not inaction; a simple failure to investigate is not "action." This is consistent with the general thrust of federal criminal law with respect to the omission/commission distinction. In federal law, absent some kind of duty created by law, *see, e.g.*, 15 U.S.C. §§ 78dd-1(f)(2)(B), 78dd-2(h)(3)(B), 78dd-3(f)(3)(B), or derived from a relationship of trust and confidence, the failure to investigate is generally not criminally culpable.

Second, the Supreme Court explicitly disclaimed recklessness as a basis for willful blindness. This should have been self-evident all long because "knowledge" and "recklessness" have always been conceived of as different mental states. *See* Model Penal Code § 2.02. If Congress meant to demand only recklessness, it could have and would have said so. Reading a statute that demands "knowledge" to be satisfied by "recklessness," then, contravenes long-established distinctions in degrees of *mens rea* as well as congressional intent. By definition, a failure to investigate in "conscious disregard of a substantial and unjustified risk" is nothing more than "reckless"; it is necessarily deals with probabilities, not "knowledge." *See* Ira P. Robbins, *The Ostrich Instruction: Deliberate Ignorance as a Criminal Mens Rea*, 81 J. Crim. L. & Criminology 191, 220-21 (1990); *see also id.* at 231 ("The high-probability... standard describes recklessness rather than knowledge, and its adoption by the judiciary instead of the legislature infringes on the legislature's province of defining criminal conduct.") Thus, "to support an inference of 'deliberate ignorance,' there must be evidence that the defendant took 'steps to make sure that he [did] not acquire full or exact knowledge of the nature and extent of' the illegal activity.' Failing to display curiosity is not enough; the defendant must affirmatively '*act* to avoid learning the truth.'" United States v. L.E. Myers Co., 562 F.3d 845, 854 (7th Cir. 2009).

When might this make a difference? Consider the following explanation from the Seventh Circuit:

> the ostrich instruction is designed for cases in which there is evidence that the defendant, knowing or strongly suspecting that he is involved in shady dealings, takes steps to make sure that he does not acquire full or exact knowledge of the nature and extent of those dealings. ... A good example of a case in which the ostrich instruction was properly given is *United States v. Diaz*, 864 F.2d 544, 550 (7th Cir. 1988). The defendant, a drug trafficker, sought 'to insulate himself from the actual drug transaction so that he could deny knowledge of it,' which he did sometimes by absenting himself from the scene of the actual delivery and sometimes by pretending to be fussing under the hood of his car. [Another case is presented where the house where illegal activity took place was a short way down a side street from the thoroughfare on which the defendant commuted to work. The government argues that he was willfully blind because it] ... would have been easy for him to drive by the house from time to time to see what was doing, and if he had done so he might have discovered its use as a wireroom. He did not do so. But this is not the active avoidance with which the ostrich doctrine is concerned. It would be if the house had been *on* the thoroughfare, and [defendant], fearful of what he would see if he drove past it, altered his commuting route to avoid it. [The defendant] failed to display curiosity, but he did nothing to prevent the truth from being communicated to him. He did not *act* to avoid learning the truth.

Macias, 786 F.3d at 1062-63 (discussing United States v. Giovannetti, 919 F.2d 1223, 1228 (7th Cir. 1990)). Does this mean that the government must prove that the defendant is more "fox" than "ostrich," and that he in fact is acting with the *purpose* of establish plausible deniability?

As a prosecutor, how would you draft a willful blindness jury instruction for the court's consideration? How would the draft instruction change if you were defense counsel?

2. *Willful Blindness and Specific Intent.* A willful blindness theory is supposed to be limited in its scope to proof of "knowledge"; it is not an instruction that should be given with respect to the government's burden of proving purposeful or willful conduct and certainly is not sufficient to prove that the defendant acted with specific intent. Where a crime requires specific intent, however, some courts hold that willful blindness can be used to assist the government in meeting its burden—although conceptually this may be difficult to swallow. For example, some courts require proof of specific intent in false statements cases. May the government prove that the defendant consciously avoided learning about the falsity of a statement he filed with the government and at the same time prove that the defendant had a specific intent to deceive the government? Is there is a certain dissonance in the argument that someone

consciously avoided learning about the falsity of a statement while at the same time harboring a specific intent to deceive by making the statement?

Courts addressing this apparent discrepancy emphasize that conscious avoidance establishes a defendant's knowledge of the falsity of a statement, which itself is relevant to the further question of intent. As the Second Circuit has explained:

> [C]onscious avoidance is not irrelevant to intent, for knowledge is one component of intent. Without … knowledge, … intent cannot exist. Thus even in a … case[] in which specific intent must be proven, [the] use of a conscious-avoidance instruction may be appropriate with respect to the defendant's knowledge.[78]

So, by assuming that conscious avoidance is proof that a person knows that his statement is false, the court converts a defendant's failure to discover the truth or falsity of a statement into partial proof that the defendant ultimately intended to deceive a governmental agency. Does this make any sense as a practical matter? Does your view depend upon whether willful blindness instructions and convictions are restricted to "foxes" or whether they will also include true "ostriches"?

In any case, are juries likely to be able to sort all this out? In recognition that these distinctions may be somewhat subtle and that the possibility exists for juries to mistakenly conclude the willful blindness is the equivalent of intent, some courts caution that instructions should be carefully crafted to "clarify for the jury to the greatest extent possible that the conscious-avoidance concept is pertinent to knowledge or sincerity of belief, or to the knowledge component of intent, but that a finding of a conscious avoidance could not alone provide the basis for finding purpose or for finding intent as a whole."[79]

3. *Willful Blindness and Reliance on Counsel Defense.* Is a conscious-avoidance charge reconcilable with a good-faith reliance on the advice-of-counsel defense, given that the Supreme Court has emphasized that an advice-of-counsel defense must rest on the defendant's good faith solicitation of advice and his complete disclosure of relevant information to his attorney?[80] Some courts have said yes,[81] reasoning:

> There is no logical reason that this instruction may not also be used in the presence of an advice-of-counsel defense, the thrust of which is that the defendant, on the basis of counsel's advice, believed his conduct to be lawful and thus could not be found to have had unlawful intent. Though a defendant who would rely on an advice-of-counsel defense is required to have disclosed all pertinent information in his possession to his attorney, there is no inherent inconsistency between his taking that action and his studious avoidance of gaining other pertinent information. Accordingly, we see no doctrinal problem with the court's giving a conscious-avoidance instruction in this case.[82]

---

[78] United States v. Gabriel, 125 F.3d 89, 98 (2d Cir. 1997); *see also* United States v. Beech-Nut Nutrition Corp., 871 F.2d 1181, 1195 (2d Cir. 1989) ("[E]ven in a conspiracy case, in which specific intent must be proven, use of a conscious-avoidance instruction may be appropriate with respect to the defendant's knowledge of the objectives of the conspiracy. The same is true of mail fraud cases.").

[79] *Beech-Nut Nutrition Corp.*, 871 F.2d at 1196.

[80] *See* Williamson v. United States, 207 U.S. 425, 453 (1908).

[81] *See Beech-Nut Nutrition Corp.*, 871 F.2d at 1194; United States v. Duncan, 850 F.2d 1104, 1118 (6th Cir. 1988).

[82] *Beech-Nut Nutrition Corp.*, 871 F.2d at 1194.

Chapter 3

U.S. SENTENCING GUIDELINES

For much of the 20th century, judges claimed the virtually unfettered power to determine a federal criminal defendant's sentence. Judges had to select a sentence within the statutory maximum penalty prescribed by Congress, but such penalties generally permitted judges a great deal of discretion. Further, judges were permitted to rely upon all manner of information in considering an appropriate sentence, were not subject to procedural constraints (such as the rules of evidence or standards of proof) in finding such information, and did not have to publicly account, at sentencing or on appeal, for the reasons or evidence upon which they based their sentencing judgments.

In 1984, Congress precipitated a profound change in the federal criminal system by establishing the U.S. Sentencing Commission and tasking it with formulating guidelines designed to control judicial discretion in sentencing. Congress was reacting to studies that showed troubling disparities among sentences judges visited upon similarly situated defendants. Its principal charge to the Commission, then, was to create guidelines that would promote uniformity and proportionality in criminal sentencing. The U.S. Sentencing Commission promulgated guidelines controlling the sentencing of individual criminal defendants, effective 1987, as well as organizational defendants, effective 2001. From 1987 through 2005, the Guidelines were a complex set of rules that, in the normal case, provided the sentencing judge with a narrow range (*e.g.*, 6-12 months) within which he or she was *required* to sentence the defendant. Judges could, in extraordinary cases, "depart" from the Guidelines range, but the U.S. Sentencing Commission had rules and policies to guide departures, and appellate courts were fairly vigorous in policing district courts' discretionary departure judgments. In short, although denominated as "guidelines," these rules were in fact *mandatory* and were expressly designed to promote uniformity and proportionality in sentencing by restricting the discretion of human actors (most notably judges) in the sentencing process.

Many defense lawyers, judges, academics, and others quite simply hated the mandatory Guidelines. Among the complaints commonly lodged were assertions that the Guidelines were unduly complicated and inflexible, that they had shifted too much power over sentencing (and thus plea bargaining) to prosecutors, and that, in reducing sentencing to mathematical formulas, they removed the humanity and individualization that should be inherent in criminal sentencing. The (less vocal) fans of the Guidelines believed that, although they were an imperfect work in progress, they had created a reasonably administrable system that promoted sentencing uniformity and proportionality better than any alternative system.

What was universally acknowledged was the Guidelines' importance. A defendant's or potential defendant's sentencing exposure under the Guidelines was an important—and often critical—factor in many decisions, including whether he would be released on bail, with what he would be charged, the types of counts to which he might plead guilty, the conduct of any trial, and strategies to be employed at sentencing. The defendant's sentence was a particularly important consideration in the plea negotiations process and, given that plea rates are hover around 97% in the federal system, the ability to use and, in some practitioners' minds, abuse the Sentencing Guidelines was essential to federal criminal practice.

The Guidelines survived a number of constitutional challenges—both to the institutional arrangement by which they were promulgated and to the operation of the Guidelines themselves. Finally, however, in January 2005, the U.S. Supreme Court held that the *mandatory* sentencing Guidelines violated the Sixth Amendment in *United States v. Booker (infra)*. The Court invalidated two statutory provisions that had the effect of making the Guidelines mandatory: 18 U.S.C. § 3553(b)(1), which required sentencing courts to impose a sentence within the guidelines range absent grounds for departure, and 18 U.S.C. § 3742(e), which set forth the applicable standards for appellate review, including a *de novo* review standard for departures. After *Booker*, only the very general guidelines provided in 18 U.S.C. § 3553(a) control criminal sentencing. Section 3553(a) provides that the U.S. Sentencing Guidelines *still operate, but they are advisory only*. Further, in lieu of the statutory appellate review standard, the *Booker* Court decreed that henceforth district court's sentencing determinations are subject only to "reasonableness" review. In 2007, the Supreme Court decided *Gall v. United States*[1] and *Kimbrough v. United States*,[2] in which it underscored that "reasonableness" means "abuse of discretion," and that it contemplates substantial appellate deference to district courts' exercises of sentencing discretion. Courts of appeals rarely reverse a sentence as "unreasonable."[3]

Post-*Booker*, then, the focus is explicitly on the factors laid out in § 3553(a). That section mandates that courts impose a criminal sentence "sufficient, but not greater than necessary,"[4] to comply with the need for the sentence imposed "to reflect the seriousness of the offense, to promote respect for the law, and to provide just punishment of the offense; ... to afford adequate deterrence to criminal conduct; ... to protect the public from further crimes of the defendant; and ... to provide the defendant with needed educational or vocational training, medical care, or other correctional treatment in the most effective manner."[5] The last clause—concerning rehabilitative concerns—was qualified by Congress in the Sentencing Reform Act when it directed that "[t]he Commission shall insure that the guidelines reflect the inappropriateness of imposing a sentence to a term of imprisonment for the purpose of rehabilitating the defendant or providing the defendant with needed educational or vocational training, medical care, or other correctional treatment." Further, in 18 U.S.C. § 3582(a), Congress decreed that in determining whether to impose a term of imprisonment and, if so, its length, courts should recognize that "imprisonment is not an appropriate means of promoting correction and rehabilitation."[6]

---

[1] 552 U.S. 38 (2007).

[2] 552 U.S. 85 (2007); *see also* Spears v. United States, 555 U.S. 261 (2009) *(per curiam)* (essentially holding that the Court meant what it said in *Kimbrough*).

[3] *But see* United States v. Singh, 877 F.3d 107 (2d Cir. 2017) (emphasizing the importance of mercy in criminal sentencing). Note that in *Rosales-Mireles*, -- U.S. --, 138 S.Ct. 1897 (2018), the Supreme Court faced a case where the sentence was founded on a miscalculation of the defendant's Guidelines but he failed to object until his appeal. His objection at that point was subject to plain error review. The Supreme Court held that a miscalculation of a Guidelines sentencing range that has been determined to be plain and to affect a defendant's substantial rights calls for a court of appeals to exercise its discretion under Fed. R. Crim. P. 52 to vacate the defendant's sentence in the ordinary case.

[4] 18 U.S.C. § 3553(a).

[5] *Id.* § 3553(a)(2).

[6] 28 U.S.C. § 994(k); 18 U.S.C. §3582(a); Tapia v. United States, 564 U.S. 319 (2011) ("Section 3582(a) precludes sentencing courts from imposing or lengthening a prison term to promote an offender's rehabilitation."). *Cf.* Pepper v. United States, 562 U.S. 476 (2011) (when a defendant's sentence has been set aside on appeal, a district court at resentencing may consider evidence of the defendant's post-sentencing rehabilitation, and such evidence may, in appropriate cases, support a downward variance from the advisory federal Sentencing Guidelines range). *Tapia* has generated circuit splits on such questions as whether rehabilitation can be considered at all at sentencing (*e.g.*, as long as it does not lengthen the resulting sentence of imprisonment), and in what circumstances. *See, e.g.*, United States v. Lemon, 777 F.3d 170 (4th Cir. 2015); United States v. Del Valle-Rodriguez, 761 F.3d 171 (1st Cir. 2014); United States v. Vandergrift, 754 F.3d 1303 (11th Cir. 2014). It appears clear, however, that a judge imposing a prison term after revoking a defendant's supervised release cannot consider the need for

Section 3553 also requires judges, in determining the particular sentence to be imposed, to consider not only the above-outlined purposes of sentencing, but also "the nature and circumstances of the offense and the history and characteristics of the defendant,"[7] "the kinds of sentences available,"[8] "the kinds of sentence and the sentencing range" applicable under the Guidelines,[9] "the need to avoid unwarranted sentence disparities among defendants with similar records who have been found guilty of similar conduct,"[10] and "the need to provide restitution to any victims of the offense."[11]

Post-*Booker*, for sentencing judges "the Guidelines have become the legal equivalent of one of the duller and slower-moving forms of movie zombie—one must take sensible precautions to avoid being bitten, but they are easily outwitted and, when troublesome, can be dispatched to oblivion without legal consequence."[12] Post-*Booker*, it appears that, for the most part, judges are following the "advisory" guidelines range—or are deviating from it at the request of the government—in about 76-80% of cases, which is about 10-14% lower than the conformance rate prior to *Booker*. It should be noted that the conformance rate dropped each year after the *Booker* decision but in the last few years appears to have stabilized at about 76%.[13] Because there is a great variation around the country in the extent to which judges are following the guidelines, however, this average conformance figure is somewhat misleading.[14] Notably, conformance also depends on the type of prosecution at

---

rehabilitation. *See* United States v. Mendiola, 696 F.3d 1033 (10th Cir. 2012).

[7] 18 U.S.C. § 3553(a)(1).

[8] *Id.* § 3553(a)(3).

[9] *Id.* § 3553(a)(4). Note that the Constitution's Ex Post Facto Clause is violated when a defendant is sentenced under current guidelines providing a higher sentencing range than the guidelines in effect at the time of the offense. *See* Peugh v. United States, 569 U.S. 530 (2013).

[10] 18 U.S.C. § 3553(a)(6).

[11] *Id.* § 3553(a)(7).

[12] Frank O. Bowman, III, *Dead Law Walking: The Surprising Tenacity of the Federal Sentencing Guidelines*, 51 Houston L. Rev. 1227, 1234 (2014).

[13] *See* "Conformance" is measured by adding the percentage of within-range sentences to the percentage of sentences that were below the range due to government-sponsored downward departures. In the pre-*Booker* period, from about October 2002 through mid-2004, the average nationwide "conformance" rate was a little over 90%. *See* U.S. Sentencing Comm'n, Final Report on the Impact of *United States v. Booker* on Federal Sentencing at vi-vii & n.9 (March 2006). The following summarizes how these percentages have changed over time, as derived from Sentencing Commission Reports and Sourcebooks: 2008, in-guidelines range (59.4%) plus government-sponsored downward departures (25.6%)=conformance rate of 85.0%; 2009: in-guidelines range (56.8%) plus government-sponsored downward departures (25.3%)=conformance rate of 82.1%; 2010: in-guidelines range (55%) plus government-sponsored downward departures (25.4%)=conformance rate of 80.4%; 2011: in-guidelines range (54.5%) plus government-sponsored downward departures (26.3%)=conformance rate of 80.8%; 2012: in-guidelines range (52.4%) plus government-sponsored downward departures (27.8%)=conformance rate of 80.2%; 2013: in-guidelines range (51.2%) plus government-sponsored downward departures (27.9%)=conformance rate of 79.1%; 2014: in-guidelines range (46%) plus government-sponsored downward departures (30.4%)=conformance rate of 76.4%; 2015: in-guidelines range (47.3%) plus government-sponsored downward departures (29.3%)=conformance rate of 76.6%; 2016: in-guidelines range (48.6%) plus government-sponsored downward departures (28.2%)=conformance rate of 76.8%.

[14] For example, in fiscal year 2017, 31.7% of cases were sentenced within the guidelines range in the D.C. Circuit, 49.5 % in the First Circuit, 65.1% in the Fifth Circuit, 37.4% in the Ninth Circuit, and 54.3% in the Eleventh Circuit. The percentage of government-sponsored below range sentences is inverse to the in-guidelines sentencing percentage, such that the overall "compliance" rates look similar. Thus, in the D.C. Circuit, 40.4% of cases had a government-sponsored departure, so that the overall compliance rate was 72.1%; in the First Circuit, such departures occurred in 26.3% of cases yielding a compliance rate of 75.8%; in the Fifth Circuit, such departures occurred in 14.0% of cases, yielding a compliance rate of 79.1%; in the Ninth Circuit, such departures occurred in 49.2% of cases, yielding a compliance rate of 86.6%; and in the Eleventh Circuit, such departures occurred in 19.5% of cases,

issue; research demonstrates that "a significant majority of defendants in major white-collar cases today receive sentences shorter than the Guidelines range."[15]

It is difficult to know whether judges will, in a substantial majority of cases (on average), continue to sentence based on guidelines ranges or government-sponsored departures from that range. Those arguing that the status quo is likely to continue point to the fact that most federal judges were appointed since the Guidelines took effect in 1987 and "have known no other regime and have considerable familiarity and facility with the Guidelines."[16] The Supreme Court's post-*Booker* decision in *United States v. Rita*[17] may have reinforced this inclination. The Supreme Court held in *Rita* that the "presumption of reasonableness" that some federal circuit courts applied when reviewing district court's within-guidelines sentences did not violate the Sixth Amendment. This presumption is only appropriate on appellate review, as the Supreme Court subsequently emphasized in *Nelson v. United States*.[18] But some in the defense bar feared that reversal-averse district court judges in those circuits that employ such a presumption will resolve all close sentencing questions in favor of the guidelines' results so as to avoid any risk of reversal for lack of reasonableness. On the other hand, one could certainly argue that *Gall* and *Kimbrough* changed the game completely. In those decisions, the Court may have encouraged district courts to put much less weight on guidelines ranges by underscoring the scope of district courts' sentencing discretion and emphasizing the substantial deference that ought to be applied on review of their decisions.

Given current practice—as well as the Supreme Court's consistent admonition in *Rita*, *Gall*, and *Kimbrough* that judges' sentencing calculus ought to at least begin with the Guidelines[19]—knowledge of these "advisory" rules continues to be essential to effective practice. It is also difficult to understand the *Booker*, *Gall*, and *Kimbrough* holdings, and thus evaluate how they will impact the criminal system going forward, without understanding how the Guidelines work. Accordingly, the following materials outline how the Guidelines are constructed as a prelude to discussions of *Booker* and the issues it has spawned.

A. REAL- VERSUS CHARGE-OFFENSE SENTENCING[20]

The U.S. Sentencing Commission ("Commission") is an independent agency in the judicial branch. The Commission, pursuant to congressional delegation, promulgated the Federal Sentencing Guidelines, which took effect for the sentencing of individuals on November 1, 1987.[21]

---

yielding a compliance rate of 73.8%. *See* U.S. Sentencing Comm'n, 2017 Sourcebook, Tbls. N-DC, N-1, N-5, N-9, N-11.

[15] Jillian Hewitt, Note, *Fifty Shades of Gray: Sentencing Trends in Major White-Collar Cases*, 125 Yale L.J. 1018, 1025 (2016).

[16] Irvin B. Nathan, *Supreme Court Gives the Defense a Boost in Plea Bargaining*, 12 Bus. Crimes Bull. 1, 2 (March 2005).

[17] 551 U.S. 338 (2007).

[18] 555 U.S. 350 (2009) (District Court erred in presuming that sentence within range was reasonable).

[19] *See, e.g., Gall*, 552 U.S. at 49; *Kimbrough*, 552 U.S. at 108-109; *Rita*, 551 U.S. at 352.

[20] Much of the following is excerpted, with some editing, renumbering, reorganizing, and rewriting, from Julie R. O'Sullivan, *In Defense of the U.S. Sentencing Guidelines' Modified Real-Offense System*, 91 Nw. U. L. Rev. 1342, 1343-61 (1997). My thanks to Northwestern University Law Review for giving me permission to use it.

[21] Congress's delegation to the Sentencing Commission survived constitutional challenges in *Mistretta v. United States*, 488 U.S. 361, 363-68 (1989).

"The efficacy of any sentencing system cannot be assessed absent agreement on the purposes and objectives of the penal system. And the responsibility for making these fundamental choices and implementing them lies with the legislature."[22] In its statement of purposes, Congress's charge to the Commission was essentially twofold.[23] First, it required that the Commission establish sentencing policies and practices designed to assure that the purposes of sentencing were met.[24] Congress decreed that those purposes are retribution (alternatively denominated "just deserts"),[25] deterrence and incapacitation (together referred to as "crime control"),[26] and, in crafting non-incarceration sentences, rehabilitation.[27] Second, it required that the Commission promote reasonable uniformity and proportionality in sentencing[28] by "narrowing the wide disparity in sentences imposed for similar criminal offenses committed by similar offenders"[29] while imposing "appropriately different sentences for criminal conduct of differing severity."[30]

The presupposition underlying these twin goals is that there are genuine differences among defendants and that those differences that correlate to the purposes of punishment isolated by Congress should be considered in formulating appropriate sentences. Traditionally, these distinctions among defendants have been considered at sentencing through what is known as "real-offense" (as opposed to "charge-offense") sentencing. In bald terms, the difference between a real-offense and a charge-offense sentencing system is simply *the amount of information that may be considered in assessing the sentence to be imposed upon a criminal defendant after conviction*. In a pure real-offense system, the sentencing authority is permitted to consider all manner of facts not necessary to the defendant's conviction on the offense actually tried ("extra-element facts"). These extra-element facts may include the circumstances leading up to and following the offense, the nature of the criminal conduct, the defendant's criminal history, the defendant's personal characteristics, and any other criminal violations committed by the defendant, whether or not charged or tried. By contrast, in a pure charge-offense system, a defendant's sentence depends entirely upon the offense of conviction, that is, the criminal statutory provision that a defendant is convicted of violating. A judge sentencing a defendant for conspiracy, for example, would look at the conspiracy statute and assess the presumptive penalty prescribed therein, say five years, without reference to facts that were not proven as elements of the offense.

---

[22] Harmelin v. Michigan, 501 U.S. 957, 998 (1991) (Kennedy, J., concurring in part and concurring in the judgment).

[23] *See* 28 U.S.C. § 994(b).

[24] *See id.* § 991(b)(1)(A).

[25] Under a "just deserts" theory of sentencing, "punishment should be scaled to the offender's culpability and the resulting harms. Thus, if a defendant is less blameworthy, he or she should receive less punishment, regardless of the danger that he or she may pose to the public and the need to deter others from committing similar crimes." Ilene H. Nagel, *Foreword, Structuring Sentencing Discretion: The New Federal Sentencing Guidelines*, 80 J. Crim. L. & Criminology 916-17 (1990) [hereinafter *Foreword*].

[26] Under a "crime control" sentencing model, defendants "should receive the punishment that most effectively lessens the likelihood of future crime, either by deterring others or incapacitating the defendant. The relationship that such sentences bear to those prescribed for other crimes committed by other offenders is of lesser importance." Nagel, *Foreword, supra* note 25, at 916-17 n.197.

[27] *See* 18 U.S.C. § 3553(a)(2); 18 U.S.C. § 3582(a).

[28] *See* 28 U.S.C. § 991(b)(1)(B); *see also id.* § 994(f); 18 U.S.C. § 3553(a)(6); S. Rep. No. 98-225, at 54, 56 (1983).

[29] U.S.S.G., ch.1, pt.A, former intro. comment. (1987); *see also* Burns v. United States, 501 U.S. 129, 133 (1991); *Mistretta*, 488 U.S. at 363-68.

[30] U.S.S.G., ch.1, pt.A, former intro. comment. (1987).

The pre-Guidelines federal sentencing system was a predominantly real-offense system.[31] Prosecutors exercised broad discretion in choosing the applicable charge. Once a conviction was obtained, sentencing judges had the discretion to choose a sentence within the penalty range set by statute.[32] Judges were permitted, and indeed encouraged, to consider all manner of "real" information regarding the offender and the offense, including proof of other criminal conduct for which the defendant had not been convicted.[33] The judge's discretion was circumscribed by only one charge-offense element: the minimum or maximum punishments prescribed in the statute(s) for whose violation the defendant was convicted provided a floor or ceiling for the judge's sentence. This element did not in practice significantly limit the effect of real-offense considerations, however, in that the statutory ranges generally were sufficiently broad to permit different sanctions to be imposed upon different defendants for the same statutory offense based upon disparities in the "real" characteristics of the offenses and the offenders.[34] "So long as the judge kept within the statutory range, there were virtually no rules about how he or she made the choice of sentence, and the sentence was effectively unreviewable by a court of appeals."[35]

The impetus behind the Sentencing Guidelines was studies that showed that the unconstrained discretion exercised by judges resulted in disparate sentencing treatment of similarly situated defendants.[36] Further, the primary rationale for wide-ranging judicial discretion—the theory that such discretion was necessary to allow judges to craft sentences that would promote the rehabilitation of the offender[37]—suffered as many (including Congress) concluded that rehabilitation was not an appropriate goal of incarceration. In the Sentencing Reform Act, Congress chose not to dictate either a charge- or real-offense based system, leaving it up to the Commission to weight the merits and demerits of each in light of the goals of the Act.

The advantages of a pure charge-offense system are its obvious simplicity, ease of administration, and procedural certainty. A defendant proved guilty beyond a reasonable doubt of violating a certain code section will receive the sentence prescribed by that section, without the need for any further litigation or fact-finding. These process-based advantages, however, come at a high cost in terms of the substantive aims of sentencing, at least given the existing federal criminal code.

The federal criminal code as presently constituted is not structured to reflect, in grades of offenses differentiated by statutory elements, the offender or offense circumstances that separate defendants in ways significant to congressional "just deserts" or "crime control" sentencing goals. Were a charge-offense system to be founded on the existing code, then, criminal sentences would have no necessary relationship to any legitimate penal goal.

For example, under such a system, all defendants would receive the same presumptive penalty upon conviction under 18 U.S.C. § 844(d) for transporting explosives "with the knowledge or intent that [they] will be used to kill ... any individual or unlawfully to ... destroy any building." Yet "it is self-evident that an internationally trained terrorist who is bent on murdering scores of innocent civilians should be sentenced far more severely than a duly

---

[31] In addition, nearly all the states allow sentencing courts to engage in real-offense sentencing although some have enacted predominantly charge-offense systems in recent years.

[32] *See, e.g., Mistretta,* 488 U.S. at 363-64.

[33] *See, e.g.,* Williams v. New York, 337 U.S. 241, 247 (1949) ("[h]ighly relevant ... to [the judge's] selection of an appropriate sentence is the possession of the fullest information possible concerning the defendant's life and characteristics").

[34] *See e.g., Mistretta,* 488 U.S. at 364.

[35] Frank O. Bowman, III, *Departing is Such Sweet Sorrow: A Year of Judicial Revolt on "Substantial Assistance" Departures Follows a Decade of Prosecutorial Indiscipline,* 29 Stetson L. Rev. 7, 9 (1999) (footnotes omitted).

[36] *See, e.g.,* Apprendi v. New Jersey, 530 U.S. 466 (2000) (O'Connor, J., dissenting).

[37] *See* Williams v. New York, 337 U.S. 241, 249-51 (1949).

licensed explosives merchant who knows that one of his customers intends to blow up an abandoned warehouse in order to commit insurance fraud, even if each of these defendants is convicted under 18 U.S.C. § 844(d)."[38] By most just deserts measures—the extent of harm threatened by the offense and the defendant's moral blameworthiness—our terrorist should receive a significantly harsher punishment than our merchant. In crime control terms, the imposition of a stiff penalty upon the terrorist is appropriate to send an unequivocal deterrent message to the terrorist, his trainers, cohorts, and others who may be tempted to employ similar means to achieve their ends. Any deterrence achieved through sentencing in the merchant's case is likely to be more localized, if not case-specific. Certainly the need to incapacitate a terrorist who willingly undertakes as a business the slaughter of innocents is greater than the need to incapacitate a merchant who looks the other way as his client destroys his own abandoned property.

As the above illustrates, imposing a uniform tariff on all persons who violate an undifferentiated criminal code section, although extremely costly in human and financial terms, will only in the most happenstantial way further the purposes of criminal sentencing. Seeking to effectuate no particular goal other than the procedurally efficient warehousing of defendants, such a sentencing system has no more principled basis than sentencing by roulette. The arbitrary tariffs this system exacts also threaten the goals of the sentencing reform movement that culminated in the Guidelines: the elimination of unwarranted disparities between like defendants and the introduction of principled proportionality in sentencing. To return to our hypothetical, the terrorist and the merchant are not similarly situated according to any principle relevant to crime control or just deserts goals. To treat them equally—that is, to pursue senseless and unprincipled uniformity—serves only to institutionalize disproportionality in sentencing.

The threat charge-offense sentencing poses to sentencing reform goals is more extreme than is suggested by a simple comparison of offense and offender characteristics with sentencing results because of the "hidden" disparities introduced by the exercise of prosecutorial discretion. The above discussion assumes that there is a single appropriate statutory charge for a given type of criminal conduct and that the prosecutor exercises little discretion in choosing the charge. In fact, federal prosecutors have long enjoyed broad discretion to choose among what may be a variety of statutory provisions applicable to particular criminal conduct. Where the charge determines the sentence, and the prosecutor chooses the charge, prosecutors' idiosyncratic practices will inevitably introduce disparities among similarly situated defendants. Although many have endorsed the idea of prosecutorial guidelines as a means of blunting this problem, others believe that the difficulties inherent in creating, and finding a means of enforcing, uniform prosecutorial charging and plea bargaining guidelines render this option impracticable.

A pure real-offense system, by contrast, offers the possibility of substantively meaningful, uniform, and proportionate sentencing but presents other serious challenges. Under a real-offense system, for example, the sentences received by our two hypothetical offenders will depend not upon the count of conviction but rather upon their disparate real-offense characteristics. The sentencing authority may factor into the sentencing calculus such extra-element facts as the nature and extent of threatened loss or harm, related but uncharged criminal episodes, the defendants' motivation, the length of their rap sheets, the degree to which they have expressed remorse or signaled their acceptance of responsibility, and the like. To the extent that the sentencing authority has successfully isolated the "real" elements that distinguish these defendants according to their relative culpability, the societal need for incapacitation in a given case, or the possibility of a sentence that will promote deterrent values, a real-offense system is capable of yielding a sentence that will promote these purposes of sentencing to a degree not presently possible under charge-offense sentencing. In this sense, real-offense sentencing has particular promise in promoting what I refer to within as penologically meaningful sentences. It also furthers the goals of sentencing reform: principled

---

[38] United States v. Kikumura, 918 F.2d 1084, 1099 (3d Cir.1990).

uniformity and proportionality. Defendants convicted of the same offense and otherwise similarly situated in terms relevant to the purposes of criminal punishment will receive like sentences, which should be proportionate to those received by other offenders with aggravating or mitigating offender and offense characteristics.

Pure real-offense sentencing also works to remove the secondary level of potential sentencing disparities by dampening or eliminating the influence of the prosecutor's choice of charge upon the eventual sentencing decision. Assuming that the sentencing authority has complete access to the "real" circumstances of the offense and is able to resolve accurately disputes regarding those facts, each defendant will receive a sentence commensurate with offenders sharing the same "real" characteristics, not just those with whom the prosecutor, for her own reasons, chooses to group the defendant through charging choices.

Pure real-offense sentencing, particularly as it has been traditionally administered, has its own significant drawbacks. Its success depends upon a number of assumptions that critics contend simply are not or cannot be validated. The principal potential drawbacks of real-offense sentencing can be summarized in three words: execution, administrability, and "fairness." First, a primarily real-offense system will succeed in promoting the purposes of sentencing and of sentencing reform only to the degree that the sentencing authority is successful in isolating and weighting those "real" elements that effectively further just deserts and crime control goals. This task is obviously an exceedingly difficult one from an empirical point of view. For example, even after years of empirical study, criminologists cannot definitively isolate those facts which will reliably forecast a defendant's future dangerousness. Further, effective execution, that is, the isolation of each and every potentially relevant "real" factor, if it is possible, may be achieved at the expense of practical administrability. The greater the number of "real" factors to be considered in sentencing, the greater the likelihood of burdensome litigation and disuniform results.

Perhaps the criticism most frequently leveled at real-offense sentencing is based on the process currently accorded in federal sentencing proceedings. Such proceedings have traditionally been conducted under procedures significantly more lax than those that apply in criminal or even civil trials. As in pre-Guidelines practice, sentencing judges need only apply a preponderance of the evidence standard to enhance a defendant's sentence on the basis of extra-element facts, including uncharged criminal conduct that the Guidelines make relevant. A defendant has no constitutional right to confront the witnesses against him or to cross-examine the sources of the "real" facts upon which his sentence rests. Finally, the Federal Rules of Evidence do not apply at sentencing, and thus "real" adjustments may be based on hearsay.[39] While these relaxed standards are not a necessary component of a "real" system, they constitute today's reality and thus must be considered in any evaluation of real-offense sentencing.

Many argue that the augmentation of sentences by discrete increments based upon consideration of "real" factors relating to criminal conduct that has not been charged or tried is fundamentally unfair. They contend first that it contravenes a variety of constitutional norms, in that it constitutes "punishment" for uncharged, unproved, or even acquitted offenses. Critics further argue that, given the limited procedural protections available to defendants at sentencing, the danger exists that inaccuracy may infect sentences that rely extensively upon "real" but uncharged information.

The above summarizes the merits and demerits of real and charge-offense sentencing in their pure, or most extreme, forms in today's charging and sentencing environment. Pure real and charge-offense sentencing, however, are not commonly viewed as "binary alternatives," but instead as "the end points of a continuum of possible sentencing information."[40] The

---

[39] *See, e.g.*, United States v. Umaña, 750 F.3d 320 (4th Cir. 2014) (Sixth Amendment's confrontation clause inapplicable at sentencing so hearsay admissible to persuade sentencers to impose the death penalty).

[40] David Yellen, *Illusion, Illogic, and Injustice: Real-Offense Sentencing and the Federal Sentencing Guidelines*, 78 Minn. L. Rev. 403, 404 (1993).

Commission adopted a compromise position on this informational continuum that, like pre-Guidelines sentencing practice, is best summarized as modified real-offense sentencing. The Guidelines contain charge-related constraints but require the consideration of a variety of "real" facts that in many cases constitute the predominant factors in determining the appropriate sentencing range. The most controversial subset of "real" information to be considered in arriving at a Guidelines range is the defendant's "non-conviction offense" conduct. "Non-conviction offense" conduct is conduct related to the offense of conviction that constitutes an independent criminal offense, or elements of such an offense, for which the defendant has not been tried or convicted and indeed for which the defendant may have been acquitted.

The Commission's "fundamental" compromise attempts to balance considerations of "procedural fairness and administrative efficiency"[41] with the need for sentencing consideration of extra-element facts that are relevant to penological goals and "protect the system from the unintended transfer of discretion from courts to prosecutors."[42] The Commission's modified real-offense system has been vigorously criticized. The U.S. Sentencing Commission, however, believes that the Guidelines have been largely effective in meeting congressional goals. In November, 2004, the Commission published a report entitled *Fifteen Years of Guidelines Sentencing: An Assessment of How Well the Federal Criminal Justice System is Achieving the Goals of Sentencing Reform*, in which the Guidelines were given good—but not perfect—scores in achieving congressional reform objectives. In particular, the Commission found that the Guidelines had "substantially achieved" the goals of the Sentencing Reform Act by increasing sentencing rationality and transparency, increasing the certainty and severity of punishment, and reducing—at least to some degree—unwarranted sentencing disparities.[43] In working their way through the following discussion of the structure of the Guidelines' modified real-offense approach, and in doing the Guidelines exercises in this and later chapters, readers should attempt to form their own conclusions regarding the fairness, effectiveness, and administrability of the Commission's compromise.

It is worth recalling that before the Guidelines, a federal sentence was the result of the discretion exercised by three actors—prosecutors who chose the charge, judges who chose a sentence within a broad statutory range, and the U.S. Parole Commission, which could parole an offender after he had served a specified portion of his sentence. The purpose and the effect of the Guidelines—*before* Booker *was decided*—was to drastically curtail judicial sentencing discretion. Indeed, in its November 2004 report, the Commission concluded that the "guidelines have succeeded in the job they were principally designed to do: reduce unwarranted disparity arising from differences among judges."[44] Further, in the same Act that delegated to the Commission the power to promulgate the Guidelines, Congress abolished parole in the federal system and substantially reduced good behavior adjustments. The only actor whose discretion was not directly limited by the congressional sentencing revolution was the prosecutor although, as we shall see, the Commission attempted to blunt the effects of prosecutorial discretion in structuring the Guidelines. Accordingly, before *Booker* was decided, there was a great deal of commentary charging that the Commission's choices had augmented, perhaps to a dangerous degree, prosecutorial power.

In *Booker*, the Supreme Court held that the Sixth Amendment jury trial right is violated where, *under a mandatory guidelines system*, a sentence is increased because of facts found by the judge that were neither admitted by the defendant nor found by the jury in arriving at a judgment of conviction (that is, the "real" facts discussed above). The *Booker* Court noted, however, that where the guidelines are *not mandatory*—that is, "when a trial judge exercises his

---

[41] United States v. Blanco, 888 F.2d 907, 910 (1st Cir. 1989) (Breyer, J.).

[42] Ilene H. Nagel & Stephen J. Schulhofer, *A Tale of Three Cities: An Empirical Study of Charging and Bargaining Practices Under the Federal Sentencing Guidelines*, 66 S. Cal. L. Rev. 501, 513 (1992).

[43] U.S. Sentencing Commission, *Fifteen Years of Guidelines Sentencing* 136-46 (Nov. 2004), at http://www.ussc.gov.

[44] *Id.* at 140.

discretion to select a specific sentence within a defined range, the defendant has no right to a jury determination of the facts that the judge deems relevant." The remedy the Supreme Court chose was to strike those portions of two statutes that make the U.S. Sentencing Guidelines binding on sentencing judges. In short, after *Booker*, the court is required by 18 U.S.C. § 3553(a) to "consider" in sentencing the U.S. Sentencing Guidelines range, but is permitted to "tailor" the sentence in light of other statutory considerations embodied in § 3553(a). The Guidelines, then, continue to be relevant but they are now *advisory only*. The Court's decision does *not* mean, however, that "real offense" sentencing is "out." Rather, the Court's decision ensures that judges can continue to consider all manner of extra-element facts now guided, but *not* bound, by the Sentencing Commission's judgments regarding what facts are important or the weight that ought to be accorded certain offense or offender circumstances.

In light of this development, readers should consider how *Booker* affects the balance of power in criminal sentencing and what consequences this shift may have for the federal criminal system as a whole.

B. GUIDELINES STRUCTURE

The following discussion is dense and may prove confusing and discouraging to some. However, a strong working knowledge of the structure of the Guidelines, and the theory that drove its construction, is important to the effective practice of federal criminal law—even post-*Booker*. For the reasons outlined above, this is, again, because the parties and the courts continue, at least for now, to begin sentencing calculations with the guidelines, and those calculations control in most cases. In short, readers are strongly encouraged to persevere. Referring to the Guidelines manual itself while reading this discussion may prove helpful.

To understand the Guidelines, one should first turn to the Sentencing Table set forth in Guidelines' Chapter Five, Part A. Before *United States v. Booker* was decided, except in unusual circumstances where a "departure" from the Guidelines was deemed appropriate, a judge *was required* to select a sentence from within the Guidelines range that lies at the intersection of the "Offense Level" (vertical axis) and the "Criminal History Category" (horizontal axis) applicable to a given defendant. For example, if a defendant had an Offense Level of 15 and a Criminal History Category of I, a judge, before *Booker*, *had* to sentence the defendant to a term of imprisonment of between 18 and 24 months (absent a departure). The bulk of the Guidelines Manual consists of instructions on how to determine what Criminal History Category and Offense Level govern in a given case. After the January 2005 decision in *Booker*, however, these Guidelines are deemed advisory only. To be clear, judges must still consult the Guidelines, among other considerations, in arriving at a sentence consistent with 18 U.S.C. § 3553(a).

The Criminal History Category "is a rough effort to determine the defendant's disposition to criminality, as reflected in the number and nature of his prior contacts with the law."[45] Calculation of this factor is concentrated in Guidelines Chapter Four.

The Offense Level, by contrast, is designed to "measure[] the seriousness of the present crime."[46] In essence, the Offense Level is determined by reference to three factors (1) the "base offense level" which is prescribed by the Chapter Two guideline applicable to the offense of conviction; (2) the "specific offense characteristics" which are again included in the applicable Chapter Two guideline; and (3) any "adjustments" from Chapter Three that are appropriately assessed given the circumstances of the offense. As Professor Frank Bowman explains:

> The base offense level is a seriousness ranking based ... on the fact of conviction of a particular statutory violation. For example, [most] ... fraud convictions carry a base

---

[45] Bowman, *supra* note 35, at 11.

[46] *Id.*

offense level of 6 [or 7]. The "specific offense characteristics" are an effort to categorize and account for commonly occurring factors that cause us to think of one crime as worse than another. They "customize" the crime. For instance, the Guidelines differentiate between a mail fraud in which the victim loses $1000 and a fraud with a loss of $1,000,000. A loss of $1000 would produce no increase in the base offense level for fraud ... , while a loss of $1,000,000 would add [14] levels and thus increase the offense level from 6 [or 7] to [20 or 21].[47]

The Chapter Three adjustments further "customize" treatment of the offense at issue, requiring courts to distinguish between offenders based upon "real," extra-element facts relating to: the nature of the victim and the defendant's motivation in selecting that victim or committing the crime;[48] the defendant's aggravating or mitigating role in the offense, abuse of a position of trust or a special skill, or use of a minor to commit an offense;[49] and the defendant's obstruction of justice during the investigation, prosecution, or sentencing of the offense, or the defendant's reckless endangerment of others in fleeing from law enforcement.[50]

To return to our "real-offense" versus "charge-offense" discussion, the Guidelines' "charge-offense" elements are confined in their effect to the *beginning* and the *end* of the Guidelines calculation. At the *beginning* of a Guidelines calculation, one must first determine which Chapter Two guideline applies. The offense of conviction presumptively determines which Chapter Two guideline will control, and thus in most cases which base offense level and which specific offense characteristics apply.[51] However, the effect of the offense of conviction is tempered by the structure of the Chapter Two guidelines. The Commission attempted to group together like offenses into discrete Chapter Two guidelines. For example, it has provided one guideline (§2B1.1) to determine the base offense level for theft, embezzlement, receipt of stolen property, and property destruction, as well as the myriad offenses that are charged under statutes relating to fraud or deceit. Thus, in many cases, the prosecutor's decision to employ one code section rather than another (for example, mail fraud rather than bank fraud) may have little sentencing consequence. To illustrate, in 2017, approximately 85.4% of all federal criminal cases were sentenced under just a few guidelines relating to drug (30.8%), immigration (30.5%), firearms (12.1%) and white-collar (12%) offenses.[52]

The Commission, however, cannot alter the determinative effect of the count of conviction at the *end* of the Guidelines process because this effect is mandated by statute.[53] Thus, the floor below which the sentence may not go, regardless of the applicable sentencing range determined under the Guidelines, is set by any statutory mandatory minimum for the offense of conviction.[54] Similarly, the ceiling that the sentence may not exceed, again

---

[47] *Id.* (footnotes omitted).

[48] U.S.S.G. §§ 3A1.1 (Hate Crime Motivation or Vulnerable Victim), 3A1.2 (Official Victim), 3A1.3 (Restraint of Victim), 3A1.4 (Terrorism).

[49] *Id.* §§ 3B1.1 (Aggravating Role), 3B1.2 (Mitigating Role), 3B1.3 (Abuse of a Position of Trust or Use of Special Skill), 3B1.4 (Using a Minor to Commit a Crime); 3B1.5 (Use of Body Armor in Drug Trafficking Crimes and Crimes of Violence).

[50] *Id.* §§ 3C1.1 (Obstructing or Impeding the Administration of Justice), 3C1.2 (Reckless Endangerment During Flight); 3C1.3 (Commission of Offense While on Release).

[51] *See id.* § 1B1.1(a) & app. A.

[52] U.S. Sentencing Comm'n, 2017 Sourcebook, Fig. A; *see also* 2017 Sourcebook, Table 17 (Percentage of cases in which the following were the primary sentencing guideline used: 30.6% Drug Trafficking (§ 2D1.1), 25.3% under Unlawful Entry into the United States (§ 2L1.2), 10.1% under Fraud/Theft (§ 2B1.1), 10.1% under Firearms (§ 2K2.1), and 4.4% under Smuggling Unlawful Aliens (§ 2L1.1)).

[53] *See* 28 U.S.C. § 994(a) (Commission to promulgate guidelines and policy statements that are "consistent with all pertinent provisions of [title 28] and title 18, United States Code").

[54] *See* U.S.S.G. § 5G1.1 (statutory maximum and minimum sentences apply where different than applicable Guidelines range); *see also id.* § 5C1.2 (limitation on applicability of statutory minimum

regardless of the Guidelines' calculus, is set by the statutory maximum sentence prescribed for the offense of conviction by Congress. So, for example, if a Guidelines' calculation yields a range of about 10 years, but the prosecutor only chooses to charge one count of conspiracy, which carries a statutory maximum of 5 years, the sentencing court *cannot* sentence the defendant to any more than 5 years. Accordingly, prosecutors have some continuing power to affect sentence through their choice among potentially applicable code sections where those sections carry maximum or mandatory minimum sentences that trump the otherwise applicable Guidelines sentencing range. It is important to recognize that *Booker* does not affect these rules: that is, judges continue to be bound by the statutory maximums and minimums set by Congress.

The Guidelines introduce "real-offense" elements primarily through five mechanisms, many of which may require the consideration of non-conviction offense conduct: (1) Chapter Two's specific offense characteristics; (2) Chapter Three's adjustments to the defendant's offense level; (3) Chapter One's relevant conduct provision, which instructs courts on what conduct may be considered in determining the applicable base offense level, specific offense characteristics, and adjustments; (4) Chapter Three's grouping rules, which control the treatment of multi-count indictments; and (5) Chapter Four's rules for computing the defendant's criminal history category.

First, Chapter Two's specific offense characteristics instruct the sentencing judge to adjust the defendant's base offense level in light of the "real" circumstances of the crime. These circumstances may reflect uncharged criminal conduct that occurs in connection with the offense of conviction. Thus, for instance, a defendant may have his base offense level for a narcotics crime increased by two levels if the judge finds that a weapons-related specific offense characteristic applies. If the sentencing judge concludes by a preponderance of the evidence that "a dangerous weapon (including a firearm) was possessed"[55] during the commission of the drug violation, the defendant's offense level may be augmented even if the defendant was not charged with or was acquitted of using or carrying a firearm during a drug trafficking offense in violation of 18 U.S.C. § 924(c).

Once the Chapter Two offense level is determined by adding the applicable Chapter Two guideline's specific offense characteristics to the base offense level, one must determine whether any of the Chapter Three adjustments are appropriately assessed in a given case. Again, these adjustments allow for the enhancement of a defendant's offense level based upon uncharged criminal conduct that is connected to the conviction offense. For example, even if a defendant is not charged with obstruction of justice or perjury or is acquitted of such an offense, a judge who finds by a preponderance of the evidence that the defendant "willfully obstructed or impeded ... the administration of justice with respect to the investigation, prosecution, or sentencing" of the offense of conviction may increase the defendant's offense level by two levels.[56]

Now for the difficult part. Chapters Two and Three tell a court what factors—such as the possession of a gun during a drug crime or a defendant's obstructive conduct—should be considered in computing a sentence. Section 1B1.3's "relevant conduct" rules tell the court what conduct of the defendant or his accomplices may be considered in applying these factors. The relevant conduct rules have three principal dimensions: the temporal dimension; the accomplice attribution dimension; and the "third" dimension.[57]

---

sentences in certain cases pursuant to 18 U.S.C. § 3553(e), (f)).

[55] U.S.S.G. § 2D1.1(b)(1).

[56] *Id.* § 3C1.1; *see, e.g.,* United States v. Akitoye, 923 F.2d 221, 228-29 (1st Cir.1991) (upholding two-point adjustment for obstruction of justice under § 3C1.1 where defendant perjured himself by denying the offense conduct on the stand at trial); *see also* United States v. Dunnigan, 507 U.S. 87, 96 (1993) (rejecting the claim that allowing sentencing adjustment for perjury chilled the exercise of the defendant's Sixth Amendment right to testify on her own behalf).

[57] William W. Wilkins, Jr. & John R. Steer, *Relevant Conduct: The Cornerstone of the Federal Sentencing Guidelines,* 41 S.C. L. Rev. 495, 503-17 (1990).

The first, temporal, dimension of relevant conduct "focuses on offense conduct as a moving picture that begins with acts in preparation for the offense and, for some purposes such as assessing whether the defendant obstructed justice or accepted responsibility for his or her conduct, extends to the time of sentencing."[58] Thus, the conduct that may be considered by a judge in applying Chapters Two and Three includes actions "that occurred during the commission of the offense of conviction, in preparation for that offense, or in the course of attempting to avoid detection or responsibility for that offense."[59]

The second, or accomplice attribution, dimension of relevant conduct provides that a defendant is responsible not only for "all acts and omissions committed, aided, abetted, counseled, commanded, induced, procured, or willfully caused by the defendant,"[60] but also all acts and omissions of others that were "within the scope of the jointly undertaken criminal activity," "in furtherance of that activity," and "reasonably foreseeable in connection with that criminal activity." This means that the defendant may be responsible for the conduct of others if that conduct was in furtherance of a criminal plan undertaken by the defendant in concert with others and was reasonably foreseeable in connection with the criminal activity the defendant agreed to undertake.[61] It should be noted that a defendant's sentencing liability for "jointly undertaken" relevant conduct considered at sentencing is not as expansive as that which the defendant may be held accountable for at trial under *United States v. Pinkerton*,[62] which is discussed, *infra*, in the Conspiracy Chapter. The Sentencing Commission recently amended the guidelines in an effort to emphasize that a defendant can only be liable for the actions of coconspirators when those acts are within the scope of the criminal activity that the *defendant agreed to jointly undertake*. The accomplice attribution dimension, then, permits the judge to consider, in sentencing a defendant on the count of conviction, an uncharged conspiracy and any reasonably foreseeable uncharged criminal actions on the part of all co-conspirators in furtherance of the criminal activity the defendant agreed to jointly undertake.

The "third" dimension of relevant conduct, contained within § 1B1.3(a)(2), is defined by reference to the Guidelines' "grouping" rules.[63] The Sentencing Chart obviously contemplates that a defendant will have only one Offense Level even though the indictment under which he is being sentenced may contain many counts. The Chapter Three grouping rules suggest how the sentencing judge may arrive at a single offense level for a defendant convicted of more than one count. In these rules, the Commission sought a way to distinguish between (1) situations in which multi-count indictments contained charges so closely intertwined—in terms of harm caused, victims affected, and temporal proximity—that the Guidelines range should not be higher for the multiple counts than it would be for a single count, and (2) situations in which the multiple counts concerned discrete harms that warranted additional punishment. For the

---

[58] *Id.* at 504.

[59] U.S.S.G. § 1B1.3(a)(1).

[60] *Id.* § 1B1.3(a)(1)(A).

[61] *Id.* § 1B1.3(a)(1)(B); *see also id.* § 1B1.3, comment. n.2.

[62] 328 U.S. 640 (1946); *see* United States v. Davison, 761 F.3d 683 (7th Cir. 2014).

[63] Section 1B1.3(a)(2) states that, in determining the applicable base offense levels, specific offense characteristics and cross-references of Chapter Two or the adjustments of Chapter Three, the judge consider, "solely with respect to offenses of a character for which § 3D1.2(d) would require grouping of multiple counts, all acts and omissions described in subdivisions (1)(A) ["all acts and omissions committed, aided, abetted, counseled, commanded, induced, procured, or willfully caused by the defendant"] and (1)(B) [relating to jointly undertaken criminal activity] above that were part of the same course of conduct or common scheme or plan as the offense of conviction." *Id.* § 1B1.3(a)(2). Section 3D1.2(d) provides that counts should be grouped for purposes of determining the offense level applicable to multi-count indictments "[w]hen the offense level is determined largely on the basis of the total amount of harm or loss, the quantity of a substance involved, or some other measure of aggregate harm, or if the offense behavior is ongoing or continuous in nature and the offense guideline is written to cover such behavior." *Id.* § 3D1.2(d).

latter group of defendants, the Commission sought to increase the defendant's punishment for the multiple criminal transactions, victims, or harms charged in a way that would fairly reflect the defendant's increased culpability but that would result in a less than proportional rate of increase in sentencing exposure for each additional transaction, victim, or harm.

Most important for present purposes, the Commission sought in the grouping rules to minimize the effect that prosecutors could have on the eventual sentence by multiplying the charges brought. Thus, for example, it sought to avoid a situation in which a prosecutor could ensure greater sentencing exposure by breaking up what was essentially a single fraud into multiple counts by charging each and every mailing in furtherance of that single scheme to defraud. In attempting to dampen the effects of prosecutorial charging and plea choices, the Commission drew a distinction in these rules between "aggregable" offenses, which should be grouped, and "non-aggregable" offenses, which are not grouped.

"Aggregable" offenses are those in which the harm caused by the defendant's conduct is based upon the amount of money or quantity of substance involved, or which involve a repetitive or continuous course of conduct.[64] Such crimes include most financial (fraud) crimes, drug offenses, firearms violations, and property crimes (except armed robberies, burglary, and extortion).[65] Where multiple counts of conviction charge such aggregable crimes, the grouping rules total the fungible items (*e.g.*, dollar amount or quantity of drugs) and punish the offender as if there were a single count involving the total amount.[66] "Since the Commission's punishments for most drug and money crimes are determined by tables that increase punishment at a rate less than proportional to the amount of drugs or money, collapsing the counts and using the tables [means that] the punishment increases, but at a less than proportional rate."[67]

"Non-aggregable" offenses, by contrast, generally involve discrete harms attributable to "single episodes of criminal behavior,"[68] such as violent offenses, robberies, burglaries, extortions, and immigration offenses. These offenses are not "grouped" and thus treated as one count, but through operation of the grouping rules, the same result is achieved. A punishment scale is assigned to these discrete offenses which yields an offense level that is higher than, but not a multiple of, the offense levels applicable to the non-aggregable offenses taken singly.[69] For example, the Guidelines dictate that a defendant convicted of six bank robberies receive more punishment than a defendant convicted of one robbery, but not six times more punishment.

The Commission defines the "third dimension" of relevant conduct by reference to these grouping rules. The relevant conduct rules and the grouping rules apparently are, in theory, designed to complement each other, with the goal of together reducing the effect of prosecutorial charging choices. Where the grouping rules ensure that a prosecutor cannot secure a more severe sentence by bringing a variety of "aggregable" counts, the relevant conduct rules prevent a prosecutor from obtaining a more lenient sentence by failing to charge or dismissing related "aggregable" counts. Thus, § 1B1.3(a)(2) states that where a defendant commits "aggregable" crimes as part of the same course of conduct or common scheme or plan as the offense of conviction, the other crimes should be considered—whether or not they were charged or proved at trial—in determining the appropriate Chapter Two offense level and specific offense characteristics and Chapter Three adjustments.[70] Given that aggregable

---

[64] *See id.* (discussing grouping rules).

[65] *See id.* § 3D1.2(d) & comment. n.6.

[66] *See id.*

[67] Stephen Breyer, *The Federal Sentencing Guidelines and the Key Compromises Upon Which They Rest*, 17 Hofstra L. Rev. 1, 25-28 (1988).

[68] U.S.S.G. ch. 3, pt. D., former intro. comment. (2004).

[69] *See id.* §§ 3D1.2-3D1.4.

[70] *See id.* § 1B1.3, comment. n.3.

offenses constitute the vast majority of federal cases sentenced, this interaction between the grouping and relevant conduct rules is designed, in a great many cases, substantially to reduce the effect of prosecutorial charging or plea bargaining choices.

To illustrate the interplay between the grouping and relevant conduct rules, assume that a defendant defrauds ten victims of approximately $1,000 each pursuant to a single ongoing scheme for a total loss of $10,000. In furtherance of the fraud, the defendant made ten mailings through the United States Postal Service. If the prosecutor chose to bring *ten* counts of mail fraud against the defendant, and the defendant were convicted, those ten counts should be grouped under § 3D1.2(d) because the offense level for fraud is determined largely on the basis of the total loss, and mail fraud is thus an aggregable offense. If the judge were to follow the Guidelines, the defendant's sentence would be determined by assessing the sentence that would be appropriate for $10,000 in losses under the fraud guideline. If the prosecutor chooses to bring only *one* count of mail fraud based on one of the mailings, the relevant conduct provision of § 1B1.3(a)(2) would permit the amounts garnered through the nine other related acts of fraud to be considered as relevant conduct in determining the defendant's offense level, *even though those acts were not charged or proved at trial*. Thus, the defendant's sentence could (again) be determined by factoring a loss of $10,000 (not just $1,000) into the fraud guideline. The linkage of the relevant conduct rules to the grouping rules in aggregable crime cases means (in theory) that *whether ten mailings are charged or simply one, the sentence available under the Guidelines would be the same*.

The symmetry of the relevant conduct and grouping rules breaks down, however, when non-aggregable offenses are considered. The grouping rules contemplate that additional, proportionate punishment will be imposed where a number of such non-aggregable offenses are charged. If the non-aggregable counts are not charged, however, the Guidelines do not contemplate that the defendant will receive these added increments of punishment because the third dimension of relevant conduct does not apply to non-aggregable offenses, regardless of their nexus to the offense of conviction. For example, assume that a defendant commits three (non-aggregable) bank robberies as a part of a common scheme or plan, but is charged with and convicted of only *one* count of robbery. The circumstances of the other crimes may *not* be considered as relevant conduct under § 1B1.3(a)(2) in determining the Chapter Two offense level or specific offense characteristics or the applicable Chapter Three adjustments because robbery is a "non-aggregable" offense that is not grouped under § 3D1.2(d). If a judge decides to follow the Guidelines, then, it is only where all three robberies are charged that the defendant will be treated in line with other similarly situated defendants and receive a proportional increase in his punishment through the operation of the grouping rules (absent a departure). Once the defendant's offense level is determined by employing the above rules, one then turns to the other principal determinant of the defendant's Guidelines range: his or her criminal history category. Because the defendant's criminal history is not normally an element of federal offenses, it is another important "real" element of Guidelines calculations. The defendant's criminal history category is determined by scoring the frequency, recency, and seriousness of the defendant's prior convictions, and may be augmented where a defendant is deemed a "career offender."[71]

In evaluating the Guidelines' modified real-offense compromise sketched out above, it may be helpful for students to understand how the Commission determined what "real" elements to select and how to weight those elements. As the Commission explained in its original introduction to the Guidelines:

> ... [The Commission took] an empirical approach that used as a starting point data estimating pre-guidelines sentencing practice. It analyzed data drawn from 10,000 presentence investigations, the differing elements of various crimes as distinguished in substantive criminal statutes, the United States Parole Commission's guidelines and statistics, and data from other relevant sources in order to determine which distinctions were important in pre-guidelines

---

[71] *See id.* § 4B1.1.

practice. After consideration, the Commission accepted, modified, or rationalized these distinctions.

This empirical approach helped the Commission solve its practical problem by defining a list of relevant distinctions that, although of considerable length, was short enough to create a manageable set of guidelines. Existing categories are relatively broad and omit distinctions that some may believe important, yet they include most of the major distinctions that statutes and data suggest made a significant difference in sentencing decisions. Relevant distinctions not reflected in the guidelines probably will occur rarely and sentencing courts may take such unusual cases into account by departing from the guidelines.

The Commission's empirical approach also helped resolve [a] philosophical dilemma. Those who adhere to a just deserts philosophy may concede that the lack of consensus might make it difficult to say exactly what punishment is deserved for a particular crime. Likewise, those who subscribe to a philosophy of crime control may acknowledge that the lack of sufficient data might make it difficult to determine exactly the punishment that will best prevent that crime. Both groups might therefore recognize the wisdom of looking to those distinctions that judges and legislators have, in fact, made over the course of time. These established distinctions are ones that the community believes, or has found over time, to be important from either a just deserts or crime control perspective.

The Commission did not simply copy estimates of pre-guidelines practice as revealed by the data, even though establishing offense values on this basis would help eliminate disparity because the data represent averages. Rather, it departed from the data at different points for various important reasons. ... [For example,] the data revealed inconsistencies in treatment, such a punishing economic crime less seriously than other apparently equivalent behavior.[72]

It should also be noted that many commentators take issue not only with the results of the Commission's empirical work, but also with its methodology in conducting that work.

C. CONSTITUTIONAL ANALYSIS

UNITED STATES v. BOOKER
543 U.S. 220 (2005)

JUSTICE STEVENS delivered the opinion of the Court in part.[73]

The question presented in each of these cases is whether an application of the Federal Sentencing Guidelines violated the Sixth Amendment. In each case, the courts below held that binding rules set forth in the Guidelines limited the severity of the sentence that the judge could lawfully impose on the defendant based on the facts found by the jury at his trial. In both cases the courts rejected, on the basis of our decision in *Blakely v. Washington*, 542 U.S. 296 (2004), the Government's recommended application of the Sentencing Guidelines because the proposed sentences were based on additional facts that the sentencing judge found by a preponderance of the evidence. We hold that both courts correctly concluded that the Sixth Amendment as construed in *Blakely* does apply to the Sentencing Guidelines. In a separate opinion authored by Justice BREYER, the Court concludes that in light of this holding, two provisions of the Sentencing Reform Act of 1984 (SRA) that have the effect of making the Guidelines mandatory must be invalidated in order to allow the statute to operate in a manner consistent with congressional intent.

---

[72] *Id.* ch.1, pt.A, former intro. comment. (1987).

[73] Justice SCALIA, Justice SOUTER, Justice THOMAS, and Justice GINSBURG join this opinion.

I

Respondent Booker was charged with possession with intent to distribute at least 50 grams of cocaine base (crack). Having heard evidence that he had 92.5 grams in his duffel bag, the jury found him guilty of violating 21 U.S.C. § 841(a)(1). That statute prescribes a minimum sentence of 10 years in prison and a maximum sentence of life for that offense. § 841(b)(1)(A)(iii).

Based upon Booker's criminal history and the quantity of drugs found by the jury, the Sentencing Guidelines required the District Court Judge to select a "base" sentence of not less than 210 nor more than 262 months in prison. See United States Sentencing Commission, Guidelines Manual §§ 2D1.1(c)(4), 4A1.1 (Nov.2003) (hereinafter USSG). The judge, however, held a post-trial sentencing proceeding and concluded by a preponderance of the evidence that Booker had possessed an additional 566 grams of crack and that he was guilty of obstructing justice. Those findings mandated that the judge select a sentence between 360 months and life imprisonment; the judge imposed a sentence at the low end of the range. Thus, instead of the sentence of 21 years and 10 months that the judge could have imposed on the basis of the facts proved to the jury beyond a reasonable doubt, Booker received a 30-year sentence.

Over the dissent of Judge Easterbrook, the Court of Appeals for the Seventh Circuit held that this application of the Sentencing Guidelines conflicted with our holding in *Apprendi v. New Jersey*, 530 U.S. 466, 490 (2000), that "[o]ther than the fact of a prior conviction, any fact that increases the penalty for a crime beyond the prescribed statutory maximum must be submitted to a jury, and proved beyond a reasonable doubt." The majority relied on our holding in *Blakely v. Washington*, 542 U.S. 296 (2004), that "the 'statutory maximum' for *Apprendi* purposes is the maximum sentence a judge may impose *solely on the basis of the facts reflected in the jury verdict or admitted by the defendant*." The court held that the sentence violated the Sixth Amendment, and remanded with instructions to the District Court either to sentence respondent within the sentencing range supported by the jury's findings or to hold a separate sentencing hearing before a jury.

Respondent Fanfan was charged with conspiracy to distribute and to possess with intent to distribute at least 500 grams of cocaine in violation of 21 U.S.C. §§ 846, 841(a)(1), and 841(b)(1)(B)(ii). He was convicted by the jury after it answered "Yes" to the question "Was the amount of cocaine 500 or more grams?" Under the Guidelines, without additional findings of fact, the maximum sentence authorized by the jury verdict was imprisonment for 78 months.

A few days after our decision in *Blakely,* the trial judge conducted a sentencing hearing at which he found additional facts that, under the Guidelines, would have authorized a sentence in the 188-to-235 month range. Specifically, he found that respondent Fanfan was responsible for 2.5 kilograms of cocaine powder, and 261.6 grams of crack. He also concluded that respondent had been an organizer, leader, manager, or supervisor in the criminal activity. Both findings were made by a preponderance of the evidence. Under the Guidelines, these additional findings would have required an enhanced sentence of 15 or 16 years instead of the 5 or 6 years authorized by the jury verdict alone. Relying not only on the majority opinion in *Blakely,* but also on the categorical statements in the dissenting opinions and in the Solicitor General's brief in *Blakely,* the judge concluded that he could not follow the particular provisions of the Sentencing Guidelines "which involve drug quantity and role enhancement." Expressly refusing to make "any blanket decision about the federal guidelines," he followed the provisions of the Guidelines that did not implicate the Sixth Amendment by imposing a sentence on respondent "based solely upon the guilty verdict in this case."

Following the denial of its motion to correct the sentence in Fanfan's case, the Government filed a notice of appeal in the Court of Appeals for the First Circuit, and a petition in this Court for a writ of certiorari before judgment. Because of the importance of the questions presented, we granted that petition, as well as a similar petition filed by the Government in Booker's case. In both petitions, the Government asks us to determine whether our *Apprendi* line of cases applies to the Sentencing Guidelines, and if so, what portions of the Guidelines remain in effect.[74]

In this opinion, we explain why we agree with the lower courts' answer to the first question. In a separate opinion for the Court, Justice BREYER explains the Court's answer to the second question.

II

It has been settled throughout our history that the Constitution protects every criminal defendant "against conviction except upon proof beyond a reasonable doubt of every fact necessary to constitute the crime with which he is charged." *In re Winship,* 397 U.S. 358, 364 (1970). It is equally clear that the "Constitution gives a criminal defendant the right to demand that a jury find him guilty of all the elements of the crime with which he is charged." *United States v. Gaudin,* 515 U.S. 506, 511 (1995). These basic precepts, firmly rooted in the common law, have provided the basis for recent decisions interpreting modern criminal statutes and sentencing procedures.

In *Jones v. United States,* 526 U.S. 227, 230 (1999), we considered the federal carjacking statute, which provides three different maximum sentences depending on the extent of harm to the victim: 15 years in jail if there was no serious injury to a victim, 25 years if there was "serious bodily injury," and life in prison if death resulted. 18 U.S.C. § 2119. In spite of the fact that the statute "at first glance has a look to it suggesting [that the provisions relating to the extent of harm to the victim] are only sentencing provisions," we concluded that the harm to the victim was an element of the crime. That conclusion was supported by the statutory text and structure, and was influenced by our desire to avoid the constitutional issues implicated by a contrary holding, which would have reduced the jury's role "to the relative importance of low-level gatekeeping." Foreshadowing the result we reach today, we noted that our holding was consistent with a "rule requiring jury determination of facts that raise a sentencing ceiling" in state and federal sentencing guidelines systems.

In *Apprendi v. New Jersey,* 530 U.S. 466 (2000), the defendant pleaded guilty to second-degree possession of a firearm for an unlawful purpose, which carried a prison term of 5-to-10 years. Thereafter, the trial court found that his conduct had violated New Jersey's "hate crime" law because it was racially motivated, and imposed a 12-year sentence. This Court set aside the enhanced sentence. We held: "Other than the fact of a prior conviction, any fact that increases the penalty for a crime beyond the prescribed statutory maximum must be submitted to a jury, and proved beyond a reasonable doubt."

The fact that New Jersey labeled the hate crime a "sentence enhancement" rather than a separate criminal act was irrelevant for constitutional purposes. As a matter of simple justice, it seemed obvious that the procedural safeguards designed to protect Apprendi from punishment for the possession of a firearm should apply equally to his violation of the hate crime statute. Merely using the label "sentence enhancement" to describe the latter did not provide a principled basis for treating the two crimes differently.

In *Ring v. Arizona,* 536 U.S. 584 (2002), we reaffirmed our conclusion that the characterization of critical facts is constitutionally irrelevant. There, we held that it was

---

[74] [Court's note 1:] The questions presented are:

"1. Whether the Sixth Amendment is violated by the imposition of an enhanced sentence under the United States Sentencing Guidelines based on the sentencing judge's determination of a fact (other than a prior conviction) that was not found by the jury or admitted by the defendant.

"2. If the answer to the first question is 'yes,' the following question is presented: whether, in a case in which the Guidelines would require the court to find a sentence-enhancing fact, the Sentencing Guidelines as a whole would be inapplicable, as a matter of severability analysis, such that the sentencing court must exercise its discretion to sentence the defendant within the maximum and minimum set by statute for the offense of conviction."

impermissible for "the trial judge, sitting alone" to determine the presence or absence of the aggravating factors required by Arizona law for imposition of the death penalty. "If a State makes an increase in a defendant's authorized punishment contingent on the finding of a fact, that fact—no matter how the State labels it—must be found by a jury beyond a reasonable doubt." Our opinion made it clear that ultimately, while the procedural error in Ring's case might have been harmless because the necessary finding was implicit in the jury's guilty verdict, "the characterization of a fact or circumstance as an 'element' or a 'sentencing factor' is not determinative of the question 'who decides,' judge or jury."

In *Blakely v. Washington*, 542 U.S. 220 (2004), we dealt with a determinate sentencing scheme similar to the Federal Sentencing Guidelines. There the defendant pleaded guilty to kidnaping, a class B felony punishable by a term of not more than 10 years. Other provisions of Washington law, comparable to the Federal Sentencing Guidelines, mandated a "standard" sentence of 49-to-53 months, unless the judge found aggravating facts justifying an exceptional sentence. Although the prosecutor recommended a sentence in the standard range, the judge found that the defendant had acted with "'deliberate cruelty'" and sentenced him to 90 months.

For reasons explained in *Jones, Apprendi,* and *Ring,* the requirements of the Sixth Amendment were clear. The application of Washington's sentencing scheme violated the defendant's right to have the jury find the existence of "'any particular fact'" that the law makes essential to his punishment. That right is implicated whenever a judge seeks to impose a sentence that is not solely based on "facts reflected in the jury verdict or admitted by the defendant." We rejected the State's argument that the jury verdict was sufficient to authorize a sentence within the general 10-year sentence for Class B felonies, noting that under Washington law, the judge was *required* to find additional facts in order to impose the greater 90-month sentence. Our precedents, we explained, make clear "that the 'statutory maximum' for *Apprendi* purposes is the maximum sentence a judge may impose *solely on the basis of the facts reflected in the jury verdict or admitted by the defendant.*" (emphasis in original). The determination that the defendant acted with deliberate cruelty, like the determination in *Apprendi* that the defendant acted with racial malice, increased the sentence that the defendant could have otherwise received. Since this fact was found by a judge using a preponderance of the evidence standard, the sentence violated Blakely's Sixth Amendment rights.

As the dissenting opinions in *Blakely* recognized, there is no distinction of constitutional significance between the Federal Sentencing Guidelines and the Washington procedures at issue in that case. See, *e.g.,* 542 U.S., at 308 (opinion of O'CONNOR, J.) ("The structure of the Federal Guidelines likewise does not, as the Government half-heartedly suggests, provide any grounds for distinction. ... If anything, the structural differences that do exist make the Federal Guidelines more vulnerable to attack"). This conclusion rests on the premise, common to both systems, that the relevant sentencing rules are mandatory and impose binding requirements on all sentencing judges.

If the Guidelines as currently written could be read as merely advisory provisions that recommended, rather than required, the selection of particular sentences in response to differing sets of facts, their use would not implicate the Sixth Amendment. We have never doubted the authority of a judge to exercise broad discretion in imposing a sentence within a statutory range. See *Apprendi,* 530 U.S., at 481; *Williams v. New York,* 337 U.S. 241, 246 (1949). Indeed, everyone agrees that the constitutional issues presented by these cases would have been avoided entirely if Congress had omitted from the SRA the provisions that make the Guidelines binding on district judges; it is that circumstance that makes the Court's answer to the second question presented possible. For when a trial judge exercises his discretion to select a specific sentence within a defined range, the defendant has no right to a jury determination of the facts that the judge deems relevant.

The Guidelines as written, however, are not advisory; they are mandatory and binding on all judges. While subsection (a) of § 3553 of the sentencing statute lists the Sentencing Guidelines as one factor to be considered in imposing a sentence, subsection (b) directs that the court "*shall* impose a sentence of the kind, and within the range" established by the Guidelines, subject to departures in specific, limited cases. Because they are binding on judges, we have consistently held that the Guidelines have the force and effect of laws.

The availability of a departure in specified circumstances does not avoid the constitutional issue, just as it did not in *Blakely* itself. The Guidelines permit departures from the prescribed sentencing range in cases in which the judge "finds that there exists an aggravating or mitigating circumstance of a kind, or to a degree, not adequately taken into consideration by the Sentencing Commission in formulating the guidelines that should result in a sentence different from that described." 18 U.S.C.A. § 3553(b)(1). At first glance, one might believe that the ability of a district judge to depart from the Guidelines means that she is bound only by the statutory maximum. Were this the case, there would be no *Apprendi* problem. Importantly, however, departures are not available in every case, and in fact are unavailable in most. In most cases, as a matter of law, the Commission will have adequately taken all relevant factors into account, and no departure will be legally permissible. In those instances, the judge is bound to impose a sentence within the Guidelines range. It was for this reason that we rejected a similar argument in *Blakely*, holding that although the Washington statute allowed the judge to impose a sentence outside the sentencing range for "'substantial and compelling reasons,'" that exception was not available for Blakely himself. The sentencing judge would have been reversed had he invoked the departure section to justify the sentence.

Booker's case illustrates the mandatory nature of the Guidelines. The jury convicted him of possessing at least 50 grams of crack in violation of 21 U.S.C. § 841(b)(1)(A)(iii) based on evidence that he had 92.5 grams of crack in his duffel bag. Under these facts, the Guidelines specified an offense level of 32, which, given the defendant's criminal history category, authorized a sentence of 210-to-262 months. See USSG § 2D1.1(c)(4). Booker's is a run-of-the-mill drug case, and does not present any factors that were inadequately considered by the Commission. The sentencing judge would therefore have been reversed had he not imposed a sentence within the level 32 Guidelines range.

Booker's actual sentence, however, was 360 months, almost 10 years longer than the Guidelines range supported by the jury verdict alone. To reach this sentence, the judge found facts beyond those found by the jury: namely, that Booker possessed 566 grams of crack in addition to the 92.5 grams in his duffel bag. The jury never heard any evidence of the additional drug quantity, and the judge found it true by a preponderance of the evidence. Thus, just as in *Blakely*, "the jury's verdict alone does not authorize the sentence. The judge acquires that authority only upon finding some additional fact." There is no relevant distinction between the sentence imposed pursuant to the Washington statutes in *Blakely* and the sentences imposed pursuant to the Federal Sentencing Guidelines in these cases.

In his dissent, Justice BREYER argues on historical grounds that the Guidelines scheme is constitutional across the board. He points to traditional judicial authority to increase sentences to take account of any unusual blameworthiness in the manner employed in committing a crime, an authority that the Guidelines require to be exercised consistently throughout the system. This tradition, however, does not provide a sound guide to enforcement of the Sixth Amendment's guarantee of a jury trial in today's world.

It is quite true that once determinate sentencing had fallen from favor, American judges commonly determined facts justifying a choice of a heavier sentence on account of the manner in which particular defendants acted. In 1986, however, our own cases first recognized a new trend in the legislative regulation of sentencing when we considered the significance of facts selected by legislatures that not only authorized, or even mandated, heavier sentences than would otherwise have been imposed, but increased the range of sentences possible for the underlying crime. See *McMillan v. Pennsylvania*, 477 U.S. 79, 87-88 (1986). Provisions for such enhancements of the permissible sentencing range reflected growing and wholly justified legislative concern about the proliferation and variety of drug crimes and their frequent identification with firearms offences.

The effect of the increasing emphasis on facts that enhanced sentencing ranges, however, was to increase the judge's power and diminish that of the jury. It became the judge, not the jury, that determined the upper limits of sentencing, and the facts determined were not required to be raised before trial or proved by more than a preponderance.

As the enhancements became greater, the jury's finding of the underlying crime became less significant. And the enhancements became very serious indeed. See, *e.g.*, *Jones*, 526 U.S., at 230 (judge's finding increased the maximum sentence from 15 to 25 years); respondent Booker (from 262 months to a life sentence).

As it thus became clear that sentencing was no longer taking place in the tradition that Justice BREYER invokes, the Court was faced with the issue of preserving an ancient guarantee under a new set of circumstances. The new sentencing practice forced the Court to address the question how the right of jury trial could be preserved, in a meaningful way guaranteeing that the jury would still stand between the individual and the power of the government under the new sentencing regime. And it is the new circumstances, not a tradition or practice that the new circumstances have superseded, that have led us to the answer first considered in *Jones* and developed in *Apprendi* and subsequent cases culminating with this one. It is an answer not motivated by Sixth Amendment formalism, but by the need to preserve Sixth Amendment substance.

III

...

The Government ... argues that four recent cases preclude our application of *Blakely* to the Sentencing Guidelines. We disagree. In *United States v. Dunnigan,* 507 U.S. 87 (1993), we held that the provisions of the Guidelines that require a sentence enhancement if the judge determines that the defendant committed perjury do not violate the privilege of the accused to testify on her own behalf. There was no contention that the enhancement was invalid because it resulted in a more severe sentence than the jury verdict had authorized. Accordingly, we found this case indistinguishable from *United States v. Grayson,* 438 U.S. 41 (1978), a pre-Guidelines case in which we upheld a similar sentence increase. Applying *Blakely* to the Guidelines would invalidate a sentence that relied on such an enhancement if the resulting sentence was outside the range authorized by the jury verdict. Nevertheless, there are many situations in which the district judge might find that the enhancement is warranted, yet still sentence the defendant within the range authorized by the jury. Thus, while the reach of *Dunnigan* may be limited, we need not overrule it.

In *Witte v. United States,* 515 U.S. 389 (1995), we held that the Double Jeopardy Clause did not bar a prosecution for conduct that had provided the basis for an enhancement of the defendant's sentence in a prior case. "We concluded that "consideration of information about the defendant's character and conduct at sentencing does not result in 'punishment' for any offense other than the one of which the defendant was convicted." Rather, the defendant is 'punished only for the fact that the present offense was carried out in a manner that warrants increased punishment ....'" *United States v. Watts,* 519 U.S. 148, 155 (1997) *(per curiam)* (emphasis omitted) (quoting *Witte,* 515 U.S., at 415, 401, 403). In *Watts,* relying on *Witte,* we held that the Double Jeopardy Clause permitted a court to consider acquitted conduct in sentencing a defendant under the Guidelines. In neither *Witte* nor *Watts* was there any contention that the sentencing enhancement had exceeded the sentence authorized by the jury verdict in violation of the Sixth Amendment. The issue we confront today simply was not presented. ...

None of our prior cases is inconsistent with today's decision. *Stare decisis* does not compel us to limit *Blakely*'s holding. ...

IV

All of the foregoing support our conclusion that our holding in *Blakely* applies to the Sentencing Guidelines. We recognize, as we did in *Jones, Apprendi,* and *Blakely,* that in some cases jury factfinding may impair the most expedient and efficient sentencing of defendants. But the interest in fairness and reliability protected by the right to a jury trial—a common-law right that defendants enjoyed for centuries and that is now enshrined in the Sixth Amendment—has always outweighed the interest in concluding trials swiftly. As Blackstone put it:

"[H]owever *convenient* these [new methods of trial] may appear at first (as doubtless all arbitrary powers, well executed, are the most *convenient*) yet let it be again remembered, that delays, and little inconveniences in the forms of justice, are the price that all free nations must pay for their liberty in more substantial matters; that these inroads upon this sacred bulwark of the nation are fundamentally opposite to the spirit of our constitution; and that, though begun in trifles, the precedent may gradually increase and spread, to the utter disuse of juries in questions of the most momentous concerns."

Accordingly, we reaffirm our holding in *Apprendi*: Any fact (other than a prior conviction) which is necessary to support a sentence exceeding the maximum authorized by the facts established by a plea of guilty or a jury verdict must be admitted by the defendant or proved to a jury beyond a reasonable doubt.

Justice BREYER delivered the opinion of the Court in part.[75] ...

The Court, in an opinion by Justice STEVENS, answers [the first question presented] ... in the affirmative. Applying its decisions in *Apprendi v. New Jersey*, 530 U.S. 466 (2000), and *Blakely v. Washington*, 542 U.S. 220 (2004), to the Federal Sentencing Guidelines, the Court holds that, in the circumstances mentioned, the Sixth Amendment requires juries, not judges, to find facts relevant to sentencing.

We here turn to the second question presented, a question that concerns the remedy. We must decide whether or to what extent, "as a matter of severability analysis," the Guidelines "as a whole" are "inapplicable ... such that the sentencing court must exercise its discretion to sentence the defendant within the maximum and minimum set by statute for the offense of conviction."

We answer the question of remedy by finding the provision of the federal sentencing statute that makes the Guidelines mandatory, 18 U.S.C.A. § 3553(b)(1), incompatible with today's constitutional holding. We conclude that this provision must be severed and excised, as must one other statutory section, § 3742(e), which depends upon the Guidelines' mandatory nature. So modified, the Federal Sentencing Act, see Sentencing Reform Act of 1984, as amended, 18 U.S.C. § 3551 *et seq.*, 28 U.S.C. § 991 *et seq.*, makes the Guidelines effectively advisory. It requires a sentencing court to consider Guidelines ranges, see 18 U.S.C.A. § 3553(a)(4), but it permits the court to tailor the sentence in light of other statutory concerns as well, see § 3553(a).

I

We answer the remedial question by looking to legislative intent. We seek to determine what "Congress would have intended" in light of the Court's constitutional holding. In this instance, we must determine which of the two following remedial approaches is the more compatible with the legislature's intent as embodied in the 1984 Sentencing Act.

One approach, that of Justice STEVENS' dissent, would retain the Sentencing Act (and the Guidelines) as written, but would engraft onto the existing system today's Sixth Amendment "jury trial" requirement. The addition would change the Guidelines by preventing the sentencing court from increasing a sentence on the basis of a fact that the jury did not find (or that the offender did not admit).

The other approach, which we now adopt, would (through severance and excision of two provisions) make the Guidelines system advisory while maintaining a strong connection between the sentence imposed and the offender's real conduct—a connection important to the increased uniformity of sentencing that Congress intended its Guidelines system to achieve.

Both approaches would significantly alter the system that Congress designed. But today's constitutional holding means that it is no longer possible to maintain the judicial factfinding

---

[75] The CHIEF JUSTICE,, Justice O'CONNOR, Justice KENNEDY, and Justice GINSBURG join this opinion.

that Congress thought would underpin the mandatory Guidelines system that it sought to create and that Congress wrote into the Act in 18 U.S.C.A. §§ 3553(a) and 3661. Hence we must decide whether we would deviate less radically from Congress' intended system (1) by superimposing the constitutional requirement announced today or (2) through elimination of some provisions of the statute. ...

II

... [W]ere the Court's constitutional requirement added onto the Sentencing Act as currently written, the requirement would so transform the scheme that Congress created that Congress likely would not have intended the Act as so modified to stand. ...

... Congress' basic statutory goal—a system that diminishes sentencing disparity—depends for its success upon judicial efforts to determine, and to base punishment upon, the *real conduct* that underlies the crime of conviction. That determination is particularly important in the federal system where crimes defined as, for example, "obstruct[ing], delay[ing], or affect[ing] commerce or the movement of any article or commodity in commerce, by ... extortion," 18 U.S.C. § 1951(a), or, say, using the mail "for the purpose of executing" a "scheme or artifice to defraud," § 1341, can encompass a vast range of very different kinds of underlying conduct. But it is also important even in respect to ordinary crimes, such as robbery, where an act that meets the statutory definition can be committed in a host of different ways. Judges have long looked to real conduct when sentencing. Federal judges have long relied upon a presentence report, prepared by a probation officer, for information (often unavailable until *after* the trial) relevant to the manner in which the convicted offender committed the crime of conviction.

Congress expected this system to continue. That is why it specifically inserted into the Act the provision cited above, which (recodifying prior law) says that

> "[n]o limitation shall be placed on the information concerning the background, character, and conduct of a person convicted of an offense which a court of the United States may receive and consider for the purpose of imposing an appropriate sentence." 18 U.S.C. § 3661.

This Court's earlier opinions assumed that this system would continue. That is why the Court, for example, held in *United States v. Watts*, 519 U.S. 148 (1997) (*per curiam*), that a sentencing judge could rely for sentencing purposes upon a fact that a jury had found *unproved* (beyond a reasonable doubt).

The Sentencing Guidelines also assume that Congress intended this system to continue. That is why, among other things, they permit a judge to reject a plea-bargained sentence if he determines, after reviewing the presentence report, that the sentence does not adequately reflect the seriousness of the defendant's actual conduct. See § 6B1.2(a).

To engraft the Court's constitutional requirement onto the sentencing statutes, however, would destroy the system. It would prevent a judge from relying upon a presentence report for factual information, relevant to sentencing, uncovered after the trial. In doing so, it would, even compared to pre-Guidelines sentencing, weaken the tie between a sentence and an offender's real conduct. It would thereby undermine the sentencing statute's basic aim of ensuring similar sentences for those who have committed similar crimes in similar ways.

Several examples help illustrate the point. Imagine Smith and Jones, each of whom violates the Hobbs Act in very different ways. See 18 U.S.C. § 1951(a) (forbidding "obstruct[ing], delay[ing], or affect[ing] commerce or the movement of any article or commodity in commerce, by ... extortion"). Smith threatens to injure a co-worker unless the co-worker advances him a few dollars from the interstate company's till; Jones, after similarly threatening the co-worker, causes far more harm by seeking far more money, by making certain that the co-worker's family is aware of the threat, by arranging for deliveries of dead animals to the co-worker's home to show he is serious, and so forth. The offenders' behavior is very different; the known harmful consequences of their actions are different; their punishments both before, and after, the Guidelines would have been different. But, under the dissenters' approach, unless prosecutors decide to charge more than the elements of the crime, the judge would have to impose similar punishments.

Now imagine two former felons, Johnson and Jackson, each of whom engages in identical criminal behavior: threatening a bank teller with a gun, securing $50,000, and injuring an innocent bystander while fleeing the bank. Suppose prosecutors charge Johnson with one crime (say, illegal gun possession, see 18 U.S.C. § 922(g)) and Jackson with another (say, bank robbery, see § 2113(a)). Before the Guidelines, a single judge faced with such similar real conduct would have been able (within statutory limits) to impose similar sentences upon the two similar offenders despite the different charges brought against them. The Guidelines themselves would ordinarily have required judges to sentence the two offenders similarly. But under the dissenters' system, in these circumstances the offenders likely would receive different punishments.

Consider, too, a complex mail fraud conspiracy where a prosecutor may well be uncertain of the amount of harm and of the role each indicted individual played until after conviction— when the offenders may turn over financial records, when it becomes easier to determine who were the leaders and who the followers, when victim interviews are seen to be worth the time. In such a case the relation between the sentence and what actually occurred is likely to be considerably more distant under a system with a jury trial requirement patched onto it than it was even prior to the Sentencing Act, when judges routinely used information obtained after the verdict to decide upon a proper sentence.

This point is critically important. Congress' basic goal in passing the Sentencing Act was to move the sentencing system in the direction of increased uniformity. See 28 U.S.C. § 991(b)(1)(B); see also § 994(f). That uniformity does not consist simply of similar sentences for those convicted of violations of the same statute—a uniformity consistent with the dissenters' remedial approach. It consists, more importantly, of similar relationships between sentences and real conduct, relationships that Congress' sentencing statutes helped to advance and that Justice STEVENS' approach would undermine. In significant part, it is the weakening of this real-conduct/uniformity-in-sentencing relationship, and not any "inexplicabl[e]" concerns for the "*manner* of achieving uniform sentences," *post* (SCALIA, J., dissenting), that leads us to conclude that Congress would have preferred *no* mandatory system to the system the dissenters envisage.

Third, the sentencing statutes, read to include the Court's Sixth Amendment requirement, would create a system far more complex than Congress could have intended. How would courts and counsel work with an indictment and a jury trial that involved not just whether a defendant robbed a bank but also how? Would the indictment have to allege, in addition to the elements of robbery, whether the defendant possessed a firearm, whether he brandished or discharged it, whether he threatened death, whether he caused bodily injury, whether any such injury was ordinary, serious, permanent or life threatening, whether he abducted or physically restrained anyone, whether any victim was unusually vulnerable, how much money was taken, and whether he was an organizer, leader, manager, or supervisor in a robbery gang? See USSG §§ 2B3.1, 3B1.1. If so, how could a defendant mount a defense against some or all such specific claims should he also try simultaneously to maintain that the Government's evidence failed to place him at the scene of the crime? Would the indictment in a mail fraud case have to allege the number of victims, their vulnerability, and the amount taken from each? How could a judge expect a jury to work with the Guidelines' definitions of, say, "relevant conduct," which includes "all acts and omissions committed, aided, abetted, counseled, commanded, induced, procured, or willfully caused by the defendant; and [in the case of a conspiracy] all reasonably foreseeable acts and omissions of others in furtherance of the jointly undertaken criminal activity"? §§ 1B1.3(a)(1)(A)-(B). How would a jury measure "loss" in a securities fraud case—a matter so complex as to lead the Commission to instruct judges to make "only ... a reasonable estimate"? § 2B1.1, comment., n. 3(C). How would the court take account, for punishment purposes, of a defendant's contemptuous behavior at trial—a matter that the Government could not have charged in the indictment? § 3C1.1.

Fourth, plea bargaining would not significantly diminish the consequences of the Court's constitutional holding for the operation of the Guidelines. Rather, plea bargaining would make matters worse. Congress enacted the sentencing statutes in major part to achieve greater uniformity in sentencing, *i.e.*, to increase the likelihood that offenders who engage in similar real conduct would receive similar sentences. The statutes reasonably assume that their efforts to move the trial-based sentencing process in the direction of greater sentencing uniformity would have a similar positive impact upon plea-bargained sentences, for plea bargaining takes place *in the shadow of* (*i.e.*, with an eye towards the hypothetical result of) a potential trial.

That, too, is why Congress, understanding the realities of plea bargaining, authorized the Commission to promulgate policy statements that would assist sentencing judges in determining whether to reject a plea agreement after reading about the defendant's real conduct in a presentence report (and giving the offender an opportunity to challenge the report). See 28 U.S.C. § 994(a)(2)(E); USSG § 6B1.2(a). This system has not worked perfectly; judges have often simply accepted an agreed-upon account of the conduct at issue. But compared to pre-existing law, the statutes try to move the system in the right direction, *i.e.*, toward greater sentencing uniformity.

The Court's constitutional jury trial requirement, however, if patched onto the present Sentencing Act, would move the system backwards in respect both to tried and to plea-bargained cases. In respect to tried cases, it would effectively deprive the judge of the ability to use post-verdict-acquired real-conduct information; it would prohibit the judge from basing a sentence upon any conduct other than the conduct the prosecutor chose to charge; and it would put a defendant to a set of difficult strategic choices as to which prosecutorial claims he would contest. The sentence that would emerge in a case tried under such a system would likely reflect real conduct less completely, less accurately, and less often than did a pre-Guidelines, as well as a Guidelines, trial.

Because plea bargaining inevitably reflects estimates of what would happen at trial, plea bargaining too under such a system would move in the wrong direction. That is to say, in a sentencing system modified by the Court's constitutional requirement, plea bargaining would likely lead to sentences that gave greater weight, not to real conduct, but rather to the skill of counsel, the policies of the prosecutor, the caseload, and other factors that vary from place to place, defendant to defendant, and crime to crime. Compared to pre-Guidelines plea bargaining, plea bargaining of this kind would necessarily move federal sentencing in the direction of diminished, not increased, uniformity in sentencing. It would tend to defeat, not to further, Congress' basic statutory goal.

Such a system would have particularly troubling consequences with respect to prosecutorial power. Until now, sentencing factors have come before the judge in the presentence report. But in a sentencing system with the Court's constitutional requirement engrafted onto it, any factor that a prosecutor chose not to charge at the plea negotiation would be placed beyond the reach of the judge entirely. Prosecutors would thus exercise a power the Sentencing Act vested in judges: the power to decide, based on relevant information about the offense and the offender, which defendants merit heavier punishment.

In respondent Booker's case, for example, the jury heard evidence that the crime had involved 92.5 grams of crack cocaine, and convicted Booker of possessing more than 50 grams. But the judge, at sentencing, found that the crime had involved an additional 566 grams, for a total of 658.5 grams. A system that would require the jury, not the judge, to make the additional "566 grams" finding is a system in which the prosecutor, not the judge, would control the sentence. That is because it is the prosecutor who would have to decide what drug amount to charge. He could choose to charge 658.5 grams, or 92.5, or less. It is the prosecutor who, through such a charging decision, would control the sentencing range. And it is different prosecutors who, in different cases—say, in two cases involving 566 grams—would potentially insist upon different punishments for similar defendants who engaged in similar criminal conduct involving similar amounts of unlawful drugs—say, by charging one of them with the full 566 grams, and the other with 10. As long as different prosecutors react differently, a system with a patched-on jury factfinding requirement would mean different sentences for otherwise similar conduct, whether in the context of trials or that of plea bargaining.

Fifth, Congress would not have enacted sentencing statutes that make it more difficult to adjust sentences *upward* than to adjust them *downward*. As several United States Senators have written in an *amicus* brief, "the Congress that enacted the 1984 Act did not conceive of—much less establish—a sentencing guidelines system in which sentencing judges were free to consider facts or circumstances not found by a jury or admitted in a plea agreement for the purpose of adjusting a base-offense level *down*, but not *up*, within the applicable guidelines range. Such a one-way lever would be grossly at odds with Congress's intent." Yet that is the system that the dissenters' remedy would create.

For all these reasons, Congress, had it been faced with the constitutional jury trial requirement, likely would not have passed the same Sentencing Act. It likely would have found the requirement incompatible with the Act as written. Hence the Act cannot remain valid in its entirety. Severance and excision are necessary.

III

We now turn to the question of *which* portions of the sentencing statute we must sever and excise as inconsistent with the Court's constitutional requirement. Although, as we have explained, see Part II, *supra*, we believe that Congress would have preferred the total invalidation of the statute to the dissenters' remedial approach, we nevertheless do not believe that the entire statute must be invalidated. Most of the statute is perfectly valid. See, *e.g.*, 18 U.S.C.A. § 3551 (describing authorized sentences as probation, fine, or imprisonment); § 3552 (presentence reports); § 3554 (forfeiture); § 3555 (notification to the victims); § 3583 (supervised release). And we must "refrain from invalidating more of the statute than is necessary." Indeed, we must retain those portions of the Act that are (1) constitutionally valid, (2) capable of "functioning independently," and (3) consistent with Congress' basic objectives in enacting the statute.

Application of these criteria indicates that we must sever and excise two specific statutory provisions: the provision that requires sentencing courts to impose a sentence within the applicable Guidelines range (in the absence of circumstances that justify a departure), see 18 U.S.C. § 3553(b)(1), and the provision that sets forth standards of review on appeal, including *de novo* review of departures from the applicable Guidelines range, see § 3742(e). With these two sections excised (and statutory cross-references to the two sections consequently invalidated), the remainder of the Act satisfies the Court's constitutional requirements.

As the Court today recognizes in its first opinion in these cases, the existence of § 3553(b)(1) is a necessary condition of the constitutional violation. That is to say, without this provision—namely the provision that makes "the relevant sentencing rules ... mandatory and impose[s] binding requirements on all sentencing judges"—the statute falls outside the scope of *Apprendi's* requirement.

The remainder of the Act "function[s] independently." Without the "mandatory" provision, the Act nonetheless requires judges to take account of the Guidelines together with other sentencing goals. See 18 U.S.C.A. § 3553(a). The Act nonetheless requires judges to consider the Guidelines "sentencing range established for ... the applicable category of offense committed by the applicable category of defendant," § 3553(a)(4), the pertinent Sentencing Commission policy statements, the need to avoid unwarranted sentencing disparities, and the need to provide restitution to victims, §§ 3553(a)(1), (3), (5)-(7). And the Act nonetheless requires judges to impose sentences that reflect the seriousness of the offense, promote respect for the law, provide just punishment, afford adequate deterrence, protect the public, and effectively provide the defendant with needed educational or vocational training and medical care. § 3553(a)(2).

Moreover, despite the absence of § 3553(b)(1), the Act continues to provide for appeals from sentencing decisions (irrespective of whether the trial judge sentences within or outside the Guidelines range in the exercise of his discretionary power under § 3553(a)). See § 3742(a) (appeal by defendant); § 3742(b) (appeal by Government). We concede that the excision of § 3553(b)(1) requires the excision of a different, appeals-related section, namely § 3742(e), which sets forth standards of review on appeal. That section contains critical cross-references to the (now-excised) § 3553(b)(1) and consequently must be severed and excised for similar reasons.

Excision of § 3742(e), however, does not pose a critical problem for the handling of appeals. That is because, as we have previously held, a statute that does not *explicitly* set forth a standard of review may nonetheless do so *implicitly*. See *Pierce v. Underwood*, 487 U.S. 552, 558-560 (1988) (adopting a standard of review, where "neither a clear statutory prescription nor a historical tradition" existed, based on the statutory text and structure, and on practical considerations). We infer appropriate review standards from related statutory language, the structure of the statute, and the "sound administration of justice." And in this instance those factors, in addition to the past two decades of appellate practice in cases involving departures, imply a practical standard of review already familiar to appellate courts: review for "unreasonable[ness]." 18 U.S.C. § 3742(e)(3). ...

As we have said, the Sentencing Commission remains in place, writing Guidelines, collecting information about actual district court sentencing decisions, undertaking research, and revising the Guidelines accordingly. The district courts, while not bound to apply the Guidelines, must consult those Guidelines and take them into account when sentencing. The courts of appeals review sentencing decisions for unreasonableness. These features of the remaining system, while not the system Congress enacted, nonetheless continue to move sentencing in Congress' preferred direction, helping to avoid excessive sentencing disparities while maintaining flexibility sufficient to individualize sentences where necessary. See 28 U.S.C. § 991(b). We can find no feature of the remaining system that tends to hinder, rather than to further, these basic objectives. Under these circumstances, why would Congress not have preferred excision of the "mandatory" provision to a system that engrafts today's constitutional requirement onto the unchanged pre-existing statute—a system that, in terms of Congress' basic objectives, is counterproductive? ...

Ours, of course, is not the last word: The ball now lies in Congress' court. The National Legislature is equipped to devise and install, long-term, the sentencing system, compatible with the Constitution, that Congress judges best for the federal system of justice. ...

Notes

1. As *Booker* makes clear, this sentencing revolution began with the Supreme Court's decision in *Apprendi v. New Jersey*, 530 U.S. 466 (2000). *Apprendi* involved a New Jersey hate-crime statute that authorized a 20-year sentence, despite the usual 10-year maximum, if the judge found the crime to have been committed "with a purpose to intimidate ... because of race, color, gender, handicap, religion, sexual orientation or ethnicity." The Supreme Court held, based on constitutional jury and due process rights, that "[o]ther than the fact of a prior conviction, any fact that increases the penalty for a crime beyond the statutory maximum must be submitted to a jury, and proved beyond a reasonable doubt."

2. The death knell for the U.S. Sentencing Guidelines was sounded in *Blakely v. Washington*, 542 U.S. 296 (2004). In *Blakely*, petitioner pled guilty to kidnapping his estranged wife. Washington State law provided a statutory maximum of 10 years for all class B felonies. Washington's Sentencing Reform Act provided for a 49-53 month sentencing range for second-degree kidnapping with a firearm. The Act provided, however, that a judge could impose a sentence above the standard range if he found "substantial and compelling reasons justifying an exceptional sentence." The Act listed aggravating factors that justify such a departure, including "deliberate cruelty." The trial court imposed upon petitioner an "exceptional" sentence of 90 months after making the judicial determination that petitioner acted with deliberate cruelty. Petitioner argued that the sentencing procedure violated his Sixth Amendment right, and the Supreme Court agreed. The critical portion of the Court's reasoning was as follows:

> In this case, petitioner was sentenced to more than three years above the 53-month statutory maximum of the standard range because he had acted with "deliberate cruelty." The facts supporting that finding were neither admitted by petitioner nor found by a jury. The State nevertheless contends that there was no *Apprendi* violation because the relevant

"statutory maximum" is not 53 months, but the 10-year maximum for class B felonies in §9A.20.021(1)(b). It observes that no exceptional sentence may exceed that limit. Our precedents make clear, however, that the "statutory maximum" for *Apprendi* purposes is the maximum sentence a judge may impose *solely on the basis of the facts reflected in the jury verdict or admitted by the defendant*. In other words, the relevant "statutory maximum" is not the maximum sentence a judge may impose after finding additional facts, but the maximum he may impose *without* any additional findings. When a judge inflicts punishment that the jury's verdict alone does not allow, the jury has not found all the facts "which the law makes essential to the punishment," and the judge exceeds his proper authority.

Id. at 303-04. Does this necessarily follow from *Apprendi*? Does it suggest that a sentencing scheme in which judges *may* but are *not required* to enhance a defendant's sentence by extra-verdict facts is unconstitutional?

3. These cases demonstrate the Supreme Court's deep unease with the extent to which Congress has increasingly denominated facts relevant to culpability "sentencing factors" rather than "elements" to be proved to the jury. The *Blakely* opinion provides perhaps the best summary of the Court's concern:

Those who would reject *Apprendi* are resigned to one of two alternatives. The first is that the jury need only find whatever facts the legislature chooses to label elements of the crime, and that those it labels sentencing factors—no matter how much they may increase the punishment—may be found by the judge. This would mean, for example, that a judge could sentence a man for committing murder even if the jury convicted him only of illegally possessing the firearm used to commit it—or of making an illegal lane change while fleeing the death scene. Not even *Apprendi's* critics would advocate this absurd result. The jury could not function as circuitbreaker in the State's machinery of justice if it were relegated to making a determination that the defendant at some point did something wrong, a mere preliminary to a judicial inquisition into the facts of the crime the State *actually* seeks to punish.

The second alternative is that legislatures may establish legally essential sentencing factors *within limits*—limits crossed when, perhaps, the sentencing factor is a "tail which wags the dog of the substantive offense." *McMillan*, 477 U.S., at 88. What this means in operation is that the law must not go *too far*—it must not exceed the judicial estimation of the proper role of the judge.

The subjectivity of this standard is obvious. Petitioner argued below that second-degree kidnaping with deliberate cruelty was essentially the same as first-degree kidnaping, the very charge he had avoided by pleading to a lesser offense. The court conceded this might be so but held it irrelevant. Petitioner's 90-month sentence exceeded the 53-month standard maximum by almost 70%; the Washington Supreme Court in other cases has upheld exceptional sentences 15 times the standard maximum. Did the court go *too far* in any of these cases? There is no answer that legal analysis can provide. With *too far* as the yardstick, it is always possible to disagree with such judgments and never to refute them.

Whether the Sixth Amendment incorporates this manipulable standard rather than *Apprendi's* bright-line rule depends on the plausibility of the claim that the Framers would have left definition of the scope of jury power up to judges' intuitive sense of how far is *too far*. We think that claim not plausible at all, because the very reason the Framers put a jury-trial guarantee in the Constitution is that they were unwilling to trust government to mark out the role of the jury.

Blakely, 542 U.S. at 304-07. Are you persuaded that there is no viable alternative to the *Blakely* rule?

4. *Apprendi's* "animating principle" is that the "preservation of the jury's historic role as a bulwark between the State and the accused at the trial for an alleged offense." Oregon v. Ice,

555 U.S. 160, 168 (2009). But this seems surreal to many of those who practice federal criminal law in that the decision seems to assume that the jury occupies a position of centrality to the process—a centrality that Congress is determined to undermine. In fact, of course, juries have very little role in the federal criminal system. Although the jury trial is the theoretical constitutional paradigm in serious criminal cases, it is not the means by which the overwhelming majority of criminal convictions are secured in state or federal proceedings. "In fiscal year 2017, the vast majority of offenders (97.2%) pleaded guilty. This high rate has been consistent for more than 15 years." U.S. Sentencing Comm'n, Overview of Federal Criminal Cases Fiscal Year 2017, at 5. Further, of those few cases resolved by trial, some were judge trials. For example, in federal criminal cases terminated in fiscal year 2017: 1,616 defendants were tried before a jury (1,420 convictions and 196 acquittals); 258 were disposed of in non-jury trials (178 convictions and 80 acquittals); and 67,418 defendants' cases were resolved by guilty plea. *See* U.S. Courts, 2017 Judicial Business Report, Tbl. D-4.

In any case, is it the jury whose prerogatives are increased through the *Booker* decision? Are juries likely to be asked to decide additional questions of fact post-*Booker*? Or does the remedy adopted by the Court ensure that, in fact, *Booker* actually gives judges far *more* discretion in making findings of fact (with far less visibility) that may have a huge impact on criminal sentencing than was the case under the Guidelines? In short, has the right to a jury trial, as read by the Justices, produced a system where the judge has almost unfettered discretion? *U.S. Sentencing Commission Hears Views On How to Go Forward in Wake of* Booker, 76 Crim. L. Rep. (BNA) 397 (Feb. 23, 2005). The best example of the extent to which *Apprendi* empowered judges at the expense of juries is demonstrated by the Supreme Court's position that a judge may consider conduct for which the defendant was acquitted by the jury if the judge concludes that the conduct was proved by a preponderance of the evidence. *See* United States v. Watts, 519 U.S. 148 (1997) (*per curiam*). This result is, of course, a consequence of the *Booker* Court's decision regarding remedy—that is, its decision to adjudge the Guidelines advisory. In light of the above, is the Court's severability analysis persuasive?

5. Justice Breyer speaks for the Court when he states that, under 18 U.S.C. § 3553(a)(4), a sentencing court is "require[d] ... to consider Guidelines ranges" but the court is permitted "to tailor the sentence in light of other statutory concerns" articulated in § 3553(a). Just how *much* weight ought the Guidelines carry? Some circuits have applied a presumption of reasonableness to within-guidelines sentences on appeal. The Supreme Court ruled in *Rita v. United States*, 551 U.S. 338 (2007) that an appellate presumption of reasonableness for within-guidelines sentences did not contravene the Sixth Amendment. The Court also noted, however, that District Courts, in making the initial sentencing decision, ought not to apply such a presumption. And it stated that the "fact that we permit courts of appeals to adopt a presumption of reasonableness does not mean that courts may adopt a presumption of unreasonableness. Even the Government concedes that appellate courts may not presume that every variance from the advisory Guidelines is unreasonable." 551 U.S. at 354-55.

6. In late 2007, the Supreme Court decided a pair of cases in which it made clear that *Booker*'s appellate "reasonableness" review was supposed to be deferential, recognizing District Courts' substantial discretion in sentencing post-*Booker*. In *Kimbrough v. United States*, 552 U.S. 85 (2007), the court held that a sentence outside the guidelines range is *not* per se unreasonable when it is based on a disagreement with the U.S. Sentencing Commission's policy determinations—in the *Kimbrough* case, the 100-to-1 sentencing disparity between the guidelines' treatment of crack versus powder cocaine. In *Gall v. United States*, 552 U.S. 38 (2007), the Court held that although the extent of the difference between the recommended guidelines range and the sentence imposed is relevant on appellate review, circuit courts must review all sentences—whether inside, just outside, or significantly outside the Guidelines range—under a deferential abuse of discretion standard. In so doing, the Court set out the applicable analysis as follows:

> As we explained in *Rita,* a district court should begin all sentencing proceedings by correctly calculating the applicable Guidelines range. As a matter of administration and to secure nationwide consistency, the Guidelines should be the starting point and the initial

benchmark. The Guidelines are not the only consideration, however. Accordingly, after giving both parties an opportunity to argue for whatever sentence they deem appropriate, the district judge should then consider all of the § 3553(a) factors to determine whether they support the sentence requested by a party. In so doing, he may not presume that the Guidelines range is reasonable. He must make an individualized assessment based on the facts presented. If he decides that an outside-Guidelines sentence is warranted, he must consider the extent of the deviation and ensure that the justification is sufficiently compelling to support the degree of the variance. We find it uncontroversial that a major departure should be supported by a more significant justification than a minor one. After settling on the appropriate sentence, he must adequately explain the chosen sentence to allow for meaningful appellate review and to promote the perception of fair sentencing.

Regardless of whether the sentence imposed is inside or outside the Guidelines range, the appellate court must review the sentence under an abuse-of-discretion standard. It must first ensure that the district court committed no significant procedural error, such as failing to calculate (or improperly calculating) the Guidelines range, treating the Guidelines as mandatory, failing to consider the § 3553(a) factors, selecting a sentence based on clearly erroneous facts, or failing to adequately explain the chosen sentence— including an explanation for any deviation from the Guidelines range. Assuming that the district court's sentencing decision is procedurally sound, the appellate court should then consider the substantive reasonableness of the sentence imposed under an abuse-of-discretion standard. When conducting this review, the court will, of course, take into account the totality of the circumstances, including the extent of any variance from the Guidelines range. If the sentence is within the Guidelines range, the appellate court may, but is not required to, apply a presumption of reasonableness. But if the sentence is outside the Guidelines range, the court may not apply a presumption of unreasonableness. It may consider the extent of the deviation, but must give due deference to the district court's decision that the § 3553(a) factors, on a whole, justify the extent of the variance. The fact that the appellate court might reasonably have concluded that a different sentence was appropriate is insufficient to justify reversal of the district court.

Practical considerations also underlie this legal principle. "The sentencing judge is in a superior position to find facts and judge their import under § 3553(a) in the individual case. The judge sees and hears the evidence, makes credibility determinations, has full knowledge of the facts and gains insights not conveyed by the record." "The sentencing judge has access to, and greater familiarity with, the individual case and the individual defendant before him than the Commission or the appeals court." Moreover, "[d]istrict courts have an institutional advantage over appellate courts in making these sorts of determinations, especially as they see so many more Guidelines sentences than appellate courts do."

"It has been uniform and constant in the federal judicial tradition for the sentencing judge to consider every convicted person as an individual and every case as a unique study in the human failings that sometimes mitigate, sometimes magnify, the crime and the punishment to ensue. The uniqueness of the individual case, however, does not change the deferential abuse-of-discretion standard of review that applies to all sentencing decisions. ...

Gall, 552 U.S. at 49-52.

7. Recall that one of the reasons for the mandatory guidelines was the disparate treatment minority and other offenders received under an indeterminate sentencing system. In March 2010, the Sentencing Commission issued a report on the sophisticated multivariate regression analysis it had performed on sentencing data from May 1, 2003 through September 30, 2009 to test the effect of the sentencing discretion *Booker* provided sentencing judges on uniformity in sentencing. U.S. Sentencing Comm'n, Demographic Differences in Federal Sentencing Practices: An Update of the Booker Report's Multivariate Regression Analysis (March 2010). Its results were troubling. After controlling for a variety of factors relevant to sentencing, the Commission observed: "[b]lack male offenders received longer sentences than

white male offenders. The differences in sentence length have increased steadily under *Booker*"; "[f]emale offenders of all races received shorter sentences than male offenders"; "[n]on-citizen offenders received longer sentences than offenders who were U.S. citizens. The differences in sentence length have increased steadily under *Booker*"; and "[o]ffenders with some college education received shorter sentences than offenders with no college education." *Id.* at 2. Is a return to the bad old days of troubling disparities in sentencing necessary? What can be done to preserve the benefits of guidelines without running afoul of the Sixth Amendment? *See, e.g.,* Stephanos Bibas, Max M. Schanzenbach & Emerson H. Tiller, *Policing Politics at Sentencing*, 103 Nw. U. L. Rev. 1371 (2009).

8. How have *Gall* and *Kimbrough* affected white-collar sentencing, if at all? It is difficult to formulate a definitive answer because comprehensive and detailed authoritative analyses of white-collar sentencing are scarce. One study of the frequency with which judges departed from the Guidelines, and the extent of those departures, in major white-collar cases in the Southern District of New York concluded that "following *Booker*, the rate at which judges impose[d] government-sponsored below-range sentences ... remained about the same. Strikingly, however, the rate at which judges impose[d] non-government-sponsored below-range sentences ... increased dramatically. As a result, a significant majority of defendants in major white-collar cases today receive sentences shorter than the Guidelines range. ... [Further,] when defendants receive[d] sentences below the Guidelines range, the sentences received [we]re, for the most part, significantly shorter than the Guidelines range." Jillian Hewitt, Note, *Fifty Shades of Gray: Sentencing Trends in Major White-Collar Cases*, 125 Yale L.J. 1018, 1024-25 (2016).

The American Lawyer studied the 440 highest-profile corporate fraud prosecutions in a five-year period and noted the marked difference in sentences imposed on those who pled out versus those who went to trial. The study demonstrates:

> Among those who pled guilty, the vast majority received sentences of 5 years or less and had a substantially greater chance to receive probation. On the other hand, among those who went to trial, the largest group received 5- to 10-year terms, with a full quarter sentenced to more than 10 years. A handful received 15-year, 20-year, or even longer terms.

Emily Barker, et al., *By the Numbers: Progress Report*, 20 Fed. Sent. Rep. 206 (2007) (reprinting *American Lawyer* study results). It appears, then, that the lengthy sentences imposed in some high-profile prosecutions—the former WorldCom ECO Bernard Ebbers' 25 years, former Enron CEO Jeffry Skilling's 24 years, Adelphia founder John Rigas' 15 years—are the exception, not the rule, and usually are visited only upon those who go to trial and lose. *See also* David Voreacos & Bob Van Voris, *Bush Fraud Probes Jail Corporate Criminals Less Than Two Years*, Bloomberg.com, Dec. 13, 2007 (reporting that 61% of "defendants sentenced during the Bush administration's crackdown on corporate fraud spent no more than two years in jail. In the past five years, 28[%] of those sentenced got no prison time and 6[%] received 10 years or more, according to a review of 1,236 white-collar convictions."). Still, even if viewed as aberrational, white-collar sentences of 100 years, in the cases of Richard Monroe Harkless and Edward Hugh Okun, seem extreme and perhaps senseless. Some view the disparities alone as troubling. *See* Breuer Cites Disparate Sentences for Financial Fraud Defendants, (BNA) 90 Crim. L. Rptr. 278 (Nov. 2011). These cases ought, at least, to provoke what some commentators believe is a much needed re-consideration of the rationality of Guidelines sentences in white-collar cases. *See, e.g.,* Daniel Richman, *Federal White Collar Sentencing in the United States: A Work in Progress*, 76 Law. & Contemp. Probs. 53 (2013); Harris & Kaminska, *supra*, 20 Fed. Sent. Rep. at 157-58; Frank O. Bowman III, *Sentencing High-Loss Corporate Insider Frauds after* Booker, 20 Fed. Sent. Rep. 167 (2008); Ellen S. Podgor, *The Challenge of White Collar* Sentencing, 97 J. Crim. L. & Criminology 731 (2007); Samuel W. Buell, *Reforming Punishment of Financial Reporting Fraud*, 28 Cardozo L. Rev. 1611 (2007).

9. In a very important decision for corporate defendants, *Southern Union Co. v. United States*, 567 U.S. 343 (2012), the Supreme Court applied *Apprendi* to criminal fines. Southern Union

was convicted of violating the Resources Conservation and Recovery Act (RCRA) by storing mercury on its premises "from on or about September 19, 2002 until on or about October 19, 2004"—a period of 762 days. Neither party requested a special interrogatory or jury verdict form to determine the precise duration of the violation. Because RCRA violations are punishable by a fine of not more than $50,000 per day of violation, the probation department computed the potential fine as up to $38.1 million, that is, $50,000 for each of the 762-day period. Southern Union argued that under *Apprendi*, because the jury had not necessarily decided how many days the violation continued, the verdict only authorized a maximum fine of $50,000 for a single-day violation. The government agreed that the jury did not make a finding about the duration of the violation but argued that *Apprendi* did not apply to criminal fines. Ultimately, the Supreme Court rejected the government's position, holding that a defendant's maximum authorized fine must be based solely on facts admitted by the defendant or found by a jury beyond a reasonable doubt. Among the questions that linger after *Southern Union* are whether restitution orders or monetary "community service" obligations imposed as a condition of probation are also subject to *Apprendi*. *See, e.g.*, David Debold & Matthew Benjamin, *A Demise Greatly Exaggerated*—Apprendi *is Extended to Criminal Fines*, 91 Crim. L. Reptr. (BNA) 797 (2012); *see also* Brynn Applebaum, Note, *Criminal Asset Forfeiture and the Sixth Amendment After* Southern Union *and* Alleyne: *State-Level Ramifications*, 68 Vand. L. Rev. 549 (2015).

10. How has *Booker* affected plea bargaining? Obviously, both sides must deal with the fact that they can no longer negotiate with a mandatory guidelines range in mind. Does this favor the government or the defense or neither? Do *Gall* and *Kimbrough* change plea bargaining incentives? *See* Stephanos Bibas & Susan Klein, *The Sixth Amendment and Criminal Sentencing*, 30 Cardozo L. Rev. 775, 788-96 (2008); U.S. Sentencing Commission, *Preliminary Findings: Federal Sentencing Practices Subsequent to the Supreme Court's Decision in* Blakely v. Washington, at http://www.ussc.gov. Some commentators believe that the *Southern Union* decision will strengthen the bargaining position of criminal defendants—and particularly organizational defendants—in negotiations over fine amounts.

11. If Congress determines that it wishes to once again constrain the discretion of sentencing judges, what can it do consistent with the *Booker* precedent? Some commentators have suggested that Congress may "fix" this problem by amending the sentencing ranges on the Chapter 5 Sentencing Table so that the top of each guideline range becomes the statutory maximum of the offense of conviction. They argued that *Booker* affected only those post-conviction judicial findings of fact that would require an increase in the *maximum* of the otherwise applicable penalty range. Accordingly, if the post-conviction judicial findings of fact merely raised the *minimum* sentence applicable to a defendant (within the congressional maximum sentence set by statute and guideline), there would be no Sixth Amendment problem with making such minimums mandatory. Judges then would be required essentially to impose minimum sentences within the statutory maximum through findings of fact. Is imposition of statutory *minimums* constitutional under the Sixth Amendment?

In *United States v. Harris*, 536 U.S. 545 (2002), the Court held that sentencing facts that raise *minimum*, but not *maximum*, sentences need not be charged in the indictment or proved to a jury beyond a reasonable doubt. But the Court overruled itself on this issue in *Alleyne v. United States*, 570 U.S. 99 (2013). In *Alleyne*, the Court concluded that *Harris* was inconsistent with *Apprendi* and with the original meaning of the Sixth Amendment. It concluded that the "elements" that under the Sixth Amendment and Due Process clauses must be proven to the jury beyond a reasonable doubt necessarily include facts that not only increase the maximum penalty, but also those that increase the minimum sentence because both affect the sentencing range to which a defendant is exposed. The Court reasoned that "[i]t is impossible to disassociate the floor of a sentencing range from the penalty affixed to the crime." *Id*. at 112. Increasing the legally prescribed "floor" indisputably aggravates the punishment and "heightens the loss of liberty associated with the crime" because the government can invoke the mandatory minimum to require a harsher punishment than would have resulted otherwise. *Id*. at 113. "This reality demonstrates that the core crime and the fact triggering the mandatory minimum sentence together constitute a new, aggravated crime, each element of which must be submitted to the jury." *Id.*

12. After *Booker*, courts struggled with the question whether "departures" had any meaning in a landscape in which judges were not bound by the guidelines range. The Commission continues to believe that those "departure" guidelines ought to be consulted when courts are considering a sentence outside the otherwise applicable guidelines range. *See, e.g.,* U.S. Sentencing Comm'n, Primer, Departures and Variances (April 2018). Accordingly, the Commission promulgated an amendment to the guidelines in 2011 that set forth a three-step process for determining sentences: (1) determining the guidelines range; (2) determining whether a departure is warranted using the instructions in guidelines Chapters 5H and 5K; and (3) applying the factors in 18 U.S.C. § 3553(a) taken as a whole to determine whether a "variance" (a sentence outside the guidelines range) is appropriate. *See* U.S. Sentencing Comm'n, Supplement to Appendix C, Amendment 741; U.S. Sentencing Comm'n, U.S. Sentencing Guidelines Manual § 1B1.1. At the same time, the Commission amended Chapter 5H to "provide sentencing courts with a framework for addressing specific offender characteristics in a reasonably consistent manner." Among other things, the Commission changed its policy statements regarding the appropriate consideration of age, mental and emotional conditions, physical condition, and military service in determining sentences. *See* U.S. Sentencing Comm'n, Supplement to Appendix C, Amendment 739; U.S. Sentencing Comm'n, U.S. Sentencing Guidelines Manual Ch. 5H. That said, it is clear that district courts are not bound by these policy statements. Thus, for example, a district court has the authority to sua sponte take into account a defendant's cooperation, even if the government did not seek a downward departure under § 5K1.1. *See* United States v. Robinson, 741 F.3d 588 (5th Cir. 2014).

13. As noted in the *Booker* opinion and above Note 4, the Supreme Court held in *United States v. Watts*, 519 U.S. 148 (1997) (*per curiam*) that a sentencing court may consider conduct for which the defendant was acquitted at trial so long as the conduct was proved by a preponderance of the evidence to the satisfaction of the sentencing judge. Recently, three Justices dissented from the denial of a petition for certiorari that asked the Court to reconsider *Watts*:

JONES v. UNITED STATES
-- U.S. --, 135 S.Ct. 8 (2014)

Justice SCALIA, with whom Justice THOMAS and Justice GINSBURG join, dissenting from denial of certiorari.

A jury convicted petitioners Joseph Jones, Desmond Thurston, and Antwuan Ball of distributing very small amounts of crack cocaine, and acquitted them of conspiring to distribute drugs. The sentencing judge, however, found that they *had* engaged in the charged conspiracy and, relying largely on that finding, imposed sentences that petitioners say were many times longer than those the Guidelines would otherwise have recommended.

Petitioners present a strong case that, but for the judge's finding of fact, their sentences would have been "substantively unreasonable" and therefore illegal. See *Rita v. United States*, 551 U.S. 338, 372 (2007) (SCALIA, J., joined by THOMAS, J., concurring in part and concurring in the judgment). If so, their constitutional rights were violated. The Sixth Amendment, together with the Fifth Amendment's Due Process Clause, "requires that each element of a crime" be either admitted by the defendant, or "proved to the jury beyond a reasonable doubt." *Alleyne v. United States*, 570 U.S. 99 (2013). Any fact that increases the penalty to which a defendant is exposed constitutes an element of a crime, *Apprendi v. New Jersey*, 530 U.S. 466, 483, n. 10 (2000), and "must be found by a jury, not a judge," *Cunningham v. California*, 549 U.S. 270, 281 (2007).[76] We have held that a substantively unreasonable

---

[76] [Dissent's footnote *:] With one exception: We held in *Almendarez-Torres v. United States*, 523 U.S. 224 (1998), that the fact of a prior conviction, even when it increases the sentence to which the defendant is

penalty is illegal and must be set aside. *Gall v. United States*, 552 U.S. 38, 51 (2007). It unavoidably follows that any fact necessary to prevent a sentence from being substantively unreasonable—thereby exposing the defendant to the longer sentence—is an element that must be either admitted by the defendant or found by the jury. It *may not* be found by a judge.

For years, however, we have refrained from saying so. In *Rita v. United States*, we dismissed the possibility of Sixth Amendment violations resulting from substantive reasonableness review as hypothetical and not presented by the facts of the case. We thus left for another day the question whether the Sixth Amendment is violated when courts impose sentences that, but for a judge-found fact, would be reversed for substantive unreasonableness. 551 U.S. 353; see also *id.*, at 366 (STEVENS, J., joined in part by GINSBURG, J., concurring) ("Such a hypothetical case should be decided if and when it arises"). Nonetheless, the Courts of Appeals have uniformly taken our continuing silence to suggest that the Constitution *does* permit otherwise unreasonable sentences supported by judicial factfinding, so long as they are within the statutory range. See, *e.g.*, *United States v. Benkahla*, 530 F.3d 300, 312 (CA4 2008); *United States v. Hernandez*, 633 F.3d 370, 374 (CA5 2011); *United States v. Ashqar*, 582 F.3d 819, 824-825 (CA7 2009); *United States v. Treadwell*, 593 F.3d 990, 1017-1018 (CA9 2010); *United States v. Redcorn*, 528 F.3d 727, 745-746 (CA10 2008).

This has gone on long enough. The present petition presents the nonhypothetical case the Court claimed to have been waiting for. And it is a particularly appealing case, because not only did no jury convict these defendants of the offense the sentencing judge thought them guilty of, but a jury *acquitted* them of that offense. Petitioners were convicted of distributing drugs, but acquitted of conspiring to distribute drugs. The sentencing judge found that petitioners had engaged in the conspiracy of which the jury acquitted them. The Guidelines, petitioners claim, recommend sentences of between 27 and 71 months for their distribution convictions. But in light of the conspiracy finding, the court calculated much higher Guidelines ranges, and sentenced Jones, Thurston, and Ball to 180, 194, and 225 months' imprisonment.

On petitioners' appeal, the D.C. Circuit held that *even if* their sentences would have been substantively unreasonable but for judge-found facts, their Sixth Amendment rights were not violated. We should grant certiorari to put an end to the unbroken string of cases disregarding the Sixth Amendment—or to eliminate the Sixth Amendment difficulty by acknowledging that all sentences below the statutory maximum are substantively reasonable.

Notes

1. The *Jones* cert petition and the amicus brief filed in support of it focused solely on the question of whether acquitted conduct ought to have a place in guidelines sentencing. Justice Scalia's dissent focuses on a different question; indeed, he mentions only fleetingly the issue of acquitted conduct as an appealing example of the larger issue that concerns him. The court of appeals cases that Justice Scalia cites as objectionable were cases in which judges made findings on the applicability of various guideline enhancements that increased the guidelines range but not beyond the statutory maximum. The courts of appeals found that as long as the guidelines are advisory, judges can and should consider the "real" facts of the case to determine a sentence within the statutorily prescribed maximum.

Is Justice Scalia in essence arguing that *any* fact that enhances the (advisory) sentencing range must be considered an element that must be proved to a jury? Is he contending that any sentence is "unreasonable" and subject to Sixth Amendment objection if any enhancement not found by a jury or admitted by the defendant is applied based on a judge's finding of fact? *See* United States v. Goossen, 723 F. App'x 608, 611 (10th Cir. 2018) (rejecting argument). Is Justice Scalia, in effect, arguing that "real" offense sentencing is forbidden?

2. In *Nelson v. Colorado*, -- U.S. --, 137 S.Ct. 1249 (2017), the issue was whether the reversal of a conviction by an appellate court on direct or collateral review entitles a defendant to reimbursement of any restitution the defendant may have paid pursuant to the sentence

---

exposed, may be found by a judge.

imposed. Colorado's Exoneration Act provides that "an innocent person who was wrongly convicted" could recover any restitution paid as a result of the conviction if the "conviction was overturned for reasons other than insufficiency of evidence or legal error unrelated to actual innocence." *Id.* at 1255. Under the Act, the exonerated defendant had to prove his actual innocence by clear and convincing evidence. The Supreme Court held that the Act violated due process by requiring defendants whose convictions have been reversed or vacated to prove their innocence by clear and convincing evidence to obtain the refund of restitution paid pursuant to the invalid conviction. The Court reasoned that "[o]nce those convictions were erased, the presumption of their innocence was restored." *Id.* at 1255. Because the *Nelson* defendants were now innocent, the Court ruled, the state had no right to retain the restitution received pursuant to the voided convictions. The *Watts* decision was founded in part on the Court's assertion that an "'acquittal on criminal charges does not prove that the defendant is innocent; it merely proves the existence of a reasonable doubt as to his guilt.'" United States v. Watts, 519 U.S. 148, 155 (1997) (*per curiam*) (quoting United States v. One Assortment of 89 Firearms, 465 U.S. 354, 362 (1984)). Is *Watts'* reasoning still valid after *Nelson*?

Chapter 4

ENTITY LIABILITY

Chapter Two (*Mens Rea*) explored in part how traditional *mens rea* requirements have been abandoned, and a species of strict liability imposed, for a variety of "public welfare" offenses. This chapter turns from examination of criminal liability "without mental fault" to a type of criminal liability for the "fault" of others: vicarious liability of organizations for the actions of their employees and agents under *respondeat superior* principles. Both strict and vicarious liability allow the criminal sanction to be imposed on one not technically at fault, but there is an important difference between the two concepts:

> With strict liability, there must be a showing that the defendant personally engaged in the necessary acts or omissions; only the requirement of mental fault is dispensed with altogether. By contrast, with vicarious liability it is the need for a personal *actus reus* that is dispensed with, and there remains the need for mental fault on the part of the employee. It is common, however, for a vicarious liability statute to also impose strict liability; in such an instance, there is no need to prove an act or omission by the defendant-employer (one by his employees will do), and there is no need to prove mental fault by anyone.[1]

These materials commence with readings in Part A discussing the wisdom of imposing vicarious *criminal* liability on corporate actors.[2] The sections that follow examine the legal rules that now control the imposition of such liability (Part B), the Department of Justice Guidelines that guide prosecutors' discretion in pursuing criminal sanctions (Part C), and the U.S. Sentencing Guidelines that apply to convicted organizations (Part D). Part E discusses a modern trend toward non-criminal dispositions in corporate crime cases. In Part F, the reasons for and conduct of corporate internal investigations are explored. Finally, this Chapter concludes in Part G with an examination of the criminal exposure of corporate actors, and particularly "responsible corporate officers," for actions taken or not taken on behalf of the corporation.

---

[1] Wayne R. LaFave, Jr., Criminal Law § 3.9(b) (West 2000).

[2] Most civil law countries long rejected the concept of corporate criminal liability. But the modern trend, at least in Western European countries, is to impose criminal liability on corporations. *See, e.g.*, Thomas Weigend, Societas delinquere non potest?: *A German Perspective*, 6 J. Intl Crim. J. 927 (2008); Sara Sun Beale & Adam G. Safwat, *What Developments in Western Europe Tell Us About American Critiques of Corporate Criminal Liability*, 8 Buff. Crim. L. Rev. 89 (2004).

A. CRIMINALIZING CORPORATE CONDUCT

We will be examining principles of vicarious liability as they apply to corporate criminal liability for the actions (or omissions where there is a duty to act) of corporate employees and agents. The rules of vicarious liability applied in this area have been transplanted from civil tort law. The issues of whether corporations ought to be subject to criminal sanction at all and, if so, under what standard, are the subject of increasing scrutiny.[3] In evaluating whether corporate criminal liability and the transplantation of the civil law's *respondeat superior* standard make sense, consider the following excerpted articles.

Harvey L. Pitt & Karl A. Groskaufmanis, *Minimizing Corporate Civil and Criminal Liability: A Second Look at Corporate Codes of Conduct*
78 Geo. L.J. 1559, 1562-74 (1990)

A corporation can act only through its employees; it is "an artificial being, invisible, intangible, and existing only in contemplation of law." This artificial person has "no soul to be damned, and no body to be kicked." As a result, corporations can be held liable for the conduct of their employees only vicariously, through the venerable doctrine of *respondeat superior*: "Let the master answer." In the last three decades, corporate civil and criminal liability has expanded well beyond its traditional boundaries. ...

A. Corporate Tort Liability

Despite the "universal adoption" of *respondeat superior* as a predicate for corporate liability, scholars have always struggled with their "inability to identify and defend its precise rationale." Scholars have advanced at least two justifications for the doctrine. The first justifies vicarious corporate tort liability as a means of distributing loss. The second justifies it as a means to promote better supervision of employees. ...

Loss distribution is the most widely accepted justification for the doctrine of *respondeat superior*. This system has proved to be "the most convenient and efficient way of ensuring that persons injured in the course of business enterprises do not go uncompensated." The law of vicarious liability, therefore, addresses the problem of judgment-proof agents. The doctrine commonly is rationalized in two ways. First, vicarious tort liability is linked to the control a company exercises over its employees. Second, tort liability provides the means to ensure that the corporation bears the costs of its conduct. The risks of an employee's misconduct "are properly allocated to the employer as a cost of engaging in the enterprise." Those who subscribe to this theory argue that the employer is in the best position to anticipate harm and insure against the resulting losses. They conclude that the melding of these factors makes it just and expedient to impose liability vicariously.

Perhaps because courts have recognized the need for some nexus between an employee's misconduct and an employer's liability, an amorphous standard has evolved: a corporation is vicariously liable for the torts that its employees commit while acting "within the scope of [their] employment." The legal standard examines, among other things, the time, place, function, and purpose of the employee's conduct. Besides raising traditional tort defenses, an employer typically argues that the employee's conduct was outside the scope of employment.

---

[3] The literature is voluminous. *See, e.g.*, Assaf Hamdani & Alon Klement, *Corporate Crime and Deterrence*, 61 Stan. L. Rev. 271 (2008); Andrew Weissmann with David Newman, *Rethinking Criminal Corporate Liability*, 82 Ind. L.J. 411 (2007); Geraldine Szott Moohr, *On the Prospects of Deterring Corporate Crime*, 2 J. Bus. & Tech. L. 25 (2007); Elizabeth K. Ainslie, *Indicting Corporations Revisited: Lessons of the Arthur Andersen Prosecution*, 43 Am. Crim. L. Rev. 107 (2006); Samuel W. Buell, *The Blaming Function of Entity Criminal Liability*, 81 Ind. L.J. 473 (2006); Sara Sun Beale & Adam G. Safwat, *What Developments in Western Europe Tell Us about American Critiques of Corporate Criminal Liability*, 8 Buff. Crim. L. Rev. 89 (2004).

Under this standard, an employer's liability for even innocuous employee acts—such as the commute from home to work—turns on very fine distinctions.

Beyond the primary concern of compensation, tort law scholars suggest that imposing vicarious liability is a way to shape employer conduct. These commentators urge that employer liability creates an incentive for management to take precautions to prevent employee accidents. The control of employees acting within the scope of their employment affords the employer the opportunity—and the obligation—to take such precautions. ...

B. Corporate Criminal Liability

Corporate criminal liability is a twentieth-century innovation, influenced by the "sweeping expansion" of common law principles. Current standards of corporate criminal liability have been borrowed directly from the doctrine of *respondeat superior*. A societal preoccupation with "white collar crime" has precipitated an increasing reliance on criminal prosecutions against corporate defendants to curb perceived corporate excesses.

At common law, a corporation could not face criminal charges. By the turn of this century, however, the Supreme Court abandoned the "old and exploded doctrine" of corporate immunity from criminal prosecution, holding instead that the Court "cannot shut its eyes to the fact that the great majority of business transactions in modern times are conducted through these bodies." Drawing liberally from civil tort principles, current standards of corporate criminal liability are premised on the notion that a corporation may, and should, be held liable for crimes committed by employees while acting in the scope of their employment with the intent to benefit the employer. ...

In adopting this standard, courts have expressly imported tort principles into the criminal forum. At the turn of the century, the Supreme Court acknowledged that it was stretching *respondeat superior* by extending it to the criminal context. The transfer has operated under an obvious tension. The primary objectives of tort law and criminal law differ: "Tort law distributes the loss of a harmful occurrence" but criminal law "coerc[es] the actual or potential wrongdoer to compliance with the set standards of society through the threat or application of sanctions." Moreover, a standard modeled on *respondeat superior* departs from the "basic premise of criminal jurisprudence that guilt requires personal fault." ...

The rationale for extending principles of *respondeat superior* to criminal prosecutions is grounded in the belief that a broad standard is needed to combat the organizational roots of white collar crime. White collar crime is attributed to pressures exerted by the corporation, which is more likely to enforce its penalties than the government is to bring criminal prosecutions. Consequently, the most commonly accepted basis for corporate criminal liability is the need to deter misconduct. A corollary to this view is that criminal liability will encourage better supervision of employee conduct.

The use of criminal sanctions against corporate defendants has expanded considerably in the last two decades. These sanctions traditionally were used to supplement civil remedies, "a last resort to punish particularly recalcitrant or egregious corporate behavior." Criminal prosecutions, for violations of laws ranging from securities and tax to environmental and safety regulations, tripled from 1970 to 1984. One commentator has suggested that this is the "Golden Age" of white collar crime prosecution. ...

* * *

In determining whether deterrence principles justify the current expansive doctrines supporting corporate vicarious liability for the actions of corporate agents, consider the following discussion.

Brent Fisse, *Reconstructing Corporate Criminal Law: Deterrence, Retribution, Fault, and Sanctions*
56 S. Cal. L. Rev. 1141, 1145-67 (1982)

Does the goal of deterrence imply the need for criminal as well as civil means of corporate regulation? This question is often answered in the negative. ...

The reasoning given ... reduces to three propositions:

1. The traditional utilitarian aims of individual criminal law are deterrence, rehabilitation, and incapacitation; of these aims, deterrence is the only one that is important in corporate criminal law;

2. Deterrence plays a more significant role in corporate than in individual criminal law because "corporate activity is normally undertaken in order to reap some economic benefit" and "corporate decisionmakers choose courses of action based on a calculation of potential costs and benefits"; and

3. Successful deterrence of corporate crime requires the threat of a sufficiently high level of monetary deprivation, a requirement which implies recourse merely to civil monetary penalties as opposed to criminal fines.

These propositions underestimate the role, both actual and potential, of corporate criminal liability in attaining utilitarian objectives. First, they take insufficient account of the deterrent value resulting from the stigma of criminal conviction and punishment. Second, they neglect important nonfinancial values in corporate decisionmaking—values which may render the use of only civil means of deterrence inadequate. Third, they do not recognize that rehabilitation and incapacitation may be subgoals of corporate deterrence that cannot be realized by civil regulation alone.

A. Deterrent Value of Criminal Stigma

The common distinction between punishment and penalty centers around the expressive nature of the sanction. In Joel Feinberg's words, "punishment is a conventional device for the expression of attitudes of resentment and indignation, and of judgments of disapproval and reprobation. ... Punishment, in short, has a *symbolic significance* largely missing from other kinds of penalties."[4] Feinberg has also stated that a theory of punishment that overlooks the expressive or denunciatory character of conviction and punishment in individual criminal law will seem "offensively irrelevant."[5]

Imposing criminal stigma on *individuals* is supportable on three primary bases: (1) the blameworthiness of the actor in causing the harm; (2) the unwantedness of the harm caused by the actor even if the victim is compensated; and (3) the deterrent effect of the stigma resulting from conviction and punishment. Three conceivable reasons for believing that imposing criminal stigma on corporations is not so readily supportable are: (1) corporations are not appropriate subjects of blame; (2) corporate offenses are not "unwanted" in the same way that crimes committed by individuals are unwanted; and (3) corporations cannot feel stigmatized by punishment. Putting aside for the moment the problems of defining corporate *mens rea* and designing sanctions against corporations, the question is whether these doubts about the applicability of the expressive function of punishment are consistent with everyday experience.

1. *Corporations as Blameworthy Agents*

People often react to corporate offenders not merely as impersonal harm-producing forces but as responsible, blameworthy agents. ...

---

[4] [Author's footnote 13:] J. Feinberg, Doing and Deserving 98 (1970) (emphasis in original).

[5] [Author's footnote 14:] J. Feinberg, *supra* note [4], at 105.

When people blame corporations, they are not merely channeling aggression against a deodand or some other symbolic object; they are condemning the fact that people within the organization collectively failed to avoid the offense to which corporate blame attaches. …

2. *"Unwantedness" of Corporate Crimes*

Criminally proscribed harm is "unwanted" in the sense that typically we do not regard crimes neutrally, as merely compensable acts. The infliction of criminal harm is unwanted even if the victim receives full compensation.

Do corporate offenses lack the unwantedness presupposed by the expressive function of punishment? In the past, corporate offenses were often spoken of as "morally neutral." One commentator has gone so far as to say: "The label 'crime' … is a misnomer in the area of corporation/economic bureaucracy. Without passion there is no need for the label 'criminal'; there is, for reasons of efficiency, only a need to bring public resources into play."[6]

Fireside inductions of this kind are now contradicted by a large body of survey evidence. In one recent unpublished study of attitudes toward the seriousness of crimes, a national sample of 8000 respondents rated white-collar crimes causing injury to persons, such as lethal toxic waste pollution, as extremely serious. Even as long ago as 1969, another national sample taken by Louis Harris revealed antipathy, rather than neutrality, toward corporate crime. A manufacturer of unsafe automobiles was regarded as a worse culprit than a mugger by sixty-eight percent of the respondents, twenty-two percent being of contrary opinion. A businessperson who illegally fixed prices was deemed more blameworthy than a burglar by fifty-four percent, while only twenty-eight percent believed a burglar to be worse.

Over the last decade, there have been numerous public outcries over actual or alleged corporate offenses. … [T]he available evidence shows that corporate offenses can be unwanted in the same way that individual crimes are unwanted, and even to a passionate degree.

3. *Corporate Stigma*

Whether corporations feel stigmatized by the imposition of corporate criminal liability has been doubted, as by Herbert Packer:

> Of course, the only punishment that can be imposed on a corporation is a fine, apart from the stigma of conviction itself. How real that stigma is may be doubted. Sociologists of the Sutherland persuasion talk about corporate recidivists; but there is very little evidence to suggest that the stigma of criminality means anything very substantial in the life of a corporation. John Doe has friends and neighbors; a corporation has none. And the argument that the fact of criminal conviction may have an adverse effect on a corporation's economic position seems fanciful.[7]

Such pessimism, however, overlooks the importance that business corporations typically attach to having a good public image. Corporations value their prestige so highly that they subsidize image-making as an extensive light industry. Moreover, in a recent empirical study of the impact of adverse publicity crises on seventeen major corporations, loss of corporate prestige, as distinct from financial loss, was found to be a significant concern of executives in all but two cases.

There is no reason to presume that criminal stigmatization is inappropriate in the context of corporations. Because society views corporations as capable of committing unwanted or morally offensive acts, and because corporations can be held blameworthy and can be stigmatized as responsible agents, the stigma of criminal punishment warrants serious

---

[6] [Author's footnote 27:] Ingber, *A Dialectic: The Fulfillment and Decrease of Passion in Criminal Law*, 28 Rutgers L.Rev. 861, 905 (1975).

[7] [Author's footnote 36:] H. Packer, [The Limits of the Criminal Sanction,] 361 [(1968)].

consideration as a device to deter corporations. Indeed, there is one important respect in which it is easier to justify the imposition of criminal stigma in punishing corporations rather than individuals. When society subjects individuals to criminal punishment, it expresses social condemnation in a way that encourages the recipients to feel outlawed, thereby driving such individuals toward further socially deviant behavior. By contrast, corporations are more likely to react positively to criminal stigma by attempting to repair their images and regain public confidence.

B. Nonfinancial Values In Organizational Decisionmaking and Deterrent Punishment

If it is assumed that monetary gain is the only significant value in organizational decisionmaking, then the implication is that deterrence can be served by imposing monetary loss through civil monetary penalties without resorting to criminal fines. Though this assumption is commonly held, it rests on a distorted view of the nature of corporate decisionmaking.

In bureaucratic practice, if not in classical economic theory, corporations are agencies having nonmonetary as well as monetary goals. Managerial motivation, like human motivation in general, is based on more than satisfaction of monetary want. Robert Gordon, an organizational theorist, has specified seven nonfinancial considerations important to the manager: the urge for power, the desire for prestige, the creative urge, the need to identify with a group, the desire for security, the urge for adventure, and the desire to serve others.[8] In some types of organizations, most notably churches and universities, nonmonetary motivations of this nature often take precedence over monetary concerns.

The primary implication of nonfinancial values is that deterrent sanctions might well be deployed to directly affect those values. A recent discussion of the potential use of probation as a sanction against corporations pointed out that probationary orders requiring corporations to rectify defective standard operating procedures or to make other structural changes within the organization may have a significant deterrent as well as rehabilitative effect because such intervention detracts from managerial autonomy. As John Kenneth Galbraith has noted, "Nothing in American business attitudes is so iniquitous as government interference in the *internal* affairs of the corporation."[9] Moreover, the value of corporate prestige in modern business suggests the relevance of stigmatization. In addition to the stigmatic potential of conviction and informal publicity in the media, it is conceivable that corporate convictions might be publicized by formal, court-ordered publicity sanctions, thereby increasing the stigma imposed.

This is not to say that the values of money, power, and prestige are disjoined; in practice, pursuit of any one tends to promote the others. Nor is a deterrent sanction aimed at any one of these values necessarily interpreted as such by decisionmakers. A fine, for example, might sometimes be perceived not as a financial blow but as a threat of shareholder challenge to managerial power. As a general rule, however, deterrence will most likely occur when the sanctions are congruent with the values on which they are intended to have an impact.

An elementary postulate of rational value maximization is that decisionmakers continuously consider the values of all relevant variables—values that provide the agenda of the organization. If the primary positive values on the corporate agenda are money, power, and prestige, but the law imposes only monetary loss as a negative value of noncompliance, then the money-biased deterrent signal transmitted within the organization may be at odds with a hypothesis of rational, multivalued corporate decisionmaking. As Christopher Stone has urged,

> To the extent that the individual managers are concerned about carrying out technology to its "logical" and dramatic limits, or being associated with a prestigious,

---

[8] [Author's footnote 45:] R. Gordon, [Business Leadership in the Large Corporation] 305 [(1945)].

[9] [Author's footnote 47:] J. Galbraith, [The New Industrial State] 77 [(1967)] (emphasis in original).

expanding, product-innovating company, the law's money threats ... aren't even striking at some of the critical motivations to begin with.

Assuming that corporations try to maximize many values in decisionmaking, deterring unwanted corporate behavior may require sanctions which, unlike monetary exactions, would be unconstitutional if characterized as civil. Preventive orders and formal publicity orders would be needed to inflict loss of corporate power and prestige directly. In serious cases calling for a convincing measure of deterrence, preventive or publicity orders would almost certainly be characterized as criminal. Intervention in the internal affairs of corporations and prestige-attacking publicity used expressly to deter certain behavior would bear the hallmarks of criminal punishment. ... By contrast, even extremely high monetary penalties may not be characterized as "criminal punishment," if assessed in accordance with an economic pricing model of deterrence.

Assume that the deterrent potential of aiming sanctions at nonfinancial values militates against relying only on civil penalties. It may then be argued that because decisionmaking occurs among subunits within the corporation that do not value maximize, the criminal law should be deployed not against corporations but against their personnel. Simeon Kriesberg's discussion of decisionmaking models and the control of corporate crime provides some support for this position.[10]

Kriesberg's analysis, which is based substantially upon Graham Allison's *Essence of Decision: Explaining the Cuban Missile Crisis*,[11] specifies three models of corporate decisionmaking. Model I, the Rational Actor Model, postulates a unitary, rational decisionmaking process derived from neoclassical economic theories of the firm; this is the model that has been described above as rational value maximization. Model II, the Organizational Process Model, describes the corporation as "a constellation of loosely allied decisionmaking units (*e.g.*, a marketing group, a manufacturing division, a research and development staff), each with primary responsibility for a narrow range of problems," the resolution of which is governed by standard operating procedures ("SOP's"), established by written or customary organizational rules. Model III, the Bureaucratic Politics Model, views corporate decisionmaking not in terms of rational process or set procedures, but rather as "a bargaining game involving a hierarchy of players and a maze of formal and informal channels through which decisions are shaped and implemented." Kriesberg has maintained that these three models, though not intended to be exhaustive, have varying implications for the design of corporate and individual criminal sanctions.

Model I implies that sanctions imposed upon the decisionmaking unit, the corporate entity, are relevant and efficacious if they relate to the particular values (such as profit, prestige, and stability) which rational corporate actors seek to maximize. Model II suggests that liability should be imposed upon the individual personnel in a position to enact and supervise SOP's. Under this Model, however, the decisionmaker is neither a corporation nor an individual, and the effects of sanctioning the corporation or certain members of its subunits are uncertain. Model III, the Bureaucratic Politics Model, strongly implies the need for sanctions against individual participants and key decisionmakers, with sanctions against the corporate entity providing only a secondary constraint.

Although Models II and III confirm the importance of individual accountability in controlling corporate crime, they do not support any need to rely heavily, much less totally, upon the deterrent capacity of individual criminal law. First, it is often impractical, unjust, or theoretically impossible to impose individual criminal responsibility for corporate crime. Models II and III support this conclusion. Second, though Models II and III indicate that individual accountability is appropriate, it does not follow that individual criminal liability is essential to achieve that accountability. Internal discipline, stimulated by corporate criminal or

---

[10] [Author's footnote 58:] Note, *Decisionmaking Models [and the Control of Corporate Crime*, 85 Yale L.J. 1091], 1100-28 [(1976)].

[11] [Author's footnote 59:] G. Allison, Essence of Decision: Explaining the Cuban Missile Crisis (1971).

civil liability, could also effectively reach the responsible individuals. Third, and above all, the Rational Actor Model need not dictate the form of sanctions targeted at the corporation itself. As Kriesberg has said, the three models discussed are "paradigmatic, not Procrustean."

Accordingly, the partial organizational truths of Models I, II, and III should be integrated in a Model IV, the Rational, Organizational, and Bureaucratic Model. Under this Model, deterrent sanctions against corporations would not be viewed as bludgeons for striking at the periphery of the corporate mass but rather as épées which, if thrust accurately, could have a deterrent effect on individual as well as corporate behavior. We can see this potential more readily if we avoid undue preoccupation with decisionmaking models and consider what organizational responses we wish to elicit through the use of corporate criminal law.

C. Deterrence As A Catalyst For Rehabilitation and Incapacitation

If deterrence is a goal distinct from rehabilitation and incapacitation—a concept which now appears to be prevalent—then rehabilitation and incapacitation are discrete civil goals that provide no foundation for corporate *criminal* law. But to treat rehabilitation and incapacitation as distinct from deterrence when applied to corporate criminal law is to entertain a misconception. Policy revision, internal disciplinary control, and procedural action—the forms of rehabilitation and incapacitation that are most practical and useful in preventing corporate crime—are subgoals of deterrence. Once this is seen, the need for criminal as well as civil means of corporate deterrence becomes apparent.

When an individual criminal is punished or threatened with punishment for a street crime, the goal of the punishment or threat is to inhibit rather than to catalyze. The message conveyed is "refrain from committing that offense," rather than "refrain from committing that offense and take such steps to improve your physiological and psychological capacity for self-control as are necessary to guard against repetition." By contrast, when a corporate offender is punished or threatened with punishment, the message is catalytic as well as inhibitory. The message conveyed, for corporate offenses of commission as well as for those of omission, is "refrain from committing that offense and take such steps as are necessary organizationally to guard against repetition."

The principal reason for this difference is that organizational offenders cannot exert self-control merely by individual self-denial. Self-denial on these offenders' parts must be embodied in corporate policy and backed by appropriate disciplinary measures and organizational procedures. Accordingly, under a scheme of corporate deterrence, punishment or a threat of punishment requires corporations to do more than merely exercise inhibition and self-restraint; they are expected to institute effective crime prevention policies, disciplinary controls and changes in standard operating procedures.

1. *Crime Prevention Policies*

Threats of punishment directed at corporations are intended to catalyze the adoption of sound policies of compliance. Although it would be most unusual to find a company with an express *non*compliance policy, companies often implement or strengthen existing compliance strategies as a result of brushes with the criminal law. ...

2. *Internal Disciplinary Controls*

Punishment or the threat of punishment should also catalyze internal disciplinary controls. Catalyzing discipline within a corporation has long been valued as a deterrent outcome of collective liability.

3. *Crime-Preventive Standard Operating Procedures*

Threats of punishment addressed to corporations are also intended to catalyze the application or modification of preventive standard operating procedures ("SOP's"). Standard operating procedures are rules prescribing day-to-day operations within an organization. Individual personnel are located by job specification in organizational subunits; their efforts within those subunits are coordinated by a set of routine procedures. These procedures may be oral or written instructions, or may evolve as a matter of custom. They are found in all forms of organizations, from large governmental departments to small private companies. ...

4. *Catalytic Deterrence and Punitive Injunctions*

If policy revision, disciplinary control, and changes in SOP's are conceived as forms of rehabilitation and incapacitation which are inherent in the goal of deterrence, that goal is transformed in such a way that civil means of regulation are not always sufficient. When it is unlikely that the threat of a fine would catalyze the internal changes necessary to achieve effective corporate self-control, or when imposing a fine is inappropriate for other reasons, it is necessary to impose structural changes directly. The type of sanction most suitable for this purpose would be a punitive mandatory injunction. As argued previously, the severity and purpose of this sanction, at least in the more serious cases, would give it a decidedly criminal character, and would require the use of criminal procedural safeguards. Although the idea of punitive mandatory injunctions may seem unusual, there is nothing odd about it from a deterrence theory standpoint. On the contrary, as John Coffee has observed, "It is a curious paradox that the civil law is better equipped at present than the criminal law to authorize [disciplinary or structural] interventions. Corporate probation could fill this gap and, at last, offer a punishment that fits the corporation."[12] This paradox exists whether or not probation or injunction is the appropriate vehicle for punitive intervention.

* * *

Finally, although the primary aim of corporate criminal liability appears to be deterrence, some commentators argue that corporations can be blameworthy actors upon whom retributive punishment is appropriately imposed. The following summarizes these arguments.

Julie Rose O'Sullivan, *Professional Discipline for Law Firms? A Response to Professor Schneyer's Proposal*
16 Geo. J. Legal Ethics 1 (2002)[13]

The case for corporate criminal liability is often founded on evidentiary or instrumental considerations: organizational liability will ease the conviction of some offender (organization or individual) for what would otherwise be difficult to prove violations. First, because of "the evidentiary difficulty of penetrating the corporate 'black box' to locate the appropriate agent or agents to prosecute for a crime," "proceeding against the enterprise is often less costly and more fruitful." This is so because, under at least the federal *respondeat superior* standard, a criminal conviction may be secured against an entity even when no one agent can be identified who both possessed the requisite guilty intent and performed the guilty act. ... Second, juries are reluctant to criminally sanction individuals where the "'bulk of harm-causing corporate conduct does not typically have, at its root, a particular agent so clearly to blame" that he or she merits'" sanction. Juries reluctant to "scapegoat" individuals may, however, be willing to convict an impersonal entity such as a corporation, thus filling a "gap in enforcement." Finally, corporate criminal liability may help the government secure sanctions against culpable

---

[12] Author's footnote 102:] Coffee, ["*No Soul to Damn: No Body to Kick": An Unscandalized Inquiry Into the Problem of Corporate Punishment*, 79 Mich. L. Rev. 386], 459 [(1981)].

[13] [Ed.:] Some of the text of this article has been revised slightly (*e.g.*, the word "entity" has been substituted for the original "firm") but the meaning has not changed. For extended analysis of imposition of criminal liability on "blameworthy" organizations, see Samuel W. Buell, *The Blaming Function of Entity Criminal Liability*, 31 Indiana L.J. 473 (2006).

individuals. The threat of criminal sanctions may force organizations to cooperate with prosecutors, identifying the malefactors in their ranks, in order to avoid liability. The potential for corporate criminal liability makes more likely, then, that the "black box" will be successfully penetrated and the culpable individuals prosecuted. At least in the federal realm, this is not an insubstantial consideration given the weight that both the Department of Justice's policy on charging corporations and the U.S. Sentencing Guidelines applicable to organizational defendants accord to corporate cooperation in the investigation and disciplining of errant employees. ...

Granting that entity liability will ease prosecutors' burden in imposing sanctions on *someone* (entities if not individuals), however, does not justify such liability. It seems to me that proponents of entity liability first need to establish that such sanctions are fair, effective, and/or necessary to further the aims of criminal law because only then are these evidentiary or instrumental considerations relevant. Stated alternatively, if vicarious entity liability will not serve the purposes of incapacitation, deterrence, retribution or rehabilitation ..., the fact that it facilitates sanctioning should be troubling rather than reassuring. ...

The ... evidentiary assertion that it is difficult to isolate and sanction an individual culprit may be correct, but "its truth may lie less in the ability of the 'true' culprit to hide his identity than in the absence of any such 'true' offender in the broad range of cases." As proponents of corporate criminal liability argue, the relevant point is that:

> Because of the diffusion of responsibility in organizations and the ways in which the individual decisions are channelled by corporate rules, policies and structures, there may in fact *be* no individual or group of individuals that is "justly to blame" for the crime. Individuals in corporations frequently operate in a kind of "twilight zone" of autonomy; they may simply exert insufficient choice or control to be suitable recipients of blame.[14] ...

[The theory is, then, that there are cases where the entity,] not the individual, is ultimately the erring actor. Focusing the sanction in the enterprise "'has appeal when ... society wishes to denounce the conduct and rehabilitate the actor, but the source of the wrongdoing seems to lie in bureaucratic shortcomings—flaws in the organizations formal and informal authority structure, or in its information pathways—rather than in the deliberate act of any particular employee.'"[15]

Some take issue with the basic premise of this rationale: they question whether an impersonal legal entity has "the capacity to have an intention and to choose"[16] that is the precondition to blameworthiness[17] and whether the "stigma" of criminal condemnation means anything when an impersonal entity is its target.[18]

It is true that a ... corporation has "no soul to be damned, and no body to be kicked." While as a philosophical matter it is difficult to see how this invisible being can manifest a will to do wrong, many scholars convincingly argue that entity intentionality is expressed through standard operating instructions, decision rules, hierarchical structures, encouraged patterns of behavior, and systems of control[19] because these policies and practices "are intended to replace

---

[14] [Author's footnote 107:] Jennifer Moore, *Corporate Culpability Under the Federal Sentencing Guidelines*, 34 Ariz. L. Rev. 743, 754 (1992).

[15] [Author's footnote 108:] [Ted Schneyer, *Professional Discipline for Law Firms?*, 77 Cornell L. Rev. 1, 25 (1992)].

[16] [Author's footnote 109:] Owen M. Fiss, *Foreward: The Forms of Justice*, 93 Harv. L. Rev. 1, 22-23 (1979); *see also Developments in the Law-Corporate Crime: Regulating Corporate Behavior Through Criminal Sanctions*, 92 Harv. L. Rev. 1227, 1241 (1979) [hereinafter *Developments*] (noting that *mens rea* "has no meaning when applied to a corporate defendant since an organization possesses no mental state").

[17] [Author's footnote 110:] *See* Paul H. Robinson, Criminal Law § 7.2, at 374-75 (1997).

[18] [Author's footnote 111:] *See* Herbert Packer, The Limits of the Criminal Sanction 361 (1968).

[19] [Author's footnote 113:] [Brent Fisse, *Reconstructing Corporate Criminal Law: Deterrence, Retribution, Fault,*

agents' decisional autonomy with an organizational decision-making process."[20] Organizational theory affirms that "[t]he behavior of individuals in corporations is not merely the product of individual choice; it is stimulated and shaped by goals, rules, policies, and procedures that are features of the corporation as an entity."[21] Research into the origins of white-collar crime demonstrates that "at least some criminal behavior usefully may be viewed not as personal deviance, but rather as a predictable product of the individual's membership in or contact with certain organizations."[22] As one researcher found, organizational cultures can constitute such a strong force as to overwhelm the significance of individual will: "In [the corporate setting,] each man's own wants, ideas—even his perceptions and emotions—are swayed and directed by an institutional structure so pervasive that it might be construed as having a set of goals and constraints (if not a mind and purpose) of *its* own."[23] The literature, then, confirms what practical experience might suggest:

> (1) each corporation is distinctive and draws its uniqueness from a complex combination of formal and informal factors; (2) the formal and informal structure of a corporation can promote, or discourage, violations of the law; and (3) this structure is identifiable, observable, and malleable.[24] ...

The above discussion may suggest that there are two potentially overlapping but analytically distinct ways in which an entity may be deemed "responsible" in a causal sense for its agents' ... misconduct. First, an entity may fail to put in place organizational policies or practices sufficient to prevent certain types of ... misconduct. Second, an entity may possess a bad "culture" or "ethos," which may in some cases explain the

---

and Sanctions, 56 S. Cal. L. Rev. 1141,1148 n.19 (1983)]; *see* also [Brent Fisse & John Braithwaite, Corporations, Crime and Accountability132 (1993)] ("Corporate responsibility may be based on corporate intentionality, in the sense of corporate policy, or corporate negligence, in the sense of an inexcusable failure to meet the standard of conduct expected of a corporation in the position of the defendant."); Peter French, Collective and Corporate Responsibility (1984); William S. Laufer & Alan Strudler, *Corporate Intentionality, Desert, and Variants of Vicarious Liability*, 37 Am. Crim. L. Rev. 1285 (2000).

[20] [Author's footnote 114:] Moore, *supra* note [14], at 767.

[21] [Author's footnote 115:] *Id.* at 753.

[22] [Author's footnote 116:] Martin Needleman & Carolyn Needleman, *Organizational Crime: Two Models of Criminogenesis*, 20 Soc. Q. 517 (1970); *see also* Moore, *supra* note [14], at 754 & n.58.

[23] [Author's footnote 117:] Christopher D. Stone, Where the Law Ends 7 (1975).

[24] [Author's footnote 118:] [Pamela H. Bucy, *Corporate Ethos: A Standard for Imposing Corporate Criminal Liability*, 75 Minn. L. Rev. 1095, 1127 (1991)]; *see also* Moore, *supra* note [14], at 755 ("there appear to be 'good' and 'bad' corporations, law-abiding corporations and recidivists, and there is a remarkable consensus as to which corporations are which"); Diane Vaughan, *Toward Understanding Unlawful Organizational Behavior*, 80 Mich. L. Rev. 1377, 1378, 1396-97 (1982). Marshall Clinard surveyed middle managers from a variety of companies, asking why some corporations are more ethical than others. He summarized their responses as follows:

> [M]ost of the executives believed that unethical corporate behavior can usually be traced to internal rather than external forces. Internally, individual ethics, personal ambition, and poor supervision by top management play major roles. The ethical history or tradition of a corporation is also important, particularly the characteristics of the founder and his influence on family participation and subsequent top management. Finally, unethical behavior is likely to result if the corporate way of life results in a tendency to push too aggressively for profits. Factors external to the corporation, such as corporate financial problems, unfair practices of competitors, or the type of industry, though mentioned by some, were not major explanations for the underlying factors that lead to some corporations being unethical and others ethical.

Marshall B. Clinard, Corporate Ethics and Crime 69-70 (1983).

above management deficiencies but which may also [actually encourage employee wrongdoing].   ...

Accepting, then, that legal entities can be responsible for wrongdoing, the next question must be how one can identify when the entity, as opposed to (or in addition to) individuals within it, should be identified as the "culprit." In framing a response to this question, two additional objections to the imposition of corporate criminal liability should be considered.

First, some argue that vicarious criminal liability is unfair because its penalties unjustly fall "on the innocent rather than the guilty—that is, the penalty is borne by stockholders and others having an interest in the corporation rather than by the guilty individual." This "flow-through" fairness argument has a second, utilitarian or consequentialist strand which contends that if the "stigma" criminal law uses to achieve its ends is applied to tar "innocent" shareholders and other corporate constituencies who did not participate in or knowingly condone the misconduct, it will create a perception that the law is unjust and thus ultimately undermine compliance with that law. Additionally, the stigma, if overused, will lose its unique force and effect. In Herbert Packer's words, "[t]he more indiscriminate we are in treating conduct as criminal, the less stigma resides in the fact that a man has been convicted of something called a crime."

... In the criminal context, the rejoinder to objections founded on the unfair "flow-through" effect of criminal penalties are many. "Innocents" to some degree suffer whenever criminal penalties are imposed, whether it is the families of individual defendants or the shareholders, bondholders, employees, or customers of corporations. Criminal penalties prevent the unjust enrichment of shareholders and other corporate constituencies; any sanctions imposed in excess of the criminal profits obtained are spread among so many shareholders as to be negligible. Shareholders have acceded to a distributional scheme in which profits and losses from corporate activities are distributed not according to "just deserts" but rather according to position in the company or type of investment. Finally, the stigma of criminal conviction does not "flow through" to shareholders. ...

[If these effects are deemed threatening,] a rule of parsimony would seem appropriate. In other words, in order to minimize unfair "flow-through" effects and thus to preserve the perceived fairness of the rule *and* the deterrent value of the sanction, entity liability should only be imposed when it is clear that the entity is actually the culprit—that is, that the entity's culture, policies or procedures caused, encouraged, or condoned the misconduct at issue.

If the fairness *and* ultimate utility of entity liability turns on the precision with which the entity is identified as the culpable party, [is] a *respondeat superior* standard of liability with no due diligence defense—that is, a standard of liability that does not permit consideration of an entity's reasonable efforts to create an [effective compliance program to prevent and detect violations of the law]— ... the answer[?] ...

If *respondeat superior* is not the appropriate standard by which to isolate corporate "culprits," what is? This issue is frequently encountered in the corporate crime literature; indeed, the question whether "it [is] possible to attribute fault to a corporation on a genuinely corporate yet workable basis" has been labeled "the blackest hole in the theory of corporate criminal law."[25] It has provoked an interesting literature in which scholars have attempted to isolate those situations in which the corporation, as opposed to individuals within it, should be deemed responsible. The answer to this query depends in part on what we are seeking to achieve in structuring the liability system because even accepting that [an entity] can be a[] ... "culprit" in that its policies or culture encouraged the misconduct at issue, we still need a principled rationale for sanctioning the entity as opposed to the individuals within it.

The underlying premise of some of the theories concerning the optimal ways to identify corporate "culprits" seems to be that corporations can be responsible for criminal misconduct in moral terms as well as in practical effect. According to some corporate crime scholars, then,

---

[25] [Author's footnote 157:] Fisse, *supra* note [19], at 1183.

the object of identifying the corporate "culprit" and imposing a criminal stigma on that "culprit" is at least in part to exact retribution.[26] ...

B. PRINCIPLES OF LIABILITY

The black letter law of corporate criminal liability is straightforward: a corporation is liable for the criminal misdeeds of its agents acting within the actual or apparent scope of their employment or authority if the agents intend, at least in part, to benefit the corporation, even though their actions may be contrary to corporate policy or express corporate order. In reviewing the following materials, which illustrate the application of this standard, the reader should consider whether these *respondeat superior* principles effectively (1) target for liability "blameworthy" *organizations* and (2) promote deterrence goals by galvanizing the organizations to address the institutional circumstances that facilitated or encouraged employee wrongdoing and to institute crime prevention policies.

1. "WITHIN THE SCOPE OF EMPLOYMENT" REQUIREMENT

NEW YORK CENTRAL & HUDSON RIVER R.R. CO. v. UNITED STATES
212 U.S. 481 (1909)

MR. JUSTICE DAY delivered the opinion of the court:

This is a writ of error to the Circuit Court of the United States for the Southern District of New York, sued out by the New York Central & Hudson River Railroad Company, plaintiff in error. In the Circuit Court the railroad company and Fred L. Pomeroy, its assistant traffic manager, were convicted for the payment of rebates to the American Sugar Refining Company and others, upon shipments of sugar from the city of New York to the city of Detroit, Michigan. The indictment was upon seven counts and was returned against the company, its general traffic manager, and its assistant traffic manager. ...

Upon the trial there was a conviction upon all of the six counts .... The assistant traffic manager was sentenced to pay a fine of $1,000 upon each of the counts; the present plaintiff in error to pay a fine of $18,000 on each count, making a fine of $108,000 in all.

The facts are practically undisputed. They are mainly established by stipulation, or by letters passing between the traffic managers and the agent of the sugar refining companies. It was shown that the established, filed, and published rate between New York and Detroit was 23 cents per 100 pounds on sugar, except during the month of June, 1904, when it was 21 cents per 100 pounds.

The sugar refining companies were engaged in selling and shipping their products in Brooklyn and Jersey City, and W. H. Edgar & Son were engaged in business in Detroit,

---

[26] [Author's footnote 158:] Fisse & Braithwaite, *supra* note [19], at 25 (asserting that "[w]hen people blame corporations, they are not merely channelling aggression against the ox that gored. Nor are they pointing the finger at individuals behind the corporate mantle. They are condemning the fact that organisations either implemented a policy of noncompliance or failed to exercise its collective capacity to avoid the offence for which blame attaches."); Fisse, *supra* note [19], at 1169-70 (arguing that retributionist "justice as fairness" ideals can be said to require that all entities compete on equal terms and that erring entities be forced to divest themselves of any undue profit or advantage accrued through wrongdoing); Moore, *supra* note [14], at 755 ("The idea of corporate culpability is not merely a product of organizational theory and research on corporate crime; it is part of ordinary moral discourse."); *Developments*, *supra* note [16], at 1241 (noting that "while the primary aim of corporate sanctions is deterrence, there may be some retributive limitations on the pursuit of this goal, and courts as well as legislatures will likely continue to require some blameworthiness on the part of the defendant in the vast majority of cases").

Michigan, where they were dealers in sugar. By letters between Palmer, in charge of the traffic of the sugar refining companies and of procuring rates for the shipment of sugar, and the general and assistant traffic managers of the railroad company, it was agreed that Edgar & Son should receive a rate of 18 cents per 100 pounds from New York to Detroit. ... [T]his concession was given to Edgar & Son to prevent them from resorting to transportation by the water route between New York and Detroit, thereby depriving the roads interested of the business, and to assist Edgar & Son in meeting the severe competition with other shippers and dealers. The shipments were made accordingly and claims of rebate made on the basis of a reduction of five cents a hundred pounds from the published rates. ...

... The principal attack in this court is upon the constitutional validity of certain features of the Elkins act. 32 Stat. 847. That act, among other things, provides:

> "(1) That anything done or omitted to be done by a corporation common carrier subject to the act to regulate commerce, and the acts amendatory thereof, which, if done or omitted to be done by any director or officer thereof, or any receiver, trustee, lessee, agent, or person acting for or employed by such corporation, would constitute a misdemeanor under said acts, or under this act, shall also be held to be a misdemeanor committed by such corporation, and upon conviction thereof it shall be subject to like penalties as are prescribed in said acts, or by this act, with reference to such persons, except as such penalties are herein changed....
>
> "In construing and enforcing the provisions of this section, the act, omission or failure of any officer, agent or other person acting for or employed by any common carrier, acting within the scope of his employment shall in every case, be also deemed to be the act, omission or failure of such carrier, as well as that of the person."

It is contended that these provisions of the law are unconstitutional because Congress has no authority to impute to a corporation the commission of criminal offenses, or to subject a corporation to a criminal prosecution by reason of the things charged. The argument is that to thus punish the corporation is in reality to punish the innocent stockholders, and to deprive them of their property without opportunity to be heard, consequently without due process of law. And it is further contended that these provisions of the statute deprive the corporation of the presumption of innocence, a presumption which is part of due process in criminal prosecutions. It is urged that, as there is no authority shown by the board of directors or the stockholders for the criminal acts of the agents of the company, in contracting for and giving rebates, they could not be lawfully charged against the corporation. As no action of the board of directors could legally authorize a crime, and as indeed the stockholders could not do so, the arguments come to this: that owing to the nature and character of its organization and the extent of its power and authority, a corporation cannot commit a crime of the nature charged in this case.

Some of the earlier writers on common law held the law to be that a corporation could not commit a crime. ... The modern authority, universally, so far as we know, is the other way. In considering the subject, Bishop's New Criminal Law, § 417, devotes a chapter to the capacity of corporations to commit crime, and states the law to be:

> "Since a corporation acts by its officers and agents, their purposes, motives, and intent are just as much those of the corporation as are the things done. If, for example, the invisible, intangible essence or air, which we term a corporation, can level mountains, fill up valleys, lay down iron tracks, and run railroad cars on them, it can intend to do it, and can act therein as well viciously as virtuously."

Without citing the state cases holding the same view, we may note *Telegram Newspaper Co. v. Com.*, 172 Massachusetts 294, in which it was held that a corporation was subject to punishment for criminal contempt, and the court, speaking by Mr. Chief Justice Field, said:

the law [handwritten margin note]

opposing Arg [handwritten margin note]

"We think that a corporation may be liable criminally for certain offenses of which a specific intent may be a necessary element. There is no more difficulty in imputing to a corporation a specific intent in criminal proceedings than in civil. A corporation cannot be arrested and imprisoned in either civil or criminal proceedings, but its property may be taken either as compensation for a private wrong or as punishment for a public wrong."...

It is now well established that in actions for tort the corporation may be held responsible for damages for the acts of its agent within the scope of his employment.

And this is the rule when the act is done by the agent in the course of his employment, although done wantonly or recklessly or against the express orders of the principal. In such cases the liability is not imputed because the principal actually participates in the malice or fraud, but because the act is done for the benefit of the principal, while the agent is acting within the scope of his employment in the business of the principal, and justice requires that the latter shall be held responsible for damages to the individual who has suffered by such conduct.

A corporation is held responsible for acts not within the agent's corporate powers strictly construed, but which the agent has assumed to perform for the corporation when employing the corporate powers actually authorized, and in such cases there need be no written authority under seal or vote of the corporation in order to constitute the agency or to authorize the act.

In this case we are to consider the criminal responsibility of a corporation for an act done while an authorized agent of the company is exercising the authority conferred upon him. It was admitted by the defendant at the trial that at the time mentioned in the indictment the general freight traffic manager and the assistant freight traffic manager were authorized to establish rates at which freight should be carried over the line of the New York Central and Hudson River Company, and were authorized to unite with other companies in the establishing, filing, and publishing of through rates, including the through rate or rates between New York and Detroit referred to in the indictment. Thus the subject-matter of making and fixing rates was within the scope of the authority and employment of the agents of the company, whose acts in this connection are sought to be charged upon the company. Thus clothed with authority, the agents were bound to respect the regulation of interstate commerce enacted by Congress, requiring the filing and publication of rates and punishing departures therefrom. Applying the principle governing civil liability, we go only a step farther in holding that the act of the agent, while exercising the authority delegated to him to make rates for transportation, may be controlled, in the interest of public policy, by imputing his act to his employer and imposing penalties upon the corporation for which he is acting in the premises.

It is true that there are some crimes which, in their nature, cannot be committed by corporations. But there is a large class of offenses, of which rebating under the Federal statutes is one, wherein the crime consists in purposely doing the things prohibited by statute. In that class of crimes we see no good reason why corporations may not be held responsible for and charged with the knowledge and purposes of their agents, acting within the authority conferred upon them. If it were not so, many offenses might go unpunished and acts be committed in violation of law, where, as in the present case, the statute requires all persons, corporate or private, to refrain from certain practices forbidden in the interest of public policy.

It is a part of the public history of the times that statutes against rebates could not be effectually enforced so long as individuals only were subject to punishment for violation of the law, when the giving of rebates or concessions enured to the benefit of the corporations of which the individuals were but the instruments. This situation, developed in more than one report of the Interstate Commerce Commission, was no doubt influential in bringing about the enactment of the Elkins law, making corporations criminally liable.

This statute does not embrace things impossible to be done by a corporation; its objects are to prevent favoritism, and to secure equal rights to all in interstate transportation, and one legal rate, to be published and posted and accessible to all alike.

We see no valid objection in law, and every reason in public policy, why the corporation, which profits by the transaction, and can only act through its agents and officers, shall be held punishable by fine because of the knowledge and intent of its agents to whom it has intrusted authority to act in the subject-matter of making and fixing rates of transportation, and whose knowledge and purposes may well be attributed to the corporation for which the agents act. While the law should have regard to the rights of all, and to those of corporations no less than to those of individuals, it cannot shut its eyes to the fact that the great majority of business transactions in modern times are conducted through these bodies, and particularly that interstate commerce is almost entirely in their hands, and to give them immunity from all punishment because of the old and exploded doctrine that a corporation cannot commit a crime would virtually take away the only means of effectually controlling the subject-matter and correcting the abuses aimed at.

There can be no question of the power of Congress to regulate interstate commerce, to prevent favoritism, and to secure equal rights to all engaged in interstate trade. It would be a distinct step backward to hold that Congress cannot control those who are conducting this interstate commerce by holding them responsible for the intent and purposes of the agents to whom they have delegated the power to act in the premises.

Notes

1. The Court also seems to found its decision in part on its determination that, absent the potential for corporate criminal liability, there would be virtually no "means of effectually controlling the subject matter and correcting the abuses aimed at." Is this statement accurate? Other countries, such as Germany, do not allow for corporate criminal liability. Couldn't the government rely on the threat of individual criminal liability and civil suits against the corporation, as do other countries? Sophisticated economic analyses of the question (which cannot be effectively summarized here) generally conclude that some mixture of both individual and corporate criminal liability is necessary for effective deterrence. *See* Jennifer Arlen, *Corporate criminal liability: theory and evidence*, in Alon Harel & Keith N. Hylton, Research Handbook on the Economics of Criminal Law (2012). Achieving the optimal mixture of individual and corporate prosecutions may be difficult as a practical matter. Many have sharply criticized the DOJ for failing to indict the individuals responsible for the recent financial crisis. *See, e.g.*, Jed S. Rakoff, *The Financial Crisis: Why have No High-Level Exeuctives Been Prosecuted?*, The New York Review of Books (Jan. 9, 2014). Others have responded by pointing out the difficulties presented by these cases and the fact that the DOJ can only charge what it can prove. *See, e.g.*, Peter J. Henning, *Why It Is Getting Harder to Prosecute Executives for Corporate Misconduct*, 41 Vt. L. Rev. 503 (2016); Samuel W. Buell, *Is the White Collar Offender Privileged?*, 63 Duke L.J. 823, 846-54 (2014). Recently, the DOJ issued a memorandum (the "Yates Memo"), which has been incorporated in the U.S. Attorney's Manual (reproduced *infra* Part C), that underscored the importance of individual accountability for corporate wrongdoing. What is the optimal mix of individual and corporate responsibility? *See* Brandon L. Garrett, *The Corporate Criminal as Scapegoat*, 101 Va. L. Rev. 1789 (2015).

2. The Court states that no good reason can be seen for not applying civil law *respondeat superior* principles in the criminal realm. Does the Court adequately consider the differences in the aims of civil and criminal law, and in particular the usual requirement that criminal liability may not be imposed vicariously and that some kind of mental fault attend the imposition of the criminal stigma?

Are *respondeat superior* principles necessarily the only theory upon which criminal liability could be based? In this case, a statute outlined the rules for entity liability. In most cases presently brought, entity liability is not expressly provided for by statute and is instead read into the statute, but courts continue to use the *respondeat superior* standard. Should courts have crafted rules for liability more attuned to the criminal context—*i.e.*, more likely to separate out those corporations that truly facilitate or encourage criminal wrongdoing by their agents from those corporations who at most are responsible for failing adequately to supervise "rogue" agents? *See generally* Brent Fisse & John Braithwaite, Corporations, Crime and Accountability 48 (1993) (proposing concept of "reactive fault" defined as "unreasonable corporate failure to devise and undertake satisfactory preventative or corrective measures in response to the commission of the *actus reus* of an offence by personnel acting on behalf of the corporation");

Pamela H. Bucy, *Corporate Ethos: A Standard for Imposing Criminal Liability*, 75 Minn. L. Rev. 1095, *passim* (1991) (proposing a corporate "ethos" standard of liability that states that a corporation should be found criminally liable only when "its ethos encourages criminal conduct by agents of the corporation"); *Developments in the Law-Corporate Crime: Regulating Corporate Behavior Through Criminal Sanctions*, 92 Harv. L. Rev. 1227, 1241-58 (1979) (identifying three different theories of corporate blameworthiness and proposing a standard of liability under which a corporation would be liable under *respondeat superior* principles but the corporation could rebut the presumption of liability created by *respondeat superior* by proving that it, as an organization, exercised due diligence to prevent the crime).

3. The Court does not in terms address the objection that to "punish the corporation is in reality to punish the innocent stockholders, and to deprive them of their property" without a hearing and thus without due process. Did the Court pay sufficient attention to the equities viewed from the shareholders' perspective? Upon whom does the punishment nominally imposed upon a corporation truly fall—and how should that affect liability rules? Consider the following perspective offered by Professor John Coffee:

> ... As a moment's reflection reveals, the costs of deterrence tend to spill over onto parties who cannot be characterized as culpable. Axiomatically, corporations do not bear the ultimate cost of the fine; put simply, when the corporation catches a cold, someone else sneezes. This overspill of the penalty initially imposed on the corporation has at least four distinct levels, each progressively more serious. First, stockholders bear the penalty in the reduced value of their securities. Second, bondholders and other creditors suffer a diminution in the value of their securities which reflects the increased riskiness of the enterprise. ... [T]he third level of incidence of a severe financial penalty involves parties even less culpable than the stockholders. As a class, stockholders can at least sometimes be said to have received unjust enrichment from the benefits of the crime; this arguably justifies their indirectly bearing a compensating fine. However, if the fine is severe enough to threaten the solvency of the corporation, the predictable response will be a cost-cutting campaign, involving reductions in the work force through layoffs of lower echelon employees who received no benefit from the earlier crime. ... Finally, there is a fourth level of incidence of a financial penalty: it may be passed onto the consumer. If the corporation competes in a product market characterized by imperfect competition (a trait of most of the "real world"), then the fine may be recovered from consumers in the form of higher prices. If this happens, the "wicked" corporation not only goes unpunished, but the intended beneficiary of the criminal statute (*i.e.*, the consumer) winds up bearing its penalty.

John C. Coffee, Jr., *"No Soul to Damn: No Body to Kick": An Unscandalized Inquiry into the Problem of Corporate Punishment*, 79 Mich. L. Rev. 386, 401-02 (1981). When the partnership Arthur Andersen LLP was indicted for obstruction based on the actions of a small subset of its employees, some questioned the wisdom of this exercise of prosecutorial discretion based on the unfair "flow-through" effect the indictment would have on many Arthur Andersen employees and customers. Consider the following critique:

> On balance, the public benefits generated by prosecuting Andersen criminally were minimal or, if they existed at all, were exceedingly subtle. No one went to jail as a result of its conviction, nor could they have under the law. The criminal fine paid by Andersen was the maximum under the criminal law but was still vastly less than the fines and penalties that might have been, and had been, levied against the firm in civil enforcement actions taken by various government agencies. Yet the indictment, the conviction, and the consequent prohibition against appearing before the [SEC] were sufficient to kill the company, a company made up not only of partners and managers, but also, of course, of lower-level employees and shareholders. In 2001, Andersen employed 85,000 people in approximately 390 offices in 85 countries. By the end of the following year, only 3000 people remained.

Elizabeth K. Ainslie, *Indicting Corporations Revisited: Lessons of the Arthur Andersen Prosecution*, 43 Am. Crim. L. Rev. 107, 109 (2006).

4. Obviously, it will be the rare case where a prosecutor uncovers a resolution by the board of directors of a corporation defining an agent's employment to include the commission of illegal acts or authorizing such acts within the course of the agent's employment. Neither is necessary to support vicarious corporate liability. The following jury instruction, approved in *United States v. American Radiator & Standard Sanitary Corp.*, 433 F.2d 174, 204-05 (3d Cir. 1970), sets forth the pertinent standard:

> A corporation, itself, cannot attend a meeting or make decisions; it must act through agents, such as its officers, directors and employees. In order for a corporation to be responsible for the acts or statements of one of its agents it is not necessary that the corporation specifically authorize the agent to commit the act or make the statement. A corporation is legally bound by the acts and statements of its agents done or made within the scope of their employment or their apparent authority. Acts within the scope of employment are acts done on behalf of the corporation and directly related to the performance of the type of duties the employee has general authority to perform. Apparent authority is the authority which outsiders could reasonably assume that the agent would have, judging from his position with the company, the responsibilities previously entrusted to him, and the circumstances surrounding his past conduct.

5. It also is not necessary that the Government show that high-ranking persons within the corporation approved, acquiesced in, or condoned the criminal activity. A corporation may be held liable under federal law for the actions of employees at the lowest rungs of its hierarchy, so long as they are acting within the scope of their employment (and the other requirements discussed below are satisfied). "'It is the *function* delegated to the corporate officer or agent which determines his power to engage the corporation in a criminal transaction' rather than the title or position he holds." Kathleen F. Brickey, *Corporate Criminal Liability: A Primer for Corporate Counsel*, 40 Bus. Lawyer, 129, 131 (1984) (citation omitted); *see also* United States v. Automated Medical Labs., Inc., 770 F.2d 399 (4th Cir.1985); United States v. Basic Construction Co., 711 F.2d 570, 573 (4th Cir.1983). For example, in *United States v. Dye Construction Co.*, a corporation was held liable for a willful violation of OSHA regulations for failing properly to shore up a trench, which failure resulted in the death of a worker. The court explained that:

> We find no merit in the ... contention that the corporation cannot be guilty of willfulness based on the acts, conduct and inferentially the states of mind of the employees. Contrary to Dye's argument, the president [of the corporation] is not the only individual whose state of mind would be relevant. The cases recognize that corporations are responsible for the acts and omissions of their authorized agents acting in the scope of their employment. There is no doubt as to the authority of the superintendent, the foreman and the back hoe operator [who had observed the trench prior to the cave-in].

510 F.2d 78, 82 (10th Cir. 1975); *see also* Steere Tank Lines v. United States, 330 F.2d 719 (5th Cir. 1963) (corporation, a motor common carrier regulated by the Interstate Commerce Commission (ICC), held vicariously liable for knowing and willful violations of ICC record-keeping regulations by its employee truck drivers).

It is important to note that although the position in the corporation of the wrongdoing agent may not be important for purposes of evaluating a corporation's legal liability, it may be an important factor in a prosecutor's decision whether to actually proceed against the corporation, *see* Justice Department Guidance on Prosecutions of Corporations, reproduced *infra*, at Part C. And it certainly will be an important factor in determining the amount of the fine to be levied on the corporation should the case go forward and should the corporation be convicted. *See* U.S. Sentencing Guidelines Manual § 8C2.5(b); *infra* Part D. Given that both prosecutors and those responsible for formulating sentencing policy believe this element to be an important part of determining corporate *culpability*, why is it not relevant to corporate criminal *liability*? What conception of the reasons for corporate criminal liability, and what model of corporate decision-making, undergird this rule?

6. A different stand of liability—the identification principle—is used in many U.S. states and countries around the world. *See, e.g.*, Cristina de Maglie, *Models of Corporate Criminal Liability in Comparative Law*, 4 Wash. U. Global Studs. L. Rev. 547 (2005). This is still a species of vicarious liability but it is narrower in its terms. For example, in the United Kingdom, subject to some limited exceptions, a corporation may be held liable for the criminal acts of those who represent its "directing mind" and will and who control what it does. The idea is that such high-ranking persons effectively *are* the company. *See* Tesco Ltd. v. Nattrass, [1962] AC 153. In Model Penal Code terms, a corporation is liable when the commission of the offense was "authorized, requested, commanded, performed or recklessly tolerated by the board of directors or by a high managerial agent acting in behalf of the corporation within the scope of his office or employment." ALI, Model Penal Code §2.07(1)(c). Consider whether this is the better approach. Does it invite difficulties in application (*e.g.*, which officers have a "directing mind"?). Might it incentivize management to avoid learning of wrongdoing within the entity? What if corporate policy effectively encouraged the lower echelon employees to commit the crime and vast harm ensued—should the entity be immune simply because management did not actually know what was going on?

7. Criminal liability issues regarding organizations other than corporations arise less frequently, but the same constitutional analysis and general principles of statutory interpretation apply. *See, e.g.*, United States v. A & P Trucking Co., 358 U.S. 121 (1958) (holding that partnerships as entities may be criminally liable for knowing violations of the Interstate Commerce Commission regulations for the safe transportation in interstate commerce of "explosives and other dangerous articles"); *cf.* Gordon v. United States, 347 U.S. 909 (1954) (holding that individual partners could not be convicted of "willfully" violating the Defense Production Act of 1950 without a showing that they had knowledge of the criminal acts of their agents).

2. "INTENTION TO BENEFIT THE CORPORATION" REQUIREMENT

Although the early view held that corporations were incapable of having an "evil intent," or *mens rea*, it is now well established that corporations may be liable for crimes requiring a culpable *mens rea*. Both the act *and* the intent of the corporate agent who committed the crime are imputed to the corporation under principles of *respondeat superior*. But does this imputation provide a rationale basis for separating culpable from non-culpable corporate actors? As Jennifer Moore has argued:

> The first troubling feature of the theory of imputed culpability is that it imputes to the corporation only the *mens rea* of the agent who committed the crime, and ignores the mental states of other corporate agents. But if corporations have "characters," ... and if corporate policies and procedures can cause crime, the culpability of the corporate entity is likely to depend on more than the intent of a single agent. By imputing only the *mens rea* of the criminal, the imputed culpability theory fails to distinguish between offenses committed with the participation or encouragement of upper management, pursuant to corporate policies or procedures, and those committed by "rogue employees" whose acts violated company policy or could not have been prevented by careful supervision. For this reason, the theory has seemed to many commentators to be unfairly overinclusive. It labels corporations "culpable" even when they do not have a "bad" character, that is, even where corporate policies and procedures bear no causal relationship to the crime.[27]

---

[27] Moore, *supra* note 14, at 759.

The "overinclusiveness" of *respondeat superior* liability is likely to be most troubling in circumstances where the wrongdoing agent's actions are not encouraged by the corporation and indeed are not necessarily in the best interests of the entity. In such cases, the corporation may look more like a victim than a truly culpable actor. The requirement that the agent must act with the intention to benefit her principal, examined in this section, is supposed to serve as "[o]ne major limitation on the imposition of corporate liability for crimes requiring *mens rea* ...."[28] At least in theory, the "intent to benefit rule serves to prevent successful prosecution of a corporation that is the victim rather than a mere vehicle for criminal conduct, by requiring that the wrongdoing agent must act with some purpose of forwarding corporate business."[29] In short, this requirement potentially could be used to bring vicarious liability more in line with assessments of *corporate* culpability.

There are scattered cases in which the conviction of a corporation has been overturned because the court concluded that there was insufficient evidence that the wrongdoing corporate agent intended to benefit the corporation.[30] More representative, however, is the result in the following case:

UNITED STATES v. SUN-DIAMOND GROWERS OF CALIFORNIA
138 F.3d 961 (D.C.Cir.1998), *aff'd on other grounds*, 526 U.S. 398 (1999)

STEPHEN F. WILLIAMS, CIRCUIT JUDGE:

Sun-Diamond is a large agricultural cooperative owned by individual member cooperatives .... It came within the sights of an independent counsel, Donald C. Smaltz, who was responsible for investigating allegations of unlawful activity by former Secretary of Agriculture Mike Espy. The independent counsel charged Sun-Diamond with making illegal gifts to Espy, committing wire fraud, and making illegal campaign contributions.

Linking Sun-Diamond and Espy was the figure of Richard Douglas. As Sun-Diamond's vice president for corporate affairs, Douglas was responsible for (among other things) representing the interests of the corporation and its member cooperatives in Washington. Given Sun-Diamond's business, the Department of Agriculture ("USDA") was naturally part of his bailiwick. According to performance evaluations signed by Sun-Diamond's president, Douglas was a diligent and able representative. He once described his approach to lobbying by paraphrasing Lord Palmerston: "We have no permanent friends or permanent enemies, only a permanent interest in Sun-Diamond Growers of California." Permanent friends aside, he had a long-time friend in Mike Espy—the two had gone to college together at Howard University and had stayed close in the years since. ...

Sun-Diamond was found guilty on Counts III and IV of committing wire fraud in violation of 18 U.S.C. §§ 1343 & 1346, and on Counts V through IX of violating the Federal Election Campaign Act, 2 U.S.C. §§ 441b(a) & 441f ("FECA"). Both sets of convictions flow from a scheme of Richard Douglas and James H. Lake to help repay the debts of the failed congressional campaign of Mike Espy's brother Henry. The following facts about the scheme come from the testimony of Lake, who was granted immunity by prosecutors in exchange for his cooperation.

Lake was one of the founding partners of a Washington based firm, Robinson Lake Sawyer & Miller ("RLSM"), which handled communications and public relations matters for Sun-Diamond. Sun-Diamond retained RLSM for a fee of $20,000 a month; Douglas oversaw Sun-Diamond's dealings with RLSM and maintained his own office there. RLSM was a wholly-owned subsidiary of Bozell Worldwide, Inc. ("Bozell").

---

28 Kathleen F. Brickey, *Corporate Criminal Liability: A Primer for Corporate Counsel*, 40 Bus.Law. 129, 134-35 (1984) (footnotes omitted).

29 *Id.*

30 *See* Standard Oil Co. v. United States, 307 F.2d 120 (5th Cir.1962).

After Mike Espy became Secretary of Agriculture, Henry Espy unsuccessfully pursued election to his brother's vacant seat in Congress, building up a sizable campaign debt in the process. In February 1994 Douglas left a telephone message at Lake's office—a crucial act for jurisdiction over one of the wire fraud counts. When Lake contacted Douglas, he learned that Secretary Espy had asked Douglas for help in retiring his brother's campaign debt. Lake immediately offered to donate $1,000, the maximum permissible individual contribution. Douglas replied that he had to raise at least $5,000 fast, and that he needed Lake's help. He then proposed a way around the campaign finance restrictions. If Lake would get five RLSM employees (including Lake himself) to write a check for $1,000 each, Douglas would find a way for Sun-Diamond to reimburse them all. Lake knew the scheme was illegal—corporations are forbidden to make contributions "in connection with any election" for Congress, 2 U.S.C. § 441b(a), and no one may make a campaign contribution in the name of another person, 2 U.S.C. § 441f—but agreed to participate anyway. Lake testified that no one else at RLSM or Bozell knew about the plan.

Lake wrote a $1,000 check in his own name and then approached the four RLSM employees identified by Douglas. Three of them agreed to pay up. (A fourth—presumably suspicious about the notion of a reimbursable campaign contribution—declined.) Lake then passed the checks worth $4,000 to Douglas, who deposited them in a "Henry Espy for Congress" account he had opened.

As the vehicle for reimbursement, Douglas settled on the Joint Center Dinner, an annual benefit for which RLSM and Lake had in the past routinely bought tickets on Sun-Diamond's behalf. Lake's staff prepared an internal RLSM document authorizing reimbursement to Lake for his supposed purchase of tickets to the dinner in the amount of $5,000 (even though he had raised only $4,000 for Henry Espy). The same document became part of the monthly invoice sent to Sun-Diamond, billing the client $5,000 for the fictitious dinner attendance on top of its $20,000 monthly retainer and other expenses. Lake received a $5,000 reimbursement check from Bozell, which he cashed and used to pay back the three other individual contributors (apparently pocketing the extra $1,000 for himself). Douglas, as part of his normal duties at Sun-Diamond, approved the payment to RLSM, which eventually went through. The net result: a $5,000 expenditure by Sun-Diamond, $4,000 of which went into Henry Espy's campaign coffers and $1,000 into James H. Lake's pocket. The independent counsel charged that the scheme worked a fraud on Bozell and RLSM, depriving the former (albeit temporarily) of $5,000, and depriving the latter of the "honest services" of its agent Lake under 18 U.S.C. § 1346. The jury convicted, evidently convinced that at least one such deprivation occurred. The jury also found Sun-Diamond guilty of making illegal campaign contributions in violation of FECA, 2 U.S.C. §§ 441b(a) & 441f.

As a threshold matter, Sun-Diamond raises a challenge which it says goes equally to the wire fraud and FECA counts. Richard Douglas's campaign contribution scheme cannot be attributed to it, Sun-Diamond argues, because Douglas was not acting with an intent to benefit the corporation. It is true, as the district court instructed the jury in this case, that an agent's acts will not be imputed to the principal in a criminal case unless the agent acts with the intent to benefit the principal. Here, Sun-Diamond says, Douglas's scheme was designed to—and did in fact—*defraud* his employer, not benefit it. In this circumstance, it strenuously argues, there can be no imputation: "[T]o establish precedent holding a principal *criminally* liable for the acts of an agent who defrauds and deceives the principal while pursuing matters within his self-interest merely because the agent's conduct *may* provide some incidental benefit to the principal serves to punish innocent principals with no countervailing policy justifications."

This argument has considerable intuitive appeal—Sun-Diamond does look more like a victim than a perpetrator, at least on the fraud charges. The facts in the record, however—that Douglas hid the illegal contribution scheme from others at the company and used company funds to accomplish it—do not preclude a valid finding that he undertook the scheme to benefit Sun-Diamond. Part of Douglas's job was to cultivate his, and Sun-Diamond's, relationship with Secretary Espy. By responding to the Secretary's request to help his brother, Douglas may have been acting out of pure friendship, but the jury was entitled to conclude that he was acting instead, or also, with an intent (however befuddled) to further the interests of his employer. The scheme came at some cost to Sun-Diamond but it also promised some benefit. *See, e.g., United States v. Automated Medical Laboratories, Inc.*, 770 F.2d 399, 406-07 (4th Cir.1985) (agent's conduct which is actually or potentially detrimental to corporation may nonetheless be imputed to corporation in criminal case if motivated at least in part by intent to benefit it); *cf. Local 1814, International Longshoremen's Association, AFL-CIO v. NLRB*, 735 F.2d 1384, 1395 (D.C.Cir.1984) ("[T]he acts of an agent motivated partly by self-interest—even where self-interest is the predominant motive—lie within the scope of employment so long as the agent is actuated by the principal's business purposes 'to any appreciable extent.'") (*quoting* Restatement (Second) of Agency § 236 & comment b (1957)). Where there is adequate evidence for imputation (as here), the only thing that keeps deceived corporations from being indicted for the acts of their employee-deceivers is not some fixed rule of law or logic but simply the sound exercise of prosecutorial discretion.

And the answer to Sun-Diamond's claim of the absence of any "countervailing policy justification" is simply the justification usually offered in support of holding corporate principals liable for the illegal acts of their agents: to increase incentives for corporations to monitor and prevent illegal employee conduct. One might well question this justification—and scholars have. Moreover, the justification may be at its weakest in cases like this one, where the offending employee breaches a duty of honesty to the very corporation whose goals he aims to advance. In any event, Sun-Diamond's argument here, whatever its merit as an issue of policy, has no real grounding in the relevant statutes. And Sun-Diamond does not invoke the Constitution, which in any event would require either an overruling of the Supreme Court's rejection of a due process attack on corporate liability, *New York Cent. & Hudson River R.R. Co. v. United States*, 212 U.S. 481 (1909), or the development of some new theory.

Sun-Diamond also raises a narrower objection concerning imputation, one which goes only to the fraud counts. To the extent Douglas's conduct is to be imputed to his employer, argues Sun-Diamond, then so must Lake's be imputed to his employers (RLSM and Bozell). Both men occupied high-level management positions in their respective firms, and both men's firms sought to establish and maintain good relations with Secretary Espy. If Douglas's knowledge can be imputed to Sun-Diamond to hold it responsible for Douglas's acts, then Lake's must be imputed to his employers, RLSM and Bozell, and they cannot be victims.

Even assuming the evidence showed the balance of private and corporate purpose in Douglas's and Lake's motivation to be identical, Sun-Diamond's argument rests on a faulty assumption—that the imputation rules must be the same on both the perpetrator and victim sides. They need not be, and indeed are not. Imputation is a legal fiction designed to assist in the allocation of liability, not a literal description of the state of a principal's knowledge. The law imputes the wrongdoer's conduct to the corporation in order to encourage monitoring, but it is not at all clear that imputation on the other side of the equation would be useful in eliciting additional caution on the part of would-be fraud victims. A rule that makes victim wariness a condition of criminally punishing the perpetrator—unlike, say, a rule of contributory negligence in tort—might not inspire much extra precaution in potential victims. However much they may benefit from the criminalization of fraud generally, potential victims (who have many incentives to avoid being gulled, independent of the criminal law) seem unlikely to step up their precautions just to increase the *ex ante* chances that their deceivers will face criminal sanctions—or so Congress could reasonably conclude. Thus, when an individual is swindled, the offender does not escape mail or wire fraud liability just because the victim was unwary, or even "gullible." Indeed, Congress's adoption of 18 U.S.C. § 1346, specifying that the term "scheme or artifice to defraud," as used in various federal criminal fraud statutes, should include schemes to deprive a principal "of the intangible right of honest services," is hard to square with an imputation rule on the victim side as broad as the one governing corporate criminal responsibility.

Notes

1. As this decision indicates, and other decisions have explicitly affirmed, the corporation need not actually receive the intended benefit. *See, e.g.*, United States v. Gold, 743 F.2d 800,

823 (11th Cir. 1984). More important, *Sun-Diamond* and other cases make clear that the corporate agent need not be acting solely, or even predominantly, with the intent to benefit the corporate principal. *See, e.g.,* United States v. Automated Medical Labs., 770 F.2d 399, 407 (4th Cir. 1985); *Gold*, 743 F.2d at 823. Given such rules, just how effective is this "intent" requirement in separating corporate offenders from corporate victims? Can we reconceptualize corporate "mens rea"? *See* Mihailis E. Diamantis, *Corporate Criminal Minds*, 91 Notre Dame L. Rev. 2049 (2016).

Do the rules contained in the Justice Department Guidance on Prosecutions of Corporations, reproduced *infra* at Part C, provide any better guidance regarding how to separate corporate victims from corporate malefactors? Should the system rely upon prosecutors to ensure that overly inclusive standards of legal liability are applied to only the most culpable organizations? *See* Moore, *supra* note 14, at 761 ("[P]rosecutorial self-restraint does not provide the inherent or legal protection against the problem of overinclusiveness that a genuine theory of corporate culpability would provide.").

2. Does the court's rationale for equating the actions of corporate agents with the corporation for one purpose—criminal liability—but not for others make sense? Why might the prosecutor have decided to charge this case as he did?

3. LIABILITY WHERE CRIMINAL ACTION IS CONTRARY TO CORPORATE POLICY/ORDERS

UNITED STATES v. HILTON HOTELS CORP.
467 F.2d 1000 (9th Cir. 1972)

BROWNING, CIRCUIT JUDGE:

This is an appeal from a conviction under an indictment charging a violation of section 1 of the Sherman Act, 15 U.S.C. § 1.

Operators of hotels, restaurants, hotel and restaurant supply companies, and other businesses in Portland, Oregon, organized an association to attract conventions to their city. To finance the association, members were asked to make contributions in predetermined amounts. Companies selling supplies to hotels were asked to contribute an amount equal to one per cent of their sales to hotel members. To aid collections, hotel members, including appellant, agreed to give preferential treatment to suppliers who paid their assessments, and to curtail purchases from those who did not....

Appellant's president testified that it would be contrary to the policy of the corporation for the manager of one of its hotels to condition purchases upon payment of a contribution to a local association by the supplier. The manager of appellant's Portland hotel and his assistant testified that it was the hotel's policy to purchase supplies solely on the basis of price, quality, and service. They also testified that on two occasions they told the hotel's purchasing agent that he was to take no part in the boycott. The purchasing agent confirmed the receipt of these instructions, but admitted that, despite them, he had threatened a supplier with loss of the hotel's business unless the supplier paid the association assessment. He testified that he violated his instructions because of anger and personal pique toward the individual representing the supplier.

Based upon this testimony, appellant requested certain instructions bearing upon the criminal liability of a corporation for the unauthorized acts of its agents. These requests were rejected by the trial court. The court instructed the jury that a corporation is liable for the acts and statements of its agents "within the scope of their employment," defined to mean "in the corporation's behalf in performance of the agent's general line of work," including "not only that which has been authorized by the corporation, but also that which outsiders could reasonably assume the agent would have authority to do." The court added:

"A corporation is responsible for acts and statements of its agents, done or made within the scope of their employment, even though their conduct may be contrary to their actual instructions or contrary to the corporation's stated policies."

Appellant objects only to the court's concluding statement.

Congress may constitutionally impose criminal liability upon a business entity for acts or omissions of its agents within the scope of their employment. Such liability may attach without proof that the conduct was within the agent's actual authority, and even though it may have been contrary to express instructions.

The intention to impose such liability is sometimes express, *New York Central & Hudson R. R. Co. v. United States*, 212 U.S. 481, ... but it may also be implied. The text of the Sherman Act does not expressly resolve the issue. For the reasons that follow, however, we think the construction of the Act that best achieves its purpose is that a corporation is liable for acts of its agents within the scope of their authority even when done against company orders. ...

The breadth and critical character of the public interests protected by the Sherman Act, and the gravity of the threat to those interests that led to the enactment of the statute, support a construction holding business organizations accountable, as a general rule, for violations of the Act by their employees in the course of their businesses. In enacting the Sherman Act, "Congress was passing drastic legislation to remedy a threatening danger to the public welfare ...." The statute "was designed to be a comprehensive charter of economic liberty aimed at preserving free and unfettered competition as the rule of trade. It rests on the premise that the unrestrained interaction of competitive forces will yield the best allocation of our economic resources, the lowest prices, the highest quality and the greatest material progress, while at the same time providing an environment conducive to the preservation of our democratic political and social institutions."

With such important public interests at stake, it is reasonable to assume that Congress intended to impose liability upon business entities for the acts of those to whom they choose to delegate the conduct of their affairs, thus stimulating a maximum effort by owners and managers to assure adherence by such agents to the requirements of the Act.

Legal commentators have argued forcefully that it is inappropriate and ineffective to impose criminal liability upon a corporation, as distinguished from the human agents who actually perform the unlawful acts .... But it is the legislative judgment that controls, and "the great mass of legislation calling for corporate criminal liability suggests a widespread belief on the part of legislators that such liability is necessary to effectuate regulatory policy." Moreover, the strenuous efforts of corporate defendants to avoid conviction, particularly under the Sherman Act, strongly suggests that Congress is justified in its judgment that exposure of the corporate entity to potential conviction may provide a substantial spur to corporate action to prevent violations by employees.

Because of the nature of Sherman Act offenses and the context in which they normally occur, the factors that militate against allowing a corporation to disown the criminal acts of its agents apply with special force to Sherman Act violations.

Sherman Act violations are commercial offenses. They are usually motivated by a desire to enhance profits. They commonly involve large, complex, and highly decentralized corporate business enterprises, and intricate business processes, practices, and arrangements. More often than not they also involve basic policy decisions, and must be implemented over an extended period of time.

Complex business structures, characterized by decentralization and delegation of authority, commonly adopted by corporations for business purposes, make it difficult to identify the particular corporate agents responsible for Sherman Act violations. At the same time, it is generally true that high management officials, for whose conduct the corporate directors and stockholders are the most clearly responsible, are likely to have participated in the policy decisions underlying Sherman Act violations, or at least to have become aware of them.

Violations of the Sherman Act are a likely consequence of the pressure to maximize profits that is commonly imposed by corporate owners upon managing agents and, in turn, upon lesser employees. In the face of that pressure, generalized directions to obey the Sherman Act, with the probable effect of foregoing profits, are the least likely to be taken seriously. And if a violation of the Sherman Act occurs, the corporation, and not the individual agents, will have realized the profits from the illegal activity.

In sum, identification of the particular agents responsible for a Sherman Act violation is especially difficult, and their conviction and punishment is peculiarly ineffective as a deterrent. At the same time, conviction and punishment of the business entity itself is likely to be both appropriate and effective.

For these reasons we conclude that as a general rule a corporation is liable under the Sherman Act for the acts of its agents in the scope of their employment, even though contrary to general corporate policy and express instructions to the agent.

Thus the general policy statements of appellant's president were no defense. Nor was it enough that appellant's manager told the purchasing agent that he was not to participate in the boycott. The purchasing agent was authorized to buy all of appellant's supplies. Purchases were made on the basis of specifications, but the purchasing agent exercised complete authority as to source. He was in a unique position to add the corporation's buying power to the force of the boycott. Appellant could not gain exculpation by issuing general instructions without undertaking to enforce those instructions by means commensurate with the obvious risks.

Notes

1. *Hilton Hotels* was decided at a time when courts thought there was no intent requirement for Sherman Act violations (imposed in *United States v. United States Gypsum Co.*, 438 U.S. 422 (1978)), but courts in subsequent cases have adopted the same rule in cases requiring proof of *mens rea. See, e.g.*, United States v. Automated Medical Labs., Inc., 770 F.2d 399 (4th Cir. 1985); United States v. Beusch, 596 F.2d 871, 877-78 (9th Cir. 1979); Steere Tank Lines, Inc. v. United States, 330 F.2d 719 (5th Cir. 1963).

2. Although the court relies heavily on the statutory (antitrust) context in *Hilton Hotels*, the rule emerging from the case has not been so limited. Is the court's rationale for this rule—in which it relies extensively on its supposition about what Congress would have done had it considered this issue—persuasive? Consider the following critique of this rule offered by H. Lowell Brown, an in-house counsel for a large corporation:

> The reluctance to recognize a violation of corporate policy as an affirmative defense may spring from several sources. One is the belief, expressed by several commentators, that some corporate cultures actually foster criminality, although others ... disagree. In any event, if it is assumed that there are corporate cultures that encourage their employees toward criminality such that the corporation can be said to be capable of criminal intent, the corollary would seem equally true. A corporation that has implemented a comprehensive compliance program, which is diligently monitored and enforced, can be said to have demonstrated an absence of criminal intent such that the corporation should not be held liable for the criminal acts of its employees—even though the acts were within the scope of employment and ostensibly intended to benefit the corporation. Another source is the suspicion that corporate policies do not necessarily represent *bona fide* efforts toward compliance but instead are merely an artifice to allow the corporation to escape liability. Still others see the recognition of corporate diligence in avoiding criminality as a significant jurisprudential shift in the criminal law.

> The concern that a corporation's compliance program is a mere sham intended only to shield the corporation from liability would seem to be assuaged if the court inquired into the corporation's diligence in enforcing its policies and instructions as a preliminary to allowing the defense to go forward. ...

H. Lowell Brown, *Vicarious Criminal Liability of Corporations for the Acts of Their Employees and Agents*, 41 Loy. L. Rev. 279, 313-15 (1995). *But see* John C. Coffee, Jr., *"No Soul to Damn: No Body to*

[handwritten margin note: Lack of affirmative defense]

Kick": An Unscandalized Inquiry into the Problem of Corporate Punishment, 79 Mich. L. Rev. 386, 401-02, 446 (1981) (consideration of "due diligence" defense only at sentencing serves the interests of general deterrence and victim compensation and gives the court a wider, more accurate, range of vision).

3. Does *Hilton Hotels* mean that corporate compliance efforts are irrelevant to liability? The answer, generally speaking, is "yes." A few cases offer some hope for corporate defendants, although the hope they offer is limited (and they seem to represent a distinctly minority view). For example, in *United States v. Beusch*, 596 F.2d 871 (9th Cir.1979), the court upheld jury instructions that, the court stated, correctly suggested that

> a corporation *may* be liable for acts of its employees done contrary to express instructions and policies, but that the existence of such instructions and policies may be considered in determining whether the employee in fact acted to benefit the corporation. Merely stating or publishing such instructions and policies without diligently enforcing them is not enough to place the acts of an employee who violates them outside the scope of his employment. It is a question of fact whether measures taken to enforce corporate policy in this area will adequately insulate the corporation against such acts ….

Id. at 878 (footnotes omitted); *see also* United States v. Basic Construction Co., 711 F.2d 570, 573 (4th Cir.1983) (holding that the trial court "properly allowed the jury to consider Basic's alleged antitrust compliance policy in determining whether the employees were acting for the benefit of the corporation"); *see generally* Kevin B. Huff, *The Role of Corporate Compliance Programs in Determining Corporate Criminal Liability: A Suggested Approach*, 96 Colum. L. Rev. 1252 (1996) (proposing modification of current vicarious liability standards to accommodate compliance programs as relevant evidence).

4. Even if prevailing legal rules make irrelevant the fact that the wrongdoing corporate agent disregarded corporate orders or policy, that fact may be considered by prosecutors in deciding whether a case should be charged and may also be factored into any eventual sentencing decisions. The Justice Department Guidance on Prosecutions of Corporations (reproduced *infra* in Part C), makes relevant the existence of corporate compliance efforts. (For the fraud section's guidelines for evaluating compliance programs, see https://www.justice.gov/criminal-fraud/page/file/937501/download).

And if a prosecutor chooses to go forward with a case despite the existence of corporate policies forbidding the conduct at issue, the U.S. Organizational Guidelines may give a corporation important sentencing relief if the corporation is able to demonstrate that it had in place an "Effective Program to Prevent and Detect Violations of Law." U.S. Sentencing Guidelines Manual § 8C2.5(f) (1999); *see also* § 8B2.1 (definition of same); *infra* Part D. Some argue that *sentencing* consideration of the existence of failed but good faith compliance efforts is insufficient:

> [L]imiting favorable treatment only to the sentencing phase is too late. … [T]he collateral consequences of indictment and conviction alone may be as severe or more so than the fine ultimately imposed. For corporations in regulated industries, indictment or conviction may be a disqualification from doing business. For companies engaged in government contracting, criminal prosecution will ordinarily result in a period of suspension and debarment during which time contracts and subcontracts cannot be awarded. In any event, the stigma and public opprobrium and the concomitant fall in employee morale which often result in defections of talent can hobble the corporations well after the financial loss from a fine has been recouped. …

Brown, *supra*, 41 Loy. L. Rev. at 321-22 (footnotes omitted).

5. What types of incentives does this rule create for corporations? Professor Jennifer Arlen presents the case that these rules create perverse incentives given the aims of corporate criminal liability:

... Many corporate crimes—such as securities fraud, government procurement fraud, and some environmental crimes—cannot be readily detected by the government. Corporations often are better positioned to detect such crimes and determine which agents committed them. In these circumstances, corporate criminal liability may affect corporate expenditures on detecting and investigating crimes committed by their employees, here described as "enforcement costs." —Should vicarious criminal liability increase corporate enforcement expenditures, it magnifies the deterrent effect of direct agent liability by increasing the probability that wrongful agents will be detected and sanctioned. Should it have the opposite effect, however, corporate crime will increase. The deterrent effect of vicarious criminal liability therefore depends on the effect of vicarious liability on corporate enforcement expenditures.

Recognizing the influence of corporate enforcement expenditures ... dramatically changes the analysis of corporate criminal liability. Previous analysis suggests that increased corporate liability necessarily reduces crime. Introducing corporate enforcement costs, however, reveals that increased corporate liability does not necessarily reduce corporate crime and, indeed, may result in increased crime. The existing legal regime governing many crimes is best approximated as a rule of "pure strict vicarious liability," under which the fine imposed for a particular crime is fixed, in that it does not vary precisely with the level of corporate enforcement expenditures. This regime of strict vicarious liability presents corporations contemplating enforcement expenditures with conflicting, potentially perverse, incentives. On the one hand, increased enforcement expenditures reduce the number of agents who commit crimes by increasing the probability of detection and thus each agent's expected cost of crime. On the other hand, these expenditures also increase the probability that the government will detect those crimes that are committed, thereby increasing the corporation's expected criminal liability for those crimes. If the expected cost to the corporation of the resulting increase in its expected criminal liability exceeds the expected benefit to the corporation of the reduction in the number of crimes, a corporation subject to strict vicarious liability will not respond by increasing its enforcement expenditures because additional enforcement would only increase the firm's expected criminal liability. In fact, in some circumstances a corporation subject to vicarious liability may spend less on enforcement than it would absent vicarious liability. Moreover, even when strict vicarious liability can induce efficient enforcement, the conflicting incentives it creates affect the efficient fine: to induce efficient enforcement, the fixed fine must exceed the net social cost of crime divided by the efficient probability of detection. These results call into question both the current trend toward increased corporate criminal liability and much of the accepted wisdom regarding strict vicarious criminal liability. This analysis also may be relevant to administrative sanctions against corporations and to vicarious civil liability, including employer liability for sexual harassment under Title VII.

In theory, the perverse incentives created by strict vicarious criminal liability can be eliminated by employing a variable fine equal to the net social cost of crime divided by the actual probability of detection (given the corporation's expenditures on enforcement). This rule would eliminate the perverse incentives otherwise present under strict vicarious liability because any increase in the probability of detection occasioned by corporate enforcement expenditures would result in an equivalent decrease in the fine imposed. Implementing this rule, however, would require a dramatic change in the current law. In particular, it would require us to abandon the goal of imposing relatively fixed fines for each type of crime—a goal that permeates the U.S. Sentencing Guidelines—in favor of a rule under which the corporate criminal fine could not be determined until after the crime was committed and investigated since only then could the corporation's precise expenditures on enforcement be determined. Perhaps more important, the precise calculations required for this rule—if feasible—would be very costly.

Accordingly, alternative rules to strict vicarious criminal liability warrant consideration. Three such rules [could be]: (1) mitigation rules, under which the fine is reduced (but not eliminated) if the firm's enforcement is efficient; (2) a "negligence" rule, under which the firm bears no liability if it incurs efficient enforcement; and (3) a modified "evidentiary privilege" (akin to use immunity) under which any information disclosed by the corporation can be used to prosecute the wrongful agents but cannot be used against the corporation in criminal or civil litigation.

Jennifer Arlen, *The Potentially Perverse Effects of Corporate Criminal Liability*, 23 J. Legal Stud. 833, 835-37 (1994); *see also* Brown, *supra*, at 324.

6. In response to concerns such as these, many commentators, judges, former prosecutors, and practitioners have criticized the current *respondeat superior* standard. A number of organizations filed an *amicus* brief (excerpted below) in United States v. Ionia Management S.A., 555 F.3d 303 (2009), asking the court to "revisit the key question of the principles and criteria that should govern the imputation of criminal misconduct by corporate employees to their employer."

The *Ionia* case involved a ship management company convicted of violating the Act to Protect Pollution from Ships, conspiracy, falsifying records in a federal investigation, and obstruction. The defendant company did not object to the District Court's *respondeat superior* jury instruction and thus the Second Circuit reviewed the challenged standard for plain error. The Circuit Court noted that the defendant did not join in the argument made by *amici*—that "in order to establish vicarious liability, [the government] should have to prove as a separate element in its case-in-chief that the corporation lacked effective policies and procedures to deter and detect criminal actions by its employees." *Id.* at 310. It ruled, however, that the "argument, whoever made it, is unavailing" in light of Second Circuit precedent. The court concluded, then, that "[a]s the District Court instructed the jury..., a corporate compliance program may be relevant to whether an employee was acting in the scope of his employment, but it is not a separate element." *Id.* Consider whether the Second Circuit should have considered intervening Supreme Court precedents, described in the following.

AMICUS BRIEF FOR THE ASSOCIATION OF CORPORATE COUNSEL, ET AL.
in United States v. Ionia Management S.A., 555 F.3d 303 (2d Cir. 2009)

Congress has clearly determined that corporations are capable of committing crimes[31] but with rare exceptions has not chosen to legislate *how* the courts are to impute to a corporation the conduct and intent of its employees or other agents. In a handful of instances in the context of regulatory regimes, Congress has explicitly set out the method of imputing the acts of an employee to the corporation for criminal purposes.[32] ...

In contrast, the statutes with which the corporate defendant was charged here contain no indication that Congress intended the misconduct of employees to be imputed to their employer through adherence to the least demanding *respondeat superior* principles. Indeed, the statutes contain no guidance whatsoever for courts to apply in determining how to impute the criminal misconduct of an employee to an employer. In the absence of any statutory authority for the application of *respondeat superior* principles to the corporate defendant below, this Court must look to recent Supreme Court precedent for the appropriate principles to apply. ...

---

[31] [Brief's footnote 1:] Unless the statute indicates otherwise, the words "person" and "whoever" in any federal statute are defined to include corporations, 1 U.S.C. § 1 (2000), and accordingly Congress has indicated that corporations may be liable for committing a wide variety of crimes. These include all four of the criminal statutes at issue in this appeal: 33 U.S.C. § 1908(a) (2000) [Act to Protect Pollution from Ships (APPS)]; 18 U.S.C. § 371 (2000) [(conspiracy)]; 18 U.S.C. § 1519 (2000) [(obstruction)]; 18 U.S.C. § 1505 (2000) [(obstruction)].

[32] [Brief's footnote 2:] Congress typically adopts *respondeat superior* principles only in regulatory-type statutes that fall outside the general Federal Criminal Code, as Title 18 of the United States Code is popularly labeled.

Remarkably, the Supreme Court has never addressed how vicarious criminal liability should be determined for corporations in the absence of a statute that explicitly includes instructions for imputing the liability of an employee to the corporation. However, recent cases in the analogous contexts of punitive damages and hostile workplace claims under Title VII of the Civil Rights Act of 1964, 42 U.S.C. § 2000(e) *et seq.* (2000), make clear that the Supreme Court would be skeptical that *respondeat superior* should be applied by default in criminal cases.

In *Faragher v. City of Boca Raton*, 524 U.S. 775 (1998), and in *Burlington Industries, Inc. v. Ellerth*, 524 U.S. 742 (1998), the Supreme Court limited the traditional applicability of *respondeat superior* in determining vicarious liability for corporate defendants in civil sexual harassment cases under Title VII. *Faragher* and *Ellerth* were companion cases, and the court explicitly noted that it was adopting the same holding for both cases. In both *Faragher* and *Ellerth*, the Court narrowed the scope of vicarious corporate liability, rejecting the usual rule in civil cases that vicarious liability arises from all acts of employees acting within the scope of their employment. The Court first restricted liability to the acts of supervisors. Additionally, the Court determined an employer is entitled to an affirmative defense if it has reasonable policies in place to deter the offending employee's conduct, and if the aggrieved employee has not availed herself of the employer's system of redress. The Court reached this result even though Congress had explicitly included "agents" in the definition of "employer" and even though the Court determined that Congress intended civil agency principles to apply to Title VII.

Importantly, the Court reached its decision primarily based on the underlying purpose of Title VII, which the Court viewed as providing incentives to prevent sexual harassment rather than the typical purpose of a civil suit, which is to redress a plaintiff's injury.

A year after *Faragher* and *Ellerth*, the Supreme Court again rejected the application of *respondeat superior* principles, this time with respect to punitive damages. In *Kolstad v. Am. Dental Ass'n*, 527 U.S. 526, 543 (1999), a discrimination case under Title VII that did not involve hostile work environment claims, the Court held that punitive damages were only available in cases where the employer ratified the tortious act of an employee or where the tortious act was performed by an employee acting in a managerial capacity. Importantly, the Court explicitly rejected the application of expansive civil agency principles, by which "even an employer who makes every effort to comply with Title VII would be held liable for the discriminatory acts of agents acting in a 'managerial capacity.'" The Court consequently held that an employer cannot be liable for punitive damages for a managerial employee's acts taken contrary to the employer's good faith efforts to comply with Title VII.

In reaching its decision, the Court relied on the fact that Title VII was not designed primarily to provide redress but instead to prevent sex discrimination through the creation by employers of effective policies and grievance mechanisms. The Court's analysis is instructive: it noted that the general common law of agency (as reflected in the Restatement (Second) of Agency (1957)) "places strict limits on the extent to which an agent's misconduct may be imputed to the principal for purposes of awarding punitive damages" beyond mere *respondeat superior* principles, but determined that those additional "strict limits" were still not demanding enough to protect against the inappropriate imposition of punitive damages in Title VII cases.

Ironically, the charge by the district court in the criminal case below did not even apply the stricter limits the common law itself provides in the *civil* punitive damages context (principally requiring that the *respondeat superior* "scope of employment" rule be applied only to agents employed at a managerial level). Instead, the jury was charged that the misconduct of Appellant's employees, regardless of their position with the company, could be imputed to the company if the acts were done within the scope of employment and to benefit the company.[33]

---

[33] [Brief's footnote 3:] The district court charged the jury that "[a] corporation may be held criminally liable for the acts of its agent done on behalf of and for the benefit of the corporation, and directly related to the performance of the duties the employee has authority to perform" and later referred to acts "'within the scope of their employment.'" The court elaborated: "[e]ven if the act or omission was not specifically authorized, it may still be within the scope of an agent's employment if (1) the agent acted for

In rejecting the common law's agency rule for punitive damages as inadequate, the *Kolstad* Court reasoned that "[a]pplying the Restatement of Agency's 'scope of employment' rule in the Title VII punitive damages context … would reduce the incentive for employers to implement antidiscrimination programs." It determined that the "scope of employment" rule, even if limited to imputing conduct of managerial level agents, would create "perverse incentives" for a corporation to avoid taking remedial measures if such measures provide no defense and may expose the corporation to liability. The Court therefore felt "compelled to modify these principles" to assure that, "in the punitive damages context, an employer may not be vicariously liable for the [misconduct] … of managerial agents where [the misconduct is] … contrary to the employer's good faith efforts to comply with Title VII."[34]

The decision in *Kolstad* is directly analogous to the application of vicarious liability in the criminal context. The Supreme Court has described punitive damages as "quasi-criminal" in nature because they are designed to punish and deter. Like punitive damages, the two primary goals of criminal law are retribution and deterrence. Thus, where a company has undertaken all reasonable measures to deter and detect the employee's criminal actions, the company has done all that can be expected, i.e., there is nothing that the criminal law is serving to deter or punish since there is no action by the *corporation* that it should have otherwise taken. If the corporation has taken all actions that can be expected, applying criminal liability would result in the same "perverse incentives" rejected by the Supreme Court in *Kolstad*.[35]

Here, the district court's instruction on vicarious liability was plainly erroneous: the instruction made it easier to impute conduct and knowledge to a corporation in a criminal case than it would be in a civil case under Title VII. Such a result is highly anomalous. The purposes of the civil justice system typically make application of *respondeat superior* principles sensible, at least when the key objective is to afford redress to the plaintiff. In contrast, the criminal justice system seeks to promote compliance with society's dictates as expressed in the criminal code. Vicarious liability principles with respect to corporate criminal liability should foster that objective; the district court's jury charge failed to do so. …

The criticism of the prevailing scope of corporate vicarious criminal liability is widespread and growing, particularly given the rise of corporate investigations and prosecutions by the federal and state governments. While the availability of corporate criminal liability is congressionally mandated, the means by which such liability is established are critical. A criminal indictment can be a life-or-death matter for a company.[36] Yet, the vast sweep of the district court's standard for the imposition of vicarious criminal liability makes corporations accountable for almost all criminal acts of any low level employees—even those acting against explicit instructions and in the face of the most robust corporate compliance program. This has caused a tremendous imbalance between the power of a prosecutor and a corporate defendant. Given the hair-trigger for corporate liability even for the most responsible corporate citizen, many corporations forego any defenses in order to resolve threatened prosecution. …

---

the benefit of the corporation and (2) the agent was acting within his authority." The court also noted: "[t]he fact that the agent's act was illegal, contrary to his employer's instructions, or against the corporation's policies will not necessarily relieve the corporation of responsibility for the agent's act." …

[34] [Brief's footnote 4:] Notably, this Court had previously held in a civil rights case under 42 U.S.C. § 1983 (2000) that "the employer himself must be shown to have acted or failed to act to prevent known or willfully disregarded actions of his employee to be liable in punitive damages."

[35] [Brief's footnote 5:] The record below includes evidence of a compliance program created by the corporate defendant. The corporate defendant should have been allowed to both present and argue such evidence to a properly instructed jury.

[36] [Brief's footnote 9:] In addition to significant reputational harm, numerous federal laws disqualify indicted corporations from participating in critical regulated activities. Such consequences include the loss of deposit insurance for banks, being unable to engage in securities transactions for broker-dealers, and suspension and debarment from government contracts for defense and other contractors.

The potential for inappropriate prosecutorial pressure is particularly heightened in the area of corporate criminal investigations that end in Draconian non-prosecution and deferred prosecution agreements, where *no* court has oversight authority. There, the prosecutor effectively serves as both judge and jury.[37] Because of the disastrous consequences of a corporate indictment and the ease with which corporations may be liable under the doctrine of *respondeat superior*, corporations are under immense pressure to agree to almost any terms. The vast majority of these negotiations go on behind closed doors, with little public scrutiny and no judicial review.[38] ...

This Court can mirror the recent Supreme Court decisions in this area, in part, by adding an additional element to criminal liability that requires the prosecution to prove that a corporation lacks "effective policies and procedures to deter and detect criminal actions by their employees."

Applying this principle has the dual benefit of encouraging effective self-policing while also protecting corporations and shareholders from rogue employees who commit crimes despite a corporation's diligence.[39] The Supreme Court has recognized that creating a limit to *respondeat superior* where a company has sought to prevent the offending employee's actions is appropriate and fair, and also serves to incentivize companies to take such measures. Indeed, promoting such compliance programs is a central goal of the United States Sentencing Guidelines.

Virtually the same approach is embraced by the Model Penal Code ("MPC"), which notably provides an affirmative defense for corporations whose officers "exercised due diligence to prevent [the crime's] commission." Model Penal Code § 2.07(5) (1962). This important principle has also been adopted in countries in both Europe and Asia.[40] In addition, the MPC generally restricts vicarious criminal liability to circumstances in which senior corporate officers are at fault. *See id.* § 2.07(1)(a), (c). This element is also necessary (but not sufficient in the absence of a due diligence defense) to ensure consistency with *Kolstad*. The majority of states have limited vicarious liability by adopting provisions similar to MPC § 2.07(1) in their criminal codes, and several states, including Illinois, Montana, New Jersey, Ohio, and Pennsylvania, have also included the due diligence defense contained in MPC § 2.07(5).[41]

---

[37] [Brief's footnote 11:] Former prosecutors have publicly acknowledged the problem, noting:

> One of the problems with the process of negotiating a deferred prosecution agreement is that it is not really a negotiation. Any pushback by the company on a provision that the government requests is not only going to be shot down, but the government may see it as a reflection that the company's claimed contrition is not genuine.

Interview of David Pitofsky, Corp. Crime Rep., Nov. 28, 2005, at 8.

[38] [Brief's footnote 12:] The use of deferred prosecution agreements and non-prosecution agreements continues to grow. From 1992 to 2002, there were a combined total of 18 corporate deferred and non-prosecution agreements. From 2003 to 2007, there were 85 of these agreements, with 20 of them in 2006 and 38 in 2007.

[39] [Brief's footnote 13:] To escape criminal liability, the company's internal compliance program would need to be an effective one, not merely a "paper" program. As a result, application of a criterion for imputing criminal liability that turns on the existence of effective measures to avoid misconduct would not have exonerated the likes of Enron, Worldcom, or other recent enterprises whose compliance programs were more "facade" than real.

[40] [Brief's footnote 14:] Italy, Austria, and Japan have created corporate criminal liability systems that provide a defense to corporations that institute effective compliance programs and take precautions to prevent their employees from committing crimes.

[41] [Brief's footnote 15:] Similarly, the National Commission on Reform of Federal Criminal Laws proposed limiting criminal liability to instances where an offense was committed by an agent whose action was authorized, commanded, or requested by the board of directors, an executive officer, a person who controls the organization, or a person otherwise considered responsible under a statute.

This alternative set of principles both encourages effective corporate compliance programs while mitigating the harsh effects of *respondeat superior*, which allows a corporation to be liable for the acts of one low-level individual employee acting against the corporation's express instructions. The application of vicarious liability principles that allows corporations to present evidence of an effective compliance programs is far more consistent with Supreme Court precedent and the purpose of corporate criminal liability than an approach based on a minimal application of *respondeat superior*.

Note

1. Commentators and practitioners who agree that compliance efforts ought to be relevant to culpability suggest a variety of ways in which this consideration may be injected into the mix. Some argue that courts ought to permit consideration of evidence of a corporate compliance program as a mitigating factor when assessing corporate criminal liability. This could be justified under a theory that an agent does not in fact operate within the scope of his employment if he acts to evade corporate compliance efforts. Some support adoption of variants Model Penal Code's approach. *See, e.g.*, Elizabeth K. Ainslie, *Indicting Corporations Revisited: Lessons of the Arthur Andersen Prosecution*, 43 Am. Crim. L. Rev. 107, 119 (2006); John Hasnas, *Rethinking Vicarious Criminal Liability: Corporate Culpability for White Collar Crime*, 1195 Web Memo, Heritage Foundation (Aug. 15, 2006). Others argue for creation of an affirmative defense in which the defense bears the burden of proving that the crime occurred despite the organization's best efforts at compliance. *See, e.g.*, Ellen S. Podgor, *A New Corporate World Mandates a "Good Faith" Affirmative Defense*, 44 Am. Crim. L. Rev. 1537 (2007). Given that most commentators concur that corporations, as a practical matter, cannot in the usual case risk a trial, how useful will any of these proposals be? *See* Larry D. Thompson, *The Blameless Corporation*, 47 Am. Crim. L. Rev. 1251 (2010) (advocating that courts be permitted to enter pre-trial judgments of acquittal based on proof of an effective compliance program affirmative defense).

Are the *Ionia* brief's authors advocating that the government bear the burden of proving that an organization lacked a good faith compliance program—that is, reformulating the *respondeat superior* standard such that noncompliance is an element relevant to culpability—or are they arguing for an affirmative defense?

4. DIFFICULTIES WHERE RESPONSIBILITY IS DEFUSED

Under *respondeat superior* principles, as traditionally employed, vicarious liability may only be imposed where there is a primary violator—that is, where an agent of the corporation has committed a crime. This requirement would seem to imply "that the corporation could not be convicted if the agent committing the *actus reus* lacked the requisite intent."[42] Conceptually, then, difficulties should arise in applying these imputation principles in cases where it is not clear which individual within an organization took the actions (or failed to take the actions) alleged to lead to corporate liability, or where the knowledge or intent necessary to prove the violations may be fragmented among many employees within a large corporate hierarchy. Thus, were *respondeat superior* principles to be strictly applied, they would be underinclusive as well as overinclusive because "[t]here are situations in which corporate policies or procedures do cause a crime, yet the doctrine of *respondeat superior* is unable to find the corporation culpable because there is no individual culpability to impute."[43] This conceptual difficulty has been obviated by the following developments:

---

[42] John C. Coffee, Jr., *Corporate Criminal Responsibility*, in Encyclopedia of Crime & Justice 253, 255 (S. Kadish ed., 1983).

[43] Moore, *supra* note 14, at 762.

... First, intent may be imputed to the corporation from a person distinct from the one who commits the *actus reus*, such as the supervisory official who realized the significance of the act. Nor has it been necessary for the prosecutor to identify the actual agent who committed the crime if the prosecutor can show that some person within the corporation must have so acted. Even more significantly, inconsistent verdicts are tolerated under which the corporation is convicted but all conceivable individual agents are acquitted. Finally, some decisions have accepted a theory of "collective knowledge," under which no single individual had the requisite knowledge to satisfy the intent requirement, but various individuals within the organization possessed all the elements of such knowledge collectively.[44]

The following case is a leading example of both toleration of inconsistent verdicts and use of aggregated *mens rea* in order to sustain corporate criminal liability that might not be sustained under a strict reading of *respondeat superior* principles.

UNITED STATES v. BANK OF NEW ENGLAND, N.A.
821 F.2d 844 (1st Cir.1987)

BOWNES, CIRCUIT JUDGE.

The Bank of New England appeals a jury verdict convicting it of thirty-one violations of the Currency Transaction Reporting Act (the [Bank Secrecy] Act). 31 U.S.C. §§ 5311-22 (1982).[45] Department of Treasury regulations promulgated under the Act require banks to file Currency Transaction Reports (CTRs) within fifteen days of customer currency transactions exceeding $10,000. 31 C.F.R. § 103.22 (1986).[46] The Act imposes felony liability when a bank willfully fails to file such reports "as part of a pattern of illegal activity involving transactions of more than $100,000 in a twelve-month period ...." 31 U.S.C. § 5322(b).

The Bank was found guilty of having failed to file CTRs on cash withdrawals made by James McDonough. It is undisputed that on thirty-one separate occasions between May 1983 and July 1984, McDonough withdrew from the Prudential Branch of the Bank more than

---

[44] Coffee, *supra* note 42, at 255-56.

[45] [Court's footnote 2:] The Act provides in relevant part:

§ 5313. Reports on domestic coins and currency transactions (a) When a domestic financial institution is involved in a transaction for the payment, receipt, or transfer of United States coins or currency (or other monetary instruments the Secretary of the Treasury prescribes), in an amount, denomination, or amount and denomination, or under circumstances the Secretary prescribes by regulation, the institution and any other participant in the transaction the Secretary may prescribe shall file a report on the transaction at the time and in the way the Secretary prescribes. A participant acting for another person shall make the report as the agent or bailee of the person and identify the person for whom the transaction is being made.

§ 5322. Criminal penalties (a) A person willfully violating this subchapter or a regulation prescribed under this subchapter (except section 5315 of this title or a regulation prescribed under section 5315) shall be fined not more than $1,000, imprisoned for not more than one year, or both. (b) A person willfully violating this subchapter or a regulation prescribed under this subchapter (except section 5315 of this title or a regulation prescribed under section 5315), while violating another law of the United States or as part of a pattern of illegal activity involving transactions of more than $100,000 in a 12-month period, shall be fined no more than $500,000, imprisoned for not more than 5 years, or both.

[46] [Court's footnote 3:] The regulations then in effect provided:

§ 103.22 Reports of currency transactions (a)(1) Each financial institution, other than a casino shall file a report of each deposit, withdrawal, exchange of currency or other payment or transfer, by, through, or to such financial institution, which involves a transaction in currency of more than $10,000.

$10,000 in cash by using multiple checks—each one individually under $10,000—presented simultaneously to a single bank teller ....

The Bank had been named in a federal grand jury indictment which was returned on October 15, 1985. Count One of the indictment alleged that between May 1983 and May 1985, James McDonough, the Bank, and Carol Orlandella and Patricia Murphy—both of whom were former head tellers with the Bank's Prudential Branch—unlawfully conspired to conceal from the IRS thirty-six of McDonough's currency transactions. The trial court directed a verdict of acquittal on this count. Defendants Murphy and Orlandella were found not guilty of charges that they individually aided and abetted the failure to file CTRs on McDonough's transactions.

The bulk of the indictment alleged that the Bank, as principal, and McDonough, as an aider and abettor, willfully failed to file CTRs on thirty-six occasions between May 1983 and July 1984. Five counts were dismissed because, on those occasions, McDonough received cashier's checks from the Bank, rather than currency. McDonough was acquitted of all charges against him. The Bank was found guilty on the thirty-one remaining counts. We affirm.

The evidence at trial revealed that from 1978 through September 1984, McDonough was a regular customer at the Prudential Branch of the Bank of New England. McDonough visited that branch several times a month to withdraw large sums of cash from various corporate accounts. On thirty-one occasions from May 1983 through July 1984, McDonough requested a number of counter checks—blank checks which a teller encodes with the customer's account number—which he would then make payable to cash for sums varying between $5,000 and $9,000. On each of the charged occasions, McDonough simultaneously presented to a teller between two and four counter checks, none of which individually amounted to $10,000. Each check was recorded separately as an "item" on the Bank's settlement sheets. Once the checks were processed, McDonough would receive in a single transfer from the teller, one lump sum of cash which always amounted to over $10,000. On each of the charged occasions, the cash was withdrawn from one account. The Bank did not file CTRs on any of these transactions until May 1985, shortly after it received a grand jury subpoena. ...

Criminal liability under 31 U.S.C. § 5322 only attaches when a financial institution "willfully" violates the CTR filing requirement. ...

The Bank contends that the trial court's instructions on knowledge and specific intent effectively relieved the government of its responsibility to prove that the Bank acted willfully. The trial judge began her instructions on this element by outlining generally the concepts of knowledge and willfulness:

> Knowingly simply means voluntarily and intentionally. It's designed to exclude a failure that is done by mistake or accident, or for some other innocent reason. Willfully means voluntarily, intentionally, and with a specific intent to disregard, to disobey the law, with a bad purpose to violate the law.

The trial judge properly instructed the jury that it could infer knowledge if a defendant consciously avoided learning about the reporting requirements. The court then focused on the kind of proof that would establish the Bank's knowledge of its filing obligations. The judge instructed that the knowledge of individual employees acting within the scope of their employment is imputed to the Bank. She told the jury that "if any employee knew that multiple checks would require the filing of reports, the bank knew it, provided the employee knew it within the scope of his employment ...."

The trial judge then focused on the issue of "collective knowledge":

> In addition, however, you have to look at the bank as an institution. As such, its knowledge is the sum of the knowledge of all of the employees. That is, the bank's knowledge is the totality of what all of the employees know within the scope of their employment. So, if Employee A knows one facet of the currency reporting requirement, B knows another facet of it, and C a third facet of it, the bank knows them all. So if you find

that an employee within the scope of his employment knew that CTRs had to be filed, even if multiple checks are used, the bank is deemed to know it. The bank is also deemed to know it if each of several employees knew a part of that requirement and the sum of what the separate employees knew amounted to knowledge that such a requirement existed.

After discussing the two modes of establishing knowledge—via either knowledge of one of its individual employees or the aggregate knowledge of all its employees—the trial judge turned to the issue of specific intent:

> There is a similar double business with respect to the concept of willfulness with respect to the bank. In deciding whether the bank acted willfully, again you have to look first at the conduct of all employees and officers, and, second, at what the bank did or did not do as an institution. The bank is deemed to have acted willfully if one of its employees in the scope of his employment acted willfully. So, if you find that an employee willfully failed to do what was necessary to file these reports, then that is deemed to be the act of the bank, and the bank is deemed to have willfully failed to file. ...
>
> Alternatively, the bank as an institution has certain responsibilities; as an organization, it has certain responsibilities. And you will have to determine whether the bank as an organization consciously avoided learning about and observing CTR requirements. The Government to prove the bank guilty on this theory, has to show that its failure to file was the result of some flagrant organizational indifference. In this connection, you should look at the evidence as to the bank's effort, if any, to inform its employees of the law; its effort to check on their compliance; its response to various bits of information that it got in August and September of '84 and February of '85; its policies, and how it carried out its stated policies. ...
>
> If you find that the Government has proven with respect to any transaction either that an employee within the scope of his employment willfully failed to file a required report or that the bank was flagrantly indifferent to its obligations, then you may find that the bank has willfully failed to file the required reports.

The Bank contends that the trial court's instructions regarding knowledge were defective because they eliminated the requirement that it be proven that the Bank violated a known legal duty. It avers that the knowledge instruction invited the jury to convict the Bank for negligently maintaining a poor communications network that prevented the consolidation of the information held by its various employees. The Bank argues that it is error to find that a corporation possesses a particular item of knowledge if one part of the corporation has half the information making up the item, and another part of the entity has the other half.

A collective knowledge instruction is entirely appropriate in the context of corporate criminal liability. The acts of a corporation are, after all, simply the acts of all of its employees operating within the scope of their employment. The law on corporate criminal liability reflects this. Similarly, the knowledge obtained by corporate employees acting within the scope of their employment is imputed to the corporation. Corporations compartmentalize knowledge, subdividing the elements of specific duties and operations into smaller components. The aggregate of those components constitutes the corporation's knowledge of a particular operation. It is irrelevant whether employees administering one component of an operation know the specific activities of employees administering another aspect of the operation:

> [A] corporation cannot plead innocence by asserting that the information obtained by several employees was not acquired by any one individual who then would have comprehended its full import. Rather the corporation is considered to have acquired the collective knowledge of its employees and is held responsible for their failure to act accordingly.

Since the Bank had the compartmentalized structure common to all large corporations, the court's collective knowledge instruction was not only proper but necessary.

Nor do we find any defects in the trial court's instructions on specific intent. The court told the jury that the concept of willfulness entails a voluntary, intentional, and bad purpose to disobey the law. Her instructions on this element, when viewed as a whole, directed the jury not to convict for accidental, mistaken or inadvertent acts or omissions. It is urged that the court erroneously charged that willfulness could be found via flagrant indifference by the Bank toward its reporting obligations. With respect to federal regulatory statutes, the Supreme Court has endorsed defining willfulness, in both civil and criminal contexts, as "a disregard for the governing statute and an indifference to its requirements." Accordingly, we find no error in the court's instruction on willfulness.

The Bank asserts that the evidence did not suffice to show that it had willfully failed to comply with the Act's reporting requirements. ...

... [T]he language of the Treasury regulations itself gave notice that cash withdrawals over $10,000 were reportable, regardless of the number of checks used. Primary responsibility for CTR compliance in the Bank's branch offices was assigned to head tellers and branch managers. Head tellers Orlandella and Murphy, who knew of the nature of McDonough's transactions, also knew of the CTR filing obligations imposed by the Bank. The jury heard testimony from former bank teller Simona Wong, who stated that she knew McDonough's transactions were reportable, and that the source of her knowledge was head teller Murphy.

Even if some Bank personnel mistakenly regarded McDonough as engaging in multiple transactions, there was convincing evidence that the Bank knew that his withdrawals were reportable. An internal memo sent in May 1983 by project coordinator Jayne Brady to all branch managers and head tellers stated that "'[r]eportable transactions are expanded to include multiple transactions which aggregate more than $10,000 in any *one day*.' This includes deposits or withdrawals by a customer to or from more than one account." The Prudential Branch Manual instructed that if Bank personnel know that a customer has engaged in multiple transactions totalling $10,000 or more, then such transactions should be regarded as a single transaction. In addition, since 1980, the instructions on the back of CTR forms have directed that reports be filed on multiple transactions which aggregate to over $10,000. Finally, a Bank auditor discussed with Orlandella and Murphy, the Bank's obligation to report a customer's multiple transactions in a single day which amount to more than $10,000. We do not suggest that these evidentiary items in themselves legally bound the Bank to report McDonough's transactions; it is the language of the regulations that impose such a duty. This evidence, however, proved that the Bank had ample knowledge that transactions like McDonough's came within the purview of the Act.

Regarding the Bank's specific intent to violate the reporting obligation, Simona Wong testified that head teller Patricia Murphy knew that McDonough's transactions were reportable, but, on one occasion, deliberately chose not to file a CTR on him because he was "a good customer." In addition, the jury heard testimony that bank employees regarded McDonough's transactions as unusual, speculated that he was a bookie, and suspected that he was structuring his transactions to avoid the Act's reporting requirements. An internal Bank memo, written after an investigation of the McDonough transactions, concluded that a "person managing the branch would have to have known that something strange was going on." Given the suspicions aroused by McDonough's banking practices and the abundance of information indicating that his transactions were reportable, the jury could have concluded that the failure by Bank personnel to, at least, inquire about the reportability of McDonough's transactions constituted flagrant indifference to the obligations imposed by the Act.

We hold that the evidence was sufficient for a finding of willfulness.

Notes

1. What is the consequence of having the "collective knowledge/flagrant organizational indifference" theory exist in tandem with traditional *respondeat superior* notions? Might

corporations find themselves "whipsawed" where such theories of liability are charged together?

2. As one commentator has noted, the "collective knowledge" approach used in this case "only makes sense if employees are viewed as aspects of a corporate entity which is distinct from each of them, and the crime is understood not as the act of an individual, but as the act of the corporate entity as such. The doctrine thus represents a step away from the concept of imputed culpability and toward a theory of genuine corporate fault." Moore, *supra* note 14, at 764. But is this a principled theory of corporate fault? Does the fault here lie in the knowledge possessed by various actors within the corporation or the corporation's apparent negligence in ensuring regulatory requirements are met?

Some state courts have not accepted the theory of collective knowledge in the absence of some specific employee who was criminally liable. *See* Commonwealth v. Life Care Centers of Am., 926 N.E.2d 206 (Mass. 2010). In one little-noticed opinion, *United States v. L.E. Myers Co.*, 562 F.3d 845 (7th Cir. 2009), the Seventh Circuit seemed to reject that idea that corporate "knowledge" may be pieced together based on the knowledge of random individuals within the corporation. In *L.E. Myers*, the corporation contested the jury charge under which it had been indicted for willful violations of OSHA regulations. The Seventh Circuit noted that the statute at issue required that the corporation have actual knowledge of both the hazardous condition in question and the associated legal obligations. *Id.* at 853. The court then rejected as too broad the jury instruction's suggestion that a corporation "knows" what any of its employees know. It held that "'the knowledge of a worker who trips over a safety hazard but does not understand or report what he has found does not count. Most federal statutes that make anything of corporate knowledge also require the knowledge to be possessed by persons authorized to do something about what they know.'" *Id.* at 853 (citation omitted). It stated that "[t]he proper inquiry is not whether the employee who acquires knowledge of a given hazard was acting within the scope of his employment when he did so but whether he was an employee with a duty to report or ameliorate such hazards." *Id.* at 854. Does this make more sense than the *Bank of New England* rule?

3. Commentators have long struggled with the notion of corporate *mens rea*. *See, e.g.,* Steven J. Sherman & Elise J. Percy, *The Psychology of Collective Responsibility: When and Why Collective Entities Are Likely to Be Held Responsible for the Misdeeds of Individual Members*, J.L. & Pol'y 137 (2010); V.S. Khanna, *Is the Notion of Corporate Fault a Faulty Notion?: The Case of Corporate Mens Rea*, 79 B.U. L. Rev. 355 (1999); Pamela H. Bucy, *Corporate Ethos: A Standard for Imposing Criminal Liability*, 75 Minn. L. Rev. 1095, 1096-1102 (1991). As Professor Brent Fisse explains:

> In virtually all United States jurisdictions, *mens rea* is vicariously attributed to a corporation on the basis of the mental state of an agent acting with intent to benefit the corporation. The reason these jurisdictions do not insist upon genuinely corporate fault is probably that none of the existing concepts of corporate *mens rea* is satisfactory. Three concepts of corporate *mens rea* have been suggested:
>
> 1. Managerial *mens rea*: *mens rea* based on the mental state of a person acting on behalf of the organization in a senior managerial capacity. This is not a concept of genuinely corporate fault and is usually very difficult to prove.
>
> 2. Composite *mens rea*: *mens rea* pieced together from the knowledge of various individuals within an organization. This mental state may be easier to prove but bears no necessary connection with corporate blameworthiness.
>
> 3. Strategic *mens rea*: *mens rea* based on express or implied organizational policy. This concept reflects genuinely corporate blameworthiness but only rarely can be proven.

Brent Fisse, *Reconstructing Corporate Criminal Law: Deterrence, Retribution, Fault, and Sanctions*, 56 S. Cal. L. Rev. 1141, 1185-86 (1982) (footnotes omitted).

4. The reader should consider, when reviewing the following materials on the Justice Department's organizational charging policy and the U.S. Organizational Sentencing Guidelines, whether the Justice Department and the U.S. Sentencing Commission correctly identified factors relevant to corporate "fault" for sentencing purposes, even if such factors are

not determinative for purposes of imposing corporate liability. *See* Moore, *supra* note 27, *passim*. The reader should also evaluate whether these rules are likely to encourage corporations to take effective steps to detect and prevent organizational crime.

C. DEPARTMENT OF JUSTICE CHARGING POLICIES

In 1999, then-Deputy Attorney General Eric Holder issued a memorandum (the Holder Memo) entitled "Federal Prosecution of Corporations," which outlined the criteria upon which the Justice Department would rely in deciding whether to charge corporations and other organizational defendants. As Mr. Holder recalls it, this Memo was drafted in response to the defense bar's request for more consistency and transparency in the government's corporate charging decisions.[47] In 2003, then-Deputy Attorney General Larry Thompson updated the charging policy (the Thompson Memo) in part to emphasize that prosecutors ought to carefully scrutinize the authenticity of a corporation's cooperation. As will be explored at greater length in Chapter 17, the Holder and Thompson memoranda generated great controversy because, according to the defense bar, the memoranda's discussion of requests for waivers of the attorney-client privilege and work product protection as evidence of corporate "cooperation" with the investigation was abused by line prosecutors. Even Mr. Holder, later in private practice, complained that "[t]oday, its maddening ... You'll go into a prosecutor's office ... and fifteen minutes into our first meeting they say, 'Are you going to waive?'"[48] (It is only fair to note that there is an empirical battle still raging over the actual extent to which prosecutors asked for privilege waivers; the defense bar contends that they were "requested" in virtually every corporate crime case as a condition of declination of charges, while the government responds that this was simply not the case.)

An "oddball alliance of business, legal and civil liberties groups," including the ACLU, the Chamber of Commerce, and the Association of Corporate Council came together to lobby against the charging policy—and particularly against the provision that permitted prosecutors to "request" waivers and to hold a corporation's decision *not* to waive against it in charging.[49] This alliance succeeded in getting the attention of sympathetic lawmakers on the Hill, as well as in persuading the U.S. Sentencing Commission to omit mention of privilege waivers in its discussion of corporate cooperation in the Organizational Sentencing Guidelines. The momentum of opponents of the policy was increased by Judge Kaplan's ruling in *United States v. Stein*, striking down the DOJ's policy to the extent that it was used to pressure corporations, under threat of indictment, to cut off legal fees to "culpable" employees. (In Chapter 18, focusing on representation issues, we will explore this decision.)

Legislation entitled the "Attorney-Client Privilege Protection Act" was introduced that would bar federal prosecutors from, *inter alia*, asking organizations to disclose information protected by the attorney-client privilege or the work product doctrine as a condition for cooperation credit or declination of criminal charges.[50] Apparently in an effort to head off congressional action, in December 2006, then-Deputy Attorney General Paul J. McNulty issued a revised set of guidelines, (McNulty Memo). The McNulty Memo altered the policies expressed in the Holder and Thompson Memoranda in two principal respects. First, in response to the *Stein* ruling, it tightened the circumstances in which prosecutors can take into

---

[47] *See* Peter Lattman, *The Holder Memo and Its Progeny*, Wall St. J. Online (Dec. 13, 2006), at http://blogs.wsj.com/2006/12/13/the-holder-memo/.

[48] *Id.*

[49] Jason McLure, *The Life and Death of the Thompson Memo*, Legal Times (Dec. 18, 2006), at http://www.nacdl.org/public.nsf/whitecollar/WCnews065.

[50] *See, e.g.,* S. 186, 110th Cong., 1st Sess. (Jan. 4, 2007), at http://thomas.loc.gov/cgi-bin/query/C?c110:./temp/~c110MfwRkl.

account whether a corporation is advancing attorney's fees to its employees or agents under investigation or indictment. Second, it put in place a more stringent internal approval and reporting regime for waiver requests. When this did not meet critics' approval, Deputy Attorney General Mark Filip issued another memorandum in August 2008 to replace the McNulty Memo (and its predecessors, the Holder and Thompson Memos). Although it has been altered since its initial release (in 2015 and 2017), it is still often referred to as the "Filip Memo."

One of the notable amendments to the policy came in response to a September 9, 2015 memorandum issued by Deputy Attorney Sally Yates that was entitled "Individual Accountability for Corporate Wrongdoing" (predictably, commonly referred to as "the Yates Memo"). In that memo, Yates outlined "six key steps to strengthen our pursuit of individual corporate wrongdoing":

> (1) in order to qualify for any cooperation credit, corporations must provide to the Department all relevant facts relating to the individuals responsible for the misconduct; (2) criminal and civil corporate investigations should focus on individuals from the inception of the investigation; (3) criminal and civil attorneys handling corporate investigations should be in routine communication with one another; (4) absent extraordinary circumstances or approved departmental policy, the Department will not release culpable individuals from civil or criminal liability when resolving a matter with a corporation; (5) Department attorneys should not resolve matters with a corporation without a clear plan to resolve related individual cases, and should memorialize any declinations as to individuals in such cases; and (6) civil attorneys should consistently focus on individuals as well as the company and evaluate whether to bring suit against an individual based on considerations beyond that individual's ability to pay.

The Yates Memo—and particularly its requirement that, to get cooperation credit, entities must provide all relevant facts regarding individual agents' culpability—potentially affects a variety of the defense's strategic choices (explored in future chapters).[51] Although the current Deputy Attorney General, Rod Rosenstein, has said that he is reevaluating the Yates Memo and the Principles below, as of this writing the Trump administration has not issued additional amendments.

Readers should also be aware that the DOJ has a Foreign Corrupt Practices Act (FCPA) Enforcement Policy[52] that some in DOJ claim serves as non-binding guidance in other areas of white-collar enforcement. This policy will be discussed in Chapter 8.

USAM § 9-28.000
PRINCIPLES OF FEDERAL PROSECUTION OF BUSINESS ORGANIZATIONS[53]

9-28.010 - Foundational Principles of Corporate Prosecution

The prosecution of corporate crime is a high priority for the Department of Justice. By investigating allegations of wrongdoing and bringing charges where appropriate for criminal misconduct, the Department promotes critical public interests. These interests include, among other things: (1) protecting the integrity of our economic and capital markets by enforcing the

---

[51] *See, e.g.*, Gideon Mark, *The Yates Memorandum*, 51 U.C. Davis L. Rev. 1589 (2018); Robert R. Stauffer & William C. Pericak, Twenty Questions Raised by the Justice Department's Yates Memorandum (May 18, 2016),   *available*   *at* https://jenner.com/system/assets/publications/15188/original/Stauffer_Pericak_Bloomberg_May_2016.pdf?1463730304.

[52] U.S.A.M. § 9-47.120.

[53] While these guidelines refer to corporations, they apply to the consideration of the prosecution of all types of business organizations, including partnerships, sole proprietorships, government entities, and unincorporated associations.

rule of law; (2) protecting consumers, investors, and business entities against competitors who gain unfair advantage by violating the law; (3) preventing violations of environmental laws; and (4) discouraging business practices that would permit or promote unlawful conduct at the expense of the public interest.

One of the most effective ways to combat corporate misconduct is by holding accountable all individuals who engage in wrongdoing. Such accountability deters future illegal activity, incentivizes changes in corporate behavior, ensures that the proper parties are held responsible for their actions, and promotes the public's confidence in our justice system.

Prosecutors should focus on wrongdoing by individuals from the very beginning of any investigation of corporate misconduct. By focusing on building cases against individual wrongdoers, we accomplish multiple goals. First, we increase our ability to identify the full extent of corporate misconduct. Because a corporation only acts through individuals, investigating the conduct of individuals is the most efficient and effective way to determine the facts and the extent of any corporate misconduct. Second, a focus on individuals increases the likelihood that those with knowledge of the corporate misconduct will be identified and provide information about the individuals involved, at any level of an organization. Third, we maximize the likelihood that the final resolution will include charges against culpable individuals and not just the corporation.

9-28.100 - Duties of Federal Prosecutors and Duties of Corporate Leaders

Corporate directors and officers owe a fiduciary duty to a corporation's shareholders (the corporation's true owners) and they owe duties of honest dealing to the investing public and consumers in connection with the corporation's regulatory filings and public statements. A prosecutor's duty to enforce the law requires the investigation and prosecution of criminal wrongdoing if it is discovered. In carrying out this mission with the diligence and resolve necessary to vindicate the important public interests discussed above, prosecutors should be mindful of the common cause we share with responsible corporate leaders who seek to promote trust and confidence. Prosecutors should also be mindful that confidence in the Department is affected both by the results we achieve and by the real and perceived ways in which we achieve them. Thus, the manner in which we do our job as prosecutors—including the professionalism and civility we demonstrate, our willingness to secure the facts in a manner that encourages corporate compliance and self-regulation, and also our appreciation that corporate prosecutions can harm blameless investors, employees, and others—affects public perception of our mission. Federal prosecutors must maintain public confidence in the way in which we exercise our charging discretion. This endeavor requires the thoughtful analysis of all facts and circumstances presented in a given case.

9-28.200 - General Considerations of Corporate Liability

A. General Principle: Corporations should not be treated leniently because of their artificial nature nor should they be subject to harsher treatment. Vigorous enforcement of the criminal laws against corporate wrongdoers, where appropriate, results in great benefits for law enforcement and the public, particularly in the area of white collar crime. Indicting corporations for wrongdoing enables the government to be a force for positive change of corporate culture, and a force to prevent, discover, and punish serious crimes.

B. Comment: In all cases involving corporate wrongdoing, prosecutors should consider the factors discussed in these guidelines.[54] In doing so, prosecutors should be aware of the public benefits that can flow from indicting a corporation in appropriate cases. For instance, corporations are likely to take immediate remedial steps when one is indicted for criminal misconduct that is pervasive throughout a particular industry, and thus an indictment can

---

[54] [Policy's footnote 1:] While these guidelines refer to corporations, they apply to the consideration of the prosecution of all types of business organizations, including partnerships, sole proprietorships, government entities, and unincorporated associations.

provide a unique opportunity for deterrence on a broad scale. In addition, a corporate indictment may result in specific deterrence by changing the culture of the indicted corporation and the behavior of its employees. Finally, certain crimes that carry with them a substantial risk of great public harm—*e.g.*, environmental crimes or sweeping financial frauds—may be committed by a business entity, and there may therefore be a substantial federal interest in indicting a corporation under such circumstances.

In certain instances, it may be appropriate to resolve a corporate criminal case by means other than indictment. Non-prosecution and deferred prosecution agreements, for example, occupy an important middle ground between declining prosecution and obtaining the conviction of a corporation. These agreements are discussed further in USAM 9-28.1100 (Collateral Consequences). Likewise, civil and regulatory alternatives may be appropriate in certain cases, as discussed in USAM 9-28.1200 (Civil or Regulatory Alternatives).

Prosecutors have substantial latitude in determining when, whom, how, and even whether to prosecute for violations of federal criminal law. In exercising that discretion, prosecutors should consider the following statements of principles that summarize the considerations they should weigh and the practices they should follow in discharging their prosecutorial responsibilities. Prosecutors should ensure that the general purposes of the criminal law— appropriate punishment for the defendant, deterrence of further criminal conduct by the defendant, deterrence of criminal conduct by others, protection of the public from dangerous and fraudulent conduct, rehabilitation, and restitution for victims—are adequately met, taking into account the special nature of the corporate "person."

9-28.210 - Focus on Individual Wrongdoers

A. General Principle: Prosecution of a corporation is not a substitute for the prosecution of criminally culpable individuals within or without the corporation. Because a corporation can act only through individuals, imposition of individual criminal liability may provide the strongest deterrent against future corporate wrongdoing. Provable individual culpability should be pursued, particularly if it relates to high-level corporate officers, even in the face of an offer of a corporate guilty plea or some other disposition of the charges against the corporation, including a deferred prosecution or non-prosecution agreement, or a civil resolution. In other words, regardless of the ultimate corporate disposition, a separate evaluation must be made with respect to potentially liable individuals.

B. Comment: It is important early in the corporate investigation to identify the responsible individuals and determine the nature and extent of their misconduct. Prosecutors should not allow delays in the corporate investigation to undermine the Department's ability to pursue potentially culpable individuals. Every effort should be made to resolve a corporate matter within the statutorily allotted time, and tolling agreements should be the rare exception. In situations where it is anticipated that a tolling agreement is unavoidable, all efforts should be made either to prosecute culpable individuals before the limitations period expires or to preserve the ability to charge individuals by tolling the limitations period by agreement or court order.

If an investigation of individual misconduct has not concluded by the time authorization is sought to resolve the case against the corporation, the prosecution authorization memorandum should include a discussion of the potentially liable individuals, a description of the current status of the investigation regarding their conduct and the investigative work that remains to be done, and, when warranted, an investigative plan to bring the matter to resolution prior to the end of any statute of limitations period. If a decision is made at the conclusion of the investigation to pursue charges or some other resolution with the corporation but not to bring criminal or civil charges against the individuals who committed the misconduct, the reasons for that determination must be memorialized and approved by the United States Attorney or Assistant Attorney General whose office handled the investigation, or their designees.

Under the doctrine of *respondeat superior*, a corporation may be held criminally liable for the illegal acts of its directors, officers, employees, and agents. To hold a corporation liable for these actions, the government must establish that the corporate agent's actions (i) were within the scope of his duties and (ii) were intended, at least in part, to benefit the corporation. In all cases involving wrongdoing by corporate agents, prosecutors should not limit their focus solely to individuals or the corporation, but should consider both as potential targets.

Agents may act for mixed reasons—both for self-aggrandizement (direct and indirect) and for the benefit of the corporation, and a corporation may be held liable as long as one motivation of its agent is to benefit the corporation. *See United States v. Potter*, 463 F.3d 9, 25 (1st Cir. 2006) (stating that the test to determine whether an agent is acting within the scope of employment is "whether the agent is performing acts of the kind which he is authorized to perform, and those acts are motivated, at least in part, by an intent to benefit the corporation."). In *United States v. Automated Medical Laboratories, Inc.*, 770 F.2d 399 (4th Cir. 1985), for example, the Fourth Circuit affirmed a corporation's conviction for the actions of a subsidiary's employee despite the corporation's claim that the employee was acting for his own benefit, namely his "ambitious nature and his desire to ascend the corporate ladder." *Id.* at 407. The court stated, "Partucci was clearly acting in part to benefit AML since his advancement within the corporation depended on AML's well-being and its lack of difficulties with the FDA." *Id.*; *see also United States v. Cincotta*, 689 F.2d 238, 241-42 (1st Cir. 1982) (upholding a corporation's conviction, notwithstanding the substantial personal benefit reaped by its miscreant agents, because the fraudulent scheme required money to pass through the corporation's treasury and the fraudulently obtained goods were resold to the corporation's customers in the corporation's name).

Moreover, the corporation need not even necessarily profit from its agent's actions for it to be held liable. In *Automated Medical Laboratories*, the Fourth Circuit stated:

> [B]enefit is not a "touchstone of criminal corporate liability; benefit at best is an evidential, not an operative, fact." Thus, whether the agent's actions ultimately redounded to the benefit of the corporation is less significant than whether the agent acted with the intent to benefit the corporation. The basic purpose of requiring that an agent have acted with the intent to benefit the corporation, however, is to insulate the corporation from criminal liability for actions of its agents which may be *inimical* to the interests of the corporation or which may have been undertaken solely to advance the interests of that agent or of a party other than the corporation.

770 F.2d at 407 (internal citation omitted) (quoting *Old Monastery Co. v. United States*, 147 F.2d 905, 908 (4th Cir. 1945)).

9-28.300 - Factors to Be Considered

A. General Principle: Generally, prosecutors apply the same factors in determining whether to charge a corporation as they do with respect to individuals. *See* USAM 9-27.220, *et seq*). Thus, the prosecutor must weigh all of the factors normally considered in the sound exercise of prosecutorial judgment: the sufficiency of the evidence; the likelihood of success at trial; the probable deterrent, rehabilitative, and other consequences of conviction; and the adequacy of noncriminal approaches. *See id.* However, due to the nature of the corporate "person," some additional factors are present. In conducting an investigation, determining whether to bring charges, and negotiating plea or other agreements, prosecutors should consider the following factors in reaching a decision as to the proper treatment of a corporate target:

1. the nature and seriousness of the offense, including the risk of harm to the public, and applicable policies and priorities, if any, governing the prosecution of corporations for particular categories of crime (*see* USAM 9-28.400);

2. the pervasiveness of wrongdoing within the corporation, including the complicity in, or the condoning of, the wrongdoing by corporate management (*see* USAM 9-28.500);

3. the corporation's history of similar misconduct, including prior criminal, civil, and regulatory enforcement actions against it (*see* USAM 9-28.600);

4. the corporation's willingness to cooperate in the investigation of its agents (*see* USAM 9-28.700);

5. the existence and effectiveness of the corporation's pre-existing compliance program (*see* USAM 9-28.800);

6. the corporation's timely and voluntary disclosure of wrongdoing (*see* USAM 9-28.900);

7. the corporation's remedial actions, including any efforts to implement an effective corporate compliance program or to improve an existing one, to replace responsible management, to discipline or terminate wrongdoers, to pay restitution, and to cooperate with the relevant government agencies (*see* USAM 9-18.1000);

8. collateral consequences, including whether there is disproportionate harm to shareholders, pension holders, employees, and others not proven personally culpable, as well as impact on the public arising from the prosecution (*see* USAM 9-28.1100);

9. the adequacy of remedies such as civil or regulatory enforcement actions (*see* USAM 9-28.1200); and

10. the adequacy of the prosecution of individuals responsible for the corporation's malfeasance (*see* USAM 9-28.1300).

B. Comment: The factors listed in this section are intended to be illustrative of those that should be evaluated and are not an exhaustive list of potentially relevant considerations. Some of these factors may not apply to specific cases, and in some cases one factor may override all others. For example, the nature and seriousness of the offense may be such as to warrant prosecution regardless of the other factors. In most cases, however, no single factor will be dispositive. In addition, national law enforcement policies in various enforcement areas may require that more or less weight be given to certain of these factors than to others. Of course, prosecutors must exercise their thoughtful and pragmatic judgment in applying and balancing these factors, so as to achieve a fair and just outcome and promote respect for the law.

9-28.400 - Special Policy Concerns

A. General Principle: The nature and seriousness of the crime, including the risk of harm to the public from the criminal misconduct, are obviously primary factors in determining whether to charge a corporation. In addition, corporate conduct, particularly that of national and multi-national corporations, necessarily intersects with federal economic, tax, and criminal law enforcement policies. In applying these Principles, prosecutors must consider the practices and policies of the appropriate Division of the Department, and must comply with those policies to the extent required by the facts presented.

B. Comment: In determining whether to charge a corporation, prosecutors should take into account federal law enforcement priorities as discussed above. *See* USAM 9-27.230. In addition, however, prosecutors must be aware of the specific policy goals and incentive programs established by the respective Divisions and regulatory agencies. Thus, whereas natural persons may be given incremental degrees of credit (ranging from immunity to lesser charges to sentencing considerations) for turning themselves in, making statements against their penal interest, and cooperating in the government's investigation of their own and others' wrongdoing, the same approach may not be appropriate in all circumstances with respect to corporations. As an example, it is entirely proper in many investigations for a prosecutor to consider the corporation's pre-indictment conduct, *e.g.*, voluntary disclosure, cooperation, remediation or restitution, in determining whether to seek an indictment. However, this would not necessarily be appropriate in an antitrust investigation, in which antitrust violations, by definition, go to the heart of the corporation's business. With this in mind, the Antitrust Division has established a firm policy, understood in the business community, that credit should not be given at the charging stage for a compliance program and that amnesty is available only to the first corporation to make full disclosure to the government. As another example, the Tax Division has a strong preference for prosecuting responsible individuals, rather than entities, for corporate tax offenses. Thus, in determining whether or not to charge a corporation, prosecutors must consult with the Criminal, Antitrust, Tax, Environmental and Natural Resources, and National Security Divisions, as appropriate.

9-28.500 - Pervasiveness of Wrongdoing Within the Corporation

A. General Principle: A corporation can only act through natural persons, and it is therefore held responsible for the acts of such persons fairly attributable to it. Charging a corporation for even minor misconduct may be appropriate where the wrongdoing was pervasive and was undertaken by a large number of employees, or by all the employees in a particular role within the corporation, or was condoned by upper management. On the other hand, it may not be appropriate to impose liability upon a corporation, particularly one with a robust compliance program in place, under a strict *respondeat superior* theory for the single isolated act of a rogue employee. There is, of course, a wide spectrum between these two extremes, and a prosecutor should exercise sound discretion in evaluating the pervasiveness of wrongdoing within a corporation.

B. Comment: Of these factors, the most important is the role and conduct of management. Although acts of even low-level employees may result in criminal liability, a corporation is directed by its management and management is responsible for a corporate culture in which criminal conduct is either discouraged or tacitly encouraged. As stated in commentary to the Sentencing Guidelines:

> Pervasiveness [is] case specific and [will] depend on the number, and degree of responsibility, of individuals [with] substantial authority ... who participated in, condoned, or were willfully ignorant of the offense. Fewer individuals need to be involved for a finding of pervasiveness if those individuals exercised a relatively high degree of authority. Pervasiveness can occur either within an organization as a whole or within a unit of an organization.

USSG § 8C2.5, cmt. (n. 4).

9-28.600 - The Corporation's Past History

A. General Principle: Prosecutors may consider a corporation's history of similar conduct, including prior criminal, civil, and regulatory enforcement actions against it, in determining whether to bring criminal charges and how best to resolve cases.

B. Comment: A corporation, like a natural person, is expected to learn from its mistakes. A history of similar misconduct may be probative of a corporate culture that encouraged, or at least condoned, such misdeeds, regardless of any compliance programs. Criminal prosecution of a corporation may be particularly appropriate where the corporation previously had been subject to non-criminal guidance, warnings, or sanctions, or previous criminal charges, and it either had not taken adequate action to prevent future unlawful conduct or had continued to engage in the misconduct in spite of the warnings or enforcement actions taken against it. The corporate structure itself (*e.g.*, the creation or existence of subsidiaries or operating divisions) is not dispositive in this analysis, and enforcement actions taken against the corporation or any of its divisions, subsidiaries, and affiliates may be considered, if germane. *See* USSG § 8C2.5(c), cmt. (n. 6).

9-28.700 – The Value of Cooperation

Cooperation is a mitigating factor, by which a corporation—just like any other subject of a criminal investigation—can gain credit in a case that otherwise is appropriate for indictment and prosecution. Of course, the decision not to cooperate by a corporation (or individual) is not itself evidence of misconduct, at least where the lack of cooperation does not involve criminal misconduct or demonstrate consciousness of guilt (*e.g.*, suborning perjury or false statements, or refusing to comply with lawful discovery requests). Thus, failure to cooperate, in and of itself, does not support or require the filing of charges with respect to a corporation any more than with respect to an individual.

A. General Principle: In order for a company to receive any consideration for cooperation under this section, the company must identify all individuals involved in or responsible for the misconduct at issue, regardless of their position, status or seniority, and provide to the Department all facts relating to that misconduct. If a company seeking cooperation credit declines to learn of such facts or to provide the Department with complete factual information about the individuals involved, its cooperation will not be considered a mitigating factor under this section. Nor, if a company is prosecuted, will the Department support a cooperation-related reduction at sentencing. *See* U.S.S.G. § 8C2.5(g), cmt. (n. 13) ("A prime test of whether the organization has disclosed all pertinent information" necessary to receive a cooperation-related reduction in its offense level calculation "is whether the information is sufficient … to identify … the individual(s) responsible for the criminal conduct.").[55] If a company meets the threshold requirement of providing all relevant facts with respect to individuals, it will be eligible for consideration for cooperation credit. To be clear, a company is not required to waive its attorney-client privilege and attorney work product protection in order satisfy this threshold. *See* USAM 9-28.720. The extent of the cooperation credit earned will depend on all the various factors that have traditionally applied in making this assessment (*e.g.*, the timeliness of the cooperation, the diligence, thoroughness and speed of the internal investigation, and the proactive nature of the cooperation).

B. Comment: In investigating wrongdoing by or within a corporation, a prosecutor may encounter several obstacles resulting from the nature of the corporation itself. It may be difficult to determine which individual took which action on behalf of the corporation. Lines of authority and responsibility may be shared among operating divisions or departments, and records and personnel may be spread throughout the United States or even among several countries. Where the criminal conduct continued over an extended period of time, the culpable or knowledgeable personnel may have been promoted, transferred, or fired, or they may have quit or retired. Accordingly, a corporation's cooperation may be critical in identifying potentially relevant actors and locating relevant evidence, among other things, and in doing so expeditiously.

This dynamic—*i.e.*, the difficulty of determining what happened, where the evidence is, and which individuals took or promoted putatively illegal corporate actions—can have negative consequences for both the government and the corporation that is the subject or target of a government investigation. More specifically, because of corporate attribution principles concerning actions of corporate officers and employees, *see* USAM 9.28-210, uncertainty about who authorized or directed apparent corporate misconduct can inure to the detriment of a corporation. For example, it may not matter under the law which of several possible executives or leaders in a chain of command approved of or authorized criminal conduct; however, that information if known might bear on the propriety of a particular disposition short of indictment of the corporation. It may not be in the interest of a corporation or the government for a charging decision to be made in the absence of such information, which might occur if, for example, a statute of limitations were relevant and authorization by any one of the officials were enough to justify a charge under the law.

---

[55] [Policy's footnote 1:] Of course, the Department encourages early voluntary disclosure of criminal wrongdoing, *see* USAM 9-28.900, even before all facts are known to the company, and does not expect that such early disclosures would be complete. However, the Department does expect that, in such circumstances, the company will move in a timely fashion to conduct an appropriate investigation and provide timely factual updates to the Department.

There may be circumstances where, despite its best efforts to conduct a thorough investigation, a company genuinely cannot get access to certain evidence or is actually prohibited from disclosing it to the government. Under such circumstances, the company seeking cooperation will bear the burden of explaining the restrictions it is facing to the prosecutor.

Moreover, a protracted government investigation of such an issue could disrupt the corporation's business operations or even depress its stock price.

For these reasons and more, cooperation can be a favorable course for both the government and the corporation. Cooperation benefits the government by allowing prosecutors and federal agents, for example, to avoid protracted delays, which compromise their ability to quickly uncover and address the full extent of widespread corporate crimes. With cooperation by the corporation, the government may be able to reduce tangible losses, limit damage to reputation, and preserve assets for restitution. At the same time, cooperation may benefit the corporation – and ultimately shareholders, employees, and other often blameless victims – by enabling the government to focus its investigative resources in a manner that will not unduly disrupt the corporation's legitimate business operations. In addition, cooperation may benefit the corporation by presenting it with the opportunity to earn credit for its efforts.

The requirement that companies cooperate completely as to individuals does not mean that Department attorneys should wait for the company to deliver the information about individual wrongdoers and then merely accept what companies provide. To the contrary, Department attorneys should be proactively investigating individuals at every step of the process – before, during, and after any corporate cooperation. Department attorneys should vigorously review any information provided by companies and compare it to the results of their own investigation, in order to best ensure that the information provided is indeed complete and does not seek to minimize the behavior or role of any individual or group of individuals.

Department attorneys should strive to obtain from the company as much information as possible about responsible individuals before resolving the corporate case. In addition, the company's continued cooperation with respect to individuals may be necessary post-resolution. If so, the corporate resolution agreement should include a provision that requires the company to provide information about all individuals involved and that is explicit enough so that a failure to provide the information results in specific consequences, such as stipulated penalties and/or a material breach.

9-28.710 - Attorney-Client and Work Product Protections

The attorney-client privilege and the attorney work product protection serve an extremely important function in the American legal system. The attorney-client privilege is one of the oldest and most sacrosanct privileges under the law. *See Upjohn v. United States*, 449 U.S. 383, 389 (1981). As the Supreme Court has stated, "[i]ts purpose is to encourage full and frank communication between attorneys and their clients and thereby promote broader public interests in the observance of law and administration of justice." *Id.* The value of promoting a corporation's ability to seek frank and comprehensive legal advice is particularly important in the contemporary global business environment, where corporations often face complex and dynamic legal and regulatory obligations imposed by the federal government and also by states and foreign governments. The work product doctrine serves similarly important goals.

For these reasons, waiving the attorney-client and work product protections has never been a prerequisite under the Department's prosecution guidelines for a corporation to be viewed as cooperative. Nonetheless, a wide range of commentators and members of the American legal community and criminal justice system have asserted that the Department's policies have been used, either wittingly or unwittingly, to coerce business entities into waiving attorney-client privilege and work-product protection. Everyone agrees that a corporation may freely waive its own privileges if it chooses to do so; indeed, such waivers occur routinely when corporations are victimized by their employees or others, conduct an internal investigation, and then disclose the details of the investigation to law enforcement officials in an effort to seek prosecution of the offenders. However, the contention, from a broad array of voices, is that the Department's position on attorney-client privilege and work product protection waivers has promoted an environment in which those protections are being unfairly eroded to the detriment of all.

The Department understands that the attorney-client privilege and attorney work product protection are essential and long-recognized components of the American legal system. What the government seeks and needs to advance its legitimate (indeed, essential) law enforcement mission is not waiver of those protections, but rather the facts known to the corporation about the putative criminal misconduct under review. In addition, while a corporation remains free to convey non-factual or "core" attorney-client communications or work product—if and only if the corporation voluntarily chooses to do so—prosecutors should not ask for such waivers and are directed not to do so. The critical factor is whether the corporation has provided the facts about the events, as explained further herein.

9-28.720 - Cooperation: Disclosing the Relevant Facts

Eligibility for cooperation credit is not predicated upon the waiver of attorney-client privilege or work product protection. Instead, the sort of cooperation that is most valuable to resolving allegations of misconduct by a corporation and its officers, directors, employees, or agents is disclosure of the relevant *facts* concerning such misconduct. In this regard, the analysis parallels that for a non-corporate defendant, where cooperation typically requires disclosure of relevant factual knowledge and not of discussions between an individual and his attorneys.

Thus, when the government investigates potential corporate wrongdoing, it seeks the relevant facts. For example, how and when did the alleged misconduct occur? Who promoted or approved it? Who was responsible for committing it? In this respect, the investigation of a corporation differs little from the investigation of an individual. In both cases, the government needs to know the facts to achieve a just and fair outcome. The party under investigation may choose to cooperate by disclosing the facts, and the government may give credit for the party's disclosures. If a corporation wishes to receive credit for such cooperation, which then can be considered with all other cooperative efforts and circumstances in evaluating how fairly to proceed, then the corporation, like any person, must disclose the relevant facts of which it has knowledge.[56]

(a) Disclosing the Relevant Facts—Facts Gathered Through Internal Investigation

Individuals and corporations often obtain knowledge of facts in different ways. An individual knows the facts of his or others' misconduct through his own experience and perceptions. A corporation is an artificial construct that cannot, by definition, have personal knowledge of the facts. Some of those facts may be reflected in documentary or electronic media like emails, transaction or accounting documents, and other records. Often, the corporation gathers facts through an internal investigation. Exactly how and by whom the facts are gathered is for the corporation to decide. Many corporations choose to collect information about potential misconduct through lawyers, a process that may confer attorney-client privilege or attorney work product protection on at least some of the information collected. Other corporations may choose a method of fact-gathering that does not have that effect—for example, having employee or other witness statements collected after interviews by non-attorney personnel. Whichever process the corporation selects, the government's key measure of cooperation must remain the same as it does for an individual: has the party timely disclosed the relevant facts about the putative misconduct? That is the operative question in assigning cooperation credit for the disclosure of information—*not* whether the corporation discloses attorney-client or work product materials. Accordingly, a corporation should receive the same credit for disclosing facts contained in materials that are not protected by the

---

[56] [Policy's footnote 1:] This section of the Principles focuses solely on the disclosure of facts and the privilege issues that may be implicated thereby. There are other dimensions of cooperation beyond the mere disclosure of facts, such as providing non-privileged documents and other evidence, making witnesses available for interviews, and assisting in the interpretation of complex business records.

attorney-client privilege or attorney work product as it would for disclosing identical facts contained in materials that are so protected.[57] ...

In short, the company may be eligible for cooperation credit regardless of whether it chooses to waive privilege or work product protection in the process, if it provides all relevant facts about the individuals who were involved in the misconduct. But if the corporation does not disclose such facts, it will not be entitled to receive any credit for cooperation.

Two final and related points bear noting about the disclosure of facts, although they should be obvious. First, the government cannot compel, and the corporation has no obligation to make, such disclosures (although the government can obviously compel the disclosure of certain records and witness testimony through subpoenas). Second, a corporation's failure to provide relevant information about individual misconduct alone does not mean the corporation will be indicted. It simply means that the corporation will not be entitled to mitigating credit for that cooperation. Whether the corporation faces charges will turn, as it does in any case, on the sufficiency of the evidence, the likelihood of success at trial, and all of the other factors identified in USAM 9-28.300. If there is insufficient evidence to warrant indictment, after appropriate investigation has been completed, or if the other factors weigh against indictment, then the corporation should not be indicted, irrespective of whether it has earned cooperation credit. The converse is also true: The government may charge even the most cooperative corporation pursuant to these Principles if, in weighing and balancing the factors described herein, the prosecutor determines that a charge is required in the interests of justice. Put differently, even the most sincere and thorough effort to cooperate cannot necessarily absolve a corporation that has, for example, engaged in an egregious, orchestrated, and widespread fraud. Cooperation is a potential mitigating factor, but it alone is not dispositive.

(b) Legal Advice and Attorney Work Product

Separate from (and usually preceding) the fact-gathering process in an internal investigation, a corporation, through its officers, employees, directors, or others, may have consulted with corporate counsel regarding or in a manner that concerns the legal implications of the putative misconduct at issue. Communications of this sort, which are both independent of the fact-gathering component of an internal investigation and made for the purpose of seeking or dispensing legal advice, lie at the core of the attorney-client privilege. Such communications can naturally have a salutary effect on corporate behavior—facilitating, for example, a corporation's effort to comply with complex and evolving legal and regulatory regimes.[58] Except as noted in subparagraphs (b)(i) and (b)(ii) below, a corporation need not disclose and prosecutors may not request the disclosure of such communications as a condition for the corporation's eligibility to receive cooperation credit.

---

[57] [Policy's footnote 2:] By way of example, corporate personnel are usually interviewed during an internal investigation. If the interviews are conducted by counsel for the corporation, certain notes and memoranda generated from the interviews may be subject, at least in part, to the protections of attorney-client privilege and/or attorney work product. To receive cooperation credit for providing factual information, the corporation need not produce, and prosecutors may not request, protected notes or memoranda generated by the interviews conducted by counsel for the corporation. To earn such credit, however, the corporation does need to produce, and prosecutors may request, relevant factual information—including relevant factual information acquired through those interviews, unless the identical information has otherwise been provided—as well as relevant non-privileged evidence such as accounting and business records and emails between non-attorney employees or agents.

[58] [Policy's footnote 3:] These privileged communications are not necessarily limited to those that occur contemporaneously with the underlying misconduct. They would include, for instance, legal advice provided by corporate counsel in an internal investigation report. Again, the key measure of cooperation is the disclosure of factual information known to the corporation, not the disclosure of legal advice or theories rendered in connection with the conduct at issue (subject to the two exceptions noted in USAM 9-28.720(b)(i-ii)).

Likewise, non-factual or core attorney work product—for example, an attorney's mental impressions or legal theories—lies at the core of the attorney work product doctrine. A corporation need not disclose, and prosecutors may not request, the disclosure of such attorney work product as a condition for the corporation's eligibility to receive cooperation credit.

(i) Advice of Counsel Defense in the Instant Context

Occasionally a corporation or one of its employees may assert an advice-of-counsel defense, based upon communications with in-house or outside counsel that took place prior to or contemporaneously with the underlying conduct at issue. In such situations, the defendant must tender a legitimate factual basis to support the assertion of the advice-of-counsel defense. *See, e.g., Pitt v. Dist. of Columbia*, 491 F.3d 494, 504-05 (D.C. Cir. 2007); *United States v. Wenger*, 427 F.3d 840, 853-54 (10th Cir. 2005); *United States v. Cheek*, 3 F.3d 1057, 1061-62 (7th Cir. 1993). The Department cannot fairly be asked to discharge its responsibility to the public to investigate alleged corporate crime, or to temper what would otherwise be the appropriate course of prosecutive action, by simply accepting on faith an otherwise unproven assertion that an attorney—perhaps even an unnamed attorney—approved potentially unlawful practices. Accordingly, where an advice-of-counsel defense has been asserted, prosecutors may ask for the disclosure of the communications allegedly supporting it.

(ii) Communications in Furtherance of a Crime or Fraud

Communications between a corporation (through its officers, employees, directors, or agents) and corporate counsel that are made in furtherance of a crime or fraud are, under settled precedent, outside the scope and protection of the attorney-client privilege. *See United States v. Zolin*, 491 U.S. 554, 563 (1989); *United States v. BDO Seidman, LLP*, 492 F.3d 806, 818 (7th Cir. 2007). As a result, the Department may properly request such communications if they in fact exist.

9-28.730 - Obstructing the Investigation

Another factor to be weighed by the prosecutor is whether the corporation has engaged in conduct intended to impede the investigation. Examples of such conduct could include: inappropriate directions to employees or their counsel, such as directions not to be truthful or to conceal relevant facts; making representations or submissions that contain misleading assertions or material omissions; and incomplete or delayed production of records.

In evaluating cooperation, however, prosecutors should not take into account whether a corporation is advancing or reimbursing attorneys' fees or providing counsel to employees, officers, or directors under investigation or indictment. Likewise, prosecutors may not request that a corporation refrain from taking such action. This prohibition is not meant to prevent a prosecutor from asking questions about an attorney's representation of a corporation or its employees, officers, or directors, where otherwise appropriate under the law.[59] Neither is it intended to limit the otherwise applicable reach of criminal obstruction of justice statutes such as 18 U.S.C. § 1503. If the payment of attorney fees were used in a manner that would otherwise constitute criminal obstruction of justice—for example, if fees were advanced on the condition that an employee adhere to a version of the facts that the corporation and the employee knew to be false—these Principles would not (and could not) render inapplicable such criminal prohibitions.

---

[59] [Policy's footnote 1:] Questions regarding the representation status of a corporation and its employees, including how and by whom attorneys' fees are paid, sometimes arise in the course of an investigation under certain circumstances—for example, to assess conflict-of-interest issues. This guidance is not intended to prohibit such limited inquiries.

Similarly, the mere participation by a corporation in a joint defense agreement does not render the corporation ineligible to receive cooperation credit, and prosecutors may not request that a corporation refrain from entering into such agreements. Of course, the corporation may wish to avoid putting itself in the position of being disabled, by virtue of a particular joint defense or similar agreement, from providing some relevant facts to the government and thereby limiting its ability to seek such cooperation credit. Such might be the case if the corporation gathers facts from employees who have entered into a joint defense agreement with the corporation, and who may later seek to prevent the corporation from disclosing the facts it has acquired. Corporations may wish to address this situation by crafting or participating in joint defense agreements, to the extent they choose to enter them, that provide such flexibility as they deem appropriate.

Finally, it may on occasion be appropriate for the government to consider whether the corporation has shared with others sensitive information about the investigation that the government provided to the corporation. In appropriate situations, as it does with individuals, the government may properly request that, if a corporation wishes to receive credit for cooperation, the information provided by the government to the corporation not be transmitted to others—for example, where the disclosure of such information could lead to flight by individual subjects, destruction of evidence, or dissipation or concealment of assets.

9-28.740 - Offering Cooperation: No Entitlement to Immunity

A corporation's offer of cooperation or cooperation itself does not automatically entitle it to immunity from prosecution or a favorable resolution of its case. A corporation should not be able to escape liability merely by offering up its directors, officers, employees, or agents. Thus, a corporation's willingness to cooperate is not determinative; that factor, while relevant, needs to be considered in conjunction with all other factors.

9-28.750 - Oversight Concerning Demands for Waivers of Attorney-Client Privilege or Work Product Protection By Corporations Contrary to This Policy

The Department underscores its commitment to attorney practices that are consistent with Department policies like those set forth herein concerning cooperation credit and due respect for the attorney-client privilege and work product protection. Counsel for corporations who believe that prosecutors are violating such guidance are encouraged to raise their concerns with supervisors, including the appropriate United States Attorney or Assistant Attorney General. Like any other allegation of attorney misconduct, such allegations are subject to potential investigation through established mechanisms.

9-28.800 - Corporate Compliance Programs

A. General Principle: Compliance programs are established by corporate management to prevent and detect misconduct and to ensure that corporate activities are conducted in accordance with applicable criminal and civil laws, regulations, and rules. The Department encourages such corporate self-policing, including voluntary disclosures to the government of any problems that a corporation discovers on its own. *See* USAM 9-28.900. However, the existence of a compliance program is not sufficient, in and of itself, to justify not charging a corporation for criminal misconduct undertaken by its officers, directors, employees, or agents. In addition, the nature of some crimes, *e.g.*, antitrust violations, may be such that national law enforcement policies mandate prosecutions of corporations notwithstanding the existence of a compliance program.

B. Comment: The existence of a corporate compliance program, even one that specifically prohibited the very conduct in question, does not absolve the corporation from criminal liability under the doctrine of *respondeat superior*. *See United States v. Basic Constr. Co.*, 711 F.2d 570, 573 (4th Cir. 1983) ("[A] corporation may be held criminally responsible for antitrust violations committed by its employees if they were acting within the scope of their authority, or apparent authority, and for the benefit of the corporation, even if ... such acts were against corporate policy or express instructions."). As explained in *United States v. Potter*, 463 F.3d 9 (1st Cir. 2006), a corporation cannot "avoid liability by adopting abstract rules" that forbid its agents from engaging in illegal acts, because "[e]ven a specific directive to an agent or employee or honest efforts to police such rules do not automatically free the company for the wrongful acts of agents." *Id.* at 25-26. *See also United States v. Hilton Hotels Corp.*, 467 F.2d 1000, 1007 (9th Cir. 1972) (noting that a corporation "could not gain exculpation by issuing general instructions without undertaking to enforce those instructions by means commensurate with the obvious risks"); *United States v. Beusch*, 596 F.2d 871, 878 (9th Cir. 1979) ("[A] corporation may be liable for acts of its employees done contrary to express instructions and policies, but ...the existence of such instructions and policies may be considered in determining whether the employee in fact acted to benefit the corporation.").

While the Department recognizes that no compliance program can ever prevent all criminal activity by a corporation's employees, the critical factors in evaluating any program are whether the program is adequately designed for maximum effectiveness in preventing and detecting wrongdoing by employees and whether corporate management is enforcing the program or is tacitly encouraging or pressuring employees to engage in misconduct to achieve business objectives. The Department has no formulaic requirements regarding corporate compliance programs. The fundamental questions any prosecutor should ask are: Is the corporation's compliance program well designed? Is the program being applied earnestly and in good faith? Does the corporation's compliance program work? In answering these questions, the prosecutor should consider the comprehensiveness of the compliance program; the extent and pervasiveness of the criminal misconduct; the number and level of the corporate employees involved; the seriousness, duration, and frequency of the misconduct; and any remedial actions taken by the corporation, including, for example, disciplinary action against past violators uncovered by the prior compliance program, and revisions to corporate compliance programs in light of lessons learned.[60] Prosecutors should also consider the promptness of any disclosure of wrongdoing to the government. In evaluating compliance programs, prosecutors may consider whether the corporation has established corporate governance mechanisms that can effectively detect and prevent misconduct. For example, do the corporation's directors exercise independent review over proposed corporate actions rather than unquestioningly ratifying officers' recommendations; are internal audit functions conducted at a level sufficient to ensure their independence and accuracy; and have the directors established an information and reporting system in the organization reasonably designed to provide management and directors with timely and accurate information sufficient to allow them to reach an informed decision regarding the organization's compliance with the law. *See, e.g.*, *In re Caremark Int'l Inc. Derivative Litig.*, 698 A.2d 959, 968-70 (Del. Ch. 1996).

Prosecutors should therefore attempt to determine whether a corporation's compliance program is merely a "paper program" or whether it was designed, implemented, reviewed, and revised, as appropriate, in an effective manner. In addition, prosecutors should determine whether the corporation has provided for a staff sufficient to audit, document, analyze, and utilize the results of the corporation's compliance efforts. Prosecutors also should determine whether the corporation's employees are adequately informed about the compliance program and are convinced of the corporation's commitment to it. This will enable the prosecutor to make an informed decision as to whether the corporation has adopted and implemented a truly effective compliance program that, when consistent with other federal law enforcement policies, may result in a decision to charge only the corporation's employees and agents or to mitigate charges or sanctions against the corporation.

Compliance programs should be designed to detect the particular types of misconduct most likely to occur in a particular corporation's line of business. Many corporations operate in complex regulatory environments outside the normal experience of criminal prosecutors. Accordingly, prosecutors should consult with relevant federal and state agencies with the

---

[60] [Policy's footnote 1:] For a detailed review of these and other factors concerning corporate compliance programs, see USSG § 8B2.1

expertise to evaluate the adequacy of a program's design and implementation. For instance, state and federal banking, insurance, and medical boards, the Department of Defense, the Department of Health and Human Services, the Environmental Protection Agency, and the Securities and Exchange Commission have considerable experience with compliance programs and can be helpful to a prosecutor in evaluating such programs. In addition, the Fraud Section of the Criminal Division, the Commercial Litigation Branch of the Civil Division, and the Environmental Crimes Section of the Environment and Natural Resources Division can assist United States Attorneys' Offices in finding the appropriate agency office(s) for such consultation.

9-28.900 - Voluntary Disclosures

In conjunction with regulatory agencies and other executive branch departments, the Department encourages corporations, as part of their compliance programs, to conduct internal investigations and to disclose the relevant facts to the appropriate authorities. Some agencies, such as the Securities and Exchange Commission and the Environmental Protection Agency, as well as the Department's Environmental and Natural Resources Division, have formal voluntary disclosure programs in which self-reporting, coupled with remediation and additional criteria, may qualify the corporation for amnesty or reduced sanctions. The Antitrust Division has a policy of offering amnesty to the first corporation that self-discloses and agrees to cooperate.

Even in the absence of a formal program, prosecutors may consider a corporation's timely and voluntary disclosure, both as an independent factor and in evaluating the company's overall cooperation and the adequacy of the corporation's compliance program and its management's commitment to the compliance program. *See* USAM 9-28.700 and 9-28.800. However, prosecution may be appropriate notwithstanding a corporation's voluntary disclosure. Such a determination should be based on a consideration of all the factors set forth in these Principles. *See* USAM 9-28.300.

9-28.1000 - Restitution and Remediation

A. General Principle: Although neither a corporation nor an individual target may avoid prosecution merely by paying a sum of money, a prosecutor may consider the corporation's willingness to make restitution and steps already taken to do so. A prosecutor may also consider other remedial actions, such as improving an existing compliance program or disciplining wrongdoers, in determining whether to charge the corporation and how to resolve corporate criminal cases.

B. Comment: In determining whether or not to prosecute a corporation, the government may consider whether the corporation has taken meaningful remedial measures. A corporation's response to misconduct says much about its willingness to ensure that such misconduct does not recur. Thus, corporations that fully recognize the seriousness of their misconduct and accept responsibility for it should be taking steps to implement the personnel, operational, and organizational changes necessary to establish an awareness among employees that criminal conduct will not be tolerated.

Among the factors prosecutors should consider and weigh are whether the corporation appropriately disciplined wrongdoers, once those employees are identified by the corporation as culpable for the misconduct. Employee discipline is a difficult task for many corporations because of the human element involved and sometimes because of the seniority of the employees concerned. Although corporations need to be fair to their employees, they must also be committed, at all levels of the corporation, to the highest standards of legal and ethical behavior. Effective internal discipline can be a powerful deterrent against improper behavior by a corporation's employees. Prosecutors should be satisfied that the corporation's focus is on the integrity and credibility of its remedial and disciplinary measures rather than on the protection of the wrongdoers

In addition to employee discipline, two other factors used in evaluating a corporation's remedial efforts are restitution and reform. As with natural persons, the decision whether or not to prosecute should not depend upon the target's ability to pay restitution. A corporation's efforts to pay restitution even in advance of any court order is, however, evidence of its acceptance of responsibility and, consistent with the practices and policies of the appropriate Division of the Department entrusted with enforcing specific criminal laws, may be considered in determining whether to bring criminal charges. Similarly, although the inadequacy of a corporate compliance program is a factor to consider when deciding whether to charge a corporation, that corporation's quick recognition of the flaws in the program and its efforts to improve the program are also factors to consider as to the appropriate disposition of a case.

9-28.1100 - Collateral Consequences

A. General Principle: Prosecutors may consider the collateral consequences of a corporate criminal conviction or indictment in determining whether to charge the corporation with a criminal offense and how to resolve corporate criminal cases.

B. Comment: One of the factors in determining whether to charge a natural person or a corporation is whether the likely punishment is appropriate given the nature and seriousness of the crime. In the corporate context, prosecutors may take into account the possibly substantial consequences to a corporation's employees, investors, pensioners, and customers, many of whom may, depending on the size and nature of the corporation and their role in its operations, have played no role in the criminal conduct, have been unaware of it, or have been unable to prevent it. Prosecutors should also be aware of non-penal sanctions that may accompany a criminal charge, such as potential suspension or debarment from eligibility for government contracts or federally funded programs such as health care programs. Determining whether or not such non-penal sanctions are appropriate or required in a particular case is the responsibility of the relevant agency, and is a decision that will be made based on the applicable statutes, regulations, and policies.

Almost every conviction of a corporation, like almost every conviction of an individual, will have an impact on innocent third parties, and the mere existence of such an effect is not sufficient to preclude prosecution of the corporation. Therefore, in evaluating the relevance of collateral consequences, various factors already discussed, such as the pervasiveness of the criminal conduct and the adequacy of the corporation's compliance programs, should be considered in determining the weight to be given to this factor. For instance, the balance may tip in favor of prosecuting corporations in situations where the scope of the misconduct in a case is widespread and sustained within a corporate division (or spread throughout pockets of the corporate organization). In such cases, the possible unfairness of visiting punishment for the corporation's crimes upon shareholders may be of much less concern where those shareholders have substantially profited, even unknowingly, from widespread or pervasive criminal activity. Similarly, where the top layers of the corporation's management or the shareholders of a closely-held corporation were engaged in or aware of the wrongdoing, and the conduct at issue was accepted as a way of doing business for an extended period, debarment may be deemed not collateral, but a direct and entirely appropriate consequence of the corporation's wrongdoing.

On the other hand, where the collateral consequences of a corporate conviction for innocent third parties would be significant, it may be appropriate to consider a non-prosecution or deferred prosecution agreement with conditions designed, among other things, to promote compliance with applicable law and to prevent recidivism. Such agreements are a third option, besides a criminal indictment, on the one hand, and a declination, on the other. Declining prosecution may allow a corporate criminal to escape without consequences. Obtaining a conviction may produce a result that seriously harms innocent third parties who played no role in the criminal conduct. Under appropriate circumstances, a deferred prosecution or non-prosecution agreement can help restore the integrity of a company's operations and preserve the financial viability of a corporation that has engaged in criminal conduct, while preserving the government's ability to prosecute a recalcitrant corporation that materially breaches the agreement. Such agreements achieve other important objectives as well, like prompt restitution for victims.[61] The appropriateness of a criminal charge against a corporation, or some lesser alternative, must be evaluated in a pragmatic and reasoned way that produces a fair outcome, taking into consideration, among other things, the Department's need to promote and ensure respect for the law.

9-28.1200 - Civil or Regulatory Alternatives

A. General Principle: Prosecutors should consider whether non-criminal alternatives would adequately deter, punish, and rehabilitate a corporation that has engaged in wrongful conduct. In evaluating the adequacy of non-criminal alternatives to prosecution—*e.g.*, civil or regulatory enforcement actions—the prosecutor should consider all relevant factors, including:

1. the sanctions available under the alternative means of disposition;
2. the likelihood that an effective sanction will be imposed; and
3. the effect of non-criminal disposition on federal law enforcement interests.

See also USAM 1-12.100 - Coordination of Corporate Resolution Penalties in Parallel and/or Joint Investigations and Proceedings Arising from the Same Misconduct.

9-28.1300 - Adequacy of the Prosecution of Individuals

A. General Principle: In deciding whether to charge a corporation, prosecutors should consider whether charges against the individuals responsible for the corporation's malfeasance will adequately satisfy the goals of federal prosecution.

B. Comment: Assessing the adequacy of individual prosecutions for corporate misconduct should be made on a case-by-case basis and in light of the factors discussed in these Principles. Thus, in deciding the most appropriate course of action for the corporation – *i.e.*, a corporate indictment, a deferred prosecution or non-prosecution agreement, or another alternative – a prosecutor should consider the impact of the prosecution of responsible individuals, along with the other factors in USAM 9-28.300 (Factors to be Considered).

9-28.1400 - Selecting Charges

A. General Principle: Once a prosecutor has decided to charge a corporation, the prosecutor at least presumptively should charge, or should recommend that the grand jury charge, the most serious offense that is consistent with the nature of the defendant's misconduct and that is likely to result in a sustainable conviction.

B. Comment: Once the decision to charge is made, the same rules as govern charging natural persons apply. These rules require "a faithful and honest application of the Sentencing Guidelines" and an "individualized assessment of the extent to which particular charges fit the specific circumstances of the case, are consistent with the purposes of the Federal criminal code, and maximize the impact of Federal resources on crime." *See* USAM 9-27.300. In making this determination, "it is appropriate that the attorney for the government consider, *inter alia*, such factors as the [advisory] sentencing guideline range yielded by the charge, whether the penalty yielded by such sentencing range ...is proportional to the seriousness of the defendant's conduct, and whether the charge achieves such purposes of the

---

[61] [Policy's footnote 1:] Prosecutors should note that in the case of national or multi-national corporations, efforts should be made to determine the existence of other matters within the Department relating to the corporation in question. In certain instances, multi-district or global agreements may be in the interest of law enforcement and the public. Such agreements may only be entered into with the approval of each affected district or the appropriate Department official. *See* USAM 9-27.641.

criminal law as punishment, protection of the public, specific and general deterrence, and rehabilitation." *Id.*

9-28.1500 - Plea Agreements with Corporations

A. General Principle: In negotiating plea agreements with corporations, as with individuals, prosecutors should generally seek a plea to an appropriate offense. In addition, the terms of the plea agreement should contain appropriate provisions to ensure punishment, deterrence, rehabilitation, and compliance with the plea agreement in the corporate context. Absent extraordinary circumstances or approved departmental policy such as the Antitrust Division's Corporate Leniency Policy, no corporate resolution should provide protection from criminal or civil liability for any individuals. *See also* USAM 9-16.050, 5-11.114.

B. Comment: Prosecutors may enter into plea agreements with corporations for the same reasons and under the same constraints as apply to plea agreements with natural persons. *See* USAM 9-27.400-530. This means, *inter alia*, that the corporation should generally be required to plead guilty to the most serious, readily provable offense charged. In addition, any negotiated departures or recommended variances from the advisory Sentencing Guidelines must be justifiable under the Guidelines or 18 U.S.C. § 3553 and must be disclosed to the sentencing court. A corporation should be made to realize that pleading guilty to criminal charges constitutes an admission of guilt and not merely a resolution of an inconvenient distraction from its business. As with natural persons, pleas should be structured so that the corporation may not later "proclaim lack of culpability or even complete innocence." *See* USAM 9-27.420(b)(4), 9-27.440, 9-27.500. Thus, for instance, there should be placed upon the record a sufficient factual basis for the plea to prevent later corporate assertions of innocence.

A corporate plea agreement should also contain provisions that recognize the nature of the corporate "person" and that ensure that the principles of punishment, deterrence, and rehabilitation are met. In the corporate context, punishment and deterrence are generally accomplished by substantial fines, mandatory restitution, and institution of appropriate compliance measures, including, if necessary, continued judicial oversight or the use of special masters or corporate monitors. *See* USSG §§ 8B1.1, 8C2.1, *et seq.* In addition, where the corporation is a government contractor, permanent or temporary debarment may be appropriate. Where the corporation was engaged in fraud against the government (*e.g.*, contracting fraud), a prosecutor may not negotiate away an agency's right to debar or delist the corporate defendant.

In negotiating a plea agreement, prosecutors must also consider the deterrent value of prosecutions of individuals within the corporation. Therefore, one factor that a prosecutor should consider in determining whether to enter into a plea agreement is whether the corporation is seeking immunity for its employees and officers or whether the corporation is willing to cooperate in the investigation of culpable individuals as outlined herein. Absent extraordinary circumstances or approved departmental policy such as the Antitrust Division's Corporate Leniency Policy, no corporate resolution should include an agreement to dismiss charges against, or provide civil or criminal immunity for, individual offices or employees. Any such release due to extraordinary circumstances must be personally approved in writing by the relevant Assistant Attorney General or United States Attorney.

Rehabilitation, of course, requires that the corporation undertake to be law-abiding in the future. It is, therefore, appropriate to require the corporation, as a condition of probation, to implement a compliance program or to reform an existing one. As discussed above, prosecutors may consult with the appropriate state and federal agencies and components of the Justice Department to ensure that a proposed compliance program is adequate and meets industry standards and best practices. *See* USAM 9-28.800.

In plea agreements in which the corporation agrees to cooperate, the prosecutor should ensure that the cooperation is entirely truthful. To do so, the prosecutor should request that the corporation make appropriate disclosures of relevant factual information and documents, make employees and agents available for debriefing, file appropriate certified financial statements, agree to governmental or third-party audits, and take whatever other steps are necessary to ensure that the full scope of the corporate wrongdoing is disclosed and that the responsible personnel are identified and, if appropriate, prosecuted. *See generally* USAM 9-28.700. In taking such steps, Department prosecutors should recognize that attorney-client communications are often essential to a corporation's efforts to comply with complex regulatory and legal regimes, and that, as discussed at length above, cooperation is not measured by the waiver of attorney-client privilege and work product protection, but rather is measured, as a threshold issue, by the disclosure of facts about individual misconduct, as well as other considerations identified herein, such as making witnesses available for interviews and assisting in the interpretation of complex documents or business records.

These Principles provide only internal Department of Justice guidance. They are not intended to, do not, and may not be relied upon to create any rights, substantive or procedural, enforceable at law by any party in any matter civil or criminal. Nor are any limitations hereby placed on otherwise lawful litigative prerogatives of the Department of Justice.

Notes

1. Some of the issues raised in this memorandum—such as how to evaluate the corporation's payment of legal fees for individuals within the entity and when, if ever, requests for waiver of attorney-client or work-product protected materials may be made—are highly controversial and shall be dealt with at greater length in future chapters. *See, e.g.*, Chapter 17 (The Attorney-Client Privilege and Work Product Doctrine in a Corporate Setting; discussion of waiver policy); Chapter 18 (Representation Issues; discussion of fee payment issues and the *Stein* decision).

2. Corporate counsel's ethical duties are owed to the entity itself, not to any of its constituencies—whether those constituencies are the Board, shareholders, or members of management. The Department of Justice may require, as a condition of declining criminal action against the company, that the entity take a very hard line with its employees, for example firing those who do not cooperate with the government's investigation. Is this the right approach? *See, e.g.*, Lisa Kern Griffin, *Compelled Cooperation and the New Corporate Criminal Procedure*, 82 N.Y.U. L. Rev. 31 (2007). Is it ethical? *See* John Hasnas, Trapped: When Acting Ethically Is Against the Law (Cato Institute 2006)).

D. U.S. SENTENCING GUIDELINES: ORGANIZATIONAL SENTENCING

1. BACKGROUND

In the Sentencing Reform Act of 1984, Congress created the U.S. Sentencing Commission and charged it with generating guidelines that would control in federal sentencing proceedings. The Commission first created sentencing guidelines applicable to individual defendants. The Commission then turned its attention to the formulation of guidelines that would control in the sentencing of organizations. The Organizational Guidelines—found in Chapter 8 of the Guidelines Manual—became effective on November 1, 1991.

As was discussed at length in Chapter 3, *supra*, the United States Supreme Court ruled in *United States v. Booker*[62] that the *mandatory* U.S. Sentencing Guidelines contravened the Sixth Amendment; accordingly, the Court struck those statutory provisions contemplating mandatory guidelines. As of the date of the *Booker* decision, January 2005, then, the Organizational Guidelines, like the individual Guidelines, became advisory only.[63] Courts are

---

[62] 543 U.S. 220 (2005).

[63] The *Booker* Court ruled that the statutes that made the guidelines mandatory violated individual

still required to consult the Guidelines, where applicable, but judges will not be required to follow them.

The following discussion traces the development of the Organizational Guidelines and their structure and operation prior to *Booker*. These materials remain relevant because these Guidelines are likely to continue to provide the framework within which the parties and courts work in formulating organizational sanctions. It is important to note, however, that judges in pre-Guidelines practice imposed much more lenient sentences on corporate defendants than is the norm in Guidelines sentencing. Defense counsel will likely push courts hard to return to the pre-Guidelines norm.

When first called upon to consider the problem of organizational sentencing, the Commission concluded that then-existing organizational sentencing practices were incoherent and inconsistent.[64] Judges struggled to find appropriate sanctions to levy on corporate wrongdoers and scholars disagreed about how best to address corporate crime.[65] Empirical research revealed that corporate offenders that engaged in similar misconduct were treated differently. Further, overall, the fines imposed on such offenders were so low as to be, on average, "*less than* the cost corporations had to pay to obey the law. This seemed to raise the specter that corporate crime did in fact 'pay,' as some had historically claimed."[66]

The Commission also concluded that corporate crime enforcement was subject to two pathologies, "speed trap enforcement" and a "circle the wagons" corporate response.[67] The former involved a reactive policy to corporate lawbreaking. The government seemed to concentrate on nabbing those offenders who came within readily available radar but little effort was made to create incentives for corporations to prevent the lawbreaking in the first instance. The "circle the wagons" response of corporations to government enforcement efforts grew out of the fact that corporations had little reason to respond in a more constructive fashion. The unpredictability and variation in the sanctions imposed upon convicted corporations meant that there was no obvious incentive to galvanize resources to avoid such sanctions. Indeed, in many cases, the sanctions were less expensive than avoiding liability in the first instance. Further, there was no guarantee that corporate cooperation or compliance efforts would be rewarded in a concrete way—either in charging decisions or at sentence.[68]

In formulating the Organizational Guidelines, the Commission considered and rejected a law and economics based "optimal penalties" approach. This approach centered upon a formula designed to achieve fines perfectly calibrated to "bring about perfectly efficient crime-avoiding responses by corporations. Under the approach, fines were to be set according to this formula: the optimal fine = monetized harm (*i.e.*, loss) [divided by] probability of conviction."[69]

---

defendants' Sixth Amendment jury trial rights. The Supreme Court has not yet decided whether corporations have a jury trial right, so one could argue that the organizational guidelines should continue to bind sentencing judges. For a discussion of this question and the law relevant to it, see Timothy A. Johnson, Note, *Sentencing Organizations After* Booker, 116 Yale L.J. 632 (2006).

[64] *See* Ilene H. Nagel & Winthrop M. Swenson, *The Federal Sentencing Guidelines for Corporations: Their Development, Theoretical Underpinnings, and Some Thoughts About Their Future*, 71 Wash. U. L.Q. 205, 214-17 (1993); Winthrop M. Swenson, *The Organizational Guidelines' "Carrot and Stick" Philosophy, and Their Focus on "Effective" Compliance* 1-3, *reprinted in* U.S. Sentencing Commission, Materials for Program on Corporate Crime in America: Strengthening the "Good Citizen" Corporation (Sept. 7, 1995).

[65] Nagel & Swenson, *supra* note 64, at 214 & n.45.

[66] Swenson, *supra* note 64, at 3; *see also* Nagel & Swenson, *supra* note 64, at 215.

[67] Swenson, *supra* note 64, at 3-4.

[68] *See id.*

[69] *Id.* at 5.

This approach was really an idealized version of the pre-existing, "speed trap" approach to corporate crime enforcement. It assumed that government policy need be little more than a commitment to catch *some* corporate wrongdoers and fine them. Fines for the unlucky corporations that were caught would then be set in inverse relationship to the likelihood of being caught, and corporate managers—carefully, coldly scrutinizing these perfectly calibrated fines and concluding that crime could not pay—would rationally choose, instead, to spend resources obeying the law.[70]

The optimal penalties approach was at last rejected for a variety of reasons, not least of which was the difficulty encountered in reducing to an administrable and consistent formula the likelihood of conviction for particular kinds of offenses.[71] In the end, the Commission adopted what some characterize as a "carrot and stick," and others term a "deterrence and just punishment," approach:

> The centerpiece of the Sentencing Guidelines structure is the fine range, from which a sentencing court selects the precise fine to impose on a convicted organization. The Commission designed the guideline provisions that established the fine range to meld the two philosophical approaches to sentencing emphasized in the enabling legislation: just punishment for the offense, and deterrence. By varying the fine based on whether, and to what extent, a company has acted "responsibly" with respect to an offense, the Guidelines embody a "just punishment for the offense" philosophy. Consistent with this paradigm, the Guidelines provide for substantial fines when a convicted organization has encouraged, or has been indifferent to, violations of the law by its employees, but impose significantly lower fines when a corporation has clearly demonstrated in specific ways its antipathy toward lawbreaking. At the same time, the guideline structure embodies principles derived from the deterrence paradigm. The specified ways in which a convicted organization may demonstrate its intolerance of criminal conduct, entitling it to a more lenient sentence, are actions that, at least theoretically, should discourage employees from committing offenses.[72]

The "carrot and stick approach" grew out of the Commission's acceptance of three propositions. First and foremost, the Commission recognized that the *respondeat superior* principles of liability studied within did not adequately respond to gradations in corporate culpability. The simple equation of the corporation with the corporate actor necessary for liability does not reflect on the relative blameworthiness of the corporation itself.[73] Second, the Commission came to believe that corporations could "hold out the promise of fewer violations in the first instance and greater detection and remediation of offenses when they occur"[74] through internal discipline, reformation of standard operating procedures, auditing standards, and the corporate culture, and institution of corporate compliance programs. Finally, and critically, the Commission concluded that it could create incentives for responsible corporate actors to foster crime control by the creation of a mandatory guidelines penalty structure that rewarded responsible corporate behavior and ensured certain and harsh sanctions for truly culpable corporations. In short, the Commission defined its objectives as: creating a model for

---

[70] *Id.*

[71] Nagel & Swenson, *supra* note 64, at 219-22.

[72] *Id.* at 210-12.

[73] Swenson, *supra* note 64, at 5 ("The Commission came to recognize that the doctrine of vicarious criminal liability for corporations operates in such a way that very different kinds of corporations can be convicted of crimes; from companies whose managers did everything reasonably possible to prevent and uncover wrongdoing, but whose employees broke the law anyway, to companies whose managers encouraged or directed the wrongdoing.").

[74] *Id.* at 6.

the good corporate citizen; using the model to make corporate sentencing fair and predictable; and ultimately employing the model to create incentives for corporations to take crime controlling steps.

2. KEY FEATURES

The Organizational Guidelines have three principal substantive parts: (1) Part B—"Remedying the Harm From Criminal Conduct"; (2) Part C—"Fines"; and (3) Part D—"Organizational Probation." Although these features do not bind sentencing judges after *Booker*, they are likely to continue to provide the structure against which organizational penalties and remedies will be measured.

a. Part B—Remedying the Harm From Criminal Conduct—Restitution

Part B, dealing with remedying the harm from the offense, and Part D, dealing with organizational probation, apply to the sentencing of all organizations[75] for felony and Class A misdemeanor offenses.[76] Part B is intended to be remedial, not punitive. Regardless of the perceived culpability of an organization, the Commission determined that all convicted organizations should be required to remedy any harm caused by the offense.[77] This will generally take the form of an order of restitution "for the full amount of the victim's loss."[78] It may also take the form of remedial orders requiring the organization "to remedy the harm caused by the offense and to eliminate or reduce the risk" that the offense will cause future harm.[79]

Although not punitive in intent, organizations may well feel that restitution or remedial orders are so onerous as to feel like punishment. For example, if an organization's wrongdoing caused $10 million in losses, it may be required to make restitution in that amount *and* to pay a fine that may amount to as much as $40 million (or more if a departure is warranted). Under the Guidelines, an order of restitution is not appropriate "when full restitution has been made" or when the court finds that "the number of identifiable victims is so large as to make restitution impracticable."[80] It is also not appropriate under the Guidelines when "determining complex issues of fact related to the cause or amount of the victim's losses would complicate or prolong the sentencing process to a degree that the need to provide restitution to any victim is outweighed by the burden on the sentencing process."[81]

b. Part C—Fines

The Guidelines' fine provisions begin by providing for an organizational "death sentence." If an organization "operated primarily for a criminal purpose or primarily by criminal means," the sentencing judge may set the fine "at an amount (subject to the statutory maximum) sufficient to divest the organization of all its net assets."[82]

---

[75] *See* U.S.S.G. § 8A1.1, Application Note 1 ("'Organization' means 'a person other than an individual'" and includes, among other entities, corporations, partnerships, unions, unincorporated organizations, governments and political subdivisions thereof, and non-profit organizations).

[76] *Id.* § 8A1.1.

[77] *Id.*, Chapter 8, Introductory Commentary.

[78] *Id.* § 8B1.1(a)(1) ("Restitution—Organizations").

[79] *Id.* § 8B1.2(a) ("Remedial Orders—Organizations").

[80] *Id.* § 8B1.1(b)(1), (2)(A).

[81] *Id.* § 8B1.1(b)(2)(B).

[82] *Id.* § 8C1.1 ("Determining the Fine—Criminal Purpose Organizations").

Before getting further into the Organizational Guidelines' fine calculations, a few important points must be understood:

1. First and foremost, keep in mind throughout these materials that, after the Supreme Court's decision in *Booker*, these computations must be considered by the sentencing court but may not bind it.

2. *It is critical to note that the balance of the fine provisions of Part C do not apply to all organizational sentencings.* While Parts B and D apply to all federal felony or Class A misdemeanor convictions, counsel must consult § 8C2.1 to determine whether the offense is one that is covered by the Part C fine guidelines. Important categories of cases, such as environmental offenses, and food and drug, RICO, and export control violations, are *not* presently covered by the fine guidelines.[83] The fines for such excluded offenses must be determined by reference to traditional criteria contained in the general sentencing provisions of Title 18.[84]

3. Another preliminary qualification is that where it is "readily ascertainable that the organization cannot and is not likely to become able (even on an installment schedule) to pay restitution," no guidelines fine calculation need be done because restitution obligations trump any fine imposed.[85] Further, where it is "readily ascertainable through a preliminary determination of the minimum of the guideline fine range" that the organization cannot pay and is unlikely to become able to pay the minimum fine, the Guidelines state that the court need not engage in further application of the fine guidelines.[86] Instead, the court would use the preliminary determination and impose a fine based on the guidelines section that provides for reductions in fines due to inability to pay.[87]

4. A final caveat is one that applies to the Guidelines generally—*the statutory maximum (or where applicable, minimum) sentence always trumps.* Thus, even if, after applying the fine guidelines, the court arrives at a fine range that exceeds the maximum set by statute, the court *may not* exceed the statutory maximum.[88] Prosecutors seeking to secure large guidelines fines after conviction of an organization, then, would be well advised to consider, when making their charging choices, applicable statutory maximums.[89]

In general, the statutory maximum for a given count if an organization is the defendant is the *greatest* of (1) the amount (if any) specified in the law setting forth the offense; (2) for an organization convicted of a felony, $500,000; or (3) "[i]f any person derives pecuniary gain from the offense, or if the offense results in pecuniary loss to a person other than the defendant, the defendant may be fined not more than the greater of twice the gross gain or twice the gross loss, unless the imposition of a fine under this subsection would unduly complicate or prolong the sentencing process."[90] This last provision, known as the twice gross gain or loss provision, is likely to be the applicable figure in many cases, especially where the dollar amount of the gain or loss is great.

* * *

If the Organizational Guidelines' fine provisions apply and there is no statutory maximum issue, the organizational fine provisions proceed through five steps, described below. In general

---

[83] *See* Nagel & Swenson, *supra* note 64, at 254 & n.268.

[84] *See* U.S.S.G. § 8C2.10 (requiring courts to apply provisions of 18 U.S.C. §§ 3553, 3572).

[85] *Id.* § 8C2.2(a); *see also id.* § 8C3.3(a).

[86] *Id.* § 8C2.2(b).

[87] *Id.*; *see also id.* § 8C3.3 (Reduction of Fine Based on Inability to Pay).

[88] *See id.* § 8C3.1(b), (c).

[89] *See* 18 U.S.C. § 3571 (Sentence of Fine).

[90] *Id.*

terms, the fine range is said to be a *product* of the *seriousness* of the offense and the *culpability* of the organization.

First, the *seriousness* of the offense committed is computed and reflected in a number called the "Base Fine."[91] Basically, this number is the greatest of (1) the amount from a table corresponding to a calculation under the individual Guidelines; (2) the pecuniary gain to the organization from the offense; or (3) the pecuniary loss from the offense caused by the organization, to the extent that the loss was intentionally, knowingly, or recklessly caused.[92] The Base Fine number often, though certainly not invariably, works out to be the loss caused by the crime.

Second, the *culpability* of the organization is assessed by adding up the organization's "Culpability Score."[93] One begins the computation with a score of 5. Points are then added or subtracted depending upon the existence or absence of certain factors that the Commission concluded aggravate or mitigate the *organization's* culpability in the crime.

Thus, a range of points are added depending upon the size of the organization (or unit of the organization within which the offense was committed) and "the hierarchical level and degree of discretionary authority" of the individuals who participated in or tolerated the illegal behavior.[94] For example, if an individual within high-level personnel of an organization with 5,000 or more employees participated in, condoned, or was willfully ignorant of the offense, 5 points will be added to the culpability score. If the organization had only 200 employees, and the same circumstances were present, only 3 points would be added.

Points would also be added to the organization's culpability score if the organization had a fairly recent prior history of similar misconduct,[95] if the commission of the offense violated a judicial order or injunction or a condition of probation,[96] and if the organization willfully obstructed or attempted to obstruct justice during the investigation, prosecution, or sentencing of the offense.[97]

There are two provisions under which organizational defendants may have points deducted from their culpability score. First, a credit of 3 points is permitted if "the offense occurred even though the organization had in place at the time of the offense a compliance and ethics program."[98] This credit is only available, however, if an organization's high-level or substantial authority personnel are not involved in the offense. The Commission heard concerns that this general prohibition operated too broadly and that internal and external reporting of criminal conduct would be better encouraged if it made an exception to this exception.[99] Thus, in 2010, the Commission amended § 8C2.5 to state that an organization qualifies for the credit, despite high-level involvement, if it meets four criteria: (1) the individual or individuals with operational responsibility for the compliance and ethics program have direct reporting obligations to the governing authority or an appropriate subgroup thereof; (2) the compliance and ethics program detected the offense before discovery outside the organization or before such discovery was reasonably likely; (3) the organization promptly

---

[91] *Id.* § 8C2.4.

[92] *Id.* § 8C2.4(a).

[93] *Id.* § 8C2.5.

[94] *See* Nagel & Swenson, *supra* note 64, at 238 (discussing rationale for selection of these factors); *see also id.* at 248-51 (discussing rationale for reliance on size of organization).

[95] U.S.S.G. § 8C2.5(c) ("Prior History").

[96] *Id.* § 8C2.5(d) ("Violation of an Order").

[97] *Id.* § 8C2.5(e) ("Obstruction of Justice").

[98] *Id.* § 8C2.5(f)(1) ("Effective Program to Prevent and Detect Violations of Law").

[99] *Id.* § 8C2.5(f)(3)(C) (eff. Nov. 1. 2010); U.S. Sentencing Comm'n, Supplement to Appendix C, Amendment 744, at 362 (Nov. 1, 2010).

reported the offense to the appropriate governmental authorities; and (4) no individual with responsibility for the compliance and ethics program participated in, condoned, or was willfully ignorant in the offense.[100]

In 2004, the Commission reworked its definition of an "effective" compliance and ethics program and included it in a separate guideline for the first time. In 2010 and 2011, this Guideline was amended. Because the Commission's original definition of an effective compliance program had an enormous impact on regulatory definitions and industry efforts to create qualifying programs, it is likely that the revised definition will also be important to the ethics and compliance community. It is therefore worth setting forth in full:

§ 8B2.1. Effective Compliance and Ethics Program

(a) To have an effective compliance and ethics program, for purposes of subsection (f) of § 8C2.5 (Culpability Score) and subsection (b)(1) of § 8D1.4 (Recommended Conditions of Probation—Organizations), an organization shall—

(1) exercise due diligence to prevent and detect criminal conduct; and
(2) otherwise promote an organizational culture that encourages ethical conduct and a commitment to compliance with the law.

Such compliance and ethics program shall be reasonably designed, implemented, and enforced so that the program is generally effective in preventing and detecting criminal conduct. The failure to prevent or detect the instant offense does not necessarily mean that the program is not generally effective in preventing and detecting criminal conduct.

(b) Due diligence and the promotion of an organizational culture that encourages ethical conduct and a commitment to compliance with the law within the meaning of subsection (a) minimally require the following:

(1) The organization shall establish standards and procedures to prevent and detect criminal conduct.

(2) (A) The organization's governing authority shall be knowledgeable about the content and operation of the compliance and ethics program and shall exercise reasonable oversight with respect to the implementation and effectiveness of the compliance and ethics program.

(B) High-level personnel of the organization shall ensure that the organization has an effective compliance and ethics program, as described in this guideline. Specific individual(s) within high-level personnel shall be assigned overall responsibility for the compliance and ethics program.

(C) Specific individual(s) within the organization shall be delegated day-to-day operational responsibility for the compliance and ethics program. Individual(s) with operational responsibility shall report periodically to high-level personnel and, as appropriate, to the governing authority, or an appropriate subgroup of the governing authority, on the effectiveness of the compliance and ethics program. To carry out such operational responsibility, such individual(s) shall be given adequate resources, appropriate authority, and direct access to the governing authority or an appropriate subgroup of the governing authority.

(3) The organization shall use reasonable efforts not to include within the substantial authority personnel of the organization any individual whom the organization knew, or should have known through the exercise of due diligence, has engaged in illegal activities or other conduct inconsistent with an effective compliance and ethics program.

---

[100] U.S.S.G. § 8C2.5(f)(3)(C).

(4)   (A) The organization shall take reasonable steps to communicate periodically and in a practical manner its standards and procedures, and other aspects of the compliance and ethics program, to the individuals referred to in subparagraph (B) by conducting effective training programs and otherwise disseminating information appropriate to such individuals' respective roles and responsibilities.

(B) The individuals referred to in subparagraph (A) are the members of the governing authority, high-level personnel, substantial authority personnel, the organization's employees, and, as appropriate, the organization's agents.

(5) The organization shall take reasonable steps—

(A) to ensure that the organization's compliance and ethics program is followed, including monitoring and auditing to detect criminal conduct;

(B) to evaluate periodically the effectiveness of the organization's compliance and ethics program; and

(C) to have and publicize a system, which may include mechanisms that allow for anonymity or confidentiality, whereby the organization's employees and agents may report or seek guidance regarding potential or actual criminal conduct without fear of retaliation.

(6) The organization's compliance and ethics program shall be promoted and enforced consistently throughout the organization through (A) appropriate incentives to perform in accordance with the compliance and ethics program; and (B) appropriate disciplinary measures for engaging in criminal conduct and for failing to take reasonable steps to prevent or detect criminal conduct.

(7) After criminal conduct has been detected, the organization shall take reasonable steps to respond appropriately to the criminal conduct and to prevent further similar criminal conduct, including making any necessary modifications to the organization's compliance and ethics program.

(c) In implementing subsection (b), the organization shall periodically assess the risk of criminal conduct and shall take appropriate steps to design, implement, or modify each requirement set forth in subsection (b) to reduce the risk of criminal conduct identified through this process.

* * *

The Commission contemplated that different organizations in different industries will have to use these general instructions to create programs that work for them. Among the relevant factors to be considered in tailoring an effective compliance program are: the size of the organization, the likelihood that certain offenses may occur because of the nature of the organization's business, and the prior history of the organization.[101] It is fair to say that professional consultation on the creation and maintenance of effective compliance programs is a growth industry.

The second way in which an organization may reduce its culpability score is by self-reporting, cooperation, and acceptance of responsibility.[102] The credits to be accrued are graduated depending upon just how much the organization is willing to do. Thus, an organization earns just 1 point for acceptance of responsibility—that is, for pleading guilty. But, if the organization is willing to "fully cooperate[] in the investigation" and plead guilty, it

---

[101] *Id.* § 8B2.1, Application Notes 2, 7.

[102] *Id.* § 8C2.5(g) ("Self-Reporting, Cooperation, and Acceptance of Responsibility").

may secure 2 credit points. Finally, if the organization, "prior to an imminent threat of disclosure or government investigation," and "within a reasonably prompt time after becoming aware of the offense," reports the offense to government authorities, fully cooperates, and then pleads guilty, the organization will gain 5 credit points.[103]

      Third, after the culpability score calculation is complete, reference should be made to the chart in which each culpability score is given a "minimum multiplier" and a "maximum multiplier."[104] These multipliers are then applied to the Base Fine amount, and the result is a fine range.

      For example, assume that the Base Fine (the loss from a criminal episode) is $10 million. Assume further that the culpability score for the organization is 9—the 5 points with which one begins, with 5 points added for the organization's size and level of management participation and 1 point off for acceptance of responsibility. Reference to the multiplier chart tells one that a culpability score of 9 means that one multiplies the base fine (here, $10 million) times the culpability multipliers that correspond to the culpability score (here, 1.80 and 3.60), to arrive at a fine range of $18 million to $36 million.

      This example may serve to illustrate the importance of the effective compliance program and cooperation credits. If in the assumed case the organization had earned a 3 point effective compliance program credit, its culpability score would have been 6, its multipliers 1.20 and 2.40, and its final fine range $12 million to $24 million. If the organization had self-reported, cooperated, and pleaded guilty, even without an effective compliance program, its culpability score would have been 5, its multipliers 1.00 and 2.00, and its fine range $10 million to $20 million.

      This example may also demonstrate the importance of prosecutorial charging choices. In many cases, the statutory maximum—which, again, trumps the Guidelines—will be set at twice the gross gain or loss.[105] Because the multipliers can be higher than 2.0 (for anything over a culpability score of 5), in some cases unless the prosecutor charges multiple counts,[106] the organizational sentence may be capped at twice the gross gain or loss regardless of the organization's culpability level or multipliers.[107]

      Fourth, the Guidelines set forth the factors the Commission believes that judges should consider in determining the amount of the fine *within* the applicable guideline range.[108] These again are factors that the Commission deemed relevant to assessment of organizational culpability, including the organization's role in the offense, any nonpecuniary loss caused or threatened by the offense, prior misconduct by the

---

[103] See *id.*

[104] *Id.* § 8C2.6 ("Minimum and Maximum Multipliers").

[105] *See* 18 U.S.C. § 3571.

[106] The statutory maximum for one charging instrument is the sum of the statutory maximums for all the counts charged in that instrument. Thus, if it appears that the organization's statutory maximum for one count will be lower than its Guidelines exposure, prosecutors may be able to cure this problem by bringing multiple counts.

[107] Assume, for example, that the defendant organization pleads guilty to one count of mail fraud, to which perhaps $1 million in losses may be attributed, but the entire fraudulent scheme reflected in part in that count caused losses of up to $10 million. Is the statutory maximum twice the gross loss from the offense of conviction—$2 million—or is it twice the gross loss attributable to all the criminal conduct at issue—$20 million? The alternative fine provision simply states that the statutory maximum may be twice the gross gain or loss caused by "the offense." The legislative history is unilluminating on this issue. *See* H.R. Rep. No. 100-390, at 1-6 (1987); H.R. Rep. No. 98-906, at 1-4 (1984). The better reading, however, seems to be that "the offense" refers only to the offense of conviction and not to the entire course of criminal conduct. This certainly seems to have been the Sentencing Commission's understanding of the term. *See* U.S. Sentencing Comm'n, Supplementary Report on Sentencing Guidelines for Organizations 11-12 (Aug. 30, 1991).

[108] U.S.S.G. § 8C2.8 ("Determining the Fine Within the Range (Policy Statement)").

organization not previously counted, and any prior criminal record of high-level personnel in the organization.[109]

One of these factors deserves particular mention. The Commission recognized the reality that organizations convicted of a federal felony are likely to be subject, in addition to criminal sanctions, to substantial collateral penalties such as debarment from government contracting, treble civil damages, shareholder derivative actions, regulatory fines, and the like.[110] "For both substantive and technical reasons," however, the Commission decided to provide "no direct offset for collateral sanctions" that might be imposed on organizational defendants but to provide means by which such sanctions may be taken into account:[111]

> The Commission designed the Guidelines' fine ranges to accommodate a "permissive offset." In general, the ranges are broad; typically, the maximum of the range is twice the minimum. Thus, the court can take collateral consequences into account in selecting the precise fine to impose. Moreover, the Guidelines explicitly direct that "the court, in setting the fine within the guideline range, should consider any collateral consequences of conviction, including civil obligations arising from the organization's conduct .... [P]unitive collateral sanctions [that] have been or will be imposed on the organization ... may provide a basis for a lower fine within the guideline fine range." The Commission designed this compromise approach to leave courts (which are best able to assess this particular factor) with sufficient flexibility to weigh collateral consequences appropriately.[112]

Fifth, consideration may be given to whether a judge should *depart from* the Guidelines fine range—either upwards or downwards. Among the express grounds upon which such a departure may be grounded are the following circumstances: substantial assistance to the authorities in the investigation or prosecution "of another organization that has committed an offense, or in the investigation or prosecution of an individual not directly affiliated with the defendant who has committed an offense";[113] risk of death or bodily injury,[114] threats to national security,[115] to the environment,[116] or to a market[117] flowing from

---

[109] *Id.*

[110] *See* Nagel & Swenson, *supra* note 64, at 245.

[111] *Id.* at 246-48. The Commission determined that, with one limited exception for fines imposed on substantial owners of closely held corporations, *see* U.S.S.G. § 8C3.4, there should be "no direct and automatic offset in the corporate fine for penalties imposed on individuals." Nagel & Swenson, *supra* note 64, at 244. It should be noted that the offset under § 8C3.4 is discretionary, and in any case must be sought before the judgment including the organization's fine becomes final. *See* United States v. Aqua-Leisure Industries, 150 F.3d 95 (1st Cir.1998).

[112] Nagel & Swenson, *supra* note 64, at 247 (quoting U.S.S.G. § 8C2.8(a)(3) & Application Note 2 (1999)) (footnotes omitted).

[113] U.S.S.G. § 8C4.1. It is important to note that the language of this rule seems to preclude corporations from obtaining substantial assistance departures merely by cooperating with the government in its prosecution of the organizational agent who is responsible for the organization's culpability. *See id.*, Application Note 1.

[114] *Id.* § 8C4.2.

[115] *Id.* § 8C4.3.

[116] *Id.* § 8C4.4.

[117] *Id.* § 8C4.5.

the offense; remedial costs that greatly exceed the gain from the offense;[118] or exceptional organizational culpability.[119]

Also, the Guidelines state that the fine should be reduced below the otherwise applicable Guidelines range "to the extent that imposition of such a fine would impair [the organizational defendant's] ability to make restitution to victims."[120] The court may impose a fine below the Guidelines range where the court finds that "the organization is not able and, even with the use of a reasonable installment schedule, is not likely to become able to pay the minimum fine."[121] The Guidelines state that "immediate" payment of any fine imposed is required if the organizational "death sentence" has been imposed.[122] "Immediate" payment is also required in any other case unless the court finds that the organization is financially unable to make such a payment or such a payment would impose an undue burden on the organization.[123]

c. Part D—Organizational Probation

Part D, dealing with organizational probation, like the restitution provisions of Part B, applies to all organizations convicted of federal felonies or Class A misdemeanors. The (now advisory) Guidelines state that a term of organizational probation is required in many circumstances—two of the most common being (1) where immediate payment is excused, if probation is necessary to ensure that restitutionary or remedial obligations are met or that the fine is paid or (2) if, at the time of sentencing, an organization having 50 or more employees does not have an effective compliance program in place.[124] The Commission also left courts substantial discretion to impose probation where the court concludes that the purposes of criminal punishment dictate[125] or where necessary to ensure that changes are made within the organization to prevent future law-breaking.[126]

The term of probation is, in the case of a felony, at least one year but not more than five years,[127] and must include conditions of probation barring the organization from committing further crimes during the probationary period and providing for restitution or community service unless it would be unreasonable to do so.[128]

The recommended conditions of probation should be a large focus of defense counsel's efforts at sentencing. "The court may order the organization, at its expense and in the format and media specified by the court, to publicize the nature of the offense committed, the fact of conviction, and the nature of the punishment imposed, and the steps that will be taken to prevent the recurrence of similar offenses."[129] If probation is imposed to ensure that the organization meets its restitutionary or fine obligations, the court may order a number of steps if it determines they are necessary to ensure payment. For example, under § 8D1.4(b)(1), the court may order the organization to make "develop and submit to the court an effective compliance and ethics program consistent with § 8B2.1." The court may also require the

---

[118] *Id.* § 8C4.9.

[119] *Id.* § 8C4.11.

[120] *Id.* § 8C3.3(a); *see* United States v. Flower Aviation, 1996 WL 38731 (D. Kan. 1996).

[121] U.S.S.G. § 8C3.3(b).

[122] U.S.S.G. § 8C3.2(a).

[123] *Id.* § 8C3.2(b).

[124] *Id.* § 8D1.1(a)(1), (2), (3).

[125] *Id.* § 8D1.1(a)(8).

[126] *Id.* § 8D1.1(a)(6).

[127] *Id.* § 8D1.2(a)(1).

[128] *Id.* § 8D1.3(a), (b).

[129] *Id.* § 8D1.4(a).

organization to make "periodic submissions to the court or probation officer, at intervals specified by the court, (A) reporting on the organization's financial conditions and results of business operations, and accounting for the disposition of all funds received and (B) reporting on the organization's progress in implementing the [effective compliance and ethics program]."[130] The court may also order that the organization submit to regular or unannounced examinations of its books and records by the probation officers or experts hired by the court (but paid by the organization) and "interrogation of knowledgeable individuals within the organization."[131]

Some of these conditions of probation may appear to organizational clients to be highly intrusive, disruptive in terms of business functioning, and expensive. A focus on the conditions of probation, then, should not be lost in the effort to reduce the fine range.

The Sentencing Commission's data demonstrates that both the mean and the median organizational fines increased significantly after the organizational guidelines became operations.[132] In short, "the impact on sentencing of the organizational guidelines has been significant and widespread."[133] But the question is not the amount of the sanctions but rather the extent to which the "carrots" and "sticks" made available by the Guidelines serve the purposes of punishment in the corporate context. At least one knowledgeable commentator, Professor Jennifer Arlen, has concluded that the Guidelines in fact provide insufficient mitigation to efficiently incentivize firms to detect, self-report, and cooperate.[134]

3. EFFECTIVE COMPLIANCE PROGRAM: THE *CAREMARK* DECISION

"Without question, the Guidelines' greatest practical effect thus far is to raise the business community's awareness of the need for effective compliance programs."[135] Although such programs are not legally mandated, some contend that "[f]or a general counsel to ignore [implementation of a compliance program under] these Guidelines is professional malpractice."[136]

Widespread interest in compliance programs has its impetus not only in the Organizational Guidelines but also in corporate law, most notably the Delaware Chancery Court decision in *In re Caremark Int'l Inc. Derivative Action*.[137] In 1995, Caremark International Inc. pleaded guilty to a mail fraud charge for illegally paying physicians for patient referrals and then falsely billing the government. Caremark agreed to reimburse various private and public parties, ultimately paying $250 million in criminal and civil fines. The important decision for the wider corporate community, however, came a year later when the Delaware

---

[130] *Id.* § 8D1.4(b)(3).

[131] *Id.* § 8D1.4(b)(5).

[132] *See, e.g.*, Hon. Diana E. Murphy, *The Federal Sentencing Guidelines for Organizations: A Decade of Promising Compliance and Ethics*, 87 Iowa L. Rev. 697, 708 n.50 (2002).

[133] *Id.* at 709; *see also* Cindy R. Alexander, et al., *Regulating Corporate Criminal Sanctions: Federal Guidelines and Sentencing of Public Firms*, 42 J. L. & Econ. 393 (1999).

[134] *See* Jennifer Arlen, *The Failure of the Organizational Sentencing Guidelines*, 66 U. Miami L. Rev. 321 (2012).

[135] Dan K. Webb & Steven F. Molo, *Some Practical Considerations in Developing Effective Compliance Programs: A Framework for Meeting the Requirements of the Sentencing Guidelines*, 71 Wash. U. L.Q. 375, 375 (1993).

[136] Michele Galen, *Keeping the Long Arm of the Law at Arm's Length*, Bus.Wk., Apr. 22, 1991, at 104 (*quoting* Professor John C. Coffee, Jr.).

[137] 698 A.2d 959 (Del.Ch.1996). The SEC has also indicated the need for management to ensure that corporate disclosure and compliance systems are strong and responsive to company needs. *See, e.g.*, Report of Investigation, Release No. 34-39,157, 65 SEC Docket 1240 (Nov. 30, 1997) (relating to investigation of W.R. Grace & Co. and certain of its former officers and directors). *See also generally* ALI Principles of Corporate Governance 4.01(a), Comment C; ABA Model Business Corporation Act 8.30(b) (1998).

Chancery Court was asked to approve the settlement of a shareholder derivative case alleging that the Caremark directors had breached their duty of care by failing to supervise the conduct of Caremark's employees. The court approved the settlement, finding that "there was a very low probability that it would be determining that the directors of Caremark breached any duty to appropriately monitor and supervise the enterprise."[138] It went on, however, to underscore the importance of compliance efforts.

The Chancery Court first noted that the case raised duty of care issues relating to directors' alleged failure to monitor, not an alleged failure to make a "good" decision. Thus the court turned to examination of the legal principles that apply where the alleged loss "eventuates not from a decision but from unconsidered inaction."[139] The court conceded that most decisions of a corporation are not the subject of director attention, pointing out that the board itself is only required to authorize the most significant corporate events. Yet, the court noted, ordinary business decisions made as a matter of course by agents deeper within the organizational structure can drastically affect the interests of the corporation, raising the question "what is the board's responsibility with respect to the organization and monitoring of the enterprise to assure that the corporation functions within the law to achieve its purposes?"[140]

The Chancery Court stated that "[m]odernly this question has been given special attention by an increasing tendency, especially under federal law, to employ the criminal law to assure corporate compliance with external legal requirements" and by the Organizational Guidelines, "which impact importantly on the prospective effect these criminal sanctions might have on business corporations."[141] The Guidelines "offer powerful incentives for corporations today to have in place compliance programs to detect violations of law, promptly to report violations to appropriate public officials when discovered, and to take prompt, voluntary remedial efforts."[142] The court went on, in distinguishing a Delaware Supreme Court opinion that could be read to state that directors have no responsibility to assure adequate reporting systems are in place,[143] to reiterate the importance of the organizational Guidelines: "Any rational person attempting in good faith to meet an organizational governance responsibility would be bound to take into account this development and the enhanced penalties and the opportunities for reduced sanctions that it offers."[144]

The court concluded that "a director's obligation includes a duty to attempt in good faith to assure that a corporate information and reporting system, which the board concludes is adequate, exists, and that failure to do so under some circumstances may, in theory at least, render a director liable for losses caused by non-compliance with applicable legal standards."[145] In applying this new standard of care to the case, however, the court indicated that the directors' default would have to be a severe one:

---

[138] 698 A.2d at 961.

[139] *Id.* at 968.

[140] *Id.* at 968-69.

[141] *Id.* at 969.

[142] *Id.* at 969.

[143] *See* Graham v. Allis-Chalmers, 188 A.2d 125 (Del. 1963).

[144] 698 A.2d at 970.

[145] *Id.* at 970.

Generally, where a claim of directorial liability for corporate loss is predicated upon ignorance of liability creating activities within the corporation, ... in my opinion only a sustained or systematic failure of the board to exercise oversight—such as an utter failure to attempt to assure a reasonable information and reporting system exists—will establish the lack of good faith that is a necessary condition to liability. Such a test of liability—lack of good faith as evidenced by sustained or systematic failure of a director to exercise reasonable oversight—is quite high.[146]

The court's remarks in *Caremark* have raised the prospect—however attenuated—of directors' derivative liability for others' failures to ensure that adequate compliance programs are in place.[147] "Consequently, *Caremark* gave the movement toward corporate self-policing—known as compliance planning—a kick in the pants."[148]

E. DEFERRED PROSECUTION AGREEMENTS

The Corporate Charging Policy, reproduced *supra*, introduces the possibility that corporate cases may be resolved through deferred prosecution ("DPA") and non-prosecution ("NPA") agreements rather than through indictment or out-right declination. Both NPAs and DPAs—referred to collectively within as deferred prosecution agreements (DPs)—are, quite simply, contracts between the government and the targeted company through which the company agrees to admit wrongdoing and take identified steps to remedy the harm it caused and put in place systems to prevent further wrongs. If the company satisfies the terms of the agreement, criminal charges that have already been filed against it in court will be dismissed (for DPAs) or no formal charges will be filed (for NPAs). Some assert that the marked increase in the use of DPAs and NPAs "is arguably the most profound development in corporate white collar criminal practice" in recent memory.[149] "Experts say the use of deferred and non-prosecution agreements ... isn't likely to recede any time soon. Indeed, recent scrutiny of DPAs and NPAs, along with subsequent guidance on how they should be implemented, should give companies and the legal department a welcomed sense of predictability to the process."[150] This practice has now become global: the United Kingdom, France, and Canada have implemented their own versions of deferred prosecution agreements.

Some defense lawyers view deferred prosecution agreements as a win-win for the government *and* for the organizational defendant.[151] In reviewing the below description of DPs,

---

[146] *Id.* at 971.

[147] *See, e.g.,* Benjamin v. Kim, 1999 WL 249706 (S.D.N.Y. 1999):

> ... [W]hile it is true ... that a director is not under a duty to "install and operate a corporate system of espionage to ferret out wrongdoing which they have no reason to suspect exists," *Graham v. Allis-Chalmers*, 188 A.2d 125, 130 (Del. 1963), a director does have a duty to be reasonably informed about the company and must make sure that appropriate information and reporting systems are in place so that the Board receives relevant and timely information necessary to satisfy its supervisory and monitoring role. *See In re Caremark Int'l Derivative Litig.*, 698 A.2d 959, 970-71 (Del.Ch. 1996) (clarifying Delaware Law after *Graham*). Thus, a claim of directorial liability "predicated upon ignorance of liability creating activities within the corporation" will lie where the plaintiff shows a "sustained or systematic failure of a director to exercise reasonable oversight."

[148] John Gibeaut, *Getting Your House in Order*, ABA Journal 66 (June 1999).

[149] Peter Spivack & Sujit Raman, *Regulating the 'New Regulators': Current Trends in Deferred Prosecution Agreements*, 45 Am. Crim. L. Rev. 159, 159 (2008).

[150] Melissa Klein Aguilar, *Hopes for More Clarity in Deferred Prosecution Deals*, Compliance Week (Jan. 27, 2009).

[151] *See, e.g.,* Jeffrey T. Green, *Make It Go Away! Deferred Prosecution for Corporations*, 10 Bus. Crimes Bull. 1 (Mar. 2003).

consider whether there be circumstances in which the availability of such an alternative works against the defense.[152] In particular, the degree of involvement, on an ongoing basis, of criminal prosecutors in the conduct of the business contemplated in the DPA described above is, viewed traditionally, extraordinary. Is this an appropriate role for prosecutors?[153]

Julie R. O'Sullivan, *How Prosecutors Apply the "Federal Prosecutions of Corporations" Charging Policy in the Era of Deferred Prosecutions, and What That Means for the Purposes of the Federal Criminal Sanction*
51 Am. Crim. L. Rev. 29 (2014)

...

Although the relevant substance of the Charging Policy has not changed, the results of prosecutors' application of that policy have. Thus, the number of criminal dispositions in cases involving large corporations has ... declined, and the rise of non-criminal dispositions in the form of DPs has skyrocketed. ...

A couple of trends are undeniable even if their precise contours are somewhat contested. First the number of federal criminal convictions of [large] corporations has declined ... over the past [fifteen] years or so. The following scorecard of organizational convictions is derived from the yearly sentencing "sourcebook" and the annual reports put out by the U.S. Sentencing Commission:[154]

2000	2001	2002	2003	2004	2005	2006	2007	2008
304	238	252	200	130	187	217	197	199

2009	2010	2011	2012	2013	2014	2015	2016	2017
177	149	160	187	172	161	181	132	131

Note, too, that the overwhelming majority of the entities sentenced under the Organizational Sentencing Guidelines are small companies ... [with] fewer than fifty employees...

In the same period that indictments have declined ... the number of dispositions of corporate cases through NPAs and DPAs has increased just as markedly, although, again, the total numbers of these agreements remains subject to some question. ...

2000	2001	2002	2003	2004	2005	2006	2007	2008
2	3	2	6	8	15	26	40	25

2009	2010	2011	2012	2013	2014	2015	2016	2017
22	40	34	38	29	30	102	39	22

---

[152] *See generally* Joseph G. Block & David L. Feinberg, *Look Before You Leap: DPAs, NPAs, And the Environmental Criminal Case*, ALI-ABA Business Law Course Materials Journal 7 (Feb. 2010); Richard M. Cooper, *Deferred Prosecution: An Added Technique for Resolving Federal Criminal Investigations of Organizations*, 10 Briefly 1, 21-22 (Nat'l Legal Center for the Public Interest Aug. 2006).

[153] *See, e.g.*, P.J. Meitl, *Who's the Boss? Prosecutorial Involvement in Corporate America*, 34 N. Ky. L. Rev. 1 (2007).

[154] [Ed.:] The statistics in this introduction have been updated since this article was published. The data on deferred- and non-prosecution agreements is derived from Gibson Dunn's website, https://www.gibsondunn.com/2017-year-end-npa-dpa-update. For an excellent resource on all types of corporate criminal resolutions, check the UVA Corporate Prosecution Registry, http://library.law.virginia.edu/corporate-prosecutions/.

Note that these figures do not include other types of non-criminal dispositions of potentially criminal charges. For example, corporate wrongdoers in the health care field and the Office of the Inspector General ("OIG") for the Department of Health and Human Services ("HHS") regularly enter into Corporate Integrity Agreements ("CIAs") to address corporate wrongdoing that could potentially be pursued criminally.[98] CIAs are "watered down versions of deferred prosecution agreements" because, although they require improvement in corporate compliance efforts as a condition of the civil settlement of corporate wrongdoing, the corporations are not required to admit guilt to criminal charges and a violation of the agreement does not automatically lead to the filing of criminal charges. The principal advantage of these agreements, like many DPs, is that they avoid the automatic debarment of drug companies from providing much needed medication in the Medicare and Medicaid programs. According to my count, based on the website of the OIG of HSS, [the number of CIAs has skyrocketed from] … one, two and three CIAs in each of the years 2003-2007 to around [329 CIAs in 2012-2016].

It seems clear … that the heightened awareness of the collateral consequences of an organizational conviction forced on the DOJ in the Arthur Andersen case was the primary impetus for the shift to DPAs and NPAs.[155] To briefly recap, on May 6, 2002, the government unsealed an indictment of Andersen for obstruction of justice. After trial, a jury found Andersen guilty in June 2002, and the company imploded. Because federal regulations bar felons from the business of auditing public companies, the conviction effectively put Andersen out of business. (Ultimately, the Supreme Court overturned the conviction because of deficient jury instructions, and the case was never retried.) The DOJ was roundly criticized for the harms inflicted on the otherwise blameless 28,000 [domestic] employees of Andersen estimated to have lost their jobs due to the initial Andersen conviction. The data bear out this correlation between Andersen's demise and an increased focus on DPs (though it does not prove a causal nexus): the escalation in deferred prosecution agreements happened shortly after the Andersen debacle.

VI. TYPICAL DP PROVISIONS (AND OBJECTIONS THERETO)

Common provisions in DPs are:

• an admission of wrongdoing by the company;
• a corporate agreement to cooperate with the government in ongoing investigations, including those in which corporate agents and employees are targeted;
• payment of monetary fines and penalties;
• a corporate undertaking to improve compliance programs, sometimes under the scrutiny of a "monitor" hired and paid for by the company in consultation with the government;
• a waiver of indictment, the statute of limitations, and the right to a speedy trial;
• a provision stating that if the company breaches the agreement, it will be subject to prosecution, and that the agreement's statement of facts, which constitutes an admission of guilt, will be admissible;
• but if the company complies with the agreement, the government will not proceed with a criminal case against it; and
• an agreement that the agreement does not bind other parties, including other federal agencies.

Many agreements go beyond these basic provisions. Indeed, "[o]ne of the most appealing aspects of both deferred- and non-prosecution agreements is the ability to tailor each one

---

[155] [Ed.:] Note that according to some sources, "no fewer than 78 of the Fortune 100 companies engage in government contracting at some level." Jeffrey T. Green, *A Terrible Trap*, Bus. Crimes Bull. (May 2013) (discussing FAR mandatory reporting rule).

according to the specific needs of the respective parties, with both sides bargaining for what they hold most dear." Perhaps as a result of a lack of DOJ guidance, however, some of the initial agreements contained ingenuous and "interesting" provisions such as "requiring a hospital to give the public millions of dollars of free health care, obligating a company to endow a chair in business ethics at the U.S. attorney's alma mater, or requiring a company to create 1,600 new jobs in the state over 10 years." This led to criticism that:

> [A]llowing prosecutors to leverage their bargaining power to compel such acts, especially when they are of local or personal significance, smacks of Tammany Hall politicking. Extraneous conditions that do not relate to the core behavior being condemned cheapens public respect for the criminal justice system by creating the perception that negotiations are unprincipled.

Recognizing this, in May 2008, DOJ issued guidance that provides that:

> Plea agreements, deferred prosecution agreements and non-prosecution agreements should not include terms requiring the defendant to pay funds to a charitable, educational, community, or other organization or individual that is not a victim of the criminal activity or is not providing services to redress the harm caused by the defendant's criminal conduct.[156]

Deferred prosecution agreements continue to contain provisions that, while appropriately aimed at reducing future criminality, have been the subject of criticism, at least in the defense community. They include:

a. Use of Monitors. The first questions to arise about the use of deferred prosecutions in lieu of corporate criminal indictments were primarily operational in nature. A great deal of controversy surrounded the DOJ's practice of requiring corporations, at their own expense, to hire outside "monitors" who would ensure that the corporation took the remedial steps identified in the deferred prosecution agreement and often would report their findings to the DOJ. The DOJ's process for selecting monitors was attacked as deficient in that these highly lucrative positions were often awarded to former colleagues and professional associates. ....

Responding to accusations of favoritism, and to stirring congressional interest, the DOJ issued guidance in March 2008 and May 2010 to ensure that the monitor selection process would be based on merit and would be more transparent. Additional complaints about monitors concerned "accountability, oversight, and costs." In recent years, DOJ appears to be much more deliberate in requiring companies to take on a monitor as part of a deferred prosecution. Thus, for example, of the 152 deferred agreements the GAO reviewed, which were entered into between 1993 and September 2009, forty-eight required the appointment of an independent monitor. By comparison ... only thirteen of sixty-eight agreements concluded in 2011-2012 required appointment of an independent monitor. A "corollary trend is the increase in self-monitoring and self-reporting requirements ...."[157]

b. Waiver provisions. Waivers of privilege protections, even if now negotiated rather than demanded under the Charging Policy, are still a common feature of deferred prosecution agreements. Obviously, those hostile to waivers argue that they have the same deleterious impact whether requested under the Filip Memo's cooperation provision or negotiated in a DP.

c. "Non-contradiction" provisions. The DOJ generally insists that the entity receiving a DP accept responsibility for wrongful conduct and agree that neither it nor its agents will make

---

[156] [Ed.:] *See also* Attorney General Sessions Memo, Prohibition on Settlement Payments to Third Parties (June 5, 2017).

[157] [Ed.:] For additional information about monitorships, see Veronica Root, *Constraining Monitors*, 85 Fordham L. Rev. 2227 (2017); Veronica Root, *Modern-Day Monitorships*, 33 Yale J. Reg. 109 (2016); Veronica Root, *The Monitor-"Client" Relationship*, 100 Va. L. Rev. 523 (2014).

statements "contradicting" anything in its statement of responsibility. This may well affect employees' ability to defend themselves in the course of the investigation: "Not only are they told they must cooperate with the government (indeed, their jobs may depend on it), but they may feel pressure to testify consistently with the agreed-upon version of facts. If an executive strays from the detailed factual statement the company has agreed to, the company's repudiation of his or her statement or testimony may be the least of his or her problems."

  d. Limitations on Business Activities and Corporate Governance Reform Requirements. Some DPs contain provisions requiring the company to change sales or compensation practices, oust executives or board members, and restrict or modify consulting, contracting, and other decisions. As Professor John Coffee has noted, "deferred corporation agreements have intruded deeply into corporate governance, requiring changes in the composition and structure of the corporation's board of directors, dismissal of specified officers and employees, replacement of auditors, and establishment of new compliance and ethics programs and even the termination of certain lines of business." Some of this may well be helpful in foreclosing future crimes. But Professor Coffee and others are concerned that "shareholders' right to choose their own directors" and other legitimate values may be sacrificed "to permit experimentation in corporate governance by a prosecutor who lacks any empirical basis for believing that these reforms will reduce the risk of future recidivism."

  e. Length of compliance. The durations of DPs vary substantially; in 2009, the [Government Accountability Office ("GAO"), in one of its reports on the use of DPs,] reported that the agreements it reviewed ranged from three months to five years. As Professor Erik Luna has argued, given the length of some of these terms,

> [i]n essence, a corporation may be held in receivership by a prosecutor, who becomes a sort of super-CEO or board chairman with the power to seek indictments should he become dissatisfied. Needless to say, the idea of state control of a private enterprise is problematic in an economy premised on free markets, even more so if the predicate crime is of doubtful validity.

  The above indicates that the content of DP agreements is not without controversy. Additional concerns are raised by: the DOJ's overstatement of the benefits of DPs; the dearth of specific Charging Policy guidance regarding when, and how, DPs ought to be used; the potential for prosecutorial overreaching and disparate treatment; and the paucity of judicial oversight into this important new law enforcement tool.

  Deputy Assistant Attorney General Gary G. Grindler, testifying before Congress, summarized the advantages flowing from the use of DPs as follows:

  1. Because a DP represents a negotiated disposition, payment of restitution to victims can be more quickly and efficiently accomplished than would be the case if criminal proceedings— e.g., formal charging, litigation, and appeals—were instituted.

  2. DPs promote the public interest in ferreting out crime more quickly by requiring corporate cooperation in the prosecution of culpable individuals.

  3. Many DPs benefit the public by requiring the corporation to initiate comprehensive ethics and compliance programs.

  4. DPs benefit the public and industries by providing guidance on what constitutes improper conduct in the publicly available DP agreement. The DPs, in identifying the remedial action required of the company, help define compliance "best practices" for particular industries.

  5. DPs achieve these benefits without incurring the collateral consequences (debarment) that might result from a conviction, thus preventing possible firm failures, loss of jobs, elimination of useful products from the market, and outsized shareholder losses.

  The problem with this list is that each of items (1) through (4) could also be achieved— and often were before the advent of DPs—through a criminal disposition. The overwhelming majority of criminal cases against corporations have long resulted in guilty pleas, meaning that they are negotiated dispositions involving virtually no litigation and with ample opportunity to provide restitution in a timely way. … [C]orporations almost always rushed to cooperate and handed over culpable individuals when required, hoping to secure a declination or at least sentencing credit. And the U.S. Sentencing Guidelines for Organizations, as well as prosecutorial Charging Policy, required a focus on implementing an effective program to prevent and detect violations of law as a part of disposition and criminal sentence. Finally, if an express summary of the wrongdoing and required remedial steps were not included in a plea agreement or as part of sentencing, certain such information could well be provided in the regulatory resolution that often paralleled the criminal case.

In short, the only item on Mr. Grindler's list that DPs may make possible that a criminal disposition may not is avoidance of collateral consequences. Unstated in Mr. Grindler's list but very important to prosecutors is the fact that the court is called upon to supervise probationary terms that require implementation of compliance programs after conviction; by contrast, DPs put prosecutors in the driver's seat, allowing them to come up with more interventionist plans for remediation of the corporation's management, compliance, and other functions, and oversight by DOJ-approved people. Thus Eugene Illovsky's summary more accurately captures the appeal of deferred prosecution agreements:

> All of the punishment, none of the guilt. What's not to like about deferred prosecution agreements for corporations? Prosecutors get another choice for disposing of a corporate other than declining or indicting. And they can still make sure wayward companies will be fined, chastised, restructured, and reformed—without unduly harming innocent constituencies. From the company side, deferred prosecution helps it avoid the distraction, risk, and often devastating consequences of indictment, trial, and conviction. The board of directors cleans house, pays money, and the company stays in business; though not without (sometimes a good bit of) pain .... Defense lawyers are happy to have another tool to help corporate clients—for whom often the only real question is how *soon* to cooperate—avoid conviction.

Both the prosecution and the defense generally applaud the opportunity this tool provides allow the parties a third way—neither indictment nor declination—to resolve cases. As then Assistant Attorney General Lanny A. Breuer explained, speaking to the New York Bar Association,

> [w]hen the only tool we had to use in cases of corporate misconduct was a criminal indictment, prosecutors sometimes had to use a sledgehammer to crack a nut. More often, they just walked away. In the world we live in now, though, prosecutors have much greater ability to hold companies accountable for misconduct that we used to—and the result has been a transformation in the culture of corporate compliance.

This novel third way is not universally applauded, however. [A number of] circumstances … make abject cooperation with the government an imperative in many cases. These circumstances also mean that targeted companies generally have to accept the disposition handed them by prosecutors. From a defense perspective, a deferred prosecution is better than an indictment, but companies would certainly prefer a declination. The introduction of this third way now means that they may be forced to accept an NPA or DPA when, formerly, they would have enjoyed a declination. "Although it is not even clear in many cases that the government would have sought indictment and conviction had the company contested the charges, companies have nevertheless entered into DPAs because fighting an indictment would simply have been too big a risk to take."

Not surprisingly, defense counsel strongly object to prosecutors' attempts to secure a DPA or NPA where the government would not otherwise be inclined to seek an indictment. Their position has some heft: deferred prosecution should not be a way of scoring a scalp where the government's theory is a stretch or it does not have the evidence to proceed. Even former prosecutors, like Randall Eliason, posit that one does not wish to make the DOJ's enforcement work *too* easy lest, freed from any worry about passing any grand jury, petit jury, or judicial scrutiny, the availability of DPs may well result "in the inappropriate pursuit of marginal cases." As James R. Copland argues:

> To be sure, prosecutors are acting upon duly enacted laws, but federal criminal provisions are often vague or ambiguous, and the fact that prosecutors and large corporations alike feel obliged to reach agreement, rather than follow an orderly regulatory process and litigate disagreements in court, denies the judiciary an opportunity to clarify the boundaries of such laws. Instead, the laws come to mean what the *prosecutors* say they mean—and companies do what the prosecutors say they must.

Former Attorney General Alberto Gonzalez made a similar observation in the context of FCPA enforcement: "[i]n an ironic twist, the more that American companies elect to settle and not force the DOJ to defend its aggressive interpretation of the [FCPA], the more aggressive DOJ has become in its interpretation of the law and its prosecution decisions."

DOJ does not appear to have adopted the view suggested by the defense. Thus, for example, Lanny Breuer asserted in a 2012 speech that "[c]ompanies now know that avoiding the disaster scenario of an indictment does not mean an escape from accountability. *They know that they will be answerable even for conduct that in years past would have resulted in a declination*." [(Emphasis added.)] This may be a defensible policy if the a prosecutor could prove that her theory of the case falls squarely within the bounds of the applicable criminal statute and has sufficient evidence to proceed, but she is reluctant to indict because the threatened collateral consequences to innocent third parties may be too grave. Where a declination would be founded on these concerns, many would argue (present company excepted, as we shall see *infra*) that it might well be appropriate for the government to seek deferred prosecution agreements rather than simply declining.

Prosecutors' bargaining advantage, combined with the Charging Policy's lack of guidance, lead to an additional problem: the potential—and many argue, the reality—that different prosecutors throughout the country will unfairly treat similarly situated companies differently. The GAO ... identified one gaping hole in the policy in this regard—that is, the fact that different offices, and even different assistants, have their own policies regarding when it is appropriate to use NPAs, which if successful involve no court filings and thus are viewed as much more attractive to targeted companies, as opposed to DPAs, in which a criminal charge is levied but then dismissed.

In sum, the DOJ ought to craft rules that delineate when a deferred prosecution is appropriate, how prosecutors ought to decide between a DPA and an NPA, and what terms are appropriately included (and when). The Charging Memo was written when the reality was that most prosecutors faced two choices in investigations of corporate wrongdoing: indict or decline. The Filip Memo, while endorsing the use of NPAs and DPAs, did not provide any additional guidance regarding the increasingly popular "third way" of using deferred prosecutions to resolve cases. That is, the Charging Policy does not give prosecutors any concrete instruction on choosing among at least four options (indict; decline; NPA; DPA) rather than two (indict or decline). At the very least, the DOJ needs to address in its Charging Policy whether deferred prosecution agreements should be available only when a decision to indict would be otherwise be appropriate, or whether should they also be an option when a declination would otherwise be the result. To ensure consistency and predictability—which are necessary both to induce companies to self-report and fully cooperate and to the perception and reality of equal treatment—the DOJ ought also to create a mechanism for Main Justice review of proposed dispositions.

Although a more detailed Charging Policy may alleviate some concerns that Assistant U.S. Attorneys ("AUSAs") are forcing companies into deferred prosecution agreements when they might not otherwise be successful in obtaining a conviction, some argue that one cannot trust AUSAs to be the only gatekeeper, given that their training and orientation may lead them to push the boundaries of the law to lengths that might not pass judicial scrutiny. Indeed, a number of commentators and at least one congressman have argued that judges should be more involved in the process so that prosecutors are not serving "unilaterally as regulator, judge, and jury."

At present, judges have no involvement in the approval of NPAs because no charges are ever filed if the agreement is successful. And there is only minimal judicial involvement with DPAs, which contemplate that charges are filed and then dismissed when the company has complied with the terms of the DP. The GAO's audit revealed that the overwhelming majority of judges presented with DPAs did not: hold hearings to review the terms of the agreement, have any involvement in the selection of monitors, or receive monitors' reports. Almost all dismissed the case upon being notified that the agreement had been satisfied without independently assessing the corporation's compliance.

Commentators have identified a second problem flowing from lack of judicial participation, and that is that prosecutors, and prosecutors alone, generally have the sole discretion under the deferred prosecution agreements to identify when a breach has occurred and what sanctions may be appropriate for that breach.

Some commentators have argued that due process considerations require federal courts to determine whether a breach has occurred. Unfortunately, however, this judicial intervention comes too late—as a practical and a legal matter. ... [E]ven accepting that courts will accept that judicial review of alleged breaches is a due process imperative, they have been unwilling to review defendants' claims that they have not breached and should not be indicted *prior to indictment*—when it really matters. ...

Very few commentators seem to believe, however, that additional judicial scrutiny—on the front or back end—is likely without congressional action. Although the deferred prosecution system might work better with judicial involvement, the government and defense in individual cases are unlikely to wish to allow judges to disrupt their negotiated agreement. Indeed, the lack of judicial oversight is viewed by the DOJ as a significant advantage, because it "does not have to worry about a judge second-guessing its terms or questioning the fairness of the resolution." Thus, the DOJ is unlikely to accept a judicial role absent a legislative imperative. Judges, too, have expressed some reluctance to becoming involved, citing already crowded dockets, inexperience, and discomfort about the appropriateness of judicial involvement given the federal rules' bar on judicial participation in plea negotiations and general concerns relating to separation of powers principles.

In conclusion, DPs' only clear advantage over criminal prosecution lies in their ability to foreclose collateral consequences to "innocent" third parties. And while many have welcomed the flexibility that DPs provide prosecutors, that flexibility carries with it the potential for abuse, unequal treatment, and overreaching. At least in the absence of greater DOJ guidance on when and how DPs ought to be used, the absence of any mechanism for accountability to a third party, like judges, is troubling.

Having laid out the current state of enforcement and addressed some of the concerns raised about the DOJ's turn toward DPs, it is time to []turn to the [central] question ...: given the factors actually driving enforcement decisions, what purposes of punishment is the DOJ seeking to pursue, and is it effective in doing so through DPs? The GAO has issued a number of reports on the DOJ's use of deferred prosecution agreements. ... [T]he GAO's work provides the best evidence available regarding the factors prosecutors actually rely upon to exercise their charging discretion. The data generated by the GAO during the course of its "audit" confirms that the Charging Policy itself has not changed; instead, it is its application—and in particular, the modern importance of collateral consequences in the charging calculus—that has changed.

The GAO interviews clearly demonstrated that prosecutors are, in fact, using the Charging Policy in making their determinations. But the GAO concluded that "[w]hile the prosecutors with whom we spoke said that many [of Charging Policy's factors] may have influenced their decision on entering into a DPA or NPA in each case, they most frequently cited" just three factors in deciding to forego criminal charges. Those three factors, which the GAO did not appear to rank in importance, are:

• Encouraging remediation of the corporate bad conduct;
• Inducing "cooperation"—meaning self-reporting, self-investigation, and cooperation against the individual wrongdoers; and
• Avoiding collateral consequences to "innocent third parties."

(Many prosecutors also predominately relied on the same three factors when deciding between a DPA and an NPA.) The question for present purposes is how—or whether—these factors serve the purposes of punishment applicable in the corporate context.

Clearly, the DOJ in practice has abandoned its stated goal of "punishment" (that is, retribution) in making charging decisions except in the most extreme cases of corporate wrongdoing (and only then when collateral consequences permit). Thus, none of the three charging factors identified as serving retributivist principles—that is, those requiring consideration of the nature and seriousness of the offense, the pervasiveness of wrongdoing within the corporation, and the corporation's history of similar misconduct—even make the top three charging considerations identified by the GAO. The conviction versus DP numbers provided above confirm this narrative. For those of us who believe there is great value in criminal prosecutors seeking to impose the criminal stigma on corporations, this is a real enforcement default. Certainly, at the very least, the first three factors laid out in the Charging Policy ought to rank higher in prosecutors' decision-making calculus.

If "just desserts" is off the table, what purposes *are* being served by prosecutors' charging choices? In my view, the evidence that DPs serve the purposes of deterrence and rehabilitation … better than criminal prosecution must be compelling to justify the DOJ's abandonment of harm, systematic criminality, and corporate recidivism in assessing the appropriateness of a given disposition. In short, the DOJ must make a compelling case that the factors upon which it concentrates serve the goals of galvanizing deterrence better than criminal convictions in order to justify its disregard of just desserts.

A. Remediation, or "Galvanizing Deterrence"

I assume that what is meant in the GAO report by "remediation" tracks the meaning contained in the Charging Policy. In the Policy, this means not just, for example, the payment of restitution (money) for damages caused by the wrongdoing, but also steps taken "to implement the personnel, operational, and organizational changes necessary to establish an awareness among employees that criminal conduct will not be tolerated." Accordingly, given the prominence of this factor, to the extent that the DOJ seeks to achieve the traditional aims of punishment through DPs, its focus appears to be on galvanizing deterrence … [This type of deterrence encompasses elements of rehabilitation and thus is aimed not just at scaring a corporation straight but also at getting rid of personnel and reforming practices and procedures that make the corporate culture ripe for recidivism. The criminal sanction is designed—as, presumably, are DPs—to help a company fix its policies and procedures, and alter its corporate culture, in such a way as to preclude future wrongdoing.]

The next question has to be whether DPs appear to be working to further the goal of galvanizing deterrence. Further, given the burden of proof I have imposed above, DPs must work better than criminal convictions in achieving this aim. Lanny Breuer, speaking for the DOJ, acknowledged that DPs have their critics, but asserted that "DPAs have had a truly transformative effect on particular companies and, more generally, on corporate culture across the globe." He claimed that the result of the use of DPs "has been, unequivocally, far greater accountability for corporate wrongdoing—and a sea change in corporate compliance efforts":

One of the reasons why deferred prosecution agreements are such a powerful tool is that, in many ways, a DPA has the same punitive, deterrent, and rehabilitative effect as a guilty plea: when a company enters into a DPA with the government, or an NPA for that matter, it almost always must acknowledge wrongdoing, agree to cooperate with the government's investigation, pay a fine, agree to improve its compliance program, and agree to face prosecution if it fails to satisfy the terms of the agreement. All of these components of DPAs are critical for accountability.

But not everyone agrees with Mr. Breuer regarding the efficacy of these agreements in enhancing accountability and compliance. For example, the GAO has noted that:

> According to DOJ, along with prosecution, DPAs and NPAs are invaluable tools in achieving its strategic objective to combat public and corporate corruption, fraud, economic crime, and cybercrime, although the public, as well as the Congress, have called into question the effectiveness of these agreements. However, DOJ cannot evaluate and demonstrate the extent to which DPAs and NPAs—in addition to other tools, such as prosecution—contribute to the department's efforts to combat corporate crime because it has no measures to assess their effectiveness. Specifically, DOJ intends for these agreements to promote corporate reform; however, DOJ does not have performance measures in place to assess whether this goal has been met. Therefore, it could be difficult for DOJ to justify its increasing use of these tools.

The 2010 Report issued by the Organization for Economic Co-operation and Development ("OECD") on the United States' enforcement of the FCPA also noted that the "actual deterrent effect [of NPAs and DPAs] has not been quantified." The DOJ responded by noting that quantifying deterrence is extremely difficult, but that one "of the best sources of anecdotal evidence demonstrating that DPAs and NPAs have a deterrent effect comes from the companies themselves," many of which have "undergone dramatic changes" in personnel, governance, compliance, training, and auditing practices as a result of a deferred prosecution agreement. One might argue, however, that these same effects likely would have resulted from a conviction. Moreover, such changes do not always guarantee law-abiding behavior going forward; entities such as the Aibel Group Inc. and Ingersoll Rand, have run into continuing FCPA problems after entering into deferred prosecution agreements with the government.

In the absence of data, I can see two interrelated reasons to question the efficacy of DPs in ensuring meaningful corporate deterrence and rehabilitation. The first concerns questions of prosecutorial competence and legitimacy in participating in corporate regulation. The second, which may flow from a lack of training or experience in compliance, relates to whether these "new regulators" are written and implemented in ways that truly can change a tainted corporate culture.

First, some question the appropriateness of federal prosecutors' assumptions of the role of "the New Regulators." Many commentators have noted that DOJ's shift to DPs represents a fundamental change in prosecutorial function:

> This shift reflects an evolving view of the purpose and function of the criminal law in the corporate context. In a post-Enron world, DOJ officials appear to believe that the principal role of corporate criminal enforcement is to reform corrupt corporate cultures— that is, to effect widespread structural reform—rather than to indict, to prosecute, and to punish. By focusing more on prospective questions of corporate governance and compliance, and less on the retrospective question of the entity's criminal liability, federal prosecutors have fashioned a new role for themselves in policing, and supervising, corporate America.

Professor Brandon Garrett has evaluated this as "structural reform prosecution" while Professors David Hess and Cristie Ford situate it within the emerging category of regulation referred to as "new governance" regulation.

For me, the fundamental concern about this new regulation, however labeled, is prosecutorial competence to identify the organizational problems to be addressed and prescribe fixes. Prosecutors will have difficulty penetrating the "black box" that is the company to identify what went wrong, let alone diagnose how to correct it. Corporate counsel, while seemingly engaged in fulsome cooperation, will always attempt to limit the future organizational and compliance burdens imposed on their clients. Even if prosecutors had full access and information, they often simply do not have the business or financial background, training, or experience to make the judgments necessary to craft a DP that has a hope of actually changing the corporation's functioning and culture.

Professor Dan Richman identifies the problem of prosecutors' institutional competence but takes solace in the fact that "prosecutors rarely act alone, and are unlikely to do so in a sustained white collar investigation." He notes that "[o]f the DPAs [Professor Brandon] Garrett studied, sixty-six percent were reached explicitly in conjunction with regulatory agencies—with the SEC leading the pack—and that figure might substantially understate agency involvement, since an agency extensively consulted by prosecutors might go unmentioned in the formal agreement." It is true that in most—but not all—cases the prosecutor will have expert agency back-up (though it should be noted that the prosecutorial and agency priorities are not always aligned). The question then becomes: if this is the case, why is the DOJ in the mix at all?

If all that the DOJ is doing in these cases is following the "expert" agency's lead (and the agencies themselves are entering into non-prosecution agreements), what value is the DOJ adding—besides the value to the DOJ in trumpeting the result and garnering some portion of the monetary award to make its bottom line look good the next time Congress scrutinizes the DOJ's budget allotment? Aren't the presence of *two* "regulators" overkill—representing a waste of scarce government resources and raising serious risks of over-deterrence and unfairness? More to the point, it would seem that the neglected factor 9—the adequacy of remedies such as civil or regulatory enforcement actions—ought to counsel that the SEC's non-prosecution agreement is just as good as the DOJ's and thus the DOJ ought to concern itself with other, *criminal*, cases.[158]

The honest answer has to be that the DOJ's presence is required to make good on the threat of a criminal prosecution if the corporation does not roll over and agree to a DP. But, again according to Professor Richman,

> [F]inding that ... regulatory agencies were using the strong norm of prosecutorial discretion to circumvent political or legal restraints on their own power so as to, say, extract structural concessions that they would not themselves have been able to achieve through rulemaking or adjudication, would raise questions about legitimacy and accountability.

The second "efficacy" problem may flow from this competency issue. According to some expert commentators, many DP agreements inappropriately focus solely on what David Hess and Cristie Ford term a corporation's "hardware," and ignore the more important "software" issues. "A corporation's hardware includes its formal structure, policies, and processes. 'Software' refers to the informal norms of behavior within an organization, which includes the ethical culture and ethical climate of the firm." It is the former that most DP agreements address; but it is reformation of the latter that is critical in most situations in which the corporate wrongdoing is systemic, as is usually the case. Thus, the Ethics Resource Center, a leading nonprofit researching organizational ethics, asserts that "[e]thical culture is the single biggest factor determining the amount of misconduct in [an] organization." And the U.S. Sentencing Guidelines controlling the sentencing of organizations have endorsed this view, recognizing the centrality of issues of culture in creating a definition of effective programs to prevent further wrongdoing. In organizational sentencing, then, a company may only receive credit for having an effective program to prevent and detect violations if its program "promote[s] an organizational culture that encourages ethical conduct and a commitment to compliance with the law."

---

[158] [Ed.: *See also* Geraldine Szott Moohr, *The Balance Among Corporate Criminal Liability, Private Civil Suits, and Regulatory Enforcement*, 46 Am. Crim. L. Rev. 1459 (2009).]

Ford and Hess believe that this new regulatory paradigm holds promise if "software" issues are made an explicit part of the DP conversation. They argue, however, that meaningful culture changes require the active presence of a third party. As noted above, many of the initial DPs required the target company to hire monitors, who would assess corporate progress toward the identified goals and notify the DOJ. But Ford and Hess warn that many monitors to date have adopted too narrow a focus, meaning that the goal of reforming corporate culture is not met:

> They rarely appear to be doing what compliance consultants would say is necessary to ensure the corporation's compliance program is effective and will result in reforming a corporation's culture over the long term. They also seem to be failing at generating the necessary self-reflective process. Even in cases where there is widespread wrongdoing within the organization, it seems the monitor is typically assuming the narrower Auditor role[—in which the monitor simply assures the DOJ that the corporation is doing what it says it is doing in terms of implementing internal controls and a new compliance program—]over the more in-depth Associate role[—in which the monitor acts as Auditor and functions more fully as a partner with the compliance officer, board, and other relevant corporate officials to turn around the corporate culture.]

Further, given the DOJ's apparent movement away from the use of monitors, one has to question whether any commitment to "software" reform in future DPs will be effected. …

All this said, mine is a comparative inquiry: are deferred prosecution agreements more likely than criminal convictions to provoke the necessary remediation? This is difficult to assess because there is also no data to show whether, in the pre-DP era, corporate convictions served the goals of galvanizing deterrence. Recognizing the theoretical nature of this assessment, then, I would posit that if prosecutors and judges were willing to pursue the goal of galvanizing deterrence in the course of criminal prosecutions, they would be at least as successful in achieving real change, and probably more so.

First, prosecutors have as much, if not more, power to ask corporations to take identified steps to remediate in a meaningful way during the course of a criminal case. The overwhelming majority of criminal cases against corporations have, traditionally and today, resulted in negotiated pleas. There is no reason that these plea agreements cannot contain the same undertakings that are required in a DP.

Second, if such plea agreements were reached, it would not be prosecutors who oversee compliance; rather, it would be federal judges. One under-examined section of the U.S. Sentencing Guidelines provides for organizational probation as part of a sentence. Such probation is actually *required* in a variety of circumstances, including where a relatively large offender lacks an effective compliance program and when probation "is necessary to ensure that changes are made within the organization to reduce the likelihood of future criminal conduct." As a condition of organizational probation, federal courts can require the organization to: develop and submit for court approval an effective program to prevent and detect violations of law; notify its employees and shareholders of the program upon court approval of it; and make periodic submissions to the court reporting on the organization's financial condition, results of its business operations, and progress in instituting its compliance program. An organization under probation "shall submit" to a reasonable number of regular or unannounced examinations of its books and records by the court's expert, who may also engage in "interrogation of knowledgeable individuals within the organization."

Some may object that courts are, if anything, at this point even less competent than prosecutors to "regulate" the rehabilitation of a corporation. But the U.S. Sentencing Guidelines also authorize the court to hire an expert, at the organization's expense, to aid the court. Thus, if one pursued galvanizing deterrence through criminal prosecution instead of DPs, one would have remediation plans that would be publicly scrutinized by third parties at the acceptance/plea stage (the court) and dispassionate third parties (court-appointed experts) reporting on efforts to revamp corporate function and culture.

We probably will not know how well corporate probation following a corporate conviction will work in furthering galvanizing deterrence in major part because prosecutors prefer to use DPs for the reasons explored above. We do not know if judges would be willing to be more interventionist than they have been in the context of DPs, although their unquestioned primacy in the approval of plea agreements and sentencing might encourage them to greater ambition. We also do not know if judges' oversight of DPs, with expert assistance, will encourage greater emphasis on "software" as opposed to "hardware" issues.

What we can say is that this alternative in theory holds as much promise as DPs and perhaps more; certainly there is no hard data to prove one is superior to the other. Readers will recall that I believe that the DOJ's abandonment of just desserts considerations in charging puts the burden of proof on it to show that its third way unequivocally serves the interest of galvanizing deterrence better than criminal prosecution. This it has not, and on this record, cannot do.

B. Cooperation

Of what relevance is "corporate cooperation" to the purposes of punishment? The emphasis on cooperation appears to relate to two issues: (1) the difficulty of criminal investigations and convictions of some organizations absent the help of the organization; and (2) the importance of corporate cooperation to identifying and convicting the individual wrongdoers within the corporation. With respect to the first issue, cooperation allows the DOJ to leverage its scarce resources to respond to more allegations of corporate wrongdoing and to overcome practical barriers to prosecution presented, in particular, in transnational cases. The fact that these cases are today generally resolved through non-criminal dispositions argues that cooperation does not lead to more criminal sanctioning of corporations. Where it does contribute to criminal enforcement is in pursuing the second aim: identifying and prosecuting individuals. Even the threat of criminal sanctions, as we have seen, often leaves organizations with little choice but to cooperate with prosecutors, identifying persons whom earlier iterations of the Charging Policy termed individual "culprits" to avoid liability.

The policies and practices discussed above suggest that the DOJ has made the judgment that prosecution of individuals, rather than the entities through which they work, offers the largest deterrent punch. The numbers tell this story pretty conclusively, as does the importance of cooperation in charging. The Charging Policy explains that "[c]orporations should not be treated leniently because of their artificial nature nor should they be subject to harsher treatment." But prosecution of responsible individuals is clearly a priority under the policy. ...

Cooperation, then, serves the DOJ's interest in deterrence as achieved through prosecutions of individuals, although many have strong reservations about the fairness and collateral consequences of this approach. The question for present purposes is whether it also serves additional goals related to *corporate* criminal sanctioning. ... [C]ooperation is only an imprecise proxy, at best, for the retributive calculus of whether the corporate culture at issue is "good" or "bad." One could argue that cooperation may have a tangential relationship to galvanizing deterrence to the extent that, as a practical matter, it is difficult to reform a company without its assent and indeed active assistance. Thus, genuine cooperation would seem to promise better odds that the company will in fact work to discipline errant employees, reform its policies and procedures to promote a law-abiding ethos, and implement a meaningful compliance regime going forward. But, again, this would be true regardless of whether the DOJ has decided on a DP or a criminal conviction. The incentive to cooperate may well be even stronger when what is at stake is a declination or sentencing credit as opposed to a DP. Certainly, corporations have felt the imperative to cooperate, and turn over culpable employees, long before the advent of DPs.

If neither of the above "factors" upon which prosecutors rely in extending the offer of a DP to a wrongdoing company clearly demonstrate that DPs are better than criminal prosecutions in serving the aims of galvanizing deterrence, it would seem the final factor must pick up the slack. And it does not.

C. Collateral Consequences

The above background demonstrates that it is the "Andersen effect" that has been the cardinal consideration in shaping DOJ disposition decisions on the ground. Indeed, the GAO study illustrated the centrality of this factor in day-to-day corporate charging decisions:

> [S]ome DOJ prosecutors explained, for example, that the potential harm that prosecution and conviction of health care companies can have on innocent third parties may be a key factor in their decision on entering into a DPA or NPA with these kinds of companies. Federal law provides for health care companies convicted of certain crimes to be debarred from—or no longer eligible to participate in—federal health care programs. Prosecutors in one office said that they chose to enter into DPAs and an NPA simultaneously with five orthopedic device companies that provided kickbacks to physicians because, combined, these companies comprised the vast majority of the market for hip and knee replacements; therefore, conviction and debarment of these companies would have severely limited doctor and patient access to replacement hips and knees.

Lanny Breuer also made this a central theme in his ... defense of the DOJ's deferred prosecution practices:

> I personally feel that it's my duty to consider whether individual employees with no responsibility for, or knowledge of, misconduct committed by others in the same company are going to lose their livelihood if we indict the corporation. In large multi-national companies, the jobs of tens of thousands of employees can be at stake. And, in some cases, the health of an industry or the markets are a real factor. Those are the kinds of considerations in white collar crime cases that literally keep me up at night, and which must play a role in responsible enforcement.[211]

But the primacy accorded collateral consequences in actual corporate charging decisions cannot be explained by any principled application of the traditional purposes of punishment. (In this respect, it is no accident that the Charging Policy frequently calls on prosecutors to exercise "pragmatism" in administering the criminal sanction). What is so interesting about prosecutors' day-to-day preoccupation with this factor is that only in the corporate context does it have so much sway. Collateral consequences are not even mentioned in the charging policies applicable to individuals. In my concededly anecdotal experience, they are almost entirely absent from charging consideration in cases involving actual human beings. Concerns, for example, about what a conviction will mean for a defendant's family or future ability to make a living enter into the picture only at sentencing, if at all. I venture to guess that even arguments that an individual defendant's conviction will lead to the failure of a family business, thus hurting innocent employees, would not persuade most prosecutors to give a clearly guilty individual a deferred prosecution agreement rather than to force a plea.

Given this reality, one has to be concerned about the double standard being liberally applied at the DOJ. As one commentator put it in explaining DOJ's apparent approach:

> [The company] can commit any crime [it] wish[es], from bribery, to corruption, to fraud. Just help us put the individual[] executives in jail, and we w[i]ll let [the company] off the hook. No conviction. No record of criminal wrongdoing. So, a double standard is being set—if not by law, then by prosecutorial discretion. On the one hand, if you are a living, breathing, human being who commits a crime, you will be prosecuted, convicted and sent to prison. On the other, if you [are] a large corporation, you will be deemed too big to convict and granted a deferred or non-prosecution agreement.

In response, many—including high-ranking prosecutors—argue that the collateral fallout from these cases is usually so great that a double standard is warranted and that corporate prosecutions should only be brought when the entity is "so sick—its culture is so sick—that it's going to re-offend, that it has to be put down and that we have to suffer the collateral consequence of the loss of all those jobs." This has momentary appeal, but closer examination reveals how utterly wrongheaded this position is.

First, an indictment does not, in fact, necessarily (or even usually) kill a company. Randall Eliason and others argue that "fears from the Andersen case are overblown. After all, it was not typical for companies to go out of business when convicted (back in the days when we used to convict companies). Exxon, Tyson Foods, General Electric, Genentech—these and scores of other corporations have been convicted of crimes and are still going strong." Indeed, as the Corporate Crime Reporter noted:

> A few years ago, we ran a list of the Top 100 Corporate Criminals of the 1990s. These were all major corporations that had been convicted of serious crimes. And few if any of them were driven out of business because they were convicted of a crime .... We get phone calls and e-mails regularly asking if we are going to update The Top 100 Corporate Criminals list. Our answer—we're not sure there will be enough convicted corporations to get to 100 in this decade [due to the frequency of deferred prosecution agreements].

Second, the drastic consequences that may flow from corporate accountability for wrongdoing are not restricted to convictions alone. Thus, as Professor Sara Sun Beale points out, debarment and de-licensing may eventuate from civil judgments as well.[218] Indeed, while mandatory statutory debarment will flow from a conviction, federal discretionary suspension or debarment may also flow from a DPA or NPA.

Third, if the magnitude of the collateral consequences are relevant, so too should be the degree of harm uniquely possible in cases of corporate wrongdoing. Corporations are "enormously powerful actors whose conduct often causes very significant harm both to individuals and to society as a whole." The Charging Policy's first criterion requires consideration of "the nature and seriousness of the offense, including the risk of harm to the public." Yet, judging from the actual application of this Policy, this factor is not treated on a par with collateral consequences in assessing how cases ought to be resolved.

Finally, and most fundamentally, the primacy of collateral consequences in the charging calculus puts the cart firmly before the horse and renders criminal enforcement random and unprincipled. The fact that various regulators—state and federal—have decided that certain consequences ought to flow from a criminal sanction ought not to have the effect of making that sanction, in practical effect, unavailable. Presumably, for example, government contracting authorities have determined that the government interest is not served by having a company that defrauded a federal agency continue to do business with that agency. Neither that entirely legitimate determination, nor a principled application of the criminal sanction, support prosecutors' decisions to forego charges for fear of these warranted consequences. A decision not to charge the company in these circumstances simply means that the company will experience a windfall due to its fortuitous market positioning and that the public interest in excluding fraudsters from doing public business will be compromised.

Prosecutors will argue that they are dealing with the cards they were dealt, and that they simply cannot be responsible, for example, for a life-saving drug being excluded from Medicaid coverage because of their charging decision or for putting 28,000 innocent people out of a job. One certainly has to sympathize with this dilemma, but the solution is not to make the happenstance of whether an entity is too big or too important to be debarred or de-licensed drive the criminal justice train. The answer, rather, is to address the real causal force here— the laws and regulations that force these false choices on prosecutors. The priority ought to be making regulators adjust the policies driving the collateral consequences to provide for consideration of equitable factors. Those responsible for making the choices controlling the collateral consequences ought also to be responsible for effects of those choices, be it excluding from federal reimbursement programs needed drugs produced only by a convicted pharmaceutical company or forcing the implosion of a company because of isolated misconduct in one of its offices.

Notes

1. Professors Jennifer Arlen and Marcel Kahan note how the use of DPAs to impose mandates—such as adopting compliance programs, internal reporting structures, modification of business practice and the like—fundamentally alters the usual assumptions underlying corporate criminal law in two ways:

> First, they impose policing duties ex post on select firms with detected wrongdoing, rather than ex ante on all firms. Indeed, not only are the mandated duties imposed after a substantive violation occurs, but the content of the mandates is often *determined* only at that time. Thus, a firm does not know beforehand what additional duties it could become subject to should it commit a substantive violation. Second, liability for violating PDA mandates is *not* harm contingent. That is, a mere violation of the firm's ex post policing mandate, without the commission of a further substantive violation, exposes the firm to liability. In combination, these two features of PDA mandates transform prosecutors into firm-specific quasi regulators. Prosecutors can impose specific duties on a subset of firms with alleged wrongdoing, and they enforce compliance with these duties through sanctions for a mere failure to comply with the duties, even if no substantive crime occurs.

Jennifer Arlen & Marcel Kahan, *Corporate Governance Regulation through Nonprosecution*, 84 U. Chi. L. Rev. 323, 326-27 (2017). Professors Arlen and Kahan argue that the mandates built into PDAs are not inevitably efficient components of a criminal liability regime. They conclude that:

> Federal authorities can best deter crime by employees of publicly held firms by inducing firms to intervene, to detect and report wrongdoing, and to cooperate to bring the individuals responsible to justice (corporate policing). [T]his goal is generally best achieved by imposing monetary sanctions for breach of generally applicable ex ante policing duties, as occurs in the traditional corporate criminal liability regime. Such duties can be enforced either by enhanced sanctions on firms that breached their policing duties and committed a substantive wrong (harm-contingent sanctions) or by sanctions on any firm that breaches these duties even if no substantive wrong occurred (non-harm-contingent sanctions).
>
> By contrast, [pre-trial diversion agreements (PDA)] mandates, which are imposed ex post on select firms with detected wrongdoing, are neither needed nor desirable, except in one particular situation: when a firm's senior managers benefit personally from deficient policing even though the firm would be better off with optimal policing. These firms are plagued by what we call "policing agency costs." Because senior managers obtain personal benefits from deficient policing, the threat of sanctions imposed *on the firm* for deficient policing may not be sufficient to induce them to ensure the firm undertakes effective policing.
>
> ... PDA mandates are a potentially effective solution to this problem. Properly designed PDA mandates can ameliorate policing agency costs by making it more difficult or more costly for senior managers to have the company undertake deficient policing. PDAs may be superior to regulation for imposing such measures because regulators cannot identify firms with severe policing agency costs ex ante. By contrast, prosecutors intervening ex post can often both identify firms with policing agency costs and employ information gained in the investigation to remedy the problem as a by-product of their criminal investigation.

Id. at 328-29.

2. The reading mentions the fact that corporate misconduct has often been sanctioned both by DOJ and by various federal agencies, notably the SEC, and questions whether such duplicative fines are "overkill." It also asks whether the threat of criminal sanctions is

inappropriately used to secure civil resolutions. Consider the following DOJ policy, issued in May 2018:

> In parallel and/or joint corporate investigations and proceedings involving multiple Department components and/or other federal, state, or local enforcement authorities, Department attorneys should remain mindful of their ethical obligation not to use criminal enforcement authority unfairly to extract, or to attempt to extract, additional civil or administrative monetary payments.
>
> In addition, in resolving a case with a company that multiple Department components are investigating for the same misconduct, Department attorneys should coordinate with one another to avoid the unnecessary imposition of duplicative fines, penalties, and/or forfeiture against the company. Specifically, Department attorneys from each component should consider the amount and apportionment of fines, penalties, and/or forfeiture paid to the other components that are or will be resolving with the company for the same misconduct, with the goal of achieving an equitable result.
>
> The Department should also endeavor, as appropriate, to coordinate with and consider the amount of fines, penalties, and/or forfeiture paid to other federal, state, local, or foreign enforcement authorities that are seeking to resolve a case with a company for the same misconduct.
>
> The Department should consider all relevant factors in determining whether coordination and apportionment between Department components and with other enforcement authorities allows the interests of justice to be fully vindicated. Relevant factors may include, for instance, the egregiousness of a company's misconduct; statutory mandates regarding penalties, fines, and/or forfeitures; the risk of unwarranted delay in achieving a final resolution; and the adequacy and timeliness of a company's disclosures and its cooperation with the Department, separate from any such disclosures and cooperation with other relevant enforcement authorities. ...

U.S.A.M. § 1-12.100.

3. Corporate deferred prosecution agreements are subject to judicial review only in limited circumstances. With respect to DPAs (not NPAs), the Speedy Trial Act permits an exclusion from the speedy trial calculation of "[a]ny period of delay during which prosecution is deferred by the attorney for the Government pursuant to a written agreement with the defendant, with the approval of the court, for the purpose of allowing the defendant to demonstrate his good conduct." 28 U.S.C. § 3161(h)(2). All agree that district court judges have the power to adjudicate speedy trial act issues with respect to DPAs, but there was uncertainty regarding whether district courts have the power to do more than that—for example, to reject a DPA or to supervise its implementation. Recently, two district court judges who asserted such authority were reversed on appeal.

In *United States v. HSBC Bank*, 2013 WL 3306161 (E.D.N.Y. July 1, 2013) (unpublished), Judge Gleeson was presented with a deferred prosecution agreement entered into in connection with charges that HSBC willfully failed to maintain an effective anti-money laundering program and facilitated financial transactions on behalf of sanctioned entities. HSBC and the government entered into a DPA that asked the court to hold the case in abeyance for five years while HSBC attempted to comply with the terms of the agreement and to exclude that time from the speedy trial clock. Judge Gleeson ruled that "[t]his Court has authority to approve or reject the DPA pursuant to its supervisory power." *Id.* at *4. At He noted that by filing criminal charges, "the contracting parties have chosen to implicate the Court in their resolution of this matter. There is nothing wrong with that, but a pending federal criminal case is not window dressing. Nor is the Court, to borrow a famous phrase, a potted plant. By placing a criminal matter on the docket of a federal court, the parties have subjected their DPA to the legitimate exercise of that court's authority." *Id.* at *5. Ultimately, however, Judge Gleeson approved the DPA. The Second Circuit, in an appeal of a related matter, held that "the district court ha[d] no freestanding supervisory power to monitor the implementation of [the] DPA," reasoning:

By *sua sponte* invoking its supervisory power at the outset of this case to oversee the government's entry into and implementation of the DPA, the district court impermissibly encroached on the Executive's constitutional mandate to "take Care that the Laws be faithfully executed." U.S. Const. art. II, §3. In the absence of evidence to the contrary, the Department of Justice is entitled to a presumption of regularity—that is, a presumption that it is lawfully discharging its duties. Though that presumption can of course be rebutted in such a way that warrants judicial intervention, it cannot be preemptively discarded based on the mere theoretical possibility of misconduct. Absent unusual circumstances not present here, a district court's role vis-à-vis a DPA is limited to arraigning the defendant, granting a speedy trial waiver if the DPA does not represent an improper attempt to circumvent the speedy trial clock, and adjudicating motions or disputes as they arise.

United States v. HSBC Bank USA, N.A., 863 F.3d 125, 129, 137 (2d Cir. 2017).

In *United States v. Fokker Servs., B.V.*, 79 F.Supp.3d 160 (D.D.C. 2015), Judge Leon went a step further by refusing to approve a speedy trial exemption. Fokker Services, a Dutch aerospace services provider, was charged with violating export laws from 2005 until 2010 by engaging in transactions with sanctioned countries including Iran, Burma, and Sudan. Fokker Services and the U.S. government entered into a DPA pursuant to which Fokker Services accepted responsibility for its conduct and agreed to pay $10,500,000. It also agreed to cooperate with the government, to implement a new compliance program, and to comply with export laws going forward. The agreement further provided that if the company were to fulfill these conditions over the course of eighteen months, the government would dismiss the charges.

Judge Leon was asked by the government and Fokker to approve the speedy trial exemption but he declined to do so. Relying on *HSBC*, Judge Leon "agreed with [Judge Gleeson's] well-reasoned conclusion that a District Court has the authority 'to approve or reject the DPA pursuant to its supervisory power.'" *Id.* at 165. "One of the purposes of the Court's supervisory powers," Judge Leon wrote, "is to protect the integrity of the judicial process." *Id.* While Judge Leon recognized the government's discretion to choose not to prosecute a case, he emphasized that the government *chose* to charge Fokker, and asked the court to lend its "judicial imprimatur" to the deferred-prosecution agreement. *Id.* He therefore found that "it is this Court's duty to consider carefully whether that approval should be given." *Id.*

Judge Leon concluded that the agreement presented in *Fokker* was not an appropriate exercise of prosecutorial discretion because the agreement was "grossly disproportionate to the gravity of Fokker Services' conduct." *Id.* at 167. He reasoned that "the integrity of the judicial proceedings would be compromised by giving the Court's stamp of approval to either overly-lenient prosecutorial action, or overly-zealous prosecutorial conduct." *Id.* at 165. Fokker Services had allegedly violated export laws for five years and earned more revenue than it agreed to pay in fines. Judge Leon objected to the short compliance period, the low fine, the lack of an independent compliance monitor, and the fact that no criminal charges were brought against individual company employees.

On appeal, the D.C. Circuit issued writ of mandamus and vacated the district court's order. *See* United States v. Fokker Servs., B.V., 818 F.3d 733 (D.C. Cir. 2016). It held that:

We vacate the district court's denial of the joint motion to exclude time under the Speedy Trial Act. We hold that the Act confers no authority in a court to withhold exclusion of time pursuant to a DPA based on concerns that the government should bring different charges or should charge different defendants. Congress, in providing for courts to approve the exclusion of time pursuant to a DPA, acted against the backdrop of long-settled understandings about the independence of the Executive with regard to charging decisions. Nothing in the statute's terms or structure suggests any intention to subvert those constitutionally rooted principles so as to enable the Judiciary to second-guess the Executive's exercise of discretion over the initiation and dismissal of criminal charges.

Id. at 738. The D.C. Circuit also noted that judicial supervisory power was at its most limited when reviewing prosecutorial charging choices. It concluded that, as a result, "'the presumption of regularity' applies to prosecutorial decisions and, in the absence of clear evidence to the contrary, courts presume that [prosecutors] have properly discharged their official duties.'" *Id.* at 741 (quoting United States v. Armstrong, 517 U.S. 456, 464 (1995)).

4. Given that the DP agreements generally include both a stipulation of guilt and a non-contradiction provision, what implications does the conclusion of a DP have for the organization's ability to withstand follow-on suits by private or public actors? For example, in the international sphere, DPs have been used to resolve a great many cases arising under the Foreign Corrupt Practices Act (FCPA). But double jeopardy (or, in international discourse, *ne bis in idem*, roughly "not twice in the same [thing]") principles often do not bar other countries with jurisdiction from bringing prosecutions for the self-same conduct. Thus, "under a multinational framework, with stipulations made known to foreign prosecutors, the company is a sitting duck as a different country with its own equivalent of the FCPA lines up. It is thus even worse for [multinational corporations (MNCs)] than double jeopardy or *ne bis in idem*, or even carbon copy prosecutions, because by admitting their guilt in one jurisdiction, these MNCs cannot retry that guilt in a new trial. They are double, triple and quadruple penalized for the same offense." Thomas J. Bussen, *Midnight in the Garden of* Ne Bis In Idem: *The New Urgency for an International Enforcement Mechanism,* 23 Cardozo J. Int'l & Comp. L. 485, 489 (2015).

5. As Professor Brandon L. Garrett has documented, "[f]oreign firms, and their employees, are increasingly convicted of a range of crimes including antitrust violations, environmental crimes, Foreign Corrupt Practices Act ("FCPA") violations, tax fraud, wire fraud, and bank fraud." Brandon L. Garrett, *Globalized Corporate Prosecutions,* 97 Va. L. Rev. 1775, 1777 (2011). He notes that foreign corporations face many of the same issues as U.S. companies, but that they generally are treated more harshly than domestic concerns, at least as measured by the availability of DPs.

> Foreign firms seek leniency to avoid potentially catastrophic consequences of a conviction at the hands of U.S. prosecutors. They do not face such consequences at home. Corporate criminal liability is a form of American Exceptionalism. Most countries in Europe and the world lack corporate criminal liability generally and only recently have enacted a handful of specific corporate crime statutes. Foreign countries impose civil regulatory fines and individuals may be prosecuted, but firms rarely face prosecution. Corporations have some incentive to cooperate with local regulators, but cooperating with U.S. prosecutors is imperative. Not only is there broad respondeat superior liability for corporations in the United States for criminal acts of employees, but federal criminal law is also broader and far more punitive than that in other countries. Federal prosecutors possess extraordinarily wide discretion as compared to their counterparts around the globe. The consequences of a criminal indictment or a conviction in the United States can sometimes be significant, though certainly not always. Firms may be debarred by regulators or from government contracting, they may face high fines, and they can suffer harm to their reputations. As a result, foreign firms often negotiate settlements when misconduct is self-reported or exposed by competitors or employees. …

> … [F]oreign firms, unlike domestic firms, often do not receive a deferred prosecution. The deferred prosecution approach, as it turns out, is dominant in certain types of prosecutions but not in others. One might expect that different types of corporate crime would be handled differently, and as it turns out, this affects foreign firms. Foreign firms typically plead guilty and receive a conviction.

Id. at 1777-79.

6. In *United States v. Saena Tech Corp.*, 140 F.Supp.3d 11 (D.D.C. 2015), Judge Sullivan also engaged in a lengthy review of the genesis of the deferred prosecution mechanism (in individual prosecutions) and concluded with the following exhortation to the DOJ:

> The Court respectfully requests the Department of Justice to consider expanding the use of deferred-prosecution agreements and other similar tools to use in appropriate circumstances when an individual who might not be a banker or business owner nonetheless shows all of the hallmarks of significant rehabilitation potential. The harm to society of refusing such individuals the chance to demonstrate their true character and avoid the catastrophic consequences of felony convictions is, in this Court's view, greater than the harm the government seeks to avoid by providing corporations a path to avoid criminal convictions. If the Department of Justice is sincere in its expressed desire to reduce over-incarceration and bolster rehabilitation, it will increase the use of deferred-prosecution agreements for individuals as well as increase the use of other available resources as discussed in this Opinion.

Id. at 46.

F. CORPORATE INTERNAL INVESTIGATIONS

As we shall see in Chapter 17, which concerns the attorney-client privilege and the work product doctrine in a corporate setting, the Supreme Court first addressed the subject of corporate internal investigations in *Upjohn Co. v. United States*.[159] In *Upjohn*, the Court permitted the corporation to resist government efforts to secure the work product of its corporate counsel generated in the course of counsel's investigation into questionable payments (i.e., bribes) that the company had made to foreign government officials. We will leave a detailed examination of the Court's holding on the issues of the scope of the attorney-client privilege and work product doctrine in this context to Chapter 17 and concentrate here instead on the activity sought to be protected—the corporate internal investigation.

Since *Upjohn* was decided, there has been an explosion in the incidence of corporate internal investigations and thus some discussion of this substantial part of white-collar practice deserves mention in this chapter. As is discussed in the DOJ's charging guidelines, in some instances defense counsel will be faced with the difficult decision whether sharing the facts necessary to earn cooperation credit will result in a waiver of the privilege protections that shield the results of (and documentation underlying) such investigations. And, as we shall learn, federal law does not recognize a "selective" waiver; that is, if a corporation should elect to turn over its attorney-client privileged material or corporate counsel's work product to the government in an effort to seek credit for full "cooperation" (and thus a declination), it may well have to turn over the same, often inculpatory, information to private litigants who seek to impose civil liability on the company. Why is this important?

Julie R. O'Sullivan, *The Last Straw: The Department of Justice's Privilege Waiver Policy and the Death of Adversarial Justice in Criminal Investigations of Corporations*
57 DePaul L. Rev. 329 (2008)

It is exceedingly difficult to conceive of the criminal process that applies to corporations today as truly "adversarial." In reality, a variety of circumstances make it nearly impossible for public companies, especially those in regulated industries or those who do significant business with the government, to mount any meaningful resistance to a criminal investigation. ...

---

[159] 449 U.S. 383 (1981).

To begin, under the federal code and regulations, the crimes that can be charged in white-collar cases are virtually limitless and shockingly malleable. The breadth and flexibility of the criminal code allows prosecutors to charge the corporation for something in almost any case in which any arguable skulduggery is uncovered. Further, the exposure of corporations to criminal sanction is even more extensive than it is for individuals, because corporations, unlike many individuals, are subject to a vast array of federal regulations. ... Corporations are more vulnerable than individuals for another reason. ... The extremely broad, judicially created standards for corporate criminal liability mean that virtually anything that a corporate agent does can be imputed to the corporation and thus result in the organization's criminal conviction. This *respondeat superior* standard has been extended to apply in situations where no one actor's conduct and *mens rea* can be imputed to the corporation. Indeed, corporations can be criminally liable even when no one agent did anything illegal under the "collective knowledge" and "flagrant organizational indifference" theories, which augment the already over-broad *respondeat superior* standards.

Even were a corporation to conclude that it has a shot at defending itself against a particular charge or theory of liability, one must recognize that its calculus regarding whether to resist a government investigation is hugely affected by the number, range, and seriousness of the sanctions available should it fail in that effort. The array of penalties to which convicted corporations may be subject is extensive and onerous. Although not every conviction is in essence a corporate death sentence—as was the case in the obstruction prosecution of Arthur Andersen LLP—the company will certainly take a pronounced pounding in a variety of ways, [including]: (1) the restitution, fine, and corporate probation obligations under the Federal Sentencing Guidelines applicable to organizations; (2) potential debarment from government contracting; (3) possibly ruinous regulatory or licensing repercussions; (4) loss of employees, customers, and financing; and (5) the application of collateral estoppel to foreclose the entity from resisting the civil damages demands of any number of potential [public and] private plaintiffs.

Corporations, unlike most individuals, will take a hard look at their bottom line and often decide that, whether or not their guilt is contestable, they have no choice but to cooperate fully with the government in hopes of avoiding the financial train wreck of a criminal conviction. This dynamic is reinforced by the incentives recent legislation and developments in corporate law have created for corporate boards—and particularly the increasingly powerful independent directors in the post-Enron era—to protect themselves against civil liability by rolling over whenever prosecutors come calling.

The above dynamic, peculiar to corporate crime cases, is compounded by the general inequality in arms between the government and persons subject to criminal investigation. The government has at its disposal some serious artillery. Subject to constitutional and other legal restraints, it can make arrests, search and seize private property, conduct surveillance in person and by wiretap, and call out all of the human, analytical, and technical resources of investigating agencies. Prosecutors can, by statute, override individuals' right to remain silent and, by statute or contract, enter into cooperation agreements by which testimony is secured by grant of immunity, dismissal of charges, sentencing discounts, or other valuable consideration. The government can force defendants to produce records and witnesses to testify through grand jury subpoenas. If that which is subpoenaed is not forthcoming, the government can ask that the contemnors be jailed until they comply. It can promise "things of value" for witnesses' help, threaten to indict their family members, and, in some circumstances, lie to get what it wants.

By contrast, those under investigation have no Sixth Amendment right to counsel until formal proceedings are launched against them. Even the Fifth Amendment right to counsel created in *Miranda* does not apply outside of the narrow context of custodial interrogations by known government actors. Subjects and targets are not entitled to any sort of pre-indictment discovery; indeed, were they to attempt to find out what the grand jury is doing, they may well face obstruction charges. The law also prohibits them from providing witnesses with any consideration in return for testimony, even for cooperation and truthful stories. Threats or lies by the subjects or targets of investigations, in many circumstances, could lead to criminal sanction. Additionally, there is no legal process in the criminal system through which putative defendants can compel third parties to give them any sort of assistance in identifying the relevant facts or in trying to fend off an indictment.

What does the adversary process provide subjects and targets of criminal investigations to even this imbalance? The sole real counterweight, at the investigative stage at least, is the Fifth Amendment privilege against [compelled] self-incrimination. It is this privilege that gives individuals the right to resist through silence—the right to not cooperate in one's own undoing. The Supreme Court has provided us with many rationales for the privilege against self-incrimination, many of which are grounded in conceptions of human dignity that do not apply comfortably to impersonal entities. The Fifth Amendment value that is critical for [these] purposes, however, is that which deals with the balance of power between the hunter and the hunted. As the Supreme Court explained, in part, in *Murphy v. Waterfront Commission*, the privilege reflects several values:

> [O]ur preference for an accusatorial rather than an inquisitorial system of criminal justice; . . . [and] our sense of fair play which dictates "a fair state-individual balance by requiring the government to leave the individual alone until good cause is shown for disturbing him and by requiring the government in its contest with the individual to shoulder the entire load."

Even this counterweight is denied to corporate subjects or targets of government inquiries. In *Hale v. Henkel*, the Supreme Court held that corporations cannot, through their agents, assert a Fifth Amendment right against [compelled] self-incrimination to resist the production of corporate books and records. Nor can corporate agents claim their own, personal Fifth Amendment right against self-incrimination when they are compelled to produce corporate records in their capacity as corporate agents.

[How do] ... corporate defense counsel operate in an environment that is heavily weighted in favor of the government[?] Two points are worth emphasis at the outset. First, because of the above-described consequences of a criminal charge, white-collar practitioners will do everything in their power to secure a disposition short of criminal indictment and, ideally, a declination from the DOJ. Most white-collar cases are viewed as won or lost in this pre-indictment phase. Second, during this phase, there are at least four challenges facing defense counsel: (1) divining what the government is investigating without the benefit of formal discovery or other means of compelling the production of most types of information; (2) tracing or, with luck, keeping a step ahead of the government in learning the facts; (3) limiting, consistent with ethical and legal constraints, government access to incriminating evidence; and (4) using the facts, law, and equitable arguments to persuade the government to decline prosecution. As the above outline reveals, information control is the central function of the defense enterprise.

Without a Fifth Amendment right, how can this central function be achieved? [T]he means that corporate counsel use to pursue this "fundamental *modus operandi* constituting [the] basic defense plan" is to shield, to the extent possible, their work in investigating and documenting corporate wrongdoing by invoking the attorney-client privilege and work-product doctrine.

* * *

As explored earlier, at one time, many DOJ prosecutors frequently asked organizations to waive the protections of the attorney-client privilege and the work product doctrine to demonstrate their "cooperation." The Filip policy now says that prosecutors cannot consider such waivers in assessing cooperation; all that is required is that the entity under investigation share all the operative facts. As a practical matter, however, it may well be difficult to disclose all the facts without raising the possibility of a waiver. Given this reality, the lack of a "selective" waiver doctrine, and the potentially onerous financial consequences, why do many public companies nonetheless regularly continue to launch internal corporate investigations at the first sign of trouble? What does an internal corporate investigation look like? The following excerpt attempts to answer these questions.

Julie R. O'Sullivan, *Does DOJ's Privilege Waiver Policy Threaten the Rationales Underlying the Attorney-Client Privilege and the Work Product Doctrine? A Preliminary "No"*
45 Am. Crim. L. Rev. 1237 (2008)

... At the most general level, companies [continue to commission corporate internal investigations because they] need to know the facts in order to defend themselves. As Nancy Kestenbaum summarizes:

> Companies ... reap numerous affirmative benefits by conducting their own investigations. Even if the government is not investigating a company, a company that conducts an internal investigation on its own gains the advantage of knowing what the facts are, and, if there is no legal requirement that such investigation be disclosed, can then take appropriate internal action and then decide whether or not to bring such results to the government's attention. Even where the government is aware of the issues, sometimes a company can persuade the government to forbear from investigating to permit the company to investigate the issues first. In those instances, occasionally the company can persuade the government not to investigate at all or to narrow the issues under investigation. Even if the government does investigate, a company that has conducted its own investigation is armed with the facts, can make informed decisions, can take appropriate remedial action and can better craft defenses—all of which will leave the company better-positioned to deal with the government, whether or not the government expressly gives the company cooperation credit for conducting its own investigation.[160]

Beyond these general considerations, a variety of external circumstances make internal investigations wise (or imperative), some of which existed at the time *Upjohn* was decided but many of which have developed since that date.

The most obvious reason to conduct an internal investigation into alleged wrongdoing is that such investigations are required, in some instances, by statute, such as the Anti-Kickback Enforcement Act of 1986,[161] the Medicare Fraud Reporting Act,[162] and federal banking regulations.[163] These statutes and other regulations were put in place only after *Upjohn*. For example, after *Upjohn*, industry regulators and associations, such as the New York Stock Exchange, the American Stock Exchange, and the National Association of Securities Dealers, put into place rules that "require ongoing investigation and/or disclosure in situations involving suspicious circumstances or allegations of wrongdoing...."[164]

Another obvious reason to investigate is to ensure that whatever wrongdoing has gone on has ceased. Especially where DOJ, regulators, or others have raised questions about the allegations, letting the conduct continue is an invitation for harsh sanctions. Even where the allegations come from within the organization—in the form of anonymous reports or questions from internal auditors or others—the corporation is risking a great deal it if

---

[160] [Author's footnote 188:] [Nancy Kestenbaum & Jason P. Criss, *Credit Where Credit is Due? The Role of Internal Investigations in the Outcome of Government Investigations*, 1564 PLI/Corp. 121, 151-52 (2006)].

[161] [Author's footnote 189:] 41 U.S.C. § 57.

[162] [Author's footnote 190:] 42 U.S.C. § 1320-a7(b)(3).

[163] [Author's footnote 191:] *See, e.g.,* 12 C.F.R. § 21.11.

[164] [Author's footnote 192:] [Sara Helene Duggin, Internal Corporate Investigations: Legal Ethics, Professionalism and the Employee Interview, 2003 Colum. Bus. L. Rev. 859, 885-86 (2003)].

determines to play ostrich, betting on its ability to contain the allegations. [Aaron R.] Marcu suggests that the

> very human and understandable reluctance to look for trouble ... is likely to be regarded by prosecutors in today's overly crime-conscious environment as indifference to or even tacit approval of wrongdoing. With scandals like Enron and WorldCom still fresh in the public memory and news stories about companies under investigation breaking every day, corporate executives do not have the luxury of hoping it goes away when the hint of criminality appears.[165]

Finally, even if the conduct itself has ceased, the organization must recognize that, unless it takes prompt remedial action, the wrongdoing may morph into other legal problems. For example, in *Upjohn*, the IRS was investigating in part to determine whether Upjohn improperly treated the "questionable payments" (i.e., bribes) as deductible business expenses. Assuming that the criminal activity is reflected in the bottom line, that bottom line may need to be restated or future accounting based on the earlier numbers may itself be misleading, and criminally actionable.

Business or regulatory considerations are often cited as critical to decisions to investigate allegations of wrongdoing. Especially today, in light of enforcement emphasis on combating corporate depredations and general public unease given global financial turmoil, investigations may be necessary to reassure various corporate stakeholders—including investors, employees, clients or customers, auditors, regulators and the like. A somewhat related—and very important—advantage of investigation is that it permits companies to meet whatever reporting requirements constrain them under state or federal law. For example, the Upjohn investigation was prompted not only by a desire to take advantage of a SEC voluntary disclosure policy that would have mitigated any criminal or civil sanctions from the wrongdoing, but also to meet Upjohn's obligations under SEC regulations controlling the disclosure requirements for publicly-traded companies.

Among the most compelling reasons to initiate internal investigations are those arising from increased federal interest in pursuing corporations civilly and criminally, the sentencing regime for organizations created by the U.S. Sentencing Commission, and the proliferation of compliance programs in part responsive to these circumstances. ... One manifestation of the organizational guidelines' underlying "carrot and stick" philosophy—which has as its object galvanizing organizational efforts to *prevent* organizational wrongdoing—is an important sentencing credit that organizations can claim for having in place an "effective program to prevent and detect violations of law." This "carrot" is critical in many corporate crime cases because of the potentially harsh restitution, fine, and corporate probation requirements that constitute the guidelines' "stick."

The guidelines have been commonly credited with creating a boom in organizational compliance efforts. As a consequence, a consulting industry has been created and significant organizational attention—in a wide variety of industries and businesses—has been devoted to determining how best to structure and maintain effective compliance programs. The organizational guidelines also undoubtedly focused prosecutorial and regulatory attention on the subject. The guidelines provided governmental actors with a template upon which to build when formulating their own policies regarding what constitutes an "effective program" for purposes of making decisions regarding the appropriate imposition of civil and criminal penalties. Finally, the organizational guidelines influenced corporate law, spurring most notably the Delaware Chancery Court, in *In re Caremark*, to authorize judicial scrutiny of directors' duties *vis-à-vis* compliance.

Compliance programs of the sort contemplated by the guidelines require that organizations faced with allegations of wrongdoing conduct some sort of internal investigation,

---

[165] [Author's footnote 193:] [Aaron R. Marcu, *Investigating Indications of Wrongdoing: Necessary and Proper in the Post-Enron Era*, 1564 PLI/Corp. 199, 202 (2006)]; *see also* Kestenbaum & Criss, *supra* note [160], at 151 (same).

stop the conduct, and remedy its effects. Other regulators such as the SEC and the New York Stock Exchange have, building on the guidelines model, issued policies stating that regulatory action will turn in part on the quality of companies' investigations of alleged malfeasance. What does all this mean? Because compliance programs generally require the initiation of an internal investigation when allegations of wrongdoing surface, such investigations are embedded in many corporations' standard operating procedures; the question is not whether to investigate, but what the scope of the investigation should be and who ought to conduct it. If a company deviates from its own compliance program and foregoes an investigation in such a situation, that itself is a huge red flag that can invite investigation.

Another reason for conducting an investigation is that such a practice generally *works* if the object is to avoid criminal sanction and minimize regulatory exposure. One informal study of available data on the effect of the conduct of an internal investigation on the government concluded:

> [T]he evidence shows a clear correlation between a specific reference by DOJ or the SEC to a company's internal investigation and a more favorable conclusion to a government investigation for the company. … [Further, t]here are presumably numerous cases—and we are aware of many from our own practice—in which, without any public mention, the government has given a company substantial credit for conducting an internal investigation and the investigation played a significant role in the government's willingness not to charge the company or to settle a case on more favorable terms.[166]

Finally, and unavoidably, there are the personal and professional imperatives faced by high-ranking individuals within the corporation. In reaction to the potential "risks posed by the criminalization of business conduct, and largely spurred by the enactment of the Sarbanes-Oxley Act, public corporations—and their Audit Committees—find themselves increasingly relying on internal investigations as both a way to ferret out potential wrongdoing and *to insulate themselves and their directors and officers from liability*."[167] Indeed, many Board members—particularly the "independent" directors—may conclude that:

> [T]he decision as to whether an internal investigation should be conducted is not really a discretionary one. Under Sarbanes-Oxley, Audit Committees and company management are required to address whistleblower complaints and other indicia of potential wrongdoing or face liability. Similarly, under Delaware and other states' corporate law, a failure to address 'red flags' may be found to constitute a breach of fiduciary duty.[168]

… [In sum, i]n the words of one lawyer: "when evidence of possible employee wrongdoing comes to management's attention, there really is no choice any more" because "[m]anagement's early and aggressive investigation of such a problem is the company's best

---

[166] [Author's footnote 200:] Kestenbaum & Criss, *supra* note [160], at 150-51; *see also* Andrew C. Hruska, *What's Really Going On in Corporate Charging Decisions?*, N.Y.L.J., Nov. 10, 2005, col. 4:

> "[A]n analysis of the Justice Department's corporate charging decisions over the past three years demonstrates that a different dynamic is at work … [I]ncreasingly often, companies that cooperate with government investigators have successfully minimized the damage even from significant criminal conduct by senior managers. In a few cases, the benefits of superlative cooperation have been so substantial as to avoid conviction even when companies initially obstructed government investigators.

[167] [Author's footnote 201:] [Paul D. Sarkozi, Internal Investigations: An Overview of the Nuts and Bolts and Key Considerations in Conducting Effective Investigations, 1564 PLI/Corp. 95, 95 (2006)] (emphasis added).

[168] [Author's footnote 202:] *Id.* at 99.

chance of maximizing control over what otherwise could become an unmanageable situation and minimizing the risk of both criminal exposure and public scandal."[169] ...

The *Upjohn* investigation was cutting-edge at the time; since then, internal corporate investigations have become commonplace, whether required by law or by corporate imperatives. Some investigations are commissioned as a prophylactic matter, but most are triggered by some circumstance that hints at corporate malfeasance, such as questionable stock trading, irregularities discovered during audits, anonymous tips, customer complaints, regulatory inspections, and, of course, the service of civil complaints or criminal grand jury subpoenas. Such circumstances are not always sufficiently serious to require the commitment of time and resources consumed by a lawyer-led investigation. And investigations can in some cases ... render the corporation more vulnerable to civil, if not criminal, liability rather than less. Nevertheless, according to much of the practice-oriented literature, "the internal investigation has become the standard of care whenever credible allegations of significant misconduct are raised in organizational settings."[170]

Some internal corporate investigations will, like Upjohn's, be conducted by in-house counsel. Increasingly, however, large-scale or particularly sensitive investigations are conducted by outside counsel from a law firm expert in such inquiries. A variety of circumstances are identified as relevant to this choice, but two stand out.

First, because it lacks a Fifth Amendment privilege, a corporation can protect the results of its investigation—at least until it chooses how it will act on the report—only by using lawyers who can shield their work under the attorney-client privilege and work product doctrine. Invocation of the attorney-client privilege and work product doctrine obviously must be based on the provision of legal services. "To the extent that an internal corporate investigation is made by management itself, there is no attorney-client privilege, and by the same token, no work-product protection." Thus, the investigation must be pursued for the purpose of securing legal advice (attorney-client) or done in anticipation of litigation (work product). While these rules are clear enough, their application may not be in the case of in-house counsel. In their case, "legal and business considerations may frequently be inextricably intertwined." "[B]ecause of their unique position as both lawyers and employees of the corporation, in-house counsel are often called upon to provide business advice as well as legal counsel. ... [Therefore] communications with in-house counsel have been subjected to stricter and more skeptical scrutiny than similar communications with outside counsel."[171]

Second, at least when the investigation is announced publicly, as it often is,[172] the company is hoping to reassure a number of constituencies beyond criminal prosecutors

---

[169] [Author's footnote 205:] Marcu, *supra* note [165] at 203. Kestenbaum & Criss noted:

> In the current enforcement environment, conducting an internal investigation is clearly the safer response to an indication of wrongful conduct by an employee. Investigating will not only leave the company in the best position to deal with the government, but the evidence is now clear that its also can help the company gain significant benefits from the federal government for having done so.

Supra note [160], at 152.

[170] [Author's footnote 206:] Duggin, *supra* note [164], at 886.

[171] [Author's footnote 211:] H. Lowell Brown, *The Crime–Fraud Exception to the Attorney–Client Privilege in the Context of Corporate Counseling*, 87 Ky. L.J. 1191, 1207-08 (1998–99)].

[172] [Author's footnote 212:] *See, e.g.,* [Marjorie J. Peerce & Peggy M. Cross, *Independent Corporate Investigations*, 14 Bus. Crimes Bull. 1, 6 (2007).]

> A company that retains outside counsel to investigate potential misconduct is likely to have announced the retention and possible scope of the investigation in a press release aimed at reassuring investors and regulators that the company has the situation under control. At the conclusion of the investigation, the company may issue another press release describing counsel's conclusions and outlining actions it plans to take in response.

Id.

regarding the corporation's remediation of the problem. For example, "[o]ne of the company's primary goals in retaining investigatory counsel is to conduct a fair, thorough and complete investigation so it can assure investors, regulators and employees that it has discovered the extent of any problems that exist and has a plan not only to correct them but to prevent their recurrence."[173] As Marjorie Peerce notes,

> Whether the company succeeds in providing these assurances depends in significant part on the degree of confidence these groups have in the outside counsel conducting the investigation. One thing is certain: unless they trust that the investigation was truly an independent one, they are not likely to have faith in the outcome. Such a lack of faith can have devastating consequences for the company: valuable employees distrustful of management may leave, investors may pull their support, and regulators may disregard the results of the internal investigation and decide to conduct their own, disrupting the company and further undermining the investing public's faith in it. And if regulators feel that the investigation was deliberately compromised by the lack of independence, they may decide to investigate the company and its senior management further.[174]

Ensuring the appearance of "true" independence often translates into hiring an outside firm to conduct the internal investigation under the control and instruction of the Board of the company or one of its subcommittees.

If the entity decides to engage an outside law firm to conduct the investigation, outside counsel and corporate representatives—usually the Board or a committee thereof—must decide on the appropriate scope of the proposed investigation and preliminarily, at least, discuss how the results are to be presented to the Board. The lawyers must then begin their work, and quickly. If the government has not yet shown an interest in the subject-matter, counsel will want to get ahead of the curve, so she can advise the company how to mitigate adverse consequences. If the government is on the case, the time pressures are magnified. There may be a rush to the courthouse among potential cooperators; certainly the benefits yielded by cooperation either at the charging phase or at sentencing decline with each passing day.

Internal investigations generally focus on two categories of information: document review (including review of computer records and financial data) and interviews of corporate employees and other agents. Generally, counsel will try to piece together the facts from the documents and then interview witnesses. Because the corporation cannot claim a Fifth Amendment privilege to resist government subpoenas *duces tecum*, and because mere review by a lawyers of pre-existing, unprivileged documents does not confer upon those documents attorney-client-privileged or work product status, documentary proof generally cannot be shielded from disclosure (although lawyers may claim as protected work product their own choice, categorization, or organization of the key documents).

Witness interviews present a variety of challenges, many of which flow from the fact that counsel's ethical duties are owed to the entity itself, not to any of its constituencies—whether those constituencies are the Board, shareholders, or members of management.[175] "That notwithstanding, legal constructs are difficult to reach on the phone, and they are highly unreliable about appearing at meetings. Thus, a lawyer representing a corporation must of necessity communicate with—and receive direction from—the client through its officers, directors, and employees."[176] Counsel may find themselves in the awkward position of

---

[173] [Author's footnote 213:] *Id.*

[174] [Author's footnote 214:] *Id.*

[175] [Author's footnote 216:] *See, e.g.,* Model Rules of Prof'l Conduct R. 1.13 (2004).

[176] [Author's footnote 217:] [William W. Horton, *A Transactional Lawyer's Perspective on the Attorney-Client Privilege: A Jeremiad for* Upjohn, 61 Bus. Law. 95, 97 (Nov. 2005)].

interrogating the very management with whom they are coordinating their investigation or the board members who engaged them on behalf of the entity.

Of great (if unquantifiable) concern to those conducting internal investigations is the question of the effect of the internal investigation—and *how it is conducted*—on employees' morale and their trust in and loyalty to the entity. On the one hand, a number of factors (including the DOJ's cooperation policy) may dictate that corporate counsel advise the entity to play hard-ball with employees (whose culpability, of course, is not proven at this point) by firing those who refuse to cooperate with them or the government. On the other hand, the corporation and its lawyers must be very careful how they treat employees or the fall-out in terms of intangibles like moral, trust, and loyalty [may be severe]; perceived heavy-handedness or "unfairness" may convince some valued employees to jump ship or move culpable employees to run to cooperate with the government. The entity's interest, then, lies in maximizing the information flow while minimizing the extent to which counsel, in pumping the well, alienate those from whom they are seeking evidence. Finally, counsel face the inevitable challenge of inducing employees to trust them enough to talk to them fully and frankly.

The results of witness interviews *are* protected under federal law, which is critical in that these interviews are "the heart of the internal investigation," through which documentary "words and numbers come to life through the stories related by real people."[177] First, at least under *Upjohn*, the communications made by corporate employees (of any rank) to counsel in furtherance of their employer's request for legal advice are protected from compelled disclosure by the attorney-client privilege. Second, to the extent that counsel memorializes employee interviews in a debriefing memorandum, that memo is protected attorney work product.

Counsel will also likely produce, during the course of an internal investigation, a variety of what can best be characterized as analytical or summary work product. One of the first tasks facing counsel will be to get a sense of the organizational hierarchy (perhaps reflected in a chart to memorialize counsel's findings or witness interview schedule) and to prepare a chronology of the relevant events (based on documents and witness interviews and probably annotated with references to the same). Counsel may catalog (perhaps in a computer program) "key" documents and other smoking guns. Certainly, counsel will prepare agendas for meetings, questions for various witnesses, "to do" lists of all sorts, and summary documentation regarding what has been learned and what remains to be uncovered. Legal memos regarding possibly applicable law will be commissioned. Finally, counsel will likely write debriefing memos to memorialize, and analyze, all interactions with government investigators. All this, if kept confidential, is protected work product.

At the conclusion of the investigation, a report in some form is generally rendered to the corporate client, whether in an oral presentation or a written summary of some sort. The report will summarize at greater or lesser length what counsel discovered after reviewing the documents and interviewing the relevant corporate agents. Note that these reports may make reference to the content of interviews with employees and may contain lawyers' assessments of credibility and the like, although they are unlikely to contain the lawyers' actual debriefing memos. The report may include some material reflecting counsel's analytical work product (*e.g.*, charts, identification of "key" documents, a form of chronology). Counsel's report will also generally contain prospective advice, such as recommended steps the corporation might take to remediate any wrongdoing or to prevent future missteps. If, as is often the case, the corporation fears imminent regulatory or prosecutorial scrutiny of the relevant events, the report may suggest a course of action to reduce the corporation's exposure. Where a government investigation has not yet been launched, counsel will have to deal with the agonizing issue of whether the corporation should self-report;[178] where an investigation has

---

[177] [Author's footnote 218:] Duggin, *supra* note [164], at 864.

[178] [Ed.:] *See, e.g.*, F. Joseph Warin, et al., To Disclose or Not to Disclose: Analyzing the Consequences of Voluntary Self-Disclosure for Financial Institutions, *available at* https://wp.nyu.edu/compliance_enforcement/2018/.

been launched, the corporation will need to quickly decide whether to cooperate with relevant authorities. Again, should a prosecutor seek to subpoena any written reports or records of the investigation, the corporation could not resist on Fifth Amendment grounds. These reports are, however, presumptively protected from disclosure as communications under the attorney-client privilege and as attorney work product.

The protected nature of such reports is critical because, absent such protection, the internal investigative report may well provide prosecutors and regulators with a roadmap to liability. Counsel will have done the government's document and computer review for it—often a huge task—and identified the important needles in the haystack. They will have gathered the statements of the relevant witnesses, at least some of whom may choose not to speak to government agents at all. With these materials, the government also will have the expert assessment of experienced criminal counsel regarding the corporation's likely exposure under federal law. ...

Notes

1. Counsel for the company will be looking for any opportunity to cooperate with the government, including providing evidence against former or existing officers or employees of the company. What does this mean for the individuals who are the subjects or targets of the investigation? We will consider a number of relevant issues in coming chapters, including representation and privilege issues. It is worth noting here, however, that commentators and lawyers are increasingly raising the alarm about whether the above-described dynamic dictates that individuals will be treated unfairly. For example, it is often the case that the government will require that the corporation seeking cooperation credit pressure its employees to waive their Fifth Amendment rights and fire those employees who decline to waive or otherwise cooperate with the government.

> Although it is understandable and even beneficial for society that corporations assist the United States government with its investigation of corporate crime, the manner in which that cooperation now occurs has eroded the Fifth Amendment rights of corporate employees. The tremendous pressure the United States government places on corporations to cooperate or face indictment—which in many cases is tantamount to a corporate death sentence—has fostered a regime where the government has corporations conduct internal investigations and then turn the results of those investigations over to the government for it to use as road maps for its prosecutions. Corporations often complain that their internal investigators have been "deputized," while the companies have been left paying the bills, but it is often the corporate employees who end up paying the greatest price. Too often, government pressure has forced companies to take action against its employees that the Constitution would prevent the government from taking directly, with the result being that the rights the Constitution was designed to secure have been eroded.

> In various investigations, the government has glossed over this issue when it has been raised, arguing that there is no constitutional problem because the rights secured by the Constitution are protections against conduct by the government, not by employers or other third-parties, but this is too convenient an excuse when it may be a corporate car that is running over the corporate employee but it is the government at the steering wheel. The reality is that corporations are not mere volunteers in these exercises, they are being compelled, and the government often is giving the corporations direction or is otherwise intertwined in how the corporate internal investigation commences. In a literal sense and at least in spirit, the corporations are acting as agents of the government.

Abbe David Lowell & Christopher D. Man, *Federalizing Corporate Internal Investigations and the Erosion of Employees' Fifth Amendment Rights*, 40 Geo. L.J. Ann. Rev. Crim. Proc. iii, iii-iv (2011); *see also* Bruce A. Green & Ellen S. Podgor, *Unregulated Internal Investigations: Achieving Fairness for Corporate Constituencies*, 54 B.C. L. Rev. 73 (2013); *cf.* Julie Rose O'Sullivan, *The DOJ Risks Killing the Golden Goose Through Computer Associates/Singleton Theories of Obstruction*, 44 Am. Crim. L. Rev. 1447 (2007).

2. In *Logos v. United States*, -- U.S. --, 138 S.Ct. 1684 (2018), the Supreme Court held that the Mandatory Victims Restitution Act of 1996 does not require a criminal defendant to pay the costs and attorneys' fees involved with an internal investigation conducted by a corporate victim.

3. For guidance on the conduct of internal corporate investigations, see Am. College of Trial Lawyers, *Recommended Practices for Companies and Their Counsel in Conducting Internal Investigations*, 46 Am. Crim. L. Rev. 73 (2009); Dan K. Webb, Robert W. Tarun & Steven F. Molo, Corporate Internal Investigations (Law Journal Press 2018).

G. MANAGERIAL LIABILITY: "RESPONSIBLE CORPORATE OFFICER" DOCTRINE

The generally-accepted wisdom is that there are three theories under which corporate officers or agents may be held liable for criminal violations that occur during the course of their employment. First, an agent who actually performs the criminal act may be liable even though he committed the act in his official or representative capacity. For example, if a corporate agent files a materially false statement with the government on behalf of his employer, he is considered liable as a principal for that criminal act.[179]

Second, corporate agents may be liable as aiders and abettors. Thus, under principles of accomplice liability, corporate agents and officers may be held accountable for crimes that they did not personally commit but which they "aid[ed], abet[ted], counsel[ed], command[ed], induce[ed] or procure[ed]" under 18 U.S.C. § 2(a). Federal law recognizes no distinction between those who act directly and those who "merely" aid and abet a criminal violation—principals and aiders and abettors are deemed equally culpable. To prove that a corporate agent aided and abetted a crime under § 2(a), the government must prove that someone committed the underlying substantive offense and that the agent "'share[d] in the intent to commit the offense ... [and] participated in some manner to assist its commission.'"[180]

Section 2(b) of Title 18 also provides that a person "who willfully causes an act to be done which if directly performed by him or another would be an offense against the United States, is punishable as a principal." This section is aimed at those who cause the commission of an offense by an innocent agent.[181] "Generally, to establish a conviction through the use of section 2(b), the government must prove that the defendant had the mental state necessary to

---

[179] Certain subordinate employees have attempted to assert a defense to criminal charges on the theory that they were just "following orders" of a superior. Not surprisingly, this defense has not met with a great deal of judicial enthusiasm. As the Eleventh Circuit explained in *United States v. Gold*, 743 F.2d 800, 823-24 (11th Cir. 1984):

[F]ollowing orders" can only be a defense where a defendant has no idea that his conduct is criminal—a critical limitation that [the defendant's] proposed instruction does not reflect. If [the defendant] was aware of the illegality of his conduct, the fact that it was authorized by a superior clearly cannot insulate him from criminal liability. If, on the other hand, [the defendant] was genuinely ignorant of the criminal nature of his actions, then he was not guilty because he lacked the knowledge and specific intent necessary to be convicted under the applicable statutes.

But cf. United States v. Natelli, 527 F.2d 311 (2d Cir. 1975) (junior accountant bore no duty to decide, and was not responsible for deciding, upon the accounting treatment of a certain item; "[a]bsent such a duty, he cannot be held to have acted in reckless disregard of the facts").

[180] United States v. Self, 2 F.3d 1071, 1088-89 (10th Cir. 1993) (*quoting* United States v. Smith, 838 F.2d 436, 441 (10th Cir. 1988)).

[181] *See* United States v. Gabriel, 125 F.3d 89, 99 (2d Cir. 1997).

violate the underlying criminal statute and that the defendant 'willfully caused' another to commit the necessary act."[182]

The third, and for purposes of this chapter, most significant theory of liability is premised upon an employee's or agent's failure to control the misconduct of others. In the following cases, the harm sought to be avoided in the applicable statute or regulation results not from a supervisor's actions in actively committing or aiding and abetting—that is doing, commanding, approving, or even acquiescing in—criminal activity, but rather from the supervisor's failure to discover or to correct a problem that lies within his managerial mandate. The "responsible corporate officer" doctrine states that "[o]ne who has control over activities that lead to a subordinate's violation of a statute may incur liability for failure to fulfill the duty, commensurate with his position of authority in the corporate hierarchy, to prevent or correct such violations."[183] It is important to stress that, at least where the statutory violation at issue is a strict liability offense, a "responsible corporate officer" may be criminally sanctioned *even though he did not personally participate in the wrongdoing* and *even though he had no personal knowledge of the misconduct perpetrated by his subordinates.*

The "responsible corporate officer" theory of liability arose, and has generally been applied, in prosecutions under the Food, Drug, and Cosmetic Act ("FDCA").[184] By its terms, it is not restricted to the FDCA context, and it has been applied to other federal statutes as well.[185] Most notably, this theory of liability has been the subject of controversy in the environmental criminal enforcement area.

Two statutes—the Clean Water Act[186] and the Clean Air Act[187]—contain explicit provisions making "responsible corporate officers" liable. Managerial liability is also possible as a matter of interpretation under other environmental statutes. The applicability of the responsible corporate officer principles developed in the FDCA context has been vigorously contested in the environmental context because the environmental statutes at issue often contemplate *felony* liability based upon some showing of *mens rea*, unlike the FDCA, which is generally read to impose strict liability for misdemeanor violations.

The dispute over whether and how the responsible corporate officer doctrine should apply in environmental prosecutions (and other situations outside the strict liability, misdemeanor context in which the doctrine was first applied) turns on the conceptualization of this exceedingly vague basis of liability. For example, if the responsible corporate officer doctrine essentially endorses imposing vicarious criminal liability upon managerial agents for the misconduct or defaults of their subordinates, it may be possible for responsible corporate officers who have no *mens rea* or *actus reus* to be convicted under a statute that requires a "knowing violation" based on the actions and knowledge of their subordinates. Alternatively, if the doctrine is not founded upon a vicarious liability theory, responsible corporate officers may

---

[182] *Id.*; *see also* United States v. Smith, 891 F.2d 703, 711 (9th Cir.1989) ("[U]nder (a) the government must prove that someone committed the crime and that another person aided and abetted without performing the criminal act himself; the second person is made 'a coprincipal with the person who takes the final step and violates a criminal statute.' In contrast, under (b) the government does not need to prove that someone other than the defendant committed the substantive crime but merely that the aider and abettor caused the act to be performed, even though the person who did the wrongful act violated no criminal statute because of the lack of criminal intent or capacity.").

[183] Kathleen F. Brickey, *Criminal Liability of Corporate Officers for Strict Liability Offenses—Another View*, 35 Vand. L. Rev. 1337, 1338-40 (1982).

[184] 21 U.S.C. §§ 301-92. For cases, see Arnold & Porter LLP Advisory, Raising the Bar: Evolving Expectations on Boards of Directors and Management Teams in Assuring Corporate Compliance at 3 (May 2009).

[185] *See, e.g.*, Kathleen F. Brickey, *Corporate Criminal Liability: A Primer for Corporate Counsel*, 40 Bus. Law. 129, 142-43 (1984) (citing statutes and cases).

[186] 33 U.S.C. § 1319.

[187] 42 U.S.C. § 7413.

not be liable under many environmental statutes unless some personal *mens rea* may be demonstrated. In considering the following cases, readers should attempt to isolate the analytical basis for the responsible corporate officer doctrine—and thus its potential limits. Is this theory of criminal liability best conceptualized as a species of aiding and abetting liability; a separate, vicarious liability theory; a definition of the *actus reus* for liability as a principal; or a hidden application of a negligence *mens rea* again for liability as a principal?[188]

UNITED STATES v. PARK
421 U.S. 658 (1975)

MR. CHIEF JUSTICE BURGER delivered the opinion of the Court.

We granted certiorari to consider whether the jury instructions in the prosecution of a corporate officer under § 301(k) of the Federal Food, Drug, and Cosmetic Act, 21 U.S.C. § 331(k), were appropriate under *United States v. Dotterweich*, 320 U.S. 277 (1943).

Acme Markets, Inc., is a national retail food chain with approximately 36,000 employees, 874 retail outlets, 12 general warehouses, and four special warehouses. Its headquarters, including the office of the president, respondent Park, who is chief executive officer of the corporation, are located in Philadelphia, Pa. In a five-count information filed in the United States District Court for the District of Maryland, the Government charged Acme and respondent with violations of the Federal Food, Drug and Cosmetic Act. Each count of the information alleged that the defendants had received food that had been shipped in interstate commerce and that, while the food was being held for sale in Acme's Baltimore warehouse following shipment in interstate commerce, they caused it to be held in a building accessible to rodents and to be exposed to contamination by rodents. These acts were alleged to have resulted in the food's being adulterated within the meaning of 21 U.S.C. §§ 342(a)(3) and (4),[189] in violation of 21 U.S.C. § 331(k).[190]

Acme pleaded guilty to each count of the information. Respondent pleaded not guilty. The evidence at trial demonstrated that in April 1970 the Food and Drug Administration (FDA) advised respondent by letter of insanitary conditions in Acme's Philadelphia warehouse. In 1971 the FDA found that similar conditions existed in the firm's Baltimore warehouse. An FDA consumer safety officer testified concerning evidence of rodent infestation and other insanitary conditions discovered during a 12-day inspection of the Baltimore warehouse in November and December 1971.[191] He also related that a second inspection of the warehouse

---

[188] *Compare, e.g.*, Brickey, *supra* note 183, *with* Norman Abrams, *Criminal Liability of Corporate Officers for Strict Liability Offenses—A Comment on* Dotterweich *and* Park, 28 UCLA L. Rev. 463 (1981). *See also* Martin Petrin, *Circumscribing the "Prosecutor's Ticket to Tag the Elite"—A Critique of the Responsible Corporate Officer Doctrine*, 84 Temp. L. Rev. 283 (2012).

[189] [Court's footnote 1:] Section 402 of the Act, 21 U.S.C. § 342, provides in pertinent part:

"A food shall be deemed to be adulterated...

"(a) ... (3) if it consists in whole or in part of any filthy, putrid, or decomposed substance, or if it is otherwise unfit for food; or (4) if it has been prepared, packed, or held under insanitary conditions whereby it may have become contaminated with filth, or whereby it may have been rendered injurious to health .... ."

[190] [Court's footnote 2:] Section 301 of the Act, 21 U.S.C. § 331, provides in pertinent part:

"The following acts and the causing thereof are prohibited: ...

"(k) The alteration, mutilation, destruction, obliteration, or removal of the whole or any part of the labeling of, or the doing of any other act with respect to, a food, drug, device, or cosmetic, if such act is done while such article is held for sale (whether or not the first sale) after shipment in interstate commerce and results in such article being adulterated or misbranded."

[191] [Court's footnote 4:] The witness testified with respect to the inspection of the basement of the "old building" in the warehouse complex:

had been conducted in March 1972.[192] On that occasion the inspectors found that there had been improvement in the sanitary conditions, but that "there was still evidence of rodent activity in the building and in the warehouses and we found some rodent-contaminated lots of food items."

The Government also presented testimony by the Chief of Compliance of the FDA's Baltimore office, who informed respondent by letter of the conditions at the Baltimore warehouse after the first inspection.[193] There was testimony by Acme's Baltimore division vice president, who had responded to the letter on behalf of Acme and respondent and who described the steps taken to remedy the insanitary conditions discovered by both inspections. The Government's final witness, Acme's vice president for legal affairs and assistant secretary, identified respondent as the president and chief executive officer of the company and read a bylaw prescribing the duties of the chief executive officer.[194] He testified that respondent functioned by delegating "normal operating duties," including sanitation, but that he retained "certain things, which are the big, broad, principles of the operation of the company," and had "the responsibility of seeing that they all work together."

At the close of the Government's case in chief, respondent moved for a judgment of acquittal on the ground that "the evidence in chief has shown that Mr. Park is not personally concerned in this Food and Drug violation." The trial judge denied the motion, stating that *United States v. Dotterweich*, 320 U.S. 277 (1943), was controlling.

Respondent was the only defense witness. He testified that, although all of Acme's employees were in a sense under his general direction, the company had an "organizational

---

"We found extensive evidence of rodent infestation in the form of rat and mouse pellets throughout the entire perimeter area and along the wall.

"We also found that the doors leading to the basement area from the rail siding had openings at the bottom or openings beneath part of the door that came down at the bottom large enough to admit rodent entry. There were also roden[t] pellets found on a number of different packages of boxes of various items stored in the basement, and looking at this document, I see there were also broken windows along the rail siding."

On the first floor of the "old building," the inspectors found:

"Thirty mouse pellets on the floor along walls and on the ledge in the hanging meat room. There were at least twenty mouse pellets beside bales of lime Jello and one of the bales had a chewed rodent hole in the product ...."

[192] [Court's footnote 5:] The first four counts of the information alleged violations corresponding to the observations of the inspectors during the November and December 1971 inspection. The fifth count alleged violations corresponding to observations during the March 1972 inspection.

[193] [Court's footnote 6:] The letter, dated January 27, 1972, included the following:

"We note with much concern that the old and new warehouse areas used for food storage were actively and extensively inhabited by live rodents. Of even more concern was the observation that such reprehensible conditions obviously existed for a prolonged period of time without any detection, or were completely ignored ...

We trust this letter will serve to direct your attention to the seriousness of the problem and formally advise you of the urgent need to initiate whatever measures are necessary to prevent recurrence and ensure compliance with the law."

[194] [Court's footnote 7:] The bylaw provided in pertinent part:

"The Chairman of the board of directors or the president shall be the chief executive officer of the company as the board of directors may from time to time determine. He shall, subject to the board of directors, have general and active supervision of the affairs, business, offices and employees of the company ....

He shall, from time to time, in his discretion or at the order of the board, report the operations and affairs of the company. He shall also perform such other duties and have such other powers as may be assigned to him from time to time by the board of directors."

structure for responsibilities for certain functions" according to which different phases of its operation were "assigned to individuals who, in turn, have staff and departments under them." He identified those individuals responsible for sanitation, and related that upon receipt of the January 1972 FDA letter, he had conferred with the vice president for legal affairs, who informed him that the Baltimore division vice president "was investigating the situation immediately and would be taking corrective action and would be preparing a summary of the corrective action to reply to the letter." Respondent stated that he did not "believe there was anything [he] could have done more constructively than what [he] found was being done."

On cross-examination, respondent conceded that providing sanitary conditions for food offered for sale to the public was something that he was "responsible for in the entire operation of the company," and he stated that it was one of many phases of the company that he assigned to "dependable subordinates." Respondent was asked about and, over the objections of his counsel, admitted receiving, the April 1970 letter addressed to him from the FDA regarding insanitary conditions at Acme's Philadelphia warehouse.[195] He acknowledged that, with the exception of the division vice president, the same individuals had responsibility for sanitation in both Baltimore and Philadelphia. Finally, in response to questions concerning the Philadelphia and Baltimore incidents, respondent admitted that the Baltimore problem indicated the system for handling sanitation "wasn't working perfectly" and that as Acme's chief executive officer he was responsible for "any result which occurs in our company."

At the close of the evidence, respondent's renewed motion for a judgment of acquittal was denied. The relevant portion of the trial judge's instructions to the jury challenged by respondent is set out in the margin.[196] Respondent's counsel objected to the instructions on the ground that they failed fairly to reflect our decision in *United States v. Dotterweich* and to define "responsible relationship." The trial judge overruled the objection. The jury found respondent

---

[195] [Court's footnote 8:] The April 1970 letter informed respondent of the following "objectionable conditions" in Acme's Philadelphia warehouse:

"1. Potential rodent entry ways were noted via ill fitting doors and door in irrepair at Southwest corner of warehouse; at dock at old salvage room and at receiving and shipping doors which were observed to be open most of the time.

"2. Rodent nesting, rodent excreta pellets, rodent stained bale bagging and rodent gnawed holes were noted among bales of flour stored in warehouse.

"3. Potential rodent harborage was noted in discarded paper, rope, sawdust and other debris piled in corner of shipping and receiving dock near bakery and warehouse doors. Rodent excreta pellets were observed among bags of sawdust (or wood shavings)."

[196] "In order to find the Defendant guilty on any count of the Information, you must find beyond a reasonable doubt on each count ...

"Thirdly, that John R. Park held a position of authority in the operation of the business of Acme Markets, Incorporated.

"However, you need not concern yourselves with the first two elements of the case. The main issue for your determination is only with the third element, whether the Defendant held a position of authority and responsibility in the business of Acme Markets....

"The statute makes individuals, as well as corporations, liable for violations. An individual is liable if it is clear, beyond a reasonable doubt, that the elements of the adulteration of the food as to travel in interstate commerce are present. As I have instructed you in this case, they are, and that the individual had a responsible relation to the situation, even though he may not have participated personally.

"The individual is or could be liable under the statute, even if he did not consciously do wrong. However, the fact that the Defendant is pres[id]ent and is a chief executive officer of the Acme Markets does not require a finding of guilt. Though, he need not have personally participated in the situation, he must have had a responsible relationship to the issue. The issue is, in this case, whether the Defendant, John R. Park, by virtue of his position in the company, had a position of authority and responsibility in the situation out of which these charges arose."

guilty on all counts of the information, and he was subsequently sentenced to pay a fine of $50 on each count.

The Court of Appeals reversed the conviction and remanded for a new trial. That court viewed the Government as arguing "that the conviction may be predicated solely upon a showing that ... [respondent] was the President of the offending corporation," and it stated that as "a general proposition, some act of commission or omission is an essential element of every crime." It reasoned that, although our decision in *United States v. Dotterweich* had construed the statutory provisions under which respondent was tried to dispense with the traditional element of "'awareness of some wrongdoing,'" the Court had not construed them as dispensing with the element of "wrongful action." The Court of Appeals concluded that the trial judge's instructions "might well have left the jury with the erroneous impression that Park could be found guilty in the absence of 'wrongful action' on his part," and that proof of this element was required by due process. It held, with one dissent, that the instructions did not "correctly state the law of the case," and directed that on retrial the jury be instructed as to "wrongful action," which might be "gross negligence and inattention in discharging ... corporate duties and obligations or any of a host of other acts of commission or omission which would 'cause' the contamination of food." ...

We granted certiorari because of an apparent conflict among the Courts of Appeals with respect to the standard of liability of corporate officers under the Federal Food, Drug, and Cosmetic Act as construed in *United States v. Dotterweich* and because of the importance of the question to the Government's enforcement program. We reverse.

The question presented by the Government's petition for certiorari in *United States v. Dotterweich* and the focus of this Court's opinion, was whether "the manager of a corporation, as well as the corporation itself, may be prosecuted under the Federal Food, Drug, and Cosmetic Act of 1938 for the introduction of misbranded and adulterated articles into interstate commerce." In *Dotterweich*, a jury had disagreed as to the corporation, a jobber purchasing drugs from manufacturers and shipping them in interstate commerce under its own label, but had convicted Dotterweich, the corporation's president and general manager. The Court of Appeals reversed the conviction on the ground that only the drug dealer, whether corporation or individual, was subject to the criminal provisions of the Act, and that where the dealer was a corporation, an individual connected therewith might be held personally only if he was operating the corporation "as his 'alter ego.'"

In reversing the judgment of the Court of Appeals and reinstating Dotterweich's conviction, this Court looked to the purposes of the Act and noted that they "touch phases of the lives and health of the people which, in the circumstances of modern industrialism, are largely beyond self-protection." It observed that the Act is of "a now familiar type," which "dispenses with the conventional requirement for criminal conduct—awareness of some wrongdoing. In the interest of the larger good it puts the burden of acting at hazard upon a person otherwise innocent but standing in responsible relation to a public danger."

Central to the Court's conclusion that individuals other than proprietors are subject to the criminal provisions of the Act was the reality that "the only way in which a corporation can act is through the individuals who act on its behalf." The Court also noted that corporate officers had been subject to criminal liability under the Federal Food and Drugs Act of 1906, and it observed that a contrary result under the 1938 legislation would be incompatible with the expressed intent of Congress to "enlarge and stiffen the penal net" and to discourage a view of the Act's criminal penalties as a "license fee for the conduct of an illegitimate business."

At the same time, however, the Court was aware of the concern which was the motivating factor in the Court of Appeals' decision, that literal enforcement "might operate too harshly by sweeping within its condemnation any person however remotely entangled in the proscribed shipment." A limiting principle, in the form of "settled doctrines of criminal law" defining those who "are responsible for the commission of a misdemeanor," was available. In this context, the Court concluded, those doctrines dictated that the offense was committed "by all who ... have ... a responsible share in the furtherance of the transaction which the statute outlaws."

The Court recognized that, because the Act dispenses with the need to prove "consciousness of wrongdoing," it may result in hardship even as applied to those who share "responsibility in the business process resulting in" a violation. It regarded as "too treacherous" an attempt "to define or even to indicate by way of illustration the class of employees which stands in such a responsible relation." The question of responsibility, the Court said, depends "on the evidence produced at the trial and its submission—assuming the evidence warrants it—to the jury under appropriate guidance." The Court added: "In such matters the good sense of prosecutors, the wise guidance of trial judges, and the ultimate judgment of juries must be trusted."

The rule that corporate employees who have "a responsible share in the furtherance of the transaction which the statute outlaws" are subject to the criminal provisions of the Act was not formulated in a vacuum. Cases under the Federal Food and Drugs Act of 1906 reflected the view both that knowledge or intent were not required to be proved in prosecutions under its criminal provisions, and that responsible corporate agents could be subjected to the liability thereby imposed. Moreover, the principle had been recognized that a corporate agent, through whose act, default, or omission the corporation committed a crime, was himself guilty individually of that crime. The principle had been applied whether or not the crime required "consciousness of wrongdoing," and it had been applied not only to those corporate agents who themselves committed the criminal act, but also to those who by virtue of their managerial positions or other similar relation to the actor could be deemed responsible for its commission.

In the latter class of cases, the liability of managerial officers did not depend on their knowledge of, or personal participation in, the act made criminal by the statute. Rather, where the statute under which they were prosecuted dispensed with "consciousness of wrongdoing," an omission or failure to act was deemed a sufficient basis for a responsible corporate agent's liability. It was enough in such cases that, by virtue of the relationship he bore to the corporation, the agent had the power to prevent the act complained of.

The rationale of the interpretation given the Act in *Dotterweich*, as holding criminally accountable the persons whose failure to exercise the authority and supervisory responsibility reposed in them by the business organization resulted in the violation complained of, has been confirmed in our subsequent cases. Thus, the Court has reaffirmed the proposition that "the public interest in the purity of its food is so great as to warrant the imposition of the highest standard of care on distributors." In order to make "distributors of food the strictest censors of their merchandise," the Act punishes "neglect where the law requires care, or inaction where it imposes a duty." "The accused, if he does not will the violation, usually is in a position to prevent it with no more care than society might reasonably expect and no more exertion than it might reasonably exact from one who assumed his responsibilities." Similarly, in cases decided after *Dotterweich*, the Courts of Appeals have recognized that those corporate agents vested with the responsibility, and power commensurate with that responsibility, to devise whatever measures are necessary to ensure compliance with the Act bear a "responsible relationship" to, or have a "responsible share" in, violations.

Thus *Dotterweich* and the cases which have followed reveal that in providing sanctions which reach and touch the individuals who execute the corporate mission—and this is by no means necessarily confined to a single corporate agent or employee—the Act imposes not only a positive duty to seek out and remedy violations when they occur but also, and primarily, a duty to implement measures that will insure that violations will not occur. The requirements of foresight and vigilance imposed on responsible corporate agents are beyond question demanding, and perhaps onerous, but they are no more stringent than the public has a right to expect of those who voluntarily assume positions of authority in business enterprises whose services and products affect the health and well-being of the public that supports them.

The Act does not, as we observed in *Dotterweich*, make criminal liability turn on "awareness of some wrongdoing" or "conscious fraud." The duty imposed by Congress on responsible corporate agents is, we emphasize, one that requires the highest standard of foresight and vigilance, but the Act, in its criminal aspect, does not require that which is objectively impossible. The theory upon which responsible corporate agents are held criminally accountable for "causing" violations of the Act permits a claim that a defendant was "powerless" to prevent or correct the violation to "be raised defensively at a trial on the merits." If such a claim is made, the defendant has the burden of coming forward with evidence, but this does not alter the Government's ultimate burden of proving beyond a reasonable doubt the defendant's guilt, including his power, in light of the duty imposed by the Act, to prevent or correct the prohibited condition. Congress has seen fit to enforce the accountability of responsible corporate agents dealing with products which may affect the health of consumers by penal sanctions cast in rigorous terms, and the obligation of the courts is to give them effect so long as they do not violate the Constitution.

We cannot agree with the Court of Appeals that it was incumbent upon the District Court to instruct the jury that the Government had the burden of establishing "wrongful action" in the sense in which the Court of Appeals used that phrase. The concept of a "responsible relationship" to, or a "responsible share" in, a violation of the Act indeed imports some measure of blameworthiness; but it is equally clear that the Government establishes a prima facie case when it introduces evidence sufficient to warrant a finding by the trier of the facts that the defendant had, by reason of his position in the corporation, responsibility and authority either to prevent in the first instance, or promptly to correct, the violation complained of, and that he failed to do so. The failure thus to fulfill the duty imposed by the interaction of the corporate agent's authority and the statute furnishes a sufficient causal link. The considerations which prompted the imposition of this duty, and the scope of the duty, provide the measure of culpability.

Turning to the jury charge in this case, it is of course arguable that isolated parts can be read as intimating that a finding of guilt could be predicated solely on respondent's corporate position. But this is not the way we review jury instructions, because "a single instruction to a jury may not be judged in artificial isolation, but must be viewed in the context of the overall charge."

Reading the entire charge satisfies us that the jury's attention was adequately focused on the issue of respondent's authority with respect to the conditions that formed the basis of the alleged violations. Viewed as a whole, the charge did not permit the jury to find guilt solely on the basis of respondent's position in the corporation; rather, it fairly advised the jury that to find guilt it must find respondent "had a responsible relation to the situation," and "by virtue of his position ... had ... authority and responsibility" to deal with the situation. The situation referred to could only be "food ... held in unsanitary conditions in a warehouse with the result that it consisted, in part, of filth or ... may have been contaminated with filth."

Moreover, in reviewing jury instructions, our task is also to view the charge itself as part of the whole trial. "Often isolated statements taken from the charge, seemingly prejudicial on their face, are not so when considered in the context of the entire record of the *trial*." The record in this case reveals that the jury could not have failed to be aware that the main issue for determination was not respondent's position in the corporate hierarchy, but rather his accountability, because of the responsibility and authority of his position, for the conditions which gave rise to the charges against him....

MR. JUSTICE STEWART, with whom MR. JUSTICE MARSHALL and MR. JUSTICE POWELL join, dissenting.

Although agreeing with much of what is said in the Court's opinion, I dissent from the opinion and judgment, because the jury instructions in this case were not consistent with the law as the Court today expounds it.

As I understand the Court's opinion, it holds that in order to sustain a conviction under § 301(k) of the Federal Food, Drug, and Cosmetic Act the prosecution must at least show that by reason of an individual's corporate position and responsibilities, he had a duty to use care to maintain the physical integrity of the corporation's food products. A jury may then draw the inference that when the food is found to be in such condition as to violate the statute's prohibitions, that condition was "caused" by a breach of the standard of care imposed upon the responsible official. This is the language of negligence, and I agree with it.

To affirm this conviction, however, the Court must approve the instructions given to the members of the jury who were entrusted with determining whether the respondent was innocent or guilty. Those instructions did not conform to the standards that the Court itself sets out today....

As the Court today recognized, the *Dotterweich* case did not deal with what kind of conduct must be proved to support a finding of criminal guilt under the Act. *Dotterweich* was concerned, rather, with the statutory definition of "person"—with what kind of corporate employees were even "subject to the criminal provisions of the Act." The Court held that those employees with "a responsible relation" to the violative transaction or condition were subject to the Act's criminal provisions, but all that the Court had to say with respect to the kind of conduct that can constitute criminal guilt was that the Act "dispenses with the conventional requirement for criminal conduct—awareness of some wrongdoing."...

The *Dotterweich* case stands for two propositions, and I accept them both. First, "any person" within the meaning of 21 U.S.C. § 333 may include any corporate officer or employee "standing in responsible relation" to a condition or transaction forbidden by the Act. Second, a person may be convicted of a criminal offense under the Act even in the absence of "the conventional requirement for criminal conduct—awareness of some wrongdoing."

But before a person can be convicted of a criminal violation of this Act, a jury must find—and must be clearly instructed that it must find—evidence beyond a reasonable doubt that he engaged in wrongful conduct amounting at least to common-law negligence. There were no such instructions, and clearly, therefore, no such finding in this case.

For these reasons, I cannot join the Court in affirming Park's criminal conviction.

Notes

1. The court below essentially had held that Park's conviction could not stand because of the absence of an *actus reus*. In affirming Park's conviction, does the Supreme Court articulate what, if any, the actionable *actus reus* was in this case? What difference does this make? Is proof of any *mens rea* required by this statutory scheme? Is the majority holding the defendant liable essentially for negligence, as Justice Stewart contends? What, if any, relevance does the responsible corporate officer doctrine have to causation principles?

2. What types of defenses are available to "responsible corporate officers"? One obvious argument would be that the defendant does not bear a "responsible relation" to the activity at issue. This raises the question of just how close a nexus there has to be between the defendant's managerial mandate and the alleged wrongdoing. In *United States v. Iverson*, 162 F.3d 1015 (9th Cir. 1998), the defendant was criminally prosecuted, among other things, for "knowing" violations of the Clean Water Act (CWA). The defendant was the founder, President, and CEO of the company whose employees made improper discharges of pollutants. The jury was instructed that the defendant could be liable under the Act as a "responsible corporate officer" if it found: that the defendant had knowledge of the fact that pollutants were being improperly discharged by his employees; that the defendant had the authority and capacity to prevent the discharges; and that the defendant failed to prevent the ongoing discharge of pollutants. *Id.* at 1022. Apparently, the defendant's knowledge of at least some of the discharges was not much of an issue. Instead, the defendant argued that "a corporate officer is 'responsible' only when the officer in fact exercises control over the activity causing the discharge or has an express corporate duty to oversee the activity." *Id.* at 1022. The Ninth Circuit rejected this "narrow" interpretation, *id.*, instead ruling that, "[u]nder the CWA, a person is a 'responsible corporate officer' if the person has authority to exercise control over the corporation's activity that is causing the discharges. There is no requirement that the officer in fact exercise such authority or that the corporation expressly vest a duty in the officer to oversee the activity." *Id.* at 1025. What implications may this broad reading have for those in the highest ranks of the corporate hierarchy?

3. Another possible defense theory is founded on the *Park* Court's statement that "[t]he theory upon which responsible corporate agents are held criminally accountable for 'causing' violations of the Act permits a claim that a defendant was 'powerless' to prevent or correct the

violation to 'be raised defensively at a trial on the merits.'" Is this an affirmative defense, or does the government bear the burden of proving the defendant's "power" once the defendant raises the issue of powerlessness? Just what might render a manager "powerless"? Is this simply a different way of saying that the defendant bore no "responsible relation" to the activity at issue, or does it mean something more? May a corporate manager defend a responsible corporate officer prosecution by arguing that she reasonably delegated responsibility for a given activity and did all that she could to monitor the performance of her subordinates, but the crime happened despite her best efforts?

UNITED STATES v. BRITTAIN
931 F.2d 1413 (10th Cir.1991)

BALDOCK, CIRCUIT JUDGE.

A jury convicted defendant-appellant, Raymond T. Brittain, of eighteen felony counts of falsely reporting a material fact to a government agency, 18 U.S.C. § 1001, and two misdemeanor counts of discharging pollutants into the waters of the United States in violation of §§ 301(a) & 309(c)(1) of the Federal Water Pollution Control Act of 1972 (Clean Water Act), codified at 33 U.S.C. §§ 1311(a) & 1319(c)(1). ... We affirm.

... The Clean Water Act prohibits the discharge of pollutants from any point source into the navigable waters of the United States unless such discharge complies with a permit issued by the EPA pursuant to the National Pollutant Discharge Elimination System (NPDES) or by an EPA authorized state agency. *See* 33 U.S.C. §§ 1311(a) & 1342. NPDES permits impose limits on the point sources and amounts of discharged pollutants, and the EPA monitors compliance through monthly discharge monitoring reports from the permittee. Defendant, as public utilities director for the city of Enid, Oklahoma, had general supervisory authority over the operations of the Enid wastewater treatment plant and was responsible for filing the plant's discharge monitoring reports. Defendant directed the plant supervisor to falsify eighteen monthly discharge monitoring reports and the supporting laboratory records by recording 25 to 30 milligrams per liter of effluent for two specific pollutants regardless of the actual measurements at the point of discharge. ...

In 1984, the city of Enid obtained a renewed NPDES permit from the EPA to discharge pollutants from the city's wastewater treatment plant into nearby Boggy Creek. The original NPDES permit provided for two discharge point sources, outfalls 001 and 002; whereas the new permit allowed for only one discharge point source, outfall 001. Discharges from outfall 002, although expressly prohibited by the renewed NPDES permit, continued during times of heavy rain. The discharges resulted from a thirty-six-inch bypass pipe which would divert raw sewage through outfall 002 when heavy rain caused excess water to flow through the sewage system. The evidence reveals that the plant supervisor informed defendant, in defendant's capacity as public utilities director, that the plant was discharging raw sewage from outfall 002, and that defendant physically observed two such discharges in January and August 1986. Moreover, the evidence reveals that defendant instructed the plant supervisor not to report the discharges to the EPA as required by the permit. The jury convicted defendant on two counts pursuant to 33 U.S.C. §§ 1311(a) & 1319(c) for the January and August 1986 permit violations.

... [Section] 1311(a) of the Clean Water Act prohibits "any person" from discharging "any pollutant" into the waters of the United States except as authorized by the EPA or an EPA authorized state agency. The EPA authorizes certain discharges pursuant to the NPDES permitting system. At the time of the indictment period, § 1319(c) provided for criminal sanctions for "any person" who "willfully or negligently" violated § 1311(a) or any NPDES permit.[197] This case involves a "willful or negligent" violation of an NPDES permit.

---

[197] [Court's footnote 3:] At the time of the indictment, the Clean Water Act provided in part:

33 U.S.C. § 1311(a) Illegality of pollutant discharges except in compliance with law:

Except as in compliance with this section and sections 1312, 1316, 1317, 1328, 1342, and 1344 of

Defendant claims: (1) he is not a "person" as contemplated by §§ 1319(c) & 1362(5) of the Clean Water Act; and (2) the government's evidence was insufficient to prove that he "willfully or negligently" discharged pollutants in violation of the city's NPDES permit. *See* § 1319(c).

Defendant's first argument calls for an interpretation of the Clean Water Act, a legal question. ... Defendant contends that the city was the only "person" chargeable for a permit violation because the city was the permittee.

As with any question of statutory interpretation, we must begin with the language of the statutes. If the statutory language "'is unambiguous and free of irrational result, that language controls.'" The plain language of the relevant statute includes "individuals" in the definition of "persons" subject to the Clean Water Act. *See* § 1362(5). Defendant certainly is an "individual." Section 1311(a) prohibits "any person"—any "individual" according to § 1362(5)—from discharging pollutants except as in accordance with an NPDES permit or other specified provisions in the Act. Section 1319(c), at the time of the indictment, provided for criminal sanctions for "any person"—"any individual"—who "willfully or negligently" caused such a violation. Thus, it appears that defendant, as an "individual," is subject to criminal liability under the Act.

Defendant, however, contends that an "individual" is subject to § 1319(c)'s criminal sanctions for NPDES permit violations only if he is the permittee. As support for this interpretation, he points to § 1319(c)(3)'s addition of "responsible corporate officers" to the Act's general definition of "persons" as contained in § 1362(5). He argues that § 1319(c)(3)'s addition of "responsible corporate officers" is meaningless if § 1362(5) already makes "persons" of "individuals" who merely are related to discharging permittees. Accordingly, he argues, he is not a "person" subject to criminal liability because the government did not prove that he was the permittee or a "responsible corporate officer" of the discharging permittee.

Section 1319(c)(3) does not define a "responsible corporate officer" and the legislative history is silent regarding Congress's intention in adding the term. The Supreme Court, however, first recognized the concept of "responsible corporate officer" in 1943. *See United States v. Dotterweich*, 320 U.S. 277 (1943). The *Dotterweich* Court held that a corporation's misdemeanor offense under the Federal Food, Drug, and Cosmetic Act of 1938 (FDCA) was committed by all corporate officers "who do have ... a responsible share in the furtherance of the transaction which the statute outlaws ... though consciousness of wrongdoing be totally wanting." *See also United States v. Park*, 421 U.S. 658, 670-73 (1975); 21 U.S.C. § 333(a) (misdemeanor criminal responsibility under FDCA does not require "consciousness of wrongdoing"). The rationale for this harsh rule lay in the type of legislative action that the *Dotterweich* Court was interpreting. Congress passed the FDCA in order to protect the public health, and, according to the Court, Congress perceived the public health interest to outweigh the hardship suffered by criminally liable responsible corporate officers who had no consciousness of wrong-doing. The same rationale applies to the Clean Water Act. Congress intended, with the Act, "to restore and maintain the chemical, physical, and biological integrity of the Nation's waters ... [and that] the discharge of pollutants into the navigable waters be eliminated by 1985." 33 U.S.C. § 1251(a). We think that Congress perceived this objective to outweigh hardships suffered by "responsible corporate officers" who are held

---

this title, the discharge of any pollutant by any person shall be unlawful.

33 U.S.C. § 1319(c) Criminal Penalties:

(1) Any person who willfully or negligently violates section 1311 ... of this title, or any permit condition or limitation implementing any of such sections in a permit issued under section 1342 [NPDES permit] of this title by the Administrator ... shall be punished ....

(3) For the purposes of this subsection, the term "person" shall mean, in addition to the definition contained in section 1362(5) of this title, any responsible corporate officer.

33 U.S.C. § 1362 Definitions:

(5) The term "person" means an individual, corporation, partnership, association, State, municipality, commission, or political subdivision of a State, or any interstate body....

criminally liable in spite of their lack of "consciousness of wrong-doing." We interpret the addition of "responsible corporate officers" as an expansion of liability under the Act rather than, as defendant would have it, an implicit limitation. The plain language of the statute, after all, states that "responsible corporate officers" are liable "in addition to the definition [of persons] contained in section 1362(5)...." § 1319(c)(3). Under this interpretation, a "responsible corporate officer," to be held criminally liable, would not have to "willfully or negligently" cause a permit violation. Instead, the willfulness or negligence of the actor would be imputed to him by virtue of his position of responsibility. This in no way limits other "persons," as defined by § 1362(5), to permittees. The statute plainly states that any "person," permittee or nonpermittee, who causes a permit violation through willful or negligent conduct, is subject to criminal sanctions. We hold that defendant, as an "individual," is a "person" subject to criminal liability under the Act....

UNITED STATES v. MacDONALD & WATSON WASTE OIL CO.
933 F.2d 35 (1st Cir. 1991)

LEVIN H. CAMPBELL, CIRCUIT JUDGE.

...

MacDonald & Watson Waste Oil Co. ("MacDonald & Watson") ... and Eugene K. D'Allesandro were convicted, on two counts each, of knowingly transporting and causing the transportation of hazardous waste, namely toluene and soil contaminated with toluene, to a facility which did not have a permit, in violation of RCRA, § 3008(d)(1), 42 U.S.C. § 6928(d)(1). ...

Located in Boston, Massachusetts, Master Chemical Company manufactured chemicals primarily for use in the shoe industry. ... Among the chemicals Master Chemical used was toluene, which it stored in a two thousand gallon underground storage tank. When Master Chemical personnel discovered in the late fall or early winter of 1982 that water was entering the tank and contaminating the toluene, the tank was emptied and its use discontinued. In 1984, Master Chemical Company was sold, and the toluene tank was excavated and removed. A Master Chemical employee testified that he found a small hole in the tank, and that the soil surrounding the tank appeared black and wet and smelled of toluene.

An environmental consulting firm, Goldberg-Zoino & Associates, Inc. ("GZA"), was retained to assist in the cleanup. GZA prepared a study of the site and solicited a bid from MacDonald & Watson for the excavation, transportation, and disposal of the toluene-contaminated soil. MacDonald & Watson, a company with offices in Johnstown, Rhode Island, was in the business of transporting and disposing of waste oils and contaminated soil. MacDonald & Watson operated a disposal facility on land in Providence, Rhode Island, known as the "Poe Street Lot," leased from appellant NIC. MacDonald & Watson operated the Poe Street Lot under NIC's Rhode Island RCRA permit, which authorized the disposal at the lot of *liquid* hazardous wastes and soils contaminated with non-hazardous wastes such as petroleum products. Neither NIC nor MacDonald & Watson held a RCRA permit authorizing them to dispose of *solid* hazardous wastes such as toluene-contaminated soil at the lot. At the Rhode Island administrative hearing held when NIC sought its permit, appellant D'Allesandro, president of MacDonald & Watson, testified that hazardous waste operations at the Poe Street Lot would be managed by MacDonald & Watson and that he would be the manager of the facility there. ...

[MacDonald & Watson's bid to remove and clean up the contaminated soil was accepted. The toluene-contaminated soil was transported by MacDonald & Watson employees from Master Chemical to the Poe Street Lot]. ... Neither NIC nor MacDonald & Watson reported the disposal of the Master Chemical wastes as a release of a hazardous substance into the environment pursuant to CERCLA § 103(b)(3)....

D'Allesandro, the President and owner of MacDonald & Watson, contends that his conviction under RCRA, § 3008(d)(1), 42 U.S.C. § 6928(d)(1), must be vacated because the district court incorrectly charged the jury regarding the element of knowledge in the case of a corporate officer. Section 3008(d)(1) penalizes "Any person who ... (1) *knowingly* transports or causes to be transported any hazardous waste identified or listed under this subchapter ... to a facility which does not have a permit ...." (Emphasis supplied.) In his closing, the prosecutor conceded that the government had "no direct evidence that Eugene D'Allesandro actually knew that the Master Chemical shipments were coming in," i.e., were being transported to the Poe Street Lot under contract with his company. The prosecution did present evidence, however, that D'Allesandro was not only the President and owner of MacDonald & Watson but was a "hands-on" manager of that relatively small firm. There was also proof that that firm leased the Poe Street Lot from NIC, and managed it, and that D'Allesandro's subordinates had contracted for and transported the Master Chemical waste for disposal at that site. The government argued that D'Allesandro was guilty of violating § 3008(d)(1) because, as the responsible corporate officer, he was in a position to ensure compliance with RCRA and had failed to do so even after being warned by a consultant on two earlier occasions that other shipments of toluene-contaminated soil had been received from other customers, and that such material violated NIC's permit. In the government's view, any failure to prove D'Allesandro's actual knowledge of the Master Chemical contract and shipments was irrelevant to his criminal responsibility under § 3008(d)(1) for those shipments.

The court apparently accepted the government's theory. It instructed the jury as follows:

> When an individual Defendant is also a corporate officer, the Government may prove that individual's knowledge in either of two ways. The first way is to demonstrate that the Defendant had actual knowledge of the act in question. The second way is to establish that the defendant was what is called a responsible officer of the corporation committing the act. In order to prove that a person is a responsible corporate officer three things must be shown.
>
> First, it must be shown that the person is an officer of the corporation, not merely an employee.
>
> Second, it must be shown that the officer had direct responsibility for the activities that are alleged to be illegal. Simply being an officer or even the president of a corporation is not enough. The Government must prove that the person had a responsibility to supervise the activities in question.
>
> And the third requirement is that the officer must have known or believed that the illegal activity of the type alleged occurred.

The court's phrasing of the third element at first glance seems ambiguous: it could be read to require actual knowledge of the Master Chemical shipments themselves. We are satisfied, however, that the court meant only what it literally said: D'Allesandro must have known or believed that illegal shipments *of the type* alleged had previously occurred. This tied into evidence that D'Allesandro had been advised of two earlier shipments of toluene-contaminated waste, and was told that such waste could not legally be received. For the court to require a finding that D'Allesandro knew of the alleged shipments themselves (i.e., the Master Chemical shipments), would have duplicated the court's earlier instruction on actual knowledge, and was not in accord with the government's theory.[198]

D'Allesandro challenges this instruction, contending that the use of the "responsible corporate officer" doctrine is improper under § 3008(d)(1) which expressly calls for proof of knowledge, i.e., requires *scienter*. The government responds that the district court properly adapted the responsible corporate officer doctrine traditionally applied to strict liability

---

[198] [Court's footnote 13:] Thus the prosecutor said, in his closing, "We can concede, Ladies and Gentlemen, that we have no direct evidence Eugene D'Allesandro ... actually knew that the Master Chemical shipments were coming in. But there is another way the Government can show that Eugene D'Allesandro was responsible for these shipments. The court will tell you what the law is but listen for the court's instruction that a corporate officer who is in a position in a company to insure that these types of actions don't occur and who knew that the company was engaged in such types of activities and did nothing to stop it can be held responsible for these actions."

offenses to this case, instructing the jury to find knowledge "that the illegal activity of the *type alleged* occurred,"—a finding that, together with the first two, made it reasonable to infer knowledge of the particular violation. We agree with D'Allesandro that the jury instructions improperly allowed the jury to find him guilty without finding he had actual knowledge of the alleged transportation of hazardous waste on July 30 and 31, 1986, from Master Chemical Company, Boston, Massachusetts, to NIC's site, knowledge being an element the statute requires. We must, therefore, vacate his conviction.

The seminal cases regarding the responsible corporate officer doctrine are *United States v. Dotterweich*, 320 U.S. 277 (1943), and *United States v. Park*, 421 U.S. 658 (1975). These cases concerned misdemeanor charges under the Federal Food, Drug, and Cosmetic Act, 21 U.S.C. §§ 301-392, as amended, relating to the handling or shipping of adulterated or misbranded drugs or food. The offenses alleged in the informations failed to state a knowledge element, and the Court found that they, in fact, dispensed with a *scienter* requirement, placing "the burden of acting at hazard upon a person otherwise innocent but standing in responsible relation to a public danger." The Court in *Park* clarified that corporate officer liability in that situation requires only a finding that the officer had "authority with respect to the conditions that formed the basis of the alleged violations." But while *Dotterweich* and *Park* thus reflect what is now clear and well-established law in respect to public welfare statutes and regulations lacking an express knowledge or other *scienter* requirement, we know of no precedent for failing to give effect to a knowledge requirement that Congress has expressly included in a criminal statute. Especially is that so where, as here, the crime is a felony carrying possible imprisonment of five years and, for a second offense, ten.

The district court, nonetheless, applied here a form of the responsible corporate officer doctrine established in *Dotterweich* and *Park* for *strict liability* misdemeanors, as a substitute means for proving the explicit knowledge element of this RCRA felony, 42 U.S.C. § 6928(d)(1). As an alternative to finding actual knowledge, the district court permitted the prosecution to constructively establish defendant's knowledge if the jury found the following: (1) that the defendant was a corporate officer; (2) with responsibility to supervise the allegedly illegal activities; and (3) knew or believed "that the illegal activity of the type alleged occurred." As previously stated, the third element did not necessitate proof of knowledge of the Master Chemical shipments charged in the indictment, but simply proof of earlier occasions when D'Allesandro was told his firm had improperly accepted toluene-contaminated soil.

Contrary to the government's assertions, this instruction did more than simply permit the jury, if it wished, to infer knowledge of the Master Chemical shipments from relevant circumstantial evidence including D'Allesandro's responsibilities and activities as a corporate executive. With respect to circumstantial evidence, the district court properly instructed elsewhere that knowledge did not have to be proven by direct evidence but could be inferred from the defendant's conduct and other facts and circumstances. The court also instructed that the element of knowledge could be satisfied by proof of willful blindness.[199] These instructions

---

[199] [Court's footnote 15:] The court instructed the jury generally regarding the element of knowledge as follows:

An act is said to be done knowingly if it is done voluntarily and intentionally and not because of ignorance, mistake, accident or some other reason. The requirement that an act be done knowingly is designed to insure that a Defendant will not be convicted for an act that he did not intend to commit or the nature of which he did not understand. Proof that a Defendant acted knowingly or with knowledge of a particular fact does not require direct evidence of what was in that Defendant's mind. Whether a Defendant acted knowingly or with knowledge of a particular fact may be inferred from that Defendant's conduct, from that Defendant's familiarity with the subject matter in question or from all of the other facts and circumstances connected with the case.

In determining whether a Defendant acted knowingly, you also may consider whether the Defendant deliberately closed his eyes to what otherwise would have been obvious. If so, the element of knowledge may be satisfied because a Defendant cannot avoid responsibility by purposefully avoiding learning the truth. However, mere negligence or mistake in not learning the facts is not sufficient to satisfy the element of knowledge.

allowed the jury to consider whether relevant circumstantial evidence established that D'Allesandro actually knew of the charged Master Chemical shipments. These would have sufficed had it merely been the court's purpose to point out that knowledge could be established by circumstantial evidence, although the court could, had it wished, have elaborated on the extent to which D'Allesandro's responsibilities and duties might lead to a reasonable inference that he knew of the Master Chemical transaction.

Instead, the district court charged, in effect, that proof that D'Allesandro was a responsible corporate officer would conclusively prove the element of his knowledge of the Master Chemical shipments. The jury was told that knowledge could be proven "in either of two ways." Besides demonstrating actual knowledge, the government could simply establish the defendant was a responsible corporate officer—the latter by showing three things, none of which, individually or collectively, necessarily established his actual knowledge of the illegal transportation charged. Under the district court's instruction, the jury's belief that the responsible corporate officer lacked actual knowledge of, and had not willfully blinded himself to, the criminal transportation alleged would be insufficient for acquittal so long as the officer knew or even erroneously believed that illegal activity of the same type had occurred on another occasion....

We agree ... that knowledge may be inferred from circumstantial evidence, including position and responsibility of defendants such as corporate officers, as well as information provided to those defendants on prior occasions. Further, willful blindness to the facts constituting the offense may be sufficient to establish knowledge. However, the district court erred by instructing the jury that proof that a defendant was a responsible corporate officer, as described, would suffice to conclusively establish the element of knowledge expressly required under 3008(d)(1). Simply because a responsible corporate officer believed that on a prior occasion illegal transportation occurred, he did not necessarily possess knowledge of the violation charged. In a crime having knowledge as an express element, a mere showing of official responsibility under *Dotterweich* and *Park* is not an adequate substitute for direct or circumstantial proof of knowledge. ...

Notes

1. Conceptually, what divides the Tenth Circuit and the First Circuit? The Tenth Circuit (at least in dicta) appears to believe that the responsible corporate officer doctrine is a rule of vicarious responsibility. Do you find the Tenth Circuit's statutory analysis persuasive? The First Circuit disclaims this view, at least in cases where the statute requires some degree of *mens rea*. *See also* Facchiano Construction Co. v. U.S. Dep't of Labor, 987 F.2d 206, 214-15 (3d Cir. 1993) (holding that district court erred in concluding that an individual could be debarred from government contracting solely on the basis of his status as a responsible corporate officer because the relevant regulations require "willful and aggravated" labor standard violations and thus the individual could not be held liable absent substantial evidence that he knew of the violations); United States v. White, 766 F. Supp. 873, 895 (E.D. Wash. 1991) (granting motion to strike portions of the bill of particulars stating that defendant is liable as a "responsible corporate officer" because that doctrine does not allow conviction without a showing of the specific intent required by statute). As the Ninth Circuit explained in a Clean Water Act case, *United States v. Iverson*, 162 F.3d 1015, 1026 (9th Cir. 1998), "the [Responsible Corporate Officer doctrine] instruction relieved the government *only* of having to prove that defendant *personally* discharged or caused the discharge of a pollutant"; "[t]he government still had to prove that the discharges violated the law and that the defendant knew that the discharges were pollutants." *See also* United States v. Hansen, 262 F.3d 1217, 1251 (11th Cir. 2001). In other

---

See generally United States v. Cincotta, 689 F.2d 238, 243 n. 2 (1st Cir. [1982]) ("The conscious avoidance principle means only that specific knowledge may be inferred when a person knows other facts that would induce most people to acquire the specific knowledge in question .... Evidence of conscious avoidance is merely circumstantial evidence of knowledge ...."); United States v. Jewell, 532 F.2d 697, 700 (9th Cir. [1976]); United States v. Rivera, 926 F.2d 1564, 1571 (11th Cir. 1991) ("deliberate ignorance and positive knowledge are equally culpable").

words, the doctrine permits vicarious liability for the *actus reus*, but not the *mens rea* (at least where the statute requires a *mens rea*). Under *Parks*, what is the correct approach?

In United States v. DeCoster, 828 F.3d 626 (8th Cir. 2016), the Eighth Circuit rejected the defendants' due process objection to the imposition of a sentence of imprisonment for a conviction founded on the responsible corporate officer doctrine. In so doing, the court made clear that it does not view this as a species of vicarious liability: "a corporate officer is held accountable not for the acts and omissions of others, but rather for his own failure to prevent or remedy the conditions which gave rise to the charges against him." *Id.* at 633 (internal quotations omitted).

2. The First Circuit required that the government prove that the responsible corporate officer had the statutorily required *mens rea* of knowledge. In so doing, it held improper a jury charge that contained a conclusive presumption of knowledge based on a defendant's position as a responsible corporate officer. The First Circuit made clear, however, that it would be appropriate to charge the jury that knowledge could be established by circumstantial evidence and by a defendant's willful blindness. It indicated that a jury could—but need not reasonably infer knowledge from a defendant's "responsibilities and duties." *See also* United States v. Johnson & Towers, Inc., 741 F.2d 662, 670 (3d Cir. 1984) (while acknowledging that the Resource Conservation and Recovery Act (RCRA) requires a "knowing" *mens rea*, holding that, for responsible corporate officers, "knowledge ... may be inferred by the jury as to those individuals who hold the requisite responsible positions within the corporate defendant"). Do such instructions potentially undermine the statutory *mens rea* requirement in these circumstances or do they simply extend established standards of proof to this context? *See* Brenda S. Hustis & John Y. Gotanda, *The Responsible Corporate Officer: Designated Felon or Legal Fiction?*, 25 Loy. U. Chi. L.J. 169, *passim* (1994).

3. In *United States v. Hong*, 242 F.3d 528 (4th Cir. 2001), the Fourth Circuit upheld Hong's misdemeanor convictions based on the defendant's *negligent* violations under the Clean Water Act on a "responsible corporate officer" theory of liability. The court held that that doctrine was appropriate applied even though Hong did not hold a formal position in the corporation at issue, ruling that the focus was not on formal title but rather on whether he "bore such a relationship to the corporation that it is appropriate to hold him criminally liable for failing to prevent the charged violations of the CWA." *Id.* at 531. Expert commentators have questioned whether "the application of the responsible corporate officer doctrine in a *negligence* case such as *Hong* raises the specter of prosecution of mere 'status offenses.'" Steven P. Solow & Ronald A. Sarachan, *Criminal Negligence Prosecutions Under the Federal Clean Water Act: A Statistical Analysis and an Evaluation of the Impact of* Hanousek *and* Hong, 32 E.L.R. 11153, 11154 (Oct.2002) (emphasis added). Because "negligence theory already encompasses situations in which the defendant can be liable for his or her failure to act, and since negligence by definition does not require proof of knowing conduct, it is unclear what more the responsible corporate officer doctrine adds to the equation. The concern is that the doctrine will be used to hold corporate officials and managers criminally negligent by virtue of their status as officials and managers without regard to their knowledge of, or causal role in, an environmental violation." *Id.*

Chapter 5

PERJURY, FALSE STATEMENTS, AND FALSE CLAIMS

A. PERJURY

Perjury undermines the appearance and reality of justice both in criminal and civil cases. "Judges, lawyers and experts on the court system worry that perjury is being committed with greater frequency and impunity than ever before."[1] There are a number of weapons with which perjurious conduct may be addressed. In some circumstances, perjurious testimony may be met with a judicial contempt sanction where there is some evidence that the perjury obstructed the court in the performance of its duty.[2] The federal sentencing guidelines provide for an enhancement of a defendant's sentence who is convicted of the crime originally charged and whose perjurious testimony at trial constituted a willful attempt to obstruct justice.[3] Finally, false testimony under oath may be prosecuted under one or more of the many federal statutes that proscribe perjury, as well as under some statutes prohibiting the obstruction of justice. Just when is it possible and appropriate to launch a criminal case charging that a witness in a civil or criminal case perjured himself?

The fallout from President Clinton's alleged perjury in the course of a civil deposition focused public attention on the extent of the problem in the civil context. As one prosecutor put it, "[i]f perjury were water, the people in civil court would be drowning."[4] Traditionally, however:

> [B]usy prosecutors often disdain involvement in civil cases. They believe (sometimes correctly) that civil litigators try to enlist prosecutors for private purposes; prosecutors do not relish being in the middle of civil disputes ... [and] ... unless civil perjury affects a government interest or an ongoing criminal investigation, prosecutors often conclude that society's interests would be better served devoting limited prosecutorial resources to pursuing other crimes, instead of promoting truth-telling in civil litigation.[5]

Another reason for prosecutors' apparent disinclination to pursue perjury cases, even when they occur in the course of criminal proceedings, is that they are perceived to be difficult cases to win. The obstacles to conviction may be overwhelming given the proof requirements (discussed within) and the perceived disinclination of juries to convict for perjury where the

---

[1] Mark Curriden, *The Lies Have It*, A.B.A.J. 68 (May 1995).

[2] *See* 18 U.S.C. § 401(1); *In re* Michael, 326 U.S. 224, 227-28 (1945).

[3] *See* U.S. Sentencing Guidelines Manual § 3C1.1 (Nov. 1, 2011) [hereinafter U.S.S.G.]; United States v. Dunnigan, 507 U.S. 87, 98 (1993).

[4] Curriden, *supra* note 1, at 70.

[5] Jonathan Liebman & Joel Cohen, *Perjury and Civil Litigation*, 20 Litigation 43, 44 (1994).

defendant's lies do not go to the heart of a significant matter or relate to a course of criminal conduct. Some argue that there is very good reason to make such prosecutions difficult: to avoid discouraging witnesses from giving evidence.[6] Stringent proof is necessary to separate those who are truly trying to mislead a court or obstruct a proceeding from those whose misstatements are attributable to "inadvertence, honest mistake, carelessness, neglect, or misunderstanding."[7]

When perjury cases are brought, it is often for reasons other than cleansing the judicial process of taint. As one expert on such cases has opined, perjury statutes

> tend to be invoked as a political weapon or as a crime-fighting weapon of last resort ("when you can't get 'em for anything else, get 'em on one of these"). Many times, the statutes are invoked to secure the "cooperation" of witnesses and secure evidence against "really bad guys." "Not so bad guys" often get caught in the crunch.[8]

The following materials focus on the two code sections under which virtually all perjuries occurring in the course of governmental inquiries, proceedings, and the federal judicial process are prosecuted: 18 U.S.C. § 1621 and § 1623.[9]

1. ELEMENTS/PRINCIPLES OF LIABILITY

Generally speaking, under either § 1621 or § 1623, the government bears the burden of showing four essential elements: (1) that the testimony was given (or, under § 1623, the described record or document was used) while the defendant was under oath; (2) the testimony (or the record or document used) was false; (3) the defendant knew when he made the statement (or gave or used the document or record) to the tribunal that it was false; and the (4) matters about which the defendant testified falsely (or the false documents or records used) were material.[10] The two sections do, however, differ in at least two important respects: their scope and the evidence required to demonstrate a violation.

Scope: Section 1623 applies only to false declarations "in any proceeding before or ancillary to any court or grand jury of the United States" which includes pre-trial civil depositions but excludes at least one important area—congressional investigations—in which perjury may be committed.[11] Section 1621 covers congressional investigations as well as much of the territory covered by § 1623, applying as it does more broadly to knowingly false statements made after the witness has "taken an oath before a competent tribunal, officer, or person, in any case in which a law of the United States authorizes an oath to be administered."[12] However, § 1621 is in one sense more limited in scope than § 1623 because a § 1621 case must rest upon false statements while § 1623 cases may lie where a witness "makes or uses" false information or false materials, including false exhibits, documents, records, or other evidence that contains a false material declaration.[13]

---

[6] *See* Bronston v. United States, 409 U.S. 352, 359 (1973).

[7] United States v. Martellano, 675 F.2d 940, 942 (7th Cir.1982).

[8] Richard H. Underwood, *Perjury! The Charges and the Defenses*, 36 Duq. L. Rev. 715, 760 (1998); *see also* Liebman & Cohen, *supra* note 5, *passim*.

[9] *See* 4 Department of Justice Manual [hereinafter U.S.A.M.]., tit. 9, § 9-69.200.

[10] *See* Kevin O'Malley, *et al.*, Federal Practice Jury Instructions § 50:08.

[11] 18 U.S.C. § 1623(a); *see also* Dunn v. United States, 442 U.S. 100 (1979) (holding that an interview in a private attorney's office at which a sworn statement is given does not constitute a "proceeding ancillary to a court or grand jury" under § 1623).

[12] 18 U.S.C. § 1621(1).

[13] *See, e.g.*, *Thirty-Third Annual Survey of White Collar Crime, Perjury*, 55 Am. Crim. L. Rev. 1537, 1555 (2018); United States v. Dudley, 581 F.2d 1193 (5th Cir. 1978) (upholding conviction of witness under § 1623(a)

Evidentiary Considerations: Congress enacted § 1623 in "response to perceived evidentiary problems in demonstrating perjury under the existing federal statute, 18 U.S.C. § 1621. As Congress noted, the strict common-law requirements for establishing falsity which had been engrafted onto the federal perjury statute often made prosecution for false statements exceptionally difficult."[14] Congress made a § 1623 case easier for the government to prove in several respects:

(1) *Proof of Falsity*: Under § 1621, the government must always prove that the defendant's statement was actually false. In § 1623, however, Congress authorized the government to meet its burden of proving the falsity of the declaration at issue by "proof that the defendant while under oath made irreconcilably contradictory declarations material to the point in question in any proceeding before or ancillary to any court or grand jury."[15] "By relieving the Government of the burden of proving which of two or more inconsistent declarations was false, Congress sought to afford 'greater assurance that testimony obtained in grand jury and court proceedings will aid the cause of truth.'"[16]

(2) *Two-Witness Rule*: Under the two-witness rule, "the uncorroborated oath of one witness is not enough to establish the falsity of the testimony of the accused."[17] Contrary to its popular name, this rule does not require that two witnesses demonstrate the falsity of the defendant's statements; rather, "what actually is needed is one witness plus some independent corroboration (that is, the uncorroborated oath of one prosecution witness is still insufficient)"[18] and "[m]ost courts appear to subscribe to the view that circumstantial evidence will do for the corroboration."[19] Section 1621 retains the two-witness rule but Congress eliminated that requirement in § 1623 cases.[20]

(3) *Mens Rea*: Both statutes require proof that the defendant made the statement or declaration, or used the information, knowing that it was false. In addition, however, § 1621 requires that the perjury be "willful" while § 1623 does not.[21]

2. DEFENSES

a. Recantation

There is no "recantation" defense to § 1621 perjury; the crime is deemed complete the moment that the false statement is uttered.[22] The correction of an innocent mistake or elaboration of an answer may, however, bear upon whether there was a willful intent to swear falsely.[23] By contrast, § 1623 contains an express recantation defense.[24] In this respect,

---

who testified regarding falsified document in grand jury); United States v. Pommerening, 500 F.2d 92 (10th Cir. 1974) (upholding convictions of defendants under § 1623(a) for relying upon falsified documents when appearing before the grand jury).

[14] *Dunn*, 442 U.S. at 108.

[15] *See* 18 U.S.C. § 1623(c).

[16] *Dunn*, 442 U.S. at 108 (*quoting* S. Rep. No. 91-617, at 59 (1969)).

[17] Hammer v. United States, 271 U.S. 620, 626 (1926); *see also* Weiler v. United States, 323 U.S. 606, 607 (1945).

[18] Underwood, *supra* note 8, at 733.

[19] *Id.*

[20] *See* 18 U.S.C. § 1623(e).

[21] *See, e.g.,* United States v. Fornaro, 894 F.2d 508, 512 (2d Cir. 1990).

[22] *See* United States v. McAfee, 8 F.3d 1010, 1017 (5th Cir. 1993).

[23] *See* United States v. Norris, 300 U.S. 564 (1937); *McAfee*, 8 F.3d at 1017.

[24] *See* 18 U.S.C. § 1623(d).

Congress gave *defendants* one evidentiary advantage in § 1623 that they do not have under § 1621—the possibility of avoiding prosecution by recanting their perjurious testimony. This advantage may be illusory, however, given the demanding preconditions for establishing the defense and the possible consequences of such a recantation.

A majority of the circuits hold that, to claim the defense, the defendant must recant in the "same continuous court or grand jury proceeding" in which the false declaration was made, the declaration must not have "substantially affected the proceeding," *and* it cannot have become "manifest that such falsity has been or will be exposed."[25] "The courts have not interpreted any of these conditions in a way that is the least bit 'defense favorable.' A virtually immediate retraction might do, but anything else probably will not do."[26] Further, as Professor Richard Underwood explains, the disparity in the treatment of recantations between sections 1621 and 1623 may lead to the anomalous result that a properly executed recantation for purposes of § 1623 may actually aid the government in pursuing the defendant for perjury under § 1621, which does not recognize recantation as a defense:

> ...The reader might reflect on the facts of *United States v. McAfee*, [8 F.3d 1010 (5th Cir.1993)]. In this case, the defendant was convicted of one count of willful perjury under section 1621 and three counts of making irreconcilable contradictory declarations under section 1623. McAfee, a cattle hide processor, had been sued in two separate civil actions for his alleged role in a stolen hides scheme. McAfee was separately deposed in each of these cases, although they were consolidated and ultimately settled. However, perceived perjury was referred to the United States Attorney by one of the plaintiff's attorneys. Section 1623(c) applies to depositions in civil cases. The three counts against McAfee under section 1623 arose from inconsistencies between his two separate depositions. As a defense to one of the section 1623 counts, McAfee argued that he recanted testimony given in his earlier deposition on the first day of his second deposition. This defense failed because the court ruled that the second deposition was not part of the same proceeding in which the false statement was made—the recantation was not sufficient under section 1623 to provide a defense to the section 1623 counts. Count 1 charged a violation of section 1621 on the ground that the testimony in the first deposition was perjured. The attempted (and in this case, legally ineffective) recantation, must have helped prove the prosecutor's point.[27]

b. *"Literal Truth" and "Ambiguity"*

"It is sometimes suggested that proof that the defendant told the literal truth, while, perhaps, hoping to mislead, is a *defense* to a perjury charge under 18 U.S.C. sections 1621 and 1623, and under 18 U.S.C. section 1001. ... However, it is important to remember that *the burden of proving falsity remains with the prosecution*."[28]

---

[25] *Id.* Although the statute places the last two conditions in the disjunctive, a majority of the circuits to address the question have held that a defendant seeking to rely on a recantation defense under § 1623(d) must show *both* that at the time he recanted the declaration had not substantially affected the proceeding *and* that it had not become manifest that the falsity had been or would be exposed. *See, e.g.*, United States v. Sherman, 150 F.3d 306, 313-18 (3d Cir. 1998); United States v. Fornaro, 894 F.2d 508, 510-11 (2d Cir. 1990); United States v. Scrimgeour, 636 F.2d 1019, 1021-24 (5th Cir. 1981). That is, these courts have read the statutory "or" to actually read "and." The Eighth Circuit, however, has held that the statute is plain on its face and that "or" truly means "or." It therefore holds that a defendant may prevail on a recantation defense by showing *either* that at the time he recanted the declaration had not substantially affected the proceeding *or* that it had not become manifest that the falsity had been or would be exposed. *See* United States v. Smith, 35 F.3d 344, 345-47 (8th Cir. 1994).

[26] Underwood, *supra* note 8, at 745.

[27] *Id.* at 744-45.

[28] *Id.* at 722 (emphasis added).

Although not technically a defense in that the government bears the burden of proving actual falsity beyond a reasonable doubt, the "literal truth" rule permits the defendant to put the government to its burden and occasionally to defeat a perjury, false declarations, or false statement prosecution. *Bronston v. United States* is the leading case describing and applying the "literal truth" "defense."[29]

BRONSTON v. UNITED STATES
409 U.S. 352 (1973)

MR. CHIEF JUSTICE BURGER delivered the opinion of the Court.

We granted the writ in this case to consider a narrow but important question in the application of the federal perjury statute, 18 U.S.C. § 1621: whether a witness may be convicted of perjury for an answer, under oath, that is literally true but not responsive to the question asked and arguably misleading by negative implication.

Petitioner is the sole owner of Samuel Bronston Productions, Inc., a company that between 1958 and 1964, produced motion pictures in various European locations. For these enterprises, Bronston Productions opened bank accounts in a number of foreign countries; in 1962, for example, it had 37 accounts in five countries. As president of Bronston Productions, petitioner supervised transactions involving the foreign bank accounts.

In June 1964, Bronston Productions petitioned for an arrangement with creditors under Chapter XI of the Bankruptcy Act, 11 U.S.C. § 701 *et seq.* On June 10, 1966, a referee in bankruptcy held a ... hearing to determine, for the benefit of creditors, the extent and location of the company's assets. Petitioner's perjury conviction was founded on the answers given by him as a witness at that bankruptcy hearing, and in particular on the following colloquy with a lawyer for a creditor of Bronston Productions:

"Q. Do you have any bank accounts in Swiss banks, Mr. Bronston?
"A. No, sir.
"Q. Have you ever?
"A. The company had an account there for about six months, in Zurich.
"Q. Have you any nominees who have bank accounts in Swiss banks?
"A. No, sir.
"Q. Have you ever?
"A. No, sir."

It is undisputed that for a period of nearly five years, between October 1959 and June 1964, petitioner had a personal bank account at the International Credit Bank in Geneva, Switzerland, into which he made deposits and upon which he drew checks totaling more than $180,000. It is likewise undisputed that petitioner's answers were literally truthful. (a) Petitioner did not at the time of questioning have a Swiss bank account. (b) Bronston Productions, Inc., did have the account in Zurich described by petitioner. (c) Neither at the time of questioning nor before did petitioner have nominees who had Swiss accounts. The Government's prosecution for perjury went forward on the theory that in order to mislead his questioner, petitioner answered the second question with literal truthfulness but unresponsively addressed his answer to the company's assets and not to his own—thereby implying that he had no personal Swiss bank account at the relevant time.

---

[29] Although *Bronston* involved a § 1621 prosecution, "its holding has equal applicability in terms of 18 U.S.C. § 1623," United States v. Reveron Martinez, 836 F.2d 684, 689 (1st Cir. 1988), except in cases sought to be proved under § 1623(c) by evidence of irreconcilably inconsistent statements.

At petitioner's trial, the District Court instructed the jury that the "basic issue" was whether petitioner "spoke his true belief." Perjury, the court stated, "necessarily involves the state of mind of the accused" and "essentially consists of wilfully testifying to the truth of a fact which the defendant does not believe to be true"; petitioner's testimony could not be found "wilfully" false unless at the time his testimony was given petitioner "fully understood the questions put to him but nevertheless gave false answers knowing the same to be false." The court further instructed the jury that if petitioner did not understand the question put to him and for that reason gave an unresponsive answer, he could not be convicted of perjury. Petitioner could, however, be convicted if he gave an answer "not literally false but when considered in the context in which it was given, nevertheless constitute[d] a false statement."[30]

...

In the Court of Appeals, petitioner contended, as he had in post-trial motions before the District Court, that the key question was imprecise and suggestive of various interpretations. In addition, petitioner contended that he could not be convicted of perjury on the basis of testimony that was concededly truthful, however unresponsive. A divided Court of Appeals held that the question was readily susceptible of a responsive reply and that it adequately tested the defendant's belief in the veracity of his answer. The Court of Appeals further held that, "[f]or the purposes of 18 U.S.C. § 1621, an answer containing half of the truth which also constitutes a lie by negative implication, when the answer is intentionally given in place of the responsive answer called for by a proper question, is perjury." In this Court, petitioner renews his attack on the specificity of the question asked him and the legal sufficiency of his answer to support a conviction for perjury. The problem of the ambiguity of the question is not free from doubt, but we need not reach that issue. Even assuming, as we do, that the question asked petitioner specifically focused on petitioner's personal bank accounts, we conclude that the federal perjury statute cannot be construed to sustain a conviction based on petitioner's answer.

The statute, 18 U.S.C. § 1621, substantially identical in its relevant language to its predecessors for nearly a century, is "a federal statute enacted in an effort to keep the course of justice free from the pollution of perjury." ... [In the bankruptcy context], as elsewhere, the perpetration of perjury "well may affect the dearest concerns of the parties before a tribunal. ..."

There is, at the outset, a serious literal problem in applying § 1621 to petitioner's answer. The words of the statute confine the offense to the witness who "willfully ... states ... any material matter which he does not believe to be true." Beyond question, petitioner's answer to the crucial question was not responsive if we assume, as we do, that the first question was directed at personal bank accounts. There is, indeed, an implication in the answer to the second question that there was never a personal bank account; in casual conversation this interpretation might reasonably be drawn. But we are not dealing with casual conversation

---

[30] [Court's footnote 3:] The District Court gave the following example "as an illustration only":

> "[I]f it is material to ascertain how many times a person has entered a store on a given day and that person responds to such a question by saying five times when in fact he knows that he entered the store 50 times that day, that person may be guilty of perjury even though it is technically true that he entered the store five times."

The illustration given by the District Court is hardly comparable to petitioner's answer; the answer "five times" is responsive to the hypothetical question and contains nothing to alert the questioner that he may be sidetracked. Moreover, it is very doubtful that an answer which, in response to a specific quantitative inquiry, baldly understates a numerical fact can be described as even "technically true." Whether an answer is true must be determined with reference to the question it purports to answer, not in isolation. An unresponsive answer is unique in this respect because its unresponsiveness by definition prevents its truthfulness from being tested in the context of the question—unless there is to be speculation as to what the unresponsive answer "implies."

and the statute does not make it a criminal act for a witness to willfully state any material matter that *implies* any material matter that he does not believe to be true.[31]

The Government urges that the perjury statute be construed broadly to reach petitioner's answer and thereby fulfill its historic purpose of reinforcing our adversary factfinding process. We might go beyond the precise words of the statute if we thought they did not adequately express the intention of Congress, but we perceive no reason why Congress would intend the drastic sanction of a perjury prosecution to cure a testimonial mishap that could readily have been reached with a single additional question by counsel alert—as every examiner ought to be—to the incongruity of petitioner's unresponsive answer. Under the pressures and tensions of interrogation, it is not uncommon for the most earnest witnesses to give answers that are not entirely responsive. Sometimes the witness does not understand the question, or may in an excess of caution or apprehension read too much or too little into it. It should come as no surprise that a participant in a bankruptcy proceeding may have something to conceal and consciously tries to do so, or that a debtor may be embarrassed at his plight and yield information reluctantly. It is the responsibility of the lawyer to probe; testimonial interrogation, and cross-examination in particular, is a probing, prying, pressing form of inquiry. If a witness evades, it is the lawyer's responsibility to recognize the evasion and to bring the witness back to the mark, to flush out the whole truth with the tools of adversary examination.

It is no answer to say that here the jury found that petitioner intended to mislead his examiner. A jury should not be permitted to engage in conjecture whether an unresponsive answer, true and complete on its face, was intended to mislead or divert the examiner; the state of mind of the witness is relevant only to the extent that it bears on whether "he does not believe [his answer] to be true." To hold otherwise would be to inject a new and confusing element into the adversary testimonial system we know. Witnesses would be unsure of the extent of their responsibility for the misunderstandings and inadequacies of examiners, and might well fear having that responsibility tested by a jury under the vague rubric of "intent to mislead" or "perjury by implication." The seminal modern treatment of the history of the offense concludes that one consideration of policy overshadowed all others during the years when perjury first emerged as a common-law offense: "that the measures taken against the offense must not be so severe as to discourage witnesses from appearing or testifying." A leading 19th century commentator, quoted by Dean Wigmore, noted that the English law "throws every fence round a person accused of perjury," for

> "the obligation of protecting witnesses from oppression, or annoyance, by charges, or threats of charges, of having borne false testimony, is far paramount to that of giving even perjury its deserts. To repress that crime, prevention is better than cure: and the law of England relies, for this purpose, on the means provided for detecting and exposing the crime at the moment of commission,—such as publicity, cross-examination, the aid of a jury, etc.; and on the infliction of a severe, though not excessive punishment, wherever the commission of the crime has been clearly proved." ...

Thus, we must read § 1621 in light of our own and the traditional Anglo-American judgment that a prosecution for perjury is not the sole, or even the primary, safeguard against errant testimony. While "the lower federal courts have not dealt with the question often," and while their expressions do not deal with unresponsive testimony and are not precisely in point, "it may be said that they preponderate against the respondent's contention." The cases support petitioner's position that the perjury statute is not to be loosely construed, nor the

---

[31] [Court's footnote 4:] Petitioner's answer is not to be measured by the same standards applicable to criminally fraudulent or extortionate statements. In that context, the law goes "rather far in punishing intentional creation of false impressions by a selection of literally true representations, because the actor himself generally selects and arranges the representations." In contrast, "under our system of adversary questioning and cross-examination the scope of disclosure is largely in the hands of counsel and presiding officer."

statute invoked simply because a wily witness succeeds in derailing the questioner—so long as the witness speaks the literal truth. The burden is on the questioner to pin the witness down to the specific object to the questioner's inquiry.

The Government does not contend that any misleading or incomplete response must be sent to the jury to determine whether a witness committed perjury because he intended to sidetrack his questioner. As the Government recognizes, the effect of so unlimited an interpretation of § 1621 would be broadly unsettling. It is said, rather, that petitioner's testimony falls within a more limited category of intentionally misleading responses with an especially strong tendency to mislead the questioner. ... [T]he Government isolates two factors which are said to require application of the perjury statute in the circumstances of this case; the unresponsiveness of petitioner's answer and the affirmative cast of that answer, with its accompanying negative implication.

This analysis succeeds in confining the Government's position, but it does not persuade us that Congress intended to extend the coverage of § 1621 to answers unresponsive on their face but untrue only by "negative implication." Though perhaps a plausible argument can be made that unresponsive answers are especially likely to mislead,[32] any such argument must, we think, be predicated upon the questioner's being aware of the unresponsiveness of the relevant answer. Yet, if the questioner is aware of the unresponsiveness of the answer, with equal force it can be argued that the very unresponsiveness of the answer should alert counsel to press on for the information he desires. It does not matter that the unresponsive answer is stated in the affirmative, thereby implying the negative of the question actually posed; for again, by hypothesis, the examiner's awareness of unresponsiveness should lead him to press another question or reframe his initial question with greater precision. Precise questioning is imperative as a predicate for the offense of perjury. ...

Notes

1. Obviously, the *Bronston* opinion errs on the side of protecting the witness and puts the burden of careful examination on counsel. Did the *Bronston* Court reach the correct result? Is the defendant's intention better left to jury determination? Note that a perjury defendant's presentation of a plausible, but not inevitable, understanding of the circumstances that would make the statements at issue "literally true" is not enough to establish an absolute defense under *Bronston* and may be left to jury determination. *See* United States v. Thomas, 612 F.3d 1107 (9th Cir. 2010).

The Court in a footnote states that an alleged perjurer's "answer is not to be measured by the same standards applicable to criminally fraudulent or extortionate statements." Are you persuaded by the reason it provides?

2. Perhaps the most famous example of a "literal truth" argument is that asserted by President Clinton in his grand jury testimony when he was asked by the prosecutor about a statement his lawyer, Mr. Bennett, made in President Clinton's civil deposition:

Q. Mr. President, I want to before I go into a new subject area .... The statement of your attorney, Mr. Bennett, at the Paul[a] Jones deposition, "counsel is fully aware ... that Ms. Lewinsky has filed, has an affidavit which they are in possession of saying that there is no sex of any kind in any manner, shape or form, with President Clinton"?

That statement was made by your attorney in front of Judge Susan Webber Wright, correct?

---

[32] [Court's footnote 5:] Arguably, the questioner will assume there is some logical justification for the unresponsive answer, since competent witnesses do not usually answer in irrelevancies. Thus the questioner may conclude that the unresponsive answer is given only because it is intended to make a statement—a negative statement—relevant to the question asked. In this case, petitioner's questioner may have assumed that petitioner denied having a personal account in Switzerland; only this unspoken denial would provide a logical nexus between inquiry directed to petitioner's personal account and petitioner's adverting, in response, to the company account in Zurich.

A. That's correct.

Q. That statement is a completely false statement. Whether or not Mr. Bennett knew of your relationship with Ms. Lewinsky, the statement that there was "no sex of any kind in any manner, shape or form, with President Clinton," was an utterly false statement. Is that correct?

A. It depends on what the meaning of the word "is" is. If the—if he—if "is" means is and never has been, that is not—that is one thing. If it means there is none, that was a completely true statement.

But, as I have testified, and I'd like to testify again, this is—it is somewhat unusual for a client to be asked about his lawyer's statements, instead of the other way around. I was not paying a great deal of attention to this exchange. I was focusing on my own testimony.

Grand Jury Testimony of President Clinton, August 17, 1998, p. 57-58. The House Committee on the Judiciary concluded in its report that "[i]t is clear to the Committee that the President perjured himself when he said that Mr. Bennett's statement that there was 'no sex of any kind' was 'completely true' depending on what the word 'is' is." *Impeachment of William Jefferson Clinton, President of the United States*, H.R. Rep. No. 105-830 (1998). Under *Bronston*, was this perjury? Is this a case that you as a prosecutor would indict? What considerations might affect your judgment?

3. A related "defense" to a prosecution under §§ 1621 and 1623 is alluded to but not addressed in *Bronston*: the contention that the question to which the defendant falsely responded was too ambiguous to serve as the basis for a perjury or false declarations count. "A fundamental ambiguity cannot be the basis for a [perjury or] false statement conviction because a person cannot knowingly give a false reply to a question that defies interpretation despite its context." United States v. Schulte, 741 F.3d 1141, 1150 (10th Cir. 2014). Generally speaking, courts will defer to the jury's determination of the meaning of the question and the truthfulness of the defendant's answer. "In other words, where a prosecutor's question is only 'arguably ambiguous,' a defendant's understanding of the question is for the jury to resolve in the first instance." United States v. Farmer, 137 F.3d 1265, 1269 (10th Cir. 1998). Where a question is "fundamentally ambiguous," however, reviewing courts have overturned convictions in order to "(1) preclude convictions grounded on surmise or conjecture; (2) prevent witnesses from unfairly bearing the risks of inadequate examination; and (3) encourage witnesses to testify (or at least not discourage them from doing so)." *Id.* A question is said to be "fundamentally ambiguous" when it "'is not a phrase with a meaning about which men of ordinary intellect could agree, nor one which could be used with mutual understanding by a questioner and answerer unless it were defined at the time it [was] sought and offered as testimony.'" *Id.* (quoting United States v. Lighte, 782 F.2d 367, 375 (2d Cir. 1986)); *see also, e.g.,* United States v. Lattimore, 127 F. Supp. 405, 412-13 (D.D.C.) (dismissing perjury indictment founded upon negative answer to ambiguous question whether defendant was "a follower of the Communist line"), *aff'd per curiam by an equally divided court*, 232 F.2d 334 (D.C. Cir. 1955). In determining what meaning could reasonably be given to a question, the jury, and the court, will examine the question in the context of the entire line of questioning and may consider extrinsic evidence that demonstrates how the defendant interpreted a question. *See Lighte*, 782 F.2d at 373.

4. Another popular defense theory in perjury or false declarations prosecutions is to move to bar the prosecution on the ground that the government improperly created a "perjury trap" into which the defendant fell, usually in the course of grand jury proceedings. "A perjury trap is created when the government calls a witness before the grand jury for the primary purpose of obtaining testimony from him in order to prosecute him later for perjury." United States v. Chen, 933 F.2d 793, 796 (9th Cir. 1991). The perjury trap defense "is based on the argument that the grand jury is the prosecutor's turf, and that the witness (who is without benefit of counsel in the grand jury room) may be led into the pit by the wily inquisitor." Underwood, *supra* note 8, at 751. Counsel have attempted to ground this essentially equitable defense in a variety of legal theories, the most popular being that such government conduct is an abuse of the grand jury process, *see* Bursey v. United States, 466 F.2d 1059, 1080 n.10 (9th Cir. 1972), or that it violates due process guarantees, *see* Wheel v. Robinson, 34 F.3d 60, 67 (2d Cir.

1994); *see also* United States v. Regan, 103 F.3d 1072, 1081 (2d Cir. 1997). Most courts hold that if there was a "legitimate basis" for an investigation and for particular questions answered falsely, a perjury trap defense must be rejected. *See, e.g., Regan*, 103 F.3d at 1079. Because most of the courts to pass on these claims have found the investigation and questions to have such a basis, they have not yet been required to pass on the validity of a perjury trap defense on any legal theory. *See, e.g., id.; Wheel*, 34 F.3d at 67-68; *Chen*, 933 F.2d at 796-97. Given that the defendants asserting perjury trap defenses are not necessarily contesting the perjurious nature of their testimony, it is a defense that is unlikely to be terribly appealing to the judiciary unless the governmental conduct involved is egregious. *See, e.g.*, Brown v. United States 245 F.2d 549, 549, 555 (8th Cir. 1957) ("Extracting the testimony from the defendant had no tendency to support any possible action of the grand jury within its competency. The purpose to get him indicted for perjury and nothing else is manifest beyond all reasonable doubt."). Indeed, some courts have rejected "perjury trap" arguments even where the prosecutor is alleged to have engaged in some misconduct of her own—by affirmatively and falsely advising the defendant that he was not a "target" of the grand jury investigation and thus inducing him to testify against his interests. *See, e.g.*, United States v. Williams, 874 F.2d 968, 975 (5th Cir. 1989). Should some variant of a perjury trap defense be available?

5. In *Johnson v. United States*, 520 U.S. 461, 465 (1997), the Supreme Court held that materiality is an element of perjury and thus must be submitted to the jury for determination. Although the magnitude of cases raising materiality challenges demonstrates that it is one of the most frequently contested issues, it is also worth noting that these challenges only infrequently are successful. The standard for materiality is the same in this context as it is in the false statements (18 U.S.C. § 1001) and mail and wire fraud statutes (18 U.S.C. §§ 1341, 1343): the statement is generally said to be material if it "has 'a natural tendency to influence, or be capable of influencing, the decision of the decisionmaking body to which it is addressed.'" United States v. Frost, 125 F.3d 346, 387 (6th Cir. 1997) (quoting United States v. Gaudin, 515 U.S. 506, 509 (1995)). The "natural tendency" test is an objective one, focused on whether the statement is "of a type capable of influencing a *reasonable* decision maker." United States v. McBane, 433 F.3d 344, 351 (3d Cir. 2005). The fact that a statement is "delusional," or "not persuasive or believable," does not make the statement immaterial. United States v. Abrahem, 678 F.3d 370, 376 (5th Cir. 2012).

How the materiality standard is applied depends to some extent upon the context in which the false statement or declaration was made. For example, as the Second Circuit explained in reviewing the materiality of a false statement made during the course of a deposition taken in connection with a civil forfeiture action filed by the government:

> We have consistently held in the grand jury context that a false declaration is "material" within the meaning of § 1623 when it has "'a natural effect or tendency to influence, impede or dissuade the grand jury from pursuing its investigation.'" We have pointed out that in a § 1623 prosecution for false declarations to a grand jury,

> > [m]atters arguably cumulative or collateral to the grand jury's objective in a given case are considered for their *potential* to aid that body, not for the *probability* of assistance from a truthful answer.

> Because the grand jury's function is investigative, materiality in that context is "broadly construed." However, we have apparently not yet addressed the issue of materiality under § 1623 in the context of a deposition in a civil matter. The purpose of civil discovery is also investigative, and the scope of discovery includes any information that "appears reasonably calculated to lead to the discovery of admissible evidence." Fed.R.Civ.P. 26(b)(1).

> The Fifth Circuit has held that for purposes of § 1623, materiality in a civil discovery deposition is not limited to evidence admissible at trial but includes matters properly the subject of and material to a deposition under Rule 26(b)(1). The Ninth and Sixth Circuits have also adapted a materiality definition under § 1623 to the civil deposition context. But

the resultant definition is considerably narrower than that of the Fifth Circuit: it requires not merely discoverability under Rule 26(b)(1), but also the tendency of the false statement itself to affect the outcome of the underlying civil suit for which the deposition was taken.

The facts of the present case favor a broad construction of the definition of materiality similar to the approach we have already used in the grand jury context. While a government deposition in a forfeiture action under 21 U.S.C. § 881 is civil in form, forfeiture actions are predicated upon a nexus between the property and criminal activity. Under the circumstances of this case, we see no persuasive reason not to apply the broad standard for materiality of whether a truthful answer might reasonably be calculated to lead to the discovery of evidence admissible at the trial of the underlying suit.

United States v. Kross, 14 F.3d 751, 753-54 (2d Cir. 1994); *see also* Underwood, *supra* note 8, at 729-30, 732 (discussing standards applied in grand jury and civil deposition context). Under a standard that concentrates on the "potential" of certain matters to aid a grand jury investigation, is it likely that anything would be immaterial?

6. The conventional wisdom is that perjury and false declarations cases are difficult to prove. There is often little physical evidence to support a perjury charge. Further, the prosecutor must prove not only that the statement was material, was made in response to a non-ambiguous question, and was actually false (not literally true), but also that the witness knew that the statement was false when it was made—that is, that the witness was not simply mistaken, absentminded, or confused. Consider how the defense in the prosecution of Vice President Dick Cheney's chief of staff, I. Lewis "Scooter" Libby, sought (ultimately unsuccessfully) to put the government to its burden on proving knowing falsity:

The defendant is charged in a five-count indictment with obstruction of justice in violation of 18 U.S.C. § 1503 (2000), two counts of false statements in violation of 18 U.S.C. § 1001(a)(2) (2000), and two counts of perjury in violation of 18 U.S.C. § 1623 (2000). All of these charges arise from a criminal investigation into the possible unauthorized disclosure of classified information—Valerie Plame Wilson's affiliation with the Central Intelligence Agency ("CIA")—to several journalists. Specifically, the charges against the defendant are predicated upon statements that the defendant allegedly made to Special Agents of the Federal Bureau of Investigation ("FBI") in October and November, 2003, and testimony he provided to a grand jury in March 2004. The alleged false statements occurred when the defendant recounted conversations he had in June and July 2003, with news reporters Tim Russert, Judith Miller, and Matthew Cooper to the FBI Agents and to the grand jury.

The defendant has made clear that in his effort to rebut these charges he will argue, in part, (1) that it is the government's witnesses, and not him, who misremembered the facts and the substance of the various conversations detailed in the indictment and (2) that any errors he may have made in describing the events were occasioned by confusion or faulty memory, not any wilful intent to misrepresent the truth. This Court has acknowledged that this "faulty memory defense" is a viable defense to the charges. Accordingly, the memory and recollection of the principal players will undoubtedly play a substantial role in the assessment of the defendant's culpability in the upcoming trial.

To support his faulty memory defense, the defendant seeks to introduce at trial the testimony of Dr. [Robert A. Bjork] "to show that it is entirely plausible, given how memory has been found to function, that Mr. Libby or the government witnesses—or both—have innocently confused or misremembered the conversations on which this case turns." Specifically, Dr. Bjork would testify about thirteen scientific principles concerning human memory ... According to the defendant, Dr. Bjork's expert testimony "will assist the jury by providing information about the findings of memory research that are not already known to the jurors." It is the admissibility of Dr. Bjork's testimony under Federal Rule of Evidence 702 that is the subject of this opinion. ...

The admissibility of expert testimony is governed by Federal Rule of Evidence 702. Central to the court's determination of whether expert testimony is admissible under Rule

702, and consistent with the Rule's purpose, is the two-prong test enunciated by the Supreme Court in *Daubert v. Merrell Dow Pharm.*, 509 U.S. 579 (1993). Under this test, a court determining the admissibility of purported expert testimony must first determine "[1] whether the reasoning or methodology underlying the testimony is scientifically valid and [2] whether that reasoning or methodology properly can be applied to the facts in issue." ...

The government does not challenge the proposed testimony of Dr. Bjork on the grounds that his testimony fails to satisfy the first prong of *Daubert*, noting that it "does not quibble with Dr. Bjork's expertise concerning research into memory, particularly with respect to the reliability of eyewitness identification." Rather, the government contends that the defendant "cannot meet his burden as the proponent of the evidence of establishing that the testimony will assist the jury in understanding or determining any of the facts at issue in this case." Thus, this is the only question the Court must resolve. For the reasons that follow, this Court agrees with the government. Therefore, Dr. Bjork will not be permitted to testify at trial. ...

... [T]he Court cannot conclude that the defendant has satisfied his burden of establishing that the expert testimony of Dr. Bjork will be helpful to the jury. Not only are the studies [regarding problems with eye-witness testimony] offered by the defendant inapposite to the situation here, but the theories upon which Dr. Bjork would testify are not beyond the ken of the average juror. And as the facts of this case unfold during the trial, the Court has no doubt that aided by the normal trial processes, and the assistance of very capable legal counsel, the jurors will have the ability to collectively draw upon their common-sense understanding of memory and render a fair and just verdict.

United States v. Libby, 461 F.Supp.2d 3, 4-5, 8-9, 18 (D.D.C. 2006).

B. FALSE STATEMENTS

Congress has outlawed the provision of false statements in about 100 different situations.[33] The code section most frequently invoked by federal prosecutors to pursue such cases is 18 U.S.C. § 1001. This statute is appealing to prosecutors for a number of reasons, not least of which is the fact that its elements are fairly simple and, in light of recent Supreme Court case law and legislative activity, open-ended. Section 1001 also provides prosecutors with a great deal of flexibility in charging choices as well as a potentially powerful instrumental weapon.[34]

First, the statute is a workhorse of a prohibition and may be used instead of, or in conjunction with, statutes covering a broad spectrum of criminal activity, including such matters as fraud, perjury, obstruction of justice, and false claims. For example, § 1001 punishes false statements but does not require that the object of the statement be to defraud the government out of money or property. Thus, it may reach frauds that are difficult to prove. As a means of addressing deceit aimed at governmental functioning, the false statement prohibition may be used when classic perjury prosecutions under 18 U.S.C. § 1621 and § 1623 would fail because § 1001 does not require, as do perjury prosecutions, that the false statements be made under oath. It may also be used to avoid some of the evidentiary strictures of § 1621; the two-witness rule applied in § 1621 cases does not control in § 1001 cases and prosecutors may avoid proving the offending statement actually false, as required in perjury cases, by charging that the defendant misled through concealment under § 1001. (Section 1001 may have a more limited role in supplanting § 1623 because that section applies only where the perjury is ancillary to a court or grand jury proceeding and § 1001's applicability at least to false statements made by parties or their counsel in judicial proceedings is limited by

---

[33] *See* United States v. Gaudin, 28 F.3d 943, 958-60 & nn.3-4 (9th Cir.1994) (Kozinski, J., dissenting), *aff'd*, 515 U.S. 506 (1995).

[34] The False Statements Accountability Act of 1996 (FSAA), Pub. L. No. 104-492, 110 Stat. 3459 (1996).

the terms of the statute.) Section 1001 may also be used to pursue activity that normally might be charged as obstruction of justice but for perceived difficulties in demonstrating the existence of elements necessary to an obstruction case, such as the defendant's knowledge of a pending proceeding, a defendant's "corrupt" motive in making the false statement, or a demonstrable "nexus" between a false statement and the due administration of justice. Finally, § 1001 is popular in addressing procurement or other instances of federal program fraud and, as is explored further, *infra*, may also be used instead of or to supplement actions under the false claims statute, 18 U.S.C. § 287.

Second, the false statements statute is often applied to simple and relatively easy to prove false statements made during a larger criminal case, or during the course of the investigation of a criminal matter. As such, it opens up the possibility that the government may secure a conviction (or plea) on a false statement count even when it does not have the proof to make its case on the underlying criminal case under investigation. This provides prosecutors with greater leverage to obtain a plea or cooperation (and defense counsel with added incentives to heed Justice Jackson's exhortation that "any lawyer worth his salt will tell the suspect in no uncertain terms to make no statement to police under any circumstances."[35]).

1. ELEMENTS/PRINCIPLES OF LIABILITY

In general terms, to make a false statement case the Government must prove beyond a reasonable doubt the following elements:

(a) the defendant either made or used a false or fraudulent statement, representation or writing; or falsified, or affirmatively concealed or covered up by trick, scheme, or device, a fact that the defendant had a legal duty to disclose;
(b) the false statement or information concealed was "material";
(c) the subject-matter involved was within the "jurisdiction";
(d) of the executive, legislative, or judicial branches of the Government of the United States (as those terms are qualified in § 1001(b), (c)); and
(e) in so doing, the defendant acted "knowingly and willfully."

a. False Statements and Affirmative Concealment of Material Facts

Courts recognize two general categories of cases under § 1001: false statement and concealment cases.[36] As the Second Circuit has explained:

It is well established that ... section [1001] encompasses within its proscription two distinct offenses, concealment of a material fact and false representation. The objective of both offenses may be the same, to create or foster on the part of a Government agency a misapprehension of the true state of affairs. What must be proved to establish each offense, however, differs significantly. False representations, like common law perjury, require proof of actual falsity; concealment requires proof of willful nondisclosure by means of a "trick, scheme or device."[37]

---

[35] Watts v. Indiana, 338 U.S. 49, 59 (1949) (Jackson, J., concurring in part and dissenting in part); *see also id.* ("Any lawyer who has ever been called into a case after his client has 'told all' and turned any evidence he has over to the Government, knows how helpless he is to protect his client against the facts thus disclosed.").

[36] *See, e.g.,* United States v. Curran, 20 F.3d 560, 566 (3d Cir. 1994); United States v. Mayberry, 913 F.2d 719, 722 n.7 (9th Cir. 1990); United States v. Diogo, 320 F.2d 898, 902 (2d Cir. 1963).

[37] *Diogo,* 320 F.2d at 902; *see also* United States v. Wright, 211 F.3d 233, 238 (5th Cir. 2000); *Curran,* 20 F.3d at 566.

With respect to the false representation aspect of the offense, § 1001 covers all false statements, "whether oral or written, sworn or unsworn, voluntary or required by law."[38] Further, "[a]lthough the statement that is the subject of a [§ 1001] violation usually concerns past or present facts, it need not be so. A present statement as to future intent, *e.g.*, a promise to do that which is not actually intended, may be a false statement of an existing fact."[39]

What is essential in a case pursued under the false representation prong (just as in a perjury case) is that the government prove that the statement was actually false. "Although a statement may be misleading, unauthorized, or even fraudulent, a conviction under this section generally cannot be sustained unless the statement also is false."[40] The government, which bears the burden of proving falsity beyond a reasonable doubt, "'must negative any reasonable interpretation that would make the defendant's statement factually correct.'"[41] Defendants often attempt to put the government to its burden in false statement cases by arguing either that the question to which a defendant responded was fundamentally "ambiguous"[42] or that the defendant's statement was "literally true."[43]

Congress has recently passed a number of statutes that are designed to attack false statements made in a given context.[44] For example, one congressional response to the corporate accounting scandals of 2002 was to create a duty on the part of certain corporate officers to certify their companies' financial statements.[45] A demonstrably false and material statement with respect to the certification made would be potentially prosecutable under § 1001. Congress, however, also created a specific statute to address such false certifications. Generally speaking, prosecutors may choose between § 1001 and the more specific statute, and may charge both if such would be consistent with double jeopardy principles (discussed within Part D).

Where a defendant may be able to argue that his statement was not actually false even if highly misleading, the Department of Justice counsels that prosecutors can avoid proof problems by charging under § 1001's concealment prong.[46] The concealment aspect of § 1001 does not require proof of a "false statement." Rather, the focus of the case is the defendant's alleged falsification or concealment of material information by trick, scheme or device. Where the § 1001 prosecution is founded upon concealment as opposed to an actual false statement,

---

[38] *Thirty-Third Annual Survey of White Collar Crime, False Statements and False Claims,* 55 Am. Crim. L. Rev. 1096, 1165 (2018).

[39] U.S.A.M., Criminal Resource Manual No. 915; *see also* United States v. Shah, 44 F.3d 285, 294 (5th Cir. 1995).

[40] U.S.A.M. Criminal Resource Manual No. 912; *see Diogo,* 320 F.2d at 905-09.

[41] United States v. Johnson, 937 F.2d 392, 399 (8th Cir.1991) (citation omitted).

[42] *See, e.g.,* United States v. Migliaccio, 34 F.3d 1517, 1525 (10th Cir.1994); United States v. Manapat, 928 F.2d 1097, 1099-1102 (11th Cir. 1991).

[43] *See, e.g.,* United States v. Stephenson, 895 F.2d 867, 873 (2d Cir. 1990).

[44] *See, e.g.,* 18 U.S.C. § 1035 ("False statements relating to health car matters") (added in the Health Insurance Portability and Accountability Act of 1996); 18 U.S.C. § 1350 (Sarbanes-Oxley Act of 2002 added this offense relating to corporate officers' failure to certify financial reports).

[45] 18 U.S.C. § 1350 ("Failure of corporate officers to certify financial reports"). The penalties for certification of periodic financial reports filed with the SEC "knowing" that the periodic report accompanying the certification statement does not comport with statutory requirements is a fine of not more than $1 million and not more than 10 years' imprisonment. The penalty for "willfully" engaging in such conduct is a fine of not more than $5 million and imprisonment of up to 20 years' imprisonment. For a (critical) commentary on this provision and its practical ramifications, see Stanley S. Arkin, *Sarbanes-Oxley and CEO/CFO Accountability,* 9 Bus. Crimes Bull. 1, 7-9 (Nov. 2002); *see also* United States v. Scrushy, 2004 WL 2713262 (N.D. Ala. 2004) (denying constitutional attack on § 1350).

[46] U.S.A.M. Criminal Resource Manual No. 912; *see, e.g., Stephenson,* 895 F.2d at 873-74.

some "affirmative act" of concealment is required.[47] Further, "[i]n order to convict under a section 1001 concealment charge, the government must show that a defendant had a legal duty to disclose the facts at the time he was alleged to have concealed them."[48] In this regard, the § 1001 case law is generally consistent with the mail, wire, and securities fraud case law examined in future chapters in treating potentially misleading silence as criminally actionable misconduct only where the defendant is subject to a disclosure duty.

The false statements prohibition obviously extends further than the perjury provisions, most importantly by applying to false statements that are *not* made under oath and even to concealment of a type that would not pass the *Bronston* test. False statements also need not be made in any official record or writing, while perjurious statements will often be recorded in some type of official record, such as a court transcript. The same statutory maximum sentence of imprisonment—five years—applies to sections 1001, 1621, and 1623. Does this make sense? Are perjury and false statement cases of equal seriousness and harmfulness?

b. Materiality

Prior to the 1996 amendment to § 1001, only one subsection contained an express materiality requirement. A circuit split developed as to whether the other two subsections of the statute also contained implicit materiality requirements.[49] Congress sought to resolve this split in 1996 by adding an explicit materiality element to each of the three subsections of § 1001(a).

The materiality element is designed to prevent the Government from prosecuting citizens for every *de minimis* false statement or concealment of information provided to the covered authorities.[50] In *United States v. Gaudin*,[51] the Supreme Court defined a statement as "material" if it has "a natural tendency to influence, or [is] capable of influencing, the decision of the decision-making body to which it was addressed."[52] Further, the Court held that—contrary to the practice in many circuits of relegating materiality questions to the judge—this element has to be proved beyond a reasonable doubt to the satisfaction of a jury.[53]

One might wonder whether this general standard provides much guidance—or protection. In terms of concrete proof, what does the Government have to show in order to demonstrate materiality?[54] What type of evidence should a prosecutor seek to introduce in support of this requirement?[55]

---

[47] *See, e.g.*, United States v. St. Michael's Credit Union, 880 F.2d 579, 589 (1st Cir. 1989); United States v. London, 550 F.2d 206, 213 (5th Cir. 1977) (*cited with approval in* United States v. Woodward, 469 U.S. 105, 108 & n. 5 (1985) (*per curiam*) (explaining that a traveler who is not asked to fill out a required currency report does not conceal material facts sought in that report by means of trick, scheme or device as required by statute and thus would not be liable under § 1001)).

[48] United States v. Curran, 20 F.3d 560, 566 (3d Cir. 1994); *see also* United States v. Safavian, 528 F.3d 957 (D.C. Cir. 2008) (no duty to disclose); United States v. Calhoon, 97 F.3d 518, 526 (11th Cir. 1996).

[49] *See, e.g.*, United States v. Gaudin, 515 U.S. 506, 524 (1995) (Rehnquist, C.J., concurring).

[50] *See, e.g.*, United States v. Baker, 626 F.2d 512, 514 (5th Cir. 1980).

[51] 515 U.S. 506 (1995).

[52] *Id.* at 509 (quoting Kungys v. United States, 485 U.S. 759, 770 (1988)).

[53] *Id.* at 522-23.

[54] In *Weinstock v. United States*, 231 F.2d 699, 701 (D.C. Cir. 1956), the D.C. Circuit explained:

"[M]aterial" when used in respect to evidence is often confused with "relevant," but the two terms have wholly different meanings. To be "relevant" means to relate to the issue. To be "material" means to have probative weight, i.e., [to be] reasonably likely to influence the tribunal in making a determination required to be made. A statement may be relevant but not material.

[55] *See* U.S.A.M., Criminal Resource Manual No. 911.

It may be helpful to note in this regard that courts have generally found that, to prove materiality, it is *not* necessary for the Government to show:

> (i) that the false statement was at all credible or was in fact believed;[56]
> (ii) that the false statement or concealment of fact was actually relied upon or actually influenced the governmental agency or department;[57]
> (iii) that there was any intended or actual financial or property loss to the federal government;[58]
> (iv) that the statements were required to be filed;[59] or
> (v) that the statement was read, or even received, by the governmental agency or department.[60]

All that the prosecutor need show is that the "statement is *capable* of influencing or affecting a federal agency."[61] In other words, "the test is the *intrinsic* capabilities of the false statement itself, rather than the possibility of the actual attainment of its end as measured by collateral consequences."[62] What types of information might *not* be material under this standard? Given the broad definition of materiality, is the fact that this is a question for the jury important? As a prosecutor or defense counsel, would you expect a jury to be more or less forgiving in making this determination than a judge? The question of materiality often is "intermixed" with that of the next element: "jurisdiction."[63]

c. *"Jurisdiction"*

Under the pre-1996 statute, the Supreme Court interpreted the term "jurisdiction" very broadly in *United States v. Rodgers*.[64] Rodgers' wife had left him and he wanted to induce federal agencies to find her. Accordingly, he "allegedly lied in telling the FBI that his wife had been kidnaped and in telling the Secret Service that his wife was involved in a plot to kill the President."[65] When he was indicted on two counts of making false statements under § 1001,

---

[56] *See, e.g.*, United States v. LeMaster, 54 F.3d 1224, 1231 (6th Cir. 1995); United States v. Parsons, 967 F.2d 452, 455 (10th Cir. 1992).

[57] *See, e.g.*, United States v. Service Deli Inc., 151 F.3d 938, 941 (9th Cir. 1998); United States v. Calhoon, 97 F.3d 518, 530 (11th Cir. 1996); United States v. Trent, 949 F.2d 998, 999 (8th Cir. 1991). For example, in *United States v. Moore*, 612 F.3d 698 (D.C. Cir. 2010), the defendant was convicted under § 1001 for signing a fake name on a postal delivery form when a postal worker dropped off a package. The D.C. Circuit upheld the conviction against a challenge of lack of materiality. The worker testified that she would not have delivered the package unless she received a signature identifying the recipient. The court explained that "the evidence was more than sufficient for a reasonable jury to conclude ... that Moore's false statement was capable of affecting the Postal Service's general function of tracking packages and identifying the recipients of packages entrusted to it." *Id.* at 702.

[58] *See, e.g.*, United States v. Campbell, 848 F.2d 846, 852 (8th Cir. 1988); United States v. Lichenstein, 610 F.2d 1272, 1278 (5th Cir. 1980).

[59] *See, e.g.*, United States v. Arcadipane, 41 F.3d 1, 4-5 (1st Cir. 1994); United States v. Dick, 744 F.2d 546, 553 (7th Cir. 1984).

[60] *See, e.g.*, United States v. Cochran, 109 F.3d 660, 668-69 (10th Cir. 1997); *Calhoon*, 97 F.3d at 530.

[61] *Service Deli Inc.*, 151 F.3d at 941; *see also Calhoon*, 97 F.3d at 530.

[62] United States v. Salinas-Ceron, 731 F.2d 1375, 1377 (9th Cir. 1984) (citations omitted), *vacated on other grounds*, 755 F.2d 726 (9th Cir. 1985).

[63] United States v. Wolf, 645 F.2d 23, 25 (10th Cir. 1981); *see also* United States v. Notarantonio, 758 F.2d 777, 785 (1st Cir. 1985).

[64] 466 U.S. 475 (1984).

[65] *Id.* at 476.

Rodgers successfully moved to dismiss on the ground that the investigation of kidnappings and the protection of the President are not matters "within the jurisdiction" of the FBI and Secret Service for purposes of § 1001. He prevailed because of circuit court precedent that read "within the jurisdiction" to refer only to "the power to make final or binding determinations."[66] The lower courts thus held that because the federal agencies involved "had no power to adjudicate rights, establishing binding regulations, compel the action or finally dispose of the problem giving rise to the inquiry," the prosecution could not proceed.

In *Rodgers*, the Supreme Court rejected this "unduly strained" interpretation, stating that "[t]he most natural, nontechnical reading of the statutory language is that it covers all matters confided to the authority of an agency or department."[67] The Court then explained:

> There are of course narrower, more technical meanings of the term "jurisdiction." For example, an alternative definition provided by Webster's is the "legal power to interpret and administer the law." See also Black's Law Dictionary 766 (5th ed. 1979). But a narrow, technical definition of this sort, limiting the statute's protections to judicial or quasi-judicial activities, clashes strongly with the sweeping, everyday language on either side of the term. It is also far too restricted to embrace some of the myriad governmental activities that we have previously concluded § 1001 was designed to protect. See, *e.g.*, *Bryson v. United States*, 396 U.S. 64 (1969) (affidavit filed by union officer with National Labor Relations Board falsely denying affiliation with Communist Party); *United States v. Bramblett*, 348 U.S. 503 (1955) (fraudulent representations by Member of Congress to Disbursing Office of House of Representatives); *United States v. Gilliland*, 312 U.S. 86 (1941) (false reports filed with Secretary of Interior on amount of petroleum produced from certain wells).
>
> In all our prior cases interpreting this statutory language we have stressed that "the term 'jurisdiction' should not be given a narrow or technical meaning for purposes of § 1001." For example, in *United States v. Gilliland*, we rejected a defendant's contention that the reach of the statute was confined "to matters in which the Government has some financial or proprietary interest." We noted that the 1934 amendment, which added the current statutory language, was not limited by any specific set of circumstances that may have precipitated its passage.
>
> > "The amendment indicated the congressional intent to protect the authorized functions of governmental departments and agencies from the perversion which might result from the deceptive practices described. We see no reason why this apparent intention should be frustrated by construction."
>
> Discussing the same amendment in *United States v. Bramblett* we concluded: "There is no indication in either the committee reports or in the congressional debates that the scope of the statute was to be in any way restricted." And in *Bryson v. United States* we noted the "valid legislative interest in protecting the integrity of official inquiries" and held that a "statutory basis for an agency's request for information provides jurisdiction enough to punish fraudulent statements under § 1001."
>
> There is no doubt that there exists a "statutory basis" for the authority of the FBI and the Secret Service over the investigations sparked by respondent Rodgers' false reports. The FBI is authorized "to detect and prosecute crimes against the United States," including kidnaping. 28 U.S.C. § 533(1). And the Secret Service is authorized "to protect the person of the President." 18 U.S.C. § 3056. It is a perversion of these authorized functions to turn either agency into a Missing Person's Bureau for domestic squabbles. The knowing filing of a false crime report, leading to an investigation and possible prosecution, can also have grave consequences for the individuals accused of crime.

---

[66] Friedman v. United States, 374 F.2d 363, 367 (8th Cir. 1967).

[67] 466 U.S. at 479.

There is, therefore, a "valid legislative interest in protecting the integrity of [such] official inquiries," an interest clearly embraced in, and furthered by, the broad language of § 1001.

Limiting the term "jurisdiction" as used in this statute to "the power to make final or binding determinations," as the Court of Appeals thought it should be limited, would exclude from the coverage of the statute most, if not all, of the authorized activities of many "departments" and "agencies" of the Federal Government, and thereby defeat the purpose of Congress in using the broad inclusive language which it did. If the statute referred only to courts, a narrower construction of the word "jurisdiction" might well be indicated; but referring as it does to "any department or agency" we think that such a narrow construction is simply inconsistent with the rest of the statutory language.[68] ...

As the Court's language indicates, the Supreme Court has chosen to interpret the "jurisdiction" requirement broadly. Does the optimal scope of § 1001 depend in part upon what its perceived purpose is intended to be?

As is explained further below, the Supreme Court overruled the *Bramblett* case (upon which the *Rodgers* Court in part relied) and read the "department or agency" language (which the *Rodgers* Court assumed to be so broad) narrowly in *Hubbard v. United States*.[69] It was in reaction to *Hubbard* that Congress enacted the current, more specific, and broader language "in any matter within the jurisdiction *of the executive, legislative, or judicial branch of the Government of the United States*." (Emphasis added). Although Congress employed the term "jurisdiction" in both iterations of the statute, could one argue that the term means different things given these developments? The Department of Justice takes the position that "[b]y including certain statutory terms (*e.g.,* "jurisdiction" and "statement") from the former section 1001 without change, Congress intended that those terms, as reenacted, continue to carry with them the body of existing judicial constructions of those terms."[70]

d. The "[E]xecutive, [L]egislative, or [J]udicial [B]ranch"

The Supreme Court was first called upon to interpret the latter part of the jurisdictional clause of § 1001 in 1955 in *United States v. Bramblett*.[71] *Bramblett* involved a false representation made by a Congressman to the House of Representatives' Disbursing Office. The Court was asked to determine whether the pre-1996 language—"within the jurisdiction *of any department or agency of the United States*"—permitted prosecutions under § 1001 for false statements made to Congress. (Emphasis added). The *Bramblett* Court rejected the argument that § 1001 was restricted to false statements made to the executive branch, holding that the word "department" "was meant to describe the executive, legislative and judicial branches of Government."[72]

"Although other federal courts ... refrained from directly criticizing *Bramblett*'s approach to statutory construction, it is fair to say that they ... greeted the decision with something less than a warm embrace."[73] Concerned in particular about the potential application of § 1001 to acts of alleged "concealment" in the course of judicial proceedings, many post-*Bramblett* lower courts adopted what became known as the "judicial function" exception to the applicability of § 1001. The D.C. Circuit planted the seeds of the exception in *Morgan v. United States*,[74] a case

---

[68] *Id.* at 480-82.

[69] 514 U.S. 695 (1995).

[70] U.S.A.M. Criminal Resource Manual No. 902.

[71] 348 U.S. 503 (1955).

[72] *Id.* at 509.

[73] *Hubbard,* 514 U.S. at 708 (1995).

[74] 309 F.2d 234 (D.C. Cir. 1962).

in which the defendant, who held himself out to be a member in good standing of the bar, was prosecuted under § 1001 for concealing from the court his name, identity, and non-admission to the bar. The circuit court affirmed the conviction but was obviously disturbed by the potential scope of § 1001. Pointing out that the statute prohibits "concealment" and "covering up" of material facts, as well as intentional falsehoods, the D.C. Circuit questioned whether the statute might be interpreted to criminalize conduct that falls well within the bounds of responsible advocacy. "Does a defendant 'cover up ... a material fact' when he pleads not guilty?" "Does an attorney 'cover up' when he moves to exclude hearsay testimony he knows to be true, or when he makes a summation on behalf of a client he knows to be guilty?"[75]

The *Morgan* court concluded with this statement, which served as the basis for the distinctions drawn under the name of the judicial function exception thereafter:

> We are certain that neither Congress nor the Supreme Court intended the statute to include traditional trial tactics within the statutory terms "conceals or covers up." We hold only, on the authority of the Supreme Court construction, that the statute does apply to the type of action with which appellant was charged, action which essentially involved the "administrative" or "housekeeping" functions, not the "judicial" machinery of the court.[76]

Another rationale for this exception was articulated by the Sixth Circuit when it reversed a conviction, relying on *Morgan*, "because [§] 1001 does not apply to the introduction of false documents as evidence in a criminal proceeding."[77] The Sixth Circuit explained that the judicial function exception also was necessary to prevent the perjury statute, with its two-witness rule, from being undermined.

The *Morgan* court's distinction between "administrative" and "judicial" functions was fleshed out by subsequent cases. Issues relating to the identity of a person before a criminal court were usually deemed "administrative,"[78] along with false statements or non-disclosures on standard court forms.[79] Such matters, then, *could* be pursued under § 1001. In contrast, falsely denying to a bankruptcy judge that one had forged a bankruptcy document, fictitious letters of recommendation for consideration by a sentencing judge,[80] and statements at bail hearings,[81] were all deemed matters that fell within the judicial function exception and thus

---

[75] *Id.* at 237.

[76] *Id.*

[77] United States v. Erhardt, 381 F.2d 173, 175 (6th Cir. 1967) (*per curiam*).

[78] *See* United States v. Plascencia-Orozco, 768 F.2d 1074 (9th Cir. 1985) (giving false name to a magistrate judge at a plea hearing interferes with the administrative function of the court; therefore § 1001 conviction was proper); *Morgan*, 309 F.2d at 237 (misrepresenting status as member of the bar impairs administrative function). *But see* United States v. Abrahams, 604 F.2d 386, 393 (5th Cir. 1979) (making false statements concerning one's identity to a magistrate judge at a bail hearing could not be prosecuted under §1001 due to judicial function exception).

[79] *See* United States v. Holmes, 840 F.2d 246, 248 (4th Cir. 1988) (giving false name to magistrate and filing a form consenting to proceed before a magistrate judge under the false name interferes with administrative function); United States v. Rowland, 789 F.2d 1169 (5th Cir. 1986) (filing a false performance bond in bankruptcy court was an administrative matter); United States v. Powell 708 F.2d 455 (9th Cir. 1983) (concealing true amount of assets in a standard affidavit for *in pauperis* status goes to administrative function), *rev'd on other grounds*, 469 U.S. 57 (1984).

[80] *See* United States v. Masterpol, 940 F.2d 760, 764-66 (2d Cir. 1991) (submitting a false letter of recommendation at a sentencing hearing impairs the judicial function; thus § 1001 is not the proper instrument for prosecution of the author).

[81] *See Abrahams*, 604 F.2d at 393 (failing to identify oneself as an escaped convict at a bail hearing impairs judicial function).

could *not* be prosecuted under § 1001.[82] Congress did not respond to the Supreme Court's *Bramblett* decision or the development of the judicial function exception. The Supreme Court was also silent for 32 years after *Morgan*—until *Hubbard v. United States*.[83]

Hubbard was charged with three § 1001 counts after filing a pair of unsworn, written documents in bankruptcy court in answer to certain filings by the trustee in the defendant's voluntary bankruptcy proceeding. On appeal, the defendant argued that his convictions were barred by the judicial function exception. Because of a split in the circuits on the availability of such a defense in the circumstances, the Court granted certiorari in *Hubbard*.

The *Hubbard* Court first determined that the terms "department" and "agency" would *not* normally be read to encompass federal court proceedings. It then recognized, however, that its decision in *Bramblett* controlled because, although the *Bramblett* case concerned a false statement made to Congress, not the courts, "the text and reasoning in the Court's opinion amalgamated all three branches of the Government."[84] The Court concluded after analysis that the *Bramblett* opinion was seriously flawed, but reasoned that "[w]hether the doctrine of *stare decisis* nevertheless requires that we accept *Bramblett*'s erroneous interpretation of § 1001 is a question best answered after reviewing the body of law directly at issue: the decisions adopting the judicial function exception."[85] The Court then reasoned:

> In this case, the[] considerations [underlying *stare decisis* principles] point in two conflicting directions. On one hand, they counsel adherence to the construction of § 1001 adopted in *Bramblett*; on the other, they argue in favor of retaining the body of law that has cut back on the breadth of *Bramblett* in Circuits from coast to coast. It would be difficult to achieve both goals simultaneously. For if the word "department" encompasses the Judiciary, as *Bramblett* stated, the judicial function exception cannot be squared with the text of the statute. A court is a court—and is part of the Judicial Branch—whether it is functioning in a housekeeping or judicial capacity. Conversely, *Bramblett* could not stand if we preserved the thrust of the judicial function exception—*i.e.*, if we interpreted 18 U.S.C. § 1001 so that it did not reach conduct occurring in federal-court proceedings. Again, although *Bramblett* involved a false representation to an office within the Legislative Branch, the decision lumped all three branches together in one and the same breath.
>
> We think the text of § 1001 forecloses any argument that we should simply ratify the body of cases adopting the judicial function exception. We are, however, persuaded that the clarity of that text justifies a reconsideration of *Bramblett*. Although such a reconsideration is appropriate only in the rarest circumstances, we believe this case permits it because of a highly unusual "intervening development of the law," and because of the absence of significant reliance interests in adhering to *Bramblett*.
>
> The "intervening development" is, of course, the judicial function exception. In a virtually unbroken line of cases, respected federal judges have interpreted § 1001 so narrowly that it has had only a limited application within the Judicial Branch. This interpretation has roots both deep and broad in the lower courts. Although the judicial function exception has not been adopted by this Court, our review of *Bramblett* supports the conclusion that the cases endorsing the exception almost certainly reflect the intent of Congress. It is thus fair to characterize the judicial function exception as a "competing legal doctrin[e]," that can lay a legitimate claim to respect as a settled body of law. Overruling *Bramblett* would preserve the essence of this doctrine and would, to that extent, promote stability in the law.
>
> *Stare decisis* has special force when legislators or citizens "have acted in reliance on a previous decision, for in this instance overruling the decision would dislodge settled rights

---

[82] *Cf.* 18 U.S.C. § 1001(b).

[83] 514 U.S. 695 (1995).

[84] *Id.* at 702.

[85] *Id.* at 708.

and expectations or require an extensive legislative response." Here, however, the reliance interests at stake in adhering to *Bramblett* are notably modest. In view of the extensive array of statutes that already exist to penalize false statements within the Judicial Branch, see, *e.g.*, 18 U.S.C. § 1621 (perjury); § 1623 (false declarations before grand jury or court); § 1503 (obstruction of justice); § 287 (false claims against the United States), we doubt that prosecutors have relied on § 1001 as an important means of deterring and punishing litigation-related misconduct.[86] But we need not speculate, for we have direct evidence on this point. The United States Attorneys' Manual states quite plainly that "[p]rosecutions should not be brought under 18 U.S.C. § 1001 for false statements submitted in federal court proceedings"; it instead directs prosecutors to proceed under the perjury or obstruction of justice statutes. United States Attorneys' Manual § 9-69.267 (1992). Clearer evidence of nonreliance can scarcely be imagined.[87] ...[88]

Accordingly, the *Hubbard* Court overruled *Bramblett* and read the terms "any department or agency of the United States" to exclude the judicial branch, thus removing from § 1001's coverage false statements made in judicial proceedings.[89] The Court's reasoning indicated that it would also read this language to exclude false statements made to the legislative branch.[90]

Congress immediately responded to the *Hubbard* decision by enacting the 1996 amendments to § 1001, which now expressly includes false statements and fraudulent concealments made "in any matter within the jurisdiction *of the executive, legislative, or judicial branch of the Government of the United States.*"[91] (Emphasis added).

As reference to the body of the statute indicates, however, Congress qualified the applicability of § 1001 to false statements made to the judicial branch by providing that the statute's prohibition "does not apply to a party to a judicial proceeding, or that party's counsel, for statements, representations, writings or documents submitted by such party or counsel to a judge or magistrate in that proceeding."[92] What is intended by this limitation—did Congress through legislation revive and reinstate the case law regarding a judicial function exception?

Note that the language of subsection (b) only carves out false statements made by "a party to a judicial proceeding, or that party's counsel." What happens if the party enlists the assistance of an accomplice? May the accomplice, as a non-party, be convicted for making a false statement during the course of a judicial proceeding while the principal, the party, escapes liability? Section 1001(b) also does not draw a distinction between "administrative" or

---

[86] [Court's footnote 14:] The perjury and false claims statutes also cover the Legislative Branch, as does 18 U.S.C. § 1505 (obstruction of justice). The existence of overlaps with other statutes does not itself militate in favor of overruling *Bramblett*; Congress may, and often does, enact separate criminal statutes that may, in practice, cover some of the same conduct. The overlaps here simply demonstrate that prosecutors cannot be said to have any significant reliance interest in *Bramblett*.

[87] [Court's footnote 15:] The absence of significant reliance interests is confirmed by an examination of statistical data regarding actual cases brought under § 1001. The Government has secured convictions under § 1001 in 2,247 cases over the last five fiscal years, but the dissent can identify only five reported § 1001 cases in that time period brought in connection with false statements made to the Judiciary and Legislature. (At least two of the five were unsuccessful, from the Government's point of view.) This tiny handful of prosecutions does not, in our view, evidence a weighty reliance interest on the part of prosecutors in adhering to the interpretation of § 1001 set forth in *Bramblett*.

[88] *Hubbard*, 514 U.S. at 712-15.

[89] *Id.* at 715.

[90] *See, e.g.*, United States v. Oakar, 111 F.3d 146, 153 (D.C. Cir. 1997).

[91] The False Statements Accountability Act of 1996, Pub. L. No. 104-292, 110 Stat. 3459, § 2 (1996); *see also* H.R. Rep. No. 104-680, *reprinted in* 6 U.S.C.C.A.N. 3935, 3935-36 (1997) ("The purpose of H.R. 3166 is to ensure that section 1001 applies to the judicial and legislative branches as well as the executive branch, thereby ensuring the integrity of legislative and judicial functions and proceedings.").

[92] 18 U.S.C. § 1001(b); *see also id.* § 1001(c) (qualifying applicability to legislative branch).

"housekeeping" matters and matters that go to the heart of the "judicial function." Did Congress in 1996 actually enlarge the scope of the judicial function exception?

Subsection (b) also states that the false statement, representation, writing, or document must be submitted to a "judge or magistrate in that proceeding." What about cases in which the party submits a false document or statement to a probation officer charged with generating a pre-sentence report for a judge,[93] or provides a false statement to an Assistant U.S. Attorney in connection with ongoing proceedings?[94] Does a grand jury investigation constitute a "judicial proceeding" such that false statements made by the party or counsel to the grand jury or its agents are exempt from prosecution under § 1001?[95] Why is this important—if the government cannot proceed under § 1001 against a defendant for (unsworn) statements made in correspondence with the Assistant U.S. Attorney or the grand jury, or in connection with fabricated documents or evidence submitted to the Assistant U.S. Attorney or the grand jury, what recourse does it have? Are the other code sections cited in *Hubbard* applicable to such cases?

Finally, what types of cases did Congress intend to carve out in subsection (c), which limits the applicability of § 1001 in cases where the false statement is addressed to the legislative branch?

The Department of Justice takes the following position on the scope of subsections (b) and (c):

> ... Section 2 of the [False Statements Accountability Act of 1996 (FSAA)] ... codifies a limited version of the "judicial function exception," which was created by the courts under the old section 1001 to avoid the chilling of advocacy that might occur if attorneys and parties were subject to prosecution for concealing facts from a court or jury. Under the codified version of the judicial function exception, parties or their counsel may be prosecuted for false submissions to other entities within the judicial branch, such as the probation office. *See* H.R. Rep. No. 104-680 at 9. Non-parties may be prosecuted for any false submission within the jurisdiction of the judicial branch.
>
> In subsection (c) of amended § 1001, Congress created a "legislative function exception." Under the new provision, false statements within the jurisdiction of the legislative branch are subject to prosecution only if they relate to administrative matters or congressional investigations conducted consistent with the applicable congressional rules. Amended § 1001 will thus reach those documents that have most often been the subject of congressional false

---

[93] *Compare* United States v. Horvath, 492 F.3d 1075 (9th Cir. 2007) (holding that defendant's false statement to a probation officer during a pretrial interview which was submitted to the judge in a presentence report constitutes a statement made by the defendant to a judge within § 1001's exception where the probation officer was by rule required to submit the defendant's statement to the judge), *with* United States v. Manning, 526 F.3d 610, 619-21 (10th Cir. 2008) (defendant's misstatement to probation officer is prosecutable). *See also* United States v. Vreeland, 684 F.3d 653 (6th Cir. 2012) (statements made to a probation officer investigating a possible violation of defendant's supervised release did not fall within judicial function exception).

[94] *Compare* United States v. Tracy, 108 F.3d 473 (2d Cir. 1997) (upholding § 1001 conviction where the defendant made false statements to Assistant U.S. Attorney during negotiations to settle seizure warrant pending in federal court because false affidavits were not requested, filed or even presented to the court and were designed to mislead or defraud the executive, not judicial branch), *with* United States v. Deffenbaugh, 957 F.2d 749 (10th Cir. 1992) (submitting allegedly false affidavit of compliance with grand jury subpoena to Assistant U.S. Attorney not prosecutable under § 1001 because grand jury proceedings are part of judicial process and prosecutor does not have "jurisdiction" in such cases).

[95] *See, e.g.,* United States v. Wood, 6 F.3d 692, 694-95 (10th Cir. 1993) (holding that false statements made to FBI agents acting under the auspices of a federal grand jury were "made in connection with a judicial proceeding" and thus fell within judicial function exception); *Deffenbaugh*, 957 F.2d at 752-53; United States v. Watt, 911 F. Supp. 538, 544 (D.D.C. 1995) (making false statements before grand jurors or in response to grand jury subpoenas are not covered by § 1001 nor are statements made to the prosecutors in lieu of the grand jury).

statement prosecutions, such as vouchers, payroll documents, and Ethics in Government Act (EIGA) financial disclosure forms. The exception was intended to protect, among other things, the free flow of constituent submissions to Congress. *See* H.R. Rep. No. 104-680 at 4-5.[96]

e. Mens Rea

The statute requires that the false statement or act of deceptive concealment be done "knowingly and willfully." At a minimum, it is clear that "[t]o establish a violation of § 1001, the Government must prove beyond a reasonable doubt that the statement was made with knowledge of its falsity."[97] The knowledge requirement is generally charged as follows: "to commit an act 'knowingly' is to do so with knowledge or awareness of the facts or situation, and not because of mistake, accident or some other innocent reason."[98]

One issue that may arise where the government brings a false statement case based on reports or claims made in an industry (such as the health care industry) that is highly regulated, is how the "knowing and willful" *mens rea* plays out with respect to applicable legal requirements. In *United States v. Whiteside*,[99] the defendants were charged with, *inter alia*, making false statements in applications for Medicare/Medicaid benefits and payments to a department of the United States, in violation of 18 U.S.C. § 1001. The case "involve[d] a single allegedly false statement which classified debt interest as 100% capital-related on cost reports submitted to the government for Medicare/Medicaid reimbursement."[100] The fundamental question was how the interest should be classified—by how the debt was being used at the time of the filing of the cost report or how the funds were used at the time that the loan originated. The government contended that the defendant's classification of the interest expense based on how the funds were used at the time of the filing was inconsistent with the Medicaid regulations. The defendants countered that no Medicare regulation or other authority indicated that their classification was in fact incorrect, much less "knowingly and willfully" false under § 1001. The Eleventh Circuit held that the government bore the burden of proving beyond a reasonable doubt that the defendant's statement was not true under a reasonable interpretation of the law.[101] It then reversed the false statement convictions, stating:

> The government cannot meet its burden in this case because, despite its contention to the contrary, no Medicare regulation, administrative ruling, or judicial decision exists that clearly requires interest expense to be reported in accordance with the original use of the loan. ...
>
> Neither the regulations nor administrative authority clearly answer the dilemma the defendants faced here. ... [U]nder current law, reasonable people could differ as to whether the debt interest was capital-related. ... This contradictory evidence lends credence to defendants' argument that their interpretation was not unreasonable. Here, "competing interpretations of the applicable law [are] far too reasonable to justify these convictions." As such, the government failed to meet its burden of proving the *actus reus* of the offense—actual falsity as a matter of law. [102]

---

[96] U.S.A.M. Criminal Resource Manual No. 902.

[97] United States v. Yermian, 468 U.S. 63, 69 (1984).

[98] U.S.A.M. Criminal Resource Manual No. 910 (quoting Fifth Circuit Pattern Jury Instruction § 1.35 (1990)); *see* United States v. Curran, 20 F.3d 560, 567 (3d Cir. 1994) ("[T]o convict a person accused of making a false statement, the government must prove not only that the statement was false, but that the accused knew it to be false. Thus, the government is required to show that the misrepresentation was not made innocently or inadvertently.").

[99] 285 F.3d 1345 (11th Cir. 2002).

[100] *Id.* at 1351.

[101] *Id.*

[102] *Id.* at 1352-53.

Despite the fact that the Supreme Court, in *United States v. Yermian*, said that § 1001 requires only knowledge and willfulness and that "[t]he statute contains no language suggesting any additional element of intent,"[103] there is a split in the circuits on the question whether this crime requires proof of a "specific intent."[104] The term "specific intent" has a number of different meanings depending upon the context in which it is used, but it seems likely that the courts using that term with respect to § 1001 prosecutions are invoking the term's "most common usage": "to designate a special mental element which is required above and beyond any mental state required with respect to the *actus reus* of the crime."[105] That is, courts requiring specific intent appear to require proof not only that the defendant knew his statement to be materially false, but also that he made the statement with the specific intention of deceiving the statement's official audience. It is worth stressing the precise nature of this further intent. Given that the defendant need not have intended to deprive the government of money or property in order to be liable under § 1001, the type of specific intent at issue is not the type usually discussed in fraud cases. As one court has explained, "[t]he statement must have been made with an *intent to deceive*, a design to induce belief in the falsity or to mislead, but § 1001 does not require an *intent to defraud*—that is, the intent to deprive someone of something by means of deceit."[106]

In many, if not most, cases, whether or not some "specific intent" is required beyond a showing of knowing publication of a materially false statement will probably make little difference. In most cases, juries will be asked to infer the existence of a specific intent to deceive from the simple fact that the defendant knowingly and materially lied; accordingly, these two mental states will merge to some extent for practical purposes. Where the presence or absence of a specific intent requirement may make a difference is in the availability of two defenses usually said to apply only to specific intent crimes: a "good faith" defense and an *un*reasonable mistake defense (*see* Chapter 2 (*Mens Rea*)).

What apparently is not in debate—among those circuits that believe § 1001 to be a specific intent crime and those that do not—is that the *mens rea* requirement in § 1001 cases may be met at least in part[107] through proof of willful blindness.[108] As the Fifth Circuit explained in affirming the conviction of a defendant who claimed not to have read the false form at issue in a case where the government was unable to prove that the defendant knew what he was signing:

---

[103] 468 U.S. 63, 73 (1984).

[104] *Compare* United States v. Geisen, 612 F.3d 471, 487 (6th Cir. 2010) (government must prove knowledge of falsity and an "intent to deceive"); United States v. Shah, 44 F.3d 285, 289 (5th Cir. 1995); United States v. Heuer, 4 F.3d 723, 732 (9th Cir. 1993); *and* Arthur Pew Construction Co. v. Lipscomb, 965 F.2d 1559, 1576 (11th Cir. 1992), *with* United States v. Jacobs, 212 F. App'x 683, 684 (9th Cir. 2006) (no need to prove specific intent); United States v. Ranum, 96 F.3d 1020, 1029 (7th Cir. 1996) (while recognizing that in dicta many circuits have held that § 1001 requires specific intent to deceive, authorities cited "strongly suggest that the knowing and willful making of a false statement are sufficient to meet the requirements of section 1001"); United States v. Leo, 941 F.2d 181, 200 (3d Cir. 1991); *cf.* United States v. Natale, 719 F.3d 719, 740-41 (7th Cir. 2013) (recognizing split).

[105] Wayne R. LaFave, Criminal Law 238 (3d ed. 2000).

[106] United States v. Lichenstein, 610 F.2d 1272, 1276-77 (5th Cir. 1980) (emphasis added); *see also* United States v. Yermian, 468 U.S. 63, 73 n.12 (1984) ("Intent to deceive and intent to defraud are not synonymous. Deceive is to cause to believe the false or mislead. Defraud is to deprive of some right, interest or property, by deceit.").

[107] *See supra*, Chapter 2, Part C(4) (*Mens Rea*) (Note on Willful Blindness and Specific Intent).

[108] *See, e.g., Brown*, 151 F.3d at 484 ("It is clear that if a defendant 'deliberately ignore[s] a high probability that [a] form contain[s] material false information,' the requisite specific intent has been established.") (citation omitted); United States v. Darrah, 119 F.3d 1322, 1328-29 (8th Cir. 1997); United States v. London, 66 F.3d 1227, 1241-42 (1st Cir. 1995) ("a false statement is made knowingly if defendant demonstrated a reckless disregard of the truth, with a conscious purpose to avoid learning the truth"); United States v. Puente, 982 F.2d 156, 159 (5th Cir. 1993); *Arthur Pew Construction Co.*, 965 F.2d at 1576.

... [Willful blindness] has been held sufficient to satisfy § 1001's scienter requirement so that a defendant who deliberately avoids learning the truth cannot circumvent criminal sanctions. Likewise, a defendant who deliberately avoids reading the form he is signing cannot avoid criminal sanctions for any false statements contained therein. Any other holding would write § 1001 completely out of existence.[109]

What danger is presented by such a theory of *mens rea*? Does it raise the possibility that if a defendant has been slapdash in filling out a student loan application or has simply signed a tax return prepared by a trusted spouse or tax advisor without examining the return's veracity, he may be convicted of making a false statement because he *should have* been more scrupulous—that is, that he was negligent?

With respect to the "willfulness" requirement, the *mens rea* materials in Chapter 2 demonstrate that the Supreme Court defines what is meant by "willful" conduct differently according to the type of criminal prohibition at issue or the type of activity regulated.[110] Recall that in Chapter 2(B), note 1 following the *Bryan* decision, the Third Circuit sketched out the three basic meanings of "willful": the lowest connotes only that an act is intentional, knowing, and voluntary as opposed to accidental; the most common meaning is that the act is done not just voluntarily, but also with a bad purpose, that is, with knowledge that the defendant's conduct is in some general sense "unlawful"; and the third, and most demanding level, is that the defendant actually knew of the specific law he was violating.

The Department of Justice has taken the position that the least demanding meaning of "willful" is not appropriate for § 1001 cases. In *United States v. Russell*,[111] the First Circuit upheld a conviction under 18 U.S.C. § 1035 for "willfully" making false statement in connection with the payment of health care benefits. The court rejected the defense argument that the government had to prove that the defendant was aware in a general sense of the unlawfulness of his conduct. Instead, the First Circuit, relying heavily on a Ninth Circuit case involving the same issue in a § 1001 case, ruled that proof that the conduct was "deliberate" was sufficient and that the "willfulness" instruction "does not necessarily require knowledge of illegality."[112] When the defendant sought certiorari, the Department of Justice took the extraordinary step of conceding error, stating:

> Petitioner contends that Section 1035's "willfully" element requires proof that the defendant knew that his false statement was unlawful. The ... government now agrees that the correct interpretation of "willfully" in Section 1035 is the one articulated in *Bryan v. United States*, 524 U.S. 184 (1998). To find that a defendant "willfully" made a false statement in violation of Section 1035, a jury must conclude "that he acted with knowledge that his conduct was unlawful." *Id.* at 193. The same interpretation should apply to 18 U.S.C. [§] 1001's materially identical prohibition on "knowingly and willfully" making a false statement in a matter within the jurisdiction of the federal government.[113]

The Supreme Court then granted certiorari and remanded to the First Circuit for reconsideration in light of the United States' confession of error.[114] Defendants have argued in

---

[109] *Puente*, 982 F.2d at 159.

[110] *See* Ratzlaf v. United States, 510 U.S. 135, 141 (1994) (holding that willful "is a 'word of many meanings,' and 'its construction [is] often ... influenced by its context.'").

[111] 728 F.3d 23, 31-32 (1st Cir. 2013).

[112] *Id.* at 32.

[113] Russell v. United States, Brief of the United States in Opposition, 2014 WL 1571932, at 6 (2014).

[114] *See* Russell v. United States, 572 U.S. 1056 (2014).

other cases that the "willfulness" element of § 1001 in fact requires the most demanding meaning of that term, requiring the government to prove that the defendant knew of the statute governing false statements and specifically intended to violate that particular law. The courts have uniformly rejected this argument.[115]

Finally, in *United States v. Yermian*,[116] the Supreme Court addressed the question whether, in addition to proving that the defendant made a statement he knew to be false, the Government must also prove that the false statement was made with actual knowledge of federal agency jurisdiction. The *Yermian* Court held:

> ...The statutory language requiring that knowingly false statements be made "in any matter within the jurisdiction of any department or agency of the United States" is a jurisdictional requirement. Its primary purpose is to identify the factor that makes the false statement an appropriate subject for federal concern. Jurisdictional language need not contain the same culpability requirement as other elements of the offense. Indeed, we have held that "the existence of the fact that confers federal jurisdiction need not be one in the mind of the actor at the time he perpetrates the act made criminal by the federal statute." Certainly in this case, the statutory language makes clear that Congress did not intend the terms "knowingly and willfully" to establish the standard of culpability for the jurisdictional element of § 1001. The jurisdictional language appears in a phrase separate from the prohibited conduct modified by the terms "knowingly and willfully." Any natural reading of § 1001, therefore, establishes that the terms "knowingly and willfully" modify only the making of "false, fictitious or fraudulent statements," and not the predicate circumstance that those statements be made in a matter within the jurisdiction of a federal agency. Once this is clear, there is no basis for requiring proof that the defendant had actual knowledge of federal agency jurisdiction. The statute contains no language suggesting any additional element of intent, such as a requirement that false statements be "knowingly made in a matter within federal agency jurisdiction," or "with the intent to deceive the Federal Government." On its face, therefore, § 1001 requires that the Government prove that false statements were made knowingly and willfully, and it unambiguously dispenses with any requirement that the Government also prove that those statements were made with actual knowledge of federal agency jurisdiction.[117]

Although the Court in *Yermian* held that proof of actual knowledge of federal agency jurisdiction is not a necessary element of a § 1001 conviction, the Court left open the issue of whether some lesser standard of culpability must be read into the statute.[118] The majority of courts to address this issue since *Yermian* have held that "no mental state is required with respect to federal involvement in order to establish a violation of § 1001."[119] Readers might wish to consider whether some *mens rea* should be required with respect to this "jurisdictional" element in light of the cases discussed below.

---

[115] *See, e.g.*, United States v. Starnes, 583 F.3d 196, 210-212 (3d Cir. 2009); United States v. Daughtry, 48 F.3d 829, 831 (4th Cir.), *vacated on other grounds*, 516 U.S. 984 (1995); United States v. Rodriguez-Rios, 14 F.3d 1040, 1048 n.21 (5th Cir. 1994) (*en banc*) (dicta); *see also* United States v. Curran, 20 F.3d 560, 567-68 (3d Cir. 1994); U.S.A.M. Criminal Resource Manual No. 910.

[116] 468 U.S. 63 (1984).

[117] *Id.* at 68-70.

[118] *Id.* at 75 n.14.

[119] United States v. Bakhtiari, 913 F.2d 1053, 1060 (2d Cir. 1990); *see also, e.g.*, United States v. Heuer, 4 F.3d 723, 734 (9th Cir. 1993); United States v. Leo, 941 F.2d 181, 190 (3d Cir. 1991).

f. Federalization

UNITED STATES v. HERRING
916 F.2d 1543 (11th Cir. 1990)

HATCHETT, CIRCUIT JUDGE:

In this case, we affirm the district court's ruling that 18 U.S.C. § 1001 is a proper statutory basis for the prosecution of one who receives Georgia Unemployment Insurance benefits as the result of filing false statements in the application for such benefits.

On January 14, 1987, Dennis D. Herring, the appellant, applied for unemployment insurance benefits from the Georgia Department of Labor. Herring stated on the application that he left his last job in Tucson, Arizona, for lack of work and was unemployed for the week prior to January 14th. Herring, however, began working for an Ohio construction company on January 12, 1987.

Based on his original application, Herring made four subsequent requests for and received unemployment compensation from the Georgia Department of Labor while he was gainfully employed. The Georgia Department of Labor paid Herring a total of $870 in unemployment insurance benefits using Georgia state funds. During a Department of Labor investigation involving State Unemployment Insurance Programs, Herring's false statements were discovered. The United States Secretary of Labor has approved Georgia's unemployment program, and Georgia receives federal funding for administrative costs from the United States Secretary of Labor.

In April, 1989, a grand jury indicted Herring on five counts of knowingly and willfully making false statements to an agency of the United States, in violation of 18 U.S.C. § 1001. ... [Herring appeals the district court's post-guilty plea refusal to dismiss the indictment.] ...

... A conviction under section 1001 requires proof of five elements: (1) a statement, (2) falsity, (3) materiality, (4) specific intent, and (5) agency jurisdiction. Only jurisdiction and materiality are at issue in this case.

A. Jurisdiction

Herring contends that the federal government lacks jurisdiction to prosecute him for false statements made to a state agency. According to Herring, jurisdiction exists under section 1001 only upon a showing of a direct relationship between the false statement and an authorized function of the federal agency or department. *United States v. Facchini*, 874 F.2d 638 (9th Cir.1989). Relying extensively on *Facchini*, Herring argues that although the Georgia Department of Labor receives federal funds from the United States Department of Labor for administrative purposes, his false statements did not affect an authorized function of the United States Department of Labor.

In *Facchini*, the Ninth Circuit, sitting en banc, addressed the application of section 1001 to a similar Department of Labor investigation involving State Unemployment Insurance Programs. The court stated that even though jurisdiction may exist under section 1001 when the false statement is not made directly to a federal agency and when the federal agency is not financially affected by the false statement, courts have refused to find jurisdiction unless a direct relationship exists between the false statement and an authorized function of a federal agency or department. The Ninth Circuit reasoned that although the state received funds from the United States Secretary of Labor, the Secretary is authorized to monitor only the administrative structure of the program and is not empowered to act on fraudulent claims for state unemployment benefits. Therefore, false statements to obtain state unemployment funds are not within the proscriptions of section 1001.

In *Facchini*, the Ninth Circuit narrowly construed the jurisdiction requirement of section 1001 to encompass only false statements with a direct nexus to an authorized function of a federal agency or department. The Ninth Circuit based its jurisdictional conclusion on the technical distinction of the Secretary of Labor's administrative involvement rather than operational involvement in the state unemployment programs. We reject the Ninth Circuit's narrow and technical definition of section 1001 jurisdiction. ...

In this case, the Georgia Department of Labor operates under an unemployment law approved by the United States Secretary of Labor. Title 42 U.S.C. § 502 requires the Secretary to pay administrative funds to approved state unemployment programs from the United States Treasury. Before paying the administrative funds, section 503(a) requires the Secretary to review the state law and find that the state unemployment plan can make full payment of unemployment compensation when due. Section 503 also provides administrative guidelines for state agencies approved under section 502(a).

The Georgia Department of Labor receives federal funds from the United States Department of Labor for administrative costs, including salaries and office expenses. The department is subject to the administrative guidelines of section 503 before receiving federal funds from the Secretary of Labor. Additionally, an unemployed worker, such as Herring, who left his job in Tucson, Arizona, may file for and receive benefits on an interstate basis.

The United States Supreme Court has stated that jurisdiction within the meaning of section 1001 should not be narrowly or technically defined. *United States v. Rodgers*, 466 U.S. 475, 480 (1984). Moreover, this court has held that false statements need not be presented to an agency of the United States and that federal funds need not actually be used to pay a claimant for federal agency jurisdiction to exist under section 1001. *United States v. Suggs*, 755 F.2d 1538, 1542 (11th Cir.1985).

In *Suggs*, the defendant was convicted of falsifying Georgia Department of Labor travel vouchers in violation of 18 U.S.C. § 1001. The defendant challenged his conviction on several grounds including lack of jurisdiction. In affirming the conviction, this court found that a state agency's use of federal funds is generally sufficient to establish jurisdiction under section 1001. *Suggs* is controlling. ...

B. Materiality

Herring next questions the material effects of his statements to the Georgia Department of Labor on the United States government. He argues that his statements did not intrinsically influence the United States Department of Labor's actions because the federal government plays only a limited role in Georgia's unemployment program. Therefore, prosecuting individuals for fraudulent receipt of state funds under section 1001 violates the notice requirement of the due process clause of the United States Constitution.

The test for determining materiality under section 1001 is whether the false statement has the capability of affecting or influencing the exercise of a government function. Materiality is satisfied even if the federal government was not actually influenced by the false statements. The false statements need not be made directly to the federal agency to sustain a section 1001 conviction as long as federal funds are involved. *United States v. Suggs*, 755 F.2d at 1542.

In the instant case, Herring received $870 in state unemployment benefits as a result of his false statements. Payment of fraudulent claims frustrates the function of the Georgia unemployment law because such claims are outside the proper and efficient administration of the law. Additionally, the administrative costs involved in processing and paying Herring's unemployment compensation were paid to the Georgia Department of Labor by the Secretary of Labor pursuant to 42 U.S.C. § 502(a). The Secretary has an obligation to ensure that the substantial sums the federal government spends to provide an unemployment compensation program are not depleted through false claims which might misdirect or corrupt the functioning of a governmental agency. Consequently, Herring's false statements to the Georgia Department of Labor had the intrinsic capability of influencing the Secretary of Labor in administering the federal unemployment funds.

We further reject Herring's lack of notice argument. As we stated in *Suggs*, notice of the federal agency's involvement in the state unemployment program is not an essential element of a section 1001 conviction. ...

Notes

1. *Herring* created a split in the circuits on the question whether prosecutions for false statements made to secure state unemployment benefits are cognizable under § 1001. *See* United States v. Holmes, 111 F.3d 463 (6th Cir. 1997) (holding that jurisdiction requirement of § 1001 not satisfied in case involving fraud upon the Michigan unemployment insurance program because federal government neither funded the fraudulently obtained state benefit payments nor has any authority to act upon discovering that the state program has been defrauded); United States v. Facchini, 874 F.2d 638, 641-42 (9th Cir. 1989) (*en banc*) (finding jurisdiction requirement of § 1001 not satisfied in case involving fraud upon the Oregon unemployment insurance program because federal agency that funded and monitored state program was not authorized to act in response to false statements made to state insurance program); *see also* United States v. Ford, 639 F.3d 718 (6th Cir. 2011). Should such cases be permitted under § 1001?

2. What is not in dispute among the circuits is that there are cases in which "jurisdiction" and materiality may exist under § 1001 even "when the false statement is not made directly to a federal agent." *Facchini*, 874 F.2d at 641. Thus, "[c]ourts have ... affirmed § 1001 convictions for false statements made to private entities receiving federal funds or subject to federal regulation or supervision." United States v. Gibson, 881 F.2d 318, 322-23 (6th Cir. 1989); *see also* United States v. St. Michael's Credit Union, 880 F.2d 579, 591 (1st Cir. 1989); United States v. Tabares, 2017 WL 1944199 (N.D. Ga. 2017). *But see* United States v. Blankenship, 382 F.3d 1110 (11th Cir. 2004).

As the *Herring* court held, "false statements need not be presented to an agency of the United States and ... federal funds need not actually be used to pay a claimant for federal agency jurisdiction to exist under section 1001." 916 F.2d at 1547; *see also* United States v. Smith, 519 F. App'x. 853 (5th Cir. 2013). However, as suggested by the *en banc* Ninth Circuit *United States v. Facchini*, some courts require that the government demonstrate some "direct relationship" between the false statement and a federal agency function. 874 F.2d at 641. The First and Seventh Circuits have stated that the government in such cases "must prove a nexus, a 'necessary link,' between the deception of the nonfederal agency and the function of a federal agency. The link may be established by showing that the concealments or "'false statements ... result in the perversion of the authorized functions of a federal department or agency.'"" *St. Michael's Credit Union*, 880 F.2d at 591 (citations omitted).

What nexus should be shown? Courts have determined that one important factor is whether federal funds are implicated. *See, e.g.*, United States v. Wright, 988 F.2d 1036, 1039 (10th Cir. 1993); United States v. Suggs, 755 F.2d 1538, 1542 (11th Cir. 1985). The requisite nexus may also be demonstrated by evidence that federal agencies retained auditing and enforcement powers. *See, e.g.*, *Wright*, 988 F.2d at 1038-39; United States v. Baker, 626 F.2d 512, 514 n.5 (5th Cir. 1980).

3. In some cases, courts have also upheld convictions under § 1001 where the false statements were contained in business documents that were not submitted to any federal (or state) agency but were subject to governmental audit or review. *See, e.g.*, United States v. Rutgard, 116 F.3d 1270 (9th Cir. 1997) (*en banc*) (upholding § 1001 conviction of doctor who kept falsified medical records in his office in furtherance of a scheme to defraud Medicare because "[false records] are criminal ... when, as here, they prevent review of payments made to a physician by the government"); United States v. Hooper, 596 F.2d 219, 221 (7th Cir. 1979) (falsifying participation rosters in federally funded student activities was sanctionable where such rosters were intended "to provide an 'audit trail' to enable federal program auditors to determine how the federal funds were disbursed").

4. Even where a statute appears largely limitless in its potential applicability, Justice Department policy can limit its actual use to instances where its enforcement is necessary to vindicate important federal interests. What factors should be important? What should the departmental policy look like for § 1001 cases?

2. DEFENSES

BROGAN v. UNITED STATES
522 U.S. 398 (1998)

JUSTICE SCALIA delivered the opinion of the Court.

This case presents the question whether there is an exception to criminal liability under 18 U.S.C. § 1001 for a false statement that consists of the mere denial of wrongdoing, the so-called "exculpatory no."

While acting as a union officer during 1987 and 1988, petitioner James Brogan accepted cash payments from JRD Management Corporation, a real estate company whose employees were represented by the union. On October 4, 1993, federal agents from the Department of Labor and the Internal Revenue Service visited petitioner at his home. The agents identified themselves and explained that they were seeking petitioner's cooperation in an investigation of JRD and various individuals. They told petitioner that if he wished to cooperate, he should have an attorney contact the U.S. Attorney's Office, and that if he could not afford an attorney, one could be appointed for him.

The agents then asked petitioner if he would answer some questions, and he agreed. One question was whether he had received any cash or gifts from JRD when he was a union officer. Petitioner's response was "no." At that point, the agents disclosed that a search of JRD headquarters had produced company records showing the contrary. They also told petitioner that lying to federal agents in the course of an investigation was a crime. Petitioner did not modify his answers, and the interview ended shortly thereafter.

Petitioner was indicted for accepting unlawful cash payments from an employer in violation of 29 U.S.C. §§ 186(b)(1), (a)(2), (d)(2), and making a false statement within the jurisdiction of a federal agency in violation of 18 U.S.C. § 1001. He was tried, along with several co-defendants, before a jury in the United States District Court for the Southern District of New York, and was found guilty. The United States Court of Appeals for the Second Circuit affirmed the convictions. We granted certiorari on the issue of the "exculpatory no."

... By its terms, 18 U.S.C. § 1001 covers "any" false statement—that is, a false statement "of whatever kind." The word "no" in response to a question assuredly makes a "statement," see, *e.g.*, Webster's New International Dictionary 2461 (2d ed.1950) (def. 2: "That which is stated; an embodiment in words of facts or opinions"), and petitioner does not contest that his utterance was false or that it was made "knowingly and willfully." In fact, petitioner concedes that under a "literal reading" of the statute he loses.

Petitioner asks us, however, to depart from the literal text that Congress has enacted, and to approve the doctrine adopted by many Circuits which excludes from the scope of § 1001 the "exculpatory no." The central feature of this doctrine is that a simple denial of guilt does not come within the statute. ...

Petitioner's argument in support of the "exculpatory no" doctrine proceeds from the major premise that § 1001 criminalizes only those statements to Government investigators that "pervert governmental functions"; to the minor premise that simple denials of guilt to Government investigators do not pervert governmental functions; to the conclusion that—§ 1001 does not criminalize simple denials of guilt to Government investigators. Both premises seem to us mistaken. As to the minor: We cannot imagine how it could be true that falsely denying guilt in a Government investigation does not pervert a governmental function. Certainly the investigation of wrongdoing is a proper governmental function; and since it is the very *purpose* of an investigation to uncover the truth, any falsehood relating to the subject of the investigation perverts that function. It could be argued, perhaps, that a *disbelieved* falsehood does not pervert an investigation. But making the existence of this crime turn upon the credulousness of the federal investigator (or the persuasiveness of the liar) would be exceedingly strange; such a defense to the analogous crime of perjury is certainly unheard of.

Moreover, as we shall see, the only support for the "perversion of governmental functions" limitation is a statement of this Court referring to the *possibility* (as opposed to the certainty) of perversion of function—a possibility that exists whenever investigators are told a falsehood relevant to their task.

In any event, we find no basis for the major premise that only those falsehoods that pervert governmental functions are covered by § 1001. Petitioner derives this premise from a comment we made in *United States v. Gilliland*, 312 U.S. 86 (1941), a case involving the predecessor to § 1001. ... The defendant in *Gilliland*, relying on the interpretive canon *ejusdem generis*,[120] argued that the statute should be read to apply only to matters in which the Government has a financial or proprietary interest. In rejecting that argument, we noted that Congress had specifically amended the statute to cover "any matter within the jurisdiction of any department or agency of the United States," thereby indicating "the congressional intent to protect the authorized functions of governmental departments and agencies from the perversion which might result from the deceptive practices described." Petitioner would elevate this statement to a holding that § 1001 does not apply where a perversion of governmental functions does not exist. But it is not, and cannot be, our practice to restrict the unqualified language of a statute to the particular evil that Congress was trying to remedy— even assuming that it is possible to identify that evil from something other than the text of the statute itself. The holding of *Gilliland* certainly does not exemplify such a practice, since it *rejected* the defendant's argument for a limitation that the text of the statute would not bear. And even the relied-upon dictum from *Gilliland* does not support restricting text to supposed purpose, but to the contrary acknowledges the reality that the reach of a statute often exceeds the precise evil to be eliminated. There is no inconsistency whatever between the proposition that Congress intended "to protect the authorized functions of governmental departments and agencies from the perversion which might result" and the proposition that the statute forbids *all* "the deceptive practices described."

The second line of defense that petitioner invokes for the "exculpatory no" doctrine is inspired by the Fifth Amendment. He argues that a literal reading of § 1001 violates the "spirit" of the Fifth Amendment because it places a "cornered suspect" in the "cruel trilemma" of admitting guilt, remaining silent, or falsely denying guilt. This "trilemma" is wholly of the guilty suspect's own making, of course. An innocent person will not find himself in a similar quandary (as one commentator has put it, the innocent person lacks even a "lemma"). And even the honest and contrite guilty person will not regard the third prong of the "trilemma" (the blatant lie) as an available option. The *bon mot* "cruel trilemma" first appeared in Justice Goldberg's opinion for the Court in *Murphy v. Waterfront Comm'n of N.Y. Harbor*, 378 U.S. 52 (1964), where it was used to explain the importance of a suspect's Fifth Amendment right to remain silent when subpoenaed to testify in an official inquiry. Without that right, the opinion said, he would be exposed "to the cruel trilemma of self-accusation, perjury or contempt." In order to validate the "exculpatory no," the elements of this "cruel trilemma" have now been altered—ratcheted up, as it were, so that the right to remain silent, which was the liberation from the original trilemma, is now *itself* a cruelty. We are not disposed to write into our law this species of compassion inflation.

Whether or not the predicament of the wrongdoer run to ground tugs at the heartstrings, neither the text nor the spirit of the Fifth Amendment confers a privilege to lie. "[P]roper invocation of the Fifth Amendment privilege against compulsory self-incrimination allows a witness to remain silent, but not to swear falsely." Petitioner contends that silence is an "illusory" option because a suspect may fear that his silence will be used against him later, or may not even know that silence is an available option. As to the former: It is well established that the fact that a person's silence can be used against him—either as substantive evidence of guilt or to impeach him if he takes the stand— does not exert a form of pressure that exonerates an otherwise unlawful lie. And as for the possibility that the person under investigation may be unaware of his right to remain silent: In the modern age

---

[120] [Court's footnote 2:] Under the principle of *ejusdem generis*, when a general term follows a specific one, the general term should be understood as a reference to subjects akin to the one with specific enumeration."

of frequently dramatized "Miranda" warnings, that is implausible. Indeed, we found it implausible (or irrelevant) 30 years ago, unless the suspect was "in custody or otherwise deprived of his freedom of action in any significant way," *Miranda v. Arizona*, 384 U.S. 436, 445 (1966).

Petitioner repeats the argument made by many supporters of the "exculpatory no," that the doctrine is necessary to eliminate the grave risk that § 1001 will become an instrument of prosecutorial abuse. The supposed danger is that overzealous prosecutors will use this provision as a means of "piling on" offenses—sometimes punishing the denial of wrongdoing more severely than the wrongdoing itself. The objectors' principal grievance on this score, however, lies not with the hypothetical prosecutors but with Congress itself, which has decreed the obstruction of a legitimate investigation to be a separate offense, and a serious one. It is not for us to revise that judgment. Petitioner has been unable to demonstrate, moreover, any history of prosecutorial excess, either before or after widespread judicial acceptance of the "exculpatory no." And finally, if there is a problem of supposed "overreaching" it is hard to see how the doctrine of the "exculpatory no" could solve it. It is easy enough for an interrogator to press the liar from the initial simple denial to a more detailed fabrication that would not qualify for the exemption.

A brief word in response to the dissent's assertion that the Court may interpret a criminal statute more narrowly than it is written: Some of the cases it cites for that proposition represent instances in which the Court did *not* purport to be departing from a reasonable reading of the text. In the others, the Court applied what it thought to be a background interpretive principle of general application. *Staples v. United States*, 511 U.S. 600 (1994) (construing statute to contain common-law requirement of *mens rea*). Also into this last category falls the dissent's correct assertion that the present statute does not "ma[ke] it a crime for an undercover narcotics agent to make a false statement to a drug peddler." Criminal prohibitions do not generally apply to reasonable enforcement actions by officers of the law.

It is one thing to acknowledge and accept such well defined (or even newly enunciated), generally applicable, background principles of assumed legislative intent. It is quite another to espouse the broad proposition that criminal statutes do not have to be read as broadly as they are written, but are subject to case-by-case exceptions. The problem with adopting such an expansive, user-friendly judicial rule, is that there is no way of knowing when, or how, the rule is to be invoked. As to the when: The only reason JUSTICE STEVENS adduces for invoking it here is that a felony conviction for this offense seems to him harsh. Which it may well be. But the instances in which courts may ignore harsh penalties are set forth in the Constitution, see Art. 1, § 9; Art. III, § 3; Amdt. 8; Amdt. 14, § 1; and to go beyond them will surely leave us at sea. And as to the how: There is no reason in principle why the dissent chooses to mitigate the harshness by saying that § 1001 does not embrace the "exculpatory no," rather than by saying that § 1001 has no application unless the defendant has been warned of the consequences of lying, or indeed unless the defendant has been put under oath. We are again at sea. ...

In sum, we find nothing to support the "exculpatory no" doctrine except the many Court of Appeals decisions that have embraced it. ... Courts may not create their own limitations on legislation, no matter how alluring the policy arguments for doing so, and no matter how widely the blame may be spread. Because the plain language of § 1001 admits of no exception for an "exculpatory no," we affirm the judgment of the Court of Appeals. ...

JUSTICE GINSBURG, with whom JUSTICE SOUTER joins, concurring in the judgment.

Because a false denial fits the unqualified language of 18 U.S.C. § 1001, I concur in the affirmance of Brogan's conviction. I write separately, however, to call attention to the extraordinary authority Congress, perhaps unwittingly, has conferred on prosecutors to manufacture crimes. I note, at the same time, how far removed the "exculpatory no" is from the problems Congress initially sought to address when it proscribed falsehoods designed to elicit a benefit from the Government or to hinder Government operations.

At the time of Brogan's offense, § 1001 made it a felony "knowingly and willfully" to make "any false, fictitious or fraudulent statements or representations" in "any matter within the jurisdiction of any department or agency of the United States." 18 U.S.C. § 1001 (1988 ed.).

That encompassing formulation arms Government agents with authority not simply to apprehend lawbreakers, but to generate felonies, crimes of a kind that only a Government officer could prompt.[121]

This case is illustrative. Two federal investigators paid an unannounced visit one evening to James Brogan's home. The investigators already possessed records indicating that Brogan, a union officer, had received cash from a company that employed members of the union Brogan served. (The agents gave no advance warning, one later testified, because they wanted to retain the element of surprise.) When the agents asked Brogan whether he had received any money or gifts from the company, Brogan responded "No." The agents asked no further questions. *After* Brogan just said "No," however, the agents told him: (1) the Government had in hand the records indicating that his answer was false; and (2) lying to federal agents in the course of an investigation is a crime. Had counsel appeared on the spot, Brogan likely would have received and followed advice to amend his answer, to say immediately: "Strike that; I plead not guilty." But no counsel attended the unannounced interview, and Brogan divulged nothing more. Thus, when the interview ended, a federal offense had been completed—even though, for all we can tell, Brogan's unadorned denial misled no one.

A further illustration. In *United States v. Tabor*, 788 F.2d 714 (C.A.11 1986), an Internal Revenue Service (IRS) agent discovered that Tabor, a notary public, had violated Florida law by notarizing a deed even though two signatories had not personally appeared before her (one had died five weeks before the document was signed). With this knowledge in hand, and without "warn[ing] Tabor of the possible consequences of her statements," the agent went to her home with a deputy sheriff and questioned her about the transaction. When Tabor, regrettably but humanly, denied wrongdoing, the Government prosecuted her under § 1001. An IRS agent thus turned a violation of state law into a federal felony by eliciting a lie that misled no one. (The Eleventh Circuit reversed the § 1001 conviction, relying on the "exculpatory no" doctrine.)

As these not altogether uncommon episodes show, § 1001 may apply to encounters between agents and their targets "under extremely informal circumstances which do not sufficiently alert the person interviewed to the danger that false statements may lead to a felony conviction." Because the questioning occurs in a noncustodial setting, the suspect is not informed of the right to remain silent. Unlike proceedings in which a false statement can be prosecuted as perjury, there may be no oath, no pause to concentrate the speaker's mind on the importance of his or her answers. As in Brogan's case, the target may not be informed that a false "No" is a criminal offense until *after* he speaks.

At oral argument, the Solicitor General forthrightly observed that § 1001 could even be used to "escalate completely innocent conduct into a felony." More likely to occur, "if an investigator finds it difficult to prove some elements of a crime, she can ask questions about other elements to which she already knows the answers. If the suspect lies, she can then use the crime she has prompted as leverage or can seek prosecution for the lie as a substitute for the crime she cannot prove." If the statute of limitations has run on an offense—as it had on four of the five payments Brogan was accused of accepting—the prosecutor can endeavor to revive the case by instructing an investigator to elicit a fresh denial of guilt. Prosecution in these circumstances is not an instance of Government "punishing the denial of wrongdoing more severely than the wrongdoing itself"; it is, instead, Government generation of a crime when the underlying suspected wrongdoing is or has become nonpunishable. It is doubtful Congress intended § 1001 to cast so large a net. ...

Even if the encompassing language of § 1001 precludes judicial declaration of an "exculpatory no" defense, the core concern persists: "The function of law enforcement is the prevention of crime and the apprehension of criminals. Manifestly, that function does not include the manufacturing of

---

[121] [Concurrence's footnote 1:] See Note, Fairness in Criminal Investigations Under the Federal False Statement Statute, 77 Colum. L. Rev. 316, 325-326 (1977) ("Since agents may often expect a suspect to respond falsely to their questions, the statute is a powerful instrument with which to trap a potential defendant. Investigators need only informally approach the suspect and elicit a false reply and they are assured of a conviction with a harsh penalty even if they are unable to prove the underlying substantive crime.") (footnotes omitted).

crime." The Government has not been blind to this concern. Notwithstanding the prosecution in this case and the others cited *supra*, the Department of Justice has long noted its reluctance to approve § 1001 indictments for simple false denials made to investigators. Indeed, the Government once asserted before this Court that the arguments supporting the "exculpatory no" doctrine "are forceful even if not necessarily dispositive." ...

...[T]he Department of Justice has maintained a policy against bringing § 1001 prosecutions for statements amounting to an "exculpatory no." At the time the charges against Brogan were filed, the United States Attorneys' Manual firmly declared: "Where the statement takes the form of an 'exculpatory no,' 18 U.S.C. § 1001 does not apply regardless who asks the question." United States Attorneys' Manual § 9-42.160 (Oct. 1, 1988). After the Fifth Circuit abandoned the "exculpatory no" doctrine in *United States v. Rodriguez-Rios*, 14 F.3d 1040 (1994) (en banc), the manual was amended to read: "It is the Department's policy that it is not appropriate to charge a Section 1001 violation where a suspect, during an investigation, merely denies his guilt in response to questioning by the government." United States Attorneys' Manual § 9-42.160 (Feb. 12, 1996).[122] ...

The Court's opinion does not instruct lower courts automatically to sanction prosecution or conviction under § 1001 in all instances of false denials made to criminal investigators. The Second Circuit, whose judgment the Court affirms, noted some reservations. That court left open the question whether "to violate Section 1001, a person must know that it is unlawful to make such a false statement." And nothing that court or this Court said suggests that "the mere denial of criminal responsibility would be sufficient to prove such [knowledge]." Moreover, "a trier of fact might acquit on the ground that a denial of guilt in circumstances indicating surprise or other lack of reflection was not the product of the requisite criminal intent," and a jury could be instructed that it would be permissible to draw such an inference. Finally, under the statute currently in force, a false statement must be "materia[l]" to violate § 1001. ...

Congress has been alert to our decisions in this area, as its enactment of the False Statements Accountability Act of 1996 (passed in response to our decision in *Hubbard v. United States*, 514 U.S. 695 (1995)) demonstrates. Similarly, after today's decision, Congress may advert to the "exculpatory no" doctrine and the problem that prompted its formulation. ...

JUSTICE STEVENS, with whom JUSTICE BREYER joins, dissenting.

Although I agree with nearly all of what JUSTICE GINSBURG has written in her concurrence—a concurrence that raises serious concerns that the Court totally ignores—I dissent for the following reasons.

The mere fact that a false denial fits within the unqualified language of 18 U.S.C. § 1001 is not, in my opinion, a sufficient reason for rejecting a well-settled interpretation of that statute. It is not at all unusual for this Court to conclude that the literal text of a criminal statute is broader than the coverage intended by Congress. Although the text of § 1001, read literally, makes it a crime for an undercover narcotics agent to make a false statement to a drug peddler, I am confident that Congress did not intend any such result. As JUSTICE GINSBURG has explained, it seems equally clear that Congress did not intend to make every "exculpatory no" a felony.

Even if that were not clear, I believe the Court should show greater respect for the virtually uniform understanding of the bench and the bar that persisted for decades with, as JUSTICE GINSBURG notes, the approval of this Court as well as the Department of Justice. Or, as Sir Edward Coke phrased it, "it is the common opinion, and *communis opinio* is of good authoritie in law." 1 E. Coke, Institutes 186a (15th ed. 1794). ...

---

[122] [Concurrence's footnote 6:] While this case was pending before us, the Department of Justice issued yet another version of the manual .... The new version reads: "It is the Department's policy not to charge a Section 1001 violation in situations in which a suspect, during an investigation, merely denies guilt in response to questioning by the government." United States Attorneys' Manual § 9-42.160 (Sept.1997).

Notes

1. *Should* there be a legal difference between lying and falsely denying? *See* Stuart P. Green, *Lying, Misleading, and Falsely Denying: How Moral Concepts Inform the Law of Perjury, Fraud, and False Statements*, 53 Hastings L.J. 157 (2001) (arguing that "falsely denying" is in a different moral category than both lying and non-lying deception, and that "falsely denying" is "associated with a defensive 'right of self-preservation,' and ... as a result, will frequently be viewed as morally 'excused,' even if not typically 'justified'"). Why would the government elect to bring charges in an "exculpatory 'no'" case? Where the government can prove a case on the underlying criminal activity, why might a prosecutor elect to also charge a false statement where such a statement is provable? As defense counsel, what advice would you give your client at the inception of a criminal investigation, especially in light of *Brogan*?

2. Does the DOJ's "exculpatory 'no'" policy, stated below, restrict the actual enforcement of § 1001 to cases in which a substantial federal interest is threatened?

> It is the Department's policy not to charge a § 1001 violation in situations in which a suspect, during an investigation, merely denies guilt in response to questioning by the government. ... This policy is to be narrowly construed, however; affirmative, discursive and voluntary statements to Federal criminal investigators would not fall within the policy. Further, certain false responses to questions propounded for administrative purposes (e.g., statements to border or United States Immigration and Naturalization Service agents during routine inquiries) are also prosecutable, as are untruthful "no's" when the defendant initiated contact with the government in order to obtain a benefit.

U.S.A.M. Criminal Resource Manual No. 916; *see also* U.S.A.M. § 9-42.160.

3. Defense counsel will also often attack prosecutors' charging choices in false statement cases. *See infra* Part D (Charging Considerations). In particular, where the false statement count is brought with or instead of other counts charged under false statement statutes that are more specific to the context, defense counsel will often argue that Congress intended that the specific statute supersede § 1001 in that context. Courts generally have been unreceptive to arguments that prosecutors may not pursue § 1001 charges in addition to or instead of other potentially applicable criminal code sections. *See, e.g.*, United States v. Curran, 20 F.3d 560, 565-66 (3d Cir. 1994). This is true more generally as well; courts are reluctant to hold that Congress impliedly repealed the applicability of a general provision by enacting a more specific prohibition. *See, e.g.*, United States v. Arif, 897 F.3d 1 (1st Cir. 2018).

C. FALSE CLAIMS

Among other sections of the United States Code employed to criminally pursue false statements to the government, the false claims statute, 18 U.S.C. § 287, is frequently cited. It, like § 1001, is often employed in pursuing procurement and government program fraud. Most particularly, it is invoked in cases involving an increasingly important criminal enforcement priority, health care fraud.

The criminal false claims statute also has a civil counterpart, the False Claims Act (FCA), 31 U.S.C. §§ 3729-3733. The "dramatic rise in *qui tam*—or whistleblower—litigation" has had a pronounced effect on criminal practice because this type of civil action "frequently brings the type of insider information to the Department of Justice that triggers criminal as well as civil investigations."[123] As one practitioner explained, this phenomenon means that "there isn't

---

[123] Jeffrey T. Green, *The Thin Line Between Civil and Criminal Proceedings*, 9 Bus. Crimes Bull. 1 (April 2002).

any decent lawyer in this town [Washington, D.C.] who isn't up on the *qui tam* statutes and looking for a *qui tam* plaintiff around every corner."[124]

The FCA encourages private citizens, known as "relators," to file suit on behalf of the government in order to recover civil damages from other private citizens for their frauds against the government. The relators who file such actions—known as *qui tam* suits—are statutorily entitled to a healthy percentage of the potentially large damages and penalties that may be recovered (with attorneys' fees) in such FCA litigation. As such, *qui tam* relators "'are motivated primarily by prospects of monetary reward rather than the public good'" and "'the government does not expect that the relator will act first and foremost with the government's interests in mind.'"[125] FCA *qui tam* cases originally were aimed predominantly at defense contracting fraud. Now they more often concern health care fraud, which is a potential goldmine for government and private litigators. Thus, "[f]rom 1987 to 1997, the number of *qui tam* cases filed increased from 33 to 534, or 1527%. From 1988 through 1997, recoveries in *qui tam* cases pursued by the DOJ increased from $355,000 to $625,000,000, or an astonishing 17828%."[126] Since 1997, the number of cases, and the recoveries, have increased, again, astronomically. In 2017, the government recovered $3.7 billion in FCA cases; 93% ($3.4 billion) came from cases filed by qui tam relators and only $266 million from cases filed by the DOJ. Relators filed 669 new qui tam cases—12 per week—during 2017 and successful relators pocketed $392 million. Healthcare continues to dominate the practice; thus 67% of the 2017 recoveries concerned the Department of Health and Human Services and 68% of the new FCA matters (90% of which were brought by relators) concerned alleged healthcare fraud and false statements.[127]

Examination of the interplay between the criminal false statement statute and its uniquely constituted civil analogue illustrates the wide-ranging powers of federal prosecutors and the challenges faced by defense counsel in responding to possible parallel criminal and civil investigations. *Qui tam* litigation spearheaded by private relators also raises fundamental questions about optimal allocation of law enforcement authority and the appropriate role of private citizens in policing fraud upon the government.

1. CRIMINAL FALSE CLAIMS CASES UNDER § 287

The criminal false claims statute was first enacted in 1863 in reaction to widespread defense contracting fraud during the Civil War. To make a § 287 case, the government must prove beyond a reasonable doubt the following elements: (1) the defendant presented a claim against the United States or any agency or department of the United States; (2) the claim was false, fictitious, or fraudulent; and (3) the defendant knew the claim was false, fictitious, or fraudulent.[128] In two respects, proof of a § 287 case may be easier than a § 1001 case, at least

---

[124] *Id.* at 6-7.

[125] Riley v. St. Luke's Episcopal Hospital, 196 F.3d 514, 528 n.39 (5th Cir. 1999) (citations omitted), *rev'd en banc*, 252 F.3d 749 (5th Cir. 2001).

[126] Robert Fabrikant & Glenn E. Solomon, *Application of the Federal False Claims Act to Regulatory Compliance Issues in the Health Care Industry*, 51 Ala. L. Rev. 105, 125 (1999) (footnotes omitted); *see also* John T. Boese, Civil False Claims and *Qui Tam* Actions 14-1 (2d ed.1993 & Supp. 2000). The rapid expansion of both criminal and civil enforcement actions under the False Claims Act has given rise to concerns that "friction exists in the manner in which the government and relators are trying to enforce the FCA, and what appears to be the unintended fallout that results from an overly expansive and inconsistent application of the statute." Robert Fabrikant, *The False Claims Act: The Dissonance Between Good Intentions and Unintended Results*, White Collar Crime Committee Report 8 (Fall 2002); *see also* Joan H. Krause, *"Promises to Keep": Health Care Providers and the Civil False Claims Act*, 23 Cardozo L. Rev. 1363 (March 2002).

[127] DOJ Press Release, Justice Department Recovered Over 37 Billion in False Claims Act Cases in Fiscal Year 2017 (Dec. 21, 2017), available at https://www.justice.gov/opa/pr/justice-department-recovers-over-37-billion-false-claims-act-cases-fiscal-year-2017.

[128] *See* United States v. Dedman, 527 F.3d 577, 594-95 (6th Cir. 2008). Just as in the false statements

in certain circuits. While a few circuits have held that § 287 requires proof of a specific intent to defraud,[129] others have stated that proof of a degree of *mens rea* higher than "knowledge" is not required.[130] Further, although materiality is clearly an element of a false statements case, most circuits to decide the issue have held that materiality is not an element of a false claims case.[131]

Obviously, the primary distinction between § 287 and § 1001 is that the former requires that a false *claim* be made and may not rest, as may the latter, on the simple provision of *any* false statement (or, in appropriate cases, concealment). Section 287 does not define a "claim," but courts have read the term broadly. "In addition to requests for direct payment or reimbursement, claims for credit and 'reverse false claims' constitute 'claims' under the FCA."[132] Although the defendant must physically present the claim to the government,[133] "there is no requirement that the claim has actually been honored"[134] or that the government actually was defrauded of property by virtue of the claim.[135] And a claim against the United States Government made through a third party may constitute a claim "upon" the United States under § 287.[136] The defendant may be liable where, for example, the claim reaches the United States Government through a state or local government, a government contractor, an insurance company, or an individual seeking federal reimbursement funding.[137]

At least where a false statement has been made in a claim upon the federal government, prosecutors may be able to proceed under either § 287 or § 1001 or both.[138] As outlined above,

---

cases, many false claims cases recognize that knowledge can be inferred from the defendant's reckless disregard for the truth, or conscious avoidance of the truth. *See, e.g.*, Commercial Contractors, Inc. v. United States, 154 F.3d 1357, 1362 (Fed. Cir. 1998); United States v. Krizek, 111 F.3d 934 (D.C. Cir. 1997). Also, as in the false statement cases, knowledge of the federal nature of the claim is not required. *See, e.g.*, United States v. Montoya, 716 F.2d 1340, 1345 (10th Cir. 1983).

[129] *See, e.g.*, United States v. Nazon, 940 F.2d 255, 260 (7th Cir. 1991); United States v. Haddon, 927 F.2d 942, 951 (7th Cir. 1991); United States v. Martin, 772 F.2d 1442, 1444-45 (8th Cir. 1985). *But see* United States v. Catton, 89 F.3d 387, 392 (7th Cir. 1996) ("It is implicit in the filing of a knowingly false claim that the claimant intends to defraud the government" but holding that specific intent to defraud is not an element of § 287 and arguing that those cases that required specific intent to defraud had made "assumptions not holdings").

[130] *See* United States v. Clarke, 801 F.3d 824, 827 (7th Cir. 2015) (proof of willfulness not required); United States v. Precision Medical Laboratories, Inc., 593 F.2d 434, 444 (2d Cir. 1978). *But see* United States v. Gumbs, 283 F.3d 128, 131 (3d Cir. 2002) (defendant must willfully cause the false claim to be presented).

[131] *Compare* United States v. Saybolt, 577 F.3d 195 (3d Cir. 2009) (Section 287's prohibition of presenting a "false, fictitious, or fraudulent" claim calls for proof of materiality only when the claim is fraudulent as opposed to false or fictitious); United States v. Nash, 175 F.3d 429, 433-34 (6th Cir. 1999) (holding materiality not an element), *with* United States v. Pruitt, 702 F.2d 152, 155 (8th Cir. 1983) (holding materiality is an element); *cf.* United States v. Cordero, 205 F.3d 1325 (2d Cir. 2000) (unpublished op.) (noting split but declining to take a position other than to note that its previous decision which stated that proof of materiality was not required, United States v. Elkin, 731 F.2d 1005, 1009-10 (2d Cir. 1984), is no longer good law after *United States v. Gaudin*, 515 U.S. 506 (1995)); United States v. Durenberger, 48 F.3d 1239, 1243 n. 2 (D.C. Cir. 1995); United States v. White, 27 F.3d 1531, 1535-35 (11th Cir. 1994).

[132] *Thirty-Third Annual Survey of White Collar Crime*, *supra* note 38, at 1078; *see also* 31 U.S.C. § 3729(c) (civil component of False Claim Act's definition of "claim").

[133] United States v. Coachman, 727 F.2d 1293, 1303 (D.C. Cir. 1984).

[134] *Id.* at 1302.

[135] United States v. Drape, 668 F.2d 22, 26 (1st Cir. 1982).

[136] *See Thirty-Third Annual Survey of White Collar Crime*, *supra* note 38, at 1079; *see also* 18 U.S.C. § 2(b); United States *ex rel.* Marcus v. Hess, 317 U.S. 537, 545 (1943).

[137] *See Thirty-Third Annual Survey of White Collar Crime*, *supra* note 38, at 1183.

[138] *See, e.g.*, United States v. Olsowy, 836 F.2d 439, 442 (9th Cir. 1987).

the two differ slightly in the proof they require, and prosecutors thus have the option of choosing that charge which best fits their case. When either count could be lodged, the Justice Department believes that its *civil* division "benefits more by a prosecution under 18 U.S.C. § 287," primarily because the government may then ease its burden of proof in collateral *civil* proceedings against the defendant under the civil False Claims Act, 31 U.S.C. § 3729. As the Department at one time advised its prosecutors, "because 18 U.S.C. § 287 and 31 U.S.C. § 3729 have much the same elements of proof[,] ...[a successful prosecution under § 287 lets] the Civil Division take advantage of the doctrines of estoppel by judgment and *res judicata*."[139] Should the prospect of civil monetary damages awards influence criminal prosecutors' charging choices?

2. CIVIL FALSE CLAIMS CASES: *QUI TAM* LITIGATION

The civil False Claims Act ("FCA"),[140] originally enacted in 1863, was also designed to address military contracting fraud. The FCA allowed private citizens, known as "relators," to bring what are known as *qui tam* suits in the name of the government, based on the individual's knowledge of fraud against the government, and to secure for their trouble a portion of the funds recovered in the suit. "The *qui tam* provisions offset inadequate law enforcement resources and encouraged 'a rogue to catch a rogue' by inducing informers 'to betray [their] coconspirators.'"[141] As the D.C. Circuit has explained the early history of the FCA:

> The [original] Act was seldom utilized ... until the 1930s and 1940s when increased government spending opened up numerous opportunities for unscrupulous government contractors to defraud the government. *Qui tam* litigation surged as opportunistic private litigants chased after generous cash bounties and, unhindered by any effective restrictions under the Act, often brought parasitic lawsuits copied from preexisting indictments or based upon congressional investigations. Such ill-motivated suits not only diminished the government's ultimate recovery without contributing any new information, but the rush to the courthouse put pressure on the government to make hasty decisions regarding whether to prosecute civil actions.
>
> When the Supreme Court decided *United States ex rel. Marcus v. Hess*, 317 U.S. 537 (1943), permitting a *qui tam* suit in which the relator copied his complaint directly from a criminal fraud indictment, Congress finally took action to prevent such piggy-back lawsuits. ...Thus, the FCA, as amended in 1943, barred *qui tam* suits that were "based upon evidence or information in the possession of the United States ... at the time such suit was brought."
>
> As amended, the Act contained no protection for those whistleblowers who furnished evidence or information to the government in the first place. Citing the fact that Congress refused in 1943 to adopt a specific provision protecting the viability of *qui tam* suits brought by an original source of the information in the government's hands, the courts barred suits brought by those original sources. But it soon became apparent that by restricting *qui tam* suits by individuals who brought fraudulent activity to the government's attention, Congress had killed the goose that laid the golden egg and eliminated the financial incentive to expose frauds against the government. The use of *qui tam* suits as a weapon for fighting fraud against the government dramatically declined. ...
>
> In 1986, Congress ... amend[ed] the Act yet another time in order to "encourage more private enforcement suits." After ricocheting between the extreme permissiveness that preceded the 1943 amendments and the extreme restrictiveness that followed,

---

[139] Former U.S.A.M. § 9-42.210.

[140] 31 U.S.C. §§ 3729-3733.

[141] United States *ex rel.* Findley v. FPC-Boron Employees' Club, 105 F.3d 675, 679 (D.C. Cir. 1997).

Congress again sought to achieve "the golden mean between adequate incentives for whistle-blowing insiders with genuinely valuable information and discouragement of opportunistic plaintiffs who have no significant information to contribute on their own." Accordingly, the 1986 amendments repealed the "government knowledge" jurisdictional bar and replaced it with a provision that restricts the subject matter jurisdiction of private plaintiff suits.[142]

Thus, the 1986 amendments, together with significant amendments in 2009 and 2010, combine in 31 U.S.C. § 3730(e)(4)(A) to dictate that:

> The court shall dismiss an action or claim under this section, unless opposed by the Government, if substantially the same allegations or transactions as alleged in the action or claim were publicly disclosed … in a Federal criminal, civil, or administrative hearing in which the Government or its agent is a party; … in a congressional, Government Accountability Office, or other Federal report, hearing, audit, or investigation; or … from the news media, unless the action is brought by the Attorney General or the person bringing the action is an original source of the information.

The statute, in 31 U.S.C. § 3730(e)(4)(B), further states that:

> For purposes of this paragraph, "original source" means an individual who either (i) prior to a public disclosure under subsection (e)(4)(a), has voluntarily disclosed to the Government the information on which allegations or transactions in a claim are based or (2) who has knowledge that is independent of and materially adds to the publicly disclosed allegations or transactions, and who has voluntarily provided the information to the Government before filing an action under this section.

The 1996 amendments gave *qui tam* relators added incentives to bring suit by increasing the relator's role in such litigation and, most important, increasing the amount that the relator may share in any money recovered in the suit.

In *Rockwell International Corp. v. United States*, the Supreme Court clarified what constitutes "original source" status—a requirement the Court deemed jurisdictional.[143] In *Rockwell*, the relator, a former Rockwell employee, had filed a *qui tam* suit, alleging in part that Rockwell had knowingly put in place a system that relator had predicted, while a Rockwell employee, would lead to substandard problems. The government eventually intervened and, with the relator, filed an amended complaint. The Supreme Court held that the relator did not qualify as the "original source" of the information upon which the FCA recovery was founded. It clarified that the original source requirement—that the relator have direct and independent knowledge of the "information on which the allegations were based"—refers to the information upon which the *relator's allegations* are based.[144] Further, the Court ruled that it had to look not just at the original allegations filed, but also the allegations as they changed throughout the litigation, including in the amended complaint. The Court concluded that the relator's "knowledge" fell short because the false claims found by the jury were based on events that Stone *predicted* but of which, because he was no longer employed by Rockwell at the time the problems actually developed, he had no *knowledge*, particularly where, as here, his predictions were premised on an engineering theory that ultimately proved to be wrong.[145]

---

[142] *Id.* at 679-81.

[143] 549 U.S. 457 (2007).

[144] *Id.* at 470-71.

[145] *Id.* at 475-76.

Under the existing statute, a civil False Claims Act suit may be initiated by either the Attorney General or by private persons.[146] The civil False Claims Act[147] contains a number of substantive prohibitions[148] but is most frequently used to recover government monies persons knowingly obtained—or improperly retained[149]—through false claims[150] or false statements.[151] Generally, a person may be liable under the FCA if the defendant presented to the government a claim that he knew to be false or fraudulent or knowingly made or used a false statement material to such a claim.

A private person may initiate a *qui tam* suit "for the person and for the United States Government" in the "name of the Government"[152] by filing a complaint under seal with the court and serving a copy on the DOJ (but not on the defendant until the court so orders). The relator is also required to provide the DOJ with a "written disclosure of substantially all material evidence and information."[153] The "relator" does not have to have alleged or suffered any personal harm—the idea is that he is suing on behalf of the harmed government. What the relator must have, however, is information not previously publicly disclosed unless the relator is the "original source" of the information.[154] A relator cannot file a *qui tam* action where he has been convicted of criminal misconduct arising from his role in the FCA violation, another *qui tam* relator alleging the same violation has filed before him, or the government is already a party to a civil or administrative procedure concerning the same conduct.[155]

Where a case is initiated by a private relator, rather than the government, the complaint remains under seal and the action is stayed for 60 days while the government determines whether to intervene—that is, take over the case as its own—or to leave the case to the relator to litigate.[156] The 60-day seal period permits the government to review the relator's allegations and evidence, to assess the suit's impact on any pending criminal investigation, and to prevent alerting potential criminal defendants of an investigation. The statute permits the court to grant the government extensions of the 60-day period during which the complaint remains under seal.[157] While the government takes over a minority of the *qui tam* actions brought by relators, it investigates all of them. As a practical matter, the Attorney General's investigation

---

[146] 31 U.S.C. § 3730(a), (b).

[147] *Id.* §§ 3729–3733. U.S. states have also passed a great number of *qui tam* statutes. *See, e.g.*, Pamela Bucy et al., *States, Statutes, and Fraud: A Study of Emerging State Efforts to Combat White Collar Crime*, 31 CARDOZO L. REV. 1523 *passim* (2010).

[148] 31 U.S.C. § 3729(a)(1)(A)–(G).

[149] *Id.* § 3729(a)(1)(G) (reverse false claims section). Section 3729(a)(1)(C) imposes liability on those who conspire to violate the FCA.

[150] *Id.* § 3729(a)(1)(A) (rendering liable any person who "knowingly presents, or causes to be presented, a false or fraudulent claim for payment or approval"). The Supreme Court, in *Universal Health Servs. v. United States ex rel. Escobar*, -- U.S. --, 136 S.Ct. 1989 (2016), held that an implied false certification theory can be the basis for FCA liability when a defendant submitting a claim makes specific representations about the goods or services provided, but fails to disclose noncompliance with material statutory, regulatory, or contractual requirements that make those representations misleading with respect to those goods or services.

[151] 31 U.S.C. § 3729(a)(1)(B) (rendering liable any person who "knowingly makes, uses, or causes to be made or used, a false record or statement material to a false or fraudulent claim").

[152] *Id.* § 3730(b)(1).

[153] *Id.* § 3730(b)(2).

[154] *Id* § 3730(e)(4)(A)–(B).

[155] *Id.* § 3730(b)(5), (d)(3), (e)(3).

[156] *Id.* § 3730(b)(2).

[157] *Id.* § 3730(b)(3).

may require multiple extensions and the mean decision time is nearly 600 days and the median is 437 days after filing.[158]

In the 1986 amendments, Congress created a special procedure known as a "civil investigative demand" (CID), which allows the Attorney General to obtain documentary evidence for the purpose of ascertaining whether any person is or has been engaged in a violation of the FCA.[159] CIDs in a civil False Claims case may include document requests, written interrogatories, and depositions.[160]

If, after investigating the matter, the government declines to intervene, the relator may litigate the case to judgment, although the relator must obtain the government's approval to settle or dismiss a case.[161] Even if the government intervenes, thus taking over primary responsibility for its prosecution,[162] relators may remain involved and must at least be heard on such matters as settlement.

If, however, the government concludes that a *qui tam* action is frivolous or not in the public interest, it has the power under the FCA to dismiss it over the relator's objection.[163] The DOJ historically has exercised this power in only approximately 4% of non-intervened *qui tam* filings.[164] This may change given a recently leaked DOJ memorandum regarding FCA enforcement. In a confidential January 10, 2018 memorandum, the DOJ emphasized its "gatekeeping role" in protecting the FCA and encouraged DOJ attorneys to consider not only their power to dismiss meritless actions brought under the FCA, but also their responsibility to do so. This memorandum emphasizes that the DOJ must use its dismissal authority to advance government interests, preserve limited resources, and avoid adverse precedent. It provides DOJ lawyers with a number of considerations that may warrant dismissal, such as curbing meritless cases and preventing interference with agency policies.[165] On January 25, 2018, Associate Attorney General Rachel Brand released another memorandum that prohibits the DOJ from relying on noncompliance with other agencies' guidance documents as evidence of a defendant's violation. This may provide DOJ attorneys additional reasons to dismiss FCA cases.[166]

Relators may, if the suit is successful, recover a maximum of 25% of the proceeds of the suit if the government chooses to intervene and conduct the litigation, and 25-30% in a case in which the government does not intervene.[167] The pot out of which the relator draws his share may be quite large by virtue of the damages provisions of the Act: a penalty of between $5,000 and $10,000 for each false claim filed may be assessed on top of the treble damages and attorneys fees awards allowable under the Act.[168] In addition to the relators' portion of the

---

[158] *See* David Kwok, *Evidence from the False Claims Act: Does Private Enforcement Attract Excessive Litigation?*, 42 Pub. Cont. L.J. 225, 247 (2013) (graphing days cases remain under seal); *see also* David Freeman Engstrom, *Private Enforcement's Pathways: Lessons from* Qui Tam *Litigation*, 114 Colum. L. Rev. 1913, 1993 (2014) (graphing investigation time by year and case type).

[159] *See* 31 U.S.C. § 3733(a)(1).

[160] *Id.* § 3733.

[161] *Id.* § 3730(b)(1).

[162] *Id.* § 3730(c)(1). In such cases, the government (*id.* § 3730(c)(2)(C)) and the defendant (*id.* § 3730(c)(2)(D)) can ask the court to limit the relator's participation.

[163] *Id.* § 3730(c)(2)(A) (2015).

[164] Kwok, *supra* note 158, at 245.

[165] *See* Michael Granston Memo to All Attorneys, Factors for Evaluating Dismissal Pursuant to 31 U.S.C. 3730(c)(2)(A).

[166] *See* Associate Attorney General Memorandum, Limiting Use of Agency Guidance Documents in Affirmative Civil Enforcement Cases (Jan. 25, 2018).

[167] 31 U.S.C. § 3730(d)(1), (d)(2).

[168] *Id.* §§ 3729(a), 3730(d)(1), (d)(2).

recovery, the Act provides relief for whistleblowing relators who are "discharged, demoted, suspended, threatened, harassed, or in any other manner discriminated against" as a result of their reporting of the false claim.[169]

The Government obviously also wins in a successful False Claims Act case, obtaining the lion's share of the recovery whether it elects to intervene or not. The Government does not have to elect how it shall proceed and may pursue civil and criminal False Claims Act cases against the same defendant(s). At one time, it appeared that dual proceedings might run afoul of the Double Jeopardy Clause by virtue of the Supreme Court's decision in *United States v. Halper*.[170] In *Halper*, the Court held that double jeopardy may bar the government from securing a criminal false claims conviction and thereafter pursing FCA awards that, although nominally civil, were so disproportionate to remedial goals as to constitute criminal punishment.[171] However, as is explained at greater length in Chapter 20 (Parallel Proceedings), the Supreme Court overruled the analytical basis for *Halper* and abandoned its efforts to conduct case-specific evaluations of the punitive nature of civil sanctions.

The FCA, measured in terms of collection of falsely or fraudulently obtained government money, has been spectacularly successful. Between 1987 and 2017, some 11,980 *qui tam* suits were filed and $40.5 billion was recovered.[172] In the same period, the government initiated FCA cases totaled 5,020 and yielded $15.6 billion. (Note that some criticize these numbers as under-inclusive because they do not include the substantial criminal penalties paid to the DOJ, nor do they include settlement amounts paid to state authorities.)

As the above statistics indicate, the overwhelming majority of FCA recoveries stemmed from actions filed by *qui tam* relators. These developments are reflected in relators' awards. From 1987 to 2017, relators were awarded more than $6.5 billion.[173] And the amount of rewards has been increasing. In fiscal year 1988, *qui tam* relators received a grand total of $97,188; by fiscal year 2017, relators' rewards totaled $393 million.[174]

Qui tam litigation provides an excellent example of some of the types of problems that the potential for parallel civil and criminal proceedings create for investigatory targets and their defense counsel. It also, however, presents its own challenges by virtue of its unique attributes. Illustrative issues are discussed generally below.

a. Practical Issues

The government may use the broad discovery devices available under the civil FCA to obtain information that ultimately may be used in either a civil or a criminal proceeding.[175] In responding to document requests, interrogatories, or deposition notices in civil FCA cases, counsel must be aware that *qui tam* cases are for all intents and purposes criminal cases. The plaintiff (either the relator or the government) is accusing the defendant of activity that is criminal: submitting a false or fraudulent claim, making or using a false record or statement material to a false or fraudulent claim, or conspiring to commit a violation of the FCA.[176]

---

[169] *Id.* § 3730(h).

[170] 490 U.S. 435 (1989).

[171] *Id.* at 449.

[172] U.S. Dep't of Justice, *Fraud Statistics—Overview: Oct. 1, 1987–Sept. 30, 2017*; *see also* Margaret H. Lemos, *Special Incentives to Sue*, 95 MINN. L. REV. 782, 802 (2011).

[173] *Id.*

[174] *See* Statistics, *supra* note 172; William McLucas, Laura Wertheimer & Adrian June, *Year Three of the SEC Whistleblower Program: Will it Turbocharge SEC Enforcement?*, 45 Sec. Reg. & L. Rep. (BNA) 3 (May 13, 2013).

[175] *See* 31 U.S.C. § 3733(i).

[176] 18 U.S.C. § 278; 31 U.S.C. § 3729; *see also* Vermont Agency of Nat'l Resources v. United States *ex rel.* Stevens, 529 U.S. 765, 771 (2000) (discussing the civil relators' standing, noting that "[i]t is beyond doubt that the complaint asserts an injury to the United States, both the injury to its sovereignty arising from

The defense of *qui tam* investigations will thus mimic the defense of any other type of criminal case. Individual targets may be required to assert their Fifth Amendment right against self-incrimination to avoid prejudicing their position in a possible criminal case, even though that assertion may harm them in the *qui tam* context. Defense counsel will attempt to master, and to the extent possible, control the facts revealed in the course of the investigation. In this, however, defense counsel will face one challenge that is not generally present in the usual criminal fraud investigation: the fact that a potential witness—often a present or former insider of the (assumedly deep-pocketed) target corporation—is the instigator of the investigation and has a financial interest in the corporation's liability. At least at the beginning stages of the case, the *qui tam* complaint is filed under seal and the relator may not be forced to disclose the existence of the case.

Defense counsel obviously will be concerned with ensuring the confidentiality of attorney-client communications and safeguarding work product materials. To that end, counsel will attempt to determine whether there is a *qui tam* relator within the targeted corporation and to identify the relator. Removing the *qui tam* relator from the information flow can be perilous, however, if the relator then alleges to have been discriminated against by virtue of his allegations or pressured into compromising the suit or changing his story, all in violation of the whistleblower protection provisions of the Act.

Another particular challenge *qui tam* counsel face in the conduct of these suits is attempting to persuade the Department of Justice not to intervene in the case. The chance of recovery if the government intervenes increases exponentially. Thus, for example, in 2017, qui tam actions yielded $3 billion in cases in which the government intervened and only $245 million where the DOJ declined.[177] The government's key considerations in determining whether to intervene are the amount of money involved and the merits of the case. These decisions can be heavily influenced by expertly investigated and convincing presentations by defense counsel. The decision to make a presentation to the government in an effort to forestall intervention involves many of the same risks that attend the decision to make a submission to regulators or to prosecutors to secure a declination of regulatory or criminal action against the defendant. In making such presentations, defense counsel will be providing the government, and possibly the relator, a roadmap of the defense. This occurs at a stage when the government may still be formulating its complaint and shaping its theory. The defense's presentation may constitute admissions that can later be used against the defendant in the civil or any subsequent criminal action. By stating a position about the factual and legal issues involved at this stage, the defense may be foregoing other defenses or arguments. At the least, staking out a position may restrict the defense's flexibility in responding to newly discovered information or theories of liability. Finally, depending upon the form and content of the presentation, the defense may later encounter arguments that, by exposing attorney-client privileged material or matters covered by the work product doctrine, the defense waived those protections.

Some argue that given the wide-ranging CID powers the Attorney General possesses, and the likelihood that the Justice Department will use those powers to investigate prior to intervening in a contested case, the practical risks of exposure of information that otherwise would remain shielded is not great. Many would conclude, then, that defense counsel will usually wish to make a presentation despite the risks of tipping off their defenses.

It is also interesting that much of the advice one would give a corporation wishing to avoid or mitigate its future criminal exposure applies equally to corporations hoping to limit their *qui tam* liability. Obviously, the best advice is to avoid false claims, but even the most well-run corporations may not always be able to prevent wrongdoing. Some would counsel corporations to institute compliance programs, which, while not infallible, may prevent problems before they occur and encourage employees to work within the corporation to

---

violation of its laws (which suffices to support a criminal lawsuit by the Government) and the proprietary injury resulting from the alleged fraud").

[177] Fraud Statistics, *supra* note 172.

remedy problems rather than filing *qui tam* suits. The existence of effective compliance programs also works to the corporation's advantage in criminal matters: prosecutors will consider the presence of an effective compliance program in determining whether to bring a criminal case in the first instance and, if charged, the corporation will earn sentencing credit by virtue of its effort to be a good corporate citizen.[178]

Self-reporting any fraud that is discovered, which will mitigate a corporation's criminal sentencing exposure under the U.S. Organizational Sentencing Guidelines, also may reduce *qui tam* exposure. The FCA statute provides for "only" double—instead of the usual treble—damages and no penalties if the fraud is promptly reported (and the responsible party cooperates) before the party knows about any investigation into the matter.[179] Those parties who operate in areas in which the responsible government agencies have amnesty programs may receive further relief.[180] Finally, depending upon the circumstances, prompt and voluntary disclosure of fraud may bar private relators from pursuing FCA claims, even if it does not foreclose the government from doing so. As noted above, there is no jurisdiction in a FCA case for a private plaintiff if substantially the same allegations or transactions as alleged in the claim were "public[ly] disclosed" unless the relator is the "original source" or the government consents to the action.[181] What all those terms mean depends upon the jurisdiction; thus, the party's ability to foreclose FCA liability to private relators based upon voluntary disclosures to the government very much depends upon where the litigation will proceed.

b. Constitutional Questions

The increase in *qui tam* suits sparked by the 1986 amendment to the False Claims Act has led to a similar increase in scrutiny of the *qui tam* statute by all levels of the federal judiciary. In 2000, the Supreme Court resolved one threshold issue: whether *qui tam* relators have Article III standing to pursue suits in federal court. The Court held in *Vermont Agency of Natural Resources v. United States ex rel. Stevens*,[182] that *qui tam* "relators do have constitutional standing to sue private defendants on behalf of the government based on relators' role as partial assignees of the government's damage claims. In the same case the Supreme Court avoided an Eleventh Amendment issue by holding that the statute does not include states as "person[s]" subject to *qui tam* liability.[183]

Other constitutional questions that have been raised but not definitively resolved include claims that *qui tam* suits violate: the Appointments Clause of Article II;[184] the Fifth Amendment Due Process Clause;[185] and general separation of powers principles.[186] Perhaps the most

---

[178] *See supra* Chapter 4 (Entity Liability).

[179] 31 U.S.C. § 3729(a)(2).

[180] For example, defense contractors may avail themselves of the Department of Defense Voluntary Disclosure Program and healthcare providers may look to the Department of Health and Human Services' "Operation Restore Trust."

[181] 31 U.S.C. § 3730(e)(4). *But see id.* § 3730(d)(1).

[182] 529 U.S. 765 (2000).

[183] *Id.* at 853.

[184] *See* United States *ex rel.* Kelly v. Boeing Co., 9 F.3d 743, 757 (9th Cir. 1993) (rejecting Appointments Clause argument); *see also Stevens*, 529 U.S. at 778 (reserving Appointments Clause issue); Steel Co. v. Citizens for a Better Environment, 523 U.S. 83, 102, n.4 (1998) (same); Riley v. St. Luke's Episcopal Hospital, 252 F.3d 749 (5th Cir. 2001) (*en banc*).

[185] *See Kelly*, 9 F.3d at 759 (rejecting argument that a *qui tam* suit violates the Due Process Clause of Fifth Amendment because it "creates a conflict of interest between a relator's desire for pecuniary gain and duty as a prosecutor performing 'government functions' to seek a just and fair result").

[186] *See Riley*, 196 F.3d 514.

interesting issue for present purpose is whether FCA *qui tam* suits initiated by relators and in which the government declines to intervene violate Article 2, section 3 of the Constitution (the "Take Care" clause).[187]

RILEY v. ST. LUKE'S EPISCOPAL HOSPITAL
252 F.3d 749 (5th Cir. 2001) (*en banc*)

CARL E. STEWART, CIRCUIT JUDGE:

We took this case en banc to reconsider the issue of whether the qui tam provisions of the False Claims Act ("FCA"), which permits private citizens, or relators, to pursue actions for fraudulent claims in the name of the federal government, violate the constitutional separation of powers doctrine under the Take Care ... Clause[] of Article II.[188] Because we find no such unconstitutional intrusion, we reverse and remand to the district court.

FACTUAL AND PROCEDURAL HISTORY

Joyce Riley ("Riley"), a former nurse at St. Luke's Episcopal Hospital ("St. Luke's"), sued eight defendants under the qui tam provisions of the FCA, claiming that they defrauded and conspired to defraud the United States Treasury in violation of the statute. Riley proceeded with the lawsuit although the government exercised its right not to intervene under 31 U.S.C. § 3730(b)(4)(B) (2000).[189] The district court subsequently dismissed Riley's lawsuit on standing grounds. On appeal, however, this Court held that although Riley had standing to sue under Article III,[190] qui tam actions pursued under the FCA in which the government does not intervene violate the doctrine of separation of powers and the Take Care Clause.

The United States intervened to defend the constitutionality of the FCA. We subsequently decided to rehear this case en banc, but delayed it pending the Supreme Court's decision in [*Vermont Agency of Natural Resources v. United States ex rel. Stevens*, 529 U.S. 765 (2000)].

DISCUSSION

I. *The Role of History*

Qui tam lawsuits have been used throughout American and English history as a means to discover and to prosecute fraud against the national treasuries. Indeed, the Founding Fathers and the First Congress enacted a number of statutes authorizing qui tam actions. After undergoing a decline in popularity and need, qui tam, under the guise of the original FCA, enjoyed a renaissance during the Civil War era. This renaissance was precipitated by a desire to combat widespread corruption and fraud amongst defense contractors who supplied the Union Army.

---

[187] *See also Stevens*, 529 U.S. at 848 (reserving issue "Take Care" clause issue); *id.* at 863 (Stevens, J., dissenting) (historical evidence sufficient to resolve Article II question). *See generally* Roger A. Fairfax, Jr., *Delegation of the Criminal Prosecution Function to Private Actors*, 43 U.C. Davis L. Rev. 411 (2009).

[188] [Ed.:] The *en banc* court, in an unexcerpted portion of this opinion, also held that the FCA does not violate the Appointments Clause of Article II.

[189] [Court's footnote 1:] In exchange, qui tam plaintiffs, such as Riley, may recover up to 30 percent of the proceeds of an action, in addition to reasonable attorneys' fees and costs, if the action is successful. 31 U.S.C. § 3730(d)(2). Relators, however, may recover a maximum of 25 percent of the proceeds in lawsuits initiated by a relator in which the government chooses to intervene. 31 U.S.C. § 3730(d)(1).

[190] [Court's footnote 3:] The United States Supreme Court subsequently held that relators have standing to bring qui tam actions under the FCA. *Vermont Agency of Natural Res. v. United States ex rel. Stevens*, 529 U.S. 765 (2000). We, therefore, pretermit discussion of this issue.

In 1986, qui tam underwent a similar surge of popularity after Congress's decision to amend the FCA in order to promote such lawsuits in the face of an ever-growing federal deficit and fears that defense contractors were once again defrauding the government. The most important amendment that Congress made to the 1986 legislation was to increase the reward offered to qui tam plaintiffs. The increase in the proceeds available to relators has resulted in an augmented number of lawsuits filed by qui tam relators. As of September 1999, more than 2900 qui tam lawsuits had been filed. Moreover, more than a billion dollars have been recovered under the FCA qui tam provisions since 1987.

The practical effects of the 1986 amendments to the FCA notwithstanding, the Supreme Court in *Stevens* gave due credence to the important historical role that qui tam lawsuits have played on both sides of the Atlantic as a means to root out corruption against national governments. Justice Scalia, writing for the 7-2 majority in *Stevens,* noted that the history of qui tam was "well nigh conclusive" with respect to resolving the question of whether qui tam relators filing suit under the FCA have Article III standing.

Although the Court in *Stevens* expressed no opinion regarding the role of history in evaluating the Article II Take Care and Appointments Clauses questions, we are persuaded that it is logically inescapable that the same history that was conclusive on the Article III question in *Stevens* with respect to qui tam lawsuits initiated under the FCA is similarly conclusive with respect to the Article II question concerning this statute. Indeed, the dissent in *Stevens* noted that history alone resolves the question of whether the qui tam provisions in the FCA violate Article II, stating "[t]hat [historical] evidence, together with the evidence that private prosecutions were commonplace in the 19th century ... is also sufficient to resolve the Article II question that the Court has introduced sua sponte." Therefore, we find that history, although not the sole definitive argument supporting the view that the FCA's qui tam provisions do not violate Article II, is certainly a "touchstone illuminating" their constitutionality. Moreover, this historical perspective provides us with a helpful bridge into the workings of the statute itself.

II. *The Executive's Control Over Qui Tam Actions Initiated Under the FCA*

That a private citizen may pursue qui tam litigation under the FCA, whether the government chooses to intervene or does not choose, does not interfere with the President's constitutionally assigned functions under Article II's Take Care Clause. Although the Clause states that the Executive must "take Care that the Laws be faithfully executed," it does not require Congress to prescribe litigation by the Executive as the *exclusive* means of enforcing federal law. U.S. Const. art. II, § 3. Thus, even though Congress has historically allowed alternative mechanisms of fraud enforcement against the federal government, this state of affairs does not therefore mean that the Executive's functions to control such litigation are necessarily impinged.

As this Court has previously noted, the Executive retains significant control over litigation pursued under the FCA by a qui tam relator. First, there is little doubt that the Executive retains such control when it intervenes in an action initiated by a relator. Second, even in cases where the government does not intervene, there are a number of control mechanisms present in the qui tam provisions of the FCA so that the Executive nonetheless retains a significant amount of control over the litigation. The record before us is devoid of any showing that the government's ability to exercise its authority has been thwarted in cases where it was not an intervenor.

Our precedent, moreover, accords with the position that this en banc court now takes. In *Searcy v. Philips Electronics N. Am. Corp., et al.,* 117 F.3d 154 (5th Cir.1997), we held that the FCA clearly permits the government to veto settlements by a qui tam plaintiff even when it remains passive in the litigation. We cited several ways in which the government may assume control over qui tam litigation in which it does not intervene under the FCA. We noted that not only may the government take over a case within 60 days of notification, but it may also intervene at a date beyond the 60-day period upon a showing of good cause. This Court also stated that the government retains the unilateral power to dismiss an action "notwithstanding the objections of the person."

In *United States ex rel. Russell v. Epic Healthcare Mgmt. Group,* we held that parties, in a qui tam suit filed under the FCA in which the United States does not intervene, have 60 days to file a notice of appeal under Rule 4(a)(1) of the Federal Rules of Civil Procedure. 193 F.3d 304, 306 (5th Cir.1999). We similarly stated in *Russell* that although the government does not intervene, its involvement in the litigation nonetheless continues. We noted, for example, that, in addition to the control mechanisms already stated in *Searcy,* the government "may request that it be served with copies of pleadings and be sent deposition transcripts ... [and it] may pursue alternative remedies, such as administrative proceedings." We also noted that despite the government's non-intervention, it "receives the larger share of any recovery," amounting to up to 70% of the proceeds of a lawsuit.[191]

Furthermore, the FCA itself describes several additional ways in which the United States retains control over a lawsuit filed by a qui tam plaintiff. In the area of settlement, for example, the government may settle a case over a relator's objections if the relator receives notice and hearing of the settlement. 31 U.S.C. § 3730(c)(2)(B). Additionally, in the area of discovery, if the government shows that discovery initiated by a qui tam plaintiff "would interfere with the Government's investigation or prosecution of a criminal or civil matter arising out of the same facts, the court may stay the discovery for sixty days or more," whether or not the government intervenes. 31 U.S.C. § 3730(c)(4).

For this reason, it is therefore apparent that the Supreme Court's decision in *Morrison v. Olson,* 487 U.S. 654 (1988), the primary case upon which the *Riley* panel majority relied to analyze the constitutionality of the qui tam provisions of the FCA under Article II,[192] is inapplicable to the present discussion. At issue in *Morrison* were the independent counsel provisions of the Ethics in Government Act ("EGA"), which permitted the delegation of "criminal prosecution functions to a judicially appointed prosecutor who could be removed only by the Attorney General, and only under a highly constrained 'good cause' requirement." The *Morrison* Court upheld the independent counsel provisions, finding that they do not violate separation of powers principles by impermissibly infringing upon the Executive's constitutional duties under either the Take Care Clause or the Appointments Clause of Article II.

Morrison, although it examined similar constitutional questions with regard to the Executive's duties under Article II, is not relevant to the present discussion of qui tam relators, which invokes civil suits filed by private plaintiffs, for two principal reasons. First, the EGA assigns the independent counsel to act as the United States itself, in contrast to the FCA's qui tam provisions, which only authorize the relator to bring a lawsuit in the name of the United States.

---

[191] [Court's footnote 7:] In *United States ex rel. Foulds v. Texas Tech Univ.,* we also held that the Eleventh Amendment barred a qui tam suit by a private plaintiff against a public university in which the government did not intervene, and we stated that there is a continuum of control that the government has in qui tam lawsuits. 171 F.3d 279, 289-90 (5th Cir.1999). On the one hand, the government has complete control when it decides to intervene. On the other hand, although we indicated that a relator has significant control over qui tam litigation when the government chooses not to intervene, we stated that the government still "retains some control over the qui tam suit." Thus, our holding in *Foulds* does not contradict our en banc position now.

[192] [Court's footnote 8:] The *Riley* majority gleaned a four-part test from *Morrison* to determine whether the Executive retains sufficient control and discretion over lawsuits filed by qui tam plaintiffs under the FCA consistent with the Take Care Clause of Article II. This test included the following inquiries: 1) whether the Executive may remove the relator for good cause; 2) whether the Executive may request the appointment of the relator; 3) whether the Executive defines the jurisdiction of the relator; and 4) whether the relator must abide by the policies of the Department of Justice. The panel majority, however, emphasized the second factor of this *Morrison* control test by focusing on two elements: 1) the Executive does not have prosecutorial discretion to prosecute a claim brought by a qui tam plaintiff; and 2) the Executive does not have sufficient control over the litigation if it does not intervene in the litigation once it is commenced.

Second, in contrast to independent counsel who undertake functions relevant to a criminal prosecution, relators are simply civil litigants. No function cuts more to the heart of the Executive's constitutional duty to take care that the laws are faithfully executed than criminal prosecution. Since the advent of public prosecutions in the United States, "no private citizen ... can subject another private citizen to the unique and virtually unfettered powers of a criminal prosecutor. ... The burdens of criminal investigation cannot be imposed on any target unless the investigator has been duly clothed with the power of the state through a process that is legally and politically accountable." Thus, because the independent counsel provisions at issue in *Morrison* and the qui tam provisions central to *Riley* involve two different types of lawsuits, the Executive must wield two different types of control in order to ensure that its constitutional duties under Article II are not impinged. Should the occasion arise, these two different types of control necessarily require the application of two different sorts of tests. Hence, the *Morrison* control test that the panel majority used to evaluate the constitutionality of the qui tam provisions in the FCA is simply not dispositive of the instant case, as it involves an entirely different lawsuit and requires entirely different control mechanisms.

There is also a credible argument that because the Court upheld the EGA's independent counsel provisions under Article II, it would similarly uphold the FCA's qui tam provisions under the same Article. Relators sue in civil capacities, involving lesser uses of traditional Executive power, in contrast to independent counsels who arguably wield greater "Executive" power because they act in criminal contexts.

Moreover, the powers of a qui tam relator to interfere in the Executive's overarching power to prosecute and to control litigation are seen to be slim indeed when the qui tam provisions of the FCA are examined in the broad scheme of the American judicial system. The prosecution of criminal cases has historically lain close to the core of the Article II executive function. The Executive Branch has extraordinarily wide discretion in deciding whether to prosecute. Indeed, that discretion is checked only by other constitutional provisions such as the prohibition against racial discrimination and a narrow doctrine of selective prosecution. Nonetheless, when the Executive has made the decision to initiate the criminal case, its large discretion is narrowed considerably and the power to dispose of the case is shared in part with the Third Branch.

For example, Rule 48(a) of the Federal Rules of Criminal Procedure clearly states that although the Executive has the power to indict an individual, it may not dismiss such an indictment without "leave of court." Fed. R. Crim. P. 48(a). Similarly, Rule 11 of the Federal Rules of Criminal Procedure requires court approval of plea bargains, a judicial check that functions in a manner similar to that of Rule 48. Fed. R. Crim. P. 11(a)(2).[193]

Thus, although our judicial system allows for these seemingly greater intrusions by the Judiciary into the Executive's paramount power to prosecute in the criminal context, Rule 48, Rule 11, and the criminal justice system have not suffered from the constitutional and systemic pitfalls that have been ascribed to the FCA's qui tam provisions. Any intrusion by the qui tam relator in the Executive's Article II power is comparatively modest, especially given the control mechanisms inherent in the FCA to mitigate such an intrusion and the civil context in which qui tam suits are pursued. Hence, the qui tam portions of the FCA do not violate the constitutional doctrine of separation of powers by impinging upon the Executive's constitutional duty to take care that the laws are faithfully executed under Article II of the Constitution.[194]

---

193 [Court's footnote 11:] Rule 11, however, is perhaps less intrusive vis-a-vis the Executive Power than judicial intervention at the indictment phase, as the guilty plea implicates the adjudication of guilt—a distinctly judicial function.

194 [Court's footnote 12:] There is also an argument that Article II's Take Care Clause and Article III's standing requirement, resolved by the Court in *Stevens*, are two different sides of the same Separation of Powers coin. In both instances, the Judiciary may not enter into the traditional sphere of Executive power, and citizens cannot enlist the judiciary in a quest to police the government absent a personal interest distinct from that of all citizens. Although we find this argument persuasive, we limit our discussion to the issues examined herein.

[Ed.: Appointments Clause discussion omitted.]

CONCLUSION

For the foregoing reasons, we hold that the qui tam provisions of the False Claims Act do not violate the principle of separation of powers by impermissibly infringing upon the constitutional duty of the Executive to take care that the laws are faithfully executed under the Take Care Clause of Article II. ...

JERRY E. SMITH, Circuit Judge, with whom DEMOSS, Circuit Judge, joins dissenting:

Allowing relators to pursue False Claims Act ("FCA") *qui tam* actions in which the government has declined to intervene violates the Take Care Clause ... of Article II.[195] Although Judge Stewart has presented a well-written, comprehensive opinion on behalf of the en banc majority, that majority fails to recognize either the encroachment on executive power that results from turning over litigation of the government's business to self-appointed relators or the consequent violations of separation of powers. Accordingly, I respectfully dissent.

I. Violations of Separation of Powers Generally.

The Constitution divides power among the three branches. "The ultimate purpose of this separation of powers is to protect the liberty and security of the governed." As former Attorney General Levi explained:

> The essence of the separation of powers concept formulated by the Founders from the political experience and philosophy of the revolutionary era is that each branch, in different ways, within the sphere of its defined powers and subject to the distinct institutional responsibilities of the others is essential to the liberty and security of the people. Each branch, in its own way, is the people's agent, its fiduciary for certain purposes. ...

Fiduciaries do not meet their obligations by arrogating to themselves the distinct duties of their master's other agents. It is the duty of the courts to police the boundaries of the separation of powers.

The branch that must be most carefully monitored against attempted encroachments on the other branches is the legislative, as James Madison explained:

> It will not be denied, that power is of an encroaching nature, and that it ought to be effectually restrained from passing the limits assigned to it. ... The founders of our republics ... seem never for a moment to have turned their eyes from the danger to liberty from the overgrown and all-grasping prerogative of an hereditary magistrate. ... They seem never to have recollected the danger from legislative usurpations; which by assembling all power in the same hands, must lead to the same tyranny as is threatened by executive usurpations. ... [I]t is against the enterprising ambition of this department, that the people ought to indulge all their jealousy and exhaust all their precautions.
>
> The legislative department derives a superiority in our governments from other circumstances. Its constitutional powers being at once more extensive and less susceptible of precise limits, it can with the greater facility, mask under complicated and indirect measures, the encroachments which it makes on the co-ordinate departments. It is not

---

[195] [Dissent's footnote 3:] Although I refer repeatedly to the constitutionality *vel non* of "the FCA," this case deals only with the small subset of FCA actions in which the United States elects not to intervene, and the relator consequently goes forward with the action on his own. There is no question that FCA claims litigated by the government are constitutional.

unfrequently a question of real-nicety in legislative bodies, whether the operation of a particular measure, will, or will not extend beyond the legislative sphere.

The Federalist No. 48, at 332-34 (J. Cooke ed.1961).

To protect against the danger of legislative encroachment, the Constitution forbids Congress to "invest itself or its Members with either executive power or judicial power." This prohibition applies not only to Congress but also to its agents, as explained in *Bowsher v. Synar*, 478 U.S. 714, 726 (1986):

> To permit the execution of the laws to be vested in an officer answerable only to Congress would, in practical terms, reserve in Congress control over the execution of the laws. ... The structure of the Constitution does not permit Congress to execute the laws; it follows that Congress cannot grant to an officer under its control what it does not possess.

Thus, the Constitution is pellucid on separation of powers. It does not permit Congress to vest executive power in one of Congress's agents. The question presented in this case is whether the Constitution also forbids Congress from vesting the executive power in a self-appointed agent who answers to no one. The answer to this question must be no, because the Constitution is violated both when one branch of government aggrandizes itself at the expense of another and when one branch "impermissibly undermine[s]" the constitutionally granted powers and functions of another, even if there is no aggrandizement.

II. Take Care Clause and Separation of Powers.

A. Violations of Take Care Clause.

The Take Care Clause states that the Executive "shall take Care that the Laws be faithfully executed." U.S. Const. art. II, § 3. It gives the Executive the power to enforce the laws, such power includes the authority "to investigate and litigate offenses against the United States."

The Take Care Clause was designed as a crucial bulwark to the separation of powers and is far from a dead letter or obsolete relic. As recently as 1997, the Supreme Court cited the Take Care Clause in striking (on other grounds) provisions of the Brady Act, explaining:

> The Constitution does not leave to speculation who is to administer the laws enacted by Congress; the President, it says, "shall take Care that the Laws be faithfully executed," Art. II, § 3, personally and through officers whom he appoints. ... The Brady Act effectively transfers this responsibility to thousands of [state law enforcement officers] in the 50 States, who are left to implement the program without meaningful Presidential control (if indeed meaningful Presidential control is possible without the power to appoint and remove). The insistence of the Framers upon unity in the Federal Executive—to insure both vigor and accountability—is well-known. ... That unity would be shattered, and the power of the President would be subject to reduction, if Congress could act as effectively without the President as with him, by simply requiring state officers to execute its laws.

Printz v. United States, 521 U.S. 898 (1997) (citations omitted).

Like the Brady Act, the FCA violates the separation of powers embodied in the Take Care Clause in a number of ways. First, it diminishes the political accountability of the Executive for enforcement of the laws by allowing any private citizen to sue on behalf of the government, even though the Attorney General—perhaps because he believes that institution of the action is inimical to the government's interests—has decided not to pursue the claim.[196] This removes

---

[196] [Dissent's footnote 9:] *See* 31 U.S.C. § 3730(c)(3) ("If the Government elects not to proceed with the action, the person who initiates the action shall have the right to conduct the action.").

from the Executive Branch the prosecutorial discretion that is at the heart of the President's power to execute the laws, and leaves no one in government who is accountable for the prosecution of government claims. Thus, the protections built into the Constitution against selective or harsh enforcement of laws are quashed in FCA suits conducted by relators.

Second, the FCA violates the separation of powers principles embodied in the Take Care Clause by both aggrandizing Congressional power and impermissibly undermining Executive power. Through this statute, Congress has invoked both its own power—to pass laws—and that of the Executive—to assign their enforcement. It does not save the Act that Congress did not give itself the enforcement power it took from the Executive, because the Act "impermissibly undermines" Executive functions by wresting control, from the President, of the initiation and prosecution of government lawsuits.

Defendants need show no more than this to establish a Take Care Clause separation-of-powers violation. Nevertheless, the FCA goes further, aggrandizing both the Legislative and Judicial branches: first, by allowing Congress to enforce laws without reliance on the Executive; second, by decreasing Executive power, which makes Congress relatively stronger; and third, by shifting some of the discretion to bring suit and to control the action from the Executive to the judiciary, as I discuss *infra*.

Third, the FCA does not provide the Executive with enough control over the relator to be able to "take care that the laws be faithfully executed." The decision to initiate the lawsuit is made by the relator, without input from the Executive.[197] The Executive has absolutely no control of the relator and therefore no way to ensure that he "take[s] care that the laws be faithfully executed." The relator does not have to follow Department of Justice ("DOJ") policies, has no agency relationship with the government, has no fiduciary or other duties to it, and has no obligation whatsoever to pursue the best interests of the United States. Instead, the relator can negotiate a settlement in his own interest rather than in the public interest. While the government must be consulted in all such settlements, there is no guarantee that it will take an active interest in these cases or that the settlements reached by a relator and approved by the DOJ will be of the same sort that the government would reach on its own for the benefit of the public.[198]

Nor may the Executive freely dismiss a qui tam action. If the relator objects to the decision to dismiss, the government must notify him of the filing of the motion to dismiss, and the court must grant him a hearing before deciding whether to permit dismissal.[199] Moreover, the Executive may not freely settle a *qui tam* action. If the relator objects to the government's attempt to settle, the government must obtain court approval, and the court may approve only

---

[197] [Dissent's footnote 13:] It is true that the government may intervene within sixty days and seek to dismiss the lawsuit. 31 U.S.C. § 3730(c)(2)(A). It cannot, however, dismiss the suit as of right. The relator has the right to be heard at a hearing before the suit is dismissed. *Id.* Unless the statutory hearing is merely *pro forma,* it follows that in some cases the Executive will be unsuccessful in overcoming the relator's objections and will be unable to dismiss the suit.

[198] [Dissent's footnote 16:] Public choice theory tells us that the reason for this is that, although the government, on its own, might not be inclined to seek the settlement negotiated by the private interest group, the fact that the public is for the most part unaware of the settlement—while the interest group lobbies the government to join the settlement—gives the government a one-sided incentive to go along with whatever agreement the private parties have made. Thus is accountability lessened and public law twisted to private purposes. ...

[199] [Dissent's footnote 17:] 31 U.S.C. § 3730(c)(2)(A). The requirement that the government obtain court permission to dismiss a *qui tam* suit raises serious questions regarding the balance of power between the Executive and Judicial Branches. *See In re Int'l Bus. Machs. Corp.,* 687 F.2d 591, 602 (2d Cir.1982) ("The district court's involvement in the executive branch's decision to abandon litigation might impinge upon the doctrine of separation of powers."). Such questions are not implicated in this case, however, because they involve potential interference with Executive prerogatives not by a relator, as here, but by the judiciary.

after it holds a hearing and finds that the settlement is "fair, adequate, and reasonable under all the circumstances."[200]

The Executive may not freely restrict the relator's participation in the *qui tam* action but first must first show the court that the relator's unrestricted participation "would interfere with or unduly delay the Government's prosecution of the case, or would be repetitious, irrelevant, or for purposes of harassment." 31 U.S.C. § 3730(c)(2)(C). Nor can the Executive control the breadth of the matter litigated by the relator. Thus, a relator may make sweeping allegations that, while true, he is unable effectively to litigate, but which nonetheless bind the government, via *res judicata*, and prevent it from suing over those concerns at a later date when more information is available. Finally, the Executive has no power to remove the relator from the litigation under any circumstances.[201]

B. Inapplicable Precedent.

In only one case has the Supreme Court allowed an encroachment on the Executive anywhere near that countenanced by the FCA. In *Morrison v. Olson,* 487 U.S. 654 (1988), the Court upheld the constitutionality of the independent counsel provisions of the Ethics in Government Act ("EGA"). The Court recognized that the special structural problems dealt with by the EGA required some encroachment on the Executive's Take Care Clause powers.

The independent counsel device was intended to address a narrow structural problem— the conflict of interest present when the Attorney General is called on to investigate criminal wrongdoing by his close colleagues in the Executive Branch. In accepting the independent counsel as an appropriate means of dealing with this intra-branch conflict, the *Morrison* Court announced that when congressional action potentially undermines the Executive's litigative function, the test of constitutionality is whether the Executive Branch retains sufficient "control" over the litigation "to ensure that the President is able to perform his constitutionally assigned duties." While acknowledging the independent counsel's special needs for independence, the *Morrison* court stressed four features of the EGA that preserved sufficient Executive control to satisfy Article II:

> Most importantly, [1] the Attorney General retains the *power to remove* the counsel for "good cause," a power that we have already concluded provides the Executive with substantial ability to ensure that the laws are "faithfully executed" by an independent counsel. [2] No independent counsel may be appointed without a specific request by the Attorney General, and *the Attorney General's decision not to request appointment if he finds "no reasonable grounds to believe that further investigation is warranted" is committed to his unreviewable discretion.* The Act thus gives the Executive a degree of *control over the power to initiate* an investigation by the independent counsel. [3] In addition, *the jurisdiction of the independent counsel is defined with reference to the facts submitted by the Attorney General,* and [4] once a counsel is appointed, the Act requires that the *counsel abide by Justice Department policy* unless it is not "possible" to do so. Notwithstanding the fact that the counsel is to some degree "independent" and free from executive supervision to a greater extent than other federal prosecutors, in our view these features of the Act give the Executive Branch sufficient

---

[200] [Dissent's footnote 18:] *Id.* § 3730(c)(2)(B). *Gravitt v. Gen. Elec. Co.,* 680 F.Supp. 1162 (S.D.Ohio 1988), illustrates how the *qui tam* provisions encroach on the Executive's control of settlements. There, the court refused to accept the government's settlement, lecturing the DOJ on the inadequacy of its investigation into the matter alleged in the relator's complaint. It turns out, however, that the fraud complained of resulted in a net undercharge to the government, and a few years later, the DOJ succeeded in settling for the sum the *Gravitt* court initially had rejected.

[201] [Dissent's footnote 19:] *See* 31 U.S.C. § 3730(c)(1) (providing that if the government intervenes, the relator "shall have the right to continue as a party to the action, subject to the limitations set forth in paragraph (2)," none of which permits removal); *id.* § 3730(c)(3) (providing that if government intervenes after initially deciding not to do so, it may not limit relator's status and rights). ...

control over the independent counsel to ensure that the President is able to perform his constitutionally assigned duties.

As the panel opinion pointed out, *not a single one* of the features of the EGA that preserved Executive control is present in the FCA's *qui tam* provisions. The Attorney General has no power to remove a relator, no matter how irresponsible the suit becomes. If he makes the proper showing to the court, the Attorney General may limit the relator's participation, *see* 31 U.S.C. § 3730(c)(2)(C), and may even dismiss the action once the court has afforded the relator with a hearing on the motion to dismiss, *see id.* § 3730(c)(2)(A), but may not simply remove the relator, *see id.* § 3730(c)(1),(3).

Perhaps more importantly, the second crucial feature present in the independent counsel statute is missing: The Attorney General loses all control over the decision whether to initiate the suit. Even if the Attorney General determines that there are "no reasonable grounds" for the fraud action, the relator may override that judgment and initiate a lawsuit.[202] The action goes forward in the government's name, under total control of the self-interested and publicly unaccountable relator, even if the Attorney General has concluded that proceeding with a lawsuit is not merited or is otherwise not in the United States's interests.

The third and fourth features also are conspicuously absent. The Attorney General has no control over the breadth of a relator's suit. Indeed, as I have already noted, a relator may make sweeping allegations that he is unable effectively to litigate, and thereby bind the government, via *res judicata,* to his failed suit. Finally, the relator, unlike the independent counsel, need not adhere to the rules and policies of the DOJ.

The majority makes two unconvincing arguments as to why it is improper to apply the analysis in *Morrison* to this case. It reasons:

> First, the EGA assigns the independent counsel to act as the United States itself, in contrast to the FCA's *qui tam* provisions, which only authorize the relator to bring a lawsuit in the name of the United States. ... Second, in contrast to independent counsel who undertake functions relevant to a criminal prosecution, relators are simply civil litigants.

As to its first point, the majority does not explain the difference between litigating "as the United States" as opposed to litigating "in the name of the United States." Nor does the majority explain how such a distinction can do away with the Court's exhortation in *Morrison* that, when congressional action threatens to encroach on Executive activities, the test of constitutionality is whether the Executive Branch retains sufficient "control" over the litigation "to ensure that the President is able to perform his constitutionally assigned duties." Certainly, different amounts of control may be appropriate depending on the role of the one litigating the government's case, but an act of Congress that uses the magic words that a person is litigating "in the name of the United States," rather than "as the United States," surely cannot strip courts of their responsibility to evaluate whether the legislation allows for the President to fulfill his duty to take care that the laws be faithfully executed.

---

[202] [Dissent's footnote 20:] The Ninth Circuit, while rejecting an Article II challenge to the FCA, admitted that, under the EGA, the "Attorney General['s] ... unreviewable discretion to request appointment of a counsel, and therefore to initiate litigation by a counsel," is an "unqualified control built into the independent counsel provisions," and that "[c]learly, the government has greater authority to prevent the initiation of prosecution by an independent counsel than by a *qui tam* relator." *United States ex rel. Kelly v. Boeing Co.,* 9 F.3d 743, 754 (9th Cir.1993). It is difficult to overstate the importance of this control, which is missing from the FCA, when one recognizes that once suit has been filed, the controls the Executive Branch may exercise—most of which require court approval of some sort—are simply not sufficient to counterbalance this major encroachment on Executive power.

The majority's second stated reason why *Morrison* is irrelevant to this case is a mere distinction between the facts of the two cases. The majority points out that independent counsel are granted criminal prosecutorial duties, whereas FCA relators "are simply civil litigants." The majority notes that criminal prosecution is at the "heart of the Executive's constitutional duty" and then, without more, asserts that "the *Morrison* control test that the panel majority used to evaluate the constitutionality of the *qui tam* provisions of the FCA is simply not dispositive of the instant case. ..." Although different controls may be needed for the Executive to take care of the execution of the laws in criminal as opposed to civil cases, nothing in the Supreme Court's jurisprudence suggests that the Take Care Clause does not apply to civil cases.[203]

Further, as the majority notes, other circuits have found the control provisions in *Morrison* useful "as a whole" in evaluating the constitutionality of the FCA "as a whole." The majority unfairly attacks the panel opinion as rigidly applying the four-factor test from *Morrison* in determining whether the FCA withstands constitutional scrutiny under Article II. In actuality, after observing that the FCA contains not a single one of the control mechanisms that the Morrison court found in the EGA, the panel went on to conclude that "[e]ven taking the *qui tam* provisions 'as a whole' and not focusing on any of the particular differences between the provisions and the independent counsel statute, *qui tam* effects a greater degree of encroachment on Executive prerogatives than does the [EGA] upheld in *Morrison*."

As I have explained above, the most crucial ways in which the FCA fails to provide the executive with sufficient control are that the FCA does not allow the Executive to initiate litigation, terminate litigation (without court approval), control the scope and pace of the litigation, or control the procedures used by the lawyer prosecuting the case. The FCA's most severe violations of the separation of powers principles embedded in the Take Care Clause include the fact that unaccountable, self-interested relators are put in charge of vindicating government rights, and that the transparency and controls of the constitutional system are not in place to influence the outcome of such litigation.

Finally, the elements of the FCA that disable effective Executive control were not drafted in response to the special intra-branch problems that the EGA sought to correct in *Morrison*.[204] Rather, the FCA was broadly drafted for the much-less-compelling purpose of being one of a number of tools available to combat fraud by government contractors. Although the majority implies otherwise, suits brought by relators in which the government does not intervene are not even particularly useful in collecting monies for the government. ...

---

[203] [Dissent's footnote 21:] Although the majority makes much of the factual distinction that the FCA only allows civil suits, whereas the Supreme Court upheld the constitutionality of criminal prosecutions brought by independent counsel, the reasoning of the majority in this case makes this a difference only in degree, not in kind. The majority articulates no rational limiting principle that allows constitutionality here but that makes it unconstitutional for Congress to pass a statute permitting relators to, say, prosecute government claims for criminal forfeiture, or for criminal fines, so long as part of the recovery was assigned to the relator. Indeed, the majority noted with approval the Fourth Circuit's statement that, in passing the FCA, "Congress has let loose a posse of ad hoc deputies to uncover and prosecute frauds against the government". Possees may have been appropriate in the Wild West, where they were deputized by the executive officer—the Sheriff—but Congress has no business forming them now.

[204] [Dissent's footnote 23:] *See Riley,* 196 F.3d at 529:

> The independent counsel device was intended to address a narrow structural problem—the perceived conflict of interest when the Attorney General is called on to investigate criminal wrongdoing by his close colleagues within the Executive Branch. The *Morrison* Court accepted the independent counsel as an appropriate means of dealing with this intra-branch conflict. The device arguably does not unduly encroach on executive power, because its very purpose is to investigate impermissible executive activity. Moreover, it is narrowly tailored to achieve its purpose: It encroaches on the Executive only to the limited extent necessary to protect against a conflict of interest, while retaining executive control consistent with that objective. ...

Given the independent counsel statute's special objective and narrow tailoring, the *Morrison* Court likely was especially forgiving of Executive encroachment.

D. CHARGING CONSIDERATIONS: DOUBLE JEOPARDY

Throughout this text, in addition to considering whether as a legal matter certain statutes may be charged and what factors, as a prudential matter, should be considered in charging, consideration will be given to *how* certain violations should be charged. One important constraint on prosecutorial charging choices is the Double Jeopardy Clause of the Fifth Amendment, which provides that no person shall "be subject for the same offence to be twice put in jeopardy of life or limb."

In evaluating whether prosecutorial charging choices are consistent with this right, the applicable legal rules depend upon whether the defendant is challenging (1) a prosecutor's decision to proceed *in a single proceeding* against the defendant on a number of charges which the defendant contends would, upon conviction, subject him to multiple punishments for the same offense ("*multiple punishment*" cases); or (2) after conviction or acquittal on some charges in one criminal case, a prosecutor's decision to bring in *another proceeding* criminal charges that the defendant alleges subject him to double jeopardy for the same offenses already adjudicated ("*successive prosecution*" cases). The Double Jeopardy Clause applies in both multiple punishment and successive prosecution cases,[205] but the interests it seeks to protect—and thus the rules that control—differ depending upon which type of case is at issue.

1. MULTIPLE PUNISHMENTS FOR THE SAME OFFENSE

UNITED STATES v. WOODWARD
469 U.S. 105 (1985)

PER CURIAM

On March 1, 1980, respondent Charles Woodward and his wife arrived at Los Angeles International Airport on a flight from Brazil. In passing through Customs, respondent was handed the usual form that included the following question:

"Are you or any family member carrying over $5,000 (or the equivalent value in any currency) in monetary instruments such as coin, currency, traveler's checks, money orders, or negotiable instruments in bearer form?"

Respondent checked the "no" box.

After questioning respondent for a brief period, customs officials decided to search respondent and his wife. As he was being escorted to a search room, respondent told an official that he and his wife were carrying over $20,000 in cash. Woodward removed approximately $12,000 from his boot; another $10,000 was found in a makeshift money belt concealed under his wife's clothing.

Woodward was indicted on charges of making a false statement to an agency of the United States, 18 U.S.C. § 1001, and willfully failing to report that he was carrying in excess of $5,000 into the United States, 31 U.S.C. §§ 1058, 1101.[206] The same conduct—answering

---

[205] *See, e.g.,* North Carolina v. Pearce, 395 U.S. 711, 717 (1969) (the Double Jeopardy Clause affords three basic protections: "It protects against a second prosecution for the same offense after acquittal. It protects against a second prosecution for the same offense after conviction. And it protects against multiple punishments for the same offense.") (footnotes omitted).

[206] [Court's footnote 2:] Title 31 U.S.C. § 1101(a) provides in pertinent part:

" ... [W]hoever ...knowingly—

"(1) transports or causes to be transported monetary instruments—

...

"no" to the question whether he was carrying more than $5,000 into the country—formed the basis of each count. A jury convicted Woodward on both charges; he received a sentence of six months in prison on the false statement count, and a consecutive 3-year term of probation on the currency reporting count. ...

The United States Court of Appeals for the Ninth Circuit, after inviting briefs on the subject, held that respondent's conduct could not be punished under both 18 U.S.C. § 1001 and 31 U.S.C. §§ 1058, 1101. The court applied the rule of statutory construction contained in *Blockburger v. United States*, 284 U.S. 299, 304 (1932)—"'whether each provision requires proof of a fact which the other does not'"—and held that the false statement felony was a lesser included offense of the currency reporting misdemeanor. In other words, every violation of the currency reporting statute necessarily entails a violation of the false statement law.[207] The court reasoned that a willful failure to file a required report is a form of concealment prohibited by 18 U.S.C. § 1001. Concluding that Congress presumably intended someone in respondent's position to be punished only under the currency reporting misdemeanor, the Court of Appeals reversed respondent's felony conviction for making a false statement.

The Court of Appeals plainly misapplied the *Blockburger* rule for determining whether Congress intended to permit cumulative punishment; proof of a currency reporting violation does *not* necessarily include proof of a false statement offense. Section 1001 proscribes the nondisclosure of a material fact only if the fact is "conceal[ed] ...by any *trick, scheme, or device*." (Emphasis added.)[208] A person could, without employing a "trick, scheme, or device," simply and willfully fail to file a currency disclosure report. A traveler who enters the country and passes through Customs prepared to answer questions truthfully, but is never asked whether he is carrying over $5,000 in currency, might nonetheless be subject to conviction under 31 U.S.C. § 1058 for willfully transporting money without filing the required currency report. However, because he did not conceal a material fact by means of a "trick, scheme, or device," (and did not make any false statement) his conduct would not fall within 18 U.S.C. § 1001.[209]

There is no evidence in 18 U.S.C. § 1001 and 31 U.S.C. §§ 1058, 1101 that Congress did not intend to allow separate punishment for the two different offenses. Sections 1058 and 1101 were enacted by Congress in 1970 as part of the Currency and Foreign Transactions Reporting Act. Section 203(k) of that Act expressly provided:

> "For the purposes of section 1001 of title 18, United States Code, the contents of reports required under any provision of this title are statements and representations in matters within the jurisdiction of an agency of the United States." 31 U.S.C. § 1052(k).[210]

> "(B) to any place within the United States from or through any place outside the United States, or
>
> " ... in an amount exceeding $5,000 on any one occasion shall file a report or reports in accordance with subsection (b) of this section."

Title 31 U.S.C. § 1058 provides:

> "Whoever willfully violates any provision of this chapter or any regulation under this chapter shall be fined not more than $1,000, or imprisoned not more than one year, or both."

Sections 1058 and 1101 were [] recodified without substantive change at 31 U.S.C. §§ 5322(a) and 5316.

[207] [Court's footnote 3:] The converse is clearly not true; 31 U.S.C. §§ 1058, 1101, but not 18 U.S.C. § 1001, involve the failure to file a currency disclosure report.

[208] [Court's footnote 4:] In Woodward's case, the Government did not have to prove the existence of a trick, scheme, or device. Woodward was charged with violating § 1001 because he made a false statement on the customs form. This type of affirmative misrepresentation is proscribed under the statute even if not accompanied by a trick, scheme, or device.

[209] [Court's footnote 5:] *See* United States v. London, 550 F.2d 206, 213 (C.A.5 1977) (§ 1001 requires "affirmative act by which means a material fact is concealed").

[210] [Court's footnote 6:] When Title 31 was recodified in 1982, this provision was eliminated as

It is clear that in passing the currency reporting law, Congress' attention was drawn to 18 U.S.C. § 1001, but at no time did it suggest that the two statutes could not be applied together. We cannot assume, therefore, that Congress was unaware that it had created two different offenses permitting multiple punishment for the same conduct.

Finally, Congress' intent to allow punishment under both 18 U.S.C. § 1001 and 31 U.S.C. §§ 1058, 1101 is shown by the fact that the statutes "are directed to separate evils." The currency reporting statute was enacted to develop records that would "have a high degree of usefulness in criminal, tax, or regulatory investigations." 31 U.S.C. § 1051. The false statement statute, on the other hand, was designed "to protect the authorized functions of governmental departments and agencies from the perversion which might result from the deceptive practices described."

All guides to legislative intent reveal that Congress intended respondent's conduct to be punishable under both 18 U.S.C. § 1001, and 31 U.S.C. §§ 1058, 1101. Accordingly, the petition for a writ of certiorari is granted, and that part of the Court of Appeals' judgment reversing respondent's 18 U.S.C. § 1001 conviction is reversed.

Notes

1. Why is the Court concerned with legislative intent in *multiple punishment* cases such as *Woodward?* As the Supreme Court has held,

> "[w]here consecutive sentences are imposed at a single criminal trial, the role of the constitutional guarantee is limited to assuring that the court does not exceed its legislative authorization by imposing multiple punishments for the same offense." Thus, the question of what punishments are constitutionally permissible is not different from the question of what punishments the Legislative Branch intended to be imposed. Where Congress intended ... to impose multiple punishments, imposition of such sentences does not violate the Constitution.

Albernaz v. United States, 450 U.S. 333, 344 (1981).

2. In order to divine the legislative intent, and thus the limits of the defendant's Double Jeopardy right in multiple punishment cases, how does the Court proceed? As the D.C. Circuit has summarized the relevant analysis:

> ...The court should first resort to the language of each provision for possible explanation of how the punishments it prescribes relate to those authorized by the other. If the provisions are silent or ambiguous on the interaction of punishments, the court should explore the legislative history of each section for legislative intent respecting multiple punishments. Should the legislative design remain obscure, the court should then invoke the judicially-fashioned *Blockburger* standard in a continuing effort to ascertain the legislative will:

> > [W]here the same act or transaction constitutes a violation of two distinct statutory provisions, the test to be applied to determine whether there are two offenses or only one, is whether each provision requires proof of a fact the other does not.

> > If, but only if, these techniques fail to reveal the legislative intent, the court should invoke the settled rule that ambiguity concerning the ambit of a criminal statute "should be resolved in favor of lenity."

"[u]nnecessary" because "Section 1001 applies unless otherwise provided."

United States v. Coachman, 727 F.2d 1293, 1299-1300 (D.C. Cir.1984) (footnotes omitted) (holding that imposition of consecutive sentences on counts charging theft of government property and false claims against the government were not double jeopardy barred).

It is important to stress that in this *multiple punishment* context (but not in the *successive prosecution* context), *Blockburger* is a rule of construction, serving merely "as a means of discerning congressional purpose." *Albernaz*, 450 U.S. at 340. Consequently, it does not override "a clear indication of contrary legislative intent," *Missouri v. Hunter*, 459 U.S. 359, 367 (1983), and may not come into play at all if that intent otherwise appears obvious. *See, e.g.*, United States v. Sutton, 700 F.2d 1078, 1081 (6th Cir. 1983) (Congress intended that a defendant could be charged with both RICO and substantive predicate offenses upon which RICO was based); United States v. Boylan, 620 F.2d 359, 361 (2d Cir. 1980)(same). Thus, for example, 18 U.S.C. § 201(e) explicitly provides that "[t]he offenses and penalties prescribed in this section are separate and in addition to those prescribed in [the obstruction statutes,] sections 1503, 1504, and 1505 of this title."

3. The *Woodward* Court found that each statute charged required proof of a fact that the other did not. What were those facts? Although the Court came up with a hypothetical situation in which the two offenses would not be violated in a given circumstance, in *Woodward* itself the same negative answer to one question "formed the basis of each count." Why, then, was the *Blockburger* test not satisfied? Again, as the D.C. Circuit has explained:

> ...The Supreme Court has consistently indicated that *Blockburger* calls for comparison of the *statutorily-prescribed elements* of the offenses, *not* the *constituent facts either as alleged or proven*. The Court has stated unqualifiedly that "application of the [*Blockburger*] test focuses on the statutory elements of the offense"; it has emphatically disavowed an attempt to apply the test "to the facts alleged in a particular indictment"; and it has declared that "[i]f each [offense] requires proof of a fact that the other does not, the *Blockburger* test is satisfied, notwithstanding a substantial overlap in the proof offered to establish the crimes." ...

Coachman, 727 F.2d at 1301 (footnotes omitted) (emphasis added).

4. *Woodward* dealt with the question of whether charging and punishing the same conduct under two *different statutes* constituted a double jeopardy problem. Sometimes, the same concerns are also present when an indictment charges a defendant with multiple counts under the *same statute* for what could be characterized as the same course of conduct. The question the parties generally ask in such a situation is what is the appropriate "unit of prosecution" for a given statute. For example, suppose a defendant mails ten letters in furtherance of a single scheme to defraud one victim. Because the "unit of prosecution" for mail fraud is each *mailing* in furtherance of the scheme to defraud, rather than each *scheme*, the government may charge ten counts in one indictment without fear of multiple punishment issues. For prosecutions under the "offense clause" of the federal conspiracy statute, however, each *agreement* is the appropriate unit of prosecution, regardless of how many *separate offenses the co-conspirators agree to commit pursuant to that single conspiracy*. In such circumstances, bringing multiple conspiracy counts relating to each crime the co-conspirators agreed to commit would pose a risk of multiple punishment; only a single conspiracy count, alleging one agreement with multiple criminal objects, would be appropriate.

In many instances, the appropriate unit of prosecution may be subject to debate or the application of the relevant rule to the facts may be unclear. For instance, where a defendant has made multiple but identical false statements to a variety of governmental actors, should he be charged in separate counts for each iteration of the false statement or should he be charged in one count for his entire course of conduct? *See, e.g.*, United States v. Graham, 60 F.3d 463, 467 (8th Cir. 1995) (examining cases and stating that they create a "unitary harm rule whereby repetition of a false statement which does not 'constitute an additional impairment of ... governmental functions' should not be charged separately in an indictment"); United States v. Salas-Camacho, 859 F.2d 788 (9th Cir. 1988) (holding that where a defendant made the same false statement to two different governmental actors, he could be prosecuted for multiple false statement counts); United States v. Olsowy, 836 F.2d 439 (9th Cir. 1987) (ruling that a number of separate but identical false statements made by a defendant to a single Secret Service agent could not be the subject of multiple convictions); *see also* United States v. Reagan, 596 F.3d 251 (5th Cir. 2010) (unit of prosecution under 18 U.S.C. § 641 for theft of federal funds is each check cashed); United States v. Tann, 577 F.3d 533 (3d Cir. 2009) (possession of both a firearm and ammunition, seized at the same time in the same location supports only one conviction and sentence under 18 U.S.C. § 922(g)(1)).

5. Often, these double jeopardy concerns will be addressed as a question of "multiplicity." Multiplicity, and its cousin, "duplicity," are considered below. These questions arise frequently, particularly in the conspiracy context. Prosecutors will obviously wish to familiarize themselves with these rules so that they may charge in a way that is both appropriate and sustainable on appeal. Defense counsel must master these rules not only because poor pleading may provide an avenue for relief from an indictment, but also because it may have serious concrete consequences for the defendant. Further, reference to the remedies for multiplicity and duplicity illustrate the importance of lodging such challenges early in order to safeguard the defendant's interests.

a. Multiplicity

"A multiplicitous indictment ... is one that charges in separate counts two or more crimes, when in fact and law, only one crime has been committed."[211] Thus, stating that an indictment is multiplicitous is a technical way of stating that it failed the test stated above in *Woodward*: "The doctrine of multiplicity "is based upon the double jeopardy clause of the Fifth Amendment, which 'assur[es] that the court does not exceed its legislative authorization by imposing multiple punishments for the same offense.'"[212] Accordingly, "[t]he test for determining if a defendant has improperly been convicted under different statutes for a single transaction is whether congress intended to authorize separate punishments for the conduct in question."[213]

It is important for counsel to focus on the way an indictment is pled because multiplicity may result in a defendant receiving more than one sentence for the same offense, in violation of the double jeopardy clause.[214] Second, a multiplicitous indictment may unfairly prejudice the defendant because "[t]he very fact that a defendant has been arrested, charged, and brought to trial on several charges may suggest to the jury that he must be guilty of at least one of those crimes."[215] Finally, "where the prosecution's evidence is weak, its ability to bring multiple charges may substantially enhance the possibility that, even though innocent, the defendant may be found guilty on one or more charges as a result of a compromise verdict."[216] That is, a "doubtful jury" is given the option "to find the defendant guilty of the less serious offense rather than to continue the debate as to his innocence."[217]

---

[211] United States v. Holmes, 44 F.3d 1150, 1153-54 (2d Cir. 1995).

[212] United States v. Harris, 79 F.3d 223, 231 (2d Cir. 1996) (citations omitted).

[213] *Holmes*, 44 F.3d at 1154 (citing Whalen v. United States, 445 U.S. 684, 688-89 (1980)); *see also* United States v. Peel, 595 F.3d 763 (7th Cir. 2010) (defendant could not be tried for both the greater offense of bankruptcy fraud and the lesser included offense of obstruction); United States v. Bonilla, 579 F.3d 1233, 1241-42 (11th Cir. 2009) (indictment charging defendant with identity theft and aggravated identity theft was multiplicitous); United States v. Hector, 577 F.3d 1099 (9th Cir. 2009) (conviction and sentencing for both receipt and possession of child pornography under 18 U.S.C §§ 2252A(a)(2) and 2252A(a)(5)(b) violated double jeopardy).

[214] *See* United States v. Reed, 639 F.2d 896, 904 (2d Cir. 1981).

[215] Missouri v. Hunter, 459 U.S. 359, 372 (1983).

[216] *Id.*

[217] *Id.* (quoting Cichos v. Indiana, 385 U.S. 76, 81 (1966)).

There are several possible remedies for multiplicity, the utility of which depend upon both the circumstances and timing of the defendant's objection. If caught early, the prosecution may be compelled to elect just one of the multiple counts and the multiplicitous counts will be dismissed.[218] This remedy, if implemented before the trial has begun, cures all three of the dangers discussed above. In certain cases, however, multiplicity claims may not be capable of resolution in the pre-trial stages because of the lack of a developed record.[219] If the dismissal is ordered after the trial has begun, courts generally believe that "[a] curative instruction can help remove any potential for prejudice stemming from the jury's awareness of the multi-charge indictment."[220] If the issue is reserved (or if the defect is left unchallenged) until after a verdict is rendered, the relief afforded is generally to vacate the defendant's conviction on the multiplicitous count(s) and, in appropriate cases, resentence, with the judge generally empowered to decide the appropriate count(s) to vacate.[221]

b. Duplicity

"An indictment is duplicitous if it joins two or more distinct crimes in a single count."[222] It is not duplicitous, however, if it alleges in a single count commission of the crime by several means.[223] Nor is a conspiracy indictment duplicitous if it alleges in a single count an agreement to commit several crimes.[224]

The policy considerations underlying the prohibition against duplicitous indictments are varied. As the Second Circuit has explained, those considerations include:

[A]voiding the uncertainty of whether a general verdict of guilty conceals a finding of guilty as to one crime and a finding of not guilty as to another, avoiding the risk that the jurors may not have been unanimous as to any one of the crimes charged, assuring the defendant adequate notice, providing the basis for appropriate sentencing, and protecting against double jeopardy in a subsequent prosecution.[225]

A duplicity objection should be raised pre-trial or it may be deemed waived.[226] If a duplicity charging error is caught in pre-trial motions, the prosecutor may simply dismiss and re-indict or seek a superseding, correct indictment (assuming no statute of limitations problems). If the error is only caught once the trial has begun, an appropriate special instruction to the jury may cure the error. Such an instruction will direct the jury that it must unanimously agree that the defendant is guilty of (at least) one of the acts charged in the

---

[218] *Reed*, 639 F.2d at 904 n.6.

[219] *See, e.g.*, United States v. Universal C.I.T. Credit Corp., 344 U.S. 218, 224 (1952); United States v. Hubbell, 177 F.3d 11, 14 (D.C. Cir. 1999).

[220] United States v. Miller, 26 F.Supp.2d 415, 423 (N.D.N.Y. 1998).

[221] *See Peel*, 595 F.3d at 767-69 (court electing, over defendant's objection, to vacate the lesser-included offense, which carried the higher penalty); *Hector*, 577 F.3d at 1099-103 (the court, not the prosecutor, decides which duplicitous count to vacate); United States v. Gore, 154 F.3d 34, 45-48 (2d Cir. 1998); United States v. Lilly, 983 F.2d 300, 305 (1st Cir. 1992).

[222] United States v. Aracri, 968 F.2d 1512, 1518 (2d Cir. 1992).

[223] *Id.*; *see also* Fed. R. Crim. P. 7(c), 8(a).

[224] Braverman v. United States, 317 U.S. 49, 53 (1942) ("Whether the object of a single agreement is to commit one or many crimes, it is in either case that agreement which constitutes the conspiracy which the statute punishes. The one agreement cannot be taken to be several agreements and hence several conspiracies because it envisages the violation of several statutes rather than one."); *Aracri*, 968 F.2d at 1518.

[225] United States v. Margiotta, 646 F.2d 729, 733 (2d Cir. 1981).

[226] *See* United States v. Trammell, 133 F.3d 1343, 1354-55 (10th Cir. 1998).

indictment.[227] In certain cases, where the special instructions are either not given or are inadequate, duplicity may require reversal of a conviction.[228]

2. SUCCESSIVE PROSECUTIONS FOR THE SAME OFFENSE

As *Woodward* indicates, in *multiple punishment* cases the Court has decreed that the Double Jeopardy Clause "does no more than prevent the sentencing court from prescribing greater punishment than the legislature intended."[229] In that context, then, the Double Jeopardy Clause is deemed a restraint upon courts and prosecutors, not on the legislature.[230] Thus, analysis in multiple punishment cases is limited to considering whether the legislature intended to endorse simultaneous convictions on different charges for the same criminal activity and legislative intent may not be second-guessed by the courts under the Double Jeopardy Clause.[231]

In *successive prosecutions* cases, the Double Jeopardy Clause is said to serve a different set of interests. In this context, the Double Jeopardy Clause prevents the government from "mak[ing] repeated attempts to convict an individual for an alleged offense, thereby subjecting him to embarrassment, expense and ordeal and compelling him to live in a continuing state of anxiety and insecurity ...."[232] In addition to the defendant's finality interests,[233] the Clause serves to bar the government from using successive prosecutions to rehearse its presentation, "honing its trial strategies and perfecting its evidence through successive attempts at conviction,"[234] because this "enhanc[es] the possibility that even though innocent [the defendant] may be found guilty."[235]

In terms of legal analysis, the Supreme Court has decreed that the *Blockburger* test applies in this context as well. Consistent with its focus not on legislative intent but on the defendant's finality interests, however, the *Blockburger* test is usually (but not always, as noted below) determinative and legislative intent should be irrelevant. If application of the *Blockburger* test reveals that the offenses successively tried have identical statutory elements or that one is a lesser included offense of the other, then the inquiry generally must cease, and the subsequent prosecution is jeopardy barred.

Because *Blockburger* requires a comparison of the facial elements of the two offenses prosecuted in successive proceedings and does not permit examination of the actual circumstances of the case or evidence sought to be introduced in support of the offenses, it is not as protective of defendants' finality interests as some would wish. For a very brief time, the Court added a second inquiry to the *Blockburger* test that was designed to cure this perceived

---

[227] *See id.*; *see also* United States v. Duncan, 850 F.2d 1104, 1112 n.8 (6th Cir. 1988).

[228] *See, e.g., Duncan*, 850 F.2d at 1114 (general unanimity instruction not sufficient where there would remain "a genuine possibility of jury confusion or that a conviction may occur as the result of different jurors concluding that the defendant committed different acts").

[229] Missouri v. Hunter, 459 U.S. 359, 366 (1983).

[230] *See* Brown v. Ohio, 432 U.S. 161, 165 (1977).

[231] *See, e.g.*, Ohio v. Johnson, 467 U.S. 493, 499 (1984) ("Because the substantive power to prescribe crimes and determine punishments is vested with the legislature, the question under the Double Jeopardy Clause whether punishments are 'multiple' is essentially one of legislative intent.") (citations and footnote omitted).

[232] Green v. United States, 355 U.S. 184, 187 (1957).

[233] *See Brown*, 432 U.S. at 165 ("Where successive prosecutions are at stake, the guarantee serves 'a constitutional policy of finality for the defendant's benefit.'") (quoting United States v. Jorn, 400 U.S. 470, 479 (1971) (plurality opinion)).

[234] Tibbs v. Florida, 457 U.S. 31, 41 (1982).

[235] *Green*, 355 U.S. at 188.

deficit. Thus, in *Grady v. Corbin*,[236] the Court held that, in addition to passing the *Blockburger* test, a subsequent prosecution must survive the "same-conduct" test to avoid the double jeopardy bar. The *Grady* test provided that, "if, to establish an essential element of an offense charged in that prosecution, the government will have to prove conduct that constitutes an offense for which the defendant has already been prosecuted," a second prosecution may not be had.[237] Three years later, the Court overruled *Grady* in *United States v. Dixon*,[238] concluding that "[t]he 'same-conduct' rule it announced is wholly inconsistent with earlier Supreme Court precedent and with the clear common-law understanding of double jeopardy."[239]

The Supreme Court has recognized exceptions to the bar on successive prosecutions of lesser and greater offenses mandated by the *Blockburger* analysis. For example,

> ... In *Jeffers v. United States*, [432 U.S. 137 (1977) (plurality opinion)], the plurality opinion rejected a claim of double jeopardy where prosecution for a greater offense followed a guilty verdict for a lesser offense, and the successive prosecution resulted from the defendant's opposition to consolidated trials. ... [In *Ohio v. Johnson*, 467 U.S. 493 (1984),] the Court relied on *Jeffers* to hold that where a court accepts, over the prosecution's objection, a defendant's guilty plea to lesser included offenses, double jeopardy does not prevent further prosecution on remaining, greater offenses. After noting the State's interest in convicting those who have violated its laws and the absence of governmental overreaching, *Johnson* observed that the defendant "should not be entitled to use the Double Jeopardy Clause as a sword to prevent the States from completing its prosecution on the remaining charges."[240]

Another instance in which the *Blockburger* rule has not been determinative is in cases where a defendant has been successively tried for a crime such as drug trafficking and then for a crime, such as engaging in a "continuing criminal enterprise" (CCE) under 21 U.S.C. § 848, that requires proof of predicate criminal acts, such as drug trafficking, for conviction. In such cases, the *Blockburger* test might yield the conclusion that prosecution on the lesser "predicate" offense should preclude later prosecution on the greater compound offense, but courts have struggled to avoid that conclusion.[241]

---

[236] 495 U.S. 508 (1990).

[237] *Id.* at 510.

[238] 509 U.S. 688 (1993).

[239] *Id.* at 704.

[240] Garrett v. United States, 471 U.S. 773, 797 (1985) (O'Connor, J., concurring).

[241] In two cases, however, the Court has found that prosecutions under criminal prohibitions which incorporate a variety of crimes as their predicates may later bar prosecutions charging the lesser crime actually chosen as the predicate in the first case. *See, e.g.*, United States v. Dixon, 509 U.S. 688 (1993) (holding that double jeopardy precluded prosecution of defendant for drug offense following conviction for criminal contempt based on violation of conditional release order that included prohibition on violation of the drug laws but that double jeopardy did not bar prosecution for assault with intent to kill and threatening to injure following prosecution for criminal contempt for violating civil protection order which prohibited assault); Harris v. Oklahoma, 433 U.S. 682 (1977) (holding that prosecution for robbery with a firearm was jeopardy barred by previous trial for felony murder based on the same underlying felony). In two other cases, the Court dealt with multiple punishments (not successive prosecution) questions presented by compound statutes and their predicate crimes. *See* Rutledge v. United States, 517 U.S. 292 (1996) (holding that a Continuing Criminal Enterprise (CCE), 21 U.S.C. § 848, prosecution bars punishment in same proceeding for lesser included offense of drug conspiracy charged under 21 U.S.C. § 846); Jeffers v. United States, 432 U.S. 137, 152 (1977) (even assuming that a drug conspiracy is a lesser included offense of CCE, holding that a defendant waives any double jeopardy claim by requesting severance of charges; examining the case as a multiple punishment rather than a successive prosecution case, then, ruling that Congress did not intend to permit cumulative punishments for these offenses). For action in the Circuit Courts in evaluating double jeopardy claims in situations

For example, in *Garrett v. United States*, the Supreme Court questioned whether the predicate drug felony was indeed a lesser-included offense of the greater CCE charge.[242] Assuming that it was, however, the Court still found that the CCE prosecution was not jeopardy-barred based on its prior ruling in *Diaz v. United States*.[243] As the *Garrett* Court explained:

> In *Diaz v. United States*, the Court had before it an initial prosecution for assault and battery, followed by a prosecution for homicide when the victim eventually died from injuries inflicted in the course of the assault. The Court rejected the defendant's claim of double jeopardy, holding that the two were not the "same offense":
>
> > "The homicide charged against the accused in the Court of First Instance and the assault and battery for which he was tried before the justice of the peace, although identical in some of their elements, were distinct offenses both in law and in fact. The death of the injured person was the principal element of the homicide, but was no part of the assault and battery. At the time of the trial for the latter the death had not ensued, and not until it did ensue was the homicide committed. Then, and not before, was it possible to put the accused in jeopardy for that offense."[244]

The *Garrett* Court concluded that the *Diaz* rule applied because the continuing criminal enterprise charged in the case had not been completed at the time of the predicate drug violation.[245] It further noted that it did not have to determine whether the government could have charged a CCE count for a different continuing criminal enterprise that ended at the time of the predicate drug violation because no "such sifting or speculation is required at the behest of one who at the time of the first indictment is returned is continuing to engage in other conduct found criminal by the jury which tried the second indictment."[246]

The Court's "guidance" in *Garrett* and similar cases has resulted in great confusion in the lower courts.[247] These double jeopardy issues are of potentially great importance as Congress continues to add to the list of predicates that may undergird prosecutions under popular statutes such as the Racketeer Influenced and Corrupt Organizations Act (RICO). What *should* be the proper analysis for determining whether a statute, like RICO, which is built upon predicate offenses is the "same offense" as the predicate crimes, some but not all of which are necessary to a conviction for the compound offense?[248]

---

involving complex statutes, see United States v. Ayala, 601 F.3d 256 (4th Cir. 2010) (double jeopardy permits a defendant to be convicted of both conspiring to participate in gang activity involving a predicate act of murder, in violation of RICO, 18 U.S.C. §§1961-1968, and of conspiring to commit murder, in violation of the Violent Crimes in Aid of Racketeering Act, 18 U.S.C. §1959, on the basis of the same course of conduct); United States v. Basciano, 599 F.3d 184 (2d Cir. 2010).

[242] *Garrett*, 471 U.S. at 788-90.

[243] 223 U.S. 442 (1912).

[244] *Garrett*, 471 U.S. at 791; *see also* United States v. Gerhard, 615 F.3d 7 (1st Cir. 2010) (relying in part on temporal factors).

[245] *Garrett*, 471 U.S. at 791.

[246] *Id.* at 792.

[247] *See* Susan R. Klein & Katherine P. Chiarello, *Successive Prosecutions and Compound Criminal Statutes: A Functional Test*, 77 Tex. L. Rev. 333, 338-39 (1998).

[248] *See id.*; *see also* United States v. Luong, 393 F.3d 913 (9th Cir. 2004); United States v. DeCologero, 364 F.3d 12 (1st Cir. 2004); United States v. Diaz, 176 F.3d 52 (2d Cir. 1998).

3. DUAL SOVEREIGNTY

Under the "dual sovereignty" doctrine enunciated by the Supreme Court, the Double Jeopardy prohibition of the Fifth Amendment does not bar concurrent or successive prosecutions by separate sovereigns. Thus, federal authorities may criminally punish a defendant for conduct that was previously prosecuted by state authorities (and vice-versa), whether or not the first case ended in conviction or acquittal.[249] As the Supreme Court reasons: "Each government in determining what shall be an offense against its peace and dignity is exercising its own sovereignty, not that of the other. It follows that an act denounced as a crime by both national and state sovereigns is an offense against the peace and dignity of both and may be punished by each."[250]

There may be an exception to this doctrine that is often claimed by defendants. As the Second Circuit has explained:

> [W]e [have] indicated that circumstances may exist in which state and federal prosecutions are so intertwined as to undermine the assumption that two supposedly independent criminal actions were prosecuted by separate sovereigns. The key criterion in determining whether the application of this exception is warranted "[is] not the extent of control exercised by one prosecuting authority over the other but rather the ultimate source of the power under which the respective prosecutions were undertaken."[251]

Although, as indicated, some courts have recognized such an exception in theory, it is rarely (if ever) found applicable.

Defendants may have more success in seeking to dissuade federal officials from pursuing a case after a prior state proceeding regarding substantially the same criminal activity. The Department of Justice follows what is known as the "Petite Policy."[252] In brief:

> This policy precludes the initiation or continuation of a federal prosecution, following a prior state or federal prosecution based on substantially the same act(s) or transaction(s) unless three substantive prerequisites are satisfied: first, the matter must involve a substantial federal interest; second, the prior prosecution must have left that interest demonstrably unvindicated; and third, applying the same test that is applicable to all federal prosecutions, the government must believe that the defendant's conduct constitutes a federal offense, and that the admissible evidence probably will be sufficient to obtain and sustain a conviction by an unbiased trier of fact.[253]

It should be noted, however, that the Department also states that the Petite Policy, like the balance of the U.S. Attorneys Manual, is promulgated solely for internal guidance and does not create any enforceable rights.[254]

In an empirical examination of two offenses (arson and robbery) that could be charged under both federal and state law over the span of a few years, investigators determined that

---

[249] *See* Abbate v. United States, 359 U.S. 187 (1959).

[250] United States v. Lanza, 260 U.S. 377, 382 (1922).

[251] United States v. Coonan, 938 F.2d 1553, 1563 (2d Cir. 1991); *see also* United States v. Pungitore, 910 F.2d 1084, 1105-06 (3d Cir. 1990).

[252] U.S.A.M. § 9-2.031 ("Dual and Successive Prosecution Policy").

[253] *Id.* § 9-2.031(A).

[254] *Id.* § 9-2.031(F).

the most significant determinants of whether a case would be brought in federal court were an investigation by a federal agency or task force, serious recidivism of the defendant (number of total prior arrests that were for violent offenses), the high value of the items stolen during a robbery, the value of the property destroyed by arson or explosion, the use of a weapon during the crime, cooperation with the government, involvement in conspiracy, cooperation with the government after arrest, involvement of a minor victim, and age of the defendant. Murder and arrests for minor offenses were factors that might point toward state charging. Neither U.S. citizenship, gender, nor black or white race was significantly related to federal versus state involvement. ... [S]entences [were] ... significantly higher at the federal level for both offenses....

...[S]cholarship and statistical information both within [this] ... study and outside of [this] ... study suggest that sentence lengths and conviction and guilty plea rates nationally are higher at the federal than the state level. That knowledge likely motivates federal actors to bring cases with a particular federal interest (e.g., crimes involving high-dollar values and professional criminals who work in groups) against the worst offenders (the ones who have already been convicted of serious felonies at the state level but are back on the streets) to federal court, where they will get a stiffer sentence and be assured of a conviction by trial or plea.[255]

With respect to international prosecutions,

[w]hile the Supreme Court has yet to address squarely whether the dual sovereignty doctrine also applies to sequential foreign and federal prosecutions, those courts of appeals addressing the issue have determined that the doctrine applies. United States v. Guzman, 85 F.3d 823, 826 (1st Cir. 1996) (trial in Netherlands Antilles did not bar U.S. prosecution); United States v. Baptista-Rodriguez, 17 F.3d 1354, 1362 (11th Cir. 1994) (Bahamian prosecution did not bar U.S. action); Chua Han Mow v. United States, 730 F.2d 1308, 1313 (9th Cir. 1984) (holding that Malaysian conviction was no bar to federal prosecution); United States v. McRary, 616 F.2d 181, 184 (5th Cir. 1980) (holding that Cuban prosecution did not bar subsequent U.S. prosecution); United States v. Richardson, 580 F.2d 946, 947 (9th Cir. 1978)(Guatemalan proceedings no bar to U.S. charges); United States v. Martin, 574 F.2d 1359, 1360 (5th Cir. 1978) (stating that "[t]he Constitution of the United States has not adopted the doctrine of international double jeopardy" and holding that U.S. prosecution not barred by Bahamian trial).[256]

---

[255] Susan R. Klein *et al.*, *Why Federal Prosecutors Charge: A Comparison of Federal and New York State Arson and Robbery Filings 2006-2010*, 51 Houston L. Rev. 1381, 1388 (2014).

[256] United States v. Rashed, 83 F. Supp.2d 96, 110 (D.D.C. 1999); *see also* United States v. Rezaq, 134 F.3d 1121, 1128 (D.C. Cir. 1998) (noting that a treaty could provide more protective double jeopardy guarantees, though the treaty at issue did not in that case).

Chapter 6

OBSTRUCTION OF JUSTICE

White-collar prosecutors are increasingly electing to rely on obstruction charges in high-profile cases such as the criminal prosecutions of Rod Blagojevich (former governor of Illinois), Frank Quattrone (former star banker for Credit Suisse First Boston), Andrew Fastow (former CFO of Enron), Martha Stewart, Sam Waksal (founder of ImClone Systems), Arthur Andersen LLP, and I. Lewis "Scooter" Libby (the former Chief of Staff for Vice President Cheney). The federal criminal code gives prosecutors a selection of statutes to work with in pursuing such cases, including 18 U.S.C. §§ 1503 (Influencing or injuring officer or juror generally), 1505 (Obstruction of proceedings before departments, agencies, and committees), 1512 (Tampering with a witness, victim, or an informant), 1519 (Destruction, alteration, or falsification of records in federal investigations and bankruptcy), and 1520 (Destruction of corporate audit records).[1] The potential activities covered by these (and other) sections of the Code are wide-ranging. Because those provisions relating to obstruction by threat of force or physical coercion are not generally relevant to our subject-matter, this chapter focuses on the two provisions traditionally used in white-collar cases: the "omnibus" clause of § 1503 and the non-coercive witness tampering prohibitions in § 1512(b). Briefer coverage is given to a less frequently invoked statute, § 1505, which has been used where obstructive activity takes place in the context of federal agency and congressional investigations and proceedings. Finally, Congress's additions to the code in the Sarbanes-Oxley Act of 2002,[2] 18 U.S.C. §§ 1512(c), 1519, and 1520, are discussed and compared with the protections already embodied in sections 1503, 1505, and 1512(b).

Examining the post-2002 state of the criminal code should illustrate that obstruction is an area in which statutes are often enacted in response to specific problems—such as the destruction of Enron audit records by Arthur Andersen LLP personnel and the resultant prosecution of Arthur Andersen. As a result, the code is fairly incoherent, often redundant, and overbroad—leaving much to the discretion of prosecutors. It is also very difficult to master. Accordingly, to assist students in working their way through these materials, charts comparing the elements (as best as I could identify them) of some of the most commonly used statutes are included at the conclusion of this chapter.

Section 1503's "omnibus clause" has been applied to sanction a great variety of non-coercive obstructive activity, including: false statements made to federal agents; false testimony before a grand jury or trial court; refusing to testify before a grand jury after immunity has been conferred; knowing concealment, falsification, or destruction of evidence to be submitted to a grand jury or court; and efforts to alter the testimony of witnesses for

---

[1] *See also* 18 U.S.C. § 1510; *id.* § 1516 (outlawing endeavors to obstruct or impede a federal auditor); 26 U.S.C. § 7212(a) (prohibiting corrupt endeavors to obstruct and impede the due administration of the Internal Revenue laws).

[2] P.L. 107-204, 116 Stat. 745 (2002).

corrupt purposes. It has also been used to pursue conduct that is not perhaps as intuitively categorizable as "obstruction," including a grand juror's or others' unauthorized disclosure of grand jury information and lawyers' efforts to obtain monies from criminal defendants by false promises to "fix" the proceedings or pay off criminal justice officials.

Until Congress amended § 1512 in 2002, that statute was more narrowly focused on witness tampering, such as defendants' efforts to compromise physical evidence or the testimony of prospective witnesses. Among other changes made in the Sarbanes-Oxley Act of 2002, Congress added a very broad obstruction prohibition in § 1512(c) that mimics in major part § 1503's omnibus provision but that is applicable in contexts outside of the judicial proceedings which § 1503 protects, such as in proceedings before federal agencies and in congressional inquiries. Congress also added a whopping potential penalty for violations of § 1512(c), meaning that § 1512(c) may eclipse § 1503 where applicable.

As these materials highlight, one of the interesting questions presented by these statutes is the degree to which otherwise legitimate legal advocacy or advisory activities may be pursued as obstruction under sections 1503, 1505 or 1512(c) or as witness tampering under § 1512(b). Two of the cases examined within, *United States v. Cueto* and the Supreme Court's decision in *Arthur Andersen LLP v. United States*, are relevant to these questions. Materials relating to the apparent theory upon which the jury convicted Arthur Andersen in its obstruction case— relating to the work product of in-house counsel—are also included as a case study on the website that supports this book, http://www.federalwhitecollarcrime.org.[3]

A. THE "OMNIBUS" CLAUSE OF 18 U.S.C. § 1503

"[T]he purpose of § 1503 is to protect not only the procedures of the criminal system but also the very goal of that system—to achieve justice."[4] "The obstruction of justice statute was drafted with an eye to 'the variety of corrupt methods by which the proper administration of justice may be impeded or thwarted, a variety limited only by the imagination of the criminally inclined.'"[5] The main body of § 1503 specifically targets conduct that interferes with the duties of a juror or court officer. The "omnibus" clause is the portion of the statute with which we are principally concerned and it states that "[w]hoever ... *corruptly* or by threats or force, or by any threatening letter or communication, *influences, obstructs, or impedes, or endeavors to influence, obstruct, or impede, the due administration of justice*, shall be punished ...." (Emphasis added.) This clause "is essentially a catch-all provision which generally prohibits conduct that interferes with the due administration of justice."[6]

The Supreme Court's *Aguilar* decision, below, illustrates the Court's concern over the potential breadth of the statute, as well as the ambiguities that exist regarding its constituent elements.

UNITED STATES v. AGUILAR
515 U.S. 593 (1995)

CHIEF JUSTICE REHNQUIST delivered the opinion of the Court.

A jury convicted United States District Judge Robert Aguilar of one count of illegally disclosing a wiretap in violation of 18 U.S.C. § 2232(c), and of one count of endeavoring to

---

[3] *See also* KC Goyer, Note, *Nancy Temple's Duty: Professional Responsibility and the* Arthur Andersen *Verdict*, 18 Geo. J. Legal Ethics 261 (2004).

[4] United States v. Griffin, 589 F.2d 200, 204 (5th Cir. 1979).

[5] *Id.* at 206-07 (quoting Anderson v. United States, 215 F.2d 84, 88 (6th Cir. 1954)).

[6] United States v. Thomas, 916 F.2d 647, 650 n. 3 (11th Cir. 1990).

obstruct the due administration of justice in violation of § 1503. ... We granted certiorari to resolve a conflict among the Federal Circuits over whether § 1503 punishes false statements made to potential grand jury witnesses ....

Many facts remain disputed by the parties. Both parties appear to agree, however, that a motion for postconviction relief filed by one Michael Rudy Tham represents the starting point from which events bearing on this case unfolded. Tham was an officer of the International Brotherhood of Teamsters, and was convicted of embezzling funds from the local affiliate of that organization. In July 1987, he filed a motion under 28 U.S.C. § 2255 to have his conviction set aside. The motion was assigned to Judge Stanley Weigel. Tham, seeking to enhance the odds that his petition would be granted, asked Edward Solomon and Abraham Chalupowitz, a.k.a. Abe Chapman, to assist him by capitalizing on their respective acquaintances with another judge in the Northern District of California, respondent Aguilar. Respondent knew Chapman as a distant relation by marriage and knew Solomon from law school. Solomon and Chapman met with respondent to discuss Tham's case, as a result of which respondent spoke with Judge Weigel about the matter.

Independent of the embezzlement conviction, the Federal Bureau of Investigation (FBI) identified Tham as a suspect in an investigation of labor racketeering. On April 20, 1987, the FBI applied for authorization to install a wiretap on Tham's business phones. Chapman appeared on the application as a potential interceptee. Chief District Judge Robert Peckham authorized the wiretap. The 30-day wiretap expired by law on May 20, 1987, but Chief Judge Peckham maintained the secrecy of the wiretap ... after a showing of good cause. During the course of the racketeering investigation, the FBI learned of the meetings between Chapman and respondent. The FBI informed Chief Judge Peckham, who, concerned with appearances of impropriety, advised respondent in August 1987 that Chapman might be connected with criminal elements because Chapman's name had appeared on a wiretap authorization.

Five months after respondent learned that Chapman had been named in a wiretap authorization, he noticed a man observing his home during a visit by Chapman. He alerted his nephew to this fact and conveyed the message (with an intent that his nephew relay the information to Chapman) that Chapman's phone was being wiretapped. ...

At this point, respondent's involvement in the two separate Tham matters converged. Two months after the disclosure to his nephew, a grand jury began to investigate an alleged conspiracy to influence the outcome of Tham's habeas case. Two FBI agents questioned respondent. During the interview, respondent lied about his participation in the Tham case and his knowledge of the wiretap. The grand jury returned an indictment; a jury convicted Aguilar of one count of disclosing a wiretap, 18 U.S.C. § 2232(c), and one count of endeavoring to obstruct the due administration of justice, § 1503. ...

Section 1503 ... is structured as follows: first it proscribes persons from endeavoring to influence, intimidate, or impede grand or petit jurors or court officers in the discharge of their duties; it then prohibits injuring grand or petit jurors in their person or property because of any verdict or indictment rendered by them; it then prohibits injury of any court officer, commissioner, or similar officer on account of the performance of his official duties; finally, the "Omnibus Clause" serves as a catchall, prohibiting persons from endeavoring to influence, obstruct, or impede the due administration of justice. The latter clause, it can be seen, is far more general in scope than the earlier clauses of the statute. Respondent was charged with a violation of the Omnibus Clause, to wit: with "corruptly endeavor[ing] to influence, obstruct, and impede the...grand jury investigation."

The first case from this Court construing the predecessor statute to § 1503 was *Pettibone v. United States*, 148 U.S. 197 (1893). There we held that "a person is not sufficiently charged with obstructing or impeding the due administration of justice in a court unless it appears that he knew or had notice that justice was being administered in such court." The Court reasoned that a person lacking knowledge of a pending proceeding necessarily lacked the evil intent to obstruct. Recent decisions of Courts of Appeals have likewise tended to place metes and bounds on the very broad language of the catchall provision. The action taken by the accused must be with an intent to influence judicial or grand jury proceedings; it is not enough that there be an intent to influence some ancillary proceeding, such as an investigation independent of the court's or grand jury's authority. Some courts have phrased this showing as a "nexus" requirement—that the act must have a relationship in time, causation, or logic with the judicial proceedings. In other words, the endeavor must have the "'natural and probable effect'" of interfering with the due administration of justice. This is not to say that the defendant's actions need be successful; an "endeavor" suffices. *United States v. Russell*, 255 U.S. 138, 143 (1921). But as in *Pettibone*, if the defendant lacks knowledge that his actions are likely to affect the judicial proceeding, he lacks the requisite intent to obstruct.

Although respondent urges various broader grounds for affirmance,[7] we find it unnecessary to address them because we think the "nexus" requirement developed in the decisions of the Courts of Appeals is a correct construction of § 1503. We have traditionally exercised restraint in assessing the reach of a federal criminal statute, both out of deference to the prerogatives of Congress and out of concern that "a fair warning should be given to the world in language that the common world will understand, of what the law intends to do if a certain line is passed." We do not believe that uttering false statements to an investigating agent—and that seems to be all that was proved here—who might or might not testify before a grand jury is sufficient to make out a violation of the catchall provision of § 1503.

The Government did not show here that the agents acted as an arm of the grand jury, or indeed that the grand jury had even summoned the testimony of these particular agents. The Government argues that respondent "understood that his false statements would be provided to the grand jury" and that he made the statements with the intent to thwart the grand jury investigation and not just the FBI investigation. The Government supports its argument with a citation to the transcript of the recorded conversation between Aguilar and the FBI agent at the point where Aguilar asks whether he is a target of a grand jury investigation. The agent responded to the question by stating:

> "[T]here is a Grand Jury meeting. Convening I guess that's the correct word. Um some evidence will be heard I'm ... I'm sure on this issue."

Because respondent knew of the pending proceeding, the Government therefore contends that Aguilar's statements are analogous to those made directly to the grand jury itself, in the form of false testimony or false documents.[8]

We think the transcript citation relied upon by the Government would not enable a rational trier of fact to conclude that respondent knew that his false statement would be provided to the grand jury, and that the evidence goes no further than showing that respondent testified falsely to an investigating agent. Such conduct, we believe, falls on the other side of the statutory line from that of one who delivers false documents or testimony to the grand jury itself. Conduct of the latter sort all but assures that the grand jury will consider the material in its deliberations. But what use will be made of false testimony given to an investigating agent who has not been subpoenaed or otherwise directed to appear before the grand jury is far more speculative. We think it cannot be said to have the "natural and probable effect" of interfering with the due administration of justice.

JUSTICE SCALIA criticizes our treatment of the statutory language for reading the word "endeavor" out of it, inasmuch as it excludes defendants who have an evil purpose but use

---

[7] [Court's footnote 1:] Respondent argues that the term "corruptly" is vague and overbroad as applied to the type of conduct at issue in this case and that Congress narrowed the scope of the Omnibus Clause when it expressly punished his conduct in 18 U.S.C. § 1512.

[8] [Court's footnote 2:] See, *e.g.*, *United States v. Mullins*, 22 F.3d 1365, 1367-1368 (C.A.6 1994) (altered records and instructed co-worker to alter records subject to subpoena *duces tecum*); *United States v. Williams*, 874 F.2d 968, 976-982 (C.A.5 1989) (uttered false testimony to grand jury); *United States v. McComb*, 744 F.2d 555, 559 (C.A.7 1984) (created false meeting minutes and voluntarily delivered them to grand jury); *United States v. Faudman*, 640 F.2d 20, 23 (C.A.6 1981) (falsified records, some of which had been sought by subpoena *duces tecum*); *United States v. Walasek*, 527 F.2d 676, 679-680 (C.A.3 1975) (falsified documents requested by subpoena *duces tecum*).

means that would "only unnaturally and improbably be successful." This criticism is unwarranted. Our reading of the statute gives the term "endeavor" a useful function to fulfill: It makes conduct punishable where the defendant acts with an intent to obstruct justice, and in a manner that is likely to obstruct justice, but is foiled in some way. Were a defendant with the requisite intent to lie to a subpoenaed witness who is ultimately not called to testify, or who testifies but does not transmit the defendant's version of the story, the defendant has endeavored to obstruct, but has not actually obstructed, justice. Under our approach, a jury could find such defendant guilty.

JUSTICE SCALIA also apparently believes that *any* act, done with the intent to "obstruct ... the due administration of justice," is sufficient to impose criminal liability. Under the dissent's theory, a man could be found guilty under § 1503 if he knew of a pending investigation and lied to his wife about his whereabouts at the time of the crime, thinking that an FBI agent might decide to interview her and that she might in turn be influenced in her statement to the agent by her husband's false account of his whereabouts. The intent to obstruct justice is indeed present, but the man's culpability is a good deal less clear from the statute than we usually require in order to impose criminal liability. ...

JUSTICE SCALIA, with whom JUSTICE KENNEDY and JUSTICE THOMAS join, concurring in part and dissenting in part. ...

The "omnibus clause" of § 1503, under which respondent was charged,   ... makes criminal not just success in corruptly influencing the due administration of justice, but also the "endeavor" to do so. We have given this latter proscription, which respondent was specifically charged with violating a generous reading: "The word of the section is 'endeavor,' and by using it the section got rid of the technicalities which might be urged as besetting the word 'attempt,' and it describes *any effort or essay* to accomplish the evil purpose that the section was enacted to prevent." *United States v. Russell*, 255 U.S. 138, 143 (1921) (emphasis added) (interpreting substantially identical predecessor statute). Under this reading of the statute, it is even immaterial whether the endeavor to obstruct pending proceedings is possible of accomplishment. In *Osborn v. United States*, 385 U.S. 323, 333 (1966), we dismissed out of hand the "impossibility" defense of a defendant who had sought to convey a bribe to a prospective juror through an intermediary who was secretly working for the Government. "Whatever continuing validity," we said, "the doctrine of 'impossibility' ... may continue to have in the law of criminal attempt, that body of law is inapplicable here."[9]

Even read at its broadest, however, § 1503's prohibition of "endeavors" to impede justice is not without limits. To "endeavor" means to strive or work for a certain end. Webster's New International Dictionary 844 (2d ed. 1950); 1 New Shorter Oxford English Dictionary 816 (1993). Thus, § 1503 reaches only *purposeful* efforts to obstruct the due administration of justice, *i.e.*, acts performed with that very object in mind. This limitation was clearly set forth in our first decision construing § 1503's predecessor statute, *Pettibone v. United States*, 148 U.S. 197 (1893), which held an indictment insufficient because it had failed to allege the intent to obstruct justice. That opinion rejected the Government's contention that the intent required to violate the statute could be found in "the intent to commit an unlawful act, in the doing of which justice was in fact obstructed"; to justify a conviction, it said, "the specific intent to violate the statute must exist." *Pettibone* did acknowledge, however—and here is the point that is distorted to produce today's opinion—that the specific intent to obstruct justice could be found where the defendant intentionally committed a wrongful act that had obstruction of justice as its "natural and probable consequence."

Today's "nexus" requirement sounds like this, but is in reality quite different. Instead of reaffirming that "natural and probable consequence" is one way of establishing intent, it

---

[9] [Justice Scalia's footnote 1:] This complete disavowal of the impossibility defense may be excessive. As *Pettibone v. United States*, 148 U.S. 197 (1893), acknowledged, an endeavor to obstruct proceedings that did not exist would not violate the statute. "[O]bstruction can only arise when justice is being administered."

substitutes "'natural and probable effect'" *for* intent, requiring that factor even when intent to obstruct justice is otherwise clear.[10] But while it is quite proper to derive an *intent* requirement from § 1503's use of the word "endeavor," it is quite impossible to derive a *"natural and probable consequence"* requirement. One would be "endeavoring" to obstruct justice if he intentionally set out to do it by means that would only unnaturally and improbably be successful. As we said in *Russell*, "any effort or essay" corruptly to influence, obstruct, or impede the due administration of justice constitutes a forbidden endeavor, even, as we held in *Osborn*, an effort that is *incapable* of having that effect.

The Court does not indicate where its "nexus" requirement is to be found in the words of the statute. Instead, it justifies its holding with the assertion that "[w]e have traditionally exercised restraint in assessing the reach of a federal criminal statute, both out of deference to the prerogatives of Congress and out of concern that a fair warning should be given ... of what the law intends to do if a certain line is passed." But "exercising restraint *in assessing the reach* of a federal criminal statute" (which is what the rule of lenity requires) is quite different from importing extratextual requirements *in order to limit the reach* of a federal criminal statute, which is what the Court has done here. By limiting § 1503 to acts having the "natural and probable effect" of interfering with the due administration of justice, the Court effectively reads the word "endeavor," which we said in *Russell* embraced "any effort or essay" to obstruct justice out of the omnibus clause, leaving a prohibition of only actual obstruction and competent attempts....

Since I find against respondent on the § 1503 count, I must consider several other grounds offered by respondent for affirming the Court of Appeals' setting aside of his conviction. First, invoking the interpretive canon of *ejusdem generis*, he argues that, since all the rest of § 1503 refers only to actions directed at jurors and court officers, the omnibus clause cannot apply to actions directed at witnesses. But the rule of *ejusdem generis*, which "limits general terms which follow specific ones to matters similar to those specified," has no application here. Although something of a catchall, the omnibus clause is *not* a general or collective term following a list of specific items to which a particular statutory command is applicable (*e.g.*, "fishing rods, nets, hooks, bobbers, sinkers, and other equipment"). Rather, it is one of the several distinct and independent prohibitions contained in § 1503 that share only the word "Whoever," which begins the statute, and the penalty provision which ends it. Indeed, given the already broad terms of the other clauses in § 1503, to limit the omnibus clause in the manner respondent urges would render it superfluous.

Respondent next contends that because Congress in 1982 enacted a different statute, 18 U.S.C. § 1512, dealing with witness tampering, and simultaneously removed from § 1503 the provisions it had previously contained specifically addressing efforts to influence or injure witnesses, see Victim and Witness Protection Act of 1982, Pub.L. 97-291, 96 Stat. 1249-1250, 1253, his witness-related conduct is no longer punishable under the omnibus clause of § 1503. The 1982 amendment, however, did nothing to alter the omnibus clause, which by its terms encompasses corrupt "endeavors to influence, obstruct, or impede, the due administration of justice." The fact that there is now some overlap between § 1503 and § 1512 is no more intolerable than the fact that there is some overlap between the omnibus clause of § 1503 and the other provisions of § 1503 itself. It hardly leads to the conclusion that § 1503 was, to the extent of the overlap, silently repealed. It is not unusual for a particular act to violate more than one criminal statute, and in such situations the Government may proceed under any

---

[10] [Justice Scalia's footnote 2:] *United States v. Thomas*, 916 F.2d 647, 651 (C.A.11 1990)], which appears to be the origin of this doctrine, made precisely the same mistake the Court does. It cited and misapplied earlier Court of Appeals cases standing for the entirely different principle—flowing from our language in *Pettibone*—that to prove an "endeavor" to obstruct justice, "all the government has to establish is that the defendant should have reasonably foreseen that the natural and probable consequence of the success of his scheme would [obstruct the due administration of justice]." *United States v. Silverman*, 745 F.2d 1386, 1393 (C.A.11 1984). This does not impose a requirement of "natural and probable consequence," but approves a manner of proof of "intent." See, *e.g.*, *United States v. Neiswender*, 590 F.2d 1269, 1273 [(CA4 1979)].

statute that applies. It is, moreover, "a cardinal principle of statutory construction that repeals by implication are not favored."

Finally, respondent posits that the phrase "'corruptly ... endeavors to influence, obstruct, or impede' may be unconstitutionally vague," in that it fails to provide sufficient notice that lying to potential grand jury witnesses in an effort to thwart a grand jury investigation is proscribed. Statutory language need not be colloquial, however, and the term "corruptly" in criminal laws has a longstanding and well-accepted meaning. It denotes "[a]n act done with an intent to give some advantage inconsistent with official duty and the rights of others .... It includes bribery but is more comprehensive; because an act may be corruptly done though the advantage to be derived from it be not offered by another." As the District Court here instructed the jury:

> "An act is done corruptly if it's done voluntarily and intentionally to bring about either an unlawful result or a lawful result by some unlawful method, with a hope or expectation of either financial gain or other benefit to oneself or a benefit of another person."

Moreover, in the context of obstructing jury proceedings, any claim of ignorance of wrongdoing is incredible. Acts specifically intended to "influence, obstruct, or impede, the due administration of justice" are obviously wrongful, just as they are necessarily "corrupt."...

Notes

1. *Elements/Source of the "Nexus" Requirement.* Courts use varying formulations to describe the elements of a prosecution under the "omnibus" clause of 18 U.S.C. § 1503. A compilation of those formulations is that the government must prove beyond a reasonable doubt that the defendant: (1) knowing that a judicial proceeding was pending; (2) corruptly; (3) endeavored; (4) to influence, obstruct, or impede the due administration of justice. *See* United States v. Quattrone, 441 F.3d 153, 170 (2d Cir. 2006); United States v. Brenson, 104 F.3d 1267, 1275 (11th Cir. 1997). Does the *Aguilar* opinion indicate that the government actually bears the burden of proving more than the above formula? Certainly, the Court indicates that an "intent to obstruct" is a "requisite"—is this a separate element to be charged and proved, or is it implicit in the above list of elements? What element does the *Aguilar* Court's "nexus" requirement modify or define—or is this a new element created by the Court?

The *Aguilar* Court seems to derive the "nexus" requirement from lower court opinions. Those opinions were themselves all over the lot with respect to where the "nexus" requirement fit in the statutory scheme. *See, e.g.,* United States v. Thomas, 916 F.2d 647, 651 n.5 (11th Cir. 1990) (explaining that various panels of the Eleventh Circuit have grafted the "nexus" requirement onto different elements of § 1503). Those decisions cited with approval by the *Aguilar* Court in support of the "nexus" requirement treated the "nexus" requirement as modifying the "due administration of justice" element. Justice Scalia's opinion is correct in noting, however, that the "natural and probable effect" language that the majority employs in its "nexus" requirement was and is often used not as an independent showing necessary to prove the impairment of the "due administration of justice," but rather as a means of lightening the government's burden of showing an intent to obstruct (more about that below). *See* United States v. Brenson, 104 F.3d 1267, 1277-78 (11th Cir. 1997). At least some judges in the Ninth Circuit believe that the "nexus" element is a materiality requirement. *See* United States v. Bond, 784 F.3d 582 (9th Cir. 2015) (*en banc*) (Smith, J., concurring; Reinhardt, J., concurring). Does it matter what element the "nexus" requirement modifies? Note that other obstruction statutes, discussed *infra*, such as § 1512, do not contain a requirement that the "due administration of justice" be impeded, obstructed, or influenced.

The Supreme Court in *Arthur Andersen LLP v. United States*, reproduced *infra*, also applied its "nexus" test to § 1512. In so doing, it seemed to characterize the "nexus" requirement as originating in the intent requirement—presumably inhering in the word "corrupt"—rather than the "due administration of justice" element.

2. *Perjury.* The "nexus" requirement has been deemed "particularly critical in section 1503 prosecutions premised on false testimony." *Thomas*, 916 F.2d at 652. Why might a prosecutor elect to charge an obstruction count together with, or in lieu of, a perjury count when pursuing false testimony? *See, e.g.*, United States v. Brown, 948 F.2d 1076, 1080 (8th Cir. 1991) (testimony of a single witness sufficient to support a conviction under § 1503).

Most courts recognize that perjury can be the basis for an obstruction prosecution, but they caution that not all false or evasive testimony constitutes obstruction, citing the Supreme Court's holding that perjurious testimony may not be the basis of a contempt sanction absent a showing that the perjury obstructed the court in the performance of its duty. *See In re* Michael, 326 U.S. 224, 227-28 (1945). To show an obstruction based on false testimony, then, courts have required the government to show that the false testimony was material. *See Thomas*, 916 F.2d at 652; *see also* United States v. Littleton, 76 F.3d 614, 619 (4th Cir. 1996). But recently an *en banc* Ninth Circuit could not agree on the definition of materiality that ought to be employed to test witness testimony before a grand jury; indeed, two of the judges were of the opinion that, notwithstanding the dicta in *Aguilar*, § 1503 does not even apply to witness testimony in grand jury proceedings. *See* United States v. Bonds, 784 F.3d 582 (9th Cir. 2015) (*en banc*). An extended discussion of the *Bonds* decision is appropriate to illustrate the indeterminacy of the statute and because the reasoning of some members of the court also has implications for the reach of the statute and the proper reading of its "corrupt" element.

In 2002, the federal government, through the Criminal Investigation Division of the Internal Revenue Service, began investigating the distribution of steroids and other performance enhancing drugs ("PEDs") to determine whether the distributors of PEDs laundered the proceeds earned by selling those drugs. The government's investigation focused on the distribution of steroids by the Bay Area Laboratory Co-operative ("BALCO"). The government raided BALCO and obtained evidence suggesting that BALCO manufactured steroids were delivered to Barry Bonds (a baseball player) and other professional athletes. The government convened a grand jury in 2003 to further investigate the sale of these drugs in order to determine whether the proceeds of the sales were being laundered. Bonds and other professional athletes were called to testify. Bonds testified under a grant of immunity that provided that, if he was not truthful, his testimony could be used in a case against him for perjury or false declarations. Bond denied knowingly using steroids or any other PEDs provided by BALCO. Bonds testified before the grand jury that he was never offered, supplied with, or administered any human growth hormone, steroids, or any substance that required injection.

Bonds was later indicted on the basis of his grand jury testimony. The jury was faced with an indictment charging Bonds with three counts of perjury before a grand jury in violation of 18 U.S.C. § 1623(a), and one count of obstruction of justice in violation of 18 U.S.C. § 1503. The jury instructions identified seven statements that the government alleged obstructed justice. The jury, however, found only one statement obstructive ("Statement C"), which the jury, on the verdict form, characterized as misleading or evasive. Thus this exchange was alone the basis of the 1503 conviction:

Question: Did Greg[, your trainer,] ever give you anything that required a syringe to inject yourself with?
Answer: I've only had one doctor touch me. And that's my only personal doctor. Greg, like I said, we don't get into each others' personal lives. We're friends, but I don't—we don't sit around and talk baseball, because he knows I don't want—don't come to my house talking baseball. If you want to come to my house and talk about fishing, some other stuff, we'll be good friends, you come around talking about baseball, you go on. I don't talk about his business. You know what I mean?
Question: Right.
Answer: *That's what keeps our friendship. You know, I am sorry, but that—you know, that—I was a celebrity child, not just in baseball by my own instincts. I became a celebrity child with a famous father. I just don't get into other people's business because of my father's situation, you see.*

The jury failed to reach a decision on the perjury counts. Bonds was sentenced to 30 days' home confinement and two years probation. A panel of the Ninth Circuit affirmed Bonds' conviction.

The Ninth Circuit granted *en banc* consideration, ultimately reversing Bonds' conviction amidst a welter of opinions. The *en banc*'s per curiam opinion's reasoning was pithy: "[d]uring a grand jury proceeding, defendant gave a rambling, non-responsive answer to a simple question. Because there is insufficient evidence that Statement C was material, defendant's conviction for obstruction of justice in violation of 18 U.S.C. § 1503 is not supported by the record. Whatever section 1503's scope may be in other circumstances, defendant's conviction here must be reversed."

Judge Kozinski filed a concurring opinion that was joined by four judges out of the eleven judges reviewing the case (O'Scannlain, Graber, Callahan, and Nguyen, JJ). He began with the query: "Can a single non-responsive answer by a grand jury witness support a conviction for obstruction of justice under 18 U.S.C. § 1503?" 784 F.3d at 582 (Kozinski, J., concurring). Judge Kozinski then went on at length about the potentially dangerous reach of the statute. He observed, for example, that, "[a]s should be apparent, section 1503's coverage is vast. By its literal terms, it applies to all stages of the criminal and civil justice process, not just to conduct in the courtroom but also to trial preparation, discovery and pretrial motions. ... Stretched to its limits, section 1503 poses a significant hazard for everyone involved in our system of justice, because so much of what the adversary process calls for could be construed as obstruction." *Id.* at 583-84 The Judge noted that "[i]t is true that any such maneuver would violate section 1503 only if it were done 'corruptly.' But it is equally true that we have given 'corruptly' such a broad construction that it does not meaningfully cabin the kind of conduct that is subject to prosecution." *Id.* at 584. Ultimately, Judge Kozinski concluded:

> We have no doubt that United States Attorneys and their Assistants would use the power to prosecute for such crimes judiciously, but that is not the point. Making everyone who participates in our justice system a potential criminal defendant for conduct that is nothing more than the ordinary tug and pull of litigation risks chilling zealous advocacy. It also gives prosecutors the immense and unreviewable power to reward friends and punish enemies by prosecuting the latter and giving the former a pass. The perception that prosecutors have such a potent weapon in their arsenal, even if never used, may well dampen the fervor with which lawyers, particularly those representing criminal defendants, will discharge their duties. The amorphous nature of the statute is also at odds with the constitutional requirement that individuals have fair notice as to what conduct may be criminal.
>
> Because the statute sweeps so broadly, due process calls for prudential limitations on the government's power to prosecute under it. Such a limitation already exists in our case law interpreting section 1503: the requirement of materiality. *See United States v. Thomas*, 612 F.3d 1107, 1129-29 (9th Cir. 2010). Materiality screens out many of the statute's troubling applications by limiting convictions to those situations where an act "has a natural tendency to influence, or was capable of influencing, the decision of the decisionmaking body." *See Kungys v. United States*, 485 U.S. 759, 770 (1988). Put another way, the government must prove beyond a reasonable doubt that the charged conduct was capable of influencing a decisionmaking person or entity—for example, by causing it to cease its investigation, pursue different avenues of inquiry or reach a different outcome.
>
> In weighing materiality, we consider "the *intrinsic* capabilities of the ... statement itself," rather than the statement's actual effect on the decisionmaker and we evaluate the statement in "the context in which [it was] made."
>
> We start with the self-evident proposition that Statement C, standing alone, did not have the capacity to divert the government from its investigation or influence the grand jury's decision whether to indict anyone. ... Statement C communicates nothing of value or detriment to the investigation. ... [T]he answer did not enlighten, obfuscate, confirm or deny anything within the scope of the question posed. ...

This is true even if, as the government now argues, Statement C is literally false. An irrelevant or wholly non-responsive answer says nothing germane to the subject of the investigation, whether it's true or false. For example, if a witness is asked, "Do you own a gun?" it makes no difference whether he answers "The sky is blue" or "The sky is green." That the second statement is false makes it no more likely to impede the investigation than the first.

Id. at 584-86. Finally, Judge Kozinski made clear that Statement C could not be considered in isolation, but rather that the court was bound to look at "the record as a whole to determine whether a rational trier of fact could have found the statement capable of influencing the grand jury's investigation, in light of defendant's entire grand jury testimony." *Id.* at 586. He reserved the possibility that, on other records, an obstruction case might succeed on the basis of unresponsive answers "[i]f, for example, a witness engages in a pattern of irrelevant statements, or launches into lengthy disquisitions that are clearly designed to waste time and preclude the questioner from continuing his examination." *Id.* Judge Kozinski, and those who joined him, simply did not find that this one statement was material and thus was incapable of influencing the grand jury.

Judge N.R. Smith filed another concurrence, which was joined by three other judges (Wardlaw, Callahan, and Friedland, JJ.). Judge Smith restated the question in light of the government's concession at trial that Statement C was not literally false, but rather only "misleading or evasive": "we must determine whether a single truthful but evasive or misleading answer could constitute evidence of obstruction of justice under § 1503." 784 F.3d at 587 & n.1. Judge Smith also answered this question "no" based on a lack of materiality, but he found the source of a materiality requirement not in Ninth Circuit caselaw, as had Judge Kozinski, but rather in *United States v. Aguilar*, 515 U.S. 593, 599 (1995). Thus, in his view the standard for materiality is not whether the statement was capable of influencing the decision of the grand jury, but rather whether the endeavor to obstruct justice had "the natural and probable effect of interfering with the due administration of justice." *Id.* at 587. Judge Smith noted that this "judicially-created materiality requirement is a primary objective limitation on § 1503's expansive reach." 784 F.3d at 588.

Judge N.R. Smith's concurrence explained that the conclusion that "Statement C could not have 'the natural and probable effect' of impeding the grand jury's investigative function stems from two sources." *Id.* The first was *Bronston v. United States*, 409 U.S. 352 (1973), in which the Supreme Court held that a nonresponsive but literally true answer that is misleading by negative implication cannot constitute perjury. The *Bronston* Court required proof of literal falsity for a perjury conviction in part because it is the questioning lawyer's job to pin down nonresponsive witnesses. Judge Smith found that, in this context as well, it was "the Government's duty to clarify merely misleading or evasive testimony." 784 F.3d at 588.

Second, the concurrence found particularly persuasive the Fifth Circuit's explanation of the materiality standard in *United States v. Griffin*, 589 F.2d 200, 204 (5th Cir. 1979), which Judge Smith read as providing that the truthful but misleading or evasive testimony must amount to a refusal to testify before it is material. 784 F.3d at 588, 589. Thus, Judge Smith explained that "[e]vasive or misleading testimony, in this light, can only obstruct the due administration of justice when it completely thwarts the investigative nature of the tribunal— when it derails the grand jury 'as effectively as if [the witness] refused to answer the question at all.'" *Id.* at 589. Taken together, these two sources lead to the conclusion that "a single truthful but evasive or misleading statement can never be material." *Id.* "In summary, the 'natural and probable effect' of a single true but evasive response to the government's questioning is not to impede the grand jury but, rather, to prompt follow-up questioning." *Id.*

Judge Reinhardt filed a concurring opinion in which he began by answering the question Judge Kozinski posed with a simple "no" "regardless of the context in which the answer was given." *Id.* at 590. Unlike Judge Kozinski, Judge Reinhardt concurred with the part of Judge N.R. Smith's opinion that would hold that "the 'natural and probable effect' test articulated in *United States v. Aguilar* constitutes the proper standard for materiality with respect to § 1503." *Id.* at 591. He concluded that Statement C could not have the "natural and probable effect" of interfering with the due administration of justice because it was non-responsive at best, and thus said nothing relevant to the grand jury's investigation. Judge Reinhardt agreed with Judges Kozinski and N.R. Smith insofar as they stated that Statement C could not have been material even if it had been false. "A non-responsive answer that is false is 'no more likely to impede the investigation than' a non-responsive answer that is true." *Id.* at 590.

But Judge Reinhardt objected to the "breadth of Judge Kozinski's opinion, its unwarranted speculation regarding context, and its use of *United States v. Thomas*, 612 F.3d 1107, 1124 (9th Cir. 2010), rather than *Aguilar*, 515 U.S. at 601, to define the materiality requirement." 784 F.3d at 591. Judge Reinhardt would not suggest, as did Judge Kozinski at the end of his opinion, "that there may be a category of non-responsive or irrelevant answers that could be characterized as evasive or misleading and thus subject to differing treatment from other kinds of nonresponsive answers." 784 F.3d at 590. As to Judge N.R. Smith's opinion, Judge Reinhardt disagreed that a flat refusal to testify may be prosecuted under § 1503. In his view, "had Bonds refused to testify or continued to answer evasively, the appropriate course would have been a contempt proceeding, not an obstruction of justice prosecution." 784 F.3d at 591. Judge Reinhardt also did not agree with Judge Smith's "unnecessary and, in my view, incorrect discussion of misleading or evasive testimony or with his implicit endorsement of *United States v. Griffin*, 589 F.2d 200 (5th Cir. 1979), as the proper rule for this circuit." 784 F.3d at 591.

Judge Reinhardt then explained his more fundamental objection to the use of § 1503 to charge witnesses testifying at court proceedings. He acknowledged that Ninth Circuit caselaw—and Supreme Court dicta in *Aguilar*—might preclude this view from prevailing in Bonds' case, but Judge Reinhardt explained the basis for his belief (shared in major part by Judge W. Fletcher in another concurrence) as follows:

> The history underlying § 1503 strongly supports the conclusion that in-court testimony is *not* a subject of criminal sanctions under that statute. The predecessor to § 1503 was originally enacted in 1831 in response to abuse of the contempt power by a federal district judge who had imprisoned a man for publishing a criticism of one of his opinions. In establishing the crime of obstruction of justice, Congress created … a "geographical" divide between the conduct constituting that crime and conduct subject to contempt: "misbehavior of any person or persons *in the presence of said courts, or so near thereto* as to obstruct the administration of justice" constituted contempt under section 1 of the Act of March 2, 1831, whereas persons *outside of court* who "corruptly, or by threats of force, obstruct, or impede, or endeavor to obstruct or impede, the due administration of justice" committed the crime of obstruction of justice under section 2. Section 1 survives today as 18 U.S.C. § 401, the contempt statute, while section 2 became the clause of § 1503 at issue in this case. Thus, the original understanding of the crime of obstruction of justice was that it applied to conduct *outside* the presence of a court. Such was and is the intent of Congress, and "[w]e cannot by process of interpretation obliterate the distinctions which Congress drew."
>
> When one considers the other criminal statutes available to punish in-court misbehavior by a witness—that is, misconduct during testimony—this "geographical" delineation, whereby only out-of-court conduct constitutes obstruction of justice under § 1503, makes sense. A false statement made during in-court testimony constitutes perjury. *See* 18 U.S.C. §§ 1621, 1623. A failure to answer a question or a material evasion that the witness refuses to correct during in-court testimony constitutes contempt. I seriously doubt that the obstruction of justice statute was intended to duplicate these crimes. Something more than a witness merely lying or being non-responsive during testimony is required in order to violate § 1503. Otherwise, the crime of obstruction of justice would be to that extent wholly superfluous.
>
> More important, the argument for coverage of such actions under § 1503 hinges entirely on the single word "corruptly." The other specified means of obstructing justice enumerated in that section—"by threats or force, or by any threatening letter or communication"—when viewed in context dictate the opposite conclusion: "corruptly"

does not describe the in-court conduct of a witness, but rather, like those enumerated means, describes the conduct of a third party who seeks to obstruct the proceedings. The specified means necessarily describe the attempts of a third party to affect the judicial proceedings by corrupt means. As Judge W. Fletcher explains, the interpretative canon *noscitur a sociis*—literally "[i]t is known from its associates"—tells us that "the meaning of questionable or doubtful words or phrases in a statute may be ascertained by reference to the meaning of other words or phrases associated with it." Black's Law Dictionary 1060 (6th ed.1990). Because obstructing proceedings by "threats or force" plainly refers to the conduct of persons outside of court who seek to obstruct the proceedings and not to the witness who is testifying in court in the proceedings, "corruptly" must similarly be understood as referring to the means used by third parties to influence, obstruct, or impede proceedings, and not to in-court testimony by a witness who may well be the object but not the subject of the corrupt tactics.

Even if 1503 covered in-court conduct, "corruptly" would, under the *noscitur a sociis* canon, as well as under any other reasonable means of statutory construction, require a greater magnitude of misconduct than simply giving a false or non-responsive answer to a question. Clearly, a mere lie or evasive answer is not akin to using threats or force to cause another to lie. Indeed, the Supreme Court has on occasion recognized that lies and evasive answers are part and parcel of the process of uncovering the truth through adversarial witness examination. The use of threats or force to impede a proceeding, by contrast, is not a customary incident of that process and constitutes a far more serious offense. "Corruptly" in the obstruction of justice statute covers conduct at the same level of obstruction as the use of threats or force and may not properly be interpreted so as to bring a mere lie or evasive answer by a witness within the scope of the statute. Although I am not certain that "corruptly" is limited to bribery as Judge W. Fletcher contends, I am wholly confident that it does describe conduct of that magnitude and not a simple lie or evasive answer by a witness during in-court testimony.

For the reasons discussed above, I would hope that the Supreme Court would revisit its dictum in *Aguilar* and would conclude that § 1503 does not cover a witness's in-court testimony. After all, Congress has enacted criminal statutes other than § 1503 that sufficiently address a witness's in-court conduct. The problems created by the misuse of § 1503 by overeager prosecutors to punish witnesses for what they say in court are all too evident from the facts of this case. It is time for them to cease using that section as a substitute for vigorous cross-examination or for the criminal statutes that properly apply to in-court testimony. ...

Id. at 592-93.

Judge W. Fletcher filed an opinion concurring in the judgment only. She disagreed with the import of Judge Kozinski's opinion, which she read as permitting the prosecution of truthful but evasive and misleading statements if they are "material." Rather than relying on a "materiality" limitation, she argued that "[t]he key to a proper understanding of the statute"—and the reason this prosecution could not succeed—is "the meaning of the word 'corruptly.'" *Id*. at 595. "As used in § 1503(a), 'corruptly' does not describe a state of mind. Rather, it describes a forbidden means of influencing, obstructing, or impeding the due administration of justice. As used in § 1503(a), 'corruptly' most likely means 'by bribery.'" *Id*. In support of this position, Judge Fletcher, like Judge Reinhardt, relied upon the text of the statute and its history, as well as a comparison to the perjury statute, 18 U.S.C. § 1621.

3. *Pending Proceeding.* Most courts believe that "*Aguilar* reaffirmed the proposition that a defendant may be convicted under section 1503 only when he knew or had notice of a pending proceeding." United States v. Frankhauser, 80 F.3d 641, 650-51 (1st Cir. 1996). There is nothing in the statute that requires proof of a pending judicial proceeding, let alone the defendant's knowledge thereof. *See, e.g.*, United States v. Novak, 217 F.3d 566 (8th Cir. 2000) (questioning existence of this requirement, which is not reflected in plain language of statute, but assuming its existence for purposes of the case). How, then, do these purported elements fit into the statutory scheme?

There is little litigation concerning the "pending proceeding" requirement where formal proceedings have commenced—for example, where the obstructive activity occurs in connection with pre-trial or trial activities. And there is relatively little call to address the question of when a proceeding ends for purposes of § 1503. Defendants commonly challenge this requirement when the obstructive activity occurs in the course of the investigation, for example when the defendant allegedly makes false statements to investigating officers or where he conceals, destroys, or falsifies documents before a designated grand jury could convene to investigate his case, hear witnesses, or in some cases, issue subpoenas. The courts have "decline[d] to establish a rule 'by which some formal act of the grand jury will be required to establish 'pendency.'" United States v. Vesich, 724 F.2d 451, 455 (5th Cir. 1984) (quoting United States v. Walasek, 527 F.2d 676, 678 (3d Cir.1975)). Instead, the courts "look to whether the investigating agency has acted 'in furtherance of an actual grand jury investigation, i.e., to secure a presently contemplated presentation of evidence before the grand jury.'" Id.

4. *Judge-Made Elements.* *Aguilar* was not an aberrational case in its attempt to secure an obstruction conviction based on false statements made to FBI agents in the course of an investigation. *See, e.g.*, United States v. Grubb, 11 F.3d 426 (4th Cir. 1993); United States v. Wood, 958 F.2d 963 (10th Cir. 1992). Why would prosecutors in such cases elect to pursue an obstruction count with, or instead of, a false statements count under § 1001? Note that *Brogan v. United States*, reproduced *supra* Chapter 5, in which the Supreme Court definitively held that an "exculpatory 'no'" *does* violate § 1001, was not decided until 1998, four years *after* the Ninth Circuit's decision in *Aguilar*. Accordingly, the Ninth Circuit below in *Aguilar* stated that the conduct alleged in the case "is governed not by section 1503 but by 18 U.S.C. § 1001. Furthermore, even under a section 1001 charge, the statute does not apply to certain situations where a truthful response would have incriminated the declarant. This is known as the 'exculpatory no' doctrine." United States v. Aguilar, 21 F.3d 1475, 1483 (9th Cir. 1994). In other words, the Ninth Circuit held that § 1001 did not cover the false statement and the Supreme Court held that § 1503 was also unavailable. What were prosecutors to do?

This situation illustrates how judge-made elements designed to rationalize the application of a given statute (such as the "exculpatory 'no'" defense under § 1001, the § 1001 "judicial function" exception, and the "nexus" requirement of § 1503), may actually work together to create unanticipated and irrational results. *See also* *Wood*, 958 F.2d 963. For example, in *Wood*, the defendant allegedly made false statements to FBI agents who were "acting under the authority of the Phoenix grand jury." *Id.* The Tenth Circuit affirmed the dismissal of the § 1001 count because the defendant's statements were made in the course of a judicial proceeding and thus were exempt from prosecution under the § 1001 "judicial function" exception. At the same time, the court affirmed the dismissal of the § 1503 count because the defendant's statement would not have the natural and probable effect of impeding the pending grand jury investigation.

5. *Civil Cases.* Pending proceedings include not only grand jury investigations and criminal cases, but also civil judicial proceedings. For example, if representatives of a party to a civil lawsuit (to which the government is not a party) were to destroy documents that might otherwise be discoverable (even though not then under court order or subpoena), those representatives may be subject to criminal prosecution for obstruction. *See, e.g.*, United States v. Lundwall, 1 F.Supp.2d 249 (S.D.N.Y. 1998).

6. *No Subpoena Needed.* At least until the Arthur Andersen case, many people (including some lawyers) mistakenly believed that if a person destroys documents or attempts to subvert witness testimony *before* a subpoena issues, that person cannot be prosecuted for obstruction under § 1503. So long as there is proof that a defendant knows of the pending proceeding, however, "the law is clear that neither a subpoena nor a court order directing the production of documents must be issued or served as a prerequisite to a § 1503 prosecution, and that the concealment and destruction of documents likely to be sought by subpoena is actionable under the statute." *See, e.g.*, *Lundwall*, 1 F.Supp.2d at 254; *see also* United States v. Ruggiero, 934 F.2d 440, 450 (2d Cir. 1991); Wilder v. United States, 143 F. 433, 442 (4th Cir. 1906) (inducing

witness not under subpoena to refuse to testify was actionable as an obstruction under the statute).

7. *Endeavor.* In reading the predecessor statute to § 1503, the Supreme Court defined an "endeavor" as "any effort or essay to accomplish the evil purpose that the section was enacted to prevent." United States v. Russell, 255 U.S. 138, 143 (1921). An individual need not succeed in actually obstructing justice to violate § 1503. Indeed, an "endeavor" is deemed "very similar to a criminal solicitation ... and does not require proof that would support a charge of attempt." United States v. Fasolino, 586 F.2d 939, 940 (2d Cir. 1978); United States v. Erickson, 561 F.3d 1150 (10th Cir. 2009) (holding that the government need not prove that fraudulent documents submitted pursuant to subpoena were relevant to the grand jury investigation because "an endeavor suffices"). Given that the "endeavor" seems to be the *actus reus* of the crime, what should suffice? Should the same concerns that require that a "substantial step" be taken in furtherance of a criminal design before attempt liability will attach control in this context? *See* ALI, Model Penal Code § 5.01(1)(c).

Justice Scalia believes that the Court's "nexus" requirement essentially reads the "endeavor" element out of the statute, "leaving a prohibition of only actual obstruction and competent attempts." If the only cases the "nexus" requirement carves out of § 1503 are those in which the obstructive activity, although intentional, "would only unnaturally and improbably be successful," is that much of a loss? Is the "nexus" requirement likely to succeed in narrowing the applicability of § 1503 to those cases in which the obstructive activity is most threatening, harmful, or blameworthy?

8. *Materiality?* In a number of high-profile cases, including the prosecutions of Matha Stewart and I. Lewis ("Scooter") Libby, the government elected to pursue the defendants for obstruction but not to charge the allegedly criminal conduct whose investigation was obstructed. Thus, for example, Martha Stewart was charged with, *inter alia*, obstruction of justice (under § 1503's kissing cousin, § 1505, considered *infra*) in connection with her sale of shares of ImClone Systems Inc. stock, allegedly after a "tip" from ImClone's founder. Although convicted for obstruction, *see* United States v. Stewart, 433 F.3d 273 (2d Cir. 2006), in connection with the false explanations she offered for her stock sale, she was never indicted for the alleged insider trading that spawned the investigation. Similarly, Scooter Libby was convicted for, *inter alia*, obstruction under § 1503 based on his lies to federal investigators and the grand jury about leaks of a CIA agent's identity, but not for the underlying alleged offense of unauthorized disclosure of classified information. *See, e.g.*, United States v. Libby, 429 F. Supp.2d 1 (D.D.C. 2006).

Some have criticized prosecutors' decisions to bring these cases; for example, one commentator argues that "it is far from clear that Stewart's trades were unlawful, let alone illegal, and it is hard to identify any harm her acts directly caused anyone." Jeanne L. Schroeder, *Envy and Outsider Trading: The Case of Martha Stewart*, 26 Cardozo L. Rev. 2023, 2023 (2004); *cf.* Daniel C. Richman, *Al Capone's Revenge: An Essay on the Political Economy of Pretextual Prosecution*, 105 Colum. L. Rev. 583 (2005) (discussing hidden costs of pretextual prosecutions). Professor Ellen Podgor, in response to cases such as these, proposes that Congress add a materiality element to the obstruction statutes—an element that is *not* presently generally required outside cases founded on perjury (and in the Ninth Circuit). *See* Ellen S. Podgor, *Arthur Andersen, LLP and Martha Stewart: Should Materiality Be an Element of Obstruction of Justice?*, 44 Washburn L.J. 583 (2005). Professor Podgor argues: "Clearly, when the obstructive conduct precludes prosecution on the underlying charge there is no choice but to use an obstruction statute to achieve justice. ... In contrast, however, when the prosecutor selects an obstruction charge and fails to charge the underlying conduct solely for expediency purposes, the choice should be subject to scrutiny." *Id.* at 584. Others argue that this objection misconceives the harm in obstruction. *See* Julie R. O'Sullivan, *The Federal Criminal "Code" Is a Disgrace: Obstruction Statutes as a Case Study*, 96 J. Crim. L. & Criminology 643, 678 (2006). What do you think?

9. *Specific Intent to Obstruct and "Corrupt" Motive.* The *Aguilar* Court talks of the "requisite intent to obstruct," and the case upon which it relies, *Pettibone v. United States*, 148 U.S. 197, 207 (1893), refers to § 1503's predecessor statute as requiring "specific intent." Once again, there is a fair amount of confusion regarding the source, definition, and application of this element.

There is also a great deal of confusion regarding the relationship between this specific intent requirement and the statutory requirement that the defendant act with a "corrupt" motive. Finally, the courts are not in agreement as to how to define a "corrupt" motive. *See generally* Eric J. Tamashasky, *The Lewis Carroll Offense: The Ever-Changing Meaning of "Corruptly" Within the Federal Criminal Law*, 31 J. Legis. 129 (2004). And that definition is critical because, as the following case illustrates, in some circuits the only thing that separates entirely lawful—and even laudable—activity from illegal obstruction is the corrupt motive of the defendant.

UNITED STATES v. CUETO
151 F.3d 620 (7th Cir.1998)

BAUER, CIRCUIT JUDGE.

...

Thomas Venezia owned B & H Vending/Ace Music Corporation ("B & H"), a vending and amusement business, and operated an illegal video gambling business through a pattern of racketeering activities and illegal gambling payouts, in violation of state and federal anti-gambling and racketeering laws. Venezia hired Amiel Cueto, an attorney, to represent him as well as to defend the tavern owners associated with B & H in the event of any arrests and/or criminal charges for their participation in the illegal gambling operation. In March of 1995, Venezia and B & H were indicted on federal racketeering charges, in addition to other related charges including illegal gambling.[11] Throughout the investigation and prior to Venezia's indictment, Cueto served as Venezia's lawyer and advisor. Cueto was not Venezia's attorney of record during the trial; nonetheless, the record indicates that Venezia continued to rely on Cueto's advice throughout the prosecution of the racketeering case.

On December 2, 1995, Venezia and B & H were convicted of racketeering, illegal gambling, and conspiracy arising out of the operation of the illegal gambling business. Seven months later, another federal grand jury returned a second indictment naming Cueto, Venezia, and Robert Romanik, a local public official and investigator who worked for Cueto and Venezia. ... This second indictment is the impetus for the current appeal.

To understand the context of the instant indictment, convictions, and appeal, we examine the nature and scope of Cueto's relationship with Venezia, his association with the illegal gambling operation, and his involvement in the investigation, indictment, and prosecution of Venezia, the illegal gambling operation, and the racketeering enterprise. In 1987, Venezia purchased a vending and amusement business, later known as B & H, which operated an illegal video gambling business for about eight years. B & H supplied video poker games to local bars in the metropolitan area of East St. Louis, Illinois, including a Veterans of Foreign Wars Post ("VFW") on Scott Air Force Base, and the tavern owners agreed to make illegal gambling payouts to its customers.[12] State agents believed the video games were being used for illegal gambling purposes, and beginning in 1992, the Illinois Liquor Control Commission ("ILCC") and the State Police initiated a joint investigation in St. Clair County, which targeted illegal gambling operations in Southern Illinois.

The ILCC has broad investigatory powers to supervise liquor licensees, and ILCC Agent Bonds Robinson worked on the task force and investigated the gambling operations in cooperation with the state police. Initially, Robinson worked in a non-undercover capacity as part of the state investigation to determine, in the course of routine liquor inspections, whether

---

[11] [Court's footnote 1:] The charges alleged that B & H supplied video poker games to various liquor-selling establishments on which the tavern owners provided illegal gambling payouts to its customers. B & H then reimbursed the tavern owners for the money they paid out on the video games and shared with the owners any profits the games earned.

[12] [Court's footnote 2:] Video games that swallow pocket change and "pay off" in game replays are unobjectionable; but if the owner of an establishment pays winners in cash or liquor, then it is a violation of Illinois anti-gambling laws.

any establishment was making illegal gambling payouts. Agents of the ILCC began to strictly enforce the gambling regulations and frequently visited the taverns to ensure compliance. Eventually, the FBI became interested in the state's investigation, and ultimately decided to use Robinson in a federal investigation of illegal gambling operations in St. Clair County, particularly Venezia's gambling operation. At some later point, Robinson assumed an undercover role for the FBI as a corrupt liquor agent in an attempt to gather evidence against Venezia and B & H. Soon thereafter, the state police raided the VFW Post, seized B & H's video poker games, and arrested two VFW employees for maintaining an illegal gambling establishment. After the raid, Venezia and B & H supplied additional video games to the VFW, which continued to provide its customers with illegal gambling payouts.

In an attempt to gather evidence, Robinson, who was present at the VFW raid, indicated that Venezia could avoid further interruptions of his illegal gambling operation if he were to offer a bribe to discourage the investigation and the interference, and he suggested to Venezia that they meet. Venezia consulted with Cueto, who instructed Venezia to meet with Tom Daley, one of his law partners at the time. In an attempt to portray Robinson as a dishonest agent, Daley reported to the ILCC that Robinson had solicited a bribe at the VFW. A meeting was then scheduled between Venezia and Robinson, who met at B & H corporate headquarters. Robinson taped the conversation at the FBI's request, and the tape was introduced into evidence in the racketeering case and at Cueto's trial. Soon after the meeting, the VFW was raided again; B & H video poker games were seized, and two employees were arrested. The ILCC issued an administrative violation to the VFW as well as a warning to remove the illegal gambling machines, otherwise, its liquor license would be revoked. Again, Venezia consulted with Cueto about the raids, the criminal charges, and the prosecutions, and they discussed available options and courses of action.

First, Cueto and Venezia drafted a letter, detailing Robinson's alleged "corrupt" conduct and accusing him of soliciting bribes, and delivered it to St. Clair County State's Attorney Robert Haida. Cueto also filed a complaint in state court against Robinson, in which Cueto alleged that Robinson was a corrupt agent. *See Venezia v. Robinson*, No. 92-CH 299. Cueto obtained a court order that required Robinson to appear for a hearing in *People v. Moore*, one of the gambling prosecutions arising from the VFW raid.[13] Pursuant to the order, Robinson appeared in state court, and Cueto immediately served him with a subpoena, which required him to appear in court within fifteen minutes for an injunction hearing in *Venezia v. Robinson*. Cueto had prepared a petition, requesting either a temporary restraining order or a preliminary and permanent injunction against alleged extortion and other vexation to prevent Robinson from interfering with the operation of Venezia's business. Robinson had not seen a copy of the complaint, had not been served with process, and was not represented by counsel.

At the hearing, Robinson's requests for an attorney were denied, and the state court judge permitted Cueto to question Robinson about the FBI's investigation (which at that point was still a covert operation) and the evidence it had obtained in the course of the investigation. Without permitting Robinson to put on a defense and without articulating any findings of fact or conclusions of law, the state court entered a preliminary injunction against Robinson, which indefinitely enjoined him from interfering with Venezia's business operations. Venezia then returned to the VFW, as well as other taverns affiliated with the gambling operation, to advise them that a state court judge had entered an injunction against Robinson and that he could no longer interfere with their establishments and the illegal gambling operation.

Notwithstanding the injunction and pursuant to instructions from the Director of ILCC to continue his routine liquor inspections, Robinson visited another establishment associated with B & H's gambling operation and discovered that the tavern owner was providing illegal gambling payouts on some of the video machines. Thereafter, Dorothy McCaw was arrested for operating and maintaining an illegal gambling establishment, and she signed a written confession for her participation in illegal gambling activities. Upon learning of the inspection

---

[13] [Court's footnote 5:] At trial, Cueto admitted that he obtained the court order for unlawful purposes and that he fraudulently used the court order to lure Robinson to court for the injunction proceedings.

and arrest, Venezia contacted Cueto, who arranged for Venezia and Romanik, the third individual charged in the instant indictment, to obtain another statement from McCaw. Cueto then drafted a letter to the ILCC, State's Attorney Haida, the Office of the United States Attorney for the Southern District of Illinois, and the FBI, claiming that his client was suffering damage as a result of Robinson's "unlawful" interference with the operation of Venezia's business and threatened that if the conduct continued, he would file suit against the ILCC, in addition to Robinson, for damages incurred. Without McCaw's knowledge, Cueto attached to that letter the statement she had given to Venezia and Romanik, which supported Cueto's allegations of interference. Cueto also filed a rule to show cause in state court, which described Robinson's violations of the injunction and requested the court to find him in contempt; McCaw's statement also was attached to the rule to show cause, again without her knowledge.

Represented by the Office of the United States Attorney for the Southern District of Illinois, Robinson filed a motion to remove the rule to show cause in *Venezia v. Robinson* to federal district court pursuant to 28 U.S.C. § 1442(a)(1). In the removal proceeding, the district court determined that Robinson had been working for the FBI under the control of a federal agent during the VFW raids, which therefore established federal jurisdiction. After removal, the district court dissolved the injunction and dismissed the complaint. Cueto filed an appeal in this court, challenging the dissolution of the injunction and the dismissal of the complaint. Recognizing that the injunction hearing had violated Robinson's rights to due process, we affirmed the district court's order. Cueto filed a petition for certiorari in the Supreme Court, which also was denied.

During the investigation, the record indicates that Cueto and Venezia developed more than a professional attorney-client relationship, entering into various financial transactions and business deals, some of which involved secret partnerships. A few examples include: (1) they purchased unimproved real estate, developed the real estate, built and managed a topless nightclub (Club Exposed), which operated some of B & H's illegal gambling machines; (2) Venezia and Cueto incorporated Millennium III, an asbestos removal company, and applied for and obtained a $600,000 line of credit to complete the purchase acquisition; and (3) Venezia purchased Cueto's office building and moved B & H corporate headquarters into it. The record demonstrates that in order to obtain financing, Venezia reported B & H as a principal asset on his financial statements and loan applications to establish the necessary credit he and Cueto needed to become joint borrowers on various loans. Moreover, the record indicates that the lender in the Millennium purchase relied upon Venezia's financial statement in its decision to loan the money for the acquisition.

About the time the Millennium purchase was finalized, state police and Robinson arrested George Vogt, a B & H customer, for gambling. At a hearing in the state's prosecution of Vogt, Robinson testified and Cueto cross-examined him. After the hearing, Cueto again approached State's Attorney Haida, provided him with the transcripts from the *Vogt* hearing, and urged Haida to indict Robinson for perjury. Thereafter, Haida commenced an investigation of Robinson's activities. Nothing came of Cueto's allegations of perjury, and the investigation ended without any charges being filed.

The investigation of Venezia and B & H began in early 1992, and the events discussed above occurred over a period of approximately three years. We briefly mentioned some of the initial business and financial dealings between Venezia and Cueto, but to avoid an even longer discussion of these background facts, we think it unnecessary to specifically discuss every financial transaction contained in the record except to point out that together Venezia and Cueto participated in various business transactions, in which millions of dollars exchanged hands to finance the purchases of various real estate interests and construction costs relating to various development projects, including certain gambling operations. The indictment specifically charged that Club Exposed, the nightclub owned by Venezia and Cueto, Millennium III, as well as other business transactions in which they were involved, depended upon the continued operation of B & H and the illegal gambling business to secure and to cover the various loans and debts they incurred in their financial ventures.

Even after Cueto became a business partner of Venezia and invested in various real estate and development projects with him, he continued to give Venezia legal advice. Although

Cueto was not an attorney of record, he participated in the preparation of Venezia's defense in the racketeering prosecution. Cueto continued to urge State's Attorney Haida to indict Robinson for perjury. He also contacted Congressman Jerry Costello, who owned an equal one-third partnership interest in a gambling development project with Cueto and Venezia, and asked the Congressman to contact Haida and to offer him a seat on the judiciary in exchange for Haida's recommendation that Cueto be appointed as the next State's Attorney. Cueto also began to publish a newspaper, the *East Side Review*, and authored an article in which he indicated that in the next election he intended to run for St. Clair County State's Attorney, and in the event he was elected, he would prosecute Robinson.[14]

In August of 1994, the government empaneled a grand jury to examine the evidence obtained in the FBI's investigation of Venezia and B & H, and the grand jury also initiated its own investigation of these allegations. In response, Cueto prepared and filed various motions to hinder the investigation and to discharge the grand jury, all of which were denied. Notwithstanding the defense tactics and delays, the grand jury indicted Venezia, among others; he was prosecuted, and ultimately, convicted for operating an illegal gambling enterprise, in addition to other related convictions.

Seven months after the racketeering convictions in July of 1996, another grand jury returned a separate nine count indictment against Cueto, Venezia, and Romanik. It is this indictment and the subsequent convictions on various counts of this indictment that are the subject of this appeal.[15] Count 1 of the indictment charged Cueto in a three-part conspiracy to defraud the United States, in violation of 18 U.S.C. § 371, alleging that he misused his office as an attorney and unlawfully and intentionally conspired with Venezia and Romanik to impede, impair, obstruct, and defeat the lawful function of the FBI, the grand jury, and the federal district court in connection with the investigation, indictment, and prosecution of Venezia, B & H, and the illegal gambling operation and racketeering enterprise. The indictment alleged that Cueto and Venezia's business relationship created Cueto's financial motive for his participation in the conspiracy, in which he endeavored to protect the illegal gambling enterprise and to maintain its continued operation in order to safeguard his personal financial interests....

Counts 2, 6, and 7 of the indictment charged obstruction of justice in violation of the omnibus clause of 18 U.S.C. § 1503, alleging that Cueto corruptly endeavored to use his office as an attorney to influence, obstruct, and impair the due administration of justice in various court proceedings in connection with the prosecution of Venezia, his illegal gambling operation, and the racketeering enterprise in *United States v. B & H Vending/Ace Music Corp. & Thomas Venezia, et al.* Specifically, Count 2 of the indictment charged that Cueto corruptly endeavored to influence the due administration of justice in *Venezia v. Robinson* by filing or causing to be filed pleadings in connection with the proceedings in federal district court, an appellate brief in this court, and a petition for certiorari to the United States Supreme Court. Count 6 involved Cueto's actions in regard to ILCC Agent Bonds Robinson, and the indictment charged that Cueto corruptly endeavored to obstruct the lawful function of the federal grand jury in his attempts to encourage and to persuade State's Attorney Haida to indict Robinson. Count 7 also focused on the filing of various court papers, and the indictment alleged that Cueto corruptly endeavored to influence, obstruct, and impede the proceedings in

---

[14] [Court's footnote 7:] In the *East Side Review*, Cueto also authored and published various articles in which he complained of prosecutorial misconduct in association with the racketeering case and attacked the integrity and reputations of various Assistant United States Attorneys involved in the indictment and prosecution of the racketeering case.

[15] [Court's footnote 8:] For purposes of this opinion, we only discuss the counts for which Cueto was convicted: Counts 1, 2, 6, and 7. Cueto was acquitted of the charges in Counts 3, 4, and 8. Romanik pleaded guilty to Count 5 of the instant indictment for lying to the grand jury. Pursuant to a deal made with the government, Venezia pleaded guilty to the crimes charged in the indictment and testified at Cueto's trial in exchange for the government's recommendation that his 15 year sentence in the illegal gambling and racketeering case be reduced to the lower end of the Sentencing Guidelines, which would result in a reduction from 15 years to 10 years.

federal district court by preparing and filing and urging defense counsel to prepare and file false pleadings and court papers in connection with the racketeering case.

After a jury trial, Cueto was convicted of the charges in Counts 1, 2, 6, and 7 and the district court ordered him to serve a prison term of 87 months, to be followed by two years of supervised release, and imposed monetary penalties. Cueto filed a timely notice of appeal. ...

Cueto asserts several arguments with respect to his convictions on Counts 2, 6, and 7 for obstruction of justice, contending that the omnibus clause of § 1503 is unconstitutionally vague as applied to the conduct charged in the indictment and, alternatively, that the evidence established at trial on these counts is insufficient to support his convictions. We address each argument in turn and begin with the constitutional challenges. Cueto argues that "much of what lawyers *do*—are attempts to influence the justice system," and that the omnibus clause of § 1503 was not intended to apply to the type of conduct charged in the indictment. ...

"[I]n determining the scope of a statute, one is to look first at its language. If the language is unambiguous, ordinarily it is to be regarded as conclusive unless there is "'a clearly expressed legislative intent to the contrary.'" The omnibus clause of § 1503 is a catch-all provision .... This clause was intended to ensure that criminals could not circumvent the statute's purpose "by devising novel and creative schemes that would interfere with the administration of justice but would nonetheless fall outside the scope of § 1503's specific prohibitions." ...

Cueto also contends that the vagueness problems are exacerbated by this court's broad construction of the term "corruptly," arguing that it fails to provide meaningful and adequate notice as to what conduct is proscribed by the statute. The Seventh Circuit has approved a jury instruction which articulates a definition for the term "corruptly," and the district court judge included this definition in its instructions to the jury:

> Corruptly means to act with the purpose of obstructing justice. *The United States is not required to prove that the defendant's only or even main purpose was to obstruct the due administration of justice.* The government only has to establish that the defendant *should have reasonably seen that the natural and probable consequences of his acts was the obstruction of justice.* Intent may be inferred from all of the surrounding facts and circumstances. *Any act, by any party, whether lawful or unlawful on its face, may violate Section 1503, if performed with a corrupt motive.*[16]

The mere fact that a term "covers a broad spectrum of conduct" does not render it vague, and the requirement that a statute must give fair notice as to what conduct is proscribed "cannot be used as a shield by one who is already bent on serious wrongdoing."

There is little case authority directly on point to consider whether an attorney acting in his professional capacity could be criminally liable under the omnibus clause of § 1503 for traditional litigation-related conduct that results in an obstruction of justice. "Correct application of Section 1503 thus requires, in a very real sense, that the factfinder discern—by direct evidence or from inference—the motive which led an individual to perform particular actions .... 'Intent may make any otherwise innocent act criminal, if it is a step in a plot.'" Therefore, it is not the means employed by the defendant that are specifically prohibited by the statute; instead, it is the defendant's corrupt endeavor which motivated the action. Otherwise lawful conduct, even acts undertaken by an attorney in the course of representing a client, can transgress § 1503 if employed with the corrupt intent to accomplish that which the statute forbids. *See* [*United States v. Cintolo*, 818 F.2d 980, 992 (1st Cir.1987)] ("means, though lawful in themselves, can cross the line of illegality if (i) employed with a corrupt motive, (ii) to hinder the due administration of justice, so long as (iii) the means have the capacity to obstruct").

We are not persuaded by Cueto's constitutional challenges, and his focus is misplaced. The government's theory of prosecution is predicated on the fact that Cueto held a personal

---

[16] [Ed.:] Italicization has been added to underscore the importance of this passage, both to the opinion and for purposes of the notes following this case.

financial interest in protecting the illegal gambling enterprise, which formed the requisite corrupt intent for his conduct to qualify as violations of the statute.[17] Cueto focuses entirely on the legality of his conduct, and not the requisite criminal intent proscribed by § 1503. It is undisputed that an attorney may use any *lawful* means to defend his client, and there is no risk of criminal liability if those means employed by the attorney in his endeavors to represent his client remain within the scope of lawful conduct. However, it is the corrupt endeavor to protect the illegal gambling operation and to safeguard his own financial interest, which motivated Cueto's otherwise legal conduct, that separates his conduct from that which is legal.

Even though courts may be hesitant, with good reason and caution, to include traditional litigation-related conduct within the scope of § 1503, the omnibus clause has been interpreted broadly in accordance with congressional intent to promote the due administration of justice and to prevent the miscarriage of justice, and an individual's status as an attorney engaged in litigation-related conduct does not provide protection from prosecution for criminal conduct. Cueto's arguments have no merit. As a lawyer, he possessed a heightened awareness of the law and its scope, and he cannot claim lack of fair notice as to what conduct is proscribed by § 1503 to shield himself from criminal liability, particularly when he was already "bent on serious wrongdoing." More so than an ordinary individual, an attorney, in particular a criminal defense attorney, has a sophisticated understanding of the type of conduct that constitutes criminal violations of the law. There is a discernable difference between an honest lawyer who unintentionally submits a false statement to the court and an attorney with specific corrupt intentions who files papers in bad faith knowing that they contain false representations and/or inaccurate facts in an attempt to hinder judicial proceedings. It is true that, to a certain extent, a lawyer's conduct influences judicial proceedings, or at least attempts to affect the outcome of the proceedings. However, that influence stems from a lawyer's attempt to advocate his client's interests *within the scope of the law*. It is the "corrupt endeavor" to influence the due administration of justice that is the heart of the offense, and Cueto's personal financial interest is the heart of his corrupt motive.

An amicus brief submitted by the National Association of Criminal Defense Lawyers ("Association") also questions the proper scope of the omnibus clause of § 1503, and the Association articulates its fears that if we affirm Cueto's convictions, criminal defense attorneys will be subject to future prosecutions not only for actual misconduct, but also for apparent and inadvertent wrongdoing, notwithstanding a lawyer's good faith advocacy. The Association believes that this type of sweeping prosecution will sufficiently chill vigorous advocacy and eventually destroy the delicate balance between prosecution and defense which is necessary to maintain the effective operation of the criminal justice system. Although the Association discusses valid policy concerns and asserts legitimate arguments, some of which we generally agree with, we are also concerned with the flipside of its argument. If lawyers are not punished for their criminal conduct and corrupt endeavors to manipulate the administration of justice, the result would be the same: the weakening of an ethical adversarial system and the undermining of just administration of the law. We have the responsibility to ensure that the integrity of the criminal justice system is maintained and that protection includes granting to both the prosecution and the defense flexibility and "discretion in the conduct of the trial and the presentation of evidence," in addition to enforcing mechanisms of punishment, which necessarily include criminal prosecution, to prevent abuses of the system.

We have carefully examined the fears articulated by the National Association of Criminal Defense Lawyers, in addition to the arguments put forth by the defendant, that a decision upholding the application of the omnibus clause of § 1503 to litigation-related conduct may

---

[17] [Court's footnote 10:] This theory of prosecution brings us some pause. With the government's emphasis on Cueto's involvement in Venezia's illegal gambling operation and the racketeering enterprise, we are puzzled why the government did not indict and prosecute Cueto in the underlying racketeering case for his participation in the illegal gambling operation. Although the government's decision not to prosecute Cueto in the previous case is fundamentally inconsequential to the instant appeal, we are concerned about the relationship between the instant appeal and the underlying prosecution of the gambling operation and the racketeering enterprise.

deter or somehow chill the criminal defense lawyers in zealous advocacy, and we find those concerns to be exaggerated, at least as considered in light of the facts in the present case. Although we appreciate that it is of significant importance to avoid chilling vigorous advocacy and to maintain the balance of effective representation, we also recognize that a lawyer's misconduct and criminal acts are not absolutely immune from prosecution. We cannot ignore Cueto's corrupt endeavors to manipulate the administration of justice and his clear criminal violations of the law. As the First Circuit recognized in *Cintolo*:

> Nothing in the caselaw, fairly read, suggests that lawyers should be plucked gently from the maddening crowd and sheltered from the rigors of 18 U.S.C. § 1503 in the manner urged by appellant and by the amici. Nor is there sufficient public policy justification favoring such a result. To the contrary, the overriding public policy interest is that "[t]he attorney-client relationship cannot ... be used to shield or promote illegitimate acts ...." "[A]ttorneys, just like all other persons, ... are not above the law and are subject to its full application under appropriate circumstances."

Accordingly, we conclude that the omnibus clause of § 1503 may be used to prosecute a lawyer's litigation-related criminality and that neither the omnibus clause of § 1503 nor this court's construction of the term "corruptly" is unconstitutionally vague as applied to the conduct charged in the indictment for which Cueto was convicted.

We now turn to Cueto's argument that his convictions on the obstruction of justice counts were not supported by sufficient evidence. Cueto's task is a formidable one, and an examination of the record illuminates that the evidence presented in this case overwhelmingly supports the jury's verdict. ...

Again the focus of Cueto's argument is misplaced; he argues that his conduct does not fall within the scope of the omnibus clause of § 1503 and that the government presented insufficient evidence to demonstrate his guilt. Cueto, however, fails to address the essence of the government's allegations and, ultimately, the basis for his convictions; it is his corrupt endeavor to obstruct the administration of justice that transforms his traditional litigation-related conduct into criminal violations of the law. ... [T]he record adequately supports the conclusion that Cueto's conduct, though nominally litigation-related conduct on behalf of his client, was undertaken with the corrupt intent to protect Venezia, Venezia's associates, and his business from criminal prosecution and to safeguard his personal financial interest in the illegal gambling operation, whatever the costs and consequences to the due administration of justice.

The charges in Count 2 of the indictment included allegations of a corrupt endeavor to obstruct the due administration of justice in *Venezia v. Robinson* by filing pleadings in federal district court and a continued attempt to hinder the proceedings by filing an appeal in this court and a petition for certiorari in the United States Supreme Court. The evidence demonstrates that Cueto successfully exposed the FBI's investigation, uncovered the evidence it had gathered, obtained the injunction against Robinson, and continued to file frivolous appeals after the district court dismissed the injunction and the complaint. Government agents, in fact, testified that the investigation was disrupted and that Cueto "blew the lid off the ongoing investigation." The jury was amply justified in concluding that Cueto's repeated filings were motivated by his attempt to protect his client from prosecution and to safeguard his financial interest. Cueto's actions may qualify as traditional litigation-related conduct in form, but not in substance, and the evidence presented at trial demonstrates that Cueto clearly intended and corruptly endeavored to obstruct the due administration of justice in *Venezia v. Robinson*.

Similar to Count 2, Count 7 includes allegations of preparing and filing and causing defense counsel to prepare and file false pleadings and other court papers; the indictment specifically charged Cueto with encouraging defense counsel in the racketeering case to file false motions and pleadings for the purpose of impeding and obstructing the administration of justice in that case. We have no doubt that Cueto in fact intended to interfere with the investigation, attempted to delay the indictment, and endeavored to obstruct the proceedings in federal district court in connection with the prosecution of Venezia. We simply are not dealing with non-corrupt, legitimate involvement in the preparation of Venezia's (and his co-defendants') defense. Nor are we dealing with inadvertent interference. From the evidence presented at trial, the jury was amply justified in concluding without a doubt that Cueto corruptly endeavored to obstruct the district court's proceedings in the gambling and racketeering prosecution. ...

Whatever the contours of the line between traditional lawyering and criminal conduct, they must inevitably be drawn case-by-case. We refuse to accept the notion that lawyers may do anything, including violating the law, to zealously advocate their clients' interests and then avoid criminal prosecution by claiming that they were "just doing their job." As the First Circuit stated in *Cintolo*, "[w]e refuse to chip some sort of special exception for lawyers into the brickwork of § 1503." We respect the importance of allowing defense counsel to perform legitimate activities without hindrance and recognize the potential dangers that could arise if prosecutors were permitted to inquire into the motives of criminal defense attorneys ad hoc. This case, however, does not create that avenue of inquiry; our conclusion is limited to the specific facts of this case. Viewing the facts and inferences most favorably to the government, as we are required to do, there was ample basis for the jury to find that Cueto corruptly endeavored to obstruct the due administration of justice. The jury was justified in concluding that Cueto had the requisite knowledge of the FBI's investigation of Venezia, the grand jury's inquiry, and the district court's proceedings and then acted in a manner that had the natural and probable effect of interfering with the lawful function of those governmental entities and the due administration of justice. His role as a defense attorney did not insulate him from the criminal consequences of his corruptly-motivated actions. Accordingly, we affirm Cueto's convictions on Counts 2, 6, and 7....

Notes

1. Judges W. Fletcher and Reinhardt, concurring in *United States v. Bond*, 784 F.3d 582 (9th Cir. 2015) (*en banc*) argued that the "corrupt" element of § 1503 does "not describe a state of mind. Rather, it describes a forbidden means of influencing, obstructing, or impeding the due administration of justice." *Id.* at 595 (Fletcher, J., concurring in the judgment). Judge Fletcher believes it means "by bribery." *See supra* Note 2 following *Aguilar*. This is a novel position, judging from the extant case law. Are you persuaded?

2. Just how far does the *Cueto* court's reasoning go? If a lawyer advises a client, or even a non-client, to assert a valid privilege—say, his or her right against self-incrimination—may that lawyer be indicted for obstruction? *See* United States v. Cintolo, 818 F.2d 980, 992 (1st Cir. 1987) (yes if done with a corrupt motive); United States v. Cioffi, 493 F.2d 1111, 1119 (2d Cir. 1974) (same); *cf.* United States v. Doss, 630 F.3d 1181 (9th Cir. 2011) (under § 1512, no but outlining split on the subject). What if defense counsel tells the prosecutor that his client is innocent because the client lacks the requisite knowledge or intent to commit the crime under investigation. If this later turns out to be erroneous information, may the prosecutor pursue the lawyer and/or the client? What if the target of a criminal investigation were to deny any wrongdoing and provide friends, family, and business associates with a false impression of what actually transpired. Would this constitute obstruction? Again, the answer may depend on the existence of a "corrupt" motive (assuming the defendant's associates' nexus to the investigation). Can we trust prosecutors and ultimately juries to be able to dispassionately assess whether such a "corrupt motive" exists? What is the possibility here for prosecutorial abuse or for a chilling of the defense function?

3. *Definition of "Corrupt" Motive.* Given the centrality of the term "corrupt" in separating entirely legal activity from activity that will warrant jail time, how satisfying is the definition of that term offered? Judging by the case law, "corruptly" is word of many meanings. *See, e.g.,* Eric J. Tamashasky, *The Lewis Carroll Offense: The Ever-Changing Meaning of "Corruptly" Within the Federal Criminal Code*, 31 J. Legis. 129 (2004); Daniel A. Shtob, *Corruption of a Term: The Problematic Nature of 18 U.S.C. § 1512(c), the New Federal Obstruction of Justice Provision*, 57 Vand. L. Rev. 1429 (2004).

Justice Scalia approved one definition in his dissent in *Aguilar*: "'An act is done corruptly if it's done voluntarily and intentionally to bring about either an unlawful result or a lawful result by some unlawful method, with a hope or expectation of either financial gain or other benefit to oneself or a benefit of another person.'" Does this definition's emphasis on financial gain or other benefit make it more apposite to public corruption cases than many obstruction cases? As the Supreme Court notes in *Arthur Andersen LLP v. United States, infra*, the Fifth Circuit Pattern Jury Instructions define "corruptly" for purposes of § 1503 as "knowingly and dishonestly, with the specific intent to subvert or undermine the integrity" of a proceeding. In *Andersen*, the Supreme Court also (for purposes of determining what "knowingly ... corruptly" meant in § 1512) noted that the dictionary defines "corrupt" and "corruptly" as normally associated with "wrongful, immoral, depraved, or evil." Probably the most common ways of expressing the meaning of "corruptly" under § 1503 is "acting with an improper motive." *See Cintolo*, 818 F.2d at 990-91; United States v. Fasolino, 586 F.2d 939, 941 (2d Cir.1978). Other popular formulations are (the circular) acting "with a corrupt motive," *Brenson*, 104 F.3d at 1278, or (the somewhat vague) with an "evil or wicked purpose," *see* United States v. Haas, 583 F.2d 216, 220 (5th Cir. 1978); Joseph V. DeMarco, Note, *A Funny Thing Happened on the Way to the Courthouse: Mens Rea, Document Destruction, and the Federal Obstruction of Justice Statute*, 67 N.Y.U. L. Rev. 570, 579 n.58 (1992).

4. Should otherwise entirely legal activities be transformed into criminal acts by a "corrupt" motive? Consider the following:

> The "corrupt" *mens rea* required under § 1503 and other obstruction statutes is nothing more than proof of an "evil" or "improper" *motive* and thus is a throw-back that requires policing. … [A]ncient notions of *mens rea* turned on "evil" motives; the modern conception, however, is that "motives" as elements should be abandoned in favor of proof of specific states of mind—such as "knowledge" or "purpose." As Jerome Hall put it in 1960, "hardly any part of penal law is more definitely settled than that motive is irrelevant" to criminal liability. [Jerome Hall, General Principles of Criminal Law 88 (2d ed. 1960).] Scholars recently have taken aim at Hall's statement and the tradition it reflects, both as a descriptive and as a normative matter. And certainly the scholars are correct that Hall's much-quoted statement is overinclusive. Thus, motive has long been relevant as *evidence* to prove matters such as intent, has traditionally been part of prosecutors' *charging* choices, and often has often been used in judges' *sentencing* determinations. Legislators have recently resurrected "motive" crimes as well, making motive an element of an offense in, for example, hate crimes statutes.
>
> Still, there remains a universal consensus that while "motive" may sometimes excuse or justify conduct that is otherwise criminal, or it may make more blameworthy that which is already criminally culpable behavior, it may *not* make a crime of an innocent act. "As a general rule, no act otherwise lawful becomes criminal because done with a bad motive. ..." A "bad" act must attend a corrupt motive for a variety of good reasons. "One basic premise of Anglo-American criminal law is that no crime can be committed by bad thoughts alone" and that basic premise applies in the obstruction context just as elsewhere. [Wayne R. LaFave, Criminal Law 303 (4th ed. 2003). First Amendment concerns play a part, as does the difficulty of "proving" thoughts unmoored from action and distinguishing "a fixed intent from mere daydream and fantasy." [*Id.* at 304.] Professor LaFave emphasizes "the notion that the criminal law should not be so broadly defined to reach those who entertain criminal schemes but never let their thoughts govern their conduct." [*Id.*]
>
> In the context of statutes that do not require proof of a specific type of obviously criminal "act" (such as killing, raping, or the like), this prohibition has another rationale. "[I]n morality there is by no means agreement on just what sort of good motives justify what sort of wrongdoing" and what sort of "improper" motives might render an innocent act criminal. While we trust our elected representatives to consider, outside of specific cases, whether particular motives should be a crime, modern legislatures have generally

done so with reasonable specificity. That is, we know what *types* of motives are "improper"—such as harming others because of their race, sex, or ethnicity. When confronted with the question of what constitutes a "corrupt" motive in the obstruction context, however, juries and judges are given no such guidance. And where all that stands between an otherwise legal act and incarceration is a "corrupt" motive, this lack of guidance constitutes an invitation to arbitrary, uneven, and potentially very unjust results depending on the "ethical" predispositions of the persons called upon to decide a given case. This is especially true when what is at issue is defense counsel's actions in defending his client. Many jurors will not understand, or if they do, sympathize with, the defense imperative of zealous advocacy even for a guilty-as-sin client. ...

Courts do not explain why it is appropriate to read this statute to violate a foundational rule of criminal law. Nothing on the face of the statute would seem to *require* a reading that allows a "corrupt" motive to render otherwise innocent conduct—like filing legal papers or advising one's client to claim his constitutional rights—criminal. It may be that judges have relied upon their moral intuitions rather than their criminal-law learning. In moral theory,

> although a good motive does not excuse a bad intention, a bad ulterior motive does render an otherwise good action impermissible. In contrast, the orthodox legal doctrine holds that motives in general are irrelevant, be they good or bad. (Thus an executioner does not do wrong in executing a man for motives of personal vengeance).

[Whitley R.P. Kaufman, *Motive, Intention, and Morality in the Criminal* Law, 28 Crim. Just. Rev. 317, 334 (2003).] While judges' judgments may be correct as a matter of moral theory, it is not their role to embody that morality in law; that job is emphatically the province of the legislature. ...

How can it be that Congress has invited judges and juries to delve into the defendant's psychology to determine his *motive* and to apply their own notions of what is "evil" or "improper" to judge his actions? How can it be that judges have decided that an "evil" or "improper" motive can convert an otherwise blameless act into something that warrants jail time? How can it be that courts are unable to arrive at a uniform and reasonably specific meaning for the word "corruptly" in § 1503 given that this one word separates entirely legal conduct from conduct that could send one away for ten years? And why *is* this a ten-year count, anyway? The same offense was punishable by a maximum of *three months* in 1892 and five years in 2005—is this incarceration inflation based on any rational judgment? My belief is that there are no satisfactory answers to these questions, and that the American public deserves better.

Julie O'Sullivan, *The Federal Criminal "Code" Is a Disgrace: Obstruction Statutes as Case Study*, 96 J. Crim. L. & Criminology 643, 698-702 (2006). *But see* Eric J. Tamashasky, *supra*, 31 J. Legis. at 129.

5. Daniel J. Hemel and Prof. Eric A. Posner have asked:

> Can a president be held criminally liable for obstruction of justice? That question took on new urgency in May 2017 after President Donald Trump fired James Comey as director of the Federal Bureau of Investigation (FBI). While the president cited Deputy Attorney General Rod Rosenstein's determination that Comey had mishandled the investigation into Hillary Clinton's disclosure of classified emails, Trump later admitted in an interview that he "was going to fire [Comey] regardless of the recommendation." Because Trump had also signaled to Comey that he was unhappy with the FBI's investigation of former National Security Advisor Michael Flynn, speculation arose that Trump had fired Comey to punish him for failing to drop the investigation of Flynn. This in turn sparked allegations that Trump had committed the crime of obstruction of justice,

which consists of interference with investigations, prosecutions, and other law enforcement actions with "corrupt" intent.

Daniel J. Hemel & Prof. Eric A. Posner, *Presidential Obstruction of Justice*, 106 Ca. L. Rev. 1277, 1278 (2018). Based (only) on press reports, Special Counsel Robert Mueller's office allegedly has been investigating the President for obstruction. Again, press reports speculate that additional fodder for such a charge may flow from the President's alleged desire to fire his Attorney General, Jeff Sessions, for allowing the Russian investigation to continue, alleged discussions about firing the Special Counsel, and alleged discussions about potential pardons for possible witnesses (such as retired Lt. General Flynn and Paul Manafort).

     President Trump is not the first president to be accused of obstruction of justice. The first article of impeachment against President Richard Nixon, which was adopted by the House Judiciary Committee in 1974, accused him of obstructing the investigation into the Watergate burglary by interfering with an FBI investigation. The article also mentioned interference with the investigation by the Watergate special prosecutor, whose firing was ordered by Nixon. High-ranking Reagan administration officials were indicted on obstruction of justice charges related to the Iran-Contra affair, and several of President Reagan's opponents suggested that he may have committed obstruction as well (though those allegations were never proven). After President George H.W. Bush pardoned former Defense Secretary Caspar Weinberger, who was one of the Reagan administration officials charged with obstruction in the Iran-Contra scandal, Bush was accused of obstructing the investigation into his own role in the scandal. The House impeached President Bill Clinton in 1998, based in part on obstruction of justice. The allegations against Clinton included charges that he had lied and withheld evidence in a civil action and lied to a grand jury. Obstruction of justice controversies also entangled the George W. Bush administration in the wake of firings of US attorneys, and the onetime chief of staff to Vice President Dick Cheney was convicted of obstruction. Amazingly, six of the last nine presidents, or their top aides, were embroiled in obstruction of justice scandals. The law of obstruction of justice has evolved into a major check on presidential power, without anyone noticing it.

     But the claim that the president can commit such a crime faces a powerful objection rooted in the Constitution. Obstruction of justice laws are normally applied to private citizens—those who bribe jurors, hide evidence from the police, or lie to investigators. The president is the head of the executive branch and therefore also the head of federal law enforcement. He can fire the FBI director, the attorney general, or any other principal officer in the executive branch who fails to maintain his confidence. If President Trump can fire an FBI director merely for displeasing him, why can't he fire an FBI director who pursues an investigation that the president wants shut down?

Id. at 1278-79. For a detailed discussion of the vulnerability of the President to an obstruction charge, see Barry H. Berke, Noah Bookbinder, & Norman L. Eisen, *Presidential Obstruction of Justice: The Case of Donald J. Trump*, Brookings Governance Studies (Oct. 10, 2017).

    6. *The Relationship between Corrupt Motive and Specific Intent.* Courts often conflate corrupt motive and specific intent—as did the *Cueto* jury instructions. *See also* United States v. Quattrone, 441 F.3d 153 (2d Cir. 2006) (stating that the "corrupt endeavor" element requires "a wrongful intent or improper motive to interfere with an agency proceeding" under § 1505). But they are in fact independent requirements. As Eric J. Tamashasky explains:

    … Justice Scalia agreed that a "corrupt" act is "[a]n act done with an intent to give some advantage inconsistent with official duty and the rights of others…." This definition comports with the traditional common law understanding and the way in which most prosecutions are brought. Justice Scalia went further and promulgated a classic mistake common among the circuits. He added, "Acts specifically intended to 'influence, obstruct, or impede, the due administration of justice' are obviously wrongful, just as they are necessarily 'corrupt.'" Under the statute, however, not all acts specifically intended to influence, obstruct, or impede are unlawful, but only those done "corruptly." While some cases conclude that acts intended to obstruct or impede the due administration of justice are tantamount to "corrupt" actions, the inclusion of "influence" makes the statement overbroad. Moreover, actions intended to "obstruct" justice need not be "necessarily corrupt." ... If the prohibited conduct is "corruptly endeavoring to impede or obstruct the due administration of justice," a construction of "corruptly" to mean "to endeavor to impede and obstruct" renders the term "corruptly" surplusage.

Tamashasky, *supra*, 31 J. Legis. at 130-32.

7. *What Does One Have to Specifically Intend?* Although the federal courts acknowledge that obstruction is a specific intent crime, there is some confusion regarding just *what* the defendant must specifically intend. *See* United States v. LaRouche Campaign, 695 F.Supp. 1265, 1270-74 (D.Mass. 1988). Does the defendant have to do the obstructive act with a specific intent *to obstruct justice*? Or will it suffice that the defendant specifically intended *to engage in the conduct alleged to be obstructive* and *should have reasonably foreseen that the natural and probable consequences of his actions* would be the obstruction of justice?

Although there is support in the caselaw for both propositions, the latter seems to be in ascendancy. *See* DeMarco, *supra*, 67 N.Y.U. L. Rev. at 576-84. The instruction in the *Cueto* case is typical of that used in jurisdictions that ascribe to the latter view. *See also* United States v. Brenson, 104 F.3d 1267, 1277-78 (11th Cir. 1997). *But see* United States v. Rasheed, 663 F.2d 843, 852 (9th Cir. 1981) ("We hold that the word 'corruptly' as used in the statute means that the act must be done with the purpose of obstructing justice").

It was in reliance on instructions such as that employed in *Cueto* that Justice Scalia argued in *Aguilar* that the Court's "nexus" requirement—which requires that the defendant's activity have the "natural and probable effect" of interfering with the due administration of justice—is correctly viewed as a means of proving intent, not an independent evidentiary requirement. Should this still be regarded as good law? The *Aguilar* majority certainly implied in its response to Justice Scalia's dissent its belief that the intent to obstruct may be present even where the requisite "nexus" is absent, thus evidencing its belief that the two proof requirements are separate. What difference does any of this make? *See also Arthur Andersen, LLP v. United States, infra.* Consider the following:

> ... The "specific intent" terminology was applied by the Supreme Court to this statute in 1893. Since that time, this term has become outmoded: it (and its cognate, "general intent") do not appear in the code and have been rejected by the Supreme Court as outdated and confusing. Yet, because of the *Pettibone* case, courts of appeals are still trying to apply this element in § 1503 cases, with (in my view) decidedly mixed results. ...
>
> Today's statutes generally include some type of express *mens rea* element, but this is a modern development. The historical meaning of "specific" versus "general" intent reflects the fact that statutes formerly did not specify the mental state necessary to be proved. Thus, "general intent" meant that the crime required a *mens rea* in the culpability sense of a blameworthy state of mind. "Specific intent" was a designation reserved for those offenses that required proof of a particular, additional state of mind [(i.e., a special motive for the conduct)]. ...
>
> In this context, then, it would appear that a specific intent to obstruct would mean that government must prove that the defendant's *purpose* was to obstruct justice—that was his special motive for acting. An apparent majority of federal courts hold, however, that a defendant can be said to have acted with a specific intent to obstruct when he specifically intended to engage in the conduct alleged to be obstructive and he should have reasonably foreseen that the natural and probable consequences of his actions would be the obstruction of justice. This means that most federal courts read the "specific intent to obstruct" element to be satisfied by proof that the defendant acted intentionally in, for example, destroying documents but *negligently* with respect to the possibility that the destruction of those documents would obstruct justice.

Substituting a negligence ("reasonably foreseeable") standard for a specific intent to obstruct requirement does not make sense. Considered together with the fact that criminal liability founded on negligence is generally only reserved for the most severe harms (such as negligent manslaughter), and that traditional notions of "specific intent" reflect the highest, not the lowest, form of culpable mental states, the majority rule seems particularly misguided. And this is not a quibble. Such a reading permits the criminal sanction to be applied to all kinds of nonculpable conduct: "[i]t is easy to imagine conduct which could foreseeably result in obstruction of justice but which lacks any sort of criminal culpability. For example, employees often ignore office memoranda; people carelessly—sometimes even recklessly—fail to preserve evidence. Section 1503 was not meant to criminalize such conduct." Judges, in relying on a misconstruction of the meaning of "specific intent," have significantly increased the power of prosecutors to pick and choose among potential defendants—only some of whom could be deemed to have been truly culpable. Why would courts wish to water down the intent to obstruct requirement, and empower prosecutors, in this way?

As it turns out, this instruction is useful to the government where the government chooses to pursue wrongful conduct as obstruction but the heart of the harm involved is something other than obstruction—usually simple fraud. Rather than forcing prosecutors to proceed on a fraud theory to prosecute this clearly wrongful activity, however, judges have acceded to prosecutors' reliance on inapposite statutes. In so doing, they have responded to bad facts by making bad law, giving prosecutors a *mens rea* instruction that can be used to prosecute the culpable *and* the not culpable.

For example, in *United States v. Neiswender*, shortly after the beginning of the criminal trial of former Maryland Governor Marvin Mandel, defendant Neiswender contacted Mandel's defense attorney and told the attorney that he had a contact with a corrupt juror and could "guarantee" an acquittal of Mandel if "proper financial arrangements were made." [590 F.2d 1269, 1270 (4th Cir. 1979).] Defense counsel promptly informed the court and prosecutor but no corrupt juror was ever identified. Neiswender, indicted for obstruction under § 1503, argued that his primary intent was to defraud, not to obstruct. He contended that his actual motivation "was directly at odds with any design to obstruct justice since a guilty verdict would have revealed Neiswender's fraud. It was in his best interests for [Mandel's defense counsel to continue] to press hard in his efforts to obtain an acquittal."

The Fourth Circuit, however, upheld the conviction, ruling that "a defendant who intentionally undertakes an act or attempts to effectuate an arrangement, the reasonably foreseeable consequence of which is to obstruct justice, violates § 1503 even if his hope is that the judicial machinery will not be seriously impaired." The court reasoned that had Neiswender convinced defense counsel that Neiswender had a juror under his control and induced defense counsel to participate in the scheme, the natural consequence would have been to reduce defense counsel's efforts in defending his client. Presumably most people would agree that this conduct is harmful—particularly the disturbing number of *Neiswender*-type cases that involve fraud by attorneys on criminal defendants involving false offers by counsel to pay off criminal justice officials to secure favorable treatment for the defendants. But they are not first and foremost the type of *purposeful* obstructive activity that is supposed to be pursued under § 1503. To allow the government to salvage these cases against (I concede) people who are committing a crime (just not obstruction) by watering down the "specific intent" instruction, courts are inviting overbroad and irresponsible applications of the statute.

O'Sullivan, *supra*, 96 J. Crim. L. & Criminology at 687–90.

B. OBSTRUCTION OF PROCEEDINGS BEFORE CONGRESS AND FEDERAL AGENCIES UNDER 18 U.S.C. § 1505

1. *Elements.* Section 1505 is the obstruction statute specifically addressed to obstruction of administrative agency proceedings and congressional inquiries. Section 1505 cases are relatively rare, at least in comparison to the frequency with which sections 1503 and 1512 are employed. The statute reads, in relevant part:

> Whoever corruptly, or by threats or force, or by threatening letter or communication influences, obstructs, or impedes or endeavors to influence, obstruct, or impede the due and proper administration of the law under which any pending proceeding is being had before any department or agency of the United States, or the due and proper exercise of the power of inquiry under which any inquiry or investigation is being had by either House, or any committee of either House or any joint committee of Congress [] shall be fined under this title or imprisoned not more than five years, or both.

The requisites for a conviction under § 1505 are that the defendant: (1) knowing that there is a proceeding pending before a department or agency of the United States or an inquiry or investigation being before either House, any committee of either House, or a joint committee of the Congress; (2) corruptly; (3) endeavors; (4) to influence, obstruct, or impede the "due and proper administration of the law" under which the pending agency proceeding is being had, or "the due and proper exercise of the power" of the congressional inquiry. *See* United States v. Johnson, 71 F.3d 139, (4th Cir. 1995) (stating elements for a congressional case); United States v. Price, 951 F.2d 1028, 1031 (9th Cir. 1991) (stating elements for an agency case); *see also* United States v. Rainey, 757 F.3d 234 (5th Cir. 2014) (statute applies to obstruction of congressional subcommittees); United States v. Mitchell, 877 F.2d 294 (4th Cir. 1989) (discussing meaning of "due and proper exercise of the power of inquiry" requirement).

This statute is very similar in structure to § 1503. How do they compare in terms of elements and coverage? *See* Chart 1, appended to this Chapter.

2. *Proceeding.* The term "proceeding" for purposes of § 1505 is very broad. Despite the statutory requirement that the defendant corruptly obstruct "the due and proper administration of the law under which any pending proceeding is being had," the reach of § 1505 is not confined to proceedings that are "juridical or administrative in nature." United States v. Fruchtman, 421 F.2d 1019, 1921 (6th Cir. 1970). Courts have instead held that the statute encompasses both the investigative and adjudicative functions of a department or agency. *See, e.g., id.* Further, the "investigative" aspect of a "proceeding" has been interpreted to include most agency activity conducted before an investigation is formally commenced. "[E]ven if the matter investigated will ultimately be tried before a criminal court, obstruction of agency investigations may be prosecutable under § 1505." *Thirty-Third Annual Survey of White Collar Crime, Obstruction of Justice,* 55 Am. Crim. L. Rev. 1497, 1515 (2018); *see also* United States v. Schwartz, 924 F.2d 410, 423 (2d Cir. 1991).

3. *"Nexus" Requirement?* Must the government demonstrate an *Aguilar* "nexus" in a § 1505 case? *See* United States v. Quattrone, 441 F.3d 153, 174 (2d Cir. 2006) (assuming without discussion that the nexus requirement applies). Whether the *Aguilar* "nexus" requirement extends to § 1505 may depend upon which element the *Aguilar* Court read the "nexus" into for purposes of § 1503. Thus, if it is a part of the "due administration of justice" element, it may not apply; if the nexus requirement inheres in the "corruptly" element, however, it may well apply. Again, the Supreme Court in *Arthur Andersen LLP v. United States,* reproduced *infra,* applied its *Aguilar* "nexus" test to § 1512. In so doing, it seemed to characterize the "nexus" requirement as originating in the intent requirement—presumably inhering in the word "corrupt"—rather than the "due administration of justice" element.

4. *"Corruptly."* In 1990, a jury convicted Admiral John Poindexter, President Reagan's National Security Advisor, *inter alia*, on two counts of obstruction of justice in violation of § 1505 for making false and/or misleading statements to congressional committees, participating in the preparation of a false chronology, deleting information from his computer, and arranging a meeting with members of Congress at which Oliver North gave false statements. In *United States v. Poindexter*, 951 F.2d 369, 379 (D.C. Cir. 1991), the D.C. Circuit reversed Poindexter's § 1505 convictions, ruling that § 1505 was unconstitutionally vague as applied to the false and misleading statements to Congress. The court found that the word "corruptly" does not meet due process standards in this context for two reasons.

First, the D.C. Circuit concluded that to apply § 1505 to Poindexter's false and misleading statements would require an "intransitive" reading of the word "corruptly" (*i.e.*, the defendant corrupts or the defendant becomes corrupt—in other words, the defendant himself does the obstruction) rather than a "transitive" meaning (*i.e.*, the defendant corrupts *another* by causing the *other* person to act corruptly—in other words, the defendant causes *others* to do his dirty work, wittingly or not). On its face, the court reasoned, the statute favored a transitive reading. That is, the court "found that the defendant could not be constitutionally convicted under § 1505 for his own independent lies. ... [T]he term 'corruptly' ... commands a 'transitive' interpretation (A corrupts B), in contrast with an "intransitive" interpretation (A is or becomes corrupt) [required by the Poindexter indictment]." *Kelley*, 36 F.3d at 1127. The court favored a transitive reading in part because "[t]he other terms in the disjunctive series in which it appears are 'by threats,' '[by] force,' and 'by any threatening letter or communication,' all of which are transitive—indeed all of which take as their object a natural person. In addition, to read 'corruptly' in an intransitive sense as 'wickedly' or 'immorally' would appear to render the other methods of violating the statute superfluous: surely the use of force to influence a congressional inquiry would always be 'wicked' or at least 'immoral.'" *Poindexter*, 951 F.2d at 379.

Second, the court, after examining various definitions of the term "corruptly," found that term was too vague to provide sufficient notice that it forbade lying to Congress. *Poindexter*, 951 F.2d at 378. The court indicated that "corruptly" might not be deemed unconstitutionally vague if applied transitively to reach the "core behavior" at which the statute was addressed, *i.e.*, a case in which the defendant, "for the purpose of influencing an inquiry, influences another person (through bribery or otherwise) *to violate a legal duty*." *Id.* at 385 (emphasis added). It concluded, however, that "[e]ven if the statute may constitutionally be applied to all attempts to influence or to obstruct a congressional inquiry by influencing another to violate his legal duty, it would still not cover the conduct at issue on this appeal—making false and misleading statements [directly] to Congress." *Id.* at 386.

Do these arguments make sense in the context of the statutory scheme as a whole? When it created § 1512 in 1982, Congress shifted "many activities that were formerly prohibited by §§ 1503 and 1505" to § 1512. *Id.* at 382. The Act "deleted the word 'witness' from § 1503 and deleted the first clause (prohibiting corruptly etc. influencing etc. a witness) from § 1505." *Id.* It left the omnibus provision of § 1505 untouched. Does it make sense, then, to hold that § 1505 was specifically and solely concerned with witness tampering of the sort § 1512 was designed to address, and lying to Congress is not covered by either § 1505 or § 1512?

Section 1503 cannot pick up the slack because it may only be invoked in the context of pending *judicial* proceedings. But isn't § 1503 subject to the same complaints? The *Poindexter* court's statutory analysis would counsel that § 1503 also apply only transitively—apparently excluding persons such as perjurers and other "intransitive" offenders heretofore regularly sanctioned under that statute. And the word "corruptly" in this statute is just as vague as the word "corruptly" in § 1505.

The D.C. Circuit, however, has rejected a vagueness challenge to § 1503's use of the term "corruptly" in a case in which the defendant was convicted under that statute for lying before a grand jury with the intent to impede the due administration of justice. United States v. Russo, 104 F.3d 431, 437 (D.C. Cir. 1997). The court did not treat *Poindexter*'s statutory construction argument or rehearse the *Poindexter* court's problems with the inherent vagueness of the word "corruptly." Rather, the *Russo* court explained that:

While the portion of § 1503 at issue here, and the portion of § 1505 at issue in *Poindexter*, are very nearly identical, the settings in which the provisions apply are vastly different. One can imagine any number of non-corrupt ways in which an individual can intend to impede the work of an agency or congressional committee. [Once example is] an executive branch official calling the chairman of a congressional committee and stating, "We both know this investigation is really designed to embarrass the President (or a Senator), not to investigate wrongdoing. Why don't you call it off?" The problem for the *Poindexter* court, then, was to discern some special meaning in the word "corruptly," some meaning "sufficiently definite as applied to the conduct at issue on this appeal, *viz.* lying to Congress, to be the basis of a criminal conviction." Otherwise, "the statute would criminalize all attempts to 'influence' congressional inquiries—an absurd result that the Congress could not have intended in enacting the statute." We have no such problem here.

Anyone who intentionally lies to a grand jury is on notice that he may be corruptly obstructing the grand jury's investigation. Whatever the limits of "corruptly" in § 1503, Russo's acts of perjury were near its center. ... [As we have said in other contexts,] "very few non-corrupt ways to or reasons for intentionally obstructing a judicial proceeding leap to mind." That is why ... "the *Poindexter* court [] drew a sharp distinction between § 1505 and § 1503, and repeatedly warned that the provisions were too 'materially different' for the construction of one to guide the other."

Id.; *see also* United States v. Brenson, 104 F.3d 1267, 1280 (11th Cir. 1997)(rejecting similar attempt to apply *Poindexter* to § 1503). Do you buy this distinction? Should the D.C. Circuit have accepted the as-applied vagueness challenge resting on the meaning of the word "corrupt" in a case in which a senior executive branch official was alleged to have (*inter alia*) knowingly lied to or misled Congress? Are there a great many "non-corrupt ways to or reasons for" impeding a congressional investigation by intentionally lying to Congress that "leap to mind"?

In 1996, Congress added § 1515(b) to the code in an effort to correct this problem. *See* 142 Cong. Rec. 11605-02, 11607-608 (1996). Section 1515(b) states that "[a]s used in Section 1505, the term 'corruptly' means acting with an improper purpose, *personally or by influencing another*, including *making a false or misleading statement*, or withholding, concealing, altering, or destroying a document or other information." (Emphasis added.) Thus, § 1515(b) puts persons chargeable under § 1505 on notice "that Congress intended the word 'corruptly' ... to be used in both the transitive and intransitive sense, that is, both a defendant who corrupts herself and a defendant who corrupts another can be prosecuted under Section 1505." United States v. Kanchanalak, 37 F.Supp.2d 1, 4 (D.D.C. 1999). It also, by specifying certain types of activity that are deemed "corrupt," gives defendants like Poindexter notice that lying to or misleading Congress is proscribed in § 1505.

C. WITNESS TAMPERING UNDER 18 U.S.C. § 1512

As a definitional note, "witness tampering" generally deals with a situation in which the defendant tampers with *another* witness, either through threats, corrupt persuasion, or misleading conduct, with the intent to cause or induce that *other* person to lie or otherwise obstruct the conduct of judicial or other proceedings (this is sometimes described as having a "transitive" meaning). This is contrasted with cases in which *the defendant* (and not some other person upon whom he is acting) is the primary actor and is altering or destroying evidence with a corrupt intent (an "intransitive" meaning).

Section 1512, at least when originally enacted, was not aimed at protecting the integrity of the whole of the justice system or the "due administration of justice." In design, § 1512 was specifically concerned with protecting witnesses and their safety.[18] These witness tampering prohibitions formerly were contained within § 1503 and § 1505. In 1982, Congress removed the express references to intimidating or influencing witnesses in § 1503 and § 1505 and created § 1512. When first enacted, § 1512 contained provisions prohibiting tampering with witnesses by intimidation, physical force, threats, misleading conduct, or harassment.[19] With the exception of misleading conduct, all the activities proscribed by the 1982 incarnation of § 1512 involved some element of coercion. This provision, then, did not cover all the non-coercive types of witness tampering that courts had, prior to 1982, recognized as falling with the "omnibus" obstruction prohibition in § 1503.

Even after passage of § 1512, then, prosecutors successfully continued to invoke § 1503 to address non-coercive witness tampering such as "efforts to urge a witness to give false testimony or withhold or destroy evidence."[20] In 1988, Congress responded to this perceived gap by amending § 1512(b) to cover non-coercive witness tampering by adding the "corruptly persuades" language.[21] Finally, in the Sarbanes-Oxley Act of 2002, Congress expanded the reach of § 1512 beyond witness tampering by including within it a general obstruction prohibition—§ 1512(c)—whose reach is not yet clear but which appears to be even broader in scope than the omnibus clause of § 1503. Again, that portion of the statute that relates to coercive activity is not as relevant for our purposes as that portion which deals with non-coercive obstruction.

As we have just seen, § 1503 and § 1505 contain a requirement that the government prove that the defendant acted "corruptly," which should help to ensure that juries find that the defendant at least acted with an "improper purpose" in knowingly engaging in the conduct alleged to be obstructive. Section 1512(c), added in 2002, also requires a "corrupt" intent. But witness tampering prosecutions under § 1512(b) are different—in purpose and effect. Under § 1512(b), only one of the proscribed activities—persuasion—requires proof of a "corrupt" motive. Instead of § 1503's broad prohibition on any type of activity that obstructs the "due administration of justice," § 1512(b) focuses more narrowly on specific types of conduct through which physical evidence can be compromised or witnesses tampered with. In short, in witness tampering cases, § 1512(b) *is said to change the focus from corrupt motives to presumptively corrupt methods*—raising concerns among the defense bar that § 1512(b) may pose an even greater threat to legitimate defense functioning than § 1503 for reasons that may become clearer as we examine, *infra*, whether all the proscribed conduct should be treated as presumptively corrupt.

ARTHUR ANDERSEN LLP v. UNITED STATES
544 U.S. 696 (2005)

REHNQUIST, C.J. delivered the opinion for a unanimous Court.

As Enron Corporation's financial difficulties became public in 2001, petitioner Arthur Andersen LLP, Enron's auditor, instructed its employees to destroy documents pursuant to its document retention policy. A jury found that this action made petitioner guilty of violating 18 U.S.C. §§ 1512(b)(2)(A) and (B). These sections make it a crime to "knowingly us[e] intimidation or physical force, threate[n], or corruptly persuad[e] another person ... with intent to ... cause" that person to "withhold" documents from, or "alter" documents for use in,

---

[18] Although not as relevant to the portions of the statute upon which these materials focus, it is worth noting that the statute protects "any person" from the types of activities proscribed. Accordingly, it extends beyond witnesses to victims, informants, and those involved with them.

[19] *See* Victim and Witness Protection Act, P.L. 97-291, 96 Stat. 1249 (1982).

[20] *See, e.g.*, United States v. Ladum, 141 F.3d 1328, 1338 (9th Cir. 1998); United States v. Lester, 749 F.2d 1288, 1294 (9th Cir. 1984).

[21] *See* United States v. Farrell, 126 F.3d 484, 488 (3d Cir. 1997).

an "official proceeding."[22] The Court of Appeals for the Fifth Circuit affirmed. We hold that the jury instructions failed to convey properly the elements of a "corrup[t] persuas[ion]" conviction under § 1512(b), and therefore reverse.

Enron Corporation, during the 1990's, switched its business from operation of natural gas pipelines to an energy conglomerate, a move that was accompanied by aggressive accounting practices and rapid growth. Petitioner audited Enron's publicly filed financial statements and provided internal audit and consulting services to it. Petitioner's "engagement team" for Enron was headed by David Duncan. Beginning in 2000, Enron's financial performance began to suffer, and, as 2001 wore on, worsened.[23] On August 14, 2001, Jeffrey Skilling, Enron's Chief Executive Officer (CEO), unexpectedly resigned. Within days, Sherron Watkins, a senior accountant at Enron, warned Kenneth Lay, Enron's newly reappointed CEO, that Enron could "implode in a wave of accounting scandals." She likewise informed Duncan and Michael Odom, one of petitioner's partners who had supervisory responsibility over Duncan, of the looming problems.

On August 28, an article in the Wall Street Journal suggested improprieties at Enron, and the SEC opened an informal investigation. By early September, petitioner had formed an Enron "crisis-response" team, which included Nancy Temple, an in-house counsel.[24] On October 8, petitioner retained outside counsel to represent it in any litigation that might arise from the Enron matter. The next day, Temple discussed Enron with other in-house counsel. Her notes from that meeting reflect that "some SEC investigation" is "highly probable."

On October 10, Odom spoke at a general training meeting attended by 89 employees, including 10 from the Enron engagement team. Odom urged everyone to comply with the firm's document retention policy.[25] He added: "'[I]f it's destroyed in the course of [the] normal policy and litigation is filed the next day, that's great. ... [W]e've followed our own policy, and whatever there was that might have been of interest to somebody is gone and irretrievable.'" On October 12, Temple entered the Enron matter into her computer, designating the "Type of Potential Claim" as "Professional Practice—Government/Regulatory Inv[estigation]." Temple also e-mailed Odom, suggesting that he "'remin[d] the engagement team of our documentation and retention policy.'"

---

[22] [Court's footnote 1:] We refer to the 2000 version of the statute, which has since been amended by Congress.

[23] [Court's footnote 2:] During this time, petitioner faced problems of its own. In June 2001, petitioner entered into a settlement agreement with the Securities and Exchange Commission (SEC) related to its audit work of Waste Management, Inc. As part of the settlement, petitioner paid a massive fine. It also was censured and enjoined from committing further violations of the securities laws. In July 2001, the SEC filed an amended complaint alleging improprieties by Sunbeam Corporation, and petitioner's lead partner on the Sunbeam audit was named.

[24] [Court's footnote 3:] A key accounting problem involved Enron's use of "Raptors," which were special purpose entities used to engage in "off-balance-sheet" activities. Petitioner's engagement team had allowed Enron to "aggregate" the Raptors for accounting purposes so that they reflected a positive return. This was, in the words of petitioner's experts, a "black-and-white" violation of Generally Accepted Accounting Principles.

[25] [Court's footnote 4:] The firm's policy called for a single central engagement file, which "should contain only that information which is relevant to supporting our work." The policy stated that, "in cases of threatened litigation, ... no related information will be destroyed." It also separately provided that, if petitioner is "advised of litigation or subpoenas regarding a particular engagement, the related information should not be destroyed. See Policy Statement No. 780-Notification of Litigation." Policy Statement No. 780 set forth "notification" procedures for whenever "professional practice litigation against [petitioner] or any of its personnel has been commenced, has been threatened or is judged likely to occur, or when governmental or professional investigations that may involve [petitioner] or any of its personnel have been commenced or are judged likely."

On October 16, Enron announced its third quarter results. That release disclosed a $1.01 billion charge to earnings.[26] The following day, the SEC notified Enron by letter that it had opened an investigation in August and requested certain information and documents. On October 19, Enron forwarded a copy of that letter to petitioner.

On the same day, Temple also sent an e-mail to a member of petitioner's internal team of accounting experts and attached a copy of the document policy. On October 20, the Enron crisis-response team held a conference call, during which Temple instructed everyone to "[m]ake sure to follow the [document] policy." On October 23, Enron CEO Lay declined to answer questions during a call with analysts because of "potential lawsuits, as well as the SEC inquiry." After the call, Duncan met with other Andersen partners on the Enron engagement team and told them that they should ensure team members were complying with the document policy. Another meeting for all team members followed, during which Duncan distributed the policy and told everyone to comply. These, and other smaller meetings, were followed by substantial destruction of paper and electronic documents.

On October 26, one of petitioner's senior partners circulated a New York Times article discussing the SEC's response to Enron. His e-mail commented that "the problems are just beginning and we will be in the cross hairs. The marketplace is going to keep the pressure on this and is going to force the SEC to be tough." On October 30, the SEC opened a formal investigation and sent Enron a letter that requested accounting documents.

Throughout this time period, the document destruction continued, despite reservations by some of petitioner's managers.[27] On November 8, Enron announced that it would issue a comprehensive restatement of its earnings and assets. Also on November 8, the SEC served Enron and petitioner with subpoenas for records. On November 9, Duncan's secretary sent an e-mail that stated: "Per Dave—No more shredding .... We have been officially served for our documents." Enron filed for bankruptcy less than a month later. Duncan was fired and later pleaded guilty to witness tampering.

In March 2002, petitioner was indicted in the Southern District of Texas on one count of violating §§ 1512(b)(2)(A) and (B). The indictment alleged that, between October 10 and November 9, 2001, petitioner "did knowingly, intentionally and corruptly persuade ... other persons, to wit: [petitioner's] employees, with intent to cause" them to withhold documents from, and alter documents for use in, "official proceedings, namely: regulatory and criminal proceedings and investigations." A jury trial followed. When the case went to the jury, that body deliberated for seven days and then declared that it was deadlocked. The District Court delivered an "*Allen* charge," and, after three more days of deliberation, the jury returned a guilty verdict. The District Court denied petitioner's motion for a judgment of acquittal.

The Court of Appeals for the Fifth Circuit affirmed. It held that the jury instructions properly conveyed the meaning of "corruptly persuades" and "official proceeding"; that the jury need not find any consciousness of wrongdoing; and that there was no reversible error. Because of a split of authority regarding the meaning of § 1512(b), we granted certiorari.

Chapter 73 of Title 18 of the United States Code provides criminal sanctions for those who obstruct justice. Sections 1512(b)(2)(A) and (B), part of the witness tampering provisions, provide in relevant part:

---

[26] [Court's footnote 5:] The release characterized the charge to earnings as "non-recurring." Petitioner had expressed doubts about this characterization to Enron, but Enron refused to alter the release. Temple wrote an e-mail to Duncan that "suggested deleting some language that might suggest we have concluded the release is misleading."

[27] [Court's footnote 6:] For example, on October 26, John Riley, another partner with petitioner, saw Duncan shredding documents and told him "this wouldn't be the best time in the world for you guys to be shredding a bunch of stuff." On October 31, David Stulb, a forensics investigator for petitioner, met with Duncan. During the meeting, Duncan picked up a document with the words "smoking gun" written on it and began to destroy it, adding "we don't need this." Stulb cautioned Duncan on the need to maintain documents and later informed Temple that Duncan needed advice on the document retention policy.

"Whoever knowingly uses intimidation or physical force, threatens, or corruptly persuades another person, or attempts to do so, or engages in misleading conduct toward another person, with intent to ... cause or induce any person to ... withhold testimony, or withhold a record, document, or other object, from an official proceeding [or] alter, destroy, mutilate, or conceal an object with intent to impair the object's integrity or availability for use in an official proceeding ... shall be fined under this title or imprisoned not more than ten years, or both."

In this case, our attention is focused on what it means to "knowingly ... corruptly persuad[e]" another person "with intent to ... cause" that person to "withhold" documents from, or "alter" documents for use in, an "official proceeding."

"We have traditionally exercised restraint in assessing the reach of a federal criminal statute, both out of deference to the prerogatives of Congress, and out of concern that 'a fair warning should be given to the world in language that the common world will understand, of what the law intends to do if a certain line is passed'." *United States v. Aguilar*, 515 U.S. 593, 600 (1995).

Such restraint is particularly appropriate here, where the act underlying the conviction—"persua[sion]"—is by itself innocuous. Indeed, "persuad[ing]" a person "with intent to ... cause" that person to "withhold" testimony or documents from a Government proceeding or Government official is not inherently malign.[28] Consider, for instance, a mother who suggests to her son that he invoke his right against compelled self-incrimination, see U.S. Const., Amdt. 5, or a wife who persuades her husband not to disclose marital confidences.

Nor is it necessarily corrupt for an attorney to "persuad[e]" a client "with intent to ... cause" that client to "withhold" documents from the Government. In *Upjohn Co. v. United States*, 449 U.S. 383 (1981), for example, we held that Upjohn was justified in withholding documents that were covered by the attorney-client privilege from the Internal Revenue Service (IRS). No one would suggest that an attorney who "persuade[d]" Upjohn to take that step acted wrongfully, even though he surely intended that his client keep those documents out of the IRS' hands.

"Document retention policies," which are created in part to keep certain information from getting into the hands of others, including the Government, are common in business. See generally Chase, To Shred or Not to Shred: Document Retention Policies and Federal Obstruction of Justice Statutes, 8 Ford. J. Corp. & Fin. L. 721 (2003). It is, of course, not wrongful for a manager to instruct his employees to comply with a valid document retention policy under ordinary circumstances.

Acknowledging this point, the parties have largely focused their attention on the word "corruptly" as the key to what may or may not lawfully be done in the situation presented here. Section 1512(b) punishes not just "corruptly persuad[ing]" another, but "*knowingly* ... corruptly persuad[ing]" another. (Emphasis added.) The Government suggests that "knowingly" does not modify "corruptly persuades," but that is not how the statute most naturally reads. It provides the *mens rea*—"knowingly"—and then a list of acts—"uses intimidation or physical force, threatens, or corruptly persuades." We have recognized with regard to similar statutory language that the *mens rea* at least applies to the acts that immediately follow, if not to other elements down the statutory chain. The Government suggests that it is "questionable whether Congress would employ such an inelegant formulation as 'knowingly ... corruptly persuades.'" Long experience has not taught us to share the Government's doubts on this score, and we must simply interpret the statute as written.

---

[28] [Court's footnote 8:] Section 1512(b)(2) addresses testimony, as well as documents. Section 1512(b)(1) also addresses testimony. Section 1512(b)(3) addresses "persuade[rs]" who intend to prevent "the communication to a law enforcement officer or judge of the United States of information" relating to a federal crime.

The parties have not pointed us to another interpretation of "knowingly ... corruptly" to guide us here.[29] In any event, the natural meaning of these terms provides a clear answer. "[K]nowledge" and "knowingly" are normally associated with awareness, understanding, or consciousness. See Black's Law Dictionary 888 (8th ed.2004) (hereinafter Black's); Webster's Third New International Dictionary 1252-1253 (1993) (hereinafter Webster's 3d); American Heritage Dictionary of the English Language 725 (1981) (hereinafter Am. Hert.). "Corrupt" and "corruptly" are normally associated with wrongful, immoral, depraved, or evil. See Black's 371; Webster's 3d 512; Am. Hert. 299-300. Joining these meanings together here makes sense both linguistically and in the statutory scheme. Only persons conscious of wrongdoing can be said to "knowingly ... corruptly persuad[e]." And limiting criminality to persuaders conscious of their wrongdoing sensibly allows § 1512(b) to reach only those with the level of "culpability ... we usually require in order to impose criminal liability." *United States v. Aguilar,* 515 U.S., at 602.

The outer limits of this element need not be explored here because the jury instructions at issue simply failed to convey the requisite consciousness of wrongdoing. Indeed, it is striking how little culpability the instructions required. For example, the jury was told that, "even if [petitioner] honestly and sincerely believed that its conduct was lawful, you may find [petitioner] guilty." The instructions also diluted the meaning of "corruptly" so that it covered innocent conduct.

The parties vigorously disputed how the jury would be instructed on "corruptly." The District Court based its instruction on the definition of that term found in the Fifth Circuit Pattern Jury Instruction for § 1503. This pattern instruction defined "corruptly" as "'knowingly and dishonestly, with the specific intent to subvert or undermine the integrity'" of a proceeding. The Government, however, insisted on excluding "dishonestly" and adding the term "impede" to the phrase "subvert or undermine." The District Court agreed over petitioner's objections, and the jury was told to convict if it found petitioner intended to "subvert, undermine, or impede" governmental factfinding by suggesting to its employees that they enforce the document retention policy.

These changes were significant. No longer was any type of "dishonest[y]" necessary to a finding of guilt, and it was enough for petitioner to have simply "impede[d]" the Government's factfinding ability. As the Government conceded at oral argument, "'impede'" has broader connotations than "'subvert'" or even "'undermine,'" and many of these connotations do not incorporate any "corrupt[ness]" at all. The dictionary defines "impede" as "to interfere with or get in the way of the progress of" or "hold up" or "detract from." Webster's 3d 1132. By definition, anyone who innocently persuades another to withhold information from the Government "get[s] in the way of the progress of" the Government. With regard to such innocent conduct, the "corruptly" instructions did no limiting work whatsoever.

The instructions also were infirm for another reason. They led the jury to believe that it did not have to find *any* nexus between the "persua[sion]" to destroy documents and any particular proceeding. In resisting any type of nexus element, the Government relies heavily on § 1512(e)(1), which states that an official proceeding "need not be pending or about to be instituted at the time of the offense." It is, however, one thing to say that a proceeding "need not be pending or about to be instituted at the time of the offense," and quite another to say a proceeding need not even be foreseen. A "knowingly ... corrup[t] persaude[r]" cannot be someone who persuades others to shred documents under a document retention policy when he does not have in contemplation any particular official proceeding in which those documents might be material.

We faced a similar situation in *Aguilar, supra.* Respondent Aguilar lied to a Federal Bureau of Investigation agent in the course of an investigation and was convicted of "'corruptly endeavor[ing] to influence, obstruct, and impede [a] ... grand jury investigation'" under §

---

[29] [Court's footnote 9:] The parties have pointed us to two other obstruction provisions, 18 U.S.C. §§ 1503 and 1505, which contain the word "corruptly." But these provisions lack the modifier "knowingly," making any analogy inexact.

1503. All the Government had shown was that Aguilar had uttered false statements to an investigating agent "who might or might not testify before a grand jury." We held that § 1503 required something more—specifically, a "nexus" between the obstructive act and the proceeding. "[I]f the defendant lacks knowledge that his actions are likely to affect the judicial proceeding," we explained, "he lacks the requisite intent to obstruct."

For these reasons, the jury instructions here were flawed in important respects. The judgment of the Court of Appeals is reversed, and the case is remanded for further proceedings consistent with this opinion.

Notes

1. *Section 1512 v. § 1503.* Defendants indicted under § 1503 for conduct that could be prosecuted under § 1512 often make the argument (as did Aguilar) that Congress' creation of § 1512, and in particular the 1988 amendment, repealed by implication the application of § 1503's "omnibus" provision to witness tampering. The Second Circuit stands alone in accepting this argument, holding that prosecutors must pursue witness tampering under § 1512, not § 1503's "omnibus" provision. *See* United States v. Bruno, 383 F.3d 65, 86-87 (2d Cir. 2004). All other circuits to consider the issue have held to the contrary. *See, e.g.,* United States v. Ladum, 141 F.3d 1328 (9th Cir. 1998); United States v. Mullins, 22 F.3d 1365, 1369 (6th Cir. 1994).

Assuming that conduct could be prosecuted under either § 1503 or § 1512, which is the "better" statute from the prosecution's and the defense's perspective? Consider the comparisons contained in Chart 2, which is appended to this Chapter.

2. *"Official Proceeding."* In terms of coverage, an important distinction between § 1503 and § 1512 concerns the type of proceedings to which the alleged obstructive activity must relate. Section 1512(b)(1), (b)(2)(A)-(D), and (c)(1)-(2) all require that the proscribed conduct occur in the context of an "official proceeding." Section 1515(a) defines "official proceeding" as a proceeding in any federal court (including those conducted before bankruptcy judges) and before a federal grand jury, "a proceeding before the Congress," "a proceeding before a Federal Government agency which is authorized by law," or a proceeding involving (interstate) insurance businesses. (For a discussion of the conflicting caselaw interpreting the term "official proceeding" in the context of agency investigations, see United States v. Ermoian, 752 F.3d 1165, 1169-72 & n.5 (9th Cir. 2013) (discussing split and holding that "official proceeding" does not include criminal investigations by the FBI); United States v. Perez, 575 F.3d 164 (2d Cir. 2009) (routine internal investigation into officers' use of force pursuant to Federal Bureau of Prison rules constitutes an "official proceeding")).

Section 1512's application to myriad "official proceedings" makes it much more broadly applicable than § 1503, which may be invoked only when the due administration of justice in *judicial* proceedings (such as grand jury or court proceedings) is threatened. Furthermore, "[i]n contrast to section 1503, 'an official proceeding need not be pending or about to be instituted at the time of the offense'" for a defendant to be convicted under § 1512(b). United States v. Frankhauser, 80 F.3d 641, 651 (1st Cir. 1996) (quoting 18 U.S.C. § 1512(f)(1), which at the time was numbered § 1512(e)(1)). "Because an official proceeding need not be pending or about to be instituted at the time of the [allegedly obstructive conduct], the statute obviously cannot require actual knowledge of the proceeding." *Id.*; *see also* United States v. Kelley, 36 F.3d 1118, 1128 (D.C. Cir. 1994)).

What *caveat* does the *Andersen* Court apply here? Does the Supreme Court require, as have some lower courts, that the government prove "at least a circumstantial showing of intent to affect the testimony [or production of physical evidence] at some particular federal proceeding that is ongoing or is scheduled to be commenced in the future"? United States v. Shively, 927 F.2d 804, 812-13 (5th Cir. 1991); *see also* United States v. Frankhauser, 80 F.3d 641, 652-53 (1st Cir. 1996). Just how proximate or foreseeable must an official proceeding be, and what degree of knowledge must the defendant have?

3. *Section 1512(b)(3).* Of all the acts proscribed in § 1512(b), only § 1512(b)(3) does not require that the allegedly obstructive activity take place in the context of an "official

proceeding." Under § 1512(b)(3) the defendant must have committed the obstructive conduct with the intent to "hinder, delay, or prevent" communication to a federal law enforcement officer or judge of information relating to the commission or *possible* commission of a federal crime. This section "do[es] not depend on the existence or immanency of a federal case or investigation but rather on the *possible* existence of a federal crime and a defendant's intention to thwart an inquiry into that crime." United States v. Veal, 153 F.3d 1233, 1250 (11th Cir. 1998); *see also* United States v. Carson, 560 F.3d 566 (6th Cir. 2009); United States v. Harris, 498 F.3d 278, 285-86 (4th Cir. 2007). Further, the defendant need not intend specifically to hinder a possible *federal* inquiry. *Harris*, 498 at 287; 18 U.S.C. § 1512(g)(2) (no state of mind need be proven with respect to the circumstance that the investigation is a federal one). Note, however, that with respect to a provision of the statute that proscribes killing or attempting to kill another person with intent to "prevent the communication by any person to a law enforcement officer or judge of the United States of information relating to the commission or possible commission of a Federal offense," 18 U.S.C. § 1512(a)(1)(C), the Supreme Court has held that where there is no evidence that the victim planned to report to any particular federal law enforcement officer,

> the Government must show *a reasonable likelihood* that, had, *e.g.*, the victim communicated with law enforcement officers, at least one relevant communication would have been made to a federal law enforcement officer. That is to say, where the defendant kills a person with an intent to prevent communication with law enforcement officers generally, that intent includes an intent to prevent communication with *federal* law enforcement officers only if it is reasonably likely under the circumstances that (in the absence of the killing) at least one of the relevant communications would have been made to a federal officer.

Fowler v. United States, 563 U.S. 668 (2011); *see also* United States v. Snyder, 865 F.3d 490 (7th Cir. 2017).

Can § 1512(b)(3) be used to pursue a defendant for obstruction—witness tampering—when the defendant lies to investigating officers? *See Veal*, 153 F.3d at 1245-47 (yes). Can § 1512(b)(3) be used to sanction an employee who lies to corporate counsel in the course of an internal corporate investigation into alleged misconduct, on the theory that the corporation may choose at some point to share what it learns in the internal investigation with federal officials in return for regulatory or prosecutorial leniency? *Cf.* United States v. Gabriel, 125 F.3d 89 (2d Cir. 1997).

4. *"Nexus"?* Must prosecutors proceeding under § 1512 satisfy the *Aguilar* "nexus" requirement to prevail? Prior to *Andersen*, the answer was "no." *See, e.g.*, United States v. Gabriel, 125 F.3d 89 (2d Cir. 1997); United States v. Veal, 153 F.3d 1233, 1250-51 (11th Cir. 1998). Given that § 1512 does not mandate that a defendant know of a pending proceeding, and indeed does not require that a pending proceeding even exist, how would a "nexus" requirement work in this context? United States v. Quattrone, 441 F.3d 153, 176 & n.22 (2d Cir. 2006). Did the Supreme Court read this element into the statute?

Although Andersen concerned only § 1512(b), courts have read the "nexus" element into § 1512(c) as well. *See* United States v. Petruk, 781 F.3d 438, 445 (8th Cir. 2015) (§ 1512(c)(2)); United States v. Friske, 640 F.3d 1288, 1292 (11th Cir. 2011); United States v. Phillips, 583 F.3d 1261, 1264 (10th Cir. 2009).

5. *Mens Rea.* Courts draw a distinction between § 1503 and § 1512 in terms of the *mens rea* they require. For example, the Sixth Circuit has explained that the *mens rea* for § 1503 is the general intent of knowledge of a pending proceeding and a specific intent or purpose to obstruct (along with a corrupt motive), while the *mens rea* for § 1512(b) is "knowing" use of obstructive methods (using intimidation, threats, corrupt persuasion or misleading conduct) with an intent to influence or prevent testimony, § 1512(b)(1), or cause or induce another person to engage in the obstructive activities outlawed by the statute, § 1512(b)(2). *See* United States v. Jeter, 775 F.2d 670, 679 (6th Cir. 1985); United States v. Scaife, 749 F.2d 338, 348

(6th Cir. 1984). Does the *Andersen* decision change this? Does it require, for example, proof in a § 1512 case of a "specific intent to obstruct"?

The *Andersen* Court focuses on the meaning of "knowingly ... corruptly persuades." Does its gloss on this language have any relevance to the *other* types of presumptively obstructive conduct covered by § 1512 (*i.e.*, using intimidation, threats, or misleading conduct)? In a case alleging "corrupt persuasion" what more, in terms of *mens rea*, must the government prove?

6. *Actus Reus.* Let us begin our examination of the *actus reus* of § 1512(b) by focusing on § 1512(b)(1) and (2)(A). This witness tampering portion of the statute makes it a crime, *inter alia*, for any person to knowingly *threaten* or *corruptly persuade* or *engage in misleading conduct* with the *intent* to "influence" the testimony of any person or to cause any person to withhold a document from an official proceeding. As the *Andersen* Court recognizes, although the intention behind § 1512(b) was to focus on *presumptively corrupt methods, rather than corrupt state of mind*, both "influencing" witnesses' testimony and causing clients to withhold documents can be entirely legitimate—and very important—defense functions.

> Whether working for the prosecution or the defense, any lawyer who has interviewed a witness prior to an appearance before a grand jury or at trial has probably sought to "influence" testimony. ... Refreshing a witness' recollection, pointing out inconsistencies in his testimony, suggesting how he might handle expected questions on cross-examination, even simply leading questions in an interview—all are proper and even necessary methods of preparing a witness, and all have the objective as well as the effect of "influencing" testimony.

William H. Jeffress, *The New Federal Witness Tampering Statute*, 22 Am. Crim. L. Rev. 1, 6 (1984) (written prior to 1986 amendment adding § 1515(c)). Similarly, defense counsel commonly will attempt to read subpoenas for documents as narrowly as ethically possible to avoid the production of damning materials; certainly, counsel will advise clients to withhold the production of privileged documents.

Returning to an earlier hypothetical, what if a defendant merely encourages another to take the Fifth? Does it matter what his or her motive is? As we know, the *Cueto* court would say that such otherwise legal conduct is criminal under § 1503 if undertaken with a corrupt motive. Is the same true under § 1512(b)? "The key issue is whether corrupt persuasion requires mere persuasion motivated by an improper purpose (such as self-interest in impeding an investigation) or persuasion that involves otherwise wrongful means (such as bribery or inducement to commit perjury)." Daniel Leddy, Note, *Interpreting the Meaning of "Corruptly Persuades": Why the Ninth Circuit Got It Right in* United States v. Doss, *630 F.3d 1181 (9th Cir. 2011)*, 92 Neb. L. Rev. 966, 968 (2014).

> At minimum, most courts—including the Fourth Circuit—conclude "that a non-coercive attempt to persuade a witness to lie to investigators constitutes a violation of § 1512(b)." However, courts are split on whether §1512 outlaws mere attempts to persuade a witness to withhold information from law enforcement officials. The Second and Eleventh Circuits hold that "corrupt persuasion" encompasses a broad range of persuasion—including efforts to encourage witnesses to withhold information—so long as a defendant is motivated by an "improper purpose." *See* United States v. Gotti, 459 F.3d 296, 342-53 (2d Cir. 2006) (finding that corrupt persuasion includes encouraging a co-conspirator to invoke his Fifth Amendment rights if the defendant was acting to ensure the co-conspirator did not implicate him in criminal activity); United States v. Shotts, 145 F.3d 1289, 1300-01 (11th Cir. 1998) (finding that corrupt persuasion includes attempts to persuade a witness to avoid talking with law enforcement); United States v. Thompson, 76 F.3d 442, 452 (2d Cir. 1996) (finding that corrupt persuasion includes efforts to persuade co-conspirators to conceal information and provide false testimony).
>
> For their part, the Third and Ninth Circuits carve out exceptions for witnesses who have a legal right to avoid cooperating with law enforcement. Specifically, this second line of cases holds that a defendant does not run afoul of § 1512 if he encourages witnesses to

invoke their Fifth Amendment rights or the marital privilege, even if the defendant intends to hinder a criminal investigation. United States v. Doss, 630 F.3d 1181, 1187-88 (9th Cir. 2011) (finding no corrupt persuasion where the defendant "appealed to his wife to exercise her marital privilege not to testify against him"); United States v. Farrell, 126 F.3d 484, 488 (3d Cir. 1997) (finding that corrupt persuasion does not include "a noncoercive attempt to persuade a co-conspirator who enjoys a Fifth Amendment right not to disclose self-incriminating information about the conspiracy to refrain, in accordance with that right, from volunteering information to investigators"). This second line of cases does not address whether the same behavior would qualify as corrupt persuasion when no privilege exists. See Farrell, 126 F.3d 489 n.3 (noting that "[i]n the absence of a privilege, society has the right to the information of citizens regarding the commission of crime, and it can be argued that discouraging another who possessed no privilege from honoring this civic duty involves some culpability not present when coconspirators with Fifth Amendment privileges converse").

United States v. Chujoy, 207 F.Supp.3d 626, 641-42 (W.D. Va. 2016).

7. *Corrupt "Persuasion."* With respect to "persuasion," this method alone among the witness tampering acts proscribed by 1512(b) requires proof of "corrupt" motive (i.e., using intimidation, threats, and engaging in misleading conduct do not require a "corrupt" intent). Attempting to persuade a witness to give false testimony and bribing a witness to withhold information are both forms of corrupt persuasion. *See, e.g.,* United States v. Khatami, 280 F.3d 907 (9th Cir. 2001); United States v. Morrison, 98 F.3d 619, 630 (D.C. Cir. 1996). Obviously, the *Andersen* Court concluded that "knowingly ... corruptly" must mean something more in the context of a § 1512(b) prosecution than "corruptly" in a § 1503 case. *Cf. Andersen, supra,* footnote 29 (the Court's footnote 9). What constitutes the "something more" that will satisfy the statute?

8. *Misleading Conduct.* With respect to "misleading conduct," Congress defined this term in § 1515(a)(3) as follows:

> (A) knowingly making a false statement;
> (B) intentionally omitting information from a statement and thereby causing a portion of such statement to be misleading, or intentionally concealing a material fact, and thereby creating a false impression by such statement;
> (C) with intent to mislead, knowingly submitting or inviting reliance on a writing or recording that is false, forged, altered, or otherwise lacking in authenticity;
> (D) with intent to mislead, knowingly submitting or inviting reliance on a sample, specimen, map, photograph, boundary mark, or other object that is misleading in a material respect; or
> (E) knowingly using a trick, scheme, or device with intent to mislead.

18 U.S.C. § 1515(a)(3). The distinction between "corruptly persuading" someone and "misleading" someone is an important one. "Misleading conduct" applies to conduct that is intended to mislead the witness, not to mislead the government. If a witness *knows* that the defendant is encouraging him or her to tell a false story, there is no "misleading" conduct. Such a case should be pursued under the "corrupt persuasion" prong of the statute.

Could the government in *Aguilar* have successfully pursued a § 1512(b)(1) case on a theory that Judge Augilar "knowingly ... engage[d] in misleading conduct toward another person, with intent to ... influence ... the testimony of any person in an official proceeding"? *See* § 1512(b)(1); § 1515(a)(3)(A) ("misleading conduct" includes "knowingly making a false statement").

Could a party who denies guilt to family, friends, and associates who may be potential witnesses be charged with witness tampering? The Second Circuit deems "[t]he most obvious example of a section 1512 violation [for "misleading" a witness] may be the situation where a defendant tells a potential witness a false story as if the story were true, intending that the witness believe the story and testify to it before the grand jury." United States v. Rodolitz, 786 F.2d 77, 81-82 (2d Cir. 1986).

What of counsel's activities under § 1515(a)(3)(B)? Would an attorney who, in closing argument, omits some facts favorable to the opposing party be chargeable with "intentionally concealing a material fact, and thereby creating a false impression"? If a witness invokes his Fifth Amendment right, is he concealing material facts? Under § 1515(a)(3)(A) and (B), could defense counsel be threatened with prosecution for witness tampering in the conduct of witness interviews? Consider the following discussion, keeping in mind that it was written regarding the pre-1986 statute (which did not contain § 1515(c), discussed below):

> It is natural for a lawyer in witness interviews, during investigations or in preparation for trial, to test the witness' recollection of the facts against the position of his client, and to seek either to minimize the areas of disagreement, or to convince the witness that he is or could be mistaken. In doing so, counsel may refer to conflicting testimony of other witnesses or documents that appear inconsistent with the witness' recollection; he may tell the witness what his own client recollects of the events in question; or he may simply suggest to the witness an alternative, non-incriminating explanation or interpretation of the occurrence. Quite likely, the prosecutor will disagree with defense counsel's position on the facts: he will contend that the defendant's account is false, and that the alternative non-incriminating explanation is a sham. Quite possibly, he will also claim that defense counsel knew it was so.

> Under prior law[, § 1503], a prosecutor in such a case would have had the burden of proving the lawyer corruptly endeavored to obtain false testimony from the witness. Under section 1512, however, the prosecutor need only prove the lawyer knowingly made a false or misleading statement, intending to influence the testimony of a witness. ... [T]hese burdens are not by any means equal; the government's burden is considerably less under section 1512.

William H. Jeffress, *The New Federal Witness Tampering Statute*, 22 Am. Crim. L. Rev. 1, 12-13 (1984).

9. *Section 1512(c).* A reform act enacted in response to the 2002 corporate accounting scandals, the Sarbanes-Oxley Act of 2002, P.L. 107-204, 116 Stat. 745 (2002), was signed into law by President Bush on July 30, 2002. Perhaps not surprisingly in light of Arthur Andersen's highly publicized destruction of audit-related documents after becoming aware of an SEC investigation into Enron's financials, Congress focused on perceived deficiencies in the existing coverage of federal obstruction statutes, adding four new crimes.

One of the most important of these new crimes is § 1512(c) (another important addition, § 1519, which is akin to § 1512(c), will be considered *infra*). Section 1512(c) "arguably has the potential to be regarded as the most expansive legislative revision of the obstruction of justice statutes in the history of the statutory scheme. Defining the parameters of this subsection will significantly impact prosecutors' ability to prove liability, courts' ability to assess a penalty, and the ability of individuals and businesses to avoid obstruction of justice charges." Daniel A. Shtob, *Corruption of a Term: The Problematic Nature of 18 U.S.C. 1512(c), the New Federal Obstruction of Justice Provision*, 57 Vand. L. Rev. 1429, 1433 (2004). This new provision reads:

> (c) Whoever corruptly—
> (1) alters, destroys, mutilates, or conceals a record, document, or other object, or attempts to do so, with the intent to impair the object's integrity or availability for use in an official proceeding; or
> (2) otherwise obstructs, influences, or impedes any official proceeding, or attempts to do so, shall be fined under this title or imprisoned not more than 20 years, or both.

10. *Comparison of new § 1512(c)(1) with § 1512(b)(2)(B) and § 1503*: Review Chart 2 appended to this Chapter. With respect to the first new subsection, § 1512(c)(1), note that the

most closely analogous pre-existing provision, § 1512(b)(2)(B), requires that the defendant tamper with *another* witness, either through threats, corrupt persuasion, or misleading conduct, with the intent to cause or induce that *other* person to alter, mutilate, or conceal an object with intent to impair the object's integrity or availability for use in an official proceeding (in the *Poindexter* court's terms, a "transitive" meaning). By contrast, the new § 1512(c)(1) would cover instances in which *the defendant* (and not some other person upon whom he is acting) is the primary actor and is altering or destroying evidence with a corrupt intent (in the *Poindexter* court's lexicon, an "intransitive" meaning). *See* § 1512(c)(1). In this respect, § 1512 is no longer a pure witness tampering statute, unless one considers the defendant or the objects he alters or destroys as the witnesses sought to be protected.

Note that the penalty under § 1512(c) is up to 20 years' imprisonment, while non-coercive tampering under § 1512(b) provides for up to 10 years' imprisonment. Should a defendant who directly destroys evidence be subject to twice the potential sentencing exposure as a defendant who causes someone else to do the destroying?

May the type of misconduct addressed in the first subsection, § 1512(c)(1), also be prosecuted under § 1503? How, if at all, do the elements needed to prove them differ? Despite the fact that some cases may be pursued under either § 1503 or § 1512(c)(1), the maximum penalty for non-coercive obstruction under § 1503 is up to 10 years' imprisonment and under § 1512(c) is up to 20 years in jail. Does this make sense?

Note that § 1512(c)(1) does not apply solely in white-collar cases. Indeed, a large portion of the prosecutions under this section have involved the destruction of an "object"—including physical evidence like guns and drugs—rather than only business records. *See, e.g.,* United States v. Johnson, 655 F.3d 594, 604 (7th Cir. 2011). As we shall see, *infra*, the Supreme Court has approved such prosecutions under § 1512(c)(1) while limiting the scope of the term "tangible object" in § 1519 prosecutions to an object that is used to record or preserve information. *See* Yates v. United States, -- U.S. --, 135 S.Ct. 1074 (2015) (a fish is not a "tangible object" under § 1519).

11. *Comparison of new § 1512(c)(2) with § 1503*: Review Chart 2. What does the second subsection, § 1512(c)(2), achieve? This omnibus provision appears to be as broad as, if not broader than, § 1503's omnibus provision in its potential scope. The omnibus provision of § 1503 penalizes a defendant who "corruptly ... influences, obstructs, or impedes," the "*due administration of justice*," or *endeavors* to do so. (Emphasis added.) The new § 1512(c)(2) penalizes a defendant who "corruptly ... obstructs, influences, or impedes *any official proceeding*, or *attempts* to do so." (Emphasis added.) In what ways, if any, do the proof requirements of the two sections differ? Could one attempt to limit the reach of this provision by arguing that its scope must be read in light of its placement after § 1512(c)(1), meaning that the activity proscribed in the new omnibus clause must also concern the compromising of physical evidence (and not, for example, false statements)? *See* United States v. Petruk, 781 F.3d 438, 445 (8th Cir. 2015) (collecting cases). Does this congressional choice make sense? Note, again, the differences in the maximum penalties applicable to each.

The circuits appear unanimous in requiring proof of a "nexus" under § 1512(c)(2), relying on *Aguilar* and *Arthur Andersen*. *See Petruk*, 781 F.3d at 445 (collecting cases).

12. *Comparison of § 1512 with § 1505*: Review Chart 3, appended to this chapter. Both § 1505 and § 1512 can be invoked in the context of congressional and federal agency proceedings. *See* § 1515(a)(1)(B), (C). Congress took witness tampering conduct that formerly had been covered by § 1505 and moved it to § 1512 when it created that statute in 1982. How do § 1505 and § 1512 compare in terms of the elements to be proved?

Note that the general statutory maximum penalty for § 1505 is up to 5 years' imprisonment while the maximum exposure for non-coercive obstruction under § 1503 and § 1512(b) is up to 10 years' and 20 years' imprisonment respectively. Is obstruction in the context of agency or congressional proceedings less dangerous or blameworthy than obstruction in other contexts (*e.g.*, judicial proceedings under § 1503)? Is witness tampering in the context of agency and congressional proceedings that may be pursued under § 1512(b) more dangerous or blameworthy than other types of obstruction prosecutable under § 1505 in the same agency or congressional context?

13. *Nexus and § 1512(c)(2)*. The DOJ brought a number of controversial prosecutions under § 1512(c)(2) that it would normally pursue under § 1503, in part in hopes of avoiding proof of the *Aguilar* "nexus" requirement. *See* Julie R. O'Sullivan, *The DOJ Risks Killing the Golden Goose Through Computer Associates/Singleton Theories of Obstruction*, 44 Am. Crim. L. Rev. 1447, 1458 (2007). As noted above, however, the circuits appear to have endorsed a "nexus" requirement in § 1512(c)(2) cases. When might this "nexus" requirement matter? Consider the following cases, which involve an obstruction theory that is deeply concerning to the white-collar bar.

In September 2004, the DOJ indicted Sanjay Kumar, the Chief Executive Officer of Computer Associates International, Inc. ("CA"), and Stephen Richards, CA's Head of Worldwide Sales. Among other charges, Kumar and Richards were charged with obstructing justice under 18 U.S.C § 1512(c)(2) based, in part, on allegations that these executives repeatedly lied when interviewed by the *company's outside law firms*. It was alleged that two outside law firms had been hired by CA to investigate allegations of accounting malfeasance and that the defendants had lied to both law firms, as well as directly to the government. Similarly, the DOJ indicted Greg Singleton, a natural gas trader at El Paso Corporation for, among other things, obstruction under § 1512(c)(2) based, again, on allegations that he *lied to corporate counsel* during counsel's internal investigation into the primary wrongdoing alleged. Notably, Singleton, unlike the CA executives, was *not* alleged to have engaged in a widespread conspiracy to obstruct that included lies to the government as well as to counsel.

Not surprisingly, Kumar, Richards, and Singleton argued that an obstruction case could not be founded on lies to the corporation's own counsel. They argued, *inter alia*, that false statements made to counsel do not bear the requisite causal connection or, in the Supreme Court's *Aguilar* terminology, "nexus," to an official proceeding. Federal prosecutors contended in response that (1) there was no "nexus" requirement under § 1512(c)(2); and (2), in any case, there was an obvious "nexus" between the executives' lies to corporate counsel and the official proceedings (grand jury and the Securities and Exchange Commission (SEC) investigations) at issue because the defendants knew (CA) or believed (Singleton) that the corporation was cooperating (CA) or might cooperate (Singleton) with the government and, in so doing, intended (CA) or at least contemplated (Singleton) that counsel would turn over the defendants' false or misleading statements to the grand jury and SEC. As the District Court in *Singleton* indicated, the proposed "nexus" was, in essence, the fact that private counsel were working as "an arm of the government" while conducting their nominally private investigations on behalf of the entity. United States v. Singleton, 2006 WL 1984467, Slip Op. at *6 (S.D. Tex. July 14, 2006).

In the Computer Associates case, the District Court did not resolve, or even mention, the question whether § 1512(c)(2) required proof of an *Aguilar* "nexus" in denying the defendants' motion to dismiss. Rather, the Court simply ruled that the allegations in the indictment, if proved, would satisfy a "nexus" requirement. *See* United States v. Kumar, Memorandum and Order, No. 04-CR-846 (ILG), slip op. at *9 (E.D.N.Y. Feb. 21, 2006). The court also did not address at all the question whether, or in what circumstances, lying to or misleading corporate counsel could be deemed actionable obstruction. In responding to the defendants' claims of a lack of the requisite "nexus," the court pointed only to the allegations that Richards knowingly lied and concealed information during his testimony before the SEC and that Kumar made false statements in an interview at the U.S. Attorneys Office. And the court relied solely on the allegations relating to the causal connection between the defendants' face-to-face lies to government agents and in the SEC's "official proceeding" to rule that the indictment was sufficient to proceed to trial. In short, the court did *not* hold that the defendants could be convicted under § 1512 for lies to corporate counsel alone. The District Court had the final word because, in April 2006, the defendants pleaded guilty to the indictment. Kumar was sentenced to twelve years in prison and Richards was sentenced to seven years in prison for both the securities fraud and the obstruction.

The District Court in Singleton's case also declined his invitation to dismiss the indictment on the ground that the indictment pled an insufficient "nexus" between Singleton's lies and an "official proceeding." Notably, the *Singleton* court, unlike the Computer Associates court, upheld the government's theory that lying to corporate counsel—even where there is no allegation that the defendant *knew* that counsel would be turning over his statements to the government—could have the requisite causal nexus to obstruction of an "official proceeding" (the grand jury investigation):

> The Indictment … alleges facts indicating that the *outside attorneys were acting as an arm of the investigating agencies*, that the investigating agencies had formally requested information from El Paso, and that Singleton *believed* that his statements to the outside attorneys would be provided to the investigating federal agencies. The indictment alleges that Singleton supplied a written response to at least one federal agency's inquiry; that he met (accompanied by his criminal defense counsel) with El Paso's outside attorneys whom he knew were performing a detailed investigation in response to the governmental inquiries; and that he "*believed* that El Paso's Outside Lawyers would inform government agencies of his statements [made] during the interview," and that, in fact, the outside attorneys did so through a memorandum of interview. These allegations—in combination—are adequate to satisfy the requirement for an official proceeding, of which Singleton was aware. The allegations, if proved . . ., could raise the inference that Singleton *expected* and thus *arguably intended* that his intentionally false statements would be supplied to the Federal government in connection with one or more of these identified official proceedings.

United States v. Singleton, 2006 WL 1984467, Slip Op. at *6 (S.D. Tex. July 14, 2006) (emphasis added). Singleton, almost alone among those charged in the overall investigation, took his case to trial. At the conclusion of the government's case, Singleton argued that the government's evidence was insufficient to sustain a conviction on the obstruction count because (1) corporate counsel testified at trial that he was not "acting as an arm of the investigating agencies"; and (2) the government failed to present evidence that the defendant knew or believed that El Paso's outside counsel "would inform government agencies of his statements during the interview." Defendant Greg Singleton's Motion for Judgement [sic] of Acquittal as to Count Ten, United States v. Singleton, Cr. No: 4:06-CR—00080, 1-2 (July 31, 2006). The trial judge granted the defense's motion without written opinion and dismissed the obstruction count. *See* Hearing Minutes and Order, United States v. Singleton, No. 4:06-CR-00080 (July 31, 2006).

14. *Affirmative Defense: §1512(e)*. There are two provisions—§ 1512(e) (which, prior to 2002, was numbered § 1512(d)) and §1515(c)—that are intended to safeguard lawyers from prosecution for allegedly "obstructive" activities related to legitimate advocacy. The first, § 1512(e) provides an affirmative defense as to which the defendant has the burden of proof by a preponderance of the evidence. Section 1512(e) provides that a person may lawfully engage in the prohibited means of influencing testimony or withholding documents if his conduct "consisted solely of lawful conduct and … the defendant's sole intention was to encourage, induce, or cause the other person to testify truthfully." Why might defense counsel be less than thrilled with this provision—especially when this statutory scheme is contrasted with § 1503?

15. *Affirmative Defense: §1515(c)*. The second, § 1515(c), was added to the statutory scheme in 1986. It provides: "This chapter does not prohibit or punish the providing of lawful, bona fide, legal representation services in connection with or anticipation of an official proceeding." Note that the "chapter" referred to includes sections 1503, 1505, 1510, 1512, 1519, and 1520. The legislative history of this enactment is exceedingly sparse. It appears to consist of one statement in the congressional record:

> The Subcommittee on Criminal Justice has received complaints of prosecutors' harassing members of the defense bar. Vigorously and zealously representing a client, however, is not a basis for charging an offense under the obstruction of justice chapter. Section 50(2) therefore amends 18 U.S.C. [§] 1515 to provide specifically that the lawful, bona fide provision of legal representation services does not constitute an offense under any of the obstruction of justice offenses in 18 U.S.C. ch. 73.

132 Cong. Rec. H32,805 (Oct. 17, 1986). Section 1515(c) has been dubbed the "safe harbor" provision by some courts. *See* United States v. Stevens, No. RWT-10-694, Transcript of Judgment of Acquittal Pursuant to Rule 29 (D. Md. May 10, 2011); United States v. Davis, 183 F.3d 231, 248 (3d Cir. 1999). One question that has arisen is whether § 1515(c) constitutes an amplification of the affirmative defense set forth in § 1512(e), an independent affirmative defense, or a negative element of an obstruction prosecution. The Eleventh Circuit has held that section 1515(c)'s "safe harbor" for legitimate attorney advocacy activities constitutes a negative element of the offense. United States v. Kloess, 251 F.3d 941 (11th Cir. 2001). It ruled that § 1515(c) provides only an affirmative defense but concluded that "[a]lthough the burden of raising Section 1515(c) as a defense is on the defendant, the burden of proof as to its non-applicability is always on the government." In *United States v. Kellington*, 217 F.3d 1084 (9th Cir. 2000), the Ninth Circuit termed § 1515(c) a "complete defense," *id.* at 1098, pointing out that testimony as to the ethical obligations of an attorney representing a client was relevant "to negate criminal intent and/or to establish a 'bona fide legal representation' defense under § 1515(c)." *Id.* at 1099. Does it matter whether this section is an affirmative defense or a negative element of the offense? Which will better protect defense counsel from the concerns discussed above?

16. *Constitutional Challenges.* Litigants have (largely unsuccessfully) lodged a variety of constitutional challenges to § 1512. For example, in *United States v. Thompson*, 76 F.3d 442, 452 (2d Cir.1996), the defendant argued that "§ 1512 violated his First Amendment rights by broadly 'proscrib[ing] persuasion' and violated his due process rights by shifting the burden of proof to him, 'compel[ling him] to prove the lack of corruption.'" The Second Circuit rejected his challenges, holding that "[b]y targeting only such persuasion as is 'corrupt[],' § 1512(b) does not proscribe lawful or constitutionally protected speech and is not overbroad" or vague. *Id.* Further, the Court ruled that the affirmative defense provided in § 1512(e) (then numbered § 1512(d)) does not improperly shift the burden of proof of elements of the offense to a defendant. While conceding that the elements of the crime and the affirmative defense overlap "'in the sense that evidence to prove the latter will often tend to negate the former,'" this overlap did not shift to the defendant the burden of disproving the element of corrupt persuasion or allow the jury to presume elements of the government's case. *Id.* (citation omitted); *see also* United States v. Johnson, 968 F.2d 208, 213 (2d Cir.1992) (rejecting burden shifting argument). *But see* William H. Jeffress, *The New Federal Witness Tampering Statute*, 22 Am. Crim. L. Rev. 1, 1 (1984).

D. SARBANES-OXLEY ACT OF 2002 PROHIBITION OF DESTRUCTION OF RECORDS AND WHISTLEBLOWER PROVISIONS: 18 U.S.C. §§ 1519, 1520, 1513, 1514a

YATES v. UNITED STATES
-- U.S. --, 135 S.Ct. 1074 (2015)

Justice GINSBURG announced the judgment of the Court and delivered an opinion, in which THE CHIEF JUSTICE, Justice BREYER, and Justice SOTOMAYOR join.

John Yates, a commercial fisherman, caught undersized red grouper in federal waters in the Gulf of Mexico. [An officer of the Florida Fish and Wildlife Conservation Commission lawfully boarded the boat, found undersized fish, and instructed Yates to bring them to shore.] To prevent federal authorities from confirming that he had harvested undersized fish, Yates ordered a crew member to toss the suspect catch into the sea. For this offense, he was charged with, and convicted of, violating 18 U.S.C. § 1519, which provides:

"Whoever knowingly alters, destroys, mutilates, conceals, covers up, falsifies, or makes a false entry in any record, document, or tangible object with the intent to impede, obstruct, or influence the investigation or proper administration of any matter within the jurisdiction of any department or agency of the United States or any case filed under title 11, or in relation to or contemplation of any such matter or case, shall be fined under this title, imprisoned not more than 20 years, or both." ...

Section 1519 was enacted as part of the Sarbanes–Oxley Act of 2002, 116 Stat. 745, legislation designed to protect investors and restore trust in financial markets following the collapse of Enron Corporation. A fish is no doubt an object that is tangible; fish can be seen, caught, and handled, and a catch, as this case illustrates, is vulnerable to destruction. But it would cut § 1519 loose from its financial-fraud mooring to hold that it encompasses any and all objects, whatever their size or significance, destroyed with obstructive intent. Mindful that in Sarbanes–Oxley, Congress trained its attention on corporate and accounting deception and cover-ups, we conclude that a matching construction of § 1519 is in order: A tangible object captured by § 1519, we hold, must be one used to record or preserve information. ...

For violating § 1519, the court sentenced Yates to imprisonment for 30 days, followed by supervised release for three years. For life, he will bear the stigma of having a federal felony conviction. ...

The Sarbanes–Oxley Act, all agree, was prompted by the exposure of Enron's massive accounting fraud and revelations that the company's outside auditor, Arthur Andersen LLP, had systematically destroyed potentially incriminating documents. The Government acknowledges that § 1519 was intended to prohibit, in particular, corporate document-shredding to hide evidence of financial wrongdoing. Prior law made it an offense to "intimidat[e], threate[n], or corruptly persuad[e] *another person*" to shred documents. § 1512(b) (emphasis added). Section § 1519 cured a conspicuous omission by imposing liability on a person who destroys records himself. See S. Rep. No. 107-146, p. 14 (2002) (describing § 1519 as "a new general anti shredding provision" and explaining that "certain current provisions make it a crime to persuade another person to destroy documents, but not a crime to actually destroy the same documents yourself"). The new section also expanded prior law by including within the provision's reach "any matter within the jurisdiction of any department or agency of the United States."

In the Government's view, § 1519 extends beyond the principal evil motivating its passage. The words of § 1519, the Government argues, support reading the provision as a general ban on the spoliation of evidence, covering all physical items that might be relevant to any matter under federal investigation.

Yates urges a contextual reading of § 1519, tying "tangible object" to the surrounding words, the placement of the provision within the Sarbanes–Oxley Act, and related provisions enacted at the same time, in particular § 1520 and § 1512(c)(1). Section 1519, he maintains, targets not all manner of evidence, but records, documents, and tangible objects used to preserve them, *e.g.,* computers, servers, and other media on which information is stored.

We agree with Yates and reject the Government's unrestrained reading. "Tangible object" in § 1519, we conclude, is better read to cover only objects one can use to record or preserve information, not all objects in the physical world.

The ordinary meaning of an "object" that is "tangible," as stated in dictionary definitions, is "a discrete ... thing," Webster's Third New International Dictionary 1555 (2002), that "possess[es] physical form," Black's Law Dictionary 1683 (10th ed. 2014). From this premise, the Government concludes that "tangible object," as that term appears in § 1519, covers the waterfront, including fish from the sea.

Whether a statutory term is unambiguous, however, does not turn solely on dictionary definitions of its component words. Rather, "[t]he plainness or ambiguity of statutory language is determined [not only] by reference to the language itself, [but as well by] the specific context in which that language is used, and the broader context of the statute as a whole." Ordinarily, a word's usage accords with its dictionary definition. In law as in life, however, the same words, placed in different contexts, sometimes mean different things. ...

In short, although dictionary definitions of the words "tangible" and "object" bear consideration, they are not dispositive of the meaning of "tangible object" in § 1519. ...

Familiar interpretive guides aid our construction of the words "tangible object" as they appear in § 1519.

We note first § 1519's caption: "Destruction, alteration, or falsification of records in Federal investigations and bankruptcy." That heading conveys no suggestion that the section prohibits spoliation of any and all physical evidence, however remote from records. Neither does the title of the section of the Sarbanes–Oxley Act in which § 1519 was placed, § 802: "Criminal penalties for altering documents." Furthermore, § 1520, the only other provision passed as part of § 802, is titled "Destruction of corporate audit records" and addresses only that specific subset of records and documents. While these headings are not commanding, they supply cues that Congress did not intend "tangible object" in § 1519 to sweep within its reach physical objects of every kind, including things no one would describe as records, documents, or devices closely associated with them. If Congress indeed meant to make § 1519 an all-encompassing ban on the spoliation of evidence, as the dissent believes Congress did, one would have expected a clearer indication of that intent.

Section 1519's position within Chapter 73 of Title 18 further signals that § 1519 was not intended to serve as a cross-the-board ban on the destruction of physical evidence of every kind. Congress placed § 1519 (and its companion provision § 1520) at the end of the chapter, following immediately after the pre-existing § 1516, § 1517, and § 1518, each of them prohibiting obstructive acts in specific contexts. See § 1516 (audits of recipients of federal funds); § 1517 (federal examinations of financial institutions); § 1518 (criminal investigations of federal health care offenses). See also S. Rep. No. 107-146, at 7 (observing that § 1517 and § 1518 "apply to obstruction in certain limited types of cases, such as bankruptcy fraud, examinations of financial institutions, and healthcare fraud"). ...

The contemporaneous passage of § 1512(c)(1), which was contained in a section of the Sarbanes–Oxley Act discrete from the section embracing § 1519 and § 1520, is also instructive. Section 1512(c)(1) provides:

"(c) Whoever corruptly—
    "(1) alters, destroys, mutilates, or conceals a record, document, or other object, or attempts to do so, with the intent to impair the object's integrity or availability for use in an official proceeding
    . . . . .
    "shall be fined under this title or imprisoned not more than 20 years, or both."

The legislative history reveals that § 1512(c)(1) was drafted and proposed after § 1519. The Government argues, and Yates does not dispute, that § 1512(c)(1)'s reference to "other object" includes any and every physical object. But if § 1519's reference to "tangible object" already included all physical objects, as the Government and the dissent contend, then Congress had no reason to enact § 1512(c)(1): Virtually any act that would violate § 1512(c)(1) no doubt would violate § 1519 as well, for § 1519 applies to "the investigation or proper administration of any matter within the jurisdiction of any department or agency of the United States ... or in relation to or contemplation of any such matter," not just to "an official proceeding."[30]

---

[30] [Court's footnote 5:] Despite this sweeping "in relation to" language, the dissent remarkably suggests that § 1519 does not "ordinarily operate in th[e] context [of] federal court[s]," for those courts are not "department[s] or agenc[ies]." That suggestion, which, as one would expect, lacks the Government's endorsement, does not withstand examination. The Senate Committee Report on § 1519, on which the dissent elsewhere relies, explained that an obstructive act is within § 1519's scope if "done 'in contemplation' of or in relation to a matter or investigation." S. Rep. No. 107-146, at 15. The Report further informed that § 1519 "is ... meant to do away with the distinctions, which some courts have read into obstruction statutes, between court proceedings, investigations, regulatory or administrative proceedings (whether formal or not), and less formal government inquiries, regardless of their title." If any doubt remained about the multiplicity of contexts in which § 1519 was designed to apply, the Report added, "[t]he intent of the provision is simple; people should not be destroying, altering, or falsifying documents to obstruct any government function."

The Government acknowledges that, under its reading, § 1519 and § 1512(c)(1) "significantly overlap." Nowhere does the Government explain what independent function § 1512(c)(1) would serve if the Government is right about the sweeping scope of § 1519. We resist a reading of § 1519 that would render superfluous an entire provision passed in proximity as part of the same Act.

The words immediately surrounding "tangible object" in § 1519—"falsifies, or makes a false entry in any record [or] document"—also cabin the contextual meaning of that term. ...[W]e rely on the principle of *noscitur a sociis*—a word is known by the company it keeps—to "avoid ascribing to one word a meaning so broad that it is inconsistent with its accompanying words, thus giving unintended breadth to the Acts of Congress."

... "Tangible object" is the last in a list of terms that begins "any record [or] document." The term is therefore appropriately read to refer, not to any tangible object, but specifically to the subset of tangible objects involving records and documents, *i.e.*, objects used to record or preserve information.

This moderate interpretation of "tangible object" accords with the list of actions § 1519 proscribes. The section applies to anyone who "alters, destroys, mutilates, conceals, covers up, *falsifies*, or *makes a false entry in* any record, document, or tangible object" with the requisite obstructive intent. (Emphasis added.) The last two verbs, "falsif[y]" and "mak[e] a false entry in," typically take as grammatical objects records, documents, or things used to record or preserve information, such as logbooks or hard drives. See, *e.g.*, Black's Law Dictionary 720 (10th ed. 2014) (defining "falsify" as "[t]o make deceptive; to counterfeit, forge, or misrepresent; esp., to tamper with (a document, record, etc.)"). It would be unnatural, for example, to describe a killer's act of wiping his fingerprints from a gun as "falsifying" the murder weapon. But it would not be strange to refer to "falsifying" data stored on a hard drive as simply "falsifying" a hard drive. Furthermore, Congress did not include on § 1512(c)(1)'s list of prohibited actions "falsifies" or "makes a false entry in." See § 1512(c)(1) (making it unlawful to "alte[r], destro[y], mutilat[e], or concea[l] a record, document, or other object" with the requisite obstructive intent). That contemporaneous omission also suggests that Congress intended "tangible object" in § 1519 to have a narrower scope than "other object" in § 1512(c)(1).[31]

A canon related to *noscitur a sociis*, *ejusdem generis*, counsels: "Where general words follow specific words in a statutory enumeration, the general words are [usually] construed to embrace only objects similar in nature to those objects enumerated by the preceding specific words." ... Had Congress intended "tangible object" in § 1519 to be interpreted so generically as to capture physical objects as dissimilar as documents and fish, Congress would have had no reason to refer specifically to "record" or "document." The Government's unbounded reading of "tangible object" would render those words misleading surplusage.

Having used traditional tools of statutory interpretation to examine markers of congressional intent within the Sarbanes–Oxley Act and § 1519 itself, we are persuaded that an aggressive interpretation of "tangible object" must be rejected. It is highly improbable that Congress would have buried a general spoliation statute covering objects of any and every kind in a provision targeting fraud in financial record-keeping. ...

---

[31] [Court's footnote 7:] The dissent contends that "record, document, or tangible object" in § 1519 should be construed in conformity with "record, document, or other object" in § 1512(c)(1) because both provisions address "the same basic problem." But why should that be so when Congress prohibited in § 1519 additional actions, specific to paper and electronic documents and records, actions it did not prohibit in § 1512(c)(1)? When Congress passed Sarbanes–Oxley in 2002, courts had already interpreted the phrase "alter, destroy, mutilate, or conceal an object" in § 1512(b)(2)(B) to apply to all types of physical evidence. See, *e.g.*, *United States v. Applewhaite*, 195 F.3d 679, 688 (C.A.3 1999) (affirming conviction under § 1512(b)(2)(B) for persuading another person to paint over blood spatter). Congress' use of a formulation in § 1519 that did not track the one used in § 1512(b)(2)(B) (and repeated in § 1512(c)(1)) suggests that Congress designed § 1519 to be interpreted apart from § 1512, not in lockstep with it.

Finally, if our recourse to traditional tools of statutory construction leaves any doubt about the meaning of "tangible object," as that term is used in § 1519, we would invoke the rule that "ambiguity concerning the ambit of criminal statutes should be resolved in favor of lenity." That interpretative principle is relevant here, where the Government urges a reading of § 1519 that exposes individuals to 20–year prison sentences for tampering with *any* physical object that *might* have evidentiary value in *any* federal investigation into *any* offense, no matter whether the investigation is pending or merely contemplated, or whether the offense subject to investigation is criminal or civil. ...[32]

For the reasons stated, we resist reading § 1519 expansively to create a coverall spoliation of evidence statute, advisable as such a measure might be. Leaving that important decision to Congress, we hold that a "tangible object" within § 1519's compass is one used to record or preserve information. The judgment of the U.S. Court of Appeals for the Eleventh Circuit is therefore reversed, and the case is remanded for further proceedings.

Justice ALITO, concurring in the judgment.

This case can and should be resolved on narrow grounds. And though the question is close, traditional tools of statutory construction confirm that John Yates has the better of the argument. Three features of 18 U.S.C. § 1519 stand out to me: the statute's list of nouns, its list of verbs, and its title. Although perhaps none of these features by itself would tip the case in favor of Yates, the three combined do so.

Start with the nouns. Section 1519 refers to "any record, document, or tangible object." The *noscitur a sociis* canon instructs that when a statute contains a list, each word in that list presumptively has a "similar" meaning. A related canon, *ejusdem generis* teaches that general words following a list of specific words should usually be read in light of those specific words to mean something "similar." Applying these canons to § 1519's list of nouns, the term "tangible object" should refer to something similar to records or documents. A fish does not spring to mind—nor does an antelope, a colonial farmhouse, a hydrofoil, or an oil derrick. All are "objects" that are "tangible." But who wouldn't raise an eyebrow if a neighbor, when asked to identify something similar to a "record" or "document," said "crocodile"?

This reading, of course, has its shortcomings. For instance, this is an imperfect *ejusdem generis* case because "record" and "document" are themselves quite general. And there is a risk that "tangible object" may be made superfluous—what is similar to a "record" or "document" but yet is not one? An e-mail, however, could be such a thing. An e-mail, after all, might not be a "document" if, as was "traditionally" so, a document was a "piece of paper with information on it," not "information stored on a computer, electronic storage device, or any other medium." Black's Law Dictionary 587–588 (10th ed. 2014). E-mails might also not be "records" if records are limited to "minutes" or other formal writings "designed to memorialize [past] events." A hard drive, however, is tangible and can contain files that are precisely akin to even these narrow definitions. Both "record" and "document" can be read more expansively, but adding "tangible object" to § 1519 would ensure beyond question that electronic files are included. To be sure, "tangible object" presumably can capture more than just e-mails; Congress enacts "catchall[s]" for "known unknowns." But where *noscitur a sociis*

---

[32] [Court's footnote 8:] The dissent cites *United States v. McRae*, 702 F.3d 806, 834-838 (C.A.5 2012), [and] *United States v. Maury*, 695 F.3d 227, 243-244 (C.A.3 2012), as cases that would not be covered by § 1519 as we read it. Those cases supply no cause for concern that persons who commit "major" obstructive acts will go unpunished. The defendant in *McRae*, a police officer who seized a car containing a corpse and then set it on fire, was also convicted for that conduct under 18 U.S.C. § 844(h) and sentenced to a term of 120 months' imprisonment for that offense. ... And the defendant in *Maury*, a company convicted under § 1519 of concealing evidence that a cement mixer's safety lock was disabled when a worker's fingers were amputated, was also convicted of numerous other violations, including three counts of violating 18 U.S.C. § 1505 for concealing evidence of other worker safety violations. For those violations, the company was fined millions of dollars and ordered to operate under the supervision of a court-appointed monitor.

and *ejusdem generis* apply, "known unknowns" should be similar to known knowns, *i.e.,* here, records and documents. This is especially true because reading "tangible object" too broadly could render "record" and "document" superfluous.

Next, consider § 1519's list of verbs: "alters, destroys, mutilates, conceals, covers up, falsifies, or makes a false entry in." Although many of those verbs could apply to nouns as far-flung as salamanders, satellites, or sand dunes, the last phrase in the list—"makes a false entry in"—makes no sense outside of filekeeping. How does one make a false entry in a fish? "Alters" and especially "falsifies" are also closely associated with filekeeping. Not one of the verbs, moreover, *cannot* be applied to filekeeping—certainly not in the way that "makes a false entry in" is always inconsistent with the aquatic.

Again, the Government is not without a response. One can imagine Congress trying to write a law so broadly that not every verb lines up with every noun. But failure to "line up" may suggest that something has gone awry in one's interpretation of a text. Where, as here, each of a statute's verbs applies to a certain category of nouns, there is some reason to think that Congress had that category in mind. Categories, of course, are often underinclusive or overinclusive—§ 1519 for instance, applies to a bomb-threatening letter but not a bomb. But this does not mean that categories are not useful or that Congress does not enact them. Here, focusing on the verbs, the category of nouns appears to be filekeeping. This observation is not dispositive, but neither is it nothing. The Government also contends that § 1519's verbs cut both ways because it is unnatural to apply "falsifies" to tangible objects, and that is certainly true. One does not falsify the outside casing of a hard drive, but one could falsify or alter data physically recorded on that hard drive.

Finally, my analysis is influenced by § 1519's title: "Destruction, alteration, or falsification of *records* in Federal investigations and bankruptcy." (Emphasis added.) This too points toward filekeeping, not fish. Titles can be useful devices to resolve "'doubt about the meaning of a statute.'" The title is especially valuable here because it reinforces what the text's nouns and verbs independently suggest—that no matter how other statutes might be read, this particular one does not cover every noun in the universe with tangible form.

Titles, of course, are also not dispositive. Here, if the list of nouns did not already suggest that "tangible object" should mean something similar to records or documents, especially when read in conjunction with § 1519's peculiar list of verbs with their focus on filekeeping, then the title would not be enough on its own. In conjunction with those other two textual features, however, the Government's argument, though colorable, becomes too implausible to accept.

Justice KAGAN, with whom Justice SCALIA, Justice KENNEDY, and Justice THOMAS join, dissenting.

A criminal law, 18 U.S.C. § 1519, prohibits tampering with "any record, document, or tangible object" in an attempt to obstruct a federal investigation. This case raises the question whether the term "tangible object" means the same thing in § 1519 as it means in everyday language—any object capable of being touched. The answer should be easy: Yes. The term "tangible object" is broad, but clear. Throughout the U.S. Code and many States' laws, it invariably covers physical objects of all kinds. And in § 1519, context confirms what bare text says: All the words surrounding "tangible object" show that Congress meant the term to have a wide range. That fits with Congress's evident purpose in enacting § 1519: to punish those who alter or destroy physical evidence—*any* physical evidence—with the intent of thwarting federal law enforcement.

The plurality instead interprets "tangible object" to cover "only objects one can use to record or preserve information." The concurring opinion similarly, if more vaguely, contends that "tangible object" should refer to "something similar to records or documents"—and shouldn't include colonial farmhouses, crocodiles, or fish. In my view, conventional tools of statutory construction all lead to a more conventional result: A "tangible object" is an object that's tangible. I would apply the statute that Congress enacted and affirm the judgment below.

…

[Ed.: I have omitted much of Justice Kagan's point-by-point rebuttal of the plurality and concurring opinions, choosing instead to focus on her discussion of the legislative history, the relationship between 1519 and 1512, and her discussion of overcriminalization concerns.]

The words "record, document, or tangible object" in § 1519 also track language in 18 U.S.C. § 1512, the federal witness-tampering law covering physical evidence in all its forms. Section 1512, both in its original version (preceding § 1519) and today, repeatedly uses the phrase "record, document, or other object"—most notably, in a provision prohibiting the use of force or threat to induce another person to withhold any of those materials from an official proceeding. 18 U.S.C. § 1512(b)(2). That language, which itself likely derived from the Model Penal Code, encompasses no less the bloody knife than the incriminating letter, as all courts have for decades agreed. And typically "only the most compelling evidence" will persuade this Court that Congress intended "nearly identical language" in provisions dealing with related subjects to bear different meanings.

And legislative history, for those who care about it, puts extra icing on a cake already frosted. Section 1519 as the plurality notes, was enacted after the Enron Corporation's collapse, as part of the Sarbanes–Oxley Act of 2002. But the provision began its life in a separate bill, and the drafters emphasized that Enron was "only a case study exposing the shortcomings in our current laws" relating to both "corporate and criminal" fraud. The primary "loophole[]" Congress identified arose from limits in the part of § 1512 just described: That provision, as uniformly construed, prohibited a person from inducing another to destroy "record[s], document[s], or other object[s]"—of every type—but not from doing so himself. Congress enacted § 1519 to close that yawning gap. But § 1519 could fully achieve that goal only if it covered all the records, documents, and objects § 1512 did, as well as all the means of tampering with them. And so § 1519 was written to do exactly that—"to apply broadly to any acts to destroy or fabricate physical evidence," as long as performed with the requisite intent. "When a person destroys evidence," the drafters explained, "overly technical legal distinctions should neither hinder nor prevent prosecution." Ah well: Congress, meet today's Court, which here invents just such a distinction with just such an effect.

As Congress recognized in using a broad term, giving immunity to those who destroy non-documentary evidence has no sensible basis in penal policy. A person who hides a murder victim's body is no less culpable than one who burns the victim's diary. A fisherman, like John Yates, who dumps undersized fish to avoid a fine is no less blameworthy than one who shreds his vessel's catch log for the same reason. Congress thus treated both offenders in the same way. It understood, in enacting § 1519, that destroying evidence is destroying evidence, whether or not that evidence takes documentary form.

… Says the plurality: If read naturally, § 1519 "would render superfluous" § 1512(c)(1), which Congress passed "as part of the same act." But that is not so: Although the two provisions significantly overlap, each applies to conduct the other does not. The key difference between the two is that § 1519 protects the integrity of "matter[s] within the jurisdiction of any [federal] department or agency" whereas § 1512(c)(1) safeguards "official proceeding[s]" as defined in § 1515(a)(1)(A). Section 1519's language often applies more broadly than § 1512(c)(1)'s, as the plurality notes. For example, an FBI investigation counts as a matter within a federal department's jurisdiction, but falls outside the statutory definition of "official proceeding" as construed by courts. See, e.g., *United States v. Gabriel*, 125 F.3d 89, 105, n. 13 (C.A.2 1997). But conversely, § 1512(c)(1) sometimes reaches more widely than § 1519. For example, because an "official proceeding" includes any "proceeding before a judge or court of the United States," § 1512(c)(1) prohibits tampering with evidence in federal litigation between private parties. See § 1515(a)(1)(A). By contrast, § 1519 wouldn't ordinarily operate in that context because a federal court isn't a "department or agency." See *Hubbard v. United States*, 514 U.S. 695, 715 (1995).[33] So the surplusage canon doesn't come into play.[34] Overlap—even

---

[33] [Dissent's footnote 3:] The plurality's objection to this statement is difficult to understand. It cannot take issue with *Hubbard*'s holding that "a federal court is neither a 'department' nor an 'agency'" in a statute referring, just as § 1519 does, to "any matter within the jurisdiction of any department or agency of the United States," 514 U.S., at 698. So the plurality suggests that the phrase "in relation to … any

significant overlap—abounds in the criminal law. This Court has never thought that of such ordinary stuff surplusage is made.

And the legislative history to which the plurality appeals only cuts against it because those materials show that lawmakers knew that § 1519 and § 1512(c)(1) share much common ground. Minority Leader Lott introduced the amendment that included § 1512(c)(1) (along with other criminal and corporate fraud provisions) late in the legislative process, explaining that he did so at the specific request of the President. Not only Lott but several other Senators noted the overlap between the President's package and provisions already in the bill, most notably § 1519. The presence of both § 1519 and § 1512(c)(1) in the final Act may have reflected belt-and-suspenders caution: If § 1519 contained some flaw, § 1512(c)(1) would serve as a backstop. Or the addition of § 1512(c)(1) may have derived solely from legislators' wish "to satisfy audiences other than courts"—that is, the President and his Justice Department. Whichever the case, Congress's consciousness of overlap between the two provisions removes any conceivable reason to cast aside § 1519's ordinary meaning in service of preventing some statutory repetition.

Indeed, the inclusion of § 1512(c)(1) in Sarbanes–Oxley creates a far worse problem for the plurality's construction of § 1519 than for mine. Section 1512(c)(1) criminalizes the destruction of any "record, document, or other object"; § 1519 of any "record, document, or tangible object." On the plurality's view, one "object" is really an object, whereas the other is only an object that preserves or stores information. But "[t]he normal rule of statutory construction assumes that identical words used in different parts of the same act," passed at the same time, "are intended to have the same meaning." And that is especially true when the different provisions pertain to the same subject. The plurality doesn't—really, can't—explain why it instead interprets the same words used in two provisions of the same Act addressing the same basic problem to mean fundamentally different things. ...[35]

If none of the traditional tools of statutory interpretation can produce today's result, then what accounts for it? The plurality offers a clue when it emphasizes the disproportionate penalties § 1519 imposes if the law is read broadly. Section 1519, the plurality objects, would then "expose[] individuals to 20–year prison sentences for tampering with *any* physical object that *might* have evidentiary value in *any* federal investigation into *any* offense." That brings to the surface the real issue: overcriminalization and excessive punishment in the U.S. Code.

Now as to this statute, I think the plurality somewhat—though only somewhat—exaggerates the matter. The plurality omits from its description of § 1519 the requirement that a person act "knowingly" and with "the intent to impede, obstruct, or influence" federal law enforcement. And in highlighting § 1519's maximum penalty, the plurality glosses over the

---

such matter" in § 1519 somehow changes *Hubbard*'s result. But that phrase still demands that evidence-tampering relate to a "matter within the jurisdiction of any department or agency"—excluding courts, as *Hubbard* commands. That is why the federal government, as far as I can tell, has never once brought a prosecution under § 1519 for evidence-tampering in litigation between private parties. It instead uses § 1512(c)(1) for that purpose.

[34] [Dissent's footnote 4:] Section 1512(c)(1) also applies more broadly than § 1519 in proceedings relating to insurance regulation. The term "official proceeding" in § 1512(c)(1) is defined to include "proceeding[s] involving the business of insurance whose activities affect interstate commerce before any insurance regulatory official or agency." § 1515(a)(1)(D). But § 1519 wouldn't usually apply in that context because state, not federal, agencies handle most insurance regulation.

[35] [Dissent's footnote 6:] As part of its lenity argument, the plurality asserts that Yates did not have "fair warning" that his conduct amounted to a felony. But even under the plurality's view, the dumping of fish is potentially a federal felony—just under § 1512(c)(1), rather than § 1519. In any event, the plurality itself acknowledges that the ordinary meaning of § 1519 covers Yates's conduct: That provision, no less than § 1512(c)(1), announces its broad scope in the clearest possible terms. And when an ordinary citizen seeks notice of a statute's scope, he is more likely to focus on the plain text than (as the plurality would have it) on the section number, the superfluity principle, and the *noscitur* and *ejusdem* canons.

absence of any prescribed minimum. (Let's not forget that Yates's sentence was not 20 years, but 30 days.) Congress presumably enacts laws with high maximums and no minimums when it thinks the prohibited conduct may run the gamut from major to minor. That is assuredly true of acts obstructing justice. Compare this case with the following, all of which properly come within, but now fall outside, § 1519: [*United States v. McRae*, 702 F.3d 806, 834-838 (C.A. 5 2012)] (burning human body to thwart murder investigation); [*United States v. Maury*, 695 F.3d 227, 243-244 (C.A.3 2012)] (altering cement mixer to impede inquiry into amputation of employee's fingers). Most district judges, as Congress knows, will recognize differences between such cases and prosecutions like this one, and will try to make the punishment fit the crime. Still and all, I tend to think, for the reasons the plurality gives, that § 1519 is a bad law—too broad and undifferentiated, with too-high maximum penalties, which give prosecutors too much leverage and sentencers too much discretion. And I'd go further: In those ways, § 1519 is unfortunately not an outlier, but an emblem of a deeper pathology in the federal criminal code.

But whatever the wisdom or folly of § 1519, this Court does not get to rewrite the law. "Resolution of the pros and cons of whether a statute should sweep broadly or narrowly is for Congress." If judges disagree with Congress's choice, we are perfectly entitled to say so—in lectures, in law review articles, and even in dicta. But we are not entitled to replace the statute Congress enacted with an alternative of our own design.

Notes

1. Section 1519 is restricted to circumstances in which the destruction or alteration of physical evidence takes place in connection with "any matter within the jurisdiction of any department or agency of the United States" or a bankruptcy case under title 11 (as opposed to § 1503, which requires knowledge of a pending judicial proceeding, or § 1512(c), which applies to obstructive activity pertinent to an "official proceeding"). Just what does this mean?

The plurality and the dissent disagree about whether § 1519 applies to judicial proceedings; Justice Alito, the deciding vote, concurs on narrower grounds and does not address the issue. Justice Kagan's dissenting opinion has the better of the argument based on existing law.

Section 1505, of course, is also restricted in application to obstruction within the jurisdiction of "any department or agency of the United States." That portion of § 1505 has been confined in application to proceedings before executive branch departments (*e.g.*, Department of Justice, IRS, Customs Service) or federal agencies (*e.g.*, SEC). As Justice Kagan points out, this language also echoes the language of § 1001 before that statute was amended in 1996. Prior to 1996, § 1001 outlawed false statements "within the jurisdiction of any department or agency of the United States." Recall that the Supreme Court, in *Hubbard v. United States*, 514 U.S. 695 (1995), read the terms "any department or agency of the United States" to *exclude* the judicial branch. The *Hubbard* Court's reasoning also indicated that the Court would read the language to exclude false statements made to the legislative branch. *See, e.g.*, United States v. Oakar, 111 F.3d 146, 153 (D.C. Cir. 1997). Congress responded to *Hubbard* in 1996 by amending § 1001 to include false statements made "in any matter within the jurisdiction of the executive, legislative, or judicial branch of the Government of the United States." 18 U.S.C. § 1001. Given this recent judicial and legislative interchange, one presumes that Congress intentionally chose language that would be read to *preclude* application of § 1519 to the judicial or legislative branches.

On such a reading, this statute is aimed at obstructive activity that affects the investigation, or proper administration, of any matter within the jurisdiction of *the executive branch or the independent agencies*. This limitation is consistent with the context in which the statute was enacted: Congress was, at least in part, concerned with the obstructive activity of Arthur Andersen that was said to impede the investigation of Enron's financials by the SEC.

The Eleventh Circuit, however, appears to agree with the plurality opinion, as it upheld a conviction based on evidence that the defendant submitted altered records in the course of a judicial proceeding, that is, a grand jury investigation. United States v. Hoffman-Vaile, 568 F.3d 1335 (11th Cir. 2009). The court attempted, however, to tie the grand jury as closely as possible to an executive agency investigation in the course of its reasoning: "Because the Department of Health and Human

Services, which is a 'department or agency of the United States,' conducted the investigation of [the defendant] and the grand jury subpoenaed the missing records 'in relation to or in contemplation of' this investigation, her failure to produce the records with the photographs intact is obstructive conduct under 1519." *Id.* at 1343.

Given the similarity in language, it seems likely that courts will turn to the Supreme Court's broad interpretation of the term "jurisdiction" under § 1001 and hold that that term includes "all matters confided to the authority of an agency or department." United States v. Rodgers, 466 U.S. 475 (1984).

2. *Comparison of new § 1519 with § 1505*: Consider Chart 4, appended to this chapter. If the correct reading is that § 1519 ought to be confined to executive or agency proceedings as is argued above, how does § 1519 compare in terms of elements to the statute specifically designed to address obstruction in federal department and agency proceedings, § 1505? Note that a violation of § 1505 warrants up to 5 years' imprisonment while a violation of § 1519 may be punished by up to 20 years' imprisonment. Does this make sense?

3. *Comparison of new § 1519 with § 1512(c)*: In structure, § 1519 owes more to § 1512 than to § 1505. The portions of § 1512 that deal, like § 1519, with efforts to compromise physical evidence are § 1512(b)(2)(B) and § 1512(c). Again, § 1519 is clearly intransitive and thus should be measured against the intransitive provisions of § 1512(c) rather than the transitive requirements of § 1512(b)(2)(B). If the above analysis in note 1, *supra*, regarding the types of proceedings in which § 1519 may be invoked is correct, how does § 1519 stack up against § 1512(c)? How do their elements compare? This statute, like § 1512(c), carries a penalty of up to 20 years' imprisonment, while a conviction for other types of non-coercive witness tampering under § 1512(b) result in exposure of up to 10 years' imprisonment. Is the destruction, alternation, or concealment of physical evidence twice as culpable or dangerous as persuading witnesses to lie under oath?

4. According to news reports, one test case for § 1519 involved a lawyer charged with destroying evidence of a pornography crime for which his client might have derivative exposure—not corporate malfeasance. Philip D. Russell, an attorney, was indicted in the District of Connecticut on charges of violating both § 1512(c)(1) and § 1519. *See* United States v. Russell, 639 F.Supp.2d 226 (D. Conn. 2007). The indictment charged that on October 6, 2006, the FBI began investigating Robert F. Tate, the choirmaster and organist at a church for 34 years, for possession of child pornography. It is further alleged that on October 7, a church employee discovered the pornography on Tate's laptop; the church hired Russell on October 8 to represent the church with respect to its employment of Tate "given that Tate's laptop computer contained images of naked boys." *Id.* at 231. On October 9, Russell and other church officials confronted Tate, provided him with the name of a defense lawyer, made arrangements for Tate to leave Connecticut, and took possession of Tate's laptop. Russell is then alleged to have "corruptly altered, destroyed, mutilated, and concealed [the laptop] by … taking it apart with the intent to impair its integrity and availability for use in an official proceeding." *Id.* at 232. The district court denied Russell's motion to dismiss. *Id.* at 240.

The indictment does not explicitly allege that Russell *knew* that the FBI had launched an investigation. Note, too, that knowing possession of child pornography is a crime, regardless of motive. So if counsel and his client could not legally hold on to the evidence, and if Russell did not know that an investigation was ongoing, what does this prosecution suggest he do, consistent with his obligation to his client? One could turn contraband over to the police but refuse (to safeguard one's client's interests) to identify the source of the contraband. Can one do that with a laptop? If one wipes out identifying information (akin to wiping the fingerprints off a gun before turning it in), is that obstruction?

The defense bar did not have a positive reaction to this prosecution. Thus, for example, Norm Pattis blogged on Crime & Federalism that:

> … Unlike pre-Sarbanes-Oxley tampering statutes, [§ 1519 does not require] an investigation in place or even imminent as a predicate for prosecution. The statute appears to criminalize what was once considered prudence by defense counsel. … Once again, the law of unintended consequences results in overcriminalization: A law designed

to prevent accountants and lawyers from shredding forms has become a tool in child pornography prosecutions. No one will care much about that. But what happens tonight if you find cocaine in your child's bedroom?

Norm Pattis, *Don't Touch That Evidence!*, Crime & Federalism Blog (posted Feb. 16, 2007), at http://federalism.typepad.com/crime_federalism/2007/02/dont_touch_ that.html.; *see also* Robert J. Ambrogi, *SOX: Unintended Consequences for Lawyers*, Law.com (Posted March 6, 2007) (quoting chief disciplinary counsel for the Connecticut Bar Association as querying "[t]he question is what's evidence and when does something become evidence? How prescient does a lawyer need to be? Now if you guess wrong you've got big problems, because it is a serious crime.").

"Under the government's sweeping interpretation of § 1519, Mr. Russell argued, it would be illegal to possess certain types of records/documents but even more illegal to destroy them." Evan T. Barr, *"Russell": Prosecuting Defense Counsel for Obstruction*, N.Y.L.J., Nov. 21, 2007, 4. Russell ended up pleading guilty to the lesser offense of misprison under 18 U.S.C. § 4, which essentially makes it a crime to conceal the commission of a felony. *Id.*

5. The Eighth Circuit has concluded that the government, seeking a conviction under § 1519 for a defendant accused of falsifying of a promissory note, must prove first that the defendant knowingly falsified the document—meaning that the "falsification must be done knowingly; an unwitting falsehood will not suffice." United States v. Yielding, 657 F.3d 688, 711 (8th Cir. 2011). Second, the court held that the intent element of the statute encompassed three possible scenarios: "(1) a defendant acts with intent to impede, obstruct, or influence the investigation or proper administration of a federal matter; (2) a defendant, in contemplation of a federal matter, acts with intent to impede, obstruct or influence the investigation or proper administration of the matter; [or] (3) a defendant, in relation to a federal matter, acts with intent to impede, obstruct, or influence the investigation or proper administration of the matter." *Id.* at 711; *see also* United States v. Hunt, 526 F.3d 739, 743 (11th Cir. 2008). The three circuits that have addressed the question have concluded that the government need not prove that the defendant specifically knew that the matter was within the jurisdiction of a federal department or agency, reasoning that *mens rea* does not normally apply to such jurisdictional elements. *See* United States v. McQueen, 727 F.3d 1144, 1152 (11th Cir. 2013) (collecting cases).

Note that the District of Maryland, in the high profile—and ultimately unsuccessful—prosecution of a lawyer under § 1519 for advice she gave to her client held that because § 1519 is a "specific intent" crime, Stevens could rely on good faith reliance of counsel as a defense. United States v. Stevens, 771 F.Supp.2d 556 (D. Md. 2011). The district court reasoned that "[o]ne cannot be said to 'knowingly … alter[], … conceal[], cover[] up, falsif[y] or make[] false entry in any record [or] document … with intent to impede, obstruct, or influence' an investigation or administration of a matter within the jurisdiction of a federal agency unless it is the individual's intent to do that which is wrongful." *Id.* at 561. *See also* Katrice Bridges Copeland, *In-House Counsel Beware*, 39 Fordham Urb. L.J. 391 (2011).

6. Moving on to non-*mens rea* elements, those circuits to address the question have held that the *Aguilar* "nexus" requirement does *not* apply in these cases. That is, the government need not prove that the defendant's actions had the natural and probable effect of impeding or obstructing the investigation or proper administration of a matter. *See, e.g.*, United Stets v. Gray, 692 F.3d 514, 519-20 (6th Cir. 2012); United States v. Gray, 642 F.3d 371, 375-78 (2d Cir. 2011); United States v. Moyer, 674 F.3d 192, 209-10 (3d Cir. 2012); *Yielding*, 657 F.3d at 711-13.

7. Section 802 of the Sarbanes-Oxley Act also added 18 U.S.C. § 1520, which states:

§ 1520. Destruction of corporate audit records

(a)(1) Any accountant who conducts an audit of an issuer of securities to which section 10A(a) of the Securities Exchange Act of 1934 (15 U.S.C. [§] 78j-1(a)) applies, shall maintain all audit or review workpapers for a period of 5 years from the end of the fiscal period in which the audit or review was concluded.

(2) The Securities and Exchange Commission shall promulgate, within 180 days, after adequate notice and an opportunity for comment, such rules and regulations, as are reasonably necessary, relating to the retention of relevant records such as workpapers, documents that form the basis of an audit or review, memoranda, correspondence, communications, other documents, and records (including electronic records) which are created, sent, or received in connection with an audit or review and contain conclusions, opinions, analyses, or financial data relating to such an audit or review, which is conducted by any accountant who conducts an audit of an issuer of securities to which section 10A(a) of the Securities Exchange Act of 1934 (15 U.S.C. [§] 78j-1(a)) applies. The Commission may, from time to time, amend or supplement the rules and regulations that it is required to promulgate under this section, after adequate notice and an opportunity for comment, in order to ensure that such rules and regulations adequately comport with the purposes of this section.

(b) Whoever knowingly and willfully violates subsection (a)(1), or any rule or regulation promulgated by the Securities and Exchange Commission under subsection (a)(2), shall be fined under this title, imprisoned not more than 10 years, or both.

(c) Nothing in this section shall be deemed to diminish or relieve any person of any other duty or obligation imposed by Federal or State law or regulation to maintain, or refrain from destroying, any document.

Section 1520 is notably different from § 1512(c) and § 1519 in that it does not penalize the obstructive act of compromising or destroying physical evidence in certain contexts. Instead, it establishes a positive duty to retain specified records and then penalizes the "knowing and willful" failure to meet that duty. Note that this provision does not require a corrupt intent for criminal liability to attach. Nor does § 1520 require that proceedings be pending or even contemplated.

Does § 1520 outlaw all accounting firms' "document retention" policies (which generally authorize the destruction of certain categories of workpapers)? Does this section put accountants at risk if they destroy *any* papers relating to a review or audit (if such destruction was done non-corruptly but knowingly and willfully) even if the evidence is not relevant to a current or future investigation or proceeding? Is there any materiality requirement implicit here? May the regulations issued under (a)(2) limit the scope of the retention duty specified in (a)(1)? For discussion of the final rules the SEC promulgated pursuant to this authority, see SEC, Final Rule: Retention of Records Relevant to Audits and Reviews, Release No. 33-8180 etc. (discussing adoption of Rule 2-06 of Regulation S-X effective March 2003).

8. Congress focused in the Sarbanes-Oxley Act on protection of whistleblowers. Thus, section 1107 of the Act amended 18 U.S.C. § 1513 to add a new subsection at the end of the statute:

(e) Whoever knowingly, with the intent to retaliate, takes any action harmful to any person, including interference with the lawful employment or livelihood of any person, for providing to a law enforcement officer any truthful information relating to the commission or possible commission of any Federal offense, shall be fined under this title or imprisoned not more than 10 years, or both.

The requirement that there be an "intent to retaliate" narrows this provision somewhat, but it is notable that the defendant need only take "*any* action harmful to any person" in order to be liable. Might this include leaving an anonymous and insulting note on the whistleblower's desk or inscribing "rat" in the snow on her car hood? *See generally* Ronald H. Levine & Michelle L. Ostrelich, *Whistleblower Retaliation Under Sarbanes-Oxley: It's a Crime!*, 10 Bus. Crimes Bull. 1 (May 2003).

Further, section 806 of the Sarbanes-Oxley Act adds 18 U.S.C. § 1514A, which creates additional whistleblower protection in the form of a civil action for employees of publicly traded companies who provide information or assist in the investigation of a fraud case and suffer retaliation as a result.

18 U.S.C. § 1503 (Omnibus Provision: Obstruction in Judicial Proceedings)	**18 U.S.C. § 1505 (Obstruction in Federal Agency Proceedings and Congressional Investigations)**
The defendant	The defendant
knowing that a judicial proceeding is pending	knowing that there is a pending proceeding before a department or agency of the United States or an inquiry or investigation being had in Congress
corruptly (probably includes *Aguilar* "nexus" requirement)	corruptly (may include *Aguilar* "nexus" requirement
endeavors	endeavors
to influence, obstruct, or impede	to influence, obstruct, or impede
the due administration of justice	the due and proper administration of the law under which the pending proceeding is being had before any department or agency of the United States or the due and proper exercise of the power of congressional inquiry
with a specific intent to obstruct	may also require a specific intent to obstruct
10 year maximum (where a killing or attempted killing is not at issue and the offense was not committed against a petit juror)	5 year maximum (if the crime does not involve terrorism)

18 U.S.C. § 1503 (Omnibus Provision: Obstruction in Judicial Proceedings)	18 U.S.C. § 1512(b) (Non-coercive Witness Tampering)	18 U.S.C. § 1512(c) (Tampering with Physical Evidence & Omnibus Provision)
knowing that a judicial proceeding is pending and corruptly (probably includes *Aguilar* "nexus" requirement)	knowingly	corruptly (includes nexus)
endeavors to influence, obstruct, or impede the due administration of justice	uses intimidation, threatens, corruptly persuades, or engages in misleading conduct toward another person (or attempts to do so) (includes nexus as per *Andersen*)	(2) otherwise obstructs, influences, or impedes any official proceeding (or attempts to do so)*
with a specific intent to obstruct	with intent to (1) influence, delay or prevent the testimony of any person in an official proceeding; (2) cause or induce any person to (A) withhold testimony or an object from an official proceeding; (B) alter, destroy, or conceal an object with intent to impair the object's integrity or availability for use in an official proceeding; (C) evade legal process summoning that person to appear or to produce an object in an official proceeding; or (D) be absent from an official proceeding despite service of legal process; or (3) hinder, delay, or prevent the communication to a law enforcement officer or U.S. judge of information relating to the commission or possible commission of a Federal offense	(1) alters, destroys, mutilates, or conceals an object (or attempts to do so) with the intent to impair the object's integrity or availability for use in an official proceeding*

*[Ed.]: These subsections have been placed out of order for purposes of comparison with § 1503.

18 U.S.C. § 1505 (Obstruction in Federal Agency Proceedings and Congressional Investigations)	18 U.S.C. § 1512(b) (Non-coercive Witness Tampering)	18 U.S.C. § 1512(c) (Tampering with Physical Evidence & Omnibus Provision)
knowing that there is a pending proceeding before a department or agency of the United States or an inquiry or investigation being had in Congress, corruptly	knowingly	corruptly (includes nexus)
endeavors to influence, obstruct, or impede the due and proper administration of the law under which the pending proceeding is being had before any department or agency of the United States or the due and proper exercise of the power of congressional inquiry	uses intimidation, threatens, corruptly persuades, or engages in misleading conduct toward another person with intent to (1) influence, delay or prevent the testimony of any person in an official proceeding; (2) cause or induce any person to (A) withhold testimony or an object from an official proceeding; (B) alter, destroy, or conceal an object with intent to impair the object's integrity or availability for use in an official proceeding; (C) evade legal process summoning that person to appear or to produce an object in an official proceeding; or (D) be absent from an official proceeding despite service of legal process; or (3) hinder, delay, or prevent the communication to a law enforcement officer or U.S. judge of information relating to the commission or possible commission of a Federal offense	(2) otherwise obstructs, influences, or impedes any official proceeding (or attempts to do so)*

(1) alters, destroys, mutilates, or conceals an object (or attempts to do so) with the intent to impair the object's integrity or availability for use in an official proceeding* |

*[Ed.]: These subsections have been placed out of order for purposes of comparison with § 1505.

18 U.S.C. § 1519 (New tampering with records in federal investigations and bankruptcy)	18 U.S.C. § 1512(c) (New omnibus provision)	18 U.S.C. § 1505 (obstruction in federal agency proceedings)
The defendant	The defendant	The defendant
		knowing that there is a pending proceeding before a department or agency of the United States ...
Knowingly (no nexus)	Corruptly (nexus)	Corruptly (nexus)
alters, destroys, mutilates, conceals, covers up, falsifies, or makes a false entry in any record, document, or tangible object (that records or preserves information)	(1) alters, destroys, mutilates, or conceals a record, document, or other object (or attempts to do so) with the intent to impair the object's integrity or availability for use in an official proceeding *or*	endeavors
with the intent to impede, obstruct, or influence	(2) otherwise obstructs, influences, or impedes	to influence, obstruct, or impede
the investigation or proper administration of any matter within the jurisdiction of any department or agency of the United States or any bankruptcy case	any official proceeding (or attempts to do so)	the due and proper administration of the law under which the pending proceeding is being had before any department or agency of the United States
20 year maximum	20 year maximum	5 year maximum

Chapter 7

MAIL AND WIRE FRAUD

Were the novice prosecutor to flip through the United States Code in search of useful provisions, she might not be tempted to linger long over §§ 1341 (mail fraud) and 1343 (wire fraud). In fact, however, as one former federal prosecutor described § 1341,

> [t]o federal prosecutors of white collar crime, the mail fraud statute is our Stradivarius, our Colt 45, our Louisville Slugger, our Cuisinart—our true love. We may flirt with RICO, show off with 10b-5, and call the conspiracy law "darling," but we always come home to the virtues of 18 U.S.C. § 1341, with its simplicity, adaptability, and comfortable familiarity. It understands us and, like many a foolish spouse, we like to think we understand it.[1]

The prosecutorial maxim used to be "[w]hen in doubt, charge mail fraud"[2]; given that snail mail has been overtaken by all manner of electronic communications, wire fraud is much more commonly charged because faxes, telephone calls, texts, and emails constitute use of the "wires." The mail and wire fraud statutes have long been among the most frequently charged federal criminal statutes for a number of reasons. First, mail and wire fraud are inchoate offenses; thus, these statutes apply to fraudulent schemes that have not necessarily come to fruition or caused any loss. Second, at bottom the offenses are very simple: their essence is to proscribe use of the mails or wires to further fraudulent activity. On their faces, the statutes contain only two elements. For mail fraud, the Government must prove beyond a reasonable doubt: "(1) a scheme to defraud, and (2) the mailing of a letter, etc., for the purpose of executing the scheme."[3] Similarly, to make out a wire fraud case, the statute requires that the Government prove only (1) a scheme to defraud and (2) the use of interstate wire communications in furtherance of the scheme.[4] Notably, the jurisdictional elements of both statutes have "become extremely attenuated," with any mailing or interstate wiring that is

---

[1] Hon. Jed Rakoff, *The Federal Mail Fraud Statute (Part I)*, 18 Duq. L. Rev. 771, 771 (1980).

[2] John C. Coffee, Jr. & Charles K. Whitehead, *The Federalization of Fraud: Mail and Wire Fraud Statutes*, in 1 Otto G. Obermaier & Robert G. Morvillo, White Collar Crime: Business and Regulatory Offenses § 9.01, at 9-2 (2018).

[3] Pereira v. United States, 347 U.S. 1, 8 (1954).

[4] The mailing or use of the wires constitute the jurisdictional element of these statutes, and that element has been interpreted slightly differently for mail and wire fraud, as the following materials will show. However, most of the caselaw concerns the meaning and applicability of the "scheme to defraud" element of these statutes and the courts have uniformly given this language the same construction in applying both the mail and wire fraud statutes.

"incidental" to an essential part of the fraudulent scheme sufficing to meet the government's burden.[5]

Mail and wire fraud charges are also popular among prosecutors because of their seemingly infinite malleability:

> At first glance, [the mail fraud statute] may seem intended only to protect the integrity of a federally administered service, the post office. Yet its key phrase, "scheme to defraud," which is common [to mail and wire fraud], has long served instead as a charter of authority for courts to decide, retroactively, what forms of unfair or questionable conduct in commercial, public and even private life should be deemed criminal. In so doing, this phrase has provided more expansive interpretations from prosecutors and judges than probably any other phrase in the federal criminal law.[6]

This expansive reading has made it possible for the federal government to attack a remarkable range of criminal activity even though some of the underlying wrongdoing does not rest comfortably within traditional notions of fraud. The statutes' "applications, too numerous to catalog, cover not only the full range of consumer frauds, stock frauds, land frauds, bank frauds, insurance frauds, and commodity frauds, but have extended even to such areas as blackmail, counterfeiting, election fraud, and bribery."[7] In particular, in the absence of a federal statute directly prohibiting state and local political corruption, the mail and wire fraud statutes have been pressed into service to address this important problem.

These statutes are attractive charges because they may serve as the foundation for more complex charges, such as money laundering and Racketeer Influenced and Corrupt Organizations Act (RICO) offenses, which can "result in more severe sanctions and can form the basis for civil or criminal forfeiture."[8]

Finally, mail and wire fraud serve as a "first line of defense. When a 'new' fraud develops—as constantly happens—the mail fraud statute becomes a stopgap device to deal on a temporary basis with the new phenomenon, until particularized legislation can be developed and passed to deal directly with the evil."[9] Even after Congress passes specific legislation to deal with these areas, prosecutors continue to charge defendants under the mail and wire fraud statutes, alone or in conjunction with the new statute, because of their simplicity and familiarity. Indeed, prosecutors may choose to "ignore the legislative trade-offs reached in these more specific statutes and instead prosecute under the more general theory of fraud codified in the mail or wire fraud statutes, thereby outflanking special defenses, minimum loss requirements or other procedural or substantive obstacles that the legislature believed were necessary to establish a fair balance of advantage."[10]

While the flexibility of the statutes is a blessing for law enforcement, it is not universally applauded. Thus, it is argued, mail and wire fraud may "be used to prosecute kinds of behavior that, albeit offensive to the morals or aesthetics of federal prosecutors, cannot reasonably be expected by the instigators to form the basis of a federal felony."[11] Congress, as we shall see, has seemingly evidenced its approval of a broad application of these statutes by increasing the statutory penalties for mail and wire fraud (and attempts and conspiracies to commit same), enacting § 1346 to enshrine "honest services fraud," and amending § 1341 to cover deliveries by private or commercial interstate carriers. Yet some judges and many commentators continue to express discomfort with the scope of

---

[5] Coffee & Whitehead, *supra* note 2, § 9.02, at 9-13.

[6] *Id.* § 9.02.

[7] Rakoff, *supra* note 1, at 772.

[8] 4 Dep't of Justice Manual [hereinafter U.S.A.M.], tit. 9, Criminal Resource Manual No. 955

[9] United States v. Maze, 414 U.S. 395, 405-06 (1974) (Burger, C.J., dissenting).

[10] Coffee & Whitehead, *supra* note 2, § 9.02, at 9-15.

[11] United States v. Czubinski, 106 F.3d 1069, 1079 (1st Cir. 1997).

these statutes. In this area more than any other area of federal white-collar enforcement, one sees judicial opinions taking special pains to question prosecutors' choices in pushing the edge of an already over-expanded envelope.[12] Some courts have attempted to limit the scope of these statutes by engrafting onto its elements—particularly the "scheme to defraud" element—certain (for lack of a better term) sub-elements that are intended to separate merely ethically suspect or very aggressive business activity from criminally proscribed conduct.

The following materials explore the elements (and sub-elements) of mail and wire fraud, and cover some of the relatively straightforward uses of these statutes—that is, cases where persons attempt to obtain money or property to which they are plainly not entitled by lying or deceit, and use the mails or wires to effectuate their schemes. The materials then focus on some of the more creative applications of the statutes: prosecution of state and local officials for "fraudulent" deprivation of citizens' intangible right to honest government; and prosecution of private employees for fraudulently depriving their employers of their intangible right to the employees' "honest services." Among other things, the materials highlight judicial attempts to define the reach of these amorphous statutes in the face of aggressive prosecutions, the dynamic between Congress and the courts demonstrated in the development of the "honest services" theory of fraud, and the number of conflicts among the circuits on critical elements of proof. They therefore should provoke some consideration of the appropriate role of the executive, judicial, and legislative branches in defining the substance of criminal prohibitions. The materials also reveal the tensions inherent in the "federalization" of the traditional state-law crime of fraud. Finally, they should underscore what a difference a sophisticated understanding of the law, and the ability to exploit that understanding in motions practice and in crafting proposed jury instructions, can make in the effective defense of a white-collar prosecution.

A. THE MAILING OR WIRING IN FURTHERANCE ELEMENT

SCHMUCK v. UNITED STATES
489 U.S. 705 (1989)

JUSTICE BLACKMUN delivered the opinion of the Court.

In August 1983, petitioner Wayne T. Schmuck, a used-car distributor, was indicted ... on 12 counts of mail fraud, in violation of 18 U.S.C. §§ 1341 and 1342.

The alleged fraud was a common and straightforward one. Schmuck purchased used cars, rolled back their odometers, and then sold the automobiles to Wisconsin retail dealers for prices artificially inflated because of the low-mileage readings. These unwitting car dealers, relying on the altered odometer figures, then resold the cars to customers, who in turn paid prices reflecting Schmuck's fraud. To complete the resale of each automobile, the dealer who purchased it from Schmuck would submit a title-application form to the Wisconsin Department of Transportation on behalf of his retail customer. The receipt of a Wisconsin title was a prerequisite for completing the resale; without it, the dealer could not transfer title to the customer and the customer could not obtain Wisconsin tags. The submission of the title-application form supplied the mailing element of each of the alleged mail frauds.

Before trial, Schmuck moved to dismiss the indictment on the ground that the mailings at issue—the submissions of the title-application forms by the automobile dealers—were not in furtherance of the fraudulent schemes and, thus, did not satisfy the mailing element of the crime of mail fraud. ...

---

[12] See, e.g., United States v. Thompson, 848 F.3d 877, 884 (7th Cir. 2007); Czubinski, 106 F.3d at 1079; United States v. Brown, 79 F.3d 1550, 1562 (11th Cir. 1996); United States v. Siegel, 717 F.2d 9, 22-23 (2d Cir. 1983); United States v. McNeive, 536 F.2d 1245, 1252 n. 13 (8th Cir. 1976).

"The federal mail fraud statute does not purport to reach all frauds, but only those limited instances in which the use of the mails is a part of the execution of the fraud, leaving all other cases to be dealt with by appropriate state law." To be part of the execution of the fraud, however, the use of the mails need not be an essential element of the scheme. It is sufficient for the mailing to be "incident to an essential part of the scheme," or "a step in [the] plot."

Schmuck, relying principally on this Court's decisions in *Kann* [*v. United States*, 323 U.S. 88 (1944)], *Parr v. United States*, 363 U.S. 370 (1960), and *United States v. Maze*, 414 U.S. 395 (1974), argues that mail fraud can be predicated only on a mailing that affirmatively assists the perpetrator in carrying out his fraudulent scheme. The mailing element of the offense, he contends, cannot be satisfied by a mailing, such as those at issue here, that is routine and innocent in and of itself, and that, far from furthering the execution of the fraud, occurs after the fraud has come to fruition, is merely tangentially related to the fraud, and is counterproductive in that it creates a "paper trail" from which the fraud may be discovered. We disagree both with this characterization of the mailings in the present case and with this description of the applicable law.

We begin by considering the scope of Schmuck's fraudulent scheme. Schmuck was charged with devising and executing a scheme to defraud Wisconsin retail automobile customers who based their decisions to purchase certain automobiles at least in part on the low-mileage readings provided by the tampered odometers. This was a fairly large-scale operation. Evidence at trial indicated that Schmuck had employed a man known only as "Fred" to turn back the odometers on about 150 different cars. Schmuck then marketed these cars to a number of dealers, several of whom he dealt with on a consistent basis over a period of about 15 years. ... Thus, Schmuck's was not a "one-shot" operation in which he sold a single car to an isolated dealer. His was an ongoing fraudulent venture. A rational jury could have concluded that the success of Schmuck's venture depended upon his continued harmonious relations with, and good reputation among, retail dealers, which in turn required the smooth flow of cars from the dealers to their Wisconsin customers.

Under these circumstances, we believe that a rational jury could have found that the title-registration mailings were part of the execution of the fraudulent scheme, a scheme which did not reach fruition until the retail dealers resold the cars and effected transfers of title. Schmuck's scheme would have come to an abrupt halt if the dealers either had lost faith in Schmuck or had not been able to resell the cars obtained from him. These resales and Schmuck's relationships with the retail dealers naturally depended on the successful passage of title among the various parties. Thus, although the registration-form mailings may not have contributed directly to the duping of either the retail dealers or the customers, they were necessary to the passage of title, which in turn was essential to the perpetuation of Schmuck's scheme. As noted earlier, a mailing that is "incident to an essential part of the scheme," satisfies the mailing element of the mail fraud offense. The mailings here fit this description.

Once the full flavor of Schmuck's scheme is appreciated, the critical distinctions between this case and the three cases in which this Court has delimited the reach of the mail fraud statute—*Kann, Parr,* and *Maze*—are readily apparent. The defendants in *Kann* were corporate officers and directors accused of setting up a dummy corporation through which to divert profits into their own pockets. As part of this fraudulent scheme, the defendants caused the corporation to issue two checks payable to them. The defendants cashed these checks at local banks, which then mailed the checks to the drawee banks for collection. This Court held that the mailing of the cashed checks to the drawee banks could not supply the mailing element of the mail fraud charges. The defendants' fraudulent scheme had reached fruition. "It was immaterial to them, or to any consummation of the scheme, how the bank which paid or credited the check would collect from the drawee bank."

In *Parr*, several defendants were charged, *inter alia*, with having fraudulently obtained gasoline and a variety of other products and services through the unauthorized use of a credit card issued to the school district which employed them. The mailing element of the mail fraud charges in *Parr* was purportedly satisfied when the oil company which issued the credit card mailed invoices to the school district for payment, and when the district mailed payment in the form of a check. Relying on *Kann*, this Court held that these mailings were not in execution of the scheme as required by the statute because it was immaterial to the defendants how the oil company went about collecting its payment.[13]

Later, in *Maze*, the defendant allegedly stole his roommate's credit card, headed south on a winter jaunt, and obtained food and lodging at motels along the route by placing the charges on the stolen card. The mailing element of the mail fraud charge was supplied by the fact that the defendant knew that each motel proprietor would mail an invoice to the bank that had issued the credit card, which in turn would mail a bill to the card owner for payment. The Court found that these mailings could not support mail fraud charges because the defendant's scheme had reached fruition when he checked out of each motel. The success of his scheme in no way depended on the mailings; they merely determined which of his victims would ultimately bear the loss.

The title-registration mailings at issue here served a function different from the mailings in *Kann*, *Parr*, and *Maze*. The intrabank mailings in *Kann* and the credit card invoice mailings in *Parr* and *Maze* involved little more than post-fraud accounting among the potential victims of the various schemes, and the long-term success of the fraud did not turn on which of the potential victims bore the ultimate loss. Here, in contrast, a jury rationally could have found that Schmuck by no means was indifferent to the fact of who bore the loss. The mailing of the title-registration forms was an essential step in the successful passage of title to the retail purchasers. Moreover, a failure of this passage of title would have jeopardized Schmuck's relationship of trust and goodwill with the retail dealers upon whose unwitting cooperation his scheme depended. Schmuck's reliance on our prior cases limiting the reach of the mail fraud statute is simply misplaced.

To the extent that Schmuck would draw from these previous cases a general rule that routine mailings that are innocent in themselves cannot supply the mailing element of the mail fraud offense, he misapprehends this Court's precedents. In *Parr* the Court specifically acknowledged that "innocent" mailings—ones that contain no false information—may supply the mailing element. In other cases, the Court has found the elements of mail fraud to be satisfied where the mailings have been routine.

We also reject Schmuck's contention that mailings that someday may contribute to the uncovering of a fraudulent scheme cannot supply the mailing element of the mail fraud offense. The relevant question at all times is whether the mailing is part of the execution of the scheme as conceived by the perpetrator at the time, regardless of whether the mailing later, through hindsight, may prove to have been counterproductive and return to haunt the perpetrator of the fraud. The mail fraud statute includes no guarantee that the use of the mails for the purpose of executing a fraudulent scheme will be risk free. Those who use the mails to defraud proceed at their peril.

For these reasons, we agree with the Court of Appeals that the mailings in this case satisfy the mailing element of the mail fraud offenses. ...

JUSTICE SCALIA, with whom JUSTICE BRENNAN, JUSTICE MARSHALL, and JUSTICE O'CONNOR join, dissenting.

. . .

---

[13] [Court's footnote 7:] *Parr* also involved a second fraudulent scheme through which the defendant school board members misappropriated school district tax revenues. The Government argued that the mailing element of the mail fraud charges was supplied by the mailing of tax statements, checks, and receipts. This Court held, however, that in the absence of any evidence that the tax levy was increased as part of the fraud, the mailing element of the offense could not be supplied by mailings "made or caused to be made under the imperative command of duty imposed by state law." No such legal duty is at issue here. Whereas the mailings of the tax documents in *Parr* were the direct product of the school district's state constitutional duty to levy taxes, and would have been made regardless of the defendants' fraudulent scheme, the mailings in the present case, though in compliance with Wisconsin's car-registration procedure, were derivative of Schmuck's scheme to sell "doctored" cars and would not have occurred but for that scheme.

The purpose of the mail fraud statute is "to prevent the post office from being used to carry [fraudulent schemes] into effect." The law does not establish a general federal remedy against fraudulent conduct, with use of the mails as the jurisdictional hook, but reaches only "those limited instances in which the use of the mails is *a part of the execution of the fraud*, leaving all other cases to be dealt with by appropriate state law." In other words, it is mail fraud, not mail and fraud, that incurs liability. This federal statute is not violated by a fraudulent scheme in which, at some point, a mailing happens to occur—nor even by one in which a mailing predictably and necessarily occurs. The mailing must be in furtherance of the fraud.

In *Kann v. United States*, we concluded that even though defendants who cashed checks obtained as part of a fraudulent scheme knew that the bank cashing the checks would send them by mail to a drawee bank for collection, they did not thereby violate the mail fraud statute, because upon their receipt of the cash "[t]he scheme ... had reached fruition," and the mailing was "immaterial ... to any consummation of the scheme." We held to the same effect in *United States v. Maze*, declining to find that credit card fraud was converted into mail fraud by the certainty that, after the wrongdoer had fraudulently received his goods and services from the merchants, they would forward the credit charges by mail for payment. These cases are squarely in point here. For though the Government chose to charge a defrauding of retail customers (to whom the innocent dealers resold the cars), it is obvious that, regardless of who the ultimate victim of the fraud may have been, the fraud was complete with respect to each car when petitioner pocketed the dealer's money. As far as each particular transaction was concerned, it was as inconsequential to him whether the dealer resold the car as it was inconsequential to the defendant in *Maze* whether the defrauded merchant ever forwarded the charges to the credit card company.

Nor can the force of our cases be avoided by combining all of the individual transactions into a single scheme, and saying, as the Court does, that if the dealers' mailings obtaining title for each retail purchaser had not occurred then the dealers would have stopped trusting petitioner for future transactions. (That conclusion seems to me a non sequitur, but I accept it for the sake of argument.) This establishes, at most, that the scheme could not technically have been consummated if the mechanical step of the mailings to obtain conveyance of title had not occurred. But we have held that the indispensability of such mechanical mailings, not strictly in furtherance of the fraud, is not enough to invoke the statute. For example, when officials of a school district embezzled tax funds over the course of several years, we held that no mail fraud had occurred even though the success of the scheme plainly depended on the officials' causing tax bills to be sent by mail (and thus tax payments to be received) every year. *Parr v. United States*, 363 U.S., at 388-392. Similarly, when those officials caused the school district to pay by mail credit card bills—a step plainly necessary to enable their continued fraudulent use of the credit card—we concluded that no mail fraud had occurred.

I find it impossible to escape these precedents in the present case. Assuming the Court to be correct in concluding that failure to pass title to the cars would have threatened the success of the scheme, the same could have been said of failure to collect taxes or to pay the credit card bills in *Parr*. And I think it particularly significant that in *Kann* the Government proposed a theory *identical* to that which the Court today uses. Since the scheme was ongoing, the Government urged, the fact that the mailing of the two checks had occurred after the defendants had pocketed the fraudulently obtained cash made no difference. "[T]he defendants expected to receive further bonuses and profits," and therefore "the clearing of these checks in the ordinary course was essential to [the scheme's] further prosecution." The dissenters in *Kann* agreed. "[T]his," they said, "was not the last step in the fraudulent scheme. It was a continuing venture. Smooth clearances of the checks were essential lest these intermediate dividends be interrupted and the conspirators be called upon to disgorge." The Court rejected this argument, concluding that "the subsequent banking transactions between the banks concerned were merely incidental and collateral to the scheme and not a part of it." I think the mailing of the title application forms equivalently incidental here.

What Justice Frankfurter observed almost three decades ago remains true: "The adequate degree of relationship between a mailing which occurs during the life of a scheme and the scheme is ... not a matter susceptible of geometric determination." All the more reason to adhere as closely as possible to past cases. I think we have not done that today, and thus create problems for tomorrow.

Notes

1. Is the Court's attempt to distinguish its prior precedents persuasive? What lesson should budding prosecutors draw from *Schmuck* when defining their theory of a mail fraud case? May defense counsel still rely on *Kann, Parr,* and *Maze* to attack an indictment? *See, e.g.,* United States v. Jinian, 725 F.3d 954 (9th Cir. 2013).

2. *Schmuck* makes clear that the jurisdictional "mailing" or "wiring" need not itself contain any fraudulent information and may, in fact, be entirely innocent. Additionally, *Schmuck* demonstrates that a defendant need not personally thrust the jurisdictional mailing into the mailbox; it is sufficient if the defendant "causes" such a mailing. "Where one does an act with knowledge that the use of the mails will follow in the ordinary course of business, or where such use can reasonably be foreseen, even though not actually intended, then he 'causes' the mail to be used." Pereira v. United States, 347 U.S. 1, 8-9 (1954); *see also* United States v. Weiss, 630 F.3d 1263, 1272 (10th Cir. 2010) (the government need not prove that the defendant reasonably foresaw a particular wiring; it need only prove that he could have reasonably foreseen that the fraudulent scheme would result in some wiring); United States v. Turner, 551 F.3d 657, 666-67 (7th Cir. 2008) (fraudulent scheme involved three janitors who worked a small fraction of their required 40-hour week but falsified their attendance logs and collected their full salaries; jurisdictional element met by wire transmission involved in the direct deposit of the inflated paychecks in the janitors' accounts). Are these standards consistent with the purported object of the mail fraud statute, that is, "to prevent the post office from being used to carry [such fraudulent schemes] into effect," Durland v. United States, 161 U.S. 306, 314 (1896)? *See* Rakoff, *supra* note 1, *passim.* Should a more rigorous causal nexus be required in order to ensure that the "mailing" and "wiring" elements are not reduced to jurisdictional hooks upon which federal prosecutors may hang what traditionally would be considered state-law fraud cases?

As subsequent cases, *infra,* made clear, mail/wire fraud is an inchoate offense in that the scheme to defraud need not reach fruition for liability to attach. When mail/wire fraud is viewed in this light, what significance can the "mailing" or "wiring" element be said to have? *See* John C. Coffee, Jr., *The Metastasis of Mail Fraud: The Continuing Story of the "Evolution" of White-Collar Crime,* 21 Am. Crim. L. Rev. 1, 10-11 (1983) [hereinafter *The Metastasis of Mail Fraud*]. Consider the following analysis by Judge Jed Rakoff:

> Aside from purely regulatory offenses (*malum prohibitum*), most federal criminal laws—at least those applicable to what are otherwise state crimes—describe a simple structure of two elements. The first or "substantive" element consists of prohibited criminal conduct, either reprehensible on its face (*e.g.,* assault, murder, rape) or made so by some reprehensible intent (*e.g.,* carrying a gun with intent to commit murder, or taking money from a bank with intent to steal). The second or "jurisdictional" element consists of some, often wholly incidental, connection between the prohibited conduct and an area of federal power or involvement sufficient to warrant the exercise of federal sovereignty over the prosecution of the crime. ...
>
> At first glance it might be thought that the mail fraud statute fits neatly into the format described above, for it likewise consists of two elements: reprehensible activity in the form of devising a scheme to defraud, and federal jurisdiction in the form of a use of the mails. On closer examination, however, neither of these elements quite accords with the general formula. The first element of federal mail fraud—devising a scheme to defraud—is not itself conduct at all (although it may be made manifest by conduct), but is simply a plan, intention, or state of mind, insufficient in itself to give rise to any kind of criminal sanctions. Accordingly, if the second element of federal mail fraud—using the mails—were nothing more than a bare jurisdictional act, having only an incidental relation to the criminal activity described in the first element and no relation whatever to

the actor's intent, it is doubtful whether the statute would state a crime (at least in any ordinary sense), since it would not be addressed to any conduct that was both overt and reprehensible. To rectify this deficiency, the language of the mail fraud statute, and the cases construing it, require that the particular mailing charged in the second element of the crime be "sufficiently closely related" to the scheme-to-defraud charged as the first element of the crime as to be fairly held to be "for the purpose of executing" it; and further, that such use of the mails in execution of the scheme be "reasonably foreseeable" to someone in the defendant's position.

These added connections between the two elements of a federal mail fraud are rather akin to the traditional requirements in a civil tort action that the ultimate injury be proximately caused by the defendant's acts and/or be a reasonably foreseeable result of the defendant's acts. But although such requirements help to define a notion of "fault" sufficient to impose civil liability for damages, they are rarely to be found in criminal statutes, which typically require as a prerequisite to imposing criminal sanctions that the defendant have actual knowledge of the commission of the injurious or forbidden act and that he not only cause but also actually intend its commission. Thus, the appearance of the "civil" requirements of proximate causation and, especially, reasonable foreseeability in the federal criminal mail fraud statute is, at the least, surprising. Moreover, whereas in tort law the requirements of proximate causation and reasonable foreseeability serve to link the defendant with the ultimate injurious act for which he is being held responsible, in the case of the federal mail fraud statute such requirements serve to link the defendant with merely an act of mailing—an act that may be perfectly innocent in itself and that, even in terms of the overall scheme that it is said to further, may be an act of minute consequence.

Rakoff, *supra* note 1, at 773-76; *see also* Jack E. Robinson, *The Federal Mail and Wire Fraud Statutes: Correct Standards for Determining Jurisdiction and Venue*, 44 Williamette L. Rev. 479 (2008).

3. Should the defense be able to seek dismissal of a case in which jurisdiction is in essence manufactured by federal agents? In *United States v. Archer*, 486 F.2d 670 (2d Cir. 1973), federal agents set up a sting operation to uncover corrupt judges and prosecutors. To ensure federal jurisdiction, the informants placed interstate calls to the targets to discuss the scheme and prompted the targets to place interstate calls. Clearly reacting to an overall course of official conduct it found profoundly disturbing, the Second Circuit ultimately threw out the case by holding that the interstate calls were insufficient to satisfy the "use of a facility in interstate commerce" element of the Travel Act, 18 U.S.C. § 1952, because "the federal officers themselves supplied the interstate element" and had "[m]anufactured federal jurisdiction." 486 F.2d at 682. More recent cases, however, have drastically limited the defense of "manufactured jurisdiction." *See, e.g.*, United States v. Wallace, 85 F.3d 1063 (2d Cir. 1996). For example, in *Wallace*, the Second Circuit noted that courts "have refused to follow *Archer* when there is any link between the federal element and a voluntary, affirmative act of the defendant. Thus, when confronted with situations in which (i) the FBI introduces a federal element into a non-federal crime and (ii) the defendant then takes voluntary actions that implicate the federal element," the Second Circuit will find that federal jurisdiction has not been improperly manufactured and the statutory element has been met. *Id.* at 1066; *see also* United States v. Peters, 952 F.2d 960, 962-63 (7th Cir. 1992) (stating that the "course of decisions casts doubt ... on the vitality of the independent principle announced [in *Archer*] that forbids the 'manufacture' of federal jurisdiction in circumstances not constituting entrapment and not canceling any element of the crime such as criminal intent"). *Cf* United States v. Sarraj, 665 F.3d 916 (7th Cir. 2012) (rejecting manufactured jurisdiction argument in firearms sting case).

4. As *Schmuck* indicates, where the jurisdictional mailing or wiring follows the point at which the defendant has obtained that which he sought to secure through fraud, prosecutors may still demonstrate that the charged mailings or wirings were done "for the purpose of executing the scheme," Kann v. United States, 323 U.S. 88, 94 (1944), by essentially redefining the scheme as an ongoing one. That is, prosecutors can, as the Court did in *Schmuck*,

characterize the scheme as a continuing one (thus deferring the point at which it can be said to have come to fruition) and demonstrate that the mailing or wiring was necessary to perpetuate the redefined scheme. *See, e.g.*, United States v. Tiller, 302 F.3d 98 (3d Cir. 2002); United States v. Woodward, 149 F.3d 46, 64-65 (1st Cir. 1998). This is not always factually possible, however. *See, e.g.*, United States v. Strong, 371 F.3d 225 (5th Cir. 2004). For example, in *United States v. Lazarenko*, 564 F.3d 1026, 1036-37 (9th Cir. 2009), the Ninth Circuit rejected the government's argument that the wire transfers charged in the indictment were part of a continuing scheme to hide the defendants' fraudulent activity where the charged transfers occurred three or four years after the defendants secured the money that was the object of the fraud.

5. Another way prosecutors may satisfy the statute when the mailing or wiring takes place after the defendant has secured his aims through fraud is to concentrate on a "lulling" theory. As the Supreme Court has said, "[m]ailings occurring after receipt of the goods obtained by fraud are within the statute if they 'were designed to lull the victims into a false sense of security, postpone their ultimate complaint to the authorities, and therefore make the apprehension of the defendants less likely than if no mailings had taken place.'" United States v. Lane, 474 U.S. 438, 451-52 (1986) (quoting United States v. Maze, 414 U.S. 395, 403 (1974)); *see also* United States v. Sampson, 371 U.S. 75 (1962); United States v. Tanke, 743 F.3d 1296 (9th Cir. 2014) (lulling letters sent as part of cover-up will only qualify where the idea of sending the letters was hatched before the fraud came to fruition); United States v. Manarite, 44 F.3d 1407 (9th Cir. 1995). When, as a prosecutor, should one define one's theory of the case regarding the jurisdictional mailings?

6. Why is *Schmuck* not covered by the "required records" exception set forth in *Parr v. United States*, 363 U.S. 370, 391 (1960) and mentioned in the *Schmuck* Court's footnote 7 (footnote 13 in this book, *supra*)? The forms constituting the "mailing" were required by state law in order to affect a valid transfer of title. As one court of appeals has explained:

> ... Both the Supreme Court and this court have rejected the claim that *Parr* holds categorically that required mailings cannot further fraud. *Schmuck* noted that while the mailings in *Parr* were solely the product of a legal duty and would have been made regardless of the defendants' fraudulent scheme, the mailings in *Schmuck* derived from Schmuck's scheme to sell modified cars. The *Schmuck* mailings would have not occurred but for the scheme.

United States v. Ashman, 979 F.2d 469, 483 (7th Cir. 1992) (government-required confirmations sent as a "direct result of fraudulent trading" satisfied mailing requirement because "[h]ad the defendants not executed the arranged transactions, those specific trades would have not occurred, obviating the need for any confirmation"); *see also* United States v. Al-Ame, 434 F.3d 614 (3d Cir. 2006).

7. The sole important distinction between the application of the mail and the wire fraud statutes relates to the jurisdictional "mailing" and "wiring" elements. Obviously, conviction under one statute requires a mailing while the other presupposes a wiring. Less obviously, the mailing that may serve as the jurisdictional basis for a § 1341 count can be an *intra*state mailing while a wiring may serve as the jurisdictional predicate for a § 1343 charge *only* when that wiring was in fact *inter*state. *See* United States v. Kieffer, 681 F.3d 1143, 1153-55 (10th Cir. 2012) (evidence that nonlawyer held himself out as a lawyer on a website that was accessed by parties in different states was sufficient proof of use of interstate wires).

The distinction is based on the constitutional foundation for the statutes. Congress had the authority to enact the mail fraud statute under its postal power, U.S. Const. art. I, § 8. In contrast, Congress's enactment of the wire fraud statute relies upon its Commerce Clause power, and thus "[t]he requirement of an interstate nexus arises from constitutional limitations on congressional power over interstate activities under the Commerce Clause." United States v. Bryant, 766 F.2d 370, 375 (8th Cir. 1985).

8. The question then arises whether the government must prove that a defendant knew or reasonably could foresee that the relevant wire was being sent interstate. Most courts to

address this issue have held that while the government must prove (1) that the defendant knew or reasonably could foresee that the *wires* would be used in furtherance of the scheme to defraud, and that (2) interstate wires were actually used, there is no further requirement that the government prove (3) that the defendant knew or could reasonably foresee that the wires would be *interstate* in character. *See* United States v. Lindemann, 85 F.3d 1232 (7th Cir. 1996); *Bryant*, 766 F.2d at 375. The articulated rationale is that the element is "only jurisdictional": "The interstate nature of the communication does not make the fraud more culpable. Thus, whether or not a defendant knows or can foresee that a communication is interstate, the offense is still every bit as grave in the moral sense." *Bryant*, 766 F.2d at 375; *see also Lindemann*, 85 F.3d at 1241.

Some jurisdictions may permit exceptions to this rule. For example, in *United States v. Bryant*, the Eighth Circuit noted that:

> The government must show that the accused knew or could have foreseen that a communication in furtherance of a fraudulent scheme was interstate, if the conduct giving rise to the scheme would not be a violation of state law and was not itself morally wrongful. In other words, if what happened was not in violation of state law or wrongful in nature, an innocent defendant could be ensnared in a federal prosecution if, unknown to him, the communication is in fact interstate.

766 F.2d at 375. How often do you think such an exception might be invoked? Readers may wish to return to this question after studying the next few sections of this chapter and reassess the potential usefulness of this exception to defense counsel.

9. Prior to 1994, fraudsters could avoid the reach of the mail fraud statute by using private couriers (such as Federal Express or United Parcel Service) in furtherance of their schemes. In 1994, the mail fraud statute was amended to include mail delivered "by the Postal Service, or ... any private or commercial interstate carrier." 18 U.S.C. § 1341. In *United States v. Photogrammetric Data Servs., Inc.*, 259 F.3d 229 (4th Cir. 2001), the Fourth Circuit held that Congress intended that the mail fraud statute would apply to *intra* and *inter*state deliveries of mail matter by private and commercial interstate carriers and that the extension of the mail fraud statute to *intra*state delivery of items by interstate private carriers is a permissible exercise by Congress of its Commerce Clause power. Must prosecutors prove that interstate nexus in each case?

10. Because the gravamen of mail/wire fraud is use of the mails or interstate wires to further a fraud, a defendant may be charged with a separate count for each mailing or wiring in furtherance of a scheme or schemes. Badders v. United States, 240 U.S. 391 (1916). That is, it is clear that the "unit of prosecution" for charging purposes is each mailing or wiring, not each "scheme to defraud." For example, suppose that a defendant engages in a fraudulent telemarketing scheme through which he makes 100 interstate telephone calls to 100 victims, using the same fraudulent pitch each time to con each victim out of $100, for a total loss of $10,000. The government could bring 100 counts if it wished to do so, even though the fraud involved one course of conduct or scheme or plan. Should that be so? *See* C.J. Williams, *What is the Gist of the Mail Fraud Statute?*, 66 Okla. L. Rev. 287 (2014).

11. What considerations would influence a prosecutor's decision regarding how many counts to bring? It is difficult comprehensively to catalogue all the factors involved but obviously the strength of the evidence and the legal sufficiency of each proposed count would be important considerations. In 2017, Attorney General Jeff Sessions issued a memorandum to all federal prosecutors overturning Obama era charging policies that had permitted prosecutors greater discretion in charging. General Sessions instructed prosecutors that:

> [I]t is a core principle that prosecutors should charge and pursue the most serious, readily provable offense. ... By definition, the most serious offenses are those that carry the most substantial guidelines sentence, including mandatory minimums.
>
> There will be circumstances in which good judgment would lead a prosecutor to conclude that a strict application of the above charging policy is not warranted. In that

case, prosecutors should carefully consider whether an exception may be justified. Consistent with longstanding Department of Justice policy, any decision to vary from the policy must be approved by a United States Attorney or Assistant Attorney General, or a supervisor designated by [such persons], and the reasons must be documented in the file.

Memorandum to Federal Prosecutors from U.S. Attorney General Sessions, Department Charging and Sentencing Policy (May 10, 2017). Although the press covered Attorney General Sessions' policy statement as though these rules were new, in fact they are not; it has been long-standing Justice Department policy to charge the "most serious, readily provable" count(s). What has changed with administrations is the degree to which individual Assistant United States Attorneys have discretion to deviate from this rule in individual cases without high level supervisory approval. Attorneys General in Republican administrations generally have taken a firm line against such exercises of discretion and Attorneys General in Democratic administrations have tended to be more open to it.

Varied resource questions could also be weighed—such as how many witnesses would have to be called, how long any trial would take, the staffing required for such an undertaking, and the like. Prosecutors might consider whether a fulsome indictment would make more likely a favorable verdict—either by permitting the introduction of evidence that might not otherwise come in or by simply persuading the jury that the sheer number of charges means that this defendant is truly a bad actor. Charges might be included so as to ensure that the venue is appropriate in the prosecutor's jurisdiction, that the indictment does not suffer statute of limitations problems, and that joinder of codefendants is possible. Charging choices might also involve numerous strategic considerations, such as whether a threatened 100 count indictment would induce the defendant to proffer needed cooperation to the government against more culpable actors or would encourage the defendant to plead out to some mutually satisfactory compromise. Are all of these factors ones that *should* affect prosecutors' judgment? How should they be weighed?

12. Congress enhanced the potential sentencing consequences of a mail or wire fraud charge in the Sarbanes-Oxley Act of 2002, P.L. 107-204, 116 Stat. 745 (2002). Section 903 of the Sarbanes-Oxley Act amended the mail and wire fraud statutes, 18 U.S.C. §§ 1341, 1343, to substitute a maximum penalty of up to 20 years' imprisonment for the pre-existing maximum of up to 5 years. Should prosecutors be responsible for determining how much sentencing exposure a defendant will face through their charging and plea bargaining choices? Should the prosecutor's decision to charge 1 count in the above case yield a substantially lesser sentence than the prosecutor's decision to charge 100 counts, given that, as courts have pointed out, the jurisdictional "mailing" or "wiring" element has no relationship to the moral culpability of a defendant? And should a sentence hinge on the accident of how many times a defendant places an interstate telephone call in pursuing a single course of wrongful conduct? As we have seen in studying and applying the Federal Sentencing Guidelines, the U.S. Sentencing Commission has attempted to blunt the effect of prosecutorial charging and plea bargaining choices in many financial crimes cases, including many mail and wire fraud cases. The "relevant conduct" and "grouping" rules that will be the subject of this chapter's guidelines exercise should demonstrate that, at least in theory, a prosecutor will achieve the same sentencing exposure under the guidelines whether or not she charges and proves at trial 1 count or 100 counts; the defendant's guidelines range will be based on the total amount of harm done—$10,000. It is worth keeping in mind, however, that the Guidelines are now advisory only and so judges can in theory sentence defendants to up to the statutory maximum. To arrive at a statutory maximum for an indictment, one simply adds up the statutory maximums for all counts. So an indictment containing 100 counts of wire fraud (not affecting a financial institution) gives the judge a sentencing range of 0 to 2,000 years.

13. Congress has singled out mail and wire fraud that "affects a financial institution" in two important ways. First, under the terms of the statutes themselves, where a mail or wire fraud "affects a financial institution," the statutory maximum skyrockets to 30 years. *See* United States v. Stargell, 738 F.3d 1018 (9th Cir. 2013) (a new or increased risk of loss is sufficient to establish that wire fraud affects a financial institution). Second, prosecutors have five extra

years to make these cases. A five-year statute of limitations applies to most non-capital federal crimes, and it usually applies to wire and mail fraud charges as well. *See* 18 U.S.C. § 3282(a). In mail or wire fraud cases "affecting a financial institution," however, 18 U.S.C. § 3293(2) doubles the statute of limitations, meaning that the prosecution has ten years to develop its case if a financial institution was targeted or exposed to increased risk of loss. *See* United States v. Mullins, 613 F.3d 1273, 1278-1279 (10th Cir. 2010); *see also* United States v. Ubakanma, 215 F.3d 421, 426 (4th Cir. 2000) ("[M]ere utilization of a financial institution" as a conduit for funds with no attendant risk of loss to the institution might not suffice).

14. In § 902 of the Sarbanes-Oxley Act of 2002, P.L. 107-204, 116 Stat. 745 (2002), Congress created 18 U.S.C. § 1349, which provides that "[a]ny person who attempts or conspires to commit any offense under this chapter shall be subject to the same penalties as those prescribed for the offense, the commission of which was the object of the attempt or conspiracy." This new section applies to all the fraud offenses in the chapter, including mail, wire, bank, securities, and health care fraud. Under prior law, the wire fraud provision did not explicitly cover "attempts" (although this was not much of an impediment in practice because, of course, the law does not require that a scheme to defraud be completed or successful to be actionable). More important, § 1349 provides that attempts and conspiracies to commit the substantive Federal fraud offenses will have the same statutory maximum as the substantive crime. Because the usual conspiracy statute (18 U.S.C. § 371) carries only a five-year maximum, while the fraud provisions carry much higher potential penalties, this gives prosecutors greater bargaining power. *See also* United States v. Roy, 783 F.3d 418 (2d Cir. 2015) (*en banc*) (conspiracy to commit wire or bank fraud does not require proof of an overt act).

B. SCHEME TO DEFRAUD ELEMENT

1. MATERIALITY AND RELIANCE

NEDER v. UNITED STATES
527 U.S. 1 (1999)

CHIEF JUSTICE REHNQUIST delivered the opinion of the Court.

...

In the mid-1980's, petitioner Ellis E. Neder, Jr., an attorney and real estate developer in Jacksonville, Florida, engaged in a number of real estate transactions financed by fraudulently obtained bank loans. ...

Neder was indicted on, among other things, 9 counts of mail fraud, in violation of 18 U.S.C. § 1341; 9 counts of wire fraud, in violation of § 1343; 12 counts of bank fraud, in violation of § 1344; and 2 counts of filing a false income tax return, in violation of 26 U.S.C. § 7206(1). The fraud counts charged Neder with devising and executing various schemes to defraud lenders in connection with ... land acquisition and development loans, totaling over $40 million. ...

We ... granted certiorari in this case to decide whether materiality is an element of a "scheme or artifice to defraud" under the federal mail fraud (18 U.S.C. § 1341), wire fraud (§ 1343), and bank fraud (§ 1344) statutes. The Court of Appeals concluded that the failure to submit materiality to the jury was not error because the fraud statutes do not require that a "scheme to defraud" employ *material* falsehoods. We disagree.

Under the framework set forth in *United States v. Wells*, 519 U.S. 482 (1997), we first look to the text of the statutes at issue to discern whether they require a showing of materiality. In this case, we need not dwell long on the text because, as the parties agree, none of the fraud statutes defines the phrase "scheme or artifice to defraud," or even mentions materiality. Although the mail fraud and wire fraud statutes contain different jurisdictional elements (§

1341 requires use of the mails while § 1343 requires use of interstate wire facilities), they both prohibit, in pertinent part, "any scheme or artifice to defraud" or to obtain money or property "by means of false or fraudulent pretenses, representations, or promises." The bank fraud statute, which was modeled on the mail and wire fraud statutes, similarly prohibits any "scheme or artifice to defraud a financial institution" or to obtain any property of a financial institution "by false or fraudulent pretenses, representations, or promises." Thus, based solely on a "natural reading of the full text," materiality would not be an element of the fraud statutes.

That does not end our inquiry, however, because in interpreting statutory language there is a necessary second step. It is a well-established rule of construction that "'[w]here Congress uses terms that have accumulated settled meaning under ... the common law, a court must infer, unless the statute otherwise dictates, that Congress means to incorporate the established meaning of these terms.'" Neder contends that "defraud" is just such a term, and that Congress implicitly incorporated its common-law meaning, including its requirement of materiality,[14] into the statutes at issue.

The Government does not dispute that both at the time of the mail fraud statute's original enactment in 1872, and later when Congress enacted the wire fraud and bank fraud statutes, actionable "fraud" had a well-settled meaning at common law. Nor does it dispute that the well-settled meaning of "fraud" required a misrepresentation or concealment of *material* fact. Indeed, as the sources we are aware of demonstrate, the common law could not have conceived of "fraud" without proof of materiality. Thus, under the rule that Congress intends to incorporate the well-settled meaning of the common-law terms it uses, we cannot infer from the absence of an express reference to materiality that Congress intended to drop that element from the fraud statutes. On the contrary, we must *presume* that Congress intended to incorporate materiality "'unless the statute otherwise dictates.'"[15]

The Government attempts to rebut this presumption by arguing that the term "defraud" would bear its common-law meaning only if the fraud statutes "indicated that Congress had codified the crime of false pretenses or one of the common-law torts sounding in fraud." Instead, the Government argues, Congress chose to unmoor the mail fraud statute from its common-law analogs by punishing, not the completed fraud, but rather any person "having devised or intending to devise a scheme or artifice to defraud." Read in this light, the Government contends, there is no basis to infer that Congress intended to limit criminal liability to conduct that would constitute "fraud" at common law, and in particular, to *material* misrepresentations or omissions. Rather, criminal liability would exist so long as the defendant *intended* to deceive the victim, even if the particular means chosen turn out to be immaterial, *i.e.*, incapable of influencing the intended victim.

---

[14] [Court's footnote 5:] The *Restatement* instructs that a matter is material if:

"(a) a reasonable man would attach importance to its existence or nonexistence in determining his choice of action in the transaction in question; or

"(b) the maker of the representation knows or has reason to know that its recipient regards or is likely to regard the matter as important in determining his choice of action, although a reasonable man would not so regard it."

Restatement (Second) of Torts § 538 (1976).

[15] [Court's footnote 7:] The Government argues that because Congress has provided express materiality requirements in other statutes prohibiting fraudulent conduct, the absence of such an express reference in the fraud statutes at issue "'speaks volumes.'" These later enacted statutes, however, differ from the fraud statutes here in that they prohibit both "false" and "fraudulent" statements or information. Because the term "false statement" does not imply a materiality requirement, *United States v. Wells*, 519 U.S. 482, 491 (1997) [(holding that materiality is not an element of the offense of making a false statement to a federally insured bank under 18 U.S.C. § 1014)], the word "material" limits the statutes' scope to material falsehoods. Moreover, these statutes cannot rebut the presumption that Congress intended to incorporate the common-law meaning of the term "fraud" in the mail fraud, wire fraud, and bank fraud statutes. That rebuttal can only come from the text or structure of the fraud statutes themselves.

The Government relies heavily on *Durland v. United States*, 161 U.S. 306 (1896), our first decision construing the mail fraud statute, to support its argument that the fraud statutes sweep more broadly than common-law fraud. But *Durland* was different from this case. There, the defendant, who had used the mails to sell bonds he did not intend to honor, argued that he could not be held criminally liable because his conduct did not fall within the scope of the common-law crime of "false pretenses." We rejected the argument that "the statute reaches only such cases as, at common law, would come within the definition of 'false pretenses,' in order to make out which there must be a misrepresentation as to some existing fact and not a mere promise as to the future." Instead, we construed the statute to "includ[e] everything designed to defraud by representations as to the past or present, or suggestions and promises as to the future." Although *Durland* held that the mail fraud statute reaches conduct that would not have constituted "false pretenses" at common law, it did not hold, as the Government argues, that the statute encompasses more than common-law fraud.

In one sense, the Government is correct that the fraud statutes did not incorporate *all* the elements of common-law fraud. The common-law requirements of "justifiable reliance" and "damages," for example, plainly have no place in the federal fraud statutes. See, *e.g.*, *United States v. Stewart*, 872 F.2d 957, 960 (C.A.10 1989) ("[Under the mail fraud statute,] the government does not have to prove actual reliance upon the defendant's misrepresentations"); *United States v. Rowe*, 56 F.2d 747, 749 (C.A.2 1932) (L. Hand, J.) ("Civilly of course the [mail fraud statute] would fail without proof of damage, but that has no application to criminal liability"). By prohibiting the "scheme to defraud," rather than the completed fraud, the elements of reliance and damage would clearly be inconsistent with the statutes Congress enacted. But while the language of the fraud statutes is incompatible with these requirements, the Government has failed to show that this language is inconsistent with a materiality requirement.

Accordingly, we hold that materiality of falsehood is an element of the federal mail fraud, wire fraud, and bank fraud statutes. Consistent with our normal practice where the court below has not yet passed on the harmlessness of any error, we remand this case to the Court of Appeals for it to consider in the first instance whether the jury-instruction error was harmless. ...

Notes

1. Materiality is often described in the fraud context as it is in the false statement and perjury contexts: a misrepresentation is material if it had a natural tendency to influence or was capable of influencing the decision maker to whom it was addressed. *See* United States v. Merrill, 685 F.3d 1002, 1012 (11th Cir. 2012). And "'a false statement can be material even if the decision maker actually knew or should have known that the statement was false.'" *Id.* (citation omitted).

2. Prior to the Court's decision in *Neder*, many courts had assumed that they were not bound by principles of common law fraud in interpreting the mail and wire fraud statute, relying, as did the government in *Neder*, upon the Court's decision in *Durland v. United States*, 161 U.S. 306 (1896). What are the consequences of the Court's apparent holding that "fraud" for purposes of sections 1341 and 1343 must be interpreted in light of common law understandings of that term? *See infra* discussion of the intent requirement; *cf.* Pasquantino v. United States, 544 U.S. 349 (2005) (holding that the wire fraud statute does not derogate from the common-law revenue rule).

The issue whether common law doctrines should be consulted in interpreting the mail and wire fraud statutes continues to arise. Thus, in *United States ex rel. O'Donnell v. Countrywide Home Loans, Inc.*, 822 F.3d 650 (2d Cir. 2016), the Second Circuit reversed a judgment against Countrywide in reliance on common law doctrine that breach of a contractual promise is insufficient to prove fraud. A *qui tam* relator filed suit against Countrywide; the Justice Department intervened and added claims under the Financial Institutions Reform, Recovery, and Enforcement Act ("FIRREA"). FIRREA allows the government to seek penalties for conduct that violates the federal fraud statutes if it affects a federally insured financial institution. The complaint alleged, and the jury found, that Fannie Mae and Freddie Mac agreed by contract to buy mortgages from Countrywide but only if such mortgages met certain quality standards. The proof showed that individuals at Countrywide knew of this contractual undertaking and knew that the loans it actually sold Fannie Mae and Freddie Mac were inconsistent with them, but they sold bad mortgages to Fannie and Freddie anyway. The government and the jury believed that this was "fraud"; indeed, Judge Rakoff, who presided at the trial, said that the program "was from start to finish the vehicle for a brazen fraud by the defendants, driven by hunger for profits and oblivious to the harms thereby visited, not just on the immediate victims but also on the financial system as a whole." United States *ex rel.* O'Donnell v. Countrywide Home Loans, Inc., 33 F.Supp.3d 494, 503 (S.D.N.Y. 2014), *rev'd,* 822 F.3d 650.

The Second Circuit, however, disagreed and vacated the $1.27 billion judgment. It cited *Neder* for the proposition that the common law is relevant in construing the reach of the mail and wire fraud statutes. It then ruled that "the common law requires proof—other than the fact of breach—that, at the time of a contractual promise was made, the promisor had no intent ever to perform the obligation." 822 F.3d at 660. "Absent such proof, a subsequent breach of that promise—even a willful and intentional one—cannot in itself transform the promise into a fraud." *Id.* at 662. The Second Circuit held that "[t]he Government did not prove—in fact, did not attempt to prove—that at the time the contracts were executed Countrywide never intended to perform its promise of investment quality. Nor did it prove that Countrywide made any later misrepresentations—*i.e.,* ones not contained in the contracts—as to which fraudulent intent could be found." *Id.* at 663. In short, the Second Circuit found that there was no actionable misrepresentation either at the time of the contract or the time of the sale. It is unclear what continuing importance this case will have because, as commentators have pointed out, the Second Circuit's opinion played fast and loose with the facts and the law. *See* Brandon Garrett, *Bad Hustle,* available at http://clsbluesky.law.columbia.edu/2016/06/13/bad-hustle/. Note that had the judgment been based on the False Claims Act, it might have survived. The implied certification doctrine available in that context holds that a request for payment from the government implicitly represents material compliance with the contract and relevant statutes and regulations. *See* Universal Health Servs. v. United States *ex rel.* Escobar, -- U.S. --, 136 S.Ct. 1989 (2016).

3. The Court in *Neder* refers to the bank fraud statute, 18 U.S.C. § 1344. The bank fraud statute provides that

> Whoever knowingly executes, or attempts to execute, a scheme or artifice—
> (1) to defraud a financial institution; or
> (2) to obtain any of the moneys, funds, credits, assets, securities, or other property owned by, or under the custody or control of, a financial institution, by means of false or fraudulent pretenses, representations, or promises
> is punishable by up to 30 years' imprisonment.

The Supreme Court, in *Shaw v. United States,* -- U.S. --, 137 S.Ct. 462 (2016), addressed a circuit split on the scope of § 1344(1). Shaw used identifying numbers of a bank account belonging to a bank customer in a scheme to transfer funds from that account to accounts at other institutions from which Shaw was able to obtain the funds. Shaw argued that subsection (1) did not apply to him because he intended only to cheat a bank depositor, not the bank. The Supreme Court rejected his argument, ruling that the bank did have property rights in its customers' bank deposits. The Court also noted that although Shaw may not have intended to cause the bank financial harm, the statute does not require a showing of such intent; nor does it require proof that the bank suffered financial losses. Shaw knew that the bank possessed the account, made false statements to the bank, believed that the false statements would cause the bank to release the account funds that ultimately and wrongfully ended up with Shaw. That, said the Court, was enough to satisfy the statute.

The Supreme Court has also addressed the reach of § 1344(2). *See* Loughrin v. United States, 573 U.S. 351, 134 S.Ct. 2384 (2014). In *Loughrin,* the defendant was charged with bank fraud after he was caught forging stolen checks, using them to buy goods at a Target store, and then returning the goods for cash. Section § 1344(2) has two elements: (1) that the defendant obtained monies in the custody or under the control of a "financial institution" (as defined in 18 U.S.C. § 20); and (2) that the obtaining of bank property occur "by means of false or fraudulent pretenses, representations, or promises." *Id.* at 2380. The defendant argued that the government had to prove an additional element: that the defendant intended to defraud the financial institution. He contended that he had no such intent because he wished only to deceive Target—not the banks upon which the altered checks were drawn. The Court rejected this suggested element, reasoning that § 1344(2) requires only that the defendant intend to obtain bank property and that this end is accomplished "by means of" a false statement. No additional requirement of intent to defraud a bank appears in the statute's text. And imposing that requirement would prevent § 1344(2) from applying to cases falling within the statute's clear terms, such as frauds directed against a third-party custodian of bank-owned property. The defendant's construction would also make § 1344(2) a mere subset of § 1344(1), which explicitly prohibits any scheme "to defraud a financial institution." Such a reading is untenable, the Court concluded, because the clauses are separated by the disjunctive "or," signaling that each is intended to have separate meaning. And to read clause (1) as fully encompassing clause (2) contravenes two related interpretive canons: that different language signals different meaning and that no part of a statute should be superfluous.

Some lower courts had required that an intent to defraud a bank be proved under § 1344(2), fearing that without such a requirement, § 1344(2) would punish—by up to 30 years—every minor fraud in which the victim happens to pay by check. In rejecting this concern, the Supreme Court reasoned that there is another textual limit on § 1344(2)'s reach: the defendant must acquire (or attempt to acquire) the bank property "*by means of*" the misrepresentation. This language limits § 1344(2)'s to cases (like Loughrin's) in which the misrepresentation had some real connection to a federally insured bank, and thus to the pertinent federal interest. "Section 1344(2)'s 'by means of' language is satisfied when ... the defendant's false statement is the mechanism naturally inducing a bank (or custodian of bank property) to part with money in its control." *Id.* at 2393. The Court cautioned that "not every but-for causes will do. If, to pick an example out of a hat, Jane traded in her car for money to take a bike trip cross-country, no one would say that she 'crossed the Rockies by means of a car,' even though her sale of the car somehow figured in the trip she took. The relation between those things would be (as the Government puts it) too 'tangential[]' to make use of the phrase at all appropriate." *Id.* Finally, Court also rejected the defendant's argument that § 1344(2) at least requires the government to prove that the defendant's scheme created a risk of financial loss to the bank. *Id.* at 2395 n.9.

It should be noted that the bank fraud statute differs from mail and wire fraud in two important respects. First, the statute of limitations is 10 years, *see* 18 U.S.C. § 3293(1), not the 5 years that normally applies to non-capital federal felonies like mail and wire fraud (that do not affect a financial institution), *see* 18 U.S.C. § 3282(a). Second, the unit of prosecution for bank fraud is not as straightforward as for mail and wire fraud, so prosecutors must carefully craft bank fraud indictments so as to avoid multiplicity. The circuits addressing multiplicity in the context of bank fraud generally agree that the bank fraud statute imposes punishment only for each "execution" of the scheme, unlike the mail and wire fraud statutes which punish each "act" (that is, each "mailing" or "wiring") undertaken in furtherance of the scheme to defraud. *See* United States v. Bruce, 89 F.3d 886, 889 (D.C. Cir. 1996). The question of what constitutes an "execution," however, is not easily answered. Some courts have defined an execution to be roughly equivalent to "acts in furtherance" as applied in the mail and wire fraud context. *See, e.g.,* United States v. Poliak, 823 F.2d 371, 372 (9th Cir. 1987) (holding each of ten checks deposited in check-kiting scheme chargeable as separate "execution," using examination of mail and wire fraud statutes for support). Other courts have defined an "execution" to constitute several acts in furtherance of a single scheme. *See, e.g.,* United States v. Lemons, 941 F.2d 309, 318 (5th Cir. 1991) (ruling each act to move funds to defendant, although they took place in separate states, were part of one execution of fraudulent scheme).

4. In addition to the holding discussed in text, the Supreme Court also ruled in *Neder* that (1) the omission of an element in the jury instructions is subject to harmless-error analysis; and (2) that, under the constitutional harmless error standard of *Chapman v. California*, 386 U.S. 18, 24 (1967) (whether it appears "beyond a reasonable doubt that the error complained of did not contribute to the verdict obtained"), the district court's failure to submit the tax offense's materiality element to the jury was harmless error. The Supreme Court granted certiorari in *United States v. Resendiz-Ponce* to determine whether the omission of an element of a criminal offense from a federal indictment can also constitute harmless error. 549 U.S. 102, 103-04 (2007). Because the Court ultimately concluded, however, that the indictment at issue was not in fact defective, it did not reach the harmless-error question. *Id.* at 109-11.

BRIDGE v. PHOENIX BOND & INDEMNITY CO.
553 U.S. 639 (2008)

THOMAS, J., delivered the opinion for a unanimous Court.

The Racketeer Influenced and Corrupt Organizations Act (RICO or Act), 18 U.S.C. §§ 1961-1968, provides a private right of action for treble damages to "[a]ny person injured in his business or property by reason of a violation" of the Act's criminal prohibitions. § 1964(c). The question presented in this case is whether a plaintiff asserting a RICO claim predicated on mail fraud must plead and prove that it relied on the defendant's alleged misrepresentations. Because we agree with the Court of Appeals that a showing of first-party reliance is not required, we affirm.

Each year the Cook County, Illinois, Treasurer's Office holds a public auction at which it sells tax liens it has acquired on the property of delinquent taxpayers. Prospective buyers bid on the liens, but not in cash amounts. Instead, the bids are stated as percentage penalties the property owner must pay the winning bidder in order to clear the lien. The bidder willing to accept the lowest penalty wins the auction and obtains the right to purchase the lien in exchange for paying the outstanding taxes on the property. The property owner may then redeem the property by paying the lienholder the delinquent taxes, plus the penalty established at the auction and an additional 12% penalty on any taxes subsequently paid by the lienholder. If the property owner does not redeem the property within the statutory redemption period, the lienholder may obtain a tax deed for the property, thereby in effect purchasing the property for the value of the delinquent taxes.

Because property acquired in this manner can often be sold at a significant profit over the amount paid for the lien, the auctions are marked by stiff competition. As a result, most parcels attract multiple bidders willing to accept the lowest penalty permissible—0%, that is to say, no penalty at all. (Perhaps to prevent the perverse incentive taxpayers would have if they could redeem their property from a winning bidder for less than the amount of their unpaid taxes, the county does not accept negative bids.) The lower limit of 0% creates a problem: Who wins when the bidding results in a tie? The county's solution is to allocate parcels "on a rotational basis" in order to ensure that liens are apportioned fairly among 0% bidders.

But this creates a perverse incentive of its own: Bidders who, in addition to bidding themselves, send agents to bid on their behalf will obtain a disproportionate share of liens. To prevent this kind of manipulation, the county adopted the "Single, Simultaneous Bidder Rule," which requires each "tax buying entity" to submit bids in its own name and prohibits it from using "apparent agents, employees, or related entities" to submit simultaneous bids for the same parcel. Upon registering for an auction, each bidder must submit a sworn affidavit affirming that it complies with the Single, Simultaneous Bidder Rule.

Petitioners and respondents are regular participants in Cook County's tax sales. In July 2005, respondents filed a complaint in the United States District Court for the Northern District of Illinois, contending that petitioners had fraudulently obtained a disproportionate share of liens by violating the Single, Simultaneous Bidder Rule at the auctions held from 2002 to 2005. According to respondents, petitioner Sabre Group, LLC, and its principal Barrett Rochman arranged for related firms to bid on Sabre Group's behalf and directed them to file false attestations that they complied with the Single, Simultaneous Bidder Rule. Having thus fraudulently obtained the opportunity to participate in the auction, the related firms collusively bid on the same properties at a 0% rate. As a result, when the county allocated liens on a rotating basis, it treated the related firms as independent entities, allowing them collectively to acquire a greater number of liens than would have been granted to a single bidder acting alone. The related firms then purchased the liens and transferred the certificates of purchase to Sabre Group. In this way, respondents allege, petitioners deprived them and other bidders of their fair share of liens and the attendant financial benefits.

Respondents' complaint contains five counts. Counts I-IV allege that petitioners violated and conspired to violate RICO by conducting their affairs through a pattern of racketeering activity involving numerous acts of mail fraud. In support of their allegations of mail fraud, respondents assert that petitioners "mailed or caused to be mailed hundreds of mailings in furtherance of the scheme," when they sent property owners various notices required by Illinois law. Count V alleges a state-law claim of tortious interference with prospective business advantage.

On petitioners' motion, the District Court dismissed respondents' RICO claims for lack of standing. It observed that "[o]nly [respondents] and other competing buyers, as opposed to the Treasurer or the property owners, would suffer a financial loss from a scheme to violate the Single, Simultaneous Bidder Rule." But it concluded that respondents "are not in the class of individuals protected by the mail fraud statute, and therefore are not within the 'zone of interests' that the RICO statute protects," because they "were not recipients of the alleged misrepresentations and, at best were indirect victims of the alleged fraud." The District Court declined to exercise supplemental jurisdiction over respondents' tortious-interference claim and dismissed it without prejudice.

The Court of Appeals for the Seventh Circuit reversed. It first concluded that "[s]tanding is not a problem in this suit" because plaintiffs suffered a "real injury" when they lost the valuable chance to acquire more liens, and because "that injury can be redressed by damages." The Court of Appeals next concluded that respondents had sufficiently alleged proximate cause under *Holmes v. Securities Investor Protection Corporation*, 503 U.S. 258 (1992), and *Anza v. Ideal Steel Supply Corp.*, 47 U.S. 451 (2006), because they (along with other losing bidders) were "immediately injured" by petitioners' scheme. Finally, the Court of Appeals rejected petitioners' argument that respondents are not entitled to relief under RICO because they did not receive, and therefore did not rely on, any false statements: "A scheme that injures D by making false statements through the mail to E is mail fraud, and actionable by D through RICO if the injury is not derivative of someone else's."

With respect to this last holding, the Court of Appeals acknowledged that courts have taken conflicting views. By its count, "[t]hree other circuits that have considered this question agree ... that the direct *victim* may recover through RICO whether or not it is the direct *recipient* of the false statements," whereas two Circuits hold that the plaintiff must show that it in fact relied on the defendant's misrepresentations.

We granted certiorari to resolve the conflict among the Courts of Appeals on "the substantial question" whether first-party reliance is an element of a civil RICO claim predicated on mail fraud.

We begin by setting forth the applicable statutory provisions. RICO's private right of action is contained in 18 U.S.C. § 1964(c), which provides in relevant part that "[a]ny person injured in his business or property by reason of a violation of section 1962 of this chapter may sue therefor in any appropriate United States district court and shall recover threefold the damages he sustains and the cost of the suit, including a reasonable attorney's fee." Section 1962 contains RICO's criminal prohibitions. Pertinent here is § 1962(c), which makes it "unlawful for any person employed by or associated with" an enterprise engaged in or affecting interstate or foreign commerce "to conduct or participate, directly or indirectly, in the conduct of such enterprise's affairs through a pattern of racketeering activity." The term "racketeering activity" is defined to include a host of so-called predicate acts, including "any act which is indictable under ... section 1341 (relating to mail fraud)." § 1961(1) (B). ...

If petitioners' proposed requirement of first-party reliance seems to come out of nowhere, there is a reason: Nothing on the face of the relevant statutory provisions imposes such a requirement. Using the mail to execute or attempt to execute a scheme to defraud is indictable as mail fraud, and hence a predicate act of racketeering under RICO, even if no one relied on any misrepresentation. See *Neder v. United States*, 527 U.S. 1, 24-25 (1999) ("The common-law requiremen[t] of 'justifiable reliance' ... plainly ha[s] no place in the [mail, wire, or bank] fraud statutes"). And one can conduct the affairs of a qualifying enterprise through a pattern of such acts without anyone relying on a fraudulent misrepresentation.

It thus seems plain—and indeed petitioners do not dispute—that no showing of reliance is required to establish that a person has violated § 1962(c) by conducting the affairs of an enterprise through a pattern of racketeering activity consisting of acts of mail fraud. If reliance is required, then, it must be by virtue of § 1964(c), which provides the right of action. But it is difficult to derive a first-party reliance requirement from § 1964(c), which states simply that "[a]ny person injured in his business or property by reason of a violation of section 1962" may sue for treble damages. The statute provides a right of action to "[a]ny person" injured by the violation, suggesting a breadth of coverage not easily reconciled with an implicit requirement that the plaintiff show reliance in addition to injury in his business or property.

Moreover, a person can be injured "by reason of" a pattern of mail fraud even if he has not relied on any misrepresentations. This is a case in point. Accepting their allegations as true, respondents clearly were injured by petitioners' scheme: As a result of petitioners' fraud, respondents lost valuable liens they otherwise would have been awarded. And this is true even though they did not rely on petitioners' false attestations of compliance with the county's rules. Or, to take another example, suppose an enterprise that wants to get rid of rival businesses mails misrepresentations about them to their customers and suppliers, but not to the rivals themselves. If the rival businesses lose money as a result of the misrepresentations, it would certainly seem that they were injured in their business "by reason of" a pattern of mail fraud, even though they never received, and therefore never relied on, the fraudulent mailings. Yet petitioners concede that, on their reading of § 1964(c), the rival businesses would have no cause of action under RICO even though they were the primary and intended victims of the scheme to defraud.

Lacking textual support for this counterintuitive position, petitioners rely instead on a combination of common-law rules and policy arguments in an effort to show that Congress should be presumed to have made first-party reliance an element of a civil RICO claim based on mail fraud. None of petitioners' arguments persuades us to read a first-party reliance requirement into a statute that by its terms suggests none.

Petitioners first argue that RICO should be read to incorporate a first-party reliance requirement in fraud cases "under the rule that Congress intends to incorporate the well-settled meaning of the common-law terms it uses." *Neder, supra*, at 23. It has long been settled, they contend, that only the recipient of a fraudulent misrepresentation may recover for common-law fraud, and that he may do so "if, but only if ... he relies on the misrepresentation in acting or refraining from action." *Restatement (Second) of Torts* § 537 (1977). Given this background rule of common law, petitioners maintain, Congress should be presumed to have adopted a first-party reliance requirement when it created a civil cause of action under RICO for victims of mail fraud. ...

[Petitioners' argument that] ... we should look to the common-law meaning of civil fraud in order to give content to the civil cause of action § 1964(c) provides for private injury by reason of a violation of § 1962(c) based on a pattern of mail fraud ... is misplaced. ... Section 1962(c) does not use the term "fraud"; nor does the operative language of § 1961(1) (B), which defines "racketeering activity" to include "any act which is indictable under ... section 1341." And the indictable act under § 1341 is not the fraudulent misrepresentation, but rather the use of the mails with the purpose of executing or attempting to execute a scheme to defraud. In short, the key term in § 1962(c)—"racketeering activity"—is a defined term, and Congress *defined* the predicate act not as fraud *simpliciter*, but mail fraud—a statutory offense unknown to the common law. In these circumstances, the presumption that Congress intends to adopt the settled meaning of common-law terms has little pull. There is simply no "reason to believe that

Congress would have defined 'racketeering activity' to include acts indictable under the mail and wire fraud statutes, if it intended fraud-related acts to be predicate acts under RICO only when those acts would have been actionable under the common law." …

As a last resort, petitioners contend that we should interpret RICO to require first-party reliance for fraud-based claims in order to avoid the "over-federalization" of traditional state-law claims. In petitioners' view, respondents' claim is essentially one for tortious interference with prospective business advantage, as evidenced by Count V of their complaint. Such claims have traditionally been handled under state law, and petitioners see no reason why Congress would have wanted to supplement traditional state-law remedies with a federal cause of action, complete with treble damages and attorney's fees, in a statute designed primarily to combat organized crime. A first-party reliance requirement, they say, is necessary "to prevent garden-variety disputes between local competitors (such as this case) from being converted into federal racketeering actions."

Whatever the merits of petitioners' arguments as a policy matter, we are not at liberty to rewrite RICO to reflect their—or our—views of good policy. We have repeatedly refused to adopt narrowing constructions of RICO in order to make it conform to a preconceived notion of what Congress intended to proscribe.

We see no reason to change course here. RICO's text provides no basis for imposing a first-party reliance requirement. If the absence of such a requirement leads to the undue proliferation of RICO suits, the "correction must lie with Congress." "It is not for the judiciary to eliminate the private action in situations where Congress has provided it."

For the foregoing reasons, we hold that a plaintiff asserting a RICO claim predicated on mail fraud need not show, either as an element of its claim or as a prerequisite to establishing proximate causation, that it relied on the defendant's alleged misrepresentations. Accordingly, the judgment of the Court of Appeals is affirmed.

Notes

1. *Fraud as a Predicate in Civil Litigation.* As noted in the introduction to this chapter, mail and wire fraud are important in part because they are frequently used as the predicate crimes upon which cases invoking complex statutes, such as RICO, are built. *Bridge* illustrates not only the difficulties that this can cause, but also the problems attendant on the fact that courts generally interpret the RICO statute as the same whether the case arises in a civil or a criminal context. With that in mind, does this case resolve the question of whether, under the fraud statutes, the government must prove in criminal cases that the victims of the fraud were also the audience of the fraudulent misrepresentations?

2. *Must the Victim Also Be the Target of the Fraud?* At least before *Bridge*, the courts were split on the question whether a mail or wire fraud conviction may rest on the deceit of a person other than the ultimate victim contemplated by the scheme. *See, e.g.*, United States v. Blumeyer, 114 F.3d 758, 768 (8th Cir. 1997). For example, in *United States v. Lew*, 875 F.2d 219, 221 (9th Cir. 1989), Bill Lew, an immigration attorney, submitted false statements to the United States Department of Labor that ultimately were designed to facilitate INS grants of permanent resident status for his clients. The government prosecuted Lew for mail fraud based on these misrepresentations on the theory that the "principal object" of the scheme was "to defraud Lew's clients of the attorneys fees they paid him." The Ninth Circuit reversed Lew's conviction because the jury instructions did not require a finding that Lew deceived his clients and there was no evidence in the record to support such a finding. *Id.* at 221-22; *see also* United States v. Sawyer, 85 F.3d 713, 734 n.18 (1st Cir. 1996) (intended victims of scheme must be the ones defrauded).

By contrast, in *Blumeyer*, the court adopted the view that "a defendant who makes false representations to a regulatory agency in order to forestall regulatory action that threatens to impede the defendant's scheme to obtain money or property from others is guilty of conducting" a cognizable fraud. 114 F.3d at 768-69; *see also* United States v. Christopher, 142 F.3d 46 (1st Cir. 1998). Similarly, the Seventh Circuit "does not interpret the mail fraud statute as requiring convergence between the misrepresentations and the defrauded victims."

United States v. Seidling, 737 F.3d 1155, 1161 (7th Cir. 2013); *see also* United States v. McMillan, 600 F.3d 434, 448-50 (5th Cir. 2010) (same).

What should be the rule? As a practical matter, how will the resolution of this issue affect a prosecutor's choices in formulating her theory of the case? *See* United States v. Howard, 619 F.3d 723, 727 (7th Cir. 2010) (the government need not prove at trial that the defendant intended to harm the particular victims identified in the indictment).

Should the fact that these cases apparently were not the focus of the *Bridge* Court—which instead chose to concentrate on civil fraud arguments—make a difference in the extent to which the *Bridge* discussion resolves this conflict? In other words, where do we stand on this issue after *Bridge*?

3. *Neder* seemed to indicate that the Supreme Court would normally look to the common law of fraud in resolving issues under the mail and wire fraud statute; indeed, as was indicated in the notes following that case, this approach was viewed as an important change in the Court's approach following the announcement of the *Neder* decision. Is *Bridge* consistent in this respect with *Neder*? Also, note that the Court declines to adopt a limiting interpretation of the RICO statute based on policy concerns regarding the federalization of areas normally left to state concern. Readers might wish to revisit this discussion after reading *McNally*, *infra*. Can the two be reconciled?

4. *Potential Reliance Requirement? The Ordinary Prudence Standard.* After *Neder* and *Bridge*, it would be impossible to argue that the fraud statutes impose an *actual* reliance standard. But what of a *potential* reliance requirement? If someone stands accused of selling snake oil to a willfully credulous market, should the criminal sanction be applied to protect those who won't or don't make reasonable efforts to protect themselves? There was a conflict among the circuits on the question whether a scheme to defraud for purposes of the mail fraud statute is proved where the misrepresentation or concealment "would not deceive a person of average intelligence and experience"—that is, where objectively reasonable "potential" reliance is not proved.

The Eleventh Circuit famously endorsed this requirement in *United States v. Brown*, 79 F.3d 1550 (11th Cir. 1996). In *Brown*, the court reversed the conviction of a former executive of a real estate development corporation, GDC, who was convicted of conspiring to defraud home buyers throughout Florida in the 1980s. The fraud alleged was that GDC, in attempting to sell second homes to customers residing in the "snowbelt" states, did not tell its customers that they might be paying more for a GDC home than they would for a largely identical home next door. GDC salespersons also falsely told prospective purchasers that the homes were safe investments, that the rental income would exceed mortgage payments, and that they would be able to sell at a profit in a year's time. The Eleventh Circuit noted that the GDC defendant did not have a relationship of special trust with his customers; thus, there was no basis in a legal relationship to infer that a reasonable person could rely on the sellers' representations. In the end, the court concluded that a reasonable juror could not have concluded that a customer of ordinary prudence would have relied on these representations because the "representation is about something which the customer should, and could, easily confirm—if they wished to do so—from readily available sources." *Id.* at 1559. It stated that, under "the circumstances of this *criminal* case, no reasonable jury could find that GDC prevented, *in a way that would make reliance on GDC's value representations reasonable,* people of ordinary prudence from discovering what houses in Florida sold for and rented for and how the price of GDC homes compared to comparable properties in Florida." *Id.* at 1561 (emphasis original).

The *Brown* decision was generally not well-received in the other circuits, particularly the Seventh. *See, e.g.*, United States v. Coffman, 94 F.3d 330 (7th Cir. 1996). After being distinguished to death, it was finally interred in *United States v. Svete*, 556 F.3d 1157 (11th Cir. 2009). The bottom line of the *Svete* reasoning was, quoting the late Judge Alvin Rubin, "The truth about virtually every scheme to defraud could be obtained if the gull were clever and diligent enough ... The laws protecting against fraud are most needed to protect the careless and the naïve from lupine predators, and they are designed for that purpose." United States v. Kreimer, 609 F.2d 126, 132 (5th Cir. 1980).

5. *"Victims" Who Do Not Feel "Victimized."* What should be the rule where the alleged "victims" do not believe themselves to have been victimized? *See* United States v. Bereano, 161 F.3d 3, 4 (4th Cir. 1998) (unpublished opinion). In *Bereano*, the defendant argued on appeal that he had relied on statements of victims that no harm had occurred and that they were satisfied with his services in arguing that no contemplated harm was present. The Fourth Circuit responded that "[s]uch issues are not decided at the whim of the perceived victim. The perception of the victim or target of the scheme is ultimately irrelevant to whether Bereano devised a scheme, or acted with the requisite intent to defraud." Similarly, in *United States v. Bryza*, 522 F.2d 414, 422 (7th Cir. 1975), the court held that an employee may be convicted of defrauding his employer of "honest and faithful services" even if the "victim" employer took no retributive action and was satisfied with defendant's performance. The Seventh Circuit concluded that "the defendant's intent must be judged by his actions, not the reaction of the mail fraud victims." *Id.* at 422. But the Second Circuit has accepted such an argument, holding that because alleged the corporate victims had no complaints about the defendant lawyer's billing or other services, perceived no fraud, and felt no harm, the lawyer, by disguising the nature of his services on bills sent to these clients, merely deceived the clients as opposed to defrauding them. United States v. D'Amato, 39 F.3d 1249, 1257 (2d Cir. 1994). Should the victims' attitude toward the wrongdoer be considered in assessing the defendant's intent to defraud? To what other element might it be relevant?

2. INTENT TO DEFRAUD: INTENT TO INJURE?

The Circuits seem to agree that a (specific) "intent to defraud" must be proved to secure a mail or wire fraud conviction. But they do not agree on how that term is defined or applied.

UNITED STATES v. REGENT OFFICE SUPPLY CO.
421 F.2d 1174 (2d Cir. 1970)

MOORE, CIRCUIT JUDGE.

...

The appellants are in the business of selling stationery supplies through salesmen (called "agents") who solicit orders for their merchandise by telephone. ... [T]hey stipulated in writing that their agents "secured sales" by making false representations to potential customers that:

    (a) the agent had been referred to the customer by a friend of the customer.
    (b) the agent had been referred to customer firms by officers of such firms.
    (c) the agent was a doctor, or other professional person, who had stationery to be disposed of.
    (d) stationery of friends of the agent had to be disposed of because of a death and that the customer would help to relieve this difficult situation by purchasing it. ...

For its defense, the accused corporations called the president of Regent, Harold Hartwig, who testified that the firms sell well-known, nationally advertised brands of stationery, such as Swingline staples, Faber pencils, Perma-Write pens, etc., and some paper to large users among which are corporations such as Goodyear, General Electric and Rexall; that many of these customers provide a large volume of reorder business; that the Regent-Oxford enterprise has over 20,000 customers; that sales are made exclusively through their customers' purchasing agents; that the false representations listed in the stipulation were made as a preliminary part of the salesmen's solicitation; that price and quality of the merchandise are always discussed honestly; that the price offered has been lower than the purchasing agent is or was paying at the time of the solicitation; that the goods could be returned if found to be unsatisfactory; and that when a complaint is made an additional discount is offered to induce the customer to keep the goods.

Cross-examination elicited that ... the "lies" were to "get by" secretaries on the telephone and to get "the purchasing agent to listen to our agent"; and that for business reasons various fictitious names were used both for their companies in different localities and for individuals. ...

The trial court found that the defendants' conduct constituted a "scheme to defraud" but that there was "no evidence that defendants intended to get 'something for nothing,' from the customer or that any of their customers failed to receive merchandise of the quality promised." However, after thoroughly analyzing the many mail fraud cases, the court found the defendants guilty as charged. They received minimal fines for their violations, but they press this appeal because they are obliged to, in their words, "as a matter of their sheer business survival." ...

The important substantive question on this appeal is: Does solicitation of a purchase by means of false representations not directed to the quality, adequacy or price of goods to be sold, or otherwise to the nature of the bargain, constitute a "scheme to defraud" or "obtaining money by false pretenses" within the prohibition of 18 U.S.C. § 1341? We hold that, as here presented, it does not and the convictions should be reversed. ... [T]he facts as stipulated in the case before us do not, in our view, constitute a scheme to defraud or to obtain money by false pretenses punishable under section 1341. But this is not to say that we could not, on different facts or more specific proof, arrive at a different conclusion.

The case presented by the Regent-Oxford operation is unique (as the government, in effect, concedes) among prosecutions for violation of section 1341. The most nearly analogous cases sustaining convictions for mail fraud have involved sales tactics and representations which have tended to mislead the purchaser, or prospective purchaser, as to the quality or effectiveness of the thing being sold, or to mislead him with regard to the advantages of the bargain which should accrue to him. Thus claims or statements in advertising may go beyond mere puffing and enter the realm of fraud where the product must inherently fail to do what is claimed for it. And promotion of an inherently useful item may also be fraud when the scheme of promotion is based on claims of additional benefits to accrue to the customer, if the benefits as represented are not realistically attainable by the customer.

The government does not contend that the Regent-Oxford agents made any false representations regarding the quality or price of their nationally advertised merchandise. Nor is there any suggestion of material benefits which the customer might expect from the transaction beyond the inherent utility of the goods purchased and the discount price at which they were offered. Thus the present case cannot fall within either of the classes of commercial fraud cases we have previously considered. We must, therefore, examine the government's theory that fraud may exist in a commercial transaction even when the customer gets exactly what he expected and at the price he expected to pay. ...

It is generally stated that there are two elements to the offense of mail fraud: use of the mails and a scheme to defraud. Since only a "scheme to defraud" and not actual fraud is required for conviction, we have said that "it is not essential that the Government allege or prove that purchasers were in fact defrauded." But this does not mean that the government can escape the burden of showing that some actual harm or injury was *contemplated* by the schemer. Proof that someone was actually defrauded is unnecessary simply because the critical element in a "scheme to defraud" is "fraudulent intent," and therefore the accused need not have succeeded in his scheme to be guilty of the crime. But the purpose of the scheme "must be to injure, which doubtless may be inferred when the scheme has such effect as a necessary result of carrying it out." Of course proof that someone was actually victimized by the fraud is good evidence of the schemer's intent.

The government has offered no direct proof that any customer was actually defrauded by the Regent-Oxford selling campaign. Instead it offers a stipulation which shows that false representations were made, and that they were made by defendants' agents with knowledge of their falsehood. As a result of the transactions of which the untrue statements were a part, money and property changed hands. With no further proof, the government urges upon us the inference that customers were induced to part with their money because of the false representations, and that such calculated inducement amounted to fraud in the terminology of section 1341. The defendants helped the government over the difficult hurdle of proving that the false representations were "reasonably calculated" to induce purchasing agents of "ordinary prudence" to buy their wares by admitting in writing that the representations were made to secure sales. On this stipulation an intent to deceive, and even to induce, may have been shown; but this does not, without more, constitute the "fraudulent intent" required by the statute.

If there is no proof that the defendants expected to get "something for nothing," or that they intended to get more for their merchandise than it was worth to the average customer, it is difficult to see any intent to injure or to defraud in the defendants' falsehoods. Instead of offering proof of some tangible injury to the objects of the Regent-Oxford promotion, the government argues in the negative that "it is not essential ... [to] ... prove that purchasers were in fact defrauded," and therefore that "pecuniary loss" need not be shown for fraud to exist. It may be true, as Judge Learned Hand stated in *United States v. Rowe*, 56 F.2d 747, 749 (2d Cir.1932), that:

> ... [a] man is none the less cheated out of his property, when he is induced to part with it by fraud, because he gets a quid pro quo of equal value. It may be impossible to measure his loss by the gross scales available to a court, but he has suffered a wrong; he has lost his chance to bargain with the facts before him.

Nevertheless, neither the *Rowe* case nor the language quoted will support the conclusion that no definable harm need be contemplated by the accused to find him guilty of mail fraud. For that is what the government is arguing: that these false representations, in the context of a commercial transaction, are *per se* fraudulent despite the absence of any proof of actual injury to any customer. In the *Rowe* case, although the court felt that it was not necessary to measure the victims' loss in pecuniary terms, the injustice done was very real and made itself felt in the victims' pocketbook. The scheme as it was outlined in the opinion showed that the defendants, on the basis of gross misrepresentations of the value of certain pieces of land as well as a complicated structure of supporting false representations, had persuaded their victims to part with substantial sums of money in return for essentially worthless property. There was no question that the principal fraud lay in the defendants' representations that the property was worth much more than they knew it was in fact worth, thereby inducing the victims to part with their money on the basis of the inflated valuation, together with the other fabrications they wove for their purchasers. Although the land sold had some inherent utility, the false representations grossly misled the victims of the scheme with regard to the bargain they were induced to enter by the representations. The defendants' representations regarding the value of the lots were unquestionably false representations of fact material to the bargain. Although the victims got something for their money—thus there was a quid pro quo—they were cheated out of the additional pecuniary benefits which the false representations led them reasonably to expect. Thus, taken in its factual context, the formulation of law stated in the *Rowe* decision was perfectly accurate in affirming that a wrong has been suffered when a man is deprived of his chance to bargain "with the facts before him" where the absent facts are facts material to the bargain he is induced thereby to enter.

We believe this to be a correct interpretation of *Rowe*, because we have found no case in which an intent to deceive has been equated with an "intent to defraud" where the deceit did not go to the nature of the bargain itself. ... Although proof that the injury was accomplished is not required to convict under 1341, we believe the statute does require evidence from which it may be inferred that some actual injury to the victim, however slight, is a reasonably probable result of the deceitful representations if they are successful.

The Regent–Oxford agents did not attempt to deceive their prospective customers with respect to the bargain they were offering; rather, they gave a false reason for being able to offer the bargain. ... The government asks us to infer some injury from the mere fact of the falseness of the representations and their connection with a commercial transaction. On the evidence before us, consisting principally of the stipulated falsehoods and the testimony of the defendants' president, we conclude that the defendants intended to deceive their customers but they did not intend to defraud them, because the falsity of their representations was not shown to be capable of affecting the customer's understanding of the bargain nor of influencing his assessment of the value of the bargain to him, and thus no injury was shown to flow from the deception. ...

Notes

1. Where does the "intent to defraud" discussed in *Regent Office Supply* fit into the statutory scheme? Why is denominating a certain proof requirement as an "element" important as a practical matter? *See, e.g.*, United States v. Ervasti, 201 F.3d 1029, 1035 (8th Cir. 2000) (noting that district court refused requested jury charge that "[t]he essence of a scheme to defraud is an intent to harm the victim" because this "language does not appear as an element in the mail fraud statute").

2. Did the *Regent Office Supply* court ultimately ground its decision on the absence of the requisite intent to defraud or was it truly imposing a materiality requirement (that is, a requirement that the Government must prove that the defendant's misrepresentation was material to the victim's willingness to engage in the bargain with the defendant)? *Compare In re* Seizure of All Funds in Accounts in Names Registry Publishing, Inc., 68 F.3d 577, 581-82 (2d Cir. 1995) (construing *Regent Office Supply* as requiring that undisclosed facts be "material to the bargain" that the defrauded party is induced to enter), *with* United States v. D'Amato, 39 F.3d 1249, 1257 (2d Cir. 1994) (relying on *Regent Office Supply* for proposition that proof of fraudulent intent, including an intent to harm, is required); *cf.* United States v. Sadler, 750 F.3d 585, 590-91 (6th Cir. 2014) (in an analogous case, reversing conviction because although defendant lied she did not deprive anyone of money or property). As we shall see within, these two concepts are closely related; indeed, materiality and intent to defraud may well be conflated in many cases because the proof of these elements may coalesce. That is, a jury may often be asked to infer intent from proof that a defendant made a clearly material misrepresentation to secure some unwarranted benefit. *See* United States v. Alston, 609 F.2d 531, 538 (D.C. Cir. 1979). And both materiality and an intent to defraud are central to the mission of the court in *Regent Office Supply*—that is, attempting to separate out cases of "puffing" or aggressive sales tactics from actionable fraud.

In a recent Seventh Circuit case, *United States v. Weimert*, 819 F.3d 351 (7th Cir. 2016), the court reversed a defendant's fraud conviction in similar circumstances. In so doing, the Seventh Circuit expressly chose to rely on a perceived lack of materiality rather than a lack of fraudulent intent. *Id.* at 358. Weimert, an employee of AnchorBank, was tasked with selling the bank's share in a commercial real estate development in Texas. He successfully arranged a sale that exceeded the bank's target price by about one third. The problem was that he also cut himself in on the deal. Weimert talked the potential buyers into including in their offer letter a term contemplating that Weimert would buy a minority interest in the property. Weimert then deliberately misled his bank's board and bank officials into believing that the buyer would not close the deal unless Weimert was a minority partner. On appeal of his conviction for fraud, the Seventh Circuit reversed because "[d]eception about negotiating positions ... should not be considered material for purposes of the mail and wire fraud statutes." *Id.* at 358. It explained:

> In commercial negotiations, it is not unusual for parties to conceal from others their true goals, values, priorities, or reserve prices in a proposed transaction. When we look closely at the evidence, the only ways in which Weimert misled anyone concerned such negotiating positions. He led the successful buyer to believe the seller wanted him to have a piece of the deal. He led the seller to believe the buyer insisted he have a piece of the deal. All the actual terms of the deal, however, were fully disclosed and subject to negotiation. There is no evidence that Weimert misled anyone about any material facts or about promises of future actions. While one can understand the bank's later decision to fire Weimert when the deception about negotiating positions came to light, his actions did not add up to federal wire fraud.

Id. at 354. The court also concluded that although Weimert engaged in self-dealing in violation of his fiduciary responsibilities to his employer, the Supreme Court has held that such self-dealing cannot be prosecuted as honest services fraud. *See* Skilling v. United States, 561 U.S. 358 (2010) (excerpted and discussed *infra*).

    3. There is agreement among the circuits that an "intent to defraud" must be proved, but a split in the circuits on whether an "intent to *defraud*" requires proof of an intent to *harm or injure*. The Second Circuit, in *Regent Office Supply* and a wealth of other cases, leads the contingent that require such proof, at least in cases where the object of the fraud is money or property rather than "honest services" under § 1346 (discussed *infra*). *See, e.g.*, United States v. Sadler, 750 F.3d 585 (6th Cir. 2014); United States v. Ervasti, 201 F.3d 1029, 1035 (8th Cir. 2000) (noting that "intent to harm is the essence of a scheme to defraud"); United States v. Walker, 191 F.3d 326, 334-36 (2d Cir. 1999); United States v. Frost, 125 F.3d 346, 368 (6th Cir. 1997); United States v. Cochran, 109 F.3d 660, 667-69 (10th Cir. 1997); United States v. Jain, 93 F.3d 436, 441 (8th Cir. 1996); United States v. Stouffer, 986 F.2d 916, 922 (5th Cir. 1993); *see also* United States v. Wynn, 684 F.3d 473, 478 (4th Cir. 2012) (the fraud statutes "have as an element the specific intent to deprive one of something of value through a misrepresentation or other similar dishonest method, which indeed would cause him harm"). (Note, however, that an "intent to *injure*" does not necessarily mean that the government need prove an intent to inflict *pecuniary* harm, *see* United States v. Treadwell, 593 F.3d 990, 997-98 (9th Cir. 2010).)

    In *United States v. Kenrick*, 221 F.3d 19 (1st Cir. 2000), however, an *en banc* First Circuit held that the "scheme to defraud" element of the bank fraud statute does not require proof of an intent to injure or harm where the object of the fraud is the bank's money or property, employing reasoning that would seem to apply in the mail and wire fraud context as well:

      [*Neder v. United States*, 527 U.S. 1 (1999)] ... requires that we look to the common-law meaning of fraud in examining the intent element of a "scheme or artifice to defraud" in violation of § 1344(1). The intent element of common-law civil fraud is well established. According to the *Restatement*, which the *Neder* Court relied on for its definition of materiality, *see* 527 U.S. at 22 n. 5, "One who fraudulently makes a misrepresentation ... for the purpose of inducing another to act or to refrain from action in reliance upon it, is subject to liability to the other in deceit ... ." *Restatement (Second) of Torts* § 525 (1976). Commentary roughly contemporary with the Congress that enacted the mail fraud statute in 1872 gives a similar definition of the intent element. "It is said that a man is liable to an action for deceit if he makes a false representation to another, knowing it to be false, but intending that the other should believe and act upon it ... ." Oliver Wendell Holmes, Jr., The Common Law 132 (1881).

      Common-law fraud thus requires an intent to induce action by the plaintiff in reliance on the defendant's misrepresentation. Commentators of the nineteenth and twentieth centuries agree that common-law fraud has no additional "intent to harm" requirement.

      The common-law element of intent to induce action by the plaintiff in reliance on the defendant's misrepresentation translates directly into the criminal bank fraud context, where a guilty defendant intends to induce the bank to act—*i.e.*, to part with money or other property—in reliance on his deceit or misrepresentation. Referring to an intent to induce reliance is potentially confusing to a jury, however, because it may erroneously suggest that actual reliance by the bank is also an element of the crime, as it is an element of common-law civil fraud. The Supreme Court has said that the common-law elements of justifiable reliance and damages "plainly have no place in the federal fraud statutes." *Neder*, 527 U.S. at 25. This potential for confusion is avoided by speaking simply of an intent to deceive the bank in order to obtain from it money or other property. We see no substantive difference between an intent to induce a bank to part with money in reliance on deceit or misrepresentation and an intent to deceive a bank in order to obtain from it money or other property.

... We hold, therefore, that the intent element of bank fraud under either subsection [of § 1344] is an intent to deceive the bank in order to obtain from it money or other property.[16] "Intent to harm" is not required.

... Although it may "ordinarily accompan[y]" a scheme to defraud a bank, an ultimate "purpose of either causing some financial loss to another or bringing about some financial gain to oneself" is not the essence of fraudulent intent. What counts is whether the defendant intended to deceive the bank in order to obtain from it money or other property, regardless of the ultimate purpose.

Kenrick, 221 F.3d at 28-29 *see also* United States v. Segal, 644 F.3d 364, 367 (7th Cir. 2011) (no intent to cause injury requirement); United States v. Howard, 613 F.3d 723, 727 (7th Cir. 2010) ("fraud does not include an element requiring a contemplated harm to a specific, identifiable victim"; the government need not prove intent to harm the victims identified in the indictment); United States v. Welch, 327 F.3d 1081 (10th Cir. 2003); United States v. Everett, 270 F.3d 986, 991 (6th Cir. 2001). Even if this holding is restricted to the bank fraud context, it is in direct conflict with Second Circuit precedent, which holds that intent to harm is an essential element of bank fraud. *See* United States v. Chandler, 98 F.3d 711, 714-15 (2d Cir. 1996).

4. May a court charge that an intent to defraud means an intent to deceive someone for the purpose of *either* causing some financial loss *or* bringing about some financial gain to oneself? The Second Circuit has concluded that it is error for a district court to instruct the jury that "it could find an intent to defraud based solely on the appellants' desire to gain a benefit for themselves." United States v. Frank, 156 F.3d 332, 336-37 (2d Cir. 1998). Other courts appear to accept such a charge. *See, e.g.*, United States v. Leahy, 464 F.3d 773, 786 (7th Cir. 2006). Thus, the Seventh Circuit explained in *Leahy* that "[t]o show the intent to defraud, we have consistently required a 'willful act by the defendant with the specific intent to deceive or cheat, usually for the purpose of getting financial gain for one's self or causing financial loss to another.'" *Id.* Why, as defense counsel, would you oppose such a charge? Would it have made a difference in *Regent Office Supply*?

5. It should be noted that the courts are unanimous at least in noting that actual injury need not be proved. The following is a representative statement: "[e]ssential to a scheme to defraud is fraudulent intent. The scheme to defraud need not have been successful or complete. Therefore, the victims of the scheme need not have been injured.'" United States v. D'Amato, 39 F.3d 1249, 1257 (2d Cir.1994).

3. VARIETIES OF FRAUD

Justice Holmes once observed that "[t]he law does not define fraud; it needs no definition; it is as old as falsehood and as versatile as human ingenuity."[17] In the context of a criminal case, however, "fraud" *does* require a definition but those definitions tendered are generally less than helpful. One oft-cited example is that "fraud" is whatever is not a "reflection of moral uprightness, of fundamental honesty, fair play and right dealing in the general and business life of members of society."[18] Although the Seventh Circuit, among others, has stated that this standard "cannot have been intended, and must not be taken, literally," it at the same time offered a formulation that is not much more precise: "[t]he legal meaning of 'fraud' is not limited to deceit or misrepresentation; it includes overreaching, undue influence, and other forms of misconduct."[19] The Supreme Court has stated that "defraud" commonly means to

---

[16] [Court's footnote 15:] Of course, this element is not applicable in a case where the alleged fraud is the deprivation of the bank's honest services under 18 U.S.C. § 1346.

[17] Weiss v. United States, 122 F.2d 675, 681 (5th Cir. 1941).

[18] Gregory v. United States, 253 F.2d 104, 109 (5th Cir. 1958).

[19] United States v. Holzer, 816 F.2d 304, 309 (7th Cir. 1987), *judgment vacated and remanded*, 484 U.S. 807 (1987).

"wrong[] someone in his property rights by dishonest methods or schemes" and typically involves "'the deprivation of something of value by trick, deceit, chicane or overreaching.'"[20]

In formulating a working definition, it may be helpful to explore the types of activities that should constitute an actionable fraud. In *Regent Office Supply*, actual lies were found not to constitute fraud within the meaning of the statute because the court was not persuaded that the lies at issue crossed the line between aggressive sales into criminal wrongdoing. In the course of the court's discussions in *Regent Office Supply*, it acknowledged, however, that there may be situations in which such falsehoods would constitute fraud and indeed where fraud would be found even in the absence of actual lies. The following case represents a species of the latter type of case, in which courts have been willing to find fraud where no express misrepresentations were made and where the defendant's wrongdoing instead consists of a misleading concealment of information. Readers should consider what circumstances must be present to make out a fraud case based on concealment.

UNITED STATES v. SIEGEL
717 F.2d 9 (2d Cir.1983)

GEORGE C. PRATT, CIRCUIT JUDGE:

Leonard S. Siegel and Martin B. Abrams appeal from judgments of conviction ... entered after a jury trial. Both defendants were found guilty of fifteen counts of wire fraud, in violation of 18 U.S.C. §§ 1343 and 2. ...

During the period covered by the indictment, [Mego International, Inc. (Mego Int'l)] was a publicly held international manufacturer and distributor of toys and games. [Mego Corporation (Mego)] was one of its wholly owned subsidiaries. Abrams was chairman of the board of Mego Int'l and its president until 1980. Siegel was secretary of Mego Int'l and executive vice president of Mego.

The fraudulent scheme underlying defendants' convictions involved unrecorded cash sales of Mego merchandise which had either been closed out and marked down for clearance or returned because of damage or defect. The evidence presented at trial showed that the scheme had been furthered in various ways. Abrams conducted some cash transactions himself. Siegel also dealt in cash transactions, supervising cash sales through a retail store of imported shirts worth over $30,000. Other cash transactions were conducted with the aid of William Stuckey, who was manager of Mego's Long Island warehouse and who became a principal witness for the government. At the direction of Abrams and Siegel, Stuckey sold Mego merchandise to various street peddlers and merchants for cash. The "off the books" sales together generated in excess of $100,000 in cash. ...

Even though ... the cash sales were not recorded on Mego's books, Siegel and Abrams told Mego's auditors that there were no unrecorded assets. In addition, no information about the cash sales was divulged to Mego's stockholders. The jury was thus entitled to find that Siegel and Abrams, top executives in Mego, generated a secret fund of over $100,000 from cash sales of company assets without disclosing their activities to their stockholders, that they used the cash in part for private benefit, in part for illegal payments to buyers, and in part for illegal payoffs to labor unions, and that they did not account for any sum that may have remained in the fund. ...

The government charged that Abrams and Siegel engaged in a scheme to defraud Mego and Mego stockholders by violating their fiduciary duties to act honestly and faithfully in the best interest of the corporation and to account for the sale of all Mego property entrusted to them. The object of the fraudulent scheme was alleged to be the misappropriation of the cash proceeds for bribery and self-enrichment.

---

[20] McNally v. United States, 483 U.S. 350, 358 (1987) (quoting Hammerschmidt v. United States, 265 U.S. 182, 188 (1924)).

... While we have described th[e wire fraud statute], as well as the mail fraud statute, 18 U.S.C. § 1341 (1976), which has been identically construed with respect to the issues before us, as "seemingly limitless," we have also recognized that "a mere breach of fiduciary duty, standing alone, may not necessarily constitute a mail fraud."

However, we have held that the statute is violated when a fiduciary fails to disclose material information "which he is under a duty to disclose to another under circumstances where the non-disclosure could or does result in harm to the other." While the prosecution must show that some harm or injury was contemplated by the scheme, it need not show that direct, tangible economic loss resulted to the scheme's intended victims. In this record there is sufficient evidence from which the jury could reasonably have concluded that defendants received the cash proceeds and used them for non-corporate purposes in breach of their fiduciary duties to act in the best interest of the corporation and to disclose material information to Mego and its stockholders. ...

Taken as a whole, and if believed, [the trial] testimony was sufficient for a jury to find that Siegel and Abrams participated in the cash sales. It was also sufficient to establish that they failed either to record the sales on the corporate books or to apprise the non-participating employees and stockholders of the transactions in some other fashion.

... Abrams argues that because the sums involved were insignificant when compared with Mego's overall sales volume, there was no affirmative duty to report the cash sales to the stockholders of Mego. While he is correct that, to prove a violation of the wire fraud statute, the government must show that the corporate officer or employee failed to disclose material information, we cannot accept as "immaterial" a failure to disclose unrecorded cash sales exceeding $100,000 over a period of nine years. Moreover, the jury was instructed, without defense objection, that "a material fact is one which would be important to a reasonable person in deciding whether to engage in a particular transaction or to engage in certain conduct," and certainly on this record the jury could reasonably have concluded that the failure to disclose the misappropriation of more than $100,000 was a fact which would be important to a Mego stockholder or corporate officer in his decisionmaking. Thus, failure to reveal the misappropriation violated defendants' fiduciary duty to disclose material information.

Defendants do not seriously contend that the wire fraud statute is not violated when a corporate officer or employee breaches his fiduciary duty to the corporation by taking the proceeds from unrecorded cash sales and using them for his own benefit. Rather, they argue that even if they did participate in the unrecorded cash sales, the record is devoid of any evidence that the money was used for other than corporate purposes and thus fails to support a finding of a breach of fiduciary duty. Defendants claim that at best the evidence merely shows that Abrams and Siegel received the proceeds from the cash sales and that Siegel periodically placed the money in the corporate safe deposit box. While neither Abrams nor Siegel testified, they argue that they received none of it for personal use and that any use of the proceeds for labor payoffs served a legitimate corporate purpose and was not in violation of any fiduciary duty. ...

... Here, the jury was presented with adequate evidence from which it could have drawn a justifiable inference that defendants used the scheme for their own benefit. ... [T]here was testimony which showed that Abrams and Siegel personally received the proceeds from the cash sales and either pocketed them or placed them in the corporate safe deposit box. Further, although the cash sales generated in excess of $100,000, the testimony concerning the use to which the money was put accounted for approximately $31,000, used mainly for illicit payoffs. The reasonable mind can think of several destinations for the more than $69,000 that was missing, and ... we conclude that the jury could have inferred that Abrams and Siegel used some or all of the remainder of the proceeds for their own benefit, and could have fairly concluded beyond a reasonable doubt that theirs was a scheme to misappropriate the proceeds from the sale of Mego assets for self-enrichment by "filch[ing] from [the corporation] its valuable property."

We do not need to consider whether use of the cash for bribery on behalf of the corporation breached defendants' fiduciary duties, for when an indictment charges acts in the conjunctive, "the verdict stands if the evidence is sufficient with respect to any one of the acts charged." Here, the acts were charged in the conjunctive: the jury was instructed that it could find the existence of a scheme if it found "beyond a reasonable doubt that a defendant breached fiduciary duties in furtherance of the unlawful or fraudulent purposes alleged in the indictment," namely, "bribes and self-enrichment." Thus, the jury's verdict establishes that it found beyond a reasonable doubt that the funds were misappropriated for both bribery and self-enrichment. We have determined that there is sufficient evidence in the record to support a finding of self-enrichment. As a result, defendants' convictions were valid, and inquiring into the question of whether the alleged use of the fund for illicit payoffs to labor officials violates the wire fraud statute is unnecessary. ...

In affirming defendants' convictions on the wire fraud counts, we in no way wish to encourage the type of indictment prosecuted here. Twenty counts were brought against five defendants, all but two of whom were acquitted of all charges. Siegel and Abrams, although convicted of the wire fraud charges (which might more properly have been redressed in a shareholder's derivative suit or in a state criminal prosecution), were acquitted on several other counts. ... While we applaud the government's concentration on unrecorded cash sales, a particularly common form of criminal activity, we nevertheless urge the government to think carefully before instituting other massive prosecutions having such slender foundations as this one.

WINTER, CIRCUIT JUDGE, dissenting in part and concurring in part:

... Today we read the wire fraud statute to create a federal law of fiduciary obligations imposed on corporate directors and officers, thereby setting the stage for the development of an expandable body of criminal law regulating intracorporate affairs.

The majority's legal theory is that wire fraud occurred because some of Mego's funds were diverted "for noncorporate purposes in breach of [the defendants'] fiduciary duties to act in the best interest of the corporation and to disclose material information to Mego and its stockholders." The evidence is that Mego, a corporation with sales ranging between $30 million and $109 million, during the relevant period, had off-book transactions engineered by the defendants averaging slightly over $11,000 per year. There is no evidence—*none*—that any of the money was diverted to the personal use of either Siegel or Abrams. The government's *prima facie* case is thus made out solely by a showing of improper corporate record keeping.

State corporate laws universally impose upon corporate directors and officers certain obligations labeled fiduciary duties which are implied from the corporate relationship. These duties are of a contractual nature. However, because of the high transaction costs of organizing numerous parties and the difficulty of spelling out precise rules to govern future transactions, fiduciary obligations are developed and applied on a case by case basis by state courts.

There is nothing in the language or legislative history of the wire fraud statute remotely suggesting that it was intended as a vehicle for the enforcement of fiduciary duties imposed upon corporate directors or officers by state law. To allow it to be so used would thus be a grave error. However, what the majority does is infinitely worse, for it holds that the wire fraud statute creates a *federal* law of fiduciary obligations. There is no pretense that the source of the fiduciary duty at issue in this case was anything but federal law. There is no reference in the majority opinion to state law or even to Mego's state of incorporation. The jury simply was told that it was up to it to decide whether, as part of the obligation "to act in the best interest of the corporation," the defendants were under a duty to disclose the off-book transactions to shareholders.

The creation of this federal fiduciary duty is no minor step. The relationship of federal and state law in the governance of corporations is a matter of great debate, in which the proponents of federal regulation have strenuously argued that state law governing the conduct of corporate directors and officers is too lax. Over the years, Congress has responded by mandating disclosure through the various securities laws, but has generally declined to enact substantive regulation of corporate transactions.

Notwithstanding the lack of even a hint of relevant Congressional intent in enacting the wire fraud laws, notwithstanding Congress' repeated rejection of pleas to strengthen the fiduciary obligations imposed on corporate directors and officers by state law, and notwithstanding the existence of precise federal legislation requiring disclosure of particular corporate matters, we read the wire fraud statute to embody a federal law of fiduciary obligations, including an undefined duty of yet further disclosure, enforceable by the sanctions of the criminal law.

It will be up to later juries and later panels to define what actions by corporate directors and officers are or are not "in the best interest of the corporation." The elasticity of the concept and the potential for infinite expansion, however, are foreshadowed by the facts of the present case. The "material" information not disclosed to shareholders in the instant case is a series of transactions of roughly $11,000 annually over nine years, a wholly trivial sum in light of Mego's sales. In holding that these transactions "would be important to a Mego stockholder," the majority simply closes its eyes to investment realities, for there is not a shred of evidence that such a sum would affect share price in the slightest. It requires little imagination to foresee future application of the theory of this case to the use of corporate airplanes, the size of executive salaries, expense accounts, etc. ...

Other aspects of the majority decision also trouble me. Adequate notice to those affected by such elastic concepts is simply not possible, for even the wisest counsel cannot foresee what corporate acts may after the fact attract a prosecutor's suspicion (or ire) and a judicial stamp of impropriety. ...

Finally, ... a crime is created which by its nature will be prosecuted infrequently and in a highly selective manner. If judges perceive a need for a catch-all federal common law crime, the issue should be addressed explicitly with some recognition of the dangers, rather than continue an inexorable expansion of the mail and wire fraud statutes under the pretense of merely discharging Congress' will.

Quite apart from the self-evident danger in creating vast areas of discretion for prosecutors to single out individuals for improper reasons, there is a real question as to whether the costs in resources equal the benefits achieved. The trial here, involving five defendants, each with his own counsel, lasted seven weeks, consuming substantial prosecutorial, private and judicial resources. Only two of the five defendants were convicted, and total jail sentences amounted to only seven months. In truth, the law enforcement results from society's point of view are as trivial as the off-book transactions were to Mego. Even had the government been more successful, however, there is reason to doubt that much would have been gained. Ill-defined crimes which are necessarily prosecuted on an infrequent and selective basis probably have little deterrent value. Were we to restrict the mail and wire fraud statutes to swindling and fraud, as originally intended, rather than extend them to perceived political or corporate improprieties, we would not only perform the judicial function correctly but probably also make a sensible policy judgment in terms of costs and benefits. ... [21]

Notes

1. What is the actionable fraud in this case? Fraud generally connotes some sort of deceit. Courts, in cases founded on a *Siegel* theory of fraud, generally insist that a simple breach of a fiduciary duty is not fraud and that "something more" is required. What is that something more? Many courts say that the "something more" is the *nondisclosure* or *concealment* of the breach that is the actual fraud:

A defendant's breach of a fiduciary duty may be a predicate for a violation of the mail fraud statute where the breach entails the violation of a duty to disclose material information. In other words, "[f]raud, for purposes of a mail fraud conviction, may be

---

[21] *See also* Lisa L. Casey, *Twenty-Eight Words: Enforcing Corporate Fiduciary Duties Through Criminal Prosecution of Honest Services Fraud*, 35 Del. J. Corp. L. 1 (2010).

proved through the defendant's non-action or non-disclosure of material facts intended to create a false and fraudulent representation." An affirmative duty to disclose need not be explicitly imposed; it may instead be implicit in the relationship between the parties.

United States v. Waymer, 55 F.3d 564, 571 (11th Cir. 1995); *see also* United States v. Silvano, 812 F.2d 754, 759 (1st Cir. 1987); United States v. Von Barta, 635 F.2d 999 (2d Cir. 1980). What gives rise to a duty to disclose, the breach of which is "fraud"? Must a fiduciary relationship be shown? Do all fiduciary relationships carry with them a duty to disclose?

Not all fiduciaries are bound by the same rules. "The words fiduciary duty are no more than a legal conclusion and the legal obligations actually imposed under that label vary greatly from relationship to relationship." United States v. Margiotta, 688 F.2d 108, 142 (2d Cir. 1982) (Winter, J., dissenting in part and concurring in part). As Justice Frankfurter noted in another context:

> to say that a man is a fiduciary only begins the analysis; it gives direction to further inquiry. To whom is he a fiduciary? What obligations does he owe as a fiduciary? In what respect has he failed to discharge these obligations? And what are the consequences of his deviation from duty?

SEC v. Chenery Corp., 318 U.S. 80, 85-86 (1943). Who should make such determinations and by reference to what body of laws? Do decisions such as this have implications for states' ability to control the content of their corporate law governing the fiduciary obligations of corporate officers and directors? *See* John C. Coffee, Jr., *From Tort to Crime: Some Reflections on the Criminalization of Fiduciary Breaches and the Problematic Line Between Law and Ethics*, 19 Am. Crim. L. Rev. 117, 154-59 (1981) [hereinafter Coffee, *From Tort to Crime*]; John C. Coffee, Jr., *Modern Mail Fraud: The Restoration of the Public/Private Distinction*, 35 Am. Crim. L. Rev. 427, 455-56 (1998) [hereinafter Coffee, *Modern Mail Fraud*].

2. In the controversial pre-*McNally* case of *United States v. Bronston*, 658 F.2d 920 (2d Cir.1981), Jack E. Bronston, an attorney, gave legal assistance to his personal client who was competing for an important bus franchise with another client represented by Bronston's law firm. The Second Circuit upheld Bronston's mail fraud conviction based on his fraudulent failure to disclose his breach of his fiduciary duty, which was, as the court described it, that he was "actively engaged in efforts designed to frustrate the precise endeavor which the [other] client had engaged the firm to pursue." *Id.* at 928. The court held that "the concealment by a fiduciary of material information which he is under a duty to disclose to another under circumstances where the non-disclosure could or does result in harm to the other is a violation of the statute." *Id.* at 926. It further stated, however, that "use or manipulation of Bronston's breach of fiduciary relationship was not a prerequisite to conviction." *Id.* at 929. Thus, under *Bronston*, a fraud case may be pursued for nondisclosure of a lawyer's conflict of interest even where there is no proof that "the defendant took advantage of or used his fiduciary relationship with firm clients to do them harm," for example by wrongfully using or disclosing the firm client's confidential information. *Id.* at 931 (Van Graafeiland, J., dissenting). Should the "something more" that converts a private fiduciary's breach into actionable fraud include proof of causation—for example, in *Bronston*, that the fiduciary breach was the proximate cause of the intended harm? *See* Coffee, *From Tort to Crime*, 19 Am. Crim. L. Rev. at 134, 163 (proposing a three-part formula to "distinguish impropriety from criminal fraud" and arguing that requiring proof of "(1) breach of duty, (2) actual or threatened loss and (3) a causal link of requisite proximity between the breach and loss gives a conceptual framework to the criminalization of fiduciary violations that prevents every ethical shortcoming from becoming a felony, but permits the state to prosecute serious deprivations").

4. It is important to recognize that although the *fraud* alleged in *Siegel* was non-disclosure of a fiduciary breach by one under a duty to disclose, the government's apparent theory was that the defendant's *object* in engaging in this fraud was self-enrichment, that is, money. The cases discussed in the next section deal with instances in which the object of the fraud is not necessarily money or other types of property but rather intangible, non-property interests,

such as the right to "honest services." *Readers should keep in mind in examining such cases that the type of fraud involved and the object of the fraud should be examined separately.* Thus, for example, the government may allege that the fraud in a given case involves straight-out lies, but that the object was an intangible right to honest services. Alternatively, the government may allege (as in *Siegel*) that the fraud was a failure to disclose a breach of fiduciary duty but that the object was property. Courts do not always separate questions of whether there was a cognizable fraud (deceit) from whether there was a cognizable object of that fraud (property or "honest services"), in part because the analysis seems to merge in cases in which the government's theory is that the defendant's failure to disclose a breach of fiduciary duty to render honest services constituted both the fraud and the object of the fraud.

C. PERMISSIBLE OBJECTS OF A SCHEME TO DEFRAUD

The garden-variety fraud involves a defendant's attempt to obtain *money or other* **tangible property** to which he is not entitled (as in *Coffman* and *Siegel*, and as charged in *Regent Office Supply*) through deceit. Courts, and Congress, have recognized, however, that mail and wire fraud prosecutions may be founded upon a defendant's fraudulent attempts to deprive others of (i) **intangible property** (such as confidential business information or a business's right to control its assets); and (ii) **intangible non-property rights**, such a right to "honest services."

The "honest services" theory has a long and tortured history, traced in the following pages. By way of background, we know that the elements of these crimes are: (1) a scheme or artifice to defraud; and (2) a mailing or interstate wiring in furtherance of the scheme. Under traditional principles, a "scheme or artifice to defraud" commonly referred to "wronging one in his *property rights* by dishonest methods or schemes"—that is, to schemes in which the defendant misled another in order to secure *money or property* to which he was not entitled.

Prosecutors sought to push beyond this traditional understanding of fraud because there was (and is) no generally-applicable federal statute available to prosecute state and local political corruption. Accordingly, federal prosecutors pursued state and local politicians under a creative theory of "honest services" fraud. And courts bought it, not just when politicians were inarguably corrupt, but also when their activities were—though disturbing to federal prosecutors—not illegal under state or local law. Thus, for decades prior to 1987, federal courts of appeals were unanimous in holding that criminal "schemes or artifices to defraud" within the meaning of the mail and wire fraud statues encompassed situations in which public officials, or politically-active persons who had no formal government position, deprived the citizenry of its rights to their "honest services." But where is the "fraud" (that is, the lies, deceit, etc.) in public corruption? The gravamen of an honest services case was not the corruption; it was the "fraud" of failing to *tell* the citizenry about the corruption or allegedly improper conduct. (If the public official *did* disclose his alleged wrongdoing, there was no case.) The government did not have to prove that the governmental entity or citizenry "victimized" by this concealment lost money or property—it was sufficient that the defendant deprived his victims of their "right to his honest services" through his *concealment* of breaches of his duty.

The "honest services" fraud theory applied in private as well as public employment cases. Thus, it was extended to employees of private companies who, prosecutors charged and courts agreed, assumed a duty to advise their employers of material breaches of their terms of employment and who were criminally responsible if they failed to make appropriate disclosures.

Forty-odd years after individuals started going to prison under this theory of liability, the Supreme Court decided *McNally v. United States*, reproduced below.

1. PROPERTY

McNALLY v. UNITED STATES
483 U.S. 350 (1987)

JUSTICE WHITE delivered the opinion of the Court.

This action involves the prosecution of petitioner Gray, a former public official of the Commonwealth of Kentucky, and petitioner McNally, a private individual, for alleged violation of the federal mail fraud statute, 18 U.S.C. § 1341. The prosecution's principal theory of the case, which was accepted by the courts below, was that petitioners' participation in a self-dealing patronage scheme defrauded the citizens and government of Kentucky of certain "intangible rights," such as the right to have the Commonwealth's affairs conducted honestly. We must consider whether the jury charge permitted a conviction for conduct not within the scope of the mail fraud statute.

We accept for the sake of argument the Government's view of the evidence, as follows. Petitioners and a third individual, Howard P. "Sonny" Hunt, were politically active in the Democratic Party in the Commonwealth of Kentucky during the 1970's. After Democrat Julian Carroll was elected Governor of Kentucky in 1974, Hunt was made chairman of the state Democratic Party and given *de facto* control over selecting the insurance agencies from which the Commonwealth would purchase its policies. In 1975, the Wombwell Insurance Company of Lexington, Kentucky (Wombwell), which since 1971 had acted as the Commonwealth's agent for securing a workmen's compensation policy, agreed with Hunt that in exchange for a continued agency relationship it would share any resulting commissions in excess of $50,000 a year with other insurance agencies specified by him. The commissions in question were paid to Wombwell by the large insurance companies from which it secured coverage for the Commonwealth.

From 1975 to 1979, Wombwell funneled $851,000 in commissions to 21 separate insurance agencies designated by Hunt. Among the recipients of these payments was Seton Investments, Inc. (Seton), a company controlled by Hunt and petitioner Gray and nominally owned and operated by petitioner McNally.

Gray served as Secretary of Public Protection and Regulation from 1976 to 1978 and also as Secretary of the Governor's Cabinet from 1977 to 1979. Prior to his 1976 appointment, he and Hunt established Seton for the sole purpose of sharing in the commissions distributed by Wombwell. Wombwell paid some $200,000 to Seton between 1975 and 1979, and the money was used to benefit Gray and Hunt. Pursuant to Hunt's direction, Wombwell also made excess commission payments to the Snodgrass Insurance Agency, which in turn gave the money to McNally.

On account of the foregoing activities, Hunt was charged with and pleaded guilty to mail and tax fraud and was sentenced to three years' imprisonment. Petitioners were charged with one count of conspiracy and seven counts of mail fraud, six of which were dismissed before trial. The remaining mail fraud count was based on the mailing of a commission check to Wombwell by the insurance company from which it had secured coverage for the State. This count alleged that petitioners had devised a scheme ... to defraud the citizens and government of Kentucky of their right to have the Commonwealth's affairs conducted honestly ... [22]

After informing the jury of the charges in the indictment, the District Court instructed that the scheme to defraud the citizens of Kentucky and to obtain money by false pretenses and concealment could be made out by either of two sets of findings: (1) that Hunt had *de facto*

---

[22] [Ed.: The pertinent count of the indictment charged that the defendants devised a scheme or artifice to "(a)(1) defraud the citizens of the Commonwealth of Kentucky and its governmental departments, agencies, officials and employees of their right to have the Commonwealth's business and its affairs conducted honestly, impartially, free from corruption, bias, dishonesty, deceit, official misconduct, and fraud."]

control over the award of the workmen's compensation insurance contract to Wombwell from 1975 to 1979; that he directed payments of commissions from this contract to Seton, an entity in which he had an ownership interest, without disclosing that interest to persons in state government whose actions or deliberations could have been affected by the disclosure; and that petitioners, or either of them, aided and abetted Hunt in that scheme; or (2) that Gray, in either of his appointed positions, had supervisory authority regarding the Commonwealth's workmen's compensation insurance at a time when Seton received commissions; that Gray had an ownership interest in Seton and did not disclose that interest to persons in state government whose actions or deliberations could have been affected by that disclosure; and that McNally aided and abetted Gray (the latter finding going only to McNally's guilt).

The jury convicted petitioners on both the mail fraud and conspiracy counts, and the Court of Appeals affirmed the convictions. In affirming the substantive mail fraud conviction, the court relied on a line of decisions from the Courts of Appeals holding that the mail fraud statute proscribes schemes to defraud citizens of their intangible rights to honest and impartial government. Under these cases, a public official owes a fiduciary duty to the public, and misuse of his office for private gain is a fraud. Also, an individual without formal office may be held to be a public fiduciary if others rely on him "'because of a special relationship in the government'" and he in fact makes governmental decisions. The Court of Appeals held that Hunt was such a fiduciary because he "substantially participated in governmental affairs and exercised significant, if not exclusive, control over awarding the workmen's compensation insurance contract to Wombwell and the payment of monetary kickbacks to Seton."

We granted certiorari, and now reverse.

The mail fraud statute clearly protects property rights, but does not refer to the intangible right of the citizenry to good government. As first enacted in 1872, as part of a recodification of the postal laws, the statute contained a general proscription against using the mails to initiate correspondence in furtherance of "any scheme or artifice to defraud." The sponsor of the recodification stated, in apparent reference to the antifraud provision, that measures were needed "to prevent the frauds which are mostly gotten up in the large cities ... by thieves, forgers, and rapscallions generally, for the purpose of deceiving and fleecing the innocent people in the country." Insofar as the sparse legislative history reveals anything, it indicates that the original impetus behind the mail fraud statute was to protect the people from schemes to deprive them of their money or property.

Durland v. United States, 161 U.S. 306 (1896), the first case in which this Court construed the meaning of the phrase "any scheme or artifice to defraud," held that the phrase is to be interpreted broadly insofar as property rights are concerned, but did not indicate that the statute had a more extensive reach. The Court rejected the argument that "the statute reaches only such cases as, at common law, would come within the definition of 'false pretenses,' in order to make out which there must be a misrepresentation as to some existing fact and not a mere promise as to the future." Instead, it construed the statute to "includ[e] everything designed to defraud by representations as to the past or present, or suggestions and promises as to the future." Accordingly, the defendant's use of the mails to sell bonds which he did not intend to honor was within the statute. The Court explained that "[i]t was with the purpose of protecting the public against all such intentional efforts to despoil, and to prevent the post office from being used to carry them into effect, that this statute was passed. ... "

Congress codified the holding of *Durland* in 1909, and in doing so gave further indication that the statute's purpose is protecting property rights. The amendment added the words "or for obtaining money or property by means of false or fraudulent pretenses, representations, or promises" after the original phrase "any scheme or artifice to defraud." The new language is based on the statement in *Durland* that the statute reaches "everything designed to defraud by representations as to the past or present, or suggestions and promises as to the future." However, instead of the phrase "everything designed to defraud" Congress used the words "[any scheme or artifice] for obtaining money or property."

After 1909, therefore, the mail fraud statute criminalized schemes or artifices "to defraud" or "for obtaining money or property by means of false or fraudulent pretenses, representation, or promises ... ." Because the two phrases identifying the proscribed schemes appear in the disjunctive, it is arguable that they are to be construed independently and that the money-or-property requirement of the latter phrase does not limit schemes to defraud to those aimed at causing deprivation of money or property. This is the approach that has been taken by each of the Courts of Appeals that has addressed the issue: schemes to defraud include those designed to deprive individuals, the people, or the government of intangible rights, such as the right to have public officials perform their duties honestly.

As the Court long ago stated, however, the words "to defraud" commonly refer "to wronging one in his property rights by dishonest methods or schemes," and "usually signify the deprivation of something of value by trick, deceit, chicane or overreaching." *Hammerschmidt v. United States*, 265 U.S. 182, 188 (1924).[23] The codification of the holding in *Durland* in 1909 does not indicate that Congress was departing from this common understanding. As we see it, adding the second phrase simply made it unmistakable that the statute reached false promises and misrepresentations as to the future as well as other frauds involving money or property.

We believe that Congress' intent in passing the mail fraud statute was to prevent the use of the mails in furtherance of such schemes. The Court has often stated that when there are two rational readings of a criminal statute, one harsher than the other, we are to choose the harsher only when Congress has spoken in clear and definite language. As the Court said in a mail fraud case years ago: "There are no constructive offenses; and before one can be punished, it must be shown that his case is plainly within the statute." Rather than construe the statute in a manner that leaves its outer boundaries ambiguous and involves the Federal Government in setting standards of disclosure and good government for local and state officials, we read § 1341 as limited in scope to the protection of property rights. If Congress desires to go further, it must speak more clearly than it has.

For purposes of this action, we assume that Hunt, as well as Gray, was a state officer. The issue is thus whether a state officer violates the mail fraud statute if he chooses an insurance agent to provide insurance for the State but specifies that the agent must share its commissions with other named insurance agencies, in one of which the officer has an ownership interest and hence profits when his agency receives part of the commissions. We note that as the action comes to us, there was no charge and the jury was not required to find that the Commonwealth itself was defrauded of any money or property. It was not charged that in the absence of the alleged scheme the Commonwealth would have paid a lower premium or secured better insurance. Hunt and Gray received part of the commissions but those commissions were not the Commonwealth's money. Nor was the jury charged that to convict it must find that the Commonwealth was deprived of control over how its money was spent. Indeed, the premium for insurance would have been paid to some agency, and what Hunt and Gray did was to assert control that the Commonwealth might not otherwise have made over

---

[23] [Court's footnote 8:] *Hammerschmidt* concerned the scope of the predecessor of 18 U.S.C. § 371, which makes criminal any conspiracy "to defraud the United States, or any agency thereof in any manner or for any purpose." *Hammerschmidt* indicates, in regard to that statute, that while "[t]o conspire to defraud the United States means primarily to cheat the Government out of property or money, ... it also means to interfere with or obstruct one of its lawful governmental functions by deceit, craft or trickery, or at least by means that are dishonest." Other cases have held that § 371 reaches conspiracies other than those directed at property interests. However, we believe that this broad construction of § 371 is based on a consideration not applicable to the mail fraud statute.

... "Quite likely the word 'defraud,' as ordinarily used in the common law, and as used in English statutes and in the statutes of our states, enacted with the object of protecting property and property rights of communities and individuals, as well as of municipal governments, which exist largely for the purpose of administering local financial affairs, has reference to frauds relating to money and property."

... "[A] statute which ... has for its object the protection of the individual property rights of the members of the civic body, is one thing; a statute which has for its object the protection and welfare of the government alone, which exists for the purpose of administering itself in the interests of the public, [is] quite another." Section 371 is a statute aimed at protecting the Federal Government alone; however, the mail fraud statute, as we have indicated, had its origin in the desire to protect individual property rights, and any benefit which the Government derives from the statute must be limited to the Government's interests as property holder.

the commissions paid by the insurance company to its agent.[24] Although the Government now relies in part on the assertion that petitioners obtained property by means of false representations to Wombwell, there was nothing in the jury charge that required such a finding. We hold, therefore, that the jury instruction on the substantive mail fraud count permitted a conviction for conduct not within the reach of § 1341. ...

JUSTICE STEVENS, with whom JUSTICE O'CONNOR joins as to [all but the last paragraph in this excerpted version], dissenting.

Congress has broadly prohibited the use of the United States mails to carry out "any scheme or artifice to defraud." 18 U.S.C. § 1341. The question presented is whether that prohibition is restricted to fraudulent schemes to deprive others of money or property, or whether it also includes fraudulent schemes to deprive individuals of other rights to which they are entitled. Specifically, we must decide whether the statute's prohibition embraces a secret agreement by state officials to place the State's workmen's compensation insurance with a particular agency in exchange for that company's agreement to share a major portion of its commissions with a list of agents provided by the officials, including sham agencies under the control of the officials themselves.

The same question of statutory construction has arisen in a variety of contexts over the past few decades. In the public sector, judges, State Governors, chairmen of state political parties, state cabinet officers, city aldermen, Congressmen and many other state and federal officials have been convicted of defrauding citizens of their right to the honest services of their governmental officials.[25] In most of these cases, the officials have secretly made governmental

---

[24] [Court's footnote 9:] JUSTICE STEVENS would affirm the convictions even though it was not charged that requiring the Wombwell agency to share commissions violated state law. We should assume that it did not. For the same reason we should assume that it was not illegal under state law for Hunt and Gray to own one of the agencies sharing in the commissions and hence to profit from the arrangement, whether or not they disclosed it to others in the state government. It is worth observing as well that it was not alleged that the mail fraud statute would have been violated had Hunt and Gray reported to state officials the fact of their financial gain. The violation asserted is the failure to disclose their financial interest, even if state law did not require it, to other persons in the state government whose actions could have been affected by the disclosure. It was in this way that the indictment charged that the people of Kentucky had been deprived of their right to have the Commonwealth's affairs conducted honestly.

It may well be that Congress could criminalize using the mails to further a state officer's efforts to profit from governmental decisions he is empowered to make or over which he has some supervisory authority, even if there is no state law proscribing his profiteering or even if state law expressly authorized it. But if state law expressly permitted or did not forbid a state officer such as Gray to have an ownership interest in an insurance agency handling the State's insurance, it would take a much clearer indication than the mail fraud statute evidences to convince us that having and concealing such an interest defrauds the State and is forbidden under federal law.

[25] [Justice Stevens' footnote 1:] See, e.g., *United States v. Holzer*, 816 F.2d 304 (C.A.7 1987) (county judge); *United States v. Silvano*, 812 F.2d 754 (C.A.1 1987) (city budget director); *United States v. Barber*, 668 F.2d 778 (C.A.4 [1982]) (State Alcoholic Beverage Control Commissioner); *United States v. Margiotta*, 688 F.2d 108 (C.A.2 1982) (party leader); *United States v. Diggs*, 198 U.S.App.D.C. 255, 613 F.2d 988 (1979) (Congressman); *United States v. Mandel*, 591 F.2d 1347 (C.A.4 1979) (Governor of Maryland); *United States v. Brown*, 540 F.2d 364 (C.A.8 1976) (city building commissioner); *United States v. Bush*, 522 F.2d 641 (C.A.7 1975) (city Director of Public Relations); *United States v. Keane*, 522 F.2d 534 (C.A.7 1975) (city alderman); *United States v. Staszcuk*, 502 F.2d 875 (C.A.7 1974) (city alderman); *United States v. Isaacs*, 493 F.2d 1124 (C.A.7 [1974]) (ex-Governor of Illinois and ex-Director of Illinois Department of Revenue); *United States v. Classic*, 35 F.Supp. 457 (E.D.La.1940) (election commissioner).

Some private defendants have also been convicted of devising schemes through which public servants defraud the public. See, e.g., *United States v. Lovett*, 811 F.2d 979 (C.A.7 1987) (bribing mayor); *United States v. Rauhoff*, 525 F.2d 1170 (C.A.7 1975) (bribing State Secretary of State).

In *Shushan v. United States*, 117 F.2d 110 (C.A.5 [1941]), the Fifth Circuit upheld the mail fraud prosecution of a member of a Louisiana parish levy board for receiving kickbacks from the underwriters of a plan to refund outstanding bonds of the levy district. Explaining why it rejected the argument that no

decisions with the objective of benefiting themselves or promoting their own interests, instead of fulfilling their legal commitment to provide the citizens of the State or local government with their loyal service and honest government. Similarly, many elected officials and their campaign workers have been convicted of mail fraud when they have used the mails to falsify votes, thus defrauding the citizenry of its right to an honest election.[26] In the private sector, purchasing agents, brokers, union leaders, and others with clear fiduciary duties to their employers or unions have been found guilty of defrauding their employers or unions by accepting kickbacks or selling confidential information.[27] In other cases, defendants have been found guilty of using the mails to defraud individuals of their rights to privacy and other nonmonetary rights.[28] All of these cases have something in common—they involved what the Court now refers to as "intangible rights." They also share something else in common. The many federal courts that have confronted the question whether these sorts of schemes constitute a "scheme or artifice to defraud" have uniformly and consistently read the statute in the same, sensible way. They have realized that nothing in the words "any scheme or artifice to defraud," or in the purpose of the statute, justifies limiting its application to schemes intended to deprive victims of money or property.

The mail fraud statute sets forth three separate prohibitions. It prohibits the use of the United States mails for the purpose of executing

> "[1] *any* scheme or artifice to defraud, [2] *or* for obtaining money or property by means of false or fraudulent pretenses, representations, or promises, [3] *or* to sell, dispose of, loan, exchange, alter, give away, distribute, supply, or furnish or procure for unlawful use any counterfeit or spurious coin, obligation, security, or other article, or anything represented to be or intimated or held out to be such counterfeit or spurious article ... ." 18 U.S.C. § 1341 (emphasis and brackets added).

As the language makes clear, each of these restrictions is independent. One can violate the second clause—obtaining money or property by false pretenses—even though one does not violate the third clause—counterfeiting. Similarly, one can violate the first clause—devising a scheme or artifice to defraud—without violating the counterfeiting provision. Until today it was also obvious that one could violate the first clause by devising a scheme or artifice to defraud, even though one did not violate the second clause by seeking to obtain money or property from his victim through false pretenses. Every court to consider the matter had so held. Yet, today, the Court, for all practical purposes, rejects this longstanding construction of

---

actual fraud had occurred because the refunding operation had actually been profitable to the levy board, the court stated:

> "No trustee has more sacred duties than a public official and any scheme to obtain an advantage by corrupting such a one must in the federal law be considered a scheme to defraud."

[26] [Justice Stevens' footnote 2:] See, *e.g.*, *United States v. Girdner*, 754 F.2d 877 (C.A.10 1985) (candidate for state legislature); *United States v. Odom*, 736 F.2d 104, 116, n. 13 (C.A.4 1984) (sheriff); *United States v. Clapps*, 732 F.2d 1148, 1153 (C.A.3 [1984]) (party chairman); *United States v. States*, 488 F.2d 761 (C.A.8 1973) (candidates for city office).

[27] [Justice Stevens' footnote 3:] See, *e.g.*, *United States v. Price*, 788 F.2d 234 (C.A.4 1986); *United States v. Boffa*, 688 F.2d 919, 930-931 (C.A.3 1982); *United States v. Curry*, 681 F.2d 406 (C.A.5 1982) (chairman of political action committee); *United States v. Bronston*, 658 F.2d 920 (C.A.2 1981) (attorney); *United States v. Von Barta*, 635 F.2d 999 (C.A.2 1980) (securities trader); *United States v. Bohonus*, 628 F.2d 1167 (C.A.9 [1980]) (insurance manager); *United States v. Bryza*, 522 F.2d 414 (C.A.7 1975) (purchasing agent); *United States v. George*, 477 F.2d 508 (C.A.7 [1973]) (purchasing agent); *United States v. Procter & Gamble Co.*, 47 F.Supp. 676 (D.Mass.1942) (attempt to bribe competitor's employee).

[28] [Justice Stevens' footnote 4:] See, *e.g.*, *United States v. Condolon*, 600 F.2d 7 (C.A.4 1979) (wire fraud conviction related to bogus talent agency designed to seduce women); *United States v. Louderman*, 576 F.2d 1383 (C.A.9 [1978]) (scheme to fraudulently obtain confidential personal information); see also *United States v. Castor*, 558 F.2d 379, 383 (C.A.7 1977) (fraudulent information on application for liquor license).

the statute by imposing a requirement that a scheme or artifice to defraud does not violate the statute unless its purpose is to defraud someone of money or property. I am at a loss to understand the source or justification for this holding. Certainly no canon of statutory construction requires us to ignore the plain language of the provision. ...

The term "defraud" is not unique to § 1341. Another federal statute, 18 U.S.C. § 371, uses the identical term in prohibiting conspiracies to "defraud the United States," and the construction we have given to that statute should be virtually dispositive here. ...   [I]n *Hammerschmidt v. United States*, 265 U.S. 182 (1924), the Court described the scope of the [predecessor to § 371] as prohibiting not only conspiracies to "cheat the Government out of property or money, but it also means to interfere with or obstruct one of its lawful governmental functions by deceit, craft or trickery, or at least by means that are dishonest." It is thus clear that a conspiracy to defraud the United States does not require any evidence that the Government has suffered any property or pecuniary loss.

There is no basis for concluding that the term "defraud" means something different in § 1341 (first enacted in 1872) than what it means in § 371 (first enacted in 1867). ...

Even if there were historical evidence of a limited definition of "fraud," the Court's holding would reflect a strange interpretation of legislation enacted by the congress in the 19th Century. Statutes like the Sherman Act, the civil rights legislation, and the mail fraud statute were written in broad general language on the understanding that the courts would have wide latitude in construing them to achieve the remedial purposes that Congress had identified. The wide open spaces in statutes such as these are most appropriately interpreted as implicit delegations of authority to the courts to fill in the gaps in the common-law tradition of case-by-case adjudication. The notion that the meaning of the words "any scheme or artifice to defraud" was frozen by a special conception of the term recognized by Congress in 1872 is manifestly untenable. As Judge Posner put it:

> "The argument depends on the view that the meaning of fraud in the mail-fraud statute was frozen by the conception of fraud held by the framers of the statute when it was first passed back in the nineteenth century. This seems to us the opposite and equally untenable extreme from arguing that fraud is whatever strikes a judge as bad, but in any event the 'intangible rights' concept that the argument attacks is too well established in the courts of appeals for us to disturb."

Finally, there is nothing in the legislative history of the mail fraud statute that suggests that Congress intended the word "fraud" to have a narrower meaning in that statute than its common meaning and the meaning that it has in § 371. ...

I recognize that there may have been some overly expansive applications of § 1341 in the past. With no guidance from this Court, the Courts of Appeals have struggled to define just when conduct which is clearly unethical is also criminal. In some instances, however, such as voting fraud cases, the criminality of the scheme and the fraudulent use of the mails could not be clearer. It is sometimes difficult to define when there has been a scheme to defraud someone of intangible rights. But it is also sometimes difficult to decide when a tangible loss was caused by fraud. The fact that the exercise of judgment is sometimes difficult is no excuse for rejecting an entire doctrine that is both sound and faithful to the intent of Congress. ...

In the long run, it is not clear how grave the ramifications of today's decision will be. Congress can, of course, negate it by amending the statute. Even without congressional action, prosecutions of corrupt officials who use the mails to further their schemes may continue since it will frequently be possible to prove some loss of money or property. But many other types of fraudulent use of the mail will now be immune from prosecution. The possibilities that the decision's impact will be mitigated do not moderate my conviction that the Court has made a serious mistake. Nor do they erase my lingering questions about why a Court that has not been particularly receptive to the rights of criminal defendants in recent years has acted so dramatically to protect the elite class of powerful individuals who will benefit from this decision. ...

Notes

1. Given the lower courts' unanimous and longstanding recognition of the so-called "intangible rights" theory of mail and wire fraud prosecutions, the Supreme Court's *McNally* decision "has been variously described as 'blockbusting,' as a 'total surprise' and as a 'wholly unexpected explication of the law of mail fraud.'" United States v. Ochs, 842 F.2d 515, 521 (1st Cir. 1988) (citations omitted). Do you find the majority's or the dissent's statutory construction more persuasive? Do you find the majority's distinction of the Court's *Hammerschmidt* precedent reasonable?

2. Review Justice Stevens' summary of the types of cases that had been pursued under the "intangible rights" theory of mail and wire fraud. *See supra* dissent footnotes 1-4 (footnotes 25-28 in this chapter) and accompanying text. Do these cases fit your conception of fraud? Are these cases that the federal government should be bringing or are they better left to state enforcement? In the context of prosecutions, such as McNally's, for violation of citizens' right to honest government, why might federal intervention be troubling? Why might it be appropriate and even necessary? Ultimately, what concern appears to be driving the majority? Is this concern applicable in all categories of cases described by Justice Stevens' dissent?

3. *Public Sector Cases*: *McNally* referred to the federalism issues in these "honest services" public employee cases. Others have pointed to other dangers potentially present in public-sector honest services cases.

For example, in the noted pre-*McNally* case of *United States v. Margiotta*, 688 F.2d 108 (2d Cir. 1982), the Second Circuit upheld the conviction of Joseph M. Margiotta, who held *no elective office* but who functioned as the Chairman of the Republican Committee in Nassau County, New York. Margiotta was convicted of fraud under an honest services theory based on his de facto control and influence over the distribution of insurance commissions on municipal properties to his political allies (in a scheme akin to the one in *McNally*). In essence, local elected officials responsible for obtaining insurance coverage for municipal properties delegated the authority for obtaining insurance to a Broker of Record. The Broker received as compensation for his services commissions consisting of a portion of the monies paid by the municipalities for the insurance policies. It was alleged that Margiotta contrived the appointment of Richard B. Williams & Sons, Inc., an insurance agency, (the "Williams Agency" or "Agency"), as Broker of Record for the Town of Hempstead and Nassau County in return for the Williams Agency kicking back 50 percent of the compensation it received to licensed insurance brokers and others designated by Margiotta.

The *Margiotta* majority held that an individual *who occupies no official public office* but nonetheless participates substantially in the operation of the government owes a fiduciary duty to the citizenry not to deprive it of intangible political rights. *Id.* at 121. It upheld the conviction on the theory that Margiotta breached his fiduciary duty to disclose this secret agreement to the public. *Id.* at 126-27. Judge Winter while concurring in part, departed from the court's analysis in *Margiotta* arguing:

> ... Reduced to essentials, the majority holds that a mail fraud conviction will be upheld when a politically active person is found by a jury to have assumed a duty to disclose material facts to the general citizenry and deliberately failed to do so. Margiotta's conviction is based upon his failure as a partisan political leader with great influence to disclose to the citizens of the Town of Hempstead and Nassau County his knowledge that the Williams Agency would have been willing to act as Broker of Record for considerably smaller commissions than were actually paid. Because those citizens might have compelled the municipalities to reduce these costs had they been given this information, it is a material fact. ...
>
> ... [N]o amount of rhetoric seeking to limit the holding to the facts of this case can conceal that there is no end to the common political practices which may now be swept within the ambit of mail fraud. Since the doctrine adopted by the majority applies to candidates as well as those holding office, a candidate who mails a brochure containing a promise which the candidate knows cannot be carried out is surely committing an even

more direct mail fraud than what Margiotta did here. An elected official who for political purposes performs an act imposing unnecessary costs on taxpayers is guilty of mail fraud if disclosure is not made to the public. A partisan political leader who throws decisive support behind a candidate known to the leader to be less qualified than his or her opponent because that candidate is more cooperative with the party organization, is guilty of mail fraud unless that motive is disclosed to the public. A partisan political leader who causes elected officials to fail to modernize government to retain jobs for the party faithful is guilty of mail fraud unless that fact is disclosed. In each of these cases the undisclosed fact is as "material" as the facts which Margiotta failed to disclose, the harm to the public is at least as substantial as the harm resulting from Margiotta's scheme, and the dishonesty, partiality, bias and deceit in failing to disclose those facts is equally present. This is not to say that Margiotta's conduct as a whole is not more odious than the conduct described in these hypotheticals. That is not the issue. The point is that the actions taken by Margiotta deemed relevant to mail fraud by the majority are present in each case: a relationship calling for disclosure, a material fact known to the candidate, official or party leader, and a failure to disclose it.

The majority is quite simply wrong in brushing aside the First Amendment issues. The theory they adopt subjects politically active persons to criminal sanctions based solely upon what they say or do not say in their discussions of public affairs. The majority explicitly bottoms Margiotta's mail fraud conviction on his failure to say something. Its logic would easily extend to the content of campaign literature. Indeed, it takes no great foresight to envision an indictment framed on the theory adopted by the majority and alleging mail fraud based on public speeches. ...

... Although the courts have, with precious little analysis, brought virtually all participants in government and politics under the rubric fiduciary, the obligations imposed are wholly the creation of recent interpretations of the mail fraud statute itself. A reading of the cases in this area, however, shows how little definition there is to these newly created obligations which carry criminal sanctions. For all one can find in the case law, no distinction is made between the fiduciary obligations of a civil servant, political appointee, elected official, candidate or partisan political leader. Juries are simply left free to apply a legal standard which amounts to little more than the rhetoric of sixth grade civics classes. One searches in vain for even the vaguest contours of the legal obligations created beyond the obligation to conduct governmental affairs "honestly" or "impartially," to ensure one's "honest and faithful participation" in government and to obey "accepted standards of moral uprightness, fundamental honesty, fair play and right dealing." The present case is no exception. While there is talk of a line between legitimate patronage and mail fraud, there is no description of its location. With all due respect to the majority, the quest for legal standards is not furthered by reference to "the right to good government" and the duty "to act in a disinterested manner."

Of course, we should all hope that public affairs are conducted honestly and on behalf of the entire citizenry. Nevertheless, we should recognize that a pluralistic political system assumes politically active persons will pursue power and self-interest. Participation in the political process is not limited to the pure of heart. Quite frankly, I shudder at the prospect of partisan political activists being indicted for failing to act "impartially" in influencing governmental acts. Where a statute, particularly a criminal statute, does not regulate specific behavior, enforcement of inchoate obligations should be by political rather than criminal sanctions. Where Congress has not passed legislation specifying particular acts by the politically active as criminal, our reliance rather should be on public debate, a free press and an alert electorate. In a pluralistic system organized on partisan lines, it is dangerous to require persons exercising political influence to make the kind of disclosure required in public offerings by the securities laws.

My concerns in this case thus extend far beyond a disagreement over statutory interpretation. The limitless expansion of the mail fraud statute subjects virtually every active participant in the political process to potential criminal investigation and prosecution. It may be a disagreeable fact but it is nevertheless a fact that political opponents not infrequently exchange charges of "corruption," "bias," "dishonesty," or deviation from "accepted standards of ... fair play and right dealing." Every such accusation is now potentially translatable into a federal indictment. I am not predicting the imminent arrival of the totalitarian night or the wholesale indictment of candidates, public officials and party leaders. To the contrary, what profoundly troubles me is the potential for abuse through selective prosecution and the degree of raw political power the freeswinging club of mail fraud affords federal prosecutors.

Margiotta, 688 F.2d at 139-43 (Winter, J., dissenting in part and concurring in part); *see also* Geraldine Szott Moohr, *Mail Fraud and the Intangible Rights Doctrine: Someone to Watch Over Us*, 31 Harv. J. on Legis. 182-83 (1994).

4. *Private sector cases*: Courts have long indicated that more should be required to prove an "honest services" case in the private employment than in the public corruption context. As the Eleventh Circuit explained in *United States v. deVegter*, 198 F.3d 1324, 1328-29 (11th Cir. 1999):

> The meaning of the "intangible right of honest services" has different implications, ... when applied to public official malfeasance and private sector misconduct. Public officials inherently owe a fiduciary duty to the public to make governmental decisions in the public's best interest. "If the official instead secretly makes his decision based on his own personal interests—as when an official accepts a bribe or personally benefits from an undisclosed conflict of interest—the official has defrauded the public of his honest services." When the prosecution can prove the other elements of the wire fraud offense, taking kickbacks or benefitting from an undisclosed conflict of interest will support the conviction of a public official for depriving his or her constituents of the official's honest services because "[i]n a democracy, citizens elect public officials to act for the common good. When official action is corrupted by secret bribes or kickbacks, the essence of the political contract is violated." Illicit personal gain by a government official deprives the public of its intangible right to the honest services of the official.
>
> On the other hand, such a strict duty of loyalty ordinarily is not part of private sector relationships. Most private sector interactions do not involve duties of, or rights to, the "honest services" of either party. Relationships may be accompanied by obligations of good faith and fair dealing, even in arms-length transactions. These and similar duties are quite unlike, however, the duty of loyalty and fidelity to purpose required of public officials. For example, "[e]mployee loyalty is not an end in itself, it is a means to obtain and preserve pecuniary benefits for the employer. An employee's undisclosed conflict of interest does not by itself necessarily pose the threat of economic harm to the employer." A public official's undisclosed conflict of interest, in contrast, does by itself harm the constituents' interest in the end for which the official serves—honest government in the public's best interest. The "intangible right of honest services" must be given an analogous interpretation in the private sector. Therefore, for a private sector defendant to have violated the victim's right to honest services, it is not enough to prove the defendant's breach of loyalty alone. Rather, as is always true in a breach of loyalty by a public official, the breach of loyalty by a private sector defendant must in each case contravene—by inherently harming—the purpose of the parties' relationship.

Are federalism concerns also present? *See* Coffee, *Modern Mail Fraud*, *supra*, 35 Am. Crim. L. Rev. at 455-56; Judge Winter's separate opinion in *Siegel*.

5. Justice Stevens expresses a concern that is rarely explicitly raised but which could be said to lurk around the edges of many of the issues discussed in this course when he says that he has "lingering questions" about why "a Court that has not been particularly receptive to the rights of criminal defendants in recent years has acted so dramatically to protect the elite class of powerful individuals who will benefit from this decision." That is, he seems to believe that courts are more willing to apply stringent legal standards in "white-collar" cases than in "white powder" cases. Is this a valid observation?

2. INTANGIBLE PROPERTY

Predictably, the Court's decision in *McNally* resulted in a great deal of litigation over the question of what constitutes cognizable "property" under the mail and wire fraud statutes. Shortly after *McNally*, the Supreme Court made clear in the following case, *Carpenter v. United States*, that the "property" it held protected by the mail fraud statute in *McNally* was not confined to "tangible" property such as cash or securities.

CARPENTER v. UNITED STATES
484 U.S. 19 (1987)

JUSTICE WHITE delivered the opinion of the Court.

Petitioners Kenneth Felis and R. Foster Winans were convicted of violating § 10(b) of the Securities Exchange Act of 1934, 48 Stat. 891, 15 U.S.C. § 78j(b), and Rule 10b-5, 17 CFR § 240.10b-5 (1987). They were also found guilty of violating the federal mail and wire fraud statutes, 18 U.S.C. §§ 1341, 1343, and were convicted for conspiracy under 18 U.S.C. § 371. Petitioner David Carpenter, Winans' roommate, was convicted for aiding and abetting.

I

In 1981, Winans became a reporter for the Wall Street Journal (the Journal) and in the summer of 1982 became one of the two writers of a daily column, "Heard on the Street." That column discussed selected stocks or groups of stocks, giving positive and negative information about those stocks and taking "a point of view with respect to investment in the stocks that it reviews." Winans regularly interviewed corporate executives to put together interesting perspectives on the stocks that would be highlighted in upcoming columns, but, at least for the columns at issue here, none contained corporate inside information or any "hold for release" information. Because of the "Heard" column's perceived quality and integrity, it had the potential of affecting the price of the stocks which it examined. The District Court concluded on the basis of testimony presented at trial that the "Heard" column "does have an impact on the market, difficult though it may be to quantify in any particular case."

The official policy and practice at the Journal was that prior to publication, the contents of the column were the Journal's confidential information. Despite the rule, with which Winans was familiar, he entered into a scheme in October 1983 with Peter Brant and petitioner Felis, both connected with the Kidder Peabody brokerage firm in New York City, to give them advance information as to the timing and contents of the "Heard" column. This permitted Brant and Felis and another conspirator, David Clark, a client of Brant, to buy or sell based on the probable impact of the column on the market. Profits were to be shared. The conspirators agreed that the scheme would not affect the journalistic purity of the "Heard" column, and the District Court did not find that the contents of any of the articles were altered to further the profit potential of petitioners' stock-trading scheme. Over a 4-month period, the brokers made prepublication trades on the basis of information given them by Winans about the contents of some 27 "Heard" columns. The net profits from these trades were about $690,000.

In November 1983, correlations between the "Heard" articles and trading in the Clark and Felis accounts were noted at Kidder Peabody and inquiries began. Brant and Felis denied knowing anyone at the Journal and took steps to conceal the trades. Later, the Securities and Exchange Commission began an investigation. Questions were met by denials both by the brokers at Kidder Peabody and by Winans at the Journal. As the investigation progressed, the conspirators quarreled, and on March 29, 1984, Winans and Carpenter went to the SEC and revealed the entire scheme. This indictment and a bench trial followed. Brant, who had pleaded guilty under a plea agreement, was a witness for the Government.

The District Court found, and the Court of Appeals agreed, that Winans had knowingly breached a duty of confidentiality by misappropriating prepublication information regarding the timing and contents of the "Heard" column, information that had been gained in the course of his employment under the understanding that it would not be revealed in advance of publication and that if it were, he would report it to his employer. It was this appropriation of confidential information that underlay both the securities laws and mail and wire fraud counts. With respect to the § 10(b) charges, the courts below held that the deliberate breach of Winans' duty of confidentiality and concealment of the scheme was a fraud and deceit on the Journal. Although the victim of the fraud, the Journal, was not a buyer or seller of the stocks traded in or otherwise a market participant, the fraud was nevertheless considered to be "in connection with" a purchase or sale of securities within the meaning of the statute and the rule. The courts reasoned that the scheme's sole purpose was to buy and sell securities at a profit based on advance information of the column's contents. The courts below rejected petitioners' submission, which is one of the two questions presented here, that criminal liability could not be imposed on petitioners under Rule 10b-5 because "the newspaper is the only alleged victim of fraud and has no interest in the securities traded."

In affirming the mail and wire fraud convictions, the Court of Appeals ruled that Winans had fraudulently misappropriated "property" within the meaning of the mail and wire fraud statutes and that its revelation had harmed the Journal. It was held as well that the use of the mail and wire services had a sufficient nexus with the scheme to satisfy §§ 1341 and 1343. The petition for certiorari challenged these conclusions.

The Court is evenly divided with respect to the convictions under the securities laws and for that reason affirms the judgment below on those counts. For the reasons that follow, we also affirm the judgment with respect to the mail and wire fraud convictions.

II

Petitioners assert that their activities were not a scheme to defraud the Journal within the meaning of the mail and wire fraud statutes; and that in any event, they did not obtain any "money or property" from the Journal, which is a necessary element of the crime under our decision last Term in *McNally v. United States*, 483 U.S. 350 (1987). We are unpersuaded by either submission and address the latter first.

We held in *McNally* that the mail fraud statute does not reach "schemes to defraud citizens of their intangible rights to honest and impartial government," and that the statute is "limited in scope to the protection of property rights." Petitioners argue that the Journal's interest in prepublication confidentiality for the "Heard" columns is no more than an intangible consideration outside the reach of § 1341; nor does that law, it is urged, protect against mere injury to reputation. This is not a case like *McNally*, however. The Journal, as Winans' employer, was defrauded of much more than its contractual right to his honest and faithful service, an interest too ethereal in itself to fall within the protection of the mail fraud statute, which "had its origin in the desire to protect individual property rights." Here, the object of the scheme was to take the Journal's confidential business information—the publication schedule and contents of the "Heard" column—and its intangible nature does not make it any less "property" protected by the mail and wire fraud statutes. *McNally* did not limit the scope of § 1341 to tangible as distinguished from intangible property rights.

Both courts below expressly referred to the Journal's interest in the confidentiality of the contents and timing of the "Heard" column as a property right, and we agree with that conclusion. Confidential business information has long been recognized as property. "Confidential information acquired or compiled by a corporation in the course and conduct of its business is a species of property to which the corporation has the exclusive right and benefit, and which a court of equity will protect through the injunctive process or other appropriate remedy." 3 W. Fletcher, Cyclopedia of Law of Private Corporations § 857.1, p. 260 (rev. ed. 1986) (footnote omitted). The Journal had a property right in keeping confidential and making exclusive use, prior to publication, of the schedule and contents of the "Heard" column. As the Court has observed before:

"[N]ews matter, however little susceptible of ownership or dominion in the absolute sense, is stock in trade, to be gathered at the cost of enterprise, organization, skill, labor, and money, and to be distributed and sold to those who will pay money for it, as for any other merchandise." *International News Service v. Associated Press*, 248 U.S. 215, 236 (1918).

Petitioners' arguments that they did not interfere with the Journal's use of the information or did not publicize it and deprive the Journal of the first public use of it, miss the point. The confidential information was generated from the business, and the business had a right to decide how to use it prior to disclosing it to the public. Petitioners cannot successfully contend based on *Associated Press* that a scheme to defraud requires a monetary loss, such as giving the information to a competitor; it is sufficient that the Journal has been deprived of its right to exclusive use of the information, for exclusivity is an important aspect of confidential business information and most private property for that matter.

We cannot accept petitioners' further argument that Winans' conduct in revealing prepublication information was no more than a violation of workplace rules and did not amount to fraudulent activity that is proscribed by the mail fraud statute. Sections 1341 and 1343 reach any scheme to deprive another of money or property by means of false or fraudulent pretenses, representations, or promises. As we observed last Term in *McNally*, the words "to defraud" in the mail fraud statute have the "common understanding" of "'wronging one in his property rights by dishonest methods or schemes,' and 'usually signify the deprivation of something of value by trick, deceit, chicane or overreaching.'" The concept of "fraud" includes the act of embezzlement, which is "'the fraudulent appropriation to one's own use of the money or goods entrusted to one's care by another.'"

The District Court found that Winans' undertaking at the Journal was not to reveal prepublication information about his column, a promise that became a sham when in violation of his duty he passed along to his co-conspirators confidential information belonging to the Journal, pursuant to an ongoing scheme to share profits from trading in anticipation of the "Heard" column's impact on the stock market. In *Snepp v. United States*, 444 U.S. 507, 515, n. 11 (1980) (*per curiam*), although a decision grounded in the provisions of a written trust agreement prohibiting the unapproved use of confidential Government information, we noted the similar prohibitions of the common law, that "even in the absence of a written contract, an employee has a fiduciary obligation to protect confidential information obtained during the course of his employment." As the New York courts have recognized: "It is well established, as a general proposition, that a person who acquires special knowledge or information by virtue of a confidential or fiduciary relationship with another is not free to exploit that knowledge or information for his own personal benefit but must account to his principal for any profits derived therefrom."

We have little trouble in holding that the conspiracy here to trade on the Journal's confidential information is not outside the reach of the mail and wire fraud statutes, provided the other elements of the offenses are satisfied. The Journal's business information that it intended to be kept confidential was its property; the declaration to that effect in the employee manual merely removed any doubts on that score and made the finding of specific intent to defraud that much easier. Winans continued in the employ of the Journal, appropriating its confidential business information for his own use, all the while pretending to perform his duty of safeguarding it. In fact, he told his editors twice about leaks of confidential information not related to the stock-trading scheme, demonstrating both his knowledge that the Journal viewed information concerning the "Heard" column as confidential and his deceit as he played the role of a loyal employee. Furthermore, the District Court's conclusion that each of the petitioners acted with the required specific intent to defraud is strongly supported by the evidence.

Lastly, we reject the submission that using the wires and the mail to print and send the Journal to its customers did not satisfy the requirement that those mediums be used to execute the scheme at issue. The courts below were quite right in observing that circulation of the "Heard" column was not only anticipated but an essential part of the scheme. Had the column not been made available to Journal customers, there would have been no effect on stock prices and no likelihood of profiting from the information leaked by Winans. ...

Notes

1. The petitioners argued that there was no "fraud" *and* that there was no cognizable "property" targeted by the fraud. How does the Court find the existence of "fraud" here—was there an actionable lie or a concealment in the face of a duty to disclose? Does the Court essentially validate the *Siegel* theory of fraud? What of the Court's "property" analysis? What kinds of sources should one look to in deciding whether a given intangible interest constitutes "property" for purposes of federal fraud law? May an employer essentially create its own "property" interest by designating a certain type of company information as "confidential" and prohibiting its use or dissemination in the employee handbook? Does *Carpenter* mean that these type of workplace rules are now enforceable through federal felony prosecution?

2. *Unissued Government Licenses:* Cleveland: There was a split in the circuits over whether various types of unissued government licenses constitute a form of property under the mail and wire fraud statutes—a split resolved in 2000 by the Supreme Court in *Cleveland v. United States*, 531 U.S. 12 (2000). Cleveland was convicted, *inter alia*, under § 1341 on the theory that he defrauded Louisiana of its "property" interest in a state license to operate video poker machines. The government's theory was that, because Cleveland had tax and financial problems that could have undermined his suitability to receive a video poker license, he fraudulently concealed that he was one of the true owners of a business in the license applications that that business mailed to the State. The *Cleveland* Court held that such a license is not "property" in the government's hands because the State's core concern is "*regulatory*" and whatever financial stake the State has in the licenses accrues only *after* they have been issued. *Id.* at 20-22. The Court also rejected the government's argument that "Cleveland frustrated the State's right to control the issuance, renewal, and revocation of video poker licenses," stating that "far from composing an interest that 'has long been recognized as property,' these intangible rights of allocation, exclusion, and control amount to no more and no less than Louisiana's sovereign power to regulate." *Id.* at 23. Finally, and perhaps most notably, the Court concluded by re-emphasizing the core concerns that drove the *McNally* Court:

> We reject the Government's theories of property rights not simply because they stray from traditional concepts of property. We resist the Government's reading of § 1341 as well because it invites us to approve a sweeping expansion of federal criminal jurisdiction in the absence of a clear statement by Congress. Equating issuance of licenses or permits with deprivation of property would subject to federal mail fraud prosecution a wide range of conduct traditionally regulated by state and local authorities. We note in this regard that Louisiana's video poker statute typically and unambiguously imposes criminal penalties for making false statements on license applications. As we reiterated last Term, "'unless Congress conveys its purpose clearly, it will not be deemed to have significantly changed the federal-state balance' in the prosecution of crimes."

Id. at 24. *Cf.* Bond v. United States, -- U.S. --, 134 S.Ct. 2077, 2089 (2014) (applying "well-established principle that it is incumbent upon the federal courts to be certain of Congress' intent before finding that federal law overrides the usual constitutional balance of federal and state powers") (internal quotations omitted).

3. *"Right to Control" Theory*: Many lower courts have also validated another intangible "property" theory alluded to in the *McNally* opinion, finding that a defendant may be convicted for "deny[ing] the victim the right to control its assets by depriving it of information necessary to make a discretionary economic decision." United States v. Rossomando, 144 F.3d 197, 201 n.5 (2d Cir. 1998). (After the Supreme Court narrowed the scope of "honest services" fraud in *Skilling*, *infra*, this theory of liability has taken on new importance.)

In *United States v. Wallach*, 935 F.2d 445 (2d Cir.1991), questionable payments were made to individuals—one of them a director of a corporation—supposedly as payment for their assistance in a public offering. The payments were disguised, in part so that they would not have to be disclosed to the SEC and to the corporation's shareholders. The individuals' convictions for mail fraud were affirmed by the Second Circuit on the basis of the defendants' fraudulent deprivation of shareholders' "right to control" how the corporation's money was spent. The court noted that although the cases approving this theory use the term "right to control," this phraseology might be confusing because shareholders actually have only limited "control" rights. Examination of the case law, the court explained, "reveals that application of the theory is predicated on a showing that some person or entity has been deprived of potentially valuable economic information." *Id.* at 462-63. The court found that "stockholders' right to monitor and to police the behavior of the corporation and its officers is a property interest," and indeed, "given the important role that information plays in the valuation of a corporation, the right to complete and accurate information is one of the most essential sticks in the bundle of rights that comprise a stockholder's property interest." *Id.* at 463.

The *Wallach* defendants had argued that the shareholders were not cheated of any property right because they received value for the money, although not perhaps the value that had been expected given the disclosures made. The court noted that even if the individuals involved did give full value in alternative services, this would not defeat a fraud claim. In support of this proposition, the Second Circuit quoted Judge Learned Hand's statement in *United States v. Rowe*, 56 F.2d 747, 749 (2d Cir. 1932) (rejected by the Second Circuit in *Regent Office Supply*, reproduced *supra*) that "'[a] man is none the less cheated out of his property, when he is induced to part with it by fraud, because he gets a quid pro quo of value. It may be impossible to measure his loss by the gross scales available to a court but he has suffered a wrong; he has lost his chance to bargain with the facts before him.'" *Id.* at 463.

In short, the court held that a scheme to defraud was made out where there was proof of a scheme to intentionally conceal the true nature of the transactions at issue: "[t]hese misrepresentations permitted the officers to pay out large sums from the corporation to undisclosed individuals for what were purportedly improper purposes, while maintaining the facade that these payments were in furtherance of legitimate corporate goals. By concealing this information, the value of the ... stock was obscured and the shareholders and the corporation were deprived of the opportunity to make informed decisions." *Id.* at 463-64. Might this theory of liability permit prosecutors and juries to subject corporate actors associated with publicly traded companies to criminal liability for failing to make disclosures that are not required by state or federal corporate or securities laws?

After *Wallach*, the Second Circuit recognized that one of the difficulties that may arise from the application of this "right to control" theory to nondisclosures by corporations or their agents is that "[w]here no rule otherwise provides, persons acting on behalf of a corporation may well find it necessary to disguise or conceal certain matters in the interests of that corporation." United States v. D'Amato, 39 F.3d 1249, 1258 (2d Cir. 1994). For example, "[a] company may ... disguise the hiring of forensic accountants in order to avoid giving warning to an undetected embezzler." *Id.*

Thus, in *United States v. D'Amato*, the Second Circuit reiterated *Regent Office Supply's* requirement of an intent to injure. The defendant in a "right to control" case must intend to injure the person misled, and that person or entity must be the specific target of the inaccurate or concealed information. *Id.* at 1257. Such a theory cannot be charged if the officer in good faith believes that his misrepresentation is otherwise legal and in the best interests of the corporation. A defendant entity and its management accused of depriving shareholders of their "right to control" may therefore defend such a charge by showing that (1) management has made an otherwise lawful decision that concealment or failure to disclose is in the corporation's best interests; and (2) management acted in good faith and did not intend to benefit personally from the deception. *Id.* at 1258. Under the *D'Amato* test, would the *Wallach* defendants have prevailed? Could the government in *Siegel* have pursued a "right to control" fraud theory even if no inference of self-enrichment had been possible and the evidence demonstrated only a failure to disclosure that the money went to "labor payoffs"? After reviewing the materials concerning the criminally enforceable "right of honest services," *infra*, you may wish to consider whether there is a continuing need for a criminally enforceable "right to control" theory of property. *See also* United States v. Finazzo, 850 F.3d 94 (2d Cir. 2017) (summarizing Second Circuit "right to control" cases).

Other circuits have embraced the "right-to-control" property theory. For example, in *United States v. Welch*, 327 F.3d 1081, 1108 (10th Cir. 2003), the defendants—the President and Senior Vice President of the Salt Lake City Bid Committee for the 2002 Olympic Winter Games (SLBC)—were indicted, *inter alia*, for mail and wire fraud. The indictment alleged that the defendants engaged in a bribery scheme to "misappropriate and misapply the monies and funds of the SLBC[] by diverting SLBC income and by giving ... money and other material benefits to influence IOC members to vote for Salt Lake City to host the Olympic Winter Games." *Id.* at 1085. Among other things, the indictment alleged Defendants instructed an SLBC "sponsor" "to make a series of payments to the defendants in cash so that the payments would not appear on the SLBC's books and records and could be diverted by the defendants for their own personal purposes." *Id.* The Government relied, in part, on a theory that the defendants' scheme to defraud deprived the SLBC of its right to control how its property was used. The Tenth Circuit upheld the government theory, reasoning as follows:

> Defendants ... assert that after *Cleveland v. United States*, 531 U.S. 12 (2000), the theory they deprived the SLBC of the right to control how its monies were used is no longer available to the Government. *Cleveland* held that because state and municipal licenses "do not rank as 'property,' for purposes of § 1341, in the hands of the official licensor[,]" a fraudulent scheme to obtain such licenses is not within the purview of the mail fraud statute. The Court explained: "It does not suffice ... that the object of the fraud may become property in the recipient's hands; for purposes of the mail fraud statute, the thing obtained must be property in the hands of the victim." *Id.*
>
> The difference between *Cleveland* and this case is readily apparent. Here, the SLBC's monies constituted "property in the hands of the victim." The Supreme Court recognized long ago that property defined in the "ordinary, everyday sense[]" is not only the tangible "thing which is the subject of ownership," but also "the owner's [intangible] right to control and dispose of that thing." *Crane v. Comm'r*, 331 U.S. 1, 6 (1947); cf. *Connecticut v. Doehr*, 501 U.S. 1, 11 (1991) (noting the intangible "property interests that attachment affects are significant"). Consistent with this view, we have recognized the intangible right to control one's property is a property interest within the purview of the mail and wire fraud statutes. *See United States v. Simpson*, [950 F.2d 1519, 1523 (10th Cir. 1991)] (approving wire fraud convictions predicated on a scheme to defraud an organization of its right to control how its assets were used). Our sister circuits agree.

Id. at 1108 (collecting cases); *see also* United States v. Gray, 405 F.3d 227 (4th Cir. 2005) (collecting cases).

4. *Tax Revenues Under Foreign Law:* Pasquantino: Most recently, the Supreme Court held in *Pasquantino v. United States*, 544 U.S. 349 (2005) that a "plot to defraud a foreign government of tax revenue violates the federal wire fraud statute." *Id.* at 352, 359. Resolving a split in the circuits, the Court also held that its conclusion did not derogate from the common-law "revenue rule," which "generally barred courts from enforcing the tax laws of foreign sovereigns." *Id.* at 352. The case involved petitioners who were indicted and convicted of wire fraud for carrying out a scheme to smuggle large quantities of liquor into Canada from the United States without paying the required Canadian excise taxes on these imports. The interstate wires upon which the prosecution was apparently premised were telephone calls Pasquantino, while in New York, made to order liquor from discount package stores in Maryland. Having purchased the liquor, the defendants drove the goods over the Canadian border without declaring the liquor at customs or paying the excise taxes that would have been due. In holding that "Canada's right to uncollected excise taxes on the liquor petitioners imported into Canada is 'property' in its hands," *id.* at 355, the Court explained:

> ... The right to be paid money has long been thought to be a species of property. See 3 W. Blackstone, Commentaries on the Laws of England 153-155 (1768) (classifying a right

to sue on a debt as personal property). Consistent with that understanding, fraud at common law included a scheme to deprive a victim of his entitlement to money. For instance, a debtor who concealed his assets when settling debts with his creditors thereby committed common-law fraud. That made sense given the economic equivalence between money in hand and money legally due. The fact that the victim of the fraud happens to be the Government, rather than a private party, does not lessen the injury.

Our conclusion that the right to tax revenue is property in Canada's hands, contrary to petitioners' contentions, is consistent with *Cleveland v. United States*. In that case, the defendant, Cleveland, had obtained a video poker license by making false statements on his license application. We held that a State's interest in an unissued video poker license was not "property," because the interest in choosing particular licensees was "'purely regulatory'" and "[could not] be economic." We also noted that "the Government nowhere allege[d] that Cleveland defrauded the State of any money to which the State was entitled by law."

Cleveland is different from this case. Unlike a State's interest in allocating a video poker license to particular applicants, Canada's entitlement to tax revenue is a straightforward "economic" interest. There was no suggestion in *Cleveland* that the defendant aimed at depriving the State of any money due under the license; quite the opposite, there was "no dispute that [the defendant's partnership] paid the State of Louisiana its proper share of revenue" due. Here, by contrast, the Government alleged and proved that petitioners' scheme aimed at depriving Canada of money to which it was entitled by law. Canada could hardly have a more "economic" interest than in the receipt of tax revenue. *Cleveland* is therefore consistent with our conclusion that Canada's entitlement is "property" as that word is used in the wire fraud statute.

Id. at 355-57. The Court then upheld the government's "fraud" theory as well, stating that

... petitioners' plot was a "scheme or artifice to defraud" Canada of its valuable entitlement to tax revenue. The evidence showed that petitioners routinely concealed imported liquor from Canadian officials and failed to declare those goods on customs forms. By this conduct, they represented to Canadian customs officials that their drivers had no goods to declare. This, then, was a scheme "designed to defraud by representations," and therefore a "scheme or artifice to defraud" Canada of taxes due on the smuggled goods.

Id. at 347. Does *Pasquantino* mean that the federal government may pursue any local, state, or federal tax evasion case as wire or mail fraud? Does it mean that *anybody, anywhere in the world*, who acts to deprive its government of tax revenues and commits a mailing or wiring in the United States can be prosecuted by U.S. federal authorities? *See* Brian Wallach, Note, *All Hands on Deck: Rescuing the Revenue Rule from the Supreme Court's Decision in* Pasquantino, 59 Tax. Law. 621 (2006).

5. The question of what constitutes a cognizable intangible property interest continues to be subject to litigation, in part because of the seemingly endless creativity of federal prosecutors in formulating novel "property" theories. *See, e.g.*, United States v. Shoss, 523 Fed. App'x. 713 (11th Cir. 2013); United States v. Ali, 620 F.3d 1062 (9th Cir. 2010); United States v. Douglas, 398 F.3d 407, 418 (6th Cir. 2005) (the "right to compete [for a skilled trades designation, and attendant wages and benefits] guaranteed by [a] collective bargaining agreement in this case is sufficient to constitute property for purposes of the mail fraud statute"); United States v. Griffin, 324 F.3d 330 (5th Cir. 2003) (unissued federal low-income housing credits were not "property" for fraud purposes); United States v. Poirier, 321 F.3d 1024 (11th Cir. 2003); United States v. Bruchhausen, 977 F.2d 464 (9th Cir. 1992) (the government's potential forfeiture interest in high technology products which defendant allegedly smuggled to Soviet Bloc countries did not constitute a "property interest," nor did manufacturer's interest in seeing that their products were not sent to the Soviet Bloc in violation of federal law).

For example, in *United States v. Henry*, 29 F.3d 112 (3d Cir. 1994), the indictment alleged corruption by public officials in the process of selecting a bank to be the repository of the Delaware River Joint Toll Bridge revenues. The indictment argued that the defendants defrauded the banks of an intangible property right: a fair opportunity to bid to receive the Commission's funds. The Third Circuit affirmed the district court's dismissal of the indictment because a fair bidding opportunity is not a traditionally recognized, enforceable property interest. Why did the government focus on the banks' alleged property interests? Could the government have instead alleged that the Commission's or the public's property rights were impaired in this case?

Also, in *United States v. Hedaithy*, 392 F.3d 580 (3d Cir. 2004), the defendants hired imposters to take their Test of English as a Foreign Language (TOEFL) for them. The TOEFL was administered by ETS, a corporation that designs and administers standardized tests. The government charged the defendants with mail fraud, based on their alleged scheme to deprive ETS of its property interest in "maintaining the integrity of its testing process." The Third Circuit found that ETS tried to protect the confidentiality and exclusivity of its exam and thus that the exam questions were confidential business information. *Id.* at 594. Further, the court noted that "indictments alleged that ETS would not have allowed the hired test-takers to sit for the exam had it known that they were not actually the Defendants, and had it known that they did not actually agree to preserve the exam's confidentiality." *Id.* at 595. Accordingly, the court held that a scheme to defraud was also properly alleged: "ETS was deprived of a recognized property interest: the 'right to decide how to use' its confidential business information, *i.e.*, the TOEFL exam" through the defendants' misrepresentations. *Id.*

6. *"Obtainable" Property?* In the context of Hobbs Act prosecutions under 18 U.S.C. § 1951, the Supreme Court has decided two cases that, some argue, may have important implications for the application of the mail and wire fraud cases in "money or property" cases. In *Scheidler v. NOW*, 537 U.S. 393 (2003), the National Organization of Women ("NOW") sued abortion protesters under the Racketeer Influenced and Corrupt Organizations Act ("RICO"), 18 U.S.C. § 1962, for engaging in a nationwide conspiracy to shut down abortion clinics through "a pattern of racketeering activity" that included acts of extortion in violation of the Hobbs Act, § 1951. The Hobbs Act subjects a person to criminal liability, *inter alia*, if he affects interstate commerce by extortion. § 1951(a). The Act defines "extortion" to mean "the *obtaining* of property from another, with his consent, induced by wrongful use of actual or threatened force, violence, or fear, or under color of official right." § 1951(b)(2) (emphasis added). NOW argued that the defendants violated the Hobbs Act by depriving abortion clinics of the right to control what medical services they offered to women. The Supreme Court stated that it was undisputed that the defendants had "interfered with, disrupted, and in some instances completely deprived [abortion clinics] of their ability to exercise their property rights." 537 U.S. at 404. The Court held, however, that such conduct did not violate the Hobbs Act because the defendants did not actually "*obtain*" the clinics' property. *Id.* at 405. "Petitioners may have deprived or sought to deprive respondents of their alleged property right to exclusive control of their business assets, but they did not acquire any such property. Petitioners neither pursued nor received 'something of value from' respondents that they could exercise, transfer, or sell." *Id.* at 405.

Subsequently, in *Sekhar v. United States*, 570 U.S. 729 (2013), the Court again struck a Hobbs Act conviction on the ground that the defendant did not "obtain" the victim's property. The general counsel of New York's Comptroller's office recommended that the State of New York's employee pension fund not invest in the defendant's investment fund. The general counsel then received a series of anonymous e-mails threatening that if he did not change his recommendation and approve investment in the defendant's fund, counsel's extramarital affair would be disclosed to his wife, government officials, and the media. The emails were traced to the defendant and he was indicted for, and convicted of, attempted extortion in violation of the Hobbs Act, 18 U.S.C. § 1951(a). On the verdict form, the jury found that the property the defendant attempted to extort was the general counsel's recommendation to approve the investment.

In *Sekhar*, The Supreme Court explained that it did not need to decide whether the "right to make a recommendation" constituted "property." 570 U.S. at 736 n.5. "*Scheidler* rested its decision, as we do, on the term 'obtaining.' The principle announced there—that a defendant must pursue something of value from the victim that can be exercised, transferred, or sold— applies with equal force here. Whether one considers the personal right at issue to be 'property' in a broad sense or not, it certainly was not *obtainable property* under the Hobbs Act." *Id.* at 736-37. In so doing, the Court relied in part on its mail fraud precedent in *Cleveland v. United States*, 531 U.S. 12 (2000), reasoning that in *Cleveland* "[w]e held that a 'license' is not "property" while in the State's hands and *so cannot be 'obtained' from the State*. Even less so can an employee's yet-to-be-issued recommendation be called obtainable property." 570 U.S. at 737 (emphasis added). The government attempted to save its case by arguing that what was truly at stake was the general counsel's "intangible property right to give his disinterested legal opinion to his client free of improper outside interference." *Id.* at 737-38. The Court responded by asking: "But *what*, exactly, would the [defendant] have obtained for himself? A right to give *his own* disinterested legal opinion to *his own* client free of improper interference? Or perhaps, a right to give *the general counsel's* disinterested legal opinion to *the general counsel's* client? Either formulation sounds absurd, because it is. Clearly, [defendant's] goal was not to acquire the general counsel's 'intangible property right to give disinterested legal advice.' It was to force the general counsel to offer advice that accorded with petitioner's wishes. ... [T]hat is coercion, not extortion." *Id.* at 738.

After *Scheidler*, defendants argued that the concept of "obtainable property" ought to apply in mail and wire fraud prosecutions as well because the statutes also address schemes "for *obtaining* money or property." (Emphasis added.) The argument is not without merit. The mail fraud statute, on its face, contains three disjunctive means of violating its dictates—"devis[ing] or intended to devise any scheme or artifice to defraud" *or* "for *obtaining* money or property by means of false or fraudulent pretenses, representations, or promises" *or* to sell or dispose of counterfeit or spurious articles. 18 U.S.C. § 1341 (emphasis added). But readers will recall that, in its *McNally* opinion, the Supreme Court read the first two disjunctive clauses of the mail fraud statute together, such that a "scheme to defraud" also required that the defendant obtain property. *See also Cleveland*, 531 U.S. 12.

So far, the lower courts have refused to accept this argument, concluding that "[u]nlike the mail fraud statute, the Hobbs Act expressly requires the Government to prove that the defendant 'obtain[ed] property from another.' 18 U.S.C. § 1951(b)(2) (defining the term 'extortion'). ... [A] mail fraud violation may be sufficiently found where the defendant has merely deprived another of a property right." United States v. Hedaithy, 392 F.3d 580, 602-03 n.21 (3d Cir. 2004); *see also* Porcelli v. United States, 404 F.3d 157, 161-62 (2d Cir. 2005); United States v. Welch, 327 F.3d 1081, 1108 & n.27 (10th Cir. 2003); *but cf.* United States v. Czubinski, 106 F.3d 1069 (1st Cir. 1997) (reversing conviction because merely accessing confidential information without doing, or intending to do, more did not "deprive" victim of intangible property right in confidential information).

These arguments have been raised anew after *Sekhar*, and again have been rebuffed. *See* Coren v. United States, 2015 WL 4937800 (E.D.N.Y. 2015) (collecting cases). Given the Supreme Court's emphasis that "obtaining" truly means "obtaining" in *Sekhar*, the Court's reading of the statute in *McNally*, and its characterization of *Cleveland's* mail fraud holding (a license is not property in the State's hands and "*so cannot be 'obtained' from the State*"), should courts revisit this question? 570 U.S. at 737 (emphasis added).

Sekhar may be read to affect also the "right-to-control" theory of property for mail and wire fraud purposes. As one commentator noted:

> ... [T]he Court was evidently unimpressed with one of the key arguments in the government's brief: that Sekhar committed extortion by attempting to exercise the general counsel's "right to control his own labor" or his "right to control the substance of his own recommendation." Many lower federal courts have accepted the theory that depriving a victim of its "right to control" what it does with its property is sufficient to meet the property requirement for mail or wire fraud. The Supreme Court, however, has

never addressed this theory. *Sekhar*'s tacit rejection of the right-to-control argument does not bode well for the government when the issue arises in the mail or wire fraud context.

The right-to-control theory does not seem consistent with *Sekhar*'s "obtainable property" test. Misrepresentations that induce a victim to do something with its property that it would not otherwise have done could logically be said to involve the *deprivation* of property. Less clear, in cases where the victim is not induced to part with any property, is how such a scheme would involve *obtaining* property. As in *Sekhar*, a right of control typically is not itself "transferrable"—the "defining feature" of obtainable property. To say that the person making the alleged misrepresentation is thereby "obtaining" the victim's right to control would, in many cases, "make nonsense of words," as Justice Scalia characterized the government's theory in *Sekhar*.

Gary Stein, *"Obtainable Property" and the Mail and Wire Fraud Statutes*, Bus. Crimes Bull. (Sept. 2013).

3. "HONEST SERVICES": SECTION 1346

Shortly after *McNally* was decided, Congress attempted to overrule that decision through legislation. Thus, in late 1988, on the last day of the 100th Congress, Congress passed a highly publicized omnibus drug bill. A provision now codified at 18 U.S.C. § 1346 was added at the last moment—and without debate or committee consideration—as one of 30 unrelated provisions attached to that bill. Section 1346 states:

For purposes of this Chapter, the term "scheme or artifice to defraud" includes a scheme or artifice to deprive another of the intangible right of honest services.

This statute applies to bank (§ 1344), health care (§ 1347), and securities (§ 1348) fraud as well as mail and wire fraud. The circuits read § 1346 as a congressional attempt to revive at least some of the pre-*McNally* "honest services" cases but there was a great deal of confusion among (and within) the circuits on the appropriate scope and application of § 1346.

The excerpted article presented below contends that § 1346 is patently and hopelessly vague; in so doing, it outlines some of the issues that divided the circuits as they attempted to find ways of limiting the potentially huge reach of the statute. The Supreme Court granted *certiorari* in three honest services fraud cases in the 2009-2010 term. Two, *Black v. United States*[29] and *Skilling v. United States*,[30] arose out of the private sector, and one, *Weyhrauch v. United States*,[31] was a public employee case. Rather than adopting the tests or principles that had developed over the 20 years of the statute's life in the circuits, the Supreme Court, in *Skilling* (reproduced in relevant part below), imposed its own limiting construction.

Julie R. O'Sullivan, *Honest-Services Fraud: A (Vague) Threat to Millions of Blissfully Unaware (and Non-Culpable) American Workers*,
63 Vand. L. Rev. En Banc 23 (2010)

It is my firm belief that if any statute is unconstitutionally vague, it is 18 U.S.C. § 1346, at least as applied to cases in which employees of private entities are prosecuted for depriving their employers of a right to their honest services (so-called "private cases"). Objections to vagueness rest on due process. "Vagueness may invalidate a criminal law for either of two independent reasons. First, it may fail to provide the kind of notice that will enable ordinary people to understand what conduct it prohibits; second, it may authorize and even encourage

---

[29] 561 U.S. 465 (2010) (vacated and remanded in light of *Skilling*).

[30] 561 U.S. 358 (2010).

[31] 561 U.S. 476 (2010) (mem.) (vacated and remanded in light of *Skilling*).

arbitrary and discriminatory enforcement." The Supreme Court's vagueness precedents do not provide much guidance regarding what objective factors one should look to in evaluating the applicability of these two concerns in a given context. Rather, the Court tends simply to reach a conclusion and explain that one or both of these reasons back up its judgment.

That said, I hope to demonstrate below that, under any standard, § 1346 fails both tests in the private cases. Fair notice concerns are certainly present when one recognizes that *anyone* could be subjected to indictment and the humiliation and stresses of a public trial, and begin serving jail time upon conviction, only to have some court of appeals decide that what she did was not, in law, a crime because of a new judicially-imposed limitation. Indeed, in the *Skilling* argument, the Chief Justice seemed very disturbed by the notion that effective notice could be provided only by lawyerly parsing of the vast—and conflicting—caselaw underlying honest services; he asserted that this common law evolution in the meaning of the term "doesn't sound like fair notice of what's criminal." More importantly, these cases demonstrate the terrifying power that such statutes give prosecutors. "Where federal prosecutors can make an 'honest services' case against *anyone* under existing 'standards'"—and I believe they can—"a vast potential for arbitrary, discriminatory, and unfair prosecutorial choices inevitably follows."

The appropriate remedy is to strike the statute, not rewrite it. For a variety of reasons—including separation of powers, the principle of legality, and the rule against retroactive lawmaking—courts are not permitted to fill in the content of otherwise vague legislation; there is not (or should not be) a common law of crime. Thus, the Court cannot fix vague statutes by "legislating" their content. ...

I. THE STATUTE REALLY IS VAGUE, AND THE LIMITING PRINCIPLES IDENTIFIED THUS FAR ARE INEFFECTIVE.

The Court's criteria in evaluating vagueness may not be clear, but when courts (let alone ordinary citizens) cannot agree on what *conduct*—attended by what *mental state* and what *attendant circumstances*—constitutes a crime, it is a vagueness trifecta. To illustrate my point, consider a hypothetical. Susan is a temp, working as an independent contractor for ABC Company. She knows that company policy mandates that employees not use ABC Company computers for personal business in the course of the workday. But the auction ends for a pair of darling shoes on eBay at 2 p.m., and she takes a few minutes out of her workday to bid on that coveted pair using her work computer. Elated in victory, she promptly pays for them using PayPal and prints out the receipt on an ABC Company printer. Is she guilty of a federal felony, subject to up to twenty years' imprisonment?

A cognizable scheme to defraud under the mail and wire fraud statutes requires (at least) proof of: (1) fraud—i.e., the defendant, acting with an intent to defraud, either made a material misstatement or failed to disclose material information in the face of a legal duty; and (2) a cognizable object of that fraud—i.e., either the deprivation of the victim's money or property (so-called "money-or-property" cases) or some right the victim claimed to the defendant's honest services (the "honest-services" cases). In honest-services cases, courts tend to (improperly) conflate these elements. That is, if they find an intentional breach of some duty the defendant owes to the public or his employer, and a failure to disclose that breach, courts will deem both the fraud and the deprivation of honest-services elements satisfied. (A head's up for purposes of future discussion: I believe that failing to separately consider these two questions has resulted in errors such as a failure to recognize that what is needed to prove fraud—including the intent to defraud—is not dependent on whatever object is alleged.) With this introduction, let us now turn to sketching out the "mess" surrounding the definition of what conduct, *mens rea*, and attendant circumstances are necessary or sufficient to anchor an honest-services conviction.

A. Conduct

Most private honest-services cases turn on whether there has been a breach of a duty of honest services and whether the defendant fraudulently failed to disclose that breach. This formulation sounds simple; in reality, it is anything but, as numerous circuit splits attest.

1. Duty of Honest Services?

Does Susan, as a temp working as an independent contractor, have a duty to render honest services to ABC Company? Federal courts are split on whether a duty of honest services can arise only out of a fiduciary relationship, but the majority seem to reject such a bright-line rule.[32] Most federal courts cite to principles of agency law—finding, for example, that *any* employment relationship creates a duty of loyalty and thus honest services—but fail to identify any basis for believing that Congress intended to criminalize the *Restatement of Agency*. If as the government contends and most circuits hold, every worker in the United States bears a duty of honest services to her employer, the scope of potential liability is breathtaking. Moreover, if agency principles are determinative in sketching out these criminally enforceable duties (as the government seems to believe), it is worth noting that principal-agent duties run both ways. Presumably the government can also criminally prosecute employers who fail to meet *their* duties to conform to their contracts with agents, to indemnify agents in specific circumstances, to disclose certain matters, and to deal with their agents "fairly and in good faith."

2. Breach?

The potential breadth of a duty of honest services raises the critical question of whether *any* breach of employer-defined rules qualifies, or if only some subset of serious breaches should suffice. That is, should courts simply accept that Susan's knowing violation of the computer-use rules is actionable, or should they attempt to restrict the scope of § 1346 to some category of breaches that are inarguably corrupt or threaten actual harm? If the former, obviously we must ask whether Congress could really have meant to delegate to private employers the power to promulgate criminally enforceable employment rules in their employee manuals. This alternative obviously creates grave problems of fair notice and, given that most workers are likely to stumble over a rule or two in the course of their employment, an enormous potential for arbitrary and discriminatory enforcement. But the latter alternative raises a serious constitutional problem: How can courts appropriately carve a heartland of honest-services cases—out of all possible violations of workplace rules—for criminal sanction without any legislative guidance?

The government argues that courts have, before *McNally* and after § 1346, identified a core of conduct that gives content to the otherwise-meaningless words "honest services." The government, and many courts of appeals, consistently say that "private-sector honest services cases fall into two general groups, cases involving bribes or kickbacks, and cases involving self-dealing"[33]—whatever "self-dealing" means. Any assertion that private honest-services cases

---

[32] [Author's footnote 30:] *See, e.g.*, United States v. Rybicki, 354 F.3d 124, 141-42 & n.17 (2d Cir.2003) (en banc) (holding that the duty that must be breached is one owed by an employee to an employer, or by "a person in a relationship that gives rise to a duty of loyalty comparable to that owed by employees to employers"); *Cf.* United States v. Frost, 125 F.3d 346, 366 (6th Cir.1997); United States v. Sun-Diamond Growers of Cal., 138 F.3d 961, 974 (D.C.Cir.1998).

[33] [Author's footnote 31:] *Rybicki*, 354 F.3d at 139. As the Second Circuit recently explained while sitting en banc:

> In the bribery or kickback cases, a defendant who has or seeks some sort of business relationship or transaction with the victim secretly pays the victim's employee (or causes such a payment to be made) in exchange for favored treatment .... In the self-dealing cases, the defendant typically causes his or her employer to do business with a corporation or other

before § 1346 only concerned bribes/kickbacks and self-dealing is untrue, and I have seen no empirical basis to substantiate the government's constant refrain that these are indeed the core of honest-services cases. Certainly prosecutors have pursued, and some courts have accepted, a variety of theories outside this "heartland." For example, prosecutors have "brought to justice," among others, a coach who improperly helped players with their coursework to ensure their eligibility to play,[34] a professor who helped his students plagiarize work to secure degrees to which they might not otherwise be entitled,[35] a lawyer who operated under an undisclosed conflict of interest,[36] and a city contractor who did not fulfill his contractual obligation to pay his workers on a city project at a certain pay scale.[37] But even if the government is correct that the caselaw reflects a core of private honest-services cases, why should the choices prosecutors have made in selecting cases in the past be determinative? And why wouldn't the Court's decision to restrict § 1346 to just these cases involve a forbidden rewriting of the statute? ...

3. Duty to Disclose?

The next question relates to whether employees have a duty to disclose. Silence is not fraud; generally a duty to disclose "arises [only] when one party has information 'that the other [party] is entitled to know because of a fiduciary or other similar relation of trust and confidence between them.'"[38] It is not clear what law or relationships are sufficient to create a duty to disclose because this is a question that rarely receives separate treatment. For reasons that are never explained, most courts appear to believe that if there is a duty of loyalty, there is an accompanying duty of disclosure as well. But this may not always be so; the *Restatement of Agency* does not contain a blanket disclosure requirement. Indeed, in *Weyhrauch*, a state statute prohibited legislator Weyhrauch's alleged conduct (negotiating for a job with a company that had business pending before the legislature). But the District Court held that the Alaska law did not attach a *disclosure requirement* to the prohibition. Thus, according to the District Court, Weyhrauch had a honest-services duty to the public that was arguably breached when he solicited employment allegedly in violation of state law, but because there was no independent disclosure requirement, there was no violation of § 1346.

B. Mental State

There is agreement among the circuits that a specific intent to defraud must be proved in mail and wire fraud cases, and that an intent to deceive through misrepresentation (or an actionable failure to disclose) is part of that intent. But there is a split in the circuits on whether an intent to defraud also requires proof of an intent to harm or injure in money-or-property cases.[39] The First Circuit sitting en banc held that the scheme-to-defraud element of the bank-

---

enterprise in which the defendant has a secret interest, undisclosed to the employer. *Id.* at 139-40.

[34] [Author's footnote 34:] United States v. Gray, 96 F.3d 769, 772 (5th Cir.1996).

[35] [Author's footnote 35:] United States v. Frost, 125 F.3d 346, 353 (6th Cir.1997) (affirming conviction).

[36] [Author's footnote 36:] United States v. Bronston, 658 F.2d 920, 922 (2d Cir.1981) (affirming conviction).

[37] [Author's footnote 37:] United States v. Handakas, 286 F.3d 92, 96 (2d Cir.2002) (overturning honest-services conviction on vagueness grounds).

[38] [Author's footnote 38:] Chiarella v. United States, 445 U.S. 222, 228 (1980), quoting Restatement (Second) of Torts §551(2)(a) (1976).

[39] [Author's footnote 43:] *Compare* United States v. Walker, 191 F.3d 326, 335 (2d Cir.1999) ("While the scheme to defraud need not have been successful, the defendant must have contemplated some actual harm or injury to the victims."), *with* United States v. Kenrick, 221 F.3d 19, 27-29 (1st Cir.2000) (holding

fraud statute does not require proof of an intent to injure or harm where the object of the fraud is the bank's money or property. That court's reasoning would apply equally to the mail and wire fraud context.[40]

The Second Circuit leads the contingent that require such proof in cases where the object of the fraud is money or property.[41] For example, in *United States v. Gabriel*, the Second Circuit held that the district court had erred (harmlessly) in instructing the jury that "a defendant acts with a[n] ... intent to defraud if he participates in the fraudulent scheme with *some realization* of its fraudulent or deceptive character and with *recognition of its capacity* to cause harm to the victims of such deception."[42] As the Second Circuit subsequently explained: "It is not sufficient that defendant realizes that the scheme is fraudulent and that it has the capacity to cause harm to its victims. Instead, the proof must demonstrate that the defendant had a conscious knowing intent to defraud ... [and] that the defendant contemplated or intended some harm to the property rights of the victim."

It is at this point that the distinction between proof of fraud and proof of the object of the fraud, discussed above, is important. Given that the specific intent to defraud is required for proof of fraud—and is common to *all* statutory schemes to defraud—its definition should be same whether the case is charged as an honest-services or a money-or-property case. Thus, circuits that require proof of an intent to injure should do so regardless of what the object of the fraud is alleged to be. This does not appear to be true (save, perhaps, in the Eighth Circuit).[43] Even in the Second Circuit, the government does not need to prove an intent to harm or injure in honest-services cases.[44]

In honest-services cases, then, the circuit courts generally express the required intent as an intent to deceive wedded to an "intent to deprive another of the intangible right of honest services."[45] Another formulation of the latter intent, perhaps a variation on a theme, is that "[t]he prosecution must prove that the employee intended to breach a fiduciary duty."[46] To return to our hypothetical, all that must be shown is that Susan's undisclosed use of a computer to buy shoes was done with full knowledge that this contravened the workplace rules (intent to breach), and that her failure to tell her employer was intentional (intent to deceive).

By definition, honest-services fraud requires no actual harm to the employer be shown (if there were economic harm, it would have been charged as a money-or-property case). Generally, in criminal law, where the harm or threatened harm flowing from the prohibited

---

that in the context of a bank fraud charge, a "scheme to defraud" does not require an intent to injure or harm), *and* United States v. Sun-Diamond Growers of Cal., 138 F.3d 961, 973-74 (D.C. Cir.1998) (same).

[40] [Author's footnote 44:] *Kenrick*, 221 F.3d at 27-29; *see also* United States v. Welch, 327 F.3d 1081, 1104-06 (10th Cir.2003); United States v. Everett, 270 F.3d 986, 991 (6th Cir. 2001).

[41] [Author's footnote 45:] *See, e.g., Walker*, 191 F.3d at 334-36; United States v. Chandler, 98 F.3d 711, 714-15 (2d Cir.1996); United States v. D'Amato, 39 F.3d 1249, 1257 (2d Cir.1994) (holding proof of fraudulent intent, including an intent to harm, is required); United States v. Regent Office Supply Co., 421 F.2d 1174, 1180 (2d Cir.1970); *see also* United States v. Ervasti, 201 F.3d 1029, 1035 (8th Cir.2000) (noting that "intent to harm is the essence of a scheme to defraud"); *Frost*, 125 F.3d at 368; United States v. Cochran, 109 F.3d 660, 667-669 (10th Cir.1997); United States v. Jain, 93 F.3d 436, 441 (8th Cir.1996); United States v. Stouffer, 986 F.2d 916, 922 (5th Cir.1993).

[42] [Author's footnote 46:] 125 F.3d 89, 96-97 (2d Cir.1997)(emphasis added); *see also* United States v. Starr, 816 F.2d 94, 98 (2d Cir.1987); *Regent Office Supply*, 421 F.2d at 1182.

[43] [Author's footnote 48:] *See* United States v. Pennington, 168 F.3d 1060, 1065 (8th Cir.1999) (describing the *mens rea* elements as "caus[ing] or intend[ing] to cause actual harm or injury, and in most business contexts, that means financial or economic harm").

[44] [Author's footnote 49:] *Rybicki*, 354 F.3d at 145.

[45] [Author's footnote 50:] *Id.*

[46] [Author's footnote 51:] *Frost*, 125 F.3d at 368.

conduct is negligible, liability attaches only upon a showing of serious mental culpability. Judged in this light, the absence of a corrupt or harmful intent requirement is troubling. Certainly it is inappropriate that a significantly lower intent standard is applied in honest-services cases than in money-or-property cases, where a threat of actual, quantifiable economic harm must also be proved.

The government repeatedly emphasized in its briefs and at oral argument that the requirement of an intent to deceive provides an ample guarantee that only truly guilty actors will be prosecuted, thus providing fair notice and restraining the discretion of federal prosecutors. This is exceedingly unlikely. First, in this context, proving an intent to deceive is not much of a burden, because such intent is usually inferred from the fact that the breach of the rule was known and not disclosed. More important, the culpability of the deception depends on the seriousness of the undisclosed conduct. Suppose that the undisclosed violation is de minimis—something, most employers would consider not worth hearing about let alone sanctioning, like Susan's two-minute computer abuse. In such cases, the deception hardly seems to merit a stint in the pen. (It may be worth adding that there is a split in the circuits on whether the views of the employer-victim are relevant, with some circuits holding that cases can be brought even if the employer expressed its belief that the services the employee rendered were of value to it and chose to overlook the infraction.[47])

Perhaps reacting to the reality that, under the government's formulation, convictions can be secured where there is no concrete or threatened tangible harm and no intent to harm, the Seventh Circuit has added an additional element requiring that the government prove that the defendant acted with the intent to secure a private or personal benefit as a result of the deprivation of honest services.[48] Presumably, this requirement is a rough proxy for some sort of corrupt intent to profit at the employer's expense.

Numerous problems attend this limitation. It too is not well-established as a core element of honest-services fraud; indeed, it appears to be operative only in the Seventh Circuit. It is also both underinclusive and overinclusive and thus ineffective in identifying those cases worthy of criminal sanction. What we may believe to be a culpable breach may not involve an intent to gain. Rather, as the pattern jury instructions recognize, it may involve an intent to harm the employer with no corresponding gain to the defendant. The intent to secure private gain limitation may also be overinclusive in that a breach of duties may ultimately result in a win-win situation, in which both the defendant and his employer gain. This may be the reason why the Second Circuit has concluded that it is error for a district court to instruct the jury that "it could find an intent to defraud based solely on the appellants' desire to gain a benefit for themselves."[49]

Finally, the Seventh Circuit's test is imprecise in its application and of limited value in limiting § 1346 to worthy cases. There is uncertainty over what private or personal gain means: Does it include gain to one's family members or other third parties? Must it be economic gain or can it relate to intangibles like enhanced reputation? The Seventh Circuit has clarified that by "'private gain' we simply mean illegitimate gain, which usually will go to the defendant, but need not."[50] Recognizing that private gain may include benefits to persons other than the defendant certainly guts this limitation, but the government would dilute it further. Its apparent theory in *Skilling*, which it concedes is novel and which has been rejected by the Seventh Circuit, is that the required private gain can relate to concerns about salary or job security. Where an employee lies about breaking an employment rule in order to safeguard his job or ensure that his salary is not docked, this would suffice. As Skilling's counsel argued

---

[47] [Author's footnote 53:] *See, e.g.*, United States v. Bereano, 161 F.3d 3, 4 (4th Cir.1998) (unpublished opinion); United States v. Bryza, 522 F.2d 414, 422 (7th Cir.1975). *But see D'Amato*, 39 F.3d at 1257.

[48] [Author's footnote 54:] *See* United States v. Bloom, 149 F.3d 649, 656-57 (7th Cir.1998). *But see Welch*, 327 F.3d at 1106-07 (rejecting this additional element).

[49] [Author's footnote 56:] United States v. Frank, 156 F.3d 332, 337 (2d Cir.1998).

[50] [Author's footnote 57:] United States v. Sorich, 523 F.3d 702, 709 (7th Cir.2008).

before the Court, such a reading of the private-gain requirement would make it applicable to virtually every employee in the country, thereby again threatening "to convert almost any lie in the workplace into an honest-services prosecution."

C. Attendant Circumstances

Many of the circuits struggling to contain the reach of honest-services cases have chosen between two competing tests: reasonably foreseeable harm and materiality. (One circuit—the Second—adopted the materiality test but also may apply the reasonably foreseeable harm test to some private honest-services cases (involving self-dealing) but not others (involving bribery or kickbacks).[51]) Neither test is grounded in statutory language or common law elements, nor are they effective in cabining the reach of the statute.

The reasonably foreseeable harm test—pressed on the Court by petitioner Black—has a number of iterations, but the gist is that the government must show that it was "reasonably foreseeable that the scheme could cause some economic or pecuniary harm to the victims" (with some courts requiring that that harm be more than de minimus).[52] This limitation has no connection to the language of the statute or the traditional elements of fraud. The reasonably foreseeable harm test is *not* a gloss on or interpretation of the fraudulent intent element: it requires "neither ... an actual economic loss *nor an intent to economically harm the employer.*"[53] Instead, the test was fabricated in an attempt to cabin § 1346's scope to cases in which the forbidden conduct has a proximate relationship to at least some potential demonstrable injury (and to preclude prosecution of cases such as the computer-misuse hypothetical posed above).

Even if this were a legitimate piece of judicial legislation, it is unlikely to be successful in its aim, as reference to the government's brief in *Black* shows. One can almost always come up with some hypothetical harm unless the employment rule in question is completely arbitrary—along the lines of forbidding left-handed persons from wearing contact lenses at work. In cases of reasonable rules whose breach should not be subject to criminal sanction, a jury could reasonably hypothesize some imagined economic peril, since actual subjective intent is not required, just some proximate relationship to potential harm. For example, in our computer-misuse hypothetical, projected harm could flow from the fact that widespread flouting of a rule prohibiting personal use of computers could result in a marked decline in worker productivity and increased exposure to costly computer viruses.

The courts that adopt materiality as a limiting principle in private honest-services cases assert that this test has the virtue of being a preexisting element of any fraud case.[54] Actually, the courts' use of materiality constitutes a questionable extension of that element. The materiality element of mail and wire fraud recognized by the Court in *Neder v United States* requires the jury to decide whether the misrepresentation or actionable failure to disclose "has the natural tendency to influence or is capable of influencing the employer to change his behavior." To be clear, under *Neder*, it is the *fraudulent misrepresentation or actionable omission* that must be material. But, as Justice Scalia pointed out in oral argument, what these courts seem to be asking is a different question: Is the undisclosed *breach of employment duties* material in the sense that a reasonable employer would believe that this particular violation of workplace rules is important?

Regardless of whether this test is an appropriate application of the materiality element, it is imprecise in its application and likely to be ineffectual in isolating those cases where

---

[51] [Author's footnote 60:] *Rybicki*, 354 F.3d 124.

[52] [Author's footnote 61:] *Id.* at 145; *see Frost*, 125 F.3d at 368; *Sun-Diamond*, 138 F.3d at 973-74.

[53] [Author's footnote 62:] United States v. Vinyard, 266 F.3d 320, 329-30 (4th Cir.2001) (emphasis added).

[54] [Author's footnote 63:] Neder v. United States, 527 U.S. 1, 25 (1999). The materiality approach has apparently been endorsed by the Second, Fourth, Fifth, Eighth, and Tenth Circuits. *See Rybicki*, 354 F.3d at 145 (collecting cases).

culpability is appropriate. First, as the Justices noted during oral argument, it is not clear what decision is the focus of the test: Must the misrepresentation or omission be material to the continued employment of the erring defendant (i.e., must it be a firing offense)? Or is it, as some courts have indicated, simply a question of whether a hypothetical employer would change its employee policies or business practices to avoid similar conduct in future? As one circuit noted in rejecting this limitation, "if a 'change in business conduct' occurs under the materiality standard when a business alters its behavior merely to avoid the *appearance* of impropriety ..., the intangible right to honest-services doctrine may lack substantive limits in the private sector."[55] Moreover, if the company took the trouble of formulating the rule and making employees aware of it, presumably juries would conclude that a reasonable employer would wish the rule enforced. Assuming again that the breach at issue does not relate to some oddly arbitrary rule, one can conclude that all breaches and nondisclosures will meet the materiality test, and indeed, I am aware of no decision in which a lack of materiality has been found.

To return to our hypothetical, most circuits would hold that the statute—read on its face—subjects Susan to criminal liability for abusing her computer access. Absent disclosure or a judicially created limitation, the result is that she, as an agent of ABC Company, would have a duty to the employer to follow the rules, as well as a duty to disclose her violations of applicable regulations. Hopefully, this hypothetical amply demonstrates the unconstitutional nature of this statute. Can anyone (not working for the government) argue with a straight face that the twenty-eight words of § 1346 give the ordinary citizen fair notice that de minimis breaches of employer-created rules such as Susan's could warrant jail time? And, contrary to the government's assertion, the caselaw does not define a core of conduct by which the average citizen can gauge her criminal exposure before the fact. In light of the many disagreements among the circuits on applicable limiting glosses, is it likely that even the most diligent layman would be able to forecast whether the caselaw would rule her workplace infraction in or out? I think not.

Finally, and most importantly, as Justice Breyer observed during oral argument, the breadth of this statute means that a federal prosecutor could bring an honest-services case against millions of working Americans: "I think there are ... 150 million workers in the United States. I think possibly 140 [million] of them would flunk" the honest-services test. With such a flexible weapon, prosecutors can choose a target and be almost certain that, with enough digging, they can find a criminal violation. If virtually anyone is vulnerable to prosecution, the potential for arbitrary and discriminatory enforcement is a given.

* * *

SKILLING v. UNITED STATES
561 U.S. 358 (2010)

JUSTICE GINSBURG delivered the opinion of the Court.

We ... consider whether Skilling's conspiracy conviction was premised on an improper theory of honest-services wire fraud. The honest-services statute, § 1346, Skilling maintains, is unconstitutionally vague. Alternatively, he contends that his conduct does not fall within the statute's compass. ...

... To satisfy due process, "a penal statute [must] define the criminal offense [1] with sufficient definiteness that ordinary people can understand what conduct is prohibited and [2] in a manner that does not encourage arbitrary and discriminatory enforcement." *Kolender v. Lawson*, 461 U.S. 352, 357 (1983). The void-for-vagueness doctrine embraces these requirements.

---

[55] [Author's footnote 67:] *Frost*, 125 F.3d at 365.

According to Skilling, § 1346 meets neither of the two due process essentials. First, the phrase "the intangible right of honest services," he contends, does not adequately define what behavior it bars. Second, he alleges, § 1346's "standardless sweep allows policemen, prosecutors, and juries to pursue their personal predilections," thereby "facilitat[ing] opportunistic and arbitrary prosecutions."

In urging invalidation of § 1346, Skilling swims against our case law's current, which requires us, if we can, to construe, not condemn, Congress' enactments. See, *e.g., Civil Service Comm'n v. Letter Carriers,* 413 U.S. 548, 571 796 (1973). See also *United States v. National Dairy Products Corp.,* 372 U.S. 29, 32 (1963) (stressing, in response to a vagueness challenge, "[t]he strong presumptive validity that attaches to an Act of Congress"). Alert to § 1346's potential breadth, the Courts of Appeals have divided on how best to interpret the statute. Uniformly, however, they have declined to throw out the statute as irremediably vague.[56]

We agree that § 1346 should be construed rather than invalidated. First, we look to the doctrine developed in pre-*McNally* cases in an endeavor to ascertain the meaning of the phrase "the intangible right of honest services." Second, to preserve what Congress certainly intended the statute to cover, we pare that body of precedent down to its core: In the main, the pre-*McNally* cases involved fraudulent schemes to deprive another of honest services through bribes or kickbacks supplied by a third party who had not been deceived. Confined to these paramount applications, § 1346 presents no vagueness problem. . . .

There is no doubt that Congress intended § 1346 to refer to and incorporate the honest-services doctrine recognized in Court of Appeals' decisions before *McNally* derailed the intangible-rights theory of fraud. Congress enacted § 1346 on the heels of *McNally* and drafted the statute using that decision's terminology. As the Second Circuit observed in its leading analysis of § 1346:

> "The definite article 'the' suggests that 'intangible right of honest services' had a specific meaning to Congress when it enacted the statute—Congress was recriminalizing mail- and wire-fraud schemes to deprive others of *that* 'intangible right of honest services,' which had been protected before *McNally,* not *all* intangible rights of honest services whatever they might be thought to be." *United States v. Rybicki,* 354 F.3d 124, 137-138 (2003) (en banc). . . .

Satisfied that Congress, by enacting § 1346, "meant to reinstate the body of pre-*McNally* honest-services law," *post* (opinion of SCALIA, J.), we have surveyed that case law. In parsing the Courts of Appeals decisions, we acknowledge that Skilling's vagueness challenge has force, for honest-services decisions preceding *McNally* were not models of clarity or consistency. While the honest-services cases preceding *McNally* dominantly and consistently applied the fraud statute to bribery and kickback schemes—schemes that were the basis of most honest-services prosecutions—there was considerable disarray over the statute's application to conduct outside that core category. In light of this disarray, Skilling urges us, as he urged the Fifth Circuit, to invalidate the statute *in toto.*

It has long been our practice, however, before striking a federal statute as impermissibly vague, to consider whether the prescription is amenable to a limiting construction. See, *e.g., Hooper v. California,* 155 U.S. 648, 657 (1895) ("The elementary rule is that *every reasonable construction* must be resorted to, in order to save a statute from unconstitutionality." (emphasis

---

[56] [Court's footnote 36:] Courts have disagreed about whether § 1346 prosecutions must be based on a violation of state law, compare, *e.g., United States v. Brumley,* 116 F.3d 728, 734-735 (C.A.5 1997) (en banc), with, *e.g., United States v. Weyhrauch,* 548 F.3d 1237, 1245-1246 (C.A.9 2008); whether a defendant must contemplate that the victim suffer economic harm, compare, *e.g., United States v. Sun-Diamond Growers of Cal.,* 138 F.3d 961, 973 (C.A.D.C.1998), with, *e.g., United States v. Black,* 530 F.3d 596, 600-602 (C.A.7 2008); and whether the defendant must act in pursuit of private gain, compare, *e.g., United States v. Bloom,* 149 F.3d 649, 655 (C.A.7 1998), with, *e.g., United States v. Panarella,* 277 F.3d 678, 692 (C.A.3 2002).

added)).[57] We have accordingly instructed "the federal courts ... to avoid constitutional difficulties by [adopting a limiting interpretation] if such a construction is fairly possible."

Arguing against any limiting construction, Skilling contends that it is impossible to identify a salvageable honest-services core; "the pre-*McNally* caselaw," he asserts, "is a hodgepodge of oft-conflicting holdings" that are "hopelessly unclear." We have rejected an argument of the same tenor before. In *Civil Service Comm'n v. Letter Carriers,* federal employees challenged a provision of the Hatch Act that incorporated earlier decisions of the United States Civil Service Commission enforcing a similar law. "[T]he several thousand adjudications of the Civil Service Commission," the employees maintained, were "an impenetrable jungle"— "undiscoverable, inconsistent, [and] incapable of yielding any meaningful rules to govern present or future conduct." [413 U.S. 548, 571 (1973).] Mindful that "our task [wa]s not to destroy the Act if we c[ould], but to construe it," we held that "the rules that had evolved over the years from repeated adjudications were subject to sufficiently clear and summary statement."

A similar observation may be made here. Although some applications of the pre-*McNally* honest-services doctrine occasioned disagreement among the Courts of Appeals, these cases do not cloud the doctrine's solid core: The "vast majority" of the honest-services cases involved offenders who, in violation of a fiduciary duty, participated in bribery or kickback schemes. *United States v. Runnels,* 833 F.2d 1183, 1187 (C.A.6 1987); see Brief for United States 42, and n. 4 (citing dozens of examples).[58] Indeed, the *McNally* case itself, which spurred Congress to enact § 1346, presented a paradigmatic kickback fact pattern. Congress' reversal of *McNally* and reinstatement of the honest-services doctrine, we conclude, can and should be salvaged by confining its scope to the core pre-*McNally* applications.

As already noted, the honest-services doctrine had its genesis in prosecutions involving bribery allegations. Both before *McNally* and after § 1346's enactment, Courts of Appeals described schemes involving bribes or kickbacks as "core ... honest services fraud precedents," *United States v. Czubinski,* 106 F.3d 1069, 1077 (C.A.1 1997); "paradigm case[s]," *United States v. deVegter,* 198 F.3d 1324, 1327-1328 (C.A.11 1999); "[t]he most obvious form of honest services fraud," *United States v. Carbo,* 572 F.3d 112, 115 (C.A.3 2009); "core misconduct covered by the statute," *United States v. Urciuoli,* 513 F.3d 290, 294 (C.A.1 2008); "most [of the] honest services cases," *United States v. Sorich,* 523 F.3d 702, 707 (C.A.7 2008); "typical," *United States v. Brown,* 540 F.2d 364, 374 (C.A.8 1976); "clear-cut," *United States v. Mandel,* 591 F.2d 1347, 1363 (C.A.4 1979); and "uniformly ... cover[ed]," *United States v. Paradies,* 98 F.3d 1266, 1283, n. 30 (C.A.11 1996).

In view of this history, there is no doubt that Congress intended § 1346 to reach *at least* bribes and kickbacks. Reading the statute to proscribe a wider range of offensive conduct, we acknowledge, would raise the due process concerns underlying the vagueness doctrine.[59] To preserve the statute without transgressing constitutional limitations, we now hold that § 1346 criminalizes *only* the bribe-and-kickback core of the pre-*McNally* case law.[60] ...

---

[57] [Court's footnote 40:] "This cardinal principle has its roots in Chief Justice Marshall's opinion for the Court in *Murray v. The Charming Betsy,* 2 Cranch 64, 118 (1804), and has for so long been applied by this Court that it is beyond debate."

[58] [Court's footnote 41:] Justice SCALIA emphasizes divisions in the Courts of Appeals regarding the source and scope of fiduciary duties. But these debates were rare in bribe and kickback cases. The existence of a fiduciary relationship, under any definition of that term, was usually beyond dispute; examples include public official-public, see, *e.g., United States v. Mandel,* 591 F.2d 1347 (C.A.4 1979); employee-employer, see, *e.g., United States v. Bohonus,* 628 F.2d 1167 (C.A.9 1980); and union official-union members, see, *e.g., United States v. Price,* 788 F.2d 234 (C.A.4 1986). See generally *Chiarella v. United States,* 445 U.S. 222, 233 (1980) (noting the "established doctrine that [a fiduciary] duty arises from a specific relationship between two parties").

[59] [Court's footnote 42:] Apprised that a broader reading of § 1346 could render the statute impermissibly vague, Congress, we believe, would have drawn the honest-services line, as we do now, at bribery and kickback schemes.

[60] [Court's footnote 43:] Justice SCALIA charges that our construction of § 1346 is "not interpretation but

The Government urges us to go further by locating within § 1346's compass another category of proscribed conduct: "undisclosed self-dealing by a public official or private employee—*i.e.,* the taking of official action by the employee that furthers his own undisclosed financial interests while purporting to act in the interests of those to whom he owes a fiduciary duty." "[T]he theory of liability in *McNally* itself was nondisclosure of a conflicting financial interest," the Government observes, and "Congress clearly intended to revive th[at] nondisclosure theory." Moreover, "[a]lthough not as numerous as the bribery and kickback cases," the Government asserts, "the pre-*McNally* cases involving undisclosed self-dealing were abundant."

Neither of these contentions withstands close inspection. *McNally,* as we have already observed, involved a classic kickback scheme: A public official, in exchange for routing Kentucky's insurance business through a middleman company, arranged for that company to share its commissions with entities in which the official held an interest. This was no mere failure to disclose a conflict of interest; rather, the official conspired with a third party so that both would profit from wealth generated by public contracts. Reading § 1346 to proscribe bribes and kickbacks—and nothing more—satisfies Congress' undoubted aim to reverse *McNally* on its facts.

Nor are we persuaded that the pre-*McNally* conflict-of-interest cases constitute core applications of the honest-services doctrine. Although the Courts of Appeals upheld honest-services convictions for "some schemes of non-disclosure and concealment of material information," they reached no consensus on which schemes qualified. In light of the relative infrequency of conflict-of-interest prosecutions in comparison to bribery and kickback charges, and the intercircuit inconsistencies they produced, we conclude that a reasonable limiting construction of § 1346 must exclude this amorphous category of cases.

Further dispelling doubt on this point is the familiar principle that "ambiguity concerning the ambit of criminal statutes should be resolved in favor of lenity." "This interpretive guide is especially appropriate in construing [§ 1346] because ... mail [and wire] fraud [are] predicate offense[s] under [the Racketeer Influenced and Corrupt Organizations Act], 18 U.S.C. § 1961(1) (1994 ed., Supp. IV), and the money laundering statute, § 1956(c)(7)(A)." Holding that honest-services fraud does not encompass conduct more wide-ranging than the paradigmatic cases of bribes and kickbacks, we resist the Government's less constrained construction absent Congress' clear instruction otherwise.

In sum, our construction of § 1346 "establish[es] a uniform national standard, define[s] honest services with clarity, reach[es] only seriously culpable conduct, and accomplish[es] Congress's goal of 'overruling' *McNally.*" "If Congress desires to go further," we reiterate, "it must speak more clearly than it has."[61] ...

---

invention." Stating that he "know[s] of no precedent for ... 'paring down'" the pre-*McNally* case law to its core, he contends that the Court today "wield[s] a power we long ago abjured: the power to define new federal crimes." As noted, cases "paring down" federal statutes to avoid constitutional shoals are legion. These cases recognize that the Court does not *legislate,* but instead *respects the legislature,* by preserving a statute through a limiting interpretation. Given that the Courts of Appeals uniformly recognized bribery and kickback schemes as honest-services fraud before *McNally,* 483 U.S. 350, and that these schemes composed the lion's share of honest-services cases, limiting § 1346 to these heartland applications is surely "fairly possible." So construed, the statute is not unconstitutionally vague. Only by taking a wrecking ball to a statute that can be salvaged through a reasonable narrowing interpretation would we act out of step with precedent.

61 [Court's footnote 44:] If Congress were to take up the enterprise of criminalizing "undisclosed self-dealing by a public official or private employee" it would have to employ standards of sufficient definiteness and specificity to overcome due process concerns. The Government proposes a standard that prohibits the "taking of official action by the employee that furthers his own undisclosed financial interests while purporting to act in the interests of those to whom he owes a fiduciary duty," so long as the employee acts with a specific intent to deceive and the undisclosed conduct could influence the victim to change its behavior. That formulation, however, leaves many questions unanswered. How direct or significant does the conflicting financial interest have to be? To what extent does the official action have to further that interest in order to amount to fraud? To whom should the disclosure be made and what

Interpreted to encompass only bribery and kickback schemes, § 1346 is not unconstitutionally vague. Recall that the void-for-vagueness doctrine addresses concerns about (1) fair notice and (2) arbitrary and discriminatory prosecutions. A prohibition on fraudulently depriving another of one's honest services by accepting bribes or kickbacks does not present a problem on either score.

As to fair notice, "whatever the school of thought concerning the scope and meaning of § 1346, it has always been "as plain as a pikestaff that" bribes and kickbacks constitute honest-services fraud," and the statute's *mens rea* requirement further blunts any notice concern.

As to arbitrary prosecutions, we perceive no significant risk that the honest-services statute, as we interpret it today, will be stretched out of shape. Its prohibition on bribes and kickbacks draws content not only from the pre-*McNally* case law, but also from federal statutes proscribing—and defining—similar crimes. See, *e.g.*, 18 U.S.C. §§ 201(b), 666(a)(2); 41 U.S.C. § 52(2) ("The term 'kickback' means any money, fee, commission, credit, gift, gratuity, thing of value, or compensation of any kind which is provided, directly or indirectly, to [enumerated persons] for the purpose of improperly obtaining or rewarding favorable treatment in connection with [enumerated circumstances].").[62] A criminal defendant who participated in a bribery or kickback scheme, in short, cannot tenably complain about prosecution under § 1346 on vagueness grounds. ...

It remains to determine whether Skilling's conduct violated § 1346. Skilling's honest-services prosecution, the Government concedes, was not "prototypical." The Government charged Skilling with conspiring to defraud Enron's shareholders by misrepresenting the company's fiscal health, thereby artificially inflating its stock price. It was the Government's theory at trial that Skilling "profited from the fraudulent scheme ... through the receipt of salary and bonuses, ... and through the sale of approximately $200 million in Enron stock, which netted him $89 million."

The Government did not, at any time, allege that Skilling solicited or accepted side payments from a third party in exchange for making these misrepresentations. It is therefore clear that, as we read § 1346, Skilling did not commit honest-services fraud. ...

Justice SCALIA, with whom Justice THOMAS joins, and with whom Justice KENNEDY ..., concurring in part and concurring in the judgment.

I agree ... that the decision upholding Skilling's conviction for so-called "honest-services fraud" must be reversed, but for a different reason. In my view, the specification in 18 U.S.C. § 1346 that "scheme or artifice to defraud" in the mail-fraud and wire-fraud statutes, §§ 1341 and 1343, includes "a scheme or artifice to deprive another of the intangible right of honest services," is vague, and therefore violates the Due Process Clause of the Fifth Amendment. The Court strikes a pose of judicial humility in proclaiming that our task is "not to destroy the Act ... but to construe it." But in transforming the prohibition of "honest-services fraud" into a prohibition of "bribery and kick-backs" it is wielding a power we long ago abjured: the power to define new federal crimes. See *United States v. Hudson*, 7 Cranch 32, 34 (1812). ...

The Court maintains that "the intangible right of honest services" means the right not to have one's fiduciaries accept "bribes or kickbacks." Its first step in reaching that conclusion is the assertion that the phrase refers to "the doctrine developed" in cases decided by lower federal courts prior to our decision in *McNally v. United States*, 483 U.S. 350 (1987). I do not contest that. I agree that Congress used the novel phrase to adopt the lower-court case law that had been disapproved by *McNally*—what the Court calls "the pre-*McNally* honest-services

---

information should it convey? These questions and others call for particular care in attempting to formulate an adequate criminal prohibition in this context.

[62] [Court's footnote 45:] Overlap with other federal statutes does not render § 1346 superfluous. The principal federal bribery statute, § 201, for example, generally applies only to federal public officials, so § 1346's application to state and local corruption and to private-sector fraud reaches misconduct that might otherwise go unpunished.

doctrine." The problem is that that doctrine provides no "ascertainable standard of guilt," and certainly is not limited to "bribes or kickbacks."

Investigation into the meaning of "the pre-*McNally* honest-services doctrine" might logically begin with *McNally* itself, which rejected it. That case repudiated the many Court of Appeals holdings that had expanded the meaning of "fraud" in the mail-fraud and wire-fraud statutes beyond deceptive schemes to obtain property. If the repudiated cases stood for a prohibition of "bribery and kickbacks," one would have expected those words to appear in the opinion's description of the cases. In fact, they do not. *Not at all.* Nor did *McNally* even provide a consistent definition of the pre-existing theory of fraud it rejected. It referred variously to a right of citizens "to have the [State]'s affairs conducted honestly," to "honest and impartial government," to "good government," and "to have public officials perform their duties honestly." It described prior case law as holding that "a public official owes a fiduciary duty to the public, and misuse of his office for private gain is a fraud."

But the pre-*McNally* Court of Appeals opinions were not limited to fraud by public officials. Some courts had held that those fiduciaries subject to the "honest services" obligation included private individuals who merely participated in public decisions, and even private employees who had no role in public decisions. Moreover, "to say that a man is a fiduciary only begins [the] analysis; it gives direction to further inquiry .... What obligations does he owe as a fiduciary?" None of the "honest services" cases, neither those pertaining to public officials nor those pertaining to private employees, defined the nature and content of the fiduciary duty central to the "fraud" offense.

There was not even universal agreement concerning the *source* of the fiduciary obligation—whether it must be positive state or federal law, or merely general principles, such as the "obligations of loyalty and fidelity" that inhere in the "employment relationship." The decision *McNally* reversed had grounded the duty in general (not jurisdiction-specific) trust law, a *corpus juris* festooned with various duties. See, *e.g.*, Restatement (Second) of Trusts §§ 169-185 (1976). Another pre-*McNally* case referred to the general law of agency, which imposes duties quite different from those of a trustee.[63] See Restatement (Second) of Agency §§ 377-398 (1957).

This indeterminacy does not disappear if one assumes that the pre-*McNally* cases developed a federal, common-law fiduciary duty; the duty remained hopelessly undefined. Some courts described it in astoundingly broad language. *Blachly v. United States*, 380 F.2d 665 (C.A.5 1967), loftily declared that "[l]aw puts its imprimatur on the accepted moral standards and condemns conduct which fails to match the 'reflection of moral uprightness, of fundamental honesty, fair play and right dealing in the general and business life of members of society.'" Other courts unhelpfully added that any scheme "contrary to public policy" was also condemned by the statute. Even opinions that did not indulge in such grandiloquence did not specify the duty at issue beyond loyalty or honesty. Moreover, the demands of the duty were said to be greater for public officials than for private employees, but in what respects (or by how much) was never made clear.

The indefiniteness of the fiduciary duty is not all. Many courts held that some *je-ne-sais-quoi* beyond a mere breach of fiduciary duty was needed to establish honest-services fraud. There was, unsurprisingly, some dispute about that, at least in the context of acts by persons owing duties to the public. And even among those courts that did require something additional where a public official was involved, there was disagreement as to what the addition should be. For example, .. the Seventh Circuit held that material misrepresentations and active concealment were enough. But ... the Eighth Circuit held that actual harm to the State was needed.

---

[63] [Justice Scalia's footnote 1:] The Court is untroubled by these divisions because "these debates were rare in bribe and kickback cases," in which "[t]he existence of a fiduciary relationship, under any definition of that term, was usually beyond dispute." This misses the point. The Courts of Appeals may have consistently found unlawful the acceptance of a bribe or kickback by one or another sort of fiduciary, but they have not consistently described (as the statute does not) any test for who is a fiduciary.

Similar disagreements occurred with respect to private employees. Courts disputed whether the defendant must use his fiduciary position for his own gain. One opinion upheld a mail-fraud conviction on the ground that the defendant's "failure to disclose his receipt of kickbacks and consulting fees from [his employer's] suppliers resulted in a breach of his fiduciary duties depriving his employer of his loyal and honest services." Another opinion, however, demanded more than an intentional failure to disclose: "There must be a failure to disclose something which in the knowledge or contemplation of the employee poses an independent business risk to the employer." Other courts required that the victim suffer some loss—a proposition that, of course, other courts rejected. The Court's statement today that there was a deprivation of honest services even if "the scheme occasioned a money or property *gain* for the betrayed party" is therefore true, except to the extent it is not.

In short, the first step in the Court's analysis—holding that "the intangible right of honest services" refers to "the honest-services doctrine recognized in Court of Appeals' decisions before *McNally*"—is a step out of the frying pan into the fire. The pre-*McNally* cases provide no clear indication of what constitutes a denial of the right of honest services. The possibilities range from any action that is contrary to public policy or otherwise immoral, to only the disloyalty of a public official or employee to his principal, to only the secret use of a perpetrator's position of trust in order to harm whomever he is beholden to. The duty probably did not have to be rooted in state law, but maybe it did. It might have been more demanding in the case of public officials, but perhaps not. At the time § 1346 was enacted there was no settled criterion for choosing among these options, for conclusively settling what was in and what was out. ...

The Court is aware of all this. It knows that adopting by reference "the pre- *McNally* honest-services doctrine" is adopting by reference nothing more precise than the referring term itself ("the intangible right of honest services"). Hence the *deus ex machina:* "[W]e pare that body of precedent down to its core." Since the honest-services doctrine "had its genesis" in bribery prosecutions, and since several cases and counsel for Skilling referred to bribery and kickback schemes as "core" or "paradigm" or "typical" examples, or "[t]he most obvious form," of honest-services fraud, and since two cases and counsel for the Government say that they formed the "vast majority," or "most" or at least "[t]he bulk" of honest-services cases, THEREFORE it must be the case that they are *all* Congress meant by its reference to the honest-services doctrine.

Even if that conclusion followed from its premises, it would not suffice to eliminate the vagueness of the statute. It would solve (perhaps) the indeterminacy of what acts constitute a breach of the "honest services" obligation under the pre-*McNally* law. But it would not solve the most fundamental indeterminacy: the character of the "fiduciary capacity" to which the bribery and kickback restriction applies. Does it apply only to public officials? Or in addition to private individuals who contract with the public? Or to everyone, including the corporate officer here? The pre-*McNally* case law does not provide an answer. Thus, even with the bribery and kickback limitation the statute does not answer the question "What is the criterion of guilt?"

But that is perhaps beside the point, because it is obvious that mere prohibition of bribery and kickbacks was not the intent of the statute. To say that bribery and kickbacks represented "the core" of the doctrine, or that most cases applying the doctrine involved those offenses, is not to say that they *are* the doctrine. All it proves is that the multifarious versions of the doctrine *overlap* with regard to those offenses. But the doctrine itself is much more. Among all the pre-*McNally* smorgasbord-offerings of varieties of honest-services fraud, *not one* is limited to bribery and kickbacks. That is a dish the Court has cooked up all on its own.

Thus, the Court's claim to "respec[t] the legislature" is false. It is entirely clear (as the Court and I agree) that Congress meant to reinstate the body of pre-*McNally* honest-services law; and entirely clear that that prohibited much more (though precisely what more is uncertain) than bribery and kickbacks. Perhaps it is true that "Congress intended § 1346 to reach *at least* bribes and kickbacks." That simply does not mean, as the Court now holds, that "§ 1346 criminalizes *only*" bribery and kickbacks.

Arriving at that conclusion requires not interpretation but invention. The Court replaces a vague criminal standard that Congress adopted with a more narrow one (included within the vague one) that can pass constitutional muster. I know of no precedent for such "paring down," and it seems to me clearly beyond judicial power. This is not, as the Court claims, simply a matter of adopting a "limiting construction" in the face of potential unconstitutionality. To do that, our cases have been careful to note, the narrowing construction must be "fairly possible," "reasonable," or not "plainly contrary to the intent of Congress." As we have seen (and the Court does not contest), *no court* before *McNally* concluded that the "deprivation of honest services" meant *only* the acceptance of bribes or kickbacks. If it were a "fairly possible" or "reasonable" construction, not "contrary to the intent of Congress," one would think that *some* court would have adopted it. The Court does not even point to a *post-McNally* case that reads § 1346 to cover only bribery and kickbacks, and I am aware of none.

The canon of constitutional avoidance, on which the Court so heavily relies, states that "when the constitutionality of a statute is assailed, if the statute be reasonably susceptible of two interpretations, by one of which it would be unconstitutional and by the other valid, it is our plain duty to adopt that construction which will save the statute from constitutional infirmity." Here there is no choice to be made between two "fair alternatives." Until today, no one has thought (and there is no basis for thinking) that the honest-services statute prohibited only bribery and kickbacks.

I certainly agree with the Court that we must, "if we can," uphold, rather than "condemn," Congress's enactments. But I do not believe we have the power, in order to uphold an enactment, to rewrite it. ...

Notes

1. All nine members of the Court concur that § 1346 is vague; they disagree on the appropriate remedy, that is, whether to restrict the scope of the statute or to strike it as unconstitutional. Who—the majority or the dissent—has the better argument regarding remedy? Is the Court legislating, or is it following tradition in construing the statute narrowly to avoid constitutional difficulties? Does the nature of the constitutional infirmity— vagueness—and the type of case—criminal—matter in deciding who is right? *See* Julie Rose O'Sullivan, Skilling: *More Blind Monks Examining the Elephant*, 39 Fordham Urb. L.J. 343 (2011).

2. Note that the Court waited 46 years to address the disarray below on the scope of honest services fraud in *McNally*, only to hold that those sent to prison all those years under that theory of fraud had not in fact committed a crime. Once Congress responded with § 1346, it waited another 22 years to resolve the many circuit splits surrounding that statute, only to find that the many people convicted of honest services fraud not based on bribery or kickbacks were also legally innocent. "Once again, the court's decision has cast doubt on a variety of investigations, prosecutions, pleas, and convictions, creating 'a wave of appeals and requests for dismissals,'" as well as collateral attacks under 28 U.S.C. § 2255 and requests for relief pursuant to the writ of *coram nobis*—a writ that is employed by convicted defendants who are no longer in custody to seek a correction of a "patent error" in their conviction. Kelly B. Kramer & Lindsey Nelson, *Déjà Vu: What Post-*McNally *Decisions Can Teach Us After* Skilling, 88 Crim. L. Rptr. 231 (2010).

3. The Court took the *Skilling*, *Black*, and *Weyhrauch* cases to decide three issues, although it ultimately failed to address them: whether the government must prove that it was reasonably foreseeable that the honest services scheme could cause some economic or pecuniary harm to victims in private sector cases (*Black*); whether the duty to disclose, the violation of which constitutes the "fraud," must arise under state law in a public sector case (*Weyhrauch*); and whether the defendant must intend to obtain private gain from the victim to whom honest services are owed (*Skilling*). The *Skilling* Court noted the existence of circuit splits on all these issues but did not resolve them. (In *United States v. Nayak*, 769 F.3d 978, 981 (7th Cir. 2014), the Seventh Circuit noted its belief that its former requirement that private gain be shown in

honest services cases did not survive *Skilling*.) Are they of continuing concern after the Court's restriction of § 1346 to bribery and kickback cases?

4. *What is the Source and Scope of the Duty Underlying Bribery and Kickbacks Prohibition?* Of all the uncertainties that have dogged the courts in determining the proper scope of § 1346, the dissent seems most concerned with the basic question—upon which certiorari was not granted but upon which there is a split below—of the source and scope of the fiduciary duties that are said to give rise to a duty of honest services. Why might the Court's failure to address the source and scope of a duty of honest services be troubling? *See* Samuel W. Buell, *The Court's Fraud Dud*, 6 Duke J. Con. L. & Pub. Policy Special Issue 31 (2010); *see also* Michelle V. Barone, Note, *Honest Services Fraud: Construing the Contours of Section 1346 in the Corporate Realm*, 38 Del. J. Corp. L. 571 (2013). Practitioners and commentators continue to be unhappy with the Court's lack of guidance on this issue: "No prosecutor, never mind the general public, has any concrete idea of what duties are owed to public and private enterprises, how those duties are defined, or from whence those duties arise in connection with Section 1346. The law remains a disastrous mess, and the line between illicit conduct and permissible behavior is more blurred than ever." Glen Austin Sproviero, *The Prosecutor's Pistol: The Genesis and State of Honest-Services Fraud*, 89 Crim. L. Rptr. 730 (2011). Nonetheless, courts have rejected defendants' continuing claims that this indeterminacy constitutes unconstitutional vagueness. *See, e.g.*, United States v. Nelson, 712 F.3d 498 (11th Cir. 2013).

The circuits continue to be split on the issue of whether, in fact, a "fiduciary duty" is necessary to give rise to an honest services case. *Compare* United States v. Milovanovic, 678 F.3d 713 (9th Cir. 2012) (*en banc*) (breach of a fiduciary duty is an element of honest services fraud but independent contractors can be fiduciaries); United States v. Ervasti, 201 F.3d 1029, 1037 (8th Cir. 2000), *with* United States v. McGeehan, 584 F.3d 560, 568 (3d Cir. 2009), *vacated in light of* Skilling, 625 F.3d 159 (3d Cir. 2010); United States v. Browne, 505 F.3d 1229, 1265 (11th Cir. 2007). The Ninth Circuit, sitting *en banc*, has explained:

> … A fiduciary is generally defined as "[a] person who is required to act for the benefit of another person on all matters within the scope of their relationship; one who owes to another the duties of good faith, trust, confidence, and candor...." Black's Law Dictionary (9th ed.). And courts have held that "fiduciary" encompasses informal fiduciaries. *See, e.g., In re Monnig's Dep't Stores, Inc. v. Azad Oriental Rugs, Inc.*, 929 F.2d 197, 201 (5th Cir. 1991) ("Confidential relationships arise not only from technical fiduciary relationships, but also from partnerships, joint ventures, and other informal relationships."); *United States v. Pappert*, 112 F.3d 1073, 1080 (10th Cir. 1997) ("[T]here is not a bright line between formal or informal fiduciary relationships, and run-of-the-mill commercial relationships.... [Courts] must carefully distinguish between those arms-length commercial relationships where trust is created by the defendant's personality or the victim's credulity, and relationships in which the victim's trust is based on defendant's position in the transaction."). This definition is broad, but intentionally so. The existence of a fiduciary duty in a criminal prosecution is a fact-based determination that must ultimately be determined by a jury properly instructed on this issue.
>
> In *Skilling*, the Supreme Court's reliance on *Chiarella v. United States*, a securities case that found "the duty to disclose arises when one party has information that the other [party] is entitled to know because of a fiduciary *or other similar relation of trust and confidence* between them," suggests that the Supreme Court interpreted the Mail Fraud Statute to mean that both formal—"fiduciary"—and informal fiduciaries—"other similar relation of trust and confidence"—are susceptible to prosecution. 445 U.S. 222, 228 (1980) (emphasis added).
>
> We therefore hold that a fiduciary duty for the purposes of the Mail Fraud Statute is not limited to a formal "fiduciary" relationship well-known in the law, but also extends to a trusting relationship in which one party acts for the benefit of another and induces the trusting party to relax the care and vigilance which it would ordinarily exercise.

Milovanovic, 678 F.3d at 723-24. Does this definition provide fair notice?

5. *International Applications.* One way to illustrate the continuing necessity of answering the question of where the duty of honest services comes from can be illustrated by reference to cases in which the defendant, or the scheme, has international aspects. In *United States v. Bahel*, 662 F.3d 610 (2d Cir. 2011), the Second Circuit upheld the conviction of a foreign employee of the United Nations who was indicted under a bribery theory of honest services. The Second Circuit rejected Bahel's argument that § 1346 does not apply to foreign nationals of international organizations. It did so without much of an explanation, simply asserting that Bahel's conduct fell within the ambit of the statute as demonstrated by a case that dealt with neither a foreign national nor an international organization. *Id.* at 632-34. Does the *Skilling* opinion stand for the proposition that whenever bribery is alleged in an employment situation, § 1346 applies? What import might this have for prosecutions of foreign officials or bribery and kickback schemes overseas?

In support of his argument, Bahel cited *United States v. Giffen*, 326 F.Supp.2d 497 (S.D.N.Y. 2004), and *United States v. Lazarenko*, No. 00 Cr. 284 (N.D. Cal. May 7, 2004), which the Second Circuit distinguished, as follows:

> *United States v. Giffen* ... involved a United States citizen who was charged with honest services fraud for bribing a government official from the Republic of Kazakhstan, resulting in the deprivation of honest services for Kazakh citizens. The district court, finding a "total absence of ... precedent supporting the Government's overseas application of the intangible rights theory, ruled that "Congress did not intend that the intangible right to honest services encompass bribery of foreign officials in foreign countries." Although Bahel urges to the contrary, *Giffen* does not dictate the outcome of this case, not only because this Court has not itself so construed Section 1346, but also because, unlike *Giffen*, the conduct at issue in this case took place within the territorial United States, and the victim was—not a foreign government's citizens—but the United Nations, an organization headquartered in the United States, and receiving its largest financial contributions from the United States.
>
> *United States v. Lazarenko* is also distinguishable. That case ... involved a former prime minister of the Republic of Ukraine, who was charged with depriving Ukranian citizens of the honest services of their government officials. At the close of evidence, the district court dismissed, inter alia, two counts of honest services fraud charged in violation of [Section 1346]. In so doing, the district court stated that, in order to establish honest services fraud, the Government would have had to plead and prove "an analogous violation of Ukraine law." This proposition has since been rejected by the Ninth Circuit. *See* United States v. Weyhrauch, 548 F.3d 1237 (9th Cir. 2008), *vacated and remanded on other grounds*, [Skilling v. United States, 561 U.S. 358 (2010)]. That is, the Ninth Circuit has rejected the notion that a deprivation of honest services requires a[n] underlying violation of state law in a domestic case. *Lazarenko* is also at odds with precedent in our Circuit [to the same effect.] Accordingly, *Lazarenko* does not provide a basis on which to vacate Bahel's conviction.

Bahel, 662 F.3d at 632-33; *see also* United States v. Lazarenko, 564 F.3d 1026 (9th Cir. 2009) (fraud counts against foreign official failed only because of deficient wiring element).

6. *What is "Bribery" Under* Skilling? Pre-*Skilling*, courts struggled with whether "*quid pro quo*" bribery had to be demonstrated in order to establish honest services fraud under a bribery theory, or whether the lesser offense of gratuities—generally simply a reward for favorable official treatment—would suffice. *See, e.g.,* United States v. Kincaid-Chauncey, 556 F.3d 923 (9th Cir. 2008); United States v. Woodward, 149 F.3d 46 (1st Cir. 1998); United States v. Brumley, 116 F.3d 728 (5th Cir. 1997) (*en banc*).

Under the federal bribery statute applicable to federal officials, 18 U.S.C. § 201, the government must prove the existence of a "*quid pro quo*"—that is, that the defendant had a specific intent to give or receive something of value to *influence* an official act. A gratuity offense is distinguished from bribery because the government need not prove a corrupt *quid pro quo*— that is that the bribe was intended to influence the official in making an official act. Rather, all this is required for a gratuity count is that the payment was a reward for an official act. Under another statute that applies in some instances to bribery on the state and local government level, 18 U.S.C. § 1951, the Supreme Court has decreed that where the corrupt payment is made in the guise of a campaign contribution, an "explicit" *quid pro quo* agreement must be proved (although there are circuit splits surrounding this question, explored in Chapter 8(C), *infra*).

Predictably, there has been extensive litigation over what, precisely, the *Skilling* Court meant by "bribery." The Seventh Circuit has explicitly held that accepting a gratuity—that is a reward for official acts without any *quid pro quo* (exchange of money with intent to influence the official actor)—does not constitute honest services fraud. *See* United States v. Hawkins, 777 F.3d 880, 883-84 (7th Cir. 2015); *see also* United States v. Johnson, 874 F.3dd 990, 999 (7th Cir. 2017); United States v. Bahel, 662 F.3d 610, 633 (2d Cir. 2011) (government conceded that honest services fraud does not encompass illegal gratuities). Other circuits deal with the question less forthrightly, holding only that proof of a *quid pro quo* is required but need not be "explicit." *See, e.g.*, United States v. Terry, 707 F.3d 607 (6th Cir. 2013); United States v. Ring, 706 F.3d 460 (D.C. Cir. 2013); United States v. Bryant, 655 F.3d 232, 245 (3d Cir. 2011) (*quid pro quo* must be proved). If expressly confronted with the question, these circuits presumably would conclude that gratuities cannot constitute honest services "bribery."

Even if a nominal *quid pro quo* requirement is identified, there may be some question whether it has any teeth. In this regard, many courts have accepted a "stream-of-payments" proof approach that significantly undercuts that requirement. Thus, for example, a number of circuits hold that one need not show that specific payments were made in exchange for particular acts; rather, it is "'sufficient if the public official understands that he or she is expected as a result of the payment to exercise particular kinds of influence—i.e., on behalf of the payor—as specific opportunities arose.'" United States v. Ganim, 510 F.3d 134, 145 (2d Cir. 2007) (citation omitted); *see also* United States v. Jefferson, 674 F.3d 332, 358-59 (4th Cir. 2012). The following is a sample jury instruction in such cases:

> A *quid pro quo* agreement may be implicit as well as explicit. The improper benefit may consist of money and other financial benefits whether given on a one time basis or as a stream of payments to the public official. In other words, when payments are accepted by a public official from a payor with the intent to obtain that official's actions on an "as needed" basis, so that when the opportunity presents itself that public official takes specific official action on the payor's behalf in return for those payments, that constitutes a breach of the public official's duty of honest services.

United States v. Bryant, 655 F.3d 232, 244 (3d Cir. 2011). Courts accepting this theory have rejected arguments that such instructions suggest to a jury that "honest services fraud include[s] accepting payments for something a public official was already planning to do or had already done, which is a gratuity (or 'reward') and not a bribe." *See id.* Are these courts correct?

7. *Kickback cases.* What is a "kickback"? In *United States v. Pelisamen*, 641 F.3d 399 (9th Cir. 2011), a defendant was convicted of wire fraud in connection with a scheme—executed with his lawyer (Arriola)—to remove funds to which the defendant was not entitled from his grandmother's estate, for which he served as the administrator. The court held that including an honest services jury instruction and jury verdict form was plainly erroneous because there "were no bribes or kickbacks alleged." *Id.* at 405. In so doing, the court rejected the government's attempt to argue that the scheme actually involved kickbacks:

> ... Black's Law Dictionary defines a "kickback" as a "*return* of a portion of a monetary sum received, esp. as a result of coercion or a secret agreement." ([E]mphasis added). The indictment nowhere mentions the term kickback or the concept of Defendant redirecting any funds to Arriola once he had received them. Moreover, Defendant never *returned* any money to Arriola because he never received any money from him. All of the stolen money was taken from ... [the] estate. The government's case has always been that

Defendant and Arriola acted together to withdraw funds that belonged to … [the] estate and its heirs. In contrast, the paradigmatic kickback is made "for the purpose of improperly obtaining or rewarding favorable treatment" in some area (*e.g.*, government contracts). 41 U.S.C. § 52(2). The Supreme Court's analysis in *Skilling* strongly suggests that what is mean by "kickbacks" was precisely this paradigmatic situation.

Id.; *see also* United States v. DeMizio, 741 F.3d 373, 381 (2d Cir. 2014) ("A kickback scheme typically involves an employee's steering business of his employer to a third party in exchange for a share of the third party's profits on that business"; "the scheme is no less a kickback scheme when the employee directs the third party to share its profits with an entity designated by the employee in which the employee has an interest"). The *Pelisamen* court concluded, however, that the defendant's substantial rights were not affected, and thus the error was harmless, because the district court had also charged the jury on a money-or-property theory and the "entire basis of the indictment was that Defendant had helped himself to money that did not belong to him." 641 F.3d at 406. The government has met with success in applying a "kick-backs" theory. *See, e.g.*, United States v. Mullins, 800 F.3d 866 (7th Cir. 2015); Jennings v. United States, 696 F.3d 759 (8th Cir. 2012); United States v. Lupton, 620 F.3d 790 (7th Cir. 2010); United States v. Cantrell, 617 F.3d 919 (7th Cir. 2010). Where all the government can prove is a gratuity (a "reward"), might it be able to recast such cases as kickbacks?

8. *Undisclosed Conflicts of Interest Cases.* In self-dealing or "conflict of interest" cases, "the defendant typically causes his or her employer to do business with a corporation or other enterprise in which the defendant has a secret interest, undisclosed to the employer." United States v. Rybicki, 354 F.3d 124, 140 (2d Cir. 2003) (*en banc*). The *Skilling* Court ruled "in" bribery and kickback cases and "out" undisclosed conflict of interest cases. *See also* United States v. Blagojevich, 794 F.3d 729 (7th Cir. 2015) ("logrolling" is not prohibited under "honest services" statute). On what principled basis? The *Skilling* Court's reluctance to accept, under the honest-services rubric, undisclosed conflicts of interest has come in for its fair share of criticism. This was a very well-established category of honest services cases—indeed, probably as well-established as the bribery and kickback theories. *See Rybicki*, 354 F.3d at 140-41 (discussing caselaw). Further, as one DOJ representative argued in a House hearing,

> As any prosecutor can attest, corrupt officials and those who corrupt them can be very ingenious, and not all corruption takes the form of flat-out bribery. Let me give you an example. If a mayor were to solicit tens of thousands of dollars in bribes in return for giving out city contracts to unqualified bidders, that mayor could be charged with bribery. But if that same mayor decides that he wants to make even more money through the abuse of his official position, he might secretly create his own company, and use the authority and power of his office to funnel city contracts to that company. This undisclosed self-dealing or conflict of interest is not bribery, and is no longer covered by the honest services fraud statute after the *Skilling* opinion. Although this second kind of scheme is plainly corrupt, and clearly undermines public confidence in the integrity of their government, it can no longer be reached by the honest services fraud statute, and there is no other Federal criminal law to address this conduct.

Statement of Mary Patrice Brown, Deputy Ass't Attorney Gen., Crim. Div., Dep't of Justice, Before the House Committee on the Judiciary, Subcomm. on Crime, Terrorism, and Homeland Security, for a Hearing entitled "H.R. 2572, The Clean Up Government Act of 2011," at 7-8 (July 26, 2011).

How might prosecutors attempt to recast their undisclosed conflicts cases to pass muster under *Skilling*? For example, could one try to characterize the corrupt mayor's undisclosed self-dealing as a species of "kickback" case? Could one attempt to recharacterize them as a "money or property" cases, perhaps under a right-to-control theory or by alleging that an employee, by serving under an undisclosed conflict, deprives his employer of his salary? *Compare* United States v. Richerson, 833 F.2d 1147, 1157-58 (5th Cir. 1987) *with Blagojevich*, 794 F.3d at 737; United States v. Ochs, 842 F.2d 515, 523-27 (1st Cir. 1988); *cf.* United States

v. Ratcliff, 488 F.3d 639 (5th Cir. 2007) (holding that election fraud could not be prosecuted under the mail fraud statute under theory that the candidate, if elected, would deprive the electorate of his salary); United States v. Turner, 465 F.3d 667 (6th Cir. 2006) (same); Westchester Co. Indep. Party v. Astorino, 137 F.Supp.3d 586 (S.D.N.Y. 2015) (same; collecting cases).

McDONNELL v. UNITED STATES
-- U.S. --, 136 S.Ct. 2355 (2016)

Chief Justice ROBERTS delivered the opinion of the Court.

...

On November 3, 2009, petitioner Robert McDonnell was elected the 71st Governor of Virginia. His campaign slogan was "Bob's for Jobs," and his focus in office was on promoting business in Virginia. As Governor, McDonnell spoke about economic development in Virginia "on a daily basis" and attended numerous "events, ribbon cuttings," and "plant facility openings." He also referred thousands of constituents to meetings with members of his staff and other government officials. According to longtime staffers, Governor McDonnell likely had more events at the Virginia Governor's Mansion to promote Virginia business than had occurred in "any other administration."

This case concerns Governor McDonnell's interactions with one of his constituents, Virginia businessman Jonnie Williams. Williams was the CEO of Star Scientific, a Virginia-based company that developed and marketed Anatabloc, a nutritional supplement made from anatabine, a compound found in tobacco. Star Scientific hoped to obtain Food and Drug Administration approval of Anatabloc as an anti-inflammatory drug. An important step in securing that approval was initiating independent research studies on the health benefits of anatabine. Star Scientific hoped Virginia's public universities would undertake such studies, pursuant to a grant from Virginia's Tobacco Commission.

Governor McDonnell first met Williams in 2009, when Williams offered McDonnell transportation on his private airplane to assist with McDonnell's election campaign. Shortly after the election, Williams had dinner with Governor and Mrs. McDonnell at a restaurant in New York. The conversation turned to Mrs. McDonnell's search for a dress for the inauguration, which led Williams to offer to purchase a gown for her. Governor McDonnell's counsel later instructed Williams not to buy the dress, and Mrs. McDonnell told Williams that she would take a rain check.

In October 2010, Governor McDonnell and Williams met again on Williams's plane. During the flight, Williams told Governor McDonnell that he "needed his help" moving forward on the research studies at Virginia's public universities, and he asked to be introduced to the person that he "needed to talk to." Governor McDonnell agreed to introduce Williams to Dr. William Hazel, Virginia's Secretary of Health and Human Resources. Williams met with Dr. Hazel the following month, but the meeting was unfruitful; Dr. Hazel was skeptical of the science behind Anatabloc and did not assist Williams in obtaining the studies.

Six months later, Governor McDonnell's wife, Maureen McDonnell, offered to seat Williams next to the Governor at a political rally. Shortly before the event, Williams took Mrs. McDonnell on a shopping trip and bought her $20,000 worth of designer clothing. The McDonnells later had Williams over for dinner at the Governor's Mansion, where they discussed research studies on Anatabloc.

Two days after that dinner, Williams had an article about Star Scientific's research e-mailed to Mrs. McDonnell, which she forwarded to her husband. Less than an hour later, Governor McDonnell texted his sister to discuss the financial situation of certain rental properties they owned in Virginia Beach. Governor McDonnell also e-mailed his daughter to ask about expenses for her upcoming wedding.

The next day, Williams returned to the Governor's Mansion for a meeting with Mrs. McDonnell. At the meeting, Mrs. McDonnell described the family's financial problems, including their struggling rental properties in Virginia Beach and their daughter's wedding expenses. Mrs. McDonnell, who had experience selling nutritional supplements, told Williams that she had a background in the area and could help him with Anatabloc. According to Williams, she explained that the "Governor says it's okay for me to help you and—but I need you to help me. I need you to help me with this financial situation." Mrs. McDonnell then asked Williams for a $50,000 loan, in addition to a $15,000 gift to help pay for her daughter's wedding, and Williams agreed.

Williams testified that he called Governor McDonnell after the meeting and said, "I understand the financial problems and I'm willing to help. I just wanted to make sure that you knew about this." According to Williams, Governor McDonnell thanked him for his help. Governor McDonnell testified, in contrast, that he did not know about the loan at the time, and that when he learned of it he was upset that Mrs. McDonnell had requested the loan from Williams. Three days after the meeting between Williams and Mrs. McDonnell, Governor McDonnell directed his assistant to forward the article on Star Scientific to Dr. Hazel.

In June 2011, Williams sent Mrs. McDonnell's chief of staff a letter containing a proposed research protocol for the Anatabloc studies. The letter was addressed to Governor McDonnell, and it suggested that the Governor "use the attached protocol to initiate the 'Virginia Study' of Anatabloc at the Medical College of Virginia and the University of Virginia School of Medicine." Governor McDonnell gave the letter to Dr. Hazel. Williams testified at trial that he did not "recall any response" to the letter.

In July 2011, the McDonnell family visited Williams's vacation home for the weekend, and Governor McDonnell borrowed Williams's Ferrari while there. Shortly thereafter, Governor McDonnell asked Dr. Hazel to send an aide to a meeting with Williams and Mrs. McDonnell to discuss research studies on Anatabloc. The aide later testified that she did not feel pressured by Governor or Mrs. McDonnell to do "anything other than have the meeting," and that Williams did not ask anything of her at the meeting. After the meeting, the aide sent Williams a "polite blow-off" e-mail.

At a subsequent meeting at the Governor's Mansion, Mrs. McDonnell admired Williams's Rolex and mentioned that she wanted to get one for Governor McDonnell. Williams asked if Mrs. McDonnell wanted him to purchase a Rolex for the Governor, and Mrs. McDonnell responded, "Yes, that would be nice." Williams did so, and Mrs. McDonnell later gave the Rolex to Governor McDonnell as a Christmas present.

In August 2011, the McDonnells hosted a lunch event for Star Scientific at the Governor's Mansion. According to Williams, the purpose of the event was to launch Anatabloc. According to Governor McDonnell's gubernatorial counsel, however, it was just lunch.

The guest list for the event included researchers at the University of Virginia and Virginia Commonwealth University. During the event, Star Scientific distributed free samples of Anatabloc, in addition to eight $25,000 checks that researchers could use in preparing grant proposals for studying Anatabloc. Governor McDonnell asked researchers at the event whether they thought "there was some scientific validity" to Anatabloc and "whether or not there was any reason to explore this further." He also asked whether this could "be something good for the Commonwealth, particularly as it relates to economy or job creation." When Williams asked Governor McDonnell whether he would support funding for the research studies, Governor McDonnell "very politely" replied, "I have limited decision-making power in this area."

In January 2012, Mrs. McDonnell asked Williams for an additional loan for the Virginia Beach rental properties, and Williams agreed. On February 3, Governor McDonnell followed up on that conversation by calling Williams to discuss a $50,000 loan.

Several days later, Williams complained to Mrs. McDonnell that the Virginia universities were not returning Star Scientific's calls. She passed Williams's complaint on to the Governor. While Mrs. McDonnell was driving with Governor McDonnell, she also e-mailed Governor McDonnell's counsel, stating that the Governor "wants to know why nothing has developed" with the research studies after Williams had provided the eight $25,000 checks for preparing grant proposals, and that the Governor "wants to get this going" at the universities. According to Governor McDonnell, however, Mrs. McDonnell acted without his knowledge or permission, and he never made the statements she attributed to him.

On February 16, Governor McDonnell e-mailed Williams to check on the status of documents related to the $50,000 loan. A few minutes later, Governor McDonnell e-mailed his counsel stating, "Please see me about Anatabloc issues at VCU and UVA. Thanks." Governor McDonnell's counsel replied, "Will do. We need to be careful with this issue." The next day, Governor McDonnell's counsel called Star Scientific's lobbyist in order to "change the expectations" of Star Scientific regarding the involvement of the Governor's Office in the studies.

At the end of February, Governor McDonnell hosted a healthcare industry reception at the Governor's Mansion, which Williams attended. Mrs. McDonnell also invited a number of guests recommended by Williams, including researchers at the Virginia universities. Governor McDonnell was present, but did not mention Star Scientific, Williams, or Anatabloc during the event. That same day, Governor McDonnell and Williams spoke about the $50,000 loan, and Williams loaned the money to the McDonnells shortly thereafter.

In March 2012, Governor McDonnell met with Lisa Hicks–Thomas, the Virginia Secretary of Administration, and Sara Wilson, the Director of the Virginia Department of Human Resource Management. The purpose of the meeting was to discuss Virginia's health plan for state employees. At that time, Governor McDonnell was taking Anatabloc several times a day. He took a pill during the meeting, and told Hicks–Thomas and Wilson that the pills "were working well for him" and "would be good for" state employees. Hicks–Thomas recalled Governor McDonnell asking them to meet with a representative from Star Scientific; Wilson had no such recollection. After the discussion with Governor McDonnell, Hicks–Thomas and Wilson looked up Anatabloc on the Internet, but they did not set up a meeting with Star Scientific or conduct any other follow-up. It is undisputed that Virginia's health plan for state employees does not cover nutritional supplements such as Anatabloc.

In May 2012, Governor McDonnell requested an additional $20,000 loan, which Williams provided. Throughout this period, Williams also paid for several rounds of golf for Governor McDonnell and his children, took the McDonnells on a weekend trip, and gave $10,000 as a wedding gift to one of the McDonnells' daughters. In total, Williams gave the McDonnells over $175,000 in gifts and loans.

B

In January 2014, Governor McDonnell was indicted for accepting payments, loans, gifts, and other things of value from Williams and Star Scientific in exchange for "performing official actions on an as-needed basis, as opportunities arose, to legitimize, promote, and obtain research studies for Star Scientific's products." The charges against him comprised one count of conspiracy to commit honest services fraud, three counts of honest services fraud, one count of conspiracy to commit Hobbs Act extortion, six counts of Hobbs Act extortion, and two counts of making a false statement. See 18 U.S.C. §§ 1343, 1349 (honest services fraud); § 1951(a) (Hobbs Act extortion); § 1014 (false statement). Mrs. McDonnell was indicted on similar charges, plus obstructing official proceedings, based on her alleged involvement in the scheme. See § 1512(c)(2) (obstruction).

The theory underlying both the honest services fraud and Hobbs Act extortion charges was that Governor McDonnell had accepted bribes from Williams. See *Skilling v. United States*, 561 U.S. 358, 404 (2010) (construing honest services fraud to forbid "fraudulent schemes to deprive another of honest services through bribes or kickbacks"); *Evans v. United States*, 504 U.S. 255, 260 (1992) (construing Hobbs Act extortion to include "'taking a bribe'").

The parties agreed that they would define honest services fraud with reference to the federal bribery statute, 18 U.S.C. § 201. That statute makes it a crime for "a public official or person selected to be a public official, directly or indirectly, corruptly" to demand, seek, receive, accept, or agree "to receive or accept anything of value" in return for being "influenced in the performance of any official act." §201(b)(2). An "official act" is defined as "any decision or action on any question, matter, cause, suit, proceeding or controversy, which may at any time be pending, or which may by law be brought before any public official, in such official's official capacity, or in such official's place of trust or profit." § 201(a)(3).

The parties also agreed that obtaining a "thing of value ... knowing that the thing of value was given in return for official action" was an element of Hobbs Act extortion, and that they would use the definition of "official act" found in the federal bribery statute to define "official action" under the Hobbs Act.

As a result of all this, the Government was required to prove that Governor McDonnell committed or agreed to commit an "official act" in exchange for the loans and gifts from Williams. See *Evans*, 504 U.S., at 268 ("the offense is completed at the time when the public official receives a payment in return for his agreement to perform specific official acts; fulfillment of the *quid pro quo* is not an element of the offense").

The Government alleged that Governor McDonnell had committed at least five "official acts":

(1) "arranging meetings for [Williams] with Virginia government officials, who were subordinates of the Governor, to discuss and promote Anatabloc";

(2) "hosting, and ... attending, events at the Governor's Mansion designed to encourage Virginia university researchers to initiate studies of anatabine and to promote Star Scientific's products to doctors for referral to their patients";

(3) "contacting other government officials in the [Governor's Office] as part of an effort to encourage Virginia state research universities to initiate studies of anatabine";

(4) "promoting Star Scientific's products and facilitating its relationships with Virginia government officials by allowing [Williams] to invite individuals important to Star Scientific's business to exclusive events at the Governor's Mansion"; and

(5) "recommending that senior government officials in the [Governor's Office] meet with Star Scientific executives to discuss ways that the company's products could lower healthcare costs."

The case proceeded to a jury trial, which lasted five weeks. Pursuant to an immunity agreement, Williams testified that he had given the gifts and loans to the McDonnells to obtain the Governor's "help with the testing" of Anatabloc at Virginia's medical schools. Governor McDonnell acknowledged that he had requested loans and accepted gifts from Williams. He testified, however, that setting up meetings with government officials was something he did "literally thousands of times" as Governor, and that he did not expect his staff "to do anything other than to meet" with Williams.

Several state officials testified that they had discussed Anatabloc with Williams or Governor McDonnell, but had not taken any action to further the research studies. A UVA employee in the university research office, who had never spoken with the Governor about Anatabloc, testified that she wrote a pro/con list concerning research studies on Anatabloc. The first "pro" was the "[p]erception to Governor that UVA would like to work with local companies," and the first "con" was the "[p]olitical pressure from Governor and impact on future UVA requests from the Governor."

Following closing arguments, the District Court instructed the jury that to convict Governor McDonnell it must find that he agreed "to accept a thing of value in exchange for official action." The court described the five alleged "official acts" set forth in the indictment, which involved arranging meetings, hosting events, and contacting other government officials. The court then quoted the statutory definition of "official act," and—as the Government had requested—advised the jury that the term encompassed "acts that a public official customarily performs," including acts "in furtherance of longer-term goals" or "in a series of steps to exercise influence or achieve an end."

Governor McDonnell had requested the court to further instruct the jury that the "fact that an activity is a routine activity, or a 'settled practice,' of an office-holder does not alone make it an 'official act,'" and that "merely arranging a meeting, attending an event, hosting a reception, or making a speech are not, standing alone, 'official acts,' even if they are settled practices of the official," because they "are not decisions on matters pending before the government." He also asked the court to explain to the jury that an "official act" must intend to or "in fact influence a specific official decision the government actually makes—such as awarding a contract, hiring a government employee, issuing a license, passing a law, or implementing a regulation." The District Court declined to give Governor McDonnell's proposed instruction to the jury.

The jury convicted Governor McDonnell on the honest services fraud and Hobbs Act extortion charges, but acquitted him on the false statement charges. Mrs. McDonnell was also convicted on most of the charges against her. Although the Government requested a sentence of at least ten years for Governor McDonnell, the District Court sentenced him to two years in prison. Mrs. McDonnell received a one-year sentence. …

II

…

According to the Government, "Congress used intentionally broad language" in § 201(a)(3) to embrace "*any* decision or action, on *any* question or matter, that may at *any time* be pending, or which may by law be brought before *any* public official, in such official's official capacity." The Government concludes that the term "official act" therefore encompasses nearly any activity by a public official. In the Government's view, "official act" specifically includes arranging a meeting, contacting another public official, or hosting an event—without more—concerning any subject, including a broad policy issue such as Virginia economic development.

Governor McDonnell, in contrast, contends that statutory context compels a more circumscribed reading, limiting "official acts" to those acts that "direct[] a particular resolution of a specific governmental decision," or that pressure another official to do so. He also claims that "vague corruption laws" such as § 201 implicate serious constitutional concerns, militating "in favor of a narrow, cautious reading of these criminal statutes."

Taking into account the text of the statute, the precedent of this Court, and the constitutional concerns raised by Governor McDonnell, we reject the Government's reading of § 201(a)(3) and adopt a more bounded interpretation of "official act." Under that interpretation, setting up a meeting, calling another public official, or hosting an event does not, standing alone, qualify as an "official act." …

The text of § 201(a)(3) sets forth two requirements for an "official act": First, the Government must identify a "question, matter, cause, suit, proceeding or controversy" that "may at any time be pending" or "may by law be brought" before a public official. Second, the Government must prove that the public official made a decision or took an action "on" that question, matter, cause, suit, proceeding, or controversy, or agreed to do so. The issue here is whether arranging a meeting, contacting another official, or hosting an event—without more—can be a "question, matter, cause, suit, proceeding or controversy," and if not, whether it can be a decision or action on a "question, matter, cause, suit, proceeding or controversy."

The first inquiry is whether a typical meeting, call, or event is itself a "question, matter, cause, suit, proceeding or controversy." …

The last four words in that list—"cause," "suit," "proceeding," and "controversy"—connote a formal exercise of governmental power, such as a lawsuit, hearing, or administrative determination. See, *e.g.*, Black's Law Dictionary 278–279, 400, 1602–1603 (4th ed. 1951) (defining "cause," "suit," and "controversy" as judicial proceedings). Although it may be difficult to define the precise reach of those terms, it seems clear that a typical meeting, telephone call, or event arranged by a public official does not qualify as a "cause, suit, proceeding or controversy."

But what about a "question" or "matter"? A "question" could mean any "subject or aspect that is in dispute, open for discussion, or to be inquired into," and a "matter" any "subject" of "interest or relevance." Webster's Third New International Dictionary 1394, 1863 (1961). If those meanings were adopted, a typical meeting, call, or event would qualify as a "question" or "matter." A "question" may also be interpreted more narrowly, however, as "a subject or point of debate or a proposition being or to be voted on in a meeting," such as a question "before the senate." Similarly, a "matter" may be limited to "a topic under active and usually serious or practical consideration," such as a matter that "will come before the committee."

To choose between those competing definitions, we look to the context in which the words appear. Under the familiar interpretive canon *noscitur a sociis,* "a word is known by the company it keeps." While "not an inescapable rule," this canon "is often wisely applied where a word is capable of many meanings in order to avoid the giving of unintended breadth to the Acts of Congress." ...

Applying ... [this] approach here, we conclude that a "question" or "matter" must be similar in nature to a "cause, suit, proceeding or controversy." Because a typical meeting, call, or event arranged by a public official is not of the same stripe as a lawsuit before a court, a determination before an agency, or a hearing before a committee, it does not qualify as a "question" or "matter" under § 201(a)(3).

That more limited reading also comports with the presumption "that statutory language is not superfluous." If "question" and "matter" were as unlimited in scope as the Government argues, the terms "cause, suit, proceeding or controversy" would serve no role in the statute— every "cause, suit, proceeding or controversy" would also be a "question" or "matter." Under a more confined interpretation, however, "question" and "matter" may be understood to refer to a formal exercise of governmental power that is similar in nature to a "cause, suit, proceeding or controversy," but that does not necessarily fall into one of those prescribed categories.

Because a typical meeting, call, or event is not itself a question or matter, the next step is to determine whether arranging a meeting, contacting another official, or hosting an event may qualify as a "decision or action" *on* a different question or matter. That requires us to first establish what counts as a question or matter in this case.

In addition to the requirements we have described, § 201(a)(3) states that the question or matter must be "pending" or "may by law be brought" before "any public official." "Pending" and "may by law be brought" suggest something that is relatively circumscribed—the kind of thing that can be put on an agenda, tracked for progress, and then checked off as complete. In particular, "may *by law* be brought" conveys something within the specific duties of an official's position—the function conferred by the authority of his office. The word "any" conveys that the matter may be pending either before the public official who is performing the official act, or before another public official.

The District Court, however, determined that the relevant matter in this case could be considered at a much higher level of generality as "Virginia business and economic development," or—as it was often put to the jury—"Bob's for Jobs." Economic development is not naturally described as a matter "pending" before a public official—or something that may be brought "by law" before him—any more than "justice" is pending or may be brought by law before a judge, or "national security" is pending or may be brought by law before an officer of the Armed Forces. Under § 201(a)(3), the pertinent "question, matter, cause, suit, proceeding or controversy" must be more focused and concrete.

For its part, the Fourth Circuit found at least three questions or matters at issue in this case: (1) "whether researchers at any of Virginia's state universities would initiate a study of Anatabloc"; (2) "whether the state-created Tobacco Indemnification and Community Revitalization Commission" would "allocate grant money for the study of anatabine"; and (3) "whether the health insurance plan for state employees in Virginia would include Anatabloc as a covered drug." We agree that those qualify as questions or matters under § 201(a)(3). Each is focused and concrete, and each involves a formal exercise of governmental power that is similar in nature to a lawsuit, administrative determination, or hearing.

The question remains whether—as the Government argues—merely setting up a meeting, hosting an event, or calling another official qualifies as a decision or action on any of those three questions or matters. Although the word "decision," and especially the word "action," could be read expansively to support the Government's view, our opinion in *United States v. Sun-Diamond Growers of Cal.,* 526 U.S. 398 (1999), rejects that interpretation.

In *Sun–Diamond*, the Court stated that it was not an "official act" under § 201 for the President to host a championship sports team at the White House, the Secretary of Education to visit a high school, or the Secretary of Agriculture to deliver a speech to "farmers concerning various matters of USDA policy." We recognized that "the Secretary of Agriculture *always* has before him or in prospect matters that affect farmers, just as the President always has before him or in prospect matters that affect college and professional sports, and the Secretary of Education matters that affect high schools." But we concluded that the existence of such pending matters was not enough to find that any action related to them constituted an "official act." It was possible to avoid the "absurdities" of convicting individuals on corruption charges for engaging in such conduct, we explained, "*through the definition of that term*," *i.e.,* by adopting a more limited definition of "official acts."

It is apparent from *Sun–Diamond* that hosting an event, meeting with other officials, or speaking with interested parties is not, standing alone, a "decision or action" within the meaning of § 201(a)(3), even if the event, meeting, or speech is related to a pending question or matter. Instead, something more is required: § 201(a)(3) specifies that the public official must make a decision or take an action *on* that question or matter, or agree to do so.

For example, a decision or action to initiate a research study—or a decision or action on a qualifying step, such as narrowing down the list of potential research topics—would qualify as an "official act." A public official may also make a decision or take an action on a "question, matter, cause, suit, proceeding or controversy" by using his official position to exert pressure on *another* official to perform an "official act." In addition, if a public official uses his official position to provide advice to another official, knowing or intending that such advice will form the basis for an "official act" by another official, that too can qualify as a decision or action for purposes of § 201(a)(3). See *United States v. Birdsall*, 233 U.S. 223, 234 (1914) (finding "official action" on the part of subordinates where their superiors "would necessarily rely largely upon the reports and advice of subordinates ... who were more directly acquainted with" the "facts and circumstances of particular cases").

Under this Court's precedents, a public official is not required to actually make a decision or take an action on a "question, matter, cause, suit, proceeding or controversy"; it is enough that the official agree to do so. The agreement need not be explicit, and the public official need not specify the means that he will use to perform his end of the bargain. Nor must the public official in fact intend to perform the "official act," so long as he agrees to do so. A jury could, for example, conclude that an agreement was reached if the evidence shows that the public official received a thing of value knowing that it was given with the expectation that the official would perform an "official act" in return. It is up to the jury, under the facts of the case, to determine whether the public official agreed to perform an "official act" at the time of the alleged *quid pro quo*. The jury may consider a broad range of pertinent evidence, including the nature of the transaction, to answer that question.

Setting up a meeting, hosting an event, or calling an official (or agreeing to do so) merely to talk about a research study or to gather additional information, however, does not qualify as a decision or action on the pending question of whether to initiate the study. Simply expressing support for the research study at a meeting, event, or call—or sending a subordinate to such a meeting, event, or call—similarly does not qualify as a decision or action on the study, as long as the public official does not intend to exert pressure on another official or provide advice, knowing or intending such advice to form the basis for an "official act." Otherwise, if every action somehow related to the research study were an "official act," the requirement that the public official make a decision or take an action on that study, or agree to do so, would be meaningless.

Of course, this is not to say that setting up a meeting, hosting an event, or making a phone call is always an innocent act, or is irrelevant, in cases like this one. If an official sets up a meeting, hosts an event, or makes a phone call on a question or matter that is or could be pending before another official, that could serve as evidence of an agreement to take an official act. A jury could conclude, for example, that the official was attempting to pressure or advise another official on a pending matter. And if the official agreed to exert that pressure or give that advice in exchange for a thing of value, that would be illegal.

The Government relies on this Court's decision in *Birdsall* to support a more expansive interpretation of "official act," but *Birdsall* is fully consistent with our reading of § 201(a)(3). We held in *Birdsall* that "official action" could be established by custom rather than "by statute" or "a written rule or regulation," and need not be a formal part of an official's decisionmaking process. That does not mean, however, that every decision or action customarily performed by a public official—such as the myriad decisions to refer a constituent to another official—counts as an "official act."...

In sum, an "official act" is a decision or action on a "question, matter, cause, suit, proceeding or controversy." The "question, matter, cause, suit, proceeding or controversy" must involve a formal exercise of governmental power that is similar in nature to a lawsuit before a court, a determination before an agency, or a hearing before a committee. It must also be something specific and focused that is "pending" or "may by law be brought" before a public official. To qualify as an "official act," the public official must make a decision or take an action on that "question, matter, cause, suit, proceeding or controversy," or agree to do so. That decision or action may include using his official position to exert pressure on another official to perform an "official act," or to advise another official, knowing or intending that such advice will form the basis for an "official act" by another official. Setting up a meeting, talking to another official, or organizing an event (or agreeing to do so)—without more—does not fit that definition of "official act." ...

In addition to being inconsistent with both text and precedent, the Government's expansive interpretation of "official act" would raise significant constitutional concerns. Section 201 prohibits *quid pro quo* corruption—the exchange of a thing of value for an "official act." In the Government's view, nearly anything a public official accepts—from a campaign contribution to lunch—counts as a *quid*; and nearly anything a public official does—from arranging a meeting to inviting a guest to an event—counts as a *quo*.

But conscientious public officials arrange meetings for constituents, contact other officials on their behalf, and include them in events all the time. The basic compact underlying representative government *assumes* that public officials will hear from their constituents and act appropriately on their concerns—whether it is the union official worried about a plant closing or the homeowners who wonder why it took five days to restore power to their neighborhood after a storm. The Government's position could cast a pall of potential prosecution over these relationships if the union had given a campaign contribution in the past or the homeowners invited the official to join them on their annual outing to the ballgame. Officials might wonder whether they could respond to even the most commonplace requests for assistance, and citizens with legitimate concerns might shrink from participating in democratic discourse.

This concern is substantial. White House counsel who worked in every administration from that of President Reagan to President Obama warn that the Government's "breathtaking expansion of public-corruption law would likely chill federal officials' interactions with the people they serve and thus damage their ability effectively to perform their duties." Six former Virginia attorneys general—four Democrats and two Republicans—also filed an *amicus* brief in this Court echoing those concerns, as did 77 former state attorneys general from States other than Virginia—41 Democrats, 35 Republicans, and 1 independent.

None of this, of course, is to suggest that the facts of this case typify normal political interaction between public officials and their constituents. Far from it. But the Government's legal interpretation is not confined to cases involving extravagant gifts or large sums of money, and we cannot construe a criminal statute on the assumption that the Government will "use it responsibly." The Court in *Sun–Diamond* declined to rely on "the Government's discretion" to protect against overzealous prosecutions under § 201, concluding instead that "a statute in this field that can linguistically be interpreted to be either a meat axe or a scalpel should reasonably be taken to be the latter."

A related concern is that, under the Government's interpretation, the term "official act" is not defined "with sufficient definiteness that ordinary people can understand what conduct is prohibited," or "in a manner that does not encourage arbitrary and discriminatory enforcement." Under the "'standardless sweep'" of the Government's reading, public officials could be subject to prosecution, without fair notice, for the most prosaic interactions.

"Invoking so shapeless a provision to condemn someone to prison" for up to 15 years raises the serious concern that the provision "does not comport with the Constitution's guarantee of due process." Our more constrained interpretation of § 201(a)(3) avoids this "vagueness shoal."

The Government's position also raises significant federalism concerns. A State defines itself as a sovereign through "the structure of its government, and the character of those who exercise government authority." That includes the prerogative to regulate the permissible scope of interactions between state officials and their constituents. Here, where a more limited interpretation of "official act" is supported by both text and precedent, we decline to "construe the statute in a manner that leaves its outer boundaries ambiguous and involves the Federal Government in setting standards" of "good government for local and state officials." *McNally v. United States*, 483 U.S. 350, 360 (1973). …

There is no doubt that this case is distasteful; it may be worse than that. But our concern is not with tawdry tales of Ferraris, Rolexes, and ball gowns. It is instead with the broader legal implications of the Government's boundless interpretation of the federal bribery statute. A more limited interpretation of the term "official act" leaves ample room for prosecuting corruption, while comporting with the text of the statute and the precedent of this Court.

Notes

1. Because the Court concluded that the jury was not correctly instructed on the meaning of "official act," and that that error was not harmless beyond a reasonable doubt, it vacated McDonnell's conviction and remanded the case to the Fourth Circuit. The Government ultimately determined not to pursue a retrial and the cases against Governor and Maureen McDonnell were both dismissed with prejudice.

2. Are you persuaded that this very narrow definition of an "official act" is wise? In future, could a Governor, without legal jeopardy, say that she will set up any meeting between a constituent and any member of her cabinet for a flat fee of $10,000?

3. There has been substantial fall-out from *McDonnell*. For example, the Second Circuit vacated and remanded the honest services and Hobbs Act extortion convictions of the former Speaker of the New York State Assembly, Sheldon Silver, after concluding that the "official act" jury instruction failed to meet *McDonnell*'s requirements. United States v. Silver, 864 F.3d 102 (2d Cir. 2017). The Second Circuit also found the "official act" jury instructions defective in the honest services fraud and Hobbs Act extortion trial of the former Majority Leader of the New York State Senate and his son, Dean and Adam Skelos; their convictions were also vacated and remanded. *See* United States v. Skelos, 707 F. App'x 733 (2d Cir. 2017).

Note that the Court's definition of an "official act" applies not just in "honest services" fraud cases but also in federal bribery and Hobbs Act extortion prosecutions (*see* Chapter 8 *infra*). In addition to threatening individuals' corruption convictions, the *McDonnell* case may well have a significant impact on the availability of the "stream of benefits" theory of *quid pro quo* bribery. *See* Chapter 8(A), *infra*; *see also* United States v. Menendez, 291 F.Supp.3d 606, 613-17 (D.N.J. 2018) (rejecting argument that *McDonnell* forecloses "stream of benefits" theory).

4. Prosecutors seeking to avoid the restrictive definition of "official acts" may turn to a heretofore little used subsection of the bribery statute: § 201(b)(1)(C). It does not require, in short, that the public official be influenced with respect to an "official act." Rather, it outlaws the corrupt payment of anything of value to a public official in return for that official's "being induced to do or omit to do any act in violation of the official duty of such official or person." *See infra* Chapter 8(A); Bridget Vuona, *Remember Me, "Part C"? Honest Services Fraud Schemes Involving Bribery Under "Part C" of the Federal Bribery Statute Post-McDonnell*, 55 Am. Crim. L. Rev. Online 35, 40-41 (2018). In short, defendants who cannot be said to have been influenced in an "official act" may well be found guilty of having bribed to violate their "official duty." *See, e.g.*, Valdes v. United States, 475 F.3d 1319, 1330 (D.C. Cir. 2007) (*en banc*) (Kavanaugh, J., concurring). As we shall see in Chapter 8(A), § 201(b)(1)(C) applies for the most part to federal officials, not state and local actors. But the *McDonnell* Court used § 201's "official act" definition to define "bribery" for purposes of honest services fraud. Can prosecutors argue that

because § 201(b)(1)(C) makes culpable bribes meant to induce public officials to violate their official duties, honest services fraud ought to extend to such cases as well? *See* Vuona, *supra*, at 41-43.

D. MAIL/WIRE FRAUD EXERCISE

UNITED STATES v. BLACKMON
839 F.2d 900 (2d Cir.1988)

MAHONEY, CIRCUIT JUDGE:

...

The indictment alleged an elaborate scheme by the appellants to defraud six victims in New York City during a period from March to November, 1985. The scheme is a variation of a street confidence game known as the "pigeon drop." The colorful details of the game are described in a portion of the district court opinion, *United States v. Jones*, 648 F.Supp. 225, 226-28 (S.D.N.Y.1986), that is set forth in the margin.[64] Essentially, the game involved persuading

---

[64] [Court's footnote 2:] In Judge Haight's words: As played in the case at bar, which covered the period April through November 1985, the game victimized elderly women (or "lames," in modern parlance). The game begins when one of the players convinces the victim that they have, fortuitously and together, found on the street a portfolio (or "pack") containing cash and securities of great value. The victim, let us say, is walking past St. Bartholomew's Church on the way to do volunteer work at the Lighthouse for the Blind. (These details are not invented for dramatic effect; they are derived from the evidence.) She is suddenly accosted by one of the con game players, who asks the victim if she dropped a leather portfolio seen lying on the street. The victim says "no." The player suggests that they open the portfolio, and does so. The victim gets a peek at what looks like bundles of cash in high denominations and negotiable securities. There is also a note making some sort of reference to the "P.L.O." or to "Iran." The player must set the hook by sustaining the prospective victim's interest, and generally exciting her desire for personal gain. If she disclaims any interest, or simply says "turn the portfolio over to the police" and departs, the game is lost and a new victim must be found. The first stage of the game is accomplished if, by fast and glib patter, the player persuades the victim that the player works for a distinguished banker or business executive, whose advice should be obtained about what to do with the "found" portfolio and its contents.

This brings the victim into telephone contact with the key con game player, the "talker." The victim never meets the talker, although she expects to, and may fruitlessly try to. Something always comes up to prevent a meeting *en face*. But what the talker says on the telephone to the victim is that he is an executive with a leading bank, or a business executive; that the cash and securities in the portfolio were destined for the P.L.O. terrorists or for Iran, in violation of humanitarian principles or legal embargo, as the case may be; that in the circumstances the owner of the valuables will never claim them, so that they may be regarded as found money; and that the total value is beyond the dreams of avarice (usually stated in the millions). The talker proposes a three-way split (victim, street player, and himself), and assures the victim that he will attend to any tax complications, in consultation with a high I.R.S. official of his acquaintance.

In the case at bar, the "talkers" pretending to be bankers or executives used the names "Mr. Goldberg" or "Mr. Goldstein." The equally fictitious I.R.S. official was "Mr. Carmichael." If the victim remains on the hook, she is next persuaded to take out a bank safe deposit box, and then rent two adjoining rooms in a motel. In one of those rooms she meets with the street player, who produces large quantities of cash (apparently quite genuine) which is "counted down" to the victim, placed in felt money bags, and then purportedly lodged, with the "assistance" of the street player, in the victim's safe deposit box.

The amount of cash counted down to the victim always corresponded to the amount the victim had in her own independent bank or securities accounts: information the con game players obtained from the victim early on. It is those assets, of course, which were the objectives of the game. The function of the cash count down, said to represent an initial distribution of the victim's share of the "found" valuables, was to make the victim feel secure about entering into the final stage of the game. That sense of security was false. The "counted down" cash (which represented, in effect, the con game players' working capital) was always switched out of the bank bags, and cut-up paper substituted for it. The victims had been

wealthy elderly women that they had "found" cash earmarked for Iran or the PLO, and then convincing the women to withdraw their *own* money from banks in an amount equivalent to their "share" of the found cash, convert that money into foreign currency, and give the foreign currency to the appellants for high-return foreign investment. The victims, of course, never saw either their share of the found money or their own money again. The six victims, who were defrauded of a total of $1,197,000, were: Gloria Rosenfeld, April, 1985; Josephine Palumbo, July, 1985; Simone Putnam, August, 1985; Peggy St. Lewis, September, 1985; Sylvia Roberts, September, 1985; and Hadassah Feit, October, 1985.

The jury found all appellants guilty on one count of conspiracy to commit wire fraud, and two counts of substantive wire fraud in connection with the fraud on Peggy St. Lewis, which involved two wire transfers of money by the victim from Florida to New York. ...

* * *

Please figure out Mr. Blackmon's guidelines exposure **based ONLY upon the two counts of wire fraud discussed in the opinion** using the following worksheet (NB: you will be asked to compute Mr. Blackmon's exposure for the conspiracy count and for the entire indictment in connection with the conspiracy class later in the semester). For purposes of this exercise:

1. Mr. Blackmon was convicted of two counts of wire fraud in connection with two wire transfers of money by Ms. St. Lewis. Assume that each wire transfer involved $100,000. (HINT: note for purposes of U.S.S.G. § 1B1.3 that the opinion states that the total loss from this *single course of fraudulent conduct* is $1,197,000).

2. Assume that Mr. Blackmon worked this scheme with four other persons.

3. Assume that Mr. Blackmon has no criminal history.

4. Note that Mr. Blackmon did not plead guilty but rather exercised his constitutional right to a jury trial.

---

instructed by "Mr. Goldberg" or "Mr. Goldstein" not to spend any of the money supposedly in the safe deposit box for several months.

All this is preamble. The game succeeds when the victim is then persuaded to take money or securities out of her own account, convert them into foreign currency, and give the foreign currency to the street player (purportedly Mr. Goldberg's employee) for delivery to Mr. Goldberg. The pretexts given to the victims for this transfer of her assets varied. Typically, "Mr. Goldberg" told the victim that, as an experienced banker or international businessman, he could produce a much higher rate of return on the victim's investments.

Chapter 8

PUBLIC CORRUPTION

A wealth of statutes proscribe bribery of federal officials and bribery in specific settings that implicate federal interests[1] but the most important statute expressly criminalizing federal public corruption is 18 U.S.C. § 201. Section 201 has two principal subparts: (1) § 201(b) criminalizes bribery, which is punishable by up to 15 years' imprisonment, a fine of up to three times the monetary equivalent of the bribe, and disqualification from any federal office; and (2) § 201(c) prohibits the payment and receipt of official gratuities, which is punishable by up to two years' imprisonment and a fine. The principal difference is said to be that bribery requires proof of a *quid pro quo*—that is, a specific intent to give or receive something of value in return for being influenced in an official act—and a gratuity offense does not. The distinction between these crimes is explored in *United States v. Sun-Diamond Growers of California*,[2] *infra*, which also outlines the "intricate web of regulations, both administrative and criminal, governing the acceptance of gifts and other self-enriching actions by [federal] public officials."[3]

"In contrast to the array of weapons available to combat corruption within the federal government, at first glance the cupboard seems virtually bare when one seeks federal laws explicitly aimed at state and local corruption."[4] Section 201 is primarily targeted at the venality of *federal* officials and has no counterpart in the federal code that specifically outlaws the provision or receipt of bribes or gratuities by state and local public officials. However, as was examined in the mail and wire fraud materials, sections 1341, 1343, and 1346 have often been pressed into service to meet this perceived gap. The Racketeering Influenced and Corrupt Organizations Act (RICO), 18 U.S.C. § 1962, which is examined *infra* in Chapter 11, is employed in all types of public corruption prosecutions. This chapter will introduce other means by which local corruption has been attacked by the federal government. The Hobbs Act, 18 U.S.C. § 1951, which outlaws as "extortion" officials' receipt of bribes "under color of official right," is often used. Bribery of local actors who receive federal funds may also be pursued under § 201 when the actors can be said to "occup[y] a position of public trust with official federal responsibilities,"[5] or under 18 U.S.C. § 666. Section 666, which outlaws theft, fraud, or bribery concerning programs receiving federal funds, was originally deemed a

---

[1] *See, e.g.*, 18 U.S.C. §§ 152 (bribery in bankruptcy proceedings), 212-13 (offer of loan or gratuity to bank examiner); 214-15 (bank bribery); 1510 (bribery of investigators).

[2] 526 U.S. 398 (1999).

[3] *Id.* at 409.

[4] Sara Sun Beale, *Comparing the Scope of the Federal Government's Authority to Prosecute Federal Corruption and State and Local Corruption: Some Surprising Conclusions and a Proposal*, 51 Hastings L.J. 699, 704-05 (2000).

[5] Dixson v. United States, 465 U.S. 482, 504 (1984).

"stealth" statute because it received little critical attention,[6] but it has come on like gangbusters and now appears to be a prosecutorial favorite.

The net result of expansive judicial interpretations, particularly in the mail/wire fraud, Hobbs Act, and § 666 federal program bribery context, "is that federal prosecutors have as broad or broader authority to prosecute state and local officials as they have to prosecute federal officials under the intricate web of statutes"[7] discussed in *Sun-Diamond*.[8] Readers may wish to consider whether the availability of these disparate avenues for redressing local corruption provide a coherent approach, and whether state and local actors are in fact subjected to different standards than are their federal counterparts.

The majority of this chapter obviously concerns domestic corruption—that is, the corruption of officials in the federal, state, or local governments in the United States. At the conclusion of this chapter, we will turn briefly to consider the laws applicable to transborder bribery. This section focuses on the U.S. legislation that outlaws certain payments to foreign officials in order to obtain business—the Foreign Corrupt Practices Act (FCPA), 15 U.S.C. §§ 78dd-1 *et seq.*

A. FEDERAL BRIBERY AND GRATUITIES UNDER § 201

UNITED STATES v. SUN-DIAMOND GROWERS OF CALIFORNIA
526 U.S. 398 (1999)

JUSTICE SCALIA delivered the opinion of the Court.

Talmudic sages believed that judges who accepted bribes would be punished by eventually losing all knowledge of the divine law. The Federal Government, dealing with many public officials who are not judges, and with at least some judges for whom this sanction holds no terror, has constructed a framework of human laws and regulations defining various sorts of impermissible gifts, and punishing those who give or receive them with administrative sanctions, fines, and incarceration. One element of that framework is 18 U.S.C. § 201(c)(1)(A), the "illegal gratuity statute," which prohibits giving "anything of value" to a present, past, or future public official "for or because of any official act performed or to be performed by such public official." In this case, we consider whether conviction under the illegal gratuity statute requires any showing beyond the fact that a gratuity was given because of the recipient's official position.

Respondent is a trade association that engaged in marketing and lobbying activities on behalf of its member cooperatives, which were owned by approximately 5,000 individual growers of raisins, figs, walnuts, prunes, and hazelnuts. Petitioner United States is represented by Independent Counsel Donald Smaltz, who, as a consequence of his investigation of former Secretary of Agriculture Michael Espy, charged respondent with, *inter alia*, making illegal gifts to Espy in violation of § 201(c)(1)(A). ...

Count One of the indictment charged Sun-Diamond with giving Espy approximately $5,900 in illegal gratuities: tickets to the 1993 U.S. Open Tennis Tournament (worth $2,295), luggage ($2,427), meals ($665), and a framed print and crystal bowl ($524). The indictment

---

[6] George D. Brown, *Stealth Statute: Corruption, the Spending Power, and the Rise of 18 U.S.C. § 666*, 73 Notre Dame L. Rev. 247 (1998).

[7] Beale, *supra* note 4, at 705.

[8] These same statutory weapons—the mail and wire fraud prohibitions, the Hobbs Act, and § 666—may in some circumstances be employed to fight federal public corruption but are less central because of the availability of § 201 in the usual case. Other statutes may also apply in appropriate cases to combat public corruption, notably the Travel Act, 18 U.S.C. § 1951, which *inter alia* allows the prosecution of persons who travel in interstate commerce or use the mails with intent to promote or carry on the unlawful activities of bribery or extortion and RICO, mentioned above.

alluded to two matters in which respondent had an interest in favorable treatment from the Secretary at the time it bestowed the gratuities. First, respondent's member cooperatives participated in the Market Promotion Plan (MPP), a grant program administered by the Department of Agriculture to promote the sale of U.S. farm commodities in foreign countries. The cooperatives belonged to trade organizations, such as the California Prune Board and the Raisin Administrative Committee, which submitted overseas marketing plans for their respective commodities. If their plans were approved by the Secretary of Agriculture, the trade organizations received funds to be used in defraying the foreign marketing expenses of their constituents. Each of respondent's member cooperatives was the largest member of its respective trade organization, and each received significant MPP funding. Respondent was understandably concerned, then, when Congress in 1993 instructed the Secretary to promulgate regulations giving small-sized entities preference in obtaining MPP funds. If the Secretary did not deem respondent's member cooperatives to be small-sized entities, there was a good chance they would no longer receive MPP grants. Thus, respondent had an interest in persuading the Secretary to adopt a regulatory definition of "small-sized entity" that would include its member cooperatives.

Second, respondent had an interest in the Federal Government's regulation of methyl bromide, a low-cost pesticide used by many individual growers in respondent's member cooperatives. In 1992, the Environmental Protection Agency announced plans to promulgate a rule to phase out the use of methyl bromide in the United States. The indictment alleged that respondent sought the Department of Agriculture's assistance in persuading EPA to abandon its proposed rule altogether, or at least to mitigate its impact. In the latter event, respondent wanted the Department to fund research efforts to develop reliable alternatives to methyl bromide.

Although describing these two matters before the Secretary in which respondent had an interest, the indictment did not allege a specific connection between either of them—or between any other action of the Secretary—and the gratuities conferred. The District Court denied respondent's motion to dismiss Count One because of this omission. The court stated:

> "[T]o sustain a charge under the gratuity statute, it is not necessary for the indictment to allege a direct nexus between the value conferred to Secretary Espy by Sun-Diamond and an official act performed or to be performed by Secretary Espy. It is sufficient for the indictment to allege that Sun-Diamond provided things of value to Secretary Espy because of his position."

At trial, the District Court instructed the jury along these same lines. It read § 201(c)(1)(A) to the jury twice (along with the definition of "official act" from § 201(a)(3)), but then placed an expansive gloss on that statutory language, saying, among other things, that "[i]t is sufficient if Sun-Diamond provided Espy with unauthorized compensation simply because he held public office," and that "[t]he government need not prove that the alleged gratuity was linked to a specific or identifiable official act or any act at all." The jury convicted respondent on, *inter alia*, Count One (the only subject of this appeal), and the District Court sentenced respondent on this count to pay a fine of $400,000.

The Court of Appeals reversed the conviction on Count One and remanded for a new trial, stating:

> "Given that the 'for or because of any official act' language in § 201(c)(1)(A) means what it says, the jury instructions invited the jury to convict on materially less evidence than the statute demands—evidence of gifts driven simply by Espy's official position."

In rejecting respondent's attack on the indictment, however, the court stated that the Government need not show that a gratuity was given "for or because of" any particular act or acts: "That an official has an abundance of relevant matters on his plate should not insulate him or his benefactors from the gratuity statute—as long as the jury is required to find the requisite intent to reward past favorable acts or to make future ones more likely."

We granted certiorari.

Initially, it will be helpful to place § 201(c)(1)(A) within the context of the statutory scheme. Subsection (a) of § 201 sets forth definitions applicable to the section—including a definition of "official act," § 201(a)(3). Subsections (b) and (c) then set forth, respectively, two separate crimes—or two pairs of crimes, if one counts the giving and receiving of unlawful gifts as separate crimes—with two different sets of elements and authorized punishments. The first crime, described in § 201(b)(1) as to the giver, and § 201(b)(2) as to the recipient, is bribery, which requires a showing that something of value was corruptly given, offered, or promised to a public official (as to the giver) or corruptly demanded, sought, received, accepted, or agreed to be received or accepted by a public official (as to the recipient) with intent, *inter alia*, "to influence any official act" (giver) or in return for "being influenced in the performance of any official act" (recipient). The second crime, defined in § 201(c)(1)(A) as to the giver, and § 201(c)(1)(B) as to the recipient, is illegal gratuity, which requires a showing that something of value was given, offered, or promised to a public official (as to the giver), or demanded, sought, received, accepted, or agreed to be received or accepted by a public official (as to the recipient), "for or because of any official act performed or to be performed by such public official."

The distinguishing feature of each crime is its intent element. Bribery requires intent "to influence" an official act or "to be influenced" in an official act, while illegal gratuity requires only that the gratuity be given or accepted "for or because of" an official act. In other words, for bribery there must be a *quid pro quo*—a specific intent to give or receive something of value *in exchange* for an official act. An illegal gratuity, on the other hand, may constitute merely a reward for some future act that the public official will take (and may already have determined to take), or for a past act that he has already taken. The punishments prescribed for the two offenses reflect their relative seriousness: Bribery may be punished by up to 15 years' imprisonment, a fine of $250,000 ($500,000 for organizations) or triple the value of the bribe, whichever is greater, and disqualification from holding government office. Violation of the illegal gratuity statute, on the other hand, may be punished by up to two years' imprisonment and a fine of $250,000 ($500,000 for organizations).

The District Court's instructions in this case, in differentiating between a bribe and an illegal gratuity, correctly noted that only a bribe requires proof of a *quid pro quo*. The point in controversy here is that the instructions went on to suggest that § 201(c)(1)(A), unlike the bribery statute, did not require any connection between respondent's intent and a specific official act. It would be satisfied, according to the instructions, merely by a showing that respondent gave Secretary Espy a gratuity because of his official position—perhaps, for example, to build a reservoir of goodwill that might ultimately affect one or more of a multitude of unspecified acts, now and in the future. The United States, represented by the Independent Counsel, and the Solicitor General as *amicus curiae*, contend that this instruction was correct. The Independent Counsel asserts that "section 201(c)(1)(A) reaches any effort to buy favor or generalized goodwill from an official who either has been, is, or may at some unknown, unspecified later time, be *in a position to act* favorably to the giver's interests." The Solicitor General contends that § 201(c)(1)(A) requires only a showing that a "gift was motivated, at least in part, by the recipient's *capacity to exercise governmental power or influence* in the donor's favor" without necessarily showing that it was connected to a particular official act.

In our view, this interpretation does not fit comfortably with the statutory text, which prohibits only gratuities given or received "for or because of *any official act* performed or to be performed" (emphasis added). It seems to us that this means "for or because of some particular official act of whatever identity"—just as the question "Do you like any composer?" normally means "Do you like some particular composer?" It is linguistically possible, of course, for the phrase to mean "for or because of official acts in general, without specification as to which one"—just as the question "Do you like any composer?" could mean "Do you like all composers, no matter what their names or music?" But the former seems to us the more natural meaning, especially given the complex structure of the provision before us here. Why go through the trouble of requiring that the gift be made "for or because of any official act performed or to be performed by such public official," and then defining "official act" (in §

201(a)(3)) to mean "any decision or action on any question, matter, cause, suit, proceeding or controversy, which may at any time be pending, or which may by law be brought before any public official, in such official's official capacity," when, if the Government's interpretation were correct, it would have sufficed to say "for or because of such official's ability to favor the donor in executing the functions of his office"? The insistence upon an "official act," carefully defined, seems pregnant with the requirement that some particular official act be identified and proved.

Besides thinking that this is the more natural meaning of § 201(c)(1)(A), we are inclined to believe it correct because of the peculiar results that the Government's alternative reading would produce. It would criminalize, for example, token gifts to the President based on his official position and not linked to any identifiable act—such as the replica jerseys given by championship sports teams each year during ceremonial White House visits. Similarly, it would criminalize a high school principal's gift of a school baseball cap to the Secretary of Education, by reason of his office, on the occasion of the latter's visit to the school. That these examples are not fanciful is demonstrated by the fact that counsel for the United States maintained at oral argument that a group of farmers would violate § 201(c)(1)(A) by providing a complimentary lunch for the Secretary of Agriculture in conjunction with his speech to the farmers concerning various matters of USDA policy—so long as the Secretary had before him, or had in prospect, matters affecting the farmers. Of course the Secretary of Agriculture *always* has before him or in prospect matters that affect farmers, just as the President always has before him or in prospect matters that affect college and professional sports, and the Secretary of Education matters that affect high schools.

It might be said in reply to this that the more narrow interpretation of the statute can also produce some peculiar results. In fact, in the above-given examples, the gifts could easily be regarded as having been conferred, not only because of the official's position as President or Secretary, but also (and perhaps principally) "for or because of" the official acts of receiving the sports teams at the White House, visiting the high school, and speaking to the farmers about USDA policy, respectively. The answer to this objection is that those actions—while they are assuredly "official acts" in some sense—are not "official acts" within the meaning of the statute, which, as we have noted, defines "official act" to mean "any decision or action on any question, matter, cause, suit, proceeding or controversy, which may at any time be pending, or which may by law be brought before any public official, in such official's official capacity, or in such official's place of trust or profit." 18 U.S.C. § 201(a)(3). Thus, when the violation is linked to a particular "official act," it is possible to eliminate the absurdities *through the definition of that term*. When, however, no particular "official act" need be identified, and the giving of gifts by reason of the recipient's mere tenure in office constitutes a violation, nothing but the Government's discretion prevents the foregoing examples from being prosecuted.

The Government insists that its interpretation is the only one that gives effect to all of the statutory language. Specifically, it claims that the "official position" construction is the only way to give effect to § 201(c)(1)(A)'s forward-looking prohibition on gratuities to persons who have been selected to be public officials but have not yet taken office. Because, it contends, such individuals would not know of specific matters that would come before them, the only way to give this provision effect is to interpret "official act" to mean "official position." But we have no trouble envisioning the application of § 201(c)(1)(A) to a selectee for federal office under the more narrow interpretation.

If, for instance, a large computer company that has planned to merge with another large computer company makes a gift to a person who has been chosen to be Assistant Attorney General for the Antitrust Division of the Department of Justice and who has publicly indicated his approval of the merger, it would be quite possible for a jury to find that the gift was made "for or because of" the person's anticipated decision, once he is in office, not to challenge the merger. The uncertainty of future action seems to us, in principle, no more an impediment to prosecution of a selectee with respect to some future official act than it is to prosecution of an officeholder with respect to some future official act.

Our refusal to read § 201(c)(1)(A) as a prohibition of gifts given by reason of the donee's office is supported by the fact that when Congress has wanted to adopt such a broadly prophylactic criminal prohibition upon gift giving, it has done so in a more precise and more administrable fashion. For example, another provision of Chapter 11 of Title 18, the chapter entitled "Bribery, Graft, and Conflicts of Interest," criminalizes the giving or receiving of any "supplementation" of an Executive official's salary, without regard to the purpose of the payment. See 18 U.S.C. § 209(a). Other provisions of the same chapter make it a crime for a bank employee to give a bank examiner, and for a bank examiner to receive from a bank employee, "any loan or gratuity," again without regard to the purpose for which it is given. See § 212-213. A provision of the Labor Management Relations Act makes it a felony for an employer to give to a union representative, and for a union representative to receive from an employer, anything of value. 29 U.S.C. § 186. With clearly framed and easily administrable provisions such as these on the books imposing gift-giving and gift-receiving prohibitions specifically based upon the holding of office, it seems to us most implausible that Congress intended the language of the gratuity statute—"for or because of any official act performed or to be performed"—to pertain to the office rather than (as the language more naturally suggests) to *particular* official acts.

Finally, a narrow, rather than a sweeping, prohibition is more compatible with the fact that § 201(c)(1)(A) is merely one strand of an intricate web of regulations, both administrative and criminal, governing the acceptance of gifts and other self-enriching actions by public officials. For example, the provisions following § 201 in Chapter 11 of Title 18 make it a crime to give any compensation to a federal employee, or for the employee to receive compensation, in consideration of his representational assistance to anyone involved in a proceeding in which the United States has a direct and substantial interest, § 203; for a federal employee to act as "agent or attorney" for anyone prosecuting a claim against the United States, § 205(a)(1); for a federal employee to act as "agent or attorney" for anyone appearing before virtually any Government tribunal in connection with a matter in which the United States has a direct and substantial interest, § 205(a)(2); for various types of federal employees to engage in various activities after completion of their federal service, § 207; for an Executive employee to participate in any decision or proceeding relating to a matter in which he has a financial interest, § 208; for an employee of the Executive Branch or an independent agency to receive "any contribution to or supplementation of salary ... from any source other than the Government of the United States," § 209; and for a federal employee to accept a gift in connection with the "compromise, adjustment, or cancellation of any farm indebtedness," § 217. A provision of the Internal Revenue Code makes it criminal for a federal employee to accept a gift for the "compromise, adjustment, or settlement of any charge or complaint" for violation of the revenue laws. 26 U.S.C. § 7214(a)(9).

And the criminal statutes are merely the tip of the regulatory iceberg. In 5 U.S.C. § 7353, which announces broadly that no "employee of the executive, legislative, or judicial branch shall solicit or accept anything of value from a person ... whose interests may be substantially affected by the performance or nonperformance of the individual's official duties," § 7353(a)(2), Congress has authorized the promulgation of ethical rules for each branch of the Federal Government, § 7353(b)(1). Pursuant to that provision, each branch of Government regulates its employees' acceptance of gratuities in some fashion. See, *e.g.*, 5 CFR § 2635.202 *et seq.* (1999) (Executive employees); Rule XXXV of the Standing Rules of the Senate, Senate Manual, S. Doc. No. 104-1 (rev. July 18, 1995) (Senators and Senate Employees); Rule XXVI of the Rules of the House of Representatives, 106th Cong. (rev. Jan. 7, 1999) (Representatives and House employees); 1 Research Papers of the National Commission on Judicial Discipline & Removal, Code of Conduct for U.S. Judges, Canon 5(C)(4), pp. 925-927 (1993) (federal judges).

All of the regulations, and some of the statutes, described above contain exceptions for various kinds of gratuities given by various donors for various purposes. Many of those exceptions would be snares for the unwary, given that there are no exceptions to the broad prohibition that the Government claims is imposed by § 201(c)(1). In this regard it is interesting to consider the provisions of 5 CFR § 2635.202 (1999), issued by the Office of Government Ethics (OGE) and binding on all employees of the Executive Branch and independent agencies. The first subsection of that provision, entitled "General prohibitions," makes unlawful approximately (if not precisely) what the Government asserts § 201(c)(1)(B) makes unlawful: acceptance of a gift "[f]rom a prohibited source" (defined to include any person who "[h]as interests that may be substantially affected by performance or nonperformance of the employee's official duties," 5 CFR § 2635.203(d)(4) (1999)) or "[g]iven because of the employee's official position," § 2635.202(a)(2). The second subsection, entitled "Relationship to illegal gratuities statute," then provides:

> "Unless accepted in violation of paragraph (c)(1) of this section [banning acceptance of a gift 'in return for being influenced in the performance of an official act'], a gift accepted under the standards set forth in this subpart *shall not constitute an illegal gratuity otherwise prohibited by 18 U.S.C. § 201(c)(1)(B)*." § 2635.202(b) (emphasis added).

We are unaware of any law empowering OGE to decriminalize acts prohibited by Title 18 of the United States Code. Yet it is clear that many gifts "accepted under the standards set forth in [the relevant] subpart" *will* violate 18 U.S.C. § 201(c)(1)(B) if the interpretation that the Government urges upon us is accepted. The subpart includes, for example—as § 201(c)(1)(B) does not—exceptions for gifts of $20 or less, aggregating no more than $50 from a single source in a calendar year, see 5 CFR § 2635.204(a) (1999), and for certain public-service or achievement awards and honorary degrees, see § 2635.204(d). We are frankly not sure that even our more narrow interpretation of 18 U.S.C. § 201(c)(1)(B) will cause OGE's assurance of nonviolation if the regulation is complied with to be entirely accurate; but the misdirection, if any, will be infinitely less.

More important for present purposes, however, this regulation, and the numerous other regulations and statutes littering this field, demonstrate that this is an area where precisely targeted prohibitions are commonplace, and where more general prohibitions have been qualified by numerous exceptions. Given that reality, a statute in this field that can linguistically be interpreted to be either a meat axe or a scalpel should reasonably be taken to be the latter. Absent a text that clearly requires it, we ought not expand this one piece of the regulatory puzzle so dramatically as to make many other pieces misfits. As discussed earlier, not only does the text here not require that result; its more natural reading forbids it. ...

We hold that, in order to establish a violation of 18 U.S.C. § 201(c)(1)(A), the Government must prove a link between a thing of value conferred upon a public official and a specific "official act" for or because of which it was given. ...

Notes

1. *Elements.* To secure a conviction for bribery under § 201(b)(1), which targets the *briber*, the government must prove that the defendant:

> (1) corruptly
> (2) directly or indirectly, gave, offered, or promised to any "public official" or person who has been selected to be a "public official"
> or offered or promised any "public official" or person who has been selected to be a public official to give "to any other person or entity"
> (3) "anything of value"
> (4) "with intent ... to influence any official act" (under § 201(b)(1)(A))
> or "to induce such public official ... to do or omit to do any act in violation of the lawful duty of such official or person" (under § 201(b)(1)(C)).

"The crime of offering a bribe is completed when a defendant expresses an ability and a desire to pay the bribe." United States v. Rasco, 853 F.2d 501, 505 (7th Cir. 1988); *see also* United States v. Jacob, 431 F.2d 754, 760 (2d Cir. 1970). Section 201(b)(1) requires "only that something of value be offered or promised, not that a bribe actually be paid. The crime is consummated whether or not the offer is accepted by the offeree." United States v.

Hernandez, 731 F.2d 1147, 1149 (5th Cir. 1984). "[I]t need not be shown that the public official to whom the bribe was offered was actually corrupted by the offer. It is not necessary to show that the official accepted the bribe, and the object of the bribe need not even be attainable to support a conviction for offering the bribe under § 201." United States v. Johnson, 621 F.2d 1073, 1076 (10th Cir.1980); *see also Jacob*, 431 F.2d at 759-60. "In fact, so long as the money is offered with corrupt intent, the official does not necessarily even need to be aware of the bribe." *Johnson*, 621 F.2d at 1076.

To secure a § 201(b)(2) conviction of the person *bribed*, the government must prove that:

(1) a "public official" or a person who has been selected to be a "public official"
(2) corruptly
(3) directly or indirectly, demanded, sought, received, accepted, or agreed to receive or accept "personally or for any other person or entity"
(4) "anything of value"
(5) "in return for ... being influenced in the performance of any official act" (under § 201(b)(2)(A))
or "being induced to do or omit to do any act in violation of the official duty of such official or person" (under § 201(b)(2)(C)).

By contrast, to secure a gratuities conviction under § 201(c)(1)(A), which targets the person making the illegal payment, the government must prove that:

(1) the defendant knowingly
(2) directly or indirectly, gave, offered, or promised
(3) "anything of value"
(4) to any "public official," former "public official," or person selected to be a "public official"
(5) "for or because of any official act performed or to be performed by such public official, former public official, or person selected to be a public official."

To convict the person to whom the gratuity was offered under § 201(c)(1)(B), the government must show that:

(1) a "public official," former "public official," or person selected to be a "public official"
(2) knowingly
(3) otherwise than as provided by law for the proper discharge of official duty, directly or indirectly demanded, sought, received, accepted, or agreed to receive
(4) "anything of value"
(5) "personally or for or because of any official act performed or to be performed by such official or person."

2. *"Public official."* Section 201 requires that the bribe or gratuity be offered, requested, or received by a "public official" or a person who has been selected to be a "public official." Section 201(a)(1) defines "public official[s]" to include not only members of Congress and federal government officers or employees, but also "person[s] acting for or on behalf of the United States, or any department, agency or branch of Government thereof ... in any official function, under or by authority of any such department, agency, or branch of Government."

This definition obviously precludes the pursuit of run-of-the-mill commercial bribery cases under § 201. Further, this definition makes clear that the primary objects of the statute are *federal* public officials.

In *Dixson v. United States*, 465 U.S. 482 (1984), however, the Supreme Court held that officers of a private, nonprofit corporation administering and expending federal community development block grants were "public officials" for purposes of the federal bribery statute. In so holding, the Court concluded:

We agree with the Government that section 201(a) has been accurately characterized as a "comprehensive statute applicable to all persons performing activities for or on behalf of the United States," whatever the form of delegation of authority. To determine whether any particular individual falls within this category, the proper inquiry is not simply whether the person had signed a contract with the United States or agreed to serve as the Government's agent, but rather whether the person occupies a position of public trust with official federal responsibilities. Persons who hold such positions are public officials within the meaning of section 201 and liable for prosecution under the federal bribery statute. ...

By finding petitioners to be public officials within the meaning of section 201(a), we do not mean to suggest that the mere presence of some federal assistance brings a local organization and its employees within the jurisdiction of the federal bribery statute or even that all employees of local organizations responsible for administering federal grant programs are public officials within the meaning of section 201(a). To be a public official under section 201(a), an individual must possess some degree of official responsibility for carrying out a federal program or policy. Our opinion today is, therefore, fully consistent with *Krichman v. United States*, 256 U.S. 363 (1921), in which this Court ruled that a baggage porter, although employed by a federally controlled railroad, could not be said to have "acted for or on behalf of the United States" because the porter lacked any duties of an official character. Similarly, individuals who work for block grant recipients and business people who provide recipients with goods and services can not be said to be public officials under section 201(a) unless they assume some duties of an official nature.

Id. at 496-500. Under *Dixson*, then, some state, local, and private actors who assume responsibility for administering federal programs may be prosecuted under § 201. The focus of subsequent cases has been on the degree to which the defendant possessed a "position of public trust with federal responsibilities." *See, e.g.*, United States v. Thomas, 240 F.3d 445 (5th Cir. 2001) (applying § 201 to guard at a private prison facility); United States v. Hang, 75 F.3d 1275 (8th Cir. 1996) (applying § 201 to eligibility technician for city public housing agency); United States v. Velazquez, 847 F.2d 140 (4th Cir. 1988) (applying § 201 to a country deputy sheriff who was responsible for supervising federal inmates).

Dixson resolved a circuit split on this issue. In reaction to this split, and without awaiting the Supreme Court's resolution of it in *Dixson*, Congress enacted 18 U.S.C. § 666, considered *infra*, which became effective while *Dixson* was pending. *See* Salinas v. United States, 522 U.S. 52, 58 (1997). Section 666, which was designed to specifically address bribery in the context of federal program administration, "supplemented § 201 to make clear that federal law prohibits 'significant acts of ... bribery involving Federal monies that are disbursed to private organizations or State and local governments pursuant to a Federal program.'" *Id.* at 1013 (quoting legislative history). If both statutes may be employed in similar circumstances, readers may wish to consider in reviewing the § 666 materials *infra* what advantages and disadvantages these statutes offer to prosecutors and defense counsel.

3. *"Thing of Value."* The bribery and gratuities statutes prohibit the giving of a "thing of value" to a public official. The definition of a "thing of value" is very broad, encompassing anything that has subjective value to the recipient. Thus, things of value include not only cash, securities, jewelry, and favorable financial consideration (*e.g.*, unsecured loans), but also items that, although worthless, were believed by the recipient to have commercial value, *see* United States v. Williams, 705 F.2d 603 (2d Cir.1983) (bogus stock offered in undercover sting was a thing of value), intangible benefits, *see* United States v. Sun-Diamond Growers, 941 F. Supp. 1262, 1269 (D.D.C. 1996) (providing official's girlfriend with plane ticket with which she could travel with the official could constitute thing of value), and future consideration, United States v. Biaggi, 909 F.2d 662, 684-85 (2d Cir. 1990) (promise of job with law firm).

4. *"Official Acts."* The term "official act" has the same definition for purposes of both bribery and gratuities offenses: it "means any decision or action on any question, matter, cause, suit, proceeding or controversy, which may at any time be pending, or which may by

law be brought before any public official, in such official's official capacity, or in such official's place of trust or profit." § 201(a)(3). "Official acts" are not limited to duties set forth in a written job description but may include as well those duties customarily associated with a particular job. United States v. Birdsall, 233 U.S. 223 (1914); United States v. Ring, 706 F.3d 460 (D.C. Cir. 2013); United States v. Jefferson, 674 F.3d 332, 351-58 (4th Cir. 2012); United States v. Parker, 133 F.3d 322 (5th Cir. 1998).

Recall from Chapter 7(D) that the Supreme Court, in *McDonnell v. United States*, -- U.S. --, 136 S.Ct. 2355 (2016), chose to read the statutory definition of an "official act" narrowly for purposes of honest services fraud, § 201 bribery, and Hobbs Act extortion. As the *McDonnell* Court summarized the required elements:

> [A]n "official act" is a decision or action on a "question, matter, cause, suit, proceeding or controversy." The "question, matter, cause, suit, proceeding or controversy" must involve a formal exercise of governmental power that is similar in nature to a lawsuit before a court, a determination before an agency, or a hearing before a committee. It must also be something specific and focused that is "pending" or "may by law be brought" before a public official. To qualify as an "official act," the public official must make a decision or take an action on that "question, matter, cause, suit, proceeding or controversy," or agree to do so. That decision or action may include using his official position to exert pressure on another official to perform an "official act," or to advise another official, knowing or intending that such advice will form the basis for an "official act" by another official. Setting up a meeting, talking to another official, or organizing an event (or agreeing to do so)—without more—does not fit that definition of "official act."

Id. at 2371-72; *see also* Valdes v. United States, 475 F.3d 1319 (D.C. Cir. 2007) (*en banc*); United States v. Muntain, 610 F.2d 964 (D.C. Cir. 1979). Governor McDonnell accepted over $175,000 in gifts and loans from Jonnie Williams in return for setting up meetings and otherwise providing Williams access to government personnel who could give Williams that which he wanted—official research studies on Williams' product. The Supreme Court's opinion indicates that such access can be purchased without legal repercussion as long as the official involved does not lean on the government personnel involved beyond arranging access. Is this the right answer?

5. *Violations of "official duty."* Prosecutors seeking to avoid the restrictive definition of "official acts" may turn to a heretofore little used subsection of the bribery statute: § 201(b)(1)(C). It does not require, in short, that the public official be influenced with respect to an "official act." Rather, it outlaws the corrupt payment of anything of value to a public official in return for that official's "being induced to do or omit to do any act in violation of the official duty of such official or person."

> Bribery offenses involving Part C's "violations of lawful duty" have rarely been prosecuted. This is surprising considering this language seems to be broader than that contained in its "official act" counterpart. In fact, some have argued that Congress specifically included Part C to catch misdeeds that would not fall under Part A's definition of official act. Of those bribery prosecutions that have been brought under Part C, the courts have uniformly interpreted the scope of an official's lawful duties broadly; the duties need not be explicitly set by statute but rather encompass those duties traditionally associated with the job. Additionally, whereas mere violations of indefinite moral or ethical codes do not constitute violations of an official's lawful duty, public officials have been convicted of bribery for failing to comply with governmental ethics codes laying out duties as broad as "[avoid] engag[ing] in criminal conduct" or "uphold the laws of all governments within the United States."

Bridget Vuona, *Remember Me, "Part C"? Honest Services Fraud Schemes Involving Bribery Under "Part C" of the Federal Bribery Statute Post-McDonnell*, 55 Am. Crim. L. Rev. Online 35, 40-41 (2018). In short, defendants who cannot be said to have been influenced in an "official act" may well be found guilty of having been bribed to violate their "official duty." *See, e.g., Valdes*, 475 F.3d at 1330 (Kavanaugh, J., concurring). Note, however, that this subsection is only available for bribery, not gratuity, prosecutions. *See* § 201(c)(1)(A) & (B).

§ 201(b)(1)(C), of course, applies for the most part to federal officials (*see supra* note 2). But the *McDonnell* Court used § 201's "official act" definition to define "bribery" for purposes of both honest services fraud and Hobbs Act extortion cases. Can prosecutors argue that because § 201(b)(1)(C) makes culpable bribes meant to induce public officials to violate their official duties, honest services fraud and Hobbs Act extortion cases ought to extend to such cases as well? *See* Vuona, *supra*, at 41-43.

6. *Bribery v. Gratuities*. Although the gratuities and bribery prohibitions share many elements, we know that they also differ in important respects, one of which has already been noted in Note 5, above. Four additional differences are notable. First, a bribery conviction carries much greater sentencing exposure than a gratuities violation. Second, "[u]nlike most of § 201's anti-bribery provisions, the anti-gratuity provision has no requirement that the payment actually 'influence[] ... the performance' of an official act. *Compare, e.g.*, 18 U.S.C. § 201(b)(2)(A)." *Valdes*, 475 F.3d at 1322. Third, the bribery statute contemplates that the thing of value may be given to the public official *or* to "any other person or entity" with the intent to influence an official act. *Cf.* United States v. Gomez, 807 F.2d 1523, 1527 (10th Cir. 1986) (where bribe was paid by check made out to a third party at defendant's own request and instructions so that in the event of discovery the money could not be linked to him, § 201(b) was satisfied). The gratuities provision does not contain similar language and thus seems to require that the gratuity be made "directly or indirectly" to the public official. Might this mean that a campaign contribution, for example, that is given to a re-election committee cannot be an actionable "gratuity"—regardless of the intent behind the contribution—because it was not personally accepted by the candidate?

Finally, perhaps the more critical distinctions between bribery and gratuities offenses concern (A) the degree of the nexus that must be shown to exist between the thing of value offered and the official act (examined in the notes below); and (B) the applicable *mens rea* element(s) of the two crimes (discussed in *United States v. Alfisi* (reproduced *infra*) and the notes that follow). *See generally* George D. Brown, *The Gratuities Debate and Campaign Reform: How Strong is the Link?*, 52 Wayne L. Rev. 1371 (2006).

7. *Nexus*. The *Sun-Diamond* Court states that the gratuities statute cannot be read as a "prohibition of gifts given by reason of the donee's office," even those given "to build a reservoir of goodwill that might ultimately affect one or more of a multitude of unspecified acts, now and in the future." Rather, "in order to establish a violation of 18 U.S.C. § 201(c)(1)(A), the Government must prove a link between a thing of value conferred upon a public official and a specific 'official act' for or because of which it was given." What is the difference between this "link" and the "*quid pro quo*" that is necessary for a conviction of the greater offense of bribery? Some argue that the *Sun-Diamond* opinion collapses an essential distinction between bribery and gratuities offenses. *See* George D. Brown, *Putting Watergate Behind Us—*Salinas, Sun-Diamond, *and Two Views of the Anticorruption Model*, 74 Tulane L. Rev. 747, 774 (2000) ("If [the *Sun-Diamond* Court's requirement of a "link" in gratuities cases] sounds like the crime of bribery, that is because it is. The Court has essentially eliminated the separate crime of unlawful gratuity and turned it into a lesser included offense of bribery."). Do you agree?

In *United States v. Schaffer*, 183 F.3d 833, 840 (D.C. Cir. 1999), the D.C. Circuit opined that even after *Sun-Diamond*, "the magnitude of the necessary link, and its proper translation into a concrete rule of decision, remains in doubt." It then tendered the following explanation of the differences between bribery and gratuities:

> The two prohibitions differ in two fundamental respects. First bribery requires a *quid pro quo*, and accordingly can be seen as having a two-way nexus. That is, bribery typically involves an intent to affect the future actions of a public official through giving something of value, and receipt of that thing of value then motivates the official act. A gratuity, by

contrast, requires only a one-way nexus; "the gratuity guideline presumes a situation in which the offender gives the gift without attaching any strings. ..."

The two provisions additionally differ in their temporal focus. Bribery is entirely future-oriented, while gratuities can be either forward or backward looking. In other words, whereas bribery involves the present giving, promise, or demand of something in return for some action in the future, an unlawful gratuity can take one of three forms. First, a gratuity can take the form of a reward for past action—*i.e.*, for a performed official act. Second, a gratuity can be intended to entice a public official who has already staked out a position favorable to the giver to maintain that position. Finally, a gratuity can be given with the intent to induce a public official to propose, take, or shy away from some future official act. This third category would additionally encompass gifts given in the hopes that, when the particular official actions move to the forefront, the public official will listen hard to, and hopefully be swayed by, the giver's proposals, suggestions, and/or concerns.

Id. at 841-42. Is this summary entirely consistent with *Sun-Diamond?* In particular, if a gratuity can take the form of a gift intended to entice a public official to take some future, favorable action, what distinguishes it from a bribe? *See* Charles B. Klein, *What Exactly Is an Unlawful Gratuity After* United States v. Sun-Diamond Growers?, 68 Geo. Wash. L. Rev. 116 (1999). In this author's opinion, the difference between a bribe and a gratuity is simply this: in a bribery prosecution, the government has to show an intent to *influence* the actions of a public official; with a gratuity, the government does not have to prove this element.

One should not confuse the "temporal focus" of the offenses discussed above with the timing of the payments. As the Fourth Circuit explained in *United States v. Jennings*, 160 F.3d 1006, 1014 (4th Cir. 1998):

[T]he timing of the payment in relation to the official act for which it is made is (in theory) irrelevant. Bribes often are paid before the fact, but "it is only logical that in certain situations the bribe will not actually be conveyed until the act is done." *United States v. Campbell*, 684 F.2d 141, 148 (D.C.Cir.1982). By this same logic, illegal gratuities, which typically follow the act for which they are paid, may be conveyed before the occurrence of the act (so long as the payor believes the official has already committed himself to the action). This can cause the distinction between bribes and illegal gratuities, which is clear in theory, to look somewhat hazy in real life.

Id. at 1014; *see also* United States v. Griffin, 154 F.3d 762, 764 (8th Cir. 1998).

8. *Stream of benefits.* In *United States v. Jennings*, 160 F.3d 1006, 1014 (4th Cir.1998), the court explained that:

... [T]he government need not show that the defendant intended for his payments to be tied to specific official acts (or omissions). Bribery requires the intent to effect an exchange of money (or gifts) for specific official action (or inaction), but each payment need not be correlated with a specific official act. Rather, it is sufficient to show that the payor intended for each payment to induce the official to adopt a specific course of action. In other words, the intended exchange in bribery can be "this for these" or "these for these," not just "this for that." Further, it is not necessary for the government to prove that the payor intended to induce the official to perform a set number of official acts in return for the payments. The quid pro quo requirement is satisfied so long as the evidence shows a "course of conduct of favors and gifts flowing to a public official *in exchange for* a pattern of official actions favorable to the donor." Thus, all that must be shown is that payments were made with the intent of securing a specific *type* of official action or favor in return. For example, payments may be made with the intent to retain the official's services on an "as needed" basis, so that whenever the opportunity presents itself the official will take specific action on the payor's behalf. This sort of "I'll scratch your back if you scratch mine" arrangement constitutes bribery because the payor made payments with the intent to exchange them for specific official action.

Id. at 1013-14. This case was decided before *Sun-Diamond* but the "stream-of-benefits" theory of *quid pro quo* approved in *Jennings* has, post-*Sun-Diamond*, been approved by other courts as well. *See, e.g.*, United States v. Jefferson, 674 F.3d 332 (4th Cir. 2012); United States v. Bryant, 655 F.3d 232, 245 (3d Cir. 2011); United States v. Whitfield, 590 F.3d 325, 337-354 (5th Cir. 2009); United States v. Gamin, 510 F.3d 134, 145 (2d Cir. 2007); United States v. Quinn, 359 F.3d 666, 673 (4th Cir. 2004). In short, these courts accept that idea that the *quid pro quo* requirement is satisfied where the defendant agrees to accept things of value in exchange for performing official acts on an "as-needed" basis, so that whenever "the opportunity presents itself, he would take specific action on the payor's behalf." *Jefferson*, 674 F.3d at 358. This "stream of benefits" theory is often used by prosecutors in public corruption cases. Can this theory be squared with *Sun-Diamond*? Does it survive the *McDonnell* ruling?

In 2015, Senator Robert Menendez was charged with, inter alia, bribery and honest services fraud. Prosecutors alleged that Menendez accepted lavish vacations, gifts, and campaign donations from Dr. Salomen Melgen, a wealthy Florida eye doctor, in exchange for using his office to benefit Melgen's personal and business interests. Menendez's lawyers argued that the gifts and vacations given to the senator were not the products of a corrupt bargain with Melgen, but rather stemmed from a decades-old friendship. Prosecutors relied on the "stream of benefits" theory. *McDonnell* was announced after the trial had started. The defense moved for a judgment of acquittal on the theory that the "stream of benefits" theory cannot be squared with *McDonnell* (or *Sun-Diamond*). The judge appeared to be sympathetic but ultimately rejected the defense argument that *McDonnell* requires that the official act that is the object of the *quid pro quo* must be specific and focused and identified at the time the agreement is made. *See* United States v. Menendez, 291 F.Supp.3d 606, 613-17 (D.N.J. 2018). In response to the defendant's reliance on *Sun-Diamond*'s requirement that the government show "a link between a thing of value conferred upon a public official and a specific 'official act' for or because of which it was given," 526 U.S. at 414, the court ruled that this language related only to the gratuities subsection of § 201, not the bribery subsection. *Id.*; *see also Ganim*, 410 F.3d at 146-47. Is this a fair reading of the relevant reasoning in *Sun-Diamond*?

After a lengthy trial, the Menendez jury was deadlocked and a mistrial declared. In response to a motion for a judgment of acquittal under Fed. R. Crim. P. 29, the Judge acquitted Menendez and Melgen of seven of the 18 charges; a week later, the government decided it would not retry the defendants and so dismissed the indictment.

9. *Rationale for Gratuities Prohibition?* Presumably, when the government has difficulty proving an express *quid pro quo*, it may charge a gratuities violation. What other rationale may there be for outlawing gratuities? As one court has explained, "[e]ven if corruption is not intended by either the donor or the donee, there is still a tendency in such a situation to provide conscious or unconscious preferential treatment of the donor by the donee, or the inefficient management of public affairs." United States v. Evans, 572 F.2d 455, 480 (5th Cir. 1978). Is this not also true of campaign contributions? Presumably, many contributors make campaign contributions intending to "entice a public official who has already staked out a position favorable to the giver to maintain that position" or "to induce a public official to propose, take, or shy away from some future official act." Do such contributions constitute illegal gratuities or, where the intent is fairly overt and reciprocal, bribery? *See* Daniel H. Lowenstein, *Political Bribery and the Intermediate Theory of Politics*, 32 UCLA L. Rev. 784 (1985); Lydia Segal, *Can We Fight the New Tammany Hall? Difficulties of Prosecuting Political Patronage and Suggestions for Reform*, 50 Rutgers L. Rev. 507 (1998); Joseph R. Weeks, *Bribes, Gratuities, and the Congress: The Institutionalized Corruption of the Political Process, The Impotence of Criminal Law to Reach It, and a Proposal for Change*, 13 J. Leg. 123 (1986).

10. *Political Theory.* What is the danger in permitting interested constituents to lavish public actors with gifts for the purpose of establishing a reserve of official good will? Does one's view of this practice depend on what theory of political representation, and model of political corruption, one adopts? Professor Daniel H. Lowenstein has examined bribery law in light of

three theories of political representation: the "trusteeship," "mandate," and "pluralism" theories. *See* Daniel H. Lowenstein, *Political Bribery and the Intermediate Theory of Politics*, 32 UCLA L. Rev. 784 (1985). The "trusteeship" theory, as its name implies, is founded on the idea that "it is the representative's function to ignore all considerations except those that truly are relevant to the public interest." *Id.* at 833. It is assumed that the public interest is objectively discernable, and that it exists independent of public opinion, the allocation of political power, or the perceived needs of special interest groups. *Id.* at 833. Under this model, the only appropriate influence on a public official's exercise of power is the provision of information; other political or special interest pressures would be deemed to interfere with the representative's proper functioning. *Id.*

Under the "mandate" theory, by contrast, the representative is supposed to "do what his constituents want, and be bound by mandates or instructions from them." Hanna Pitkin, The Concept of Representation 145 (1967). Only those outside influences or pressures that reflect the popular preference aid effective representation under this theory. Finally, under the "pluralist" ideology, "government officials are essentially nullities. Their sole function is to register the opposing strengths of the competing interest groups and to record the result in the form of government policy." Lowenstein, *supra*, at 838. Under this theory, the pressures and influence exerted by constituents and interest groups are not only acceptable, they are necessary to effective governance.

The above sketch is obviously highly simplified (interested readers are encouraged to read the entirety of Professor Lowenstein's article). It may, however, provide readers with some basis for thinking about how one's view of what the law *should* be may differ depending on which theory one adopts. Under which theory will bribery and gratuity prohibitions be broadly interpreted and applied? Under which theory might one argue that we should assume that special interest groups "will attempt to influence government officials, and [that] these attempts can be a valuable part of the system"? *See* George D. Brown, *Putting Watergate Behind Us*—Salinas, Sun-Diamond, *and Two Views of the Anticorruption Model*, 74 Tulane L. Rev. 747, 763 (2000) (outlining "counterrevolutionary critique" of post-Watergate "hard line" corruption model). What view, if any, could be said to be reflected in *Sun-Diamond*?

10. *Practical Concerns.* In assessing what the law of bribery and particularly gratuities *should* be, one might also wish to consider the practical as well as the theoretical implications of those prohibitions. Could one argue that even if one believes that gratuities and other ethical violations by public officials below the level of actual bribery are wrong and harmful, that criminalization is not the answer? Some argue that tighter ethics regulation is not necessarily better regulation in that it has a "devastating effect on public employees," may make "public service so encumbered with layers of rules as to harm recruitment," "leads to an emphasis on compliance for its own sake," and may even be counterproductive in that, far from enhancing public trust, the "scandal machine" fueled by criminalization of ethical lapses actually undermines confidence in public actors. *See* George D. Brown, *Putting Watergate Behind Us*—Salinas, Sun-Diamond, *and Two Views of the Anticorruption Model*, 74 Tulane L. Rev. 747, 756-57 (2000).

UNITED STATES v. ALFISI
308 F.3d 144 (2d Cir. 2002)

WINTER, Circuit Judge.

Mark Alfisi appeals from a conviction by a jury ... on counts of: (i) bribery of a public official in violation of 18 U.S.C. § 201(b)(1)(A); (ii) paying an unlawful gratuity to a public official in violation of 18 U.S.C. § 201(c)(1)(A); and (iii) engaging in a conspiracy to commit bribery in violation of 18 U.S.C. § 371. ...

[The scheme alleged concerned payoffs to USDA inspectors responsible for inspecting produce at the Hunt's Point Market Terminal Market. Commercial brokers act as agents of the growers and sell produce to wholesalers at the market. The contracts between the brokers and the wholesalers set the price and the expected quality of the produce. If, upon delivery, the wholesaler claims that the produce does not meet the contractual standard, the parties may call for an USDA inspector to verify the quality and condition of the produce. An investigation revealed that USDA inspectors routinely accepted money from wholesalers falsely to downgrade their assessment of the grade level of the produce lot, thus allowing the wholesalers to renegotiate the price of the lot downward. One inspector, William Cashin, was arrested and agreed to cooperate with government investigators. Afisi, who worked for a wholesaler, agreed to pay Cashin $50 in cash per inspection. Cashin testified in that in exchange for the payments, he would falsely downgrade his inspection report except where the produce was already "legitimately bad."]

[At his trial,] Alfisi did not testify but did present evidence in support of his defense that he did not make the payoffs to obtain false inspection results. Rather, he argued that Cashin and other USDA officials at the market were operating an extortion scheme and that Alfisi was coerced into paying Cashin solely to ensure that Cashin would do his job properly. In that regard, Alfisi offered evidence from three produce brokers that some of Cashin's inspections yielded accurate grade levels. Cashin could not specify at trial whether particular certifications that caused specific loads of produce to fail "good delivery" standards had been falsely downgraded or were "legitimately bad."

... [T]he jury convicted Alfisi of seven counts of bribery, six counts of paying unlawful gratuities as a lesser-included offense to bribery, and one count of conspiracy to commit bribery. The district court sentenced Alfisi to a prison term of a year and a day, two years of supervised release, and a fine of $6,000. ...

As we understand Alfisi's argument, he claims first that the instruction given by the district court failed to explain sufficiently the difference between bribery, which requires a *quid pro quo* element, and paying unlawful gratuities, which does not. Second, he argues that the instruction erroneously allowed the jury to convict him for bribery even if the jury found that the payments were a *quid pro quo* exchange for Cashin to perform his job faithfully.

... We are satisfied that the district court's jury instructions, viewed in their entirety, were correct.

We begin by examining the pertinent elements of bribery and paying unlawful gratuities. ... Bribery ... requires that the payor intend "to influence" an official act "corruptly" while the payment of an unlawful gratuity requires only that the payment be "for or because of" an official act.

The "corrupt" intent necessary to a bribery conviction is in the nature of a *quid pro quo* requirement; that is, there must be "a specific intent to give ... something of value *in exchange* for an official act." [*United States v. Sun-Diamond Growers of California*, 526 U.S. 398, 404-05 (1999)]. Putting it only slightly differently, bribery involves the giving of value to procure a specific official action from a public official. The element of a *quid pro quo* or a direct exchange is absent from the offense of paying an unlawful gratuity. ...

Turning to the instructions in the present case, ... [in] defining "corruptly," the district court stated that the term entailed a "specific intent to influence Inspector Cashin's official acts of performing inspections and certifying the condition and grade of fruits and vegetables." The payment of an unlawful gratuity was described as the giving of money "for or because of official acts performed or to be performed by William Cashin." More specifically, the district court told the jury that to prove the payment of an unlawful gratuity, the government must show a link between the payment and some official act, but not corrupt intent as earlier defined. ...

The jury evidently found the instructions somewhat ambiguous with regard to the difference between bribery and paying unlawful gratuities and asked the court for clarification. In response, the court described bribery as the giving of money to a public official "for or because of an official act [and] with a corrupt intention specifically to influence the outcome of the official act." This instruction clearly set out the *quid pro quo* requirement, and, accordingly, any ambiguity in the original jury instructions was cured. The events here suggest that it might be well to add similar language in the future for such jury instructions.

Alfisi also argues that he should not be found guilty of bribery if he paid money to Cashin solely to induce him to perform his job faithfully. Put another way, Alfisi contends that the term "corruptly" requires evidence of an intent to procure a violation of the public official's duty. For this reason, he contends, it was not "corrupt" for him to give Cashin money to ensure that Cashin inspect and report accurately on the produce because that was Cashin's legal duty. We are not persuaded.[9]

First, Alfisi's suggested reading of the bribery statute does not rest comfortably within the statutory language. Subsection (b)(1)(A), the basis for Alfisi's bribery convictions, outlaws payments made with a corrupt intent—to procure a *quid pro quo* agreement—"to influence any official act."[10] It cannot be seriously argued that Alfisi's payments did not fall within that broad language, even if he was paying Cashin solely to make accurate inspections.[11]

Second, there is no lack of sound legislative purpose in defining bribery to include payments in exchange for an act to which the payor is legally entitled. On the one hand, there is of course a danger of overinclusion in a broad definition, in particular the risk here that marginally culpable conduct by those facing insistent extortionists will be criminalized. That danger is eliminated or at least minimalized, however, by the existence of the economic coercion defense, which the jury rejected in the present case.

On the other hand, a danger of underinclusion inheres in the narrow definition suggested by Alfisi. This is particularly so in cases where the official duties require the exercise of some

---

[9] [Court's footnote 1:] The dissent argues that the statute's use of "corruptly" precludes a conviction for bribery if the defendant paid a public official only for the performance of a legal duty. In that regard, it relies upon *United States v. Barash*, 365 F.2d 395 (2d Cir. 1966) ("*Barash I*"), which stated that, "if a government officer threatens serious economic loss unless paid for giving a citizen his due, the latter is entitled to have the jury consider this ... as bearing on the specific intent required for the commission of bribery." However, *Barash I* does not state that the existence of economic coercion negates a "corrupt" intent. Instead, it recognizes more generally that economic coercion is relevant to the culpability of the intent of a defendant charged with bribery. *Barash I* does not limit the kinds of *quid pro quo* exchanges that qualify as bribery.

Moreover, our ruling in the present matter is based on precedent subsequent to *Barash I*. In *United States v. Kahn*, 472 F.2d 272 (2d Cir.1973), we upheld a jury charge that treated the issue of economic coercion separately from the object of bribery, i.e., what is sought by the payor. The district court's instructions in this case closely match those addressed in *Kahn*, where the jury was told that bribery required the intent to influence a "public officer with respect to *any official act*." *Id.* (emphasis in original). We simply adhere to that precedent. As a policy matter, the dissent's position ignores *Kahn*'s concern that "[t]he proper response to coercion by corrupt public officials should be to go to the authorities, not to make the payoff."

Finally, we emphasize that Alfisi requested and received instructions to the jury regarding an economic coercion defense. However, he failed to convince the jury. Thereafter, he was convicted of bribery for his *quid pro quo* arrangement with Cashin. This outcome is entirely consistent with our holding in *United States v. Barash*, 412 F.2d 26 (2d Cir. 1969) ("*Barash II*"), a case addressing an appeal from the second trial mandated by *Barash I*. *Barash II* makes it clear that economic coercion is not an issue derived from the term "corruptly" in the statute but is instead a defense for which separate instructions are to be given. Once the defense of economic coercion has been rejected, a defendant may properly be convicted for paying bribes to a public official for any kind of a quid pro quo exchange.

[10] [Court's footnote 2:] The dissent argues that defining "corruptly" to include the intent to engage in a *quid pro quo* exchange renders the term surplusage because the *quid pro quo* element is established in the statutory language "with intent ... to influence any official act. ..." 18 U.S.C. § 201(b)(1)(A). However, that language, standing alone, can just as easily describe the motivation for paying an unlawful gratuity, e.g., with the hope of buying general goodwill that "influences" an official's future act. Therefore, far from being a surplusage, the term "corruptly" distinguishes between the nature of the influence sought by a person who commits bribery and another who pays an unlawful gratuity. We believe this view sustained by the comparison of bribery and unlawful gratuity in *Sun-Diamond*, 526 U.S. at 404-05.

[11] [Court's footnote 3:] Section (b)(1)(C) outlaws payments with the same corrupt intent "to induce [a] public official ... to do or omit to do any act in violation of the lawful duty of such official or person." Subsections (A) and (C) undoubtedly overlap in some considerable measure, although resort to (A) seems most appropriate in the case of bribes regarding decisions involving the exercise of judgment or discretion, such as judicial decisions or produce inspections, while use of (C) would be most appropriate in the case of bribes to induce actions that directly violate a specific duty, such as a prison guard's duty to prevent the smuggling of contraband.

judgment or discretion. In such cases, if the government must prove beyond a reasonable doubt actual or intended violations of official duties, many highly culpable payments would go underpunished as unlawful gratuities, or unpunished altogether.[12]

For example, if a party to litigation were to pay a judge money in exchange for a favorable decision, that conduct would—and should—constitute bribery, even if a trier of fact might conclude *ex post* that the judgment was on the merits legally proper. This principle was at stake and upheld in a decision arising from the most lamentable episode in this court's history. *See United States v. Manton,* 107 F.2d 834, 845-46 (2d Cir.1939) (rejecting Chief Circuit Judge's defense that payments in exchange for particular decisions were not obstruction of justice where decisions rendered were legally correct). In such a case, the key element of the offense is the intent of the payor to purchase a particular decision "without regard to the merits," as opposed to an impartial judgment.[13] The legal merits, or lack thereof, of the judgment rendered is not an element of the offense. ...

SACK, Circuit Judge, dissenting:

Because I think that the district court's jury instruction regarding the "corruptly" element of the bribery statute was incorrect ... I respectfully dissent.

The first question challenging the Court is whether, as the majority holds, a defendant acts "corruptly" so as to violate the bribery statute if he intends his payment to influence a public official in *any* manner, or, as I think, only if he intends the public official to do what the official should not do, or to refrain from doing what he should. I thus do not disagree with the majority that a bribe payer is looking for a *quid pro quo*; unlike the majority, however, I think that the nature of the *quid pro quo* the payer is looking for matters. The "corruptly" element indicates that the bribe payer seeks not any manner of benefit, but seeks, rather, to corrupt. ...

Bribery under 18 U.S.C. § 201(b)(1)(A) requires the jury to find that the defendant "directly or indirectly, *corruptly* g[a]ve[], offer[ed] or promised [some]thing of value to [a] public official ... with intent ... to influence any official act performed or to be performed." *Id.* (emphasis added). ... Alfisi contended in the district court that because he paid Cashin to do his job properly, the payment was not made "corruptly"; a person acts "corruptly" only if he intends to cause an official to breach a public duty. Thus, Alfisi argued, if an official threatens to abuse his position in a way that will harm an individual, and that individual then makes a payment to avoid the abuse, the individual does not act "corruptly" because his intent is not to corrupt, but only to avoid the effects of corruption. Accordingly, Alfisi requested an instruction providing that "to act 'corruptly' is to act with the specific intent to secure an unlawful advantage or benefit."

Alfisi's requested instruction accurately reflects the law as I understand it. The mere presence of lawlessness or corruption in the circumstances of a payment to an official is not enough to make it "corrupt" and therefore a bribe. Rather, an unlawful or corrupt result must be that which the payer specifically seeks to achieve.

Bribery is a crime of specific intent. *United States v. Barash,* 365 F.2d 395, 402 (2d Cir.1966). A person therefore does not commit bribery unless he intends to bring about "the

---

[12] [Court's footnote 4:] We do not agree that *Sun-Diamond* requires us to define the crime of bribery narrowly. The dissent selectively quotes from text spanning multiple paragraphs on four pages of that opinion and omits important distinguishing details. As we understand *Sun-Diamond,* the offense of paying unlawful gratuity should not be broadly construed because there are other laws and regulations *specifically dealing with the problem of public officials receiving unlawful gratuities. Sun-Diamond,* however, says nothing about bribery, especially with regard to how the term "corruptly" should be interpreted.

[13] [Court's footnote 5:] The dissent's response to our analysis here supports our conclusion. The dissent states that paying a judge for a favorable, albeit legally proper, decision would nonetheless constitute bribery because the judge would be deciding the case based on the identities of the parties rather than the merits of the case. However, precisely the same description applies to Alfisi's payments to Cashin. Even if Alfisi merely paid Cashin to perform a proper and honest inspection, Cashin would nonetheless be improperly carrying out his function according to the identities of the parties.

evil sought to be prevented" by the bribery statute, *United States v. Jacobs*, 431 F.2d 754, 759 (2d Cir.1970). The evil of bribery that the criminal law seeks to prevent, we have said, is

> the aftermath suffered by the public when an official is corrupted and thereby perfidiously *fails to perform his public service and duty.* Thus the purpose of the statute is to discourage one from seeking an advantage by attempting to influence an official to depart from conduct deemed essential to the public interest.

Id. (emphasis added). *Jacobs* thus stands for the proposition that a bribe payer seeks advantage or benefit by attempting to influence an official to breach a public duty. We have repeatedly reaffirmed this principle. "As is evident in many of our cases dealing with bribery, a fundamental concept of a 'corrupt' act is a breach of some official duty owed to the government or the public at large."

Our cases thus provide that a payment made in the course of a shakedown where the public official demands payment as a *quid pro quo* for proper execution of his duty is *not* a bribe. A person who makes a payment pursuant to such extortion intends not to cultivate corruption, but only to avoid the tendrils of a corruption already sprouted. Such a person does not act "corruptly" within the meaning of the statute because he does not seek the lawlessness that the bribery statute aims to prevent.

We recognized this principle in *Barash*, a case in which we dismissed an argument that economic coercion is merely an affirmative defense to the bribery statute:

> We think that if a government officer threatens serious economic loss unless paid for giving a citizen his due, the latter is entitled to have the jury consider this, not as a complete defense like duress but as bearing on the specific intent required for the commission of bribery.

Barash, 365 F.2d at 401-02. If a person could violate the bribery statute even if he hoped only to influence a public official to give him "his due," then the fact that the person was under pressure to pay for "his due" would not bear on the question of specific intent. But *Barash* holds the opposite, and thus supports Alfisi's position. To act corruptly and therefore to commit bribery, a person must do more than merely seek to secure some benefit or *quid pro quo.* Rather, the benefit sought must entail a breach of duty or trust. I therefore conclude that the jury instruction that Alfisi requested was correct as a matter of law.

The jury instructions submitted by the district court, on the other hand, not only seem to me to be at odds with our caselaw, they also appear to me to violate principles of statutory construction. The district court's instructions defined "corruptly" as "*specific intent to influence ... official acts. ...*" (emphasis added). Inserting this definition of "corruptly" into the terms of the bribery statute, the district court effectively instructed the jury that Alfisi committed bribery if he "directly or indirectly, *with specific intent to influence official acts* [the court's definition of "corruptly"], [gave], offer[ed] or promise[d] [some]thing of value to [a] public official *with intent to influence any official act.*" (emphasis added). The district court merely used the statute's other terms to define "corruptly," thus effectively reading "corruptly" out of the statute. I think that this was clearly an error. It is a "well-settled rule of statutory construction that all parts of a statute, if at all possible, are to be given effect." Alfisi's definition of "corruptly," unlike the district court's, gives separate meaning to each of the terms of the statute.[14]

---

[14] [Dissent's footnote 2:] In response to a subsequent query from the jury, the district court gave an instruction defining bribery as the giving of money to a public official "for or because of an official act [and] with a corrupt intention specifically to influence the outcome of the official act." This did little to cure the problem with the first instruction because it continued to beg the question of the meaning of the word "corrupt." If "corrupt" means what the district court said it meant when it first instructed the jury, then, substituting that definition of "corrupt" into this new instruction, bribery consists of paying a public official "for or because of an official act [and] with specific intent to influence ... official acts ... [and the] intention specifically to influence the outcome of the official act." The result is redundant and still gives no separate meaning to the term "corruptly."

I find unpersuasive the majority's attempts to correct the district court's error and its reasons for dismissing Alfisi's interpretation of the statute. As indicated, it seems to me that the district court's definition of "corruptly" rendered that term surplusage. The majority attempts to salvage the district court's instructions by holding that they gave meaning to the term "corruptly" by defining it as connoting a "*quid pro quo*." As noted, I agree that bribery involves the seeking of a *quid pro quo*, that is, an advantage in exchange for a payment. But attributing the *quid pro quo* element to the word "corruptly" does not avoid the surplusage because the words of the statute indicate that the *quid pro quo* element is established not by the term "corruptly," but rather by the other terms, i.e., a payment "with intent ... to influence any official act." That seems to me to be the import of *United States v. Sun-Diamond Growers of Cal.*, 526 U.S. 398 (1999), upon which the majority relies for the proposition that a bribe payer seeks a *quid pro quo*. In comparing a bribe with an illegal gratuity, *Sun-Diamond* does not address the fact that the bribery statute contains the term "corruptly" while the illegal gratuity statute does not; it addresses instead the fact that the bribery statute requires intent "to influence an official act" while the illegal gratuity statute does not. *Sun-Diamond* then holds what plain meaning suggests: The *quid pro quo* element arises not from the term "corruptly," but rather from the term "to influence." ... In holding that the "'corrupt' intent necessary to a bribery conviction is in the nature of a *quid pro quo* requirement," the majority's construction of the statute seems not only at odds with *Sun-Diamond*, but also renders the term "to influence" surplusage by attributing its meaning to the term "corruptly." ...

[A]n argument similar to the majority's "underinclusion" argument was rejected by the Supreme Court in *Sun-Diamond*. There the government sought to define the crime of paying an illegal gratuity broadly to cover gifts not associated with a specific official act. The Supreme Court rejected that argument in part because:

> [A] narrow, rather than a sweeping, prohibition is more compatible with the fact that [the illegal gratuity statute] is merely one strand of an intricate web of regulations, both administrative and criminal, governing the acceptance of gifts and other self-enriching actions by public officials. ... [T]his is an area where precisely targeted prohibitions are commonplace, and where more general prohibitions have been qualified by numerous exceptions. Given that reality, a statute in this field that can linguistically be interpreted to be either a meat axe or a scalpel should reasonably be taken to be the latter.

Id. at 409, 412. The top strand in the "intricate web" is the bribery statute, and so defendants loosed by a narrow construction of it will not fall far without tangling on other provisions. Specifically, individuals who pay public officials to avoid a threatened abuse rather than to engage in abuse will still be guilty of paying an illegal gratuity, a felony.

Finally, the majority argues that "if a party to litigation were to pay a judge money in exchange for a favorable decision, that conduct would—and should—constitute bribery, even if a trier of fact might conclude *ex post* that the judgment was on the merits legally proper." But such a payment would constitute bribery even under Alfisi's construction of the statute because the hypothetical payer specifically intends to influence the judge to breach his duties by deciding the case based on the identity of the parties rather than the merits. The majority rightly notes that "[t]he legal merits, or lack thereof, of the judgment rendered is not an element of the offense." But I do not understand Alfisi to argue otherwise. He asserts that "to act 'corruptly' is to act with the specific intent to secure an unlawful advantage or benefit." Under both the majority's *and* Alfisi's construction, all that matters is the payer's intent, which can be decided based upon the circumstances of the payment and need not depend on the payment's effect. A jury following Alfisi's statutory construction in the hypothetical case would no more need to decide whether a judgment was actually meritorious than would a jury following the majority's approach. ...

Notes

1. Does the majority or dissent have the better of the statutory construction argument? What about the policy dispute? Interestingly, the word "corruptly" for purposes of the Foreign Corrupt Practices Act is understood to carry the meaning endorsed by the dissent. *See infra* Chapter 8(D).

Note that the government proceeded under § 201(b)(1)(A), which requires proof of an intent "to influence any official act." Recall that an alternative means of proving bribery is to show, under § 201(b)(1)(C), that the corrupt payment was made "to induce such public official ... to do or omit to do any act in violation of the lawful duty of such official or person." Although § 201(b)(1)(C) was not charged in this case, how might this subsection be relevant to the statutory construction argument in *Alfisi?*

2. Traditionally, courts discussing the differing intent required for bribery and gratuity point to the fact that bribery requires a "corrupt" motive, while the gratuity provision does not. *See, e.g.*, United States v. Jennings, 160 F.3d 1006, 1013-14 (4th Cir. 1998).

Recall our discussion of the confusion among the circuits in the obstruction context regarding the relationship between the "corrupt" motive requirement and the specific intent to obstruct requirement (and the accepted wisdom that motives should not be relevant to criminal liability). *See supra* Chapter 6. Recall, too, that the courts differ in their definitions of the word "corrupt."

It would seem that the "corrupt" motive requirement *should* be separate and in addition to the *quid pro quo* element that requires proof of a "specific intent to give or receive something of value in exchange for an illegal act." The latter requirement flows from the element of the statute which dictates that the thing of value be tendered with intent to "influence an official act" or to induce the public official "to do or omit to do any act in violation of the lawful duty" of the public official. However, many courts, like the *Alfisi* court, seem to meld the two requirements. Typical is the D.C. Circuit's explanation:

> A central difference between accepting a bribe and accepting a gratuity is the degree of culpable intent on the part of the recipient; to convict a defendant for accepting a bribe a jury must find that the defendant acted "corruptly," whereas to convict for accepting a gratuity the jury need only find that the defendant acted "knowingly and willingly." Given the equation of bribery with a *quid pro quo*, "corruptly" in the context of the bribery statute would appear to mean that the defendant accepts money with the specific intent of performing an official act in return.

United States v. Gatling, 96 F.3d 1511, 1522 (D.C. Cir. 1996); *see generally* David Mills & Robert Weisberg, *Corrupting the Harm Requirement in White Collar Crime*, 60 Stanford L. Rev. 1371, 1384-94 (2008).

3. Where the treatment of the "corrupt" intent language as nothing more than restating the *quid pro quo* requirement is important is in cases, like *Alfisi*, where the defense asserts that what took place was extortion, not bribery. If the requirement that the defendant act "corruptly" means no more than to act with the intent to exchange money for the public official's performance of his job, then a defendant who succumbs to a public official's extortionate demands will be guilty of bribery; where, however, the "corrupt" intent requires further proof that the defendant intended to secure through such payments consideration to which he is not otherwise entitled, then extortion may not be coextensive with bribery. Is the defendant's real claim here that the government improperly charged him, a *victim* of extortion, as a *perpetrator* of bribery? How does the majority address this issue?

4. How would the government prove that the parties to a transaction had a "corrupt" intent or, if the two elements are read as one, a "specific intent to give or receive something of value in exchange for an official act"? Assuming that neither the donor nor the donee is willing to cooperate with the government, how difficult is it for the government to prove that the parties understood and intended that the money was given in exchange for an official act? Would a jury's willingness to infer a "corrupt" agreement depend on the type of consideration

given (cash in brown paper bags versus purported campaign contributions)? What other facts might one look to, either in prosecuting or defending a corruption case, particularly in the campaign contribution context?

5. Might prosecutors avoid the proof requirements of § 201 by proceeding under a "right to honest services" mail or wire fraud prosecution under §§ 1341, 1343, and 1346? As discussed in the mail and wire fraud chapter, the courts are struggling to define what the appropriate limits of an "honest services" bribery case are after *Skilling*. Should courts rely on the caselaw under § 201? Professor Sara Sun Beale argues:

> [I]n construing the honest services prong of the mail fraud statute, federal courts should look to the scope of the criminal statutes regulating federal officials and to the line that Congress has drawn in that context between criminal violations and mere ethical lapses. If adopted, this proposal would serve two purposes. First, by providing content to the definition of "honest services" it would rein in federal prosecutions at the state and local level, limiting such prosecutions to conduct that has been defined by Congress and identified as sufficiently serious to warrant criminal punishment. It would also address, at least partially, federalism concerns. Second, and perhaps equally important, this proposal would also have significant implications for the prosecution of *federal* officers and employees. This proposal would eliminate the incentive for federal prosecutors to prosecute federal officials under the mail and wire fraud statute, using the undefined and elastic phrase "honest services" to evade the carefully drawn limitations in the statute that regulates the conduct of federal officials.

Beale, *supra* note 4, at 701; *see also* Randall D. Eliason, *Surgery with a Meat Axe: The Growing and Troubling Use of Honest Services Fraud to Prosecute Federal Corruption*, 99 J. Crim. L. & Criminology 929 (2009). Note that the Court in *McDonnell v. United States*, -- U.S. --, 136 S.Ct. 2355 (2016), read the an "official act" requirement into honest services fraud and defined it by reference to § 201.

6. Note that § 201 also prohibits the offering of a thing of value to a federal witness for or because of his testimony. 18 U.S.C. § 201(c)(2); *see also* United States v. Blaszak, 349 F.3d 881 (6th Cir. 2003) (affirming conviction under § 201(c) where the witness "sold" his *truthful* testimony in a civil case).

Does a prosecutor who offers a cooperating witness immunity or leniency offer a witness a "thing of value" for his testimony? A panel of the Tenth Circuit shocked the federal criminal bar by answering this question in the affirmative in *United States v. Singleton*, 144 F.3d 1343 (10th Cir.1998). The panel decision was quickly overturned *en banc*, 165 F.3d 1297 (10th Cir.1999), and every circuit to consider the question since has rejected the panel's holding. This subject will be treated at greater length in Chapter 19 (Plea Bargaining and Cooperation).

B. EXTORTION UNDER COLOR OF OFFICIAL RIGHT UNDER § 1951 (THE HOBBS ACT)

EVANS v. UNITED STATES
504 U.S. 255 (1992)

JUSTICE STEVENS delivered the opinion of the Court.

We granted certiorari to resolve a conflict in the Circuits over the question whether an affirmative act of inducement by a public official, such as a demand, is an element of the offense of extortion "under color of official right" prohibited by the Hobbs Act, 18 U.S.C. § 1951. We agree with the Court of Appeals for the Eleventh Circuit that it is not, and therefore affirm the judgment of the court below.

I

Petitioner was an elected member of the Board of Commissioners of DeKalb County, Georgia. During the period between March 1985 and October 1986, as part of an effort by the Federal Bureau of Investigation (FBI) to investigate allegations of public corruption in the Atlanta area, particularly in the area of rezonings of property, an FBI agent posing as a real estate developer talked on the telephone and met with petitioner on a number of occasions. Virtually all, if not all, of those conversations were initiated by the agent and most were recorded on tape or video. In those conversations, the agent sought petitioner's assistance in an effort to rezone a 25-acre tract of land for high-density residential use. On July 25, 1986, the agent handed petitioner cash totaling $7,000 and a check, payable to petitioner's campaign, for $1,000. Petitioner reported the check, but not the cash, on his state campaign-financing disclosure form; he also did not report the $7,000 on his 1986 federal income tax return. Viewing the evidence in the light most favorable to the Government, as we must in light of the verdict, we assume that the jury found that petitioner accepted the cash knowing that it was intended to ensure that he would vote in favor of the rezoning application and that he would try to persuade his fellow commissioners to do likewise. Thus, although petitioner did not initiate the transaction, his acceptance of the bribe constituted an implicit promise to use his official position to serve the interests of the bribegiver.

In a two-count indictment, petitioner was charged with extortion in violation of 18 U.S.C. § 1951 and with failure to report income in violation of 26 U.S.C. § 7206(1). He was convicted by a jury on both counts. With respect to the extortion count, the trial judge gave the following instruction:

"The defendant contends that the $8,000 he received from agent Cormany was a campaign contribution. The solicitation of campaign contributions from any person is a necessary and permissible form of political activity on the part of persons who seek political office and persons who have been elected to political office. Thus, the acceptance by an elected official of a campaign contribution does not, in itself, constitute a violation of the Hobbs Act even though the donor has business pending before the official.

"However, if a public official demands or accepts money in exchange for [a] specific requested exercise of his or her official power, such a demand or acceptance does constitute a violation of the Hobbs Act regardless of whether the payment is made in the form of a campaign contribution."

In affirming petitioner's conviction, the Court of Appeals noted that the instruction did not require the jury to find that petitioner had demanded or requested the money, or that he had conditioned the performance of any official act upon its receipt. The Court of Appeals held, however, that "passive acceptance of a benefit by a public official is sufficient to form the basis of a Hobbs Act violation if the official knows that he is being offered the payment in exchange for a specific requested exercise of his official power. The official need not take any specific action to induce the offering of the benefit."

This statement of the law by the Court of Appeals for the Eleventh Circuit is consistent with holdings in eight other Circuits. Two Circuits, however, have held that an affirmative act of inducement by the public official is required to support a conviction of extortion under color of official right. Because the majority view is consistent with the common-law definition of extortion, which we believe Congress intended to adopt, we endorse that position.

II

It is a familiar "maxim that a statutory term is generally presumed to have its common-law meaning." ...

At common law, extortion was an offense committed by a public official who took "by colour of his office" money that was not due to him for the performance of his official duties.[15] A demand, or request, by the public official was not an element of the offense. Extortion by the public official was the rough equivalent of what we would now describe as "taking a bribe." It is clear that petitioner committed that offense. The question is whether the federal statute, insofar as it applies to official extortion, has narrowed the common-law definition.

Congress has unquestionably *expanded* the common-law definition of extortion to include acts by private individuals pursuant to which property is obtained by means of force, fear, or threats. It did so by implication in the Travel Act, 18 U.S.C. § 1952, see *United States v. Nardello*, 393 U.S. 286, 289-296 (1969), and expressly in the Hobbs Act. ...

Although the present statutory text is much broader[16] than the common-law definition of extortion because it encompasses conduct by a private individual as well as conduct by a public official, the portion of the statute that refers to official misconduct continues to mirror the common-law definition. There is nothing in either the statutory text or the legislative history that could fairly be described as a "contrary direction," from Congress to narrow the scope of the offense. ...

The two courts that have disagreed with the decision to apply the common-law definition have interpreted the word "induced" as requiring a wrongful use of official power that "begins with the public official, not with the gratuitous actions of another." If we had no common-law history to guide our interpretation of the statutory text, that reading would be plausible. For two reasons, however, we are convinced that it is incorrect.

First, we think the word "induced" is a part of the definition of the offense by the private individual, but not the offense by the public official. In the case of the private individual, the victim's consent must be "induced by wrongful use of actual or threatened force, violence or fear." In the case of the public official, however, there is no such requirement. The statute merely requires of the public official that he obtain "property from another, with his consent, ... under color of official right." The use of the word "or" before "under color of official right" supports this reading.

Second, even if the statute were parsed so that the word "induced" applied to the public officeholder, we do not believe the word "induced" necessarily indicates that the transaction must be *initiated* by the recipient of the bribe. Many of the cases applying the majority rule have concluded that the wrongful acceptance of a bribe establishes all the inducement that the statute requires. They conclude that the coercive element is provided by the public office itself. And even the two courts that have adopted an inducement requirement for extortion under color of official right do not require proof that the inducement took the form of a threat or demand.

Petitioner argues that the jury charge with respect to extortion allowed the jury to convict him on the basis of the "passive acceptance of a contribution."[17] He contends

---

[15] [Court's footnote 5:] The dissent says that we assume that "common-law extortion encompassed any taking by a public official of something of value that he was not 'due.'" That statement, of course, is incorrect because, as stated in the text above, the payment must be "for the performance of his official duties."

[16] [Court's footnote 12:] This Court recognized the broad scope of the Hobbs Act in Stirone v. United States, 361 U.S. 212, 215 (1960):

> "That Act speaks in broad language, manifesting a purpose to use all the constitutional power Congress has to punish interference with interstate commerce by extortion, robbery or physical violence. The Act outlaws such interference 'in any way or degree.'"

[17] [Court's footnote 18:] Petitioner also makes the point that "[t]he evidence at trial against [petitioner] is more conducive to a charge of bribery than one of extortion." Although the evidence in this case may have supported a charge of bribery, it is not a defense to a charge of extortion under color of official right that the defendant could also have been convicted of bribery. Courts addressing extortion by force or fear have occasionally said that extortion and bribery are mutually exclusive; while that may be correct when the victim was intimidated into making a payment (extortion by force or fear), and did not offer it voluntarily (bribery), that does not lead to the conclusion that extortion under color of official right and

that the instruction did not require the jury to find "an element of duress such as a demand," and it did not properly describe the *quid pro quo* requirement for conviction if the jury found that the payment was a campaign contribution.

We reject petitioner's criticism of the instruction, and conclude that it satisfies the *quid pro quo* requirement of *McCormick v. United States*, 500 U.S. 257 (1991), because the offense is completed at the time when the public official receives a payment in return for his agreement to perform specific official acts; fulfillment of the *quid pro quo* is not an element of the offense. We also reject petitioner's contention that an affirmative step is an element of the offense of extortion "under color of official right" and need be included in the instruction. As we explained above, our construction of the statute is informed by the common-law tradition from which the term of art was drawn and understood. We hold today that the Government need only show that a public official has obtained a payment to which he was not entitled, knowing that the payment was made in return for official acts.[18] ...

III

An argument not raised by petitioner is now advanced by the dissent. It contends that common-law extortion was *limited* to wrongful takings under a false pretense of official right. It is perfectly clear, however, that although extortion accomplished by fraud was a well-recognized type of extortion, there were other types as well. As the court explained in *Commonwealth v. Wilson*, 30 Pa.Super. 26 (1906), an extortion case involving a payment by a would-be brothel owner to a police captain to ensure the opening of her house:

> "The form of extortion most commonly dealt with in the decisions is the corrupt taking by a person in office of a fee for services which should be rendered gratuitously; or when compensation is permissible, of a larger fee than the law justifies, or a fee not yet due; but this is not a complete definition of the offense, by which I mean that it does not include every form of common-law extortion." ...

The dissent's theory notwithstanding, not one of the cases it cites holds that the public official is innocent unless he has deceived the payor by representing that the payment was proper. Indeed, none makes any reference to the state of mind of the payor, and none states that a "false pretense" is an element of the offense. Instead, those cases merely support the proposition that the services for which the fee is paid must be official and that the official must not be entitled to the fee that he collected—both elements of the offense that are clearly satisfied in this case. The complete absence of support for the dissent's thesis presumably explains why it was not advanced by petitioner in the District Court or the Court of Appeals, is not recognized by any Court of Appeals, and is not advanced in any scholarly commentary.

[JUSTICE O'CONNOR joined Parts I and II of the Court's opinion but declined to express a view on the issue raised by the dissent and discussed in Part III of the Court's opinion because it was not raised, briefed, or argued]

---

bribery are mutually exclusive under either common law or the Hobbs Act. ... We agree with the Seventh Circuit in *United States v. Braasch*, 505 F.2d 139, 151, n. 7 (1974), that "'the modern trend of the federal courts is to hold that bribery and extortion as used in the Hobbs Ac[t] are not mutually exclusive.'"

18 [Court's footnote 20:] The dissent states that we have "simply made up" the requirement that the payment must be given in return for official acts. On the contrary, that requirement is derived from the statutory language "under color of official right," which has a well-recognized common-law heritage that distinguished between payments for private services and payments for public services.

JUSTICE KENNEDY, concurring in part and concurring in the judgment.

The Court gives a summary of its decision in these words: "We hold today that the Government need only show that a public official has obtained a payment to which he was not entitled, knowing that the payment was made in return for official acts." In my view the dissent is correct to conclude that this language requires a *quid pro quo* as an element of the Government's case in a prosecution under 18 U.S.C. § 1951, and the Court's opinion can be interpreted in a way that is consistent with this rule. Although the Court appears to accept the requirement of a *quid pro quo* as an alternative rationale, in my view this element of the offense is essential to a determination of those acts which are criminal and those which are not in a case in which the official does not pretend that he is entitled by law to the property in question. Here the prosecution did establish a *quid pro quo* that embodied the necessary elements of a statutory violation. I join Part III of the Court's opinion and concur in the judgment affirming the conviction. I write this separate opinion to explain my analysis and understanding of the statute.

With regard to the question whether the word "induced" in the statutory definition of extortion applies to the phrase "under color of official right," 18 U.S.C. § 1951(b)(2), I find myself in substantial agreement with the dissent. Scrutiny of the placement of commas will not, in the final analysis, yield a convincing answer, and we are left with two quite plausible interpretations. Under these circumstances, I agree with the dissent that the rule of lenity requires that we avoid the harsher one. We must take as our starting point the assumption that the portion of the statute at issue here defines extortion as "the obtaining of property from another, with his consent, induced ... under color of official right."

I agree with the Court, on the other hand, that the word "induced" does not "necessarily indicat[e] that the transaction must be *initiated* by the" public official. Something beyond the mere acceptance of property from another is required, however, or else the word "induced" would be superfluous. That something, I submit, is the *quid pro quo*. The ability of the official to use or refrain from using authority is the "color of official right" which can be invoked in a corrupt way to induce payment of money or to otherwise obtain property. The inducement generates a *quid pro quo*, under color of official right, that the statute prohibits. The term "under color of" is used, as I think both the Court and the dissent agree, to sweep within the statute those corrupt exercises of authority that the law forbids but that nevertheless cause damage because the exercise is by a governmental official.

The requirement of a *quid pro quo* means that without pretense of any entitlement to the payment, a public official violates § 1951 if he intends the payor to believe that absent payment the official is likely to abuse his office and his trust to the detriment and injury of the prospective payor or to give the prospective payor less favorable treatment if the *quid pro quo* is not satisfied. The official and the payor need not state the *quid pro quo* in express terms, for otherwise the law's effect could be frustrated by knowing winks and nods. The inducement from the official is criminal if it is express or if it is implied from his words and actions, so long as he intends it to be so and the payor so interprets it.

The criminal law in the usual course concerns itself with motives and consequences, not formalities. And the trier of fact is quite capable of deciding the intent with which words were spoken or actions taken as well as the reasonable construction given to them by the official and the payor. In this respect a prosecution under the statute has some similarities to a contract dispute, with the added and vital element that motive is crucial. For example, a *quid pro quo* with the attendant corrupt motive can be inferred from an ongoing course of conduct. In such instances, for a public official to commit extortion under color of official right, his course of dealings must establish a real understanding that failure to make a payment will result in the victimization of the prospective payor or the withholding of more favorable treatment, a victimization or withholding accomplished by taking or refraining from taking official action, all in breach of the official's trust.

Thus, I agree with the Court, that the *quid pro quo* requirement is not simply made up, as the dissent asserts. Instead, this essential element of the offense is derived from the statutory requirement that the official receive payment under color of official right, as well as the inducement requirement. And there are additional principles of construction which justify this interpretation. First is the principle that statutes are to be construed so that they are constitutional. As one Court of Appeals Judge who agreed with the construction the Court today adopts noted, "the phrase 'under color of official right,' standing alone, is vague almost to the point of unconstitutionality." By placing upon a criminal statute a narrow construction, we avoid the possibility of imputing to Congress an enactment that lacks necessary precision.

Moreover, the mechanism which controls and limits the scope of official right extortion is a familiar one: a state of mind requirement. Hence, even if the *quid pro quo* requirement did not have firm roots in the statutory language, it would constitute no abuse of judicial power for us to find it by implication. ...

... As I have indicated, and as the jury instructions in this case made clear, an official violates the statute only if he agrees to receive a payment not due him in exchange for an official act, knowing that he is not entitled to the payment. ... In short, a public official who labors under the good-faith but erroneous belief that he is entitled to payment for an official act does not violate the statute. That circumstance is not, however, presented here.

The requirement of a *quid pro quo* in a § 1951 prosecution such as the one before us, in which it is alleged that money was given to the public official in the form of a campaign contribution, was established by our decision last Term in *McCormick v. United States*, 500 U.S. 257 (1991). Readers of today's opinion should have little difficulty in understanding that the rationale underlying the Court's holding applies not only in campaign contribution cases, but in all § 1951 prosecutions. That is as it should be, for, given a corrupt motive, the *quid pro quo*, as I have said, is the essence of the offense.

Because I agree that the jury instruction in this case complied with the *quid pro quo* requirement, I concur in the judgment of the Court.

JUSTICE THOMAS, with whom THE CHIEF JUSTICE and JUSTICE SCALIA join, dissenting.

The Court's analysis is based on the premise, with which I fully agree, that when Congress employs legal terms of art, it "'knows and adopts the cluster of ideas that were attached to each borrowed word in the body of learning from which it was taken and the meaning its use will convey to the judicial mind.'" Thus, we presume, Congress knew the meaning of common-law extortion when it enacted the Hobbs Act, 18 U.S.C. § 1951. Unfortunately, today's opinion misapprehends that meaning and misconstrues the statute. I respectfully dissent.

Extortion is one of the oldest crimes in Anglo-American jurisprudence. Hawkins provides the classic common-law definition: "[I]t is said, that Extortion in a large Sense signifies any Oppression *under Colour of Right*; but that in a strict Sense it signifies the Taking of Money by any Officer, *by Colour of his Office*, either where none at all is due, or not so much is due, or where it is not yet due." Blackstone echoed that definition: "[E]xtortion is an abuse of public justice, which consists in any officer's unlawfully taking, *by colour of his office*, from any man, any money or thing of value, that is not due to him, or more than is due, or before it is due."

These definitions pose, but do not answer, the critical question: What does it mean for an official to take money "by colour of his office"? The Court fails to address this question, simply assuming that common-law extortion encompassed *any* taking by a public official of something of value that he was not "due."

[After surveying numerous sources, Justice Thomas concludes that extortion under color of office, at common law, required that the money or property was obtained "under the pretense that the officer was entitled thereto by virtue of his office."] ...

Perhaps because the common-law crime—as the Court defines it—is so expansive, the Court, at the very end of its opinion, appends a qualification: "We hold today that the Government need only show that a public official has obtained a payment to which he was not entitled, *knowing that the payment was made in return for official acts*." (emphasis added). This *quid pro quo* requirement is simply made up. The Court does not suggest that it has any basis in the common law or the language of the Hobbs Act, and I have found no treatise or dictionary that refers to any such requirement in defining "extortion."

Its only conceivable source, in fact, is our opinion last Term in *McCormick v. United States*, 500 U.S. 257 (1991). Quite sensibly, we insisted in that case that, unless the Government established the existence of a *quid pro quo*, a public official could not be convicted of extortion under the Hobbs Act for accepting a campaign contribution. We did not purport to discern that requirement in the common law or statutory text, but imposed it to prevent the Hobbs Act from effecting a radical (and absurd) change in American political life. ...

Because the common-law history of extortion was neither properly briefed nor argued in *McCormick*, the *quid pro quo* limitation imposed there represented a reasonable first step in the right direction. Now that we squarely consider that history, however, it is apparent that that limitation was in fact overly modest: at common law, McCormick was innocent of extortion *not* because he failed to offer a *quid pro quo* in return for campaign contributions, but because he did not take the contributions under color of official right. Today's extension of *McCormick*'s reasonable (but textually and historically artificial) *quid pro quo* limitation to *all* cases of official extortion is both unexplained and inexplicable—except insofar as it may serve to rescue the Court's definition of extortion from substantial overbreadth.

As serious as the Court's disregard for history is its disregard for well-established principles of statutory construction. The Court chooses not only the harshest interpretation of a criminal statute, but also the interpretation that maximizes federal criminal jurisdiction over state and local officials. I would reject both choices.

The Hobbs Act defines "extortion" as "the obtaining of property from another, with his consent, *induced* by wrongful use of actual or threatened force, violence, or fear, or *under color of official right*." 18 U.S.C. § 1951(b)(2) (emphasis added). Evans argues, in part, that he did not "induce" any payment. The Court rejects that argument, concluding that the verb "induced" applies *only* to the first portion of the definition. ...

The more natural construction is that the verb "induced" applies to *both* types of extortion described in the statute. Thus, the unstated "either" belongs *after* "induced": "The term 'extortion' means the obtaining of property from another, with his consent, induced *either* [1] by wrongful use of actual or threatened force, violence, or fear, *or* [2] under color of official right." This construction comports with correct grammar and standard usage by setting up a parallel between two prepositional phrases, the first beginning with "by"; the second with "under." ... Given the text of the statute and the rule of lenity, I believe that inducement is an element of official extortion under the Hobbs Act.

Perhaps sensing the weakness of its position, the Court suggests an alternative interpretation: even if the statute *does* set forth an "inducement" requirement for official extortion, that requirement is always satisfied, because "the coercive element is provided by the public office itself." I disagree. A particular public official, to be sure, may wield his power in such a way as to coerce unlawful payments, even in the absence of any explicit demand or threat. But it ignores reality to assert that *every* public official, in *every* context, automatically exerts coercive influence on others by virtue of his office. If the chairman of General Motors meets with a local court clerk, for example, whatever implicit coercive pressures exist will surely not emanate from the clerk. ...

The Court's construction of the Hobbs Act is repugnant not only to the basic tenets of criminal justice reflected in the rule of lenity, but also to basic tenets of federalism. Over the past 20 years, the Hobbs Act has served as the engine for a stunning expansion of federal criminal jurisdiction into a field traditionally policed by state and local laws—acts of public corruption by state and local officials. That expansion was born of a single sentence in a Third Circuit opinion: "[The 'under color of official right' language in the Hobbs Act] repeats the common law definition of extortion, a crime which could only be committed by a public official, and which did not require proof of threat, fear, or duress." *United States v. Kenny*, 462 F.2d 1205, 1229. As explained above, that sentence is not necessarily incorrect in its description of what common-law extortion did *not* require; unfortunately, it omits an important part of what common-law extortion *did* require. By overlooking the traditional meaning of "under color of official right," *Kenny* obliterated the distinction between extortion and bribery, essentially creating a new crime encompassing both.

"As effectively as if there were federal common law crimes, the court in *Kenny* ... amend[ed] the Hobbs Act and [brought] into existence a new crime—local bribery affecting interstate commerce. Hereafter, for purposes of Hobbs Act prosecutions, such bribery was to be called extortion. The federal policing of state corruption had begun." J. Noonan, Bribes 586 (1984).

After *Kenny*, federal prosecutors came to view the Hobbs Act as a license for ferreting out *all* wrongdoing at the state and local level—"'a special code of integrity for public officials.'" In short order, most other Circuits followed *Kenny*'s lead and upheld, based on a bribery rationale, the Hobbs Act extortion convictions of an astonishing variety of state and local officials, from a State Governor down to a local policeman.

Our precedents, to be sure, suggest that Congress enjoys broad constitutional power to legislate in areas traditionally regulated by the States—power that apparently extends even to the direct regulation of the qualifications, tenure, and conduct of state governmental officials. As we emphasized only last Term, however, concerns of federalism require us to give a *narrow* construction to federal legislation in such sensitive areas unless Congress' contrary intent is "unmistakably clear in the language of the statute." *Gregory v. Ashcroft*, 501 U.S. 452, 460 (1991). ...

The reader of today's opinion, however, will search in vain for any consideration of the principles of federalism that animated *Gregory* ... It is clear, of course, that the Hobbs Act's proscription of extortion "under color of official right" applies to all public officials, including those at the state and local level. As our cases emphasize, however, even when Congress has clearly decided to engage in *some* regulation of the state governmental officials, concerns of federalism play a vital role in evaluating the *scope* of the regulation. The Court today mocks this jurisprudence by reading two significant limitations (the textual requirement of "inducement" and the common-law requirement of "under color of office") *out* of the Hobbs Act's definition of official extortion. ...

Whatever evils today's opinion may redress, in my view, pale beside those it will engender. "Courts must resist th[e] temptation [to stretch criminal statutes] in the interest of the long-range preservation of limited and even-handed government." All Americans, including public officials, are entitled to protection from prosecutorial abuse. The facts of this case suggest a depressing erosion of that protection.

Petitioner Evans was elected to the Board of Commissioners of DeKalb County, Georgia, in 1982. He was no local tyrant—just one of five part-time commissioners earning an annual salary of approximately $16,000. The board's activities were entirely local, including the quintessentially local activity of zoning property. The United States does not suggest that there were any allegations of corruption or malfeasance against Evans.

In early 1985, as part of an investigation into "allegations of public corruption in the Atlanta area," a Federal Bureau of Investigation agent, Clifford Cormany, Jr., set up a bogus firm, "WDH Developers," and pretended to be a land developer. Cormany sought and obtained a meeting with Evans. From March 1985 until October 1987, a period of some *two and a half years*, Cormany or one of his associates held 33 conversations with Evans. Every one of these contacts was initiated by the agents. During these conversations, the agents repeatedly requested Evans' assistance in securing a favorable zoning decision, and repeatedly brought up the subject of campaign contributions. Agent Cormany eventually contributed $8,000 to Evans' reelection campaign, and Evans accepted the money. There is no suggestion that he claimed an official entitlement to the payment. Nonetheless, he was arrested and charged with Hobbs Act extortion. ...

Our criminal justice system runs on the premise that prosecutors will respect, and courts will enforce, the boundaries on criminal conduct set by the legislature. Where, as here, those boundaries are breached, it becomes impossible to tell where prosecutorial discretion ends and prosecutorial abuse, or even discrimination, begins. The potential for abuse, of course, is particularly grave in the inherently political context of public corruption prosecutions. ...

Notes

1. Does the Court's analysis mean that extortion is indistinguishable from bribery? Conceptually, as the Third Circuit has summarized, "[t]he essence of the crime of bribery is voluntariness, while the essence of extortion is duress." United States v. Addonizio, 451 F.2d 49, 77 (3d Cir. 1971). Bribery involves a person who uses his wealth to "buy" favors from a public official. Extortion, by contrast, generally involves the use of duress or coercion to induce the wrongful taking of property. In a "color of official right" case, the coercion inheres in the power of the public office. See United States v. Buffis, 867 F.3d 230, 235 (1st Cir. 2017) (Hobbs Act extortion under claim of official right does not require proof that the victims were afraid when they made the payments to the public official); United States v. Manzo, 636 F.3d 56 (3d Cir. 2011) (candidate for public office who loses cannot be prosecuted for "color of official right" extortion). Because of this duress or coercion, in an extortion case the person who is paying the public official is the victim; in a bribery case, he is just as culpable as the corrupt public official receiving the money. (Another important distinction between extortion and bribery is the extent of the potential penalty: while bribery under § 201 is punishable by up to 15 years' imprisonment, extortion under § 1951 is punishment by up to 20 years' imprisonment.)

In light of this distinction, what problems might arise from treating extortion as equivalent to bribery? If the person paying the money in an extortion case is the "victim," can she be liable as a coconspirator in the extortion scheme? Logic may say "no," but the Supreme Court said "yes" in United States v. Ocasio, -- U.S. --, 136 S.Ct. 1423 (2016). Ocasio, a former a police officer, participated in a kickback scheme in which he and other officers routed damaged vehicles from accident scenes to an auto repair shop in exchange for payments from the shop owners. He was charged with obtaining money from the shop owners under color of official right, in violation of § 1951, and conspiring to violate the Hobbs Act under § 371. At trial, the district court rejected Ocasio's argument that—because the Hobbs Act prohibits the obtaining of property "from another"—a Hobbs Act conspiracy requires proof that the conspirators agreed to obtain property form someone outside the conspiracy. The Supreme Court agreed, relying on the fundamental principles of conspiracy law. Under established law, "a conspiracy is a joint commitment to an 'endeavor which, if completed, would satisfy all the elements of [the underlying substantive] criminal offense.'" 136 S.Ct. at 1429 (quoting Salinas v. United States, 522 U.S. 52, 65 (1997)). A defendant must reach "an agreement with the 'specific intent that the underlying crime be committed'" by some member of the conspiracy. Id. (citation omitted). The government does not need to prove that the defendant intended to commit the underlying offense himself, and a conspirator may be convicted even though he was incapable of committing the substantive crime himself. See id. at 1429-30.

Ocasio argued that the shop owners did not have the same criminal purpose because they did not share the officers' objective of obtaining money "from another" because the money in question was their own. Id. at 1433. The Court rejected this position, reasoning that the defendant and the shop owners "did have a common criminal objective. The objective was not that each conspirator, including the [shop owners], would obtain money 'from another' but rather that [Ocasio] and other Baltimore officers would do so." Id. at 1434. Finally, the Court said that the subtext of Ocasio's argument is that "it seems unnatural to prosecute bribery on the basis of a statute prohibiting 'extortion.'" The Court responded that it had already held that § 1951 prohibits the rough equivalent of bribery in Evans, and it was unwilling to reconsider that. Id. at 1435.

Justice Thomas pointed out the obvious: "Today the Court holds that an extortionist can conspire to commit extortion with the person whom he is extorting." His view was that Evans, which equated bribery with extortion, was incorrectly decided.

2. What function would an "inducement" requirement serve in Hobbs Act cases? Evans was a case in which the extortionate payment took the form of a campaign contribution. The petitioner argued that the jury instruction permitted conviction on the basis of "passive acceptance of a contribution." Would an "inducement" element serve as an effective means of distinguishing between legitimate campaign contributions and illegal extortion (or bribery)?

3. A number of courts have read the "under color of official right" element broadly to include cases in which the defendant public official actually did not have the power to control the decision for which he was being paid. *See, e.g.*, United States v. Bencivengo, 749 F.3d 205 (3d Cir. 2014). *McDonnell v. United States*, excerpted in Chapter 7(C) and discussed *supra* (Part A) with respect to bribery under § 201, applies to the Hobbs Act as well. In *McDonnell*, the Court indicated that an "official act" can include using the defendant official's position to exert pressure on another official to perform an official act or advising another official, knowing that such advice will serve as the basis for that other official's official act.

4. May gratuities cases be pursued as color of official right Hobbs Act cases? How do the proof requirements of a Hobbs Act case differ from the proof requirements of a § 201 case?

Evans is important not only for its rejection of an "inducement" element in color of official right cases, but also for its discussion (albeit limited) of the *quid pro quo* requirement of *McCormick v. United States*, 500 U.S. 257 (1991). Justice Kennedy, in his concurring opinion, states his belief that this *quid pro quo* requirement is "the essence of the offense," while the three dissenting Justices question the legitimacy of the *McCormick* Court's holding that proof of a *quid pro quo* is a necessary element of a Hobbs Act prosecution, at least outside the context of campaign contribution cases.

In *McCormick*, petitioner, a member of the West Virginia House of Delegates in 1984, was a leading advocate of a legislative program allowing foreign medical school graduates to practice under temporary permits while studying for the state licensing exams. Some doctors practiced for years under the program, as they repeatedly failed the licensing exams. McCormick sponsored a bill, sought by an organization of those doctors, extending the program's expiration date. He later agreed to sponsor legislation in the 1985 session that would grant the doctors a permanent license by virtue of their years of experience. After advising the doctors' lobbyist, during his 1984 reelection campaign, that he had heard nothing from the doctors, McCormick received four cash payments from them, which he neither listed as campaign contributions nor reported as income on his 1984 federal income tax return. In 1985, he sponsored the permanent licensing legislation, and, after it was enacted, he received another payment from the doctors. Subsequently, he was indicted on five counts of violating the Hobbs Act by extorting payments under color of official right.

McCormick was convicted of one Hobbs Act count and the Court of Appeals affirmed. The Supreme Court reversed McCormick's conviction, holding that a *quid pro quo* is necessary for a conviction when an official receives a campaign contribution, regardless of whether it is a legitimate contribution. The Court explained:

> Serving constituents and supporting legislation that will benefit the district and individuals and groups therein is the everyday business of a legislator. It is also true that campaigns must be run and financed. Money is constantly being solicited on behalf of candidates, who run on platforms and who claim support on the basis of their views and what they intend to do or have done. Whatever ethical considerations and appearances may indicate, to hold that legislators commit the federal crime of extortion when they act for the benefit of constituents or support legislation furthering the interests of some of their constituents, shortly before or after campaign contributions are solicited and received from those beneficiaries, is an unrealistic assessment of what Congress could have meant by making it a crime to obtain property from another, with his consent, "under color of official right." To hold otherwise would open to prosecution not only conduct that has long been thought to be well within the law but also conduct that in a very real sense is unavoidable so long as election campaigns are financed by private contributions or expenditures, as they have been from the beginning of the Nation. It would require statutory language more explicit than the Hobbs Act contains to justify a contrary conclusion.
>
> This is not to say that it is impossible for an elected official to commit extortion in the course of financing an election campaign. Political contributions are of course vulnerable if induced by the use of force, violence, or fear. The receipt of such contributions is also vulnerable under the Act as having been taken under color of official right, but only if the

payments are made in return for *an explicit promise or undertaking* by the official to perform or not to perform an official act. In such situations the official asserts that his official conduct will be controlled by the terms of the promise or undertaking. This is the receipt of money by an elected official under color of official right within the meaning of the Hobbs Act. [Ed: emphasis added.]

This formulation defines the forbidden zone of conduct with sufficient clarity. As the Court of Appeals for the Fifth Circuit observed in *United States v. Dozier*, 672 F.2d 531, 537 (1982):

> "A moment's reflection should enable one to distinguish, at least in the abstract, a legitimate solicitation from the exaction of a fee for a benefit conferred or an injury withheld. Whether described familiarly as a payoff or with the Latinate precision of *quid pro quo*, the prohibited exchange is the same: a public official may not demand payment as inducement for the promise to perform (or not to perform) an official act." ...

We thus disagree with the Court of Appeals' holding in this case that a *quid pro quo* is not necessary for conviction under the Hobbs Act when an official receives a campaign contribution. ...

McCormick, 500 U.S. at 272-74. The *McCormick* Court, however, noted that "McCormick's sole contention in this case is that the payments made to him were campaign contributions. Therefore, we do not decide whether a *quid pro quo* requirement exists in other contexts, such as when an elected official receives gifts, meals, travel expenses, or other items of value." *Id.* at 274 n.10.

5. In response to the question left open in *McCormick*, the circuits seem in accord in holding that a *quid pro quo* requirement applies in all Hobbs Act "under color of official right" extortion prosecutions, not just to those involving campaign contributions. United States v. Abbey, 560 F.3d 513, 517-18 (6th Cir. 2009); United States v. Hairston, 46 F.3d 361, 365 (4th Cir. 1995); United States v. Martinez, 14 F.3d 543 (11th Cir. 1994). The circuits appear to be in disarray, however, on just what that requirement means. In particular, the question is whether the government has to prove an "explicit promise or undertaking" in the language of *McCormick* or whether the relevant standard is that stated in *Evans*—that "the Government need only show that a public official has obtained a payment to which he was not entitled, knowing that the payment was made in return for official acts." *Evans*, 504 U.S. at 268. Must the government show an actual agreement between the parties or can "a *quid pro quo* with the attendant corrupt motive ... be inferred from an ongoing course of conduct," *Evans*, 504 U.S. at 274 (Kennedy, J., concurring)?

Some courts to address this issue have held that "proof of an explicit promise to perform the official acts in return for the payment is not required." United States v. Delano, 55 F.3d 720, 731 (2d Cir. 1995); *see also* United States v. Kincaid-Chauncey, 556 F.3d 923, 936-938 (9th Cir. 2009) ("[a]lthough we agree that the government must prove the existence of a *quid pro quo* to obtain a conviction under the Hobbs Act for non-campaign related payments, we reject the notion that the *quid pro quo* needs to be explicitly stated"); United States v. Bradley, 173 F.3d 225, 231-32 (3d Cir. 1999). As the Sixth Circuit reasoned in *United States v. Blandford*, 33 F.3d 685, 696 (6th Cir. 1994), "*Evans* provided a gloss on the *McCormick* Court's use of the word 'explicit' to qualify its *quid pro quo* requirement. Explicit, as explained in *Evans*, speaks not to the form of the agreement between the payor and payee, but to the degree to which the payor and payee were aware of its terms, regardless of whether those terms were articulated. Put simply, *Evans* instructed that by 'explicit,' *McCormick* did not mean 'express.'" *See also* United States v. Siegelman, 640 F.3d 1159, 1172 (11th Cir. 2011). The rationale for this rule is that articulated by Justice Stevens in his dissenting opinion in *McCormick*, 500 U.S. at 282: "In my opinion there is no statutory requirement that illegal agreements, threats, or promises be in writing, or in any particular form. Subtle extortion is just as wrongful—and probably much more common—than the kind of express understanding that the Court's opinion seems to require."

Others courts have indicated that, under *McCormick* and *Evans* "an explicit promise by a public official to act or not act is an essential element of Hobbs Act extortion." United States v. Davis, 30 F.3d 108, 109 (11th Cir. 1994). As the Seventh Circuit has explained: "Because of the realities of the American political system, and the fact that the Hobbs Act's language did not justify making commonly accepted political behavior criminal, the Supreme Court in *McCormick* added to this definition of extortion the requirement that the connection between the payment and the exercise of office—the *quid pro quo*—be explicit." United States v. Allen, 10 F.3d 405, 411 (7th Cir. 1993) (dicta). As a practical matter, how would the government bear the burden of proving such a promise? What are the dangers of permitting a jury to infer such an agreement?

Some courts have expressed, at least in dicta, a preference for a two-tiered standard. They have indicated that the more rigorous "explicit promise" requirement should apply in campaign contribution cases but, in the apparent belief that *Evans* "modified this standard for non-campaign contribution cases," *Martinez*, 14 F.3d at 553, employ in non-campaign cases the *Evans* statement that "the Government need only show that a public official has obtained a payment to which he was not entitled, knowing that the payment was made in return for official acts," *Evans*, 504 U.S. at 268. *See Abbey*, 560 F.3d at 517-18; *Martinez*, 14 F.3d at 552-53. Given that *Evans* was itself a campaign contribution case, does this make sense? Consider the *Blandford* court's reasoning:

> [A] strong argument could be advanced for treating campaign contribution cases and non-campaign contribution cases disparately. Campaign contributions, as the *McCormick* Court noted, enjoy what might be labeled a presumption of legitimacy. Although legitimate campaign contributions, not unlike Hobbs Act extortion payments, are given with the hope, and perhaps the expectation, that the payment will make the official more likely to support the payor's interests, we punish neither the giving nor the taking presumably because we have decided that the alternative of financing campaigns with public funds is even less attractive than the current arrangement. Conversely, if any presumption is to be accorded to payments that occur outside of the campaign contribution context, the presumption would be the antithesis of the one described above. Stated another way, where, as in this case, a public official's primary justification for receiving, with relative impunity, cash payments from private sources, *i.e.*, our present campaign financing system, is not available, that public official is left with few other means of rationalizing his actions.

33 F.3d at 697. Assuming that this is a reasonable rationale for a distinction between campaign contribution cases and other types of "color of official right" cases, can such a distinction find a principled basis in the statutory language?

6. A *quid pro quo* element serves as one potential limitation on prosecutors' ability to pursue the crime of bribery as extortion under a Hobbs Act "color of official right" theory. A second possible constraint is the fact that the statute may only be invoked where the activity at issue "in any way or degree obstructs, delays, or affects commerce or the movement of any article or commodity in commerce." 18 U.S.C. § 1951(a). The Act defines "commerce" broadly to include "all ... commerce over which the United States has jurisdiction." *Id.* § 1951(b)(3). The *Evans* Court quoted with apparent approval in footnote 12 its statement in *Stirone v. United States*, 361 U.S. 212, 214 (1960), that the Hobbs Act "speaks in broad language, manifesting a purpose to use all the constitutional power Congress has to punish interference with interstate commerce by extortion, robbery or physical violence." As Professor Sara Sun Beale has noted, this element does not in fact act as much of a limitation on Hobbs Act public corruption prosecutions:

> The courts have upheld convictions where the effect or potential effect on commerce is negligible. For example, [in *United States v. Stillo*, 57 F.3d 553 (7th Cir. 1995),] the Seventh Circuit upheld the conviction of a state judge who agreed to accept a bribe to fix a sham

case, but then, fearing a trap, backed out before the bribe was paid. The court found that payment of a bribe of $1,000-$2,000 would have depleted the law firm's assets, reducing its ability to purchase goods in interstate commerce, such as document covers and calculators. Unless the Supreme Court imposes a more restrictive reading, the jurisdictional requirements will not significantly limit the reach of the Hobbs Act as a mechanism to prosecute state and local corruption in federal the courts.

Beale, *supra* note 4, at 707-08. Some defendants have argued that after the Supreme Court's decision in *United States v. Lopez*, 514 U.S. 549 (1995) (holding that Gun-Free School Zones Act, which made it a federal crime to possess a firearm within 1,000 feet of a school, exceeded Congress' power to regulate commerce), the government must prove that the extortion had a "substantial effect" on interstate commerce, rather than the "de minimis effect" previously required. *See, e.g.*, United States v. Smith, 182 F.3d 452, 456 (6th Cir. 1999). The Supreme Court rejected this position in *United States v. Taylor*, -- U.S. --, 136 S.Ct. 2074 (2016). The Court reasoned that in *Gonzales v. Raich*, 545 U.S. 1 (2005), it had held that Congress had the power to regulate the national market for marijuana, including the authority to proscribe purely intrastate production, possession and sale. Because Congress may regulate these intrastate activities based on their aggregate economic effect on interstate commerce, "it follows that Congress may also regulate intrastate drug *theft*." *Id.* at 2077. Accordingly, proof that Taylor attempted to rob local marijuana dealers of their drugs and money was sufficient to satisfy the Hobbs Act's commerce element.

7. The Supreme Court's addressed the Hobbs Act's requirement that the defendant must "obtain" property in *Scheidler v. National Organization for Women, Inc.*, 537 U.S. 393 (2003) (*Scheidler II*). In *Scheidler II*, the defendants were anti-abortion protestors who had attempted to shut down abortion clinics. The plaintiffs argued that these defendants—"by using or threatening to use force, violence, or fear to cause respondents 'to give up' property rights, namely, 'a woman's right to seek medical service from a clinic, the right of the doctors, nurses, or other clinic staff to perform their jobs, and the right of the clinics to provide medical services free from wrongful threats, violence, coercion, and fear'"—had committed extortion under the Hobbs Act. The Seventh Circuit agreed, stating that "the defendants assert that, even if 'property' was involved, the defendants did not 'obtain' that property; they merely forced the plaintiffs to part with it ... [but] this argument is contrary to a long line of precedent in this circuit." *Nat'l Org. for Women, Inc. v. Scheidler*, 267 F.3d 687, 709 (7th Cir. 2001).

The Supreme Court reversed. Initially, the Court noted that on appeal, the respondents "had shifted the thrust of their theory" with regard to precisely which property rights had been extorted from them. *Scheidler II*, 537 U.S. at 401. It stated that although the respondents had argued below that the extorted property rights were those of the women and the clinics to receive and perform medical services, they

now assert that petitioners violated the Hobbs Act by "seeking to get control of the use and disposition of respondents' property." They argue that because the right to control the use and disposition of an asset is property, petitioners, who interfered with, and in some instances completely disrupted, the ability of the clinics to function, obtained or attempted to obtain respondents' property.

The United States offers a view similar to that of respondents, asserting that "where the property at issue is a business's intangible right to exercise exclusive control over the use of its assets, [a] defendant obtained that property by obtaining control over the use of those assets."

The Court then concluded that even this revised construction was inconsistent with the Hobbs Act's explicit reference to "obtaining of property from another," 18 U.S.C. s 1951(b)(2). It stated that

[w]e need not now trace what are the boundaries of extortion liability under the Hobbs Act, so that liability might be based on obtaining something as intangible as another's

right to exercise exclusive control over the use of a party's business assets. ... Whatever the outer boundaries may be, the effort to characterize petitioners' actions here as an 'obtaining of property from' respondents is well beyond them.

Id. at 402. The Court went on conclude that

[t]here is no dispute in these cases that petitioners interfered with, disrupted, and in some instances completely deprived respondents of their ability to exercise their property rights. ... But even when their acts of interference and disruption achieved their ultimate goal of "shutting down" a clinic that performed abortions, such acts did not constitute extortion because petitioners did not "obtain" respondents' property. Petitioners may have deprived or sought to deprive respondents of their alleged property right of exclusive control of their business assets, but they did not acquire any such property. Petitioners neither pursued nor received something of value from respondents that they could exercise, transfer, or sell. To conclude that such actions constituted extortion would effectively discard the statutory requirement that property must be obtained from another, replacing it instead with the notion that merely interfering with or depriving someone of property is sufficient to constitute extortion.

Id. at 404-05.

SEKHAR v. UNITED STATES
570 U.S. 729 (2013)

JUSTICE SCALIA delivered the opinion of the Court.

We consider whether attempting to compel a person to recommend that his employer approve an investment constitutes "the obtaining of property from another" under 18 U.S.C. § 1951(b)(2).

New York's Common Retirement Fund is an employee pension fund for the State of New York and its local governments. As sole trustee of the Fund, the State Comptroller chooses Fund investments. When the Comptroller decides to approve an investment he issues a "Commitment." A Commitment, however, does not actually bind the Fund. For that to happen, the Fund and the recipient of the investment must enter into a limited partnership agreement.

Petitioner Giridhar Sekhar was a managing partner of FA Technology Ventures. In October 2009, the Comptroller's office was considering whether to invest in a fund managed by that firm. The office's general counsel made a written recommendation to the Comptroller not to invest in the fund, after learning that the Office of the New York Attorney General was investigating another fund managed by the firm. The Comptroller decided not to issue a Commitment and notified a partner of FA Technology Ventures. That partner had previously heard rumors that the general counsel was having an extramarital affair.

The general counsel then received a series of anonymous e-mails demanding that he recommend moving forward with the investment and threatening, if he did not, to disclose information about his alleged affair to his wife, government officials, and the media. The general counsel contacted law enforcement, which traced some of the e-mails to petitioner's home computer and other e-mails to offices of FA Technology Ventures.

Petitioner was indicted for, and a jury convicted him of, attempted extortion, in violation of the Hobbs Act, 18 U.S.C. § 1951(a). That Act subjects a person to criminal liability if he "in any way or degree obstructs, delays, or affects commerce or the movement of any article or commodity in commerce, by robbery or extortion or attempts or conspires so to do." § 1951(a). The Act defines "extortion" to mean "the obtaining of property from another, with his consent, induced by wrongful use of actual or threatened force, violence, or fear, or under color of official right." § 1951(b)(2). On the verdict form, the jury was asked to specify the property that petitioner attempted to extort: (1) "the Commitment"; (2) "the Comptroller's approval of the Commitment"; or (3) "the General Counsel's recommendation to approve the Commitment." The jury chose only the third option.

The Court of Appeals for the Second Circuit affirmed the conviction. The court held that the general counsel "had a property right in rendering sound legal advice to the Comptroller and, specifically, to recommend—free from threats—whether the Comptroller should issue a Commitment for [the funds]." The court concluded that petitioner not only attempted to deprive the general counsel of his "property right," but that petitioner also "attempted to exercise that right by forcing the General Counsel to make a recommendation determined by [petitioner]." ...

Whether viewed from the standpoint of the common law, the text and genesis of the statute at issue here, or the jurisprudence of this Court's prior cases, what was charged in this case was not extortion.

It is a settled principle of interpretation that, absent other indication, "Congress intends to incorporate the well-settled meaning of the common-law terms it uses." *Neder v. United States*, 527 U.S. 1, 23 (1999)....

The Hobbs Act punishes "extortion," one of the oldest crimes in our legal tradition, see E. Coke, The Third Part of the Institutes of the Laws of England 148–150 (1648) (reprint 2008). The crime originally applied only to extortionate action by public officials, but was later extended by statute to private extortion. As far as is known, no case predating the Hobbs Act—English, federal, or state—ever identified conduct such as that charged here as extortionate. Extortion required the obtaining of items of value, typically cash, from the victim. It did not cover mere coercion to act, or to refrain from acting.

The text of the statute at issue confirms that the alleged property here cannot be extorted. Enacted in 1946, the Hobbs Act defines its crime of "extortion" as "the *obtaining of property from another,* with his consent, induced by wrongful use of actual or threatened force, violence, or fear, or under color of official right." 18 U.S.C. § 1951(b)(2) (emphasis added). Obtaining property requires "not only the deprivation but also the acquisition of property." *Scheidler v. National Organization for Women, Inc.*, 537 U.S. 393, 404 (2003). That is, it requires that the victim "part with" his property and that the extortionist "gain possession" of it, *Scheidler, supra,* at 403. The property extorted must therefore be *transferable*—that is, capable of passing from one person to another. The alleged property here lacks that defining feature.[19] ...

And finally, this Court's own precedent similarly demands reversal of petitioner's convictions. In *Scheidler*, we held that protesters did not commit extortion under the Hobbs Act, even though they "interfered with, disrupted, and in some instances completely deprived" abortion clinics of their ability to run their business. We reasoned that the protesters may have deprived the clinics of an "alleged property right," but they did not pursue or receive "'something of value from'" the clinics that they could then "exercise, transfer, or sell" themselves. The opinion supported its holding by citing the three New York coercion cases discussed above.

This case is easier than *Scheidler*, where one might at least have said that physical occupation of property amounted to obtaining that property. The deprivation alleged here is far more abstract. *Scheidler* rested its decision, as we do, on the term "obtaining." The principle announced there—that a defendant must pursue something of value from the victim that can be exercised, transferred, or sold—applies with equal force here. Whether one considers the personal right at issue to be "property" in a broad sense or not, it certainly was not *obtainable property* under the Hobbs Act.[20]

---

[19] [Court's footnote 2:] It way well be proper under the Hobbs Act for the Government to charge a person who obtains money by threatening a third party, who obtains funds belonging to a corporate or governmental entity by threatening the entity's agent, or who obtains "goodwill and customer revenues" by threatening a market competitor, see, *e.g., United States v. Zemek*, 634 F.2d 1159, 1173 (C.A.9 1980). Each of these might be considered "obtaining property from another." We need not consider those situations, however, because the Government did not charge any of them here.

[20] [Court's footnote 5:] The concurrence contends that the "right to make [a] recommendation" is not property. We are not sure of that. If one defines property to include anything of value, surely some rights

The Government's shifting and imprecise characterization of the alleged property at issue betrays the weakness of its case. According to the jury's verdict form, the "property" that petitioner attempted to extort was "the General Counsel's recommendation to approve the Commitment." But the Government expends minuscule effort in defending that theory of conviction. And for good reason—to wit, our decision in *Cleveland v. United States*, 531 U.S. 12 (2000), which reversed a business owner's mail-fraud conviction for "obtaining money or property" through misrepresentations made in an application for a video-poker license issued by the State. We held that a "license" is not "property" while in the State's hands and so cannot be "obtained" from the State. Even less so can an employee's yet-to-be-issued recommendation be called obtainable property, and less so still a yet-to-be-issued recommendation that would merely approve (but not effect) a particular investment.

Hence the Government's reliance on an alternative, more sophisticated (and sophistic) description of the property. Instead of defending the jury's description, the Government hinges its case on the general counsel's "intangible property right to give his disinterested legal opinion to his client free of improper outside interference." But *what*, exactly, would the petitioner have obtained for himself? A right to give *his own* disinterested legal opinion to *his own* client free of improper interference? Or perhaps, a right to give *the general counsel's* disinterested legal opinion to *the general counsel's* client?

Either formulation sounds absurd, because it is. Clearly, petitioner's goal was not to acquire the general counsel's "intangible property right to give disinterested legal advice." It was to force the general counsel to offer advice that accorded with petitioner's wishes. But again, that is coercion, not extortion. No fluent speaker of English would say that "petitioner *obtained and exercised* the general counsel's right to make a recommendation," any more than he would say that a person "*obtained and exercised* another's right to free speech." He would say that "petitioner *forced* the general counsel to make a particular recommendation," just as he would say that a person "*forced* another to make a statement." Adopting the Government's theory here would not only make nonsense of words; it would collapse the longstanding distinction between extortion and coercion and ignore Congress's choice to penalize one but not the other. That we cannot do.

JUSTICE ALITO, with whom JUSTICE KENNEDY and JUSTICE SOTOMAYOR join, concurring in the judgment.

The question that we must decide in this case is whether "the General Counsel's recommendation to approve the Commitment"—or his right to make that recommendation—is property that is capable of being extorted under the Hobbs Act. In my view, they are not.

The jury in this case returned a special verdict form and stated that the property that petitioner attempted to extort was "the General Counsel's recommendation to approve the Commitment." What the jury obviously meant by this was the general counsel's internal suggestion to his superior that the state government issue a nonbinding commitment to invest in a fund managed by FA Technology Ventures. We must therefore decide whether this nonbinding internal recommendation by a salaried state employee constitutes "property" within the meaning of the Hobbs Act, which defines "extortion" as "the obtaining of property from another, with his consent, induced by wrongful use of actual or threatened force, violence, or fear, or under color of official right." § 1951(b)(2).

The Hobbs Act does not define the term "property," but even at common law the offense of extortion was understood to include the obtaining of any thing of value. 2 E. Coke, The First Part of the Institutes of the Laws of England 368b (18th English ed. 1823) ("Extortion ... is

---

to make recommendations would qualify—for example, a member of the Pulitzer Prize Committee's right to recommend the recipient of the prize. I suppose that a prominent journalist would not give up that right (he cannot, of course, transfer it) for a significant sum of money—so it must be valuable. But the point relevant to the present case is that it cannot be transferred, so it cannot be the object of extortion under the statute.

a great misprison, by wresting or unlawfully taking by any officer, by colour of his office, any money or valuable thing of or from any man").

At the time Congress enacted the Hobbs Act, the contemporary edition of Black's Law Dictionary included an expansive definition of the term. See Black's Law Dictionary 1446 (3d ed. 1933). It stated that "[t]he term is said to extend to every species of valuable right and interest. ... The word is also commonly used to denote everything which is the subject of ownership, corporeal or incorporeal, tangible or intangible, visible or invisible, real or personal; everything that has an exchangeable value or which goes to make up wealth or estate." And the lower courts have long given the term a similarly expansive construction. See, e.g., *United States v. Tropiano*, 418 F.2d 1069, 1075 (C.A.2 1969) ("The concept of property under the Hobbs Act ... includes, in a broad sense, any valuable right considered as a source or element of wealth").

Despite the breadth of some of these formulations, however, the term "property" plainly does not reach everything that a person may hold dear; nor does it extend to everything that might in some indirect way portend the possibility of future economic gain. I do not suggest that the current lower court case law is necessarily correct, but it seems clear that the case now before us is an outlier and that the jury's verdict stretches the concept of property beyond the breaking point. ...

Our decision in *Cleveland v. United States*, 531 U.S. 12 (2000), supports the conclusion that internal recommendations regarding government decisions are not property. In *Cleveland*, we vacated a business owner's conviction under the federal mail fraud statute, 18 U.S.C. § 1341, for "obtaining money or property" through misrepresentations made in an application for a video poker license issued by the State. We held that a video poker license is not property in the hands of the State. I do not suggest that the concepts of property under the mail fraud statute and the Hobbs Act are necessarily the same. But surely a video poker license has a stronger claim to be classified as property than a mere internal recommendation that a state government take an initial step that might lead eventually to an investment that would be beneficial to private parties....[21]

The Second Circuit recharacterized the property that petitioner attempted to obtain as the general counsel's "right to make a recommendation consistent with his legal judgment." And the Government also presses that theory in this Court. According to the Government, the general counsel's property interest in his recommendation encompasses the right to make the recommendation. But this argument assumes that the recommendation itself is property. If an internal recommendation regarding a government decision does not constitute property, then surely a government employee's right to make such a recommendation is not property either (nor could it be deemed a *property* right). ...

The Court holds that petitioner's conduct does not amount to attempted extortion, but for a different reason: According to the Court, the alleged property that petitioner pursued was not transferrable and therefore is not capable of being "obtained." Because I do not believe that the item in question constitutes property, it is unnecessary for me to determine whether or not petitioner sought to obtain it. ...

Notes

1. The majority chose not to decide whether the case involved "property" ("w[e] are not sure about that"). Instead it focused on the word "obtain" and ruled that the defendant "must pursue something of value from the victim that can be exercised, transferred, or sold." The

---

[21] [Dissent's footnote 5:] To recognize that an internal recommendation regarding a government decision is not property does not foreclose the possibility that threatening a government employee, as the government's agent, in order to secure government property could qualify as Hobbs Act extortion. Here, after all, petitioner's ultimate goal was to secure an investment of money from the government. But the jury found only that petitioner had attempted to obtain the general counsel's recommendation, so I have no occasion to consider whether a Hobbs Act conviction could have been sustained on a different legal theory.

concurrence would have decided the case on the basis that the extortion did not have any "property" as its aim. What is the scope of "property" within the meaning of the Hobbs Act? For example, consider the facts of a case cited in the concurrence, *United States v. Tropiano*, 418 F.2d 1069 (2d Cir. 1969). The *Tropiano* defendants were partners in a garbage collection company who wished to prevent new competitor, Caron Refuse Removal, Inc. ("Caron"), from soliciting business in their vicinity and taking away their customers. They then used threats of violence to force Caron to stop recruiting their customers and to agree not to solicit any business in the area. On appeal, the Second Circuit upheld the *Tropiano* defendants' Hobbs Act extortion convictions, rejecting their argument that "nothing more than 'the right to do business' in the Milford area was surrendered by Caron and that such a right was not 'property' 'obtained' by the appellants." *Id.* at 1075. The court explained:

> The concept of property under the Hobbs Act, as devolved from its legislative history and numerous decisions, is not limited to physical or tangible property or things but includes, in a broad sense, any valuable right considered as a source or element of wealth and does not depend upon a direct benefit being conferred on the person who obtains the property.
>
> Obviously, Caron had a right to solicit business from anyone in any area without any territorial restrictions by the appellants and only by the exercise of such a right could Caron obtain customers whose accounts were admittedly valuable. Some indication of the value of the right to solicit customers appears from the fact that when the [Tropiano defendants' company's] accounts were sold for $53,135, [the] agreement [obtained from Caron] not to solicit those customers was valued at an additional $15,000. ... Caron's right to solicit accounts in Milford, Connecticut constituted property within the Hobbs Act definition.

Id. at 1075-76. The Second Circuit ruled that *Tropiano* survived *Scheidler II* in *United States v. Gotti*, 459 F.3d 296, 320-324 (2d Cir. 2006), but did it survive *Sekhar*? What about a more recent Second Circuit ruling that "[t]he right of the members of a union to democratic participation in a union election is property; that the right is intangible does not divest it of protection under the Hobbs Act."? *United States v. Bellomo*, 176 F.3d 580, 592-93 (2d Cir. 1999). On that basis, the court held that the crime families who sought to replace control of the union could be found guilty of conspiracy to commit extortion.

2. Both *Sekhar* opinions relied on *Cleveland v. United States*, 531 U.S. 12 (2000), a mail/wire fraud precedent. What implication, if any, does the *Sekhar* Court's ruling have for the definition of "property" under the mail and wire fraud statutes? Note that post-*Scheidler II* several circuits held that neither of these fraud statutes requires that the defendant "obtain" property; it is enough that the defendant merely deprived another of the property. *See, e.g.*, Porcelli v. United States, 404 F.3d 157, 161-62 (2d Cir. 2005); United States v. Hedaithy, 392 F.3d 580, 601-02 & n.21 (3d Cir. 2004). Should they reconsider? What about the "right to control" theory of property? Does the Court's refusal to accept the government's argument that the extortion consisted of the defendant's attempting to exercise the general counsel's "right to control his own labor," or his "right to control the substance of his own recommendation," mean that the lower courts have been mistaken in accepting the "right to control" as a species of property in the mail/wire fraud context?

3. Consider the Seventh Circuit's application of these precedents to a case involving "log-rolling"—that is, the trading of political favors—by then-Governor of Illinois, Rod Blagojevich. *See* United States v. Blagojevich, 794 F.3d 729, 734 (7th Cir. 2015). The Seventh Circuit concluded that "a proposal to trade one public act for another, a form of logrolling, is fundamentally unlike the swap of an official act for a private payment." Do you agree?

> The events leading to Blagojevich's arrest began when Barack Obama, then a Senator from Illinois, won the election for President in November 2008. When Obama took office in January 2009, Blagojevich would appoint his replacement, to serve until the time set by a writ of election. Before the 2008 election, federal agents had been

investigating Blagojevich and his associates. Evidence from some of those associates had led to warrants authorizing the interception of Blagojevich's phone calls. ... Interceptions revealed that Blagojevich viewed the opportunity to appoint a new Senator as a bonanza.

Through intermediaries (his own and the President-elect's), Blagojevich sought a favor from Sen. Obama in exchange for appointing Valerie Jarrett, who Blagojevich perceived as the person Sen. Obama would like to have succeed him. Blagojevich asked for an appointment to the Cabinet or for the President-elect to persuade a foundation to hire him at a substantial salary after his term as Governor ended, or find someone to donate $10 million and up to a new "social-welfare" organization that he would control. The President-elect was not willing to make a deal, and Blagojevich would not appoint Jarrett without compensation, saying: "They're not willing to give me anything except appreciation. Fuck them."

Blagojevich then turned to supporters of Rep. Jesse Jackson, Jr., offering the appointment in exchange for a $1.5 million "campaign contribution." (We put "campaign contribution" in quotation marks because Blagojevich was serving his second term as Governor and had decided not to run for a third. A jury was entitled to conclude that the money was for his personal benefit rather than a campaign.) Blagojevich broke off negotiations after learning about the wiretaps, and he was arrested before he could negotiate with anyone else. ...

... The indictment charged Blagojevich with the "color of official right" version of extortion [under the Hobbs Act], but none of the evidence suggests that Blagojevich claimed to have an "official right" to a job in the Cabinet. He did have an "official right" to appoint a new Senator, but unless a position in the Cabinet is "property" from the President's perspective, then seeking it does not amount to extortion. Yet a political office belongs to the people, not to the incumbent (or to someone hankering after the position). *Cleveland v. United States*, 531 U.S. 12 (2000), holds that state and municipal licenses, and similar documents, are not "property" in the hands of a public agency. That's equally true of public positions. The President-elect did not have a property interest in any Cabinet job, so an attempt to get him to appoint a particular person to the Cabinet is not an attempt to secure "property" from the President (or the citizenry at large).

Sekhar v. United States, [570 U.S. 729] (2013), shows that the phrase "obtaining of property" in the Hobbs Act must not be extended just to penalize shady dealings. *Sekhar* holds that a recommendation about investments is not "property" under § 1951(b)(2) for two principal reasons: first, in the long history of extortion law it had never before been so understood (similarly, political logrolling has never before been condemned as extortion); second, the making of a recommendation is not transferrable. The Court restricted "property" to what one owner can transfer to another. By that standard a job in the Cabinet (or any other public job) is not "property" from the employer's perspective. It is not owned by the person with appointing power, and it cannot be deeded over. The position may be *filled* by different people, but the position itself is not a transferrable property interest. A position is "held" or "occupied" but not "obtained," and under *Sekhar* something that cannot be "obtained" also cannot be the subject of extortion. ...

Id. at 733, 735-36. The Seventh Circuit also concluded that this conduct also did not constitute honest services fraud under 18 U.S.C. § 1346 or program fraud under 18 U.S.C. § 666.

C. FEDERAL PROGRAM BRIBERY, THEFT, AND FRAUD UNDER § 666

Section 666 applies when governmental or other entities receive federal program assistance "benefits" exceeding $10,000 in any one year. The statute contains two principal prohibitions. The first, contained within § 666(a)(1)(A), permits conviction of (1) an agent of the entity receiving the federal assistance (2) who "embezzles, steals, obtains by fraud or otherwise without authority knowingly converts" (3) property valued at $5,000 or more of the recipient entity.

The second, contained in § 666(a)(1)(B) and 666(a)(2), is addressed to program bribery rather than theft and fraud and at present seems the prohibition more often invoked. Section 666(a)(1)(B) penalizes (1) an agent of the entity receiving the federal assistance (2) who corruptly solicits, accepts, or agrees to accept "anything of value" from any person, (3) "intending to be influenced or rewarded in connection with any business, transaction, or series of transactions" of the receiving entity involving anything of value of $5,000 or more. Section 666(a)(2) essentially replicates the above prohibition and authorizes the prosecution of the briber, as well as the bribed. The following cases, *Fischer* (a fraud case) and *Sabri* (a bribery case), illustrate how many issues are raised by the above elements, and the implications of broad readings of the statute's terms.

FISCHER v. UNITED STATES
529 U.S. 667 (2000)

JUSTICE KENNEDY delivered the opinion of the Court.

The federal bribery statute prohibits defrauding organizations which "receiv[e], in any one year period, benefits in excess of $10,000 under a Federal program." 18 U.S.C. § 666(b). We granted certiorari to determine whether the statute covers fraud perpetrated on organizations participating in the Medicare program. Upon consideration of the role and regulated status of hospitals as health care providers under the Medicare program, we hold they receive "benefits" within the meaning of the statute. We affirm petitioner's convictions.

Petitioner Jeffrey Allan Fischer was president and partial owner of Quality Medical Consultants, Inc. (QMC), a corporation which performed billing audits for health care organizations. In 1993 petitioner, on QMC's behalf, negotiated a $1.2 million loan from West Volusia Hospital Authority (WVHA), a municipal agency responsible for operating two hospitals located in West Volusia County, Florida. Both hospitals participate in the Medicare program, and in 1993 WVHA received between $10 and $15 million in Medicare funds.

A February 1994 audit of WVHA's financial affairs raised questions about the QMC loan. An investigation revealed QMC used the loan proceeds to repay creditors and to raise the salaries of its five owner-employees, including petitioner. It was determined that petitioner had arranged for QMC to advance at least $100,000 to a private company owned by an individual who had assisted QMC in securing a letter of credit in connection with the WVHA loan. QMC, at petitioner's directive, also committed portions of the loan proceeds to speculative securities. These investments yielded losses of almost $400,000. The investigation further uncovered use of the loan proceeds to pay, through an intermediate transfer, a $10,000 kickback to WVHA's chief financial officer, the individual with whom petitioner had negotiated the loan in the first instance. QMC defaulted on its obligation to WVHA and filed for bankruptcy.

In 1996 petitioner was indicted by a federal grand jury on 13 counts, including charges of defrauding an organization which receives benefits under a federal assistance program, 18 U.S.C. § 666(a)(1)(A), and of paying a kickback to one of its agents, § 666(a)(2). A jury convicted petitioner on all counts charged, and the District Court sentenced him to 65 months' imprisonment and a 3-year term of supervised release. Petitioner, in addition, was ordered to pay $1.2 million in restitution.

On appeal petitioner argued that the Government failed to prove WVHA, as the organization affected by his wrongdoing, received "benefits in excess of $10,000 under a Federal program," as required by 18 U.S.C. § 666(b). Rejecting the argument, the United States Court of Appeals for the Eleventh Circuit affirmed the convictions. ...

We granted certiorari, and we affirm.

The nature and purposes of the Medicare program give us essential instruction in resolving the present controversy. Established in 1965 as part of the Social Security Act, 42

U.S.C. § 1395 *et seq.* (1994 ed. and Supp. III), Medicare is a federally funded medical insurance program for the elderly and disabled. In fiscal 1997 some 38.8 million individuals were enrolled in the program, and over 6,100 hospitals were authorized to provide services to them. Medicare expenditures for hospital services exceeded $123 billion in 1998, making the Federal Government the single largest source of funds for participating hospitals. This amount constituted 32% of the hospitals' total receipts.

Providers of health care services, such as the two hospitals operated by WVHA, qualify to participate in the program upon satisfying a comprehensive series of statutory and regulatory requirements, including particular accreditation standards. Hospitals, for instance, must satisfy licensing standards; possess a governing body to "ensure that there is an effective, hospital-wide quality assurance program to evaluate the provision of patient care"; and employ a "well organized" medical staff accountable on matters relating to "the quality of the medical care provided to patients." ... Compliance with these standards provides the Government with assurance that participating providers possess the capacity to fulfill their statutory obligation of providing "medically necessary" services "of a quality which meets professionally recognized standards of health care." Peer review organizations monitor providers' compliance with these and other obligations. Sanctions for noncompliance include dismissal from the program.

Medicare attains its objectives through an elaborate funding structure. Participating health care organizations, in exchange for rendering services, receive federal funds on a periodic basis. The amounts received reflect the "reasonable cost" of services rendered, defined as "the costs necessary in the efficient delivery of needed health services to individuals covered [by the program]." Necessary costs are not limited to the immediate costs of an individual treatment procedure. Instead they are defined in broader terms: "Necessary and proper costs are costs that are appropriate and helpful in developing and maintaining the operation of patient care facilities and activities." ...

In the normal course Medicare disbursements occur on a periodic basis, often in advance of a provider's rendering services. The payment system serves to "protect providers' liquidity," thereby assisting in the ongoing provision of services. The program, then, establishes correlating and reinforcing incentives: The Government has an interest in making available a high level of quality of care for the elderly and disabled; and providers, because of their financial dependence upon the program, have incentives to achieve program goals. The nature of the program bears on the question of statutory coverage.

Section 666 of Title 18 of the United States Code prohibits acts of theft and fraud against organizations receiving funds under federal assistance programs. ...

Liability for the acts prohibited by subsection (a) is predicated upon a showing that the defrauded organization "receive[d], in any one period, benefits in excess of $10,000 under a Federal program." § 666(b). Those benefits can be in the form of "a grant, contract, subsidy, loan, guarantee, insurance, or other form of Federal assistance." All agree Medicare is a federal assistance program, and that WVHA, as the organization defrauded by petitioner's actions, received in excess of $10,000 in payments under the program. The sole point in contention is whether those payments constituted "benefits," within the meaning of subsection (b).

Petitioner argues that the Medicare program provides benefits to the elderly and disabled but not to the health care organizations. Provider organizations, in petitioner's view, do no more than render services in exchange for compensation. Under petitioner's submission the Medicare program envisions a single beneficiary, the qualifying patient. The Government, in opposition, urges that a determination whether an organization receives "benefits" within the meaning of § 666(b) turns on whether the Federal Government was the source of the payment. Funds received under a federal assistance program, the Government asserts, can be traced from federal coffers, often through an intermediary or carrier, to the health care provider. Under its view, the "federal-program source of the funds" satisfies the benefits definition.

We reject petitioner's reading of the statute but without endorsing the Government's broader position. We conclude Medicare payments are "benefits," as the term is used in its ordinary sense and as it is intended in the statute. The noun "benefit" means "something that guards, aids, or promotes well-being: advantage, good"; "useful aid"; "payment, gift [such as]" financial help in time of sickness, old age, or unemployment"; or "a cash payment or service provided for under an annuity, pension plan, or insurance policy." Webster's Third New International Dictionary 204 (1971). These definitions support petitioner's assertion that qualifying patients receive benefits under the Medicare program. ...

That one beneficiary of an assistance program can be identified does not foreclose the existence of others, however. In this respect petitioner's construction would give incomplete meaning to the term "benefits." Medicare operates with a purpose and design above and beyond point-of-sale patient care, and it follows that the benefits of the program extend in a broader manner as well. The argument limiting the term "benefits" to the program's targeted or primary beneficiaries would exclude, for example, a Medicare intermediary (such as Blue Cross and Blue Shield), a result both parties disavow. For present purposes it cannot be disputed the providers themselves derive significant advantage by satisfying the participation standards imposed by the Government. These advantages constitute benefits within the meaning of the federal bribery statute, a statute we have described as "expansive," "both as to the [conduct] forbidden and the entities covered."

Subsection (b) identifies several sources as providing benefits under a federal program—"a grant, contract, subsidy, loan, guarantee, insurance, or other form of Federal assistance." 18 U.S.C. § 666(b). This language indicates that Congress viewed many federal assistance programs as providing benefits to participating organizations. Coupled with the broad substantive prohibitions of subsection (a), the language of subsection (b) reveals Congress' expansive, unambiguous intent to ensure the integrity of organizations participating in federal assistance programs.

Subsection (c) of the statute bears on the analysis. The provision removes from the statute's coverage any "bona fide salary, wages, fees, or other compensation paid, or expenses paid or reimbursed, in the usual course of business." § 666(c). Petitioner argues that the subsection operates to exclude the payments in question because they are either "compensation" or "expenses paid or reimbursed," or some combination of the two, and that the payments are made in the "usual course of business." We disagree. ...

We do not accept the view that the Medicare payments here in question are for the limited purposes of compensating providers or reimbursing them for ordinary course expenditures. The payments are made for significant and substantial reasons in addition to compensation or reimbursement, so that neither these terms nor the usual course of business conditions set forth in subsection (c) are met here. The payments in question have attributes and purposes well beyond those described in subsection (c). These attributes and purposes are consistent with the definition of "benefit." While the payments might have similarities to payments an insurer would remit to a hospital quite without regard to the Medicare program, the Government does not make the payment unless the hospital complies with its intricate regulatory scheme. The payments are made not simply to reimburse for treatment of qualifying patients but to assist the hospital in making available and maintaining a certain level and quality of medical care, all in the interest of both the hospital and the greater community.

Here ... the provider itself is the object of substantial Government regulation. Medicare is designed to the end that the Government receives not only reciprocal value from isolated transactions but also long-term advantages from the existence of a sound and effective health care system for the elderly and disabled. The Government enacted specific statutes and regulations to secure its own interests in promoting the well being and advantage of the health care provider, in addition to the patient who receives care. The health care provider is receiving a benefit in the conventional sense of the term, unlike the case of a contractor whom the Government does not regulate or assist for long-term objectives or for significant purposes beyond performance of an immediate transaction. Adequate payment and assistance to the health care provider is itself one of the objectives of the program. These purposes and effects suffice to make the payment a benefit within the meaning of the statute.

The structure and operation of the Medicare program reveal a comprehensive federal assistance enterprise aimed at ensuring the availability of quality health care for the broader community. Participating health care organizations ... must satisfy a series of qualification and accreditation requirements, standards aimed in part at ensuring the provision of a certain quality of care. By reimbursing participating providers for a wide range of costs and expenses, including medical treatment costs, overhead costs, and education costs, Medicare's reimbursement system furthers this objective. This scheme is structured to ensure that providers possess the capacity to render, on an ongoing basis, medical care to the program's qualifying patients. The structure, moreover, proves untenable petitioner's assertion that Congress has no interest in the financial stability of providers once services are rendered to patients. Payments are made in a manner calculated to maintain provider stability. Incentives are given for long-term improvements, such as capital costs and education. Subsidies, defined as "special treatment," are awarded to certain providers. In short, provider organizations play a vital role and maintain a high level of responsibility in carrying out the program's purposes. Medicare funds, in turn, provide benefits extending beyond isolated, point-of-sale treatment transactions. The funds health care organizations receive for participating in the Medicare program constitute "benefits" within the meaning of 18 U.S.C. § 666(b).

Our discussion should not be taken to suggest that federal funds disbursed under an assistance program will result in coverage of all recipient fraud under § 666(b). Any receipt of federal funds can, at some level of generality, be characterized as a benefit. The statute does not employ this broad, almost limitless use of the term. Doing so would turn almost every act of fraud or bribery into a federal offense, upsetting the proper federal balance. To determine whether an organization participating in a federal assistance program receives "benefits," an examination must be undertaken of the program's structure, operation, and purpose. The inquiry should examine the conditions under which the organization receives the federal payments. The answer could depend, as it does here, on whether the recipient's own operations are one of the reasons for maintaining the program. Health care organizations participating in the Medicare program satisfy this standard. ...

JUSTICE THOMAS, with whom JUSTICE SCALIA joins, dissenting.

In my view, the only persons who receive "benefits" under Medicare are the individual elderly and disabled Medicare patients, not the medical providers who serve them. Payments made by the Federal Government to a Medicare health care provider to reimburse the provider for the costs of services rendered, rather than to provide financial aid to the hospital, are not "benefits." I respectfully dissent.

... As the Court notes, an organization is not a beneficiary of a federal program merely because the organization receives federal funds. Rather, as the Court admits, a "benefit" is something that "guards, aids, or promotes well-being"; "useful aid"; or a "payment, gift [as] financial help in time of sickness, old age, or unemployment." Webster's Third New International Dictionary 204 (1971). Therefore, the Court acknowledges, an organization "receives ... benefits" within the meaning of § 666(b) only if the federal funds are designed to guard, aid, or promote the well-being of the organization, to provide useful aid to the organization, or to give the organization financial help in time of trouble. In my view, payments made by the Federal Government to a Medicare health care provider as part of a market transaction are not "benefits."[22]

The statutory and regulatory scheme governing Medicare reimbursements leaves no doubt that hospitals do not receive "benefits" from the Federal Government within this meaning of the term, but merely receive payments for costs pursuant to a market transaction. ...

Although the statutory provisions and regulations ... demonstrate that Medicare operates as a reimbursement scheme with respect to health care providers, and not as a means of providing them "useful aid" or "financial help," the Court finds in the statute and regulations

---

[22] [Dissent's footnote 1:] Even if I thought that, under a reading of § 666(b) standing alone, a market exchange of payment for services might amount to "benefits," § 666(c) would eliminate that doubt. Section 666(c) makes clear that "bona fide ... expenses paid or reimbursed, in the usual course of business," are not covered by the statute. As discussed below, Medicare payments to health care providers are precisely this type of payment.

evidence that health care providers are, along with the individual elderly and disabled patients, also target beneficiaries of the program. I think that the Court's reasoning is both unpersuasive and boundless; any funds flowing from a federal assistance program could be deemed "benefits" under the Court's rationale, notwithstanding the Court's concluding disclaimer of such a result. Thus, although the Court purports to reject the Government's argument that "benefits" means "funds that originate in a federal assistance program," the Court, in practice, adopts it.

First, the Court describes Medicare's elaborate funding structure and notes that Medicare's reasonable cost recovery system allows recovery of certain capital costs and the costs of education and training. These provisions of Medicare do not establish that hospitals receive "benefits." To the contrary, the capital costs recoverable under those provisions of Medicare are the costs tied to the treatment of Medicare patients. In this sense, the cost provisions of Medicare expressly defeat any suggestion that they are meant to provide a "benefit" to the hospital. These provisions are not designed to provide financial assistance to the hospital; they are designed to ensure that Medicare beneficiaries receive quality medical care. And again, the Medicare program picks up only the portion of the costs attributable to the care of Medicare beneficiaries. In fact, the Court does not grapple with the evidence that Medicare systematically *under*-compensates health care providers, evidence that would further undermine the notion that hospitals are receiving some form of financial assistance from the program.

Second, the Court relies on the numerous obligations imposed on health care providers participating in Medicare. The Court notes that health care providers must satisfy licensing standards, provide a laundry list of particular health care services, and ensure an effective quality-assurance program. I assume, however, that the same could be said of most Government contractors. The defense contractor who agrees to build the military's equipment is, no doubt, subject to an extensive list of statutory and regulatory requirements, not because the Government intends to provide "benefits" to the contractor, but because the Federal Government intends to place controls on the expenditure of federal dollars. Similarly, private insurers no doubt impose various requirements on those who receive reimbursements from them. In requiring hospitals to meet certain standards, the Federal Government is no different from these private insurers, except that the Federal Government exercises vastly greater market power. In other words, the imposition on health care providers of an intricate regulatory scheme is irrelevant to the question whether funds paid pursuant to that scheme are benefits. ...

Finally, the Court concludes, based on its observations of Medicare, that "Medicare operates with a purpose and design above and beyond point-of-sale patient care," namely, "ensuring the availability of quality health care for the broader community." According to the Court, Medicare guarantees that "providers possess the capacity to render, on an on-going basis, medical care to the program's qualifying patients." In other words, Medicare exists to guarantee patients' access to quality medical care. Quality medical care is available only if medical providers remain financially viable. Medicare payments create demand for medical services and, therefore, provide "benefits" to health care providers. This syllogism, however, amounts to nothing more than the self-evident point that Medicare aims to ensure that the beneficiaries of the program—patients—are able to receive the program's intended benefits. It does not establish that Medicare exists to put hospitals on the dole.

In short, none of the components of Medicare cited by the Court establishes that benefits flow to hospitals. It is significant that, although the Court repeatedly invokes, mantra-like, its conclusion that Medicare exists for a purpose above and beyond reimbursing hospitals for treating Medicare patients, when the Court comes around to actually identifying this purpose, it can only state: "The structure and operation of the Medicare program reveal a comprehensive federal assistance enterprise aimed at ensuring the availability of quality health care for the broader community." The Court cannot bring itself to say, as it must, that Medicare exists for the *hospital*. ...

I doubt that there is any federal assistance program that does not provide "benefits" to organizations under the Court's expansive rationale, but will illustrate my point with just one example employed by two lower courts. See *United States v. Wyncoop*, 11 F.3d 119, 123 (C.A.9 1993); *United States v. LaHue*, 998 F.Supp. 1182, 1187 (D.Kan.1998), aff'd, 170 F.3d 1026 (C.A.10 1999). Many grocery stores accept more than $10,000 per annum in food stamps distributed to individual beneficiaries as part of the Federal Food Stamp and Food Distribution Program. Like Medicare providers, stores participating in the Food Stamp Program are required to satisfy a comprehensive series of statutory and regulatory requirements. For example, stores are qualified to participate only if they sell an adequate percentage of staple foods such as meat, cereal, and dairy products. Stores must document an ability to attract food stamp business and demonstrate the business integrity and reputation of the store owners and managers. Like Medicare, the Food Stamp Program monitors the providers' compliance with the program's requirements. Like Medicare, the Food Stamp Program sanctions noncompliance with dismissal from the program. And, the Food Stamp Program is like Medicare in that it can be described as having "a purpose and design above and beyond point-of-sale" of food. Undoubtedly, the Food Stamp program helps to address the "grocery gap," that is, the lack of availability of reasonably priced nutritional foods in some low-income and rural areas. There is ample evidence on the face of the statute and regulations that Congress and the agency had in mind the need to ensure that low-income communities have access to grocery stores. It could be said, therefore, that the grocery store's "own operations are one of the reasons for maintaining the program."

To my mind, the reason that a corner grocery does not receive "benefits" is simply that it merely receives payment from the Government in a market transaction. I fail to see, however, how the Court could reach the same conclusion that I would. ...

Notes

1. The *Fischer* decision is an important one in the health care fraud area, which has become a federal enforcement priority. What implications does it have outside that area?

Take the dissent's hypothetical. Could a defendant be prosecuted under § 666 for stealing from or defrauding a grocery store that participates in the Food Stamp Program (assuming the jurisdictional amounts were satisfied)? What about the defense contractor example posited by the dissent? *See* United States v. Copeland, 143 F.3d 1439 (11th Cir. 1998) (pre-*Fischer* case reversing § 666 conviction based on bribery of Lockheed employee because Lockheed, with whom federal government engaged in ordinary commercial transactions, did not receive benefits pursuant to a federal assistance program).

What about a case in which a defendant is prosecuted for embezzling from a college that does not directly receive federal funding but rather receives the proceeds of students' federal college loans? *See* United States v. Wyncoop, 11 F.3d 119 (9th Cir. 1993) (pre-*Fischer* case reversing § 666 conviction based on embezzlement by private college employee because although federal student-loan program required the college to monitor the continued enrollment and eligibility of loan recipients and the banks often issued the loan checks jointly to the students and the school, the school itself received no federal funds directly and received only the indirect benefits associated with increased enrollment of students receiving private loans).

How about nursing homes that receive social security payments as fiduciaries for incapacitated residents? *See* United States v. Zyskind, 118 F.3d 113 (2d Cir. 1997) (pre-*Fischer* case affirming § 666 conviction of administrator of home for handicapped adults for theft of residents' Veteran's Administration benefits checks which were provided directly to the home as fiduciary for the residents).

Can a "benefit" include a government loan? *See* United States v. Rooney, 986 F.2d 31 (2d Cir. 1993) (upholding indictment charging real estate developer who received a market rate federal government loan exceeding $10,000 with bribery for offering to apply for additional loans and with them to make prompt payment to contractor if contractor would provide the developer with free services), *rev'd after trial*, 37 F.3d 847 (2d Cir. 1994) (concluding that solicitation of contractor was not "corrupt").

Note that in United States v. Bahel, 662 F.3d 610, 627 (2d Cir. 2011), the Second Circuit applied *Fischer* to uphold the conviction of a foreign national employed by the United Nations on a bribery theory under § 666. In so doing, the court held that the United Nations Participation Act, 22 U.S.C. § 287e, which authorizes payment of the United States' dues to the U.N., can be considered a 'benefit' program. *Id.* at 627. The Second Circuit reasoned that because Congress authorized such payments, the United States' payments "are made under 'a specific statutory scheme' that aims to advance the government's foreign policy objectives, specifically, the policy of participating in collective endeavors to secure the benefits of world peace." *Id.* Further, the U.S. funding of the U.N. is "subject to several conditions designed in part to promote broader objectives related to national security while ensuring that any money contributed to the U.N. is responsibly expended and accounted for." *Id.*

2. Even if the "benefits" element were deemed satisfied in the Food Stamp hypothetical by virtue of the Court's holding in *Fischer*, would the government need to prove that there was a nexus between the things of value obtained through theft or fraud and the federal program funding—that is, that items obtained either are traceable to the federal funding or that the theft or fraud somehow impaired federal governmental interests? Must any bribery cognizable under the statute affect the disbursement of the federal funding or the federal program that is funded? Consider the following.

SABRI v. UNITED STATES
541 U.S. 600 (2004)

JUSTICE SOUTER delivered the opinion of the Court.

The question is whether 18 U.S.C. § 666(a)(2), proscribing bribery of state, local, and tribal officials of entities that receive at least $10,000 in federal funds, is a valid exercise of congressional authority under Article I of the Constitution. We hold that it is.

Petitioner Basim Omar Sabri is a real estate developer who proposed to build a hotel and retail structure in the city of Minneapolis. Sabri lacked confidence, however, in his ability to adapt to the lawful administration of licensing and zoning laws, and offered three separate bribes to a city councilman, Brian Herron, according to the grand jury indictment that gave rise to this case. At the time the bribes were allegedly offered (between July 2, 2001, and July 17, 2001), Herron served as a member of the Board of Commissioners of the Minneapolis Community Development Agency (MCDA), a public body created by the city council to fund housing and economic development within the city.

Count 1 of the indictment charged Sabri with offering a $5,000 kickback for obtaining various regulatory approvals, and according to Count 2, Sabri offered Herron a $10,000 bribe to set up and attend a meeting with owners of land near the site Sabri had in mind, at which Herron would threaten to use the city's eminent domain authority to seize their property if they were troublesome to Sabri. Count 3 alleged that Sabri offered Herron a commission of 10% on some $800,000 in community economic development grants that Sabri sought from the city, the MCDA, and other sources.

The charges were brought under 18 U.S.C. § 666(a)(2), which imposes federal criminal penalties on anyone who

"corruptly gives, offers, or agrees to give anything of value to any person, with intent to influence or reward an agent of an organization or of a State, local or Indian tribal government, or any agency thereof, in connection with any business, transaction, or series of transactions of such organization, government, or agency involving anything of value of $5,000 or more."

For criminal liability to lie, the statute requires that

"the organization, government, or agency receiv[e], in any one year period, benefits in excess of $10,000 under a Federal program involving a grant, contract, subsidy, loan, guarantee, insurance, or other form of Federal assistance." § 666(b).

In 2001, the City Council of Minneapolis administered about $29 million in federal funds paid to the city, and in the same period, the MCDA received some $23 million of federal money.

Before trial, Sabri moved to dismiss the indictment on the ground that § 666(a)(2) is unconstitutional on its face for failure to require proof of a connection between the federal funds and the alleged bribe, as an element of liability. The Government responded that "even if an additional nexus between the bribery conduct and the federal funds is required, the evidence in this case will easily meet such a standard" because Sabri's alleged actions related to federal dollars. Although Sabri did not contradict this factual claim, the District Court agreed with him that the law was facially invalid. A divided panel of the Eighth Circuit reversed, holding that there was nothing fatal in the absence of an express requirement to prove some connection between a given bribe and federally pedigreed dollars, and that the statute was constitutional under the Necessary and Proper Clause in serving the objects of the congressional spending power. ...

We granted certiorari to resolve a split among the Courts of Appeals over the need to require connection between forbidden conduct and federal funds. We now affirm.

Sabri raises what he calls a facial challenge to § 666(a)(2): the law can never be applied constitutionally because it fails to require proof of any connection between a bribe or kickback and some federal money. It is fatal, as he sees it, that the statute does not make the link an element of the crime, to be charged in the indictment and demonstrated beyond a reasonable doubt. Thus, Sabri claims his attack meets the demanding standard set out in *United States v. Salerno*, 481 U.S. 739, 745 (1987), since he says no prosecution can satisfy the Constitution under this statute, owing to its failure to require proof that its particular application falls within Congress's jurisdiction to legislate.

We can readily dispose of this position that, to qualify as a valid exercise of Article I power, the statute must require proof of connection with federal money as an element of the offense. We simply do not presume the unconstitutionality of federal criminal statutes lacking explicit provision of a jurisdictional hook, and there is no occasion even to consider the need for such a requirement where there is no reason to suspect that enforcement of a criminal statute would extend beyond a legitimate interest cognizable under Article I, § 8.

Congress has authority under the Spending Clause to appropriate federal monies to promote the general welfare, Art. I, § 8, cl. 1, and it has corresponding authority under the Necessary and Proper Clause, Art. I, § 8, cl. 18, to see to it that taxpayer dollars appropriated under that power are in fact spent for the general welfare, and not frittered away in graft or on projects undermined when funds are siphoned off or corrupt public officers are derelict about demanding value for dollars. See generally *McCulloch v. Maryland*, 4 Wheat. 316 (1819) (establishing review for means-ends rationality under the Necessary and Proper Clause). Congress does not have to sit by and accept the risk of operations thwarted by local and state improbity. See, *e.g., McCulloch, supra*, at 417 (power to "'establish post-offices and post-roads'" entails authority to "punish those who steal letters"). Section 666(a)(2) addresses the problem at the sources of bribes, by rational means, to safeguard the integrity of the state, local, and tribal recipients of federal dollars.

It is true, just as Sabri says, that not every bribe or kickback offered or paid to agents of governments covered by § 666(b) will be traceably skimmed from specific federal payments, or show up in the guise of a *quid pro quo* for some dereliction in spending a federal grant. Cf. *Salinas v. United States*, 522 U.S. 52, 56-57 (1997) (The "expansive, unqualified" language of the statute "does not support the interpretation that federal funds must be affected to violate § 666(a)(1)(B)"). But this possibility portends no enforcement beyond the scope of federal interest, for the reason that corruption does not have to be that limited to affect the federal interest. Money is fungible, bribed officials are untrustworthy stewards of federal funds, and corrupt contractors do not deliver dollar-for-dollar value. Liquidity is not a financial term for nothing; money can be drained off here because a federal grant is pouring in there. And officials are not any the less threatening to the objects behind federal spending just because they may accept general retainers. It is certainly enough that the statutes condition the offense on a threshold amount of federal dollars defining the federal interest, such as that provided here, and on a bribe that goes well beyond liquor and cigars.

For those of us who accept help from legislative history, it is worth noting that the legislative record confirms that § 666(a)(2) is an instance of necessary and proper legislation. The design was generally to "protect the integrity of the vast sums of money distributed through Federal programs from theft, fraud, and undue influence by bribery," see S.Rep. No. 98-225, p. 370 (1983), in contrast to prior federal law affording only two limited opportunities to prosecute such threats to the federal interest: 18 U.S.C. § 641, the federal theft statute, and § 201, the federal bribery law. Those laws had proven inadequate to the task. The former went only to outright theft of unadulterated federal funds, and prior to this Court's opinion in *Dixson v. United States*, 465 U.S. 482 (1984), which came after passage of § 666, the bribery statute had been interpreted by lower courts to bar prosecution of bribes directed at state and local officials. Thus we said that § 666 "was designed to extend federal bribery prohibitions to bribes offered to state and local officials employed by agencies receiving federal funds," thereby filling the regulatory gaps. Congress's decision to enact § 666 only after other legislation had failed to protect federal interests is further indication that it was acting within the ambit of the Necessary and Proper Clause.

Petitioner presses two more particular arguments against the constitutionality of § 666(a)(2), neither of which helps him. First, he says that § 666 is all of a piece with the legislation that a majority of this Court held to exceed Congress's authority under the Commerce Clause in *United States v. Lopez*, 514 U.S. 549 (1995), and *United States v. Morrison*, 529 U.S. 598 (2000). But these precedents do not control here. In *Lopez* and *Morrison*, the Court struck down federal statutes regulating gun possession near schools and gender-motivated violence, respectively, because it found the effects of those activities on interstate commerce insufficiently robust. The Court emphasized the noneconomic nature of the regulated conduct, commenting on the law at issue in *Lopez*, for example, "that by its terms [it] has nothing to do with 'commerce' or any sort of economic enterprise, however broadly one might define those terms." The Court rejected the Government's contentions that the gun law was valid Commerce Clause legislation because guns near schools ultimately bore on social prosperity and productivity, reasoning that on that logic, Commerce Clause authority would effectively know no limit. In order to uphold the legislation, the Court concluded, it would be necessary "to pile inference upon inference in a manner that would bid fair to convert congressional authority under the Commerce Clause to a general police power of the sort retained by the States."

No piling is needed here to show that Congress was within its prerogative to protect spending objects from the menace of local administrators on the take. The power to keep a watchful eye on expenditures and on the reliability of those who use public money is bound up with congressional authority to spend in the first place, and Sabri would be hard pressed to claim, in the words of the *Lopez* Court, that § 666(a)(2) "has nothing to do with" the congressional spending power.

Sabri next argues that § 666(a)(2) amounts to an unduly coercive, and impermissibly sweeping, condition on the grant of federal funds as judged under the criterion applied in *South Dakota v. Dole*, 483 U.S. 203 (1987). This is not so. Section 666(a)(2) is authority to bring federal power to bear directly on individuals who convert public spending into unearned private gain, not a means for bringing federal economic might to bear on a State's own choices of public policy. ...

JUSTICE THOMAS, concurring in the judgment.

Title 18 U.S.C. § 666(a)(2) is a valid exercise of Congress' power to regulate commerce, at least under this Court's precedent. Cf. *Perez v. United States*, 402 U.S. 146, 154 (1971). I continue to doubt that we have correctly interpreted the Commerce Clause. But until this

Court reconsiders its precedents, and because neither party requests us to do so here, our prior case law controls the outcome of this case.

I write further because I find questionable the scope the Court gives to the Necessary and Proper Clause as applied to Congress' authority to spend. In particular, the Court appears to hold that the Necessary and Proper Clause authorizes the exercise of any power that is no more than a "rational means" to effectuate one of Congress' enumerated powers. This conclusion derives from the Court's characterization of the seminal case *McCulloch v. Maryland*, 4 Wheat. 316 (1819), as having established a "means-ends rationality" test, a characterization that I am not certain is correct. ...

Under the *McCulloch* formulation, I have doubts that § 666(a)(2) is a proper use of the Necessary and Proper Clause as applied to Congress' power to spend. ... All that is necessary for § 666(a)(2) to apply is that the organization, government, or agency in question receives more than $10,000 in federal benefits of any kind, and that an agent of the entity is bribed regarding a substantial transaction of that entity. No connection whatsoever between the corrupt transaction and the federal benefits need be shown.

The Court does a not-wholly-unconvincing job of tying the broad scope of § 666(a)(2) to a federal interest in federal funds and programs. But simply noting that "[m]oney is fungible," for instance, does not explain how there could be any federal interest in "prosecut[ing] a bribe paid to a city's meat inspector in connection with a substantial transaction just because the city's parks department had received a federal grant of $10,000," *United States v. Santopietro*, 166 F.3d 88, 93 (C.A.2 1999). It would be difficult to describe the chain of inferences and assumptions in which the Court would have to indulge to connect such a bribe to a federal interest in any federal funds or programs as being "plainly adapted" to their protection. And, this is just one example of many in which any federal interest in protecting federal funds is equally attenuated, and yet the bribe is covered by the expansive language of § 666(a)(2). Overall, then, § 666(a)(2) appears to be no more plainly adapted to protecting federal funds or federally funded programs than a hypothetical federal statute criminalizing fraud of any kind perpetrated on any individual who happens to receive federal welfare benefits. ...

Notes

1. Does *Sabri* mean that if a governmental entity receives qualifying benefits, *for any purpose*, that receipt subjects *all* that governmental entity's agents to liability for *any* substantial theft, fraud, or bribery affecting the entity's business? If, as it seems, the answer is "yes," the sweep of this statute is "truly stunning" Beale, *supra* note 4, at 710. As Professor Beale notes, "[i]t seems fair to assume that every state and virtually every city and county receive federal funds of more than $10,000 per year. Indeed, the reported prosecutions involve not only states and large cities, but cities with populations of less than 10,000." *Id.* Thus, the breadth of this statute may turn § 666 "into something of a national anti-corruption statute. Such a statute has long been the holy grail of federal prosecutors. Perhaps they already had it" in § 666. George D. Brown, *Carte Blanche: Federal Prosecution of State and Local Officials After* Sabri, 54 Catholic Univ. L. Rev. 403, 406 (2005).

Defense counsel, however, assert that all is not lost, and that redemption may be found in limiting opinions various circuits have issued on other statutory terms. *See* Michael J. Leotta, *Supreme Court Overrules the Nexus Requirement*, 11 No. 7 Bus. Crimes Bull. 1, 6, 8 (2004). Thus, Michael Leotta advises attorneys defending a § 666 case to

> consider whether the defendant is an "agent" of the particular entity that received the federal funds, as the Fifth and Ninth Circuits require, and whether the "structure, operation and purpose" of the federal payments were sufficiently comprehensive to deem them "benefits," as the Eleventh Circuit requires. *Sabri* does not prevent lower courts from construing the words of § 666 to answer federalism concerns.

Id. at 8; *see also* United States v. Edgar, 304 F.3d 1320, 1325 (11th Cir. 2002); United States v. Phillips, 219 F.3d 404, 413-15 (5th Cir. 2000).

2. *Who Is An "Agent"?* Section 666 prohibits bribery of an "agent" of an "organization, government or agency" that receives yearly federal program funds in excess of $10,000. The statute defines an "agent" as a "person authorized to act on behalf of another person or a government and, in the case of an organization or government, [the term] includes a servant or employee, and a partner, director, officer, manager, and representative." 18 U.S.C. § 666(d)(1). Whether a defendant is an "agent" for purposes of the statute is a question of federal law, not contract interpretation. Thus, even where a state contractor operated under a state contract that stated that he "shall act in the capacity of an independent contractor and not as an officer, employee, or agent of the state," he was an "agent" for § 666 purposes because he was "authorized to act" on behalf of the state. United States v. Lupton, 620 F.3d 790, 801 (7th Cir. 2010). Some courts, however, look to state law in determining whether a given defendant is a state agent. United States v. Langston, 590 F.3d 1226 (11th Cir. 2009) (official paid by state commission with money from the state treasury was not an agent of the state because under state law he was an employee of the commission, not the state).

The Supreme Court having squelched lower court efforts to contain the reach of the statute by rejecting a "nexus" requirement in *Sabri*, defense counsel may ask courts to use the "agency" requirement to limit the statute's scope. It appears, however, that courts are largely inclined to read the "agency" requirement broadly. *See, e.g.*, United States v. Shoemaker, 746 F.3d 614, 621-622 & n.7 (5th Cir. 2014) ("agent" need not have direct authority over the ultimate decision targeted by the bribe; "agent" need only have general authority to act for the organization and to control its funds); United States v. Keen, 676 F.3d 981, 990 (11th Cir. 2012) (to qualify as an "agent," an individual need only be authorized to act on behalf of that entity; the person need not be authorized to act with respect to the entity's funds); United States v. Fernandez, 722 F.3d 1, 9-12 (1st Cir. 2013). Courts also have rejected related arguments that § 666 contains an "official act" requirement akin to that required in § 201 cases. *See, e.g.*, United States v. Garrido, 713 F.3d 985, 999-1002 (9th Cir. 2013) (collecting cases).

3. *What is a "Thing of Value"?* Section 666 outlaws bribery of federally funded organizations "in connection with any business, transaction, or series of transactions ... involving anything of value of $5,000 or more." *See also* United States v. Smith, 804 F.3d 724 (5th Cir. 2015). Thus, "the *subject matter* of the bribe must be valued at $5,000 or more; the *bribe* itself need only be 'anything of value.'" United States v. Robinson, 663 F.3d 265, 271 (7th Cir. 2011). The "business" or "transaction" for which the bribe is paid can be intangible in value. For example, the Seventh Circuit upheld a conviction under § 666 based on a drug trafficker's offer of payments to a police officer to divert attention away from his illegal operation. *See Robinson*, 663 F.3d at 273-74. In such cases, courts have held that "[w]here the bribe-giver receives an intangible benefit, ... the bribe amount [may be used] as a proxy to stand for the value of the business or transaction." United States v. McNair, 605 F.3d 1152, 1186, n.38 (11th Cir. 2010). Thus, in *United States v. Townsend*, 630 F.3d 1003, 1006 (11th Cir.), "a drug dealer indicted on state charges who was released pending trial bought himself more freedom by bribing the officer whose duty it was to supervise his release." The court, explicitly rejecting the view that "'[f]reedom's just another word for nothin' left to lose/And nothin' ain't worth nothin', but its free,'" adopted a "non-lyrical, free-market approach that peg[ged] the value of freedom and other intangible benefits to the price settled upon by the bribe-giver and the bribe-taker," which exceeded $5,000. *Id.* at 1006. *But see* United States v. Owens, 697 F.3d 657 (7th Cir. 2012) (insufficient proof that occupancy permits were worth $5,000 or more).

4. *Gratuities v. Bribery.* Section 666 makes it illegal to "corruptly" offer or give anything of value "with intent to influence or reward." Many courts have held that the statute extends to illegal gratuities as well as to bribery, reasoning that the "intent to reward" language is broad enough to encompass gratuities. *See* United States v. Jackson, 688 Fed. App'x 685 (11th Cir. 2017); United States v. Mullins, 800 F.3d 866, 870 (7th Cir. 2015) ("An agent acts corruptly when he understands that the payment given is a bribe, reward, or gratuity" under § 666); United States v. Bahel, 662 F.3d 610, 636 (2d Cir. 2011) (to the extent that the defendant "had been convicted on a gratuities theory (i.e., 'intent to be rewarded' for official acts), Section 666 is broad enough to encompass an illegal gratuity theory of liability"); *McNair*, 605 F.3d at 1186;

United States v. Zimmerman, 509 F.3d 920, 927 (8th Cir. 2007); United States v. Gee, 432 F.3d 713, 714 (7th Cir. 2005); United States v. Bonito, 57 F.3d 167, 171 (2d Cir.1995).

But the First Circuit has squarely held that gratuities are not criminalized under § 666. *See* United States v. Fernandez, 722 F.3d 1 (1st Cir. 2013). And the Fourth Circuit has questioned whether gratuities are proscribed in language that suggests that, if squarely faced with the issue, that court would restrict § 666 to bribery cases. In so doing, it focused on the fact that "corrupt intent" traditionally applies only in bribery cases. *See* United States v. Jennings, 160 F.3d 1006, 1015 n. 4 (4th Cir. 1998); *see also* United States v. Hamilton, 701 F.3d 404 (4th Cir. 2012); United States v. Siegelman, 640 F.3d 1159, 1172 (4th Cir. 2011); Lauren Garcia, Note, *Curbing Corruption or Campaign Contributions? The Ambiguous Prosecution of "Implicit" Qui Pro Quos Under the Federal Funds Bribery Statute,* 65 Rutgers L. Rev. 1 (2012); Artur G. Davis & Thomas R. Miller, *Bribery by Any Other Name? The Undecided Quid Pro Quo Element in Section 666 Federal Bribery Cases,* 88 Crim. L. Rptr. 820 (2011).

If the statute applies to gratuities, may the application of this section be broader than the gratuities provision of § 201? In light of the different statutory maximum penalties available under § 666 and § 201, what consequence could such a holding have? *See* Brown, *supra* note 6, at 307-11. And what does it mean to "intentionally misappl[y]" state property? *See* United States v. Jimenez, 705 F.3d 1305 (11th Cir. 2013); United States v. Thompson, 484 F.3d 877 (7th Cir. 2007).

5. When might prosecutors choose to proceed against state and local corruption under § 666 rather than under the mail or wire fraud statutes, § 201 (where appropriate under *Dixson*), or the Hobbs Act? Which statute might defense counsel prefer?

6. Does § 666 apply extraterritorially? The D.C. District Court said "yes" in a case in which the defendant was charged with solicitation of a bribe by an agent of an organization receiving more than $10,000 in federal funds in connection with his work for a contractor on contracts in Afghanistan that were funded by the U.S. Agency for International Development. *See* United States v. Campbell, 798 F.Supp.2d 293 (D.D.C. 2011). But another district court has held that § 666 did not apply extraterritorially in a case involving foreign defendants charged with violating the statute for foreign acts involving a foreign governmental entity. *See* United States v. Sidorenko, 102 F.Supp.3d 1124 (N.D. Ca. 2015).

D. THE FOREIGN CORRUPT PRACTICES ACT

As former U.N. Secretary-General Kofi Annan explained upon the conclusion of the U.N. Convention Against Corruption:

> Corruption is an insidious plague that has a wide range of corrosive effects on societies. It undermines democracy and the rule of law, leads to violations of human rights, distorts markets, erodes the quality of life, and allows organized crime, terrorism and other threats to human security to flourish.
>
> This evil phenomenon is found in all countries big and small, rich and poor but it is in the developing world that its effects are most destructive. Corruption hurts the poor disproportionately by diverting funds intended for development, undermining government's ability to provide basic services, feeding inequality and injustice, and discouraging foreign investment and aid. Corruption is a key element in economic under-performance, and a major obstacle to poverty alleviation and development.[23]

We have seen, both in examining the corruption cases, *supra,* and in studying "honest services" fraud in Chapter 7, "corrupt" activities encompass a wide variety of behavior by public and private actors who misuse their positions of trust for personal gain of some sort. Our focus for

---

[23] Kofi Annan, Statement on the Adoption by the General Assembly of the United Nations Convention Against Corruption (Oct. 31, 2003), http://www.un.org/press/en/2003/sgsm8977.doc.htm.

purposes of this brief foray into transborder corruption, like that of the international community at present, is principally on bribery of public officials by those seeking to obtain or retain business.[24]

Most countries have outlawed the type of "domestic" bribery—that is, corruption of their *own* government officials under national law—that we have studied thus far in this chapter. But for many years the United States was alone in prohibiting corrupt payments to *foreign* officials ("transnational" or "transborder" bribery). The United States' decision to criminalize such conduct resulted from the disclosure in the 1970's that hundreds of U.S. corporations had been involved in hundreds of millions of dollars in corrupt payments to foreign officials. Congress determined that such bribes were "counter to the moral expectations and values of the American public," "erode[d] public confidence in the integrity of the free market system," "embarrass[ed] friendly governments, lower[ed] the esteem for the United States among the citizens of foreign nations, and len[t] credence to the suspicions sown by foreign opponents of the United States that American enterprises exert a corrupting influence on the political processes of their nations."[25] Thus, Congress passed the Foreign Corrupt Practices Act (FCPA), 15 U.S.C. §§ 78dd-1 *et seq.*, in 1977 in an effort to establish criminally-enforceable standards for U.S. companies that operate in foreign countries.

The United States has lobbied the world community to join it in outlawing transborder corruption (in part to level the playing field for U.S. companies engaged in international business). Since 1996, in recognition of the dangers corruption poses to development, stability, and peace, many significant anti-corruption regional conventions have come into effect: the Convention on Combating Bribery of Foreign Public Officials in the Organization for Economic Cooperation and Development (OECD Convention), the Inter-American Convention Against Corruption negotiated in the Organization of American States, and the Criminal and Civil Law Conventions on Corruption in the Council of Europe. Most significantly, a United Nations Convention Against Corruption (UNCAC) entered into force on December 14, 2005.

The United States' FCPA regime is very complex. Many U.S. companies operating overseas rely heavily on expert counsel to ensure that they are compliant. To implement its obligations under the OECD Convention, moreover, the United States expanded the reach of the FCPA to include non-U.S. companies and actors previously not regulated; the amended FCPA, then, significantly increases the criminal peril of foreign businesses and their agents. It is worth noting that this is an area of practice in which there is not a great deal of case law. Until recently, not many criminal FCPA criminal cases were brought, and what cases were brought did not often go to trial or result in a published opinion regarding the scope of the statute.

"In a brief couple of decades, American's enforcement of the [FCPA]—civilly by the [SEC] and criminally by the [DOJ]—has gone from practically nonexistent to one of the largest and busiest fields of corporate crime practice in the world. ... No other area has expanded so rapidly nor so expensively for corporate defendants as enforcement under the

---

[24] The World Bank has "conservative[ly] estimate[d]" that the dollar value of bribes paid by the private sector to the public sector annually is $1 trillion." *See* http://www.worldbank.org/wbi/governance/briefs.html (follow "Six Questions on the Cost of Corruption with World Bank Institute Global Governance Director Daniel Kaufmann" hyperlink). This figure does not include the embezzlement of public funds, the theft or misuse of public assets, or the dollars lost to nepotism and other such misuses of office. Thus, for example, it does not include what Transparency International has estimated as the between $15-35 billion President Suharto embezzled in Indonesia and the $5 billion each that Presidents Marcos, Mobutu, Abacha stole from the Philippines, Zaire, and Nigeria, respectively. *Id.*

[25] H.R.Rep. No. 95-640, at 4-5 (1977); *see also* S.Rep. No. 95-114, at 3-4 (1977), *reprinted in* 1977 U.S.C.C.A.N. 4098, 4100-01; Susan Rose Ackerman & Sinead Hunt, *Transparency and Business Advantage: The Impact of International Anti-Corruption Policies on the United States National Interest,* 67 N.Y.U. Ann. Surv. Am. L. 433 (2012); Kevin E. Davis, *Why Does the United States Regulate Foreign Bribery: Moralism, Self-Interest, or Altruism?,* 67 N.Y.U. Ann. Surv. Am. L. 497 (2012).

umbrella of the FCPA."[26] The numbers bear this out. "In the nearly quarter century from the statute's enactment in 1977 through the year 2000, the federal government pursued only fifty-two FCPA enforcement actions. No more than five such actions were bought in a single year, and in four of those years, zero actions were commenced. Then, from 2001 through 2015, the government initiated 379 FCPA cases, reaching an annual high of 56 cases in 2010."[27]

FCPA practice involves consulting with companies at every stage up to and including the moment a subpoena arrives. Practitioners are called upon to advise: on the companies' potential FCPA exposure if they undertake proposed joint ventures, acquisitions, contracts, consulting arrangements, and mergers;[28] on structuring business arrangements, like contracts and transactions, so as to avoid FCPA difficulties; on whether and how to conduct internal corporate investigations into possible FCPA wrongdoing within the company; on implementation of FCPA compliance programs; on how to avoid civil or criminal enforcement actions; and on how to resolve such actions if they are threatened or brought. Because of the dearth of definitive judicial guidance on the meaning of the FCPA's terms, experience in this area of practice—meaning knowledge of how similar cases have been dealt with below the public waterline—is at a premium. (It also often means that the regulators and enforcement officials' interpretation is often, for all practical purposes, the definitive one.) In November 2012, the DOJ and SEC jointly issued *A Resource Guide to the U.S. Foreign Corrupt Practices Act* ("*Resource Guide*") that provides helpful and reasonably concrete guidance on prior applications of the statute as well as the government's enforcement policies.

This is likely to continue to be a "growth" area in white-collar crime because of the conclusion of the treaties noted above that require their states parties to implement anti-corruption legislation akin to the FCPA to bar at least some forms of transnational corruption. Many countries have passed implementing legislation. And "[f]oreign bribery actions brought by non-U.S. actors increased 71 percent between 2012 and 2013 alone. Of all the cases ever brought by non-U.S. actors through 2013, more than 36 percent of the cases have been brought since 2008. While the FCPA for years stood alone as the only serious foreign bribery law, 26 countries and three international organizations have now brought actions for foreign bribery."[29]

Assuming that states parties actively enforce their anti-corruption regimes, this international movement may signal a "sea change in the way that business will have to be

---

[26] Rachel Brewster & Samuel W. Buell, *The Market for Global Anticorruption Enforcement*, 80 Law & Contemp. Probs. 193, 193 (2017) (exploring the reasons for this explosion in anticorruption enforcement).

[27] *Id.*

[28] *See, e.g.*, Daniel J. Grimm, *The Foreign Corrupt Practices Act in Merger and Acquisition Transactions: Successor Liability and Its Consequences*, 7 N.Y.U. L. & Bus. 247 (2010).

[29] Thomas J. Bussen, *Midnight in the Garden of* Ne Bis In Idem: *The New Urgency for an International Enforcement Mechanism*, 23 Cardozo J. Int'l & Comp. Law 486, 495-96 (2015).

> However, enforcement actions are primarily initiated by Western countries. Outside of Europe and the U.S., only a handful of other countries have ever brought foreign bribery actions. Transparency International says, "People are not seeing the results" of increased legislation and promises to combat corruption. Even enforcement within Europe is somewhat deceiving, as smaller countries such as Denmark and Switzerland make up a disproportionate number of global enforcement cases. For many countries, anti-bribery laws are paper tigers perhaps implemented to satisfy the demands of foreign trade partners, influential non-governmental organizations (NGOs), or domestic citizenry.

Id. at 496; *see also* Rachel Brewster, *The Domestic and International Enforcement of the OECD Anti-Bribery Convention*, 15 Chi. J. Int'l L. 84 (2014). This is unfortunate because "MNC's from Russia, China, Mexico, Indonesia, and the UAE, respectively, were the most likely to pay bribes abroad in 2011." Bussen, *supra*, at 502.

conducted around the world."[30] Thus, U.S. companies, and their lawyers, may need to worry not just about FCPA compliance, but also about meeting anti-corruption measures that other nations put into place to implement these international treaties, some of which—like the United Kingdom's Act (discussed *infra*)—may be more restrictive than the FCPA. Certainly

> [t]he quilt work of the international anti-bribery landscape is more complex than at any time before. While anti-bribery laws are similar across jurisdictions, they are not identical. For example, the U.K.'s Bribery Act forbids all facilitation payments, which are permissible under the FCPA, but it also provides a complete defense to firms with adequate procedures in place meant to prevent violations; China, Japan, Indonesia, South Korea and several African countries implicitly or expressly permit gift giving in the business context, which may violate the FCPA; and Azerbaijan eliminates liability for a corrupt payment as long as it is reported to governmental authorities. Companies thus have to expend resources understanding the different laws, including varying cultural interpretations and approaches to enforcement, while ... coordinat[ing] multiple investigations.[31]

Perhaps most significantly, the new treaties and the domestic law enacted to implement them will strengthen international law enforcement by facilitating cross-border evidence gathering, asset seizures, extradition, and other cooperation. The legal difficulties the DOJ and SEC encountered when attempting to secure evidence abroad will be greatly diminished. One can, in short, expect that there will be substantially more cooperative, and successful, international enforcement of anti-corruption norms. Not surprisingly, then, one of the hallmarks of recent DOJ efforts has been the increasingly international nature if its investigations.

UNITED STATES v. KAY
359 F.3d 738 (5th Cir. 2004)

WIENER, Circuit Judge:

... [T]he United States appeals the district court's grant of the motion of defendants-appellees David Kay and Douglas Murphy to dismiss the Superseding Indictment that charged them with bribery of foreign officials in violation of the Foreign Corrupt Practices Act ("FCPA")[, 15 U.S.C. § 78dd-1 *et seq.*] In their dismissal motion, defendants contended that the indictment failed to state an offense against them. The principal dispute in this case is whether, if proved beyond a reasonable doubt, the conduct that the indictment ascribed to defendants in connection with the alleged bribery of Haitian officials to understate customs duties and sales taxes on rice shipped to Haiti to assist American Rice, Inc. in obtaining or retaining business was sufficient to constitute an offense under the FCPA. ...

American Rice, Inc. ("ARI") is a Houston-based company that exports rice to foreign countries, including Haiti. Rice Corporation of Haiti ("RCH"), a wholly owned subsidiary of ARI, was incorporated in Haiti to represent ARI's interests and deal with third parties there. As an aspect of Haiti's standard importation procedure, its customs officials assess duties based

---

[30] Michael F. Zeldin & Carlo V. Di Floro, *Effective Corporate Governance Under Emerging Global Anti-Corruption Laws*, 6 No. 5 Bus. Crimes Bull. 1, 1 (June 1999). Note, however, that Transparency International (TI) is discouraged by the lack of overall progress, and loss of momentum, in recent international enforcement efforts. As of 2015, TI reported that only about half of the 41 OECD countries have not brought a transnational bribery case since 1999. Only four OECD countries actively enforced their anti-corruption legislation (United States, Germany, the United Kingdom, and Switzerland) and only six moderately enforced the legislation (Italy, Canada, Australia, Austria, Norway, and Finland). Transparency International, Progress Report 2015: Enforcement of the OECD Anti-Bribery Convention.

[31] Bussen, *supra* note 29, at 504-05.

on the quantity and value of rice imported into the country. Haiti also requires businesses that deliver rice there to remit an advance deposit against Haitian sales taxes, based on the value of that rice, for which deposit a credit is eventually allowed on Haitian sales tax returns when filed.

In 2001, a grand jury charged Kay with violating the FCPA and subsequently returned the indictment, which charges both Kay and Murphy with 12 counts of FCPA violations. As is readily apparent on its face, the indictment contains detailed factual allegations about (1) the timing and purposes of Congress's enactment of the FCPA, (2) ARI and its status as an "issuer" under the FCPA, (3) RCH and its status as a wholly owned subsidiary and "service corporation" of ARI, representing ARI's interest in Haiti, and (4) defendants' citizenship, their positions as officers of ARI, and their status as "issuers" and "domestic concerns" under the FCPA. The indictment also spells out in detail how Kay and Murphy allegedly orchestrated the bribing of Haitian customs officials to accept false bills of lading and other documentation that intentionally understated by one-third the quantity of rice shipped to Haiti, thereby significantly reducing ARI's customs duties and sales taxes. In this regard, the indictment alleges the details of the bribery scheme's machinations, including the preparation of duplicate documentation, the calculation of bribes as a percentage of the value of the rice not reported, the surreptitious payment of monthly retainers to Haitian officials, and the defendants' purported authorization of withdrawals of funds from ARI's bank accounts with which to pay the Haitian officials, either directly or through intermediaries—all to produce substantially reduced Haitian customs and tax costs to ARI. Further, the indictment alleges discrete facts regarding ARI's domestic incorporation and place of business, as well as the particular instrumentalities of interstate and foreign commerce that defendants used or caused to be used in carrying out the purported bribery.

In contrast, without any factual allegations, the indictment merely paraphrases the one element of the statute that is central to this appeal, only conclusionally accusing defendants of causing payments to be made to Haitian customs officials:

> for purposes of influencing acts and decisions of such foreign officials in their official capacities, inducing such foreign officials to do and omit to do acts in violation of their lawful duty, and to obtain an improper advantage, in order to assist American Rice, Inc. in *obtaining and retaining* business for, and directing business to American Rice, Inc. and Rice Corporation of Haiti.   (Emphasis added).

Although it recites in great detail the discrete facts that the government intends to prove to satisfy each other element of an FCPA violation, the indictment recites no particularized facts that, if proved, would satisfy the "assist" aspect of the business nexus element of the statute, i.e., the nexus between the illicit tax savings produced by the bribery and the assistance such savings provided or were intended to provide in *obtaining or retaining business* for ARI and RCH. Neither does the indictment contain any factual allegations whatsoever to identify just *what* business in Haiti (presumably some rice-related commercial activity) the illicit customs and tax savings assisted (or were intended to assist) in obtaining or retaining, or just *how* these savings were supposed to assist in such efforts. In other words, the indictment recites no facts that could demonstrate an actual or intended cause-and-effect nexus between reduced taxes and obtaining identified business or retaining identified business opportunities. ...

Because an offense under the FCPA requires that the alleged bribery be committed for the purpose of inducing foreign officials to commit unlawful acts, the results of which will assist in obtaining or retaining business in their country, the question[] before us in this appeal [is] ... whether bribes to obtain illegal but favorable tax and customs treatment can ever come within the scope of the statute...

B. Words of the FCPA ...

The FCPA prohibits payments to foreign officials for purposes of:

(i) influencing any act or decision of such foreign official in his official capacity, (ii) inducing such foreign official to do or omit to do any act in violation of the lawful duty of such official, or (iii) securing any improper advantage ... in order to assist [the company making the payment] in obtaining or retaining business for or with, or directing business to, any person. [15 U.S.C. § 78dd-1(a)(1).]

None contend that the FCPA criminalizes every payment to a foreign official: It criminalizes only those payments that are intended to (1) influence a foreign official to act or make a decision in his official capacity, or (2) induce such an official to perform or refrain from performing some act in violation of his duty, or (3) secure some wrongful advantage to the payor. And even then, the FCPA criminalizes these kinds of payments only if the result they are intended to produce—their *quid pro quo*—will *assist* (or is intended to assist) the payor in efforts to get or keep some *business* for or with "any person." Thus, the first question of statutory interpretation presented in this appeal is whether payments made to foreign officials to obtain unlawfully reduced customs duties or sales tax liabilities can ever fall within the scope of the FCPA, i.e., whether the illicit payments made to obtain a reduction of revenue liabilities can *ever* constitute the kind of bribery that is proscribed by the FCPA. ...

The principal thrust of the defendants' argument is that the business nexus element, i.e., the "assist ... in obtaining or retaining business" element, narrowly limits the statute's applicability to those payments that are intended to obtain a foreign official's approval of a bid for a new government contract or the renewal of an existing government contract. In contrast, the government insists that, in addition to payments to officials that lead directly to getting or renewing business contracts, the statute covers payments that indirectly advance ("assist") the payor's goal of obtaining or retaining foreign business with or for some person. The government reasons that paying reduced customs duties and sales taxes on imports, as is purported to have occurred in this case, is the type of "improper advantage" that always will assist in obtaining or retaining business in a foreign country, and thus is *always* covered by the FCPA.

In approaching this issue, the district court concluded that the FCPA's language is ambiguous, and proceeded to review the statute's legislative history. We agree with the court's finding of ambiguity for several reasons. Perhaps our most significant statutory construction problem results from the failure of the language of the FCPA to give a clear indication of the exact scope of the business nexus element; that is, the proximity of the required nexus between, on the one hand, the anticipated results of the foreign official's bargained-for action or inaction, and, on the other hand, the assistance provided by or expected from those results in helping the briber to obtain or retain business. ...

Second, the parties' diametrically opposed but reasonable contentions demonstrate that the ordinary and natural meaning of the statutory language is genuinely debatable and thus ambiguous. For instance, the word "business" can be defined at any point along a continuum from "a volume of trade," to "the purchase and sale of goods in an attempt to make a profit," to "an assignment" or a "project." Thus, dictionary definitions can support both (1) the government's broader interpretation of the business nexus language as encompassing any type of commercial activity, and (2) defendants' argument that "obtain or retain business" connotes a more pedestrian understanding of establishing or renewing a particular commercial arrangement. Similarly, although the word "assist" suggests a somewhat broader statutory scope,[32] it does not connote specificity or define either how proximate or how remote the foreign official's anticipated actions that constitute assistance must or may be to the business obtained or retained. ...

Neither does the remainder of the statutory language clearly express an exclusively broad or exclusively narrow understanding of the business nexus element. The extent to which the

---

[32] [Court's footnote 18:] Invoking basic economic principles, the SEC reasoned in its amicus brief that securing reduced taxes and duties on imports through bribery enables ARI to reduce its cost of doing business, thereby giving it an "improper advantage" over actual or potential competitors, and enabling it to do more business, or remain in a market it might otherwise leave.

exception for routine governmental action ("facilitating payments" or "grease") is narrowly drawn reasonably suggests that Congress was carving out very limited categories of permissible payments from an otherwise broad statutory prohibition.[33] As defendants suggest, however, another plausible implication for including an express statutory explanation that routine governmental action does not include decisions "to award new business to or to continue business with a particular party," [15 U.S.C. § 78dd-1(f)(3)(B),] is that Congress was focusing entirely on identifiable decisions made by foreign officials in granting or renewing specific business arrangements in foreign countries, and not on a more general panoply of competitive business advantages. ...

C. FCPA Legislative History

As the statutory language itself is amenable to more than one reasonable interpretation, it is ambiguous as a matter of law. We turn therefore to legislative history in our effort to ascertain Congress's true intentions.

1. 1977 Legislative History

Congress enacted the FCPA in 1977, in response to recently discovered but widespread bribery of foreign officials by United States business interests. Congress resolved to interdict such bribery, not just because it is morally and economically suspect, but also because it was causing foreign policy problems for the United States. In particular, these concerns arose from revelations that United States defense contractors and oil companies had made large payments to high government officials in Japan, the Netherlands, and Italy. Congress also discovered that more than 400 corporations had made questionable or illegal payments in excess of $300 million to foreign officials for a wide range of favorable actions on behalf of the companies.

In deciding to criminalize this type of commercial bribery, the House and Senate each proposed similarly far-reaching, but non-identical, legislation. In its bill, the House intended "broadly [to] prohibit[] transactions that are *corruptly* intended to induce the recipient to use his or her influence to affect *any* act or decision of a foreign official. ..." Thus, the House bill contained no limiting "business nexus" element. Reflecting a somewhat narrower purpose, the Senate expressed its desire to ban payments made for the purpose of inducing foreign officials to act "so as to direct business to any person, maintain an established business opportunity with any person, divert any business opportunity from any person or influence the enactment or promulgation of legislation or regulations of that government or instrumentality."

At conference, compromise language "clarified the scope of the prohibition by requiring that the purpose of the payment must be to influence any act or decision of a foreign official ... so as to assist an issuer in obtaining, retaining or directing business to any person." In the end,

---

[33] [Court's footnote 19:] Section 78dd-1(b) excepts from the statutory scope "any facilitating or expediting payment to a foreign official ... the purpose of which is to expedite or to service the performance of a routine governmental action by a foreign official. ..." 15 U.S.C. § 78dd-1(b). Section 78dd-1(f)(3)(A), in turn, provides that:

[T]he term "routine governmental action" means only an action which is ordinarily and commonly performed by a foreign official in—

(i) obtaining permits, licenses, or other official documents to qualify a person to do business in a foreign country;

(ii) processing governmental papers, such as visas and work orders;

(iii) providing police protection, mail pick-up and delivery, or scheduling inspections associated with contract performance or inspections related to transit of goods across country;

(iv) providing phone service, power and water supply, loading and unloading cargo, or protecting perishable products or commodities from deterioration; or

(v) actions of a similar nature. 15 U.S.C. § 78dd-1(f)(3)(A).

then, Congress adopted the Senate's proposal to prohibit only those payments designed to induce a foreign official to act in a way that is intended to facilitate ("assist") in obtaining or retaining of business.

Congress expressly emphasized that it did not intend to prohibit "so-called grease or facilitating payments," such as "payments for expediting shipments through customs or placing a transatlantic telephone call, securing required permits, or obtaining adequate police protection, transactions which may involve even the proper performance of duties." Instead of making an express textual exception for these types of non-covered payments, the respective committees of the two chambers sought to distinguish permissible grease payments from prohibited bribery by only prohibiting payments that induce an official to act "corruptly," i.e., actions requiring him "to misuse his official position" and his discretionary authority, not those "essentially ministerial" actions that "merely move a particular matter toward an eventual act or decision or which do not involve any discretionary action."

In short, Congress sought to prohibit the type of bribery that (1) prompts officials to misuse their discretionary authority and (2) disrupts market efficiency and United States foreign relations, at the same time recognizing that smaller payments intended to expedite ministerial actions should remain outside of the scope of the statute. ...

To divine the categories of bribery Congress did and did not intend to prohibit, we must look to the Senate's proposal, because the final statutory language was drawn from it, and from the SEC Report on which the Senate's legislative proposal was based. In distinguishing among the types of illegal payments that United States entities were making at the time, the SEC Report identified four principal categories: (1) payments "made in an effort to procure special and unjustified favors or advantages in the enactment or *administration of the tax* or other *laws*" of a foreign country; (2) payments "made with the intent to assist the company in obtaining or retaining government contracts"; (3) payments "to persuade low-level government officials to perform functions or services which they are obliged to perform as part of their governmental responsibilities, but which they may refuse or delay unless compensated" ("grease"), and (4) political contributions. The SEC thus exhibited concern about a wide range of questionable payments (explicitly including the kind at issue here) that were resulting in millions of dollars being recorded falsely in corporate books and records.

As noted, the Senate Report explained that the statute should apply to payments intended "to *direct business* to any person, *maintain an established business opportunity* with any person, divert any business opportunity from any person *or influence the enactment or promulgation of legislation or regulations* of that government or instrumentality." We observe initially that the Senate only loosely addressed the categories of conduct highlighted by the SEC Report. Although the Senate's proposal picked up the SEC's concern with a business nexus, it did not expressly cover bribery influencing the administration of tax laws or seeking favorable tax treatment. It is clear, however, that even though the Senate was particularly concerned with bribery intended to secure new business, it was also mindful of bribes that influence legislative or regulatory actions, and those that maintain established business opportunities, a category of economic activity separate from, and much more capacious than, simply "directing business" to someone.

The statute's ultimate language of "obtaining or retaining" mirrors identical language in the SEC Report. But, whereas the SEC Report highlights payments that go toward "obtaining or retaining *government contracts*," the FCPA, incorporating the Senate Report's language, prohibits payments that assist in obtaining or retaining *business*, not just government contracts. Had the Senate and ultimately Congress wanted to carry over the exact, narrower scope of the SEC Report, they would have adopted the same language. We surmise that, in using the word "business" when it easily could have used the phraseology of SEC Report, Congress intended for the statute to apply to bribes beyond the narrow band of payments sufficient only to "obtain or retain government contracts." The Senate's express intention that the statute apply to corrupt payments that *maintain* business opportunities also supports this conclusion.

For purposes of deciding the instant appeal, the question nevertheless remains whether the Senate, and concomitantly Congress, intended this broader statutory scope to encompass the administration of tax, customs, and other laws and regulations affecting the revenue of foreign states. To reach this conclusion, we must ask whether Congress's remaining expressed desire to prohibit bribery aimed at getting assistance in retaining business or maintaining business opportunities was sufficiently broad to include bribes meant to affect the administration of revenue laws. When we do so, we conclude that the legislative intent was so broad.

Congress was obviously distraught not only about high profile bribes to high-ranking foreign officials, but also by the pervasiveness of foreign bribery by United States businesses and businessmen. Congress thus made the decision to clamp down on bribes intended to prompt foreign officials to misuse their discretionary authority for the benefit of a domestic entity's business in that country. This observation is not diminished by Congress's understanding and accepting that relatively small facilitating payments were, at the time, among the accepted costs of doing business in many foreign countries.

In addition, the concern of Congress with the immorality, inefficiency, and unethical character of bribery presumably does not vanish simply because the tainted payments are intended to secure a favorable decision less significant than winning a contract bid. Obviously, a commercial concern that bribes a foreign government official to award a construction, supply, or services contract violates the statute. Yet, there is little difference between this example and that of a corporation's lawfully obtaining a contract from an honest official or agency by submitting the lowest bid, and—either before or after doing so—bribing a different government official to reduce taxes and thereby ensure that the under-bid venture is nevertheless profitable. Avoiding or lowering taxes reduces operating costs and thus increases profit margins, thereby freeing up funds that the business is otherwise legally obligated to expend. And this, in turn, enables it to take any number of actions to the disadvantage of competitors. Bribing foreign officials to lower taxes and customs duties certainly *can* provide an unfair advantage over competitors and thereby be of assistance to the payor in obtaining or retaining business. This demonstrates that the question whether the defendants' alleged payments constitute a violation of the FCPA truly turns on whether these bribes were intended to lower ARI's cost of doing business in Haiti enough to have a sufficient nexus to garnering business there or to maintaining or increasing business operations that ARI already had there, so as to come within the scope of the business nexus element as Congress used it in the FCPA. Answering this fact question, then, implicates a matter of proof and thus evidence.

In short, the 1977 legislative history, particularly the Senate's proposal and the SEC Report on which it relied, convinces us that Congress meant to prohibit a range of payments wider than only those that directly influence the acquisition or retention of government contracts or similar commercial or industrial arrangements. ... The congressional target was bribery paid to engender assistance in improving the business opportunities of the payor or his beneficiary, irrespective of whether that assistance be direct or indirect, and irrespective of whether it be related to administering the law, awarding, extending, or renewing a contract, or executing or preserving an agreement. In light of our reading of the 1977 legislative history, the subsequent 1988 and 1998 legislative history is only important to our analysis to the extent it confirms or conflicts with our initial conclusions about the scope of the statute.

2. 1988 Legislative History

After the FCPA's enactment, United States business entities and executives experienced difficulty in discerning a clear line between prohibited bribes and permissible facilitating payments. As a result, Congress amended the FCPA in 1988, expressly to clarify its original intent in enacting the statute. Both houses insisted that their proposed amendments only clarified ambiguities "without changing the basic intent or effectiveness of the law."

In this effort to crystallize the scope of the FCPA's prohibitions on bribery, Congress chose to identify carefully two types of payments that are not proscribed by the statute. It expressly excepted payments made to procure "routine governmental action" (again, the grease exception[in 15 U.S.C. §§ 78dd-1(b) & (f)(3)(A), reproduced *supra* in court's footnote 19; footnote 33 in this chapter]), and it incorporated an affirmative defense for payments that are legal in the country in which they are offered or that constitute bona fide expenditures directly relating to promotion of products or services, or to the execution or performance of a contract with a foreign government or agency.[34] We agree with the position of the government that these 1988 amendments illustrate an intention by Congress to identify very limited exceptions to the kinds of bribes to which the FCPA does not apply. ... [R]outine governmental action does not include the issuance of *every* official document or *every* inspection, but only (1) documentation that qualifies a party to do business and (2) scheduling an inspection—very narrow categories of largely non-discretionary, ministerial activities performed by mid- or low-level foreign functionaries. In contrast, the FCPA uses broad, general language in prohibiting payments to procure assistance for the payor in obtaining or retaining business, instead of employing similarly detailed language, such as applying the statute only to payments that attempt to secure or renew particular government contracts. ...

Defendants argue, nevertheless, that Congress's decision to reject House-proposed amendments to the business nexus element constituted its implicit rejection of such a broad reading of the statute. The House bill proposed new language to explain that payments for "obtaining or retaining business" also includes payments made for the "procurement of legislative, judicial, regulatory, or other action in seeking more favorable treatment by a foreign government." Indeed, defendants assert, the proposed amendment itself shows that Congress understood the business nexus provision to have narrow application; otherwise, there would have been no need to propose amending it.

Contrary to defendants' contention, the decision of Congress to reject this language has no bearing on whether "obtaining or retaining business" includes the conduct at issue here. In explaining Congress's decision not to include this proposed amendment in the business nexus requirement, the Conference Report stated that the "retaining business" language was

> not limited to the renewal of contracts or other business, but also includes a prohibition against corrupt payments related to the execution or performance of contracts or the carrying out of existing business, *such as a payment to a foreign official for the purpose of obtaining more favorable tax treatment*. ... The term should not, however, be construed so broadly as to include lobbying or other normal representations to government officials. ...

3. 1998 Legislative History

In 1998, Congress made its most recent adjustments to the FCPA when the Senate ratified and Congress implemented the Organization of Economic Cooperation and Development's Convention on Combating Bribery of Foreign Public Officials in International Business Transactions (the "Convention"). Article 1.1 of the Convention prohibits payments to a foreign public official to induce him to "act or refrain from acting in relation to the performance of official duties, in order to obtain or retain business or *other improper advantage* in the conduct of international business." When Congress amended the language of the FCPA, however, rather than inserting "any improper advantage" immediately following "obtaining or retaining business" within the business nexus requirement (as does the Convention), it chose to add the "improper advantage" provision to the original list of abuses of discretion in

---

[34] [Court's footnote 44:] 15 U.S.C. § 78dd-1(c). The subsection provides in full:

It shall be an affirmative defense to actions under subsections (a) or (g) of this section that—

(1) the payment, gift, offer, or promise of anything of value that was made, was lawful under the written laws and regulations of the foreign official's, political party's, party official's, or candidate's country; or

(2) the payment, gift, offer, or promise of anything of value that was made, was a reasonable and bona fide expenditure, such as travel and lodging expenses, incurred by or on behalf of a foreign official, party, party official, or candidate and was directly related to—

(A) the promotion, demonstration, or explanation of products or services; or

(B) the execution or performance of a contract with a foreign government or agency thereof.

consideration for bribes that the statute proscribes. Thus, as amended, the statute now prohibits payments to foreign officials not just to buy any act or decision, and not just to induce the doing or omitting of an official function "to assist ... in obtaining or retaining business for or with, or directing business to, any person," but also the making of a payment to such a foreign official to secure an "improper advantage" that will assist in obtaining or retaining business.

The district court concluded, and defendants argue on appeal, that merely by adding the "improper advantage" language to the two existing kinds of prohibited acts acquired in consideration for bribes paid, Congress "again declined to amend the 'obtain or retain' business language in the FCPA." In contrast, the government responds that Congress's choice to place the Convention language elsewhere merely shows that Congress already intended for the business nexus requirement to apply broadly, and thus declined to be redundant.

The Convention's broad prohibition of bribery of foreign officials likely includes the types of payments that comprise defendants' alleged conduct. The commentaries to the Convention explain that "'[o]ther improper advantage' refers to something to which the company concerned was not clearly entitled, for example, an operating permit for a factory which fails to meet the statutory requirements." Unlawfully reducing the taxes and customs duties at issue here to a level substantially below that which ARI was legally obligated to pay surely constitutes "something [ARI] was not clearly entitled to," and was thus potentially an "improper advantage" under the Convention.

As we have demonstrated, the 1977 and 1988 legislative history already make clear that the business nexus requirement is not to be interpreted unduly narrowly. We therefore agree with the government that there really was no need for Congress to add "or other improper advantage" to the requirement.[35] In fact, such an amendment might have inadvertently swept grease payments into the statutory ambit—or at least created new confusion as to whether these types of payments were prohibited—even though this category of payments was excluded by Congress in 1977 and remained excluded in 1988; and even though Congress showed no intention of adding this category when adopting its 1998 amendments. That the Convention, which the Senate ratified without reservation and Congress implemented, would also appear to prohibit the types of payments at issue in this case only bolsters our conclusion that the kind of conduct allegedly engaged in by defendants can be violative of the statute.[36]

4. Summary

... [W]e hold that Congress intended for the FCPA to apply broadly to payments intended to assist the payor, either directly or indirectly, in obtaining or retaining business for some

---

[35] [Court's footnote 66:] Although Congress intended to expand the scope of the FCPA in its implementation of the Convention, such expansion did not clearly implicate the business nexus element. Obviously, Congress added "any improper advantage" to the *quid pro quo* requirement. Other ways in which Congress intended to expand FCPA coverage included: (1) amending the statute to apply to "any person," instead of the more limited category of issuers registered under the 1934 Act and domestic concerns; (2) expanding the definition of "foreign official" to include officials of public international organizations; and (3) extending the FCPA to cover "acts of U.S. businesses and nationals in furtherance of unlawful payments that take place wholly outside the United States." S.Rep. No. 105-277, at 2-3.

[36] [Court's footnote 68:] ... We recognize that there may be some variation in scope between the Convention and the FCPA. The FCPA prohibits payments inducing official action that "assist[s] ... in obtaining or retaining business"; the Convention prohibits payments that induce official action "to obtain or retain business or other improper advantage in the conduct of international business." Potential variation exists because it is unclear whether the Convention's "other improper advantage in the conduct of international business" language requires a business nexus to the same extent as does the FCPA. This case, however, does not require us to address potential discrepancies (including whether they exist) between the scope of the Convention and the scope of the statute, i.e., payments that clearly fall outside of the FCPA but clearly fall within the Convention's prohibition or vice versa, because we have already concluded that the type of bribery engaged in by defendants has the potential of violating the statute.

person, and that bribes paid to foreign tax officials to secure illegally reduced customs and tax liability constitute a type of payment that can fall within this broad coverage. ...

... We hasten to add, however, that this conduct does not automatically constitute a violation of the FCPA: It still must be shown that the bribery was intended to produce an effect—here, through tax savings—that would "assist in obtaining or retaining business." ...

Notes

1. *Elements.* To win a conviction under the FCPA's anti-bribery provisions, the government must prove beyond a reasonable doubt the following:

> a. The defendant falls within one of three categories of persons covered by the FCPA (we will return to this complicated equation below in note 3);
> b. The defendant made a payment, or an offer, authorization, or promise to pay, money or anything of value, directly or indirectly (through a third party);
> c. The defendant made the payment or promise to pay to a covered recipient, meaning:
> (i)   any foreign official
> (ii)   any foreign political party or party official
> (iii)   any candidate for foreign political office, or
> (iv)   any other person while "knowing" that the payment or promise to pay will be passed on to one of the above
> d. In furtherance of the bribe or offer to bribe, "corruptly" committed the *actus reus* of the crime. The proscribed act differs depending upon which subsection is invoked (that is, who the defendant is) and whether the defendant is a U.S. national (we will return to this complex question below in Note 4, below)
> e. For the purpose of influencing an official act or decision of that person to do or omit to do any act in violation of his or her lawful duty, securing any improper advantage, or inducing that person to use his influence with a foreign government to affect or influence any government act or decision
> f. In order to assist in obtaining or retaining business for, with, or to any person.

2. *Nexus Between Bribe and Maintaining or Obtaining Business.* The *Kay* court obviously was trying to identify the relationship or nexus that must exist between elements (e) and (f). The district court in *Kay* had held that the bribes paid in that case did not qualify as covered payments under the FCPA. The Fifth Circuit reversed, ruling that although the language of the statute is "ambiguous," the payments may in fact be covered in some circumstances. The Fifth Circuit thought that the ambiguity necessitated a review of the legislative history. Should the court instead of employed the rule of lenity?

The bar and business community viewed this as a *very* important case because many payments may be made to covered persons that do not directly relate to securing or retaining a particular business opportunity, but rather simply permit the company to operate more efficiently or cost-effectively than its competitors. FCPA lawyers and business people were eagerly awaiting the Fifth Circuit's *Kay* decision in hopes that it would provide some clarity regarding just how direct a nexus must exist between the payment and the business sought to be secured or maintained. Many practitioners found the *Kay* opinion deeply disappointing in this respect. Irvin Nathan concluded, for example, that the *Kay* decision "leaves American companies and their counsel at sea as to whether or not certain types of payments to foreign officials violate the statute ... Unless [a proposed] payment is designed to secure or retain a contract, no brightline guidance can be given in the wake of the *Kay* decision." Irvin B. Nathan, *Is Bribing Foreign Tax Collectors a Federal Crime? The Fifth Circuit Says Maybe Yes, Maybe No,* 11 Bus. Crimes Bull. 1, 4 (2004).

3. *Three Categories of Covered Persons.* Before launching into the persons covered by the FCPA, an important definitional note is necessary: throughout these notes, the term "U.S.

companies" is used to refer to companies that are organized under the laws of the United States (including, as is usually the case, under the law of any U.S. state).

There are three categories of covered persons under the FCPA. Note that the *Kay* court is careful to describe the jurisdictional elements that were pled in the indictment. Under which of these categories did the defendants in *Kay* fall?

First, 15 U.S.C. § 78dd-1 covers "issuers" and "any officer, director, employee, or agent of such issuer[s] or any stockholder thereof acting on behalf of such issuer[s]." An issuer is an entity whose securities are registered in the United States or that is required to file periodic reports with the SEC. *Id.* Note that under § 78dd-1, companies that are "issuers" may be prosecuted even if they are not U.S. companies and are not "resident" in the United States. Further, the agents acting on behalf of an "issuer" need not be nationals of, or resident in, the United States to be themselves covered.

Second, 15 U.S.C. § 78dd-2 covers "domestic concerns" and "any officer, director, employee, or agent of such domestic concern or any stockholder thereof acting on behalf of such domestic concern." A "domestic concern" means "(A) any individual who is a citizen, national, or resident of the United States; and (B) any corporation, partnership, association, joint stock company, business trust, unincorporated organization, or sole proprietorship which has its principal place of business in the United States ..." *Id.* § 78dd-2(h)(1). Companies having their principal place of business in the United States are considered "domestic concerns" even if they are not U.S. companies or agents of U.S. companies. Individuals who are not U.S. nationals are nonetheless "domestic concerns" if they are resident in the United States. Note also that non-U.S. companies not having their principal place of business in the United States and foreign nationals who are not resident in the United States may be prosecuted under this provision if they are acting as agents of a "domestic concern."

Third, under 15 U.S.C. § 78dd-3, foreign nationals or businesses (or agents of such nationals or businesses) who are neither "issuers" nor "domestic concerns" but who perform a qualifying act in furtherance of the illicit bribe in U.S. territory may be liable. For ease of reference, this category of persons is described as "§ 78dd-3 persons" within. This provision was added to the statute in 1998 to implement the Convention on Combating Bribery of Foreign Officials in International Business Transactions adopted by the OECD (the OECD Convention), to which the U.S. Senate gave its advice and consent in 1998. The Convention requires all states parties to make it a criminal offense for "any person" to bribe a foreign official and requires signatories "to take such measures as may be necessary to establish its jurisdiction over the bribery of a foreign public official when the offense is committed in whole or in part in its territory." As a result, Congress acted in 1998 to extend the FCPA's coverage to persons who are not issuers or domestic concerns but who commit an offense, at least in part, in the United States.

This is the section that significantly increases the jeopardy of non-U.S. companies and their agents because it reaches individuals who are not U.S. nationals or residents, and companies that are not regulated by the SEC, whose securities are not registered in the United States, and who are neither U.S. companies nor businesses having their principal place of business in the United States. *See, e.g., id.* § 78dd-3(f)(1). Section 78dd-3 persons may be prosecuted under the FCPA's anti-bribery provisions *if*, "*while in the territory of the United States*," they "corruptly ... make use of the mails or any other means or instrumentality of interstate commerce *or* ... do *any act* in furtherance" of the offer to bribe or illicit payment. (Emphasis added.) In short, any person (natural or juridical) (who is not an "issuer" or a "domestic concern") who takes any act in furtherance of a corrupt offer or payment in the territory of the United States is subject to U.S. prosecution—whether or not that "person" has any other connection to the United States.

How broadly can this be construed? Is it sufficient that the foreign person "caused" an act in the United States or does it require physical presence in U.S. territory? Although the Second Circuit did not expressly interpret this phrase in *United States v. Hoskins*, -- F.3d --, 2018 WL 4038192 (2d Cir. 2018), the import of the opinion is that the latter must be proved. In *Hoskins*,

The government allege[d] that several defendants, including Hoskins, were part of a scheme to bribe officials in Indonesia so that their company could secure a $118 million contract from the Indonesian government. Hoskins worked for Alstom S.A. ("Alstom"), a global company headquartered in France that provides power and transportation services During the relevant time … Hoskins was employed by Alstom's UK subsidiary, but was assigned to work with another subsidiary called Alstom Resources Management, which is in France.

The alleged bribery scheme center[ed] on Alstom's American subsidiary, Alstom Power, Inc. ("Alstom U.S."), headquartered in Connecticut. The allegations [we]re that Alstom U.S. and various individuals associated with Alstom S.A. retained two consultants to bribe Indonesian officials who could help secure the $118 million power contract for the company and its associates. Hoskins never worked for Alstom U.S. in a direct capacity. But the government allege[d] that Hoskins, while working from France for Alstom Resources Management, was "one of the people responsible for approving the selection of, and authorizing payments to, [the consultants], knowing that a portion of the payments to [the consultants] was intended for Indonesian officials in exchange for their influence and assistance in awarding the [contract.]"

The government allege[d] that several parts of the scheme occurred within the United States. The indictment allege[d] that one of the consultants kept a bank account in Maryland. In some cases, funds for bribes allegedly were paid from bank accounts held by Alstom and its business partners in the United States, and deposited in the consultant's account in Maryland, for the purpose of bribing Indonesian officials. The indictment also state[d] that several executives of Alstom U.S. held meetings within the United States regarding the bribery scheme and discussed the project by phone and email while present on American soil.

The government concede[d] that, although Hoskins "repeatedly e-mailed and called … U.S.-based coconspirators" regarding the scheme "while they were in the United States," Hoskins "did not travel here" while the bribery scheme was ongoing.

Id. at *1-2. The Second Circuit explained that "[t]he central question of the appeal is whether Hoskins, a foreign national who never set foot in the United States or worked for an American company during the alleged scheme, may be held liable, under a conspiracy or complicity theory, for violating FCPA provisions targeting American persons and companies and their agents, officers, directors, employees, and shareholders, and persons physically present within the United States. In other words, can a person be guilty as an accomplice or a co-conspirator for an FCPA crime that he or she is incapable of committing as a principal?" *Id.* at *5. In short, the assumption underlying the Second Circuit's statement of the case was that Hoskins could not be liable as a § 78dd-3 person because he was never physically present in the United States, even though he could be said to have "caused" actions in the United States that facilitated the corrupt payments. *See* 2018 WL 4038192, at *24.

With respect to the issue presented, the Second Circuit held that Hoskins could not be prosecuted as a conspirator or aider and abettor because he could not be convicted as a principle under § 78dd-3. The court acknowledged that "the firm baseline rule with respect to both conspiracy and complicity is that where the crime is so defined that only certain categories of persons, such as employees of a particular sort of entity, may commit the crime through their own acts, persons not within those categories can be guilty of conspiring to commit the crime or of the substantive crime itself as an accomplice." 2018 WL 4038192, at *6. The Court relied on an exception to this general rule articulated in *Gebardi v. United States*, 287 U.S. 112 (1932), in which the Supreme Court held that where Congress enacts a substantive criminal statute that excludes a class of individuals from liability, prosecutors cannot evade congressional intent by charging those same individuals with conspiring to violate the statute. The *Hoskins* court concluded that "the carefully tailored text of the statute, read against the backdrop of a well-established principle that U.S. law does not apply extraterritorially without express congressional authorization and a legislative history reflecting that Congress drew lines in the FCPA out of specific concern about the scope of extraterritorial application of the statute, persuades us that Congress did not intend for persons outside of the statute's carefully delimited categories to be subject to conspiracy or complicity liability." 2018 WL 4038192, at *11. The court did, however, allow the government to go forward on an alternate theory: that Hoskins could be convicted as an agent of a domestic concern (Alstom U.S.).

4. *Jurisdictional Element.* Note again the *Kay* court's description of the allegations of the indictment. The jurisdictional act necessary to an FCPA prosecution depends on who the defendant is. What jurisdictional act was the government required to prove in *Kay* given the status of the defendants? There are three categories of such persons (unfortunately, however, this break-down of persons does not correspond to that described in note 3 above):

First, "United States persons," defined as the subset of "issuers" and "domestic concerns" (and their agents) who are U.S. nationals or U.S. companies, will be liable if they make use of the mails or any means or instrumentalities of interstate commerce corruptly in furtherance of the corrupt payment *or* take *any* act *outside the United States* in furtherance of a corrupt payment.

Liability for use of the mails or any means or instrumentalities of interstate commerce corruptly in furtherance of the corrupt payment applies to all issuers and domestic concerns, regardless of their nationality. "Interstate commerce" is defined as "trade, commerce, transportation, or communication among the several States, or between any foreign country and any State or between any State and any place or ship outside thereof...." 15 U.S.C. §§ 78dd-2(h)(5), 78dd-3(f)(5); *see also id.* § 78c(a)(17). According to the DOJ, "placing a telephone call or sending an e-mail, text message, or fax from, to, or through the United States involves interstate commerce—as does sending a wire transfer from or to a U.S. bank or otherwise using the U.S. banking system, or traveling across state borders or internationally to or from the United States." *Resource Guide* at 11. Indeed, in *S.E.C. v. Straub*, 921 F.Supp.2d 244, 262(S.D.N.Y. 2013), a civil enforcement action brought by the SEC, the court ruled that the complaint sufficiently pled the interstate commerce element for purposes of the FCPA by alleging that the defendants sent emails in furtherance of the corrupt scheme that were "sent from locations outside the United States, but were routed through and/or stored on network servers located within the United States." The court ruled that the defendants did not have to know that their emails would be so routed, because no *mens rea* attends this jurisdictional element. *Id.* at 262-64.

The "alternative jurisdiction" provisions tucked onto the end of § 78dd-1 and § 78dd-2, however, further provides that, where "issuers" and "domestic concerns" that *are* U.S. nationals or U.S. companies are implicated in the scheme, they need take *no* action *within the United States* in furtherance of the scheme and *indeed need not use the mails or other instrumentalities of interstate commerce* because any *act in furtherance of the bribery scheme overseas* will suffice to satisfy the jurisdictional act requirement. Assuming that some act accompanied the alleged offer to pay, or the payment to, a foreign official overseas, it seems difficult to imagine that the jurisdictional requirement will not be met in any case involving a United States person.

Second, "issuers" and "domestic concerns" (and their agents) who are not U.S. nationals or U.S. companies will be liable if they "make use of the mails or any means or instrumentalities of interstate commerce corruptly in furtherance" of the corrupt payment to a foreign official. 15 U.S.C. §§ 78dd-1(a), 78dd-2(a).

This subsection would apply, in particular, to non-U.S. nationals resident in the United States and non-U.S. companies that have listed securities or SEC filing obligations under U.S. law, as well as non-U.S. companies resident in, or having their principal place of business in, the United States. Note that the jurisdictional act is restricted to using the mails or means or instrumentalities of "interstate commerce." By omitting reference to "foreign commerce," is Congress requiring that the jurisdictional act must take place in the United States?

Third, persons who are neither "issuers" nor "domestic concerns" (and their agents) can be prosecuted if "*while in the territory of the United States*," they corruptly "make use of the mails or any means or instrumentality of interstate commerce *or* ... do *any* other act in furtherance of" the illicit payment. (Emphasis added).

5. Compare the jurisdictional act defined for foreign "issuers" or "domestic concerns" (category 2) with that applied to foreign companies with no ties to the United States (category

3). Does the FCPA allow for *more* expansive jurisdiction over companies with *fewer* connections to the United States?

6. *Jurisdictional Reach.* What are the implications of these jurisdictional provisions?

The 1998 amendments to the FCPA allowed U.S. courts to exercise jurisdiction for FCPA violations over U.S. persons for actions occurring anywhere on Earth. For foreign nationals, there is similarly unlimited jurisdiction where the alleged violation involved some action in "interstate commerce." This requirement is met by such simple acts as making a telephone call, sending an email or text message, sending a wire transfer from a U.S. bank, or travelling across state borders or internationally to or from the U.S. For example, if the employee of a foreign company authorized a payment to a foreign official using a U.S. licensed cellular phone, or using funds held in a U.S. bank, the U.S. may exercise jurisdiction over both the foreign employee and company. Consequently, the U.S. can bring actions against all U.S. citizens and companies, and many foreign nationals and companies, acting anywhere in the world.

Historically, 25 percent of all FCPA enforcement actions were initiated against foreign [multinational corporations (MNCs)]. The DOJ has moreover shown a recent willingness to take an extremely broad interpretation of extra-territorial jurisdiction pertaining to related legislation. For example, on June 30, 2014, BNP Paribas pled guilty to violating U.S. trade sanctions by doing business with Iran, Sudan and Cuba, and agreed to pay a fine of almost $9 billion. It is the tenuous link to U.S. jurisdiction that makes this case unique, controversial, and worrisome to many. BNP Paribas is a French MNC not ordinarily subject to U.S. law. But the DOJ determined it had jurisdiction because the agreements at issue were denominated in the U.S. dollar—as is often the case for international transactions—and thus, the transactions were completed by accessing the U.S. financial system. This case shows a willingness to apply U.S. jurisdiction to a foreign MNC with only minimal links to the U.S.

Bussen, *supra* note 29, at 488-89.

7. *What About Gratuities?* Does the FCPA cover what, under 18 U.S.C. § 201, would constitute a gratuity as well as out-and-out bribes? Note that bribery, in the *Kay* court's words, involves "seeking to induce a foreign official to act in consideration of a bribe *(quid pro quo)*." Does this mean that the FCPA only proscribes "bribes" and does not cover "gratuities"?

8. *Qualifying recipients of a bribe.* The recipient of the corrupt payment or offer to pay must be a "foreign official," a "foreign political party or official thereof or any candidate for foreign political office," or any other "person, while knowing that all or a portion of such money ... will be offered ... directly or indirectly, to any foreign official, to any foreign political party or official thereof, or to any candidate for foreign political office." 15 U.S.C. §§ 78dd-1(a), 78dd-2(a), 78dd-3(a). Congress expanded the definition of "foreign official" in 1998 to include officers, employees or those acting on behalf of public international organizations. *Id.* §§ 78dd-1(f)(1), 78dd-2(h)(2), 78dd-3(f)(2). Note that among the organizations whose employees would be "foreign officials" are the International Monetary Fund, the Organization of American States, the United Nations, the World Trade Organization, and the Organization for Economic Cooperation and Development (OECD).

9. *"State-Owned Entity" Issue.* Of late, there has been a great deal of litigation over the question of when employees of government-owned or government-controlled commercial entities can be deemed "public officials" within the meaning of the FCPA. This is important given how many countries own large parts of the country's infrastructure (e.g., utilities, airlines, etc.), as well as the fact that in countries like China almost everything can be deemed government owned or controlled. Indeed, as Professor Mike Koehler pointed out in 2015, 60% of the "foreign officials" identified in 2014 corporate enforcement actions involved, in whole or in part, employees of alleged state-owned or state-controlled entities, "ranging from power and electric companies, hospitals and labs, an oil and gas company, and an aluminum smelter." Mike Koehler, FCPA Professor Blog, A Summary of FCPA Enforcement Statistics (Jan. 28, 2015), *available at* http://www.fcpaprofessor.com/a-summary-of-fcpa-enforcement-

statistics (last visited August 2018). To date, the only circuit to formulate a test for when employees of state-owned or controlled entities qualify as "public officials" is the Eleventh; that court summarized its standard in *United States v. Duperval*, 777 F.3d 1324, 1333-34 (2015):

> ... The Act prohibits officers of a domestic concern from making corrupt payments to a "foreign official." [15 U.S.C. §§ 78dd-2(a)(1),] A "foreign official" includes "any officer or employee of a foreign government or any department, agency or instrumentality thereof." *Id.* § 78dd-2(h)(2)(A). ...
>
> Although the Act does not define "instrumentality," we recently explained that an instrumentality is "an entity controlled by the government of a foreign country that performs a function the controlling government treats as its own." United States v. Esquenazi, 752 F.3d 912, 925 (11th Cir. 2014). In *Esquenazi*, we explained that "what constitutes control and what constitutes a function the government treats as its own are fact-bound questions," and we "provide[d] a list of some factors that may be relevant." To determine if the government controls the entity, the fact-finder should consider the following several factors:
>
>> the foreign government's formal designation of that entity; whether the government has a majority interest in the entity; the government's ability to hire and fire the entity's principals; the extent to which the entity's profits, if any, go directly into the governmental fisc, and by the same token, the extent to which the government funds the entity if it fails to break even; and the length of time these indicia have existed.
>
> And to determine if the entity performs a function that the government treats as its own, the fact-finder should consider the following several factors:
>
>> whether the entity has a monopoly over the function it exists to carry out; whether the government subsidizes the costs associated with the entity providing services; whether the entity provides services to the public at large in the foreign country; and whether the public and the government of that foreign country generally perceive the entity to be performing a governmental function.
>
> The government introduced sufficient evidence that Haiti controlled Teleco and treated that entity as its own. Our review of the sufficiency of the evidence is controlled by our recent decision in the appeal by Duperval's co-conspirators. In *Esquenazi* and this appeal, the government introduced almost identical evidence about Teleco. That evidence included that the Central Bank of Haiti owned 97 percent of the shares of Teleco; the government had owned its interest since about 1971; the government appointed the board of directors and the general director of Teleco; the government granted Teleco a monopoly over telecommunication services; and the "government, officials, everyone consider[ed] Teleco as a public administration." As in *Esquenazi*, the jury could have reasonably found that Teleco was an instrumentality of Haiti.

See also, e.g., United States v. Aguilar, 783 F.Supp.2d 1108 (C.D. Ca. 2011) (holding that employees of Comisión Federal de Electricidad ("CFE"), an electric utility company owned by the Mexican government, were "foreign officials" because they were "employees" of an "instrumentality" of a foreign government); United States v. Carson, SACR 09-00077-JVS, Criminal Minutes, at 4-5 (C.D. Ca. May 18, 2011); United States v. Goodyear Int'l Corp., CR No. 89-0156 (D.D.C. 1989); U.S. v. Crawford Enter., Inc., CR No. 82-224 (S.D. Tex. 1982).

10. *Mens Rea.* The government must prove that the defendant had a "corrupt" motive in acting in furtherance of the bribery scheme. Readers have struggled with meaning of the term "corruptly" both in this chapter for purposes of § 201, and in Chapter 6 on obstruction of justice. The Eighth Circuit upheld a conviction obtained based on the following jury instruction for the word "corruptly":

> [T]he offer, promise to pay, payment or authorization of payment, must be intended to induce the recipient to misuse his official position or to influence someone else to do so .... [A]n act is "corruptly" done if done "voluntarily [a]nd intentionally, and with a bad purpose of accomplishing either an unlawful end or result, or a lawful end or result by some unlawful method or means."

United States v. Liebo, 923 F.2d 1308, 1312 (8th Cir. 1991). The Second Circuit approved the same instruction with a final sentence stating: "The term 'corruptly' is intended to connote that the offer, payment, and promise was intended to influence an official to misuse his official position." United States v. Kozeny, 667 F.3d 122, 135 (2d Cir. 2011); *see also* United States v. Bourke, Jury Charge, S2 05 Cr. 518, at 25 (SAS) (S.D.N.Y.)

The *Kay* court believes that Congress included the requirement of a "corrupt" intent to separate actionable bribes from "grease" payments, which originally were intended to be exempted from the 1977 FCPA's coverage but were not explicitly exempted until the 1988 amendments. In other words, the *Kay* court thought that the legislative history established that a "corrupt" intent required proof that the payments were designed to prompt an official to deviate from his official duty; payments that simply ensured that an official properly performed his ministerial duties would not be "corrupt." Does the above jury instruction capture this meaning of "corrupt"? Has this element, at least as explained by the *Kay* court, essentially been rendered superfluous by the addition in 1988 of an express exemption of "grease" payments? Given this background, does this mean that in the context of the FCPA, the *Alfisi* case would have come out differently?

Although the term does not appear in the substantive anti-bribery prohibition, the penalty provisions of the FCPA require that, to receive a criminal sentence, natural persons must be convicted of "willful" violations of the anti-bribery provisions. 15 U.S.C. §§ 78ff(c)(2)(A), 78dd-2(g)(2)(A), 78dd-3(e)(2)(A). Again, as we know from our studies in Chapter 2, the word "willfully" is "'a word of many meanings'" whose construction is "often dependent on the context in which it appears." Bryan v. United States, 524 U.S. 184, 191 (1998) (quoting Spies v. United States, 317 U.S. 492, 497 (1943)). The Second Circuit upheld the following instruction in an FCPA case:

> A person acts willfully if he acts deliberately and with the intent to do something that the law forbids, that is, with a bad purpose to disobey or disregard the law. The person need not be aware of the specific law and rule that his conduct may be violating, but he must act with the intent to do something that the law forbids.

Kozeny, 667 F.3d at 135; *see also* United States v. Bourke, Jury Charge, S2 05 Cr. 518, at 25 (SAS) (S.D.N.Y.). Courts appear to be in agreement that the government need not prove that the defendant was specifically aware of the FCPA or knew he was violating the FCPA. *See, e.g.*, Stichting Ter Behartiging Van de Belangen Van Oudaandeelhouders in Het Kapitaal Van Saybolt Int'l B.V. v. Schreiber, 327 F.3d 173, 181 (2d Cir. 2003).

11. *Use of Third Parties and Willful Blindness.* A company or its agents may be criminally liable for payments actually made by another agent or intermediary if the company authorized the payment or "knew" that it would be offered or made. The FCPA prohibits such indirect payments by stating that it is unlawful for covered persons to offer or give a thing of value to "any person, while knowing that all or a portion of such ... thing of value will be offered, given, or promised, directly or indirectly, to any foreign official, to any foreign political party or official thereof, or to any candidate for foreign political office" for purposes of obtaining or retaining business. 15 U.S.C. §§ 78dd-1(a)(3), 78dd-2(a)(3), 78dd-3(a)(3).

Notably, the FCPA defines a "knowing" state of mind to include willful blindness as well as actual subjective knowledge:

> (2) (A) A person's state of such mind is "knowing" with respect to conduct, a circumstance, or a result if—

(i) such person is aware that such person is engaging in such conduct, that such circumstance exists, or that such result is substantially certain to occur; or

(ii) such person has firm belief that such circumstance exists or that such result is substantially certain to occur.

(B) when knowledge of the existence of a particular circumstance is required for an offense, such knowledge is established if a person is aware of a high probability of the existence of such circumstance, unless the person actually believes that such circumstance does not exist.

Id. §§ 78dd-1(f)(2), 78dd-2(h)(3), 78dd-3(f)(3). The willful blindness provision is one of the more significant features of the statute because it makes the application of the statute broader and more uncertain. It is also significant in that it appears to be a more forgiving (for the government) standard than that approved by the Supreme Court in *Global-Tech Appliances, Inc. v. SEB, S.A.*, 563 U.S. 754 (2011). *See supra* Chapter 2(C)(4). Congress appears to have imposed a duty of investigation under this provision that does not apply under *Global Tech* because liability under these provisions can be founded only on a defendant's awareness of a "high probability" of the relevant circumstances and does not require, as does *Global Tech*, an affirmative act of avoidance.

A willful blindness charge was used to secure a conviction of Frederic Bourke for his role in an ultimately unsuccessful conspiracy to bribe government officials in Azerbaijan to take over the state-owned oil company, SOCAR. Bourke lost a great deal of money and there was no proof that Bourke directly engaged in the bribery efforts. Instead, according to one commentator, "the government's proof centered on Bourke's failure to act in response to his knowledge of the allegedly corrupt political environment and Bourke's knowledge of the actions of others who were alleged to be acting on his behalf." Brian Whisler, *Heightened FCPA Exposure for Executives*, 17 Bus. Crimes Bull. 3 (March 2010). In denying a motion for a judgment of acquittal, the judge indicated that Bourke's liability was founded on willful blindness; she stated that there was sufficient evidence for the jury to find a "high probability that payments to Azeri officials were illegal and that Bourke deliberately avoided confirming this fact." *Id.*

12. *Non-Covered Payments and Affirmative Defenses.* As is discussed at length in *Kay*, the FCPA does not criminalize "facilitating" or "grease" payments to foreign officials who perform "routine governmental actions." 15 U.S.C. §§ 78dd-1(b), 78dd-2(b), 78dd-3(b); *see also Kay*, court's footnote 19; footnote 33 of this chapter, *supra* (reproducing text); United States v. Duperval, 777 F.3d 1324, 1334 (11th Cir. 2015).

The FCPA also provides for two affirmative defenses. *See Kay*, court's footnote 44; footnote 34 of this chapter, *supra*. First, a defendant may assert that the payment was lawful "under the written laws and regulations" of the State at issue. 15 U.S.C. §§ 78dd-1(c), 78dd-2(c), 78dd-39(c). Why do you suppose that this defense has never been successfully asserted? *See, e.g.*, United States v. Kozeny, 582 F.Supp.2d 535, 537-40 (S.D.N.Y. 2008). Second, the FCPA permits a defendant to assert as an affirmative defense that the payment was a reasonable and bona fide expenditure (such as travel and lodging expenses) incurred by or on behalf of a foreign official, party official, or candidate, and was made in connection with the promotion, demonstration, or explanation of the defendant's products or services, or the execution or performance of a contract with a foreign government (or agency). *Id.* For guidance on the DOJ's interpretation of this exception, see *Resource Guide* at 14-15, 24.

13. *Record-keeping Violations.* The FCPA imposes certain record-keeping and internal control requirements on issuers (but not domestic concerns or other persons), which require that publicly-traded companies maintain accurate books and records. 15 U.S.C. § 78m(b)(2). To facilitate discovery of improper transactions, the record-keeping provisions have three targets: "ensuring that businesses accurately report transactions; preventing the falsification of records to conceal illegal transactions; and promoting the correct characterization of all transactions so that financial statements conform to accounting principles." *Thirty-Third Annual Survey of White Collar Crime, Foreign Corrupt Practices Act*, 55 Am. Crim. L. Rev. 1269, 1276 (2018). The internal control measures require reasonable assurances that transactions are properly

authorized, recorded, and audited. These accounting provisions generally fall within the civil enforcement authority of the SEC. They are important to criminal practice, however, for at least two reasons. First, counsel may be able to resolve potential criminal charges by agreeing to a civil settlement using these provisions as its foundation. Second, the Justice Department can bring criminal charges if it can prove that the defendant *willfully* circumvented or failed to implement a system of internal accounting controls or *willfully* falsified an issuer's books and records.

Should the DOJ elect to proceed on these "willful" books and records violations, they carry the potential for hefty criminal penalties: for individuals, fines of up to the greater of $5 million or twice the gross gain or loss flowing from the offense and imprisonment up to 20 years; for corporations, fines of up to the greater of $25 million or twice the gross gain or loss flowing from the offense. 15 U.S.C. § 78ff(a); 18 U.S.C. § 3571(d). By contrast, under the FCPA and the alternative minimum fine statute, juridical "persons" who violate the anti-bribery provisions of the FCPA are subject to a fine of the greater of $2 million or twice the gross gain or loss flowing from the offense. 15 U.S.C. §§ 78ff(c)(1)(A), 78dd-2(g)(1)(A), 78dd-3(e)(1)(A); 18 U.S.C. § 3571(d). Natural persons who willfully violate the anti-bribery provisions are subject to a criminal fine of not more than the greater of $250,000 or twice the gross gain or loss flowing from the offense, and imprisonment of not more than 5 years. 15 U.S.C. §§ 78ff(c)(2)(A), 78dd-2(g)(2)(A), 78dd-3(e)(2)(A); 18 U.S.C. § 3571(b)(3), (d). Criminal fines imposed on individuals may not be paid by their employer or principal. *See* 15 U.S.C. §§ 78dd-2(g)(3), 78dd-3(e)(3), 78ff(c)(3). Any property, real or personal, "which constitutes or is derived from proceeds traceable to a violation of the FCPA, or a conspiracy to violate the FCPA, may be forfeited." U.S.A.M., Criminal Resource Manual § 1019; *see* 18 U.S.C. §§ 981(a)(1)(C), 1956(c)(7).

14. *Foreign Subsidiaries.* In *Kay*, could prosecutors have prosecuted RCH, a company organized under Haitian law but that is a wholly-owned subsidiary of ARI? The House version of the FCPA in 1977 defined "domestic concerns" to include foreign subsidiaries of U.S. companies "both because of the extensive use of subsidiaries as conduits for improper payments and because the extension of U.S. jurisdiction [to] foreign subsidiaries was necessary in order to avoid 'a massive loophole ... through which millions of bribery dollars will continue to flow.'" H. Lowell Brown, *Parent-Subsidiary Liability under the Foreign Corrupt Practices Act*, 50 Baylor L. Rev. 1, 29 (1998). The Senate's more restrictive definition did not include foreign subsidiaries and, at conference, the House acceded to the Senate on this issue in recognition of "'the inherent jurisdictional, enforcement, and diplomatic difficulties raised by inclusion of foreign subsidiaries of U.S. companies in the direct prohibitions of the bill.'" *Id.* at 33. Might subsequent amendments to the FCPA, as well as the availability of a number of common law doctrines, have increased the potential that a U.S. company will be liable for the misconduct of its subsidiaries organized under the laws of foreign countries?

If the foreign subsidiary acted as an agent of the U.S. company, and the U.S. company had knowledge of, or was willfully blind, to the offending conduct, the U.S. company may be liable. *See* Note 11, *supra*. "The fundamental characteristic of agency is control. Accordingly, the DOJ and SEC evaluate the parent's control—including the parent's knowledge and direction of the subsidiary's actions, both generally and in the context of the specific transaction—when evaluating whether a subsidiary is an agent of the parent." *Resource Guide* at 27. FCPA liability may be also grounded in common law doctrines, such as piercing the corporate veil or application of *respondeat superior* principles to render a corporate parent liable for the activities of its subsidiary alter ego or agent. Brown, *supra*, 50 Baylor L. Rev. at 38. Certainly the addition of the alternative jurisdiction provisions of § 78dd-1 and § 78dd-2 mean that a U.S. parent company will be liable under the FCPA if it takes any action abroad in furtherance of the bribery scheme. And although before 1998 foreign subsidiaries were used precisely to avoid their being deemed "issuers" or "domestic concerns" under the FCPA, the addition of § 78dd-3 means that foreign subsidiaries may be liable under the FCPA if any act in furtherance of the illicit bribe takes place in U.S. territory. Under what theory or theories could the foreign subsidiary in *Kay* have been prosecuted?

15. *Successor Liability*. One of the reasons that FCPA advice is often required when companies are contemplating mergers or acquisitions, especially of companies operating overseas, is that the successor company may assume the predecessor company's liabilities, including FCPA violations. *See Resource Guide* at 28. This is why the "DOJ and SEC encourage companies to conduct pre-acquisition due diligence and improve compliance programs and internal controls after acquisition." *Id*. The Resource Guide reports that "[i]n a significant number of instances, DOJ and SEC have declined to take action against companies that voluntarily disclosed and remediated conduct and cooperated with DOJ and SEC in the merger and acquisition context. And DOJ and SEC have only taken action against successor companies in limited circumstances, generally in cases involving egregious and sustained violations or where the successor company directly participated in the violations or failed to stop the misconduct from continuing after acquisition." *Id*.

16. *Opinion Procedure*. The FCPA provides issuers and domestic concerns with a process through which they can obtain Department of Justice review and an opinion regarding proposed, specific, and non-hypothetical business activities that raise FCPA concerns. *See* 15 U.S.C. §§ 78dd-1(d),(e); 78dd-2(e), (f); *see also* 28 C.F.R. § 80.1 *et seq*. (DOJ Opinion Procedure). "The Opinion Procedure provides a mechanism by which any U.S. company or national may request a statement of the Justice Department's present enforcement intentions, under the antibribery provisions of the FCPA, regarding any proposed business conduct." U.S. Attorney's Manual, Criminal Resource Manual, Title 9, § 1016. "A favorable opinion from the Department of Justice creates a rebuttable presumption, applicable in any subsequent enforcement action, that the conduct described in the request conformed with the FCPA." *Id*.

17. *Passive Bribery*. The term "active bribery" is used to describe offenses that target the persons who make the corrupt payment or offer to pay—that is, cases in which the *briber* is in the dock. "Passive bribery" describes offenses outlawing the receipt of bribes—that is, cases in which the *bribee* is subject to prosecution. The FCPA has long been read to cover only active bribery. The leading case is *United States v. Castle*, 925 F.2d 831, 834 (5th Cir. 1991), in which the Fifth Circuit, noting the "overwhelming evidence of a Congressional intent to exempt foreign officials from prosecution for receiving bribes," ruled that the foreign officials receiving the bribes could not be prosecuted under the FCPA. The *Castle* decision was handed down in 1991—seven years before § 78dd-3 was added to the FCPA scheme; at that point, the Fifth Circuit explained,

> The drafters of the statute knew that they could, consistently with international law, reach foreign officials in certain circumstances. But they were equally well aware of, and actively considered, the "inherent jurisdictional, enforcement, and diplomatic" difficulties raised by application of the bill to non-citizens of the United States. In the conference report, the conferees indicated that the bill would reach as far as possible, and listed all the persons or entities who could be prosecuted. The list includes virtually every person or entity involved, including foreign nationals who participated in the payment of the bribe when the U.S. courts have jurisdiction over them. But foreign officials were not included.
> ...
> Most likely Congress made this choice because U.S. businesses were perceived to be the aggressors, and the efforts expended in resolving the diplomatic, jurisdictional, and enforcement difficulties that would arise upon the prosecution of foreign officials was not worth the minimal deterrent value of such prosecutions. Further minimizing the deterrrent value of a U.S. prosecution was the fact that many foreign nations already prohibited the receipt of a bribe by an official. In fact, whenever a nation permitted such payments, Congress allowed them as well. *See* 15 U.S.C. § 78dd-2(c)(1).

Id. at 835. Most of the international anti-corruption conventions also do not require their states parties to outlaw passive transnational bribery. Why? Shouldn't deterrent considerations compel the criminalization of the "demand" side of these corrupt transactions as well as the "supply" side?

18. *Other Statutes Potentially Applicable?* As discussed above, in *Gebardi v. United States*, 287 U.S. 112 (1932), the Supreme Court held that where Congress enacts a substantive criminal statute that excludes a class of individuals from liability, prosecutors cannot evade congressional intent by charging those same individuals with conspiring to violate the statute. In *United States v. Castle*, 925 F.2d 831 (5th Cir. 1991), the Fifth Circuit determined that Congress intended to exempt foreign officials from the coverage of the FCPA and thus, under *Gebardi*, such officials could not be charged with conspiracy to violate the FCPA. *Id.* at 836. Where the elements of money laundering are met, however, those who may not be reachable under the FCPA may still find themselves subject to U.S. criminal prosecution. *See* 18 U.S.C. §§ 1956(c)(7), 1957(f)(3); *see also* United States v. Bodmer, 342 F.Supp.2d 176 (S.D.N.Y. 2004). A violation of the FCPA may also qualify as "racketeering activity" upon which a prosecution (or treble damages civil liability) under the Racketeering Influenced and Corrupt Organizations (RICO) statute can be built. *See* 18 U.S.C. §§ 1961(1)(A); *see also* Env'l Tectronics v. W.S. Kirkpatrick, 847 F.2d 1052, 1063 (3d Cir. 1988), *aff'd on other grounds*, 493 U.S. 400; Rotec Indus., Inc. v. Mitsubishi Corp., 163 F.Supp.2d 1268, 1278 (D.Or. 2001).

19. *Honest Services Mail and Wire Fraud.* A mail or wire fraud charge is another alternative, at least where money or property can be charged as the object of the scheme. What of "honest services" mail and wire fraud? Should federal prosecutors be able to pursue foreign officials for depriving foreign citizens and governments of the officials' "honest services" under § 1346? In *United States v. Giffen*, 326 F. Supp.2d 497 (S.D.N.Y. 2004), the district court rejected such a prosecution. *Giffen* involved a defendant who was charged with making unlawful payments totaling more than $78 million to Nurlan Balgimaev, the former Prime Minister and Oil Minister of the Republic of Kazakhstan, and Nursultan Nazarbaev, the President of Kazakstan, in violation of, *inter alia*, the FCPA, 15 U.S.C. § 78dd-2, and the mail and wire fraud statutes, 18 U.S.C. §§ 1341, 1343, 1346.

Giffen did not challenge the indictment's reliance on the mail and wire fraud statute to the extent that the indictment charged a scheme to deprive Kazakhstan of property (that is, "tens of millions of dollars"). However, he moved for dismissal of the mail and wire fraud counts charging that his alleged scheme defrauded the citizens of Kazakhstan of the honest services of their government officials. The district court held that Congress did not intend the "honest services" provision of § 1346 to apply to schemes to defraud foreign citizens of their right to the honest services of foreign officials. *Id.* at 504-506. The court also ruled that any such application would be unconstitutionally vague because the statute did not provide sufficient notice that such schemes would be covered by § 1346. *Id.* at 506-07. Finally, the district court considered Giffen's argument that the application of the "honest services" theory to prosecute him was "non-justiciable" and violated considerations of "international comity":

> The concept of the Kazakh people's intangible right to honest services by their government officials requires definition. The indictment does not allege any facts or law regarding the meaning of honest services by Kazakh officials to the Kazakh people. The Government's argument that "[t]he notion that government officials owe a duty to provide honest services to the public is not so idiosyncratically American as to have no application at all to Kazakhstan" is inapposite and begs the question. In a jarring disconnect, the Government acknowledges that "Kazakhstan has sought to derail the investigation and eventual prosecution of this matter by numerous appeals to officials ... in the executive branch including ... [the] Departments of State and Justice." Implicit in the Government's observation is the suggestion that Kazakhstan itself is unable to define "honest services" within its own polity.
>
> In effect, the Government urges that American notions of honesty in public service developed over two centuries be engrafted on Kazakh jurisprudence. "While admittedly some ... countries do not take their [anti-corruption] responsibilities seriously, the correct answer to such a situation is not the extraterritorial application of United States law but rather cooperation between [the appropriate] home and host country ... authorities." "An argument in favor of the export of United States law represents not only a form of legal imperialism but also embodies the essence of sanctimonious chauvinism." While well

intentioned, the Government's suggestion that American legal standards be exported to Kazakhstan is simply a bridge too far.

"Because the principle of comity does not limit the legislature's power and is, in the final analysis, simply a rule of construction, it has no application where Congress has indicated otherwise." Until Congress authorizes an expansion of Section 1346 beyond pre-*McNally* precedent, this Court may not consider such an extraterritorial enlargement.

Id. at 507–08; *see also* United States v. Sidorenko, 102 F.Supp.3d 1124 (N.D. Ca. 2015) (dismissing honest services prosecution in a case involving prosecution of foreign defendants for foreign acts involving a foreign governmental entity); United States v. Lazarenko, No. CR 00-0284(MJJ) (dismissing honest services prosecution of the former president of the Republic of Ukraine because the government failed to prove that the defendant violated any provision of Ukrainian law analogous to § 1346).

20. *Travel Act.* The government has also relied on the Travel Act, 18 U.S.C. § 1952, in corruption cases—both domestic and transborder—because it can reach corrupt conduct not chargeable under 18 U.S.C. § 201 or the FCPA. As relevant here, the elements of a Travel Act violation include: (1) travel in interstate or foreign commerce or use of the mail or any facility in interstate or foreign commerce, (2) with the intent to promote, manage, establish, carry on, or facilitate the promotion, management, establishment, or carrying on, of any "unlawful activity," followed by (3) performance of or an attempt to perform an act of promotion, management, establishment, carrying on, or facilitation of the enumerated "unlawful activity." 18 U.S.C. § 1952(a)(3). "Unlawful activity" is defined to include "extortion, bribery, or arson in violation of the laws of the State in which committed or of the United States." 18 U.S.C. § 1952(b). Basically, this statute makes the act of traveling, or using the wires or mails, in furtherance of a bribery or extortion scheme punishable by not more than five years.

The majority of U.S. states outlaw commercial bribery. Because "unlawful activity" under the Travel Act includes "bribery ... in violation of the laws of the State in which committed," the DOJ can, and has, used this statute to attack transnational commercial bribery. *See* Perrin v. United States, 444 U.S. 37 (1979) (bribery of private employees prohibited by state criminal statutes violates the Travel Act); United States v. Welch, 327 F.3d 1081 (10th Cir. 2003). For example, Control Components, Inc. (CCI) was charged with violating the FCPA and the Travel Act by bribing government officials and employees of private companies. CCI was a California corporation and the California code outlaws commercial bribery. The district court rejected CCI's argument that the Travel Act should not be applied extraterritorially, for two reasons. First, it held that the Travel Act does have extraterritorial reach. Second, it ruled that, in any case, all elements of the Travel Act violation happened in California and that the offense "was complete the moment the Defendants used a channel of foreign commerce allegedly to offer a 'corrupt payment' to an employee and thereafter effectuated the payment to that employee." United States v. Carson, 2011 WL 7416975, *5 (C.D. Ca. 2011).

Can the Travel Act also be used to address passive as well as active bribery—that is, to indict the bribee as well as the briber?

21. *Private Suits.* A number of courts have held that there is no private right of action under the FCPA. *See* Republic of Iraq v. ABB AG, 768 F.3d 145 (2d Cir. 2014); Lamb v. Phillip Morris, Inc., 915 F.2d 1024 (6th Cir. 1980). When a company discloses an FCPA problem in its public filings or an investigation is made public, shareholder derivative and other suits against the company and its officers and directors will almost inevitably be filed. As Professor Mike Koehler notes

Particularly in the last few years, private plaintiffs firms representing shareholders have brought civil causes of action for securities fraud alleging that the company's securities lost value upon disclosure of an FCPA issue or derivative claims against officers and directors alleging breach of fiduciary duty for allowing the conduct to occur and/or for failure to effectively monitor the company's operations. ... In addition, if a company is the subject of FCPA scrutiny or has resolved an FCPA enforcement action, competitor companies may bring RICO claims in which an FCPA offense may be a predicate act or antitrust claims and/or federal and state law unfair competition claims in an attempt to hold a company accountable for alleged FCPA violations.

Mike   Koehler,   FCPA   Professor   Blog,   FCPA   101,   *available*   *at* http://www.fcpaprofessor.com/fcpa-101#q21 (last visited August 2018).

U.S. ATTORNEY'S MANUAL, 9-47.120 - FCPA CORPORATE ENFORCEMENT POLICY

1. <u>Credit for Voluntary Self-Disclosure, Full Cooperation, and Timely and Appropriate Remediation in FCPA Matters</u>

Due to the unique issues presented in FCPA matters, including their inherently international character and other factors, the FCPA Corporate Enforcement Policy is aimed at providing additional benefits to companies based on their corporate behavior once they learn of misconduct. When a company has voluntarily self-disclosed misconduct in an FCPA matter, fully cooperated, and timely and appropriately remediated, all in accordance with the standards set forth below, there will be a presumption that the company will receive a declination absent aggravating circumstances involving the seriousness of the offense or the nature of the offender. Aggravating circumstances that may warrant a criminal resolution include, but are not limited to, involvement by executive management of the company in the misconduct; a significant profit to the company from the misconduct; pervasiveness of the misconduct within the company; and criminal recidivism.

If a criminal resolution is warranted for a company that has voluntarily self-disclosed, fully cooperated, and timely and appropriately remediated, the Fraud Section:

--will accord, or recommend to a sentencing court, a 50% reduction off of the low end of the U.S. Sentencing Guidelines (U.S.S.G.) fine range, except in the case of a criminal recidivist; and

--generally will not require appointment of a monitor if a company has, at the time of resolution, implemented an effective compliance program.

To qualify for the FCPA Corporate Enforcement Policy, the company is required to pay all disgorgement, forfeiture, and/or restitution resulting from the misconduct at issue.

2. <u>Limited Credit for Full Cooperation and Timely and Appropriate Remediation in FCPA Matters Without Voluntary Self-Disclosure</u>

If a company did not voluntarily disclose its misconduct to the Department of Justice (the Department) in accordance with the standards set forth above, but later fully cooperated and timely and appropriately remediated in accordance with the standards set forth above, the company will receive, or the Department will recommend to a sentencing court, up to a 25% reduction off of the low end of the U.S.S.G. fine range.

3. <u>Definitions</u>

a. *Voluntary Self-Disclosure in FCPA Matters*

In evaluating self-disclosure, the Department will make a careful assessment of the circumstances of the disclosure. The Department will require the following items for a company to receive credit for voluntary self-disclosure of wrongdoing:

--The voluntary disclosure qualifies under U.S.S.G. § 8C2.5(g)(1) as occurring "prior to an imminent threat of disclosure or government investigation";

--The company discloses the conduct to the Department "within a reasonably prompt time after becoming aware of the offense," with the burden being on the company to demonstrate timeliness; and

--The company discloses all relevant facts known to it, including all relevant facts about all individuals involved in the violation of law.

b. *Full Cooperation in FCPA Matters*

In addition to the provisions contained in the Principles of Federal Prosecution of Business Organizations, the following items will be required for a company to receive credit for full cooperation for purposes of USAM 9-47.120(1) (beyond the credit available under the U.S.S.G.):

--... [D]isclosure on a timely basis of all facts relevant to the wrongdoing at issue, including: all relevant facts gathered during a company's independent investigation; attribution of facts to specific sources where such attribution does not violate the attorney-client privilege, rather than a general narrative of the facts; timely updates on a company's internal investigation, including but not limited to rolling disclosures of information; all facts related to involvement in the criminal activity by the company's officers, employees, or agents; and all facts known or that become known to the company regarding potential criminal conduct by all third-party companies (including their officers, employees, or agents);

---Proactive cooperation, rather than reactive; that is, the company must timely disclose facts that are relevant to the investigation, even when not specifically asked to do so, and, where the company is or should be aware of opportunities for the Department to obtain relevant evidence not in the company's possession and not otherwise known to the Department, it must identify those opportunities to the Department;

---Timely preservation, collection, and disclosure of relevant documents and information relating to their provenance, including (a) disclosure of overseas documents, the locations in which such documents were found, and who found the documents, (b) facilitation of third-party production of documents, and (c) where requested and appropriate, provision of translations of relevant documents in foreign languages;

Note: Where a company claims that disclosure of overseas documents is prohibited due to data privacy, blocking statutes, or other reasons related to foreign law, the company bears the burden of establishing the prohibition. Moreover, a company should work diligently to identify all available legal bases to provide such documents;

--Where requested, de-confliction of witness interviews and other investigative steps that a company intends to take as part of its internal investigation with steps that the Department intends to take as part of its investigation; and

--Where requested, making available for interviews by the Department those company officers and employees who possess relevant information; this includes, where appropriate and possible, officers, employees, and agents located overseas as well as former officers and employees (subject to the individuals' Fifth Amendment rights), and, where possible, the facilitation of third-party production of witnesses

c. *Timely and Appropriate Remediation in FCPA Matter*

The following items will be required for a company to receive full credit for timely and appropriate remediation for purposes of USAM 9-47.120(1) (beyond the credit available under the U.S.S.G.):

--Demonstration of thorough analysis of causes of underlying conduct (i.e., a root cause analysis) and, where appropriate, remediation to address the root causes;

--Implementation of an effective compliance and ethics program, the criteria for which will be periodically updated and which may vary based on the size and resources of the organization, but may include:

--The company's culture of compliance, including awareness among employees that any criminal conduct, including the conduct underlying the investigation, will not be tolerated;

--The resources the company has dedicated to compliance;

--The quality and experience of the personnel involved in compliance, such that they can understand and identify the transactions and activities that pose a potential risk;

--The authority and independence of the compliance function and the availability of compliance expertise to the board;

--The effectiveness of the company's risk assessment and the manner in which the company's compliance program has been tailored based on that risk assessment;

--The compensation and promotion of the personnel involved in compliance, in view of their role, responsibilities, performance, and other appropriate factors;

--The auditing of the compliance program to assure its effectiveness; and

--The reporting structure of any compliance personnel employed or contracted by the company.

--Appropriate discipline of employees, including those identified by the company as responsible for the misconduct, either through direct participation or failure in oversight, as well as those with supervisory authority over the area in which the criminal conduct occurred;

--Appropriate retention of business records, and prohibiting the improper destruction or deletion of business records, including prohibiting employees from using software that generates but does not appropriately retain business records or communications; and

--Any additional steps that demonstrate recognition of the seriousness of the company's misconduct, acceptance of responsibility for it, and the implementation of measures to reduce the risk of repetition of such misconduct, including measures to identify future risks.

Comment

Cooperation Credit: Cooperation comes in many forms. ... [T]he Department will assess the scope, quantity, quality, and timing of cooperation based on the circumstances of each case when assessing how to evaluate a company's cooperation under the FCPA Corporate Enforcement Policy.

"De-confliction" is one factor that the Department may consider in determining the credit that a company will receive for cooperation. The Department's requests to defer investigative steps, such as the interview of company employees or third parties, will be made for a limited period of time and will be narrowly tailored to a legitimate investigative purpose (e.g., to prevent the impeding of a specified aspect of the Department's investigation). Once the justification dissipates, the Department will notify the company that the Department is lifting its request.

Where a company asserts that its financial condition impairs its ability to cooperate more fully, the company will bear the burden to provide factual support for such an assertion. The Department will closely evaluate the validity of any such claim and will take the impediment into consideration in assessing whether the company has fully cooperated.

... [E]ligibility for full cooperation credit is not predicated upon waiver of the attorney-client privilege or work product protection, and none of the requirements above require such waiver. Nothing herein alters that policy, which remains in full force and effect. Furthermore, not all companies will satisfy all the components of full cooperation for purposes of USAM 9-47.120(2) and (3)(b), either because they decide to cooperate only later in an investigation or they timely decide to cooperate but fail to meet all of the criteria listed above. In general, such companies will be eligible for some cooperation credit if they meet the criteria of [the Principles of Federal Prosecution of Business Organizations], but the credit generally will be markedly less than for full cooperation, depending on the extent to which the cooperation was lacking.

Remediation: In order for a company to receive full credit for remediation and avail itself of the benefits of the FCPA Corporate Enforcement Policy, the company must have effectively remediated at the time of the resolution.

The requirement that a company pay all disgorgement, forfeiture, and/or restitution resulting from the misconduct at issue may be satisfied by a parallel resolution with a relevant regulator (e.g., the United States Securities and Exchange Commission).

Public Release: A declination pursuant to the FCPA Corporate Enforcement Policy is a case that would have been prosecuted or criminally resolved except for the company's voluntary disclosure, full cooperation, remediation, and payment of disgorgement, forfeiture, and/or restitution. If a case would have been declined in the absence of such circumstances, it is not a declination pursuant to this Policy. Declinations awarded under the FCPA Corporate Enforcement Policy will be made public.

Notes

1. In late 2017, the Department of Justice adopted this new enforcement policy with respect to FCPA cases and incorporated it into the U.S. Attorney's Manual. The policy seeks to give companies more concrete assurance that self-reporting, cooperation, and remediation will result in tangible benefits. Its aim, then, is to increase the volume of voluntary disclosures and enhance the DOJ's ability to identify and punish culpable individuals. (The DOJ has had great difficulty pursuing individuals for FCPA violations in the past.)

Up to this point, the DOJ (and to some extent the SEC) has used deferred prosecution agreements (DPAs) and non-prosecution agreements (NPAs) as the carrot for corporate self-reporting and cooperation. These agreements are essentially contracts under which the government undertakes to refrain from bringing charges or to dismiss existing charges if certain conditions are satisfied in return for consideration that usually includes an acknowledgement of wrongdoing, cooperation in the investigation of the activities at issue, payment of penalties, and agreed-upon corporate reforms. Reforms will generally involve putting in place an effective compliance program to prevent and detect future FCPA violations. Does the new policy's offer of the possibility of a declination, as opposed to an NPA or a DPA, significantly increase corporate incentives to self-report?

2. The policy, while welcomed by the practice community, has been subjected to some criticisms. First, the policy is non-binding, because it, like the rest of the U.S. Attorney's Manual, creates no private rights and is not enforceable in court. Second, the SEC has not signed on to it, so an enforcement action against issuers may still be possible from that quarter. Third, even with a declination, the company will have to pay disgorgement, forfeiture and/or restitution resulting from the misconduct. And the policy does nothing to reduce the most costly component of an FCPA case—pre-enforcement action professional (legal) fees and expenses. "In nearly every instance of FCPA scrutiny, [these costs are] the largest financial hit to a business organization." Mike Koehler, *Grading the DOJ's "FCPA Enforcement Policy"*, Bloomberg BNA Criminal Law Reporter (Dec. 20, 2017). For example, Avon resolved an FCPA enforcement action for $135 million in payments to the SEC and DOJ but it spent approximately $550 million in pre-enforcement action professional fees and expenses. *See id.* Hyperdynamics resolved an FCPA enforcement action for $375,000 but paid approximately $12.7 million in professional fees and expenses. *See id.*

Fourth, the benefits of the program are heavily dependent on the discretion of prosecutors in evaluating, for example, "full cooperation" and "timely and appropriate remediation." Fifth, the announcement of the declination may well cause some of the same collateral effects that a settlement provokes: loss of market capitalization, shareholder litigation, and the like. Finally, this policy does nothing to address the possibility of other, foreign regulators pursuing the case, as is discussed below. Professor Koehler and others argue that a statutory amendment providing an affirmative defense for companies that have an effective compliance program would be more effective in inducing self-reporting and cooperation. *See id.*

3. *Multiple Jurisdictions?* By definition, FCPA-type corruption crosses borders and may involve multiple jurisdictions, which may mean not only a multitude of investigations but also

many fines and other sanctions being assessed by different national actors. Until recently, other governments "seemed happy to let the DOJ and SEC serve as the world's corruption police. But when they saw DOJ's mega-settlements, they decided to claim a piece of the action." Laurence A. Urgenson *et al.*, *New Bumps and Tolls Along the Road to FCPA Settlements*, 17 Bus. Crimes Bull. 1 (Nov. 2009). What does this mean as a practical matter?

The FCPA is the inspiration for many anti-bribery conventions and the domestic anti-bribery laws of individual countries. Therefore, expansive jurisdictional reach by U.S. prosecutors and courts are feeding a chain reaction in which foreign jurisdictions similarly draft their own anti-bribery laws to include broad jurisdictional reach. For example, whereas the FCPA requires a link between the *bribe* itself and the U.S., under the U.K.'s Bribery Act jurisdiction extends to *anyone* with a "close connection" to the U.K., regardless of nationality, place of incorporation, and even regardless of whether the bribe itself implicates U.K. territory.

In many domestic settings, such as the U.S. and parts of Europe, double jeopardy or *ne bis in idem*, respectively, would bar ["give me the money too" or *da mihi quoque*] prosecutions. In the unfettered world of international law, however, no such mechanism exists. The U.S., for example, does not extend the concept of double jeopardy to the international arena. To the contrary, past U.S. settlements suggest a willingness to foster an environment in which MNCs are not merely subject to multiple prosecutions, but to multiple findings of guilt. And while several European states do apply *ne bis in idem* to international prosecutions, these principles are undeveloped and riddled with loopholes.

With the U.S. first adopting extra-territorial jurisdictional claims, the stage was set for other prosecutorial agencies to similarly assert extra-territorial jurisdiction. U.S. precedent thus created a preliminary condition to *da mihi quoque* prosecutions.

Bussen, *supra* note 29, at 498; see also Micheál Ó Floinn, *The Concept of Idem in European Courts: Extricating the Inextricable Link in European Double Jeopardy Law*, 24 Colum. J. of Europ. L. 75 (2017); Frederick T. Davis, *International Double Jeopardy: U.S. Prosecutions and the Developing Law in Europe*, 31 Am. U. Int'l L. Rev. 57 (2016). Multi-national subjects and targets of investigations will increasingly be working to achieve "global settlements" with multiple jurisdictions. *See id.*; *see also* Andrew S. Boutros & T. Markus Funk, *"Carbon Copy" Prosecutions: A Growing Anticorruption Phenomenon inta Shrinking World*, 2012 Univ. of Chi. Legal Forum 259 (2012).

4. *The U.K. Act.* The United Kingdom's recent efforts on the anti-bribery front have garnered a great deal of attention. The U.K. Bribery Act of 2010, which went into effect in July 2011, is in some significant respects broader in application than the FCPA. *See* U.K. Bribery Act, 2010, c. 23. On March 30, 2011, the U.K. Ministry of Justice issued an interpretive release which clarified certain aspects of the Act's scope and operation. *See* U.K. Ministry of Justice, *The Bribery Act of 2010: Guidance about procedures which relevant commercial organisations can put into place to prevent persons associated with them from bribing* (March 2011) [hereinafter "Guidance"]. The head of the U.K. Serious Fraud Office (SFO), which is charged with enforcing the new statute, has served notice that he intends to prosecute bribery cases aggressively to level the playing field for British companies relative to foreign competitors.

The Act creates four offenses: bribing another person (Section 1), being bribed (Section 2), bribing a foreign public official (Section 6), and a strict liability offense for the failure of a commercial organization to prevent bribery (Section 7).

(A) *FCPA Analog: Section 6.* To begin with the provision most like the FCPA, section 6 criminalizes bribery of foreign officials and is similar in scope to the FCPA. Thus, this section outlaws directly or through a third party offering, promising, or giving a financial or other advantage to a foreign public official with the intention to influence the official in her official capacity and to obtain or retain business or an advantage in the conduct of business. U.K. Bribery Act, 2010, c. 23, §6(1)-(3). No offence is deemed committed if the official is permitted or required by written law to be so influenced. *Id.* § 5(2), (3); *cf.* § 6(3)(b). The FCPA, of course, provides for two additional outs—for reasonable and bona fide corporate hospitality expenditures and for "grease" or facilitation payments. *See* 15 U.S.C. §§ 78dd-1(b), 78dd-2(b),

78dd-3(b). Similar exceptions were not provided for in the UK Act, although such matters are expected to be taken into account in exercising prosecutorial discretion in charging. *See* Guidance ¶¶ 26-32, 44-47, 49-50. The UK penalties are stiffer than those prescribed by the FCPA: the Act provides that, on conviction on indictment, a sanction of an unlimited fine and jail time up to 10 years can be imposed. U.K. Bribery Act, 2010, c. 23, §11(1)-(2).

The UK Act is potentially much broader than the FCPA in application in at least two further respects: (1) the potential application of the nominally non-transnational bribery provisions (Sections 1 and 2) to foreign nationals, businesses, and transactions; and (2) the controversial strict liability provision for commercial organizations who fail to prevent bribery (Section 6).

(B) *Commercial and Public Bribery Provisions with Transnational Scope: Sections 1 and 2.* Sections 1 and 2 are intended to be applied both domestically (in that they are akin to 18 U.S.C. § 201) and extraterritorially. Notably, they also are not restricted to the bribery of public officials, foreign or domestic. Sections 1 and 2 cover bribery of any "person," regardless of whether the person is a foreign official or a government official. UK Bribery Act, 2010, c. 23, § 3. Thus, these sections cover commercial bribery, which in the United States is principally addressed on the state level (with the exception of § 1346 private-sector honest services cases and a very few industry-specific commercial bribery provisions in the U.S. Code).

A person is guilty of active bribery under Section 1 when the person offers, promises, or gives a financial or other advantage to another person, and he either (1) intends the advantage to induce a person to perform a relevant function or activity improperly, or to reward a person for performing a relevant function or activity improperly, or (2) the person knows or believes that acceptance of the advantage would itself constitute improper performance of a relevant function or activity. *Id.* § 1(1)-(3). In both cases, Section 1 applies whether a bribe is offered directly or indirectly through a third party. *Id.* § 1(4)-(5).

Section 2 of the Act proscribes the offense of accepting or requesting a bribe. In this it is akin to 18 U.S.C. §201 but different than the FCPA, which does not cover passive bribery. A person can run afoul of Section 2 in four ways. A person who requests, agrees to receive, or accepts a financial or other advantage is guilty under Section 2 if: first, he intends, as a consequence, to perform a relevant function or activity improperly; second, the request, agreement, or acceptance itself constitutes the improper performance of a relevant function or activity; or third, the financial or other advantage is a reward for improper performance of a relevant function or activity. U.K. Bribery Act, 2010, c. 23, §2(1)-(4). Fourth, a person who performs a relevant function or activity improperly or assents to the improper performance of a relevant function or activity by another in anticipation of or in consequence of requesting, agreeing to receive, or accepting a financial or other advantage is also guilty under Section 2 of the Act. *Id.* § 2(5).

For Section 1 and Section 2 offenses, relevant "functions" and "activities" include any function of a public nature, and any activity connected with a business (including a trade or profession), performed in the course of a person's employment, or performed by or on behalf of a body of persons, whether corporate or unincorporated. *Id.* §§ 3(2), (7). The function list ensures that these Sections apply to public and private sector activities equally. *See id.* § 3(2). Note that, because Sections 1 and 2 are, unlike the FCPA, general public and private corruption prohibitions, they focus on "improper performance" and do not require the intention to obtain or retain business that is the hallmark of transnational bribery statutes like the FCPA and, indeed, Section 6 of the U.K. Act.

The performance of the "function" or "activity" must also meet one of the following conditions: (1) the person performing the function or activity is expected to perform it in good faith; (2) the person performing the function or activity is expected to perform it impartially; or (3) the person performing the function or activity is in a position of trust by virtue of performing it. *Id.* at §§ 3(1), (3)-(5). For the purposes of the Act, "good faith," "impartiality," and "trust" are defined by a reasonable (British) person's expectations and "and local custom or practice is to be disregarded" unless written into law. *Id.* § 5(1), (2). The conditions exclude from the scope of the Act defective performances of a function or activity that does not amount to corruption. *Id.* § 3(3)-(5).

Perhaps most important for present purposes, Sections 1 and 2 have wide applicability outside the United Kingdom. A "relevant function or activity" compromised by bribery qualifies under the Act even if it "has no connection with the United Kingdom," and "is performed in a country or territory outside the United Kingdom." *Id.* § 3(6). Thus, presumably corruption of a public official's "function" or a private executive's business "function" in the United States, China, or Russia (to name three random countries) could be prosecuted under these sections. The only limitation—applicable to prosecutions under Sections 1, 2, or 6—is that the defendant "person" must have "close connection" with the U.K. *Id.* § 12(2), (3). A "close connection" is defined to include those with British citizenship, residents of the United Kingdom, and entities incorporated under British law. *Id.* § 12(4).

(C) *Strict Liability for Failure to Prevent: Section 7.* Recall that liability under the FCPA for payments to intermediaries is restricted to cases in which a company pays or authorizes payment to a third party or intermediary knowing (or willfully blind to the fact) that some of the payment will go to a foreign official. 15 U.S.C. §§ 78dd-1(a)(3), 78dd-2(a)(3), 78dd-3(a)(3). Thus, under the FCPA, a company generally cannot be held liable for bribes by its foreign agents made without its knowledge. In contrast, the U.K. Act, in Section 7, creates a strict liability offence for covered commercial organizations who to fail to prevent their "associated persons" from committing offenses under Sections 1 or 6 anywhere in the world. Section 7 provides that a "relevant commercial organisation" commits an offense if "a person associated with" the organization bribes another intending "to obtain or retain business" or a "business advantage" for the organization. U.K. Bribery Act, 2010, c. 23, §7(1). Upon a showing that a person associated with such an organization has committed a bribery offense under Sections 1 or 6, the burden shifts to the organization to prove, by a "balance of probabilities," that it had in place adequate compliance procedures to prevent bribery. Guidance ¶ 33; U.K. Bribery Act, 2010, c. 23, § 7(2). Note that liability under Section 7 is in addition to, and does not displace, liability that may arise under Sections 1 or 6.

Obviously, it is critically important to understand who is an "associated person" for whose activities an entity may be strictly liable, subject to the compliance defense. The difficulty is that the definitions provided are somewhat amorphous. A person is "associated with" a commercial organization "if (disregarding any bribe under consideration), … [the] person … performs services for or on or behalf of" the organization. *Id.* § 8(1). We know that the capacity in which the person performs services for or on behalf of the entity does not matter, and whether or not a person is "associated with" the organization "is to be determined by reference to all the relevant circumstances and not merely be reference to the nature of the relationship" between the agent and the entity. *Id.* § 8(2), (4). An employee of the organization is "presumed" to be "associated with" his or her employer "unless the contrary is show." *Id.* § 8(5). Persons associated with an organization can also include agents and subsidiaries. *Id.* § 8(3). Foreign sales agents and other third party intermediaries may arguably fall within this category. The UK Ministry of Justice is not inclined to read the term restrictively, noting that "[t]he concept of a person who 'performs services for or on behalf of' the organisation is intended to give section 7 broad scope so as to embrace the whole range of persons connected to an organisation who might be capable of committing bribery on the organisation's behalf." Guidance ¶ 37.

Jurisdiction under Section 7 is also very expansive. An offense is committed under Section 7 "irrespective of whether the acts or omissions which form part of the offence take place in the United Kingdom or elsewhere." U.K. Bribery Act, 2010, c. 23, § 12(5). The requirement that the defendant person have a "close connection" with the United Kingdom, applicable in Section 1, 2 or 6 cases, does not apply to Section 7 prosecutions. *See* Guidance, ¶¶ 15-16. Further, it is critical to note that the "relevant commercial organizations" that may be strictly liable for public or private bribery under Section 7 include not just organizations formed under U.K. law, but also any body corporate or partnership—wherever formed—that "*carries on a business, or part of a business,*" in any part of the United Kingdom; note that "business" in this context also includes trade and professions. U.K. Bribery Act, 2010, c. 23, § 7(5) (emphasis added). Thus, a company that is not formed in the United Kingdom and has its principal place of business elsewhere can be found strictly liable for failing to prevent bribery by its agents in any country around the globe, so long as that company "carries on a business, or part of a business," in the United Kingdom.

Given the strict liability nature of this offense and the Sections' broad jurisdictional reach, the central question obviously becomes what is meant by "carrying on a business" in the United Kingdom? The term "carries on a business," however, is not a defined term. The Ministry of Justice's March 2011 guidance adopts a "common sense approach," Guidance ¶ 36, and commentators read the document as endorsing a narrow version of the term. The guidance, for example, indicates that "organisations that do not have a demonstrable business presence in the United Kingdom would not be caught" by the Act. Guidance ¶ 36. Merely listing securities on the London Stock Exchange would not alone qualify as "carrying on a business" under the U.K. Act. *Id.* "[H]aving a UK subsidiary will not, in itself, mean that a parent company is carrying on a business in the UK, since a subsidiary may act independently of its parent or other group companies." *Id.*

Although the written guidance indicates that the term "carries on a business" may not be expansive, the head of the SFO has indicated that the office will take a very aggressive stance in enforcing the Act outside the United Kingdom's borders, which may mean that in practice the term will be read broadly. A former Director of the SFO noted that "proceeding against foreign corporations under the Bribery Act for corruption committed in other countries is a high priority for the SFO. What we are actively looking for is a case where a foreign corporation, with a UK business presence, has disadvantaged a good ethical UK company by using corruption in another country." Covington & Burling, LLP, Advisory: Anti-Corruption, UK Serious Fraud Office Director Outlines Bribery Act Enforcement Agenda at Covington Anti-Corruption Summit (Oct. 14, 2011).

23. The U.K. Ministry of Justice has provided guidance in the administration of the U.K. Bribery Act and, in particular, Section 7 of that Act. In its guidance, it outlined the "six principles" entities should follow in creating compliance programs:

> Principle 1: Proportionate procedures. A commercial organisation's procedures to prevent bribery by persons associated with it are proportionate to the bribery risks it faces and to the nature, scale and complexity of the commercial organisation's activities. They are also clear, practical, accessible, effectively implemented and enforced.
>
> Principle 2: Top-level commitment. The top-level management of a commercial organisation (be it a board of directors, the owners or any other equivalent body or person) are committed to preventing bribery by persons associated with it. They foster a culture within the organisation in which bribery is never acceptable.
>
> Principle 3: Risk assessment. The commercial organisation assesses the nature and extent of its exposure to potential external and internal risks of bribery on its behalf by persons associated with it. The assessment is periodic, informed and documented.
>
> Principle 4: Due diligence. The commercial organisation applies due diligence procedures, taking a proportionate and risk based approach, in respect of persons who perform or will perform services for or on behalf of the organisation, in order to mitigate identified bribery risks.
>
> Principle 5: Communication (including training). The commercial organisation seeks to ensure that its bribery prevention policies and procedures are embedded and understood throughout the organization through internal and external communication, including training, that is proportionate to the risks it faces.
>
> Principle 6: Monitoring and review. The commercial organisation monitors and reviews procedures designed to prevent bribery by persons associated with it and makes improvements where necessary.

Guidance, pp. 20-43. Note, too, that the U.K.'s Serious Fraud Office is now authorized to enter into deferred prosecution agreements. *See* Serious Fraud Office, Deferred Prosecution Agreements Code of Practice: Crime and Courts Act 2013; *see generally* Daniel Huynh, *Preemption v. Punishment: A Comparative Study of White Collar Crime Prosecution in the United States and the United Kingdom*, 9 J. Int'l Bus. & L. 105 (2010).

Chapter 9

SECURITIES FRAUD

Rather than surveying all potential types of criminal securities violations,[1] this chapter focuses primarily on one highly visible subset of such violations—those involving "insider trading." Professor Don Langevoort advises that:

> "Insider trading" is a term of art that refers to unlawful trading in securities by persons who possess material nonpublic information about the company whose shares are traded or the market for its shares. Two points are worthy of note at the outset about this term. First, it is a misnomer. The prohibition against insider trading applies to a larger class of persons than those traditionally considered corporate insiders. Potentially, it reaches anyone who has access to privileged information. Second, there is a circularity to the definition, insofar as the term is generally used to refer only to *unlawful* trading. There are numerous instances where persons who possess material nonpublic information can trade lawfully. Only after reaching a legal conclusion, then, can its applicability be determined.[2]

This area of securities enforcement has waxed and waned, but the U.S. Attorney's Office for the Southern District of New York has made insider trading cases a priority in the last decade. The impact of these prosecutions has been called seismic due in part to the novel—and exceedingly effective—use of wiretaps in a white-collar investigation. At the conclusion of the chapter is a brief treatment of the securities fraud that has also dominated the news in recent years: accounting fraud.

Insider trading has long been prohibited by securities law statute and by Securities and Exchange Commission (SEC) rule. The relevant statutory prohibition, § 10(b) of the Securities and Exchange Act of 1934 (1934 Act), states that "[i]t shall be unlawful for any person ... [t]o use or employ, in connection with the purchase or sale of any security ..., any manipulative or deceptive device or contrivance in contravention of such rules and regulations as the Commission may prescribe ... ."[3] The principal rule relied on by the SEC in insider trading cases, Rule 10b-5, is not much more specific. In relevant part, Rule 10b-5 renders it unlawful

---

[1] For a more ambitious attempt to define the conceptual underpinnings of "securities fraud," see Samuel W. Buell, *What is Securities Fraud?*, 61 Duke L.J. 511 (2011).

[2] Donald C. Langevoort, Insider Trading: Regulation, Enforcement, and Prevention, § 1:1, at 1-10 (2015).

[3] 15 U.S.C. § 78j(b). The jurisdictional element of the statute is rarely contested and simply requires that the offender "use ... any means or instrumentality of interstate commerce or of the mails, or of any facility of any national securities exchange" in effecting the prohibited deceptive device or contrivance. Rule 10b-5 has contains a similar requirement. See 17 C.F.R. § 240.10b-5.

for any person "[t]o employ any device, scheme, or artifice to defraud" or "[t]o engage in any act, practice, or course of business which operates or would operate as a fraud or deceit upon any person," "in connection with the purchase or sale of any security."[4] The SEC may bring an enforcement action to address a violation of § 10(b) and Rule 10b-5, and defrauded participants in securities transactions may pursue civil damages for such violations. The only element necessary to convert a civil fraud under § 10(b) and Rule 10b-5 into a criminal violation is proof that the defendant acted "willfully" in violating the securities laws.[5]

In the following materials, the Supreme Court gives content to the general proscriptions reflected in § 10(b) and Rule 10b-5, defining in what circumstances individuals should be sanctioned for buying or selling securities based on material information that is not available to the public generally. In particular, the Supreme Court has "interpreted" the above laws to provide standards controlling when corporate "insiders" (*e.g.*, controlling shareholders, directors, and officers), "misappropriators" (those who have improperly obtained the material inside information), and "tippees" (those to whom such insiders or misappropriators have provided material non-public information) must disclose the non-public information generally, abstain from trading, or face liability.

In response to the corporate accounting scandals that erupted in 2002, Congress passed the Sarbanes-Oxley Act of 2002,[6] which was signed into law by President Bush on July 30, 2002. These materials therefore include some consideration of the potentially significant but relatively untested crime of "securities fraud" (codified at 18 U.S.C. § 1348) that Congress crafted in the Sarbanes-Oxley Act. This statute may remove certain of the proof requirements that control in criminal securities law cases, including the requirement that a defendant act "willfully" in violating the securities laws and, in some cases, that the defendant's misuse of inside information be in connection with "the purchase or sale" of securities. Finally, President Obama signed into law the Dodd-Frank Wall Street Reform and Consumer Protection Act on July 10, 2010; this Act effected numerous changes in the financial regulatory landscape. Most significantly for present purposes, the statute created a new SEC whistleblower program under which a whistleblower who voluntarily provides the SEC with original information that leads to the SEC recovering more than $1 million in a successful enforcement action can receive up to 10-30% of these multi-million dollar awards. The final section of this chapter summarizes the new whistleblower legislation and discusses the potential unintended consequences it may have for internal compliance efforts, as well as the SEC's attempt to forestall those consequences through regulation.[7]

To give readers some basis upon which to evaluate Congress' and the Supreme Court's efforts, this Chapter commences with an excerpt from a work by Professor Donald Langevoort. The cases that follow explore two distinct legal theories under which insider trading has been prosecuted—"traditional" theory and "misappropriation" theory—as well as the legal requisites of "tippee" liability.

---

[4] 17 C.F.R. § 240.10b-5.

[5] *See* 15 U.S.C. § 78ff(a); *see also* United States v. O'Hagan, 521 U.S. 642 (1997).

[6] P.L. 107-204, 116 Stat. 745 (2002).

[7] The press uncovered that 130 members of Congress or their families traded stocks collectively worth hundreds of millions of dollars in companies lobbying on bills that came before their committees. *See, e.g.*, Dan Keating *et al.*, *Members of Congress Trade in Companies While Making Laws that Affect Those Same Firms*, Wash. Post (June 23, 2012). As a result, Congress enacted the Stop Trading on Congressional Knowledge Act of 2012 ("STOCK Act"), Pub. L. 112-105, S. 2038, 126 Stat. 291, which applies federal prohibitions on insider trading to members of Congress, congressional staff, executive branch officials, and judicial officers and employees.

A. RATIONALE FOR INSIDER TRADING PROHIBITION

DONALD C. LANGEVOORT, INSIDER TRADING: REGULATION, ENFORCEMENT, AND PREVENTION
§ 1:2 to 1:6, at 1-8 to 1-17 (West 2002)

Why Is Insider Trading Prohibited?

Many people argue that there is nothing wrong with insider trading—that it is one of the rightful "perks" of executive status. [For example, there is a scene from the movie, *The Big Chill*, in which the founder of a regional chain of sporting goods stores is out jogging with an old college friend. During the run, he mentions to the friend that a much larger company is planning to acquire his company, and will be paying a handsome premium for the shares. The obvious implication is that the friend should buy some of the sporting goods company's shares now, and make a quick profit.] In the example from *The Big Chill*, [many people] would say, the company's founder was just doing a favor for a friend. He was sharing some good fortune, to no one's harm. Perhaps this explains an August 1986 *Business Week* poll which found that 53 percent of the respondents said that they would trade if given material nonpublic information; 82 percent thought that most other people would trade under the same circumstances.[8] ...

Investor and Marketplace Impact

On a more considered level, a number of legal commentators have also seriously questioned whether there should be any prohibition at all. Critics of the insider trading prohibition make a number of points, all of which have some merit. First and foremost, they challenge the notion that anyone is seriously harmed by insider trading. Take the example from above, and assume that the stock of the small sporting goods chain is trading at around $7 per share on the over-the-counter market. Unknown to the public, the acquiring company is prepared to pay $12 per share in a friendly merger. Suppose that the friend buys 1,000 shares at $7 as a result of the tip, and thus stands to make a quick $5,000 profit. Where is the harm?

The economics of the securities marketplace are complicated, and some oversimplification here is necessary. Certainly, the person (or persons) who sold the 1,000 shares that the friend bought made what later turned out to be a bad choice; he almost surely would not have sold at $7 had he known of the impending merger. But, in all likelihood, he would have sold at $7 (or thereabouts) to someone, insider trading or not. That is to say, his investment decision was probably wholly independent of the insider trading. It is hard to see, therefore, that such trading *caused* his bad fortune.

Of course, it is possible that some sellers were induced to come into the market by the insider trading. That would happen if bids for shares by insiders and their associates led to a rise in the price of the stock, and that price rise caused others to decide to sell. Here, again, however, it is very hard to say that the insiders actually *harmed* the sellers, except in a very abstract sense. All that the insiders did was bid for shares in the anonymous marketplace just like anyone else. Such a bid carries with it no representations or warranties; in responding to it, sellers took an inevitable and foreseeable risk that subsequent events would, in retrospect, render $7 too low a selling price. That sort of harm (if it is harm at all) hardly seems by itself to rise to the level that calls for costly and aggressive federal protection, and might well be discounted by the marketplace. If this discounting were significant, in turn, firms might be

---

[8] [Author's footnote 1:] Bus. Wk., Aug. 25, 1986, at 74. Nonetheless, 52 percent of the respondents stated that they believed that insider trading should be illegal. ... [Ed.: *see also* Stuart P. Green & Matthew B. Kugler, *When Is It Wrong to Trade Stocks on the Basis of Non-Public Information? Public Views of the Morality of Insider Trading*, 39 Ford. Urb. L.J. 445 (2011).]

expected to be more aggressive in eliminating insider trading, in order to lower their cost of capital.

Critics of the insider trading prohibition do not rest their argument solely on the idea that insider trading is harmless to the marketplace. The more sophisticated commentators suggest that in fact insider trading is socially valuable. In our example, the true intrinsic value of the smaller company is $12 per share, not $7. Trading at the misinformed price misallocates capital resources. Anything that causes the price to move toward the true value—including purchases by insiders and their associates—is proper, and should not be discouraged.[9]

Impact on the Company and Its Operations

Much of the debate over insider trading has to do with the likely impact of permitting such trading on the company itself, i.e., its profitability. To the critics of the insider trading prohibition, the bar against trading is a costly one. They see the profits from insider trading as a useful form of management compensation (lowering the salaries or bonuses that would otherwise be paid), and as creating a mechanism to make managers more willing to take risks in order to enhance profitability.

This assertion has been criticized on a number of grounds. First, using trading profits as compensation appears grossly inefficient given their essential randomness and the secrecy that surrounds them. A rational employer and manager would find it much more sensible to use stock and options as compensatory mechanisms designed to align the interests of the manager and the company—and these raise far smaller issues of informational advantage. Second, permitting insider trading invites managers to devote some significant portion of the time and attention that they might otherwise devote to running the business to identifying trading profit opportunities, and creates an unfortunate level of competition among managers to exploit information. As to the risk-taking argument, a number of commentators have observed that this proves too much: insiders who see that they can profit from price movements will simply want to introduce volatility into the market price—without regard to whether it is up or down. Finally, there is the obvious point that under some circumstances, insider trading could harm the very same interest in maintaining secrecy that led corporate officials not to make prompt public disclosure of the information in question, by focusing marketplace attention and scrutiny on the issuer as a result of leaks from tipping or the price movements from the trading itself. In sum, there is ample reason to see insider trading as at least a threat to corporate self-interest. ...

Disclosure Incentives

From the perspective of federal securities regulation, probably the most important direction that the rational debate over insider trading has taken is toward the question of what impact freely permitting insider trading would have on the prompt disclosure of new information. Intuitively, there seems to be a strong argument to be made that were insiders permitted to profit from trading, they would have an incentive to delay disclosure of information until their personal profit from the information has been captured (as well as to

---

[9] [Author's footnote 7:] This view has been subject to criticism on a number of grounds. First, there is no reason to believe that insider trading will automatically move the market price in any significant fashion. That will occur only where other marketplace participants can "decode" the trading as involving an insider with a significant informational advantage, and such decoding may or may not occur in a given case. Second, such movement is clearly a second best to prompt disclosure of the information. In addition, it seems clear that short-run allocational efficiency may be overstated as an objective—i.e., the value of market movements during the short periods between information creation and disclosure may be relatively insignificant. ...

overstate its significance upon disclosure). This disincentive might well even extend to disclosure within the company hierarchy, as lower-level employees delay transmission of new data to others in order to gain the greatest advantage from it. In either event, a marketplace perception that current and accurate information was not readily available about a particular issuer might well dampen its market price.

To this, the critics of the prohibition reply that any time lag between the discovery of information and its disclosure because of the manager's conflict of interest will be minimal, since insiders are pressured to act quickly to exploit information before it is discovered by a significant number of their colleagues. Moreover, there are strong countervailing forces—legal and marketplace—that lead toward both prompt and accurate disclosure. In addition, secrets are hard to keep—especially if there is no strong justification for keeping them. Thus, while some disincentive may indeed be present, they argue that it is not likely to be of dispositive significance in the overall debate over the pros and cons of insider trading.

Fairness and Politics

In light of the foregoing ambiguity, the desirability of a prohibition against insider trading seems, at the very least, a legitimately debatable question. It is odd, then, that the prohibition takes such prominence in American securities regulation and has quickly been replicated throughout the world. Yet it does. ...

Why? Even though the rational arguments against insider trading seem correct, these seem much too subtle and intellectual to be the source of the intense political sentiment behind the law of insider trading.[10] Descriptively, most people who oppose insider trading seem to believe that quite apart from any harm caused to specific investors, insider trading is simply an *unfair* exploitation of information that properly belongs to someone else. Corporate executives are fiduciaries, charged with acting on behalf of the corporation and its stockholders. The idea, long ingrained in the common law, that an executive's self-interest should be subordinate to the interests of the shareholders seems to be turned on its head if insiders are allowed (either directly or indirectly) to profit from their special knowledge at the same time that shareholders who are buying or selling are disadvantaged by their ignorance. Confidence in the securities marketplace, the argument goes, is diminished if shareholders believe that only those "in the know" can profit in the stock market. And building confidence in the securities marketplace—what SEC officials have described as the "mantra of market integrity" of which insider trading enforcement is "symbolically, and in a very real sense" a major part—is the overriding objective of the federal securities laws. An American Bar Association task force report has stated:

> In our society, we traditionally abhor those who refuse to play by the rules, that is, the cheaters and the sneaks. The spitball pitcher or card shark with an ace up his sleeve, may win the game but not our respect. And if we know such a person is in the game, chances are we won't play.[11]

---

[10] [Author's footnote 21:] Indeed, many of the rational arguments against insider trading suggest that the disincentives and problems could best be dealt with by state corporation law or private contracting. At the very least, the current legal structure extends far beyond the settings that most clearly deserve regulation (e.g., disclosure incentives). Another possibility that is worth noting, however, is some special interest pressure in this direction. Probably the most direct beneficiaries of the prohibition against insider trading are investment professionals, for they are "next in line" to corporate insiders with respect to the opportunity to benefit from newly discovered information. Hence, the investment community might well be expected to push for legislation banning trading by true insiders (but less aggressive with respect to "outsider" trading).

[11] [Author's footnote 23:] American Bar Association, Report of the Task Force on the Regulation of Insider Trading, Committee on Federal Regulation of Securities, *reprinted in* 41 Bus. Law, 223, 227 (1985). The fairness rationale is at the heart of the SEC's enforcement philosophy. *See* McLucas, Walsh &

That same thought was a prominent part of the Supreme Court's most pro-regulatory insider trading decision, *United States v. O'Hagan*, where the Court said that "[a]lthough informational disparity is inevitable in the securities markets, investors likely would hesitate to venture their capital in a market where trading based on misappropriated nonpublic information is unchecked by law."[12]

This sentiment is, no doubt, based as much on emotion as logic, and probably felt by many people who do not invest at all. It may be rooted in the vague feeling of jealousy directed against persons of status whose already lucrative positions give them opportunities for profit systematically denied to most investors—a sentiment that perhaps explains the public and legal fascination with the most recent stories of insider trading by young Wall Street professionals whose compensation was already, by contrast to others of similar age and experience, exorbitant. ...

Understanding the emotional motivation behind the prohibition is essential to understanding the law of insider trading, for both the "fiduciary duty" and "fair play" concepts are building blocks in the development of doctrine in this area. Indeed, breach of fiduciary duty has become the principal key to developing a coherent theory of "abstain or disclose" liability. At the same time, however, the subjectivity of the law's motivation is also a source of confusion. Neither fair play nor fiduciary duty is a particularly well-defined concept; there is much room for disagreement over whether given trading instances contravene these standards. The desire to have an expansive and flexible reach to the prohibition in order to remedy all perceived wrongs, however, is inevitably in tension with another strong desire given prominence in recent securities law jurisprudence, the need for predictability and clarity in the law. Much of the complexity of the law of insider trading—something long recognized as a problem in this area—is a product of quixotic attempts by the courts to resolve this tension.

B. TRADITIONAL THEORY

CHIARELLA v. UNITED STATES
445 U.S. 222 (1980)

MR. JUSTICE POWELL delivered the opinion of the Court.

The question in this case is whether a person who learns from the confidential documents of one corporation that it is planning an attempt to secure control of a second corporation violates § 10(b) of the Securities Exchange Act of 1934 if he fails to disclose the impending takeover before trading in the target company's securities.

Petitioner is a printer by trade. In 1975 and 1976, he worked as a "markup man" in the New York composing room of Pandick Press, a financial printer. Among documents that petitioner handled were five announcements of corporate takeover bids. When these documents were delivered to the printer, the identities of the acquiring and target corporations were concealed by blank spaces or false names. The true names were sent to the printer on the night of the final printing.

The petitioner, however, was able to deduce the names of the target companies before the final printing from other information contained in the documents. Without disclosing his knowledge, petitioner purchased stock in the target companies and sold the shares immediately after the takeover attempts were made public. By this method, petitioner realized a gain of

---

Fortune, *"Settlement of Insider Trading Cases with the SEC,"* 48 Bus. Law. 79, 79-80 (1992). [Ed.: *see also* Sung Hui Kim, *Insider Trading as Private Corruption,* 61 UCLA L. Rev. 928 (2014).]

[12] [Author's footnote 24:] United States v. O'Hagan, 521 U.S. 642, 658 (1997).

slightly more than $30,000 in the course of 14 months. Subsequently, the Securities and Exchange Commission (Commission or SEC) began an investigation of his trading activities. In May 1977, petitioner entered into a consent decree with the Commission in which he agreed to return his profits to the sellers of the shares. On the same day, he was discharged by Pandick Press.

In January 1978, petitioner was indicted on 17 counts of violating § 10(b) of the Securities Exchange Act of 1934 (1934 Act) and SEC Rule 10b-5. After petitioner unsuccessfully moved to dismiss the indictment, he was brought to trial and convicted on all counts.

The Court of Appeals for the Second Circuit affirmed petitioner's conviction. We granted certiorari, and we now reverse. ...

This case concerns the legal effect of the petitioner's silence. The District Court's charge permitted the jury to convict the petitioner if it found that he willfully failed to inform sellers of target company securities that he knew of a forthcoming takeover bid that would make their shares more valuable. In order to decide whether silence in such circumstances violates § 10(b), it is necessary to review the language and legislative history of that statute as well as its interpretation by the Commission and the federal courts.

Although the starting point of our inquiry is the language of the statute, § 10(b) does not state whether silence may constitute a manipulative or deceptive device. Section 10(b) was designed as a catch-all clause to prevent fraudulent practices. But neither the legislative history nor the statute itself affords specific guidance for the resolution of this case. When Rule 10b-5 was promulgated in 1942, the SEC did not discuss the possibility that failure to provide information might run afoul of § 10(b).

The SEC took an important step in the development of § 10(b) when it held that a broker-dealer and his firm violated that section by selling securities on the basis of undisclosed information obtained from a director of the issuer corporation who was also a registered representative of the brokerage firm. In *Cady, Roberts & Co.*, 40 S.E.C. 907 (1961), the Commission decided that a corporate insider must abstain from trading in the shares of his corporation unless he has first disclosed all material inside information known to him. The obligation to disclose or abstain derives from

> "[a]n affirmative duty to disclose material information[, which] has been traditionally imposed on corporate 'insiders,' particularly officers, directors, or controlling stockholders. We, and the courts have consistently held that insiders must disclose material facts which are known to them by virtue of their position but which are not known to persons with whom they deal and which, if known, would affect their investment judgment."

The Commission emphasized that the duty arose from (i) the existence of a relationship affording access to inside information intended to be available only for a corporate purpose, and (ii) the unfairness of allowing a corporate insider to take advantage of that information by trading without disclosure.[13]

That the relationship between a corporate insider and the stockholders of his corporation gives rise to a disclosure obligation is not a novel twist of the law. At common law, misrepresentation made for the purpose of inducing reliance upon the false statement is fraudulent. But one who fails to disclose material information prior to the consummation of a

---

[13] [Court's footnote 8:] In *Cady, Roberts*, the broker-dealer was liable under § 10(b) because it received nonpublic information from a corporate insider of the issuer. Since the insider could not use the information, neither could the partners in the brokerage firm with which he was associated. The transaction in *Cady, Roberts* involved sale of stock to persons who previously may not have been shareholders in the corporation. The Commission embraced the reasoning of Judge Learned Hand that: "the director or officer assumed a fiduciary relation to the buyer by the very sale; for it would be a sorry distinction to allow him to use the advantage of his position to induce the buyer into the position of a beneficiary although he was forbidden to do so once the buyer had become one."

transaction commits fraud only when he is under a duty to do so. And the duty to disclose arises when one party has information "that the other [party] is entitled to know because of a fiduciary or other similar relation of trust and confidence between them."[14] In its *Cady, Roberts* decision, the Commission recognized a relationship of trust and confidence between the shareholders of a corporation and those insiders who have obtained confidential information by reason of their position with that corporation.[15] This relationship gives rise to a duty to disclose because of the "necessity of preventing a corporate insider from ... tak[ing] unfair advantage of the uninformed minority stockholders."

The federal courts have found violations of § 10(b) where corporate insiders used undisclosed information for their own benefit. The cases also have emphasized, in accordance with the common-law rule, that "[t]he party charged with failing to disclose market information must be under a duty to disclose it." Accordingly, a purchaser of stock who has no duty to a prospective seller because he is neither an insider nor a fiduciary has been held to have no obligation to reveal material facts. ...

Thus, administrative and judicial interpretations have established that silence in connection with the purchase or sale of securities may operate as a fraud actionable under § 10(b) despite the absence of statutory language or legislative history specifically addressing the legality of nondisclosure. But such liability is premised upon a duty to disclose arising from a relationship of trust and confidence between parties to a transaction. Application of a duty to disclose prior to trading guarantees that corporate insiders, who have an obligation to place the shareholder's welfare before their own, will not benefit personally through fraudulent use of material, nonpublic information.

In this case, the petitioner was convicted of violating § 10(b) although he was not a corporate insider and he received no confidential information from the target company. Moreover, the "market information" upon which he relied did not concern the earning power or operations of the target company, but only the plans of the acquiring company. Petitioner's use of that information was not a fraud under § 10(b) unless he was subject to an affirmative duty to disclose it before trading. In this case, the jury instructions failed to specify any such duty. In effect, the trial court instructed the jury that petitioner owed a duty to everyone; to all sellers, indeed, to the market as a whole. The jury simply was told to decide whether petitioner used material, nonpublic information at a time when "he knew other people trading in the securities market did not have access to the same information."

The Court of Appeals affirmed the conviction by holding that "[a]nyone—corporate insider or not—who regularly receives material nonpublic information may not use that information to trade in securities without incurring an affirmative duty to disclose." Although the court said that its test would include only persons who regularly receive material, nonpublic information, its rationale for that limitation is unrelated to the existence of a duty to disclose.[16] The Court of Appeals, like the trial court, failed to identify a relationship between petitioner and the sellers that could give rise to a duty. Its decision thus rested solely upon its belief that the federal securities laws have "created a system providing equal access to information necessary for reasoned and intelligent investment decisions." The use by anyone of material information not generally available is fraudulent, this theory suggests, because such information gives certain buyers or sellers an unfair advantage over less-informed buyers and sellers.

---

[14] [Court's footnote 9:] Restatement (Second) of Torts § 551(2)(a) (1976). ...

[15] [Court's footnote 10:] *See* 3 W. Fletcher, Cyclopedia of the Law of Private Corporations § 838 (rev. 1975); 3A *id.*, §§ 1168.2, 1171, 1174; 3 L. Loss, Securities Regulation 1446-1448 (2d ed. 1961); 6 *id.*, at 3557-3558 (1969 Supp.).

[16] [Court's footnote 14:] The Court of Appeals said that its "regular access to market information" test would create a workable rule embracing "those who occupy ... strategic places in the market mechanism." These considerations are insufficient to support a duty to disclose. A duty arises from the relationship between parties, and not merely from one's ability to acquire information because of his position in the market. ...

This reasoning suffers from two defects. First not every instance of financial unfairness constitutes fraudulent activity under § 10(b). Second, the element required to make silence fraudulent—a duty to disclose—is absent in this case. No duty could arise from petitioner's relationship with the sellers of the target company's securities, for petitioner had no prior dealings with them. He was not their agent, he was not a fiduciary, he was not a person in whom the sellers had placed their trust and confidence. He was, in fact, a complete stranger who dealt with the sellers only through impersonal market transactions.

We cannot affirm petitioner's conviction without recognizing a general duty between all participants in market transactions to forgo actions based on material, nonpublic information. Formulation of such a broad duty, which departs radically from the established doctrine that duty arises from a specific relationship between two parties, should not be undertaken absent some explicit evidence of congressional intent.

As we have seen, no such evidence emerges from the language or legislative history of § 10(b). Moreover, neither the Congress nor the Commission ever has adopted a parity-of-information rule. Instead the problems caused by misuse of market information have been addressed by detailed and sophisticated regulation that recognizes when use of market information may not harm operation of the securities markets. ...

We see no basis for applying such a new and different theory of liability in this case. As we have emphasized before, the 1934 Act cannot be read "'more broadly than its language and the statutory scheme reasonably permit.'" Section 10(b) is aptly described as a catchall provision, but what it catches must be fraud. When an allegation of fraud is based upon nondisclosure, there can be no fraud absent a duty to speak. We hold that a duty to disclose under § 10(b) does not arise from the mere possession of nonpublic market information. The contrary result is without support in the legislative history of § 10(b) and would be inconsistent with the careful plan that Congress has enacted for regulation of the securities markets.

In its brief to this Court, the United States offers an alternative theory to support petitioner's conviction. It argues that petitioner breached a duty to the acquiring corporation when he acted upon information that he obtained by virtue of his position as an employee of a printer employed by the corporation. The breach of this duty is said to support a conviction under § 10(b) for fraud perpetrated upon both the acquiring corporation and the sellers. ...

The jury instructions demonstrate that petitioner was convicted merely because of his failure to disclose material, nonpublic information to sellers from whom he bought the stock of target corporations. The jury was not instructed on the nature or elements of a duty owed by petitioner to anyone other than the sellers. Because we cannot affirm a criminal conviction on the basis of a theory not presented to the jury, we will not speculate upon whether such a duty exists, whether it has been breached, or whether such a breach constitutes a violation of § 10(b). ...

MR. CHIEF JUSTICE BURGER, dissenting.

I believe that the jury instructions in this case properly charged a violation of § 10(b) and Rule 10b-5, and I would affirm the conviction.

As a general rule, neither party to an arm's-length business transaction has an obligation to disclose information to the other unless the parties stand in some confidential or fiduciary relation. See W. Prosser, Law of Torts § 106 (2d ed. 1955). This rule permits a businessman to capitalize on his experience and skill in securing and evaluating relevant information; it provides incentive for hard work, careful analysis, and astute forecasting. But the policies that underlie the rule also should limit its scope. In particular, the rule should give way when an informational advantage is obtained, not by superior experience, foresight, or industry, but by some unlawful means. One commentator has written:

"[T]he way in which the buyer acquires the information which he conceals from the vendor should be a material circumstance. The information might have been acquired as the result of his bringing to bear a superior knowledge, intelligence, skill or technical judgment; it might have been acquired by mere chance; or it might have been acquired by means of some tortious action on his part. ... *Any time information is acquired by an illegal act it would seem that there should be a duty to disclose that information.*" Keeton, Fraud—Concealment and Non-Disclosure, 15 Texas L.Rev. 1, 25-26 (1936).

I would read § 10(b) and Rule 10b-5 to encompass and build on this principle: to mean that a person who has misappropriated nonpublic information has an absolute duty to disclose that information or to refrain from trading.

The language of § 10(b) and of Rule 10b-5 plainly supports such a reading. By their terms, these provisions reach *any* person engaged in *any* fraudulent scheme. This broad language negates the suggestion that congressional concern was limited to trading by "corporate insiders" or to deceptive practices related to "corporate information."[17] Just as surely Congress cannot have intended one standard of fair dealing for "white collar" insiders and another for the "blue collar" level. The very language of § 10(b) and Rule 10b-5 "by repeated use of the word 'any' [was] obviously meant to be inclusive."

The history of the statute and of the Rule also supports this reading. The antifraud provisions were designed in large measure "to assure that dealing in securities is fair and without undue preferences or advantages among investors." These provisions prohibit "those manipulative and deceptive practices which have been demonstrated to fulfill no useful function." An investor who purchases securities on the basis of misappropriated nonpublic information possesses just such an "undue" trading advantage; his conduct quite clearly serves no useful function except his own enrichment at the expense of others. ...

The Court's opinion, as I read it, leaves open the question whether § 10(b) and Rule 10b-5 prohibit trading on misappropriated nonpublic information. Instead, the Court apparently concludes that this theory of the case was not submitted to the jury. In the Court's view, the instructions given the jury were premised on the erroneous notion that the mere failure to disclose nonpublic information, however acquired, is a deceptive practice. And because of this premise, the jury was not instructed that the means by which Chiarella acquired his informational advantage—by violating a duty owed to the acquiring companies—was an element of the offense. ...

... [E]ven assuming the instructions were deficient in not charging misappropriation with sufficient precision, on this record any error was harmless beyond a reasonable doubt. Here, Chiarella, himself, testified that he obtained his informational advantage by decoding confidential material entrusted to his employer by its customers. He admitted that the information he traded on was "confidential," not "to be use[d] ... for personal gain." In light of this testimony, it is simply inconceivable to me that any shortcoming in the instructions could have "possibly influenced the jury adversely to [the defendant]." ...

In sum, the evidence shows beyond all doubt that Chiarella, working literally in the shadows of the warning signs in the printshop misappropriated—stole to put it bluntly—valuable nonpublic information entrusted to him in the utmost confidence. He then exploited his ill-gotten informational advantage by purchasing securities in the market. In my view, such conduct plainly violates § 10(b) and Rule 10b-5. Accordingly, I would affirm the judgment of the Court of Appeals.

Notes

1. Under *Chiarella*, when may "outsiders" be liable for insider trading? The Court makes clear that silence (that is, trading on the basis of material non-public information without

---

[17] [Dissent's footnote 1:] Academic writing in recent years has distinguished between "corporate information"—information which comes from within the corporation and reflects on expected earnings or assets—and "market information." It is clear that § 10(b) and Rule 10b-5 by their terms and by their history make no such distinction.

disclosing that information generally) is not actionable absent some kind of a duty to disclose. The Court further emphasizes that "mere possession" of the information, even by those "outsiders" who "regularly receive" such information, does not create a duty to disclose. Rather, the duty must arise from a "relationship." What types of relationships give rise to a duty to disclose? With whom must the trader have the relationship?

2. Professor Langevoort, in the reading excerpted above, discusses two concepts that seem to be the "building blocks in the development of doctrine in this area": "fiduciary duty" and "fair play." The Court appears to adopt the former while rejecting the latter in this opinion. In particular, the Court rejects the Second Circuit's approach, which was founded on the belief that the securities laws have "created a system providing equal access to information necessary for reasoned and intelligent investment decisions," and emphasized the "unfair advantage" that those in possession of material non-public information have in securities transactions. On what basis does the Supreme Court make this determination regarding the rationale behind the insider trading prohibition?

3. Chiarella's conviction was overturned because he did not have a relationship with the shareholders in the stocks in which he traded that gave rise to a duty to disclose or abstain from trading. Chiarella did, however, have a relationship with his employer and perhaps by extension with his employer's client corporation, from whom he could be said to have "misappropriated" the information upon which he traded. Under the mail and wire fraud precedents considered in Chapter 7, *supra*, Chiarella's misappropriation for his own use of business information that he knew his employer wished to keep confidential could constitute "fraud." *See* Carpenter v. United States, 484 U.S. 19 (1987). Both Section 10(b) and Rule 10b-5 require, however, that such fraud be "in connection with the purchase or sale of any security." Would Chiarella's fraud on the *source* of the misappropriated information (*e.g.*, his employer), as opposed to *the shareholders with whom he was trading*, satisfy the "in connection with" requirement? Isn't there a disconnect between the person defrauded (the employer) and those presumably suffering a securities-related harm (the shareholders with whom he is trading)?

The government advanced the argument that Chiarella's conviction could be upheld on the basis of the fraud he perpetrated on his employer's client, under what is known as the "misappropriation" theory of insider trading. If Chiarella's misappropriation of information were deemed to be a fraud on his employer's client, there would be a stronger case that there was some securities-related harm at issue. Should the government have to demonstrate the potential for such harm in order to satisfy the "in connection with" requirement? Or is it just enough to show that the misappropriated information was used to purchase securities? The *Chiarella* Court declined to pass on the government's "misappropriation" theory because it had not been charged to the jury. (That theory is considered in *United States v. O'Hagan, infra*.) Is this "misappropriation" theory the basis for Chief Justice Burger's dissenting opinion?

4. On July 30, 2002, President Bush signed into law a reform act, the Sarbanes-Oxley Act of 2002, P.L. 107-204, 116 Stat. 745 (2002), passed in response to the corporate accounting scandals. Section 1106 of the Sarbanes-Oxley Act increases the penalties provided by 15 U.S.C. § 78ff(a), which sets forth the maximum criminal penalties for many securities violations, including false or misleading statements. The maximum fine and prison term for individuals is raised from $1 million and up to 10 years' imprisonment to $5 million and up to 20 years' imprisonment. For entities, the maximum fine is raised from $2.5 million to $25 million. One should recall, however, that the alternative minimum fine provision remains applicable and may provide for even higher fines in some cases. *See* 18 U.S.C. § 3571(d).

C. MISAPPROPRIATION THEORY

UNITED STATES v. O'HAGAN
521 U.S. 642 (1997)

JUSTICE GINSBURG delivered the opinion of the Court.

This case concerns the interpretation and enforcement of § 10(b) ... of the Securities Exchange Act of 1934, and [the] rule[] made by the Securities and Exchange Commission pursuant to th[at] provision[], Rule 10b-5 ... . [The question presented] ... relates to the misappropriation of material, nonpublic information for securities trading ... . In particular, we address and resolve th[is] issue[]: ... Is a person who trades in securities for personal profit, using confidential information misappropriated in breach of a fiduciary duty to the source of the information, guilty of violating § 10(b) and Rule 10b-5?[18] ... Our answer to th[is] ... question is yes. ...

Respondent James Herman O'Hagan was a partner in the law firm of Dorsey & Whitney in Minneapolis, Minnesota. In July 1988, Grand Metropolitan PLC (Grand Met), a company based in London, England, retained Dorsey & Whitney as local counsel to represent Grand Met regarding a potential tender offer for the common stock of the Pillsbury Company, headquartered in Minneapolis. Both Grand Met and Dorsey & Whitney took precautions to protect the confidentiality of Grand Met's tender offer plans. O'Hagan did no work on the Grand Met representation. Dorsey & Whitney withdrew from representing Grand Met on September 9, 1988. Less than a month later, on October 4, 1988, Grand Met publicly announced its tender offer for Pillsbury stock.

On August 18, 1988, while Dorsey & Whitney was still representing Grand Met, O'Hagan began purchasing call options for Pillsbury stock. Each option gave him the right to purchase 100 shares of Pillsbury stock by a specified date in September 1988. Later in August

---

[18] [Ed.:] The above excerpted opinion omits reference to a second issue addressed by the *O'Hagan* Court: whether the SEC, in adopting Rule 14e-3(a), 17 C.F.R. § 240.14e-3(a), exceeded the Commission's rulemaking authority under § 14(e) of the 1934 Act, 15 U.S.C. § 78n(e). Section 14(e) prohibits "fraudulent ... acts ... in connection with any tender offer" and authorizes the SEC to "define, and prescribe means reasonably designed to prevent, such acts." Under that mandate, the SEC adopted Rule 14e-3(a), which provides that if a tender offer has been launched, or substantial steps have been taken to commence such an offer, "it shall be deemed a fraudulent ... practice" for any person in possession of material information relating to such offer that he knows or has reason to know is non-public and has been acquired from an insider of the offeror or issuer, to buy or sell the stock sought in the tender offer unless within a reasonable time before any purchase or sale such information and its source are publicly disclosed. The controversy regarding Rule 14e-3 was its imposition of a duty to disclose or abstain from trading on persons who owe no fiduciary duty to respect the confidentiality of the information. The court of appeals below had invalidated Rule 14e-3(a), *inter alia*, on the theory that § 14(e) empowers the SEC to identify and regulate "fraudulent" acts but not to create its own definition of "fraud," that the § 10(b) precedents control the construction of § 14(e), and that the SEC's rule, which would have proscribed trading in absence of a disclosure duty arising out of a fiduciary relationship, therefore exceeded § 14(e)'s rulemaking authority. The *O'Hagan* Court reversed. It stated that it need not resolve whether the SEC's § 14(e)'s "fraud-defining" authority is broader than its like authority under § 10(b), holding instead that "Rule 14e-3(a), as applied to cases of this genre, qualifies under § 14(e) as a 'means reasonably designed to prevent' fraudulent trading on material, non-public information in the tender offer context." The Court therefore ruled that "under § 14(e), the Commission may prohibits acts, not themselves fraudulent under the common law or § 10(b), if the prohibition is 'reasonably designed to prevent ... acts and practices [that] are fraudulent.'" The Court deferred to the Commission's determination that this requirement was so designed, finding that its determination was not "arbitrary, capricious, or manifestly contrary to the statute," within the meaning of *Chevron U.S.A. Inc. v. Nat'l Resources Defense Council, Inc.*, 467 U.S. 837, 844 (1984).

and in September, O'Hagan made additional purchases of Pillsbury call options. By the end of September, he owned 2,500 unexpired Pillsbury options, apparently more than any other individual investor. O'Hagan also purchased, in September 1988, some 5,000 shares of Pillsbury common stock, at a price just under $39 per share. When Grand Met announced its tender offer in October, the price of Pillsbury stock rose to nearly $60 per share. O'Hagan then sold his Pillsbury call options and common stock, making a profit of more than $4.3 million.

The Securities and Exchange Commission (SEC or Commission) initiated an investigation into O'Hagan's transactions, culminating in a 57-count indictment. The indictment alleged that O'Hagan defrauded his law firm and its client, Grand Met, by using for his own trading purposes material, nonpublic information regarding Grand Met's planned tender offer.[19] According to the indictment, O'Hagan used the profits he gained through this trading to conceal his previous embezzlement and conversion of unrelated client trust funds. O'Hagan was charged with 20 counts of mail fraud, in violation of 18 U.S.C. § 1341; 17 counts of securities fraud, in violation of § 10(b) of the Securities Exchange Act of 1934 (Exchange Act), and SEC Rule 10b-5; 17 counts of fraudulent trading in connection with a tender offer, in violation of § 14(e) of the Exchange Act, and SEC Rule 14e-3(a); and 3 counts of violating federal money laundering statutes, 18 U.S.C. §§ 1956(a)(1)(B)(i), 1957. A jury convicted O'Hagan on all 57 counts, and he was sentenced to a 41-month term of imprisonment.

A divided panel of the Court of Appeals for the Eighth Circuit reversed all of O'Hagan's convictions. Liability under § 10(b) and Rule 10b-5, the Eighth Circuit held, may not be grounded on the "misappropriation theory" of securities fraud on which the prosecution relied. ... The Eighth Circuit further concluded that O'Hagan's mail fraud and money laundering convictions rested on violations of the securities laws, and therefore could not stand once the securities fraud convictions were reversed. ...

Decisions of the Courts of Appeals are in conflict on the propriety of the misappropriation theory under § 10(b) and Rule 10b-5 ... . We granted certiorari and now reverse the Eighth Circuit's judgment. ...

Under the "traditional" or "classical theory" of insider trading liability, § 10(b) and Rule 10b-5 are violated when a corporate insider trades in the securities of his corporation on the basis of material, nonpublic information. Trading on such information qualifies as a "deceptive device" under § 10(b), we have affirmed, because "a relationship of trust and confidence [exists] between the shareholders of a corporation and those insiders who have obtained confidential information by reason of their position with that corporation." *Chiarella v. United States*, 445 U.S. 222, 228 (1980). That relationship, we recognized, "gives rise to a duty to disclose [or to abstain from trading] because of the 'necessity of preventing a corporate insider from ... tak[ing] unfair advantage of ... uninformed ... stockholders.'" The classical theory applies not only to officers, directors, and other permanent insiders of a corporation, but also to attorneys, accountants, consultants, and others who temporarily become fiduciaries of a corporation. See *Dirks v. SEC*, 463 U.S. 646, 655, n. 14 (1983).

The "misappropriation theory" holds that a person commits fraud "in connection with" a securities transaction, and thereby violates § 10(b) and Rule 10b-5, when he misappropriates confidential information for securities trading purposes, in breach of a duty owed to the source of the information. Under this theory, a fiduciary's undisclosed, self-serving use of a principal's

---

[19] [Court's footnote 1:] As evidence that O'Hagan traded on the basis of nonpublic information misappropriated from his law firm, the Government relied on a conversation between O'Hagan and the Dorsey & Whitney partner heading the firm's Grand Met representation. That conversation allegedly took place shortly before August 26, 1988. O'Hagan urges that the Government's evidence does not show he traded on the basis of nonpublic information. O'Hagan points to news reports on August 18 and 22, 1988, that Grand Met was interested in acquiring Pillsbury, and to an earlier, August 12, 1988, news report that Grand Met had put up its hotel chain for auction to raise funds for an acquisition. O'Hagan's challenge to the sufficiency of the evidence remains open for consideration on remand.

information to purchase or sell securities, in breach of a duty of loyalty and confidentiality, defrauds the principal of the exclusive use of that information. In lieu of premising liability on a fiduciary relationship between company insider and purchaser or seller of the company's stock, the misappropriation theory premises liability on a fiduciary-turned-trader's deception of those who entrusted him with access to confidential information.

The two theories are complementary, each addressing efforts to capitalize on nonpublic information through the purchase or sale of securities. The classical theory targets a corporate insider's breach of duty to shareholders with whom the insider transacts; the misappropriation theory outlaws trading on the basis of nonpublic information by a corporate "outsider" in breach of a duty owed not to a trading party, but to the source of the information. The misappropriation theory is thus designed to "protec[t] the integrity of the securities markets against abuses by 'outsiders' to a corporation who have access to confidential information that will affect th[e] corporation's security price when revealed, but who owe no fiduciary or other duty to that corporation's shareholders."

In this case, the indictment alleged that O'Hagan, in breach of a duty of trust and confidence he owed to his law firm, Dorsey & Whitney, and to its client, Grand Met, traded on the basis of nonpublic information regarding Grand Met's planned tender offer for Pillsbury common stock. This conduct, the Government charged, constituted a fraudulent device in connection with the purchase and sale of securities.[20]

We agree with the Government that misappropriation, as just defined, satisfies § 10(b)'s requirement that chargeable conduct involve a "deceptive device or contrivance" used "in connection with" the purchase or sale of securities. We observe, first, that misappropriators, as the Government describes them, deal in deception. A fiduciary who "[pretends] loyalty to the principal while secretly converting the principal's information for personal gain," "dupes" or defrauds the principal.

We addressed fraud of the same species in *Carpenter v. United States*, 484 U.S. 19 (1987), which involved the mail fraud statute's proscription of "any scheme or artifice to defraud," 18 U.S.C. § 1341. Affirming convictions under that statute, we said in *Carpenter* that an employee's undertaking not to reveal his employer's confidential information "became a sham" when the employee provided the information to his co-conspirators in a scheme to obtain trading profits. A company's confidential information, we recognized in *Carpenter*, qualifies as property to which the company has a right of exclusive use. The undisclosed misappropriation of such information, in violation of a fiduciary duty, the Court said in *Carpenter*, constitutes fraud akin to embezzlement—"'the fraudulent appropriation to one's own use of the money or goods entrusted to one's care by another.'" *Carpenter*'s discussion of the fraudulent misuse of confidential information, the Government notes, "is a particularly apt source of guidance here, because [the mail fraud statute] (like Section 10(b)) has long been held to require deception, not merely the breach of a fiduciary duty."

Deception through nondisclosure is central to the theory of liability for which the Government seeks recognition. As counsel for the Government stated in explanation of the theory at oral argument: "To satisfy the common law rule that a trustee may not use the property that [has] been entrusted [to] him, there would have to be consent. To satisfy the requirement of the Securities Act that there be no deception, there would only have to be disclosure." [S]ee generally Restatement (Second) of Agency §§ 390, 395 (1958) (agent's disclosure obligation regarding use of confidential information).[21]

---

[20] [Court's footnote 5:] The Government could not have prosecuted O'Hagan under the classical theory, for O'Hagan was not an "insider" of Pillsbury, the corporation in whose stock he traded. Although an "outsider" with respect to Pillsbury, O'Hagan had an intimate association with, and was found to have traded on confidential information from, Dorsey & Whitney, counsel to tender offeror Grand Met. Under the misappropriation theory, O'Hagan's securities trading does not escape Exchange Act sanction, as it would under the dissent's reasoning, simply because he was associated with, and gained nonpublic information from, the bidder, rather than the target.

[21] [Court's footnote 6:] Under the misappropriation theory urged in this case, the disclosure obligation

... [F]ull disclosure forecloses liability under the misappropriation theory: Because the deception essential to the misappropriation theory involves feigning fidelity to the source of information, if the fiduciary discloses to the source that he plans to trade on the nonpublic information, there is no "deceptive device" and thus no § 10(b) violation—although the fiduciary-turned-trader may remain liable under state law for breach of a duty of loyalty.[22]

We turn next to the § 10(b) requirement that the misappropriator's deceptive use of information be "in connection with the purchase or sale of [a] security." This element is satisfied because the fiduciary's fraud is consummated, not when the fiduciary gains the confidential information, but when, without disclosure to his principal, he uses the information to purchase or sell securities. The securities transaction and the breach of duty thus coincide. This is so even though the person or entity defrauded is not the other party to the trade, but is, instead, the source of the nonpublic information. A misappropriator who trades on the basis of material, nonpublic information, in short, gains his advantageous market position through deception; he deceives the source of the information and simultaneously harms members of the investing public.

The misappropriation theory targets information of a sort that misappropriators ordinarily capitalize upon to gain no-risk profits through the purchase or sale of securities. Should a misappropriator put such information to other use, the statute's prohibition would not be implicated. The theory does not catch all conceivable forms of fraud involving confidential information; rather, it catches fraudulent means of capitalizing on such information through securities transactions.

The Government notes another limitation on the forms of fraud § 10(b) reaches: "The misappropriation theory would not ... apply to a case in which a person defrauded a bank into giving him a loan or embezzled cash from another, and then used the proceeds of the misdeed to purchase securities." In such a case, the Government states, "the proceeds would have value to the malefactor apart from their use in a securities transaction, and the fraud would be complete as soon as the money was obtained." In other words, money can buy, if not anything, then at least many things; its misappropriation may thus be viewed as sufficiently detached from a subsequent securities transaction that § 10(b)'s "in connection with" requirement would not be met.

The dissent's charge that the misappropriation theory is incoherent because information, like funds, can be put to multiple uses, misses the point. The Exchange Act was enacted in part "to insure the maintenance of fair and honest markets," 15 U.S.C. § 78b, and there is no question that fraudulent uses of confidential information fall within § 10(b)'s prohibition if the fraud is "in connection with" a securities transaction. It is hardly remarkable that a rule suitably applied to the fraudulent uses of certain kinds of information would be stretched beyond reason were it applied to the fraudulent use of money.

The dissent does catch the Government in overstatement. Observing that money can be used for all manner of purposes and purchases, the Government urges that confidential information of the kind at issue derives its value *only* from its utility in securities trading. Substitute "ordinarily" for "only," and the Government is on the mark.[23] ...

---

runs to the source of the information, here, Dorsey & Whitney and Grand Met. Chief Justice Burger, dissenting in *Chiarella*, advanced a broader reading of § 10(b) and Rule 10b-5; the disclosure obligation, as he envisioned it, ran to those with whom the misappropriator trades. 445 U.S., at 240 ("a person who has misappropriated nonpublic information has an absolute duty to disclose that information or to refrain from trading"). The Government does not propose that we adopt a misappropriation theory of that breadth.

[22] [Court's footnote 7:] Where, however, a person trading on the basis of material, nonpublic information owes a duty of loyalty and confidentiality to two entities or persons—for example, a law firm and its client—but makes disclosure to only one, the trader may still be liable under the misappropriation theory.

[23] [Court's footnote 8:] The dissent's evident struggle to invent other uses to which O'Hagan plausibly might have put the nonpublic information is telling. It is imaginative to suggest that a trade journal would

The misappropriation theory comports with § 10(b)'s language, which requires deception "in connection with the purchase or sale of any security," not deception of an identifiable purchaser or seller. The theory is also well-tuned to an animating purpose of the Exchange Act: to insure honest securities markets and thereby promote investor confidence. See 45 Fed.Reg. 60412 (1980) (trading on misappropriated information "undermines the integrity of, and investor confidence in, the securities markets"). Although informational disparity is inevitable in the securities markets, investors likely would hesitate to venture their capital in a market where trading based on misappropriated nonpublic information is unchecked by law. An investor's informational disadvantage vis-a-vis a misappropriator with material, nonpublic information stems from contrivance, not luck; it is a disadvantage that cannot be overcome with research or skill.

In sum, considering the inhibiting impact on market participation of trading on misappropriated information, and the congressional purposes underlying § 10(b), it makes scant sense to hold a lawyer like O'Hagan a § 10(b) violator if he works for a law firm representing the target of a tender offer, but not if he works for a law firm representing the bidder. The text of the statute requires no such result.[24] The misappropriation at issue here was properly made the subject of a § 10(b) charge because it meets the statutory requirement that there be "deceptive" conduct "in connection with" securities transactions. ...

... [T]he misappropriation theory, as we have examined and explained it in this opinion, is both consistent with the statute and with our precedent. Vital to our decision that criminal liability may be sustained under the misappropriation theory, we emphasize, are two sturdy safeguards Congress has provided regarding scienter. To establish a criminal violation of Rule 10b-5, the Government must prove that a person "willfully" violated the provision. See 15 U.S.C. § 78ff(a).[25] Furthermore, a defendant may not be imprisoned for violating Rule 10b-5 if he proves that he had no knowledge of the rule. See *ibid.* O'Hagan's charge that the misappropriation theory is too indefinite to permit the imposition of criminal liability thus fails not only because the theory is limited to those who breach a recognized duty. In addition, the statute's "requirement of the presence of culpable intent as a necessary element of the offense

---

have paid O'Hagan dollars in the millions to publish his information. Counsel for O'Hagan hypothesized, as a nontrading use, that O'Hagan could have "misappropriat[ed] this information of [his] law firm and its client, deliver[ed] it to [Pillsbury], and suggest[ed] that [Pillsbury] in the future ... might find it very desirable to use [O'Hagan] for legal work." But Pillsbury might well have had large doubts about engaging for its legal work a lawyer who so stunningly displayed his readiness to betray a client's confidence. Nor is the Commission's theory "incoherent" or "inconsistent," for failing to inhibit use of confidential information for "personal amusement ... in a fantasy stock trading game."

[24] [Court's footnote 9:] As noted earlier, however, the textual requirement of deception precludes § 10(b) liability when a person trading on the basis of nonpublic information has disclosed his trading plans to, or obtained authorization from, the principal—even though such conduct may affect the securities markets in the same manner as the conduct reached by the misappropriation theory. Contrary to the dissent's suggestion, the fact that § 10(b) is only a partial antidote to the problems it was designed to alleviate does not call into question its prohibition of conduct that falls within its textual proscription. Moreover, once a disloyal agent discloses his imminent breach of duty, his principal may seek appropriate equitable relief under state law. Furthermore, in the context of a tender offer, the principal who authorizes an agent's trading on confidential information may, in the Commission's view, incur liability for an Exchange Act violation under Rule 14e-3(a).

[25] [Court's footnote 12:] In relevant part, § 32 of the Exchange Act, as set forth in 15 U.S.C. § 78ff(a), provides:

"Any person who willfully violates any provision of this chapter ... or any rule or regulation thereunder the violation of which is made unlawful or the observance of which is required under the terms of this chapter ... shall upon conviction be fined not more than $1,000,000, or imprisoned not more than 10 years, or both ... ; but no person shall be subject to imprisonment under this section for the violation of any rule or regulation if he proves that he had no knowledge of such rule or regulation."

does much to destroy any force in the argument that application of the [statute]" in circumstances such as O'Hagan's is unjust. ...

Based on its dispositions of the securities fraud convictions, the Court of Appeals also reversed O'Hagan's convictions, under 18 U.S.C. § 1341, for mail fraud. Reversal of the securities convictions, the Court of Appeals recognized, "d[id] not as a matter of law require that the mail fraud convictions likewise be reversed." But in this case, the Court of Appeals said, the indictment was so structured that the mail fraud charges could not be disassociated from the securities fraud charges, and absent any securities fraud, "there was no fraud upon which to base the mail fraud charges."

The United States urges that the Court of Appeals' position is irreconcilable with *Carpenter*. Just as in *Carpenter*, so here, the "mail fraud charges are independent of [the] securities fraud charges, even [though] both rest on the same set of facts." We need not linger over this matter, for our rulings on the securities fraud issues require that we reverse the Court of Appeals judgment on the mail fraud counts as well.[26] ...

JUSTICE THOMAS, with whom THE CHIEF JUSTICE joins, concurring in the judgment in part and dissenting in part.

Today the majority upholds respondent's convictions for violating § 10(b) of the Securities Exchange Act of 1934, and Rule 10b-5 promulgated thereunder, based upon the Securities and Exchange Commission's "misappropriation theory." Central to the majority's holding is the need to interpret § 10(b)'s requirement that a deceptive device be "use[d] or employ[ed], in connection with the purchase or sale of any security." Because the Commission's misappropriation theory fails to provide a coherent and consistent interpretation of this essential requirement for liability under § 10(b), I dissent. ...

I do not take issue with the majority's determination that the undisclosed misappropriation of confidential information by a fiduciary can constitute a "deceptive device" within the meaning of § 10(b). Nondisclosure where there is a pre-existing duty to disclose satisfies our definitions of fraud and deceit for purposes of the securities laws. See *Chiarella v. United States*, 445 U.S. 222, 230 (1980).

Unlike the majority, however, I cannot accept the Commission's interpretation of when a deceptive device is "use[d] ... in connection with" a securities transaction. Although the Commission and the majority at points seem to suggest that *any* relation to a securities transaction satisfies the "in connection with" requirement of § 10(b), both ultimately reject such an overly expansive construction and require a more integral connection between the fraud and the securities transaction. The majority states, for example, that the misappropriation theory applies to undisclosed misappropriation of confidential information "for securities trading purposes," thus seeming to require a particular intent by the misappropriator in order to satisfy the "in connection with" language. The Commission goes further, and argues that the misappropriation theory satisfies the "in connection with" requirement because it "depends on an *inherent* connection between the deceptive conduct and the purchase or sale of a security."

The Commission's construction of the relevant language in § 10(b), and the incoherence of that construction, become evident as the majority attempts to describe why the fraudulent theft of information falls under the Commission's misappropriation theory, but the fraudulent

---

[26] [Court's footnote 25:] The dissent finds O'Hagan's convictions on the mail fraud counts, but not on the securities fraud counts, sustainable. Under the dissent's view, securities traders like O'Hagan would escape SEC civil actions and federal prosecutions under legislation targeting securities fraud, only to be caught for their trading activities in the broad mail fraud net. If misappropriation theory cases could proceed only under the federal mail and wire fraud statutes, practical consequences for individual defendants might not be large; however, "proportionally more persons accused of insider trading [might] be pursued by a U.S. Attorney, and proportionally fewer by the SEC." Our decision, of course, does not rest on such enforcement policy considerations.

performance obligations." But the more obvious forms of financial statement fraud also are the ones where accounting literature is relatively unambiguous. A "parking" transaction, for example, where the "sale" transfers mere temporary ownership or control to the buyer, ordinarily would not meet the tests of SFAS No. 48, "Sales with a Right of Return." Similarly, a large sale to a "shell" entity with no resources to make good on its obligation to the seller other than through resale of the goods ordinarily would run afoul of the "significant uncertainties" regarding "ability to pay" restraints of GAAP. *See, e.g., Accounting Principles Board Opinion (APBO) No. 10, "Omnibus Opinion", footnote 8 (1966).*

Example:
Seven officers of KnowledgeWare, Inc., a computer software company, were accused of improper revenue recognition techniques to meet sales quotas. The alleged fraud was implemented by placing or "parking" inventory with customers and resellers who were informed either orally or through "side letters" that they did not need to pay for the goods when they were delivered. *SEC v. Tarkenton, Accounting and Auditing Enforcement Release No. 1179*. Defendant settled.

b. <u>Round Trippers</u>: A "round tripper" takes place where Company A and Company B agree to buy each others' products or services (usually in approximately equal amounts) to boost the revenues—and sometimes reported profits—of each. These transactions are particularly attractive where the "outgoing" transaction (the purchase) can be treated as a capital cost. The cash makes a "round trip", leaving both companies out-of-pocket for little or nothing but transaction costs. The purchase ends up on the balance sheet as infrastructure or other types of deferred costs that are amortized or depreciated over relatively long periods. Note however, that there is no authoritative GAAP that prohibits revenue recognition for these sorts of transactions, per se. The real issues most often are either a lack of business purpose, or a disclosure deficiency.

Example:
A senior vice president of AOL/Time Warner (AOLTW) purportedly assisted in alleged sham transactions with Homestore. The transactions allegedly entailed recording advertising revenue by using "three-legged round trip" deals. Homestore would buy products from a third-party that they purportedly did not need. That same third party would then purchase advertising from AOLTW using the money that Homestore paid them for products in the first part of the roundtrip. To complete the roundtrip transaction, AOLTW would purchase advertising from Homestore in the same amount that Homestore had paid the third-party. *In re AOL Time Warner Securities Litigation, 2004 U.S. Dist. Lexis 7917, (S.D.N.Y. 2004)*. Motion to dismiss amended complaint deferred.

c. <u>Barter Transactions</u>: Barter, or "non-monetary" transactions are a special version of round trippers where the transaction involves little or no exchange of cash. Once largely confined to the advertising business (where they long have been common) the '90s saw them spread to a host of other businesses and proliferate in the new area of internet advertising. A few public companies were actually in the barter business as a principle source of revenue.

Example:
Itex Corp. allegedly overstated its financial condition by entering into sham barter transactions where unregistered Itex stock was issued to related entities at substantial discounts or in exchange for other assets. "The barter deals involved difficult-to-value assets, such as artwork, pre-paid advertising due bills and worthless stocks in public companies. Some Itex deals involved purely bogus assets such as leases on vacant property, a non-existent stamp collection, and highly-questionable unpatented and undeveloped mineral claims." *SEC v. Itex Corp. et al., Accounting and Auditing Enforcement Releases No. 1175*. Defendants subsequently settled.

The SEC staff has taken a highly skeptical view of barter transactions for some time, often challenging whether the exchange is the "culmination of an earning process." *Accounting Principles Board Opinion No. 29, "Non-monetary Transactions", ¶21 (FASB 1973).*

d. Channel Stuffing: This usually occurs where a manufacturer that sells through distributors "makes forecast" by unusually large sales to those distributors. These transactions often take place at or near quarter end and result in the distributors carrying an unusually large inventory of the manufacturer's goods. The distribution channel is thus "stuffed" in the same sense as the aggressive eater at Thanksgiving. The process may be aided by one time offers of special pricing or other incentives to the customers.

Assuming that the stuffing is not subject to other revenue recognition issues (e.g., special "right of return" privileges), GAAP generally does not prohibit recording the sales. There can be, however, disclosure issues that arise, either because of the unusual nature of the arrangements that produced the incremental sales or because those sales "steal" revenues from the next quarter in a relatively predictable fashion. *See, e.g., Regulation S-K, Item 303(a) regarding "unusual trends, events or uncertainties" in the annual Management's Discussion and Analysis.*

Example:
A Vice President of Sunbeam Corp. was charged with improper boosting of revenues in 1997 through channel stuffing. The SEC alleged Sunbeam overloaded "the channels of distribution by offering discounts and other inducements in order to sell product now", but did not disclose that practice. Sunbeam allegedly experienced further difficulties in meeting revenue goals in 1998, due to the prior year over-demand scheme. *SEC v. Dunlap, 2002 U.S. Dist. LEXIS 10769 (S.D. Fla. 2002).* Motion to dismiss SEC complaint denied. *See also Accounting and Auditing Enforcement Release No. 1623.*

e. Keeping the Books Open: A rather blatant form of revenue based fraudulent financial reporting is the simple technique of keeping the books open at quarter end long enough to report results in line with forecasts. This is almost always done with legitimate sales; they are simply recorded in an earlier quarter than otherwise would be the case. However, unless business picks up dramatically so that the shortfall disappears in the following quarter, management can end up digging an ever deeper hole for itself. The thirty-two day month becomes the thirty-three day month and so on. This often requires somewhat sophisticated document forgeries at year-end to conceal the matter from the auditors.

Example:
Minuteman International Inc. allegedly recognized quarterly revenue by leaving its sales registers open for several days after quarter end, improperly recording sales. Minuteman's "keeping its books open" also purportedly entailed backdating of invoices, shipment documents, and daily sales registers. *In the matter of Minuteman International Inc. et al., Accounting and Auditing Enforcement Release No. 1786 (2003).* Defendants settled.

2. Cost Deferrals

When increasing the revenue is not practicable, deferring costs may be the next best choice. While there are numerous legitimate (and often required) ways in which costs are deferred, the number of areas where there are *choices* about whether to defer has become smaller. *See, e.g., SOP 98-5 "Reporting on the Costs of Start-Up Activities" (April 1998).* With fewer options available, the more traditional repositories for deferred costs have seen increased attention in attempts to falsify financial statements.

a. Inventory: In a manufacturing or distribution company, inventory often is the largest number on the balance sheet. That attribute can make it a tempting target for financial reporting fraud. The *really* old fashioned way to falsify financial statements using inventory is to simply invent some inventory. Using the formula: Beginning Inventory + Purchases - Ending Inventory = Cost of Sales, every dollar of invented year-end inventory becomes a dollar of pretax profit. But that particular approach has become relatively rare in recent years, except for falsifications involving relatively small companies. Modern accounting systems almost always include a perpetual inventory feature. A big gap between what the accounting system reflects and an inflated physical "count" is too likely to grab the attention of the auditors. The technique is still sometimes used to falsify interim financial statements, however.

Example:

Chipwich, a distributor of frozen snacks, allegedly overstated inventories by recording large volume fruits and vegetables at outside warehouses where the external auditors were unlikely to perform physical inventories. Personnel at the warehouse familiar with Chipwich employees were then contacted and requested to send confirmation of inventory amounts to the external auditors. *Accounting and Auditing Enforcement Release No. 909*. Defendant settled.

But a variety of other techniques can and have been used to inflate reported inventory, usually by capitalizing what otherwise would be cost of sales or selling, general and administrative (SG&A) expenses. These techniques include:

• Various versions of "full absorption" costing where everything short of the CEO's salary becomes "eligible" for treatment as "manufacturing overhead."
• Creation of "inventory in transit" from suppliers, sometimes by falsifying receiving or payables records.
• Falsifying production or other records that are inputs to a manufacturing costing system.
• Inflating prices of purchased goods in the system used to price inventory.
• Mischaracterizing payments to suppliers or others (e.g., for cooperative advertising) as deposits or "prepaid inventory."
• Altering unit sales records to make "dogs" look like hot sellers, and avoid writing down obsolete inventory.

The possibilities are not limitless, of course, but they mostly are limited by the imaginations of the corporate officials who devise these techniques.

b. <u>Property, Plant and Equipment (PP&E)</u>: Costs of PP&E, including costs incurred to prepare the asset for its intended use, are deferred and amortized over the asset's estimated life. Spreading those costs over periods of 3 to 30 years has a far less dramatic impact on the income statement than immediate expensing. Hence there is an incentive to "recharacterize" ordinary operating expenses as part of PP&E. This can be done in a number of ways, including:

• Treating repairs and maintenance activities as overhaul or replacement costs that extend the life of the assets.
• Characterizing unrelated costs as moving, installation or testing expenses.
• Calling small parts and equipment (that normally would be expensed) "fixed assets."
• Obtaining false appraisal or other information to justify assigning excessive costs to PP&E in connection with a business combination or barter transaction.

In the telecommunications world and similar businesses, a whole class of fixed assets sometimes lends itself well to use as a repository for what should be period costs. These "infrastructure" assets, even when entirely legitimate, often are a hodgepodge of "hard" asset costs (e.g., fiber optic cable), site preparation expenditures, rights of way, payments for installations and other subcontractor costs, licenses, connecting charges, legal fees, costs of launching satellites and amounts paid for access to or use if other companies' infrastructure. A few extra millions of dollars in deferred costs easily can go unnoticed.

Example:

If the allegations turn out to be true, Worldcom looks like the hands down favorite in the race for the world record in inappropriate deferral of operating expenses as PP&E. Several billion dollars of what should have been period expenses purportedly were treated as "capital assets". *See, e.g., SEC v. Scott D. Sullivan, Accounting and Enforcement Release No. 1966.* Defendant settled.

       c. Other Deferrals: Even companies not in contention for world record status have made use of various devices to put costs in the balance sheet rather than the income statement. Contract acquisition, pre-opening, organizational and other costs sometimes include what should be current expenses.

Example:

In an attempt to manufacture its own line of photocopiers, Savin Corporation allegedly violated GAAP by improperly deferring research and development costs as "deferred start-up cost." The engagement partner and manager, who performed the audits of Savin Corporation from 1981-84, were accused of allowing the improper accounting. *SEC v. David Checkosky & Norman Aldrich, Accounting and Auditing Enforcement Releases Nos. 412, 628 and 871; See also Checkosky & Aldrich v. SEC, 23 F.3d 452.* Defendants suspended from practice before the Commission for two years.

3. Cookie Jars

In an often quoted speech, then SEC Chairman Arthur Levitt referred to "Cookie Jar" reserves as one of the devices used for "earnings management". *Arthur Levitt, "A Financial Partnership", Remarks to the Financial Executives Institute, New York (Nov. 16, 1998).* But "earnings management" is an unfortunately ambiguous term, since in many respects, corporate executives should be managing earnings, or at least managing the company to produce earnings. It is when earnings management becomes earnings manipulation that the line is crossed and fraudulent financial statements result. The basic distinction is concealment of the manipulation.

Imagine an MD&A paragraph that said:

"We achieved our corporate goal this year of 20% earning growth. That growth primarily was the result of an overly conservative bad debt allowance recorded last year. When we corrected the estimate in this year's fourth quarter by reversing part of the reserve, we added $21.4 million to earnings (net of tax) accounting for $.15 of the $.23 in year-over-year earnings per share increase."

Now *that* would take the fun out of "earnings management"!

Of course, none of us likely have seen such a disclosure. The manipulator buries the truth and honest management has no need for cookie jars. And, some estimating accruals that turn out to be overdone simply reflect inherent imprecision or evolving circumstances that cause estimates to change (e.g., the plaintiff was willing to settle for one half of where the company reasonably thought the settlement negotiations would end up).

But the fact that a reasonable estimate was made in the first instance does not necessarily change disclosure obligations. Not disclosing material reversals may still be a financial reporting sin, and that sin can be compounded by reversing the accrual through an inappropriate income statement line item—generally any line other than the one that was charged when the original accrual was made. Further, "transferring" the reserve to "cover" another necessary contingency accrual may not obviate the need for disclosure, even where both are reflected in the same financial statement line items. *See SAB No. 100, "Restructuring and Impairment Charges."*

Cookie jar reserves can be created in a variety of ways using both routine and not-so-routine accrual (liability) and allowance (contra asset) accounts, including

- Bad debt allowances
- Accruals for sales returns and warranties
- Litigation accruals
- Inventory lower of cost or market (LOCOM) reserves
- Deferred revenue accounts
- General (unspecified) reserves

Example:

In connection with alleged inflation of InaCom's earnings by its CFO and corporate controller, a "cookie jar" reserve was created by improperly accruing general reserves during the first two quarters of 1999. During the third quarter, $7.1 million of these excess reserves allegedly were reversed into income to inflate earnings. *SEC v. Guenthner, 212 F.R.D. 531 (D. Ne. 2003)*. Motion to dismiss denied.

But the king and queen of the cookie jar kingdom historically have been reserves created in connection with business combinations and "restructurings." Sheer size accounts for much of this popularity, as does the (until recently) less than rigorous accounting rules governing which parts of the kitchen sink might be included. For those intent on anything from the mildest forms of earnings management to systematic falsification of financial statements, merger and restructuring reserves often have proven irresistible.

Example:

Sunbeam allegedly overstated restructuring reserves by expensing in 1996 what should have been expensed in 1997, blaming its 1996 net loss on the effects of restructuring charges. The restructuring charge was purportedly overstated because it included costs that were related to future periods and costs unrelated to restructuring. *In re Sunbeam Sec. Litig. No. 89, F. Supp.2d 1326 (S.D. Fla. 1999)*. Officers considered directly involved with day-to-day operations; motions to dismiss were denied.

On occasion, these reserves have offered a sort of triple whammy. As a hypothetical, suppose an inflated merger reserve was first created for all sorts of real and imagined costs that purportedly would result from integration and rationalization of an acquired business. The offsetting goodwill created was amortizable either over relatively long periods of time (if prior to implementation of *SFAS No. 142, "Goodwill and Other Intangible Assets"*) or not at all (if after such implementation). Second, all manner of "excess" costs were then charged to the merger reserve instead of against current earnings, in some cases without much regard to whether those costs were specifically identified when the reserve was created. Third, any "left over" reserve amounts were reversed in a subsequent period against some uncomfortably large income statement caption, with little or no disclosure of the impact. Some companies might even go for a quadruple. When the acquired business heads south, a "restructuring" is implemented, giving rise to impairment of the inflated goodwill which is then written off as part of a "restructuring charge."

Many of the perceived abuses associated with "restructuring" reserves were curtailed with the issuance of *SFAS No. 146, "Accounting for Costs Associated with Exit or Disposal Activities."* The FASB determined that obligations associated with these activities should be recognized when the liability is incurred, not the earlier date of an entity's commitment to an exit plan. There is as yet no comparable new accounting principles for merger reserves, although the SEC staff's *SAB No. 100, "Restructuring and Impairment Charges"* has had a similar curtailing effect.

4.   Related Party Transactions

Perhaps the most interesting aspect of related party transactions is the fact that (with rare exceptions) there are no special accounting rules that govern them, other than disclosure requirements. This leaves open the possibilities that such transactions were not "carried out on an arm's length basis" and that transactions among entities under common control "could result in operating results or financial position of the reporting enterprise significantly different from those that would have been obtained if the enterprises were autonomous ..." *SFAS No. 57, "Related Party Disclosures", ¶ 3-4 (FASB 1982)*. In short, negotiating with yourself can and sometimes does produce peculiar results.

Related party transactions sometimes are a means to an end, and that end sometimes is fraudulent financial statements. This can be the result where one or more of the following occur:

• There is no substance to the transaction. Its only "business purpose" is to create income or avoid a loss. For example, "selling" an uncollectible receivable to a related party may effectively park the problem "off books" until the auditors (or regulatory examiners) go away.

• Entity A provides goods or services to related Entity B at inflated prices (to boost revenues and earnings of Entity A) or at artificially low prices (to boost earnings of Entity B).

• Entity A makes a non-reciprocal transfer of assets to a joint venture (JV) controlled by related Entity B. The transfer is recorded as an "investment" even though the JV has no real business and the transfer really is a preferential dividend to the owners of Entity B.

• Almost any transaction occurs with a purportedly unrelated entity that is in fact controlled by the counterparty or its senior executives.

The focus on disclosure is, more often than not, the trap for fraudsters using related party transactions as a vehicle. In many cases the transactions probably would not have taken place in the face of a truthful and complete "description of the transactions ... and such other information deemed necessary to an understanding of the effects of the transactions on the financial statements." *Id.*, ¶ 2.b.

Example:

An SEC complaint alleged Medi-Hut violated GAAP by failing to disclose material related party transactions, namely drug sales totaling approximately $1 million (13% of total revenues) to a wholesale pharmaceutical company owned and operated by its vice president of sales. *Securities and Exchange Comm'n Litigation Release No. 18296 (August 19, 2003); see also Securities and Exchange Commission v. Medi-Hut Company, Inc., Joseph A. Sanpietro, Laurence M. Simon and Lawrence P. Marasco, Civil Action No. 03 Civ 3921 (Jose L. Linares) (D.N.J. filed August 19, 2003)*.

5. Topside Entries

This isn't really a "category" of fraudulent financial statements, but rather a means of accomplishing a variety of financial reporting misstatements. "Topside" refers to entries made at the last stages of converting books and records into financial statements. Sometimes the entries are not posted to the general ledger at all, but rather are integrated with (or hidden within) the often complex series of consolidating and other entries needed to convert the trial balances of several subsidiaries or operating units into consolidated financial statements. Such entries also are "topside" in the sense that neither the operating nor accounting people at business units need to be aware, much less a part of, the process that results in falsified financial results.

There is nothing inherently improper about topside entries. They often are necessary to get the financial statements right. But a number of significant financial reporting frauds have been accomplished using topside entries.

Example:

Findings of the Securities and Exchange Commission's investigation into accounting improprieties at Cendant Corporation include, among other things, the allegation that CUC's (the membership-based consumer services section of Cendant's businesses) management made top side adjustments to the company's actual results to insure the results met analyst expectations. "No journal entries were made, the company's general ledger was not altered and the changes were not carried down to the books of the company's divisions." *In the matter of Cendant Corporation, Accounting and Auditing Enforcement Release No. 1272 (2000).* Defendant settled.

B. Some Not-So-Old Fashioned Ways:

1. Hiding the Debt

While manipulation or falsification of revenues and/or earnings is the goal of most financial reporting fraud, sometimes the goal is simply to hide debt. Analysts often focus on debt levels (or "financial leverage" if you are inclined to be more obtuse) simply because creditors are a burden on both earnings (in the form of interest expense) and cash flows (because creditors like to get their principal back, as well).

"Off balance sheet financing" has become a popular buzzword for any arrangement that permits payment for assets or expenses over relatively extended periods without the ratio damaging effects of recording a liability for the entire obligation. The two most popular legitimate means of accomplishing this are operating leases and properly structured securitizations. The GAAP required disclosures in both of those cases ordinarily assure that the related obligations are not concealed, and financial reporting fraud is only rarely associated with these financing mechanisms.

That said, it is worth noting that the financial Accounting Standards Board (FASB) arguably has done the business and financial communities a disservice with respect to accounting for securitizations. *SFAS No. 140, "Accounting for Transfers and Servicing of Financial Assets and Extinguishments of Liabilities"* (and its predecessor, *SFAS No. 125*) quite blatantly elevates form over substance by requiring "derecognition" of assets (most often, receivables) and "nonrecognition" of liabilities in such highly structured transactions. Never mind that these arrangements look, feel, smell, and taste like collateralized borrowings. The liability is "off balance sheet" so long as the transaction is structured so that the related assets have been "put presumptively beyond the reach of the transferor and its creditors, even in bankruptcy or other receivership", and certain other conditions are met. *SFAS No. 140, ¶ 9.* Some believe that puts at least a large dent in the notion that

> "[r]epresentational faithfulness of reported measurements lies in the closeness of their correspondence with the economic transactions, events or circumstances that they represent." *Statement of Financial Accounting Concepts (CON) No. 2, "Qualitative Characteristics of Accounting Information", ¶ 86.*

The connection to financial statement fraud is not all that tenuous. Special purpose entities (SPEs) like those used to structure securitizations also have been a favored vehicle for less than legitimate attempts to achieve "off balance sheet" treatment.

Example:

J.P Morgan Chase, Citigroup and Barclay's, allegedly helped to structure and finance one or more of Enron's off balance sheet partnerships or purported "special purpose entities", purportedly allowing Enron to hide billions of dollars of debt. *Conn. Res. Recovery Auth. v. Lay, 292 B.R. 484; 2003 U.S Dist. LEXIS 10511.*

Other means of concealing debt have (allegedly at least) included use of unconsolidated affiliates and debt disguised as equity investments.

Example:

The SEC alleged Adelphia fraudulently excluded bank debt from its financial statements by: (1) moving debt from its books and onto the books of an unconsolidated affiliate in violation of GAAP and (2) creating fictitious documents to give the appearance that Adelphia had repaid the debts. The SEC further claims Adelphia misrepresented that its Company's financial statements included all outstanding debt. *See Accounting and Audting Enforcement Release No. 1802 (SEC v. Adelphia Communications Corp. complaint filed in Southern District of New York).*

Disguising debt as equity not only gets the debt "off books", it also improves the debt/equity ratio, among other things.

Example:

The class action complaint filed against Parmalat Finanziaria S.p.A. alleges Parmalat understated its liabilities, in part, using one transaction where Citigroup provided Parmalat a $137 million cash infusion via a Delaware LLC dubbed Buconero, or the "black hole." The cash obtained was actually a loan and should have been included as a liability on Parmalat's financial statements, but was reported as equity. *Class Action Complaint for Violations of the Federal Securities Laws, Southern Alaska Carpenters Fund v. Bonlat Financing Corporation; see also Accounting and Enforcement Release No. 1936.*

2. Fabricated (Non-existent and Non-substantive) Transactions

Non-existent transactions probably are the most flagrant variety of revenue related financial reporting fraud. Desperate to "make the numbers", management simply resorts to creating transactions from whole cloth, sometimes with actual counterparties, sometimes with imaginary ones. This often leads quickly to a need for a second fraudulent transaction to conceal the first, since there is then an imaginary receivable or other asset sitting on the books. This is sometimes accomplished by having the receivable "paid" by diverting cash from an unrecorded debt or by "rolling" or refreshing the fraudulent receivable with newly minted imaginary transactions.

Example:

The Court entered judgment against former officers and directors of WIZ Technology, Inc. for using "accounting gimmicks, sham sales, and backdated agreements artificially to inflate WIZ's publicly reported sales." Sham sales included a fictitious distributorship and barter transactions involving obsolete products. *SEC v. Mar-Jeanne Tendler, Arthur Tendler, and Billie M. Jolson, D.C.C.D.Cal., SA CV 99-1200. See also Accounting and Auditing Enforcement Release No. 1168.*

Non-substantive transactions are a close cousin. There is a real transaction with a real customer, but the substance of the transaction is concealed through use of side letters or outright collusion with the customer. Some resemble round trippers, where concessions granted to the customer in apparently unrelated arrangements in a different accounting period effectively nullify the original arrangement. Consignment arrangements disguised as legitimate sales are another route to a similar result.

Example:

A former vice-president of Peregrine Systems, Inc. (a San-Diego based software company) allegedly recorded revenue for sales with resellers where side letters or other agreements evidenced an understanding with the resellers that they did not have to pay for the goods ("parked in their warehouses") until the goods were sold to an end-user. *SEC v. Steven S. Spitzer, Civil Action No. 03 CV 1178 filed in United States District Court for the Southern District of California; see also Accounting and Auditing Enforcement Release No. 1802.*

3. "Alternative" Performance Measures

If a healthy profit can't be shown by conventional performance measures (e.g., GAAP earnings), one approach to looking marvelous is to move the investors' attention to a different performance measure. "Pro forma earnings" was a label many companies used for their peculiar (and, not infrequently, self invented) performance measure.

This is not to say that all alternative performance measures or all "pro forma earnings" formulations are fraudulent. Many serve a legitimate purpose and, so long as disclosure is adequate to keep them from being misleading, usually are harmless. But fraudulent use of such alternative measures can be substantially easier than with GAAP basis financial statements or earnings releases.

First, there are no "rules" for this sort of information. The relatively rigorous framework of GAAP is missing; there are no widely accepted definitions of what "pro forma earnings" are, much less what should be included or excluded, or how those elements are to be measured.

Second, the "pro forma" part can be a means of excluding ill-defined categories of transactions and events on the premise that they are "one time" or "non cash" or "nonrecurring." The result occasionally is reminiscent of the good/bad old days (depending on your perspective) when "extraordinary items" were anything you wanted them to be. And, as then, the "nonrecurring" items almost always seem to be charges, rarely credits. Companies that view restructurings like birthdays (never let a year go by without one) nevertheless characterize the restructuring *costs* as "nonrecurring" in pro forma earnings formulations. This sort of loosey-goosey approach can invite creative characterizations of various sorts.

Example:
Ashford.com allegedly misstated its pro forma results to meet analysts' pro forma earnings estimates by classifying marketing expenses as "depreciation and amortization." *In the matter of Ashford.com, Inc. et al., Accounting and Auditing Release No. 1574*. Defendants settled.

Inside the financial statements, reporting of "segments" also can be used as an alternative performance measure. The only real constraint on what constitutes an operating segment is that it is supposed to be a business activity where the "operating results are regularly reviewed by the enterprise's chief operating decision maker to make decisions about resources to be allocated to the segment and assess its performance ...." *SFAS No. 131, "Disclosures about Segments of an Enterprise and Related Information", ¶ 18 (FASB 1997)*.

This is not a difficult state of affairs to create where there is a desire to isolate some aspect of the business whose prospects can be portrayed as bright. Internet related and "hot topic" products and services often are the "segment" chosen to be touted. While these efforts may well be legitimate, segment reporting provides sufficient flexibility (in allocating joint costs, for example) that some fraudulent financial reporting is almost inevitable.

Example:
The former Chief Accounting Officer of Enron allegedly concealed losses by "reorganizing" the company's business segment reporting in order to meet internal budget targets. *SEC v. Richard A. Causey, Civil Action No. H-04-0284; See Accounting and Auditing Enforcement Release No. 1947*.

II. Wherefore Art Thou, Internal Control

For more than 25 years it has been against the law (and potentially a criminal offense) for a public company to fail to "devise and maintain a system of internal accounting controls" that meets certain objectives, including providing reasonable assurance that its financial statements can be prepared in accordance with GAAP. *Securities Exchange Act of 1934 § 13(b)(2)(B)*. Since at least the time of the Treadway Commission report, internal control has been a continuing focus of attention as at least a significant part of the "solution" to fraudulent financial statements. The most recent legislative initiative came in the form of Sarbanes-Oxley Section 404, which requires the Public Company Accounting Oversight Board (PCAOB) to establish professional standards for auditors to attest to management's formal assessment of internal control effectiveness.

Here is the awful truth: *internal control has little to do with financial statement fraud.* The vast majority of financial statement frauds are not the result of some weakness in the corporate control structure, or its exploitation. Rather, these frauds mostly are perpetrated by senior management who circumvent or override the controls. The exceptions generally are cases restricted to a subsidiary or operating division. In some of these cases, the finger of blame legitimately can be pointed at the corporate control structure for failing to include mechanisms that should have at least raised a flag that something might be amiss.

In the real world, people and position usually are the major factors. Senior executives of a corporation have the authority and the means to simply ignore the control structure—and to direct others to do so as well. In particular, if the CEO and CFO are intent on falsifying the financial statements, they can do so, and often for extended periods of time.

While internal controls per se are of limited utility in preventing financial reporting fraud, the control environment—really part of the corporate culture—can and sometimes does play a role. That role seldom is one of preventing the fraud. Rather, it works on the positive side to help surface intentional misstatements (via a whistleblower, for example) and on the negative side to help prolong the problem (because those who know about it consider it "normal").

If the corporate culture is "make the numbers no matter what" most employees, at all levels of the organization, will behave accordingly. But even where the control environment/corporate culture is basically one of honest dealing, and a strong control structure is functioning effectively, senior management intent on falsification quickly learns to circumvent the system. Hence the popularity of "side letters", which ordinarily never get in the system to start with.

III. Beware the Ides of March (when most Forms 10-K are now due); Warning Sign Season is Here

Much has been written about the "warning signs" of financial statement fraud. There are in fact such things as "warning signs", and by and large they are not that hard to spot. But there is a huge caveat that goes with that observation. Almost all of the warning signs easily could be warning of far more innocuous matters than financial statement fraud.

Having provided that caveat, the following situations each are worthy of at least further inquiry for those intent on trying their hand as forensic accountants (notice we didn't say "analysts").

- Operating cash flows that appear to be out of kilter with reported profitability.
- Substantial lengthening of "days sales outstanding" (DSO).
- Steadily worsening inventory turnover.
- A history of significant fourth quarter "adjustments."
- A highly generalized MD&A narrative, particularly where the "analysis" is simplistic and reveals little about real operational issues.
- Significant transactions that appear to be unnecessarily complex.
- Problematic performance measures, particularly "pro forma" earnings that are not clearly explained.
- A business that by its nature should have at least modest volatility, but where management always seems to hit the "guidance" or street consensus numbers dead on.
- An industry where most of the players that are not bleeding profusely are at least in extreme pain—except this one, which is blessed with "superior management skills."
- Indecipherable financial statement notes.

• Any company where management seems intent on persuading the world that GAAP earnings don't count.

Identification of these warning signs is the beginning of the inquiry, not the end. Most of them also can be indicia of things like industry conditions, effects of marketing initiatives or (gasp!) even inept management. With all due respect to Mssrs. Freud and Clinton, keep in mind that sometimes a cigar is just a good smoke.

IV. The Audit Committee as "Mr. Clean" (Denial is not just a river in Egypt)

When the suspicion of financial reporting fraud first raises its ugly head, it usually falls to the Audit Committee to fashion an appropriate response. While a treatise on the roles and responsibilities of audit committees is well beyond the scope of this paper, we will venture a few basic pointers for an audit committee (and its counsel) to ponder.

Here are the basics:

• Ignoring the issue is a no-win proposition. If the SEC (or some other regulator) doesn't get wind of it, the auditors probably will. You need to get to the truth and deal with it. "Tis a knavish piece of work, but what of that?"

• Don't count on the auditors to do the investigative work. Most will not undertake it, and their objectivity may be subject to challenge under even the best of circumstances.

• Some "suspicions" can be handled by the GC and internal audit staff (e.g. disgruntled former employees who obviously don't have any real clue)

• More serious matters often are best handled by the audit committee's counsel and an outside forensic accounting team.

• A partially baked internal investigation may be worse than none at all. Serial investigations (or worse yet, serial restatements) virtually guarantee massive corporate credibility problems.

• Keep in mind that "cooperation" (with regulators and law enforcement) counts, but the price of that "cooperation" may be extraordinarily high.

• Don't fall into the trap of giving short shrift to disclosure issues.

• Maintain open lines of communication with the auditors and, where appropriate, the SEC. Keep in mind that "we don't know" is rarely an acceptable answer to the inevitable question: "Who done it?"

UNITED STATES v. EBBERS
458 F.3d 110 (2d Cir. 2006)

WINTER, CIRCUIT JUDGE.

Bernard J. Ebbers appeals from his conviction by a jury on nine counts of conspiracy, securities fraud, and related crimes and from the 25-year jail sentence imposed by Judge Jones.

Ebbers was the Chief Executive Officer ("CEO") of WorldCom, Inc., a publicly traded global telecommunications company. During the pertinent times-from the close of the fourth quarter of the 2000 fiscal year through the first quarter of the 2002 fiscal year-he engineered a scheme to disguise WorldCom's declining operating performance by falsifying its financial reports. Although the scheme was multi-faceted, the fraud primarily involved the treating of hundreds of millions of dollars of what had always been recorded operating costs as capital expenditures for several fiscal quarters. After a seven week trial, the jury convicted Ebbers on all counts. He was sentenced to 25 years' imprisonment, to be followed by 3 years' supervised release.

On appeal, Ebbers ... [contends, *inter alia*,] that the government should have been required to allege and prove violations of Generally Accepted Accounting Principles

("GAAP"). ... [He also] challenges his sentence as based on an inaccurate calculation of losses to investors, as significantly greater than those imposed on his co-conspirators, and as unreasonable in length. We affirm. ...

a) Beginnings

There is an element of tragedy here in that it was not a lack of legitimate entrepreneurial skills that caused Ebbers to resort to fraud. Before WorldCom, he was, among other things, a teacher, coach, and warehouse manager. He was a motel operator when, in 1983, he first invested in Long Distance Discount Services ("LDDS"), a small long distance company in Mississippi. When LDDS was in danger of failing in 1985, Ebbers agreed to become its CEO and led it to profitability by merging with other long distance providers. In 1989, LDDS went public by merging with Advantage Companies, another telecommunications company that was listed on NASDAQ. In 1995, LDDS changed its name to WorldCom, Inc. After WorldCom acquired MCI, Inc., in 1998, it was a global company with subsidiaries in Brazil, Mexico, and Canada. WorldCom then tried to acquire Sprint, but the Justice Department and the European Union stopped the merger on antitrust grounds. Having exhausted the market for acquisition targets in the long distance business, WorldCom began to acquire web hosting services. By 2000, WorldCom had about 90,000 employees in 65 countries, and reported revenues of $39 billion.

As part of its business, WorldCom built a global network of fiber-optic cables and telephone wires to transmit data and telephone calls. It also leased capacity on other companies' network facilities to transmit data and calls. The cost of the leasing was WorldCom's single largest expense-styled "line costs." When the "dot-com bubble" burst in early 2000, WorldCom's business slowed dramatically as some of its dot-com customers were unable to pay their bills and demand for WorldCom's internet services declined. Anticipating growth rather than declining demand, WorldCom had added 10,000 new employees, continued to invest heavily in new equipment, and had taken on long-term line leases with fixed monthly payments. By the end of the third quarter of 2000, as its revenue growth decreased and its expenses increased, the company could no longer meet investors' expectations of revenue and profit growth.

b) Ebbers' Personal Finances

By this time, Ebbers had powerful personal as well as occupational motives to see that investors' expectations were met and that WorldCom's stock price did not fall. Although Ebbers had become very wealthy since his earlier days, his consumption and investment habits outpaced his income. Ebbers had accumulated millions of shares of WorldCom stock but had borrowed over $400 million from banks, using his stock in WorldCom as collateral. As WorldCom's stock price began to drop in 2000, Ebbers received margin calls from the banks, requiring him either to put up more stock as collateral or to pay back a portion of the money he owed. Because he had used much of the borrowed money to buy relatively illiquid assets, such as a ranch, timber lands, and a yacht-building company, Ebbers could not use those assets to meet the margin calls. As WorldCom's stock price continued to fall, Ebbers pledged more of his WorldCom stock until every share he owned was collateral for the loans. By October 2000, Ebbers entered into a forward sale transaction, allowing Bank of America to sell some of his WorldCom stock at a future date in exchange for $70.5 million in cash to pay off his margin debts. WorldCom assumed the liability for the debts to the banks in October 2000, requiring Ebbers to make payments directly to WorldCom in the amount the company owed the banks; the debts to WorldCom and to the banks were still secured by Ebbers' WorldCom stock.

c) Third Quarter 2000

As a public company, WorldCom was required to file quarterly financial statements and annual reports with the SEC. When it became clear that the company would be unable to meet analysts' expectations in the third quarter of 2000, Ebbers and WorldCom's Chief Financial Officer ("CFO") Scott Sullivan reviewed the monthly revenue reports and discussed the company's options. Sullivan told Ebbers that WorldCom's financial performance had deteriorated and that they should issue an earnings warning to investors. Ebbers refused. Sullivan then told Ebbers that to meet expectations the company would have to make an improper adjustment to the revenue figure. Ebbers replied that "[W]e have to hit our numbers." Sullivan instructed others to increase the publicly reported revenues by adding $133 million in anticipated under-usage penalties to the revenue calculation, even though he believed that those penalties were not likely to be collected.

Soon after, Sullivan learned that line cost expenses would be almost $1 billion greater than expected. He reported that to Ebbers, who reiterated that the company had to hit its quarterly earnings estimates. Sullivan instructed Controller David Myers and his subordinates Buford Yates, Betty Vinson, and Troy Normand to reduce line cost expense accounts in the general ledger while also reducing reserves in the same amounts, which lowered the reported line costs by about $828 million. As a result, WorldCom's reported earnings were increased by the same amount.

Vinson and Normand believed the entries were wrong and considered resigning. When Sullivan told Ebbers that the accounting staff might quit, Ebbers told Sullivan that "we shouldn't be making adjustments; we've got to get the operations of this company going; we shouldn't be putting people in this position." Ebbers then spoke to Controller Myers, apologizing for the position that Myers and his staff were put in. In November 2000, WorldCom lowered its future earnings estimates and offered new guidance to analysts.

d) Fourth Quarter 2000

WorldCom's revenues and line costs did not improve in the fourth quarter of 2000. In January 2001, Ebbers and Sullivan agreed that WorldCom would not be able to meet even the analysts' revised expectations if it reported its actual results. Sullivan asked Ebbers if he would again reduce the earnings estimate given to analysts, but Ebbers refused to do so. Sullivan asked Myers to alter the reported revenue and expense numbers to meet expectations. The commissions paid to airlines as part of a marketing partnership were no longer removed from the reported revenues, increasing the revenue reported by about $42 million.

WorldCom's line cost expenses were $800 million above analysts' expectations. Sullivan directed Myers to bring the reported line costs in line with expectations. Myers and his staff then reduced the income tax reserve by $407 million, and altered other accounts until they were able to reduce the reported line costs by $797 million for the fourth quarter. Monthly reports sent to Ebbers, referred to at trial as the Monthly Budget Variation Reports ("MBVRs"), detailed the company's financial results and included the reduced line costs, giving the company an apparent gross margin of 78% in September 2000 and 74% in December 2000-margins that had never been achieved by WorldCom before. The 2000 annual report and Form 10-K also contained the false information.

e) First Quarter 2001

In early 2001, WorldCom's line costs were still hundreds of millions of dollars higher than the company had predicted, again making it impossible to meet analysts' expectations without further manipulation of the company's financial reports. The staff had been asked to find ways to reduce line costs, but the proposed cost savings were far smaller than needed to meet expectations. When the first quarter ended, reserves had been largely exhausted and could no longer be used to reduce line costs. Sullivan suggested capitalization of the line costs, that is, shifting a portion of the costs out of reported current expenses into capital expenses. Because line costs had always been treated as operating expenses, their unannounced treatment as capital expenses would disguise the decline in earnings. Myers and his staff agreed to capitalize about $771 million in line costs, although they believed it to be improper. At a dinner in Washington in March 2001, Sullivan and Ebbers discussed the line cost problem. Sullivan told Ebbers that the planned allocation of current expenses to capital expenses-in an amount over $500 million-"wasn't right." Ebbers did not deter him from the allocation.

Ebbers approved the capitalization of line costs in a later conversation with Sullivan. He told Sullivan that "[w]e have to grow our revenue and we have to cut our expenses, but we have to hit the numbers this quarter." Sullivan told Myers to change the general ledger to capitalize a portion of the line cost expenses in an amount totaling hundreds of millions of dollars. Ebbers later told Sullivan to change the format of the reports to remove the line cost figures. When Ebbers spoke to analysts and the public about WorldCom's first quarter performance in the earnings conference call, he did not mention the change in how the company was booking line costs. Instead, he said "there were no storms on the horizon," urging them to "go out and buy stock."

f) Second Quarter 2001

Capitalizing WorldCom's line cost expenses left another problem unaddressed: revenues were not growing at the 12% annual rate that Ebbers had predicted. Missing the revenue growth target was likely to lower WorldCom's stock price. Sullivan, Ebbers, and a handful of other executives created a new program called "Close the Gap" to "get [the] operating performance ... up to the market guidance expectations" by finding new items to include in revenue. Each month, and sometimes more often, the business operations group presented revenue data to Ebbers in detail as part of the "Close the Gap" program. Sullivan told Ebbers that there was no basis for including many of the opportunities presented in the "Close the Gap" program in reported revenues. In a voicemail to Ebbers, Sullivan described some of the items eventually included in reported revenues as "accounting fluff," "one-time stuff," and "junk." In July 2001, Ebbers sent a memorandum to Chief Operating Officer ("COO") Ron Beaumont, who was involved in the "Close the Gap" program, asking him "[w]here we stand on those one time events that had to happen in order for us to have a chance to make our numbers." Ebbers and Sullivan were aware that the company's true results fell far short of analysts' expectations, but ordered the improper revenue accounting so that those expectations would be met.

Once again, Sullivan told Ebbers that the company could reach the analysts' estimates only by capitalizing a portion of its line costs. Ebbers attended one of the line cost meetings around this time, and explained to the employees there that his "lifeblood was in the stock of the company" and that if the price fell below about $12 per share, he would be wiped out financially by margin calls. Although the line costs had improved slightly since the previous quarter, the accounting staff still had to capitalize over $610 million in line costs in order to meet earnings estimates.

g) Third Quarter 2001

In the third quarter of 2001, WorldCom's actual revenue growth rate, as reported internally to Ebbers, had fallen to about 5.5%. However, Ebbers announced that WorldCom had sustained its 12% revenue growth rate when the third quarter results were reported. The "Close the Gap" program added several new revenue items, largely one-time items not previously counted in revenue. Sullivan told Ebbers that the purpose of the adjustments to revenue was to reach the 12% growth target. WorldCom's press release announcing the quarterly results quoted Ebbers as saying the company had "delivered excellent growth this quarter." During the earnings conference call with analysts, Ebbers said "[w]e were able to achieve very solid growth." However, over $700 million in line costs had to be capitalized to create the appearance of meeting the earnings target for the quarter.

At the time, WorldCom was in merger negotiations with Verizon. Concerned that Verizon might discover the capitalization of line costs and the revenue adjustments in the course of a due diligence inquiry, Ebbers abruptly ended the merger negotiations.

At the board meeting in June 2001, board members began to ask about the "Close the Gap" program when COO Ron Beaumont presented several slides on it to them. One board member approached Sullivan privately to question the program. When Sullivan broached the subject with Ebbers, Ebbers told Beaumont and Sullivan that the next board presentation should be at a higher level and not include "Close the Gap" information. Beaumont's next board presentation, in September 2001, did not include any information about the "Close the Gap" program.

h) Fourth Quarter 2001

By the fourth quarter of 2001, even the "Close the Gap" program could not generate enough one-time revenue opportunities to create double-digit revenue growth. Nor could the staff find ways to adjust the line cost expenses sufficient to hit the earnings target. After Myers capitalized over $941 million in line costs, the accounting staff still had to adjust the SG & A (sales, general, and administrative) expenses in order to reach the target. On the fourth quarter earnings conference call, Ebbers assured investors that "[w]e stand by our accounting," and later said in a CNBC interview that "[w]e've been very conservative on our accounting."

i) First Quarter 2002

WorldCom's revenue declined in the first quarter of 2002. The accounting staff added new sources of revenue to improve the results but were unable to bring the revenue up to analysts' expectations. Sullivan informed Ebbers that even with the improper revenue adjustments and the capitalization of line costs, the company would be unable to meet investors' expectations that quarter. The accounting staff capitalized about $818 million in line costs, but WorldCom still had to announce that its results had fallen below investors' expectations.

j) Investigation, Trial, and Sentence

In March 2002, the Securities and Exchange Commission ("SEC") began to investigate WorldCom. At the end of April 2002, WorldCom's board asked Ebbers to resign, which he did on April 29th. Ebbers began to liquidate some of his assets in order to pay back his debts, but during May 2002 he also bought three million more shares of WorldCom stock. A month after Ebbers' departure, WorldCom's Internal Audit Department learned of the line cost capitalization, and alerted the new CEO. Sullivan was soon fired, and WorldCom disclosed the fraud to the public on June 25, 2002. WorldCom's stock collapsed, losing 90% of its value, and the company filed for bankruptcy.

On September 15, 2004, Ebbers was charged in a superseding indictment with one count of conspiracy to commit securities fraud and related crimes, one count of securities fraud, and seven counts of making false filings with the SEC. See 18 U.S.C. § 371 (conspiracy); 15 U.S.C. §§ 78j (b) & 78ff (securities fraud); 15 U.S.C. §§ 78m(a) & 78ff (false filings).

A jury convicted Ebbers on all counts on March 15, 2005. The pre-sentence report ("PSR") recommended a base offense level of six, plus sentencing enhancements of 26 levels for a loss over $100 million, of four levels for involving more than 50 victims, of two levels for receiving more than $1 million from financial institutions as a result of the offense, of four levels for leading a criminal activity involving five or more participants, and of two levels for abusing a position of public trust, bringing the total offense level to 44 levels. The government also sought a two-level enhancement for obstruction of justice on the basis of Ebbers' having testified contrary to the jury's verdict. With Ebbers' criminal history category of I, the Guidelines range calculated in the PSR was life imprisonment. The Probation Department recommended a 30-year sentence. Judge Jones declined to apply the enhancements for deriving more than $1 million from financial institutions or for obstruction of justice. She also denied Ebbers' motions for downward departures based on the claims that, inter alia, the loss overstated the seriousness of the offense, his medical condition was poor, and he had performed many beneficial community services and good works. She determined that his total offense level was 42 and that the advisory Guidelines range would be 30 years to life. She then sentenced Ebbers to 25 years' imprisonment and three years' supervised release, and imposed a $900 special assessment but no fines.

This appeal followed.

DISCUSSION

Ebbers argues that ... the government should have been required to allege and prove violations of GAAP; and ... the sentence imposed is unreasonable. ...

Ebbers argues that the indictment was flawed because it did not allege that the underlying accounting was improper under GAAP,[35] and that the district court should have required the government to prove violations of GAAP at trial. He claims that where a fraud charge is based on improper accounting, the impropriety must involve a violation of GAAP, because financial statements that comply with GAAP necessarily meet SEC disclosure requirements. *See Ganino v. Citizens Utilities Co.*, 228 F.3d 154, 160 n. 4 (2d Cir.2000) ("The SEC treats the FASB's standards as authoritative."); 17 C.F.R. § 210.4-01(a)(1) ("Financial statements filed with the [SEC] which are not prepared in accordance with generally accepted accounting principles will be presumed to be misleading or inaccurate...."). ...

We addressed a similar argument in *United States v. Simon*, 425 F.2d 796, 805-06 (2d Cir.1969) (Friendly, J.), when three accountants asked for a jury instruction that they could not be found guilty of securities fraud if the financial statements in question were in compliance with GAAP. We ruled that the district court properly refused to give the instruction.

We see no reason to depart from *Simon*. To be sure, GAAP may have relevance in that a defendant's good faith attempt to comply with GAAP or reliance upon an accountant's advice regarding GAAP may negate the government's claim of an intent to deceive. *Id.* at 805. Good faith compliance with GAAP will permit professionals who study the firm and understand GAAP to accurately assess the financial condition of the company. This can be the case even when the question of whether a particular accounting practice complies with GAAP may be subject to reasonable differences of opinion.

However, even where improper accounting is alleged, the statute requires proof only of intentionally misleading statements that are material, i.e., designed to affect the price of a security. 15 U.S.C. § 78ff. If the government proves that a defendant was responsible for financial reports that intentionally and materially misled investors, the statute is satisfied. The government is not required in addition to prevail in a battle of expert witnesses over the application of individual GAAP rules.

For example, an addition to revenue used in the "Close the Gap" program may or may not have been improper under particularized GAAP rules. However, where an addition intentionally involved funds that had not previously been used to calculate revenue and were a one-time addition to revenue, investors would not have been alerted to the fact that revenue as previously calculated was actually down. Such an intentionally misleading financial statement violates the statute. For similar reasons, the addition of underusage penalties to revenue may or

---

[35] Generally Accepted Accounting Principles ("GAAP") are the official standards adopted by the American Institute of Certified Public Accountants (the "AICPA"), a private professional organization, through three successor groups it established: the Committee on Accounting Procedure, the Accounting Principles Board (the "APB"), and the Financial Accounting Standard Board (the "FASB").

may not have been proper under some GAAP rule, but was intentionally misleading because the penalties were not expected to be realized. Finally, appellant claims that capitalization of some leases may have been proper under GAAP, but the capitalization of line costs—again an unannounced change in bookkeeping—was based not on an examination of particular leases but on the financial targets needed to keep share price high.

In a real sense, by alleging and proving that the financial statements were misleading, the government did, in fact, allege and prove violations of GAAP. According to the AICPA's Codification of Statements on Accounting Standards, AU § 312.04, "[f]inancial statements are materially misstated when they contain misstatements whose effect, individually or in the aggregate, is important enough to cause them not to be presented fairly, in all material respects, in compliance with GAAP." Thus, GAAP itself recognizes that technical compliance with particular GAAP rules may lead to misleading financial statements, and imposes an overall requirement that the statements as a whole accurately reflect the financial status of the company.

To be sure-and to repeat-differences of opinion as to GAAP's requirements may be relevant to a defendant's intent where financial statements are prepared in a good faith attempt to comply with GAAP. The rules are no shield, however, in a case such as the present one, where the evidence showed that accounting methods known to be misleading-although perhaps at times fortuitously in compliance with particular GAAP rules-were used for the express purpose of intentionally misstating WorldCom's financial condition and artificially inflating its stock price.

f) Reasonableness of Sentence

With regard to his sentence, Ebbers urges that the district court's loss calculation was incorrect and that his sentence was unreasonably long. After *Booker*, we review a district court's conclusions of law de novo, its application of the Guidelines on issues of fact for clear error, and its exercise of discretion with respect to departures for abuse of that discretion.

1. Loss Calculation

The district court applied the loss calculation from then-applicable the fraud Guidelines at U.S.S.G. § 2B1.1 (2001). No detailed definition of loss relevant to the issues before us is set out in the Guidelines. The Commentary does state, "The court need only make a reasonable estimate of the loss." U.S. Sentencing Guidelines Manual § 2B1.1 cmt. 2(c) (2001). Moreover, where fraud in investments is concerned, the loss to a buyer or seller who relied upon the fraud is not to be reduced by the gain to an innocent seller or buyer on the other side of the transaction. *Id.* at cmt. 2(F)(iv). In this case, therefore, the loss is that suffered by those investors who bought or held WorldCom stock during the fraud period either in express reliance on the accuracy of the financial statements or in reliance on what *Basic, Inc. v. Levinson* described as the "integrity" of the existing market price. 485 U.S. 224, 247 (1988).

Determining this amount is no easy task. One version of the so-called market capitalization test would, in its simplest form, take the share price on the date of a fraudulent statement—X-day, we shall call it—subtract from it the share price on the day after the fraud is revealed—Y-day—and multiply that amount by the number of outstanding shares.

There is a problem, however, with this simplistic analysis. If the truth had been told on X-day, shareholder A would have suffered an immediate loss commensurate with the fraud loss because potential buyers at the earlier price would have immediately disappeared upon the bad news. When perpetrated, therefore, the fraud would not damage A any more than the truth, at least immediately. However, were investor B to buy the stock after the fraudulent statement and in reliance upon the integrity of the market price, B would suffer a loss in the amount of the price paid less the intrinsic value, which, under the market capitalization test, would usually be deemed to be the price after the disclosure of the fraud on Y-day.

While shareholder A is as damaged by the truth as by the fraud on X-day, many frauds are ongoing, and, contrary to the testimony of Ebbers' expert, shareholder A may suffer a loss over time in being misled in assessing whether to hold or sell the stock. While A can be said not to have lost anything as a result of the fraud on X-day—assuming no prior disclosure obligation on the defendant's part—if new fraudulent statements are issued on X+1, X+2, etc., and the company's true value has further diminished on each occasion, the succeeding X-day frauds would have the effect of preventing A from making an informed judgment about holding the stock.

The securities laws are intended to allow investors to buy, sell, or hold based on accurate information. An investor who buys securities before an extended fraud begins, and holds them during the period of the fraud, may therefore be little different from one why buys in mid-fraud.

For example, the ongoing fraud here involved a series of periodic, fraudulent financial reports that systematically inflated WorldCom's operating profits. If the first report had been accurate, some decrease in fundamental value would have been revealed, but the decrease would have been far less than that revealed in June 2002 after several more fraudulent reports. Investors who held their stock throughout the fraud period were therefore denied the opportunity to reassess and perhaps sell according to their own informed estimates of the declining performance.

The loss to investors who hold during the period of an ongoing fraud is not easily quantifiable because we cannot accurately assess what their conduct would have been had they known the truth. However, some estimate must be made for Guidelines' purposes, or perpetrators of fraud would get a windfall. Moreover, revelation of an extended period of fraudulent financial statements may cause losses beyond that resulting from the restatement of financial circumstances because confidence in management and in even the truthful portions of a financial statement will be lost. *AUSA Life Ins. Co. v. Ernst & Young*, 206 F.3d 202, 230 (2d Cir.2000) (Winter, C.J., dissenting) ("Reasonable investors surely view firms with an untrustworthy management and auditor far more negatively than they view financially identical firms with honest management and a watch-dog auditor."). Credit may become totally unavailable even where an otherwise viable firm remains.

Worse, there is another variable. The loss must be the result of the fraud. *United States v. Olis*, 429 F.3d 540, 547 (5th Cir.2005). Many factors causing a decline in a company's performance may become publicly known around the time of the fraud and be one cause in the difference in price between X-day and Y-day. *Id.* at 548 (explaining that numerous factors, not just defendant's fraud, contributed to stock price decline). For example, the dot-com bubble burst and its likely negative future effect on WorldCom's business was public knowledge. The effect of that knowledge would be a downward pressure on share price not attributable to the defendant. Losses from causes other than the fraud must be excluded from the loss calculation.

Other complications would undoubtedly appear in a case where more than the grossest calculation is needed. This is not such a case. All of Ebbers' arguments with regard to the loss calculation encounter a hard fact. A 26-level loss calculation has a $100 million threshold, which is easily surpassed under any calculation. For example, the Probation Office calculated the loss at $2.23 billion, based on a price of $0.83/share on June 25, 2002, when the company announced the improper accounting and restated its results, and the price on July 1, 2002, $0.06. There were about 2.9 billion shares of WorldCom stock outstanding on June 25, 2002. Even excluding the 20,436,193 shares owned by Ebbers, the 5,000 shares owned by Sullivan, and shares owned by other guilty executives, there was still a $2.2 billion loss to investors not involved in the conspiracy, using the Probation Office's estimate of 77 cents loss per share.

To be sure, this calculation is flawed. Ebbers' expert testified that at least some of the decline in WorldCom's stock price immediately after June 25, 2002, was attributable to factors other than accounting fraud, citing "(1) planned sharp reductions in capital expenditures, (2) lay-offs affecting 17,000 employees, (3) the abandonment of non-core businesses, and (4) the deferral or elimination of dividends." His expert estimated that these other factors might have been responsible for 35% or more of the stock decline.

Even so, the loss amount is still well above $1 billion, or ten times greater than the $100 million dollar threshold for the 26-level enhancement. U.S. Sentencing Guidelines Manual § 2B1.1 (2001). Moreover, it is probably the case that large numbers of investors holding shares on June 25, 2002, had either held the shares during the period when the repeated fraudulent financial statements were used or had bought them during the scheme at prices much higher than 83¢ per share. And neither their loss nor those of bondholders-estimated by the Probation Office at $10 billion-is included in the Probation Office's calculations. Even a loss calculation of $1 billion is therefore almost certainly too low, and there is no reasonable calculation of loss to investors that would call for a remand.[36]

2. Sentence Disparities

Ebbers argues that his sentence should have been closer to those imposed on his co-defendants: CFO Scott Sullivan, who received five years; Controller David Myers, who received one year and one day; Accounting Director Buford Yates, who received one year and one day; Director of Management Reporting Betty Vinson, who received five months; and Director of Legal Entity Accounting Troy Normand, who received three years on probation.

District courts must consider "the need to avoid unwarranted sentence disparities among defendants with similar records who have been found guilty of similar conduct," 18 U.S.C. § 3553(a)(6), and we may remand cases where a defendant credibly argues that the disparity in sentences has no stated or apparent explanation. *See United States v. McGee*, 408 F.3d 966, 988 (7th Cir.2005) (remanding for reconsideration of sentencing disparities between equally culpable codefendants). However, a reasonable explanation of the different sentences here is readily apparent, namely, the varying degrees of culpability and cooperation between the various defendants. All of those named above cooperated and pled guilty. Ebbers did not. Moreover, each was a subordinate of Ebbers. Ebbers, as CEO, had primary responsibility for the fraud.

3. Reasonableness

At oral argument, the overall reasonableness of the sentence was raised by the court. Twenty-five years is a long sentence for a white collar crime, longer than the sentences routinely imposed by many states for violent crimes, including murder, or other serious crimes such as serial child molestation. However, Congress has directed that the Guidelines be a key component of sentence determination. Under the Guidelines, it may well be that all but the most trivial frauds in publicly traded companies may trigger sentences amounting to life imprisonment—Ebbers' 25-year sentence is actually below the Guidelines level. Even the threat of indictment on wafer-thin evidence of fraud may therefore compel a plea. For example, a 15¢ decline in share price in a firm with only half the number of outstanding shares that WorldCom had would constitute a loss of $200 million. No matter how many reasons other than the fraud may arguably account for the decline, a potential defendant would face an enormous jeopardy, given the present loss table, and enhancements for more than 250 victims, for being a leader of a criminal activity involving 5 or more participants, and for being an officer of the company.[37] However, the Guidelines reflect Congress' judgment as to the

---

[36] [Court's footnote 3:] Ebbers relies upon United States v. Canova, 412 F.3d 331, 355-56 (2d Cir.2005), for the proposition that a $5 million error in the calculation of the loss amount is sufficient to support a remand for resentencing. However, in that case the total loss alleged by the government was $5 million, which would have enhanced the defendant's offense level by thirteen levels, and the district court erred in declining to add any loss enhancement. While a $5 million calculation error is obviously significant in such a case, no putative error here is of remotely comparable significance. See U.S. Sentencing Guidelines Manual § 2B1.1 (2001).

[37] [Court's footnote 4:] U.S. Sentencing Guidelines Manual § 2B1.1 (2005) (setting the offense level of 28 for a loss of $200 million or more, 6 levels for a crime involving 250 or more victims, and 4 levels for

appropriate national policy for such crimes, *United States v. Rattoballi*, 452 F.3d 127, 2006 WL 1699460, at *5 (2d Cir. June 21, 2006) (stating that the court will "continue to seek guidance from the Sentencing Commission as expressed in the Sentencing Guidelines and authorized by Congress."), and Ebbers does not argue otherwise.

Moreover, the securities fraud here was not puffery or cheerleading or even a misguided effort to protect the company, its employees, and its shareholders from the capital-impairing effects of what was believed to be a temporary downturn in business. The methods used were specifically intended to create a false picture of profitability even for professional analysts that, in Ebbers' case, was motivated by his personal financial circumstances. Given Congress' policy decisions on sentences for fraud, the sentence is harsh but not unreasonable.

G. DODD-FRANK WHISTLEBLOWER PROGRAM

On July 10, 2010, the Dodd-Frank Wall Street Reform and Consumer Protection Act ("Dodd-Frank" or the "Act") was signed into law.[38] It was a reaction to the regulatory failures that contributed to the severe economic downturn in about 2008. It effected broad changes in the rules governing a wide array of areas, including systemic risk, derivatives, securitization, private equity, hedge funds, insurance, credit rating agencies, and corporate governance. For present purposes, it suffices to concentrate on the portion of the Act that replaced the SEC's largely unsuccessful whistleblower reward program with one that is modeled after the more successful program created by the IRS[39] and that borrows (but differs in significant part) from the False Claims Act's *qui tam* provisions.[40]

What some have coined the SEC "bounty program" creates incentives for tipping the government to violations of the securities laws, rules, and regulations—and to violations of the Sarbanes-Oxley Act and the Foreign Corrupt Practices Act. In sum, a whistleblower who voluntarily provides "original information" regarding a possible violation of the securities laws that leads to a successful SEC enforcement action in which the government recovers more than $1 million is entitled to 10-30% of the total recovery—the precise amount being determined by the SEC. Because recoveries in securities law cases and settlements often reach into the hundreds of millions of dollars, the incentives for whistleblowing are now huge— which may have negative consequences for companies seeking to resolve problems internally and head off regulatory action.

---

being the officer of a publicly traded company); § 3B1.1 (2005) (adding 4 levels for leading a criminal activity with five or more participants); Sentencing Table (2005) (setting the sentence at thirty years to life for an offense level of 42 for an offender in criminal history category I).

[38] Pub. Law No. 111-203 (July 21, 2010) (codified in sections of Title 7, 12, and 15). Section 21F of the Act amends the Securities Exchange Act of 1934, 15 U.S.C. § 78a, *et seq.* to establish the new SEC whistleblower program. The Act also creates a similar whistleblower program by amending the Commodities Exchange Act, 7 U.S.C. § 1, *et seq.*, administered by the Commodities Futures Trading Commission (CFTC). The Act further makes some changes in the False Claims Act and provides whistleblower protections to those who tip to the new Bureau of Consumer Financial Protection. For a summary of the Dodd-Frank whistleblower legislation, see Allen B. Roberts, *The Sounds of New Whistleblower Awards and Protections under the Dodd-Frank Wall Street Reform and Consumer Protection Act*, Bloomberg Law Reports (Securities Law) (2010).

[39] *See* 26 U.S.C. § 7623.

[40] *See* 31 U.S.C. §§ 3729-33 (and Chapter 5(C)(2), *infra*). For a comparison of the SEC's program and the False Claims Act's *qui tam* provisions, see Julie Rose O'Sullivan, *"Private Justice" and FCPA Enforcement: Should the SEC Whistleblower Program Include a* Qui Tam *Provision?*, 53 Am. Crim. L. Rev. 67 (2016).

As in the *qui tam* context, the devil is in the details—and much litigation can be expected over the language of the statute and the SEC's implementing regulations ("regulations").[41] "Original information" is defined as information derived from the whistleblower's direct and independent knowledge or analysis. If the information is derived from public sources, or the SEC already has the information from other sources, the whistleblower may not recover unless he or she was the "original source" of the information. The whistleblower is precluded from recovering if the whistleblower was convicted of a crime related to the enforcement action, obtained the information as a result of auditing responsibilities, failed to disclose the information in required SEC filings, or received the information while an employee of a law enforcement or regulatory authority.

Whistleblower protections against retaliation are also augmented. Thus, employee whistleblowers are protected against discharge, demotion, suspension, threat, harassment, and other forms of discrimination. To avoid the potential of retaliation, whistleblowers may remain anonymous, although the whistleblower must disclose his or her identity to the SEC to obtain the reward. The SEC is prohibited from revealing the whistleblower's identity, with some exceptions. The Act creates a civil cause of action for whistleblowers who are subject to retaliation, allowing them to file immediately in district court. The Act permits whistleblowers who successfully sue for retaliation to secure reinstatement with equal seniority and twice their lost wages, as well as attorney's fees and certain other expenses.

The Dodd-Frank Act's new SEC whistleblower program has raised a number of concerns among defense lawyers and counsel for companies. As Pamela Rogers Chepiga and Sarah Cox explained in a presentation to the White-Collar Bar:

> … [A]s drafted, the Dodd-Frank Act whistleblower provisions creates a disincentive for employees to report a problem internally before approaching the SEC. To ensure that their information is "original" and that they are first in line to collect the bounty, employees may well decide to bypass the internal corporate whistleblower programs the SEC has been promoting.
>
> …[T]he new SEC bounty program also creates a risk that companies will be more reluctant to conduct internal investigations into possible securities law violations, and be less thorough when they do perform an investigation. An internal investigation usually requires interviewing witnesses and gathering documents, processes that inevitably raise suspicions and ruffle feathers among employees, thereby increasing the risk of premature disclosure to the SEC. Once an internal investigation has begun, categories of potential whistleblowers include witnesses, compliance officers tasked with conducting interviews, external experts and consultants, paralegals, and even attorneys. Faced with this risk, companies may simply choose not to pursue an investigation. Moreover, investigations that do occur could be more limited in scope because the company's counsel may sensibly shy away from sharing relevant information and documents with witnesses, each of whom is a potential whistleblower.[42]

The SEC, in its implementing regulations, attempted to address these concerns. Below is the SEC's summary of its rules; do you think that the SEC has done enough to counter these concerns?

---

[41] See Rules 21F-1 through 21F-17; Implementation of the Whistleblower Provisions of Section 21F of the Securities Exchange Act of 1934, Release No. 34-64545, File No. S7-33-10 (eff. August 12, 2011).

[42] Allen & Overy, *The Dodd-Frank Act: A New SEC Bounty Program*, in ABA White Collar Crime 2011, at C-4 (Jan. 24, 2011).

SEC Adopts Rules to Establish Whistleblower Program
SEC Press Release, Fact Sheet (May 25, 2011)

… The new SEC whistleblower program … is primarily intended to reward individuals who act early to expose violations and who provide significant evidence that helps the SEC bring successful cases.

To be considered for an award, the SEC's rules require that a whistleblower must voluntarily provide the SEC with original information that leads to the successful enforcement by the SEC of a federal court or administrative action in which the SEC obtains monetary sanctions totaling more than $1 million. …

Rules Requirement

The final rules define a whistleblower as a person who provides information to the SEC relating to a possible violation of the securities laws that has occurred, is ongoing, or is about to occur.

To be considered for an award, the final rules require that a whistleblower must:

Voluntarily provide the SEC …

In general, a whistleblower is deemed to have provided information voluntarily if the whistleblower has provided information before the government, a self-regulatory organization or the Public Company Accounting Oversight Board asks for it directly from the whistleblower or the whistleblower's representative.

… with original information …

Original information must be based upon the whistleblower's independent knowledge or independent analysis, not already known to the Commission and not derived exclusively from certain public sources.

… that leads to the successful enforcement by the SEC of a federal court or administrative action …

A whistleblower's information can be deemed to have led to a successful enforcement action if:

1. The information is sufficiently specific, credible and timely to cause the Commission to open a new examination or investigation, reopen a closed investigation, or open a new line [of] inquiry in an existing examination or investigation.
2. The conduct was already under investigation when the information was submitted, and the information significantly contributed to the success of the action.
3. The whistleblower reports original information through his or her employer's internal whistleblower, legal, or compliance procedures before or at the same time it is passed along to the Commission; the employer provides the whistleblower's information (and any subsequently-discovered information) to the Commission; and the employer's report satisfies prongs (1) or (2) above.

… in which the SEC obtains monetary sanctions totaling more than $1 million.

The rules permit aggregation of multiple Commission cases that arise out of a common nucleus of operative facts as a single action. These may include proceedings involving the same or similar parties, factual allegations, alleged violations of the federal securities laws, or transactions or occurrences.

The final rules further define and explain these requirements.

Key Concepts

Avoiding Unintended Consequences

Certain people generally will not be considered for whistleblower awards under the final rules.

These include:

> People who have a pre-existing legal or contractual duty to report their information to the Commission.
>
> Attorneys (including in-house counsel) who attempt to use information obtained from client engagements to make whistleblower claims for themselves (unless disclosure of information is permitted under SEC rules or state bar rules).
>
> People who obtain the information by means or in a manner that is determined by a U.S. court to violate federal or state criminal law.
>
> Foreign government officials.
>
> Officers, directors, trustees or partners of an entity who are informed by another person (such as by an employee) of allegations of misconduct, or who learn the information in connection with the entity's processes for identifying, reporting and addressing possible violations of law (such as through the employee hotline).
>
> Compliance and internal audit personnel.
>
> Public accountants working on SEC engagements, if the information relates to violations by the engagement client.

However, in certain circumstances, compliance and internal audit personnel as well as public accountants could become whistleblowers when:

> The whistleblower believes disclosure may prevent substantial injury to the financial interest or property of the entity or investors.
>
> The whistleblower believes that the entity is engaging in conduct that will impede an investigation.
>
> At least 120 days have elapsed since the whistleblower reported the information to his or her supervisor or the entity's audit committee, chief legal officer, chief compliance officer—or at least 120 days have elapsed since the whistleblower received the information, if the whistleblower received it under circumstances indicating that these people are already aware of the information.

Certain other people—such as employees of certain agencies and people who are criminally convicted in connection with the conduct—are already excluded by Dodd-Frank.

Under the final rules, the Commission also will not pay culpable whistleblowers awards that are based upon either:

The monetary sanctions that such culpable individuals themselves pay in the resulting SEC action.

The monetary sanctions paid by entities whose liability is based substantially on conduct that the whistleblower directed, planned, or initiated.

The purpose of this provision is to prevent wrongdoers from benefitting by, in effect, blowing the whistle on themselves.

Providing Information to the Commission and Seeking a Reward:

The rules also describe the procedures for submitting information to the SEC and for making a claim for an award after an action is brought. The claim procedures provide opportunities for whistleblowers to fairly present their claim before the Commission makes a final award determination.

Under the final rules, the SEC also will pay an award based on amounts collected in related actions brought by certain agencies that are based upon the same original information that led to a successful SEC action.

Clarifying the Anti-Retaliation Protection:

Under the rules, a whistleblower who provides information to the Commission is protected from employment retaliation if the whistleblower possesses a reasonable belief that the information he or she is providing relates to a possible securities law violation that has occurred, is ongoing, or is about to occur. In addition, the rules make it unlawful for anyone to interfere with a whistleblower's efforts to communicate with the Commission, including threatening to enforce a confidentiality agreement.

Supporting Internal Compliance Programs:

The final rules do not require that employee whistleblowers report violations internally in order to qualify for an award. However, the rules strengthen incentives that have been proposed and add certain additional incentives intended to encourage employees to utilize their own company's internal compliance programs when appropriate to do so.
For instance, the rules:

Make a whistleblower eligible for an award if the whistleblower reports internally and the company informs the SEC about the violations.

Treat an employee as a whistleblower, under the SEC program, as of the date that employee reports the information internally—as long as the employee provides the same information to the SEC within 120 days. Through this provision, employees are able to report their information internally first while preserving their "place in line" for a possible award from the SEC.

Provide that a whistleblower's voluntary participation in an entity's internal compliance and reporting systems is a factor that can increase the amount of an award, and that a whistleblower's interference with internal compliance and reporting is a factor that can decrease the amount of an award.

* * *

Chapter 10

CONSPIRACY

A great number of federal statutes address the problem of group criminality, the foremost of which is the general conspiracy statute, 18 U.S.C. § 371.[1] The elements of a § 371 conspiracy are exceedingly simple: "(1) the existence of an agreement to achieve an unlawful objective; (2) the defendant's knowing and voluntary participation in the conspiracy; and (3) the commission of an overt act in furtherance of the conspiracy."[2]

Conspiracy is an inchoate offense. Because there is no general federal attempts statute, conspiracy is one way in which the government may attack planned criminal activity that does not come to fruition, at least where a multiplicity of actors can be proved. It is important to note, however, that even when the coconspirators are able to complete the crime that they have conspired to achieve, the "conspiracy to commit an offense and the subsequent commission of that crime normally do not merge into a single punishable act."[3] Thus, "it is well recognized that in most cases separate sentences can be imposed for conspiracy to do an act and for the subsequent accomplishment of that end."

These materials explore the reasons why conspiracy is treated as a crime separate and apart from the offenses that are the illegal objectives or means employed by the criminal partnership. They should also illustrate the expansive reach of conspiracy liability—a crime that some view as "so vague that it almost defies definition."[4] Finally, these readings should make clear why, as a practical matter, the government views the conspiracy statute as the "darling of the modern prosecutor's nursery"[5] and why many defense lawyers concur with

---

[1] Although this Chapter focuses on § 371, readers should be aware that there are literally dozens of federal code provisions that address conspiracies to commit particular types of substantive offenses, with some of the most important being conspiracy to violate the Hobbs Act, 18 U.S.C. § 1951, conspiracy to violate the Racketeer Influenced and Corrupt Organizations Act (RICO) provisions, 18 U.S.C. § 1962(d), conspiracy to commit money laundering, 18 U.S.C. § 1956(h), conspiracy to restrain trade, 15 U.S.C. § 1, conspiracy to monopolize, 15 U.S.C. § 2, and conspiracy to traffic in or import drugs, 21 U.S.C. §§ 846, 963. Courts usually apply the same general conspiracy law principles whether they are addressing § 371 or these more specific conspiracy statutes. It is important to note, however, that not all of the specific conspiracy statutes contained in the United States Code precisely mirror § 371. For example, neither the RICO conspiracy provision nor the drug trafficking or importing conspiracy statutes require proof of an overt act to secure a conviction. *See, e.g.*, Salinas v. United States, 522 U.S. 52 (1997) (RICO); United States v. Pool, 660 F.2d 547, 559-60 (5th Cir. 1981) (21 U.S.C. § 963); United States v. Pringle, 576 F.2d 1114, 1120 (5th Cir. 1978) (21 U.S.C. § 846).

[2] United States v. Cure, 804 F.2d 625, 628 (11th Cir. 1986).

[3] Iannelli v. United States, 420 U.S. 770, 777 (1975).

[4] *See, e.g.*, Krulewitch v. United States, 336 U.S. 440, 446 (1949) (Jackson, J., concurring) (discussing some of the troubling attributes of conspiracy prosecutions).

[5] Harrison v. United States, 7 F.2d 259, 263 (2d Cir. 1925) (per J. Learned Hand); *see also* United States v. Reynolds, 919 F.2d 435 (7th Cir. 1990) ("[P]rosecutors seem to have conspiracy on their word processors as Count I; rare is the case omitting such a charge").

Clarence Darrow's observation that "if there are still any citizens interested in protecting human liberty, let them study the conspiracy law of the United States."[6]

A. PRACTICAL CONSEQUENCES OF A CONSPIRACY CHARGE

Some of the battles fought in the ensuing materials regarding such matters as the definition of the conspiratorial agreement and the appropriate scope of a conspiracy may only be completely understood by recognizing the practical consequence of such battles.

1. FED. R. EVID. 801(d)(2)(E)

Fed.R.Evid. 801(c) provides that hearsay is "a statement, other than one made by the declarant while testifying at the trial or hearing, offered in evidence to prove the truth of the matter asserted." Rule 801(d)(2)(E) goes on to provide, however, that a statement is not hearsay if it is offered against a party and is "a statement by a coconspirator of a party during the course and in furtherance of the conspiracy." Coconspirators' statements, if believed, can be very damaging to the defense because they often constitute the only direct evidence regarding such central issues as the defendant's knowledge or intent. Although the alleged coconspirators generally need not be included in the indictment for their damning statements to be admitted under Rule 801(d)(2)(E), proof of a conspiracy is necessary and charging the conspiracy may ease the admission of this proof (as well as ensuring the introduction of other relevant evidence).[7]

There are two fairly low hurdles that the government must surmount in order to secure the admission of coconspirator statements. To get a coconspirator's statement admitted against a defendant, the government must establish that a conspiracy existed and that the defendant against whom it is sought to be admitted and the declarant were parties to that conspiracy. The existence of a conspiracy is a question for determination, under a preponderance of evidence standard, by the trial court.[8] The Supreme Court has held that in determining whether a conspiracy existed and whether the defendant was a member of it, courts may consider the proffered hearsay statement itself and need not look only to independent evidence (that is, evidence other than the statement sought to be admitted).[9] In 1997, Fed. R. Evid. 801(d)(2) was amended to make clear, however, that "[t]he contents of the statement shall be considered but are not alone sufficient to establish ... the existence of a conspiracy and the participation therein by the declarant and the party against whom the statement is offered under subdivision (E)."

Further, the statement must be made during the course and in furtherance of the conspiracy. Where the record demonstrates that the "central aim of the alleged conspiracy ... had either never existed or had long since ended in success or failure when and if the alleged

---

[6] John R. Wing & Michael J. Bresnick, *Curbing Conspiracy Charges: Effective Legal Arguments for White Collar Defendants*, 7 Bus. Crimes Bull. 1 (Jan. 2001) (quoting Clarence Darrow's biography); *see also* Benjamin E. Rosenberg, *Several Problems in Criminal Conspiracy Laws and Some Proposals for Reform*, 43 Crim. L. Bull. Art. 1 (2007).

[7] *See* 4 Dep't of Justice Manual, tit. 9 [hereinafter U.S.A.M.], § 9-27.320(B)(3) (In considering whether to bring additional charges, "[i]t is proper to consider the evidentiary consequences of failing to seek certain charges. For example, in a case in which a substantive offense was committed pursuant to an unlawful agreement, inclusion of a conspiracy count is permissible and may be desirable to ensure the introduction of all relevant evidence at trial.").

[8] Bourjaily v. United States, 483 U.S. 171 (1987).

[9] *Id.*

coconspirator made the statement attributed to her," the statement is inadmissible.[10] Governmental attempts to extend the temporal course of the conspiracy by alleging that later efforts to conceal the crime were a part of the ongoing scheme have met with limited success in the Supreme Court.[11] "[A]fter the central criminal purposes of a conspiracy have been attained, a subsidiary conspiracy to conceal may not be implied from circumstantial evidence showing merely that the conspiracy kept a secret and that the conspirators took care to cover up their crime in order to escape detection and punishment."[12] To extend the length of the conspiracy and thus have admitted coconspirators' statements made after at least some of the conspiratorial aims have been achieved, the government must define the objectives of the conspiracy in such a way as to necessitate the concealing activity.[13]

2. JOINDER

The federal joinder and severance rules are found in Fed. R. Crim. P. 8 ("Joinder of Offenses and Defendants") and 14 ("Relief from Prejudicial Joinder"). As examination of Rule 8(b) reveals, joinder of defendants in one trial may be substantially eased by inclusion of a conspiracy charge, particularly where the activities at issue involve disparate crimes by many defendants. Where joinder appears proper under Rule 8(b), the battle becomes one of whether the defense can secure a severance under Rule 14.

In *Zafiro v. United States*,[14] the Supreme Court refused to adopt a rule mandating severance whenever co-defendants have conflicting defenses. The *Zafiro* Court set forth the standard by which severance requests are to be judged:

There is a preference in the federal system for joint trials of defendants who are indicted together. Joint trials "play a vital role in the criminal justice system." They promote efficiency and "serve the interests of justice by avoiding the scandal and inequity of inconsistent verdicts." For these reasons, we repeatedly have approved of joint trials. But Rule 14 recognizes that joinder, even when proper under Rule 8(b), may prejudice either a defendant or the Government. ...

We believe that, when defendants properly have been joined under Rule 8(b), a district court should grant a severance under Rule 14 only if there is a serious risk that a joint trial would compromise a specific trial right of one of the defendants, or prevent the jury from making a reliable judgment about guilt or innocence.[15]

In theory, the defendant can meet his burden of showing sufficient prejudice flowing from a joint trial by demonstrating that the jury will be unable to sift through all the evidence (some of it admitted pursuant to Fed. R. Evid. 801(d)(2)(E)) and make an individualized determination as to each defendant.[16] However, "[t]he mere fact that there may be an 'enormous disparity in the evidence admissible against [one coconspirator] compared to the other defendants' is not a

---

[10] Krulewitch v. United States, 336 U.S. 440, 442 (1949).

[11] *See id.* at 443-44 (co-conspirators' statements not admissible because they were made after the conspiracy had ended); Lutwak v. United States, 344 U.S. 604, 616-18 (1953) (same).

[12] Grunewald v. United States, 353 U.S. 391, 401-02 (1957) (refusing to accept government's argument that concealment lengthened the duration of the conspiracy and thus saved the crime from statute of limitations difficulties).

[13] *See, e.g.*, Forman v. United States, 361 U.S. 416 (1960); *see also* United States v. Upton, 559 F.3d 3 (1st Cir. 2009) (concealment of conspiracy can in qualifying cases extend the statute of limitations period).

[14] 506 U.S. 534 (1993).

[15] *Id.* at 538-39 (citations omitted).

[16] *See id.*; *see also* United States v. Schlei, 122 F.3d 944, 984 (11th Cir. 1997).

sufficient basis" for a severance.[17] Further, courts often find that any fear of prejudicial spill-over may be cured by provision of appropriate limiting instructions to the jury. As a practical matter, then, the existence of inconsistent defenses or fears that the jury will not be able to follow limiting instructions regarding what evidence may be considered against which defendants in a sprawling conspiracy trial are generally insufficient to win a severance. "In the context of conspiracy, severance will rarely, if ever, be required."[18]

Prosecutors may prefer group trials in conspiracy cases for a variety of reasons, not all of which relate to efficiency and the evidentiary advantages of the vicarious admissions rule of Fed. R. Evid. 801(d)(2)(E). As the Model Penal Code commentary notes,

> The most obvious and probably the greatest service to prosecutors of joint trials in cases of organized criminality lies in permitting the presentation in one trial of all aspects of the entire scheme. In the case of complex and far-flung networks of crime, such a presentation may be essential to an understanding of the entire operation and the role played by each participant, and even in simpler cases the purport of each actor's behavior may be clarified by his cohorts. There are concomitant dangers to the defendant in such joint trial, for he may suffer from jury confusion in the face of a long and complicated trial involving scores of defendants and from being associated in the jurors' minds with more nefarious criminals. ...[20]

3. VENUE

One very basic question that may influence charging choices is whether venue is appropriate for a given charge in the district at issue. The government bears the burden of proving by a preponderance of the evidence that venue is proper.[19] As the Supreme Court explained in *United States v. Cabrales*,[20]

> Proper venue in criminal proceedings was a matter of concern to the Nation's founders. Their complaints against the King of Great Britain, listed in the Declaration of Independence, included his transportation of colonists "beyond Seas to be tried." The Constitution twice safeguards the defendant's venue right: Article III, § 2, cl. 3 instructs that "Trial of all Crimes ... shall be held in the State where the Crimes shall have been committed"; the Sixth Amendment calls for trial "by an impartial jury of the State and district wherein the crime shall have been committed." Rule 18 of the Federal Rules of Criminal Procedure, providing that "prosecution shall be in a district in which the offense was committed," echoes the constitutional commands.[21]

Venue is anything but a mere technical issue—poor venue choices may unfairly burden defendants and may impair government interests. The Supreme Court has explained that constitutional venue provisions were intended to protect defendants against the "unfairness and hardship" of being prosecuted far from home, with all the attendant expense and emotional and physical hardships that may entail for the defendant and for his family.[22] At the

---

[17] *Schlei*, 122 F.3d at 984.

[18] United States v. Searing, 984 F.2d 960, 965 (8th Cir. 1993); *see also* United States v. DiMarzo, 80 F.3d 656, 659 (1st Cir. 1996).

[19] *See, e.g.*, United States v. Lanoue, 137 F.3d 656, 661 (1st Cir. 1998).

[20] 524 U.S. 1 (1998).

[21] *Id.* at 6; *see also* United States v. Johnson, 323 U.S. 273, 275 (1944).

[22] United States v. Cores, 356 U.S. 405, 407 (1958).

same time, the venue provisions ensure that the trial is held in a location convenient to the crime and where the witnesses and other evidence would normally be found.[23]

As the above-quoted sources dictate, the determination of proper venue usually turns on where the crime is deemed to have been "committed." This is "determined from the nature of the crime alleged and the location of the act or acts constituting it."[24] Because many white-collar crimes are often "continuing offenses," *i.e.* offenses consisting of a series of two or more acts that occur over a period of time, and because they are often committed jointly by multiple parties located in different districts, the question of venue may be particularly complicated. Some of the difficulty in such cases is removed by 18 U.S.C. § 3237(a), which provides:

> Except as otherwise expressly provided by enactment of Congress, any offense against the United States begun in one district and completed in another, or committed in more than one district, may be inquired of and prosecuted in any district in which such offense was begun, continued, or completed.

A conspiracy under § 371 is deemed "committed" not only where the agreement is formed but also where the overt acts occurred. Thus, "[a] conspiracy may be prosecuted in the district where it was formed or in any district where an overt act was committed in furtherance of its objects."[25] For example, in a case in which a conspiratorial agreement was reached in California and none of the defendants had entered the District of Columbia as part of the conspiracy, the Supreme Court nevertheless found that venue was appropriate in the District of Columbia based on the overt acts of a coconspirator.[26]

4. STATUTE OF LIMITATIONS

Generally, the five-year federal statute of limitations for non-capital offenses governs in § 371 prosecutions.[27] However, where a defendant is charged with conspiracy, the limitations period commences upon the occurrence of the last overt act committed in furtherance of the conspiracy.[28] Even if the agreement, most of the overt acts, and even crimes that were the object of the conspiracy would be time-barred if pursued independently, a criminal conspiracy prosecution based on the same evidence is still viable if one overt act occurred within the statutory period.

---

[23] *Johnson*, 323 U.S. at 278.

[24] United States v. Anderson, 328 U.S. 699, 703 (1946).

[25] United States v. Schlei, 122 F.3d 944, 975 (11th Cir. 1997); *see also* Hyde v. United States, 225 U.S. 347 (1912).

[26] *Hyde*, 225 U.S. at 363; *see also* United States v. Fahnbulleh, 752 F.3d 470, 477 (D.C. Cir. 2014) (all acts committed overseas but venue proper in D.C. because the defendants caused fraudulent reports to be sent to Washington in furtherance of the scheme); United States v. Rommy, 506 F.3d 108, 119-20 (2d Cir. 2007) (telephone call from a government actor to a member of a conspiracy will provide venue to prosecute the conspiracy in the caller's district as long as the conspirator receiving the call believes the conversation promotes the conspiracy).

[27] 18 U.S.C. § 3282. However, in tax cases, the six-year period provided in 26 U.S.C. § 6531 may apply. *See* United States v. Waldman, 941 F.2d 1544 (11th Cir. 1991).

[28] *See, e.g.*, United States v. Ngige, 780 F.3d 497, 502 (1st Cir. 2015); United States v. Salmonese, 352 F.3d 608, 614 (2d Cir. 2003).

B. ELEMENTS/PRINCIPLES OF LIABILITY

1. DEFRAUD AND OFFENSE CLAUSES

UNITED STATES v. ARCH TRADING CO.
987 F.2d 1087 (4th Cir. 1993)

NIEMEYER, CIRCUIT JUDGE:

On August 2, 1990, Iraq invaded Kuwait. On that same day President Bush invoked the emergency powers provided to him by Congress and issued executive orders prohibiting United States persons from, among other things, traveling to Iraq and dealing with the government of Iraq and its agents. In the present appeal, Arch Trading Company, Inc., a Virginia corporation, challenges its convictions for various crimes arising from violations of these prohibitions. The company was convicted of conspiring to commit an offense against the United States, in violation of 18 U.S.C. § 371; of disobeying the emergency executive orders, in violation of the International Emergency Economic Powers Act (IEEPA), 50 U.S.C. § 1701 *et seq.*, and of lying to the Department of Treasury's Office of Foreign Assets Control (OFAC) about its conduct, in violation of 18 U.S.C. § 1001. ...

Arch Trading contends principally that ... the indictment charging it with conspiracy to *commit an offense* under § 371 was defective because in the circumstances the company could only have been charged with conspiracy *to defraud* .... After carefully considering each of Arch Trading's arguments, we affirm.

In November 1988 Arch Trading entered into a $1.9 million contract with Agricultural Supplies Company, a "quasi-governmental body owned by the government of Iraq" (Agricultural of Iraq), to ship to Iraq and install there laboratory equipment, including a "virology fermenter" and a "bacteriology machine," purportedly for veterinary use. Payment by Agricultural of Iraq to Arch Trading was assured by a $2 million irrevocable letter of credit issued by Rafidain Bank of Iraq and performance by Arch Trading was guaranteed by a letter of credit issued by the Commercial Bank of Kuwait. To secure that letter of credit, Arch Trading was required to deposit $200,000 with the Kuwaiti bank.

From April 1990 through July 1990 Arch Trading acquired the equipment and related chemicals and arranged for their delivery to Iraq. By early August 1990, five of a planned six shipments had arrived in Iraq, but none had been installed. The sixth shipment, which was never actually delivered, was en route. On August 2, 1990, when Iraq invaded Kuwait, President Bush, invoking the powers given him under the IEEPA, issued Executive Order No. 12722, 55 Fed.Reg. 31,803 (1990), prohibiting United States persons from, among other things, exporting goods, technology, or services to Iraq; performing any contract in support of an industrial, commercial or governmental project in Iraq; and engaging in any transaction related to travel to Iraq by United States persons. At Arch Trading's request, that same day the Treasury Department's OFAC faxed a copy of the Executive Order to Arch Trading's offices. A week later the President issued a slightly more detailed order, Executive Order No. 12724, 55 Fed.Reg. 33,089 (1990). Both executive orders were formally implemented through regulations published in the Code of Federal Regulations.

Notwithstanding the prohibitions of the first executive order, two executives of Arch Trading immediately attempted to enter Iraq via Cyprus to install the laboratory equipment that had already been delivered. When that effort failed, Arch Trading retained a Jordanian firm, Biomedical Technologies, Inc., to perform the installation. One of the Arch Trading executives who had earlier attempted to enter Iraq later joined Biomedical employees in Baghdad to help coordinate the installation, which was accomplished between October 24 and November 2, 1990. The travel expenses of both the Arch Trading executive and the Biomedical Technologies employees were reimbursed by Arch Trading, on authority of its president, Kamal Sadder, and upon completion of the installation, Biomedical Technologies was paid a bonus.

Arch Trading then sought to recover the $200,000 which had been deposited with the Kuwaiti bank to secure the letter of credit guaranteeing contractual performance, submitting backdated documents which falsely represented that contractual performance was completed on July 24, 1990, before the embargo of August 2 was imposed. Arch Trading also asked Biomedical Technologies to backdate its confirmation of performance. The Kuwaiti bank nevertheless denied the request for return of the funds "until [Arch Trading] obtain[ed] a license from the Office of Foreign Assets Control of the Department of the Treasury (OFAC)." To obtain the license, Arch Trading wrote a letter, dated April 3, 1991, to the Treasury Department's OFAC explaining the company's position. The letter stated: "We have performed our contract *prior to August 2d, 1991* [1990], and stopped any contact with Iraq in conformity with the presidential executive [order]." Noting that the Kuwaiti bank said it required a license before the $200,000 deposit could be released, the letter concluded, "At this time we would like your office to inform us if such license is necessary for the release of our funds. *If so, kindly issue us this license at the earliest possible time.*" The OFAC replied by letter, erroneously advising Arch Trading that no license was required. ...

Arch Trading first contends that it was improperly charged under 18 U.S.C. § 371. That section criminalizes conspiracies of two sorts: conspiracies *to commit an offense* against the United States and conspiracies *to defraud* the United States. Arch Trading was charged with, and convicted of, conspiring to commit an "offense" against the United States government. It asserts, however, it could only have been charged, if at all, with having conspired to "defraud" the United States, because violations of executive orders and regulations do not constitute an "offense." Arch Trading argues that the conspiracy count must therefore be dismissed ....

We reject this argument because we do not agree that violation of an executive order cannot constitute an offense as that term is used in 18 U.S.C. § 371. While it may be that executive orders cannot alone establish crimes, when such orders are duly authorized by an act of Congress and Congress specifies a criminal sanction for their violation, the consequence is different. In this case the IEEPA authorized the President to issue executive orders proscribing conduct, and 50 U.S.C. § 1705(b) makes criminal the disobedience of an order issued under the Act. There is no question that violation of a federal criminal statute may properly be charged under the "offense" clause. We therefore hold that when Congress provides criminal sanctions for violations of executive orders that it empowers the President to issue, such violation constitutes an "offense" for the purposes of 18 U.S.C. § 371.

While Arch Trading's conduct could arguably have been charged also as a conspiracy "to defraud," the two prongs of § 371 are not mutually exclusive. Because of the broad interpretation which has been given the "defraud" clause, § 371's two clauses overlap considerably. The wide breadth of the "defraud" clause has long been established:

> To conspire to defraud the United States means to cheat the government out of property or money, but it also means to interfere with or obstruct one of its lawful functions by deceit, craft or trickery, or at least by means that are dishonest. It is not necessary that the government shall be subjected to property or pecuniary loss by the fraud, but only that its legitimate official actions and purpose shall be defeated by misrepresentation, chicane, or the overreaching of those charged with carrying out the governmental intention.

Hammerschmidt v. United States, 265 U.S. 182, 188 (1924).

Because of this overlap, given conduct may be proscribed by both of the section's clauses. In such a situation, the fact that a particular course of conduct is chargeable under one clause does not render it immune from prosecution under the other. When both prongs of § 371 apply to the conduct with which a particular defendant is charged, the government enjoys considerable latitude in deciding how to proceed. Convictions under the "defraud" clause for conspiracies *to commit particular offenses* are commonly upheld. Conversely, convictions under the "offense" clause for conspiracy to engage in conduct which would defraud the United States are also proper. Many courts have even found it permissible to list both prongs of § 371 in a single indictment count rather than specifying whether the alleged conspiracy was one to defraud or one to commit an offense. ...

In short, the evidence in this case against Arch Trading would have supported conviction under either the "offense" or the "defraud" clause, and absent an improper motive, which is not alleged here, the government's choice of invoking the offense clause was an appropriate exercise of discretion. ...

Notes

1. Under federal law, a conspiracy obviously may consist of an agreement to do an unlawful act. Such conspiracies are commonly charged as an agreement to violate a specific federal statute under the offense clause of § 371 although, as the court above notes, the government may also elect in appropriate cases to proceed under the defraud clause. Are there cases that may not be brought under the offense clause because there has been no violation of a specific prohibition in the Code but where the government may nonetheless proceed under the defraud clause? In other words, may a criminal conspiracy be charged where the object of the conspiracy is *lawful*? What potential dangers might the availability of a "defraud clause" charge raise? *See* ALI, Model Penal Code § 5.03, Comment, at 395-97 (recommending that conspiracy definition be limited to cases where a specific substantive offense is the objective of the agreement).

As the *Arch Trading Co.* court indicated, the Supreme Court has stated that "[t]o conspire to defraud the United States means primarily to cheat the Government out of property or money, but it also means *to interfere with or to obstruct one of its lawful governmental functions* by deceit, craft or trickery, or at least by means that are dishonest." Hammerschmidt v. United States, 265 U.S. 182, 188 (1924) (emphasis added). *This may include agreements to engage in activities that are not necessarily illegal.* Under the defraud clause, "so long as deceitful or dishonest means are employed to obstruct governmental functions, the impairment 'need not involve the violation of a separate statute.'" United States v. Ballistrea, 101 F.3d 827, 832 (2d Cir. 1996); United States v. Tuohey, 867 F.2d 534, 537 (9th Cir. 1989). Note, however, that the fraud must be addressed to the federal government; an electric cooperative receiving federal funds and supervision could not, for example, be treated as the "United States" under the defraud clause. *See* Tanner v. United States, 483 U.S. 107 (1987).

Courts have summarized the four elements of a § 371 conspiracy-to-defraud clause case as follows: "[T]he government need only show (1) [that defendant] entered into an agreement (2) to obstruct a lawful function of the government (3) by deceitful or dishonest means and (4) at least one overt act in furtherance of the conspiracy." *Tuohey*, 867 F.2d at 537 (quoting United States v. Caldwell, 989 F.2d 1056, 1059 (9th Cir. 1993)). Further,

> The fraud need not be common law fraud. It may involve misrepresentation or use of any means that are dishonest. The conspirators do not have to intend to prevent government action. The government need not suffer any pecuniary or property loss. The conspiracy may involve defrauding the United States by violating the customary practices or duties of a particular governmental agency or office. No showing of actual contact between the conspirators and the government is required.

Mark F. Pomerantz & Otto G. Obermaier, *Defending Charges of Conspiracy*, in 1 Otto G. Obermaier et al., White Collar Crime: Business and Regulatory Offenses § 4.02[2], at 4-18 (2018) (footnotes omitted).

2. Among the types of cases that have been successfully pursued under the "defraud" clause are:

> conspiracies that have among their objects (1) to interfere with the performance of official duties by government officials; (2) to make payments to government officials, usually to influence some matter pending before a government agency; (3) to deprive the United States of its proper governmental functions; (4) to embezzle or improperly obtain and use

governmental funds; (5) to fail to pay taxes; and (6) to deprive the Internal Revenue Service of information.

Pomerantz & Obermaier, *supra*, § 4.02[2], at 4-19 (footnotes omitted); *see also* U.S.A.M., *supra* note 7, Criminal Resource Manual No. 923. One notable recent example of a "defraud clause" charge involves the so-called Russian Investigation by Special Counsel Robert Mueller. The Special Counsel's office secured a grand jury indictment of 13 Russians and 3 Russian organizations accused of conducting a covert operation to manipulate social media during the U.S. presidential election and to help President Trump win the White House. *See* United States v. Internet Research Agency, *et al.*, Case 1:18-cr-00032-DLF (filed Feb. 16, 2018). The first count charged a conspiracy to defraud the United States under § 371. The alleged object of the conspiracy was "to enable the Defendants to interfere with U.S. political and electoral processes, including the 2016 presidential election." *Id.* ¶ 28. Specifically, the defendants were accused of conspiring to, through deceit, "impair[], obstruct[], and defeat[] the lawful functions of the Federal Election Commission [(FEC)], the U.S. Department of Justice, and the U.S. Department of State in administering federal requirements for disclosure of foreign involvement in certain domestic activities." *Id.* ¶ 9. Those lawful functions allegedly impaired included: the FEC's responsibility to enforce limits on foreign campaign contributions and to ensure accurate campaign finance reporting; the DOJ's responsibility for administering the Foreign Agent Registration Act (FARA), which establishes a registration, reporting, and disclosure regime for agents of foreign principals; and the State Department's visa issuance process.

3. The two clauses of § 371 raise potential charging challenges. To begin with the known, suppose that two persons enter into an agreement to pursue a single scheme to defraud a number of banks and are successful in executing their scheme through the mails and interstate wires. Should the government charge the case as one conspiracy, or may it charge a separate offense clause conspiracy count for each mail fraud, wire fraud, and bank fraud?

In *Braverman v. United States*, 317 U.S. 49 (1942), the defendants were indicted and convicted on seven counts, each charging a conspiracy to violate a different provision of the internal revenue code. They were sentenced to eight years' imprisonment, although the maximum penalty for each single violation of the conspiracy statute was (then) two years. Before the Supreme Court, the government conceded that only a single agreement had been proved, but claimed that separate punishments could constitutionally be imposed for the separate counts. The Court rejected the government's argument, stating that "the precise nature and extent of the conspiracy must be determined by reference to the agreement which embraces and defines its objects." *Id.* at 53. It then reasoned:

> Whether the object of a single agreement is to commit one or many crimes, it is in either case that agreement which constitutes the conspiracy which the statute punishes. The one agreement cannot be taken to be several agreements and hence several conspiracies because it envisages the violation of several statutes rather than one. The allegation in a single count of a conspiracy to commit several crimes is not duplicitous, for "The conspiracy is the crime, and that is one, however diverse its objects." A conspiracy is not the commission of the crimes which it contemplates, and neither violates nor "arises under" the statute whose violation is its object. ... The single agreement is the prohibited conspiracy, and however diverse its objects it violates but a single statute, [§ 371] of the Criminal Code. For such a violation only the single penalty prescribed by the statute can be imposed.

Id. at 53-54. The *Braverman* ruling assists the defense in eliminating the possibility of cumulation of statutory maximum penalties that a contrary ruling would have permitted. However,

> [b]y holding that a single conspiracy may embrace a multiplicity of criminal objectives the rule affects the determination of the conspiracy's scope for all purposes. Consequently it operates to the defendant's disadvantage insofar as these purposes involve a conspirator's

accountability for all the activities of all the persons embraced in the conspiracy, for example, with respect to his liability for substantive crimes, the admissibility against him of hearsay acts and declarations, and satisfaction of the overt act requirement or statutes of limitations or rules of venue and jurisdiction.

ALI, Model Penal Code § 5.03, Comment at 438. Additionally, the Supreme Court has held that where in a multiple-object conspiracy case the evidence is determined to be inadequate as to one of the objects, a general verdict of guilty should still be sustained if the evidence is adequate to support conviction as to any one of the objects. *See* Griffin v. United States, 502 U.S. 46 (1991).

4. Where the government wishes to pursue a given agreement under both the offense clause and the defraud clause, should the agreement be charged as a single conspiracy with multiple criminal objects or as two different conspiracies? The *Arch Trading* court indicates that the former is appropriate, but there is an apparent disagreement among the circuits on the issue whether the two clauses of § 371 should be treated as separate offenses or as alternative means of commission of the same crime. *Compare* United States v. Ervasti, 201 F.3d 1029, 1040 & n.9 (8th Cir. 2000) (upholding government's decision to pursue in two counts the same agreement because offense and defraud clause are distinct offenses for double jeopardy purposes), *with* United States v. Rigas, 605 F.3d 194 (3d Cir. 2010) (*en banc*) (double jeopardy forbids separate punishments for violating the "offense" and "fraud" clauses of § 371); United States v. Smith, 891 F.2d 703, 711-12 (9th Cir. 1989) (holding that because § 371 creates alternative means of commission, not separate offenses, count charging both clauses was not defective on duplicity grounds).

Prosecutors contemplating a "defraud clause" charge should also be careful to include sufficient language describing the conduct deemed criminal so as to adequately inform the defendant of the crime with which he is charged, especially where a more specific statute applies to the conduct at issue. *See* United States v. Minarik, 875 F.2d 1186 (6th Cir. 1989) (reversing conviction under defraud clause because the defendant was charged with defrauding the Treasury by impeding its functions but the indictment did not spell out the functions impeded); *see also* U.S.A.M., *supra* note 7, Criminal Resource Manual No. 923.

2. AGREEMENT

a. Plurality

UNITED STATES v. STEVENS
909 F.2d 431 (11th Cir.1990)

RONEY, SENIOR CIRCUIT JUDGE:

In this criminal conspiracy case, we hold that a sole stockholder who completely controls a corporation and is the sole actor in performance of corporate activities, cannot be guilty of a criminal conspiracy with that corporation in the absence of another human actor. We therefore reverse the conspiracy conviction of defendant Gary S. Stevens. ... The indictment alleged the following scheme: Stevens formed four separate corporations in the state of Florida for the purpose of performing government contract work. The corporations entered into a government contract with the U.S. Navy to build an automated storage and retrieval system at the Portsmouth Naval Shipyard in Kittery, Maine. The contract provided for periodic progress payments from the Government as designated aspects of the project were completed.

Stevens was the sole shareholder of these corporations and exercised sole control over them. He was also the only agent of the corporations who executed forms relating to these contracts. Stevens misrepresented that certain work had been performed in several requests for progress payments. Stevens applied for both personal and commercial loans at several federally insured banks, duplicitously listing as security the income derived from this contract.

The jury focused on the issue, presented by this appeal, concerning the alleged conspiracy between Stevens and his corporations. During deliberations, it submitted several written questions to the district court, including the following:

> Can a person conspire with his own corporation, realizing that he is the primary (only) agent of his own corporation?
> Can we have a definition of conspiracy as it applies to wholly owned corporations?

The district court judge responded in writing that a person was legally able to conspire with his wholly owned corporation, and that the general definition of conspiracy applies to both humans and corporations.

Although a conspiracy under 18 U.S.C.A. § 371 requires an agreement between two or more persons, we have held that a corporation may be held criminally liable under § 371 when conspiring with its officers or employees. In so holding, we rejected the "single entity" theory that all agents of a corporation engaging in corporate conduct form a single, collective legal person—that is, the corporation—and that the acts of each agent constitute the acts of the corporation. The single entity theory shielded intracorporate associations of individuals from conspiracy liability on the rationale that a corporation cannot conspire with itself any more than a private individual can.

Distinguishing the antitrust context in which the single entity theory first arose, this Court decided that in the context of a criminal conspiracy to defraud the Government, the single entity theory contravened "the underlying purpose that led to the creation of the fiction of corporate personification. It originated to broaden the scope of corporate responsibility; we will not use it to shield individuals or corporations from criminal liability." *United States v. Hartley*, 678 F.2d 961, 972 (11th Cir. 1982).

Hartley makes two important holdings in the field of intracorporate conspiracy. *First*, it holds that a group of conspirators cannot escape conspiracy responsibility merely because they all act on behalf of a corporation. *Second*, *Hartley* holds that liability for a conspiracy may be imputed to the corporation itself on a respondeat superior theory.

> The [corporate] fiction was never intended to prohibit the imposition of criminal liability by allowing a corporation or its agents to hide behind the identity of the other. We decline to expand the fiction only to limit corporate responsibility in the context of the criminal conspiracy now before us.
> ... In these situations, the action by an incorporated collection of individuals creates the 'group danger' at which conspiracy liability is aimed, and the view of the corporation as a single legal actor becomes a fiction without a purpose.

In this case, we confront a different situation: there is only one human actor, acting for himself and for the corporate entity which he controls. In the great majority of reported decisions involving intracorporate conspiracies under § 371, there were multiple human conspirators in addition to the corporate coconspirator. Some cases have expressly indicated that multiple actors must be involved.

The argument that a single human actor can be convicted of conspiracy under § 371 under the circumstances of this case flies in the face of the traditional justification for criminal conspiracies. Conspiracy is a crime separate from the substantive criminal offense which is the purpose of the conspiracy. This separate punishment is targeted not at the substantive offenses themselves, but at the danger posed to society by combinations of individuals acting in concert.

> This settled principle derives from the reason of things in dealing with socially reprehensible conduct: collective criminal agreement—partnership in crime—presents a greater potential threat to the public than individual delicts. Concerted action both increases the likelihood that the criminal object will be successfully attained and decreases the probability that the individuals involved will depart from their path of criminality. Group association for criminal purposes often, if not normally, makes possible the

attainment of ends more complex than those which one criminal could accomplish. Nor is the danger of a conspiratorial group limited to the particular end toward which it has embarked. Combination in crime makes more likely the commission of crimes unrelated to the original purpose for which the group was formed. In sum, the danger which a conspiracy generates is not confined to the substantive offense which is the immediate aim of the enterprise.

The threat posed to society by these combinations arises from the creative interaction of two autonomous minds. It is for this reason that the essence of a conspiracy is an *agreement*. The societal threat is of a different quality when one human simply uses the corporate mechanism to carry out his crime. The danger from agreement does not arise.

Even if it can be said that Stevens made up his mind as an individual to pursue fraudulent ends and at the same time made up the "minds" of his corporations to pursue these same ends, this case lacks any interaction between multiple autonomous actors. The basis for punishing Stevens for the separate offense of conspiracy, in addition to the substantive offenses he committed, is not present in this case.

Although it takes three incorporators to form a corporation in Florida, the Government does not assert that the incorporators, other than Stevens, were in any way involved in the criminal objective.

We accordingly reverse Stevens's conviction for conspiracy under § 371. ...

Notes

1. What, according to the court, is the reason why the "agreement" is the central element of conspiracy? Why may conspiracy be punished separate and apart from the criminal objective of the conspiracy? Professor Neal Katyal identifies two reasons why conspiracies are more harmful than simply the crimes that are their object: "specialization of labor/economies of scale and the development of a pernicious group identity." He argues:

> The former is easily understood by thinking about how difficult it is for an individual to rob a bank alone. Several individuals are needed to carry weapons and provide firepower (economies of scale), someone needs to be the "brains behind the operation" (a form of specialization of labor), another should serve as a lookout (specialization again). Conspiracy creates obvious efficiencies... .
>
> What are somewhat less obvious, but are at least as important, are psychological accounts of the dangers of group activity. Advances in psychology in the past thirty years have demonstrated that groups cultivate a special social identity. This identity often encourages risky behavior, leads individuals to behave against their self-interest, solidifies loyalty, and facilitates harm against non-members. The psychological and economic accounts explain why law treats conspiracy in a distinctive way. The law focuses on "agreement" because that decision has drastic consequences. The law seeks to attach a broad and potentially uncognizable set of penalties at this early stage to deter many from becoming conspirators.

Neal Kumar Katyal, *Conspiracy Theory*, 112 Yale L.J. 101, 104 (2003). What implications do these rationales have for the formulation of the elements of, and defenses to, conspiracy liability? In the context of *Stevens*, are you persuaded by the court's explanation for why the dangers presented by criminal agreements are not present here?

2. Another purpose underlying a stand-alone conspiracy offense is to provide the government with a means of nipping criminal activity in the bud. As the Second Circuit explained in *United States v. Wallach*, 935 F.2d 445 (2d Cir. 1991):

> "It is well settled that the law of conspiracy serves ends different from, and complementary to, those served by criminal prohibitions of the substantive offense." The law of conspiracy serves two independent values: (1) it protects society from the dangers of

concerted criminal activity, and (2) it serves a preventive function by stopping criminal conduct in its early stages of growth before it has a full opportunity to bloom. As the applicable law has been summarized:

> The law of conspiracy identifies the agreement to engage in a criminal venture as an event of sufficient threat to social order to permit the imposition of criminal sanctions for the agreement alone, plus an overt act in pursuit of it, regardless of whether the crime agreed upon actually is committed. Criminal intent has crystallized, and the likelihood of actual, fulfilled commission warrants preventive action.

Id. at 470 (quoting United States v. Feola, 420 U.S. 671, 694 (1975)).

3. *Stevens* treats the recurring issue of what constitutes a plurality of actors for criminal conspiracy purposes where one or more corporate agents scheme to commit a crime. *See generally* Sarah N. Welling, *Intracorporate Plurality in Criminal Conspiracy Law*, 33 Hastings L.J. 1155 (1982). Readers should bear in mind that the *Stevens* holding constitutes an exception to the general rule, which states that when two or more agents of a corporation conspire together on behalf of the corporation, this is an actionable conspiracy, *see, e.g.*, United States v. Hartley, 678 F.2d 961, 972 (11th Cir. 1982); United States v. Ames Sintering Co., 927 F.2d 232 (6th Cir. 1990), and may subject the corporation to liability along with the corporate agents, *see id.*; United States v. Hughes Aircraft Co., Inc., 20 F.3d 974, 978-79 (9th Cir. 1994).

4. This general rule is inapplicable in another context—civil suits under the Sherman Act, 15 U.S.C. § 1 ("Every contract, combination ... or conspiracy, in restraint of trade or commerce ... is ... unlawful [and] [e]very person who shall make any contract or engage in any combination or conspiracy hereby declared to be illegal shall be deemed guilty of a felony"). Individual officers, employees, or directors within a corporation, acting on behalf of the corporation, are legally incapable of conspiring with each other or the corporation for § 1 purposes. *See, e.g.*, Nelson Radio & Supply v. Motorola, 200 F.2d 911, 914 (5th Cir. 1952). Further, in *Copperweld Corp. v. Independence Tube Corp.*, 467 U.S. 752 (1984), the Supreme Court held that a corporation and its wholly owned subsidiary are incapable of conspiring with each other for purposes of § 1. Why does this make sense in the Sherman Act context but not in a criminal § 371 case?

5. In many cases, the question is not whether the two parties are legally capable of constituting an actionable conspiracy, but rather whether the alleged coconspirators in fact had an *agreement*. How does the government prove that two or more individuals got together and agreed to commit a crime? Rarely do coconspirators reduce their criminal plans to writing. Absent cooperation from one or more coconspirators, or evidence in the form of vicarious admissions by coconspirators, the evidence will generally be circumstantial. The following is a fairly typical statement of the law:

> The existence of—and a particular defendant's participation in—a conspiracy may be established entirely by circumstantial evidence. Moreover, the conspiratorial agreement itself may be established by evidence of a tacit understanding among the participants, rather than by proof of an explicit agreement ....
>
> An individual defendant's membership in a conspiracy may not be established simply by his presence at the scene of a crime, nor by the fact he knows that a crime is being committed. Instead, membership requires proof of purposeful behavior aimed at furthering the goals of the conspiracy.

United States v. Desimone, 119 F.3d 217, 223 (2d Cir. 1997); *see also* United States v. Migliaccio, 34 F.3d 1517 (10th Cir. 1994) (insufficient proof of agreement).

b. Intent, Impossibility, and Withdrawal

UNITED STATES v. RECIO

537 U.S. 270 (2003)

Justice BREYER delivered the opinion of the Court.

We here consider the validity of a Ninth Circuit rule that a conspiracy ends automatically when the object of the conspiracy becomes impossible to achieve—when, for example, the Government frustrates a drug conspiracy's objective by seizing the drugs that its members have agreed to distribute. In our view, conspiracy law does not contain any such "automatic termination" rule.

In *United States v. Cruz*, 127 F.3d 791, 795 (C.A.9 1997), the Ninth Circuit ... wrote that a conspiracy terminates when "'there is affirmative evidence of abandonment, withdrawal, disavowal *or defeat of the object of the conspiracy*'" (emphasis added). It considered the conviction of an individual who, the Government had charged, joined a conspiracy (to distribute drugs) after the Government had seized the drugs in question. The Circuit found that the Government's seizure of the drugs guaranteed the "defeat" of the conspiracy's objective, namely, drug distribution. The Circuit held that the conspiracy had terminated with that "defeat," *i.e.*, when the Government seized the drugs. Hence the individual, who had joined the conspiracy after that point, could not be convicted as a conspiracy member.

In this case the lower courts applied the *Cruz* rule to similar facts ....

In *Cruz*, the Ninth Circuit held that a conspiracy continues "'until there is affirmative evidence of abandonment, withdrawal, disavowal or defeat of the object of the conspiracy.'" The critical portion of this statement is the last segment, that a conspiracy ends once there has been "defeat of [its] object." The Circuit's holdings make clear that the phrase means that the conspiracy ends through "defeat" when the Government intervenes, making the conspiracy's goals impossible to achieve, even if the conspirators do not know that the Government has intervened and are totally unaware that the conspiracy is bound to fail. In our view, this statement of the law is incorrect. A conspiracy does not automatically terminate simply because the Government, unbeknownst to some of the conspirators, has "defeat[ed]" the conspiracy's "object."

Two basic considerations convince us that this is the proper view of the law. First, the Ninth Circuit's rule is inconsistent with our own understanding of basic conspiracy law. The Court has repeatedly said that the essence of a conspiracy is "an agreement to commit an unlawful act." That agreement is "a distinct evil," which "may exist and be punished whether or not the substantive crime ensues." The conspiracy poses a "threat to the public" over and above the threat of the commission of the relevant substantive crime—both because the "[c]ombination in crime makes more likely the commission of [other] crimes" and because it "decreases the probability that the individuals involved will depart from their path of criminality." See also *United States v. Rabinowich*, 238 U.S. 78, 88 (1915) (conspiracy "sometimes quite outweigh[s], in injury to the public, the mere commission of the contemplated crime"). Where police have frustrated a conspiracy's specific objective but conspirators (unaware of that fact) have neither abandoned the conspiracy nor withdrawn, these special conspiracy-related dangers remain. Cf. 2 W. LaFave & A. Scott, Substantive Criminal Law §6.5,p. 85 (1986) ("[i]mpossibility" does not terminate conspiracy because "criminal combinations are dangerous apart from the danger of attaining the particular objective"). So too remains the essence of the conspiracy—the agreement to commit the crime. That being so, the Government's defeat of the conspiracy's objective will not necessarily and automatically terminate the conspiracy.

Second, the view we endorse today is the view of almost all courts and commentators but for the Ninth Circuit. No other Federal Court of Appeals has adopted the Ninth Circuit's rule. Three have explicitly rejected it. In *United States v. Wallace*, 85 F.3d 1063, 1068 (C.A.2 1996), for example, the court said that the fact that a "conspiracy cannot actually be realized because of facts unknown to the conspirators is irrelevant." One treatise, after surveying lower court conspiracy decisions, has concluded that "[i]mpossibility of success is not a defense." And the American Law Institute's Model Penal Code §5.03, p. 384 (1985), would find that a conspiracy "terminates when the crime or crimes that are its object are committed" or when the relevant "agreement ... is abandoned." It would not find "impossibility" a basis for termination.

The *Cruz* majority argued that the more traditional termination rule threatened "endless" potential liability. To illustrate the point, the majority posited a sting in which police instructed an arrested conspirator to go through the "telephone directory ... [and] call all of his acquaintances" to come and help him, with the Government obtaining convictions of those who did so. The problem with this example, however, is that, even though it is not necessarily an example of entrapment itself, it draws its persuasive force from the fact that it bears certain resemblances to entrapment. The law independently forbids convictions that rest upon entrapment. And the example fails to explain why a different branch of the law, conspiracy law, should be modified to forbid entrapment-like behavior that falls outside the bounds of current entrapment law. Cf. *United States v. Russell*, 411 U.S. 423, 435 (1973) ("defense of entrapment ... not intended to give the federal judiciary ... veto" over disapproved "law enforcement practices"). At the same time, the *Cruz* rule would reach well beyond arguable police misbehavior, potentially threatening the use of properly run law enforcement sting operations. See *Lewis v. United States*, 385 U.S. 206, 208-209 (1966) (Government may "use decoys" and conceal agents' identity); see also M. Lyman, Criminal Investigation 484-485 (2d ed. 1999) (explaining the importance of undercover operations in enforcing drug laws). ...

Notes

1. *Impossibility.* The Supreme Court in *Recio* recognizes that impossibility is not a defense to conspiracy, referencing a Second Circuit case, *United States v. Wallach*, 85 F.3d 1063 (2d Cir. 1996), as support. In *Wallach*, the defendant entered into a consulting agreement with a company, Wedtech, under which the defendant was to assist the company in selling its products to the U.S. government. His consulting compensation, however, was paid prematurely, and the accompanying documentation falsely portrayed that the payment was for services that he had not, in fact, rendered. This was arranged because the defendant informed the company that he would be receiving an appointment to a position in the U.S. Department of Justice from his close friend, then-Attorney General Edwin Meese. Wallach advised Wedtech that he wished to continue lobbying for the company while a full-time government officer. This, of course, is illegal under 18 U.S.C. § 203, which prohibits the receipt of or the agreement to receive any compensation for services to be rendered at a time when the intended recipient is an officer of the United States. Wallach ultimately did *not* receive a federal appointment, but he was charged with and convicted of, inter alia, conspiracy to violate § 203. The Second Circuit upheld his conviction, stating:

> ... [T]o establish the existence of a conspiracy the government need only establish the existence of an agreement and an overt act in furtherance of the agreement. "Whether the substantive crime itself is, or is likely to be, committed is irrelevant." Conspiracy is a crime separate and apart from the substantive offense that is the object of the conspiracy. Because it is the conspiratorial plan itself that is the focus of the charge, the illegality of the agreement is not dependent on the actual achievement of its goal. Indeed, "it does not matter that the ends of the conspiracy were from the beginning unattainable." ... Impossibility, therefore, is not a defense to a conspiracy charge. "[I]t is the intent of the defendants to violate the law which matters, not whether their conduct would actually violate the underlying substantive statute." The central question becomes whether the government's proof could establish that the accused planned to commit a substantive offense which, if attainable, would have violated a federal statute, and that at least one overt step was taken to advance the conspiracy's purpose.

Id. at 470-71; *see also* United States v. Min, 704 F.3d 314, 321-22 (4th Cir. 2013) (factual impossibility not a defense).

2. *Mens Rea.* If it is the conspirators' "intent" that is central, just what does that intent have to be? To be convicted of conspiracy, the government must prove that the defendant entered into an agreement with others "with *knowledge* of the criminal purpose of the scheme" and "with the *specific intent* to aid in the accomplishment of those unlawful ends." United States v. Svoboda, 347 F.3d 471, 477 (2d Cir. 2003) (emphasis added). Although these *mens rea* elements are demanding ones, it is important to note that they are often proven through inference. As the *Svoboda* court explained, "[c]onspiracies are secretive by their very nature, and it is well-settled that the elements of a conspiracy may be proved by circumstantial evidence." *Id.* The Second Circuit also holds that a defendant's *knowledge* of the aims of the conspiracy can be satisfied through willful blindness, although conscious avoidance cannot be used to prove the requisite intent to participate. *Id.* at 478-79.

3. *Withdrawal.* Finally, the *Recio* Court clarifies the rules concerning the termination of a conspiracy. Thus, a conspiracy may end where "*the defendant* abandoned, withdrew from, or disavowed the conspiracy *or defeated its purpose*," but not when that purpose is defeated by the government.

The general rule is that *before* any of the coconspirators engage in an overt act in furtherance of the conspiracy, or the crime that is the object of the conspiracy is committed, a party to the conspiratorial agreement may withdraw from the conspiracy and thus avoid liability. The question, however, is what acts are necessary to constitute an effective "withdrawal." As the Supreme Court noted in *United States v. U.S. Gypsum Co.*, 438 U.S. 422, 464-65 (1978), "[a]ffirmative acts inconsistent with the object of the conspiracy and communicated in a manner reasonably calculated to reach coconspirators have generally been regarded as sufficient to establish withdrawal or abandonment." *See also* Hyde v. United States, 225 U.S. 347, 369 (1912). Such affirmative acts could include, but are not limited to, notifying each member of the conspiracy that the former coconspirator will no longer participate or disclosure of the illegal scheme to law enforcement authorities. *See Gypsum*, 438 U.S. at 464-65; *see also* United States v. Bergman, 852 F.3d 1046 (11th Cir. 2017); United States v. Grimmett, 236 F.3d 452, 456 (8th Cir. 2001) (conspiracy charge time barred because defendant had withdrawn from the conspiracy more than five years previously when, after the killing of her drug-dealing boyfriend, she immediately and voluntarily disclosed to authorities enough incriminating information about the conspiracy to permit its defeat). "'Mere inaction would not be enough to demonstrate abandonment'" or withdrawal. *Gypsum*, 438 U.S. at 464-65. And it is the defendant's burden to establish an effective withdrawal. *See* Smith v. United States, 568 U.S. 106 (2013).

c. Defining the "Essential Nature" of the Agreement

UNITED STATES v. STAVROULAKIS
952 F.2d 686 (2d Cir.1992)

McLaughlin, Circuit Judge:

Nick Stavroulakis appeals from his convictions on all counts of a four-count indictment. Count One charged, pursuant to 18 U.S.C. § 371, that Stavroulakis conspired with Kostas Giziakis to violate the money laundering statute (18 U.S.C. § 1956) by attempting to conceal the source of certain money alleged to be the proceeds of unlawful activity, and to avoid the currency reporting requirements of Title 31. ...

In February 1989, a confidential government informant introduced Stavroulakis to an undercover FBI agent, David Maniquis, who said he was connected with organized-crime figures eager to launder substantial amounts of cash derived from narcotics transactions. Stavroulakis took the bait and agreed to introduce Maniquis to his accountant, Charlie Kirkelis, assuring Maniquis that if Kirkelis could not help, Stavroulakis had other ways to launder the cash.

When Kirkelis eventually demurred, Stavroulakis agreed to enlist the help of an acquaintance, Kostas Giziakis, an officer at the National Mortgage Bank of Greece ("NMBG"). Agent Maniquis was amenable to laundering the money through the NMBG, if, besides concealing the source of the money, Giziakis would also be willing to circumvent any currency reporting requirements. Maniquis stressed to Stavroulakis the need for secrecy because of the illegal source of the cash. Stavroulakis agreed that secrecy was paramount, and, with Maniquis' blessing, proceeded to contact Giziakis.

Soon thereafter, in May 1989, Stavroulakis and Agent Maniquis ventured to the NMBG branch in Astoria, Queens, to meet Giziakis. Prior to entering the bank, Stavroulakis outlined an elaborate scheme—which he and Giziakis had already concocted—for laundering the money: Stavroulakis would open an account at the NMBG in his own name, the money would be deposited in that account and then transferred to Greece, where it would be funneled through a fictitious corporation and returned to the NMBG, ostensibly as legitimate corporate earnings. Stavroulakis also told Maniquis that Giziakis was under the impression that the money was derived from gambling, rather than narcotics transactions. Stavroulakis explained that when he had first broached the subject with Giziakis, he had decided to tell Giziakis the money came from gambling because Giziakis appeared to have scruples about laundering narcotics money.

Once inside the NMBG, the three individuals ironed out the scheme to launder the money. Agent Maniquis represented to Giziakis that the cash was the product of a numbers operation run by his alleged associates. He informed Giziakis that his associates obtained hundreds of thousands of dollars per month in small bills from gambling, and that they wanted to make the cash appear to come from a legitimate source. Giziakis agreed to accommodate Maniquis, and said he could launder large amounts of cash through the NMBG.

Several weeks later the three of them met again at the NMBG. Because Stavroulakis was late for this meeting, Maniquis and Giziakis spoke privately for a few minutes. After handing Giziakis $2,000 in cash as the initial deposit, Maniquis warned Giziakis that gambling proceeds were almost always in small denominations, and told Giziakis of his concern over toting the money into the bank in a large gym bag. Giziakis assured Maniquis that this would be no problem. His concerns assuaged, Maniquis then told Giziakis that he would soon deposit $30,000 for the first month. At that point, Stavroulakis arrived and signed the account-opening card. The stage was now set to execute the scheme. ...

Stavroulakis argues that his conviction for conspiracy to violate the money laundering statute cannot stand because there was no agreement on the essential nature of the plan. More precisely, he claims that because he believed the money came from narcotics while Giziakis—his co-conspirator—believed it came from gambling, no conspiratorial agreement existed. We disagree.

The money laundering statute provides in pertinent part:

(3) Whoever, with the intent—
(A) to promote the carrying on of specified unlawful activity;
(B) to conceal or disguise the nature, location, source, ownership, or control of property believed to be the proceeds of specified unlawful activity; or
(C) to avoid a transaction reporting requirement under State or Federal law, conducts or attempts to conduct a financial transaction involving property represented by a law enforcement officer to be the proceeds of specified unlawful activity, or property used to conduct or facilitate specified unlawful activity, shall be fined under this title or imprisoned for not more than 20 years, or both.

18 U.S.C. § 1956(a)(3). Subsection (c)(7) of this statute then defines the term "specified unlawful activity," and it enumerates a myriad of activities that are illegal under either federal or state law, including *both* felony-level gambling and narcotics transactions. 18 U.S.C. § 1956(c)(7).

The issue, therefore, is whether a conspiracy to violate 18 U.S.C. § 1956(a)(3) requires that the co-conspirators believe that the money to be laundered is derived from the *same* specified unlawful activity. To be more specific, is there a conspiracy to launder money when one of the conspirators believes the cash stems from narcotics transactions while the other believes the money came from illegal gambling? We believe the answer must be yes.

A conspiracy involves an agreement by at least two parties to achieve a particular illegal end. While the conspirators need not agree on every detail of their venture, there must be proof beyond a reasonable doubt that they agreed on the "essential nature of the plan." It is not required that they agree on the ancillary aspects of a scheme not running to the heart of the agreement. The policies underlying conspiratorial liability could easily be thwarted by the careful compartmentalization of information, and "conspirators would go free by their very ingenuity," if it were required that they agree on all details of the scheme. To vindicate these policies, we focus on the essence of the underlying illegal objective to determine whether the conspirators agreed on "what kind of criminal conduct was in fact contemplated." Where, as here, the indictment charges a conspiracy under the "offense" clause of the conspiracy statute, the conspirators must have agreed to commit the same offense to satisfy the rule that they have agreed on the essential nature of the plan.

The issue can be distilled, therefore, to the question whether, as part of the "essential nature" of a conspiracy to launder unlawfully acquired money, it is necessary that the conspirators agree on where the unlawful money will come from. We think not. We hold that, so long as the unlawful source is proven to be one of the illegal activities enumerated in § 1956(c)(7), it is not essential that the conspirators agree on the same illegal activity.

Section 1956 creates the crime of money laundering, and it takes dead aim at the attempt to launder dirty money. Why and how that money got dirty is defined in other statutes. Section 1956 does not penalize the underlying unlawful activity from which the tainted money is derived. That the money is represented to be the proceeds of one of the listed, illegal sources is, of course, essential to culpability. The statute, however, does not distinguish among these specified unlawful activities either in degrees of importance or levels of criminal culpability. All the specified unlawful activities are clustered, almost willy-nilly, under a single definition section of the statute. So long as the cash is represented to have come from *any* of these activities, a defendant is guilty of the substantive offense of money laundering.

Defendant's argument would require us to accept that one who launders illegal gambling money has engaged in a course of conduct essentially different from that of someone who launders narcotics money. Congress has made clear that concealing the source of illegal gambling proceeds is just as detrimental to society as concealing the source of narcotics money. The crime is the same: money laundering; the *particular* underlying activity specified by Congress is a necessary, but ancillary, concern.

Defendant makes the policy argument that because some individuals—such as Giziakis—might be willing to launder gambling money but not narcotics money, the *particular* specified unlawful activity is an essential element of the crime. Again, we need look only to the language of the statute to reject this argument. Congress did not distinguish among the specified unlawful activities; both gambling and narcotics proceeds trigger the money laundering statute.

The legislative history, while scant, supports our view that the focal point of the statute is the laundering process, not the underlying unlawful conduct that soiled the money. ...

Because individuals who are willing to conceal the source of illegal booty have become so necessary to the secrecy that organized-crime figures and drug dealers cherish, Congress decided to criminalize the laundering activity. The statute was designed to create a new federal crime, rather than to further penalize the underlying criminal conduct. In 1988, Congress added subsection (a)(3) to the money laundering statute. At that time, Senator Biden emphasized that the purpose of this amendment was to enhance the ability of law-enforcement officers "to obtain evidence necessary to convict *money launderers*." Thus, while not overwhelming, the legislative history supports our view that the essential nature of a conspiracy to violate Section 1956 is an agreement to launder money, regardless of which particular specified unlawful activity is the source. ...

Notes

1. How does the court go about determining what the essential nature of the agreement was? *See also* United States v. Tum, 707 F.3d 68, 75 (1st Cir. 2013). Should the focus be on the legislation or the parties' actual intention? Why is defining the "essential nature" of the agreement important as a practical matter?

2. If the court had come out the other way and determined that the parties' differing understandings of that which was being laundered precluded a finding that they had entered into a conspiracy, could the government have proceeded on the theory that each conspired with the undercover agent? Once again, the question is what constitutes a plurality of actors in this circumstance. The money laundering statute contemplates, in a discrete section addressed specifically to "sting" operations, that a prosecution may proceed on substantive money laundering (not conspiracy) charges even though the defendant never dealt with a "real" coconspirator, only undercover agents. *See* 18 U.S.C. § 1956(a)(3).

Under prevailing federal conspiracy law, however, courts endorse a "bilateral" approach under which there can be no conspiracy between a defendant and a government informer or undercover agent because "it takes two to conspire and the government informer is not a true conspirator." United States v. Portela, 167 F.3d 687, 700 n. 8 (1st Cir. 1999). The courts reason that the government agent "lacks the criminal intent necessary to render him a bona fide coconspirator," United States v. Desimone, 119 F.3d 217, 223 (2d Cir. 1997), and that "[t]here is neither a true agreement nor a meeting of the minds when an individual 'conspires' to violate the law with only one other person and that person is a government agent." United States v. Schmidt, 947 F.2d 362, 367 (9th Cir. 1991). The Model Penal Code takes the alternative, "unilateral," approach, under which it is "immaterial to the guilt of a conspirator whose culpability has been established that the person or all of the persons with whom he conspired had not been or cannot be convicted." *See* ALI, Model Penal Code § 5.03 & commentary at 399.

Given the reasons why conspiracy is viewed as a crime distinct from the criminal activity that underlies it, what is the correct resolution of this question? Have the criminal project's chances of success been heightened by the agreement with an undercover agent? What relevance should the defendant coconspirator's firm intent to commit a crime have?

3. At one time, the common law "rule of consistency" held sway in federal and state courts. *See* United States v. Tyson, 653 F.3d 192, 207 (3d Cir. 2011). That rule required that where all possible co-conspirators are jointly tied, and all but one are acquitted, the conviction of the remaining alleged co-conspirator cannot stand. *Id.* But the Supreme Court hastened the demise of this rule by its reasoning on a related issue in *United States v. Powell*, 469 U.S. 57 (1984). The defendant in *Powell* was tried alone, thus the "rule of consistency" was not applicable. But Powell was found guilty of using a telephone to facilitate the drug conspiracy for which she was acquitted. As the Third Circuit has explained in declaring the "rule of consistency" dead:

> The [*Powell*] Court held that although this result was inconsistent, it was not for a judge to go behind the jury's decision in such circumstances. True, the verdict may have been the product of juror error or plain irrationality. But an inconsistent verdict may also be the product of juror lenity, which historically has operated "as a check against arbitrary or oppressive exercises of power by the Executive Branch." The point, according to *Powell*, is that a reviewing court cannot know why the jury reached its verdict. Rather than task courts with the responsibility to find out, the *Powell* Court held that inconsistent verdicts are not reviewable merely because they are inconsistent.
>
> *Powell* does not directly address inconsistency among jointly tried co-conspirators, but every court of appeals to consider the question has held that *Powell's* logic fatally undermines the rule of consistency. ... [U]nder *Powell*, "the acquittal of all but one co-conspirator during the same trial does not necessarily indicate that the jury found no agreement to act." Instead, the verdict may represent a manifestation of lenity, which *Powell* clearly held was not subject to judicial review.

Tyson, 653 F.3d at 207-08 (collecting cases).

3. DEFINING THE SCOPE OF THE CONSPIRACY

In many cases the question is not whether the defendant committed or conspired to commit crimes; the evidence may amply demonstrate the defendant's individual wrongdoing. Rather, the issue that frequently is litigated is whether the government has appropriately charged *the scope* of the conspiracy—that is, whether the defendant is a conspirator with each of the persons alleged in a large, single conspiracy or whether the criminal activity at issue involves several smaller conspiracies. Among defense lawyers' greatest concerns regarding the use (or alleged misuse) of conspiracy charges is prosecutors' perceived tendency to fold as much criminal conduct as possible under the umbrella of a single overarching conspiracy rather than charging defendants individually for the crimes they personally committed or breaking a group of wrongdoers into more appropriate, smaller alleged conspiracies for charging and trial purposes. As defense counsel express the problem:

> One reason why a conspiracy charge remains "the darling of the modern prosecutor's nursery" is the seemingly limitless breadth of conspiracy charges found in federal indictments—a practice the evolved in the prosecution of large-scale narcotics conspiracies. As a result, a white-collar defendant also can find himself lumped together with a host of alleged co-conspirators charged with conspiring to commit a vast range of financial crimes—some or most of which he had nothing to do with.[29]

The following materials explain the principles applied to determine the proper scope of a charged conspiracy, as well as the implications that flow from that determination. In so doing, they should illustrate the reasons why prosecutors largely prefer, and defense counsel generally abhor, charges that include a broader rather than narrower conspiracy count.

UNITED STATES v. GATLING
96 F.3d 1511 (D.C. Cir. 1996)

WALD, CIRCUIT JUDGE:

...

Section 8 is a federal housing assistance program administered through local public housing authorities. Under the section 8 program, qualified applicants can obtain subsidies in the form of vouchers or certificates to help cover their rent. From 1988 through 1992, section 8 subsidies were distributed in the District of Columbia by the Section 8 Division of [the District of Columbia's Department of Public and Assisted Housing ("DPAH")]. [Appellant Cheryl Walker ("Walker")] began working at DPAH in 1989 as Chief of the Section 8 Division, and became Acting Administrator of the Subsidized Housing Administration at DPAH in 1992. From 1989 to 1993, [appellant Jennifer Gatling ("Gatling")] was a Housing Specialist in the Section 8 Division. Both Walker and Gatling were suspended from their positions at DPAH in 1993.

Under federal and D.C. regulations in effect from 1989 to 1993, section 8 subsidies were only available to D.C. residents who met certain income requirements and were on a wait list for subsidies. The wait list was necessary because only a limited number of subsidies were given to DPAH and other local housing authorities each year, and the demand for section 8 subsidies far outstripped the supply of available subsidies. The wait list was divided into several categories based on different need criteria, such as "homeless and living in a D.C. shelter" or "living in a unit unfit for habitation," and within each category applicants were listed by the date and time of their application. The regulations established preferences among these need

---

[29] Wing & Bresnick, *supra* note 6, at 1.

categories and required that subsidies be offered first to applicants in the highest need category. Only when everyone in this category had received a subsidy could subsidies be offered to individuals in the next highest need category, and so on. Within each category, subsidies were to be offered to applicants in accordance with their position on the wait list. The regulations also provided that 10 percent of the subsidies could be allocated to lower preference need categories even if individuals in higher preference categories had not received subsidies. Individuals were required to apply in person for section 8 subsidies unless they were elderly or disabled, and applicants often remained on the wait list for several years before they obtained subsidies.

... On September 9, 1994, a grand jury charged Walker and Gatling with conspiring to accept bribes in return for section 8 subsidies. Walker and Gatling were also charged with several counts of accepting bribes, mail fraud, and making false statements. Trial began on November 29, 1994, and lasted more than six weeks.

At trial, the government claimed that in exchange for bribes Walker and Gatling gave section 8 subsidies to individuals who were not eligible to receive them because they were not D.C. residents and were not on the wait list, or, if they were on the wait list, were not next in line in the appropriate need category. The government offered evidence indicating that several Chicago residents had applied for and received section 8 subsidies through DPAH by mail, using false D.C. addresses, and then transferred the subsidies to Chicago. A critical witness for the government regarding subsidies received by Chicago residents was Anthony Bufford ("Bufford"), who pled guilty to attempted bribery. Bufford, who knew Walker's sister, testified that he contacted Walker about arranging a section 8 subsidy for his former wife, Veronica Bufford. He stated that Walker told him to contact Walker's assistant, Gatling, to get help on filling out the section 8 application, even though Walker knew that Veronica Bufford was a Chicago resident. Veronica Bufford testified that Gatling assisted her in submitting a section 8 application which falsely claimed that Veronica Bufford lived and worked in D.C. Bufford also reported that he told Walker he would "make it worth her while," that he offered Walker $1,000 after Walker had said she would arrange for Veronica Bufford to receive a subsidy, and that he sent Walker $1,000 when the section 8 voucher arrived in the mail. A copy of Veronica Bufford's section 8 voucher, dated June 28, 1991, was introduced into evidence.

Bufford further testified that he later contacted Walker about arranging a section 8 subsidy for Camilla Perkins-Henry ("Perkins-Henry"), the widow of a friend of Bufford's. According to Bufford, he told Walker that Perkins-Henry was a Chicago resident and Walker stated that she "would do basically what she had done" for Veronica Bufford. Bufford also stated that he offered to make the same payment of $1,000, that Walker suggested he make the check out to Gatling because Gatling needed the money, and that Perkins-Henry was referred to Gatling for help in filling out the application. Perkins-Henry testified that she spoke to Gatling in regard to her section 8 application and gave Bufford a check for $1,000 made out to Gatling. The government introduced a copy of Perkins-Henry's section 8 voucher, dated March 9, 1992, and a copy of a canceled check for $1,000 she made out to Gatling, dated March 20, 1992, that had been deposited to Gatling's account.

The government also offered substantial evidence on section 8 subsidies that were issued to D.C. residents in exchange for money. The evidence consisted mainly of testimony from individuals who had obtained subsidies in this fashion from September 1991 through April 1992. According to these witnesses, they had heard through either Darnell Jackson ("Jackson") or Rodney Knight ("Knight") that section 8 subsidies were available for $500, and that once they had the $500 in cash, either Jackson or Knight, or both, drove them to DPAH. Several of these witnesses also testified that Jackson told them what documents to bring, such as their children's birth certificates, and instructed them to carry the money in an envelope. At DPAH, Gatling took the applicants back to her office and filled out the necessary paperwork. The section 8 subsidies were usually provided at the same meeting, after the paperwork was completed and the applicants had given Gatling the $500. Most witnesses testified that they put the envelope containing $500 on Gatling's desk and that Gatling put the envelope in a desk drawer. One witness testified that she gave the $500 to Jackson and thought she saw Jackson slip the money to Gatling when he hugged her goodbye. There was also evidence that the individuals who testified to receiving section 8 subsidies in this fashion either were not on the section 8 wait list at the time or, if they were on the list, were not next in line for subsidies.

Jackson, who was charged with conspiracy to accept bribes and with aiding and abetting the acceptance of a bribe, did not testify at trial. Knight, who pled guilty to attempted bribery, did testify and his testimony corroborated that of the D.C. residents who had obtained section 8 subsidies with Gatling's help. Knight stated that Jackson was a friend of Gatling's and that on several occasions he heard Jackson tell recipients that Gatling was "splitting the money" with Walker. According to Knight, Jackson made this statement "to convince whoever was getting a Section 8 voucher that it was all good." Knight's niece Judy Johnson, one of the witnesses who paid Gatling for a section 8 subsidy, testified that she asked Jackson how Gatling could arrange the subsidies and he responded that Walker, "her supervisor[,] was in doing it with her." Judy Johnson also testified that Gatling spoke with Walker about whether Johnson's section 8 certificate should be for a two or three bedroom apartment, and Cynthia Knight, who paid Gatling for a section 8 certificate for her handicapped sister, testified that Walker helped Gatling photocopy the documents that Knight had brought. The government also introduced evidence that Walker had deposited over $6,000 to her children's savings accounts between July 1991 and October 1992.

The defense's evidence consisted primarily of Walker's testimony, in which she acknowledged arranging section 8 subsidies for Veronica Bufford and Perkins-Henry but denied receiving any money in exchange. She stated that she believed she was authorized to provide section 8 subsidies to non-D.C. residents and to individuals not on the wait list in allocating the 10 percent of subsidies that did not go automatically to individuals in the highest preference need category. She also claimed that the money in her children's accounts came from relatives. …

At the close of the government's case Walker made a motion for judgment of acquittal on the conspiracy and substantive bribery counts. The court first denied the motion, but later granted it in regard to the substantive bribery counts involving D.C. residents when the motion was renewed at the close of all evidence. On January 18, 1995, the jury convicted Walker of conspiracy to accept bribes and on one of the false statements counts. The jury acquitted Walker on all the other counts, except for one mail fraud count on which they were unable to reach a verdict. Gatling was convicted of conspiracy to accept bribes and four counts of accepting a bribe, and acquitted on all other counts. On May 30, 1995, Gatling received a 40 month jail sentence and on June 6, 1995, Walker received a 41 month jail sentence. …

The indictment charged Walker and Gatling with engaging in a single conspiracy to commit bribes which covered the issuance of subsidies to ineligible residents in both Chicago and D.C. Walker contends that the evidence at trial established at most the existence of two conspiracies, one involving Chicago residents and the other involving D.C. residents. If Walker's claim were correct, then there would have been a variance between the indictment and the evidence offered at trial. Such a variance can be grounds for reversal if it substantially prejudices the defendant, as, for example, if the jury were "substantially likely to transfer evidence from one conspiracy to a defendant involved in another." Walker argues that the variance she believes existed substantially prejudiced her because there was no evidence linking her to the D.C. conspiracy and it was extremely likely that the evidence on the D.C. conspiracy, which dominated the trial, spilled over into the jury's consideration of her role in the Chicago conspiracy. …

In determining whether the evidence supports a finding of a single conspiracy or instead only demonstrates multiple conspiracies, we look at whether the defendants "shared a common goal," any "interdependence between the alleged participants," and "any overlap among alleged participants," such as the presence of core participants linked to all the defendants. Both the Chicago and D.C. schemes shared a common purpose, namely obtaining money in exchange for section 8 subsidies. The differences between the two schemes—that Bufford contacted the appellants by phone to see if he could procure subsidies for two Chicago residents and sent the appellants $1,000 for each subsidy, whereas Jackson brought numerous D.C. residents to DPAH where they gave Gatling $500 in an envelope in exchange for their subsidies—are simply differences in their *modus operandi* and not differences in their underlying objective. Our case law makes clear that a conspiracy's purpose should not be defined in too narrow or specific terms. *See, e.g.*, [*United States v. Graham*, 83 F.3d 1466, 1471-72 (D.C.Cir.1996)] (drug distributing cliques that were in competition with one another were still part of a single conspiracy in part because they shared the common goal of selling one defendant's cocaine for profit). In any event, the two schemes do not appear to have been significantly dissimilar in operation; both involved section 8 subsidies issued through the DPAH office in Washington, D.C. and took advantage of the lax controls at that office over the issuance of subsidies.

In addition, there were significant overlaps between the timing and participants in the Chicago and D.C. schemes. Both occurred during the same period; the Chicago subsidies were provided in June 1991 and March 1992, while the D.C. subsidies were provided on ten occasions between September 1991 and April 1992. *Cf.* [*United States v. Childress*, 58 F.3d 693, 710 (D.C.Cir.1995)] (noting that some courts have been reluctant to find a single conspiracy "when certain participants are involved in the enterprise during radically different time periods"). In addition, Walker and Gatling were the main figures in both schemes. As discussed above, the testimony and documentary evidence at trial clearly indicated that Gatling was involved in both the Chicago and D.C. schemes, as well as that Walker was involved in the Chicago scheme. There was also evidence suggesting Walker's participation in the D.C. scheme. Walker made significant cash deposits to her children's accounts during the period, and two D.C. residents who illegally procured section 8 subsidies testified that Walker assisted Gatling in completing the paperwork on their subsidies. More significantly, Knight and his niece, Judy Johnson, testified that Jackson repeatedly stated that Walker and Gatling were splitting the money Gatling collected from D.C. residents.

Walker argues that the district court erred in admitting evidence of Jackson's statements against Walker because the statements constituted inadmissible hearsay. Federal Rule of Evidence 801(d)(2)(E) provides that an out-of-court statement by a co-conspirator during and in furtherance of a conspiracy is not hearsay, and therefore evidence of such a statement is admissible to prove the truth of any matter asserted therein. In order to admit a statement under Rule 801(d)(2)(E), the district court must find by a preponderance of the evidence that the person making the statement was a co-conspirator and that the statement was made during and in furtherance of the conspiracy. *Bourjaily v. United States*, 483 U.S. 171, 175-76 (1987). This circuit additionally requires that there be independent evidence of the conspiracy apart from the statement, although the content of the statement itself can also be considered in determining whether such independent evidence exists. ...

The district court did not clearly err in admitting Jackson's statement against Walker because there was independent evidence indicating Walker and Jackson were co-conspirators. This independent evidence takes two forms. First, there was some evidence, albeit weak, suggesting Walker's participation in the issuance of subsidies to D.C. residents, namely that she made significant unexplained deposits to her children's accounts during the period and that she assisted Gatling with some details of two illegal D.C. subsidies. Second, as discussed above, the common purpose and timing of the Chicago and D.C. schemes and the participation of Gatling in both provide grounds for concluding that the two schemes were one single conspiracy. There is also substantial independent evidence indicating that both Walker and Jackson were participants in this single conspiracy, namely Bufford's testimony that Walker agreed to provide section 8 subsidies to Veronica Bufford and Perkins-Henry and the testimony from numerous D.C. residents that Jackson told them how they could buy section 8 subsidies and brought them to DPAH. ... Furthermore, once the content of Jackson's statements is considered there was clearly a sufficient basis for the court to find by a preponderance of the evidence that Rule 801(d)(2)(E)'s requirements were met. The statements clearly linked Walker to the issuance of subsidies to D.C. residents and were made to reassure individuals that they would in fact receive a subsidy for their $500 payments.

It is true that the Chicago and D.C. schemes were not interdependent in the way that the separate groups involved in many drug "chain" conspiracies are, where each group is dependent on the actions of other groups for the venture as a whole to succeed. Here, the principal actions required for the success of the Chicago scheme—identifying individuals seeking subsidies, completing the applications, issuing the subsidies and transferring them to Chicago and receiving money—were unrelated to the actions necessary for the success of the D.C. scheme, and vice versa. Yet even in that regard there was some interdependence between the two schemes; given the overlap in participation and timing and the fact that all illegal subsidies were issued by DPAH, accusations relating to one of the schemes could trigger an investigation that would lead to exposure of both. We have previously found interdependence to exist when the assistance one branch of a conspiracy provides to another is fairly minimal. *Graham*, 83 F.3d at 1471-72 (interdependence exists when members of different and competing drug cliques occasionally assisted one another, even though this assistance was not significant to each clique's success); cf. *United States v. Macchia*, 35 F.3d 662, 667-68 (2d Cir.1994) (in determining whether two conspiracies amount to the same offense for double jeopardy purposes, court considers factors such as common purpose, overlap of participants and time, location where acts occurred, and interdependence but "no dominant factor or single touchstone" determines if two conspiracies are one offense); *United States v. Daily*, 921 F.2d 994, 1008 (10th Cir.1990) ("Generally, it is sufficient for purposes of a single-conspiracy finding that a conspirator knowingly participated with a core conspirator in achieving a common objective with knowledge of the larger venture.").

In sum, we find that this evidence of the common purpose, participants, timing and interdependence of the Chicago and D.C. schemes more than sufficient for a reasonable juror to conclude that a single conspiracy existed. ...

Notes

1. What are some of the advantages that flowed to the government from charging this case as a single overarching conspiracy? Some potential advantages include those discussed above, relating to joinder, statute of limitations, venue, and evidentiary advantages. Perhaps more important, as a consequence of such a charging choice, the defendant will not only be exposed to punishment for what he did, but he may also be punished for the conspiracy and, as we shall when discussing the *Pinkerton* doctrine, *infra*, all reasonably foreseeable substantive crimes committed by his co-conspirators in furtherance of the conspiracy, even if he was unaware of those crimes.

Defense counsel often lack confidence that a jury will adequately understand and apply an instruction that requires the jury to determine the appropriate contours of the conspiracy charged. "However fairly [a multiple conspiracy jury charge] may be presented, it is clearly not a sufficient or appropriate cure for the legal problem—particularly given the practical reality that such a charge is inevitably buried amid many complicated, mind-numbing instructions on other aspects of conspiracy law." Wing & Bresnick, *supra* note 6, at 9. And, as the Ninth Circuit has cautioned, "there is a tendency in conspiracy cases for the jury to believe that a defendant must have been involved in the alleged over-all conspiracy once it finds that the defendant committed one of the minor acts which the prosecution contends is but an extension of the greater conspiracy." United States v. Bailey, 607 F.2d 237, 245 (9th Cir. 1979). In light of these circumstances, should courts such as the *Gatling* court, apply a more stringent standard to test whether one conspiracy has been proved?

2. Two Supreme Court precedents are often employed in analyzing the single/multiple conspiracy question, the analysis of one of which is alluded to in *Gatling*. First, in *Kotteakos v. United States*, 328 U.S. 750 (1946), one individual, Simon Brown, undertook to act as a broker in securing for a variety of other persons loans on the basis of false and fraudulent information. Brown was the central and key figure in all the transactions proven. Brown and 32 others were indicted for a single conspiracy to violate the National Housing Act by fraudulently inducing lending institutions to make loans. The Supreme Court held, however, that the evidence proved eight or more different conspiracies by separate groups of defendants:

Except for Brown, the common figure, no conspirator was interested in whether any loan except his own went through. And none aided in any way, by agreement or otherwise, in procuring another's loan. The conspiracies therefore were distinct and disconnected, not parts of a larger general scheme, both in the phase of agreement with Brown and also in the absence of any aid given to others as well as in the specific object and result. ...

Blumenthal v. United States, 332 U.S. 539, 558 (1947) (explaining *Kotteakos*). The *Kotteakos* Court noted that the "pattern was 'that of separate spokes meeting in a common center,' though, we may add, without the rim of the wheel to enclose the spokes." *Kotteakos*, 328 U.S. at 755. The Supreme Court ultimately reversed the petitioner codefendants' conspiracy convictions, finding that their rights were substantially prejudiced by the fact that the case was charged as one conspiracy. In subsequent cases, courts have explained the *Kotteakos* "wheel" conspiracy theory as follows:

> For a [single] wheel conspiracy to exist those people who form the wheel's spokes must have been aware of each other and must do something in furtherance of some single, illegal enterprise. Otherwise the conspiracy lacks "the rim of the wheel to enclose the spokes." If there is not some interaction between those conspirators who form the spokes of the wheel as to at least one common illegal object, the "wheel" is incomplete, and two conspiracies rather than one are charged.

United States v. Levine, 546 F.2d 658, 663 (5th Cir. 1977).

Second, in *Blumenthal v. United States*, 332 U.S. 539 (1947), the indictment charged a single conspiracy to sell whiskey at prices above the ceiling set by the Office of Price Administration. The owner of the whiskey, through a series of middlemen, conducted a complex scheme pursuant to which he was able to conceal the true price for which he was selling the whiskey. Some of the middlemen had no contact with each other, and did not even know the identity of the owner of the whiskey. However, the Supreme Court determined, they had to know that they were indispensable cogs in the machinery through which the illegal scheme was executed:

> All [the defendants] intended to aid the owner ... to sell the whiskey unlawfully, though the two groups of defendants differed on the proof in knowledge and belief concerning the owner's identity. All ... sought a common end, to aid in disposing of the whiskey. True, each salesman aided in selling only his part. But he knew the lot to be sold was larger and thus that he was aiding in a larger plan. ...

Id. at 559. The Court thus concluded that "in every practical sense the unique facts of this case reveal a single conspiracy of which the several agreements were essential and integral steps." *Id.* The *Blumenthal* Court thus gave birth to the "chain" conspiracy. As subsequent courts have explained:

> The essential element of a chain conspiracy—allowing persons unknown to each other and never before in contact to be jointly prosecuted as co-conspirators—is interdependence. The scheme which is the object of the conspiracy must depend on the successful operation of each link in the chain. "An individual associating himself with a 'chain' conspiracy knows that it has a 'scope' and that for its success it requires an organization wider than may be disclosed by his personal participation". "Thus, in a 'chain' conspiracy prosecution, the requisite element—knowledge of the existence of remote links—may be inferred solely from the nature of the enterprise."

United States v. Elliott, 571 F.2d 880, 901 (5th Cir. 1978). The "chain" conspiracy theory is most often relied upon in drug cases but, as is demonstrated in *Blumenthal* itself, it may also be employed in large, complex white-collar crime cases.

3. In a case in which the theory of the prosecution is neither a classic chain nor a typical wheel conspiracy, what general factors do courts look to in evaluating whether a single or multiple conspiracies has been proven? What other factors might be relevant here and might counsel against a single conspiracy finding? Of what practical significance is the definition of a criminal course of conduct as a single or multiple conspiracy case?

4. Post-conviction challenges to the definition of the scope of the conspiracy, although very frequently lodged, are very rarely successful. *But see* Wing & Bresnick, *supra* note 6, at 1, 8-9 (discussing successful challenges). The following is a representative discussion:

> The essence of the crime of conspiracy is the agreement. "'[I]n order to prove a single conspiracy, the government must show that each alleged member agreed to participate in what he knew to be a collective venture directed toward a common goal.'" The government need not prove that each defendant "knew every other member or was aware of all acts committed in furtherance of" the conspiracy. Moreover, "'a single conspiracy is not transported into a multiple one simply by lapse of time, change in membership, or a shifting emphasis on its locale of operations.'" "Finally, a single conspiracy is not transformed into multiple conspiracies merely by virtue of the fact that it may involve two or more phases or spheres of operation, so long as there is sufficient proof of mutual dependence and assistance."

United States v. Aracri, 968 F.2d 1512, 1521 (2d Cir. 1992) (citations omitted). Indeed, a single conspiracy may be found where the coconspirators are demonstrably at odds:

> ... "[I]t is not at all uncommon for disagreements to occur in a common enterprise." Nor is it "inconsistent with such an ongoing, unitary conspiracy that disputes might arise ... and that switches in affiliation might occur from time to time." [United States v. Beech-Nut Nutrition Corp., 871 F.2d 1181, 1192 (2d Cir. 1989)] ("'That certain defendants were eager to cheat each other for a large slice of the spoils does not obscure the unifying means used by all of them to defraud the public.'"); [United States v. Nersesian, 824 F.2d 1294, 1303 (2d Cir. 1987)] ("That conspirators may have problems or difficulties in dealing with one another which result in angry accusations or heated discussions does not necessarily negate the existence of a single conspiracy").

Aracri, 968 F.2d at 1522; *see also* United States v. Marino, 277 F.3d 11 (1st Cir. 2002) (holding that statements by rival faction of organized-crime family were admissible as co-conspirators' statements against members of the faction with which they were at war).

5. Even where a defendant establishes to a reviewing court's satisfaction that he was not, as charged, party to a single overarching conspiracy, he does not automatically secure reversal of his conspiracy conviction. As the Second Circuit has explained:

> It is the law of this Circuit that when a defendant is charged with a single conspiracy among multiple members, and the proof at trial shows that he conspired with some, but not all, of those members, the variance is subject to the harmless error rule. In order to merit a reversal, "the variance must have caused the defendant 'substantial prejudice' at trial." Substantial prejudice is shown if the defendant can "prove that the evidence in support of the conspiracy ... in which he did not participate prejudiced the case against him with respect to the conspiracy to which he was a party."

United States v. McDermott, 277 F.3d 240, 242 (2d Cir. 2002) (holding defendant not prejudiced because virtually all the evidence received in support of the larger charged conspiracy would have been admitted in a trial of smaller conspiracy to which he was a party, and the "sensational highlight" of the government's evidence regarding his participation was his own SEC deposition testimony).

4. OVERT ACTS

Proof of an overt act is an element of a § 371 prosecution. The statute essentially "fixes the point of legal intervention at agreement to commit a crime ... coupled with an overt act."[30] It is

---

[30] ALI, Model Penal Code § 5.03, cmt. at 387.

not necessary that the overt act be the substantive crime charged as the object of the conspiracy. In fact, the overt act need not be an act that is in and of itself criminal in character.[31] Thus, the overt act may be a mailing, a meeting, a telephone call, or other facially innocent acts done in furtherance of the conspiracy. "Once a conspiracy is established, and an individual is linked to that conspiracy, an overt act committed by any conspirator is sufficient" to support liability for all.[32] Finally, a number of circuits have upheld conspiracy convictions where the government proves a different overt act than the act alleged in the indictment, finding such a variance did not affect the defendants' substantial rights; indeed, the Second Circuit has held that the jurors can convict under § 371 even if they do not unanimously agree on which overt act the government has proved.[33] Although the burden of proving an overt act beyond a reasonable doubt rests on the government, the above should indicate that it is rarely a difficult element to establish. Indeed, this requirement actually aids the government in many cases because it provides multiple bases for venue, as well as potentially extending the duration of the conspiracy for statute of limitations and evidentiary purposes.

Because the overt act may have little significance, conspiracy "reaches further back into preparatory conduct than attempt" liability.[34] Should this be so? Recall that impossibility is not a defense to conspiracy and that the focus is on the culpable intent of the parties, not on their likelihood of success. What dangers does this raise? Should the overt act requirement be beefed up to remove the potential that defendants will be jailed for evil thoughts/intentions alone?

Earlier cases debating the legal significance of the overt act (since settled to be an element of the offense) posited various reasons for the requirement. It can be seen as a way of proving that "'the conspiracy is at work' and is neither a project still resting solely in the minds of the conspirators nor a fully completed operation no longer in existence."[35] Alternatively, the requirement that "there must be an act done to effect the object of the conspiracy merely affords a *locus penitentice*, so that before the act [is] done, either one or all of the parties may abandon their design, and thus avoid the penalty prescribed by the statute."[36] Given the rationale(s) for such a proof requirement, why is an overt act an element of § 371 but not of Racketeer Influenced and Corrupt Organization Act (RICO) conspiracies or drug trafficking or importation conspiracies?

5. *PINKERTON* LIABILITY

PINKERTON v. UNITED STATES
328 U.S. 640 (1946)

MR. JUSTICE DOUGLAS delivered the opinion of the Court

Walter and Daniel Pinkerton are brothers who live a short distance from each other on Daniel's farm. They were indicted for violations of the Internal Revenue Code. The indictment contained ten substantive counts and one conspiracy count. The jury found Walter

---

[31] Braverman v. United States, 317 U.S. 49, 53 (1942).

[32] United States v. Schlei, 122 F.3d 944, 975 (11th Cir. 1997).

[33] *See* United States v. Kozeny, 667 F.3d 122, 130-32 (2d Cir. 2011) (no unanimity); United States v. Stoner, 98 F.3d 527, 531-33 (10th Cir. 1996) (no variance). Where the overt act alleged in the indictment is time-barred, however, the government may not revive its case at trial by proving a non-time-barred overt act. *See id.*

[34] ALI, Model Penal Code § 5.03, cmt. at 387.

[35] Yates v. United States, 354 U.S. 298, 334 (1957); *see also* Hyde v. United States, 225 U.S. 347, 388 (1912) (Holmes, J., dissenting) ("The overt act is simply evidence that the conspiracy has passed beyond words and is on foot when the act is done.").

[36] United States v. Britton, 108 U.S. 199, 205 (1883).

guilty on nine of the substantive counts and on the conspiracy count. It found Daniel guilty on six of the substantive counts and on the conspiracy count. ...

A single conspiracy was charged and proved. Some of the overt acts charged in the conspiracy count were the same acts charged in the substantive counts. Each of the substantive offenses found was committed pursuant to the conspiracy. Petitioners therefore contend that the substantive counts became merged in the conspiracy count, and that only a single sentence not exceeding the maximum two-year penalty provided by the conspiracy statute could be imposed. ...

[We cannot] ... accept the proposition that the substantive offenses were merged in the conspiracy. ... The common law rule that the substantive offense, if a felony, was merged in the conspiracy, has little vitality in this country. It has been long and consistently recognized by the Court that the commission of the substantive offense and a conspiracy to commit it are separate and distinct offenses. ... A conviction for the conspiracy may be had though the substantive offense was completed. ...

There is ... no evidence to show that Daniel participated directly in the commission of the substantive offenses on which his conviction has been sustained, although there was evidence to show that these substantive offenses were in fact committed by Walter in furtherance of the unlawful agreement or conspiracy existing between the brothers. The question was submitted to the jury on the theory that each petitioner could be found guilty of the substantive offenses, if it was found at the time those offenses were committed petitioners were parties to an unlawful conspiracy and the substantive offenses charged were in fact committed in furtherance of it.

... We have here a continuous conspiracy. There is here no evidence of the affirmative action on the part of Daniel which is necessary to establish his withdrawal from it. ... "[H]aving joined in an unlawful scheme, having constituted agents for its performance, scheme and agency to be continuous until full fruition be secured, until he does some act to disavow or defeat the purpose he is in no situation to claim the delay of the law. As the offense has not been terminated or accomplished, he is still offending. And we think, consciously offending,—offending as certainly, as we have said, as at the first moment of his confederation, and consciously through every moment of its existence." And so long as the partnership in crime continues, the partners act for each other in carrying it forward. It is settled that "an overt act of one partner may be the act of all without any new agreement specifically directed to that act." Motive or intent may be proved by the acts or declarations of some of the conspirators in furtherance of the common objective. A scheme to use the mails to defraud, which is joined in by more than one person, is a conspiracy. Yet all members are responsible, though only one did the mailing. The governing principle is the same when the substantive offense is committed by one of the conspirators in furtherance of the unlawful project. The criminal intent to do the act is established by the formation of the conspiracy. Each conspirator instigated the commission of the crime. The unlawful agreement contemplated precisely what was done. It was formed for the purpose. The act done was in execution of the enterprise. The rule which holds responsible one who counsels, procures, or commands another to commit a crime is founded on the same principle. That principle is recognized in the law of conspiracy when the overt act of one partner in crime is attributable to all. An overt act is an essential ingredient of the crime of conspiracy under [this statute]. If that can be supplied by the act of one conspirator, we fail to see why the same or other acts in furtherance of the conspiracy are likewise not attributable to the others for the purpose of holding them responsible for the substantive offense. ...

MR. JUSTICE RUTLEDGE, dissenting in part.

The judgment concerning Daniel Pinkerton should be reversed. In my opinion it is without precedent here and is a dangerous precedent to establish.

Daniel and Walter, who were brothers living near each other, were charged in several counts with substantive offenses, and then a conspiracy count was added naming those offenses as overt acts. The proof showed that Walter alone committed the substantive crimes. There was none to establish that Daniel participated in them, aided and abetted Walter in committing them, or knew that he had done so. Daniel in fact was in the penitentiary, under sentence for other crimes, when some of Walter's crimes were done.

There was evidence, however, to show that over several years Daniel and Walter had confederated to commit similar crimes concerned with unlawful possession, transportation, and dealing in whiskey, in fraud of the federal revenues. On this evidence both were convicted of conspiracy. Walter also was convicted on the substantive counts on the proof of his committing the crimes charged. Then, on that evidence without more than the proof of Daniel's criminal agreement with Walter and the latter's overt acts, which were also the substantive offenses charged, the court told the jury they could find Daniel guilty of those substantive offenses. They did so.

I think this ruling violates both the letter and the spirit of what Congress did when it separately defined the three classes of crime, namely, (1) completed substantive offenses; (2) aiding, abetting or counseling another to commit them; and (3) conspiracy to commit them. Not only does this ignore the distinctions Congress has prescribed shall be observed. It either convicts one man for another's crime or punishes the man convicted twice for the same offense.

The three types of offense are not identical. Nor are their differences merely verbal. The gist of conspiracy is the agreement; that of aiding, abetting or counseling is in consciously advising or assisting another to commit particular offenses, and thus becoming a party to them; that of substantive crime, going a step beyond mere aiding, abetting, counseling to completion of the offense.

These general differences are well understood. But when conspiracy has ripened into completed crime, or has advanced to the stage of aiding and abetting, it becomes easy to disregard their differences and loosely to treat one as identical with the other, that is, for every purpose except the most vital one of imposing sentence. And thus the substance, if not the technical effect, of double jeopardy or multiple punishment may be accomplished. Thus also may one be convicted of an offense not charged or proved against him, on evidence showing he committed another.

The old doctrine of merger of conspiracy in the substantive crime has not obtained here. But the dangers for abuse, which in part it sought to avoid, in applying the law of conspiracy have not altogether disappeared. There is some evidence that they may be increasing. The looseness with which the charge may be proved, the almost unlimited scope of vicarious responsibility for others' acts which follows once agreement is shown, the psychological advantages of such trials for securing convictions by attributing to one proof against another, these and other inducements require that the broad limits of discretion allowed to prosecuting officers in relation to such charges and trials be not expanded into new, wider and more dubious areas of choice. If the matter is not generally of constitutional proportions, it is one for the exercise of this Court's supervisory power over the modes of conducting federal criminal prosecutions....

I think that power should be exercised in this case with respect to Daniel's conviction. If it does not violate the letter of constitutional right, it fractures the spirit. ... Daniel has been held guilty of the substantive crimes committed only by Walter on proof that he did no more than conspire with him to commit offenses of the same general character. There was no evidence that he counseled, advised or had knowledge of those particular acts or offenses. There was, therefore, none that he aided, abetted or took part in them. There was only evidence sufficient to show that he had agreed with Walter at some past time to engage in such transactions generally. As to Daniel this was only evidence of conspiracy, not of substantive crime.

The court's theory seems to be that Daniel and Walter became general partners in crime by virtue of their agreement and because of that agreement without more on his part Daniel became criminally responsible as a principal for everything Walter did thereafter in the nature of a criminal offense of the general sort the agreement contemplated, so long as there was not clear evidence that Daniel had withdrawn from or revoked the agreement. Whether or not his commitment to the penitentiary had that effect, the result is a vicarious criminal responsibility as broad as, or broader than, the vicarious civil liability of a partner for acts done by a co-partner in the course of the firm's business.

Such analogies from private commercial law and the law of torts are dangerous, in my judgment, for transfer to the criminal field. Guilt there with us remains personal, not vicarious, for the more serious offenses. It should be kept so. ...

Notes

1. What *is* the rule? Is it founded on agency notions arising from the conspiratorial agreement? Is it a rule of vicarious liability? Does the rule require any consideration of the role of the particular defendant in the conspiracy? *See* United States v. Alvarez, 755 F.2d 830, 849 (11th Cir.1985) (generally, no). Should it? What practical consequences might this rule have in terms of increasing the likelihood or consequences of conviction? *See generally* Neal Kumar Katyal, *Conspiracy Theory*, 112 Yale L.J. 101, 156-69 (2003). Professor Neal Katyal defends *Pinkerton* liability by arguing that: it encourages "information extraction" from cooperating (former) co-conspirators; may discourage some potential coconspirators from joining a conspiracy due to uncertainty about the scope of their liability; undermines trust among the group which may inhibit its effective functioning; and will make conspiracies more difficult to operate because of the level of "monitoring" needed to offset uncertainty about coconspirators' loyalty. *See also* Jens David Ohlin, *Group Think: The Law of Conspiracy and Collective Reason*, 98 J. Crim. L. & Criminology 147 (2007).

2. The most common category of *Pinkerton* case is the one where the substantive crime that is the subject of the *Pinkerton* charge is also one of the primary goals of the alleged conspiracy. *See Alvarez*, 755 F.2d at 850 n.24. A *Pinkerton* theory is also frequently invoked when the "substantive crime is not a primary goal of the alleged conspiracy, but directly facilitates the achievement of one of the primary goals." *Id.* (citing Shockley v. United States, 166 F.2d 704, 715 (9th Cir. 1948) (conspiracy to escape by violent means from federal penitentiary; substantive crime of first degree murder of prison guard)).

3. *Recio* and the notes that follow that decision discuss the rules controlling when a defendant has made a legally effective withdrawal from a conspiracy. Timely withdrawal may also limit a coconspirator's *Pinkerton* liability for the substantive offenses committed by his coconspirators pursuant to the conspiracy. It is important to stress, however, that affirmative acts of withdrawal, not "mere inaction" or the passage of time without active participation in an ongoing conspiracy, are necessary. Thus, for example, in the *Pinkerton* case itself, one of the coconspirators was held liable for some of the foreseeable substantive crimes of his coconspirator committed in furtherance of a pre-existing conspiracy even though the defendant was in prison at the time that the coconspirator alone committed those crimes. What does *Pinkerton* liability and the withdrawal rule's requirement of an affirmative act mean for defendants who have a minor role at the beginning of a large-scale criminal conspiracy but whose active participation ends fairly early on?

4. As the dissent notes, an aiding and abetting charge, like a conspiracy charge, permits the government to indict persons who may not have taken any personal act that satisfies an element of the object crime. Like conspiracy, the application of aiding and abetting standards has come in for its fair share of criticism. *See, e.g.*, Adam Harris Kurland, *To "Aid, Abet, Counsel, Command, Induce, or Procure the Commission of an Offense": A Critique of Federal Aiding and Abetting Principles*, 57 S.C. L. Rev. 85 (2005). Aiding and abetting is distinguished from conspiracy because it does not require proof of an agreement or an overt act. The *actus reus* of aiding and abetting is not a criminal agreement, but rather the defendant's aiding, abetting, commanding, inducing or procuring the commission of the object offense. *See* 18 U.S.C. § 2. With respect to *mens rea*, "[t]he words "aids, abets, counsels, commands, induces or procures" all suggest that a person violates section 2 only if the person has 'chosen, with full knowledge, to participate in the illegal scheme.'" United States v. Ford, 821 F.3d 63, 69 (1st Cir. 2017) (quoting Rosemond v. United States, 572 U.S. 65, 72 (2014)). A person may only be convicted of aiding and abetting a crime when that object crime is actually committed, while conspiracy permits the

government to pursue persons for inchoate crimes. Consider the Supreme Court's latest word on the requisites of aiding and abetting liability.

ROSEMOND v. UNITED STATES
572 U.S. 65 (2014)

Justice Kagan delivered the opinion of the Court.

A federal criminal statute, § 924(c) if Title 18, prohibits "us[ing] or carr[ying]" a firearm "during and in relation to any crime of violence or drug trafficking crime." In this case, we consider what the Government must show when it accuses a defendant of aiding or abetting that offense. We hold that the Government makes its case by proving that the defendant actively participated in the underlying drug trafficking or violent crime with advance knowledge that a confederate would use or carry a gun during the crime's commission. We also conclude that the jury instructions given below were erroneous because they failed to require that the defendant knew in advance that one of his cohorts would be armed.

[Three persons, including Justus Rosemond, arrived at a local park to sell a pound of marijuana to two other individuals. One of the buyers, rather than handing over money, fled with the drugs. One of the dealers—which one was not clear—fired on the fleeing buyers. They gave chase to the buyers-turned-robbers but were pulled over and arrested by the police.] ...

The Government charged Rosemond with, *inter alia*, violating § 924(c) by using a gun in connection with a drug trafficking crime, or aiding and abetting that offense under § 2 of Title 18. Section 924(c) provides that "any person who, during and in relation to any crime of violence or drug trafficking crime[,] ... uses or carries a firearm," shall receive a five-year mandatory-minimum sentence, with seven- and ten-year minimums applicable, respectively, if the firearm is also brandished or discharged. 18 U.S.C. § 924(c)(1)(A). Section 2, for its part, is the federal aiding and abetting statute: It provides that "[w]hoever commits an offense against the United States or aids, abets, counsels, commands, induces or procures its commission is punishable as a principal."

Consistent with the indictment, the Government prosecuted the § 924(c) charge on two alternative theories. The Government's primary contention was that Rosemond himself used the firearm during the aborted drug transaction. But recognizing that the identity of the shooter was disputed, the Government also offered a back-up argument: Even if it was [another dealer] who fired the gun as the drug deal fell apart, Rosemond aided and abetted the § 924(c) violation.

... The verdict form was general: It did not reveal whether the jury found that Rosemond himself had used the gun or instead had aided and abetted a confederate's use during the marijuana deal. As required by § 924(c), the trial court imposed a consecutive sentence of 120 months of imprisonment for the statute's violation. ...

We granted certiorari to resolve the Circuit conflict over what it takes to aid and abet a § 924(c) offense. ... [W]e find that the trial court erred in instructing the jury. We therefore vacate the judgment below.

The federal aiding and abetting statute, 18 U.S.C. § 2, states that a person who furthers—more specifically, who "aids, abets, counsels, commands, induces or procures"—the commission of a federal offense "is punishable as a principal." That provision derives from (though simplifies) common-law standards for accomplice liability. See, *e.g., Standefer v. United States*, 447 U.S. 10, 14-19 (1980); *United States v. Peoni*, 100 F.2d 401, 402 (C.A.2 1938) (L. Hand, J.). And in so doing, § 2 reflects a centuries-old view of culpability: that a person may be responsible for a crime he has not personally carried out if he helps another to complete its commission. We have previously held that under § 2 "those who provide knowing aid to persons committing federal crimes, with the intent to facilitate the crime, are themselves committing a crime." Both parties here embrace that formulation, and agree as well that it has two components. As at common law, a person is liable under § 2 for aiding and abetting a crime if (and only if) he (1) takes an affirmative act in furtherance of that offense, (2) with the intent of facilitating the offense's commission. See 2 W. LaFave, Substantive Criminal Law § 13.2, p. 337 (2003) (hereinafter LaFave) (an accomplice is liable as a principal when he gives "assistance or encouragement ... with the intent thereby to promote or facilitate commission of the crime"); *Hicks v. United States*, 150 U.S. 442, 449 (1893) (an accomplice is liable when his acts of assistance are done "with the intention of encouraging and abetting" the crime).

The questions that the parties dispute, and we here address, concern how those two requirements—affirmative act and intent—apply in a prosecution for aiding and abetting a § 924(c) offense. Those questions arise from the compound nature of that provision. Recall that § 924(c) forbids "us[ing] or carr [ying] a firearm" when engaged in a "crime of violence or drug trafficking crime." The prosecutor must show the use or carriage of a gun; so too he must prove the commission of a predicate (violent or drug trafficking) offense. For purposes of ascertaining aiding and abetting liability, we therefore must consider: When does a person act to further this double-barreled crime? And when does he intend to facilitate its commission? We address each issue in turn.

A.

Consider first Rosemond's account of his conduct (divorced from any issues of intent). Rosemond actively participated in a drug transaction, accompanying two others to a site where money was to be exchanged for a pound of marijuana. But as he tells it, he took no action with respect to any firearm. He did not buy or borrow a gun to facilitate the narcotics deal; he did not carry a gun to the scene; he did not use a gun during the subsequent events constituting this criminal misadventure. His acts thus advanced one part (the drug part) of a two-part incident—or to speak a bit more technically, one element (the drug element) of a two-element crime. Is that enough to satisfy the conduct requirement of this aiding and abetting charge, or must Rosemond, as he claims, have taken some act to assist the commission of the other (firearm) component of § 924(c)?

The common law imposed aiding and abetting liability on a person (possessing the requisite intent) who facilitated any part—even though not every part—of a criminal venture. As a leading treatise, published around the time of § 2's enactment, put the point: Accomplice liability attached upon proof of "*[a]ny* participation in a general felonious plan" carried out by confederates. 1 F. Wharton, Criminal Law § 251, p. 322 (11th ed. 1912) (hereinafter Wharton) (emphasis added). Or in the words of another standard reference: If a person was "present abetting while *any* act necessary to constitute the offense [was] being performed through another," he could be charged as a principal—even "though [that act was] *not the whole thing necessary*." 1 J. Bishop, Commentaries on the Criminal Law § 649, p. 392 (7th ed. 1882) (emphasis added). And so "[w]here several acts constitute[d] together one crime, if each [was] separately performed by a different individual[,] ... all [were] principals as to the whole." Indeed, as yet a third treatise underscored, a person's involvement in the crime could be not merely partial but minimal too: "The quantity [of assistance was] immaterial," so long as the accomplice did "*something*" to aid the crime. After all, the common law maintained, every little bit helps—and a contribution to some part of a crime aids the whole.

That principle continues to govern aiding and abetting law under § 2: As almost every court of appeals has held, "[a] defendant can be convicted as an aider and abettor without proof that he participated in each and every element of the offense." In proscribing aiding and abetting, Congress used language that "comprehends all assistance rendered by words, acts, encouragement, support, or presence"—even if that aid relates to only one (or some) of a crime's phases or elements. So, for example, in upholding convictions for abetting a tax evasion scheme, this Court found "irrelevant" the defendants' "non-participation" in filing a false return; we thought they had amply facilitated the illegal scheme by helping a confederate conceal his assets. *United States v. Johnson*, 319 U.S. 503, 515 (1943). "[A]ll who shared in [the overall crime's] execution," we explained, "have equal responsibility before the law, whatever may have been [their] different roles." And similarly, we approved a conviction for abetting mail fraud even though the defendant had played no part in mailing the fraudulent documents; it was enough to satisfy the law's conduct requirement that he had in other ways aided the deception. See *Pereira v. United States*, 347 U.S. 1, 8-11 (1954). The division of labor between two (or more) confederates thus has no significance: A strategy of "you take that element, I'll take this one" would free neither party from liability.

Under that established approach, Rosemond's participation in the drug deal here satisfies the affirmative-act requirement for aiding and abetting a § 924(c) violation. As we have previously described, the commission of a drug trafficking (or violent) crime is—no less than the use of a firearm—an "essential conduct element of the § 924(c) offense." In enacting the statute, "Congress proscribed both the use of the firearm *and* the commission of acts that constitute" a drug trafficking crime. Rosemond therefore could assist in § 924(c)'s violation by facilitating either the drug transaction or the firearm use (or of course both). In helping to bring about one part of the offense (whether trafficking drugs or using a gun), he necessarily helped to complete the whole. And that ends the analysis as to his conduct. It is inconsequential, as courts applying both the common law and § 2 have held, that his acts did not advance each element of the offense; all that matters is that they facilitated one component.   ...

B.

Begin with (or return to) some basics about aiding and abetting law's intent requirement, which no party here disputes. As previously explained, a person aids and abets a crime when (in addition to taking the requisite act) he intends to facilitate that offense's commission. An intent to advance some different or lesser offense is not, or at least not usually, sufficient: Instead, the intent must go to the specific and entire crime charged—so here, to the full scope (predicate crime plus gun use) of § 924(c).[37] And the canonical formulation of that needed state of mind—later appropriated by this Court and oft-quoted in both parties' briefs—is Judge Learned Hand's: To aid and abet a crime, a defendant must not just "in some sort associate himself with the venture," but also "participate in it as in something that he wishes to bring about" and "seek by his action to make it succeed." *Nye & Nissen v. United States*, 336 U.S. 613, 619 (1949) (quoting *Peoni*, 100 F.2d, at 402).

We have previously found that intent requirement satisfied when a person actively participates in a criminal venture with full knowledge of the circumstances constituting the charged offense. In *Pereira*, the mail fraud case discussed above, we found the requisite intent for aiding and abetting because the defendant took part in a fraud "know[ing]" that his confederate would take care of the mailing. Likewise, in *Bozza v. United States*, 330 U.S. 160, 165 (1947), we upheld a conviction for aiding and abetting the evasion of liquor taxes because the defendant helped operate a clandestine distillery "know[ing]" the business was set up "to violate Government revenue laws." And several Courts of Appeals have similarly held— addressing a fact pattern much like this one—that the unarmed driver of a getaway car had the requisite intent to aid and abet armed bank robbery if he "knew" that his confederates would use weapons in carrying out the crime. So for purposes of aiding and abetting law, a person who actively participates in a criminal scheme knowing its extent and character intends that scheme's commission.[38]

The same principle holds here: An active participant in a drug transaction has the intent needed to aid and abet a § 924(c) violation when he knows that one of his confederates will

---

[37] [Court's footnote 7:] Some authorities suggest an exception to the general rule when another crime is the "natural and probable consequence" of the crime the defendant intended to abet. That question is not implicated here, because no one contends that a § 924(c) violation is the natural and probable consequence of simple drug trafficking. We therefore express not view on the issue.

[38] [Court's footnote 8:] We did not deal in these cases, nor do we here, with defendants who incidentally facilitate a criminal venture rather than actively participate in it. A hypothetical case is the owner of a gun store who sells a firearm to a criminal, knowing but not caring how the gun will be used. We express no view about what sort of facts, if any, would suffice to show that such a third party has the intent necessary to be convicted of aiding and abetting.

carry a gun. In such a case, the accomplice has decided to join in the criminal venture, and share in its benefits, with full awareness of its scope—that the plan calls not just for a drug sale, but for an armed one. In so doing, he has chosen (like the abettors in *Pereira* and *Bozza* or the driver in an armed robbery) to align himself with the illegal scheme in its entirety—including its use of a firearm. And he has determined (again like those other abettors) to do what he can to "make [that scheme] succeed." He thus becomes responsible, in the typical way of aiders and abettors, for the conduct of others. He may not have brought the gun to the drug deal himself, but because he took part in that deal knowing a confederate would do so, he intended the commission of a § 924(c) offense—*i.e.,* an armed drug sale.

For all that to be true, though, the § 924(c) defendant's knowledge of a firearm must be advance knowledge—or otherwise said, knowledge that enables him to make the relevant legal (and indeed, moral) choice. When an accomplice knows beforehand of a confederate's design to carry a gun, he can attempt to alter that plan or, if unsuccessful, withdraw from the enterprise; it is deciding instead to go ahead with his role in the venture that shows his intent to aid an *armed* offense. But when an accomplice knows nothing of a gun until it appears at the scene, he may already have completed his acts of assistance; or even if not, he may at that late point have no realistic opportunity to quit the crime. And when that is so, the defendant has not shown the requisite intent to assist a crime involving a gun. As even the Government concedes, an unarmed accomplice cannot aid and abet a § 924(c) violation unless he has "foreknowledge that his confederate will commit the offense with a firearm." For the reasons just given, we think that means knowledge at a time the accomplice can do something with it—most notably, opt to walk away.[39] ...

Under these principles, the District Court erred in instructing the jury, because it did not explain that Rosemond needed advance knowledge of a firearm's presence. ... [T]he court stated that Rosemond was guilty of aiding and abetting if "(1) [he] knew his cohort used a firearm in the drug trafficking crime, and (2) [he] knowingly and actively participated in the drug trafficking crime." We agree with that instruction's second half: As we have explained, active participation in a drug sale is sufficient for § 924(c) liability (even if the conduct does not extend to the firearm), so long as the defendant had prior knowledge of the gun's involvement. The problem with the court's instruction came in its description of that knowledge requirement. In telling the jury to consider merely whether Rosemond "knew his cohort used a firearm," the court did not direct the jury to determine *when* Rosemond obtained the requisite knowledge. So, for example, the jury could have convicted even if Rosemond first learned of the gun when it was fired and he took no further action to advance the crime. ... The court's statement failed to convey that Rosemond had to have advance knowledge, of the kind we have described, that a confederate would be armed.

C. U.S. SENTENCING GUIDELINES: CONSPIRACY EXERCISE

As the above materials make clear, conspiracy is viewed as a crime separate and apart from the criminal objectives of the partnership in crime. Where the criminal objective has been achieved, it is thus permissible, and perhaps appropriate in view of the dangers said to be presented by a conspiracy, to impose punishment for both the completed crime and the conspiracy. In performing the following guidelines analysis, consider whether the Sentencing Commission authorizes such compound punishment or instead dictates that a conspiracy charge generally is transparent (*i.e.,* does not add to the sentence imposed for the completed substantive crime that is the object of the conspiracy). Does the Sentencing Commission's

---

[39] [Court's footnote 9:] Of course, if a defendant continues to participate in a crime after a gun was displayed or used by a confederate, the jury can permissibly infer from his failure to object or withdraw that he had such knowledge. In any criminal case, after all, the factfinder can draw inferences about a defendant's intent based on all the facts and circumstances of a crime's commission.

result make sense in light of the purposes of criminalizing conspiratorial activity? Should the Sentencing Commission be responsible for making such judgments?

Please determine Mr. Blackmon's sentencing guidelines exposure for both counts of wire fraud *and* for conspiracy using the opinion and the assumptions previously provided.

Chapter 11

THE RACKETEER INFLUENCED AND CORRUPT ORGANIZATIONS ACT ("RICO")

Congress passed the Racketeer Influenced and Corrupt Organizations statute[1] in 1970 as part of the Organized Crime Control Act.[2] That Act was designed to "'seek the eradication of organized crime in the United States by ... establishing new penal prohibitions, and by providing enhanced sanctions and new remedies to deal with the unlawful activities of those engaged in organized crime.'"[3] Criminal RICO has become an important prosecutorial tool in pursuing group criminality but has generated a great deal of controversy, literature, and case law[4] in part because the statute has regularly been applied to conduct which in no way resembles the traditional organized crime "racketeering" that it was intended to address. In defining the prohibited activities outlawed in 18 U.S.C. § 1962, Congress's major purpose was "to address the infiltration of legitimate business by organized crime."[5] However, the two provisions most pertinent to this effort—§§ 1962(a) and (b)—are the provisions least frequently invoked.[6] Indeed, one commentator concluded after reviewing the cases in which RICO is regularly employed that "RICO has been a nearly total failure as a weapon against the kind of [infiltration] activity that led Congress to enact it."[7]

The following materials concentrate on the more popular subsections: § 1962(c), which makes it unlawful for "any person employed by or associated with any enterprise engaged in, or the activities of which affect, interstate ... commerce, to conduct or participate ... in the conduct of such enterprise's affairs through a pattern of racketeering activity"; and § 1962(d) which makes it unlawful for a person to conspire to violate subsections (a), (b), or (c) of § 1962. These are the subsections most frequently employed in white-collar cases. A large percentage of such RICO cases concern public corruption, most of it by state and local actors.[8] RICO is

---

[1] 18 U.S.C. §§ 1961-68.

[2] Pub. L. No. 91-452, 84 Stat. 941 (1970).

[3] United States v. Turkette, 452 U.S. 576, 589 (1981) (quoting 84 Stat. 923).

[4] *See, e.g.*, Paul E. Coffey, *The Selection, Analysis, and Approval of Federal RICO Prosecutions*, 65 Notre Dame L. Rev. 1035, 1035-37 (1990) (documenting sources).

[5] *Turkette*, 452 U.S. at 591.

[6] *See Thirty-Third Annual Survey of White Collar Crime, RICO*, 55 Am. Crim. L. Rev. 1619, 1639-40 (2018).

[7] Hon. Gerard E. Lynch, *RICO: The Crime of Being a Criminal, Parts I & II*, 87 Colum. L. Rev. 661, 726 (1987); *see also* Daniel R. Fischel & Alan O. Sykes, *Civil RICO After Reves: An Economic Commentary*, 1993 Sup. Ct. Rev. 157, 157. *But cf.* Coffey, *supra* note 4, at 1039, 1040 ("RICO is an essential component of the government's strategy of attacking organized crime" and "is an effective weapon against corrupt public officials.").

[8] *See, e.g.*, Coffey, *supra* note 4, at 1040 ("Between 1984 and 1989, for example, public corruption was the

also frequently invoked to pursue business crime,[9] although "[t]here is no clearly identifying feature in the white collar cases in which federal prosecutors have elected to use RICO":

> [B]y far the greater number of RICO indictments in the white collar area have no connection whatever to organized crime. Rather, they run the gamut of ordinary business and regulatory offenses. Businesses overcharging their customers or underpaying their suppliers, con artists selling dubious commodities and securities or obtaining financing for nonexistent equipment sales, businessmen trying to salvage a bit more from a bankruptcy than the law allows—the whole range of fraudulent activity usually associated with the mail fraud statute—all have been prosecuted under RICO.[10]

Prosecutors, and civil litigants, have aggressively sought to invoke RICO outside the organized crime context in major part because of the "enhanced sanctions and new remedies" made available in that statute. RICO has fueled a litigation bonanza by providing for treble civil damages, and awards of costs and attorneys fees, for "[a]ny person injured in his business or property by reason" of a § 1962 violation.[11] For prosecutors, it offers not only criminal penalties but also criminal forfeiture of, inter alia, any interest acquired or maintained in violation of § 1962, any interest in any enterprise operated in violation of § 1962, and any property constituting, or derived from, the proceeds of racketeering activity in violation of § 1962.[12] Finally, upon application of the government, RICO provides for civil remedies such as divestiture, corporate dissolution, and reorganization.[13] Notably, these civil remedies give prosecutors a means to secure pre-trial and even pre-indictment "injunctions that bar a defendant from using available [tainted] assets to obtain legal representation or prepare a defense."[14]

These sanctions are not the only reasons that RICO has been termed the "*new* darling of the prosecutor's nursery."[15] When RICO is charged along with federal substantive crimes alleged to be the "racketeering activity" upon which the RICO charge is predicated, defendants face much higher cumulative maximum statutory penalties and the possibility of consecutive sentences. A wide variety of crimes may serve as the predicates for a RICO case, including: mail, wire, and bank fraud; obstruction of justice and witness tampering; Hobbs and Travel Act violations; money laundering; and "fraud in the sale of securities." Given the malleability of many of these predicates, prosecutors often have a great deal of discretion in determining whether to invoke RICO's arsenal of sanctions. RICO charges may also be based on an array of criminal acts chargeable under state law but included by Congress within the definition of actionable "racketeering activity."[16] RICO thus permits prosecutors to "federalize" traditionally state-law crimes like murder, kidnaping, extortion, robbery, bribery, and dealing in obscene materials.[17] Such cases may proceed regardless of whether the

---

underlying criminal conduct in twenty-six percent of all approved RICO prosecutions.").

[9] *See id.* at 1042 n.33 ("On average, 39% of RICO prosecutions involve only white-collar businessmen.").

[10] Lynch, *RICO: The Crime of Being a Criminal, Parts I & II, supra* note 7, at 750 (footnotes omitted).

[11] 18 U.S.C. § 1964(c); *see also* Anza v. Ideal Steel Supply Corp., 547 U.S. 451 (2006).

[12] 18 U.S.C. § 1963.

[13] *Id.* § 1964(a), (b); *see, e.g.*, United States v. Local 30, 871 F.2d 401 (3d Cir. 1989).

[14] Barry Tarlow, *RICO: The New Darling of the Prosecutor's Nursery*, 49 Fordham L. Rev. 165, 170 (1980); *cf. also* Luis v. United States, -- U.S. --, 136 S.Ct. 1083 (2016); United States v. Monsanto, 491 U.S. 600 (1989); Caplin & Drysdale v. United States, 491 U.S. 617 (1989).

[15] Tarlow, *supra* note 14, at 170 (emphasis added).

[16] *See* 18 U.S.C. § 1961(1).

[17] *See id.* § 1961(1)(A).

defendant has been criminally prosecuted (and acquitted or convicted) in state court for the same conduct because of the double jeopardy clause's dual sovereignty exception.[18] Indeed, RICO is so powerful that it is capable of reviving the dead: even where the predicate "racketeering activity" would be time-barred, prosecutors may proceed with a RICO case built upon those crimes assuming the requisites of the RICO statute are satisfied.[19] RICO charges also potentially lend prosecutors significant venue, joinder, and evidentiary advantages.[20] Finally, charging a defendant with "racketeering" carries with it a stigma that may well cow defendants and adversely affect juries.[21] That stigma and RICO's onerous remedies certainly provide prosecutors a large club with which to force pleas, especially from corporate actors.[22]

Studying all aspects of the RICO statute could consume the rest of students' careers. The following materials, then, necessarily provide a fairly limited overview. They outline the general elements of a RICO criminal prosecution and illustrate the types of situations in which the various RICO provisions may apply. In reflecting on these materials, readers should consider the appropriate use of this powerful instrument. Is the statute simply a penalty-enhancement, or recidivist, statute or does it in fact address unique dangers created by a certain type of organized criminal activity? When is prosecution for the predicate crimes and for conspiracy enough to punish and deter the activity at issue and when should the great guns of the RICO "super-conspiracy" be brought to bear on criminal partnerships? Other issues that pervade any study of RICO are: the extent to which the decisions of courts plagued with a deluge of *civil* RICO cases should bind courts interpreting the scope and application of the statute in *criminal* cases; what approach federal courts should take in defining the reach of this very broad and, many argue, very vague criminal prohibition; whether RICO's federalization of many state law crimes is wise; and whether RICO gives federal prosecutors too much discretion in charging and too much power in bargaining.

---

[18] *See supra* Chapter 5(D) (Double Jeopardy); *see, e.g.*, United States v. Coonan, 938 F.2d 1553, 1562-63 (2d Cir. 1991).

[19] *See, e.g.*, United States v. Licavoli, 725 F.2d 1040, 1046-47 (6th Cir. 1984); United States v. Malatesta, 583 F.2d 748, 757-58 (5th Cir. 1978). Generally, RICO cases may be brought based on predicate acts, no matter when committed, if "the government ... demonstrate[s] that a defendant committed at least one predicate racketeering act within the [five-year RICO criminal] statute of limitations." United States v. Wong, 40 F.3d 1347, 1367 (2d Cir. 1994); *see also* Agency Holding Corp. v. Malley-Duff & Assocs., Inc., 483 U.S. 143, 155-56 (1987) (in the course of holding that four-year statute of limitations controlled in RICO civil enforcement action, noting that five-year statute of limitations applies to criminal RICO prosecutions). The Second Circuit upheld a RICO conspiracy conviction under § 1962(d) even though the two predicate acts the jury found were outside the limitations period because the government proved that the conspiracy of which the defendant was a member continued into the limitations period. United States v. Pizzonia, 577 F.3d 455 (2d Cir. 2009).

Although not a statute of limitations, the definition of a "pattern of racketeering activity" also injects a temporal limitation on RICO cases. Thus, § 1961(5) requires that the government demonstrate "at least two acts of racketeering activity, one of which occurred after the effective date of this chapter and the last of which occurred within ten years (excluding any period of imprisonment) after the commission of a prior act of racketeering activity."

[20] *See, e.g.*, Hon. Gerard E. Lynch, *RICO: The Crime of Being a Criminal, Parts III & IV*, 87 Colum. L. Rev. 920, 940-41 (1987).

[21] *See, e.g.*, John C. Coffee, Jr., *"No Soul to Damn: No Body to Kick"; An Unscandalized Inquiry Into the Problem of Corporate Punishment*, 79 Mich. L. Rev. 386, 427 n.111 (1981); Tarlow, *supra* note 14, at 170.

[22] *See, e.g.*, Lynch, *RICO: The Crime of Being a Criminal, Parts I & II*, *supra* note 7, at 725.

A. ELEMENTS/PRINCIPLES OF LIABILITY

1. ENTERPRISE

UNITED STATES v. TURKETTE
452 U.S. 576 (1981)

JUSTICE WHITE delivered the opinion of the Court.

... The question in this case is whether the term "enterprise" as used in RICO encompasses both legitimate and illegitimate enterprises or is limited in application to the former. ...

Count Nine of a nine-count indictment charged respondent and 12 others with conspiracy to conduct and participate in the affairs of an enterprise engaged in interstate commerce through a pattern of racketeering activities, in violation of 18 U.S.C. § 1962(d). The indictment described the enterprise as "a group of individuals associated in fact for the purpose of illegally trafficking in narcotics and other dangerous drugs, committing arsons, utilizing the United States mails to defraud insurance companies, bribing and attempting to bribe local police officers, and corruptly influencing and attempting to corruptly influence the outcome of state court proceedings ... ." The other eight counts of the indictment charged the commission of various substantive criminal acts by those engaged in and associated with the criminal enterprise, including possession with intent to distribute and distribution of controlled substances, and several counts of insurance fraud by arson and other means. The common thread to all counts was respondent's alleged leadership of this criminal organization through which he orchestrated and participated in the commission of the various crimes delineated in the RICO count or charged in the eight preceding counts.

After a 6-week jury trial, in which the evidence focused upon both the professional nature of this organization and the execution of a number of distinct criminal acts, respondent was convicted on all nine counts. ...

On appeal, respondent argued that RICO was intended solely to protect legitimate business enterprises from infiltration by racketeers and that RICO does not make criminal the participation in an association which performs only illegal acts and which has not infiltrated or attempted to infiltrate a legitimate enterprise. The Court of Appeals agreed. We reverse.

In determining the scope of a statute, we look first to its language. ...

Section 1962(c) makes it unlawful "for any person employed by or associated with any enterprise engaged in, or the activities of which affect, interstate or foreign commerce, to conduct or participate, directly or indirectly, in the conduct of such enterprise's affairs through a pattern of racketeering activity or collection of unlawful debt." The term "enterprise" is defined as including "any individual, partnership, corporation, association, or other legal entity, and any union or group of individuals associated in fact although not a legal entity." § 1961(4). There is no restriction upon the associations embraced by the definition: an enterprise includes any union or group of individuals associated in fact. On its face, the definition appears to include both legitimate and illegitimate enterprises within its scope; it no more excludes criminal enterprises than it does legitimate ones. Had Congress not intended to reach criminal associations, it could easily have narrowed the sweep of the definition by inserting a single word, "legitimate." But it did nothing to indicate that an enterprise consisting of a group of individuals was not covered by RICO if the purpose of the enterprise was exclusively criminal.

The Court of Appeals, however, clearly departed from and limited the statutory language. It gave several reasons for doing so, none of which is adequate. First, it relied in part on the rule of *ejusdem generis*, an aid to statutory construction problems suggesting that where general words follow a specific enumeration of persons or things, the general words should be limited to persons or things similar to those specifically enumerated. The Court of Appeals ruled that because each of the specific enterprises enumerated in § 1961(4) is a "legitimate" one, the final catchall phrase—"any union or group of individuals associated in fact"—should also be limited to legitimate enterprises. There are at least two flaws in this reasoning. The rule of *ejusdem generis* is no more than an aid to construction and comes into play only when there is some uncertainty as to the meaning of a particular clause in a statute. Considering the language and structure of § 1961(4), however, we not only perceive no uncertainty in the meaning to be attributed to the phrase, "any union or group of individuals associated in fact" but we are convinced for another reason that *ejusdem generis* is wholly inapplicable in this context.

Section 1961(4) describes two categories of associations that come within the purview of the "enterprise" definition. The first encompasses organizations such as corporations and partnerships, and other "legal entities." The second covers "any union or group of individuals associated in fact although not a legal entity." The Court of Appeals assumed that the second category was merely a more general description of the first. Having made that assumption, the court concluded that the more generalized description in the second category should be limited by the specific examples enumerated in the first. But that assumption is untenable. Each category describes a separate type of enterprise to be covered by the statute—those that are recognized as legal entities and those that are not. The latter is not a more general description of the former. The second category itself not containing any specific enumeration that is followed by a general description, *ejusdem generis* has no bearing on the meaning to be attributed to that part of § 1961(4).

A second reason offered by the Court of Appeals in support of its judgment was that giving the definition of "enterprise" its ordinary meaning would create several internal inconsistencies in the Act. With respect to § 1962(c), it was said:

> "If 'a pattern of racketeering' can itself be an 'enterprise' for purposes of section 1962(c), then the two phrases 'employed by or associated with any enterprise' and 'the conduct of such enterprise's affairs through [a pattern of racketeering activity]' add nothing to the meaning of the section. The words of the statute are coherent and logical only if they are read as applying to legitimate enterprises."

This conclusion is based on a faulty premise. That a wholly criminal enterprise comes within the ambit of the statute does not mean that a "pattern of racketeering activity" is an "enterprise." In order to secure a conviction under RICO, the Government must prove both the existence of an "enterprise" and the connected "pattern of racketeering activity." The enterprise is an entity, for present purposes a group of persons associated together for a common purpose of engaging in a course of conduct. The pattern of racketeering activity is, on the other hand, a series of criminal acts as defined by the statute. 18 U.S.C. § 1961(1). The former is proved by evidence of an ongoing organization, formal or informal, and by evidence that the various associates function as a continuing unit. The latter is proved by evidence of the requisite number of acts of racketeering committed by the participants in the enterprise. While the proof used to establish these separate elements may in particular cases coalesce, proof of one does not necessarily establish the other. The "enterprise" is not the "pattern of racketeering activity"; it is an entity separate and apart from the pattern of activity in which it engages. The existence of an enterprise at all times remains a separate element which must be proved by the Government.

Apart from § 1962(c)'s proscription against participating in an enterprise through a pattern of racketeering activities, RICO also proscribes the investment of income derived from racketeering activity in an enterprise engaged in or which affects interstate commerce as well as the acquisition of an interest in or control of any such enterprise through a pattern of racketeering activity. 18 U.S.C. §§ 1962(a) and (b). The Court of Appeals concluded that these provisions of RICO should be interpreted so as to apply only to legitimate enterprises. If these two sections are so limited, the Court of Appeals held that the proscription in § 1962(c), at issue here, must be similarly limited. Again, we do not accept the premise from which the Court of Appeals derived its conclusion. It is obvious that § 1962(a) and (b) address the infiltration by organized crime of legitimate businesses, but we cannot agree that these sections were not also aimed at preventing racketeers from investing or reinvesting in wholly illegal enterprises and from acquiring through a pattern of racketeering activity wholly illegitimate enterprises such as an illegal gambling business or a loan-sharking operation. There is no inconsistency or anomaly in recognizing that § 1962 applies to both legitimate and illegitimate enterprises. Certainly the language of the statute does not warrant the Court of Appeals' conclusion to the contrary.

Similarly, the Court of Appeals noted that various civil remedies were provided by § 1964, including divestiture, dissolution, reorganization, restrictions on future activities by violators of RICO, and treble damages. These remedies it thought would have utility only with respect to legitimate enterprises. As a general proposition, however, the civil remedies could be useful in eradicating organized crime from the social fabric, whether the enterprise be ostensibly legitimate or admittedly criminal. The aim is to divest the association of the fruits of its ill-gotten gains. Even if one or more of the civil remedies might be inapplicable to a particular illegitimate enterprise, this fact would not serve to limit the enterprise concept. Congress has provided civil remedies for use when the circumstances so warrant. It is untenable to argue that their existence limits the scope of the criminal provisions.

Finally, it is urged that the interpretation of RICO to include both legitimate and illegitimate enterprises will substantially alter the balance between federal and state enforcement of criminal law. This is particularly true, so the argument goes, since included within the definition of racketeering activity are a significant number of acts made criminal under state law. 18 U.S.C. § 1961(1). But even assuming that the more inclusive definition of enterprise will have the effect suggested, the language of the statute and its legislative history indicate that Congress was well aware that it was entering a new domain of federal involvement through the enactment of this measure. Indeed, the very purpose of the Organized Crime Control Act of 1970 was to enable the Federal Government to address a large and seemingly neglected problem. The view was that existing law, state and federal, was not adequate to address the problem, which was of national dimensions. That Congress included within the definition of racketeering activities a number of state crimes strongly indicates that RICO criminalized conduct that was also criminal under state law, at least when the requisite elements of a RICO offense are present. As the hearings and legislative debates reveal, Congress was well aware of the fear that RICO would "mov[e] large substantive areas formerly totally within the police power of the State into the Federal realm." In the face of these objections, Congress nonetheless proceeded to enact the measure, knowing that it would alter somewhat the role of the Federal Government in the war against organized crime and that the alteration would entail prosecutions involving acts of racketeering that are also crimes under state law. There is no argument that Congress acted beyond its power in so doing. That being the case, the courts are without authority to restrict the application of the statute.

Contrary to the judgment below, neither the language nor structure of RICO limits its application to legitimate "enterprises." Applying it also to criminal organizations does not render any portion of the statute superfluous nor does it create any structural incongruities within the framework of the Act. The result is neither absurd nor surprising. On the contrary, insulating the wholly criminal enterprise from prosecution under RICO is the more incongruous position.

Section 904(a) of RICO directs that "[t]he provisions of this Title shall be liberally construed to effectuate its remedial purposes." With or without this admonition, we could not agree with the Court of Appeals that illegitimate enterprises should be excluded from coverage. We are also quite sure that nothing in the legislative history of RICO requires a contrary conclusion. ...

... [I]t was the declared purpose of Congress [in enacting the Organized Crime Control Act of 1970] "to seek the eradication of organized crime in the United States by strengthening the legal tools in the evidence-gathering process, by establishing new penal prohibitions, and by providing enhanced sanctions and new remedies to deal with the unlawful activities of those engaged in organized crime." ...

Considering this statement of the Act's broad purposes, the construction of RICO suggested by respondent and the court below is unacceptable. Whole areas of organized criminal activity would be placed beyond the substantive reach of the enactment. For example, associations of persons engaged solely in "loan sharking, the theft and fencing of property, the importation and distribution of narcotics and other dangerous drugs," would be immune from prosecution under RICO so long as the association did not deviate from the criminal path. Yet these are among the very crimes that Congress specifically found to be typical of the crimes committed by persons involved in organized crime, see 18 U.S.C. § 1961(1), and as a major source of revenue and power for such organizations. ... In view of the purposes and goals of the Act, as well as the language of the statute, we are unpersuaded that Congress nevertheless confined the reach of the law to only narrow aspects of organized crime, and, in particular, under RICO, *only* the infiltration of legitimate business.

This is not to gainsay that the legislative history forcefully supports the view that the major purpose of Title IX is to address the infiltration of legitimate business by organized crime. The point is made time and again during the debates and in the hearings before the House and Senate. But none of these statements requires the negative inference that Title IX did not reach the activities of enterprises organized and existing for criminal purposes.

On the contrary, these statements are in full accord with the proposition that RICO is equally applicable to a criminal enterprise that has no legitimate dimension or has yet to acquire one. Accepting that the primary purpose of RICO is to cope with the infiltration of legitimate businesses, applying the statute in accordance with its terms, so as to reach criminal enterprises, would seek to deal with the problem at its very source. Supporters of the bill recognized that organized crime uses its primary sources of revenue and power—illegal gambling, loan sharking and illicit drug distribution—as a springboard into the sphere of legitimate enterprise. ...

As a measure to deal with the infiltration of legitimate businesses by organized crime, RICO was both preventive and remedial. Respondent's view would ignore the preventive function of the statute. If Congress had intended the more circumscribed approach espoused by the Court of Appeals, there would have been some positive sign that the law was not to reach organized criminal activities that give rise to the concerns about infiltration. The language of the statute, however—the most reliable evidence of its intent—reveals that Congress opted for a far broader definition of the word "enterprise," and we are unconvinced by anything in the legislative history that this definition should be given less than its full effect. ...

Notes

1. *Turkette*'s holding—that a group of persons "associated in fact" to pursue entirely illegitimate purposes can constitute a RICO enterprise—is a critical one. "Prosecutions of such associations have quickly become the leading use of the statute. It can be reliably estimated that more than forty percent of the reported appellate cases involving RICO indictments concern prosecutions in which the alleged enterprise was such an illicit association." Lynch, *RICO: The Crime of Being a Criminal, Parts III & IV, supra* note 20, at 920. What distinguishes such an "association-in-fact" enterprise from a run-of-the-mill conspiracy like those examined in Chapter 10? Does the *Turkette* holding mean that RICO is simply a "super-conspiracy" statute that permits prosecutors to secure the many advantages of the RICO statute in cases such as *Arch Trading, Gatling,* or *Pinkerton*? Are you persuaded that this was Congress' intent?

2. In distinguishing an "association-in-fact" RICO "enterprise" from its "racketeering activity," the *Turkette* Court notes that "[t]he enterprise is an entity, for present purposes a group of persons associated together for a common purpose of engaging in a course of conduct." The Court further states that the enterprise "is proved by evidence of an ongoing organization, formal or informal, and by evidence that the various associates function as a continuing unit." Finally, the Court states that while proof of the predicate racketeering acts and the enterprise itself "may in particular cases coalesce, proof of one does not necessarily establish the other. The 'enterprise' is not the 'pattern of racketeering activity'; it is an entity separate and apart from the pattern of activity in which it engages."

The *Turkette* Court appears to be attempting to separate out the types of truly "organized" criminal activity at which RICO is aimed from run-of-the-mill criminal conspiracies. Is it successful? Note that criminologists, law enforcement personnel, and academics have long struggled to define "organized crime." They have come up with a number of attributes of organized crime, including: (1) organized crime groups are normally motivated by money or power, not ideology; (2) an organized crime group is ongoing in nature and is designed to exist beyond the lifetimes of existing members; (3) an organized crime syndicate typically has a limited membership and is bound by understood rules, which often involve discipline, obedience, and secrecy, and may include rites such as initiation; (4) the power structure is hierarchical, with defined ranks; (5) organized crime groups promote specialization, so that they will have enforcers, "fixers," and the like; (6) violence and bribery are routinely used to achieve the group's ends; and (7) the group will seek a monopolistic position within its spheres of business or geographical location. Could these attributes be used to help the courts craft a legal definition for RICO purposes?

3. *Boyle v. United States.* Recall the *Turkette* Court's final directive: while proof of the predicate racketeering acts and the enterprise itself "may in particular cases coalesce, proof of one does not necessarily establish the other. The 'enterprise' is not the 'pattern of racketeering activity'; it is an entity separate and apart from the pattern of activity in which it engages." This "separate and apart" language raised the question whether the existence of an "enterprise" could be inferred solely from the pattern of racketeering in which it engaged, or whether some additional showing—such as an "ascertainable structure beyond that inherent in the pattern of racketeering activity"—had to be made.

This question provoked a pronounced circuit split. *See* Odom v. Microsoft Corp., 486 F.3d 541, 548-52 (9th Cir. 2007) (collecting cases). The Supreme Court resolved the question in *Boyle v. United States*, 556 U.S. 938 (2009). Justice Alito, writing for the majority, held that no additional proof was required, explaining that while an association-in-fact enterprise must have a "structure," it need not be an ascertainable structure beyond that inherent in the pattern of racketeering in which it engages. The Court held that, "[f]rom the terms of RICO,"

> it is apparent that an association-in-fact enterprise must have at least three structural features: a purpose, relationships among those associated with the enterprise, and longevity sufficient to permit these associates to pursue the enterprise's purpose. As we succinctly put it in *Turkette*, an association-in-fact enterprise is "a group of persons associated together for a common purpose of engaging in a course of conduct."

Id. at 946. This structure must be proved as an element of the offense, but there is no need to prove that there was a definite structure beyond that inherent in the pattern of racketeering. That is, the existence of an enterprise may be inferred from the evidence demonstrating a pattern of racketeering activity. *See id.* at 947.

In so holding, the Court rejected petitioner's argument that an association-in-fact enterprise must have additional structural attributes, such as a hierarchy, role differentiation, or a unique *modus operandi. See id.*

> … Such a group need not have a hierarchical structure or a "chain of command"; decisions may be made on an ad hoc basis and by any number of methods—by majority vote, consensus, a show of strength, etc. Members of the group need not have fixed roles; different members may perform different roles at different times. The group need not have a name, regular meetings, dues, established rules and regulations, disciplinary procedures, or induction or initiation ceremonies. While the group must function as a continuing unit and remain in existence long enough to pursue a course of conduct, nothing in RICO exempts an enterprise whose associates engage in spurts of activity punctuated by periods of quiescence. Nor is the statute limited to groups whose crimes are sophisticated, diverse, complex, or unique; for example, a group that does nothing but engage in extortion through old-fashioned, unsophisticated, and brutal means may fall squarely within the statute's reach.

Id. at 948.

The *Boyle* majority also rejected the petitioner's argument that an inclusive reading of "association-in-fact enterprise" would make substantive RICO violations under 18 U.S.C. § 1962(c) indistinguishable from conspiracies to commit the RICO predicates under § 371:

> Under § 371, a conspiracy is an inchoate crime that may be completed in the brief period needed for the formation of the agreement and the commission of a single overt act in furtherance of the conspiracy. Section 1962(c) demands much more: the creation of an "enterprise"—a group with a common purpose and course of conduct—and the actual commission of a pattern of predicate offenses.

Boyle, 556 U.S. at 950. The Court similarly disregarded the plaintiff's argument that a broad definition of association-in-fact would effectively merge the substantive RICO violation in § 1962(c) with RICO conspiracy in § 1962(d), stating that although the elements of the two offenses are similar "this overlap would persist even if petitioner's conception of an association-in-fact enterprise were accepted." *Id.*

Justice Stevens, in dissent, contended that Congress intended the term "enterprise" "to refer only to business-like entities that have an existence apart from the predicate acts committed by their employees or associates." *Boyle*, 556 U.S. at 952 (Stevens, J., dissenting). He argued that in order to prove a § 1962(c) association-in-fact enterprise "the Government [should have to] ... prov[e] that an alleged enterprise has an existence separate from the pattern of racketeering activity undertaken by its constituents." *Id.* at 956. He objected that, under the majority's reading of the statute, juries are invited to find an association-in-fact enterprise in "every case involving a pattern of racketeering activity undertaken by two or more associates." *Id.* at 957. The majority "renders the enterprise requirement essentially meaningless in association-in-fact cases." *Id.*

The facts of *Boyle* demonstrate that the evidentiary bar of proving an association-in-fact is low. The defendant and a group of other individuals committed a series of bank thefts over a five-year period. *See Boyle*, 129 S.Ct. at 2241. Each theft was planned on an ad hoc basis, with the participants meeting beforehand to plan the crime, gather tools, and assign roles. *See id.* "The group was loosely and informally organized. It does not appear to have had a leader or hierarchy; nor does it appear that the participants ever formulated any long-term master plan or agreement." *Id.* Yet the Supreme Court affirmed Boyle's conviction under § 1962(c). Does virtually any "association-in-fact" allegation fly after *Boyle*? *See, e.g.*, United States v. Bergrin, 650 F.3d 257 (3d Cir. 2011)?

4. Many courts have indicated that the burden of proving an "association-in-fact" enterprise may be eased when a legal entity, such as a corporation, is injected into the mix. Does this necessarily make sense? A corporation may itself be alleged to be the enterprise through which racketeering was conducted, or a corporation may be one of a number of persons who together are alleged to comprise an "association-in-fact" enterprise. In studying the balance of this Chapter, readers may wish to think about what considerations would affect their charging choices in this regard. That is, what are the advantages of alleging, where possible on the facts, that a corporation or other legal entity is the "enterprise"? And when might a prosecutor or plaintiff wish to allege instead that the corporation is part of an "association-in-fact" enterprise that includes, again where possible, other corporate or individual actors?

CEDRIC KUSHNER PROMOTIONS, LTD. v. KING
533 U.S. 158 (2001)

JUSTICE BREYER delivered the opinion of the Court.

The Racketeer Influenced and Corrupt Organizations Act, 18 U.S.C. § 1961 *et seq.*, makes it "unlawful for any person employed by or associated with any enterprise ... to conduct or participate ... in the conduct of such enterprise's affairs" through the commission of two or more statutorily defined crimes—which RICO calls "a pattern of racketeering activity." §

1962(c). The language suggests, and lower courts have held, that this provision foresees two separate entities, a "person" and a distinct "enterprise."

This case focuses upon a person who is the president and sole shareholder of a closely held corporation. The plaintiff claims that the president has conducted the corporation's affairs through the forbidden "pattern," though for present purposes it is conceded that, in doing so, he acted within the scope of his authority as the corporation's employee. In these circumstances, are there two entities, a "person" and a separate "enterprise"? Assuming, as we must given the posture of this case, that the allegations in the complaint are true, we conclude that the "person" and "enterprise" here are distinct and that the RICO provision applies.

Petitioner, Cedric Kushner Promotions, Ltd., is a corporation that promotes boxing matches. Petitioner sued Don King, the president and sole shareholder of Don King Productions, a corporation, claiming that King had conducted the boxing-related affairs of Don King Productions in part through a RICO "pattern," i.e., through the alleged commission of at least two instances of fraud and other RICO predicate crimes. The District Court, citing Court of Appeals precedent, dismissed the complaint. And the Court of Appeals affirmed that dismissal. In the appellate court's view, § 1962(c) applies only where a plaintiff shows the existence of two separate entities, a "person" and a distinct "enterprise," the affairs of which that "person" improperly conducts. In this instance, "it is undisputed that King was an employee" of the corporation Don King Productions and also "acting within the scope of his authority." Under the Court of Appeals' analysis, King, in a legal sense, was part of, not separate from, the corporation. There was no "person," distinct from the "enterprise," who improperly conducted the "enterprise's affairs." And thus § 1962(c) did not apply.

Other Circuits, applying § 1962(c) in roughly similar circumstances, have reached a contrary conclusion. See, e.g., *Jaguar Cars, Inc. v. Royal Oaks Motor Car Co.*, 46 F.3d 258, 265, 269 (C.A.3 1995). We granted certiorari to resolve the conflict. We now agree with these Circuits and hold that the Second Circuit's interpretation of § 1962(c) is erroneous.

We do not quarrel with the basic principle that to establish liability under § 1962(c) one must allege and prove the existence of two distinct entities: (1) a "person"; and (2) an "enterprise" that is not simply the same "person" referred to by a different name. The statute's language, read as ordinary English, suggests that principle. The Act says that it applies to "person[s]" who are "employed by or associated with" the "enterprise." § 1962(c). In ordinary English one speaks of employing, being employed by, or associating with others, not oneself. In addition, the Act's purposes are consistent with that principle. Whether the Act seeks to prevent a person from victimizing, say, a small business, S.Rep. No. 91-617, p. 77 (1969), or to prevent a person from using a corporation for criminal purposes, *National Organization for Women, Inc. v. Scheidler*, 510 U.S. 249, 259 (1994), the person and the victim, or the person and the tool, are different entities, not the same.

The Acting Solicitor General reads § 1962(c) "to require some distinctness between the RICO defendant and the RICO enterprise." And she says that this requirement is "legally sound and workable." We agree with her assessment, particularly in light of the fact that 12 Courts of Appeals have interpreted the statute as embodying some such distinctness requirement without creating discernible mischief in the administration of RICO. Indeed, this Court previously has said that liability "depends on showing that the defendants conducted or participated in the conduct of the '*enterprise*'s affairs,' not just their *own* affairs." *Reves v. Ernst & Young*, 507 U.S. 170, 185 (1993).

While accepting the "distinctness" principle, we nonetheless disagree with the appellate court's application of that principle to the present circumstances—circumstances in which a corporate employee, "acting within the scope of his authority," allegedly conducts the corporation's affairs in a RICO-forbidden way. The corporate owner/employee, a natural person, is distinct from the corporation itself, a legally different entity with different rights and responsibilities due to its different legal status. And we can find nothing in the statute that requires more "separateness" than that. Cf. *McCullough v. Suter*, 757 F.2d 142, 144 (C.A.7 1985) (finding either formal or practical separateness sufficient to be distinct under § 1962(c)).

Linguistically speaking, an employee who conducts the affairs of a corporation through illegal acts comes within the terms of a statute that forbids any "person" unlawfully to conduct an "enterprise," particularly when the statute explicitly defines "person" to include "any individual ... capable of holding a legal or beneficial interest in property," and defines "enterprise" to include a "corporation." 18 U.S.C. §§ 1961(3), (4). And, linguistically speaking, the employee and the corporation are different "persons," even where the employee is the corporation's sole owner. After all, incorporation's basic purpose is to create a distinct legal entity, with legal rights, obligations, powers, and privileges different from those of the natural individuals who created it, who own it, or whom it employs.

We note that the Second Circuit relied on earlier Circuit precedent for its decision. But that precedent involved quite different circumstances which are not presented here. This case concerns a claim that a corporate employee is the "person" and the corporation is the "enterprise." It is natural to speak of a corporate employee as a "person employed by" the corporation. § 1962(c). The earlier Second Circuit precedent concerned a claim that a corporation was the "person" and the corporation, together with all its employees and agents, were the "enterprise." See *Riverwoods Chappaqua Corp. v. Marine Midland Bank, N. A.*, 30 F.3d 339, 344 (1994). It is less natural to speak of a corporation as "employed by" or "associated with" this latter oddly constructed entity. And the Second Circuit's other precedent also involved significantly different allegations compared with the instant case. See[, e.g.,] *Discon, Inc. v. NYNEX Corp.*, 93 F.3d 1055, 1064 (1996) (involving complaint alleging that corporate subsidiaries were "persons" and subsidiaries, taken together as parent, were "enterprise"), *vacated on other grounds*, 525 U.S. 128 (1998). We do not here consider the merits of these cases, and note only their distinction from the instant case.

Further, to apply the RICO statute in present circumstances is consistent with the statute's basic purposes as this Court has defined them. The Court has held that RICO both protects a legitimate "enterprise" from those who would use unlawful acts to victimize it, *United States v. Turkette*, 452 U.S. 576, 591 (1981), and also protects the public from those who would unlawfully use an "enterprise" (whether legitimate or illegitimate) as a "vehicle" through which "unlawful ... activity is committed," *National Organization for Women, Inc.*, 510 U.S., at 259. A corporate employee who conducts the corporation's affairs through an unlawful RICO "pattern ... of activity," § 1962(c), uses that corporation as a "vehicle" whether he is, or is not, its sole owner.

Conversely, the appellate court's critical legal distinction—between employees acting within the scope of corporate authority and those acting outside that authority—is inconsistent with a basic statutory purpose. Cf. *Reves, supra*, at 184 (stating that an enterprise is "'operated,'" within § 1962(c)'s meaning, "not just by upper management but also by lower rung participants in the enterprise *who are under the direction of upper management*" (emphasis added)). It would immunize from RICO liability many of those at whom this Court has said RICO directly aims—*e.g.*, high-ranking individuals in an illegitimate criminal enterprise, who, seeking to further the purposes of that enterprise, act within the scope of their authority. Cf. *Turkette, supra*, at 581 (Congress "did nothing to indicate that an enterprise consisting of a group of individuals was not covered by RICO if the purpose of the enterprise was exclusively criminal").

Finally, we have found nothing in the statute's history that significantly favors an alternative interpretation. That history not only refers frequently to the importance of undermining organized crime's influence upon legitimate businesses but also refers to the need to protect the public from those who would run "organization[s] in a manner detrimental to the public interest." This latter purpose, as we have said, invites the legal principle we endorse, namely, that in present circumstances the statute requires no more than the formal legal distinction between "person" and "enterprise" (namely, incorporation) that is present here.

In reply, King argues that the lower court's rule is consistent with (1) the principle that a corporation acts only through its directors, officers, and agents, (2) the principle that a corporation should not be liable for the criminal acts of its employees where Congress so intends, and (3) the Sherman Act principle limiting liability under 15 U.S.C. § 1 by excluding "from unlawful combinations or conspiracies the activities of a single firm," *Copperweld Corp. v. Independence Tube Corp.*, 467 U.S. 752, 769-770, n. 15 (1984). The alternative that we endorse, however, is no less consistent with these principles. It does not deny that a corporation acts through its employees; it says only that the corporation and its employees are not legally identical. It does not assert that ordinary *respondeat superior* principles make a corporation legally liable under RICO for the criminal acts of its employees; that is a matter of congressional intent not before us. See, *e.g.,* [*Gasoline Sales, Inc. v. Aero Oil Co.,* 39 F.3d 70, 73 (C.A.3 1994)] (holding that corporation cannot be "vicariously liable" for § 1962(c) violations committed by its vice president). Neither is it inconsistent with antitrust law's intracorporate conspiracy doctrine; that doctrine turns on specific antitrust objectives. See *Copperweld Corp., supra,* at 770-771. Rather, we hold simply that the need for two distinct entities is satisfied; hence, the RICO provision before us applies when a corporate employee unlawfully conducts the affairs of the corporation of which he is the sole owner—whether he conducts those affairs within the scope, or beyond the scope, of corporate authority. ...

Notes

1. To understand the issue presented in *Cedric Kushner,* it may help to understand the unanimous rule prevailing in the circuits (and seemingly approved by the Supreme Court) which provides that a corporate "person" charged under § 1962(c) cannot also be the "enterprise" under that section. See United States v. Goldin Indus., Inc., 219 F.3d 1268 (11th Cir. 2000) (overruling the sole decision to the contrary in *United States v. Hartley,* 678 F.2d 961 (11th Cir. 1982)). This is sometimes referred to as the distinctiveness requirement of § 1962(c). To illustrate, assume that corporate employees, using their positions in the corporation, defraud the corporation's customers for corporate gain and personal advancement. The customers in a civil RICO suit, and perhaps the prosecutor in a criminal case, may wish to go after the "deep-pocket" corporation. How would they charge the case?

Corporations fall within the statutory definition of both defendant "person" and "enterprise." See 18 U.S.C. § 1961(3) ("person"), (4) ("enterprise"). But if the case is charged under § 1962(c), does it make sense to say that the defendant "person" (the corporation) can be "employed by or associated with" an enterprise that is the corporation? Can a person be employed by or associated with itself? The courts say "no," relying primarily on plain language, *see, e.g.,* United States v. Computer Sciences Corp., 689 F.2d 1181, 1190 (4th Cir. 1982) (a "defendant could [not] conspire with his right arm"), and on policy. *See also Cedric Kushner Promotions, supra;* Schoedinger v. United Healthcare of Midwest, Inc., 557 F.3d 872, 878 (8th Cir. 2009). As the Seventh Circuit explained in *Haroco, Inc. v. American Nat'l Bank & Trust Co.,* 747 F.2d 384 (7th Cir. 1984):

> At the policy level of the dispute, there are several significant competing arguments. The Eleventh Circuit argued in *Hartley* [, since overruled in *Goldin,* 219 F.3d at 1271,] that where the defendant corporation is the central figure in a criminal scheme, as it was in that case, Congress could not have meant to let the central perpetrator escape RICO liability while subjecting only the sidekicks to RICO's severe penalties. Similarly, plaintiffs here argue that Congress intended to make a "deep pocket" (in the person of the corporation) liable where corporate agents engage in a pattern of racketeering activity redounding to the benefit of the corporation. ...
>
> In our view, the RICO provisions have already taken into account these competing policies in different situations, and a careful parsing of section 1962 reveals a sensible balance among these policies. We find helpful here Professor Blakey's discussion in [*The Rico Civil Fraud Action in Context,* 58 Notre Dame L. Rev. 237, 307-25 (1982)]. Blakey points out that under the subsections of section 1962, the enterprise may play the various roles of victim, prize, instrument or perpetrator. The RICO liability of the enterprise should depend on the role played. In our view, the plaintiffs here and the court in *Hartley* are correct when they argue that the corporate enterprise should be liable where it is the perpetrator, or the central figure in the criminal scheme. In that situation, the corporate deep pocket should certainly be subject to RICO liability. At the same time, the defendants here ... are surely correct in saying that the corporation-enterprise should not

be liable when the corporation is itself the victim or target, or merely the passive instrument for the wrongdoing of others.

In our view, the tensions between these policies may be resolved sensibly and in accord with the language of section 1962 by reading subsection (c) together with subsection (a). As we read subsection (c), the "enterprise" and the "person" must be distinct. However, a corporation-enterprise may be held liable under subsection (a) when the corporation is also a perpetrator. As we parse subsection (a), a "person" (such as a corporation-enterprise) acts unlawfully if it receives income derived directly or indirectly from a pattern of racketeering activity in which the person has participated as a principal within the meaning of 18 U.S.C. § 2, and if the person uses the income in the establishment or *operation* of an enterprise affecting commerce. Subsection (a) does not contain any of the language in subsection (c) which suggests that the liable person and the enterprise must be separate. Under subsection (a), therefore, the liable person may be a corporation using the proceeds of a pattern of racketeering activity in its operations. This approach to subsection (a) thus makes the corporation-enterprise liable under RICO when the corporation is actually the direct or indirect beneficiary of the pattern of racketeering activity, but not when it is merely the victim, prize, or passive instrument of racketeering. This result is in accord with the primary purpose of RICO, which, after all, is to reach those who ultimately profit from racketeering, not those who are victimized by it.

Id. at 401-02. When should a corporation be deemed a perpetrator and when should it be deemed the victim, prize, or passive instrument in a § 1962(c) case? Given that corporations may only act through their agents, and the rules underlying *respondeat superior* liability, aren't most corporate "instruments" also reasonably termed "perpetrators"? Because the plain language of § 1962(c) may preclude charging the corporation as the defendant "person" and the "enterprise" even where the corporation is the perpetrator, how should plaintiffs or prosecutors proceed? Why might prosecutors or plaintiffs be unwilling or unable to proceed under § 1962(a) in some cases?

2. The *Cedric Kushner* Court also alludes to, without definitively resolving, the issue whether plaintiffs or prosecutors could avoid § 1962(c)'s plain language bar by using vicarious liability principles. For example, could one charge that a corporation is the RICO "enterprise" and that it is also liable under *respondeat superior* principles for the actions of the individual "persons" within the corporation who committed the racketeering activity? Many courts have permitted civil plaintiffs to pursue a corporation under vicarious liability principles under subsections (a) and (b) of § 1962 where the plaintiffs can demonstrate that the corporation in fact derived some benefit from its agent's racketeering activity. *See, e.g.*, Crowe v. Henry, 43 F.3d 198, 206 (5th Cir. 1995); Landry v. Air Line Pilots Ass'n, 901 F.2d 404, 425 (5th Cir. 1990); Liquid Air Corp. v. Rogers, 834 F.2d 1297, 1306-07 (7th Cir. 1987); Petro-Tech, Inc. v. Western Co., 824 F.2d 1349, 1360-62 (3d Cir. 1987). By contrast, the weight of authority seems to be that, at least in civil cases, a plaintiff may not use vicarious liability principles to escape the rule that a corporation may not be both the defendant "person" and the "enterprise" under § 1962(c). *See, e.g.*, Miller v. Yokohama Tire Corp., 358 F.3d 616, 620 (9th Cir. 2004); Miranda v. Ponce Federal Bank, 948 F.2d 41, 45 (1st Cir. 1991); *Landry*, 901 F.2d at 425; *Liquid Air Corp.*, 834 F.2d at 1306-07; *Petro-Tech, Inc.*, 824 F.2d at 1360-62; Schofield v. First Commodity Corp., 793 F.2d 28, 32-33 (1st Cir. 1986).

3. Some courts, however, hold that "an employer that is benefitted by its employee or agent's violations of § 1962(c) may be held liable under the doctrine of *respondeat superior* and agency when the employer is distinct from the enterprise" (that is, when the enterprise alleged is not the corporation). Brady v. Dairy Fresh Prods. Co., 974 F.2d 1149, 1154 (9th Cir. 1992); *see also* Davis v. Mutual Life Ins. Co., 6 F.3d 367, 378-80 (6th Cir. 1993); Ashland Oil v. Arnett, 875 F.2d 1271, 1281 (7th Cir. 1989). *But see* D & S Auto Parts, Inc. v. Schwartz, 838 F.2d 964 (7th Cir. 1988) (seemingly rejecting vicarious liability under any section of § 1962). How would one charge a case so as to fit within the *Brady* rule? Could one get around the bar on charging corporations as both the defendant "person" and the "enterprise" by charging the

corporation as the defendant "person" and as one of a number of actors who together constitute an "association-in-fact" enterprise?

4. An "association-in-fact" enterprise may be made up of a number of different corporate or other entities and individuals who together fit the other requirements of an "enterprise." *See, e.g.*, United States v. Philip Morris USA, Inc., 566 F.3d 1095, 1110-1116 (D.C. Cir. 2009). May prosecutors or plaintiffs seek to go after the deep pocket company, while avoiding the restraints of the distinctiveness requirement, by alleging that the defendant "person" corporation operated through an association-in-fact comprised of the corporation and other (legal or natural) persons?

Some courts have permitted cases to go forward where the "enterprise" is charged as an association-in-fact of entities and individuals, and the entities are also the defendant "persons." *See, e.g., Philip Morris USA, Inc.*, 566 F.3d at 111; Odom v. Microsoft Corp., 486 F.3d 541, 552-553 (9th Cir. 2007); United States v. Najjar, 300 F.3d 466, 484-85 (4th Cir. 2002); United States v. Goldin Indus. Inc., 219 F.3d 1271, 1275-1277 (11th Cir. 2000); Atlas Pile Driving Co. v. DiCON Financial, 886 F.2d 986, 995 (8th Cir. 1989).

Other courts have held that where a *corporation* is alleged to be both the defendant "person" and a part of an "association-in-fact" enterprise that consists of the corporation and its errant employees or the corporation and affiliated corporate entities, there is an insufficient distinction between the corporate defendant "person" and the RICO "enterprise" for purposes of § 1962(c). *See, e.g.*, Fitzgerald v. Chrysler Corp., 116 F.3d 225, 226 (7th Cir. 1997); Jaguar Cars, Inc. v. Royal Oaks Motor Car Co., 46 F.3d 258, 268 (3d Cir. 1995); Riverwoods Chappaqua Corp. v. Marine Midland Bank, N.A., 30 F.3d 339, 343-45 (2d Cir. 1994); *cf.* St. Paul Mercury Ins. Co. v. Williamson, 224 F.3d 425, 445-47 (5th Cir. 2000). The courts reason that plaintiffs or prosecutors should not be permitted to "circumvent" the plain language bar merely by alleging that the corporation and its errant employees or affiliates constitute an "association-in-fact" enterprise. Cedric Kushner Promotions, Ltd. v. King, 219 F.3d 115, 116 (2d Cir.2000) (*per curiam*), *rev'd*, 533 U.S. 158 (2001). More fundamentally, they appear to be troubled by the potential such pleadings hold for allowing every commercial dispute alleging corporate fraud to be brought under RICO in federal court. *See Fitzgerald*, 116 F.3d at 226-27. The Supreme Court in *Cedric Kushner* notes this issue but, again, does not resolve it. What is the right result?

On what basis do these courts (and the Second Circuit in *Cedric Kushner*) determine that a case that appears to fit within the language of the statute may not proceed because of "policy" concerns? Then Chief Judge Posner explained in *Fitzgerald v. Chrysler Corp.*, 116 F.3d 225 (7th Cir. 1997):

> Read literally, RICO would encompass every fraud case against a corporation, provided only that a pattern of fraud and some use of the mails or of telecommunications to further the fraud were shown; the corporation would be the RICO person and the corporation plus its employees the "enterprise." The courts have excluded this far-fetched possibility by holding that an employer and its employees cannot constitute a RICO enterprise. We do not understand the plaintiffs to be quarreling with this exclusion, even though it doesn't emerge from the statutory language; it emerges from a desire to make the statute make sense and have some limits.
>
> When a statute is broadly worded in order to prevent loopholes from being drilled in it by ingenious lawyers, there is a danger of its being applied to situations absurdly remote from the concerns of the statute's framers. Courts find it helpful, in interpreting such statutes in a way that will avoid absurd applications—a conventional office of statutory interpretation, even under "plain language" approaches—first to identify the prototype situation to which the statute is addressed. That need not be the most common case to which it is applied; the prototype may be effectively deterred because its legal status is clear. The second step is to determine how close to the prototype the case before the court is—how close, in other words, the family resemblance is between the prototypical case and the case at hand.

Id. at 226-27. Is this an appropriate role for courts to undertake in interpreting vague statutes? Does it comport with the Supreme Court's analysis in *Turkette*? Shouldn't the fact that RICO has both criminal and civil applications militate against such an approach?

5. Does this rule mean that *individual* defendant "persons" who are alleged to be participants in the "association-in-fact" enterprise also are insufficiently "distinct" from the enterprise for purposes of § 1962(c)? The answer appears to depend upon the nature of the case, and on the circuit in which suit is filed. Many courts hold that an individual *can* be both a defendant "person" and one of a group of persons alleged to be the "association-in-fact" enterprise; indeed, *Turkette* was such a case. The reasoning is, as the Eighth Circuit has explained:

> "A collective entity is something more than the members of which it is comprised." Although a defendant may not be both a person and an enterprise, a defendant may be both a person and a part of an enterprise. In such a case, the individual defendant is distinct from the organizational entity.

United States v. Fairchild, 189 F.3d 769, 777 (8th Cir. 1999); *see also* St. Paul Mercury Ins. Co. v. Williamson, 224 F.3d 425, 445-47 (5th Cir. 2000) (apparently overruling two Fifth Circuit decisions to the contrary in *In re* Burzynski, 989 F.2d 733, 743 (5th Cir. 1993) and Crowe v. Henry, 43 F.3d 198, 206 (5th Cir. 1995)). Why doesn't this same reasoning compel the conclusion that a *corporation* "may be both a person and a part of an enterprise"?

6. The above cases deal with situations in which the corporation is best viewed as either the instrument or perpetrator of the misconduct. What about where the corporation truly is the victim? For example, may a corporate victim of employee embezzlement sue the employee claiming that the employee "person" conducted the affairs of the plaintiff "enterprise" through a pattern of racketeering? Is there any plain language bar on the corporation being the *plaintiff* and the "enterprise"? Despite the fact that this situation appears to fall within the language of the statute, and that many courts thought at least for a time that § 1962(c) was designed to prevent victimization of legitimate entities, some courts have recently suggested that it would *not* be possible for the corporation to pursue such a suit. *See, e.g.*, LaSalle Bank Lake View v. Seguban, 54 F.3d 387, 393-94 (7th Cir. 1995). For example, in the Third Circuit's decision in *Jaguar Cars, Inc. v. Royal Oaks Motor Car Co.*, 46 F.3d 258 (3d Cir. 1995), cited by the Supreme Court in *Cedric Kushner*, the court explained that "a victim 'drained of its own money' by pilfering officers and employees could not reasonably be viewed as the enterprise through which employed persons carried out their racketeering activity. Rather, in such an instance, the proper enterprise would be the association of employees who are victimizing the corporation, while the victim corporation would not be the enterprise, but instead the § 1962(c) claimant." *Id.* at 267.

7. May an individual be both the RICO "person" and a one-man "enterprise"? On the reasoning of the above cases, the answer is "no" because one cannot be employed by or associated with oneself for purposes of § 1962(c). May a sole proprietorship be the "enterprise" through which the proprietor can be "associated"? If the sole proprietorship is a "one-man show," the answer would be "no" but if the sole proprietorship has employees or other associates, the courts answer "yes." *See* United States v. Benny, 786 F.2d 1410 (9th Cir. 1986); McCullough v. Suter, 757 F.2d 142, 143-44 (7th Cir. 1985). But, under *Cedric Kushner*, if an individual adopts the corporate form to run a "one-man show," that one-man corporation may be deemed an enterprise through which the incorporator is associated under § 1962(c).

8. In public corruption cases, prosecutors often charge that the RICO "enterprise" is a legitimate public entity through which corrupt defendants are said to have conducted racketeering activities such as bribery or extortion. *See, e.g.*, United States v. Davis, 707 F.2d 880 (6th Cir. 1983) (Country Sheriff's Office); United States v. Thompson, 685 F.2d 993 (6th Cir. 1982) (Office of the Governor of the state); United States v. Angelilli, 660 F.2d 23 (2d Cir. 1981) (New York City Civil Court); United States v. Grzywacz, 603 F.2d 682 (7th Cir. 1979) (city police department). Some courts believe that the practice of naming a government entity as a RICO "enterprise" should be discouraged. *See Thompson*, 685 F.2d at 994-95, 100. Why?

Reves v. Ernst & Young, reproduced *infra*, set limits on the extent to which "outsiders" of a legal enterprise may be held liable under § 1962(c). Readers may wish to reconsider the wisdom of alleging that a government entity is the RICO "enterprise" in corruption cases that target the "outside" corruptors as well as the "insider" who is corrupted after reviewing *Reves*.

9. Instead of creating policy-based pleading rules not reflected in the language of the statute, may courts troubled by the federalization of state-law commercial disputes instead rely on RICO's jurisdictional requirements to limit its scope? Section 1962(c) states that it shall be unlawful for a person employed by or associated with "any enterprise engaged in, or the activities of which affect, interstate or foreign commerce" to conduct the affairs of the enterprise through a pattern of racketeering activity. Thus, the statute requires that it be the *enterprise* that satisfies the statute's jurisdictional requirement. *See, e.g.*, United States v. Robertson, 514 U.S. 669 (1995); *see also* National Org. for Women v. Scheidler, 510 U.S. 249, 257-58 (1994); United States v. Gray, 137 F.3d 765, 772 (4th Cir. 1998). The jurisdictional proof courts require mirrors that required in public corruption cases, *see supra* Chapter 8, and little generally need be shown to establish this element. *See, e.g.*, United States v. Nascimento, 491 F.3d 25 (1st Cir. 2007); *Gray*, 137 F.3d at 773; United States v. Miller, 116 F.3d 641, 674 (2d Cir. 1997). *But see* Waucaush v. United States, 380 F.3d 251, 256 (6th Cir. 2004) ("where the enterprise itself did not engage in economic activity, a minimal effect on commerce will not do"). Why should defense counsel remain vigilant with respect to this element? In what kinds of cases could it make a difference?

2. PATTERN OF RACKETEERING ACTIVITY

H.J. INC. v. NORTHWESTERN BELL TEL. CO.
492 U.S. 229 (1989)

JUSTICE BRENNAN delivered the opinion of the Court.

The Racketeer Influenced and Corrupt Organizations Act (RICO or Act), 18 U.S.C. §§ 1961-1968, imposes criminal and civil liability upon those who engage in certain "prohibited activities." Each prohibited activity is defined in 18 U.S.C. § 1962 to include, as one necessary element, proof either of "a pattern of racketeering activity" or of "collection of an unlawful debt." "Racketeering activity" is defined in RICO to mean "any act or threat involving" specified state-law crimes, any "act" indictable under various specified federal statutes, and certain federal "offenses," 18 U.S.C. § 1961(1); but of the term "pattern" the statute says only that it "requires at least two acts of racketeering activity" within a 10-year period, 18 U.S.C. § 1961(5). We are called upon in this civil case to consider what conduct meets RICO's pattern requirement. ...

Petitioners, customers of respondent Northwestern Bell Telephone Co., filed this putative class action in 1986 in the District Court for the District of Minnesota. Petitioners alleged violations of §§ 1962(a), (b), (c), and (d) by Northwestern Bell and the other respondents—some of the telephone company's officers and employees, various members of the Minnesota Public Utilities Commission (MPUC), and other unnamed individuals and corporations—and sought an injunction and treble damages under RICO's civil liability provisions, §§ 1964(a) and (c).

The MPUC is the state body responsible for determining the rates that Northwestern Bell may charge. Petitioners' five-count complaint alleged that between 1980 and 1986 Northwestern Bell sought to influence members of the MPUC in the performance of their duties—and in fact caused them to approve rates for the company in excess of a fair and reasonable amount—by making cash payments to commissioners, negotiating with them regarding future employment, and paying for parties and meals, for tickets to sporting events and the like, and for airline tickets. Based upon these factual allegations, petitioners alleged in their first count a pendent state-law claim, asserting that Northwestern Bell violated the Minnesota bribery statute, as well as state common law prohibiting bribery. They also raised four separate claims under § 1962 of RICO. Count II alleged that, in violation of § 1962(a), Northwestern Bell derived income from a pattern of racketeering activity involving predicate acts of bribery and used this income to engage in its business as an interstate "enterprise." Count III claimed a violation of § 1962(b), in that, through this same pattern of racketeering activity, respondents acquired an interest in or control of the MPUC, which was also an interstate "enterprise." In Count IV, petitioners asserted that respondents participated in the conduct and affairs of the MPUC through this pattern of racketeering activity, contrary to § 1962(c). Finally, Count V alleged that respondents conspired together to violate §§ 1962(a), (b), and (c), thereby contravening § 1962(d).

The District Court granted respondents' Federal Rule of Civil Procedure 12(b)(6) motion, dismissing the complaint for failure to state a claim upon which relief could be granted. The court found that "[e]ach of the fraudulent acts alleged by [petitioners] was committed in furtherance of a single scheme to influence MPUC commissioners to the detriment of Northwestern Bell's ratepayers." It held that dismissal was therefore mandated by the Court of Appeals for the Eighth Circuit's decision in *Superior Oil Co. v. Fulmer*, 785 F.2d 252 (1986), which the District Court interpreted as adopting an "extremely restrictive" test for a pattern of racketeering activity that required proof of "multiple illegal schemes." The Court of Appeals for the Eighth Circuit affirmed the dismissal of petitioners' complaint, confirming that under Eighth Circuit precedent "[a] single fraudulent effort or scheme is insufficient" to establish a pattern of racketeering activity, and agreeing with the District Court that petitioners' complaint alleged only a single scheme. ... Most Courts of Appeals have rejected the Eighth Circuit's interpretation of RICO's pattern concept to require an allegation and proof of multiple schemes, and we granted certiorari to resolve this conflict. We now reverse.

In *Sedima, S.P.R.L. v. Imrex Co.*, 473 U.S. 479 (1985), this Court rejected a restrictive interpretation of § 1964(c) that would have made it a condition for maintaining a civil RICO action both that the defendant had already been convicted of a predicate racketeering act or of a RICO violation, and that plaintiff show a special racketeering injury. In doing so, we acknowledged concern in some quarters over civil RICO's use against "legitimate" businesses, as well as "mobsters and organized criminals"—a concern that had frankly led to the Court of Appeals' interpretation of § 1964(c) in *Sedima*. But we suggested that RICO's expansive uses "appear to be primarily the result of the breadth of the predicate offenses, in particular the inclusion of wire, mail, and securities fraud, and the failure of Congress and the courts to develop a meaningful concept of 'pattern'"—both factors that apply to criminal as well as civil applications of the Act. Congress has done nothing in the interim further to illuminate RICO's key requirement of a pattern of racketeering; and as the plethora of different views expressed by the Courts of Appeals since *Sedima* demonstrates, developing a meaningful concept of "pattern" within the existing statutory framework has proved to be no easy task.

It is, nevertheless, a task we must undertake in order to decide this case. Our guides in the endeavor must be the text of the statute and its legislative history. We find no support in those sources for the proposition, espoused by the Court of Appeals for the Eighth Circuit in this case, that predicate acts of racketeering may form a pattern only when they are part of separate illegal schemes. Nor can we agree with those courts that have suggested that a pattern is established merely by proving two predicate acts, or with *amici* in this case who argue that the word "pattern" refers only to predicates that are indicative of a perpetrator involved in organized crime or its functional equivalent. In our view, Congress had a more natural and commonsense approach to RICO's pattern element in mind, intending a more stringent requirement than proof simply of two predicates, but also envisioning a concept of sufficient breadth that it might encompass multiple predicates within a single scheme that were related and that amounted to, or threatened the likelihood of, continued criminal activity.

We begin, of course, with RICO's text, in which Congress followed a "pattern [of] utilizing terms and concepts of breadth." As we remarked in *Sedima*, the section of the statute headed "definitions," 18 U.S.C. § 1961, does not so much define a pattern of racketeering activity as state a minimum necessary condition for the existence of such a pattern. Unlike other provisions in § 1961 that tell us what various concepts used in the Act "mean," 18 U.S.C. § 1961(5) says of the phrase "pattern of racketeering activity" only that it "requires at least two acts of racketeering activity, one of which occurred after [October 15, 1970,] and the last of which occurred within ten years (excluding any period of imprisonment) after the commission of a prior act of racketeering activity." It thus places an outer limit on the concept of a pattern of racketeering activity that is broad indeed.

Section 1961(5) does indicate that Congress envisioned circumstances in which no more than two predicates would be necessary to establish a pattern of racketeering—otherwise it would have drawn a narrower boundary to RICO liability, requiring proof of a greater number of predicates. But, at the same time, the statement that a pattern "requires at least" two predicates implies "that while two acts are necessary, they may not be sufficient." Section 1961(5) concerns only the minimum *number* of predicates necessary to establish a pattern; and it assumes that there is something to a RICO pattern *beyond* simply the number of predicate acts involved. ...

The legislative history ... shows that Congress ... had a fairly flexible concept of a pattern in mind. A pattern is not formed by "sporadic activity," and a person cannot "be subjected to the sanctions of title IX simply for committing two widely separated and isolated criminal offenses." Instead, "[t]he term 'pattern' itself requires the showing of a relationship" between the predicates and of "'the threat of continuing activity.'" "It is this factor of *continuity plus relationship* which combines to produce a pattern." RICO's legislative history reveals Congress' intent that to prove a pattern of racketeering activity a plaintiff or prosecutor must show that the racketeering predicates are related, *and* that they amount to or pose a threat of continued criminal activity.

For analytic purposes these two constituents of RICO's pattern requirement must be stated separately, though in practice their proof will often overlap. The element of relatedness is the easier to define, for we may take guidance from a provision elsewhere in the Organized Crime Control Act of 1970 (OCCA). OCCA included as Title X the Dangerous Special Offender Sentencing Act. Title X provided for enhanced sentences where, among other things, the defendant had committed a prior felony as part of a pattern of criminal conduct or in furtherance of a conspiracy to engage in a pattern of criminal conduct. ... Congress defined Title X's pattern requirement solely in terms of the *relationship* of the defendant's criminal acts one to another: "[C]riminal conduct forms a pattern if it embraces criminal acts that have the same or similar purposes, results, participants, victims, or methods of commission, or otherwise are interrelated by distinguishing characteristics and are not isolated events." We have no reason to suppose that Congress had in mind for RICO's pattern of racketeering component any more constrained a notion of the relationships between predicates that would suffice.

RICO's legislative history tells us, however, that the relatedness of racketeering activities is not alone enough to satisfy § 1962's pattern element. To establish a RICO pattern it must also be shown that the predicates themselves amount to, or that they otherwise constitute a threat of, *continuing* racketeering activity. ... It is this aspect of RICO's pattern element that has spawned the "multiple scheme" test adopted by some lower courts, including the Court of Appeals in this case. But although proof that a RICO defendant has been involved in multiple criminal schemes would certainly be highly relevant to the inquiry into the continuity of the defendant's racketeering activity, it is implausible to suppose that Congress thought continuity might be shown *only* by proof of multiple schemes. The Eighth Circuit's test brings a rigidity to the available methods of proving a pattern that simply is not present in the idea of "continuity" itself; and it does so, moreover, by introducing a concept—the "scheme"—that appears nowhere in the language or legislative history of the Act.[23] We adopt a less inflexible approach that seems to us to derive from a commonsense, everyday understanding of RICO's language and Congress' gloss on it. What a plaintiff or prosecutor must prove is continuity of

---

23 [Court's footnote 3:] Nor does the multiple scheme approach to identifying continuing criminal conduct have the advantage of lessening the uncertainty inherent in RICO's pattern component, for "'scheme' is hardly a self-defining term." A "scheme" is in the eye of the beholder, since whether a scheme exists depends on the level of generality at which criminal activity is viewed. For example, petitioners' allegation that Northwestern Bell attempted to subvert public utility commissioners who would be voting on the company's rates might be described as a single scheme to obtain a favorable rate, or as multiple schemes to obtain favorable votes from individual commissioners on the ratemaking decision. ...

racketeering activity, or its threat, *simpliciter*. This may be done in a variety of ways, thus making it difficult to formulate in the abstract any general test for continuity. We can, however, begin to delineate the requirement.

"Continuity" is both a closed- and open-ended concept, referring either to a closed period of repeated conduct, or to past conduct that by its nature projects into the future with a threat of repetition. It is, in either case, centrally a temporal concept—and particularly so in the RICO context, where *what* must be continuous, RICO's predicate acts or offenses, and the *relationship* these predicates must bear one to another, are distinct requirements. A party alleging a RICO violation may demonstrate continuity over a closed period by proving a series of related predicates extending over a substantial period of time. Predicate acts extending over a few weeks or months and threatening no future criminal conduct do not satisfy this requirement: Congress was concerned in RICO with long-term criminal conduct. Often a RICO action will be brought before continuity can be established in this way. In such cases, liability depends on whether the *threat* of continuity is demonstrated.

Whether the predicates proved establish a threat of continued racketeering activity depends on the specific facts of each case. Without making any claim to cover the field of possibilities—preferring to deal with this issue in the context of concrete factual situations presented for decision—we offer some examples of how this element might be satisfied. A RICO pattern may surely be established if the related predicates themselves involve a distinct threat of long-term racketeering activity, either implicit or explicit. Suppose a hoodlum were to sell "insurance" to a neighborhood's storekeepers to cover them against breakage of their windows, telling his victims he would be reappearing each month to collect the "premium" that would continue their "coverage." Though the number of related predicates involved may be small and they may occur close together in time, the racketeering acts themselves include a specific threat of repetition extending indefinitely into the future, and thus supply the requisite threat of continuity. In other cases, the threat of continuity may be established by showing that the predicate acts or offenses are part of an ongoing entity's regular way of doing business. Thus, the threat of continuity is sufficiently established where the predicates can be attributed to a defendant operating as part of a long-term association that exists for criminal purposes. Such associations include, but extend well beyond, those traditionally grouped under the phrase "organized crime." The continuity requirement is likewise satisfied where it is shown that the predicates are a regular way of conducting defendant's ongoing legitimate business (in the sense that it is not a business that exists for criminal purposes), or of conducting or participating in an ongoing and legitimate RICO "enterprise." ...

We turn now to the application of our analysis of RICO's pattern requirement. ...

Petitioners' complaint alleges that at different times over the course of at least a 6-year period the noncommissioner respondents gave five members of the MPUC numerous bribes, in several different forms, with the objective—in which they were allegedly successful—of causing these commissioners to approve unfair and unreasonable rates for Northwestern Bell. RICO defines bribery as a "racketeering activity," 18 U.S.C. § 1961(1), so petitioners have alleged multiple predicate acts.

Under the analysis we have set forth above, and consistent with the allegations in their complaint, petitioners may be able to prove that the multiple predicates alleged constitute "a pattern of racketeering activity," in that they satisfy the requirements of relationship and continuity. The acts of bribery alleged are said to be related by a common purpose, to influence commissioners in carrying out their duties in order to win approval of unfairly and unreasonably high rates for Northwestern Bell. Furthermore, petitioners claim that the racketeering predicates occurred with some frequency over at least a 6-year period, which may be sufficient to satisfy the continuity requirement. Alternatively, a threat of continuity of racketeering activity might be established at trial by showing that the alleged bribes were a regular way of conducting Northwestern Bell's ongoing business, or a regular way of conducting or participating in the conduct of the alleged and ongoing RICO enterprise, the MPUC.

The Court of Appeals thus erred in affirming the District Court's dismissal of petitioners' complaint for failure to plead "a pattern of racketeering activity." The judgment is reversed, and the case is remanded for further proceedings consistent with this opinion.

JUSTICE SCALIA, with whom THE CHIEF JUSTICE, JUSTICE O'CONNOR, and JUSTICE KENNEDY join, concurring in the judgment.

... It is clear to me ... that the word "pattern" in the phrase "pattern of racketeering activity" was meant to import some requirement beyond the mere existence of multiple predicate acts. ... But what that something more is, is beyond me. ... [I]t is also beyond the Court. Today's opinion has added nothing to improve our prior guidance, which has created a kaleidoscope of circuit positions ...

That situation is bad enough with respect to any statute, but it is intolerable with respect to RICO. For it is not only true ... that our interpretation of RICO has "quite simply revolutionize[d] private litigation" and "validate[d] the federalization of broad areas of state common law of frauds," so that clarity and predictability in RICO's civil applications are particularly important; but it is also true that RICO, since it has criminal applications as well, must, even in its civil applications, possess the degree of certainty required for criminal laws. No constitutional challenge to this law has been raised in the present case, and so that issue is not before us. That the highest Court in the land has been unable to derive from this statute anything more than today's meager guidance bodes ill for the day when that challenge is presented. ...

Notes

1. Before *H.J., Inc.*, the Courts of Appeals were faced with "an extraordinary number of cases" raising the issue of what constitutes a cognizable "pattern of racketeering activity." Ashland Oil, Inc. v. Arnett, 875 F.2d 1271, 1276 (7th Cir. 1989). One reason for the recurrence of the issue is the scope and nature of the predicate racketeering activities identified by Congress. For example, mail and wire fraud, which as we have seen may be applied to an extraordinary variety of activities, are RICO predicates. As the Seventh Circuit explained:

> RICO includes as "racketeering activity" any act indictable under the mail and wire fraud statutes. In mail and wire fraud, each mailing or interstate communication is a separate indictable offense, even if each relates to the same scheme to defraud, and even if the defendant did not control the number of mailings or communications. Thus, the number of offenses is only tangentially related to the underlying fraud, and can be a matter of happenstance. ...
>
> Because of this peculiarity, when the crimes of mail and wire fraud are alleged as RICO predicate acts, any fraud which generates mailings or wire communications involves as many acts of "racketeering activity" as mailings or communications which further the scheme. This encourages bootstrapping ordinary civil fraud cases into RICO suits.

Id. at 1278; *see also* United States v. Computer Sciences Corp., 689 F.2d 1181, 1189-90 (4th Cir. 1982) (expressing similar concern in criminal case). Can you see why the court below may have required proof of "multiple schemes" in order to demonstrate a pattern of racketeering? The *H.J., Inc.* Court rejected the lower court's approach, instead requiring proof of "relatedness" and "continuity." Are these requirements effective to separate out those organized criminal activities that deserve RICO treatment from ordinary fraud cases involving multiple mailings or wirings that should not warrant punishment under RICO? Does the Court provide sufficient guidance to the lower courts required to administer these standards? *See Thirty-Third Annual Survey of White Collar Crime, supra* note 6, 1627-29 (surveying different approaches taken by the circuits post-*H.J., Inc.*). Rather than tailoring the list of predicate crimes, it has been Congress' wont to constantly add to that list. For example, in 2001,

Congress made terrorism crimes RICO predicates. In 2016, Congress added theft of trade secrets and economic espionage (18 U.S.C. §§ 1831, 1832) to the list of predicate acts.

2. Some courts of appeals have attempted to graft onto the statute additional proof requirements in an effort to cabin the reach of RICO to the problems it was created to address. The Supreme Court, bowing to the congressional mandate to read the statute expansively, has generally rebuffed these efforts.

For example, as the Court indicated in *H.J., Inc.*, the lower court in *Sedima, S.P.R.L. v. Imrex Co.*, 473 U.S. 479 (1985), had, "in response to what it perceived to be misuse of civil RICO by private plaintiffs, ... construed § 1964(c) to permit private actions only against defendants who had been convicted on criminal charges, and only where there had occurred a 'racketeering injury.'" *Id.* at 481. The *Sedima* Court rejected this attempt.

More recently, in *National Org. for Women v. Scheidler*, 510 U.S. 249 (1994), NOW and a number of abortion clinics had brought an action against a coalition of anti-abortion groups alleging that defendants were members of nationwide conspiracy to shut down abortion clinics through a pattern of racketeering activity in violation of RICO. The Supreme Court reversed the lower courts' dismissal of the action, holding that RICO does not require proof that either the racketeering enterprise or the predicate acts of racketeering be motivated by an *economic purpose*. In April 1998, a jury awarded the plaintiff abortion clinics $86,000 upon finding that "the Pro-Life Action League and Operation Rescue committed acts of extortion against abortion clinics throughout the country, using intimidation and violence against clinic employees and patients to shut down the clinics." *Seventeenth Survey of White Collar Crime*, 39 Am. Crim. L. Rev. 977, 1030 (2002). In *Scheidler v. Nat'l Organization for Women, Inc.*, 267 F.3d 687 (7th Cir. 2001), the Seventh Circuit held that injunctive relief is available to private plaintiffs under RICO's civil remedy provisions, 18 U.S.C. § 1964. The Supreme Court granted *certiorari* to hear this and a question related the predicate Hobbs Act violations alleged. In *Scheidler v. Nat'l Org. for Women, Inc.*, 537 U.S. 393 (2003) (discussed *supra*, Chapter 8 (Public Corruption)), the Supreme Court held that because the defendants did not "obtain" or attempt to obtain property from the plaintiffs, they did not commit extortion under the Hobbs Act. It reversed the RICO judgment because the predicate acts were based upon the claimed extortion. The Court therefore did not address the second question presented—whether a private plaintiff in a civil RICO action is entitled to injunctive relief under 18 U.S.C. § 1964.

3. Justice Scalia's concurrence essentially invited constitutional vagueness challenges, which were duly brought by eager defendants and universally rejected by lower courts. *See Thirty-Third Annual Survey of White Collar Crime*, *supra* note 6, at 1649-53. *Is* the statute unconstitutionally vague? What terms are particularly troubling? Is the true problem here vagueness—that is, the lack of precision in the definition of statutory terms—or is it rather overbreadth—that is, that the terms of the statute, while defined, cover too large an expanse of conduct?

As noted in Chapter 2 (*Mens Rea*), courts often find that the *mens rea* element of a statutory scheme saves it from attack on vagueness grounds. They in fact use the possible vagueness of the statute in absence of a high level of *mens rea* to justify reading such a heightened *mens rea* into the statutory scheme. For example, in *Posters 'N' Things, Ltd. v. United States*, 511 U.S. 513, 526 (1994), the Court stated that it "has recognized that a scienter requirement may mitigate a law's vagueness, especially with respect to the adequacy of notice ... that [the] conduct is proscribed.'" The RICO statute offers no such possibility because the only *mens rea* requirement that need be proven to obtain a RICO conviction is the *mens rea* required by the underlying predicate acts. *See, e.g.*, Bruner Corp. v. R.A. Bruner Co., 133 F.3d 491, 494 n. 3 (7th Cir.1998); United States v. Biasucci, 786 F.2d 504, 512 (2d Cir. 1986).

4. In *RJR Nabisco v. The European Community*, -- U.S. --, 136 S.Ct. 2090 (2016), the Supreme Court ruled that RICO has limited extraterritorial application. The *RJR Nabisco* Court applied a strong presumption against extraterritorial application of the statute, requiring that Congress "affirmatively and unmistakably instruct[] that the statute" will apply extraterritorially. *Id.* at 2100. The Court found an "obvious textual clue" in the fact that some RICO predicates, by their express terms, apply extraterritorially. *Id.* at 2101. Indeed, "[a]t least one predicate—the prohibition against 'kill[ing] a national of the United States, while such national is outside the

United States'—applies *only* to conduct occurring outside the United States." *Id.* at 2102 (citing 18 U.S.C. § 2332(a) (2012)). Congress's incorporation of extraterritorial predicates into RICO, the Court concluded, "gives a clear, affirmative indication that § 1962 applies to foreign racketeering activity." *Id.* Thus, RICO's unique structure made it "the rare statute that clearly evidences extraterritorial effect despite lacking an express statement of extraterritoriality." *Id.* at 2103. But the *RJR Nabisco* Court held that RICO has extraterritorial application only where Congress has made the predicate statutes upon which the RICO case is built extraterritorial.

RJR Nabisco was a civil case in which the European Community (EC) sued RJR for treble damages for racketeering activity allegedly committed in Europe. The Court went on to hold that even if RICO itself applies to conduct that occurs outside the United States, the section of RICO (18 U.S.C. § 1964) that allows private plaintiffs like the EC to file civil suits in U.S. courts does not apply to injuries outside the United States. Instead, to maintain its lawsuit against RJR, the EC would have to show that it was injured in the United States.

For more on the question of the extraterritorial application of federal criminal statutes, see *infra* Chapter 21; Julie Rose O'Sullivan, *The Extraterritorial Application of Federal Criminal Statutes: Analytical Roadmap, Normative Conclusions, and a Plea to Congress for Direction*, 106 Geo. L.J. 1021 (2018).

3. CONDUCT OF ENTERPRISE'S AFFAIRS

REVES v. ERNST & YOUNG
507 U.S. 170 (1993)

JUSTICE BLACKMUN delivered the opinion of the Court.

[This case involved a suit arising out of the bankruptcy of The Farmer's Cooperative of Arkansas and Oklahoma, Inc. ("Co-op"). Jack White, the Co-op's general manager, took large loans from the Co-op to finance his own business venture, White Flame Fuels, Inc. White and Gene Kuykendall, the accountant for both the Co-op and White Flame, were indicted on federal tax fraud charges. White then proposed that the Co-op purchase White Flame, and the Co-op eventually agreed. White and Kuykendall were convicted of tax fraud. The Co-op then retained the accounting firm (later merged with Arthur Young) headed by an individual who had testified for the defense at White's trial to conduct the Co-op's 1981 audit. In auditing the Co-op's books, the Arthur Young accounting firm, later merged with Ernst & Young, determined that the value of White Flame on the Co-op's books depended on when it was acquired. Thus, if the Co-op were deemed to have owned the venture from its inception, its value would be its fixed-asset value of $4.5 million. If, however, the Co-op had purchased White Flame from White, it would have to be given its fair market value at the time of purchase, which was between $444,000 and $1.5 million. If White Flame were valued at less than $1.5 million, the Co-op was insolvent. After consulting with White and Kuykendall, the accountant chose to treat White Flame as having been owned by the Co-op from its inception and thus valued the asset on the Co-op's books at $4.5 million. When Arthur Young presented its 1981 and 1982 audits to the Co-op board, it did not tell the board of its conclusion that the Co-op always had owned White Flame or that without that conclusion the Co-op was insolvent.]

[In 1984, the Co-op filed for bankruptcy, and its bankruptcy trustee filed suit against 40 individuals and entities, including Arthur Young, on behalf of the Co-op and certain noteholders. The District Court granted summary judgment in favor of Arthur Young on the RICO claim. It applied the test established in *Bennett v. Berg*, 710 F.2d 1361, 1364 (8th Cir.1983) (*en banc*), that § 1962(c) requires "some participation in the operation or management of the enterprise itself." The court ruled: "Plaintiffs have failed to show anything more than that the accountants reviewed a series of completed transactions, and certified the Co-op's records as fairly portraying its financial status as of a date three or four months preceding the meetings of the directors and the shareholders at which they presented their reports. We do not hesitate to declare that such activities fail to satisfy the degree of management required by

Bennett v. Berg." The case went to trial, however, on other claims. The jury then found Arthur Young had committed both state and federal securities fraud and awarded approximately $6.1 million in damages.] ...

The narrow question in this case is the meaning of the phrase "to conduct or participate, directly or indirectly, in the conduct of such enterprise's affairs." The word "conduct" is used twice, and it seems reasonable to give each use a similar construction. As a verb, "conduct" means to lead, run, manage, or direct. Webster's Third New International Dictionary 474 (1976). Petitioners urge us to read "conduct" as "carry on," so that almost any involvement in the affairs of an enterprise would satisfy the "conduct or participate" requirement. But context is important, and in the context of the phrase "to conduct ... [an] enterprise's affairs," the word indicates some degree of direction.

The dissent agrees that, when "conduct" is used as a verb, "it is plausible to find in it a suggestion of control." The dissent prefers to focus on "conduct" as a noun, as in the phrase "participate, directly or indirectly, in the conduct of [an] enterprise's affairs." But unless one reads "conduct" to include an element of direction when used as a noun in this phrase, the word becomes superfluous. Congress could easily have written "participate, directly or indirectly, in [an] enterprise's affairs," but it chose to repeat the word "conduct." We conclude, therefore, that as both a noun and a verb in this subsection "conduct" requires an element of direction.

The more difficult question is what to make of the word "participate." This Court previously has characterized this word as a "ter[m] ... of breadth." Petitioners argue that Congress used "participate" as a synonym for "aid and abet." That would be a term of breadth indeed, for "aid and abet" "comprehends all assistance rendered by words, acts, encouragement, support, or presence." Black's Law Dictionary 68 (6th ed. 1990). But within the context of § 1962(c), "participate" appears to have a narrower meaning. We may mark the limits of what the term might mean by looking again at what Congress did *not* say. On the one hand, "to participate ... in the conduct of ... affairs" must be broader than "to conduct affairs" or the "participate" phrase would be superfluous. On the other hand, as we already have noted, "to participate ... in the conduct of ... affairs" must be narrower than "to participate in affairs" or Congress' repetition of the word "conduct" would serve no purpose. It seems that Congress chose a middle ground, consistent with a common understanding of the word "participate"—"to take part in." Webster's Third New International Dictionary 1646 (1976).

Once we understand the word "conduct" to require some degree of direction and the word "participate" to require some part in that direction, the meaning of § 1962(c) comes into focus. In order to "participate, directly or indirectly, in the conduct of such enterprise's affairs," one must have some part in directing those affairs. Of course, the word "participate" makes clear that RICO liability is not limited to those with primary responsibility for the enterprise's affairs, just as the phrase "directly or indirectly" makes clear that RICO liability is not limited to those with a formal position in the enterprise,[24] but *some* part in directing the enterprise's affairs is required. The "operation or management" test expresses this requirement in a formulation that is easy to apply. ...

... [T]he legislative history confirms what we have already deduced from the language of § 1962(c)—that one is not liable under that provision unless one has participated in the operation or management of the enterprise itself. ...

Petitioners argue that the "operation or management" test is flawed because liability under § 1962(c) is not limited to upper management but may extend to "any person employed by or associated with [the] enterprise." We agree that liability under § 1962(c) is not limited to upper management, but we disagree that the "operation or management" test is inconsistent with this proposition. An enterprise is "operated" not just by upper management but also by lower-rung participants in the enterprise who are under the direction of upper management.[25]

---

[24] [Court's footnote 4:] For these reasons, we disagree with the suggestion of the Court of Appeals for the District of Columbia Circuit that § 1962(c) requires "*significant control*" over or within an enterprise."

[25] [Court's footnote 9:] At oral argument, there was some discussion about whether low-level employees

An enterprise also might be "operated" or "managed" by others "associated with" the enterprise who exert control over it as, for example, by bribery.

The United States also argues that the "operation or management" test is not consistent with § 1962(c) because it limits the liability of "outsiders" who have no official position within the enterprise. The United States correctly points out that RICO's major purpose was to attack the "infiltration of organized crime and racketeering into legitimate organizations," but its argument fails on several counts. First, it ignores the fact that § 1962 has four subsections. Infiltration of legitimate organizations by "outsiders" is clearly addressed in subsections (a) and (b), and the "operation or management" test that applies under subsection (c) in no way limits the application of subsections (a) and (b) to "outsiders." Second, § 1962(c) is limited to persons "employed by or associated with" an enterprise, suggesting a more limited reach than subsections (a) and (b), which do not contain such a restriction. Third, § 1962(c) cannot be interpreted to reach complete "outsiders" because liability depends on showing that the defendants conducted or participated in the conduct of the "*enterprise's* affairs," not just their *own* affairs. Of course, "outsiders" may be liable under § 1962(c) if they are "associated with" an enterprise and participate in the conduct of *its* affairs—that is, participate in the operation or management of the enterprise itself—but it would be consistent with neither the language nor the legislative history of § 1962(c) to interpret it as broadly as petitioners and the United States urge.

In sum, we hold that "to conduct or participate, directly or indirectly, in the conduct of such enterprise's affairs," § 1962(c), one must participate in the operation or management of the enterprise itself. ...

Notes

1. "Because RICO awards successful plaintiffs their attorneys fees and contains a mandatory treble damages provision, plaintiffs have strong incentives to proceed under RICO whenever possible. Outside professionals such as law and accounting firms—perennial deep pocket defendants—have been sued routinely under the RICO statute." Fischel & Sykes, *supra* note 7, at 157. Does the *Reves* "operation or management" test provide such outsiders, and lower-level employees, some protection against RICO charges? Should it? In light of the jury's apparent conclusion that Arthur Young was involved in the fraud, should it be shielded from RICO liability under § 1962(c)?

2. Just what *does* the *Reves* test mean? At the inception of the opinion, the Court emphasizes the need for evidence of "direction." "This language suggests that an outside professional can know about a fraud, by its actions facilitate the fraud, but still not be liable under RICO because it does not 'direct the enterprise's affairs.'" Fischel & Sykes, *supra* note 7, at 191. The Court then goes on to state that defendants may only be liable upon proof that they had "participate[d] in the operation or management" of the enterprise's affairs. Prior to *Reves*, lower courts had generally ruled that lower-level employees could be liable under § 1962(c) because, as the *Elliott* court explained *infra*, "the RICO net is woven tightly to trap even the smallest fish, those peripherally involved with the enterprise." United States v. Elliott, 571 F.2d 880, 903 (5th Cir. 1978). The Department of Justice, as an amicus in *Reves*, contended that the Court should not limit § 1962(c) liability to control persons or upper management. Fischel & Sykes, *supra* note 7, at 192. In an apparent response to these concerns, the *Reves* Court stated that "[a]n enterprise is 'operated' not just by upper management but also by lower-rung participants in the enterprise who are under the direction of upper management." Does this statement seem in tension with the Court's earlier emphasis on direction? How can lower-level employees both direct and be directed? Does the *Reves* opinion,

---

could be considered to have participated in the conduct of an enterprise's affairs. We need not decide in this case how far § 1962(c) extends down the ladder of operation because it is clear that Arthur Young was not acting under the direction of the Co-op's officers or board.

at bottom, provide much clarity, or protection, to those who do not hold formal office within a legal entity, or to lower-level employees within it?

3. The courts have experienced some confusion in applying the *Reves* standard to lower-level employees. *See, e.g.*, United States v. Owens, 167 F.3d 739, 754 (1st Cir. 1999) ("*Reves*' analysis does not apply where a party is determined to be inside a RICO enterprise."); United States v. Allen, 155 F.3d 35, 42 (2d Cir. 1998); United States v. Oreto, 37 F.3d 739, 750 (1st Cir. 1994) (a defendant may participate in an enterprise by "knowingly implementing decisions, as well as by making them"); United States v. Viola, 35 F.3d 37, 41 (2d Cir. 1994) ("Since *Reves*, it is plain that the simple taking of directions and performance of tasks that are 'necessary or helpful' to the enterprise, without more, is insufficient to bring a defendant within the scope of § 1962(c)."); University of Maryland v. Peat, Marwick, Main & Co., 996 F.2d 1534, 1538-39 (3d Cir. 1993) ("Under [*Reves*], not even action involving some degree of decisionmaking constitutes participation in the affairs of an enterprise."). One student of these opinions provided the following attempted synthesis:

> In the wake of *Reves* and countless decisions interpreting its "easy to apply" rule, a few things are clear. First, *Reves* appears to have absolved tangentially related white collar professionals from RICO liability, as courts have found the provision of professional services to a RICO enterprise, even if necessary or helpful, insufficient to demonstrate operation or management. In this vein, the Seventh Circuit has stated that "simply performing services for an enterprise, even with knowledge of the enterprise's illicit nature, is not enough." Second, the distinction between insiders and outsiders appears to have persisted with some vigor: A much more exacting standard, generally requiring actual evidence of active control, is commonly applied to "unaffiliated persons outside the chain of command." And one final thing is certain: Very little is certain. The Second Circuit has appropriately concluded that "the only principle to be drawn from th[e] array of holdings and statements is that the commission of crimes by lower level employees of a RICO enterprise may be found to indicate participation in the operation or management … but does not compel such a finding." Thus the operation or management test has come to hinge on several amorphous distinctions and characterizations—and, of course, a great deal of artful pleading by prosecutors and plaintiffs.

Adam B. Weiss, Note, *From the Bonannos to the Bin Ladens: The* Reves *Operation or Management Test and the Viability of Civil RICO Suits Against Financial Supporters of Terrorism*, 110 Colum. L. Rev. 1123, 1139 (2010). How helpful is this guidance, especially in giving "fair notice" in criminal cases?

4. The Court believes that it was "clear" that Arthur Young "was not acting under the direction of the Co-op's officers or board." Was it? There did not appear to be direct evidence that the officers or board instructed Arthur Young to use the allegedly inflated numbers. Should that be determinative? The alleged fraud benefitted the Co-op, not Arthur Young. "Why else would Arthur Young knowingly participate and assist in the Co-op's fraud except at the behest of management? And even if Arthur Young somehow decided to participate in the fraud independently as opposed to being directed to do so by management, why should this be exonerating?" Fischel & Sykes, *supra* note 7, at 192.

5. May litigants get around the *Reves* "operation or management" test by redefining the enterprise? *See id.* at 193-94. That is, in *Reves*, rather than alleging that the enterprise was the Co-op, could the plaintiffs instead have alleged that the enterprise was an "association-in-fact" of the Co-op, Arthur Young, and Jack White? Wouldn't proof that Arthur Young "operated or managed" this "association-in-fact" be far easier?

6. Liability under § 1962(c) requires that an individual "conduct or participate, directly or indirectly, in the conduct of such enterprise's affairs through a pattern of racketeering activity." *Reves* interpreted this provision to mean that "one must have some part in directing those affairs," or, put alternatively, that "one must participate in the operation or management of the enterprise itself." Recall that the Court in *Boyle v. United States*, 556 U.S. 938 (2009), discussed *supra*, rejected efforts to require that proof of an "association-in-fact" enterprise require some

"ascertainable structure beyond that inherent in the pattern of racketeering in which it engages" and held that the existence of the "enterprise" can be inferred simply from the pattern of racketeering in which it engages. Does *Reves*'s holding render the argument over the structural attributes of the enterprise in question moot? That is, is it possible for an individual to participate in the operation or management of an association-in-fact enterprise that is completely lacking in any of the structural attributes argued for by the plaintiff in *Boyle*?

7. "The principal legitimate institution the corruption of which federal prosecutors have attacked through the RICO statute has been government itself—more particularly, state and local government. *See, e.g.*, Lynch, *RICO: The Crime of Being a Criminal, Parts I & II, supra* note 7, at 734-35 (survey revealed that "corruption of government officials was the essence of the activity alleged" in thirty percent of the sampled cases). And "[t]he principal motivating factor in the use of RICO in public corruption cases seems to be the unavailability of an alternative simple theory of federal jurisdiction in prosecuting local officials for bribery." *Id.* at 741. What implications does *Reves* have for such cases, when (as was noted above) the enterprise is often alleged to be a state governmental entity that is corrupted by outside actors?

In *United States v. Castro*, 89 F.3d 1443 (11th Cir. 1996), the Eleventh Circuit addressed this issue in the context of a § 1962(d) conspiracy prosecution. In *Castro*, two state court judges repeatedly took kickbacks from the defendant lawyers in return for appointing the lawyers as special assistant public defenders for their court, the Circuit Court of the Eleventh Judicial Circuit of Dade County, Florida. These lawyers asserted that the evidence was insufficient to establish that they conspired to participate in the "operation or management" of the RICO enterprise, alleged to be the Circuit Court.

> ... Appellants argue that under *Reves v. Ernst & Young*, 507 U.S. 170 (1993), the government was required to produce evidence showing that appellants agreed to exercise control or direction in the management of the Circuit Court of the Eleventh Judicial Circuit. Appellants suggest that as outsiders they could not have exerted the requisite degree of control over the "operation or management" of the Circuit Court of the Eleventh Judicial Circuit to meet the requirements of *Reves*.
>
> ... [W]e reject appellants' limited reading of *Reves*. Under *Reves*, section 1962(c) liability is not limited to insiders or upper management as appellants suggests. In *Reves*, the Supreme Court emphasized that because the statute includes the phrase "to participate directly or indirectly," RICO liability is not confined to those with a formal position in the enterprise. The language in *Reves* indicates that persons in appellants' position fall within the scope of section 1962(c)'s coverage because "an enterprise might be operated or managed by others associated with the enterprise who exert control over it as, for example, by *bribery*."

Id. at 1452.

8. As we shall see *infra*, § 1962(d) makes it unlawful "for any person to conspire to violate any of the provisions of subsection (a), (b), or (c) of this section." The *Castro* court further reasoned:

> We reject the appellants' narrow reading of *Reves* and their attempt to infuse the *Reves* analysis into this case. In this case, the indictment charged the appellants with RICO conspiracy under section 1962(d), and not a substantive RICO offense under section 1962(c). This court recently decided that the *Reves* "operation or management" test does not apply to section 1962(d) convictions. Our view of the evidence in the light most favorable to the government indicates that more than sufficient evidence existed to demonstrate that appellants "agreed" to affect the operation or management of the Circuit Court of the Eleventh Judicial Circuit through paying kickbacks.

Id. There is a split in the circuits on the issue whether the *Reves* operations or control requirement applies to a RICO *conspiracy* charge. Should a defendant who exercises insufficient "operation or management" over the RICO enterprise to be directly liable under § 1962(c) nevertheless be held liable under § 1962(d) for conspiring with those who do? Consider the Third Circuit's discussion in *United States v. Antar*, 53 F.3d 568 (3d Cir. 1995):

> RICO's conspiracy section, section 1962(d), makes it unlawful for any person to conspire to violate sections 1962(a), (b), or (c). Despite *Reves*, a number of courts have held that even if a person may not be held directly liable for violating section 1962(c), he or she still may be liable for conspiring to violate section 1962(c). In *United States v. Quintanilla*, 2 F.3d 1469 (7th Cir.1993), for example, Gutierrez participated in a scheme to defraud a corporation of money by submitting false funding proposals to a corporate program designed to fund various social events. It appears from the court of appeals' discussion that Gutierrez, while assisting her boyfriend in submitting the false proposals, did not operate or manage the enterprise in any way, and therefore did not violate section 1962(c). Nonetheless, she was charged with and was convicted of conspiring to violate section 1962(c) pursuant to section 1962(d). On appeal, Gutierrez argued that *Reves* barred her conviction under section 1962(d). The court of appeals disagreed, reasoning as follows:

>> The defendant confuses her conviction for conspiracy (an agreement to commit a crime) with a conviction for a substantive crime. She was charged in Count One of the superseding indictment with violating 18 U.S.C. § 1962(d) .... . Section 1962(d), unlike § 1962(c), is not a substantive RICO offense; rather, § 1962(d) merely makes it illegal to conspire to violate any of the preceding sections of the statute.

> *Quintanilla*, 2 F.3d at 1484. Thus, "[o]ne violates § 1962(d) ... when she agrees to violate a substantive RICO offense, regardless of whether she personally agreed to commit the predicate crimes or actually participated in the commission of those crimes." *Id.* Other courts have used similar reasoning in upholding section 1962(d) liability when section 1962(c) liability proved unavailing.

> Nonetheless, Mitchell's argument that courts risk eviscerating *Reves* by blanketly approving conspiracy convictions when substantive convictions under section 1962(c) are unavailable has some merit. There is no question that a broad reading of the cases cited above would be problematic. As one commentator has explained, "[i]f Congress' restriction of section 1962(c) liability to those who operate or manage the enterprise can be avoided simply by alleging that a defendant aided and abetted or conspired with someone who operated or managed the enterprise, then *Reves* would be rendered almost nugatory." David B. Smith & Terrance G. Reed, *Civil RICO*, § 5.04 at 5-39 (1994). But we believe that a distinction can be drawn between, on the one hand, conspiring *to* operate or manage an enterprise, and, on the other, conspiring *with* someone who is operating or managing the enterprise. Liability under section 1962(d) would be permissible under the first scenario, but, without more, not under the second. This is because in the former situation, the defendant is conspiring to do something for which, if the act was completed successfully, he or she would be liable under section 1962(c). But in the latter scenario, the defendant is not conspiring to do something for which he or she could be held liable under the substantive clause of the statute. Therefore, liability should not attach. The distinction we draw derives directly from 18 U.S.C. § 1962(d) which provides that it is "unlawful for any person *to conspire to violate*" sections 1962(a), (b), or (c). (Emphasis added.) Of course, under section 1962(d) a "person" is not limited to a person "employed by or associated with any enterprise" as is the case under section 1962(c).

Id. at 580-81. What is the right result?

4. RICO CONSPIRACY

UNITED STATES v. ELLIOTT
571 F.2d 880 (5th Cir. 1978)

SIMPSON, CIRCUIT JUDGE:

... THE SUBSTANTIVE RICO VIOLATION

[John Clayburn "J.C."] Hawkins and Recea Hawkins contend that their acts, while arguably violative of other criminal statutes, are not proscribed by the substantive RICO provision under which they were charged, 18 U.S.C. § 1962(c), in that they were not committed in furtherance of the affairs of an "enterprise" as required by the Act. At best, they say, the facts disclosed that two brothers confederated to commit a few, isolated criminal acts over a period of six years. Neither the facts nor the law support this contention. ...

Here, the government proved beyond a reasonable doubt the existence of an enterprise comprised of at least five of the defendants. This enterprise can best be analogized to a large business conglomerate. Metaphorically speaking, J. C. Hawkins was the chairman of the board, functioning as the chief executive officer and overseeing the operations of many separate branches of the corporation. An executive committee in charge of the "Counterfeit Title, Stolen Car, and Amphetamine Sales Department" was comprised of J. C., [Robert Ervin Delph], and [John Frank Taylor], who supervised the operations of lower level employees such as [Marvin] Farr, the printer [who produced counterfeit titles for stolen cars], and [Billy Royce Jackson, James A. Green, and Kenneth Sutton Boyd], the car thieves. Another executive committee, comprised of J. C., Recea, and [William Marion Foster], controlled the "Thefts From Interstate Commerce Department," arranging the purchase, concealment, and distribution of such commodities as meat, dairy products, "Career Club" shirts, and heavy construction equipment. An offshoot of this department handled subsidiary activities, such as murder and obstruction of justice, intended to facilitate the smooth operation of its primary activities. Each member of the conglomerate, with the exception of Foster, was responsible for procuring and wholesaling whatever narcotics could be obtained. The thread tying all of these departments, activities, and individuals together was the desire to make money. J. C. might have been voicing the corporation's motto when he told Bob Day, in May, 1976, "if it ain't a pretty damn good bit of money, I ain't going to fuck with it."

A jury is entitled to infer the existence of an enterprise on the basis of largely or wholly circumstantial evidence. Like a criminal conspiracy, a RICO enterprise cannot be expected to maintain a high profile in the community. Its affairs are likely to be conducted in secrecy and to involve a minimal amount of necessary contact between participants. Thus, direct evidence of association may be difficult to obtain; a jury should be permitted to draw the natural inference arising from circumstantial evidence of association. ...

Additionally, although the target of the RICO statute is not "sporadic activity," we find nothing in the Act excluding from its ambit an enterprise engaged in diversified activity. ... While earlier cases have considered enterprises engaged in only one type of prohibited activity, a single enterprise engaged in diversified activities fits comfortably within the proscriptions of the statute and the dictates of common sense ... We would deny society the protection intended by Congress were we to hold that the Act does not reach those enterprises nefarious enough to diversify their criminal activity.

The evidence in this case demonstrated the existence of an enterprise—a myriopod criminal network, loosely connected but connected nonetheless. By committing arson, actively assisting a car theft ring, fencing thousands of dollars worth of goods stolen from interstate commerce, murdering a key witness, and dealing in narcotics, J. C. and Recea Hawkins directly and indirectly participated in the enterprise's affairs through a pattern, indeed a plethora, of racketeering activity. We therefore affirm their convictions [on the substantive RICO count].

... THE RICO CONSPIRACY COUNT

All six defendants were convicted under 18 U.S.C. § 1962(d) of having conspired to violate a substantive RICO provision, § 1962(c). In this appeal, all defendants, with the exception of Foster, argue that while the indictment alleged but one conspiracy, the government's evidence at trial proved the existence of several conspiracies, resulting in a variance which substantially prejudiced their rights and requires reversal, citing *Kotteakos v. United States*, 328 U.S. 750 (1946). Prior to the enactment of the RICO statute, this argument would have been more persuasive. However, as we explain below, RICO has displaced many of the legal precepts traditionally applied to concerted criminal activity. Its effect in this case is to free the government from the strictures of the multiple conspiracy doctrine and to allow the joint trial of many persons accused of diversified crimes.

A. Prior Law: Wheels and Chains

1. Kotteakos *and the Wheel Conspiracy Rationale*: The Court in *Kotteakos* held that proof of multiple conspiracies under an indictment alleging a single conspiracy constituted a material variance requiring reversal where a defendant's substantial rights had been affected. At issue was "the right not to be tried *en masse* for the conglomeration of distinct and separate offenses committed by others." *Kotteakos* thus protects against the "spill-over effect," the transference of guilt from members of one conspiracy to members of another.

... [The Court in *Kotteakos* found that the indictment charged not one conspiracy, but rather several conspiracies. Its analysis spoke] in terms of a "wheel conspiracy", in which one person, the "hub" of the wheel, was accused of conspiring with several others, the "spokes" of the wheel. As we [have] explained [*Kotteakos*]:

> For a [single] wheel conspiracy to exist those people who form the wheel's spokes must have been aware of each other and must do something in furtherance of some single, illegal enterprise. Otherwise the conspiracy lacks "the rim of the wheel to enclose the spokes." If there is not some interaction between those conspirators who form the spokes of the wheel as to at least one common illegal object, the "wheel" is incomplete, and two conspiracies rather than one are charged.

2. Blumenthal *and the Chain Conspiracy Rationale*: The impact of *Kotteakos* was soon limited by the Court in *Blumenthal v. United States*, 332 U.S. 539 (1947), where the indictment charged a single conspiracy to sell whiskey at prices above the ceiling set by the Office of Price Administration. The owner of the whiskey, through a series of middlemen, had devised an intricate scheme to conceal the true amount he was charging for the whiskey. Although some of the middlemen had no contact with each other and did not know the identity of the owner, they had to have realized that they were indispensible cogs in the machinery through which this illegal scheme was effectuated. The Court concluded that "in every practical sense the unique facts of this case reveal a single conspiracy of which the several agreements were essential and integral steps." Thus the "chain conspiracy" rationale evolved.

The essential element of a chain conspiracy—allowing persons unknown to each other and never before in contact to be jointly prosecuted as co-conspirators—is interdependence. The scheme which is the object of the conspiracy must depend on the successful operation of each link in the chain. "An individual associating himself with a 'chain' conspiracy knows that it has a 'scope' and that for its success it requires an organization wider than may be disclosed by his personal participation." "Thus, in a 'chain' conspiracy prosecution, the requisite element—knowledge of the existence of remote links—may be inferred solely from the nature of the enterprise."

3. *Limits of the Chain Conspiracy Rationale*: The rationale of *Blumenthal* applies only insofar as the alleged agreement has "a common end or single unified purpose." Generally, where the government has shown that a number of otherwise diverse activities were performed to

achieve a single goal, courts have been willing to find a single conspiracy. This "common objective" test has most often been used to connect the many facets of drug importation and distribution schemes. The rationale falls apart, however, where the remote members of the alleged conspiracy are not truly interdependent or where the various activities sought to be tied together cannot reasonably be said to constitute a unified scheme. ...

Applying pre-RICO conspiracy concepts to the facts of this case, we doubt that a single conspiracy could be demonstrated. Foster had no contact with Delph and Taylor during the life of the alleged conspiracy. Delph and Taylor, so far as the evidence revealed, had no contact with Recea Hawkins. The activities allegedly embraced by the illegal agreement in this case are simply too diverse to be tied together on the theory that participation in one activity necessarily implied awareness of others. Even viewing the "common objective" of the conspiracy as the raising of revenue through criminal activity, we could not say, for example, that Foster, when he helped to conceal stolen meat, had to know that J. C. was selling drugs to persons unknown to Foster, or that Delph and Taylor, when they furnished counterfeit titles to a car theft ring, had to know that the man supplying the titles was also stealing goods out of interstate commerce. The enterprise involved in this case probably could not have been successfully prosecuted as a single conspiracy under the general federal conspiracy statute, 18 U.S.C. § 371.

B. RICO to the Rescue: The Enterprise Conspiracy

In enacting RICO, Congress found that "organized crime continues to grow" in part "because the sanctions and remedies available to the Government are unnecessarily limited in scope and impact." Thus, one of the express purposes of the Act was "to seek the eradication of organized crime ... by establishing new penal prohibitions, and by providing enhanced sanctions and new remedies to deal with the unlawful activities of those engaged in organized crime." Against this background, we are convinced that, through RICO, Congress intended to authorize the single prosecution of a multi-faceted, diversified conspiracy by replacing the inadequate "wheel" and "chain" rationales with a new statutory concept: the enterprise.

To achieve this result, Congress acted against the backdrop of hornbook conspiracy law. Under the general federal conspiracy statute,

> the precise nature and extent of the conspiracy must be determined by reference to the agreement which embraces and defines its objects. Whether the object of a single agreement is to commit one or many crimes, it is in either case that agreement which constitutes the conspiracy which the statute punishes.

In the context of organized crime, this principle inhibited mass prosecutions because a single agreement or "common objective" cannot be inferred from the commission of highly diverse crimes by apparently unrelated individuals. RICO helps to eliminate this problem by creating a substantive offense which ties together these diverse parties and crimes. Thus, the object of a RICO conspiracy is to violate a substantive RICO provision—here, to conduct or participate in the affairs of an enterprise through a pattern of racketeering activity—and not merely to commit each of the predicate crimes necessary to demonstrate a pattern of racketeering activity. The gravamen of the conspiracy charge in this case is not that each defendant agreed to commit arson, to steal goods from interstate commerce, to obstruct justice, and to sell narcotics; rather, it is that each agreed to participate, directly and indirectly, in the affairs of the enterprise by committing two or more predicate crimes. Under the statute, it is irrelevant that each defendant participated in the enterprise's affairs through different, even unrelated crimes, so long as we may reasonably infer that each crime was intended to further the enterprise's affairs. To find a single conspiracy, we still must look for agreement on an overall objective. What Congress did was to define that objective through the substantive provisions of the Act.

C. Constitutional Considerations

The "enterprise conspiracy" is a legislative innovation in the realm of individual liability for group crime. We need to consider whether this innovation comports with the fundamental demand of due process that guilt remain "individual and personal."

The substantive proscriptions of the RICO statute apply to insiders *and outsiders*—those merely "associated with" an enterprise—who participate directly *and indirectly* in the enterprise's affairs through a pattern of racketeering activity. Thus, the RICO net is woven tightly to trap even the smallest fish, those peripherally involved with the enterprise. This effect is enhanced by principles of conspiracy law also developed to facilitate prosecution of conspirators at all levels. Direct evidence of agreement is unnecessary: "proof of such an agreement may rest upon inferences drawn from relevant and competent circumstantial evidence—ordinarily the acts and conduct of the alleged conspirators themselves." Additionally, once the conspiracy has been established, the government need show only "slight evidence" that a particular person was a member of the conspiracy. Of course, "a party to a conspiracy need not know the identity, or even the number, of his confederates."

Undeniably, then, under the RICO conspiracy provision, remote associates of an enterprise may be convicted as conspirators on the basis of purely circumstantial evidence. We cannot say, however, that this section of the statute demands inferences that cannot reasonably be drawn from circumstantial evidence or that it otherwise offends the rule that guilt be individual and personal. The Act does not authorize that individuals "be tried *en masse* for the conglomeration of distinct and separate offenses committed by others." Nor does it punish mere association with conspirators or knowledge of illegal activity; its proscriptions are directed against conduct, not status. To be convicted as a member of an enterprise conspiracy, an individual, by his words or actions, must have objectively manifested an agreement to participate, directly or indirectly, in the affairs of an enterprise *through the commission of two or more predicate crimes*.[26] One whose agreement with the members of an enterprise did not include this vital element cannot be convicted under the Act. Where, as here, the evidence establishes that each defendant, over a period of years, committed several acts of racketeering activity in furtherance of the enterprise's affairs, the inference of an agreement to do so is unmistakable.

It is well established that "[t]he government is not required to prove that a conspirator had full knowledge of all the details of the conspiracy; knowledge of the essential nature of the plan is sufficient." The Supreme Court explained the policy behind this rule in *Blumenthal v. United States*, 332 U.S. at 556-57:

> For it is most often true, especially in broad schemes calling for the aid of many persons, that after discovery of enough to show clearly the essence of the scheme and the identity of a number participating, the identity and the fact of participation of others remain undiscovered and undiscoverable. Secrecy and concealment are essential features of successful conspiracy. The more completely they are achieved, the more successful the crime. Hence the law rightly gives room for allowing the conviction of those discovered upon showing sufficiently the essential nature of the plan and their connections with it, without requiring evidence of knowledge of all its details or of the participation of others. Otherwise the difficulties, not only of discovery, but of certainty in proof and of correlating proof with pleading would become insuperable, and conspirators would go free by their very ingenuity.

In the instant case, it is clear that "the essential nature of the plan" was to associate for the purpose of making money from repeated criminal activity. Defendant Foster, for example, hired J. C. Hawkins to commit arson, helped him to conceal large quantities of meat and shirts stolen from interstate commerce, and bought a stolen forklift from him. It would be "a

---

[26] [Ed.:] To the extent that the *Elliott* court is suggesting that each co-conspirator must personally commit two predicate acts, it was made clear by the Supreme Court in *Salinas v. United States*, 522 U.S. 52 (1997) (reproduced *infra*) that this is not so.

perversion of natural thought and of natural language" to deny that these facts give rise to the inference that Foster knew he was directly involved in an enterprise whose purpose was to profit from crime. As we noted in *United States v. Gonzalez*, 491 F.2d 1202, 1206 (5th Cir.1974), "persons so associating and forming organizations for furthering such illicit purposes do not normally conceive of the association as engaging in one unlawful transaction and then disbanding. Rather the nature of such organizations seems to be an ongoing operation ... ." Foster also had to know that the enterprise was bigger than his role in it, and that others unknown to him were participating in its affairs. He may have been unaware that others who had agreed to participate in the enterprise's affairs did so by selling drugs and murdering a key witness. That, however, is irrelevant to his own liability, for he is charged with agreeing *to participate* in the enterprise through his own crimes, not with agreeing *to commit* each of the crimes through which the overall affairs of the enterprise were conducted. We perceive in this no significant extension of a co-conspirator's liability. When a person "embarks upon a criminal venture of indefinite outline, he takes his chances as to its content and membership, so be it that they fall within the common purposes as he understands them." ...

We do not lightly dismiss the fact that under this statute four defendants who did not commit murder have been forced to stand trial jointly with, and as confederates of, two others who did. Prejudice inheres in such a trial; great Neptune's ocean could not purge its taint. But the Constitution does not guarantee a trial free from the prejudice that inevitably accompanies any charge of heinous group crime; it demands only that the potential for transference of guilt be minimized to the extent possible under the circumstances in order "to individualize each defendant in his relation to the mass." The RICO statute does not offend this principle. Congress, in a proper exercise of its legislative power, has decided that murder, like thefts from interstate commerce and the counterfeiting of securities, qualifies as racketeering activity. This, of course, ups the ante for RICO violators who personally would not contemplate taking a human life. Whether there is a moral imbalance in the equation of thieves and counterfeiters with murderers is a question whose answer lies in the halls of Congress, not in the judicial conscience. ...

Notes

1. *Elliott*, in which the court "construed section 1962(d) as establishing an offense fundamentally different from the traditional form of conspiracy," was a controversial decision that has been criticized on numerous grounds. Tarlow, *supra* note 14, at 245, 248-54. In explaining how RICO conspiracy differs from traditional conspiracy, the *Elliott* court noted that the diversified activities of the coconspirators could not have been pursued in a single § 371 count. Why not?

If the government had a tape recording of a meeting at which all the participants had gathered in a room and agreed to together engage in a scheme to make money through all the varied criminal activities undertaken in *Elliott*, the government certainly could have successfully prosecuted the defendants for a single conspiratorial agreement to engage in diverse criminal objects. What the *Elliott* court seems to be saying then is that, in the absence of such (unusual) direct evidence, a single conspiratorial agreement is normally proved through an inference drawn from the nature of the criminal scheme and the interdependence of the persons engaging in it. Such an inference would not be available under § 371 in a case such as this because there is little evidence of interaction among the defendants and the varied nature of their activity precludes an inference that they knew that they were simply cogs in a larger criminal machine. The court, however, seems to believe that such an inference is available in RICO cases. Why? As Hon. Gerard Lynch asked:

> ... [I]f there was insufficient proof to infer a single agreement to "rais[e] revenue through criminal activity," how can the proof in turn be sufficient—as the court says it must be— to permit finding an "agreement on an overall objective" to "further the enterprise's affairs"? After all, the enterprise in this case consists of nothing more than an association to raise revenue by committing crimes. Conversely, if it is permissible to infer from a

defendant's participation in particular concrete crimes that he simultaneously agreed to participate in the affairs of an overarching enterprise, why not just rename the "enterprise" a "conspiratorial agreement with multiple criminal objects" and infer his agreement to that?

Lynch, *RICO: The Crime of Being Criminal, Parts III & IV, supra* note 20, at 951. In response to these questions, Michael Goldsmith argues that "the enterprise itself is an important link in the evidentiary chain: a defendant's knowledge of the enterprise's existence is probative of a central purpose. Thus, upon proof that such an enterprise exists, the enterprise itself provides the basis for inferring one large conspiracy instead of many smaller ones." Michael Goldsmith, *RICO and Enterprise Criminality: A Response to Gerard E. Lynch*, 88 Colum. L. Rev. 774, 798 (1988). Do you find this explanation persuasive?

2. How does the *Elliott* court define the *scope* of the conspiratorial agreement? Some have contended that the "primary flaw in the *Elliott* view is the court's assumption that the scope of a RICO substantive offense or a RICO conspiracy is defined by the *enterprise*. The court believed that, although the defendants must agree to commit a pattern of racketeering activity, they need not agree to commit the same pattern as long as the defendants' patterns involve the *same enterprise*." Tarlow, *supra* note 14, 251-52 (emphasis added). Why would such a focus potentially be troubling? Recall that RICO is often used to attack state and local corruption. Assume that various actors conduct similar, parallel but not interdependent types of racketeering acts through the same legitimate government enterprise, for example by each bribing a municipal official for assistance in fixing their traffic tickets. Because they are conducting their similar but unrelated criminal acts through the same "enterprise," are they now punishable together as a RICO conspiracy?

In *United States v. Sutherland*, 656 F.2d 1181 (5th Cir. 1981), the Fifth Circuit attempted to correct the impression left by *Elliott* that the scope of such a conspiracy is determined by reference only to the enterprise. In *Sutherland*, Glen Sutherland, a municipal court judge, was alleged to have conspired with two others, Grace Walker and Edward Maynard, to fix traffic tickets. The case was charged as a conspiracy to violation § 1962(c), with the enterprise being the Municipal Court of the City of El Paso, and the racketeering acts being bribery of a state official in violation of state law. Neither Walker nor Maynard knew of each other's activities. In this respect, the case mirrored *Kotteakos* in that it was a wheel, having at its hub the corrupt judge, and having two spokes, Walker and Maynard, not joined by a rim. The Government, relying on *Elliott*, argued that "so long as the object of each conspiracy is participation in the same enterprise [, here, the municipal court,] in violation of RICO, it matters not that the different conspiracies are otherwise unrelated." *Id.* at 1191. The Fifth Circuit rejected this argument, reasoning:

> *Elliott* does indeed hold that on the facts of that case a series of agreements that under pre-RICO law would constitute multiple conspiracies could under RICO be tried as a single "enterprise" conspiracy. But the language of *Elliott* explains that what ties these conspiracies together is not the mere fact that they involve the same enterprise, but is instead—as in any other conspiracy—an "agreement on an overall objective." What RICO does is to provide a new criminal objective by defining a new substantive crime. In *Elliott*, as here, that crime consists of participation in an enterprise through a pattern of racketeering activity. The defendants in *Elliott* could not have been tried on a single conspiracy count under pre-RICO law because the defendants had not agreed to commit any particular crime. They were properly tried together under RICO only because the evidence established an agreement to commit a substantive RICO offense, *i.e.*, an agreement to participate in an enterprise through a pattern of racketeering activity.
>
> To be sure, the government did not prove in *Elliott* that each of the conspirators had explicitly agreed with all of the others to violate the substantive RICO provision at issue. However, the government did prove that, as in a traditional "chain" conspiracy, the nature of the scheme was such that each defendant must necessarily have known that others were also conspiring to participate in the same enterprise through a pattern of

racketeering activity. We found the facts sufficient to demonstrate that the defendants knew they were "directly involved in an enterprise whose purpose was to profit from crime," and that each knew "that the enterprise was bigger than his role in it, and that others unknown to him were participating in its affairs." The agreement among all of the defendants in *Elliott* was an implicit one, but it was an agreement nonetheless. ...

... *Elliott* does not stand for the proposition that multiple conspiracies may be tried on a single "enterprise conspiracy" count under RICO merely because the various conspiracies involve the same enterprise. What *Elliott* does state is two-fold: (1) a pattern of agreements that absent RICO would constitute multiple conspiracies may be joined under a single RICO conspiracy count if the defendants have agreed to commit a substantive RICO offense; and (2) such an agreement to violate RICO may, as in the case of a traditional "chain" or "wheel" conspiracy, be established on circumstantial evidence, *i.e.*, evidence that the nature of the conspiracy is such that each defendant must necessarily have known that others were also conspiring to violate RICO.

In this case the government has not attempted to prove that Walker and Maynard agreed with each other to participate in a bribery scheme with Sutherland, nor has it contended that the nature of each defendant's agreement with Sutherland was such that he or she must necessarily have known that others were also conspiring to commit racketeering offenses in the conduct of the Municipal Court. We must conclude, therefore, that the multiple conspiracy doctrine precluded the joint trial of the two multiple conspiracies involved in this case on a single RICO conspiracy count. In accordance with *Kotteakos* and its progeny, we must reverse the defendants' convictions if this error affected their substantial rights.

Id. at 1192-95. Does the *Sutherland* court accurately report the reasoning of the *Elliott* opinion?

3. It should be noted that while many courts (including the Fifth Circuit) have in words repudiated *Elliott*'s apparent emphasis on the "enterprise" in defining the scope of the conspiracy, some courts have required very little to demonstrate that otherwise unconnected "spokes" are joined in a RICO conspiracy other than some proof that the "spokes" are acting through the same enterprise and are on notice that other actors are engaging in parallel conduct. Consider in this regard *United States v. Castro*, discussed above in the Note following *Reves*, in which the Eleventh Circuit reasoned:

A material variance between an indictment and the government's proof at trial occurs if the government proves multiple conspiracies under an indictment alleging only a single conspiracy. In order to prove a RICO conspiracy, the government must show an agreement to violate a substantive RICO provision. Specifically, the government must prove that the conspirators agreed to participate directly or indirectly in the affairs of an enterprise through a pattern of racketeering activity.

The government may prove the existence of an "agreement" to participate in a RICO conspiracy through showing (1) the existence of an agreement on an overall objective, or (2) in the absence of an agreement on an overall objective, that the defendant agreed personally to commit two or more predicate acts. In meeting its burden of proof on showing an agreement on an overall objective, the government must offer direct evidence of an explicit agreement on an overall objective or, in the absence of direct evidence, the government must offer circumstantial evidence demonstrating "that each defendant must necessarily have known that others were also conspiring to participate in the same enterprise through a pattern of racketeering activity."

In this case, the indictment charged a single RICO conspiracy, and the government presented evidence that adequately proved the existence of a single conspiracy. At trial, [Judge] Gelber testified that he informed the [lawyer-]appellants that they would not only receive appointments from him but also from another judge in the circuit court. In light of this testimony, each appellant knew that at least two circuit judges agreed to use the Circuit Court of the Eleventh Judicial Circuit to engage in a kickback scheme. In addition to Gelber's testimony, other evidence adduced at trial indicates appellants' agreement to participate in and awareness that others also participated in a single conspiracy. For example, when Gelber's secretary asked appellant Boehme to enroll in the kickback scheme, she asked him whether he wished to join the "preferred list" for court appointments. Similarly, appellant Lechtner was informed that a kickback scheme was "something that's being done" in the Circuit Court of the Eleventh Judicial Circuit. Appellant Castro actually recruited another lawyer to join the kickback scheme. In light of this evidence, we find that each appellant agreed on an overall objective and agreed personally to commit two or more predicate acts by paying kickbacks for SAPD appointments.

Additionally we note that, contrary to appellants' assertions, in proving the existence of a single RICO conspiracy, the government does not need to prove that each conspirator agreed with every other conspirator, knew of his fellow conspirators, was aware of all of the details of the conspiracy, or contemplated participating in the same related crime. In viewing the evidence in the light most favorable to the government, a jury could have reasonably concluded that one common agreement on a single overall objective existed. Consequently, we find that no material variance occurred.

Castro, 89 F.3d at 1450-51; *see also* United States v. Alkins, 925 F.2d 541, 554 (2d Cir. 1991) (holding that although the various defendants seemed to have operated independently if corruptly in doing their jobs at the DMV, creating the appearance of a *Kotteakos* wheel conspiracy, there was only one conspiracy because the clerks at the DMV "cooperated with one another in communicating how to process the fraudulent documents" and "each was aware of the 'nature and extent' of the enterprise and that their role was only part of a larger scheme" to "operate the [DMV] for private gain through a pattern of racketeering activity" (*i.e.*, taking bribes to issue unlawful registration forms and drivers licenses)).

What practical difference does this make? Why is the question of the appropriate "scope" of the conspiracy important to the defense?

SALINAS v. UNITED STATES
522 U.S. 52 (1997)

JUSTICE KENNEDY delivered the opinion of the Court.

The case before us [presents the question] ... does the conspiracy prohibition contained in the Racketeer Influenced and Corrupt Organizations Act (RICO) apply only when the conspirator agrees to commit two of the predicate acts RICO forbids? ...

This federal prosecution arose from a bribery scheme operated by Brigido Marmolejo, the Sheriff of Hidalgo County, Texas, and petitioner Mario Salinas, one of his principal deputies. In 1984, the United States Marshals Service and Hidalgo County entered into agreements under which the county would take custody of federal prisoners. ...

Homero Beltran-Aguirre was one of the federal prisoners housed in the jail under the arrangement negotiated between the Marshals Service and the county. ... Beltran paid Marmolejo a series of bribes in exchange for so-called "contact visits" in which he remained alone with his wife or, on other occasions, his girlfriend. Beltran paid Marmolejo a fixed rate of six thousand dollars per month and one thousand dollars for each contact visit, which occurred twice a week. Petitioner Salinas was the chief deputy responsible for managing the jail and supervising custody of the prisoners. When Marmolejo was not available, Salinas arranged for the contact visits and on occasion stood watch outside the room where the visits took place. In return for his assistance with the scheme, Salinas received from Beltran a pair of designer watches and a pickup truck.

... Salinas was charged with one count of violating RICO, 18 U.S.C. § 1962(c), one count of conspiracy to violate RICO, § 1962(d), and two counts of bribery in violation of § 666(a)(1)(B). The jury acquitted Salinas on the substantive RICO count but convicted him on the RICO conspiracy count and the bribery counts. ...

The RICO conspiracy statute, simple in formulation, provides:

"It shall be unlawful for any person to conspire to violate any of the provisions of subsection (a), (b), or (c) of this section." 18 U.S.C. § 1962(d).

There is no requirement of some overt act or specific act in the statute before us, unlike the general conspiracy provision applicable to federal crimes, which requires that at least one of the conspirators have committed an "act to effect the object of the conspiracy." § 371. The RICO conspiracy provision, then, is even more comprehensive than the general conspiracy offense in § 371.

In interpreting the provisions of § 1962(d), we adhere to a general rule: When Congress uses well-settled terminology of criminal law, its words are presumed to have their ordinary meaning and definition. The relevant statutory phrase in § 1962(d) is "to conspire." We presume Congress intended to use the term in its conventional sense, and certain well-established principles follow.

A conspiracy may exist even if a conspirator does not agree to commit or facilitate each and every part of the substantive offense. The partners in the criminal plan must agree to pursue the same criminal objective and may divide up the work, yet each is responsible for the acts of each other. See *Pinkerton v. United States*, 328 U.S. 640, 646 (1946) ("And so long as the partnership in crime continues, the partners act for each other in carrying it forward"). If conspirators have a plan which calls for some conspirators to perpetrate the crime and others to provide support, the supporters are as guilty as the perpetrators. As Justice Holmes observed: "[P]lainly a person may conspire for the commission of a crime by a third person." A person, moreover, may be liable for conspiracy even though he was incapable of committing the substantive offense.

The point Salinas tries to make is in opposition to these principles, and is refuted by *Bannon v. United States*, 156 U.S. 464 (1895). There the defendants were charged with conspiring to violate the general conspiracy statute, which requires proof of an overt act. One defendant objected to the indictment because it did not allege he had committed an overt act. We rejected the argument because it would erode the common-law principle that, so long as they share a common purpose, conspirators are liable for the acts of their co-conspirators. We observed in *Bannon*: "To require an overt act to be proven against every member of the conspiracy, or a distinct act connecting him with the combination to be alleged, would not only be an innovation upon established principles, but would render most prosecutions for the offence nugatory." The RICO conspiracy statute, § 1962(d), broadened conspiracy coverage by omitting the requirement of an overt act; it did not, at the same time, work the radical change of requiring the Government to prove each conspirator agreed that he would be the one to commit two predicate acts. ...

A conspirator must intend to further an endeavor which, if completed, would satisfy all of the elements of a substantive criminal offense, but it suffices that he adopt the goal of furthering or facilitating the criminal endeavor. He may do so in any number of ways short of agreeing to undertake all of the acts necessary for the crime's completion. One can be a conspirator by agreeing to facilitate only some of the acts leading to the substantive offense. It is elementary that a conspiracy may exist and be punished whether or not the substantive crime ensues, for the conspiracy is a distinct evil, dangerous to the public, and so punishable in itself.

It makes no difference that the substantive offense under [§ 1962](c) requires two or more predicate acts. The interplay between subsections (c) and (d) does not permit us to excuse from the reach of the conspiracy provision an actor who does not himself commit or agree to commit the two or more predicate acts requisite to the underlying offense. True, though an "enterprise" under § 1962(c) can exist with only one actor to conduct it, in most instances it will be conducted by more than one person or entity; and this in turn may make it somewhat difficult to determine just where the enterprise ends and the conspiracy begins, or, on the other hand, whether the two crimes are coincident in their factual circumstances. In some cases the connection the defendant had to the alleged enterprise or to the conspiracy to further it may be tenuous enough so that his own commission of two predicate acts may become an important part of the Government's case. Perhaps these were the considerations leading some of the Circuits to require in conspiracy cases that each conspirator himself commit or agree to commit two or more predicate acts. Nevertheless, that proposition cannot be sustained as a definition of the conspiracy offense, for it is contrary to the principles we have discussed.

In the case before us, even if Salinas did not accept or agree to accept two bribes, there was ample evidence that he conspired to violate subsection (c). The evidence showed that Marmolejo committed at least two acts of racketeering activity when he accepted numerous bribes and that Salinas knew about and agreed to facilitate the scheme. This is sufficient to support a conviction under § 1962(d). ...

B. PROSECUTORIAL POWERS AND POLICIES

1. CHARGING AND EVIDENTIARY CONSIDERATIONS

The above should illustrate the malleability of RICO's provisions, and thus the extent of prosecutors' discretion in choosing whether or not to levy such a charge instead of, or in addition to, the predicate "racketeering activities." From a prosecutor's perspective, RICO charges carry with them significant advantages. As Hon. Gerard E. Lynch has explained:

... Since section 1962(c) defines participating in the affairs of an enterprise through a pattern of racketeering as a crime separate and apart from the predicate acts, it does not merely enhance the statutory penalty for the predicate acts, but rather permits the imposition of consecutive sentences for the RICO offense and the predicates. Because the RICO offense is a separate crime, the statute of limitations runs only from its completion; thus, every additional racketeering offense committed in furtherance of the enterprise's affairs within ten years of a previous one extends the statute of limitations for another five years for prosecution of the entire pattern. A RICO indictment thus may hold a defendant accountable for acts that took place twenty or more years before the date of the indictment—not for the penalty attached to the predicate crime, but for the separately defined RICO offense.

Even within the ordinary limits of the double jeopardy principle and the statute of limitations, a prosecutor can use section 1962(c) to place before a single jury in a single trial offenses that could not otherwise be included in the same indictment or admitted into evidence at the same trial. Suppose, for example, the authorities develop evidence that the same defendant from whom they have recently made an undercover purchase of narcotics is a member of an organized crime family who committed a contract killing three years earlier. Under our ordinary, transaction-bound rules of procedure and evidence, the defendant would have to be tried separately for each offense. Since the earlier crime is plainly not part of the same course of events as the later, joinder of the two crimes would not be possible; if the homicide had taken place in another state, jurisdictional or venue problems would also prevent joinder.

In a trial on the narcotics charge alone, moreover, the evidence of a prior homicide committed by the defendant would likely be excluded as irrelevant and highly prejudicial. Evidence that the defendant in a narcotics trial was part of the "Mafia" would surely be excluded as merely prejudicial evidence of the defendant's character and associations. And the prosecutor presumably would not even think about trying to elicit evidence of crimes that some *other* member of the same crime family had committed, in which this particular defendant was not personally involved. Evidence of the defendant's involvement in organized crime or of the murder he may have committed might finally surface after the defendant's conviction, as part of an argument for a severe sentence.

If the case could be indicted and tried under RICO, however, all of the evidence regarding this defendant's activities could easily be presented in the same trial. Since the government would have to allege and prove a pattern of racketeering activity, the murder and the narcotics offense could be alleged as elements of the same crime, the violation of section 1962(c). The rules precluding admission of evidence of other crimes, consequently, would simply have no application—evidence of the homicide would not be evidence of a *prior* crime, but evidence of the very offense charged in the indictment.

Jurisdictional and venue problems disappear, as well. It is irrelevant that the federal government lacks jurisdiction to prosecute ordinary homicides; the crime charged here is racketeering that affects interstate commerce, not murder. The single crime of racketeering, like any other crime, can be prosecuted in any district where a portion of the crime was committed, so any venue problem with combining crimes committed in different districts disappears.

The government would also have to allege and prove that the crimes were committed in furtherance of the affairs of an enterprise, so the prosecution would be permitted to show the existence, purposes and structure of the organized crime family, and the defendant's membership in it. Even if no other defendant were on trial, this may necessitate reference to criminal activities committed by other members of the organization, as examples of its continuing nature, hierarchical structure, or purposes as an entity; if the defendant were indicted along with several other alleged members of the same organized crime family, as is commonly done in RICO prosecutions, their crimes would of course have to be proved too. Joining those defendants in the same indictment would automatically be proper, of course; since the defendants were all jointly charged with the same crime—the RICO violation—we are faced not with the joinder of several separate offenses by different actors, but with a single offense all the defendants are alleged to have committed together.[27]

It is safe to say that defense counsel will never wish for a RICO charge, but are there any downsides to indicting under RICO from the government's perspective?

2. CRIMINAL FORFEITURE

In terms of sanctions, RICO permits prosecutors the ability to rack up statutory maximums. More significantly, a RICO charge opens up the possibility of criminal forfeiture. Asset forfeiture provisions have been a favored tool of prosecutors seeking to impose penalties that will not only punish offenders, but will also limit the ability of criminal organizations to function after one of its members has been convicted of a crime. Federal criminal forfeiture may be had under three statutes: (1) 21 U.S.C. § 853, which deals with drug-related crimes; (2) 18 U.S.C. § 1963, which concerns RICO violations; and (3) 18 U.S.C. § 982, which relates to several crimes, including money laundering. The language of the three statutes overlaps considerably, though there are important differences among them in the scope of property subject to forfeiture. Forfeiture law is exceedingly complex; a comprehensive analysis of these provisions and the issues they raise is not possible in these pages.[28] The following should serve, however, to give readers some sense of the power of the forfeiture remedy.

A criminal forfeiture must be based on a conviction for the underlying substantive criminal offense. The forfeiture is viewed as part of the sentence imposed on the defendant because of his violation. In this way, *in personam* criminal forfeitures differ from civil forfeitures, which are *in rem* actions against the specific items sought to be forfeited. If a prosecutor wishes to seek forfeiture, she must include a demand for forfeiture in the indictment against the

---

[27] Lynch, *RICO: The Crime of Being a Criminal, Parts III & IV, supra* note 20, at 940-41 (footnotes omitted).

[28] For further guidance, see Steven L. Kessler, Civil and Criminal Forfeiture: Federal and State Practice (West Group 2018); J. Kelly Strader & Diana Parker, *Civil and Criminal Forfeitures* in 1 Otto G. Obermaier & Robert G. Morvillo, White Collar Crime: Business and Regulatory Offenses ch. 6A (Law Journal Press 2018); 2 Sarah N. Welling, Sara Sun Beale & Pamela Bucy, Federal Criminal Law and Related Actions: Crimes, Forfeiture, The False Claims Act and RICO, Chapter 29 (West Group); Stefan D. Cassella, *Criminal Forfeiture Procedure: An Analysis of Developments in the Law Regarding the Inclusion of a Forfeiture Judgment in the Sentence Imposed in a Criminal Case*, 32 Am. J. Crim. L. 55 (2004); *see also* Brian Fork, *The Federal Seizure of Attorneys' Fees in Criminal Forfeiture Actions and the Threat to the American System of Criminal Defense*, 83 N.C. L. Rev. 205 (2004).

defendant.[29] The government bears the burden of proof beyond a reasonable doubt both as to the defendant's guilt and as to the forfeitability of the subject property. Section 1963 dictates that defendants who violate § 1962 "shall" forfeit any interest in the RICO enterprise, including a legitimate business, and any property constituting or derived from the racketeering activity, including proceeds, direct or indirect, which were generated by or connected to the racketeering activity.

The property subject to forfeiture is exceedingly broad. For example, "[a]ssets subject to forfeiture under RICO include real property, cash, stock, and other interests in property that a RICO defendant may have. Even assets of the enterprise that are not tainted by use in connection with the racketeering activity may be subject to forfeiture. All property that constitutes an interest in a criminal enterprise or property constituting proceeds of a racketeering activity, regardless of whether the property was tainted by the racketeering activity, is subject to forfeiture."[30] Also, RICO permits courts to order forfeiture of "substitute assets" of a defendant when, due to the defendant's action, the property that would have been subject to forfeiture cannot be located, has been transferred to a third party, is beyond the jurisdiction of the court, or has been substantially diminished in value or irrevocably commingled with other property.[31] But the Supreme Court held in *Honeycutt v. United States* that a defendant may not be held jointly and severally liable for property that co-conspirator derived from the crime but that defendant himself did not acquire, at least under the drug forfeiture provision, § 853.[32]

Because of the possibility that defendants may seek to transfer or hide assets during the period before forfeiture is ordered, RICO permits the government to obtain pre-conviction injunctions preventing defendants from using or dissipating potentially forfeitable property.[33] The government may also seek *pre-indictment* restraining orders or injunctions. Such orders generally issue only after notice and a hearing, at which the government must prove that: (1) there is a substantial likelihood that the government will prevail on the issue of forfeiture and that the failure to issue an order would likely result in the property being made unavailable for forfeiture; and (2) the need to preserve the property outweighs the hardship on any party against whom the order will be entered.[34] The scope of pre-conviction injunctions vary with the underlying criminal offense and the circumstances, but can be quite broad.

Because the government's rights in the property relate back to the date of the commission of the crime,[35] and because the government may obtain pre-indictment or pre-trial restraints on potentially forfeitable assets,[36] the government may preclude defendants from using potentially forfeitable assets to pay attorney's fees. Statutory and constitutional challenges to such restraints have been unsuccessful. In *United States v. Monsanto*,[37] the Supreme Court ruled, under the substantially identical criminal forfeiture statute 21 U.S.C. § 853 that "there is no exemption from § 853's forfeiture or pretrial restraining order provisions for assets which a defendant wishes to use to retain an attorney."[38] Further, the Court held, relying upon its

---

[29] *See* Fed. R. Crim. P. 7(c)(2).

[30] Kessler, *supra* note 28, § 4:28, at 4-87 (footnotes omitted).

[31] *See* 18 U.S.C. § 1963(m); Kessler, *supra* note 28, § 4:28, at 4-89.

[32] -- U.S. --, 137 S.Ct. 1626 (2017).

[33] *See* 18 U.S.C. § 1963(d).

[34] *See id.* § 1963(d)(1)(B).

[35] *See* 18 U.S.C. § 1963(c).

[36] *See* 18 U.S.C. § 1963(d)(1)(A), (B).

[37] United States v. Monsanto, 491 U.S. 600 (1989).

[38] *Id.* at 614.

contemporaneous decision in *Caplin & Drysdale, Chartered v. United States*,[39] that "neither the Fifth nor the Sixth Amendment to the Constitution requires Congress to permit a defendant to use assets adjudged to be forfeitable to pay that defendant's legal fees."[40]

In *Caplin*, announced the same day as *Monsanto*, the Court determined that "whatever discretion § 853(e) provides district court judges to refuse to enter pretrial restraining orders, it does not extend so far as" to allow a defendant "to withhold assets to pay bona fide attorneys fees."[41] Nor, the Court held, "does the exercise of that discretion 'immunize' nonrestrained assets from *subsequent forfeiture* under § 853(c), *if they are transferred to an attorney to pay legal fees.*"[42] *Caplin* makes clear, then, the government's statutory authority to forfeit legal fees already paid upon a conviction of a defendant. Moreover, the Court rejected the defendant's contention that the statute so construed infringed on his Sixth Amendment right to counsel of choice and upset the "balance of power" between the government and the accused in a manner contrary to due process. Note, however, that the Supreme Court has held, under a different statute, that the Sixth Amendment prohibits the pretrial restraint of a defendant's legitimate, *un*tainted assets (*i.e.*, funds not traceable to a criminal offense) needed to retain counsel of choice even if that would result in the defendant having insufficient funds to pay restitution and other financial penalties if convicted.[43]

A defendant may claim that the RICO forfeiture violates the Eighth Amendment's prohibition against excessive fines.[44] As is explored at greater length in Chapter 20 (Parallel Proceedings), the Supreme Court has held that a "punitive forfeiture violates the Excessive Fines Clause if it is grossly disproportional to the gravity of a defendant's offense."[45]

It will be difficult for defense counsel to resist fee forfeitures under the third-party defenses provided by statute. The attorney will argue that she is a bona fide purchaser but it will be difficult for her to establish that she was reasonably without knowledge that the property was subject to forfeiture. Indeed, all lawyers are on notice that property, and perhaps their fee, may be subject to forfeiture once the indictment is rendered.[46]

3. DOJ APPROVAL REQUIREMENTS AND CHARGING DIRECTIONS

Perhaps in recognition of RICO's power and potential for abuse, the Department of Justice requires approval by the Department's Criminal Division prior to the initiation of any RICO criminal information or indictment, or the filing of any civil complaint.[47] It has also responded to the forfeiture of attorneys' fees problem discussed above by requiring approval from main Justice before such forfeitures may be sought and has issued guidelines for attorney's fee forfeitures.[48] As a result, the Justice Department has not frequently pursued fee forfeiture actions, though it has made exceptions in extraordinary circumstances.[49]

---

[39] 491 U.S. 617 (1989).

[40] *Monsanto*, 491 U.S. at 614.

[41] *Caplan*, 491 U.S. at 623.

[42] *Id.* (emphasis added).

[43] *See* Luis v. United States, -- U.S. --, 136 S.Ct. 1083 (2016) (18 U.S.C. § 1345(a)).

[44] *See, e.g.*, United States v. Bajakajian, 524 U.S. 321 (1998) (involving § 982 forfeiture); Alexander v. United States, 509 U.S. 544 (1993) (involving § 1963 forfeiture).

[45] *Bajakajian*, 524 U.S. at 334.

[46] *See, e.g.*, United States v. Moffitt, Zwerling & Kemler, 83 F.3d 660 (4th Cir. 1996) (finding attorney did not qualify under bona fide purchaser exception, and affirming forfeiture of funds still held by the firm).

[47] *See* Dep't of Justice Manual, tit. 9, §§ 9-110.101, 9-110.210 [hereinafter U.S.A.M.].

[48] *Id.* §§ 9-120.100 through 9-120.116.

[49] *See, e.g.*, *Moffitt*, 83 F.3d at 660 (pursuing fee forfeiture where fee of $103,800 was paid mainly in $100 bills stacked inside shoeboxes).

The Department has also attempted to provide prosecutors some guidance in determining when RICO charges are appropriate. In your view, are these (unenforceable) guidelines sufficient to constrain prosecutorial discretion? Do they effectively separate those types of cases in which RICO should be invoked from those cases in which it is unnecessary or excessive?

The decision to institute a federal criminal prosecution involves balancing society's interest in effective law enforcement against the consequences for the accused. Utilization of the RICO statute, more so than most other federal criminal sanctions, requires particularly careful and reasoned application, because, among other things, RICO incorporates certain state crimes. One purpose of these guidelines is to reemphasize the principle that the primary responsibility for enforcing state laws rests with the state concerned. Despite the broad statutory language of RICO and the legislative intent that the statute "shall be liberally construed to effectuate its remedial purpose," it is the policy of the Criminal Division that RICO be selectively and uniformly used. It is the purpose of these guidelines to make it clear that not every proposed RICO charge that meets the technical requirements of a RICO violation will be approved. Further, the Criminal Division will not approve "imaginative" prosecutions under RICO which are far afield from the congressional purpose of the RICO statute. A RICO count which merely duplicates the elements of proof of traditional Hobbs Act, Travel Act, mail fraud, wire fraud, gambling or controlled substances cases, will not be approved unless it serves some special RICO purpose. Only in exceptional circumstances will approval be granted when RICO is sought merely to serve some evidentiary purpose.[50]

By way of example, the guidelines provide:

Except as hereafter provided, a government attorney should seek approval for a RICO charge only if one or more of the following requirements is present:
1. RICO is necessary to ensure that the indictment adequately reflects the nature and extent of the criminal conduct involved in a way that prosecution only on the underlying charges would not;
2. A RICO prosecution would provide the basis for an appropriate sentence under all the circumstances of the case in a way that prosecution only on the underlying charges would not;
3. A RICO charge could combine related offenses which would otherwise have to be prosecuted separately in different jurisdictions;
4. RICO is necessary for a successful prosecution of the government's case against the defendant or a codefendant;
5. Use of RICO would provide a reasonable expectation of forfeiture which is proportionate to the underlying criminal conduct;
6. The case consists of violations of State law, but local law enforcement officials are unlikely or unable to successfully prosecute the case, in which the federal government has a significant interest;
7. The case consists of violations of State law, but involves prosecution of significant or government individuals, which may pose special problems for the local prosecutor.
The last two requirements reflect the principle that the prosecution of state crimes is primarily the responsibility of state authorities. RICO should be used to prosecute what are essentially violations of state law only if there is a compelling reason to do so.[51]

---

[50] U.S.A.M. § 9-110.200.

[51] *Id.* § 9-110.310; *see also id.* § 9-110.330 (charging RICO where the predicate acts consist only of state offenses).

C. U.S. SENTENCING GUIDELINES: RICO EXERCISE

Recall the case of Mr. Blackmon (*see* Chapter 7 Guidelines Exercise). Assume that:

    1. Mr. Blackmon was convicted of six counts of wire fraud, each of which related to one of the victims described in the opinion.

    2. Mr. Blackmon, and his cohorts, were charged with a § 1962(c) count, alleging that they conducted an "enterprise" consisting of an "association-in-fact" of themselves, through a pattern of wire fraud.

    3. Mr. Blackmon was convicted of one count charging a RICO violation (Count Seven) in addition to the six counts of wire fraud. Those six wire fraud counts served as the predicate racketeering acts underlying the RICO charge.

    4. Mr. Blackmon has a criminal history category of I.

What is Mr. Blackmon's sentencing range?

Chapter 12

MONEY LAUNDERING

"Money laundering" is often described as "the process by which one conceals the existence, illegal source, or illegal application of income, and disguises that income to make it appear legitimate."[1] Laundering, under this conception, is simply a process designed to *conceal* the source, location, or ownership of criminally tainted money. A related conception—again focusing on *concealment*—focuses on the use of laundering techniques to avoid applicable currency reporting, record-keeping, or tax laws. The concealment conception may be most familiar to American readers in that it is associated with attempts to cleanse the illegal taint from the proceeds of the drug trade and organized criminal activity. "Money laundering is a crucial financial underpinning of organized crime and narcotics trafficking. Without [it], drug traffickers would literally drown in cash. ... [They] need money laundering to conceal the billions of dollars in cash generated annually in drug sales and to convert [their] cash into manageable form."[2] Laundering allows criminals to enjoy the proceeds of their crimes without worrying that their "dirty" money will serve as the evidentiary trail through which their illegal activity can be identified and prosecuted. It also helps criminals avoid taxes and the possible confiscation of the fruits of their crimes.[3]

Another, perhaps less intuitive, conception of money laundering is using tainted (and sometimes untainted funds) to *facilitate or promote* criminal activity. This may involve the reinvestment of the proceeds of crime to support further crimes. It may also, however, include the use of "innocent" funds to promote criminal activity. Some would conceptualize this as "criminal financing," not money laundering, but one could explain it as a form of concealment: "[a] person financing a crime such as terrorism with clean money might still be engaged in some sort of laundering (or obscuring of the source of funds) in order to achieve anonymity or at least pseudonymity, but the soil being washed away is not the crime that produced the money, but the person who finances it."[4]

---

[1] President's Comm'n on Organized Crime, Interim Report to the President and Attorney General, The Cash Connection: Organized Crime, Financial Institutions, and Money Laundering 7 (1984).

[2] S. Rep. No. 99-433, at 4 (1986); *see also* Scott Sultzer, *Money Laundering: The Scope of the Problem and Attempts to Combat It,* 63 Tenn. L. Rev. 143, 145-48 (1995); Patrick T. O'Brien, Comment, *Tracking Narco-Dollars: The Evolution of a Potent Weapon in the Drug War,* 21 U. Miami Inter-Am. L. Rev. 637, 643 n.29 (1990) ("A million dollars, composed of an equal mix of [$5, $10, and $20 dollar bills] would consist of 85,715 individual bills weighing 189 pounds ... One hundred billion dollars would weigh approximately nine tons. These bills, if new, unwrinkled, and put in a single stack, would reach more than 600 miles high.") (*citing* Bureau of Engraving and Printing, U.S. Dep't of the Treasury, Pub. No. 15, Production of Government Securities 5 (1985)).

[3] *See* Rajeev Saxena, *Cyberlaundering: The Next Step for Money Laundering,* 10 St. Thomas L. Rev. 685, 685 (1998).

[4] Mariano-Florentino Cuellar, *The Tenuous Relationship Between the Fight Against Money Laundering and the Disruption of Criminal Finance,* 93 J. Crim. & Criminology 311, 337 (2003).

A final conception of money laundering describes the use of the proceeds of criminal activity when one knows of the criminal origins of those funds. This type of laundering is essentially a tainted *money-spending* prohibition, not an effort to prevent the *concealment* of past crimes or the *promotion* of future ones.

All three conceptions are of concern in the United States and abroad. All three are covered in U.S. money laundering legislation, and the first two, at least, have received a great deal of attention on the international and regulatory planes, as well as in criminal cases. The second—"promotion" money laundering or "criminal finance"—has become particularly important post-9/11 because of the government's efforts to stop the flow of money to support terrorist organizations.[5] Because of the criminal focus of our studies, and space constraints, we will not be able to examine all that is going on domestically and internationally to address money laundering; instead, we will focus on the primary U.S. criminal money laundering prohibitions.

The congressional response to money laundering has evolved over time. Outlawing the underlying criminal activity giving rise to the "dirty" funds (such as drug trafficking), and imposing currency reporting requirements on financial institutions did not achieve the desired effect of curbing the discrete activity of money laundering.[6] Accordingly, in 1986, Congress enacted the Money Laundering Control Act, intending in so doing to create "a separate crime distinct from the underlying offense that generated the money to be laundered."[7]

The Money Laundering Control Act of 1986 prohibits money laundering activities in two sections, 18 U.S.C. §§ 1956 and 1957. Section 1956, which is the primary focus of this chapter, contains three distinct offenses. Subsection 1956(a)(1) was intended to address primarily domestic money laundering and prohibits knowing participation in *transactions* with criminal proceeds with the object of promoting crime or knowing that the transaction is designed to conceal the provenance of the money. Subsection 1956(a)(2) is targeted at international money laundering and prohibits knowing *transportation* of monetary instruments or funds across U.S. borders for certain ends, including the promotion of criminal activity or the concealment of ill-gotten gains.

Throughout these materials a distinction has been drawn between § 1956(a)(1) "transaction" and § 1956(a)(2) "transportation" offenses but it should be clear to readers that a "transportation" offense does not have to involve the physical movement of property. Indeed, the "transportation" prohibition can apply to financial transactions such as the wiring of money. The use of the word "transportation," then, is not meant to evoke images of someone carrying a bag full of cocaine-crusted $20's; rather, it is intended to underscore that what *is* required in "transportation" offenses is the movement—by wire as well as by physical means—of monetary instruments or funds over U.S. borders. Finally, § 1956(a)(3) explicitly authorizes the use of government sting operations to expose criminal activity.

Section 1957, which carries lesser penalties and is less frequently invoked, outlaws engaging in monetary transactions with property derived from specified unlawful activity. It, then, is in the nature of a "money spending" prohibition.

A more recently enacted statute, and the "stealth" candidate for the money laundering statute of the future, 18 U.S.C. § 1960, is one that nominally sanctions unlicensed money transmitting businesses. Antiterrorism legislation entitled "Uniting and Strengthening America by Providing Appropriate Tools Required to Intercept and Obstruct Terrorism" (also known as the "USA PATRIOT" Act)[8] was signed into law by President Bush on October 26, 2001.

---

[5] *See, e.g.*, Herbert V. Morais, *Fighting International Crime and Its Financing: The Importance of Following a Coherent Global Strategy Based on the Rule of Law*, 50 Vill. L. Rev. 583 (2005); Bruce Zagaris, *The Merging of the Counter-Terrorism and Anti-Money Laundering Regimes*, 34 Law. & Pol'y Int'l Bus. 45 (2002).

[6] *See, e.g.*, *Thirty-Third Annual Survey of White Collar Crime, Money Laundering*, 55 Am. Crim. L. Rev. 1469, 1470 (2018); Maura E. Fenningham, Note, *A Full Laundering Cycle is Required: Plowing Back the Proceeds to Carry on Crime is the Crime Under 18 U.S.C. § 1956(a)(1)(A)(I)*, 70 Notre Dame L. Rev. 891, 892-93 (1995).

[7] United States v. Edgmon, 952 F.2d 1206, 1213 (10th Cir. 1991).

[8] Pub. L. No. 107-56, 115 Stat. 272 (2001).

That Act amended, and substantially expanded, the reach of § 1960, arguably making it "now the broadest money laundering statute on the books."[9]

Why is familiarity with these money laundering prohibitions important to white-collar practice? First, money laundering is *big, big* business. Laundering by its nature, demands secrecy and deception; as a consequence, it is often difficult to detect. "[L]ooking for evidence of money laundering is not merely like looking for a needle in a haystack, but rather for 'a needle in a needlestack.'"[10] This same quality renders it difficult to quantify, but the United Nations Office on Drugs and Crime estimates that the amount of money laundered globally in one year is "2-5% of global GDP, or $800 billion-$2 trillion in current US dollars. Though the margin between those figures is huge, even the lower estimate underlines the seriousness of the problem governments have pledged to address."[11]

> Laundering has grown hand-in-hand with globalisation, and particularly with the lifting of capital controls and the development of international payment systems. These allow money to be shifted in seconds between banks in different parts of the world that may not even be aware of each other's existence. The sums of money being transferred are huge. Bank of America, for example, sees nearly $1 trillion pass through its internal wires every day. As Alan Greenspan, the [former] chairman of America's Federal Reserve Board, has put it, the international payment system is "crucial to the integrity and stability" of the world's financial markets. But it also provides big opportunities for crooks to hide their money by shuffling it around the globe.[12]

A second reason that study of money laundering makes sense in a white-collar course is that the laundering problem extends far beyond the financial shenanigans of drug lords. A number of high-profile cases in the recent past "have laid to rest any lingering doubts that money laundering ... is something that involves only drug dealers and unknown banks in banana republics, though such banks are certainly part of the story. Whether wittingly or not, many of the world's best-known banks have become a central element in the process by which crooks clean up their ill-gotten gains."[13] Further, in 1993, a Treasury Department official testified that "[w]hile drug money laundering captures the most public attention, money laundering sustains every criminal activity engaged in for profit, which is to say all crime but crimes of passion or vengeance."[14] (Recent events have demonstrated that even this expansive statement was underinclusive; in particular, one of the lessons of September 11, 2001 is that money laundering is also employed by those whose crimes apparently have political or ideological, rather than strictly profit-driven, roots.)

Finally, these statutes are very important to white-collar practice because prosecutors have made them so. In 1990, a Justice Department spokesman commented "that U.S. attorneys around the country see the future as lying in the money-laundering statutes, rather than RICO," because "Section 1956 gets you everything that RICO gets you, and more."[15] In late 2001, amendments to the sentencing guidelines became effective that dampened the formerly

---

[9] *Money Laundering: Panelists Explore USA PATRIOT Act's Effects on Anti-Money Laundering Laws*, 70 Crim. L. Reporter (BNA) 536-37 (March 20, 2002).

[10] *Money Laundering: Through the Wringer*, The Economist 64 (Apr. 14, 2001).

[11] UNODC, Money Laundering and Globalization, *available at* https://www.unodc.org/unodc/en/money-luandering/globilization.html (last visited Sept. 10, 2018).

[12] *Money Laundering: Through the Wringer, supra* note 10.

[13] *Id.*

[14] *Federal Government's Response to Money Laundering: Hearings Before the Committee on Banking, Finance, & Urban Affairs*, 103d Cong., 1st Sess. 200-01 (1993) (statement of Ronald K. Noble, Assistant Secretary for Enforcement, U.S. Dep't of the Treasury).

[15] Barry Tarlow, *RICO Report*, The Champion 32 (Aug.1990).

disproportionate sentencing kick that a money laundering charge could bring in a white-collar case. Although the laundering statutes, as a result, lost some of their allure for the government, they retain many of their advantages from a prosecutor's point of view. Sections 1956 and 1957 are broadly worded and flexible in their reach. These sections have an even more extensive list of predicates than does RICO. Money laundering may also be easier, or at least less complicated, to prove to the satisfaction of a jury. It carries with it many of the collateral advantages of a RICO case, most notably the forfeiture of any property involved in a money laundering offense or any property traceable to such property.[16] And, unlike RICO prosecutions, not all money laundering cases require prior Department of Justice approval.[17]

These circumstances have in fact given prosecutors an incentive to call upon these statutory weapons to sanction conduct far removed from the type of laundering that was the apparent target of congressional efforts. While the money laundering statutes were intended primarily to halt the laundering of organized crime proceeds or drug money, their proscriptions are sufficiently broad to apply to transactions involving funds derived from most serious federal crimes, a large number of state crimes, and a variety of offenses against foreign nations. "Money laundering" therefore can include everything from the international transportation of millions of dollars in drug proceeds to the deposit of a bribe into a corrupt official's bank account or the purchase of a vacation home with funds obtained through fraud. Indeed, a 1992 U.S. Sentencing Commission study "demonstrated that 40 percent of the crimes for which money laundering sentences were imposed were not related to drug trafficking but were characterized as 'white collar.'"[18] A DOJ study released in 2003 noted that between 1994 and 2001, 60 percent of the laundering cases prosecuted involved an underlying property offense (embezzlement or fraud); by contrast, only about 17 percent involved drug trafficking.[19]

A. "TRANSACTION" OFFENSES UNDER § 1956(a)(1) and § 1957

1. "CONCEALMENT" OFFENSE UNDER § 1956(a)(1)(B)(i)

UNITED STATES v. CAMPBELL
977 F.2d 854 (4th Cir.1992)

ERVIN, CHIEF JUDGE:

The United States appeals from the district court's grant of Ellen Campbell's motion for judgment of acquittal on charges of money laundering, 18 U.S.C. § 1956(a)(1)(B)(i), and engaging in a transaction in criminally derived property, 18 U.S.C. § 1957(a). Campbell had been convicted of the charges by a jury in the Western District of North Carolina. We reverse the judgment of acquittal. ...

... In the summer of 1989, Ellen Campbell was a licensed real estate agent working at Lake Norman Realty in Mooresville, North Carolina. During the same period, Mark Lawing was a drug dealer in Kannapolis, North Carolina. Lawing decided to buy a house on Lake

---

[16] *See* 18 U.S.C. §§ 981 (providing for civil *in rem* forfeiture), 982 (providing for criminal *in personam* forfeiture).

[17] *See* 4 Dep't of Justice Manual, tit. 9 [hereinafter U.S.A.M.], § 9-105.300.

[18] Robert G. Morvillo & Barry A Bohrer, *Checking the Balance: Prosecutorial Power in an Age of Expansive Legislation*, 32 Am. Crim. L. Rev. 137, 145 & n.41 (1995).

[19] Dep't of Justice, Bureau of Justice Statistics, *Money Laundering Offenders, 1994-2001* 1 (July 2003).

Norman. He obtained Campbell's business card from Lake Norman Realty's Mooresville office, called Campbell, and scheduled an appointment to look at houses.

Over the course of about five weeks, Lawing met with Campbell approximately once a week and looked at a total of ten to twelve houses. Lawing and Campbell also had numerous phone conversations. Lawing represented himself to Campbell as the owner of a legitimate business, L & N Autocraft, which purportedly performed automobile customizing services. When meeting with Campbell, Lawing would travel in either a red Porsche he owned or a gold Porsche owned by a fellow drug dealer, Randy Sweatt, who would usually accompany Lawing. During the trips to look at houses, which occurred during normal business hours, Lawing would bring his cellular phone and would often consume food and beer with Sweatt. At one point, Lawing brought a briefcase containing $20,000 in cash, showing the money to Campbell to demonstrate his ability to purchase a house.

Lawing eventually settled upon a house listed for $191,000 and owned by Edward and Nancy Guy Fortier. The listing with the Fortiers had been secured by Sara Fox, another real estate agent with Lake Norman Realty. After negotiations, Lawing and the Fortiers agreed on a price of $182,500, and entered into a written contract. Lawing was unable to secure a loan and decided to ask the Fortiers to accept $60,000 under the table in cash and to lower the contract price to $122,500.[20] Lawing contacted Campbell and informed her of this proposal. Campbell relayed the proposal to Fox, who forwarded the offer to the Fortiers. The Fortiers agreed, and Fox had the Fortiers execute a new listing agreement which lowered the sales price and increased the commission percentage (in order to protect the realtors' profits on the sale).

Thereafter Lawing met the Fortiers, Fox and Campbell in the Mooresville sales office with $60,000 in cash. The money was wrapped in small bundles and carried in a brown paper grocery bag. The money was counted, and a new contract was executed reflecting a sales price of $122,500. Lawing tipped both Fox and Campbell with "a couple of hundred dollars."

William Austin, the closing attorney, prepared closing documents, including HUD-1 and 1099-S forms, reflecting a sales price of $122,500, based on the information provided by Campbell. Campbell, Fox, Austin, Lawing, Lawing's parents and the Fortiers were all present at the closing. The closing documents were signed, all reflecting a sales price of $122,500.

Campbell was indicted on a three count indictment alleging: 1) money laundering, in violation of 18 U.S.C. § 1956(a)(1)(B)(i); 2) engaging in a transaction in criminally derived property, in violation of 18 U.S.C. § 1957(a); and 3) causing a false statement (the HUD-1 form) to be filed with a government agency, in violation of 18 U.S.C. § 1001. She was tried and convicted by a jury on all three counts. After the verdict, the district court granted Campbell's motion for judgment of acquittal with respect to the money laundering and transaction in criminally derived property counts. The district court also conditionally ordered a new trial on these counts if the judgment of acquittal was reversed on appeal. The Government appeals. ...

The money laundering statute under which Campbell was charged applies to any person who:

> knowing that the property involved in a financial transaction represents the proceeds of some form of unlawful activity, conducts or attempts to conduct such a financial transaction which in fact involves the proceeds of specified unlawful activity ... knowing that the transaction is designed in whole or in part ... to conceal or disguise the nature, the location, the source, the ownership, or the control of the proceeds of specified unlawful activity. ...

---

[20] [Court's footnote 1:] Lawing's explanation to Campbell of this unorthodox arrangement was that the lower purchase price would allow Lawing's parents to qualify for a mortgage. Lawing would then make the mortgage payments on his parent's behalf. Lawing justified the secrecy of the arrangement by explaining that his parents had to remain unaware of the $60,000 payment because the only way he could induce their involvement was to convince them he was getting an excellent bargain on the real estate.

18 U.S.C. § 1956(a)(1). The district court found, and Campbell does not dispute, that there was adequate evidence for the jury to find that Campbell conducted a financial transaction which in fact involved the proceeds of Lawing's illegal drug activities. The central issue in contention is whether there was sufficient evidence for the jury to find that Campbell possessed the knowledge that: (1) Lawing's funds were the proceeds of illegal activity, and (2) the transaction was designed to disguise the nature of those proceeds.

In assessing Campbell's culpability, it must be noted that the statute requires actual subjective knowledge. Campbell cannot be convicted on what she objectively should have known. However, this requirement is softened somewhat by the doctrine of willful blindness. In this case, the jury was instructed that:

> The element of knowledge may be satisfied by inferences drawn from proof that a defendant deliberately closed her eyes to what would otherwise have been obvious to her. A finding beyond a reasonable doubt of a conscious purpose to avoid enlightenment would permit an inference of knowledge. Stated another way, a defendant's knowledge of a fact may be inferred upon willful blindness to the existence of a fact.

> It is entirely up to you as to whether you find any deliberate closing of the eyes and inferences to be drawn from any evidence. A showing of negligence is not sufficient to support a finding of willfulness or knowledge.

> I caution you that the willful blindness charge does not authorize you to find that the defendant acted knowingly because she should have known what was occurring when the property at 763 Sundown Road was being sold, or that in the exercise of hindsight she should have known what was occurring or because she was negligent in failing to recognize what was occurring or even because she was reckless or foolish in failing to recognize what was occurring. Instead, the Government must prove beyond a reasonable doubt that the defendant purposely and deliberately contrived to avoid learning all of the facts.

Neither party disputes the adequacy of these instructions on willful blindness or their applicability to this case.

As outlined above, a money laundering conviction under section 1956(a)(1)(B)(i) requires proof of the defendant's knowledge of two separate facts: (1) that the funds involved in the transaction were the proceeds of illegal activity; and (2) that the transaction was designed to conceal the nature of the proceeds. In its opinion supporting the entry of the judgment of acquittal, the district court erred in interpreting the elements of the offense. After correctly reciting the elements of the statute, the court stated, "in a prosecution against a party other than the drug dealer," the Government must show "*a purpose of concealment*" and "knowledge of the drug dealer's activities." This assertion misstates the Government's burden. The Government need not prove that the defendant had the *purpose* of concealing the proceeds of illegal activity. Instead, as the plain language of the statute suggests, the Government must only show that the defendant possessed the *knowledge* that the transaction was designed to conceal illegal proceeds.[21]

This distinction is critical in cases such as the present one, in which the defendant is a person other than the individual who is the source of the tainted money. It is clear from the record that Campbell herself did not act with the purpose of concealing drug proceeds. Her motive, without question, was to close the real estate deal and collect the resulting commission, without regard to the source of the money or the effect of the transaction in concealing a portion of the purchase price. However, Campbell's motivations are irrelevant. Under the

---

21 [Court's footnote 3:] The other portion of the district court's statement, that the Government must show Campbell possessed "knowledge of the drug dealer's activities," is also incorrect. The statute requires only a showing that the defendant had knowledge that "the property involved in a financial transaction represents the proceeds of *some form of illegal activity*." 18 U.S.C. § 1956(a)(1). This issue is addressed *infra*.

terms of the statute, the relevant question is not Campbell's purpose, but rather her knowledge of Lawing's purpose.[22]

The sufficiency of evidence regarding Campbell's knowledge of Lawing's purpose depends on whether Campbell was aware of Lawing's status as a drug dealer. Assuming for the moment that Campbell knew that Lawing's funds were derived from illegal activity, then the under the table transfer of $60,000 in cash would have been sufficient, by itself, to allow the jury to find that Campbell knew, or was willfully blind to the fact, that the transaction was designed for an illicit purpose. *See United States v. Massac*, 867 F.2d 174, 177-78 (3rd Cir.1989) (knowledge that funds were drug-related, coupled with irregular nature of financial transactions, sufficient to permit jury to infer defendant's knowledge of the purpose of such transactions). Only if Campbell was oblivious to the illicit nature of Lawing's funds could she credibly argue that she believed Lawing's explanation of the under the table transfer of cash and was unaware of the money laundering potential of the transaction. In short, the fraudulent nature of the transaction itself provides a sufficient basis from which a jury could infer Campbell's knowledge of the transaction's purpose, if, as assumed above, Campbell also knew of the illegal source of Lawing's money.[23] As a result, we find that, in this case, the knowledge components of the money laundering statute collapse into a single inquiry: Did Campbell know that Lawing's funds were derived from an illegal source?

The Government emphasizes that the district court misstated the Government's burden on this point as well, by holding that the Government must show Campbell's "knowledge of the drug dealer's activities." As the text of the statute indicates, the Government need only show knowledge that the funds represented "the proceeds of some form of unlawful activity." 18 U.S.C. § 1956(a)(1); *see also* 18 U.S.C. § 1956(c)(1) (money laundering provision requires "that the person knew the property involved in the transaction represented proceeds from some form, though not necessarily which form, of [specified unlawful] activity"). Practically, this distinction makes little difference. All of the Government's evidence was designed to show that Campbell knew that Lawing was a drug dealer. There is no indication that the jury could have believed that Lawing was involved in some form of criminal activity other than drug dealing. As a result, the district court's misstatement on this point is of little consequence.

The evidence pointing to Campbell's knowledge of Lawing's illegal activities is not overwhelming. First, we find that the district court correctly excluded from consideration testimony by Sweatt that Lawing was a "known" drug dealer. Kannapolis, where Lawing's operations were located, is approximately fifteen miles from Mooresville, where Campbell

---

[22] [Court's footnote 4:] We have no difficulty in finding that *Lawing's* purpose satisfied the statutory requirement that the transaction be "designed in whole or in part ... to conceal or disguise the nature, the location, the source, the ownership, or the control of the proceeds of specified unlawful activity. ..." 18 U.S.C. § 1956(a)(1)(B). The omission of $60,000 from all documentation regarding the sales price of the property clearly satisfies this standard—concealing both the nature and the location of Lawing's illegally derived funds. *See United States v. Lovett*, 964 F.2d 1029, 1034 (10th Cir.1992) (money laundering transaction need not necessarily conceal the *identity* of the participants in the transaction; concealment of the funds themselves is sufficient). Accordingly, we need not address the Government's alternative argument that Lawing concealed ownership of the funds by placing title to the Lake Norman property in the name of his parents.

[23] [Court's footnote 5:] In this respect the present case is completely distinguishable from the principal case relied upon by the district court, *United States v. Sanders*, 929 F.2d 1466 (10th Cir.[1992]). In that case, the court overturned two money laundering convictions of a defendant who, with funds admittedly derived from an illegal source, had purchased two automobiles. Unlike the present case, there was nothing irregular about the transactions themselves. The court found the transactions to be devoid of any attempt "to conceal or disguise the source or nature of the proceeds" and found that application of the money laundering statute to "ordinary commercial transactions" would "turn the money laundering statute into a 'money spending statute,'" a result clearly not intended by Congress. The present case, by contrast, presents a highly irregular financial transaction which, by its very structure, was designed to mislead onlookers as to the amount of money involved in the transaction.

lived and worked, and, as the district court pointed out, there was no indication that Lawing's reputation extended over such an extensive "community."

However, the district court also downplayed evidence that we find to be highly relevant. Sara Fox, the listing broker, testified at trial that Campbell had stated prior to the sale that the funds "may have been drug money." The trial court discounted this testimony because it conflicted with Fox's grand jury testimony that she did not recall Campbell ever indicating that Lawing was involved with drugs. In evaluating the testimony in this manner, the trial court made an impermissible judgment on witness credibility—a judgment that was clearly within the exclusive province of the jury. When ruling on a motion for judgment of acquittal the district court is obligated to weigh the evidence in the light most favorable to the Government. Under that standard, Fox's testimony regarding Campbell's statement that the funds "may have been drug money" should have been accepted as completely true.

In addition, the Government presented extensive evidence regarding Lawing's lifestyle. This evidence showed that Lawing and his companion both drove new Porsches, and that Lawing carried a cellular phone, flashed vast amounts of cash, and was able to be away from his purportedly legitimate business for long stretches of time during normal working hours. The district court conceded that this evidence "is not wholly [*sic*] irrelevant" to Campbell's knowledge of Lawing's true occupation, but noted that Lawing's lifestyle was not inconsistent with that of many of the other inhabitants of the affluent Lake Norman area who were not drug dealers. Again, we find that the district court has drawn inferences from the evidence which, while possibly well-founded, are not the only inferences that can be drawn. It should have been left to the jury to decide whether or not the Government's evidence of Lawing's lifestyle was sufficient to negate the credibility of Campbell's assertion that she believed Lawing to be a legitimate businessman.

We find that the evidence of Lawing's lifestyle, the testimony concerning Campbell's statement that the money "might have been drug money," and the fraudulent nature of the transaction in which Campbell was asked to participate were sufficient to create a question for the jury concerning whether Campbell "deliberately closed her eyes to what would otherwise have been obvious to her." As a result, we find that a reasonable jury could have found that Campbell was willfully blind to the fact that Lawing was a drug dealer and the fact that the purchase of the Lake Norman property was intended, at least in part, to conceal the proceeds of Lawing's drug selling operation. Accordingly, we reverse the judgment of acquittal on the money laundering charge.

The statute under which Campbell was charged in Count 2 provides:

> Whoever ... knowingly engages or attempts to engage in a monetary transaction in criminally derived property that is of a value greater than $10,000 and is derived from specified unlawful activity, shall be punished as provided in subsection (b).

18 U.S.C. § 1957(a). The parties do not dispute that Campbell engaged in a monetary transaction in property of a value in excess of $10,000 or that the property was derived from "specified unlawful activity" as defined by the statute. Once again, the dispositive question is whether Campbell knew that Lawing's funds were the proceeds of criminal activity. As such, the discussion above with regard to the money laundering charge is completely applicable here. Because a jury could reasonably find that Campbell knew of, or was willfully blind to, Lawing's true occupation, it was error for the district court to grant a judgment of acquittal on this count as well. ...

Notes

1. *Elements of a § 1956(a)(1) "transaction" money laundering case*: To prove a "transaction" money laundering offense under § 1956(a)(1), the government must demonstrate beyond a reasonable doubt that a defendant:

(a) conducted or attempted to conduct a financial transaction;

(b) knowing that the property involved in the transaction represented the proceeds of unlawful activity;

(c) the transaction in fact "involv[ed]" the proceeds of "specified unlawful activity"; and

(d) the defendant acted with the requisite knowledge or purpose.

Although § 1956(a)(1) sets forth four *alternative* means by which the government can demonstrate that the defendant acted with the requisite knowledge or purpose, these materials focus only on two:

(i) cases in which the government charges that the defendant conducted the financial transaction "with the intent to promote the carrying on of specified unlawful activity" (a "promotion" transaction offense under § 1956(a)(1)(A)(i)); and

(ii) cases in which the government alleges that the defendant knew that the transaction was "designed in whole or in part ... to conceal or disguise" the nature, location, source, ownership, or control of the proceeds of "specified unlawful activity" (a "concealment" transaction offense under § 1956(a)(1)(B)(i)).

(The other two alternatives, not explored in this text, are: (iii) cases in which the government contends that the defendant conducted the financial transaction with the intent to engage in tax fraud (§ 1956(a)(1)(A)(ii)); and (iv) cases in which the government alleges that the defendant knew that the transaction was designed to avoid a transaction reporting requirement under State or Federal law (§ 1956(a)(1)(B)(ii)).

For individuals, violations of § 1956(a)(1) are felonies punishable by a fine of not more than $500,000 or twice the value of the property involved in the transaction, whichever is greater, and up to 20 years' imprisonment.

2. *Financial transaction.* The foundation of any money laundering case under § 1956(a)(1) is a proscribed "financial transaction." The statute defines a "financial transaction" very broadly. *See* 18 U.S.C. § 1956(c)(3), (4). A "transaction" is defined in § 1956(c)(3) to include a "purchase, sale, loan, pledge, gift, transfer, delivery, or other disposition, and with respect to a financial institution includes a deposit, withdrawal, transfer between accounts, exchange of currency, loan, extension of credit, purchase or sale of any stock, bond, certificate of deposit, or other monetary instrument, use of a safe-deposit box, or any other payment, transfer, or delivery by, through, or to a financial institution." The term "financial transaction" contains a jurisdictional element. It is defined in § 1956(c)(4) as:

(A) a transaction which in any way or degree affects interstate or foreign commerce (i) involving the movement of funds by wire or other means or (ii) involving one or more monetary instruments or (iii) involving the transfer of title to any real property, vehicle, vessel, or aircraft, or

(B) a transaction involving the use of a financial institution which is engaged in, or the activities of which affect, interstate or foreign commerce in any way or degree.

The relationship that a given transaction or financial institution must have to interstate or foreign commerce is generally characterized in the caselaw as "de minimis." *See* United States v. Tarkoff, 242 F.3d 991 (11th Cir. 2001). For example, in *Tarkoff*, a defense lawyer's conviction for money laundering was upheld because a "financial transaction" was proven under § 1956(c)(4)(A) by virtue of defendant's and a coconspirator's travel to Israel to transact business with a bank there, as well as their international phone calls arranging for funds transfers and, under § 1956(c)(4)(B), because the transactions involved an Israeli bank that was engaged in and affected foreign commerce. *Id.*; *see also* United States v. Villarini, 238 F.3d 530, 533 (4th Cir. 2001); United States v. Wilkinson, 137 F.3d 214, 220-21 (4th Cir. 1998).

As should be obvious, "[t]he definition of 'financial transaction' is not limited to transactions with banking or financial institutions. Virtually any exchange of money between two parties constitutes a financial transaction subject to criminal prosecution under § 1956, provided that the transaction has at least a minimal effect on interstate commerce and satisfies at least one of the four intent requirements of § 1956(a)(1)(A) [or] (B)." *Thirty-Third Annual Survey of White Collar Crime, supra* note 6, at 1484 1374 (footnotes omitted).

The USA PATRIOT Act's money laundering title, the "International Money Laundering Abatement and Anti-Terrorist Financing Act," is primarily directed to the banking industry but makes a number of adjustments of interest to criminal law practitioners. *See Broad Anti-Terrorism Package Passed by Congress, Signed by President,* 70 Crim. L. Rep. (BNA) 93, at 94-95 (Oct. 31, 2001) (summarizing money laundering changes). In the Act, Congress expanded § 1956(c)(6)'s definition of a "financial institution" to include foreign banks. *See* 18 U.S.C. § 1956(c)(6)(B).

3. Mens rea *regarding the nature of the proceeds involved in the transaction.* The statute makes clear that the element of "knowing that property involved in a financial transaction represents the proceeds of some form of unlawful activity" means only that "the person knew the property involved in the transaction represented proceeds from some form, though not necessarily which form, of activity that constitutes a felony under State, Federal, or foreign law, regardless of whether or not such activity is [specified unlawful activity]." 18 U.S.C. § 1956(c)(1).

It is worth underscoring the implications of this definition. The "some form of unlawful activity" standard defines the required scope of the defendant's knowledge with respect to the nature of the "proceeds." Thus, "some form of unlawful activity" means only that the defendant has to know that the money was the dirty proceeds of some type of felony, but it does not have to be a crime that is listed in any section of the money laundering statute and indeed the defendant does not even have to know the actual nature of the crime that spun off the money. By contrast, to be "specified unlawful activity," an offense must actually appear on the laundry list of offenses in the statutory definition of that term; "specified unlawful activity," then, although it is very broadly defined, is still a far narrower category than the "some form of unlawful activity" standard.

4. *Concealment. Campbell* is a "concealment" prosecution under § 1956(a)(1)(B)(i). Campbell did not contest that the financial transaction—the house purchase—in fact involved the proceeds of illegal drug activities. What evidence demonstrated that the transaction was intended to conceal the nature and location of those tainted funds?

For purposes of a § 1956(a)(1)(B)(i) "concealment" prosecution, a variety of activity has been held to demonstrate an intent to conceal or disguise the nature, location, source, ownership, or control of the proceeds of specified unlawful activity. As the Fifth Circuit explained in *United States v. Willey,* 57 F.3d 1374 (5th Cir. 1995), "while a showing of simply spending money in one's own name will generally not support a money laundering conviction, using a third party, for example, a business entity or a relative, to purchase goods on one's behalf or from which one will benefit usually constitutes sufficient proof of a design to conceal." *Id.* at 1385. Similarly, "[e]vidence that the defendant commingled illegal proceeds with legitimate business funds has been held to be sufficient to support the design element." *Id.* at 1386. "Moving money through a large number of accounts has, in the light of other evidence, also been found to support the design element of this offense, even when all the accounts to which the defendant transferred the money and from which he withdrew it were in his name." *Id.* Evidence that a defendant repeatedly deposited fraudulently obtained reimbursement checks into his own checking account before withdrawing the entire amount in cash has been held enough to prove an intent to conceal. *See* United States v. Dvorak, 617 F.3d 1017 (8th Cir. 2010).

In sum, the cases "demonstrate that in order to establish the design element of money laundering, it is not necessary to prove with regard to any single transaction that the defendant removed all traces of his involvement with the money or that the particular transaction charged is itself highly unusual, although either of these elements might be sufficient to support a money laundering conviction." *Willey,* 57 F.3d at 1386; *see also* United States v. Naranjo, 634 F.3d 1198 (11th Cir. 2011); United States v. Adefehinti, 510 F.3d 319 (D.C. Cir. 2007); *see generally* Helen Gredd & Karl D. Cooper, *Money Laundering* in 1 Otto G. Obermaier, *et al.,*

White Collar Crime: Business and Regulatory Offenses § 2A.02[1][d][iii], at 2A-44 to 2A-45 (2018).

Some courts, however, have reversed convictions where the government's theory would convert § 1956 into a "money spending" statute. Thus, for example, in *United States v. Rockelman*, 49 F.3d 418, 422 (8th Cir. 1995), the Eighth Circuit reversed a money laundering conviction for lack of concealment because the defendant purchased a cabin with cash, which consisted of illegal proceeds, placed the title in the name of his business, and made no attempt to conceal either his own identity or the source of the funds. *See also* United States v. Shoff, 151 F.3d 889 (8th Cir. 1998) (holding that purchase of two cars with the proceeds of fraudulent activities did not support a "concealment" money laundering conviction); United States v. Herron, 97 F.3d 234 (8th Cir. 1996).

5. Mens Rea*: Intent to Conceal and* Cuellar v. United States. In a "concealment" prosecution under either the "transaction" or the "transportation" prongs, the government must prove an intent to conceal—that is, that the "animating purpose" of the transaction or transportation was to conceal the nature, source, or location of illicit funds. United States v. Faulkenberry, 614 F.3d 573, 586 (6th Cir. 2010); *see also* United States v. Demmitt, 706 F.3d 665 (5th Cir. 2013); *Naranjo*, 634 F.3d at 1208.

The Supreme Court addressed the design-to-conceal element in a "transportation" prosecution in *Cuellar v. United States*, 553 U.S. 550 (2008). In that case, the defendant took substantial trouble to conceal $81,000 in a car that he planned to drive over the United States-Mexico border. The Supreme Court reversed his conviction under 1956(a)(2)(B)(i), ruling that a concealment money laundering conviction required proof that the transportation's *purpose*—not merely its effect—was to conceal or disguise one of the listed attributes. In other words, the defendant had to transport in order to conceal; it was not sufficient to show simply that he concealed in the course of transporting.

6. For a conviction under the "transaction" concealment prong, does every defendant have to share this intent to conceal? That is, in this case, did Campbell have to *share* Lawing's intent to conceal in order to be convicted under § 1956(a)(1)(B)(i)? What does the government have to prove to demonstrate her culpability? Campbell's "knowledge" is obviously critical but just what did she have to "know" (or what did she have to consciously avoid knowing)? Does the government have to prove that she knew that the property represented proceeds of *a certain type of criminal conduct—that is "specified unlawful activity"*—or merely that she knew that the transaction was designed to conceal or disguise the nature of the money? *See, e.g.*, United States v. Richardson, 658 F.3d 333 (3d Cir. 2011) (vacating conviction because evidence was insufficient to establish that the defendant knew that the transaction was designed to conceal); United States v. Carr, 25 F.3d 1194, 1206 (3d Cir. 1994) (holding in a §1956(a)(2) concealment case that the statute requires only that "[the defendant] knew his act of transporting the funds was designed to disguise or conceal its nature, source, ownership, or control.").

7. *Actual nature of the proceeds.* The financial transaction must "in fact involve[]" the proceeds of specified unlawful activity in a § 1956(a)(1) "transaction" prosecution. *See* United States v. Harris, 666 F.3d 905 (5th Cir. 2012).

The issues that arise with respect to this element include: (1) the degree to which the government may rely on circumstantial evidence to demonstrate this "fact," *see* Gredd & Cooper, *supra*, § 2A.02[1][b][iii], and (2) whether tracing is required when the transaction "involves" dollars from an account where proceeds of specified unlawful activity have been commingled with legitimate funds, *id.* § 2A.02[1][b][i]. In general, the present state of the law with respect to first, evidentiary, issue may be summarized as follows:

> In a § 1956 prosecution the government does not have to trace proceeds involved in a scheme back to a particular offense. The government need only present evidence that the defendant engaged in conduct typical of criminal activity and had no other legitimate source of funds. While some courts hold that evidence of a lack of a legitimate source of income standing alone is insufficient to support a conviction, others have held a jury's inference that the proceeds could only have been derived from an illegal source. The lack

of a tracing requirement allows the government to prosecute a predicate offense through the use of circumstantial, rather than direct, evidence.

Thirty-Third Annual Survey of White Collar Crime, supra note 6, at 1480 (footnotes omitted); *see also* United States v. Monaco, 194 F.3d 381, 387 (2d Cir. 1999).

With regard to the second, tracing, issue:

> Courts have looked to the "involve" language in the statute and the broad remedial intent of the money laundering statute to hold that requiring *direct* tracing is contrary to the statutory language and would allow criminals to avoid conviction by commingling dirty money in accounts with other funds. Commingling itself has been held to be indicative of intent to launder funds. No circuit has required the government to *directly* trace proceeds to specified unlawful activity in a § 1956 case ... .

Joseph R. Miller, Note, *Federal Money Laundering Crimes-Should Direct Tracing of Funds Be Required?*, 90 Ky. L.J. 441, 448 (2001-02) (footnotes omitted) (emphasis added). However,

> [t]he circuits have taken various approaches with regard to the *amount* of tracing that is required. First, some courts have held that any transaction out of a commingled account constitutes laundering. Second, some courts have suggested that defendants will be responsible only for those transactions from a commingled account that do not exceed the total amount of illegitimate funds. Finally, other courts have decided to treat spending from commingled accounts as involving "proportional fractions of clean and dirty money."

United States v. Braxtonbrown-Smith, 278 F.3d 1348, 1353 n.1 (D.C. Cir. 2002) (emphasis added).

The federal circuit courts of appeals are in disagreement as to the commingling issue in § 1957 prosecutions:

> A majority of circuits have held that the government is not required to trace criminally derived funds in commingled accounts to prove that the subject funds were derived from specified unlawful activity. Some of the circuits have utilized the reasoning used in § 1956 cases to arrive at this result. However, the Ninth Circuit, in *United States v. Rutgard*, [116 F.3d 1270 (9th Cir. 1997),] held that direct tracing is required.

Miller, *supra*, at 449 (footnotes omitted); *see also* United States v. Silver, 864 F.3d 102 (2d Cir. 2017). Upon what basis can a distinction between § 1956 and § 1957 regarding tracing be justified?

8. *Undercover operations.* A situation in which the government may have difficulty demonstrating that a transaction "in fact involves" the proceeds of specified unlawful activity, even under the forgiving tracing standards discussed above, is when the funds "are not actually derived from a real crime; they are undercover funds supplied by the Government." U.S. Dep't of Justice, Criminal Resource Manual No. 2101. Section 1956(a)(3) may be invoked where the money "laundered" does not in fact "involve" the proceeds of illegal activity because the money is actually government money used in a sting operation designed to flush out money launderers.

Under § 1956(a)(3), a defendant may be convicted who, with the intent to promote the carrying on of a specified unlawful activity, to conceal the nature, location, source, ownership or control of property *believed* to be the proceeds of specified unlawful activity, or to avoid a transaction reporting requirement, conducts a financial transaction involving property *represented* to be the proceeds of specified unlawful activity. The statute specifically provides that "[for] purposes of this paragraph ... , the term 'represented' means any representation made by a law enforcement officer or by another person at the direction of, or with the approval of, a

Federal official authorized to investigate or prosecute violations of this section." § 1956(a)(3). Violations of § 1956(a)(3) are felonies punishable by a fine and up to 20 years' imprisonment.

It should be noted that the specific intent provisions of § 1956(a)(3) are different from those in § 1956(a)(1). As the Department of Justice has explained:

> First, the intent to violate the tax laws is *not* included in this subsection. Second, subsections 1956(a)(3)(B) and (C) require that the transaction be conducted with the *intent* to conceal or disguise the nature location, source, ownership or control of the property and to avoid a transaction reporting requirement, respectively, in contrast to the subsections 1956(a)(1)(B)(i) and (ii), which only require that [the] defendant *know* that the transaction is designed, in whole or in part, to accomplish one of those ends.

U.S. Dep't of Justice, Criminal Resource Manual No. 2101. Why do you think Congress enhanced the intent requirements of § 1956(a)(3)?

9. *Specified unlawful activity.* The requirement that the transaction involve the proceeds of "specified unlawful activity" (and, under § 1956(a)(1)(A)(i), be intended to promote the carrying on of "specified unlawful activity") does little to limit the reach of the statute. "Specified unlawful activity" may include not only a range of drug-related activity, but also a wide variety of white-collar crimes (*e.g.*, 18 U.S.C. §§ 201 (federal public corruption), 666 (federal program theft, fraud or bribery), 1341 (mail fraud), 1343 (wire fraud), 1344 (bank fraud), 1503 (obstruction of justice), 1512 (witness tampering), 1951 (Hobbs Act), 1952 (Travel Act), 2314-15 (interstate transportation of stolen property), certain environmental violations, fraud in the sale of securities, "any felony violation of the Foreign Corrupt Practices Act," and "[a]ny act or activity constituting an offense involving a Federal health care offense"). 18 U.S.C. § 1956(c)(7). In the USA PATRIOT Act, Congress added offenses relating to the provision of material support to terrorists (18 U.S.C. §§ 2339, 2339A, 2339B) and computer fraud and abuse violations (18 U.S.C. § 1030) to the list of "specified unlawful activities." § 1956(c)(7)(D).

Notably, § 1956(c)(7)(B) includes in the list of specified unlawful activities certain offenses against *foreign* nations. "Thus, proceeds of certain crimes committed in another country may constitute proceeds of a specified unlawful activity for purposes of the money laundering statutes." U.S. Dep't of Justice, Criminal Resource Manual No. 2101. The statute has for some time stated that, "with respect to financial transactions occurring in whole or in part in the United States," an offense against a foreign nation involving controlled substances violations, certain serious crimes (*e.g.*, murder, kidnapping, arson, and extortion), and bank fraud perpetrated against a foreign bank constitute "specified unlawful activity." § 1956(c)(7)(B)(i)-(iii). In the USA PATRIOT Act, Congress added to the list "bribery of a public official, or the misappropriation, theft, or embezzlement of public funds by or for the benefit of a public official," § 1956(c)(7)(B)(iv), "smuggling or export control violations" involving certain controlled materials, § 1956(c)(7)(B)(v), and "an offense with respect to which the United States would be obligated by a multilateral treaty, either to extradite the alleged offender or to submit the case for prosecution, if the offender were found within the territory of the United States." § 1956(c)(7)(B)(vi). (It is worth underscoring, however, that these offenses against foreign nations only qualify as "specified unlawful activity" with respect to "a financial transaction occurring in whole or in part in the United States." § 1956(c)(7)(B).)

Do these additions make sense? Should the United States be in the business of prosecuting corrupt foreign officials for their attempts to launder the proceeds of their corruption if not the corruption itself?

10. *Proceeds.* As noted above, the defendant must believe that the property involved in the transaction was the "proceeds" of unlawful activity. And the property must also in fact involve the "proceeds" of specified unlawful activity under § 1962(a)(1). For twenty years, the statute did not define the critical term "proceeds." A circuit split developed over the meaning of the term "proceeds," and the Supreme Court attempted, without much success, to resolve the issue in *United States v. Santos*, 553 U.S. 507 (2007). In *Santos*, the defendant was convicted of money laundering based on his acceptance of a salary paid from the commission generated from an illegal lottery. A plurality of the Supreme Court reversed his conviction, holding that,

at least in the circumstances of an illegal gambling business, "proceeds" under 1956(a)(1)(A)(i) of the money laundering statute meant "profits" and not simply "gross receipts." The dissent argued that "proceeds" simply meant "gross receipts," not just "profits." Justice Stevens essentially split the baby, providing the plurality the fifth vote necessary for the judgment, but opining that "proceeds" could mean different things in different cases.

Congress reacted to the *Santos* decision by amending § 1956 to define "proceeds" as "any property derived from or obtained or retained, directly or indirectly, through some form of unlawful activity, including the gross receipts of such activity." 18 U.S.C. § 1956(c)(9).

Another issue that arose regarding the meaning of "proceeds" prior to the amendment was whether "indirect" proceeds could serve as the predicate for a money laundering conviction. *See, e.g.*, United States v. Yusuf, 536 F.3d 178 (3d Cir. 2008) (holding that unpaid taxes that are unlawfully disguised and retained by means of the filing of false tax returns through the mail constitute "proceeds" of mail fraud); United States v. Boscarino, 437 F.3d 634 (7th Cir.2006) ("proceeds" constituted the ill-gotten gains flowing from the scheme to defraud defendant's employer of its right to his honest services). Does the amendment resolve this question?

11. *Temporal Question: "Merger" Issue.* Courts have struggled to identify the temporal relationship that must exist between the underlying criminal conduct and the money laundering. The issue arises when there is arguably is too close a nexus between the crime and the laundering—that is, where the money laundering is difficult to distinguish from the criminal activity alleged to have spun off the "proceeds" laundered. This "merger" issue can arise in both concealment and promotion cases, although it may be more often a problem in promotion cases (discussed in Note 7 after *United States v. Piervinanzi*, reproduced *infra*).

Some courts have indicated that the defendant first must acquire the "proceeds" of a specified unlawful activity to then engage in a financial transaction to launder those proceeds. *See, e.g.*, United States v. Butler, 211 F.3d 826, 830 (4th Cir. 2000) ("Put plainly, the laundering of funds cannot occur in the same transaction through which those funds first became tainted by crime."); United States v. Napoli, 54 F.3d 63, 68 (2d Cir. 1995). Courts have on occasion concluded that use of the money laundering statute is inappropriate where the successful consummation of a fraud is the very transaction that is alleged to also constitute the laundering of the "proceeds" of that fraud. For example, in *United States v. Christo*, 129 F.3d 578 (11th Cir.1997), the Eleventh Circuit reversed a money laundering conviction where the "withdrawal of funds charged as money laundering was one and the same as the underlying criminal activity of bank fraud and misapplication of bank funds." *Id.* at 580-81. The court concluded that the crimes of bank fraud and misapplication of bank funds were, until the alleged laundering transaction, "incomplete and had generated no proceeds." *Id.* at 581; *see also* Gredd & Cooper, *supra*, § 2A.02[1][b][ii].

"In the case of complex, ongoing frauds, however, a number of courts have hesitated to adhere to this strict temporal approach, and have suggested that the act of money laundering may occur simultaneously with the fraudulent scheme as long as some phase of the scheme has been completed." *Id.* § 2A.02[1][b][ii], at 2A-24; *see also* United States v. Omoruyi, 260 F.3d 291 (3d Cir. 2001); *Butler*, 211 F.3d at 830; United States v. Ross, 210 F.3d 916 (8th Cir. 2000). Indeed, in one Seventh Circuit case involving a charged laundering of the "proceeds" of a mail fraud, the court held that the government did not have to prove that the jurisdictional mailing had occurred prior to the money laundering activity that was purportedly removing the taint from the "proceeds" of the mail fraud. *See* United States v. Mankarious, 151 F.3d 694, 703 (7th Cir.1998). Some commentators conclude that "if current trends continue, there may well be few mail or wire fraud schemes that could not be prosecuted as money laundering offenses as well." Gredd & Cooper, *supra*, § 2A.02[1][b][ii], at 2A-21.

12. *Conspiracy.* In *Whitfield v. United States*, 543 U.S. 209 (2005), the Supreme Court held that a conviction for conspiracy to commit money laundering under 18 U.S.C. § 1956(h) does not require proof of an overt act in furtherance of the conspiracy. It also made clear that this conspiracy offense is a stand-alone crime, separate from the substantive money laundering offenses in the same statute. Congress enacted this specialized conspiracy provision in part to

ensure a greater sanction applied to money laundering conspiracies than run-of-the-mill conspiracies charged under § 371.

13. *Elements of a § 1957 case*: Campbell was also charged under § 1957, which carries lesser penalties, and is less frequently invoked, than § 1956(a)(1). To secure a conviction under § 1957, the government must prove beyond a reasonable doubt that the defendant:

(a) knowingly engaged or attempted to engage;
(b) in a monetary transaction;
(c) in criminally derived property with a value of more than $10,000;
(d) knowing that the property was derived from unlawful activity; and
(e) the property was, in fact, derived from "specified unlawful activity."

Violations of § 1957 are felonies punishable by a fine and up to 10 years' imprisonment.

14. *Section 1957: monetary transaction.* A monetary transaction under § 1957 means the deposit, withdrawal, transfer, or exchange in or affecting interstate or foreign commerce of funds or a monetary instrument by, through, or to a "financial institution." Like § 1956, this definition includes a jurisdictional element but, unlike § 1956, the definition requires that the transaction involve a "financial institution." Does the requirement that a "financial institution" be involved limit the scope of this prohibition?

Consider the *Campbell* case in the light of this requirement. Campbell seems to have conceded the existence of a "monetary transaction" in her case—should she have done so? The $60,000 in cash, which appears to be the only proceeds of a specified unlawful activity at issue in the case, was passed directly from Lawing, the drug dealer, to the home's owners at closing. This may be a "financial transaction" within the meaning of § 1956, but is it a "monetary transaction" within the meaning of § 1957? How about the mortgage amount? It clearly went though a "financial institution," but were those funds the proceeds of unlawful activity?

The answer may lie in the breadth of the term "financial institution." A "financial institution" includes "such institutions as banks, thrifts, securities dealers or brokers and currency exchanges," as well as "a broad array of other businesses and entities, such as insurance companies, credit card systems, pawnbrokers, travel agencies, telegraph companies, certain casinos, car, airplane and boat dealers, persons involved in real estate closings, and the United States Postal Service." Gredd & Cooper, *supra*, § 2A.03[2], at 2A-73; *see also* 18 U.S.C. §§ 1956(c)(6), 1957(f)(1). Further, courts have interpreted the term to include "individuals engaged in the business of exchanging cash for cashier's checks, a husband and wife who engaged in 'warehouse banking services,' and two bank officers who arranged the exchange of cash for a bank check." Gredd & Cooper, *supra*, § 2A.03[2], at 2A-73 (footnotes omitted).

15. *Section 1957: criminally derived property with a value exceeding $10,000.* "Criminally derived property" is "any property constituting, or derived from, proceeds obtained from a criminal offense." § 1957(f)(2). Generally, the term "proceeds" is interpreted in much the same way as it is under § 1956(a)(1), and it raises many of the same issues (*e.g.*, the question of merger where the monetary transaction is difficult to distinguish from the underlying criminal transaction).

16. *Section 1957: "knowledge" of illicit nature of the property.* Section 1957 requires that the defendant "knowingly" engage in the transaction involving criminally derived property but it does not require the government to prove that the defendant knew that the criminal activity was "specified unlawful activity." *See* §1957(c). Further, as *Campbell* illustrates, proof of "knowledge" of the illicit nature of the funds may be based upon a defendant's "willful blindness" or "conscious avoidance" of positive knowledge. Although most defense counsel will strenuously resist a "willful blindness" jury charge out of a fear that the jury will convict for negligence, a "willful blindness" charge does not (at least in theory) permit a jury to convict upon proof that the defendant "should have known." The circuit courts are seemingly united in the belief that the "willful blindness" standard is a subjective one (not an objective standard sounding in negligence); the *Campbell* charge reflects this consensus. The courts have been split, however, on the actual basis for equating willful blindness with knowledge. Some courts refer to willful blindness as grounded in a defendant's reckless behavior, *see* United States v. Ramsey,

785 F.2d 184, 189 (7th Cir. 1986), while others, like the *Campbell* trial court, require more stringent proof essentially demonstrating a defendant's willful decision to turn a blind eye in order to create a defense of ignorance.

Recall that in *Global-Tech Appliances, Inc. v. SEB, S.A.*, 563 U.S. 764 (2011), discussed *supra* Chapter 2, the Supreme Court clarified its understanding of the elements of willful blindness as follows:

> While the Courts of Appeals articulate the doctrine of willful blindness in slightly different ways, all appear to agree on two basic requirements: (1) the defendant must subjectively believe that there is a high probability that a fact exists and (2) the defendant must take deliberate actions to avoid learning of that fact. We think these requirements give willful blindness an appropriately limited scope that surpasses recklessness and negligence. Under this formulation, a willfully blind defendant is one who takes deliberate actions to avoid confirming a high probability of wrongdoing and who can almost be said to have actually known the critical facts.

Is the *Campbell* court's discussion consistent with this understanding?

17. *Section 1957: property in fact derived from specified unlawful activity.* The definition of "specified unlawful activity" is the same in sections 1956 and 1957. *See* §1957(f)(3). The requirement that the property "is derived from specified unlawful activity" (like the inclusion of the element in §1956(a)(1)), means that the statute may not be used for prosecuting persons caught up in a government sting operation, at least where the money supposedly laundered consists entirely of government (and thus presumably untainted) money.

18. *Section 1957: Scope.* To understand the potential scope of § 1957, it may be helpful to think about what that section does *not* require in the way of proof. It does *not* require the government to show that the defendant actually laundered the funds or intended to promote or conceal unlawful activity. Indeed, it does not require that the defendant even know that others are engaging in the transaction to promote or conceal unlawful activity. As the Department of Justice has summarized: "The most significant difference [between § 1957 cases and] § 1956 prosecutions is the intent requirement. Under § 1957, the four intents have been replaced with a $10,000 threshold amount for each ... transaction and the requirement that a financial institution be involved in the transaction. ... [T]he prosecutor need not prove any intent to promote, conceal or avoid the reporting requirements." U.S. Dep't of Justice, Criminal Resource Manual No. 2101. In light of the fact that such proof is *not* required, as well as the fact that a conviction may be founded upon "willful blindness" (and the equivocal nature of some of the "red flags" the Department of Justice relies upon to prove such conscious avoidance), some have expressed concern that § 1957 potentially criminalizes seemingly "innocent" acts or commercial transactions. *See* United States v. Allen, 129 F.3d 1159, 1165 (10th Cir. 1997); Larry D. Thompson & Elizabeth B. Johnson, *Money Laundering: Business Beware*, 44 Ala. L. Rev. 703, 719 (1993).

"Congress intended § 1957 to dissuade people from engaging in even ordinary commercial transactions with people suspected of involvement in criminal activity." *Thirty-Third Annual Survey of White Collar Crime, supra* note 6, at 1475. The Act makes the *use* of criminal proceeds in any transaction illegal—seemingly into perpetuity—and certainly long after the statute of limitations has run on the criminal conduct that spawned the tainted proceeds. Thus, as the Ninth Circuit has explained:

> [§ 1957] is a powerful tool because it makes any dealing with a bank potentially a trap for the drug dealer or any other defendant who has a hoard of criminal cash derived from the specified crimes. If he makes a "deposit, withdrawal, transfer or exchange" with this cash, he commits the crime; he's forced to commit another felony if he wants to use a bank. This draconian law, so powerful by its elimination of criminal intent, freezes the proceeds of specific crimes out of the banking system.

United States v. Rutgard, 116 F.3d 1270, 1291-92 (9th Cir. 1997); *see also* United States v. Huff, 641 F.3d 1228 (10th Cir. 2011).

B. "TRANSPORTATION" OFFENSES UNDER § 1956(a)(2)

1. "PROMOTION" OFFENSE UNDER § 1956(a)(2)(A)

UNITED STATES v. PIERVINANZI
23 F.3d 670 (2d Cir. 1994)

MAHONEY, CIRCUIT JUDGE:

Michael Piervinanzi and Daniel Tichio appeal from judgments of conviction entered July 31, 1992 in the United States District Court for the Southern District of New York, Peter K. Leisure, *Judge,* after an eleven-day jury trial. The jury found Piervinanzi and Tichio guilty of conspiracy, attempted bank fraud, and attempted money laundering charges arising from a scheme to fraudulently transfer funds overseas from an account at Irving Trust Company ("Irving Trust"). The jury also convicted Piervinanzi of wire fraud, attempted bank fraud, attempted money laundering, and money laundering charges stemming from a separate but related scheme targeting an account at Morgan Guaranty Trust Company ("Morgan Guaranty"). The district court sentenced Piervinanzi to concurrent terms of 210 months imprisonment on each of seven counts of conviction, imposed a five-year term of supervised release for one attempted money laundering count and concurrent three-year terms of supervised release on the six other counts, and fined him $10,000. The court sentenced Tichio to concurrent terms of 135 months imprisonment on each of his three counts of conviction, and to concurrent three-year terms of supervised release.

We vacate Piervinanzi's conviction for money laundering under 18 U.S.C. § 1957, and remand both cases to the district court for resentencing. We affirm the convictions in all other respects. ...

This case involves two separate but related schemes to transfer funds electronically out of banks and overseas. The basic facts are not in dispute.

A. *The Irving Trust Scheme.*

From 1982 to 1988, Lorenzo DelGiudice was an auditor and computer operations specialist for Irving Trust. DelGiudice was responsible for monitoring and improving the security of the bank's wire transfer procedures to prevent unauthorized transfers. In March 1988, Anthony Marchese told DelGiudice that he and Piervinanzi were planning to rob an armored car. DelGiudice suggested a less violent alternative—an unauthorized wire transfer of funds from Irving Trust into an overseas account. DelGiudice explained that he could use his position at Irving Trust to obtain the information necessary to execute such a transfer. DelGiudice also explained that it would be necessary to obtain an overseas bank account for the scheme to succeed, because (1) United States banking regulations made the rapid movement of proceeds difficult, and (2) a domestic fraudulent transfer could, if detected, be readily reversed.

Marchese then introduced DelGiudice to Tichio. After DelGiudice explained the wire transfer scheme to Tichio, Tichio said that he could provide a foreign account to receive the stolen funds. Tichio made arrangements with Dhaniram Rambali, a business associate, to use Rambali's personal account at First Home Bank in the Cayman Islands to receive the stolen funds. Tichio then told DelGiudice that he would be able to provide access to accounts in the Cayman Islands, and emphasized that the strong bank secrecy laws there would prevent tracing of the purloined funds. Tichio told DelGiudice that the $10 million they were then planning to steal could be repatriated in monthly amounts of $200,000.

DelGiudice and Marchese distrusted Tichio's commitment to repatriate the money to them and feared for their safety, especially in view of the protracted payout schedule that Tichio had proposed. Marchese suggested that Piervinanzi be recruited to provide security for the operation; Piervinanzi's reputed ties to organized crime, he suggested, would deter Tichio from treachery or violence. Marchese and Tichio then met with Piervinanzi, who agreed to participate in the scheme and ensure that no one would "be hurt." Piervinanzi thereafter asked his brother, Robin Piervinanzi ("Robin"), to make the telephone call to Irving Trust that would initiate the transfer of funds to the Cayman Islands. Primarily in order to compensate Piervinanzi for his efforts, the conspirators increased the amount they planned to steal from $10 million to $14 million, of which DelGiudice and Marchese would receive $4 million each, and Tichio and Piervinanzi would receive $3 million each.

Despite Piervinanzi's participation, DelGiudice remained concerned about his safety, and decided to "sabotage [the] deal." However, DelGiudice did not want his coconspirators to know that he was intentionally frustrating their efforts. Accordingly, when he created the script that Robin would read when calling Irving Trust, DelGiudice left one necessary piece of information out of it: the name of a bank in the United States that would serve as the correspondent bank of First Home Bank in the Cayman Islands.[24] DelGiudice knew that if this information was not provided by the caller, it was likely that the transaction would not be consummated.

On July 6, 1988, Robin called Irving Trust and identified himself as "Joseph Herhal," an officer at Beneficial Corporation ("Beneficial"), whose Irving Trust account had been selected by DelGiudice for the transfer. Robin instructed a clerk to wire $14.2 million from the Beneficial account to Rambali's account at First Home Bank in the Cayman Islands. Reading from the script provided by DelGiudice, Robin supplied all required information except the identity of the correspondent bank. In the course of processing the transaction, the clerk contacted Beneficial to ask the identity of the American correspondent bank for First Home Bank. The clerk then learned that Beneficial had not requested the wire transfer, and halted the transaction. To deflect suspicion from himself, DelGiudice told Marchese that Irving Trust had stopped the transfer because First Home Bank was a "fly by night" operation.

B. *The Morgan Guaranty Scheme.*

In July 1988, in a move unrelated to the attempted bank fraud, DelGiudice left his job at Irving Trust and accepted a "better position" at Morgan Guaranty as audit manager. His first assignment at Morgan Guaranty was to perform an audit of the bank's wire transfer department. During the autumn of 1988, DelGiudice, Marchese, and Piervinanzi began planning a fraudulent wire transfer from Morgan Guaranty. DelGiudice agreed to acquire the necessary information for the transfer; Marchese and Piervinanzi took responsibility for arranging other aspects of the scheme, such as locating an overseas bank account to receive the stolen funds, recruiting a "caller" to initiate the wire transfer, and arranging for the distribution of the proceeds. They agreed that Tichio would not be involved in the Morgan Guaranty scheme.

Marchese and Piervinanzi contacted Philip Wesoke, a self-styled "financial consultant" who had previously invested (and lost) money for Piervinanzi. Marchese and Piervinanzi told Wesoke that they represented individuals who wanted to invest $14 to $20 million discreetly in a liquid, unregistered asset. Marchese and Piervinanzi told Wesoke that the investment could be "settled" overseas, and Piervinanzi mentioned the Cayman Islands, saying that he and Marchese had recently completed a transaction there. Having learned from the aborted Irving Trust scheme that correspondent bank information was necessary to transfer funds out of the country, Piervinanzi told Wesoke to provide the identity of a correspondent bank.

Wesoke recommended, and Piervinanzi and Marchese agreed, that they invest in diamonds. Wesoke accordingly arranged for a syndicate of Israeli diamond dealers to assemble a portfolio of diamonds for the conspirators. Wesoke also provided Piervinanzi with the necessary account and correspondent bank information for the planned recipient bank.

---

[24] [Court's footnote 2:] Under banking practice, money cannot be transferred overseas directly, but must instead go through a correspondent bank where the recipient offshore bank has an account.

DelGiudice had selected an account of Shearson Lehman Hutton, Inc. ("Shearson") at Morgan Guaranty as his target, and compiled the necessary information for the transfer. Piervinanzi gave DelGiudice the information that Wesoke had provided concerning the recipient bank and its American correspondent bank. DelGiudice then met with Robin, who again was chosen to make the call that would trigger the fraudulent transfer. DelGiudice provided Robin with the appropriate Morgan Guaranty telephone number, dictated a script for him to use, and told him when to make the call.

On February 23, 1989, Robin telephoned Morgan Guaranty and, purporting to be Shearson employee William Cicio, directed a wire transfer of $24 million to the selected account in London, with Bankers Trust Company in New York ("Bankers Trust") serving as the correspondent bank. Although Robin supplied all the information needed to complete the transfer, Morgan Guaranty's clerk became suspicious because she had spoken with Cicio previously, and discerned that the voice on the telephone was not Cicio's. The clerk processed the transfer, but reported her suspicions to a supervisor. Either the supervisor or the clerk then contacted Shearson and learned that the transaction had not been authorized. Although the $24 million had already reached Bankers Trust, the wire transfer was stopped and reversed.

C. *The Proceedings Below*

The FBI arrested Piervinanzi on March 2, 1989 for his participation in the Morgan Guaranty scheme. On March 20, 1989, the original indictment was filed in this case, charging Piervinanzi alone with one count of wire fraud in violation of 18 U.S.C. §§ 1343 and 2. A twenty-three count superseding indictment was filed on December 18, 1990. This indictment was redacted to seven counts at trial. Counts one through three involved the Irving Trust scheme, while counts four through seven involved the Morgan Guaranty scheme. Count one charged Piervinanzi and Tichio with conspiracy to commit wire fraud, bank fraud, and money laundering in violation of 18 U.S.C. § 371. Count two charged Piervinanzi and Tichio with attempted bank fraud in violation of 18 U.S.C. §§ 1344 and 2. Count three charged Piervinanzi and Tichio with attempted money laundering in violation of 18 U.S.C. § 1956(a)(2) and 2. Count four charged Piervinanzi with wire fraud in violation of 18 U.S.C. §§ 1343 and 2. Count five charged Piervinanzi with attempted bank fraud in violation of 18 U.S.C. §§ 1344 and 2. Count six charged Piervinanzi with attempted money laundering in violation of 18 U.S.C. §§ 1956(a)(2) and 2. Count seven charged Piervinanzi with money laundering in violation of 18 U.S.C. §§ 1957(a) and 2. Trial commenced on May 1, 1991 and concluded on May 17, 1991, when the jury returned a verdict convicting Piervinanzi and Tichio on all counts...

Discussion ...

A. *Money Laundering Conviction of Piervinanzi under § 1957(a).*

Piervinanzi was convicted on count seven of the indictment of violating 18 U.S.C. § 1957(a) for his participation in the Morgan Guaranty scheme. This statute provides in relevant part:

> (a) Whoever ... knowingly engages or attempts to engage in a monetary transaction in criminally derived property that is of a value greater than $10,000 and is derived from specified unlawful activity, shall be punished as provided in subsection (b). ... .
> (f) As used in this section— ...
>> (2) the term "criminally derived property" means any property constituting, or derived from, proceeds obtained from a criminal offense; and
>> (3) the term "specified unlawful activity" has the meaning given that term in section 1956 of this title.

As defined in § 1956, "specified unlawful activity" includes bank fraud. *See* § 1956(c)(7)(D).

Count seven charged that Piervinanzi violated § 1957 by fraudulently causing the transfer of approximately $24 million from Morgan Guaranty. Piervinanzi argues that the language of the statute only encompasses transactions in which a defendant first obtains "criminally derived property," and then engages in a monetary transaction with that property. Because the funds transferred from Morgan Guaranty were not yet property derived from the wire fraud and bank fraud scheme, Piervinanzi contends, his actions did not come within the purview of § 1957. The government does not dispute this reading of the statute, and joins Piervinanzi's request to vacate his conviction on this count.

The language of § 1957 supports Piervinanzi's interpretation of that statute. The ordinary meaning of the word "obtained" entails possession of a thing. *See* Webster's Third New International Dictionary 1559 (1986). Similarly, the word "property" implies ownership, or the "exclusive right to possess, enjoy, and dispose of a thing." *Id.* at 1818. The use of such language demonstrates a congressional intent that the proceeds of a crime be in the defendant's possession before he can attempt to transfer those proceeds in violation of § 1957. *See United States v. Johnson*, 971 F.2d 562, 569 (10th Cir.1992) ("both the plain language of § 1957 and the legislative history behind it suggest that Congress targeted only those transactions occurring after proceeds have been obtained from the underlying unlawful activity"); *United States v. Lovett*, 964 F.2d 1029, 1042 (10th Cir.) ("Congress intended [§ 1957] to separately punish a defendant for monetary transactions that follow in time the underlying specified unlawful activity that generated the criminally derived property in the first place.") (citing H.R.Rep. No. 855, 99th Cong., 2d Sess., pt. 1, at 7 (1986) (the "House Report")).

Piervinanzi and his colleagues succeeded in transferring $24 million from Morgan Guaranty to Bankers Trust, but these funds never came into the possession or under the control of the conspirators. Thus, Piervinanzi was improperly convicted of money laundering in violation of § 1957, and we reverse his conviction on count seven.

B. *Money Laundering Convictions under § 1956(a)(2).*

Piervinanzi contends that the proof at trial did not establish the elements of money laundering or attempted money laundering under 18 U.S.C. § 1956(a)(2), and therefore that his convictions under counts three and six of the indictment must be reversed. He argues that § 1956(a)(2) is not violated unless there is some "secondary laundering activity not previously made criminal by pre-existing criminal statutes." Accordingly, he contends, because the asserted criminal laundering activity, the overseas transfer of the bank funds, was simply a component of the bank frauds that the conspirators attempted to perpetrate against Irving Trust and Morgan Guaranty, there was no analytically distinct "secondary" activity, and thus no criminal laundering violative of § 1956(a)(2).... .

Piervinanzi contends that the language of § 1956(a)(2) (1988), its legislative history, [and] pertinent case law ... all support the conclusion that this provision proscribes only "laundering" activity that is analytically distinct from the underlying criminal activity that it promotes, and that the overseas fund transfers intended in this case do not satisfy this statutory requirement. For the reasons that follow, we reject his reading of § 1956(a)(2). ...The statutory language at issue requires that there be a transmission of funds "with the intent to promote the carrying on of specified unlawful activity." § 1956(a)(2)(A). As previously noted, "specified unlawful activity" includes bank fraud. The counts (three and six) of the indictment that charge violations of § 1956(a)(2) both specify that the overseas fund transfers were designed to further "a fraudulent scheme in violation of 18 U.S.C. § 1344 [i.e., bank fraud]."

Piervinanzi contends that in this case, the overseas transmission of funds "merges" with the underlying bank fraud, precluding independent liability under § 1956(a)(2). In our view, however, the conduct at issue in this case falls within the prohibition of the statute. The conspirators understood the use of overseas accounts to be integral to the success of both the Irving Trust and Morgan Guaranty schemes. DelGiudice explained to the other conspirators that use of foreign accounts would make the fraudulently obtained funds more difficult to trace. Tichio obtained access to Rambali's Cayman Islands bank account because he understood that bank secrecy laws there would hamper official efforts to recover the stolen funds. Similarly, Piervinanzi and Marchese told Wesoke that they wished to "settle[]" their transaction overseas. Because transferring the funds overseas (and beyond the perceived reach of U.S. officials) was integral to the success of both fraudulent schemes, it is undeniable that the attempted transfers were designed to "promote" the underlying crime of bank fraud. Contrary to Piervinanzi's assertion, this reading of the statute does not "merge" the underlying criminal activity and promotion through laundering into one. The act of attempting to fraudulently transfer funds out of the banks was analytically distinct from the attempted transmission of those funds overseas, and was itself independently illegal. *See* 18 U.S.C. § 1344.

Analysis of the overall structure of § 1956 confirms this interpretation. Section 1956(a)(1),[25] the domestic money laundering statute, penalizes financial transactions that "involv[e] ... the proceeds of specified unlawful activity." The provision requires first that the proceeds of specified unlawful activity be generated, and second that the defendant, knowing the proceeds to be tainted, conduct or attempt to conduct a financial transaction with these proceeds with the intent to promote specified unlawful activity.[26] By contrast, § 1956(a)(2) contains no requirement that "proceeds" first be generated by unlawful activity, followed by a financial transaction with those proceeds, for criminal liability to attach. Instead, it penalizes an overseas transfer "with the intent to promote the carrying on of specified unlawful activity." § 1956(a)(2)(A).

The fact that Congress uses different language in defining violations in a statute indicates that Congress intentionally sought to create distinct offenses. The clearly demarcated two-step requirement which Piervinanzi advocates in the construction of § 1956(a)(2) is apparent in other provisions of the federal money laundering statutes, but not in § 1956(a)(2). We have no authority to supply the omission.

Piervinanzi also contends that the prohibition in § 1956(a)(2)(A) of "carrying on" underlying criminal activity would be meaningless, and the phrase rendered superfluous, unless it connotes continuous criminal activity that is not presented by the discrete bank frauds in this case. (This argument could be presented even more strongly by Tichio, who engaged in only one of the attempted frauds.) The "specified unlawful activity" that must be "carried on" to result in a § 1956(a)(2) violation, however, is consistently defined in each paragraph of § 1956(c)(7) as including discrete, singular offenses, as follows: "*any act* or activity constituting an offense" (paragraph (A), emphasis added); "*an offense*"(paragraph (B), emphasis added); "*any act*" or acts constituting a continuing criminal enterprise" (paragraph (C), emphasis added); and "*an offense*" (paragraph (D), emphasis added). Thus, we conclude, § 1956(a)(2) can be satisfied by the "carrying on" of a single offense of "bank fraud," and "carrying on" in § 1956(a)(2), rather than connoting continuous criminal activity, has essentially the same meaning as "conducts" in § 1956(a)(1). Indeed, this is the primary meaning of "carry on." *See* Webster's Third New International Dictionary 344. ...

The relatively scanty legislative history of § 1956(a)(2), *see United States v. Stavroulakis*, 952 F.2d 686 (2d Cir.[1992]), supports this analysis. The Senate report on the version of the bill reported to the Senate explains that § 1956(a)(2) is "designed to illegalize international money laundering transactions," and "covers situations in which money is being laundered ... by transferring it out of the United States." S.Rep. No. 433, 99th Cong., 2d Sess. 11 (1986) (the "Senate Report"). The Senate Report's discussion of § 1956(a)(2) is conspicuously silent about

---

[25] [Court's footnote 7:] Section 1956(a)(1) provides in relevant part:

> Whoever, knowing that the property involved in a financial transaction *represents the proceeds of some form of unlawful activity,* conducts or attempts to conduct such a financial transaction which in fact involves the proceeds of specified unlawful activity--

> (A)(i) with the intent to promote the carrying on of specified unlawful activity, ...

> shall be sentenced to a fine ... or imprisonment for not more than twenty years, or both.

Emphasis added.

[26] [Court's footnote 8:] In this respect, § 1956(a)(1) is similar to § 1957(a), which requires the separate obtention of "criminally derived property" followed by a monetary transaction with that property.

any requirement that the funds be proceeds of some distinct activity, merely stating that the statute is violated when a defendant "engage[s] in an act of transporting or attempted transporting and either intend[s] to facilitate a crime or know[s] that the transaction was designed to facilitate a crime."[27] By contrast, the Senate Report explains that § 1956(a)(1) "requires that the property involved in a transaction must in fact be proceeds of 'specified unlawful activity' ... ."

Piervinanzi points out that a pertinent House report states in general terms that "[t]his bill ... will punish transactions that are undertaken with the proceeds of crimes or that are designed to launder the proceeds of crime." However, the version of the statute upon which this report comments was substantially different from that ultimately enacted. Rather than prohibiting overseas transfers made "with the intent to promote the carrying on of specified illegal activity," as the enacted § 1956(a)(2) provides, the version of the bill discussed in the House Report would have applied to overseas transfers made "to conceal *criminally derived property* that is derived from a designated offense, or ... to disguise the source of ownership of, or control over, *criminally deprived property* that is derived from a designated offense." The House Report thus discusses a version of the money laundering bill too different from that enacted to be of any use in divining congressional intent with respect to the enacted provisions of § 1956. Indeed, the broader language that Congress ultimately adopted bespeaks an intention not to be constrained to punishing laundering activity involving separately derived criminal property.

...

Nor do the precedents invoked by Piervinanzi sustain his position. He points, for example, to the following statement in *Stavroulakis*:

Section 1956 creates the crime of money laundering, and it takes dead aim at the attempt to launder dirty money. Why and how that money got dirty is defined in other statutes. *Section 1956 does not penalize the underlying unlawful activity from which the tainted money is derived.*

952 F.2d at 691 (emphasis added). In the context of this case, the emphasized language is a truism that begs the question whether the intended overseas transfers should be considered as separate secondary "laundering" or a component of the underlying bank fraud.

Our opinion in *United States v. Skinner*, 946 F.2d 176 (2d Cir.1991), is considerably more relevant. Concededly, in that case we construed § 1956(a)(1), which requires that separate proceeds be utilized in a financial transaction. *See supra* note 7. Our focus in *Skinner*, however, was upon the statutory requirement, identical in this respect to § 1956(a)(2)(A), that a financial transaction be undertaken "with the intent to promote the carrying on of specified unlawful activity." § 1956(a)(1)(A)(i). We concluded that this language applied to the transportation of money orders to pay for purchases of cocaine. Although the transactions "in reality represented only the completion of the sale" of cocaine, we concluded that they were made to facilitate the sale of cocaine and thus were made "with the intent to promote the carrying on of specified unlawful activity."

A number of cases from other circuits support this view. In *United States v. Cavalier*, 17 F.3d 90 (5th Cir.1994), the Fifth Circuit ruled that the transfer of a single check to complete a mail fraud "promote[d] the carrying on" of that fraud within the meaning of § 1956(a)(1)(A)(i). The Ninth Circuit ruled similarly with respect to the deposit of a single check to complete a violation of the Hobbs Act. *See United States v. Montoya*, 945 F.2d 1068, 1076 (9th Cir.1991). And the Third Circuit held that the cashing of government checks to complete mail frauds perpetrated against the Internal Revenue Service constituted a § 1956(a)(1) violation, although the proceeds of the fraud were concededly spent for personal purposes and not "plowed back" into the criminal venture. *See United States v. Paramo*, 998 F.2d 1212, 1216-18 (3d Cir.1993).

---

[27] [Court's footnote 9:] As Piervinanzi points out, the language of § 1956(a)(2) was subsequently amended prior to its enactment to substitute "promotes" for "facilitates." We do not regard this amendment as altering the outcome in this case. The overseas transfers contemplated by the conspirators would clearly have both facilitated and promoted the underlying bank fraud that they hoped to achieve.

Similarly, we are not persuaded by Piervinanzi's references to *United States v. Jackson*, 935 F.2d 832 (7th Cir.1991), and *United States v. Hamilton*, 931 F.2d 1046 (5th Cir.1991). *Jackson* comments that § 1956(a)(1)(A)(i) is "aimed at ... the practice of plowing back proceeds of 'specified unlawful activity' to promote that activity." 935 F.2d at 842. *Hamilton* states that § 1956(a)(2) is meant to criminalize the transfer of funds "that would contribute to the growth and capitalization of the drug trade or other unlawful activities." In both cases, the same statutory language ("promote the carrying on of specified unlawful activity," § 1956(a)(1)(A)(i) and (a)(2)(A)) is construed.

The *Jackson* comment faithfully reflects the facts of that case, in which a violation of § 1956(a)(1) was premised upon the use of proceeds from drug sales to purchase beepers for use by participants in the criminal drug enterprise. We agree with *Paramo*, however, that *Jackson* did not intend "either to delineate the universe of conduct prohibited under section 1956(a)(1)(A)(i), or to decide whether a defendant could violate that section other than by plowing back the proceeds of unlawful activity." The focus in *Hamilton* was upon the violation of § 1956(a)(2) involved in a hypothetical transfer of legitimately derived funds from a foreign source to the United States to capitalize a domestic drug enterprise.

Neither case establishes that a defendant may be deemed to "promote the carrying on of specified unlawful activity" *only* when the laundering would promote subsequent criminal activity. As previously discussed, such a reading would not accord with the plain meaning of the statute. Further, *Hamilton* involved a scheme similar to that in *Skinner,* in which the proceeds of drug sales were sent through the mails to pay for a drug purchase. As in *Skinner,* the defendant was convicted of violating § 1956(a)(1), although there was no indication that the transferred proceeds were to be invested in subsequent illegal activities. ...

Notes

1. *Jurisdiction*: Section 1956 provides for extraterritorial jurisdiction. Section 1956(f) states:

> There is extraterritorial jurisdiction over the conduct prohibited by this section if—(1) the conduct is by a United States citizen or, in the case of a non-United States citizen, the conduct occurs in part in the United States; and (2) the transaction or series of related transactions involves funds or monetary instruments of a value exceeding $10,000.

Congress sought to limit extraterritorial jurisdiction "to situations in which the interests of the United States are involved, either because the defendant is a U.S. citizen or because the transaction occurred in whole or in part in the United States." S. Rep. 99-433, at 14 (1986). The $10,000 jurisdictional limit was intended to ensure that extraterritorial jurisdiction "is confined to significant cases." *Id.* (For the jurisdiction provision applicable to § 1957 cases, see § 1957(a).)

The Department of Justice requires its prosecutors to secure prior approval from the Asset Forfeiture and Money Laundering Section of the Criminal Division prior to commencing an investigation based solely on the extraterritorial jurisdiction provisions of sections 1956 and 1957. *See* U.S.A.M. § 9-105.300(1). Why might this requirement be imposed in extraterritorial, but not domestic, cases? Where the illegal conduct charged is clearly within the statutorily prescribed extraterritorial jurisdiction, what considerations, if any, might counsel the Department of Justice to withhold approval of a prosecution?

2. *Elements of a § 1956(a)(2) "transportation" money laundering offense*: In some circumstances international money laundering may be charged either as a "transaction" offense under § 1956(a)(1) or as a "transportation" offense under § 1956(a)(2), or as both. What are the differences in proof necessary to prove a "transportation" as opposed to a "transaction" offense? In what circumstances might a prosecutor choose one subsection over the other?

To prove a "transportation" money laundering offense under § 1956(a)(2), the government has to prove certain common elements for all such violations (as well as additional elements for some, but not all offenses—as we shall see *infra*):

The defendant

(a) transported, transmitted, or transferred (or attempted to do so);

(b) monetary instruments or funds;

(c) across the border of the United States; and

(d) acted with the requisite knowledge or purpose.

Although § 1956(a)(2) sets forth three *alternative* means by which the government can demonstrate that the defendant acted with the requisite knowledge or purpose, these materials focus only on two:

(i) cases in which the government charges that the defendant transported the funds "with the intent to promote the carrying on of specified unlawful activity" (a "promotion" transaction offense under § 1956(a)(2)(A)); and

(ii) cases in which the government alleges that the defendant transported funds knowing that the funds involved in the transportation represent the proceeds of some form of unlawful activity and knowing that such transfer is designed in whole or in part to conceal or disguise the nature, location, source, ownership, or control of the proceeds of specified unlawful activity (a "concealment" transaction offense under § 1956(a)(2)(B)(i)).

(The other alternative, not covered in text, is: (iii) cases in which the government alleges that the defendant knew that the transaction was designed to avoid a transaction reporting requirement under State or Federal law (§ 1956(a)(2)(B)(ii)). Unlike § 1956(a)(1)(A)(ii), a transportation case under § 1956(a)(2) cannot be made based upon a transportation of funds with the intent to engage in tax fraud).

Violations of § 1956(a)(2) are felonies punishable by a fine of not more than $500,000 or twice the value of the property involved in the transaction, whichever is greater, and up to 20 years' imprisonment.

3. *Transport, transmit, or transfer.* Most obviously, while the *actus reus* or culpable act at the heart of a § 1956(a)(1) case is conducting a "financial transaction" (or an attempt to conduct a qualifying transaction), the culpable act at the core of a § 1956(a)(2) case is the transport, transmission, or transfer (or attempt to do so) of a "monetary instrument or funds from a place in the United States to or through a place outside the United States or to a place in the United States from or through a place outside the United States." Section 1956(a)(2), as originally enacted, prohibited only the international "transportation" of funds. The statute was amended in 1988 to expressly add the terms "transmit" and "transfer." The amendment was intended to clarify what most courts had already read into the statute—that is, that the section prohibited international wire transfers as well as the physical transportation of monetary instruments or funds.

4. *Monetary instruments or funds.* Courts generally define "funds" to mean "moneys held on account at banks." Gredd & Cooper, *supra*, § 2A.02[2][b], at 2A-54. The statute defines "monetary instruments" to include coin and currency (of any country), traveler's checks, personal checks, bank checks, money orders, and investment securities or negotiable instruments. *See* § 1956(c)(5).

5. *Trans-border.* The transborder element requires that the funds or monetary instruments cross a U.S. border—"either originating or terminating in the United States." U.S. Dep't of Justice, Criminal Resource Manual No. 2101. Thus, for example, in *United States v. Kramer*, 73 F.3d 1067 (11th Cir. 1995), the Eleventh Circuit held that a defendant could not be convicted under § 1956(a)(2) where he transferred funds from one location outside the United States to another country outside the United States because none of the money transferred crossed the U.S. border. Strangely enough, then, the "international" money laundering prohibition is not applicable where the conduct is truly (or entirely) "international" in scope. Note that at least one court has held that the nominally domestic "transaction" money laundering provision of 1956(a)(1) *may* be used where the laundering transaction occurs entirely abroad, assuming the other elements of the offense are proved. *See, e.g.*, United States v. Tarkoff, 242 F.3d 991 (11th Cir. 2001) (holding that transfers from Curacao to Israel and between accounts in Israel

constitute "financial transactions" under 1956(c)(4) and were within the reach of § 1956(a)(1)(B)(i)).

6. *"Promotion"* mens rea *element in either transaction or transportation cases.* For purposes of a "promotion" offense under § 1956(a)(1)(A)(i) or § 1956(a)(2)(A), the government must show that the defendant conducted a financial transaction or transported monetary instruments or funds with the intent to promote the carrying on of specified unlawful activity. The Fifth Circuit has explained:

> It is not enough to show that a money launderer's actions *resulted* in promoting the carrying on of specified unlawful activity. Nor may the government rest on proof that the defendant engaged in "knowing promotion" of the unlawful activity. Instead, there must be evidence of *intentional* promotion. In other words, the evidence must show that the defendant's conduct not only promoted a specified unlawful activity but that he engaged in it *with the intent* to further the progress of that activity. The justification for this rigorous *mens rea* requirement is that, in enacting the statute, Congress meant to create a *separate* crime of money laundering, discrete and apart from the underlying substantive offense.

United States v. Trejo, 610 F.3d 308, 314 (5th Cir. 2010).

The language requiring proof of an "intent to promote the carrying on of specified unlawful activity" is identical in "transaction" offenses under § 1956(a)(1)(A)(i) and "transportation" offenses under § 1956(a)(2)(A). As noted above, because the list of crimes included in "specified unlawful activity" is long (and growing), it is not usually the case that the government has difficulty identifying a particular qualifying crime that is sought to be promoted.

7. *Temporal Issue #1: Merger Issues.* To illustrate the nature of this issue, assume that our defendant engaged in a classic Ponzi scheme whereby he attracts investors by offering higher returns on their investments than are otherwise available and then pays returns to investors using new capital from new investors, rather than from profits earned by investing the sums received. Such payments obviously require an ever-increasing flow of money from new investors to keep the scheme from collapsing. If our defendant paid his co-defendants to solicit new investors and authorized the payment of lulling returns to the investors, those transactions constitute part of the fraud. But couldn't they also be charged as money laundering transactions designed to "promote" the defendant's criminal scheme? If that is true, does every transaction necessary to sustain a criminal venture also constitute money laundering? What if the money laundering charge carries much more sentencing exposure than the underlying crime? This is identified as the "merger" problem.

As discussed *supra* Note 10 following *Campbell*, the Supreme Court decided in *United States v. Santos*, 553 U.S. 507 (2007), that, at least in some cases, "proceeds" should be read to mean "profits," not gross "receipts." (Recall, too, that Congress subsequently overruled the Court, defining "proceeds" by statute to include "gross receipts," 18 U.S.C. § 1956(c)(9)). It was in part in reaction to the merger problem that the *Santos* plurality decided that "proceeds" meant "profits," not "receipts." Justice Scalia's plurality opinion explained that "if 'proceeds' meant 'receipts,' nearly every violation of the illegal-lottery statute would also be a violation of the money-laundering statute" because most, if not all, lotteries pay their winners and all of those payments, which could be deemed to promote the carrying on of the illegal lottery if proceeds meant "receipts," would violate both statutes. *Santos*, 553 U.S. at 515. Justice Scalia argued that the merger issue arose in many cases, not just those involving illegal gambling. "Generally speaking, any specified unlawful activity, an episode of which includes transactions which are not elements of the offense and in which a participant passes receipts on to someone else, would merge with money laundering." *Id.* at 516. Justice Scalia reasoned the reading "proceeds" to mean "profits" ameliorated the merger problem because money laundering transactions "promoting" the carrying on of illegal activity would be limited to payments made over and above expenses paid to support the underlying criminal activity. Thus, prosecutors could not charge defendants with "promoting" the underlying unlawful activity by paying expenses—rent, employee salaries—necessary to the predicate crime. *Id.* Justice Breyer, in dissent, agreed that the merger issue was a problem but adopted a solution that Justice Scalia rejected: interpreting promotion money laundering to apply only where the money laundering transaction occurs separately and after the underlying offense is committed. *Id.* at 530 (Breyer, J., dissenting). In Justice Breyer's view, promoting the carrying on of an underlying offense can only happen after that offense is complete. *Id.* at 530.

Now that Congress has determined that "proceeds" means "gross receipts," how can these merger problems be avoided? What ought to be relevant to a court addressing such concerns? *See* Leslie A. Dickinson, Note, *Revisiting the "Merger Problem" in Money Laundering Prosecutions Post-*Santos *and the Fraud Enforcement and Recovery Act of 2009*, 28 Notre Dame J. L. Ethics & Pub. Pol'y, 579 (2014).

8. *Temporal Issue #2: Can one promote an ongoing or completed crime in transaction or transportation cases?* Another issue that has arisen under the "transaction" money laundering provision of § 1956(a)(1)(A)(i) concerns whether a defendant can be convicted for "promoting" a *completed* crime, or whether he can only be convicted where there is proof that he is seeking to "promote" the commission of a *future* "specified unlawful activity."

A representative case is *United States v. Paramo*, 998 F.2d 1212 (3d Cir.1999). In *Paramo*, Paramo's coconspirator, who worked for the IRS, sent fictitious tax refund checks through the mails to payees in New York. Paramo then picked up the checks and deposited them. Paramo challenged his money laundering conviction, which was founded on the deposit of the embezzled checks, arguing that the underlying offense that generated the proceeds—the mail fraud—was complete as of the mailing of the checks and thus that he could not be convicted of money laundering for "promoting" a completed crime. The Third Circuit disagreed, holding that Paramo promoted the carrying on of the completed crime of mail fraud when he cashed the checks because Paramo believed that the embezzled checks would be worthless unless cashed. Should courts require proof that the targeted transaction actually promote an *ongoing* or *future* crime? Under *Paramo*, is there any real distinction between the money laundering and the underlying predicate fraud?

The circuits are split on the question whether, under the promotion prong of § 1956(a)(1)(A)(i), a defendant can be said to have conducted a financial transaction with the intent to "promote the carrying on" of an already *completed* criminal activity. *Compare, e.g.*, United States v. Valuck, 286 F.3d 221 (5th Cir. 2002) ("we categorically reject any suggestion ... that a financial transaction cannot promote a completed illegal activity for purposes of section 1956(a)(1)(A)(i)"); United States v. King, 169 F.3d 1035 (6th Cir. 1999) (holding that payments for drugs already delivered may constitute "promotion" for purposes of the money laundering statute when such payment encourages further drug transactions); United States v. Paramo, 998 F.2d 1212 (3d Cir. 1993); United States v. Montoya, 945 F.2d 1068 (9th Cir. 1991), *with* United States v. Jolivet, 224 F.3d 902 (8th Cir.2000) ("We find no logic in the government's suggestion that Jolivet could promote the carrying on of an already completed crime."); United States v. Heaps, 39 F.3d 479 (4th Cir.1994) (holding that a cash payment for the sale of drugs did not constitute the "promotion" of a drug offense, at least where no subsequent sales were proven); Jimmy Gurule, *The Money Laundering Control Act of 1986: Creating a New Federal Offense or Merely Affording Federal Prosecutors An Alternative Means of Punishing Specified Unlawful Activity?*, 32 Am. Crim. L. Rev. 823, 846-50 (1995).

9. The Second Circuit finds in *Piervinanzi* that there is no "merger" problem because the bank fraud concerns the defendants' efforts to get the money (improperly) out of the bank while the money laundering concerns their efforts to send the money overseas. As *Piervinanzi* illustrates, the question whether one can "promote" a completed crime also arises under the transportation prohibition (§ 1956(a)(2)(A)). If the bank fraud is accomplished when the money is improperly transferred out of a client's account, how can the overseas transfer of the funds "promote" this completed fraud? The Second Circuit reasons that the use of the foreign accounts was designed in part to "hamper official efforts to recover the stolen funds" and thus served to "promote" the underlying (completed) bank fraud. Is this an inference that could credibly be drawn in almost all cases where international transfers of stolen or embezzled funds occur? Does this holding effectively remove crime "promotion" as an element of the crime? Why might the Second Circuit's holding in *Piervinanzi* be even more helpful to the government than *Paramo* and the cases discussed in relation to "transportation" offenses, *supra*?

10. *Transaction promotion case v. transportation promotion case: difference #1.* One reason may be the differences in the proof required under § 1956(a)(2)(A) as opposed to § 1956(a)(1)(A)(i). The *Pievinanzi* court held that, unlike other portions of the statute (and, for that matter, § 1957), § 1956(a)(2)(A) "contains no requirement that 'proceeds' first be generated by unlawful activity, followed by a financial transaction with those proceeds." Does this mean that a defendant can be prosecuted under a transportation theory for "laundering" money *that is not derived from criminal activity?* The Department of Justice says "yes":

> If the transportation, transmission or transfer was conducted with the intent to conceal the proceeds of specified unlawful activity or to avoid a reporting requirement, the prosecutor must show that the defendant knew the monetary instrument or funds represented the proceeds of some form of unlawful activity. *However*, if the transportation, transmission or transfer was conducted with the intent to promote the carrying on of specified unlawful activity, the prosecutor need not show that the funds or monetary instruments were actually derived from any criminal activity.

U.S. Dep't of Justice, Criminal Resource Manual No. 2101.

What are the implications of a holding that a defendant can be convicted of "promoting" a specified unlawful activity through transfers of innocent funds abroad, or the repatriation of innocent funds from abroad? In such cases, is any dirty money being "laundered"? Or is the focus of the criminality the aiding and abetting of the specified unlawful activity? Why not charge it as such? Might jurisdictional concerns force prosecutors to seek a money laundering charge rather than a charge founded on the illegal conduct sought to be promoted? Is this an appropriate exercise of prosecutorial discretion?

11. *Transaction promotion case v. transportation promotion case: difference #2.* What is the other potentially important difference between transportation and transaction "concealment" offenses? Unlike its counterpart transaction offense, § 1956(a)(2)(B)(i) does *not* expressly require that the property involved *in fact* represents the proceeds of specified unlawful activity. *See Carr*, 25 F.3d at 1204-05. Indeed, § 1956(a)(2)(B)(i) states only that the defendant must know that the monetary instrument or funds involved in the transportation "represent" the proceeds of some form of unlawful activity and § 1956(a)(2) provides that "[f]or the purpose of the offense described in subparagraph (B), the defendant's knowledge may be established by proof that a law enforcement officer represented the matter specified in subparagraph (B) as true, and the defendant's subsequent statements or actions indicate that the defendant believed such representations to be true." *See also* § 1956(a)(3)(C) (defining the term "represented" for purposes of § 1956(a)(2) to mean "any representation made by a law enforcement officer or by another person at the direction of, or with the approval of, a Federal official authorized to investigate or prosecute violations of this section.")

12. *Transportation concealment cases.* Subsection 1956(a)(2)(B)(i) obviously *does* require that "proceeds" be laundered, providing as it does that the government must prove that the defendant knew both that the transfer represents the "proceeds of some form of unlawful activity" and that the transfer is designed in whole or in part to conceal or disguise the nature, location, source or ownership of the "proceeds" of specified unlawful activity. Because the requirements of this subsection are largely identical to § 1956(a)(1)(B)(i), the courts generally interpret them identically. Thus, for example, a defendant may be convicted not only where he personally designed the concealing transaction, but also (as in *Campbell*) where the defendant knew someone else designed the transaction with concealment in mind. *See* United States v. Carr, 25 F.3d 1194, 1206 (3d Cir. 1994).

C. NON-BANKING SYSTEMS: CHALLENGES FOR FUTURE?

At least since 1992, Congress has prohibited illegal money transmitting businesses in 18 U.S.C. § 1960. This section was generally aimed at money transmitters who failed to secure the requisite state license for their business.[28] In the USA PATRIOT Act, however, Congress made a number of changes to the statute which earned § 1960 at least one commentator's vote for the measure that would emerge out of the Act as the new "prosecutor's darling."[29]

Section 1960 now provides that whoever knowingly conducts, controls, manages, supervises, directs, or owns all or part of an unlicensed money transmitting business is guilty of a felony punishable by fine and up to 5 years' imprisonment. This section (both before the USA PATRIOT Act and after) includes within the definition of "money transmitting" a wealth of activity, according to some going "way beyond what you would think of as a money transmitting business."[30] Thus, the term "money transmitting" is defined to "include[] transferring funds on behalf of the public by any and all means including but not limited to transfers within this country or to locations abroad by wire, check, draft, facsimile, or courier."[31] Further, in the USA PATRIOT Act, Congress expanded the definition of the proscribed "unlicensed money transmitting business." It states, in part:

> the term "unlicensed money transmitting business" means a money transmitting business which affects interstate or foreign commerce in any manner or degree and ... involves the transportation or transmission of funds that are known to the defendant to have been derived from a criminal offense or are intended to be used to promote or support unlawful activity.[32]

Note that unlike sections 1956 and 1957, § 1960 is not tied to a list of "specified unlawful activities" and thus potentially applies to defendants who transmit funds derived from, or in support of, *all* types of federal (and perhaps state or foreign) crimes.

After you have read the materials concerning hawala transactions, below, consider whether this system could be considered a network of "money transmitting" businesses.

Hawala and Underground Terrorist Financing Mechanisms, Prepared Statement of Mr. Patrick Jost, SRA International
U.S. Senate Committee on Banking, Housing, and Urban Affairs,
Subcommittee on International Trade and Finance (Nov. 14, 2001)

...[T]here are two essential characteristics of hawala—the first is a network of hawala brokers or dealers, called hawaladars in Hindi and Urdu and often referred to as "hawala operators" in the English language South Asian press, and the second is the trust that exists not only between hawaladars but between hawaladars and their clients.

With this context, let me proceed with an example of a typical hawala transaction. Suppose an individual in a large US city wishes to remit the sum of $5,000 to a relative living in South Asia. This individual contacts a hawaladar, and they negotiate terms. These terms

---

[28] *See Panelists Explore USA PATRIOT Act's Effects on Anti-Money Laundering Laws, supra* note 9, 536.

[29] *Id.* ("Commenting that a prosecutor reading the statute should 'feel like a kid in a candy store,' [Faith E. Gay, of White & Case, Miami] said her criteria for 'prosecutor's darling' are that the measure can encompass a large variety of financial activities and be easy for juries to understand.").

[30] *Id.*

[31] 18 U.S. C. § 1960(b)(2) (emphasis added).

[32] *Id.* § 1960(b)(1)(C); *see also* United States v. Mazza-Alauf, 621 F.3d 205 (2d Cir. 2010).

often include the rate of exchange and the manner of delivery of the money. The hawaladar will take the money, and make contact with an associate in or near the place where the money is to be delivered. This second hawaladar will make the necessary delivery arrangements. This can be done by sending a courier to the person with the money, or by providing a phone number to be called to arrange delivery.

It is useful to think of the above example as a hawala "theme"; and what actually happens, is, as in improvised music the "variations" on the theme. The hawala system is very flexible, so many variations occur. This can be seen in the ways hawaladars settle their debts. Sometimes, the flow between two hawaladars is balanced, so, in a reasonable amount of time, debts are settled automatically.

Another possibility is that the hawaladar has money in a country and cannot remove it due to measures designed to counter capital flight. These measures can be circumvented via hawala. The hawaladar accepts money in his current country of residence, and has an associate "drain" the supply of money in the other country until it is gone.

Some hawaladars utilize invoice manipulation schemes to settle their debts. These schemes are often necessary because of remittance controls. For example, a hawaladar operating in the United States could send an associate $ 100,000 by purchasing $200,000 worth of goods that his associate wants. He ships the merchandise with an invoice for $ 100,000. The associate receives the merchandise and pays the first hawaladar $100,000. This payment appears to be legitimate because of the shipment and the invoice. The associate has $200,000 worth of merchandise for which only $100,000 was paid. This technique, known as "under invoicing" is one way of circumventing remittance controls as well as settling debts between hawaladars.

The inverse of this, "over invoicing" also exists. It would, for example, be used to transfer money to the United States. A hawaladar operating in the United States would purchase $ 100,000 worth of goods that his associate wants. He would ship the goods with an invoice for $300,000. Payment of this amount would allow the associate to move $200,000 to the United States. Like "under invoicing" this technique can be used to circumvent remittance controls and settle debts between hawaladars.

What might be termed "debt assignment" also takes place. If hawaladar A owes money to hawaladar B, and hawaladar B owes money to hawaladars C and D, hawaladar B might ask A to settle the debts with C and D, settling his debt with B. As with other aspects of hawala transactions, there is a great deal of flexibility. Hawaladars will use these settlement methods— or variations on them—as needed and dictated by circumstances.

The majority of hawala transfers out of the United States are remittances by South Asians living and working here to friends or relatives still in South Asia. There are several reasons for this. The first is a cultural preference for hawala. Hawala was developed as a remittance mechanism in South Asia before the appearance of "western" style banking, and continues to be used. The second is cost effectiveness. Since hawaladars do not necessarily respect official exchange rates, they can often deliver more rupees per dollar than an institution that respects official exchange rates. This is an important part of hawala; hawaladars make a certain amount of their profit off of exchange rate speculation, and much "colorful language" is often used while bargaining over very small differences in exchange rates! A third is speed—many hawaladars offer service "in two hours" even though 24 hours is more realistic, given time differences, but is, in any case, almost always faster than bank transfers. The final consideration is reliability, closely related to the trust component of hawala-transfers are not "lost in the mail" or "held up at the bank"; when someone places an order with a hawaladar, there is little if any doubt that the money will be delivered.

In some respects, the hawala system is self-regulating. Hawaladars form an extended community, and it is rare for them to defraud one another or their clients. In the rare cases where this has happened, other hawaladars have been known to make good on the debts of their colleague. While it is possible that some sort of "disciplinary action" will be taken, a hawaladar who commits fraud is one who cannot be trusted. Without the trust of other hawaladars, he can no longer function effectively.

To summarize, hawala is a system that is cost effective, quick, reliable and secure. These characteristics of hawala account, in large part, for its use instead of other remittance systems. There are also places, like Afghanistan, where hawala is the only viable remittance system. These factors also account for the use of hawala by certain terrorist organizations. Osama bin Ladin is a Saudi with connections to Afghanistan and Somalia. All of these are countries where hawala is the preferred means of remitting money.

Terrorists, drug traffickers and other criminals also exploit another characteristic of hawala. This is its frequent lack of a complete paper trail documenting all parties to a transaction. It is not uncommon for hawaladars to maintain only logs of debts with other hawaladars. Records of remittance clients and beneficiaries are kept only long enough to facilitate the transaction, and the debt logs are often kept until the debts have been settled.

The lack of a paper trail is but one of several difficulties in investigating the criminal use of hawala. Even when records are available, they are rarely in English, necessitating translation. Even though the records may contain names of other hawaladars, the names are rarely, if ever complete enough to facilitate proper identification-references to "Ali Hussein" or "Shahbhai" are typical.

The most significant investigative barrier is probably the fact that "hawala behavior" lies well outside the cultural experience of most US investigators. Hawala is a system where large amounts of money are handed over without receipts, confirmation numbers, or identification. Hawala transactions take place in the context of a large network unlike a "traditional" corporate structure. The business of hawala is conducted informally, with little in the way of overhead and almost nothing in the way of a regulatory infrastructure, making it, in this respect, nearly the antithesis of banking.

I would like to devote the remainder of my remarks to possible solutions to the problems posed by hawala.

Recent legislative changes calling for the registration and supervision of hawaladars, as well as for identifying hawala transactions as potentially suspicious are commendable first steps, but I do believe that much remains to be done.

There are two areas that I believe need to be addressed. First, I believe that it is essential for banks and other financial institutions already required to file Suspicious Activity Reports (SARs) to develop an understanding of "what hawala looks like" and act accordingly. This will help in the identification of hawaladars. If a bank has a client who is conducting hawala transactions, and this client is identified as doing so, and a SAR is filed, this can be used by the authorities to determine whether or not the hawaladar is licensed appropriately ....

Even though it is certainly possible for terrorists and other criminals to move vast amounts of money into the United States via hawala with little or no trace, some of this money is useless unless it can be converted into an acceptable form. This necessitates a relationship between banks and hawala. This relationship is a potential vulnerability in a hawala money laundering or terrorist financing scheme, and this vulnerability should be exploited ....

The second area deals with the difference between money laundering and terrorist financing. In brief, money laundering is the process of taking money from "dirty" sources and making it "clean" so that it can be used for what are often legitimate purposes.

This is not always the case with terrorist financing. In many cases, terrorist money has a "clean" origin and a "dirty" purpose. Some terrorists, such as Osama bin Ladin are wealthy, and use their own funds—often derived from legitimate sources—to finance acts of terror. Other terrorists make use of funds received from charities; some of these organizations appear to have been established solely for the purpose of raising money for terrorists, others are possible unwitting participants in terrorism.

In both of these cases, the money comes from legitimate sources—business dealings or charitable contributions—so what happens with it is not money laundering.

What happens in many instances of terrorist financing can almost be seen as the inverse of money laundering. "Clean money" becomes "dirty money"—money used to finance acts of terror.

So, from one perspective, and with a certain amount of simplification, money laundering and terrorist financing are opposites. In money laundering, dirty money becomes clean; in terrorist financing, clean money becomes dirty. From another perspective, however, the processes have much in common. ... I believe that it is essential that what is known about terrorist financing be made available to financial institutions to assist them not only in complying with reporting requirements but to aid them in developing new information about methods. Even though a certain amount of what has been learned about money laundering can be used, terrorist financing is not always the same, so new indicators will have to be developed.

Note

1. Another new problem for anti-money laundering efforts is the development of a digital, decentralized currency in the form of bitcoin. For discussions of the nature of this currency and the challenges it presents in this context, see, e.g., Catherine Martin Christopher, *Whack-A-Mole: Why Prosecuting Digital Currency Exchanges Won't Stop Online Money Laundering*, 18 Lewis & Clark L. Rev. 1 (2014).

D. MONEY LAUNDERING: CASE STUDY IN INSTITUTIONAL INTERACTION IN SENTENCING

In the 1990s, money laundering charges gained great popularity with federal prosecutors. Money laundering was punished much more harshly under the U.S. Sentencing Guidelines than (generally) the underlying criminal conduct that generated the proceeds—particularly in white collar criminal cases. For example, the Sentencing Commission has noted that "from 1992 through 1996, the election to pursue a money laundering charge in addition to an underlying fraud-related offense would raise the guideline penalty in 85 to 95 percent of the cases."[33] And in 1991, a Justice Department spokesman explained that money laundering statutes are attractive to prosecutors, especially in white-collar cases, because the "sentence for money laundering is, except in drug cases, generally about *four times* the sentence for the crime that generates the proceeds."[34] The Department used the significant sentencing consequences of a money laundering charge as a bargaining chip with which to pressure pleas on other charges. Thus, "[b]y the mid-1990s, DOJ statistics suggested that up to half of all money laundering charges returned by grand juries were subsequently dropped in connection with plea agreements."[35]

The U.S. Sentencing Commission, which is charged with generating (subject to congressional approval) the guidelines that formerly controlled but now guide felony sentencing in federal court, became concerned about the possibility that the onerous sentences available for money laundering cases had created unwarranted disparities between similarly situated defendants due to the Department of Justice's use of the statute in unforeseen ways. The Commission noted that the sentencing structure for money-laundering offenses had been promulgated less than six months after sections 1956 and 1957 had become effective, and thus "no actual prosecutorial experience or judicial guidance existed to inform the Commission's formulation of the initial money laundering guidelines."[36] The Commission set the "relatively high" base offense levels "to penalize the conduct about which Congress seemed most concerned when it enacted the money laundering statutes, namely: 1) situations in which the

---

[33] U.S. Sentencing Comm'n, Report to Congress: Sentencing Policy for Money Laundering Offenses, including Comments on Department of Justice Report 8 (Sept. 18, 1997) [hereinafter 1997 Commission Report].

[34] *Money Laundering Conference Focuses on Additions to Government's Arsenal*, 49 Crim. L. Rep. (BNA) 1018, 1019 (Apr. 13, 1991) (emphasis added).

[35] Jefferson M. Gray, *Sentencing Comm'n Revises Money Laundering Guidelines*, Bus. Crimes Bull. 5 (Aug. 2001).

[36] 1997 Commission Report, *supra* note 33, at 3.

'laundered' funds derived from serious underlying criminal conduct such as a significant drug trafficking operation or organized crime; and 2) situations in which the financial transaction was separate from the underlying crime and was undertaken to either: a) make it appear that the funds were legitimate, or b) promote additional criminal conduct by reinvesting the proceeds in additional criminal conduct."[37]

But, after reviewing the types of cases that the Department of Justice was pursuing under the money laundering statutes, the Commission concluded that "money laundering sentences are being imposed for a much broader scope of offense conduct, including some conduct that is substantially less serious than the conduct contemplated when the money laundering guidelines were first formulated."[38] In articulating this concern, the Commission pointed to two types of cases that have been examined within: (1) "receipt and deposit" cases in which a "person convicted of a specified unlawful activity, such as mail fraud, deposits the proceeds in a financial institution, does virtually nothing to camouflage either the source of the funds or the identity of the depositor, and is nonetheless convicted of money laundering";[39] and (2) "merger" cases in which "the conduct comprising the money laundering conviction is virtually indistinguishable from the conduct comprising the specified unlawful activity."[40]

After Congress rejected a commission-sponsored amendment to the money laundering guidelines in 1995, the Commission reviewed the steps taken by the Department of Justice to ensure that money-laundering offenses were being prosecuted uniformly, but concluded that the Department's efforts, without a "properly restructured money laundering guideline," were not adequate to avoid "unwarranted sentencing disparity."[41] The Commission "continue[d] to see money laundering sentences imposed where the money laundering conduct is so attenuated as to be virtually unrecognizable as the type of conduct for which the original money laundering sentencing guidelines were drafted."[42] The Commission also objected to the Justice Department's use of the money laundering guidelines to pressure pleas. It concluded that "[t]he problem with the current money laundering guideline structure, vis-a-vis the threat by prosecutors to add a money laundering charge, is that the incremental guideline penalty associated with that charge often does not reasonably relate to the seriousness of either the underlying conduct or the money laundering activity engaged in by the defendant. Hence, the prosecutor's 'club' may be disproportionate to the defendant's conduct."[43]

The judicial response to these disparities was not, for the most part, to narrow the scope of the money laundering statute. Rather, some judges reacted to prosecutors' "creative" money laundering theories (for example, in the "receipt and deposit" and "merger" cases) by attempting to eliminate disparities in treatment at sentencing. In an effort to dampen the sentencing consequences of a money laundering charge, some judges "grouped" the money laundering charge with the underlying criminal conduct when the judges concluded that the charges involved substantially the same harm and victims. Further, "[j]udicial dissatisfaction with the broad reach of the money laundering guidelines ... often resulted in a determination that the actual conduct for which the defendant was convicted was outside the 'heartland' of the money laundering guidelines as drafted by the Commission, thus justifying a substantial downward departure."[44] While some courts were willing to make these adjustments in some

---

[37] *Id.* at 4.

[38] *Id.* at 5.

[39] *Id.* at 14 n.36.

[40] *Id.*

[41] *Id.* at 13.

[42] *Id.* at 6-7 (footnote omitted).

[43] *Id.* at 14-15 n.37.

[44] *Id.* at 8; *see also id.* at 9 (noting that in 1997, "the average judicial departure rate [excluding substantial assistance departures] for non-drug money laundering convictions for the past five years is 32 percent higher than the overall departure rate").

cases, others were not; even those courts willing to "group" or make downward departures in order to alleviate perceived inequities in charging did not always isolate the same criteria in doing so. In short, the judicial response to the deficiencies in the structure of the money laundering guideline ultimately exacerbated unwarranted sentencing disparities among similarly situated defendants.

Finally, in 1997, the Commission concluded that "its multi-year analysis of money laundering sentencing found that the broad and inconsistent use of money laundering charges, coupled with an inflexible, arbitrarily determined guideline structure, is resulting in substantial unwarranted disparity and disproportionality in the sentencing of money laundering conduct."[45] The Commission's efforts to respond to this problem were "stymied in the late 1990s by the multiple vacancies on the seven-member commission. Once these positions were filled, the commission's staff revisited this issue, and the commission voted to adopt" a comprehensive restructuring of the money laundering guidelines.[46] This time, Congress acquiesced in the amendment and it became effective November 1, 2001.

The money laundering guidelines, as amended, are founded on a new distinction, which may have been an outgrowth of prosecutorial charging choices, between those who launder the proceeds of their own criminal conduct ("direct" or "first-party" money launderers) and those who launder others' criminal proceeds ("indirect" or "third-party" launders).[47] The Commission abandoned some of the distinctions that had previously been incorporated in the guidelines. For example, a defendant convicted of a promotion offense under § 1956(a)(1)(A)(i) will only receive a one-level enhancement over a defendant convicted under § 1957, rather than the six-level distinction drawn under the pre-existing guidelines. Similarly, a defendant convicted of a promotion offense will be treated the same as a defendant convicted of a concealment offense, while, under the pre-existing guideline, promotion offenses were treated much more harshly (by three levels) than concealment violations.[48]

With respect to "direct" money launders (who comprised 86% of the money laundering defendants at the time of the amendment), a defendant's sentence will generally be the sentence he would have received for the underlying offense plus an adjustment for the statute under which he was convicted (one level for § 1957 and two levels for § 1956).[49] A further two-level adjustment is authorized for those "direct" launderers who are convicted under § 1956 and whose offense involved "sophisticated" laundering.[50] Finally, the Commission decreed that in cases in which the defendant "is convicted of a count of laundering funds and a count for the underlying offense from which the laundered funds were derived, the counts shall be grouped."[51] This structure significantly dampens the sentencing consequences of a money laundering conviction for a defendant alleged to have laundered the proceeds of his own criminal activity, thus addressing the type of "receipt and deposit" and "merger" cases about which the Commission was concerned.

Those who are "indirect" launderers are potentially subject to much higher penalties. The amount of their sentence will hinge to a great extent on the amount of money they laundered.[52] They will be subjected to a very large (6-level) enhancement if they knew or believed that the laundered funds were the proceeds of, or were intended to promote, drug

---

[45] *Id.* at 9.

[46] Gray, *supra* note 35, at 5.

[47] *See id.* at 5-6; U.S. Sentencing Commission, Revised Proposed Amendment: Money Laundering, Synopsis of Proposed Amendment, http://www.ussc.gov.

[48] Gray, *supra* note 35, at 6.

[49] *See* U.S. Sentencing Guideline § 2S1.1(a)(1), (b)(2).

[50] *Id.* § 2S1.1(b)(3).

[51] *Id.* § 2S1.1, Application Note 6.

[52] *Id.* § 2S1.1(a)(2).

manufacture, importation or distribution, a crime of violence, firearms, explosives, national security, or terrorism offenses, or the sexual exploitation of a minor.[53] They will also receive the greatest of an adjustment for the statute under which they were convicted (one level for § 1957 and two levels for § 1956) or a significant (four-level) increase if they were in the business of laundering funds.[54] Finally, a two-level adjustment is authorized for those "indirect" launderers who are convicted under § 1956 and whose offense involved "sophisticated" laundering.[55]

The practical effect of these amendments is that those who launder their own criminal proceeds will receive *much* less of a sentencing "kick" from the lodging of a money laundering charge than was the case prior to the amendments. Those who launder others' money, and particularly those who are in the business of laundering drug money, will receive a significantly higher sentence than would be the case if they were simply charged with facilitating the underlying criminal conduct.[56]

Money laundering charges are also popular among federal prosecutors because they permit the government to seek civil or criminal forfeiture under 18 U.S.C. §§ 981 and 982. Because this has not changed, it may be that prosecutors continue to have a significant incentive to bring money laundering counts even though the Sentencing Commission has blunted the disproportionate sentencing impact of those counts in "direct" laundering cases. In particular, in criminal cases, § 982 provides that "[t]he court in imposing sentence on a person convicted of an offense in violation of section 1956, 1957, or 1960 of this title, *shall* order that the person forfeit to the United States any property, real or personal, involved in such offense, or any property traceable to such property" (emphasis added). The law of civil and criminal forfeiture under these provisions (like the RICO forfeiture precedents) is highly complex.

---

[53] *Id.* § 2S1.1(b)(1).

[54] *Id.* § 2S1.1(b)(2).

[55] *Id.* § 2S1.1(b)(3).

[56] *See id.* § 2S1.1.

Chapter 13

GRAND JURY

These materials on grand jury practice and the materials that follow on discovery are obviously designed to provide the reader with some insight into these important areas of practice. They also, however, demonstrate the decided imbalance between the prosecution and defense in access to the commodity that can make or break a case: information. The materials both on the grand jury and on discovery, then, highlight the unique, dual nature of prosecutorial obligations.

Prosecutors have very broad powers over the conduct of grand jury investigations, and their actions are not likely to be subjected to examination by defense counsel or oversight by courts. Accordingly, it is particularly important in this context that prosecutors are aware of their obligations both as zealous advocates on behalf of their client *and* as "ministers of justice." The Department of Justice's United States Attorneys' Manual provides the following description of the role of the prosecutor before the grand jury:

> In dealing with the grand jury, the prosecutor must always conduct himself or herself as an officer of the court whose function is to ensure that justice is done and that guilt shall not escape nor innocence suffer. The prosecutor must recognize that the grand jury is an independent body, whose functions include not only the investigation of crime and the initiation of criminal prosecution but also the protection of the citizenry from unfounded criminal charges. The prosecutor's responsibility is to advise the grand jury on the law and to present evidence for its consideration. In discharging these responsibilities, the prosecutor must be scrupulously fair to all witnesses and must do nothing to inflame or otherwise improperly influence the grand jurors.[1]

Readers should consider whether the Department of Justice's policies discussed within regarding the conduct of grand jury investigations comport with this overarching mandate. Consideration should also be given to whether the courts and Congress, in shaping the legal rules that govern grand jury practice, have struck the appropriate balance between ensuring that the grand jury's investigative mandate is unimpaired and guarding the grand jury's role as "a protective bulwark standing solidly between the

---

[1] 4 Dep't of Justice Manual, tit. 9 [hereinafter U.S.A.M.], § 9-11.010. A federal grand jury may not indict without the concurrence of the attorney for the government. For an indictment to be valid, the prosecutor must sign it. *See* Fed. R. Crim. P. 7(c). The judiciary cannot compel the attorney for the government to sign any indictment, at the request of the grand jury or otherwise, because the attorney for the government is not just complying with Rule 7; the prosecutor is exercising a power belonging to the executive branch of the government. *See* Smith v. United States, 375 F.2d 243 (5th Cir. 1967); United States v. Cox, 342 F.2d 167, 171 (5th Cir. 1965).

ordinary citizen and an overzealous prosecutor."[2] Finally, readers may wish to reflect upon the possibilities for grand jury reform—a subject that arises with some frequency even if it rarely eventuates in a statute. In particular, consider the following wishlist contained in a grand jury "Bill of Rights" proposed by the National Association of Criminal Defense Lawyers:

A. "Any grand jury witness not receiving immunity has the right to be accompanied by counsel."

B. "A prosecutor must disclose to the grand jury any evidence which exonerates the target or subject of the offense."

C. "A prosecutor shall not present evidence to a grand jury known to be constitutionally inadmissible at trial because of a court ruling on the matter."

D. "A target or subject of a grand jury investigation shall have the right to testify before the grand jury."

E. "Grand jury witnesses shall have the right to receive a transcript of their testimony."

F. "Before questioning any non-immunized subject or target called before a grand jury, the prosecutor shall give the warnings from *Miranda v. Arizona*."

G. "Grand jurors shall be given meaningful jury instructions, on the record, about their duties and powers as grand jurors, and the charges they are to consider."

H. "A prosecutor shall not call before the grand jury any subject or target who has stated personally or through an attorney an intent to invoke the constitutional privilege against self-incrimination."[3]

A. GRAND JURY FUNCTION

The Fifth Amendment provides that in federal cases "no person shall be held to answer for a capital, or otherwise infamous crime, unless on a presentment or indictment of a grand jury …."[4] A grand jury is a very different creature from the petit jury with which most readers will be familiar. A federal grand jury consists of between 16 and 23 members,[5] has a quorum with 16 members,[6] and may return an indictment (also called a "true bill") only if at least 12 jurors concur.[7] On the rare occasions when 12 or more jurors do not vote for indictment

---

[2] United States v. Dionisio, 410 U.S. 1, 17 (1973).

[3] *NACDL Commission Issue Report Calling For Reform of Federal Grand Jury System*, 67 Crim. L. Rep. (BNA) 3309 (May 24, 2000); *see also* NACDL, Evaluating Grand Jury Reform in Two States: The Case for Reform (Nov. 2011); The District of Columbia Grand Jury Study Committee of the Council for Court Excellence, *The Grand Jury of Tomorrow* (2001), at http://www.courtexcellence.org. For a very thoughtful discussion of the limitations (and possible unforeseen consequences of) proposed grand jury reforms and a cry for caution, see Prof. Andrew D. Leipold, *Constitutional Rights and the Grand Jury*, Testimony Before the House Judiciary Comm., Subcomm. on the Constitution (July 27, 2000).

[4] U.S. Const. amend. V. Indictments are required in all federal capital cases. Fed. R. Crim. P. 7(a). Federal felonies must be prosecuted by indictment unless the defendant waives indictment and agrees to prosecution by information, which is a charging document signed by the prosecutor and not submitted to a grand jury. *Id.* Federal misdemeanors may be prosecuted by information. *Id.* A defendant has a right to a prompt preliminary hearing, *see* Fed. R. Crim. P. 5.1 (c) (specifying time limitations), at which the magistrate will determine the existence of probable cause to believe that an offense has been committed and that the defendant committed it, *see* Fed. R. Crim. P. 5.1. If the defendant is indicted by a grand jury (or waives indictment and an information is filed by the prosecutor) prior to the date set for the preliminary examination, the preliminary hearing shall not be held. Fed. R. Crim. P. 5.1(a). For the applicable (statutory) speedy trial limitations upon the timing of the indictment, see 18 U.S.C. § 3161.

[5] Fed. R. Crim. P. 6(a)(1).

[6] *Id.*

[7] *Id.* Rule 6(f).

(returning what is known as a "no true bill" or, in earlier times, an "ignoramus"), there is no double jeopardy or other legal bar to re-presentation of the same matter (*i.e.*, the same transaction or event and the same putative defendant) to the same or another grand jury.[8]

The grand jury can be said to have two functions: screening and investigation:

Screening: "[T]he grand jury's principal function is to determine whether or not there is *probable cause* to believe that one or more persons committed a certain Federal offense within the venue of the district court."[9] In this regard, the task of the grand jury is to "serv[e] the invaluable function in our society of standing between the accuser and the accused, whether the latter be an individual, minority group, or other, to determine whether a charge is founded upon reason or dictated by an intimidating power or by malice and personal ill will."[10]

Although the standard applied—probable cause—is low, this screening function is important for a number of reasons. First, given that the plea rate in federal criminal cases hovering around 95%, it may be the only process by which evidence of guilt is ever formally tested. Second, "[f]or an innocent suspect charged with a crime, there are only two possible outcomes: bad and really bad. The really bad outcome is a wrongful conviction. ... For wrongfully charged defendants ... an acquittal or dismissal is such a relief that they may not realize—at first—how bad their remaining problems are."[11]

As Professor Andrew D. Leipold explains the consequences of a wrongful indictment:

> [W]hile innocent people who are arrested, charged, and acquitted of crimes have far fewer problems than the wrongfully convicted, their burdens are still substantial and still worthy of attention. Many of these problems, such as cost and the risk of an erroneous outcome, are faced by every party in any legal proceeding, but others are unique. In particular, a factually innocent defendant confronts the problem of being publicly accused by the government of criminal behavior with no real prospect of ever being officially vindicated [as "innocent" rather than simply "not guilty"]. An innocent suspect may have the charges dismissed or may be acquitted, but the sequella of an indictment may leave the defendant's reputation, personal relationships, and ability to earn a living so badly damaged that he may never be able to return to the life he knew before being accused. More subtly, a person who was once charged with a crime is put on a different (and far less desirable) track in the legal system than someone who has never been arrested. A later acquittal or dismissal does surprisingly little to relieve an innocent defendant of the resulting burdens.[12]

---

[8] "The protections afforded by the [Double Jeopardy] Clause are implicated only when the accused has actually been placed in jeopardy. This state of jeopardy attaches when a jury is empaneled and sworn, or, in a bench trial, when the judge begins to receive evidence." United States v. Martin Linen Supply Co., 430 U.S. 564, 569 (1977); *see also* Martinez v. Illinois, -- U.S. --, 134 S.Ct. 2070 (2014) (per curiam) (jeopardy attached when jury was sworn). Once a grand jury has returned a "no-true bill" or has otherwise declined to return an indictment on the merits, however, Department of Justice policy provides that the same matter "should not be presented to another grand jury or resubmitted to the same grand jury without first securing the approval of the responsible United States Attorney." U.S.A.M. § 9-11.120(A).

[9] U.S.A.M. § 9-11.101 (emphasis added); *see also* United States v. Calandra, 414 U.S. 338, 343 (1974).

[10] United States v. Mechanik, 475 U.S. 66, 74 (1986) (O'Connor, J., concurring in the judgment) (quoting Wood v. Georgia, 370 U.S. 375, 390 (1962)).

[11] Andrew D. Leipold, *The Problem of the Innocent, Acquitted Defendant*, 94 Nw. L. Rev. 1297, 1301 (2000).

[12] *Id.* at 1299; *see also* United States v. Serubo, 604 F.2d 807, 817 (3d Cir. 1979) ("[W]hile in theory a trial provides a defendant with a full opportunity to contest and disprove the charges against him, in practice, the handing up of an indictment will often have a devastating personal and professional impact that a later dismissal or acquittal can never undo."); *In re* Fried, 161 F.2d 453, 458-59 (2d Cir. 1947) ("[A] wrongful indictment is no laughing matter; often it works a grievous, irreparable injury to the person indicted. The stigma cannot easily be erased. In the public mind, the blot a man's escutcheon,

1. RULES APPLICABLE TO WITNESSES

"It is clear that a subpoena to appear [and testify] before a grand jury is not a 'seizure' in the Fourth Amendment sense, even though that summons may be inconvenient or burdensome."[40] Thus, there is no requirement that the Government make any preliminary showing of reasonableness prior to issuing an ad testificandum subpoena.[41] A person subpoenaed to appear before the grand jury, however, has a right to claim certain recognized evidentiary privileges. She may assert the shield of the work product doctrine or the attorney-client privilege. Most importantly, the witness may assert her Fifth Amendment right against self-incrimination if the answers to the questions at issue might provide a link in the chain of evidence used to criminally incriminate her. (The scope of the Fifth Amendment privilege is examined in Chapters 15 (compelled testimony) and 16 (forced production of tangible items)).

Given the dictates of grand jury secrecy, how will a target of the grand jury investigation know whether her statements may tend to incriminate her? Do the targets have a right to appear before the grand jury to present their side of the story? May the Government subpoena a target, and if it does, need it provide *Miranda* warnings? If the target intends to assert her Fifth Amendment privilege, may the Government force the target to assert that right in front of the grand jurors (thus prejudicing the target in the jurors' eyes)? The following are the Department of Justice's policies on these matters.

U.S.A.M. § 9-11.150 Subpoenaing Targets of the Investigation

A grand jury may properly subpoena a subject or a target of the investigation and question the target about his or her involvement in the crime under investigation. *See United States v. Wong*, 431 U.S. 174, 179 n. 8 (1977); *United States v. Washington*, 431 U.S. 181, 190 n. 6 (1977); *United States v. Mandujano*, 425 U.S. 564, 573-75 and 584 n. 9 (1976); *United States v. Dionisio*, 410 U.S. 1, 10 n. 8 (1973). However, in the context of particular cases such a subpoena may carry the appearance of unfairness. Because the potential for misunderstanding is great, before a known "target" (as defined in U.S.A.M. § 9-11.151) is subpoenaed to testify before the grand jury about his or her involvement in the crime under investigation, an effort should be made to secure the target's voluntary appearance. If a voluntary appearance cannot be obtained, the target should be subpoenaed only after the grand jury and the United States Attorney or the responsible Assistant Attorney General have approved the subpoena. In determining whether to approve a subpoena for a "target," careful attention will be paid to the following considerations:

--The importance to the successful conduct of the grand jury's investigation of the testimony or other information sought;

--Whether the substance of the testimony or other information sought could be provided by other witnesses; and

--Whether the questions the prosecutor and the grand jurors intend to ask or the other information sought would be protected by a valid claim of privilege.

U.S.A.M. § 9-11.151 Advice of "Rights" of Grand Jury Witnesses

It is the policy of the Department of Justice to advise a grand jury witness of his or her rights if such witness is a "target" or "subject" of a grand jury investigation. ...

A "target" is a person as to whom the prosecutor or the grand jury has substantial evidence linking him or her to the commission of a crime and who, in the judgment of the prosecutor, is a putative defendant. An officer or employee of an organization which is a target is not automatically considered a target even if such officer's or employee's conduct contributed to the commission of the crime by the target organization. The same lack of

---

[40] United States v. Dionisio, 410 U.S. 1, 9 (1973).

[41] *Id.*

automatic target status holds true for organizations which employ, or employed, an officer or employee who is a target.

A "subject" of an investigation is a person whose conduct is within the scope of the grand jury's investigation.

The Supreme Court declined to decide whether a grand jury witness must be warned of his or her Fifth Amendment privilege against compulsory self-incrimination before the witness's grand jury testimony can be used against the witness. *See United States v. Washington*, 431 U.S. 181, 186 and 190-191(1977); *United States v. Wong*, 431 U.S. 174 (1977); *United States v. Mandujano*, 425 U.S. 564, 582 n. 7 (1976). In *Mandujano* the Court took cognizance of the fact that Federal prosecutors customarily warn "targets" of their Fifth Amendment rights before grand jury questioning begins. Similarly, in *Washington*, the Court pointed to the fact that Fifth Amendment warnings were administered as negating "any possible compulsion to self-incrimination which might otherwise exist" in the grand jury setting.

Notwithstanding the lack of a clear constitutional imperative, it is the policy of the Department that an "Advice of Rights" form be appended to all grand jury subpoenas to be served on any "target" or "subject" of an investigation. *See* the advice of rights list below.

In addition, these "warnings" should be given by the prosecutor on the record before the grand jury and the witness should be asked to affirm that the witness understands them.

Although the Court in *Washington, supra*, held that "targets" of the grand jury's investigation are entitled to no special warnings relative to their status as "potential defendant(s)," the Department of Justice continues its longstanding policy to advise witnesses who are known "targets" of the investigation that their conduct is being investigated for possible violation of Federal criminal law. This supplemental advice of status of the witness as a target should be repeated on the record when the target witness is advised of the matters discussed in the preceding paragraphs. ...

Advice of Rights

The grand jury is conducting an investigation of possible violations of Federal criminal laws involving: (State here the general subject matter of inquiry, e.g., conducting an illegal gambling business in violation of 18 U.S.C. § 1955).

--You may refuse to answer any question if a truthful answer to the question would tend to incriminate you.

--Anything that you do say may be used against you by the grand jury or in a subsequent legal proceeding.

--If you have retained counsel, the grand jury will permit you a reasonable opportunity to step outside the grand jury room to consult with counsel if you so desire.

Additional Advice to be Given to Targets. If the witness is a target, the above advice should also contain a supplemental warning that the witness's conduct is being investigated for possible violation of federal criminal law.

U.S.A.M. § 9-11.152 Requests by Subjects and Targets to Testify Before the Grand Jury

It is not altogether uncommon for subjects or targets of the grand jury's investigation, particularly in white-collar cases, to request or demand the opportunity to tell the grand jury their side of the story. While the prosecutor has no legal obligation to permit such witnesses to testify, a refusal to do so can create the appearance of unfairness. Accordingly, under normal circumstances, where no burden upon the grand jury or delay of its proceedings is involved, reasonable requests by a "subject" or "target" of an investigation, as defined above, to testify personally before the grand jury ordinarily should be given favorable consideration, provided that such witness explicitly waives his or her privilege against self-incrimination, on the record before the grand jury, and is represented by counsel or voluntarily and knowingly appears without counsel and consents to full examination under oath.

Such witnesses may wish to supplement their testimony with the testimony of others. The decision whether to accommodate such requests or to reject them after listening to the testimony of the target or the subject, or to seek statements from the suggested witnesses, is a matter left to the sound discretion of the grand jury. When passing on such requests, it must be kept in mind that the grand jury was never intended to be and is not properly either an adversary proceeding or the arbiter of guilt or innocence.

U.S.A.M. § 9-11.153 Notification of Targets

When a target is not called to testify pursuant to U.S.A.M. § 9-11.150, and does not request to testify on his or her own motion (*see* U.S.A.M. § 9-11.152), the prosecutor, in appropriate cases, is encouraged to notify such person a reasonable time before seeking an indictment in order to afford him or her an opportunity to testify before the grand jury, subject to the conditions set forth in U.S.A.M. § 9-11.152. Notification would not be appropriate in routine clear cases or when such action might jeopardize the investigation or prosecution because of the likelihood of flight, destruction or fabrication of evidence, endangerment of other witnesses, undue delay or otherwise would be inconsistent with the ends of justice.

U.S.A.M. § 9-11.154 Advance Assertions of an Intention to Claim the Fifth Amendment Privilege Against Compulsory Self-Incrimination

A question frequently faced by Federal prosecutors is how to respond to an assertion by a prospective grand jury witness that if called to testify the witness will refuse to testify on Fifth Amendment grounds. If a "target" of the investigation and his or her attorney state in a writing, signed by both, that the "target" will refuse to testify on Fifth Amendment grounds, the witness ordinarily should be excused from testifying unless the grand jury and the United States Attorney agree to insist on the appearance. In determining the desirability of insisting on the appearance of such a person, consideration should be given to the factors which justified the subpoena in the first place, i.e., the importance of the testimony or other information sought, its unavailability from other sources, and the applicability of the Fifth Amendment privilege to the likely areas of inquiry.

Some argue that unless the prosecutor is prepared to seek an order pursuant to 18 U.S.C. § 6003, the witness should be excused from testifying. However, such a broad rule would be improper and make it too convenient for witnesses to avoid testifying truthfully to their knowledge of relevant facts. Moreover, once compelled to appear, the witness may be willing and able to answer some or all of the grand jury's questions without incriminating himself or herself. ...

Notes

1. Are these rules consistent with the overarching Department of Justice policy regarding the prosecutorial role in grand jury investigations quoted at the beginning of this chapter? Generally speaking, the above rules are not enforceable by the investigatory target against the government. If an Assistant fails to comply with Department of Justice policy regarding the provision of warnings, however, he or she may be threatened at least with departmental discipline, especially in the First, Second, and Third Circuits. *See, e.g.*, United States v. Pacheco-Ortiz, 889 F.2d 301 (1st Cir. 1989) (although declining to suppress grand jury testimony secured without DOJ-required warnings, cautioning that the court will refer future violations of the U.S.A.M. to the Justice Department for internal review).

2. Subjects or targets often wish to put their story before the grand jury, believing that they can sway the jurors to reject any indictment proposed by the prosecutor. The generally-accepted wisdom among the defense bar, however, is that unless they have been immunized, "subjects" or "targets" should avoid the grand jury, claiming their Fifth Amendment right whenever possible. *See, e.g.*, Dan K. Webb, Robert W. Tarun & Steven F. Molo, Corporate Internal Investigations § 12.03[1][d], at 12-24 (Law Journal Press 2018). The reasons

underlying this rule are many. First, it is thought that a grand jury appearance rarely will succeed in winning over a grand jury that is usually under the control and direction of the prosecutor. It is often said that "'a grand jury would indict a ham sandwich if the prosecutor asked it to.'" R. Michael Cassidy, *Toward a More Independent Grand Jury: Recasting and Enforcing the Prosecutor's Duty to Disclose Exculpatory Evidence*, 13 Geo. J. Legal Ethics 361, 361 (2000). Although perhaps not conclusive evidence, Justice Department statistics certainly substantiate this belief. Those statistics show that "99.9 percent of the defendants called before federal grand juries are indicted." Sam Skolnick, *Lawmaker's Vow to Give Defendants Clout Is Likely to Draw Heat*, Legal Times, Apr. 12, 1999, at 1. "From fiscal years 1994 through 1998, federal prosecutors secured 122,879 indictments, according to DOJ records. During the same period, prosecutors failed to get indictments in only 83 cases." *Id.* at 6.

Further, subjects or targets will be examined without their lawyers present. Thus, defense counsel will not be able to: object to confusing or misleading questions; bring out facts necessary to put the testimony in its proper context; caution the witness against responding to questions that threaten a waiver of the protections of the work product doctrine or the attorney-client privilege; or limit the scope of examination to avoid questioning on irrelevant, prejudicial, or inculpatory collateral topics. Any statements that the subject or target makes may be used at trial, either admitted as evidence against him or employed to impeach should the subject or target take the stand. At the least, the testimony will likely reveal and "lock in" the defense theory, giving the government the ability to develop a rebuttal to that theory. Finally, should the uncounseled witness misspeak, he may open himself up to prosecution for perjury and, possibly, obstruction of justice.

As with any general rule, that which counsels that targets and subjects stay out of the grand jury is subject to exceptions. For example, defense counsel who knows the prosecutor and trusts her to be open-minded and fair, and who believes her to be truly on the fence about whether to indict, may conclude in unusual cases that a target has a good chance of avoiding prosecution if he testifies. Further, many clients (such as politicians and corporate executives) conclude that, for reputational, public relations, professional licensure, or employment reasons, they simply cannot assert their Fifth Amendment right in response to a subpoena or a grand jury "invitation" to appear. Clients may also insist on appearing to protest their actual innocence.

If one's client decides to testify, counsel should prepare him for his appearance within an inch his life. *See* Webb *et al., supra*, § 12.04[1], [2], at 12-29 to 12-32 (discussing preparation of client for grand jury appearance). Among the matters that should be stressed are, first, that lying to the grand jury can only exacerbate the witness's difficulties. *See id.* § 12.04[1][a], at 12-29. In this regard, it may be helpful to note that convenient failures of recollection may constitute perjury and that there is no exception to the perjury statute for lying to protect family or friends. *See id.* Second, clients should not, before or after the grand jury appearance, talk about their testimony with anyone other than counsel. Even honest attempts by a witness to clarify their recollection of the facts with other potential witnesses may be misconstrued as attempts to suborn perjury, "cook a story," or otherwise obstruct justice. *See id.* Third, witnesses should not create, destroy, or alter documents. Not only is such conduct likely to be fruitless in a world filled with Xerox machines and computers and itself independently indictable as obstruction, it also may demonstrate the client's "consciousness of guilt" and thus cinch the government's case. *See id.* For a discussion of the difficulties of, and ethical issues surrounding, witness preparation, see Peter J. Henning, *The Pitfalls of Dealing with Witnesses in Public Corruption Prosecutions*, 23 Geo. J. Legal Ethics 351 (2010).

3. Under Department of Justice policy, certain types of subpoenas, such as subpoenas addressed to members of the news media for information relating to the news gathering function, *see* U.S.A.M. §§ 9-11.255, 9-13.400; 28 C.F.R. § 50.10 (2006), and attorneys, *see id.* § 9-11.255, 9-13.410, must be cleared with supervisory Department of Justice personnel before they may be issued. *See also* U.S.A.M. § 9-2.032; *id.* Criminal Resource Manual No. 86 (policy regarding prosecutions of attorneys). As discussed in Chapter 1 (Introduction), Congress has enacted a statute, 28 U.S.C. § 530B(a) (the "McDade Amendment"), which provides that "[a]n attorney for the Government shall be subject to State laws and rules, and local Federal court

This standard is not self-explanatory. As we have observed, "what is reasonable depends on the context." In *Nixon*, this Court defined what is reasonable in the context of a jury trial. We determined that, in order to require production of information prior to trial, a party must make a reasonably specific request for information that would be both relevant and admissible at trial. But, for the reasons we have explained above, the *Nixon* standard does not apply in the context of grand jury proceedings. In the grand jury context, the decision as to what offense will be charged is routinely not made until after the grand jury has concluded its investigation. One simply cannot know in advance whether information sought during the investigation will be relevant and admissible in a prosecution for a particular offense.

To the extent that Rule 17(c) imposes some reasonableness limitation on grand jury subpoenas, however, our task is to define it. In doing so, we recognize that a party to whom a grand jury subpoena is issued faces a difficult situation. As a rule, grand juries do not announce publicly the subjects of their investigations. A party who desires to challenge a grand jury subpoena thus may have no conception of the Government's purpose in seeking production of the requested information. Indeed, the party will often not know whether he or she is a primary target of the investigation or merely a peripheral witness. Absent even minimal information, the subpoena recipient is likely to find it exceedingly difficult to persuade a court that "compliance would be unreasonable." ...

Our task is to fashion an appropriate standard of reasonableness, one that gives due weight to the difficult position of subpoena recipients but does not impair the strong governmental interests in affording grand juries wide latitude, avoiding minitrials on peripheral matters, and preserving a necessary level of secrecy. We begin by reiterating that the law presumes, absent a strong showing to the contrary, that a grand jury acts within the legitimate scope of its authority. Consequently, a grand jury subpoena issued through normal channels is presumed to be reasonable, and the burden of showing unreasonableness must be on the recipient who seeks to avoid compliance. Indeed, this result is indicated by the language of Rule 17(c), which permits a subpoena to be quashed only "on motion" and "if *compliance* would be unreasonable." To the extent that the Court of Appeals placed an initial burden on the Government, it committed error. Drawing on the principles articulated above, we conclude that where, as here, a subpoena is challenged on relevancy grounds, the motion to quash must be denied unless the district court determines that there is no reasonable possibility that the category of materials the Government seeks will produce information relevant to the general subject of the grand jury's investigation. Respondents did not challenge the subpoenas as being too indefinite nor did they claim that compliance would be overly burdensome. The Court of Appeals accordingly did not consider these aspects of the subpoenas, nor do we.

It seems unlikely, of course, that a challenging party who does not know the general subject matter of the grand jury's investigation, no matter how valid that party's claim, will be able to make the necessary showing that compliance would be unreasonable. After all, a subpoena recipient "cannot put his whole life before the court in order to show that there is no crime to be investigated." Consequently, a court may be justified in a case where unreasonableness is alleged in requiring the Government to reveal the general subject of the grand jury's investigation before requiring the challenging party to carry its burden of persuasion. We need not resolve this question in the present case, however, as there is no doubt that respondents knew the subject of the grand jury investigation pursuant to which the business records subpoenas were issued. In cases where the recipient of the subpoena does not know the nature of the investigation, we are confident that district courts will be able to craft appropriate procedures that balance the interests of the subpoena recipient against the strong governmental interests in maintaining secrecy, preserving investigatory flexibility, and avoiding procedural delays. For example, to ensure that subpoenas are not routinely challenged as a form of discovery, a district court may require that the Government reveal the subject of the investigation to the trial court *in camera*, so that the court may determine whether the motion to quash has a reasonable prospect for success before it discloses the subject matter to the challenging party.

Applying these principles in this case demonstrates that the District Court correctly denied respondents' motions to quash. It is undisputed that all three companies—Model, R.

Enterprises, and MFR—are owned by the same person, that all do business in the same area, and that one of the three, Model, has shipped sexually explicit materials into the Eastern District of Virginia. The District Court could have concluded from these facts that there was a reasonable possibility that the business records of R. Enterprises and MFR would produce information relevant to the grand jury's investigation into the interstate transportation of obscene materials. Respondents' blanket denial of any connection to Virginia did not suffice to render the District Court's conclusion invalid. A grand jury need not accept on faith the self-serving assertions of those who may have committed criminal acts. Rather, it is entitled to determine for itself whether a crime has been committed. …

Notes

1. What is the standard articulated by the Court? Given this standard, how often are those seeking to quash or modify a subpoena duces tecum likely to be successful? Why might such motions be filed even if the chances of prevailing are dim?

2. One of the most important developments in white-collar practice is the creation, through technology, of an entirely new body of potential evidence—the electronic "document" and, in particular, records of text and e-mail communications. Now when the government serves a wide-ranging grand jury subpoena duces tecum (which, of course, will be difficult to resist under the *R. Enterprises* standard), the search for relevant evidence may be much more onerous, expensive, and, ultimately, damaging. And, as we shall see below, some of the controlling rules are unclear; the existing Fourth Amendment doctrines and rules of criminal procedure are ill-suited in some respects to the new digital world. *See, e.g.*, Orin S. Kerr, *Applying the Fourth Amendment to the Internet: A General Approach*, 62 Stan. L. Rev. 1005 (2010); Orin S. Kerr, *Digital Evidence and the New Criminal Procedure*, 105 Colum. L. Rev. 279 (2005).

But the penalties for failure to guess correctly, and thus to comply, with electronic discovery requests can be disastrous. *See, e.g.*, Andrew P. Gaillard, *Document Destruction Horror Stories*, 11 Bus. Crimes Bull. 1 (Nov. 2004); Steven F. Reich, *The Duty to Preserve Electronic Business Records*, 11 Bus. Crimes Bull. 1 (Sept. 2004). We begin with some advice regarding how counsel ought to navigate in this new terrain.

Robert J. Giuffra, Jr., *E-Mail: The Prosecutor's New Best Friend*
10 Bus. Crimes Bull. 1 (July 2003)[43]

Over the past 10 years, e-mail has replaced the telephone as the favored method of communication within Fortune 500 companies. The typical employee might send or receive dozens of e-mails per day, with the amount of e-mail traffic growing exponentially the higher up the employee sits on the corporate ladder. In a large company, the CEO might receive hundreds of e-mails daily, leaving to an assistant the task of "screening" them. This explosive growth in e-mail has not been lost on prosecutors. In case after case, prosecutors are securing convictions with carelessly written e-mail. Because e-mail is a form of almost instantaneous communication, it has replaced the wiretap as the best source of incriminating evidence in white-collar prosecutions. … People write things in e-mail that they would never write in a memo or letter—and with far less concern about content and accuracy. E-mail is viewed as only slightly more formal than speaking on the telephone, and encourages a stream-of-consciousness style that easily can be misconstrued when viewed out of context.

Most employees still don't realize that e-mail can survive indefinitely within the bowels of a company's computer system. An employee may delete an e-mail, but it can survive on his or

---

[43] Reproduced with the permission of the publisher from Robert J. Giuffra, Jr., "E-mail: The Prosecutor's New Best Friend," 10 Business Crimes Bulletin 1 (July 2003). Published by Law Journal Press, a division of ALM. © ALM Properties, Inc. All rights reserved. Copies of the complete work may be ordered from Law Journal Press, Book Fulfillment Department, 105 Madison Avenue, New York, New York 10016 or at www.lawcatalog.com or by calling 800-537-2128, ext. 9300.

her computer's hard drive, the company's server and, through transmission to others, on multiple hard drives and servers. In fact, contrary to what many employees believe, e-mail tends to be harder to purge than paper documents, including documents typed on an individual PC.

E-mail is particularly susceptible to "immortalizing" what would otherwise never be written down. One or two inflammatory e-mails can be powerful stuff in front of a jury, particularly in cases turning on an executive's intent. A single e-mail, believed to have been deleted long ago, can be a ticking time bomb inside a company.

Over the past several years, e-mail evidence has generated headlines. New York Attorney General Eliot Spitzer's investigation of Wall Street investment banks accelerated after the disclosure of private e-mail by prominent stock analysts seeming to contradict their public research. The prosecution of former CSFB investment banker Frank Quattrone rests on a series of e-mails sent to and from Quattrone regarding document retention. And, the events leading to the conviction of accounting giant Arthur Andersen began with an e-mail from an in-house lawyer regarding compliance with the firm's document retention policy.

As a result, some prosecutors and enforcement staff at agencies like the SEC have started seeking all e-mail of a company's key employees, regardless of subject matter, even including personal e-mail to family and friends. Such broad subpoenas encourage fishing expeditions that were not possible when prosecutors sought paper documents concerning specified subjects.

Prosecutors now insist that e-mail be produced on searchable CD-roms and require companies to go to the enormous expense of restoring "deleted" e-mail. With thousands of e-mails to comb through, prosecutors can count on finding a stray statement or comment that supports their pet theory. For example, prosecutors can try to build a conscious avoidance case on the fact that a top executive was copied on an e-mail that the executive never read, or deleted after glancing at the "subject" line. In a securities fraud case, an e-mail indicating that an executive had questions about the quality of a company's public disclosures can be evidence of criminal intent.

When a government investigation or private litigation requires it, restoring and reviewing e-mail is difficult and expensive. The volume of e-mail in a large corporation can reach into the millions. It can take dozens of lawyers working around the clock for weeks, if not months, to review e-mail for production to government regulators. Because computer soft- and hardware rapidly become obsolete and are replaced, restoring old e-mail sometimes requires reconstructing old servers—a considerable expense.

The best way to avoid having a careless e-mail convict a company or its executives is to take action long before a subpoena arrives. Companies should train employees in the proper use of e-mail, including on-line training sessions. Employees should be reminded not to send business e-mail when they are angry or rushed. Only a very small portion of all the e-mail sent is of any value after a few weeks have passed. Employees should be encouraged to print out and save on paper any essential e-mail. Unnecessary e-mail should not be stored on hard drives. Employees must understand that e-mail is just as likely as a letter or memo to be scrutinized in a government investigation or private lawsuit.

Companies must make clear to employees that company e-mail is not private, and that the company reserves the right to review employee e-mail. Companies should make use of computer programs that identify senders and receivers of inappropriate e-mail. Employees should not be permitted to send e-mail indiscriminately outside of the company. As with paper records, companies should develop written policies for e-mail retention. The creation of such a policy requires understanding the company's computer systems, including the methods used to reconstruct e-mail. To the extent permitted by law, companies can implement a computer program that permanently deletes or "overwrites" e-mail after (for example) 30 days.

These programs can be configured to automatically delete old e-mail, thereby avoiding the risk that some employees will ignore retention requirements. Procedures can be implemented for excepting certain e-mail and other electronic documents from the program. For example, important e-mail can be copied to a specified directory on the company's server used to store "permanent" files.

Prior to implementing an e-mail retention program, it is critical that counsel carefully determine whether applicable laws and regulations require the preservation of paper and electronic documents for specified time periods. Even after a seemingly long mandated retention period, it is still worth the effort of purging old e-mail to eliminate the danger that an ancient e-mail will be misconstrued by a zealous government regulator.

E-mail retention policies must be regularly enforced. Prosecutors are likely to view any sporadic enforcement with suspicion, and a retention policy should never be adopted when a government investigation is looming. At the same time, the regular enforcement of an e-mail retention policy can eliminate the need for a company to go to the potentially enormous expense of restoring back-ups tapes and reviewing irrelevant e-mail.

Timing is critical with regard to the implementation of document retention policies. The conviction of Arthur Andersen demonstrates the risk of complying with a retention policy on the eve of an investigation. When a company receives a subpoena or has constructive notice of a pending or threatened government investigation, the company must take steps to preserve all potentially relevant e-mail and electronic information. The proper notices must be sent to employees, especially those involved in the matters under investigation and in the company's IT department.

Counsel must remember that information can be stored on different computer servers and stored on tape for varying periods of time. Programs that permanently delete electronic data must be stopped. Employees must be reminded to preserve business e-mail on home computers and Blackberrys.

Before producing e-mail to prosecutors, counsel must review the e-mail for privilege and relevance. Litigation systems should be put in place to permit the searching of e-mail for purposes of identifying helpful or problematic e-mail and for witness preparation. ...

...[I]n the wake of Sarbanes-Oxley, corporate counsel clearly must take steps to preserve e-mail whenever a company learns that a government investigation is reasonably foreseeable. With prosecutors and government regulators empowered to ferret out wrongdoing, real and imagined, a company that purges e-mail and other electronic information at the wrong time could be put out of business. The safest course, then, is to create a corporate culture where e-mail communication is viewed as almost on a par with a memorandum to the CEO. Employees who write careless e-mails should be warned and, when the abuse of e-mail is especially egregious, terminated. For most companies, the risk of even a single careless e-mail is simply too great.

Notes

1. The above advice should be applied to text messaging and employees' use of social media as well.

2. What are the implications of these policies for individuals, as well as for the corporate employer? If companies put in place policies that make clear that employees have no reasonable expectation of privacy in the materials they communicate or store on employers' electronic systems, employees may find that their culpable communications can easily be turned over to the government when the employer decides to cooperate with the government. *See, e.g.*, Marjorie J. Peerce & Elizabeth S. Weinstein, *Employee Communications and Loss of Privilege*, Bus. Crimes Bull. (Oct. 2011).

3. What about personal email information that is routed through an Internet service provider? The Stored Communications Act (SCA), 18 U.S.C. § 2701, *et seq.* permits the government to compel a service provider to disclose the contents of electronic communications in certain circumstances.

The compelled-disclosure provisions give different levels of privacy protection based on whether the e-mail is held with an electronic communication service or a remote computing service and based on how long the e-mail has been in electronic storage. The government may ask about the contents of e-mails that are "in electronic storage" with an electronic communication service for 180 days or less "only pursuant to warrant." 18

U.S.C. § 2703(a). The government has three options for obtaining communications stored with a remote computing service and communications that have been in electronic storage with an electronic service provider for more than 180 days: (1) obtain a warrant; (2) use an administrative subpoena; or (3) obtain a court order under § 2703(d). *Id.* § 2703(a), (b).

United States v. Warshak, 631 F.3d 266 (6th Cir. 2011); *see also* Orin S. Kerr, *A User's Guide to the Stored Communications Act, and a Legislator's Guide to Amending It*, 72 Geo. Wash. L. Rev. 1208 (2004). Note that in certain circumstances, the government can obtain much content information through a simple administrative subpoena. Does this statutory scheme pass constitutional muster?

Congress recently clarified the extraterritorial reach of the Stored Communications Act in the Clarifying Lawful Overseas Use of Data (CLOUD) Act (passed as part of the Consolidated Appropriations Act, 2018, Pub. L. 115-141). The Act provides that U.S. authorities can compel providers of electronic communications services like email service providers and social media networks to produce data stored outside the United States. The CLOUD Act also puts in place new rules that facilitate foreign law enforcement access to data stored in the United States.

The Supreme Court "consistently has held that a person has no legitimate expectation of privacy in information he voluntarily turns over to third parties." Smith v. Maryland, 442 U.S. 735, 743-44 (1979) (numbers dialed through telephone company). "[T]he Fourth Amendment does not prohibit the obtaining of information revealed to a third party and conveyed by him to the Government authorities, even if the information is revealed on the assumption that it will be used only for a limited purpose and the confidence placed in the third party will not be betrayed." United States v. Miller, 425 U.S. 435, 443 (1976) (bank records). The Court recently appeared to limit the applicability of this third-party doctrine in holding, in *Carpenter v. United States*, -- U.S. --, 138 S.Ct. 2206 (2018), that an individual has a legitimate expectation of privacy for Fourth Amendment purposes in the record—maintained by third parties—of his physical movement obtained through cell site location information. The Supreme Court has not addressed the question whether an individual retains a reasonable expectation of privacy in the *content* of data sent through an Internet Service Provider (ISP). *Cf.* City of Ontario v. Quon, 560 U.S. 746 (2010) (assuming, without deciding, that a city employee had an expectation of privacy in the text messages he sent on a pager provided him by the city, the search was reasonable under the "special needs" doctrine). Some circuits have been reluctant to address the issue. *See* Rehberg v. Paulk, 611 F.3d 828, 842-47 (11th Cir.2010), *aff'd on other grounds*, 566 U.S. 356 (2012).

In *United States v. Warshak*, 631 F.3d 266 (6th Cir. 2011), however, the Sixth Circuit held that a defendant did have a reasonable expectation of privacy, protected by the Fourth Amendment, in his email vis-à-vis his ISP, and government agents violated his rights by compelling his ISP to turn over his email without first obtaining a warrant even if authorized to do so by the SCA. The court ultimately concluded, however, that the information so obtained did not have to be excluded because the agents relied in good faith on the SCA.

4. If a warrant is obtained, how particular need the government be in describing the materials to be searched or seized in the context of computer searches? This is a question that is vexing the lower courts. *See, e.g.*, United States v. Richards, 659 F.3d 527 (6th Cir. 2011); United States v. Stabile, 633 F.3 219 (3d Cir. 2011); United States v. Comprehensive Drug Testing, Inc., 621 F.3d 1162 (9th Cir. 2010); United States v. Mann, 592 F.3d 779 (7th Cir. 2010); United States v. Williams, 592 F.3d 511 (4th Cir. 2010); United States v. Burgess, 576 F.3d 1078 (10th Cir. 2009). The question of the permissible scope of a computer search also arises in the context of plain-view and consent searches. *See, e.g.*, *Stabile*, 633 F.3d 219; United States v. Lucas, 640 F.3d 168 (6th Cir. 2011); *Mann*, 592 F.3d 779; *Williams*, 592 F.3d 511. As the *Richards* court summarized:

We recently observed, in the context of determining that the scope of a defendant's laptop computer did not exceed the scope of his consent to search his home, that analogizing computers to other physical objects when applying Fourth Amendment law is not an exact fit because computers hold so much personal and sensitive information touching on many private aspects of life … [T]here is a far greater potential "for the 'intermingling' of documents and a consequent invasion of privacy when police execute a search for evidence on a computer."

Courts that have addressed the permissible breadth of computer-related searches have grappled with how to balance two interests that are in tension with each other:

> On one hand, it is clear that because criminals can—and often do—hide, mislabel, or manipulate files to conceal criminal activity, a broad, expansive search of the hard drive may be required…. One the other hand, … granting the Government a *carte blanche* to search *every* file on the hard drive impermissibly transforms a limited search into a general one.

… Ultimately, … given the unique problem encountered in computer searches, and the practical difficulties inherent in implementing universal search methodologies, the majority of federal courts have eschewed the use of a specific search protocol and, instead, have employed the Fourth Amendment's bedrock principle of reasonableness on a case-by-case basis: "While officers must be clear as to what it is they are seeking on the computer and conduct the search in a way that avoids searching files of types not identified in the warrant, … a computer search may be as extensive as reasonably required to locate the items described in the warrant based on probably cause." We agree with the Tenth Circuit's succinct assessment … that

> it is folly for a search warrant to attempt to structure the mechanics of a search and a warrant imposing such limits would unduly restrict legitimate search objectives. One would not ordinarily expect a warrant to search filing cabinets for evidence of drug activity to prospectively restrict the search to "file cabinets in the basement" or to file folders labeled "Meth Lab" or "Customers." And there is no reason to so limit computer searches. But that is not to say methodology is irrelevant.
>
> A warrant may permit only the search of particularly described places and only particularly described things may be seized. As the description of such places and things becomes more general, the method by which the search is executed become[s] more important—the search method must be tailed to meet allowed ends. And those limits must be functional. For instance, unless specifically authorized by the warrant there would be little reason for officers searching for evidence of drug trafficking to look at tax returns (beyond verifying the folder labeled "2002 Tax Return" actually contains tax returns and not drug files or trophy pictures).
>
> Respect for legitimate rights to privacy in papers and effects requires an officer executing a search warrant to first look in the most obvious places and as it become necessary to progressively move from the obvious to the obscure. That is the purpose of a search protocol which structures the search by requiring an analysis of the file structure, next looking for suspicious file folders, then looking for files and types of files most likely to contain the objects of the search by doing keyword searches.
>
> But in the end, there may be no practical substitute for actually looking in many (perhaps all) folders and sometimes at the documents contained within those folders, and that is true whether the search is of computer files or physical files. It is particularly true with image files.

Richards, 659 F.3d at 537-39 (quoting *Burgess,* 576 F.3d at 1094).

3. EVIDENTIARY RULES

The evidentiary rules governing grand jury proceedings are much less stringent than those that apply at trial. As the Court explained in *R. Enterprises*:

This Court has emphasized on numerous occasions that many of the rules and restrictions that apply at a trial do not apply in grand jury proceedings. This is especially true of evidentiary restrictions. The same rules that, in an adversary hearing on the merits, may increase the likelihood of accurate determinations of guilt or innocence do not necessarily advance the mission of a grand jury, whose task is to conduct an *ex parte* investigation to determine whether or not there is probable cause to prosecute a particular defendant. In *Costello v. United States*, 350 U.S. 359 (1956), this Court declined to apply the rule against hearsay to grand jury proceedings. Strict observance of trial rules in the context of a grand jury's preliminary investigation "would result in interminable delay but add nothing to the assurance of a fair trial." In *United States v. Calandra*, 414 U.S. 338 (1974), we held that the Fourth Amendment exclusionary rule does not apply to grand jury proceedings. Permitting witnesses to invoke the exclusionary rule would "delay and disrupt grand jury proceedings" by requiring adversary hearings on peripheral matters, and would effectively transform such proceedings into preliminary trials on the merits. The teaching of the Court's decisions is clear: A grand jury "may compel the production of evidence or the testimony of witnesses as it considers appropriate, and its operation generally is unrestrained by the technical procedural and evidentiary rules governing the conduct of criminal trials."[44]

The following represents the Department of Justice's policy with respect to the admission of illegally seized evidence, hearsay evidence, and exculpatory evidence during grand jury proceedings.

U.S.A.M. § 9-11.231 Motions to Dismiss Due to Illegally Obtained Evidence Before a Grand Jury

A prosecutor should not present to the grand jury for use against a person whose constitutional rights clearly have been violated evidence which the prosecutor personally knows was obtained as a direct result of the constitutional violation.

U.S.A.M. § 9-11.232 Use of Hearsay in a Grand Jury Proceeding

As a general rule, it is proper to present hearsay to the grand jury, *United States v. Calandra* 414 U.S. 338 (1974). Each United States Attorney should be assured that hearsay evidence presented to the grand jury will be presented on its merits so that the jurors are not misled into believing that the witness is giving his or her personal account.

U.S.A.M. § 9-11.233 Presentation of Exculpatory Evidence

In *United States v. Williams*, 504 U.S. 36 (1992), the Supreme Court held that the Federal courts' supervisory powers over the grand jury did not include the power to make a rule allowing the dismissal of an otherwise valid indictment where the prosecutor failed to introduce substantial exculpatory evidence to a grand jury. It is the policy of the Department of Justice, however, that when a prosecutor conducting a grand jury inquiry is personally aware of substantial evidence that directly negates the guilt of a subject of the investigation, the prosecutor must present or otherwise disclose such evidence to the grand jury before seeking

---

[44] 498 U.S. at 298.

an indictment against such a person. While a failure to follow the Department's policy should not result in dismissal of an indictment, appellate courts may refer violations of the policy to the Office of Professional Responsibility for review. ...

Notes

1. Why would prosecutors use illegally seized evidence to obtain an indictment when they may not rely upon that evidence to secure a conviction on the indictment? Should such evidence be admissible in grand jury proceedings? The question of whether prosecutors should be required to present exculpatory evidence to the grand jury will be treated *infra* in *United States v. Williams*. Should hearsay be admissible in grand jury proceedings? As Professor Daniel Richman explains:

> The government may present hearsay evidence to the grand jury, and will often do so, because it facilitates the presentation of a seamless case, limits the burden on non-government witnesses, and limits the effectiveness of cross-examination should the out-of-court declarants later testify at trial. These are not necessarily good reasons, *see* Andrew D. Leipold, *Why Grand Juries Do Not (and Cannot) Protect the Accused*, 80 Cornell L. Rev. 260, 292 n.157 (1995), but they are reasons just the same.

Richman, *supra*, at 342 n.21. Are the above-quoted standards consistent with the Departmental policy quoted at the beginning of this chapter? Are they enforceable?

2. Given that the overwhelming majority (generally estimated at about 97%) of all federal criminal cases never go to trial and are resolved by plea, one could certainly argue that greater procedural protections should be accorded targets in the grand jury process. As some defense lawyers contend, "the grand jury has in effect become the last resort for many accused in the federal criminal justice system." *NACDL Commission Issue Report Calling For Reform of Federal Grand Jury System*, 67 Crim. L. Rep. (BNA) 3309 (May 24, 2000). Should the rules governing this ancient device be responsive to modern developments and needs?

3. In *Kaley v. United States*, 571 U.S. 320 (2014), the Supreme Court held that the defendants were not entitled to revisit the grand jury's probable cause determination in a pre-trial hearing challenging the restraint of potentially forfeitable assets needed to hire counsel of choice. In so ruling, the Court explained:

> This Court has often recognized the grand jury's singular role in finding the probable cause necessary to initiate a prosecution for a serious crime. "[A]n indictment 'fair upon its face,' and returned by a 'properly constituted grand jury,'" we have explained, "conclusively determines the existence of probable cause" to believe the defendant perpetrated the offense alleged. And "conclusively" has meant, case in and case out, just that. We have found no "authority for looking into and revising the judgment of the grand jury upon the evidence, for the purpose of determining whether or not the finding was founded upon sufficient proof." To the contrary, "the whole history of the grand jury institution" demonstrates that "a challenge to the reliability or competence of the evidence" supporting a grand jury's finding of probable cause "will not be heard." The grand jury gets to say—without any review, oversight, or second-guessing—whether probable cause exists to think that a person committed a crime.

> And that inviolable grand jury finding, we have decided, may do more than commence a criminal proceeding (with all the economic, reputational, and personal harm that entails); the determination may also serve the purpose of immediately depriving the accused of her freedom. If the person charged is not yet in custody, an indictment triggers "issuance of an arrest warrant without further inquiry" into the case's strength. Alternatively, if the person was arrested without a warrant, an indictment eliminates her Fourth Amendment right to a prompt judicial assessment of probable cause to support any detention. In either situation, this Court—relying on the grand jury's "historical role of protecting individuals from unjust persecution"—has "let [that body's] judgment

substitute for that of a neutral and detached magistrate." The grand jury, all on its own, may effect a pre-trial restraint on a person's liberty by finding probable cause to support a criminal charge.

The same result follows when, as here, an infringement on the defendant's property depends on a showing of probable cause that she committed a crime. If judicial review of the grand jury's probable cause determination is not warranted (as we have so often held) to put a defendant on trial or place her in custody, then neither is it needed to freeze her property. The grand jury that is good enough—reliable enough, protective enough—to inflict those other grave consequences through its probable cause findings must needs be adequate to impose this one too. ... [T]he probable cause standard, once selected, should work no differently for the single purpose of freezing assets than for all others. So the longstanding, unvarying rule of criminal procedure we have just described applies here as well: The grand jury's determination is conclusive.

Id. at 328-31.

D. JUDICIAL POLICING AND PROSECUTORIAL MISCONDUCT

BANK OF NOVA SCOTIA v. UNITED STATES
487 U.S. 250 (1988)

JUSTICE KENNEDY delivered the opinion of the Court.

The issue presented is whether a district court may invoke its supervisory power to dismiss an indictment for prosecutorial misconduct in a grand jury investigation, where the misconduct does not prejudice the defendants.

In 1982, after a 20-month investigation conducted before two successive grand juries, eight defendants, including petitioners William A. Kilpatrick, Declan J. O'Donnell, Sheila C. Lerner, and The Bank of Scotia, were indicted on 27 counts....

... After 10 days of hearings, Judge Kane dismissed all 27 counts of the indictment. The District Court held that dismissal was required for various violations of Federal Rule of Criminal Procedure 6. Further, it ruled dismissal was proper under the "totality of the circumstances," including the "numerous violations of Rule 6(d) and (e), Fed.R.Crim.P., violations of 18 U.S.C. §§ 6002 and 6003, violations of the Fifth and Sixth Amendments to the United States Constitution, knowing presentation of misinformation to the grand jury and mistreatment of witnesses." We shall discuss these findings in more detail below.

The District Court determined that "[a]s a result of the conduct of the prosecutors and their entourage of agents, the indicting grand jury was not able to undertake its essential mission" to act independently of the prosecution. In an apparent alternative holding, the District Court also ruled that

> "[t]he supervisory authority of the court must be used in circumstances such as those presented in this case to declare with unmistakable intention that such conduct is neither 'silly' nor 'frivolous' and that it will not be tolerated." ...

We hold that, as a general matter, a district court may not dismiss an indictment for errors in grand jury proceedings unless such errors prejudiced the defendants.

In the exercise of its supervisory authority, a federal court "may, within limits, formulate procedural rules not specifically required by the Constitution or the Congress." Nevertheless, it is well established that "[e]ven a sensible and efficient use of the supervisory power ... is invalid if it conflicts with constitutional or statutory provisions." To allow otherwise "would confer on the judiciary discretionary power to disregard the considered limitations of the law it is charged with enforcing." ...

We now hold that a federal court may not invoke supervisory power to circumvent the harmless-error inquiry prescribed by Federal Rule of Criminal Procedure 52(a). Rule 52(a) provides that "[a]ny error, defect, irregularity or variance which does not affect substantial rights shall be disregarded." ... Rule 52 is, in every pertinent respect, as binding as any statute duly enacted by Congress, and federal courts have no more discretion to disregard the Rule's mandate than they do to disregard constitutional or statutory provisions. The balance struck by the Rule between societal costs and the rights of the accused may not casually be overlooked "because a court has elected to analyze the question under the supervisory power." ...

Having concluded that our customary harmless-error inquiry is applicable where, as in the cases before us, a court is asked to dismiss an indictment prior to the conclusion of the trial, we turn to the standard of prejudice that courts should apply in assessing such claims. We adopt for this purpose, at least where dismissal is sought for nonconstitutional error, the standard articulated by JUSTICE O'CONNOR in her concurring opinion in *United States v. Mechanik*[, 475 U.S. 66 (1986)]. Under this standard, dismissal of the indictment is appropriate only "if it is established that the violation substantially influenced the grand jury's decision to indict," or if there is "grave doubt" that the decision to indict was free from the substantial influence of such violations. This standard is based on our decision in *Kotteakos v. United States*, 328 U.S. 750, 758-759 (1946), where, in construing a statute later incorporated into Rule 52(a), we held that a conviction should not be overturned unless, after examining the record as a whole, a court concludes that an error may have had "substantial influence" on the outcome of the proceeding.

To be distinguished from the cases before us are a class of cases in which indictments are dismissed, without a particular assessment of the prejudicial impact of the errors in each case, because the errors are deemed fundamental. These cases may be explained as isolated exceptions to the harmless-error rule. We think, however, that an alternative and more clear explanation is that these cases are ones in which the structural protections of the grand jury have been so compromised as to render the proceedings fundamentally unfair, allowing the presumption of prejudice. These cases are exemplified by *Vasquez v. Hillery*, 474 U.S. 254, 260-264 (1986), where we held that racial discrimination in selection of grand jurors compelled dismissal of the indictment. In addition to involving an error of constitutional magnitude, other remedies were impractical and it could be presumed that a discriminatorily selected grand jury would treat defendants unfairly. We reached a like conclusion in *Ballard v. United States*, 329 U.S. 187 (1946), where women had been excluded from the grand jury. The nature of the violation allowed a presumption that the defendant was prejudiced, and any inquiry into harmless error would have required unguided speculation. Such considerations are not presented here, and we review the alleged errors to assess their influence, if any, on the grand jury's decision to indict in the factual context of the cases before us. ...

The District Court found that the Government had violated Federal Rule of Criminal Procedure 6(e) by: (1) disclosing grand jury materials to Internal Revenue Service employees having civil tax enforcement responsibilities; (2) failing to give the court prompt notice of such disclosures; (3) disclosing to potential witnesses the names of targets of the investigation; and (4) instructing two grand jury witnesses, who had represented some of the defendants in a separate investigation of the same tax shelters, that they were not to reveal the substance of their testimony or that they had testified before the grand jury. The court also found that the Government had violated Federal Rule of Criminal Procedure 6(d) in allowing joint appearances by IRS agents before the grand jury for the purpose of reading transcripts to the jurors.

The District Court further concluded that one of the prosecutors improperly argued with an expert witness during a recess of the grand jury after the witness gave testimony adverse to the Government. It also held that the Government had violated the witness immunity statute, 18 U.S.C. §§ 6002, 6003, by the use of "pocket immunity" (immunity granted on representation of the prosecutor rather than by order of a judge), and that the Government caused IRS agents to mischaracterize testimony given in prior proceedings. Furthermore, the District Court found that the Government violated the Fifth Amendment by calling a number of witnesses for the sole purpose of having them assert their privilege against self-incrimination and that it had violated the Sixth Amendment by conducting postindictment interviews of several high-level employees of The Bank of Nova Scotia. Finally, the court concluded that the Government had caused IRS agents to be sworn as agents of the grand jury, thereby elevating their credibility.

As we have noted, no constitutional error occurred during the grand jury proceedings. The Court of Appeals concluded that the District Court's findings of Sixth Amendment postindictment violations were unrelated to the grand jury's independence and decisionmaking process because the alleged violations occurred *after* the indictment. We agree that it was improper for the District Court to cite such matters in dismissing the indictment. The Court of Appeals also found that no Fifth Amendment violation occurred as a result of the Government's calling seven witnesses to testify despite an avowed intention to invoke their Fifth Amendment privilege. We agree that, in the circumstances of these cases, calling the witnesses was not error. The Government was not required to take at face value the unsworn assertions made by these witnesses outside the grand jury room. Once a witness invoked the privilege on the record, the prosecutors immediately ceased all questioning. Throughout the proceedings, moreover, the prosecution repeated the caution to the grand jury that it was not to draw any adverse inference from a witness' invocation of the Fifth Amendment.

In the cases before us we do not inquire whether the grand jury's independence was infringed. Such an infringement may result in grave doubt as to a violation's effect on the grand jury's decision to indict, but we did not grant certiorari to review this conclusion. We note that the Court of Appeals found that the prosecution's conduct was not "a significant infringement on the grand jury's ability to exercise independent judgment," and we accept that conclusion here. Finally, we note that we are not faced with a history of prosecutorial misconduct, spanning several cases, that is so systematic and pervasive as to raise a substantial and serious question about the fundamental fairness of the process which resulted in the indictment.

We must address, however, whether, despite the grand jury's independence, there was any misconduct by the prosecution that otherwise may have influenced substantially the grand jury's decision to indict, or whether there is grave doubt as to whether the decision to indict was so influenced. Several instances of misconduct found by the District Court—that the prosecutors manipulated the grand jury investigation to gather evidence for use in civil audits; violated the secrecy provisions of Rule 6(e) by publicly identifying the targets and the subject matter of the grand jury investigation; and imposed secrecy obligations in violation of Rule 6(e) upon grand jury witnesses—might be relevant to an allegation of a purpose or intent to abuse the grand jury process. Here, however, it is plain that these alleged breaches could not have affected the charging decision. We have no occasion to consider them further.

We are left to consider only the District Court's findings that the prosecutors: (1) fashioned and administered unauthorized "oaths" to IRS agents in violation of Rule 6(c); (2) caused the same IRS agents to "summarize" evidence falsely and to assert incorrectly that all the evidence summarized by them had been presented previously to the grand jury; (3) deliberately berated and mistreated an expert witness for the defense in the presence of some grand jurors; (4) abused its authority by providing "pocket immunity" to 23 grand jury witnesses; and (5) permitted IRS agents to appear in tandem to present evidence to the grand jury in violation of Rule 6(d). We consider each in turn.

The Government administered oaths to IRS agents, swearing them in as "agents" of the grand jury. Although the administration of such oaths to IRS agents by the Government was unauthorized, there is ample evidence that the jurors understood that the agents were aligned with the prosecutors. At various times a prosecutor referred to the agents as "my agent(s)," and, in discussions with the prosecutors, grand jurors referred to the agents as "your guys" or "your agents." There is nothing in the record to indicate that the oaths administered to the IRS agents caused their reliability or credibility to be elevated, and the effect, if any, on the grand jury's decision to indict was negligible.

The District Court found that, to the prejudice of petitioners, IRS agents gave misleading and inaccurate summaries to the grand jury just prior to the indictment. Because the record does not reveal any prosecutorial misconduct with respect to these summaries, they provide no ground for dismissing the indictment. The District Court's finding that the summaries offered by IRS agents contained evidence that had not been presented to the grand jury in prior testimony boils down to a challenge to the reliability or competence of the evidence presented to the grand jury. We have held that an indictment valid on its face is not subject to such a challenge. *United States v. Calandra*, 414 U.S. 338, 344-345 (1974). To the extent that a challenge is made to the accuracy of the summaries, the mere fact that evidence itself is unreliable is not sufficient to require a dismissal of the indictment. In light of the record, the finding that the prosecutors knew the evidence to be false or misleading, or that the Government caused the agents to testify falsely, is clearly erroneous. Although the Government may have had doubts about the accuracy of certain aspects of the summaries, this is quite different from having knowledge of falsity.

The District Court found that a prosecutor was abusive to an expert defense witness during a recess and in the hearing of some grand jurors. Although the Government concedes that the treatment of the expert tax witness was improper, the witness himself testified that his testimony was unaffected by this misconduct. The prosecutors instructed the grand jury to disregard anything they may have heard in conversations between a prosecutor and a witness, and explained to the grand jury that such conversations should have no influence on its deliberations. In light of these ameliorative measures, there is nothing to indicate that the prosecutor's conduct toward this witness substantially affected the grand jury's evaluation of the testimony or its decision to indict.

The District Court found that the Government granted "pocket immunity" to 23 witnesses during the course of the grand jury proceedings. Without deciding the propriety of granting such immunity to grand jury witnesses, we conclude the conduct did not have a substantial effect on the grand jury's decision to indict, and it does not create grave doubt as to whether it affected the grand jury's decision. Some prosecutors told the grand jury that immunized witnesses retained their Fifth Amendment privilege and could refuse to testify, while other prosecutors stated that the witnesses had no Fifth Amendment privilege, but we fail to see how this could have had a substantial effect on the jury's assessment of the testimony or its decision to indict. The significant point is that the jurors were made aware that these witnesses had made a deal with the Government.

Assuming the Government had threatened to withdraw immunity from a witness in order to manipulate that witness' testimony, this might have given rise to a finding of prejudice. There is no evidence in the record, however, that would support such a finding. The Government told a witness' attorney that if the witness "testified for Mr. Kilpatrick, all bets were off." The attorney, however, ultimately concluded that the prosecution did not mean to imply that immunity would be withdrawn if his client testified for Kilpatrick, but rather that his client would be validly subject to prosecution for perjury. Although the District Court found that the Government's statement was interpreted by the witness to mean that if he testified favorably for Kilpatrick his immunity would be withdrawn, neither Judge Winner nor Judge Kane made a definitive finding that the Government improperly threatened the witness. The witness may have felt threatened by the prosecutor's statement, but his subjective fear cannot be ascribed to governmental misconduct and was, at most, a consideration bearing on the reliability of his testimony.

Finally, the Government permitted two IRS agents to appear before the grand jury at the same time for the purpose of reading transcripts. Although allowing the agents to read to the grand jury in tandem was a violation of Rule 6(d), it was not prejudicial. The agents gave no testimony of their own during the reading of the transcripts. The grand jury was instructed not to ask any questions and the agents were instructed not to answer any questions during the readings. There is no evidence that the agents' reading in tandem enhanced the credibility of the testimony or otherwise allowed the agents to exercise undue influence.

In considering the prejudicial effect of the foregoing instances of alleged misconduct, we note that these incidents occurred as isolated episodes in the course of a 20-month investigation, an investigation involving dozens of witnesses and thousands of documents. In view of this context, those violations that did occur do not, even when considered cumulatively, raise a substantial question, much less a grave doubt, as to whether they had a substantial effect on the grand jury's decision to charge.

Errors of the kind alleged in these cases can be remedied adequately by means other than dismissal. For example, a knowing violation of Rule 6 may be punished as a contempt of court. See Fed. Rule Crim. Proc. 6(e)(2). In addition, the court may direct a prosecutor to show cause why he should not be disciplined and request the bar or the Department of Justice to initiate disciplinary proceedings against him. The court may also chastise the prosecutor in a published opinion. Such remedies allow the court to focus on the culpable individual rather than granting a windfall to the unprejudiced defendant.

We conclude that the District Court had no authority to dismiss the indictment on the basis of prosecutorial misconduct absent a finding that petitioners were prejudiced by such misconduct. The prejudicial inquiry must focus on whether any violations had an effect on the grand jury's decision to indict. If violations did substantially influence this decision, or if there is grave doubt that the decision to indict was free from such substantial influence, the violations cannot be deemed harmless. The record will not support the conclusion that petitioners can meet this standard. The judgment of the Court of Appeals is affirmed. ...

JUSTICE MARSHALL, dissenting.

I cannot concur in the Court's decision to apply harmless-error analysis to violations of Rule 6 of the Federal Rules of Criminal Procedure. I already have outlined my objections to the Court's approach, which converts "Congress' command regarding the proper conduct of grand jury proceedings to a mere form of words, without practical effect." *United States v. Mechanik*, 475 U.S. 66, 84 (1986) (Marshal, J., dissenting). Because of the strict protection of the secrecy of grand jury proceedings, instances of prosecutorial misconduct rarely come to light. This is especially true in the pretrial setting, because defendants' chief source of information about grand jury proceedings is governmental disclosures under the Jencks Act, 18 U.S.C. § 3500, which do not occur until trial is underway. The fact that a prosecutor knows that a Rule 6 violation is unlikely to be discovered gives the Rule little enough bite. To afford the occasional revelation of prosecutorial misconduct the additional insulation of harmless-error analysis leaves Rule 6 toothless. Moreover, as I argued in *Mechanik*, in this context "[a]ny case-by-case analysis to determine whether the defendant was actually prejudiced is simply too speculative to afford defendants meaningful protection, and imposes a difficult burden on the courts that outweighs the benefits to be derived." Given the nature of grand jury proceedings, Rule 6 violations can be deterred and redressed effectively only by a *per se* rule of dismissal. Today's decision reduces Rule 6 to little more than a code of honor that prosecutors can violate with virtual impunity. I respectfully dissent.

Notes

1. Are you persuaded that a harmless error analysis makes sense in the grand jury context? Do you agree that the laundry list of problems uncovered in this case could not have "substantially influenced the grand jury's decision to indict" or raised "grave doubt as to whether the decision to indict was so influenced"? The *Nova Scotia* Court, in articulating a stringent standard for dismissal of an indictment based on prosecutorial abuse, declined to address two additional challenges to an indictment that may be made but were not at issue in this case. As to the first, what types of prosecutorial (or grand juror) misconduct might raise substantial questions regarding potentially sanctionable infringement of "the grand jury's independence"? As to the second, how would defense counsel prove "a history of prosecutorial misconduct, spanning several cases, that is so systematic and pervasive as to raise a substantial and serious question about the fundamental fairness of the process which resulted in the indictment"?

2. The knowing use of perjured testimony by prosecutors violates due process. *See* Mooney v. Holohan, 294 U.S. 103, 110, 112 (1935). Will a prosecutor's use of perjured testimony in the grand jury warrant dismissal of an indictment? "[C]ourts will let an indictment stand, even when supported by false evidence or perjured testimony, as long as the indictment is facially valid and the alleged error is harmless. If a defendant is able to show, however, that the prosecutor knowingly presented false evidence or perjured testimony to the grand jury and there is no other inculpatory evidence, the court has adequate grounds to find that introduction of the evidence amounted to harmful error." *Seventeenth Survey of White Collar Crime*, 39 Am. Crim. L. Rev. 923, 930 (2002) (footnotes omitted) (collecting cases); *see, e.g.*, United States v. Strouse, 286 F.3d 767 (5th Cir. 2002) (holding that perjury before the grand jury that was not knowingly sponsored by the government may not form the basis for a district court's dismissal of an indictment under its limited supervisory power over the grand jury process).

3. Defendants must lodge any objections to the indictment prior to trial unless the challenge is based on jurisdiction or the indictment's failure to charge a crime. *See* Fed. R. Crim. P. 12(b)(2). As noted in *Nova Scotia*, in federal court, an "indictment valid on its face is not subject to challenge" on the grounds of the alleged unreliability, incompetence, or insufficiency of the evidence presented to the grand jury. *See* United States v. Calandra, 414 U.S. 338, 344-45 (1974); *see also* Kaley v. United States, 571 U.S. 320 (2014). A defendant seeking dismissal of an indictment on the basis of asserted prosecutorial abuses faces many obstacles, most notably the difficulty of discovering problems in the grand jury process given the absence of discovery rights and the grand jury secrecy rules, the fact that applicable evidentiary standards permit prosecutors substantial leeway, and a manifest judicial reluctance to dismiss facially valid indictments. If cognizable misconduct is uncovered, prosecutors may be able to cure the problem by superseding the indictment before another grand jury or re-indicting after an indictment is dismissed. Obviously, the application of the *Novia Scotia* harmless error standard further limits the likelihood that the defense will succeed in derailing a prosecution based on prosecutorial abuse of the grand jury process, including violations of Rule 6(e).

It should also be noted that the Supreme Court has held that "an order denying a motion to dismiss an indictment for an alleged violation of Rule 6(e) does not satisfy our 'stringent conditions for qualification as an immediately appealable collateral order,'" and thus cannot be the subject of an interlocutory appeal if the District Court denies the motion prior to trial. Midland Asphalt Corp. v. United States, 489 U.S. 794 (1989). And where the defense's motion for dismissal of an indictment due to non-constitutional grand jury abuses is not decided until after trial (whether because belatedly lodged or because the judge took the defense's pre-trial motion under advisement), the Supreme Court has held that a conviction necessarily demonstrates that the error occurring before the grand jury is harmless beyond a reasonable doubt. *See* United States v. Mechanik, 475 U.S. 66 (1986). Does this combination of rules render prosecutorial "abuses" in grand jury practice largely immune from effective sanction? May judges seek to prevent grand jury abuse by prescribing, under their supervisory powers, rules governing prosecutorial practices in the grand jury?

UNITED STATES v. WILLIAMS
504 U.S. 36 (1992)

JUSTICE SCALIA delivered the opinion of the Court.

The question presented in this case is whether a district court may dismiss an otherwise valid indictment because the Government failed to disclose to the grand jury "substantial exculpatory evidence" in its possession.

On May 4, 1988, respondent John H. Williams, Jr., a Tulsa, Oklahoma, investor, was indicted by a federal grand jury on seven counts of "knowingly mak[ing] [a] false statement or report ... for the purpose of influencing ... the action [of a federally insured financial institution]," in violation of 18 U.S.C. § 1014 (1988 ed., Supp. II). According to the indictment, between September 1984 and November 1985 Williams supplied four Oklahoma banks with "materially false" statements that variously overstated the value of his current assets and interest income in order to influence the banks' actions on his loan requests.

Williams' misrepresentation was allegedly effected through two financial statements provided to the banks, a "Market Value Balance Sheet" and a "Statement of Projected Income and Expense." The former included as "current assets" approximately $6 million in notes receivable from three venture capital companies. Though it contained a disclaimer that these assets were carried at cost rather than at market value, the Government asserted that listing them as "current assets"—*i.e.*, assets quickly reducible to cash—was misleading, since Williams knew that none of the venture capital companies could afford to satisfy the notes in the short term. The second document—the Statement of Projected Income and Expense—allegedly misrepresented Williams' interest income, since it failed to reflect that the interest payments received on the notes of the venture capital companies were funded entirely by Williams' own loans to those companies. The Statement thus falsely implied, according to the Government, that Williams was deriving interest income from "an independent outside source."

Shortly after arraignment, the District Court granted Williams' motion for disclosure of all exculpatory portions of the grand jury transcripts. See *Brady v. Maryland*, 373 U.S. 83 (1963). Upon reviewing this material, Williams demanded that the District Court dismiss the indictment, alleging that the Government had failed to fulfill its obligation ... to present "substantial exculpatory evidence" to the grand jury. His contention was that evidence which the Government had chosen not to present to the grand jury—in particular, Williams' general ledgers and tax returns, and Williams' testimony in his contemporaneous Chapter 11 bankruptcy proceeding—disclosed that, for tax purposes and otherwise, he had regularly accounted for the "notes receivable" (and the interest on them) in a manner consistent with the Balance Sheet and the Income Statement. This, he contended, belied an intent to mislead the banks, and thus directly negated an essential element of the charged offense.

The District Court initially denied Williams' motion, but upon reconsideration ordered the indictment dismissed without prejudice. It found, after a hearing, that the withheld evidence was "relevant to an essential element of the crime charged," created " 'a reasonable doubt about [respondent's] guilt,'" and thus "render[ed] the grand jury's decision to indict gravely suspect." Upon the Government's appeal, the Court of Appeals affirmed the District Court's order. ... It first sustained as not "clearly erroneous" the District Court's determination that the Government had withheld "substantial exculpatory evidence" from the grand jury. It then found that the Government's behavior "'substantially influence[d]'" the grand jury's decision to indict, or at the very least raised a "'grave doubt that the decision to indict was free from such substantial influence.'" Under these circumstances, the Tenth Circuit concluded, it was not an abuse of discretion for the District Court to require the Government to begin anew before the grand jury. We granted certiorari. ...

Respondent does not contend that the Fifth Amendment itself obliges the prosecutor to disclose substantial exculpatory evidence in his possession to the grand jury. Instead, building on our statement that the federal courts "may, within limits, formulate procedural rules not specifically required by the Constitution or the Congress," *United States v. Hasting*, 461 U.S. 499, 505 (1983), he argues that imposition of the Tenth Circuit's disclosure rule is supported by the courts' "supervisory power." We think not. *Hasting*, and the cases that rely upon the principle it expresses, deal strictly with the courts' power to control their *own* procedures. That power has been applied not only to improve the truth-finding process of the trial, but also to prevent parties from reaping benefit or incurring harm from violations of substantive or procedural rules (imposed by the Constitution or laws) governing matters apart from the trial itself. Thus, *Bank of Nova Scotia v. United States*, 487 U.S. 250 (1988), makes clear that the supervisory power can be used to dismiss an indictment because of misconduct before the grand jury, at least where that misconduct amounts to a violation of one of those "few, clear rules which were carefully drafted and approved by this Court and by Congress to ensure the integrity of the grand jury's functions."[45]

---

[45] [Court's footnote 6:] Rule 6 of the Federal Rules of Criminal Procedure contains a number of such rules, providing, for example, that "no person other than the jurors may be present while the grand jury

We did not hold in *Bank of Nova Scotia*, however, that the courts' supervisory power could be used, not merely as a means of enforcing or vindicating legally compelled standards of prosecutorial conduct before the grand jury, but as a means of *prescribing* those standards of prosecutorial conduct in the first instance—just as it may be used as a means of establishing standards of prosecutorial conduct before the courts themselves. It is this latter exercise that respondent demands. Because the grand jury is an institution separate from the courts, over whose functioning the courts do not preside, we think it clear that, as a general matter at least, no such "supervisory" judicial authority exists, and that the disclosure rule applied here exceeded the Tenth Circuit's authority.

"[R]ooted in long centuries of Anglo-American history," the grand jury is mentioned in the Bill of Rights, but not in the body of the Constitution. It has not been textually assigned, therefore, to any of the branches described in the first three Articles. It "'is a constitutional fixture in its own right.'" In fact the whole theory of its function is that it belongs to no branch of the institutional Government, serving as a kind of buffer or referee between the Government and the people. Although the grand jury normally operates, of course, in the courthouse and under judicial auspices, its institutional relationship with the Judicial Branch has traditionally been, so to speak, at arm's length. Judges' direct involvement in the functioning of the grand jury has generally been confined to the constitutive one of calling the grand jurors together and administering their oaths of office.

The grand jury's functional independence from the Judicial Branch is evident both in the scope of its power to investigate criminal wrongdoing and in the manner in which that power is exercised. "Unlike [a] [c]ourt, whose jurisdiction is predicated upon a specific case or controversy, the grand jury 'can investigate merely on suspicion that the law is being violated, or even because it wants assurance that it is not.'" It need not identify the offender it suspects, or even "the precise nature of the offense" it is investigating. The grand jury requires no authorization from its constituting court to initiate an investigation, nor does the prosecutor require leave of court to seek a grand jury indictment. And in its day-to-day functioning, the grand jury generally operates without the interference of a presiding judge. It swears in its own witnesses, and deliberates in total secrecy.

True, the grand jury cannot compel the appearance of witnesses and the production of evidence, and must appeal to the court when such compulsion is required. And the court will refuse to lend its assistance when the compulsion the grand jury seeks would override rights accorded by the Constitution, or even testimonial privileges recognized by the common law. Even in this setting, however, we have insisted that the grand jury remain "free to pursue its investigations unhindered by external influence or supervision so long as it does not trench upon the legitimate rights of any witness called before it." Recognizing this tradition of independence, we have said that the Fifth Amendment's "constitutional guarantee *presupposes* an investigative body 'acting independently of either prosecuting attorney *or judge*' ..."

No doubt in view of the grand jury proceeding's status as other than a constituent element of a "criminal prosecutio[n]," U.S. Const., Amdt. 6, we have said that certain constitutional protections afforded defendants in criminal proceedings have no application before that body. The Double Jeopardy Clause of the Fifth Amendment does not bar a grand jury from returning an indictment when a prior grand jury has refused to do so. We have twice suggested, though not held, that the Sixth Amendment right to counsel does not attach when

---

is deliberating or voting," Rule 6(d), and placing strict controls on disclosure of "matters occurring before the grand jury," Rule 6(e). Additional standards of behavior for prosecutors (and others) are set forth in the United States Code. See 18 U.S.C. §§ 6002, 6003 (setting forth procedures for granting a witness immunity from prosecution); § 1623 (criminalizing false declarations before grand jury); § 2515 (prohibiting grand jury use of unlawfully intercepted wire or oral communications); § 1622 (criminalizing subornation of perjury). That some of the misconduct alleged in *Bank of Nova Scotia v. United States*, 487 U.S. 250 (1988), was not specifically proscribed by Rule, statute, or the Constitution does not make the case stand for a judicially prescribable grand jury code, as the dissent suggests. All of the allegations of violation were dismissed by the Court—without considering their validity in law—for failure to meet *Nova Scotia*'s dismissal standard.

an individual is summoned to appear before a grand jury, even if he is the subject of the investigation. See *United States v. Mandujano*, 425 U.S. 564, 581 (1976) (plurality opinion); *In re Groban*, 352 U.S. 330, 333 (1957). And although "the grand jury may not force a witness to answer questions in violation of [the Fifth Amendment's] constitutional guarantee" against self-incrimination, our cases suggest that an indictment obtained through the use of evidence previously obtained in violation of the privilege against self-incrimination "is nevertheless valid."

Given the grand jury's operational separateness from its constituting court, it should come as no surprise that we have been reluctant to invoke the judicial supervisory power as a basis for prescribing modes of grand jury procedure. Over the years, we have received many requests to exercise supervision over the grand jury's evidence-taking process, but we have refused them all, including some more appealing than the one presented today. In *United States v. Calandra*, a grand jury witness faced questions that were allegedly based upon physical evidence the Government had obtained through a violation of the Fourth Amendment; we rejected the proposal that the exclusionary rule be extended to grand jury proceedings, because of "the potential injury to the historic role and functions of the grand jury." In *Costello v. United States*, we declined to enforce the hearsay rule in grand jury proceedings, since that "would run counter to the whole history of the grand jury institution, in which laymen conduct their inquiries unfettered by technical rules."

These authorities suggest that any power federal courts may have to fashion, on their own initiative, rules of grand jury procedure is a very limited one, not remotely comparable to the power they maintain over their own proceedings. It certainly would not permit judicial reshaping of the grand jury institution, substantially altering the traditional relationships between the prosecutor, the constituting court, and the grand jury itself. As we proceed to discuss, that would be the consequence of the proposed rule here.

Respondent argues that the Court of Appeals' rule can be justified as a sort of Fifth Amendment "common law," a necessary means of assuring the constitutional right to the judgment "of an independent and informed grand jury." Respondent makes a generalized appeal to functional notions: Judicial supervision of the quantity and quality of the evidence relied upon by the grand jury plainly facilitates, he says, the grand jury's performance of its twin historical responsibilities, *i.e.*, bringing to trial those who may be justly accused and shielding the innocent from unfounded accusation and prosecution. We do not agree. The rule would neither preserve nor enhance the traditional functioning of the institution that the Fifth Amendment demands. To the contrary, requiring the prosecutor to present exculpatory as well as inculpatory evidence would alter the grand jury's historical role, transforming it from an accusatory to an adjudicatory body.

It is axiomatic that the grand jury sits not to determine guilt or innocence, but to assess whether there is adequate basis for bringing a criminal charge. That has always been so; and to make the assessment it has always been thought sufficient to hear only the prosecutor's side. ...

Imposing upon the prosecutor a legal obligation to present exculpatory evidence in his possession would be incompatible with this system. If a "balanced" assessment of the entire matter is the objective, surely the first thing to be done—rather than requiring the prosecutor to say what he knows in defense of the target of the investigation—is to entitle the target to tender his own defense. To require the former while denying (as we do) the latter would be quite absurd. It would also be quite pointless, since it would merely invite the target to circumnavigate the system by delivering his exculpatory evidence to the prosecutor, whereupon it would *have* to be passed on to the grand jury—unless the prosecutor is willing to take the chance that a court will not deem the evidence important enough to qualify for mandatory disclosure.

Respondent acknowledges (as he must) that the "common law" of the grand jury is not violated if the *grand jury itself* chooses to hear no more evidence than that which suffices to convince it an indictment is proper. Thus, had the Government offered to familiarize the grand jury in this case with the five boxes of financial statements and deposition testimony alleged to contain exculpatory information, and had the grand jury rejected the offer as pointless, respondent would presumably agree that the resulting indictment would have been valid. Respondent insists, however, that courts must require the modern prosecutor to alert the grand jury to the nature and extent of the available exculpatory evidence, because otherwise the grand jury "merely functions as an arm of the prosecution." We reject the attempt to convert a nonexistent duty of the grand jury itself into an obligation of the prosecutor. The authority of the prosecutor to seek an indictment has long been understood to be "coterminous with the authority of the grand jury to entertain [the prosecutor's] charges." If the grand jury has no obligation to consider all "substantial exculpatory" evidence, we do not understand how the prosecutor can be said to have a binding obligation to present it. ...

... [R]espondent argues that a rule requiring the prosecutor to disclose exculpatory evidence to the grand jury would, by removing from the docket unjustified prosecutions, save valuable judicial time. That depends, we suppose, upon what the ratio would turn out to be between unjustified prosecutions eliminated and grand jury indictments challenged—for the latter as well as the former consume "valuable judicial time." We need not pursue the matter; if there is an advantage to the proposal, Congress is free to prescribe it. For the reasons set forth above, however, we conclude that courts have no authority to prescribe such a duty pursuant to their inherent supervisory authority over their own proceedings. ...

JUSTICE STEVENS, with whom JUSTICE BLACKMUN and JUSTICE O'CONNOR join, and with whom JUSTICE THOMAS joins as to [excerpted portion], dissenting.

The Court's opinion announces [an] important change[] in the law. ... [I]t concludes that a federal court has no power to enforce the prosecutor's obligation to protect the fundamental fairness of proceedings before the grand jury. ...

It is ... clear that the prosecutor has ... [a] duty to refrain from improper methods calculated to produce a wrongful indictment. Indeed, the prosecutor's duty to protect the fundamental fairness of judicial proceedings assumes special importance when he is presenting evidence to a grand jury. As the Court of Appeals for the Third Circuit recognized, "the costs of continued unchecked prosecutorial misconduct" before the grand jury are particularly substantial because there

> "the prosecutor operates without the check of a judge or a trained legal adversary, and virtually immune from public scrutiny. The prosecutor's abuse of his special relationship to the grand jury poses an enormous risk to defendants as well. For while in theory a trial provides the defendant with a full opportunity to contest and disprove the charges against him, in practice, the handing up of an indictment will often have a devastating personal and professional impact that a later dismissal or acquittal can never undo. Where the potential for abuse is so great, and the consequences of a mistaken indictment so serious, the ethical responsibilities of the prosecutor, and the obligation of the judiciary to protect against even the appearance of unfairness, are correspondingly heightened." ...

In an opinion that I find difficult to comprehend, the Court today ... seems to suggest that the court has no authority to supervise the conduct of the prosecutor in grand jury proceedings so long as he follows the dictates of the Constitution, applicable statutes, and Rule 6 of the Federal Rules of Criminal Procedure. The Court purports to support this conclusion by invoking the doctrine of separation of powers and citing a string of cases in which we have declined to impose categorical restraints on the grand jury. Needless to say, the Court's reasoning is unpersuasive.

Although the grand jury has not been "textually assigned" to "any of the branches described in the first three Articles" of the Constitution, it is not an autonomous body completely beyond the reach of the other branches. Throughout its life, from the moment it is convened until it is discharged, the grand jury is subject to the control of the court. As Judge Learned Hand recognized over 60 years ago, "a grand jury is neither an officer nor an agent of the United States, but a part of the court." This Court has similarly characterized the grand jury:

"A grand jury is clothed with great independence in many areas, but it remains an appendage of the court, powerless to perform its investigative function without the court's aid, because powerless itself to compel the testimony of witnesses. It is the court's process which summons the witness to attend and give testimony, and it is the court which must compel a witness to testify if, after appearing, he refuses to do so."

This Court has, of course, long recognized that the grand jury has wide latitude to investigate violations of federal law as it deems appropriate and need not obtain permission from either the court or the prosecutor. Correspondingly, we have acknowledged that "its operation generally is unrestrained by the technical procedural and evidentiary rules governing the conduct of criminal trials." But this is because Congress and the Court have generally thought it best not to impose procedural restraints on the grand jury; it is not because they lack all power to do so.[46]

To the contrary, the Court has recognized that it has the authority to create and enforce limited rules applicable in grand jury proceedings. Thus, for example, the Court has said that the grand jury "may not itself violate a valid privilege, whether established by the Constitution, statutes, or the common law." And the Court may prevent a grand jury from violating such a privilege by quashing or modifying a subpoena, or issuing a protective order forbidding questions in violation of the privilege. Moreover, there are, as the Court notes, a series of cases in which we declined to impose categorical restraints on the grand jury. In none of those cases, however, did we question our power to reach a contrary result.

Although the Court recognizes that it may invoke its supervisory authority to fashion and enforce privilege rules applicable in grand jury proceedings, and suggests that it may also invoke its supervisory authority to fashion other limited rules of grand jury procedure, it concludes that it has no authority to *prescribe* "standards of prosecutorial conduct before the grand jury," because that would alter the grand jury's historic role as an independent, inquisitorial institution. I disagree.

We do not protect the integrity and independence of the grand jury by closing our eyes to the countless forms of prosecutorial misconduct that may occur inside the secrecy of the grand jury room. After all, the grand jury is not merely an investigatory body; it also serves as a "protector of citizens against arbitrary and oppressive governmental action." ... It blinks reality to say that the grand jury can adequately perform this important historic role if it is intentionally misled by the prosecutor—on whose knowledge of the law and facts of the underlying criminal investigation the jurors will, of necessity, rely.

Unlike the Court, I am unwilling to hold that countless forms of prosecutorial misconduct must be tolerated—no matter how prejudicial they may be, or how seriously they may distort the legitimate function of the grand jury—simply because they are not proscribed by Rule 6 of the Federal Rules of Criminal Procedure or a statute that is applicable in grand jury proceedings. Such a sharp break with the traditional role of the federal judiciary is unprecedented, unwarranted, and unwise. Unrestrained prosecutorial misconduct in grand jury proceedings is inconsistent with the administration of justice in the federal courts and should be redressed in appropriate cases by the dismissal of indictments obtained by improper methods.

What, then, is the proper disposition of this case? I agree with the Government that the prosecutor is not required to place all exculpatory evidence before the grand jury. A grand jury proceeding is an *ex parte* investigatory proceeding to determine whether there is probable cause to believe a violation of the criminal laws has occurred, not a trial. Requiring the prosecutor to ferret out and present all evidence that could be used at trial to create a reasonable doubt as to the defendant's guilt would be inconsistent with the purpose of the grand jury proceeding and would place significant burdens on the investigation. But that does not mean that the prosecutor may mislead the grand jury into believing that there is probable cause to indict by

---

[46] [Dissent's footnote 10:] Indeed, even the Court acknowledges that Congress has the power to regulate the grand jury, for it concedes that Congress "is free to prescribe" a rule requiring the prosecutor to disclose substantial exculpatory evidence to the grand jury.

withholding clear evidence to the contrary. I thus agree with the Department of Justice that "when a prosecutor conducting a grand jury inquiry is personally aware of substantial evidence which directly negates the guilt of a subject of the investigation, the prosecutor must present or otherwise disclose such evidence to the grand jury before seeking an indictment against such a person." U.S. Dept. of Justice, United States Attorneys' Manual § 9-11.233, p. 88 (1988). ...

Notes

1. Who has the better of the supervisory power debate? What implications does the majority's holding have for judicial efforts to respond to prosecutorial abuses?

2. The Court apparently believes that Congress, at least, has the power to regulate the conduct of prosecutors practicing before this fourth branch of government. *Should* Congress codify the policy articulated in the U.S. Attorney's Manual? *See* Michael Cassidy, *Toward a More Independent Grand Jury: Recasting and Enforcing the Prosecutor's Duty to Disclose Exculpatory Evidence*, 13 Geo. J. Legal Ethics 361, 385-92 (2000) (surveying state law approaches). Should Congress alternatively provide that defense counsel may accompany witnesses into the grand jury room and in some circumstances may produce evidence for the grand jury's consideration? *See id.* at 384 (same). What difficulties might accompanying witnesses into the grand jury present for defense counsel?

3. Another McDade Amendment issue raised in the grand jury context is whether state rules may require prosecutors to present any exculpatory evidence in their possession to the grand jury. Model Rule of Professional Conduct 3.8, which sets for the "special responsibilities of a prosecutor," requires a prosecutor to "refrain from prosecuting a charge that the prosecutor knows is not supported by probable cause." Model Rule of Professional Conduct 3.3(d), which concerns lawyers' duty of candor to the tribunal, states that "[i]n an ex parte proceeding, a lawyer shall inform the tribunal of all material facts known to the lawyer which will enable the tribunal to make an informed decision, whether or not the facts are adverse." Do these ethical rules mandate that prosecutors provide substantially exculpatory evidence to a grand jury? *See* Cassidy, *supra*, at 377-83. Some jurisdictions have ethical rules specifically addressing this subject. For example, D.C. Rules of Prof'l Conduct R. 3.8(e) provides that prosecutor, in presenting case to grand jury, shall not "intentionally interfere with the independence of the grand jury, preempt a function of the grand jury, abuse the processes of the grand jury, or fail to bring to the attention of the grand jury material facts tending substantially to negate the existence of probable cause." Should prosecutorial abuses in the grand jury be policed by ethics authorities? Are these standards enforceable only through state bar disciplinary proceedings or does the McDade Amendment give federal courts the authority, even under *Williams*, to enforce these rules through dismissal of an indictment?

4. In 1997, Congress enacted the so-called "Hyde Amendment," 18 U.S.C. § 3006A, which authorizes courts in federal criminal cases to award "to a prevailing party, other than the United States, a reasonable attorney's fee and other litigation expenses, where the court finds that the position of the United States was vexatious, frivolous or in bad faith." *See generally* Irvin B. Nathan & John C. Massaro, *Shekels & Hyde: Little Money But Many Lessons From the Early Years of the Hyde Amendment*, White Collar Crime 2000, at C-1 (ABA 2000). "Prevailing parties" include not only defendants who prevail after trial, but also those who are successful in challenging an indictment. *See id.* at C2-C3. As the Third Circuit explained in 2013:

> [T]he Hyde Amendment "places a daunting obstacle before defendants who seek to obtain attorneys fees and costs from the government following a successful defense of criminal charges." In particular, a defendant must show that the government's position underlying the prosecution amounts to prosecutorial misconduct—a prosecution brought vexatiously, in bad faith, or so utterly without foundation in law or fact as to be frivolous."
> "The defendant bears the burden of meeting any one of three grounds under the statute, and acquittal by itself does not suffice."

That burden is made more difficult by the approach courts take in assessing the government's litigation position. In determining whether a position is vexatious, frivolous or in bad faith, courts "make only one finding, which should be based on the case as an inclusive whole. A count-by-count analysis is inconsistent with this approach." In addition, when the legal issue is one of first impression, a court should be wary of awarding fees and costs so as not to "chill the ardor of prosecutors and prevent them from prosecuting with earnestness and vigor." ...

With respect to the three grounds for relief under the statute, courts have held that a "vexatious" position is one that is "without reasonable or probable cause or excuse." ... Courts have interpreted a "frivolous" action as one that is "groundless[,] with little prospect of success." ... Finally, "bad faith" means "not simply bad judgment or negligence, but rather it implies the conscious doing of a wrong because of dishonest purpose or moral obliquity...."

United States v. Manzo, 712 F.3d 805, 810-11 (3d Cir. 2013); *see also* United States v. Shaygan, 676 F.3d 1237 (11th Cir. 2012).

Does this avenue for relief provide an effective means of ensuring that prosecutors police their own? *See* Peter J. Henning, *Prosecutorial Misconduct in Grand Jury Investigations*, 51 S.C. L. Rev. 1 (1999).

Chapter 14

DISCOVERY

Chapter 13 highlights the power that prosecutors wield in investigating white-collar cases through the grand jury. In particular, it illustrates prosecutors' ability to range freely in their pre-indictment search for information potentially relevant to the prosecution or defense of a case, subject only to claims of privilege and the very permissive limits set by the Constitution and federal rules. This Chapter concentrates on the much more limited opportunities open to defense counsel to obtain information that may be critical to their effectiveness in heading off a prosecution or in defending against any eventual indictment.

As outlined in Chapter 1 (Introduction), pre-indictment practice is often the critical phase of white-collar defense work. Yet prior to indictment, the defense has no entitlement to discovery under the Constitution or federal law. At this stage, counsel must rely on informal or collateral legal mechanisms to secure the information needed to mount an effective defense. Such means may include: entering into a "joint defense" with other subjects or targets of the investigation, pursuant to which the joint defense participants may pool information without fear that such sharing will expose the information to discovery by the government or others (*see* Chapter 18 (Representation)); attempting to garner from communications with the prosecutor what is being investigated and the evidence that has and has not been found; lodging Freedom of Information Act ("FOIA") requests;[1] using whatever concurrent civil proceedings may be ongoing to obtain discovery pertinent to the criminal case (*see* Chapter 20 (Parallel Proceedings)); and depending on the kindness of witnesses to voluntarily share the information (testimonial and documentary) upon which the government is seeking to build a case.

After indictment, the playing field becomes slightly more even, but the government's pre-indictment informational advantage certainly is not erased by existing disclosure rules. The following materials cover three principal post-indictment disclosure mechanisms: (1) the government's obligations under *Brady v. Maryland*,[2] which provides that prosecutors may not suppress materially exculpatory evidence in the government's possession; (2) Fed. R. Crim. P. 16, which governs (reciprocal) pre-trial discovery obligations; and (3) the Jencks Act[3] and Fed. R. Crim. P. 26.2, which govern the (reciprocal) disclosure of witness statements.[4] In many

---

[1] 5 U.S.C. § 552.

[2] 373 U.S. 83 (1963).

[3] 18 U.S.C. § 3500. In this statute, Congress codified, with certain alterations, the Supreme Court's decision in *Jencks v. United States*, 353 U.S. 657 (1957) (holding under Court's supervisory power that federal criminal defendants are entitled under certain circumstances to receive, for impeachment purposes, relevant statements of a government witness in possession of the government).

[4] Two other avenues for securing information from the government deserve mention. First, the defense may move for a bill of particulars under Fed. R. Crim. P. 7(f). *See* John R. Wing & Michael J. Bresnick,

white-collar cases, information potentially helpful to the defense may be held by persons or entities who are not involved in the prosecution and who are not subject to the above disclosure rules. Accordingly, these materials touch upon some of the challenges facing defense counsel in obtaining needed evidence from third parties under Fed. R. Crim. P. 17.

Readers are cautioned that there are many levels of rules applicable in the discovery realm and a great deal of variation in those rules among jurisdictions. Thus, for example, although Supreme Court precedents and federal statutes and rules provide some common parameters, how those precedents, statutes, and rules are interpreted and applied vary in important respects among the circuits. Further, many districts, U.S. Attorneys Offices, and even individual prosecutors follow their own policies and practices.[5] Potentially applicable ethical standards may differ with the jurisdiction. Accordingly, both prosecutors and defense counsel must be careful to familiarize themselves with the law and the practice prevailing in their jurisdiction.[6] Prosecutors, in particular, however, must focus on their discovery obligations, as an ethical and a professional matter.

Recently, there has been a drumbeat for reform of Department of Justice policy and procedures regarding criminal disclosure, spurred in part by a number of well-publicized instances in which Assistants did not meet their *Brady* or other disclosure obligations. The most visible of these failures led to the decision by Attorney General Eric Holder to drop all charges against Senator Ted Stevens after he had been convicted following a lengthy jury trial. The judge in the case issued a blistering denunciation of the government's practices, and commissioned an independent investigation of the shortcomings of the Stevens prosecution. That investigation concluded that the investigation and prosecution of Senator Stevens were "'permeated by the systematic concealment of significant exculpatory evidence which would have independently corroborated his defense and his testimony, and seriously damaged the testimony and credibility of the government's key witness.'"[7] As a consequence of this case and other prosecutorial missteps, The Department issued additional guidance to prosecutors, which is examined within.

Defense Tool Extraordinaire—Bill of Particulars, 7 Bus. Crimes Bull. 1 (May 2000). Rule 7(f) "permits a defendant to seek a bill of particulars to identify with sufficient particularity the nature of the charge pending against him, thereby enabling the defendant to prepare for trial, to prevent surprise, and to interpose a plea of double jeopardy should he be prosecuted a second time for the same offense." United States v. Bortnovsky, 820 F.2d 572, 574 (2d Cir. 1987). Trial courts have a great deal of discretion in passing on a motion for a bill of particulars, *see* United States v. Davidoff, 845 F.2d 1151, 1154 (2d Cir. 1988), and generally are reluctant to accede to defense requests to transform the bill of particulars into a discovery device. Second, upon the request of the accused, prosecutors are also required to "provide reasonable notice in advance of trial, or during trial if the court excuses pretrial notice on good cause shown, of the general nature" of any evidence it "intends to introduce at trial" of the defendant's other crimes, wrongs or acts under Fed. R. Evid. 404(b). This requirement applies to the prosecution "regardless of how it intends to use the extrinsic act evidence at trial, i.e., during its case-in-chief, for impeachment, or for possible rebuttal." Fed. R. Evid. 404(b), 1991 Amendment Advisory Committee Notes.

[5] *See, e.g.*, Laurie L. Levenson, *Working Outside the Rules: The Undefined Responsibilities of Federal Prosecutors*, 26 Fordham Urb. L.J. 553, 562-63 (1999).

[6] *See Panel Discussion: Criminal Discovery in Practice*, 15 Ga. St. U. L. Rev. 781, 795, 789 (1999).

[7] *In re* Special Proceedings, Order, Misc. No. 09-0198 (EGS) (Nov. 21, 2011) (quoting report of independent investigators Henry F. Schuelke, III, William B. Shields); *see also* Robert M. Cary, *Exculpatory Evidence: A Call for Reform after the Unlawful Prosecution of Senator Ted Stevens*, 36 Litig. 34 (Summer 2010). For an excellent discussion of the entire Stevens prosecution, see Rob Cary, Not Guilty: The Unlawful Prosecution of U.S. Senator Ted Stevens (Thomson Reuters 2014).

A. "BRADY" MATERIAL

BRADY v. MARYLAND
373 U.S. 83 (1963)

Opinion of the Court by MR. JUSTICE DOUGLAS, announced by MR. JUSTICE BRENNAN.

Petitioner and a companion, Boblit, were found guilty of murder in the first degree and were sentenced to death, their convictions being affirmed by the Court of Appeals of Maryland. Their trials were separate, petitioner being tried first. At his trial Brady took the stand and admitted his participation in the crime, but he claimed that Boblit did the actual killing. And, in his summation to the jury, Brady's counsel conceded that Brady was guilty of murder in the first degree, asking only that the jury return that verdict "without capital punishment." Prior to the trial petitioner's counsel had requested the prosecution to allow him to examine Boblit's extrajudicial statements. Several of those statements were shown to him; but one dated July 9, 1958, in which Boblit admitted the actual homicide, was withheld by the prosecution and did not come to petitioner's notice until after he had been tried, convicted, and sentenced, and after his conviction had been affirmed. ...

We now hold that the suppression by the prosecution of evidence favorable to an accused upon request violates due process where the evidence is material either to guilt or to punishment, irrespective of the good faith or bad faith of the prosecution.

The principle ... is not punishment of society for misdeeds of a prosecutor but avoidance of an unfair trial to the accused. Society wins not only when the guilty are convicted but when criminal trials are fair; our system of the administration of justice suffers when any accused is treated unfairly. An inscription on the walls of the Department of Justice states the proposition candidly for the federal domain: "The United States wins its point whenever justice is done its citizens in the courts." A prosecution that withholds evidence on demand of an accused which, if made available, would tend to exculpate him or reduce the penalty helps shape a trial that bears heavily on the defendant. That casts the prosecutor in the role of an architect of a proceeding that does not comport with standards of justice, even though, as in the present case, his action is not "the result of guile," to use the words of the Court of Appeals.

UNITED STATES v. BAGLEY
473 U.S. 667 (1985)

JUSTICE BLACKMUN announced the judgment of the Court and delivered an opinion of the Court except as to Part III.[8]

In *Brady* v. *Maryland*, 373 U.S. 83, 87 (1963), this Court held that "the suppression by the prosecution of evidence favorable to an accused upon request violates due process where the evidence is material either to guilt or punishment." The issue in the present case concerns the standard of materiality to be applied in determining whether a conviction should be reversed because the prosecutor failed to disclose requested evidence that could have been used to impeach Government witnesses.

I

---

[8] [Ed.:] Only Justice O'Connor joined Part III of Justice Blackmun's opinion. Three justices joined an opinion concurring in part and concurring in the judgment, in which they agreed with the definition of "materiality" Justice Blackmun announced in Part III.

In October 1977, respondent Hughes Anderson Bagley was indicted in the Western District of Washington on 15 charges of violating federal narcotics and firearms statutes. On November 18, 24 days before trial, respondent filed a discovery motion. The sixth paragraph of that motion requested:

> "The names and addresses of witnesses that the government intends to call at trial. Also the prior criminal records of witnesses, and any deals, promises or inducements made to witnesses in exchange for their testimony." ...

The Government's two principal witnesses at the trial were James F. O'Connor and Donald E. Mitchell. O'Connor and Mitchell were state law-enforcement officers employed by the Milwaukee Railroad as private security guards. Between April and June 1977, they assisted the federal Bureau of Alcohol, Tobacco and Firearms (ATF) in conducting an undercover investigation of respondent.

The Government's response to the discovery motion did not disclose that any "deals, promises or inducements" had been made to O'Connor or Mitchell. ...

Respondent waived his right to a jury trial and was tried before the court in December 1977. At the trial, O'Connor and Mitchell testified about both the firearms and the narcotics charges. On December 23, the court found respondent guilty on the narcotics charges, but not guilty on the firearms charges.

In mid-1980, respondent filed requests for information pursuant to the Freedom of Information Act and to the Privacy Act of 1974, 5 U.S.C. §§ 552 and 552a. He received in response copies of ATF form contracts that O'Connor and Mitchell had signed on May 3, 1977. Each form was entitled "Contract for Purchase of Information and Payment of Lump Sum Therefor." The printed portion of the form stated that the vendor "will provide" information to ATF and that "upon receipt of such information by the Regional Director, Bureau of Alcohol, Tobacco and Firearms, or his representative, and upon the accomplishment of the objective sought to be obtained by the use of such information to the satisfaction of said Regional Director, the United States will pay to said vendor a sum commensurate with services and information rendered." Each form contained the following typewritten description of services:

> "That he will provide information regarding T–I and other violations committed by Hughes A. Bagley, Jr.; that he will purchase evidence for ATF; that he will cut [sic] in an undercover capacity for ATF; that he will assist ATF in gathering of evidence and testify against the violator in federal court."

The figure "$300.00" was handwritten in each form on a line entitled "Sum to Be Paid to Vendor."

Because these contracts had not been disclosed to respondent in response to his pretrial discovery motion,[9] respondent moved under 28 U.S.C. § 2255 to vacate his sentence. He alleged that the Government's failure to disclose the contracts, which he could have used to impeach O'Connor and Mitchell, violated his right to due process under *Brady* v. *Maryland*, [373 U.S. 83 (1963)].

The motion came before the same District Judge who had presided at respondent's bench trial. An evidentiary hearing was held before a Magistrate. The Magistrate found that the printed form contracts were blank when O'Connor and Mitchell signed them and were not signed by an ATF representative until after the trial. He also found that on January 4, 1978, following the trial and decision in respondent's case, ATF made payments of $300 to both O'Connor and Mitchell pursuant to the contracts. ...

---

[9] [Court's footnote 4:] The Assistant United States Attorney who prosecuted respondent stated in stipulated testimony that he had not known that the contracts existed and that he would have furnished them to respondent had he known of them.

The District Court adopted each of the Magistrate's findings except for the last one to the effect that "[n]either O'Connor nor Mitchell expected to receive the payment of $300 or any payment from the United States for their testimony." Instead, the court found that it was "probable" that O'Connor and Mitchell expected to receive compensation, in addition to their expenses, for their assistance, "though perhaps not for their testimony." The District Court also expressly rejected the Magistrate's conclusion that:

> "Because neither witness was promised or expected payment for his testimony, the United States did not withhold, during pretrial discovery, information as to any 'deals, promises or inducements' to these witnesses. Nor did the United States suppress evidence favorable to the defendant, in violation of *Brady* v. *Maryland*."

The District Court found beyond a reasonable doubt, however, that had the existence of the agreements been disclosed to it during trial, the disclosure would have had no effect upon its finding that the Government had proved beyond a reasonable doubt that respondent was guilty of the offenses for which he had been convicted. The District Court reasoned: Almost all of the testimony of both witnesses was devoted to the firearms charges in the indictment. Respondent, however, was acquitted on those charges. The testimony of O'Connor and Mitchell concerning the narcotics charges was relatively very brief. On cross-examination, respondent's counsel did not seek to discredit their testimony as to the facts of distribution but rather sought to show that the controlled substances in question came from supplies that had been prescribed for respondent's personal use. The answers of O'Connor and Mitchell to this line of cross-examination tended to be favorable to respondent. Thus, the claimed impeachment evidence would not have been helpful to respondent and would not have affected the outcome of the trial. Accordingly, the District Court denied respondent's motion to vacate his sentence. ...

II

The holding in *Brady* v. *Maryland* requires disclosure only of evidence that is both favorable to the accused and "material either to guilt or to punishment." The Court explained in *United States* v. *Agurs*, 427 U.S. 97, 104 (1976): "A fair analysis of the holding in *Brady* indicates that implicit in the requirement of materiality is a concern that the suppressed evidence might have affected the outcome of the trial." The evidence suppressed in *Brady* would have been admissible only on the issue of punishment and not on the issue of guilt, and therefore could have affected only Brady's sentence and not his conviction. Accordingly, the Court affirmed the lower court's restriction of Brady's new trial to the issue of punishment.

The *Brady* rule is based on the requirement of due process. Its purpose is not to displace the adversary system as the primary means by which truth is uncovered, but to ensure that a miscarriage of justice does not occur. Thus, the prosecutor is not required to deliver his entire file to defense counsel,[10] but only to disclose evidence favorable to the accused that, if suppressed, would deprive the defendant of a fair trial:

> "For unless the omission deprived the defendant of a fair trial, there was no constitutional violation requiring that the verdict be set aside; and absent a constitutional violation, there was no breach of the prosecutor's constitutional duty to disclose. ...
> " ... But to reiterate a critical point, the prosecutor will not have violated his constitutional duty of disclosure unless his omission is of sufficient significance to result in the denial of the defendant's right to a fair trial."

---

[10] [Court's footnote 7:] An interpretation of *Brady* to create a broad, constitutionally required right of discovery "would entirely alter the character and balance of our present systems of criminal justice." Furthermore, a rule that the prosecutor commits error by any failure to disclose evidence favorable to the accused, no matter how insignificant, would impose an impossible burden on the prosecutor and would undermine the interest in the finality of judgments.

In *Brady* and *Agurs*, the prosecutor failed to disclose exculpatory evidence. In the present case, the prosecutor failed to disclose evidence that the defense might have used to impeach the Government's witnesses by showing bias or interest. Impeachment evidence, however, as well as exculpatory evidence, falls within the *Brady* rule. See *Giglio* v. *United States*, 405 U.S. 150, 154 (1972). Such evidence is "evidence favorable to an accused," so that, if disclosed and used effectively, it may make the difference between conviction and acquittal. ...

This Court has rejected any ... distinction between impeachment evidence and exculpatory evidence. In *Giglio* v. *United States*, the Government failed to disclose impeachment evidence similar to the evidence at issue in the present case, that is, a promise made to the key Government witness that he would not be prosecuted if he testified for the Government. This Court said:

> "When the 'reliability of a given witness may well be determinative of guilt or innocence,' nondisclosure of evidence affecting credibility falls within th[e] general rule [of *Brady*]. We do not, however, automatically require a new trial whenever 'a combing of the prosecutors' files after the trial has disclosed evidence possibly useful to the defense but not likely to have changed the verdict. ... 'A finding of materiality of the evidence is required under *Brady*. ... A new trial is required if 'the false testimony could ... in any reasonable likelihood have affected the judgment of the jury. ...'" ...

III

It remains to determine the standard of materiality applicable to the nondisclosed evidence at issue in this case. Our starting point is the framework for evaluating the materiality of *Brady* evidence established in *United States* v. *Agurs*. The Court in *Agurs* distinguished three situations involving the discovery, after trial, of information favorable to the accused that had been known to the prosecution but unknown to the defense. The first situation was the prosecutor's knowing use of perjured testimony or, equivalently, the prosecutor's knowing failure to disclose that testimony used to convict the defendant was false. The Court noted the well-established rule that "a conviction obtained by the knowing use of perjured testimony is fundamentally unfair, and must be set aside if there is any reasonable likelihood that the false testimony could have affected the judgment of the jury." Although this rule is stated in terms that treat the knowing use of perjured testimony as error subject to harmless-error review, it may as easily be stated as a materiality standard under which the fact that testimony is perjured is considered material unless failure to disclose it would be harmless beyond a reasonable doubt. The Court in *Agurs* justified this standard of materiality on the ground that the knowing use of perjured testimony involves prosecutorial misconduct and, more importantly, involves "a corruption of the truth-seeking function of the trial process."

At the other extreme is the situation in *Agurs* itself, where the defendant does not make a *Brady* request and the prosecutor fails to disclose certain evidence favorable to the accused. The Court rejected a harmless-error rule in that situation, because under that rule every nondisclosure is treated as error, thus imposing on the prosecutor a constitutional duty to deliver his entire file to defense counsel. At the same time, the Court rejected a standard that would require the defendant to demonstrate that the evidence if disclosed probably would have resulted in acquittal. The Court reasoned: "If the standard applied to the usual motion for a new trial based on newly discovered evidence were the same when the evidence was in the State's possession as when it was found in a neutral source, there would be no special significance to the prosecutor's obligation to serve the cause of justice." The standard of materiality applicable in the absence of a specific *Brady* request is therefore stricter than the harmless error standard but more lenient to the defense than the newly-discovered evidence standard.

The third situation identified by the Court in *Agurs* is where the defense makes a specific request and the prosecutor fails to disclose responsive evidence. The Court did not define the standard of materiality applicable in this situation, but suggested that the standard might be more lenient to the defense than in the situation in which the defense makes no request or only a general request. The Court also noted: "When the prosecutor receives a specific and relevant request, the failure to make any response is seldom, if ever, excusable."

The Court has relied on and reformulated the *Agurs* standard for the materiality of undisclosed evidence in two subsequent cases arising outside the *Brady* context. In neither case did the Court's discussion of the *Agurs* standard distinguish among the three situations described in *Agurs*. In *United States* v. *Valenzuela-Bernal*, 458 U.S. 858, 874 (1982), the Court held that due process is violated when testimony is made unavailable to the defense by Government deportation of witnesses "only if there is a reasonable likelihood that the testimony could have affected the judgment of the trier of fact." And in *Strickland* v. *Washington*, 466 U.S. 668 (1984), the Court held that a new trial must be granted when evidence is not introduced because of the incompetence of counsel only if "there is a reasonable probability that, but for counsel's unprofessional errors, the result of the proceeding would have been different." The *Strickland* Court defined a "reasonable probability" as "a probability sufficient to undermine confidence in the outcome."

We find the *Strickland* formulation of the *Agurs* test for materiality sufficiently flexible to cover the "no request," "general request," and "specific request" cases of prosecutorial failure to disclose evidence favorable to the accused: The evidence is material only if there is a reasonable probability that, had the evidence been disclosed to the defense, the result of the proceeding would have been different. A "reasonable probability" is a probability sufficient to undermine confidence in the outcome.

The Government suggests that a materiality standard more favorable to the defendant reasonably might be adopted in specific request cases. The Government notes that an incomplete response to a specific request not only deprives the defense of certain evidence, but also has the effect of representing to the defense that the evidence does not exist. In reliance on this misleading representation, the defense might abandon lines of independent investigation, defenses, or trial strategies that it otherwise would have pursued.

We agree that the prosecutor's failure to respond fully to a *Brady* request may impair the adversary process in this manner. And the more specifically the defense requests certain evidence, thus putting the prosecutor on notice of its value, the more reasonable it is for the defense to assume from the nondisclosure that the evidence does not exist, and to make pretrial and trial decisions on the basis of this assumption. This possibility of impairment does not necessitate a different standard of materiality, however, for under the *Strickland* formulation the reviewing court may consider directly any adverse effect that the prosecutor's failure to respond might have had on the preparation or presentation of the defendant's case. The reviewing court should assess the possibility that such effect might have occurred in light of the totality of the circumstances and with an awareness of the difficulty of reconstructing in a post-trial proceeding the course that the defense and the trial would have taken had the defense not been misled by the prosecutor's incomplete response.

In the present case, we think that there is a significant likelihood that the prosecutor's response to respondent's discovery motion misleadingly induced defense counsel to believe that O'Connor and Mitchell could not be impeached on the basis of bias or interest arising from inducements offered by the Government. Defense counsel asked the prosecutor to disclose any inducements that had been made to witnesses, and the prosecutor failed to disclose that the possibility of a reward had been held out to O'Connor and Mitchell if the information they supplied led to "the accomplishment of the objective sought to be obtained ... to the satisfaction of [the Government]." The possibility of a reward gave O'Connor and Mitchell a direct, personal stake in respondent's conviction. The fact that the stake was not guaranteed through a promise or binding contract, but was expressly contingent on the Government's satisfaction with the end result, served only to strengthen any incentive to testify falsely in order to secure a conviction. Moreover, the prosecutor disclosed affidavits that stated that O'Connor and Mitchell received no promises of reward in return for providing information in the affidavits implicating respondent in criminal activity. In fact, O'Connor and Mitchell signed the last of these affidavits the very day after they signed the ATF contracts. While the Government is technically correct that the blank contracts did not constitute a "promise of reward," the natural effect of these affidavits would be misleadingly to induce defense counsel to believe that O'Connor and Mitchell provided the information in the affidavits, and ultimately their testimony at trial recounting the same information, without any "inducements."

... Accordingly, we reverse the judgment of the Court of Appeals and remand the case to that court for a determination whether there is a reasonable probability that, had the inducement offered by the Government to O'Connor and Mitchell been disclosed to the defense, the result of the trial would have been different. ...

JUSTICE MARSHALL, with whom JUSTICE BRENNAN joins, dissenting.

... We have long recognized that, within the limit of the state's ability to identify so-called exculpatory information, the state's concern for a fair verdict precludes it from withholding from the defense evidence favorable to the defendant's case in the prosecutor's files.

This recognition no doubt stems in part from the frequently considerable imbalance in resources between most criminal defendants and most prosecutors' offices. Many, perhaps most, criminal defendants in the United States are represented by appointed counsel, who often are paid minimal wages and operate on shoestring budgets. In addition, unlike police, defense counsel generally is not present at the scene of the crime, or at the time of arrest, but instead comes into the case late. Moreover, unlike the government, defense counsel is not in the position to make deals with witnesses to gain evidence. Thus, an inexperienced, unskilled, or unaggressive attorney often is unable to amass the factual support necessary to a reasonable defense. When favorable evidence is in the hands of the prosecutor but not disclosed, the result may well be that the defendant is deprived of a fair chance before the trier of fact, and the trier of fact is deprived of the ingredients necessary to a fair decision. This grim reality, of course, poses a direct challenge to the traditional model of the adversary criminal process, and perhaps because this reality so directly questions the fairness of our longstanding processes, change has been cautious and halting. Thus, the Court has not gone the full road and expressly required that the state provide to the defendant access to the prosecutor's complete files, or investigators who will assure that the defendant has an opportunity to discover every existing piece of helpful evidence. Instead, in acknowledgment of the fact that important interests are served when potentially favorable evidence is disclosed, the Court has fashioned a compromise, requiring that the prosecution identify and disclose to the defendant favorable material that it possesses. This requirement is but a small, albeit important, step toward equality of justice.

Brady v. *Maryland*, 373 U.S. 83 (1963), of course, established this requirement of disclosure as a fundamental element of a fair trial by holding that a defendant was denied due process if he was not given access to favorable evidence that is material either to guilt or punishment. Since *Brady* was decided, this Court has struggled, in a series of decisions, to define how best to effectuate the right recognized. To my mind, the *Brady* decision, the reasoning that underlay it, and the fundamental interest in a fair trial, combine to give the criminal defendant the right to receive from the prosecutor, and the prosecutor the affirmative duty to turn over to the defendant, *all* information known to the government that might reasonably be considered favorable to the defendant's case. Formulation of this right, and imposition of this duty, are "the essence of due process of law. It is the State that tries a man, and it is the State that must insure that the trial is fair." If that right is denied, or if that duty is shirked, however, I believe a reviewing court should not automatically reverse but instead should apply the harmless-error test the Court has developed for instances of error affecting constitutional rights.

My view is based in significant part on the reality of criminal practice and on the consequently inadequate protection to the defendant that a different rule would offer. To implement *Brady*, courts must of course work within the confines of the criminal process. Our system of criminal justice is animated by two seemingly incompatible notions: the adversary model, and the state's primary concern with justice, not convictions. *Brady*, of course, reflects the latter goal of justice, and is in some ways at odds with the competing model of a sporting event. Our goal, then, must be to integrate the *Brady* right into the harsh, daily reality of this apparently discordant criminal process.

At the trial level, the duty of the state to effectuate *Brady* devolves into the duty of the prosecutor; the dual role that the prosecutor must play poses a serious obstacle to implementing *Brady*. The prosecutor is by trade, if not necessity, a zealous advocate. He is a trained attorney who must aggressively seek convictions in court on behalf of a victimized public. At the same time, as a representative of the state, he must place foremost in his hierarchy of interests the determination of truth. Thus, for purposes of *Brady*, the prosecutor must abandon his role as an advocate and pore through his files, as objectively as possible, to identify the material that could undermine his case. Given this obviously unharmonious role, it is not surprising that these advocates oftentimes overlook or downplay potentially favorable evidence, often in cases in which there is no doubt that the failure to disclose was a result of absolute good faith. Indeed, one need only think of the Fourth Amendment's requirement of a neutral intermediary, who tests the strength of the policeman-advocate's facts, to recognize the curious status *Brady* imposes on a prosecutor. One telling example, offered by Judge Newman when he was a United States Attorney, suffices:

> "I recently had occasion to discuss *[Brady]* at a PLI Conference in New York City before a large group of State prosecutors ... I put to them this case: You are prosecuting a bank robbery. You have talked to two or three of the tellers and one or two of the customers at the time of the robbery. They have all taken a look at your defendant in a line-up, and they have said, 'This is the man.' In the course of your investigation you also have found another customer who was in the bank that day, who viewed the suspect, and came back and said, 'This is *not* the man.'
>
> "The question I put to these prosecutors was, do you believe you should disclose to the defense the name of the witness who, when he viewed the suspect, said 'that is not the man'? In a room of prosecutors not quite as large as this group but almost as large, only two hands went up. There were only two prosecutors in that group who felt they should disclose or would disclose that information. Yet I was putting to them what I thought was the easiest case—the clearest case for disclosure of exculpatory information!" J. Newman, A Panel Discussion before the Judicial Conference of the Second Judicial Circuit (Sept. 8, 1967), reprinted in Discovery in Criminal Cases, 44 F.R.D. 481, 500–501 (1968) (hereafter Newman).

While familiarity with *Brady* no doubt has increased since 1967, the dual role that the prosecutor must play, and the very real pressures that role creates, have not changed.

The prosecutor surely greets the moment at which he must turn over *Brady* material with little enthusiasm. In perusing his files, he must make the often difficult decision as to whether evidence is favorable, and must decide on which side to err when faced with doubt. In his role as advocate, the answers are clear. In his role as representative of the state, the answers should be equally clear, and often to the contrary. Evidence that is of doubtful worth in the eyes of the prosecutor could be of inestimable value to the defense, and might make the difference to the trier of fact.

Once the prosecutor suspects that certain information might have favorable implications for the defense, either because it is potentially exculpatory or relevant to credibility, I see no reason why he should not be required to disclose it. After all, favorable evidence indisputably enhances the truth-seeking process at trial. And it is the job of the defense, not the prosecution, to decide whether and in what way to use arguably favorable evidence. In addition, to require disclosure of all evidence that might reasonably be considered favorable to the defendant would have the precautionary effect of assuring that no information of potential consequence is mistakenly overlooked. By requiring full disclosure of favorable evidence in this way, courts could begin to assure that a possibly dispositive piece of information is not withheld from the trier of fact by a prosecutor who is torn between the two roles he must play. A clear rule of this kind, coupled with a presumption in favor of disclosure, also would facilitate the prosecutor's admittedly difficult task by removing a substantial amount of unguided discretion.

If a trial will thereby be more just, due process would seem to require such a rule absent a countervailing interest. I see little reason for the government to keep such information from the defendant. Its interest in nondisclosure at the trial stage is at best slight: the government apparently seeks to avoid the administrative hassle of disclosure, and to prevent disclosure of inculpatory evidence that might result in witness intimidation and manufactured rebuttal evidence. Neither of these concerns, however, counsels in favor of a rule of nondisclosure in close or ambiguous cases. To the contrary, a rule simplifying the disclosure decision by definition does not make that decision more complex. Nor does disclosure of favorable evidence inevitably lead to disclosure of inculpatory evidence, as might an open file policy, or to the anticipated wrongdoings of defendants and their lawyers, if indeed such fears are warranted. We have other mechanisms for disciplining unscrupulous defense counsel; hamstringing their clients need not be one of them. I simply do not find any state interest that warrants withholding from a presumptively innocent defendant, whose liberty is at stake in the proceeding, information that bears on his case and that might enable him to defend himself.

Under the foregoing analysis, the prosecutor's duty is quite straightforward: he must divulge all evidence that reasonably appears favorable to the defendant, erring on the side of disclosure.

The Court, however, offers a complex alternative. It defines the right not by reference to the possible usefulness of the particular evidence in preparing and presenting the case, but retrospectively, by reference to the likely effect the evidence will have on the outcome of the trial. Thus, the Court holds that due process does not require the prosecutor to turn over evidence unless the evidence is "material," and the Court states that evidence is "material" "only if there is a reasonable probability that, had the evidence been disclosed to the defense, the result of the proceeding would have been different." Although this looks like a post-trial standard of review, it is not. Instead, the Court relies on this review standard to define the contours of the defendant's constitutional right to certain material prior to trial. By adhering to the view articulated in *United States* v. *Agurs*, 427 U.S. 97 (1976)—that there is no constitutional duty to disclose evidence unless nondisclosure would have a certain impact on the trial—the Court permits prosecutors to withhold with impunity large amounts of undeniably favorable evidence, and it imposes on prosecutors the burden to identify and disclose evidence pursuant to a pretrial standard that virtually defies definition. ...

... Besides legitimizing the nondisclosure of clearly favorable evidence, the standard set out by the Court also asks the prosecutor to predict what effect various pieces of evidence will have on the trial. He must evaluate his case and the case of the defendant—of which he presumably knows very little—and perform the impossible task of deciding whether a certain piece of information will have a significant impact on the trial, bearing in mind that a defendant will later shoulder the heavy burden of proving how it would have affected the outcome. At best, this standard places on the prosecutor a responsibility to speculate, at times without foundation, since the prosecutor will not normally know what strategy the defense will pursue or what evidence the defense will find useful. At worst, the standard invites a prosecutor, whose interests are conflicting, to gamble, to play the odds, and to take a chance that evidence will later turn out not to have been potentially dispositive. One Court of Appeals has recently vented its frustration at these unfortunate consequences:

> "It seems clear that those tests [for materiality] have a tendency to encourage unilateral decision-making by prosecutors with respect to disclosure .... [T]he root of the problem is the prosecutor's tendency to adopt a retrospective view of materiality. Before trial, the prosecutor cannot know whether, after trial, particular evidence will prove to have been material .... Following their adversarial instincts, some prosecutors have determined unilaterally that evidence will not be material and, often in good faith, have disclosed it neither to defense counsel nor to the court. If and when the evidence emerges after trial, the prosecutor can always argue, with the benefit of hindsight, that it was not material."

The Court's standard also encourages the prosecutor to assume the role of the jury, and to decide whether certain evidence will make a difference. In our system of justice, that decision properly and wholly belongs to the jury. The prosecutor, convinced of the guilt of the defendant and of the truthfulness of his witnesses, may all too easily view as irrelevant or unpersuasive evidence that draws his own judgments into question. Accordingly he will decide the evidence need not be disclosed. But the ideally neutral trier of fact, who approaches the case from a wholly different perspective, is by the prosecutor's decision denied the opportunity to consider the evidence. The reviewing court, faced with a verdict of guilty, evidence to support that verdict, and pressures, again understandable, to finalize criminal judgments, is in little better position to review the withheld evidence than the prosecutor. ...

Notes

1. To prevail on a *Brady* claim, a defendant must demonstrate three things: (1) "the evidence at issue must be favorable to the accused"; (2) "that evidence must be suppressed by the State, either willfully or inadvertently"; and (3) "prejudice must have ensued," that is, the suppressed evidence must have been "material." Strickler v. Greene, 527 U.S. 263, 281–82 (1999). In the notes that follow, we will explore how these elements have been interpreted.

With respect to the first element, as the *Bagley* Court made clear, information coming within the scope of the *Brady* mandate "includes not only evidence that is exculpatory, *i.e.*, going to the heart of the defendant's guilt or innocence, but also evidence that is useful for impeachment, *i.e.*, having the potential to alter the jury's assessment of the credibility of a significant prosecution witness." United States v. Avellino, 136 F.3d 249, 255 (2d Cir.1998); *see also* Kyles v. Whitley, 514 U.S. 419, 433 (1995). *Brady*'s application to impeachment material was made clear in *Giglio v. United States*, 405 U.S. 150 (1972), and thus such *Brady* impeachment material is often called "*Giglio* material." In *Giglio*, the defendant was convicted of passing forged money orders but, while his appeal was pending, his attorney discovered that the government had not disclosed to the defense a promise of immunity made to a key government witness. The Supreme Court ordered a new trial, stating that "[w]hen the 'reliability of a given witness may well be determinative of guilt or innocence,' nondisclosure of evidence affecting credibility falls within" the *Brady* rule. *Id.* at 154. Certainly formal cooperation agreements must be turned over, but a number of circuits have also "found a duty to disclose under *Brady* where there was a tacit agreement promising potential or actual leniency." Douglas v. Workman, 560 F.3d 1156, 1185-86 (10th Cir. 2009); *see also* Bell v. Bell, 512 F.3d 223, 233 (6th Cir. 2008); Wisehart v. Davis, 408 F.3d 321, 323-24 (7th Cir. 2005).

Similarly, the government's *Brady* obligation exists when the suppressed evidence would be favorable to the defense with respect to either guilt *or* punishment. Note that *Brady* was a case in which the Supreme Court affirmed a state court order granting a new trial limited solely to the issue of punishment. "Despite its sentencing origins, practitioners have largely focused on *Brady* as a tool to obtain exculpatory evidence for trial or guilt phase purposes—and not evidence that would reduce the penalty or affect punishment. In doing so, defense lawyers and courts have overlooked the critical mitigation implications of *Brady* to the U.S. Sentencing Guidelines." Robert W. Tarun, Brady v. Maryland*: Underused Landmark Sentencing Sword*, 8 Bus. Crimes Bull. 1 (Feb.2001).

2. With respect to the second element, what is meant by "suppression" of evidence by the government? One thing it does not connote is intentionality: *Brady* itself made clear that the due process disclosure obligation exists "irrespective of the good faith or bad faith of the prosecution." "Suppression" questions instead generally turn on issues of access. As the Seventh Circuit has explained, evidence is suppressed for *Brady* purposes when "(1) the prosecution failed to disclose evidence that it or law enforcement was aware of before it was too late for the defendant to make use of the evidence, and (2) the evidence was not otherwise available to the defendant through the exercise of reasonable diligence." Boss v. Pierce, 263 F.3d 734, 740 (7th Cir. 2001) (holding that reasonable diligence does not require defense counsel to ask defense alibi witness about matters of which counsel could not have reasonably expected the witness to know).

Thus, for example, the prosecution cannot be charged with "suppressing" materially exculpatory evidence in violation of *Brady* if the defendant actually had the information prior to trial, either by virtue of government production or through some independent means. *See, e.g.*, Tate v. Wood, 963 F.2d 20, 25–26 (2d Cir. 1992); United States v. Wilson, 901 F.2d 378,

380 (4th Cir. 1990); United States v. Gaggi, 811 F.2d 47, 59 (2d Cir. 1987). White-collar prosecutions often are exceedingly paper-intensive. Prosecutors sometimes invite defense counsel to peruse filing cabinet after filing cabinet stuffed with documents and to mark what materials they want for copying by the government. Why might prosecutors elect to permit such "open-file" discovery? Consider the testimony of Beth Wilkinson, former Chief of the DOJ Terrorism and Violent Crime Section, before Congress on her high-profile Oklahoma City bombing cases: "what really saved our conviction at the very end was that we did have open-file discovery and that the defense had access to all information and that, honestly, we couldn't have known at some points whether it was *Brady* or not. And only by sharing all of it with the other side were we able to know that they could pursue whatever they thought was appropriate during the pre-trial phase." The Justice Project, *Expanded Discovery in Criminal Cases: A Policy Review* 15 (May 31, 2007). (NB: the DOJ frowns on the use of the term "open file discovery": "because the concept of the 'file' is imprecise, such a representation exposes the prosecutor to broader disclosure requirements than intended" and it is possible that a prosecutor will inadvertently omit something from the production, opening the assistant to accusations of misrepresentation, *see* U.S. DOJ, U.S. Attorney's Manual, Criminal Resource Manual No. 165 (Jan. 2010)).

Does "open-file" discovery bar any subsequent claim that the government "suppressed" *Brady* materials sprinkled throughout the thousands of documents made available for defense review? Although actual access in such circumstances may defeat a "suppression" claim, *see, e.g.*, United States v. Morris, 80 F.3d 1151, 1168 (7th Cir. 1996), some courts, recognizing the difficulties present in such cases, have ordered the government to identify *Brady* material. *See, e.g.*, United States v. Hsia, 24 F.Supp.2d 14, 29–30 (D.D.C. 1998). Other courts have declined such motions, citing the impossibility of determining in advance of trial whether exculpatory evidence is material and, therefore, whether a *Brady* violation has occurred. *See, e.g.*, United States v. Stein, 2005 WL 3058644 (S.D.N.Y. 2005). Finally, the Fifth Circuit has steered a middle path, seemingly looking to the reasons prosecutors elected open-file discovery. It stated that, "[a]s a general rule, the government is under no duty to direct a defendant to exculpatory evidence within a larger mass of disclosed evidence." United States v. Skilling, 554 F.3d 529, 576 (5th Cir. 2009), *aff'd in part and rev'd in part on other grounds*, 561 U.S. 358 (2010). However, the court went on to state:

> We do not hold that the use of voluminous open file can never violate *Brady*. For instance, evidence that the government "padded" an open file with pointless or superfluous information to frustrate a defendant's review of the file might raise serious *Brady* issues. Creating a voluminous file that is unduly onerous to access might raise similar concerns. And it should go without saying that the government may not hide *Brady* material of which it is actually aware in a huge open file in the hope that the defendant would never find it. These scenarios would indicate that the government was acting in bad faith in performing its obligations under *Brady*. But considering the additional steps the government took beyond merely providing [the defendant] with the open file, the equal access that [the defendant] and the government had to the open file, the complexity of [the defendant's] case, and the absence of evidence that the government used the open file to hide potentially exculpatory evidence or otherwise acted in bad faith, we hold that the government's use of open file did not violate *Brady*.

Id. at 577. The Sixth Circuit apparently agrees. *See* United States v. Warshak, 631 F.3d 266, 297-98 (6th Cir. 2010). Does this inquiry into prosecutorial motives square with the *Brady* decision?

Note, however, that where the question is not whether the government complied with its disclosure obligations, but rather the form, format, or manner in which the government produced voluminous electronic records, as to which the Federal Rules of Criminal Procedure do not speak, courts have looked to the Federal Rules of Civil Procedure for guidance. *See, e.g.*, United States v. Briggs, 831 F. Supp.2d 623 (W.D.N.Y. 2011); United States v. Briggs, Slip op., 2011 WL 4024766 (W.D.N.Y. 2011); United States v. O'Keefe, 537 F. Supp.2d 14 (D.D.C. 2008); *see also Warshak*, 631 F.3d 295-96.

3. As noted above, many courts require some due diligence from the defense prior to finding that the government is "suppressing" *Brady* materials. Thus, courts have held that evidence is not "suppressed" by the government if counsel could have discovered it through exercise of reasonable diligence. *See, e.g.*, United States v. Georgiou, 777 F.3d 125 (3d Cir. 2015); United States v. Dimas, 3 F.3d 1015, 1018-19 (7th Cir. 1993); United States v. Ellender, 947 F.2d 748, 756-57 (5th Cir. 1991). For example, courts have held the government is under no obligation to "disclose" information that is a matter of public record or is easily obtained by the defense. *See, e.g.*, United States v. Newman, 849 F.2d 156, 161 (5th Cir. 1988); United States v. McMahon, 715 F.2d 498, 501 (11th Cir. 1983). And, at least in some jurisdictions, "[i]t is well settled that defendants cannot base a *Brady* claim on information that could have been obtained from other sources via subpoena." United States v. Boyd, 833 F.Supp. 1277, 1357 (N.D. Ill. 1993), *aff'd*, 55 F.3d 239 (7th Cir. 1995); *see also Ellender*, 947 F.2d at 756-57. These courts hold that "where counsel is on notice that a witness may have exculpatory information, and has an opportunity to subpoena that witness, there is no obligation for the prosecutor to seek out and provide information." United States v. Lockhart, 956 F.2d 1418, 1426 (7th Cir. 1992); *see also* United States v. Bond, 552 F.3d 1092 (9th Cir. 2009). *But see In re* Sealed Case No. 99-3096 (Brady Obligations), 185 F.3d 887, 897 (D.C. Cir. 1999) (holding that the fact that defense counsel could have subpoenaed withheld materials did not defeat government's *Brady* obligation because the "appropriate way for defense counsel to obtain such information was to make a *Brady* request of the prosecutor, just as he did").

Recall that Part III of the *Bagley* opinion ruled that the same standard of materiality applies regardless of whether the defense has made a request for *Brady* material. Although Part III of the Court's opinion technically did not have precedential force in that it was joined by only two Justices, it has been treated as binding by subsequent courts, including the Supreme Court. *See, e.g.*, Kyles v. Whitley, 514 U.S. 419, 433 (1995). Indeed, the Court has made clear that "the duty to disclose [*Brady* material] is applicable *even though there has been no request by the accused*." Strickler v. Greene, 527 U.S. 263, 280 (1999) (emphasis added) (citing United States v. Agurs, 427 U.S. 97, 107 (1976)). In light of the fact that the defense does not even have to ask for *Brady* material to trigger the government's duty, do the above cases make sense? Should the extent of a prosecutor's *Brady* obligation be contingent upon the due diligence of counsel in seeking out alternative sources of exculpatory materials? *See* Kate Weisburd, *Prosecutors Hide, Defendants Seek: The Erosion of* Brady *Through the Defendant Due Diligence Rule*, 60 UCLA L. Rev. 138 (2012). What is the rationale underlying these cases? *See* People v. Chenault, 845 N.W.2d 731 (Mich. 2014) (abandoning "due diligence" rule).

4. With respect to what information is deemed to be within the possession of the "government" for *Brady* purposes, the Supreme Court has explained that the *Brady* "rule encompasses evidence 'known only to police investigators and not to the prosecutor.' In order to comply with *Brady*, therefore, 'the individual prosecutor has a duty to learn of any favorable evidence known to the others acting on the government's behalf in th[e] case, including the police.'" *Strickler*, 527 U.S. at 280-81 (quoting *Kyles*, 514 U.S. at 437, 438). Thus, "[i]t is well settled that information possessed by any member of the United States Attorneys Office will be attributed, for these purposes, to the 'prosecution.' ... This rule encompasses not only Assistant United States Attorneys not working on the case, but also other Assistant United States Attorney's Office personnel, such as paralegals. Likewise, it is also clear that the 'prosecution' includes police officers, federal agents and other investigatory personnel who participated in the investigation and prosecution of the case." *Boyd*, 833 F. Supp. at 1353; *see also* United States v. Brooks, 966 F.2d 1500, 1503 (D.C. Cir. 1992). There is uncertainty among the circuits, however, on the precise scope of a prosecutor's duty to search outside of the prosecution team for *Brady* not personally known to the prosecutor. *See, e.g.*, Mark D. Villaverde, *Structuring the Prosecutor's Duty to Search the Intelligence Community for* Brady *Material*, Note, 88 Cornell L. Rev. 1471 (2003).

An important question in white-collar cases is whether the knowledge of agencies charged with civil enforcement of a particular statutory regime, or other persons who engage in parallel civil investigations of the same misconduct for which the defendant was indicted, are deemed to be part of the prosecution team for *Brady* purposes. As Professor Peter J. Henning explains:

> The extent of economic regulation by federal and state governments has undergone an enormous expansion, especially since the 1970s. Prosecutors now give much greater attention to white collar crime, and investigations take place over a broad range of activity, from bank and securities fraud to public corruption to abuses of the health care system. The expanding jurisdiction of regulatory agencies to monitor markets and investigate possible abuses, with the concomitant increase in the staff needed to conduct extensive regulatory oversight, has created the well-known problem of the so-called "parallel proceeding." A number of federal statutes have both a civil and a criminal component, raising the possibility of concurrent investigations of the same conduct by different arms of the government. ... The regulatory agencies are limited to civil enforcement of their statutes, and those proceedings usually entail an extensive investigation by the agency staff before the institution of proceedings. While the civil regulatory agencies cannot bring criminal charges, they are empowered to compel individuals and organizations to produce documents and appear for testimony under oath.
>
> The dual nature of many regulatory provisions means that a course of conduct may be subject to investigation by both the civil and criminal authorities. It is quite common for the regulatory agency to conduct a preliminary investigation of the conduct because it has greater expertise in the area and will often receive the information from regulated entities regarding possible wrongdoing at an early stage. In the course of that investigation, the agency staff can refer the matter to the criminal authorities if it appears that there is a possible criminal violation. At that point, the civil agency's investigation need not stop, and the two cases can proceed in tandem, hence a parallel proceeding. These types of parallel investigations are particularly common in cases involving banking, securities and commodities trading, antitrust, and environmental violations. ...
>
> The effect of these proliferating proceedings is that documents relevant to the criminal prosecution may be housed in a number of locations and held by self-regulatory organizations or agencies at different levels of government. In many instances, a regulatory agency or executive department develops evidence of possible criminal conduct that it refers to the prosecutor to determine whether criminal charges should be filed. But even without a formal referral, prosecutors can seek information from other arms of the government to assess whether to pursue the criminal case, relying on the expertise of an agency's staff to ascertain the nature and effect of conduct. While the regulators provide valuable information and expertise, a prosecutor may not be aware of all the documents held by agencies and other regulatory organizations that relate to the potential criminal activity.

Peter J. Henning, *Defense Discovery in White Collar Criminal Prosecutions*, 15 Ga. St. U. L. Rev. 601, 604-06 (1999) (footnotes omitted); *see also* Michael Kendall & Scott Murray, *How to Make the SEC Disgorge Exculpatory Evidence*, 11 Bus. Crimes Bull. 1 (June 2004). Should prosecutors be charged with possession of materials held by other investigating agencies for *Brady* purposes? *Compare, e.g.*, United States v. Morris, 80 F.3d 1151, 1169-70 (7th Cir.1996) (refusing to find *Brady* violation where materials were in the possession of government agencies (the Office of Thrift Supervision, the IRS and the SEC) that had no involvement in the investigation or prosecution at issue), *with* United States v. Wood, 57 F.3d 733, (9th Cir. 1995) ("We hold ... that under *Brady* the agency charged with administration of the statute, which has consulted with the prosecutor in the steps leading to prosecution, is to be considered as part of the prosecution in determining what information must be made available to the defendant charged with violation of the statute").

Perhaps more important, what should be the standard to evaluate the "question of how much knowledge possessed by various arms of the State should be imputed to the prosecution"? United States v. Combs, 267 F.3d 1167, 1174 (10th Cir. 2001) (discussing various circuits' conflicting standards). Note that in 2010 the Department of Justice issued discovery guidance to federal prosecutors that includes factors to be considered in reviewing potentially discoverable information from a federal agency. U.S. DOJ, U.S. Attorney's Manual, Criminal Resource Manual No. 165, Step 1(A) (Jan. 2010) ("Where to look—the Prosecution Team").

5. Courts may be willing to attribute possession of information to the prosecution which is held by other governmental actors with whom the prosecutor is working closely, even if the particular prosecutor responsible for the case does not have actual knowledge of that information. However, if that universe of governmental actors do not have the information sought, courts generally hold that the prosecutor is under no obligation to seek it out. As the Eighth Circuit has explained, "[t]he government has no 'affirmative duty ... to take action to discover information which it does not possess.' ... In addition, the 'prosecutor has no duty to undertake a fishing expedition in other jurisdictions in an effort to find impeaching evidence.'" United States v. Jones, 34 F.3d 596, 599 (8th Cir. 1994). Why? Should prosecutors, in their role as "ministers of justice," be tasked with this obligation or is it unwise to impose such a duty on prosecutors? Given this rule, the question of whether prosecutors are deemed in "possession" of information obviously takes on greater import. As we shall see, absent such a finding of "possession," and a concomitant governmental obligation to disclose either under *Brady* or the Fed. R. Crim. P. 16 discovery rules, defense counsel may not be able to secure the needed information through other means, such as Fed. R. Crim. P. 17 trial subpoenas (considered *infra*).

6. Often, the claim that the government improperly withheld *Brady* material turns on the third element of the *Brady* test outlined in note 1 above—"prejudice," more often termed materiality. *See, e.g.*, Turner v. United States, -- U.S. --, 137 S.Ct. 1885 (2017); United States v. Bartko, 728 F.3d 327 (4th Cir. 2013); United States v. Olsen, 704 F.3d 1172 (9th Cir. 2013). The *Bagley* Court articulated this definition of materiality: "evidence is material only if there is a reasonable probability that, had the evidence been disclosed to the defense, the result of the proceeding would have been different. A 'reasonable probability' is a probability sufficient to undermine confidence in the outcome." Although the Court's test sounds like a harmless error standard, and is in fact the means by which *Brady* claims are tested on appeal, it was intended to be the standard by which prosecutors must make their *forward-looking* decisions whether or not to turn over potentially exculpatory information. Does Justice Marshall persuade you that the test is unworkable? What are the policies or considerations that counsel for and against Justice Marshall's more generous disclosure standard?

Some district courts have determined that the "materiality" standard articulated in *Bagley* and other cases makes sense for the backward-looking evaluation performed on appeal but is not helpful for resolving *Brady* issues in the course of pretrial discovery motions. *See* United States v. Peitz, 2002 WL 226865, at *3 (N.D. Ill. 2002); United States v. Sudikoff, 36 F. Supp.2d 1196, 1198-99 (C.D. Cal. 1999); United States v. Glover, 1995 WL 151823, at *2 (N.D. Ill. 1995). Thus, some courts have held that "[i]n the pretrial context, 'the government is obligated to disclose *all evidence relating to guilt or punishment which might reasonably be considered favorable to a defendant's case*,' with doubts as to usefulness resolved in favor of disclosure.'" *Peitz*, 2002 WL 226865, at *3 (quoting *Sudikoff*, 36 F. Supp.2d at 1199) (emphasis added); *see also* United States v. Arosta, 357 F. Supp.2d 1228 (D. Nev. 2005); Christopher Deal, Note, *Materiality Before Trial: The Scope of the Duty to Disclose and the Right to a Trial by Jury*, N.Y.U. L. Rev. 1780, 1785 (2007). Can this approach be squared with *Bagley*?

7. One problem referred to by Justice Marshall is the difficulty prosecutors may have in discerning what *the defense* may judge to be important exculpatory or impeachment evidence. Many prosecutors, by virtue of their training, experience, and investment in a particular case, simply may not recognize that certain evidence is exculpatory. G. Douglas Jones, former U.S. Attorney for the Northern District of Alabama, has asserted that "the biggest problem I've always had with criminal discovery both as an Assistant, as

a defense lawyer, and now as United States Attorney, [is] I have a real hard time convincing ... Assistant U.S. Attorneys that they often don't know what may be material to the defense. They just don't get it." *Panel Discussion: Criminal Discovery in Practice, supra* note 6, 785-86. Similarly, Christina Arguedas has argued that prosecutors are not necessarily unethical in generally failing to provide good *Brady* material; rather, "it's a 'point of view problem'—prosecutors and defense counsel simply do not see materials the same way." *Program Explores Recent* Brady *Cases, Defense Strategies in Seeking Disclosure*, 68 Crim. L. Rep. (BNA) 533 (Mar.21, 2001). Defense lawyer and prosecutor Earl Silbert has opined that prosecutors are not more forthcoming with *Brady* because there is little deterrent under existing law to not turning *Brady* over and "it is psychologically difficult for a prosecutor who sincerely believes in the defendant's guilt to turn over information that might adversely impact a result the prosecutor considers to be just." *Id.; see also* Alafair S. Burke, *Improving Prosecutorial Decision Making: Some Lessons of Cognitive Science*, 47 Wm. & Mary L. Rev. 1587 (2006).

Prosecutors who do not know what the defense's theory will be may not be able to effectively judge the worth of evidence in its possession to that defense. *See id.* at 797. As the district court explained in *United States v. McVeigh*, 954 F.Supp. 1441 (D. Colo. 1997):

> ... [T]he materiality of information depends on the judgment of persons having knowledge of all of the other information necessary for evaluation of it. The trial judge does not have that knowledge before trial. The government lawyers may also lack some necessary information known to the defendant's lawyers. Accordingly, to expect a reliable response, defense counsel must be willing to provide what is known to them that may affect this evaluation. ...
>
> There is an obligation of fairness required of defense counsel in making requests for information from the government. These requests must be sufficiently clear and directed to give reasonable notice about what is sought and why the information may be material to the case. To the extent that materiality may depend upon something that only the defendant knows, the Fifth Amendment privilege against self-incrimination must, of course, be protected. Beyond that, the basis for refusal is not apparent. ...

Id. at 1451. Why might defense counsel be reluctant to be specific in their *Brady* requests? What is the better practice? *See, e.g., Program Explores Recent* Brady *Cases, Defense Strategies in Seeking Disclosure*, 68 Crim. L. Rep. (BNA) 533 (Mar.21, 2001).

8. In *Kyles v. Whitley*, 514 U.S. 419 (1995), the Supreme Court explained that "[f]our aspects of materiality under *Bagley* bear emphasis":

> ... [First,] [a]lthough the constitutional duty is triggered by the potential impact of favorable but undisclosed evidence, a showing of materiality does not require demonstration by a preponderance that disclosure of the suppressed evidence would have resulted ultimately in the defendant's acquittal (whether based on the presence of reasonable doubt or acceptance of an explanation for the crime that does not inculpate the defendant). *Bagley*'s touchstone of materiality is a "reasonable probability" of a different result, and the adjective is important. The question is not whether the defendant would more likely than not have received a different verdict with the evidence, but whether in its absence he received a fair trial, understood as a trial resulting in a verdict worthy of confidence. A "reasonable probability" of a different result is accordingly shown when the government's evidentiary suppression "undermines confidence in the outcome of the trial."
>
> The second aspect of *Bagley* materiality bearing emphasis here is that it is not a sufficiency of evidence test. A defendant need not demonstrate that after discounting the inculpatory evidence in light of the undisclosed evidence, there would not have been enough left to convict. The possibility of an acquittal on a criminal charge does not imply an insufficient evidentiary basis to convict. One does not show a *Brady* violation by demonstrating that some of the inculpatory evidence should have been excluded, but by

showing that the favorable evidence could reasonably be taken to put the whole case in such a different light as to undermine confidence in the verdict.

Third, we note that, contrary to the assumption made by the Court of Appeals, once a reviewing court applying *Bagley* has found constitutional error there is no need for further harmless-error review. ...

The fourth and final aspect of *Bagley* materiality to be stressed here is its definition in terms of suppressed evidence considered collectively, not item by item. As Justice Blackmun emphasized in the portion of his [*Bagley*] opinion written for the Court, the Constitution is not violated every time the government fails or chooses not to disclose evidence that might prove helpful to the defense. We have never held that the Constitution demands an open file policy (however such a policy might work out in practice), and the rule in *Bagley* (and, hence, in *Brady*) requires less of the prosecution than the ABA Standards for Criminal Justice, which call generally for prosecutorial disclosures of any evidence tending to exculpate or mitigate. See ABA Standards for Criminal Justice, Prosecution Function and Defense Function 3-3.11(a) (3d ed. 1993) ("A prosecutor should not intentionally fail to make timely disclosure to the defense, at the earliest feasible opportunity, of the existence of all evidence or information which tends to negate the guilt of the accused or mitigate the offense charged or which would tend to reduce the punishment of the accused"); ABA Model Rule of Prof'l Conduct R.3.8(d) (1984) ("The prosecutor in a criminal case shall ... make timely disclosure to the defense of all evidence or information known to the prosecutor that tends to negate the guilt of the accused or mitigates the offense").

While the definition of *Bagley* materiality in terms of the cumulative effect of suppression must accordingly be seen as leaving the government with a degree of discretion, it must also be understood as imposing a corresponding burden. On the one side, showing that the prosecution knew of an item of favorable evidence unknown to the defense does not amount to a *Brady* violation, without more. But the prosecution, which alone can know what is undisclosed, must be assigned the consequent responsibility to gauge the likely net effect of all such evidence and make disclosure when the point of "reasonable probability" is reached. This in turn means that the individual prosecutor has a duty to learn of any favorable evidence known to the others acting on the government's behalf in the case, including the police. But whether the prosecutor succeeds or fails in meeting this obligation (whether, that is, a failure to disclose is in good faith or bad faith), the prosecution's responsibility for failing to disclose known, favorable evidence rising to a material level of importance is inescapable. ...

This means, naturally, that a prosecutor anxious about tacking too close to the wind will disclose a favorable piece of evidence. See [*United States v. Agurs*, 427 U.S. 97, 108 (1976)] ("[T]he prudent prosecutor will resolve doubtful questions in favor of disclosure"). This is as it should be. Such disclosure will serve to justify trust in the prosecutor as "the representative ... of a sovereignty ... whose interest ... in a criminal prosecution is not that it shall win a case, but that justice shall be done." And it will tend to preserve the criminal trial, as distinct from the prosecutor's private deliberations, as the chosen forum for ascertaining the truth about criminal accusations. The prudence of the careful prosecutor should not therefore be discouraged.

The *Kyles* Court concluded that the favorable evidence the state had failed to disclose would have made a different result "reasonably probable" in that capital murder prosecution and accordingly reversed.

Another instance in which a defendant was able to meet the materiality standard was *Smith v. Cain*, 565 U.S. 73 (2012). Because the witness's testimony was the "*only*" evidence linking the defendant to the crime, and the undisclosed statements "directly contradict[ed]" the witness's trial testimony, the Court reversed and remanded.

9. In contrast, in *Strickler v. Greene*, 527 U.S. 263 (1999), the Court declined to find a *Brady* violation where the government had failed to turn over what the district court found to be "potentially devastating impeachment material" relating to an important government witness,

Anne Stoltzfus. *Id.* at 289. Stoltzfus gave detailed and vivid eyewitness testimony about the crimes and petitioner's role as one of the perpetrators. The prosecution failed, however, to disclose notes taken by a detective of interviews with Stoltzfus and letters written by her contained in police files that cast serious doubt on significant portions of her testimony. The Court noted that

> ... Without a doubt, Stoltzfus' testimony was prejudicial in the sense that it made petitioner's conviction more likely than if she had not testified, and discrediting her testimony might have changed the outcome of the trial.
>
> That, however, is not the standard that petitioner must satisfy in order to obtain relief. He must convince us that "there is a reasonable probability" that the result of the trial would have been different if the suppressed documents had been disclosed to the defense. As we stressed in *Kyles*,
>
> > "[T]he adjective is important. The question is not whether the defendant would more likely than not have received a different verdict with the evidence, but whether in its absence he received a fair trial, understood as a trial resulting in a verdict worthy of confidence." ...
>
> The District Court was surely correct that there is a reasonable *possibility* that either a total, or just a substantial, discount of Stoltzfus' testimony might have produced a different result, either at the guilt or sentencing phases. ... As the District Court recognized, however, petitioner's burden is to establish a reasonable *probability* of a different result."

Id. at 289-91. Is this result reconcilable with the Court's analysis in *Bagley*? Given the district court's findings in *Bagley* regarding the substance of the agents' testimony, could the impeachment material in that case have been characterized as "potentially devastating"?

Justice Souter, who authored the *Kyles* opinion, dissented in part in *Greene*. He began by noting that, "[l]ike the Court, I think it clear that the materials withheld were exculpatory as devastating ammunition for impeaching Stoltzfus." *Id.* at 296. In analyzing the materiality question, Justice Souter explained:

> Despite our repeated explanation of the shorthand formulation in these words, the continued use of the term "probability" raises an unjustifiable risk of misleading courts into treating it as akin to the more demanding standard, "more likely than not." While any short phases for what the cases are getting at will be "inevitably imprecise," I think "significant possibility" would do better at capturing the degree to which the undisclosed evidence would place the actual result in question, sufficient to warrant overturning a conviction or sentence.

Id. at 298. Justice Souter concluded that while he and the majority applied the same standard, they arrived at a different conclusion with respect to the materiality of the impeachment to the jury's sentencing recommendation largely because they differed in assessing the significance the jurors probably ascribed to Stoltzfus' testimony. *Id.* at 302. Did the majority and Justice Souter in fact apply the same standard?

In a capital case such as this, where the withheld information was deemed by all to have been "devastating" impeachment material, what justification could the prosecution possibly have had for not looking through the police files and for failing to turn this impeachment material over? What standard *should* prosecutors follow? Hon. Gerrilyn G. Brill has proposed an "ouch test": "If a prosecutor is looking at its case and says 'Ouch, that hurts,' it means it would be turned over to the defense. ... [I]n most cases, if it hurts the prosecution's case, it's going to be favorable to the defense, and should be turned over. You shouldn't need to read a whole bunch of cases to figure that out if you are a prosecutor." *Panel Discussion: Criminal Discovery in Practice, supra* note 6, at 793-94. Art Leach, an Assistant U.S. Attorney, abides by the following rule: "when you are looking at *Brady*, if you have to think about whether it should be disclosed, it probably needs to be disclosed. ... [I]f you have to think about it, disclose it." *Id.* at 806, 808.

10. If information appears exculpatory, but is not admissible, can it fall within the *Brady* standard for materiality? That is, does the suppressed material have to be "evidence" or could it simply be information that may lead the defendant to exculpatory or impeachment evidence? In *Wood v. Bartholomew*, 516 U.S. 1 (1995), the government did not turn over to the defense the results of polygraph examinations it had administered to two of its witnesses. Those results showed, with respect to one witness, deception as to certain questions. The Ninth Circuit granted a writ of habeas corpus holding that, even though under state law the polygraphic examinations were inadmissible in evidence even for impeachment purposes, the information could have been material under *Brady* because it could have affected defense counsel's pretrial investigation and strategic decisionmaking. In a *per curiam* opinion, the Supreme Court reversed, reasoning:

> ... [E]vidence is "material" under *Brady*, and the failure to disclose it justifies setting aside a conviction, only where there exists a "reasonable probability" that had the evidence been disclosed the result at trial would have been different. To begin with, on the Court of Appeals' own assumption, the polygraph results were inadmissible under state law, even for impeachment purposes, absent a stipulation of the parties, and the parties do not contend otherwise. The information at issue here, then—the results of a polygraph examination of one of the witnesses—is not "evidence" at all. Disclosure of the polygraph results, then, could have had no direct effect on the outcome of the trial, because respondent could have made no mention of them either during argument or while questioning witnesses. To get around this problem, the Ninth Circuit reasoned that the information, had it been disclosed to the defense, might have led respondent's counsel to conduct additional discovery that might have led to some additional evidence that could have been utilized. ...
>
> ... It is difficult to see [however] on what basis the Ninth Circuit concluded that respondent's counsel would have prepared in a different manner, or (more important) would have discovered some unspecified additional evidence, merely by disclosure of polygraph results that, as to two questions, were consistent with respondent's preestablished defense. ...
>
> In short, it is not "reasonably likely" that disclosure of the polygraph results—inadmissible under state law—would have resulted in a different outcome at trial. Even without [the testimony of the witness polygraphed], the case against respondent was overwhelming. ... [In the face of such evidence], it should take more than supposition on the weak premises offered by respondent to undermine a court's confidence in the outcome.

Id. at 10-11. Unfortunately, "[r]eactions to *Wood* have been as varied as the pre-*Wood* jurisprudence." Felder v. Johnson, 180 F.3d 206, 212 n.7 (5th Cir. 1999); *see also* Paradis v. Arave, 240 F.3d 1169, 1178-79 (9th Cir. 2001) (discussing circuit split but determining that it need not resolve that possible conflict because under Ninth Circuit law evidence can be material if it can be used to impeach, even if it is inadmissible even to impeach). For example, one circuit has read *Wood* to hold that inadmissible statements are immaterial under *Brady* "as a matter of law." Hoke v. Netherland, 92 F.3d 1350, 1356 n.3 (4th Cir. 1996). Others have found that inadmissible evidence can be material if it "would have led to admissible evidence." Wright v. Hopper, 169 F.3d 695, 703 & n.1 (11th Cir. 1999); *see also* Ellsworth v. Warden, 333 F.3d 1, 5 (1st Cir. 2003); United States v. Gil, 297 F.3d 93, 104-05 (2d Cir. 2002); Madsen v. Dormire, 137 F.3d 602, 604 (8th Cir. 1998).

11. In 2010, after a government working group conducted a "thorough review" of DOJ practices, Deputy Attorney General David W. Ogden mandated that U.S. Attorney's Offices implement discovery policies that reflect circuit and district court precedent and local rules and practice. *See* David W. Ogden, Dep'y Att. Gen'l, Memorandum for Heads of Dep't Litigating Components Handling Criminal Matters, Requirement for Office Discovery Policies in

Criminal Matters (Jan. 4, 2010). He also issued new guidance for prosecutors regarding criminal discovery. *See* U.S. DOJ, U.S. Attorney's Manual, Criminal Resource Manual No. 165 (Jan. 2010). The DOJ standards purportedly were not intended to establish new discovery obligations. Rather, "[b]y following the steps [laid out in the new directive]... and being familiar with the laws and policies regarding discovery obligations, prosecutors are more likely to meet all legal requirements, to make considered decisions about disclosures in a particular case, and to achieve a just result in every case." Resource Manual No. 165, *supra*, at 1. The current policy, however, repeatedly exhorts prosecutors to produce more than the Supreme Court's *Brady* caselaw would require:

U.S.A.M. § 9-5.001 ("Policy Regarding Disclosure of Exculpatory and Impeachment Information) (last updated July 2014)

B. *Constitutional obligation to ensure a fair trial and disclose material exculpatory and impeachment evidence. ...*

1. *Materiality and Admissibility.* Exculpatory and impeachment evidence is material to a finding of guilt—and thus the Constitution requires disclosure—when there is a reasonable probability that effective use of the evidence will result in an acquittal. *United States v. Bagley*, 475 U.S. 667, 676 (1985). Recognizing that it is sometimes difficult to assess the materiality of evidence before trial, prosecutors generally must take a broad view of materiality and err on the side of disclosing exculpatory and impeaching evidence. While ordinarily, evidence that would not be admissible at trial need not be disclosed, this policy encourages prosecutors to err on the side of disclosure if admissibility is a close question.

2. *The prosecution team.* It is the obligation of federal prosecutors, in preparing for trial, to seek all exculpatory and impeachment information from all the members of the prosecution team. Members of the prosecution team include federal, state, and local law enforcement officers and other government officials participating in the investigation and prosecution of the criminal case against the defendant.

C. *Disclosure of exculpatory and impeachment information beyond that which is constitutionally and legally required.* Department policy recognizes that a fair trial will often include examination of relevant exculpatory or impeachment information that is significantly probative of the issues before the court but that may not, on its own, result in an acquittal or, as is often colloquially expressed, make the difference between guilt and innocence. As a result, this policy requires disclosure by prosecutors of information beyond that which is "material" to guilt .... The policy recognizes, however, that a trial should not involve the consideration of information which is irrelevant or not significantly probative of the issues before the court and should not involve spurious issues or arguments which serve to divert the trial process from examining the genuine issues. Information that goes only to such matters does not advance the purpose of a trial and thus is not subject to disclosure.

1. *Additional exculpatory information that must be disclosed.* A prosecutor must disclose information that is inconsistent with any element of any crime charged against the defendant or that establishes a recognized affirmative defense, regardless of whether the prosecutor believes such information will make the difference between conviction and acquittal of the defendant for a charged crime.

2. *Additional impeachment information that must be disclosed.* A prosecutor must disclose information that either casts a substantial doubt upon the accuracy of any evidence—including but not limited to witness testimony—the prosecutor intends to rely on to prove an element of any crime charged, or might have a significant bearing on the admissibility of prosecution evidence. This information must be disclosed regardless of whether it is likely to make the difference between conviction and acquittal of the defendant for a charged crime.

3. *Information.* Unlike the requirements of *Brady* and its progeny, which focus on evidence, the disclosure requirement of this section applies to information regardless of whether the information subject to disclosure would itself constitute admissible evidence.

4. *Cumulative impact of items of information.* While items of information viewed in isolation may not reasonably be seen as meeting the standards outlined in paragraphs 1 and 2 above, several items together can have such an effect. If this is the case, all such items must be disclosed. ...

F. *Comment.* This policy establishes guidelines for the exercise of judgment and discretion by attorneys for the government in determining what information to disclose to a criminal defendant pursuant to the government's disclosure obligation as set out in *Brady v. Maryland* and *Giglio v. United States* and its obligation to seek justice in every case. ... As the Supreme Court has explained, disclosure is required when evidence in the possession of the prosecutor or prosecution team is material to guilt, innocence or punishment. This policy encourages prosecutors to err on the side of disclosure in close questions of materiality and identifies standards that favor greater disclosure in advance of trial through the production of exculpatory information that is inconsistent with any element of any charged crime and impeachment information that casts a substantial doubt upon either the accuracy of any evidence the government intends to rely on to prove an element of any charged crime or that might have a significant bearing on the admissibility of prosecution evidence. This expanded disclosure policy, however, does not create a general right of discovery in criminal cases. Nor does it provide defendants with any additional rights or remedies. Where it is unclear whether evidence or information should be disclosed, prosecutors are encouraged to reveal such information to defendants or to the court for inspection *in camera* and, where applicable, seek a protective order from the Court. By doing so, prosecutors will ensure confidence in fair trials and verdicts.

Is this policy enforceable in any practical way? *See, e.g.,* Connick v. Thompson, 563 U.S. 51 (2011) (denying damages for failure to train Assistant DAs on *Brady* obligations); George A. Weiss, *Prosecutorial Accountability after* Connick v. Thompson, 60 Drake L. Rev. 199 (2011).

13. The Supreme Court recognized in *Kyles* that the *Brady* standard is less favorable to the defense than reigning ethical standards. That is, Model Rule 3.8(d) requires a prosecutor to "make timely disclosure to the defense of all evidence or information known to the prosecutor that tends to negate guilt of the accused or mitigates the offense, and, in connection with sentencing, [to] disclose to the defense and to the tribunal all unprivileged mitigating information known to the prosecutor." Should the constitutional and ethical standards be different?

In 1998, Congress enacted the Citizens Protection Act (CPA), sometimes referred to as the "McDade Amendment." 28 U.S.C. § 530B(a). Section 530B is entitled "Ethical Standards for Attorneys for the Government" and provides in relevant part that "[a]n attorney for the Government shall be subject to State laws and rules, and local Federal court rules, governing attorneys in each State where such attorney engages in that attorney's duties, to the same extent as other attorneys in that State." As noted above, ABA Model Rule of Professional Conduct 3.8(d) states that a prosecutor shall make timely disclosure of all evidence or information known to the prosecutor "that *tends* to negate the guilt of the accused or mitigates the offense." (Emphasis added.) *Brady* provides a constitutional floor below which federal prosecutors may not go. But in those jurisdictions that have adopted Rule 3.8(d), are federal prosecutors now obliged by § 530B(a) to follow this more demanding disclosure standard? (In the District of Columbia, the answer is "yes." *See In re* Kline, 113 A.3d 202 (D.C. Ct. Apps. 2015) (professional conduct rule requires prosecutors to disclose all potentially exculpatory information in their possession regardless of materiality)).

That the ethical standard *is* more demanding in most jurisdictions was underscored by the ABA Standing Committee on Ethics and Professional Responsibility in its 2009 opinion on Rule 3.8(d) of the Model Rules of Professional Conduct, which most states have adopted as part of their binding lawyer conduct rules. *See* ABA Standing Comm. on Ethics and

Professional Responsibility, Formal Op. 09-454 (July 8, 2009). The Committee emphasized that the disclosure duty under Rule 3.8(d) is separate from rules derived from state or federal constitutions, statutes, or rules. *Id.* at 1. Rule 3.8(d) does not simply codify prosecutors' *Brady* obligations; the disclosure rules under 3.8(d) are more demanding. *Id.* at 1-2, 4. For example, Rule 3.8(d) requires disclosure of evidence or information favorable to the accused whether or not it is material—that is, regardless of what impact it might have on the trial result. *Id.* at 2. The duty to disclose extends beyond "evidence" to "information" that may lead to admissible evidence or help the defense in other ways, such as in plea negotiations. *Id.* at 5.

The ABA Formal Opinion does note that Rule 3.8(d) only requires disclosure of evidence and information "known to the prosecutor" and that the rule "does not establish a duty to undertake an investigation in search of exculpatory evidence." *Id.* at 5-6. Once favorable information is known to the prosecutor, however, he or she must disclose it as soon as "reasonably practical." *Id.* at 6. If disclosure would undermine the investigation or jeopardize a witness, the prosecutor's recourse is requesting a protective order. *Id.*

The Formal Opinion noted that the prosecutor's duty to disclose runs to the court as well as the defense, so that duty requires that disclosure of information that would lead to a lesser sentence. *Id.* at 7-8. Finally, under Model Rule 5.1, supervisory and managerial personnel in the prosecutors' offices are obligated to ensure that subordinate lawyers comply with their disclosure duties under Rule 3.8(d). *Id.* at 8.

Note that this opinion states that because defense counsel need this type of information to advise the defendant whether to take a plea, prosecutors must disclose favorable evidence prior to a guilty plea proceeding even if that proceeding comes at an early point. *Id.* at 6. The prosecutor cannot escape the mandates of Rule 3.8(d) by negotiating a disclosure waiver; that is, a prosecutor and defendant may not agree that, as a condition of leniency, the defendant will forego evidence and information that would otherwise have to be revealed. *Id.* at 7. Indeed, a prosecutor may not "solicit, accept, or rely on the defendant's consent." *Id.* Consider, by contrast, the Supreme Court's decision on the permissible scope of constitutional *Brady* waivers.

UNITED STATES v. RUIZ
536 U.S. 622 (2002)

Justice Breyer delivered the opinion of the Court.

In this case we primarily consider whether the Fifth and Sixth Amendments require federal prosecutors, before entering into a binding plea agreement with a criminal defendant, to disclose "impeachment information relating to any informants or other witnesses." We hold that the Constitution does not require that disclosure.

After immigration agents found 30 kilograms of marijuana in Angela Ruiz's luggage, federal prosecutors offered her what is known in the Southern District of California as a "fast track" plea bargain. That bargain—standard in that district—asks a defendant to waive indictment, trial, and an appeal. In return, the Government agrees to recommend to the sentencing judge a two-level departure downward from the otherwise applicable United States Sentencing Guidelines sentence. In Ruiz's case, a two level departure downward would have shortened the ordinary Guidelines-specified 18-to-24-month sentencing range by 6 months, to 12-to-18 months.

The prosecutors' proposed plea agreement contains a set of detailed terms. Among other things, it specifies that "any [known] information establishing the factual innocence of the defendant" "has been turned over to the defendant," and it acknowledges the Government's "continuing duty to provide such information." At the same time it requires that the defendant "[waive] the right" to receive "impeachment information relating to any informants or other witnesses" as well as the right to receive information supporting any affirmative defense the defendant raises if the case goes to trial. Because Ruiz would not agree to this last-mentioned waiver, the prosecutors withdrew their bargaining offer. The Government then indicted Ruiz for unlawful drug possession. And despite the absence of any agreement, Ruiz ultimately pleaded guilty.

At sentencing, Ruiz asked the judge to grant her the same two-level downward departure that the Government would have recommended had she accepted the "fast track" agreement. The Government opposed her request, and the District Court denied it, imposing a standard Guideline sentence instead.

... [On appeal] the Ninth Circuit pointed out that the Constitution requires prosecutors to make certain impeachment information available to a defendant before trial. It decided that this obligation entitles defendants to receive that same information before they enter into a plea agreement. The Ninth Circuit also decided that the Constitution prohibits defendants from waiving their right to that information. And it held that the prosecutors' standard "fast track" plea agreement was unlawful because it insisted upon that waiver. ...

The constitutional question concerns a federal criminal defendant's waiver of the right to receive from prosecutors exculpatory impeachment material—a right that the Constitution provides as part of its basic "fair trial" guarantee. See U.S. Const., Amdts. 5, 6. See also *Brady v. Maryland*, 373 U.S. 83, 87 (1963).

When a defendant pleads guilty he or she, of course, forgoes not only a fair trial, but also other accompanying constitutional guarantees. *Boykin v. Alabama*, 395 U.S. 238, 243 (1969) (pleading guilty implicates the Fifth Amendment privilege against self-incrimination, the Sixth Amendment right to confront one's accusers, and the Sixth Amendment right to trial by jury). Given the seriousness of the matter, the Constitution insists, among other things, that the defendant enter a guilty plea that is "voluntary" and that the defendant must make related waivers "knowing[ly], intelligent[ly], [and] with sufficient awareness of the relevant circumstances and likely consequences." *Brady v. United States*, 397 U.S. 742, 748 (1970).

In this case, the Ninth Circuit in effect held that a guilty plea is not "voluntary" (and that the defendant could not, by pleading guilty, waive his right to a fair trial) unless the prosecutors first made the same disclosure of material impeachment information that the prosecutors would have had to make had the defendant insisted upon a trial. We must decide whether the Constitution requires that preguilty plea disclosure of impeachment information. We conclude that it does not.

First, impeachment information is special in relation to the *fairness of a trial*, not in respect to whether a plea is *voluntary* ("knowing," "intelligent," and "sufficient[ly] aware"). Of course, the more information the defendant has, the more aware he is of the likely consequences of a plea, waiver, or decision, and the wiser that decision will likely be. But the Constitution does not require the prosecutor to share all useful information with the defendant. *Weatherford v. Bursey*, 429 U.S. 545, 559 (1977) ("There is no general constitutional right to discovery in a criminal case"). And the law ordinarily considers a waiver knowing, intelligent, and sufficiently aware if the defendant fully understands the nature of the right and how it would likely apply *in general* in the circumstances—even though the defendant may not know the *specific detailed* consequences of invoking it. A defendant, for example, may waive his right to remain silent, his right to a jury trial, or his right to counsel even if the defendant does not know the specific questions the authorities intend to ask, who will likely serve on the jury, or the particular lawyer the State might otherwise provide.

It is particularly difficult to characterize impeachment information as critical information of which the defendant must always be aware prior to pleading guilty given the random way in which such information may, or may not, help a particular defendant. The degree of help that impeachment information can provide will depend upon the defendant's own independent knowledge of the prosecution's potential case—a matter that the Constitution does not require prosecutors to disclose.

Second, we have found no legal authority embodied either in this Court's past cases or in cases from other circuits that provide significant support for the Ninth Circuit's decision. To the contrary, this Court has found that the Constitution, in respect to a defendant's awareness of relevant circumstances, does not require complete knowledge of the relevant circumstances, but permits a court to accept a guilty plea, with its accompanying waiver of various constitutional rights, despite various forms of misapprehension under which a defendant might labor. See *Brady v. United States*, 397 U.S., at 757 (defendant "misapprehended the quality of the State's case"); *ibid.* (defendant misapprehended "the likely penalties"); *ibid.* (defendant failed to "anticipate a change in the law regarding" relevant "punishments"); *McMann v. Richardson*, 397 U.S. 759, 770 (1970) (counsel "misjudged the admissibility" of a "confession"); *United States v. Broce*, 488 U.S. 563, 573 (1989) (counsel failed to point out a potential defense); *Tollett v. Henderson*, 411 U.S. 258, 267 (1973) (counsel failed to find a potential constitutional infirmity in grand jury proceedings). It is difficult to distinguish, in terms of importance, (1) a defendant's ignorance of grounds for impeachment of potential witnesses at a possible future trial from (2) the varying forms of ignorance at issue in these cases.

Third, due process considerations, the very considerations that led this Court to find trial-related rights to exculpatory and impeachment information in *Brady* and *Giglio*, argue against the existence of the "right" that the Ninth Circuit found here. This Court has said that due process considerations include not only (1) the nature of the private interest at stake, but also (2) the value of the additional safeguard, and (3) the adverse impact of the requirement upon the Government's interests. Here, as we have just pointed out, the added value of the Ninth Circuit's "right" to a defendant is often limited, for it depends upon the defendant's independent awareness of the details of the Government's case. And in any case, as the proposed plea agreement at issue here specifies, the Government will provide "any information establishing the factual innocence of the defendant" regardless. That fact, along with other guilty-plea safeguards, see Fed. Rule Crim. Proc. 11, diminishes the force of *Ruiz*'s concern that, in the absence of impeachment information, innocent individuals, accused of crimes, will plead guilty.

At the same time, a constitutional obligation to provide impeachment information during plea bargaining, prior to entry of a guilty plea, could seriously interfere with the Government's interest in securing those guilty pleas that are factually justified, desired by defendants, and help to secure the efficient administration of justice. The Ninth Circuit's rule risks premature disclosure of Government witness information, which, the Government tells us, could "disrupt ongoing investigations" and expose prospective witnesses to serious harm. And the careful tailoring that characterizes most legal Government witness disclosure requirements suggests recognition by both Congress and the Federal Rules Committees that such concerns are valid.

Consequently, the Ninth Circuit's requirement could force the Government to abandon its "general practice" of not "disclos[ing] to a defendant pleading guilty information that would reveal the identities of cooperating informants, undercover investigators, or other prospective witnesses." It could require the Government to devote substantially more resources to trial preparation prior to plea bargaining, thereby depriving the plea-bargaining process of its main resource-saving advantages. Or it could lead the Government instead to abandon its heavy reliance upon plea bargaining in a vast number—90% or more—of federal criminal cases. We cannot say that the Constitution's due process requirement demands so radical a change in the criminal justice process in order to achieve so comparatively small a constitutional benefit. These considerations, taken together, lead us to conclude that the Constitution does not require the Government to disclose material impeachment evidence prior to entering a plea agreement with a criminal defendant.

In addition, we note that the "fast track" plea agreement requires a defendant to waive her right to receive information the Government has regarding any "affirmative defense" she raises at trial. We do not believe the Constitution here requires provision of this information to the defendant prior to plea bargaining—for most (though not all) of the reasons previously stated. That is to say, in the context of this agreement, the need for this information is more closely related to the *fairness* of a trial than to the *voluntariness* of the plea; the value in terms of the defendant's added awareness of relevant circumstances is ordinarily limited; yet the added burden imposed upon the Government by requiring its provision well in advance of trial (often before trial preparation begins) can be serious, thereby significantly interfering with the administration of the plea bargaining process. ...

JUSTICE THOMAS, concurring in the judgment.

I agree with the Court that the Constitution does not require the Government to disclose either affirmative defense information or impeachment information relating to informants or other witnesses before entering into a binding plea agreement with a criminal defendant. The Court, however, suggests that the constitutional analysis turns in some part on the "degree of help" such information would provide to the defendant at the plea stage, a distinction that is neither necessary nor accurate. To the extent that the Court is implicitly drawing a line based on a flawed characterization about the usefulness of certain types of information, I can only concur in the judgment. The principle supporting *Brady* was "avoidance of an unfair trial to the accused." That concern is not implicated at the plea stage regardless.

Notes

1. Given the number of federal criminal cases resolved by guilty pleas, the question whether the government is required to make pre-plea *Brady* disclosures is a very important one. Generally the issue arises when a defendant seeks to withdraw a guilty plea on the basis of the prosecutor's failure to turn over *Brady* material prior to the plea. Before the Court decided *Ruiz*, the Ninth Circuit had taken the position that "a defendant can argue that his guilty plea was not voluntary and intelligent because it was made in absence of withheld *Brady* material." Sanchez v. United States, 50 F.3d 1448, 1453 (9th Cir. 1995). The Ninth Circuit reasoned in *Sanchez* that this exception to the general rule that a defendant who pleads guilty waives independent claims of constitutional violations was sensible

> because a defendant's decision whether or not to plead guilty is often heavily influenced by his appraisal of the prosecution's case. A waiver cannot be deemed "intelligent and voluntary" if "entered without knowledge of material information withheld by the prosecution." Moreover, if a defendant may not raise a *Brady* claim after a guilty plea, prosecutors may be tempted to deliberately withhold exculpatory information as part of an attempt to elicit guilty pleas.

50 F.3d at 1453. The *Sanchez* court concluded, however, that failure to disclose information of which the government is aware constitutes grounds for a plea withdrawal only where "there is a reasonable probability that but for the failure to disclose *Brady* material, the defendant would have refused to plead and would have gone to trial." *Id.* at 1454. Does the *Ruiz* Court adequately address the concerns underlying the rule it rejects?

2. Did the Supreme Court in *Ruiz* categorically hold that there is no due process right to pre-plea *Brady*? A careful reading reveals that the Court consistently referred to the materials at issue in that case—impeachment (often called *Giglio*) material. Could those precedents that require pre-plea disclosure of *Brady* material that negates actual guilt or that goes to punishment survive? Note that the government's proposed *Brady* waiver in the plea agreement (unlike such waivers used in other districts) specified that "any [known] information establishing the factual innocence of the defendant" "has been turned over to the defendant," and it acknowledged the Government's "continuing duty to provide such information."

3. The *Ruiz* Court's explicit balancing analysis is a new development in *Brady* case law. Does the Court's treatment of impeachment material indicate that it is creating a hierarchy of *Brady* material or imposing a higher burden on defendants to demonstrate the materiality of such impeachment materials? Is the Court's treatment of impeachment material consistent with its existing precedents? *Should* impeachment material be treated differently?

4. Does the *Ruiz* Court's discussion of the types of mistakes that may be countenanced in the course of a valid guilty plea undermine one's confidence that such pleas involve a truly knowing, intelligent, and voluntary surrender of vital constitutional trial rights? Does this discussion undermine the Court's conclusion that the guilty-plea safeguards (as well as the government's commitment to provide disclosure of information regarding the factual innocence of the defendant) "diminishes the force of Ruiz's concern

that, in the absence of impeachment information, innocent individuals, accused of crimes, will plead guilty"?

5. What of the Court's treatment of the government's interest in the course of its constitutional balancing? Throughout its discussion of that interest, the Court consistently notes what "could" result from a contrary ruling. Should the Court require more concrete evidence regarding the burdens that a contrary rule would entail?

The Court appears to be very concerned with the possibility that the Ninth Circuit's holding could force more trials. Should the fact that a practice might induce more defendants to exercise their constitutional trial rights weigh against such a rule? The Court emphasizes that the information required to be waived goes more to the "*fairness* of a trial than to the *voluntariness* of the plea." What does the Court mean by the "fairness" of the trial? If it means that the information will ensure that the trial verdict is fairly achieved and reliable, shouldn't this mean that the provision of pre-plea *Brady* is necessary for a fair and reliable plea process, regardless of the voluntariness of the plea? Should the Court's balancing come out the same for information relating to a defendant's affirmative defense?

6. As this case demonstrates, in response to court rulings that defendants may in some cases withdraw a guilty plea upon learning of suppressed *Brady* material, prosecutors are increasingly requiring defendants, as a condition of a plea deal, to agree to what are known as *Brady* waivers, one of which was obviously required in *Ruiz*. Such waivers are further considered in Chapter 19 (Plea Bargaining and Cooperation). Does the Supreme Court, implicitly if not explicitly, resolve the issue of the propriety of such required waivers?

B. PRETRIAL DISCOVERY: FED. R. CRIM. P. 16

"There is no general constitutional right to discovery in a criminal case, and *Brady* did not create one"; as the Court has explained, "the Due Process Clause has little to say regarding the amount of discovery which the parties must be afforded ...."[11] Accordingly, the parties' rights to pretrial discovery in criminal cases are determined by the controlling federal rule: Fed. R. Crim. P. 16. "Rule 16's mandatory discovery provisions were designed to contribute to the fair and efficient administration of justice by providing the defendant with sufficient information upon which to base an informed plea and litigation strategy; by facilitating the raising of objections to admissibility prior to trial; by minimizing the undesirable effect of surprise at trial; and by contributing to the accuracy of the fact-finding process."[12]

Rule 16 is broader than *Brady* in that it is obviously not limited to materially exculpatory evidence. Further, as the district court explained in *United States v. McVeigh*:

> The differences between discovery available upon request [by] the defendant under Rule 16 and the prosecutor's duty to disclose exculpatory information under *Brady* are important, both in determining what the government must produce and in the procedure to be followed in so doing. Rule 16 is applicable only when the defense chooses to invoke it by making a request. Compliance with such a request triggers a defense obligation to make reciprocal discovery under Rule 16(b). Both parties are then under a continuing duty to disclose any additional evidence or material as they discover it. Rule 16(c). Disputes about rule discovery are brought to the court by a motion for a protective order under Rule 16(d)(1) or a motion to compel or for

---

[11] Weatherford v. Bursey, 429 U.S. 545, 559 (1977). The Court also "reads the Sixth Amendment rights to compulsory process and confrontation narrowly, rejecting an interpretation of those provisions as requiring the Government to provide discovery to the defendants." Peter J. Henning, *Defense Discovery in White Collar Criminal Prosecutions*, 15 Ga. St. U. L. Rev. 601, 611 (1999); *see also* Pennsylvania v. Ritchie, 480 U.S. 39, 52-53 (1987).

[12] United States v. Lanoue, 71 F.3d 966, 976 (1st Cir. 1995).

sanctions under Rule 16(d)(2). Rule 12(b)(4) requires requests for Rule 16 discovery to be made before trial and the court may control the timing of discovery motions under Rule 12(c).[13]

Compare what the government and the defense will be required to turn over and on what conditions under Rule 16. Are their obligations equal? Why not? What rationale(s) would explain why these particular categories of materials were selected for pretrial disclosure? Rule 16 also expressly excludes from discovery certain materials. What are they? Why are these materials exempted from pretrial disclosure?

Readers should bear in mind that Rule 16 defines the universe of mandated discovery and that courts generally refuse to permit defense counsel to secure discovery not permitted under Rule 16 through other means, such as Fed. R. Crim. P. 17 trial subpoenas or Fed. R. Crim. P. 7(f) bills of particular. Should additional discovery be provided? In particular, should the discovery tools regularly employed in civil cases (*e.g.*, interrogatories, depositions, and the like) be made available in criminal cases? As Justice Brennan asked in 1963, in terms that apply today:

> Should we extend to criminal prosecutions the civil pre-trial discovery techniques which force both sides of a civil law suit to put all cards on the table before trial, and tend to reduce the chance that surprise or maneuver, rather than truth, may determine the outcome of the trial? Or, as Glanville Williams asked recently, shall we continue to regard the criminal trial as "in the nature of a game or sporting contest" and not "a serious inquiry aiming to distinguish between guilt and innocence"?[14]

Justice Brennan identified, and rejected, three asserted grounds for the dearth of discovery provided in criminal cases: (1) "pretrial discovery would inevitably result in a perjured defense";[15] (2) "an accused, knowing the names of witnesses against him, may see to it that they are silenced before the trial";[16] and (3) "our constitutional privilege against self-incrimination prevents discovery being a two-way street."[17] Are these reasons persuasive? Might the discovery rules be tailored to account for at least some of these possibilities?

Notes

1. The most important subsection of Rule 16 in document-intensive white-collar practice is Rule 16(a)(1)(E)(ii). That rule provides that the government must permit the defense access to documents and other objects if the government "intends to use the item in its case-in-chief at trial." In other words, the government must make pretrial disclosure of its intended exhibits. The rule further requires the government to give the defense access to documents which the government does not intend to use in its case in chief but which are "material to preparing the defense" and are in its possession, custody, or control. Fed. R. Crim. P. 16(a)(1)(E)(i); *see also* 16(a)(1)(F) (relating to reports of examinations or tests). What is meant by evidence in the government's "possession" that is "material" to the preparation of the defendant's "defense"?

2. Many courts read the term "material" for Rule 16 purposes to mean "material" in the *Brady* sense of potentially exculpatory rather than "material" in the sense of "important." For example, in *United States v. Stevens*, 985 F.2d 1175 (2d Cir. 1993), the Second Circuit explained:

---

[13] 954 F. Supp. 1441, 1449 (D. Colo. 1997).

[14] Hon. William J. Brennan, Jr., *The Criminal Prosecution: Sporting Event or Quest for Truth?*, 1963 Wash. U. L.Q. 279, 279 (1963).

[15] *Id.* at 290.

[16] *Id.* at 292.

[17] *Id.* at 293.

Evidence that the government does not intend to use in its case is material if it could be used to counter the government's case or to bolster a defense; information not meeting either of those criteria is not to be deemed material within the meaning of the Rule merely because the government may be able to use it to rebut a defense position. ... Nor is it to be deemed material merely because it would have dissuaded the defendant from proffering easily impeached testimony.

Id. at 1180; *see also* United States v. Ross, 511 F.2d 757, 762-63 (5th Cir. 1975). However, the D.C. Circuit, in *United States v. Marshall*, 132 F.3d 63 (D.C. Cir. 1998), adopted a different standard:

> ... [Rule 16(a)(1)(E)(i)] covers evidence which is material "to *the preparation of* the defendant's defense." (Emphasis added). The government ignores the words we have just italicized, reading the rule to refer to evidence which is "favorable or helpful to a defendant's defense." The rule as written does not compel the conclusion that inculpatory evidence is immune from disclosure. Inculpatory evidence, after all, is just as likely to assist in "the preparation of the defendant's defense" as exculpatory evidence. In other words, it is just as important to the preparation of a defense to know its potential pitfalls as it is to know its strengths. ...
>
> Additionally, we note that the discovery obligations mandated by Rule 16 "contribute[] to the fair and efficient administration of criminal justice by providing the defendant with enough information to make an informed decision as to plea." Fed.R.Crim.P. 16 advisory committee note to 1974 amendment. The government's interpretation of Rule 16 is at loggerheads with this policy. If the government is excused from its obligation to disclose incriminating evidence (and does not intend to introduce such evidence during its case-in-chief), the defense must make any pre-trial plea decisions without knowing the true strength of the government's evidence.

Id. at 67-68; *see also* United States v. Baker, 453 F.3d 419, 424-25 (7th Cir. 2006). (Note that in 2002, after *Marshall*, certain stylistic but not substantive changes were made to this rule, which is now numbered Rule 16(a)(1)(E)(i) and calls for disclosure of items "material to preparing the defense.") Which interpretation of the rule makes the most sense? Should "material" mean the same thing under *Brady* and Rule 16? *See* Henning, *supra* note 11, at 618-28.

3. Courts generally state that the defendant cannot rely on conclusory allegations or on a general description of the requested information under Rule 16(a)(1)(E), but must make a prima facie showing of materiality to obtain the requested information. *See, e.g.*, United States v. Thompson, 944 F.2d 1331, 1341 (7th Cir. 1991). Representative is the Ninth Circuit's admonition that "[n]either a general description of the information sought nor conclusory allegations of materiality suffice; a defendant must present facts which would tend to show that the Government is in possession of information helpful to the defense." United States v. Mandel, 914 F.2d 1215, 1219 (9th Cir. 1990). What challenges does this requirement present for defense counsel? Consider the following explanation by Professor Peter J. Henning:

> Allegations of white collar crime generally involve economic transactions that ostensibly appear to be ordinary business events. In most cases, the crucial question is not whether the defendant engaged in the conduct at issue—that is usually conceded—but whether the conduct rises to the level of being criminal. To establish a white collar case, government agents often pore over voluminous documents to determine whether the transactions show a pattern of criminality from which a jury can infer the requisite knowledge and intent on the part of the defendant. ... White collar prosecutions are "paper cases," in the sense that the Government's principle proof of criminality comes from comparing what a document discloses with witness statements and other records. Without the paper, it is unlikely that the Government could establish the elements of many white collar crimes, especially those involving fraud, bribery, or conflicts of interest.

Unlike a street crime, there is no real physical evidence of the white collar criminal's violation, much less a scene of the crime.

If the Government must rely on the paper trail to establish its case, then certainly a defendant needs access to the documents related to the transactions to mount a defense. ... [A] defendant in a white collar prosecution usually does not know exactly what documents exist, or how they will affect the case. The defendant's lack of knowledge can make the discovery of documents a complicated dance because the burden is on the defendant to establish the prosecutor's "possession" of the documents and their "materiality" to a defense before gaining access to them. The federal approach to discovery can be a "heads I win, tails you lose" situation because the defendant must show what is in the records *before* being permitted to review them.

Henning, *supra* note 11, at 602-03.

4. In *United States v. Armstrong*, 517 U.S. 456 (1996), the Supreme Court gave a narrow interpretation to the meaning of the term "defense" for purposes of Rule 16(a)(1)(E)(i) (which, at the time of the decision, was numbered 16(a)(1)(C)). In *Armstrong*, the defendants were indicted for drug and firearms offenses. They then filed a motion for discovery or for dismissal of the indictment, alleging that they were selected for federal prosecution because of their race. Over the government's opposition, the district court granted the motion and ordered the government to (1) to provide a list of all cases from the last three years in which the Government charged both cocaine and firearms offenses, (2) to identify the race of the defendants in those cases, (3) to identify what levels of law enforcement were involved in the investigations of those cases, and (4) to explain its criteria for deciding to prosecute those defendants for federal cocaine offenses. The Supreme Court held that the discovery order was not authorized by Fed. R. Crim. P. 16(a)(1)(E). It ruled that "in the context of Rule 16 'the defendant's defense' means the defendant's response to the Government's case-in-chief." *Id.* at 462. Thus, the Court held that "Rule 16(a)(1)([E]) authorizes defendants to examine Government documents material to the preparation of their defense against the Government's case-in-chief, but not to the preparation of selective-prosecution claims." *Id.* at 463.

5. The government is only required to produce those documents that are material to the preparation of the defendant's defense that are in the "possession, custody or control of the government." *See* United States v. Libby, 429 F. Supp.2d 1 (D.D.C. 2006). Should the cases concerning what is deemed within the possession of the government for *Brady* purposes control in this context? *See* Henning, *supra* note 11, at 612-18 (stating that "[t]he answer should be no, despite the fact that defendants and courts sometimes treat them as equivalent means to the same end, and, therefore subject to the same interpretation"). As was noted above in the *Brady* materials, the question of what is in the possession, custody, or control of the government may be critical in some white-collar cases because of the increasing incidence of parallel criminal and regulatory enforcement proceedings. As the discussion of the availability of subpoenas under Fed. R. Crim. P. 17, *infra*, illustrates, materials gathered in such parallel proceedings may be difficult for the defense to access absent a governmental discovery obligation.

One court has held that where the government and a target entity have entered into a deferred prosecution agreement (DPA) that gives the government "the unqualified right to demand production by [the entity] of any documents it wishes for purposes of [the] case," subject to a "limited privilege carve-out," the entity's documents are "within the possession, custody or control of the government" for purposes of Rule 16 discovery. United States v. Stein, 488 F. Supp.2d 350, 360-64 (S.D.N.Y. 2007). As was explored further in Chapter 4, *supra*, the government increasingly relies on the use of DPAs to resolve charges of corporate criminality. The *Stein* court was unsympathetic to the argument that such a ruling would have a broad compass given the numbers of deferred prosecution agreements extant between the DOJ and corporate actors. The court explained:

The plain language of Rule 16 makes clear that documents material to the defense that are within the government's control are producible. That the government has begun making broad use of agreements of this sort only in comparatively recent years or that it might regard compliance with the rule in such cases to be inconvenient warrants no different conclusion. If it is uncomfortable with the consequences of such provisions, it need not insist upon them in future.

Id. at 364; *see also* United States v. Buske, 2011 WL 2912707 (E.D. Wis. 2011) (distinguishing *Stein*); United States v. Norris, 753 F.Supp.2d 492, 529-31 (E.D. Pa. 2010) (same). *But see* United States v. Carson, Order Granting in Part and Denying in Part Defendants' Motion to Compel, No. 8:09-Cr-00077-JVS (C.D. Ca. Dec. 8, 2009) (rejecting *Stein* analysis).

6. Where the government engages in "open file" discovery in a case involving thousands of documents, defense counsel may be hampered by the overabundance rather than the dearth of materials made available by the government. As one attorney expressed it, "having too much information is sometimes as dangerous or harmful or unproductive as having not enough information." *Panel Discussion: Criminal Discovery in Practice, supra* note 6, at 801. In such circumstances, may the defense force the government at least to identify that which it proposes to use as exhibits at trial? *Compare* United States v. Weissman, No. S2 94 Cr. 760 (CSH), 1996 WL 751385 (S.D.N.Y. 1996) (yes), *with* United States v. Skilling, 554 F.3d 529, 576-77 (5th Cir. 2009); United States v. Savin, 2001 WL 243533, at *6 (S.D.N.Y. 2001) (no) *and* United States v. Nachamie, 91 F. Supp.2d 565 (S.D.N.Y. 2000) (no); *cf.* United States v. Bortnovsky, 820 F.2d 572, 575 (2d Cir. 1987) (reversing conviction for abuse of discretion in denying bill of particulars and stating that "[t]he government does not fulfill its obligation merely by providing mountains of documents to defense counsel who were left unguided as to which documents would be proven" to be falsified at trial); United States v. Davidoff, 845 F.2d 1151, 1155 (2d Cir. 1988); *Savin*, 2001 WL 243533, at *2-*6.

7. In a case of first impression, *United States v. Maury*, 695 F.3d 227 (3d Cir. 2012), the Third Circuit interpreted narrowly that portion of Rule 16 that mandates disclosure to organizational defendants of employees' statements. The court held that there are two classes of individuals who can made statements that are sufficient to constitute corporate admissions, "which are thus discoverable under Rule 16(a)(1)(C): (1) representatives, or individuals who have the power to bind an organization by virtue of their authority to make statements on the subject on behalf of the organization, see Fed. R. Crim. P. 16(a)(1)(C)(i); and (2) employees who engage in illegal conduct within the scope of their jobs and then make some statement about having done so, see Fed. R. Crim. P. 16(a)(1)(C)(ii)." *Maury*, 695 F.3d at 253. The defendants had argued on appeal that the government was required to disclose all statements given by employees covered by the rule, even if their statements were unrelated to the conduct at issue. The court rejected their position, reasoning:

> we think the second category, which references "the conduct constituting the offense" *and* the ability "to bind the defendant in respect to that alleged conduct," contemplates that the statements governed by Rule 16(a)(1)(C)(ii) are tethered to the conduct itself. In keeping with traditional notions of agency and vicarious liability, it is only in this context that the employee "speaks" on the behalf of the Company as concerns the charged conduct against which the organizational defendant must defend itself.

Id.

8. Both the government and the defense are increasingly mining social media for evidence and impeachment material. The defense may sometimes be entitled to obtain such information in the government's possession when it constitutes *Brady* or *Giglio* material. *But see* United States v. Meregildo, 920 F.Supp.2d 920 (S.D.N.Y. 2013) (no *Brady* obligation to turn over Facebook posts of cooperating witness because the witness was not a member of the "prosecution team"). Often, when the social media information relates to non-parties, the defense will have to try to use a Rule 17 subpoena to obtain it. *See generally* Justin P. Murphy & Adrian Fontecilla, *Social Media Evidence in Government Investigations and Criminal Proceedings: A Frontier of New Legal Issues,* 19 Richmond J.L. & Tech. 11 (2013).

9. In 2012, the DOJ and the Administrative Office (AO) of U.S. Courts announced the results of a joint effort to address e-discovery in criminal cases:

> The digital revolution is producing increasingly complex litigation and discovery issues in federal criminal cases. Most challenging for federal court practitioners are cases involving electronic discovery, also known as "electronically stored information" (ESI).
>
> After 18 months of negotiation, the Administrative Office (AO) and the Department of Justice jointly have developed a set of recommendations aimed at making the production or exchange of ESI discovery between prosecutors and defense counsel more efficient and cost-effective.
>
> "An expansion in the amount of digital data, the number of devices on which it can be created and stored, and the declining cost of storing such information have resulted in the increased presence of ESI in federal criminal litigation," said Theodore Lidz, the AO's Assistant Director for the Office of Defender Services. "Often the amount of information ranges from tens of thousands to millions of pages. While difficult to quantify, the expectation is that use of the recommendations will limit overall criminal justice discovery costs, reduce the number of discovery disputes, and shorten the time for processing complex cases."
>
> ... [T]he *Recommendations for Electronically Stored Information Discovery Production* were sent by the deputy attorney general to all U.S. attorney offices, and by the AO to all federal defenders and Criminal Justice Act (CJA) panel attorneys. Training also has begun for defender and prosecutorial personnel. ...
>
> The recommendations are built on 10 principles:
>
> --Lawyers have a responsibility to have an adequate understanding of electronic discovery.
>
> --In the process of planning, producing, and resolving disputes about ESI discovery, the parties should include individuals with sufficient technical knowledge and experience regarding ESI.
>
> --At the outset of a case, the parties should meet and confer about the nature, volume, and mechanics of producing ESI discovery. Where the ESI discovery is particularly complex or produced on a rolling basis, an ongoing dialogue may be helpful.
>
> --The parties should discuss what formats of production are possible and appropriate, and what formats can be generated. Any format selected for producing discovery should maintain the ESI's integrity, allow for reasonable usability, reasonably limit costs, and, if possible, conform to industry format standards.
>
> --When producing ESI discovery, a party should not be required to take on substantial additional processing or format conversion costs and burdens beyond what the party has already done or would do for its own case preparation or discovery production.
>
> --Following the "meet and confer," the parties should notify the court of ESI discovery production issues or problems that they reasonably anticipate will significantly affect the handling of the case.
>
> --The parties should discuss ESI discovery transmission methods and media that promote efficiency, security, and reduced costs. The producing party should provide a general description and maintain a record of what was transmitted.
>
> --In multi-defendant cases, the defendants should authorize one or more counsel to act as the discovery coordinator(s) or seek appointment of a coordinating discovery attorney.
>
> --The parties should make good-faith efforts to discuss and resolve disputes over ESI discovery, involving those with the requisite technical knowledge when necessary, and they should consult with a supervisor, or obtain supervisory authorization, before seeking judicial resolution of an ESI discovery dispute or alleging misconduct, abuse, or neglect concerning the production of ESI.
>
> --All parties should limit dissemination of ESI discovery to members of their litigation team who need and are approved for access, and they should also take reasonable and appropriate measures to secure ESI discovery against unauthorized access or disclosure.
>
> ...

AO, Justice Department Jointly Recommend ESI Discovery Practices (April 23, 2012), *available at* http://www.uscourts.gov/news/2012/04/23/ao-justice-department-jointly-recommend-esi-discovery-practices; *see also* Recommendations, *available at* http://www.foxrothschild.com/content/uploads/2015/05/usdoj_intro_recommendations_esi_discovery.pdf.

C. JENCKS ACT OR "3500" MATERIAL: WITNESS STATEMENTS

Although the Jencks Act[18] mandates that, upon request, witnesses' prior statements must be disclosed, it is in essence an anti-discovery statute. That is, the Jencks Act is designed to make clear that the government cannot be forced to produce this critical category of materials prior to the conclusion of the witnesses' direct examination at trial. Fed. R. Crim. P. 26.2 largely mirrors the Jencks Act, but extends its coverage by providing for reciprocal disclosures by the defense of witness statements, and by requiring the provision of witness statements not only at trial, but also at various types of hearings.[19] Like Fed. R. Crim. P. 16, the disclosure obligations of the Jencks Act and Fed. R. Crim. P. 26.2 are triggered only by a timely request for witness statements (often called "Jencks" or "3500" material).

It is important to note that the Jencks Act is also the exclusive means by which witness statements may be obtained.[20] Thus, if a witness shares her story with investigators, but those investigators do not take her story down in a form that fits within the statutory definition of a "statement,"[21] the defense ordinarily is held to have no entitlement to it. Not surprisingly, then,

> [a] host of controversies has developed in interpreting the Jencks Act and Rule 26.2. Courts often are left to resolve whether an item is in fact a "statement," whether it is "signed, adopted, or approved," and whether the statement is "substantially verbatim." Jencks is limited to statements of government witnesses. The Government routinely contests whether FBI reports constitute a statement. Further, a defendant is entitled only to statements that relate to the witnesses' testimony and, therefore, questions also arise as to whether that relationship exists. Finally, cases have discussed whether the statement is in the prosecutor's possession in that courts have required the Government only to produce that which is in its possession.[22]

---

[18] 18 U.S.C. § 3500.

[19] *See* Ellen S. Podgor, *Criminal Discovery of Jencks Witness Statements: Timing Makes a Difference*, 15 Ga. St. U. L. Rev. 651, 660-61 (1999); *see also* United States v. Rosa, 891 F.2d 1074 (3d Cir. 1989) (Jencks applies at sentencing hearing).

[20] *See* Palermo v. United States, 360 U.S. 343, 349 (1959) (agents' written summary (consisting of approximately 600 words) of an hour conference with a government witness, was not a "statement" within the meaning of Jencks Act because it "clearly was not a virtually verbatim narrative of the conference").

[21] 18 U.S.C. § 3500(e); Fed.R.Crim.P. 26.2(f); *see also* United States v. Brimage, 115 F.3d 73 (1st Cir. 1997) ("For the purposes of the Jencks Act, we have already recognized that ... the Act, which requires the production of all statements by government witnesses relating to the substance of their testimony, does not require the government to record all aspects of interviews with witnesses.").

[22] Podgor, *supra* note 19, at 663 (footnotes omitted).

Recently courts have wrestled with such issues as whether emails and text messages between government agents and witnesses can be Jencks material (they can).[23]

One notable issue arising under the Jencks Act concerns the timing of disclosure. In many white-collar cases, the "Jencks" or "3500" material may be voluminous. If it is in fact turned over to the defense at the conclusion of a witness's direct examination, there may be insufficient time for the defense to read, digest, and effectively use it in cross-examining the witness.[24] Courts may grant counsel a continuance to review the material, but such continuances disrupt the trial proceedings and burden all involved. Accordingly, some judges have attempted to order the government to make early disclosure of Jencks material. "Appellate courts have ruled that efforts by a court to promote efficiency and avoid delays do not warrant avoiding the timing requirements of the Jencks Act. When contested by prosecutors in appellate tribunals, judicial orders requiring an early release of Jencks material have been reversed as beyond the mandates of the timing requirements explicitly provided in the Jencks Act."[25]

Courts, however, can and do strongly "encourage" early disclosure.[26] Prosecutors of course have the discretion to make early disclosure and sometimes do so. There appears to be very little consistency in federal practice in this regard.[27] What factors should be relevant to a prosecutor's decision whether to make early disclosure of Jencks material?

One recurring issue relating to the timing of Jencks disclosure arises when information constitutes both *Brady* material (in that it is, for example, materially impeaching) and Jencks material. Some courts hold that "[w]hen *Brady* material sought by a defendant is covered by the Jencks Act, 18 U.S.C. § 3500, the terms of that Act govern the timing of the government's disclosure."[28] As the Sixth Circuit has explained:

> ... Preserving the defendant's ability to defend himself effectively at trial is the underlying purpose of the criminal discovery rules. Therefore, so long as the defendant is given impeachment material, even exculpatory impeachment material, in time for use at trial, we fail to see how the Constitution is violated. Any prejudice the defendant may suffer as a result of disclosure of the impeachment evidence during trial can be eliminated by the trial court ordering a recess in the proceedings in order to allow the defendant time to examine the material and decide how to use it.[29]

At the other end of the spectrum, some courts "that hold that *Brady* material must be provided to the defense sooner than the time requirements outlined in the Jencks Act support their position by arguing that *Brady* is premised on the constitutional right to due process."[30] Some courts adopt a balancing approach in which they weigh "the potential dangers of early discovery against the need that *Brady* purports to serve of avoiding wrongful convictions."[31]

---

[23] *See* United States v. Suarez, 2010 WL 4226524 (D. N.J. 2010).

[24] *See, e.g.*, United States v. Holmes, 722 F.2d 37 (4th Cir. 983).

[25] Podgor, *supra* note 19, at 669; *see, e.g.*, United States v. Lewis, 35 F.3d 148, 151 (4th Cir. 1994).

[26] *See, e.g.*, *Lewis*, 35 F.3d at 151.

[27] *See* Podgor, *supra* note 19, at 678-92.

[28] United States v. Bencs, 28 F.3d 555, 561 (6th Cir. 1994); United States v. Scott, 524 F.2d 465, 467-68 (5th Cir. 1975) ("*Brady* is not a pretrial remedy and was not intended to override the mandate of the Jencks Act.").

[29] United States v. Presser, 844 F.2d 1275, 1283-84 (6th Cir. 1988).

[30] Podgor, *supra* note 19, at 676.

[31] United States v. Pollack, 534 F.2d 964, 974 (D.C. Cir. 1976); *see also, e.g.*, United States v. Levasseur, 826 F.2d 158 (1st Cir. 1987) (*per curiam*); United States v. Beckford, 962 F. Supp. 780 (E.D. Va. 1997).

D. WITNESS LISTS

In general, the Government has no obligation to provide the defense with a witness list in federal criminal trials.[32] Obviously, however, if the Government elects to provide Jencks material prior to the witness taking the stand, the defense will have advance notice of the Government's witness list. The following is the Department of Justice's policy regarding the pretrial disclosure of witness identity:

Insuring the safety and cooperativeness of prospective witnesses, and safeguarding the judicial process from undue influence, are among the highest priorities of federal prosecutors. *See* the Victim and Witness Protection Act of 1982, P.L. 97-291, § 2, 96 Stat. 1248-9. The Attorney General Guidelines for Victim Witness Assistance 2000 provide that prosecutors should keep in mind that the names, addresses, and phone numbers of victims and witnesses are private and should reveal such information to the defense only pursuant to Federal Rule of Procedure 16, any local rules, customs or court orders, or special prosecutorial need.

Therefore, it is the Department's position that pretrial disclosure of a witness' identity or statement should not be made if there is, in the judgment of the prosecutor, any reason to believe that such disclosure would endanger the safety of the witness or any other person, or lead to efforts to obstruct justice. Factors relevant to the possibility of witness intimidation or obstruction of justice include, but are not limited to, the types of charges pending against the defendant, any record or information about the propensity of the defendant or the defendant's confederates to engage in witness intimidation or obstruction of justice, and any threats directed by the defendant or others against the witness. In addition, pretrial disclosure of a witness' identity or statements should not ordinarily be made against the known wishes of any witness.

However, pretrial disclosure of the identity or statements of a government witness may often promote the prompt and just resolution of the case. Such disclosure may enhance the prospects that the defendant will plead guilty or lead to the initiation of plea negotiations; in the event the defendant goes to trial, such disclosure may expedite the conduct of the trial by eliminating the need for a continuance.

Accordingly, with respect to prosecutions in federal court, a prosecutor should give careful consideration, as to each prospective witness, whether absent any indication of potential adverse consequences of the kind mentioned above reason exists to disclose such witness' identity prior to trial. It should be borne in mind that a decision by the prosecutor to disclose pretrial the identity of potential government witnesses may be conditioned upon the defendant's making reciprocal disclosure as to the identity of the potential defense witnesses. Similarly, when appropriate in light of the facts and circumstances of the case, a prosecutor may determine to disclose only the identity, but not the current address or whereabouts of a witness.

Prosecutors should be aware that they have the option of applying for a protective order if discovery of the private information may create a risk of harm to the victim or witness and the prosecutor may seek a temporary restraining order under 18 U.S.C. § 1514 prohibiting harassment of a victim or witness.

---

[32] *See, e.g.*, United States v. Perkins, 994 F.2d 1184, 1190 (6th Cir. 1993).

In sum, whether or not to disclose the identity of a witness prior to trial is committed to the discretion of the federal prosecutor, and that discretion should be exercised on a case-by-case, and witness-by-witness basis. Considerations of witness safety and willingness to cooperate, and the integrity of the judicial process are paramount.[33]

E. TRIAL SUBPOENAS: FED. R. CRIM. P. 17

As outlined above, materials important to the formulation of an effective defense may be held by government actors who are not directly involved in the prosecution of the criminal case. Further, it may often be the case that important documents are held by non-governmental third parties. As Professor Henning notes:

> White collar crimes often involve economic transactions that involve third parties, such as banks, brokerage firms, suppliers, and insurance companies. Misconduct by an employee may be investigated by the organization first to determine the scope of the activity and the company's potential criminal and civil exposure. The federal Sentencing Guidelines create a powerful incentive for organizations to cooperate with the government by alerting it to misconduct by employees. Whether or not the organization is involved in the conduct, it can have valuable information regarding the defendant's activities.[34]

These third-party materials may not only provide fodder for the defense theory and possible impeachment material, but they may also yield critical information about the government's theory of the case when they are obtained from regulatory enforcement authorities whose investigation parallels prosecutorial efforts. However, "'[d]iscovery' for the purposes of a criminal prosecution is much more limited than in a civil proceeding. Discovery of documents under Rule 16(a)(1)([E]) does not reach documents held by nonparties except insofar as the Government might have gathered material from them for use in its investigation."[35]

Fed. R. Crim. P. 17 governs the issuance of subpoenas—both grand jury subpoenas and trial subpoenas—in criminal cases. It is the primary means by which the defense may seek to obtain materials from persons not subject to *Brady*, Rule 16, or Jencks Act requirements.[36] Readers will recall that in *United States v. R. Enterprises*[37] (reproduced in Chapter 13 (Grand Jury)), the Supreme Court articulated a very forgiving standard for assessing the reasonableness of grand jury subpoenas. In so doing, the Court rejected application in the

---

[33] 4 Dep't of Justice Manual, tit. 9, § 9-6.200.

[34] Henning, *supra* note 11, at 606 (footnotes omitted); *see also id.* at 608-10.

[35] *Id.* at 612.

[36] Defense counsel may seek to use the civil discovery mechanism of the Freedom of Information Act ("FOIA"), 5 U.S.C. § 552, to obtain materials from relevant governmental agencies, but there are exceptions to FOIA through which prosecutors and agencies may refuse to provide materials relevant to an ongoing criminal investigation. *See id.* § 552(b)(1)(A) (national security exemption), § 552(b)(7) (law enforcement investigation). Courts may also be reluctant to order, at the behest of a criminal defendant, broader governmental disclosure through FOIA than is available under the criminal discovery rules. *See, e.g.*, United States v. United States District Court, 717 F.2d 478, 480 (9th Cir. 1983) ("We hold that in criminal cases the Freedom of Information Act does not extend the scope of discovery permitted under Rule 16."); *see generally* Jonathan S. Feld & Andrew N. Gentin, *Using the Freedom of Information Act in Enforcement Cases*, 2 Bus. Crimes Bull. 2 (Feb.1999).

[37] 498 U.S. 292 (1991).

grand jury context of the more rigorous standard the Court imposed in *United States v. Nixon*[38] on the pretrial issuance of Rule 17 trial subpoenas.

In *Nixon*, the Court stated:

> A subpoena for documents may be quashed [under Rule 17(c)] if their production would be "unreasonable or oppressive," but not otherwise. The leading case in this Court interpreting this standard is *Bowman Dairy Co. v. United States*, 341 U.S. 214 (1951). This case recognized certain fundamental characteristics of the subpoena *duces tecum* in criminal cases: (1) it was not intended to provide a means of discovery for criminal cases; (2) its chief innovation was to expedite the trial by providing a time and place *before* trial for the inspection of subpoenaed materials. As both parties agree, cases decided in the wake of *Bowman* have generally followed Judge Weinfeld's formulation in *United States v. Iozia*, 13 F.R.D. 335, 338 (S.D.N.Y.1952), as to the required showing. Under this test, in order to require production prior to trial, the moving party must show: (1) that the documents are evidentiary and relevant; (2) that they are not otherwise procurable reasonably in advance of trial by exercise of due diligence; (3) that the party cannot properly prepare for trial without such production and inspection in advance of trial and that the failure to obtain such inspection may tend unreasonably to delay the trial; and (4) that the application is made in good faith and is not intended as a general "fishing expedition."[39]

Courts have applied *Nixon* to require the defense to show "(1) relevancy; (2) admissibility; (3) specificity"[40] even when the defense seeks to subpoena persons other than the prosecutorial team from whom it has no entitlement to *Brady* or Jencks Act disclosure or Rule 16 discovery. This broad application of the *Nixon* standard makes it difficult for the defense to compel disclosure of materials potentially important to the defense that are held by third-parties. For example, courts regularly hold that Rule 17 subpoenas may only be used to secure materials that themselves would be admissible as evidence. Notably, "[c]ourts have consistently interpreted the admissibility standard of Rule 17(c) to preclude production of materials whose evidentiary use is limited to impeachment."[41] "In this respect, Rule 17(c) can be contrasted with the civil rules which permit the issuance of subpoenas to seek production of documents or other materials which, although not themselves admissible, could lead to admissible evidence."[42] Should the scope of discovery aimed at third parties be more limited in criminal cases than civil cases? Does application of the *Nixon* standard in this context make sense?[43]

---

[38] 418 U.S. 683 (1974).

[39] *Id.* at 698-700.

[40] *Id.* at 700.

[41] United States v. Cherry, 876 F. Supp. 547, 552 (S.D.N.Y. 1995) (collecting cases).

[42] *Id.* at 553.

[43] *See* Henning, *supra* note 11, at 630-49 ("arguing that the Supreme Court's analysis of the scope of the authority to compel the production of records [under Rule 17] misconstrues the nature of the Rule and the contrasting positions of the criminal defendant and the federal prosecutor" and concluding that "a fair reading of Rules 16(a)(1)([E]) and 17(c) would reveal that they are complementary provisions that permit defendants to engage in discovery of relevant documents that, while not permitting 'fishing expeditions,' must allow the white collar criminal defendant sufficient access to mount a credible defense"). *But see* United States v. Ferguson, 2007 WL 2815068 (D. Conn. 2007).

Note that *Bowman Dairy Co. v. United States*,[44] the case often cited for the proposition that a Rule 17 trial subpoena is not a discovery device, involved the defendants' attempt to subpoena the prosecution for documents not then subject to discovery under Rule 16. In *United States v. Nixon*,[45] the Special Prosecutor issued a trial subpoena to President Nixon for tapes that it wished to use in the trial of certain of the President's aides; the Special Prosecutor apparently knew of the tapes during the grand jury proceedings but did not attempt to secure them until after indictment.[46] Finally, recall that in *R. Enterprises*, the Supreme Court noted:

> In this case, the focus of our inquiry is the limit imposed on a grand jury by Federal Rule of Criminal Procedure 17(c), which governs the issuance of subpoenas *duces tecum* in federal criminal proceedings. The Rule provides that "[t]he court on motion made promptly may quash or modify the subpoena if compliance would be unreasonable or oppressive."
>
> This standard is not self-explanatory. As we have observed, "what is reasonable depends on the context." In *Nixon*, this Court defined what is reasonable in the context of a jury trial. We determined that, in order to require production of information prior to trial, a party must make a reasonably specific request for information that would be both relevant and admissible at trial. But, for the reasons we have explained above, the *Nixon* standard does not apply in the context of grand jury proceedings. In the grand jury context, the decision as to what offense will be charged is routinely not made until after the grand jury has concluded its investigation. One simply cannot know in advance whether information sought during the investigation will be relevant and admissible in a prosecution for a particular offense.[47]

Given the above, how would you persuade a court that the *Nixon* standard is inapplicable in the context of third-party subpoenas? What *should* be the standard? Should Rule 17 in such a context be recognized as a discovery device?

F. DISCOVERY HYPOTHETICAL

Daniel McGuigan, the former General Manager of a wastewater treatment plant, tells government investigators that the plant has been discharging in excess of permitted amounts into navigable waters. He turns over to the government drafts of reports required by regulation upon which appear handwritten directions to alter the amounts of the actual discharges to meet permit requirements. The documents, he says, establish that the President of plant, Patrick O'Sullivan, directed McGuigan to file false reports with the government. An FBI agent goes to O'Sullivan's house one evening and asks him about the discharges. O'Sullivan denies any wrongdoing, informs the agents that he was out of town on business during the relevant periods, and notes that McGuigan was fired and thus has it out for O'Sullivan and the plant. O'Sullivan later provided, pursuant to subpoena, handwriting exemplars (Assume that there are no constitutional or other problems with the interview or compelled production of the handwriting exemplar).

1. Assume that the agent is prepared to testify from memory as to the content of O'Sullivan's remarks. Under Rule 16, is the defense team entitled to interview the agent before

---

[44] 341 U.S. 214 (1951).

[45] 418 U.S. 683 (1974).

[46] *See* Henning, *supra* note 11, at 639-40.

[47] 498 U.S. at 299-300.

trial to explore what he recalls about O'Sullivan's statements? Must the government make a record of the agent's recollection and turn it over to the defense?

2. Assume that, shortly after the agent's interview with O'Sullivan, the agent returns to his office and writes out (pursuant to FBI policy) a short summary of O'Sullivan's statements on a form 302. Is the defense entitled to this memo?

3. Assume that the agent surreptitiously taped the entire interview with O'Sullivan. Is the recording discoverable? If so, in what form? Assume that the U.S. Attorneys Office staff makes a transcript of the interview tape. Is the defense entitled to a copy of the transcript?

4. Assume that McGuigan files suit against O'Sullivan and the plant, claiming that he was fired because he refused to comply with O'Sullivan's illegal orders. (How is the government likely to feel about this suit?) O'Sullivan responds to the complaint, denying all allegations, and appears for a deposition. (How is O'Sullivan's criminal counsel likely to feel about that?) Must the government turn over to the defense these materials?

5. Assume that the government has no record of any past criminal conduct by O'Sullivan. Defense counsel knows about a marital battery conviction in another state. Does the defense have to turn over this information over to the government?

6. Is the defense entitled to access to the draft reports turned over to the government by McGuigan?

7. Assume that both the government and the defense have submitted the reports to their own expert document examiners for handwriting and other analyses, and that those experts have submitted written reports of their findings. The government's report reaches an indeterminant result based on O'Sullivan's alleged malingering. Must the government turn over its report? Assume that the government does so. The defense expert detects fingerprints on the report that were not noted in the government report. Defense counsel fears that the fingerprints are O'Sullivan's. Must defense counsel give a copy of the defense's expert's report to the government?

McGuigan agreed to plead guilty to a misdemeanor offense in a cooperation agreement with the government. McGuigan has completed his direct examination. Defense counsel earlier filed a motion for Jencks material.

8. Is the defense entitled to discover McGuigan's prior criminal record, if any, to use to impeach McGuigan at trial? Must the government turn over to the defense McGuigan's cooperation agreement? Plea colloquy? Pleadings and depositions in McGuigan's civil action?

9. Assume that during the course of their investigation, the agents met on a number of occasions with McGuigan, spending a total of about 9 days with him. At the conclusion of these debriefing meetings, the agents took about 25 pages of handwritten notes generally summarizing McGuigan's information. Is the defense entitled to discover these notes?

10. Assume that at the conclusion of the debriefing meetings, the case agent returned to his office and (pursuant to FBI policy) dictated a 20-page memorandum on form 302 describing the interviews with McGuigan. He used his handwritten notes to prompt his memory of the interview. Must the government turn over this memorandum? How about the dictation tape?

11. Assume that in the grand jury, the case agent testified extensively regarding McGuigan's statements to the agents. Must the grand jury transcript be produced to the defense?

12. Assume that, just before trial, the government received a letter from McGuigan, complaining about the government's failure to follow through on promises it had allegedly made to him in terms of protecting him from the media fall-out of the investigation and prosecution. Must the government turn this over?

13. Assume that you are the Assistant U.S. Attorney who is trying this case. After speaking with McGuigan in prep sessions and after reviewing the agent's memorandum, you prepared a draft "script" for your examination of McGuigan, summarizing his likely testimony on 6 typed pages. Must you disclose this to the defense?

Chapter 15

FIFTH AMENDMENT: TESTIMONY AND IMMUNITY

This chapter focuses on the Fifth Amendment right against self-incrimination in relation to government attempts to secure the testimony of witnesses. In this context, the Fifth Amendment privilege protects individuals from being compelled by the government to make statements that would furnish a link in the chain of evidence needed to criminally prosecute them absent a grant of immunity coextensive with the scope of the privilege. Some pertinent aspects of the Fifth Amendment right will be treated in the next chapter, which explores the privilege against self-incrimination in relation to government efforts to compel the production of documents and other tangible evidence. Because immunity grants are commonly employed in white-collar cases to secure the testimony—and often cooperation—of witnesses, the following materials concentrate primarily on the rules and practice surrounding the provision of statutory immunity under 18 U.S.C. §§ 6002-05 and informal (or "pocket" or "letter") immunity through negotiated agreements between the prosecution and defense. These materials contain a variety of excerpts that are designed to reveal the thinking of prosecutors on the theory that prosecutors, by and large, have the upper hand in immunity negotiations and students may not intuit the considerations that inform their thinking on immunity issues.

A. FORMAL IMMUNITY PURSUANT TO 18 U.S.C. §§ 6002-05

1. CONSTITUTIONAL STANDARDS

KASTIGAR v. UNITED STATES
406 U.S. 441 (1972)

MR. JUSTICE POWELL delivered the opinion of the Court.

This case presents the question whether the United States Government may compel testimony from an unwilling witness, who invokes the Fifth Amendment privilege against compulsory self-incrimination, by conferring on the witness immunity from use of the compelled testimony in subsequent criminal proceedings, as well as immunity from use of evidence derived from the testimony.

Petitioners were subpoenaed to appear before a United States grand jury in the Central District of California on February 4, 1971. The Government believed that petitioners were likely to assert their Fifth Amendment privilege. Prior to the scheduled appearances, the Government applied to the District Court for an order directing petitioners to answer questions and produce evidence before the grand jury under a grant of immunity conferred pursuant to 18 U.S.C. §§ 6002-6003. Petitioners opposed issuance of the order, contending primarily that the scope of the immunity provided by the statute was not coextensive with the scope of the privilege against self-incrimination, and therefore was not sufficient to supplant the privilege and compel their testimony. The District Court rejected this contention, and ordered petitioners to appear before the grand jury and answer its questions under the grant of immunity.

Petitioners appeared but refused to answer questions, asserting their privilege against compulsory self-incrimination. They were brought before the District Court, and each persisted in his refusal to answer the grand jury's questions, notwithstanding the grant of immunity. The court found both in contempt, and committed them to the custody of the Attorney General until either they answered the grand jury's questions or the term of the grand jury expired. The Court of Appeals for the Ninth Circuit affirmed. This Court granted certiorari to resolve the important question whether testimony may be compelled by granting immunity from the use of compelled testimony and evidence derived therefrom ("use and derivative use" immunity), or whether it is necessary to grant immunity from prosecution for offenses to which compelled testimony relates ("transactional" immunity).

The power of government to compel persons to testify in court or before grand juries and other governmental agencies is firmly established in Anglo-American jurisprudence. ...While it is not clear when grand juries first resorted to compulsory process to secure the attendance and testimony of witnesses, the general common-law principle that "the public has a right to every man's evidence" was considered an "indubitable certainty" that "cannot be denied" by 1742. ...

> "Among the necessary and most important of the powers of the States as well as the Federal Government to assure the effective functioning of government in an ordered society is the broad power to compel residents to testify in court or before grand juries or agencies. Such testimony constitutes one of the Government's primary sources of information."

But the power to compel testimony is not absolute. There are a number of exemptions from the testimonial duty, the most important of which is the Fifth Amendment privilege against compulsory self-incrimination. The privilege reflects a complex of our fundamental values and aspirations, and marks an important advance in the development of our liberty. It can be asserted in any proceeding, civil or criminal, administrative or judicial, investigatory or adjudicatory; and it protects against any disclosures that the witness reasonably believes could be used in a criminal prosecution or could lead to other evidence that might be so used. This Court has been zealous to safeguard the values that underlie the privilege.

Immunity statutes, which have historical roots deep in Anglo-American jurisprudence, are not incompatible with these values. Rather, they seek a rational accommodation between the imperatives of the privilege and the legitimate demands of government to compel citizens to testify. The existence of these statutes reflects the importance of testimony, and the fact that many offenses are of such a character that the only persons capable of giving useful testimony are those implicated in the crime. Indeed, their origins were in the context of such offenses, and their primary use has been to investigate such offenses. Congress included immunity statutes in many of the regulatory measures adopted in the first half of this century. Indeed, prior to the enactment of the statute under consideration in this case, there were in force over 50 federal immunity statutes. In addition, every State in the Union, as well as the District of Columbia and Puerto Rico, has one or more such statutes. The commentators, and this Court on several occasions, have characterized immunity statutes as essential to the effective enforcement of various criminal statutes. ...

Petitioners contend, first, that the Fifth Amendment's privilege against compulsory self-incrimination, which is that "[n]o person ...shall be compelled in any criminal case to be a witness against himself," deprives Congress of power to enact laws that compel self-incrimination, even if complete immunity from prosecution is granted prior to the compulsion of the incriminatory testimony. In other words, petitioners assert that no immunity statute, however drawn, can afford a lawful basis for compelling incriminatory testimony. They ask us to reconsider and overrule *Brown v. Walker*, [161 U.S. 591 (1896),] and *Ullmann v. United States*, [350 U.S. 422 (1956),] decisions that uphold the constitutionality of immunity statutes.[1] We find no merit to this contention and reaffirm the decisions in *Brown* and *Ullmann*.

Petitioners' second contention is that the scope of immunity provided by the federal witness immunity statute, 18 U.S.C. § 6002, is not coextensive with the scope of the Fifth Amendment privilege against compulsory self-incrimination, and therefore is not sufficient to supplant the privilege and compel testimony over a claim of the privilege. The statute provides that when a witness is compelled by district court order to testify over a claim of the privilege:

> "the witness may not refuse to comply with the order on the basis of his privilege against self-incrimination; but no testimony or other information compelled under the order (or any information directly or indirectly derived from such testimony or other information) may be used against the witness in any criminal case, except a prosecution for perjury, giving a false statement, or otherwise failing to comply with the order." 18 U.S.C. § 6002.

The constitutional inquiry, rooted in logic and history, as well as in the decisions of this Court, is whether the immunity granted under this statute is coextensive with the scope of the privilege. If so, petitioners' refusals to answer based on the privilege were unjustified, and the judgments of contempt were proper, for the grant of immunity has removed the dangers against which the privilege protects. If, on the other hand, the immunity granted is not as comprehensive as the protection afforded by the privilege, petitioners were justified in refusing to answer, and the judgments of contempt must be vacated.

Petitioners draw a distinction between statutes that provide transactional immunity and those that provide, as does the statute before us, immunity from use and derivative use. They

---

[1] [Ed.:] The referenced decisions basically decided that the Fifth Amendment right against self-incrimination is not a right to silence but rather a right against the use of one's compelled statements against one in a criminal case. In *Brown v. Walker*, 161 U.S. 591 (1896), the Supreme Court held that a statute that secures the witness against a criminal prosecution that might be aided directly or indirectly from his compelled statements may be employed to compel an individual to speak despite his assertion of a Fifth Amendment privilege. In *Ullmann v. United States*, 350 U.S. 422 (1956), the Court reaffirmed this ruling in a case in which the defendant was found in contempt for continuing to assert his Fifth Amendment right, over a grant of immunity, in response to grand jury questioning regarding, inter alia, his and other persons' membership in the Communist Party. The Supreme Court rejected Ullmann's argument that a different rule should obtain in his case because "the impact of the disabilities imposed by federal and state authorities and the public in general [for one's status as a Communist] ... is so oppressive that the statute does not give him true immunity." *Id.* at 430. In dissent, Justice Douglas noted that "there are numerous disabilities created by federal law that attach to a person who is a Communist. These disabilities include ineligibility for employment in the Federal Government and in defense facilities, disqualification for a passport, risk of internment ...—to mention only a few." *Id.* at 440. He further contended:

> There is great infamy involved in the present case apart from the loss of rights of citizenship under federal law which I have already mentioned. The disclosure that a person is a Communist practically excommunicates him from society. School boards will not hire him. A lawyer risks exclusion from the bar; a doctor, the revocation of his license to practice. If an actor, he is on a black list. And he will find no employment in our society except at the lowest level, if at all. ... It is no answer to say that a witness who exercises his Fifth Amendment right to silence and stands mute may bring himself into disrepute. If so, that is the price he pays for exercising the right of silence granted by the Fifth Amendment. The critical point is that the Constitution places the right of silence beyond the reach of the government. The Fifth Amendment stands between the citizen and his government. When public opinion casts a person into the outer darkness, as happens today when a person is exposed as a Communist, the government brings infamy on the head of the witness when it compels disclosure. This is precisely what the Fifth Amendment prohibits.

Id. at 453-54.

contend that a statute must at a minimum grant full transactional immunity in order to be coextensive with the scope of the privilege. In support of this contention, they rely on *Counselman v. Hitchcock*, 142 U.S. 547 (1892), the first case in which this Court considered a constitutional challenge to an immunity statute. The statute, a re-enactment of the Immunity Act of 1868, provided that no "evidence obtained from a party or witness by means of a judicial proceeding ... shall be given in evidence, or in any manner used against him ...in any court of the United States ..." Notwithstanding a grant of immunity and order to testify under the revised 1868 Act, the witness, asserting his privilege against compulsory self-incrimination, refused to testify before a federal grand jury. He was consequently adjudged in contempt of court. On appeal, this Court construed the statute as affording a witness protection only against the use of the specific testimony compelled from him under the grant of immunity. This construction meant that the statute "could not, and would not, prevent the use of his testimony to search out other testimony to be used in evidence against him." Since the revised 1868 Act, as construed by the Court, would permit the use against the immunized witness of evidence derived from his compelled testimony, it did not protect the witness to the same extent that a claim of the privilege would protect him. Accordingly, under the principle that a grant of immunity cannot supplant the privilege, and is not sufficient to compel testimony over a claim of the privilege, unless the scope of the grant of immunity is coextensive with the scope of the privilege, the witness' refusal to testify was held proper. In the course of its opinion, the Court made the following statement, on which petitioners heavily rely:

> "We are clearly of opinion that no statute which leaves the party or witness subject to prosecution after he answers the criminating question put to him, can have the effect of supplanting the privilege conferred by the Constitution of the United States. [The immunity statute under consideration] does not supply a complete protection from all the perils against which the constitutional prohibition was designed to guard, and is not a full substitute for that prohibition. In view of the constitutional provision, a statutory enactment, to be valid, must afford absolute immunity against future prosecution for the offence to which the question relates."

Sixteen days after the *Counselman* decision, a new immunity bill was introduced by Senator Cullom, who urged that enforcement of the Interstate Commerce Act would be impossible in the absence of an effective immunity statute. The bill, which became the Compulsory Testimony Act of 1893, was drafted specifically to meet the broad language in *Counselman* set forth above. The new Act removed the privilege against self-incrimination in hearings before the Interstate Commerce Commission and provided that:

> "no person shall be prosecuted or subjected to any penalty or forfeiture for or on account of any transaction, matter or thing, concerning which he may testify, or produce evidence, documentary or otherwise ...."

This transactional immunity statute became the basic form for the numerous federal immunity statutes until 1970, when, after re-examining applicable constitutional principles and the adequacy of existing law, Congress enacted the statute here under consideration. The new statute, which does not "afford [the] absolute immunity against future prosecution" referred to in *Counselman*, was drafted to meet what Congress judged to be the conceptual basis of *Counselman*, as elaborated in subsequent decisions of the Court, namely, that immunity from the use of compelled testimony and evidence derived therefrom is coextensive with the scope of the privilege.

The statute's explicit proscription of the use in any criminal case of "testimony or other information compelled under the order (or any information directly or indirectly derived from such testimony or other information)" is consonant with Fifth Amendment standards. We hold that such immunity from use and derivative use is coextensive with the scope of the privilege against self-incrimination, and therefore is sufficient to compel testimony over a claim of the privilege. While a grant of immunity must afford protection commensurate with that afforded by the privilege, it need not be broader. Transactional immunity, which accords full immunity from prosecution for the offense to which the compelled testimony relates, affords the witness considerably broader protection than does the Fifth Amendment privilege. The privilege has never been construed to mean that one who invokes it cannot subsequently be prosecuted. Its sole concern is to afford protection against being "forced to give testimony leading to the infliction of 'penalties affixed to ... criminal acts.'" Immunity from the use of compelled testimony, as well as evidence derived directly and indirectly therefrom, affords this protection. It prohibits the prosecutorial authorities from using the compelled testimony in *any* respect, and it therefore insures that the testimony cannot lead to the infliction of criminal penalties on the witness.

Our holding is consistent with the conceptual basis of *Counselman*. The *Counselman* statute, as construed by the Court, was plainly deficient in its failure to prohibit the use against the immunized witness of evidence derived from his compelled testimony. ... The basis of the Court's decision was recognized in *Ullmann*, in which the Court reiterated that the *Counselman* statute was insufficient:

> "because the immunity granted was incomplete, in that it merely forbade the use of the testimony given and failed to protect a witness from future prosecution *based on knowledge and sources of information obtained from the compelled testimony*."

The broad language in *Counselman* relied upon by petitioners was unnecessary to the Court's decision, and cannot be considered binding authority.

In *Murphy v. Waterfront Comm'n*, 378 U.S. 52 (1964), the Court carefully considered immunity from use of compelled testimony and evidence derived therefrom. The *Murphy* petitioners were subpoenaed to testify at a hearing conducted by the Waterfront Commission of New York Harbor. After refusing to answer certain questions on the ground that the answers might tend to incriminate them, petitioners were granted immunity from prosecution under the laws of New Jersey and New York. They continued to refuse to testify, however, on the ground that their answers might tend to incriminate them under federal law, to which the immunity did not purport to extend. They were adjudged in civil contempt, and that judgment was affirmed by the New Jersey Supreme Court.

The issue before the Court in *Murphy* was whether New Jersey and New York could compel the witnesses, whom these States had immunized from prosecution under their laws, to give testimony that might then be used to convict them of a federal crime. Since New Jersey and New York had not purported to confer immunity from federal prosecution, the Court was faced with the question what limitations the Fifth Amendment privilege imposed on the prosecutorial powers of the Federal Government, a nonimmunizing sovereign. After undertaking an examination of the policies and purposes of the privilege, the Court overturned the rule that one jurisdiction within our federal structure may compel a witness to give testimony which could be used to convict him of a crime in another jurisdiction. The Court held that the privilege protects state witnesses against incrimination under federal as well as state law, and federal witnesses against incrimination under state as well as federal law. Applying this principle to the state immunity legislation before it, the Court held the constitutional rule to be that:

> "[A] state witness may not be compelled to give testimony which may be incriminating under federal law unless the compelled testimony and its fruits cannot be used in any manner by federal officials in connection with a criminal prosecution against him. We conclude, moreover, that in order to implement this constitutional rule and accommodate the interests of the State and Federal Government in investigating and prosecuting crime, the Federal Governments must be prohibited from making any such use of compelled testimony and its fruits."[2]

---

[2] [Court's footnote 45:] At this point the Court added the following note: "Once a defendant demonstrates that he has testified, under a state grant of immunity, to matters related to the federal

The Court emphasized that this rule left the state witness and the Federal Government, against which the witness had immunity only from the *use* of the compelled testimony and evidence derived therefrom, "in substantially the same position as if the witness had claimed his privilege in the absence of a state grant of immunity."

It is true that in *Murphy* the Court was not presented with the precise question presented by this case, whether a jurisdiction seeking to compel testimony may do so by granting only use and derivative-use immunity, for New Jersey and New York had granted petitioners transactional immunity. The Court heretofore has not squarely confronted this question, because post-*Counselman* immunity statutes reaching the Court either have followed the pattern of the 1893 Act in providing transactional immunity, or have been found deficient for failure to prohibit the use of all evidence derived from compelled testimony. But both the reasoning of the Court in *Murphy* and the result reached compel the conclusion that use and derivative-use immunity is constitutionally sufficient to compel testimony over a claim of the privilege. Since the privilege is fully applicable and its scope is the same whether invoked in a state or in a federal jurisdiction, the *Murphy* conclusion that a prohibition on use and derivative use secures a witness' Fifth Amendment privilege against infringement by the Federal Government demonstrates that immunity from use and derivative use is coextensive with the scope of the privilege. As the *Murphy* Court noted, immunity from use and derivative use "leaves the witness and the Federal Government in substantially the same position as if the witness had claimed his privilege" in the absence of a grant of immunity. The *Murphy* Court was concerned solely with the danger of incrimination under federal law, and held that immunity from use and derivative use was sufficient to displace the danger. This protection coextensive with the privilege is the degree of protection that the Constitution requires, and is all that the Constitution requires even against the jurisdiction compelling testimony by granting immunity.

Although an analysis of prior decisions and the purpose of the Fifth Amendment privilege indicates that use and derivative-use immunity is coextensive with the privilege, we must consider additional arguments advanced by petitioners against the sufficiency of such immunity. We start from the premise, repeatedly affirmed by this Court, that an appropriately broad immunity grant is compatible with the Constitution.

Petitioners argue that use and derivative-use immunity will not adequately protect a witness from various possible incriminating uses of the compelled testimony: for example, the prosecutor or other law enforcement officials may obtain leads, names of witnesses, or other information not otherwise available that might result in a prosecution. It will be difficult and perhaps impossible, the argument goes, to identify, by testimony or cross-examination, the subtle ways in which the compelled testimony may disadvantage a witness, especially in the jurisdiction granting the immunity.

This argument presupposes that the statute's prohibition will prove impossible to enforce. The statute provides a sweeping proscription of any use, direct or indirect, of the compelled testimony and any information derived therefrom:

> "[N]o testimony or other information compelled under the order (or any information directly or indirectly derived from such testimony or other information) may be used against the witness in any criminal case ...." 18 U.S.C. § 6002.

This total prohibition on use provides a comprehensive safeguard, barring the use of compelled testimony as an "investigatory lead," and also barring the use of any evidence obtained by focusing investigation on a witness as a result of his compelled disclosures.

---

prosecution, the federal authorities have the burden of showing that their evidence is not tainted by establishing that they had an independent, legitimate source for the disputed evidence." If transactional immunity had been deemed to be the "constitutional rule" there could be no federal prosecution.

A person accorded this immunity under 18 U.S.C. § 6002, and subsequently prosecuted, is not dependent for the preservation of his rights upon the integrity and good faith of the prosecuting authorities. As stated in *Murphy*:

> "Once a defendant demonstrates that he has testified, under a state grant of immunity, to matters related to the federal prosecution, the federal authorities have the burden of showing that their evidence is not tainted by establishing that they had an independent, legitimate source for the disputed evidence."

This burden of proof, which we reaffirm as appropriate, is not limited to a negation of taint; rather, it imposes on the prosecution the affirmative duty to prove that the evidence it proposes to use is derived from a legitimate source wholly independent of the compelled testimony.

This is very substantial protection, commensurate with that resulting from invoking the privilege itself. The privilege assures that a citizen is not compelled to incriminate himself by his own testimony. It usually operates to allow a citizen to remain silent when asked a question requiring an incriminatory answer. This statute, which operates after a witness has given incriminatory testimony, affords the same protection by assuring that the compelled testimony can in no way lead to the infliction of criminal penalties. The statute, like the Fifth Amendment, grants neither pardon nor amnesty. Both the statute and the Fifth Amendment allow the government to prosecute using evidence from legitimate independent sources. ...

There can be no justification in reason or policy for holding that the Constitution requires an amnesty grant where, acting pursuant to statute and accompanying safeguards, testimony is compelled in exchange for immunity from use and derivative use when no such amnesty is required where the government, acting without colorable right, coerces a defendant into incriminating himself.

We conclude that the immunity provided by 18 U.S.C. § 6002 leaves the witness and the prosecutorial authorities in substantially the same position as if the witness had claimed the Fifth Amendment privilege. The immunity therefore is coextensive with the privilege and suffices to supplant it. ...

Notes

1. Should the government ever, by grant of any kind of immunity, be able to override a defendant's assertion of his Fifth Amendment privilege? If so, does the Court make a persuasive case that the Constitution requires only the provision of use and derivative use, as opposed to transactional, immunity? As we shall see, the fact that the statute provides only use and derivative use immunity does not bar the government from granting a defendant transactional immunity in a negotiated agreement.

2. How will state grants of immunity affect federal prosecutors, and vice versa? *See* Zicarelli v. New Jersey State Comm'n of Investigation, 406 U.S. 472 (1972); Murphy v. Waterfront Comm'n, 378 U.S. 52 (1964). Is there a potential for conflict here among state and federal enforcement officials? The federal immunity statute also contemplates that Congress may secure grants of immunity for witnesses in congressional investigations. In the prosecution of Oliver North, Congress "granted witness immunity over objection by Independent Counsel that 'any grant of use and derivative use immunity would create serious—and perhaps insurmountable—barriers to the prosecution of the immunized witness.'" United States v. North, 920 F.2d 940, 945 (D.C. Cir. 1990) ("*North II*"). In what types of circumstances should Congress grant a witness immunity even if it may mean complicating or foreclosing a subsequent criminal prosecution? *Id.* at 945 ("The decision as to whether the national interest justifies that institutional cost in the enforcement of the criminal laws is, of course, a political one to be made by Congress.").

3. Given the increasing incidence of international cooperation to confront cross-border criminality, another question is how a foreign sovereign's grants of immunity will affect U.S. prosecutors seeking to bring cases against those so immunized. In *United States v. Allen*, 864 F.3d 63 (2d Cir. 2017), the Second Circuit held that the Fifth Amendment's prohibition on the use

of compelled testimony applied even when it was a foreign sovereign who compelled that testimony. This case is excerpted and discussed further in Chapter 21(B), *infra*.

4. A related question is whether a witness can assert a Fifth Amendment privilege against self-incrimination based on his real and substantial fear of criminal prosecution in *another country*. *See* United States v. Balsys, 524 U.S. 666 (1998) (generally, no). For a comparative analysis of the developing jurisprudence regarding a right against self-incrimination in the European Court of Human Rights and European states, see Mark Berger, *Europeanizing Self-Incrimination: The Right to Remain Silent in the European Court of Human Rights*, 12 Colum. J. Eur. L. 339 (2006).

5. Does statutory immunity shield from use or derivative use statements the witness makes during the course of informal debriefing sessions or does it only cover those statements made during the course of formal grand jury, trial, or congressional testimony? In *Dunn v. United States*, 442 U.S. 100 (1979), the Supreme Court held that, under the perjury statute, 18 U.S.C. § 1623, an interview in a private attorney's office at which a sworn statement is given does not constitute a "proceeding ... ancillary to any court or grand jury of the United States." In explaining this result, the Court relied by analogy on the substantially identical language in § 6002, stating that "[a]lthough neither the House nor Senate Report defines the precise scope of § 6002, they both specify pretrial depositions as the sole example of what would constitute an ancillary proceeding under that provision." 442 U.S. at 111 (citing H.R. Rep. No. 91-1549, at 42 (1970); S. Rep. No. 91-617, at 145 (1969)). Why is this limited scope potentially important?

6. The *Kastigar* Court sought to make meaningful a promise of use and derivative use immunity by constructing certain procedural safeguards. Although there are splits among the circuits on many important issues relating to the scope and application of *Kastigar*, the following discussion of procedural points appears to command a substantial consensus:

> When the government proceeds to prosecute a previously immunized witness, it has "the heavy burden of proving that all of the evidence it proposes to use was derived from legitimate independent sources." [*Kastigar v. United States*, 406 U.S. 441, 461-62 (1972)]. The Court characterized the government's affirmative burden as "heavy." Most courts following *Kastigar* have imposed a "preponderance of the evidence" evidentiary burden on the government. ...
>
> A trial court must normally hold a hearing (a "*Kastigar* hearing") for the purpose of allowing the government to demonstrate that it obtained all of the evidence it proposes to use from sources independent of the compelled testimony. ... [A] trial court may hold a *Kastigar* hearing pre-trial, post-trial, mid-trial (as evidence is offered), or it may employ some combination of these methods. A pre-trial hearing is the most common choice.
>
> Whenever the hearing is held, the failure of the government to meet its burden can have most drastic consequences. One commentator has stated that "[i]f the tainted evidence was presented to the grand jury, the indictment will be dismissed; when tainted evidence is introduced at trial, the defendant is entitled to a new trial. ..."
>
> Dismissal of the indictment or vacation of the conviction is not necessary where the use is found to be harmless beyond a reasonable doubt.
>
> A district court holding a *Kastigar* hearing "must make specific findings on the independent nature of this proposed [allegedly tainted] evidence." Because the burden is upon the government, the appellate court "may not infer findings favorable to it on these questions."

United States v. North, 910 F.2d 843, 854-55 ("*North I*"), *modified*, *North II*, 920 F.2d 940 (D.C. Cir. 1990). Further, a prosecutor's or agent's representations that he did not make any use of the immunized testimony, standing alone, are generally found inadequate to meet the government's burden. *See, e.g.*, United States v. Allen, 864 F.3d 63 (2d Cir. 2017); United States v. Schmidgall, 25 F.3d 1523, 1528 (11th Cir. 1994); United States v. Harris, 973 F.2d 333, 337 (4th Cir. 1992). As a practical matter, how would the government go about meeting its "affirmative duty to prove that the evidence it proposes to use is derived from a legitimate source wholly independent of the compelled testimony"? When should defense counsel raise any *Kastigar* issues, and why?

7. In light of the above, how difficult will it be to prosecute a witness given use and derivative use immunity? The answer may depend in part on just how far use and derivative use immunity extends. The caselaw discusses two types of contested potential "uses" of immunized testimony: "indirect evidentiary" use and "non-evidentiary" use. Unfortunately, just what is encompassed by those terms is subject to some dispute. *See, e.g., Harris*, 973 F.3d at 337 n.2; *North I*, 910 F.2d at 857-58. The following discussion employs the categorizations commonly used by courts, and does not attempt to formulate a rigorous definition of either term.

8. One type of "indirect evidentiary" use that has generated some controversy is the use of immunized testimony "by witnesses to refresh their memories, or otherwise to focus their thoughts." *North I*, 910 F.2d at 860. The D.C. Circuit, in *North I*, held that "[i]f the government uses immunized testimony to refresh the recollection of a witness (or to sharpen his memory or focus his thoughts) when the witness testifies before a grand jury considering the indictment of a citizen for acts as to which the citizen was forced to testify, then the government has clearly used the immunized testimony." *Id.* at 861. In the D.C. Circuit, then, the prosecution must make a two-part showing to meet its *Kastigar* burden in these circumstances: (1) the prosecutor must prove that there is an independent source for all matters on which the witness testifies; and (2) the prosecutor must prove that any witness exposed to the compelled statement has not shaped or altered her testimony in any way, either directly or indirectly, as result of that exposure. *North II*, 920 F.2d at 942; *North I*, 910 F.2d at 860-63, 872-73. The D.C. Circuit appears to adhere to this rule even if the refreshment is employed to promote truthful testimony, *see id.* at 861, and even if the witnesses themselves undertook to immerse themselves in the immunized testimony for the purpose of defeating the prosecution by tainting their own testimony, *see id.* at 864-65. In *United States v. Allen*, 864 F.3d 63 (2d Cir. 2017), the Second Circuit faced a situation in which a cooperating witness was exposed to the compelled testimony of other witnesses. The court relied upon the *North* decision to hold that "the Government is required to prove that his exposure to the compelled testimony did not shape, alter, or affect the information that he provided and that the Government used." *Id.* at 93.

In *United States v. Koon*, 34 F.3d 1416 (9th Cir. 1994), by contrast, the Ninth Circuit declined to impose the second part of the *North* test, holding that "it is the law of our circuit that the prosecutor's *Kastigar* burden is met if the substance of the exposed witness's testimony is based on a legitimate source that is independent of the immunized testimony. Ensuring that the content of a witness's testimony is based on personal knowledge provides the required Fifth Amendment protections and meets the *Kastigar* requirement that the defendant's compelled statements shall not be used against him in subsequent criminal proceedings." *Id.* at 1432-33.

What implications does the D.C. Circuit's rule have for the successful criminal prosecution of witnesses who are immunized and testify in highly publicized cases or congressional investigations? Does the *North* or the *Koon* decision make more sense given the language and reasoning of *Kastigar*?

9. "Non-evidentiary" use is a potentially broader category which concentrates on the effect that immunized testimony may have on prosecutors' thought processes and strategic decision-making. It has been said to include use of immunized testimony for "assistance in focusing the investigation, deciding to initiate prosecution, refusing to plea bargain, interpreting evidence, planning cross-examination, and otherwise generally planning trial strategy." United States v. Serrano, 870 F.2d 1, 16 (1st Cir. 1989) (quoting United States v. McDaniel, 482 F.2d 305, 311 (8th Cir. 1973)). It also may include use of immunized testimony to: "help explicate evidence heretofore unintelligible"; to "expose as significant facts once thought irrelevant (or vice versa)"; to "indicate which witnesses to call, and in what order"; and to assist in "in developing opening and closing arguments." *North I*, 910 F.2d at 857-58. "*Kastigar* does not define, except perhaps by implication, what non-evidentiary use of compelled testimony might be nor does it expressly discuss the permissible scope of such use." *Id.* at 857 (declining to decide these issues). The issue of whether and in what circumstances non-evidentiary use is proscribed has divided courts, *see id.*, as well as commentators, *see, e.g.*,

Gary S. Humble, *Nonevidentiary Use of Compelled Testimony: Beyond the Fifth Amendment*, 66 Tex. L. Rev. 351, 355-56 (1987); Kristine Strachan, *Self-Incrimination, Immunity, and Watergate*, 56 Tex. L. Rev. 791, 820 (1978).

The form in which this "non-evidentiary" use debate manifests itself in many of the reported cases is in courts' discussion of what the government must show to demonstrate that even though its prosecutor or agent may have been exposed to immunized testimony, that exposure did not irrevocably taint an indictment or trial. *See, e.g.*, United States v. Crowson, 828 F.2d 1427, 1429 (9th Cir. 1987). At bottom, the issue is whether the government must merely show an independent basis for all its evidence, or whether it must go further and demonstrate that government agents' thought processes were unaffected. The debate is important because in most cases it may be impossible for the government affirmatively to demonstrate that a prosecutor's or agent's exposure to immunized testimony has not consciously or unconsciously affected her strategic decision-making other than by a simple representation that it has not—and, as noted above, such representations generally are insufficient to carry the day. A requirement that the government bear this further burden essentially translates, then, into a bar on non-evidentiary use and thus a bar on the participation of government agents whose thought processes have been "tainted" by exposure to the immunized testimony in the subsequent indictment or prosecution of the immunized witness.

Two cases—*United States v. McDaniel*, 482 F.2d 305 (8th Cir. 1973) and *United States v. Semkiw*, 712 F.2d 891 (3d Cir. 1983)—are often read to imply such a bar—*i.e.*, that once a prosecuting attorney is exposed to a defendant's immunized testimony, she cannot thereafter participate in the trial of the defendant, even where all the evidence to be introduced was derived from legitimate independent sources. *See, e.g.*, United States v. Mariani, 851 F.2d 595, 600 (2d Cir. 1988); United States v. Byrd, 765 F.2d 1524, 1530 (11th Cir. 1985). At the very least, these cases "suggest[] that the government cannot meet its burden of showing that there was no non-evidentiary use of the immunized testimony merely by proving a prior, independent source for the information." *Crowson*, 828 F.2d at 1430.

Other courts have rejected any *per se* rule of exclusion, holding that the simple fact that a prosecutor received or was exposed to immunized testimony does not constitute a bar to that prosecutor's participation in at least some aspects of the subsequent prosecution of the immunized witness. *See Harris*, 973 F.2d at 337; *Serrano*, 870 F.2d at 16 (dicta); *Crowson*, 828 F.2d at 1429; *Byrd*, 765 F.2d at 1528-31; United States v. Pantone, 634 F.2d 716, 720 (3d Cir. 1980). For example, the Second Circuit has stated that "to the extent that *McDaniel* can be read to foreclose the prosecution of an immunized witness where his immunized testimony might have tangentially influenced the prosecutor's thought processes in preparing the indictment and preparing for trial, we decline to follow that reasoning." *Mariani*, 851 F.2d at 600-01. A few courts have indicated that the government need only produce affirmative evidence that it had a prior, independent source. *See, e.g.*, *Byrd*, 765 F.2d at 1529-31; *Mariani*, 851 F.2d at 600-01; *see also United States v. Schmidgall*, 25 F.3d 1523, 1529 (11th Cir. 1994). The Eleventh Circuit, in discussing one non-evidentiary use of immunized testimony—the decision to indict—stated:

> We do not read *Kastigar* to require a court to inquire into a prosecutor's motives in seeking indictment. So long as all the evidence presented to the grand jury is derived from legitimate sources independent of the defendant's immunized testimony, and the grand jury finds that independent evidence sufficient to warrant a return of an indictment, the defendant's privilege against self-incrimination has not been violated. At a minimum, the existence of independent evidence sufficient to establish probable cause to indict must be deemed to raise a presumption that the decision to indict was not tainted. Any other result would be the equivalent of transactional immunity, for it is almost impossible to conceive of a method whereby the government could demonstrate by a preponderance of the evidence that the immunized testimony did not indirectly enter into a subsequent decision to prosecute. It is our view that the privilege against self-incrimination is concerned with direct and indirect evidentiary uses of compelled testimony, and not with the exercise of

prosecutorial discretion. If the contrary views of *McDaniel* and *Semkiw* were adopted, the realistic difference between transactional immunity and use immunity would become hopelessly blurred if not totally extinguished, thus negating the plain import of *Kastigar* that "both [18 U.S.C. § 6002] and the Fifth Amendment allow the government to prosecute using evidence from legitimate independent sources."

Byrd, 765 F.2d at 1530. *Should* some or all non-evidentiary uses be proscribed under the reasoning of *Kastigar*?

10. Many of the above difficulties may be avoided by use of procedures that foreclose any suggestion of taint. In the United States Attorneys Manual, Criminal Resource Manual No. 726 ("Steps to Avoid Taint"), the Department of Justice states that in order to ensure that prosecutors are able to meet their *Kastigar* burden, "prosecutors should take the following precautions in the case of a witness who may possibly be prosecuted for an offense about which the witness may be questioned during his/her compelled testimony":

> 1. Before the witness testifies, prepare for the file a signed and dated memorandum summarizing the existing evidence against the witness and the date(s) and source(s) of such evidence;
> 2. Ensure that the witness's immunized testimony is recorded verbatim and thereafter maintained in a secure location to which access is documented; and
> 3. Maintain a record of the date(s) and source(s) of any evidence relating to the witness obtained after the witness has testified pursuant to the immunity order.

Is this sufficient? Departmental policy formerly "recommend[ed] that prosecution of a compelled witness be handled by an attorney unfamiliar with the substance of the compelled testimony." *Harris*, 973 F.2d at 337 (citing former U.S.A.M. §1-11.400); *see also Crowson*, 828 F.2d at 1429. This policy is apparently no longer in force. *See* U.S.A.M. §§ 9-23.100 through 9-23.400; U.S.A.M. Criminal Resource Manual Nos. 716-728. Should the department institute such a requirement in light of the above uncertainty over the constitutionality of non-evidentiary use?

11. Although the Supreme Court has yet to address the lingering *Kastigar* questions outlined above, it has provided some clarification of the scope of the immunity grant in other contexts. In *New Jersey v. Portash*, 440 U.S. 450 (1979), the defendant testified before a New Jersey grand jury under a state statutory grant of use and derivative use immunity. The Supreme Court held that "a person's testimony before a grand jury under a grant of immunity cannot constitutionally be used to impeach him when he is a defendant in a later criminal trial." *Id.* at 459-60.

Subsequently, in *United States v. Apfelbaum*, 445 U.S. 115 (1980), the Supreme Court dealt with the scope of the statutory exception to § 6002's protections, which provides that the testimony of a witness immunized under § 6002 *may* be used in "a prosecution for perjury, giving a false statement, or otherwise failing to comply" with the immunity order. Apfelbaum conceded that the government could use that portion of his immunized testimony that the government contended was false in any subsequent prosecution. He objected, however, to the government's attempt to use other portions of his immunized testimony—not alleged to have been false—to prove that he knowingly made the charged false statements. The Supreme Court upheld the government's use of all the immunized testimony—including that which was not alleged to be false—ruling that "neither the immunity statute nor the Fifth Amendment precludes the use of respondent's immunized testimony at a subsequent prosecution for false statements, so long as that testimony conforms to otherwise applicable rules of evidence." *Id.* at 131.

12. One questions that has arisen is what constitutes a "criminal case" for Fifth Amendment purposes. Thus, for example, if testimony is compelled, the government may not use it at trial but can it use it in suppression hearings, arraignments, and probable cause hearings? There is a split in the circuits on this question:

The U.S. Supreme Court has not conclusively defined the scope of a "criminal case" under the Fifth Amendment. In dicta, the Supreme Court suggested in a 1990 opinion, *United States v. Verdugo-Urquidez*, that the right against self-incrimination is only a trial right. 494 U.S. 259, 264 (1990).

But the Supreme Court later appeared to retreat from that dicta. In *Mitchell v. United States*, for instance, the Court held that the right against self-incrimination extends to sentencing hearings. 526 U.S. 314, 320-21, 327 (1999). The Court reasoned that "[t]o maintain that sentencing proceedings are not part of 'any criminal case' is contrary to the law and to common sense."

Even more recently, the Court again addressed the scope of the Fifth Amendment in *Chavez v. Martinez*, 538 U.S. 760 (2003). In *Chavez*, the plaintiff sued a police officer under 1983, alleging coercion of self-incriminating statements in violation of the Fifth Amendment. Writing for himself and two other justices, Justice Thomas concluded that (1) the plaintiff had failed to state a valid claim because he had not been charged with a crime and (2) the plaintiff's statements had not been used in a criminal case.

Though the Court did not produce a majority opinion on the Fifth Amendment issue, Justice Thomas's plurality opinion explained that "mere coercion does not violate the text of the Self-Incrimination Clause absent use of the compelled statements in a criminal case against the witness." Justice Thomas added that "[a] 'criminal case' at the very least requires the initiation of legal proceedings." Two other justices agreed with the outcome, reasoning that the Fifth Amendment's text "focuses on *courtroom use* of a criminal defendant's compelled, self-incriminating testimony." ([E]mphasis added).

The *Chavez* Court did not decide "the precise moment when a 'criminal case' commences." Justice Thomas cited *Verdugo-Urquidez*, but apparently did not read it to limit the Fifth Amendment to use at trial.

Three other justices stated that a violation of the Self-Incrimination Clause is complete the moment a confession is compelled. Thus, even in light of *Verdugo-Urquidez*, these three justices concluded that the Fifth Amendment extended beyond use of a compelled statement at trial.

Following *Chavez*, a circuit split developed over the definition of a "criminal case" under the Fifth Amendment. The Third, Fourth, and Fifth Circuits have stated that the Fifth Amendment is only a trial right.

In contrast, the Second, Seventh, and Ninth Circuits have held that certain pretrial uses of compelled statements violate the Fifth Amendment. For example, the Second Circuit has applied *Chavez* to hold that a bail hearing is part of a criminal case under the Fifth Amendment. The Seventh Circuit has similarly held that a criminal case under the Fifth Amendment includes not only bail hearings but also suppression hearings, arraignments, and probable cause hearings. And the Ninth Circuit has concluded that a Fifth Amendment violation occurs when "[a] coerced statement ... has been relied upon to file formal charges against the declarant, to determine judicially that the prosecution may proceed, and to determine pretrial custody status."

Vogt v. City of Hayes, 844 F.3d 1235, 1239-1240 (10th Cir. 2017) (holding that Fifth Amendment right applies to use in a probable cause hearing as well as at trial).

13. The obvious object of a grant of immunity is securing a witness's evidence and, in many cases, active cooperation. In discussing cooperation deals in general, Professor Graham Hughes notes, "[m]ost cooperation agreements would be difficult to fit into any concept of repentance or rehabilitation. These are agreements to sell a commodity—knowledge. The witness usually gains that knowledge through participation in criminal conduct, and the offer of testimony is a calculated attempt to gain immunity or leniency. Freeing such a person can powerfully excite the public's sense of injustice." Graham Hughes, *Agreements for Cooperation in Criminal Cases*, 45 Vand. L. Rev. 1, 13 (1992). When, if ever, should the Department of Justice give a clearly guilty individual a "walk" in return for his cooperation?

14. Before seeking a judicial immunity order pursuant to §§ 6002-03, Assistant U.S. Attorneys must secure Department of Justice approval. The following is the departmental policy regarding such grants:

U.S.A.M. § 9-23.210 Decision to Request Immunity—The Public Interest

Section 6003(b) of Title 18, United States Code, authorizes a United States Attorney to request immunity when, in his/her judgment, the testimony or other information that is expected to be obtained from the witness "may be necessary to the public interest." Some of the factors that should be weighed in making this judgment include:

A. The importance of the investigation or prosecution to effective enforcement of the criminal laws;

B. The value of the person's testimony or information to the investigation or prosecution;

C. The likelihood of prompt and full compliance with a compulsion order, and the effectiveness of available sanctions if there is no such compliance;

D. The person's relative culpability in connection with the offense or offenses being investigated or prosecuted, and his or her criminal history;

E. The possibility of successfully prosecuting the person prior to compelling his or her testimony;

F. The likelihood of adverse collateral consequences to the person if he or she testifies under a compulsion order.

These factors are not intended to be all-inclusive or to require a particular decision in a particular case. They are, however, representative of the kinds of factors that should be considered when deciding whether to seek immunity.

U.S.A.M. § 9-23.212 Decision to Request Immunity—Conviction Prior to Compulsion

It is preferable as a matter of policy to punish offenders for their criminal conduct prior to compelling them to testify. While this is not feasible in all cases, a successful prosecution of the witness, or obtaining a plea of guilty to at least some of the charges against the witness, will avoid or mitigate arguments of co-defendants made to the court or jury that the witness "cut a deal" with the government to avoid the witness's own conviction and punishment.

* * *

15. Assuming that the public interest demands an immunity deal, great care must be taken in effecting such deals. Again, in discussing cooperation deals generally, Professor Hughes argues that "[t]he chief dangers of cooperation agreements are: (1) improper or imprudent selection of the beneficiaries of informal immunity or lenient bargains; (2) presentation of unacceptably tainted or suspect testimony [as] … evidence against defendants; (3) agreements with cooperators that may impose unconscionable obligations on cooperators, confer unacceptable license to commit future crimes, or excessively forgive their past crimes; and (4) vindictive or excessively harsh retaliations against cooperators who, in a prosecutor's opinion, have not satisfied their obligations." Hughes, *supra*, at 67. Just how immediate are these dangers in the immunity context? Can the Department of Justice obviate these concerns through effective training of novice prosecutors? What procedures or practices might be effective?

16. Many of the above-listed dangers concern prosecutorial abuses or lack of judgment. The following excerpt discusses the dangers of cooperating witnesses (raising some of the same concerns) from the perspective of a prosecutor. These words of warning offered by Judge

Stephen Trott, a former prosecutor who now sits on the Ninth Circuit, for future prosecutors ought to be equally enlightening to future defense lawyers. (Future practitioners, particularly aspiring prosecutors, are encouraged to read the entirety of Judge Trott's article).

Hon. Stephen S. Trott, *Words of Warning for Prosecutors Using Criminals as Witnesses*
47 Hastings L.J. 1381 (1996)

In the early stages of a prosecutor's career, most prosecution witnesses are normal citizens who, by virtue of some misfortune, have been either the victim of, or a witness to, a criminal act. ...

Sooner or later, however, another type of not-so-reliable witness starts to make an occasional appearance on the subpoena list, and the prosecutor begins to venture out onto a totally different sea where he or she is frequently ill-prepared to navigate—the watery and treacherous straits of the accomplice, the co-conspirator, the snitch, and the informer. ...

The usual defense to ... [a] criminally involved witness is never just a polite assertion that he is mistaken. Not surprisingly, the rejoinder ordinarily mounted amidst loud, indignant, and sometimes even enraged accusations is that the witness is lying through his teeth for reasons that should be patently obvious to every decent person in the courtroom.

The prosecutor on such occasions will be surprised to discover that his or her own personal integrity is on the line. Such an unexpected turn of events is not a laughing matter. It is neither helpful to a prosecutor's case nor very comforting personally to have the defense persuasively arguing to the court and jury, for example, that you, as a colossal idiot, have given immunity to the real killer in order to prosecute an innocent man. Alan Dershowitz in his book, *The Best Defense*, describes this tactic as follows:

> In representing criminal defendants—especially guilty ones—it is often necessary to take the offense against the Government; to put the Government on trial for *its* misconduct. In law as in sports, the best defense is often a good offense. ...

There are two principal reasons why this type of frontal offensive can be marshaled against these kinds of witnesses. ...

The first of the two reasons relates to the general nature of a witness predisposed to criminality. Read it and commit the message to memory:

> 1. Criminals are likely to say and do almost anything to get what they want, especially when what they want is to get out of trouble with the law. ...

The second of the two reasons why converted criminals as witnesses come under such heavy fire pertains to the general disposition of people who become jurors towards informers. To a prosecutor, it is of equal importance as the first.

> 2. Ordinary decent people are predisposed to dislike, distrust, and frequently despise criminals who "sell out" and become prosecution witnesses. Jurors suspect their motives from the moment they hear about them in a case, and they frequently disregard their testimony altogether as highly untrustworthy and unreliable, openly expressing disgust with the prosecution for making deals with such "scum." ...

With the foregoing in mind, let me put a different spin on this and confront you with some observations that color the answer to the threshold question of whether or not to use accomplices or snitches as witnesses in the trial of any particular case.

First, calling to the stand an actual participant/eyewitness to the crime who knows the criminals and can easily identify them—normally a devastating witness—can backfire and have the unintended effect of making your case worse rather than better if the eyewitness is a crook who has bartered for some sort of consideration in return for his testimony.

Second, evidence amounting to a complete confession—normally the end of a defendant's chances with a jury—can actually have the unanticipated effect of making your case weaker rather than stronger if the witness upon whom the jury has to rely for the truth of the testimony is a person they will not trust.

Why? Because in the hands of a skillful defense tactician, all the liabilities and the unseverable baggage that such a witness brings to your case, along with the "confession" or the "identification," become the elements of reasonable doubt the defense is looking for and the brush with which the rest of your case is tarred. The issue of the defendant's guilt can seep away ... while the prosecutor attempts to defend against the forceful assertions of deceit and misconduct on the part of the government's witnesses. Once a prosecutor loses control and begins in desperation to defend rather than prosecute, disaster is right around the corner! The defense will go after these witnesses with everything it can find, hoping to make them the vulnerable links in your chain. ...

Notwithstanding all the problems that accompany using criminals as witnesses, however, the fact of the matter is that police and prosecutors cannot do without them—period. Often they do tell the truth, and on occasion they must be used in court. ...

The appropriate questions, therefore, are not really whether criminals should ever be used as government witnesses, but when and if so, how? [T]he two main goals of a prosecutor and an investigator [are]:

(1) To discover the truth, the whole truth, and nothing but the truth; and
(2) To present persuasively what you have unearthed to a jury and convince them to rely on it in arriving at a just verdict.

In this regard, there are a few important rules of thumb that should normally be observed. ...

A. Use Little Fish

Make agreements with "little fish" to get "big fish." Jurors will understand this approach, but they may reject out of hand anything that smacks of giving a fat deal to a "big fish" to get a "little fish." It will offend their notion of basic fairness and will play into the hands of the defense. ...

B. Drive a Hard Deal

Do not give up more to make a deal than you have to. This is a temptation to which too many prosecutors succumb. If you have to give up anything at all, a plea to a lesser number of counts, a reduction in the degree of a crime, or a limitation on the number of years that an accomplice will serve is frequently sufficient to induce an accomplice to testify; and it sounds better to jurors when they discover that both fish are still in the net. ...

C. Stay in Control

You must always be in control, not the witness! The moment you sense that the witness is dictating terms and seizing control of the situation, you are in very deep trouble and you must reverse what has happened. ... Do not fix their parking tickets, smooth over their rental car defalcations, or intervene in all their problems with the law without expecting repercussions later on. Inexperienced prosecutors tend to coddle such witnesses for fear of losing their testimony. This fear stems from not understanding what drives them. The basic deal is all you need to keep them on board. ...

D. Keep Your Distance from the Witness

If you decide to call an informer as a witness, you will end up spending much time with him preparing for his testimony. Not all such witnesses are hard core street criminals, and some of them are affable and will try to ingratiate themselves in your good favor. Remain courteous, but do not let down your guard and share the kind of information with them you might share with a friend or colleague. Today, he might be testifying for you, but ... tomorrow he may decide to turn against you. Never say anything to a witness ... that you would not repeat yourself in open court ....

* * *

2. DEFENSE WITNESS IMMUNITY

Can the *defense* compel the prosecution to grant a *defense* witness formal statutory immunity where the defense contends that the witness has exculpatory information and is necessary to an effective defense but where the witness has expressed an intention, if called by the defense, to assert the Fifth? Under existing caselaw, the defense has no right to compel witness immunity on the basis of the Sixth Amendment right to compulsory process:

> The established content of the Sixth Amendment does not support a claim for defense witness immunity. Traditionally, the Sixth Amendment's Compulsory Process Clause gives the defendant the right to bring his witness to court and have the witness's non-privileged testimony heard, but does no[t] carry with it the additional right to displace a proper claim of privilege, including the privilege against self-incrimination. While the prosecutor may not prevent or discourage a defense witness from testifying, it is difficult to see how the Sixth Amendment of its own force places upon either the prosecutor or the court any affirmative obligation to secure testimony from a defense witness by replacing the protection of the self-incrimination privilege with a grant of use immunity.[3]

Most courts to address the issue have also held that the defendant has no due process entitlement to defense witness immunity.[4] As the Second Circuit explained in *United States v. Turkish*:

> The ... argument [that defense witness immunity is required by due process because of] the need to pursue the truth, [while weighty, does not persuade us]. As a general rule the Government is properly obliged to divulge exculpatory evidence. *Brady v. Maryland*, 373 U.S. 83 (1963). That principle, however, has heretofore been limited to evidence in the Government's possession and has not been extended to create a Government obligation to assist the defense in extracting from others evidence the Government does not have. Moreover the concept of a trial as a search for the truth has always failed of full realization whenever important facts are shielded from disclosure because of a lawful privilege. ... However, the grant of use immunity does implicate public interests, and any assessment of a claim for defense witness use immunity must reckon with those public concerns.
>
> In the first place, while the prosecution remains theoretically free under *Kastigar* to prosecute a witness granted use immunity, the obstacles to a successful prosecution can be substantial. The Government has a "heavy burden" to prove that its evidence against the

---

[3] United States v. Turkish, 623 F.2d 769, 773 (2d Cir. 1980).

[4] *See, e.g.*, Autry v. McKaskle, 465 U.S. 1085 (1984) (Marshall, J., dissent from denial of certiorari); United States v. Thevis, 665 F.2d 616, 639 (5th Cir. 1982).

immunized witness has not been obtained as a result of his immunized testimony. While this burden can be met by cataloguing or "freezing" the evidence known to the Government prior to the immunized testimony, that technique is not available when continuing investigations disclose vital evidence after, though not resulting from, the immunized testimony. Moreover, to meet its burden of proving that prosecution of the immunized witness was not benefitted in any way by his immunized testimony the prosecutors most knowledgeable about an investigation may in some circumstances be obliged to forgo any further contact with the witness and arrange for a new team of investigators and prosecutors to pursue the case against him.

Secondly, awareness of the obstacles to successful prosecution of an immunized witness may force the prosecution to curtail its cross-examination of the witness in the case on trial to narrow the scope of the testimony that the witness will later claim tainted his subsequent prosecution. While the witness cannot prevent prosecution and secure an immunity "bath" by broadening the scope of his answers, as he could if testifying under a grant of transactional immunity, his fulsome answers may substantially lessen the likelihood of any successful prosecution.

Finally, there is considerable force to the Government's apprehension that defense witness immunity could create opportunities for undermining the administration of justice by inviting cooperative perjury among law violators. Co-defendants could secure use immunity for each other, and each immunized witness could exonerate his co-defendant at a separate trial by falsely accepting sole responsibility for the crime, secure in the knowledge that his admission could not be used at his own trial for the substantive offense. The threat of a perjury conviction, with penalties frequently far below substantive offenses, could not be relied upon to prevent such tactics. Moreover, this maneuver would substantially undermine the opportunity for joint trials, with consequent expense, delay, and burden upon disinterested witnesses and the judicial system. How these substantial concerns are to be weighed against the defendant's interest in securing truthful exculpatory testimony through defense witness immunity turns in large part upon whether the balancing of these interests is appropriately a judicial function. The Government suggests it is not, contending that the granting of immunity is pre-eminently a function of the Executive Branch. ...

... [A] court cannot determine whether any constitutional provision requires a judicial grant of use immunity without assessing the implications upon the Executive Branch, both those that flow from a grant of use immunity and those that flow from an adjudication of whether such immunity might be appropriate in a particular case. The concerns previously expressed about the risk to other successful prosecutions are matters normally better assessed by prosecutors than by judges. Surely a court is in no position to weigh the public interest in the comparative worth of prosecuting a defendant or his witness, although if a court decides that immunity is required, it can always leave that ultimate assessment with the prosecutor by advising that trial of the defendant will continue only if the witness's testimony is immunized. But confronting the prosecutor with a choice between terminating prosecution of the defendant or jeopardizing prosecution of the witness is not a task congenial to the judicial function.[5]

Are you persuaded by the above reasoning? Should there ever be cases where the court may grant a defense witness immunity over prosecutorial objection? In what sorts of circumstances?

---

[5] *Turkish*, 623 F.2d at 775-76. *But see* Reid H. Weingarten & Brantt Heberlong, *The Defense Witness Immunity Doctrine: The Time Has Come to Give it Strength to Address Prosecutorial Overreaching*, 43 Am. Crim. L. Rev. 1189 (2006). One way of examining this issue is to consider the larger issue of why the government should be permitted to "buy" witness testimony with grants of immunity or other consideration of value while defense counsel is not only generally unable to secure defense immunity but is also barred from giving other things of value to prospective defense witnesses. For such a discussion, see the article by Prof. David Sklansky excerpted *infra* in Chapter 19 (Plea Bargaining and Cooperation).

In 2008, the Ninth Circuit upheld a due process claim founded on the government's failure to grant a defense witness immunity.[6] In *United States v. Straub*, Straub was convicted of narcotics crimes and an attempted robbery and shooting. He had unsuccessfully sought immunity for a proposed defense witness, Mike Baumann, who the defense alleged would contradict the testimony of the government's star (immunized) witness, Straub's co-conspirator, David Adams. The Ninth Circuit explained:

> ...We now hold that for a defendant to compel use immunity the defendant must show that: (1) the defense witness's testimony was relevant; and (2) either (a) the prosecution intentionally caused the defense witness to invoke the Fifth Amendment right against self-incrimination with the purpose of distorting the fact-finding process; or (b) the prosecution granted immunity to a government witness in order to obtain that witness's testimony, but denied immunity to a defense witness whose testimony would have directly contradicted that of the government witness, with the effect of so distorting the fact-finding process that the defendant was denied his due process right to a fundamentally fair trial. ...
>
> ...The district court found that Adams's testimony was "crucial" to the prosecution's case. Adams was the only witness who testified Straub was armed that evening. Adams was also the only witness who put Straub at the location of the crime. The court found that, "if a jury believed that Adams lied about this, and was shifting the blame to Straub for his own actions, it would seriously weaken the government's case" ... These findings of fact suggest that for the government to grant use immunity for Adams while denying use immunity to the one witness who could possibly portray Adams as a perjurer and the true perpetrator of the crime had the effect of distorting the fact-finding process.
>
> In addition to considering the fact that Adams was granted use immunity, we may consider how the prosecution exercised its discretion to provide use immunity and other incentives to secure the testimony of its other witnesses. ... Of thirteen witnesses described, all but one of the prosecution's twelve witnesses received either formal immunity, informal immunity, or other substantial incentives such as cash compensation or a reduction of sentence in exchange for their testimony. ... Six government witnesses ... received incentives for their testimony, including one who was paid $8,300 for providing assistance, and another whose sentence was reduced from 24 months in prison to three years probation. Only one government witness ... appears to have received no incentives or immunity. All but one of the eleven government witnesses who received either immunity or another incentive testified to having committed crimes involving the

---

[6] United States v. Straub, 538 F.3d 1147 (9th Cir. 2008); *see also* United States v. Wilkes, 662 F.3d 524 (9th Cir. 2011). The Third and the Second Circuits have left the door slightly ajar to the possibility that judicial grants of defense witness immunity might be appropriate in select cases. *See, e.g., id.*; Government of the Virgin Islands v. Smith, 615 F.2d 964 (3d Cir. 1980) (a defendant may attempt to claim defense witness immunity as a matter of due process upon a showing that (1) the government refused to grant such an immunity pursuant to a "deliberate intention of distorting the judicial factfinding process" or (2) where the proffered testimony is "clearly exculpatory" and "essential" and there are "no strong governmental interests which countervail against a grant of immunity"); *see also* United States v. Brooks, 681 F.3d 678, 711 (5th Cir. 2012) (district courts have no inherent power to grant immunity; leaving open the possibility, "[a]t most," that immunity "may be necessary to stem government abuse"); Carter v. United States, 684 A.2d 331 (D.C. App. 1996); *see generally* Amicus Curiae Brief of NACDL Lawyers in Support of Petitioners, Brooks v. United States, Nos. 12-218, 12-5847 (2012). The Department of Justice's policy, contained in U.S.A.M. § 9-23.214, is as follows:

> As a matter of policy, 18 U.S.C. § 6002 will not be used to compel the production of testimony or other information on behalf of a defendant except in extraordinary circumstances where the defendant plainly would be deprived of a fair trial without such testimony or other information. This policy is not intended to preclude compelling a defense witness to testify if the prosecutor believes that to do so is necessary to a successful prosecution.

sale or manufacture of drugs; several admitted to sales totaling hundreds of thousands of dollars.

The only defense witness listed, Mike Baumann, was denied use immunity.

The prosecution granted Adams use immunity, and Adams' testimony was crucial to the conviction for the attempted robbery with a firearm. The prosecution denied use immunity to the one defense witness who could have discredited Adams' testimony, even though the prosecution claimed it had no interest in prosecuting that witness. Meanwhile, the prosecution granted use and informal immunity, gave cash, and issued sentence reductions to eleven other admitted drug offenders, all for the purpose of securing evidence against Straub. We conclude that this exercise of discretion by the prosecution impermissibly distorted the fact-finding process, in violation of the Due Process Clause. A trial under these circumstances is not fundamentally fair. The district court erred when it denied Straub's request to compel use immunity.[7]

B. PROFFERS

1. RATIONALE

To evaluate both the value of the prospective immunized witness's testimony and his worth as a witness, most prosecutors will insist upon an "offer of proof," oftentimes called a "proffer," prior to concluding a deal. (This is also true in circumstances where the defendant agrees to plead guilty and cooperate in return for the government's consideration in charging or sentencing, discussed in Chapter 19 (Plea Bargaining and Cooperation).) At the outset of negotiations, counsel may make preliminary proffers on behalf of the defendant, attempting to persuade the government of his client's worth to the prosecution of others ("hypothetical" proffer) and to provide the government with sufficient specific information to attest to the client's value and veracity as a witness ("subject matter" proffer).[8] Note that even these preliminary proffers are not without risk. Arguments may subsequently be made that the attorney was acting as the defendant's agent and, as such, made "admissions" that may be used against the client[9] and that "a client's communications of proposed testimony made with the intent that the lawyer relay the communications to the government are not protected by the lawyer-client privilege."[10]

In many cases, if a prosecutor is sufficiently intrigued by the attorney's proffer, she will insist upon a proffer from the potential cooperating witness as well. As Judge Stephen Trott advises prosecutors:

The first problem that usually arises is the "Catch 22" situation where you want to know exactly what the witness has to offer before committing yourself to a "deal," but the witness, even though desirous of cooperating, is afraid to talk for fear of incriminating himself unless he is promised something first. When you get into such a situation, never buy a pig in a poke! If you first give a criminal absolute immunity from prosecution or commit irrevocably to a generous deal and then ask him what he knows, the probability is

---

[7] *Straub*, 538 F.3d at 1162, 1163-64.

[8] *See, e.g.*, Dan K. Webb, Robert W. Tarun, & Steven F. Molo, Corporate Internal Investigations § 15.08[1], at 15-23 (Law Journal Press 2018).

[9] *Cf.* United States v. Catena, 500 F.2d 1319, 1326-27 (3d Cir. 1974) (upholding trial court's admission into evidence of a written statement made by counsel denying any wrongdoing by the defendant in the course of a meeting with investigators at which the defendant was present).

[10] United States v. Sudikoff, 36 F.Supp.2d 1196, 1205 (C.D. Cal. 1999) (so holding in a case in which a defendant sought information relating to the proffer and plea negotiations between the government and the government's cooperating witness as *Brady* material and witness statements under 18 U.S.C. § 3500).

that you will get nothing but hot air. Remove the witness' incentive to cooperate and you will lose all the fish, both big and little. ...

The answer to this seeming dilemma is very simple. Get a proffer! Promise the witness in writing that you will not use what he tells you at this stage of the proceedings against him, but make it equally clear that your decision whether or not to make a deal will not be made until after you have had the opportunity to assess both the value and the credibility of the information.[11]

What are the dangers to the defendant of such a proffer? When might the government be persuaded to forgo a proffer, or accept an attorney's proffer of his client's likely testimony? In the conduct of a proffer, what are the objectives of both sides? Consider discussion of the usual purpose and conduct of proffer sessions, offered by Judge John Gleeson, a former prosecutor and former judge on the U.S. District Court for the Eastern District of New York:

The purpose of the proffer session is to get all of the information necessary to a plea offer (or to determine whether one will be made) on the negotiating table. The prosecutor needs to know several things before she can make an informed offer. Some relate to the crime or crimes under investigation. Initially, the prosecutor wants to know the defendant's version of his or her own role in the crime. This will be measured against the information already available to the investigators in an effort to determine whether the prospective witness will tell the truth (or at least what the prosecutor then believes to be the truth) about his or her own conduct. Prospective cooperators rarely deny their criminality, but the temptation to minimize it is strong, and for some it is insurmountable. Some proffer sessions end abruptly, without any plea offer, because the defendant cannot pass even this first test.

Some also fail the next test as well, which is to talk about the conduct of the others involved in the crime. Certain defendants who genuinely want to be government witnesses are simply unable to testify against other people, and do not get offered cooperation agreements as a result.

The prosecutor also uses proffer sessions to determine what "baggage" a witness will bring to the witness stand at trial. Because future cross-examinations of the witness will not be limited to the crimes under investigation, the prosecutor needs to know about all of the criminal activity in the witness's past, whether or not the government is aware of it. Prior crimes that are disclosed during the proffer session will be covered by any resulting plea agreement, so the terms of the government's offer (and, indeed, whether there will be an offer at all) depend in part on the other criminal activity disclosed during the proffer session.[12] Thus, at bottom, the prospective cooperating witness is asked in a proffer session to tell a prosecutor about crimes the prosecutor has no knowledge of, which may result in a worse deal (or no deal at all) for the witness.[13] Needless to say, this sort of disclosure does not come naturally to experienced criminals.

---

[11] Hon. Stephen S. Trott, *Words of Warning for Prosecutors Using Criminals as Witnesses*, 47 Hastings L.J. 1381, 1401-02 (1996).

[12] [Article's footnote 109:] For example, prospective witnesses who are arrested on mail fraud charges may enter a proffer session with the reasonable expectation that prosecutors will "allow" them to plead guilty to a single five-year maximum mail fraud count in exchange for cooperation. [Ed.: The statutory maximum for mail fraud has, since this article was written, been changed to 20 years.] If the proffer session, however, reveals that the witness killed Jimmy Hoffa, the prosecutor may require a guilty plea that carries the potential for longer imprisonment as a condition of cooperation. This is only natural; simply as a matter of right and wrong, the prosecutor may feel uncomfortable with allowing a plea of guilty to a five-year count to satisfy the defendant's criminal exposure for a murder. More selfishly, the prosecutor will worry that some future jury will conclude that the government paid too high a price for the testimony, and thus reject the testimony and perhaps the entire case.

[13] [Article's footnote 110:] This practice of obtaining a full proffer of all prior crimes prevails in many districts, including the Eastern and Southern Districts of New York, but is not universal. For example,

The attorney for the prospective witness plays a crucial role during the proffer sessions. These are the client's first face-to-face contacts with the prosecutor and case agent. There is every reason to be nervous "because the interview process intimidates" and because the client is expected to incriminate "people who may be predisposed to commit violence against him or his family." The lawyer often helps the client resist the natural temptation to minimize the client's involvement in the crimes under investigation and plays the central role in persuading the client to reveal prior crimes, as criminals simply do not trust a prosecutor who says that it is in the client's interest to do so.[14] The lawyer must "keep her client focused on the fact that while he is seeking the assistance and protection of the government, that entity does not share the defendant's interests." Indeed, the adversarial posture of the prosecutor is at its most acute during proffer sessions. The typical proffer agreement provides only limited protection to the prospective witness if no plea agreement results from the sessions, and does not prohibit the derivative use of the defendant's statements to pursue further investigation. Thus, a prospective witness who fails this audition and gets no agreement may well be helping the government strengthen its existing case and, perhaps, to add new charges as well.

> To borrow a phrase from [*United States v. Ming He,*][15] "to send a defendant into this perilous setting without his attorney is ... inconsistent with the fair administration of justice." That is why it does not happen; defense attorneys invariably attend proffer sessions ....[16]

The above excerpt makes clear that defense counsel's job is particularly delicate in the proffer context. She must negotiate zealously on behalf of her client, ensuring that the proffer is made subject to appropriate safeguards and that she makes the best possible deal for her client. At the same time, she must press the client to fully and completely respond to the government's inquiries in the proffer—a role that may alienate her client unless she is able to communicate to the client the reasons why a less than fulsome or honest account may not only derail any potential deal but may well exacerbate the client's exposure.[17] Finally, a few recent cases raise the specter that defense counsel may become a witness by virtue of her participation in the proffer. Thus, courts have indicated (without expressly deciding) that counsel may be called upon to serve as a government witness regarding any false statements her client made

---

some United States Attorney's offices will enter into cooperation agreements that do not cover prior crimes of violence. A proffer session leading up to such an agreement will therefore be limited—employing a "don't ask, don't tell" approach to violent crimes.

[14] [Article's footnote 112:] As counterintuitive as it seems to these clients to tell the government about crimes no one knows about, defense counsel will frequently advise them that it is in their best interests to do so. Because the prosecutor's principal goal is to enlist testimony against someone else, it is often a good time to clean all the past skeletons out of the closet and wrap them up in one favorable plea agreement. Also, few defendants are worse off than one who has pleaded guilty under a cooperation agreement, claiming to have disclosed all prior crimes to the government, only to have an undisclosed crime come to light after the agreement is reached. That defendant can both lose the § 5K1.1 motion with regard to the sentence on a guilty plea and, because the undisclosed crime is not covered by the plea agreement, be prosecuted separately for that crime.

[15] [Ed.:] 94 F.3d 782, 790 (2d Cir.1996) (creating rule, criticized in the above-quoted article, that during the course of criminal investigations cooperating witnesses are entitled to have counsel present during the debriefing sessions that generally follow a successful proffer and conclusion of a cooperation deal unless they explicitly waive such assistance).

[16] Hon. John Gleeson, *Supervising Criminal Investigations: The Proper Scope of the Supervisory Power of Federal Judges,* 5 J.L. & Pol'y 423, 447-50 (1997).

[17] *See* United States v. Wood, 780 F.2d 929 (11th Cir.1986).

during the course of the proffer[18] or may be required to turn over her notes for disclosure to the defendant against whom her client will testify at trial.[19]

2. FED. R. CRIM. P. 11(f) AND FED. R. EVID. 410

Fed. R. Crim. P. 11(f) and Fed. R. Evid. 410 state that the content of the defendant's statements during such proffer sessions is inadmissible for most purposes against the defendant. In what circumstances may statements made in the course of plea negotiations come in? What is the purpose of excluding from evidence statements the defendant or his counsel make during the course of plea discussions?

Most importantly for present purposes, may a defendant waive the protections of this rule? In *United States v. Mezzanatto*,[20] the Supreme Court held that a defendant may waive the bar, found in Fed. R. Evid. 410 and Fed. R. Crim. P. 11(f), on the admissibility of statements made in the course of plea discussions for purposes of impeachment or rebuttal. It is noteworthy, however, that three justices who joined the majority—Justices Ginsburg, O'Connor, and Breyer—said in a concurrence that a waiver allowing prosecutors to introduce proffer statements during the government's case-in-chief presented different concerns and that extending *Mezzanatto* to that context might "more severely undermine a defendant's incentive to negotiate, and thereby inhibit plea bargaining."[21] Justice Souter, joined in dissent by Justice Stevens, argued that the majority opinion contained no principled limitation upon what waivers prosecutors could seek and therefore gave the government an incentive to seek even broader waivers—which is precisely what the government has done (*see infra*).[22]

3. SAMPLE PROFFER AGREEMENT

In fact, most proffer agreements provide for some type of waiver of the protections of Fed. R. Crim. P. 11(f) and Fed. R. Evid. 410. The following is a sample of one type of proffer agreement, sometimes referred to as a "Queen for a Day" agreement, that was employed in the Southern District of New York circa 2005 (the names have, obviously, been altered).

AGREEMENT

With respect to the meeting of JOE WITNESS ("Client") and his attorney, DUDLEY DORIGHT, Esq., with Assistant United States Attorney BUSTER O. CRIME to be held at the Office of the United States Attorney for the Southern District of New York on September 1, 2018 ("the meeting"), the following understandings exist:

(1) THIS IS NOT A COOPERATION AGREEMENT. The Client has agreed to provide the Government with information, and to respond to questions, so that the Government may evaluate Client's information and responses in making prosecutive decisions. By receiving Client's proffer, the Government does not agree to make a motion on Client's behalf or to enter into a cooperation agreement, plea agreement, immunity or non-

---

[18] *See In re* Grand Jury Subpoena Dated Oct. 22, 2001, 282 F.3d 156 (2d Cir. 2002) (upholding the claim that the work product privilege bars a subpoena compelling an attorney to testify to her client's admissions to an IRS agent during an interview as evidence of the client's commission of the offenses of fraud and tax evasion, on which the attorney was representing the client during the interview; noting, however, that the court does not resolve the issue of what would occur if the government issued a new subpoena summoning the attorney before a different grand jury investigating whether at the interview the client committed new false statement offenses).

[19] United States v. Sudikoff, 36 F. Supp.2d 1196, 1205 (C.D. Cal. 1999).

[20] 513 U.S. 196 (1995).

[21] *Id.* at 211 (Ginsburg, J., concurring).

[22] *Id.* at 217-18 (Souter, J., dissenting).

prosecution agreement. The Government makes no representation about the likelihood that any such agreement will be reached in connection with this proffer.

(2) In any prosecutions brought against Client by this Office, except as provided below, the Government will not offer in evidence on its case-in-chief, or in connection with any sentencing proceeding for the purpose of determining an appropriate sentence, any statements made by Client at the meeting, except in a prosecution for false statements, obstruction of justice or perjury with respect to any acts committed or statements made during or after the meeting or testimony given after the meeting.

(3) Notwithstanding item (2) above: (a) the Government may use information derived directly or indirectly from the meeting for the purpose of obtaining leads to other evidence, which evidence may be used in any prosecution of Client by the Government; (b) in any prosecution brought against Client, the Government may use statements made by Client at the meeting and all evidence obtained directly or indirectly therefrom for the purpose of cross-examination should Client testify; and (c) the government may also use statements made by Client at the meeting to rebut any evidence or arguments offered by or on behalf of Client (including arguments made or issues raised *sua sponte* by the District Court) at any stage of the criminal prosecution (including bail, all phases of trial, and sentencing) in any prosecution brought against Client.

(4) The Client understands and agrees that in the event the Client seeks to qualify for a reduction in sentence under Title 18, United States Code, Section 3553(f) or United States Sentencing Guidelines, Section 2D1.1(b)(7) or 5C1.2, the Office may offer in evidence, in connection with the sentencing, statements made by the Client at the meeting and all evidence obtained directly or indirectly therefrom.

(5) To the extent that the Government is entitled under this Agreement to offer in evidence any statements made by Client or leads obtained therefrom, Client shall assert no claim under the United States Constitution, any statute, Rule 410 of the Federal Rules of Evidence, or any other federal rule that such statements or any leads therefrom should be suppressed. It is the intent of the Agreement to waive all rights in the foregoing respects.

(6) If this Office receives a request from another prosecutor's office for access to information obtained pursuant to this Proffer Agreement, this Office may furnish such information but will do so only on the condition that the requesting office honor the provisions of this Agreement.

(7) It is further understood that this Agreement is limited to the statements made by Client at the meeting and does not apply to any oral, written or recorded statements made by Client at any other time. No understandings, promises, agreements and/or conditions have been entered into with respect to the meeting other than those set forth in this Agreement and none will be entered into unless in writing and signed by all parties.

(8) The understandings set forth in paragraphs 1 through 7 above extend to the continuation of this meeting on dates that appear below.

(9) Client and Attorney acknowledge that they have fully discussed and understand every paragraph and clause in this Agreement and the consequences thereof. ...

Notes

1. Contract principles control the interpretation of proffer agreements. *See, e.g.*, United States v. Chiu, 109 F.3d 624, 625 (9th Cir. 1997); United States v. Liranzo, 944 F.2d 73, 77 (2d Cir. 1991). What legal entitlements is the witness waiving under this proffer agreement? May the government use the witness's statements to prepare another government witness? *See Chiu*, 109 F.3d at 625 (yes). May the government share the witness's statements with other governmental actors, such as regulators conducting parallel civil enforcement actions or a government employer pursuing disciplinary action against the witness/employee? The answer appears to be "yes" unless the agreement provides otherwise. The same is true of sharing with foreign governments: if a proffer agreement does not bar the U.S. government from sharing a defendant's proffer statements, the government is free to give the statements to other interested sovereigns. *See* McKnight v. Torres, 563 F.3d 890 (9th Cir. 2009).

What is the government giving up? For other examples of proffer agreements, see Webb, *et al.*, *supra* note 8, § 15.08[2], at 15-23 through 15-30.1.

2. At the time that the parties enter into this agreement, both may be fairly certain that some kind of immunity or other cooperation agreement is in the offing. Both sides must keep firmly in mind, however, that the circumstances may change, the proposed deal may break down, and the parties may find themselves at trial. Defense counsel, in particular, should be particularly cautious in evaluating proffer language drafted by the government. Given the heavy weight that jurors give to admissions or prior inconsistent statements by a defendant, whether such statements come in may well change the outcome of a trial. *See, e.g.*, Frederick P. Hafetz & Burt M. Garson, *The 'Queen for a Day Agreement': A High-Risk Venture*, 8 Bus. Crimes Bull. 1 (April 2001). What avenues of attack are open to the defense? Consider, in that respect, the following case.

UNITED STATES v. VELEZ
354 F.3d 190 (2d Cir. 2004)

José A. Cabranes, Circuit Judge.

José Velez appeals from a judgment of conviction and sentence entered against him in the United States District Court for the Southern District of New York … for one count of possession of a firearm transported in interstate commerce, after a felony conviction, pursuant to 18 U.S.C. § 922(g)(1). …

On November 21, 2001, defendant was indicted for being a convicted felon in possession of a firearm shipped and transported in interstate commerce, in violation of 18 U.S.C. § 922(g)(1). The charge was based on the observations of three New York Police Department officers—namely, that on August 18, 2001 the officers saw defendant pull a gun from his waistband, heard the sound of metal hitting pavement, and then recovered a gun from the ground where defendant had been standing.

Shortly after being charged, defendant participated in two proffer sessions. In a first session on January 14, 2002, defendant, accompanied by counsel, asserted his innocence, claiming that he did not possess the gun found on the ground where he had been standing. The Government did not credit defendant's statements.

On May 9, 2002, defendant, again accompanied by counsel, participated in a second proffer session, which he had requested. (At this session, defendant was represented by his second attorney, because the District Court had granted defendant's request that he be relieved of his prior counsel.) Before participating in the meeting, defendant signed an agreement in which he waived, in certain circumstances, the protection otherwise applicable to his proffer statements that prohibits use of those statements as evidence against him. Relevant to this appeal, the waiver provision to which defendant agreed provides:

> [T]he Government may … use statements made by [defendant] at the meeting to rebut any evidence or arguments offered by or on behalf of [defendant] (including arguments made or issues raised *sua sponte* by the District Court) at any stage of the criminal prosecution (including bail, all phases of trial, and sentencing) in any prosecution brought against [defendant].

Accordingly, by signing the proffer agreement that included this waiver provision, defendant authorized the Government to introduce defendant's proffer statements at trial if defendant introduced evidence or arguments that were inconsistent with his proffer statements.

In the second proffer session, defendant recanted his claims of innocence at the initial session and admitted facts pertaining to one element of the charged offense—namely, that he owned and possessed the firearm that the officers found on the ground near him.

Defendant thereafter requested a third proffer session, which the Government scheduled, but defendant canceled the meeting and elected to proceed to trial.

Before the start of trial, however, defendant presented two issues to the District Court. First, he requested that the Court again appoint new defense counsel, on the ground that he would not receive a fair trial because his current (second) counsel had stated that he was "limited to attack[ing] certain areas," which, as defendant contended, was due to counsel's presence at the proffer session. The District Court denied defendant's request.

Second, through his attorney at a pretrial conference and in an *in limine* motion, defendant sought a preliminary ruling from the District Court on the scope of the defense's arguments and defense witness testimony that would open the door to the Government's use of defendant's proffer statements. In response to defendant's argument at the pretrial conference, the Government informed the Court that it did not seek to introduce defendant's proffer statements in its case-in-chief, but that it reserved the right "to introduce such statements if they are deemed necessary to rebut testimony or arguments made by or on behalf of the defendant that are inconsistent with statements made by the defendant during the proffer session."

The District Court initially did not rule on defendant's motion, but it noted that certain anticipated defense witness testimony would "come 'close' to opening the door to [the Government's] introduction of [defendant's] proffer statements." When defense counsel informed the Court that it would not elicit that testimony, the District Court provided additional time for the defense to reconsider its decision. However, later in the day, the District Court stated that if the anticipated defense witness testimony were introduced, the Court would indeed permit the Government to introduce defendant's proffer admissions, thereby implicitly finding that the proffer agreement was enforceable. Defendant did not introduce the anticipated testimony.

After a three-day trial, the jury convicted defendant of the sole count of the indictment, which yielded a sentencing range of 100 to 125 months' imprisonment under applicable guidelines. At sentencing, in the context of offering mitigation to warrant a sentence at the low end of the range, defendant stated that he had been "trap[ped]" into making his admissions at the second proffer session.[23] The District Court declined to credit defendant's statement as relevant to mitigation, and on December 16, 2002, sentenced defendant principally to 120 months' imprisonment.

1.   Challenge to the Waiver Provision in the Proffer Agreement

On appeal, defendant argues that the waiver provision in the proffer agreement—which permits the Government to offer a proffer admission by the defendant in rebuttal to contradictory evidence or argument—violates defendant's constitutional rights to mount a defense, to the effective assistance of counsel, and to a fair trial. We disagree. ...

Ordinarily, statements made by a defendant during plea negotiations, including proffer sessions, are inadmissible at trial. Fed.R.Evid. 410; *see also* Fed.R.Crim.P. 11(f) (referring to Federal Rule of Evidence 410).[24] However, a defendant can waive the protection afforded by

---

[23] [Court's footnote 2:] Defendant's exact statement was the following:

> I signed a proffer statement which says I was innocent the first time I went there, and I explained the story to them, and it was innocent. And the second time, it became a totally different story because they offer you something that I want to go home, I want to be with my family, and they trap me into saying something which cut the ring short at my trial.

[24] [Court's footnote 5:] Federal Rule of Evidence 410 provides in relevant part:

> Except as otherwise provided in this rule, evidence of the following is not, in any civil or criminal proceeding, admissible against the defendant who made the plea or was a participant in the plea discussions:

> (1) a plea of guilty which was later withdrawn;

> (2) a plea of nolo contendere;

> (3) any statement made in the course of any proceedings under Rule 11 of the Federal Rules of

Rule 410 as long as there is no "affirmative indication that the agreement [to waive] was entered into unknowingly or involuntarily." [*United States v. Mezzanatto*, 513 U.S. 196, 210 (1995)]. In *Mezzanatto*, as defendant correctly points out, the Supreme Court considered and enforced a narrow waiver provision in which the defendant permitted the Government to use his plea-negotiation statements only when responding to contrary testimony by the defendant himself. Here we face a more expansive waiver of Rule 410 because, in the proffer agreement at issue, defendant waived his exclusionary privilege in all circumstances in which the defense presents contradictory testimony, evidence, or arguments—whether or not defendant himself testifies. We agree with the District Court's implicit decision that the agreement is enforceable.

In contending that the agreement is unenforceable, defendant relies principally on *United States v. Duffy*, 133 F.Supp.2d 213 (E.D.N.Y.2001), in which the district court refused to enforce a waiver provision in a proffer agreement similar to the one we consider here. The *Duffy* ruling determined that the waiver provision "prevent[ed defense counsel] from making any sort of *meaningful* defense," and that it "exploit[ed]" a disparity of bargaining power between the Government and the defendant. The court stated: "After signing the standard proffer agreement, the terms of which are dictated by the government, the only thing that a defendant is guaranteed is the chance to convince the prosecutor to enter a deal. At the same time, the defendant bears all of the risk." Concluding that the waiver provision effectively forfeited the defendant's fundamental rights to present a defense and to the effective assistance of counsel and, in doing so, implicated important public interests, the district court held the waiver provision unenforceable.

For the reasons that follow, we respectfully decline to adopt the position advanced in *Duffy*, and we note with approval the recent, contrasting opinion in *United States v. Gomez*, 210 F.Supp.2d 465 (S.D.N.Y.2002), which found enforceable a proffer agreement containing a waiver provision identical to the one at issue in this case.

As the *Gomez* ruling points out, "fairness dictates that the agreement be enforced." *Id.* at 475. "If the proffer agreement is not enforced, a defendant will have less incentive to be truthful, for he will know that his proffer statements cannot be used against him at trial as long as he does not testify, even if he presents inconsistent evidence or arguments." *Id.*; *see also United States v. Krilich*, 159 F.3d 1020, 1025 (7th Cir.1998) (stating that, in proffer sessions, "a prosecutor needs assurance that the defendant is being candid" and that "[f]or this strategy to work the conditional waiver must be enforceable; its effect depends on making deceit *costly*").

In addition, invalidating a waiver provision like the one before us would clearly interfere with plea bargaining and cooperation efforts—in direct contravention of the criminal justice system's legitimate goal of encouraging plea bargaining in appropriate circumstances. The Supreme Court has noted that, "[i]f prosecutors were precluded from securing [waiver] agreements, they might well decline to enter into cooperation discussions in the first place and might never take this potential first step toward a plea bargain." *See also Gomez*, 210 F.Supp.2d at 475 ("Prosecutors will be reluctant to enter into cooperation agreements if they cannot obtain some assurance that the defendant will tell the truth.").

We do not lightly dismiss the observation in *Duffy* that the Government holds significant bargaining power in arranging proffer sessions and securing a waiver provision as a prerequisite for a defendant's participation. However, "[t]he mere potential for abuse of prosecutorial bargaining power is an insufficient basis for foreclosing negotiation altogether." *Mezzanatto*, 513 U.S. at 210 (rejecting the argument that "'gross disparity' in the relative bargaining power" renders waiver of Rule 410 in plea negotiations so "inherently unfair and coercive" that waiver should be prohibited). Indeed, to the extent there is a disparity between

---

Criminal Procedure or comparable state procedure regarding either of the foregoing pleas; or

(4) *any statement made in the course of plea discussions with an attorney for the prosecuting authority which do not result in a plea of guilty or which result in a plea of guilty later withdrawn.* (Emphasis added.)

Federal Rule of Criminal Procedure 11(f) provides: "The admissibility or inadmissibility of a plea, a plea discussion, and any related statement is governed by Federal Rule of Evidence 410."

the parties' bargaining positions, it is likely attributable to the Government's evidence of the defendant's guilt. *See Gomez*, 210 F.Supp.2d at 475 ("[A]lthough the Government does have significant bargaining power in these situations, it is because the Government has substantial evidence to prove the defendant's guilt."). We thus reject the argument that defendant, relying on *Duffy*, makes in this case—that the asserted disparity of power between the Government and a defendant in proffers renders waiver provisions in proffer agreements unenforceable.

Finally, a defendant remains free to present evidence inconsistent with his proffer statements, with the fair consequence that, if he does, "the Government [is] then ... permitted to present the defendant's own words in rebuttal." With this avenue open to him, a defendant who has consented to a waiver provision like the one at issue here has not forfeited his constitutional right to present a defense, to the effective assistance of his counsel, or to a fair trial.

Accordingly, we reject defendant's claim that the waiver provision is unconstitutional, and we hold that, where a proffer agreement is entered into knowingly and voluntarily, a provision in which defendant waives his exclusionary privilege under Federal Rule of Evidence 410 by permitting the Government to introduce defendant's proffer statements to rebut contrary evidence or arguments presented by the defense, whether or not defendant testifies, is enforceable.

Having concluded that the waiver provision in this proffer agreement is enforceable as long as it was entered into knowingly and voluntarily, we review the facts in that regard.

As noted above, before the waiver can be deemed unenforceable, the trial judge must find "some affirmative indication that the agreement [to waive] was entered into unknowingly or involuntarily." *Mezzanatto*, 513 U.S. at 210. A waiver is made knowingly if the defendant has "a full awareness of both the nature of the right being abandoned and the consequences of the decision to abandon it," and it is voluntary if it is "the product of a free and deliberate choice rather than intimidation, coercion, or deception."

Defendant does not contend that he failed to understand the right being waived or the consequences of the waiver. Instead, he claims, as he did at sentencing, that, when he participated in the second proffer session, he changed his story because the prosecution "trap[ped]" him into making admissions. Defendant contends that this statement—by him, at a sentencing hearing held four months after the end of the trial, *see* note 2, *ante*—is evidence of coercion at the proffer session.

We find no merit in defendant's claim of coercion. Defendant's explanation of his participation in the second proffer session fails to demonstrate that his consent to the terms of the proffer agreement was a product of coercion, rather than a normal consequence of his decision to participate in the proffer session—which defendant himself had requested.

In sum, we hold that the District Court did not err in implicitly finding enforceable the waiver provision in the proffer agreement.

2.   Claim of Ineffective Assistance of Counsel

Defendant, represented on appeal by still another attorney (his third), also asserts that trial counsel's continued representation of him following the attorney's presence at the second proffer session, in which defendant made partial admissions of guilt, constitutes a conflict of interest between defendant and attorney that deprived defendant of the effective assistance of counsel guaranteed by the Sixth Amendment to the United States Constitution. Defendant essentially argues that his attorney's continued representation created a potential conflict of interest by placing the attorney under inconsistent duties in the future—namely, that the attorney was a potential witness to the proffer session in the event that defendant claimed that his participation and statements in the session were a product of coercion.

Defendant argues that "this Court [should] announce a new rule for the Circuit and mandate the assignment of new counsel in situations such as confronted the defendant at bar," that is, where the trial court knows that the defendant, accompanied by counsel, attended a proffer session and made damaging admissions but did not receive a cooperation agreement. "At the least," defendant contends, "the rule should be that a post-proffer, pre-trial hearing should be conducted to ascertain the extent of any conflict that appears from a claim of the kind made by the defendant in the case at bar."

Defendant's contention is meritless. He would have us rule that whenever the district court learns that a defendant has made admissions at a proffer session with his lawyer present, and still faces trial, the court should assume the defendant may at some time in the future contend that he was coerced and will need the testimony of his lawyer to prove the coercion, which will be unavailable unless the lawyer is relieved of the representation.

We see no reason why a trial court should assume that a conflict arose from a proffer session. Every time a communication occurs between a defendant and counsel, the possibility exists that the communication gives rise to some conflict or potential conflict. There is nothing about a proffer session that makes it particularly likely that such a conflict will arise. Defendant presents no basis for devising a rule that requires the trial court to hold a hearing, much less replace counsel, merely because one can imagine unlikely events that may give rise to a conflict.

We have previously ruled that "an initial inquiry is required when 'the trial court knows or reasonably should know that a particular conflict exists.'" In these holdings, we did not suggest that the court was under a duty to inquire whenever, as a result of creative speculation, one could imagine a situation in which a conflict may have arisen. … The Supreme Court has specifically counseled against requiring inquiry whenever "the trial court is aware of a vague, unspecified possibility of conflict." *Mickens v. Taylor*, 535 U.S. 162, 168-69 (2002). Furthermore, our prior rulings require the trial court to conduct a *Curcio* hearing—to determine whether the defendant knowingly and intelligently waives his right to conflict-free representation, *see United States v. Curcio*, 680 F.2d 881, 888-90 (2d Cir.1982)—only if, "through this inquiry, the court determines that the attorney suffers from an actual or potential conflict of interest." We see no reason to change the rules in the manner the defendant suggests. …

Notes

1. Defense counsel representing defendants who proffered under a plea agreement like that in *Velez* and then proceed to trial will often have to attempt to determine in advance (through pretrial motions *in limine*) just what type of argument or cross-examination might be considered "contradictory evidence or argument" that would permit the government to use the defendant's proffer statements in rebuttal. *See* United States v. Oluwanisola, 605 F.3d 124 (2d Cir. 2010).

2. Despite five justices' apparent disquiet in *Mezzanatto* with waivers that go beyond use of proffers statements for impeachment purposes, courts after *Velez* have approved an even more aggressive waiver term that is not restricted to impeachment or rebuttal evidence. For example, in *United States v. Sylvester*, 583 F.3d 285 (5th Cir. 2009), the court upheld a proffer agreement in which the defendant agreed that the government could use a defendant's statement in its case-in-chief. *See also* United States v. Mitchell, 633 F.3d 997, 1002-06 (10th Cir. 2011) (same) (collecting cases). The difficult question for trial courts in applying these waivers is determining what defense counsel may and may not say, for example, in opening so as to avoid "opening the door" to statements clients made during proffer sessions. *See, e.g.*, United States v. Roberts, 660 F.3d 149 (2d Cir. 2011); United States v. Oluwanisola, 605 F.3d 124 (2d Cir. 2010).

3. Might defendants refuse to proffer under Queen for a Day agreements and simply proceed without any waivers under the fuller protections of Rules 410 and 11(f)? *See* Richard B. Zabel & James J. Benjamin, Jr., *Are 'Queen for a Day' Pacts Courtesans?*, N.Y. L.J. p. 1, col. 1 (June 13, 2001) ("Our experience … is that this option is simply unavailable. Prosecutors generally refuse to tinker with the language of, much less forego, their proffer agreements. Thus, a defendant who chooses not to sign the proffer agreement in effect chooses not to proffer.").

4. The government has argued that a defendant who contradicts his proffer may be perpetrating a "fraud on the court" that requires admission of the proffer statements. Zabel &

Benjamin, *supra*, at p. 1, col. 1. Some commentators take issue with this argument, contending that:

> ... Congress could not have drafted Rules [11(f)] and 410 without understanding that if the plea process breaks down, the defendant's admission of guilt will be excluded and the defendant's admission of guilt will be excluded and the defendant will likely contradict that admission at trial. Congress presumably did not view itself as licensing rampant fraud on the federal courts. Rather, it struck a compromise that encourages guilty pleas yet preserves a viable defense when plea negotiations break down.

Id. Are prosecutors who require the types of waivers at issue in *Velez* countermanding congressional wishes? As a practical matter, might expansive waivers required prior to a proffer be counterproductive *from the government's perspective* in that they may discourage cooperation? *See, e.g.*, Frederick P. Hafetz & Burt M. Garson, *The 'Queen for a Day Agreement': A High-Risk Venture*, 8 Bus. Crimes Bull. 1, 8 (April 2001) ("Because the downside [of the new proffer agreement requirements] is so great, defense counsel should consider a Queen for a Day agreement only when the client cannot risk a trial and is forced to seek a plea-cooperation agreement."); *see also* Benjamin A. Naftalis, Note, *"Queen for a Day" Agreements and the Proper Scope of Permissible Waiver of the Federal Plea Statement Rules*, 37 Colum. J.L. & Soc. Probs. 1 (2003). Might the Supreme Court have gotten it wrong in *Mezzanato*?

C. INFORMAL IMMUNITY AGREEMENTS

A U.S. Attorney may determine that, rather than seeking a formal immunity order pursuant to statute, she will confer some form of informal (or "pocket" or "letter") immunity. These informal agreements may provide for conditional use and derivative use immunity or for what is essentially conditional transactional immunity as to specified crimes (reflected in what are called non- or no-prosecution agreements), or for some combination of the two. Because they are not statutory immunity grants but rather are contractual in nature, their terms are subject to negotiation between the parties. The government's object is to secure the defendant's cooperation in the investigation or prosecution of others and the defense's objective it to secure for the defendant the greatest possible protection against potential criminal liability. Informal immunity agreements provide both parties flexibility in furthering these goals, and may secure for both the government and the defendant significant advantages. They also, however, may carry important disadvantages, especially for the unwary defendant or ill-prepared defense counsel.

> Unlike formal statutory grants of immunity ... where the Fifth Amendment is necessarily implicated, informal immunity agreements are "bargained for" immunity agreements in which the State agrees to limit its rights in prosecuting the defendant in return for the defendant's cooperation or testimony. In an informal immunity agreement, the State is not bound by the procedures and requirements of the immunity statute, and ordinary contract principles apply when interpreting the informal agreements. In contrast to statutory immunity, these informal agreements are contractual in nature and do not as a general proposition, bind prosecutorial authorities who are not a party to the agreement. Informal immunity agreements are enforced not because of the self-incrimination clause but because the due process clause requires prosecutors to scrupulously adhere to commitments made to suspects in which they induce the suspects to surrender their constitutional rights in exchange for the suspects giving evidence that the government needs against others which simultaneously implicates themselves.[25]

---

[25] State v. Edmondson, 714 So.2d 1233, 1237-38 (La. 1998); *see also* Jason M. Freier, *How To Obtain Immunity: A Risky Minuet for an Attorney*, Bus. Crimes Bull. 6 (May 1998).

1. DOJ POLICY

U.S.A.M. § 9-27.600 Entering into Non-Prosecution Agreements in Return for Cooperation—Generally

A. Except as hereafter provided, the attorney for the government may, with supervisory approval, enter into a non-prosecution agreement in exchange for a person's cooperation when, in his/her judgment, the person's timely cooperation appears to be necessary to the public interest and other means of obtaining the desired cooperation are unavailable or would not be effective.

B. Comment.

    1. *Fifth Amendment Privilege.* In many cases, it may be important to the success of an investigation or prosecution to obtain the testimonial or other cooperation of a person who is himself/herself implicated in the criminal conduct being investigated or prosecuted. However, because of his/her involvement, the person may refuse to cooperate on the basis of his/her Fifth Amendment privilege against compulsory self-incrimination. In this situation, there are several possible approaches the prosecutor can take to render the privilege inapplicable, to induce its waiver, or to otherwise obtain the testimony or cooperation.

        a. First, if time permits, the person may be charged, tried, and convicted before his/her cooperation is sought in the investigation or prosecution of others.

        b. Second, the person may be willing to cooperate if the charges or potential charge against him/her are reduced in number or degree in return for his/her cooperation and his/her entry of a guilty plea to the remaining charges. An agreement to file a motion pursuant to Sentencing Guideline 5K1.1 or Rule 35 of the Federal Rules of Criminal Procedure after the defendant gives full and complete cooperation is the preferred method for securing such cooperation. Usually such a concession by the government will be all that is necessary, or warranted, to secure the cooperation sought. Since it is certainly desirable as a matter of policy that an offender be required to incur at least some liability for his/her criminal conduct, government attorneys should attempt to secure this result in all appropriate cases, following the principles set forth in USAM 9-27.430 to the extent practicable.

        c. The third method for securing the cooperation of a potential defendant is by means of a court order under 18 U.S.C. §§ 6001-6003. Those statutory provisions govern the conditions under which uncooperative witnesses may be compelled to testify or provide information notwithstanding their invocation of the privilege against compulsory self incrimination. In brief, under the so-called "use immunity" provisions of those statutes, the court may order the person to testify or provide other information, but neither his/her testimony nor the information he/she provides may be used against him/her, directly or indirectly, in any criminal case except a prosecution for perjury or other failure to comply with the order. Ordinarily, these "use immunity" provisions should be relied on in cases in which attorneys for the government need to obtain sworn testimony or the production of information before a grand jury or at trial, and in which there is reason to believe that the person will refuse to testify or provide the information on the basis of his/her privilege against compulsory self-incrimination. *See* USAM 9-23.000. Offers of immunity and immunity agreements should be in writing. Consideration should be given to documenting the evidence available prior to the immunity offer.

        d. Finally, there may be cases in which it is impossible or impractical to employ the methods described above to secure the necessary information or other assistance, and in which the person is willing to cooperate only in return for an agreement that he/she will not be prosecuted at all for what he/she has done. The provisions set forth hereafter describe the conditions that should be met before such an agreement is made, as well as the procedures recommended for such cases.

It is important to note that these provisions apply only if the case involves an agreement with a person who might otherwise be prosecuted. If the person reasonably is viewed only as a potential witness rather than a potential defendant, and the person is willing to cooperate, there is no need to consult these provisions.

USAM 9-27.600 describes three circumstances that should exist before government attorneys enter into non-prosecution agreements in return for cooperation: the unavailability or ineffectiveness of other means of obtaining the desired cooperation; the apparent necessity of the cooperation to the public interest; and the approval of such a course of action by an appropriate supervisory official.

2. *Unavailability or Ineffectiveness of Other Means.* As indicated above, non-prosecution agreements are only one of several methods by which the prosecutor can obtain the cooperation of a person whose criminal involvement makes him/her a potential subject of prosecution. Other methods—seeking cooperation after trial and conviction, bargaining for cooperation as part of a plea agreement, and compelling cooperation under a "use immunity" order—involve prosecuting the person or at least leaving open the possibility of prosecuting him/her on the basis of independently obtained evidence. Since these outcomes are clearly preferable to permitting an offender to avoid any liability for his/her conduct, the possible use of an alternative to a non-prosecution agreement should be given serious consideration in the first instance.

Another reason for using an alternative to a non-prosecution agreement to obtain cooperation concerns the practical advantage in terms of the person's credibility if he/she testifies at trial. If the person already has been convicted, either after trial or upon a guilty plea, for participating in the events about which he/she testifies, his/her testimony is apt to be far more credible than if it appears to the trier of fact that he/she is getting off "scot free." Similarly, if his/her testimony is compelled by a court order, he/she cannot properly be portrayed by the defense as a person who has made a "deal" with the government and whose testimony is, therefore, suspect; his/her testimony will have been forced from him/her, not bargained for.

In some cases, however, there may be no effective means of obtaining the person's timely cooperation short of entering into a non-prosecution agreement. The person may be unwilling to cooperate fully in return for a reduction of charges, the delay involved in bringing him/her to trial might prejudice the investigation or prosecution in connection with which his/her cooperation is sought and it may be impossible or impractical to rely on the statutory provisions for compulsion of testimony or production of evidence. One example of the latter situation is a case in which the cooperation needed does not consist of testimony under oath or the production of information before a grand jury or at trial. Other examples are cases in which time is critical, or where use of the procedures of 18 U.S.C. §§ 6001-6003 would unreasonably disrupt the presentation of evidence to the grand jury or the expeditious development of an investigation, or where compliance with the statute of limitations or the Speedy Trial Act precludes timely application for a court order.

Only when it appears that the person's timely cooperation cannot be obtained by other means, or cannot be obtained effectively, should the attorney for the government consider entering into a non-prosecution agreement.

3. *Public Interest.* If he/she concludes that a non-prosecution agreement would be the only effective method for obtaining cooperation, the attorney for the government should consider whether, balancing the cost of foregoing prosecution against the potential benefit of the person's cooperation, the cooperation sought appears necessary to the public interest. This "public interest" determination is one of the conditions precedent to an application under 18 U.S.C. § 6003 for a court order compelling testimony. Like a compulsion order, a non-prosecution agreement limits the

government's ability to undertake a subsequent prosecution of the witness. Accordingly, the same "public interest" test should be applied in this situation as well. ...

4. *Supervisory Approval.* Finally, the prosecutor should secure supervisory approval before entering into a non-prosecution agreement. ...

U.S.A.M. § 9-27.620 Entering into Non-Prosecution Agreements in Return for Cooperation—Considerations to be Weighed

In determining whether, a person's cooperation may be necessary to the public interest, the attorney for the government, and those whose approval is necessary, should weigh all relevant considerations, including:

1. The importance of the investigation or prosecution to an effective program of law enforcement, or consideration of other national security or governmental interests;
2. The value of the person's cooperation to the investigation or prosecution;
3. The person's relative culpability in connection with the offense or offenses being investigated or prosecuted and his/her history with respect to criminal activity; and
4. The interests of any victims.

Comment. This paragraph is intended to assist Federal prosecutors, and those whose approval they must secure, in deciding whether a person's cooperation appears to be necessary to the public interest. The considerations listed here are not intended to be all-inclusive or to require a particular decision in a particular case. Rather they are meant to focus the decision-maker's attention on factors that probably will be controlling in the majority of cases.

1. *Importance of Case.* Since the primary function of a Federal prosecutor is to enforce the criminal law, he/she should not routinely or indiscriminately enter into non-prosecution agreements, which are, in essence, agreements not to enforce the law under particular conditions. Rather, he/she should reserve the use of such agreements for cases in which the cooperation sought concerns the commission of a serious offense or in which successful prosecution is otherwise important in achieving effective enforcement of the criminal laws, including national security-related enforcement and prevention efforts. The relative importance or unimportance of the contemplated case is therefore a significant threshold consideration.

2. *Value of Cooperation.* An agreement not to prosecute in return for a person's cooperation binds the government to the extent that the person carries out his/her part of the bargain. *See Santobello v. New York*, 404 U.S. 257 (1971); *Wade v. United States*, 504 U.S. 181 (1992). Since such an agreement forecloses enforcement of the criminal law against a person who otherwise may be liable to prosecution, it should not be entered into without a clear understanding of the nature of the quid pro quo and a careful assessment of its probable value to the government. In order to be in a position adequately to assess the potential value of a person's cooperation, the prosecutor should insist on an "offer of proof" or its equivalent from the person or his/her attorney. The prosecutor can then weigh the offer in terms of the investigation or prosecution in connection with which cooperation is sought. In doing so, he/she should consider such questions as whether the cooperation will in fact be forthcoming, whether the testimony or other information provided will be credible, whether it can be corroborated by other evidence, whether it will materially assist the investigation or prosecution, and whether substantially the same benefit can be obtained from someone else without an agreement not to prosecute. After assessing all of these factors, together with any others that may be relevant, the prosecutor can judge the strength of his/her case with and without the person's cooperation, and determine whether it may be in the public interest to agree to forego prosecution under the circumstances.

3. *Relative Culpability and Criminal History.* In determining whether it may be necessary to the public interest to agree to forego prosecution of a person who may have violated the law in

return for that person's cooperation, it is also important to consider the degree of his/her apparent culpability relative to others who are subjects of the investigation or prosecution as well as his/her history of criminal involvement. Of course, ordinarily it would not be in the public interest to forego prosecution of a high-ranking member of a criminal enterprise in exchange for his/her cooperation against one of his/her subordinates, nor would the public interest be served by bargaining away the opportunity to prosecute a person with a long history of serious criminal involvement in order to obtain the conviction of someone else on less serious charges. These are matters with regard to which the attorney for the government may find it helpful to consult with the investigating agency or with other prosecuting authorities who may have an interest in the person or his/her associates.

4. *The Interests of Any Victims.* When considering whether it is in the public interest to forego prosecution, it is also important to consider the economic, physical, and psychological impact of the offense on any victims. In this connection, it is appropriate for the prosecutor to take into account such matters as the victim's desire for prosecution, the victim's age or health, and whether full or partial restitution has been made.

It is also important to consider whether the person has a background of cooperation with law enforcement officials, either as a witness or an informant, and whether he/she has previously been the subject of a compulsion order under 18 U.S.C. §§ 6001-6003 or has escaped prosecution by virtue of an agreement not to prosecute. ...

U.S.A.M. § 9-27.630 Entering into Non-Prosecution Agreements in Return for Cooperation—Limiting the Scope of Commitment

In entering into a non-prosecution agreement, the attorney for the government should, if practicable, explicitly limit the scope of the government's commitment to:

1. Non-prosecution based directly or indirectly on the testimony or other information provided; or
2. Non-prosecution within his/her district with respect to a pending charge, or to a specific offense then known to have been committed by the person.

<u>Comment</u>. The attorney for the government should exercise extreme caution to ensure that his/her non-prosecution agreement does not confer "blanket" immunity on the witness. To this end, he/she should, in the first instance, attempt to limit his/her agreement to non-prosecution based on the testimony or information provided. Such an "informal use immunity" agreement has two advantages over an agreement not to prosecute the person in connection with a particular transaction: first, it preserves the prosecutor's option to prosecute on the basis of independently obtained evidence if it later appears that the person's criminal involvement was more serious than it originally appeared to be; and second, it encourages the witness to be as forthright as possible since the more he/she reveals the more protection he/she will have against a future prosecution. To further encourage full disclosure by the witness, it should be made clear in the agreement that the government's forbearance from prosecution is conditioned upon the witness's testimony or production of information being complete and truthful, and that failure to testify truthfully may result in a perjury prosecution.

Even if it is not practicable to obtain the desired cooperation pursuant to an "informal use immunity" agreement, the attorney for the government should attempt to limit the scope of the agreement in terms of the testimony and transactions covered, bearing in mind the possible effect of his/her agreement on prosecutions in other districts.

It is important that non-prosecution agreements be drawn in terms that will not bind other Federal prosecutors or agencies without their consent. Thus, if practicable, the attorney for the government should explicitly limit the scope of his/her agreement to non-prosecution within his/her district. If such a limitation is not practicable and it can reasonably be anticipated that the agreement may affect prosecution of the person in other districts, the attorney for the government contemplating such an agreement shall communicate the relevant facts to the Assistant Attorney General with supervisory responsibility for the subject matter. United States Attorneys may not make agreements which prejudice other litigating divisions, without the agreement of all affected divisions. ...

Notes

1. U.S.A.M. § 27.600 makes clear that informal immunity grants should be the last resort for prosecutors seeking to secure a defendant's testimony or cooperation and that other means should at least be considered as a preliminary matter. Going down the list of options, why does a defendant who has been prosecuted and convicted lose his Fifth Amendment right? Why is this the preferred prosecutorial alternative and why might it be, in many cases, impractical? The possibility of trading cooperation for negotiated pleas of guilty is discussed at length in Chapter 19 (Plea Bargaining and Cooperation). Why might the Department of Justice prefer deals involving a plea to something in return for cooperation to grants of immunity?

Why does the DOJ advocate formal immunity over informal immunity? What are the potential pitfalls of an informal immunity grant for the government? For example, if a court grants immunity, that order may be enforceable by a civil or criminal contempt sanction and ultimately by jailing the witness. *See* 28 U.S.C. §§ 401, 1826; Fed. R. Crim. P. 42. Are such sanctions available for violations of an informal agreement?

What potential advantages does informal immunity hold for the government? Will a potential subject be likely to provide the same degree of cooperation under a use and derivative use statutory grant as he would under a negotiated nonprosecution agreement? Can a prosecutor force a statutorily immunized witness to appear for debriefing or preparation sessions outside the grand jury or trial setting? Why might individual prosecutors—if not the Department itself—prefer to proceed under an informal, rather than a formal, immunity grant?

2. The DOJ policy explores some of the reasons for prosecutors to consider long and hard before they offer a witness immunity. One additional reason that may not be obvious is the potential trial consequences of an immunity offer that is *rejected*. In *United States v. Biaggi*, 909 F.2d 662 (2d Cir. 1990), the court held that it constituted reversible error to exclude evidence of immunity negotiations that the defendant contended demonstrated his "consciousness of innocence." In *Biaggi*, the defendant sought to prove at trial that the government offered him immunity if he would give what the government regarded as truthful information regarding wrongdoing by others. The defendant contended that, in response to this offer, he denied knowledge of such wrongdoing, thereby "rejecting" immunity. The court reasoned that

> When a defendant rejects an offer of immunity on the ground that he is unaware of any wrongdoing about which he could testify, his action is probative of a state of mind devoid of guilty knowledge. Though there may be reasons for rejecting the offer that are consistent with guilty knowledge, such as fear of reprisal from those who would be inculpated, a jury is entitled to believe that most people would jump at the chance to obtain an assurance of immunity from prosecution and to infer from rejection of the offer that the accused lacks knowledge of wrongdoing.

Id. at 690; *see also* United States v. Maloof, 205 F.3d 819 (5th Cir. 2000). *But see* United States v. Geisen, 612 F.3d 471 (6th Cir. 2010) (refusing to permit evidence of rejection of deferred prosecution agreement). In the more usual circumstance where a defendant rejects an offer to plead guilty to reduced charges or in exchange for sentencing leniency, should this same inference be available? *See, e.g.*, United States v. Greene, 995 F.2d 793, 798-99 (8th Cir. 1993) (evidence of rejection of plea offer is inadmissible). Why?

3. Is defense counsels' preferred order of proceeding the reverse of the Department's? What are the possible advantages and disadvantages to the defendant of informal immunity? Much depends upon the actual terms of the agreement. For example, informal immunity (unlike formal statutory immunity) does not necessarily bind other actors in the state and federal system who are not parties to the agreement. *See, e.g.*, United States v. Bryant, 750 F.3d

642 (7th Cir. 2014) (statements given to state authorities pursuant to state agreement could be used by federal prosecutors). Whether other persons are bound will depend upon whether the government agent had the authority to bind other parts of the government and the reasonable inferences to be drawn from the language of the agreement itself. *See, e.g.*, United States v. Johnson, 199 F.3d 1015, 1020-22 (9th Cir. 1999); United States v. Igbonwa, 120 F.3d 437, 442-44 (3d Cir. 1997); Thomas v. INS, 35 F.3d 1332, 1337-42 (9th Cir. 1994).

If the defendant breaches his informal immunity/cooperation agreement, what are the consequences? Due process requires that prosecutors must keep their promises; how are the extent of those promises determined? "Plea agreements are typically construed according to the principles of contract law. "'To determine whether a plea agreement is violated, the court must look to what the parties "reasonably understood to be the terms of the agreement."' Typically the government must bear responsibility for any lack of clarity in those terms." *Johnson*, 199 F.3d at 1020 (citations omitted). It is important to stress that a defendant who voluntarily enters into an informal immunity agreement and thereby gives up his Fifth Amendment right is not "compelled" to speak and thus does not automatically secure any protection against the use and derivative use of his statements or against eventual prosecution. Thus, the protections of *Kastigar* do not apply unless those protections are included as part of the contract between the government and the immunized party. It is due process, not the Fifth Amendment, that is the source of law defendants must rely upon to secure enforcement of their contract rights. *See, e.g.*, Taylor v. Singletary, 148 F.3d 1276, 1283 n.7 (11th Cir. 1998) (informally immunized witness retains his Fifth Amendment privilege, cannot later claim he was "compelled" to testify simply because he fulfilled his promise to the prosecutor and did not invoke his privilege, and therefore is not entitled, under the Fifth Amendment, to a *Kastigar* hearing); United States v. Kilroy, 27 F.3d 679, 683-85 (D.C. Cir. 1994) (whether defendant should be entitled to relief for government's claimed improper use of testimony secured through informal "use" immunity agreement should be analyzed under *Santobello v. New York*, 404 U.S. 257 (1971) (due process analysis of government's obligations under plea agreement), rather than *Kastigar v. United States*, 406 U.S. 441 (1972), although determination of whether government breached the agreement under *Santobello* required reference to *Kastigar* rules deemed incorporated in agreement).

2. SAMPLE AGREEMENT

AGREEMENT

This is an agreement ("Agreement") between Monica S. Lewinsky and the United States, represented by the Office of the Independent Counsel ("OIC"). The terms of the Agreement are as follows:

1. Ms. Lewinsky agrees to cooperate fully with the OIC, including special agents of the Federal Bureau of Investigation ("FBI") and any other law enforcement agencies that the OIC may require. This cooperation will include the following:

A. Ms. Lewinsky will provide truthful, complete and accurate information to the OIC. She will provide, upon request, any documents, records, or other tangible evidence within her custody or control relating to the matters within the OIC's jurisdiction. She will assist the OIC in gaining access to such materials that are not within her custody and control, and she will assist in locating and gaining the cooperation of other individuals who possess relevant information. Ms. Lewinsky will not attempt to protect any person or entity through false information or omission, and she will not attempt falsely to implicate any person or entity.

B. Ms. Lewinsky will testify truthfully before grand juries in this district and elsewhere, at any trials in this district and elsewhere, and in any other executive, military, judicial or congressional proceedings. Pending a final resolution of this matter, neither Ms. Lewinsky nor her agents will make any statements about this matter to witnesses, subjects, or targets of the OIC's investigation, or their agents, or to representatives of the news media, without first obtaining the OIC's approval.

C. Ms. Lewinsky will be fully debriefed concerning her knowledge of and participation in any activities within the OIC's jurisdiction. This debriefing will be conducted by the OIC, including its attorneys, law enforcement agents, and representatives of any other institutions as the OIC may require. Ms. Lewinsky will make herself available for any interviews upon reasonable request.

D. Ms. Lewinsky acknowledges that she has orally proffered information to the OIC on July 27, 1998, pursuant to a proffer agreement. Ms. Lewinsky further represents that the statements she made during that proffer session were truthful and accurate to the best of her knowledge. She agrees that during her cooperation, she will truthfully elaborate with respect to these and other subjects.

E. Ms. Lewinsky agrees that, upon the OIC's request, she will waive any evidentiary privileges she may have, except for the attorney-client privilege.

2. If Ms. Lewinsky fully complies with the terms and understandings set forth in this Agreement, the OIC: 1) will not prosecute her for any crimes committed prior to the date of this Agreement arising out of the investigations within the jurisdiction of the OIC; 2) will grant her derivative use immunity within the meaning and subject to the limitations of 18 United States Code, Section 6002, and will not use, in any criminal prosecution against Ms. Lewinsky, testimony or other information provided by her during the course of her debriefing, testimony, or other cooperation pursuant to this agreement, or any information derived directly or indirectly from such debriefing, testimony, information, or other cooperation; and 3) will not prosecute her mother, Marsha Lewis, or her father, Bernard Lewinsky, for any offenses which may have been committed by them prior to this Agreement arising out of the facts summarized above, provided that Ms. Lewis and Mr. Lewinsky cooperate with the OIC's investigation and provide complete and truthful information regarding those facts.

3. If the OIC determines that Ms. Lewinsky has intentionally given false, incomplete, or misleading information or testimony, or has otherwise violated any provision of this Agreement, the OIC may move the United States District Court for the District of Columbia which supervised the grand jury investigating this matter for a finding that Ms. Lewinsky has breached this Agreement, and, upon such a finding by the Court, Ms. Lewinsky shall be subject to prosecution for any federal criminal violation of which the OIC has knowledge, including but not limited to perjury, obstruction of justice, and making false statements to government agencies. In such a prosecution, the OIC may use information provided by Ms. Lewinsky during the course of her cooperation, and such information, including her statements, will be admissible against her in any grand jury, court, or other official proceedings.

4. Pending a final resolution of this matter, the OIC will not make any statements about this Agreement to representatives of the news media.

5. This is the entire agreement between the parties. There are no other agreements, promises or inducements.

If the foregoing terms are acceptable, please sign, and have your client sign, in the spaces indicated below.

Notes

1. What obligations do the signatories to this agreement undertake? In what respects does the protection afforded by the above agreement differ from the protections afforded by a formal immunity order? What would you add to the agreement if you were defense counsel? The government?

2. Under this agreement what constitutes a breach? What are the remedies for a breach? Who bears the burden of any ambiguity?

3. Among the terms that should be considered carefully in drafting these agreements are: (1) the scope of the agreement (*i.e.*, does the agreement bar the government from providing the

information obtained through cooperation to other state or federal actors, *see, e.g.*, Taylor v. Singletary, 148 F.3d 1276, 1284 (11th Cir. 1998)); and (2) the conditions that constitute a breach and the consequences that flow from that breach (*e.g.*, is the commission of any future crime a breach; does the witness's lack of candor on *any* issue constitute a breach; what are the crimes for which the defendant may be prosecuted in the event of a breach; can any and all information and statements provided by the immunized witness be used in the event of a breach, *see, e.g.*, *Fitch*, 964 F.2d at 571; United States v. Pelletier, 898 F.2d 297 (2d Cir. 1990); United States v. Irvine, 756 F.2d 708 (9th Cir. 1985); United States v. Skalsky, 857 F.2d 172 (3d Cir. 1988)). One important and recurring issue is the temporal limitation of the agreement, that is, whether the breach of a condition of the agreement (*e.g.*, that the defendant will commit no further crimes) after the defendant's cooperation *is complete* permits the government to void the entire agreement. *See, e.g.*, United States v. Brown, 801 F.2d 352 (8th Cir. 1986). The legal complexity of some of these issues means that counsel's assistance in the course of plea negotiations is indispensable.

Chapter 16

FIFTH AMENDMENT: DOCUMENTS AND TANGIBLE OBJECTS

This chapter focuses on governmental attempts to force persons to turn over to the government documents and other tangible things rather than governmental attempts to compel individuals to give testimony. In this context, it is helpful to keep in mind the following summary: The Fifth Amendment's privilege against self-incrimination protects (1) *natural persons* (and sole proprietorships) from being (2) *compelled* (3) to make a *testimonial communication* (and, when the testimonial communication is a fact implicitly communicated by an "act of production," that fact is not a *foregone conclusion*) that (4) is *incriminating* (5) absent a grant of governmental *immunity*. Unless all these elements are present, a claim of privilege will not be sustained. The following materials serve to illustrate the meaning of these terms in the corporate crime context.

A. NATURAL PERSONS (AND SOLE PROPRIETORSHIPS)

In *Hale v. Henkel*,[1] the Supreme Court refused to permit the custodian of records of a corporation to resist the compelled production of corporate records on Fifth Amendment grounds. The custodian himself was assured of immunity from criminal prosecution. With respect to the corporation, the Court held that the custodian could not assert the Fifth Amendment rights of a third-party, *i.e.*, the corporation. It reasoned that "[t]he amendment is limited to a person who shall be compelled in any criminal case to be a witness against *himself*; and if he cannot set up the privilege of a third person, he certainly cannot set up the privilege of a corporation." (It should be noted that in the self-same opinion, the Court did permit the corporate agent to assert the corporation's Fourth Amendment right.) Although the *Hale* Court did not explicitly hold that a corporation has no Fifth Amendment privilege, subsequent decisions have read *Hale* to say that a corporation indeed has no right against compelled self-incrimination.[2] Why not?

---

[1] 201 U.S. 43 (1906).

[2] *See, e.g.*, Braswell v. United States, 487 U.S. 99 (1988). For the comparable rules in Australia, Canada, New Zealand, and the United Kingdom, see Norman M. Garland, *The Unavailability to Corporations of the Privilege Against Self-Incrimination: A Comparative Examination*, 16 N.Y. L. Sch. J. Int'l & Comp. L. 55 (1996).

Corporations are protected by the Fourth Amendment's right to be free from unreasonable searches and seizures (thus making them part of the American "people" to whom the Amendment applies), the Fifth Amendment's prohibitions against double jeopardy and against takings of property without just compensation, and the Sixth and Seventh Amendments' respective rights to a jury trial in criminal and civil cases. Likewise, corporations have free-speech rights under the First Amendment, including the rights to engage in political and commercial speech and to abstain from association with the speech of others. Corporations also enjoy rights to equal protection under the Fourteenth Amendment and to due process under the Fifth (against the federal government) and Fourteenth (against the state governments) Amendments. There are strikingly few individual constitutional rights that corporations do not share. ... In some commentators' views, the apotheosis of corporate legal personhood is the recent First Amendment corporate campaign-funding case, *Citizens United v. FEC*, [558 U.S. 310 (2010)].[3]

What, then, accounts for the Court's Fifth Amendment holding?

Many have pointed to passages in the *Hale* opinion that indicate that the Court's decision was dictated by pure practical exigency. For example, after concluding that appellants, as agents, could not assert the rights of their corporate principal for Fifth Amendment purposes, the *Hale* majority reasoned as follows:

As the combination or conspiracies provided against by the Sherman Anti Trust Act can ordinarily be proved only by the testimony of the parties thereto, in the person of their agents or employees, the privilege claimed would practically nullify the whole act of Congress. Of what use would it be for the legislature to declare these combinations unlawful if the judicial power may close the door of access to every available source of information upon the subject?

This reading seems correct.[4]

The Supreme Court has extended its *Hale* ruling to hold that other "collective entities," including an unincorporated labor union,[5] a three-partner law firm,[6] and a one-man corporation,[7] have no Fifth Amendment right against the compulsory production of the entities' books and records.

The Supreme Court's precedents also hold that an individual who is a custodian of records for a collective entity and is compelled by subpoena to produce entity records in his capacity as an entity representative cannot resist production on the ground that the records (or, as we shall see *infra*, his production of the records) may incriminate him personally.[8] By contrast, a sole proprietor—who the Court apparently believes is more akin to a natural person than to a collective entity—is entitled to assert his Fifth Amendment privilege when called upon to produce his business records.[9]

---

[3] Andrew E. Taslitz, *Reciprocity and the Criminal Responsibility of Corporations*, 41 Stetson L. Rev. 73, 75-76 (2011); *see also* Joan MacLeod Heminway, *Thoughts on the Corporation as a Person for Purposes of Corporate Criminal Liability*, 41 Stetson L. Rev. 140 (2011).

[4] Julie R. O'Sullivan, *The Last Straw: The Department of Justice's Privilege Waiver Policy and the Death of Adversarial Justice in Criminal Investigations of Corporations*, 57 DePaul L. Rev. 329, 357-58 (2008).

[5] United States v. White, 322 U.S. 694 (1944).

[6] Bellis v. United States, 417 U.S. 85 (1974).

[7] *Braswell*, 487 U.S. 99; *see also* In re Grand Jury Subpoena Issued June 18, 2009 (Account Services Corp. v. United States, 593 F.3d 155 (2d Cir. 2010).

[8] *See, e.g.*, *White*, 322 U.S. 694 (1944).

[9] United States v. Doe, 465 U.S. 605 (1984) (holding that sole proprietor may assert act of production

B. WHAT CONSTITUTES "COMPULSION"

A little background may be necessary to understand the importance of the next case, *Fisher v. United States*.[10] In particular, it may be helpful to review the Supreme Court's analysis in *Boyd v. United States*,[11] which is discussed at some length in *Fisher*. *Boyd* presents a competing, and broader, view of what constitutes "compelled" self-incrimination for Fifth Amendment purposes when physical evidence is at issue. The Supreme Court has overruled *Boyd* in every respect save one, but it haunts the Court still. Indeed, as recently as 2000, Justices Scalia and Thomas indicated in *United States v. Hubbell*[12] (excerpted *infra*, Part F) that they might be willing to reconsider *Fisher* (and perhaps revive *Boyd*) in a proper case.

Boyd "involved a civil forfeiture proceeding brought by the Government against two partners for fraudulently attempting to import 35 cases of glass without paying the prescribed duty."[13] At trial, the Government obtained a court order directing the partners to produce an invoice the partnership had received from the shipper.[14] "The invoice was disclosed, offered in evidence, and used, over the objection of the partners, to establish that the partners were fraudulently claiming a greater exemption from duty than they were entitled to under the contract."[15] The Supreme Court ruled the invoice inadmissible, and reversed the judgment that had been entered for the government.[16] The *Boyd* Court ruled that:

> (1) The Fourth Amendment applies to court orders in the nature of subpoenas *duces tecum* in the same manner that it applies to search warrants; both are subject to the requirement that "seizures" (whether effected by physical seizure or by subpoena) must be "reasonable."[17]

This is the only ruling in *Boyd* that is still good law. It is important to note because, although we do not deal in terms with the Fourth Amendment in this chapter, a Fourth Amendment objection is open to those who receive grand jury subpoenas for the production of *documents and other tangible things* even where there is no Fifth Amendment privilege applicable.[18] Note, however, that an *ad testificandum* subpoena requiring an *individual to give testimony* before the grand jury is not deemed to be a Fourth Amendment "search or seizure" of the person and thus no Fourth Amendment objection is possible.[19]

> (2) "The Government may not, consistent with the Fourth Amendment, seize a person's documents or other property as evidence unless it can claim a proprietary interest in the

---

privilege with respect to business documents).

[10] 425 U.S. 391 (1976).

[11] 116 U.S. 616 (1886).

[12] 530 U.S. 27 (2000).

[13] *Fisher*, 425 U.S. at 405.

[14] *Id.* at 406.

[15] *Id.*

[16] *Id.*

[17] *See id.*

[18] *See supra* Chapter 13 (Grand Jury: Rules Applicable to Documents/Tangible Objects).

[19] *See* United States v. Dionisio, 410 U.S. 1, 9 (1973) ("It is clear that a subpoena to appear before a grand jury is not a 'seizure' in the Fourth Amendment sense, even though that summons may be inconvenient or burdensome.").

property superior to that of the person from whom the property is obtained."[20] The government is deemed to have a superior interest in contraband or the fruits or instrumentalities of crime, but not in materials of solely evidentiary value.

The pronouncement in *Boyd* that the seizure of purely "evidentiary" materials (as opposed to fruits or instrumentalities of crime or contraband) violated the Fourth Amendment because the government had no property interest in such evidentiary materials superior to the person subpoenaed was overruled in *Warden v. Hayden*.[21]

(3) The accused in a criminal case or the defendant in a forfeiture action could not be forced to produce evidentiary items without violating the Fifth Amendment as well as the Fourth. In the course of its decision on the Fourth Amendment issue, the *Boyd* Court made clear its belief that "any forcible and compulsory extortion of a man's own testimony, or *of his private papers to be used as evidence to convict him of a crime*, or to forfeit his goods, is within the condemnation of" the Fifth Amendment.[22] It added that, "[i]n this regard the fourth and fifth amendments run almost into each other."[23] Thus, the *Boyd* Court concluded, "a compulsory production of the private books and papers of the owner of goods sought to be forfeited in such a suit is compelling him to be a witness against himself, within the meaning of the fifth amendment to the constitution, and is the equivalent of a search and seizure—and an unreasonable search and seizure—within the meaning of the fourth amendment."[24]

In the subsequent case of *Hale v. Henkel*,[25] the Supreme Court separated Fourth and Fifth Amendment analysis, making clear that the Fourth Amendment "reasonableness" of a "seizure" of documents pursuant to subpoena was no longer to be judged by what might run afoul of Fifth Amendment standards.[26] That is, after *Hale*, the "reasonableness" of the "seizure" does not turn on whether the papers are incriminating or are "private papers" protected by the Fifth Amendment. Instead of an absolute bar on the compelled production of certain types of materials ("evidentiary" materials or incriminating "private papers"), the Fourth Amendment "reasonableness" of a subpoena turns instead on whether it is "too sweeping in its terms to be regarded as reasonable."[27] In *See v. City of Seattle*,[28] the *Hale* rule of reasonableness was described as "requir[ing] that the subpoena be sufficiently limited in scope, relevant in purpose, and specific in directive so that compliance will not be unreasonably burdened."

Finally, recall that the documents at issue in *Boyd* were *partnership* records. Thus, under the "collective entity doctrine" that evolved after *Boyd*, these documents should not have been sheltered by the individual Fifth Amendment privileges of the partners.

This, then, is the foundation from which we will work forward.

---

[20] *Fisher*, 425 U.S. at 406 (quoting *Boyd*, 116 U.S. at 623-24).

[21] 387 U.S. 294 (1967).

[22] 116 U.S. at 630 (emphasis added).

[23] *Id.*

[24] *Id.* at 634-35.

[25] 201 U.S. 43 (1906).

[26] *Id.* at 72 (noting that the cases after *Boyd* "treat the 4th and 5th Amendments as quite distinct, having different histories, and performing separate functions").

[27] *Id.* at 76.

[28] 387 U.S. 541, 544 (1967).

FISHER v. UNITED STATES
425 U.S. 391 (1976)

MR. JUSTICE WHITE delivered the opinion of the Court.

In these two cases we are called upon to decide whether a summons directing an attorney to produce documents delivered to him by his client in connection with the attorney-client relationship is enforceable over claims that the documents were constitutionally immune from summons in the hands of the client and retained that immunity in the hands of the attorney.

In each case, an Internal Revenue agent visited the taxpayer or taxpayers and interviewed them in connection with an investigation of possible civil or criminal liability under the federal income tax laws. Shortly after the interviews ... the taxpayers obtained from their respective accountants certain documents relating to the preparation by the accountants of their tax returns. Shortly after obtaining the documents ... the taxpayers transferred the documents to their lawyers ... each of whom was retained to assist the taxpayer in connection with the investigation. Upon learning of the whereabouts of the documents, the Internal Revenue Service served summonses on the attorneys directing them to produce documents listed therein. [Those documents included the accountants' work papers, the accountants' analyses of the taxpayers' income and expenses, retained copies of income tax returns, and the accountants' copies of correspondence between the accounting firm and the taxpayer] ... In each case, the lawyer declined to comply with the summons directing production of the documents, and enforcement actions were commenced by the Government. ...

All of the parties in these cases and the Court of Appeals for the Fifth Circuit have concurred in the proposition that if the Fifth Amendment would have excused a *taxpayer* from turning over the accountant's papers had he possessed them, the *attorney* to whom they are delivered for the purpose of obtaining legal advice should also be immune from subpoena. Although we agree with this proposition ... we are convinced that, under our decision in *Couch v. United States*, 409 U.S. 322 (1973), it is not the taxpayer's Fifth Amendment privilege that would excuse the attorney from production.

The relevant part of that Amendment provides:

"No person ... shall be *compelled* in any criminal case to be a *witness against himself.*" (Emphasis added.)

The taxpayer's privilege under this Amendment is not violated by enforcement of the summonses involved in these cases because enforcement against a taxpayer's lawyer would not "compel" the taxpayer to do anything and certainly would not compel him to be a "witness" against himself. The Court has held repeatedly that the Fifth Amendment is limited to prohibiting the use of "physical or moral compulsion" exerted on the person asserting the privilege. In *Couch v. United States*, we recently ruled that the Fifth Amendment rights of a taxpayer were not violated by the enforcement of a documentary summons directed to her accountant and requiring production of the taxpayer's own records in the possession of the accountant. We did so on the ground that in such a case "the ingredient of personal compulsion against an accused is lacking."

Here, the taxpayers are compelled to do no more than was the taxpayer in *Couch*. The taxpayers' Fifth Amendment privilege is therefore not violated by enforcement of the summonses directed toward their attorneys. This is true whether or not the Amendment would have barred a subpoena directing the taxpayer to produce the documents while they were in his hands.

The fact that the attorneys are agents of the taxpayers does not change this result. *Couch* held as much, since the accountant there was also the taxpayer's agent, and in this respect reflected a longstanding view. In *Hale* v. *Henkel*, 201 U.S. 43, 69-70 (1906), the Court said that the privilege "was never intended to permit [a person] to plead the fact that some third person might be incriminated by his testimony, even though he were the agent of such person ... .

[T]he Amendment is limited to a person who shall be compelled in any criminal case to be a witness against *himself*." "It is extortion of information from the accused himself that offends our sense of justice." Agent or no, the lawyer is not the taxpayer. The taxpayer is the "accused," and nothing is being extorted from him.

Nor is this one of those situations, which *Couch* suggested might exist, where constructive possession is so clear or relinquishment of possession so temporary and insignificant as to leave the personal compulsion upon the taxpayer substantially intact. In this respect we see no difference between the delivery to the attorneys in these cases and delivery to the accountant in the *Couch* case. As was true in *Couch*, the documents sought were obtainable without personal compulsion on the accused. ...

The Court of Appeals for the Fifth Circuit suggested that because legally and ethically the attorney was required to respect the confidences of his client, the latter had a reasonable expectation of privacy for the records in the hands of the attorney and therefore did not forfeit his Fifth Amendment privilege with respect to the records by transferring them in order to obtain legal advice. It is true that the Court has often stated that one of the several purposes served by the constitutional privilege against compelled testimonial self-incrimination is that of protecting personal privacy. But the Court has never suggested that every invasion of privacy violates the privilege. Within the limits imposed by the language of the Fifth Amendment, which we necessarily observe, the privilege truly serves privacy interests; but the Court has never on any ground, personal privacy included, applied the Fifth Amendment to prevent the otherwise proper acquisition or use of evidence which, in the Court's view, did not involve compelled testimonial self-incrimination of some sort.

The proposition that the Fifth Amendment protects private information obtained without compelling self-incriminating testimony is contrary to the clear statements of this Court that under appropriate safeguards private incriminating statements of an accused may be overheard and used in evidence, if they are not compelled at the time they were uttered; and that disclosure of private information may be compelled if immunity removes the risk of incrimination. If the Fifth Amendment protected generally against the obtaining of private information from a man's mouth or pen or house, its protections would presumably not be lifted by probable cause and a warrant or by immunity. The privacy invasion is not mitigated by immunity; and the Fifth Amendment's strictures, unlike the Fourth's, are not removed by showing reasonableness. The Framers addressed the subject of personal privacy directly in the Fourth Amendment. They struck a balance so that when the State's reason to believe incriminating evidence will be found becomes sufficiently great, the invasion of privacy becomes justified and a warrant to search and seize will issue. They did not seek in still another Amendment—the Fifth—to achieve a general protection of privacy but to deal with the more specific issue of compelled self-incrimination.

We cannot cut the Fifth Amendment completely loose from the moorings of its language, and make it serve as a general protector of privacy—a word not mentioned in its text and a concept directly addressed in the Fourth Amendment. We adhere to the view that the Fifth Amendment protects against "compelled self-incrimination, not [the disclosure of] private information." ...

Our above holding is that compelled production of documents from an attorney does not implicate whatever Fifth Amendment privilege the taxpayer might have enjoyed from being compelled to produce them himself. The taxpayers in these cases, however, have from the outset consistently urged that they should not be forced to expose otherwise protected documents to summons simply because they have sought legal advice and turned the papers over to their attorneys. The Government appears to agree unqualifiedly. The difficulty is that the taxpayers have erroneously relied on the Fifth Amendment without urging the attorney-client privilege in so many words. They have nevertheless invoked the relevant body of law and policies that govern the attorney-client privilege. In this posture of the case, we feel obliged to inquire whether the attorney-client privilege applies to documents in the hands of an attorney which would have been privileged in the hands of the client by reason of the Fifth Amendment.

Confidential disclosures by a client to an attorney made in order to obtain legal assistance are privileged. The purpose of the privilege is to encourage clients to make full disclosure to their attorneys. As a practical matter, if the client knows that damaging information could more readily be obtained from the attorney following disclosure than from himself in the absence of disclosure, the client would be reluctant to confide in his lawyer and it would be difficult to obtain fully informed legal advice. However, since the privilege has the effect of withholding relevant information from the fact-finder, it applies only where necessary to achieve its purpose. Accordingly it protects only those disclosures—necessary to obtain informed legal advice—which might not have been made absent the privilege. This Court and the lower courts have thus uniformly held that pre-existing documents which could have been obtained by court process from the client when he was in possession may also be obtained from the attorney by similar process following transfer by the client in order to obtain more informed legal advice. The purpose of the privilege requires no broader rule. Pre-existing documents obtainable from the client are not appreciably easier to obtain from the attorney after transfer to him. Thus, even absent the attorney-client privilege, clients will not be discouraged from disclosing the documents to the attorney, and their ability to obtain informed legal advice will remain unfettered. It is otherwise if the documents are not obtainable by subpoena *duces tecum* or summons while in the exclusive possession of the client, for the client will then be reluctant to transfer possession to the lawyer unless the documents are also privileged in the latter's hands. Where the transfer is made for the purpose of obtaining legal advice, the purposes of the attorney-client privilege would be defeated unless the privilege is applicable." It follows, then, that *when the client himself would be privileged* from production of the document, either as a party at common law ... or as exempt from self-incrimination, the attorney having possession of the document is not bound to produce." ...

Since each taxpayer transferred possession of the documents in question from himself to his attorney in order to obtain legal assistance in the tax investigations in question, the papers, if unobtainable by summons from the client, are unobtainable by summons directed to the attorney by reason of the attorney-client privilege. We accordingly proceed to the question whether the documents could have been obtained by summons addressed to the taxpayer while the documents were in his possession. The only bar to enforcement of such summons asserted by the parties or the courts below is the Fifth Amendment's privilege against self-incrimination. ...

The proposition that the Fifth Amendment prevents compelled production of documents over objection that such production might incriminate stems from *Boyd* v. *United States*, 116 U.S. 616 (1886). *Boyd* involved a civil forfeiture proceeding brought by the Government against two partners for fraudulently attempting to import 35 cases of glass without paying the prescribed duty. ... At trial, the Government obtained a court order directing the partners to produce an invoice the partnership had received from the shipper ... . The invoice was disclosed, offered in evidence, and used, over the Fifth Amendment objection of the partners, to establish that the partners were fraudulently claiming a greater exemption from duty than they were entitled to under the contract. This Court held that the invoice was inadmissible and reversed the judgment in favor of the Government. The Court ruled that the Fourth Amendment applied to court orders in the nature of subpoenas *duces tecum* in the same manner in which it applies to search warrants, and that the Government may not, consistent with the Fourth Amendment, seize a person's documents or other property as evidence unless it can claim a proprietary interest in the property superior to that of the person from whom the property is obtained. The invoice in question was thus held to have been obtained in violation of the Fourth Amendment. The Court went on to hold that the accused in a criminal case or the defendant in a forfeiture action could not be forced to produce evidentiary items without violating the Fifth Amendment as well as the Fourth. More specifically, the Court declared, "a compulsory production of the private books and papers of the owner of goods sought to be forfeited ... is compelling him to be a witness against himself, within the meaning of the Fifth Amendment of the Constitution." Admitting the partnership invoice into evidence had violated both the Fifth and Fourth Amendments.

Among its several pronouncements, *Boyd* was understood to declare that the seizure, under warrant or otherwise, of any purely evidentiary materials violated the Fourth Amendment and that the Fifth Amendment rendered these seized materials inadmissible. That rule applied to documents as well as to other evidentiary items— "[t]here is no special sanctity in papers, as distinguished from other forms of property, to render them immune from search and seizure, if only they fall within the scope of the principles of the cases in which other property may be seized ... ." Private papers taken from the taxpayer, like other "mere evidence," could not be used against the accused over his Fourth and Fifth Amendment objections.

Several of *Boyd*'s express or implicit declarations have not stood the test of time. The application of the Fourth Amendment to subpoenas was limited by *Hale* v. *Henkel* ... Purely evidentiary (but "nontestimonial") materials, as well as contraband and fruits and instrumentalities of crime, may now be searched for and seized under proper circumstances, *Warden* v. *Hayden*, 387 U.S. 294(1967). Also, any notion that "testimonial" evidence may never be seized and used in evidence is inconsistent with *Katz* v. *United States*, 389 U.S. 347 (1967), approving the seizure under appropriate circumstances of conversations of a person suspected of crime.

It is also clear that the Fifth Amendment does not independently proscribe the compelled production of every sort of incriminating evidence but applies only when the accused is compelled to make a *testimonial* communication that is incriminating. We have, accordingly, declined to extend the protection of the privilege to the giving of blood samples; to the giving of handwriting exemplars, voice exemplars; or the donning of a blouse worn by the perpetrator. Furthermore, despite *Boyd*, neither a partnership nor the individual partners are shielded from compelled production of partnership records on self-incrimination grounds. *Bellis* v. *United States*, 417 U.S. 85 (1974). It would appear that under that case the precise claim sustained in *Boyd* would now be rejected for reasons not there considered.

The pronouncement in *Boyd* that a person may not be forced to produce his private papers has nonetheless often appeared as dictum in later opinions of this Court. To the extent, however, that the rule against compelling production of private papers rested on the proposition that seizures of or subpoenas for "mere evidence," including documents, violated the Fourth Amendment and therefore also transgressed the Fifth, the foundations for the rule have been washed away. In consequence, the prohibition against forcing the production of private papers has long been a rule searching for a rationale consistent with the proscriptions of the Fifth Amendment against compelling a person to give "testimony" that incriminates him. Accordingly, we turn to the question of what, if any, incriminating testimony within the Fifth Amendment's protection, is compelled by a documentary summons.

A subpoena served on a taxpayer requiring him to produce an accountant's workpapers in his possession without doubt involves substantial compulsion. But it does not compel oral testimony; nor would it ordinarily compel the taxpayer to restate, repeat, or affirm the truth of the contents of the documents sought. Therefore, the Fifth Amendment would not be violated by the fact alone that the papers on their face might incriminate the taxpayer, for the privilege protects a person only against being incriminated by his own compelled testimonial communications. The accountant's workpapers are not the taxpayer's. They were not prepared by the taxpayer, and they contain no testimonial declarations by him. Furthermore, as far as this record demonstrates, the preparation of all of the papers sought in these cases was wholly voluntary, and they cannot be said to contain compelled testimonial evidence, either of the taxpayers or of anyone else.[29] The taxpayer cannot avoid compliance with the subpoena

---

[29] [Court's footnote 11:] The fact that the documents may have been written by the person asserting the privilege is insufficient to trigger the privilege. And, unless the Government has compelled the subpoenaed person to write the document, *cf.* Marchetti v. United States, 390 U.S. 39 (1968); Grosso v. United States, 390 U.S. 62 (1968), the fact that it was written by him is not controlling with respect to the Fifth Amendment issue. Conversations may be seized and introduced in evidence under proper safeguards if not compelled. In the case of a documentary subpoena the only thing compelled is the act of producing the document and the compelled act is the same as the one performed when a chattel or document not authored by the producer is demanded.

merely by asserting that the item of evidence which he is required to produce contains incriminating writing, whether his own or that of someone else.

The act of producing evidence in response to a subpoena nevertheless has communicative aspects of its own, wholly aside from the contents of the papers produced. Compliance with the subpoena tacitly concedes the existence of the papers demanded and their possession or control by the taxpayer. It also would indicate the taxpayer's belief that the papers are those described in the subpoena. The elements of compulsion are clearly present, but the more difficult issues are whether the tacit averments of the taxpayer are both "testimonial" and "incriminating" for purposes of applying the Fifth Amendment. These questions perhaps do not lend themselves to categorical answers; their resolution may instead depend on the facts and circumstances of particular cases or classes thereof. In light of the records now before us, we are confident that however incriminating the contents of the accountant's workpapers might be, the act of producing them—the only thing which the taxpayer is compelled to do—would not itself involve testimonial self-incrimination.

It is doubtful that implicitly admitting the existence and possession of the papers rises to the level of testimony within the protection of the Fifth Amendment. The papers belong to the accountant, were prepared by him, and are the kind usually prepared by an accountant working on the tax returns of his client. Surely the Government is in no way relying on the "truth-telling" of the taxpayer to prove the existence of or his access to the documents. The existence and location of the papers are a foregone conclusion and the taxpayer adds little or nothing to the sum total of the Government's information by conceding that he in fact has the papers. Under these circumstances by enforcement of the summons "no constitutional rights are touched. The question is not of testimony but of surrender."

When an accused is required to submit a handwriting exemplar he admits his ability to write and impliedly asserts that the exemplar is his writing. But in common experience, the first would be a near truism and the latter self-evident. In any event, although the exemplar may be incriminating to the accused and although he is compelled to furnish it, his Fifth Amendment privilege is not violated because nothing he has said or done is deemed to be sufficiently testimonial for purposes of the privilege. This Court has also time and again allowed subpoenas against the custodian of corporate documents or those belonging to other collective entities such as unions and partnerships and those of bankrupt businesses over claims that the documents will incriminate the custodian despite the fact that producing the documents tacitly admits their existence and their location in the hands of their possessor. The existence and possession or control of the subpoenaed documents being no more in issue here than in the above cases, the summons is equally enforceable.

Moreover, assuming that these aspects of producing the accountant's papers have some minimal testimonial significance, surely it is not illegal to seek accounting help in connection with one's tax returns or for the accountant to prepare workpapers and deliver them to the taxpayer. At this juncture, we are quite unprepared to hold that either the fact of existence of the papers or of their possession by the taxpayer poses any realistic threat of incrimination to the taxpayer.

As for the possibility that responding to the subpoena would authenticate the workpapers, production would express nothing more than the tax payer's belief that the papers are those described in the subpoena. The taxpayer would be no more competent to authenticate the accountant's workpapers or reports by producing them than he would be to authenticate them if testifying orally. The taxpayer did not prepare the papers and could not vouch for their accuracy. The documents would not be admissible in evidence against the taxpayer without authenticating testimony. Without more, responding to the subpoena in the circumstances before us would not appear to represent a substantial threat of self-incrimination. Moreover, [in a series of cases], the custodian of corporate, union, or partnership books or those of a bankrupt business was ordered to respond to a subpoena for the business' books even though doing so involved a "representation that the documents produced are those demanded by the subpoena."

Whether the Fifth Amendment would shield the taxpayer from producing his own tax records in his possession is a question not involved here; for the papers demanded here are not his "private papers." We do hold that compliance with a summons directing the taxpayer to produce the accountant's documents involved in these cases would involve no incriminating testimony within the protection of the Fifth Amendment. ...

MR. JUSTICE BRENNAN, concurring in the judgment.

I concur in the judgment. Given the prior access by accountants retained by the taxpayers to the papers involved in these cases and the wholly business rather than personal nature of the papers, I agree that the privilege against compelled self-incrimination did not in either of these cases protect the papers from production in response to the summonses. I do not join the Court's opinion, however, because of the portent of much of what is said of a serious crippling of the protection secured by the privilege against compelled production of one's private books and papers. ... [I]t is but another step in the denigration of privacy principles settled nearly 100 years ago in *Boyd* v. *United States*, 116 U.S. 616 (1886). According to the Court, "[w]hether the Fifth Amendment would shield the taxpayer from producing his own tax records in his possession is a question not involved here; for the papers demanded here are not his 'private papers.'" This implication that the privilege might not protect against compelled production of tax records that are his "private papers" is so contrary to settled constitutional jurisprudence that this and other like implications throughout the opinion prompt me to conjecture that once again the Court is laying the groundwork for future decisions that will tell us that the question here formally reserved was actually answered against the availability of the privilege. ...

Expressions are legion in opinions of this Court that the protection of personal privacy is a central purpose of the privilege against compelled self-incrimination. ...

The Court pays lip service to this bedrock premise of privacy in the statement that "[w]ithin the limits imposed by the language of the Fifth Amendment, which we necessarily observe, the privilege truly serves privacy interests." But this only makes explicit what elsewhere highlights the opinion, namely, the view that protection of personal privacy is merely a by product and not, as our precedents and history teach, a factor controlling in part the determination of the scope of the privilege. This cart-before-the-horse approach is fundamentally at odds with the settled principle that the scope of the privilege is not constrained by the limits of the wording of the Fifth Amendment but has the reach necessary to protect the cherished value of privacy which it safeguards. ... History and principle, not the mechanical application of its wording, have been the life of the Amendment. ...

History and principle teach that the privacy protected by the Fifth Amendment extends not just to the individual's immediate declarations, oral or written, but also to his testimonial materials in the form of books and papers. ...

... An individual's books and papers are generally little more than an extension of his person. They reveal no less than he could reveal upon being questioned directly. Many of the matters within an individual's knowledge may as easily be retained within his head as set down on a scrap of paper. I perceive no principle which does not permit compelling one to disclose the contents of one's mind but does permit compelling the disclosure of the contents of that scrap of paper by compelling its production. Under a contrary view, the constitutional protection would turn on fortuity, and persons would, at their peril, record their thoughts and the events of their lives. The ability to think private thoughts, facilitated as it is by pen and paper, and the ability to preserve intimate memories would be curtailed through fear that those thoughts or events of those memories would become the subjects of criminal sanctions however invalidly imposed. Indeed, it was the very reality of those fears that helped provide the historical impetus for the privilege. ...

Notes

1. At the outset of the opinion, the Supreme Court states that the Fisher's Fifth Amendment right did not protect the documents at issue in the hands of his attorney. What element of the Fifth Amendment formula recited at the inception of this chapter was missing? Why, then, does the Court engage in a prolonged analysis of Fisher's entitlement to the Fifth

Amendment privilege with respect to the documents at issue? Say that you write in your diary "I shot the Sheriff but I did not kill the Deputy." Assume that, after federal agents come calling, you turn your diary over to a friend who is not a lawyer, a priest, or your spouse. If the grand jury subpoenas your friend, requiring production of the diary, can you or your friend resist the subpoena on the basis of your Fifth Amendment right?

2. *Search Warrants: No "Compulsion."* Let us change the facts slightly. Assume that you retain possession of the diary and that federal agents seize it pursuant to a valid search warrant for your home. Can you successfully petition a court for its return, claiming that its seizure violated your Fifth Amendment privilege? *See* Andresen v. Maryland, 427 U.S. 463, 473 (1976) (holding that Fifth Amendment not violated by use against criminal defendant of personal business records seized pursuant to lawful search because the records had been "voluntarily committed to writing" and because the defendant had not been forced to produce or authenticate them).

3. *Contents Not "Compelled."* Assume now that either you are subpoenaed for the diary while it is still in your hands or that, after you gave the diary to your lawyer for the purpose of securing legal advice, your lawyer receives a subpoena for the diary. The *contents* of the document are certainly "testimonial" in that, unlike the work papers at issue in *Fisher*, they were written *by you* and reflect the contents of *your mind*. The contents are also clearly "incriminating." But are they "compelled" within the meaning of *Fisher*? *Fisher* stands for the proposition that the *contents* of any *pre-existing* documents, that is, documents the government did not *force* one to write, are not "compelled" within the meaning of the Fifth Amendment and thus the *contents* of the documents are not relevant to the Fifth Amendment analysis regardless of how "testimonial" or "incriminating" they may be.

Boyd v. United States, 116 U.S. 616 (1886), which the *Fisher* Court attempts to bury (but which, as we shall see, at least one Justice presently sitting may not be inclined to inter), was commonly cited for the proposition that the Fifth Amendment protects against the compelled production of *pre-existing* "private papers" whose *contents* were incriminating. Is there any basis upon which one could argue that *Boyd* lives at least as far as clearly "private" papers, such as diaries, are concerned even if does not apply to business-related papers such as those at issue in *Fisher*? Would a privacy-based theory of the Fifth Amendment work after *Fisher*? *See, e.g.,* United States v. Doe, 465 U.S. 605, 618 (1984) (O'Connor, J., concurring) ("I write separately ... just to make explicit what is implicit in [the Court's] opinion: that the Fifth Amendment provides absolutely no protection for the contents of private papers of any kind. The notion that the Fifth Amendment protects the privacy of papers originated in *Boyd v. United States* but our decision in *Fisher v. United States* sounded the death knell for *Boyd*."); *see also* Baltimore City Dep't of Social Servs. v. Bouknight, 493 U.S. 549, 555 (1990) (citing Justice O'Connor's *Doe* concurrence and stating that "a person may not claim the Amendment's protections based upon the incrimination that may result from the contents or nature of the thing demanded").

4. *The "Act of Production" is "Compelled" But is it "Testimonial"?* The government is not forcing one to record the contents of the records when it serves a subpoena, but it *is* compelling the subject to do something: it is forcing the subpoena's subject to make an "act of production" of the required documents or other physical evidence called for in the subpoena. But to be protected, that "compelled" act must be deemed "testimonial."

Although the Fifth Amendment privilege is often referred to as a "privilege against self-incrimination," this "is not an entirely accurate description of a person's constitutional protection against being 'compelled in any criminal case to be a witness against himself.'" *United States v. Hubbell*, 530 U.S. 27 (2000). As the Court explained in *Hubbell*,

> The word "witness" in the constitutional text limits the relevant category of compelled incriminating communications to those that are "*testimonial*" in character. As Justice Holmes observed, there is a significant difference between the use of compulsion to extort *communications* from a defendant and compelling a person to engage in *conduct* that may be incriminating. Thus, even though the *act* may provide incriminating evidence, a criminal suspect may be compelled to put on a shirt, to provide a blood sample or handwriting exemplar, or to make a recording of his voice. The *act* of exhibiting such

physical characteristics is not the same as a *sworn communication by a witness that relates either express or implied assertions of fact or belief. ...*

Id. (emphasis added). Revisiting our diary hypothetical, although the government did not "compel" the *contents* of the diary, the subpoena would "compel" the diary's author to *act—that is, to physically produce the diary.* Can such an "act of production" be deemed a "testimonial communication" or is it, like the provision of handwriting exemplars or blood samples, not deemed sufficiently "testimonial" in character? The *Fisher* Court states that a compelled "act of production" of pre-existing documents may indeed constitute an implicit "testimonial communication" regarding the existence, possession, or authenticity of the documents, or the responsiveness of the documents to the subpoena.

5. *Foregone Conclusion: Insufficiently "Testimonial"?* The *Fisher* Court further notes, however, that a valid Fifth Amendment claim may not be made in all instances in which one or more of those facts are implicitly communicated by the act of production. Where these facts are "foregone conclusions" by virtue of the Government's prior knowledge, an "act of production" is "insufficiently testimonial" and no Fifth Amendment privilege may be asserted. Returning to our diary example, if the government has been told by your roommate that you keep a diary and that roommate is prepared to take the stand to authenticate the diary, what remains of your Fifth Amendment "act of production" privilege?

6. *Is the Compelled, Testimonial "Act of Production" Incriminating?* What about the "incrimination" element? Even if the facts of possession, existence, authenticity, or responsiveness were not "foregone conclusions," the fact that the *contents* of the diary are incriminating *does not* satisfy this element because the contents are not compelled. One would need to show that the testimonial act that *is* compelled is also incriminating—that is, that *conceding possession, existence, authenticity, or responsiveness* would be incriminating. In *Fisher*, the court stated that "it is not illegal to seek accounting help ... [and] we are quite unprepared to hold either the fact of existence of the papers or of their possession by the taxpayer poses any realistic threat of incrimination to the taxpayer." Is keeping a diary or possession of a diary illegal or incriminating? Can you posit a case in which conceding the existence, or one's possession, of a document or tangible thing will be incriminating?

If a diary is not protected, what is? Consider *People v. Havrish*, in which the New York Court of Appeals upheld a defendant's claim that turning over a gun pursuant to a protective order would be both testimonial and incriminating. 8 N.Y.3d 389, 866 N.E.2d 1009 (2007). In *Havrish*, the defendant was charged with assault in connection with an incident of domestic violence. Prior to trial on this charge, the court issued a protective order directing the defendant to stay away from the victim and to surrender any firearms. The defendant, in complying with the order, turned over to the police his "long guns" and an unlicensed revolver. The state subsequently charged the defendant with criminal possession of an unlicensed handgun. New York's highest court ruled, however, that the defendant's surrender of the firearm was compelled by court order, was testimonial in that the police did not of his possession of the gun prior to the surrender, and was incriminating in that "the act of production involved the commission of a crime in the presence of the police." *Id.* at 396-97. The Court suppressed the handgun, and thus was required to dismiss the weapons charge for lack of evidence.

7. Does the *Fisher* Court's approach make sense given the rationale underlying the Fifth Amendment privilege? What *is* that rationale after *Fisher*?

C. THE CONTINUING VIABILITY OF THE COLLECTIVE ENTITY DOCTRINE AFTER *FISHER*

BRASWELL v. UNITED STATES
487 U.S. 99 (1988)

CHIEF JUSTICE REHNQUIST delivered the opinion of the Court.

This case presents the question whether the custodian of corporate records may resist a subpoena for such records on the ground that the act of production would incriminate him in violation of the Fifth Amendment. We conclude that he may not.

[A federal grand jury issued a subpoena *duces tecum* to petitioner Braswell as the president of two corporations, Worldwide Machinery, Inc. and Worldwide Purchasing. Although both corporations had three directors—petitioner, his wife, and his mother—only petitioner had authority over the business affairs of the corporations. Petitioner moved to quash the subpoena, arguing that the act of producing the records would constitute a violation of his Fifth Amendment rights. The district court denied the motion, and the Fifth Circuit affirmed.]
...

There is no question but that the contents of the subpoenaed business records are not privileged. Similarly, petitioner asserts no self-incrimination claim on behalf of the corporations; it is well established that such artificial entities are not protected by the Fifth Amendment. Petitioner instead relies solely upon the argument that his act of producing the documents has independent testimonial significance, which would incriminate him individually, and that the Fifth Amendment prohibits Government compulsion of that act. The bases for this argument are extrapolated from the decisions of this Court in *Fisher* and *United States v. Doe*, 465 U.S. 605 (1984).

In *Fisher*, the Court was presented with the question whether an attorney may resist a subpoena demanding that he produce tax records which had been entrusted to him by his client. ... After explaining that the Fifth Amendment prohibits "compelling a person to give 'testimony' that incriminates him," the Court rejected the argument that the contents of the records were protected. The Court, however, went on to observe:

> "The act of producing evidence in response to a subpoena nevertheless has communicative aspects of its own, wholly aside from the contents of the papers produced. Compliance with the subpoena tacitly concedes the existence of the papers demanded and their possession or control by the taxpayer. It also would indicate the taxpayer's belief that the papers are those described in the subpoena. The elements of compulsion are clearly present, but the more difficult issues are whether the tacit averments of the taxpayer are both 'testimonial' and 'incriminating' for purposes of applying the Fifth Amendment. These questions perhaps do not lend themselves to categorical answers; their resolution may instead depend on the facts and circumstances of particular cases or classes thereof."

The Court concluded that under the "facts and circumstances" there presented, the act of producing the accountants' papers would not "involve testimonial self-incrimination."

Eight years later, in *United States v. Doe, supra*, the Court revisited the question, this time in the context of a claim by a sole proprietor that the compelled production of business records would run afoul of the Fifth Amendment. After rejecting the contention that the contents of the records were themselves protected, the Court proceeded to address whether respondent's act of producing the records would constitute protected testimonial incrimination. The Court concluded that respondent had established a valid Fifth Amendment claim. It deferred to the lower courts, which had found that enforcing the subpoenas at issue would provide the

Government valuable information: By producing the records, respondent would admit that the records existed, were in his possession, and were authentic.

Had petitioner conducted his business as a sole proprietorship, *Doe* would require that he be provided the opportunity to show that his act of production would entail testimonial self-incrimination. But petitioner has operated his business through the corporate form, and we have long recognized that, for purposes of the Fifth Amendment, corporations and other collective entities are treated differently from individuals. This doctrine—known as the collective entity rule—has a lengthy and distinguished pedigree.

The rule was first articulated by the Court in the case of *Hale v. Henkel*, 201 U.S. 43 (1906). Hale, a corporate officer, had been served with a subpoena ordering him to produce corporate records and to testify concerning certain corporate transactions. Although Hale was protected by personal immunity, he sought to resist the demand for the records by interposing a Fifth Amendment privilege on behalf of the corporation. The Court rejected that argument: "[W]e are of the opinion that there is a clear distinction ... between an individual and a corporation, and ... the latter has no right to refuse to submit its books and papers for an examination at the suit of the State." The Court explained that the corporation "is a creature of the State," with powers limited by the State. As such, the State may, in the exercise of its right to oversee the corporation, demand the production of corporate records. ...

Although *Hale* settled that a corporation has no Fifth Amendment privilege, the Court did not address whether a corporate officer could resist a subpoena for corporate records by invoking his personal privilege—Hale had been protected by immunity. ...

The plain mandate of [this Court's decisions in *United States* v. *White*, 322 U.S. 694 (1944) (holding that a labor union is a collective entity unprotected by the Fifth Amendment), and *Bellis* v. *United States*, 417 U.S. 85 (1974) (ruling that a partner in a small partnership could not properly refuse to produce partnership records)] is that without regard to whether the subpoena is addressed to the corporation, or as here, to the individual in his capacity as a custodian, a corporate custodian such as petitioner may not resist a subpoena for corporate records on Fifth Amendment grounds. Petitioner argues, however, that this rule falls in the wake of *Fisher v. United States*, 425 U.S. 391 (1976), and *United States v. Doe*, 465 U.S. 605 (1984). In essence, petitioner's argument is as follows: In response to *Boyd v. United States*, 116 U.S. 616 (1886), with its privacy rationale shielding personal books and records, the Court developed the collective entity rule, which declares simply that corporate records are not private and therefore are not protected by the Fifth Amendment. The collective entity decisions were concerned with the contents of the documents subpoenaed, however, and not with the act of production. In *Fisher* and *Doe*, the Court moved away from the privacy-based collective entity rule, replacing it with a compelled-testimony standard under which the contents of business documents are never privileged but the act of producing the documents may be. Under this new regime, the act of production privilege is available without regard to the entity whose records are being sought.

To be sure, the holding in *Fisher*—later reaffirmed in *Doe*—embarked upon a new course of Fifth Amendment analysis. We cannot agree, however, that it rendered the collective entity rule obsolete. The agency rationale undergirding the collective entity decisions, in which custodians asserted that production of entity records would incriminate them personally, survives. ... [T]he Court has consistently recognized that the custodian of corporate or entity records holds those documents in a representative rather than a personal capacity. Artificial entities such as corporations may act only through their agents, and a custodian's assumption of his representative capacity leads to certain obligations, including the duty to produce corporate records on proper demand by the Government. Under those circumstances, the custodian's act of production is not deemed a personal act, but rather an act of the corporation. Any claim of Fifth Amendment privilege asserted by the agent would be tantamount to a claim of privilege by the corporation—which of course possesses no such privilege. ...

We note further that recognizing a Fifth Amendment privilege on behalf of the records custodians of collective entities would have a detrimental impact on the Government's efforts to prosecute "white-collar crime," one of the most serious problems confronting law enforcement authorities.[30] "The greater portion of evidence of wrongdoing by an organization or its representatives is usually found in the official records and documents of that organization. Were the cloak of the privilege to be thrown around these impersonal records and documents, effective enforcement of many federal and state laws would be impossible." If custodians could assert a privilege, authorities would be stymied not only in their enforcement efforts against those individuals but also in their prosecutions of organizations. In *Bellis*, the Court observed: "In view of the inescapable fact that an artificial entity can only act to produce its records through its individual officers or agents, recognition of the individual's claim of privilege with respect to the financial records of the organization would substantially undermine the unchallenged rule that the organization itself is not entitled to claim any Fifth Amendment privilege, and largely frustrate legitimate governmental regulation of such organizations." ...

Although a corporate custodian is not entitled to resist a subpoena on the ground that his act of production will be personally incriminating, we do think certain consequences flow from the fact that the custodian's act of production is one in his representative rather than personal capacity. Because the custodian acts as a representative, the act is deemed one of the corporation and not the individual. Therefore, the Government concedes, as it must, that it may make no evidentiary use of the "individual act" against the individual. For example, in a criminal prosecution against the custodian, the Government may not introduce into evidence before the jury the fact that the subpoena was served upon and the corporation's documents were delivered by one particular individual, the custodian. The Government has the right, however, to use the corporation's act of production against the custodian. The Government may offer testimony—for example, from the process server who delivered the subpoena and from the individual who received the records—establishing that the corporation produced the records subpoenaed. The jury may draw from the corporation's act of production the conclusion that the records in question are authentic corporate records, which the corporation possessed, and which it produced in response to the subpoena. And if the defendant held a prominent position within the corporation that produced the records, the jury may, just as it would had someone else produced the documents, reasonably infer that he had possession of the documents or knowledge of their contents. Because the jury is not told that the defendant produced the records, any nexus between the defendant and the documents results solely from the corporation's act of production and other evidence in the case.[31]

Notes

1. Should a collective entity, such as a corporation, have a Fifth Amendment right against self-incrimination? *See* Robert E. Wagner, *Miranda, Inc.: Corporations and the Right to Remain Silent*, 11 Va. L. & Bus. Rev. 499 (2017).

2. It has long been established that a corporate custodian required to produce corporate records could not assert his personal Fifth Amendment privilege to resist production, even if the contents of the documents incriminated him personally. How did Braswell attempt to escape the force of these precedents? The subpoenas at issue in *Braswell* were served on petitioner Braswell in his capacity as president of the corporate entities whose records were sought. But the result is no different if the subpoenas are directed at the individuals personally and call for the production of corporate records in their personal possession. *See In re* Grand

---

[30] [Court's footnote 9:] White-collar crime is "the most serious and all-pervasive crime problem in America today." Conyers, *Corporate and White-Collar Crime: A View by the Chairman of the House Subcommittee on Crime*, 17 Am. Crim. L. Rev. 287, 288 (1980). Although this statement was made in 1980, there is no reason to think the problem has diminished in the meantime.

[31] [Court's footnote 11:] ... We leave open the question whether the agency rationale supports compelling a custodian to produce corporate records when the custodian is able to establish, by showing for example that he is the sole employee and officer of the corporation, that the jury would inevitably conclude that he produced the records.

Jury Subpoena Issued June 18, 2009, 593 F.3d 155, 157-58 (2d Cir. 2010) (corporation that has one shareholder, officer, and employee may not assert the Fifth); *In re* Grand Jury Witnesses, 92 F.3d 710 (8th Cir.1996).

May the act of production incriminate the custodian personally? Does the limited immunity the Court formulates in the last paragraph of its opinion undercut its agency theory? Should the dangers of white-collar crime and the enforcement difficulties that may arise from a contrary rule inform the Court's constitutional analysis? Might the government get what it sought, even under a contrary ruling, through "act of production" immunity? Why might such immunity create as many problems for law enforcement as it solves? *See United States v. Hubbell,* reproduced *infra.*

3. Where a corporate employee leaves his job or is fired after a grand jury investigation has commenced and, seeking to protect himself, takes with him corporate records that might incriminate him, may he be compelled to turn over the records under *Braswell?* There is a split in the circuits on this question. The Second Circuit has held that an ex-employee may assert his personal privilege in such circumstances because "once the agency relationship terminates, the former employee is no longer an agent of the corporation and is not a custodian of the corporate records. When such an individual produces records in his possession he cannot be acting in anything other than his personal capacity. In no sense can it be said, as *Braswell* requires, that 'the corporation produced the records subpoenaed.'" *In re* Three Grand Jury Subpoenas Duces Tecum Dated Jan. 29, 1999, 191 F.3d 173 (2d Cir. 1999). By contrast, the Eleventh Circuit has held that it is the "immutable character of the records as corporate which requires their production and which dictates that they are held in a representative capacity." *In re* Grand Jury Subpoena Dated Nov. 12, 1991, 957 F.2d 807, 810-13 (11th Cir. 1992). Under *Braswell,* what is the correct result? To the extent that policy considerations are relevant, what would they counsel?

4. The *Braswell* analysis also applies where a government employee seeks to claim an "act of production" privilege for the production of governmental records. Thus, for example, the D.C. Circuit has held that, in a grand jury investigation of federal officials, a former official could not assert his Fifth Amendment right against self-incrimination with respect to his act of production of governmental records. *See In re* Sealed Case (Government Records), 950 F.2d 736 (D.C. Cir. 1991). As the court explained:

> Federal law makes the taking, concealing, or destroying of government property or government records a criminal offense. 18 U.S.C. §§ 641, 2071. Appellee cites these specific provisions in urging that the very production of the subpoenaed documents indeed can be an incriminating act. That may be true, but under *Braswell,* it is not material. The rationale of *Braswell,* we think, encompasses government records. Just as corporate records belong to the corporation and are held for the entity by the custodian only in an agency capacity, so government records do not belong to the custodian, in this case the appellee, but to the government agency. Their production thus falls outside the Fifth Amendment privilege, which is a personal one.

Id. at 740.

5. One remaining argument in support of a custodian's refusal to turn over certain records is the contention that the records subpoenaed are personal, not business or governmental records, and thus that an individual custodian cannot be required to produce them in her representative capacity. In *In re Sealed Case (Governmental Records),* 950 F.2d 736 (D.C. Cir. 1991), the District of Columbia Circuit held that the district court was required to review documents about which the parties had a dispute regarding the appropriate characterization (private records v. governmental records). It explained:

> The precise scope of the government records exception—what is a government record and what remains a personal record—is not elaborated in case law. The collective entity, or corporate records, cases, however, provide a useful guide.

In determining whether a document belongs in the corporate or the personal category, courts employ a functional test. Under this approach, a pocket calendar kept by a business executive for her personal convenience, and to which not even her secretary had daily access, may qualify as a personal record, while a desk calendar maintained jointly by the executive and her secretary, kept open on the executive's desk, would more likely qualify as a corporate record. The proper characterization turns less on the ownership of the calendar than on its use: a Brooks Brothers diary used to record an executive's conduct of business meetings and transactions has been held a corporate record; a diary containing an individual's end-of-the-day reflections on social and business experiences, not used in conducting office affairs, ordinarily would rank as a personal item.

The corporate record cases also show that a "mixed" document containing both personal and corporate notations may qualify as a corporate record. On the other hand, a diary or calendar may remain essentially "private" and therefore shielded from compulsory production even if it contains an occasional notation of a corporate appointment or activity. Furthermore, the contents of "mixed" records should be culled so as to delete or excise purely private notations from a corporate record, or corporate materials mingled with private papers. A witness retains the right to assert her Fifth Amendment privilege as to personal materials contained in government records; conversely, she may not shield from production government material in personal papers. The witness, we note, bears the burden of proving the nature of the documents and their various contents.

In sum, to determine whether a document is a government record, inquiry into the nature, purpose, and use of the document is in order, and the precedent set in the context of corporate records should analogously apply. In addition, agency regulations regarding the treatment of certain records are relevant to the inquiry. For example, where either a collective entity or a government agency directs employees to keep certain papers or notes in performing assigned work, the direction counts as evidence that the document is job-related and not simply or principally a personal record. Office procedures, such as a secretary's or co-workers' access to and use of a document, can also help inform the court as to the nature of the document.

Id. at 740-41.

D. WHAT CONSTITUTES A "TESTIMONIAL COMMUNICATION"

DOE v. UNITED STATES
487 U.S. 201 (1988)

JUSTICE BLACKMUN delivered the opinion of the Court.

This case presents the question whether a court order compelling a target of a grand jury investigation to authorize foreign banks to disclose records of his accounts, without identifying those documents or acknowledging their existence, violates the target's Fifth Amendment privilege against self-incrimination.

Petitioner, named here as John Doe, is the target of a federal grand jury investigation .... Doe appeared before the grand jury pursuant to a subpoena that directed him to produce records of transactions in accounts at three named banks in the Cayman Islands and Bermuda. Doe produced some bank records and testified that no additional records responsive to the subpoena were in his possession or control. When questioned about the existence or location of additional records, Doe invoked the Fifth Amendment privilege against self-incrimination.

The United States branches of the three foreign banks also were served with subpoenas commanding them to produce records of accounts over which Doe had signatory authority. Citing their governments' bank-secrecy laws, which prohibit the disclosure of account records without the customer's consent, the banks refused to comply. ...

[The Government filed a motion with the District Court, asking that court to order Doe to sign forms consenting to the disclosure of specified bank records. After its initial consent directive was rejected by the District Court, the Government] submitted to the court a revised proposed consent directive. ... The form purported to apply to any and all accounts over which Doe had a right of withdrawal, without acknowledging the existence of any such account.[32] The District Court denied this motion also, reasoning that compelling execution of the consent directive might lead to the uncovering and linking of Doe to accounts that the grand jury did not know were in existence. The court concluded that execution of the proposed form would "admit signatory authority over the speculative accounts [and] would implicitly authenticate any records of the speculative accounts provided by the banks pursuant to the consent."

The Court of Appeals for the Fifth Circuit reversed. ...

On remand, the District Court ordered petitioner to execute the consent directive. He refused. The District Court accordingly found petitioner in civil contempt and ordered that he be confined until he complied with the order. ...

... We conclude that a court order compelling the execution of such a directive as is at issue here does not implicate the [Fifth] Amendment.

It is undisputed that the contents of the foreign bank records sought by the Government are not privileged under the Fifth Amendment. There also is no question that the foreign banks cannot invoke the Fifth Amendment in declining to produce the documents; the privilege does not extend to such artificial entities. Similarly, petitioner asserts no Fifth Amendment right to prevent the banks from disclosing the account records, for the Constitution "necessarily does not proscribe incriminating statements elicited from another." Petitioner's sole claim is that his execution of the consent forms directing the banks to release records as to which the banks believe he has the right of withdrawal has independent testimonial significance that will incriminate him, and that the Fifth Amendment prohibits governmental compulsion of that act.

... The execution of the consent directive at issue in this case obviously would be compelled, and we may assume that its execution would have an incriminating effect.[33] The question on which this case turns is whether the act of executing the form is a "testimonial communication." The parties disagree about both the meaning of "testimonial" and whether the consent directive fits the proposed definitions.

Petitioner contends that a compelled statement is testimonial if the Government could use the content of the speech or writing, as opposed to its physical characteristics, to further a

---

[32] [Court's footnote 3:] The revised consent form reads: "I, _____, of the State of Texas in the United States of America, do hereby direct any bank or trust company at which I may have a bank account of any kind or at which a corporation has a bank account of any kind upon which I am authorized to draw, and its officers, employees and agents, to disclose all information and deliver copies of all documents of every nature in your possession or control which relate to said bank account to Grand Jury 84-2, empaneled May 7, 1984 ... , and to give evidence relevant thereto, in the investigation conducted by Grand Jury 84-2 in the Southern District of Texas, and this shall be irrevocable authority for so doing. This direction has been executed pursuant to that certain order of the United States District Court for the Southern District of Texas issued in connection with the aforesaid investigation, dated _____. This direction is intended to apply to the Confidential Relationships (Preservation) Law of the Cayman Islands, and to any implied contract of confidentiality between Bermuda banks and their customers which may be imposed by Bermuda common law, and shall be construed as consent with respect thereto as the same shall apply to any of the bank accounts for which I may be a relevant principal."

[33] [Court's footnote 5:] As noted above, the District Court concluded that the consent directive was incriminating in that it would furnish the Government with a link in the chain of evidence leading to Doe's indictment. Because we ultimately find no testimonial significance in either the contents of the directive or Doe's execution of it, we need not, and do not, address the incrimination element of the privilege.

criminal investigation of the witness. The second half of petitioner's "testimonial" test is that the statement must be incriminating, which is, of course, already a separate requirement for invoking the privilege. Thus, Doe contends, in essence, that every written and oral statement significant for its content is necessarily testimonial for purposes of the Fifth Amendment. Under this view, the consent directive is testimonial because it is a declarative statement of consent made by Doe to the foreign banks, a statement that the Government will use to persuade the banks to produce potentially incriminating account records that would otherwise be unavailable to the grand jury.

The Government, on the other hand, suggests that a compelled statement is not testimonial for purposes of the privilege, unless it implicitly or explicitly relates a factual assertion or otherwise conveys information to the Government. It argues that, under this view, the consent directive is not testimonial because neither the directive itself nor Doe's execution of the form discloses or communicates facts or information. Petitioner disagrees.

The Government's view of the privilege, apparently accepted by the Courts of Appeals that have considered compelled consent forms, is derived largely from this Court's decisions in *Fisher* and *Doe*. The issue presented in those cases was whether the act of producing subpoenaed documents, not itself the making of a statement, might nonetheless have some protected testimonial aspects. The Court concluded that the act of production could constitute protected testimonial communication because it might entail implicit statements of fact: by producing documents in compliance with a subpoena, the witness would admit that the papers existed, were in his possession or control, and were authentic. Thus, the Court made clear that the Fifth Amendment privilege against self-incrimination applies to acts that imply assertions of fact.

We reject petitioner's argument that this test does not control the determination as to when the privilege applies to oral or written statements. While the Court in *Fisher* and *Doe* did not purport to announce a universal test for determining the scope of the privilege, it also did not purport to establish a more narrow boundary applicable to acts alone. To the contrary, the Court applied basic Fifth Amendment principles. An examination of the Court's application of these principles in other cases indicates the Court's recognition that, in order to be testimonial, an accused's communication must itself, explicitly or implicitly, relate a factual assertion or disclose information.[34] Only then is a person compelled to be a "witness" against himself.

This understanding is perhaps most clearly revealed in those cases in which the Court has held that certain acts, though incriminating, are not within the privilege. Thus, a suspect may be compelled to furnish a blood sample, to provide a handwriting exemplar, or a voice exemplar; to stand in a lineup; and to wear particular clothing. These decisions are grounded on the proposition that "the privilege protects an accused only from being compelled to testify against himself, or otherwise provide the State with evidence of a testimonial or communicative nature." The Court accordingly held that the privilege was not implicated in each of those cases, because the suspect was not required "to disclose any knowledge he might have," or "to speak his guilt." It is the "extortion of information from the accused," the attempt to force him "to disclose the contents of his own mind," that implicates the Self-Incrimination Clause. "Unless some attempt is made to secure a communication—written, oral or otherwise—upon which reliance is to be placed as involving [the accused's] consciousness of the facts and the operations of his mind in expressing it, the demand made upon him is not a testimonial one."

It is consistent with the history of and the policies underlying the Self-Incrimination Clause to hold that the privilege may be asserted only to resist compelled explicit or implicit disclosures of incriminating information. Historically, the privilege was intended to prevent the

---

[34] [Court's footnote 9:] We do not disagree with the dissent that "[t]he expression of the contents of an individual's mind" is testimonial communication for purposes of the Fifth Amendment. We simply disagree with the dissent's conclusion that the execution of the consent directive at issue here forced petitioner to express the contents of his mind. In our view, such compulsion is more like "be[ing] forced to surrender a key to a strongbox containing incriminating documents" than it is like "be[ing] compelled to reveal the combination to [petitioner's] wall safe."

use of legal compulsion to extract from the accused a sworn communication of facts which would incriminate him. ...

We are not persuaded by petitioner's arguments that our articulation of the privilege fundamentally alters the power of the Government to compel an accused to assist in his prosecution. There are very few instances in which a verbal statement, either oral or written, will not convey information or assert facts. The vast majority of verbal statements thus will be testimonial and, to that extent at least, will fall within the privilege. ...

The difficult question whether a compelled communication is testimonial for purposes of applying the Fifth Amendment often depends on the facts and circumstances of the particular case. This case is no exception. We turn, then, to consider whether Doe's execution of the consent directive at issue here would have testimonial significance. We agree with the Court of Appeals that it would not, because neither the form, nor its execution, communicates any factual assertions, implicit or explicit, or conveys any information to the Government.

The consent directive itself is not "testimonial." It is carefully drafted not to make reference to a specific account, but only to speak in the hypothetical. Thus, the form does not acknowledge that an account in a foreign financial institution is in existence or that it is controlled by petitioner. Nor does the form indicate whether documents or any other information relating to petitioner are present at the foreign bank, assuming that such an account does exist. The form does not even identify the relevant bank. Although the executed form allows the Government access to a potential source of evidence, the directive itself does not point the Government toward hidden accounts or otherwise provide information that will assist the prosecution in uncovering evidence. The Government must locate that evidence "'by the independent labor of its officers.'" As in *Fisher*, the Government is not relying upon the "'truth-telling'" of Doe's directive to show the existence of, or his control over, foreign bank account records.

Given the consent directive's phraseology, petitioner's compelled act of executing the form has no testimonial significance either. By signing the form, Doe makes no statement, explicit or implicit, regarding the existence of a foreign bank account or his control over any such account. Nor would his execution of the form admit the authenticity of any records produced by the bank. Not only does the directive express no view on the issue, but because petitioner did not prepare the document, any statement by Doe to the effect that it is authentic would not establish that the records are genuine. Authentication evidence would have to be provided by bank officials.

Finally, we cannot agree with petitioner's contention that his execution of the directive admits or asserts Doe's consent. The form does not state that Doe "consents" to the release of bank records. Instead, it states that the directive "shall be construed as consent" with respect to Cayman Islands and Bermuda bank-secrecy laws. Because the directive explicitly indicates that it was signed pursuant to a court order, Doe's compelled execution of the form sheds no light on his actual intent or state of mind. The form does "direct" the bank to disclose account information and release any records that "may" exist and for which Doe "may" be a relevant principal. But directing the recipient of a communication to do something is not an assertion of fact or, at least in this context, a disclosure of information. In its testimonial significance, the execution of such a directive is analogous to the production of a handwriting sample or voice exemplar: it is a nontestimonial act. In neither case is the suspect's action compelled to obtain "any knowledge he might have."[35]

---

[35] [Court's footnote 15:] Petitioner apparently maintains that the performance of every compelled act carries with it an implied assertion that the act has been performed by the person who was compelled, and therefore the performance of the act is subject to the privilege. In [the cases upholding the compelled production of handwriting or voice exemplars or blood samples], the Court implicitly rejected this argument. It could be said in those cases that the suspect, by providing his handwriting or voice exemplar, implicitly "acknowledged" that the writing or voice sample was his. But as the holdings make clear, this kind of simple acknowledgment—that the suspect in fact performed the compelled act—is not "sufficiently testimonial for purposes of the privilege." Similarly, the acknowledgment that Doe directed the bank to disclose any records the bank thinks are Doe's—can acknowledgment implicit in Doe's placing his signature on the consent directive—is not sufficiently testimonial for purposes of the privilege.

We read the directive as equivalent to a statement by Doe that, although he expresses no opinion about the existence of, or his control over, any such account, he is authorizing the bank to disclose information relating to accounts over which, in the bank's opinion, Doe can exercise the right of withdrawal. When forwarded to the bank along with a subpoena, the executed directive, if effective under local law, will simply make it possible for the recipient bank to comply with the Government's request to produce such records. As a result, if the Government obtains bank records after Doe signs the directive, the only factual statement made by anyone will be the *bank's* implicit declaration, by its act of production in response to the subpoena, that *it* believes the accounts to be petitioner's. The fact that the bank's customer has directed the disclosure of his records "would say nothing about the correctness of the bank's representations." ...

Because the consent directive is not testimonial in nature, we conclude that the District Court's order compelling petitioner to sign the directive does not violate his Fifth Amendment privilege against self-incrimination. ...

JUSTICE STEVENS, dissenting.

A defendant can be compelled to produce material evidence that is incriminating. Fingerprints, blood samples, voice exemplars, handwriting specimens, or other items of physical evidence may be extracted from a defendant against his will. But can he be compelled to use his mind to assist the prosecution in convicting him of a crime? I think not. He may in some cases be forced to surrender a key to a strongbox containing incriminating documents, but I do not believe he can be compelled to reveal the combination to his wall safe—by word or deed.

The document the Government seeks to extract from John Doe purports to order third parties to take action that will lead to the discovery of incriminating evidence. The directive itself may not betray any knowledge petitioner may have about the circumstances of the offenses being investigated by the grand jury, but it nevertheless purports to evidence a reasoned decision by Doe to authorize action by others. The forced execution of this document differs from the forced production of physical evidence just as human beings differ from other animals.[36]

If John Doe can be compelled to use his mind to assist the Government in developing its case, I think he will be forced "to be a witness against himself." The fundamental purpose of the Fifth Amendment was to mark the line between the kind of inquisition conducted by the Star Chamber and what we proudly describe as our accusatorial system of justice. It reflects "our respect for the inviolability of the human personality." "[I]t is an explicit right of a

---

The dissent apparently disagrees with us on this point, although the basis for its disagreement is unclear. Surely, the fact that the executed form creates "a new piece of evidence that may be used against petitioner" is not relevant to whether the execution has testimonial significance, for the same could be said about the voice and writing exemplars the Court found were not testimonial in nature. ...

[36] [Dissent's footnote 1:] The forced production of physical evidence, which we have condoned, see *Gilbert* v. *California*, 388 U.S. 263 (1967) (handwriting exemplar); *United States* v. *Wade*, 388 U.S. 218 (1967) (voice exemplar); *Schmerber* v. *California*, 384 U.S. 757 (1966) (blood test); *Holt* v. *United States*, 218 U.S. 245 (1910) (lineup), involves no intrusion upon the contents of the mind of the accused. See *Schmerber*, 384 U.S., at 765 (forced blood test permissible because it does not involve "even a shadow of testimonial compulsion upon or enforced communication by the accused"). The forced execution of a document that purports to convey the signer's authority, however, does invade the dignity of the human mind; it purports to communicate a deliberate command. The intrusion on the dignity of the individual is not diminished by the fact that the document does not reflect the true state of the signer's mind. Indeed, that the assertions petitioner is forced to utter by executing the document are false, causes an even greater violation of human dignity. For the same reason a person cannot be forced to sign a document purporting to authorize the entry of judgment against himself, I do not believe he can be forced to sign a document purporting to authorize the disclosure of incriminating evidence. In both cases the accused is being compelled "to be a witness against himself"; indeed, here he is being compelled to bear false witness against himself.

The expression of the contents of an individual's mind falls squarely within the protection of the Fifth Amendment. ...

natural person, protecting the realm of human thought and expression." In my opinion that protection gives John Doe the right to refuse to sign the directive authorizing access to the records of any bank account that he may control. ...

Notes

1. Why is there no question about "compulsion" in this case? How is Doe's case distinguishable from Fisher's in this respect? In arguing this case, how did the parties try to work around existing Supreme Court precedents?

2. The government is seeking to force Doe to say something in writing as opposed to speaking. Is that the reason why Doe loses? May the government force the defendant to write, rather than relate through testimony, a confession? Why did the Supreme Court believe that the forced action in this case was more akin to a compelled handwriting exemplar than to compelled testimony (oral or written)?

3. Do you believe that this case is more analogous to forcing a defendant "to surrender a key to a strongbox containing incriminating documents" or to compelling him "to reveal the combination to his wall safe"? Although even the dissent accepts that the former is not a violation of the Fifth Amendment, should it be—at least on these facts? *See United States v. Hubbell, infra* (Thomas, J., concurring) ("A substantial body of evidence suggests that the Fifth Amendment privilege protects against compelled production not just of incriminating testimony, but of any incriminating evidence."). Does it trouble you that the government can force an investigatory target to endorse a document that purports to give a consent that the target vigorously denies in hopes of securing evidence to convict the target?

4. Can the government force an individual to de-encrypt the contents of his computers? Would the act of de-encryption be a "testimonial communication"? *See, e.g., In re* Grand Jury Subpoena Duces Tecum, 670 F.3d 1335 (11th Cir. 2012) (yes); Commonwealth v. Gelfgatt, 11 N.E.2d 605 (Mass. 2014) (yes but foregone conclusion doctrine applied). Would it make a difference if one de-encrypted through use of a fingerprint as opposed to a code?

E. HOW "INCRIMINATING" MUST THE COMMUNICATION BE

HOFFMAN v. UNITED STATES
341 U.S. 479 (1951)

MR. JUSTICE CLARK delivered the opinion of the Court.

Petitioner has been convicted of criminal contempt for refusing to obey a federal court order requiring him to answer certain questions asked in a grand jury investigation. He raises here important issues as to the application of the privilege against self-incrimination under the Fifth Amendment, claimed to justify his refusal.

A special federal grand jury was convened at Philadelphia on September 14, 1950, to investigate frauds upon the Federal Government, including violations of the customs, narcotics and internal revenue liquor laws of the United States, the White Slave Traffic Act, perjury, bribery, and other federal criminal laws, and conspiracy to commit all such offenses. In response to subpoena petitioner appeared to testify on the day the grand jury was empaneled, and was examined on October 3. The pertinent interrogation, in which he refused to answer, follows:

> "Q. What do you do now, Mr. Hoffman?
> "A. I refuse to answer.
> "Q. Have you been in the same undertaking since the first of the year?
> "A. I don't understand the question.

"Q. Have you been doing the same thing you are doing now since the first of the year?

"A. I refuse to answer.

"Q. Do you know Mr. William Weisberg?

"A. I do.

"Q. How long have you known him?

"A. Practically twenty years, I guess.

"Q. When did you last see him?

"A. I refuse to answer.

"Q. Have you seen him this week?

"A. I refuse to answer.

"Q. Do you know that a subpoena has been issued for Mr. Weisberg?

"A. I heard about it in Court.

"Q. Have you talked with him on the telephone this week?

"A. I refuse to answer.

"Q. Do you know where Mr. William Weisberg is now?

"A. I refuse to answer."

It was stipulated that petitioner declined to answer on the ground that his answers might tend to incriminate him of a federal offense. ...

The privilege afforded [by the Fifth Amendment] not only extends to answers that would in themselves support a conviction under a federal criminal statute but likewise embraces those which would furnish a link in the chain of evidence needed to prosecute the claimant for a federal crime. But this protection must be confined to instances where the witness has reasonable cause to apprehend danger from a direct answer. The witness is not exonerated from answering merely because he declares that in so doing he would incriminate himself—his say-so does not of itself establish the hazard of incrimination. It is for the court to say whether his silence is justified, and to require him to answer if "it clearly appears to the court that he is mistaken." However, if the witness, upon interposing his claim, were required to prove the hazard in the sense in which a claim is usually required to be established in court, he would be compelled to surrender the very protection which the privilege is designed to guarantee. To sustain the privilege, it need only be evident from the implications of the question, in the setting in which it is asked, that a responsive answer to the question or an explanation of why it cannot be answered might be dangerous because injurious disclosure could result. The trial judge in appraising the claim "must be governed as much by his personal perception of the peculiarities of the case as by the facts actually in evidence."

What were the circumstances which the District Court should have considered in ruling upon petitioner's claim of privilege? This is the background as indicated by the record:

The judge who ruled on the privilege had himself impaneled the special grand jury to investigate "rackets" in the district. He had explained to the jury that "the Attorney General's office has come into this district to conduct an investigation ... [that] will run the gamut of all crimes covered by Federal statute." ... Subpoenas had issued for some twenty witnesses, but only eleven had been served; as the prosecutor put it, he was "having trouble finding some big shots." ... The prosecutor had requested bench warrants for eight of the nine who had not appeared the first day of the session, one of whom was William Weisberg. Petitioner had admitted having known Weisberg for about twenty years. In addition, counsel for petitioner had advised the court that "It has been broadly published that [petitioner] has a police record."   ...

... [T]he court should have recognized, in considering the Weisberg questions, that one person with a police record summoned to testify before a grand jury investigating the rackets might be hiding or helping to hide another person of questionable repute sought as a witness. To be sure, the Government may inquire of witnesses before the grand jury as to the whereabouts of unlocated witnesses; ordinarily the answers to such questions are harmless if not fruitless. But of the seven questions relating to Weisberg (of which three were answered), three were designed to draw information as to petitioner's contacts and connection with the fugitive witness; and the final question, perhaps an afterthought of the prosecutor, inquired of

Weisberg's whereabouts at the time. All of them could easily have required answers that would forge links in a chain of facts imperiling petitioner with conviction of a federal crime. The three questions, if answered affirmatively, would establish contacts between petitioner and Weisberg during the crucial period when the latter was eluding the grand jury; and in the context of these inquiries the last question might well have called for disclosure that Weisberg was hiding away on petitioner's premises or with his assistance. Petitioner could reasonably have sensed the peril of prosecution for federal offenses ranging from obstruction to conspiracy.

In this setting it was not "*perfectly clear*, from a careful consideration of all the circumstances in the case, that the witness is mistaken, and that the answer[s] *cannot possibly* have such tendency" to incriminate. ...

Notes

1. A defendant does not forfeit or waive her ability to rely on her Fifth Amendment right when she denies all culpability. *See* Ohio v. Reiner, 532 U.S. 17 (2001) (*per curiam*). In *Reiner*, the Supreme Court stated:

> We have held that the privilege's protection extends only to witnesses who have "reasonable cause to apprehend danger from a direct answer." That inquiry is for the court; the witness' assertion does not by itself establish the risk of incrimination. A danger of "imaginary and unsubstantial character" will not suffice. But we have never held, as the Supreme Court of Ohio did, that the privilege is unavailable to those who claim innocence. To the contrary, we have emphasized that one of the Fifth Amendment's "basic functions ... is to protect *innocent* men ... 'who otherwise might be ensnared by ambiguous circumstances.'" [We have] recognized that truthful responses of an innocent witness, as well as those of a wrongdoer, may provide the government with incriminating evidence from the speaker's own mouth.

Id. at 21.

F. "ACT OF PRODUCTION" IMMUNITY: *FISHER* REVISITED

UNITED STATES v. HUBBELL
530 U.S. 27 (2000)

JUSTICE STEVENS delivered the opinion of the Court.

The two questions presented concern the scope of a witness' protection against compelled self-incrimination: (1) whether the Fifth Amendment privilege protects a witness from being compelled to disclose the existence of incriminating documents that the Government is unable to describe with reasonable particularity; and (2) if the witness produces such documents pursuant to a grant of immunity, whether 18 U.S.C. § 6002 prevents the Government from using them to prepare criminal charges against him.

This proceeding arises out of the second prosecution of respondent, Webster Hubbell, commenced by the Independent Counsel appointed in August 1994 to investigate possible violations of federal law relating to the Whitewater Development Corporation. The first prosecution was terminated pursuant to a plea bargain. In December 1994, respondent pleaded guilty to charges of mail fraud and tax evasion arising out of his billing practices as a member of an Arkansas law firm from 1989 to 1992, and was sentenced to 21 months in prison. In the plea agreement, respondent promised to provide the Independent Counsel with "full, complete, accurate, and truthful information" about matters relating to the Whitewater investigation.

The second prosecution resulted from the Independent Counsel's attempt to determine whether respondent had violated that promise. In October 1996, while respondent was incarcerated, the Independent Counsel served him with a subpoena *duces tecum* calling for the production of 11 categories of documents before a grand jury sitting in Little Rock, Arkansas. On November 19, he appeared before the grand jury and invoked his Fifth Amendment privilege against self-incrimination. In response to questioning by the prosecutor, respondent initially refused "to state whether there are documents within my possession, custody, or control responsive to the Subpoena." Thereafter, the prosecutor produced an order, which had previously been obtained from the District Court pursuant to 18 U.S.C. § 6003(a), directing him to respond to the subpoena and granting him immunity "to the extent allowed by law." Respondent then produced 13,120 pages of documents and records and responded to a series of questions that established that those were all of the documents in his custody or control that were responsive to the commands in the subpoena, with the exception of a few documents he claimed were shielded by the attorney-client and attorney work-product privileges.

The contents of the documents produced by respondent provided the Independent Counsel with the information that led to this second prosecution. On April 30, 1998, a grand jury in the District of Columbia returned a 10-count indictment charging respondent with various tax-related crimes and mail and wire fraud. The District Court dismissed the indictment relying, in part, on the ground that the Independent Counsel's use of the subpoenaed documents violated § 6002 because all of the evidence he would offer against respondent at trial derived either directly or indirectly from the testimonial aspects of respondent's immunized act of producing those documents. Noting that the Independent Counsel had admitted that he was not investigating tax-related issues when he issued the subpoena, and that he had "'learned about the unreported income and other crimes from studying the records' contents,'" the District Court characterized the subpoena as "the quintessential fishing expedition."

The Court of Appeals vacated the judgment and remanded for further proceedings. The majority concluded that the District Court had incorrectly relied on the fact that the Independent Counsel did not have prior knowledge of the contents of the subpoenaed documents. The question the District Court should have addressed was the extent of the Government's independent knowledge of the documents' existence and authenticity, and of respondent's possession or control of them. It explained:

> "On remand, the district court should hold a hearing in which it seeks to establish the extent and detail of the [G]overnment's knowledge of Hubbell's financial affairs (or of the paperwork documenting it) on the day the subpoena issued. It is only then that the court will be in a position to assess the testimonial value of Hubbell's response to the subpoena. Should the Independent Counsel prove capable of demonstrating with reasonable particularity a prior awareness that the exhaustive litany of documents sought in the subpoena existed and were in Hubbell's possession, then the wide distance evidently traveled from the subpoena to the substantive allegations contained in the indictment would be based upon legitimate intermediate steps. To the extent that the information conveyed through Hubbell's compelled act of production provides the necessary linkage, however, the indictment deriving therefrom is tainted."

In the opinion of the dissenting judge, the majority failed to give full effect to the distinction between the contents of the documents and the limited testimonial significance of the act of producing them. In his view, as long as the prosecutor could make use of information contained in the documents or derived therefrom without any reference to the fact that respondent had produced them in response to a subpoena, there would be no improper use of the testimonial aspect of the immunized act of production. In other words, the constitutional privilege and the statute conferring use immunity would only shield the witness from the use of any information resulting from his subpoena response "beyond what the prosecutor would receive if the documents appeared in the grand jury room or in his office unsolicited and unmarked, like manna from heaven." ...

Acting pursuant to 18 U.S.C. § 6002, the District Court entered an order compelling respondent to produce "any and all documents" described in the grand jury subpoena and granting him "immunity to the extent allowed by law." In *Kastigar v. United States*, 406 U.S. 441 (1972), we upheld the constitutionality of § 6002 because the scope of the "use and derivative-use" immunity that it provides is coextensive with the scope of the constitutional privilege against self-incrimination. ...

The "compelled testimony" that is relevant in this case is not to be found in the contents of the documents produced in response to the subpoena. It is, rather, the testimony inherent in the act of producing those documents. The disagreement between the parties focuses entirely on the significance of that testimonial aspect.

The Government correctly emphasizes that the testimonial aspect of a response to a subpoena *duces tecum* does nothing more than establish the existence, authenticity, and custody of items that are produced. We assume that the Government is also entirely correct in its submission that it would not have to advert to respondent's act of production in order to prove the existence, authenticity, or custody of any documents that it might offer in evidence at a criminal trial; indeed, the Government disclaims any need to introduce any of the documents produced by respondent into evidence in order to prove the charges against him. It follows, according to the Government, that it has no intention of making improper "use" of respondent's compelled testimony.

The question, however, is not whether the response to the subpoena may be introduced into evidence at his criminal trial. That would surely be a prohibited "use" of the immunized act of production. But the fact that the Government intends no such use of the act of production leaves open the separate question whether it has already made "derivative use" of the testimonial aspect of that act in obtaining the indictment against respondent and in preparing its case for trial. It clearly has.

It is apparent from the text of the subpoena itself that the prosecutor needed respondent's assistance both to identify potential sources of information and to produce those sources. Given the breadth of the description of the 11 categories of documents called for by the subpoena, the collection and production of the materials demanded was tantamount to answering a series of interrogatories asking a witness to disclose the existence and location of particular documents fitting certain broad descriptions. The assembly of literally hundreds of pages of material in response to a request for "any and all documents reflecting, referring, or relating to any direct or indirect sources of money or other things of value received by or provided to" an individual or members of his family during a 3-year period is the functional equivalent of the preparation of an answer to either a detailed written interrogatory or a series of oral questions at a discovery deposition. Entirely apart from the contents of the 13,120 pages of materials that respondent produced in this case, it is undeniable that providing a catalog of existing documents fitting within any of the 11 broadly worded subpoena categories could provide a prosecutor with a "lead to incriminating evidence," or "a link in the chain of evidence needed to prosecute."

Indeed, the record makes it clear that that is what happened in this case. The documents were produced before a grand jury sitting in the Eastern District of Arkansas in aid of the Independent Counsel's attempt to determine whether respondent had violated a commitment in his first plea agreement. The use of those sources of information eventually led to the return of an indictment by a grand jury sitting in the District of Columbia for offenses that apparently are unrelated to that plea agreement. What the District Court characterized as a "fishing expedition" did produce a fish, but not the one that the Independent Counsel expected to hook. It is abundantly clear that the testimonial aspect of respondent's act of producing subpoenaed documents was the first step in a chain of evidence that led to this prosecution. The documents did not magically appear in the prosecutor's office like "manna from heaven." They arrived there only after respondent asserted his constitutional privilege, received a grant of immunity, and—under the compulsion of the District Court's order—took the mental and physical steps necessary to provide the prosecutor with an accurate inventory of the many sources of potentially incriminating evidence sought by the subpoena. It was only through respondent's truthful reply to the subpoena that the Government received the incriminating documents of which it made "substantial use ... in the investigation that led to the indictment."

For these reasons, we cannot accept the Government's submission that respondent's immunity did not preclude its derivative use of the produced documents because its "possession of the documents [was] the fruit *only* of a simple physical act—the act of producing the documents." It was unquestionably necessary for respondent to make extensive use of "the contents of his own mind" in identifying the hundreds of documents responsive to the requests in the subpoena. The assembly of those documents was like telling an inquisitor the combination to a wall safe, not like being forced to surrender the key to a strongbox. The Government's anemic view of respondent's act of production as a mere physical act that is principally non-testimonial in character and can be entirely divorced from its "implicit" testimonial aspect so as to constitute a "legitimate, wholly independent source" (as required by *Kastigar*) for the documents produced simply fails to account for these realities.

In sum, we have no doubt that the constitutional privilege against self-incrimination protects the target of a grand jury investigation from being compelled to answer questions designed to elicit information about the existence of sources of potentially incriminating evidence. That constitutional privilege has the same application to the testimonial aspect of a response to a subpoena seeking discovery of those sources. Before the District Court, the Government arguably conceded that respondent's act of production in this case had a testimonial aspect that entitled him to respond to the subpoena by asserting his privilege against self-incrimination. On appeal and again before this Court, however, the Government has argued that the communicative aspect of respondent's act of producing ordinary business records is insufficiently "testimonial" to support a claim of privilege because the existence and possession of such records by any businessman is a "foregone conclusion" under our decision in *Fisher v. United States*, 425 U.S., at 411. This argument both misreads *Fisher* and ignores our subsequent decision in *United States v. Doe*, 465 U.S. 605 (1984).

... *Fisher* involved summonses seeking production of working papers prepared by the taxpayers' accountants that the IRS knew were in the possession of the taxpayers' attorneys. In rejecting the taxpayers' claim that these documents were protected by the Fifth Amendment privilege, we stated:

> "It is doubtful that implicitly admitting the existence and possession of the papers rises to the level of testimony within the protection of the Fifth Amendment. The papers belong to the *accountant*, were prepared by him, and are the kind usually prepared by an accountant working on the tax returns of his client. Surely the Government is in no way relying on the 'truthtelling' of the *taxpayer* to prove the existence of or his access to the documents.... The existence and location of the papers are a foregone conclusion and the taxpayer adds little or nothing to the sum total of the Government's information by conceding that he in fact has the papers." ([E]mphases added).

Whatever the scope of this "foregone conclusion" rationale, the facts of this case plainly fall outside of it. While in *Fisher* the Government already knew that the documents were in the attorneys' possession and could independently confirm their existence and authenticity through the accountants who created them, here the Government has not shown that it had any prior knowledge of either the existence or the whereabouts of the 13,120 pages of documents ultimately produced by respondent. The Government cannot cure this deficiency through the overbroad argument that a businessman such as respondent will always possess general business and tax records that fall within the broad categories described in this subpoena. The *Doe* subpoenas also sought several broad categories of general business records, yet we upheld the District Court's finding that the act of producing those records would involve testimonial self-incrimination.

Given our conclusion that respondent's act of production had a testimonial aspect, at least with respect to the existence and location of the documents sought by the Government's subpoena, respondent could not be compelled to produce those documents without first receiving a grant of immunity under § 6003. As we construed § 6002 in *Kastigar*, such immunity is coextensive with the constitutional privilege. *Kastigar* requires that respondent's motion to dismiss the indictment on immunity grounds be granted unless the Government proves that the evidence it used in obtaining the indictment and proposed to use at trial was derived from legitimate sources "wholly independent" of the testimonial aspect of respondent's immunized conduct in assembling and producing the documents described in the subpoena. The Government, however, does not claim that it could make such a showing. Rather, it contends that its prosecution of respondent must be considered proper unless someone—presumably respondent—shows that "there is some substantial relation between the compelled testimonial communications implicit in the act of production (as opposed to the act of production standing alone) and some aspect of the information used in the investigation or the evidence presented at trial." We could not accept this submission without repudiating the basis for our conclusion in *Kastigar* that the statutory guarantee of use and derivative-use immunity is as broad as the constitutional privilege itself. This we are not prepared to do.

CHIEF JUSTICE REHNQUIST dissents and would reverse the judgment of the Court of Appeals in part, for the reasons given by Judge Williams in his dissenting opinion in that court, 167 F.3d 552, 597 (C.A.D.C.1999).

JUSTICE THOMAS, with whom JUSTICE SCALIA joins, concurring.

Our decision today involves the application of the act-of-production doctrine, which provides that persons compelled to turn over incriminating papers or other physical evidence pursuant to a subpoena *duces tecum* or a summons may invoke the Fifth Amendment privilege against self-incrimination as a bar to production only where the act of producing the evidence would contain "testimonial" features. I join the opinion of the Court because it properly applies this doctrine, but I write separately to note that this doctrine may be inconsistent with the original meaning of the Fifth Amendment's Self-Incrimination Clause. A substantial body of evidence suggests that the Fifth Amendment privilege protects against the compelled production not just of incriminating testimony, but of any incriminating evidence. In a future case, I would be willing to reconsider the scope and meaning of the Self-Incrimination Clause. ...

This Court has not always taken the approach to the Fifth Amendment that we follow today. The first case interpreting the Self-Incrimination Clause—*Boyd v. United States*—was decided, though not explicitly, in accordance with the understanding that "witness" means one who gives evidence. In *Boyd*, this Court unanimously held that the Fifth Amendment protects a defendant against compelled production of books and papers. And the Court linked its interpretation of the Fifth Amendment to the common-law understanding of the self-incrimination privilege.

But this Court's decision in *Fisher v. United States*, 425 U.S. 391 (1976), rejected this understanding, permitting the Government to force a person to furnish incriminating physical evidence and protecting only the "testimonial" aspects of that transfer. In so doing, *Fisher* not only failed to examine the historical backdrop to the Fifth Amendment, it also required—as illustrated by extended discussion in the opinions below in this case—a difficult parsing of the act of responding to a subpoena *duces tecum*.

None of the parties in this case has asked us to depart from *Fisher*, but in light of the historical evidence that the Self-Incrimination Clause may have a broader reach than *Fisher* holds, I remain open to a reconsideration of that decision and its progeny in a proper case.[37]

---

[37] [Concurrence's footnote 6:] To hold that the Government may not compel a person to produce incriminating evidence (absent an appropriate grant of immunity) does not necessarily answer the question whether (and, if so, when) the Government may secure that same evidence through a search or seizure. The lawfulness of such actions, however, would be measured by the Fourth Amendment rather than the Fifth.

Notes

1. *Foregone Conclusion Doctrine.* Recall that *Fisher* holds that the contents of pre-existing records are irrelevant because they are not "compelled" and the Fifth Amendment is not a general guarantor of any privacy interests individuals may have in such records. All that is "compelled" under *Fisher* is the act of production. If that act of production is not sufficiently "testimonial" because the facts of existence, possession, authenticity, or responsiveness are "foregone conclusions" due to the government's knowledge of those facts, there is no valid claim of privilege. Late in the *Hubbell* opinion the Court rejects an argument that Hubbell essentially had no Fifth Amendment privilege and that the immunity grant was therefore unnecessary because the existence and location of the documents at issue were "foregone conclusions." What was the government's argument, and what does the Court's response suggest as to the scope of the "foregone conclusion" exception?

Since *Hubbell*, a number of circuits have employed a "reasonable particularity" standard in testing whether the "foregone conclusion" doctrine applies. For example, in *In re* Grand Jury Subpoena, Dated April 18, 2003, 383 F.3d 905 (9th Cir. 2004), the Ninth Circuit stated that "[t]he government was not required to have actual knowledge of the existence and location of each and every responsive document; the government was required, however, to establish the existence of the documents sought and and Doe's possession of them with 'reasonable particularity' before the existence and possession of the documents could be considered a foregone conclusion and production therefore would not be testimonial." *Id.* at 910; *see also, e.g.,* United States v. Sideman & Bancroft, LLP, 704 F.3d 1197, 1203 (9th Cir. 2013); *In re* Grand Jury Subpoena Duces Tecum Dated March 25, 2011, 670 F.3d 1335 (11th Cir. 2012); United States v. Pond, 454 F.3d 313, 324-27 (D.C.Cir. 2006).

2. *Derivative Use Problems.* Hubbell was given statutory "act of production" immunity under § 6002. That section, of course, bars "use and derivative use" of the testimonial communication compelled by the immunity grant. The government was therefore clearly barred from making any "use" of Hubbell's act of producing the documents and of the implied assertions of fact underlying that production (*i.e.,* existence, possession, authenticity, responsiveness, and, apparently after *Hubbell,* location of the records requested). The question here is whether the government made "derivative use" of the documents in preparing its case against Hubbell, a question the Court answered in the affirmative. What was that "derivative use"? Was it relying on the *contents* of those documents (even if the government said it would not make *evidentiary* use of those contents)?

Note that although this case was decided in the context of determining the scope of use and derivative use "act of production" immunity, it also has relevance to the questions that confront lawyers *before* the grant of any immunity. The relevance is that, as the Supreme Court constantly reiterates, the scope of use and derivative use immunity is co-extensive with the scope of the Fifth Amendment right itself. The *Hubbell* decision is relevant to the issue of whether the subject of a subpoena duces tecum has a right to resist production in at least two respects (explored further in notes 4 and 5 below): (1) in providing a new ground upon which to argue that the "act of production" is "testimonial"; and (2) extending the scope of what will be deemed an "incriminating" act of production.

3. *What is "Testimonial" About an Act of Production?* The Court repeatedly references the fact that the very broad subpoena required Hubbell to use the contents of his mind to identify and then to disclose the existence and location of particular documents responsive to the subpoena. The subpoena in this case was not unusual—at least in many white-collar cases—in its breadth or in the quantity of records sought to be produced. *See, e.g.,* Lance Cole, *The Fifth Amendment and Compelled Production of Personal Documents After United States v. Hubbell-New Protection for Private Papers?,* 29 Am. J. Crim. L. 123, 164-65 (2002). The Court's determination that Hubbell had to use the contents of his mind to assemble the documents responsive to the subpoena, then, would seem to be applicable to many subpoena productions in white-collar cases. In each such case, the subpoena recipient should be able to argue, based on *Hubbell,* that her act of production is necessarily "testimonial" (regardless of whether it communicates information the government already had with respect to existence, possession, authenticity, location, etc.)

because she used the contents of her mind to determine what was and what was not responsive the subpoena.

4. *What was "Incriminating"?* Readers will recall that in *Fisher* the Court indicated that if the possession, existence, etc. of business records—without regard to their content—was not "incriminating," that that element would not be satisfied. And because, as in *Fisher*, it is almost never "incriminating" to have, for example, possession of tax worksheets (again, without reference to their content), this was always fatal the Fifth Amendment claim. *See Fisher, infra* (concluding that "it is not illegal to seek accounting help ... [and] we are quite unprepared to hold either the fact of existence of the papers or of their possession by the taxpayer poses any realistic threat of incrimination to the taxpayer").

Hubbell radically changed this result by transplanting *Hoffman's* "link in the chain" analysis—previously only employed in cases of actual witness testimony—to document production cases. Thus, the *Hubbell* Court noted, the "testimonial aspect of respondent's act of producing subpoenaed documents was the first step in a chain of evidence that led to this prosecution" apparently because it led the Independent Counsel to additional "sources of potentially incriminating information."

Justice Stevens, writing for the majority in *Hubbell*, returned to the analogy he employed in his dissent in *Doe, supra*. He concluded that "[t]he assembly of ... documents [responsive to the subpoena] was like telling an inquisitor the combination to a wall safe, not like being forced to surrender the key to the strongbox." The majority opinion further states that, "[i]n sum, we have no doubt that the constitutional privilege against self-incrimination protects the target of a grand jury investigation from being compelled to answer questions designed to elicit information about the existence of sources of potentially incriminating evidence. That constitutional privilege has the same application to the testimonial aspect of a response to a subpoena seeking discovery of those sources." Is this summary inconsistent with the reasoning of the *Doe* majority?

5. *Relevance of "Contents"?* Note that it must be the compelled testimonial communication at issue that is the link in the chain. Was it Hubbell's *use of the contents of his mind to identify documents responsive to the subpoena* that was a "link in the chain" to this derivative evidence, or was it the *contents* of those documents that gave the government leads? Did the *Hubbell* decision make the *contents* of subpoenaed records relevant once more?

As noted, the opinion focuses on the fact that the use of the contents of Hubbell's mind in compiling the documents produced derivatively led the government to other sources of information. But those sources were only revealed by reading the *contents* of the documents, correct? One will find no statement to that effect in the *Hubbell* decision itself, but other courts since *Hubbell* have made the connection. In *United States v. Ponds*, 454 F.3d 313 (D.C. Cir. 2006), for example, the D.C. Circuit explained:

> With act-of-production immunity, the key question is whether, despite the compelled testimony implicit in the production, the government remains free to use the *contents* of the (non-testimonial) produced documents. In *Hubbell*, the Supreme Court rejected the "manna from heaven" theory by holding the use of the *contents* of produced documents to be a barred derivative use of the compelled testimonial act of production. ... In context, [the Court's] statements indicate that the Supreme Court understands the *contents* of the documents to be off-limits because they are a derivative use of the compelled testimony regarding the existence, location, and possession of the documents.

Id. at 321 (emphasis added). In short, the "contents" of the subpoenaed records *are* once again relevant under *Hubbell*—if the required production is testimonial, that testimonial communication will provide a "link in the chain" to incriminating *contents*, thus enabling the subject of the subpoena to assert her Fifth Amendment right. It would seem, then, that we are back to pre-*Fisher* results, if not reasoning. Why didn't the Court save us all a great deal of bother and simply overrule *Fisher*?

6. *Law Enforcement.* What are the implications of the Court's decision for law enforcement? Professor Lance Cole has argued that, after *Fisher*, the common understanding was that the

privilege against self-incrimination did not protect the contents of documentary evidence that pre-existed the issuance of the subpoena and thus was not said to be "compelled" within the meaning of the Fifth Amendment. The "conventional wisdom in white collar criminal investigations [was] that most documents are not within the protections of the Fifth Amendment privilege against self-incrimination. Documents [were] routinely produced to grand juries by individuals who [were] the subjects or targets of the grand jury's investigation in response to subpoenas duces tecum without any assertion of Fifth Amendment privilege—whether as to the contents of the documents or the act of producing the documents." Cole, *supra*, at 126-27.

As a practical matter, then, the Fifth Amendment provided no more protection to documents called for by subpoena than those seized pursuant to a search warrant. Accordingly, white-collar prosecutors relied predominantly on subpoenas, rather than search warrants, to seize relevant evidence except in cases where there was some reason to fear that the evidence was at risk of destruction or the government did not trust the grand jury subjects and their counsel to respond honestly to the subpoena. *See id.* at 127. The advantages of proceeding by subpoena from the government's perspective are many, and include the fact that subpoenas can be issued by a prosecutor without the approval of any judicial officer, do not carry with them the probable cause and particularity requirements that apply to search warrants under the Fourth Amendment, and generally require much less time and effort to issue than warrants. *See id.* Professor Lance suggests, however, that

> when private documents in the possession of an individual are sought by the government, neither of these assumptions[—that the contents of pre-existing documents generally are not protected by the Fifth Amendment privilege against self-incrimination and that subpoenas are the easiest and best way for prosecutors to obtain documentary evidence—]necessarily remains valid after the Supreme Court's decision in *United States v. Hubbell.* ... [T]he *Hubbell* decision effectively, if not explicitly, overruled *Fisher* in cases where prosecutors are seeking private documents from an individual. After *Hubbell*, prosecutors no longer can use a grand jury subpoena duces tecum and a grant of "act of production immunity" to compel production of documents by an individual who is a subject or target of a grand jury investigation without risking the loss of their ability to prosecute that individual.
>
> Therefore, contrary to conventional wisdom, after *Hubbell*, prosecutors in many cases may be better off using search warrants to obtain personal documents from individuals who are subjects or targets of an investigation—if, that is, they can satisfy the Fourth Amendment's particularity and probable cause requirements. If prosecutors cannot satisfy these Fourth Amendment requirements, then after *Hubbell* they cannot use the contents of truly private, personal documents in a prosecution of the individual whom they compel to produce the documents. These changes flow directly from the *Hubbell* decision, and they represent a major "power shift" from prosecutors to defense counsel in white-collar criminal investigations and prosecutions.

Id. at 129-30; *see also* Aaron M. Clemens, *The Pending Reinvigoration of* Boyd: *Personal Papers are Protected by the Privilege Against Self-Incrimination*, 25 N. Ill. U. L. Rev. 75 (2004).

7. Justices Thomas and Scalia reserve a fundamental question—whether the Fifth Amendment privilege "protects against the compelled production not just of incriminating testimony, but of any incriminating evidence." They cite *Boyd* for the proposition that "witness" within the meaning of the Fifth Amendment "means one who gives evidence," not just one who makes "testimonial communications." If the Court were to revisit this issue and adopt this approach, would it be forced to overrule *Fisher? Doe?* Would it affect the collective entity doctrine and cases such as *Braswell?* Would it prohibit the government from forcing the targets of investigations to provide handwriting exemplars, blood samples, or other physical evidence?

The Chabots' additional contention that no accountholder keeps records of the maximum annual values of his overseas accounts is unpersuasive. Maximum annual account values are simply account balances, and account owners typically keep these numbers on record.

The Chabots further argue that even if there are some accountholders who maintain the records that § 1010.420 requires them to keep, they do not retain these records for the five-year period that § 1010.420 mandates. The Chabots, however, misunderstand the inquiry that this prong of the required records exception entails. The "customarily kept" analysis simply asks whether individuals typically would maintain the information that the law requires them to keep, not the length of time for which they normally would do so absent the requirement. The Chabots fail to cite any case in which the length of time for which someone usually kept a document affected the court's holding on whether or not the document was customarily kept, and we have been unable to identify any such case. Furthermore, here, we do not deal with an extraordinarily long time period, but rather one that seems appropriate for taxation and similar purposes. ...

3. Public Aspects

The Chabots contend that their account records do not have public aspects because owning a foreign bank account is not a public activity. It is undeniable that an individual who holds an overseas account normally does not think of his account records as being equivalent to public records. Nevertheless, "[t]he fact that documents have privacy protections elsewhere does not transform those documents into private documents" for all purposes. We note that several circuits have reasoned that records required to be kept under a valid, civil regulatory scheme (i.e., meet prong one of the *Grosso* test) automatically have "public aspects" sufficient to meet the third prong. We need not adopt such a broad holding to conclude that the documents requested here have sufficient "public aspects" to meet the third prong of the *Grosso* test.

As discussed earlier under the first prong of the *Grosso* test, § 1010.420 is a valid, civil regulatory scheme, and the Chabots voluntarily participated in the regulated activity, namely foreign banking. When accountholders such as the Chabots voluntarily engage in foreign banking, they effectively waive their Fifth Amendment privilege to prevent the government's compelled disclosure of their account records. *See M.H.*, 648 F.3d at 1078 (relying on this consent theory in concluding that the appellant's account records satisfied the public aspects prong of the *Grosso* test); [*In re Special Feb. 2011-1 Grand Jury Subpoena*, 691 F.3d 903, 909 (7th Cir. 2012)] ("The voluntary choice to engage in an activity that imposes record-keeping requirements under a valid civil regulatory scheme carries consequences, perhaps the most significant of which ... is the possibility that those records might have to be turned over upon demand, notwithstanding any Fifth Amendment privilege."); *cf. Smith v. Richert*, 35 F.3d 300, 303 (7th Cir. 1994) (holding that production of certain documents necessary to determine personal income tax liability were not within required records exception, because "[t]he decision to become a taxpayer cannot be thought voluntary ... [as] [a]lmost anyone who works is a taxpayer, along with many who do not"). The government circulates the data from these records to several government agencies, which use this information for a number of important noncriminal purposes. *See Under Seal*, 737 F.3d at 335, 337 (concluding that the records kept pursuant to § 1010.420 possess public aspects given the Treasury Department's circulation of this data to other government agencies for the purpose of implementing economic, monetary, and regulatory public policies). Through these processes, the Chabots' account records acquire public aspects.

The Chabots contend that the absence of a licensing requirement for foreign banking necessarily means that their account records do not have public aspects. This argument, however, does nothing to advance the Chabots' case, because private activities that do not require licenses still may be subject to the required records exception. We conclude that the records sought in this case are sufficiently imbued with "public aspects" to satisfy the third prong of the required records exception.[38] Thus all three prongs are met.

Conclusion

The Chabots have failed to raise valid policy or other reasons as to why their account records should not be included in the required records exception to the Fifth Amendment privilege. Because § 1010.420 is essentially regulatory, requires account owners to retain records that they customarily keep, and requires retention of records that have public aspects, we will affirm the District Court's grant of the IRS's petition.

Note

1. Since 2009, the IRS and DOJ have been launching civil and criminal investigations targeting foreign bank account reporting as a result of the 2009 landmark deferred prosecution agreement the United States reached with Switzerland's largest bank, UBS AG. Under the federal Bank Secrecy Act every "resident or citizen of the United States or a person in, and doing business in, the United States" is required to keep records and file reports about transactions with foreign financial institutions. 31 U.S.C. § 5314(a); 31 C.F.R. §§ 1010.350 (reporting requirement), 1010.420 (required record keeping). U.S. taxpayers are required to file these reports on what is known as an "FBAR" annually. Failure to file the FBAR form carries draconian civil penalties. Willful failure to file a FBAR can also be prosecuted criminally and carries the potential for up to five years' imprisonment for each year that the account holder failed to file. Given these penalties, persons with foreign bank accounts who have not filed FBAR forms are reluctant to concede the existence of such accounts by complying with government subpoenas for the type of account records they are required by law to keep. U.S. taxpayers have fought production on Fifth Amendment grounds, arguing that complying with the summons effectively forced them to incriminate themselves, as the requested information was all the IRS needed to charge them with willful failure to report overseas accounts.

At least six circuits agree with the *Chabot* holding—in cases that, unlike *Chabot*, concern grand jury subpoenas designed to further a criminal investigation. Obviously, under these decisions, individuals who have foreign bank accounts will have to produce account records even if this production seals their fate. This is because the "required records" doctrine is conceptualized as an "exception" to the Fifth Amendment's protection—that is, it is by definition applied when the person asserting the Fifth has otherwise satisfied all elements of the privilege against compelled self-incrimination. *In re* Special Feb. 2011-1 Grand Jury Subpoena, 691 F.3d 903, 908 (7th Cir. 2012).

Most taxpayers have unsuccessfully argued that the "public"/"private" records distinction central to the required records doctrine is obsolete after *Fisher* dispensed with the *Boyd* doctrine. *See, e.g., In re* Grand Jury Subpoena Dated Feb. 2, 2012, 741 F.3d 339, 345-47 (2d Cir. 2013). What is the modern rationale for the doctrine? What are its limits? Do you agree with Justice Frankfurter, in dissent in *Shapiro*, that "[i]f Congress by the easy device of requiring a man to keep the private papers that he has customarily kept can render such papers 'public' and nonprivileged, there is little left to either the right of privacy or the constitutional privilege"? 335 U.S. at 70 (Frankfurter, J., dissenting).

---

[38] [Court's footnote 8:] As the interstate commerce power gives Congress the authority to prohibit foreign banking, Congress could impose the lesser restriction of a licensing requirement on foreign banking. Obviously, this kind of scheme would be considerably more burdensome than § 1010.420's current recordkeeping requirements.

Does the required records exception apply to public employees called upon to produce public records? *See, e.g.,* N.J. Legislative Select Comm. on Investigation v. Kelly, Docket No. L-350-14, Opinion (N.J. Superior Ct., Mercer Co. April 9, 2014) ("BridgeGate" investigation).

Chapter 17

THE ATTORNEY-CLIENT PRIVILEGE AND THE WORK PRODUCT DOCTRINE IN A CORPORATE SETTING

In part because entities lack a Fifth Amendment privilege against compelled self-incrimination, the protections offered by the attorney-client privilege and the work product doctrine are of critical importance in white-collar defense practice, particularly in the context of internal corporate investigations. The following material explores when these protections may be invoked, and how they may be lost, in the corporate setting. It is worth noting that, quite apart from the legal rules considered below, recent developments in the policies and practices of federal prosecutors and the institution of the federal organizational sentencing guidelines may profoundly affect the practical availability of attorney-client or work product protections in this setting. Many defense counsel believe that "[t]he sound you hear coming from the corridors of the Department of Justice is a requiem marking the death of privilege in corporate criminal investigations."[1] Increasingly frequent governmental suggestions—explicit or implicit—that corporations waive otherwise applicable privileges if they wish to avoid indictment[2] or gain credit at sentencing for cooperating with the government[3] are cited as the principal impetus for the "death" of corporate privileges. Readers should consider the wisdom of these policies given the legal standards and policies discussed throughout this chapter.

In this context, as in any other, the attorney-client privilege applies only if:

(1) the asserted holder of the privilege is or sought to become a client; (2) the person to whom the communication was made (a) is a member of the bar of a court, or his subordinate and (b) in connection with this communication is acting as a lawyer; (3) the communication relates to a fact of which the attorney was informed (a) by his client (b) without the presence of strangers (c) for the purpose of securing primarily either (i) an opinion on law or (ii) legal services or (iii) assistance in some legal proceeding, and not (d) for the purpose of committing a crime or tort; and (4) the privilege has been (a) claimed and (b) not waived by the client.[4]

---

[1] David M. Zornow & Keith D. Krakaur, *On the Brink of a Brave New World: The Death of Privilege in Corporate Criminal Investigations*, 37 Am. Crim. L. Rev. 147, 147 (2000).

[2] *See* Chapter 4 (Entity Liability; DOJ Corporate Charging Policy; "Filip Memo" (aka Principles of Federal Prosecution of Business Organizations (2008)).

[3] *See id.* (U.S. Sentencing Guidelines: Organizational Sentencing).

[4] United States v. United Shoe Machinery Corp., 89 F.Supp. 357, 358-59 (D. Mass. 1950).

"There may be some overlap, but the work product doctrine 'is distinct from and broader than the attorney-client privilege.'"[5] It is not restricted to "communications" between client and counsel, encompassing material "obtained or prepared by an adversary's counsel" in the course of his legal work, provided that the work was done "with an eye toward litigation."[6] "And because it looks to promote the vitality of the adversary system rather than simply seeking to promote communication through confidentiality, the work product privilege is not automatically waived by any disclosure to a third party."[7] Finally, "only the client may assert the attorney-client privilege while both the attorney and the client may invoke the work product doctrine."[8]

In addition to discussing the question of the scope and availability of these protections in different contexts, this chapter addresses the critical question of waiver and, in so doing, focuses on Federal Rule of Evidence 502. As the Advisory Committee that drafted the rule summarized:

- *Limitations on Scope of Waiver.* Subdivision (a) provides that if a waiver is found, it applies only to the information disclosed, unless a broader waiver is made necessary by the holder's intentional and misleading use of privileged or protected communications or information.

- *Protections Against Inadvertent Disclosure.* Subdivision (b) provides that an inadvertent disclosure of privileged or protected communications or information, when made at the federal level, does not operate as a waiver if the holder took reasonable steps to prevent such a disclosure and employed reasonably prompt measures to retrieve the mistakenly disclosed communications or information.

- *Effect on State Proceedings and Disclosures Made in State Courts.* Subdivision (c) provides that 1) if there is a disclosure of privileged or protected communications or information at the federal level, then state courts must honor Rule 502 in subsequent state proceedings; and 2) if there is a disclosure of privileged or protected communications or information in a state proceeding, then admissibility in a subsequent federal proceeding is determined by the law that is most protective against waiver.

- *Orders Protecting Privileged Communications Binding on Non-Parties.* Subdivision (d) provides that if a federal court enters an order providing that a disclosure of privileged or protected communications or information does not constitute a waiver, that order is enforceable against all persons and entities in any federal or state proceeding. This provision allows parties in an action in which such an order is entered to limit their costs of pre-production privilege review.

- *Agreements Protecting Privileged Communications Binding on Parties.* Subdivision (e) provides that parties in a federal proceeding can enter into a confidentiality agreement providing for mutual protection against waiver in that proceeding. While those agreements bind the signatory parties, they are not binding on non-parties unless incorporated into a court order.[9]

---

[5] *In re* Antitrust Grand Jury, 805 F.2d 155, 163 (6th Cir. 1986) (*quoting* United States v. Nobles, 422 U.S. 225, 238 n. 11 (1975)).

[6] Hickman v. Taylor, 329 U.S. 495, 511 (1947).

[7] *In re* Sealed Case, 676 F.2d 793, 809 (D.C. Cir. 1982); *see also In re* Grand Jury Proceedings, 43 F.3d 966, 970 (5th Cir. 1994).

[8] *In re* Antitrust Grand Jury, 805 F.2d at 163.

[9] Federal Rule of Evidence 502, Advisory Comm. Notes, Explanatory Note (Rev. 11/28/07).

Finally, the chapter concludes with an inquiry into the crime-fraud exception and the rules governing assertions of privilege by governmental actors.

A. QUALIFYING FOR PROTECTION

UPJOHN CO. v. UNITED STATES
449 U.S. 383 (1981)

JUSTICE REHNQUIST delivered the opinion of the Court.

...

Petitioner Upjohn Co. manufactures and sells pharmaceuticals here and abroad. In January 1976 independent accountants conducting an audit of one of Upjohn's foreign subsidiaries discovered that the subsidiary made payments to or for the benefit of foreign government officials in order to secure government business. The accountants so informed petitioner Mr. Gerard Thomas, Upjohn's Vice President, Secretary, and General Counsel. Thomas is a member of the Michigan and New York Bars, and has been Upjohn's General Counsel for 20 years. He consulted with outside counsel and R. T. Parfet, Jr., Upjohn's Chairman of the Board. It was decided that the company would conduct an internal investigation of what were termed "questionable payments." As part of this investigation the attorneys prepared a letter containing a questionnaire which was sent to "All Foreign General and Area Managers" over the Chairman's signature. The letter began by noting recent disclosures that several American companies made "possibly illegal" payments to foreign government officials and emphasized that the management needed full information concerning any such payments made by Upjohn. The letter indicated that the Chairman had asked Thomas, identified as "the company's General Counsel," "to conduct an investigation for the purpose of determining the nature and magnitude of any payments made by the Upjohn Company or any of its subsidiaries to any employee or official of a foreign government." The questionnaire sought detailed information concerning such payments. Managers were instructed to treat the investigation as "highly confidential" and not to discuss it with anyone other than Upjohn employees who might be helpful in providing the requested information. Responses were to be sent directly to Thomas. Thomas and outside counsel also interviewed the recipients of the questionnaire and some 33 other Upjohn officers or employees as part of the investigation.

On March 26, 1976, the company voluntarily submitted a preliminary report to the Securities and Exchange Commission on Form 8-K disclosing certain questionable payments. A copy of the report was simultaneously submitted to the Internal Revenue Service, which immediately began an investigation to determine the tax consequences of the payments. Special agents conducting the investigation were given lists by Upjohn of all those interviewed and all who had responded to the questionnaire. On November 23, 1976, the Service issued a summons pursuant to 26 U.S.C. § 7602 demanding production of:

> "All files relative to the investigation conducted under the supervision of Gerard Thomas to identify payments to employees of foreign governments and any political contributions made by the Upjohn Company or any of its affiliates since January 1, 1971 and to determine whether any funds of the Upjohn Company had been improperly accounted for on the corporate books during the same period.
> "The records should include but not be limited to written questionnaires sent to managers of the Upjohn Company's foreign affiliates, and memorandums or notes of the interviews conducted in the United States and abroad with officers and employees of the Upjohn Company and its subsidiaries."

The company declined to produce the documents specified in the second paragraph on the grounds that they were protected from disclosure by the attorney-client privilege and constituted the work product of attorneys prepared in anticipation of litigation. [The government sought enforcement of the summons, and the District Court ordered that] ... the summons should be enforced. Petitioners appealed to the Court of Appeals for the Sixth Circuit which rejected the Magistrate's finding of a waiver of the attorney-client privilege, but agreed that the privilege did not apply "[t]o the extent that the communications were made by officers and agents not responsible for directing Upjohn's actions in response to legal advice ... for the simple reason that the communications were not the 'client's.'" The court reasoned that accepting petitioners' claim for a broader application of the privilege would encourage upper-echelon management to ignore unpleasant facts and create too broad a "zone of silence." Noting that Upjohn's counsel had interviewed officials such as the Chairman and President, the Court of Appeals remanded to the District Court so that a determination of who was within the "control group" could be made. ...

Federal Rule of Evidence 501 provides that "the privilege of a witness ... shall be governed by the principles of the common law as they may be interpreted by the courts of the United States in light of reason and experience." The attorney-client privilege is the oldest of the privileges for confidential communications known to the common law. Its purpose is to encourage full and frank communication between attorneys and their clients and thereby promote broader public interests in the observance of law and administration of justice. The privilege recognizes that sound legal advice or advocacy serves public ends and that such advice or advocacy depends upon the lawyer's being fully informed by the client. ... "The lawyer-client privilege rests on the need for the advocate and counselor to know all that relates to the client's reasons for seeking representation if the professional mission is to be carried out." ... [W]e [have] recognized the purpose of the privilege to be "to encourage clients to make full disclosure to their attorneys." ... Admittedly complications in the application of the privilege arise when the client is a corporation, which in theory is an artificial creature of the law, and not an individual; but this Court has assumed that the privilege applies when the client is a corporation, *United States v. Louisville & Nashville R. Co.*, 236 U.S. 318, 336 (1915), and the Government does not contest the general proposition.

The Court of Appeals, however, considered the application of the privilege in the corporate context to present a "different problem," since the client was an inanimate entity and "only the senior management, guiding and integrating the several operations, ... can be said to possess an identity analogous to the corporation as a whole." The first case to articulate the so-called "control group test" adopted by the court below, *Philadelphia v. Westinghouse Electric Corp.*, 210 F.Supp. 483, 485 (E.D.Pa.[1962]), reflected a similar conceptual approach:

> "Keeping in mind that the question is, Is it the corporation which is seeking the lawyer's advice when the asserted privileged communication is made?, the most satisfactory solution, I think, is that if the employee making the communication, of whatever rank he may be, is in a position to control or even to take a substantial part in a decision about any action which the corporation may take upon the advice of the attorney, ... then, in effect, *he is (or personifies) the corporation* when he makes his disclosure to the lawyer and the privilege would apply." (Emphasis supplied.)

Such a view, we think, overlooks the fact that the privilege exists to protect not only the giving of professional advice to those who can act on it but also the giving of information to the lawyer to enable him to give sound and informed advice. The first step in the resolution of any legal problem is ascertaining the factual background and sifting through the facts with an eye to the legally relevant. See ABA Code of Professional Responsibility, Ethical Consideration 4-1:

> "A lawyer should be fully informed of all the facts of the matter he is handling in order for his client to obtain the full advantage of our legal system. It is for the lawyer in the exercise of his independent professional judgment to separate the relevant and important from the irrelevant and unimportant. The observance of the ethical obligation of a lawyer to hold inviolate the confidences and secrets of his client not only facilitates the full development of facts essential to proper representation of the client but also encourages laymen to seek early legal assistance."

In the case of the individual client the provider of information and the person who acts on the lawyer's advice are one and the same. In the corporate context, however, it will frequently be employees beyond the control group as defined by the court below— "officers and agents ... responsible for directing [the company's] actions in response to legal advice"—who will possess the information needed by the corporation's lawyers. Middle-level—and indeed lower-level—employees can, by actions within the scope of their employment, embroil the corporation in serious legal difficulties, and it is only natural that these employees would have the relevant information needed by corporate counsel if he is adequately to advise the client with respect to such actual or potential difficulties. ...

The control group test adopted by the court below thus frustrates the very purpose of the privilege by discouraging the communication of relevant information by employees of the client to attorneys seeking to render legal advice to the client corporation. The attorney's advice will also frequently be more significant to noncontrol group members than to those who officially sanction the advice, and the control group test makes it more difficult to convey full and frank legal advice to the employees who will put into effect the client corporation's policy.

The narrow scope given the attorney-client privilege by the court below not only makes it difficult for corporate attorneys to formulate sound advice when their client is faced with a specific legal problem but also threatens to limit the valuable efforts of corporate counsel to ensure their client's compliance with the law. In light of the vast and complicated array of regulatory legislation confronting the modern corporation, corporations, unlike most individuals, "constantly go to lawyers to find out how to obey the law," particularly since compliance with the law in this area is hardly an instinctive matter.[10] The test adopted by the court below is difficult to apply in practice, though no abstractly formulated and unvarying "test" will necessarily enable courts to decide questions such as this with mathematical precision. But if the purpose of the attorney-client privilege is to be served, the attorney and client must be able to predict with some degree of certainty whether particular discussions will be protected. An uncertain privilege, or one which purports to be certain but results in widely varying applications by the courts, is little better than no privilege at all. The very terms of the test adopted by the court below suggest the unpredictability of its application. The test restricts the availability of the privilege to those officers who play a "substantial role" in deciding and directing a corporation's legal response. Disparate decisions in cases applying this test illustrate its unpredictability.

---

[10] [Court's footnote 9:] The Government argues that the risk of civil or criminal liability suffices to ensure that corporations will seek legal advice in the absence of the protection of the privilege. This response ignores the fact that the depth and quality of any investigations to ensure compliance with the law would suffer, even were they undertaken. The response also proves too much, since it applies to all communications covered by the privilege: an individual trying to comply with the law or faced with a legal problem also has strong incentive to disclose information to his lawyer, yet the common law has recognized the value of the privilege in further facilitating communications.

The communications at issue were made by Upjohn employees to counsel for Upjohn acting as such, at the direction of corporate superiors in order to secure legal advice from counsel. As the Magistrate found, "Mr. Thomas consulted with the Chairman of the Board and outside counsel and thereafter conducted a factual investigation to determine the nature and extent of the questionable payments *and to be in a position to give legal advice to the company with respect to the payments.*" (Emphasis supplied.) Information, not available from upper-echelon management, was needed to supply a basis for legal advice concerning compliance with securities and tax laws, foreign laws, currency regulations, duties to shareholders, and potential litigation in each of these areas. The communications concerned matters within the scope of the employees' corporate duties, and the employees themselves were sufficiently aware that they were being questioned in order that the corporation could obtain legal advice. The questionnaire identified Thomas as "the company's General Counsel" and referred in its opening sentence to the possible illegality of payments such as the ones on which information was sought. A statement of policy accompanying the questionnaire clearly indicated the legal implications of the investigation. The policy statement was issued "in order that there be no uncertainty in the future as to the policy with respect to the practices which are the subject of this investigation." It began "Upjohn will comply with all laws and regulations," and stated that commissions or payments "will not be used as a subterfuge for bribes or illegal payments" and that all payments must be "proper and legal." Any future agreements with foreign distributors or agents were to be approved "by a company attorney" and any questions concerning the policy were to be referred "to the company's General Counsel." This statement was issued to Upjohn employees worldwide, so that even those interviewees not receiving a questionnaire were aware of the legal implications of the interviews. Pursuant to explicit instructions from the Chairman of the Board, the communications were considered "highly confidential" when made, and have been kept confidential by the company. Consistent with the underlying purposes of the attorney-client privilege, these communications must be protected against compelled disclosure.

The Court of Appeals declined to extend the attorney-client privilege beyond the limits of the control group test for fear that doing so would entail severe burdens on discovery and create a broad "zone of silence" over corporate affairs. Application of the attorney-client privilege to communications such as those involved here, however, puts the adversary in no worse position than if the communications had never taken place. The privilege only protects disclosure of communications; it does not protect disclosure of the underlying facts by those who communicated with the attorney:

> "[T]he protection of the privilege extends only to *communications* and not to facts. A fact is one thing and a communication concerning that fact is an entirely different thing. The client cannot be compelled to answer the question, 'What did you say or write to the attorney?' but may not refuse to disclose any relevant fact within his knowledge merely because he incorporated a statement of such fact into his communication to his attorney."

Here the Government was free to question the employees who communicated with Thomas and outside counsel. Upjohn has provided the IRS with a list of such employees, and the IRS has already interviewed some 25 of them. While it would probably be more convenient for the Government to secure the results of petitioner's internal investigation by simply subpoenaing the questionnaires and notes taken by petitioner's attorneys, such considerations of convenience do not overcome the policies served by the attorney-client privilege. As Justice Jackson noted in his concurring opinion in *Hickman v. Taylor*, [329 U.S. 495, 516 (1947)]: "Discovery was hardly intended to enable a learned profession to perform its functions ... on wits borrowed from the adversary."

Needless to say, we decide only the case before us, and do not undertake to draft a set of rules which should govern challenges to investigatory subpoenas. Any such approach would violate the spirit of Federal Rule of Evidence 501. While such a "case-by-case" basis may to some slight extent undermine desirable certainty in the boundaries of the attorney-client privilege, it obeys the spirit of the Rules. At the same time we conclude that the narrow "control group test" sanctioned by the Court of Appeals, in this case cannot, consistent with "the principles of the common law as ... interpreted ... in the light of reason and experience," Fed. Rule Evid. 501, govern the development of the law in this area.

Our decision that the communications by Upjohn employees to counsel are covered by the attorney-client privilege disposes of the case so far as the responses to the questionnaires and any notes reflecting responses to interview questions are concerned. The summons reaches further, however, and Thomas has testified that his notes and memoranda of interviews go beyond recording responses to his questions. To the extent that the material subject to the summons is not protected by the attorney-client privilege as disclosing communications between an employee and counsel, we must reach the ruling by the Court of Appeals that the work-product doctrine does not apply to summonses issued under 26 U.S.C. § 7602.

... [T]he work-product doctrine does apply to IRS summonses. This doctrine was announced by the Court over 30 years ago in *Hickman v. Taylor*. In that case the Court rejected "an attempt, without purported necessity or justification, to secure written statements, private memoranda and personal recollections prepared or formed by an adverse party's counsel in the course of his legal duties." The Court noted that "it is essential that a lawyer work with a certain degree of privacy" and reasoned that if discovery of the material sought were permitted

> "much of what is now put down in writing would remain unwritten. An attorney's thoughts, heretofore inviolate, would not be his own. Inefficiency, unfairness and sharp practices would inevitably develop in the giving of legal advice and in the preparation of cases for trial. The effect on the legal profession would be demoralizing. And the interests of the clients and the cause of justice would be poorly served." ...

... While conceding the applicability of the work-product doctrine, the Government asserts that it has made a sufficient showing of necessity to overcome its protections. The Magistrate apparently so found. The Government relies on the following language in *Hickman*:

> "We do not mean to say that all written materials obtained or prepared by an adversary's counsel with an eye toward litigation are necessarily free from discovery in all cases. Where relevant and nonprivileged facts remain hidden in an attorney's file and where production of those facts is essential to the preparation of one's case, discovery may properly be had .... And production might be justified where the witnesses are no longer available or can be reached only with difficulty."

The Government stresses that interviewees are scattered across the globe and that Upjohn has forbidden its employees to answer questions it considers irrelevant. The above-quoted language from *Hickman*, however, did not apply to "oral statements made by witnesses ... whether presently in the form of [the attorney's] mental impressions or memoranda." As to such material the Court did "not believe that any showing of necessity can be made under the circumstances of this case so as to justify production .... If there should be a rare situation justifying production of these matters petitioner's case is not of that type." Forcing an attorney to disclose notes and memoranda of witnesses' oral statements is particularly disfavored because it tends to reveal the attorney's mental processes.

Rule 26 accords special protection to work product revealing the attorney's mental processes. The Rule permits disclosure of documents and tangible things constituting attorney work product upon a showing of substantial need and inability to obtain the equivalent without undue hardship. This was the standard applied by the Magistrate. Rule 26 goes on, however, to state that "[i]n ordering discovery of such materials when the required showing has been made, the court shall protect against disclosure of the mental impressions, conclusions, opinions or legal theories of an attorney or other representative of a party concerning the litigation." Although this language does not specifically refer to memoranda based on oral statements of witnesses, the *Hickman* court stressed the danger that compelled disclosure of such memoranda would reveal the attorney's mental processes. It is clear that this is the sort of material the draftsmen of the Rule had in mind as deserving special protection.

Based on the foregoing, some courts have concluded that *no* showing of necessity can overcome protection of work product which is based on oral statements from witnesses. Those courts declining to adopt an absolute rule have nonetheless recognized that such material is entitled to special protection.

We do not decide the issue at this time. It is clear that the Magistrate applied the wrong standard when he concluded that the Government had made a sufficient showing of necessity to overcome the protections of the work-product doctrine. The Magistrate applied the "substantial need" and "without undue hardship" standard articulated in the first part of Rule 26(b)(3). The notes and memoranda sought by the Government here, however, are work product based on oral statements. If they reveal communications, they are, in this case, protected by the attorney-client privilege. To the extent they do not reveal communications, they reveal the attorneys' mental processes in evaluating the communications. As Rule 26 and *Hickman* make clear, such work product cannot be disclosed simply on a showing of substantial need and inability to obtain the equivalent without undue hardship.

While we are not prepared at this juncture to say that such material is always protected by the work-product rule, we think a far stronger showing of necessity and unavailability by other means than was made by the Government or applied by the Magistrate in this case would be necessary to compel disclosure. ...

Notes

1. The *Upjohn* court accepted, based on the government's concession, the foundational proposition that corporations should be able to claim the attorney-client privilege. Is this a question that deserved greater consideration? *See, e.g.*, Radiant Burners, Inc. v. American Gas Ass'n, 320 F.2d 314 (7th Cir. 1963) (holding that corporation could claim the attorney-client privilege and discussing sources debating the question). "In large part, the Court based its analysis on two critical, yet unsupported, assumptions about the behavior of corporate actors: first, that application of the privilege in the corporate setting does, in fact, induce corporate clients to provide their attorneys with information that, absent the privilege, they would not provide and second, that once attorneys inform corporate decisionmakers of the demands of the law, the decisionmakers will conform their behavior to those demands voluntarily." John E. Sexton, *A Post-*Upjohn *Consideration of the Corporate Attorney-Client Privilege*, 57 N.Y.U. L. Rev. 443, 444 (1982). Are these assumptions valid? The Court also rejects in a footnote the government's argument that "the risk of civil or criminal liability suffices to ensure that corporations will seek legal advice in the absence of the protection of the privilege." Is the Court's reasoning persuasive? Readers should assess these questions in light of the discussion of corporate internal investigations in Chapter 4, *supra*, as well as the rules (especially the waiver standards) and recent developments outlined throughout this chapter. *See also* Julie R.

O'Sullivan, *Does the DOJ's Compelled-Voluntary Privilege Waivers Policy Threaten the Rationales Underlying the Attorney-Client Privilege or the Word Product Doctrine? A Preliminary "No"*, 45 Am. Crim. L. Rev. 1237 (2008); Julie R. O'Sullivan, *The Last Straw: The Department of Justice's Privilege Waiver Policy and the Death of Adversarial Justice in Criminal Investigations of Corporations*, 57 DePaul L. Rev. 329 (2008).

2. The *Upjohn* Court rejected the "control group" test employed by some courts to determine, in the corporate context, just who constitutes the client for attorney-client privilege purposes. What, if any, "test" did the Court adopt in its stead? What factors were important to the Court's conclusion that the privilege applied in *Upjohn*? *See, e.g.*, Baxter Travenol Labs., Inc. v. Lemay, 89 F.R.D. 410 (S.D. Ohio 1981).

When evidence of corporate wrongdoing is discovered, a corporation may undertake a formal internal investigation into the matter, often under the instruction and direction of the Board of Directors or a subcommittee thereof. Many will mirror the internal investigation in *Upjohn*, although large-scale or particularly sensitive investigations are often conducted by outside rather than in-house counsel. The primary reasons for such investigations are: the increase in enforcement actions against corporate actors; the need to uncover and stop illegal employee conduct; the belief that an investigation will allow the corporation to respond quickly to any government investigation, to formulate its defenses, and effectively to weigh the merits and demerits of disclosing the wrongdoing or cooperating with any government investigation; and the perceived willingness of the government to treat more leniently organizations that actively seek to investigate and respond appropriately to employee wrongdoing. At the conclusion of the investigation, a report in some form is generally rendered to the corporate client. Assuming that the *Upjohn* requirements have been satisfied, normally the report of an internal corporate investigation, and the materials underlying it, will be protected by the attorney-client privilege and/or the work product doctrine.

The protected nature of such reports is critical because, absent such protection, the reports may well provide prosecutors and regulators with a roadmap to corporate liability. Further, "such information will be welcome fodder for the use of plaintiffs' counsel in what surely will be endlessly ensuing civil litigation and massive attorneys' fees for a company. ... There is a real danger that the release of privileged information could trigger a 'feeding frenzy' of civil litigation." *Counsel Group Assails Prosecution Policy Compelling Corporations to Waive Privileges*, 67 Crim. L. Rep. (BNA) 391, 393 (June 14, 2000) (quoting letter of American Corporate Counsel Association).

3. Who is the "client" when the shareholders of a corporation sue the corporation and seek attorney-client privileged materials? In the seminal case of *Garner v. Wolfinbarger*, 430 F.2d 1093 (5th Cir. 1970), the court addressed the question of "the availability to a corporation of the privilege against disclosure of communications between it and its attorney, when access to the communications is sought by stockholders of the corporation ... charging the corporation and its officers with acts injurious to their interests as stockholders." *Id.* at 1095. The Fifth Circuit declined to adopt an absolute rule—either the absolute bar on disclosure sought by the corporation or the absolute access claimed by the stockholders. *Id.* at 1098. In so doing, it recognized legitimate corporate interests against disclosure: "The managerial preference [that it confer with counsel without the risk of having the communications revealed at the instance of dissatisfied stockholders] is a rational one, because it is difficult to envision the management of any sizable corporation pleasing all of its stockholders all of the time, and management desires protection from those who might second-guess or even harass in matters purely of judgment." *Id.* at 1101. On the other hand, the court reasoned, "it must be borne in mind that management does not manage for itself and that the beneficiaries of its action are the stockholders. ... [M]anagement judgment must stand on its merits, not behind an ironclad veil of secrecy which under all circumstances preserves it from being questioned by those for whom it is, at least in part, exercised." *Id.* at 1101. The Fifth Circuit concluded:

... The attorney-client privilege still has viability for the corporate client. The corporation is not barred from asserting it merely because those demanding information enjoy the status of stockholders. But where the corporation is in a suit against its stockholders on charges of acting inimically to stockholder interests, protection of those interests as well as those of the corporation and of the public require that the availability of the privilege be subject to the right of the stockholders to show cause why it should not be invoked in a particular instance.

Id. at 1103-04; *see also id.* at 1104 (articulating criteria for assessing whether good cause has been shown). Does this rule make sense? The circuits seem in accord in applying the *Garner* analysis to stockholders' attempts to pierce the corporate attorney-client privilege, although some apply *Garner* only where the suit at issue is a shareholder derivative suit, *see, e.g.*, Weil v. Investment/Indicators, Research & Management, 647 F.2d 18 (9th Cir. 1981), while others permit plaintiffs to pursue a *Garner* disclosure theory even where the suit is brought by individuals for their own benefit rather than on behalf of the corporation. *See, e.g.*, Fausek v. White, 965 F.2d 126, 129 (6th Cir. 1992); Ward v. Succession of Freeman, 854 F.2d 780, 786 (5th Cir. 1988); *cf.* Cox v. Administrator U.S. Steel & Carnegie, 17 F.3d 1386, 1413-16 (11th Cir. 1994) (examining applicability of *Garner* in context where union asserts privilege against plaintiff union members). Some courts also refuse to apply the *Garner* analysis to work product, reasoning that "[t]he work product privilege is based on the existence of an adversarial relationship, not the quasi-fiduciary relationship analogized in *Garner*." *In re* Int'l Sys. & Controls Corp. Sec. Litig., 693 F.2d 1235, 1239 (5th Cir. 1982); *see also Cox*, 17 F.3d 1386.

    4. The *Upjohn* Court notes, but does not resolve, the question of what showing, if any, will be sufficient to force disclosure of "opinion" work product—that is, "the mental impressions, conclusions, opinions, or legal theories ... of [a party or its representative] concerning the litigation." The Circuits appear to be split on this issue. *Compare* Duplan Corp. v. Moulinage et Retorderie de Chavanoz, 509 F.2d 730, 734 (4th Cir. 1974) (opinion work product never discoverable), *with* Holmgren v. State Farm Mut. Auto. Ins. Co., 976 F.2d 573, 577 (9th Cir. 1992) (rejecting *Duplan* bar). Given the rationale underlying the work product doctrine, what *should* be the result?

    5. Invocation of the attorney-client privilege and work product doctrine must be founded on the provision of legal services. For example, in *In re Grand Jury Subpoenas Date March 9, 2001*, 179 F. Supp.2d 270 (S.D.N.Y. 2001), Judge Chin in the U.S. District Court for the Southern District of New York held that lawyers representing Marc Rich in connection with his presidential pardon application could not rely on the work product doctrine or attorney-client privilege to withhold testimony or documentary evidence. The court explained:

Here, once Rich and Green decided to seek presidential pardons, the Marc Rich Lawyers ceased providing legal services in an adversarial context. They faced no opposing parties or adversaries and the pardon proceedings were entirely *ex parte*. Rich and Green had been fugitives for some 17 years, the parties had reached an impasse, and it was clear that there would be no further litigation of the criminal charges. The Marc Rich Lawyers were acting principally as lobbyists, working with public relations specialists and individuals—foreign government officials, prominent citizens, and personal friends of the President—who had access to the White House. They were not acting as lawyers or providing legal advice in the traditional sense. Accordingly, the objections based on the work product doctrine and the attorney-client privilege are overruled. ...

Id. at 274.

    It is worth stressing that, to be protected by the attorney-client privilege and work product doctrine, internal corporate investigations of the type employed in *Upjohn* must be pursued for the purpose of securing legal advice (attorney-client) or done in anticipation of litigation (work product). "To the extent that an internal corporate investigation is made by management itself, there is no attorney-client privilege, and by the same token, no work-product protection." *In re* Grand Jury Subpoena Dated Dec. 19, 1978, 599 F.2d 504, 510 (2d Cir. 1979). Even where attorneys are involved in the investigation, the attorney-client privilege "is triggered only by a client's request for legal, as contrasted with business, advice." *In re* Grand Jury Subpoena Duces Tecum (Marc Rich & Co.), 731 F.2d 1032, 1037 (2d Cir. 1984); *see also* H. Lowell Brown, *The Crime-Fraud Exception to the Attorney-Client Privilege in the Context of Corporate Counseling*, 87 Ky. L.J. 1191, 1204-06 & n.38 (1998-99). Similarly, "'[m]aterials assembled in the ordinary course of business ... or for other nonlitigation purposes'" do not qualify for work product protection. *See, e.g.,* Simon v. G.D. Searle & Co., 816 F.2d 397, 401 (8th Cir. 1987) (quoting Fed. R. Civ. P. 26(b)(3) advisory committee notes). Although the pendency of litigation is not necessary for a finding that a certain document was prepared in anticipation of litigation, the prospect of litigation must be real and specific, rather than speculative. *See, e.g.,* United States v. Adlman, 68 F.3d 1495, 1501-02 (2d Cir. 1995); National Union Fire Ins. Co. v. Murray Sheet Metal Co., Inc., 967 F.2d 980, 984 (4th Cir. 1992).

Problems often arise because "legal and business considerations may frequently be inextricably intertwined." Coleman v. American Broadcasting Co., 106 F.R.D. 201, 206 (D.D.C. 1985). The intersection between business and legal considerations becomes particularly problematic in two recurring situations: where non-attorney third parties are brought in to assist in the formulation of legal advice or in the context of an internal corporate investigation; and where legal advice or investigations are sought both in contemplation of litigation and for business purposes. The following notes consider these issues, first in regard to the attorney-client privilege and second in relation to the work product doctrine.

6. In the attorney-client context, a question often presented is whether the attorney-client privilege will extend to counsel's consultations with expert third parties, such as accountants or investment bankers, in the course of an internal corporate investigation of past wrongdoing or as part of counsel's evaluation of proposed business activities or transactions. "When disclosure to a third party is necessary for the client to obtain informed legal advice, courts have recognized exceptions to the rule that disclosure waives the attorney-client privilege." Westinghouse Electric Corp. v. Republic of the Philippines, 951 F.2d 1414, 1424 (3d Cir. 1991). There is a "small circle of 'others' with whom information may be shared without loss of the privilege (*e.g.,* secretaries, interpreters, counsel for a cooperating co-defendant, a parent present when a child consults a lawyer)." United States v. MIT, 129 F.3d 681, 684 (1st Cir. 1997). Outside this "magic circle," however, courts generally find that disclosure to third parties means that the holder of the privilege has "breached the confidentiality needed to shield its attorney-client communications." United States v. El Paso Co., 682 F.2d 530, 542 (5th Cir. 1982); *see also* United States v. Ruehle, 583 F.3d 600 (9th Cir. 2009) (CFO's statements to corporate attorneys were not made in confidence when it was clear that the information would go to, among others, the auditors).

In the corporate context, the exception made for "interpreters" has been especially important. In a situation such as that presented in *Upjohn*, corporations and their counsel may require expert assistance—particularly forensic accounting expertise—to conduct an internal investigation into alleged corporate wrongdoing. Corporations and their counsel also often seek the assistance of accountants and investment bankers to assist them in determining whether to undertake a given transaction which is likely to be subjected to regulatory scrutiny and eventuate in litigation. *See, e.g.,* United States v. Ackert, 169 F.3d 136 (2d Cir. 1999); United States v. Adlman, 68 F.3d 1495 (2d Cir. 1995) ("*Adlman I*"). The question arises whether communications with such third-party consultants is protected from disclosure.

In *United States v. Kovel*, 296 F.2d 918 (2d Cir. 1961), the court recognized that the attorney-client privilege extended to communications by an attorney's client to an accountant hired by the attorney to assist the attorney in understanding the client's financial information. The court analogized the case to one in which an attorney hires an interpreter to converse with a client who speaks only a language foreign to the attorney. It reasoned that "[a]ccounting concepts are a foreign language to some lawyers in almost all cases, and to almost all lawyers in some cases. Hence, the presence of an accountant ... while the client is relating a complicated tax story to the lawyer, ought not destroy the privilege." *Id.* at 922. The court concluded that "[w]hat is vital to the privilege is that the communication be made *in confidence* for the purpose of obtaining *legal* advice *from the lawyer.* If what is sought is not legal advice but only accounting service ... or if the advice sought is the accountant's rather than the lawyer's, no privilege exists." *Id.*

"Since *Kovel*, the use of outside consultants of all kinds has become so common that counsel routinely speak of 'Kovelling' accountants, investigators and experts. There is now a cottage industry of 'Kovel accountants,' meaning forensic accountants who work with lawyers." Lawrence S. Bader & John J. Tigue, Jr., *Are Corporate Counsel's Talks With Third Parties Privileged?*, 6 Bus. Crimes Bull. No. 6, at 3 (July 1999). The Second Circuit decision in *United States v. Ackert*, 169 F.3d 136 (2d Cir. 1999), however, indicates that there are limits to permissible "Kovelling." In *Ackert*, an investment banking firm, Goldman, Sachs, and Co., approached a corporation with a proposed investment designed to reduce the corporation's tax liability. In-house counsel for the corporation discussed with a Goldman banker (who was also a lawyer but not acting as such), *inter alia*, the potential tax consequences of the deal "so that [counsel] could advise his client ... about the legal and financial complications of the transaction." *Id.* at 138. The corporation paid Goldman $1.5 million for its services rendered in connection with its proposal. *Id.*

The Second Circuit upheld enforcement of an IRS summons for the testimony of the Goldman banker, holding that the attorney-client privilege did not apply. In so doing, the *Ackert* court found that *Kovel* held only that the "inclusion of a third party in attorney-client communications does not destroy the privilege if the purpose of the third party's participation is to improve the comprehension of the communications between attorney and client." *Id.* at 139. Because in-house counsel was not relying on the Goldman banker "to translate or interpret information" given to counsel or his client, but rather "for information [the corporation] did not have about the proposed transaction and its tax consequences," *Kovel* did not apply. *Id.* at 139-40; *see also In re* Lindsey (Grand Jury Testimony), 158 F.3d 1263, 1280-81 (D.C. Cir. 1998). In short, "a communication between an attorney and a third party does not become shielded by the attorney-client privilege solely because the communication proves important to the attorney's ability to represent the client." *Ackert*, 169 F.3d at 139. It is only protected if counsel can demonstrate that third-party expert assistance was needed to permit counsel to communicate effectively with her client.

The government often attempts to characterize the assistance of accounting firms or investment banks as consultants to management, rather than as "interpreters" necessary to allow corporate lawyers to render legal advice. *See, e.g.*, *Adlman I*, 68 F.3d 1495, 1499 (2d Cir. 1995). The burden is on the party seeking the protection of the privilege to make a sufficient record to demonstrate that the expert assistance was provided to allow the lawyer to communicate informed legal advice. *See id.* at 1500. Some have suggested that it may be easier for outside counsel, as opposed to in-house counsel, to carry this burden. *See* Bader & Tigue, *supra*. "The privilege has been held to attach equally to both in-house counsel and outside counsel. However, because of their unique position as both lawyers and employees of the corporation, in-house counsel are often called upon to provide business advice as well as legal counsel. ... [Therefore] communications with in-house counsel have been subjected to stricter and more skeptical scrutiny than similar communications with outside counsel." H. Lowell Brown, *The Crime-Fraud Exception to the*

Attorney-Client Privilege in the Context of Corporate Counseling, 87 Ky. L.J. 1191, 1207-08 (1998-99). Evidence generated at the inception or during the course of the relationship, such as retainer agreements between outside counsel (rather than the client) and the consultant and billing statements evidencing that the work was primarily for legal rather than business purposes, will carry much more weight than after-the-fact affidavits by counsel as to their intentions in seeking expert assistance. *See id.*; see also Sandra T.E. v. South Berwyn School District 100, 600 F.3d 612, 619 (7th Cir. 2010).

7. The work product doctrine may protect the product of communications with third parties even when assertions of attorney-client privilege fail. "The work-product rule shields from disclosure materials prepared 'in anticipation of litigation' by a party, *or the party's representative*, absent a showing of substantial need." *Adlman I*, 68 F.3d at 1501 (emphasis added); *see also In re* Cendant Corp. Secs. Litig., 343 F.3d 658 (3d Cir. 2003). In *Adlman I*, the Second Circuit held that a memorandum prepared by an accounting firm which advised the client corporation on the tax consequences of a proposed corporate reorganization was not protected by the attorney-client privilege. It ruled that the corporation had failed to bear its burden under *Kovel* of establishing that the accounting firm's advice was sought for the purpose of securing legal, as opposed to business, counsel. Subsequently, however, in *United States v. Adlman*, 134 F.3d 1194 (2d Cir. 1998) ("*Adlman II*"), the Second Circuit held that the same memorandum was protected by the work product privilege. In that case, it addressed the specific issue of whether "documents which, although prepared because of expected litigation, are intended to inform a business decision influenced by the prospect of litigation," are prepared "in anticipation of litigation" within the meaning of the work product doctrine. *Id.* at 1197-98.

The *Adlman II* court rejected the standard adopted by some courts that requires that litigation had to be "the primary motivating purpose behind the creation of the document." United States v. Davis, 636 F.2d 1028, 1040 (5th Cir. 1981); *cf.* United States v. Textron Inc., 577 F.3d 21 (1st Cir .2009). Under this standard, the document generally must be prepared to *aid* in litigation to warrant work product protection. The *Adlman II* court instead adopted what appears to be the majority rule, which asks whether the documents were prepared "*because of*" existing or expected litigation. *See Adlman II*, 134 F.3d at 1200-02 (emphasis added). As the *Adlman II* court explained, "[w]here a document is created because of the prospect of litigation, analyzing the likely outcome of that litigation, it does not lose protection under this formulation merely because it is created in order to assist with a business decision." *Id.* at 1202; *see also In re* Grand Jury Subpoena (Mark Torf/Torf Env'l Management), 357 F3d 900, 908 (9th Cir. 2004). Is there a real difference between these two standards? *See id.* at 1199-1200. The Second Circuit's *Adlman II* ruling should assist those entities that enlist expert assistance in situations in which a business issues are inextricably intertwined with litigation considerations.

Adlman II will be of less assistance in another recurring situation alluded to above. Often, internal corporate investigations of alleged wrongdoing may have both litigation and business objectives. That is, they may be conducted *both* to assist in contemplated litigation with the government *and* to serve business interests, such as persuading regulators, customers, suppliers, competitors, or the general public that the wrongdoing was the act of a rogue employee and that the corporation is acting diligently to prevent future occurrences of misconduct. The *Adlman II* court cautioned that "it should be emphasized that the 'because of' formulation that we adopt here withholds protection from documents that are prepared in the ordinary course of business or *that would have been created in essentially similar form irrespective of the litigation.*" *Id.* at 1202 (emphasis added). Does this require that the investigation will not be privileged unless it would not have happened "but for" anticipated litigation?

In a recent high-profile case, *In re* Kellogg Brown & Root Inc., 756 F.3d 754 (D.C. Cir. 2014), the D.C. Circuit answered with an emphatic "no." In that case, a *qui tam* action against a defense contractor under the False Claims Act, the plaintiff relator sought documents relating to the contractor's internal investigation into the alleged fraud. The District Court ordered the production of the materials in part because the internal investigation was undertaken in part to comply with Department of Defense regulations that require defense contractors to maintain compliance programs and conduct internal investigations into allegations of wrongdoing. As the D.C. Circuit explained:

> The District Court began its analysis by reciting the "primary purpose" test, which many courts (including this one) have used to resolve privilege disputes when attorney-client communications may have had both legal and business purposes. But in a key move, the District Court then said that the primary purpose of a communication is to obtain or provide legal advice only if the communication would not have been made "but for" the fact that legal advice was sought. In other words, if there was any other purpose behind the communication, the attorney-client privilege apparently does not apply. The District Court went on to conclude that [the contractor's] internal investigation was "undertaken pursuant to regulatory law and corporate policy rather than for the purpose of obtaining legal advice." Therefore, in the District Court's view, "the primary purpose of" the internal investigation "was to comply with federal defense contractor regulations, not to secure legal advice."
>
> The District Court erred because it employed the wrong legal test. The but-for test articulated by the District Court is not appropriate for attorney-client privilege analysis. Under the District Court's approach, the attorney-client privilege apparently would not apply unless the sole purpose of the communication was to obtain or provide legal advice. That is not the law. ...
>
> In the context of an organization's internal investigation, if one of the significant purposes of the internal investigation was to obtain or provide legal advice, the privilege will apply. That is true regardless of whether an internal investigation was conducted pursuant to a company compliance program required by statute or regulation, or was otherwise conducted pursuant to company policy.

Id. at 758-60.

B. LOSING THE PRIVILEGE: WAIVER

As the First Circuit has noted, "waiver" is a "loose and misleading label for what is in fact a collection of different rules addressed to different problems":[11]

> Cases under this "waiver" heading include situations as divergent as an express and voluntary surrender of the privilege, partial disclosure of a privileged document, selective disclosure.[12]

For ease of analysis, the following sections break many of these waiver cases into three categories:

> (a) cases concerning asserted *"inadvertent"* waivers, in which "unintended" or mistaken disclosures were made of privileged communications or work product and the privilege-holders sought either to reclaim the privileged materials or to restrict the scope of any implied waiver;

---

[11] United States v. MIT, 129 F.3d 681, 684 (1st Cir. 1997).

[12] *Id.*

(b) cases concerning asserted *"partial"* waivers, in which the privilege-holders contended that they waived only a portion of privileged communications or work product by intentionally using or disclosing that portion and that the balance of the communication or work product should be protected; and

(c) cases concerning asserted *"selective"* waivers, in which the privilege-holders asserted that they could intentionally disclose the privileged communications or work product to some persons but not to others.

It should be noted that while some courts use the above terms and draw similar distinctions in analyzing waiver issues,[13] other courts use a variety of labels to describe different types of waivers. Further, courts often do not distinguish for analytical purposes between these different types of waiver theories. Finally, some cases may well fall into a number of different categories where, for example, assertions are made of both "partial" and "selective" waivers.[14] These distinctions may, however, be important if not determinative in determining what waiver standard will be employed.[15]

1. WHO MAY WAIVE?

The first question in the corporate context is who may waive the protections of the attorney-client privilege or the work product doctrine on behalf of the client corporation? In *Commodity Futures Trading Commission v. Weintraub*,[16] the Supreme Court explained that:

> The parties in this case agree that, for solvent corporations, the power to waive the corporate attorney-client privilege rests with the corporation's management and is normally exercised by its officers and directors. The managers, of course, must exercise the privilege in a manner consistent with their fiduciary duty to act in the best interests of the corporation and not of themselves as individuals.
>
> The parties also agree that when control of a corporation passes to new management, the authority to assert and waive the corporation's attorney-client privilege passes as well. New managers installed as a result of a takeover, merger, loss of confidence by shareholders, or simply normal succession, may waive the attorney-client privilege with respect to communications made by former officers and directors. Displaced managers may not assert the privilege over the wishes of current managers, even as to statements that the former might have made to counsel concerning matters within the scope of their corporate duties.[17]

In *Weintraub*, the issue was whether the trustee of a corporation in bankruptcy had the power to waive the debtor corporation's attorney-client privilege with respect to communications that took place before the filing of the bankruptcy petition. The Court held that the trustee had the power to waive, reasoning that in light of the extensive powers and responsibilities of trustees in bankruptcy, "it is clear that the trustee plays the role most closely analogous to that of a solvent corporation's management."[18] Is the *Weintraub* Court's emphasis on the powers and position of the person seeking to waive inconsistent with the Court's

---

[13] *See, e.g.*, Westinghouse Electric Corp. v. Republic of the Philippines, 951 F.2d 1414 (3d Cir. 1991).

[14] *See e.g.*, *In re* Sealed Case, 676 F.2d 793 (D.C. Cir. 1982).

[15] *See, e.g.*, *Westinghouse*, 951 F.2d at 1430-31.

[16] 471 U.S. 343 (1985).

[17] *Id.* at 348.

[18] *Id.* at 353.

rejection of the "control person" test for determining the existence of the privilege in the first instance?

Weintraub dealt with an *express* waiver—the only issue was whether the person seeking to make the waiver was competent to do so on behalf of the corporation. But what rules apply when the government asserts that a court should *imply* a waiver—over the corporation's assertions that no waiver was intended or made—based on the disclosure of privileged information by corporate officers or agents?

The Second Circuit addressed this question in *In re Grand Jury Proceedings (United States v. Doe)*, ultimately concluding that the District Court had applied too liberal a waiver standard and remanding for consideration of additional factors.[19] The *Doe* court declined to adopt a bright-line rule, employing instead a "fairness" approach to determine whether the disclosure of privileged communications by a corporate actor should be imputed to the corporation as an implied waiver. (Such a case-specific approach may be equitable in the circumstances of a given case, but does it ultimately undermine the purposes of the attorney-client privilege and work product doctrine?)

As the Second Circuit explained its approach:

> This court has recognized that implied waiver may be found where the privilege holder "asserts a claim that *in fairness* requires examination of protected communications." We have stated in *In re von Bulow*, [828 F.2d 94, 103 (2d Cir.1987)], and in [*United States v. Bilzerian*, 926 F.2d 1285, 1292 (2d Cir.1991), that fairness considerations arise when the party attempts to use the privilege both as "a shield and a sword." In other words, a party cannot partially disclose privileged communications or affirmatively rely on privileged communications to support its claim or defense and then shield the underlying communications from scrutiny by the opposing party. "The quintessential example is the defendant who asserts an advice-of-counsel defense and is thereby deemed to have waived his privilege with respect to the advice that he received."
>
> Whether fairness requires disclosure has been decided by the courts on a case-by-case basis, and depends primarily on the specific context in which the privilege is asserted. Thus, in *Bilzerian*, we held that a defendant who intended to testify as to his "good faith" reliance on legal advice could not prevent the government from cross-examining him on advice received from counsel. Because the defendant raised the advice-of-counsel defense and sought to rely on privileged information in a judicial setting, the court found that if defendant so testified a broad waiver would be appropriate. By contrast, the D.C. Circuit declined to find a waiver when defendant testified at trial that he lacked the intent to commit the crime because, after meeting with his lawyers, he believed that his actions were lawful. *United States v. White*, 887 F.2d 267, 270-71 (D.C.Cir.1989) (Ginsburg, J.). The *White* court, citing our decision in *In re von Bulow*, concluded that mere denial of *mens rea* through "[a]n averment that lawyers have looked into a matter does not imply an intent to reveal the substance of the lawyers' advice. Where a defendant neither reveals substantive information, nor prejudices the government's case, nor misleads a court by relying on an incomplete disclosure, fairness and consistency do not require the inference of waiver."
>
> We have also recognized that a more limited form of implied waiver may be appropriate where disclosure occurred in a context that did not greatly prejudice the other party in the litigation. Thus, in *In re von Bulow*, we limited the scope of the waiver to

---

19 219 F.3d 175 (2d Cir. 2000); *see also* Velsicol Chemical Corp. v. Parsons, 561 F.2d 671, 675 (7th Cir. 1977) (holding that in-house counsel for the corporation under investigation waived, in his grand jury testimony, the corporation's attorney-client privilege as to conversations with outside counsel even though the corporation had not authorized him to do so). On remand from the Second Circuit, the District Court applied the factors set forth by the Second Circuit in *Doe* and concluded that there was no waiver of attorney client or work product protection by the testimony of either Doe Corp.'s CFO or counsel. *In re* Grand Jury Proceedings, 2001 WL 237377, at *15 (S.D.N.Y. 2001).

only those communications already revealed to the public because the context of the disclosure—publication of a tell-all book about the high-profile defense of Claus von Bulow—was extrajudicial. The scope of waiver has also been limited where "the disclosure occurred early in the proceedings, was made to opposing counsel rather than to the court, and was not demonstrably prejudicial to [the] other party." Further, when waiver occurs as a result of inadvertent document disclosure, courts have limited the scope of that waiver based on the circumstances involved and overall fairness. See, e.g., *United States v. Gangi*, 1 F.Supp.2d 256, 264 (S.D.N.Y.1998) (describing flexible, "middle of the road" approach).

The general rules governing waiver are more complicated when the issue arises in the context of corporate entities. ...

The cases on which the government relies to support application of the implied waiver doctrine to corporations are, for the most part, quite distinguishable from the case at hand. For instance, in *In re Sealed Case*, 29 F.3d 715, 717-18 (D.C.Cir.1994), the court held that voluntary disclosure during a plea proffer could result in waiver. Similarly, in *In re Martin Marietta Corp.*, 856 F.2d 619, 623-25 (4th Cir.1988), the court found that voluntary disclosure to the government during settlement negotiations resulted in waiver. Disclosures made to the Securities and Exchange Commission (SEC) in the context of its voluntary disclosure program have also been held to result in waiver. See, e.g., *In re Sealed Case*, 676 F.2d 793, 824 (D.C.Cir.1982). Finally, where a corporation has disseminated information to the public that reveals parts of privileged communications or relies on privileged reports, courts have found the privilege waived. In each case, the corporation waiving the privilege made a deliberate decision to disclose privileged materials in a forum where disclosure was voluntary and calculated to benefit the disclosing party. Clearly, when the corporation as an entity makes the strategic decision to disclose some privileged information, the courts may find implied waiver, as they do in cases involving individuals. [In *Doe*, however, the reverse is true—Doe Corp. made no such decision and indeed vehemently and repeatedly asserted the privilege.][20]

In *Doe*, Doe Corp.'s founder, chairman, and controlling shareholder (Witness) testified before the grand jury in such a way, the government claimed, as to waive the corporations' privilege. In an effort to provide guidance to the District Court on remand, the Second Circuit identified a number of considerations that ought to be considered in the corporation's favor when testing whether the actions of its agent ought to be imputed to it. The key consideration, implicit in the various factors identified by the court, was whether Witness's disclosure was intentional or inadvertent; that is, whether Witness sought to use the information to exculpate *the corporation*, while seeking at the same time to hide behind the privilege.

First, the court noted that "we have here a corporation that has asserted its privilege, has not deliberately disclosed (so far as the record before us indicates) any privileged material to the government or to other parties, but whose officer, in contravention of the corporation's instructions, has arguably waived that privilege in his grand jury testimony."[21] Second, the corporate agent was subpoenaed individually:

Although Witness was called to the grand jury because he was a Doe Corp. officer, his testimony in the grand jury was not affirmatively offered by Doe Cxorp. on its own behalf. Doe Corp. is a publicly held corporation; it has a board of directors, numerous shareholders, and a large number of employees. It is far from being Witness's "alter-ego." It is true that Witness and Doe Corp. share many of the same interests: an indictment of Doe Corp. would likely harm Witness's financial prospects, not to mention his reputation.

---

[20] 219 F.3d at 182-184.

[21] *Id.* at 184.

However, even if we accept the government's position that Witness's reference to advice-of-counsel was self-interested, it does not necessarily follow that, as a result, the corporation itself should be penalized. While it may be that Witness intended to abide by Doe Corp.'s decision not to waive its attorney-client privilege, the corporation had no direct means of controlling Witness's testimony while he was in the grand jury room. At oral argument, Doe Corp. made the significant suggestion that Witness's interest in exculpating his own conduct may override his fidelity to the corporation, including its interest in preserving the privilege. We believe the district court should consider this possibility.

Third, the Second Circuit thought it significant that the corporate officer "was compelled to appear and to testify before the grand jury. Because the corporation does not enjoy the protection of the Fifth Amendment, Witness could not assert the Fifth Amendment on its behalf. Consequently, Witness's alleged waiver occurred in the context of purely compelled testimony. ... In that sense, the 'shield and sword' analogy used by the government to justify waiver may be inappropriate."[22] Relatedly, the fact that Witness, who was not a lawyer, had to appear before the grand jury unaided by counsel was another factor. "Witness here was not proffered by Doe Corp., but was compelled to testify before the grand jury. He was answering the government's questions, not putting up his own defense."[23]

What other factors may be relevant to a claim of implied waiver of a corporate privilege by a corporate agent?

2. FED. R. EVID. 502

The Judicial Conference Advisory Committee on Evidence Rules recommended a new rule of Evidence, 502, first to "resolve some of the longstanding disputes in the courts about the effect of certain disclosures of communications or information protected by the attorney-client privilege or as work product—specifically those disputes involving inadvertent disclosure" and partial waivers.[24] (A proposed provision on selective waivers was ultimately not included in the rule.) The new rule also responds to the widespread complaint that litigation costs necessary to protect against waivers "have been come prohibitive due to the concern that any disclosure (however innocent or minimal) will operate as a subject matter waiver of all protected communications or information. This concern is especially troubling in cases involving electronic discovery."[25]

RULE 502. ATTORNEY-CLIENT PRIVILEGE AND WORK PRODUCT; LIMITATIONS ON WAIVER

The following provisions apply, in the circumstances set out, to disclosure of a communication or information covered by the attorney-client privilege or work-product protection.

(a) Disclosure made in a Federal proceeding or to a Federal office or agency; scope of a waiver.--When the disclosure is made in a Federal proceeding or

---

[22] *Id.* at 185.

[23] *Id.* at 186.

[24] Federal Rule of Evidence 502, Judicial Conference Advisory Comm. on Evidence Rules, Explanatory Note on Evidence Rule 502.

[25] *Id.* (citing Hopson v. City of Baltimore, 232 F.R.D. 228, 244 (D. Md. 2005) (electronic discovery may encompass "millions of documents" and to insist upon "record-by-record pre-production privilege review, on pain of subject matter waiver, would impose upon parties costs of production that bear no proportion to what is at stake in the litigation").

to a Federal office or agency and waives the attorney-client privilege or work-product protection, the waiver extends to an undisclosed communication or information in a Federal or State proceeding only if:

(**1**) the waiver is intentional;

(**2**) the disclosed and undisclosed communications or information concern the same subject matter; and

(**3**) they ought in fairness to be considered together.

(**b**) **Inadvertent disclosure.**--When made in a Federal proceeding or to a Federal office or agency, the disclosure does not operate as a waiver in a Federal or State proceeding if:

(**1**) the disclosure is inadvertent;

(**2**) the holder of the privilege or protection took reasonable steps to prevent disclosure; and

(**3**) the holder promptly took reasonable steps to rectify the error, including (if applicable) following Federal Rule of Civil Procedure 26(b)(5)(B).

(**c**) **Disclosure made in a State proceeding.**--When the disclosure is made in a State proceeding and is not the subject of a State-court order concerning waiver, the disclosure does not operate as a waiver in a Federal proceeding if the disclosure:

(**1**) would not be a waiver under this rule if it had been made in a Federal proceeding; or

(**2**) is not a waiver under the law of the State where the disclosure occurred.

(**d**) **Controlling effect of a court order.**--A Federal court may order that the privilege or protection is not waived by disclosure connected with the litigation pending before the court—in which event the disclosure is also not a waiver in any other Federal or State proceeding.

(**e**) **Controlling effect of a party agreement.**--An agreement on the effect of disclosure in a Federal proceeding is binding only on the parties to the agreement, unless it is incorporated into a court order.

(**f**) **Controlling effect of this rule.**--Notwithstanding Rules 101 and 1101, this rule applies to State proceedings and to Federal court-annexed and Federal court-mandated arbitration proceedings, in the circumstances set out in the rule. And notwithstanding Rule 501, this rule applies even if State law provides the rule of decision.

(**g**) **Definitions.**--In this rule:

(**1**) "attorney-client privilege" means the protection that applicable law provides for confidential attorney-client communications; and

(**2**) "work-product protection" means the protection that applicable law provides for tangible material (or its intangible equivalent) prepared in anticipation of litigation or for trial.

ADVISORY COMMITTEE NOTES
Explanatory Note (Revised 11/28/2007)

... The [new] rule seeks to provide a predictable, uniform set of standards under which parties can determine the consequences of a disclosure of a communication or information covered by the attorney-client privilege or work-product protection. Parties to litigation need to know, for example, that if they exchange privileged information pursuant to a confidentiality order, the court's order will be enforceable. Moreover, if a federal court's confidentiality order is not enforceable in a state court then the burdensome costs of privilege review and retention are unlikely to be reduced.

The rule makes no attempt to alter federal or state law on whether a communication or information is protected under the attorney-client privilege or work-product immunity as an initial matter. Moreover, while establishing some exceptions to waiver, the rule does not purport to supplant applicable waiver doctrine generally.

The rule governs only certain waivers by disclosure. Other common-law waiver doctrines may result in a finding of waiver even where there is no disclosure of privileged information or work product. *See, e.g., Nguyen v. Excel Corp.*, 197 F.3d 200 (5th Cir. 1999) (reliance on an advice of counsel defense waives the privilege with respect to attorney-client communications pertinent to that defense); *Ryers v. Burleson*, 100 F.R.D. 436 (D.D.C. 1983) (allegation of lawyer malpractice constituted a waiver of confidential communications under the circumstances). The rule is not intended to displace or modify federal common law concerning waiver of privilege or work product where no disclosure has been made. ...

The rule is intended to apply in all federal court proceedings, including court-annexed and court-ordered arbitrations, without regard to any possible limitations of Rules 101 and 1101. This provision is not intended to raise an inference about the applicability of any other rule of evidence in arbitration proceedings more generally.

The costs of discovery can be equally high for state and federal causes of action, and the rule seeks to limit those costs in all federal proceedings, regardless of whether the claim arises under state or federal law. Accordingly, the rule applies to state law causes of action brought in federal court.

Subdivision (g). The rule's coverage is limited to attorney-client privilege and work product. The operation of waiver by disclosure, as applied to other evidentiary privileges, remains a question of federal common law. Nor does the rule purport to apply to the Fifth Amendment privilege against compelled self-incrimination.

The definition of work product "materials" is intended to include both tangible and intangible information. *See In re Cendant Corp. Sec. Litig.*, 343 F.3d 658, 662 (3d Cir. 2003) ("work product protection extends to both tangible and intangible work product").

Notes

1. *Federalism issues.* The effect of Rule 502 on existing waiver standards will be examined in subsequent sections. This note will concentrate on the question of *where* these rules apply. The Advisory Committee explained as follows:

> **Subdivision (c).** Difficult questions can arise when 1) a disclosure of a communication or information protected by the attorney-client privilege or as work product is made in a state proceeding, 2) the communication or information is offered in a subsequent federal proceeding on the ground that the disclosure waived the privilege or protection, and 3) the state and federal laws are in conflict on the question of waiver. The Committee determined that the proper solution for the federal court is to apply the law that is most protective of privilege and work product. If the state law is more protective (such as where the state law is that an inadvertent disclosure can never be a waiver), the holder of the privilege or protection may well have relied on that law when making the disclosure in the state proceeding. Moreover, applying a more restrictive federal law of waiver could impair the state objective of preserving the privilege or work-product protection for disclosures made in state proceedings. On the other hand, if the federal law is more protective, applying the state law of waiver to determine admissibility in federal court is likely to undermine the federal objective of limiting the costs of production. ...
>
> **Subdivision (f).** The protections against waiver provided by Rule 502 must be applicable when protected communications or information disclosed in federal proceedings are subsequently offered in state proceedings. Otherwise the holders of

protected communications and information, and their lawyers, could not rely on the protections provided by the Rule, and the goal of limiting costs in discovery would be substantially undermined. Rule 502(f) is intended to resolve any potential tension between the provisions of Rule 502 that apply to state proceedings and the possible limitations on the applicability of the Federal Rules of Evidence otherwise provided by Rules 101 [(rules apply to proceedings in U.S. courts)] and 1101 [(explaining which federal courts and proceedings to which the evidence rules apply)].

2. Note that the Rules of Evidence generally are consulted for determination of the admissibility of evidence in a federal judicial proceeding. Obviously, Congress determined that the waiver rules would have effect in state courts as well. Given that many of the waiver cases involve submission of protected materials to executive branch agencies or departments, what force do they have in that context?

During the legislative process by which Congress enacted Rule 502, Pub. L. 110-322, 122 Stat. 3537 (Sept. 19, 2008), the Judicial Conference agreed to provide an additional note to the new rule that was entered into the Congressional Record and was entitled "Statement of Congressional Intent Regarding Rule 502 of the Federal Rules of Procedure." *See* 154 Cong. Rec. H7818-H7819 (Sept. 8, 2008) [hereinafter "Statement"]. That Statement provided, in part, as follows:

> Subdivisions (a) and (b)--Disclosures to Federal Office or Agency
>
> This rule, as a Federal Rule of Evidence, applies to admissibility of evidence. While subdivisions (a) and (b) are written broadly to apply as appropriate to disclosures of information to a federal office or agency, they do not apply to uses of information—such as routine use in government publications—that fall outside the evidentiary context. Nor do these subdivisions relieve the party seeking to protect the information as privileged from the burden of proving that the privilege applies in the first place.

Id. at H7818.

3. INADVERTENT WAIVER

Every litigator's nightmare involves the waiver of the privilege through "inadvertent" production of privileged materials. Prior to Rule 502, some courts—particularly the D.C. Circuit—applied a very unsympathetic standard in reviewing such cases. The D.C. Circuit stated, for example, that: "[I]f a client wishes to preserve the privilege, it must treat the confidentiality of attorney-client communications like jewels—if not crown jewels. Short of court-compelled disclosure, or other equally extraordinary circumstances, we will not distinguish between various degrees of 'voluntariness' in waivers of ... privilege."[26] Other circuits employed a "fairness" approach.[27] Among the factors that the courts taking a "fairness" approach looked to in assessing whether a waiver should be found (and the extent of any waiver) were: (1) "the extent to which reasonable precautions were taken to avoid disclosure of privileged documents"; (2) "the scope of discovery as compared to the amount of privileged documents disclosed"; (3) "the amount of time taken to correct the error"; and (4) "the overreaching issue of fairness."[28]

---

[26] *In re* Sealed Case, 877 F.2d 976, 980 (D.C. Cir. 1989).

[27] *See, e.g.,* Gray v. Bicknell, 86 F.3d 1472, 1484 (8th Cir. 1996); Alldread v. City of Grenada, 988 F.2d 1425, 1434 (5th Cir. 1993).

[28] United States v. Gangi, 1 F. Supp.2d 256, 264 (S.D.N.Y. 1998); *see also Gray* 86 F.3d at 1484; *Alldread,* 988 F.2d at 1433; *In re* Natural Gas Commodity Litig., 229 F.R.D. 82 (S.D.N.Y. 2005).

In Rule 502, the Advisory Committee explained the approach it chose to take:

Subdivision (b). Courts are in conflict over whether an inadvertent disclosure of a communication or information protected as privileged or work product constitutes a waiver. A few courts find that a disclosure must be intentional to be a waiver. Most courts find a waiver only if the disclosing party acted carelessly in disclosing the communication or information and failed to request its return in a timely manner. And a few courts hold that any inadvertent disclosure of a communication or information protected under the attorney-client privilege or as work product constitutes a waiver without regard to the protections taken to avoid such a disclosure. *See generally Hopson v. City of Baltimore*, 232 F.R.D. 228 (D.Md. 2005), for a discussion of this case law.

The rule opts for the middle ground: inadvertent disclosure of protected communications or information in connection with a federal proceeding or to a federal office or agency does not constitute a waiver if the holder took reasonable steps to prevent disclosure and also promptly took reasonable steps to rectify the error. This position is in accord with the majority view on whether inadvertent disclosure is a waiver.

Cases such as *Lois Sportswear, U.S.A., Inc. v. Levi Strauss & Co.*, 104 F.R.D. 103, 105 (S.D.N.Y. 1985) and *Hartford Fire Ins. Co. v. Garvey*, 109 F.R.D. 323, 332 (N.D.Cal. 1985), set out a multi-factor test for determining whether inadvertent disclosure is a waiver. The stated factors (none of which is dispositive) are the reasonableness of precautions taken, the time taken to rectify the error, the scope of discovery, the extent of disclosure and the overriding issue of fairness. The rule does not explicitly codify that test, because it is really a set of non-determinative guidelines that vary from case to case. The rule is flexible enough to accommodate any of those listed factors. Other considerations bearing on the reasonableness of a producing party's efforts include the number of documents to be reviewed and the time constraints for production. Depending on the circumstances, a party that uses advanced analytical software applications and linguistic tools in screening for privilege and work product may be found to have taken "reasonable steps" to prevent inadvertent disclosure. The implementation of an efficient system of records management before litigation may also be relevant.

The rule does not require the producing party to engage in a post-production review to determine whether any protected communication or information has been produced by mistake. But the rule does require the producing party to follow up on any obvious indications that a protected communication or information has been produced inadvertently.

The rule applies to inadvertent disclosures made to a federal office or agency, including but not limited to an office or agency that is acting in the course of its regulatory, investigative or enforcement authority. The consequences of waiver, and the concomitant costs of pre-production privilege review, can be as great with respect to disclosures to offices and agencies as they are in litigation.

The Judicial Conference Statement entered into the Congressional Record provides as follows:

The Tenth Circuit has employed a similar test when determining the extent of "inadvertent waiver" even in a case in which the assertedly privileged material was seized pursuant to a search warrant—that is, where the surrender of the materials was not truly voluntary. *See, e.g.*, United States v. Ary, 518 F.3d 775 (10th Cir. 2008).

Subdivision (b)--Fairness Considerations

The standard set forth in this subdivision for determining whether a disclosure operates as a waiver of the privilege or protection is ... the majority rule in the federal courts. The majority rule has simply been distilled here into a standard designed to be predictable in its application. This distillation is not intended to foreclose notions of fairness from continuing to inform application of the standard in all aspects as appropriate in particular cases—for example, as to whether steps taken to rectify an erroneous inadvertent disclosure were sufficiently prompt under subdivision (b)(3) where the receiving party has relied on the information disclosed.[29]

Note

1. Do inadvertent waiver cases raise questions regarding receiving counsel's ethical obligations? "Courts, state bar committees and the American Bar Association have all reached different conclusions on the question of what use counsel may make of privileged material produced by an opposing party." Joseph F. Savage, Jr. & Melissa M. Longo, *'Waive' Goodbye to Attorney-Client Privilege*, 7 No. 9 Bus. Crimes Bull. 1 (Oct.2000). Should a lawyer who receives privileged or confidential information mistakenly transmitted to him return the information unread? *See* ABA Comm. on Ethics and Prof'l Responsibility Op. 94-382 (1994) (yes). Or should lawyers, given their obligation to zealously represent the interests of their clients, refuse to return inadvertently produced privileged material? *See* Mass. Bar Ass'n, Comm. on Prof'l Ethics Op. No. 99-4 (1999) (yes); *see also* Amgen Inc. v. Hoechst Marion Roussel, Inc., 190 F.R.D. 287, 290 n.2 (D. Mass. 2000) (applauding receiving law firm's ethical conduct in returning inadvertently produced materials but finding the privilege to be waived due to negligence). What should be the right answer?

4. PARTIAL WAIVER

One important area in which waiver questions arise is in the context of internal corporate investigations. It is normally considered vital to conduct an internal investigation in such a way as to preserve the work product or attorney-client status of materials generated in the course, or at the conclusion, of the investigation. Corporations may, however, wish to disclose some or all of the results of the investigation, and at times the underlying documentation, to selected government officials in the hopes that such disclosure will secure for the corporation a declination of official action or at least sentencing consideration. Corporations may also feel pressured to share the results of their internal investigation with third parties who, for business reasons, want to see them. Thus, for example, a company's independent auditors may demand to see the report before certifying a corporation's financial statements. Underwriters and others who propose to engage in important financial transactions with the corporation may also condition their participation on access to the results of the internal investigation.

In considering whether to disclose part or all of an internal investigation, corporations must consider the possibility of a waiver of otherwise applicable privileges. In particular, they must consider: (1) whether disclosing selected parts of a report or its underlying documentation waives the privilege as to the entirety of the report and documentation or whether courts will accept an assertion of *"partial"* waiver; and (2) whether courts will accept a *"selective"* waiver argument that disclosure of the report to a government agency, prosecutor, or grand jury does not waive the privilege or work product doctrine when *other* parties (*e.g.*, other governmental entities or private plaintiffs) seek to secure the same materials. (Selective waivers will be considered in the following section.)

---

[29] 154 Cong. Rec. H7818, H7818 (Sept. 8, 2008).

"Partial" waiver issues arise when the privilege-holder discloses, publishes, or attempts to use selected portions of protected materials, or documents that are built on privileged information, while protecting the balance of the protected materials, or underlying documents, from disclosure. This issue comes up in a variety of situations beyond the internal investigation context discussed above. For example, "partial" waiver questions also frequently arise when the privilege-holder relies, directly or indirectly, on a privileged communication or piece of work product in the course of litigation.[30]

Another important context in which partial waiver is an issue is in connection with defense "white papers" or "submissions." In an effort to head off threatened regulatory or criminal action, defense counsel often make what are referred to as "submissions" to government actors. Submissions may take the form of written documents, or may consist of one or more oral presentations. Counsel will generally argue that the law, the facts, and the equities preclude government action. Some of the information conveyed in a submission may be derived, directly or indirectly, from attorney-client privileged or work product materials. Thus, the government and others may argue that the defense's use of protected materials, directly or indirectly, to substantiate the defense's submission constituted a waiver as to the entire subject matter discussed.[31]

Generally, the issue in "partial" waiver cases is not whether the protections attaching to the materials actually disclosed have been waived—that much is clear. Thus, for example, courts have found that the attorney-client privilege was waived when the results of internal investigations into corporate wrongdoing were revealed to: independent auditors verifying the company's financial statements;[32] counsel for underwriters;[33] government contract performance auditors;[34] government regulators, either to secure approval of a proposed corporate action;[35] or to avert regulatory enforcement action;[36] and grand juries or prosecutors.[37] The important question in these cases is the *scope of any additional waiver*, that is, whether the privilege-holder may argue for a finding of a "partial" waiver of only the materials disclosed.

Prior to Rule 502, with respect to the *attorney-client privilege*, the standard was generally that the privilege was waived as to all communications concerning the same "subject matter" as the disclosed communications.[38] Courts generally employed a "fairness" analysis to determine how broadly or narrowly to define the "subject matter" of the waiver.[39] In the litigation context, most courts found a broad waiver appropriate where "a litigant place[d] information protected by it in issue through some affirmative act for his

---

[30]*See, e.g.*, Cox v. Administrator U.S. Steel & Carnegie, 17 F.3d 1386, 1417-18 (11th Cir. 1994); Weil v. Investment/Indicators, Research & Management, Inc., 647 F.2d 18, 24 (9th Cir. 1981).

[31] *See, e.g.*, *In re* John Doe Co. v. United States, 350 F.3d 299 (2d Cir. 2003); *In re* Weatherford Int'l Secs. Litig., 2013 WL 6628964 (S.D.N.Y. 2013).

[32] *See, e.g.*, *In re* John Doe Corp., 675 F.2d 482, 488 (2d Cir. 1982); United States v. El Paso Co., 682 F.2d 530, 539-42 (5th Cir. 1982).

[33] *See, e.g.*, *In re* John Doe Corp., 675 F.2d at 488-89.

[34] *See, e.g.*, United States v. MIT, 129 F.3d 681, 683 (1st Cir. 1997).

[35] *See, e.g.*, Permian Corp. v. United States, 665 F.2d 1214, 1216 (D.C. Cir. 1981).

[36] *See, e.g.*, Westinghouse Electric Corp. v. Republic of the Philippines, 951 F.2d 1414, 1417-18 (3d Cir. 1991); *In re* Subpoenas Duces Tecum, 738 F.2d 1367, 1369-75 (D.C. Cir. 1984).

[37] *See, e.g.*, *id.*; *In re* Martin Marietta Corp., 856 F.2d 619, 623-24 (4th Cir.1988).

[38] *See, e.g.*, *In re Martin Marietta*, 856 F.2d at 623-24; *In re* Sealed Case, 676 F.2d at 809; *Weil*, 647 F.2d at 24.

[39] *See, e.g.*, *In re* Keeper of the Records (Grand Jury Subpoena to XYZ Corp.), 348 F.3d 16 (1st Cir. 2003).

own benefit, and to allow the privilege to protect against [further] disclosure of such information would be manifestly unfair to the opposing party."[40] Where, however, an extrajudicial disclosure of protected communications did not greatly prejudice the other party in litigation, a narrower waiver is deemed appropriate.[41]

The dominant approach in determining the scope of waiver in the *work product context* prior to Rule 502 was again one of "fairness" in determining the appropriate scope of waiver. Courts looked to whether the disclosing party was seeking to gain an advantage to the prejudice of others and ultimately to whether "a party seeks greater advantage from its control over work product than the law must provide to maintain a healthy adversary system."[42]

The Advisory Committee explained its approach, reflected in Rule 502:

> **Subdivision (a).** The rule provides that a voluntary disclosure in a federal proceeding or to a federal office or agency, if a waiver, generally results in a waiver only of the communication or information disclosed; a subject matter waiver (of either privilege or work product) is reserved for those unusual situations in which fairness requires a further disclosure of related, protected information, in order to prevent a selective and misleading presentation of evidence to the disadvantage of the adversary. *See, e.g., In re United Mine Workers of America Employee Benefit Plans Litig.*, 159 F.R.D. 307, 312 (D.D.C. 1994) (waiver of work product limited to materials actually disclosed, because the party did not deliberately disclose documents in an attempt to gain a tactical advantage). Thus, subject matter waiver is limited to situations in which a party intentionally puts protected information into the litigation in a selective, misleading and unfair manner. It follows that an inadvertent disclosure of protected information can never result in a subject matter waiver. *See* Rule 502(b). The rule rejects the result in *In re Sealed Case*, 877 F.2d 976 (D.C. Cir. 1989), which held that inadvertent disclosure of documents during discovery automatically constituted a subject matter waiver.
>
> The language concerning subject matter waiver—"ought in fairness"—is taken from Rule 106 [(rule of completeness)], because the animating principle is the same. Under both Rules, a party that makes a selective, misleading presentation that is unfair to the adversary opens itself to a more complete and accurate presentation.
>
> To assure protection and predictability, the rule provides that if a disclosure is made at the federal level, the federal rule on subject matter waiver governs subsequent state court determinations on the scope of the waiver by that disclosure.

The Statement that the Judicial Conference provided Congress, and that was entered into the Congressional Record, also clarified the intent behind subsection (a) of Rule 502:

---

[40] *Cox*, 17 F.3d at 1417-18) (*quoting* Conkling v. Turner, 883 F.2d 431, 434 (5th Cir. 1989)); *Westinghouse*, 951 F.2d 1414, 1426; *Weil*, 647 F.2d at 25.

[41] *See, e.g., In re* Von Bulow, 828 F.2d 94 (2d Cir. 1987).

[42] *In re* Sealed Case, 676 F.2d at 818; *see also, e.g., In re* Perrigo, 128 F.3d 430, 438-41 (6th Cir. 1997); *Westinghouse*, 951 F.2d at 1430; *In re* Subpoenas Duces Tecum, 738 F.2d at 1371-74; *In re* Sealed Case, 676 F.2d at 817-24. The Fourth Circuit drew a distinction between opinion and non-opinion work product, holding that the waiver extended to "all *non*-opinion work-product on the same subject matter as that disclosed" but wss limited to only those opinion work product documents actually disclosed. *In re Martin Marietta*, 856 F.2d at 624-27; *but see Westinghouse*, 951 F.2d at 1431 n.17 (holding that a corporation that had shown the report of an internal corporate investigation to the SEC and, subject to a protective order, had produced the report (and, apparently, the documents accumulated in connection with that investigation) to a grand jury waived any attorney-client or work product protection even as to opinion work product).

Subdivision (a)—Disclosure v. Use

This subdivision does not alter the substantive law regarding when a party's strategic use in litigation of otherwise privileged information obliges that party to waive the privilege regarding other information concerning the same subject matter, so that the information being used can be fairly considered in context. One situation in which this issue arises [is] the assertion as a defense in patent-infringement litigation that a party was relying on advice of counsel .... In this and similar situations, under subdivision (a)(1) the party using an attorney-client communication to its advantage in the litigation has, in so doing, intentionally waived the privilege as to other communications concerning the same subject matter, regardless of the circumstances in which the communication being so used was initially disclosed.[43]

Note

1. In the internal corporate investigation context, the question often arises whether disclosure or use of the results of an internal corporate investigation waives the attorney-client privilege with respect to the notes and memoranda of counsel who prepared the report, even if privileged communications or work product are not expressly quoted in it. Some courts have held that merely repeating non-privileged facts in a report does not waive the privilege as to the communications underlying those facts. *See, e.g., In re* Woolworth Corp. Sec. Class Action Litig., 1996 WL 306576 (S.D.N.Y. 1996). Other courts have ordered at least some disclosure of the underlying documentation on a wider "fairness" waiver theory. *See, e.g.,* United States v. Billmyer, 57 F.3d 31, 37 (1st Cir. 1995) (finding waiver where "counsel informed the client of detailed evidence and allegations concerning possible bribes of its employees, and the client chose to make this same information available to the government"); *In re* Martin Marietta Corp., 856 F.2d at 623-24 (disclosure of position paper to U.S. Attorney that described why the company should not face indictment and contained statements that characterized witnesses' likely testimony and other evidence waived the attorney-client privilege as to audit papers and witness statements upon which the assertions in the position paper were based). *But see* Diversified Indus., Inc. v. Meredith, 572 F.2d 596, 611 (8th Cir. 1977) (*en banc*) (ruling that disclosure to SEC of report of investigation conducted (and, apparently, underlying documentation) did not constitute waiver of report and underlying memoranda and correspondence for all purposes).

By contrast, in *John Doe Co. v. United States*, 350 F.3d 299 (2d Cir. 2003), the government made the argument that, by submitting a lengthy "submission" to the government in an effort to talk it out of indicting, the company had effected a waiver of the privilege as to the attorney work product paraphrased within it. The District Court held that this submission did constitute a waiver and ordered Doe Corp. to produce all non-opinion portions of notes of Doe Corp. contacts with the government. On appeal, the Second Circuit reversed, holding that, by sending a letter to the government in which it made claims about the advice it had received from the government and about its innocent state of mind, the company did not involuntarily waive or forfeit the work product protection applicable to attorneys' notes.

Will Rule 502 change these rules? *See, e.g., In re* General Motors LLC Ignition Switch Litig., 80 F.Supp.3d 521 (S.D.N.Y. 2015); United States v. Treacy, 2009 WL 812033 (S.D.N.Y. 2009) (unpublished).

---

[43] 154 Cong. Rec. H7818 (Sept. 8, 2008).

5. SELECTIVE WAIVER

The issue in these cases is whether the waiver found—of whatever scope was determined above—may be limited to the party to whom disclosure was made or whether the waiver as to one person waives the protections of the attorney-client privilege or work product doctrine as to all other persons. Courts employ different analyses with respect to attorney-client, as opposed to work product, materials, but the result is often the same: a refusal to permit a "selective waiver."

With respect to the *attorney-client privilege*, all the circuits to consider the issue except the Eighth Circuit have rejected a "selective" waiver theory. They have ruled that where otherwise privileged materials are shown to third-parties—either in an attempt to head off regulatory or criminal action against the corporation, in the conduct of the corporation's business, or in the conduct of litigation—the protections of the attorney-client privilege are waived *as to any other person.*[44] Only the Eighth Circuit has adopted a limited doctrine of "selective" waiver whereby voluntary disclosure to a government agency constitutes a waiver of the attorney-client privilege *only* as to that agency.[45] These courts do not apply a "fairness" or "balancing" approach to "selective" waiver cases.[46] They simply hold that the disclosure to one third party requires a disclosure to all because the initial disclosure exploded any expectation of confidentiality.[47]

Under the *work product doctrine*, exposure of protected materials to third parties does not automatically waive the doctrine's protection.[48] "[A] party who discloses documents protected by the work-product doctrine may continue to assert the doctrine's protection only when the disclosure furthers the doctrine's underlying goal."[49] Generally, this inquiry turns on whether the disclosure was made to one deemed an "adversary," in which case work product protection is lost, or whether it is turned over to one with a "common interest" under circumstances that indicate a legitimate expectation of continued confidentiality, in which case the work product protections will be sustained.[50] "[T]he presence of an adversarial relationship does not depend on the existence of litigation."[51] Where the disclosing party knows that an investigation is ongoing by the recipient entity, that will certainly suffice to demonstrate an adversary relationship.[52] All the circuits to consider this issue have rejected a "selective" waiver theory or a "fairness" analysis.[53]

---

[44] *See, e.g., In re* Pacific Pictures Corp., 679 F.3d 1121 (9th Cir. 2012) (collecting cases); *In re* Quest Communications Int'l Inc., 450 F.3d 1179 (10th Cir. 2006) (collecting cases).

[45] *See* Diversified Indus. Inc. v. Meredith, 572 F.2d 596, 611 (8th Cir. 1977) (*en banc*) (attorney-client privilege *not* waived as to civil plaintiff where documents had been voluntarily disclosed to SEC).

[46] *See Westinghouse*, 9501 F.2d at 1430. Note that the Second Circuit, in *In re* Steinhardt Partners, L.P., 9 F.3d 230, 236 (2d Cir. 1993), stated that it declined to adopt a per se rule that all voluntary disclosures to the government waive the privilege, and seemingly carved out a potential exception where the disclosing party turns the privileged materials over to the government pursuant to an express agreement that the government will maintain the confidentiality of the materials. *But see* Gruss v. Zwirn, 2013 WL 3481350 (S.D.N.Y. 2013) (arguing that in light of more recent precedents, the Second Circuit would be unlikely to apply this exception).

[47] *See, e.g., Permian Corp.*, 665 F.2d at 1220.

[48] *See MIT*, 129 F.3d at 687 & n.6.

[49] *Westinghouse*, 951 F.2d at 1429.

[50] *See, e.g., MIT*, 129 F.3d at 687; *In re* Steinhardt Partners, 9 F.3d at 234-36.

[51] *In re* Steinhardt Partners, L.P., 9 F.3d at 234.

[52] *Id.*; *Westinghouse*, 951 F.2d at 1428.

[53] *See* United States v. Williams Cos., Inc. 562 F.3d 387 (D.C. Cir. 2009); *In re* Quest Communications Int'l Inc., 450 F.3d 1179.

They hold that disclosure of work product to one adversary is sufficient to waive the doctrine as to all adversaries.[54]

Having examined the rules, perhaps it is time to reflect on the policy underlying the rules. Should some kind of "selective" waiver doctrine apply where corporations seek to cooperate with government authorities in investigations of corporate wrongdoing?[55] A "selective" waiver doctrine may promote voluntary cooperation with the government because companies need not fear that their factual findings and legal theories will be handed over to future adversaries.[56] It may also encourage companies to police their operations more carefully and to conduct internal investigations where necessary. Even if it does not promote such efforts, it at least does not discourage them. As the Eighth Circuit argued in recognizing a "selected" waiver theory in the attorney-client context, a contrary ruling "may have the effect of thwarting the developing procedure of corporations to employ independent outside counsel to investigate and advise them in order to protect, stockholders, potential stockholders, and customers."[57] Finally, "loss of the privilege may discourage frank exchange between attorney and client in future cases, wherever the client anticipates making a disclosure to at least one government agency."[58]

On the other hand, courts rejecting a "selective" waiver doctrine reason that selective waiver does not promote the interests that underlie the attorney-client and work product doctrines: it neither helps foster attorney-client relationships, nor better enables counsel to "prepare a client's case without fear of intrusion by an adversary."[59] As the Third Circuit has argued, "selective waiver does not serve the purpose of encouraging full disclosure to one's attorney in order to obtain informed legal assistance; it merely encourages voluntary disclosure to government agencies, thereby extending the privilege beyond its intended purpose."[60] The D.C. Circuit has also pointed to the concerns often relied on in the "partial" waiver context: "[f]airness and consistency require that [parties] not be allowed to gain the substantial advantages" accruing through selective voluntary disclosure of protected materials in one proceeding but not another.[61] The Third Circuit rejects this particular rationale in the "selective" waiver context because "when a client discloses privileged information to a government agency, the private litigant in subsequent proceedings is no worse off than it would have been had the disclosure to the agency not occurred."[62]

Courts further argue that, as an empirical matter, companies have continued to conduct internal investigations and cooperate with government agencies despite near universal judicial rejection of a "selective" waiver doctrine.[63] It must be, then, that the incentives to cooperate—avoidance of burdensome inquiries by the government and the prospect of more lenient treatment—are sufficient to promote such cooperation.[64] Further, "such agencies usually have

---

[54] *See, e.g., Westinghouse*, 951 F.2d at 1428-1429.

[55] *See generally In re* Quest Communications Int'l Inc., 450 F.3d 1179.

[56] *See In re Steinhardt*, 9 F.3d at 235.

[57] *Meredith*, 572 F.2d at 611.

[58] *MIT*, 129 F.3d at 685.

[59] *In re* Steinhardt, 9 F.3d at 234.

[60] *Westinghouse*, 951 F.2d at 1425.

[61] *In re* Subpoena Duces Tecum, 738 F.2d 1367, 1372 (D.C. Cir. 1984); *see also Permian*, 665 F.2d at 1221.

[62] *Westinghouse*, 951 F.2d at 1426 n.13.

[63] *See, e.g., In re* Steinhardt, 9 F.3d at 235; *Westinghouse*, 951 F.2d at 1425.

[64] *See In re* Steinhard, 9 F.3d at 235.

means to secure the information they need and, if not, can seek legislation from Congress."[65] Finally, "the general principle that disclosure normally negates the privilege is worth maintaining. To maintain it here makes the law more predictable and certainly eases its administration. Following the Eighth Circuit's approach would require, at the very least, a new set of difficult line-drawing exercises that would consume time and increase uncertainty."[66] Which side of this debate do you find more persuasive?

The Advisory Committee undertook to write a rule to deal with selective waivers along with the inadvertent and selective waiver standards discussed above. It drafted a provision, which would have been Rule 502(c), that stated that "[i]n a federal or state proceeding, a disclosure of a communication or information covered by the attorney-client or work product protection—when made to a federal public office or agency in the exercise of its regulatory, investigative, or enforcement authority—does not operate as a waiver of the privilege or protection in favor of non-governmental persons or entities."[67]

This provision of the proposed rule was not adopted. As the author of the proposed selective waiver provision, Professor Daniel Capra, has explained, "'[t]he committee thought it was doing corporations a favor by giving them some protection when they cooperated with the government. ... We knew we'd get grief from the plaintiffs' counsel, but it turns out the defense bar has objected the most."[68] According to Capra, "defense attorneys do not like the provision because it eliminates a common excuse for not cooperating with government investigators."[69]

Professor Lonnie Brown proposes one creative and sensible solution to corporations' cooperation dilemma: implementation (presumably through legislation) of the "control group" test for corporate privilege assertions rejected by the Supreme Court in *Upjohn*. This approach, he argues, has a number of advantages, one of which is that "the proposed corporate attorney-client privilege will protect that about which corporations are primarily concerned—legal advice and incriminating statements attributable to the corporation—while leaving unprotected that which is reportedly of most interest to the government—factual information. The result is that corporations can be deemed 'cooperative' by turning over the unprotected factual materials without the necessity of waiver and the related concerns that accompany it—i.e., ... waiver as to third parties."[70]

6. COURT ORDERS AND CONFIDENTIALITY AGREEMENTS

May the disclosing party increase the chances of maintaining attorney-client or work product protection by securing a confidentiality agreement or court order prior to disclosure? Why might government actors seeking to obtain reports of internal investigations assist corporations in their efforts to limit the possibility of collateral waivers?

Until Rule 502 went into effect, it was not clear whether those wishing to disclose otherwise protected information could limit the scope of any waiver by entering into an agreement with the receiving part and/or by securing a court order limiting the extent of their exposure. Rule 502 seeks to provide additional guidance, and protection. As the Advisory Committee explained:

---

[65] *MIT*, 129 F.3d at 685.

[66] *Id.*

[67] Proposed Fed. R. Evid. 502(c).

[68] *Provision on Selective Privilege Waiver Likely to Be Pulled From Proposed Rules of Evidence*, 80 Crim. L. Rep. (BNA) 464 (Jan. 31, 2007).

[69] *Id.*

[70] Lonnie T. Brown, Jr., *Reconsidering the Corporate Attorney-Client Privilege: A Response to the Compelled-Voluntary Waiver Paradox*, 34 Hofstra L. Rev. 897, 956 (2006).

Subdivision (d). Confidentiality orders are becoming increasingly important in limiting the costs of privilege review and retention, especially in cases involving electronic discovery. But the utility of a confidentiality order in reducing discovery costs is substantially diminished if it provides no protection outside the particular litigation in which the order is entered. Parties are unlikely to be able to reduce the costs of pre-production review for privilege and work product if the consequence of disclosure is that the communications or information could be used by non-parties to the litigation.

There is some dispute on whether a confidentiality order entered in one case is enforceable in other proceedings. *See generally Hopson v. City of Baltimore*, 232 F.R.D. 228 (D.Md. 2005), for a discussion of this case law. The rule provides that when a confidentiality order governing the consequences of disclosure in that case is entered in a federal proceeding, its terms are enforceable against non-parties in any federal or state proceeding. For example, the court order may provide for return of documents without waiver irrespective of the care taken by the disclosing party; the rule contemplates enforcement of "claw-back" and "quick peek" arrangements as a way to avoid the excessive costs of pre-production review for privilege and work product. *See Zubulake v. UBS Warburg LLC*, 216 F.R.D. 280, 290 (S.D.N.Y. 2003) (noting that parties may enter into "so-called 'claw-back' agreements that allow the parties to forego privilege review altogether in favor of an agreement to return inadvertently produced privilege documents"). The rule provides a party with a predictable protection from a court order—predictability that is needed to allow the party to plan in advance to limit the prohibitive costs of privilege and work product review and retention.

Under the rule, a confidentiality order is enforceable whether or not it memorializes an agreement among the parties to the litigation. Party agreement should not be a condition of enforceability of a federal court's order.

Under subdivision (d), a federal court may order that disclosure of privileged or protected information "in connection with" a federal proceeding does not result in waiver. But subdivision (d) does not allow the federal court to enter an order determining the waiver effects of a separate disclosure of the same information in other proceedings, state or federal. If a disclosure has been made in a state proceeding (and is not the subject of a state-court order on waiver), then subdivision (d) is inapplicable. Subdivision (c) would govern the federal court's determination whether the state-court disclosure waived the privilege or protection in the federal proceeding.

Subdivision (e). Subdivision (e) codifies the well-established proposition that parties can enter an agreement to limit the effect of waiver by disclosure between or among them. Of course such an agreement can bind only the parties to the agreement. The rule makes clear that if parties want protection against non-parties from a finding of waiver by disclosure, the agreement must be made part of a court order.

Notes

1. The rule does not explicitly address whether a state court confidentiality order is enforceable in federal proceedings, but the Advisory Committee, in its Notes, stated:

"that question is covered both by statutory law and principles of federalism and comity. *See* 28 U.S.C. § 1738 (providing that state judicial proceedings "shall have the same full faith and credit in every court within the United States ... as they have by law or usage in the courts of such State ... from which they are taken"). *See also Tucker v. Ohtsu Tire & Rubber Co.*, 191 F.R.D. 495, 499 (D. Md. 2000 (noting that a federal court considering the enforceability of a state confidentiality order is "constrained by principles of comity, courtesy, and ... federalism"). Thus, a state court order finding no waiver in connection with a disclosure made in a state court proceeding is enforceable under existing law in subsequent federal proceedings.

2. Recall that the proposed "selective waiver" provision was not included in the final rule. Prior to the Rule's enactment, in those circuits that have rejected the "selective" waiver doctrine, the law was unsettled as to the significance of an express assurance of confidentiality by the government agency to which the original disclosure was made. The D.C., Third and Ninth Circuits have held that even an express agreement by the government agency to preserve the confidentiality of the disclosures offers no protection against waiver of the *attorney-client privilege*. *See In re* Pacific Pictures Corp., 679 F.3d 1121, 1128-29 (9th Cir. 2012); Westinghouse Electric Corp. v. Republic of Philippines, 951 F.2d 1414, 1426-27 (3d Cir.1991); Permian Corp. v. United States, 665 F.2d 1214, 1219-1222 (D.C. Cir.1981). The D.C. Circuit, however, upheld a disclosing party's claim of *work product protection* because an agreement with the SEC established a protective attitude of confidentiality which demonstrated the disclosing party's intent to preserve its work product as against another government "adversary." *See Permian*, 665 F.2d at 1217-19; *see also In re* Subpoenas Duces Tecum, 738 F.2d 1367, 1374 n.12 (D.C. Cir.1984). The Second Circuit has also indicated that an express assurance of confidentiality by the government agency would bar a finding of waiver in the work product context. *See In re* Steinhardt Partners, L.L.P., 9 F.3d 230, 236 (2d Cir.1993); *In re* Subpoena Duces Tecum, 738 F.2d at 1375; *see also* United States v. Billmyer, 57 F.3d 31, 37 (1st Cir.1995). The Third Circuit, by contrast, has ruled that the existence of a confidentiality agreement between the disclosing party and the "adversary" agencies to whom the work product was disclosed would not change its determination that the disclosure effected a waiver. *Westinghouse*, 951 F.2d at 1430.

Can parties hoping to essentially create a selective waiver rule seek a court order under the authority of Rule 502(d)? That is, can the parties make an agreement between themselves that disclosure of protected information will not constitute a waiver with regard to anyone except those entering into it, have a judge "so order" the agreement, and expect that that order will be enforceable in state or federal court? That was not the intent of the Advisory Committee, as revealed in its Statement included in the Congressional Record:

Subdivision (d)—Court Orders

This subdivision authorizes a court to enter orders only in the context of litigation pending before the court. And it does not alter the law regarding waiver of privilege resulting from having acquiesced in the use of otherwise privileged information. *Therefore, this subdivision does not provide a basis for a court to enable parties to agree to a selective waiver of the privilege, such as to a federal agency conducting an investigation, while preserving the privilege as against other parties seeking the information.* This subdivision is designed to enable a court to enter an order, whether on motion of one or more parties or on its own motion, that will allow the parties to conduct and respond to discovery expeditiously, without the need for exhaustive pre-production privilege reviews, while still preserving each party's right to assert the privilege to preclude use in litigation of information disclosed in such discovery. While the benefits of a court order under this subdivision would be equally available in government enforcement actions as in private actions, acquiescence by the disclosing party in use by the federal agency of information disclosed pursuant to such an order would still be treated as under current law for purposes of determining whether the acquiescence in use of the information, as opposed to its mere disclosure, effects a waiver of the privilege. The same applies to acquiescence in use by another private party.

Moreover, whether the order is entered on motion of one or more parties, or on the court's own motion, the court retains its authority to include the conditions it deems appropriate in the circumstances.

Subdivision (e)—Party Agreements

This subdivision simply makes clear that while parties to a case may agree among themselves regarding the effect of disclosures between each other in a federal proceeding, it is not binding on others unless it is incorporated into a court order. This subdivision does not confer any authority on a court to enter any order regarding the effect of disclosures. That authority must be found in subdivision (d), or elsewhere.

154 Cong. Rec. H7818-7819 (Sept. 8, 2008) (emphasis added). Note, however, that the fact that the court order provision was not intended to be used to approve selective waivers appears to be not well recognized. *See, e.g.*, SEC v. Bank of America Corp., Order Approving Disclosure Stipulation and Proposed Protective Order, 09 Civ. 6829 (JSR) (Oct. 14, 2009).

7. INDIVIDUALS' ATTEMPTS TO CLAIM THE CORPORATE PRIVILEGE

When a corporate employee makes a communication to counsel for the corporation and the corporation later decides to waive applicable privileges, may the individual employee assert a privilege to shield his communication from disclosure? In *United States v. International Brotherhood of Teamsters*,[71] the Second Circuit explained that "[r]ecognizing that entities can act only through agents, courts have held that any privilege that attaches to communications on corporate matters between corporate employees and corporate counsel belongs to the corporation, not to the individual employee, and that employees generally may not prevent a corporation from waiving the attorney-client privilege arising from such communications."[72] While some courts "have been willing to allow corporate employees to assert a personal privilege with respect to conversations with corporate counsel, despite the fact that the privilege generally belongs to the corporation,"[73] the employees bear a heavy burden in making such a claim. A popular test was articulated by the Third Circuit in *The Matter of Bevill*:

First, … [the employees] must show they approached [counsel] for the purpose of seeking legal advice. Second, they must demonstrate that when they approached [counsel] they made it clear that they were seeking legal advice in their individual rather than in their representative capacities. Third, they must demonstrate that the [counsel] saw fit to communicate with them in their individual capacities, knowing that a possible conflict could arise. Fourth, they must prove that their conversations with [counsel] were confidential. And, fifth, they must show that the substance of their conversations with [counsel] did not concern matters within the company or the general affairs of the company.[74]

---

[71] 119 F.3d 210 (2d Cir. 1997).

[72] *Id.* at 215; *see also* United States v. Graf, 610 F.3d 1148 (9th Cir. 2010); United States v. Ruehle, 583 F.3d 600 (9th Cir. 2009); *The Matter of* Bevill, Bresler & Schulman Asset Mgmt. Corp., 805 F.2d 120, 124 (3d Cir. 1986); *Meredith*, 572 F.2d at 611 n. 5.

[73] *Teamsters*, 119 F.3d at 215.

[74] *Bevill*, 805 F.2d at 123 (quoting *In re* Grand Jury Investigation No. 83-30557, 575 F. Supp. 777, 780 (N.D. Ga. 1983)); *see also* United States v. Merida, 828 F.3d 1203, 1210 (10th Cir. 2016); *In re* Grand Jury Subpoena: Under Seal, 415 F.3d 333 (4th Cir. 2005).

Other courts concur that, if such a privilege is to be claimed, the onus is on the employee to make it clear to corporate counsel that he seeks legal advice on personal matters.[75]

Teamsters makes clear that an employee's unarticulated "reasonable belief" is not sufficient to confer upon the employee control of the privilege.[76] The rationale is that "[t]his standard would provide employees seeking to frustrate internal investigations with an exceedingly powerful weapon, and would stray quite far from the principle that the attorney-client privilege should be 'strictly confined' in order to allow public access to 'every man's evidence.'"[77]

Even where a corporate employee is able to demonstrate the existence of an individual attorney-client relationship running between the employee and corporate counsel, and claims that he and the corporation had a joint defense privilege, the individual may find that a corporate waiver also may explode the privilege he enjoys.[78] The First Circuit has stated (arguably in dicta) that "we hold that a corporation may unilaterally waive the attorney-client privilege with respect to communications made by a corporate officer in his corporate capacity, notwithstanding the existence of an individual attorney-client relationship between him and the corporation's counsel."[79]

While a corporate employee bears the burden of demonstrating an entitlement to the privilege under the above standards, does counsel bear an ethical obligation to make clear who constitutes the client and who "owns" the privilege during interviews of corporate employees? ABA Model Rule of Professional Conduct 1.13(d) provides that "[i]n dealing with an organizations's directors, officers, employees, members, shareholders or other constituents, a lawyer shall explain the identity of the client when it is apparent that the organization's interests are adverse to those of the constituents with whom the lawyer is dealing."[80]

8. *UPJOHN* WARNING

There is widespread agreement among white-collar practitioners that corporate counsel, before interviewing corporate employees, *must* give what is commonly referred to as an *"Upjohn* warning." The content of that warning is subject to debate; some practitioners are more thorough than others. That said, the elements of the warning can include the following: (1) counsel represents the company—not the employee—and is interviewing the employee to gather information in order to provide legal advice to the company; (2) the interview is confidential and covered by the attorney-client privilege; (3) but the privilege belongs to and is controlled by the company; (4) because the company—not the employee—owns the privilege, the company, but not the employee, may elect in future to waive any privilege and provide information derived from the interview to third parties, including prosecutors or regulators.[81] In some circumstances, this warning is

---

[75] *See, e.g., In re* Grand Jury Subpoena, 274 F.3d 563, 571 (1st Cir. 2001); In re Grand Jury Subpoenas, 144 F.3d 653, 658-59 (10th Cir. 1998). *Cf.* United States v. Ruehle, 583 F.3d 600, 608 n.7 (9th Cir. 2009) (summarizing different approaches but concluding that, on the facts of the case, it need not adopt a standard); Ross v. City of Memphis, 423 F.3d 596, 605 (6th Cir. 2005) (civil, public employment context).

[76] *Teamsters*, 119 F.3d at 214-16.

[77] *Id.* at 216 n.2.

[78] *See In re* Grand Jury Subpoena, 274 F.3d 563 (1st Cir. 2001).

[79] *Id.* at 573.

[80] *See also Teamsters*, 119 F.3d at 217.

[81] *See, e.g.,* Lonnie T. Brown, Jr., *Reconsidering the Corporate Attorney-Client Privilege: A Response to the Compelled-Voluntary Waiver Paradox,* 34 Hofstra L. Rev. 897, 938-39; Sara Helene Duggin, *Internal Corporate Investigations: Legal Ethics, Professionalism and the Employee Interview,* 2003 Colum. Bus. L. Rev.

dictated by ethical rules, at least where corporate counsel's client's interests are adverse to those of the employee being interviewed. In most cases, it is also required to serve the organizational client's overall interests.

As noted above, some courts have said that, in very narrow circumstances, they may allow corporate employees to assert a personal privilege over conversations with corporate counsel despite the fact that the privilege generally belongs to the corporation (although the employees bear a heavy burden in making such a claim and generally are unsuccessful). Thus, the "*Upjohn* warning" is given to preclude an employee from claiming to have believed that the attorney represented the employee during the interview, so as to claim control of the attorney-client privilege and prevent the company from disclosing the employee's statements to others.

With the advent of the Yates Memorandum (discussed in Chapter 4(C)) and its insistence that, to gain cooperation credit, organizations must turn over all relevant facts regarding individual corporate agents' culpability, some in the defense bar have questioned whether "enhanced *Upjohn* warnings may be a best practice, whether or not it rises to the level of an ethical obligation":

> Recall the first directive of the Memorandum—to be eligible for any cooperation credit, corporations must provide to the DOJ all relevant facts about the individuals involved in corporate misconduct. This specifically includes facts obtained from witness interviews, even if those interviews are privileged. The standard pre-Yates *Upjohn* warning should be supplemented to reflect this directive by making clear that (1) Corporation A may decide to cooperate with the DOJ in order to resolve the government's investigation of, or charges against, A, and (2) Corporation A may choose to disclose the entirety of a witness interview to government attorneys and/or investigators without consulting the witness. Indeed, it may be wise to make clear to the witness that if he or she discloses incriminating information during the interview that it is highly likely—and not just possible—that the corporation will disclose that information to the DOJ in order to obtain cooperation credit.
>
> The provision of enhanced *Upjohn* warnings may chill the constituent's candor and thereby undermine the truth-finding function of an internal investigation. Moreover, the DOJ may view enhanced *Upjohn* warnings as unnecessary and potentially a subterfuge designed to allow the company to assert its cooperation while ensuring that it will be unable to fully describe its misconduct to the DOJ. But this risk is likely unsubstantial, because constituents typically cooperate with investigations even when it is contrary to their self-interest—probably because many companies have "walk or talk" policies that deem non-cooperation a fireable offense, at least if the interview is conducted in the United States. This situation is unlikely to change if enhanced *Upjohn* warnings are given, unless employees decide that losing their jobs is a superior alternative to risking prison sentences that may result from disclosures during interviews. Conversely, if enhanced warnings are not provided, the constituent may be more likely to believe he or she has an attorney-client relationship with the company lawyer, which may lead the constituent to block disclosure to the government of information gleaned during the investigatory interview. In turn, this could both impede the company's ability to comply with the Yates Memorandum's requirement that all relevant facts be disclosed and "optically align the interests of the individual wrongdoer with the corporation."

The post-Yates environment may justify four additional modifications to pre-Yates *Upjohn* practice. First, counsel may be wise to develop a formal script for the delivery of *Upjohn* warnings. Second, while it is counterproductive to provide constituent witnesses with written warnings, it may be useful post-Yates to provide them with a written summary of the key points that comprise the oral warnings. Third, it also may be useful to require constituent witnesses to acknowledge in writing that they received *Upjohn* warnings and they understand the basic scope of the attorney-client privilege. Fourth, corporate counsel may have an ethical obligation to conform their *Upjohn* warnings to the standard policy of the DOJ with respect to targets of criminal investigations who testify to grand juries. The DOJ's policy is to advise such targets before they testify that their conduct is being investigated for possible violations of federal criminal law. Corporations that plan to interview employees suspected of illegal activity for the purpose of disclosing to the DOJ information gleaned during the interviews may have an ethical obligation to provide similar target warnings before the interviews begin. But the provision of such an enhanced warning increases the chances of a substantial chilling effect, which may reduce the company's capacity to gather relevant facts or identify culpable individuals.[82]

What other possible cautions might be added to the *Upjohn* warning? In light of the obstruction prosecutions of individuals for lying to corporate counsel in the course of an internal investigation (*see supra* Chapter 6(C)), should corporate counsel warn interviewees that the company is cooperating with the government? That if the interviewee lies she may face obstruction charges? That she ought to consult with a lawyer before deciding whether to go forward with the interview?

C. DOJ's "COMPELLED-VOLUNTARY" WAIVER POLICY

As noted in Chapter 4 (Entity Liability; DOJ Charging Policy), various Deputy Attorneys General have issued policies that outline the criteria upon which federal prosecutors must rely in deciding whether to criminally charge an organization. The DOJ organizational charging policy was first set forth in a 1999 DOJ Memorandum issued by then-Deputy Attorney General Eric Holder (the "Holder Memo").[83] One of the ten factors prosecutors were instructed to examine in making these decisions was identified as the corporation's "cooperation and voluntary disclosure," and the following was the stated policy with respect to privilege waivers in service of cooperation credit:

> One factor the prosecutor may weigh in assessing the adequacy of a corporation's cooperation is the completeness of its disclosure including, if necessary, a waiver of the attorney-client and work product protections, both with respect to its internal investigation and with respect to communications between specific officers, directors and employees and counsel. Such waivers permit the government to obtain statements of possible witnesses, subjects, and targets, without having to negotiate individual cooperation or immunity agreements. In addition, they are often critical in enabling the government to evaluate the completeness of a corporation's voluntary disclosure and cooperation. Prosecutors may, therefore, request a waiver in appropriate circumstances. The Department does not, however, consider waiver of a

---

[82] Gideon Mark, *The Yates Memorandum*, 51 U.C. Davis L. Rev. 1589, 1614-17 (2018).

[83] *See* Peter Lattman, *The Holder Memo and Its Progeny*, Wall St. J.Online (Dec. 13, 2006), at http://blogs.wsj.com/2006/12/13/the-holder-memo/.

corporation's attorney-client and work product protection an absolute requirement, and prosecutors should consider the willingness of a corporation to waive such protection when necessary to provide timely and complete information as one factor in evaluating the corporation's cooperation.

In a footnote, the following caution was added:

This waiver should ordinarily be limited to the factual internal investigation and any contemporaneous advice given to the corporation concerning the conduct at issue. Except in unusual circumstances, prosecutors should not seek a waiver with respect to communications and work product related to advice concerning the government's criminal investigation.

Mr. Holder's memo was updated in 2003 by then-Deputy Attorney General Larry Thompson, in major part to emphasize that prosecutors ought to scrutinize carefully the authenticity of a corporation's cooperation, but with no change to substance of the above-stated policy.

The Holder/Thompson policy on its face does not "require" privilege waivers as a condition for cooperation credit. The defense bar asserted, however, that prosecutors used the language of the standard to request waivers in virtually every corporate investigation. They objected that a policy that requires, in essence, regular waivers will thwart the rationales underlying the attorney-client privilege and work product doctrine, resulting in fewer internal investigations into corporate wrong-doing, less able investigations in cases where some inquiry is undertaken, and a likelihood that corporate employees will be less willing to share what they know with investigators. Counsel argued that the affect of the waiver policy was exacerbated by the absence of a "selective" waiver privilege. Thus, if corporations are forced to waive to the government in every case, they will be required to turn over whatever roadmap to liability their internal investigations reveal to civil plaintiffs.[84]

It is important to note that there was a serious contest over the issue of the frequency of waiver requests.[85] According to defense practitioners, "[w]aiver of the privilege is now a routine part of discussing a corporate resolution" of a criminal investigation.[86] Predictably, the DOJ responded, just as emphatically, that its prosecutors had been judicious in requesting privilege waivers,[87] doing so only where necessary to determine

---

[84] *See, e.g.*, Counsel Group Assails Prosecution Policy Compelling Corporations to Waive Privileges, 67 Crim. L. Rep. (BNA) 391, 393 (June 14, 2000).

[85] *Compare, e.g.*, Mary Beth Buchanan, *Effective Cooperation by Business Organizations and the Impact of Privilege Waivers*, 39 Wake Forest L. Rev. 587, 597-98 (2004) (discussing survey of 94 U.S. Attorney's Offices conducted in 2002, which indicated that "requests for waivers simply are not the norm"), *with* Am. Chemistry Council, Ass'n of Corp. Counsel, et al., *The Decline of the Attorney-Client Privilege in the Corporate Context: Survey Results* (March 2006); Ass'n of Corp Counsel, *Executive Summary, Association n of Corporate Counsel Survey: Is the Attorney/Client Privilege Under Attack?* (Apr. 2005); Nat'l Ass'n of Criminal Defense Lawyers, *Executive Summary, National Association of Criminal Defense Lawyers Survey: The Attorney-Client Privilege is Under Attack* (Apr. 2005).

[86] Joseph F. Savage, Jr. & Melissa M. Longo, *'Waive' Goodbye to Attorney–Client Privilege*, 7 Bus. Crimes Bull. No. 9, at 1 (Oct. 2000).

[87] *See, e.g.*, Buchanan, *supra* note 85; Joan C. Rodgers, *DOJ Official Suggests Corporate Defendants Do Not Have to Waive Privilege But It Helps*, 21 Laws. Man. on Prof. Conduct (BNA) 391, 391 (July 27, 2005) (noting Acting Assistant Attorney General John C. Richter's claim that "waiver of privilege is not a requirement and is not a litmus test for cooperation with the government"); Philip Urofsky, *Interview with United States Attorney James B. Comey Regarding Department of Justice's Policy on Requesting Corporations Under Criminal Investigation to Waive the Attorney Client Privilege and Work Product Protection*, in Corp. Couns. F. 2004, at 639, 642 (PLI Corp. Law & Practice, Course Handbook Series No. B-1421,

the underlying facts and to test the completeness of corporate efforts to cooperate. There also appears to be less than full information about just *what* the government requested—that is, the scope of the requested waivers and thus the extent of the solicited invasion.

The government said that it was only looking for the *facts*[88]—which corporate counsel could provide more effectively, quickly, and efficiently in many cases. Prosecutors noted that the cooperation policy did not *require* that corporations cooperate, let alone waive. Prosecutors asserted that because the corporation and their counsel were seeking a significant dispensation from the government, that dispensation should not be cost-free, particularly if the "cost" (waiver) was intended not to punish but rather to permit the government to get to the bottom of criminal conduct.

An "oddball alliance of business, legal, and civil liberties groups," including the ACLU, the Chamber of Commerce, and the Association of Corporate Council, lobbied Congress against the policy. This alliance was successful in pursuing its cause, for example, by securing an amendment to the U.S. Sentencing Guidelines for Organizations deleting a reference to privilege waivers in the context of assessing corporate cooperation efforts.[89] More important, the defense bar and its allies were able to get the attention of some in Congress, which proposed "fixing" the problem in legislation that would bar federal prosecutors from asking for or considering corporate privilege waivers when deciding whether to bring criminal or civil charges.[90]

Most notably, this alliance's success in gaining the attention of lawmakers pressured the DOJ to adopt a revised policy, reflected in the "McNulty Memo."[91] This Memo continued to authorize requests for corporate privilege waivers, but it required prosecutors to consider identified factors before requesting waivers, was more detailed regarding the types of materials that could be requested, and mandated that requests be considered, and in some cases, approved at the highest levels of Main Justice. The DOJ's olive branch was promptly rejected by the American Bar Association, whose President,

---

2004).

[88] *See* Buchanan, *supra* note 85, at 596-97. U.S. Attorney Mary Beth Buchanan asserted, for example, that:

> [T]he information disclosed pursuant to a waiver is nearly always attorney work product concerning the underlying facts, rather than privileged communications. [Further,] the work product protection, as opposed to the attorney-client privilege, is not absolute, so that disclosure to a civil litigant may be ordered upon a showing of substantial need, pursuant to Federal Rule of Civil Procedure 26(b)(3). Even with respect to work product, the government rarely seeks the attorney's mental impressions of witness interviews. To avoid any such disclosure unnecessarily, experienced attorneys will refrain from including mental impressions and strategy in their notes of witness interviews. While disclosure of the underlying facts may in some cases reveal some of the questions asked of employees by counsel for the organization, any such intrusion into counsel's mental processes is minimal.

Id.

[89] U.S. Sentencing Comm'n, Amendments to the Sentencing Guidelines, May 18, 2006, at 45 (eliminating final sentence of Application Note 12 to § 8C2.5, which stated "[w]aiver of attorney-client privilege and of work product protections is not a prerequisite to a reduction in culpability score[] unless such waiver is necessary in order to provide timely and thorough disclosure of all pertinent information known to the organization") (effective Nov. 1, 2006).

[90] *See also* Proposed (but not adopted) Fed. R. Evid. 502(c) ("In a federal or state proceeding, a disclosure of a communication or information covered by the attorney-client or work product protection–when made to a federal public office or agency in the exercise of its regulatory, investigative, or enforcement authority–does not operate as a waiver of the privilege or protection in favor of non-governmental persons or entities."), transmission letter from Advisory Comm. (May 16, 2006).

[91] Jason McLure, *The Life and Death of the Thompson Memo*, Legal Times (Dec. 18, 2006).

Karen J. Mathis, issued a press release stating that the McNulty guidelines fell "far short of what is needed to prevent further erosion of fundamental attorney-client privilege, work product, and employee protections during government investigations."[92] And the DOJ did not satisfy those on the Hill who expressed interest in intervening to ban DOJ privilege waiver requests. One month after issuance of the McNulty Memo, Senator Arlen Specter introduced a bill, the "Attorney-Client Privilege Protection Act of 2007," which would bar federal actors from demanding or requesting, or conditioning lenient treatment on, privilege waivers.[93]

With this not-so-subtle reminder of congressional concern, DOJ, in the person of Deputy Attorney General Mark Filip, finally issued another revision of its policy in August 2008.[94] This third iteration of DOJ policy on the substance and effect of corporate "cooperation" in criminal charging decisions is now referred to as the "Filip Memo."[95] The Filip Memo seems to simplify matters considerably, at least measured against the detailed—and now apparently obsolete—guidelines and approval requirements embedded in the McNulty policy. Its bottom line is clear: (1) privilege waivers are not (and assertedly have never been) a prerequisite for cooperation credit or for declination of criminal charges; (2) a corporation may freely waive its privileges if it wishes; (3) *but* that waiver may not be considered when a prosecutor decides whether to give a corporation credit for its cooperation in charging; (4) rather, the critical determinant is *whether the entity has provided prosecutors with the facts necessary for them to investigate the matter fairly and responsibly.*[96]

Some in practice have correctly summarized the ultimate DOJ message as: "we don't care if you waive, just provide the relevant facts," leaving it to practitioners to sort out if and how that can be achieved while maintaining the privilege protections.[97] Although the above appears to respond to the proposed legislation, the revised policy does not institute Congress's proposed bar on prosecutorial requests for waivers. The policy seemingly permits prosecutors to ask for waivers of "fact" work product and privileged communications, but it does provide that corporations "need not produce, and prosecutors may not request," such "core" work product and attorney-client privileged materials as attorneys' notes of witness interviews and advice given to the client concerning the legal implications of the putative misconduct at issue "as a condition for the corporation's eligibility to receive cooperation credit."[98] In assessing the merits of this debate, and the value of the proposed litigation, consider the following:

---

[92] *Id.*

[93] *See* S. 445, 111th Cong., 1st Sess. (Feb. 13, 2009); *see also* S. 186, 110th Cong., 1st Sess. (Jan. 4, 2007); Margaret Aulino, *House Subcommittee Wants to Bolster Means to Combat Forced Waiver of Privilege,* Corporate Accountability & Fraud Daily (BNA).

[94] *See* Principles of Federal Prosecution of Business Organizations §§ 9.28.000 to 9.28.1300 (2018).

[95] *See id.*

[96] *Id.* at 10.

[97] Davis Polk & Wardwell, White Collar Update (Sept. 5, 2008), *available at* http://www.dpw.com.

[98] *See* Filip Memo, cited *supra* note 94. This last injunction is subject to the standard exceptions: where the advice of counsel defense is asserted; where the communications at issue are subject to the crime-fraud exception to privilege rules; and where the conduct at issue constitutes criminal obstruction.

Julie R. O'Sullivan, *The Last Straw: The Department of Justice's Privilege Waiver Policy And the Death of Adversarial Justice in Criminal Investigations of Corporations*
57 DePaul L. Rev. 329 (2008)

The white-collar criminal defense bar has never been reticent to complain about U.S. Department of Justice (DOJ) policies that threaten its clients or the viability of its practice. But nothing—at least in the author's twenty-plus years of involvement in white-collar issues—has consumed the bar as much as the threats posed to the corporate attorney-client privilege and work product doctrine.[99] While commentators have identified a variety of assaults on these protections,[100] the bar is most vocally outraged by the DOJ policy, pursuant to which, it charges, federal prosecutors regularly insist that corporations waive these protections to secure cooperation credit, declination of criminal action against the corporate actor, and consideration at sentencing. For some time now, the defense objections to this particular policy have been unusually sustained, widespread, and passionate. Until recently, very few outside the DOJ have questioned the bona fides of these objections.[101] ...

Why has this issue energized the corporate defense bar as never before and seemingly resonated with the judicial and political establishments? At the outset, let me state what I do *not* think is going on. The rationale most often used to explain the bar's aversion to the DOJ's compelled-voluntary waiver policy is that it undermines the policies underlying the attorney-client privilege and work product doctrine.[102] [It is my position that] ... the attorney-client privilege is *not* necessary to ensure that public corporations continue conducting competent internal investigations when allegations of wrongdoing arise; and ... that the corporate privilege is *not* effective in inducing rational employees to disclose to corporate counsel information that they otherwise would not.

Public corporations essentially have no choice but to investigate when confronted with possible corporate malfeasance. Internal investigations certainly have their costs, but given the imperatives created by statutory, regulatory, prosecutorial, sentencing, civil liability, and corporate law pressures, "the internal investigation has become the standard of care whenever credible allegations of significant misconduct are raised in

---

[99] [Article footnote 1:] *See, e.g.*, Lance Cole, *Revoking Our Privileges: Federal Law Enforcement's Multi-Front Assault on the Attorney-Client Privilege (And Why it is Misguided)*, 48 Vill. L. Rev. 469 (2003); David M. Zornow & Keith D. Krakaur, *On the Brink of a Brave New World: The Death of Privilege in Corporate Criminal Investigations*, 37 Am. Crim. L. Rev. 147 (2000). *See also* Am. College of Trial Lawyers, *The Erosion of the Attorney-Client Privilege and Work Product Doctrine in Federal Criminal Investigations*, 41 Duq. L. Rev. 307 (2003); *Counsel Group Assails Prosecution Policy Compelling Corporations to Waive Privileges*, 67 Crim. L. Rep. (BNA) 391 (June 14, 2000); Joseph F. Savage, Jr. & Melissa M. Longo, *'Waive' Goodbye to Attorney–Client Privilege*, 7 Bus. Crimes Bull., Oct. 2000, at 1; Breckinridge L. Wilcox, *Attorney/Client Privilege Waiver: Wrongheaded Practice?*, 6 Bus. Crimes Bull., Jan. 2000, at 1.

[100] [Article footnote 2:] *See* Cole, *supra* note [99]; *Counsel Group Assails Prosecution Policy Compelling Corporations to Waive Privileges*, *supra* note [99].

[101] [Article footnote 4:] *See, e.g.*, Lonnie T. Brown, Jr., *Reconsidering the Corporate Attorney-Client Privilege: A Response to the Compelled-Voluntary Waiver Paradox*, 34 Hofstra L. Rev. 897, 897-900 (2006); Daniel Richman, *Decisions About Coercion: The Corporate Attorney-Client Privilege Waiver Problem*, 57 DePaul L. Rev. 295 (2008).

[102] [Article footnote 13:] *See, e.g.*, [The McNulty Memorandum's Effect on the Right to Counsel in Corporate Investigations: Before the Subcomm. on Crime, Terrorism, and Homeland Security of the H. Comm. on the Judiciary, 110 Cong. 11-12 (2007) (Statement of Karen J. Mathis, President, ABA).]

organizational settings."[103] Corporations, then, have compelling incentives to investigate allegations of potential criminal wrongdoing, whether or not the attorney-client privilege will ultimately shield the facts revealed by their investigative efforts.

Some object that, if work product waivers are encouraged, corporate counsel will respond by compromising the depth or quality of their investigation. In particular, counsel will refuse to record incriminating evidence. However, given the dynamics of internal corporate investigations and the regulatory environment, this author does not think that competent lawyers will compromise the quality of either their investigations or their eventual advice to clients because of the potential for government-induced privilege waivers. If they do so, it is malpractice. First, serious corporate investigations require papering; if counsel decides not to write down facts she finds troubling to the corporation, she is necessarily going to do a shoddy job. Counsel needs all the facts to adequately advise the client, and ignoring certain facts will necessarily disserve the client. In addition to compromising the quality of counsel's advice, such actions would more generally run contrary to the entity's interests.

Criminal prosecutors are certainly one audience for internal investigations, but far from the only, or even most crucial. In fact, one of the "primary goals in retaining investigatory counsel is to conduct a fair, thorough and complete investigation so [companies] can assure investors, regulators and employees that [they have] discovered the extent of any problems that exist and [have] a plan not only to correct them but to prevent their recurrence."[104] As Marjorie Peerce and Peggy Cross have further explained this goal:

> Whether the company succeeds in providing these assurances depends in significant part on the degree of confidence these groups have in the outside counsel conducting the investigation. One thing is certain: unless they trust that the investigation was truly an independent one, they are not likely to have faith in the outcome. Such a lack of faith can have devastating consequences for the company: valuable employees distrustful of management may leave, investors may pull their support, and regulators may disregard the results of the internal investigation and decide to conduct their own, disrupting the company and further undermining the investing public's faith in it. And if regulators feel that the investigation was deliberately compromised by the lack of independence, they may decide to investigate the company and its senior management further.[105]

Accordingly, some practitioners, far from cautioning counsel to stop taking notes of potentially inculpatory statements made in witness interviews, actually stress that such material *must* be included in the final report counsel renders to the entity's board because "[i]f the company decides to disclose the report to the Government a report that presents the incriminating evidence as well as the exculpatory evidence is more likely to be credited by law enforcement officials; government officials are likely to discount a report that ignores incriminating evidence."[106]

The report will also be ignored, or worse, by the other regulatory and business constituencies noted above. In the eyes of prosecutors, a selective, biased, or sloppy

---

[103] [Article footnote 15:] Sara Helene Duggin, *Internal Corporate Investigations: Legal Ethics, Professionalism and the Employee Interview*, 2003 Colum. Bus. L. Rev. 859, 886 (2003).

[104] [Article footnote 16:] [Marjorie J. Peerce & Peggy M. Cross, *Independent Corporate* Investigations, 14 Bus. Crimes Bull., Jan. 2007, at 6.]

[105] [Article footnote 17:] *Id.*

[106] [Article footnote 18:] Kenneth B. Winer *et al*, *Internal Investigations and the Foreign Corrupt Practices Act*, 1588 PLI/Corp. 286, 334 (2007)].

investigative effort is worse than no effort at all, because the government is likely to view it as a whitewash, an attempt to protect management, or, at worst, an actionable obstruction. If it is in the corporate client's best interests to investigate—as it will almost always be—it will also be in the entity's best interest that the investigation is unbiased, fair, and thorough.

Finally, the existence of a privilege owned by the corporation does not create incentives for the rational individual employee to share information with corporate counsel *that he or she otherwise would not.* Some employees will provide corporate counsel with the details of their wrongdoing even after being given the so-called *Upjohn* warning informing them that counsel does not represent them and that the corporation owns the privilege shielding their conversation. But those employees' irrational choices certainly cannot be attributed to the existence of a corporate attorney-client privilege; rather, it is likely precipitated by corporate threats to fire uncooperative employees. Indeed, to the extent that the extension of the corporate privilege to these circumstances carries an obligation to warn the witness that she does not own or control the privilege and that her statement is confidential only so long as the corporation wants it to be, the privilege may actually inhibit fulsome communication.

If privilege waivers do not unduly undermine the rationales for the attorney-client privilege and work product protection, why is the bar so distraught? There are, no doubt, a complex of factors, some of them self-interested, that contribute to this phenomenon. But, after numerous conferences, discussions, and informal talks with white-collar practitioners, my sense of the predominant "why" of this is difficult to footnote but very clear: these advocates are genuinely outraged by the feeling that the government has stepped over the line and made it virtually impossible for them function as defenders of corporate clients in an adversary confrontation with the government.

[My] thesis turns on a circumstance that is rarely raised in this debate, but which is central to it: collective entities, such as corporations, cannot claim the Fifth Amendment right against self-incrimination. The attorney-client privilege and the work product doctrine are critical, not because they encourage self-correction or candid communication between corporate client and counsel, but rather because they serve as a substitute for the Fifth Amendment in criminal investigations of corporations in two senses.

First, from a systemic point of view, the lack of a Fifth Amendment privilege strips a company of the only weapon it has in the pre-indictment stage to counterbalance the weighty advantages the government enjoys at this point: the power to refuse to provide evidence that will be a link in the chain to its own conviction. Second, and more concretely, these protections are the only means through which corporations, deprived of any privilege against self-incrimination, may shield from government scrutiny that which the government truly wants and often needs to make its case: the informed conclusions of counsel regarding what records are relevant and the witness statements to which counsel will be privy. Demands for this analytical and evidentiary material—in effect, in many cases, a roadmap for liability—forces counsel not only to lay her client open for the government, but also to be the engineer of the case against it. Counsel's ultimate aim, of course, is to persuade the government that such extraordinary efforts warrant a declination of prosecution.

Practitioners do not analyze the waiver issue in the above terms, but the general objections contained in some of their literature are entirely consistent with this thesis. In particular, two related themes emerge from a survey of practitioners' writings on this and related issues. First, practitioners seem to object to the pervasive presuppositions underlying the DOJ's policy—and the policies of a wide array of federal institutions—that corporations have duties not visited upon individuals to self-report potential wrongdoing within the company, cooperate fully with government investigators, remedy any damage, and act aggressively to prevent recurrence of the objectionable behavior. The assumption is that the proper role of corporations confronted with allegations of wrongdoing, is, quite simply, to roll over. Individual defendants can fight like hell, but corporations should self-report, remediate harm, cooperate fully, and take whatever prosecutors and regulators believe they have coming. Zealous defense counsel find this assumption beyond galling.

The second theme resonating throughout the literature flows from the first. The bar argues that the waiver policy essentially "deputizes" corporate counsel in furtherance of this "crime-fighting partnership" between corporate America and the government. By definition, the reigning conception of what corporations *ought* to do when confronted by allegations of criminal wrongdoing means that counsel are no longer conceived of as the corporation's champions, poised to defend their clients in an adversarial joust. Rather, they are simply functionaries charged with exposing whatever wrongdoing has occurred, and advocates only in trying to talk the government into taking the least damaging avenue—such as regulatory sanction rather than criminal prosecution—in response to whatever is uncovered. In short, zealous advocates feel that they have become junior g-men, and they hate it.

What prevents corporate counsel and their clients from simply saying "no" to this new paradigm? The answer is that they would if they could, but a variety of circumstances conspire to make such choices exceedingly difficult. The same coercive forces that make the adversary system a myth in the context of corporate criminal liability also take away the bargaining leverage of corporations in attempting to resist DOJ privilege waiver "requests." These circumstances ... include the malleable nature of the federal criminal code, the overbroad standards of corporate criminal liability, and the range and harshness of sanctions applicable upon conviction. The DOJ and other regulators could talk about "crime-fighting partnerships with corporate American"[107] all they wish and could attempt to "deputize" defense counsel to work on their behalf, but absent these circumstances, the defense could quite simply say "no" or "prove it," as is at least their hypothetical privilege in an adversary system. Given the existence of these coercive factors, however, counsel have few options in resisting government inquiries.

... [W]hy [are] "requests" for waiver of a corporation's attorney-client privilege and work product doctrine ... viewed both as virtually irresistible and as the critical "tipping point" in the balance of power between the government and the defense and the evisceration of defense counsel's role[?] To mix metaphors, the coercive factors mentioned above are the lever that DOJ prosecutors and other government agents have used to move the corporate boulder up to the precipice overlooking the Sea of Complete Capitulation. Once the "last straw" of privilege waivers is laid on, the lever sends the boulder over the cliff to be smothered in that Sea. ...

The DOJ would argue that it can, and should, do everything possible to quickly and efficiently nip corporate crime in the bud and that corporate cooperation in this regard, through waivers of privilege and other means, is in the best interests of the public, as well as the entity and its shareholders. Prosecutors' positions are not irrational. Corporate crime can be exceedingly costly to society—whether that cost is assessed in financial terms, as collateral damage (for example, to the environment or to public safety), or by reference to public confidence in markets, financial institutions, and the like. Viewed from the perspective of punishing and deterring corporate crime through the most efficient and effective allocation of government resources, a "crime-fighting partnership" between the government and corporate America makes sense, as does enlistment of experienced corporate counsel as investigating arms of the government.

The only problem is that a similar balancing could be made for rapists, drug dealers, and murderers. Individual defendants' rights to resist the government to the bitter end are also costly and counterproductive measured by law enforcement imperatives. Yet the

---

[107] [Article footnote 22:] *See, e.g.,* John F. Savarese & David B. Anders, *DOJ Adopts Revised Polices on Corporate Prosecution* (Dec. 13, 2006). The McNulty Memo does not "[change] the fundamental principle that corporations are liable, in virtually all cases, for criminal misconduct by their employees. Thus, prosecutors will continue to have enormous leverage over corporations and corporations will, in turn, continue to have powerful incentives to try to appear as cooperative as possible to prosecutors." *Id.*

government has not structured its policies, at least as explicitly or comprehensively, with the clear expectation that individuals are wrong or irrational to stand on their rights. The assumption that corporations should engage in a "crime-fighting partnership" with the government, even if it means criminal prosecution and hefty penalties, is such a constant that its foundation is rarely, if ever, examined. But it does require justification and I have not heard a convincing one.

... [I]f society truly believes that the adversary system is the best and fairest way to test criminal charges when individuals are in the government's cross-hairs, it is not at all clear why legal entities such as corporations should be denied its benefits. ... That being the case, the DOJ could at least ameliorate the "justice" imbalance by reconsidering its "compelled-voluntary" waiver policy. ...

D. LOSING THE PRIVILEGE: CRIME/FRAUD EXCEPTION

IN RE SEALED CASE
107 F.3d 46 (D.C.Cir.1997)

RANDOLPH, CIRCUIT JUDGE:

This appeal arises out of ongoing grand jury proceedings. The grand jury is investigating violations of federal election laws. The record is sealed. The appellant is a corporation, which we shall call the "Company." The Company refused to produce two subpoenaed documents, for which it was held in contempt. One of the documents is a memorandum from a Company vice president to the president, with a copy to the Company's general counsel. The memorandum reflects a conversation between the vice president and the Company's general counsel about campaign finance laws. The Company withheld it on the basis of the attorney-client privilege. The other document is a memorandum written by the general counsel, apparently at the request of outside counsel. The Company withheld it on the basis of the attorney-client privilege and work product immunity.

The district court examined both documents *in camera*, and, without deciding whether they were covered by the privilege or the work product doctrine, ordered the Company to turn them over. The court found that the crime-fraud exception applied because of these circumstances. In late June 1994, the Company's political action committee contributed the maximum amount permitted by law to a former candidate for federal office who was seeking to retire his campaign debt. The vice president wrote his memorandum and had his discussion with the general counsel in early August 1994. Later in the same month, the vice president called two individuals who did business with the Company and asked them to contribute to the former candidate. The individuals and their wives made the contributions. After several weeks had passed, the vice president authorized checks to be drawn from his department's budget to reimburse these individuals not only for the amount of their contributions, but also to make up for the additional taxes they would incur from reporting the reimbursement as income. The vice president's solicitation may have been permissible but, according to the government, this use of corporate funds was illegal.

The other subpoenaed document—the general counsel's memorandum to the file— was written more than a year later. It mentions dates in November 1995, and according to the Company's appellate counsel, recites actions the Company took to correct the vice president's use of corporate funds to reimburse the donors.

In addition to appealing from the order to produce the documents and the contempt citation, the Company appeals the district court's order compelling the vice president to testify in the grand jury about a late August 1994 meeting between him, the Company's president, and its general counsel. The participants at the meeting discussed certain facts and the general counsel gave legal advice about federal election laws. In the grand jury, the vice president—who had been granted immunity—invoked the attorney-client privilege on behalf of the Company. Again, the district court ruled that the crime-fraud exception applied and ordered him to testify about the late August 1994 meeting. The vice president then signed an affidavit stating that he would honor the court's directive. The court stayed its order pending the outcome of the Company's appeal.

We will take up first the vice president's early August 1994 memorandum and his meeting in late August 1994 with the president and general counsel. Both the memorandum and the meeting, as the Company sees it, are covered by the attorney-client privilege. Since the district court has yet to pass on this question, we will assume the Company is correct. ... In modern society, legal advice and assistance is often essential. To provide effective representation, attorneys need "full and frank" disclosures from their clients. Clients, it has been thought, might not be forthright if their lawyers could be turned into witnesses against them or if they could be forced to disclose their conversations with their lawyers.

The relationship between client and counsel may, however, be abused. And so the attorney-client privilege is subject to what is known as the crime-fraud exception. Two conditions must be met. First, the client must have made or received the otherwise privileged communication with the intent to further an unlawful or fraudulent act.[108] Second, the client must have carried out the crime or fraud. In other words, the exception does not apply even though, at one time, the client had bad intentions. Otherwise "it would penalize a client for doing what the privilege is designed to encourage—consulting a lawyer for the purpose of achieving law compliance." *See* Restatement of the Law Governing Lawyers § 142 cmt. c, at 461 (Proposed Final Draft No. 1, 1996).[109]

The privilege is the client's, and it is the client's fraudulent or criminal intent that matters. A third party's bad intent cannot remove the protection of the privilege. For example, a stenographer hired to record a meeting between an attorney and a client might intend to use his notes to commit some kind of crime—say extortion—but the contents of the meeting would not therefore cease to be privileged. Otherwise, existence of the attorney-client privilege would be unpredictable and the interest of "full and frank communication" between client and counsel would be undermined.

As the party seeking to overcome the privilege, the government had the burden of showing that the crime-fraud exception applied to the memorandum and the meeting. What was the nature of that burden? Here we encounter some confusion. This court and others have described the required showing in terms of establishing a "prima facie" case. The formulation can be traced to the Supreme Court's opinion in *Clark v. United States*, 289 U.S. 1, 14 (1933). The problem is, as the Supreme Court mentioned in [*United States v. Zolin*, 491 U.S. 554, 565 n. 7 (1989)], that "prima facie" evokes the concept, familiar in civil litigation, of shifting the burden from one party to another. Yet it is altogether clear where the burden in these cases lies—on the party invoking the crime-fraud exception. In

---

[108] [Court's footnote 2:] In nearly all cases, a client's innocence will bar application of the crime-fraud exception. We say "nearly all" because there may be rare cases—this is not one of them—in which the attorney's fraudulent or criminal intent defeats a claim of privilege even if the client is innocent.

[109] [Court's footnote 3:] To this the *Restatement* drafters added: "By the same token, lawyers might be discouraged from giving full and candid advice to clients about legally questionable courses of action." This seems to us rather doubtful. Why would a lawyer put his client—and himself—at such risk? Fully advising the client may prevent possibly unlawful action. On the other hand, if the lawyer gives less than "full and candid" advice, the client may rely on it, wind up violating the law and thus lose the privilege anyway. A lawyer representing such a client would have reason to be concerned about his own personal civil and criminal liability. Rather than discouraging full advice, that prospect plus the danger to the client provides a strong incentive for the lawyer to advise the client clearly and firmly.

terms of the level of proof, is a "prima facie showing" a preponderance of the evidence, clear and convincing evidence, or something else?

Our opinion in [*In re* Sealed Case, 754 F.2d 395 (D.C.Cir.1985) (hereinafter *Sealed Case II*)] contains this answer: "The government satisfies its burden of proof if it offers evidence that if believed by the trier of fact would establish the elements of an ongoing or imminent crime or fraud." We appended a footnote to this statement explaining that although the Second Circuit had "framed the test in terms of probable cause to believe that a crime or fraud had been committed and that the communications were in furtherance thereof," there was "little practical difference" between that standard and the one just quoted from *Sealed Case II*. We confess some difficulty in understanding why the differences between the two formulations were considered slight, but there is no reason to dwell on the matter.[110] It is apparent here that the government failed to make the sort of probable cause showing the Second Circuit would demand, or the showing *Sealed Case II* contemplated.

The critical consideration is that the government's presentation had to be aimed at the intent and action of the client. It was not enough for the government to show that the vice president committed a crime after he wrote his memorandum and attended the late August meeting with Company counsel. The holder of the privilege is the client and, in this case, the client was the Company, not the vice president. Unless the government made some showing that the Company intended to further and did commit a crime, the government could not invoke the crime-fraud exception to the privilege.

As to the late August meeting, the government's evidence reveals that the participants discussed campaign finance laws. That is not enough. One cannot reasonably infer from the meeting that the Company was consulting its general counsel with the intention of committing a crime, or even that the vice president was then doing so. Companies operating in today's complex legal and regulatory environments routinely seek legal advice about how to handle all sorts of matters, ranging from their political activities to their employment practices to transactions that may have antitrust consequences. There is nothing necessarily suspicious about the officers of this corporation getting such advice. True enough, within weeks of the meeting about campaign finance law, the vice president violated that law. But the government had to demonstrate that the Company sought the legal advice with the intent to further its illegal conduct. Showing temporal proximity between the communication and a crime is not enough.

Moreover, from the material before the district court, there was no way of knowing or even guessing whether the vice president was on a frolic of his own, against the advice of Company counsel, when he reimbursed the donors with corporate funds. The government suggested at oral argument that even if he was, the Company still could be held criminally liable. There are circumstances under which corporations are responsible for the crimes of their agents. But neither in this court nor in the district court did the government offer anything in terms of evidence or law to support the idea that the Company bore criminal responsibility for the acts of this officer. The government therefore did not sustain its burden. ...

Many of the same points can be made about the vice president's memorandum. Like the district court, we have examined this document, which the Company submitted *in camera* and *ex parte*. From the memorandum and the other information the government presented, all that can be discerned is that the Company's vice president and its general counsel discussed federal election laws in early August 1994, perhaps at the suggestion of the Company's president. The

---

[110] [Court's footnote 6:] *Zolin* left the standard of proof question for another day. The Supreme Court decided only that the crime-fraud exception need not be established entirely with independent evidence; that courts may review allegedly privileged materials *in camera* in order to determine whether the crime-fraud exception applies; and that before "engaging in *in camera* review ..., the judge should require a showing of a factual basis adequate to support a good faith belief by a reasonable person that *in camera* review of the materials may reveal evidence to establish the claim that the crime-fraud exception applies."

memorandum reflected that discussion. Again, given the need for corporations and their officers to seek legal advice about activities like political contributions, there is nothing suspect about this discussion. And the fact that the vice president broke the law weeks later does not, without more, demonstrate the validity of the government's assumption that the Company intended or probably intended to further that crime.

This brings us to the second of the two documents the Company withheld. We have examined the document. It is a memorandum by the Company's general counsel, written to the file and relating to matters that occurred one year after the vice president's illegal action. As Company counsel seemed to agree at oral argument, the document is covered by work product immunity rather than the attorney-client privilege. The protection for attorney work product is broader than the attorney-client privilege, but less absolute. Work product immunity covers not only confidential communications between the attorney and client. It also attaches to other materials prepared by attorneys (and their agents) in anticipation of litigation. Like the attorney-client privilege, work product immunity promotes the rendering of effective legal services. And as with the privilege, the interests in favor of work product immunity are overcome when the client uses the attorney to further a crime or fraud.

With respect to work product immunity, the crime-fraud exception calls for a somewhat different inquiry than with the attorney-client privilege. The focus is not on the client's intent regarding a particular communication, but on the client's intent in consulting the lawyer or in using the materials the lawyer prepared. The question is: Did the client consult the lawyer or use the material for the purpose of committing a crime or fraud?[111]

In light of these principles, the government's argument for invoking the crime-fraud exception goes nowhere. As is apparent from the nature of the inquiry, the crime-fraud exception for work product immunity cannot apply if the attorney prepared the material after his client's wrongdoing ended. Here, the general counsel wrote the memorandum long after the vice president committed the offenses. The government points out that work product might still be in furtherance of a crime or fraud even if the client's original offense was complete. The client could be using the attorney to cover up or conceal his first crime. The trouble is that the government has made no such allegation here and, even if it did, we have spotted nothing in the record that would support it. And if the government cannot show that the Company or any of its officers tried to or intended to cover up the vice president's illegality, it surely cannot show that the Company used its general counsel for that purpose. ...

Notes

1. The circuits seem to be in agreement that those seeking to obtain otherwise protected documents using the crime-fraud exception must prove a prima facie case that "(1) the client was committing or intending to commit a fraud or crime, and (2) the attorney-client communications were in furtherance of that alleged crime or fraud." *In re* Grand Jury Subpoena, 223 F.3d 213, 217 (3d Cir. 2000); *see also In re* Richard Roe, Inc., 168 F.3d 69, 71 (2d Cir. 1999); *In re* Grand Jury Investigation (Schroeder), 842 F.2d 1223, 1226 (11th Cir. 1987); *In re* Int'l Sys. & Controls Corp., 693 F.2d 1235, 1242 (5th Cir. 1982); *In re* Sealed Case, 676 F.2d 793, 814-15 (D.C. Cir. 1982). It is in applying these principles that the courts have created "a patchwork of standards." Geraldine Gauthier, Note, *Dangerous Liaisons: Attorney-Client Privilege, the Crime-Fraud Exception, ABA Model Rule 1.6 and Post-September 11 Counter-Terrorism*

---

111 [Court's footnote 7:] So long as the client had the requisite intent, the proposed Restatement removes work product immunity—but not the attorney-client privilege—even if the client never carries out the crime or fraud. Compare § 132 with § 142 of the Restatement of the Law Governing Lawyers, *supra*. Why the crime-fraud exception differs in these two contexts is not explained in the draft's commentary or in the reporter's notes.

Measures, 68 Brooklyn L. Rev. 351 (2002); *see also* Thomas M. DiBiagio, *Federal Criminal Law and the Crime-Fraud Exception: Disclosure of Privileged Communications and Documents Should Not Be Compelled Without the Government's Factual Foundation Being Tested By the Crucible of Meaningful Adversarial Testing*, 62 Md. L. Rev. 1 (2003). *Cf.* Cary Bricker, *Revisiting the Crime-Fraud Exception to the Attorney-Client Privilege: A Proposal to Remedy the Disparity in Protections for Civil and Criminal Privilege Holders*, 82 Temp. L. Rev. 149 (2009) (noting disparity in procedure applied in civil versus criminal cases).

2. With respect to the first prong, the Eleventh Circuit has explained that "there must be a prima facie showing that the client was engaged in criminal or fraudulent activity when he sought the advice of counsel, that he was planning such conduct when he sought the advice of counsel, or that he committed a crime or fraud subsequent to receiving the benefit of counsel's advice." *Schroeder*, 842 F.2d at 1226. In the above case, the D.C. Circuit states that "the client must have carried out the crime or fraud" in order to avoid penalizing the client's "bad intentions." The Second Circuit has rejected the argument that the crime-fraud exception will only apply if the crime or fraud has actually taken place, stating that "[t]he crime or fraud need not have occurred for the exception to be applicable; it need only have been the objective of the client's communication. ... [T]he client need not have succeeded in his criminal or fraudulent scheme for the exception to apply. If a fraudulent plan were ineffective, the client's communications would not thereby be protected from disclosure." *In re* Grand Jury Subpoena Duces Tecum (Marc Rich & Co.), 731 F.2d 1032, 1039 (2d Cir. 1984); *see also In re* Grand Jury Subpoena, 745 F.3d 681 (3d Cir. 2014). At the very least, however, even where the crime was never completed, there must have been a criminal or fraudulent intent at the time of the attorney-client communication. H. Lowell Brown, *The Crime-Fraud Exception to the Attorney-Client Privilege in the Context of Client Counseling*, 87 Ky. L.J. 1191, 1226 (1998-99). And it is very clear that while "[a]dvice sought in furtherance of a future or ongoing fraud is unprivileged," "communications with respect to advice as to past or completed frauds is within the privilege." 731 F.2d at 1041; *see also In re* Grand Jury Proceedings (FMC Corp.), 604 F.2d 798, 803 (3d Cir. 1979).

3. With respect to the second prong, courts vary in how they express the degree of relatedness required between the criminal or fraudulent intent of the client and the communication sought to be revealed. *See, e.g., In re* Grand Jury Subpoena, 745 F.3d 681 (3d Cir. 2014) (legal advice must be used "in furtherance" of the crime or fraud; more relaxed "related to" standard is rejected); *In re* Grand Jury Investigation, 445 F.3d 266, 276-280 (3d Cir. 2006); *Schroeder*, 842 F.2d at 1227 (citing cases articulating degree of nexus to be "reasonably relate," "close relationship," "potential relationship"); *In re* Sealed Case, 676 F.2d at 815 & n.91. Why require a demonstrated nexus between the intended crime and the communications at issue? As the Third Circuit has explained:

> We must always keep in mind that the purpose of the crime-fraud exception is to assure that the "seal of secrecy" between lawyer and client does not extend to communications from the lawyer to the client made by the lawyer for the purpose of giving advice for the commission of a fraud or crime. The seal is broken when the lawyer's communication is meant to facilitate future wrongdoing by the client. Where the client commits a fraud or crime for reasons completely independent of legitimate advice communicated by the lawyer, the seal is not broken, for the advice is, as logicians explain, *non causa pro causa*. The communication condemned and unprotected by the attorney-client privilege is advice that is illicit because it gives direction for the commission of future fraud or crime. The advice must relate to future illicit conduct by the client; it is the *causa pro causa*, the advice that leads to the deed.

Haines v. Liggett Group, Inc., 975 F.2d 81, 90 (3d Cir. 1992); *see also In re* Richard Roe, 168 F.3d at 71 (rejecting a "test for the crime-fraud exception that examine[s] only whether the material sought might provide evidence of a crime or fraud, *i.e.*, a 'relevant evidence' test.").

According to the *In re* Sealed Case court, just which element was not proved as to each of the documents at issue? In a case in which the corporation is the client whose privilege is sought to be pierced by a showing of crime or fraud, what additional elements must the government demonstrate?

4. The answer to the last question depends in part on what quantum of proof must be adduced in support of the above elements. The prima facie standard employed by the courts is derived from *Clark v. United States*, 289 U.S. 1, 15 (1933), which described the evidence needed to meet this standard as "something to give colour to the charge ... that has some foundation in fact." *Id.* The problem is that "'[p]rima facie' is among the most rubbery of all legal phrases; it usually means little more than a showing of whatever is required to permit some inferential leap sufficient to reach a particular outcome." *In re* Grand Jury Proceedings, 417 F.3d 18, 22-23 (1st Cir. 2005). The Third Circuit provided this taxonomy of the various ways in which the circuits interpret the term "prima facie":

> Courts of appeals have articulated the proper measure of proof in different ways. Some require there to be probable cause or a reasonable basis to suspect or believe that the client was committing or intending to commit a crime or fraud and that the attorney-client communications were used in furtherance of the alleged crime or fraud. *See In re Grand Jury Proceedings*, [417 F.3d 18, 23 & n.4 (1st Cir. 2005)]; *United States v. Jacobs*, 117 F.3d 82, 87 (2d Cir. 1997); *United States v. Collis*, 128 F.3d 313, 321 (6th Cir. 1997); *In re Grand Jury Proceedings*, 87 F.3d 377, 381 (9th Cir. 1996). Other courts call for evidence sufficient to compel the party asserting the privilege to come forward with an explanation for the evidence offered against the privilege. *See United States v. Boender*, 649 F.3d 650, 655-56 (7th Cir. 2011); *In re Grand Jury Subpoena*, 419 F.3d 329, 336 (5th Cir. 2005). Still other courts demand a showing of evidence that, if believed by a trier of fact, would establish that some violation was ongoing or about to be committed and that the attorney-client communications were used in furtherance of that scheme. *See In re Grand Jury*, 475 F.3d 1299, 1305 (D.C. Cir. 2007); *In re Grand Jury Proceedings #5 Empanelled January 28, 2004*, 401 F.3d 247, 251 (4th Cir. 2005); In re grand Jury Investigation, 842 F.2d 1223, 1226-27 (11th Cir. 1987). ...Today, we clarify that our precedent is properly captured by the reasonable basis standard.

In re Grand Jury, 705 F.3d 133, 152 (3d Cir. 2012).

In *In re* Sealed Case, the D.C. Circuit stated that "[t]he government satisfies its burden of proof if it offers evidence that if believed by the trier of fact would establish the elements" of the crime fraud exception. 676 F.2d at 815; *see also In re* Grand Jury Investigation, 445 F.3d 266, 274 (3d Cir. 2006). In discussing this "prima facie evidence" standard in case excerpted above, the D.C. Circuit notes that its formulation is different than the Second Circuit's "probable cause" standard, and indicates that, although it had previously stated that there was no real difference between these formulations, there might in fact be a difference. Is there?

The D.C. Circuit has applied its prima facie standard in a much more rigorous fashion than have other courts, most particularly the Seventh Circuit. As the Seventh Circuit has noted, the formulations employed by the D.C. and some other Circuits suggest that "prima facie evidence" means "enough to support a verdict in favor of the person making the claim." In the Matter of Feldberg, 862 F.2d 622, 625 (7th Cir. 1988). The Seventh Circuit rejects such an approach, as (in its view) do the Second and Sixth Circuits. *See Mark Rich & Co.*, 731 F.2d at 1039; *In re* Antitrust Grand Jury (Advance Publications, Inc.), 805 F.2d 155, 166 (6th Cir. 1986). In *Feldberg*, the Seventh Circuit explained that "[t]he question here is not whether the evidence supports a verdict but whether it calls for inquiry. Courts often use 'prima facie evidence' to refer to enough to require explanation rather than evidence that by itself satisfies a more-likely-than-not standard. ... Here, ... a prima facie case must be defined by regard to its function: to require the adverse party, the one with superior access to the evidence and in the best position to explain things, to come forward with that explanation." 862 F.2d at 625-26.

Contrasting Seventh Circuit precedent with the analysis in *In re* Sealed Case illustrates that the difference in these formulations is not meaningless. In *In the Matter of Feldberg*, 862 F.2d 622 (7th Cir. 1988), a grand jury investigating a sports agent who signed amateur athletes to undisclosed contracts issued a subpoena to a corporation calling for the production of all contracts between the corporation and college football players. Counsel for the corporation and its president initially turned over 51 contracts. At the grand jury's further request, counsel produced an additional 7 contracts, six of which had been post-dated to make it appear that they had been signed after the players' college careers had ended. The corporation and its president were indicted for mail fraud. The prosecutor, believing that the failure to produce the 7 contracts in response to the subpoena may have been obstruction of justice, subpoenaed the lawyer to testify about how he obtained the initial batch of contracts. The lawyer was not suspected of complicity in the alleged obstruction. Although the district court found that the government had failed to make out a prima facie case of fraud or obstruction of justice, the Seventh Circuit on appeal determined that the district court had abused its discretion in so ruling. The sole basis of the Seventh Circuit's determination seems to be its "logical inferences" from the facts that the files were probably not voluminous and the contracts should probably have been "ready to hand": "Disclosing 51 innocent-seeming contracts, while retaining six highly suspicious ones, is not a common result of random errors, and the compact nature of [the corporate] files makes it doubtful that one box was overlooked during a trudge through a mile-long warehouse." *Id.* at 625. The court noted that "[t]here may of course be an innocent explanation for the problem" but concluded that "[w]e need not try to figure out whether an innocent explanation is more likely than a culpable one" given the low threshold presented by the prima facie evidence standard.

Where the government has introduced nothing except logically supportable speculation to satisfy its burden of proving the applicability of the crime-fraud exception, should a court find that a prima facie case has been made? Does the client or lawyer have the opportunity to rebut this showing by tendering an innocent explanation or is the matter over once the court has ruled that a prima facie case has been made out? "Although ... *ex parte, in camera* proceedings appear to be the norm, courts have exercised their discretion to allow the party opposing disclosure to offer contrary evidence or at least to argue that the privilege should be maintained." Brown, *supra*, at 1260. "Operation of the crime-fraud exception has the effect of transforming the attorney into a witness against the client." *Id.* at 1222. Is the lawyer now conflicted from further representation in this matter? *See also* United States v. Davis, 1 F.3d 606 (7th Cir. 1993).

What are the potential consequences of choosing one standard over the other? One court has reasoned that "[r]equiring only a *prima facie* showing may lead to the disclosure of confidential communications that do not reflect a genuine crime or fraud. Presumably, this would occur infrequently. The alternative—requiring actual proof of the crime or fraud in lieu of the *prima facie* showing—imposes an impracticable and unduly burdensome standard that tips the balance too far in favor of confidentiality and against the 'full and free discovery of the truth.'" *See* X Corp. v. Doe, 805 F.Supp. 1298, 1307 (E.D. Va. 1992). Do you agree?

5. In general, the prima facie standard may not be met by conclusory allegations. *See, e.g., Schroeder*, 842 F.2d at 1226. However, the government may carry its burden by "a good faith statement by the prosecutor as to what evidence is before the grand jury," *Schroeder*, 842 F.2d at 1226, or by *ex parte* submissions to the court. *See, e.g.,* United States v. Zolin, 491 U.S. 554 (1989); *In re* Grand Jury Subpoena, 223 F.3d 213, 218-19 (3d Cir. 2000). Further, the contents of the allegedly privileged communications sought to be revealed may be used to provide the evidentiary basis for application of the crime-fraud exception. *See Zolin*, 491 U.S. at 574 & n.12. Should such evidence suffice, particularly in circuits such as the Seventh?

6. The crime-fraud exception applies to work product as well. *See, e.g. In re* Green Grand Jury Proceedings, 492 F.3d 976, 979-80 (8th Cir. 2007).

However, "[n]umerous courts have agreed that, in the specific context of the work product privilege, an innocent attorney may invoke the privilege even if a prima facie case of fraud or criminal activity has been made as to the client." *In re* Grand Jury Proceedings, 43 F.3d 966, 972 (5th Cir. 1994); *see also In re* Green Grand Jury Proceedings, 492 F.3d 976, 979-82 (8th Cir. 2007) (noting that this rule is generally restricted to opinion work product). "In contrast to the attorney-client privilege, the work product privilege belongs to both the client and the attorney, either one of whom may assert it. Thus, a waiver by the client of the work product privilege will not deprive the attorney of his own work product privilege, and vice versa." *See id.*

E. PRIVILEGES OF GOVERNMENTAL ACTORS

IN RE GRAND JURY INVESTIGATION
399 F.3d 527 (2d Cir. 2005)

JOHN M. WALKER, JR., CHIEF JUDGE.

. . .

On February 19, 2004, in the course of investigating possible criminal violations by Connecticut public officials and employees, and by private parties with whom the state had done business, a federal grand jury subpoenaed the testimony of Anne C. George, former chief legal counsel to the Office of the Governor of Connecticut. George served in that position from August 2000 to December 2002 and before that as deputy legal counsel. During the period leading up to issuance of the subpoena, the U.S. Attorney's Office ("the Government") had been investigating, in particular, whether Governor Rowland and members of his staff had received gifts from private individuals and entities in return for public favors, including the favorable negotiation and awarding of state contracts. The Government had sought, through direct contact with Governor Rowland, to gain access to specified communications between Rowland, his staff, and legal counsel, all to no avail. The Government had also asked George herself to submit to a voluntary interview. She declined, however, after the Office of the Governor notified her that it believed that the information the Government was seeking was protected by the attorney-client privilege.

On March 3, 2004, prior to George's appearance before the grand jury, the Government moved in the district court to compel George to testify about the contents of confidential communications between George and Governor Rowland and members of his staff. The district court withheld decision pending George's actual appearance and assertion of the privilege before the grand jury.

On April 7, 2004, when George appeared before the grand jury, she testified that in her capacity as legal counsel to the Governor she had engaged in numerous conversations with Rowland and other members of his staff on the subject of the receipt of gifts and the meaning of related state ethics laws. George also stated that she had spoken with Rowland's former co-Chief of Staff about a practice of state contracts being sent to the Governor's Office for approval. She testified, however, that because all of these conversations were in confidence and conducted for the purpose of providing legal advice, the Office of the Governor was of the view that they were protected by the attorney-client privilege, which it declined to waive. Accordingly, asserting the privilege on behalf of her client, George refused to answer questions pertaining to the content of the conversations.

On April 26, 2004, the district court entered an order compelling George's testimony. After noting that it was "undisputed that the grand jury need[ed] the information it [sought] to obtain from Ms. George," the district court concluded that "[r]eason and experience dictate that, in the grand jury context, any governmental attorney-client privilege must yield because the interests served by the grand jury's factfinding process clearly outweigh the interest served by the privilege." The district court distinguished the "governmental" attorney-client privilege from the privilege in the context of a private attorney-client relationship, by explaining that "unlike a private lawyer's duty of loyalty to an individual client, a government lawyer's duty does not lie solely with his or her client agency," but also with the public.

Both the Office of the Governor and Rowland, as interested parties, appealed the district court's decision. We granted the Government's motion to expedite the appeal.

On June 21, 2004, one day prior to oral argument, Governor Rowland announced that he would resign as Governor, effective July 1, 2004. At argument, we asked the parties to address the question of whether Rowland's resignation would affect our disposition of the appeal. The Government subsequently informed us that it had asked Rowland's successor, Governor M. Jodi Rell, to consider waiving the privilege insofar as the privilege was held by the Office of the Governor, and requested that we defer our disposition of the appeal pending Governor Rell's decision. On August 6, 2004, the newly appointed counsel to the Office of the Governor informed us that Governor Rell declined to waive the privilege. ...

DISCUSSION

Federal Rule of Evidence 501 governs the nature and scope of a privilege claimed in proceedings before a federal grand jury. The rule instructs that " the privilege of a witness, person, government, State, or political subdivision thereof shall be governed by the principles of the common law as they may be interpreted by the courts of the United States in the light of reason and experience." Fed.R.Evid. 501. Our determination of whether the Office of the Governor may claim a privilege, then, requires us to ascertain "the principles of the common law" and to apply them "in the light of reason and experience." In doing so, while we may draw on the law of privilege as it has developed in state courts, we are not bound by it. In criminal cases, Rule 501 plainly requires that we apply the federal law of privilege.

Although there is little case law addressing the application of the attorney-client privilege in the specific circumstances presented here, we are nonetheless dealing with a well-established and familiar principle. "The attorney-client privilege is one of the oldest recognized privileges for confidential communications." Today, the generally acknowledged purpose of the privilege is "to encourage 'full and frank communication between attorneys and their clients and thereby promote broader public interests in the observance of law and the administration of justice.'"

The idea that a robust attorney-client privilege will in fact "promote broader public interests" does not mean that application of the privilege will render justice in every single case. Nevertheless, courts have by reason and experience concluded that a consistent application of the privilege over time is necessary to promote the rule of law by encouraging consultation with lawyers, and ensuring that lawyers, once consulted, are able to render to their clients fully informed legal advice. ...

There is no dispute in this case that these principles and assumptions apply to government lawyers and their clients under certain circumstances. The Government concedes, for instance, both that a governmental attorney-client privilege exists generally, and that it may be invoked in the civil context. Ample authority supports both propositions. In 1972, the Supreme Court promulgated Federal Rules of Evidence setting forth nine specific categories of privileges, including an attorney-client privilege. Proposed Federal Rule 503, defining the privilege, included public officers and public entities within its definition of "client," *see* Proposed Fed.R.Evid. 503(a)(1), *reprinted in* 56 F.R.D. 183, 235 (1972); commentary accompanying the proposed rule, moreover, provided that the "definition of 'client' includes governmental bodies," *id.* at 236. While Proposed Rule 503 was not adopted by Congress, courts and commentators have treated it as a source of general guidance regarding federal common law principles. Similarly, section 74 of the

Restatement (Third) of the Law Governing Lawyers provides that the "attorney-client privilege extends to a communication of a governmental organization" as it would to a private organization. The commentary to that section notes that "[t]he privilege aids government entities and employees in obtaining legal advice founded on a complete and accurate factual picture." *Id.* cmt. b. While these authorities are not conclusive as to the existence at common law of a governmental attorney-client privilege, they demonstrate that serious legal thinkers, applying "reason and experience," have considered the privilege's protections applicable in the government context.

The case law, as well, while not extensively addressing the issue, generally assumes the existence of a governmental attorney-client privilege in civil suits between government agencies and private litigants. ...

There is, then, substantial authority for the view that the rationale supporting the attorney-client privilege applicable to private entities has general relevance to governmental entities as well. The Government argues that while this authority may establish a privilege of some kind, recent case law in other circuits supports its view that the attorney-client privilege in the government context is weaker than in its traditional form. It cites *In Re: A Witness Before the Special Grand Jury*, 288 F.3d 289 (7th Cir.2002) ("*Ryan*"); *In re* Lindsey, 158 F.3d 1263 (D.C.Cir.1998) ("*Lindsey*"); and *In re* Grand Jury Subpoena Duces Tecum, 112 F.3d 910 (8th Cir. 1997) ("*Grand Jury*"), for the proposition that the "governmental" attorney-client privilege must give way where a federal grand jury seeks access to otherwise privileged statements in order to further a criminal investigation. While *Lindsey* and *Grand Jury* involved applications of the privilege to communications by a *federal* executive, and thus involved statutes and considerations unrelated to this case, all three decisions broadly questioned the relevance of the traditional rationale supporting the privilege to the government context.

Drawing on these decisions, the Government contends that the reasons for the traditional attorney-client privilege do not apply with the same force in the circumstances presented by this case: a federal grand jury investigation into potentially criminal government conduct. It argues, first, that George, as a government attorney, has a fundamentally different relationship with her client, the Office of the Governor, than does a private attorney representing a private individual. George's client is a public entity, accountable to the general citizenry. As the Office of the Governor serves the public, the Government argues, so too must George as counsel to that office. Her loyalty to the Governor, the Government contends, must yield to her loyalty to the public, to whom she owes ultimate allegiance when violations of the criminal law are at stake. Accordingly, the Government argues that the privilege should not be used as a shield to permit George, as a government attorney, to withhold client confidences, when revealing them would be in the public interest. Implicit in the Government's argument is the presumption that the public interest in the present circumstances lies with disclosure and the furtherance of the "truth-seeking" function of the grand jury. "[T]o allow the Governor's Office to interpose a testimonial privilege 'as a shield against the production of information relevant to a federal criminal investigation,'" the Government concludes, "'would represent a gross misuse of public assets.'"

We cannot accept the Government's unequivocal assumption as to where the public interest lies. To be sure, it is in the public interest for the grand jury to collect all the relevant evidence it can. However, it is also in the public interest for high state officials to receive and act upon the best possible legal advice. Indeed, the people of Connecticut have deemed the latter interest more important than the former: if *state* prosecutors had sought to compel George to reveal the conversations at issue, there is little doubt that the conversations would be protected. The Connecticut legislature has enacted a statute specifically providing that

> [i]n any civil or criminal case or proceeding or in any legislative or administrative proceeding, all confidential communications shall be privileged and a government

attorney shall not disclose any such communications unless an authorized representative of the public agency consents to waive the privilege and allow such disclosure.

Conn. Gen.Stat. § 52-146r(b). The people of Connecticut, then, acting through their representatives, have concluded that the public interest is advanced by upholding a governmental privilege even in the face of a criminal investigation. We do not suggest, of course, that federal courts, charged with formulating federal common law, must necessarily defer to state statutes in determining whether the public welfare weighs in favor of recognizing or dissolving the attorney-client privilege. But we cite the Connecticut statute to point out that the public interest is not nearly as obvious as the Government suggests. One could as easily conclude, with the Connecticut legislature, that the protections afforded by the privilege ultimately promote the public interest, even when they might impede the search for truth in a particular criminal investigation.

We believe that, if anything, the traditional rationale for the privilege applies with special force in the government context. It is crucial that government officials, who are expected to uphold and execute the law and who may face criminal prosecution for failing to do so, be encouraged to seek out and receive fully informed legal advice. Upholding the privilege furthers a culture in which consultation with government lawyers is accepted as a normal, desirable, and even indispensable part of conducting public business. Abrogating the privilege undermines that culture and thereby impairs the public interest. *See* 1 Paul R. Rice, *Attorney-Client Privilege in the United States*, § 4:28, at 4 (2d ed. 1999) ("If the government attorney is required to disclose [internal communications with counsel] upon grand jury request, it is sheer fantasy to suggest that it will not make internal governmental investigations more difficult, to the point of being impossible. ... To the extent that the protection of the privilege is justified in any corporate context, the need within the government is equal, if not greater.").

We are aware, of course, that the relationship between a government attorney and a government official or employee is not the same as that between a private attorney and his client. For one, in the government context, the individual consulting with his official attorney may not control waiver of the privilege. Even if he does control waiver during his time in government, the possibility remains that a subsequent administration might purport to waive the privilege exercised by a predecessor. Thus, some commentators (and presumably the Government, here) question whether application of the attorney-client privilege in the government context will in fact encourage public officials and employees to confide in counsel. *See, e.g.,* Melanie B. Leslie, *Government Officials as Attorneys and Clients: Why Privilege the Privileged?*, 77 Ind. L.J. 469, 507 (2002). While encouraging little in the way of legal consultation and disclosure, their argument goes, the privilege engenders significant costs by frustrating the "search for truth."

Whatever merit there is to this reasoning, we think it insufficient to jettison a principle as entrenched in our legal tradition as that underlying the attorney-client privilege. Such reasoning amounts to little more than speculation over the way in which the privilege functions in the government context. We also reject the idea that because government employees can confer with private counsel to represent their own, individual interests, the privilege is somehow less important when applied to government counsel. The privilege serves to promote the free flow of information to the attorney (and thereby to the client entity) as well as to the individual with whom he communicates. The government attorney requires candid, unvarnished information from those employed by the office he serves so that he may better discharge his duty to that office.

Having determined that the attorney-client privilege applies to the communications at issue in this case, we decline to fashion a balancing test, or otherwise establish a rule whereby a "generalized assertion of privilege must yield to the demonstrated, specific need for evidence ...." [United States v. Nixon, 418 U.S. 683, 713 (1974)] (establishing balancing test with regard to executive privilege). The Supreme Court has instructed that, where the attorney-client privilege applies, its protections must be reliably enforced in order to effectuate its goal of promoting compliance with the law.

We see no persuasive reason to abandon that logic here. Of course, nothing we hold today derogates from traditional doctrines, such as the crime-fraud exception, that apply to the private attorney-client relationship and that courts have developed, through reason and experience, to limit egregious abuses of the protections that the privilege affords.

In arguing that we ought not "extend" the attorney-client privilege to the present situation, the Government asks us, in essence, to assign a precise functional value to its protections and then determine whether, and under what circumstances, the costs of these protections become too great to justify. We find the assumptions underlying this approach to be illusory, and the approach itself potentially dangerous. The Government assumes that "the public interest" in disclosure is readily apparent, and that a public official's willingness to consult with counsel will be only "marginally" affected by the abrogation of the privilege in the face of a grand jury subpoena. Because we cannot accept either of these assumptions, we decline to abandon the attorney-client privilege in a context in which its protections arguably are needed most.[112] In the end, we do not view the question before us as whether to " extend" the privilege to the government context, and our decision today does no such thing. Rather, we have simply refused to countenance its abrogation in circumstances to which its venerable and worthy purposes fully pertain.

Notes

1. Upon whom does the court put the burden here? Is that burden consistent with the normal rules of construing the scope of an evidentiary privilege? As the court indicates in footnote 4, the Second Circuit placed itself in conflict with the D.C. and Eighth Circuits. Which result makes the most sense?

Some argue that the D.C. and Eighth Circuit decisions create an incentive for government officials to seek out the advice of private counsel on sensitive matters that may involve their public duties. W. Neil Eggleston and Timothy Armstrong argue:

> Private attorneys ... may make poor civil servants. They would necessarily lack the institutional familiarity with the mission and operations of the client agency that agency counsel would provide. Indeed, in sensitive cases ... officials of the client agency may be severely restricted by federal law or other considerations of the public interest from disclosing all material facts to a private attorney. More fundamentally, retained private counsel have no ethical obligation to serve any interests beyond those of their individual client. They are not necessarily well suited to advise an official on what course of action is best for the agency, branch, or Nation as a whole.

W. Neil Eggleston & Timothy K. Armstrong, *Attorney-Client Privilege When the Client is a Public Official: Litigating the Opening Act of the Impeachment Drama*, White Collar Crime 1999, at A–9 (ABA 1999); *see also* Adam M. Chud, Note, *In Defense of the Government Attorney–Client Privilege*, 84 Cornell L. Rev. 1683 (1999).

---

[112] [Court's footnote 4:] Our decision is in conflict with the Seventh Circuit's decision in *Ryan*, and is in sharp tension with the decisions of the Eighth (*Grand Jury*) and the D.C. Circuits (*Lindsey*). We are mindful that uniformity among the circuits fosters predictability in the invocation of the privilege and suppresses forum shopping. We are in no position, however, to resolve this tension in the law.

2. There are almost "40,000 federal government lawyers" including those employed by Congress, the federal courts, and the executive branch. Chud, *supra*, at 1683. Do the D.C. and Eighth Circuit's ruling potentially affect all of them?

And just how far-reaching are the implications of these decisions? For example, do the D.C. and Eighth Circuits' precedents mean that a *defendant* in a criminal case may claim access to materials the government claims are protected by the attorney-client privilege? *See* United States v. Peitz, 2002 WL 31101681 (N.D. Ill. 2002). In *Peitz*, the court rejected the defendant's reliance on these cases for the proposition that the attorney-client privilege does not apply to a communication with a government attorney when the information is being requested for a criminal case. It reasoned that, at most, the government's attorney-client privilege in a criminal case is not absolute and that the court may balance the defendant's need for disclosure against the agency's interest in confidentiality. Finally, the court held that an SEC action memorandum, which included an exculpatory statement regarding the defendant, would hold limited value for the defendant and that the circumstances therefore did not call for overriding the government's attorney-client privilege.

3. Representing clients in congressional investigations requires a particular expertise: "a congressional investigation is a procedural hybrid, part political circus and seemingly little order, and part legal process with unique and explicit rules and procedures." James Hamilton, Robert F. Muse & Kevin R. Amer, *Congressional Investigations: Politics and* Process, 44 Am. Crim. L. Rev. 1115 (2007). One of the ways in which congressional investigations are unique is the status of privilege claims:

> The availability of the attorney-client privilege in the context of congressional investigations has been the subject of considerable debate. Very few judicial decisions have addressed this issue, and those that have done so fail to resolve the matter conclusively. However, in recent decades a number of congressional committees have taken the position that the attorney-client and other common law privileges do not apply as of right in their proceedings but instead fall within the committee's discretion.

Id. at 1147-48; *see also* Steven R. Ross & Raphael A. Prober, *Attorney-Client Privilege in Congressional Investigations*, 16 Bus. Crimes Bull. 1 (Jan. 2009).

Chapter 18

REPRESENTATION ISSUES

A great variety of representation and conflicts issues may arise when acts undertaken in a business context become the focus of a criminal investigation and the business (generally a corporation) and certain of its officers, directors, employees, or agents are possible subjects or targets. At the inception of the investigation, one lawyer's or firm's representation of the corporation *and* the individuals involved (usually termed "multiple" or "joint" representation) may have many advantages. Counsel can maintain greater control over the matter, track the investigation more efficiently and inexpensively, and present a common, united defense to possible prosecution. However, this type of multiple representation may—as the investigation progresses or after indictment and at trial—raise a number of ethical, legal, and practical difficulties, some of which are discussed within. Accordingly, the subjects or targets of a white-collar investigation often hire separate counsel but form what is known as a "joint defense." Pursuant to a joint defense agreement, counsel for each client may work together and pool information without fear that such sharing will expose their communications or work product to examination by third parties, such as the grand jury or litigants in collateral civil cases. These materials cover some of the issues surrounding the effective creation and conduct of a joint defense.

A. ETHICAL RULES

Because there are significant variations in the ethical standards that apply in different jurisdictions, counsel must examine the propriety of a particular representation under the rules prevailing in her own jurisdiction. Further, most applicable ethical rules are not exclusively tailored for criminal cases and, to the extent that they speak specifically to criminal issues, focus on conflicts that may arise in the course of pleas or trial proceedings. They generally provide little specific guidance in cases in which representation issues arise in the pre-trial, criminal investigative setting—a common event in white-collar practice. With these caveats in mind, readers should be familiar with the following rules reflected in ABA model standards.

The fundamental challenges facing counsel are, in the words of the Model Code of Professional Responsibility: to "exercise independent professional judgment on behalf of a client"—and in the case of multiple clients—each client;[1] to "preserve the confidences and secrets of [each] client;"[2] and to "represent [each] client zealously within the bounds of the

---

[1] ABA Model Code of Prof'l Responsibility Canon 5.

[2] *Id.* Canon 4

law."[3] In this context, the most important provisions of the ABA Model Rules of Professional Conduct for conflicts purposes are Rules 1.7, 1.13(e), and 1.8.

Model Rule of Professional Conduct 1.7 provides a general rule with respect to determining whether a disabling conflict of interest exists:

> (a) Except as provided in paragraph (b), a lawyer shall not represent a client if the representation involves a concurrent conflict of interest. A current conflict of interest exists if:
>> (1) the representation of one client will be directly adverse to another client; or
>> (2) there is a significant risk that the representation of one or more clients will be materially limited by the lawyer's responsibilities to another client, a former client or a third person or by a personal interest of the lawyer.
> (b) Notwithstanding the existence of a concurrent conflict of interest under paragraph (a), a lawyer may represent a client if:
>> (1) the lawyer reasonably believes that the lawyer will be able to provide competent and diligent representation to each affected client;
>> (2) the representation is not prohibited by law;
>> (3) the representation does not involve the assertion of a claim by one client against another client represented by the lawyer in the same litigation or other proceeding before a tribunal; and
>> (4) each affected client gives informed consent, confirmed in writing.[4]

The comment to Rule 1.7 talks about joint representation in criminal trials and cautions:

> ... The potential for conflict of interest in representing multiple defendants in a criminal case is so grave that ordinarily a lawyer should decline to represent more than one co-defendant.[5] ...

Where the organization is a client, Model Rule of Professional Conduct 1.13(e) states that "a lawyer representing an organization may also represent any of its directors, officers, employees, members, shareholders or other constituents, subject to the provisions of Rule 1.7."

Finally, Model Rule of Professional Conduct 1.8(g) states, in pertinent part:

> A lawyer who represents two or more clients shall not participate in making ... in a criminal case an aggregated agreement as to guilty or nolo contendere pleas, unless each client gives informed consent, in a writing signed by the client. The lawyer's disclosure shall include the existence and nature of all the claims or pleas involved and of the participation of each person in the settlement.

Because the defense of individual as well as corporate targets of an investigation is often funded by the corporation under investigation, reference should be made to ABA Model Rule of Professional Conduct 1.8(f), which states:

> A lawyer shall not accept compensation for representing a client from one other than the client unless:

---

[3] *Id.* Canon 7.

[4] *See also* ABA Model Code of Prof'l Responsibility DR 5-105 ("Refusing to Accept or Continue Employment if the Interests of Another Client May Impair the Independent Professional Judgment of the Lawyer").

[5] Model Rule of Prof'l Conduct 1.7, Comment ("Conflicts in Litigation").

(1) the client gives informed consent;

(2) there is no interference with the lawyer's independence of professional judgment or with the client-lawyer relationship; and

(3) information relating to representation of a client is protected as required by Rule 1.6.[6]

The ABA has also promulgated standards that are specifically designed for criminal cases (ABA Standards for Criminal Justice). One such standard, Defense Function Standard 4-1.7, provides a very strict conflicts rule:

> (d) Except where necessary to secure counsel for preliminary matters such as initial hearings or applications for bail, a defense counsel (or multiple counsel associated in practice) should not undertake to represent more than one client in the same criminal case. When there is not yet a criminal case, such multiple representation should be engaged in only when, after careful investigation and consideration, it is clear either that no conflict is likely to develop at any stage of the matter, or that multiple representation will be advantageous to each of the clients represented and that foreseeable conflicts can be waived.
>
> (e) In instances of permissible multiple representation:
>
> > (i) the clients should be fully advised that the lawyer may be unable to continue if a conflict develops, and that confidentiality may not exist between the clients;
> >
> > (ii) informed written consent should be obtained from each of the clients, and
> >
> > (iii) if the matter is before a tribunal, such consent should be made on the record with appropriate inquiries by counsel and the court.

To understand the following materials, readers should be aware of two other standards. First, ABA Model Rule of Professional Conduct 1.6 provides:

> (a) A lawyer shall not reveal information relating to the representation of a client unless the client gives informed consent, [or] the disclosure is impliedly authorized in order to carry out the representation ... .[7]

Second, ABA Model Rule of Professional Conduct 1.9 states:

> (a) A lawyer who has formerly represented a client in a matter shall not thereafter represent another person in the same or a substantially related matter in which that

---

[6] *See also* Model Code of Prof'l Responsibility DR 5-107 ("Except with the consent of his client after full disclosure, a lawyer shall not ... [a]ccept compensation for his legal services from one other than his client. ... A lawyer shall not permit a person who recommends, employs, or pays him to render legal services for another to direct or regulate his professional judgment in rendering such legal services."). The New Jersey Supreme Court has articulated six conditions that must be met to satisfy conflict-of-interest concerns when a company retains lawyers for individual employees during a criminal investigation. *See In re* State Grand Jury, 200 N.J. 481, 495-97 983 A.2d 1097, 1105-06 (2009).

[7] *See also* Model Rules of Prof'l Conduct DR 4-101 ("[A] lawyer shall not knowingly: (1) reveal a confidence or secret of his client; [or] (2) use a confidence or secret of his client to the disadvantage of his client"; "confidence" refers to information protected by the attorney-client privilege and "secret" refers to other information gained in the professional relationship that the client has requested by held inviolate or the disclosure of which would be embarrassing or would be likely to be detrimental to the client).

person's interests are materially adverse to the interests of the former client unless the former client gives informed consent, confirmed in writing.

B. "MULTIPLE" OR "JOINT" REPRESENTATION

1. CONSTITUTIONAL ISSUES

In *Holloway v. Arkansas*,[8] the Supreme Court held that appointing one lawyer to represent at trial three codefendants was unconstitutional in a case where counsel had informed the trial court of a conflict among his clients, but the court failed to take adequate steps to ascertain whether the risk of conflict was likely or remote. *Holloway* recognizes that the effective assistance of counsel guaranteed by the Sixth Amendment includes a right to conflict-free counsel: "the 'Assistance of Counsel' guaranteed by the Sixth Amendment contemplates that such assistance be untrammeled and unimpaired by a court order requiring that one lawyer should simultaneously represent conflicting interests."[9] The *Holloway* Court was careful to note, however, that not all multiple representations imperil Sixth Amendment interests, stating:

> Requiring or permitting a single attorney to represent codefendants, often referred to as [multiple or] joint representation, is not *per se* violative of constitutional guarantees of effective assistance of counsel. This principle recognizes that in some cases multiple defendants can appropriately be represented by one attorney; indeed, in some cases, certain advantages might accrue from joint representation. In Mr. Justice Frankfurter's view: "Joint representation is a means of insuring against reciprocal recrimination. A common defense often gives strength against a common attack."[10]

The Supreme Court has also held that the Sixth Amendment includes "a presumption in favor of ... counsel of choice."[11] May a defendant waive his right to conflict-free counsel in the interests of exercising his right to counsel of choice—a counsel through whom he and his codefendants intend to pursue a common defense against common attack?

WHEAT v. UNITED STATES
486 U.S. 153 (1988)

CHIEF JUSTICE REHNQUIST delivered the opinion of the Court.

The issue in this case is whether the District Court erred in declining petitioner's waiver of his right to conflict-free counsel and by refusing to permit petitioner's proposed substitution of attorneys.

[Petitioner Mark Wheat, with numerous codefendants, was charged with participating in a complex drug distribution scheme. Also charged in the conspiracy were Juvenal Gomez-Barajas and Javier Bravo, who were represented by attorney Eugene Iredale. Gomez-Barajas was tried first and acquitted on drug charges overlapping with those lodged against petitioner. To avoid a second trial on other charges, however, Gomez-Barajas offered to plead to certain counts. As of the commencement of petitioner's trial, the District

---

[8] 435 U.S. 475 (1978).

[9] *Id.* at 482 (quoting Glasser v. United States, 315 U.S. 60, 70 (1942)).

[10] *Id.* at 482-83.

[11] Wheat v. United States, 486 U.S. 153, 164 (1988).

Court had not accepted Gomez-Barajas's plea. Bravo, a lesser player, pleaded guilty to one count of transporting marijuana.]

[Shortly before his trial, petitioner contacted Iredale and asked him to represent petitioner. The government objected, saying that Iredale's representation of Gomez-Barajas and Bravo created a serious conflict of interest arising from two facts: (1) if the District Court rejected Gomez-Barajas' proposed plea and Gomez-Barajas then elected to proceed to trial, petitioner was in the government's view likely to be called as a witness for the government; and (2) the government had asked that Bravo be made available as a witness to testify against petitioner in exchange for sentencing consideration.] ...

In response, petitioner emphasized his right to have counsel of his own choosing and the willingness of Gomez-Barajas, Bravo, and petitioner to waive the right to conflict-free counsel. Petitioner argued that the circumstances posited by the Government that would create a conflict for Iredale were highly speculative and bore no connection to the true relationship between the co-conspirators. If called to testify, Bravo would simply say that he did not know petitioner and had no dealings with him; no attempt by Iredale to impeach Bravo would be necessary. Further, in the unlikely event that Gomez-Barajas went to trial on the charges of tax evasion and illegal importation, petitioner's lack of involvement in those alleged crimes made his appearance as a witness highly improbable. Finally, and most importantly, all three defendants agreed to allow Iredale to represent petitioner and to waive any future claims of conflict of interest. In petitioner's view, the Government was manufacturing implausible conflicts in an attempt to disqualify Iredale, who had already proved extremely effective in representing Gomez-Barajas and Bravo.

After hearing argument from each side, the District Court noted that it was unfortunate that petitioner had not suggested the substitution sooner, rather than two court days before the commencement of trial. The court then ruled:

> "[B]ased upon the representation of the Government in [its] memorandum that the Court really has no choice at this point other than to find that an irreconcilable conflict of interest exists. I don't think it can be waived, and accordingly, Mr. Wheat's request to substitute Mr. Iredale in as attorney of record is denied."

Petitioner proceeded to trial with his original counsel and was convicted. ...

The Sixth Amendment to the Constitution guarantees that "[i]n all criminal prosecutions, the accused shall enjoy the right ... to have the Assistance of Counsel for his defence." ... [T]his right [i]s designed to assure fairness in the adversary criminal process. Realizing that an unaided layman may have little skill in arguing the law or in coping with an intricate procedural system, we have held that the Sixth Amendment secures the right to the assistance of counsel, by appointment if necessary, in a trial for any serious crime. We have further recognized that the purpose of providing assistance of counsel "is simply to ensure that criminal defendants receive a fair trial," and that in evaluating Sixth Amendment claims, "the appropriate inquiry focuses on the adversarial process, not on the accused's relationship with his lawyer as such." Thus, while the right to select and be represented by one's preferred attorney is comprehended by the Sixth Amendment, the essential aim of the Amendment is to guarantee an effective advocate for each criminal defendant rather than to ensure that a defendant will inexorably be represented by the lawyer whom he prefers.

The Sixth Amendment right to choose one's own counsel is circumscribed in several important respects. Regardless of his persuasive powers, an advocate who is not a member of the bar may not represent clients (other than himself) in court. Similarly, a defendant may not insist on representation by an attorney he cannot afford or who for other reasons declines to represent the defendant. Nor may a defendant insist on the counsel of an attorney who has a previous or ongoing relationship with an opposing party, even when the opposing party is the Government. The question raised in this case is the extent to which a criminal defendant's right under the Sixth Amendment to his chosen attorney is qualified by the fact that the attorney has represented other defendants charged in the same criminal conspiracy.

In previous cases, we have recognized that multiple representation of criminal defendants engenders special dangers of which a court must be aware. While "permitting a single attorney to represent codefendants ... is not *per se* violative of constitutional guarantees of effective assistance of counsel," *Holloway v. Arkansas*, 435 U.S. 475, 482 (1978), a court confronted with and alerted to possible conflicts of interest must take adequate steps to ascertain whether the conflicts warrant separate counsel. As we said in *Holloway*:

> "Joint representation of conflicting interests is suspect because of what it tends to prevent the attorney from doing ... . [A] conflict may ... prevent an attorney from challenging the admission of evidence prejudicial to one client but perhaps favorable to another, or from arguing at the sentencing hearing the relative involvement and culpability of his clients in order to minimize the culpability of one by emphasizing that of another."

Petitioner insists that the provision of waivers by all affected defendants cures any problems created by the multiple representation. But no such flat rule can be deduced from the Sixth Amendment presumption in favor of counsel of choice. Federal courts have an independent interest in ensuring that criminal trials are conducted within the ethical standards of the profession and that legal proceedings appear fair to all who observe them. Both the American Bar Association's Model Code of Professional Responsibility and its Model Rules of Professional Conduct, as well as the rules of the California Bar Association (which governed the attorneys in this case), impose limitations on multiple representation of clients. See ABA Model Code of Professional Responsibility DR5-105(C) (1980); ABA Model Rules of Professional Conduct, Rule 1.7 (1984). Not only the interest of a criminal defendant but the institutional interest in the rendition of just verdicts in criminal cases may be jeopardized by unregulated multiple representation.

For this reason, the Federal Rules of Criminal Procedure direct trial judges to investigate specially cases involving joint representation. In pertinent part, Rule 44(c) provides:

> "[T]he court shall promptly inquire with respect to such joint representation and shall personally advise each defendant of his right to the effective assistance of counsel, including separate representation. Unless it appears that there is good cause to believe no conflict of interest is likely to arise, the court shall take such measures as may be appropriate to protect each defendant's right to counsel."

Although Rule 44(c) does not specify what particular measures may be taken by a district court, one option suggested by the Notes of the Advisory Committee is an order by the court that the defendants be separately represented in subsequent proceedings in the case. This suggestion comports with our instructions in *Holloway* and in *Glasser v. United States*, 315 U.S. 60 (1942), that the trial courts, when alerted by objection from one of the parties, have an independent duty to ensure that criminal defendants receive a trial that is fair and does not contravene the Sixth Amendment.

To be sure, this need to investigate potential conflicts arises in part from the legitimate wish of district courts that their judgments remain intact on appeal. As the Court of Appeals accurately pointed out, trial courts confronted with multiple representations face the prospect of being "whip-sawed" by assertions of error no matter which way they rule. If a district court agrees to the multiple representation, and the advocacy of counsel is thereafter impaired as a result, the defendant may well claim that he did not receive effective assistance. On the other hand, a district court's refusal to accede to the multiple representation may result in a challenge such as petitioner's in this case. Nor does a waiver by the defendant necessarily solve the problem, for we note, without passing judgment on, the apparent willingness of Courts of Appeals to entertain ineffective-assistance claims from defendants who have specifically waived the right to conflict-free counsel.

Thus, where a court justifiably finds an actual conflict of interest, there can be no doubt that it may decline a proffer of waiver, and insist that defendants be separately represented.

...

Unfortunately for all concerned, a district court must pass on the issue whether or not to allow a waiver of a conflict of interest by a criminal defendant not with the wisdom of hindsight after the trial has taken place, but in the murkier pre-trial context when relationships between parties are seen through a glass, darkly. The likelihood and dimensions of nascent conflicts of interest are notoriously hard to predict, even for those thoroughly familiar with criminal trials. It is a rare attorney who will be fortunate enough to learn the entire truth from his own client, much less be fully apprised before trial of what each of the Government's witnesses will say on the stand. A few bits of unforeseen testimony or a single previously unknown or unnoticed document may significantly shift the relationship between multiple defendants. These imponderables are difficult enough for a lawyer to assess, and even more difficult to convey by way of explanation to a criminal defendant untutored in the niceties of legal ethics. Nor is it amiss to observe that the willingness of an attorney to obtain such waivers from his clients may bear an inverse relation to the care with which he conveys all the necessary information to them.

For these reasons we think the district court must be allowed substantial latitude in refusing waivers of conflicts of interest not only in those rare cases where an actual conflict may be demonstrated before trial, but in the more common cases where a potential for conflict exists which may or may not burgeon into an actual conflict as the trial progresses. In the circumstances of this case, with the motion for substitution of counsel made so close to the time of trial, the District Court relied on instinct and judgment based on experience in making its decision. We do not think it can be said that the court exceeded the broad latitude which must be accorded it in making this decision. Petitioner of course rightly points out that the Government may seek to "manufacture" a conflict in order to prevent a defendant from having a particularly able defense counsel at his side; but trial courts are undoubtedly aware of this possibility, and must take it into consideration along with all of the other factors which inform this sort of a decision.

Here the District Court was confronted not simply with an attorney who wished to represent two coequal defendants in a straightforward criminal prosecution; rather, Iredale proposed to defend three conspirators of varying stature in a complex drug distribution scheme. The Government intended to call Bravo as a witness for the prosecution at petitioner's trial.[12] The Government might readily have tied certain deliveries of marijuana by Bravo to petitioner, necessitating vigorous cross-examination of Bravo by petitioner's counsel. Iredale, because of his prior representation of Bravo, would have been unable ethically to provide that cross-examination.

Iredale had also represented Gomez-Barajas, one of the alleged kingpins of the distribution ring, and had succeeded in obtaining a verdict of acquittal for him. Gomez-Barajas had agreed with the Government to plead guilty to other charges, but the District Court had not yet accepted the plea arrangement. If the agreement were rejected, petitioner's probable testimony at the resulting trial of Gomez-Barajas would create an ethical dilemma for Iredale from which one or the other of his clients would likely suffer.

Viewing the situation as it did before trial, we hold that the District Court's refusal to permit the substitution of counsel in this case was within its discretion and did not violate petitioner's Sixth Amendment rights. Other district courts might have reached differing or opposite conclusions with equal justification, but that does not mean that one conclusion was "right" and the other "wrong[."] The District Court must recognize a presumption in favor of petitioner's counsel of choice, but that presumption may be overcome not only by

---

[12] [Court's footnote 4:] Bravo was in fact called as a witness at petitioner's trial. His testimony was elicited to demonstrate the transportation of drugs that the prosecution hoped to link to petitioner.

a demonstration of actual conflict but by a showing of a serious potential for conflict. The evaluation of the facts and circumstances of each case under this standard must be left primarily to the informed judgment of the trial court. ...

JUSTICE MARSHALL, with whom JUSTICE BRENNAN joins, dissenting.

This Court today concludes that the District Court did not commit reversible error by denying the motion of petitioner Mark Wheat to add or substitute counsel of his choice. In the course of discussing the District Court's ruling, the Court sets forth several principles with which I agree. The Court acknowledges, as it must, that the Sixth Amendment's guarantee of assistance of counsel comprehends the right to select one's own attorney. The Court also states that, although this constitutional right is not absolute, it mandates a presumption in favor of accepting a criminal defendant's choice of counsel. Having articulated these principles, however, the Court unaccountably grants broad discretion to the trial court to decide whether this presumption has been overcome. As a consequence of this unwarranted deference to a trial court's decision respecting a constitutional right, the Court countenances a ruling that is patently incorrect. Because I believe that the potential for a conflict of interest in this case did not overcome petitioner's right to choose his own counsel, I dissent. ...

The Court's resolution of the instant case flows from its deferential approach to the District Court's denial of petitioner's motion to add or substitute counsel; absent deference, a decision upholding the District Court's ruling would be inconceivable. Indeed, I believe that even under the Court's deferential standard, reversal is in order. The mere fact of multiple representation, as the Court concedes, will not support an order preventing a criminal defendant from retaining counsel of his choice. As this Court has stated on prior occasions, such representation will not invariably pose a substantial risk of a serious conflict of interest and thus will not invariably imperil the prospect of a fair trial. The propriety of the District Court's order thus depends on whether the Government showed that the particular facts and circumstances of the multiple representation proposed in this case were such as to overcome the presumption in favor of petitioner's choice of counsel. I believe it is clear that the Government failed to make this showing. Neither Eugene Iredale's representation of Juvenal Gomez-Barajas nor Iredale's representation of Javier Bravo posed any threat of causing a conflict of interest.

At the time of petitioner's trial, Iredale's representation of Gomez-Barajas was effectively completed. As the Court notes, Iredale had obtained an acquittal for Gomez-Barajas on charges relating to a conspiracy to distribute marijuana. Iredale also had negotiated an agreement with the Government under which Gomez-Barajas would plead guilty to charges of tax evasion and illegal importation of merchandise, although the trial court had not yet accepted this plea arrangement. Gomez-Barajas was not scheduled to appear as a witness at petitioner's trial; thus, Iredale's conduct of that trial would not require him to question his former client. The only possible conflict this Court can divine from Iredale's representation of both petitioner and Gomez-Barajas rests on the premise that the trial court would reject the negotiated plea agreement and that Gomez-Barajas then would decide to go to trial. In this event, the Court tells us, "petitioner's probable testimony at the resulting trial of Gomez-Barajas would create an ethical dilemma for Iredale."

This argument rests on speculation of the most dubious kind. The Court offers no reason to think that the trial court would have rejected Gomez-Barajas' plea agreement; neither did the Government posit any such reason in its argument or brief before this Court. The most likely occurrence at the time petitioner moved to retain Iredale as his defense counsel was that the trial court would accept Gomez-Barajas' plea agreement, as the court in fact later did. Moreover, even if Gomez-Barajas had gone to trial, petitioner probably would not have testified. The record contains no indication that petitioner had any involvement in or information about crimes for which Gomez-Barajas might yet have stood trial. The only alleged connection between petitioner and Gomez-Barajas sprang from the conspiracy to distribute marijuana, and a jury already had acquitted Gomez-Barajas of that charge. It is therefore disingenuous to say that representation of both petitioner and Gomez-Barajas posed a serious potential for a conflict of interest.

Similarly, Iredale's prior representation of Bravo was not a cause for concern. The Court notes that the prosecution intended to call Bravo to the stand at petitioner's trial and asserts that Bravo's testimony could well have "necessitat[ed] vigorous cross-examination ... by petitioner's counsel." The facts, however, belie the claim that Bravo's anticipated testimony created a serious potential for conflict. Contrary to the Court's inference, Bravo could not have testified about petitioner's involvement in the alleged marijuana distribution scheme. As all parties were aware at the time, Bravo did not know and could not identify petitioner; indeed, prior to the commencement of legal proceedings, the two men never had heard of each other. Bravo's eventual testimony at petitioner's trial related to a shipment of marijuana in which petitioner was not involved; the testimony contained not a single reference to petitioner. Petitioner's counsel did not cross-examine Bravo, and neither petitioner's counsel nor the prosecutor mentioned Bravo's testimony in closing argument. All of these developments were predictable when the District Court ruled on petitioner's request that Iredale serve as trial counsel; the contours of Bravo's testimony were clear at that time. Given the insignificance of this testimony to any matter that petitioner's counsel would dispute, the proposed joint representation of petitioner and Bravo did not threaten a conflict of interest.[13]

Moreover, even assuming that Bravo's testimony might have "necessitat[ed] vigorous cross-examination," the District Court could have insured against the possibility of any conflict of interest without wholly depriving petitioner of his constitutional right to the counsel of his choice. Petitioner's motion requested that Iredale either be substituted for petitioner's current counsel or be added to petitioner's defense team. Had the District Court allowed the addition of Iredale and then ordered that he take no part in the cross-examination of Bravo, any possibility of a conflict would have been removed. Especially in light of the availability of this precautionary measure, the notion that Iredale's prior representation of Bravo might well have caused a conflict of interest at petitioner's trial is nothing short of ludicrous. ...

[13] [Dissent's footnote 3:] The very insignificance of Bravo's testimony, combined with the timing of the prosecutor's decision to call Bravo as a witness, raises a serious concern that the prosecutor attempted to manufacture a conflict in this case. The prosecutor's decision to use Bravo as a witness was an 11th-hour development. Throughout the course of plea negotiations with Bravo, the prosecutor never had suggested that Bravo testify at petitioner's trial. At Bravo's guilty-plea proceedings, when Iredale notified the District Court of petitioner's substitution motion, the prosecutor conceded that he had made no plans to call Bravo as a witness. Only after the prosecutor learned of the substitution motion and decided to oppose it did he arrange for Bravo's testimony by agreeing to recommend to the trial court a reduction in Bravo's sentence. Especially in light of the scarce value of Bravo's testimony, this prosecutorial behavior very plausibly may be viewed as a maneuver to prevent Iredale from representing petitioner at trial. Iredale had proved to be a formidable adversary; he previously had gained an acquittal for the alleged kingpin of the marijuana distribution scheme. As the District Court stated in considering petitioner's motion: "Were I in [petitioner's] position I'm sure I would want Mr. Iredale representing me, too. He did a fantastic job in that [Gomez-Barajas] trial ... ." The prosecutor's decision to call Bravo as a witness may well have stemmed from a concern that Iredale would do an equally fantastic job at petitioner's trial. As the Court notes, governmental maneuvering of this kind is relevant to a trial court's decision as to whether to accept a criminal defendant's chosen counsel. The significant possibility that the prosecutor was engaging in such bad-faith conduct provides yet another reason to dispute the Court's resolution of this case.

Notes

1. What is the likelihood that this potential conflict would blossom into an actual conflict? Is the better course to guard the defendant's right to conflict-free counsel at the expense of his right to counsel of choice? Why is the right to counsel of choice important?

2. Where codefendants are jointly represented at trial or sentencing, the potential for prejudicial conflicts is perhaps greatest. For example, in *United States v. Curcio*, 680 F.2d 881 (2d Cir. 1982), the court explained:

> "[A] possible conflict inheres in almost every instance of multiple representation," in part because the interests of the defendants may diverge at virtually every stage of the proceeding. Thus, the joint attorney may have to prefer the interests of one defendant over the other in deciding, for example, ... whether or not to present a defense that helps one defendant more than the other; whether or not to cross-examine a witness whose testimony may help one defendant and hurt the other; whether to have one defendant testify while the other remains silent; whether to have neither defendant testify because one would be a poor or vulnerable witness; whether or not to emphasize in summation that certain evidence is admitted only against (or is less compelling against) one defendant rather than the other; whether or not to argue at sentencing that one defendant's role in the criminal enterprise was shown only to be subordinate to that of the other defendant. These dilemmas are insidious because it often is not clear that the conflict of interests, and not pure trial strategy, are the reasons for the tactics adopted—or forgone—at trial. As the Supreme Court observed in *Holloway v. Arkansas*, "[j]oint representation of conflicting interests is suspect because of what it tends to prevent the attorney from doing"; "in a case of joint representation of conflicting interests the evil—it bears repeating—is in what the advocate finds himself compelled to *refrain* from doing, not only at trial but also as to possible pretrial plea negotiations and in the sentencing process."

Id. at 887.

3. Where two defendants are jointly represented in a criminal case, plea bargaining raises another obvious potential for disqualifying conflicts of interest:

> When one attorney represents multiple defendants, ... plea bargain negotiations are fraught with danger of conflicts of interests. For example, where an attorney represents two clients, one of whom is substantially more culpable than the other, he may forego altogether an attempt to bargain for the less culpable defendant out of a fear that the defendant's cooperation with the prosecution may undermine the defense of his more culpable client. ... Recognizing this potential detriment to the interests of the other defendants, the attorney may be inclined to dissuade him from accepting the proffered bargain. But if his advice to one defendant is influenced by concern for other defendants, the lawyer suffers an impairment of loyalty violative of the former's sixth amendment rights.

John Stewart Geer, *Representation of Multiple Criminal Defendants: Conflicts of Interest and the Professional Responsibilities of the Defense Attorney*, 62 Minn. L. Rev. 119, 125 (1978); *see also Holloway*, 435 U.S. at 489-90. Thus, for example, when the same lawyer represents two defendants and negotiates immunity for one defendant, an actual conflict is likely to be found, particularly when the immunity agreement contemplates that one jointly represented defendant will testify against the other. *See, e.g.,* Burden v. Zant, 24 F.3d 1298 (11th Cir. 1994). *But see* Yeck v. Goodwin, 985 F.2d 538 (11th Cir. 1993) (finding no adverse effect upon counsel's representation because the testimony of the codefendant for whom counsel negotiated a plea agreement actually supported the accused's defense of consent); In the Matter of the Special Feb. 1977 Grand Jury, 581 F.2d 1262 (7th Cir. 1978) (upholding denial of disqualification where counsel represented two immunized witnesses and there was no evidence to suggest that the immunized witnesses would implicate counsel's other clients).

4. The *Wheat* Court mentions the possibility that the trial court will be "whip-sawed" in making these determinations. That is, a defendant who insists upon his right to counsel of choice and thus states that he waives conflict-free counsel may, after conviction, raise an ineffective assistance of counsel claim on appeal.

In *Strickland v. Washington*, 466 U.S. 668 (1984), the Supreme Court set forth the standard for constitutional ineffective assistance. It held that the defendant must meet a two-part burden. First, he must demonstrate counsel's ineffectiveness (*i.e.*, that counsel's representation fell below an objective standard of reasonableness under prevailing professional norms). Second, the defendant must establish prejudice, defined to mean a reasonable probability that, but for counsel's unprofessional errors, the result of the proceeding would have been different. *See id.* at 687.

With respect to the second part of the *Strickland* test—the prejudice inquiry—the *Strickland* Court noted, however, that the usual showing is not required when the ineffective assistance of counsel claim is grounded in an actual conflict of interest. It explained the relevant standard as follows:

> ... In *Cuyler v. Sullivan*, 446 U.S. 335 (1980), the Court held that *prejudice is presumed when counsel is burdened by an actual conflict of interest.* In those circumstances, counsel breaches the duty of loyalty, perhaps the most basic of counsel's duties. Moreover, it is difficult to measure the precise effect on the defense of representation corrupted by conflicting interests. Given the obligation of counsel to avoid conflicts of interest and the ability of trial courts to make early inquiry in certain situations likely to give rise to conflicts, *see, e.g.*, Fed. Rule. Crim. Proc. 44(c), it is reasonable for the criminal justice system to maintain a fairly rigid rule of presumed prejudice for conflicts of interest. Even so, the rule is not quite the *per se* rule of prejudice that exists for the Sixth Amendment claims [of actual or constructive denial of counsel or state interference with counsel's assistance]. Prejudice is presumed *only if the defendant demonstrates that counsel "actively represented conflicting interests" and that "an actual conflict of interest adversely affected his lawyer's performance."*

Strickland, 466 U.S. at 692 (1984) (emphasis added). In short, where counsel was burdened by an actual conflict of interest, a defendant, to prevail on an ineffective assistance of counsel claim, need only show that the conflict "adversely affected his lawyer's performance," *not* that "but for counsel's unprofessional errors, the result of the proceeding would have been different."

5. In *Mickens v. Taylor*, 535 U.S. 162 (2002), Mickens was convicted of the premeditated murder of Timothy Hall and sentenced to death. Mickens sought to attack his conviction on habeas alleging that he was denied the effective assistance of counsel because one of his court-appointed attorneys had a conflict of interest at trial. Habeas counsel had discovered that the judge before whom Mickens was tried had appointed Mickens' lead trial counsel to represent Timothy Hall—the victim of the alleged murder—in a prior juvenile proceeding. Thus, at the time of the murder, Mickens' counsel was representing Mickens' victim. Counsel did not disclose to the court, to his co-counsel, or to Mickens that he had represented Mickens' victim.

The Supreme Court rejected Mickens' suggestion that the Court should employ a rule of automatic reversal under the Sixth Amendment where there existed a conflict that the judge knew or should have known about but did not explore further, regardless of whether the conflict affected counsel's performance. Instead, the Court held that to demonstrate a Sixth Amendment violation where the trial court failed to inquire into possible conflicts of interest about which he knew or reasonably should have known, defendant must establish that this conflict of interest adversely affected counsel's performance. Because the Fourth

Circuit found no such effect, the Supreme Court affirmed the Fourth Circuit's denial of habeas relief.

In conclusion, the *Mickens* Court also noted that the case was presented and argued on the assumption that the same standard (requiring a showing of defective performance but not the type of prejudice normally required under *Strickland*) applies when (1) as here, the problem was a potential conflict arising from a previous representation and (2) cases in which the conflict arises by virtue of two substantially contemporaneous representations. The Court pointedly stated that it did not rule upon the correctness of that assumption. Since that time, a split has (predictably) developed regarding whether the presumed prejudice rule of *Cuyler* or the *Strickland* standard ought to apply to conflicts of interest other than those arising out of concurrent multiple representation. *See, e.g.,* Stewart v. Wolfenbarger, 468 F.3d 338 (6th Cir. 2006) (collecting cases); Schwab v. Crosby, 451 F.3d 1308 (11th Cir. 2006) (same); United States v. Esparza-Serrano, 81 Fed. Appx. 111 (9th Cir. 2003) (same).

6. One could argue that *Wheat* values the judicial system's interest in conflict-free, effective counsel more than the defendant's right to choice of counsel, at least when these two Sixth Amendment values come into conflict; that is, that the right to counsel ultimately serves primarily the system's interest in a fair trial. In 2006, however, the Supreme Court made clear in *United States v. Gonzalez-Lopez*, 548 U.S. 140 (2006), the value that counsel of choice holds where there is no prospective conflict alleged. In that case, all agreed on the fact that the District Court had erred in disqualifying the defendant's counsel of choice. The Supreme Court then held that no additional showing of prejudice was required to make the Sixth Amendment violation complete *and* that the erroneous deprivation of the defendant's right to choice of counsel was a "structural error" not subject to harmless error review. In so holding, the Court rejected the government's argument that this right is valued not for its own sake, but rather for the affect it will have on the ability of the accused to receive a fair trial. *Id.* at 144-46. The Court instead ruled that the Sixth Amendment's right to counsel of choice "commands, not that a trial be fair, but that a particular guarantee of fairness be provided—to wit, that the accused be defended by the counsel he believes to be best." *Id.* at 146. The Court also noted in conclusion, however, that "[n]othing we have said today casts any doubt or places any qualification upon our previous holdings that limit the right to counsel of choice," including the fact that "the right to counsel of choice does not extend to defendants who require counsel to be appointed for them." *Id.* at 151.

2. MULTIPLE REPRESENTATION DECISIONS IN THE CORPORATE CONTEXT

> If those summoned in the investigation work for an entity, the entity may retain counsel to represent itself and its employees and officers ... . If the investigation comes to naught this works out well; if the investigation culminates in indictment of some of those jointly represented[,] hindsight often—perhaps almost invariably—indicates that separate representation from the outset would have been advisable. [14]

How does an entity and those associated with it avoid the heartbreak of hindsight? As the following article makes clear, entities and their directors, officers, employees, and agents must carefully weigh three principal factors in making a decision about whether to engage in multiple representation or to hire separate counsel: ethical rules, tactical considerations, and prosecutorial responses.

---

[14] United States v. Turkish, 470 F. Supp. 903, 907-08 (S.D.N.Y. 1978).

Gregory J. Wallance, *Can You Represent Both Company and Employees After Receiving Grand Jury Subpoenas?*
6 Bus. Crimes Bull. 1, 5-6 (Nov. 1999)[15]

Nearly every grand jury investigation of a corporate entity and its current or former employees raises tricky and potentially treacherous issues of multiple representation. Many white collar defense attorneys advocate that a company's outside counsel should represent company employees and obtain separate counsel for employees who receive grand jury subpoenas. As with any sensible rule, there are limited exceptions, which this article addresses. ...

Ethical Considerations

Rule 1.13(e) (organization as client) of the Model Rules of Professional Conduct expressly permits a lawyer representing an organization to represent its officers and employees as well, with the critical qualification that such multiple representation must be permissible under Model Rule 1.7 (conflict of interest). In substance, Model Rule 1.7, without distinguishing between civil and criminal representations, permits joint representation even if the clients have adverse positions as long as the clients consent after full disclosure, including an explanation of the advantages and risks of common representation, and the lawyer reasonably believes that he can adequately represent both.

The comment to Model Rule 1.7 addresses representation of multiple defendants in a criminal case and states that an impermissible conflict can arise as a result of substantial discrepancy in the witness' testimony, inconsistent positions regarding an adversary party, or the existence of different possibilities of resolution of the liabilities in question. The comment then states that, because the potential for conflict of interest in representing multiple defendants in a criminal case is "so grave," ordinarily a lawyer should decline to represent more than one co-defendant. The comment is silent on the question of joint representation of a company and its employees in a grand jury investigation. See County Lawyers Association, Op. 707, N.Y. (1995) ("Joint representation [of] multiple clients having differing interests in a criminal investigation is disfavored even with consent of each client.") (Interpreting the Code of Professional Responsibility).

There are two types of conflicts: actual and potential. Some courts hold that a knowing and intelligent waiver of either type of conflict is possible, while others rule that actual conflicts of interest cannot be waived. In the post-indictment period, an actual conflict exists, for example, where a particular attorney has represented a witness or a co-defendant and has gained confidential knowledge from that representation that could impede his advocacy on behalf of the defendant in, for example, cross-examining the witness or co-defendant.

At the outset of a grand jury investigation, the concern usually is with potential conflicts. No charges have been brought, and the direction the investigation may take is not apparent to outsiders. Is it a serious investigation? What information does the prosecutor have? What is he after? Whom is he after? Which employee needs immunity as a condition for testifying? Sometimes, even the prosecutor cannot answer these questions.

The dilemma is that while at the outset there may be no apparent differing interests between company and employees, their alignment can easily become adverse as the investigation progresses. In that case, by representing employees whose interests have

---

become adverse to the corporation—i.e., an actual conflict of interest—the company counsel risks disqualification of its outside counsel in the event of an indictment and trial, if not earlier. The result is that the company may find itself without knowledgeable counsel just when it needs him or her the most *and* incurs the additional cost of hiring and educating new counsel. ...

There are gray areas where multiple representation inevitably carries unquantifiable but real risks. For example, at the outset of the investigation, the prosecutor may disclose only that the company and its senior officers are subjects and that its theory of criminal wrongdoing applies equally to both. At first glance, the company and the officers appear to have no differing interests, particularly if the company's exposure results directly from a decision made by the senior officers. If the company is a closely held one, and the officers are the shareholders, then multiple representation may be appropriate. In this scenario, it is unlikely that the company can obtain lenient treatment at the expense of the officers or vice versa.

This is certainly not necessarily the case with large publicly held companies. While it is unusual for a senior officer such as the president to obtain immunity or leniency in exchange for testifying against the company, in our modern era of leniency and amnesty programs, companies can and do obtain better terms by cooperating with the prosecution against senior officers. To be sure, such cooperation is usually preceded by the departure of the senior officer, which may moot the issue of multiple representation. But at the early stages of most grand jury investigations of major companies, no one can really be sure whether such differing interests may later arise. A decision in favor of multiple representation of the company and its senior officers is, therefore, an act of faith.

The company's inside counsel, after having done as thorough a fact investigation as possible, satisfying itself that "differing interests are not present," and recognizing the risk that unanticipated facts might create an actual conflict of interest that could disqualify the company's outside counsel at a trial, if not during the grand jury investigation, may opt for the benefit of joint representation. If so, the company's outside counsel should make certain that both company and other employees fully understand the risks of multiple representation and obtain their consent in writing.

The minimum elements of the written waiver include:

--An explanation of the existence and focus of the grand jury investigation.
--An expression that neither party is aware of any wrongdoing by the employee, and
--A warning that if additional facts come to light suggesting that the employee was involved in wrongdoing, the employee will have to retain separate counsel and will not object to continued representation by joint counsel of the company.

The lawyer should be careful to obtain consent from an officer authorized by the company to waive conflicts of interest. The waiver should also warn the company that the waiver by the officer or employee will not necessarily prevent disqualification of the company's counsel at trial or even at the grand jury stage.

The Prosecution's Response

Prosecutors do not like multiple representations at the grand jury stage any better than at trial and typically threaten disqualification when presented with such representations. In their view, multiple representation raises obstruction-of-justice concerns and reduces the likelihood of obtaining cooperation of the company employees. From the perspective of the company's counsel, the likely prosecution reaction is an important consideration, particularly where the company seeks to demonstrate that it has fully cooperated with the investigation. In that situation, multiple representation may be inadvisable because, by distancing itself from an employee under suspicion, the company projects a "nothing to hide" attitude and will not be held responsible if the employee refuses to cooperate or provides false testimony.

But if a company appropriately has opted for multiple representation, then it should be prepared to stand its ground. To disqualify a lawyer from representing multiple clients, a prosecutor must demonstrate either a potential or actual conflict of interest. At the early stage of a grand jury investigation, this burden may not be easy for a prosecutor to meet. More typically, prosecutors raise potential conflicts of interest by suggesting that, absent multiple representation, the employee would be under consideration for immunity. Once such a suggestion is made, however, the company counsel will have to reconsider whether the employee should have his own counsel even if the employee continues to insist that he has no information damaging to the company. It is difficult to envision how the company's lawyer can ethically represent an employee in immunity negotiations in which the likelihood of immunity increases in direct proportion to the employee's willingness to inculpate the company. ...

Tactical Consideration When Considering Multiple Representation

Are there any circumstances in which the attendant risks may be worth the benefits to be gained by multiple representation? Such benefits include:

--A coordinated strategy in pooling information to the benefit of all witnesses, which likely will be more complete (and certainly more efficient) than exchanges of information among multiple defense counsel pursuant to joint defense agreements.

--Maintenance of morale of lower-level company employees, who are less likely to believe that they are being abandoned by their company.

--At the senior level, a clear signal to the prosecutors that the company does not believe that its senior executives have engaged in wrongdoing.

--Cost savings.

How does a company judge when multiple representation is or is not cost beneficial? Some circumstances in which multiple representation is inadvisable and/or unethical are easy to recognize. These include an investigation where:

--The company is neither a target nor a subject and where the employee's alleged criminal acts furthered no company interests and may have harmed it.

--The company is a target and the employee is a nontarget witness with knowledge that inculpates the company.

--The employee is a candidate for immunity in exchange for providing assistance to the investigation.

--The company is fully cooperating with the investigation in the hope of leniency or amnesty and the information it provides inculpates the employee.

At the other extreme, the best case for multiple representation exists where the prosecutor assures the company counsel that neither the company nor its employees are targets or subjects, or where the facts are such that the company counsel is fully (and happily) satisfied that neither the company nor its employees committed any crimes, or where a settled legal doctrine such as the statute of limitations precludes prosecution. ...

Note

1. The Yates Memo, discussed in Chapter 4(C), has had an impact on the decision whether to provide employees with separate counsel:

[T]he Yates Memorandum has resulted in the retention by employees of separate counsel both more often and earlier in the investigative process. While the use by employees of counsel separate from counsel representing the business organization has typically been an option (albeit a costly one) during investigations, pre-Yates it was not commonly exercised. The Yates Memorandum changes the calculation in two respects. First, if an employee has apparent exposure and knows that corporate counsel are required to report all relevant facts regarding the employee's involvement in the misconduct in order to obtain any cooperation credit for the corporation, then the employee may be much more reticent to participate in interviews without separate counsel. Indeed, many European nations have domestic laws that require companies to utilize works councils to protect the interests of employees, and European or other foreign employees may be entitled to have an attorney or a works council representative present during their interviews. This can restrict a company's ability to interview its foreign employees and collect personal data during internal investigations. Second, insofar as the provision of cooperation credit hinges on the DOJ's belief that the organization has provided all relevant facts about individual culpability, the decision to bifurcate the legal representation can enhance the credibility of corporate counsel when it asserts that no individual is culpable.

The overall result has been the increased retention of separate counsel, often at an early stage of the investigation, and longer, more complicated, and more costly internal investigations. This can create a snowball effect—once a few employees obtain separate counsel, others in the same company are likely to seek the same protection—that can lead to exhaustion of directors' and officers' liability insurance policy limits. One upside, at least from the perspective of the DOJ, is that employees are more likely to give more complete and truthful answers during investigations when they have separate counsel.

Gideon Mark, *The Yates Memorandum*, 51 U.C. Davis L. Rev. 1589, 1617-19 (2018).

C. PRE-INDICTMENT SIXTH AMENDMENT PROTECTION? *UNITED STATES v. STEIN*

Wheat discusses various attributes of the Sixth Amendment counsel right but that right "does not attach until the initiation of adversary judicial proceedings," generally through indictment.[16] What rules apply at the grand jury stage? This is a critical question for our purposes because, as a white-collar practitioner, one must confront these issues at the investigative stage, when it may be difficult to forecast the potential for conflicts ahead. If one does not adequately predict potential conflicts, counsel later found to be conflicted may be disqualified from representing *all* the clients.[17] The timing of such disqualification may seriously imperil the clients' interests, coming as it usually does fairly late in the day after both counsel and her clients have invested a great deal in the representation.

Few cases have addressed the scope of any right to counsel in pre-charge proceedings. A couple of courts have recognized that a grand jury witness "has a right to consult with an attorney outside the grand jury room and has a general due process right to legal assistance."[18] And some courts have been willing to entertain government disqualification

---

[16] United States v. Gouveia, 467 U.S. 180, 188 (1984); *see also* United States v. Mandujano, 425 U.S. 564, 581 (1976); *In re* Grand Jury Investigation, 182 F.3d 668, 671 (9th Cir. 1999).

[17] *See, e.g.*, United States v. Moscony, 927 F.2d 742, 748–51 (3d Cir. 1991).

[18] Dan K. Webb, Robert W. Tarun & Steven F. Molo, Corporate Internal Investigations § 5.02[2], at 5-7 (Law Journal Press 2018); *see also In re* Grand Jury Subpoena, 567 F.2d 1183 (2d Cir. 1977).

motions based upon a lawyer's potential conflict of interest in representing a number of persons, including investigatory targets, at the grand jury stage, though those motions are not generally successful in absence of some evidence of a strong potential or an actual conflict of interest.[19] In two 2012 cases the Supreme Court ruled that defendants have a Sixth Amendment right to counsel during plea negotiations, but both those cases involved defendants against who adversary proceedings had commenced.[20] The Second Circuit issued some guidance on this question in a very high-profile case, *United States v. Stein*. (The *Stein* decision is also relevant to a number of other topics, including: (1) the discussion of the DOJ's policy on charging corporations in Chapter 4; and (2) discussion of the implications of the "state action" decision in this case on other constitutional issues—discussed in part in Chapter 20).

UNITED STATES v. STEIN
541 F.3d 130 (2d Cir. 2008)

DENNIS JACOBS, CHIEF JUDGE:

The United States appeals from an order of the United States District Court for the Southern District of New York (Kaplan, *J.*), dismissing an indictment against thirteen former partners and employees of the accounting firm KPMG, LLP. Judge Kaplan found that, absent pressure from the government, KPMG would have paid defendants' legal fees and expenses without regard to cost. Based on this and other findings of fact, Judge Kaplan ruled that the government deprived defendants of their right to counsel under the Sixth Amendment by causing KPMG to impose conditions on the advancement of legal fees to defendants, to cap the fees, and ultimately to end payment. *See United States v. Stein*, 435 F.Supp.2d 330, 367–73 (S.D.N.Y. 2006) ("*Stein I*"). Judge Kaplan also ruled that the government deprived defendants of their right to substantive due process under the Fifth Amendment.[21]

We hold that KPMG's adoption and enforcement of a policy under which it conditioned, capped and ultimately ceased advancing legal fees to defendants followed as a direct consequence of the government's overwhelming influence, and that KPMG's conduct therefore amounted to state action. We further hold that the government thus unjustifiably interfered with defendants' relationship with counsel and their ability to mount a defense, in violation of the Sixth Amendment, and that the government did not cure the violation. Because no other remedy will return defendants to the *status quo ante*, we affirm the dismissal of the indictment as to all thirteen defendants. In light of this disposition, we do not reach the district court's Fifth Amendment ruling.

---

[19] *See, e.g.*, *In re* Grand Jury Subpoena, 567 F.2d at 1186–87; *In re* Grand Jury Proceedings, 859 F.2d 1021 (1st Cir.1988); *In re* Investigation Before the Feb. 1977, Lynchburg Grand Jury, 563 F.2d 652 (4th Cir. 1977).

[20] Lafler v. Cooper, 566 U.S. 156 (2012); Missouri v. Frye, 566 U.S. 134 (2012).

[21] [Court's footnote 1:] In later decisions, Judge Kaplan ruled that defendants Richard Smith and Mark Watson's proffer session statements were obtained in violation of their Fifth Amendment privilege against self-incrimination, and that their statements would be suppressed, *see United States v. Stein*, 440 F.Supp.2d 315 (S.D.N.Y. 2006) ("*Stein II*"); that the court had ancillary jurisdiction over Defendants-Appellees' civil suit against KPMG for advancement of fees, *see United States v. Stein*, 452 F.Supp.2d 230 (S.D.N.Y. 2006) ("*Stein III*"), *vacated*, Stein v. KPMG, LLP, 486 F.3d 753 (2d Cir. 2007); and that dismissal of the indictment is the appropriate remedy for those constitutional violations, *see United States v. Stein*, 495 F.Supp.2d 390 (S.D.N.Y. 2007) ("*Stein IV*").

BACKGROUND

The Thompson Memorandum

In January 2003, then-United States Deputy Attorney General Larry D. Thompson promulgated a policy statement, *Principles of Federal Prosecution of Business Organizations* (the "Thompson Memorandum"), which articulated "principles" to govern the Department's discretion in bringing prosecutions against business organizations. The Thompson Memorandum was closely based on a predecessor document issued in 1999 by then-U.S. Deputy Attorney General Eric Holder, *Federal Prosecution of Corporations*. Along with the familiar factors governing charging decisions, the Thompson Memorandum identifies nine additional considerations, including the company's "timely and voluntary disclosure of wrongdoing and its willingness to cooperate in the investigation of its agents." The Memorandum explains that prosecutors should inquire

> whether the corporation appears to be protecting its culpable employees and agents [and that] a corporation's promise of support to culpable employees and agents, either *through the advancing of attorneys fees*, through retaining the employees without sanction for their misconduct, or through providing information to the employees about the government's investigation pursuant to a joint defense agreement, may be considered by the prosecutor in weighing the extent and value of a corporation's cooperation.

(emphasis added). A footnote appended to the highlighted phrase explains that because certain states require companies to advance legal fees for their officers, "a corporation's compliance with governing law should not be considered a failure to cooperate." In December 2006—after the events in this prosecution had transpired—the Department of Justice replaced the Thompson Memorandum with the McNulty Memorandum, under which prosecutors may consider a company's fee advancement policy only where the circumstances indicate that it is "intended to impede a criminal investigation," and even then only with the approval of the Deputy Attorney General. Mem. from Paul J. McNulty, Deputy Att'y Gen., U.S. Dep't of Justice, *Principles of Federal Prosecution of Business Organizations* (Dec. 12, 2006), at VII n. 3.

Commencement of the Federal Investigation

After Senate subcommittee hearings in 2002 concerning KPMG's possible involvement in creating and marketing fraudulent tax shelters, KPMG retained Robert S. Bennett of the law firm Skadden, Arps, Slate, Meagher & Flom LLP ("Skadden") to formulate a "cooperative approach" for KPMG to use in dealing with federal authorities. Bennett's strategy included "a decision to 'clean house'—a determination to ask Jeffrey Stein, Richard Smith, and Jeffrey Eischeid, all senior KPMG partners who had testified before the Senate and all now [Defendants-Appellees] here—to leave their positions as deputy chair and chief operating officer of the firm, vice chair-tax services, and a partner in personal financial planning, respectively." Smith was transferred and Eischeid was put on administrative leave. Stein resigned with arrangements for a three-year $100,000-per-month consultancy, and an agreement that KPMG would pay for Stein's representation in any actions brought against Stein arising from his activities at the firm. KPMG negotiated a contract with Smith that included a similar clause; but that agreement was never executed.

In February 2004, KPMG officials learned that the firm and 20 to 30 of its top partners and employees were subjects of a grand jury investigation of fraudulent tax shelters. On February 18, 2004, KPMG's CEO announced to all partners that the firm was aware of the United States Attorney's Office's ("USAO") investigation and that "[a]ny present or former members of the firm asked to appear will be represented by competent coun[sel] *at the firm's expense.*"

The February 25, 2004 Meeting

In preparation for a meeting with Skadden on February 25, 2004, the prosecutors—including Assistant United States Attorneys ("AUSAs") Shirah Neiman and Justin Weddle—decided to ask whether KPMG would advance legal fees to employees under investigation. Bennett started the meeting by announcing that KPMG had resolved to "clean house," that KPMG "would cooperate fully with the government's investigation," and that its goal was not to protect individual employees but rather to save the firm from being indicted. AUSA Weddle inquired about the firm's plans for advancing fees and about any legal obligation to do so. Later on, AUSA Neiman added that the government would "take into account" the firm's legal obligations to advance fees, but that "the Thompson Memorandum [w]as a point that had to be considered." Bennett then advised that although KPMG was still investigating its legal obligations to advance fees, its "common practice" was to do so. However, Bennett explained, KPMG would not pay legal fees for any partner who refused to cooperate or "took the Fifth," so long as KPMG had the legal authority to do so.

Later in the meeting, AUSA Weddle asked Bennett to ascertain KPMG's legal obligations to advance attorneys' fees. AUSA Neiman added that "misconduct" should not or cannot "be rewarded" under "federal guidelines." One Skadden attorney's notes attributed to AUSA Weddle the prediction that, if KPMG had discretion regarding fees, the government would "look at that under a microscope."

Skadden then reported back to KPMG. In notes of the meeting, a KPMG executive wrote the words "[p]aying legal fees" and "[s]everance" next to "not a sign of cooperation."

Communications Between the Prosecutors and KPMG

On March 2, 2004, Bennett told AUSA Weddle that although KPMG believed it had no legal obligation to advance fees, "it would be a big problem" for the firm not to do so given its partnership structure. But Bennett disclosed KPMG's tentative decision to limit the amount of fees and condition them on employees' cooperation with prosecutors.

Two days later, a Skadden lawyer advised counsel for Defendant-Appellee Carol G. Warley (a former KPMG tax partner) that KPMG would advance legal fees if Warley cooperated with the government and declined to invoke her Fifth Amendment privilege against self-incrimination.

On a March 11 conference call with Skadden, AUSA Weddle recommended that KPMG tell employees that they should be "totally open" with the USAO, "even if that [meant admitting] criminal wrongdoing," explaining that this would give him good material for cross-examination. That same day, Skadden wrote to counsel for the KPMG employees who had been identified as subjects of the investigation. The letter set forth KPMG's new fees policy ("Fees Policy"), pursuant to which advancement of fees and expenses would be

[i] capped at $400,000 per employee;
[ii] conditioned on the employee's cooperation with the government; and
[iii] terminated when an employee was indicted.

The government was copied on this correspondence.

On March 12, KPMG sent a memorandum to certain other employees who had not been identified as subjects, urging them to cooperate with the government, advising them that it might be advantageous for them to exercise their right to counsel, and advising that KPMG would cover employees' "reasonable fees."

The prosecutors expressed by letter their "disappoint[ment] with [the] tone" of this memorandum and its "one-sided presentation of potential issues," and "demanded that KPMG send out a supplemental memorandum in a form they proposed." The government's alternative language, premised on the "assum[ption] that KPMG truly is committed to fully cooperating with the Government's investigation," Letter of David N. Kelley, United States Attorney, Southern District of New York, March 17, 2004, advised employees that they could "meet with investigators without the assistance of counsel." KPMG complied, and circulated a memo advising that employees "may deal directly with government representatives without counsel."

At a meeting in late March, Skadden asked the prosecutors to notify Skadden in the event any KPMG employee refused to cooperate. Over the following year, the prosecutors regularly informed Skadden whenever a KPMG employee refused to cooperate fully, such as by refusing to proffer or by proffering incompletely (in the government's view). Skadden, in turn, informed the employees' lawyers that fee advancement would cease unless the employees cooperated. The employees either knuckled under and submitted to interviews, or they were fired and KPMG ceased advancing their fees. For example, Watson and Smith attended proffer sessions after receiving KPMG's March 11 letter announcing the Fees Policy, and after Skadden reiterated to them that fees would be terminated absent cooperation. They did so because (they said, and the district court found) they feared that KPMG would stop advancing attorneys fees—although Watson concedes he attended a first session voluntarily.[22] As Bennett later assured AUSA Weddle: "Whenever your Office has notified us that individuals have not ... cooperat[ed], KPMG has promptly and without question encouraged them to cooperate and threatened to cease payment of their attorney fees and ... to take personnel action, including termination."

KPMG Avoids Indictment

In an early-March 2005 meeting, then-U.S. Attorney David Kelley told Skadden and top KPMG executives that a non-prosecution agreement was unlikely and that he had reservations about KPMG's level of cooperation: "I've seen a lot better from big companies." Bennett reminded Kelley how KPMG had capped and conditioned its advancement of legal fees. Kelley remained unconvinced.

KPMG moved up the Justice Department's chain of command. At a June 13, 2005 meeting with U.S. Deputy Attorney General James Comey, Bennett stressed KPMG's pressure on employees to cooperate by conditioning legal fees on cooperation; it was, he said, "precedent[] setting." KPMG's entreaties were ultimately successful: on August 29, 2005, the firm entered into a deferred prosecution agreement (the "DPA") under which KPMG admitted extensive wrongdoing, paid a $456 million fine, and committed itself to cooperation in any future government investigation or prosecution.

Indictment of Individual Employees

On August 29, 2005—the same day KPMG executed the DPA—the government indicted six of the Defendants-Appellees (along with three other KPMG employees): Jeffrey Stein; Richard Smith; Jeffrey Eischeid; John Lanning, Vice Chairman of Tax Services; Philip Wiesner, a former tax partner; and Mark Watson, a tax partner. A superseding indictment filed on October 17, 2005 named ten additional employees, including seven of the Defendants-Appellees: Larry DeLap, a former tax partner in charge of professional practice; Steven Gremminger, a former partner and associate general counsel; former tax

---

[22] [Court's footnote 3:] As discussed above, in a decision that is the subject of the summary order filed today, the district court held that Defendants-Appellees Smith and Watson's proffer statements were obtained in violation of their Fifth Amendment privilege against self-incrimination and that their statements would be suppressed.

partners Gregg Ritchie, Randy Bickham and Carl Hasting; Carol G. Warley; and Richard Rosenthal, a former tax partner and Chief Financial Officer of KPMG.[23] Pursuant to the Fees Policy, KPMG promptly stopped advancing legal fees to the indicted employees who were still receiving them.

Procedural History

On January 12, 2006, the thirteen defendants (among others) moved to dismiss the indictment based on the government's interference with KPMG's advancement of fees. In a submission to the district court, KPMG represented that

> the Thompson memorandum in conjunction with the government's statements relating to payment of legal fees affected KPMG's determination(s) with respect to the advancement of legal fees and other defense costs to present or former partners and employees. ... In fact, KPMG is prepared to state that the Thompson memorandum substantially influenced KPMG's decisions with respect to legal fees. ...

At a hearing on March 30, 2006, Judge Kaplan asked the government whether it was "prepared at this point to commit that [it] has no objection whatsoever to KPMG exercising its free and independent business judgment as to whether to advance defense costs to these defendants and that if it were to elect to do so the government would not in any way consider that in determining whether it had complied with the DPA?" The AUSA responded: "That's always been the case, your Honor. That's fine. We have no objection to that. ... They can always exercise their business judgment. As you described it, your Honor, that's always been the case. It's the case today, your Honor."

Judge Kaplan ordered discovery and held a three-day evidentiary hearing in May 2006 to ascertain whether the government had contributed to KPMG's adoption of the Fees Policy. The court heard testimony from two prosecutors, one IRS agent, three Skadden attorneys, and one lawyer from KPMG's Office of General Counsel, among others. Numerous documents produced in discovery by both sides were admitted into evidence.

Stein I

Judge Kaplan's opinion and order of June 26, 2006 noted, as the parties had stipulated, that KPMG's past practice was to advance legal fees for employees facing regulatory, civil and criminal investigations without condition or cap. Starting from that baseline, Judge Kaplan made the following findings of fact. At the February 25, 2004 meeting, Bennett began by "test[ing] the waters to see whether KPMG could adhere to its practice of paying its employees' legal expenses when litigation loomed [by asking] for [the] government's view on the subject." It is not clear what AUSA Neiman intended to convey when she said that "misconduct" should not or cannot "be rewarded" under "federal guidelines"; but her statement "was understood by both KPMG and government representatives as a reminder that payment of legal fees by KPMG, beyond any that it might legally be obligated to pay, could well count against KPMG in the government's decision whether to indict the firm." "[W]hile the USAO did not say in so many words that it did not want KPMG to pay legal fees, no one at the meeting could have failed to draw that conclusion."

Based on those findings, Judge Kaplan arrived at the following ultimate findings of fact, all of which the government contests on appeal:

---

[23] [Court's footnote 4:] The superseding indictment filed on October 17, 2005 charged 19 defendants in 46 counts for conspiring to defraud the United States and the IRS, tax evasion and obstruction of the internal revenue laws (although not every individual was charged with every offense).

[1] "the Thompson Memorandum caused KPMG to consider departing from its long-standing policy of paying legal fees and expenses of its personnel in all cases and investigations even before it first met with the USAO" and induced KPMG to seek "an indication from the USAO that payment of fees in accordance with its settled practice would not be held against it";

[2] the government made repeated references to the Thompson Memo in an effort to "reinforce[] the threat inherent in the Thompson Memorandum";

[3] "the government conducted itself in a manner that evidenced a desire to minimize the involvement of defense attorneys"; and

[4] but for the Thompson Memorandum and the prosecutors' conduct, KPMG would have paid defendants' legal fees and expenses without consideration of cost.

Against that background, Judge Kaplan ruled that a defendant has a fundamental right under the Fifth Amendment to fairness in the criminal process, including the ability to get and deploy in defense all "resources lawfully available to him or her, free of knowing or reckless government interference" and that the government's reasons for infringing that right in this case could not withstand strict scrutiny. Judge Kaplan also ruled that the same conduct deprived each defendant of the Sixth Amendment right "to choose the lawyer or lawyers he or she desires and to use one's own funds to mount the defense that one wishes to present." He reasoned that "the government's law enforcement interests in taking the specific actions in question [do not] sufficiently outweigh the interests of the KPMG Defendants in having the resources needed to defend as they think proper against these charges." "[T]he fact that advancement of legal fees occasionally might be part of an obstruction scheme or indicate a lack of full cooperation by a prospective defendant is insufficient to justify the government's interference with the right of individual criminal defendants to obtain resources lawfully available to them in order to defend themselves. ..."

Judge Kaplan rejected the government's position that defendants have no right to spend "other people's money" on high-priced defense counsel: "[T]he KPMG Defendants had at least an expectation that their expenses in defending any claims or charges brought against them by reason of their employment by KPMG would be paid by the firm," and "any benefits that would have flowed from that expectation—the legal fees at issue now—were, in every material sense, their property, not that of a third party." He further determined that defendants need not show how their defense was impaired: the government's interference with their Sixth Amendment "right to be represented as they choose," "like a deprivation of the right to counsel of their choice, is complete irrespective of the quality of the representation they receive."

As to remedy, Judge Kaplan conceded that dismissal of the indictment would be inappropriate unless other avenues for obtaining fees from KPMG were first exhausted. To that end, Judge Kaplan invited defendants to file a civil suit against KPMG under the district court's ancillary jurisdiction. The suit was commenced, and Judge Kaplan denied KPMG's motion to dismiss. However, this Court ruled that the district court lacked ancillary jurisdiction over the action.

Stein IV

Judge Kaplan dismissed the indictment against the thirteen defendants on July 16, 2007. He reinforced the ruling in *Stein I* that the government violated defendants' right to substantive due process by holding that the prosecutors' conduct also "independently shock[s] the conscience." Judge Kaplan concluded that no remedy other than dismissal of the indictment would put defendants in the position they would have occupied absent the government's misconduct.

The government appeals the dismissal of the indictment.

We review … whether the promulgation and enforcement of KPMG's Fees Policy amounted to state action under the Constitution and … whether the government deprived defendants of their Sixth Amendment right to counsel. …

Judge Kaplan found that "KPMG's decision to cut off all payments of legal fees and expenses to anyone who was indicted and to limit and to condition such payments prior to indictment upon cooperation with the government *was the direct consequence* of the pressure applied by the Thompson Memorandum and the USAO." The government protests that KPMG's adoption and enforcement of its Fees Policy was private action, outside the ambit of the Sixth Amendment. …

Actions of a private entity are attributable to the State if "there is a sufficiently close nexus between the State and the challenged action of the … entity so that the action of the latter may be fairly treated as that of the State itself." The "close nexus" test is not satisfied when the state "[m]ere[ly] approv[es] of or acquiesce[s] in the initiatives" of the private entity, or when an entity is merely subject to governmental regulation. "The purpose of the [close-nexus requirement] is to assure that constitutional standards are invoked only when it can be said that the State is *responsible* for the specific conduct of which the plaintiff complains." *Blum v. Yaretsky*, 457 U.S. 991, 1004 (1982). Such responsibility is normally found when the State "has exercised coercive power or has provided such significant encouragement, either overt or covert, that the choice must in law be deemed to be that of the State."

Although Supreme Court cases on this issue "have not been a model of consistency," some principles emerge. "A nexus of state action exists between a private entity and the state when the state exercises coercive power, is entwined in the management or control of the private actor, or provides the private actor with *significant encouragement,* either overt or covert, or when the private actor operates as a *willful participant in joint activity* with the State or its agents, is controlled by an agency of the State, has been delegated a public function by the state, or is *entwined with governmental policies.*"

The government argues: KPMG simply took actions in the shadow of an internal DOJ advisory document (the Thompson Memorandum) containing multiple factors and caveats; the government's approval of KPMG's Fees Policy did not render the government responsible for KPMG's actions enforcing it; even if the government had specifically *required* KPMG to adopt a policy that penalized non-cooperation, state action would still have been lacking because KPMG would have retained the power to apply the policy; and although the prosecutors repeatedly informed KPMG when employees were not cooperating, they did so at KPMG's behest, without knowing how KPMG would react. We disagree.

KPMG's adoption and enforcement of the Fees Policy amounted to "state action" because KPMG "operate[d] as a willful participant in joint activity" with the government, and because the USAO "significant[ly] encourage[d]" KPMG to withhold legal fees from defendants upon indictment.[24] The government brought home to KPMG that its survival depended on its role in a joint project with the government to advance government prosecutions. The government is therefore legally "responsible for the specific conduct of which the [criminal defendants] complain[]." …

State action is established here as a matter of law because the government forced KPMG to adopt its constricted Fees Policy. The Thompson Memorandum itself—which prosecutors stated would be considered in deciding whether to indict KPMG—emphasizes that cooperation will be assessed in part based upon whether, in advancing counsel fees, "the corporation appears to be protecting its culpable employees and agents." Since defense counsel's objective in a criminal investigation will virtually always be to protect the client,

---

[24] [Court's footnote 8:] As explained in section IV.A, *infra,* the government's pre-indictment conduct was designed to have an effect once defendants were indicted, and it is therefore proper to consider such conduct for purposes of evaluating state action.

KPMG's risk was that fees for defense counsel would be advanced to someone the government considered culpable. So the only safe course was to allow the government to become (in effect) paymaster.

The prosecutors reinforced this message by inquiring into KPMG's fees obligations, referring to the Thompson Memorandum as "a point that had to be considered," and warning that "misconduct" should not or cannot "be rewarded" under "federal guidelines." The government had KPMG's full attention. It is hardly surprising, then, that KPMG decided to condition payment of fees on employees' cooperation with the government and to terminate fees upon indictment: only that policy would allow KPMG to continue advancing fees while minimizing the risk that prosecutors would view such advancement as obstructive.

To ensure that KPMG's new Fees Policy was enforced, prosecutors became "entwined in the ... control" of KPMG. They intervened in KPMG's decisionmaking, expressing their "disappoint[ment] with [the] tone" of KPMG's first advisory memorandum and declaring that "[t]hese problems must be remedied" by a proposed supplemental memorandum specifying that employees could meet with the government without being burdened by counsel. Prosecutors also "made plain" their "strong preference" as to what the firm should do, and their "desire to share the fruits of such intrusions." They did so by regularly "reporting to KPMG the identities of employees who refused to make statements in circumstances in which the USAO knew full well that KPMG would pressure them to talk to prosecutors." (The government's argument that it could not have known how KPMG would react when informed that certain employees were not cooperating is at best plausible only vis-a-vis the first few employees.) The prosecutors thus steered KPMG toward their preferred fee advancement policy and then supervised its application in individual cases. Such "overt" and "significant encouragement" supports the conclusion that KPMG's conduct is properly attributed to the State.[25] ...

We therefore conclude that KPMG's adoption and enforcement of the Fees Policy (both before and upon defendants' indictment) amounted to state action. The government may properly be held "responsible for the specific conduct of which the [criminal defendants] complain[]," *i.e.*, the deprivation of their Sixth Amendment right to counsel, if the violation is established. ...

The district court's ruling on the Sixth Amendment was based on the following analysis (set out here in precis). The Sixth Amendment protects "an individual's right to choose the lawyer or lawyers he or she desires," and "to use one's own funds to mount the defense that one wishes to present." The goal is to secure "a defendant's right to spend his own money on a defense." Because defendants reasonably expected to receive legal fees from KPMG, the fees "were, in every material sense, their property." The government's interest in retaining discretion to treat as obstruction a company's advancement of legal fees "is insufficient to justify the government's interference with the right of individual criminal defendants to obtain resources lawfully available to them in order to defend themselves." Defendants need not make a "particularized showing" of how their defense was impaired because "[v]irtually everything the defendants do in this case may be influenced by the extent of the resources available to them," such as selection of counsel and "what the KPMG Defendants can pay their lawyers to do." Therefore, the Sixth Amendment violation "is complete irrespective of the quality of the representation they receive."[26]

---

[25] [Court's footnote 9:] Because the Sixth Amendment attaches only upon indictment, the KPMG conduct attributable to the government is relevant only insofar as it contributed to KPMG's decision to withhold legal fees *upon* defendants' indictment. *See* Part IV, *infra*. Many of KPMG's actions occurred prior to the August and October 2005 indictments. Nevertheless, when the defendants were indicted, KPMG had been so schooled by the government in the necessity of enforcing a particular fee advancement policy that KPMG understood what was expected of it once the indictments came down.

[26] [Court's footnote 10:] In *Stein IV*, Judge Kaplan nevertheless expanded his findings as to Sixth

A

Most of the state action relevant here—the promulgation of the Thompson Memorandum, the prosecutors' communications with KPMG regarding the advancement of fees, KPMG's adoption of a Fees Policy with caps and conditions, and KPMG's repeated threats to employees identified by prosecutors as being uncooperative—pre-dated the indictments of August and October 2005. (Of course, *after* the indictments were filed KPMG ceased advancing fees to all thirteen of the present defendants who were still receiving fees up to that point. As explained in Part III, this was also state action.) So we must determine how this pre-indictment conduct may bear on defendants' Sixth Amendment claim.

"The Sixth Amendment right of the 'accused' to assistance of counsel in 'all criminal prosecutions' is limited by its terms: it does not attach until a prosecution is commenced." "Attachment" refers to "*when* the [Sixth Amendment] right may be asserted"; it does not concern the separate question of "*what* the right guarantees," *i.e.*, "what the substantive guarantee of the Sixth Amendment" is at that stage of the prosecution. The Supreme Court has "pegged commencement [of a prosecution] to 'the initiation of adversary judicial criminal proceedings—whether by way of formal charge, preliminary hearing, indictment, information, or arraignment.'" "The rule is not 'mere formalism,' but a recognition of the point at which 'the government has committed itself to prosecute,' 'the adverse positions of government and defendant have solidified,' and the accused 'finds himself faced with the prosecutorial forces of organized society, and immersed in the intricacies of substantive and procedural criminal law.'" …

… Although defendants' Sixth Amendment rights attached only upon indictment, the district court properly considered pre-indictment state action that affected defendants post-indictment. When the government acts prior to indictment so as to impair the suspect's relationship with counsel post-indictment, the pre-indictment actions ripen into cognizable Sixth Amendment deprivations upon indictment.[27] As Judge Ellis explained in *United States v. Rosen*, 487 F.Supp.2d 721 (E.D.Va.2007), "it is entirely plausible that pernicious effects of the pre-indictment interference continued into the post-indictment period, effectively hobbling defendants' Sixth Amendment rights to retain counsel of choice with funds to which they had a right.... [I]f, as alleged, the government coerced [the employer] into halting fee advances on defendants' behalf and the government did so for the purpose of

---

Amendment harms suffered by particular defendants: defendants Gremminger, Hasting and Watson were deprived of their chosen counsel, "lawyers who had represented them as long as KPMG was paying the bills"; and defendant Ritchie was deprived of the services of Cadwalader Wickersham & Taft, "which was to have played an integral role in his defense." In addition:

> All of the [present] KPMG Defendants ... say that KPMG's refusal to pay their post-indictment legal fees has caused them to restrict the activities of their counsel, limited or precluded their attorneys' review of the documents produced by the government in discovery, prevented them from interviewing witnesses, caused them to refrain from retaining expert witnesses, and/or left them without information technology assistance necessary for dealing with the mountains of electronic discovery. The government has not contested these assertions. The Court therefore has no reason to doubt, and hence finds, that all of them have been forced to limit their defenses in the respects claimed for economic reasons and that they would not have been so constrained if KPMG paid their expenses subject only to the usual sort of administrative requirements typically imposed by corporate law departments on outside counsel fees.

Judge Kaplan explained that even though many defendants had net assets ranging from $1 million to $5 million, their resources were inadequate "to defend this case as they would have defended it absent the government's actions."

[27] [Court's footnote 12:] As Judge Kaplan recognized, the pre-indictment conduct is separately constrained by the Fifth Amendment.

undermining defendants' relationship with counsel once the indictment issued, the government violated defendants' right to expend their own resources towards counsel once the right attached."

Since the government forced KPMG to adopt the constricted Fees Policy—including the provision for terminating fee advancement upon indictment—and then compelled KPMG to enforce it, it was virtually certain that KPMG would terminate defendants' fees upon indictment. We therefore reject the government's argument that its actions (virtually all pre-indictment) are immune from scrutiny under the Sixth Amendment.[28]

B

We now consider "*what* the [Sixth Amendment] right guarantees."

The Sixth Amendment ensures that "[i]n all criminal prosecutions, the accused shall enjoy the right ... to have the Assistance of Counsel for his defence." U.S. Const. amend. VI. Thus "the Sixth Amendment guarantees the defendant the right to be represented by an otherwise qualified attorney whom that defendant can afford to hire, or who is willing to represent the defendant even though he is without funds." "[A]n element of this right is the right of a defendant who does not require appointed counsel to choose who will represent him."[29]

The government must "honor" a defendant's Sixth Amendment right to counsel:

This means more than simply that the State cannot prevent the accused from obtaining the assistance of counsel. The Sixth Amendment also imposes on the State an affirmative obligation to respect and preserve the accused's choice to seek this assistance.... [A]t the very least, the prosecutor and police have an affirmative obligation not to act in a manner that circumvents and thereby dilutes the protection afforded by the right to counsel.

This is intuitive: the right to counsel in an adversarial legal system would mean little if defense counsel could be controlled by the government or vetoed without good reason.

Consistent with this principle of non-interference, courts have identified violations of the Sixth Amendment right to counsel where the government obtains incriminating statements from a defendant outside the presence of counsel and then introduces those statements at trial. Likewise, the government violates the Sixth Amendment when it intrudes on the attorney-client relationship, preventing defense counsel from "participat[ing] fully and fairly in the adversary factfinding process." *Herring v. New York*, 422 U.S. 853, 858 (1975); *see, e.g., id.* at 858–59 (holding that a New York statute allowing judges in a criminal bench trial to deny counsel the opportunity to make a closing argument deprived defendant of his Sixth Amendment right to the assistance of counsel); *Geders v. United States*, 425 U.S. 80, 91 (1976) (holding that a trial court's order that defendant not consult with his attorney during an overnight recess during trial violated the Sixth Amendment).

---

[28] [Court's footnote 13:] We need not decide whether KPMG's pre-indictment conditioning and capping of fees-conduct we have determined was state action-establishes a Sixth Amendment violation by itself. As discussed below, KPMG's termination of fees upon indictment deprived defendants of their Sixth Amendment right to counsel.

[29] [Court's footnote 14:] Although the Sixth Amendment right to counsel of choice "has been regarded as the root meaning of the constitutional guarantee," the right is qualified: the attorney must be admitted to the bar, willing to represent the defendant, free from certain conflicts of interest, compliant with the rules of the court, and so on, *see Wheat v. United States*, 486 U.S. 153, 159-60 (1988).

Defendants-Appellees do not say that they were deprived of constitutionally effective counsel. Their claim is that the government unjustifiably interfered with their relationship with counsel and their ability to mount the best defense they could muster.

The government, relying on *Caplin & Drysdale, Chartered v. United States*, 491 U.S. 617 (1989), contends that a defendant has no Sixth Amendment right to a defense funded by someone else's money. In that case, the Supreme Court ruled that a defendant's Sixth Amendment right to retain counsel of choice was not violated when the funds he earmarked for defense were seized under a federal forfeiture statute, because title to the forfeitable assets had vested in the United States. *[S]ee also United States v. Monsanto*, 491 U.S. 600, 616 (1989) (holding that pretrial restraining order based on showing of probable cause that property is forfeitable "does not 'arbitrarily' interfere with a defendant's 'fair opportunity' to retain counsel").

The government focuses on the following passage from *Caplin & Drysdale*:

> Whatever the full extent of the Sixth Amendment's protection of one's right to retain counsel of his choosing, that protection does not go beyond 'the individual's right to spend his own money to obtain the advice and assistance of ... counsel.' *A defendant has no Sixth Amendment right to spend another person's money for services rendered by an attorney, even if those funds are the only way that that defendant will be able to retain the attorney of his choice.* A robbery suspect, for example, has no *Sixth Amendment* right to use funds he has stolen from a bank to retain an attorney to defend him if he is apprehended. The money, though in his possession, is not rightfully his. ...

The holding of *Caplin & Drysdale* is narrow: the Sixth Amendment does not prevent the government from reclaiming its property from a defendant even though the defendant had planned to fund his legal defense with it. It is easy to distinguish the case of an employee who reasonably expects to receive attorneys' fees as a benefit or perquisite of employment, whether or not the expectation arises from a legal entitlement. As has been found here as a matter of fact, these defendants *would* have received fees from KPMG but for the government's interference. Although "there is no Sixth Amendment right for a defendant to obtain counsel using tainted funds, [a defendant] still possesses a qualified Sixth Amendment right to use *wholly legitimate funds* to hire the attorney of his choice."

It is axiomatic that if defendants had already received fee advances from KPMG, the government could not (absent justification) deliberately interfere with the use of that money to fuel their defenses. And the government concedes that it could not prevent a lawyer from furnishing a defense gratis. And if the Sixth Amendment prohibits the government from interfering with such arrangements, then surely it also prohibits the government from interfering with financial donations by others, such as family members and neighbors—and employers. In a nutshell, the Sixth Amendment protects against unjustified governmental interference with the right to defend oneself using whatever assets one has or might reasonably and lawfully obtain. ...

Judge Kaplan found that defendants Gremminger, Hasting, Ritchie and Watson were unable to retain the counsel of their choosing as a result of the termination of fee advancements upon indictment. The government does not contest this factual finding, and we will not disturb it. A defendant who is deprived of counsel of choice (without justification) need not show how his or her defense was impacted; such errors are structural and are not subject to harmless-error review. "[T]he right at stake here is the right to counsel of choice, ... and that right was violated because the deprivation of counsel was erroneous. No additional showing of prejudice is required to make the violation 'complete.'" ...

The remaining defendants—Bickham, DeLap, Eischeid, Lanning, Rosenthal, Smith, Stein, Warley, and Wiesner—do not claim they were deprived of their chosen counsel. Rather, they assert that the government unjustifiably interfered with their relationship with counsel and their ability to defend themselves. In the district court, the government conceded that these defendants are also entitled to dismissal of the indictment, assuming the correctness of *Stein I*. We agree: these defendants can easily demonstrate interference in their relationships with counsel and impairment of their ability to mount a defense based on Judge Kaplan's non-erroneous findings that the post-indictment termination of fees "caused them to restrict the activities of their counsel," and thus to limit the scope of their pre-trial investigation and preparation. Defendants were indicted based on a fairly novel theory of criminal liability; they faced substantial penalties; the relevant facts are scattered throughout over 22 million documents regarding the doings of scores of people; the subject matter is "extremely complex"; technical expertise is needed to figure out and explain what happened; and trial was expected to last between six and eight months. As Judge Kaplan found, these defendants "have been forced to limit their defenses ... for economic reasons and ... they would not have been so constrained if KPMG paid their expenses." We therefore hold that these defendants were also deprived of their right to counsel under the Sixth Amendment.[30]

Notes

1. Why are the actions of KMPG deemed to be state action, and what implications does this ruling have? *Cf.* United States v. Brooks, 681 F.3d 678 (5th Cir. 2012) (no *Stein* error given lack of evidence of direct government influence over corporate decisions regarding payment of attorneys' fees and fact that corporate policy regarding payment of fees was discretionary). Thus, for example, if the government threatened to fire someone if they asserted their Fifth Amendment rights, that would constitute a constitutional violation; is KPMG now estopped from doing so as well? The defendants also had no legally enforceable right to KPMG's payment of attorney's fees. How, then, did the government's actions affect their legal rights? The Sixth Amendment normally attaches when adversary proceedings have commenced against a given individual. In *Stein*, the court held that the government had violated the Sixth Amendment—warranting the unusual step of dismissing an indictment—because of its pre-indictment interaction with KPMG. Why did the defendants have any Sixth Amendment right to assert?

Does an uncharged suspect have a right to counsel in plea negotiations based on *Stein*? In *Turner v. United States*, 885 F.3d 949 (6th Cir. 2018) (*en banc*), *cert. filed*, No. 18-106 (July 24, 2018), the en banc Sixth Circuit said "no," holding that because the Sixth Amendment right to counsel is not triggered until the commencement of adversarial proceedings, a defendant may not attack a plea based on the allegedly ineffective assistance his retained counsel gave him in pre-indictment plea negotiations. This is not clearly in conflict with cases in other circuits but it is in conflict with a few district court opinions. At this writing, a petition for certiorari is pending. Given the fact that the *en banc Turner* court issued five different opinions and in light of the number of amici who have weighed in at the cert stage, this may be a potential "grant."

2. Note that the Thompson Memorandum has been supplanted by the Filip Memo, which is reproduced in full in Chapter 4(C). In the Filip Memo, at § 9-28.730, the DOJ instructs:

> In evaluating cooperation, ... prosecutors should not take into account whether a corporation is advancing or reimbursing attorneys' fees or providing counsel to employees, officers, or directors under investigation or indictment. Likewise,

---

[30] [Court's footnote 15]: This case does not raise, and therefore we have no occasion to consider, the application of our holding to the following scenario: A defendant moves unsuccessfully in the district court to dismiss the indictment on the same Sixth Amendment theory. The defendant proceeds to trial with his or her chosen attorney, and the attorney is forced to limit the scope of his or her efforts due to the defendant's financial constraints. The defendant is convicted based on overwhelming evidence of his or her guilt.

prosecutors may not request that a corporation refrain from taking such action. This prohibition is not meant to prevent a prosecutor from asking questions about an attorney's representation of a corporation or its employees, officers, or directors, where otherwise appropriate.

In a footnote, the DOJ further advises that "[r]outine questions regarding the representation status of a corporation and its employees, including how and by whom attorneys' fees are paid, sometimes arise in the course of an investigation under certain circumstances—to take on example, to assess conflict-of-interest issues. Such questions can be appropriate and this guidance is not intended to prohibit such limited inquiries." *Id.* at n.6.

3. Note that although this chapter is primarily concerned with issues of conflicts and representation decisions, the Supreme Court has also imposed Sixth Amendment effective assistance obligations on defense counsel at least in the post-charging period. In *Missouri v. Frye*, 566 U.S. 134 (2012) and *Lafler v. Cooper*, 566 U.S. 156 (2012), the Court accepted that defendants have a Sixth Amendment right to counsel in the plea-bargaining process and that the two-part *Strickland v. Washington* test applies to challenges to guilty pleas based on ineffective assistance of counsel in that context.

In *Frye*, the lawyer had failed to communicate to the defendant a plea offer sent to counsel by the government, and that plea offer subsequently expired. The defendant ultimately entered a guilty plea and received a harsher sentence than he would have under the proposed plea deal. With respect to the first prong of the *Strickland* test, the *Frye* Court ruled that "as a general rule, defense counsel has the duty to communicate formal offers from the prosecution to accept a plea on terms and conditions that may be favorable to the accused. … When defense counsel allowed the offer to expire without advising the defendant or allowing him to consider it, defense counsel did not render the effective assistance the Constitution requires." 566 U.S. at 145. Second, the Court adapted the *Strickland* prejudice test to these circumstances, ruling that where a plea offer has lapsed or been rejected because of counsel's deficient performance, a defendant must demonstrate: a reasonable probability that he would have accepted the earlier plea offer if he had effective assistance; that there is a reasonable probability that the plea would have been entered without the prosecution withdrawing it or the trial court refusing to accept it; and that there is a reasonable probability that the end result of the criminal process would have been more favorable by reason of a plea to a lesser charge or a sentence of less jail time. *Id.* at 147.

Lafler, by contrast, involved a situation in which counsel had communicated the plea offer to the defendant but persuaded the defendant to reject it and go to trial based on a reading of the law and facts that everyone in the case conceded fell below an objective standard of reasonableness. The question in the case was whether the defendant could establish the *Strickland* prejudice prong after having received a fair trial and a jury determination of guilt. The Court ultimately held that "[e]ven if the trial itself is free from constitutional flaw, the defendant who goes to trial instead of taking a more favorable plea may be prejudiced from either a conviction on more serious counts or the imposition of a more severe sentence." 566 U.S. at 166. The test for *Strickland* prejudice applicable in this situation is the same one identified in *Frye*. *Id.* at 165. If the defendant carries his burden, the appropriate relief will vary with the type of injury he suffered; he may receive reconsideration of his sentence or the government may be forced to reoffer the rejected plea proposal.

D. "JOINT DEFENSES"

Instead of having one counsel (or firm) represent a number of different subjects, targets, or defendants, the subjects/targets/defendants may each hire individual counsel and form a "joint defense." Pursuant to a joint defense, subjects/targets/defendants may share information that: may permit each to better evaluate his position and to craft an individual defense; may allow the group more effectively to track the direction and status of the government's investigative efforts; may make possible the formulation of a common, coherent defense theory and strategy; and may facilitate the division and efficient allocation of investigative or trial preparation responsibilities. At the same time, the government and other potential adversaries may not access the shared materials, which are treated by the courts as maintaining their attorney-client privileged or work product status despite being shared among joint defense participants. In short, joint defenses may achieve many of the advantages of multiple representation while potentially avoiding disqualifying conflict of interest and other problems.

"Prosecutors have emphasized, however, that joint defense arrangements can present two significant problems. A joint defense arrangement allows its members to shape testimony and perhaps even coordinate perjury. Moreover, ... a joint defense arrangement can effectively keep innocent or less culpable subordinates in line with a 'stonewall' defense."[31] For these (and perhaps less admirable) reasons, "government prosecutors have attacked joint defense agreements and the joint defense privilege in the white-collar criminal arena with increasing vigor in recent years."[32] Most often government challenges are lodged when one member of the joint defense turns government witness, creating a real possibility that counsel for the remaining members of the joint defense will be required to cross-examine the cooperating witness. In such circumstances, the government argues that "trial counsel who is in possession of privileged joint defense communications from prospective witnesses must be disqualified."[33] The continuing viability of the joint defense privilege in the face of such government assaults may depend upon its conceptualization. If, as many courts appear to believe, the joint defense privilege "is an extension of the attorney-client privilege" pursuant to which "an implied attorney-client relationship" develops between all the participants and all the lawyers in the joint defense,[34] the government's efforts may yield fruit. Conceptualized in this way, the same considerations that would potentially disqualify counsel in multiple representation situations may apply in the joint defense context as well. The following report discusses the legal and theoretical underpinnings of the joint defense privilege and the rules governing the effective conduct of a joint defense effort. In so doing, it challenges this conception of the joint defense privilege.[35]

---

[31] Matthew D. Forsgren, Note, *The Outer Edge of the Envelope: Disqualification of White Collar Criminal Defense Attorneys Under the Joint Defense Doctrine*, 78 Minn. L. Rev. 1219, 1232-33 (1994).

[32] Ronald J. Nessim, *Joint Defense Privilege and Conflicts of Interest*, 3 L.A. Law. 34, 36 (May 1992).

[33] *Id.*

[34] United States v. Henke, 222 F.3d 633, 637 (9th Cir. 2000).

[35] *See also* Deborah Stavile Bartel, *Reconceptualizing the Joint Defense Doctrine*, 65 Fordham L. Rev. 871, 880 (1996).

Ethical Implications of Joint Defense/Common Interest Agreements, Committee on Professional Responsibility of the Association of the Bar of the City of New York (1996)[36]

...

Agreements among separately represented persons to exchange factual information and share legal strategy regarding civil or criminal matters of common interest—so-called "joint defense agreements"—have become increasingly prevalent in recent years. By entering such agreements, the parties seek to shield their joint communications from discovery by adversaries or third parties, thereby facilitating a complete discussion of common issues, defenses and strategies.[37]

Although joint defense agreements are often entered informally or using standardized form language, recent government challenges to these agreements in criminal cases have revealed that the ethical issues posed by these agreements require serious consideration in both the civil and criminal context. In particular, these challenges have raised questions about the nature of the relationship formed between the parties and their respective counsel and what obligations an attorney for one participant owes to other participants in the joint defense. Conflicting interests between joint defense participants and their counsel naturally emerge in sharper focus when a participant elects to "change sides," an event which happens with great frequency in criminal investigations involving multiple targets, and not infrequently in civil cases where one or more parties settle.

The likelihood that a joint defense participant may elect to cooperate with and testify for the opponent requires joint defense counsel to confront difficult issues that directly affect the quality and effectiveness of their advocacy: To what extent may joint defense counsel use confidential information obtained from a participant during the course of the joint defense against the participant in cross examination? In such circumstances, does the joint defense agreement interfere with the attorney's ability to represent effectively the attorney's client and thus require the attorney's disqualification? Can these conflicts be effectively addressed in written joint defense agreements through prospective waivers? Are such waivers of a participant's right to seek disqualification of an attorney or to prevent the use of such confidential joint defense disclosures enforceable? ...

I. THE UNDERPINNINGS OF THE JOINT DEFENSE DOCTRINE

The joint defense privilege (or "common interest rule," as some courts prefer to call it),[38] has received wide acceptance by courts in situations where confidential information is shared by persons with common or joint interests, typically in litigation or in advance of expected litigation.[39] It is not necessary for actual litigation to be pending for the doctrine to apply. The doctrine protects both communications between attorneys for joint defense participants and communications between a participant and attorneys for other participants. Although the doctrine protects communications "made in the course of an

---

[36] 51 Rec. Ass'n B. City N.Y. 115 (1996).

[37] [Committee's footnote 1:] These agreements may be entered by either plaintiffs or defendants in civil cases, as well as defense counsel in criminal cases. For simplicity of terminology, they are collectively referred to as "joint defense agreements" throughout this Report. For the same reason, the governing legal doctrine is uniformly referred to as the "joint defense"—rather than the "common interest"—doctrine.

[38] [Committee's footnote 2:] See United States v. Schwimmer, 892 F.2d 237 (2d Cir.1989).

[39] [Ed.:] See In re Santa Fe Int'l Corp., 272 F.3d 705, 713 (5th Cir. 2001) (denying common interest privilege where the materials were created not in anticipation of litigation, but rather were "circulated for the purpose of ensuring compliance with the antitrust laws and minimizing any potential risk associated with the exchange of wage and benefit information").

ongoing common enterprise and intended to further the enterprise,"[40] the participants' interests must only be "common," not "identical."[41] A written agreement is not legally necessary to assert the privilege and, at common law, the privilege could be waived to permit disclosure of joint defense communications only with the unanimous consent of all the parties.[42]

The modern judicial construct of the joint defense doctrine, while offering protection similar to that provided by the attorney-client privilege, is different in one key conceptual respect. The attorney-client privilege is founded on the principle that protecting the confidentiality of discussions between a client and an attorney is essential to insuring free and candid disclosure of information. By contrast, the joint defense doctrine is not intended to promote the free flow of information between client and attorney, but to further the efficient representation of a client by allowing similarly situated persons—typically represented by different lawyers or proceeding *pro se*—to exchange information without running the risk that the information will be revealed to parties of adverse interest.

The close relationship between the joint defense doctrine and the attorney-client privilege has long jurisprudential roots. In *Chahoon v. Commonwealth*,[43] a multi-defendant criminal case in which the defendants pooled information, the court held that the communications were privileged by analogizing to cases where a single counsel represented multiple parties:

> The parties were jointly indicted for a conspiracy ... they might have employed the same counsel, or they might have employed different counsel as they did. But whether they did the one thing or the other, the effect is the same, as to their right of communication to each and all of the counsel, and as to the privilege of such communication. They had the same defence to make, the act of one in furtherance of the conspiracy, being the act of all, and the counsel of each was in effect the counsel of all. ... They had a right, all the accused and their counsel, to consult together about the case and the defence, and it follows as a necessary consequence that all the information, derived by any of the counsel from such consultation is privileged ... .

Descriptions of the joint defense doctrine as an "extension" of the attorney-client privilege have persisted into recent jurisprudence, creating considerable confusion as to the doctrine's underpinnings. For example, some courts have protected joint communications by asserting that they constitute exceptions to the general rule that disclosure to third parties will destroy the attorney-client privilege. In one case in which parties shared confidential information, the court deemed joint defense participants to be "representatives" of the sharing party's counsel.[44] Other courts have found that the attorney-client privilege itself encompasses "communications [that] are engendered solely in the interests of a joint defense effort."[45]

The problem with viewing the joint defense doctrine as an extension of the attorney-client privilege is that this analysis might suggest that the joint defense doctrine

---

[40] [Committee's footnote 5:] *See Schwimmer*, 892 F.2d at 243 (citing Eisenberg v. Gagnon, 766 F.2d 770, 787 (3d Cir. 1985)).

[41] [Committee's footnote 6:] *See* Weinstein's Evidence § 503(b)[06], at 503-100 to 503-101.

[42] [Ed.:] *But see In re* Grand Jury Subpoena, 274 F.3d 563 (1st Cir. 2001), reproduced *infra*.

[43] [Committee's footnote 9:] 62 Va. (21 Gratt) 1036 (1871). ...

[44] [Committee's footnote 11:] *See* Continental Oil Co. v. United States, 330 F.2d 347, 350 (9th Cir. 1964).

[45] [Committee's footnote 12:] *See* In re Grand Jury Subpoena Duces Tecum, 406 F.Supp. 381, 389 (S.D.N.Y. 1975).

hinges on the existence of an attorney-client relationship between each attorney in the joint defense and each participant. This view would find such a relationship notwithstanding the absence of any independent contractual relationship between attorneys and participants and the absence of any promise by the participants (or expectation by the attorneys) that the participants would jointly pay each attorney's fees. It would also import the notion that an attorney owed a fiduciary duty to every participant, not merely to those who had formally retained the attorney and to whom the attorney had presumably rendered advice regarding entering the joint defense agreement.

Recognizing this concern, many courts and commentators consider the joint defense doctrine to be separate and apart from the attorney-client privilege. This approach confirms that no attorney-client relationship is necessarily formed among each participant and each attorney. Nevertheless, other than making clear that the relationship formed does not rise to the level of attorney and client, these authorities do not precisely define what duties and obligations an attorney for one participant owes to the other participants in the joint defense arrangement. Nor do they define what obligations an attorney owes a joint defense participant who withdraws and cooperates with an adversary such as the government. May an attorney cross-examine a former participant? If so, to what extent may the attorney use, directly or indirectly, admissions made under the cloak of the joint defense privilege?

At least one court that has considered these issues has made it clear that an attorney seeking to cross-examine a former joint defense participant runs a decided risk of disqualification. In *United States v. Anderson*, 790 F.Supp. 231 (W.D. Wash. 1992), Anderson and other employees of a company were charged criminally with conspiracy, mail fraud and making false statements to the government. After Anderson and his co-defendants entered a written joint defense agreement, some of the co-defendants pleaded guilty and others had agreed to cooperate and testify for the government at trial.

In language common to many joint defense agreements, the Anderson agreement limited the lawyers' use of the information they gained through communications vis-à-vis the agreement. The agreement stated:

> Any counsel who receives "joint defense communications"[46] may disclose the same to his client and to those individuals assisting counsel in the preparation and defense of his case, *but may not disclose such "joint defense communications" to any other person without the consent of all the signatories to this Agreement.*

The Agreement also provided that the confidential nature of the communications would withstand any potential conflicts of interest: [T]he confidentiality prescribed above will not become retrospectively inoperative if adversity should subsequently arise between the signatories or their clients (or any of them), irrespective of any claim that the joint defense privilege may otherwise become prospectively inoperative by virtue of such claimed adversity.

The Agreement also prohibited the signatories who decided to plead guilty or cooperate from disclosing any information they obtained pursuant to the Agreement without the consent of the other signatories. Essentially, the Agreement insulated all information gained pursuant to it: all participants were prohibited from disclosing the joint defense information, regardless of whether they cooperated, pleaded guilty or went to trial.

After Anderson chose to take the case to trial, the government sought to disqualify his attorneys on various grounds, including that they had a conflict of interest arising from their inability to cross-examine withdrawn participants using information obtained during the joint defense. The court ordered a hearing on the issue and ultimately appointed a

---

[46] [Committee's footnote 15:] "Joint defense communication" is defined in the agreement as any information that a signatory to the agreement receives from any other signatories, their law firms, representatives or outside consultants.

special counsel to assess the participants' understanding and interpretation of the agreement. The court reasoned that: [A]n attorney who acquires information from a potential witness pursuant to a joint defense agreement is in no different position than would be an attorney who acquires such information from a prior or jointly represented client.

The *Anderson* court then concluded that Anderson's attorneys were conflicted because they could not use information they had obtained from the cooperating witnesses against them, to Anderson's detriment. The court further found, however, that counsel would not be disqualified because Anderson had waived his right to conflict-free counsel, at least with respect to the cross-examination issue, by entering the agreement knowing that some of the participants would become government witnesses.[47]

The *Anderson* court thus implied that a joint defense agreement creates an attorney-client relationship between every attorney and every participant in the joint defense. The result, according to the court, is that an attorney's obligation to zealously defend the attorney's original client by impeaching a cooperating witness conflicts with the lawyer's Canon 4 obligations to preserve the confidences of a former client and to avoid taking an adverse position to a former client in a substantially related matter. The existence of an attorney-client relationship also invokes the analysis set forth in *Wheat v. United States*, 486 U.S. 153, 164 (1988), which requires courts to investigate carefully the potential for conflict in a multiple or joint representation situation and affords "substantial latitude in refusing waivers of conflicts."

Although the *Anderson* analysis was criticized by the private bar, at least one court has followed it to the extent of questioning participants as to whether they understood that "there might be a potential for conflict" arising from the joint defense.[48] That neither *Anderson* nor any other reported decision has resulted in disqualification of an attorney based on participating in a joint defense does not eliminate the chilling effect that the threat of disqualification and the necessity of judicial questioning of participants may have upon a joint defense arrangement.[49]

---

[47] [Committee's footnote 16:] Thereafter, on motion by the government, the court required Anderson to consult with independent counsel about other potential conflicts of interest concerning Anderson's cooperation with the government in light of Anderson's employer paying his legal fees.

[48] [Committee's footnote 17:] However, the court in United States v. Bicoastal Corp., 92-CR-261 (N.D.N.Y., September 28, 1992) appeared to do so reluctantly, describing the potential conflict as "very attenuated." The court recognized that "defendants with common interests in multi-defendant actions are entitled to share information protected by the attorney-client privilege without that danger that the privilege will be waived ... ." The court also noted that the existence of a written agreement "does not change the character of the privilege and raises no conflict that would not otherwise exist."

[49] [Ed.:]In *United States v. Henke*, 222 F.3d 633 (9th Cir. 2000), the Ninth Circuit held that the government's use of a cooperating witness who had formerly been in a joint defense with the defendants created a conflict of interest for defendants' counsel. The Ninth Circuit found that, by virtue of the joint defense agreement, the defendants' counsel had "an attorney-client relationship" with the cooperating witness. It noted that defendants' counsel had heard the cooperating witness give information at a joint defense meeting that was at odds with his trial testimony for the government. "This put the two defense attorneys in a difficult position. Had they pursued the material discrepancy in some other way, a discrepancy they learned about in confidence, they could have been charged with using it against their one-time client." *Id.* at 637-38. *Defense counsel* then asked for leave to withdraw, citing this problem. The district court denied the motion to withdraw, stating that "any privileged impeaching information counsel learned about [the cooperating witness] would not be known to new counsel and the defendants were therefore no worse off for being represented by their original counsel." *Id.* at 637. On appeal of their convictions, the Ninth Circuit held that the district court should have permitted counsel to withdraw and ordered a new trial. In so holding, however, the court noted that "[n]othing in our holding today is intended to suggest ... that joint defense meetings are in and of themselves disqualifying. We stress that it was defense counsel in this case that timely moved for disqualification. ... There may be cases in which defense counsel's possession of

In response to *Anderson*, some practitioners have attempted to avoid the possibility of disqualification or the necessity of judicial questioning by including in joint defense agreements language such as the following:

> Nothing contained [in this agreement] shall be deemed to create an attorney-client relationship between any attorney and anyone other than the client of that attorney ... and no attorney who has entered into this Agreement shall be disqualified from examining or cross-examining any joint defense participant who testifies at any proceeding, whether under a grant of immunity or otherwise, because of such attorney's participation in this agreement, and it is herein represented that each party to this agreement has specifically advised his or her client of this clause.

Some criminal lawyers have suggested a model joint defense agreement that incorporates not only language reflecting the absence of an attorney-client relationship, but includes the parties' consent to an attorney's use on cross-examination of confidential communications made by a withdrawn participant (while at the same time precluding the withdrawn participant from disclosing to a third party such as the government other participants' confidential communications). Under this model agreement, which is appended as Appendix A to this Report, a participant would be deemed to have prospectively consented to a partial waiver—permitting disclosure of that participant's confidential communications—upon leaving the joint defense.

There have been no reported decisions as to the effect of this model agreement,[50] but regardless of their effectiveness—considered below—the Committee notes the practical flaw that this model would likely discourage the open dialogue among participants that the doctrine is designed to protect. It is also likely that prosecutors, and aggressive civil lawyers, who have long viewed joint defense agreements as obstructionist and against public policy, would consider the model agreement with particular displeasure because of its perceived one-sided position on the use of confidential communications.

II. THE ETHICAL IMPLICATIONS OF JOINT DEFENSE AGREEMENTS

The Committee believes that *Anderson* mistakes the purpose of the joint defense doctrine in finding that an attorney who participates in a joint defense takes on the equivalent of an attorney-client relationship with each participant. A joint defense is designed to facilitate each individual attorney's representation of that attorney's client by means of free-flowing discussions with persons situated similarly. Indeed, a participant in a joint defense may wish merely to brainstorm with others on common strategy. The notion that, merely because of the desire to engage in such brainstorming, an attorney takes on a duty to zealously represent *each* participant and owes *each* participant the highest duty of loyalty far exceeds what either the attorney or the individual participant could reasonably expect, particularly given the absence of any retainer agreement between them.

In the absence of an agreement specifically delineating the nature of the relationship among joint defense participants, an attorney should be presumed to maintain an attorney-client relationship only with those whom the attorney represented at the time the joint defense was formed. Unless otherwise stated, the duty owed to other participants in the joint defense is principally to keep their communications confidential, except with

---

information about a former codefendant/government witness learned through joint defense meetings will not impair defense counsel's ability to represent the defendant or breach the duty of confidentiality to the former codefendant. Here, however, counsel told the district court that this was not a situation where they could avoid reliance on the privileged information and still fully uphold their ethical duty to represent their clients." *Id.* at 638.

[50] [Ed.:] *But see* United States v. Almeida, 341 F.3d 1318 (11th Cir. 2003); United States v. Stepney, 246 F.Supp.2d 1069 (N.D. Ca. 2003), discussed *infra* in the notes following this reading.

unanimous consent. Naturally, where a client elects to "change sides" (thereby destroying the common interest underlying the agreement), the attorney should cease participating in joint defense discussions and communications. Continuing such contact without notifying other joint defense members of the client's radically changed circumstances may raise issues under DR 1-102(4) (requiring attorneys to avoid deceitful behavior).[51] Written joint defense agreements will typically require notice and withdrawal.

The Committee also questions *Anderson's* conclusion that a lawyer is unable to represent a client zealously (and is therefore necessarily conflicted) because the lawyer's obligations under the joint defense prevent the use of a withdrawn participant's confidential statements for purposes of cross-examination or impeachment. Had the attorney never joined the joint defense, the confidential information would not have been disclosed and no issue would be raised as to its use. It is hard to discern why a client is better off with an attorney who is unaware of admissions by the withdrawn participant as opposed to an attorney who knows of the admissions but cannot use them.

The situation is conceptually distinct from cases in which courts have found that permitting an attorney to cross-examine a former client might bestow an "unfair advantage" and violate "fundamental fairness."[52] Particularly where a joint defense agreement expressly anticipates that one or more participants may withdraw, and that adversity may exist, the participants have no legitimate expectation that they will not in the future confront one another as adversaries—represented by the same persons who had represented each client.

By the same token, an attorney's obligation to zealously represent a client does not justify using confidential communications against a withdrawn participant. This is so not merely because the attorney would breach a valid agreement, but because—notwithstanding the absence of a "client" relationship that would trigger a Canon 4 obligation to keep client confidences and secrets inviolate—an attorney who uses confidential information obtained under the joint defense may violate DR 7-102 (conduct involving fraud and deceit) and the spirit of EC 7-25 ("a lawyer is not justified in consciously violating" rules of evidence and procedure). Some courts have also held that an attorney should not take improper advantage of knowledge gained in a joint defense setting by using it as a springboard to obtain the information from other, non-privileged sources.[53]

The Committee believes that the concerns raised by *Anderson* have greater validity where no written joint defense agreement exists. In such cases, the expectations and understandings of participants may be unclear and an attorney who seeks to cross-examine a withdrawn participant may have a far less persuasive basis to contend

---

[51] [Committee's footnote 18:] There may well be cases where an attorney may be justifiably reticent about disclosing directly or indirectly his client's cooperation with the opponent; for example, in a criminal case, where such disclosure would pose a risk to his client's safety or where the government either discourages or prohibits such disclosure. Where the physical safety of the client is at stake, that consideration obviously must take precedence. Arbitrary requests by the government to conceal the cooperation of a client, however, cannot ethically provide a basis for continued participation in joint defense meetings.

[52] [Committee's footnote 20:] *See* United States v. James, 708 F.2d 40, 45-46 (2d Cir.1983); United States v. Cunningham, 672 F.2d 1064 (2d Cir.1982). *See also* Wheat v. United States, 486 U.S. 153, 164 (1988) (noting that attorney's prior representation of a witness made him "unable ethically to provide" necessary vigorous cross-examination on his client's behalf).

[53] [Committee's footnote 21:] *See* United States v. James, 708 F.2d at 44 n.3, 45 (attorney is barred from disclosing not only the confidential communications, but also facts he learned only from the confidential communications; however, there is "no vice in the proposed questioning of a former client that springs from sources independent of the client"); *see also* People v. Pennachio, [637 N.Y.S.2d 633 (1995)] (under New York law, which does not codify the joint defense privilege, evidence derived from withdrawn participant's voluntary disclosure of privileged communications to prosecutor was not suppressible).

that the nature of the prior relationship permits cross-examination by that attorney. As a practical matter, the existence of a written agreement clarifies such questions as whether the communications involve issues of common interest; the time frame of the joint defense; and the precise purpose of the communication. *See United States v. Sawyer*, 878 F.Supp. 295, 297-98 (D. Mass. 1995) (rejecting efforts to show unwritten joint defense). Given the complexity of the ethical issues raised, a prudent practitioner embarking on a joint defense should create a written joint defense agreement and insure that all participants and their counsel sign.[54]

With respect to the extent to which participants can prospectively waive rights in a joint defense agreement, the Committee believes that it is not unethical or inappropriate for participants expressly to agree in advance that: (a) no new attorney-client relationships are created by the joint defense; (b) no conflict of interest exists merely because an attorney may not be able to use certain information obtained in the joint defense in the future; and (c) a participant will not seek disqualification of any attorney in the joint defense based on that attorney's cross-examination or attempted impeachment of the participant. This type of language should in most cases avoid the necessity of the inquiry involved in *Anderson*. The attached model joint defense agreement contains language that, in the Committee's view, comports with the attorney's ethical obligations to other participants in the joint defense.

Similarly, the Committee does not believe it is unethical for lawyers to enter a joint defense agreement in which participants agree in advance that confidential communications can be used to cross-examine or impeach a withdrawn participant. Such a prospective, limited waiver by a participant will presumably be knowing, intelligent and voluntary if each participant is clearly apprised in advance of the benefits, risks and potential conflicts inherent in participating in a joint defense. This provision appears consistent with the common law requirement that disclosure of confidential information in a joint defense be by "unanimous consent." Still unclear is the level of judicial scrutiny such agreements will receive.[55] ...

APPENDIX A: MODEL JOINT DEFENSE/COMMON INTEREST AGREEMENT

Privileged and Confidential Attorney Work Product Joint Defense Agreement

This Joint Defense Agreement is entered into by and between the undersigned clients and their counsel on this ___ day of _____, [*year*].

WHEREAS the undersigned, clients and their counsel alike, believe that there are [*describe pending or future administrative, civil or criminal investigations or proceedings*] being conducted by [*agency or party*] with regard to [*describe general subject matter of investigations or proceedings*] (the "Matter"); and

WHEREAS, the undersigned clients and their counsel believe and anticipate that, on the basis of currently available information, the nature of the Matter and the relationship

---

[54] [Committee's footnote 22:] We note that courts in New York and elsewhere have declined to order discovery of joint defense agreements in the face of motions to compel by adverse parties on the grounds that they may intrude upon a privileged relationship. *See Bicoastal, supra* note [48]; *Matter of Two Grand Jury Subpoenas Duces Tecum*, N.Y.L.J., July 14, 1995, at 26, col. 6 (Sup. Ct. N.Y. Co.).

[55] [Committee's footnote 23:] In *Wheat*, the Supreme Court viewed with skepticism proffered waivers from jointly represented clients, noting that potential conflicts may be difficult to explain to a "criminal defendant untutored in the niceties of legal ethics." The Court also noted that an attorney's willingness to obtain such waivers from his clients "may bear an inverse relation to the care with which he conveys all the necessary information to them." Although these concerns would appear to center primarily on situations in which an attorney has multiple clients, it is uncertain whether the latitude extended to the courts under *Wheat* to reject conflict waivers in cases of joint *representation* will apply to prospective waivers under a joint *defense*.

among the clients will present various common legal and factual issues and a mutuality of interest in a joint defense in connection with the Matter; and

WHEREAS, the undersigned counsel wish to continue to pursue their separate but common interests, and to avoid any suggestion of waiver of the confidentiality or immunity of communications and documents protected by the attorney-client privilege, the attorney's work product doctrine or any other privilege or immunity vis-à-vis potentially adverse parties; and

WHEREAS, it is the intention and understanding of the undersigned that past and future communications among and between the undersigned, and any joint interviews of prospective witnesses or any interviews obtained by counsel for a party hereto with the knowledge, consent, and on behalf of the other signatories to the agreement, are and shall remain confidential and shall continue to be protected from disclosure to any third party by applicable privileges and immunities, except as set forth herein; and

WHEREAS, in order to pursue a joint defense effectively, the undersigned have also each concluded that, from time to time, their interests will be best served by sharing documents, factual material, mental impressions, memoranda, interview reports, litigation strategies and other information, including the confidences of each client—all of which will hereafter be referred to as the "Defense Materials" (but only to the extent that such material and/or information was not already in the possession of the recipient before the communication of such material and/or information by a signatory to this Agreement or was thereafter independently obtained); and

WHEREAS, it is the purpose of this Agreement to ensure that any exchange and/or disclosure of the Defense Materials contemplated herein does not diminish in any way the confidentiality of the Defense Materials and does not constitute a waiver of any privilege or immunity otherwise available;

IT IS THEREFORE AGREED as follows:

1. Except as expressly stated in writing to the contrary, any and all Defense Materials obtained by any of the undersigned counsel from each other and/or each other's client are being provided solely for internal use of the clients and their counsel and shall remain confidential and shall be protected from disclosure to any third party by the joint-defense privilege, the clients' attorney-client privilege, the attorneys' work product doctrine and other applicable privileges and immunities. All Defense Materials shall be used solely in connection with the Matter.

2. Neither the undersigned counsel nor their respective clients shall disclose Defense Materials or the contents thereof to anyone not a signatory to this Agreement (except the undersigned counsel's firms, or undersigned counsel's employees or agents) without first obtaining the written consent of all counsel who are parties to this Agreement. It is expressly understood that nothing contained in this Agreement shall limit the right of any of the undersigned to disclose to anyone as they see fit any of their own documents or information, or any documents or information obtained independently and not pursuant to this Agreement, by the undersigned.

3. All persons permitted access to Defense Materials shall be advised that the Defense Materials are privileged and subject to the terms of this Agreement.

4. If any person or entity requests or demands, by subpoena or otherwise, any Defense Materials from any of the undersigned or their clients, that counsel will immediately notify all counsel who are parties to this Agreement whose clients or who themselves may have rights in said materials, and each counsel so notified will take all steps necessary to permit the assertion of all applicable rights, privileges and immunities with respect to such Defense Materials, including permitting the other affected parties a reasonable opportunity to intervene and be heard, and otherwise cooperating fully with the other affected parties in any judicial proceedings relating to the disclosure of Defense Materials.

5. Nothing contained herein shall be deemed to create an attorney-client relationship between any attorney and anyone other than the client of that attorney and the fact that any attorney has entered this Agreement shall not in any way preclude that attorney from representing any interest that may be construed to be adverse to any other party to this Agreement or be used as a basis for seeking to disqualify any counsel from representing any other party in this or any other proceeding; and no attorney who has entered into this Agreement shall be disqualified from examining or cross-examining any client who testifies at any proceeding, whether under a grant of immunity or otherwise, because of such attorneys participation in this Agreement; [*and the signatories further agree that a signatory attorney examining or cross-examining any client who testifies at any proceeding, whether under a grant of immunity or otherwise, may use any Defense Materials or other information contributed by such client during the joint defense;*][56] and it is herein represented that each undersigned counsel to this Agreement has specifically advised his or her respective client of this clause.

6. Nothing in this Agreement shall obligate any signatory to share or communicate any Defense Materials or independently obtained or created materials with any other signatory hereto.

7. In the event any undersigned counsel determines that his or her client no longer has, or will no longer have, a mutuality of interest in a joint defense, such counsel will promptly notify the other undersigned counsel of his or her withdrawal from this Agreement, which will thereupon be terminated as to that client; provided, however, that such termination shall not affect or impair the obligations of confidentiality with respect to Defense Materials previously furnished pursuant to this Agreement;

8. Should any client choose to withdraw from this Agreement, he or she shall provide prior written notice to the other clients, in which case this Agreement shall no longer be operative as to the withdrawing client and his or her counsel, but shall continue to protect all joint defense materials disclosed to the withdrawing client and its counsel prior to such withdrawal. The withdrawing client and his or her counsel shall promptly return all Defense Materials and shall continue to be bound by the obligations of confidentiality with respect to Defense Materials previously furnished pursuant to this Agreement.

9. This Agreement memorializes any earlier oral agreements and incorporates any prior written agreements, between or among any of the undersigned pursuant to which defense materials have been exchanged.

10. This Agreement may not be amended or modified except by a written agreement signed by each signatory hereto.

Notes

1. If the joint defense privilege is not an outgrowth of the attorney-client privilege, what is it? Do you agree that as a policy matter, courts should recognize such a privilege? *See* Craig S. Lerner, *Conspirators' Privilege and Innocents' Refuge: A New Approach to Joint Defense Agreements*, 77 Notre Dame L. Rev. 1449, 1454 (2002) (arguing "that the joint defense privilege, especially in the context of criminal investigations, is of doubtful social utility"); Mark Miller, Note, *A Privileged Character? The President and Joint Defense*, 85 Geo. L.J. 1979 (1997).

This question of what relationship is established between joint defense participants is one that arises with some frequency in the context of determining whether and to what

---

[56] [Committee's footnote 28:] As set forth in the accompanying report of the Committee on Professional Responsibility: (1) it is unclear how courts will treat challenges by adverse parties to a provision that permits use of Defense Materials against a withdrawn participant, but precludes corresponding disclosure or use by the withdrawn participant; (2) this model is therefore likely to discourage open dialogue among participants; and (3) prosecutors and aggressive civil lawyers are likely to consider this model obstructionistic and contrary to public policy because of its apparently one-sided position on the use of confidential communication.

extent firms are barred from undertaking future representations adverse to members of a joint defense group who were never clients of the firm. Thus, the D.C. Bar Legal Ethics Committee, in response to numerous inquiries, issued an opinion that joint defense agreements do not create former-client conflicts of interest, but a lawyer who participates in a joint defense arrangement may acquire contractual and fiduciary obligations to members of the joint defense group who are not the lawyer's client. *See* D.C. Bar Legal Ethics Comm., Op. 349 (Sept. 2009).

2. Most joint defense agreements contemplate that the confidentiality obligations they impose survive the defection of a joint defense member to the government's camp. Thus, until recently, it was assumed that, unless the joint defense agreement provided otherwise, joint defense counsel could not use materials learned through the joint defense to cross-examine cooperating joint defense defectors. Joint defense protection could not be waived without the consent of all parties to the agreement, it was argued, because a contrary rule would "whittle away" the privilege and make joint defense participants reluctant to share as fulsomely as they otherwise might. *See* United States v. Weissman, 1996 WL 737042 at *26 (S.D.N.Y. 1996). More recently, however, two important decisions have come down that call into question whether such provisions will be enforceable; in both cases, the court held that a party to a joint defense agreement who testifies for the government may be cross-examined with the statements he made pursuant to the joint defense agreement—whether or not the agreement at issue contained such a provision.

First, in *United States v. Stepney*, 246 F.Supp.2d 1069, 1086 (N.D. Cal. 2003), Chief Judge Patel of the Northern District of California required defense counsel to write down any joint defense agreement they had and submit it to the court for *in camera* review. Judge Patel ruled that the obligations created by joint defense agreements are distinct from those created by actual attorney-client relationships. She noted that while these agreements might impose a duty of confidentiality, joint defense counsel do not have a duty of loyalty to other joint defense clients, and that no such duty could be created by joint defense contract. *Id.* at 1079-1080. The Judge noted, in particular, that "courts have ... consistently ruled that where an attorney represents a client whose interests diverge from a party with whom the attorney has previously participated in a joint defense agreement, no conflict of interest arises unless the attorney actually obtained relevant confidential information," a position inconsistent with the general duty of loyalty owed to former clients under Model Rule of Professional Conduct 1.9. *Id.* at 1080. The Judge also ruled that "[e]ach joint defense Agreement must contain provisions conditionally waiving confidentiality by providing that a signatory attorney cross-examining any defendant who testifies at any proceeding, whether under a grant of immunity or otherwise, may use any material or other information contributed by such client during the joint defense." *Id.* at 1086.

Subsequently, in *United States v. Almeida*, 341 F.3d 1318 (11th Cir. 2003), one of two parties to a joint defense agreement decided to cooperate with the government. At trial, the trial court sustained the government's objection to defense counsel's effort to cross-examine the defecting joint defense participant with statements he had made during the joint defense meetings. After the defendant was convicted, the cooperator claimed that the defendant was not guilty and that he had told the defendant's lawyer so during a joint defense meeting. The Eleventh Circuit reversed the conviction, ruling:

> We hold that when each party to a joint defense agreement is represented by his own attorney, and when communications by one co-defendant are made to the attorneys of other co-defendants, such communications do not get the benefit of the attorney-client privilege in the event that the co-defendant decides to testify on behalf of the government in exchange for a reduced sentence.

Id. at 1326. The court also noted that "[i]n the future, defense lawyers should insist that their clients enter into written joint defense agreements that contain a clear statement of the waiver rule enunciated in this case, thereby allowing each defendant the opportunity to fully understand his rights prior to entering into the agreement." *Id.* at 1326 n.21. Should courts be dictating the provisions of joint defense agreements? What affect are these rulings likely to have?

3. As a practical matter, what are the potential downsides of entering into a joint defense? Should it be reduced to writing? May prosecutors force counsel to turn over the above agreement? As a prosecutor, how might you feel about joint defense agreements in general and the above in particular?

4. Once again, the Yates Memo may have consequences for joint defense agreement ("JDA") practice as well:

> First, while some evidence suggests that *requests* by employees for JDAs have become more common post-Yates Memorandum, actual agreements are likely to become less frequent. JDAs, like joint representation, could signal to the DOJ that a company is not committed to producing all relevant evidence of employee misconduct and instead prefers to keep its interests synchronized with those of its employees. Post-Yates JDAs could further impede a corporation's ability to obtain cooperation credit if one or more constituents seek to block the company from unilaterally disclosing joint defense materials to the government. In the years before the Yates Memorandum was issued it was fairly common for companies to include in joint defense agreements language expressly allowing the company to make unilateral disclosures. If companies continue to insist on antiblocking provisions—and it appears that such provisions are being included in post-Yates JDAs—then constituents will have less incentive to join a joint defense agreement as their fears of being sacrificed by the leniency-seeking corporation are magnified. Indeed, the DOJ may seek to leverage the Yates Memorandum to discourage JDAs expressly or impliedly, given prosecutors' general aversion to such agreements. The government could persuasively argue that a common interest sufficient to support a JDA never existed, if a company decides early in an investigation to cooperate by divulging all facts about individual employee misconduct in order to obtain credit. This cooperation would undercut or destroy an alleged common interest between the company and an individual target. Employees could make the same argument and then freely use against the company confidential or privileged information obtained through the joint defense relationship.
>
> Second, those JDAs which do form post-Yates Memorandum are likely to be more complex than those which previously formed. While constituents will be less likely to enter into JDAs with their companies they will retain their incentives to enter into joint agreements with their fellow constituents, to the exclusion of the company. This is because the Yates Memorandum's policy concerning eligibility for cooperation credit applies to organizational entities but not to individuals. This could lead to a "web of multiple, overlapping JDAs that would only compound the complexity of tracking common interests and confidentiality obligations."

Gideon Mark, *The Yates Memorandum*, 51 U.C. Davis L. Rev. 1589, 1622-23 (2018).

In re GRAND JURY SUBPOENA et al.
274 F.3d 563 (1st Cir. 2001)

SELYA, CIRCUIT JUDGE.

This appeal requires us to traverse largely unexplored terrain concerning the operation of the attorney-client and work product privileges. The underlying controversy arises out of a subpoena duces tecum issued by a federal grand jury to a corporation, seeking records pertaining to the affairs of a subsidiary. Although the corporation and the subsidiary waived all claims of privilege, the subsidiary's former attorney and two of its former officers intervened and moved to quash the subpoena. They claimed that the subsidiary had entered into a longstanding joint defense agreement with the former officers and contended that the subpoenaed materials were privileged (and, thus, not amenable to disclosure). The district court eschewed an evidentiary hearing and denied the motion to quash, but stayed production of the documents pending appeal.

We affirm the district court's order. We hold that an individual privilege may exist in these circumstances only to the extent that communications made in a corporate officer's personal capacity are separable from those made in his corporate capacity. Because the intervenors do not allege that any of the subpoenaed documents are solely privileged to them but rest instead on the theory that all the documents are jointly privileged, their claim, as a matter of law, does not survive the subsidiary's waiver. The joint defense agreement does not demand a different result: privileges are created, and their contours defined, by operation of law, and private agreements cannot enlarge their scope. Moreover, this particular joint defense agreement is unenforceable.

We have a second, independently sufficient ground for our decision. The denial of the motion to quash must be upheld in all events because the intervenors failed to generate a descriptive list of the documents alleged to be privileged. ...

We start by recounting the events leading to this appeal. Consistent with the secrecy that typically attaches to grand jury matters, *see, e.g.,* Fed. R. Crim. P. 6(e), this case has gone forward under an order sealing the proceedings, the briefs, and the parties' proffers. To preserve that confidentiality, we use fictitious names for all affected persons and corporations.

On March 26, 2001, Oldco—a Massachusetts corporation in the business of processing, packaging, and distributing food products—entered into a plea agreement with the United States Attorney for the District of Massachusetts. Under the agreement's terms, Oldco pled guilty to charges of conspiracy to defraud the Internal Revenue Service and agreed to cooperate with the government's ongoing investigation of certain present and former officers, employees, and customers. As part of this cooperation, Oldco expressly waived applicable attorney-client and work product privileges. Soon thereafter, a federal grand jury issued a subpoena duces tecum to Oldco's parent corporation, Newparent, Inc., demanding the production of documents relating to its "rebate program"—a program under which, according to the government, Oldco would charge certain complicit customers more than the going rate for its products, but would then refund the difference by payments made directly to principals of these customers.

At the time the subpoena was served, Oldco was a wholly-owned subsidiary of Newparent. Its records were in the possession of Newparent's counsel, a law firm that we shall call Smith & Jones. Newparent had acquired Oldco in June of 1998, but the grand jury investigation focused on conduct that occurred prior to the acquisition date. During that earlier period, Oldco had operated as a closely held corporation, owned by a number of members of a single family; one family member (Richard Roe) served as its board chairman and chief executive officer, and another (Morris Moe) served on the board and as executive vice-president for sales and marketing. A. Nameless Lawyer was Oldco's principal outside counsel. These three individuals—Roe, Moe, and Lawyer—intervened in the proceedings and filed a motion to quash the subpoena.

The factual premise for the motion to quash is derived largely from Lawyer's affidavit. He states that while representing Oldco he also represented Roe and Moe in various individual matters. Moreover, he claims to have conducted this simultaneous representation of corporate and individual clients under a longstanding joint defense agreement. According to Lawyer, this agreement, although never committed to writing, provided that communications among the three clients were jointly privileged and could not be released without unanimous consent. Despite the absence of any reference to this agreement in the corporate records—there was no resolution or other vote of the board of directors authorizing Oldco to participate in such an arrangement—the intervenors assert that Roe, as chief executive officer, had the authority to commit the corporation to it.

Pertinently, Lawyer claims to have represented Oldco and its officers in connection with the grand jury investigation from and after October 1997 (when the grand jury served Oldco with an earlier subpoena requesting the production of certain customer records). He says that the oral joint defense agreement applies to this multiple-party representation and that he told the government that he represented Oldco and "all of its executives."

There is, to be sure, a written joint defense agreement entered into by and between Lawyer, as counsel for Roe/Moe, and Smith & Jones, as counsel for Newparent/Oldco.[57] However, that agreement was not executed until the fall of 1999 (by which time Lawyer was no longer representing Oldco). There is no evidence in the voluminous record (apart from Lawyer's affidavit) that any joint defense agreement existed before that time. Moreover, the intervenors neglected to mention the existence of an oral joint defense agreement when Newparent acquired Oldco and likewise failed to incorporate any reference to such a pact into the subsequent written agreement.

Notwithstanding these discrepancies, the intervenors solemnly maintain that the oral joint defense agreement existed from 1990 forward; that its terms apply to the grand jury investigation; and that it gives them a joint privilege—they mention both attorney-client and work product privileges—in the Oldco documents currently in the hands of Smith & Jones. But they do not identify any particular documents as privileged, nor do they specify the reasons why certain communications should be considered privileged. Thus, like soothsayers scrutinizing the entrails of a goat, we are left to scour the record for indications of what these documents might be and what they might contain. As best we can tell, some of the documents comprise transcripts of interviews with Oldco employees (including Roe and Moe); others comprise Lawyer's written summaries of Oldco's internal investigation into the rebate program.

Not surprisingly, the government and Oldco both filed oppositions to the intervenors' motion to quash. In response, the intervenors sought leave to present immunized evidence with respect to the privilege claims. They also filed a formal offer of proof and requested an evidentiary hearing. The district court denied the motion to quash at a non-evidentiary hearing held on July 2, 2001, thereby implicitly denying the intervenors' other requests. This expedited appeal ensued. ...

This appeal presents a smorgasbord of legal issues, but we must forgo the temptation to sample them all. Instead, we masticate only those issues that are necessary to a principled resolution of the matter.

We begin by discussing the ramifications of Roe's and Moe's claim that they were individual clients of Lawyer with respect to the grand jury investigation. We conclude that although such individual representation might have occurred in theory, no individual privilege exists as to documents in which Oldco also has a privilege. Because no independently enforceable privilege is alleged here, the corporation's waiver is effective for all communications covered by the subpoena, notwithstanding the existence *vel non* of the oral joint defense agreement. In all events, the intervenors failed adequately to inform the district court of the particular communications to which their claims of privilege allegedly attached. In the pages that follow, we proceed to discuss these issues one by one.

A. *Privilege Claims.*

Because the attorney-client and work product privileges differ, we treat them separately.

1. *Individual Attorney-Client Privilege Claims.* The attorney-client privilege protects communications made in confidence by a client to his attorney. Because it stands in the way of a grand jury's right to every man's evidence, the privilege applies only to the extent

---

[57] [Court's footnote 1:] The written joint defense agreement need not concern us as the grand jury has limited its request to documents predating the execution of that agreement.

necessary to achieve its underlying goal of ensuring effective representation through open communication between lawyer and client.

Roe and Moe can mount a claim of attorney-client privilege only if, and to the extent that, Lawyer represented them individually. If the only attorney-client privilege at stake is that of their corporate employer, then Oldco's waiver defeats the claim of privilege. After all, the law is settled that a corporation's attorney-client privilege may be waived by current management. *See CFTC v. Weintraub*, 471 U.S. 343, 349 (1985) ("[W]hen control of a corporation passes to new management, the authority to assert and waive the corporation's attorney client privilege passes as well.").

It is often difficult to determine whether a corporate officer or employee may claim an attorney-client privilege in communications with corporate counsel. The default assumption is that the attorney only represents the corporate entity, not the individuals within the corporate sphere, and it is the individuals' burden to dispel that presumption. This makes perfect sense because an employee has a duty to assist his employer's counsel in the investigation and defense of matters pertaining to the employer's business.

To determine when this presumption bursts, several courts have adopted the test explicated in *In re Bevill, Bresler & Schulman Asset Mgmt. Corp.*, 805 F.2d 120 (3d Cir.1986). That test enumerates five benchmarks that corporate employees seeking to assert a personal claim of attorney-client privilege must meet:

> First, they must show they approached [counsel] for the purpose of seeking legal advice. Second, they must demonstrate that when they approached [counsel] they made it clear that they were seeking legal advice in their individual rather than in their representative capacities. Third, they must demonstrate that the [counsel] saw fit to communicate with them in their individual capacities, knowing that a possible conflict could arise. Fourth, they must prove that their conversations with [counsel] were confidential. And fifth, they must show that the substance of their conversations with [counsel] did not concern matters within the company or the general affairs of the company.

Id. at 123; *accord Grand Jury Proceedings v. United States*, 156 F.3d 1038, 1041 (10th Cir.1998); *United States v. Int'l Bhd. of Teamsters*, 119 F.3d 210, 215 (2d Cir.1997); *In re Sealed Case*, 29 F.3d 715, 719 n.5 (D.C.Cir.1994).

We think that *Bevill's* general framework is sound. Of course, the first four elements of its test are most relevant when an attorney disputes a corporate officer's claim of individual privilege. Here, however, Lawyer's affidavit makes it clear that he represented both Roe and Moe in their personal capacities. Thus, even though the intervenors' brief does not specifically address the *Bevill* factors, we assume for argument's sake that the first four prongs of the test are satisfied.

With respect to the final prong, the government claims that all of Roe's and Moe's communications were within the orbit of Oldco's general affairs, and therefore could not be individually privileged. In the government's view, *Bevill* precludes a finding of individual representation with respect to matters—such as the grand jury investigation into the rebate program—that involve the corporation. We do not read *Bevill* so grudgingly. As the Tenth Circuit explained:

> The fifth prong of *In Matter of Bevill*, properly interpreted, only precludes an officer from asserting an individual attorney client privilege when the communication concerns the *corporation's* rights and responsibilities. However, if the communication between a corporate officer and corporate counsel specifically focuses upon the *individual officer's* personal rights and liabilities, then the fifth prong of *In Matter of Bevill* can be satisfied even though the general subject matter of the conversation pertains to matters within the general affairs of the company.

Grand Jury Proceedings, 156 F.3d at 1041. We adopt this interpretation and conclude that, theoretically, Lawyer could have represented Roe and Moe individually with respect to the grand jury investigation. Still, this attorney-client relationship would extend only to those communications which involved Roe's and Moe's individual rights and responsibilities arising out of their actions as officers of the corporation.

2. *The Corporation's Right to Waive the Attorney-Client Privilege.* Having concluded that there are potentially some communications protected by the attorney-client privilege, we next consider the effect of Oldco's waiver of that privilege. The major difficulty—there are others, but we need not discuss them here—is that the individuals' allegedly protected communications with Lawyer do not appear to be distinguishable from discussions between the same parties in their capacities as corporate officers and corporate counsel, respectively, anent matters of corporate concern. The intervenors propose that such "dual" communications be treated as jointly privileged such that the consent of all parties would be required to waive the privilege. But they fail to cite authority supporting this position, and we ultimately decline to accept it: permitting a joint privilege of this type would unduly broaden the attorney-client privilege by allowing parties outside a given attorney-client relationship to prevent disclosure of statements made by the client.

The reference to an alleged joint defense agreement does little to advance the intervenors' argument on this point. "The joint defense privilege protects communications between an individual and an attorney for another when the communications are 'part of an ongoing and joint effort to set up a common defense strategy.'" Because the privilege sometimes may apply outside the context of actual litigation, what the parties call a "joint defense" privilege is more aptly termed the "common interest" rule. Even when that rule applies, however, a party always remains free to disclose his own communications. Thus, the existence of a joint defense agreement does not increase the number of parties whose consent is needed to waive the attorney-client privilege; it merely prevents disclosure of a communication made in the course of preparing a joint defense by the third party to whom it was made.

In the clamor over the existence *vel non* of a joint defense agreement, the parties tend to overlook case law dealing directly with the circumstances under which statements made in a joint conference remain privileged. Although these cases do not speak with one voice, they inform our resolution of the issue. They establish that joint communications with a single attorney are privileged with respect to the outside world because clients must be entitled to the full benefit of joint representation undiluted by fear of waiving the attorney-client privilege. Nevertheless, the privilege does not apply in subsequent litigation between the joint clients; in that sort of situation, one client's interest in the privilege is counterbalanced by the other's interest in being able to waive it.

The instance of a criminal investigation in which one former co-client is willing to aid in the prosecution of the other lies in the wasteland between these two doctrinal strands, and courts have split on whether the target of the prosecution may block disclosure in this context. *See McCormick on Evidence,* § 91 at 365 n.13 (John W. Strong ed., 5th ed. 1999) ("Whether the privilege is effective where one joint client is prosecuted and the other is willing to testify as to the joint consultations is a question which has divided the courts."); *see also Conn. v. Cascone,* 195 Conn. 183, 487 A.2d 186, 189-90 (1985) (collecting cases on both sides of the issue).

Although the instant case arises as a motion to quash a subpoena, rather than as an attempt to block a former co-client's testimony, the issue of privilege is entirely congruent. But there is another difference here—a significant one that cuts against the intervenors. In this iteration, the former co-clients were not independent actors, but, rather, corporate officers who owed a fiduciary duty to the corporation. Faced with an analogous assertion of privilege by corporate managers, the Fifth Circuit has held that the managers' interest must yield to the shareholders' interest in disclosure of the privileged materials. *Garner* v. *Wolfinbarger,* 430 F.2d 1093, 1101- 04 (5th Cir.1970). Taking a similar tack, we hold that a corporation may unilaterally waive the attorney-client privilege with respect to any communications made by a corporate officer in his corporate capacity, notwithstanding the existence of an individual attorney-client relationship between him and the corporation's counsel.

The line we draw parallels the holding of *Bevill*, 805 F.2d at 124 (rejecting the contention that "because [corporate officers'] personal legal problems were inextricably intertwined with those of the corporation, disclosure of discussions of corporate matters would eviscerate their personal privileges"). In this regard, we think it significant that the fifth prong of the *Bevill* test is stated in the negative: communications may be individually privileged only when they "*[do] not* concern matters within the company or the general affairs of the company," rather than when they *do* concern an individual's rights.

On this view, it follows that Roe or Moe may only assert an individual privilege to the extent that communications regarding individual acts and liabilities are segregable from discussions about the corporation. When one bears in mind that a corporation is an incorporeal entity and must necessarily communicate with counsel through individuals, the necessity for such a rule becomes readily apparent. Holding otherwise would open the door to a claim of jointly held privilege in virtually every corporate communication with counsel.

Here, neither Roe nor Moe have even attempted to make any showing of segregability. On the contrary, their main argument in the district court and on appeal appears to be that the documents at issue do not lend themselves to separation into individual and corporate categories. The intervenors' brief is replete with references to "joint privilege," but contains no allegation that any particular communication related solely to the representation of Roe or Moe. Given the absence of such an allegation and the allocation of the burden of proof (which, on this issue, rests with the intervenors), we perceive no error in the district court's explicit finding that "all communications in this case are corporate communications." That dooms the intervenors' claim of attorney-client privilege, and renders moot the question of whether Roe and Moe also possessed an attorney-client privilege in these documents.

3. *The Work Product Privilege.* The claim of work product privilege raises a similar set of issues anent joint privilege. The work product rule protects work done by an attorney in anticipation of, or during, litigation from disclosure to the opposing party. The rule facilitates zealous advocacy in the context of an adversarial system of justice by ensuring that the sweat of an attorney's brow is not appropriated by the opposing party. Although the record does not include an index of allegedly privileged documents—a shortcoming to which we shall return—it appears that at least two categories of files contemplated by the subpoena might qualify as work product: Lawyer's interviews of employees during Oldco's internal investigation into the rebate program, and his notes and mental impressions of the investigation.

Roe, Moe, and Lawyer as their attorney may, at least in theory, invoke the work product privilege as to work done exclusively for Roe and Moe as individuals. Yet, their argument does not claim exclusivity,[58] but, rather, amounts to an insistence that they should have a veto over the disclosure of documents produced for the joint benefit of the individuals and the corporation. As in the case of the attorney-client privilege, however, the intervenors may not successfully assert the work product privilege with respect to such documents. Because they effectively conceded that the work was performed, at least in part, for the corporation, Oldco's waiver of all privileges negates their potential claim of privilege. In these circumstances, therefore, the work product privilege does not preclude disclosure of the documents sought by the subpoena.

Undaunted, the intervenors argue that the presence of the oral joint defense agreement demands a different result. We do not agree. Although a valid joint defense agreement may protect work product, one party to such an agreement may not preclude disclosure of work product by another party on whose behalf the work originally was performed. Nor can the

---

[58] [Court's footnote 2:] For example, with respect to the employee interviews conducted by Lawyer, the intervenors argued to the lower court that the work product privilege does not belong exclusively to Oldco because the work was performed on behalf of all three clients.

parties, by agreement, broaden the scope of the privilege that the law allows. Such an agreement would contravene public policy (and, hence, would be unenforceable).[59]

We add, moreover, that the type of joint defense agreement described in Lawyer's affidavit would be null and void. After all, a primary requirement of a joint defense agreement is that there be something against which to defend. In other words, a joint defense agreement may be formed only with respect to the subject of potential or actual litigation. Lawyer's affidavit avers that his three clients (Oldco, Roe, and Moe) entered into an oral joint defense agreement in 1990, at which time no particular litigation or investigation was in prospect. The agreement thereafter remained in effect, Lawyer says, attaching *ex proprio vigore* to all matters subsequently arising (including the current grand jury investigation). The law will not countenance a "rolling" joint defense agreement of this limitless breadth.

The rationale for recognizing joint defense agreements is that they permit parties to share information pertinent to each others' defenses. In an adversarial proceeding, a party's entitlement to this enhanced veil of confidentiality can be justified on policy grounds. But outside the context of actual or prospective litigation, there is more vice than virtue in such agreements. Indeed, were we to sanction the intervenors' view, we would create a judicially enforced code of silence, preventing attorneys from disclosing information obtained from other attorneys and other attorneys' clients. Common sense suggests that there can be no joint defense agreement when there is no joint defense to pursue. We so hold.[60]

B. *Fed. R. Civ. P. 45(d)(2).*

As an alternate ground for our decision, we note that the motion to quash was properly denied because the intervenors failed to present sufficient information with respect to the items to which their claim of privilege attaches. The Civil Rules specifically provide that:

> When information subject to a subpoena is withheld on a claim that it is privileged or subject to protection as trial preparation materials, the claim shall be made expressly and shall be supported by a description of the nature of the documents, communications or things not produced that is sufficient to enable the demanding party to contest the claim.

Fed. R. Civ. P. 45(d)(2). The operative language is mandatory and, although the rule does not spell out the sufficiency requirement in detail, courts consistently have held that the rule requires a party resisting disclosure to produce a document index or privilege log. Although most of the reported cases arise in the context of a claim of attorney-client privilege, the "specify or waive" rule applies equally in the context of claims of work product privilege.

In a somewhat indirect fashion, the intervenors suggest that they were hampered in their ability to present a list of privileged documents by the district court's refusal to hold an evidentiary hearing. This suggestion does not withstand scrutiny. After all, the intervenors were not without knowledge of the communications to which the subpoena pertained; Lawyer originally had possession of them and turned them over to Smith & Jones only when Newparent decided to change counsel. Despite this knowledge, the intervenors made no effort to prepare a privilege log. That omission is fatal.

---

[59] [Court's footnote 3:] This same reasoning applies to defeat the intervenors' claim that the parties' understanding, at the time they entered into the oral joint defense agreement, somehow serves to trump the normal operation of the attorney-client privilege.

[60] [Court's footnote 4:] Given this holding, we need not address other potential problems with the purported joint defense agreement in this case (e.g., the absence of any indicium of corporate authority and the related question of whether corporate officers have the power to bind a corporation to such agreements when a conflict of interest plainly exists).

Privilege logs do not need to be precise to the point of pedantry. Thus, a party who possesses some knowledge of the nature of the materials to which a claim of privilege is addressed cannot shirk his obligation to file a privilege log merely because he lacks infinitely detailed information. To the contrary, we read Rule 45(d)(2) as requiring a party who asserts a claim of privilege to do the best that he reasonably can to describe the materials to which his claim adheres. ...

We need go no further. We hold that the intervenors' claims of privilege fail because the oral joint defense agreement on which they rely cannot defeat Oldco's express waiver of privilege, and, alternatively, because the intervenors failed without justification to produce a privilege log (thereby waiving the underlying attorney-client and work product privileges). ...

Note

1. This case is a good example of the many issues that can arise when, as is increasingly the case, a corporate actor is pressured into waiving applicable privileges as a means of getting credit for "cooperating," and thus a potential declination of criminal charges against the entity. Wasn't this a case of multiple representation? Why, then, were those seeking to resist disclosure of the subpoenaed documents relying on a joint defense or common interest privilege? Does the First Circuit suggest (arguably in dicta) that "the corporation could waive the joint-defense privilege as to any statements made to its counsel by individual employees about corporate matters, because those statements were effectively statements by the corporation itself"? John J. Falvey, Jr. & Valerie K. Frias, *The Corporate Joint-Defense Privilege: For Defense Lawyers, a Shield or a Sieve?* Bus. Crimes Bull. 3, 4 (Feb. 2002). If read this broadly, this case "raises questions as to whether an employee speaking to corporate counsel under a [joint defense agreement] has any assurance that the corporation will not later waive the privilege and disclose the employee's statement." *Id.* Would such a reading create appropriate incentives? The court provided a second basis for its ruling: that the intervenors had not demonstrated the existence of a valid joint defense agreement. What were the shortcomings identified by the court? Finally, *must* those seeking to withhold documents on a claim of privilege provide a privilege log? Of what relevance are the rules of *civil* procedure?

Chapter 19

PLEA BARGAINING AND COOPERATION AGREEMENTS

Once charged, defendants in the federal system have a variety of plea options. Most obviously, they may plead not guilty or guilty.[1] A defendant may, in pleading guilty, concede guilt or, in appropriate cases, enter what is known as an *Alford*[2] plea pursuant to which he continues to maintain his innocence. A defendant may also enter a plea of nolo contendere,[3] which constitutes a judgment of conviction but cannot be used against a defendant as an admission in subsequent criminal or civil cases.[4] Accordingly, nolo contendere pleas may be entered only with the consent of the court after the court has considered the views of the parties and the public interest.[5] Finally, the federal rules provide for a conditional plea of guilty or nolo contendere.[6] This device was created because normally a defendant entering a guilty plea waives all nonjurisdictional[7] objections to the

---

[1] *See* Fed. R. Crim. P. 11(a)(1).

[2] *See* North Carolina v. Alford, 400 U.S. 25 (1970) (holding that where evidence of actual guilt provided a strong factual basis for the plea, court did not err in accepting represented defendant's guilty plea despite defendant's claim of innocence). The Department of Justice policy states that "[d]espite the constitutional validity of *Alford* pleas, such pleas should be avoided except in the most unusual circumstances." Dep't of Justice Manual, tit. 9 [hereinafter U.S.A.M.], § 9-27.440.

[3] *See* Fed. R. Crim. P. 11(a)(1), (3).

[4] *See* Fed. R. Evid. 410(a)(2).

[5] *See* Fed. R. Crim. P. 11(a)(3). Department of Justice policy also frowns on nolo pleas. *See* U.S.A.M. § 9-27.500 ("The attorney for the government should oppose the acceptance of a plea of nolo contendere unless the United States Attorney and the appropriate Assistant Attorney General conclude that the circumstances of the case are so unusual that acceptance of such a plea would be in the public interest.").

[6] *See* Fed. R. Crim. P. 11(a)(2).

[7] In *United States v. Cotton*, 535 U.S. 625 (2002), the Supreme Court clarified that "jurisdiction" in this context refers to the "'courts' statutory or constitutional power to adjudicate the case.'" *Id.* at 630 (citation omitted). The Court held that "defects in an indictment do not deprive a court of its power to adjudicate a case," and that the question whether the indictment "'does not charge a crime against the United States goes only to the merits of the case.'" *Id.* at 630-31 (citation omitted); *see also* United States v. Brown, 752 F.3d 1344 (11th Cir. 2014) (guilty plea waived defendant's argument that the indictment was defective for failure to allege *mens rea*); United States v. Yousef, 750 F.3d 254 (2d Cir. 2014) (guilty plea waived due process argument that there was an insufficient nexus between the

prosecution.[8] Thus, a defendant who loses potentially dispositive pre-trial motions—such as motions to suppress—may go to trial solely to preserve these pre-trial issues for appellate review. To avoid this drain on prosecutorial and judicial resources, the federal rules permit a defendant, with the consent of the government and the court, to enter a conditional plea, reserving the right to appeal the adverse pre-trial ruling and, if successful on appeal, to withdraw the guilty or nolo contendere plea.

The overwhelming majority of federal criminal prosecutions are resolved by a plea of guilty. Some of those guilty pleas are "straight" pleas to an indictment, entered without any bargaining or concessions by the prosecutor. Many, however, involve some type of bargained-for disposition. The following materials concentrate on these latter types of pleas and, in particular, on one type of increasingly important plea bargain—an agreement by a defendant to cooperate in return for leniency in charging or for sentencing consideration. As Fed. R. Crim. P. 11 indicates, the parties may bargain in a number of currencies in addition to cooperation, including particular charges, sentences or sentencing ranges, or the application of guidelines policies, factors, or provisions. This chapter also examines the rules that apply to such deals under Fed. R. Crim. P. 11, DOJ rules, and the Guidelines. As in the Immunity Chapter, the reader should note that many of the materials excerpted within are authored by former prosecutors. Again, this was a choice founded on the reality that prosecutors generally have more power in determining the shape of any plea or cooperation deal and on the belief that most students are not privy to the perspectives and types of considerations that inform prosecutorial judgments on these matters.

Plea negotiations are conducted by the government and the defense. Fed. R. Crim. P. 11(c)(1) provides that the "court must not participate in these discussions." "The prohibition of participation by the district court in plea discussions is a 'bright line rule' and constitutes 'an absolute prohibition on all forms of judicial participation in or interference with the plea negotiation process.'"[9]

Once a deal is struck that involves a plea of guilty, however, Rule 11 requires the judge to accept or reject the plea and any plea agreement after a review of all the relevant factors set forth in the rule. The court's participation at this stage is essential because without it, a judgment of conviction cannot be entered. The district court has the obligation to ensure that the defendant's plea is knowing, intelligent, and voluntary. If the plea is entered pursuant to an agreement, judges have wide discretion in refusing to accept the deal/plea.

---

defendant's conduct and the United States and thus statute could not apply extraterritorially); United States v. Rubin, 743 F.3d 31 (2d Cir. 2014) (guilty plea waived defendant's argument that indictment failed to state an offense). A guilty plea bars some antecedent constitutional violations related to events that occur prior to the entry of the guilty plea; thus, for example, a guilty plea precludes a defendant from appealing the disposition of Fourth Amendment suppression claims and challenges related to the grand jury. *See, e.g,* Class v. United States, -- U.S. --, 138 S.Ct. 798, 804–05 (2018). But a guilty plea does not extinguish due process vindictive prosecution claims, *see* Blackledge v. Perry, 417 U.S. 21 (1974), double jeopardy claims of double punishment, *see* Menna v. New York, 423 U.S. 61 (1975) (per curiam), or challenges to the constitutionality of the statute of conviction on direct appeal, *see Class,* 138 S.Ct. 803.

[8] United States v. Castillo, 496 F.3d 947, 954 (9th Cir. 2007). At least in the Ninth Circuit, however, if the defendant enters an unconditional plea, then appeals, and the government does not object to the appeal, the court can hear the case. The Ninth Circuit ruled that Rule 11 does not divest the court of subject-matter jurisdiction to hear the appeal. *Id.*

[9] United States v. Hemphill, 748 F.3d 666, 672 (5th Cir. 2014). "First and foremost, [this prohibition] serves to diminish the possibility of judicial coercion of a guilty plea, regardless of whether the coercion would cause an involuntary, unconstitutional plea." *Id.* (internal quotation omitted). Second, the rule safeguards the court's impartiality because the court has no personal stake in any deal struck. *Id.* And participation by the court may give rise to the misimpression that the court is not a neutral arbiter but rather an advocate for the agreement. *Id.; see also* United States v. Braxton, 784 F.3d 240, 243 (4th Cir. 2015).

This chapter discusses the Guidelines' policies regarding when judges ought, and ought not, to accept negotiated deals.

A. PLEA BARGAINING: CONSTITUTIONAL STANDARDS

BRADY v. UNITED STATES
397 U.S. 742 (1970)

MR. JUSTICE WHITE delivered the opinion of the Court.

In 1959, petitioner was charged with kidnaping in violation of 18 U.S.C. § 1201(a). Since the indictment charged that the victim of the kidnaping was not liberated unharmed, petitioner faced a maximum penalty of death if the verdict of the jury should so recommend. [Under the law prevailing at the time of petitioner's plea, a defendant could only be sentenced to death if a jury so recommended. Thus, only by waiving a jury trial could a petitioner ensure that a capital sentence would not be imposed.] Petitioner, represented by competent counsel throughout, first elected to plead not guilty. Apparently because the trial judge was unwilling to try the case without a jury, petitioner made no serious attempt to reduce the possibility of a death penalty by waiving a jury trial. Upon learning that his codefendant, who had confessed to the authorities, would plead guilty and be available to testify against him, petitioner changed his plea to guilty. His plea was accepted after the trial judge twice questioned him as to the voluntariness of his plea. Petitioner was sentenced to 50 years' imprisonment, later reduced to 30.

In 1967, petitioner sought relief under 28 U.S.C. § 2255, claiming that his plea of guilty was not voluntarily given because § 1201(a) operated to coerce his plea. ...

That a guilty plea is a grave and solemn act to be accepted only with care and discernment has long been recognized. Central to the plea and the foundation for entering judgment against the defendant is the defendant's admission in open court that he committed the acts charged in the indictment. He thus stands as a witness against himself and he is shielded by the Fifth Amendment from being compelled to do so—hence the minimum requirement that his plea be the voluntary expression of his own choice. But the plea is more than an admission of past conduct; it is the defendant's consent that judgment of conviction may be entered without a trial—a waiver of his right to trial before a jury or a judge. Waivers of constitutional rights not only must be voluntary but must be knowing, intelligent acts done with sufficient awareness of the relevant circumstances and likely consequences. On neither score was Brady's plea of guilty invalid. ...

The voluntariness of Brady's plea can be determined only by considering all of the relevant circumstances surrounding it. One of these circumstances was the possibility of a heavier sentence following a guilty verdict after a trial. It may be that Brady, faced with a strong case against him and recognizing that his chances for acquittal were slight, preferred to plead guilty and thus limit the penalty to life imprisonment rather than to elect a jury trial which could result in a death penalty. But even if we assume that Brady would not have pleaded guilty except for the death penalty provision of § 1201(a), this assumption merely identifies the penalty provision as a "but for" cause of his plea. That the statute caused the plea in this sense does not necessarily prove that the plea was coerced and invalid as an involuntary act.

The State to some degree encourages pleas of guilty at every important step in the criminal process. For some people, their breach of a State's law is alone sufficient reason for surrendering themselves and accepting punishment. For others, apprehension and charge, both threatening acts by the Government, jar them into admitting their guilt. In still other cases, the post-indictment accumulation of evidence may convince the defendant and his counsel that a trial is not worth the agony and expense to the defendant and his family. All these pleas of guilty are valid in spite of the State's responsibility for some of the factors motivating the pleas; the pleas are no more improperly compelled than is the decision by a defendant at the close of the State's evidence at trial that he must take the stand or face certain conviction.

Of course, the agents of the State may not produce a plea by actual or threatened physical harm or by mental coercion overbearing the will of the defendant. But nothing of the sort is claimed in this case; nor is there evidence that Brady was so gripped by fear of the death penalty or hope of leniency that he did not or could not, with the help of counsel, rationally weigh the advantages of going to trial against the advantages of pleading guilty. Brady's claim is of a different sort: that it violates the Fifth Amendment to influence or encourage a guilty plea by opportunity or promise of leniency and that a guilty plea is coerced and invalid if influenced by the fear of a possibly higher penalty for the crime charged if a conviction is obtained after the State is put to its proof.

Insofar as the voluntariness of his plea is concerned, there is little to differentiate Brady from (1) the defendant, in a jurisdiction where the judge and jury have the same range of sentencing power, who pleads guilty because his lawyer advises him that the judge will very probably be more lenient than the jury; (2) the defendant, in a jurisdiction where the judge alone has sentencing power, who is advised by counsel that the judge is normally more lenient with defendants who plead guilty than with those who go to trial; (3) the defendant who is permitted by prosecutor and judge to plead guilty to a lesser offense included in the offense charged; and (4) the defendant who pleads guilty to certain counts with the understanding that other charges will be dropped. In each of these situations,[10] as in Brady's case, the defendant might never plead guilty absent the possibility or certainty that the plea will result in a lesser penalty than the sentence that could be imposed after a trial and a verdict of guilty. We decline to hold, however, that a guilty plea is compelled and invalid under the Fifth Amendment whenever motivated by the defendant's desire to accept the certainty or probability of a lesser penalty rather than face a wider range of possibilities extending from acquittal to conviction and a higher penalty authorized by law for the crime charged.

The issue we deal with is inherent in the criminal law and its administration because guilty pleas are not constitutionally forbidden, because the criminal law characteristically extends to judge or jury a range of choice in setting the sentence in individual cases, and because both the State and the defendant often find it advantageous to preclude the possibility of the maximum penalty authorized by law. For a defendant who sees slight possibility of acquittal, the advantages of pleading guilty and limiting the probable penalty are obvious—his exposure is reduced, the correctional processes can begin immediately, and the practical burdens of a trial are eliminated. For the State there are also advantages— the more promptly imposed punishment after an admission of guilt may more effectively attain the objectives of punishment; and with the avoidance of trial, scarce judicial and prosecutorial resources are conserved for those cases in which there is a substantial issue of the defendant's guilt or in which there is substantial doubt that the State can sustain its burden of proof. It is this mutuality of advantage that perhaps explains the fact that at present well over three-fourths of the criminal convictions in this country rest on pleas of guilty,[11] a great many of them no doubt motivated at least in part by the hope or assurance of a lesser penalty than might be imposed if there were a guilty verdict after a trial to judge or jury.

---

[10] [Court's footnote 8:] We here make no reference to the situation where the prosecutor or judge, or both, deliberately employ their charging and sentencing powers to induce a particular defendant to tender a plea of guilty. In Brady's case there is no claim that the prosecutor threatened prosecution on a charge not justified by the evidence or that the trial judge threatened Brady with a harsher sentence if convicted after trial in order to induce him to plead guilty.

[11] [Court's footnote 10:] It has been estimated that about 90%, and perhaps 95%, of all criminal convictions are by pleas of guilty; between 70% and 85% of all felony convictions are estimated to be by guilty plea.

Of course, that the prevalence of guilty pleas is explainable does not necessarily validate those pleas or the system which produces them. But we cannot hold that it is unconstitutional for the State to extend a benefit to a defendant who in turn extends a substantial benefit to the State and who demonstrates by his plea that he is ready and willing to admit his crime and to enter the correctional system in a frame of mind that affords hope for success in rehabilitation over a shorter period of time than might otherwise be necessary.

A contrary holding would require the States and Federal Government to forbid guilty pleas altogether, to provide a single invariable penalty for each crime defined by the statutes, or to place the sentencing function in a separate authority having no knowledge of the manner in which the conviction in each case was obtained. In any event, it would be necessary to forbid prosecutors and judges to accept guilty pleas to selected counts, to lesser included offenses, or to reduced charges. The Fifth Amendment does not reach so far. ...

The standard as to the voluntariness of guilty pleas must be essentially that defined by Judge Tuttle of the Court of Appeals for the Fifth Circuit:

> "[A] plea of guilty entered by one fully aware of the direct consequences, including the actual value of any commitments made to him by the court, prosecutor, or his own counsel, must stand unless induced by threats (or promises to discontinue improper harassment), misrepresentation (including unfulfilled or unfulfillable promises), or perhaps by promises that are by their nature improper as having no proper relationship to the prosecutor's business (e.g. bribes)."

Under this standard, a plea of guilty is not invalid merely because entered to avoid the possibility of a death penalty.

The record before us also supports the conclusion that Brady's plea was intelligently made. He was advised by competent counsel, he was made aware of the nature of the charge against him, and there was nothing to indicate that he was incompetent or otherwise not in control of his mental faculties; once his confederate had pleaded guilty and became available to testify, he chose to plead guilty, perhaps to ensure that he would face no more than life imprisonment or a term of years. Brady was aware of precisely what he was doing when he admitted that he had kidnaped the victim and had not released her unharmed. ...

This is not to say that guilty plea convictions hold no hazards for the innocent or that the methods of taking guilty pleas presently employed in this country are necessarily valid in all respects. This mode of conviction is no more foolproof than full trials to the court or to the jury. Accordingly, we take great precautions against unsound results, and we should continue to do so, whether conviction is by plea or by trial. We would have serious doubts about this case if the encouragement of guilty pleas by offers of leniency substantially increased the likelihood that defendants, advised by competent counsel, would falsely condemn themselves. But our view is to the contrary and is based on our expectations that courts will satisfy themselves that pleas of guilty are voluntarily and intelligently made by competent defendants with adequate advice of counsel and that there is nothing to question the accuracy and reliability of the defendants' admissions that they committed the crimes with which they are charged. In the case before us, nothing in the record impeaches Brady's plea or suggests that his admissions in open court were anything but the truth.

Although Brady's plea of guilty may well have been motivated in part by a desire to avoid a possible death penalty, we are convinced that his plea was voluntarily and intelligently made and we have no reason to doubt that his solemn admission of guilt was truthful.

Notes

1. In other contexts, the Supreme Court has held that Due Process constrains the ability of the government to punish individuals for exercise of a constitutionally protected interest and restricts the government's power to condition the grant of benefits on the

recipient's decision to forgo exercise of a constitutional right. *See* Thomas R. McCoy & Michael J. Mirra, *Plea Bargaining as Due Process in Determining Guilt*, 32 Stan. L. Rev. 887 (1980); *see also* Bordenkircher v. Hayes, 434 U.S. 357, 363 (1978) ("To punish a person because he has done what the law plainly allows him to do is a due process violation of the most basic sort."). How can these rules be squared with the Court's analysis in *Brady*? Is there "a difference of constitutional dimension between giving someone a discount for *waiving* a constitutional right as opposed to punishing someone for *exercising* a constitutional right"? Daniel Givelber, *Punishing Protestations of Innocence: Denying Responsibility and Its Consequences*, 37 Am. Crim. L. Rev. 1363, 1366 (2000). Professor Givelber argues that:

> There may well be other distinctions in the law as ephemeral as the distinction between the acceptable practice of discounting for guilty pleas and the unacceptable practice of punishment for insisting upon trial, but one hopes not. ... In both law and practice, the Sixth Amendment right to trial now means that the state cannot *deny* a criminal trial to a defendant who is prepared to pay a price in terms of additional prison time if he receives a trial and is convicted. What the Sixth Amendment does not mean, apparently, is what it seems to say—that the defendant has an unencumbered *right* to trial by jury in every case.

Id. at 1370-71. "Could a state legislature provide that the penalty for every criminal offense to which a defendant pleads guilty is to be one-half the penalty to be imposed upon a defendant convicted of the same offense after a not-guilty plea?" Corbitt v. New Jersey, 439 U.S. 212, 227-28 (1978) (Stewart, J., concurring) (arguing that statutes that provide differing sentences based only on the plea entered would be unconstitutional); *see also* United States v. Jackson, 390 U.S. 570 (1968) (holding that a statute which permits the imposition of the death penalty only in cases where the defendant demands a jury trial violates the Sixth Amendment).

2. The *Brady* Court stated in concluding that "[w]e would have serious doubts about this case if the encouragement of guilty pleas by offers of leniency substantially increased the likelihood that defendants, advised by competent counsel, would falsely condemn themselves." *Are* there some types of prosecutorial offers that are *so* inherently coercive as to unduly threaten to coerce the innocent to plead guilty? What types of inducements may legitimately be offered in return for a plea? *See, e.g.,* Corcoran v. Wilson, 651 F.3d 611, 613-14 (7th Cir. 2011) (no constitutional violation where prosecutors in a capital case offered to withdraw their request for the death penalty if the defendant waived his right to a jury trial).

Consider *Miles v. Dorsey*, 61 F.3d 1459 (10th Cir. 1995), in which the defendant pleaded no contest to state charges of murder and first-degree criminal sexual penetration. On habeas review, he challenged the voluntariness of his plea, citing the fact that one of the inducements for the plea was the state's undertaking to ensure that his family (parents, two sisters, brother, and sister-in-law) would not serve jail time as a result of the multiple offenses for which they had been charged arising out of their attempts to hide or destroy evidence that would have potentially inculpated the defendant for his crimes. In refusing his challenge to the voluntariness of this guilty plea, the Tenth Circuit stated:

> "The Supreme Court has specifically reserved judgment on 'the constitutional implications of a prosecutor's offer during plea bargaining of adverse or lenient treatment for some persons *other* than the accused.'" [*Bordenkircher v. Hayes*, 434 U.S. 357, 364 n. 8 (1978).] Because "[a]lmost anything lawfully within the power of a prosecutor acting in good faith can be offered in exchange for a guilty plea," we have ruled that a plea is not per se involuntary if entered under a plea agreement that includes leniency for a third party. Instead, a third party benefit in a plea agreement presents "a factor for the court to consider when evaluating the voluntariness of the defendant's plea." "[B]ecause such bargaining 'can pose a danger of coercion' and

'increase the leverage possessed by prosecutors,' the government must abide by 'a high standard of good faith' in its use of such tactics."

The government acts in good faith when it offers leniency for an indicted third party or threatens to prosecute an unindicted third party in exchange for a defendant's plea when the government has probable cause to prosecute the third party. Consequently, so long as the government has prosecuted or threatened to prosecute a defendant's relative in good faith, the defendant's plea, entered to obtain leniency for the relative, is not involuntary. *See* [*Mosier v. Murphy*, 790 F.2d 62, 66 (10th Cir. 1986)] (plea offered by man to protect his validly indicted wife and mother-in-law from prosecution held not involuntary); [*United States v. Marquez*, 909 F.2d 738, 741-42 (2d Cir. 1990)] (plea entered by man to protect his wife from prosecution held not involuntary).

Miles, 61 F.3d at 1468. Should prosecutors' good faith be the focus of this analysis?

3. Consider another practice—that of the "wired" or "package deal" plea. Under such agreements, several confederates plead together and the government gives them a "volume discount—a better deal than each could have gotten separately." United States v. Caro, 997 F.2d 657, 658 (9th Cir. 1993). The nature of the deal is that all must plead or no one gets the deal. The Ninth Circuit has explained that:

> Though package deal plea agreements are not per se impermissible, they pose an additional risk of coercion not present when the defendant is dealing with the government alone. Quite possibly, one defendant will be happier with the package deal than his codefendant(s); looking out for his own best interests, the lucky one may try to force his codefendant(s) into going along with the deal. The Supreme Court has therefore observed that tying defendants' plea decisions together "might pose a greater danger of inducing a false guilty plea by skewing the assessment of the risks a defendant must consider.' *Bordenkircher v. Hayes*, 434 U.S. 357, 364 n. 8 (1978) (dictum). We, in turn, have recognized that "the trial court should make a more careful examination of the voluntariness of the plea when [it might have been] induced by ... threats or promises" from a third party. We make it clear today that, in describing a plea agreement under Rule 11[(c)](2), the prosecutor must alert the district court to the fact that codefendants are entering a package deal.

Caro, 997 F.2d at 659-60. A number of circuits, like the Ninth, require that package plea deals to be disclosed to the court and that district courts conduct colloquies with the pleading defendants "with special care." United States v. Hodge, 412 F.3d 479, 489-90 (3d Cir. 2005) (collecting cases). Prosecutors would argue that "wired" plea agreements are justified by reasons other than simply forcing pleas, including an interest in conducting joint trials or none at all because the trial of one defendant may consume nearly as much time and resources as a trial of both. *See* United States v. Hernandez, 79 F.3d 1193, 1195 n.* (D.C. Cir. 1996). What rationale, if any, would justify plea agreements offered to four co-defendants that are conditioned on each refraining from testifying at the trial of any of the others? *See* People v. Dixon, 939 N.Y.S.2d 199 (2012) (upholding such agreements where there was nothing in the record to indicate that the co-defendants would have agreed to testify if asked and would have had anything exculpatory to say).

4. The literature concerning the merits and demerits of plea bargaining is rich and lengthy. Because it is difficult to summarize the entirety of it, the following constitutes an attempt to set forth some of the most common arguments made. Those who question the legitimacy of plea bargaining do so on a number of grounds. One obvious ground is that rejected in the cases discussed above—that plea bargaining essentially coerces defendants into waiving fundamental rights or permits sentencing courts to penalize those who exercise those rights by going to trial. Another important ground is that alluded to but dismissed by the *Brady* Court: the concern that prosecutors, through plea bargaining,

may offer defendants such stark choices between a lenient plea offer and a threat of harsh charges if the plea offer is rejected that risk-averse but innocent defendants will be coerced into a guilty plea.

Plea bargaining also obviously short circuits formal fact-finding and adjudication mechanisms; in some cases, it may be that the negotiated result does not comport with the actual facts that would be found had trial-type procedural safeguards been employed. Thus, some ask how "a civilized country [can] send people to prison for many years based on such a perfunctory judicial analysis of facts and law" and argue that the lack of procedure accorded plea bargaining defendants is entirely inadequate to avoid mistaken convictions. Gerard E. Lynch, *Our Administrative System of Criminal Justice*, 66 Fordham L. Rev. 2117, 2122 (1998) (summarizing arguments); *see also* Stephanos Bibas, *Designing Plea Bargaining from the Ground Up: Accuracy and Fairness Without Trials as Backstops*, 57 Wm. & Mary L. Rev. 1055 (2016). Others contend that plea bargaining undermines the goals of criminal punishment because it permits sentences that are unduly lenient given the conduct at issue. A corresponding concern is that bargained-for and presumptively lenient sentences undermine public confidence in the criminal justice system. Finally, many argue that, to the extent that some defendants are receiving charging or sentencing "breaks" while others are not, plea bargaining potentially increases irrational disparities and discrimination in the administration of criminal justice.

5. The primary justification often advanced for plea bargaining is at bottom practical: absent plea bargaining, the system would be overwhelmed with trials and all would suffer as the justice system ground to a halt. It is argued that even if the practice were overtly banned, it would through necessity be resurrected in clandestine dealing. Plea bargaining also provides the parties flexibility that might not otherwise be available were the case go to trial and obviates putting victims and others through the burdens of litigation. It is also argued that plea bargaining allows for an efficient allocation of scarce resources through which both parties secure important advantages. The government gains prompt, final, and risk-free convictions and frees up the resources to pursue other cases. The (presumably guilty) defendant eliminates the risk, expense, and potential embarrassment of a criminal trial in return for certainty regarding the adjudicated level of his culpability and sentencing or other concessions of value. *See generally* Fred C. Zacharias, *Justice in Plea Bargaining*, 39 Wm. & Mary L. Rev.1121 (1998) (examining justifications for plea bargaining); *but see* David S. Abrams, *Is Pleading Really a Bargain?*, 8 J. Empirical Legal Stud. (Special Issue) 200 (2011) (concluding based on empirical work in Cook County state courts that risk-neutral defendants seeking to minimize expected sentences would do substantially better by rejecting plea bargains).

6. Judge Gerard Lynch has argued that the widespread practice of plea bargaining has resulted in a system of justice that American lawyers would view as more akin to an inquisitorial system than to the idealized adversary system described in textbooks. He has suggested that this system should be judged on its own merits and demerits rather than simply as a "perversion of the classic due process model." Lynch, *supra*, 66 Fordham L. Rev. *passim*; *see also* Máximo Langer, *Rethinking Plea Bargaining: The Practice and Reform of Prosecutorial Adjudication in American Criminal Procedure*, 33 Am. J. Crim. L. 223 (2006).

7. It appears that the Supreme Court is beginning to recognize this reality, as is demonstrated in *Missouri v. Frye*, 566 U.S. 134 (2012) and *Lafler v. Cooper*, 566 U.S. 156 (2012). In *Frye*, the government sent defendant Frye's lawyer a plea offer that expired on an identified date. Frye's lawyer never told Frye about the offer and it expired. Frye ultimately pleaded guilty without a plea agreement and received a significantly higher sentence than he would have had he known about, and accepted, the government's initial offer.

The Supreme Court had long recognized a right to effective assistance of counsel in the "critical" plea stage, but the cases concerned claims that the plea was invalid because counsel had provided constitutionally deficient advice relative to the plea (*i.e.*, counsel misinformed the defendant of the immigration consequences of a conviction, Padilla v.

Kentucky, 559 U.S. 356 (2010), or counsel misled the defendant regarding the amount of time he would have to serve before being eligible for parole, Hill v. Lockhart, 474 U.S. 52 (1985)). *Frye* was different because the guilty plea was accepted and there was no contention that the plea was based on inaccurate advice and information from counsel. "The challenge is not to the advice pertaining to the plea that was accepted but rather to the course of legal representation that preceded it with respect to other potential pleas and plea offers." 566 U.S. at 141-42.

The state in *Frye* argued, inter alia, that defendants have no right to a plea offer or a plea bargain and thus that Frye was not deprived of any legal benefit to which he was entitled. The wrongful or mistaken action of counsel with respect to the elapsed plea offer is simply irrelevant given the defendant's confession of guilt in his plea. The Court responded:

> The State's contentions are neither illogical nor without some persuasive force, yet they do not suffice to overcome a simple reality. Ninety-seven percent of federal convictions and ninety-four percent of state convictions are the result of guilty pleas. The reality is that plea bargains have become so central to the administration of the criminal justice system that defense counsel have responsibilities in the plea bargain process, responsibilities that must be met to render the adequate assistance of counsel that the Sixth Amendment requires in the criminal process at critical stages. Because ours "is for the most part a system of pleas, not a system of trials," it is insufficient simply to point to the guarantee of a fair trial as a backstop that inoculates any errors in the pretrial process. "To a large extent ... horse trading [between prosecutor and defense counsel] determines who goes to jail and for how long. This is what plea bargaining is. It is not some adjunct to the criminal justice system; it *is* the criminal justice system." In today's criminal justice system, therefore, the negotiation of a plea bargain, rather than the unfolding of a trial, is almost always the critical point for a defendant.

Id. at 143-44 (citations omitted).

To test whether counsel had rendered ineffective assistance within the meaning of the Sixth amendment, the *Frye* Court applied the two-prong standard the Court articulated in *Strickland v. Washington*, 466 U.S. 668 (1984). First, the *Frye* Court ruled that "as a general rule, defense counsel has the duty to communicate formal offers from the prosecution to accept a plea on terms and conditions that may be favorable to the accused. ... When defense counsel allowed the offer to expire without advising the defendant or allowing him to consider it, defense counsel did not render the effective assistance the Constitution requires." 566 U.S. at 145. Second, the Court adapted the *Strickland* prejudice test to these circumstances, ruling that where a plea offer has lapsed or been rejected because of counsel's deficient performance, a defendant must demonstrate a reasonable probability that he would have accepted the earlier plea offer if he had effective assistance; that the plea would have been entered without the prosecution withdrawing it or the trial court refusing to accept it; and that the end result of the criminal process would have been more favorable by reason of a plea to a lesser charge or a sentence of less jail time. *Id.* at 148-49.

In *Lafler v. Cooper*, defendant Cooper was advised of a plea offer from the government and wanted to accept it, but his lawyer convinced him, based on a laughable reading of the law and facts, to go to trial. After a trial and guilty verdict, Cooper received a sentence harsher than that offered in the plea deal. The Court accepted, as in *Frye*, that "[d]efendants have a Sixth Amendment right to counsel, a right that extends to the plea-bargaining process" and that "'the two-part *Strickland v. Washington* test applies to challenges to guilty pleas based on ineffective assistance of counsel.'" 566 U.S. at 162-63 (citation omitted). The parties in *Lafler* agreed that the first *Strickland* prong had been satisfied; that is, there was no dispute that Cooper's lawyer's representation fell below an objective standard of reasonableness. *Id*. The question, then, was how to apply the second, prejudice prong of the *Strickland* test.

The government and *Lafler* dissent argued there simply can be no showing of *Strickland* prejudice arising from plea bargaining if the defendant is later convicted after a fair trial. *Id*. at 164-65. But the majority rejected this view, arguing that the Sixth Amendment counsel right is not designed solely to guarantee the fairness of the trial itself; rather, it requires effective assistance at all critical stages, including plea bargaining. The majority summarized the government's arguments as essentially saying that "[a] fair trial wipes clean any deficient performance by defense counsel during plea bargaining." *Id*. at 169-70. To this, the Court responded: "That position ignores the reality that criminal justice today is for the most part a system of pleas, not a system of trials. ... [T]he right to adequate assistance of counsel cannot be defined or enforced without taking account of the central role that plea bargaining plays in securing convictions and determining sentences." *Id*.

The Court ultimately held that "[e]ven if the trial itself is free from constitutional flaw, the defendant who goes to trial instead of taking a more favorable plea may be prejudiced from either a conviction on more serious counts or the imposition of a more severe sentence." *Id*. at 166. The test for *Strickland* prejudice applicable in this situation is the same one identified in *Frye*. *Id*. at 164. If the defendant carries his burden, the appropriate relief will vary with the type of injury he suffered; he may receive reconsideration of his sentence or the government may be forced to reoffer the rejected plea proposal.

Consider Professor Stephanos Bibas' explanation of the significance of these two decisions:

> For many years, plea bargaining has been a gray market. Courts are rarely involved, leaving prosecutors unconstrained by judges or juries. Prosecutors' plea offers largely set sentences, checked only by defense lawyers. In this laissez-faire bargaining system, defense lawyers, not judges or juries, are the primary guarantors of fair bargains and equal treatment for their clients. But the quality of defense lawyering varies widely. Bargaining can be a shadowy process, influenced not only by the strength of the evidence and the seriousness of the crime but also by irrelevant factors such as counsel's competence, compensation, and zeal. And because bargaining takes place off the record and is conveyed to clients in confidence, it is not easy to verify that defense counsel have represented their clients zealously and effectively.
>
> Nevertheless, criminal procedure has long focused on jury trials. Even though guilty pleas resolve roughly ninety-five percent of adjudicated criminal cases, the Supreme Court has usually treated plea bargaining as an afterthought, doing little to regulate it. When it has regulated pleas, the Court has largely focused on the procedures for waiving trial rights, not the substantive pros and cons of striking a deal. This past Term, the Court for the first time addressed how the Sixth Amendment's guarantee of effective assistance of counsel applies to defendants who reject bargains and receive heavier sentences after fair trials ... [i]n *Lafler v. Cooper* and *Missouri v. Frye*.
> ...
>
> The majority and dissenting opinions almost talked past each other, reaching starkly different conclusions because they started from opposing premises: contemporary and pragmatic versus historical and formalist. The dissenters would have limited the Sixth Amendment to the jury trials with which the Framers were concerned and proceedings ancillary to those trials. As Justice Scalia put it at oral argument, a jury trial is "the 24-karat test of fairness," and defendants who fail to plead guilty cannot complain that they received "the best thing [that] our legal system" has to offer. Justice Kennedy's majority opinions, by contrast, rested heavily on the dominance of plea bargaining today and its central role in setting sentences as well as convictions. Even a fair trial cannot wipe away an earlier tactical decision that results in a much longer sentence after trial.

Belatedly, the Court noticed that "ours 'is for the most part a system of pleas, not a system of trials.'" The Court, like Rip Van Winkle, has at last awoken from its long slumber and sees the vast field it has left all but unregulated. Justice Scalia, in dissent, repeatedly assailed the majority for "open[ing] a whole new field of ... plea-bargaining law," but it is about time. Now the big question is which institutions can and will ameliorate poor defense lawyering retrospectively or prospectively. The upshot, I predict, will depend on semi-private ordering: few reversals in court, but much more prospective extrajudicial reform.

Lafler and *Frye* will not cause courts of appeals to invalidate many convictions for constitutional error. Courts are poorly equipped to remedy woefully inadequate defense lawyering on their own. Plea bargaining creates little record, after-the-fact review is cumbersome and expensive, and courts are reluctant to reverse final judgments, intrude on prosecutors' prerogatives to bargain, or subject defense counsel's performance to searching review. *Lafler* and *Frye* will loosen these cautions a bit but will not open the floodgates. Moreover, judges cannot fix the massive underfunding and overwork that plague indigent defense counsel. The good news is that *Lafler* and *Frye* will probably have much bigger effects indirectly, in prompting solutions beyond the courts. Plea bargaining's semiprivatized justice is best suited to semiprivatized remedies and reforms, backstopped by judges but driven by other actors. Other actors have the incentives and power to achieve, prospectively and flexibly, much that after-the-fact judicial review cannot. In the real world of plea bargaining, the parties' stances are no longer antagonistic. Counterintuitively, even prosecutors and defendants have strong incentives to collaborate in explaining, promoting, and bulletproofing plea bargains. ...

[I] predict[] that nonjudicial actors (especially prosecutors) will do much to solve plea bargaining's problems prospectively, [because these decisions give them] ... the incentives to do so. ... While courts can do little on their own, they can create incentives for other market participants to explain offers and shore up their bargains.

Stephanos Bibas, Comment: *Incompetent Plea Bargaining and Extrajudicial Reforms*, 126 Harv. L. Rev. 150, 150-52 (2012); *see also* Cynthia Alkon, *The U.S. Supreme Court's Failure to Fix Plea Bargaining: The Impact of* Lafler *and* Frye, 41 Hastings Const. L.Q. 561 (2014).

There remains a question whether an unindicted suspect has a right to counsel in plea negotiations. Most recently, in *Turner v. United States*, 885 F.3d 949 (6th Cir. 2018) (*en banc*), *cert. filed*, No. 18-106 (July 24, 2018), the *en banc* Sixth Circuit said "no," holding that because the Sixth Amendment right to counsel is not triggered until the commencement of adversarial proceedings, a defendant may not attack a plea based on the allegedly ineffective assistance his retained counsel gave him in pre-indictment plea negotiations. At this writing, a petition for certiorari is pending.

BORDENKIRCHER v. HAYES
434 U.S. 357 (1978)

MR. JUSTICE STEWART delivered the opinion of the Court.

The question in this case is whether the Due Process Clause of the Fourteenth Amendment is violated when a state prosecutor carries out a threat made during plea negotiations to reindict the accused on more serious charges if he does not plead guilty to the offense with which he was originally charged.

[Paul Hayes was indicted in Fayette County, Kentucky, on a charge of uttering a forged instrument in the amount of $88.30, punishable by two to ten years in prison. Hayes and his retained counsel met with the prosecutor who offered to recommend a sentence of five years if Hayes would plead guilty and added that if Hayes did not plead guilty he would seek an indictment under the Kentucky Habitual Criminal Act, which would subject Hayes to a mandatory sentence of life imprisonment by reason of his two prior felony convictions. Hayes chose not to plead guilty, and the prosecutor did obtain such an indictment. A jury found Hayes guilty on the principal charge of uttering a forged instrument and, in a separate proceeding, further found that he had twice before been convicted of felonies. As required by the habitual offender statute, he was sentenced to life imprisonment. The Kentucky Court of Appeals rejected Hayes' constitutional objections to the enhanced sentence, and on Hayes' petition for a federal writ of habeas corpus the district court agreed that there had been no constitutional violation in the sentence or the indictment procedure. The Court of Appeals for the Sixth Circuit reversed on the ground that the prosecutor's conduct violated the principles of *Blackledge v. Perry*, 417 U.S. 21 (1974), which "protect defendants from the vindictive exercise of a prosecutor's discretion."]

It may be helpful to clarify at the outset the nature of the issue in this case. While the prosecutor did not actually obtain the recidivist indictment until after the plea conferences had ended, his intention to do so was clearly expressed at the outset of the plea negotiations. Hayes was thus fully informed of the true terms of the offer when he made his decision to plead not guilty. This is not a situation, therefore, where the prosecutor without notice brought an additional and more serious charge after plea negotiations relating only to the original indictment had ended with the defendant's insistence on pleading not guilty. As a practical matter, in short, this case would be no different if the grand jury had indicted Hayes as a recidivist from the outset, and the prosecutor had offered to drop that charge as part of the plea bargain.

The Court of Appeals nonetheless drew a distinction between "concessions relating to prosecution under an existing indictment," and threats to bring more severe charges not contained in the original indictment—a line it thought necessary in order to establish a prophylactic rule to guard against the evil of prosecutorial vindictiveness. Quite apart from this chronological distinction, however, the Court of Appeals found that the prosecutor had acted vindictively in the present case since he had conceded that the indictment was influenced by his desire to induce a guilty plea. The ultimate conclusion of the Court of Appeals thus seems to have been that a prosecutor acts vindictively and in violation of due process of law whenever his charging decision is influenced by what he hopes to gain in the course of plea bargaining negotiations.

... "[W]hatever might be the situation in an ideal world, the fact is that the guilty plea and the often concomitant plea bargain are important components of this country's criminal justice system. Properly administered, they can benefit all concerned." The open acknowledgment of this previously clandestine practice has led this Court to recognize the importance of counsel during plea negotiations, the need for a public record indicating that a plea was knowingly and voluntarily made, and the requirement that a prosecutor's plea-bargaining promise must be kept. The decision of the Court of Appeals in the present case, however, did not deal with considerations such as these, but held that the substance of the plea offer itself violated the limitations imposed by the Due Process Clause of the Fourteenth Amendment. For the reasons that follow, we have concluded that the Court of Appeals was mistaken in so ruling.

This Court held in *North Carolina v. Pearce*, 395 U.S. 711, 725 (1969), that the Due Process Clause of the Fourteenth Amendment "requires that vindictiveness against a defendant for having successfully attacked his first conviction must play no part in the sentence he receives after a new trial." The same principle was later applied to prohibit a prosecutor from reindicting a convicted misdemeanant on a felony charge after the defendant had invoked an appellate remedy, since in this situation there was also a "realistic likelihood of 'vindictiveness.'" *Blackledge v. Perry*, 417 U.S. 21, 27 (1974).

In those cases the Court was dealing with the State's unilateral imposition of a penalty upon a defendant who had chosen to exercise a legal right to attack his original conviction— a situation "very different from the give-and-take negotiation common in plea bargaining between the prosecution and defense, which arguably possess relatively equal bargaining power." The Court has emphasized that the due process violation in cases such as *Pearce* and

Perry lay not in the possibility that a defendant might be deterred from the exercise of a legal right, but rather in the danger that the State might be retaliating against the accused for lawfully attacking his conviction.

To punish a person because he has done what the law plainly allows him to do is a due process violation of the most basic sort, and for an agent of the State to pursue a course of action whose objective is to penalize a person's reliance on his legal rights is "patently unconstitutional." But in the "give-and-take" of plea bargaining, there is no such element of punishment or retaliation so long as the accused is free to accept or reject the prosecution's offer.

Plea bargaining flows from "the mutuality of advantage" to defendants and prosecutors, each with his own reasons for wanting to avoid trial. Defendants advised by competent counsel and protected by other procedural safeguards are presumptively capable of intelligent choice in response to prosecutorial persuasion, and unlikely to be driven to false self-condemnation. Indeed, acceptance of the basic legitimacy of plea bargaining necessarily implies rejection of any notion that a guilty plea is involuntary in a constitutional sense simply because it is the end result of the bargaining process. By hypothesis, the plea may have been induced by promises of a recommendation of a lenient sentence or a reduction of charges, and thus by fear of the possibility of a greater penalty upon conviction after a trial.

While confronting a defendant with the risk of more severe punishment clearly may have a "discouraging effect on the defendant's assertion of his trial rights, the imposition of these difficult choices [is] an inevitable"—and permissible—"attribute of any legitimate system which tolerates and encourages the negotiation of pleas." It follows that, by tolerating and encouraging the negotiation of pleas, this Court has necessarily accepted as constitutionally legitimate the simple reality that the prosecutor's interest at the bargaining table is to persuade the defendant to forgo his right to plead not guilty.

It is not disputed here that Hayes was properly chargeable under the recidivist statute, since he had in fact been convicted of two previous felonies. In our system, so long as the prosecutor has probable cause to believe that the accused committed an offense defined by statute, the decision whether or not to prosecute, and what charge to file or bring before a grand jury, generally rests entirely in his discretion.[12] Within the limits set by the legislature's constitutionally valid definition of chargeable offenses, "the conscious exercise of some selectivity in enforcement is not in itself a federal constitutional violation" so long as "the selection was [not] deliberately based upon an unjustifiable standard such as race, religion, or other arbitrary classification." ...

There is no doubt that the breadth of discretion that our country's legal system vests in prosecuting attorneys carries with it the potential for both individual and institutional abuse. And broad though that discretion may be, there are undoubtedly constitutional limits upon its exercise. We hold only that the course of conduct engaged in by the prosecutor in this case, which no more than openly presented the defendant with the unpleasant alternatives of forgoing trial or facing charges on which he was plainly subject to prosecution, did not violate the Due Process Clause of the Fourteenth Amendment. ...

Notes

1. *Brady* concerned a claim that the defendant was coerced into waiving fundamental constitutional rights by operation of the statute. How does this case differ? Should the factual distinctions between these cases make a constitutional difference? *See* Corbitt v. New Jersey, 439 U.S. 212, 227-28 (1978) (Stewart, J., concurring).

---

[12] [Court's footnote 8:] This case does not involve the constitutional implications of a prosecutor's offer during plea bargaining of adverse or lenient treatment for some person *other* than the accused, which might pose a greater danger of inducing a false guilty plea by skewing the assessment of the risks a defendant must consider.

The Court asserts that "[d]efendants advised by competent counsel and protected by other procedural safeguards are presumptively capable of intelligent choice in response to prosecutorial persuasion, and unlikely to be driven to false self-condemnation." Are they? *See* Stephanos Bibas, *The Myth of the Fully Informed Rational Actor*, 31 St. Louis U. Pub. L. Rev. 79 (2011).

2. "Legal vindictiveness does not refer to a prosecutor's generic ill feeling toward, or even his desire to harm, a defendant. Rather, as defined by the Supreme Court, vindictiveness means that a prosecutor has retaliated against a defendant for the exercise of a legal right, denying her due process. One might think, then, that pursuing more severe charges or a harsher sentence after a defendant exercises her right to a jury trial would constitute vindictiveness. But it doesn't. The law specifically permits severely penalizing defendants for going to trial in an effort to induce a guilty plea—or, in the Court's words, 'openly present[ing] the defendant with the unpleasant alternatives of forgoing trial or facing charges on which he was plainly subject to prosecution.'" Doug Lieb, Note, *Vindicating Vindictiveness: Prosecutorial Discretion and Plea Bargaining, Past and Future*, 123 Yale L.J. 1014, 1017 (2014).

The Court examines cases in which it has applied a presumption of vindictiveness to governmental action and found that action wanting as a matter of due process. The Supreme Court distinguishes the plea bargaining context at issue here from cases in which a presumption of vindictiveness is appropriate by characterizing the former as the permissible presentation of "unpleasant" alternatives to a defendant in the "give-and-take" of bargaining and the latter as the forbidden imposition of unilateral penalties on those who exercise constitutional rights. Is this a distinction that you find persuasive?

3. After *Bordenkircher*, the Supreme Court held in *United States v. Goodwin*, 457 U.S. 368 (1982), that a presumption of prosecutorial vindictiveness was not warranted in a case in which the defendant was indicted and convicted of a felony charge arising from the same incident as previously pending misdemeanor charges after the defendant decided to plead not guilty and requested trial by jury on the misdemeanor charges. In so doing, the Court strongly indicated a disinclination to apply a presumption of vindictiveness to prosecutors' *pretrial* decisions:

> A prosecutor should remain free before trial to exercise the broad discretion entrusted to him to determine the extent of the societal interest in prosecution. An initial decision should not freeze future conduct. As we made clear in *Bordenkircher*, the initial charges filed by a prosecutor may not reflect the extent to which an individual is legitimately subject to prosecution.

Id. at 382; *see also* United States v. Tingle, 880 F.3d 850 (7th Cir. 2018). *Cf.* United States v. LaDeau, 734 F.3d 561 (6th Cir. 2013); State v. Knowles, 357 Mont. 272, 239 P.3d 129 (2010) (distinguishing *Goodwin* in the course of concluding that a prosecutor's decision to increase the charges because the defendant rejected a plea offer after a mistrial constituted vindictiveness).

4. The *Bordenkircher* Court concludes by noting that "the decision whether or not to prosecute, and what charge to file or bring before a grand jury, generally rests" in the prosecutor's broad discretion. It further states that there are undoubtedly some limits on prosecutors' exercises of their broad discretion. What are those limits? Two constitutional limitations are alluded to in *Bordenkircher*: due process prohibitions against prosecutorial vindictiveness and equal protection safeguards against selectivity in enforcement on the basis of "an unjustifiable standard such as race, religion, or other arbitrary classification." *Bordenkircher* indicates the limitations of the first, due process, ground for attack. *See also* Jordan v. Epps, 756 F.3d 395, 406-411 (5th Cir. 2014). Equal protection claims are also exceedingly difficult to make out.

In *United States v. Armstrong*, 517 U.S. 456, 465 (1996), the Court stated as follows:

In order to dispel the presumption that a prosecutor has not violated equal protection, a criminal defendant must present "clear evidence to the contrary."... Judicial deference to the decisions of these executive officers rests in part on an assessment of the relative competence of prosecutors and courts. ... It also stems from a concern not to unnecessarily impair the performance of a core executive constitutional function.

The requirements for a selective-prosecution claim draw on "ordinary equal protection standards." The claimant must demonstrate that the federal prosecutorial policy "had a discriminatory effect and that it was motivated by discriminatory purpose." To establish a discriminatory effect in a race case, the claimant must show that similarly situated individuals of a different race were not prosecuted.

In *Armstrong*, the defendants, who were indicted for selling crack and using guns in relation to a drug trafficking offense, moved for discovery on a claim that they had been selected for federal, as opposed to state, prosecution because they are African-American. The Court held that to establish an entitlement to discovery on a claim of selective prosecution based on race, the defendants had to produce credible evidence regarding discriminatory effect—that is, that the government could have prosecuted similarly situated defendants of a different race for the offense but did not. The Supreme Court rejected the Ninth Circuit's presumption that "people of *all* races commit *all* types of crimes" and that no crime is the exclusive province of any particular racial or ethnic group. 517 U.S. at 469. The Court cited federal sentencing statistics that showed that more than 90% of the persons sentenced in 1994 for crack cocaine trafficking were African-American. *Id.* (Given that these defendants alleged that they were selected for federal prosecution for crack offenses because of their race, should this sentencing statistic be deemed probative?) The Court went on to find the study the defendants tendered to show discriminatory effect insufficient, *id.* at 470, leaving defendants with the obvious Catch-22 of not being able to find sufficient evidence (most of which will be in the government's possession) of discriminatory effect absent discovery but not being able to obtain discovery absent an ability to compile sufficient evidence.

The Supreme Court underscored its intent to enforce this stringent discovery standard when it summarily overturned a Sixth Circuit decision affirming a district court discovery order in *United States v. Bass*, 536 U.S. 862 (2002). Bass had been indicted for the intentional killings of two individuals. The federal government filed a notice of an intent to seek the death penalty. Bass, who is African-American, alleged that the government had determined to seek the death penalty against him because of his race. He moved to dismiss the death penalty notice and, in the alternative, for discovery of information relating to the government's capital charging practices. The defendant introduced in support of his discovery motion a report released by the Department of Justice in September 2000 entitled *The Federal Death Penalty System: A Statistical Survey (1988-2000)*. He also put into evidence public comments regarding the survey on the day of its release by then-Attorney General Janet Reno and then-Deputy Attorney General Eric Holder. The district court ordered that the government provide discovery and, when it refused, dismissed the death penalty notice.

The Sixth Circuit upheld the discovery order, finding that the defendant had met the test articulated in *Armstrong*. United States v. Bass, 266 F.3d 532 (6th Cir. 2001). In particular, the court identified three sets of statistics in the DOJ survey "tending to show that selective prosecution taints the [DOJ's] death penalty protocol." *Id.* at 536. The statistics identified showed (1) "a significant difference between the percentage of white and black prisoners in the general federal prison population (white: fifty-seven percent; black: thirty-eight percent) and those charged by the United States with death-eligible crimes (white: twenty percent; black: forty-eight percent)," *id.* at 537; (2) "the United States entered into a plea bargain with forty-eight percent of the white defendants against whom it sought the death penalty, compared with twenty-five percent of similarly situated black defendants," *id.*; and (3) "two of the three death-eligible offenses charged most frequently against whites and blacks were the same, but … the percentages by race of those charged with each crime were vastly different." *Id.* Finally, the court also noted the evidence introduced from other official sources indicating that blacks are no more likely to commit violent federal offenses than are whites. *Id.* The court also summarized the comments of DOJ officials on the Statistical Survey as follows:

> [T]he top Department of Justice officials have taken the position that, although the Survey's results do not conclusively show intentional racial bias, neither do they conclusively show the lack of bias. Rather, in Reno's and Holder's view, the results demonstrate a clear racial disparity and raise questions warranting further study to determine whether that disparity is caused by intentional racial discrimination.

Id. at 538.

Deputy Attorney General Eric Holder stated, with respect to the statistics revealed in the survey, that "no one reading this report can help but be disturbed, troubled, by this disparity." *Id.* No one, that is, except, perhaps, the Supreme Court of the United States. The Supreme Court granted review in *Bass* and, without briefing or oral argument, summarily reversed in a *per curiam* decision. United States v. Bass, 536 U.S. 862 (2002). The Court's one-paragraph analysis consisted of the following:

> In *United States v. Armstrong*, 517 U.S. 456 (1996), we held that a defendant who seeks discovery on a claim of selective prosecution must show some evidence of both discriminatory effect and discriminatory intent. We need go no further in the present case than consideration of the evidence supporting discriminatory effect. As to that, *Armstrong*, says that the defendant must make a "credible showing" that "similarly situated individuals of a different race were not prosecuted." The Sixth Circuit concluded that respondent had made such a showing based on nationwide statistics demonstrating that "[t]he United States charges blacks with a death-eligible offense more than twice as often as it charges whites" and that the United States enters into plea bargains more frequently with whites than it does with blacks. 266 F.3d, at 538-539 (citing U.S. Dept. of Justice, The Federal Death Penalty System: A Statistical Survey (1988-2000), p. 2 (Sept. 12, 2000)). Even assuming that the *Armstrong* requirement can be satisfied by a nationwide showing (as opposed to a showing regarding the record of the decisionmakers in respondent's case), raw statistics regarding overall charges say nothing about charges brought against *similarly situated defendants*. And the statistics regarding plea bargains are even less relevant, since respondent *was* offered a plea bargain but declined it. Under *Armstrong*, therefore, because respondent failed to submit relevant evidence that similarly situated persons were treated differently, he was not entitled to discovery.

Id. at 863-64. If the DOJ's own statistics—and an Attorney General's and Deputy Attorney General's own conclusions—do not suffice to satisfy *Armstrong*, what does?

RICKETTS v. ADAMSON
483 U.S. 1 (1987)

JUSTICE WHITE delivered the opinion of the Court.

[Shortly after commencement of his first-degree murder trial, Adamson agreed to plead guilty to second-degree murder and testify against his accomplices in exchange for a specified prison term. The agreement provided that if he refused to testify "this entire agreement is null and void and the original charge will be automatically reinstated" and the parties "returned to the positions they were in before this agreement." The court accepted the plea agreement and sentenced Adamson accordingly, and he thereafter testified against the others, who were convicted of first-degree murder. Upon reversal of those convictions and remand, Adamson refused to testify again on the ground that his obligation under the agreement had terminated. Adamson was then charged with first-degree murder, and after the trial court rejected his double jeopardy claim, the Arizona Supreme Court vacated the second-degree murder conviction and reinstated the original charge on the ground that the plea agreement contemplated use of his testimony upon retrial. The state declined Adamson's subsequent offer to testify, and he was then convicted of first-degree murder and sentenced to death.] ...

We may assume that jeopardy attached at least when respondent was sentenced in December 1978, on his plea of guilty to second-degree murder. Assuming also that under Arizona law second-degree murder is a lesser included offense of first-degree murder, the Double Jeopardy Clause, absent special circumstances, would have precluded prosecution of respondent for the greater charge on which he now stands convicted. The State submits, however, that respondent's breach of the plea arrangement to which the parties had agreed removed the double jeopardy bar to prosecution of respondent on the first-degree murder charge. We agree with the State.

Under the terms of the plea agreement, both parties bargained for and received substantial benefits. The State obtained respondent's guilty plea and his promise to testify against "any and all parties involved in the murder of Don Bolles" and in certain specified other crimes. Respondent, a direct participant in a premeditated and brutal murder, received a specified prison sentence accompanied with a guarantee that he would serve actual incarceration time of 20 years and 2 months. He further obtained the State's promise that he would not be prosecuted for his involvement in certain other crimes.

... The terms of the agreement could not be clearer: in the event of respondent's breach occasioned by a refusal to testify, the parties would be returned to the *status quo ante*, in which case respondent would have *no* double jeopardy defense to waive. And, an agreement specifying that charges may be *reinstated* given certain circumstances is, at least under the provisions of this plea agreement, *precisely* equivalent to an agreement waiving a double jeopardy defense. The approach taken by the Court of Appeals would render the agreement meaningless: first-degree murder charges could not be reinstated against respondent if he categorically refused to testify after sentencing even if the agreement specifically provided that he would so testify, because, under the Court of Appeals' view, he never waived his double jeopardy protection. Even respondent, however, conceded at oral argument that "a waiver could be found under those circumstances ... ."

We are also unimpressed by the Court of Appeals' holding that there was a good-faith dispute about whether respondent was bound to testify a second time and that until the extent of his obligation was decided, there could be no knowing and intelligent waiver of his double jeopardy defense. But respondent knew that if he breached the agreement he could be retried, and it is incredible to believe that he did not anticipate that the extent of his obligation would be decided by a court. Here he sought a construction of the agreement in the Arizona Supreme Court, and that court found that he had failed to live up to his promise. The result was that respondent was returned to the position he occupied prior to execution of the plea bargain: he stood charged with first-degree murder. Trial on that charge did not violate the Double Jeopardy Clause. ...

[The defendant's choice was voluntary.] He could submit to the State's request that he testify at the retrial, and in so doing risk that he would be providing testimony that pursuant to the agreement he had no obligation to provide, or he could stand on his interpretation of the agreement, knowing that if he were wrong, his breach of the agreement would restore the parties to their original positions and he could be prosecuted for first-degree murder. Respondent chose the latter course, and the Double Jeopardy Clause does not relieve him from the consequences of that choice.

Respondent cannot escape the Arizona Supreme Court's interpretation of his obligations under the agreement. The State did not force the breach; respondent chose, perhaps for strategic reasons or as a gamble, to advance an interpretation of the agreement that proved erroneous. And, there is no indication that respondent did not fully understand the potential seriousness of the position he adopted. In the April 3 letter, respondent's counsel advised the prosecutor that respondent "is fully aware of the fact that your office may feel that he has not completed his obligations under the plea agreement ... and, further, that your office may attempt to withdraw the plea agreement from him, [and] that he may be prosecuted for the killing of Donald Bolles on a first degree murder charge." This statement of respondent's awareness of the operative terms of the plea agreement only underscores that which respondent's plea hearing made evident: respondent clearly appreciated and understood the consequences were he found to be in breach of the agreement.

Finally, it is of no moment that following the Arizona Supreme Court's decision respondent offered to comply with the terms of the agreement. At this point, respondent's second-degree murder conviction had already been ordered vacated and the original charge reinstated. The parties did not agree that respondent would be relieved from the consequences of his refusal to testify if he were able to advance a colorable argument that a testimonial obligation was not owing. The parties could have struck a different bargain, but permitting the State to enforce the agreement the parties actually made does not violate the Double Jeopardy Clause. ...

Notes

1. Where, as is the usual case, the government drafts the plea agreement, wouldn't contract principles normally dictate that ambiguity in the document be construed against the government? *See, e.g.,* Connecticut v. Rivers, 283 Conn. 713, 725, 931 A.2d 185, 193 (2007). For a discussion of the applicability of contract norms to "contracts" reached in the criminal justice context, see Candace Zierdt & Ellen S. Podgor, *Corporate Deferred Prosecutions Through the Looking Glass of Contract Policing*, 96 Ky. L.J. 1 (2008).

Is it possible to cover every eventuality in the course of drafting such an agreement? What terms and conditions, at a minimum, should be covered in detail? May the parties provide for a mechanism by which disagreements regarding the terms of the plea may be resolved? *See* Lewinsky Agreement, reproduced *supra* Chapter 15, at ¶ 3.

2. The Supreme Court has also made clear that due process requires that the terms of plea bargains be enforced against the government. In *Santobello v. New York*, 404 U.S. 257 (1971), the defendant agreed to plead guilty pursuant to a deal in which one prosecutor agreed to make no recommendation as to sentence. A new prosecutor recommended the maximum at defendant's sentencing, which the judge imposed. The Supreme Court held that even if the prosecutor's lapse was inadvertent and even though the judge stated that he was not influenced by the prosecutor's recommendation, the "interests of justice and appropriate recognition of the duties of the prosecution in relation to promises made in the negotiation of pleas of guilty will be best served by remanding" the case. *Id.* at 262. In terms of remedy, the Court left it up to the court on remand to determine whether "the circumstances of this case require only that there be specific performance of the agreement on the plea, in which case petitioner should be resentenced by a different judge, or whether, in the view of the state court, the circumstances require granting the relief sought by petitioner, *i.e.*, the opportunity to withdraw his plea of guilty." *Id.* at 263; *see also* United States v. Hodge, 412 F.3d 479 (3d Cir. 2005).

Although the government's due process obligations are clear, the mechanics required to implement it are often in dispute. For example, the circuits are split as to whether the government must first establish a defendant's breach of an agreement by a preponderance of the evidence before repudiating its own promises under a plea agreement, *see* United States v. Benjamin, 138 F.3d 1069, 1074 (6th Cir. 1998), or whether a defendant seeking enforcement of a plea agreement bears the burden of first establishing by a preponderance of the evidence that he had fulfilled his obligations under the agreement, *see* United States

v. Snow, 234 F.3d 187, 189 & n.2 (4th Cir. 2000). Similarly, there is a split among *all* courts, state and federal, over who controls the choice of which of the two equitable remedies recognized by the *Santobello* Court—specific performance or rescission—should apply in a given case. *Compare, e.g.,* Roye v. United States, 772 A.2d 837, 839-41 (D.C. 2001), *with* State v. Munoz, 305 Mont. 139, 23 P.3d 922, 925-27 (2001). Some courts hold that the choice of remedy is for the court to decide, others hold that the defendant should be permitted to elect the remedy, and still others reason that the matter is for judicial determination but that "considerable weight" should be accorded to the defendant's preference. *See Munoz,* 23 P.3d at 926 (citing cases); *cf.* United States v. Purser, 747 F.3d 284 (5th Cir. 2014) (government can "cure" breach).

Note, however, that if the defendant does not timely object to the government's breach of its plea agreement, Fed. R. Crim. P's 52(b)'s plain error test applies to the forfeited claim that the government filed to meet its contractual obligations. *See* Puckett v. United States, 556 U.S. 129 (2009).

3. The *Ricketts* Court enforced against the defendant a provision of the plea agreement that it found was "equivalent to an agreement waiving a double jeopardy defense." Controversy has arisen over other types of prospective waivers that federal prosecutors are increasingly demanding of defendants in plea negotiations.

First, some federal prosecutors had insisted that defendants surrender any potential claims of ineffective assistance of counsel (IAC) as a condition of accepting a plea bargain. Although some courts have ruled that such waivers are not per se invalid, United States v. Grimes, 739 F.3d 125 (3d Cir. 2014), this type of waiver has been viewed with serious disapproval by state ethics enforcers. For example, in 2014, the Supreme Court of Kentucky, in examining an ethics advisory opinion by the Kentucky Bar Association that outlawed such IAC waivers, ruled that embedding an IAC waiver in a plea agreement constitutes professional misconduct by a federal prosecutor. United States v. Ky. Bar Ass'n, 439 S.W.3d 136 (Ky. 2014); *see also* Susan R. Klein et al., *Waiving the Criminal Justice System: An Empirical and Constitutional Analysis,* 52 Am. Crim. L. Rev. 73 (2015). A few months after this decision was handed down, the Department of Justice issued a policy statement that, although asserting that IAC waivers are ethical and legal, nonetheless instructed federal prosecutors as follows: "Federal prosecutors should no longer seek in plea agreements to have a defendant waive claims of ineffective assistance of counsel whether those claims are made on collateral attack or, when permitted by circuit law, made on direct appeal." James M. Cole, Deputy Att'y Gen., Memo. For All Federal Prosecutors re: Dep't Policy on Waivers of Claims of Ineffective Assistance of Counsel (Oct. 14, 2014).

4. Second, many U.S. Attorneys Offices have incorporated into plea agreements *Brady* waivers. A representative example states:

> The defendant understands that discovery may not have been completed in this case, and that there may be additional discovery to which he would have access if he elected to proceed to trial. The defendant agrees to waive his right to receive additional discovery which may include, among other things, evidence tending to impeach the credibility of potential witnesses.

Raymond Banoun, *Preface: The Year in Review, reprinted in* White Collar Crime 2000 at x (ABA 2000) (quoting San Francisco U.S. Attorney's Office plea agreement provision). One office has also used waiver provisions further limiting the prosecutor's continuing obligation to give the defense information that establishes the defendant's "factual innocence"; providing that the defendant waives his right to impeaching information that he would obtain at trial; and providing that the defendant will not collaterally attack the plea. *See* Erica G. Franklin, Note, *Waiving Prosecutorial Disclosure in the Guilty Plea Process: A Debate on the Merits of "Discovery" Waivers,* 51 Stan. L. Rev. 567, 568-69 (1999).

The practice of insisting on such waivers was adopted in response to rulings in a number of circuits that a defendant may be entitled to withdraw a guilty plea upon learning of withheld *Brady* materials relevant to a defendant's decision to plead guilty. *See, e.g., Sanchez v. United States*, 50 F.3d 1448, 1454 (9th Cir. 1995); *see also* Chapter 14 (Discovery). The Supreme Court held, however, in *United States v. Ruiz*, 536 U.S. 622 (2002), that the Fifth and Sixth Amendments do not require federal prosecutors, before entering into a binding plea agreement with a criminal defendant, to disclose "impeachment information relating to any informants or other witnesses." *See* Chapter 14 (reprinting *Ruiz*). Thus, at least as to impeachment materials, there is no right to "waive" and thus presumably no question about the validity of express waiver provisions in plea agreements. Might there be some value in an express waiver provision despite *Ruiz*? *See* John G. Douglass, *Fatal Attraction? The Uneasy Courtship of* Brady *and Plea Bargaining*, 50 Emory L.J. 437, 514 (2001) (arguing, pre-*Ruiz*, that there was no right to "trial-related" *Brady* and concluding in any case that "[t]he principal effect of an explicit '*Brady* waiver' ... may be to inform the defendant of another trial-related right that he is giving up by pleading guilty. As a result, and somewhat ironically, explicit *Brady* waivers may actually lead to better informed pleas.").

Does *Ruiz* extend to other categories of *Brady* material, such as evidence that may establish the defendant's "factual innocence"? If *Ruiz* does not foreclose claims to such evidence in connection with plea proceedings, might those precedents, such as *Sanchez*, that authorize the defendant to withdraw from a guilty plea upon finding that such materials were withheld continue in force? Should such waivers be upheld? What challenges does prosecutorial insistence on such waivers present for defense counsel? *See* Franklin, *supra*, at 567.

What challenges do such waivers potentially present for prosecutors? Recall, in this regard, the discussion in Chapter 14 (Discovery) of the ABA Standing Committee on Ethics and Professional Responsibility's Formal Opinion 09-454 (July 8, 2009), which opines that ABA Model Rule of Professional Responsibility 3.8(d) requires prosecutors to disclose favorable evidence to the accused prior to a guilty plea and that prosecutors may not, consistent with ethical standards applicable in most states, "solicit, accept or rely on" a defendant's waiver of this ethical disclosure requirement. *Id*. at. 7

5. Third, some U.S. Attorneys Offices have inserted into their plea agreements sentencing appeal waivers that take a variety of forms. *See* U.S.A.M., Criminal Resource Manual No. 626. According to a study by Professors Nancy J. King and Michael E. O'Neill, in nearly two-thirds of 971 randomly selected cases sentenced under the Guidelines that were resolved by plea agreement, the defendants waived their rights to review. *See* Nancy J. King & Michael E. O'Neill, *Appeal Waivers and the Future of Sentencing Policy*, 55 Duke L.J. 209, 209-210 (2005). The study disclosed that the frequency of such waivers, however, varies substantially among the districts. *Id*. The study also showed that "the government appears to provide some sentencing concessions more frequently to defendants who sign waivers than to defendants who do not, including agreeing to 'C' pleas (binding sentencing terms), downward departures, safety-valve credits, and a variety of stipulations." *Id*. The authors concluded that the "observed trend of increased use of stipulations combined with no review raises the risk that sentences not in compliance with the law can proliferate without scrutiny. The uneven practice of trading sentencing concessions for waivers among cases and courts also suggests that waivers are undercutting efforts to advance consistency in federal sentencing." *Id*.; *see also* Nancy J. King, *Regulating Settlement: What Is Left of the Rule of Law in the Criminal Process?*, 56 DePaul L. Rev. 389 (2007).

6. With respect to the substantive issue of the enforceability of appeals waivers, a couple of District Court judges have struck such provisions as contrary to public policy and void but were rebuffed on appeal. Their reasoning, however, should be considered. In *United States v. Raynor*, 989 F. Supp. 43 (D.D.C. 1997), *overruled*, United States v. Guillen, 561 F.3d 527, 529 (D.C. Cir. 2009), the court refused to accept the defendants' pleas because of the inclusion in the plea agreements of the following appeal waiver:

Your client understands and acknowledges that Title 18, United States Code, Section 3742 affords a defendant the right to appeal the sentence imposed after a plea of guilty or trial. After consultation with counsel, and in exchange for the concessions made by this Office in this plea agreement, your client voluntarily and knowingly waives the right to appeal any sentence within the maximum provided in the statute(s) of conviction, or the manner in which that sentence was determined, on the grounds set forth in Title 18, United States Code, Section 3742 or on any ground whatever. Your client also voluntarily and knowingly waives your client's right to challenge the sentence or the manner in which it was determined in any collateral attack, including but not limited to a motion brought under Title 28, United States Code, Section 2255. Your client further acknowledges and agrees that this agreement does not limit the Government's right to appeal a sentence, as set forth in Title 18, United States Code, Section 3742(b).

989 F. Supp. at 43. The district court concluded that:

> The condition sought to be imposed by the government is inherently unfair; it is a one-sided contract of adhesion; it will undermine the error correcting function of the courts of appeals in sentencing; it will create a sentencing regime where courts of appeals will never have the opportunity to review an illegal or unconstitutional sentence, or a sentence that has no basis in fact, unless those sentencing errors work to the disadvantage of the government. Such a result is inconsistent with what Congress intended when it created the Sentencing Commission and the Sentencing Guidelines. It is inconsistent with the express terms of 18 U.S.C. § 3742, and it is inconsistent with the scheme of Rule 11 of the Federal Rules of Criminal Procedure. A defendant cannot knowingly, intelligently and voluntarily give up the right to appeal a sentence that has not yet been imposed and about which the defendant has no knowledge as to what will occur at the time of sentencing. This Court therefore will accept no plea agreements containing waiver provisions of this kind.

Id. at 49; *see also* United States v. Medina-Carrasco, 815 F.3d 457, 463 (9th Cir. 2015) (Friedman, J., dissenting); United States v. Perez, 46 F. Supp.2d 59, 61 (D.Mass.1999), *overruled,* United States v. Teeter, 257 F.3d 14, 25-26 (1st Cir. 2001). Another judge rejected an appeal waiver embedded in a plea agreement in part because the circuit courts accepted the validity of such waivers before the Guidelines were held to be merely advisory, not mandatory, in *United States v. Booker,* 543 U.S. 220, 247 (2005). *See* United States v. Vanderwerff, Crim. Action 12-cr-00069, at 7-8 (Kane, J.) (D. Colo. June 28, 2012), *rev'd,* 788 F.3d 1266, 1271 (10th Cir. 2015). The judge then reasoned:

> Sentencing, post-*Booker,* requires a trial court to consider context and to apply criteria rather than perform a mechanical or clerical entry of a matrixed judgment. Ethical and moral values inevitably infuse the decision-making process, but they must be justified by being drawn from governing texts in statutes and judicial opinions and established principles of fairness generally accepted by the community affected by the criminal conduct, *i.e.,* the fundamental values widely accepted by society and identifiable as such.
>
> The responsibility of appellate review is to decide how well the sentencing judge has established the sentence within this described discipline. That is fundamentally dissimilar to the pre-*Booker* function of determining whether an arithmetic calculation has been executed correctly. Rather, reviewing sentences under an abuse of discretion standard is a complex inquiry meant to assure that the judicial administration of justice is relevant to the values and expectations of society.
>
> Indiscriminate acceptance of appellate waivers undermines the ability of appellate courts to ensure the constitutional validity of convictions and to maintain consistency and reasonableness in sentencing decisions...

All the circuits have held, however, that waivers of appeal are generally permissible and enforceable, *see* United States v. Khattak, 273 F.3d 557, 560-61 (3d Cir. 2001) (collecting cases), although some state Supreme Courts have ruled otherwise, at least in certain types of cases. *See, e.g.,* Spann v. State, 704 N.W.2d 486 (Minn. 2005); State v. Ethington, 121 Ariz. 572, 592 P.2d 768 (1979). Many circuits to address the question have adopted the same rule with respect to another very common waiver provision: defendants' waivers of their rights to seek collateral relief under 28 U.S.C. § 2255 (remedies on motion attacking sentence for those in federal custody). *See, e.g.,* Moon v. United States, 181 F.Supp.2d 596, 599 (E.D. Va. 2002) (collecting cases).

The reasoning of the court in *United States v. Khattack* is representative. 273 F.3d at 560-61. In that case, the defendant sought on direct appeal to challenge a sentencing determination made by the district court. He argued that "waiver-of-appeals provisions are void as contrary to public policy, because defendants cannot ever knowingly and voluntarily waive their rights to appeal future errors." *Id.* at 560. The court rejected his contention, ruling that "waivers of appeals are generally permissible if entered into knowingly and voluntarily, unless they work a miscarriage of justice." *Id.* at 558. It explained:

> As the Supreme Court has stated, "A criminal defendant may knowingly and voluntarily waive many of the most fundamental protections afforded by the Constitution." *United States v. Mezzanatto,* 513 U.S. 196, 201 (1995). In every plea agreement, the defendant waives the right to a jury trial, the right to confront and cross-examine witnesses, and the right against self-incrimination. In addition, a defendant can waive his rights against double jeopardy and his Sixth Amendment right to counsel.
>
> The United States Constitution does not guarantee a right to appeal. *Jones v. Barnes,* 463 U.S. 745, 751 (1983). The right to appeal a criminal conviction is created by statute. *See* 18 U.S.C. § 3742. The ability to waive statutory rights, like those provided in 18 U.S.C. § 3742, logically flows from the ability to waive constitutional rights. If done knowingly and voluntarily, a statutorily created right to appeal is generally held to be waiveable. ...
>
> Khattak's arguments have been rejected by each appellate court to consider them. Waivers of the legal consequences of unknown future events are commonplace. A defendant waiving a right to trial by jury, for example, waives a procedural protection that might result in a favorable verdict. But the "prospective nature" of waivers has "never been thought to place [waivers] off limits or to render a defendant's act 'unknowing.'" These waivers "preserve the finality of judgments and sentences imposed pursuant to valid pleas of guilty." Allowing defendants to retract waivers would prolong litigation, affording defendants the benefits of their agreements while shielding them from their self-imposed burdens.
>
> Khattak relies on *United States v. Raynor,* 989 F.Supp. 43, 44 (D.D.C. 1997), where the trial court determined a defendant could not knowingly or intelligently waive the right to challenge a yet-imposed sentence, as that might result in an "illegal, unconstitutional or otherwise improper" sentence. *Id.* But by waiving the right to appeal, a defendant necessarily waives the opportunity to challenge the sentence imposed, regardless of the merits. As the Court of Appeals for the Eleventh Circuit explained:
>
> > A waiver of the right to appeal includes a waiver of the right to appeal difficult or debatable legal issues—indeed, it includes a waiver of the right to appeal blatant error. Waiver would be nearly meaningless if it included only those appeals that border on the frivolous. ... While it may appear unjust to allow criminal defendants

to bargain away meritorious appeals, such is the necessary consequence of a system in which the right to appeal may be freely traded. …

Moreover, Khattak's argument ignores that waivers of appeals may assist defendants in making favorable plea bargains. The government often looks favorably on the opportunity to conserve resources necessary to prosecute an appeal, providing defendants a valuable bargaining chip in the plea process. [*United States v. Teeter*, 257 F.3d 14, 22 (1st Cir. 2001)] (suggesting the benefit of avoiding a lengthy, costly appeal is "very real," and that "in some cases, the government, without such a waiver, might not be willing to plea-bargain at all"). Furthermore, as in this case, a defendant can bargain for a sentence range or ceiling.

In view of these considerations, we do not believe the waiver of appellate rights in criminal cases contravenes public policy. At the same time, we believe waivers of appeals should be strictly construed. Thus, we hold that waivers of appeals, if entered into knowingly and voluntarily, are valid.

Id. at 561-62. Which position do you find more persuasive—*should* such agreements be enforced? If so, how?

Normally the remedy is dismissal of the appeal. But the Third Circuit has held that where a defendant breached his plea agreement by appealing his sentence despite a plea waiver, the defendant should be subject to sentencing de novo in the District Court and the government would be relieved of its obligation to recommend a bargained-for downward departure. *See* United States v. Erwin, 765 F.3d 219 (3d Cir. 2014).

7. Although the courts appear unanimous on the basic viability of appeal waivers, a great number of circuits have also indicated (often in dicta) that such waivers are not necessarily enforceable in all cases. One obvious ground for invalidating a waiver is if the defendant establishes that the waiver in the plea agreement was not made knowingly, intelligently, and voluntarily. *See, e.g.*, United States v. Rollings, 751 F.3d 1183, 1187 (10th Cir. 2014); United States v. Schmidt, 47 F.3d 188, 190 (7th Cir. 1995); Jones v. United States, 167 F.3d 1142, 1145 (7th Cir. 1999). Relatedly, the majority view appears to be that "a waiver of appeal may not be enforced against a [defendant] who claims that ineffective assistance of counsel rendered *that waiver* unknowing or involuntary." United States v. White, 307 F.3d 336, 341 (5th Cir. 2002). There is a split in the circuits, however, on the further question whether ineffective assistance claims directed to counsel's performance at sentencing or in other activities that do not relate to the execution of the waiver or the plea agreement survive appeal waivers.

Some circuits have also indicated that certain challenges to sentencing decisions *other* than ineffective assistance claims will be entertained despite an otherwise valid waiver, and the list of permissible challenges seems to be getting longer. Thus, some courts have stated that they will not enforce an appeal waiver if the sentence was imposed in excess of the maximum penalty provided by law, *see* Dowell v. United States, 694 F.3d 898, 902 (7th Cir. 2012); United States v. Brown, 232 F.3d 399, 403 (4th Cir. 2000); United States v. Black, 201 F.3d 1296, 1301 (10th Cir. 2000), where the sentence was based on a constitutionally impermissible factor such as race, *see Brown*, 232 F.3d at 403, where the sentence violates a material term of the plea agreement, *see* DeRoo v. United States, 223 F.3d 919, 923 (8th Cir. 2000), or where a sentence was predicated on subsequently overruled circuit law, United States v. Torres-Rosario, 658 F.3d 110, 115-16 (1st Cir. 2011); United States v. Gonzalez-Melchor, 648 F.3d 959, 964 (9th Cir. 2011) (waiver invalid due to judicial participation in the negotiation of the waiver).

A number of circuits have declined to delineate specific instances in which waivers will be unenforceable, opting instead for a more general "miscarriage of justice" standard. *See* United States v. Castro, 704 F.3d 125 (3rd Cir. 2013); United States v. Andis, 333 F.3d 886, 891-92 (8th Cir. 2003) (*en banc*); *Teeter*, 257 F.3d at 25-26. Thus, in these circuits, "if denying a right of appeal would work a miscarriage of justice, the appellate court, in its sound discretion, may refuse to honor the waiver." *Id.* at 25; *Khattack*, 273 F.3d at 562. "'To successfully invoke the miscarriage of justice exception, a garden-variety error will not suffice, rather there must be, at a bare minimum, an increment of error more glaring than routine reversible error.'" United States v. Del Valle-Cruz, 785 F.3d 48, 54 (1st Cir. 2015) (citation omitted).

The First Circuit has explained that "[t]his category is infinitely variable, but, by way of illustration, we would include within it situations in which appellants claim that their sentences were based on constitutionally impermissible factors (say, race or ethnicity), or that the plea proceedings were tainted by ineffective assistance of counsel." *Teeter*, 257 F.3d at 25 n.9. The First Circuit has also made express its belief that as "a subset of this premise, we think that the same flexibility ought to pertain when the district court plainly errs in sentencing." *Id.* at 25. It added that "we do not think that a waiver should be construed to bar an appeal if the trial court imposes a sentence exceeding the maximum penalty permitted by law, or one that violates a material term of the plea agreement." *Id.* at 25 n.10. Among the factors to be considered before "reliev[ing] the defendant of the waiver" are:

> [T]he clarity of the error, its gravity, its character (e.g., whether it concerns a fact issue, a sentencing guideline, or a statutory maximum), the impact of the error on the defendant, the impact of correcting the error on the government, and the extent to which the defendant acquiesced in the result.

Id. at 25-26; *see also Khattack*, 273 F.3d at 563. Does a totality of circumstances test deprive the government of the benefit of its bargain? That is, given that the government must apparently brief the appeal at least in part on the merits to make its case for the enforceability of a waiver, what good does the waiver truly do it—whether ultimately enforced or not?

8. Some plea agreements define the "cooperation" required by the agreement as including a defendant's agreement not only affirmatively to aid the government in its efforts to prosecute others, but also to refrain from certain activity and waive certain rights. For example, defendants may undertake not to commit any further crimes, to waive statute of limitations defenses to any future prosecution that may flow from a defendant's breach of the agreement, to waive any claim that the defendant is a "prevailing party" entitled to file a claim under the Hyde Amendment (discussed *supra* Chapter 13 (Grand Jury)), to waive any possibility of avoiding fine or restitution obligations through bankruptcy, and to waive any possible protections for statements made in the course of the defendant's cooperation that could be claimed under *Kastigar* or the federal rules of evidence or criminal procedure.

B. FED. R. CRIM. P. 11 AND GUIDELINES BARGAINING

1. FED. R. CRIM. P. 11

Should a defendant elect to plead guilty, the district court will hold a plea hearing, also known as a Rule 11 proceeding. Fed. R. Crim. P. 11 details the requisites for a valid plea. The judge will normally inquire of the defendant whether circumstances exist that may undermine the "knowing" character of the plea (such as the defendant being on drugs or otherwise intoxicated). Before a court may accept a plea of guilty, the court must inform the defendant of, and determine that the defendant understands, the constitutional rights he is giving up by pleading (*e.g.*, the right to a jury trial, to be represented by counsel at trial, to confront and cross-examine witnesses, to call witnesses in his own behalf and the like).[13] The court must make sure that the defendant understands the charges to which he is pleading, including any maximum and minimum sentences and other potentially applicable penalties or obligations.[14] The court is entitled to rely on counsel's representation that he or she advised the defendant of the nature of the charges and the elements of the crimes to which he is pleading guilty.[15] Among the matters about which the judge must advise the defendant under Rule 11, and ensure he understands, are the terms of any appeal waiver in the plea agreement.[16]

Defense counsel must be vigilant that all of the appropriate warnings are given because if the defendant does not object and seeks a reversal of his conviction on the ground that the district court committed plain error under Rule 11 in connection with advice or warnings omitted, the defendant must show a reasonable probability that he would not have pleaded guilty but for the error.[17] At bottom, because the "guilty plea operates as a waiver of important rights," the court's most important function in a Rule 11 guilty plea proceeding is to ensure that the defendant's plea is "done voluntarily, knowingly, and intelligently, 'with sufficient awareness of the relevant circumstances and likely consequences.'"[18]

During the course of a plea allocution under Rule 11(b)(3), the court "must determine that there is a factual basis for the plea." This may entail the defendant personally acknowledging guilt. The court may put the defendant under oath, and if it does, the court must warn the defendant of the government's right to use against the defendant any statement he makes in a prosecution for perjury or false statements.[19] In *Mitchell v. United States*,[20] however, the Supreme Court held that a guilty plea does not waive the defendant's Fifth Amendment privilege in the sentencing phase of the case, either as a result of the plea colloquy or by operation of law when the plea is entered. Moreover, the Court ruled that a trial court, in determining facts about the crime which bear upon the severity of the sentence under the Sentencing Guidelines, may not draw an adverse inference from the defendant's silence.

A defendant may, of course, enter a straight plea to the indictment or information— without any agreement with the government. If the government agrees to give the defendant some consideration in return for a plea, this should be reflected in a written plea agreement. Rule 11 also provides the basic parameters for such plea bargaining. The rule contemplates three types of plea agreements: (1) a "charge" bargain under Fed. R. Crim. P. 11(c)(1)(A); (2) a "recommended sentence" bargain under Fed. R. Crim. P. 11(c)(1)(B); and (3) a "specific sentence" bargain under Fed. R. Crim. P. 11(c)(1)(C). Sometimes the judge will want more information before accepting a plea agreement. For example, she

---

[13] *See* Fed. R. Crim. P. 11(b)(1)(B)-(F).

[14] *Id.* Rule 11(b)(1)(G)-(M); *see also* United States v. Ortiz-Garcia, 665 F.3d 279 (1st Cir. 2011) (a federal judge's failure to ensure that a defendant who pled guilty was aware of the maximum sentence he faced rendered the defendant's waiver of his appeal rights involuntary and constituted plain error requiring a change-of-plea hearing).

[15] *See, e.g.*, Bradshaw v. Stumpf, 545 U.S. 175 (2005).

[16] Fed. R. Crim. P. 11(b)(1)(N).

[17] United States v. Dominguez Benitez, 542 U.S. 74 (2004).

[18] *Bradshaw*, 545 U.S. at 183 (quoting *Brady*, 397 U.S. at 748); *see also* Fed. R. Crim. P. 11(b)(2). *But see* United States v. Diaz-Ramirez, 646 F.3d 653 (9th Cir. 2011) (conducting a group plea hearing during which over 60 defendants pleaded guilty did not violate due process).

[19] Fed. R. Crim. P. 11(b)(1)(A); *see also* United States v. Self, 596 F.3d 245 (5th Cir. 2010) (Rule 11 does not allow "piecemeal" acceptance or rejection of the terms of the plea agreement).

[20] 526 U.S. 314 (1999).

may be concerned that the bargain constrains her sentencing discretion in ways she suspects she will not like once the Probation Department has done an investigation and come up with the Pre-Sentence Report (PSR). Accordingly, the judge may accept the guilty plea but defer acceptance of the plea bargain itself until after receipt of the PSR. With respect to the first type of plea bargain (charge bargains) and the third (specific sentence bargains), if the judge decides to reject the plea agreement, the defendant can elect to withdraw his plea under Fed. R. Crim. P. 11(c)(5)(B). But a defendant may not withdraw a plea entered pursuant to a recommended sentence bargain under Rule 11(c)(1)(B) even if the court ultimately rejects the sentencing recommendation or request; accordingly, the court must advise the defendant of this fact at the get-go.[21]

What if the defendant gets cold feet between the time he enters his guilty plea and the court's deferred decision on whether to accept or reject the plea agreement? In *United States v. Hyde*,[22] the Court held that where a defendant enters a guilty plea pursuant to a plea agreement, but the court reserves decision on whether to accept the plea agreement pending preparation of a PSR, the defendant may not change his mind and *as of right* withdraw his plea at any time prior to the judge's decision on the plea agreement. *Hyde* involved a charge bargain under Rule 11(c)(1)(A).

The Supreme Court ruled that the provisions of Federal Rule of Criminal Procedure 32(e) control. Thus, a defendant may only withdraw his guilty plea pending judicial acceptance of the plea bargain, in the words of Rule 32(e), "if the defendant shows any fair and just reason." Absent such a showing, a defendant who has entered into a recommended sentence bargain under Rule 11(c)(1)(B) is bound by the plea. Where a defendant has entered into a charge bargain under Rule 11(c)(1)(A) or a specific sentence bargain under Rule 11(c)(1)(C) and the court ultimately accepts the plea agreement, the defendant again is bound by his plea absent demonstration of a "fair and just reason" for a plea withdrawal. If the court rejects the Rule 11(c)(1)(A) charge bargain or a Rule 11(c)(1)(C) specific sentence agreement, however, the defendant is entitled by Rule 11(c)(5) to withdraw his plea without proffering any further reason. The *Hyde* holding has since been included in the text of Rule 11(d).

As noted, Federal Rule 11 and the U.S. Sentencing Guidelines contemplate that judges may defer formal acceptance of a plea until after the preparation of a PSR which will permit the judge to evaluate the "deal" being offered by the government in light of the sentence that would otherwise be applied to the defendant and those similarly situated. Where a judge has conducted a "thorough Rule 11 colloquy" but defers formal acceptance of the *guilty plea* (not, as in *Hyde*, of the plea agreement) until after the preparation of a pre-sentence report, should Rule 32(e)'s "fair and just reason" requirement apply? Most circuits have determined that even where the judge "defers" acceptance of the plea until after provision of a PSR, the judge's "provisional acceptance" after all Rule 11 findings have been made is sufficient to require application of Rule 32's requirements to a defendant who seeks to withdraw his plea; others refuse to construe deferral as a conditional acceptance.[23]

---

[21] Fed. R. Crim. P. 11(c)(3)(B).

[22] 520 U.S. 670 (1997).

[23] *See* United States v. Shaker, 279 F.3d 494, 497 (7th Cir. 2002) (accepting latter view and laying out circuit split).

2. GUIDELINES BARGAINING[24]

Prior to January 2005, and the Supreme Court's decision in *United States v. Booker*,[25] judges were bound by law to follow the U.S. Sentencing Guidelines. The Guidelines provide, among other things, certain policies that were designed to constrain judges in their decisions whether to accept or reject plea agreements. These policy statements, contained in Chapter 6 of the Guidelines, generally required judges to reject plea agreements tendered by the government and defense where those agreements would subvert the uniformity goals of sentencing reform. The Guidelines, when mandatory, also provided the structure within which the parties worked in negotiating and concluding deals. As outlined in Chapter 3, *Booker* revolutionized sentencing—and perhaps plea—practices. After *Booker*, the Guidelines are not binding in sentencing, although they continue to be one factor among many that judges should look to in determining sentence.

How has *Booker* affected plea bargaining? This is a critical question, but one that is, at this point, difficult to answer definitively. One might make the case that *Booker* necessarily introduces a greater degree of uncertainty into sentencing. That is, the parties can no longer be *confident* that the judge will follow the Guidelines and accordingly will be bargaining in the face of greater uncertainty regarding the sentencing result that would follow after any trial. Judges' sentencing choices are no longer as transparent as they were under the Guidelines. That is, it may be difficult to know just what factors the judge will consider important—and what quantum of evidence the judge will rely upon in finding those factors—in imposing sentence in a case. Finally, two 2007 Supreme Court decisions, *Gall v. United States*[26] and *Kimbrough v. United States*,[27] introduce further flexibility but also additional uncertainty into sentencing. In those cases, the Court underscored that its "reasonableness" standard of appellate review truly meant "abuse of discretion," and that the Court contemplates substantial appellate deference to district courts' exercises of sentencing discretion. One might forecast that these circumstances may dampen plea rates over time as defendants decide that there is insufficient certainty regarding whether they will in fact receive bargained-for sentencing dispensations. One could also argue, however, that judges' ability to be more flexible in sentencing may benefit defendants who plead out.

After *Booker*, the parties continued to bargain and plead, largely using the Guidelines construct to do so. Plea rates—which range around 97%—remained the same after *Booker*; indeed, plea rates have stayed within this range from at least 2002 to 2017.[28] Post-*Booker*, it appears that, for the most part, judges are following the "advisory" Guidelines range—or are deviating from it at the request of the government—in about 76-80% of cases, which is about 10-14% lower than the conformance rate prior to *Booker*. It should

---

[24] Much of the following is derived from a discussion included in an article, Julie R. O'Sullivan, *In Defense of the U.S. Sentencing Guidelines' Modified Real-Offense System*, 91 Nw. U. L. Rev. 1342 (1997). Thanks to Northwestern University Law Review for copyright permission to reprint and change portions of the text.

[25] 543 U.S. 220 (2005).

[26] 552 U.S. 38 (2007).

[27] 552 U.S. 85 (2007); *see also* Spears v. United States, 555 U.S. 261 (2009) (*per curiam*) (essentially holding that the Court meant what it said in *Kimbrough*).

[28] *See* U.S. Sentencing Comm'n, 2017 Sourcebook of Federal Sentencing Statistics, Fig. C (2017: 97.2%, 2016: 97.3%; 2015: 97.1%); U.S. Sentencing Comm'n, 2014 Sourcebook of Federal Sentencing Statistics, Fig. C (2014: 97.1%; 2013: 96.9%; 2012: 97.0%; 2011: 96.9%; 2010: 96.8%); U.S. Sentencing Comm'n, 2010 Annual Report, at 31; (96.8%); U.S. Sentencing Comm'n, 2009 Annual Report, at 36 (96.3%); U.S. Sentencing Comm'n, 2008 Sourcebook of Federal Sentencing Statistics, Fig. C (2008: 96.3%; 2007: 95.8%; 2006: 95.7%).

be noted that the conformance rate dropped each year after the *Booker* decision but appears to have stabilized at about 76%.[29] (Because there is a great variation around the country in the extent to which judges are following the Guidelines, however, this average conformance figure is somewhat misleading.)

When considering the effect of *Booker* on plea practices, departures become a critical focus because before *Booker* they were the principal means through which defendants could secure sentences outside the otherwise applicable Guidelines range. As we shall see, a government motion (under U.S.S.G. § 5K1.1) for "substantial assistance" in the investigation and prosecution of others was a particularly valuable bargaining chit, and one that, before *Booker*, could only be secured on government motion under the Guidelines. Some circuits have taken the position that, after *Booker*, "departures are beside the point"[30] and that *Booker* "rendered the departure apparatus and terminology archaic."[31] That said, the Sentencing Commission's data indicates that district courts continue to look to the Guidelines' departure rules to guide their sentencing choices. In particular, although the Sentencing Commission reports that, in some cases, district courts have sentenced below the otherwise applicable Guidelines range to recognize a defendant's "substantial assistance" even in absence of a government motion, it appears that this is not commonplace. The government continues to make substantial assistance and other departure motions. Although the number of substantial assistance motions dipped slightly post-*Booker*, the national average over the last few years is 11-12% of cases (but again, one must, in considering these statistics, understand that these numbers represent national averages and that there are variations by district in the government's substantial assistance motion practice).[32]

Perhaps the most important reason to believe that the parties will continue to look to the Guidelines and to pre-*Booker* government policies to structure plea bargaining practices is because the DOJ evidently believes that this is the correct way to proceed. In 2017, Attorney General Sessions instructed prosecutors that:

---

[29]"Conformance" is measured by adding the percentage of within-range sentences to the percentage of sentences that were below the range due to government-sponsored downward departures. In the pre-*Booker* period, from about October 2002 through mid-2004, the average nationwide "conformance" rate was a little over 90%. *See* U.S. Sentencing Comm'n, Final Report on the Impact of *United States v. Booker* on Federal Sentencing at vi-vii & n.9 (March 2006). The following summarizes how these percentages have changed over time, as derived from Sentencing Commission Reports and Sourcebooks: 2008, in-guidelines range (59.4%) plus government-sponsored downward departures (25.6%)=conformance rate of 85.0%; 2009: in-guidelines range (56.8%) plus government-sponsored downward departures (25.3%)=conformance rate of 82.1%; 2010: in-guidelines range (55%) plus government-sponsored downward departures (25.4%)=conformance rate of 80.4%; 2011: in-guidelines range (54.5%) plus government-sponsored downward departures (26.3%)=conformance rate of 80.8%; 2012: in-guidelines range (52.4%) plus government-sponsored downward departures (27.8%)=conformance rate of 80.2%; 2013: in-guidelines range (51.2%) plus government-sponsored downward departures (27.9%)=conformance rate of 79.1%; 2014: in-guidelines range (46%) plus government-sponsored downward departures (30.4%)=conformance rate of 76.4%; 2015: in-guidelines range (47.3%) plus government-sponsored downward departures (29.3%)=conformance rate of 76.6%; 2016: in-guidelines range (48.6%) plus government-sponsored downward departures (28.2%)=conformance rate of 76.8%.

[30] United States v. Laufle, 433 F.3d 981, 987 (7th Cir. 2006); *see also* United States v. Zolp, 479 F.3d 715, 722 (9th Cir. 2007).

[31] United States v. Hewlett, 453 F.3d 876, 881-82 (7th Cir. 2006) (Easterbrook, J., concurring).

[32] The Sentencing Commission's Sourcebooks and Annual Reports indicate that the national rate of substantial assistance departures on government motion post-*Booker* were 14.4% in 2007, 13.5% in 2008, 12.5% in 2009, and 11.5% in 2010; 11.2% in 2011; 11.7% in 2012; 12.1% in 2013; and 12.8% in 2014 (as compared, *e.g.*, with a rate of 15.9% in 2003).

[I]t is a core principle that prosecutors should charge and pursue the most serious, readily provable offense. ... By definition, the most serious offenses are those that carry the most substantial [G]uidelines sentence, including mandatory minimum sentences.

There will be circumstances in which good judgment would lead a prosecutor to conclude that a strict application of the above charging policy is not warranted. In that case, prosecutors should carefully consider whether an exception may be justified. Consistent with longstanding Department of Justice policy, any decision to vary from the policy must be approved by a United States Attorney or Assistant Attorney General, or a supervisor designated by [such persons], and the reasons must be documented in the file.

Memorandum to Federal Prosecutors from U.S. Attorney General Sessions, Department Charging and Sentencing Policy (May 10, 2017). Although the press covered Attorney General Sessions' policy statement as though these rules were new, in fact that are not; it has been long-standing Justice Department policy to charge the "most serious, readily provable" count(s). What has changed with administrations is the degree to which individual Assistant United States Attorneys have discretion to deviate from this rule in individual cases without high level supervisory approval. Attorneys General in Republican administrations generally took a firm line against such exercises of discretion while Attorneys General in Democratic administrations tended to be more open to it.

As discussed in Chapter 3, the U.S. Sentencing Commission adopted a modified real-offense sentencing system. The Commission's decision to lean toward a real-offense, as opposed to a charge-offense system, was motivated in part by its desire to inhibit the extent to which prosecutors could manipulate sentencing results through their charging and plea bargaining decisions. The Guidelines' modified real-offense system was designed not to interfere with traditional prosecutorial charging criteria but rather to dampen the extent to which prosecutors may bargain in the currency of sentence to accommodate those criteria. In theory, at least with respect to the aggregable offenses that constitute the majority of federal criminal cases, a prosecutor often could not, based upon her evaluation of the imperatives of her caseload or her need for the defendant's cooperation, offer sentence discounts to induce pleas or provide differing incentives to different defendants (aside from § 5K1.1 motions, discussed *infra*). A prosecutor could allocate her resources as she deemed fit and pursue whatever instrumental or other goals she wished, but the power to affect certain results—*e.g.*, to induce a plea or cooperation—by manipulating the defendant's sentence was *in theory* denied her by operation of the "real" elements of the Guidelines system. *Booker*, of course, rendered these rules, as all others, advisory only; accordingly, if judges do not elect to follow the Guidelines' rules they may allow the government additional leeway.

Obviously, the U.S. Sentencing Commission's intent here was to reduce the extent to which prosecutors may reintroduce sentencing disparities through their idiosyncratic charging and plea bargaining choices. When a judge sentences a defendant on the basis of what he "really" did as opposed to simply what the prosecutor chose to charge, disparities among similarly situated defendants that may flow from prosecutorial decisions are, again in theory, avoided.

If prosecutors under the mandatory Guidelines system were unable to affect sentencing results through their charging and plea bargaining decisions, what tools were left to them to induce pleas and cooperation? Deprived of the ability to deal in the commodity that defendants often value most (certain and calculable sentencing concessions), with what could prosecutors bargain under the Guidelines? The following gives an overview of some common bargaining techniques, both before and after *Booker*.

a. Acceptance of Responsibility

The Guidelines do not entirely ignore the resource constraints under which federal prosecutors operate. They provide an incentive to plead guilty, but state that that incentive should be the same for all defendants: the approximately 35% reduction in sentence that can be achieved through the combination of a two-level credit for "acceptance of responsibility" and the imposition of a sentence at the lowest portion of the resultant Guidelines range. The guilty plea rate appeared to have remained roughly constant from pre-Guidelines practice through the mandatory Guidelines era and now to the post-*Booker* era. If one accepts that prosecutors were manipulating the mandatory Guidelines to provide additional discounts in only a minority of cases, this statistic indicates that the mandatory Guidelines' plea discount was normally sufficient to allow prosecutors to secure a satisfactory conviction rate, allocate resources rationally given local needs, and pursue instrumental goals (*i.e.*, induce cooperation). Thus, through substitution of a uniform concession for bargaining, the mandatory Guidelines removed a potential source of disuniformity but apparently not at an undue cost, in the usual case, to executive prerogatives.

Although it is difficult to generalize because the extent and type of pre-*Booker* Guidelines subversion varied from district to district, the available study results indicate that this accommodation broke down principally in cases where potentially applicable penalties were perceived to be too high. In these cases—particularly those in which mandatory sentence enhancements or mandatory minimum penalties applied—the pre-*Booker* evidence suggests that prosecutors engaged in Guidelines manipulation either because they felt that the principled application of the Guidelines would result in an unconscionably high sentence, or because they believed that the uniform plea concession was insufficient to induce pleas at an efficient rate or to secure defendants' cooperation. There is no post-*Booker* data, but one presumes that the same impetus yields the same result under an advisory Guidelines system.

b. Charge Bargaining

Where the choice of charge could affect sentence under the mandatory Guidelines, prosecutors sometimes sought to bargain away counts—either forgoing them (pre-indictment) or agreeing to drop them (post-indictment)—in return for a plea or an agreement to cooperate. This is commonly known as "charge bargaining" of a type still contemplated in Fed. R. Crim. P. 11(c)(1)(A). If the Commission had embraced a pure real-offense system, presumably charge-bargaining would have been fairly useless. However, the mandatory Guidelines continued to contain "charge" elements and thus charge bargaining was still possible:

i. *Manipulation of mandatory minimums, statutory maximums.* Because the statutory maximums and minimums trump the Guidelines, a prosecutor who, given the evidence, could bring a count containing a mandatory minimum sentence could bargain away that count if the defendant was willing to plead to a lesser count that did not carry a mandatory minimum. Similarly, prosecutors could agree to drop a statutory charge that carried a mandatory sentence enhancement (for example, a mandatory 5 year penalty for violating 18 U.S.C. § 924(c) (using or carrying a gun in connection with a crime of violence or drug trafficking offense)) in return for a plea to other counts.

More important in most white-collar cases (where applicable statutes generally do not carry mandatory minimums or mandatory sentence enhancements), the parties could manipulate the sentencing result by agreeing on a charge or charges for which the maximum statutory penalty was less than the sentencing range that would result from application of the mandatory Guidelines to the facts of the criminal conduct at issue. For example, assume that a defendant, with others, committed a series of mail frauds. Assume further that the defendant's Guidelines exposure was well over five years because of the large amount of loss involved. In such circumstances, the parties could bargain to "cap" the defendant's exposure to five years by agreeing to a plea to only one conspiracy count under 18 U.S.C. § 371 (which continues to carry a 5-year maximum sentence) rather than conspiracy to commit mail fraud under 18 U.S.C. § 1349 (which carries a 20-year maximum and would not therefore operate to "cap" the defendant's Guidelines exposure).

ii. *Manipulation of charging with respect to nonaggregable offenses.* Recall that nonaggregable offenses are not subject to the Guidelines' relevant conduct provisions. Thus, a prosecutor could induce pleas by agreeing to forgo or drop certain nonaggregable counts.[33]

iii. *Manipulation where Guidelines results differ depending upon the statute charged.* In certain cases, one statutory charge could yield a longer sentence than another under the mandatory Guidelines. For example, a defendant who was charged with money laundering often was, under the mandatory Guidelines, subject to greater sentencing exposure than a defendant who was simply charged with the underlying offenses that generated the money laundered. Thus, a prosecutor could bargain away a money laundering count in return, for example, for pleas to the wire frauds that gave rise to the tainted cash.

Booker obviously made statutory maxima the most important constraint on sentences; accordingly, *Booker* makes prosecutorial charging choices—and charge bargaining—exceedingly important. Prosecutors may have the power to charge bargain, but DOJ policy, in theory, may constrain them in some instances. Once a decision has been made to initiate a prosecution, DOJ policy instructs prosecutors to charge, or recommend that the grand jury charge, "the most serious offense that is consistent with the nature ... of the defendant's conduct and likely to result in a sustainable conviction."[34] In requiring that prosecutors "initially charge the most serious, readily provable offense or offenses consistent with the defendant's conduct," the DOJ cautions that "[c]harges should not be filed simply to exert leverage to induce a plea, nor should charges be abandoned in an effort to arrive at a bargain that fails to reflect the seriousness of the defendant's conduct."[35]

Importantly, the Department of Justice still defines the "most serious" offenses as "those that carry the *most substantial guidelines sentence.*"[36] If multiple violations can be levied, the Department of Justice requires that federal prosecutors bring all charges necessary to ensure that the information or indictment: "[a]dequately reflects the nature and extent of the criminal conduct involved" and "[p]rovides the basis for an appropriate

---

[33] As we know, the § 1B1.3(a)(2) relevant conduct rule applies only to those offenses groupable under § 3D1.2(d)—that is, aggregable offenses (such as drug and financial crimes). Thus, where a defendant commits three (non-aggregable) bank robberies as a part of a common scheme or plan but is charged with and convicted of only one count of robbery, the circumstances of the other crimes may not be considered as relevant conduct under § 1B1.3(a)(2) in determining the Chapter Two offense level, Chapter Two specific offense characteristics, or the applicable Chapter Three adjustments. Absent an upward departure to reflect related but uncharged non-aggregable offenses, it is only where all three robberies are charged that the defendant will be treated in line with other similarly situated defendants and receive a proportional increase in his punishment through the operation of the grouping rules under the (advisory) Guidelines regime.

[34] U.S.A.M. § 9-27.300(A).

[35] *Id.* § 9-27.300(B).

[36] *Id.* § 9-27.300(A) (emphasis added); *see also id.* § 9-27.300(B).

sentence" or "[w]ill significantly enhance the strength of the government's case against the defendant or a co-defendant."[37]

In considering whether to agree to a disposition of a case by negotiated plea, the prosecutor must assess not only sentencing-related factors, but also such criteria as "the defendant's willingness to cooperate against others, the defendant's criminal record, the nature and seriousness of the offense, the defendant's remorse or contrition, the desirability of a prompt and certain disposition of the case, the likelihood of obtaining a conviction at trial, the probable effect on witnesses, the probable sentence or consequence if the defendant is convicted, the public interest in having a trial as opposed to a plea, the expense of trial and appeal, the need to avoid delay in the disposition of other pending cases, and the effect on the victim's right to restitution."[38] However, once a determination is made based upon all these considerations that a plea agreement is worthwhile, a prosecutor generally must require a defendant to plead to a charge: "[t]hat is the most serious readily provable charge consistent with the nature and extent of his/her criminal conduct;" "[t]hat has an adequate factual basis;" "[t]hat makes likely the imposition of an appropriate sentence and order of restitution, if appropriate;" and "[t]hat does not adversely affect the investigation or prosecution of others."[39] It should be noted, however, that the DOJ believes that the "requirement that a defendant plead to a charge that is consistent with the nature and extent of his/her criminal conduct is not inflexible" and may be bent when necessary to secure necessary cooperation.[40]

In charge negotiations, the DOJ continues, post-*Booker*, to caution prosecutors to "take care to avoid a 'charge agreement' that would unduly restrict the court's sentencing authority" by imposing a statutory cap on the otherwise applicable Guidelines range.[41] It also states generally that:

> Charge agreements envision dismissal of counts in exchange for a plea. As with the indictment decision, the prosecutor should seek a plea to the most serious readily provable offense(s) charged. Should a prosecutor determine in good faith after indictment that, as a result of a change in the evidence or for another reason (e.g., a need has arisen to protect sources and methods, including the identity of a particular witness until he or she testifies against a more significant defendant), a charge is not readily provable or that an indictment exaggerates the seriousness of an offense or offenses, a plea bargain may reflect the prosecutor's reassessment.[42]

There are limited exceptions to the "basic policy ... that charges are not to be bargained away or dropped."[43] The two most relevant in white-collar practice provide that prosecutors can drop readily provable charges where (1) dropping the charges will not affect the sentencing calculus; or (2) upon the approval of the U.S. Attorney or a designated supervisor where extraordinary considerations exist—"[f]or example, ... the United States Attorney's office is particularly over-burdened, the case would be time-consuming to try, and proceeding to trial would significantly reduce the total number of cases disposed of by

---

[37] *Id.* § 9-27.320(A).

[38] *Id.* § 9-27.420(A).

[39] *Id.* § 9-27.430(A).

[40] *Id.* § 9-27.430(B)(1).

[41] *Id.* § 9-27.430(B)(3).

[42] *Id.* § 9-27.400(B).

[43] *Id.*

the office."[44] In short, in recognition of the fact that "the aims of the Sentencing Reform Act must be sought without ignoring other, critical aspects of the federal criminal justice system,"[45] the Department of Justice reserves to its prosecutors the right—in exceptional cases and only with high level approval—to override the highest readily provable count policy where necessary to induce pleas that will permit an Office to order its resources consistent with law enforcement imperatives in that district.

As noted above, although these provisions of the U.S. Attorney's Manual appear to severely cabin individual prosecutor's charging choices where those choices affect sentencing results, various administrations have, while formally endorsing the rules, indicated that line assistants may in fact have more discretion than the rules suggest. Attorney General Sessions' 2017 instruction to federal prosecutors demonstrates that he will tolerate far less discretion than was the case under Attorney General Eric Holder.[46]

Studies conducted before *Booker* was decided revealed that prosecutors charge bargained in contravention of these policies in a minority of cases. As noted above, the bargaining away of mandatory minimum counts and charges carrying mandatory sentence enhancements was a particularly common practice. Two ways in which the parties evaded these policies while appearing to comply was first, classification of count(s) as "not readily provable" (an inherently subjective standard), and second, use of the resource exception noted above.

c. Guidelines "Fact" or "Factor" Bargaining

In those cases in which the "real" circumstances of the offense drive sentence, prosecutors in some cases sought to bargain away aggravating "real" facts or Guidelines factors in order to induce a plea. This is commonly known as Guidelines "fact" or "factor" bargaining and is still reflected in Fed. R. Crim. P. 11(c)(1)(B) and (C). For example, under the mandatory Guidelines, prosecutors might agree that a certain amount of the loss potentially chargeable should not be used ("fact" bargaining) or they might stipulate that an otherwise appropriate Chapter Three adjustment should not be assessed in a given case ("factor" bargaining). An implicit or explicit part of this bargain was sometimes an agreement not to discuss with the probation department or the sentencing judge the facts or factors bargained away.

Again, prosecutors are constrained in "fact" or "factor" bargaining by a variety of potentially applicable rules. A prosecutor who misrepresents the true scope of the defendant's relevant conduct or the factual or legal applicability of other aggravating factors in order to affect the applicable Guidelines range or departure analysis risks professional and ethical censure.[47] Such misrepresentations are certainly contrary to Guidelines

---

[44] *Id.*

[45] *Id.*

[46] Eric H. Holder, Jr., Attorney General, Memorandum to all Federal Prosecutors, Dep't Policy on Charging and Sentencing (May 19, 2010).

[47] *See, e.g.*, Memorandum for All Federal Prosecutors from Attorney General Sessions, Department Charging and Sentencing Policy (May 10, 2017) ("prosecutors must disclose to the sentencing court all facts that impact the sentencing guidelines or mandatory minimum sentences"); U.S.A.M. § 9-27.430(B)(2) ("[T]he Department's policy is only to stipulate to facts that accurately reflect the defendant's conduct. If a prosecutor wishes to support a departure from the guidelines, he or she should candidly do so and not stipulate to facts that are untrue. *Stipulations to untrue facts are unethical. If a prosecutor has insufficient facts to contest a defendant's effort to seek a downward departure or to claim an adjustment, the prosecutor can say so.*") (emphasis added); *id.* § 9-27.400(B); Hon. John Gleeson, *Sentence Bargaining Under the Guidelines*, 8 No. 6 Fed. Sentencing Rep. 314 (May/June 1996) ("[L]ying to a court, or deceiving it by withholding relevant facts, is wrong, period, and there is never a valid justification for it."); Am. Bar Ass'n Standards for Criminal Justice: Prosecution Function and Defense Function Standard 3-2.8(a) (1993) ("A prosecutor should not intentionally misrepresent matters of fact or law

policy.[48] The most common way such agreements were justified under the mandatory Guidelines regime was to label the bargained-away "facts" or "factors" as "not readily provable"—an assertion that is not susceptible to ready second-guessing by the probation department, courts, or the Sentencing Commission.[49]

d. Sentencing Bargaining

Fed. R. Crim. P. 11(c)(1)(B) and (C) permit the parties to agree to a recommended or specific sentence. The DOJ contemplates that prosecutors have a number of options regarding sentence negotiation: "taking no position regarding the sentence; not opposing the defendant's request; requesting a specific type of sentence (*e.g.*, a fine or probation), a specific fine or term of imprisonment, or not more than a specific fine or term of imprisonment; and requesting concurrent rather than consecutive sentences."[50] It states that "[a]greement to any such option must be consistent with the guidelines."[51] The DOJ notes that specific or recommended sentence bargains come in two basic types: those in which prosecutors bargain for a sentence that is within the Guidelines range, and those in which prosecutors bargain in departures from the applicable Guidelines range. The latter type of bargain involves a prosecutor agreeing to stipulate to, or at least not to oppose, a given departure.

Under the mandatory Guidelines, the ultimate decision to make a departure, and if a departure was made, the extent of the departure, were matters within the district judge's sole discretion. Accordingly, as a practical matter the parties in the pre-*Booker* period generally found this to be a less appealing bargaining tool than those noted above because it did not involve a certain and calculable sentencing concession. The parties sometimes attempted to ensure that the departure was a "done deal" by hiding it in a charge bargain or a stipulation to facts that were not true. The DOJ was unusually emphatic in forbidding this practice.[52]

---

to the court."); Model Rule of Prof'l Conduct 3.1 ("A lawyer shall not bring or defend a proceeding, or assert or controvert an issue therein, unless there is a basis in law or fact for doing so that is not frivolous."); *id.* Rule 8.4(c), (d) ("It is professional misconduct for a lawyer to ... engage in conduct involving dishonesty, ... deceit or misrepresentation; ... [or to] engage in conduct that is prejudicial to the administration of justice."); Model Code of Prof'l Responsibility DR 1-102(A)(4), (5) (1983) (A lawyer shall not "[e]ngage in conduct involving dishonesty, ... deceit, or misrepresentation ... [or] [e]ngage in conduct that is prejudicial to the administration of justice.").

[48] *See* U.S.S.G. § 6B1.4, comment. ("[I]t is not appropriate for the parties to stipulate to misleading or non-existent facts, even when both parties are willing to assume the existence of such 'facts' for purposes of the litigation. Rather, the parties should fully disclose the actual facts and then explain to the court the reasons why the disposition of the case should differ from that which such facts ordinarily would require under the guidelines.").

[49] Prosecutors may read DOJ policy to allow them to hold back from the Probation Department and the court those facts or issues that they determine are not "readily provable." However, it is clear that "readily provable" determinations should be made on the basis of a "good faith" doubt as to the legal or evidentiary sufficiency of a sentencing fact or factor. *See, e.g.*, U.S.A.M. § 9-27.400(B).

[50] *Id.* § 9-27.400(B)(2).

[51] *Id.*

[52] *Id.* ("Department policy requires transparency and honesty in sentencing; federal prosecutors are expected to identify for the court departures when they agree to support them. For example, it would be improper for a prosecutor to agree that a departure is in order, but to conceal the agreement in a charge bargain that is presented to a court as a fait accompli so that there is neither a record of nor judicial review of the departure."); *see also id.* § 9-27.430(B)(2) (departures should not be hidden in untrue factual stipulations).

The pre-*Booker* evidence also indicated that the parties had increasingly been using as a bargaining tool departures under Federal Sentencing Guidelines § 5K1.1 for "substantial assistance" the defendant (purportedly) provided the government in the investigation and prosecution of others. Although the parties could not guarantee that a judge would make such a departure, when the government lodged a substantial assistance motion judges generally paid attention. The downside of this approach, from the parties' perspective, was that once a motion was made, the extent of the departure was within the district judge's sole discretion.

As was discussed above, the degree to which the parties and judges feel the need to even discuss departures after *Booker* made the Guidelines advisory is subject to some question. This may not, then, be the most fruitful area for negotiation going forward, at least in some districts.

e. Enforcement

Where both parties agree to a bargain that contravenes Guidelines principles or DOJ policy, how can such subversion of uniformity goals be prevented? First, the probation department is charged with independently investigating the facts of the offense in preparing its pre-sentence report (PSR). Thus, for example, if the prosecutor stipulates to a lesser amount of loss than the facts would support, the probation department in theory will bring this to the sentencing judge's attention. This safeguard is not always effective. The probation department primarily relies upon the parties—and particularly the prosecutor—to supply the facts of the case and thus its "independent" inquiry may be thwarted by parties eager to conclude the bargain.

Second, courts are supposed to police the parties' attempts to subvert the Guidelines through their power under Fed. R. Crim. P. 11 and Guidelines Chapter Six to approve plea agreements. Congress directed the Commission to "issue policy statements for consideration by Federal judges in deciding whether to accept a plea agreement," in the belief that "[t]his guidance will assure that judges can examine plea agreements to make certain that prosecutors have not used plea bargaining to undermine the sentencing guidelines."[53] Pursuant to this congressional mandate, the Commission provided standards to which judges should refer in deciding whether to accept a plea bargain under Rule 11. These policy statements, found in Guidelines Chapter Six, contemplate that the judge will compare the Guidelines sentence that the defendant would receive under the plea bargain with that which would be applicable to the defendant and other offenders similarly situated in absence of a plea.

The Guidelines advise that where a plea agreement contemplates the dismissal of charges or an undertaking not to pursue potential charges,[54] a judge should accept the agreement only if "the remaining charges adequately reflect the seriousness of the actual offense behavior and ... accepting the agreement will not undermine the statutory purposes of sentencing or the sentencing guidelines."[55] In cases where the plea agreement contains a nonbinding sentence recommendation[56] or an agreement on a specific sentence,[57] the judge should accept the deal only if the recommended or agreed "sentence is within the

---

[53] S. Rep. No. 98-225, at 63 (1983); *see* 28 U.S.C. § 994(a)(2)(E).

[54] *See* Fed. R. Crim. P. 11(c)(1)(A).

[55] U.S.S.G. § 6B1.2(a).

[56] *See* Fed. R. Crim. P. 11(c)(1)(B).

[57] *See id.* Rule 11(c)(1)(C).

applicable guideline range"[58] or the recommended or agreed sentence "is outside the applicable guideline range for justifiable reasons."[59]

After *Booker*, of course, these rules are advisory only. How is *Booker* likely to affect judges' practices in scrutinizing proposed pleas for their compliance with guideline standards? The available evidence from the pre-*Booker* era suggests that judges have been reluctant to use their Rule 11 and Chapter Six plea rejection power to police the extent to which prosecutors are subverting uniformity goals through their charging and plea bargaining powers. There are a number of reasons for this reluctance, including many judges' objection to the perceived unfairness or excessiveness of Guidelines sentences, and their sense that judicial supervision of prosecutorial plea choices is inappropriate or unconstitutional. It remains to be seen how the freedom *Booker* gives sentencing judges will affect this judicial reluctance to second-guess plea agreements proffered for the court's approval.

C. COOPERATION AGREEMENTS

Cooperation agreements are one type of plea agreement. (Some cooperation agreements confer immunity, require no plea of guilty from the defendant, and thus are not truly plea agreements; such cooperation deals are treated in Chapter 15 (Fifth Amendment: Testimony and Immunity).) Typically, in cooperation plea agreements, the defendant agrees to plead guilty to specified charges and to cooperate with the government. In return, the government often undertakes to dismiss or forgo other possible counts and/or to ask a judge to consider the defendant's cooperation in sentencing.

1. POLICY DISCUSSION: *UNITED STATES v. SINGLETON*

"The prosecutorial prerogative to recommend leniency in exchange for testimony dates back to the common law in England and has been recognized and approved by Congress, the courts, and the Sentencing Commission of the United States."[60] Despite its historical pedigree, however, it is a practice that continues to discomfit many commentators, and some judges. In 1998, a unanimous panel of the Tenth Circuit sent a shock wave through the federal criminal bar by overturning the conviction of a defendant convicted of money laundering and conspiring to distribute cocaine on a theory that threatened a frontal assault on the practice of bargained-for testimony. The panel held in *United States v. Singleton (Singleton I)*[61] that the testimony of a codefendant should have been suppressed because the prosecuting attorney violated the federal gratuities statute, 18 U.S.C. § 201(c)(2), in offering the codefendant leniency ("something of value") in return for his truthful testimony.[62] This panel decision was quickly reversed by the Tenth Circuit sitting en banc (*Singleton II*).[63] (The Tenth Circuit has since also rejected a claim that allowing testimony of unindicted co-conspirators whose testimony has been induced by

---

[58] U.S.S.G. § 6B1.2(b)(1), (c)(1).

[59] *Id.* § 6B1.2(b)(2), (c)(2).

[60] United States v. Ware, 161 F.3d 414, 419 (6th Cir. 1998).

[61] 144 F.3d 1343 (10th Cir. 1998).

[62] Section 201(c)(2) states: "Whoever ... directly or indirectly, gives, offers, or promises anything of value to any person, for or because of the testimony under oath or affirmation given or to be given by such person as a witness upon a trial ... before any court ... shall be fined under this title or imprisoned for not more than two years, or both."

[63] United States v. Singleton, 165 F.3d 1297 (10th Cir. 1999) (*en banc*).

offers of lenient treatment violates due process.[64]) The *en banc* court, over the dissent of the original panel members, held that § 201(c)(2) does not apply to the United States or an Assistant United States Attorney functioning within the official scope of her office.[65] The rejection of *Singleton I* by the other circuits has been aptly characterized as a "stampede."[66]

Most courts to address the issue have focused on the question whether "Whoever" within the meaning of the gratuities statute includes Assistant U.S. Attorneys who obtain testimony from cooperating witnesses by promises of leniency, and have concluded that it does not.[67] In doing so, they have relied on a canon of construction recognized by the Supreme Court in *Nardone v. United States*.[68] In *Nardone*, the Court ruled that a statute should not be read to apply to the government when doing so would (1) deprive the sovereign of a recognized or established prerogative, or (2) lead to absurd results.[69]

Representative is the Third Circuit's reasoning in *United States v. Hunte*.[70] That court noted first that "construing section 201(c)(2) to preclude the government from offering leniency in exchange for truthful testimony would deprive the sovereign of an established and recognized prerogative" in that "'[t]he prosecutorial prerogative to recommend leniency in exchange for truthful testimony arises from English common law, and has been repeatedly approved by the United States Supreme Court.'"[71] Second, the court noted "application of section 201(c)(2) to the government in cases such as this would work an obvious absurdity" because "interpreting section 201(c)(2) to forbid promises of leniency in exchange for truthful testimony would 'preclude enforcement or limit the efficacy of the terms of several more recent—and more specific—statutes [or Rules or Guidelines enacted pursuant to statute], all of which presuppose the potential use of testimony in exchange for non-prosecution agreements, leniency recommendations, and/or other valuable promises.'"[72] The court noted that "[n]umerous statutes adopted after the anti-gratuity law, for example, authorize sentence reductions for defendants who have provided 'substantial assistance' in the investigation or prosecution of others," including U.S.S.G. § 5K1.1 (allowing government motion for a sentence reduction below the applicable sentencing range when a defendant provides substantial assistance) and Fed. R. Crim. P. 35(b) (allowing government motion for a sentence reduction based on post-sentencing substantial assistance).[73] Finally, the court concluded that "we reject the holding of *Singleton I* because it is completely implausible to us that Congress, in enacting section 201(c)(2), intended to sub silentio overrule the government's long-standing practice of entering into leniency-for-testimony agreements."[74]

---

[64] United States v. Fria Vazquez Del Mercado, 223 F.3d 1213 (10th Cir. 2000) (relying on Hoffa v. United States, 385 U.S. 293, 310-11 (1966)).

[65] *Singleton*, 165 F.3d 1297.

[66] United States v. Lowery, 166 F.3d 1119, 1123 (11th Cir. 1999).

[67] *See* United States v. Smith, 196 F.3d 1034 (9th Cir. 1999); United States v. Albanese, 195 F.3d 389 (8th Cir. 1999); United States v. Hunte, 193 F.3d 173 (3d Cir. 1999); United States v. Stephenson, 183 F.3d 110 (2d Cir. 1999); United States v. Lara, 181 F.3d 183, 197 (1st Cir. 1999); *Singleton II*, 165 F.3d at 1298; United States v. Ramsey, 165 F.3d 980 (D.C .Cir. 1999).

[68] 302 U.S. 379 (1937).

[69] *Id.* at 383-84.

[70] 193 F.3d 173.

[71] *Id.* at 175.

[72] *Id.*

[73] *Id.* at 176.

[74] *Id.*

One circuit, the Seventh, took a different path to the same result. The Seventh Circuit held that "a promise not to prosecute a witness (or to secure a lower sentence for the witness) is not a 'thing of value' under § 201(c)(2)."[75] The court expressed some reservation about embracing the *Singleton II* court's holding—that the term "Whoever" does not include federal prosecutors—reasoning that such an approach, "if taken seriously, would permit prosecutors to pay cash for favorable testimony, a practice that lacks the statutory and historical support of immunity and sentence reduction."[76] While some courts have reserved this issue,[77] others have expressly held that the government does not violate the gratuities statute by paying an informant for his assistance and testimony.[78]

The members of the *Singleton I* panel, in dissent in *Singleton II*, obviously disagreed with the *en banc* court in assessing the meaning of the word "Whoever." They argued, in essence, that "'Whoever' means Whoever."[79] In responding to the majority's reasoning and to the criticism the *Singleton I* decision received, however, the *Singleton II* dissent articulated a much more fundamental disagreement regarding the necessity and value of bargained-for testimony:

> In holding that § 201(c)(2) simply does not apply to the government, the court does not hold that leniency in exchange for testimony does not constitute "anything of value." To be sure, the investigation and prosecution of criminal wrongdoing is an important societal function. Yet, largely missing from the debate since the panel opinion was issued is any concern for the other deeply held values that § 201(c) was intended to protect and which, I believe, the panel opinion honored by applying § 201(c) as Congress wrote it. Those concerns center on maintaining the integrity, fairness, and credibility of our system of criminal justice. ...
>
> Contrary to the concerns expressed by some commentators and courts, a straight-forward interpretation of § 201(c), which encompasses a prohibition against the government buying witness testimony with leniency, actually aids the search for truth. In theory, the leniency is only in exchange for "truthful" testimony. But as the Supreme Court has recognized: "Common sense would suggest that [an accused accomplice] often has a greater interest in lying in favor of the prosecution rather than against it, especially if he is still awaiting his own trial or sentencing. To think that criminals will lie to save their fellows but not to obtain favors from the prosecution for themselves is indeed to clothe the criminal class with more nobility than one might expect to find in the public at large." *Washington v. Texas*, 388 U.S. 14, 22-23 (1967). To be sure, there are devices that partially ameliorate the problem. The government is required to disclose exculpatory information, including impeachment information, to a defendant. Testifying accomplices may be cross-examined. Their credibility may be impeached, and the jury is instructed that it may regard such testimony with caution. However, all of these devices have limitations. In the real world of trial and uncertain proof, and in view of § 201(c), a witness's demeanor and actual testimony are simply too important to hinge upon promises of leniency. Although the court notes that a prosecutor who procures false testimony could be prosecuted for subornation of perjury, 18 U.S.C. § 1622, such a remedy offers little practical advantage to a defendant facing trial. By barring an exchange of leniency for testimony, Congress in § 201(c) has sought to eliminate, *at the source*, the most obvious incentive for false testimony.

---

[75] United States v. Condon, 170 F.3d 687, 689 (7th Cir. 1999).

[76] *Id.*

[77] *See, e.g., Hunte*, 193 F.3d at 176 n.4.

[78] *See, e.g.*, United States v. Anty, 203 F.3d 305 (4th Cir. 2000); *Albanese*, 195 F.3d 389.

[79] *Singleton II*, 165 F.3d at 1310 (dissenting opinion).

On the other side of the ledger is my concern for the institutional role of Article III courts. Much of this case has been about policy. I accept the government's position that accomplices can provide important information and interpreting § 201(c) to include prosecutors might require some changes to elicit testimony of some witnesses. While it would be up to the Department of Justice to devise ways of compliance, the government is not precluded from offering leniency in exchange for information and assistance short of actual testimony at trial. Likewise, the government could prosecute accomplices first, then compel their testimony by subpoena against co-conspirators.[80] Finally, the government could request that the district court order an accomplice to testify under a grant of immunity. Surely the Department has the ability and resources to come up with effective and lawful means for procuring necessary accomplice testimony. However, I also accept the defense attorneys' position that government leniency in exchange for testimony can create a powerful incentive to lie and derail the truth-seeking purpose of the criminal justice system. The very nature and complexity of this policy debate reinforces my initial belief that this is an argument better left to Congress. This court must perform its constitutional duties and no more. Ours is not to explore the farthest meanings that the term "whoever" can bear so as to effectuate the policy we think best. ... I continue to believe that meaning is clear: § 201(c), as written, applies to prosecutors and criminal defendants alike. If the balance struck by § 201 is to be reweighed, that reweighing should be done by the policymaking branch of government—the Congress, and not the courts. ... [81]

Which side has the better of the statutory interpretation debate? To the extent that "policy" differences are driving that debate, which side do you find more persuasive?[82] Are

---

[80] [Dissent's footnote 3:] One way prosecutors could obtain information and assistance short of actual testimony at trial is to enter into a plea agreement with a defendant under Fed.R.Crim.P. 11(c). Section 201(c) does not prohibit Rule 11(e) plea agreements in which the defendant pleads in exchange for *information* helpful to the prosecution if the plea agreement is not conditioned on the defendant testifying. However, the prosecutor could record the plea discussions to preserve the information provided by the defendant. After the defendant enters his guilty plea and is sentenced, the prosecutor could subpoena him as a witness in a trial of the other participants in the crime. If the defendant testified contrary to the statements he made during the plea negotiations, the government could impeach him with the record of his prior statements. *See United States v. Mezzanatto*, 513 U.S. 196 (1995) (upholding waiver of exclusionary provisions of Rule 11(e)). It is important to note that the defendant's trial testimony in this situation is compelled through subpoena, and is not given in exchange for anything of value. Such a practice protects every legitimate prosecutorial concern expressed in this case by the government and refutes its contention that the criminal justice system would be crippled if it could not offer leniency to a defendant in exchange for testimony.

[81] *Singleton II*, 165 F.3d at 1308-10 (dissenting opinion).

[82] With respect to the central concern—the potential for perjury—it is extremely difficult to study the extent of such perjury in an empirical way. However, Professor Ellen Yaroshefsky conducted extensive interviews with prosecutors and defense lawyers who practiced in the Southern District of New York, addressing such topics as "the extent to which prosecutors believe that they are able to obtain truthful information from cooperators and the basis for those beliefs, safeguards and techniques utilized to assure the truthfulness of cooperators, and perceived problems with obtaining truthful information from cooperators." Ellen Yaroshefsky, *Cooperation with Federal Prosecutors: Experiences of Truth Telling and Embellishment*, 68 Fordham L. Rev. 917, 921 (1999). She concludes that:

The interviews that form the basis of this article expose the reasons that prosecutors may believe unreliable information provided by cooperators. These reasons are: lack of corroboration for cooperator information, particularly in small narcotics and historical gang cases; lack of thorough investigation; insufficient evidence; unwarranted trust of cooperators; the development of a rigid theory of a given case; cultural barriers between defendants and prosecutors; attitudes of individual assistants; and lack of experience of many assistants. Many of these problems are reflected in the conduct of proffer sessions where additional psychological factors and dynamics

cooperating witnesses the only types of witnesses who may be perceived as "interested" and who thus may be inclined to embellish or manufacture evidence? Can we rely on the means generally employed to defeat perjury by interested witnesses—full disclosure of cooperation deals, adversarial cross-examination, summation arguments, and strong charges to juries warning of the dangers of cooperating witness testimony—or do cooperating witnesses present a unique case?[83] As a practical matter, how viable are the alternatives suggested by the *en banc* dissent? Is the suggestion posed in footnote 3 of the dissenting opinion (footnote 80 in this chapter) workable and does it obviate the concerns regarding perjured testimony that so concerned the dissent?

One way of examining this issue is to consider why a ban on giving things of value to witnesses should apply to the defense but not the government. As Professor David Sklansky asks:

> Among the acts by President Clinton that the Referral [submitted to Congress by Independent Counsel Kenneth Starr] suggested "may constitute grounds for impeachment" were [the President's] efforts to help Monica Lewinsky find a job while discovery was underway in the Paula Jones case. Starr suggested that these efforts may have constituted "witness tampering," depending on the President's intent: "The question ... is whether the President's efforts in obtaining a job for Ms. Lewinsky were to influence her testimony or simply to help an ex-intimate without concern for her testimony." And Starr concluded that the President's intent appeared to have been criminal: "There is substantial and credible information that the President assisted Ms. Lewinsky in her job search motivated at least in part by his desire to keep her 'on the team' in the Jones litigation."
>
> Of course Starr's office made its own considerable efforts to get and to keep Lewinsky "on the team." In return for her written agreement "to cooperate fully," by among other things "testify[ing] truthfully," the Independent Counsel gave her use immunity (a promise not to use her statements, or evidence derived from her statements, against her in any criminal case), transactional immunity (a promise not to prosecute her for any previous offenses within Starr's jurisdiction), and transactional immunity for her parents (conditioned on their own cooperation). These concessions went beyond the "plain vanilla" inducements [normally offered to cooperating witnesses]. Why were they permissible, if the President's help was, in Starr's view, not only felonious, but possible grounds for impeachment?[84]

Are the two cases distinguishable because "Starr wanted the truth, and the President allegedly wanted perjury"?[85] Because the cooperating witnesses were not paid anything, but rather simply obtained promises regarding particular exercises of prosecutorial discretion?[86]

Professor Sklansky concludes the following—do you agree?

> If the prosecutors' promises to ... Lewinsky differ critically from ... the President's alleged efforts to find Lewinsky a job, it cannot be simply because the prosecutors seek

---

of the process may lead prosecutors to falsely believe the testimony of cooperators.

Id. at 962-63; *see also* Saul M. Kassin, *Human Judges of Truth, Deception, and Credibility: Confident But Erroneous*, 23 Cardozo L. Rev. 809 (2002).

[83] *See* Graham Hughes, *Agreements for Cooperation in Criminal Cases*, 45 Vand. L. Rev. 1, 29-40 (1992).

[84] David A. Sklansky, *Starr, Singleton, and the Prosecutor's Role*, 26 Fordham Urb. L.J. 509, 517-18 (1999); *see also* infra Chapter 15 (containing text of Lewinsky cooperation agreement).

[85] *Id.* at 518.

[86] *Id.* at 523.

the truth. Defense attorneys are not allowed to pay for truthful testimony. Nor can the difference be that prosecutors offer immunity instead of money. That distinction is too arbitrary—and underinclusive to boot. The difference is neither what is bargained *for*, nor what is bargained *with*. It is who does the bargaining.

Why should prosecutors have a freedom denied to defense attorneys, particularly a freedom that threatens to bias testimony in one direction? I think the answer is that prosecutors serve a different role and shoulder different responsibilities: they represent not "an ordinary party to a controversy," but "a sovereignty ... whose interest ... is not that it shall win a case, but that justice shall be done." And I think this answer, as hoary as it sounds, has implications that are not always recognized. But before I discuss these, I need to dispose of two red herrings.

The first is that prosecutors should be allowed to barter for testimony because they are required to reveal what they have promised. ... "Unlike defense lawyers or other members of the public, prosecutors have an affirmative obligation to disclose benefits they confer on a witness, and defendants are entitled to cross-examine witnesses concerning any benefits they received from the government." This is true, and perhaps it should inform interpretation of the statutory ban on witness gratuities. But as a matter of policy the government's discovery burdens offer little reason to continue to allow prosecutors but not defense attorneys to reward witnesses. If defense attorneys could pay for testimony, most would gladly assume the obligation to disclose the payments.

The other red herring is simple necessity. ... The government [has argued] that it "relies on witnesses who testify in return for leniency in literally thousands of cases each year, including major cases such as the Oklahoma City bombing prosecutions." Without this testimony, the government argued, it "could not enforce the drug laws, could not prosecute organized crime figures under RICO, and could not prosecute many other cases 'of such a character that the only persons capable of giving useful testimony are those implicated in the crime.'"

Although unproven, this claim also may be true. It certainly has been conventional wisdom for generations. The problem, again, is that by itself it cannot justify different rules for prosecutors and defense attorneys. Defense attorneys, too, might be able to obtain more candid and more complete testimony, from law enforcement officers as well as other witnesses, if they were allowed to pay for it. Defense attorneys cannot claim that the missing testimony cripples law enforcement, but they can argue credibly that it would assist justice. And we ordinarily do not take the position that, in the interest of law enforcement, evidence too unreliable to be used by criminal defendants may nonetheless be used by prosecutors.

The government's claim of necessity becomes persuasive only when it is coupled with recognition of the distinctive responsibilities of prosecutors. Unlike defense attorneys, prosecutors are not simply advocates, nor should they be. They are and should be adjudicators as well as litigants, and their "twofold aim ... is that guilt shall not escape nor innocence suffer." The notion that prosecutors serve a different role than ordinary advocates can sound like an embarrassing homily. When invoked to justify special powers for prosecutors, it can also sound self-serving. ... But it is manifestly true that prosecutors have different obligations than defense attorneys, and the differences have important implications. Inattention to those implications is what has made a bromide of the prosecutor's "twofold aim."

[The original *Singleton* panel], it may be recalled, reasoned that the special role of prosecutors was all the more reason they should not give rewards for testimony: "[b]ecause prosecutors bear a weighty responsibility to do justice and observe the law in the course of a prosecution, it is particularly appropriate to apply the strictures of [the gratuity prohibition] to their activities." This works as a rhetorical flourish, but not as a serious argument. No one contends that prosecutors should break the law. Instead, the question is what the law is with respect to prosecutors. After all, judges have, if anything, an even weightier responsibility than prosecutors "to do justice and observe the law." But not even the *Singleton* panel suggested that federal law bars sentencing judges from taking into account a defendant's candor on the witness stand, despite the fact that ... the plain language of 18 U.S.C. § 201—"whoever ... gives ... anything of value"—applies to judges no less than to prosecutors. Of course judges typically do not *promise* particular sentences in exchange for testimony, but, as the *Singleton* panel stressed, the statute "prohibits even the rewarding of testimony after it is given." "One obvious purpose," [the *Singleton* panel] explained, "is to keep testimony free of *all* influence so that its truthfulness is protected." But even [the panel] seemed to recognize that rewards from judges are different, notwithstanding their preeminent duty "to do justice and observe the law." Rewards from judges are less objectionable precisely *because* judges are assumed to be impartial. We trust them to reward true candor, not partisanship.

Prosecutors of course are not as impartial as judges, nor are they asked to be. But they *are* asked to be more impartial than defense attorneys. If that request is taken seriously—if prosecutors value justice above convictions, and truthful testimony above helpful testimony—then they may sensibly be granted some tools denied to defense attorneys. The point is not that prosecutors are more ethical than defense attorneys, but that their ethical obligations are different.

Many people scoff at the notion that prosecutors have a "twofold aim." Prosecutorial impartiality, they suggest, is an oxymoron, an institutional impossibility. If these skeptics are right, allowing prosecutors but not defense attorneys to pay for testimony cannot be justified. But like most prosecutors and former prosecutors, I think the skeptics are wrong.[87]

Since *Singleton II*, a number of defendants have argued that the admission of co-conspirator's testimony induced through governmental promises of leniency violates their due process rights because § 201(c)(2) precludes them from "similarly making enticing offers in exchange for testimony, thus generating an unfair procedural imbalance whereby the prosecution may obtain and present testimony in a manner unavailable to the defendant."[88] Thus far courts have rejected such claims, relying on "the myriad procedural safeguards to which a defendant is entitled when the government plans to introduce testimony obtained through offers of value" and the fact that "the role of assessing witness credibility belongs to the jury."[89] *Should* the playing field be leveled—perhaps by repealing § 201(c)(2) and allowing the defense to provide inducements to its witnesses, subject to the same "procedural safeguards"?[90]

The courts' and Professor's Sklansky's arguments notwithstanding, the issue of the propriety of prosecutorial provisions of leniency or other consideration in exchange for testimony is not yet settled. As noted in Chapter 1 (Introduction), the McDade Amendment makes federal prosecutors "subject to State laws and rules, and local Federal court rules, governing attorneys in each State where such attorney engages in that attorney's duties, to

---

[87] *Id.* at 525-28.

[88] United States v. Fria Vazquez Del Mercado, 223 F.3d 1213, 1215 (10th Cir. 2000).

[89] *Id.*; *see also* United States v. Abrego, 141 F.3d 142, 151-52 (5th Cir. 1998).

[90] *See* H. Richard Uviller, *No Sauce for the Gander: Valuable Consideration for Helpful Testimony From Tainted Witnesses in Criminal Cases*, 23 Cardozo L. Rev. 771 (2002); Korin K. Ewing, Note, *Establishing an Equal Playing Field for Criminal Defendants in the Aftermath of* United States v. Singleton, 49 Duke L.J. 1371, 1373 (2000) (proposing repeal of subsection 201(c)(2) altogether, "allowing prosecutors and defendants alike to exchange consideration for testimony and requiring only that both sides fully disclose any such arrangement to the jury").

the same extent and in the same manner as other attorneys in that State."[91] "[A] reasonable argument can be made that plea bargaining inducements do constitute 'compensation' under the state ethics rules. The CPA may provide a stronger basis than the federal bribery statute for defense attorneys to seek the exclusion of testimony procured through plea bargains."[92]

2. U.S.S.G. 5K1.1

Prior to the Supreme Court's decision in *United States v. Booker*, when federal prosecutors contemplated entering into a cooperation arrangement, the usual inducement they offered a defendant was the potential for a motion made pursuant to Federal Sentencing Guidelines § 5K1.1 ("Substantial Assistance to Authorities"). Section 5K1.1 provides that "[u]pon motion of the government stating that the defendant has provided substantial assistance in the investigation or prosecution of another person who has committed an offense, the court may depart from the guidelines." Section 5K1.1 was by far the most common ground for departure from the otherwise applicable sentencing ranges. "The number of § 5K1.1 motions filed by federal prosecutors increased steadily in the years following 1987, and by 1994, the government made substantial assistance motions in nearly 20% of all federal prosecutions."[93] Although not presently at that historic high, government substantial assistance motions appear to be maintaining their importance in the bargaining process. Thus, while the Sentencing Commission reports that some district courts have recognized a defendant's "substantial assistance" without government motion post-*Booker*,[94] departures pursuant to government § 5K1.1 motions are made in about 11% of cases nationally.[95]

Section 5K1.1 also, in the view of many observers, significantly increased the incentives for cooperation.[96] For defendants against whom the government had a strong case, a § 5K1.1 constituted their only chance to substantially reduce or eliminate the possibility of jail time. Section 5K1.1 was controversial, for two principal reasons:

> The overarching concern of many critics is that in the Guidelines era the incentives to cooperate are now so powerful that they dramatically increase the risk of perjury that always exists whenever the government rewards witnesses for testimony. For many critics, this general concern about excessive government leverage is exacerbated by a pivotal procedural component of the substantial assistance

---

[91] 28 U.S.C. § 530B.

[92] Fred C. Zacharias & Bruce A. Green, *The Uniqueness of Federal Prosecutors*, 88 Geo. L.J. 207, 221 & n.87 (2000); *see, e.g.*, Del. Rules of Prof'l Conduct 3.4(b) & n.2 (limiting compensation for fact witnesses, but not expert witnesses); Ill. Rules of Prof'l Conduct 3.4(b) & n.3 (permitting lawyers to pay fact witnesses expenses and reimbursement for lost compensation and permitting payment of reasonable fee to expert witnesses); Pa. Rule of Prof'l Conduct 3.4b(1)-(3) (limiting fact witness compensation).

[93] Frank O. Bowman, III, *Departing is Such Sweet Sorrow: A Year of Judicial Revolt on "Substantial Assistance" Departures Follows a Decade of Prosecutorial Indiscipline*, 29 Stetson L. Rev. 7, 14 (1999).

[94] *See, e.g.,* United States v. Robinson, 741 F.3d 588 (5th Cir. 2014).

[95] *See supra* note 32.

[96] *See, e.g.,* Steven M. Cohen, *What is True? Perspectives of a Former Prosecutor*, 23 Cardozo L. Rev. 817, 817-20 (2002); Yaroshefsky, *supra* note 84, at 103-04 & n.7; G. Adam Schweickert, III, Comment, *Third-Party Cooperation: A Welcome Addition to Substantial Assistance Departure Jurisprudence*, 30 Conn. L. Rev. 1445, 1449 (1993) ("The implementation of the United States Sentencing Guidelines and mandatory minimum sentencing has led to a ten-fold increase in cooperation from indicted individuals.").

mechanism—the requirement of a government motion as a prerequisite for a substantial assistance sentence reduction.[97]

The problem of perjury inheres in any discussion of cooperation. Thus, for example, Professor R. Michael Cassidy writes:

> It is now widely accepted that the practice of conditioning leniency on cooperation in criminal cases is rife with the potential for abuse. The frequency of fabrication by witnesses who have made "deals" with the government, while impossible to ascertain with accuracy, is potentially staggering. To cite but one recent study, members of the Innocence Project at Cardozo Law School analyzed sixty-seven cases in which defendants were wrongfully convicted, incarcerated, and later exonerated by DNA evidence. In a remarkable 21 percent of these cases, false testimony by a government informant contributed to the wrongful conviction.[98]

The question for present purposes is whether the threat of perjury was unacceptably exacerbated in a mandatory Guidelines environment that enhanced prosecutors' bargaining power and created substantial pressures to cooperate. It is exceedingly difficult to test this question empirically. Is it reasonable to assume that the fact that there were more "cooperating" defendants necessarily means that there was more perjury? Is it reasonable to further assume that an increase in cooperating witness perjury translates into an increase in erroneous convictions? Professor Frank Bowman, a former prosecutor, argues as follows—do you agree?

> It would be foolish and naive to dismiss the very real possibility that lying informants will sometimes convict the innocent, or still more commonly, make small fries appear more culpable than they are. The prisons produce some very plausible liars. On the other hand, much of the criticism of witness cooperation agreements seems to proceed from the even more naive assumption that juries consist of credulous bumpkins who automatically convict on the uncorroborated testimony of a defendant's "flipped" accomplice. ... As a rule, such testimony helps the government only where it is woven into a fabric of corroborating detail from untainted sources, and as I can attest from painful personal experience, a "dirty" witness can actually harm an otherwise strong case. In short, although accomplice testimony presents undeniable risks, there is reason for faith in the law's conventional mechanisms for testing its veracity.[99]

Professor Bowman's conclusion is that, while witness cooperation agreements should not be abolished (or criminalized), the "ineradicable fact" that the risk of perjury cannot be eliminated "strongly suggest[s] a principle of parsimony in wielding this uniquely powerful prosecutorial tool. That is, the Department of Justice should employ cooperation agreements whenever necessary, *but not more than necessary*, to apprehend and convict serious violators of federal criminal law."[100]

The other major controversy surrounding § 5K1.1 before the Supreme Court's decision in *Booker* concerned the requirement that sentencing departures for cooperation could *only* be triggered by government motion. The § 5K1.1 departure is, by the terms of that section, contingent on a government motion. Courts generally held that they could

---

[97] Bowman, *supra* note 93, at 15-16.

[98] R. Michael Cassidy, *"Soft Words of Hope:" Giglio, Accomplice Witnesses, and the Problem of Implied Inducements*, 98 Nw. U. L. Rev. 1129, 1130 (2004) (footnotes omitted).

[99] Bowman, *supra* note 93, at 45.

[100] *Id.* at 46.

not, in the absence of a government motion, base a downward departure for a defendant's substantial assistance to federal prosecutors on other provisions of the Guidelines, including the general departure provision, § 5K2.0.[101] Finally, judicial review of the government's refusal to file a § 5K1.1 motion was extremely limited.[102]

The government motion requirement has been heavily criticized and a variety of proposals were made to eliminate or qualify it.[103] It appears that *Booker* has done what Congress did not—that is, because the Guidelines are now only advisory, it appears that the government motion requirement no longer binds courts seeking to reward defendants—over government opposition—for cooperation with government investigators.[104] As noted, however, it does not appear that district courts are embracing this freedom in many cases; government-sponsored § 5K1.1 departures appear to be the norm at present.

Is the elimination of this requirement wise? What was its purpose? Professor Frank Bowman's defense of the government motion requirement, below, appeared to represent a minority view (at least of those outside the government). Do the concerns he identifies have continued force in the post-*Booker* environment?

The primary criticisms of the government motion requirement are that it gives the government too much power, that it deprives sentencing courts of authority properly theirs, and that it risks unfairness because prosecutors may refuse to make the motion for defendants whose assistance really has been substantial. One of the principle flaws in the critics' position flows from a miscategorization of the substantial assistance mechanism as merely another of the myriad Guidelines rules whose function is to control unwarranted sentencing disparity. Section 3553(e) of Title 18 and § 5K1.1 of the Guidelines are not rules about sentencing equity. They are grants of power to prosecutors to perform a difficult and sometimes unappetizing task—coercing criminals to do a doubly unpleasant thing: admit their own guilt, and then violate a basic human taboo by informing on their friends, associates, or even blood relatives. "Turning" accomplices into witnesses is rough business. Fair arguments can be made that as a society we ought not do it at all. However, if we are to do it, then the rules governing the process must ensure that society gets the benefit of its bargain in the form of full, complete, truthful information and testimony.

Cooperating witnesses do not like either to give incriminating information about or to testify against their friends. Overcoming their initial resistance to helping the government at all takes immense leverage. The Guidelines and statutory minimum mandatory sentences provide the initial leverage by creating a level of certainty about the unpleasant consequences of conviction that never existed in the pre-Guidelines indeterminate sentencing system. It is one thing to be facing a sentence that *could* range anywhere from probation to forty years depending on the whim of the judge. It is another thing altogether to have your lawyer sit you down in front of a chart that says you *will* be sentenced to 121–151 months unless a ground for departure can be found. Before the Guidelines, it was psychologically easy to gamble on the sentencing judge's

---

[101] *See In re* Sealed Case, 181 F.3d 128, 136 (D.C. Cir. 1999); United States v. Alegria, 192 F.3d 179, 189 (1st Cir. 1999).

[102] *See* Wade v. United States, 504 U.S. 181 (1992); United States v. Abuhouran, 161 F.3d 206, 211-12 (3d Cir. 1998).

[103] *See, e.g.,* Am. College of Trial Lawyers, Proposal, *Report and Proposal on Section 5K1.1 of the U.S. Sentencing Guidelines,* 38 Am. Crim. L. Rev. 1503 (2001): Cynthia Kwei Yung Lee, *Prosecutorial Discretion, Substantial Assistance, and the Federal Sentencing Guidelines,* 42 UCLA L. Rev. 105 (1994).

[104] *See, e.g.,* Jonathan S. Feld & Fritz E. Berckmueler, *The Benefits of Booker for Cooperating Defendants,* 12 Bus. Crimes Bull. 1 (June 2005).

generosity. Now defendants reach much faster for the only escape hatch, an agreement to cooperate with the government.

Nevertheless, even after defendants cross the first hurdle of agreeing to cooperate, they would still prefer, naturally enough, to give as little information as possible, to conceal facts that show themselves in a discreditable light, and to do as little damage to their former friends as they can. The severity and certainty of Guidelines sentences provide the initial impetus for witness cooperation, but it is the government monopoly on the substantial assistance motion that ensures candor, completeness, and continued cooperation until the job is done. In a system where the sentencing judge can act at the defendant's request and over the objection of the government, even partial, grudging cooperation stands a fair chance of earning at least some sentence reduction.
...

Finally, given that sentencing levels under the Guidelines are indeed quite substantial, judges have plenty of leeway to grant some sentence reduction for disputed or half-hearted cooperation without completely forgoing punishment. By contrast, under the current system, unless the prosecutor, who knows the case better than anyone and has both the knowledge and incentive to detect lies, half-truths, and incomplete disclosure, is satisfied that defendant is truthful and completely forthcoming, no motion will be filed and no reduction is possible. Thus, under a substantial assistance system in which the prosecutor is stripped of the doorkeeper function, the incentive to cooperate some would remain, but the imperative of complete and candid cooperation would be dramatically diminished. ...

The complaint that the government motion requirement improperly deprives judges of sentencing authority is also misconceived. It tends to glide over the fact that, once the government makes its motion, the district court has essentially unlimited discretion either to grant or deny it, and unlimited discretion as to the amount of any resulting departure. The critics would certainly respond that the motion requirement deprives the court of power to redress the injustice that results when the government refuses to seek a substantial assistance departure for a defendant whose efforts on the government's behalf entitle him to a reduction.

There are two answers to this critique. First, as discussed above, judges are ill-suited for making the determination of whether a defendant provided genuine, and substantial, assistance to the government. The best judge of whether a defendant has been of substantial assistance to the government is the government itself. Second, and more importantly, common sense (buttressed by some statistical evidence) demonstrate that the risk of prosecutors frequently refusing to seek sentence reductions for those who genuinely cooperate is vanishingly small.

In the first place, the claim that prosecutors would behave this way ignores the powerful systemic incentives that favor reliably rewarding witness cooperation. Understanding this reality requires an appreciation of some of the subtleties of substantial assistance negotiations. The relationship between witness and prosecutor does not begin with an exchange of unconditional promises. At her first meeting with a potential cooperator, the AUSA does not say, "If you talk to me today, I promise to move to reduce your sentence." Instead, the prosecutor says, "Start talking today. Today, and all the other times we will meet, tell me everything you know. Testify truthfully at trial. Once you have done all those things, I will evaluate your performance, and *if*, in my sole discretion, I conclude that you have provided substantial assistance, *then* I will move to reduce your sentence. Trust me." From the government's perspective, this one-sided arrangement is absolutely necessary to ensure complete cooperation until the end of the case. From the defendant's perspective, it makes no sense to accept such a lopsided deal *unless your lawyer tells you that you can trust the prosecutor to do the right thing.*

If a prosecutor uses a cooperating defendant in any significant way, and then refuses without powerful justification to make a substantial assistance motion, she risks lasting damage to her credibility that will markedly impair her capacity to turn other defendants in future cases. The federal criminal bar, even in very large cities, is a limited and insular fraternity. Word gets around. All experienced federal criminal lawyers understand this reality.

In addition, when evaluating the claim that prosecutors commonly withhold "deserved" substantial assistance motions, one must remember one fact of prosecutorial life that has remained constant before and after the advent of the Sentencing Guidelines—the ever-present need to manage caseloads by securing guilty pleas in the vast majority of indicted cases. The substantial assistance motion is not only a useful tool for its intended purpose of obtaining necessary testimony from reluctant accomplices, it is also a marvelous method of securing a guilty plea from the cooperator himself. Thus, the persistent temptation for prosecutors is not to withhold § 5K1.1 motions from the deserving, but to distribute them liberally in order to facilitate easy guilty pleas.[105]

Finally, the sheer plenitude of substantial assistance departures is a powerful refutation of the contention that AUSAs are unfairly parsimonious in rewarding cooperators. ... [R]oughly one-fifth of all federal defendants nationwide are the beneficiaries of substantial assistance motions. ... When the statistical evidence suggests that substantial assistance departures are, if anything, over-recommended by federal prosecutors, the solution is hardly to abandon the government motion requirement and give carte blanche to courts to hand out even more such departures.[106]

Assume that one were to accept in principle the argument that the government motion requirement is sensible, given the plea bargaining dynamics described above and prosecutors' better positioning to evaluate the worth of tendered cooperation. What if it could be demonstrated, however, that federal prosecutors were not using their § 5K1.1 powers in a principled or at least an even-handed way? What if the statistics indicated that prosecutors were over-using the device and thus introducing unnecessary and unjustified disparities among defendants? As Professor Bowman notes:

Sentencing Commission statistics establish two undeniable facts. First, there are quite astonishing differences among U.S. Attorney's Offices in the rates at which they make substantial assistance motions. In contrast to the 47.5% rate in the Eastern District of Pennsylvania, federal prosecutors in the Eastern District of Virginia and the Central District of California make such motions in only 7.2 and 6.9 percent of their cases respectively. Although not quite as stark as the inter-district disparities, there are also marked regional differences in substantial assistance departure rates among federal circuits. In FY 1998, the rate varied from a low of 11.3% in the Ninth Circuit to a high of 31.5% in the Third Circuit (home of the Eastern District of Pennsylvania). Second, the very high substantial assistance departure rates in districts like the Eastern District of Pennsylvania are plainly inconsistent with both the text and spirit of § 5K1.1, and cannot be explained by reference to the conventional justification for the substantial assistance device. It simply strains credulity to suggest that half the federal defendants in Philadelphia provide genuinely "substantial" help to the government, or

---

[105] [Author's footnote 226:] The impetus to use § 5K1.1 to secure pleas from cooperators also stems from what I perceive to be a common psychological truth about prosecutors. In my experience, prosecutors tend to measure their success by convictions, not by the length of sentences obtained. ... With this mindset, prosecutors can find it very easy to rationalize exchanging a sentencing concession, even a concession not permitted by the letter of the Guidelines, for the certainty of a guilty plea.

[106] Bowman, *supra* note 93, at 54–58.

that Philadelphia prosecutors need to offer substantial assistance departures to half the people indicted in the district in order to secure an acceptable rate of convictions. ...

Even if large inter-district disparities in substantial assistance motion rates did not exist, *excessive* substantial assistance departure rates, such as those in Philadelphia, which are far higher than can possibly be justified by any genuine need to obtain accomplice testimony, would lend force to the allegation that the government is routinely manipulating the Guidelines to achieve the sentencing outcomes it desires rather than those that would be produced by neutral application of Guidelines rules.[107]

One thing that has not changed with the *Booker* decision is this disparity. The Sentencing Commission reported that, in its fiscal year 2017, the incidence of § 5K1.1 motions varied from 7.1% (9th Cir.) and 7.3% (5th Cir.) to 17.9% (2d Cir.) and 24.9% (CA9); the national average was 10.8%.[108] Given that the Department of Justice has apparently failed to police its own, is *Booker*'s apparent elimination of the government motion requirement problematic?

3. SAMPLE AGREEMENT

Prior to entering into a cooperation agreement, like an immunity deal, the government will normally demand a proffer from the defendant. Some of the issues surrounding defendant proffers are covered *supra* in Chapter 15 (Immunity).

At the culmination of a successful proffer, the government and the cooperating witness may conclude a cooperation deal which, like any plea or immunity agreement, should always be reduced to writing.[109] The following is the cooperation agreement entered into between the Special Counsel Robert Mueller's office and Lieutenant Michael T. Flynn (Ret.).

November 30, 2017

Robert K. Kelner Stephen P. Anthony
Covington & Burling LLP
One City Center, 850 Tenth Street, NW
Washington, DC 20001-4956

Re: <u>United States v. Michael T. Flynn</u>

Dear Counsel:

This letter sets forth the full and complete plea offer to your client, Lieutenant General Michael T. Flynn (Ret.) (hereinafter referred to as "your client" or "defendant"), from the Special Counsel's Office (hereinafter also referred to as "the Government" or "this Office"). If your client accepts the terms and conditions of this offer, please have your client execute this document in the space provided below. Upon

---

[107] *Id.* at 59-62.

[108] U.S. Sentencing Comm'n, Interactive Sourcebook, Sentencing Information, Departures & Variances, Departures, available at ussc.gov.

[109] *See, e.g.,* U.S.A.M. § 9-27.450A ("All negotiated plea agreements to felonies or to misdemeanors negotiated from felonies shall be in writing and filed with the court."); United States v. McQueen, 108 F.3d 64, 66 (4th Cir. 1997) (stating that "we believe it behooves the government to reduce all oral pleas to writing" and "suggest[ing] that lower courts require all future plea agreements be reduced to writing").

receipt of the executed document, this letter will become the Plea Agreement (hereinafter referred to as "this Agreement"). The terms of the offer are as follows:

1. Charges and Statutory Penalties

Your client agrees to plead guilty to the Criminal Information, a copy of which is attached, charging your client with making false statements to the Federal Bureau of Investigation in violation of 18 U.S.C. § 1001.

Your client understands that a violation of 18 U.S.C. § 1001 carries a maximum sentence of 5 years' imprisonment; a fine of $250,000, pursuant to 18 U.S.C. § 3571(b)(3); a term of supervised release of not more than 3 years, pursuant to 18 U.S.C. § 3583(b)(2); and an obligation to pay any applicable interest or penalties on fines and restitution not timely made.

In addition, your client agrees to pay a special assessment of $100 per felony conviction to the Clerk of the United States District Court for the District of Columbia. Your client also understands that, pursuant to 18 U.S.C. § 3572 and § 5El.2 of the United States Sentencing Guidelines, *Guidelines Manual* (2016) (hereinafter "Sentencing Guidelines," "Guidelines," or "U.S.S.G."), the Court may also impose a fine that is sufficient to pay the federal government the costs of any imprisonment, term of supervised release, and period of probation.

2. Factual Stipulations

Your client agrees that the attached "Statement of the Offense" fairly and accurately describes your client's actions and involvement in the offense to which your client is pleading guilty. Please have your client sign and return the Statement of the Offense as a written proffer of evidence, along with this Agreement.

3. Additional Charges

In consideration of your client's guilty plea to the above offense, your client will not be further prosecuted criminally by this Office for the conduct set forth in the attached Statement of the Offense.

4. Sentencing Guidelines Analysis

Your client understands that the sentence in this case will be determined by the Court, pursuant to the factors set forth in 18 U.S.C. § 3553(a), including a consideration of the applicable guidelines and policies set forth in the Sentencing Guidelines. Pursuant to Federal Rule of Criminal Procedure 11(c)(l)(B), and to assist the Court in determining the appropriate sentence, the parties agree to the   following:

A. Estimated Offense Level Under the Guidelines

The parties agree that the following Sentencing Guidelines sections apply:

U.S.S.G. §2Bl.l(a)(2)	Base Offense Level:	6
Total:		6

B. Acceptance of Responsibility

The Government agrees that a 2-level reduction will be appropriate, pursuant to U.S.S.G. § 3E1.1, provided that your client clearly demonstrates acceptance of responsibility, to the satisfaction of the Government, through your client's allocution, adherence to every provision of this Agreement, and conduct between entry of the plea and imposition of sentence.

Nothing in this Agreement limits the right of the Government to seek denial of the adjustment for acceptance of responsibility, pursuant to U.S.S.G. § 3El. l, and/or imposition of an adjustment for obstruction of justice, pursuant to U.S.S.G. § 3C1.1, regardless of any agreement set forth above, should your client move to withdraw your client's guilty plea after it is entered, or should it be determined by the Government that your client has either (a) engaged in conduct, unknown to the Government at the time of the signing of this Agreement, that constitutes obstruction of justice, or (b) engaged in additional criminal conduct after signing this Agreement.

In accordance with the above, the applicable Guidelines Offense Level will be at least 4.

C.   Estimated Criminal History Category

Based upon the information now available to this Office, your client has no criminal convictions.

Accordingly, your client is estimated to have zero criminal history points and your client's Criminal History Category is estimated to be I. Your client acknowledges that if additional convictions are discovered during the pre-sentence investigation by the United States Probation Office, your client's criminal history points may increase.

D.   Estimated Applicable Guidelines Range

Based upon the agreed total offense level and the estimated criminal history category set forth above, your client's estimated Sentencing Guidelines range is zero months to six months' imprisonment (the "Estimated Guidelines Range"). In addition, the parties agree that, pursuant to U.S.S.G. § 5El.2, should the Court impose a fine, at Guidelines level 4, the estimated applicable fine range is $500 to $9,500. Your client reserves the right to ask the Court not to impose any applicable fine.

The parties agree that, solely for the purposes of calculating the applicable range under the Sentencing Guidelines, neither a downward nor upward departure from the Estimated Guidelines Range set forth above is warranted, subject to the paragraphs regarding cooperation below. Accordingly, neither party will seek any departure or adjustment to the Estimated Guidelines Range, nor will either party suggest that the Court consider such a departure or adjustment, except as provided in the preceding sentence. Moreover, your client understands and acknowledges that the Estimated Guidelines Range agreed to by the parties is not binding on the Probation Office or the Court. Should the Court determine that a different guidelines range is applicable, your client will not be permitted to withdraw his guilty plea on that basis, and the Government and your client will still be bound by this Agreement.

Your client understands and acknowledges that the terms of this section apply only to conduct that occurred before the execution of this Agreement. Should your client commit any conduct after the execution of this Agreement that would form the basis for an increase in your client's base offense level or justify an upward departure (examples of which include, but are not limited to, obstruction of justice, failure to appear for a court proceeding, criminal conduct while pending sentencing, and false statements to law enforcement agents, the probation officer, or the Court), the Government is free under this Agreement to seek an increase in the base offense level based on that post-agreement conduct.

5. Agreement us to Sentencing Allocution

Based upon the information known to the Government at the time of the signing of this Agreement, the parties further agree that a sentence within the Estimated Guidelines Range would constitute a reasonable sentence in light of all of the factors set forth in 18 U.S.C. § 3553(a), should such a sentence be subject to appellate review notwithstanding the appeal waiver provided below.

6. Reservation of Allocution

The Government and your client reserve the right to describe fully, both orally and in writing, to the sentencing judge, the nature and seriousness of your client's misconduct, including any misconduct not described in the charges to which your client is pleading guilty.

The parties also reserve the right to inform the presentence report writer and the Court of any relevant facts, to dispute any factual inaccuracies in the presentence report, and to contest any matters not provided for in this Agreement. In the event that the Court considers any Sentencing Guidelines adjustments, departures, or calculations different from any agreements contained in this Agreement, or contemplates a sentence outside the Guidelines range based upon the general sentencing factors listed in 18 U.S.C. § 3553(a}, the parties reserve the right to answer any related inquiries from the Court. In addition, if in this Agreement the parties have agreed to recommend or refrain from recommending to the Court a particular resolution of any sentencing issue, the parties reserve the right to full allocation in any post-sentence litigation. The parties retain the full right of allocution in connection with any post-sentence motion which may be filed in this matter and/or any proceeding(s) before the Bureau of Prisons. In addition, your client acknowledges that the Government is not obligated and currently does not intend to file any post-sentence downward departure motion in this case pursuant to Rule 35(b) of the Federal Rules of Criminal Procedure.

7. Court Not Bound by this Agreement or the Sentencing Guidelines

Your client understands that the sentence in this case will be imposed in accordance with 18 U.S.C. § 3553(a), upon consideration of the Sentencing Guidelines. Your client further understands that the sentence to be imposed is a matter solely within the discretion of the Court. Your client acknowledges that the Court is not obligated to follow any recommendation of the Government at the time of sentencing or to grant a downward departure based on your client's substantial assistance to the Government, even if the Government files a motion pursuant to Section 5K1.1 of the Sentencing Guidelines. Your client understands that neither the Government's recommendation nor the Sentencing Guidelines are binding on the Court.

Your client acknowledges that your client's entry of a guilty plea to the charged offense authorizes the Court to impose any sentence, up to and including the statutory maximum sentence, which may be greater than the applicable Guidelines range. The Government cannot, and does not, make any promise or representation as to what sentence your client will receive. Moreover, it is understood that your client will have no right to withdraw your client's plea of guilty should the Court impose a sentence that is outside the Guidelines range or if the Court does not follow the Government's sentencing recommendation. The Government and your client will be bound by this Agreement, regardless of the sentence imposed by the Court. Any effort by your client to withdraw the guilty plea because of the length of the sentence shall constitute a breach of this Agreement.

8.   Cooperation

Your client agrees to cooperate with this Office on the following terms and conditions:

Your client shall cooperate fully, truthfully, completely, and forthrightly with this Office and other Federal, state, and local law enforcement authorities identified by this Office in any and all matters as to which this Office deems the cooperation relevant. Your client acknowledges that your client's cooperation may include, but will not necessarily be limited to: answering questions; providing sworn written statements; taking government-administered polygraph examination(s); and participating in covert law enforcement activities. Any refusal by your client to cooperate fully, truthfully, completely, and forthrightly as directed by this Office and other Federal, state, and local law enforcement authorities identified by this Office in any and all matters in which this Office deems your client's assistance relevant will constitute a breach of this Agreement by your client, and will relieve this Office of its obligations under this Agreement, including, but not limited to, its obligation to inform this Court of any assistance your client has provided. Your client agrees, however, that such breach by your client will not constitute a basis for withdrawal of your client's plea of guilty or otherwise relieve your client of your client's obligations under this Agreement.

(a)   Your client shall promptly turn over to this Office, or other law enforcement authorities, or direct such law enforcement authorities to, any and all evidence of crimes about which your client is aware; all contraband and proceeds of such crimes; and all assets traceable to the proceeds of such crimes. Your client agrees to the forfeiture of all assets which are proceeds of crimes or traceable to such proceeds of crimes.

(b)   Your client shall submit a full and complete accounting of all your client's financial assets, whether such assets are in your client's name or in the name of a third party.

(c)   Your client acknowledges and understands that, during the course of the cooperation outlined in this Agreement, your client will be interviewed by law enforcement agents and/or Government attorneys. Your client waives any right to have counsel present during these interviews and agrees to meet with law enforcement agents and Government attorneys outside of the presence of counsel. If, at some future point, you or your client desire to have counsel present during interviews by law enforcement agents and/or Government attorneys, and you communicate this decision in writing to this Office, this Office will honor this request, and this change will have no effect on any other terms and conditions of this Agreement.

(d)   Your client shall testify fully, completely and truthfully before any and all Grand Juries in the District of Columbia and elsewhere, and at any and all trials of cases or other court proceedings in the District of Columbia and elsewhere, at which your client's testimony may be deemed relevant by the Government.

(e)   Your client understands and acknowledges that nothing in this Agreement allows your client to commit any criminal violation of local, state or federal law during the period of your client's cooperation with law enforcement authorities or authorities or at any time in this case. The commission of a criminal offense during the period of your client's cooperation or at any time prior to sentencing will constitute a breach of this Agreement and will relieve the Government of all of its obligations under this Agreement, including, but not limited to, its obligation to inform this Court of any assistance your client has provided. However, your client acknowledges and agrees that such a breach of this Agreement will not entitle your client to withdraw your client's plea of guilty or relieve your client of the obligations under this   Agreement.

(f)   Your client agrees that the sentencing in this case may be delayed until your client's efforts to cooperate have been completed, as determined by the Government, so that the Court will have the benefit of all relevant information before a sentence is imposed.

9.   Waivers

A. Venue

Your client waives any challenge to venue in the District of Columbia.

B. Statute of Limitations

Your client agrees that, should the conviction following your client's plea of guilty pursuant to this Agreement be vacated for any reason, any prosecution, based on the conduct set forth in the attached Statement of the Offense, that is not time-barred by the applicable statute of limitations on the date of the signing of this Agreement (including any counts that the Government has agreed not to prosecute or to dismiss at sentencing pursuant to this Agreement) may be commenced or reinstated against your client, notwithstanding the expiration of the statute of limitations between the signing of this Agreement and the commencement or reinstatement of such prosecution. It is the intent of this Agreement to waive all defenses based on the statute of limitations with respect to any prosecution of conduct set forth in the attached Statement of the Offense that is not time-barred on the date that this Agreement is signed.

C.   Trial Rights

Your client understands that by pleading guilty in this case your client agrees to waive certain rights afforded by the Constitution of the United States and/or by statute or rule. Your client agrees to forgo the right to any further discovery or disclosures of information not already provided at the time of the entry of your client's guilty plea. Your client also agrees to waive, among other rights, the right to be indicted by a Grand Jury, the right to plead not guilty, and the right to a jury trial. If there were a jury trial, your client would have the right to be represented by counsel, to confront and cross-examine witnesses against your client, to challenge the admissibility of evidence offered against your client, to compel witnesses to appear for the purpose of testifying and presenting other evidence on your client's behalf, and to choose whether to testify. If there were a jury trial and your client chose not to testify at that trial, your client would have the right to have the jury instructed that your client's failure to testify could not be held against your client. Your client would further have the right to have the jury instructed that your client is presumed innocent until proven guilty, and that the burden would be on the United States to prove your client's guilt beyond a reasonable doubt. If your client were found guilty after a trial, your client would have the right to appeal your client's conviction. Your client understands that the Fifth Amendment to the Constitution of the United States protects your client from the use of compelled self-incriminating statements in a criminal prosecution. By entering a plea of guilty, your client knowingly and voluntarily waives or gives up your client's right against compelled self-incrimination.

Your client acknowledges discussing with you Rule 11(f) of the Federal Rules of Criminal Procedure and Rule 410 of the Federal Rules of Evidence, which ordinarily limit the admissibility of statements made by a defendant in the course of plea discussions or plea proceedings if a guilty plea is later withdrawn. Your client knowingly and voluntarily waives the rights that arise under these rules in the event your client withdraws your client's guilty plea or withdraws from this Agreement after signing it.

Your client also agrees to waive all constitutional and statutory rights to a speedy sentence and agrees that the plea of guilty pursuant to this Agreement will be entered at a time decided upon by the parties with the concurrence of the Court. Your client understands that the date for sentencing will be set by the Court.

D. Appeal Rights

Your client understands that federal law, specifically 18 U.S.C. § 3742, affords defendants the right to appeal their sentences in certain circumstances. Your client agrees to waive the right to appeal the sentence in this case, including but not limited to any term of imprisonment, fine, forfeiture, award of restitution, term or condition of supervised release, authority of the Court to set conditions of release, and the manner in which the sentence was determined, except to the extent the Court sentences your client above the statutory maximum or guidelines range determined by the Court or your client claims that your client received ineffective assistance of counsel, in which case your client would have the right to appeal the illegal sentence or above-guidelines sentence or raise on appeal a claim of ineffective assistance of counsel, but not to raise on appeal other issues regarding the sentencing. In agreeing to this waiver, your client is aware that your client's sentence has yet to be determined by the Court.

Realizing the uncertainty in estimating what sentence the Court ultimately will impose, your client knowingly and willingly waives your client's right to appeal the sentence, to the extent noted above, in exchange for the concessions made by the Government in this Agreement.

E. Collateral Attack

Your client also waives any right to challenge the conviction entered or sentence imposed under this Agreement or otherwise attempt to modify or change the sentence or the manner in which it was determined in any collateral attack, including, but not limited to, a motion brought under 28 U.S.C. § 2255 or Federal Rule of Civil Procedure 60(b), except to the extent such a motion is based on newly discovered evidence or on a claim that your client received ineffective assistance of counsel. Your client reserves the right to file a motion brought under 18 U.S.C. § 3582(c)(2), but agrees to waive the right to appeal the denial of such a motion.

F. Privacy Act and FOIA Rights

Your client also agrees to waive all rights, whether asserted directly or by a representative, to request or receive from any department or agency of the United States any records pertaining to the investigation or prosecution of this case, including and without limitation any records that may be sought under the Freedom of Information Act, 5 U.S.C. § 552, or the Privacy Act, 5 U.S.C. § 552a, for the duration of the Special Counsel's investigation.

10. Restitution

Your client understands that the Court has an obligation to determine whether, and in what amount, mandatory restitution applies in this case under 18 U.S.C. § 3663A. The Government and your client agree that mandatory restitution does not apply in this case.

11. Breach of Agreement

Your client understands and agrees that, if after entering this Agreement, your client fails specifically to perform or to fulfill completely each and every one of your client's obligations under this Agreement, or engages in any criminal activity prior to sentencing, your client will have breached this Agreement. In the event of such a breach: (a) the Government will be free from its obligations under this Agreement; (b) your client will not have the right to withdraw the guilty plea; (c) your client will be fully subject to criminal prosecution for any other crimes, including perjury and obstruction of justice; and (d) the Government will be free to use against your client, directly and indirectly, in any criminal or civil proceeding, all statements made by your client and any of the information or materials provided by your client, including such statements, information, and materials provided pursuant to this Agreement or during the course of any debriefings conducted in anticipation of, or after entry of, this Agreement, whether or not the debriefings were previously characterized as "off-the-record" debriefings, and including your client's statements made during proceedings before the Court pursuant to Rule 11 of the Federal Rules of Criminal Procedure.

Your client understands and agrees that the Government shall be required to prove a breach of this Agreement only by a preponderance of the evidence, except where such breach is based on a violation of federal, state, or local criminal law, which the Government need prove only by probable cause in order to establish a breach of this Agreement.

Nothing in this Agreement shall be construed to permit your client to commit perjury, to make false statements or declarations, to obstruct justice, or to protect your client from prosecution for any crimes not included within this Agreement or committed by your client after the execution of this Agreement. Your client understands and agrees that the Government reserves the right to prosecute your client for any such offenses. Your client further understands that any perjury, false statements or declarations, or obstruction of justice relating to your client's obligations under this Agreement shall constitute a breach of this Agreement. In the event of such a breach, your client will not be allowed to withdraw your client's guilty plea.

12. Government's Obligations

The Government will bring to the Court's attention at the time of sentencing the nature and extent of your client's cooperation or lack of cooperation. The Government will evaluate the full nature and extent of your client's cooperation to determine whether your client has provided substantial assistance in the investigation or prosecution of another person who has committed an offense. If the Government determines that your client has provided such substantial assistance, this Office shall file a departure motion pursuant to Section 5K1.1 of the Sentencing Guidelines, which would afford your client an opportunity to persuade the Court that your client should be sentenced to a lesser period of incarceration and/or fine than indicated by the Sentencing Guidelines. The determination of whether your client has provided substantial assistance warranting the filing of a motion pursuant to Section 5K1.1 of the Sentencing Guidelines is within the sole discretion of the Government and is not reviewable by the Court. In the event your client should fail to perform specifically and fulfill completely each and every one of your client's obligations under this Agreement, the Government will be free from its obligations under this

Agreement, and will have no obligation to present your client's case to the Departure Guideline Committee or file a departure motion pursuant to Section 5Kl.1 of the Sentencing Guidelines.

13. Complete Agreement

No agreements, promises, understandings, or representations have been made by the parties or their counsel other than those contained in writing herein, nor will any such agreements, promises, understandings, or representations be made unless committed to writing and signed by your client, defense counsel, and the Special Counsel's Office.

Your client further understands that this Agreement is binding only upon the Special Counsel's Office. This Agreement does not bind any other United States Attorney's Office, nor does it bind any other state, local, or federal prosecutor. It also does not bar or compromise any civil, tax, or administrative claim pending or that may be made against your client.

If the foregoing terms and conditions are satisfactory, your client may so indicate by signing this Agreement and the Statement of the Offense, and returning both to me no later than November 30, 2017.

Sincerely yours,

ROBERT S. MUELLER. III
Special Counsel

Zainab N. Ahmad
Senior Assistant Special Counsel
The Special Counsel's Office

DEFENDANT'S ACCEPTANCE

I have read every page of this Agreement and have discussed it with my attorneys, Robert K. Kelner and Stephen P. Anthony. I fully understand this Agreement and agree to it without reservation. I do this voluntarily and of my own free will, intending to be legally bound. No threats have been made to me nor am I under the influence of anything that could impede my ability to understand this Agreement fully. I am pleading guilty because I am in fact guilty of the offense identified in this Agreement.

I reaffirm that absolutely no promises, agreements, understandings, or conditions have been made or entered into in connection with my decision to plead guilty except those set forth in this Agreement. I am satisfied with the legal services provided by my attorneys in connection with this Agreement and matters related to it.

Date: 11/30/17

/s/
Lieutenant General Michael T. Flynn (Ret.)
Defendant

ATTORNEYS' ACKNOWLEDGEMENT

I have read every page of this Agreement, reviewed this Agreement with my client, Lieutenant General Michael T. Flynn (Ret.), and full discussed the provisions of this Agreement with my client. These pages accurately and completely set forth the entire Agreement. I concur in my client's desire to plead guilty as set forth in this Agreement.

Date: 11/30/17

/s/
Robert K. Kelner
Attorney for Defendant

Stephen P. Anthony
Attorney for Defendant

* * *

**UNITED STATES DISTRICT COURT
FOR THE DISTRICT OF COLUMBIA**

UNITED STATES OF AMERICA	Criminal No.:
v.	Violation: 18 U.S.C. § 1001 (False Statements)
MICHAEL T. FLYNN, Defendant.	

STATEMENT OF THE OFFENSE

Pursuant to Federal Rule of Criminal Procedure 11, the United States of America and the defendant, MICHAEL T. FLYNN, stipulate and agree that the following facts are true and accurate. These facts do not constitute all of the facts known to the parties concerning the charged offense; they are being submitted to demonstrate that sufficient facts exist that the defendant committed the offense to which he is pleading guilty.

1. The defendant, MICHAEL T. FLYNN, who served as a surrogate and national security advisor for the presidential campaign of Donald J. Trump ("Campaign"), as a senior member of President-Elect Trump's Transition Team ("Presidential Transition Team"), and as the National Security Advisor to President Trump, made materially false statements and omissions during an interview with the Federal Bureau of Investigation ("FBI") on January 24, 2017, in Washington, D.C. At the time of the interview, the FBI had an open investigation into the Government of Russia's ("Russia") efforts to interfere in the 2016 presidential election, including the nature of any links between individuals associated with the Campaign and Russia, and whether there was any coordination between the Campaign and Russia's efforts.

2. FLYNN's false statements and omissions impeded and otherwise had a material impact on the FBI's ongoing investigation into the existence of any links or coordination between individuals associated with the Campaign and Russia's efforts to interfere with the 2016 presidential election.

False Statements Regarding FLYNN's Request to the Russian Ambassador that Russia Refrain from Escalating the Situation in Response to US. Sanctions against Russia

3. On or about January 24, 2017, FLYNN agreed to be interviewed by agents from the FBI ("January 24 voluntary interview"). During the interview, FLYNN falsely stated that he did not ask Russia's Ambassador to the United States ("Russian Ambassador") to

refrain from escalating the situation in response to sanctions that the United States had imposed against Russia. FLYNN also falsely stated that he did not remember a follow-up conversation in which the Russian Ambassador stated that Russia had chosen to moderate its response to those sanctions as a result of FLYNN's request. In truth and in fact, however, FLYNN then and there knew that the following had occurred:

a. On or about December 28, 2016, then-President Barack Obama signed Executive Order 13757, which was to take effect the following day. The executive order announced sanctions against Russia in response to that government's actions intended to interfere with the 2016 presidential election ("U.S. Sanctions").

b. On or about December 28, 2016, the Russian Ambassador contacted FLYNN.

c. On or about December 29, 2016, FLYNN called a senior official of the Presidential Transition Team ("PTT official"), who was with other senior members of the Presidential Transition Team at the Mar-a-Lago resort in Palm Beach, Florida, to discuss what, if anything, to communicate to the Russian Ambassador about the U.S. Sanctions. On that call, FLYNN and the PTT official discussed the U.S. Sanctions, including the potential impact of those sanctions on the incoming administration's foreign policy goals. The PTT official and FLYNN also discussed that the members of the Presidential Transition Team at Mar-a-Lago did not want Russia to escalate the situation.

d. Immediately after his phone call with the PTT official, FLYNN called the Russian Ambassador and requested that Russia not escalate the situation and only respond to the U.S. Sanctions in a reciprocal manner.

e. Shortly after his phone call with the Russian Ambassador, FLYNN spoke with the PTT official to report on the substance of his call with the Russian Ambassador, including their discussion of the U.S. Sanctions.

f. On or about December 30, 2016, Russian President Vladimir Putin released a statement indicating that Russia would not take retaliatory measures in response to the U.S. Sanctions at that time.

g. On or about December 31, 2016, the Russian Ambassador called FLYNN and informed him that Russia had chosen not to retaliate in response to FLYNN's request.

h. After his phone call with the Russian Ambassador, FLYNN spoke with senior members of the Presidential Transition Team about FLYNN's conversations with the Russian Ambassador regarding the U.S. Sanctions and Russia's decision not to escalate the situation.

False Statements Regarding FLYNN's Request that Foreign Officials Vote Against or Delay a United Nations Security Council Resolution

4. During the January 24 voluntary interview, FLYNN made additional false statements about calls he made to Russia and several other countries regarding a resolution submitted by Egypt to the United Nations Security Council on December 21, 2016. Specifically FLYNN falsely stated that he only asked the countries' positions on the vote, and that he did not request that any of the countries take any particular action on the resolution. FLYNN also falsely stated that the Russian Ambassador never described to him Russia's response to FLYNN's request regarding the resolution. In truth and in fact, however, FLYNN then and there knew that the following had occurred:

a. On or about December 21, 2016, Egypt submitted a resolution to the United Nations Security Council on the issue of Israeli settlements ("resolution"). The United Nations Security Council was scheduled to vote on the resolution the following day.

b. On or about December 22, 2016, a very senior member of the Presidential Transition Team directed FLYNN to contact officials from foreign governments, including Russia, to learn where each government stood on the resolution and to influence those governments to delay the vote or defeat the resolution.

c. On or about December 22, 2016, FLYNN contacted the Russian Ambassador about the pending vote. FLYNN informed the Russian Ambassador about the incoming administration's opposition to the resolution, and requested that Russia vote against or delay the resolution.

d. On or about December 23, 2016, FLYNN again spoke with the Russian Ambassador, who informed FLYNN that if it came to a vote Russia would not vote against the resolution.

Other False Statements Regarding FLYNN's Contacts with Foreign Governments

5. On March 7, 2017, FLYNN filed multiple documents with the Department of Justice pursuant to the Foreign Agents Registration Act ("FARA") pertaining to a project performed by him and his company, the Flynn Intel Group, Inc. ("FIG"), for the principal benefit of the Republic of Turkey ("Turkey project"). In the FARA filings, FLYNN made materially false statements and omissions, including by falsely stating that (a) FIG did not know whether or the extent to which the Republic of Turkey was involved in the Turkey project; (b) the Turkey project was focused on improving U.S. business organizations' confidence regarding doing business in Turkey; and (c) an op-ed by FLYNN published in *The Hill* on November 8, 2016, was written at his own initiative; and by omitting that officials from the Republic of Turkey provided supervision and direction over the Turkey project.

ROBERT S. MUELLER, III
Special Counsel

By: /s/
Brandon L. Van Grack
Zainab N. Ahmad
Senior Assistant Special Counsels
The Special Counsel's Office

Notes

1. What type of Rule 11 plea agreement is this? Does the defendant secure, under this agreement, any definite and measurable sentencing consideration? How may a defendant breach such an agreement, and what is the remedy for such a breach? What are the government's obligations under the agreement? Who would adjudicate any differences in opinion regarding the relative obligations of the parties under this model?

2. Many commentators concluded that Michael Flynn got a very sweet plea deal, either because Special Counsel Robert Mueller's evidence on the other accusations of criminal conduct was weak or, more likely, because Flynn could offer very significant cooperation. *See, e.g.*, Kate Brannan, Asha Rangappa & Alex Whiting, *What Does Flynn Plea Deal Mean?*, *available at* https://www.justsecurity.org/47552/flynn-plea-deal-mean/ (last visited August 30, 2018); Susan Hennessey & Benjamin Wittes, *The Unsolved Mystery of Michael Flynn's Plea Deal*, *available at* https://foreignpolicy.com/2017/12/08/the-unsolved-mystery-of-michael-flynns-plea-deal/ (last visited August 30, 2018). But does the fact that the plea deal involved only one count of false statements in fact mean that Flynn got a good deal? Consider section 3 ("Additional Charges") of the plea agreement; then read the Statement

of the Offense. What, exactly, did Mueller give up in this agreement? For example, does this plea agreement foreclose further prosecution for Flynn's alleged failure to register as a Foreign Agent under the Foreign Agents Registration Act (FARA)?

3. Note that this agreement conditions the receipt of a § 5K1.1 motion on the defendant's compliance with the terms of the agreement and on the defendant's provision of "substantial assistance" to law enforcement authorities. In other words, it does not condition the government's leniency on the defendant's ability to ensure certain results, such as the indictment or conviction of another person. Although some courts have found that cooperation agreements that condition prosecutorial leniency on the defendant's provision of specific testimony or results violate due process, the weight of authority seems to find such agreements unobjectionable. *See* Hughes, *supra* note 83, at 23-29. What are the dangers of such a practice?

4. One way of attempting to contain the dangers of perjured testimony is to require that the government deliver on its promises to the witness before he testifies, thus mitigating to some extent the perceived pressure felt by a witness to shape his testimony to please a prosecutor who still holds the power to deny the witness the benefit of the deal. This would mean that the cooperating witness would plead guilty and be sentenced prior to testifying in the grand jury or at any trial. This sequence is not, however, the general federal practice. Often the cooperating witness will plead guilty pursuant to a cooperation agreement, and the government and the cooperating witness will then both seek to defer sentencing until after the witness's cooperation is complete (*i.e.*, after he has testified in the grand jury or at trial). "[T]he great weight of modern authority, particularly in the federal courts, is that, in guilty-plea cases, the postponement of plea and sentence is unobjectionable. Federal courts consistently have refused to find a due process violation in this practice and have viewed the traditional safeguards of cross-examination, summation, and the court's charge to the jury as adequate for exposing the possibilities of perjury." Hughes, *supra* note 83, at 25. Why is this sequence in the best interests of the government *and* the cooperating witness? Why might counsel for the defendant against whom this cooperating witness will testify wish for a prompt sentencing?

5. Some judges refuse to defer a cooperating witness's sentencing until after the completion of his cooperation. In this case and other instances in which a defendant provides post-sentencing cooperation, the parties may use Fed. R. Crim. P. 35(b), to obtain post-sentencing credit for cooperation.

6. For an exploration of the considerations facing cooperating defendants and the challenges faced by defense counsel in advising their clients contemplating cooperation, see Daniel C. Richman, *Cooperating Clients*, 56 Ohio St. L.J. 69 (1995). Future prosecutors concerned with whether and how to use cooperating witnesses (as well as for future defense counsel seeking to discredit such witnesses) should consult the following article: Hon. Stephen S. Trott, *Words of Warning for Prosecutors Using Criminals as Witnesses*, 47 Hastings L.J. 1381, 1381-96 (1996).

7. In negotiating the terms of a cooperation agreement, defense counsel should be aware that certain of the information provided in the course of cooperation may impact the defendant's sentencing exposure. Counsel may wish, then, to negotiate for the exclusion of such information authorized in U.S.S.G. § 1B1.8(a). That section states that "[w]here a defendant agrees to cooperate with the government by providing information concerning unlawful activities of others, and as part of that cooperation agreement the government agrees that self-incriminating information provided pursuant to the agreement will not be used against the defendant, then such information shall not be used in determining the applicable Guidelines range, except to the extent provided in the agreement." This exemption is subject to important qualifications, including the inoperability of the exclusion in a prosecution for perjury or giving a false statement and in the event there is a breach of the cooperation agreement by the defendant. *Id.* § 1B1.8(b)(3), (4).

Chapter 20

PARALLEL PROCEEDINGS

In the white-collar context, it will not be unusual for alleged criminal misconduct to be investigated by a number of jurisdictions and parties. These materials concentrate on *civil* investigations and litigation collateral to a criminal proceeding. The potential plaintiffs in such parallel civil actions may include a wide variety of actors, from private litigants, to shareholders bringing derivative suits, to *qui tam* relators suing on behalf of the government, to a range of local, state, and federal governmental agencies. When involved in the defense of concurrent civil and criminal investigations or litigation, defense counsel face the difficult task of attempting to coordinate responses and to ensure that actions taken in one proceeding do not prejudice the client in another. While these materials do not attempt comprehensively to survey all the legal, practical, and strategic issues potentially involved, they should serve to illustrate some of the difficulties encountered in the effective defense of parallel proceedings.

In 2012, the Department of Justice issued a policy stressing that "Department prosecutors and civil attorneys handling white collar matters should timely communicate, coordinate, and cooperate with one another and with agency attorneys to the fullest extent appropriate to the case and permissible by law, whenever an alleged offense or violation of federal law gives rise to the potential for criminal, civil, regulatory, and/or agency administrative parallel (simultaneous or successive proceedings."[1] In her 2015 Memo regarding Individual Accountability for Corporate Wrongdoing, discussed *supra* Chapter 4, Deputy Attorney General Yates stressed that cooperation between civil and criminal DOJ attorneys should "happen early" and that civil attorneys, like criminal prosecutors, should focus on individual wrongdoing early and often. It appears likely, then, that more concurrent or sequential DOJ civil and criminal actions can be expected.

A. CONSTITUTIONALITY

Due process does not require that the government choose how it will proceed against a malefactor: it generally may proceed civilly, administratively, and criminally against a single

---

[1] U.S. Attorneys Manual (U.S.A.M.) § 1-12.000; *see also* Attorney General Memorandum to All United States Attorneys et al. Regarding Coordination of Parallel Criminal, Civil, Regulatory, and Administrative Proceedings (Jan. 30, 2012).

defendant concurrently or sequentially.[2] The leading case in this area is *United States v. Kordel,*[3] in which a corporation, its president, and its vice-president were simultaneously subjected to a criminal prosecution for violations of the Federal Food, Drug and Cosmetic Act and to a civil enforcement action by the Food and Drug Administration (FDA) based upon the same events. The Supreme Court held that the vice-president, who answered interrogatories addressed to the corporation in the civil enforcement proceeding, could have invoked his individual Fifth Amendment privilege against compulsory self-incrimination. It further ruled that, having failed to do so, the vice-president could not assert that he was "compelled" to give testimony against himself as a ground for overturning his conviction, even if information supplied in his answers provided evidence or leads useful to the government in the criminal prosecution. In the course of so holding, the Supreme Court rejected the individual defendants' argument that the government's conduct "reflected such unfairness and want of consideration for justice as independently to require the reversal of their convictions."[4] The Court stated:

> On the record before us, we cannot agree that the respondents have made out either a violation of due process or a departure from proper standards in the administration of justice requiring the exercise of our supervisory power. The public interest in protecting consumers throughout the Nation from misbranded drugs requires prompt action by the agency charged with responsibility for administration of the federal food and drug laws. But a rational decision whether to proceed criminally against those responsible for the misbranding may have to await consideration of a fuller record than that before the agency at the time of the civil seizure of the offending products. It would stultify enforcement of federal law to require a governmental agency such as the FDA invariably to choose either to forgo recommendation of a criminal prosecution once it seeks civil relief, or to defer civil proceedings pending the ultimate outcome of a criminal trial.[5]

Although it declined to hold that the maintenance of simultaneous parallel proceedings constitutes a *per se* violation of due process, the Court left open the possibility that under certain "special circumstances" such proceedings would be impermissible:

> We do not deal here with a case where the Government has brought a civil action solely to obtain evidence for its criminal prosecution or has failed to advise the defendant in its civil proceeding that it contemplates his criminal prosecution; nor with a case where the defendant is without counsel or reasonably fears prejudice from adverse pretrial publicity or other unfair injury; nor with any other special circumstances that might suggest the unconstitutionality or even the impropriety of this criminal prosecution.[6]

Defendants are rarely successful in relying on *Korbel* to attack parallel proceedings, as the following case demonstrates. The court's discussion of relevant precedents indicates,

---

[2] *See* United States v. Kordel, 397 U.S. 1 (1970); Sec. and Exch. Comm'n v. Dresser Indus., 628 F.2d 1368 (D.C. Cir. 1980) (*en banc*). In the tax context, see 26 U.S.C. § 7602 (1994); United States v. LaSalle Nat'l Bank, 437 U.S. 298 (1978); United States v. Michaud, 907 F.2d 750, 752 (7th Cir. 1990); *see also* United States v. Stuart, 489 U.S. 353 (1989).

[3] 397 U.S. 1.

[4] *Id.* at 11.

[5] *Id.*

[6] *Id.* at 11-12 (footnotes omitted).

however, that a *Korbel* objection is meeting with more success of late—a fact (if not yet a trend) of which prosecutors and regulators need to be aware.[7]

UNITED STATES v. MAHAFFY

446 F. Supp.2d 115 (E.D.N.Y. 2006)[8]

GLASSER, SENIOR DISTRICT JUDGE.

In this case, [defendant Michael A. Picone has] … been indicted for [inter alia] conspiracy to commit securities fraud. … Picone moves to suppress statements he made to the SEC, and dismiss Count Forty[-]One for making false statements in a government investigation …

It is well-established that as a general rule, "[t]he prosecution may use evidence acquired in a civil action in a subsequent criminal proceeding unless the defendant demonstrates that such use would violate his constitutional rights or depart from the proper administration of criminal justice." *United States v. Teyibo*, 877 F.Supp. 846, 855 (S.D.N.Y.1995) … (citing *United States v. Kordel*, 397 U.S. 1 (1970). In dicta, *Kordel* hypothesizes that there may be instances in which the Government's conduct "reflect[s] such unfairness and want of consideration for justice" as to warrant the court's reversal of a conviction or a dismissal of an indictment. … *See also United States v. Parrott*, 248 F.Supp. 196 (D.D.C.1965) (noting that "the Supreme Court has made it clear that Federal courts do have supervisory authority … over the manner in which Federal agents exercise their powers.") [citation omitted]. For example, *Kordel* suggests that "where the Government has brought a civil action solely to obtain evidence for its criminal prosecution or has failed to advise the defendant in its civil proceeding that it contemplates his criminal prosecution," such a departure has occurred.

Picone acknowledges that there is "concededly sparse precedent where such violations have been found." Nonetheless, analogizing to *United States v. Stringer*, 408 F.Supp.2d 1083 (D.Ore.2006) and *United States v. Scrushy*, 366 F.Supp.2d 1134 (N.D.Ala.2005), he moves to suppress statements he made to the SEC and to dismiss Count Forty-One, which charges him with making false statements to a government investigator. Picone asserts that the methods employed by the government to obtain his testimony before the SEC, and the failure of the government to promptly advise his counsel of a potential conflict of interest in his representation, violated his constitutional rights under the Fifth and Sixth Amendments to the United States Constitution.

In *Stringer*, the defendants were subjected to a securities fraud investigation by the SEC, lasting more than two years, which was orchestrated by the United States Attorney's Office ["USAO"] as a means of "conceal[ing] the criminal investigation from [the] defendants." *Stringer*, 408 F.Supp.2d at 1088. Evidence showed that several years prior to the criminal indictment, the Assistant United States Attorney and the SEC investigators had "extensive discussions" about the case, and, rather than initiating parallel proceedings, used the SEC investigation in order to "suppress the presence of the USAO." This, despite the fact that a decision had already been made that the case warranted prosecution. Moreover, when the defendant testified before the SEC, his attorney asked if the SEC was "working in conjunction with any other department of the United States, such as the United States Attorney's Office," and received a response that was "evasive and misleading, particularly

---

[7] *But see* United States v. Posada Carriles, 541 F.3d 344 (5th Cir. 2008) (reversing District Court's dismissal of the indictment founded on its findings of deception and outrageous governmental conduct and concluding, on the facts, that there was "no basis for a finding of outrageous conduct here").

[8] [Ed.:] This decision was affirmed by a summary, unpublished order. *See* United States v. Mahaffy, 2008 WL 2645493 (2d Cir. 2008).

B. FIFTH AMENDMENT IMPLICATIONS

As the above indicates, individuals may assert their Fifth Amendment privilege not only in the course of a criminal investigation or prosecution, but also in the course of civil proceedings:

> The [Fifth] Amendment not only protects the individual against being involuntarily called as a witness against himself in a criminal prosecution but also privileges him not to answer official questions put to him in any other proceeding, civil or criminal, formal or informal, where the answers might incriminate him in future criminal proceedings. *McCarthy v. Arndstein*, 266 U.S. 34, 40 (1924), squarely held that "[t]he privilege is not ordinarily dependent upon the nature of the proceeding in which the testimony is sought or is to be used. It applies alike to civil and criminal proceedings, wherever the answer might tend to subject to criminal responsibility him who gives it. The privilege protects a mere witness as fully as it does one who is also a party defendant."[10]

Further, to assert the privilege, the witness need not implicitly concede participation in criminal conduct. Indeed, the Supreme Court has held, in *Ohio v. Reiner*, that a defendant does not forfeit or waive her ability to rely on her Fifth Amendment right when she denies all culpability.[11] What considerations ought counsel to consider in the course of advising a defendant whether to assert a Fifth Amendment privilege in civil litigation?

1. WAIVER

Assume that your client is the subject of parallel criminal and civil proceedings. If your client testifies in one proceeding—for example, to resist a civil claim against him—will the client have waived his Fifth Amendment right against self-incrimination when asked to testify on the same subject before a criminal grand jury?

First, it is critical to understand that the warning requirements and stringent waiver standards set forth by the Supreme Court in *Miranda v. Arizona*[12] apply only when a defendant is subjected to a *"custodial interrogation"* by government agents. In that discrete context, a defendant's statements will be found *not* to constitute a waiver of his Fifth Amendment rights absent proof that the defendant was given *Miranda* warnings and that he knowingly, intelligently, and voluntarily waived his rights within the meaning of *Johnson v. Zerbst*.[13] In all other contexts, *including when a client is being deposed, testifying at trial, or even in the grand jury*,[14] courts generally do not require the provision of full *Miranda* warnings[15] and do not apply the *Zerbst* standard to test whether a defendant's otherwise voluntary statements comport with the Fifth Amendment. Thus, "an individual may lose the benefit of the privilege without making a *knowing* and *intelligent* waiver."[16]

The issue outside the custodial interrogation context will be not whether the witness received warnings or knowingly waived his or her rights, but rather whether his statement

---

[10] Lefkowitz v. Turley, 414 U.S. 70, 77 (1973).

[11] Ohio v. Reiner, 532 U.S. 17, 21 (2001) (*per curiam*); *see also supra* Chapter 15 (Fifth Amendment, Testimony).

[12] 384 U.S. 436 (1966).

[13] 304 U.S. 458 (1938).

[14] *See* United States v. Mandujano, 425 U.S. 564 (1976).

[15] *See supra* Chapter 13 (Grand Jury).

[16] Garner v. United States, 424 U.S. 648, 654 n.9 (1976) (footnote omitted) (emphasis added).

was *voluntary* as opposed to *compelled*. "The [Fifth] Amendment speaks of compulsion. It does not preclude a witness from testifying voluntarily in matters which may incriminate him. If, therefore, he desires the protection of the privilege, he must claim it or he will not be considered to have been 'compelled' within the meaning of the Amendment."[17] With certain exceptions (discussed in *LaSalle Bank Lake View v. Seguban, infra*), a witness who answers a question, even if the witness is not aware of the danger of incrimination or possibility of waiver, will not be deemed to have been "compelled" to be a witness against himself. In sum, a witness under examination outside of a custodial interrogation generally must use the privilege or lose it.[18]

Second, in testing the consequences of a defendant's decision to speak in one forum on his ability later to claim the privilege, *Rogers v. United States,*[19] while not on point, is the closest Supreme Court precedent. In *Rogers*, a witness testified before a federal grand jury that as Treasurer of the Communist Party of Denver she had turned membership records over to another person. The witness then refused to name the person to whom she had given the records, grounding her refusal upon her Fifth Amendment privilege against self-incrimination. The Supreme Court rejected her claim of privilege, compelling her to reveal the name of the person in possession of the records. The Court held that "[d]isclosure of a fact waives the privilege as to details," and found that, on these facts, the witness's privilege was not implicated because answering the question would not incriminate her further.[20]

Although *Rogers* concerned the scope of a waiver in the context of sequential questions in a *single* grand jury appearance, courts often reference the *Rogers* analysis in determining whether a witness's statement in one proceeding constitutes a waiver for purposes of *subsequent* proceedings. Under *Rogers*, courts hold that "where criminating facts have been voluntarily revealed, the privilege cannot be invoked to avoid disclosure of the details."[21] Accordingly, "[a]s to each question to which a claim of privilege is directed, the court must determine whether the answer to that particular question would subject the witness to a 'real danger' of further crimination."[22] In making this determination, however, a clear majority of courts apply an irrebuttable presumption of further incrimination where the witness is asked to reiterate his earlier statement in a "separate proceeding." Indeed, in most jurisdictions it is "hornbook law"[23] that "[t]he waiver involved is limited to the particular proceeding in which the witness volunteers the testimony."[24]

> The policy behind the majority rule that the privilege is 'proceeding specific' and not waived in a subsequent proceeding by waiver in an earlier one, rests on the thought that during the period between the successive proceedings conditions might have changed creating new grounds for apprehension, *e.g.*, the passage of new criminal law, or that the witness might be subject to different interrogation for different purposes at a subsequent proceeding, or that repetition of testimony in an independent proceeding

---

[17] Minnesota v. Murphy, 465 U.S. 420, 427 (1984) (quoting United States v. Monia, 317 U.S. 424, 427 (1943)).

[18] *But see* United States v. McLaughlin, 126 F.3d 130, 133-35 (3d Cir. 1997).

[19] 340 U.S. 367 (1951).

[20] *Id* at 373.

[21] *Id.*

[22] *Id.* at 374.

[23] United States v. Gary, 74 F.3d 304, 312 (1st Cir. 1996).

[24] United States v. Johnson, 488 F.2d 1206, 1210 (1st Cir. 1973) (guilty plea at Fed. R. Crim. P. 11 plea hearing held not to be a waiver of privilege defendant may claim when compelled to give testimony at codefendant's trial); *see also* United States v. James, 609 F.2d 36, 45 (2d Cir. 1979).

might itself be incriminating, even if it merely repeated or acknowledged the witness' earlier testimony, because it could constitute an independent source of evidence against him or her.[25]

Courts have construed "separate proceedings" to include separate legal actions as well as, in some instances, distinct phases of related litigation. Thus, for example, courts have held that: testimony in a deposition in one civil case does not preclude a Fifth Amendment assertion when the witness is called for a deposition in another case;[26] statements made to law enforcement officials do not bar a witness from asserting his privilege in a subsequent grand jury examination or at trial;[27] testimony before a grand jury or at some type of preliminary hearing does not bar assertion of the privilege at trial;[28] testimony in a trial does not waive assertion of the privilege in a subsequent grand jury investigation;[29] disclosures made in pleadings or affidavits prior to trial do not preclude a witness from asserting his privilege at a later trial[30] or before a legislative committee;[31] disclosures made to a grand jury do not bar the witness from asserting the privilege before the same grand jury when his appearances were separated by indictment and conviction for crimes related to the original disclosures and the passage of nearly a year.[32] Although not relying upon the above rule, the Supreme Court also has made clear that the privilege against self-incrimination survives a guilty plea, holding that a defendant who had pleaded guilty could assert her Fifth Amendment right not to testify at sentencing and that a sentencing judge could not draw an adverse inference from her assertion of her right.[33]

As the above examples may illustrate, it is not always clear whether sequential hearings at which the witness is asked to make statements constitute two separate "proceedings" or the same "proceeding."[34] Courts are much more likely to find that two hearings are parts of a single proceeding where they are two sequential civil hearings, as opposed to a civil then criminal hearing or two sequential criminal hearings.

When a court finds that the proceedings are the same, either the *Rogers* further incrimination test or a permutation of that test articulated by the Second Circuit in *Klein v. Harris*[35] is applied. Under *Klein*, the court is to "indulge every reasonable presumption" in favor of the party seeking to invoke the privilege and the court should presume waiver only if "(1) the witness' prior [sworn] statements have created a significant likelihood that the finder of fact will be left with and prone to rely on a distorted view of the truth, and (2) the witness had reason to know that his prior statements would be interpreted as a waiver of the fifth amendment's

---

[25] *In re* Morganroth, 718 F.2d 161, 165 (6th Cir. 1983) (holding that witness's previous testimony in civil deposition did not waive privilege as to deposition in later civil suit because new testimony could subject him to danger of perjury charges); *see also* United States v. Miranti, 253 F.2d 135, 140 (2d Cir. 1958).

[26] *See, e.g.*, Carter-Wallace, Inc. v. Hartz Mountain Indus. Inc., 553 F.Supp. 45, 49 (S.D.N.Y. 1982).

[27] *See, e.g.*, United States v. Goodman, 289 F.2d 256, 259 (4th Cir.1961); *Miranti*, 253 F.2d at 138; *James*, 609 F.2d at 45.

[28] *See, e.g.*, *In re* Neff, 206 F.2d 149, 152-53 (3d Cir. 1953).

[29] *See, e.g.*, United States v. Field, 193 F.2d 109, 110 (2d Cir. 1951).

[30] *See, e.g.*, United States v. Trejo-Zambrano, 582 F.2d 460, 464 (9th Cir. 1978).

[31] *See, e.g.*, Poretto v. United States, 196 F.2d 392, 396 (5th Cir. 1952).

[32] *Miranti*, 253 F.2d at 140.

[33] Mitchell v. United States, 526 U.S. 314 (1999).

[34] *See, e.g.*, *In re* Gi Yeong Nam, 245 B.R. 216 (Bankr. E.D. Pa. 2000).

[35] 667 F.2d 274 (2d Cir. 1981).

privilege against self-incrimination."[36] The *Klein* test is most frequently applied, with *Rogers,* in cases in which a defendant answers some questions in a deposition but refuses to answer others,[37] and in bankruptcy cases when several sequential proceedings relate to one bankruptcy petition.[38] Regardless of the posture of the case, the courts are reluctant to find a waiver of the privilege against self-incrimination. This is in line with Supreme Court precedent that holds that "waiver of constitutional rights … is not lightly to be inferred."[39]

A distinct minority view was articulated by the D.C. Circuit in *Ellis v. United States.*[40] In *Ellis,* the court held that "where a non-indicted witness has waived his Fifth Amendment privilege by testifying before a grand jury voluntarily and with knowledge of his privilege, his waiver extends to a subsequent trial based on an indictment returned by the grand jury that heard his testimony."[41] In so ruling, the *Ellis* court rejected a "mechanical" presumption that successive proceedings or a lapse in time between different instances of testimony during the same proceeding create a real danger of further incrimination. [42] Instead, courts adopting *Ellis*'s minority approach look at the actual circumstances of the testimony and hold that the waiver will carry through to a subsequent proceeding unless there actually has been a material change in circumstances between the two proceedings.[43]

2. ADVERSE INFERENCES AND OTHER "PENALTIES"

The above discussion concerned whether a witness will be required to testify in a subsequent proceeding to facts previously the subject of testimony in a prior or related proceeding. The discussion did *not* address whether the previous testimony will *itself* be admissible in a subsequent proceeding. Even if the court finds no waiver and thus refuses to compel the witness to reiterate his statements, the prior statements may well be independently admissible on a number of grounds, most commonly as a party admission[44] or coconspirator's statement.[45] Given that counsel may easily win the waiver battle but lose the admissibility war, these evidentiary issues are often critical.

Further, the dangers of making statements in collateral civil litigation extend beyond the potential for evidentiary use of such statements in a criminal case. The government may also use any information revealed in developing its criminal case or rebutting a defense. Finally, the defendant may be cross-examined on the basis of statements made in a civil action which are inconsistent with his criminal trial testimony.

If, to sidestep these and other difficulties, the criminal defendant asserts his Fifth Amendment right to avoid making testimonial communications in the course of the civil

---

[36] *Id.* at 287.

[37] *See, e.g.,* Uni Supply, Inc. v. Government of Israel, 1993 WL 6204 (S.D.N.Y. 1993); Dogan Enters., Inc. v. Hubsher, 1987 WL 20312 (E.D.N.Y. 1987); *see also* SEC v. Cayman Islands Reinsurance Corp., 551 F.Supp. 1056 (S.D.N.Y. 1982).

[38] *See, e.g., In re* Blan, 239 B.R. 385, 394-96 (Bankr. W.D. Ark. 1999); *In re* A & L Oil Co., 200 B.R. 21, 24-25 (Bankr. D. N.J. 1996).

[39] Smith v. United States, 337 U.S. 137, 150 (1949).

[40] 416 F.2d 791 (D.C.Cir. 1969); *see also* United States v. Miller, 904 F.2d 65 (D.C. Cir. 1990) (reaffirming rule).

[41] 416 F.2d at 805.

[42] *Id.* at 801.

[43] *Id.* at 805.

[44] *See* Fed. R. Evid. 801(d)(2)(A) (party's prior statement offered against that party is not hearsay; statement need not be against the party's interest or made under oath).

[45] *See* Fed. R. Evid. 801(d)(2)(E).

proceeding, what are the consequences? May adverse inferences in the civil litigation be based upon his assertion of his right against self-incrimination? May a court impose sanctions (*e.g.*, judgment on the pleadings or dismissal of a complaint) based upon the criminal defendant's failure to respond to a complaint or discovery requests?

The prevailing rule in *criminal cases* is that no adverse inference may constitutionally be drawn from a defendant's failure to testify.[46] However, the Supreme Court "has recognized 'the prevailing rule that the Fifth Amendment does not forbid adverse inferences against parties to *civil actions* when they refuse to testify in response to probative evidence offered against them,' at least where refusal to waive the privilege does not lead 'automatically and without more to [the] imposition of sanctions.'"[47] The following case illustrates the principles employed to determine whether relief or sanctions may be ordered where a defendant relies on his Fifth Amendment rights in the course of collateral civil proceedings.

LASALLE BANK LAKE VIEW v. SEGUBAN
54 F.3d 387 (7th Cir. 1995)

ILANA DIAMOND ROVNER, CIRCUIT JUDGE.

LaSalle Bank Lake View has sued its former Assistant Teller Manager, Ellen Seguban, under the Racketeer Influenced and Corrupt Organizations Act ("RICO"), 18 U.S.C. § 1962(c) & (d), asserting that she embezzled $940,000 from the bank during twelve years of her employment there. The action, which was filed on September 29, 1993, also named as a defendant Ellen's husband, Rafael Seguban, alleging that he accepted and used the funds with full knowledge of their illegal source. Along with its RICO claims, the bank brought supplemental state law claims for breach of fiduciary duty, conversion, and fraud.

In addition to this civil action, the Bank's allegations spawned a criminal investigation by the United States Attorney for the Northern District of Illinois. That investigation was underway on February 4, 1994, when the Bank moved for summary judgment in this action. The Segubans therefore asserted their Fifth Amendment privilege against self-incrimination in response to the Bank's motion and offered no evidence to rebut the Bank's statement of material facts. Finding that the Segubans had thereby failed to show the existence of a material factual dispute, the district court granted the Bank's motion and entered judgment against the Segubans in the amount of $2,820,000, three times the Bank's damages of $940,000, in accordance with RICO's trebling provision, 18 U.S.C. § 1964(c). The Segubans now appeal, arguing that the district court improperly drew an inference of guilt based on their assertion of the Fifth Amendment privilege, and that without that inference the evidence did not entitle the bank to judgment as a matter of law. We reverse and remand for further proceedings.

The Northern District of Illinois' Local Rule 12(M) requires that a movant for summary judgment file "a statement of material facts as to which the moving party contends there is no genuine issue and that entitle the moving party to a judgment as a matter of law ... ." In response to that statement, Local Rule 12(N) requires the opposing party to file "a response to each numbered paragraph in the moving party's statement, including, in the case of any disagreement, specific references to the affidavits, parts of the record, and other supporting materials relied upon" and "a statement, consisting of short numbered paragraphs, of any additional facts that require the denial of summary judgment ... ," also supported by record

---

[46] *See* Griffin v. California, 380 U.S. 609, 614 (1965); *see also* Mitchell v. United States, 526 U.S. 314, 326 (1999) (holding that bar on adverse inferences extends to judge's consideration of defendant's silence at sentencing).

[47] *Mitchell*, 526 U.S. at 326 (emphasis added) (quoting Baxter v. Palmigiano, 425 U.S. 308, 318 (1976) and Lefkowitz v. Cunningham, 431 U.S. 801, 808, n. 5 (1977)); *see also* Ohio Adult Parole Auth. v. Woodard, 523 U.S. 272, 286 (1998) (holding that adverse inference may be drawn from refusal to answer in "civil" clemency proceeding before Ohio Adult Parole Authority).

citations. Finally, Rule 12(N) admonishes that "[a]ll material facts set forth in the statement required of the moving party will be deemed to be admitted unless controverted by the statement of the opposing party." We have on numerous occasions upheld a district court's strict adherence to that rule. Thus, if the party opposing summary judgment fails to respond to the facts set out by the movant, the court may assume those facts to be admitted and use them in determining whether the movant is entitled to judgment as a matter of law. The first question posed by this appeal is whether the normal operation of Rule 12(N) is precluded here because the Segubans' failure to file a 12(N) response was based on their assertion of the Fifth Amendment privilege.[48]

The Fifth Amendment provides that "[n]o person ... shall be compelled in any criminal case to be a witness against himself ... ." Not limited to the criminal context, the privilege protects the individual from being compelled "'to answer official questions put to him in any ... proceeding, civil or criminal, formal or informal, where the answers might incriminate him in future criminal proceedings.'" *Baxter v. Palmigiano*, 425 U.S. 308, 316 (1976) (quoting *Lefkowitz v. Turley*, 414 U.S. 70, 77 (1973)). If required to answer, the individual "must be offered 'whatever immunity is required to supplant the privilege' and may not be required to 'waive such immunity.'" In addition to direct compulsion, the Supreme Court has prohibited practices that are coercive in that they make the exercise of the privilege "costly." *Spevack v. Klein*, 385 U.S. 511, 515 (1967). Into that category the Court has placed sanctions with serious economic consequences, such as the loss of employment or state contracts. *See Lefkowitz*, 414 U.S. 70 (architects may not be forced to choose between loss of state contracts and self-incrimination); *Uniformed Sanitation Men Ass'n v. Commissioner of Sanitation*, 392 U.S. 280 (1968) (public employees may not be forced to chose [sic] between discharge from employment and self-incrimination); *Gardner v. Broderick*, 392 U.S. 273 (1968) (same); *Spevack*, 385 U.S. 511 (attorney may not be disbarred for exercising the privilege); *Garrity v. New Jersey*, 385 U.S. 493 (1967) (testimony compelled by threatened loss of employment cannot be used in subsequent criminal prosecution).

In *Baxter v. Palmigiano*, 425 U.S. 308 (1976), the Court discussed whether the drawing of an adverse inference from Fifth Amendment silence in a civil proceeding imposed too high a cost on the exercise of the privilege. In that case, a prison inmate had been brought before a prison disciplinary board on charges of inciting a disturbance. Informed that state criminal charges might also be brought against him, the inmate was advised that he could remain silent at the disciplinary proceeding, but that his silence "would be held against him" in that forum. At the hearing, Palmigiano was confronted with incriminating evidence and remained silent. The board placed him in segregation for thirty days and downgraded his institutional status. The Court held that the rule it had articulated in the *Garrity-Lefkowitz* line of cases did not prohibit the drawing of an adverse inference from Fifth Amendment silence in a prison disciplinary proceeding when incriminating evidence had also been presented. Such an inference did not, in other words, impose an unconstitutional cost on the exercise of the privilege. The rule that adverse inferences may be drawn from Fifth Amendment silence in civil proceedings has been widely recognized by the circuit courts of appeals, including our own, in the two decades since *Baxter* was decided.[49]

But while holding that factual inferences based on the assertion of the privilege do not place too high a cost on its exercise, the *Baxter* Court was just as clear that the rule of *Lefkowitz* and its predecessors would be violated if the failure to testify alone were taken as an admission of guilt, without regard to other evidence:

---

[48] [Court's footnote 2:] The Segubans did not move the district court to stay the Bank's civil action until the criminal investigation was concluded. We therefore need not consider the propriety of such a course, which is sometimes taken to avoid the dilemma faced by defendants like the Segubans.

[49] [Court's footnote 4:] Notably, the party asserting the privilege is not the only one whose case is consequently impaired. The opponent, unable to obtain discovery, is also disadvantaged.

[T]his case is very different from the circumstances before the Court in the *Garrity-Lefkowitz* decisions, where refusal to submit to interrogation and to waive the Fifth Amendment privilege, standing alone and without regard to the other evidence, resulted in loss of employment or opportunity to contract with the State. There, failure to respond to interrogation was treated as a final admission of guilt. Here, Palmigiano remained silent at the hearing in the face of evidence that incriminated him; and, as far as this record reveals, his silence was given no more evidentiary value than was warranted by the facts surrounding this case.

Thus, although "the Fifth Amendment does not forbid adverse inferences against parties to civil actions when they refuse to testify in response to probative evidence offered against them," an analysis of that evidence is nonetheless required. Silence is a relevant factor to be considered in light of the proffered evidence, but the direct inference of guilt from silence is forbidden. The Court reiterated that limitation on *Baxter* the following year in *Lefkowitz v. Cunningham*, which characterized *Baxter*'s holding in this way:

> *Baxter* did no more than permit an inference to be drawn in a civil case from a party's refusal to testify. Respondent's silence in *Baxter* was only one of a number of factors to be considered by the finder of fact in assessing a penalty, and was given no more probative value than the facts of the case warranted; here, refusal to waive the Fifth Amendment privilege leads automatically and without more to imposition of sanctions.

We further explored the constitutionally acceptable inference that could be drawn from the assertion of the Fifth Amendment privilege in [*National Acceptance Co. v. Bathalter*, 705 F.2d 924, 924 (7th Cir.1983)], when we held that the failure to answer the allegations of a civil complaint based on an assertion of the Fifth Amendment privilege[50] could not be construed as an admission of those allegations even though Fed.R.Civ.P. 8(d)[51] would otherwise require that result. We distinguished *Baxter* on the ground that it had considered silence in response to adverse evidence rather than to the mere allegations of a complaint. We concluded:

> It is our best judgment, in the light of *Baxter*, that even in a civil case a judgment imposing liability cannot rest solely upon a privileged refusal to admit or deny at the pleading stage. We conclude that defendant's claim of privilege should not have been deemed an admission, and that plaintiff should have been put to its proof, either by way of evidentiary support for a motion for summary judgment or at trial.

Thus, deeming an allegation of a complaint to be admitted based on the invocation of the Fifth Amendment privilege without requiring the complainant to produce evidence in support of its allegations would impose too great a cost and exceed the authorization of *Baxter*.

How does the admission of properly supported 12(M) facts, effected automatically by operation of Rule 12(N), fare in light of these cases? It seems to us much closer to the inference permitted by *Baxter* than to the admission prohibited by *National Acceptance*. *Baxter*'s concern, after all (as is clear not only from *Baxter* but from *Cunningham* and *National Acceptance* as well), is that the defendant's silence be weighed in light of other evidence rather than leading directly and without more to the conclusion of guilt or liability. And it was the absence of such other

---

[50] [Court's footnote 5:] Like the Segubans, Bathalter's assertion of the privilege was based on the fact that an investigation by federal prosecutors was simultaneously underway.

[51] [Court's footnote 6:] Rule 8(d), which has not changed since the issuance of *National Acceptance*, provides that "[a]verments in a pleading to which a responsive pleading is required ... are admitted when not denied in the responsive pleading."

proof that underlay our rejection of the automatic admission effected by Fed.R.Civ.P. 8(d) in *National Acceptance*:

> A complaint, ... no matter how detailed, is not evidence. It contains only averments and claims which, unless admitted, must be proved in order to support a judgment.

Unlike Rule 8(d), Local Rule 12(N), which deems admitted unrebutted Rule 12(M) facts that are evidentiarily supported, does no more than operationalize an inference that could in any event be reasonably drawn from Fifth Amendment silence in the face of such evidence—that the facts it reveals are true. This particular inference seems to us clearly permissible under *Baxter*,[52] and the fact that the admission is achieved automatically through operation of a rule rather than subjectively by a finder of fact does not, in our view, overstep the bounds of constitutional acceptability.[53]

Baxter's limitation, however, bears repetition at this point: although inferences based on the assertion of the privilege are permissible, the entry of judgment based only on the invocation of the privilege and "without regard to the other evidence" exceeds constitutional bounds. Our holding regarding Rule 12(N), then, is conditioned on the fact that the admission it effects does not lead directly and without more to the entry of summary judgment, but merely establishes the factual basis from which the Rule 56 analysis will proceed. As we recently explained ... ,

> "[S]trict enforcement of Rule 12(n) does not mean that a party's failure to submit a timely filing automatically results in summary judgment for the opposing party." ... Rule 56(e) permits judgment for the moving party only "if appropriate—that is, if the motion demonstrates that there is no genuine issue of material fact and that the movant is entitled to judgment as a matter of law." ... Thus, even where many or all of the material facts are undisputed, the court still must ascertain that judgment is proper "as a matter of governing law." ...

... The onus on the district court to engage in the second step of the summary judgment analysis is particularly weighty here, where that analysis alone distinguishes a constitutional from an unconstitutional approach. ...

---

[52] [Court's footnote 7:] The "inference" effected by Rule 12(N)—that the facts revealed by the opponent's evidence are true—seems to be among the more conservative of inferences that might be drawn from Fifth Amendment silence, because it does not give any separate and additional evidentiary weight to the silence itself. The propriety in the summary judgment context of drawing any additional inferences from silence (such as that the withheld testimony would have been harmful to the defendant's case) poses a more difficult question. Treating the Segubans' silence as a separate piece of evidence supporting the Bank's motion for summary judgment and drawing inferences against the Segubans on the basis of that fact seems to be in tension with the ordinary summary judgment rule that all reasonable inferences must be drawn in favor of the nonmovant. We need not address that question here, as the district court does not appear to have made any such inference and the Bank has not suggested that it should have done so.

[53] [Court's footnote 8:] We also note that the Fifth Amendment is in any event least implicated in a civil suit, like this one, between two private parties. As Justice Brennan noted when he dissented from the Court's holding in *Baxter*:

> I would have difficulty holding such an inference impermissible in civil cases involving only private parties ... . In a civil suit involving only private parties, no party brings to the battle the awesome powers of the government, and therefore to permit an adverse inference to be drawn from exercise of the privilege does not implicate the policy considerations underlying the privilege.

Notes

1. Is the rule permitting a (nondeterminative) adverse inference to be drawn in civil cases based on a witness's assertion of his Fifth Amendment right consistent with the purposes underlying that right? Should the availability of the inference depend upon the circumstances—for example, the amount of the judgment at stake or the fact that the plaintiffs are relying on the self-same statute and theory that prosecutors will likely use in a subsequent criminal case? Should the identity of the parties or the imminency of criminal proceedings matter? "[D]ecisions by federal courts have established that an adverse inference is equally to be drawn where the government is a party to the civil proceeding ... [and] in enforcement actions brought by the SEC." SEC v. Tome, 638 F.Supp. 629, 632 (S.D.N.Y. 1986). Also, "federal courts have held that the pendency of related criminal proceedings is irrelevant in determining whether to draw an adverse inference, and many decisions have drawn an adverse inference when criminal charges are pending." *Id.*

2. As discussed in earlier materials, collective entities, including corporations, have no Fifth Amendment privilege. Fed. R. Evid. 801(d)(2)(D) provides that a statement "made by the party's agent or employee on a matter within the scope of that relationship while it existed" is not hearsay and is therefore admissible against a corporate party. Suppose that, rather than speaking, the corporate agent legitimately asserts her Fifth Amendment right. May an adverse inference based on that assertion be drawn against the *corporation* in civil proceedings?

> ... [I]t is permissible to draw a negative inference against the corporation based upon the corporate agent's assertion of his Fifth Amendment privilege. Although it may seem unfair to hold the employee's assertion of this personal right against the company, courts have not been reluctant to do so.
>
> The more difficult situation for corporations is when an employee has been terminated and invokes his Fifth Amendment privilege when called by the adverse party in a civil proceeding. Courts have held that even though the agency relationship between the company and the former employee has ended, the trier of fact is still free to draw a negative inference against the company based upon the *former* employee's assertion of the privilege.

Dan K. Webb, Robert W. Tarun & Steven F. Molo, Corporate Internal Investigations § 14.08[2], at 14-38 to 39 (Law Journal Press 2018) (footnotes omitted). The Third Circuit has reasoned: "An employee's self-interest would counsel him to exculpate his employer, if possible. The witness, as well, would know the facts about which he is called to testify since they relate to the scope of his employment. The employer, moreover, could rebut any adverse inference that might attend the employee's silence, by producing contrary testimonial or documentary evidence." Rad Services, Inc. v. Aetna Cas. & Sur. Co., 808 F.2d 271, 275 (3d Cir. 1986); *see also* Robert Heidt, *The Conjurer's Circle—The Fifth Amendment Privilege in Civil Cases*, 91 Yale L.J. 1062 (1982). Do you agree? Is the rule more troubling with respect to former employees?

3. *"State Action": Private Self-Regulatory Organizations.* Note that the "compulsion" must be visited upon the defendant by state actors to waive his Fifth Amendment rights. Courts generally are reluctant to extend the category of "state actors" to include others, such as professional self-regulatory organizations, who may also be investigating the defendant. *D.L. Cromwell Investments, Inc. v. NASD Regulation, Inc.*, 279 F.3d 155 (2d Cir. 2002), is representative. In that case, plaintiffs, all members of the National Association of Securities Dealers, Inc. (NASD), sued to enjoin the investigatory arm of the NASD from compelling them—under threat of sanctions authorized by NASD rule—to submit to on-the-record interviews "arguing that [the NASD investigators were] a willing tool of the prosecutors and that the compelled interviews would therefore violate their Fifth Amendment privilege

against self-incrimination." *Id.* at 156-57. The NASD is a private, not-for-profit, self-regulatory organization registered with the SEC. The investigating arm of the NASD is responsible for investigating and commencing disciplinary proceedings against NASD members relating to their compliance with the federal securities laws and regulations. The NASD division of enforcement conducts hearings and imposes sanctions that are subject, ultimately, to review by the SEC.

In this case, the NASD investigators, FBI, and U.S. Attorneys office were all investigating the plaintiffs. In the course of their parallel investigations, they cooperated extensively. For example, the NASD investigators turned documents and other information over to the FBI. They also assisted the U.S. Attorneys Office in preparing a grand jury subpoena and in receiving the information produced by the subpoena recipient in response to that subpoena. *Id.* at 158. The U.S. Attorneys Office shared with the NASD information (including that generated through a confidential informant) and allowed NASD investigators access to documents seized pursuant to a search warrant. *Id.*

The Second Circuit, however, affirmed the district court's denial of relief, reasoning:

> To establish a Fifth Amendment violation, a plaintiff must demonstrate "that in denying the plaintiff's constitutional rights, the defendant's conduct constituted state action." That is because the Fifth Amendment restricts only governmental conduct, and will constrain a private entity only insofar as its actions are found to be "fairly attributable" to the government.
>
> Actions are "fairly attributable" to the government where "there is a sufficiently close nexus between the State and the challenged action of the regulated entity." That nexus exists either (1) where the state "has exercise coercive power [over a private decision] or has provided such significant encouragement, either over or covert, that the choice must in law be deemed to be that of the State"; or (2) where "the private entity has exercised powers that are 'traditionally the exclusive prerogative of the State.'"
>
> Under [this] test, even heavily-regulated private entities generally are held not to be state actors. ... It has been found, repeatedly, that the NASD itself is not a government functionary. ... Testimony in an NASD proceeding may entail exposure to criminal liability, but that in itself is not enough to establish the requisite governmental nexus. ... Here, the district court found "no direct evidence of such governmental involvement," and that finding is not clearly erroneous.

Id. at 161-62.

4. *"State Action": Cooperating Corporations.* In *United States v. Stein*, 440 F. Supp. 2d 315 (S.D.N.Y. 2006), Judge Kaplan issued a ruling attributing to the government the actions of private counsel conducting an internal corporate investigation in an effort to cooperate with the prosecution—a ruling that has received *great* attention. In *Stein*, individual employees of KPMG argued that they were coerced into speaking to the government by KPMG's policy decreeing that the company would cease paying attorneys' fees to employees' individual defense attorneys if the employees refused to cooperate with the government. This corporate policy was instituted with the object of securing for KPMG credit for fulsome cooperation with the government and, accordingly, declination of criminal charges. Recall the discussion, *supra*, in Chapter 4 (Entity Liability) of the Holder/Thompson/McNulty/Filip memos, which outline the DOJ's charging policy for organizations. Recall, too, the importance of corporate cooperation in the DOJ's decision-making under that policy. In assessing whether KPMG's "coercive" action was attributable to the government for constitutional purposes, the court explained:

> [Defendants] point to the [Filip Memo's predecessor, the] Thompson Memorandum, which quite specifically tells a company under investigation, as was KPMG, that a failure to ensure that its employees tell prosecutors what they know may contribute to a decision

to indict and, in this case, likely destroy the company. And they point also to the [U.S. Attorney's Office's (USAO's)] close involvement in KPMG's decision making process by, among other things, pointedly reminding KPMG that it would consider the Thompson Memorandum in deciding whether to indict, saying that payment of employee legal fees would be viewed "under a microscope," and reporting to KPMG the identities of employees who refused to make statements in circumstances in which the USAO knew full well that KPMG would pressure them to talk to prosecutors.

Id. at 336-37. Judge Kaplan ruled that "the government, both through the Thompson Memorandum and the actions of the USAO, quite deliberately coerced, and in any case significantly encouraged, KPMG to pressure its employees to surrender their Fifth Amendment rights. There is a clear nexus between the government 'and the specific conduct of which'" the defendants were complaining. *Id.* at 337. Having found that KMPG's actions in this regard were "fairly attributable" to the government, the court ruled that "the coerced statements and their fruits must be suppressed." *Id.* at 337-38.

The Second Circuit upheld the District Court's findings of fact as well as its legal conclusion regarding state action. *See* excerpted decision, *supra*, Chapter 18. In so doing, the court explained:

> KPMG's adoption and enforcement of the Fees Policy amounted to "state action" because KPMG "operate[d] as a willful participant in joint activity" with the government, and because the USAO "significant[ly] encourage[d]" KPMG to withhold legal fees from defendants upon indictment. The government brought home to KPMG that its survival depended on its role in a joint project with the government to advance government prosecutions. The government is therefore legally "responsible for the specific conduct of which the [criminal defendants] complain[]." ...

United States v. Stein, 541 F.3d 130, 147 (2d Cir. 2008).

Note that the DOJ has changed its policy with respect to requests for fee cut-offs in the newest iteration of the DOJ corporate charging policy, the Filip Memo (*see supra* Chapter 4), and accordingly (hopefully) these particular facts may not recur. But wouldn't the *Stein* decision apply equally to corporate threats to fire employees who assert their Fifth Amendment rights—a practice that continues?

5. Recall our discussion in Chapter 6 (Obstruction) of the cases in which the DOJ has prosecuted corporate officers for lying to corporate counsel, on the apparent theory that corporate counsel are acting as "arms of the government" while conducting internal corporate investigations aimed at securing for the corporation cooperation credit and declination of criminal charges. The defense in those cases argued that there was an insufficient "nexus" between the lies and the government investigation for purposes of liability under the obstruction statutes. The government countered that there was an obvious "nexus" between the executives' lies to corporate counsel and the official proceedings (grand jury and the Securities and Exchange Commission (SEC) investigations) at issue because the defendants believed that the corporation might cooperate with the government and at least contemplated that counsel would turn over the defendants' false or misleading statements to the grand jury and SEC. These prosecutions are perfectly consistent with the government's conception of the proper role of the corporation and corporate counsel when allegations of wrongdoing erupt. But might they be counterproductive in terms of the "state action" question discussed above? Might courts take the government theory to heart and decide that if corporate lawyers are indeed acting as "arms of the government," they must abide by the same constitutional restraints that bind state actors? Consider the following:

> While arguing that there is a sufficient "nexus" between lies to counsel and the conduct of the official investigation for purposes of the obstruction statutes, the DOJ

has, at the same time, resisted attempts to impute to it the actions corporations take to secure the benefits of the cooperation policy. These actions, prosecutors contend, lack a sufficient "nexus" to the government's investigation and thus cannot constitute "state action" for constitutional purposes. It is difficult to credit the government's contention that a "nexus" sufficient to secure up to twenty years in jail for obstruction is not a "nexus" for purposes of constraining government action. And if the actions of counsel are deemed "state action," the information they secure, for example by threatening employees who do not cooperate with the government with employment termination, may well be suppressed and thus unusable by the government.

Julie Rose O'Sullivan, *The DOJ Risks Killing the Golden Goose Through Computer Associates/Singleton Theories of Obstruction*, 44 Am. Crim. L. Rev. 1447, 1451 (2007).

C. OBTAINING A STAY OF CIVIL OR ADMINISTRATIVE PROCEEDINGS

As suggested by the court in *LaSalle Bank Lake View*, a defendant facing parallel proceedings may consider applying for a stay of civil or administrative proceedings. The arguments for such an attempt may be obvious—to avoid the problems discussed above and the burdens of having to fight on multiple fronts. Sometimes, however, defendants may actually wish to proceed with the civil litigation in hopes that it will provide them with much more fulsome discovery than will the criminal proceeding. Which, of course, is one of the reasons the government may move for a stay even if the defendant does not. The government's primary argument in such motions is generally that the civil discovery process may provide the defendant discovery to which he would not otherwise be entitled under the criminal procedure rules. While defendants generally have difficulty securing a stay, once an indictment has been returned the government "often moves for and frequently obtains relief preventing a criminal defendant from using parallel civil proceedings to gain premature access to evidence and information pertinent to the criminal case,"[54] although some recent cases indicate that this circumstance may be changing.[55] The staying of civil or administrative proceedings until the conclusion of a prospective or pending criminal case is generally considered an extraordinary measure (at least when requested by the defendant). As explained by Dan K. Webb, Robert W. Tarun, and Steven F. Molo, courts will generally consider four factors in deciding whether to grant a stay:[56]

---

[54] SEC v. Doody, 186 F.Supp.2d 379, 381 (S.D.N.Y. 2002); *see also* Mem. of Law in Supp. of Government's Appl. to Intervene and for a Stay of Disc., Semon v. Stewart, 2003 WL 22850066 (S.D.N.Y. Sept. 29, 2003) (government motion to intervene and seek a limited stay in a civil suit in which Martha Stewart sought discovery).

[55] *See, e.g.,* Jodi Misher Peikin & James R. Stovall, *Stays in Parallel Proceedings*, 17 Bus. Crimes Bull. 3 (April 2010); Stanley S. Arkin & Charles Sullivan, *DOJ Requests to Stay Civil Discovery: Recent Trends*, Bus. Crimes Bull. 3, 4 (Aug. 2004) (noting that some courts have been more willing to "scrutinize carefully government assertions of prejudice and potential witness tampering and defendants' claims of hardship and prejudice").

[56] Reproduced with the permission of the publisher from Section 14.04[3] of Chapter 14, "Parallel Proceedings," as it appears in *Corporate Internal Investigations* by Dan K. Webb, Robert W. Tarun & Steven F. Molo. Published by Law Journal Press, a division of ALM. © ALM Properties, Inc. All rights reserved. Copies of the complete work may be ordered from Law Journal Press, Book Fulfillment Department, 105 Madison Avenue, New York, New York 10016 or at www.lawcatalog.com or by calling 800-537-2128, ext. 9300.

[a]—The Effect on the Plaintiff's Interests. ... The types of prejudice that a plaintiff may suffer if a stay is granted include the general weakening of evidence over time ... and the dissipation of assets that would be the subject of the civil proceedings.

[b]—The Effect on the Defendant's Interests. ... [C]ourts focus primarily on the risk to a defendant's Fifth Amendment privilege and ability to present a defense. This risk is almost always present and courts rarely find it sufficient to justify granting a stay. ... Another prejudice courts have recognized is the possibility that adverse publicity from the civil case will inhibit a defendant's ability to impanel an impartial jury in a criminal case. ... The argument of prejudice to the defendant takes on substantially more weight if an indictment already has been returned in the criminal proceedings. ...

[c]—The Convenience to the Courts. Granting a stay for the convenience of the court is a factor based in judicial economy. Courts do not want to duplicate each other's efforts. A court may be more inclined to stay a civil case if the result can be determined or aided substantially at a later date through the collateral estoppel assertion of a conviction in a pending parallel criminal case. ...

[d]—The Public Interest. In considering the public interest, courts look to whether the matter involves important policy considerations such as environmental damage, consumer safety, or the integrity of a market. If an ongoing harm to a significant public interest can be remedied through an injunction or another civil order, a court may be inclined to allow the civil proceedings to go forward. However, a potential harm to a large group of individuals—as opposed to the general public—may not be sufficient to tip the balance in favor of allowing the civil case to proceed.[57]

D. OBTAINING A PROTECTIVE ORDER IN CIVIL OR ADMINISTRATIVE PROCEEDINGS

Where the extraordinary relief of a complete stay of the concurrent civil litigation is denied, the parties may seek more easily obtainable protective orders. Such orders will commonly be sought in an attempt to bar the litigants from turning evidence revealed in the course of civil discovery over to the government and, more particularly, to the grand jury.

IN RE GRAND JURY SUBPOENA SERVED ON MESERVE, MUMPER & HUGHES
62 F.3d 1222 (9th Cir.1995)

WIGGINS, CIRCUIT JUDGE:

Janet Greeson's A Place For Us, Inc., et al., (including Janet Greeson) ("APFU"), appeal a district court's denial of their motion to quash a grand jury subpoena, which ordered them to produce documents sealed by a protective order in an earlier, settled civil litigation. We affirm.

Various medical insurance companies brought a civil suit against APFU, alleging fraudulent billing by APFU. According to the insurance companies, APFU submitted bills for the provision of psychiatric care, when in truth APFU operated weight-loss clinics that were not covered by the relevant insurance policies. The insurance companies alleged that they were fraudulently billed in excess of one hundred million dollars. After very lengthy

---

[57] Dan K. Webb, Robert W. Tarun & Steven F. Molo, Corporate Internal Investigations § 14.04[3], at 14-13 to 14-17 (Law Journal Press 2018) (discussing issues relevant to obtaining stays of parallel proceedings); *see also* Fed. Savings & Loan Ins. Corp. v. Molinaro, 889 F.2d 899 (9th Cir. 1989).

discovery, but before trial, the parties settled the suit. As part of the settlement, the district court granted a protective order concerning the discovery that had already been taken.

A grand jury, in connection with a criminal investigation, subsequently subpoenaed Blue Cross' law firm, Meserve, Mumper & Hughes ("MMH"), requesting copies of all documents produced during discovery in the settled civil action. APFU moved to intervene in order to file a motion to quash the subpoena, arguing against modification of the protective order. The district court granted APFU's motion to intervene, but denied the motion to quash the subpoena. ...

The question of whether a grand jury subpoena trumps a district court's protective order is one of first impression in the Ninth Circuit. Three other circuits have addressed the question, however. Their cases provide a comprehensive background against which we evaluate this issue.

I. The Second Circuit's Compelling Need/Extraordinary Circumstances Test

In *Martindell v. ITT*, 594 F.2d 291 (2d Cir.1979), the Second Circuit held that in order to enforce a grand jury subpoena, and gain access to civil discovery protected by a protective order, the Government must demonstrate either "improvidence in the grant of a Rule 26(c) protective order or some extraordinary circumstance or compelling need." The Second Circuit based its compelling need test on its belief that the most important factor to be weighed in deciding whether to modify a protective order was "the vital function of a protective order issued under Rule 26(c), Fed. R. Civ. P., which is to 'secure the just, speedy, and inexpensive determination' of civil disputes, Rule 1, Fed. R. Civ. P., by encouraging full disclosure of all evidence that might conceivably be relevant." The court went on to note that this process would be undermined if witnesses were reluctant to testify out of a fear that their testimony would later be used by the Government for criminal investigatory purposes.

The *Martindell* court recognized that there was a countervailing consideration, namely the "public interest in obtaining all relevant evidence required for law enforcement purposes," which favored allowing access to the protected materials. The court determined that this factor was outweighed by the aforementioned goals of the civil procedure system, however, because "'the Government as investigator has awesome powers' which render unnecessary its exploitation of the fruits of private litigation." ...

II. The Fourth and Eleventh Circuits' *Per Se* Rule

The Fourth and Eleventh Circuits have taken quite a different approach to this question, and adopted a *per se* rule that protective orders cannot shield discovery from grand jury subpoenas. *In re Grand Jury (Williams)*, 995 F.2d 1013 (11th Cir.1993); *In re Grand Jury Subpoena*, 836 F.2d 1468 (4th Cir.[1988]). Both courts, in cases very similar to the one before us, specifically rejected the compelling need test adopted by the Second Circuit in *Martindell*.

A. The Fourth Circuit

The Fourth Circuit, in *In re Grand Jury Subpoena*, identified three interests that potentially are at stake when protective orders butt up against grand jury subpoenas. First, the grand jury has important, independent constitutional status, and is not generally subject to the direction of the courts. It has "sweeping power" to compel the production of evidence. Second, Fifth Amendment rights of deponents may be implicated. Third, protective orders aid civil courts in facilitating resolution of private disputes, thereby furthering Fed. R. Civ. P. 1's goal of "secur[ing] the just, speedy, and inexpensive determination" of civil disputes. If deponents cannot rely upon such protective orders, and instead assert their Fifth Amendment privilege, litigation can be prolonged and its costs increased.

The *In re Grand Jury Subpoena* court first explained that the second concern, the Fifth Amendment rights of deponents, is not truly implicated "because the deponents' fifth amendment right against self-incrimination did not require, nor may it depend on, the shield of civil protective orders." Deponents are entitled, instead, to rely on their own silence or upon a grant of immunity to protect against self-incrimination. As to the corollary concern that "the burden of silence in civil litigation may unduly punish an individual for asserting the right," the court answered that "the burden placed on an individual's right to avoid self-incrimination by the institution of a civil lawsuit by a private party does not implicate values protected by the fifth amendment." The Fourth Circuit cited, in support, the Supreme Court's statement that "the fifth amendment does not forbid adverse inferences against parties to civil actions when they refuse to testify in response to probative evidence offered against them." (citing *Baxter v. Palmigiano*, 425 U.S. 308, 318 (1976)).

The Fourth Circuit then carefully explained why, in balancing the remaining two interests—the grand jury's authority to gather all relevant evidence versus the district court's interest in facilitating resolution of civil disputes—it favored the former:

1) A grand jury has a right to all relevant evidence. Protective orders, if enforced at the expense of grand jury subpoenas, would be "significant impediment[s]" to grand jury investigations. Further, protective orders can keep a grand jury from obtaining not only important and relevant information, but also evidence of impeachment, should deponents testify inconsistently with their depositions in future criminal trials. Protective orders also can "absurd[ly]" shield deponents from perjury charges.

2) If protective orders were allowed to stand against grand jury subpoenas, district courts would effectively be given the authority to grant immunity to civil deponents. The power to grant immunity, however, is limited by federal law to the executive branch. 18 U.S.C. §§ 6002, 6003.

3) The countervailing benefits of enforcing protective orders at the expense of grand jury subpoenas are limited. Protective orders are not "a substitute for invocation of the [Fifth Amendment] privilege and [they] should not be afforded that status.":

a) Individuals cannot totally rely on protective orders, for at least three reasons:

i) there is always the risk of a leak. And, unlike immunity, there is no assurance that incriminating statements will not later be used against the deponent.

ii) Protective orders are subject to modification under Fed. R. Civ. P. 26.

iii) Protective orders are often only stopgap measures. Incriminating information effectively suppressed prior to trial is normally disclosed at that time.

b) Deponents can, despite protective orders, assert their Fifth Amendment privilege. (Note that fearful deponents are now especially likely to do so, after the rulings of the Fourth and Eleventh Circuits have shown that protective orders are not adequate substitutes for invoking the Fifth Amendment).

4) Civil courts have available other tools besides protective orders to "ensure successful resolution of a civil action which is threatened by a deponent's privileged silence."

a) The court can delay discovery until a pending grand jury investigation is completed.

b) The court can hold a pretrial hearing to weed out frivolous assertions of the privilege.

c) The court can shift the burden of proof "in accordance with the doctrine that the burden of proof should be placed on the party who is in the best position to provide relevant proof."

      d) The court can exclude testimony given at a subsequent trial if the same information had been withheld during discovery, pursuant to the privilege, in an effort to thwart discovery.

      The Fourth Circuit ultimately determined that the costs of enforcing protective orders against grand jury subpoenas were great, while the benefits were small. The court thus concluded that a reasonable balancing of the respective interests at stake "favors enforcement of a grand jury subpoena despite the existence of an otherwise valid protective order."

      The court then explained why it was adopting a *per se* rule in favor of grand jury subpoenas, rather than "a case-by-case approach of balancing these competing interests." The court explained that even assuming courts were "capable of fairly examining the disparate interests of law enforcement and of the civil courts in individual cases," the adoption of a case-by-case approach would actually "have the effect of *undermining both of these interests*." (emphasis added). On the one side, grand juries would often be deprived of relevant evidence. And on the other, parties would be unlikely to rely on protective orders, knowing that if the Government could show a compelling need for the evidence in the future, the orders would be modified accordingly.

      Further, the Fourth Circuit reiterated its belief that even if courts could properly conduct such a balancing test, they do not have the constitutional authority to do so. The executive branch, alone, has the right to determine when to immunize a witness. Lastly, the court noted that a rule permitting a protective order to prevail over a grand jury subpoena "could easily become a tool for delaying criminal investigations." That is, all parties who were subject to a grand jury investigation at the same time as a civil dispute would seek protective orders in the latter, forcing the Government to attempt to intervene.

B. The Eleventh Circuit

      The Eleventh Circuit has subsequently joined the Fourth Circuit in adopting a *per se* rule favoring grand jury subpoenas over protective orders, explicitly rejecting the Second Circuit's *Martindell* test. In *Williams*, the Eleventh Circuit ruled that "the essential and historic purpose served by the grand jury outweighs the utility served by Rule 26(c) protective orders." The court described at length the grand jury's historical status, its sweeping powers, citizens' duty to appear before it when summoned, and courts' responsibility to compel those subpoenaed to appear. The Eleventh Circuit also explained that courts are not to interfere in the operations of a grand jury.

      The Eleventh Circuit found that civil courts' interest in using protective orders to help dispose of cases could not compete with the interests in a powerful and independent grand jury. Refuting the Second Circuit's *Martindell* language that securing the speedy resolution of civil cases was a "vital function" and "the cornerstone of our administration of civil justice," the *Williams* court stated that "[p]rotective orders are merely a facilitating device and should not be used to shield relevant information from a valid grand jury subpoena." Turning to the text of the underlying Rule, the court stated: "We find absolutely nothing in Rule 26(c) or its advisory committee notes to support the notion that Congress, in passing on and enacting the Rule, intended to circumscribe the grand jury's authority and subpoena power as the Second Circuit has done."

      After echoing the Fourth Circuit's concerns about the judiciary infringing upon the executive branch's authority to grant immunity, the *Williams* court added another reason to reject a balancing test and adopt a *per se* rule: the *Martindell* test is inherently unworkable. The court noted that the Second Circuit had never defined the terms "compelling need," "extraordinary circumstances," or "improvidence in the original grant of the [protective] order." Further, the Second Circuit had never indicated how prosecutors are supposed to demonstrate "compelling need" when they have a duty to keep grand jury proceedings secret. Lastly, judges, as well, are put in a difficult position by the balancing test:

[T]he Second Circuit approach creates a Hobson's choice when, after the judge has induced a witness to incriminate himself by promising to enforce a protective order, the government demonstrates compelling need for the witness' testimony. The judge must choose between (1) going back on his word (thus breeding disrespect for the law in the eyes of the witness, if not the public in general) by honoring the grand jury subpoena, and (2) denying the public its "right to every man's evidence." Either way, the public suffers.

III. Adoption of the *Per Se* Rule

We adopt the *per se* rule of the Fourth and Eleventh Circuits. *In re Grand Jury Subpoena* and *Williams*, in their discussions of the factors weighing on both sides, convincingly explain that a grand jury subpoena should, as a matter of course, prevail over a protective order. …

Notes

1. Obviously, there is a split in the circuits on whether a protective order issued under Fed. R. Civ. P. 26(c) may shield evidence given in a civil suit from a subsequent federal grand jury subpoena. The First Circuit has weighed in on this controversy, adopting yet another standard. *See In re* Grand Jury Subpoena (Served Upon Stephen A. Roach), 138 F.3d 442 (1st Cir. 1998). That court determined that the Second Circuit's approach was flawed in that "its creation of a presumption favoring the sanctity of civil protective orders tilts the scales in exactly the wrong direction. By establishing a presumption in favor of civil protective orders, *Martindell* fails to pay proper respect to what we deem an issue of great importance: society's profound interest in the thorough investigation of potential criminal wrongdoing." *Id*. at 445. At the same time, the First Circuit rejected the *per se* approach of the Fourth, Ninth and Eleventh Circuits as too inflexible. *Id*. It ultimately held that:

[a] grand jury's subpoena trumps a Rule 26(c) protective order unless the person seeking to avoid the subpoena can demonstrate the existence of exceptional circumstances that clearly favor subordinating the subpoena to the protective order. … How this presumption in favor of a grand jury subpoena plays out in each individual case will depend upon the particular facts and circumstances. When called upon to adjudicate a motion to quash a grand jury subpoena in the face of a civil protective order, a district court may mull factors such as the government's need for the information (including the availability of other sources), the severity of the contemplated criminal charges, the harm to society should the alleged criminal wrongdoing go unpunished, the interests served by continued maintenance of complete confidentiality in the civil litigation, the value of the protective order to the timely resolution of that litigation, the harm to the party who sought the protective order if the information is revealed to the grand jury, the severity of the harm alleged by the civil-suit plaintiff, and the harm to society and the parties should the encroachment upon the protective order hamper the prosecution or defense of the civil case. In the end, society's interest in the assiduous prosecution of criminal wrongdoing almost always will outweigh its interest in the resolution of a civil matter between private parties.

Id. The Third Circuit has joined the First Circuit "in concluding that a strong but rebuttable presumption in favor of a grand jury subpoena best accommodates the sweeping powers of the grand jury and the efficient resolution of civil litigation fostered by protective orders." *In re* Grand Jury, 286 F.3d 153, 158 (3d Cir. 2002).

Does a rule permitting civil protective orders to trump grand jury subpoenas truly impede the grand jury's function in all circumstances? Is it true that the Second Circuit's rule is the equivalent of permitting judges to give witnesses immunity in the guise of civil protective orders? Quite apart from the policy considerations involved, what advantages does a *per se* rule have over a balancing test?

Would your conclusion be different if the facts of the case were more compelling? For example, in a Second Circuit case in which that court again declined to adopt a *per se* rule that grand jury investigations trumped civil protective orders, *In re* Grand Jury Subpoena Duces Tecum Dated April 19, 1991, 945 F.2d 1221 (2d Cir. 1991), the facts were described as follows:

> In March 1989, [Eastern Airlines, Inc. ("Eastern")] filed a voluntary petition for relief under Chapter 11 of the Bankruptcy Code in the United States Bankruptcy Court for the Southern District of New York. At the time, Eastern was involved in a labor dispute with various striking unions. Shortly after the petition was filed, Chief Bankruptcy Judge Burton R. Lifland denied without prejudice a motion for appointment of a trustee to replace Eastern's management. Judge Lifland determined, however, that an examiner should be appointed to investigate and review allegedly fraudulent pre-Chapter 11 transactions involving Eastern, its affiliate corporation Continental Airlines and their then-mutual parent Texas Air Corporation, and to consider whether a trustee should be appointed to manage Eastern's affairs. In April 1989, the United States Trustee appointed [David I. Shapiro] as examiner.

> According to the record before us, counsel for Eastern, Texas Air and Continental Airlines told Shapiro that they would not voluntarily produce documents or witnesses unless the information obtained would be kept confidential and used only in the bankruptcy proceeding. We are informed that the striking unions and Eastern's management were in a bitter dispute over the pre-petition transactions, which were already the subject of litigation, and that the examiner's investigation would have been seriously delayed had the bankruptcy court not approved the assurance of confidentiality. We are also told that all parties to the bankruptcy proceeding, including the unions, and the bankruptcy judge felt that time was of the essence, and that Eastern was a wasting asset. In addition, according to the record, Shapiro was under enormous pressure to expedite his investigation in the interests of creditors who were owed billions of dollars, the traveling public and thousands of Eastern employees whose jobs depended on a prompt reorganization.

> Accordingly, the United States Trustee, the examiner, and the respective counsel for Eastern, various unions and the creditors' committee signed a stipulation to keep confidential the information obtained during the depositions taken by the examiner. ... Judge Lifland signed an order dated May 3, 1989, placing under seal the matters referred to in the stipulation and stating that the order was "in the best interests of the Debtor's estate and the requirements of justice ... ." ...

Id. at 1222. Pursuant to the protective order, David Shapiro took testimony from over 100 witnesses. The deposition transcripts were subpoenaed by a federal grand jury. How would the First Circuit rule in this case?

2. If your client, a defendant in concurrent civil and criminal cases, were subpoenaed for his civil deposition and the civil litigation was being conducted under a protective order barring dissemination of deposition materials to the government, what would you advise him to do? If he refuses to testify on Fifth Amendment grounds, he cannot be held in contempt because only a statutory grant of immunity can overcome the privilege and a Rule 26(c) protective order is inadequate. *See* Andover Data Servs. v. Statistical Tabulating Corp., 876 F.2d 1080 (2d Cir. 1989). Even if the witness, prior to the deposition, were given

statutory use and derivative use by the government, that witness may not be compelled to answer deposition questions that track his immunized grand jury testimony. *See* Pillsbury Co. v. Conboy, 459 U.S. 248 (1983). In *Pillsbury*, the Court held that a deponent's civil deposition testimony repeating verbatim or closely tracking his prior immunized grand jury testimony is not, without duly authorized assurance of immunity at the time, immunized testimony within the meaning of 18 U.S.C. § 6002 and therefore may not be compelled over a valid assertion of his Fifth Amendment privilege.

3. Note that for non-U.S. companies, or companies that are not resident in the United States, a rule that privileges grand jury subpoenas over civil protective orders may well complicate their decision-making in responding to civil litigation in the United States. For example, in *In re Grand Jury Subpoena*, 646 F.3d 159, 162 (4th Cir. 2011), a foreign company sued by a U.S. company produced documents to the domestic concern under a protective order that provided that the covered documents "shall not be used or disclosed for any purposes other than the litigation of this action." The government subpoenaed covered documents as part of a criminal investigation. The Fourth Circuit recognized that the documents at issue could not otherwise have been secured by the government under Fed. R. Crim. P. 17(e)(2) and 18 U.S.C. § 1783, which provide that a grand-jury subpoena may be served in the United States or, if the subpoenaed party is a U.S. national or resident, in a foreign country. If a company, such as the defendant, was neither a U.S. national nor a resident, the government could not serve a subpoena on the company overseas. *Id.* at 165. (Other means of securing evidence abroad—letters rogatory and requests under Mutual Legal Assistance Treaty—are more cumbersome and may be subject to the discovery rules of the foreign nation.) But because the defendant foreign company had voluntarily produced the documents to a U.S. company subject to a protective order, and because in the Fourth Circuit a protective order is always trumped by a grand jury subpoena, the court ruled that the documents were discoverable by the government. The Ninth Circuit ruled similarly in *In re Grand Jury Subpoenas*, 627 F.3d 1143, 1144 (9th Cir. 2010), explaining that "[b]y a chance of litigation, the documents have been moved from outside the grasp of the grand jury to within its grasp. No authority forbids the government from closing its grip on what lies within the jurisdiction of the grand jury."

E. USE OF GRAND JURY MATERIALS

Primarily due to the protections of Fed. R. Crim. P. 6(e), a party subjected to parallel proceedings usually does not have the same concern about information flowing in the opposite direction—that is, the government sharing grand jury information with civil adversaries. Once grand jury information is disclosed (at trial, or through other authorized means) and becomes part of the record in a criminal case, however, the rule of confidentiality does not apply and the information may be used in a civil proceeding.[58] Further, under certain circumstances, civil litigants may secure orders modifying Rule 6(e)'s protections even where the grand jury information does not become a matter of public record.

Rule 6(e) prohibits any disclosure of matters occurring before the grand jury except in limited circumstances specifically enumerated in the rule. Generally, disclosure may be made to a civil agency or litigant involved in a parallel proceeding only when ordered by a court preliminary to, or in connection with, a judicial proceeding upon a showing of particularized need for the materials.

If a party seeks to gain access to evidence developed through the grand jury process, it must do so upon a motion, pursuant to Rule 6(e), before the judge supervising the

---

[58] *Id.* § 14.06[1], at 14-23.

grand jury. Usually, this is the chief judge for the district in which the grand jury sits. The court will then consider the following factors: (1) whether the material sought is a "matter occurring before the grand jury"; (2) whether the material sought is "preliminary to, or connected with, a judicial proceeding"; and (3) whether the party seeking access has demonstrated a "particularized need" for the material. The movant must meet all three criteria.[59]

DOUGLAS OIL CO. OF CAL. v. PETROL STOPS NORTHWEST
441 U.S. 211 (1979)

MR. JUSTICE POWELL delivered the opinion of the Court.

This case presents ... [the question of] what justification for disclosure must a private [civil litigant] show in order to overcome the presumption of grand jury secrecy applicable to [transcripts of federal criminal grand jury proceedings]. ...

We consistently have recognized that the proper functioning of our grand jury system depends upon the secrecy of grand jury proceedings. In particular, we have noted several distinct interests served by safeguarding the confidentiality of grand jury proceedings. First, if preindictment proceedings were made public, many prospective witnesses would be hesitant to come forward voluntarily, knowing that those against whom they testify would be aware of that testimony. Moreover, witnesses who appeared before the grand jury would be less likely to testify fully and frankly, as they would be open to retribution as well as to inducements. There also would be the risk that those about to be indicted would flee, or would try to influence individual grand jurors to vote against indictment. Finally, by preserving the secrecy of the proceedings, we assure that persons who are accused but exonerated by the grand jury will not be held up to public ridicule.

For all of these reasons, courts have been reluctant to lift unnecessarily the veil of secrecy from the grand jury. At the same time, it has been recognized that in some situations justice may demand that discrete portions of transcripts be made available for use in subsequent proceedings. Indeed, recognition of the occasional need for litigants to have access to grand jury transcripts led to the provision in Fed. R. Crim. Proc. 6(e)(2)(C)(i) that disclosure of grand jury transcripts may be made "when so directed by a court preliminarily to or in connection with a judicial proceeding."

In *United States v. Procter & Gamble Co.*, [356 U.S. 677 (1958),] the Court sought to accommodate the competing needs for secrecy and disclosure by ruling that a private party seeking to obtain grand jury transcripts must demonstrate that "without the transcript a defense would be greatly prejudiced or that without reference to it an injustice would be done." Moreover, the Court required that the showing of need for the transcripts be made "with particularity" so that "the secrecy of the proceedings [may] be lifted discretely and limitedly."

In *Dennis v. United States*, 384 U.S. 855 (1966), the Court considered a request for disclosure of grand jury records in quite different circumstances. It was there held to be an abuse of discretion for a District Court in a criminal trial to refuse to disclose to the defendants the grand jury testimony of four witnesses who some years earlier had appeared before a grand jury investigating activities of the defendants. The grand jury had completed its investigation, and the witnesses whose testimony was sought already had testified in public concerning the same matters. The Court noted that "[n]one of the reasons traditionally advanced to justify nondisclosure of grand jury minutes" was significant in those circumstances, whereas the defendants had shown it to be likely that the witnesses' testimony at trial was inconsistent with their prior grand jury testimony.

From *Procter & Gamble* and *Dennis* emerges the standard for determining when the traditional secrecy of the grand jury may be broken: Parties seeking grand jury transcripts

---

[59] *Id.* § 14.06[2], at 14-24 (footnotes omitted); *see also* Fed. R. Crim. P. 6(e)(2).

under Rule 6(e) must show that the material they seek is needed to avoid a possible injustice in another judicial proceeding, that the need for disclosure is greater than the need for continued secrecy, and that their request is structured to cover only material so needed.[60] Such a showing must be made even when the grand jury whose transcripts are sought has concluded its operations, as it had in *Dennis*. For in considering the effects of disclosure on grand jury proceedings, the courts must consider not only the immediate effects upon a particular grand jury, but also the possible effect upon the functioning of future grand juries. Persons called upon to testify will consider the likelihood that their testimony may one day be disclosed to outside parties. Fear of future retribution or social stigma may act as powerful deterrents to those who would come forward and aid the grand jury in the performance of its duties. Concern as to the future consequences of frank and full testimony is heightened where the witness is an employee of a company under investigation. Thus, the interests in grand jury secrecy, although reduced, are not eliminated merely because the grand jury has ended its activities.[61]

It is clear from *Procter & Gamble* and *Dennis* that disclosure is appropriate only in those cases where the need for it outweighs the public interest in secrecy, and that the burden of demonstrating this balance rests upon the private party seeking disclosure. It is equally clear that as the considerations justifying secrecy become less relevant, a party asserting a need for grand jury transcripts will have a lesser burden in showing justification. In sum, as so often is the situation in our jurisprudence, the court's duty in a case of this kind is to weigh carefully the competing interests in light of the relevant circumstances and the standards announced by this Court. And if disclosure is ordered, the court may include protective limitations on the use of the disclosed material, as did the District Court in this case. Moreover, we emphasize that a court called upon to determine whether grand jury transcripts should be released necessarily is infused with substantial discretion. ...

Notes

1. The inquiry into particularized need is fact-intensive but among the factors that may be relevant are the following: "the passage of time; whether the grand jury investigation had terminated; whether the witness in question had testified in a public forum already; the nature of the materials sought (documents vs. grand jury testimony); whether the witness whose testimony or documents are being sought objects to disclosure; and whether the proceedings for which the materials are being sought would in some way benefit the public interest generally." Webb *et. al.*, *supra* note 57, §§ 14.06[2], at 14-25 (footnotes omitted.)

2. Fed. R. Crim. P. 6(e)(3)(A)(i) provides that disclosure of materials occurring before the grand jury may be made (without court order) to "an attorney for the government for use in performing that attorney's duty." "Attorney for the government" is defined in Fed. R. Crim. P. 54(c). Such attorneys do *not* include government attorneys concerned only with civil matters. Thus, disclosure to government attorneys and their assistants for use in a civil suit is permissible only with a court order under Rule 6(e)(3)(E)(i). United States v. Sells Engineering, Inc., 463 U.S. 418 (1983). In *Sells*, the Supreme Court held that government civil attorneys seeking grand jury materials are held to the same "particularized need" standard as private parties. However, in *United States v. John Doe, Inc. I*, 481 U.S. 102 (1987), the Supreme Court held that the

---

[60] [Court's footnote 12:] As noted in *United States v. Procter & Gamble Co.*, 356 U.S. at 683, the typical showing of particularized need arises when a litigant seeks to use "the grand jury transcript at the trial to impeach a witness, to refresh his recollection, to test his credibility and the like." Such use is necessary to avoid misleading the trier of fact. Moreover, disclosure can be limited strictly to those portions of a particular witness' testimony that bear upon some aspect of his direct testimony at trial.

[61] [Court's footnote 13:] The transcripts sought by respondents already had been given to the target companies in the grand jury investigation. Thus, release to respondents will not enhance the possibility of retaliatory action by employers in this case. But the other factors supporting the presumption of secrecy remain and must be considered.

government attorney involved in a grand jury investigation may make *continued* use of grand jury materials if the attorney is subsequently involved in the civil phase of the same (or a related) matter without having to obtain court approval under Fed. R. Crim. P. 6(e)(3)(E). The Court, relying on the plain language of the rule, held that the government attorney's continued use of the grand jury information did not constitute a "disclosure" within the meaning of Rule 6(e).

As noted above, DOJ's policy regarding coordination between civil and criminal investigations stresses that such cooperation ought to take place "to the fullest extent appropriate and permissible by law." Likely in recognition of the *Sells* limit on the sharing of grand jury materials, the policy counsels that attorneys ought to consider investigative strategies that "maximize the government's ability to share information among criminal, civil, and agency administrative teams …, including the use of investigative means other than grand jury subpoenas for documents or witness testimony." U.S.A.M. § 1-12.000.

3. The government's investigative file may well contain materials not subject to Rule 6(e). Federal prosecutors as well as administrative agencies generally treat even non-grand jury investigative materials as highly confidential. Civil litigants may seek the production of materials held by administrative agencies or the Executive Branch through civil discovery processes or requests submitted under the Freedom of Information Act (FOIA), 5 U.S.C. § 552. Civil litigants may encounter difficulties extracting such materials from the government under FOIA because it contains a number of disclosure exemptions, the most important of which for present purposes is an investigatory files exemption, *see* 5 U.S.C. § 552(b); *see generally* Webb *et. al.*, *supra* note 57, § 14.07[1], at 14-26.1 to 14-28.

F. COLLATERAL ESTOPPEL

Collateral estoppel principles generally provide that "a party who has had issues of fact determined against him after a full and fair opportunity to litigate … is collaterally estopped from obtaining a subsequent … trial of these same issues of fact."[62] The Court in *Parklane Hosiery v. Shore*[63] held that where an issue of fact—the falsity of defendants' proxy statements—was resolved against a defendant in the course of an enforcement proceeding brought by the SEC, the defendant was collaterally estopped from relitigating the issue in a derivative suit brought by shareholders. The Court, in deciding that "a litigant who was not a party to a prior judgment may nevertheless use that judgment 'offensively' to prevent a defendant from relitigating issues resolved in the earlier proceeding,"[64] ruled as follows:

> We have concluded that the preferable approach for dealing with these problems in the federal courts is not to preclude the use of offensive collateral estoppel, but to grant trial courts broad discretion to determine when it should be applied. The general rule should be that in cases where a plaintiff could easily have joined in the earlier action or where … the application of offensive estoppel would be unfair to a defendant, a trial judge should not allow the use of offensive collateral estoppel.

> In the present case, however, none of the circumstances that might justify reluctance to allow the offensive use of collateral estoppel is present. The application of offensive collateral estoppel will not here reward a private plaintiff who could have joined in the previous action, since the respondent probably could not have joined in the injunctive action brought by the SEC even had he so desired. Similarly, there is no unfairness to the petitioners in applying offensive collateral estoppel in this case. First, in light of the serious allegations made in the SEC's complaint against the petitioners, as well as the foreseeability

---

[62] Parklane Hosiery Co. v. Shore, 439 U.S. 322, 325 (1979).

[63] *Id.*

[64] *Id.* at 326.

of subsequent private suits that typically follow a successful Government judgment, the petitioners had every incentive to litigate the SEC lawsuit fully and vigorously. Second, the judgment in the SEC action was not inconsistent with any previous decision. Finally, there will in the respondent's action be no procedural opportunities available to the petitioners that were unavailable in the first action of a kind that might be likely to cause a different result.

    We conclude, therefore, that none of the considerations that would justify a refusal to allow the use of offensive collateral estoppel is present in this case. Since the petitioners received a "full and fair" opportunity to litigate their claims in the SEC action, the contemporary law of collateral estoppel leads inescapably to the conclusion that the petitioners are collaterally estopped from relitigating the question of whether the proxy statement was materially false and misleading.[65]

Although *Parklane Hosiery* holds that mutuality of parties need not exist under federal collateral estoppel principles as applied to private litigants, *there must be mutuality of parties* for collateral estoppel to be asserted successfully *against* the federal government.[66]

    Accordingly, collateral estoppel is largely a concern for defense counsel. Under *Parklane Hosiery*, issues of fact tried and conclusively determined against a defendant in a criminal case are generally binding on a defendant in a subsequent civil proceeding brought by the government or outside parties based upon the same acts or transactions:

A criminal conviction—whether by guilty plea or trial verdict—is assumed determinative in a later civil or administrative proceeding because proof beyond a reasonable doubt is required in a criminal case. Conversely, an acquittal in a criminal case is not determinative in a later civil or administrative action because an acquittal demonstrates only that the defendant was not proved guilty beyond a reasonable doubt. The defendant has not proven by a preponderance of the evidence, which is the standard in most civil proceedings, that he did *not* commit the acts charged in the indictment.[67]

    May a judge's findings at *sentencing* in a criminal case later be used by civil litigants to collaterally estop a defendant on the extent of civil damages caused by his criminal wrong? In *SEC v. Monarch Funding Corp.*,[68] the Second Circuit held that it was "presumed improper" for the district court to preclude relitigation of a sentencing judge's findings of securities fraud (a crime for which the defendant had not been convicted).[69] After an analysis of the merits and demerits of according preclusive effect to sentencing findings, the court chose not to impose a *per se* bar on according collateral estoppel effect to sentencing findings. Instead, it adopted an approach akin to that followed in *Parklane Hosiery*, leaving it up to district courts to determine "those circumstances where it is clearly fair and efficient" to do so.[70] However, it expressly put

---

[65] *Id.* at 331-32.

[66] *See* United States v. Mendoza, 464 U.S. 154, 158 (1984) ("*Parklane Hosiery*'s approval of nonmutual offensive collateral estoppel is not to be extended to the United States."); *cf.* United States v. Stauffer Chem. Co., 464 U.S. 165 (1984) (the doctrine of mutual defensive collateral estoppel is applicable against the government to preclude relitigation of the same issue already litigated against the same party in another case involving virtually identical facts).

[67] Webb *et. al.*, *supra* note 57, § 14.10[1], at 14-70 (footnote omitted).

[68] 192 F.3d 295 (2d Cir.1999).

[69] *Id.* at 306.

[70] *Id.*

the burden on those seeking the benefit of a collateral estoppel rule to justify its imposition in a given case.[71]

A defendant who works out a plea with the government obviously must take into account the possibility that whatever plea is entered may preclude the defendant from resisting liability in collateral civil suits. What can a defendant do to minimize the collateral effect of a plea decision?[72]

It may be worth reiterating that even if a prior proceeding has resulted in a judgment that may not be employed to estop a party (for example, a plea of *nolo contendere*[73]), testimony given, statements made, or pleadings filed in the earlier action may be deemed "admissions" by the defendant and thus may be admissible when offered against him in subsequent civil *or* criminal cases.[74]

G. GLOBAL SETTLEMENTS

Parties subjected to parallel proceedings may attempt to secure what is termed a "global settlement" of all the various criminal, civil, and administrative proceedings against them. The advantages of such settlements may be substantial: "obtaining complete 'peace' and leaving no remaining uncertainties or contingencies"; "eliminating the risk of collateral estoppel issues in subsequent proceedings"; "minimizing the length of time the company must be in a defense mode and minimizing the time the corporation must carry a reserve on its books"; and "reducing the amount of adverse publicity associated with a series of adverse resolutions."[75] Global settlements may be difficult to achieve, however, for a variety of reasons. On a general level, the parties sought to be brought together in one deal— prosecutors, plaintiffs, and agencies—operate independently of each other and often have different priorities and goals in investigating and litigating. "[C]onflicting policies among various governmental agencies, or a general unwillingness on the part of the government to coordinate actions ... , often results in piecemeal or temporary settlements."[76]

"For a global settlement to occur, it is essential that the lead criminal prosecutorial agency involved in the investigation—usually the Department of Justice—be in agreement."[77] "The primary limitation [on global settlements]—general prosecutorial reluctance to enter into agreements binding agencies other than their own—is founded on both legal and practical concerns. As a practical matter, government officials often

---

[71] *Id.*

[72] *See, e.g.*, Robert Plotkin, *After the Guilty Plea*, 10 Bus. Crimes Bull. 1 (2003).

[73] *Nolo contendere* pleas have no collateral estoppel effect and, under Fed. R. Evid. 410 may not be offered as evidence against a party in any later proceeding. Some courts have also held that collateral estoppel does not apply to *Alford* pleas. *See, e.g.*, Blohm v. Comm'r, 994 F.2d 1542 (11th Cir. 1993).

[74] *See also supra* Chapter 19 (Plea Bargaining and Cooperation Agreements).

[75] Lawrence B. Pedowitz & Carol Miller, Confronting the Criminal Investigation, 161 PLI/CRIM 133, 175 (1991); *see also* Richard Marmaro & John W. Crumpacker, Government Procurement: The Ever-Expanding Scope of Liability and Methods of Damage Control, 161 PLI/CRIM 361, 426 (1991).

[76] Gary P. Naftalis, *Overview of Government Procurement Liability*, 161 PLI/CRIM 321, 355 (1991).

[77] Webb *et al.*, *supra* note 57, § 14.12, at 14-65. The Department of Justice has issued various policy statements regarding the coordination of parallel criminal, civil, and administrative proceedings. Those policies encourage greater cooperation and coordination by criminal prosecutors and other governmental actors conducting parallel proceedings. U.S.A.M. Criminal Resource Manual No. 2464. They also emphasize that "last-minute" global settlements are disfavored and that criminal plea agreements must be handled by criminal attorneys and civil settlements by civil attorneys. *Id.* Directive No. 99-20; *see also* Directive 99-21.

try to avoid 'stepping on the feet' of their compatriots and fear having to justify their existence subsequent to 'giving a case away.'"[78] As a legal matter, prosecutors must be sensitive to potential charges that they used the power of the criminal sanction to extort a civil settlement.[79] "Counsel also may encounter other bureaucratic obstacles to global settlements due to the dispersal of responsibility and the refusal or inability of the prosecutor or any other one government agency to assert control over other government agencies."[80] In short, while often desirable, "[n]egotiating a global settlement is rarely possible [and] [s]eparate negotiations with each agency involved are the norm."[81]

H. DOUBLE JEOPARDY AND EXCESSIVE FINES PROVISIONS

The Double Jeopardy Clause reads: "[N]or shall any person be subject for the same offence to be twice put in jeopardy of life or limb. ..."[82] The Double Jeopardy Clause has traditionally been read to preclude only successive *criminal* actions by the same sovereign based upon the same offense. As a general rule, then, one cannot argue that double jeopardy precludes successive criminal and civil actions.[83] Moreover, until 1989 and the Supreme Court's decision in *United States v. Halper*,[84] courts were disinclined to accept defendants' arguments that a nominally civil sanction actually constituted "criminal punishment" for double jeopardy purposes.

In 1989, the *Halper* Court began a litigation landslide by holding that in certain circumstances courts should look through the nominally "civil" nature of certain types of penalties and treat them as criminal punishment for purposes of double jeopardy analysis:

> [The defendant in *Halper*] worked as manager of New City Medical Laboratories, Inc., a company which provided medical service in New York City for patients eligible for benefits under the federal Medicare program. In that capacity, Halper submitted to Blue Cross and Blue Shield of Greater New York, a fiscal intermediary for Medicare, 65 separate false claims for reimbursement for service rendered. Specifically, on 65 occasions ... Halper mischaracterized the medical service performed by New City, demanding reimbursement at the rate of $12 per claim when the actual service rendered entitled New City to only $3 per claim. Duped by these misrepresentations, Blue Cross overpaid New City a total of $585; Blue Cross passed these overcharges along to the Federal Government.[85]

The Government indicted Halper on 65 counts of violating the criminal false claims statute[86] which prohibits "mak[ing] or present[ing] ... any claim upon or against the United States, or any department or agency thereof, knowing such claim to be false, fictitious, or fraudulent." Halper was convicted on all 65 counts, as well as on 16 counts of mail fraud. He was sentenced to imprisonment for two years and fined $5,000.

---

[78] Marmaro & Crumpacker, *supra* note 75, at 426.

[79] *See id.*; *see also* United States v. Litton Sys., Inc., 573 F.2d 195 (4th Cir. 1978).

[80] Webb *et al.*, *supra* note 57, § 14.12, at 14-65.

[81] Naftalis, *supra* note 76, at 355; *see also* Marmaro & Crumpacker, *supra* note 75, at 425 (global settlements are "generally difficult to obtain").

[82] U.S. Const. amend. V.

[83] *See, e.g.*, One Lot Emerald Cut Stones v. United States, 409 U.S. 232 (1972).

[84] 490 U.S. 435 (1989).

[85] *Id.* at 437.

[86] 18 U.S.C. § 287.

The Government then brought a *civil* action against Halper under the False Claims Act.[87] Halper was found liable under that Act. A person liable under the civil Act is "liable to the United States Government for a civil penalty of not less than $5000 ... plus 3 times the amount of damages which the Government sustains because of the action of that person."[88] Having violated the Act 65 separate times, Halper thus appeared to be subject to a statutory civil penalty of more than $130,000. The District Court, however, concluded that in light of Halper's previous criminal punishment, an additional penalty this large would violate the Double Jeopardy Clause. "In the District Court's view, the authorized recovery of more than $130,000 bore no rational relation to the sum of the Government's $585 actual loss plus its costs in investigating and prosecuting Halper's false claims. The court therefore ruled that imposition of the full amount would violate the Double Jeopardy Clause by punishing Halper a second time for the same conduct."[89]

The Supreme Court agreed, although it remanded to allow the district court to determine what portion of the statutory penalty could be sustained as compensation for the government's actual damages. The *Halper* Court held that in assessing whether the Double Jeopardy Clause's proscription of multiple punishments has been violated:

> ... [T]he labels "criminal" and "civil" are not of paramount importance. It is commonly understood that civil proceedings may advance punitive as well as remedial goals, and, conversely, that both punitive and remedial goals may be served by criminal penalties. The notion of punishment, as we commonly understand it, cuts across the division between the civil and the criminal law, and for the purposes of assessing whether a given sanction constitutes multiple punishment barred by the Double Jeopardy Clause, we must follow the notion where it leads. To that end, the determination whether a given civil sanction constitutes punishment in the relevant sense requires a particularized assessment of the penalty imposed and the purposes that the penalty may fairly be said to serve. Simply put, a civil as well as a criminal sanction constitutes punishment when the sanction as applied in the individual case serves the goals of punishment.
>
> These goals are familiar. We have recognized in other contexts that punishment serves the twin aims of retribution and deterrence. *See, e.g., Kennedy v. Mendoza-Martinez,* 372 U.S. 144, 168 (1963) (these are the "traditional aims of punishment"). Furthermore, "[r]etribution and deterrence are not legitimate nonpunitive governmental objectives." From these premises, it follows that a civil sanction that cannot fairly be said solely to serve a remedial purpose, but rather can only be explained as also serving either retributive or deterrent purposes, is punishment, as we have come to understand the term. We therefore hold that under the Double Jeopardy Clause a defendant who already has been punished in a criminal prosecution may not be subjected to an additional civil sanction to the extent that the second sanction may not fairly be characterized as remedial, but only as a deterrent or retribution. ...
>
> ... What we announce now is a rule for the rare case, the case such as the one before us, where a fixed-penalty provision subjects a prolific but small-gauge offender to a sanction overwhelmingly disproportionate to the damages he has caused. The rule is one of reason: Where a defendant previously has sustained a criminal penalty and the civil penalty sought in the subsequent proceeding bears no rational relation to the goal of compensating the Government for its loss, but rather appears to qualify as

---

[87] 31 U.S.C. §§ 3729-3731. In pertinent part, the Act provided that "[a] person not a member of an armed force of the United States" violates the act when, *inter alia*, he "knowingly makes, uses, or causes to be made or used, a false record or statement material to an obligation to pay or transmit money or property." *Id.* § 3729(a)(1)(G).

[88] 31 U.S.C. § 3729(a)(1).

[89] *Halper*, 490 U.S. at 439.

"punishment" in the plain meaning of the word, then the defendant is entitled to an accounting of the Government's damages and costs to determine if the penalty sought in fact constitutes a second punishment. We must leave to the trial court the discretion to determine on the basis of such an accounting the size of the civil sanction the Government may receive without crossing the line between remedy and punishment. While the trial court's judgment in these matters often may amount to no more than an approximation, even an approximation will go far towards ensuring both that the Government is fully compensated for the costs of corruption and that, as required by the Double Jeopardy Clause, the defendant is protected from a sanction so disproportionate to the damages caused that it constitutes a second punishment.[90]

After *Halper*, the Supreme Court underscored its willingness to reexamine the nominally civil nature of certain governmental assessments by holding that the Double Jeopardy Clause can, under certain circumstances, bar the imposition of a state tax. In *Department of Revenue of Montana v. Kurth Ranch*,[91] the Court held that a Montana tax on the possession of illegal drugs constituted criminal "punishment" for double jeopardy purposes. The *Kurth Ranch* Court explained that "tax statutes serve a purpose quite different from civil penalties, and *Halper's* method of determining whether the exaction was remedial or punitive 'simply does not work in the case of a tax statute.' Subjecting Montana's drug tax to *Halper's* test for civil penalties is therefore inappropriate."[92] It held, however, that the tax constituted criminal punishment based on a variety of factors: (1) "a high tax rate and deterrent purpose len[d] support to the characterization of the drug tax as punishment";[93] (2) "the so-called tax [was] conditioned on the commission of a crime," which is "'significant of penal and prohibitory intent rather than the gathering of revenue'";[94] (3) the tax is "exacted only after the taxpayer has been arrested for the precise conduct that gives rise to the tax obligation in the first place";[95] and (4) although the tax purported to be "a species of property tax," "it is levied on goods that the taxpayer neither owns nor possesses when the tax is imposed. Indeed, the State presumably *destroyed* the contraband goods in this case before the tax on them was assessed."[96]

The Supreme Court's holdings under the Eighth Amendment Excessive Fines Clause are also important to understanding the development of this line of double jeopardy cases. The Eighth Amendment states that "[e]xcessive bail shall not be required, nor excessive fines imposed, nor cruel and unusual punishments inflicted."[97] In *Austin v. United States*,[98] the defendant was convicted in state court of a drug offense. The United States then instituted an action under 21 U.S.C. §§ 881(a)(4) and (a)(7), seeking civil *in rem* forfeiture of Austin's mobile home and auto body shop. The Supreme Court held that the Excessive Fines Clause of the Eighth Amendment applies to civil *in rem* forfeitures under 21 U.S.C. § 881 and remanded the case for consideration of whether the forfeiture at issue was "excessive." The *Austin* Court reasoned that the question for analysis was not "whether forfeiture under §§ 881(a)(4) and (a)(7) is civil or criminal, but rather whether it is

---

90 *Id.* at 447-50.

91 511 U.S. 767 (1994).

92 *Id.* at 784.

93 *Id.* at 781.

94 *Id.*

95 *Id.*

96 *Id.* at 783.

97 U.S. Const. amend. VIII.

98 509 U.S. 602 (1993).

punishment."[99] It then surveyed the history of the Eighth Amendment as well as the statutes at issue and concluded that "nothing in these provisions or their legislative history ... contradict[s] the historical understanding of forfeiture as punishment."[100]

Courts after *Austin* reasoned that because *Austin* held that civil *in rem* forfeitures may constitute "punishment" for Eighth Amendment purposes, such forfeitures also constituted "punishment" for double jeopardy purposes under *Halper*. Some courts therefore held that a civil *in rem* forfeiture could bar, on double jeopardy grounds, subsequent *criminal* prosecutions based on the same underlying behavior. One such case came before the Supreme Court in *United States v. Ursery*.[101] The *Ursery* Court reasoned that although civil *in rem* forfeiture may constitute "punishment" for Eighth Amendment purposes, "this does not mean, however, that those forfeitures are so punitive as to constitute punishment for the purposes of double jeopardy. The holding of *Austin* was limited to the Excessive Fines Clause of the Eighth Amendment, and we decline to import the analysis of *Austin* into our double jeopardy jurisprudence."[102]

The *Ursery* Court concluded that "nothing in *Halper, Kurth Ranch,* or *Austin* purported to replace our traditional understanding that civil forfeiture does not constitute punishment for the purpose of the Double Jeopardy Clause."[103] It held that *Halper's* case-by-case balancing test, "in which a court must compare the harm suffered by the Government against the size of the penalty imposed, is inapplicable to civil forfeiture."[104] Instead of applying its *Halper* analysis, the *Ursery* Court applied a two-part test set forth in prior forfeiture decisions: (1) whether Congress intended forfeiture proceedings under the statutes at issue to be criminal or civil and (2) whether the proceedings are so punitive in fact as to persuade the court that the forfeiture proceedings may not legitimately be viewed as civil in nature despite Congress's intent.[105] The Court ultimately ruled that the *in rem* forfeitures at issue were neither "punishment" nor criminal for purposes of the Double Jeopardy Clause.[106]

In 1997, the Court's obvious discomfort with the unforeseen consequences of its *Halper* analysis, reflected in *Ursery*, was made explicit in *Hudson v. United States*.[107] The *Hudson* Court implicitly, if not explicitly, overruled *Halper*. In *Hudson*, the Office of the Comptroller of the Currency had administratively imposed monetary penalties and occupational debarment on bank officers for violation of federal banking statutes. The *Hudson* Court held that the subsequent criminal indictment of the bank officers for misapplication of bank funds was not barred by the Double Jeopardy Clause because Congress intended the monetary penalties and occupational debarment to be civil penalties and those penalties were not so punitive in form or effect as to render them criminal for double jeopardy purposes.[108]

Notably, the Supreme Court stated that "[o]ur reasons for so holding in large part disavow the method of analysis used in *United States v. Halper,* ... and reaffirm the previously

---

[99] *Id.* at 610.

[100] *Id.* at 619.

[101] 518 U.S. 267 (1996).

[102] *Id.* at 287.

[103] *Id.*

[104] *Id.* at 284 (appearing to limit *Halper* analysis to the context of fixed civil-penalty provision cases).

[105] *Id.* at 288 (applying analysis from *United States v. One Assortment of 89 Firearms,* 465 U.S. 354 (1984)).

[106] *Ursery,* 518 U.S. at 292.

[107] 522 U.S. 93 (1997).

[108] *Id.* at 103-04.

established rule exemplified in *United States v. Ward*."[109] *United States v. Ward*[110] was a 1980 precedent in which the Supreme Court had held that a monetary penalty under the Federal Water Pollution Control Act against the owner or operator of a vessel from which substances are discharged in violation of the Act is civil in nature and does not trigger the constitutional protections afforded to criminal defendants. In *Hudson*, the Court embraced the two-part test laid out in Ward[111] to determine whether a sanction is civil or criminal.

In applying the *Ward* test, a court first must determine whether the legislature intended to establish a civil or criminal penalty.[112] Second, the court must decide whether the nominally civil statutory penalties are "'so punitive in form and effect as to render them criminal despite Congress' intent to the contrary.'"[113] Importantly, courts are to evaluate the statute on its face, and only the "clearest proof" will suffice to override legislative intent and transform what has been denominated a civil remedy into a criminal penalty.[114] That proof should include reference to seven nonexhaustive factors outlined in the Court's 1963 decision in *Kennedy v. Mendoza-Martinez*,[115] in which the Supreme Court struck as unconstitutional statutes in which "Congress has plainly employed the sanction of deprivation of nationality as a punishment—for the offense of leaving or remaining outside the country to evade military service—without affording the procedural safeguards guaranteed by the Fifth and Sixth Amendments."[116] The seven factors relied upon in *Kennedy* and again by the *Hudson* Court are: "(1) '[w]hether the sanction involves an affirmative disability or restraint'; (2) 'whether it has historically been regarded as punishment'; (3) 'whether it comes into play only on a finding of scienter'; (4) 'whether its operation will promote the traditional aims of punishment—retribution and deterrence'; (5) 'whether the behavior to which it applies is already a crime'; (6) 'whether an alternative purpose to which it may rationally be connected is assignable for it'; (7) 'whether it appears excessive in relation to the alternative purpose assigned.'"[117]

Although *Hudson* did not in so many words overrule *Halper*, the Court's methodology represented a repudiation of the *Halper* analysis and a return to the reasoning of prior cases such as *Ward* and *Kennedy*. In particular, the Court stated:

> The analysis applied by the *Halper* Court deviated from our traditional double jeopardy doctrine in two key respects. First, the *Halper* Court bypassed the threshold question: whether the successive punishment at issue is a "criminal" punishment. Instead, it focused on whether the sanction, regardless of whether it was civil or criminal, was so grossly disproportionate to the harm caused as to constitute "punishment." In so doing, the Court elevated a single *Kennedy* factor—whether the sanction appeared excessive in relation to its nonpunitive purposes—to dispositive status. But as we emphasized in *Kennedy* itself, no one factor should be considered controlling as they "may often point in different directions." The second significant departure in *Halper* was the Court's decision to "assess the character of the actual

---

[109] *Id.* at 96.

[110] 448 U.S. 242 (1980) (holding that reporting requirement, as used to support this civil penalty, does not violate the reporter-violator's right against self-incrimination).

[111] *Id.* at 248-49.

[112] *Hudson*, 522 U.S. at 99.

[113] *Id.* at 104 (quoting *Ursery*, 518 U.S. at 290).

[114] *See id.* at 100, 101, 104, 105.

[115] 372 U.S. 144, 168-69 (1963).

[116] *Id.* at 165-66.

[117] *Hudson*, 522 U.S. at 99-100 (quoting *Kennedy*, 372 U.S. at 168-69).

sanctions imposed," rather than, as *Kennedy* demanded, evaluating the "statute on its face" to determine whether it provided for what amounted to a criminal sanction.[118]

Obviously, *Hudson* renders arguments that sanctions are jeopardy-barred, or in fact jeopardy-bar subsequent criminal proceedings, much more difficult to win. In effect, the Court has made near-dispositive (once more) the legislative label affixed to a given sanction and has further insulated nominally civil sanctions from scrutiny by permitting only facial challenges.[119] The Court, seeming to sense that its decision would have closed the door to such worthy petitioners as Mr. Halper, whose case would have come out very differently under the *Hudson* analysis, concluded that:

> ... [I]t should be noted that some of the ills at which *Halper* was directed are addressed by other constitutional provisions. The Due Process and Equal Protection Clauses already protect individuals from sanctions which are downright irrational. The Eighth Amendment protects against excessive civil fines, including forfeitures. The additional protection afforded by extending double jeopardy protections to proceedings heretofore thought to be civil is more than offset by the confusion created by attempting to distinguish between "punitive" and "nonpunitive" penalties.[120]

With the probable demise of the Double Jeopardy Clause as a source of relief from apparently repetitive and punitive sanctions, the Eighth Amendment's Excessive Fines Clause looks more promising. After *Austin*, the Supreme Court reaffirmed in *Alexander v. United States*[121] that the Eighth Amendment's Excessive Fines Clause applies to both civil and criminal forfeitures. In *Alexander*, the Court rejected a First Amendment challenge to an *in personam* criminal forfeiture under RICO's forfeiture penalty, 18 U.S.C. § 1963, of numerous businesses dealing in sexually explicit materials. It ruled, however, that "the *in personam* criminal forfeiture at issue here is clearly a form of monetary punishment no different, for Eighth Amendment purposes, from a traditional 'fine.' Accordingly, the forfeiture in this case should be analyzed under the Excessive Fines Clause."[122] The Court ultimately remanded the case for consideration of whether the forfeiture was "excessive" under the Eighth Amendment.[123]

Generally, to determine whether the Excessive Fines Clause has been violated, the Court first determines whether the governmental action is "punishment" for Eighth Amendment purposes.[124] A conclusion that a civil *in rem* forfeiture is not a criminal penalty for purposes of the Double Jeopardy Clause is not controlling under the Excessive Fines

---

[118] *Id.* at 101.

[119] *See* United States v. $273,969.04 U.S. Currency, 164 F.3d 462 (9th Cir. 1999) (holding that an *in rem* forfeiture of $273,969.04 following defendant's conviction for making false statements to customs officials was not barred by Double Jeopardy Clause); Herbert v. Billy, 160 F.3d 1131 (6th Cir. 1998) (holding that convictions for driving under the influence of alcohol after the defendants' drivers' licenses had been revoked was not barred by the Double Jeopardy Clause); *see also* United States v. Lippert, 148 F.3d 974 (8th Cir. 1998) (holding that a statutory civil penalty of double damages under the civil Anti-Kickback statute, 41 U.S.C. § 55, was not barred by prior conviction under criminal Anti-Kickback statute, 41 U.S.C. § 54).

[120] *Hudson*, 522 U.S. at 102-03.

[121] 509 U.S. 544 (1993).

[122] *Id.* at 558-59.

[123] *Id.* at 559.

[124] *See* United States v. Bajakajian, 524 U.S. 321 (1998).

Clause.[125] Upon a finding that a forfeiture is at least in part punitive, a court must then determine whether the forfeiture is "excessive."

The Court, in *United States v. Bajakajian,* held that a punitive forfeiture is excessive when that "forfeiture is grossly disproportional to the gravity of the defendant's offense."[126] In *Bajakajian,* the defendant pleaded guilty to a violation of 31 U.S.C. § 5316(a)(1)(A) for failing to report that he was attempting to leave the United States with more than $10,000 in currency. The United States Government also sought criminal forfeiture under 18 U.S.C. § 982(a)(1) of the currency—$357,144—that the defendant was carrying. The Supreme Court first concluded that full forfeiture of $357,144 was punitive.[127] The court articulated the test for Eighth Amendment excessiveness as whether "a punitive forfeiture ... is grossly disproportional to the gravity of a defendant's offense."[128] In then determining that forfeiture of $357,144 was "grossly disproportional" to the gravity of the defendant's offense, the Court listed six factors: (1) the violation was unrelated to any other illegal activities; (2) the harm caused was minimal; (3) the violation affected only one party, the United States Government; (4) the violation affected that one party in a relatively minor way; (5) the forfeiture was larger than the $5,000 forfeiture ordered by the District Court by many orders of magnitude; and (6) the forfeiture bore no articulable correlation to any injury suffered by the United States Government.[129]

---

[125] *See Hudson,* 522 U.S. at 102-03; *Ursery,* 518 U.S. at 287; *United States v. $273,969.04,* 164 F.3d at 466; *Lippert,* 148 F.3d at 977.

[126] 524 U.S. at 337.

[127] *Id.* at 328.

[128] *Id.* at 334.

[129] *Id* at 337-40.

Chapter 21

EXTRATERRITORIAL APPLICATION OF FEDERAL CRIMINAL LAW

White collar practice is increasingly transnational—that is, some or all of the conduct deemed criminal may happen outside the United States, essential witnesses and evidence may be found abroad, and the government may need a way to compel defendants who are located overseas to come to the United States for trial. One chapter cannot exhaustively catalog all the issues, and law, raised by the increasingly extraterritorial nature of the practice. Accordingly, this chapter is designed as a sort of primer to expose students to the sorts of questions they may face and to give them a sense of how to contextualize and analyze issues raised in this new practice world.

To begin with a definitional note, this Chapter focuses on *transnational criminal law*. This consists of that part of a nation's domestic criminal law that "regulates actions or events that transcends national frontiers."[1] So, for example, assume that representatives of a U.S. company file fraudulent claims for payment under a contract with the U.S. Department of Defense for work supposedly performed in Connecticut. This is a purely domestic crime, with no transnational element. Now suppose that a French company bribes an Indonesian public official to secure a contract to build a bridge in Indonesia and the bribe is paid by wire transfer from a U.S. bank. Efforts of U.S. prosecutors to bring to justice the responsible French citizens in U.S. courts under U.S. law would constitute a transnational application of U.S. law.[2]

Foreign law may be relevant to transnational criminal prosecutions both substantively and procedurally. Thus, for example, some U.S. statutes incorporate the laws of other jurisdictions. The Lacey Act makes it a federal crime to import fauna or flora in violations of another country's laws.[3] The money laundering statute, 18 U.S.C. § 1956, outlaws the laundering of the proceeds of violations of certain foreign laws (e.g.,

---

[1] Phillp C. Jessup, Transnational Law 2 (1956).

[2] *Transnational* criminal law should be distinguished from *international* criminal law. An example of an international criminal law prosecution would be an effort to bring an individual to justice in an international tribunal governed by international law—such as efforts to try persons who commit genocide, crimes against humanity, or war crimes in the treaty-based International Criminal Court. Transnational crimes, by contrast, are outlawed under States' domestic law and tried in domestic courts, even if the conduct at issue is international in scope.

[3] *See* 16 U.S.C. §§3371-78; *see also* 18 U.S.C. § 546 (prohibiting smuggling goods into another State in violation of its laws); 19 U.S.C. § 1527 (Prohibiting the importation of wild mammals and birds in violation of another State's laws); 21 U.S.C. § 960(d)(2) (prohibiting the export of listed chemicals in violation of a another State's laws). For a discussion of such practices, see Paul J. Larkin, Jr., *The Dynamic Incorporation of Foreign Law and the Constitutional Regulation of Federal Lawmaking*, 38 Harv. J.L. & Pub. Pol'y 337 (2015); Ellen S. Podgor, *A New Dimension to the Prosecution of White Collar Crime: Enforcing Extraterritorial Social Harms*, 37 McGeorge L. Rev. 83 (2006).

against corruption). On the procedural side, foreign law issues arise regularly in determining what types of evidence can be gathered, and how, and certainly will be relevant in extradition proceedings seeking the transfer of a person to U.S. soil from abroad. The differences between foreign and domestic law—in areas such as privilege law, Fifth Amendment protections, and the like—will create challenges for counsel conducting transnational investigations.

International law also must be consulted on a regular basis. Treaty law[4] is also relevant both to substance and procedure. For example, there are an increasing number of treaty-based domestic crimes. Countries (in international parlance "States") may come together and create a treaty that requires those States that join it ("States-Parties") to criminalize certain conduct under their domestic law. For example, we saw in Chapter 8 (Corruption), Part D (FCPA) that the United States became a State-Party to the Convention on Combating Bribery of Foreign Officials in International Business Transactions adopted by the OECD. Because that treaty required its States-Parties to "take such measures as may be necessary to establish its jurisdiction over bribery of a foreign official when the offense is committed in whole or in part in its territory," the United States was bound by the treaty to implement this undertaking in U.S. domestic law, which the United States did by legislation expanding the reach of the FCPA.[5] Prosecutions under this expanded version of the FCPA can be seen as a sort of hybrid in that they are clearly applications of transnational criminal law because they proceed under U.S. domestic law and in U.S. courts, but that domestic law was implemented to

---

[4] Two influential authorities on the sources of international law recognize "international conventions" or "international agreement[s]" as a source of international law: the Statute of the International Court of Justice, Art. 38(1)(a) (hereinafter *ICJ Statute*) and the *Restatement (Third) of the Foreign Relations Law of the United States* § 102(1)(b) (1987) (hereinafter *Restatement*). An international agreement (also known as a treaty, convention, covenant, protocol, or pact) is an explicit agreement among its States-Parties. The rules governing treaties are themselves contained in a treaty, the Vienna Convention on the Law of Treaties (VCLT). The United States is not a party to the VCLT but accepts that many of its provisions have become binding customary international law. *See infra* note 7. The VCLT's two most basic rules are: "Every state possesses the capacity to conclude treaties" and "[e]very treaty in force is binding upon the parties to it and must be performed by them in good faith." VCLT, Arts. 6, 25.

The U.S. Constitution is the highest source of law in the United States so that "a provision of an international agreement of the United States will not be given effect as law in the United States if it is inconsistent with the United States Constitution." *Restatement* § 115(3). Treaties are treated on a par with federal statutes so that if a conflict arises between a treaty provision and an act of Congress, the "last in time" prevails. *Id.* § 115(1)(a), (2). (But even if a later-in-time statute supersedes a treaty, the United States is still bound by its treaty obligations under international law, *id.* 115(1)(b)). Treaties, under the Supremacy Clause, are "supreme over the law of the several states." *Id.* 111(1). A ratified self-executing treaty, then, would nullify inconsistent state law.

[5] There are two types of treaties under U.S. law—"self-executing" and "non-self-executing." As the Supreme Court has explained, "[t]he label 'self-executing' has on occasion been used to convey different meanings." Medellín v. Texas, 552 U.S. 491, 505 n.2 (2008). In the Court's latest word on the subject, in *Medellín*, it explained that a "self-executing" treaty is one that "has automatic domestic effect as federal law upon ratification" while a "non-self-executing" treaty does not "by itself give rise to domestically enforceable federal law." *Id.*; *see also id.* at 504 (non-self-executing treaties "do not of their own force create domestic law"). Although this distinction is both important and sometimes tricky to apply, for present purposes it does not create difficulties. For example, treaties under which the United States undertakes to criminalize certain activity, such as the OECD Convention, clearly require implementing legislation. Because their obligations are in essence addressed to Congress, they cannot be "self-executing"; by definition, they require Congress to "execute" them by passing the contemplated criminal legislation. By contrast, other types of treaties that we will be discussing—extradition treaties and mutual legal assistance treaties (MLATs)—are generally deemed to be self-executing. They become enforceable as federal law upon ratification.

satisfy international law (i.e., treaty) obligations.[6] Treaties will also be procedurally critical in determining how prosecutors can gather evidence and in extradition cases.

Customary international law[7] is less relevant but may still play a potentially important role, for example in determining whether a U.S. statute that is silent on the question of its extraterritorial application should be construed to have transnational scope.

A great many questions arise when U.S. prosecutors attempt to apply U.S. domestic law transnationally, some of which are:

a.   If the criminal conduct crosses borders, where is the crime "committed"?

b.   If the crime is deemed to have been "committed" abroad, does the U.S. statute apply extraterritorially? This question, in turn, can be broken down into a number of inquiries: Does the Constitution give Congress the authority to regulate this overseas conduct? Where the statute is silent on the subject of its reach, did Congress intend the statute to apply extraterritorially? Would such an extraterritorial reach be consistent with

---

[6] *See also* United States v. Ali, 718 F.3d 929, 943 (D.C. Cir. 2013) (hostage-taking statute, 18 U.S.C. § 1203, fulfills U.S. treaty obligations under the International Convention Against the Taking of Hostages); United States v. Shi, 525 F.3d 709, 719-20 (9th Cir. 2008) (prohibition on certain acts of violence that endanger maritime navigation, 18 U.S.C. § 2280, implements the Convention for the Suppression of Unlawful Acts Against the Safety of Maritime Navigation).

[7] "Customary international law" (formerly referred to as the "law of nations") is also a source of international law. *See ICJ Statute, supra* note 4, Art. 1(b) ("international custom, as evidence of a general practice accepted as law"); *Restatement, supra* note 4, § 102(1)(a) ("customary law"). "Customary international law results from a general and consistent practice of states followed by them from a sense of legal obligation." *Restatement* § 102(2). This type of international law requires two things: custom *and* a sense of legal obligation (often referred to as "*opinio juris*"). With respect to custom, the *Restatement* explains:

> The practice necessary to create customary law may be of comparatively short duration, but ... it must be "general and consistent." A practice can be general even if is not universally followed; there is no precise formula to indicate how widespread a practice must be, but it should reflect wide acceptance among the statutes particularly involved in the relevant activity ... A principle of customary international law not binding on a state that declares its dissent from the principle during its development."

Id. § 102, comment (b). With respect to *opinion juris*,

> For a practice of states to become a rule of customary international law it must appear that the states follow the practice from a sense of legal obligation...; a practice that is generally followed but which states feel legally free to disregard does not contribute to customary law. A practice initially followed by states as a matter of courtesy or habit may become law when states generally come to believe that they are under a legal obligation to comply with it. It is often difficult to determine when that transformation into law has taken place. ... An international agreement creates obligations binding between the states under international law. International agreements may contribute to customary law.

Id. § 102 comments (c), (f). The Supremacy Clause does not mention customary international law but the Supreme Court holds that it is part of federal law. In *The Pacquete Habana*, the Court explained that "where there is no treaty, and no controlling executive or legislative act or judicial decision, resort must be had to the customs and usages of civilized nations." 175 U.S. 677, 700 (1900). In 2004, the Court reaffirmed that customary international law controls in U.S. courts, stating "[f]or two centuries we have affirmed that the domestic law of the United States recognizes the law of nations. ... It would take some explaining to say now that federal courts must avert their gaze entirely from any international norm intended to protect individuals." Sosa v. Alvarez-Machain, 542 U.S. 692, 752 (2004).

customary international law? Would application of the statute to the defendant violate constitutional due process norms?

c. What rules apply and issues arise when a company attempts to conduct a transnational internal investigation? Where criminal conduct occurs in multiple countries what should companies do to limit their global liability?

d. How can U.S. prosecutors investigate activity that occurs overseas and secure competent evidence admissible in U.S. courts? How can defense counsel find and introduce exculpatory materials that may be found abroad?

e. Given that the U.S. generally forbids prosecutions *in absentia*—that is, the defendant must at some point be brought to court in the United States—how can the government secure the presence in a U.S. courtroom of defendants living overseas?

To comprehensively survey all the potentially applicable issues would require another volume; accordingly, the ambition of this Chapter is simply to give students some basic grounding in applicable law and a sense of the issues that must be considered in transnational criminal law cases.

A. EXTRATERRITORIAL APPLICATION OF U.S. CRIMINAL STATUTES

We have studied statutes that expressly provide for extraterritorial application. For example, Congress explicitly permits the extraterritorial application of the money laundering statute, 18 U.S.C. § 1956(f), where the conduct prohibited by the statute "is by a United States citizen or, in the case of a non-United States citizen, the conduct occurs in part in the United States" and "the transaction or series of related transactions involves funds or monetary instruments of a value exceeding $10,000." Perjury is defined as lying under oath about material facts "before a competent tribunal, officer, or person, in any case in which a law of the United States authorizes an oath to be administered," or the equivalent in written declarations. The perjury statute explicitly provides that these false statements under oath are prosecutable "whether the statement or subscription is made within or without the United States."[8]

The difficulty is that most federal criminal statutes do not contain such explicit direction, including many of the prohibitions we have studied (such as false statements, mail, wire, bank, and securities fraud, various obstruction and corruption offenses, conspiracy, RICO, etc.). Where a statute is silent as to its extraterritorial application, how can courts resolve the question?

1. RECENT SUPREME COURT EXTRATERRITORIALITY CASES

A discussion of the modern Supreme Court's extraterritoriality jurisprudence must begin with *Morrison v. National Australia Bank*.[9] *Morrison* was a blockbuster because it overruled decades of courts of appeals case law and seriously limited the transnational scope of the civil remedies available to private plaintiffs under the federal securities fraud laws. National Australia Bank (National), a non-U.S. bank whose shares were not traded on any U.S. exchange, purchased HomeSide Lending, a company headquartered in

---

[8] 18 U.S.C. § 1621. Other statutes that clearly provide for extraterritorial application include 18 U.S.C. § 1651 (piracy); 46 U.S.C. § 70503(a), (b) (the Maritime Drug Law Enforcement Act (MDLEA)); and 18 U.S.C. § 2340A (torture).

[9] 561 U.S. 247 (2010).

Florida. After a few years, National was forced to write down the value of Homeside's assets, which caused a drop in National's share price. Petitioner Morrison and other Australians who had purchased National's stock before the write-down sued National, Homeside, and officers of both companies in federal district court alleging violations of §§ 10(b) and 20(a) of the Securities and Exchange Act of 1934 and SEC Rule 10b-5. They claimed that HomeSide and its officers, with the connivance of National and its chief executive, altered their financial models to make the company appear more valuable than it was. The alleged fraud, then, was said to have happened in part in Florida. Although the shares were listed, and purchased, on a foreign exchange by Australians, petitioners believed that because the fraudulent conduct took place, at least in part, in the United States, their civil securities fraud suit belonged in a U.S. court.

The district court dismissed the case for want of subject-matter jurisdiction, and the Second Circuit affirmed." The Supreme Court affirmed the dismissal of the complaint, making three critical rulings.

First, until *Morrison*, all the circuits treated extraterritoriality as a question going to the courts' subject-matter jurisdiction. In *Morrison*, however, the Supreme Court ruled that extraterritoriality is not a jurisdictional question; rather, it concerns only whether a case can be made on the merits:

> [T]o ask what conduct § 10(b) reaches is to ask what conduct § 10(b) prohibits, which is a merits question. Subject-matter jurisdiction, by contrast, refers to a tribunal's power to hear a case. It presents an issue quite separate from the question whether the allegations the plaintiff makes entitle him to relief. The District Court here had jurisdiction under 15 U.S.C. § 78aa to adjudicate the question whether § 10(b) applies to National's conduct.[10]...

Second, the *Morrison* Court, again overruling decades of lower court precedent, held that § 10(b) applies only to transactions in securities listed on domestic exchanges and domestic transactions in other securities—in short, to domestic securities transactions. The Court applied a strong presumption against extraterritoriality it derived from a 1991 case, *EEOC v. Arabian American Oil Co.*[11] It scrutinized the language and history of § 10(b) and identified "no affirmative indication in the Exchange Act that § 10(b) applies extraterritorially" and thus found nothing to rebut the presumption.[12] Accordingly, the Court ruled that the securities fraud provisions at issue did not apply extraterritorially.

Having lost the battle of extraterritoriality, the petitioners attempted to win the war by arguing that they sought only *domestic* application of § 10(b). Petitioners contended that, given that the fraud was hatched in Florida and false statements were made there, the fraud was committed in the United States.

Addressing this third issue, the Court acknowledged that "it is a rare case of prohibited extraterritorial application that lacks all contact with the territory of the United States." To answer the question of "where" the securities violation happened, the Court applied a "focus" test, which asks what conduct is the "object[] of the statute's solicitude."[13] This test examines "those transactions that the statute seeks to 'regulate'" and the "parties to those transactions that the statute seeks to 'protec[t].'"[14] The Court

---

[10] 561 U.S. at 254 (internal quotation marks and citations omitted).

[11] 499 U.S. 244 (1991).

[12] 561 U.S. at 265.

[13] *Id.* at 255 at 266–67.

[14] *Id.* at 267 (citations omitted).

argued that § 10(b) does not "punish deceptive conduct, but only deceptive conduct 'in connection with the purchase or sale of any security registered on a national securities exchange or any security not so registered.'"[15] Thus, the Court ruled that § 10(b) applies "only [to] transactions in securities listed on domestic exchanges, and domestic transactions in other securities"[16]; all other cases constitute improper extraterritorial applications of the statute. To be clear, where the fraudulent acts took place are irrelevant; unless the case concerns a domestic securities transaction, it constitutes a forbidden extraterritorial application of the statute.

After *Morrison* was announced, Congress amended the jurisdictional provisions of a number of securities laws in the Dodd–Frank Wall Street Reform and Consumer Protection Act (Dodd–Frank Act).[17] The amendments left *Morrison*'s holding untouched in private civil securities suits.[18] But with respect to securities fraud cases brought by the SEC and Department of Justice, the Act provides the government jurisdiction to pursue securities violations where the "conduct within the United States . . . constitutes significant steps in furtherance of the violation, even if the securities transaction occurs outside the United States and involves only foreign investors; or . . . conduct occurring outside the United States . . . has a foreseeable substantial effect within the United States."[19]

The Court's next extraterritoriality case, *Kiobel v. Royal Dutch Petroleum Co.*,[20] addressed whether the Alien Tort Statute (ATS) confers federal-court jurisdiction over causes of action alleging international-law violations committed overseas. In *Kiobel*, Nigerian nationals resident in the United States sued Dutch, British, and Nigerian corporations under the ATS. They alleged that Royal Dutch Petroleum aided and abetted the Nigerian government in committing violations of the law of nations in Nigeria. The Court granted certiorari to decide whether corporations can be held liable under the ATS for violations of the law of nations. The Court then asked for additional briefing on whether the ATS applies to violations occurring within the territory of another State.

The *Kiobel* Court, acknowledging that the presumption against extraterritoriality is "typically" applied to statutes "regulating conduct," nonetheless determined that the principles supporting the presumption should "similarly constrain courts considering causes of action that may be brought under the ATS."[21] The Court applied its strong presumption, holding that the ATS statute did not apply extraterritorially because the

---

[15] *Id.* at 266 (quoting 15 U.S.C. § 78j(b)).

[16] *Id.* at 267.

[17] Dodd–Frank Wall Street Reform and Consumer Protection Act, Pub. L. No. 111-203, § 929P(b)(2)(A), 124 Stat. 1376, 1865–66 (2010) (codified as amended at 15 U.S.C. § 78aa).

[18] *See* Liu Meng-Lin v. Siemens AG, 763 F.3d 175, 180–81 (2d Cir. 2014) (noting that section 929P(b) applies only to government-initiated claims).

[19] *Id.* (quoting 15 U.S.C. § 78aa (2010)). Some argue that this provision was not effective in overruling *Morrison* with respect to the statutes' extraterritorial reach in government-initiated securities fraud suits. The question whether this provision was sufficient to overrule *Morrison* arises because Congress included its conduct-and-effects test in the Act's subject-matter jurisdiction provisions. *Morrison*, however, held that the extraterritorial limitation was a merits question and Congress did not amend the substantive portions of the statutes. *See, e.g.*, SEC v. Chi. Convention Ctr., LLC, 961 F. Supp. 2d 905, 909–17 (N.D. Ill. 2013); Richard W. Painter, *The Dodd-Frank Extraterritorial Jurisdiction Provision: Was It Effective, Needed or Sufficient?*, 1 HARV. BUS. L. REV. 195, 199–205 (2011).

[20] 569 U.S. 108 (2013).

[21] *Id.* at 116.

statute lacked any clear indication that Congress intended it to extend to the sorts of foreign violations alleged in that case.[22]

In 2016, the Court in *RJR Nabisco, Inc. v. European Community*[23] ruled on the extraterritorial scope of the Racketeer Influenced and Corrupt Organizations Act (RICO).[24] RICO complaints generally allege that the defendants conducted an "enterprise" through a "pattern of racketeering activity."[25] Such patterns require proof of two or more violations of qualifying federal or state statutes (aka "predicate acts").[26] In *RJR Nabisco*, the Court held that RICO has extraterritorial application only where Congress has made the predicate statutes upon which the RICO case is built extraterritorial.[27] *RJR Nabisco* shows that the Court's presumption is not irrebuttable, but its discussion also illustrates how difficult it is to overcome the presumption.

The *Morrison* Court required that congressional intent for a statute's extraterritorially be "clearly expressed."[28] The *RJR Nabisco* Court required that Congress "affirmatively and unmistakably instruct[] that the statute" will apply extraterritorially.[29] It found an "obvious textual clue" in the fact that some RICO predicates, by their express terms, applied extraterritorially.[30] The Court pointed out that "[a]t least one predicate—the prohibition against 'kill[ing] a national of the United States, while such national is outside the United States'—applies *only* to conduct occurring outside the United States."[31] Congress's incorporation of extraterritorial predicates into RICO, the Court concluded, "gives a clear, affirmative indication that § 1962 applies to foreign racketeering activity."[32] Thus, RICO's unique structure made it "the rare statute that clearly evidences extraterritorial effect despite lacking an express statement of extraterritoriality."[33]

The Court ruled that it did not have to decide the third issue presented in *Morrison*: that is, where the violation occurred using the "focus" test. It explained:

> *Morrison* and *Kiobel* reflect a two-step framework for analyzing extraterritoriality issues. At the first step, we ask whether the presumption against extraterritoriality has been rebutted—that is, whether the statute gives a clear, affirmative indication that it applies extraterritorially. We must ask this question regardless of whether the statute in question regulates conduct, affords relief, or merely confers jurisdiction. If the statute is not extraterritorial, then at the second step we determine whether the case involves a domestic application of the statute, and we do this by looking to the statute's "focus." If the conduct relevant to the statute's focus occurred in the United States, then the case involves a permissible domestic application even if other

---

[22] *See id.* at 118–24.

[23] *See* -- U.S. --, 136 S. Ct. 2090 (2018).

[24] 18 U.S.C. §§ 1961–68.

[25] *Id.* § 1962(c).

[26] *See id.* § 1961(1), (5).

[27] 136 S. Ct. at 2101–03.

[28] *Morrison*, 561 U.S. at 255.

[29] 136 S. Ct. at 2100.

[30] *Id.* at 2101.

[31] *Id.* at 2102 (citing 18 U.S.C. § 2332(a)).

[32] *Id.*

[33] *Id.* at 2103.

conduct occurred abroad; but if the conduct relevant to the focus occurred in a foreign country, then the case involves an impermissible extraterritorial application regardless of any other conduct that occurred in U.S. territory.

What if we find at step one that a statute clearly *does* have extraterritorial effect? Neither *Morrison* nor *Kiobel* involved such a finding. But we addressed this issue in *Morrison*, explaining that it was necessary to consider § 10(b)'s "focus" only because we found that the statute does not apply extraterritorially: "If § 10(b) did apply abroad, we would not need to determine which transnational frauds it applied to; it would apply to all of them (barring some other limitation)." The scope of an extraterritorial statute thus turns on the limits Congress has (or has not) imposed on the statute's foreign application, and not on the statute's "focus."[34]

The *RJR Nabisco* case involved a civil suit by the European Community against RJR Nabisco alleging that RJR Nabisco had directed a global money laundering scheme with organized crime groups. The European Community sought treble damages under § 1964(c), which is the statutory provision that creates a private RICO cause of action. The Supreme Court determined that whether that section applies extraterritoriality presented a question distinct from whether the substantive sections of § 1962 could be applied to overseas conduct. The Court applied the presumption against extraterritoriality and ruled that § 1964(c) does not apply extraterritorially; thus, § 1964(c) "requires a civil RICO plaintiff to allege and prove a domestic injury to business or property and does not allow recovery for foreign injuries."[35]

Finally, in 2017, the Supreme Court granted certiorari in *United States v. Microsoft Corp.*[36] In that case, the government obtained a Stored Communications Act (SCA) warrant under 18 U.S.C. § 2703 that required Microsoft to disclose emails and other information associated with one of its customers. After the warrant was served, Microsoft moved to quash because the relevant data was stored in Microsoft's datacenter in Dublin, Ireland. The district court upheld the warrant, but the Second Circuit reversed, ruling that requiring Microsoft to disclose the electronic communications in question would be an unauthorized extraterritorial application of § 2703. After the case was fully briefed and argued, Congress passed the Clarifying Lawful Overseas Use of Data Act (CLOUD Act) as part of the Consolidated Appropriations Act, 2018.[37] The CLOUD Act amended the SCA as follows:

> A [service provider] shall comply with the obligations of this chapter to preserve, backup, or disclose the contents of a wire or electronic communication and any record or other information pertaining to a customer or subscriber within such provider's possession, custody, or control, regardless of whether such communication, record, or other information is located within or outside the United States.[38]

Because the government obtained, pursuant to the new law, a renewed § 2703 warrant covering the required information, the Court directed that the case be dismissed as moot.[39]

---

[34] *Id.* at 2101 (citations omitted).

[35] *Id.* at 2111.

[36] -- U.S. --, 138 S.Ct. 356 (2017).

[37] Pub. L. 115-141.

[38] CLOUD Act § 103(a)(1).

[39] -- U.S. --, 138 S.Ct. 1186 (2018).

2. EXTRATERRITORIALITY IN CRIMINAL CASES

All four cases discussed above were civil cases, although *Morrison* and *RJR Nabisco* involved statutes that can be enforced civilly or criminally ("hybrid" statutes). What analysis ought to apply in criminal cases? Note that "all fifteen cases decided since 1818 in which criminal conduct did not occur within U.S. territory or territorial waters, the Court did not apply a presumption against extraterritoriality. No presumption was applied in an additional five cases that questioned the scope or meaning of federal statutes where the crime occurred in United States waters or at least partially in the United States."[40] Further, "[d]espite the modern Supreme Court's strong presumption against extraterritoriality, it is relatively rare for courts of appeals to find that a federal criminal statute does *not* have extraterritorial purchase. The Second Circuit has twice asserted that the presumption against extraterritoriality does not apply in criminal cases … although a subsequent panel of the court attempted to walk back that assertion."[41]

Consider the following effort to provide a roadmap to the extraterritoriality issues presented in criminal cases and to explore the wisdom of a presumption against extraterritoriality in both contexts.

Julie Rose O'Sullivan, *Extraterritorial Criminal Jurisdiction*
1 Reforming Criminal Justice: Introduction and Criminalization 229 (Erik Luna ed., 2017)[42]

---

[40] *See* Julie Rose O'Sullivan, *The Extraterritorial Application of Federal Criminal Statutes: Analytical Roadmap, Normative Conclusions, and a Plea to Congress for Direction*, 106 Geo. L.J. 1021, 1047-48 (2018).

[41] *Id.* at 1027 (emphasis added); *compare* United States v. Siddiqui, 699 F.3d 690, 700 (2d Cir. 2012) ("The ordinary presumption that laws do not apply extraterritorially has no application to criminal statutes."), *and* United States v. Al Kassar, 660 F.3d 108, 118 (2d Cir. 2011) ("The presumption that ordinary acts of Congress do not apply extraterritorially does not apply to criminal statutes.") (internal citations omitted), *with* United States v. Vilar, 729 F.3d 62, 72 (2d Cir. 2013) (presumption applies in criminal cases).

[42] [Ed.:] Many citations were omitted from the excerpted version of this article but it is important to note that I relied on the excellent work of others throughout this piece, including: Gary B. Born, *A Reappraisal of the Extraterritorial Reach of U.S. Law*, 24 Law & Pol'y Int'l Bus. 1 (1992); Curtis A. Bradley, *Territorial Intellectual Property Rights in an Age of Globalism*, 37 Va. J. Int'l L. 505, 507 (1997); Lea Brilmayer, *The Extraterritorial Application of American Law: A Methodological and Constitutional Appraisal*, 50 Law & Contemp. Probs. 11, 33–34 (1987); Zachary D. Clopton, *Replacing the Presumption Against Extraterritoriality*, 94 B.U. L. Rev. 1 (2014); Anthony J. Colangelo, *A Unified Approach to Extraterritoriality*, 97 Va. L. Rev. 1019, 1028 (2011); Anthony J. Colangelo, *Constitutional Limits on Extraterritorial Jurisdiction: Terrorism and the Intersection of National and International Law*, 48 Harv. Int'l L.J. 121 (2007); William S. Dodge, *Extraterritoriality and Conflict-of-Laws Theory: An Argument for Judicial Unilateralism*, 39 Harv. Int'l L.J. 101 (1998); William S. Dodge, *Understanding the Presumption Against Extraterritoriality*, 16 Berkeley J. Int'l. L. 85, 89-90 (1998); John H. Knox, *A Presumption Against Extrajurisdictionality*, 104 Am. J. Int'l L. 351, 351–52, 396 (2010); Larry D. Kramer, *Vestiges of Beale: Extraterritorial Application of American Law*, 1991 Sup. Ct. Rev. 179 (1991); Larry Kramer, *Extraterritorial Application of American Law After the Insurance Antitrust Case: A Reply to Professsors Lowenfeld and Trimble*, 89 Am. J. Int'l L. 750, 752 (1995); Jeffrey A. Meyer, *Dual Illegality and Geoambiguous Law: A New Rule for Extraterritorial Application of U.S. Law*, 95 Minn. L. Rev. 110 (2010); Austen Parrish, *The Effects Test: Extraterritoriality's Fifth Business*, 61 Vand. L. Rev. 1455, 1458-1461 (2008); Dan E. Stigall, *International Law and Limitations on the Exercise of Extraterritorial Jurisdiction in U.S. Domestic Law*, 35 Hastings Int'l & Comp. L. Rev. 323 (2012); and Jonathan Turley, *"When in Rome": Multinational Misconduct and the Presumption Against Extraterritoriality*, 84 Nw. L. Rev. 598, 599–601 (1990).

Assume that a Russian citizen hacked into the e-mail of the Democratic National Committee and then provided masses of stolen DNC e-mails to WikiLeaks for publication. This type of unauthorized access and release is unlawful in many countries (which will be referred to within as "States"). But where was the crime "committed"? At the hacker's keyboard in Russia? Where the DNC's servers are—presumably somewhere in the United States? Where WikiLeaks' servers are—presumably *not* in the United States? Or perhaps where the actual and intended effect of the criminal activity was felt? If it is concluded that this criminal activity took place outside the territory of the United States—that is, extraterritorially—further critical questions include whether Congress has the constitutional power to regulate such conduct, whether Congress intended the anti-hacking statute to apply extraterritorially, and what, if any, due process limits exist on such exercises of criminal jurisdiction.

These questions have increasing importance in a world where criminal activity and criminals regularly cross national borders. The question of whether U.S. laws can or should apply to such transborder criminal activity, then, is one that courts encounter frequently. The difficulty is that the applicable analysis is unclear, particularly in criminal cases. Scholars agree that "the case law is so riddled with inconsistencies and exceptions that [attempting to bring coherence to the law on extraterritoriality] … is probably futile and maybe even counterproductive." It will not surprise, then, that "the only thing courts and scholars seem to agree on is that the law in this area is a mess."

Despite this consensus, I will first attempt to summarize the analytical steps applied to extraterritoriality decisions, highlighting uncertainties and questions. I will then attempt to summarize the deep and rich literature on the modern Supreme Court's presumption against extraterritoriality, which is today the predominant factor in extraterritoriality decisions in the usual case where the statute does not explicitly specify its geographic applicability. The Supreme Court originally applied this strong presumption against application of U.S. federal law to conduct outside U.S. territory in the 1991 case of *EEOC v. Arabian American Oil Co. (Aramco)*,[43] and it has applied the presumption with vigor in its most recent extraterritoriality precedents, all of which were civil cases. …

I. PRESCRIPTIVE JURISDICTION

To begin, readers must have some understanding of the most generally relevant[44] international law principles that control prescriptive—here, legislative—jurisdiction in criminal cases. The prescriptive principles of international law delineate the legislative power "to make its law applicable to the activities, relations, or status of persons, or the interests of persons in things."[45] [The actual function of these principles is to determine whether the action of a State in prescribing or enforcing its laws abroad gives another State a claim for violation of its rights. Congress has the power under our constitutional structure to pass laws that exceed the limits of these principles. They do not limit the power of Congress; they simply give other States a basis for objection if Congress exceeds the prescriptive principles by legislation.]

Although Congress has the power to specify that statutes apply beyond the limits set by international law, the Supreme Court, in many of its pre-1991 cases, was reluctant to

---

[43] [Article's footnote 4:] 499 U.S. 244 (1991).

[44] [Article's footnote 7:] Because Congress rarely uses it, I will not here discuss "universal jurisdiction." RESTATEMENT (THIRD) OF THE FOREIGN RELATIONS LAW OF THE UNITED STATES § 404 (Am. Law Inst. 1987) [hereinafter RESTATEMENT]. …

[45] [Article's footnote 8:] [*Id.*] § 401.

ascribe such a purpose to Congress absent expressed congressional intent. Thus, where a statute did not on its face speak to its extraterritorial application, the Supreme Court often applied the *Charming Betsy* canon of construction (named after an early 19th-century case), which dictates that "an act of Congress ought never to be construed to violate the law of nations if any other possible construction remains."[46] The Supreme Court's extraterritoriality decisions have not been a model of consistency, but it is fair to say that the Court, prior to 1991, frequently referenced the customary international law prescriptive principles in ascertaining the scope of federal statutes pursuant to *Charming Betsy*.

The most traditional and important basis for prescriptive jurisdiction is territorial. The *Restatement (Third) of Foreign Relations Law of the United States (Restatement)* recognizes that there are two types of territorial principles. First, a State has jurisdiction to prescribe law with respect to "*conduct* that, wholly or in substantial part, takes place within its territory"[47] ("subjective" territorial jurisdiction). The second type of territorial jurisdiction gives a State the power to regulate "conduct outside its territory that has or is intended to have *substantial effect* within its territory"[48] ("objective" territorial jurisdiction or "effects" jurisdiction). One might logically ask: How can a given claim or prosecution be founded on "territorial" jurisdiction if it may not involve actionable conduct (only effects) on the territory of the State seeking to address the crime? One answer is that effects jurisdiction was intended to capture situations such as the following (frequently used) example: In an illegal duel, Jones, on the Canadian side of the border, shoots with intent to kill Smith, who dies on the United States' side of the border. In such a case, elements of the crime are committed in both jurisdictions: Firing the gun with intent to kill occurred in one country, but without the death in the other, there could be no murder prosecution. ... [Modern "effects" jurisdiction, however, does not require that an element of the crime occur within the territory of the State seeking to assert jurisdiction as long as a "substantial effect" can be demonstrated. Perhaps as a result, the American Law Institute's draft *Restatement (Fourth) of the Foreign Relations Law of the United States* no longer includes "effects" as a subset of territorial jurisdiction, delineating it instead as a discrete jurisdictional basis.][49]

For many years, the lower courts accepted the *Restatement*'s view that both domestic conduct and domestic effects could mean that a claim constituted a territorial, as opposed to extraterritorial, application of a statute. They therefore employed a "conduct-and-effects" test founded both on subjective and objective territorial principles to discern when a suit concerned territorial claims and thus was unobjectionable, as opposed to extraterritorial claims that would require an analysis of whether the statute was intended to be employed extraterritorially. With respect to effects jurisdiction, for example, the D.C. Circuit, in *United States v. Philip Morris USA Inc.*, explained that:

> Because conduct with substantial domestic effects implicates a state's legitimate interest in protecting its citizens within its borders, Congress's regulation of foreign conduct meeting this "effects" test is "*not* an *extraterritorial* assertion of jurisdiction."

---

[46] [Article's footnote 10:] Murray v. Schooner Charming Betsy (Charming Betsy), 6 U.S. (2 Cranch) 64, 118 (1804); *see also* RESTATEMENT, *supra* note [44], § 114 ("Where fairly possible, a United States statute is to be construed so as not to conflict with international law or with an international agreement of the United States.").

[47] [Article's footnote 12:] RESTATEMENT, *supra* note [44], § 402(1)(a) (emphasis added).

[48] [Article's footnote 13:] *Id.* § 402(1)(c) (emphasis added).

[49] [Ed.:] *See* RESTATEMENT (FOURTH) OF THE FOREIGN RELATIONS LAW OF THE UNITED STATES, Tentative Draft No. 2, §201(b) & cmts. 3, f (Am. Law Inst. March 22, 2016).

Thus, when a statute is applied to conduct meeting the effects test, the presumption against extraterritoriality does not apply.[50]

As we shall see, however, the Supreme Court's modern presumption against extraterritoriality is keyed only to the subjective territoriality principle—that is, to conduct occurring on U.S. soil—and excludes the objective territorial principle—that is, reference to the effects of foreign conduct on the U.S. territory and population.

Another very traditional basis for jurisdiction concerns nationality. Thus, a State has prescriptive jurisdiction over "the activities, interests, status, or relations of its nationals outside as well as within its territory."[51] A less widely accepted basis for jurisdiction that relates to nationality, passive personality jurisdiction, "asserts that a state may apply law—particularly criminal law—to an act committed outside its territory by a person not its national where the victim of the act was its national."[52] Many civil law countries make extensive use of nationality and passive personality jurisdiction, but the United States traditionally has been sparing in its use of these principles. Finally, a State also has the prescriptive jurisdiction to address "certain conduct outside its territory by persons not its nationals that is directed against the security of the state or against a limited class of other state interests."[53] This so-called "protective principle" is intended to be limited to offenses directed against the security of the State or the integrity of governmental functions, involving crimes such as espionage, counterfeiting the State currency, and the like.

II. STATE OF PLAY: GENERAL

A. THE "WHERE" QUESTION

Logically, the first question is when a given application of a statute is "domestic," and thus unexceptional, as opposed to "extraterritorial," and thus questionable. If, as in the above WikiLeaks example, conduct occurs both in the United States and abroad, or if conduct abroad has concrete and harmful effects in the United States, where is the crime deemed to have been "committed"? When all the elements of a crime occur on one State's territory, that crime is clearly "committed" domestically. Where, however, the elements of the crime occur in different States, as in our dueling case, it may be that two (or more) States will claim territorial jurisdiction. A critical difficulty in applying the territoriality principle is the question of just what, and how much, activity must occur on a State's territory for a transborder crime to be deemed committed within that State and thus justified by the subjective territorial principle.

The Supreme Court did not address the question of what, or how much, conduct must occur in the territorial United States before a given claim or prosecution could be deemed domestic as opposed to extraterritorial until its 2010 decision in *Morrison v. National Australia Bank*.[54] Before *Morrison*, at least in securities and antitrust cases, the lower courts applied their conduct-and-effects test to determine whether they could adjudicate a case where the claim was founded on conduct that spanned borders.

The conduct-and-effects test, pioneered by the Second Circuit and adopted by other circuits, did not require a global inquiry into whether a certain statute was intended to

---

[50] [Article's footnote 16:] [United States v. Philip Morris USA, Inc., 566 F.3d 1095, 1130 (D.C. Cir. 2009) (citation omitted).]

[51] [Article's footnote 17:] RESTATEMENT, *supra* note [44], § 402(2).

[52] [Article's footnote 18:] *Id.* § 402 cmt. g.

[53] [Article's footnote 19:] *Id.* § 402(3).

[54] [Article's footnote 20:] Morrison v. National Australia Bank Ltd., 561 U.S. 247 (2010).

apply extraterritorially or only domestically because the test *assumed* that only territorial cases could proceed. The courts assessed the facts of each case—the extent of the alleged conduct and effects—to determine whether "Congress would have wished the precious resources of United States courts and law enforcement agencies to be devoted to them rather than leave the problem to foreign countries."[55] If the answer was yes, the case proceeded; if the answer was no, the case was dismissed. In other words, the courts assumed that if the conduct-and-effects test was not satisfied, the claim concerned an extraterritorial application of the statute *and* that such extraterritorial claims could not proceed.

The Supreme Court emphatically rejected the use of the conduct-and-effects test, at least as applied in securities fraud cases, in *Morrison*.[56] ... [T]he conduct-and-effects test can be abused; it is subject to inconsistent results and can be manipulated. Certainly this was an argument that won the day with the *Morrison* Court. ...

In any case, the Court's rejection of the conduct-and-effects test meant that it had to come up with a global solution to the question of how to determine where a crime is committed. That is, given that the Court rejected use of an effects test, it had to decide what conduct must occur in a State for the crime to be considered domestic as opposed to extraterritorial. The *Morrison* Court articulated a "focus" test under which courts must evaluate what "territorial event" or "relationship" is the "focus" of the statute—that is, the "object[] of the statute's solicitude"—to identify the conduct that must occur in the United States for the suit to be deemed territorial.[57] In the *Morrison* case, the question concerned when a violation would be deemed domestic as opposed to extraterritorial when a civil securities fraud claim was based on conduct both in the United States and abroad. The Court identified one element of the claim to be decisive based on its "focus" test. It decreed that subjective territoriality is only present in civil securities fraud cases involving "transactions in securities listed on domestic exchanges, and domestic transactions in other securities."[58] Under *Morrison*'s transactional focus, the place where the fraudulent activity occurred and the location of the harm flowing from the fraud are all irrelevant.

Because *Morrison* was relatively recently decided, it is unclear how one determines a statute's "focus," which is not something Congress normally identifies and which appears to be an extremely subjective, and manipulable, determination. The Court's decision to focus on the location of the securities transaction, to the exclusion of the site of the fraud, seems arbitrary. The focus test was also an unnecessary innovation because more logical and well-developed references were available—venue, for example. "The Constitution makes it clear that the determination of proper venue in a criminal case requires determination of where the crime was *committed*."[59] When federal courts have been asked to determine where a criminal securities fraud was committed for venue purposes, they have recognized that criminal securities fraud happens both where the transactions are consummated and where the fraud is hatched. Indeed, in identifying the site of the

---

[55] [Article's footnote 21:] Bersch v. Drexel Firestone, Inc., 519 F.2d 974, 985 (2d Cir. 1975) (Friendly, J.).

[56] [Article's footnote 22:] *Morrison*, 561 U.S. at 255–61.

[57] [Article's footnote 25:] *Id.* at 266–67.

[58] [Article's footnote 26:] *Id.* at 267.

[59] [Article's footnote 29:] United States v. Cores, 356 U.S. 405, 407 (1958) (emphasis added); *see* U.S. CONST. Art. III, § 2, cl. 3 ("The Trial of all Crimes . . . shall be held in the State where the said Crimes shall have been committed); *Id.* Amend. VI ("In all criminal prosecutions, the accused shall enjoy the right to a speedy and public trial, by an impartial jury of the State and district wherein the crime shall have been committed.").

securities transaction as the only relevant factor in determining subjective territorial jurisdiction, the *Morrison* Court ignored the fact that Congress had, by statute, expressly provided that a criminal securities fraud is committed (for venue purposes) where "*any act or transaction constituting the violation occurred.*"[60]

B. ARTICLE I CHALLENGES

If a situation is deemed to concern an extraterritorial application of the relevant statute, and if prompted (many litigants do not press this objection), courts will then ask whether Congress had the power under Article I of the U.S. Constitution to reach the overseas conduct. The most popular Article I powers invoked to justify extraterritorial extensions of criminal prohibitions are the foreign or domestic Commerce Clause, the power given Congress to define and punish piracies and felonies committed on the high seas and offenses against the law of nations, and the Necessary and Proper Clause when employed by Congress to implement a treaty that requires the States that join it to enact criminal legislation pursuant to its terms.

Assuming Congress has the constitutional power to extend a statute's coverage to extraterritorial conduct, courts will follow any direction provided in the statute as to its extraterritorial reach. Congress' instructions in this regard vary with the statute. More commonly, Congress has not spoken to the issue of extraterritorially in the criminal statute itself. The inquiry then becomes whether Congress intended to give the statute extraterritorial effect.

C. JURISDICTION VERSUS MERITS

One threshold question is whether the issue of the geographic scope of a statute goes to the subject-matter jurisdiction of the court or goes only to whether a plaintiff or prosecutor has made out a case on the merits. For decades, the courts of appeals treated the issue as going to the courts' subject-matter jurisdiction, which meant, among other things, that it was a non-waivable issue that was reserved for judicial determination. In *Morrison*, the Court clarified that, unless Congress specifies otherwise, whether a statute applies extraterritorially is a merits question and does not go to jurisdiction.[61] This determination means that persons who plead guilty or who fail to timely object to the extraterritorial application of a statute will waive that objection.[62] But other consequences are less clear. For example, as a "merits" question, is extraterritoriality now an element of the crime, and thus an issue that must be proven beyond a reasonable doubt to a jury? And, if so, just what would the jury be asked to decide?

D. CONGRESSIONAL INTENT

Where the statute is ambiguous as to its extraterritorial application, lower federal courts generally apply two canons of interpretation. The first is the presumption against extraterritoriality that the Supreme Court first articulated in its modern form in the 1991 case, *EEOC v. Arabian American Oil Co. (Aramco).*[63] In *Aramco* and subsequent cases, the

---

[60] [Article's footnote 31:] 15 U.S.C. § 78aa(a) (emphasis added); *see also* United States v. Johnson, 510 F.3d 521, 524 (4th Cir. 2007).

[61] [Article's footnote 37:] *See* Morrison v. National Australia Bank Ltd., 561 U.S. 247, 253-254 (2010).

[62] [Article's footnote 38:] *See* United States v. Miranda, 780 F.3d 1185, 1191 (D.C. Cir. 2015).

[63] [Article's footnote 39:] 499 U.S. 244 (1991).

Court decreed that unless a statute gives a "'clear indication'"[64] that Congress intended it to apply outside the "territorial jurisdiction"[65] of the United States, it does not. The presumption has become something approaching a clear statement rule (although the Court disclaims this reality[66]). To be clear, the presumption assumes that Congress acts only with subjective territoriality in mind and thus intends statutes to apply only to conduct in the territory over which the United States is sovereign unless Congress affirmatively indicates otherwise.

The second canon of construction that lower courts reference is the *Charming Betsy* canon, in reliance upon the Court's pre-1991 case law. ... "For most of U.S. history, the Supreme Court determined the reach of federal statutes in light of international law— specifically, the international law of legislative jurisdiction. In effect, it applied a ... presumption that federal law does not extend beyond the jurisdictional limits set by international law. This presumption was an offshoot of the long-standing *Charming Betsy* canon." Lower courts continue to ask, in cases raising extraterritoriality questions, whether the extraterritorial application of a statute will exceed the prescriptive jurisdiction of Congress under international law.

The historical reality is that the Court employed the the *Charming Betsy* canon in its pre-*Aramco* cases but has only referenced it in one extraterritoriality decision since.[67] The Court, in its most recent extraterritoriality decision, *RJR Nabisco, Inc. v. European Community* (2016),[68] was explicit about its preferred analysis. First, the Supreme Court advised that courts must determine whether a statute has any extraterritorial purchase, and it again emphasized the strength of the presumption against extraterritoriality.[69] If the statute does *not* apply extraterritorially, the courts must take a second step and "determine whether the case involves a domestic application of the statute, and we do this by looking to the statute's 'focus.'"[70] Nowhere was the *Charming Betsy* canon referenced or applied. It seems likely, then, that the *Charming Betsy* canon currently applied in extraterritoriality cases by the lower courts is akin to the human appendix—a vesitigial structure that has lost its original function.

---

[64] [Article's footnote 40:] Kiobel v. Royal Dutch Petroleum Co., 133 S. Ct. 1659, 1664 (2013) (quoting *Morrison*, 561 U.S. at 255).

[65] [Article's footnote 41:] EEOC v. Arabian Am. Oil Co. (Aramco), 499 U.S. 244, 248 (1991) (quoting Foley Bros., Inc. v. Filardo, 336 U.S. 281, 285 (1949)).

[66] [Article's footnote 42:] *See Morrison*, 561 U.S. at 265. It is true that the Court has stated that there need not be "an express statement of extraterritoriality" and that "'context can be consulted as well.'" RJR Nabisco, Inc. v. European Community, 136 S. Ct. 2090, 2102 (2016) (quoting *Morrison*, 561 U.S. at 265). And the "presumption" is not irrebuttable, as is demonstrated by *RJR Nabisco* .... That said, the *Morrison* Court required that congressional intent to apply a statute extraterritorially be "clearly expressed," *Morrison*, 561 U.S. at 255, and the *RJR Nabisco* Court took it up a notch by requiring that Congress "affirmatively and unmistakably instruct[] that the statute" will apply extraterritorially. *RJR Nabisco*, 136 S. Ct. at 2100.

[67] [Article's footnote 44:] *See* F. Hoffman La Roche Ltd. v. Empagrn, S.A., 542 U.S. 155, 165 (2004).

[68] [Article's footnote 45:] 136 S. Ct. 2090 (2016).

[69] [Article's footnote 46:] *Id.* at 2101.

[70] [Article's footnote 47:] *Id.*

III. STATE OF PLAY: CRIMINAL CASES

A. *BOWMAN*

It is notable that, at least until recently, the lower federal courts have been very willing to find that federal statutes apply extraterritorially in criminal cases. They have resisted application of the Court's modern strong presumption in two ways. First, until recently, many courts did so by employing a fairly forgiving (from the government's point of view) conduct-and-effects test in a variety of cases, most notably antitrust and securities fraud cases. Lower courts' willingness to use this test has receded after they were taken to task for using it in no uncertain terms by the *Morrison* Court. But it is worth noting that even the Supreme Court, post-*Aramco*, has recognized that the conduct-and-effects test still controls in antitrust cases without reference to any presumption.[71] Due to the post-*Morrison* congressional attempt to reinstitute the conduct-and-effects test in government-initiated securities fraud cases, this test may well also apply in criminal securities fraud cases despite *Morrison*.

Second, in criminal cases, the lower federal courts escaped the presumption by relying on a Supreme Court opinion hailing from 1922, *United States v. Bowman*.[72] *Bowman* involved a scheme hatched on the high seas and brought to fruition in Rio de Janeiro pursuant to which a U.S. government-owned corporation was defrauded. The Court acknowledged that punishment of crimes against private individuals or their property "must, of course, be committed within the territorial jurisdiction of the government where it may properly exercise it."[73] But, the Court stated:

> The same rule of interpretation should not be applied to criminal statutes which are, as a class, not logically dependent on their locality for the government's jurisdiction, but are enacted because of the right of the government to defend itself against obstruction, or fraud wherever perpetrated, especially if committed by its own citizens, officers, or agents. Some such offenses can only be committed within the territorial jurisdiction of the government because of the local acts required to constitute them. Others are such that to limit their locus to the strictly territorial jurisdiction would be greatly to curtail the scope and usefulness of the statute and leave open a large immunity for frauds as easily committed by citizens on the high seas and in foreign countries as at home. In such cases, Congress has not thought it necessary to make specific provision in the law that the locus shall include the high seas and foreign countries, but allows it to be inferred from the nature of the offense.[74]

Bowman is widely used—and some say misused—by lower courts looking to justify the extraterritorial application of criminal statutes. Some lower courts question whether, in light of *Bowman*, the presumption even applies in criminal cases, although those appear to be in the minority.[75] *Bowman* has never been overruled but it is arguably inconsistent with

---

[71] [Article's footnote 48:] Hartford Fire Ins. Co. v. California, 509 U.S. 764 (1993).

[72] [Article's footnote 50:] United States v. Bowman, 260 U.S. 94 (1922).

[73] [Article's footnote 51:] *Id.* at 98.

[74] [Article's footnote 52:] *Id.*

[75] [Article's footnote 53:] *Compare* United States v. Siddiqui, 699 F.3d 690, 700 (2d Cir. 2012), *and* United States v. Al Kassar, 660 F.3d 108, 118 (2d Cir. 2011), *with* United States v. Vilar, 729 F.3d 62, 72 (2d Cir. 2013).

today's Court's emphatic embrace of the presumption against application of statutes in any circumstances other than where justified by the subjective territorial principle.

B. DUE PROCESS

A final step in the extraterritoriality analysis in criminal cases deals with the potential application of the Due Process Clause. Although no decision of the Supreme Court has yet addressed the issue of whether constitutional due process limitations apply in transborder federal criminal cases, the courts of appeals have found that such limitations do exist. The difficulty, however, is that the courts are split on the applicable test—that is, whether due process requires only that the extraterritorial prosecution not be arbitrary and unfair, or whether the Due Process Clause also requires proof of a sufficient "nexus" between defendant and the United States.

The odds of succeeding on such a due process claim are vanishingly small; out of the hundreds of extraterritoriality cases I have read, I have found only one case in which a due process challenge succeeded.[76]

IV. THE PRESUMPTION AGAINST EXTRATERRITORIALITY

The above attempt to summarize the governing extraterritoriality analysis illustrates the extent to which the law is underdeveloped (*e.g.*, What does the Court mean by a statutory "focus" and how can one divine that focus? If extraterritoriality is a merits question, does that mean it is an element of the crime that must be proved beyond a reasonable doubt to the jury?). It also shows important areas of uncertainty (*e.g.*, What is the status of the *Charming Betsy* canon of construction? Does the presumption apply in criminal cases? What is the status of *Bowman*? Is there a due process limit on extraterritorial prosecutions, can it be invoked by non-U.S. nationals, and, if so, what is the applicable due process standard?).

Perhaps the only thing that is clear is the Court's commitment to a very strong presumption against extraterritoriality—one founded only on subjective territorial jurisdiction—and the generally case-determinative effect of that presumption. This raises the question many scholars have struggled with: does this presumption make sense?

To the extent that the modern presumption against extraterritoriality is founded upon 19th-century convictions about the absolute nature of territorial sovereignty, such notions can no longer be entertained. The United States—and the rest of the world—has long since recognized that in fact a State may legitimately extend its jurisdiction beyond its borders where effects, nationality, passive personality, and protective jurisdictional principles permit. Then what, if anything, justifies the presumption against extraterritoriality upon which the modern Court is so insistent? Instead of adopting a default presumption, why not instead … "determine what policy a law was enacted to achieve in wholly domestic cases and ask whether there are connections between the case and the nation implicating that policy"? The Court's explanation for why a presumption against extraterritoriality is appropriately applied has changed over time and even today has a certain shape-shifting quality.

---

[76] [Article's footnote 54:] *See* United States v. Perlaza, 439 F.3d 1149, 1168–69 (9th Cir. 2006); *see also* United States v. Ali, 885 F. Supp. 2d 55 (D.D.C. 2012) (dismissing on due process grounds), *rev'd*, 718 F.3d 929 (D.C. Cir. 2013) (reversing due process determination).

A. CONFLICT WITH FOREIGN LAW

Probably the most consistent rationalization for the modern presumption against extraterritoriality is that it is necessary "to protect against unintended clashes between our laws and those of other nations which could result in international discord." There is undoubtedly a potential for conflict where one sovereign seeks to enforce its laws on a non-national whose conduct occurred on the territory of another sovereign. Subjecting foreign nationals to U.S. law for conduct that occurred on the territory of another State can create political controversies as well as retaliatory actions. … [T]he overextension of U.S. jurisdiction has provided a justification for other countries to aggressively use extraterritorial jurisdiction "for their own ends" and generated a number of other costs.

But most commentators find that the conflicts argument is overstated and unpersuasive. First, … the presumption against extraterritoriality "unduly elevates Congress's presumed desire to avoid conflicts with foreign laws over other important legislative goals. Much more important, in the real world, are legislators' desires to assist local constituencies, to further domestic legislative programs and interests, and to make statements of political or moral principle."

The presumption also underestimates Congress's appetite for conflict with other nations. Commentators generally concur that conflict with other States is most pronounced when the United States is exercising effects jurisdiction. Yet Congress has responded to the Supreme Court's application of the presumption and other extraterritoriality decisions in important regulatory areas—including areas, such as antitrust and securities law enforcement, most likely to generate international consternation—by expressly endorsing a conduct-and-effects test. Thus, Congress responded to lower courts' application of the conduct-and-effects test in antitrust cases by codifying it in the Foreign Trade Antitrust Improvements Act (FTAIA).[77] The FTAIA excludes from the Sherman Act's reach "conduct involving trade or commerce … with foreign nations," other than import trade or import commerce, unless "such conduct has a direct, substantial, and reasonably foreseeable effect" on domestic or import commerce.[78] And as noted previously, shortly after *Morrison* was announced, Congress amended the jurisdictional provisions in various securities statutes with the apparent intention to codify the conduct-and-effects test in government-initiated securities fraud actions.

The conflict-avoidance rationale also appears to be disingenuous at worst and under- and over-inclusive at best. The Court does not actually inquire into whether a threat of conflict exists in each case. The Court has recognized that this concern does not arise in all cases in which it chooses to apply the presumption.[79] It has applied the presumption in cases in which it acknowledged that no conflict was possible[80] and has not applied the presumption where conflicts might well eventuate.[81] Where there is no potential for conflict, yet the Court has applied the presumption, the result may well be that no

---

[77] [Article's footnote 62 :] 15 U.S.C. § 6a.

[78] [Article's footnote 63:] *Id.* § 6a(1)(A).

[79] [Article's footnote 65:] *See, e.g.*, RJR Nabisco, Inc. v. European Community, 136 S. Ct. 2090, 2100 (2016); Morrison v. National Australia Bank Ltd., 561 U.S. 247, 255 (2010); Smith v. United States, 507 U.S. 197, 206-07 (1993); Sale v. Haitian Centers Council, Inc., 509 U.S. 155, 174 (1993).

[80] [Article's footnote 66:] *See Sale*, 509 U.S. at 173-174 (U.S. ship on the high seas); *see also Smith*, 507 U.S. 197 (Antarctica).

[81] [Article's footnote 67:] *See* Hartford Fire Ins. Co. v. California, 509 U.S. 764 (1993).

national law applies to objectionable conduct (as in a case arising in the Antarctic).[82] Indeed, in failing to apply U.S. law to situations where only U.S. law might apply, the Court may actually create conflicts.[83] Thus, for example, in *Sale v. Haitian Centers Council, Inc.*, the Court refused to apply restrictions Congress put in place to comply with U.S. treaty obligations to a U.S. vessel over which no other nation could exercise sovereignty—a result that disappointed, rather than mollified, the international community.

Additionally, the Court draws no distinction in its application of the presumption between cases in which U.S. law would be applied to U.S. nationals as opposed to non-nationals abroad even though there is far greater potential for conflict in the latter cases than the former. And the Court does not seem to recognize that conflict-creation may occur whether or not U.S. statutes apply abroad. Many States employ all the prescriptive principles, including effects jurisdiction and expansive nationality and passive personality jurisdiction. Even where U.S. law is being applied strictly territorially, then, there may still be a potential for conflict because other States may, consistent with international law norms, apply their laws extraterritorially—for example, to their own nationals even if those nationals are acting on U.S. territory.

Finally, the presumption overstates the potential for conflict. While it is true that, for example, many in the international community weighed in through amicus briefs in *Morrison* to argue against allowing civil securities actions in cases where extraterritorial elements predominate, it is also true that in *RJR Nabisco*, it was the European Community itself seeking damages in a civil RICO case against American cigarette companies. In that case, the European Community aggressively argued *for* extraterritorial application of U.S. law.

B. DOMESTIC CONCERNS

A rationale for the presumption against extraterritoriality that appears to have gained traction in the Court's most recent cases is that "Congress ordinarily legislates with respect to domestic, not foreign matters." [84] This is the weakest of the Court's justifications. It is questionable whether Congress in fact is primarily concerned only with conduct occurring on U.S. soil given the increasingly globalized nature of many problems and certainly given the explosion in cross-border criminality. Indeed, as noted above, Congress has repeatedly overruled judicial decisions limiting the reach of statutes to the shores of the United States.[85]

Second, and more importantly, there is a fundamental indeterminacy here—what, exactly, is a "domestic concern"? The assumption appears to be that Congress is concerned only with conduct that occurs on U.S. territory, while conduct that occurs abroad but has concrete, harmful effects in U.S. territory or on its citizens is not a

---

[82] [Article's footnote 68:] *Smith*, 507 U.S. 197.

[83] [Article's footnote 69:] *See, e.g., Sale*, 509 U.S. 155.

[84] [Article's footnote 72:] Morrison v. National Australia Bank Ltd., 561 U.S. 247, 258–61, 255 (2010); *see also* RJR Nabisco, Inc. v. European Community, 136 S. Ct. 2090, 2100 (2016); Microsoft Corp. v. AT&T Corp., 550 U.S. 437, 454–55 (2007); Smith v. United States, 507 U.S. 197, 204 n.5 (1993); EEOC v. Arabian Am. Oil Co. (Aramco), 499 U.S. 244, 248 (1991); Foley Bros. v. Filardo, 336 U.S. 281, 285 (1949).

[85] [Article's footnote 74:] ... Congress also overruled *Aramco* by amending Title VII to extend protection to United States citizens working overseas. *See* Civil Rights Act of 1991, Pub. L. No. 102-166, § 109(a), 105 Stat. 1077, codified at 42 U.S.C. § 2000e(f) ("With respect to employment in a foreign country," the term "employee" "includes an individual who is a citizen of the United States.").

"domestic concern." But as Professor Knox points out, "domestic concerns" "may include not only actions taken within U.S. borders, but also actions taken outside it when they either affect the United States or are taken by the U.S. government or even, in some cases, its nationals." Further, even if one assumes that Congress is concerned only with circumstances affecting the territory of the United States, "[f]oreign actions can and often do affect conditions within U.S. borders so that, at least under certain conditions, legislation must address foreign conduct in order to regulate domestic concerns." ...

C. LEGISLATIVE EFFICIENCY

A third modern rationale for the presumption is the Court's stated belief that Congress knows of the Court's devotion to the presumption, and thus "legislates against the backdrop of the presumption against extraterritoriality."[86] This, the Court asserts, "preserv[es] a stable background against which Congress can legislate with predictable effects."[87]

Many question the implicit assumption underlying this rationale: that the presumption is value-neutral and that, like "driving a car on the right-hand side of the road," it "is not so important to choose the best convention as it is to choose one convention and stick to it."[88] Professor Eskridge explains that, to justify the presumption against extraterritoriality on this basis, three conditions must be met: (1) Congress must be "institutionally capable of knowing and working from an interpretive regime that the Court is institutionally capable of devising and transmitting in coherent form"; (2) the application of the interpretive regime must be "transparent" to Congress; and (3) the interpretive regime should not change in unpredictable ways. He concludes that while the presumption established in *Aramco* may have satisfied the first of these conditions, it failed the second and "dramatically flunk[ed]" the third. Many question whether the presumption is sufficiently transparent, coherent, and consistently applied to be a useful guide to Congress. ...

Finally, it is difficult to deny that the presumption has allocational effects. The presumption advantages those, like transnational companies, who would rather avoid regulation whenever possible because the heavy burden of galvanizing Congress to overrule the Court after it has applied the presumption lies on advocates of regulation. In part because of these obvious allocational effects, many commentators believe that the presumption is best understood as a disguised judicial normative preference. This can be read as a commitment to territorial sovereignty or as a hostility to certain types of suits. For example, Justice Scalia, writing for the majority in *Morrison*, noted that one should be "repulsed" by the potential adverse consequences of a ruling permitting civil securities liability in cases like *Morrison* because this would lead to a "Shangri-La of class-action litigation for lawyers representing those allegedly cheated in foreign securities markets."

D. SEPARATION OF POWERS/JUDICIAL COMPETENCY

Professor Bradley asserts that "the determination of whether and how to apply federal legislation to conduct abroad raises difficult and sensitive policy questions that tend to fall outside both the institutional competence and constitutional prerogatives of

---

[86] [Article's footnote 79:] EEOC v. Arabian American Oil Co. (Aramco), 499 U.S. 244, 248 (1991); *see also* Smith v. United States, 507 U.S. 197, 204 (1993).

[87] [Article's footnote 80:] Morrison v. National Australia Bank Ltd., 561 U.S. 247, 261 (2010).

[88] [Article's footnote 81:] WILLIAM N. ESKRIDGE, JR., DYNAMIC STATUTORY INTERPRETATION 277 (1994).

the judiciary."[89] Arguably this rationale encompasses two concerns: judicial interference with the executive's conduct of foreign policy and judicial meddling with congressional prerogatives in determining the scope of federal statutes.[90]

In criminal cases, there is no legitimate concern over interference with executive prerogatives because it is, of course, the executive who determines whether to launch a given case. The Department of Justice's own policies reflect that it recognizes the sensitivity of transnational prosecutions and applies increased scrutiny to their appropriateness. For example, only money-laundering prosecutions that involve extraterritorial application of the relevant statutes require Main Justice approval.[91]

With respect to arguments founded on avoiding judicial intrusion on congressional decisions, these arguments assume that Congress actually has a view on extraterritoriality when it legislates, but as Professor Brilmayer notes, "in the vast majority of cases, legislatures *have* no actual intent on territorial reach." Further, "[t]he presumption against extraterritoriality is supposed to be used only when congressional intent is unclear, so by definition it is ambiguous whether applying the statute territorially or extraterritorially would be the 'activist' position." One may legitimately question whether the presumption, which "always sacrific[es] legislative aims in order to avoid conflict with foreign law," is truly the best way to limit judicial intrusion. "A court attempting to carry out congressional intent should apply a statute extraterritorially whenever doing so would advance the domestic purposes that Congress sought to achieve with the statute. To constrain the extraterritorial application of a statute on the basis of a court's intuition that conflict with foreign law is undesirable is—to borrow a phrase—judicial activism." Congress can, of course, respond to a mistaken judicial decision to deny a statute extraterritorial application by legislatively expanding the scope of the statute; but the reverse is true as well. Professor Dodge queries whether the Court should apply a presumption designed to "force Congress to reveal its preferences by adopting a rule that Congress would not want," noting that this argument seems strongly counter-majoritarian and contrary to separation of powers.

Finally, "if the presumption is intended to respect the decisions of the political branches—legislative and executive—it needs work." Courts applying the Supreme Court's strong presumption have rejected the views of the executive-branch departments or agencies charged with interpretation and application of the relevant statutes. And given the strength of the modern presumption, the Court has arguably ignored strong, but less than "clear," evidence of a congressional intent to apply statutes extraterritorially.

Notes

1. This author has attempted to answer some of the questions posed within the above reading. First, because the geographical appropriateness of a given prosecution is now a "merits" question, it—like venue—should be a treated as an element of the offense:

> It is unlikely that courts will ask juries to answer the legal question whether, applying the presumption against extraterritoriality, a given geoambiguous criminal statute has extraterritorial application. But ... at least the factual issues underlying extraterritoriality ought to be considered an element to be charged in the indictment and proven to a jury. In cases where the statute is held to have no extraterritorial application, juries should be tasked with determining whether the relevant conduct (identified by the focus test) occurred on U.S. territory. And in cases in which the

---

[89] [Article's footnote 89:] [Curtis A. Bradley, *Territorial Intellectual Property Rights in an Age of Globalism*, 37 Va. J. Int'l L. 505, 516 (1997).]

[91] [Article's footnote 92:] *See* U.S. Attorney's Manual § 9-105.300(1).

statute does apply extraterritorially, juries should be charged with determining whether the statutory requisites are satisfied. For example, if a statute states that it applies extraterritorially when the defendant is a U.S. national or the criminal conduct occurred in whole or in part in the United States, the jury should be required to make the findings of fact relevant to that requirement.

O'Sullivan, *supra* note 40, at 1066. Second, this article offers a rebuttal to the near-universal conclusion, by courts and commentators, that extraterritoriality analysis should be the same in civil and criminal cases. It argues that the presumption of extraterritoriality is applied where it should not be—in civil cases—but that courts are avoiding the presumption where it should apply—in criminal cases:

> Fundamental separation of powers considerations and criminal law's foundational legality principle require that Congress, not courts, clearly and prospectively specify the content of criminal prohibitions. The Supreme Court has decreed that the issue of extraterritoriality goes to the merits of a case, not to courts' subject-matter jurisdiction. Where there is ambiguity regarding this element—that is, whether a statute applies extraterritorially and in what circumstances—the operational arms of the legality principle, the rule of lenity, and (perhaps) the vagueness doctrine demand that this ambiguity be resolved in favor of the defendant. In short, where a criminal statute is geoambiguous, it should not be construed to apply extraterritorially. The Supreme Court has not had full briefing and argument on the issue of extraterritoriality in a criminal case in the post-*Aramco* period, and thus has not been forced to consider the applicability of the rule of lenity and the vagueness doctrine. The lower courts, looking for the most part to *Bowman* for answers in criminal cases, have ignored this seemingly fundamental and obvious issue.
>
> A rule of strict construction or the vagueness doctrine may not be enough, however, to satisfy the imperative that Congress specify in advance the scope of federal criminal statutes. This is because many important statutory schemes are hybrids, meaning that they are also capable of civil and criminal enforcement. Thus, for example, the Supreme Court held in *Morrison* that the securities fraud prohibitions of § 10(b) of the Securities and Exchange Act of 1934 and SEC Rule 10b-5 do not have extraterritorial application. The Court ruled in *RJR Nabisco* that the Racketeer Influenced and Corrupt Organizations Act (RICO) has limited extraterritorial purchase. Both *Morrison* and *RJR Nabisco* were civil cases, yet these statutes are also capable of criminal enforcement. The principle of legality and the interpretive tools that operationalize it are not generally consulted in civil cases. But the question of extraterritoriality ought not turn on the happenstance of whether a case regarding a hybrid statute's scope arrives before the Court in a civil or criminal context. The presumption against extraterritoriality, then, should be used when examining both criminal and hybrid statues as a means of honoring the legality principle, and as a proxy for the rule of lenity and the vagueness doctrine, requiring Congress to specify, in advance, the extraterritorial scope of a statute that has criminal applications.

Id. at 1028-29.

2. How can *Morrison's* "presumption of territoriality" and the Court's *Bowman* precedent be harmonized? Is the *Bowman* "exception" applicable only in criminal cases, while *Morrison* is the rule in civil cases? *See* United States v. Leija-Sanchez, 602 F.3d 797, 798-00 (7th Cir. 2010) (using *Bowman* and holding that statute barring violent crime in aid of racketeering activity, 18 U.S.C. § 1959, applies extraterritorially).

3. The only criminal case in which extraterritoriality arguably has been discussed by the Supreme Court post-*Aramco* is *Pasquantino v. United States*, 544 U.S. 349 (2005).

The defendants were indicted for wire fraud for carrying out a scheme to smuggle large quantities of liquor from the United States into Canada, thereby depriving the Canadian government of the required excise taxes. The Court took the case to decide whether the Canadian excise taxes could be considered "property" under the wire fraud statute as charged in the indictment (they could), and whether the common law revenue rule—which precludes enforcement of tax liabilities of one sovereign in the courts of another—applied to bar the prosecution (it did not). The question whether this was an extraterritorial application of the wire fraud statute "was not pressed or passed upon below and was raised only as an afterthought in petitioners' reply brief."

The best reading of *Pasquantino* is that the Court rejected the petitioner's argument by determining that this was a domestic, not an extraterritorial, application of the wire fraud statute. The statute has only two elements: a scheme to defraud and an interstate wiring in furtherance of that scheme. It does not require that the scheme be consummated, that a discrete false statement be proven, or that damage to the defendant ensue. The scheme was apparently hatched in the United States. And the Court held that the offense "was complete the moment [the defendants] executed the scheme inside the United States" through their domestic, interstate use of the wires—that is, their use of a telephone in New York to place orders with liquor stores in Maryland. The Court referred to the defendants' use of U.S. interstate wires as the "domestic element of [their] conduct . . . [that] the Government is punishing in this prosecution."

Granted, the case had significant transnational circumstances: The victim was a foreign sovereign, the object of the fraud was the Canadian tax revenues due, and the actual fraud concerned misrepresentations made to Canadian officials. But none of these circumstances are elements of the crime. The Court focused on where the elements of the crime occurred, determining that all of them (that is the formation of a scheme to defraud and wirings in furtherance of that scheme) were satisfied in the United States. When all elements of an offense take place in the United States, the statute will be deemed to apply domestically, requiring no inquiry into the extraterritorial reach of the statute.

The only difficulty with this characterization of *Pasquantino* is the Court's cryptic concluding sentence: "In any event, the wire fraud statute punishes frauds executed 'in interstate and foreign commerce,' so this is surely not a statute in which Congress had only 'domestic concerns in mind.'" The modern Court justifies its presumption against extraterritoriality in part by contending that Congress "is primarily concerned with domestic conditions." This, then, can be read as a coded statement that extraterritorial applications of the statute are appropriate. It is difficult to believe, however, that this one sentence represented a holding that the wire fraud statute applies extraterritorially, although at least one court has so read it.

The wire fraud statute is among the most frequently invoked statutes in the federal criminal code, so its scope is of more than passing interest. The issue of the wire fraud statute's extraterritorial reach was not even fully briefed, much less the subject of a decision below. And the Court has made clear in the past that "even statutes that contain broad language in their definitions of 'commerce' . . . do not apply abroad." Thus, the premise of this critical sentence—that the foreign commerce element was itself conclusive evidence of a congressional intent that the statute apply extraterritorially—cannot be reconciled with precedent. Finally, the presumption, which is so prominent in the Court's recent cases, was not even mentioned, much less distinguished. My own view is that this throw away was dicta.

> *Pasquantino* is best understood as a case in which the Court determined that because all the elements of the crime occurred in the United States, the prosecution was domestic—not extraterritorial—in nature.

O'Sullivan, *supra* note 40, at 1073-75; *compare* United States v. Georgiou, 777 F.3d 125, 137–38 (3d Cir. 2015) (wire fraud statute applies extraterritorially), *and* United States v. Lyons, 740 F.3d 702, 718 (1st Cir. 2014) (the Wire Act, 18 U.S.C. § 1084, applies extraterritorially), *with* European Cmty. v. RJR Nabisco, Inc., 764 F.3d 129, 140–41 (2d Cir. 2014) (wire fraud not extraterritorial), *rev'd on other grounds*, -- U.S. --, 136 S. Ct. 2090 (2016); United States v. All Assets Held at Bank Julius, 251 F. Supp. 3d 82, 101–02 (D.D.C. 2017); Elsevier, Inc. v. Grossman, 199 F. Supp.3d 768, 783 (S.D.N.Y. 2016); United States v. Sidorenko, 102 F. Supp. 3d 1124, 1132 (N.D. Cal. 2015); United States v. Hayes, 99 F. Supp. 3d 409, 420 (S.D.N.Y. 2015); United States v. Hijazi, 845 F. Supp. 2d 874, 906 (C.D. Ill. 2011).

In *Pasquantino* the Court looked to see where the elements of the crime took place to determine whether the case was domestic or transnational. In *Morrison*, by contrast, the Court applied a "focus" test to resolve that issue. So in determining whether a given case is domestic or extraterritorial, should one employ the *Paquantino* "elements" test in criminal cases but the *Morrison* "focus" test in civil cases? Can one employ different tests when the same statute is capable of criminal and civil enforcement (e.g., securities fraud, antitrust, and RICO)?

B. TRANSNATIONAL INTERNAL INVESTIGATIONS

Lucian E. Dervan, *International White Collar Crime and The Globalization of Internal Investigations*
39 Fordham Urb. L.J. 361 (2011)

On April 14, 2010, Russian authorities raided Hewlett-Packard's (HP's) Moscow company offices in search of information regarding an alleged scheme by employees in Germany to bribe Russian officials. HP's German subsidiary allegedly paid kickbacks in Russia to obtain a €35 million contract for the delivery and installation of an information technology network to a Russian public prosecutor's office. By September 2010, HP publicly disclosed through its securities filings that the criminal investigations into the scheme had spread well beyond Germany and Russia and now included an investigation by the U.S. Department of Justice (DOJ) and Securities and Exchange Commission (SEC). Further, HP revealed that the investigation by the United States' government had expanded to include Germany, Russia, Austria, Serbia, and the Netherlands. The proliferation of an alleged bribe in Germany into subsequent government investigations in as many as twelve countries around the globe demonstrates the truly international nature of white collar crime in the twenty-first century. With this internationalization of white collar crime and increase in global enforcement initiatives and cooperatives comes an inevitable byproduct: the globalization of internal corporate investigations. ...

Much has been written about the methods by which counsel may efficiently, thoroughly, and credibly conduct internal investigations. Given the globalization of such matters, however, this Article seeks to focus on the challenges present when conducting an internal investigation of potential international white collar criminal activity. ...

I. Selecting the Investigators in International Matters

One of the most important initial considerations when launching an internal investigation is determining who will conduct the inquiry. Several options exist, including utilizing corporate human resources, internal compliance officers, in-house counsel, or outside counsel. In the context of potential international white collar criminal activity, however, it is clear that independent counsel should be retained as soon as possible to achieve two important goals. First, retention of outside counsel makes investigative findings more credible, because the government often looks with suspicion upon the statements and conclusions of insiders who may either be involved in the underlying misconduct or, at a minimum, who have a significant financial stake in the investigation's outcome. Second, utilization of attorneys to conduct the investigation, rather than corporate employees or officers, shields investigative memoranda, reports, and conclusions from involuntary disclosure to third parties, including the government, because of the application of the attorney-client privilege and work product protections. While it appears at first glance that the issue of who will conduct the investigation is a simple one in the context of international white collar crime, the reality of international multi-jurisdictional inquiries makes this a complex and precarious area in which several potential pitfalls exist.

On February 10, 2003, the European Union's (EU) Commission, charged with developing antitrust rules for the EU and investigating alleged violations of EU competition provisions, ordered Akzo Nobel Chemicals Ltd. (Akzo) and Akcros Chemicals Ltd. (Akcros) to submit to an inquiry regarding potential anti-competitive practices. On February 12 and 13, 2003, the Commission carried out a dawn raid on the companies' Manchester, Britain, offices in search of documents relevant to the governmental investigation. During the search, Commission officials discovered two emails that appeared to contain relevant information. The emails were an exchange regarding antitrust issues between a general manager and Akzo's in-house counsel, who was in charge of coordinating competition law and who was a licensed practitioner in the Netherlands. Though company officials protested, the Commission's representatives took the emails after concluding that the documents were not protected by the attorney-client privilege.

The basis for the Commission representatives' decision to seize the documents was a 1982 European Court of Justice decision entitled *AM&S v. Commission*. In *AM&S*, the Commission sought documents regarding potential price-fixing from AM&S's Bristol, England, offices that the company claimed were protected by the attorney-client privilege. In considering the application of privilege to the documents, the court held that an EU rule of privilege, rather than a country specific rule, applied in all Commission investigations of anti-competitive practices. To fall within the protection of the EU rule of privilege, two elements were required to be satisfied. "First, the communication must have been given for purposes of the client's defense. Second, the communication must have been with an independent lawyer, which would not include in-house counsel." As the emails seized in the *Akzo Nobel* case involved communications between an in-house attorney and a company manager, the Commission believed they were not protected from disclosure, even though privilege rules in the Netherlands would have protected the exchange. ...

In its *Akzo Nobel* decision rejecting the companies' claims of privilege, the European Court of Justice reaffirmed its earlier, narrow interpretation of the applicability of privilege in the corporate context. In particular, the court stated, "It follows, both from the in-house lawyer's economic dependence and the close ties with his employer, that he does not enjoy a level of professional independence comparable to that of an external lawyer," resulting in a failure to satisfy the second prong of the *AM&S* test. Importantly, however, the court noted that the EU privilege standard established in *AM&S* and reiterated in *Akzo Nobel* applies only to EU investigations, such as those conducted by the Commission regarding anti-competitive practices. As such, in other legal situations the various laws of each individual country of the EU apply, some of which take similar views of in-house counsel.

As the *Akzo Nobel* decision makes strikingly clear, one must be familiar with privilege laws in the jurisdictions, both regional and national, involved in an international internal investigation as the rules vary dramatically by country and subject matter. While the different variations of privilege can have a myriad of impacts on an internal inquiry, two will be mentioned here specifically. First, the role of in-house counsel, including a corporation's general counsel, must be closely examined. While it is common for in-house counsel in the United States to perform a preliminary inquiry to determine whether outside counsel is required for a more extensive investigation, in some jurisdictions the materials and information collected during this initial appraisal of the situation might not be protected from compulsory disclosure. Further, to the extent in-house counsel seeks to assist outside counsel during the performance of the internal investigation, consideration must be given to whether such activity would be covered by privilege. While an argument exists that any such assistance by in-house counsel would be at the direction of a recognized outside "attorney," this argument may be defeated in jurisdictions that interpret privilege in a narrow fashion. Second, counsel must be aware of the possibility that attorneys from one region of the globe might not enjoy any privilege protections in certain jurisdictions, even if they are independent outside counsel. As has been noted by some commentators, the European Court of Justice's decision on the issue of privilege in *Akzo Nobel* contains language indicating attorneys unlicensed within the EU itself may not enjoy privilege when working for clients within its borders. While grappling with the difficulties presented by these divergent privilege rules is challenging, conducting an international internal investigation without consideration of their impact on the course and conduct of the inquiry could be fatal.

II. Collecting, Reviewing and Transferring Investigatory Documents from Abroad

The starting place for any internal investigation is the collection of relevant documentary evidence for review and analysis. Such an undertaking allows counsel to begin the process of compartmentalizing information, piecing together facts, identifying issues for further analysis, and preparing for employee interviews. In the international context, however, collection, review, and transfer of documentation can present unique challenges to counsel because of the growing prevalence of data protection laws around the globe. First, some data protection laws prevent companies from collecting and reviewing information, including company emails, that are deemed "personal" without consent from the affected employee. Further, in securing such consent, the corporation may be required to provide the employee access to the material and an opportunity to correct any inaccuracies. …

[Ed.: The European Union's General Data Protection Regulation (GDPR) took effect on May 25, 2018. Like the EU Data Protection Directive that preceded it, the GDPR protects a very broad range of personal data: "any information relating to an identified or identifiable natural person." As a result, most of the EU-based employee communications—including emails and IMs—gathered during an internal investigation will be protected. (Note that the GDPR provides the floor for data protection; States may impose more stringent protections.) Many companies rely on consent to support evidence gathering in internal investigations, but the GDPR not raises the bar for what constitutes valid consent. And some national courts have ruled that an employee cannot give free and valid consent in the context of an internal corporate investigation.]

... [S]ome data protection laws prevent or hinder the transfer of certain data outside the country of origin, including transfers back to corporate headquarters or affiliates located in other countries. ... A failure to satisfy the stringent EU data protection requirements may result in substantial liability for the breaching entity, including criminal liability for investigating counsel.

One company that likely navigated the challenges presented by the growing cadre of data protection laws is Avon Products Inc., ... [conducted] an international internal investigation regarding allegations of bribery by its officials in numerous countries, including China. China has strong data protection laws, including the Law of the People's Republic of China on Guarding State Secrets (Chinese State Secrets Law), which was first passed in 1989 and revised in 2010. The Chinese State Secrets Law broadly defines state secrets to include "matters that relate to state security and national interests," a statement that leaves much ambiguity and uncertainty regarding what types of data may be collected and transferred out of the country during an investigation. As one set of practitioners has noted, "[T]he [international internal] investigative team must ensure that the data and information being exported from China does not constitute state secrets. This can be difficult given that the categories of state secrets remain vague and open to subjective interpretation." Further, the penalties for failing to abide by the Chinese State Secrets Law are severe, including capital punishments for intentional misappropriations and lesser punishments for other disclosures, including the strict liability offense of "stealing" state secrets.

... As it becomes increasingly common for countries around the globe to create restrictive and varying laws protecting data, internal investigators must recognize that utilization of a standard Americanized investigatory strategy can result in significant collateral consequences and liabilities for both client and counsel. As such, internal investigators must be cognizant of the difficulties data collection and review present in the international setting and be proactive in determining the most appropriate procedures in each individual jurisdictional setting.

III. Dealing with Employees in an International Context

There are two particularly defining encounters with employees during an internal investigation. The first is when investigating counsel interviews employees as part of the inquiry. When conducting such interviews, counsel must be cognizant of her ethical and legal duty to clarify the relationship between herself and the interviewee through the delivery of an *Upjohn* warning.

The warning typically includes the following elements: the attorney represents the corporation and not the individual employee; the interview is covered by the attorney-client privilege, which belongs to and is controlled by the corporation, not the individual employee; the corporation may decide, in its sole discretion, whether to waive the privilege and disclose information from the interview to third parties, including the government.

Often, during internal investigations in the United States, little else need be done beyond giving the targeted employee this preliminary instruction and proceeding with the questioning. In foreign jurisdictions, however, investigating counsel must be alert to the possibility that local laws may restrict one's ability to conduct employee interviews or, at a minimum, may curtail the manner in which any such interview may occur. As one commentator notes, several European nations restrict in total the ability of counsel conducting an international internal investigation to interview witnesses if there are parallel proceedings.

[M]any European countries have what are called blocking statutes, which prohibit the interview of witnesses. In a potential civil or criminal investigation in that jurisdiction, of which France is a good example, you are not allowed to interview a witness who was also a witness in a French criminal investigation. So if you have a multi-jurisdictional insider trading investigation, you are not allowed to go to France and interview that witness without the permission of the French authorities.

Even where such onerous blocking statutes are not applicable, local labor laws and related regulations may impede one's ability to quickly conduct employee interviews in an informal one-on-one setting. For example, the employee may have the right to consult with representatives before being interviewed or to have such representatives present during the interview itself.

The second defining encounter with employees during an internal investigation occurs when employees are disciplined either because they have failed to cooperate with the inquiry or the investigation has revealed that they have committed wrongful conduct. When disciplining employees in the United States under either of these scenarios, corporations and their counsel have significant discretion in determining the appropriate procedures and punishments, up to and including termination. This, however, is not the case in most other jurisdictions around the world. First, employees in many countries are not required to cooperate with internal investigations and, therefore, may not be disciplined for such refusals. Second, employees in foreign jurisdictions are often entitled to damages or severance pay when terminated, even for good cause, and must be afforded certain procedural rights during the disciplinary process. In this context, some countries even impose strict temporal limitations on disciplinary actions, which can create significant difficulties for internal investigators examining complex matters.

In Belgium, for example, an employee termination for good cause "must occur within three working days from the moment the facts are known to the [employer]; the facts must be notified to the dismissed [employee] by registered mail within three working days from the date of dismissal." The clock here can start as soon as an employer gets a credible allegation, not after it completes a full-blown internal investigation.

While such restrictions on disciplinary procedures and determinations seem unnaturally intrusive in the American corporate context, counsel must be aware of the impact of these laws on the course of an international internal investigation.

The breadth of laws in foreign jurisdictions regarding disciplinary procedures is exemplified by a series of communications … released as part of the … investigations of phone-hacking by the now defunct *News of the World*. While much attention is currently centered on hacking from recent years, this is not the first time the newspaper had dealt with this issue. In 2007, Clive Goodman, a former *News of the World* reporter in Britain pleaded guilty to phone-hacking charges and was imprisoned. Shortly after his guilty plea, he received a letter from company officials:

I am sorry to have to be writing this letter, but am afraid that events of the last few days and months provide us no choice but to terminate your employment with News Group Newspapers Limited. This action, I know you understand, is the consequence of your plea of guilty, and subsequent imprisonment on 26 January, in relation to conspiracy to intercept voicemail messages. This obviously constitutes a very serious breach of your obligations as an employee, such as to warrant dismissal without any warning. In the circumstances of your plea and the court's sentence, it is reasonable for us to dismiss you without any further enquiries.

In response, Goodman sent a letter to the company containing numerous allegations, including the following statement: "The dismissal is automatically unfair as the company failed to go through the minimum required statutory dismissal procedures."

The newspaper responded to Goodman's allegations as follows:

> I would like to request your attendance at an appeal hearing on Tuesday, 20th March 2007 at 10:00 am at the offices of News Magazine Limited. ... The purpose of the hearing is to consider, under the News International disciplinary procedure, your appeal against your dismissal on 5th February, on the grounds raised in your letter of 2nd March. ... You are entitled to be accompanied as specified in the Company's Disciplinary procedures. Please let me know in advance if you decide to bring a companion and their name and contact details. If there are any documents you wish to be considered at the appeal hearing, please provide copies as soon as possible. If you do not have those documents, please provide details so that they can be obtained.

While such an exchange and appeals process might appear absurd in the United States, particularly given the serious criminal conviction of the employee and the criminal offense's direct relation to his work at the corporation, British law imposes strikingly different obligations on employers.

Since 2004, the United Kingdom has imposed an extensive "Code of Practice for Disciplinary and Grievance Procedures" on employers that dictates the manner in which all manner of significant discipline may be imposed, including terminations. At its most basic, the law requires a three-step process of notice and meeting prior to any disciplinary action, a disciplinary hearing at which the employee may respond to the allegations, and an appeals process to challenge the corporation's disciplinary decision. Failure to abide by these requirements can result in serious penalties for the corporation.

As with the other unique aspects and challenges of conducting international internal investigations, counsel must be aware of the significant differences that exist between jurisdictions regarding disciplinary procedures and options. Even in situations where the conduct of the employee under review clearly violates corporate standards and rules of conduct, local labor laws may dictate the manner in which disciplinary action may be taken. Proceeding without an understanding of the constraints and deadlines imposed by such requirements may lead to additional exposure for clients and limiting of options in response to troubling conduct by employees.

IV. Disclosure and Settlement After International Internal Investigations

One of the most challenging decisions faced by corporations at the conclusion of an internal investigation where the government is, as of yet, unaware of the conduct under examination is determining whether to disclose the investigatory findings. While some disclosures are required by law, there can also be several advantages to disclosure even where it is permissive, including receipt of cooperation credit from the DOJ when determining the appropriate governmental response and potential application of amnesty programs. As an example, in 2008 the U.S. government alleged that Siemens had engaged in widespread bribery overseas. In response, the company hired an outside law firm to conduct a thorough internal investigation. The inquiry covered thirty-four countries, included over 1750 interviews, and resulted in the collection of more than one-hundred million documents. Throughout this extensive investigation, Siemens cooperated fully with the government and provided documents and other information as requested. As a result, Siemens was rewarded with significantly less punishment than might otherwise have been exacted on the corporation for its conduct:

Though Siemens could have been fined as much as $2.7 billion in the criminal prosecution, the Justice Department and SEC settled for a combined U.S. total of $800 million. The Justice Department has not prosecuted any of the company's executives or employees for the violations. Based partly on Siemens' cooperation in the case, the U.S. government decided that the firm could remain eligible for federal contracts, a priority for Siemens.

For Siemens, disclosure and cooperation proved to be valuable tools in resolving its case in a satisfactory manner with both American and European authorities.

As was true in the Siemens case, many internal corporate investigations today involve examination of international conduct. Therefore, potential resolution of the matter requires consideration of not only American disclosure obligations and advantages, but such obligations and advantages on a global scale. In this regard, it is important to note first that the United States is not the only country that rewards disclosure and cooperation. A significant example is the EU's amnesty program in anti-trust cases. Under the European program, the first corporation to reveal its involvement in anti-competitive practices receives immunity.

> [The Commission] will grant immunity from any fine which would otherwise have been imposed to an undertaking disclosing its participation in an alleged cartel affecting the Community if that undertaking is the first to submit information and evidence which in the Commission's view will enable it to:
>   (a) carry out a targeted inspection in connection with the alleged cartel; or
>   (b) find an infringement of Article 81 EC in connection with the alleged cartel.

Importantly, under the EU anti-trust amnesty program, corporations that are not the first through the door can still achieve significant advantages from self-reporting the discovered conduct.

> Companies which do not qualify for immunity may benefit from a reduction of fines if they provide evidence that represents "significant added value" to that already in the Commission's possession and have terminated their participation in the cartel. Evidence is considered to be of a "significant added value" for the Commission when it reinforces its ability to prove the infringement. The first company to meet these conditions is granted 30 to 50% reduction, the second 20 to 30% and subsequent companies up to 20%.

Without carefully examining the unique aspects of disclosure obligations and advantages in the various jurisdictions affected, counsel may inadvertently create additional liability for a corporation or forfeit a potentially significant advantage.

It is also important to note that while numerous countries offer advantages to those who disclose investigatory findings and cooperate with governmental inquiries, the globalization of white collar crime and the international nature of modern internal investigations also present significant challenges to successful resolution and settlement of such matters. Two particular reasons for this challenge will be noted herein. First, different jurisdictions and varying enforcement agencies may be unwilling to operate in a uniform timeframe or approach the issue of resolution in a similar manner. As such, while the DOJ may be pressuring a corporation to settle a matter quickly, a parallel proceeding in the EU might only just be starting. Where such multijurisdictional inquires are operating at different speeds or one or more entities are unwilling to enter into negotiations, it becomes difficult to settle any of the matters for fear that admissions made during one agreement will simply become incriminating admissions for another. Second, even where all of the governmental entities involved may be willing and prepared to enter into negotiations, significant differences regarding what modes of settlement are appropriate may exist. For example, while non-prosecution and deferred prosecution agreements are extremely popular mechanisms by which to settle matters involving potential corporate criminal liability, they are rejected forms of resolution in many jurisdictions outside the United States.

For any corporation embroiled in a significant global white collar criminal matter, a keen awareness of the challenges regarding disclosure and settlement alternatives on an international scale is invaluable. In 2010, BAE Systems settled a long-standing criminal bribery investigation that had spanned several continents. The settlement included guilty pleas by the corporation in both the United States and the United Kingdom. Though the case involved complex international issues, BAE was successful in resolving the matter in a universally agreeable manner by utilizing the institutions and mechanisms available in each of the affected jurisdictions. According to the United Kingdom Serious Fraud Office (UK SFO), the agreement between the DOJ, the UK SFO, and BAE was a "ground breaking global agreement." As the globalization of white collar crime continues to bring internal investigations into various international jurisdictions, the necessity of striving for such truly global settlement will only continue to become of greater importance.

Conclusion

Though this Article only begins to touch on the various types of challenges one might experience as a result of the globalization of internal investigations, it does reveal one constant in such matters. Counsel must avoid the temptation of utilizing a standard American-style investigatory technique when undertaking multi-jurisdictional investigations. As the above examples demonstrate, different jurisdictions and regions of the world view the tools and techniques of such inquiries in strikingly different ways. Through realization of the types of challenges that exist in this field and a willingness to conduct particularized investigations that are flexible to the demands of differing jurisdictions, the achievement of successful and thorough internal investigations can continue even in the testing context of growing globalization.

Notes

1. This reading touches upon one privilege issue: the fact that many European jurisdictions do not extend the attorney-client privilege to in-house counsel. (It is also the case that the EU only recognizes as privileged communications between a client and a lawyer who is a member of a bar in one of the member States of the EU.)

There may be other important differences as well. For example, in the United Kingdom, the "legal advice privilege" is akin to the U.S. attorney client privilege, but there is at least one important difference. Under English law, only communications between a lawyer and a client are protected by this privilege. In the corporate context, U.K. courts hold that the "client" consists of only those individuals who are authorized to give instructions to and receive legal advice from the lawyer in relation to the matter at hand. The privilege does not, as in the United States, extend communications between a lawyer and any employee of the company who is interviewed by the lawyer for the purpose of giving the corporation legal advice in the course of an authorized investigation. In other words, the U.K. adheres to the rule that the Supreme Court rejected in *Upjohn Co. v. United States*, 449 U.S. 383 (1981) (discussed in Chapter 17(A)). *See* Three Rivers DC v. Bank of England [2003] EWCA Civ 474. The United Kingdom's functional equivalent of the work product doctrine is known as the "litigation privilege." Until very recently, the scope of protection offered by that privilege in the context of internal investigations was unclear. In two cases the English High Court of Justice ruled that notes and interview memoranda created during internal investigation enjoyed no privilege protection. *See* Serious Fraud Office v. Eurasian Nat'l Resources Corp., Ltd. [2017] EWHC 1017 (QB); The RBS Rights Issue Litig. [2016] EWHC 3161 (Ch). These courts reasoned that the "litigation privilege" did not apply until prosecutors had initiated a formal criminal investigation or prosecution. These cases were overruled by England's Court of Appeal in *The Director of the Serious Fraud Office v. Eurasian Natural Resources Corp., Ltd.* [2018], EWCA Civ. 2006. The Appeals Court held that the documents at issue in that case had been brought into existence for the dominant purpose of resisting or avoiding the contemplated criminal proceedings, which was sufficient to qualify as being "for the purposes of litigation" as required by English law.

2. We examined in some depth the many circumstances that make it "exceedingly difficult to conceive of the criminal process that applies to corporations today as truly 'adversarial.' In reality, a variety of circumstances make it nearly impossible for public companies, especially those in regulated industries or those who do significant business with the government, to mount any meaningful resistance to a criminal investigation." O'Sullivan, *supra* pages 230-31. One of the most important factors pushing corporations to (virtually inevitably) cooperate with government investigators is the extremely broad standard of liability that applies under federal law. Almost anything that a corporate agent does can be imputed to the corporation under the judge-made *respondeat superior* principle; if no one agent can be identified, the corporation may still be convicted under the *Bank of New England* theory.

Except in the United Kingdom and the Netherlands, corporate criminal liability came late to Europe; Germany still does not recognize it. France recognized corporate criminal liability in 1994, followed by Belgium (1999), Italy (2001), Poland (2003), Romania (2006), Luxembourg and Spain (2010), and the Czech Republic (2012). Counsel must be attentive to the standards of liability in those States. In some, corporate liability is only triggered by those with management responsibilities acting within the scope of their employment. In such countries, corporations may not have the same incentives to cooperate with local authorities because corporations can only be held liable under limited circumstances. This may create culture issues if foreign corporations abroad are being pursued by the DOJ. U.S. Counsel, then, may have difficulty persuading foreign corporations that their best interests would be served by cooperation rather than combat.

3. Counsel must also be aware of the important differences in ethical standards governing lawyers around the globe. For example, in the United States it verges on malpractice not to prepare one's client for interviews or one's witnesses for proceedings (this practice is variously referred to as witness preparation, witness familiarization, or witness proofing). *See, e.g.*, D.C. Ethics Op. No. 79 (1979) ("a lawyer who did not prepare his or her witness for testimony, having had an opportunity to do so, would not be doing his or her professional job properly") Restatement (Third) Law Governing Lawyers § 116, comment (b). Lawyers cannot, of course, suborn perjury or otherwise solicit false testimony. But they can and do suggest how clients ought to best present themselves (in dress and demeanor), warn them about likely areas of inquiry and "moot" them on their responses, and even suggest language (so long as the answer is truthful).

In many parts of Europe, however, such practices would be unethical and even illegal. For example, the Code of Conduct of the Bar Council of England and Wales does not permit barristers to "rehearse, practice, or coach a witness in relation to his evidence" (§705); *see also* R. v. Momodou [2005] EWCA Crim.177. Indeed, according to the Pre-Trial Chamber of the International Criminal Court (ICC), witness proofing would be "either unethical or unlawful in jurisdictions as different as Brazil, Spain, France, Belgium, Germany, Scotland, Ghana, England and Wales and Australia, to give just a few examples." Prosecutor v. Lubanga, Case No. ICC-01/04-01/06, Decision on the Practices of Witness Familiarisation and Witness Proofing, Pre-Trial Chamber I, ¶37 (Nov. 8, 2006). What would happen if U.S. lawyers prepare a witness who is then called to testify in one of these jurisdictions? Is that witness now hopelessly tainted?

C. OBTAINING EVIDENCE ABROAD AND EXTRADITION

1. THE PROSECUTION

Turning to the scope of the jurisdiction to enforce, the *Restatement (Third) of the Foreign Relations Law of the United States* cautions that "[l]aw enforcement officers of the United States may exercise their functions in the territory of another state only (a) with the consent of the other state and if duly authorized by the United States; and (b) in compliance with the laws both of the United States and of the other state."[92] Thus, "[i]t is universally recognized, as a corollary of state sovereignty, that officials of one state may not exercise their functions in the territory of another state without the latter's consent. Thus, [a State's] law enforcement officers cannot arrest [a person] in another state, and can engage in criminal investigations in that state only with that state's consent."[93] These rules obviously create challenges for prosecutors investigating and prosecuting transnational crimes, as discussed below.

Hon. Thomas G. Snow, *The Investigation and Prosecution of White Collar Crime: International Challenges and the Legal Tools Available to Address Them*
11 Wm. & Mary Bill of Rights J. 209 (2002)

Increasingly, white collar crimes targeting American victims are committed by persons located in the United States who then flee the country or hide their illicitly derived proceeds abroad, or by persons located physically outside the United States who utilize the telephone, mail, Internet, and the international financial system to perpetrate their crimes and launder their profits. Put another way, much contemporary white collar crime is also transnational crime. Consequently, a twenty-first century prosecutor responsible for the investigation and prosecution of such offenses must, by necessity, be a public international lawyer. He must understand and be capable of utilizing the various international legal tools available to address the challenges posed by criminals whose activities touch on more than one sovereign state.[94] Specifically, he must know how to obtain, often in a form admissible in U.S. courts, information or evidence located outside the United States. And he must know how to secure the legal rendition of fugitives wanted for prosecution in this country, but who carefully avoid crossing U.S. borders.

The primary international legal tools available for the rendition of international fugitives and the acquisition of overseas evidence are, respectively, extradition and mutual

---

[92] *Restatement, supra* note 49, § 433(1).

[93] *Id.* §432, Comment b.

[94] [Article's footnote 4:] Among those legal tools are bilateral extradition treaties and mutual legal assistance treaties (MLATs). However, while not addressed in this article, an increasing number of multilateral law enforcement conventions contain articles designed to facilitate extradition and mutual legal assistance in cases involving the type of criminality covered by the conventions. *See, e.g.,* United Nations Convention Against Transnational Organized Crime, Nov. 15, 2000, arts. 16-18, 40 I.L.M. 335; United Nations Convention Against Illicit Traffic in Narcotic Drugs and Psychotropic Substances, Dec. 20., 1998, arts. 6-7, U.N. Doc. NO. E/CONF.82/15, 28 I.L.M. 493; Inter-American Convention Against Corruption, Mar. 29, 1996, arts. 13-14, 35 I.L.M. 724.

legal assistance treaties. Many such treaties are already in force,[95] and the number is increasing. Although highly successful in providing U.S. prosecutors with international fugitives to prosecute[96] and crucial extraterritorial evidence with which to convict them,[97] such treaties are not always available. Either no treaty exists with the foreign country from which assistance is needed,[98] or the treaty in force fails to provide for the specific assistance required.[99] As a result, the contemporary white collar crime prosecutor must also be conscious of alternative, and sometimes internationally sensitive, legal means available to bring fleeing defendants into the jurisdiction of their courts or to gain access to evidence located beyond U.S. territory.[100]

Finally, even when extradition and mutual legal assistance treaties are in force, and when their terms appear to provide for the foreign assistance needed in a particular case, their utilization can generate vexing legal, policy, and practical issues which at times frustrate, or at a minimum slow, the acquisition of the requested assistance. ...

I. International Extradition

A. Treaties and Their Contents

When a U.S. prosecutor seeks the return of an international fugitive wanted for prosecution on fraud charges, for some other white collar crime such as money laundering, or for any other criminal offense, the primary legal tool for securing the rendition of such a fugitive is the international extradition treaty. Most countries, like the

---

[95] [Article's footnote 5:] According to records maintained by the U.S. Justice Department's Office of International Affairs, as of July 11, 2002, there were bilateral United States extradition treaties in force with 126 foreign jurisdictions and bilateral U.S. mutual legal assistance treaties in force with forty-six foreign jurisdictions.

[96] [Article's footnote 7:] According to U.S. Justice Department statistics submitted to Congress, in the five year period from 1995 to 2000, over six hundred extradition requests were granted by foreign countries, and more than two hundred other requests resulted in the return of fugitives to the U.S. via deportation or expulsion.

[97] [Article's footnote 8:] The U.S. Justice Department does not maintain publicly available records of the specific number of cases in which foreign evidence has actually been obtained in response to formal U.S. requests for international assistance. However, hundreds of such requests are made and executed each year.

[98] [Article's footnote 9:] While bilateral United States extradition and mutual legal assistance treaties are in force with a majority of the countries in Latin America, the Caribbean, and Europe, no such treaties yet exist with significant numbers of countries in the Middle East, Sub-Sahara Africa, and Asia.

[99] [Article's footnote 10:] For example, many modern criminal offenses are not included in older "list" extradition treaties, and thus are not extraditable, and while many MLATs do not make dual criminality a prerequisite for obtaining evidentiary assistance, some do contain such a requirement. Thus, depending on the crime being prosecuted or investigated by the U.S. prosecutor, there may be instances when an extradition or mutual legal assistance treaty exists with a foreign country, but in which the prosecutor may be unable to effectively utilize such treaties for securing the return of an international fugitive or obtaining overseas evidence.

[100] [Article's footnote 11:] For example, U.S. prosecutors may seek the expulsion or deportation of fugitives from foreign countries to the United States, or "lure" them from a country of refuge to the United States or to a place from which extradition or deportation to the U.S. is possible. U.S. prosecutors may rely upon unilateral compulsory measures, such as subpoenas with extraterritorial application, compelled customer consents, or searches and seizures conducted abroad, in order to obtain foreign financial records needed for U.S. criminal investigations.

United States,[101] cannot extradite fugitives absent such a treaty. Extradition treaties set out the crimes that are "extraditable": those crimes that the parties to the treaties have agreed to grant extradition.

Most older U.S. extradition treaties contain a list or schedule of extraditable offenses.[102] More modern U.S. extradition treaties, including most of those negotiated in the past generation, contain a "dual criminality" provision. Instead of a list or schedule of crimes, such treaties define extraditable offenses as those which are punishable under the laws of both countries by deprivation of liberty, by some agreed upon minimum term, or by a more severe penalty.[103] A few U.S. extradition treaties utilize both approaches, and contain a list of extraditable offenses combined with a dual criminality provision. The modern dual criminality approach is preferred not only by the United States but has also been embraced by the international community. This approach provides for growth and development in criminal law and obviates the need to re-negotiate an extradition treaty in order to capture new forms of criminality.[104]

A variety of "standard" provisions exist in modern U.S. extradition treaties. For example, in addition to defining the offenses for which extradition is available, extradition treaties set out the supporting documents which must be submitted by the "requesting state,"—the country seeking extradition. Among such documents are copies of the arrest warrant, the charging document, and information on the identify of the fugitive. In addition to information establishing the charges for which the fugitive is being sought, extradition treaties also identify the requisite evidentiary standard the requesting state must meet.

Extradition treaties contain articles which can limit the requested state's obligation to extradite. For example, despite the strong U.S. policy interest in negotiating extradition treaties that obligate the parties to surrender their own nationals,[105] some treaties make

---

[101] [Article's footnote 14:] 18 U.S.C. § 3184 sets out the procedure for extradition of fugitives from the United States: "Whenever there is a treaty or convention for extradition between the United States and any foreign government ...." *Id.*; *see also* Factor v. Laubenheimer, 290 U.S. 276, 287 (1933) ("While a government may, if agreeable to its own constitution and laws, voluntarily exercise its power to surrender a fugitive from justice to the country from which he had fled ... the legal right to demand his extradition and the correlative duty to surrender him to the demanding country exist only when created by treaty.").

[102] [Article's footnote 15:] The U.S. extradition treaty with Egypt, for example, dates from the time of the Ottoman Empire and contains a short list of offenses that includes murder, rape, arson, piracy, mutiny, burglary, robbery, forgery, counterfeiting, and embezzlement. Convention on Extradition, Aug. 11, 1874, U.S-Ottoman Empire, art. 2, 19 Stat. 572. ...

[103] [Article's footnote 16:] [For example,] Article 2(1) of the U.S. extradition treaty with India states: "An offense shall be an extraditable offense if it is punishable under the laws in both Contracting States by deprivation of liberty, including imprisonment, for a period of more than one year or by a more severe penalty." Extradition Treaty, June 25, 1997, U.S.-India, art. 2(1), S. Treaty Doc. 105-30 (1997).

[104] [Article's footnote 19:] Thus, if only one party to such a treaty criminalizes money laundering, insider trading on the securities markets, or international parental kidnaping at the time the extradition treaty enters into force, those offenses will not be extraditable between the treaty partners. Once the other party also criminalizes such behavior those offenses will become extraditable under the terms of the existing treaty, and an obligation to surrender persons wanted for such offenses will be created.

[105] [Article's footnote 22:] Senior U.S. Department of Justice officials routinely urge foreign officials to change the laws or policies which prevent them from extraditing their nationals. The Department of Justice position is that justice is usually best served when a case is prosecuted in the country whose citizens or interests were harmed and where the witnesses and other evidence are located. The assertion of extraterritorial jurisdiction and domestic prosecution by the country of the

such surrender discretionary. As a practical matter, many countries still do not extradite their nationals, often based upon a constitutional prohibition against doing so.

Extradition treaties often provide a basis to deny extradition when the crime is deemed a "political offense,"[106] the relevant statute of limitations has run, or the person has already been prosecuted and either convicted or acquitted of the same offense for which extradition is being sought.[107]

Extradition treaties even limit the requesting state's actions with respect to a fugitive after his surrender. The "rule of specialty" prohibits a country from prosecuting or punishing an extradited person for crimes other than those for which the requested state granted extradition. However, specialty can be waived by the requested state, providing the possibility of prosecution for crimes in addition to those for which extradition was provided. The rule of specialty in modern extradition treaties often limits the re-extradition of a person to a third state. Other exceptions exist for extradited persons who leave the requesting state and later return to it, or who remain in the requesting state after they are free to leave.

Finally, there are a variety of other fairly standard provisions in modern U.S. extradition treaties. They cover everything from the procedures for making urgent requests for "provisional arrest," to the language of the documents submitted in support of extradition, bases for the temporary or deferred surrender of a fugitive, how to prioritize competing requests for extradition from several countries, the "waiver" by a fugitive of formal extradition, how to arrange for "transit" through the territory of one of the parties to the treaty of a person being extradited to the other treaty partner from a third state, and how legal representation and the costs of extradition are handled.

B.   *The Extradition Process*

Formal, fully documented requests for extradition are made through the diplomatic channel, normally under cover of diplomatic note. Requests for provisional arrest made under urgent circumstances typically go through the diplomatic channel as well. Yet some modern extradition treaties permit provisional arrest requests to be made directly between the U.S. Justice Department and the comparable Ministry of our treaty partner. Interpol may be utilized for the transmission of such requests.

As a practical matter, a United States prosecutor who wishes to seek the extradition of an international fugitive must first contact the Justice Department's Office of International Affairs (OIA) in Washington, D.C. Country experts in that office work with the prosecutor to obtain the information and supporting material necessary to initiate the

---

perpetrator's nationality, while occasionally successful as a last resort, has not been a viable, routine alternative to the extradition of nationals.

[106] [Article's footnote 25:] Extradition treaties do not define what constitutes a political offense. Consequently, how that term is interpreted will depend on the law of the requested state. Yet some modern U.S. extradition treaties exclude various agreed upon crimes from the definition of a political offense—such as those covered by certain multilateral conventions to which both extradition treaty partners are also parties.

[107] [Article's footnote 27:] …[A]n example of a "prior prosecution," or *non bis in idem* provision, [is] "Extradition shall not be granted when the person sought has been convicted or acquitted in the Requested State for the offense for which extradition is requested." Of course, if personal jurisdiction can be obtained over a fugitive previously prosecuted in a foreign country (a separate sovereign) without relying upon extradition, his subsequent prosecution and punishment in the United States would not be prohibited by the Fifth Amendment prohibition against double jeopardy. *See* United States v. Rashed, 234 F.3d 1280 (D.C. Cir. 2000); Chan Han Mow v. United States, 730 F.2d 1308 (9th Cir. 1984); United States v. McRary, 615 F.2d 181 (5th Cir. 1980).

provisional arrest and/or extradition process. Once the requisite information and supporting materials are obtained, OIA then works directly with the U.S. State Department, which in turn transmits the information to the relevant U.S. Embassy and directs the Embassy to submit the request to the government of the country in which the fugitive is located. Prior to the submission of a formal request for extradition to a foreign country, the supporting documents are translated, at the cost of the requesting prosecutor's office, into the language of the other country.

What happens next depends on the other country's substantive laws and procedural rules relating to international extradition. In many countries, as with the United States[108] both the judicial and executive branches of government have a role to play. Often, an extradition hearing in a foreign court is held to determine whether the requirements of the treaty have been complied with, and some form of judicial review of the initial finding of extraditability is provided.[109] The final decision to surrender the person found extraditable by the courts is ultimately made by a high ranking executive branch official of the foreign government.[110] ...

II. Mutual Legal Assistance

A. Treaties and Their Contents

When a prosecutor in the United States needs evidence or other formal assistance from a foreign country for use in a white collar crime case,[111] or for the investigation or prosecution of any other type of criminal offense, the primary legal tool for obtaining such evidence is the mutual legal assistance treaty (MLAT).[112] Such treaties provide for a wide range of evidential assistance. Consider, for example, a U.S. white collar crime prosecutor investigating a complex fraud and money laundering scheme. The prosecutor

---

[108] [Article's footnote 46:] *See* 18 U.S.C. §§ 3181-3190.

[109] [Article's footnote 47:] This is usually accomplished by direct appeal to a superior court or by petition for writ of habeas corpus, depending the foreign country's law.

[110] [Article's footnote 48:] For example, in the United Kingdom the decision to surrender the person found extraditable is made by the Secretary of State. U.K. Home Office, Extradition Procedures in the United Kingdom (2002), *at* http://www.homeoffice.gov.uk/oicd/jcu/extranote.htm).

[111] [Article's footnote 50:] Usually, the United States must make formal requests when (1) the information, evidence, or other required assistance can only be obtained via compulsory process in the other country, such as a foreign search warrant or subpoena; (2) the foreign country, based upon its domestic laws or principles of sovereignty, demands a formal request before it will provide the information, evidence, or assistance; or (3) the foreign evidence must be obtained in a particular form or following a particular procedure in order to better ensure its admissibility in U.S. courts. As a practical matter, much evidence, information, and criminal intelligence can and should be obtained without the need for formal requests, without relying upon MLATs, letters of request, or letters rogatory. Rather, what is desired from a foreign country may be more quickly and efficiently obtained through police or regulatory channels—for example, through the International Criminal Police Organization (Interpol); through law enforcement liaison agents stationed at U.S. Embassies abroad; through Financial Intelligence Units (FIUs) such as the U.S. Treasury Department's Financial Crimes Enforcement Network (FinCEN); or through Memoranda of Understanding (MOUs) such as those utilized by the U.S. Securities and Exchange Commission and the U.S. Customs Service with their overseas counterparts.

[112] [Article's footnote 52:] In the absence of a bilateral MLAT or an applicable multilateral convention with a mutual legal assistance article, prosecutors utilize letters of request or letters rogatory when seeking formal international assistance. *See* 18 U.S.C. § 1781 (2000); Fed. R. Civ. P. 28(b); Restatement (Third) of Foreign Relations Law of the United States § 474 cmt. h (1987).

may determine that he needs the testimony of victim-witnesses in Hong Kong who are unwilling or unable to travel to the United States, copies of authenticated bank records from the Cayman Islands, the freezing of illegally derived assets secreted in Swiss banks, and the temporary transfer in custody to the United States of a cooperating defendant in Italy in order to testify at the U.S. trial. Mutual legal assistance treaties provide for all of these forms of assistance and more.

In addition to the wide variety of assistance available to prosecutors pursuant to MLATs, there are other benefits to such treaties. For example, they create an international treaty obligation to provide the types of assistance set out in the agreement. When prosecutors seek such evidence using the traditional letters rogatory approach, the requested countries provide the assistance, if at all, simply as a matter of comity. Under an MLAT, if the requested assistance is not forthcoming, the United States may cite the other country's obligation to execute the request, perhaps resulting in a more prompt response by the country to the U.S. prosecutors' request.

Many United States MLATs do not require dual criminality as a prerequisite for obtaining assistance. This means that it is often not necessary that the crime being investigated or prosecuted in the United States, and for which mutual legal assistance is sought, would also be considered a criminal offense in the requested country. This differs dramatically from extradition treaties, which virtually always capture the dual criminality principle.[113] For example, the absence of a dual criminality requirement in MLATs may prove helpful to U.S. white collar crime prosecutors seeking evidence in support of their export control cases even when the foreign countries from which they need evidence lack similar criminal laws restricting the export of controlled goods or technologies.

As with extradition treaties, MLATs contain provisions which limit the requested state's obligation to provide assistance. For example, many MLATs state that assistance may be denied if the request relates to a "political offense," or that assistance may be postponed if execution of the request would interfere with an ongoing criminal investigation or prosecution in the country from which assistance has been sought. Although dual criminality is often not a prerequisite to the obligation to grant assistance, most MLATs permit a country to refuse to execute a request if doing so would prejudice the security or similar essential interests of the requested state. Many MLATs contain provisions that are somewhat analogous to the rule of specialty in extradition treaties, because they limit the use of the provided evidence to the particular investigation or prosecution set out in the request.

B. The Mutual Legal Assistance Process

MLAT requests are made directly between the "Central Authorities" as identified in the applicable treaty. For the United States, the Central Authority is always the United States Attorney General or his designee. The Office of International Affairs in the Criminal Division of the U.S. Department of Justice serves as the designee of the United States Attorney General for purposes of making and receiving MLAT requests. The Central Authority for the treaty partner is most often the Minister of Justice, Attorney General, Minister of Interior, or other person responsible for international criminal assistance matters in that country, or a person designated by such an official.

The existence of law enforcement Central Authorities, which make and receive requests directly without the need to rely upon the slower, more cumbersome diplomatic

---

[113] [Article's footnote 56:] Older "list" treaties usually delineate extraditable offenses as only those acts deemed criminal by both contracting states at the time the treaties were negotiated. More modern "dual criminality" treaties define extraditable offenses as those acts deemed criminal by both contracting states, and punishable in both states by an agreed upon minimum penalty.

channel, and provide for direct consultations on cases, issues, and problems, constitutes one of the most important improvements of MLATs over the traditional letters rogatory process.

As with extradition, when a state, local, or federal prosecutor needs overseas evidence, the first contacts one of the country experts in the Justice Department's Office of International Affairs (OIA). The OIA attorney will then work with the prosecutor throughout the process of drafting the mutual legal assistance request. It is not unusual for the prosecutor and the OIA attorney to exchange several drafts by e-mail or fax before the MLAT request is put in final form. Such requests must state clearly what is being investigated in the United States, what specific assistance is needed from the other country, how that assistance relates to the U.S. investigation or prosecution, and any procedures for obtaining or authenticating the foreign evidence that will assist in its admissibility in the United States.

Once any necessary translation of the request is obtained, OIA forwards the MLAT request directly to the other country's Central Authority. The requested country's response depends on its domestic laws and procedures for executing international requests for assistance. Many countries have detailed mutual legal assistance statutes, which set out how to execute foreign MLAT requests. Often the process is for prosecutors in the foreign countries to seek the assistance of their domestic courts to obtain the necessary subpoenas or other compulsory orders required to collect the evidence sought in the U.S. request. The United States proceeds in a similar fashion when foreign authorities make an MLAT request for evidence.[114]

Many relatively simple MLAT requests can be executed without further involvement by U.S. authorities including most requests for foreign business or official records. However, more complicated requests[115] require continued involvement by the OIA attorney and the prosecutor to manage the legal and logistical issues necessary for the successful execution of the request. Once the requested evidence is obtained by the foreign authorities, it is returned by the Central Authority of the requested country to the United States Central Authority—the Office of International Affairs. The Office of International Affairs then transmits the evidence directly to the United States prosecutor.

III. Alternatives to Formal Extradition and Mutual Legal Assistance

A. Securing the Rendition of International Fugitives

White collar crime prosecutors sometimes find themselves interested in effecting the return of an accused or convicted defendant who is outside the United States even when formal extradition is not available. There may be no extradition treaty in force with the country of refuge, the extant treaty may not make the offense for which the defendant is wanted extraditable, or the defendant may be a citizen of the other country and that country may refuse to extradite its own nationals. In such circumstances, prosecutors sometimes explore legal alternatives to formal extradition.

Prosecutors may work with the Office of International Affairs, which in turn works with the U.S. State Department, to seek the deportation or expulsion of a fugitive from another country back to the United States. If the fugitive is a U.S. citizen, OIA relies

---

[114] [Article's footnote 71:] 28 U.S.C. § 1782.

[115] [Article's footnote 72:] For example, a Fed. R. Crim. P. 15 deposition in the foreign country at which the U.S. desires the presence of the defendant and full direct and cross examination by the prosecutor and defense counsel. Such depositions are sometimes used in a criminal case to obtain the testimony of a witness unable or unwilling to travel to the United States.

upon the U.S. arrest warrant to have his passport cancelled.[116] At OIA's request, the State Department then sends a cable to the U.S. Embassy in the country in which the fugitive is located, explaining that the U.S. citizen is a fugitive without a valid travel document, and requests that the other country use its domestic immigration law or other available legal means to return him, perhaps in the custody of U.S. Marshals, to the United States. Whether and under what circumstances a foreign country is willing to execute such requests varies, and depends both on its domestic law, and its willingness to utilize immigration procedures to accomplish a purpose more often pursued via international extradition.[117]

Sometimes white collar crime and other prosecutors will attempt to "lure" an international fugitive from a jurisdiction where his extradition cannot readily be obtained, whether directly to the United States or to a third country where extradition or deportation to the United States is possible. Lures usually involve some sort of subterfuge, trick, or other deception, often by undercover law enforcement agents or informants in communication with the fugitive, which convince the wanted person to voluntarily leave the country of refuge.

International fugitive lures are a legitimate, increasingly important law enforcement technique and do not violate U.S. Constitutional due process. That said, a foreign country may view any U.S. law enforcement activity necessary to effect the lure of a fugitive from its soil—even if that activity consists of nothing more than telephone calls or e-mails into the country—as an infringement upon its sovereignty unless specifically approved by that country. In fact, lures can even be prohibited by foreign criminal law. To ensure that broader law enforcement and other U.S. interests are fully considered prior to implementation of an international fugitive lure,[118] federal prosecutors interested in utilizing this technique must first consult with the Office of International Affairs.

Countries which refuse to extradite their own nationals usually can assert jurisdiction over crimes committed by their citizens no matter where in the world those crimes were committed by relying upon the nationality principle. Consequently, the U.S. white collar crime prosecutor should be aware that a country that refuses to surrender one of its nationals for prosecution in the U.S. may be willing to assert jurisdiction over that individual and prosecute him there. However, this alternative may provide more of a theoretical than a practical solution depending on how much of, and in what form, the U.S. evidence of the crime must be produced in order to support such a foreign prosecution, and whether the other country has the resources and political will to actually undertake such prosecutions.

B. Obtaining Financial Information From Abroad

Prosecutors may also resort to using unilateral legal measures to obtain extraterritorial evidence when cooperative measures such as formal MLATs or letters rogatory are not likely to secure needed bank records or other financial information from

---

[116] [Article's footnote 74:] 22 C.F.R. §§ 51.70-.72.

[117] [Article's footnote 75:] *See, e.g.,* United States v. Usama Bin Laden, 156 F.Supp.2d 359 (S.D.N.Y. 2001) (discussing a South African Supreme Court decision that analyzed the distinction between extradition and deportation, and found that the delivery of Khalfan Mohamed to U.S. authorities for his alleged role in the 1998 U.S. Embassy bombings in Africa constituted a deportation in violation of South African immigration law).

[118] [Article's footnote 80:] For example, a lure operation, although perfectly legal as a matter of U.S. law, may not be advisable if the country from which the fugitive is lured will object and take measures seriously adverse to other important U.S. law enforcement or foreign policy interests with that country.

abroad.[119] For example, sometimes U.S. prosecutors need financial records from a foreign country with strict bank secrecy laws or blocking statutes. If an MLAT exists with the other country, the records should be accessible. During the negotiation process, U.S. negotiators routinely ensure that provisions in our MLATs obligating the parties to provide testimony, documents, and other evidence will provide U.S. prosecutors with access to bank and other foreign business records regardless of the limiting provisions of foreign domestic law. Without an MLAT or comparable executive agreement in force, however, no such obligation exists. A country may or may not be willing and able to provide copies of a customer's bank records sought by letters rogatory or a letter of request. Absent customer consent, a release of bank records may actually constitute a criminal violation under the law of the foreign country. In such cases, U.S. prosecutors may consider serving a grand jury subpoena on a branch of the bank in the U.S., demanding records from the branch in the foreign bank-secrecy jurisdiction.

Such extraterritorial subpoenas[120]—often referred to as Bank of Nova Scotia subpoenas or "BNS" subpoenas after the Canadian banks involved in the seminal U.S. court cases upholding the government's authority to use them[121]—compel a foreign bank doing business in the United States to obtain records from its overseas branch or branches when needed in connection with a U.S. grand jury investigation, or the banks face contempt and fines for failure to do so. Given the conflicting U.S. and foreign legal obligations the subpoenas generate when served—for example, compliance with the U.S. grand jury subpoena may require a violation of foreign penal laws—courts have sometimes conducted a balancing test addressing several factors in order to determine whether to enforce such subpoenas. Among those factors are the "vital national interests" of the United States and the other sovereign state and the "extent and the nature of the hardship that inconsistent enforcement actions would impose upon the [bank]." U.S. courts, in upholding the use of BNS subpoenas, have determined that the U.S. interest in investigating crime is greater than the foreign interest in bank secrecy and that banks must comply with the subpoenas regardless of the potential hardship they may suffer due to the conflict with foreign law.

However, BNS subpoenas can be viewed by foreign governments as an improper assertion of extraterritorial power by the United States which infringes upon state sovereignty, and use of the subpoenas has sometimes led to diplomatic criticism and complaints. Consequently, as with international-fugitive lures, federal prosecutors must obtain Office of International Affairs approval in Washington prior to issuing or enforcing such subpoenas. As a practical matter, with the increasing number of MLATs that provide a less coercive and less controversial means to obtain foreign bank records, the need to resort to BNS subpoenas has diminished somewhat, and they are utilized less often today.[122]

---

[119] [Article's footnote 87:] For example, with countries with which the U.S. does not have an MLAT or in which a foreign letters rogatory request will not pierce domestic bank secrecy laws.

[120] [Article's footnote 94:] Such subpoenas are "extraterritorial" in the sense that, while served on a bank with a domestic U.S. presence, they seek records located outside the United States.

[121] [Article's footnote 95:] *In re* Grand Jury Proceedings Bank of Nova Scotia (*Bank of Nova Scotia II*), 740 F.2d 817 (11th Cir. 1984); *In re* Grand Jury Proceedings (*Bank of Nova Scotia I*), 691 F.2d 1384 (11th Cir. 1982).

[122] [Article's footnote 99:] However, if important evidence cannot be obtained through more cooperative means, unilateral measures will still be considered, and in some cases authorized. In addition to the established "BNS subpoena" mechanism, Congress recently passed a new statute permitting U.S. prosecutors to seek foreign bank records. Section 319(b) of the USA PATRIOT Act permits subpoenas to be issued to foreign banks that maintain correspondent accounts in the United States. Uniting and Strengthening America by Providing Appropriate Tools Required to

Prosecutors may also seek U.S. court ordered, compelled customer consent directives. Essentially, the prosecutor asks the court to order a person subject to its jurisdiction—often the target of a criminal investigation—to sign a consent directive authorizing banks to disclose records of any and all accounts over which the person has a right of withdrawal and turn those records over to the U.S. grand jury.[123] Presented with a signed directive demonstrating the customer's consent to the release of his account information, foreign banks will often produce records that would otherwise be protected by bank secrecy laws.

Carefully worded compelled customer consent directives have been held not to violate the Fifth Amendment privilege against self-incrimination.[124] Specifically, while clearly compelled and potentially self-incriminating, the directives are not "testimonial" in nature. However, their utility is only as good as a foreign country's willingness to honor them. Some foreign jurisdictions refuse to recognize such directives, viewing them as failing to represent free and voluntary consent to disclosure by the account holder.

Finally, a white collar crime or other prosecutor in the United States may rely upon the U.S. agents with whom he is working to obtain foreign financial information or other useful evidence located abroad. In other words, sometimes a U.S. prosecutor may forgo the use of formal MLAT or letters rogatory requests and simply rely upon U.S. law enforcement authorities, acting unilaterally or with the cooperation of foreign police authorities, to secure the extraterritorial evidence he needs.

Unilateral extraterritorial investigative action by U.S. law enforcement personnel without the knowledge, permission, or assistance of the host country's law enforcement authorities is not common. Principles of international law[125] and foreign law may restrict it. In addition, as a general matter, U.S. law enforcement agencies seek to conduct investigative activities in foreign countries in a manner that will not undermine the future law enforcement cooperation of those countries. However, it is quite common for U.S. law enforcement agencies to obtain informal, "police to police" assistance from their overseas counterparts. If evidence is obtained in such a manner, U.S. prosecutors must be cognizant of relevant Fourth Amendment jurisprudence that may effect their ability to use it.

A search and seizure of evidence abroad as part of a "joint venture" between U.S. and foreign law enforcement authorities may need to be "reasonable" under the Fourth Amendment in order to overcome an eventual motion to suppress the evidence by a U.S. citizen defendant. To determine "reasonableness," courts may look to see whether the evidence was obtained in a manner consistent with the law of the foreign country. However, when the evidence is to be introduced in a trial in this country against a criminal defendant who is a nonresident alien without significant voluntary connection to the United States, he is not entitled to the protection of the Fourth Amendment at all.[126]

Intercept and Obstruct Terrorism Act of 2001 (codified at 31 U.S.C. § 5318(k). It is anticipated that federal prosecutors' ability to utilize this statute will be governed by the same or similar *U.S. Attorneys' Manual* rules that govern the issuance and enforcement of BNS Subpoenas.

[123] [Article's footnote 100:] Such consent directives are often referred to as *"Ghidoni* waivers," after the seminal case in which a consent directive was unsuccessfully challenged on Fifth Amendment grounds. United States v. Ghidoni, 732 F.2d 814 (11th Cir. 1984).

[124] [Article's footnote 103:] Doe v. United States, 487 U.S. 201 (1988).

[125] [Article's footnote 107:] Restatement (Third) on Foreign Relations Law of the United States § 432(2) (1987) ("A state's law enforcement officers may exercise their functions in the territory of another state only with the consent of the other state, given by duly authorized officials of that state.").

[126] [Article's footnote 113:] United States v. Verdugo-Urquidez, 494 U.S. 259 (1990).

So long as the evidence was obtained from abroad in a manner that does not "shock the conscience" of the U.S. court, prosecutors may use it against defendants without concern over Fourth Amendment restrictions.

IV. Challenges Faced When Utilizing International Law Enforcement Treaties

A. Extradition Treaties

When an extradition treaty exists with a country through which a white collar crime fugitive is transiting or in which he has taken extended refuge, the U.S. prosecutor usually relies upon the treaty to obtain the arrest and extradition of the fugitive to the United States. Yet requests for extradition can generate a wide variety of interesting legal and political hurdles that may slow or frustrate the return of the person being sought for prosecution or punishment. While it is impossible to detail all such hurdles, a few of the more common may be usefully highlighted.

For one, even with a modern dual criminality treaty, a foreign country will only extradite if the acts leading to the crime or crimes for which the United States is seeking extradition would be deemed a criminal offense under the laws of the other country (had those acts taken place within the jurisdiction of that country). Yet acts that constitute some serious white collar crimes under U.S. law—such as export control violations—are not recognized as criminal offenses under the laws of every other country. In such circumstances, extradition may not be possible.

Alternatively, in a particular case there may exist no direct foreign counterpart to the U.S. white collar crime—computer fraud, for example—but the same acts that constitute the U.S. criminal violation would constitute some differently denominated offense under foreign law—perhaps a general fraud or obtaining property by deception statute—if committed within that country's jurisdiction. In such circumstances U.S. authorities argue that the dual criminality requirement is satisfied, and that, for purposes of extradition, it shouldn't matter whether the parties to the treaty place the crime within the same category of offenses or describe the offense by the same terminology.

Similarly, sometimes the fact that the federal government enjoys only those powers that the U.S. Constitution expressly or impliedly grants to it, with the remaining powers reserved to the fifty states, can complicate the international extradition of a person wanted for prosecution on federal charges. For example, the use of mail or wire as elements of the federal mail or wire fraud statutes, essential to the assertion of U.S. federal jurisdiction over fraud, have proven confusing to foreign extradition courts. Yet again, the usually prevailing U.S. position in such cases is that a purely jurisdictional element should not hinder the dual criminality analysis, and concomitantly, it should not undermine the extraditability of the offense.

A white collar crime prosecutor seeking the extradition of a fugitive may encounter other challenges as well. For example, even when dual criminality otherwise exists, if the United States is asserting extraterritorial jurisdiction over the offense for which extradition is being sought, that alone may affect a country's ability to surrender the fugitive. In other words, if the fugitive is not only located in a foreign country, but the behavior for which he is criminally charged occurred partially or entirely outside the United States, that may make a difference to whether his extradition can be obtained. Whether extradition can or will occur depends on the country of refuge and the language of the applicable U.S. extradition treaty. Many modern U.S. extradition treaties make clear that extradition shall be granted regardless of where the act or acts constituting the offense were committed. Several older U.S. extradition treaties are silent on this point. Others contain language indicating that extradition will be granted when the country from which extradition is requested would enjoy extraterritorial jurisdiction in similar circumstances.

As noted above, many U.S. extradition treaties contain provisions prohibiting extradition when the person sought has been convicted or acquitted for the same offense in the country from which extradition is sought or in a third country. The increased international mobility of many of today's white collar criminals, combined with the inherently transnational nature of much contemporary white collar crime, creates a growing need for the interpretation of such provisions. Yet their texts do not make clear just how a foreign government or extradition court will determine whether the crime for which a person is wanted in the U.S. constitutes the "same offense" for which he has already been prosecuted in the requested state.[127] In modern extradition treaties the United States negotiators attempt to ensure that such clauses will be interpreted narrowly. As a practical matter, however, if there exists no clear, mutually accepted *traveaux prepatoires* or negotiating history to the treaty which sheds light on this issue, the answer will likely turn upon the requested state's interpretation of the clause and its applicable domestic law.

A final example of a potential obstacle to extradition is the possible punishment that the fugitive may receive in the United States. While as a practical matter the issue does not arise in U.S. white collar crime cases,[128] many modern extradition treaties contain separate articles dealing with capital punishment. These treaties often permit the requested state, when extradition is sought for a crime potentially punishable by death in the requesting state and not so punishable in the requested state, to demand promises or assurances from the requesting state that, if the fugitive is extradited, he will not be executed. Absent the provision of such assurances, the requested state is under no obligation to surrender the fugitive. However, recently a very small number of countries, without a valid treaty basis for doing so, have put the United States on notice that they will refuse to extradite fugitives to this country absent assurances that the extraditees will not be subjected to life imprisonment,[129] or even to an indeterminate sentence. Thus, depending on the country in which the fugitive has taken refuge, it is at least possible that some of the most serious U.S. white collar crime cases could generate demands for such assurances.

---

[127] [Article's footnote 130:] As indicated above, U.S. constitutional double jeopardy principles do not prohibit the United States from prosecuting a person for the same offense for which he has been tried, convicted, and even punished in a foreign country, assuming personal jurisdiction can be obtained, through extradition or some alternative means.

[128] [Article's footnote 132:] Although white collar crimes are not punishable by death in the United States, such is not the case in every country in the world. Thus, while U.S. white collar crime prosecutors may never need to decide whether to forgo capital punishment in order to secure the return of an international fugitive, it is possible the United States Government could find itself in a position where it must decide whether to demand "death penalty assurances" from a requesting extradition treaty partner in a white collar crime case. For example, if the United States ever enters into an extradition treaty with the People's Republic of China, that country may seek the extradition of a fugitive wanted for taking bribes. *See* Charles Hutzler, *China Executes Official for Bribery*, Plain Dealer (Cleveland, Ohio), Mar. 9, 2000, at A3.

[129] [Article's footnote 135:] On October 2, 2001, the Mexican Supreme Court ruled that a sentence of life imprisonment constitutes inhumane punishment under the Mexican constitution, which permits only a sentence of finite years. Subsequently, lower courts in Mexico began demanding assurances from the United States that fugitives extradited to this country will not be imprisoned for life. The Mexican Supreme Court decision, and the subsequent demand for life imprisonment assurances by the Mexican Government and lower courts, has created a host of challenging legal, policy, and practical problems with which the U.S. Justice Department officials and prosecutors throughout the United States are still wrestling. ...

B. Mutual Legal Assistance Treaties

While requests pursuant to mutual legal assistance treaties (MLATs) are now made regularly on behalf of white collar crime prosecutors in the United States who need evidence located abroad, and while increasingly such requests are executed fully and successfully, various hurdles can delay or frustrate acquisition of the requested assistance. Just as with international extradition cases, the hurdles which can arise in MLAT cases are too varied to always anticipate, much less identify specifically. However, a few representative examples are worth noting.

One unfortunate reality in the MLAT process is the time it takes for the execution of requests made to a foreign country: often weeks or months, and occasionally longer. While the Central Authorities named in MLATs provide for direct communication between the law enforcement authorities of the requesting and requested states, once a request is made, it can still take a considerable amount of time for the foreign authorities to obtain any necessary compulsory process in the foreign court, collect the requested evidence, and send it back to the United States. Of course, if the foreign resources devoted to handling incoming requests for assistance are limited or overtaxed, the execution of such requests will be further delayed.

This time delay can frustrate a U.S. prosecutor who needs to obtain and analyze the overseas evidence in order to determine which, if any, U.S. charges to bring, as well as a U.S. prosecutor who has already brought criminal charges against a defendant, but views the foreign evidence as a critical link in his chain of proof. Federal statutes exist that recognize the time-consuming nature of international evidence gathering and provide for the relaxation of traditional statutes of limitations[130] and speedy trial rules[131] in such cases. Yet white collar crime prosecutors who seek evidence located outside the United States, especially in cases in which such evidence is located in several foreign jurisdictions, must be both careful planners and patient people.

When the requested foreign assistance includes computer related information or records, the time it takes to make and execute an MLAT request can prove even more problematic. As a commentator from the U.S. Department of Justice Criminal Division's Computer Crimes and Intellectual Property Section has put it:

> One characteristic of electronic evidence is that it can be altered, transferred or destroyed almost instantaneously, and from remote locations, often with a single keystroke. These changes to evidence may result from a criminal trying to cover his tracks, or a system administrator routinely clearing old e-mails or other data from a company's servers. Whatever the case, criminal evidence can be lost—long before an international request for evidence is ever transmitted.

Efforts are being made to address the challenges to international mutual legal assistance posed by new technology. On a bilateral level, MLAT requests are often sent by facsimile or the Internet directly from the Office of International Affairs (the U.S. Central Authority) to the Central Authority in the requested state. In addition, many modern MLATs contain a provision indicating that while requests are to be made in writing, the Central Authority of the requested state may accept a request made otherwise—for example, by telephone—in urgent circumstances. On the multilateral

---

[130] [Article's footnote 141:] 18 U.S.C. § 3292.

[131] [Article's footnote 142:] 18 U.S.C. § 3161(h)(9).

level, in recent years organizations such as the G-8, the Council of Europe, and the European Union have focused extensively on computer and high-tech crimes and have agreed upon everything from "action plans" to actual multilateral conventions designed in part to facilitate more effective international cooperation in such cases.

Today U.S. prosecutors handle cases involving not only the extradition of international white collar crime fugitives and the acquisition of overseas evidence needed to effectively prosecute them, but also cases in which they want to effect the freeze, forfeiture, and repatriation of the proceeds of crimes which have been laundered through or hidden in foreign banks. Most U.S. MLATs have articles providing for assistance in forfeiture matters. For the most part, the wording of those articles does not obligate the requested parties to do any more than what their domestic laws permit. While the progressive domestic laws of some countries enable them in some circumstances to actually immobilize, confiscate, and even return all or a portion of the illegally derived proceeds to the United States, other countries are quite limited in what forfeiture related assistance they can provide. Thus, even with an MLAT in place containing an article on forfeiture assistance, U.S. prosecutors should be prepared for mixed results when actually seeking such assistance.

Last, while rarely utilized, most MLATs contain a provision that authorizes the requested state to deny assistance when execution would prejudice the security or similar essential interests of that state. For example, if as part of a criminal investigation a United States MLAT request were to seek sensitive national security related information, the treaty partner could deny the request. United States treaty negotiators try to ensure that such "essential interests" provisions will be applied narrowly. Interpreted too broadly, they could undermine the fundamental obligation to provide mutual assistance which is the cornerstone to effective MLAT practice. Yet to the extent it is the requested state's own view that controls whether a foreign request for assistance implicates such essential interests, U.S. prosecutors could face the denial of a request which would otherwise appear to fall within the proper scope of the treaty.

* * *

UNITED STATES v. ALLEN
864 F.3d 63 (2d Cir. 2017)

José A. Cabranes, Circuit Judge.

This case—the first criminal appeal related to the London Interbank Offered Rate ("LIBOR") to reach this (or any) Court of Appeals—presents the question, among others, whether testimony given by an individual involuntarily under the legal compulsion of a foreign power may be used against that individual in a criminal case in an American court. As employees in the London office of Coöperatieve Centrale Raiffeisen–Boerenleenbank B.A. ("Rabobank") in the 2000s, defendants–appellants Anthony Allen and Anthony Conti ("Defendants") played roles in that bank's LIBOR submission process during the now–well–documented heyday of the rate's manipulation. [Ed.: the court's discussion of the particulars of the LIBOR scandal are omitted as irrelevant for these purposes.] Allen and Conti were, for unrelated reasons, no longer employed at Rabobank by 2008 and 2009, respectively. By 2013, they were among the persons being investigated by enforcement agencies in the United Kingdom ("U.K.") and the United States for their roles in setting LIBOR.

The U.K. enforcement agency, the Financial Conduct Authority ("FCA"), interviewed Allen and Conti (each a U.K. citizen and resident) that year, along with several of their coworkers. At these interviews, Allen and Conti were compelled to testify and given "direct use"—but not "derivative use"—immunity. In accordance with

U.K. law, refusal to testify could result in imprisonment. The FCA subsequently decided to initiate an enforcement action against one of Defendants' coworkers, Paul Robson, and, following its normal procedures, the FCA disclosed to Robson the relevant evidence against him, including the compelled testimony of Allen and Conti. Robson closely reviewed that testimony, annotating it and taking several pages of handwritten notes.

For reasons not apparent in the record, the FCA shortly thereafter dropped its case against Robson, and the Fraud Section of the United States Department of Justice (the "DOJ") promptly took it up. Robson soon pleaded guilty and became an important cooperator, substantially assisting the DOJ with developing its case. Ultimately, Robson was the sole source of certain material information supplied to the grand jury that indicted Allen and Conti and, after being called as a trial witness by the Government, Robson provided significant testimony to the petit jury that convicted Defendants.

In October 2014, a grand jury returned an indictment charging Defendants with one count of conspiracy to commit wire fraud and bank fraud, ... as well as several counts of wire fraud, in violation... Following a trial held in October 2015 in the United States District Court for the Southern District of New York, a jury convicted on all counts. The District Court sentenced Allen principally to two years' imprisonment and Conti to a year–and–a–day's imprisonment. ... We address only their Fifth Amendment challenge ... and conclude as follows.

... [T[he Fifth Amendment's prohibition on the use of compelled testimony in American criminal proceedings applies even when a foreign sovereign has compelled the testimony. ...

... [I]n this prosecution, Defendants' compelled testimony was "used" against them, and this impermissible use before the petit and grand juries was not harmless beyond a reasonable doubt. ...

A. Applicability of the Fifth Amendment

In arguing that Fifth Amendment protections apply in this case, Defendants rely on our cases pertaining to foreign and cross–border law enforcement, which have consistently held that "in order to be admitted in our courts, inculpatory statements obtained overseas by foreign officials must have been made voluntarily." In so holding, we joined our sister circuits that have considered the issue. Defendants contend that these cases are sufficient to resolve the present dispute regarding whether compulsion by a foreign power implicates the Fifth Amendment. We agree.

1. The Requirement of Voluntariness

The Supreme Court has "recognized two constitutional bases for the requirement that a confession be voluntary to be admitted into evidence: the Fifth Amendment right against self–incrimination and the Due Process Clause of the Fourteenth Amendment." Of these two potential "constitutional bases," our precedents applying such a requirement to confessions procured by foreign law enforcement have been grounded in the Self–Incrimination Clause and *Bram v. United States*, 168 U.S. 532 (1897). This constitutional footing is significant.

The freedom from self–incrimination guaranteed by the Fifth Amendment is a personal trial right of the accused in any American "criminal case." To that end, "a violation of the Fifth Amendment's right against self–incrimination occurs *only* when a compelled statement is offered at trial against the defendant." Whatever may occur prior to trial, the right not to testify against oneself *at trial* is "absolute." Even a negative comment by a judge or prosecutor on a defendant's silence violates that defendant's constitutional right.

These features of the Self–Incrimination Clause distinguish it from the exclusionary rules attached to unreasonable searches and seizures and to otherwise–valid confessions given without *Miranda* warnings. As the Supreme Court has explained, the Fourth Amendment's exclusionary rule "is a judicially created remedy designed to safeguard Fourth Amendment rights generally through its deterrent effect, rather than a personal constitutional right of the party aggrieved." So too with the exclusionary rule buttressing *Miranda* warnings, which "were primarily designed to prevent United States police officers from relying upon improper interrogation techniques." Such exclusionary rules "have little, if any, deterrent effect upon *foreign* police officers." Accordingly, we do not apply the strictures of our Fourth Amendment and *Miranda* jurisprudence to foreign authorities.

The Supreme Court has taken care, however, to distinguish extraterritorial applications of the Fourth Amendment from those of the Self–Incrimination Clause of the Fifth Amendment. The Fourth Amendment "prohibits unreasonable searches and seizures *whether or not* the evidence is sought to be used in a criminal trial," such that "a violation of the Amendment is fully accomplished at the time of an unreasonable governmental intrusion." By contrast, in the case of the Fifth Amendment's Self–Incrimination Clause, "a constitutional violation occurs *only at trial*," even if "conduct by law enforcement officials prior to trial may ultimately impair that right." In light of that distinction, "it naturally follows that, regardless of the origin— *i.e.*, domestic or foreign—of a statement, it cannot be admitted at trial in the United States if the statement was 'compelled.'"

Thus, the Self–Incrimination Clause's prohibition of the use of compelled testimony arises from the text of the Constitution itself, and directly addresses what happens in American courtrooms, in contrast to the exclusionary rules that are crafted as remedies to deter unconstitutional actions by officers in the field. Its protections therefore apply in American courtrooms even when the defendant's testimony was compelled by foreign officials.

Moreover, for much the same reasons, the Clause applies in American courtrooms even where, as here, the defendant's testimony was compelled by foreign officials *lawfully*—that is, pursuant to foreign legal process—in a manner that does not shock the conscience or violate fundamental fairness. The Clause flatly prohibits the use of compelled testimony and is not based on any matter of misconduct or illegality on the part of the agency applying the compulsion.

In short, compelled testimony cannot be used to secure a conviction in an American court. This is so even when the testimony was compelled by a foreign government in full accordance with its own law.

It is true that, with respect to statements taken abroad by foreign agents, we have often referred to the Fifth Amendment's prohibition against illicit use as encompassing "involuntary," rather than "compelled," statements. But this semantic distinction does not bear significant, much less dispositive, weight. Accordingly, we agree with Defendants that our cases applying a voluntariness test in the context of physical coercion extend to the present context of lawful compulsion.

2. The Government's Counterarguments

... The Government's ... counterargument extends from the premise that foreign governments are on the same footing as private employers when it comes to compelled testimony. In particular, the Government points to the fact that *private* employers may question an employee under threat of discharge without Fifth Amendment consequence, whereas in certain circumstances courts have found that the same threat by an American *government* employer rendered an employee's testimony "compelled" and excludable under the Fifth Amendment. "For purposes of the Fifth Amendment," the

Government submits, "the British government is on the same footing as a private entity such as the New York Stock Exchange." We disagree.

Only sovereign power exposes "'those suspected of crime to the cruel trilemma of self–accusation, perjury or contempt.'" Only the U.K. *government* could have immunized Defendants (neither of whom were employed by Rabobank at the time), compelling them to testify or go to jail. To the extent there may be an "official/private action spectrum," when foreign authorities compel testimony they are acting in the quintessence of their sovereign authority, not in their capacity as a mere employer, and thus their compulsion is cognizable by the Fifth Amendment (when testimony so compelled is used in a U.S. trial). ...

... [T]he Government's [final] ... counterargument is that testimony is only "compelled" for purposes of the Self–Incrimination Clause if the compelling sovereign is bound by the Fifth Amendment. Here, too, we disagree. The Government's argument relies on the so–called "same–sovereign" principle, under which Fifth Amendment protections apply only if the same sovereign (or, at least, a Fifth–Amendment–bound sovereign) both compelled and used testimony. This "same–sovereign" principle has never been fully abandoned; it still applies, for example, where the prosecuting sovereign is not bound by the Fifth Amendment (*i.e.*, where the prosecuting authority is a foreign government). But where, as here, the prosecuting sovereign *is* bound by the Fifth Amendment, the "same–sovereign" principle no longer has force. As already explained, it is now clear that the Fifth Amendment is a personal *trial* right—one violated only at the time of "use" rather than at the time of "compulsion." Accordingly, the Government's reliance on the "same–sovereign" principle in the circumstances of this case is unavailing.

3. The Consequences of Our Holding

The Government also asserts that a prohibition on its use in U.S. courts of testimony compelled by a foreign authority "could seriously hamper the prosecution of criminal conduct that crosses international borders." In particular, the Government submits:

A foreign government could inadvertently scuttle prosecutions in the U.S. by compelling testimony and then making the testimony available to potential witnesses or the public. Worse yet, a hostile government bent on frustrating prosecution of a defendant would have to do no more than compel [that defendant] to testify and then publicize the substance of that testimony, unilaterally putting the United States to its heavy *Kastigar* burden.

The Government's first concern—that foreign powers could inadvertently or negligently obstruct federal prosecutions—fails to account for the fact that this risk already exists within our own constitutional structure. In our system—composed of "State and National Governments," with the latter government further divided into separate co–equal branches—the DOJ does not control the granting or handling of witness immunity by the States or by the U.S. Congress. Similarly, and "[f]or better or for worse, we live in a world of nation–states in which our Government must be able to 'function effectively in the company of sovereign nations.'"

We are confident the Government is able to do so. Indeed, in a March 2016 address that specifically discussed the immunity issue in this case, Leslie Caldwell, then–Assistant Attorney General for the Criminal Division, observed that

as we and our [foreign] counterparts work together more frequently and better understand our respective systems, we are having ... conversations [about double jeopardy and Fifth Amendment protections] earlier, so that individuals are much less likely to be caught in the middle of last minute turf battles over where and by whom a prosecution should be brought.

In the present case, the Government was plainly aware from the outset—well before the FCA transmitted the Defendants' compelled testimony to Robson—of the need for close coordination of its efforts with those of the U.K. authorities. The practical outcome of our holding today is that the risk of error in coordination falls on the U.S. Government (should it seek to prosecute foreign individuals), rather than on the subjects and targets of cross-border investigations.

As to the Government's concerns that a hostile foreign government might hypothetically endeavor to sabotage U.S. prosecutions by immunizing a suspect and publicizing his or her testimony—that, of course, is not this case. *This* case raises no questions regarding the legitimacy or regularity of the procedures employed by the U.K. government or the U.K. government's investigation more generally. We thus need only say here that should U.S. prosecutors or judges face the situation suggested by the Government, our holding today would not necessarily prevent prosecution in the United States. That is true not only if the U.S. prosecution navigated any resulting *Kastigar* issues by meeting its burden or by not using exposed witnesses. It is true for another reason as well. Specifically, should the circumstances in a particular case indicate that a foreign defendant had faced no real threat of sanctions by his foreign government for not testifying, then that defendant's testimony might well not be considered involuntary. In short, the situation hypothesized by the Government is not before us today, and our resolution of this case on the facts that are before us leaves open the issue of foreign efforts to sabotage a U.S. prosecution.

On the other hand, the Government nowhere responds to the troubling consequences of accepting its argument. As conceded at oral argument, the Government's rule would remove any bar to introducing compelled testimony directly in U.S. prosecutions similar to this one—as in, "Your honor, we offer Government Exhibit 1, the defendant's compelled testimony." To be sure, the Government did not introduce Defendants' compelled testimony directly and appears to have generally sought in good faith to respect the principles underlying the Fifth Amendment. But it is well established that a defendant's "preservation of his rights" does not turn "upon the integrity and good faith of the prosecuting authorities." We cannot entertain a rule that discards the most basic Fifth Amendment right simply because prosecutors can be expected to respect its objectives generally.

The concerns that we express here are not idle. However unusual this particular prosecution may prove to be, so-called cross-border prosecutions have become more common. Such prosecutions necessarily entail intimate coordination between the United States and foreign authorities. As then-Assistant Attorney General Caldwell put it in the address to which we referred earlier, "[c]ollaboration and coordination among multiple regulators in cross-border matters is the future of major white collar criminal enforcement." Perhaps the most striking development in cooperative conduct is the embedding of U.S. prosecutors in foreign law enforcement. According to Caldwell, the DOJ "recently placed Criminal Division prosecutors with Eurojust in The Hague and INTERPOL in France" and was "exploring the possibility of embedding prosecutors with other foreign law enforcement as well." In a more recent address, Acting Principal Deputy Assistant Attorney General Trevor N. McFadden announced that DOJ will be detailing one of its anti-corruption prosecutors to work at the U.K. FCA—"the first time the Criminal Division ... will detail a prosecutor to work in a foreign regulatory agency on white collar crime issues."

One area in particular where intimate cooperation and coordination will be needed between U.S. prosecutors and foreign authorities (or, perhaps, between U.S. prosecutors and U.S. prosecutors on detail to foreign authorities) is the securing of witness testimony.

As the Government explained in a letter to the District Court in this case, "large scale economic crime conspiracies that harm U.S. markets, such as LIBOR rigging and the manipulation of the foreign exchange spot, often occur, in large part, overseas and *successful prosecutions of these matters frequently rely on evidence provided by witnesses who live in foreign countries.*" And as this case illustrates, foreign authorities may conduct compulsory witness interviews, including interviews of those who end up being—or are already—the targets of U.S. prosecution.

We do not presume to know exactly what this brave new world of international criminal enforcement will entail. Yet we are certain that these developments abroad need not affect the fairness of our trials at home. If as a consequence of joint investigations with foreign nations we are to hale foreign men and women into the courts of the United States to fend for their liberty we should not do so while denying them the full protection of a "*trial* right" we regard as "fundamental" and "absolute."

Accordingly, we adhere to our precedent in assessing the voluntariness of inculpatory testimony compelled abroad by foreign governments. In the instant appeal, there is no question that the Defendants' testimony was compelled and, thus, involuntary. We therefore conclude in this case that the Fifth Amendment prohibited the Government from using Defendants' compelled testimony against them.

Notes

1. The Supreme Court has held that a witness whose testimony is sought in a U.S. proceeding cannot assert a Fifth Amendment privilege against compelled self-incrimination based on his real and substantial fear of criminal prosecution in *another country*. *See* United States v. Balsys, 524 U.S. 666 (1998). Is this consistent with *Allen*?

2. Counsel should be aware that most countries do not have the same rules relating to a right against compelled self-incrimination that the U.S. does. For a comparative analysis of the developing jurisprudence regarding a right against self-incrimination in the European Court of Human Rights and European states, see Mark Berger, *Europeanizing Self-Incrimination: The Right to Remain Silent in the European Court of Human Rights*, 12 Colum. J. Eur. L. 339 (2006).

3. As the *Allen* court indicates, the rules that apply in the Fourth Amendment context are different than those that apply to the Fifth Amendment.

In *United States v. Verdugo-Urquidez*, 494 U.S. 259, 274 (1990), the Supreme Court made clear that U.S.-issued search warrants have no potency overseas; they are "dead letters" outside the United States. This follows from two circumstances. First, in Fed. R. Crim. P. 41, Congress has not authorized extraterritorial warrants except in very specific cases:

> (b) ... (5) a magistrate judge having authority in any district where activities related to the crime may have occurred, or in the District of Columbia, may issue a warrant for property that is located outside the jurisdiction of any state or district, but within any of the following:
>
> (A) a United States territory, possession, or commonwealth;
>
> (B) the premises—no matter who owns them—of a United States diplomatic or consular mission in a foreign state, including any appurtenant building, part of a building, or land used for the mission's purposes; or
>
> (C) a residence and any appurtenant land owned or leased by the United States and used by United States personnel assigned to a United States diplomatic or consular mission in a foreign state.

Second, under international law, the service of such subpoenas abroad—at least without the consent of the State in question—would constitute a breach of that State's sovereignty and would violate the customary international law norms of enforcement jurisdiction.

Even where Fed. R. Crim. P. 41 authorizes a search or seizure abroad, however, there are limitations on those who may "claim" the Fourth Amendment in U.S. courts. Where the property subject to the search and seizure is abroad, only persons with a substantial and voluntary connection with the United States can seek its suppression in U.S. criminal proceedings. *Verdugo-Urquidez*, 494 U.S. 259.

Note too that the Fourth Amendment and the Due Process Clause of the Fourteenth Amendment only bind U.S. federal and state official actors. It is universally agreed that the substantive prohibitions in the Fourth Amendment, as well as the exclusionary rule that is applied to deter future abuses, are *not* applicable to the actions of the foreign law enforcement officers. This rule, often called the international "silver platter" rule, means that evidence collected by foreign officials on their own territory under their own law and turned over to U.S. officials is admissible in U.S. courts, even though it was gathered in a manner that would not have violated the Fourth Amendment if done in the United States.

There are a couple of narrowly drawn exceptions to the international silver platter rule. First, if the circumstances of the foreign search and seizure "shock the conscience," the federal courts may exercise their supervisory authority to exclude the fruits *in federal court. See, e.g.*, United States v. Barona, 56 F.3d 1087, 1091 (9th Cir. 1995). (One might also argue that due process provides a basis for excluding such evidence in state trials.) Second, evidence illegally seized by foreign agents may be excluded in U.S. courts where the cooperation between U.S. and foreign law enforcement agencies is designed to evade constitutional requirements applicable to officials. *See* United States v. Maturo, 982 F.2d 57, 61 (2d Cir. 1992). Finally, and most importantly, evidence seized by non-U.S. agents may still be excluded if the "[f]ederal agents so substantially participate in the raids so as to convert them into joint ventures between the United States and the foreign officials." Stonehill v. United States, 405 F.2d 738, 743 (9th Cir. 1968); *see also* United States v. Stokes, 726 F.3d 880, 891 (7th Cir. 2013). It is very difficult to prevail on this ground. *See, e.g.*, United States v. Hawkins, 661 F.2d 436, 455-456 (5th Cir. 1981); United States v. Heller, 625 F.2d 594, 599-600 (5th Cir. 1980); Birdsell v. United States, 346 F.2d 775, 782 (5th Cir. 1965).

Even if a joint venture is found, however, "the law of the foreign country must be consulted at the outset as part of the determination whether or not the search was reasonable." *Barona*, 56 F.3d at 1091. If foreign law was complied with, then the search is considered "reasonable" within the meaning of the Fourth Amendment and the exclusionary rule cannot be invoked in U.S. courts. If the foreign law was *not* complied with, the good faith exception to the exclusionary rule becomes part of the analysis. Thus, if the defendant shows that the United States and foreign officials were engaged in a joint venture *and* that a violation of foreign law occurred making the search unreasonable, the evidence may still be admissible if the United States demonstrates that its agents relied in good faith upon the foreign officials' representations that their law was being complied with. *Id.* at 1092.

This rule applies not only in prosecutions against non-U.S. nationals who have a sufficient connection to the United States to claim the protection of the Fourth Amendment, but also where U.S. citizens' property is searched or seized abroad. For example, in *United States v. Barona*, 56 F.3d 1087, U.S. and Danish officials conducted a joint investigation of a U.S. citizen in Denmark. The Ninth Circuit held that the evidence seized abroad in this investigation did not have to be excluded unless the search violated Danish law (thus rendering it "unreasonable" under the United States' Fourth Amendment) and U.S. officials did not rely in good faith on Danish assertions that the search comported with foreign law.

There has been an explosion in cooperation in international law enforcement, through informal contacts as well as through bilateral or multinational cooperation agreements. Given the increasing extent of joint law enforcement investigations, does this stringent test constitute, as Judge Reinhardt argued in dissent, a "substantial step toward the elimination of what was once a firmly established constitutional right, the right of American citizens to be free from unreasonable searches and seizures conducted by their own government"? *Id.* at 1099 (Reinhardt, J., dissenting).

2. THE DEFENSE

We have previously discussed the advantages the government has vis-à-vis the defense in terms of securing information and evidence.[132] For example, the government can obtain search warrants, confer immunity to secure needed testimony, and effectively depose witnesses in the grand jury; the defense does not have access to these discovery mechanisms. Prosecutors bemoan the difficulties they face in securing competent evidence in transnational investigations but, once again, the defense faces even greater challenges. Defense counsel must surmount the same legal obstacles to information gathering abroad in the form of data privacy laws and blocking statutes. But they have no ability to ask for the extradition or deportation of relevant witnesses. They cannot seek to force persons to sign so-called "*Ghidoni* waivers" (the type of "consent directives" discussed above by Judge Snow and *supra*, Chapter 16, in *Doe v. United States*[133]). And the defense generally do not have access to the informal mechanisms of information collection, such as "police to police" contacts discussed above.

Most importantly, MLATs concluded between the United States and other countries are unavailable to individuals. As Michael Abbell, notes:

> Three of the earliest United States mutual assistance treaties do not contain a provision regulating the use of the treaties by criminal defendants and other persons. The next group of treaties negotiated by the United States provides that the treaties are intended "solely" for mutual assistance between the governmental or law enforcement authorities of the contracting parties. Several of them add that they are not intended or designed to provide assistance to private parties. The more recent treaties go beyond this second group by expressly providing that they do "not give rise to a right on the part of private parties to obtain ... any evidence."[134]

The defense, then, cannot use these "primary tools" of prosecutorial transborder investigation. Courts also have rejected the contention that, because the government has the power to secure materials through an MLAT, it should be tasked with doing so to comply with its discovery obligations under Fed. R. Crim. P. 16. For example, the D.C. Circuit has held that "[h]aving the authority 'to seek' tapes or transcripts through a treaty is not the same as having 'the power to secure them,'" nor does it make those materials within the government's "possession custody, or control" for Rule 16 purposes.[135] Indeed, courts have concluded that defense cannot even object to perceived government

---

[132] *See, e.g., supra* Chapters 13 (Grand Jury), 14 (Discovery), 15 (Fifth Amendment: Testimony and Immunity).

[133] 487 U.S. 201 (1988).

[134] Michael Abbell, Obtaining Evidence Abroad in Criminal Cases 2010 (Martinus Nijhoff Pub. 2010).

[135] United States v. Mejia, 448 F.3d 436, 444 (D.C. Cir. 2006).

violations of the MLAT's requirements.[136] To add insult to injury, prosecutors can seek extensions of otherwise applicable statute of limitations or speedy trial provisions while seeking evidence under MLATs.[137] So what *can* defense counsel do?

a. Domestic Criminal Process: Fed. R. Crim. P. 17 Subpoena Power

Defense counsel do have subpoena power, but readers will recall that in *United States v. Nixon*[138] (discussed in Chapter 14(E)) the Supreme Court seriously limited the availability of such subpoenas:

> ... [In] *Bowman Dairy Co. v. United States*, 341 U.S. 214 (1951)[, this Court] ... recognized certain fundamental characteristics of the subpoena *duces tecum* in criminal cases: (1) it was not intended to provide a means of discovery for criminal cases; (2) its chief innovation was to expedite the trial by providing a time and place *before* trial for the inspection of subpoenaed materials. [C]ases ... have generally followed Judge Weinfeld's formulation in *United States v. Iozia*, 13 F.R.D. 335, 338 (S.D.N.Y.1952), as to the required showing. Under this test, in order to require production prior to trial, the moving party must show: (1) that the documents are evidentiary and relevant; (2) that they are not otherwise procurable reasonably in advance of trial by exercise of due diligence; (3) that the party cannot properly prepare for trial without such production and inspection in advance of trial and that the failure to obtain such inspection may tend unreasonably to delay the trial; and (4) that the application is made in good faith and is not intended as a general "fishing expedition."[139]

Thus, courts have applied *Nixon* to require the defense to show "(1) relevancy; (2) admissibility; (3) specificity"[140] even when the defense seeks to subpoena persons other than the prosecutorial team from whom it has no entitlement to *Brady*, Jencks Act disclosure, or Rule 16 discovery.

This broad application of the *Nixon* standard makes it difficult for the defense to compel disclosure of materials potentially important to the defense that are held by third-parties. For example, courts regularly hold that Rule 17 subpoenas may only be used to secure materials that themselves would be admissible as evidence. Notably, "[c]ourts have consistently interpreted the admissibility standard of Rule 17(c) to preclude production of materials whose evidentiary use is limited to impeachment."[141]

More importantly for present purposes, the subpoena power extends only to witnesses and evidence within the United States pursuant to Fed. R. Crim. P. 17(e)(1) or to U.S. nationals or U.S. residents in foreign countries under Fed. R. Crim. P. 17(e)(2)

---

[136] *See, e.g., In re* Request from the United Kingdom, 685 F.3d 1, 9 (1st Cir. 2012) (MLAT did not create private rights to suppress evidence or to impede execution of requests under MLAT); United States v. Rommy, 506 F.3d 108, 129-31 (2d Cir. 2007).

[137] *See* 18 U.S.C. §§ 3292, 3161(h)(9).

[138] 418 U.S. 683 (1974).

[139] *Id.* at 698-700.

[140] *Id.* at 700.

[141] United States v. Cherry, 876 F. Supp. 547, 552 (S.D.N.Y. 1995) (collecting cases).

and 28 U.S.C. § 1783.[142] To be clear, the federal courts' subpoena power does not extend to foreign nationals located abroad.[143]

As noted by Judge Thomas Snow, *supra*, however, a species of "extraterritorial subpoenas—often referred to as Bank of Nova Scotia subpoenas or 'BNS' subpoenas after the Canadian banks involved in the seminal U.S. court cases upholding the government's authority to use them—compel a foreign bank doing business in the United States to obtain records from its overseas branch or branches when needed in connection with a U.S. grand jury investigation, or the banks face contempt and fines for failure to do so."[144] The government has also used BNS subpoenas to require U.S. companies to repatriate records they maintain overseas.[145] This obviously may create problems for defense counsel employed to defend companies against a BNS subpoena. Indeed, courts enforcing BNS subpoenas have forced companies to produce records that are maintained overseas, even where the law of the jurisdiction in which those materials reside mandate that the materials subpoenaed are protected from disclosure by law or privilege.[146]

Can the defense use BNS subpoenas?

b. Letters Rogatory

A letter rogatory is the traditional means of obtaining evidence located abroad. It is an official request from a court in one country to the appropriate judicial authority in another requesting that certain testimony, evidence, or legal process be ordered. Letters rogatory are "the medium, in effect, whereby one country, speaking through one of its courts, requests another country acting through its own courts and by methods of court procedure peculiar thereto and entirely within the latter's control, to assist the administration of justice in the former country; such requests being made, and being usually granted, by reason of the comity existing between nations in ordinary peaceful times."[147] The State Department has long been authorized under 18 U.S.C. § 1781 to process outgoing letters rogatory issued by U.S. courts, to transmit them to foreign or

---

[142] *See* 28 U.S.C. § 1783 ("A court of the United States may order the issuance of a subpoena requiring the appearance as a witness before it, or before a person or body designed by it, of a national or resident of the United States who is in a foreign country.").

[143] *See* United States v. Moussaoui, 382 F.3d 453, 463-64 (4th Cir. 2004); United States v. Filippi, 918 F.2d 244 (1st Cir. 1990); United States v. Padilla, 869 F.2d 372, 377 (8th Cir. 1989); United States v. Ismaili, 828 F.2d 153, 159 n.2 (3d Cir. 1987); United States v. Korogodsky, 4 F. Supp.2d 262, 268 (S.D.N.Y. 1998).

[144] *See, e.g., In re* Grand Jury Proceedings Bank of Nova Scotia, 740 F.2d 817 (11th Cir. 1984); *In re* Grand Jury Proceedings, 691 F.2d 1384 (11th Cir. 1982).

[145] *See, e.g., In re* Grand Jury Subpoena Dated Aug. 9, 2000, 218 F. Supp.2d 544 (S.D.N.Y. 2002) (requiring U.S. company to produce documents maintained abroad even though foreign nation asserted they were protected by executive privilege); *see generally Restatement, supra* note 49, § 442 ("Requests for Disclosure: Law of the United States"). *But see In re* Sealed Case, 825 F.2d 494 (D.C. Cir. 1987) (reversing order to produce documents protected under foreign law); United States v. First Nat'l Bank of Chicago, 699 F.2d 341 (7th Cir. 1983) (reversing order enforcing tax summons against U.S. company for documents in Greece where compliance with subpoena (production of documents) would subject Greek employees to criminal sanctions).

[146] *See supra* authorities cited in notes 144 and 145.

[147] The Signe, 37 F. Supp. 819, 820 (E.D. La. 1941). For the rules applicable to authentication of evidence obtained from overseas, and special rules of admissibility, see 18 U.S.C. §§ 3491-3494, 3505; Fed. R. Evid. 902(3).

international tribunals, and to return them after execution.[148] Both the government and the defense can use letters rogatory, although prosecutors prefer to proceed under the more efficient MLAT process, where available, because there is no obligation, other than considerations of comity, for the receiving state to comply with U.S. letters rogatory—in contrast to MLATs, where cooperation of foreign authorities is required if the terms of the treaty are met.

Securing evidence through letters rogatory is by no means certain, given their discretionary nature, and in any event will assuredly take valuable time. Defendants wishing a more efficient alternative have asked the DOJ to use its MLAT powers to assist in their investigations. The DOJ opposes such assistance. Courts generally side with the DOJ, holding that MLATs do not invest individuals with rights under the treaty, and insisting that defendants instead avail themselves of the letters rogatory process and Rule 15 depositions (discussed *infra*) where available to them.[149]

It must be noted that letters rogatory are a two-edged sword for the defense. Obviously, they may be used by the defense to secure evidence overseas. But they can also be used by foreign governments seeking evidence found in the United States to use in foreign criminal prosecutions of U.S. persons. The same statute, 18 U.S.C. § 1781, authorizes the State Department to process incoming letters rogatory from foreign courts, transmit them to the appropriate body in the United States, and to return the responses. Under 28 U.S.C. § 1782, federal district courts are authorized to require the giving of testimony and the production of documents or other evidence "for use in a proceeding in a foreign or international tribunal, including criminal investigations conducted before formal accusation." The order may be made pursuant to a letter rogatory issued, or request made, by a foreign or international tribunal or upon the application of any interested person and may direct that the testimony or statement be given, or the document or other thing be produced, before a person appointed by the court."[150] Note, however, that, under 28 U.S.C. § 1782, "[a] person may not be compelled to give his testimony or statement or to produce a document or other thing in violation of any legally

---

[148] The State Department's website provides advice on the letter rogatory process. *See* https://travel.state.gov/content/travel/en/legal-considerations/judicial/obtaining-evidence/preparation-letters-rogatory.html.

[149] *See Mejia*, 448 F.3d at 444-45 (where the defendants did not use the letters rogatory process open to them, holding that the government's obligations under Fed. R. Crim. P. 16 did not extend to using MLAT to obtain materials requested by the defense).

[150] 18 U.S.C. § 1782. This section goes on to provide:

> … By virtue of his appointment, the person appointed has power to administer any necessary oath and take the testimony or statement. The order may prescribe the practice and procedure, which may be in whole or part the practice and procedure of the foreign country or the international tribunal, for taking the testimony or statement or producing the document or other thing. To the extent that the order does not prescribe otherwise, the testimony or statement shall be taken, and the document or other thing produced, in accordance with the Federal Rules of Civil Procedure. …

Predictably, there has been a great deal of litigation regarding the scope of this authorization. *See, e.g.,* Intel Corp. v. Advanced Micro Devices, Inc., 542 U.S. 241 (2004) (complainant was an "interested person" and Directorate General-Competition Commission of the European Communities was a "tribunal" under the statute; proceeding before foreign tribunal did not have to be imminent; applicant need not show that U.S. law would allow discovery in domestic litigation analogous to the foreign proceedings; district court need not grant order under statute just because it has the authority to do so); *In re* Application of Dubey, 949 F. Supp.2d 990 (C.D. Ca. 2013) (private arbitrations are not "foreign or international tribunals" within the meaning of the statute).

applicable privilege." The decision whether to issue a discovery order under § 1782 lies in the sound discretion of the district court.[151]

In 2009, to streamline the process for handling foreign requests for assistance in criminal cases, Congress enacted the Foreign Evidence Request Efficiency Act, codified at 18 U.S.C. § 3512.[152] Congress intended this section to augment, not replace, requests under § 1782.[153] Section 3512(a)(1) provides:

> Upon application, duly authorized by an appropriate official of the Department of Justice, of an attorney for the Government, a Federal judge may issue such orders as may be necessary to execute a request from a foreign authority for assistance in the investigation or prosecution of criminal offenses, or in proceedings related to the prosecution of criminal offenses, including proceedings regarding forfeiture, sentencing, and restitution.

Such orders can include issuance of a search warrant, a warrant or order for the contents of stored wire or electronic communications or for related records, an order for a pen register or trap and trace device, or an order requiring the appearance of a person for the purpose of providing testimony or a statement or requiring the production of documents or other things, or both.[154]

c. Deposition to Preserve Evidence under Fed. R. Crim. P. 15

A court cannot compel foreign nationals to come to the United States to testify, but it can authorize, pursuant to Fed. R. Crim. P. 15, the taking of depositions to preserve the witnesses' testimony for trial, at least if the country at issue permits such depositions (China, for example, does not). Fed. R. Crim. P. 15 states:

> A party may move that a prospective witness be deposed in order to preserve testimony for trial. The court may grant the motion because of exceptional circumstances and in the interests of justice. If the court orders the deposition to be taken, it may also require the deponent to produce at the deposition any designated material that is not privileged, including any book, paper, document, record, recording, or data.

Courts are conservative in granting Rule 15 depositions because "[d]epositions are disfavored in criminal cases. In particular, because of the absence of procedural safeguards afforded parties in the United States, foreign depositions are suspect and, consequently, not favored."[155] The burden is on the moving party to establish exceptional

---

[151] *See Intel Corp.*, 542 U.S. at 264 (listing factors to be considered).

[152] Pub. L. 111-79, § 2(4), Oct. 19, 2009, 123 Stat. 2087. For a discussion of the relationship between 18 U.S.C. § 1792 and § 3512, see *In re* Premises Located at 840 140th Avenue, NE, 634 F.3d 557 (9th Cir. 2011).

[153] 18 U.S.C. § 3512(g).

[154] *Id.* § 3512(a)(2). "The term 'foreign authority' means a foreign judicial authority, a foreign authority responsible for the investigation or prosecution of criminal offenses or for proceedings related to the prosecution of criminal offenses, or an authority designated as a competent authority or central authority for the purpose of making requests for assistance pursuant to an agreement or treaty with the United States regarding assistance in criminal matters." *Id.* § 3512(h)(2).

[155] United States v. Drogoul, 1 F.3d 1546, 1551 (11th Cir. 1993); *see also* United States v. Alvarez, 837 F.2d 1024, 1029 (11th Cir. 1988).

circumstances justifying the taking of a deposition,[156] and the decision whether to order such a deposition "rests within the sound discretion of the trial court and will not be disturbed absent clear abuse of that discretion."[157] The deposition procedure is governed by Fed. R. Civ. P. 28(b)(2) and must comply with the domestic law of the country in which it is taken. To be admissible under Fed. R. Evid. 804(b)(1), the party against whom the testimony is offered must have the opportunity to examine or cross-examine the declarant at the time of the deposition.

"[E]xceptional circumstances" generally boil down to whether: (1) the witness is unavailable for trial, (2) the testimony of the witness is material, and (3) the testimony is necessary to prevent a failure of justice.[158] In practice, "the 'exceptional circumstances' requirement of Rule 15 is met 'if [the] witness's testimony is material to the case and if the witness is unavailable to appear at trial.'" [159] "Courts will sometimes weigh countervailing factors against authorizing the deposition. Countervailing factors include: (1) the fact finder's inability to observe the demeanor of the deposition witness, (2) whether the laws where the deposition will be held restrict cross-examination of the witness, and (3) if the witnesses are placed under oath, whether the significance of that oath is diminished because there is no realistic perjury sanction."[160]

d. Fifth and Sixth Amendment Objections/Arguments?

The Sixth Amendment guarantees that "[i]n all criminal prosecutions, the accused shall enjoy the right … to have compulsory process for obtaining witnesses in his favor."[161] But, "the Sixth Amendment can give the right to compulsory process only where it is within the power of the federal government to provide it."[162] In particular, the "compulsory process right is circumscribed by the ability of the district court to obtain the presence of a witness through service of process."[163] The courts, then, have held that, because federal courts have "no power to compel the presence of a foreign national residing outside the Unite States, … a Sixth Amendment violation … cannot rest on the failure to issue a subpoena,"[164] even where the "witness could provide testimony that is

---

[156] *Drogoul*, 1 F.3d at 1552.

[157] United States v. Johnpoll, 739 F.2d 702, 708 (2d Cir. 1984); *see also Drogoul*, 1 F.3d at 1552.

[158] *See, e.g.*, United States v. Sanford, Ltd., 860 F. Supp.2d 1 (D.D.C. 2012); United States v. Jefferson, 594 F. Supp.2d 655, 665 (E.D. Va. 2009).

[159] Linda Friedman Ramirez, *Federal Law Issues in Obtaining Evidence Abroad—Part Two: Witness Entry to the United States*, 31 The Champion 38, 39 (July 2007) (quoting *Johnpoll*, 739 F.2d at 708-09); *see also* United States v. Sanchez-Llama, 161 F.3d 545, 547-48 (9th Cir. 1998); *Drogoul*, 1 F.3d at 1552; United States v. Ismaili, 828 F.2d 153, 159 (3d Cir. 1987); United States v. Vo, 53 F. Supp.3d 77, 80 (D.D.C. 2014).

[160] Ramirez, *supra*, note 159; *see also* United States v. Ramos, 45 F.3d 1519 (11th Cir. 1995); *Drogoul*, 1 F.3d at 1552; *Alvarez*, 837 F.2d at 1029; United States v. Oudovenko, 2001 WL 253027 (E.D.N.Y. 2001).

[161] U.S. Const. amend. VI.

[162] United States v. Greco, 298 F.2d 247, 251 (2d Cir. 1962).

[163] *Moussaoui*, 382 F.3d at 463.

[164] *Filippi*, 918 F.2d at 247; *see also* United States v. Zabaneh, 837 F.2d 1249, 1259-60 (5th Cir. 1988) ("It is well established … that convictions are not unconstitutional under the Sixth Amendment even though the United States courts lack power to subpoena witnesses, (other than American citizens) from foreign countries.") (citing cases). Note that, "[e]ven where it is the government's actions that prohibit a witness from testifying, a defendant may compel the presence

material and favorable to the defendant."[165] The reasoning is that Sixth Amendment gives the right to compulsory process only where it is in the power of the federal government to provide it, "[o]therwise any defendant could forestall trial simply by specifying that a certain person living where he could not be forced to come to this country was required as a witness in his favor."[166] Accordingly, courts have consistently held that a defendant's inability to subpoena foreign witnesses does not implicate the Sixth Amendment's compulsory process right.[167]

Defendants have not had much more success in arguing that their inability call foreign witnesses deprives them of their due process rights,[168] at least where the government is not responsible for the unavailability of the witness,[169] or the defendant had not sought court permission to depose the witness pursuant to Fed. R. Crim. P. 15(a) or asked the district court to issue letters rogatory to the foreign court requesting its assistance in gathering evidence from the foreign witnesses.[170]

Defendants may, however, have a Fifth or Sixth Amendment claim where "the government unreasonably denies a visa to a willing witness or has made a witness unavailable by physically removing the witness from the United States."[171] Some also argue that at least where the defense has succeeded in securing a Rule 15 order for a deposition, the Constitution requires that the government use its MLAT powers to enforce the order. According to Michael Abbel, an expert on obtaining evidence abroad,

> MLATs provide the government with *de facto* compulsory process. Therefore, if DOJ were to refuse to use an MLAT to execute a Rule 15 court order authorizing a criminal defendant to obtain evidence from abroad, the denial would appear to violate the defendant's rights under the Compulsory Process clause of the Sixth Amendment. That clause obligates the government to provide criminal defendants with the same means to obtain evidence from abroad as it affords itself through the MLATs—especially where that means is markedly superior to the alternative methods available to defendants.[172]

---

of the witness only if he can 'make some plausible showing of how their testimony would [be] both material and favorable to his defense.'" United States v. Campbell, 874 F.2d 838, 851 (1st Cir. 1989) (quoting United States v. Valenzuela-Bernal, 458 U.S. 858, 867 & n.7 (1982)).

[165] *Korogodsky*, 4 F. Supp.2d at 268.

[166] *Greco*, 298 F.2d at 251.

[167] *See, e.g.*, United States v. Sensi, 879 F.2d 888, 898, 899 (D.C. Cir. 1989) (In a case where the defendant did not ask for a Rule 15 deposition or letters rogatory, denying compulsory process and due process claims, explaining that the defendant "does not argue as a general matter that the United States must ensure criminal defendants access to witnesses outside the jurisdiction of the United States, nor could he. ... It is well settled that a defendant's inability to subpoena foreign witnesses is not a bar to criminal prosecution."); *Zabaneh*, 837 F.2d at 1259-60; *Greco*, 298 F.2d at 251 (in a case in which the defendant never identified prospective foreign witnesses and did not apply to take testimony abroad, denying Sixth Amendment compulsory process claim).

[168] *See Sensi*, 879 F.2d at 898.

[169] *See* United States v. White, 51 F. Supp.2d 1008 (E.D. Ca. 1997).

[170] *See Sensi*, 879 F.2d at 899; *see also* United States v. Yousef, 327 F.3d 56, 112-13 (2d Cir. 2003).

[171] Linda Friedman Ramirez, *Federal Law Issues in Obtaining Evidence Abroad—Part I*, 31 The Champion 28, 29 (June 2007); *see also Sanchez-Lima*, 161 F.3d at 548; *Fillipi*, 918 F.2d at 247-48.

[172] Michael Abbell, *DOJ Renews Assault on Defendant's Right to Use Treaties to Obtain Evidence from Abroad*, 21 The Champion 20 (1997); *see also* Abbell, *supra* note 134, at 22-23; Note, *Compulsory Process in a Globalized Era: Defendant Access to Mutual Legal Assistance Treaties*, 47 Va. J. Int'l L. 261 (2006); *cf.* United States v. Des Marteau, 162 F.R.D. 364, 372 n.5 (M.D. Fla. 1995) (indicating that DOJ

Generalized arguments that compulsory process mandates that the government use its MLAT powers to secure evidence for the defense have failed, however.[173]

It is troubling that although Congress regularly proscribes extraterritorial conduct, and prosecutors, armed with the fruits of MLATs, seek to imprison defendants based only on acts they take abroad, these same defendants are not regularly afforded extra-territorial compulsory process to defend themselves. Abbell believes that, despite some adverse caselaw, all is not lost:

> ...[I]n at least one case in which a defendant sought to use a United States mutual legal assistance treaty in criminal matters to obtain evidence from a United States treaty party pursuant to a treaty which was silent with respect to a defendant's right to seek evidence under it, the trial court directed the Department of Justice to make a treaty request on behalf of the defendant threatening to dismiss the case with prejudice if the government failed to do so. Other United States courts may also seek to avoid Compulsory Process Clause questions under treaties containing a provision restricting their use by private parties either by making the request themselves, and directing the U.S. Department of Justice to transmit it to the appropriate authority in the requested country for execution pursuant to the treaty, or by ordering the U.S. Department of Justice to make the request on behalf of the defendant.[174]

e. Extradition

Judge Snow describes the general requisites and procedures for extradition, *supra*. If the defendant is attempting to avoid extradition to the United States, counsel will use whatever mechanisms are afforded in that foreign jurisdiction, under the relevant treaty and foreign law, to resist the return of the defendant. Often the defense will attempt to argue that: the required documentation is flawed, the dual criminality requirement has not been met, the crime at issue concerns a "political offense," the statute of limitations has run, double jeopardy precludes the prosecution, and the like. If the defendant is lucky enough to be a foreign national residing in a country that does not extradite its own nationals, the defense will press that case (and strongly advise the defendant not to leave his haven and travel to other countries that have extradition treaties with the United States). Because the ultimate decision to extradite often lies in the executive, not the courts, political, rather than legal, approaches to head off the defendant's extradition may also be helpful.

If the defendant is unsuccessful and is returned to the United States, he may have difficulty re-litigating the question of whether dual criminality exists in the U.S. criminal proceeding. Some courts have held that U.S. courts are obliged to defer to the sending state's determination of whether dual criminality is satisfied in a particular case.[175] There

---

approved the use of Canadian MLAT to take testimony of witnesses where Rule 15 depositions had been ordered).

[173] *See, e.g.,* United States v. Sedaghaty, 728 F.3d 885, 916-17 (9th Cir. 2013); United States v. Rosen, 240 F.R.D. 204, 213 (E.D. Va. 2007) (after denying motion for Rule 15 deposition, holding that defendants were not deprived of their right to compulsory process by the government's refusal, in response to defense request, to use its MLAT to secure the testimony of three government officials).

[174] Abbell, *supra* note 134, at 22-23.

[175] *See, e.g.,* United States v. Campbell, 300 F.3d 202, 209 (2d Cir. 2002) ("the question of whether an extradition treaty allows prosecution for a particular crime that is specified in the extradition

is also some question whether the defendant can assert the rule of specialty in U.S. courts after extradition. As Judge Snow explained, *supra*, the rule of specialty bars the federal government from seeking to bring additional charges not contemplated in the extradition proceedings and from sending the extradited person on to a third country for prosecution. Some courts have suggested that the rule of specialty exists only to protect the interests of the foreign requested State and, therefore, "[t]he right to insist on the application of the principle of specialty belongs to the requested state, not to the individual whose extradition is requested."[176] Others allow the defendant the standing to raise specialty issues. But the defendant only "enjoys this right at the sufferance of the requested state. As a sovereign, the requested nation may waive its right to object to a treaty violation and thereby deny the defendant standing to object to such an action."[177]

---

request is a matter for the extraditing country to determine"); United States v. Salinas Doria, 2008 WL 4684229, at *3 (S.D.N.Y. 2008); *see also* Johnson v. Browne, 205 U.S. 309, 316 (1907).

[176] Demjanjuk v. Petrovsky, 776 F.2d 571, 584 (6th Cir. 1985); *see also* United States v. Kaufman, 874 F.2d 242, 243 (5th Cir. 1980).

[177] United States v. Puentes, 50 F.3d 1567, 1572 & n.2 (11th Cir. 1995); *see also* United States v. Stokes, 726 F.3d 880 (7th Cir. 2013).

Index

References are to Pages

Accounting Fraud, 578-599

Actus Reus
    Definition, 57
    Relation to "responsible corporate officer" doctrine, 241-42

Aiding and Abetting Liability (18 U.S.C. § 2)
    Distinction from conspiracy, 605-09
    Generally, 240-42

Appeals Waivers
    Brady or discovery, 780-81, 993-94
    Sentencing, 994-97

Attorney Subpoenas
    Citizens Protection Act (28 U.S.C. § 530B), 42-43, 733-34
    Department of Justice policy, 732-33

Attorney–Client Privilege and Work Product Doctrine (*see also* "Entity Liability"; "Joint Defense"; "Representation Issues")
    Availability in grand jury, 729
    Citizens Protection Act aka "McDade Amendment" (28 U.S.C. § 530B)
        Applicability to attorney-client privilege standards, 42-43
    Claims by government actors, 920-25
    Corporate context
        Communications made to secure both legal and business guidance, 880-84
        Consultation with expert third parties ("*Kovelling*"), 882-84
        Crime/fraud exception to, 913-20
        Internal corporate investigations, 34, 188-91, 230-40, 871-84, 905-13
        Prepared both in anticipation of litigation and for business purposes, 880-84
        Waiver Issues Generally, Ch. 17
        Who is the client
            For waiver purposes, 884-905
            Internal corporate investigations, 905-13
            Shareholder suits against the corporation, 879-80
    Elements generally
        Attorney-client privilege, 871-73
        Work product doctrine, 872
    Joint defenses
        Importance in white-collar practice, 32-33, 956
        Sample agreement, 963-65
        Underpinnings and rules applicable to, 957-61
    Opinion work product, 877-78, 880
    Waiver
        Corporate internal investigations, 188-91
        Court Orders & Confidentiality Agreements, 899-902
        Federal Rule of Evidence 502, 888-891
        Flowing from submissions, 34
        Government demands for as precondition for cooperation credit, 32-34, 180-81, 188-92, 230-40
        Inadvertent, 891-93
        Individual Attempts to Claim the Corporate Privilege, 902-03
        Partial, 893-96
        Selective, 897-899
        Upjohn Warning, 903-05
        Who may waive in corporate context, 885-88

Bank Fraud (18 U.S.C. § 1344), 405-06

Bills of Particulars (*see* "Discovery, Bills of particulars")

Brady Obligations (*see* "Discovery, *Brady* obligations")

Bribery (*see* "Public Corruption, Bribery")

Causation
   Importance in white-collar cases, 34
   Relation to "responsible corporate officer" doctrine, 254-55

Citizens Protection Act (aka the "McDade Amendment") (28 U.S.C. § 530B)
   Application to attorney subpoenas, 42-43, 733-34
   Application to discovery rules, 42-43, 777
   Application of no-misrepresentation rules to undercover operations and plea bargaining, 42-43
   Application to "no-contact" rule, 42-43
   Application to plea bargaining inducements, 42-43
   Application to rules barring public comment by law enforcement, 42-43
   Application to rules limiting prosecution's attempt to discourage witnesses from cooperating with defense, 42-43
   Application to submission of exculpatory evidence to grand jury, 42-43, 755-56
   Effect of state rules and decisions, 42-43
   General, 42-43

Civil Alternatives
   Department of Justice Corporate Charging Guidelines, 196
   General, 36

Civil Investigative Demands ("CID"s)
   Health care context (31 U.S.C. § 3733), 297-98

Clean Water Act (*see also* "Environmental Crimes")(33 U.S.C. § 1251, *et seq.*)
   Mens Rea, 64-65, 79-85
   "Responsible corporate officer" doctrine, 240-42, 249-51

Co-conspirators' Statement (*see* "Conspiracy, Hearsay/co-conspirators' statements rule")

Collateral Estoppel, 34, 1061-63

Common Interest Privilege (*see* "Joint Defense")

Compliance Programs (*see* "Entity Liability, Compliance programs")

Conflicts of Interest (*see* "Representation Issues")

Conscious Avoidance (*see* "*Mens Rea*, Conscious avoidance/willful blindness/ ostrich jury instructions")

Conspiracy (18 U.S.C. § 371)
   Agreement, 614-17
   Agreement with undercover or cooperating witness, 606-07, 623-34
   Charging, 614
   Defraud and Offense Clauses 607-08
   Elements, 605
   Generally, Ch.10
   Hearsay/co-conspirators' statements rule, 607-08
   Impossibility, 618-20
   Joinder/Severance, 607-08
   Mens Rea, 620
   Money laundering, 696-97
   Other conspiracy code sections, 605 n.1
   Overt acts, 630-31
   Pinkerton liability, 631-38
   Plurality of actors, 614-17, 620-24
   Principles of liability, 610-38
   Public Corruption, 605 n.1
   RICO, 668-69

Scope of
>   Chain conspiracy, 628-29, 668-77
>   Defining, 624-30
>   Wheel conspiracy, 628-29, 668-77
Statute of limitations, 609
Venue, 608-09
Withdrawal from, 620

Cooperation (*see also* "Entity Liability, Voluntary disclosure and cooperation";
>   "Fifth Amendment, Immunity"; "Plea Bargaining"; "Proffers")
Bargaining for limitations on use of information tendered by the cooperating witness, 813-23, 1034
Cooperation departures
>   Individuals (U.S.S.G. § 5K1.1), 1017-22
Post-sentencing cooperation, 1034
Privilege waivers as a condition to, 189-91
Proffers, 813-23, 1022
Timing of sentencing of cooperating witness, 1034

Corporate Criminal Liability (*see* "Entity Liability")

Corporate Internal Investigations (*see* "Entity Liability, Voluntary disclosure and cooperation")

Corruption (*see* "Public Corruption")

Crime Definition
Congressional role, 9-36
Judicial role, 17-18, 19-21
Prosecutorial role, 21-23

Criminal Code, Federal
Difficulties of constructing charge-offense sentencing system based on, 112-13
Number of prohibitions, 11-15
Redundancy of prohibitions, 10-11, 14-15
Vagueness of prohibitions, 15-21

Criminal Punishment
Distinction between criminal and civil law, 7-9, 144-45
Purposes, congressional definition, 7 n.17

Currency Transaction Reporting Act (31 U.S.C. §§ 5311–22), 174-78

Defense Counsel Role (*see also* "Attorney–Client Privilege and Work Product Doctrine"; "Ethical Obligations, Defense"; "Representation Issues"; "White–Collar Crime")
Attributes of white-collar practice, 25-36
Challenges presented by appeals waivers in proposed plea bargains, 778-82, 994-98
Challenges presented by false claims civil cases, 291-310
Challenges presented by parallel proceedings, 34, Ch.20
Challenges presented by representation of corporate client, 32-34
Conduct of proffers, 813-23
Conflicts of interest issues generally, 927-38
Crime/fraud exception to privileges, 913-20
Defense activity as obstruction, 321, 337-49, 358-66, 376
Defense witness immunity, 810-13
Discovery, 292-321, 324-25, Ch. 14
Forfeiture of fees, 678-80
Grand jury
>   Advance assertions of the witness's privilege, 730-31
>   Defense requests to testify, 731-32
>   Subpoenas to attorneys, 43, 732-34
Internal corporate investigations, 34, 189-91, 230-40
Joint defense, 32-33, 192, 956
Obtaining grand jury material, 722-24, 1058-61
Privilege questions where dual business and legal role undertaken, 880-83
Reliance on counsel defense, 98-99, 105
Right to counsel
>   Application in grand jury, 942-55

When attaches, 942-55
Sentencing guidelines bargaining, 30-31, Ch. 19

Deferred Prosecution Agreements, 34, 173, 182-83, 194-95, 211-30

Definition of Crimes (*see* "Crime Definition")

Department of Justice
    Corporate Charging Guidelines, 180-211
        Privilege waivers, 34, 180-81, 189-91, 230-40
    Policies—Appeals waivers 778-82, 994-98
    Policies—Charging general
        Factors, 311-16, 392-93, 998-1010
        Petite policy, 320-21
    Policies—Charging particular statutes
        False statements; "exculpatory 'no'" cases, 286-291
        Money laundering, 687-88, 705
        RICO, 680-81
    Policies—Discovery
        Witness lists, 790-91
    Policies—Grand jury
        Advance assertions of Fifth Amendment right, 732
        Advice of rights to witnesses before, 730-31
        Conduct of prosecutors in, 717-18
        Defense requests to testify before, 731-32
        Enforcement of, 728
        Notification of "target" status, 732
        Presentation of exculpatory evidence to, 742-43, 749-55
        Presentation of hearsay to, 742
        Presentation of illegally seized evidence to, 742
        Subpoenas to attorneys, 43, 732-33
        Subpoenas to media, 733-34
    Policies—Immunity and non-prosecution
        Decision to request immunity, 807-10
        Defense witness immunity, 812 & n.6
        Entering into non-prosecution agreements, 824-28
        Steps to avoid taint, 805
    Policies—Pleas and plea bargaining
        Alford pleas, 975 & n.2
        Charge bargains, 1004-7
        Cooperation departures (U.S.S.G. §§ 5K1.1), 1008-09, 1010-22
        Guidelines bargaining generally, 1001-10
        Guidelines' "fact" or "factor" bargains, 1007-08
        Nolo contendere pleas, 975 & n.5
        Privilege waivers, 34, 180-81, 188-92, 230-40
        Sentence (and departure) bargains, 1008-09
    Sample cooperation agreement, 816-17, 1022-33
    Sample informal immunity agreement. 829-30
    Sample proffer agreement, 816-17
    U.S. Attorneys, 37-39

Deposition (Fed. R. Crim. P. 15), 1127-28

Disclosure Obligations
    Regulatory, 233-34

Discovery
    Appeals waivers in plea agreements, 782, 994-98
    Bills of particulars, 757 n.4, 786
    Brady obligation, 757-82
        Ethical rules, 771-75, 777-78
        Inadmissible but exculpatory materials, 775
        Materiality, 759-67, 771-78
        No duty to create, 771
        "Possession" by the government, 769-71
        Pre-plea disclosure, 778-82

Prosecutors' difficulties in distinguishing, 771-73
"Suppression" by the government, 767-69
Fed. R. Crim. P. 16 pre-trial discovery, 782-88
Comparison with civil discovery, 782-83
Contrast with *Brady*, 782-83
"Defense", 785
Exclusivity, 782-83
"Material" to the defense, 783-85
No constitutional entitlement, 782-83
"Possession" of the government, 785-86
Rationales for limited scope, 783
Fed. R. Crim. P. 17(c) trial subpoenas, 734-37, 771, 783, 791-93
Fed. R. Evid. 404(b) "other acts" notice, 757 n.4
Freedom of Information Act (5 U.S.C. § 552), 757, 791 n.36, 1061
Jencks Act (18 U.S.C. § 3500) and Fed. R. Crim. P. 26.2 rules regarding witness statements
Controversies in interpreting, 788-89
Exclusivity, 788
General, 788-89
Timing of disclosure, 788-89
Pre-indictment discovery, 30-33, 757
Variation in rules and practices regarding, 758-69
Witness lists, 790-91

"Do–Justice" Obligation (*see* "Prosecutorial Role, 'Ministers of Justice' ")

Dodd-Frank Wall Street Reform & Consumer Protection Act Whistleblower Program, 599-603

Double Jeopardy
Application to successive criminal and civil proceedings (*Halper* issue), 1064-70
Blockburger standard, 311-19
Dual sovereignty doctrine, 320-21
Multiple punishments for the same offense, 311-117
Multiplicity, 315-16
Petite policy, 320-21
Successive prosecutions for the same offense, 317-19
When jeopardy attaches, 719 n.8

Dual Sovereignty Doctrine, 320-21

Duplicity, 316-17

Entity Liability (*see also* "Parallel Proceedings")
Adverse inference against corporation from employee's assertion of privilege, 34, 1048
Effect of corporate liability on others, 154, 159-60
Caremark decision, 209-11
Collective knowledge theory, 175-80
Compliance programs, 165-74, 192-94, 203-16, 209-11
Deferred Prosecution Agreements, 33-34, 211-30, 173, 182-83, 211-30
Department of Justice Corporate Charging Guidelines, 180-98
Generally, 19-20, 32-34, Ch. 4
Global settlements, 1063-64, 1099-1102
Inconsistent verdicts, 175-80
"Intention to benefit" element, 161-65
Internal corporate investigations, 34, 189-91, 230-40, 873-84, 905-13, 1094-1102
Liability for acts of subsidiaries, 160-61
Liability of partnerships, 160-61
Liability where actions contrary to corporate policy/orders, 165-74
Principles of liability, 155-80
Privilege waivers as a condition for cooperation/declination, 34, 180-81, 188-92, 230-40
Rationale for corporate criminal liability, 144-55
Respondeat superior, 20, 32-34, Ch. 4
SEC Charging Policy, 230-40
Transnational Internal Investigations, 1094-1102
Transplantation from tort context, 145-46, 155-59, 170-75
U.S. Organizational Sentencing Guidelines, 198-211
Background, 198-201

Key features, 201-09
    Fines, 201-08
    Probation, 208-09
    Restitution, 201
Voluntary disclosure and cooperation
    Affect on *qui tam* liability, 294-301
    Amnesty programs, 185-86, 194
    Collateral consequences, 34, 195-96
    Debarment and suspension, 168,172 n.36, 195-96
    Internal corporate investigations, 33-34, 189-91, 230-40, 881-92, 912-19, 1098-1105
"Within the scope of employment" element, 155-61
    Evidence of authority, 160
    Persons who may subject entity to liability, 160

Environmental Crimes (*see also* "Clean Water Act")
    Clean Water Act (33 U.S.C. § 1251, et seq.), 79-87, 241-42, 249-55
    Harms, 4-5
    Mens rea issues, 64-65, 79-87
    Prosecutions of responsible corporate officers, 241-42, 249-55

Ethical Obligations
    Defense counsel (*see also* "Representation Issues")
        Citizens Protection Act (28 U.S.C. § 530B), 42-43
        Discussion in light of attributes of white-collar practice, 55-56
        Discussion of issues relating to joint defenses, 32-34, 192, 956-67
        Inadvertent production of privileged material, 872, 888-93
        "No-contact" rule, 42-43
        Role, ABA Standards for Criminal Justice 4-1.2(b), 39-41
        Rules relating to "multiple" or "joint" representation, 927-28
    Prosecutors (*see also* "Citizens Protection Act")
        Advice to witnesses regarding discussions with the defense, 728
        Discovery obligations, 776-78
        Discussions with press, 726 n.27, 727
        Role, ABA Model Rule of Prof'l Conduct 3.8, 40-41, 49
        Role, ABA Standards for Criminal Justice 3-1.2(b), (c), 39 n.101

Excessive Fines Clause, 1064-70

Exculpatory Evidence, Submission to Grand Jury (*see* "Grand Jury, Exculpatory Evidence"; "Citizens Protection Act")

"Exculpatory 'No' Defense (*see* "False Statements, Defenses")

Extortion (*see* "Public Corruption, Hobbs Act extortion under color of official right")

Extradition and alternatives, 1104-07, 1109-10, 1113-14, 1130-31

Extraterritoriality
    Antitrust law, 1088
    Application to U.S. criminal statutes, 1074-94
    Constitutional authority, 1084
    Extradition, 1106-07, 1130-31
    Generally, Ch. 21
    Internal investigations, 1094-1102
    Mutual Legal Assistance Process, 1108-09, 1115-16
    RICO, 1077-78
    Securities law, 1074-76

Fair Notice
    Federal criminal code, 9-35
    Relation to rule of lenity and vagueness standard, 18-19

Fair Warning (*see* "Fair Notice")

False Claims Act, Civil (31 U.S.C. §§ 3729–3733)
    Constitutional issues regarding, 300-10

Discussion of statute, 291-300
Evolution of statute, 294-98
Parallel proceedings, 34, Ch. 20
Practical issues in defense of, 295-300
Qui tam litigation, 291-301
Use in health care fraud cases, 291-92

False Claims Act, Criminal (18 U.S.C. § 287), 292-94
Application to health care fraud, 291-92
Principles of liability, 292-94

False Statements (18 U.S.C. § 1001) (*see also* "Perjury, Defenses")
Charging considerations, 268-71, 311-21
Concealment cases, 238-39
Defenses, 286-91
"Exculpatory 'no'", 286-91
Mens rea, 279-82, 289
Principles of liability, 268-85
Jurisdiction, 272-74
Materiality, 271-72

Federal Criminal Code (*see* "Criminal Code, Federal")

Federal Program Theft, Fraud, and Bribery (18 U.S.C. § 666)
(*see* "Public Corruption, Federal program theft, fraud, and bribery")

"Federalization" of crime
ABA Task Force conclusion, 11-13
False statement cases, 268-71
Importance to white-collar enforcement, 14-15
Increased federal presence, 2-3 & n.7

Fifth Amendment Privilege Against Self–Incrimination (*see also* "Cooperation"; "Entity Liability, voluntary
disclosure and self-reporting"; "Plea Bargaining"; "Proffers")
Adverse inferences and other penalties, 34, 1040-51
Applicability to materials seized pursuant to warrant, 843
Availability in grand jury, 29, 732
Claims by attorneys in possession of client records, 837-43
Considerations in target's/subject's decision whether to assert in grand jury, 732-34
Contexts in which privilege may be asserted, 1040
Documents and tangible objects, generally, Ch.16
Elements
"Act of production", 840-44, 847-49
"Compulsion", 840-44, 847-49
"Foregone conclusion" rule, 841, 859-60, 861
"Incriminating", 841-42, 854-56, 858, 862
"Testimonial communication", 843-44, 849-54, 856-63
Entity (corporate) context
Claims by corporate custodians, 846-48
Claims by former employees, 848
"Collective entity" doctrine, 834, 836, 845-49
Private versus business records, 848-49
Foreign prosecution, threat of, 802
Government context
Government employee as custodian, 848-49
Immunity, generally, Ch.15
"Act of production", 856-63
Congressional grants, 801
Constitutional standard, 795-801
Defense witness, 810-13
Department of Justice policies, 805, 807-10, 812 & n.6, 814-15, 824-29
Effect of state grant of, 799-801
Enforcement, 800-01
Indirect evidentiary use (witness refreshment), 803
"Informal"/ "pocket"/ "letter", 823-31
Kastigar procedural safeguards, 795-805

                    Non-evidentiary use (various types), 803-05
                    Often used in white-collar cases, 29, 31, 795
                    Proffers, 813-23
                    Statutory, 795-813
                    Use of immunized testimony for impeachment, 805
                    Use of immunized testimony to prosecute for perjury, 805
          Protective order in civil or administrative proceedings, 1052-58
          Required Records Exception, 864-70
          Sample informal immunity agreement, 829-30
          Sample proffer agreement, 816-17
          Testimony, generally, Ch.15
          Waivers
                    Effect of guilty plea, 975-77
                    Effect of statements made in same or prior proceeding, 1040-43

Food, Drug, and Cosmetic Act (FDCA) (21 U.S.C. §§ 301–92)
          Responsible corporate officer doctrine, 240-42

Foreign Corrupt Practices Act (FCPA) (15 U.S.C. §§ 78dd-1, *et seq.*), 515-45

Forfeiture
          Money laundering, 686 & n.16, 716
          RICO, 642, 678-80

Fourth Amendment
          Applied transnationally, 1112-13, 1121-22
          Subpoenas ad testificandum, 730-32
          Subpoenas duces tecum, 730, 835

Freedom of Information Act (5 U.S.C. § 552), 757, 791 n.36, 1061
          (*see also* "Discovery")

General Intent (*see* "*Mens Rea*, Specific and general intent")

Global Settlements, 1063-64

Good Faith Defense (*see* "*Mens Rea*, Good faith defense")

Good Faith Reliance on Counsel Defense (*see* "*Mens Rea*, Good faith reliance on counsel defense")

Grand Jury
          Advance assertions of Fifth Amendment privilege, 732
          Advice of rights, 730-31
          Challenges to sufficiency or competency of evidence before, 749
          Charging the law to, 734
          Generally, 29, Ch.13
          Citizens Protection Act (28 U.S.C. § 530B)
                    Submission of exculpatory evidence, 755-56
                    Subpoenas to attorneys, 43, 733-34
          Composition, 718-19
          Considerations in subject's/target's decision whether to appear before, 732-33
          Constitutional guarantee, 718 n.4
          Defense requests to testify, 731-32
          Evidentiary rules
                    Exclusionary rule, 742-43
                    Hearsay, 742
          Exculpatory evidence, 742-43, 749-55
          Function, 717-20
          Hyde Amendment (18 U.S.C. § 3006A), 755-56, 998
          Investigative function, 720
          Jeopardy not attached, 719 n.8
          Notification of target status, 732
          Persons authorized to be present, 722
          Privilege assertions, 730
          Reform proposals, 717-18
          Reports by, 720 n.16

Right to Financial Privacy Act (12 U.S.C. §§ 3401–22), 722 n.18
Screening function, 719-20
Secrecy, 717-27
    Attorneys for the government, 722-24, 1060-61
    "Disclosure" of grand jury material, 723-24, 1058-61
    Enforcement of, 728
    "Matters occurring before the grand jury", 724-28
    Obtaining transcripts in parallel proceedings, 1058-61
    Obtaining transcripts of witnesses' own testimony, 723 n.23
    Rationale, 725-26, 1059-61
    Supplementation of, 729
    Those not bound by, 722-23
"Subject" of investigation, definition, 731
Subpoenas
    Ad testificandum, 729
    Addressed to attorneys, 43, 733
    Addressed to media, 733-34
    Addressed to "targets", 729-32
    Duces tecum, 729
    Reasonableness standard (constitutional and Fed. R. Crim. P. 17), 734-37
    When used in lieu of warrant, 721-22 & n.19
"Target" of investigation, definition, 730
Witness preparation, 732-34

Gratuities (*see* "Public Corruption, Gratuities")

"Grouping" (*see* "Sentencing Guidelines, Grouping")

Harmless Error
    Failure to charge element of offense to the jury, 397-98
    Prosecutorial misconduct in grand jury, 744-49

Health Care Fraud
    False Claims Act use, 292
    Federal program theft, fraud, and bribery, 503-515

Hearsay (*see* "Conspiracy, Hearsay/co-conspirators' statements rule")

Hobbs Act (18 U.S.C. § 1951) (*see* "Public Corruption, Hobbs Act")

Honest Services (*see* "Mail and Wire Fraud")

Hyde Amendment (18 U.S.C. § 3006A), 755-56, 998

Ignorance or Mistake of Fact (*see* "*Mens Rea*, Ignorance or mistake of fact")

Ignorance or Mistake of Law (*see* "*Mens Rea*, Ignorance or mistake of law")

Immunity (*see* "Fifth Amendment, Immunity")

Impossibility
    Conspiracy context, 618-19

Inconsistent verdicts
    Conspiracy, 623-24
    Corporate liability, 175-80

Indictment
    Prosecutorial misconduct, 744-49
    Sufficiency or competency of evidence before grand jury, 743-44
    Waiver of non-jurisdictional defects through guilty plea, 975-76
Insider Trading (*see* "Securities Fraud: Insider Trading")

Intent (*see* "*Mens Rea*")

Internal Corporate Investigation (*see* "Entity Liability, Voluntary disclosure and cooperation")

International law
       Customary International Law, 1073 n.7
       Treaties. 1072 nn. 4-5
       Jurisdiction, 1081-82, 1084

Jencks Act (18 U.S.C. § 3500) (*see* "Discovery, Jencks Act")

Joinder/Severance
       Conspiracy, 607-08
       Generally, 607-08
       RICO, 668-69, 672-73, 677-78

Joint Defenses
       Consideration by government in determining whether to charge, 33, 192, 956-57
       Generally, 956-67
       Importance in white-collar practice, 32-33, 956-57
       Joint defense privilege, 33, 192, 956-57
       Sample agreement, 963-65

Justice Department (*see* "Department of Justice")

Legality Principle, 20-21

Lenity, Rule of, 61, 76, 83-84

Letters Rogatory, 1109, 1125-27

"Literal Truth" Defense (*see* "Perjury, Defenses")

Mail and Wire Fraud (18 U.S.C. §§ 1341, 1343, 1346)
       Charging, 392-93
       Extraterritorial application, 1093-94
       Generally, Ch.7
       Manufactured jurisdiction, 390
       Popularity with prosecutors, 383-85
       Principles of liability, 385-462
              Intent to defraud/harm, 387-409
              Interstate wiring in furtherance, 383, 415
              Mailing in furtherance, 383-394
                   Continuing scheme, 385-390
                   Lulling mailings, 391
                   Private couriers, 392
                   Required mailings, 391-92
              Materiality, 394-404
              Objects of a scheme to defraud
                   Confidential business information, 425-28
                   Foreign tax revenues, 430-31
                   Intangible, non-property rights, 415, 425-34
                   Intangible property rights, 415, 425-434
                   Property, 415-423
                   "Right to control", 415, 428-30
                   Right to "honest services" (18 U.S.C. § 1346), 415, 434-48
                   Unissued government licenses, 428
              Relevance of victim's identity, 432-33
              Relevance of victim's potential reliance, 394-404
              Varieties of fraud, 409-415

Malum in se, 16, 63

Malum prohibitum, 16-17, 63

"McDade Amendment" (*see* "Citizens Protection Act")

Mens Rea
       Conscious avoidance/willful blindness/ostrich jury instructions, 98-107, 531-33, 678, 686-90

Conspiracy, 620
Construction to save statute from vagueness challenge, 79, 661
Definition, 57
Difficulties in ascertaining, 16-18, 57-58
Entity liability (*mens rea* in *respondeat superior* context)
    "Collective knowledge" and flagrant organizational indifference, 175-198
    "Intention to benefit" requirement, 161-65
General, Ch.2
Good faith defense, 96-97
Good faith reliance on counsel defense, 98-99, 105
Ignorance or mistake of fact, 58, 63-64
Ignorance or mistake of law, 58, 60-64, 87-94
Ignorance or mistake of legal fact, 58, 79-85
Importance in white-collar cases, 34-35
Issues in environmental cases, 63-66, 85-86
Model Penal Code, 58-59
Presumption existence of, 67, 73
"Public welfare" offenses and doctrine, 17-18, 60-87
Relevance of perceptions of moral culpability, 73, 78-79, 93-94
Reliance on official interpretation, 87 & n.11
Specific and general intent, 94-96, 104-05
    False statement cases, 239-40
    Obstruction cases, 337-44
Tax cases, heightened standard, 87-93

"Ministers of Justice" (*see* "Prosecutorial Role, 'Ministers of Justice'")

Mistake of Fact (*see* "*Mens Rea*, Ignorance or mistake of fact")

Mistake of Law (*see* "*Mens Rea*, Ignorance or mistake of law")

Model Penal Code, 58-59

Money Laundering (18 U.S.C. §§ 1956, 1957), Ch. 12
    Concealment offenses, 686-90, 692-93, 709
    Conscious avoidance/willful blindness/ostrich instruction, 688-90, 697-98
    Conspiracy, 696-97
    Definitions, 683-86
    Department of Justice policy, 685-86, 705, 713-16
    Engaging in financial transactions with criminally derived property (18 U.S.C. § 1957), 684-85, 690, 697-98
    Extraterritorial application, 705-07
    "Financial transaction", 691-92
    Forfeiture, 686 & n.16, 705, 716
    Generally, Ch.12
    Hawala, 710-13
    Mens rea, 688-90, 692-93, 707
    Monetary Transaction, 697
    Principles of liability, 686-709
    "Proceeds", 693-94
    "Proceeds of some form of unlawful activity", 688-89, 692
    Promotion offenses, 699-709
    Reasons prosecutors use, 684-86, 713-16
    Sentencing guidelines, 713-16
    "Specified unlawful activity", 695
    Tracing, 693-95
    Transaction offenses, 684, 686-98
    Transportation offenses, 684, 699-709
    Undercover operations, 694-95
    Unlicensed transmitting businesses (18 U.S.C. § 1960), 684, 710-13

Multiplicity, 315-16

Mutual Legal Assistance Treaties (MLATs), 1104-09, 1115-16, 1123-24, 1128-30

"No–Contact" Rule (*see* "Ethical Obligations, 'No-contact' rule"; "Citizens Protection Act")

Obstruction of Justice (18 U.S.C. §§ 1503, 1512, 1515, 1519, 1520), Ch.6
        Application to defense counsel, 321, 337-49, 356-66, 374-76
        Defenses, 365-66
        Perjury as, 330
        Principles of liability under omnibus clause (18 U.S.C. § 1503), 324-49
        Principles of liability under witness tampering (18 U.S.C. § 1512), 352-66
        Principles of liability under 18 U.S.C. § 1505, 350-52
        Principles of liability under 18 U.S.C. § 1519, 366-76
        Principles of liability under 18 U.S.C. § 1520, 377-78

Organizational Sentencing Guidelines (*see* "Entity Liability, U.S. Organizational Sentencing Guidelines")

Ostrich Jury Instructions (*see* "*Mens Rea*, Conscious avoidance/willful blindness/ ostrich jury instructions")

Parallel Proceedings
        Collateral estoppel, 34, 1061-63
        Constitutionality, 1035-39
        Double Jeopardy and Excessive Fines Clauses protections, 1064-70
        Fifth Amendment implications
                Adverse inferences and other penalties, 34, 1043-51
                Contexts in which privilege may be asserted, 1040
                Waiver by statements in same or prior proceeding, 1040-43
        General, Ch.20
        Global settlements, 1063-64
        Protective order in civil or administrative proceedings, 1052-58
        Stays of civil or administrative proceedings, 1051-52
        Use of civil discovery as pre-indictment discovery device, 1052

Perjury (18 U.S.C. §§ 1621, 1623)
        Charged as obstruction, 330
        Charging considerations, 257-58, 267-68
        Civil context, 257-58
        Defenses
                Ambiguity, 260-68
                Literal truth, 260-68
                Recantation, 259-60
        Materiality, 286-87
        Principles of liability, 259-68
        "Perjury trap", 265-66

Pinkerton liability (*see* "Conspiracy, *Pinkerton* liability")

Plea Bargaining (*see also* "Cooperation"; "Entity Liability, Voluntary disclosure and cooperation"; "Fifth
Amendment Right Against Self–Incrimination, Immunity")
        Application of bribery statute to prosecutors who offer witnesses immunity or leniency for testimony,
        485, 1010-17
        Arguments regarding legitimacy and wisdom of, 981-82
        Bargaining for limitations on use of information tendered by the cooperating witness, 813-23, 1034
        Breach
                Defendant's, 990-92
                Government's, 992-93
        Citizens Protection Act (28 U.S.C. § 530B)
                Application of no-misrepresentation rules to undercover operations and plea bargaining,
                43, 1017
                Application to plea bargaining inducements, 1017
        Constitutional considerations, 977-98
        Distinguished from vindictive prosecution, 985-87
        Fed. R. Crim. P. 11 and Guidelines Bargaining, 998-1010
                Charge bargains, 1004-07
                Cooperation departures (U.S.S.G. § 5K1.1), 1008-09, 1010-14
                Enforcement of guideline policies, 1009-10
                Guidelines' "fact" or "factor" bargains, 1007-08
                Sentence bargains, 1008-09
                Standards for judicial acceptance of bargains, 1009-10
        Proffers, 813-23
        Sample cooperation agreements, 816-17, 1022-33

Types of deals or conditions (*see also* Fed. R. Crim. P. 11 and
  Brady or discovery appeals waivers, 778-82, 993-94
  Guidelines Bargaining, above)
  Sentencing appeal waivers, 994-97
  Third-party, 980-81
  "Wired" or "package", 981
  Withdrawal of plea prior to acceptance of agreement, 998-1000

Pleas,

  Alford, 975 & n.2
  Conditional, 975-76
  Implications for Fifth Amendment waiver at sentencing, 999-1000
  Nolo contendere, 975 & n.5
  Withdrawal, 999-1000

Policies of United States Department of Justice (*see* "Department of Justice, Policies")

Privilege Against Self–Incrimination (*see* "Fifth Amendment Privilege Against Self–Incrimination")

Proffers

  Bargaining for limitations on use of information tendered by the cooperating witness, 800-11
  Generally, 813-23
  Negotiation, 818-23
  Rationale, 813-16
  Sample agreement, 816-17
  Waivers of protections of Fed. R. Crim. P. 11(e)(6) and Fed. R. Evid. 410, 816

Prosecutorial Discretion
  Criticisms of, 21-28, 33
  Federal Sentencing Guidelines augmentation of, 115-16
  Suggested means of containing, 23
  Systemic attributes that contribute to, 21-23, 35-36

Prosecutorial Misconduct (*see also* "Citizens Protection Act"; "Ethical Obligations, Prosecutor")
  Advice to witnesses regarding discussions with the defense, 728-29
  Appealability of adverse determination in grand jury context, 749
  Breach of plea agreement, 992-93
  Conduct of grand jury, 744-49
  Harmless error test applicable to misconduct in grand jury, 749
  Vindictive prosecution, 985-89

Prosecutorial Role (*see also* "Citizens Protection Act"; "Ethical Obligations, Prosecutor")
  Adversary role, 38-43
  Conduct of proffers, 813-23
  Discussions with the press, 727
  "Do justice" obligation and role as "minister of justice", 39-43
      Grand jury context, 717-18
  Effect of the Citizens Protection Act (28 U.S.C. § 530B), 42-43, 732-433, 755-56, 777, 1017
  Grand jury
      Function, 718-20
      Misconduct, 728-29, 744-56

Protective Order (*see* "Parallel Proceedings, Protective orders")

Public Corruption
  Applicability of federal statutes to state actors, 472-73, 503-515
  Application to prosecutors who offer witnesses immunity or leniency for testimony, 485, 1010-22
  Bribery (18 U.S.C. § 201(b)(1), (2)), 466-85
      "Corrupt", 478-85
      Quid pro quo, 475-76
      "Thing of value", 473, 485
  Campaign contributions, 485-496
  Conspiracy, 605 n.1
  Federal program theft, fraud, and bribery (18 U.S.C. § 666), 503-15
      "Benefits", 504-09
      "Nexus", 510-15

Foreign Corrupt Practices Act (FCPA) (18 U.S.C. §§ 78dd-1, *et seq.*), 515-45
    Generally, Ch.8
    Gratuities offense (18 U.S.C. § 201(c)(1)(A), (B)), 465-85
    Hobbs Act extortion under color of official right (18 U.S.C. § 1951), 485-503
        Inducement, 485-95
        Interstate commerce element, 496-97
        "Property" "obtained", 501-02
        Quid pro quo, 485-497
    Mail and wire fraud prosecutions for, 415-24, 428, 434-48, 465, 484-85
    RICO prosecutions for, 466 n.8, 641 & n.8, 655-56, 666
    Travel Act (18 U.S.C. § 1952), 642, 681

"Public welfare" offenses and doctrine (*see* "*Mens Rea*, 'Public welfare' offenses and doctrine")

Purposes of Criminal Punishment (*see* "Criminal Punishment, Purposes")

Qui tam Litigation (*see* "False Claims, Civil")

Quid pro quo (*see* "Public Corruption")

Racketeer Influenced and Corrupt Organizations Act (*see* "RICO")

Relators, *Qui Tam* (*see* "False Claims, Civil")

"Relevant Conduct" (*see* Sentencing Guidelines, Relevant conduct")

Reliance on Counsel Defense (*see* "*Mens Rea*, Good faith reliance on counsel defense")

Representation Issues
    Conflicts of interest, 930-38
    Ethical rules, 927-30
    Generally, Ch. 18
    Joint defenses, 956-57
        Generally, 956-67
        Sample joint defense agreement, 963-65
    Multiple or joint representation, 930-42
        Constitutional issues, 930-38
        In the corporate context, 938-42
    Right to counsel, 927
    Sixth Amendment issues, 930-38

Respondeat Superior (*see* "Entity Liability")

Responsible Corporate Officer Doctrine, 240-55

RICO (Racketeer Influenced and Corrupt Organizations Act) (18 U.S.C. §§ 1961–68), Ch. 11
    Attorneys' fees, 642, 664
    Civil remedies, 642, 646, 661, 664
    Civil suits under, 642, 664
    "Conduct" of enterprise's affairs (*Reves*) element, 662-67
        Application in conspiracy cases, 666-67
        Application to low-level employees, 664-65
    Conspiracy, 605 n.1, 668-77
        Application of "conduct" (*Reves*) test to, 667, 674-75
        Scope of agreement, 668-69
    Department of Justice requirements and policies, 680-81
    Dual sovereignty, 643
    Economic purpose, 661
    "Enterprise" element, 644-56
        Applicability to corporate actors, 654-56
    Federalization of state crimes, 642-43
    Forfeiture, 642, 678-80
    Interstate commerce element, 644-45
    Mens Rea, 661
    "Pattern" of racketeering activity, 656-61
    "Person", 647-56

Applicability to corporate actors, 647-56
Predicate acts of racketeering, 643, 661-62
Principles of liability, 644-77
Public corruption, 466 n.8, 641 & n.8, 655-56, 666
Purpose, 641-42
"Racketeering activity", 647-48, 656-62
Racketeering injury, 661
Reasons prosecutors use, 641-43, 677-81
Statute of limitations, 643 n.19
Transnational application, 1077-78

Right to Counsel (*see* "Representation Issues, Right to Counsel")

Right to Financial Privacy Act (12 U.S.C. §§ 3401-22), 722 n.18

Rule of Lenity (*see* "Lenity, Rule of")

Scienter (*see* "*Mens Rea*")

Securities Fraud: Insider Trading (15 U.S.C. §§ 78ff(a); 78j(b); 17 C.F.R. § 240.10b-5; 18 U.S.C. § 1348)
18 U.S.C. § 1348, 577-78
Accounting fraud, 578-99
Dodd-Frank Wall Street Reform & Consumer Protection Act Whistleblower Program, 599-603
Generally, Ch. 9
Misappropriation theory, 556-57, 558-77
Quasi- or temporary insider, 562 n.31, 577
Rationale for prohibition, 549-52
Statutes, 547-48, 556-57, 577-78
Tippee liability, 568, 570-77
Traditional theory, 552-57
Transnational application, 1074-76

Sentencing Guidelines, United States (*see also* "Entity Liability, U.S. Organizational Sentencing Guidelines")
Acceptance of responsibility credit, 1004
Appeals waivers, 994-97
Bargaining
Charge bargains, 1004-07
Enforcement of guideline policies, 1009-10
Guidelines' "fact" or "factor" bargains, 1007-08
Sentence bargains, 1008-09
Standards for judicial acceptance of bargains, 1009-10
Commission methodology, 107-16, 116-22
Departures
Departure bargaining, 1008-09
Individuals (U.S.S.G. § 5K1.1), 1017-22
Evidentiary rules applicable at sentencing, 114
Generally, Ch. 3
Grouping, 119-21
Limitations on use of information disclosed in plea bargaining or cooperation, 1034
Money laundering, 713-16
Organizational Sentencing Guidelines, 198-211
Purposes, 107-10, 198-201
Real- versus charge-offense sentencing, 110-16, 117-19
Relevant conduct, 107-22, 118-22
Structure, 116-22, 204-19

Separation of Powers
Prosecutorial role, 19-23, 300-04
Rationale for bar on judicial lawmaking, 19-21

Severance (*see* "Joinder/Severance")

Specific Intent (*see* "*Mens Rea*, Specific and general intent")

Statute of Limitations
Conspiracy, 609

General, 609
RICO, 643 n.19

Stays (*see* "Parallel Proceedings, Stays")

Stored Communications Act, 1078

"Subject" of Investigation
    Definition, 731

Submissions, 298-300

Subpoenas
    Ad testificandum, 730
    Addressed to attorneys, 43, 733-34
    Addressed to media, 733-34
    Addressed to "targets", 730-32
    BNS Subpoenas, 1111, 1125
    Duces tecum, 730, 835
    Fed. R. Crim. P. 17 subpoenas, 734-37
    Grand jury, 717
    In transnational cases, 1110-11, 1124-25
    Trial, 734-37, 771, 783, 791-93
    Reasonableness standard (constitutional and Fed. R. Crim. P. 17), 734-37
    When used in lieu of warrant, 721-22 & n.19

"Target" of Investigation
    Definition, 730
    Notification of status, 732

Tax Offenses
    Heightened *mens rea* standard, 89-94

Transcripts of Grand Jury Testimony
    Obtaining grand jury materials, 723-24, 1058-61
    Witnesses' prior testimony, 723 n.23

Travel Act (18 U.S.C. § 1952), 642, 681

United States Criminal Code (*see* "Criminal Code, Federal")

United States Department of Justice (*see* "Department of Justice")

Vagueness
    Federal Criminal Code, 15-18
    Reading *mens rea* elements to avoid, 79, 661

Venue
    Conspiracy, 608-09
    Continuing offenses, 608-09

Vicarious Liability (*see also* "Entity Liability"; "Responsible Corporate Officer")
    General, 143-45

Vindictive Prosecution, 985-87

Voluntary Disclosure (*see* "Entity Liability, Voluntary disclosure and cooperation")

Waiver (*see* "Attorney Client Privilege and Work Product Doctrine, Waiver"; "Fifth Amendment Privilege Against Self–Incrimination, Waiver")

"White-Collar" Crime
    Costs, 1 n.3
    Defense counsel role, 55-56
    Definition, 3-6

References are to Pages

Description of practice attributes, 25-36
Empirical study, 25-36
Grand jury use, 29-32, 717-22
Growth industry, 25-28
History of development of practice, 25-28
Importance of information control, 29-33, 55
Organizational presence, 32-34

Willful Blindness (*see* "*Mens Rea*, Conscious avoidance/willful blindness/ ostrich jury instructions")

Wire Fraud (*see* "Mail and Wire Fraud")

Work Product Doctrine (*see* "Attorney–Client Privilege and Work Product Doctrine"